New England Marriages

Prior to 1700

New England Marriages

Prior to 1700

Clarence Almon Torrey

With a revised Introduction by
Gary Boyd Roberts

Prepared for Publication by Elizabeth P. Bentley

Baltimore
GENEALOGICAL PUBLISHING CO., INC.

Published by Genealogical Publishing Co., Inc.
Baltimore, 1985
Second printing, 1987
Third printing, 1990
Fourth printing, 1992
Fifth printing, 1994
Library of Congress Catalogue Card Number 84-81867
International Standard Book Number 0-8063-1102-9
Made in the United States of America

Introduction

I

CLARENCE ALMON TORREY'S *New England Marriages Prior to 1700* is one of the greatest genealogical manuscripts of the twentieth century. The major successor to James Savage's *Genealogical Dictionary of the First Settlers of New England*, published 1860-1862 and reprinted frequently since, Torrey's compilation is both (1) a nearly comprehensive listing of, and bibliography for, the married population of seventeenth-century New England; and (2) a summary and index, for its subject, of the best American genealogical scholarship, 1860-1960. Acquired by the New England Historic Genealogical Society (henceforth NEHGS) after Torrey's death in 1962, used almost hourly by its librarians and members to find sources for, and identify, Pilgrim and Great Migration immigrants, their children and grandchildren, *New England Marriages Prior to 1700* was published on microfilm by NEHGS in 1979. Although Torrey's own rather difficult handwriting and his hundreds of cryptic source abbreviations were merely photographed, this microfilm — in seven reels — proved so immediately and universally useful that Genealogical Publishing Company of Baltimore (henceforth GPC) asked Elizabeth Petty Bentley, the well-known compiler of census indexes, to prepare a book version as well. Requiring two years to transcribe, this volume contains that portion of Torrey's work that can serve as a guide to the remainder — the listing, but not the bibliography, of the 37,000 couples who resided in colonial New England during its first eight decades. Included as well, whenever known, are the wife's maiden name, the marriage date or birth year of a first child, the birth and death years of both partners, and question marks to indicate unproved assertions. Most importantly, this volume also lists all residences of every couple, so that the geographical spread of any surname can be easily surmised, and the index includes all surname variations (since Torrey was not always strictly alphabetical), all known seventeenth-century New England wives, and each of their *other* husbands.

Clarence Almon Torrey, whose obituary appears in *The New England Historical and Genealogical Register* (hereafter the *Register*), 116 (1962):158-159, was born in Manchester, Iowa August 28, 1869 and died in Newton, Massachusetts February 5, 1962. A graduate of Cornell College at Mount Vernon, a member of the library staff of the University of Chicago from

1893 to 1920, a resident of Boston after 1921, a contributing editor to *The American Genealogist* (henceforth *TAG*) from July 1932 until his death, and the twenty-second elected fellow of the American Society of Genealogists, Torrey was one of the major genealogical scholars of his generation. An elder member of the "Jacobus school" that revolutionized standards of evidence in the first decades of this century (see *The Connecticut Nutmegger* 12(1979):371-373), Torrey published a David Roe of Flushing, Long Island genealogy in 1924, co-authored two genealogies, in 1953 and 1959 respectively, that definitively cover almost all New England Gilberts, and compiled book-length typescript genealogies as well of the early progeny of John Heald and Edward Wright of Concord and of John Young of Eastham (a nephew-in-law of John Howland of the *Mayflower*). His similar study of the colonial descendants of Stephen Gates of Hingham was published in volumes 120 and 121 of the *Register* and reprinted in Volume I of *Genealogies of Connecticut Families from NEHGR* (Baltimore: GPC, 1983). Of Torrey's over fifty *TAG* articles, "Some Ancestral Lines of President John Quincy Adams" and "Some Ancestral Lines of President William Howard Taft"(21(1944-5):167-169 and 22 (1945-6):205-210 respectively), together with his manuscript outline charts of this ancestry, have been the cornerstone of my own work on the ancestry and various connections of these presidents, notably *Ancestors of American Presidents*, revised edition (Santa Clarita, Calif., 1989). Four of Torrey's TAG articles, on Thomas Ford, Maj. Aaron Cooke, John Thompson, and Mrs. Alice Freeman Thompson Parke, cover ancestors of the Princess of Wales and are cited in *American Ancestors and Cousins of the Princess of Wales* by Gary Boyd Roberts and William Addams Reitwiesner (Baltimore: GPC, 1984). Other immigrants whose English ancestry, origins, or marriages are treated in Torrey's TAG corpus include Edmund Hobart of Hingham, his son, Rev. Peter Hobart, and two sons-in-law, John Beal and Thomas Chubbuck; Edward Gilman, also of Hingham, and his Jacob, Lincoln, Peck, and Cooper kinsmen; Francis Chickering, James Draper, and Jonathan Fairbanks, all of Dedham; the Howland brothers and Nicholas Snow (son-in-law of Stephen Hopkins) among *Mayflower*-connected families; the Cheevers, Stephen Kinsley, and John Parker of Boston; Valentine Prentice and Nathaniel Wilson of Roxbury; Richard Lyman and the Spencer brothers of Hartford; Bygod Eggleston and Philip Randall of Windsor; William Cowdrey of Reading; Lt. Robert Feake of Watertown; Charles Gott of Salem; Thomas Hale of Newbury; Thomas Olney of Providence; Brian Pendleton of Maine; and Humphrey Turner of Scituate.

Clarence Almon Torrey was an almost daily reader at NEHGS for many years. His manuscript collection, totalling thirteen cartons, was given to the Society after his death. *New England Marriages Prior to 1700,* his major life's work, begun in 1927, lists every married seventeenth-century New Englander of whom he could find *any* record in *any* printed work and a few NEHGS typescripts or manuscripts (notably those of Mrs. Holman, mentioned below), through roughly 1960. Including probably 99% of this population that left issue (a few marriages of the 1690s are omitted), this compendium indicates not only — as transcribed herein and abstracted originally from what Torrey considered the best printed treatments of both partners — their full names, birth and death years, marriage date, and residences; it also lists, under each couple, every source in which he found data on either spouse — in effect, a bibliography of every married seventeenth-century New Englander compiled from virtually everything in print through 1960. These references, to volume and page number, are over 100,000 in number. For most couples with a large modern progeny there are at least five, for many over ten, such references.

The more than 2,500 works thus indexed for seventeenth-century New Englanders by Torrey fall into five general categories. Indexed and abstracted firstly are the genealogical dictionaries — the works of James Savage, C. H. Pope, J. O. Austin, and Sybil Noyes, C. T. Libby, and W. G. Davis, all several times reissued in recent years by GPC. Also thoroughly combed was the pertinent periodical literature, most notably the *Register, TAG,* and *The New York Genealogical and Biographical Record* through 1960, early decades of the *Essex Institute Historical Collections,* and all volumes of, among other defunct journals, *The Mayflower Descendant, Putnam's Historical Magazine* (variously titled), *The Essex Antiquarian,* and *The Genealogical Advertiser.* The third category of sources surveyed by Torrey is the single-family genealogy, usually treating the agnate (male-line only) descendants of a Puritan or Great Migration immigrant. Hundreds of these works were published between the Civil War and 1930 (their "golden age"), and the popularity of this form continues still. When there are several genealogies tracing the progeny of different or various immigrants sharing the same surname, Torrey has indicated each work's year of publication for every reference. For the most common surnames, moreover, he has listed all available genealogies and assigned each a number (Smith 1, for example) by which it is easily identified. A fourth category covered by Torrey is the town history or "town genealogy" covering all residents through 1850 or even 1900. The "golden age" of these works was also 1865-1930, but they are often more authoritative than nineteenth-century genealogies and sometimes contain unexpected data on the families of wives, daughters, or non-resident parents of later townsmen. The best pre-1960 town histories or town genealogies — Paige's and Mrs. Gozzaldi's *Cambridge*, Wyman's *Charlestown*, Lincoln's *Hingham*, Hudson's *Lexington*, Banks' *Martha's Vineyard*, Starbuck's *Nantucket*, Davis' *Plymouth*, Blodgett and Jewett's *Rowley*, Perley's *Salem*, Hoyt's *Salisbury and Amesbury*, Bond's *Watertown*, Chamberlain's *Weymouth*, Stiles' *Windsor and Wethersfield, Ct.*, Jacobus' *New Haven and Fairfield, Ct.*, and Bowen's *Woodstock, Ct.* — are cited repeatedly. Most of those just listed, moreover, have been reprinted in the last two decades — largely by GPC or New England History Press.

Probably the most useful sources so indexed by Torrey, however, are the various multi-ancestor compendia, usually tracing all known forebears of a given couple or individual, in which some of the best research of twentieth-century scholars on immigrant origins, and much of the best revision of the early generations of nineteenth-century genealogies, is "buried." Sixty such works are listed and subject-indexed by immigrant in "My Own Index", an appendix to Volume III of Donald Lines Jacobus' *Index to Genealogical Periodicals* (a set most recently reissued, by GPC, in a single volume, in 1981); seventy more are listed, but not indexed, in "Seventy Multi-Ancestor Genealogies," an appendix I compiled for "Genealogical Research in Massachusetts: A Survey and Bibliographical Guide," in the Register, 135(1981):196-198, reprinted, with corrections, in *Genealogical Research in New England* (Baltimore: GPC, 1984), pp. 110-112, 114. All of these 130 works published through 1960, plus many others, are fully indexed for married seventeenth-century New Englanders by Torrey. So covered, then, are most of the volumes by Walter Goodwin Davis (author of sixteen books outlining the full known ancestry of each of his great-great-grandparents; only one was published after 1960), Herbert Furman Seversmith (*Colonial Families of Long Island, New York, and Connecticut*), M. A. S. Anderson, C. H. Cory, Louis Effingham deForest, J. R. Delafield, Mary Walton Ferris, Ernest Flagg (*Genealogical Notes on the Founding of New England*, also reprinted by GPC), Mrs. Josephine C. Frost, Mrs. Mary Lovering Holman and her daughter, Mrs. Winifred Lovering Holman Dodge (friends of Torrey and parts of whose enormous manuscript collection, given to NEHGS in 1974, he also surveyed and indexed), J. W. Hook, Donald Lines Jacobus (the collaborations with E. F. Waterman — notably *Hale, House and Related Families*, also a GPC reprint — and N. G. Parke especially), J. W. Linzee, Belle Preston, E. E. Salisbury, L. L. M. Selleck, N. E. Snow, F. F. Starr, Edith Bartlett Sumner, R. M. Tingley, L. A. W. Underhill, J. A. Vinton, and Frederick Chester Warner (the typescript "Ancestry of Samuel, Freda, and John Warner," 1949, which Torrey calls "Warner-Harrington"). Among these works Torrey cites the Davis, deForest,

Frost, Jacobus, and Warner volumes, Mrs. Ferris' magnificent *Dawes-Gates Ancestral Lines* (of U.S. Vice-President Charles Gates Dawes), and the equally definitive Pillsbury and Stevens-Miller sets by the Holmans (covering the New England ancestry of the Pillsbury flour family of Minneapolis), literally hundreds of times.

Torrey's references may at first seem idiosyncratically abbreviated but are both logical and consistent. "Sv" (for Savage's *Genealogical Dictionary*), "Pope" or "Pope's Pioneers" (for *The Pioneers of Massachusetts* and *The Pioneers of Maine and New Hampshire*), "Austin's Dict." (for *Genealogical Dictionary of Rhode Island*), and "Libby's Gen. Dict." or "Libby's Dict."(for *Genealogical Dictionary of Maine and New Hampshire*) cover the genealogical dictionaries. "Reg." (for the *Register*), "Am. Gen." (for *TAG*; "NHGM" indicates the first eight volumes, known as the *New Haven Genealogical Magazine* and reprinted by GPC as *Families of Ancient New Haven*), "N.Y.G.B.Rec." or "N.Y.Rec." (for *The New York Genealogical and Biographical Record*), "E.I.H.C." (for *Essex Institute Historical Collections*), "M.D." (for *The Mayflower Descendant*), "Essex Ant." (for *The Essex Antiquarian*), and "Gen. Adv." (for *The Genealogical Advertiser*) cover most periodical literature. Genealogies are abbreviated, as indicated above, by surname and date of publication or surname and assigned number; town histories by the town name only (few towns have more than one major pre-1960 book-length history with a genealogical "register" in back); and multi-ancestor compendia usually by two hyphenated surnames, those of the man and wife mentioned in the title, or of the parents of the figure whose ancestry the book treats (Smith-Hale, Bassett-Preston, Snow-Estes, Goodwin-Morgan, Tingley-Meyers, etc.). One abbreviation that often puzzles initial users of *New England Marriages* is "L.B.D.F.P." for *Lineage Books of the National Society of the Daughters of Founders and Patriots of America*, the major hereditary society publication that Torrey combed. A full bibliography of the works Torrey indexed, alphabetically arranged *by his abbreviations*, was compiled several years ago by Alicia Crane Williams, editor of the newly revived doyen of Pilgrim publications, *The Mayflower Descendant*. This bibliography is also available at NEHGS in Boston.

II

Four further uses of Torrey's great opus merit discussion. So, too, do various post-1960 works, in effect useful supplements to *New England Marriages* and the literature it abstracts, that contain or index additional data on seventeenth-century New Englanders. With Torrey's references and often with just the listings provided herein (see below) the skillful researcher can quickly locate the best printed material on any given New Englander who married before 1700. In addition, using the dictionaries by Savage, Pope, Austin, and Noyes, Libby and Davis as a guide, he can frequently see at a glance whether any major monograph on the family has appeared since 1860, and what it may have added — an English or "old world" origin if the birth year or likely pre-American marriage is listed; a wife's maiden name; earlier or later marriages; or earlier or later residences in New England. The marriages and later residences of sons or likely children or grandchildren of immigrants, so long as these descendants married before 1700, may be readily gleaned as well. Most importantly, since Torrey identified the maiden name of 70% or so of the wives herein listed, with the index to this volume the researcher can determine, often for the first time, the husbands of sisters, daughters, and many granddaughters of immigrants, and of immigrant sisters or kinswomen. Thus the first major additional use of *New England Marriages* is the extensive construction of seventeenth-century pedigrees and "family group sheets".

Researchers can also find such information on the numerous early New Englanders who migrated to Long Island, New Jersey, or elsewhere, for Torrey included these as well. Because his work lists all known marriages of the 1680s and most of the 1690s, plus the post-1700 residences and death dates of both partners, it can greatly aid eighteenth-century research also. Most New Englanders born in the 1720s or 1730s will be grandchildren, and many revolutionary soldiers great-grandchildren, of seventeenth-century residents of the same surname in the same or nearby towns. From a list of such earlier probable kinsmen and (if the microfilm is used as well) the sources in which they are treated, a large amount of genealogical data on early and mid-eighteenth-century New Englanders can also be quickly located. The researcher can then usually begin work in eighteenth-century primary sources or among the various guides to "pioneer" (i.e., post 1750, or 1750-1850) genealogy with either proved or probable seventeenth-century forebears, or with some confidence that at least the pre-1960 genealogical literature offers few clues to the origin of his eighteenth-century New England ancestor. For any genealogist beginning a search for the English origins of a seventeenth-century New Englander, the first sources to check, among American works, are C.E. Banks' *Topographical Dictionary of 2885 English Emigrants to New England, 1620-1650* (1931), H.F. Waters' *Genealogical Gleanings in England,* 2 vols. (1901) (both of these titles were most recently reissued by GPC in 1981), and both series of *English Origins of New England Families from The New*

England Historical and Genealogical Register (Baltimore: GPC, 1984-1985). Immediately after checking these works, however, and before surveying pertinent British pedigrees listed in the guides by G.W. Marshall, J. B. Whitmore, G. B. Barrow, and Margaret Stuart, researchers should thoroughly canvass all sources listed by Torrey. For immigrant origin studies, reconstruction of seventeenth-century pedigrees, eighteenth-century research, and work, too, on early New Englanders who moved elsewhere, *New England Marriages Prior to 1700* is essential.

Among major post-1960 publications *Founders of Early American Families: Emigrants from Europe, 1607-1657*, Revised Edition, by Meredith B. Colket, Jr. (Cleveland, 1985) subject-indexes for pre-1657 immigrants whose agnate progeny still probably survives, most, but not all, pertinent articles in the *Register, TAG, The New York Genealogical and Biographical Record*, and the *National Genealogical Society Quarterly*. Mrs. Jean D. Worden has compiled subject indexes for the *Register*, volumes 51-142 (1897-1988), *TAG*, volumes 1-60 (1922-84) and the *Record*, volumes 1-113 (1870-1982). The genealogical columns of the *Boston Evening Transcript*, 1901-1941 (but not 1894-1900) are being indexed in the second series of the *American Genealogical-Biographical Index (AGBI)*, over 170 volumes to date, now into the letter "T" alphabetically. *Transcript* index entries for the remainder of the alphabet can be obtained from the Godfrey Memorial Library in Middletown, Connecticut, from which *AGBI* is produced. Torrey occasionally lists a *Transcript* entry but made no systematic index. GPC's splendid ongoing periodical extraction program, reviewed in the Register, 137 (1984):46-51, has so far yielded, among New England-area compilations, *Genealogies of Rhode Island Families from Rhode Island Periodicals*, 2 vols. (1983); *Genealogies of Connecticut Families from NEHGR*, 3 vols. (1983); *English Origins of New England Families from NEHGR*, two series, 6 vols. (1984-1985); *Genealogies of Mayflower Families from NEHGR*, 3 vols. (1985); [Early] *Suffolk County* [Mass.] *Wills. . .from NEHGR* (1984); *Mayflower Source Records from NEHGR* (1986); *Genealogies of Long Island Families from NYGBR*, 2 vols. (1987); *Long Island Source Records from NYGBR* (1987); and *Genealogies of Rhode Island Families from NEHGR*, 2 vols. (1989), with an updated version of "A Bibliography for 100 Colonial Rhode Island Families." Another useful work, with a highly selective (and therefore partial) bibliography-by-subject, is *Plymouth Colony Probate Guide: Where to Find Wills and Related Data for 800 People of Plymouth Colony, 1620-1691* (1983), compiled by Ruth Wilder Sherman and Robert S. Wakefield.

Microfilm collections published or acquired by NEHGS since 1960 include, in addition to *New England Marriages, The Corbin Collection:* [Genealogical and] *Historical Material Relating to Central and Western*

Massachusetts, 1650-1850 (55 reels, NEHGS, 1982. Compiled by Walter E. and Lottie S. Corbin, this enormous corpus of vital records, cemetery inscriptions, etc., for ninety-seven Massachusetts towns, includes compiled genealogies of early families of Belchertown, Northampton, Pittsfield, Southampton, and Wales); Waldo Chamberlain Sprague's *Genealogies of the Families of Braintree, Massachusetts, 1640-1850* (NEHGS, 1984); *The* (George Ernest) *Bowman Files,* 229 microfiche cards containing data on *Mayflower* families (Massachusetts Society of Mayflower Descendants, 1983); *Genealogical Notes of Cape Cod Families,* eight reels, compiled by Lydia Brownson, Grace Held, and Doris Norton (largely, however, from sources covered by Torrey); Charles Dyer Parkhurst's *Early Families of New London* [Conn.] *and Vicinity,* nine reels; and Agnes P. Bartlett's *Portsmouth* [N.H.] *Family Records,* three reels. Town histories or genealogies of the last three decades include three major works published by GPC and the Connecticut Society of Genealogists — Lucius Barnes Barbour's *Families of Early Hartford, Connecticut* (1977, but compiled in the 1910s and 1920s), Susan Woodruff Abbott's *Families of Early Milford, Connecticut* (1979), and Alvan Talcott's *Families of Early Guilford, Connecticut* (1984, compiled by 1890) — for which see *The Connecticut Nutmegger,* 12 (1979):371-385; plus Benjamin Franklin Wilbour's *Little Compton* [R.I.] *Families* (Little Compton, 1967; rev. ed., 1974). Major manuscript collections of "town genealogies" not covered by Torrey include Charlotte Helen Abbott's notes on Andover families and Hamilton Wilson Welch's almost 300 notebooks (undocumented, however) on Scituate-area families, both at NEHGS. NEHGS has also recently acquired microfilm copies of most available vital records for New England and the Canadian Maritimes, including Massachusetts, 1841-1900, Connecticut through 1850 (the Barbour Collection, for which we have both individual town volumes and the consolidated microfilm), New Hampshire through 1900, Vermont through 1908, Maine through 1955 (only 80 towns submitted pre-1892 data), and the Newport Monthly Meeting records for Rhode Island (in addition to the Arnold, Beaman, and Providence volumes).

The best post-1960 multi-ancestor compendia are listed, as stated earlier, on pages 110-112 and 114 of *Genealogical Research in New England.* Note especially the multiple works by Carl Boyer III, J.S. Elston, and H.M. Pitman, and single studies by G.E. Bates, S. W. McArthur, P.W. Prindle, and H.M. Stryker-Rodda, the last two of whom have written widely elsewhere. Single-family genealogies of the past thirty years are, of course, far too numerous to list. One further collective work, however, deserves special mention. This is *Mayflower Families Through Five Generations,* the long-planned and eagerly awaited compilation of the seventeenth and early eighteenth-century progeny of the twenty-three *Mayflower* progenitors who left American descendants. Seven volumes of this set have appeared so far, along with about a dozen pamphlets of four-generation "in progress" studies. The seven volumes (1975, 1978, 1980, 1990, 1991 and two in 1992), with addenda, cover the progeny of twelve of the twenty-three: John Billington, Peter Brown, James Chilton, Francis Eaton, Edward and Samuel Fuller, Stephen Hopkins, Richard More, Thomas Rogers, George Soule, William White and Edward Winslow. The pamphlets cover nine more — all except John Alden, William Brewster and John Howland. The pamphlets for Myles Standish and Degory Priest also extend coverage through the fifth generation, and two volumes of the separately published *John Howland of the Mayflower: The First Five Generations* (Camden, Maine, 1990, 1993), by Elizabeth Pearson White, definitively cover Howland's early progeny through his eldest daughter and son.

III

Having reviewed Torrey's life, the scope and uses of *New England Marriages Prior to 1700*, the genealogical literature it indexes, and recent works that supplement it, we may now examine the volume at hand. This consists, as stated before, of the listing, but not the bibliography, of 37,000 married couples of seventeenth-century New England. From the works discussed above and a few other guides, however, many of the sources Torrey cites can be readily inferred or discovered. From a concise list of married residents, moreover, the early geographical distribution of any New England surname can be seen immediately, so that researchers now know where the families or forebears of pioneer ancestors are likely to have originated. And the listing and indexing of wives not only summarizes much post-1860 scholarship and suggests many in-law connections between immigrants; it also covers the hitherto difficult-of-access marital history of many seventeenth-century women "not further treated" in other sources. For these reasons, and given the sheer convenience of a typed book over a microfilmed manuscript, NEHGS and GPC have cooperated in producing this second listing-only, book edition of Clarence Almon Torrey's *New England Marriages Prior to 1700*.

For each of the 37,000 couples herein covered, the husband's full name (roughly alphabetical, with variant spellings grouped under the most common) is followed sometimes by a superscript to indicate generation (usually first or second), then by birth and death years, if known, in parenthesis. "(1654-)" indicates a birth in 1654 and an unknown death year; "(-1700)" indicates an unknown birth year and a death in 1700. "Ca" for "circa" means "about" and "ae 35 in 1674" indicates aged 35 in 1674, a fact recorded probably in a court deposition. After an ampersand, "&", the wife's full name is given, with any known birth or death years likewise in parenthesis. "1/wf" or "2/wf" indicates first or second wife, any surname in parenthesis is a maiden name (in general, if there are two surnames, one or both in parenthesis, the first is a maiden surname, the second that of a first husband; if there are three surnames, however the parenthesis are placed, the last two are those of previous husbands in chronological order), a blank line (within or outside parenthesis) indicates that the wife's maiden name is unknown, a surname in brackets is one not derived from a marriage record, "w Daniel" indicates "widow of Daniel", whose last name is given earlier, and "m/2" or "m/3", followed by a man's full name and often a year, indicates a second or third marriage. After the data on husband and wife is a semi-colon, then a date. If the date is exact — 25 Nov. 1674 — it is a marriage (or marriage intention) date; if it is a year only, preceded by *"b", it is the birth date of a first child, not the birthdate of either partner,* and the marriage can be assumed to have taken place a year or more earlier. Often these "first child" birthdates are approximate. Following this date is a list of residences, from marriage through usually the death of the husband, in chronological order. Question marks alongside any data indicate doubt, of course, "+" after a date means "following", "–" means "before", and stray kinships that might provide clues to origins are sometimes noted as well. Since marriages of men with the same name are also roughly chronological, and each marriage is listed separately, data on a man's second marriage (including residence only after it) often does not immediately follow the listing for his first.

Once a researcher has culled a list of ancestors — proved, probable, or likely — from this edition of *New England Marriages Prior to 1700*, and is looking, of course, for further information on them, he can first determine if the major genealogical library nearby has purchased the microfilm edition. Copies are now in at least one library in most states with significant New England-derived populations. He can also purchase any one or more reels of the microfilm from the New England Historic Genealogical Society, 101 Newbury Street, Boston, Massachusetts 02116. NEHGS will also, for a fee, photocopy pages from Torrey's original manuscript that contain the references he seeks. At present the Society can only send pages from *New England Marriages* — not from the sources it cites; and fees for such copies are determined by the number of couples for whom references are requested. By himself and in many local libraries, however, the researcher can find many of the sources Torrey combed. After checking the genealogical dictionaries by Savage, Pope, Austin, and Noyes, Libby and Davis, plus the entries in *Founders of Early American Families* and *AGBI*, one should next examine any printed genealogies covering New Englanders with either husband's or wife's surname, plus any definitive work on the family of an earlier or later spouse. Researchers can next peruse pertinent town histories and town genealogies (for *each* town in which the couple resided). Even the periodical literature and multi-family compendia can be usefully surveyed without prior references. For periodicals through 1953 check Jacobus' already cited *Index to Genealogical Periodicals;* for later articles check firstly the already-mentioned *Register, TAG*, and *Record* subject indexes by Jean Worden, and then try either the *Genealogical Periodical Annual Index*, which now covers, selectively, the years 1962-1969 and 1974-1989, or *Periodical Source Index, 1847-1985*, 8 vols. (1988, 1990), with eight annual supplements to date. Every-name indexes exist for volumes 1-34 of *The Mayflower Descendant*, volumes 1-105 (through 1969) of the *Essex Institute Historical Collections*, and volumes 1-50 of the *Register* (a multi-volume index of volumes 51-145 of the *Register* is now being prepared by editor Jane Fletcher Fiske, assisted by Margaret F. Costello and Mark Choquet). With several or many ancestors in mind one can finally examine in depth the 130 major multi-ancestor compendia discussed above. Sixty were immigrant-subject-indexed by Jacobus; the remainder should be combed individually. Almost everyone with more than a few colonial New England forebears will find a few, and perhaps many, of his ancestors treated in these 130 works. If a researcher uses all of these techniques he can himself identify probably two-thirds of the sources for his forebears that Torrey cites.

Lastly, this volume should also be used in conjunction with Melinde Lutz Sanborn's 1991 *Supplement* to it, also published by GPC, the first I hope of several such works that will either correct or add to the entries herein (a second volume is expected in 1994). This *Supplement* summarizes post-1960 data for approximately 700 couples and is abstracted mostly from periodicals but also from some printed source records, unpublished primary data, and the private research of several genealogists (especially Andrew B.W. MacEwen, David Curtis Dearborn, George Freeman Sanborn Jr., and Robert Charles Anderson). Each new reference is cited, and the index covers wives and their other husbands.

IV

Clarence Almon Torrey's *New England Marriages Prior to 1700* is *the* seminal compendium on seventeenth-century New Englanders. Superseding, despite its form, Savage's *Genealogical Dictionary*, summarizing 100 years of scholarship, listing probably 99% of the married population of the eight decades it covers, Torrey's opus also leads us, with or without its magnificent bibliography, to much of the best modern work in American genealogy as a whole. For any seventeenth-century research — on immigrant origins, the first several generations here, or New England migrations south — and for much eighteenth-century delving as well, the volume in hand is indispensable. Long-time users of Torrey's manuscript at NEHGS and readers of the microfilm elsewhere cannot imagine high-quality results without continual reference to this work. Neither, too, I predict, will genealogists who consult this long-needed edition in book form.

Gary Boyd Roberts

New England Marriages

Prior to 1700

NEW ENGLAND MARRIAGES PRIOR TO 1700

ABBE, John[1] & 1/wf Mary __?__ (-1672); ?ca 1635; Salem/Wenham

ABBE, John[2] & 1/wf __?__ ; b 1665; Wenham

ABBIE, John[1] & 2/wf Marah/Mary (?PERKINS) GOLDSMITH, w Richard; 25 Nov 1674; Wenham

ABBEY, John[2] (-1700) & 2/wf Hannah [KILLAM?] GOLDSMITH?, wid, m/3 Jonathan JENNINGS; b 1683?; Wenham/Windham, CT

ABBY, Joseph (1673-1706/7) & 1/wf __?__ ; ?b 1700; Wenham

ABBE, Obadiah & Sarah (TIBBALLS) (COLLINS) [WARRINER], w Daniel, w Joseph; aft 21 Aug 1697, no issue; Enfield, CT

ABBY, Samuel (ca 1648-1698) & Mary KNOWLTON (1654-), m/2 Abraham MITCHELL 1699; 12 Oct 1672; Wenham/Salem/Windham, CT

ABBY, Thomas (-1728) & Sarah (FAIRFIELD) [NEEDHAM], wid; 17 Dec 1683/16 Dec 1683; Marblehead, Wenham

ABBOTT, Arthur & __?__ ; b 1638?; Marblehead, Ipswich

ABBOTT, Arthur (1639-) (ae 35 in 1674) & Elizabeth WHITE (1648-1738); 26 Apr 1669; Ipswich

ABBOTT, Benjamin (1661-1703) & Sarah FARNAM/FARNHAM (1661-); 22 Apr 1685; Andover

ABBOTT, Daniel (-1647) & Mary __?__ (-1643); by 1634; Cambridge/Providence

ABBOTT, Daniel (-1709) & Margaret (WHITE) (CALDWELL) WALLING (-1717+), div w of Robert, w Thomas; 25 Dec 1678; Providence

ABBOTT, Daniel (1654-) & Hannah [BROOKS]; b 1694; New Haven/Branford, CT

ABBOTT, Daniel (1672-) & __?__ ; b 1701?; Norwalk, CT

ABBOTT, George (-1647) (wid Jane BROCKLEBANK his sister-in-law) & __?__ ; in Eng by 1630; Rowley

ABBOTT, George (1617-1681) (ae 50 in 1662, 54 in 1669, 40 in 1656) (see George of Rowley) & Hannah CHANDLER (-1711, ae 82), m/2 Francis DANE ca 1690; 12 Dec 1646; Roxbury

ABBOTT, George & 1/wf Mary [WEED] (ca 1639-1672+); ca 1657/8; Windsor, CT/Wethersfield, CT/Norwalk, CT

ABBOTT, George (?1632-1689) (ae 30 in 1661, 26 in 1656) & Sarah FARNUM/FARNHAM, m/2 Henry INGALLS 1689; 26 Apr 1658; Andover

ABBOTT, George & 2/wf Joanna (LINN) [WILLIAMS] (-1682), w William; aft 1676; Norwalk, CT

ABBOTT, George (1655-1736) & Dorcas GRAVES (-1740); 17 Apr 1678; Andover

ABBOTT, George & 1/wf Elizabeth BALLARD (-1706); 13 Sept 1689; Andover

ABBOTT, George (?1669-1731) & Hannah [?HAYES]; ca 1690/97?; Norwalk

ABBOTT, John (-1721) & Sarah BARKER (-1729); 17 Nov 1673; Andover

ABBOTT, John & 1/wf __?__ ; b 1676; Portsmouth, NH

ABBOTT, John & Mercy __?__ , m/2 Edmund CHAMBERLAIN ?1690 or 1691; b 1684; Woburn

ABBOTT, John (1659-) & 1/wf Ruth [RUSCOE]; ca 1684/91?; Norwalk, CT

ABBOTT, John & 1/wf Abigail NASON; 3 Jan 1694, 1694/5, York Co., ME; Kittery, ME/Biddeford, ME/Saco, ME

ABBOTT, John & Christian __?__ ; b 9 Oct 1694; Manchester

ABBOTT, John & Jemima [?JOHNSON] (?GRAY), m/2 John BEEKS; b 1699; Sudbury/Watertown

ABBOTT, John (1676-) & 1/wf __?__ [WEBBER?]; ca 1700; Portsmouth, NH

ABBOTT, Jonathan & Sarah OLMSTEAD; 5 June 1696; Norwalk, CT

ABBOTT, Joseph (1666?-) & Alice [NASON]; b 1693; Kittery, ME

ABBOTT, Joseph (1652-) & [?Anna SANFORD?] (1675-1721+); b 1700; East Haven, CT

ABBOTT, Joseph & Sarah [DEVEREUX]; b 1701; Marblehead

ABBOTT, Josiah & Hannah [FARRINGTON]; b 1687; Boston

ABBOTT, Nathaniel (-1749) & Dorcas HIBBERT (-1743); 22 Oct 1695; Andover

ABBOTT, Nehemiah (-1707) & Mary HOW; 14 Dec 1659; Ipswich

ABBOTT, Nehemiah (-1736) & Remember FISKE (-1703); 21 Jan [1689/90?], 1685?; Ipswich

ABBOTT, Nehemiah & Abigail **LOVEJOY**; 9 Apr 1691; Andover

ABBOTT, Peter (-1667) & Elizabeth [**EVARTS**] (killed by her husband); b 1658; Branford, CT/Fairfield, CT

ABBOTT, Peter & _?_ ; b 1675; Saco, ME

ABBOTT, Philip (1672-) & Mary _?_ (-1730); b 1694; Ipswich

ABBOTT, Richard & 1/wf Elizabeth _?_ ; b 1676; Kittery, ME

ABBOTT, Richard & 2/wf Mary **GRAFTON** [**GRAFFAM**], w Stephen; Kittery, ME

ABBOTT, Robert[1] (-1658) & Mary _?_, m/2 John **ROBBINS** 1659; b 1636?; Watertown/Wethersfield/Branford, CT

ABBOTT, Thomas (-1659) & Dorothy **SWAN** (?1636-1710), m/2 Edward **CHAPMAN**, m/3 Archelaus **WOODMAN** 1678; 13 July 1655; Rowley

ABBOTT, Thomas (?1643-1713) & Elizabeth [**GREEN**]; b 1664; Kittery, ME/Berwick, ME

ABBOTT, Thomas (-1695) & Sarah **STEWARD/STEWART** (-1716, ae 69); 15 Dec 1664; Andover

ABBOTT, Thomas & Hannah **GREY/GRAY**; 7 Dec 1697; Andover

ABBOTT, Timothy (-1730) & Hannah **GROVES** (-1726); 27 Dec 1689; Andover

ABBOTT, Walter (-1667) & Sarah _?_ (1617-) (ae 64 in 1681), m/2 Henry **SHERBURN** ca 1675?; b 1639; Exeter, NH/Portsmouth, NH

ABBOTT, Walter?, Jr.

ABBOTT, Walter & Elizabeth **KEY**; 3 Jan 1694, York Co., ME; Kittery, ME

ABBOTT, William (1657-1713) & Elizabeth **GEERY/GARY** (1661-1712); 19 June 1682; Andover

ABBOTT, _?_ & Bethiah **MOTT** (1664)

ABBOTT, _?_ & Lidia **WING** (1647), m _?_ **MOTH**?

ABDA, Matthew (1620-) (ae 40 June 1669) & 1/wf Tabitha [**REYNOLDS**] (-1661); b 1648; Boston/Cambridge

ABDY, Matthew (?1620-) & 2/wf Alice **COX**; 24 May 1662; Boston

ABDY, Matthew (1654-1730) & Deborah (**STIMPSON**) **WILSON**, w Robert; 10 Apr 1688; Cambridge

ABELL, Benjamim (-1699) & Hannah [?**BALDWIN**], m/2 David **CAULKINS**; b 1683; Norwich, CT

ABELL, Caleb (ca 1647-1731) & 1/wf Margaret **POST** (1653-1700); July 1669; Norwich, CT

ABELL, Joshua (-1725) & 1/wf [Mehitable] **SMITH** (1655-1685); 1 Nov 1677; Norwich, CT

ABELL, Joshua & 2/wf Bethiah **GAGER** (1657-1723); - Nov 1685; Norwich, CT

ABELL, Preserved (1644-1724) & 1/wf Martha **REDAWAY/REDWAY** (1648-1686); 27 Sept 1667, 27 Nov; Rehoboth

ABELL, Preserved (1644-1724) & 2/wf Sarah **BOWEN** (1656-1703); 27 Dec 1686; Rehoboth

ABELL, Robert[1] (-Jun 1663) & Joanna _?_ (-1682+), m/2 William **HYDE** of Norwich, CT, 1667; b 1639; Weymouth/Rehoboth

ABELL, Samuel & Elizabeth **SLUMAN**; 3 Nov 1696; Rehoboth

ABERNETHY, William (-1718) & 1/wf Sarah **DOOLITTLE**; 17 Feb 1673, [1672/3]; Wallingford, CT

ABERNETHY, William (1675-) & Mary [**PECK**] (1677-); b 1700; Wallingford, CT

ABOURN, George (-1654) & Susanna _?_ ; Hampton, NH

EBBORNE, Moses (1645/6-1735/6) (ae 21 in 1666/7) & 1/wf Sarah **HAINES** (-1676); 9 Sept 1671; Salem/Marblehead/Lynn

ABOURNE, Moses (ca 1646-1735/6) & 2/wf Abigail [**GILBERT**] (d aft 8 May 1735); b 1680; Lynn

ABORNE, Samuel (1619/20-) (ae 52 in 1666, 80 in 1707) & Catherine [**SMITH**]; b 1639; Salem/Lynn

EBBORNE, Samuel (1639-1721) (ae 78 in 1717) & Susanna **TRASK** (1638-); 19 Feb 1663/4; Salem

EBURNE, Rev. Samuel & _?_ ; b 1685, aft 1681; Brookhaven, LI

ABORN, Thomas (-1642) & (Did he marry?); Salem

ABORNE, William (1666-) & Sarah _?_ ; b 1701; Salem

EBURNE, _?_ & Elizabeth (**LEWIS**) **PHILLIPS** (1669-), w Israel; ?Portsmouth, NH

AKERLY, Henry (-1658) & Ann _?_ (ae 75 in 1662); Wethersfield, CT

AKERLY, Robert & _?_ ; b 1640; Southold, LI/Brookhaven

AKERLY, _?_ & Hannah **BENTON** (1640)

AKERLY, Samuel & _?_ ; by 1655/60?; Brookhaven, LI

ACKERMAN, Stephen & 1/wf Sarah (**MORSE**) **STICKNEY** (-1711), w Amos; 17 Dec 1684?; Newbury

ACKLEY, John (ca 1666-1736) & Rebecca SPENCER (1666/7-); 23 May 1699; Hartford/Haddam, CT

ACKLEY, Nicholas (-1695) & 2/wf Hannah/?Miriam __?__ (was widow); ca 1656; Hartford/Haddam, CT

ACKLEY, Samuel (-1745) & Bethia __?__ ; ca 1700?, b 1703; Haddam, CT

ACKLEY, Thomas (-1704) & Hannah __?__ , m/2 Benjamin TROWBRIDGE 1705; ca 1695; East Haddam, CT

ACRES, Henry & Hannah SILVER (1655-); 13 Mar 1673/4; Newbury

AKORS, John & Desiretruth (Desire ye Truth) [THORNE]; b 1664?, b 1666;. Boston/Roxbury/Dunstable

ACRES/AKAS, John & Margery __?__ ; b 1665; New Shoreham, RI

AKERS, Thomas (-1650, 1651?) & Priscilla __?__ , m/2 William KNAPP 1654; b 1643; Charlestown

ACKERS, Thomas & Lydia WHITTELL, m/2 William WEST; 26 Dec 1699; Salem

ACY, John (-1690) & Hannah GREEN (-1718), m/2 John SHEPARD by 1698; 5 June 1678, 1676; Hampton, NH

ACY, William (1596-1690) & Margaret HAITON (-1675); 25 Mar 1620, 25 Jan 1620, 1620/21/1; Rowley

ADAMS, Abraham (1642-1700) & 1/wf Sarah [MACWORTH]; by 1665; Falmouth, ME/Boston

ADAMS, Abraham (?1639-1714) & Mary PETTINGILL (-1705); 16 Nov 1670; Newbury

ADAMS, Abraham (1650-1729) & 1/wf [?Sarah LOCKWOOD] ([1651/2]-); ca 1677; Fairfield, CT

ADAMS, Abraham (1642-1700) & 2/wf Abigail [WILMOT] (1657-), m/2 Joseph LORD 1700; b 27 Sept 1684, b 1680; Boston, etc.

ADAMS, Alexander (1614-1678) & Mary [COFFIN] (?1620-); b 1646; Boston/Dorchester

ADAMS, Archelaus & 1/wf Sarah (COKER) MARCH, w Hugh; 18 March 1697/8; Newbury

ADAMS, Benjamin (?1649-) & Elizabeth [DICKINSON] (1668-); ca 1690/1; Wethersfield, CT

ADAMS, Charles (-1695) & Rebecca [SMITH]; ca 1660; ?Oyster River, NH/Dover, NH

ADAMS, Charles (?1668-1695) & Temperance [BENMORE]; ca 1690?; Dover, NH

ADAMS, Christopher (-1687) & Margaret [HAMBURG] (-1722); ca 1655/62?; Braintree

ADAMS, Daniel (-1713) & Mary PHELPS (1658-); 20 Sep 1677; Windsor, CT

ADAMS, Daniel (-1750, ae 65) & 1/wf Sarah __?__ ; b 1664(5?); Boston

ADAMS, David (-1705) & 2/wf Hannah [?GANNETT]; b 1672; Boston

ADAMS, David (?1676) & Lois/Loues [COLLINS], m/3 William WATERS; 15 Dec 1698; Boston

ADAMS, Edward (-1671) & Mary __?__ , m/2 Anthony BEERS; b 1647; New Haven/Milford, CT

ADAMS, Edward (1629-1716) & 1/wf Lydia [PENNIMAN] ROCKWOOD? (prob wrong) (-1676); b 1653; Medfield

ADAMS, Edward (-1683) & Elizabeth BUCKLAND (1641-1683); 25 May 1660; Windsor, CT

ADAMS, Edward (1629-1716) & 2/wf Abigail (CRAFTS) (RUGGLES) DAY (1634-1707,1709?), w John, w Ralph; 7 Dec 1678; Dedham/Medfield

ADAMS, Edward & Elizabeth WALLEY; 19 May 1692; Bristol, RI

ADAMS, Eleazer (1644-1710 (1701 in Gen. wrong)) & Elizabeth HARDING (-1708); 20 Nov 1667; Medfield

ADAMS, Eliah (-1708) & 1/wf Priscilla [WINTHROP] (1669-), dau Deane; b 1702, b 1701?, b 1698; Boston

ADAMS, Eliashib/Elisha? (-1698) & Mehitable CARY (1670-), m/2 Myles STANDISH 1700; 18 Dec 1689; Bristol, RI

ADAMS, Ferdinando (returned to England) & Ann __?__ ; b 1638; Dedham

ADAMS, Freegrace (?1675) & Mary GALPIN; 8 Jan 1700, 1700/01?; Stratford,CT

ADAMS, George (-1696) & Frances __?__ ; b 1645; Watertown/Cambridge/Lexington

ADAMS, George & 1/wf __?__ ; b 1657; Branford, CT

ADAMS, George & 2/wf [?Mary] BRADFIELD, w Leslie or Lesly; 5 Sep 1657; Branford, CT

ADAMS, George & Martha FISKE (1666-); 28 Jan 1683, 20 Jan 1683/4; Cambridge/Lexington

ADAMS, Henry[1] (1583?-1646) & Edith SQUIRE (1587-1673), m/2 John FUSSELL b 1650?; in Eng, 19 Oct 1609; Braintree

ADAMS, Henry (1610-1676) & Elizabeth PAINE (1620-1676); 17 Oct 1643; Braintree

ADAMS, Henry & Mary PITTEY (1642-); 10 May 1660; Boston

ADAMS, Henry (1657-1733) & Prudence FRARY (1662-1750); 19 Dec 1679; Medfield

ADAMS, Henry & 1/wf Patience ELLIS (-1695); 10 Dec 1691; Medfield

ADAMS, Henry & Martha (TRISCOTT) HEWEN/HEWING (1661-), w Jacob; 10 Jan 1694; Boston

ADAMS, Henry (1663-) & 2/w Ruth [ELLIS]; ca 1698; Providence

ADAMS, Hugh/John? & Avis __?__ (-1699); b 1676; Ireland/Boston

ADAMS, Isaac (1673-1732) & Martha STOCKER; 4 Jan 1699; Boston

ADAMS, Jacob (1654-1717) & Anna ELLEN?/?Anne ALLEN? (1658-); 7 Apr 1677; Newbury/Suffield, CT

ADAMS, James (-1667) & Frances VASSALL (-1673+); 16 Jun 1646, 15 Jul 1646, 16 Jul 1646; Scituate/Marshfield

ADAMS, James & Priscilla RAMSDEN; 7 May 1662; Concord

ADAMS, James & Mary [ALLEN]; 3 Jan, 4 Jan 1689; Bristol, RI

ADAMS, James & Priscilla SHORE; 17 Feb 1690/1; Concord

ADAMS, James & Katharine/?Catharine FORD; 5 Jan 1696/7; Charlestown

ADAMS, James & Honor [HALL]; b 1698, ca 1697; Westerly, RI

ADAMS, Jeremiah (1664-1735) & __?__ ; ca 1685/92?; ?Huntington, LI/Great Egg Harbor, NJ

ADAMS, Jeremy (1606, ?1604-1683) & Rebecca (_?_) [GREENHILL] (-1678), w Samuel; ca 1636?; Braintree/Cambridge/Hartford

ADAMS, Jeremy (-1683) & 2/wf Rebecca (FLETCHER) [WARNER] (-1715), w Andrew; aft 26 Jan 1681; Hartford

ADAMS, John (-1633) & Eleanor/Ellen? [NEWTON]/?WORDEN (-1681, ae 83), m/2 Kenelm WINSLOW; ca 1623-4; Plymouth

ADAMS, John (1622-1706) & Ann __?__ (ca 1627-1714+); in Eng?, ca 1649; Cambridge

ADAMS, John & 1/wf Jane JAMES; 27 Dec 1654; Marshfield

ADAMS, John (?1638-1670) & Abigail SMITH, m/2 John BETTS 1673; ca 26 Aug 1657, ?1 Sep; Hartford

ADAMS, John (-1690+) & 2/wf Elizabeth __?__ (-1690+); ca 1663; Marshfield/Flushing, LI

ADAMS, John (?1631-) (ae 60 in 1692) & 1/wf Rebecca __?__ (-31 Dec 1666); ca 1665; Ipswich

ADAMS, John & Mary __?__ ; b 1666(7?); Boston

ADAMS, John (?1631-) & 2/w Sarah (WOODMAN) [BROCKLEBANK] (-1676), w John; [1667]; Ipswich

ADAMS, John (-1703) & 3/w Dorcas (WATSON) DWIGHT (-1707), w Timothy; 8 May 1677; Ipswich/Medfield

ADAMS, John & Abigail PINNEY; 6 Dec 1677; Windsor, CT/Simsbury, CT

ADAMS, John & Avis __?__ (-1699); in Scotland?, b 1673; Boston

ADAMS, John (1655-1733/36) & 1/wf Hannah BENT (1661-); 26 Feb 1680, 1680/1?; Sudbury

ADAMS, John & Sarah [BROWN] (1661-), m/2 Henry HARVEY 1700; b 1682; Salem

ADAMS, John (1652-1717+) & (Did he marry?)

ADAMS, John (1657-) & 1/wf Deborah PARTRIDGE, 4 Apr 1682; Medfield

ADAMS, John (1661-1702) & 1/wf Hannah [WEBB] (-1694); ca 1683-4, b 1683?; Bramton/Boston

ADAMS, John (-1724) & Michall BLOICE, 2 Apr 1685; Medfield

ADAMS, John (-1718) & Hannah TREADWELL (-1733); 22 May 1690; Ipswich

ADAMS, John & Elizabeth BARNES; 11 Oct 1692; Marblehead

ADAMS, John (-1742+) & 2/wf Hannah CHICKLEY (1674-), m/2 Samuel WINKLEY; 19 Oct 1693, 1694 in Boston records (wrong); Boston

ADAMS, John (1657-) & 2/wf Susanna [BRECK] (1667-); ca 1695; Medway

ADAMS, John & Esther FORD (1675-); 11 Nov 1696; Charlestown

ADAMS, John (1674-1735) & 1/wf Amy [DENNETT] (1679-); b 1699; Kittery, ME

ADAMS, Jonathan (?1614-1690) & 1/wf Joane CLOSE; Baltonsborough, Somersetshire, 7 Feb 1638/9; Medfield

ADAMS, Jonathan (?1614-1690) & 2/wf Elizabeth [HOLMAN] (1644-); b 1666; Medfield

ADAMS, Jonathan (-1707) & Rebecca [ANDREWS]; b 1672; Boston

ADAMS, Jonathan & 1/wf Mary ELLIS (-1717); 20 Mar 1677/8; Medfield

ADAMS, Jonathan (1646-1712) & Leah GOOLD/GOULD (1663-); 29 Aug 1681; Chelmsford

ADAMS, Jonathan (1668-1727) & Barbara __?__ ; ca 1692?; Huntington, LI/Great Egg Harbor, NJ

ADAMS, Jonathan & Tamerson SHOFELD/Thomasine/Thamasine/SCOFIELD (1673-); 1 Feb 1696/7; Dedham

ADAMS, Joseph[2] (1626-1694, ae 68) & Abigail BAXTER (1634-1692); 2 Nov 1650, 20 Nov, 26? Nov; Braintree

ADAMS, Joseph (-1737) & 1/wf Mary CHAPIN (1662-1687); 1682; Braintree

ADAMS, Joseph (?1664, ?1658/9-1701) & Margaret EAMES (1668-), m/2 Daniel DEAN 1705; 21 Feb 1687/8; Cambridge

ADAMS, Joseph[3] (1654-1737) & 2/wf Hannah [BASS] (1667-1705); ca 1688; Braintree

ADAMS, Joseph (1663-1737) & Elizabeth **HEWES** (-1729; 3 May 1694; Boston
ADAMS, Joseph (1672-1717) & Mary **JONES** (1677-); 26 Sep 1696?, 1695?; Concord/Chelmsford
ADAMS, Joseph & 2/wf Elizabeth **ANDREWS;** 12 Jun 1699; Marblehead
ADAMS, Moses (-1724) & 1/wf Mary **FAIRBANKS** (-1681); 14 May 1680; Medfield
ADAMS, Moses (-1729) & 2/wf Lydia **WHITNEY** (1657-1719); 15 Apr 1684; Sherborn
ADAMS, Nathan (-1749?, 1750) & 1/wf Mary [**JAMES**]; b 5 Dec 1687; Fairfield, CT
ADAMS, Nathaniel (?1601±-1675) & Sarah __?__ (-1685); b 1638; Weymouth/Boston
ADAMS, Nathaniel (-1690) & [Mary] **PURMOTT/PORMOTT** (Elizabeth in m rec wrong); 24 Nov 1652; Boston
ADAMS, Nathaniel (-1693+) & Mercy **DICKINSON;** 30 Jun 1688; Ipswich
ADAMS, Nathaniel (1653-1710) & 1/wf Hannah [**WILMOT**] (1660-1699, ae 39); b 1681; Charlestown
ADAMS, Nathaniel & Abigail **KIMBALL;** - Jan 1693, 1693/4?; Ipswich
ADAMS, Nathaniel (-1692) & Margadelen [**HILTON**], m/2 Elias **WEARE** 1696, m/3 John **WEBBER;** b 1691; York, ME
ADAMS, Nathaniel (-1710) & 2/wf Anna **COOLIDGE** (1671±-1718), m/2 Benjamin **LAWRENCE** 1716; 1700; Charlestown
ADAMS, Peletiah (1646-1725) & Ruth **?PARKER** (1719); b 1673; Chelmsford
ADAMS, Peter (?1622, 1621-1690±) & Rachel [**?NEWCOMB**], ?dau Francis; ca 1650/2; Medfield
ADAMS, Peter & Experience **COOK** (1662-); 27 May 1680; Medfield
ADAMS, Peter & Mary **LONG;** 4 Jan 1682; Dorchester
ADAMS, Peter & Mary **WEBB;** 12 Feb 1694/5, 17 Jan 1694/5, 13 Feb 1694/5; Braintree
ADAMS, Philip & Elizabeth [**TURPIN**]; b 1648; York, ME
ADAMS, Richard (1606-) (?Batcombe, Somerset) (Related to Thomas **BIBBLE** of Boston & Malden) & 1/wf Mary [**CHEAME**]? (1609-), wid; in Eng, b 1635?, b 1637; Weymouth/Malden/Salem
ADAMS, Richard & 2/wf Elizabeth __?__ (-1656); b 1651?; Malden
ADAMS, Richard & 3/wf Elizabeth __?__ ; aft Nov 1656; Malden
ADAMS, Richard & Mary [**PARNELL**]; b 1677 in Eng
ADAMS, Richard & Rebecca **DAVIS;** 24 Jun 1679; Sudbury/Norwich, CT
ADAMS, Richard & Martha (**TOMPKINS**) **FOSTER,** w John; m cont 16 Nov 1688; Salem
ADAMS, Robert (?1602-1682) & 1/wf Eleanor [**?WILMOT**] (-1677); b 1633; Ipswich/Newbury
ADAMS, Robert (-1682, ae 80) & 2/wf Sarah (**GLOVER**) **SHORT** (-1697), w Henry; 6 Feb 1677, 1677/8; Newbury
ADAMS, Robert (1674-) & Rebecca **KNIGHT;** m int 13 Jul 1695, ?m in Aug?; Newbury
ADAMS, Roger (-1714) & Mary [**BAKER**] (1653-1710); b 1675; Roxbury/Brookline
ADAMS, Samuel & __?__ ; b 1632; York, ME
ADAMS, Samuel (1616?, 1618?-1689) & 1/wf Mary [**EGLESFIELD**] (-1650); in Eng, b 1646; Charlestown
ADAMS, Samuel (1616?, 1618?-1689) & 2/wf Rebecca [**GRAVES**] (1631-1664, 1663?); 1650 or 1651; Charlestown/Chelmsford
ADAMS, Samuel & Mehitable **NORTON;** 20 Dec 1664; Ipswich
ADAMS, Samuel (1616?, 1618?-1689) & 3/wf Esther **SPARHAWK** (1636-1692); 7 May 1668; Chelmsford
ADAMS, Samuel (-1694) & Mary **MEEKER** m/2 Moses **LYON** 1694+, m/3 John **THORPE** 1698+; 15 Jul 167_, 1675?, 1677; Fairfield, CT
ADAMS, Samuel & Hannah, Mary? __?__ ; b 1678 (seems doubtful); Cambridge
ADAMS, Samuel (ca 1652-1727) & Mary __?__ (-1718), b 1681; Charlestown/Canterbury, CT
ADAMS, Samuel & Elizabeth [**HILL**]; b 1687; Simsbury
ADAMS, Samuel (-1694) & __?__ ; ca 1689?; Durham, NH
ADAMS, Samuel & Deborah (**BARTLETT**) **GILLET,** w Jeremiah; 23 Apr 1694; Windsor, CT
ADAMS, Samuel (-1729, ae 60) & Jane **ANDERSON;** 24 Oct 1694; Charlestown
ADAMS, Simon (?1654-1723) (ae 35 in 1692) ("cousin of Simon **STACY,** Ipswich (?nephew)) & Hannah __?__ ; ca 1689?; Ipswich
ADAMS, Thomas (1612-1688?, 1690) (cousin of Rev. Zachariah **SYMES or SYMMS**) (see below m in 1680) & Mary [**BLACKMORE?**] (1694/5, ae 82); b 1643; Braintree/Concord/Chelmsford
ADAMS, Thomas (-1697) & Alice **ROPER** (-1698); 2 Dec 1656; Charlestown
ADAMS, Thomas & Rebecca **POTTER;** 27 Nov 1667; New Haven
ADAMS, Thomas (-1726) & Hannah [**PARKER**]; b 1676; York, ME

ADAMS, Thomas (-1684, 1686?) & Mary **BLACKMORE**, w H. **BLACKMORE**?, m/3 J. **SMITH**, m/4 Thomas **WALKER**; 28 Apr 1680; Boston/Barbados

ADAMS, Thomas (-1698) & Margaret **WATTS**; 24 May 1686; Charlestown

ADAMS, Thomas (1672-1729) & Bethiah [**BLANCHARD**?]; b 1694; Ipswich

ADAMS, Timothy (1648-1708) & Mary __?__; b 1675; Chelmsford

ADAMS, Timothy & Dorothy **CHAMBERLAIN**; 11 Aug 1699; Chelmsford

ADAMS, Walter & 1/wf Hannah **MOULTON** (1641-); 15 Dec 1657; Charlestown/Malden

ADAMS, Walter & Mary (**BRADEN**) [**OAKMAN**] (1634-), w Samuel d 1676; by 1687; Charlestown

ADAMS, William (-1661) & __?__; ca 1620/4; Cambridge/Ipswich

ADAMS, William (1620-1659) & Elizabeth [**STACY**] (1655); ca 1647/49?; Ipswich

ADAMS, William (-1655) & Elizabeth [**HICKOK**] (-1655), wid __?__ ?**HEACOCK**; b 1649; Hartford/Farmington, CT

ADAMS, William & Elizabeth __?__; b 1674; Sudbury/Concord

ADAMS, William (1650-1685) & 1/wf Mary **MANNING** (-1679); 15 Oct 1674, 21? Oct; Dedham

ADAMS, William (1650-1685) & 2/wf Alice **BRADFORD** (1661?, ?1662-1741), m/2 James **FITCH** 1689; 29 Mar 1680; Dedham

ADAMS, William & Susanna __?__; b 1686; Weymouth

ADAMS, William & Sarah **NOSTOCK**; 10 Dec 1691; Boston

ADAMS, William (1673-1742) & Abigail [**OVIATT**] (1674-); b 1699; Milford, CT

ADAMS, [Joseph?] & Mary **HOWARD** (1673-) Chelmsford; Charlestown

ADAMS, __?__ & Sarah [**RICE**] (1662-)

ADDINGTON, Isaac (-1652) & Anne [**LEVERETT**] (1619-); 1642/44, b 1645; Boston

ADDINGTON, Isaac (1645-1715) & 1/wf Elizabeth [**BOWEN**] (1646-1712/13); on or bef 7 Apr 1669; Boston

ADDIS/ADDES, William & __?__; in Eng, b 1626; Gloucester/New London, CT

ADEWITTE, Bryan & Rachel __?__; b 1692; Salem/Bristol, RI

ADGATE, Thomas (1620?, 1621-1707) & 1/wf __?__; b 1651; Saybrook, CT/Norwich, CT

ADGATE, Thomas (1620?, 1621-1707) & 2/wf Mary (**MARVIN**) [**BUSHNELL**] (1628-1713), w Richard; ca 1660; Saybrook, CT/Norwich, CT

ADGATE, Thomas (1670-1760) & 1/wf Ruth **BREWSTER** (1671-1734); 15 Jun 1692; Norwich, CT

ADJETT/ATCHET/ADJET, John (-1712+) Hartford, Block Island & Sarah [**HOWARD**]/HAYWARD (1653-); b 1688; Wethersfield, CT

ADKINS, Josiah (-1690) & 1/wf Elizabeth [**ANDREWS**?], dau Edward; b 1669?; Middletown, CT (calls Nathaniel **STOWE** "brother")

ADKINS, Josiah (-1690) & Elizabeth **WETHMER/WHITMORE** (-1700); 8 Oct 1673; Middletown, CT

ADKINS, Josiah (-1724) & Mary [**WHEELER**], m/2 [John?] **STEDMAN**; b 1701?, 16 Dec 1708; Middletown, CT

ADKINS, Thomas (-1694) & 1/wf Elizabeth __?__/**ANDREWS** d 1693; b 1672?; Hartford

ADKINS, Thomas & Mary (__?__) **HILLS**, w John

ADKINS, William & __?__; b 1650?; Hartford

ADLINGTON/?ADDINGTON, James & Elizabeth __?__; b 1684; Boston

ADONIS, James & __?__; b 1696; Bristol, RI

ADVARD/ADVERD/ADFORD, Henry (-1653) & Thomasine **MAUSON/MANSON**; 6 Oct 1643; Scituate/Rehoboth

AGER/AGUR, Benjamin[2] (1636-1671) & Ann [**CROMWELL**], m/2 David **PHIPPEN** 1672; b 1671; Salem

AGER, Benjamin[3] (-1690/1) & Ann [**PHIPPEN**]; b 1689; Salem

AUGER/ANGER, John & Hannah __?__; b 1652; Boston

AGARD, John & Esther __?__, m/2 Samuel **STOWS** 1695; b 1683, b 1687; Boston

AGER, Jonathan (1639-1716+) (ae 65 in 1704, ae 73 in 1713) & Rebecca **HIDE** (1644-); 27 Jun 1661; Salem

AGER/EAGER, Richard (1668±-1719) & Abigail [**NASH**] (1673-); b 1698; Weymouth

AUGUR, Robert & 1/wf Mary **GILBERT** (1651-); 20 Nov 1673, ?21 Nov; New Haven

AUGER, Thomas & Elizabeth **PACKER**; 14 Nov 1665; Dover

AUGUR, Thomas & __?__; b 1665(6?); New Haven

AGER, William (-1654) & Alice __?__ (-1654+), m/2 Henry **TOTINGHAM** 1654; b 1636; Salem

AUGUR, William & Ruth **HILL** (1640-); 7 Dec 1659; Malden

AGER, __?__ & Martha __?__; b 1685; Gloucester

AGNEW, Nivan & _?_ BARROW/BARRY, w James; b 1676; Berwick, ME
AIKEN, John (1663-1740) & Mary [BRIGGS] (1671-); b 1689; Dartmouth
AIKEN, _?_ & Mary _?_; b 1663; Newport
AINSWORTH, Daniel (-1680) & Alice _?_ (-1685); b 1647; Roxbury/Dedham
AINSWORTH, Edward (-1741) & Joanna HEMENWAY (1670-1748); 11 Jan 1687, 1687/8; Roxbury/Woodstock, CT
ALBEE/ALBIE, Benjamin[1] & Hannah _?_; b 1641; Braintree/Medfield
ALBE, Benjamin[3] & Abial _?_; b 1694; Mendon
ALBIE, James[2] (-1717+) & Hannah COOKE; 18 Oct 1671; Medfield/Mendon
ALBIE, John (-1675) & Jane HOLBROOKE; 18 Oct 1671; Medfield/Mendon/Rehoboth
ALBERRY, Joseph & Mary _?_; b 1687; Boston
ALBERTSON, Derrick & Dinah [COLES] (-1739+); b 12 Sep 1693; Oyster Bay, LI
ALBERTSON, Garret/Garrett & Abigail _?_; Oyster Bay, LI
ALBERSON, John & Elizabeth TOLLAND; 16 Mar 1696/7; Yarmouth
ALBESON/ALBERSON?, Nicholis & _?_; Scituate
ALBERTSON, William & Mary [WILLMAN]; ca 1670/2?; Oyster Bay, LI
ALBARDSON, William & Esther WILLIS; 9 Oct 1695; Westbury, LI
ALBERTSON, William (-1732) & Barbara [SIMKINS] (-1754); b 1701?; Musketa Cove, LI
ALBERTUS, Arthur (-1692) & Elizabeth [?BURROUGHS]; 1669/72?; Hempstead, LI
ALBERTUS, John (1643-1691) & Elizabeth SCUDDER/_?_ [?SCUDDER], m/2 William LAWRENCE; b 1669?; Newtown, LI
ALBERTUS, John[3] (-1709) & Sarah GRAVES
ALBERTUS, Pietro Cesare & _?_
ALBRO, John (1617-1712) & Dorothy [POTTER] (1617-1696), w Nathaniel; b 1644; Portsmouth, RI
ALBROUGH, John & Mary STOKES; 27 Apr 1693; Portsmouth, RI
ALBRO, Samuel (1644-1789) & Isabel [LAWTON] (-1730); ca 1670?; Portsmouth/North Kingston, RI
ALCOCK, George (?1604-1640) & 1/wf [?Anne] HOOKER (-?Aug 1629?, 1630 or 1631); in Eng, b 1625; Roxbury/Charlestown
ALCOCK, George (-1640) & 2/wf Elizabeth _?_ (-Apr 1641), m/2 Henry DEENGRINE/DINGHAM/DENGAYNE 1641; ca 1632?; Roxbury
ALCOCK, Job (1638-1716) & Dorothy [REYNER]; ca 1660/5?, no issue; York, ME
ALCOCK, John (-ca 1675) & Elizabeth _?_; b 1632?; York, ME
ALCOCK, John (1627-1667) & Sarah [PALSGRAVE] (ca 1621-1665, ae 44) (dau Joanna m Ephraim HUNT, dau Elizabeth m/1 Timothy DWIGHT, m/2 Joseph GALLOP 1694); 1648?, ca 1645/8; Charlestown/Roxbury
ALCOCK/ALCOTT, John (1651-1690) (son Thomas) & Constance [MYLAM]/MILAM?; b 29 Nov 1677; Boston
ALCOCK, John (1659-1693) & Joanna [AMEREDITH]; ca 1682?; Kittery, ME
ALCOTT/ALCOCK, John & Susanna HEATON, 8 May 1698; ?New Haven
ALCOCK, Joseph (-1678) & Abigail [LEVER?]/PAUL?, m/2 Robert ROWSLEY ca 1680; b 1657?; Kittery/York, ME
ALCOCK, Palsgrave (1662-1710) & Esther [BRIGHTMAN], ?m/2 John CHANDLER 1711; ?, no issue; Roxbury
ALCOCK/ALIACK, Samuel (1637-1677, 1676) & Sarah (STEDMAN) BRACKETT (1644-1730), w John, m/3 Thomas GRAVES 1682, m/4 Hon. John PHILLIPS 1701; 24 Mar 1667/8; Cambridge
ALCOCK, Samuel (1665-1708) & Elizabeth [CHADBOURNE]/WELLS? (1667-); ca 1690/5; Portsmouth, NH
ALCOCK, Thomas see ALCOTT
ALCOTT/ALCOCK?, John & Susanna HEATON, 8 May 1698; New Haven
ALCOTT/ALCOCK?, Philip (ca 1648-1715) & 1/wf Elizabeth MITCHELL (1751-); 5 Dec 1672; New Haven
ALCOTT, Philip (ca 1648-1715) & 2/wf Sarah (_?_) BUTLER, w Nathaniel; 4 Apr 1699; Wethersfield, CT
ALCOTT/ALCOCK, Thomas (-1657) & Margery _?_ (-1638), m/2 John BENHAM 1660, 1659?, m/3 Richard PRITCHARD 1667; b 1635; Boston/Dedham
ALDEN, David[2] (1646-1719?) & Mary [SOUTHWORTH] (-1718+); ca 1670?; Duxbury
ALDEN, Henry (-1729?) & Deborah _?_; b 1694; Bellerica/Roxbury/Needham

ALDEN, Isaac[3] (-1727) & Mehitable ALLEN (1665-); 2 Dec 1685; Bridgewater

ALDEN, John_2 (?1599-1687) & Priscilla [MULLINS] (-1680+); b Jun 1621; Plymouth

ALDEN, John[2] (1626-1702) & Elizabeth (PHILLIPS) EVERILL (-1696), w Abiell; 1 Apr 1660, should be 1659; Boston

ALDEN, John (1663-1730) & 1/wf Elizabeth [?PHELPS] (-1719, ae 50); ca 1684, b 1687; Boston

ALDEN, Jonathan (?1632-1698) & Abigail HALLETT (1644-1725); 10 Dec 1672; Duxbury

ALDEN, Joseph (?1622-1697) & Mary [SIMMONS]; ca 1660; Bridgewater

ALDEN, Joseph (1667-1747) & Hannah [DUNHAM] (?1670-1748); prob 1690; Bridgewater

ALDEN, Nathaniel (-1702) & Hepzibah MOUNTJOY, m/2 Edward MORTIMER; 1 Oct 1691; Boston

ALDEN, William (1669-1728) & Mary DRURY (1672-1732+); 21 May 1690; Boston

ALDEN, Zachariah (1673-1709) & Mary [VIALL] (1676-); 13 Jan 1700; Duxbury

ALDERMAN, John (-1657) & Jane __?__ ; b 1636?; Salem

ALDERMAN, William (-1697) & Mary [CASE] (1660, 1666-1725), m/2 James HILLYER/HIL-LIARD 1699; b 1680, 1675?; Simsbury/Farmington, CT

ALDIS, Daniel (-1717) & Sarah PAYNE (1666-1711); 23 Nov 1685; Dedham

ALDIS, John (-1700) & Sarah ELLIOTT (1629-1686); 27 Sep 1650; Dedham

ALDIS, John (1655-) & Mary (_?_) WINCHESTER, w Jonathan; 28 May 1682; Wrentham/Rox-bury/Dedham

ALDIS, Nathan (1596-1676) & Mary __?__ (-1677); in Eng, ca 1624; Dedham

ALDRICH, Ephraim & Barbara __?__ ; b 1701?; Providence/Glouster, RI

ALDRIDGE, George[1] (-1683) & Catherine [SEOLD]? (no evidence); ?Derbyshire, 3 Sep 1629; Dorchester/Braintree/Mendon

ALDRIDGE, Henry (-1646) & Mary __?__, m/2 Samuel JUDSON 1646, m/3 John HAYWARD 1656; b 1643; Dedham

ALDRIDG, Jacob (1653-1695) & Huldah THARE/THAYER (1657-), m/2 Samuel WILKERSON of Providence 1697; 25 Jun 1675; Medfield

ALDRICH, Jacob[3] (1677-) & 1/wf Margery HAYWARD/HEYWARD?; 15 Sep 1699; Mendon

ALDRIDGE, John[2] (1644-) & 1/wf Sarah TOMPSON/THOMPSON (-1678); 9 Jun 1670; Mendon

ALDRIDGE, John (1644-) & 2/wf Sarah LEACH; 31 Oct 1678; Braintree

ALDRICH, John (-1735) & Martha EVANS (-1735+); 20 Mar 1698/9; Providence

ALDRIDGE, Joseph (1635-1701) (ae 32 in 1667) & Patience OSBORN (-1705+); 26 Feb 1661/2?, 1662; Braintree

ALDRICH, Joseph (1663-1705) & Mary __?__ (-1713+); ca 1685?, ca 1682?; Providence

ALDRICH, Peter & Mehitable SWAZEY (?Elizabeth [COOKE]? of Mendon, wrong); b 1686, b 12 Nov 1692, by 1673?; Southold, LI

ALDRICH, Samuel (-1747) & Jane [PUFFER?] (-1747+); b 1681?, b 1691?; Providence

ALDRICH, Seth (1679-1737 Uxbridge) & 1/wf Deborah HAYWARD (1682-); 3 Sep 1700; Mendon/Uxbridge

ALDRIDG, Thomas (1643-1694) & 1/wf Elizabeth PRENTICE (1650-1676); 4 May 1675; Dedham

ALDRIDGE, Thomas (1643-1694) & 2/wf Hannah COLBURN (1653-1728); 16 Jan 1677, 1677/8; Dedham

ALDRICH, __?__ & __?__, w; b 1638; Plymouth

ALEWELL, Thomas & __?__ ; b 1687; Lynn

ALEXANDER, David (-1704) & 1/wf Elizabeth (COPLEY/COOLEY?) (TURNER) [LANGTON], w Praisever, w Samuel; aft 11 Aug 1683; Deerfield

ALEXANDER, Francis & Sarah KIRK; 13 Mar 1699; Boston

ALEXANDER, George & Susanna [?SAGE] (-1684); 18 Mar 1644; Windsor, CT/Northampton/etc.

ALEXANDER, John[1] & __?__ (doubtful); Deerfield

ALEXANDER, John (-1696) & Beatrix/Beatrice __?__ ; b 1653; Cambridge/Newton

ALEXANDER, John (1645-1733) & Sarah GAYLORD (1652-1732); 29 Nov 1671, 28 Nov Northampton; Windsor, CT

ALEXANDER, Nathaniel (1652-1742) Northampton & Hannah ALLEN, Northampton; 19 Jun 1679?, 20? Jun 1679, 20 Jan 1680?, 1679?

ALFORD/ALVORD?, Benjamin (-1710, 1709? New London) & Mary [RICHARDS] (1663-); b 1683; Boston

ALFORD, Elisha & Bethiah __?__ ; b 9 Jul 1676; Salem

ALFORD, John & Charity [DIKE]; Salem

ALFORD, William (1603-1677) & 1/wf Mary __?__ ; b 1636; Salem

ALFORD, William (1603-1677, 1676?) & 2/wf Ann _?_; b 1658; Boston
ALFORD, _?_ & Mary _?_, m/2 John CRAWFORD 1692; Charlestown
ALFRED, Jonathan & Hannah BROWN; 28 Dec 1682; Westfield
ALGER, Andrew (?1610-1675) & [Agnes]/[Ann] _?_ (1621-); b 1641; Charlestown/Scarboro, ME/Weymouth
ALGER, Andrew (-1694) & _?_; b 1669; Cape Porpoise/Duxbury
ALGER, Andrew (-1689) & Jane ANDREWS, m/2 Robert DAVIS 1698; ca 1684; Falmouth, ME
ALGER, Arthur (1622/5-1675) & Ann [SHELDON]/ROBERTS (1634-1716) dau Giles?, m/2 Samuel WALKER 1676; no issue?; Scarboro, ME/Black Point, ME
ALGER, Israel & Patience [HAYWARD], dau Nathaniel, (Patience called "dau" of John WILDER Bridgewater, correction grand dau); b 1689; Bridgewater
ALGER, John & Mary [WILMOT] (1650-); b 1669; Charlestown/Scarboro, ME
AULGAR, John & Hannah [BAKER] (1644-); b 1679; Boston
AULGAR, John & Sarah [MYLAM] (-1697); b 1682; Boston
AULGAR, Matthew (-1690) & Martha [CARVER] (-1718, ae ca 62), wid; b 1680/1; Boston
ALGER, Roger & _?_
AUGER, Thomas, Taunton & Elizabeth PACKER/PACKARD, Bridgewater; 14 Nov 1665; Taunton/Boston
ALGER, Tristram & _?_; Scarboro, ME (wife in Eng)
ALKIN, Robert & Patience (FIRNOLD) [EVANS], w Ebenezer; 9 Nov 1686; Kittery, ME
ALIBON/ALLIBONE?, John (1653-1750) & Hannah _?_ (1656-1748); Southold, LI
ALLABEN, John & Tabitha? _?_; ca 1694?; Southold, LI
ALLAIRE, Lewise & Abigail _?_; b 1689; Boston
ALLARD, Hugh (1639?-) & Grace [TUCKER], w William; ca 1660/2?, aft Oct 1666; Isles of Shoals, ME
ALLARD, James & Oner/Honor? [WALLIS?]; ca 1682?; Isles of Shoals, ME
ALLARD, Mathurton & _?_; b 1681; Oxford
ALLEN, Abel (1669-1756) & 1/wf Sarah _?_ (-1786); b 1694; Watertown/Sudbury/Weston
ALLYN, Alexander (1659-1708) & 1/wf Mary GRANT (-1703); 21 Sep 1693; Windsor, CT
ALLYN, Andrew (-1690) & Faith [INGALLS] (?1623-); b 28 Aug 1648; Andover
ALLEN, Andrew (1657-1690) & Elizabeth RICHARDSON (1665-); 1 Jan 1681, 1681/2; Andover
ALLEN, Arnold & Mary _?_ (?sister of Richard TUCKER's wife); Casco Bay
ALLIEN, Benjamin (-1678) & Hannah BULLARD; 6 Mar 1668/9; Medfield/Lancaster
ALLIN, Benjamin & 1/wf Rachel (SQUIRE) WHEELER (-1694), w Henry; 3 Sep 1686; Salisbury
ALLEN, Benjamin (-1703/4) & Mary _?_ (-1704); b 1687; Salem
ALLEN, Benjamin (1662-1721) & Frances [RICE] (1671-1767); b 1690; Watertown/Weston
ALLEN, Benjamin (1652-1723) & Hopestill LEONARD; 18 Nov 169-, 1695; Rehoboth
ALLEN, Benjamin & Mary FAIRBANKS; 16 Apr 1696; Dedham
ALLEN, Benjamin (-1742) & Mercy TOWSLEY; 4 Oct 1699; Suffield, CT
ALLEN, Benoni & _?_; b 1660; Milford
ALLEN, Bozoan (-1652, Boston) & Ann _?_ (-1661), m/2 Joseph JEWETT 1653; b 1638; Hingham
ALLEN, Bozoan & 1/wf Rachel [HOUCHIN]; [1673?], b 1677; Boston
ALLEN, Bozoan & 2/wf Lydia [BALSTON], dau Jonathan; b 1679; Boston
ALLEN, Caleb (1648-) & Elizabeth SISSON; ?8 Apr 1680, ?28 Sep; Sandwich
ALLEN, Charles (?1627-) & 1/wf _?_; Portsmouth, NH/Greenland, NH
ALLEN, Charles & 2/wf Susanna HUGGINS (1640-); m cont 13 Feb 1666; Portsmouth, NH
ALLEN, Christopher (1664-1734) & Elizabeth [SEYANCHE/SEGOUCHE/LEGORGE/SEYMONE] (1668-) Little Compton, RI; b 1688, m bond 19 Jan 1687/[8], at Boston; N. Kings Town, RI
ALLEN, Daniel & Mary [WILDER]?/BABCOCK?/SHERMAN? (see Daniel ELLEN) (1642-), m/2 Lewis ALLEN; b 1659; Watertown
ALLEN, Daniel & Mary DEXTER; 12 Oct 1670; Swansea
ALLIN, Daniel (-1693) & Mary/Mariana [BENDALL], w _?_ RICHARDSON?, m/2 Samuel [LYNDE?] 1698; b 1680; Boston
ALLEN, Daniel (1663-) & [Bathena] [HOXIE]; ca 1685; Sandwich
ALLEN, Daniel & [Sarah] _?_; by 1690?
ALLEN, Daniel (1669-) & Hannah [BERRY]; [1699]; Greenland, NH
ALLEN, Ebenezer & Abigail [HILL]; b 1682; Dartmouth
ALLEN, Ebenezer & Lydia [HASTINGS] (1671-); ca 1690/6?; Cambridge
ALLEN, Ebenezer (-1730) & Rebecca RUSSELL; 14 Apr 1698; Barnstable/Bridgewater

ALLEN, Ebenezer (1674-) & Rebecca SCATE/SKEATH (1679-) Boston; 11 Oct 1698; Bridgewater
ALLEN, Ebenezer (?1677-1770) & 1/wf Elizabeth EDDY (-1712); 2 Apr 1700; Watertown
ALLEN, Edward & Martha WAYE/WAY; 7 May 1652; Boston
ALLEN, Edward (-1696) & Sarah KIMBALL (-1696); 24 Nov 1658; Ipswich/Suffield, CT
ALLEN, Edward (ca 1650-ca 1690) & Sarah __?__ (-ca 1720; b 1670, 1671; Boston/Berwick, ME
ALLEN, Edward & Lydia [LUDKIN]; b 1671, b 1669?; Boston
ALLEN, Edward (1663-1740) & Mercy PAINTER (1664±-); 14 Nov 1683; Suffield, CT/Deerfield
ALLYN, Edward (-1724) & 1/wf Rachel [STEELE]; b 1689(90?); Hartford
ALLEN, Edward (1671-) & Ann [COLEMAN] (1675-); b 1698; Nantucket
ALLIN, Eleazer & Hannah LEVERETT, m/2 Thomas DAVIS 1689; 14 Jun 1681? (1691 in record wrong); Boston
ALLEN, Elnathan (1666-1735) & Mercy/Mary [RICE] (1670-1727); b 1695; Watertown/Sudbury/Hopkinton/Shrewsbury, NJ?
ALLEN, Francis (-1697) & Mary BARLOW; 20 Jul 1662; Sandwich
ALLEN, Francis & Hannah [JENKINS]; b 1680; Kittery, ME
ALLEN, George[1] (-1648) & 1/wf __?__ ; in Eng, b 1619, b 1609?; Lynn/Sandwich
ALLEN, George[1] (-1648, ae 70) & 2/wf Catherine [STARKES?] (1605-), m/2 John COLLINS ca 1648; London, ?5 Nov 1624; Lynn/Sandwich
ALLEN, George[1] (-1653+) & Susan __?__ (-1653+); b 1644?, 1645?; Boston
ALLEN, George[2] & 1/wf Hannah __?__ ; b 1648, b 1646?; Sandwich
ALLEN, George[2] & 2/wf Sarah __?__ ; b 1657; Sandwich
ALLEN, George[3] (1672-) & Elizabeth HULETT/HEWLETT; 22 Feb 1694; Sandwich/Shrewsbury, NJ
ALLEN, Gideon (-1693?) & Sarah [PRUDDEN] (1650-); b 1671; Boston/Swansea/Milford, CT
ALLEN, Gideon & 1/wf Ann/Anna? BURR (-1748); 20 Jan 1696, 1695/6?; Fairfield, CT?
ALLEN, Gideon & Mary [WRIGHT] (1674?-); ca 1699; New Haven Co., CT
ALLEN, Henry (1620-1696, 1695?) (ae 47 in 1667) & 1/wf Anne [TEFFE], w William; aft 2 Nov 1648; Boston
ALLEN, Henry (-1690) & Sarah [HILL] (-1680), dau John of Guilford; b 1663; Milford, CT/Stratford, CT
ALLEN, Henry (1620-1696, 1695?) (ae 47 in 1667) & 2/wf Judith [BEERS] (1646-); b 1673, ?Milford, CT; Boston
ALLEN, Henry (-1690) & 2/wf Rebecca (__?__) ROSE, w Robert; 1685
ALLEN, Henry (1674-) & [Mercy TIBBALS] (1671-); b 1700; Milford, CT
ALLEN, Henry & Mary [UDALL]; b 1701; Hempstead, LI
ALLEN, Hope (-1677) & 1/wf Rachel __?__ (-ca 1667); b 1653; Boston
ALLEN, Hope (-1677) & 2/wf Mary __?__ (-1670); b 1670; Boston
ALLEN, Hope (-1677) & 3/wf Hannah (TOWNSEND) [HALLS] (1641-1721+), w Thomas, m/3 Richard KNIGHT 1679?, m/4 Richard WAY 1689; b 1672; Boston
ALLEN, Increase (-1724) & Rachel __?__ (1658-1731); b 1682; Dartmouth
ALLEN, Isaac & Mary BOWEN; 30 May 1673; Rehoboth
ALLEN, Isaac & Catherine [BALCOM], m/2 Daniel JENKS bef 1692?; b 1683; Rehoboth
ALLEN, Jacob (1654-) & 1/wf Elizabeth [CLIFFORD]; b 1676; Salem/Lynn/LI
ALLEN, James[1] (-1676) & Ann GUILD (-1673); 16 Mar 1637/8; Dedham
ALLEN, James (1636-1714) & Elizabeth [PARTRIDGE] (not PERKINS) (1644-1722); b 1663; Braintree/Sandwich/Chilmark
ALLEN, James & 1/wf Hannah DUMMER (-1668); 18 Aug 1663; Boston
ALLEN, James & 2/wf Elizabeth (HOUCHIN) ENDICOTT (-1673), w John; 31 Aug 1668; Boston
ALLEN, James & 3/wf Sarah (HAWKINS) BRICK, w Robert; 11 Sep 1673; Boston
ALLEN, James (-1691) & Lydia ADAMS, m/2 Joseph DANIELS 1697?; 12 Dec 1673; Medfield
ALLEN, James & Dorothy [BARSHAM] (1674-); b 1701?; Portsmouth, NH
ALLEN, James (1674-1724) & Mary [BOURNE] (1678-); b 1701?; Martha's Vineyard
ALLEN, Jedediah (1646-1712) & Elizabeth [HOWLAND] (-1733+); ca 1668; Sandwich/Shrewsbury, NJ
ALLEN, Jeremiah/Jeremy (1658-) & Ann [BRADBURY] (1666-1733); bet 1686 & 1689; Salisbury/Wells, ME
ALLEN, Jeremiah & Mary CABALL/CABLE; 25 Jun 1695; Boston

ALLIN, John (1597-1671) & 1/wf Margaret [MORSE] (-1653); Wrentham, Eng, 10 Oct 1622, 22 Oct?; Dedham

ALLEN, John & Elizabeth [GREENWAY]

ALLEN, John (1605-) & Ann __?__ (1605-); in Eng, b 1635; Plymouth

ALLEN, John (1609/10-1690) & Christian __?__ (-1690+); ca 1735?; Swamsea

ALLEN, John (1615-1675) & 1/wf Sarah __?__ (-1643+); b 1640; Charlestown

ALLEN, John (1615-1675) & 2/wf Mary __?__ ; aft 1644; Charlestown

ALLEN, John (-1662, 1663?) & Ann [JAMES]?, wid?, m/2 Capt. Michael PIERCE; b 1649; Scituate

ALLEN, John (-1708) & Elizabeth [BULL] BACON; 14 Oct 1650, 10? Oct, 10 Oct 1650; Newport/Kings Town, RI

ALLYN, John (1630-1696, Hartford) & 1/wf Hannah/Ann? SMITH; 19 Nov 1651; Springfield/Hartford

ALLIN, Rev. John (1597, ?1596-1671) & 2/wf Katharine (DIGHTON) (HAGBOURNE) DUDLEY (-1671), w Samuel, w Thomas; 8 Nov 1653; Dedham/Cambridge

ALLEN, John & Sarah __?__ (-1701/2); b 1656; Newbury/Sudbury

ALLEN, John (1615-1675) & 3/wf Sarah __?__ (-1675); b 1657?; Charlestown

ALLEN, John (1642-1709) & 1/wf Elizabeth/Mary GAGER (1649-); 24 Dec 1668; New London, CT

ALLEN, John (-1675) & Mary HANNUM; 8 Dec 1669, 16? Dec; Northampton

ALLEN, John (1641-) & __?__ (-29 Aug 1671); Hingham

ALLEN, John & Bethiah [PENNIMAN] (?1643-); b 1673, no issue; Swansea

ALLYN, John (1646-) & Mary [HOWLAND] (-1703+); b 1674, b 1671?; Barnstable

ALLIN, John (-1697) & Mary (PIKE) ANDROS/ANDREWS? (-1695), w Jedidiah; 24 Aug 1674, ca 30 Aug; Salisbury

ALLEN, John (-1678, 1679, Malden) & Mercy (CALL) LEE, w Samuel; 25 Aug 1677?; Charlestown

ALLEN, John & Hannah [MOSS]; ca 1678/80, 4 ch bapt 1685; Marblehead

ALLEYN, John & Mary (GENT/JENT) MASON, w John; ?ca 1680; Sherbscot, ME

ALLEN, John (?1659-1704) & Elizabeth PRICHARD (?1654-1704); 22 Feb 1681, 1681/2; Suffield, CT/Deerfield

ALLEN, John & Elizabeth __?__ ; b 1686; Boston

ALLEN, John & Mercy PETERS; 22 May 1686; Andover

ALLEN, John (1666-) & 1/wf Elizabeth __?__ ; b 1690; Manchester

ALLYN, John (1642-1709) & 2/wf Hester (ALLEN) ANDREWS (1647-), w John, m/3 Samuel FOX 1715; ?ca 1690?; Norwich, CT/Groton, CT?

ALLEN, John (1670-1739) & 1/wf Bridget BOOTH (ca 1668, 1670-1714); 3 May 1694; Windsor, CT/Deerfield/Enfield, CT

ALLYN, John (-1696) & 2/wf Hannah (LAMBERTON) [WELLS/WELLES] (1676/7?-), w Samuel; b 1696, aft 1675, b 6 Nov 1696?; Hartford

ALLEN, John (?1654-1706) & Rebecca __?__, m/2 [?Richard] LAUNDERS; ca 1696?; Sandwich

ALLEN, John & Elizabeth EDWARDS; 22 Jul 1697; Boston

ALLEN, John & Mary BROADWAY; May 169-, ?28 Apr 1698, ?30 May 1698; Gloucester/Salem

ALLEN, John & Mary FARGO; 20 Jun 1700; Windham, CT

ALLEN, Joseph & 1/wf Sarah HOLLEY; Jul 1662; Newport/Dartmouth

ALLEN, Joseph (-1721) & Ann BRAZIER -1720); 11 Oct 1667; Watertown

ALLEN, Joseph & 1/wf Ruth LEADER (1652-); 30 Jan 1670/1; Braintree

ALLEN, Joseph & 2/wf Sarah [HULL] (1650-); ?aft 10 Aug 1673; Dartmouth/Shrewsbury, NJ

ALLEN, Joseph (1652-) & Hannah SABIN (1654-); 10 Nov 1678; Rehoboth/Pomfret, CT

ALLEN, Joseph (-1682) & Bethia __?__, m/2 Richard PETERS 1684; b 1678; Salem

ALLEN, Joseph (-1724) & 1/wf Rachel GRIGS/GRIGGS; 29 Jul 1680; Gloucester

ALLEN, Joseph & 2/wf Rose HEYWOOD/HOWARD; 20 Nov 1684; Gloucester

ALLEN, Joseph, Sudbury & 1/wf Abigail MYRICK (1660-); 5 May 1687; Watertown/Sudbury/Rehoboth

ALLEN, Joseph & Anne [WILMOT]; b 1689, by 1696; Boston

ALLEN, Joseph (1672-1703) & Elizabeth MUDGE (1673-); 27 Sep 1695; Northampton

ALLEN, Joseph (1672-1740) & 2/wf? Abigail [HILL?]/[HUTCHINSON?]/LAKE? (?1667-); b 1696; Salem

ALLIN, Joseph (1673) & 1/wf Caturn/Catharine LEACH (1680-); 28 Oct 1696; Manchester

ALLYN/ALLEN, Joseph & Mary DOTY; 21 Dec, 26 Dec 1699; Plymouth

ALLEN, Joseph (1668-) & 1/wf Rachel _?_; b 1700; Dartmouth

ALLEN, Joseph & Elizabeth ROBBINS (-1712); 19 Dec 1700; Cambridge/Watertown

ALLEN, Joshua (-1699 Windham) & Mary _?_ (-1727), m/2 William MOORE 1700; b 1672, b 1688?; Yarmouth/Mansfield, CT/Windham, CT

ALLEN, Lewis (-1708) & 1/wf Sarah IVES; 6 Apr 1664, 1665?; Billerica

ALLEN, Lewis (-1708) & 2/wf Mary (SHERMAN) FREEMAN (-1703), w Henry; aft 12 Nov 1672, bef 6 Dec 1677; Watertown/Billerica

ALLEN, Lewis (-1733+) & Margaret _?_; b 1685?; Wells, ME

ALLYN, Matthew[1] (1605-1671) (a cousin of William SPENCER) & Margaret WYOTT/WYATT (-1671+, 1675?); Braunton, Eng, 2 Feb 1626/7; Cambridge/Hartford/Windsor, CT

ALLEN, Matthew (1629-1695) & Sarah KIRBY (-1688); 6 Jun 1657; Sandwich/Dartmouth

ALLYN, Matthew & Elizabeth WOLCOTT (-1784); 5 Jan 1686, 1686/7; Windsor, CT

ALLEN, Matthew (1675-) & Phebe COOK (1677-); 2 May 1700; Portsmouth, RI/Warwick, RI

ALLEN, Matthew (1677-) & Elizabeth [PROCTOR]; b 1701; Dartmouth/N. Kingstown, RI

ALLEN, Nathaniel (1648-) & 1/wf Mary SABIN (1652-1675); - Apr 1674; Rehoboth

ALLEN, Nathaniel[2] (1648-) & 2/wf Mary FRIZZELL/FRISALL (1656-); 10 Apr 1677; Medfield

ALLEN, Nathaniel (1672-) & Bethiah CONET/CONANT (1677-); 14 Dec 1696; Bridgewater

ALLEN, Nehemiah (?1634-1684) & Sarah WOODFORD (1649-1712, 1713), m/2 Richard BURKE 1687, m/3 Judah WRIGHT 1706; 21 Sep 1664; Northampton/Salisbury, CT

ALLEN/ELLEN?, Nicholas & Margaret _?_; b 1693(4?); Boston

ALLEN, Obadiah (ca 1644-1712) & 1/wf Elizabeth SANFORD; 21 Oct 1669, 28 Oct 1669, 26 Oct 1669, 23 Oct; Milford, CT/Middletown, CT

ALLEN, Obadiah (-1712) & 2/w Mary (SAVAGE) WHITMORE (1663-1723), w John, ?m/3 Benjamin ANDREWS?; aft 31 Aug 1696, by 1707; Middletown, CT

ALLYN, Obadiah (1670-1702) & Dorcas WRIGHT, m/2 Nathaniel WITMORE 1703, ?m/3 Benjamin ANDREWS; 23 Nov 1699, 29 Nov 1699; Middletown, CT

ALIN/ALLEN, Onesiphorus (1642-) & Martha _?_; b 1670; Manchester

ALLEN, Peter (1668-1728) & Mary SMETHURST; 5 Mar 1690/1; Watertown/Roxbury

ALLEN, Ralph[1] & 1/wf Hester ENGLISH; St. Mary le Bos, London, 6 May 1619; Newport/Rehoboth/Sandwich

ALLEN, Ralph[2] (-1698) & ?Susannah _?_; b 1640?; Sandwich

ALLEN, Ralph[1] & 2/wf Esther [SWIFT]; b 1646(7?); Sandwich

ALLEN, Richard (-1664, 1665) & Ruth _?_, m/2 Philip KNEALE/KNELL? 1666; b 1662; Charlestown

ALLEN, Richard (1673-1731) & Hannah [BUTLER]; b 1696; Sandwich

ALLEN, Robert (ca 1616-1683) & Sarah _?_ (-1683+); b 1642; Salem/New London, CT/Norwich, CT

ALLEN, Robert (-1701) & Hannah [WHITE]; ca 1670?; Kittery, ME

ALLYN, Robert (1671-) & Deborah AVERY (1670-); 29 Jun 1691; Groton, CT

ALLEN, Robert & Sarah (LYDSTON/LITTON) [LARY], w John; 1700?; Kittery, ME

ALLEN, Samuel (-1669) & 1/wf Ann [?WHITMORE] (-1641); b 1632; Braintree/etc.

ALLEN, Samuel (-1648) & Ann _?_ (-1687), m/2 William HURLBURT; b 1634; Windsor, CT/?Dorchester

ALLEN, Samuel (-1669) & 2/wf Margaret (FRENCH) [LAMB], w Edward; b 1650; Braintree

ALLEN, Samuel (?1634-1718, 1719) & Hannah WOODFORD (ca 1638-); 29 Nov 1659; Northampton

ALLEN, Samuel (-1703, ae 71) (1705 probate) & Sarah [PARTRIDGE] (1639-); ca 1659, b 1663; Bridgewater

ALLEN, Samuel (1632-1709) & 2/wf? Sarah [TUCK]?; ca 1660; Manchester

ALLEN, Samuel & Mary _?_; b 1663; Fairfield, CT

ALLYN, Samuel (1643/4-1726) & Hannah WALLEY (-1711); 10 May 1664; Barnstable

ALLEN, Samuel (?1636-1705) & Elizabeth [DOWSE]; ca 1665/70, 2 Jan 1672/3

ALLEN, Samuel & 1/wf Jane ROSS; 4 Jan 1683; Sudbury

ALLEN, Samuel (1664-) (had 2/wf Lydia HASTINGS) & Elizabeth GROUT (-1694); 22 Dec 1683; Sudbury

ALLEN, Samuel (1660-1750) & 1/wf Rebecca CAREY (1665-1697); 2 Dec 1685; Bridgewater

ALLIN, Samuel & 1/wf Abigail WILLIAMS; 17 Mar 1686/7; Marblehead/Salem

ALLEN, Samuel & Mary BALDWIN; 14 Jul 1687; Northampton

ALLEN, Samuel (1661-1717) & Elizabeth [?WODELL]/[SANFORD] (1663-1743); ca 1688?; Newport
ALLEN, Samuel (1665-1718, 1717) & Mercy [WRIGHT] (1669-1728); ?15 Dec 1692, 1692?; Northampton/Deerfield/Coventry, CT
ALLEN, Samuel & Abigail WEBB; 26 May 1698; Braintree
ALLEN, Samuel (1675-1739) & Sarah RUST; 28 Feb 1699?, 20 Feb; Deerfield
ALLEN, Samuel (1673-1735) & Hannah [BURROUGHS] (1675-); 29 May 1700; Northampton/Enfield, CT
ALLEN, Samuel (1660-1750) & 2/wf? Mary [ALDEN?]/PRATT? (?1667-), dau Matthew, had son Matthew; b 1701; Bridgewater
ALLIN, Silence & Esther/Hester WISWALL (1669-); 20 Jan 1692; Dorchester
ALLEN, Stillson & Margaret _?_ ; b 1697; Salisbury
ALLEN, Rev. Thomas (returned to Eng) & 1/wf Anna (SADLER/SULLER) HARVARD, w John; ca 1638/9; Charlestown
ALLEN, Thomas (-1680) & 1/wf Winifred (CRAWFORD) [WOLCOTT], w _?_, w John; b 1644; Watertown/Barnstable
ALLYN, Thomas² (-1696) & Abigail WARHAM (1638-bef 1696); 21 Oct 1658; Windsor, CT
ALLYN, Thomas & 1/wf [Isabella] _?_ ; by 1668; Cambridge/Hartford/Middletown, CT
ALLIN, Thomas & Elizabeth _?_ ; b 1669; Boston
ALLYN, Thomas (-1680) & 2/wf _?_ ; by 1676; Barnstable
ALLEN, Thomas & Mary _?_, m/2 Jonathan STEVENSON 1684, m/3 John BOUTON; ?ca 1680; Fairfield, CT
ALLYN, Thomas (-1688/9) & 2/wf Martha (MORRIS) [GIBSON/GIPSON] (-1690), w Roger; b Sep 1682; Middleton, CT
ALLYN, Thomas, Jr. (1662-1709) & 1/wf Martha WOLCOTT (1664-1687 Windsor); 6 Jan 1686/7, 6 Jan 1686; Windsor, CT
ALLYN, Thomas (-1696) & Elizabeth OTIS, m/2 David LORING 1699; 9 Oct 1688; Barnstable
ALLEN, Thomas (1668-1719) & Anna/Anne BARNES (-1719+); 24 Sep 1694; Swansea
ALLEN, Thomas (1673-1733) & Hannah LEEK (1674-); 4 May 1698; Middletown, CT
ALLEN, Thomas & Elizabeth (ROBERTS) [DUNN], w Nicholas; ca 1700?; ?Durham, NH
ALLEN, Timothy & Elizabeth _?_ ; b 1660; Lynn/Groton/Marblehead
ALLEN, Walter¹ (-1681) & 1/wf Rebecca _?_ ; b 1635, b 1631?; Newbury/Charlestown/Watertown
ALLEN, Walter (1643/46-) & 1/wf Elizabeth? _?_ ; b 1671; Kittery, ME
ALLEN, Walter (-1681) & 2/wf, ?3/wf Abigail ROGERS; 29 Nov 1678; Charlestown
ALLEN, Walter & Elizabeth MIDDLETON; 11 Dec 1693; Boston
ALLEN, Walter & 2/wf Mary [HOLMES]; by 1694; Kittery, ME
ALLEN, William (1602-1679, 1678?) & 1/wf Alice _?_ (-8 Mar 1631/2); b 1630; Salem
ALLEN, William (1602-1679, 1678?) (ae 62 in 1664) (called "brother-in-law" by John BRADLEY in 1642) & 2/wf? Elizabeth [BRADLEY]; ca 1633; Salem
ALLEN, William (-1686) & 1/wf Ann [GOODALE] (-1678); b 1640, by 1638?, b 1639?; Salisbury
ALLEN, William (-1705) & Priscilla BROWN (1698+); 21 Mar 1649, 1649/50, no issue; Sandwich
ALLYN, William (-1671) & _?_ in Eng, ca 1650?; Providence
ALLEN, William (?1640-1685) & Elizabeth _?_ (-1685+); b 1664; Portsmouth, RI/Swansea
ALLEN, William (1646-1696) & Hannah _?_, m/2 Samuel FISKE 1697; b 1668; Salem/Manchester
ALLIEN, William & Elizabeth TWICHELL; 15? Feb 1668/9; Medfield
ALLEN, William & Rebecca [JOHNSON]; b 1670; Boston
ALLEN, William (1650-1700) & Mary HARRIS (-1717+); 5 Jul 1674; Salisbury
ALLEN, William (1629-1718) & Patience (CLIFTON) BEERE, w John; 16 May 1677; Newport, RI
ALLEN, William (-1686) & 2/wf Alice (_?_) (ROPER) [DICKINSON] (-1687), w John, w John; after May 1678, 1684?; Salisbury
ALLEN, William (?1664-) & _?_ COOK/?Martha SWEET; ?ca 1688; Portsmouth, RI
ALLEN, William (-1711) & Joanna DIBBLE, Susanna in some records, m/2 David BURT 1715; 20 Dec 1692, 29 Dec 1692; Suffield, CT
ALLEN, William (1670-1747) & 1/wf Elizabeth SMALL (1675-); 13 Mar 1694/5; Salem
ALLEN, William & Sarah WALKER; 19 Nov 1700; Manchester
ALLEN, _?_ & Sarah (CHANDLER) (CLEAVES) (STEVENS) (PARKER), w Wm., w _?_, w John, m _?_ ; b 1691; Sandwich
ALLEN, _?_ & Mercy [LEWIS]; by 1701; Boston

ALLEN, _?_ & Mary (PARMENTER) BURKE, w Richard; aft 1694
ALLEN, _?_ & Elizabeth _?_, m/2 Samuel STONE 1691?
ALLERTON, Isaac[1] (ca 1586-1659) & 1/wf Mary NORRIS (-1621); 4 Nov 1611; Plymouth
ALLERTON, Isaac[1] (ca 1586-1659) & 2/wf Fear [BREWSTER] (-1634); b 22 May 1627; Plymouth
ALLERTON, Isaac[1] (-1659) & 3/wf Joanna _?_ (-1682); aft 1634, by 1644; NY/NJ
ALLERTON, Isaac[2] (1630-1702 Virginia) & 1/wf Elizabeth _?_ (-ca 1660); b 1653; New Haven
ALLERTON, Isaac[2] & 2/wf Elizabeth [WILLOUGHBY]/COLCLOUGH; 1663
ALLERTON, Isaac[3] (1655-) & Elizabeth _?_ ; b 1685; New Haven/Norwich, CT
ALLEY, Hugh (1608-1673/4) (ae 53 in 1662) & Mary [?GRAVES] (-1674+); b 1641/[2]; Lynn
ALLEY, Hugh (1653-) & Rebecca HOOD; 9 Dec 1681; Lynn
ALLEY, Jacob (1663-1707+) & Anna _?_ (-1707+); b 1687; Charlestown
ALLEY, John (1646-) & Joanna FURNILL/FURNELL; middle of Aug 1670; Lynn
ALLEY/AEALY, Philip (-1655) & Susanna _?_, m/2 William PITTS 1655; Boston/Marblehead
ALLEY/ALIE/ELSE, Roger & Jane _?_ ; b 1659; Charlestown
ALLY, Thomas (-1699) & 1/wf Sarah SILVER; 9 Feb 1670, 6 Feb 1670; Newbury/Rowley
ALLEY, Thomas & 2/wf Abigail KILLIM/KILHAM, m/2 William THOMSON 1700; 10 Oct 1681; Rowley
ALLING, Abraham[1] & [?Mary] _?_ (no evidence); Oyster Bay, LI
ALLING, Abraham[2] & ?1/wf Mary (HAWXHURST) [TOWNSEND], w George; & 2/wf Meribah HARCOURT?; aft winter of 1696/7 or 97/8; Oyster Bay, LI
ALLING/ALLEN, Rev. James (1657-1696) & Elizabeth COTTON?, Plymouth, NH, (1668, 1665?-1743), m/2 Rev. Caleb CUSHING 1699; 2 Jun 1690? (no), 14 Mar 1699; Plymouth/Salisbury
ALLING, James (1673-1752) & Abigail [PECK] (1674-); b 1701; Wallingford, CT
ALLING, John (-1691) & Ellen BRADLEY; 14 Oct 1652; New Haven
ALLING, John, New Haven (-1717) & Susanna COE, Stratford (1653-); 11 Jan 1671; New Haven
ALLING/ALLEN, John (1671-) & Abigail GRANNIS; 20 Mar 1688/9; New Haven
ALLING, Roger (1612-1674) & Mary [NASH] (-1683); ca 1642; New Haven/Salisbury
ALLING, Samuel (1645-1707?, 1709?) & 1/wf Elizabeth WINSTON (1649-1682); 24 Oct 1667; New Haven
ALLING, Samuel (-1707?, 1709?) & 2/wf Sarah CHIDSEY (1653-); 26 Oct 1683; New Haven
ALLING, Samuel (1668-1732) & Sarah [?CURRY]; ca 1690; New Haven/Newark, NJ
ALLING, Samuel & [Sarah SACKETT]; b 1696(7?), b 1696; New Haven
ALLING, Thomas & Elizabeth [WEEKS]; Oyster Bay
ALLIS, Ichabod (1675-1747) & 1/wf Mary [BELDING/BELDEN] (1679-1724); ca 1698; Hadley
ALLIS, John (-1691) & Mary (MEEKINS) CLARK, w Nathaniel, m/3 Samuel BELDEN 1691, 1692; 14 Dec 1669; Northampton
ALLIS, Samuel (1647-1691) & Alice _?_, m/2 John HAWKS 1696; b 1677; Hadley
ALLIS, William (?1613-1678) & 1/wf Mary _?_ (-1677); b 1641(2?); Braintree/Hadley/Hatfield
ALLIS, William (-1678) & 2/wf Mary (BRONSON) (WYATT) GRAVES, w John, w John, m/4 Samuel GAYLORD 1681; 25 Jun 1678; Hatfield
ALLISET, John (1651-) & Grace [DYER]; ca 1683; Boston
ALLISON, James & Christian _?_, m/2 Nathaniel FRYER b 1653; b 1650; Boston
ALLISON, James & Elizabeth VEAZIE; 28 May 1674; Dorchester/Boston
ALLISON, John (-1733) & Mary JEFFERIES (1669-1730); 4 Aug 1698, no issue; Deerfield
ALLISON/ALLISTON?, Joseph & Comfort [WILKINS]; b 1693; Boston (his daus were neices of Mrs. Susannah THATCHER)
ALLISON, Ralph (1622±-1676+) & [Anne DIXON]; Scarboro, ME
ALLISON, Richard (1633-) (brother-in-law Thomas CARR, John ALBERTUS) & [Elizabeth GRAVES]; in Eng, b 1662
ALLISON, Thomas & Cornelia JOHNSON, m/2 John GILBERT; m lic 4 Jul 1698
ALMARY, Robert & [Hannah PARTRIDGE]; b 1694
ALMY, Christopher (1632-1713) & Elizabeth CORNELL (-1708+, 1715); 9 Jul 1661; Portsmouth, RI
ALMY, Christopher & 1/wf Joanna SLOCUM (1672-); 16 Apr 1690; Portsmouth/Newport
ALMY, Job (-1684) & Mary [UNTHANK] (-1724+), m/2 Thomas TOWNSEND; b 1664; Portsmouth, RI
ALMY, Job (1675-1743) & 1/wf Ann LAWTON (-1739); Mar 1696; Portsmouth, RI

ALMY, John (-1676) & Mary [COLE], m/2 John POCOCKE 1677±; no issue; Plymouth/Portsmouth, RI

ALMY, William[1] (?1591, ?1601-1676) & Audrey [BARLOW?] (1603-1676+); in Eng; b 1627, m 1626; Lynn/Sandwich/Portsmouth, RI

ALMY, William (1665-1747) & 1/wf Deborah [COOK] (1666-); b 1689; Tiverton, RI/Portsmouth, RI

ALSOP, Joseph (1621-1698) & Elizabeth [PRESTON] (?1623-1693); b 9 Jul 1647; New Haven/Stratford

ALSOP, Joseph (-1691) & Abigail THOMPSON, m/2 John MILES 1691+; 25 Nov 1672, no issue; New Haven

ALSOP, Key (-30 Apr 1672) & Mary _?_, m/2 Capt. William TURNER; Boston

ALSOP, Richard (?1660-1718) & Hannah [UNDERHILL] (1666-1757); ca 1685, b 1687; Newtown, RI

ALTON, Erasmus & Elizabeth [QUINBY]; b 1698; Westchester, NY

ALVORD, _?_ & [Isabell HOSKINS] (1675); Hartford

ALVORD, Alexander (1627-1687) & Mary VORE?; 2? Oct, 29 Oct 1646; Windsor, CT/Northampton

ALVORD, Benedictus (-1683) & Jane NEWTON (-1715); 26 Nov 1640; Windsor, CT

ALVORD, Benjamin (-1715) & Deborah STEBBINS (1672-), m/2 Henry BURT 1716; ca 1690; Northampton

ALVORD, Ebenezer (1665-1738) & 1/wf Ruth BAKER (1668-1706); 1691?, 1692?; Northampton

ALVORD, Jeremiah (1663-1709) & 1/wf Mehitable (FRARY) [ROOT] (-1698), w Hezekiah; 1691; Deerfield/Windsor, CT

ALVORD, Jeremiah/Jeremy? (1663-1709) & Jane [HOSKINS] (1671-1715); b 1688; Windsor, CT

ALVORD, Jeremiah & 2/wf Mercy [GULL] (1668-); after 7 Nov 1698, bef 1703, b 1701?; Hadley

ALVORD, John (1649-1727) & Abigail [PHELPS] (1655-1756, ae 101-4-11); ca 1675/80?, no issue; Northampton

ALVORD, Jonathan, Westfield (1645-) & Hannah [BROWN]; 1681, no issue; Windham, CT/Milford

ALVORD, Jonathan (1669-1729) & Thankful MILLER (1669-1738); 12 Jan 1693; Northampton

ALVORD, Josiah/Josias? (1649-1722?) & Hannah WESTOVER; 22 May 1693; Simsbury

ALVORD, Thomas (1653-1688) & Johannah/Joanna TAYLOR (1665-1738), m/2 Samuel KING, ca 1690, m/3 Deliverence BALSOMON; 22 Mar 1681; Northampton

ALWAY/ALWAYS, Francis & Elizabeth _?_; b 1697; Braintree

AMAZEEN, John & Mary [WALFORD], w Jeremiah; aft 5 Nov 1660, b 1666, b 1663, b 26 Jun 1666; Portsmouth, NH/Kennebec

AMBECK, John/(Johannes) & Mary [VARLEET], m/2 Paulus SCHRICK 1658; b 1654; Hartford

AMBLER, Abraham (1642-1699) & 1/wf Mary BATES (1675+); 25 Dec 1662; Stamford, CT

AMBLER, Abraham (1665/6-) & Hannah GOLD, m/2 Jeremiah ANDREWS 1697; 12 Jan 1692, 1692/3; Stamford, CT

AMBLER, Abraham (-1699) & 2/wf Hannah _?_ (-1699+); b 1699; Stamford, CT

AMBLER, John (-1711) & Martha [WILDMAN]; b 1695(6?); Stamford, CT

AMBLER, John & 1/wf Hannah (?KENT) [WATSON], w Robert; aft 9 Jan 1695/6, bef 2 Mar 1702/3; Durham, NH

AMBLER, Richard (1611-1699+) & 1/wf Sarah _?_; b 1639; Watertown/Stamford, CT

AMBLER, Richard (1611-1699+) & 2/wf Elizabeth _?_ (-1685); Stamford, CT

AMBROSE, Henry (?1613-1658) & Susanna _?_, m/2 John SEVERANCE 1663; b 1640; Charlestown/Salisbury/Boston

AMBROSS, Henry (1649-) & Susannah (_?_) WORCESTER, w Timothy; last week in Oct 1672; Salisbury

AMBRUSS, Nathaniel & Sarah EASTMAN, m int 8 Dec 1697; Salisbury

AMBROSE, Samuel (1646-) (He went to LI, married again) & Hope [LAMBERTON?], m/2 _?_ HERBERT by 1687, m/3 William CHENEY; b 1666, div 1678; Salisbury

AMBROSS, William & Elizabeth MATTOCK; 6 Jan 1697; Boston

AMBROSE, _?_ & _?_, wid in 1644; ?Lynn

AMERIDETH, John (1615-1691) & Joanna/Joan [TREVOROYE] (-1690+); Kittery, ME

EIMES/EAMES?, Daniel (he deserted his wife) & Lydia WHEELER, prob m/2 John KELLY 1716; 15? Apr, 25 Apr 1683; Andover/Boxford

EMMS/EAMES?, Jacob (1677-) & Mary VAUGHAN; 4 Jun 1700; Boston

AMES, John (1610-1698±) & Elizabeth [HAYWARD]; ?20 Oct 1645, no issue; Duxbury

AMES, John, Jr. (1647-1726) & Sarah [WILLIS], dau John; b 1672; Bridgewater

AMES/EAMES?, John (1670-1724) & Prisselah KIMBOL/Priscilla KIMBALL; 3 Nov 16[88-92?], b 1693; Boxford

AMES, John (1672-1756) & Sarah WASHBURN; 12 Jan 1696/7; Bridgewater

EMES, John (-1735) & Abigail MORGAN; 1 Feb 1698/9; New London

AMES/EIMES/EAMES?, Robert (-1693) (ae 31 in 1671) & Rebecca [BLAKE] (-1691), dau George; b 1661, 1661; Andover

AMES/EAMES? (1667-) & Bathiah GATCHEL/Bethiah GATCHELL; 20 Apr [1695]; Boxford

AMES, William & 1/wf _?_ BURGESS

AMES, Rev. William (1576-1633 in Eng), Rotterdam & 2/wf Joanna [FLETCHER?] (?1587-1644), Cambridge; in Eng, b 1619; Cambridge

AMES, William (?1605-1655, 1654) & Hannah _?_, m/2 John NILES 1660; b 1641; Braintree

AMES, William (1673-) & Mary HAYWARD/HAYWOOD? (1672-); 13 Dec 1698; Bridgewater

AMBERY/AMSBERY/AMBREY, Robert (-1656) & _?_; b 1649; New Haven/Stamford, CT

AMEY/EAMES, John & Martha JOHNSON (1631-); 18 Mar 1650, 1649/50; Woburn/Boston/Barbados

AMEE, John (1654-) & Desire _?_; b 1678; Boston

AMEE, John & Sarah [GULLISON]; b 1695; Kittery, ME

AMY, John & Mary SHAW, m int 2 Oct 1695; Boston

AMY, John & Mary SHOAR, m int 1 Nov 1695; Boston

AMY _?_ & Lydia [NAYLOR] (1668-); Boston

AMLET, Charles & Mary _?_; b 1694; Salem

AMMIDOWNE, Philip (1669/70-) & 1/wf Mehittabel PERRIN; 27 May 1698; Rehoboth

AMMIDOWNE, Philip (1669/70-) & 2/wf Ithamar WARFIELD; 16 Sep 1700; Rehoboth/Windsor/Oxford

AMADOWNE, Roger (-1673) & 1/wf Sarah _?_ (-1668); b 1640; Salem/Weymouth/Boston/Rehoboth

AMMIDOWNE, Roger (-1673) & 2/wf Joanna [HARROD/HARWOOD] (-1711); ?27 Dec 1668

AMORY/EMERY?, Joseph (-1712 Inv.) (gr son of Anthony) & Rebecca _?_/Elizabeth WASHBURN; b 1682; Little Compton, RI

AMORY, Simon (-1677) & Mary _?_; b 1673; Boston

AMOS, Hugh (-1707) & Anne _?_; b 1665; Norwich, CT/Boston

AMOS, John (?1665, 1658-1758) & Sarah MORGAN (1678-); Apr 1694; Preston, CT

AMSDEN, Isaake[1] (-1659) & Frances PERRIMAN, m/2 Richard CUTTER 1662; 8 Jun 1654; Cambridge

AMSDEN, Isaac (1655-1727) & Jane RUTTER (-1739); 17 May 1677; Cambridge/Marlboro

AMSDEN, Jacob (1657-1701) & Susanna [MARRET] (-1707); ca 1681?, no issue; Cambridge

AMSDEN, John (-1696) & Elizabeth _?_ (-1689); b 1686; Hatfield

ANDERSON, David (-1677) & 1/wf Hannah NICHOLS (1647-1671); 5 Jun 1667; Charlestown

ANDERSON, David (-1677) & 2/wf Katharine RICHESON/RICHARDSON (1655-), m/2 Richard SPRAGUE; 12 Sep 1672; Charlestown

ANDERSON, David (1677-1701) & Hannah PHILLIPS, Boston, m/2 Habijah SAVAGE 1703; 4 Jan 1699/1700, 5 Jan 1699; Charlestown/Boston

ANDERSON, Gowen & Alice _?_; b 1639?; Roxbury

ANDERSON, John (-1677) & 1/wf Jane _?_ (-4 May 1654); b 1639; Boston

ANDERSON, John (-1677), Boston & 2/wf Mary (DAVISON, sister of Nicholas)/ MILLER? HODGES, w John (-1693); 3 Jan 1654/5; Charlestown

ANDERSON/ANDRUESON, Thomas (-1746) & Hannah PECK; 25 Jun 1696; Lyme, CT

ANDREWS, Abraham (-1731) & Rebecca [CARRINGTON]; b 1672; Farmington, CT

ANDREWS/ANDRUS, Abraham (1648-1693) & Sarah [PORTER] (1657-), ?m/2 James BENEDICT 1707; ca 1676?, 1682?; Farmington, CT/Waterbury, CT

ANDREWS/ANDRUSS, Benjamin (ca 1659-1727) & 1/wf Mary SMITH (-1707); ca 26 May 1682; Farmington, CT

ANDREWS, Daniel (1649-1731) & Mary [PECK] (ca 1652-); ca 1671-2; Farmington, CT

ANDREWS, Daniel (-1703) (ae 28 in 1671) & Sarah [PORTER] (1649-); b 1677; Salem

ANDROS, Gov. Edmund (1637-1714) & Sarah _?_ (-1688); NY/Boston/etc.

ANDREWS, Edward & _?_ [DOLTERIS], wid; b 1637

ANDREWS, Edward (1628-1673) & Ann [?ADKINS] (-1708); b 1653?; Hartford

ANDREWS, Edward & Bridget __?_; b 1654; Portsmouth, RI

ANDREWS, Edward & __?__

ANDREWS, Elisha & Eleanor (BRACHETT) [FOXWELLS?], w Philip, m/3 Richard PULLEN/ PULLING?; b 1698; Boston

ANDREWS, Francis (-1663) & Anne/Anna __?_, m/2 [?Henry] SMITH ca 1664; ca 1639/43; Hartford

ANDREWS, Gideon & 1/wf Lydia [JOHNSON] (1681-); ca 1699; NH

ANDREWS, Henry (-1654, 1653?) & Mary [WADSWORTH/?WILLIAMS] (?1611-1655); ?in Eng, b 1631, b 1629; Taunton

ANDREWS, Henry² & 1/wf Hannah [STREET], m/2 William CORBETT?; b 1659, ca 1652

ANDREWS, Henry (-1676) & 2/wf Mary [WADSWORTH] (-ca 1693/4); b 1664, ca 1659; Taunton/Duxbury

ANDREWS, Henry (1660/2-1733) & 1/wf Mary DEAN (-1687); 17 Feb 1685/6; Taunton/Duxbury

ANDREWS, Henry (-1733) & 2/wf Mary WILLIAMS (1664-1736); 4 Jul 1688; Taunton

ANDREWS, James (1625-1704, ae 79) & 1/wf Dorcas [MILTON] (-1696); b 1650?; Falmouth, ME/Saco, ME

ANDREWS, James & __?_; b 1675; Falmouth, ME

ANDREWS, James (1625-1704) & 2/wf Margaret (PHIPPS) HALSE/HALSEY; m int 6 Aug 1696; Boston

ANDREWS/ANDROS?, Jedediah (-1673) & Mary [PIKE], m/2 John ALLEN 1674; b 1670; Salisbury/Dover, NH

ANDREWS, Jeremiah (-1713) & Hannah (GOLD) AMBLER, w Abraham; 8 Sep 1697; Stamford, CT/Bedford, NY

ANDREWS, John (1600-1671) & Joan __?_ (1621-), m/2 Philip ATWELL by 1672; ca 1640; Kittery, ME

ANDREWS, John (?1616-1681/2) & Mary __?_ (-1694); b 1643; Farmington, CT

ANDREWS, John (1614?, 1621-1708) (ae 70 in 1692, 40 in 1659, 80 in 1701) & Jane [JORDAN] (1622-1705+); b 1646; Ipswich

ANDREWS, John² (-1662) (ae 31 in 1659) & Sarah [HOLYOKE] (-1666?); ca 1650/2?; Ipswich

ANDREWS, John (-1679) & 1/wf Lucy __?_ (-1653); b 1653; Boston

ANDREWS, John (-1679) & 2/wf Hannah [JACKSON] (1636-), m/2 John DICKINSON; b 1656; Boston

ANDREWS, John (-1690) & Mary [LILLY?], m/2 Isaac CAKEBREAD?; b 1667; Hartford

ANDREWS, John & 1/wf __?_; b 1671; Kings Town, RI

ANDREWS, John (1645-) & Hester [ALLEN] (?1647-), m/2 John ALLYN ca 1690?, m/3 Samuel FOX; b 1672; ?Plymouth/?Norwich, CT

ANDREWS, John & Elizabeth [STRICKLAND] (1648, 1647-); ca 1672?, by 1675, b 21 Jun 1670; Hartford

ANDREWS, John (?ae 36 in 1684) & Margaret __?_; by 1672; Kittery, ME/Braveboat Harbor

ANDREWS, John & Bethiah [KIRBY] (1658-); ca 1678; Middletown, CT

ANDREWS, John & Mary [PECK] (1662-1752); b 1682; Hartford

ANDREWS, John & Judith [?BELCHER] (1658-); ca 1680/2; Ipswich

ANDREWS, John & Sarah DICKINSON; 18 Apr 1683, 1684; Boxford/Rowley/Topsfield

ANDREWS, John³ & Anne [JACOBS]; b 1685; Salem

ANDREWS, John (-1695) & Patience NICHOLS, m/2 Joseph BEAL 1696; 21 Dec 1685; Hingham

ANDREWS, John (1662-1742) & 1/wf Alice [SHAW] (1666-1735); b 1686; Mendon/Bristol, RI

ANDREWS, John & Rebecca __?_, m/2 John NICHOLS; b 1693; E. Greenwich, RI

ANDREWS, John (-1693) & 2/wf Mary [RIDGLY]; b 22 Aug 1693; Kings Town, RI

ANDREWS/ANDROS, John & Mary __?_; b 1696; Plymouth

ANDREWS?, John & Rachel __?_; 2 Dec 1696; Lyme, CT

ANDREWS, Joseph (1597-1680) & Elizabeth __?_ (-1688); in Eng, b 1622?; Hingham/Duxbury

ANDREWS, Joseph (1651-1706) & Rebecca __?_ (-1709, 1710); ca 1677; Farmington, CT/Wethersfield

ANDREWS, Joseph (1657-1725) & Sarah RING (-1714+); 16 Feb 1680, 1680/1; Ipswich

ANDREWS, Joseph (1657-1732±) & 1/wf Sarah PERLEY (1665-1694); 1 Feb 1681; Topsfield

ANDREWS, Joseph (1657-1732±) & 2/wf Mary GIRDLER; 15 Nov 1694; Marblehead

ANDREWS, Joseph (1657-1732±) & 2/wf Mary DICKINSON; 13 Mar 1696, 30 Mar 1696; Boxford/Rowley

ANDREWS, Nathan (1639-) & 1/wf Deborah ABBOTT (-1672); Oct 1661; New Haven

ANDREWS, Nathan (1639-) & 2/wf Phebe GIBBARD (1647-1720); 6 Jan 1675, 1675/6?; New Haven

ANDREWS, Nathan (1662-) & 1/wf Elizabeth MILES (?1665, 1666-); 21 Jan 1686; New Haven/Wallingford

ANDREWS, Nathan (1662-) & Mary [MARTIN], div; b 1697; New Haven

ANDREWS, Nathaniel & Hannah [TYLER]; b 1690, m 13 Dec 1705; Wallingford

ANDREWS, Nathaniel & Mary MOSS; 8 Sep 1698; Hartford

ANDREWS, Nicholas (-1698) & Elizabeth [NICHOLSON]; b 1672; Marblehead

ANDREWS, Nicholas & Mary FAIRFIELD; 27 Jun 1695; Lynn/Marblehead

ANDREWS, Ralph & Abigail VERY; 12 Dec 1682; Gloucester

ANDREWS, Richard & 1/wf _?_ ; b 1678; Hampton

ANDREWS, Richard & 2/wf Joan AVELLY, w Thomas, some uncertainty; aft Sep 1681, in 1682; Hampton

ANDREWS, Robert[1] (-1643?) & Elizabeth _?_ (-1644+, 1647+); in Eng, ca 1620?; Ipswich

ANDREWS, Robert (-1668) & Grace _?_ ; ca 1637?; Boxford/Topsfield

ANDREWS, Robert (-1718) & Susannah _?_ ; b 1701?; Isles of Shoals

ANDREWS, Samuel (1598-1637/8?) & Jane _?_ (1605-), m/2 Arthur MACKWORTH; in Eng, b 1625; Biddeford, ME/Saco, ME

ANDREWS, Samuel (-1659) & _?_ ; Charlestown/etc.

ANDREWS, Samuel (-1701, ae ca 80) & Elizabeth WHITE (-1687, ae 57); 22 Sep 1652; Cambridge

ANDREWS, Samuel (ca 1635-1704, ae 69) & Elizabeth [PECK] (1643-1704+); ca 1660?; New Haven/Wallingford, CT

ANDREWS, Samuel & Mary WRIGHT; 30 Oct 1663; Oyster Bay, LI/Mansfield, NJ

ANDREWS, Samuel (1645-1712) & Elizabeth [SPENCER] (1648-); ca 1667/8; Hartford/?Wallingford, CT

ANDREWS, Rev. Samuel (1656-1737/8) & 1/wf Abigail [TREAT] (?1660-1727, 1724?); b 1686; Milford, CT

ANDREWS, Samuel (1663-1727) & Anna HALL (1661-1746); 27 Aug 1686; Wallingford, CT

ANDREWS, Samuel (1668-ca 1725) & Elizabeth (SMITH) LUDDEN (1667-), w Joseph; 5 Feb 1690/1; Hingham

ANDREWS, Stephen & Bethia STETSON (1675-); 23 Jun 1697; Scituate

ANDREWS, Thomas (-1643) & _?_ ; in Eng, b 1597; Hingham

ANDREWS, Thomas (-1667, 1673?) & Ann _?_ (-1684, 1685?); b 1639; Dorchester

ANDREWS, Thomas (-1647±) & Rebecca _?_ , m/2 Nicholas WYETH ca 1648, m/3 Thomas FOX 1685; b 1641; Watertown/Cambridge

ANDREWS, Thomas (1632-1690) & Ruth _?_ (-1732, in 97th y.); b 1656; Hingham

ANDREWS, Thomas (-1704) & Phebe GOURD/GOARD; 31 Dec 1667; Dorchester/Roxbury

ANDREWS, Thomas & 1/wf Martha (BAKER) ANTROME/ANTRIM, w Obadiah; 22 Jun 1670; Topsfield

ANDREWS, Thomas & Hannah [KIRBY] (1649/50-1717), m/2 Alexander ROLLO 1693?, m/3 William STONE; ca 1670/2; Middletown, CT

ANDREWS, Thomas (1641-) & Martha ECCLES; 30 Oct 1673; Cambridge

ANDREWS, Thomas (1648-1718) & Elizabeth [PORTER?] (1654-); b 1678; Milford, CT

ANDREWS, Thomas & 2/w Mary BELCHER; 9 Feb 1681, 1681/2; Ipswich

ANDREWS, Thomas & 3/wf Rebecca _?_ ; b 1686; Boxford

ANDREWS, Thomas & Abigail LINCOLN; 12 Apr 1693; Hingham

ANDREW, William (-1652) & 1/wf Mary _?_ (-1640) (no according to Mr. Jacobus); b 1621; Cambridge

ANDREWS, William (-1676) & 1/wf _?_ (-1663?); b 1628; New Haven

ANDREWS, William (-1659) & Abigail [GRAVES]?, m/2 Nathaniel BARDING/BEARDING?; by 1635?; Hartford

ANDREW, William (-1652) & 2/wf Reana (?) JAMES, w Edmund, m/3 Robert DANIEL 1654, m/4 Edmund FROST bef 1669; m cont 11 Aug 1640; Cambridge

ANDREWS, William (deserted his wife: m/2 in Ireland) & Mary CHANDLER; 31 Jan 1649, div 1661; New Haven

ANDREWS, William & 2/wf Anna (TAPP) GIBBARD, w William; 7 Dec 1665; New Haven

ANDREWS, William (-1717) & Margaret WOODWARD (1655-); 20 Oct 1672; Ipswich

ANDREWS, William & Esther/Hester (ARNOLD) DEXTER (1647-1688+), w James, m/3 Edward HAWKINS b 1685; 30 Oct 1680; Warwick, RI

ANDREW, William (-1702) & Seeth _?_, m/2 Zechariah HICKS 1704; b 1684; Salem/Cambridge

ANDREWS, William (166?-1726) & Hannah PARKER, m/2 Bartholomew FOSTER; 12 Jan 1692; Wallingford, CT

ANDREWS, William (1679-1762) & Anne/Anna SEARLE; 25 Sep 1700; E. Greenwich, RI

ANDREWS, _?_ & Abigail (COLE) NORMAN, w Timothy; 24 May 1695; Salem

ANDREWS, _?_ & Hannah [PHILLIPS?], Dedham, dau Henry, m/2 _?_ NEGUS?

ANDREWS, _?_ & [?Hannah] [STREET]; b 1674

ANGELL, James (-1711) & Abigail DEXTER (1655-); 3 Sep 1678, 30? Sep; Providence

ANGELL, John (1646-1720) & Ruth FIELD (-1727+); 7 Jan 1669, 1669/70; Providence

ANGELL, Thomas (-1694) & Alice [ASHTON] (1618-1695); b 1646; Providence

ANGELL, Thomas (1672-) & Sarah BROWN (1677-), dau James; 4 Apr 1700; Providence/Scituate, RI

ANGIER, Edmund (?1612-1692) & 1/wf Ruth [AMES] (-1656); b 1645; Cambridge

ANGIER, Edmund (1612-1692) & 2/wf Ann/Anne?/Anna BATT (1630-1688); 12 Jun 1657; Cambridge

ANGER/AUGER?, John (called "cousin by Rev. John COTTON, 1652) & Hannah/Anna? [ASPINWALL] (1631-) (ae 41 in 1672); b 1652; Boston

ANGIER, Joseph (-1718) & Elizabeth _?_ (-1732); b 1694; Dorchester/Framingham

ANGIER, Sampson & 1/wf Susannah ISAACKE; Lezant, Eng?, 17 Jul 1666; York, ME

ANGIER, Sampson & 2/wf Sarah _?_, m/2 Arthur HEWES by 1694; by 1672; York, ME

ANGIER, Samuel (1655-1719), Watham & Hannah OAKE/OAKES (-1714); 2 Sep 1680; Rehoboth

ANNABLE, Anthony (-1674) & 1/wf Jane MOUMFORD/MOMFORD (-1643); All Saints, Cambridge, Eng, 26 Apr 1619; Plymouth/Scituate/Barnstable

ANNABLE, Anthony (-1674) & 2/wf Anne CLARCK?/ALCOCKE/ELCOCK?/ALCORD (-1645/6, 1651); 1 Mar 1645, 3 Mar 1644, 1644/5; Barnstable

ANNABLE, Anthony (-1674) & 3/wf Ann/?Hannah [BARKER] (-1658); b 1653; Barnstable

ANNABLE, John[1] (-1664) & Anna [WHIPPLE?], had Matthew, m/2 Nicholas CLAPP; b [1648], b 1649; Ipswich

ANNABLE, John (1649-1718) & Mary [PERKINS] (1658-), dau Jacob; b 1678(9?); Ipswich

ANNABLE, John (1673-) & Experience TAYLER/TAYLOR (1672-); 16 Jun 1692; Barnstable

ANNABLE, Joseph & Mary _?_; b 1694; Ipswich

ANNABLE, Robert (1659-1717) & Susanna [SPARKS]; b 1690, b 1701?

ANNABLE, Samuel (1646-1678) & Mehitable ALLYN (1648), m/2 Cornelius BRIGGS 1683; 1 Jun 1667; Barnstable

ANNABLE, Samuel (1669-) & Patience DOGGED/DOGGETT (1670-), dau Thomas; 11 Apr 1695; Barnstable

ANNIS, Abraham (1668-) & Hannah [?OSGOOD]; b 1694; Newbury

ANNIS, Anthony & Jane RUNDLETT; 24 Feb 1699; Hampton, NH

ANNIS, Carmac alias Charles (1638-1717) & Sara/Sarah CHASE (-1726?); 15 May 1666; Newbury

ANNIS, Isaac (1672-1712) & Rebecca _?_, m/2 Shimuel GRIFFIN; b 1701; Newbury

ANNIS, Joseph (?1667-1758) & Dorothy [OSGOOD] (1671-1740); b 1692; Newbury

ANSELL, Thomas & Mary _?_; b 1686; Boston

ANTHONY, Abraham (1650-1727) & Alice WODELL/WOODELL (1650-1734); 26 Dec 1671; Portsmouth, RI

ANTHONY, John[1] (1607-1675) & Susanna [POTTER?]; b 1642; Portsmouth, RI

ANTHONY, John (1642-1715) & 1/wf Frances WODELL/WOODELL (1652-1692?); 23 Nov 1669; Portsmouth, RI

ANTHONY, John[3] (1671-1699) & Sarah HICKS (-1694); 2 May 1693; Portsmouth, RI

ANTHONY, John (1642-1715) & 2/wf Susanna ALBRO (-1715+); 3 Jan 1694, 1693/4; ?Portsmouth, RI

ANTHONY, John (?1672-1703) & Jane RUDLETT/RUNKET (1676-), dau Charles; 24 Feb 1699; Hampton, NH

ANTHONY, Joseph (-1728) & Mary WAIT (-1713+); 5 Apr 1676); Portsmouth, RI/Dartmouth

ANTHONY, William & Mary COGGESHALL; 14 Mar 1695, 1694/5?; Portsmouth, RI

ANTHONY, William (1676-1737) & Patience FREEBORN (1676-1757); 26 Jul 1698, 7 Sep 1698; Portsmouth, RI

ANTRIM/ANTRUM, Obadiah (1640-1665) & Martha [BAKER], m/2 Thomas ANDREWS 1670; b 1664; Ipswich

ANTRUM, Thomas (-1663) & Jane BATTER; 24 May 1630; Salem

APPLEBY/APLEBEE, William & Deborah JOHNSON; 24 Nov 1680; Gravesend, LI

APPLEGATE, John (-1712, ae 82) & Avis _?_ (-1717, ae 80); Gravesend, LI

APPLEGATE, Thomas & Elizabeth _?_ ; b 1630?; Weymouth

APPLETON, Isaac (1664-1747) & Priscilla [BAKER] (1674-1731); b 1697(8?), 1695(?); Ipswich

APPLETON, John (1622-1699) (ae ca 36 in 1659, ae 50 in 1672) & Priscilla GLOVER (-1697/8); ?14 Oct 1651, Oct 1651; ?Ipswich

APPLETON, John (1652-1739) & Elizabeth ROGERS (1661-1754); 28 Nov 1681, 1680?; Ipswich

APPLETON, John (1660-1724) & 1/wf Rebecca RUCK; 1 Apr 1689?, 1 Apr 1698?, b 1695; Ipswich/Salem

APPLETON, John (-1724) & 2/wf Elizabeth (BAKER) DUTCH, w Benjamin; m int 31 Aug 1700; Ipswich

APPLETON, Samuel (1586-1670) (?m/2 Martha _?_, very doubtful) & Judith EVERARD; Preston, Eng, 24 Jan 1615/16; Ipswich

APPLETON, Samuel (1624-1696) & 1/wf Hannah/Anna? PAINE (1630-1656?); 2 Apr 1651; Ipswich

APLETON, Samuel (1624-1696) & 2/wf Mary OLIVER (1640-1698); 8 Dec 1656; Newbury

APPLETON, Samuel, Jr. (-1725) & Elizabeth WHITINGHAM, m/2 Edward PAYSON 1726; 19 Jun 1682; Lynn

APPLETON, Samuel (-1693) & Mary [WOODBRIDGE] (-1712); b 1684?; Ipswich

APPLIN, John & Bethshuah BARTLITT/?Bathsheba BARTLETT (-1692); 23 Nov 1671; Watertown

APPLIN, John (-1725+) & 2/wf Sarah [SMITH] (1675-1718); b 1701?, aft 1692; Littleton/Watertown

APPLY/?APPLEY, [?Daniel], Preston, CT, & Abigail [SWIFT] (1676-), Dorchester; b 1701?, b 1711

ARCHER, Benjamin & Sarah NEAL, m/2 Gilbert TAPPLEY 1707, m/3 _?_ WILKINS; 13 Jul 1693; Beverly

ARCHER, Henry (ae 66 in 1671) & Elizabeth STOW (1617-1669); 4 Dec 1639; Roxbury/Ipswich

ARCHER, John & Catherine [CARLES]?; b 2 Jun 1659; Stamford, CT

ARCHER, John (-1685) & Mary [FOWLER?]; Westchester, NY

ARCHER, John & _?_ [THEOLE?]/[UFFORD?]; Stamford, CT

ARCHER, John (-1693) (called "son" by Matthew WOODWELL, 1669) & Bethiah [WEEKS] (1642-1684+); b 1664; Salem

ARCHER, John, Westchester & Sarah ODELL, Westchester; m lic 7 Oct 1686, cert Dec 1686; ?Westchester, NY/Fordham, NY

ARCHER, John & Mehitable SHEARS; 5 Jan 1692, ?5 Jun; Bristol, RI

ARCHER, Jonathan & Abigail (MASSEY)/MANCY? WILLIAMS, w Hilliard; ?8 Nov 1699, ?Dec 1699; Salem

ARCHARD/ARCHER?, Nicholas & Hannah CARRELL; 12 Jan 1699; Salem

ARCHER, Richard, Portsmouth, NH & Mary WEST, Portsmouth, NY; 16 Jul 1688, 19 Jul 1688; Portsmouth, NH

ARCHARD, Samuel (1608-1667, 1668?) (ae 50 in 1668, ae 58 in 1666) & ?1/wf [Alice ALLAN?]; b 1632?, b 1639; Salem

ARCHARD, Samuel (1608?-) & Susanna [TUCK?] FELTON?, m/3? Richard HUTCHINSON 1668; b 1632, b 12 Feb 1649/50; Salem

ARCHER, Samuell (-1717+) (ae 65 in 1700) & Hannah OSGOOD (-1706+); 22 May 1659, 22 May 1660; Andover

ARCHER, Stephen & Sarah HODGES (1670-); 14 Oct 1697; Salem

ARCHER, _?_ & Sarah [HOLBROOK], Braintree, m Tristam DAVIS 1695, (ae 24 in 1690)

ARCHER, [?John] & Sarah [TRASK] (1656-), dau Henry, m/2 Abraham WHITICAR/WHITTIER? 7 Sep 1694; 18 Jun 1694; Salem

ARDELL, William & Mary SANDERSON, w Joseph, div wife of Augustine LINDON; 27 Feb 1681/2, ca 21 Dec 1681; Boston/Exeter, NH/Newmarket, NH

ARDEN, James & Hannah BALDEN (1667-); 9 May 1689; Beverly, MA

AREY, Richard (-1669) & [?Elizabeth CROUCH], sister Richard; b 1640; Martha's Vineyard

AREY, Richard (1640-1689) & Sarah [MARCHANT], m/2 Thomas HARLOCK 1696; ca 1676; Edgartown

ARMITAGE, Eleazer (-1673(probate)) & Hana/Hannah NEEDHAM, m/2 John DIVEN b 1675; 18 Oct 1669; Lynn/Boston
ARMITAGE, Godfrey (-1675) & 1/wf Sarah [WEBB]; b 1645; Boston
ARMITAGE, Godfrey (-1675) & 2/wf Mary [COGSWELL] (1619-1677+); b 1651, 1649?; Boston
ARMITAGE, Jonathan & Elizabeth __?__; b 1674; Boston
ARMITAGE, Joseph (1601-1680) (60 in 1661, 60 in 1670?) & Jane __?__ (-1677); b 1643; Lynn
ARMITAGE, Thomas (1611?-1680, ae 80) & 1/wf __?__; ?b 1641; Lynn/Sandwich/Stamford, CT/Hempstead, LI
ARMITAGE, Thomas (1611?-1680, ae 80) & 2/wf Martha __?__; b 1650?
ARMITAGE, Timothy & Joanna [RICHARDSON] (1658-); b 1688(9?), ?b Jul 1686; Boston
ARMS, William (-1731, ae 71) & Joanna HAWKS (-1729, ae 76); 21 Nov 1677; Hatfield/Hadley/Deerfield
ARMSTRONG, Benjamin (-1718) & Rachel __?__; b 1674; Norwich, CT
ARMSTRONG, Gregory (-1650) & Eleanor [BILLINGTON] (-1643+), w John; ?Sep 1638; ?Plymouth/Yarmouth
ARMSTRONG, Jonathan & __?__; ca 1669?; Westerly, RI/Stonington, CT/Norwich, CT/Roxbury, CT
ARMSTRONG, Matthew (ae 27 in 1661) & Hannah __?__; b 1664; Boston
ARMSTRONG, Matthew (1666-) & Margaret HALCE/HALSEY; 7 Jun 1694; Boston
ARMSTRONG, William & Deborah __?__; b 1671; Boston
ARNOLD, Benedict (1615-1678) & Damaris WESTCOTT (ca 1620-1671+); 17 Dec 1640; Providence
ARNOLD, Benedict (1641-1727) & 1/wf Mary TURNER (-1690); 9 Mar 1671, 1670/1; Newport
ARNOLD, Benedict (1641-1727) & 2/wf Sarah [MUMFORD] (1668-1746); b 1695; Newport
ARNOLD, Berachiah/Barachiah (1654-1703) & Abigail [FRARY] (1662, ?1663-); b 1688?, b 1692; Boston
ARNOLD, Caleb (1644-1719) & Abigail WILBUR (-1730); 10 Jun 1666; Portsmouth, RI
ARNOLD, Daniel (-1691) & Elizabeth [OSBORN] (1647-); ca 1663; Hartford
ARNOLD, Edward (-1657) & Martha __?__; b 1653?; Boston
ARNOLD, Eleazer (1651-1722) & Eleanor [SMITH]; b 1672; Providence
ARNOLD, Elisha (1662-1741) & Susanna [CARPENTER] (ca 1662-); b 1685?, b 1690; Providence
ARNOLD, Ephraim (1664-1697) & Mary __?__, m/2 Thomas COPELAND, m/3 __?__ NEWCOMB; [ca 1687]; Braintree
ARNOLD, Henry & [Elizabeth COLFAX]; b 9 Mar 1680/1; Hartford
ARNOLD, Isaac & __?__ [SYLVESTER]?; b 1640?; Southold, LI
ARNOLD, Isaac & 2/wf Sarah (CORNELL) WASHBURN, w John; 30? Oct 1641 m lic; ?Southold, LI
ARNOLD, Israel (1649-1717) & Mary (BAKER/BARBER) SMITH, w Elisha; 16 Apr 1677; Providence/Warwick, RI
ARNOLD, Israel & Elizabeth SMITH; 28 Feb 1698/9, 1698; Warwick, RI
ARNOLD, Jasper (1595-) & Ann __?__ (?1591-); b 1635
ARNOLD, John (-1664) & Susanna __?__ (1598-); b 1635; Cambridge/Hartford
ARNOLD, John & Mary [?BOWLEY]; b 1674?, b 1673?; Newark, NJ/Killingworth/Norwich, CT/Windham, CT
ARNOLD, John (1655-) & Mary __?__ (-1701); b 1678; Braintree/Weymouth/Boston
ARNOLD, John (?1648-1723) & Hannah __?__ (-1723+); b 1687?; ?Providence/Haddam, CT
ARNOLD, John (1670-1756) & 1/wf Mary [MOWRY] (1675-1742); b 1699, b 1695; ?Providence/Smithfield, RI
ARNOLD, Jonathan (?1679-) & Elizabeth __?__; 14 Aug 1699; Haddam, CT
ARNOLD, Joseph (-aft 5 Nov 1696, 1701) & Rebecca (__?__) CURTIS (-1693), w Diodatus; 8 June 1648, Aug 4; Braintree
ARNOLD, Joseph (?1637-1691?) & Elizabeth [WAKEMAN]/WILLETT? (1633?-), m/2 Daniel? BRAINERD 1693; b 1662?, by 1659, b 6 Sept 1662; Haddam, CT/Newark, NJ
ARNOLD, Joseph & Elizabeth [BATEMAN?] [GRIDLEY] (1647-), wid; b 1679; Boston
ARNOLD, Joseph (1666-) & Susanna SMITH; 28 Jan 1695, 1695/6; Haddam, CT
ARNOLD, Josiah & 1/wf Sarah MILLS/?MILLER (1664-1704); 4 Sept 1683; Jamestown, RI
ARNOLD, Josiah (-1724) & Mary (SMITH?/WELLS?/WARD?); b 1691; Providence/Jamestown, RI
ARNOLD, Josiah (1670-1712) & Mary [WELLS?] (-1714?); b 1694; Haddam
ARNOLD, Josiah & 2/wf Mary (SANFORD) BRINLEY (1674-1721), w Wm.; 12 Feb 1705, b 1701?; Jamestown, RI

ARNOLD, Oliver (1655-1697) & Phoebe [COOK] (1665-1732), m/2 Jonathan MARSH 1700, m/3 Robert BARKER 1705; b 1680; Jamestown, RI

ARNOLD, Richard (1642-1710) & 1/wf Mary [ANGELL]; ca 1665?; Providence/Smithfield, RI/Woonsocket

ARNOLD, Richard (-1710) & 2/wf Sarah [SMITH?] (-1712); ca 1685, ca 1695, aft 22 May 1685; Providence

ARNOLD, Richard (-1745) & 1/wf Mary [WOODWARD]; b 1701?; Providence/Smithfield, RI/?Woonsocket, RI

ARNOLL, Samuel (-1693, ae 71) & Elizabeth _?_; b 1649; Yarmouth/Marshfield

ARNOLD, Samuel (1649-1709?) & Sarah _?_; Marshfield/Rochester

ARNOLD, Samuel & Susannah _?_?; b 1700; New Shoreham, RI

ARNOLD, Seth & Elizabeth [GRAY] (1658-); b 1680; Marshfield

ARNOLD, Sion (1674-1753) & Mary WARD (1679-1754); 7 Feb 1700; Newport

ARNOLD, Stephen (1622-1699) & Sarah SMITH (1629-1713); 24 Nov 1646; Providence

ARNOLD, Stephen, Jr. (1654-) & [?Mary SHELDON]?; 12 Jan 1688?; Woodstock

ARNOLD, Thomas (1599-1674) & 1/wf _?_; in Eng, b 1625, b 1634?; Watertown/Providence

ARNOLD, Thomas (1599-1674) & 2/wf Phebe [PARKHURST] (1612-1688+); b 1640; Watertown/Providence

ARNOLD, Thomas & Mary _?_; b 1697; Boston

ARNOLD, William (1587-1676±) & Christian/?Elizabeth [PEAKE] (1583/4-); in Eng, b 1610/11; Hingham/Providence

ARNOLL, William & _?_; b 1655; Boston

ARNOLD, William (?1649-1697) & Elizabeth [CLARK] (1659-1695), dau Thomas; b 1676; Reading

ARNOLD/ARNOLL, William & Phillis _?_; b 1688; Boston

ARNOLD, William & Mary _?_; b 1689; Boston

ARNOLL, William & Phillippi _?_; b 1691; Boston

ARNOLL, William & Hannah NICHOLS; 22 Feb 1694/5; Portsmouth, RI

ARTHER, Benjamin & Sarah NEAL; 13 July 1643 doubtful, 1743?

ARTHUR, John & Elizabeth _?_ (1616-1677+); Isles of Shoals

ARTHUR, John & Priscilla [GARDNER] (1656-); 2m-20-1676?; Nantucket

ARTHUR, [Robert?] & Mary [SANDERS]; b 1686; Huntington, LI

ARTHER, Richard, Portsmouth, NH & Mary WEST, Portsmouth; 16 July 1688; York Co., ME

ASBURY?/ASHBURY, John (-1736) & 1/wf Eleanor GRIFFEN (-1718), w Matthew; 18 Oct 1699; Boston

ASH, Edward & _?_; b 1676; Boston

ASH, John & Mary BARTLETT; 14 Aug 1667; Salisbury

ASH, Thomas & 1/wf Hannah [CHESLEY]; ca 1696?; Dover, NH/Durham, NH/Portsmouth, NH

ASH, Thomas & Mary (TIBBETS) [ROLLINS], w Ichabod; ca 1698?, b 1700, aft 1707?; Durham, NH

ASH, William & Millicent (ADDIS) [SOUTHMEADE/SOUTHMAYD], w William, m/3 Thomas BEEBE b 1663; bet 1649 & 1651; Glouster

ASH, William (-1675) & _?_; b 1671?; Berwick, ME

ASHBOURNE, Joseph & Mary [SANFORD] (1620-1750), m/2 Joshua HOTCHKISS, m/3 Eleazer HOLT; ca 1688?; Milford, CT

ASHBY, Anthony & Abigail (HUTCHINSON) [LAMBERT] (bpt 1636-), w John; aft 6 Nov 1667, bef Dec 1670, bef 12 June 1670; Salem

ASHBY, Benjamin (-1713) & Hannah _?_ (-1731+); ca 1668?; Salem

ASHBY, Benjamin (-1718) & Elizabeth PRIEST (1680-); 27 Dec 1700; Salem

ASHBY, Edmund (-1733) & Ellen/Eleanor _?_; b 1680; Gloucester/Beverly

ASHCRAFT/ASCRAFT/ASHCROFTE, John & Hannah OSBORNE; 12 Sept 1670; Stonington, CT

ASHCRAFT, John, Jr. & _?_; 12 Dec 1670, b 1696; Stonington

ASHFIELD, William (-bef 1695) & Jane [LARRABEE] (-1695); b 1688?, b 1691; Malden/North Yarmouth, ME

ASHLEY, David (1642-1718) & Hannah GLOVER (1646-); 24 Nov 1663; New Haven, CT/Springfield/Westfield

ASHLEY, David (1667-1744) & Mary DEWEY (-1731); 11 July 1688; Westfield/Deerfield/Wethersfield, CT

ASHLEY, Edward & Mary [HALLOWAY/HOLLOWELL] (1653-), m/2 John WEBB; b 1674; Boston/Salem

ASHLEY, John (1669-1759) & 1/wf Sarah DEWEY (1672-1708); 8 Sep 1692; Westfield/Deerfield

ASHLEY, Jonathan (1646-1705) & Sarah WADSWORTH, Hartford; 10 Nov 1669; Springfield/ Hartford

ASHLEY, Jonathan & Abigail STEBBINS; 1 Feb 1699/1700; Springfield/Deerfield

ASHLEY, Joseph (1652-1698) & Mary PARSONS, Northampton (1661-), m/2 Joseph MILLISTON 1699; 16 Oct 1685, 15(?) Oct; Springfield/Deerfield/Wethersfield

ASHLEY, Joseph (1671-) & Abigail DEWEY, m/2 Thomas DEWEY; 12 Apr 1699; Westfield/Deer- field

ASHLEY, Robert (-1682) & Mary (_?_) HORTON (-1683), w Thomas; m cont 7 Aug 1641; Springfield/Deerfield

ASHLEY, Samuel & Sarah KELLOGG; 27 Apr 1686; Westfield/Hadley/Deerfield

ASHLEY, Thomas (1616-) & 1/wf Joanna _?_ (1661); b 1661; Boston

ASHLEY, Thomas & 2/wf Hannah BROOME? BROWNE?, w George; last of Jan 1661/2; Boston

ASHLEY, Thomas & Rebecca _?_; b 1678

ASHLEY, Thomas & Mary (FOSDICK?)/[BRANSON] (1651-1691, 1697); b 1681; Boston/Charles- town

ASHLEY, William & 2/wf? Elizabeth [BATSON]; b 1674?; ?Wells, ME

ASHLEY, William (-1694) & Sarah _?_ (-1695+); Providence

ASHMAN, John & Phebe [WASHBURN] (-1665); LI

ASHMAN, Robert (-1683) & [Katrina] [ARMITAGE?]; ca 1650?; Hempstead, LI/Jamaica, LI

ASHTON, James (1604?-1687+) & _?_ ; Providence

ASHTON, James & Deliverance THROCKMARTON/THROCKMORTON (?1645-); 25 May 1669, b 1665; Providence/Middletown, NJ

ASHTON, John (1638-1714+) & 1/wf _?_ [ALGER]; Scarborough, ME

ASHTON, John & 2/wf Susannah [FOXWELL], b 1666; Scarborough, ME

ASHTON, John & 3/wf Mary (EDGECOMB) PAGE, w George; 30 Jul 1691; Marblehead

ASHTON, Joseph & 1/wf Mary PAGE; 4 Aug 1700; Marblehead

ASHTON, Samuel & Mary SANDEN (-1730), Marblehead; 15 Jul 1686; Scarborough, ME

ASLET, John (?1614-1671) (ae 50 in 1664) & Rebecca AYER/AYRES, m/2 George KEYSER 1617+; ca 8 Oct 1648; Newbury/Andover

ASLETT, John (1656-1728), Boston & Mary OSGOOD (1656-1740); 8 Jul 1680; Andover

ASPINWALL, Joseph (-1743?) & 1/wf Hannah DEAN (-1712+); m lic 6 Jun 1700; New York City

ASPINWALL, Nathaniel (1666-1713) & Abigail BOWEN; 11 Nov 1698; Woodstock, CT

ASPINWALL, Peter (1612-1687) (called "cousin" by James CLARK of Boston, 1667) & 1/wf Alice [SHARP]/MORRILL?; b 30 Mar 1645, no issue, b 8 Jun 1645; Dorchester/Boston

ASPINWALL, Peter (1612-1687) & 2/wf Remember PALFREY (1638-); 12 Feb 1661, [1661/2]; Reading/Boston/Roxbury

ASPINWALL, Peter (1664-1749+) & Elizabeth (PRESTON) LEAVENS, w John; 24 Mar 1699, [1698/9]; Woodstock, CT

ASPINWALL, Samuel (1662-1727) & [Sarah STEVENS] (1668-1710); ca 1689; Roxbury?

ASPINWALL, William & Elizabeth [?STANLEY]; b 1630, b 1628; RI/New Haven/Boston

ASPINWALL, William & Elizabeth GOODYEAR (very doubtful); 5 Feb 1628; Manchester

ASTWOOD, James (-1653) & Sarah _?_; b 1637?; Roxbury/Boston

ASTWOOD, John (-1654, England) & 1/wf Martha _?_; b 1635; Roxbury/Milford, CT

ASTWOOD, John (-1654, England) & 2/wf Sarah (BRYAN?/BRUEN) [BALDWIN] (-1669), w Sylvester; 1640?, aft 1638; Milford, CT

ATCHINSON/?ATCHISON, John (-1677), Hatfield & Deliverance _?_ ; b 1672; Hadley

ATHEARN, Simon (-1714, ae 71) & Mary BUTLER; 4 Oct 1665; Tilbury/Martha's Vineyard

ATHERTON, Consider (-1690) & Anna ANNIBALL/ANNABLE (-1687); 19 Dec 1671; Dorchester

ATHERTON, Rev. Hope (1646-1677) & Sarah [HOLLISTER] (ca 1654-1691), Wethersfield, CT, m/2 Timothy BAKER 1680; 1674/5; Hatfield/Hadley/Wentworth

ATHERTON, Humphrey & Mary [WALES?] (doubtful); in Eng, ca 1629/30; Dorchester

ATHERTON, Humphrey (1673-1748) & Elizabeth [WORTHINGTON] (1676-); b 1701; Dorchester

ATHERTON, James (-1707, 1710?) & Hannah _?_ (-1713); b 1654; Dorchester/Lancaster/Milton

ATHERTON, James (1654-) & Abigail HUDSON/WATERS?; 6 Jun 1684; Lancaster

ATHERTON, Jonathan & Mary GULLIVER?/Sarah FENBREAD (1663, London?); 17 March 1679 (see Joshua); Milton

ATHERTON, Joseph (1675-) & 1/wf Mary [TAYLOR] (1673-1729); b 1701?; Northampton

ALTHERTON, Joshua (1656-1721) & Mary [GULLIVER?] (1656-1704) (dau Anthony?, had Stephen 30 Oct 1680), ?17 Mar 1679 (see Jonathan); Milton

ATHERTON, Watching (1651-) & Elizabeth RIGBEE; 23 Jan 1678, 1678/9?, 1677/8?, 28 Jan 1678/9 wrong; Dorchester/Bristol, RI

ATHY, Mark & Martha SMITH, w Abraham; 13 Aug 1685; Charlestown

ATKINS, Henry (-1700) & 1/wf Elizabeth WELLS (-1662); m cont 9 Jul 1647; Barnstable/Eastham

ATKINS, Henry (-1700) & 2/wf Bethiah LINNELL?/LENNETT (-1726), m/2 Stephen HOPKINS 1701; 25 Mar 1664; Eastham

ATKINS, Isaac (1657-1729) & Mercy _?_ ; ca 1680/85?; ?Eastham/Harwick

ATKINS, James & Margaret (CLEAVES) [PARKER], w Thomas; b 1682?; Roxbury

ATKINS/ADKINS, James & _?_ ; b 1691; Sandwich

ATKINS, John (1674-1733) & Elizabeth NEWCOMB (1681-1743); 5 Mar 1699/1700; Edgartown/Eastham/Chatham

ATKINS, Joseph (1669-) & Martha [PEASE] (1682?-); b 1701; Eastham/Wellfleet

ATKINS, Nathaniel (1667-) & Winifred [CHICK]; b 1694; Eastham/Truro

ATKINS/ALBINS, Robert (see ELKINS) & Patience (FENOLD) EVANS, w Ebenezer; 9 Nov 1686; Kittery, ME

ATKINS, Thomas & Elizabeth [?SCAMMON]; b 1645; Salisbury/Bath, ME

ATKINS, Thomas (-1709, ae 66) & Mary _?_ ; b 1672; Boston

ATKINS, Thomas (-1709), Boston & Abigail (WAITE) JONES, Charlestown, w Thomas; 11 Aug 1687; Charlestown/Boston

ATKINS, Thomas (1671-) & _?_ ; ca 1703?, b 1701; Charlestown

ATKINS/ADKINS?, Tobias & Anne [STRATTON] (1662-); b 1684; Boston

ATKINSON, John (1636-1715) (calls Theodore A. uncle 1655) (ae 28 in 1668) & 1/wf Sarah MIRRICKE/MYRICK?; 27 Apr 1664; Newbury

ATKINSON, John & Sarah [WOODMAN] (1670-); b 1694; Newbury

ATKINSON, John (1636-1715) & 2/wf Hannah (NOYES) CHENEY (1643-1705), w Peter; 3 Jun 1700; Newbury

ATKINSON, Joseph (1634±-1678) & Ann _?_ ; Portsmouth, NH

ATKINSON/ATCHINSON?, Luke (-1665/6) & 2/w? Mary PLOTT/PLATT (-1669), m/2 Thomas WHITMORE/WETMORE 1666/7; 1 May 1651; New Haven/Middletown

ATKINSON, Marmaduke & Mary [JENKINS], m/2 William COX? 1676 (see Robert COOKE); 1670, 1668?, div 1674, he deserted her, div 1 Mar 1674/5; Scituate

ATKINSON, Theodore (1611-1701?) & 1/wf Abigail _?_ (-1667?); b 1642, b 1634?; Boston/Charlestown

ATKINSON, Theodore (1611-1701, ae 89), Boston & 2/wf Mary (WHEELWRIGHT) LYDE, w Edward; 2 Oct 1667; Salisbury/Boston

ATKINSON, Theodore (1645?-1675) & Elizabeth [MITCHELSON], dau Edward, m/2 Henry DEERING 1676; b 1665; Boston/Cambridge

ATKINSON, Theodore (1669-1719) & Mary _?_ (cousin of Ruth TARLETON); b 1692; Boston/New Castle, NH?

ATKINSON, Thomas (-1646) & Susan/Susanna? _?_, m/2 William ALMY?/ALLME; b 1641, b 1636; Concord

ATKINSON, Thomas & Rebecca FALLET; m int 27 Dec 1695; Boston

ADKINSON, William & Sarah WHITE; 31 Aug 1698; Boston

ATWATER, David (1615-1692) & Damaris SAYRE? (1592-1691); 10 Mar 1646/7, ca 1645; New Haven

ATWATER, David (1651-1735/6) & Joanna _?_ ; b 1682(3?); New Haven

ATWATER, Ebenezer (1667-) & Abigail HEATON, m/2 John GILBERT; - Dec 1691; New Haven

ATWATER, John (1654-1748) & 1/wf Abigail MANSFIELD (1665-1717); 13 Sep 1682; New Haven

ATWATER, John (-1692/3) & Mehitable WAINWRIGHT (-1693+), dau Francis; b 1687; Salem

ATWATER, Jonathan (1656-1736) & Ruth PECK (1661-); 1 Jun 1681; New Haven

ATWATER, Joshua (-1676) & Mary BLACKMAN (-1709), m/2 John HIGGINSON 1676+; 6 May 1651; New Haven/Milford, CT/Boston

ATWATER, Joshua & Lydia ROCKWELL (1656-1681); 24 Jun 1680; Wallingford, CT

ATWATER, Joshua (1658-) & Mary (MAVERICK) [SMITH], w Samuel; b 1686(7?); Boston

ATWATER, Samuel (1668-) & Sarah ALLING; 7 Jul 1691; New Haven

ATWATER, [John?], Salem & Maria COTTON (doubtful) (1670-1729), m/2 Samuel PARTRIDGE; Hampton, NH

ATWELL, Benjamin & Dorothy __?__, prob m/2 Richard MARTIN; ca 1640-43, b 1640?; ?Falmouth, ME

ATWELL, Benjamin (-1676) & Alice [LEWIS]; ca 1667-8; Scarboro, ME

ATWELL, Benjamin (-1683) & Mary __?__, m/2 Joseph INGHAMS bet 1683 & 1686; b 1668, b 1670; New London, CT

ATWELL, Benjamin (1668-1723) & Mary __?__; b 1701?; New London, CT

ATWELL, John & Elizabeth (MAINE/MAINS)?; b 1648?, b 1668?; N. Yarmouth, ME

ATWELL, John & Margaret MAXE; 19 Jun 1693, 12 Dec (wrong); Topsfield/Killingly, CT

ATWELL, Philip (-1695+) & [Joan] [ANDREWS], w John; by 1672; ?Kittery, ME

ATWOOD see WOOD

ATWOOD, Eldad & Anna SNOW (1656-1715); 14 Feb 1683, 1683/4; Eastham

ATWOOD, Herman/Harman (-1651) & Ann COPP (-1661), m/2 Thomas SAXTON 1651/2; 11 Aug 1646; Boston

ATWOOD/WOOD?, John (-1644) (William CROWE was a nephew) & Ann [?LEE]; b 1636?, no issue; Plymouth

WOOD/ATWOOD, John & Sarah [MASTERSON]; b 1645; Plymouth

ATWOOD, John (1647-1714) & 1/wf Sarah [?CROWE]; b 1671; Boston

ATWOOD, John (-1714) & Mary (LONG) SMITH (-1729), w Francis; 27 Oct 1690; Boston

WOOD/?ATWOOD, Joseph (-1697, ae 47) & Hester WALKER (-1696, ae 46); 1 Jan 1679, 1679/80?; ?Taunton

ATWOOD, Machiel/Malchiel & Prudence (HARDING)? ROGERS (1676-), w Joseph; 25 Oct 1700; Eastham/Truro

ATWOOD, Medad (1659-) & Esther/Hester [COLE], dau Daniel; b 1686; Eastham

ATWOOD/?WOOD, Nathaniel (1652-1724) & Mary [MOREY] (1660-); b 1684; Plymouth

ATWOOD, Oliver (1671-) & Anna BETTS (1681-); 30 Mar 1699; Malden/Boston

ATWOOD, Philip & 1/wf Rachel [BATCHELDER]; b 1653; Malden/Charlestown

ATWOOD, Philip & 2/wf Elizabeth GROVER (-1676), w Thomas; 7 Apr 1675; Malden

ATWOOD, Philip & 3/wf Elizabeth __?__ (-1688); Malden

ATWOOD, Philip (1658-1722) & Sarah TENNEY, Bradford; 23 Jul 1684, Salem; Bradford/Malden

ATWOOD/WOOD?, Stephen (-1694) & Abigail DUNHAM; 11 Nov; Plymouth?/Eastham

ATWOOD/WOOD?, Stephen (-1722) & Apphia (BANGS) KNOWLES (1651-), w John; aft 1675, b 1677; Eastham

ATWOOD, Stephen & Martha PIKE; 26 Jun 1700; Eastham

ATWOOD, Thomas (-1682) & Abigail __?__ (1645/8-1713); b 1668; Wethersfield, CT

ATWOOD, Thomas (-1694) & Elizabeth __?__ (-1720), m/2 John WEST 1697; ?ca 1675; Ipswich

ATWOOD, Thomas & Mary __?__; b 1687; Boston

ATWOOD, __?__ & Mehitable __?__, m/2 Thomas COPELAND 1692; Braintree

AUBREY/AWBREY, William & Rachel RAWSON; 18 Jan 1652/3; Boston

AULT, John (?1601-) (ae 73 in 1678) & Remembrance [TIBBETTS] (1607-); b 1640; Dover, NH

AUSTIN, Anthony (1636-1708) (ae 27 in 1663, 35 in 1671) & Esther HUGGINS (-1694, 1698); 19 Oct 1664; Rowley/Suffield, MA

AUSTIN, Anthony & Abigail HOLCOMB, Windsor, CT; 4 Oct 1699; Suffield, CT

AUSTIN, David (1670-1713) & Abigail [PECK] (1682-1741); b 1699; New Haven

AUSTIN, Ebenezer (1662-1723) & 1/wf Thankful (STOW) BENJAMIN (-1699), w Joshua; 8 Jul 1685; Charlestown

AUSTIN, Ebenezer (1662-1723) & 2/wf Rebecca SPRAGUE (?1666, 1675-1709); 27 Jan 1691/2; Malden/Charlestown

AUSTIN, Francis (-1642) & Isabel/Isabella BLAND, alias SMITH?, m/2 Thomas LEAVITT by 1644; b 1633?; Dedham/Hampton, NH

AUSTIN, Jeremiah (-1754) & Elizabeth __?__ (-1752+); b 1687?; Kingston, RI/Exeter, RI

AUSTIN, John (-1657) & Katerine __?__, ?m/2 William HUBBARD; ?ca 1647; New London, CT/Stamford, CT

AUSTIN, John & 1/wf Mercy ATWATER (1648-1683); 5 Nov 1667; New Haven

AUSTIN, John & Mercy [OSBURNE]; b 1673; New Haven

ASTIN, John (-1699) & Hannah [HARDY] (-1710?), dau Richard; b 1679; Stamford, CT

AUSTIN, John (-1690) & 2/wf Elizabeth (BARNES) BROCKETT (1650-), w Benjamin; 21 Jan 1684, [1684/5]; New Haven

AUSTIN, John (1676-1767) & 1/wf Agnes KING (1681-1732); 5 Oct 1699; Suffield, CT
AUSTIN, John (1671-) & Sarah HALL; 23 Nov 1699; Taunton/Norton
AUSTIN/ALLEN, Jonah[1]/Jonas? (-1683?) & 1/wf Constance [ROBINSON] (-1667), w William; b 1636, b 1635, 22 Jan 1626/7; Cambridge/Hingham/Taunton
AUSTIN, Jonah[2]/Jonas? (-1676) & [Esther] _?_ ; b 1662; Taunton
AUSTIN/ALLEN, Jonah[1]/Jonas? (-1683) & 2/wf Frances HILL? (-1676), w John?; 14 Dec 1667; Taunton
AUSTIN, Jonah/Jonas? (1667-1755) & Tamason LINCOLN (1667-); 20 Apr 1692; Taunton
AUSTIN, Joseph (-1663) & Sarah (STARBUCK), w William, m/3 Humphrey VARNEY 1668/9; by Oct 1649; Dover, NH
AUSTIN, Joseph (-1739) & Elizabeth PITTS; 10 Nov 1692; Charlestown
AUSTIN, Joshua (1673-1760) & 1/wf Silence [FRISBIE] (1672-); b 1701?, b 1714; ?Bramford, CT/New Haven
AUSTIN, Matthew (1620±-) & 1/wf _?_ [CANNEY]; b 1658, b 1654?; Hampton, NH
AUSTIN, Matthew & 2/wf Mary (DAVIS) [DODD], w George, m/3 William WRIGHT; b 1667?; York, ME
AUSTIN, Matthew[2] & Mary [LITTLEFIELD]; b 1675, b 1701; York, ME
AUSTIN, Richard (1598-1638) & (?Elizabeth) _?_ ; b 1638, b 1632?; Charlestown
AUSTIN, Richard (1632-1703, ae 71) & Abigail BACHELDER (-1694, ae 56 or 67); 11 Nov 1659; Charlestown
AUSTIN, Richard (1665-1694) & Mehitable WELSTED, m/2 Benjamin GIBSON 1699/1700; 27 Nov 1691; Charlestown
AUSTIN, Richard (1666-1733) & Dorothy ADAMS (1679-); 12 Jan 1698, 1698/9; Suffield, CT
AUSTIN, Robert (?1634-1687-) & _?_ ; b 1661; Kingston, RI
AUSTIN, Samuel (-1716) & Sarah [STORER]; ca 1660, b 27 Jun 1661; Dover, NH/Mills, ME/Charlestown
AUSTIN, Samuel & [Elizabeth GOOCH]; b 1667; Salisbury
AUSTINS, Samuel & Hopestill _?_ ; b 1669; Boston
AUSTIN, Samuel (?1660-1716) & Sarah [RIDGWAY] (-1728+); b 1689; Charlestown
ASTIN, Samuel & Lucy POOR; 11 Oct 1691; Andover
AUSTIN, Thomas & Ann [OTIS]; b 1678, nr 1677; Dover, NH
ASTIN, Thomas (-1712) & Hannah FOSTER; 15 Sep 1690; Andover
AUSTIN/ASHTON?, William (-1687) & Hannah _?_ ; b 1673; Providence
AUSTIN, William & Hannah TRERICE (1664-); 3 Jun 1696, 30? Jun; Charlestown
AVERILL, Ebenezer (1669-) & 1/wf Susannah HOVEY (-1699); 30 Nov 1687; Topsfield
AVERIL, Ebenezer & 2/wf Mehitable FOSTER (1675-); 31 Dec 1700; Ipswich/Topsfield
AVERILL, Job (1671-1726) & Mary [RUBLE]; 1701?, 26 Apr 1700?; York Co., ME
AVERILL, Nathaniel (1664-) & 1/wf Sarah HOWLETT (-1729); 31 Dec 1698; Topsfield
AVERILL, Thomas (1630-1714) & Frances COLLINGS; 8 Dec 1657; Ipswich/York Co., ME
AVERILL, Thomas & Hannah _?_ ; by 1672; York Co., ME
AVERILL, William (-1652/3) & Abigail [HINTON] (-1655), in Eng, b 1630, 26 Nov 1618; Chipping Norton, Oxfordshire/Ipswich/Topsfield
AVERILL, William (?1637-1691) & Hannah JACKSON; 31 Jul 1661; Ipswich/Topsfield
AVERILL, William (1662-) & Mary _?_ (-1729); ca 1688; Topsfield
AVERY, Christopher (-1630) & Margery STEPHENS, d in Eng; Ippledon, Devonshire 26 Aug 1616 m lic.; Gloucester/Boston/New London, CT
AVERY, Edward (-1759) & Joanna ROSE (ca 1681-1760?); 3 Jun 1699; Preston, CT/Stonington, CT
AVERY, James (1620-1700) & Joane/?Joanna GREENSLADE; 10 Nov 1643; Gloucester/New London, CT
AVERY, James (1646-1728) & Deborah STALLION/?STERLING; 20 Feb 1669; New London, CT
AVERY, James & Mary [GRISWOLD], E. Windsor; b 1696; Stonington, CT
AVERY, James & 2/wf Abigail (?INGRAHAM) CHESEBROUGH HOLMES (-1715), w Samuel, w Joshua; 4 Jul 1698; Groton, CT/Stonington, CT
AVERY, John (lived in London, Eng) & Sarah BROWN; 21 Aug 1663; Charlestown
AVERY, John (1654-) & Abigail CHESEBROUGH; 29 Nov 1675; Stonington, CT
AVERY, Jonathan (-1690) & Sybil SPARHAWKE, m/2 Michael WIGGLESWORTH; 22 Jul 1679; Dedham
AVERY, Joseph (-1635) & _?_

AVERY, Matthew (-1643, London) & Anna _?_, m/2 William ROBERTS; b 20 Apr 1642; Charlestown

AVERY, Robert & Elizabeth LANE; 3 Apr 1677; Billerica/Dedham

AVERY, Samuel (1664-1723) & Susannah PALMES (ca 1665-1747); 25 Oct 1686; Swansea

AVERY, Thomas (-1681) & Joan?/Susanna? _?_ (?sister of Mrs. Rebecca BACON); b 1657; Portsmouth, NH

AVERY, Thomas (1651-1737) & Hannah MINOR (1655-1692?); 22 Oct 1677; Stonington, CT

AVERY, Thomas & Hannah (RAYMOND) BULKLEY, w Charles; 13 Mar 1693; Wethersfield/New London

AVERY, Thomas (-1744) & Abigail COOMBS, wid; 8 Oct 1697; Dover, NH

AVERY, William[1] (ca 1622-1687) & Margaret [ALBRIGHT] (ca 1628-1678); b 1645; Dedham

AVERY, William & _?_ ; b 1637

AVERY, William (1647-1708) & 1/wf Mary [LANE] (-1681); 21 Sep 1673; Dedham

AVERY, William (-1686/7) & 2/wf Mary (WOODMANSEY) TOPPING (ca 1628-1707), w John; bef 8 Nov 1679; ?Boston

AVERY, William (-1708) & 2/wf Elizabeth WHITE (-1690); 29 Aug 1682; Dedham

AVERY, William (-1708) & 3/wf Mehitable (HINCKLEY) WORDEN/WARDEN? (1659-), w Samuel; 25 Aug 1698; Dedham/Boston

AVERY, William (1678-1750) & Esther HUNTING (1677-1745); 26 Jun 1700; Dedham

AVES/AVIS, Samuel (1674-) & Mary POMRY; m int 30 Apr 1696; Boston

AVIS, William & Mehetable MARTAIN/MARTIN; 25 Jul 1662; Charlestown/Boston

AWKLEY, Miles & Mary _?_ ; b 1635; Boston

AXALL, Humphrey & Mary (JENKINS) GREEN, w John; aft 1693?; Portsmouth, NH/York, ME/Eliot Neck, ME

AXEY, James (-1667, 1669?) & Frances _?_ (-1670); ca 1630-40?; Lynn

AXTEL, Henry (1641-1676) & Hannah [MERRIAM] (1645?-1683?), m/2 William TAYLOR 1677; 14 Jun 1665; Marlborough

AXDELL, Thomas (1619-1646) & Mary _?_ (d bef 1653), m/2 John MAYNARD 1646; b 1639; Sudbury

AXTELL, Thomas (1672-1750) & Sarah BARKER (-1747); 2 Nov 1697; Concord/Grafton

AYRES, Edward (1658/9-) & Alice [SHAPLEIGH?]; b 1680?; Kittery, ME/Portsmouth, NH

AYRES, Henry & Ann _?_ ; b 1660; Portsmouth, RI

AYER, John (?1590-1657) & Hannah [?WEBB] (-1688), EVERED alias WEBB; b 1622?, Norwich, Eng, ca 1620?; Salisbury/Haverhill

AYER, John (-1694+) & 1/wf Sarah WILLIAMS (-1662); 5 May 1646; Haverhill

AYER, John (-1675) & Susanna [SYMONDS] (1617-1653); ca 1644, ca 1642?; Ipswich/Brookfield

AYERS, John & Abigail [HOVEY]; b 1658/[9?]; Ipswich

AYER, John (-1694+) & 2/wf Mary WOODDAM/WOODHAM (ae 34 in 1668); 26 Mar 1663; Haverhill

AYRES, John (1647-1683?) & Mary _?_ ; b 1670?, b 1677; Salisbury/Boston/Ipswich

AIRES, John & Bridget _?_ ; b 1679; Boston

AYERS, John (1657-1743) & Hannah TRAVERS/TRAVIS? (1661-); 13 Sept 1683; Haverhill

AYRES, John (1663-1732) & Mary WALKER (-1739); 24 Feb 1689/90; ?Woodbridge, NJ

AYRE, John & Ruth BROWN; 31 Oct 1698; Newbury

AYERS, Joseph & Sarah CALDWELL (1658-1700+); 9 Jun 1684; Ipswich

AYERS, Joseph & Sarah CORLES/CORLISS; 24 Nov 1686; Amesbury/Haverhill

AYERS, Joseph & Margery _?_/FISKE?; b 1694; Ipswich

AYERS, Mark & Sarah _?_ ; b 169[3]?; Portsmouth, NH

AYRES/EYRES, Moses & 1/wf Bethiah MILLS (-1669); 3 Aug 1666, 26 Mar 1666; ?Dorchester

AYRES, Moses & 2/wf Elizabeth TOLMAN; 28 Oct 1692; Dorchester

AYER, Nathaniel (-1717) & Tamasin TURLOAR/TURLAND?/THURLOW? (-1700); 10 May 1670; Haverhill/Hampton, NH

AYER, Nathaniel & Ann SWAN (1658-); 31 Aug 1683; Haverhill/Stonington, CT

AYRES, Nathaniel (1674-1731?) & Amy (COWELL) (SHERBURN) [FURBER], w Joseph, w Jethro; b 26 Dec 1692; Portsmouth, NH/Boston

AYER, Obadiah (-1691) & Hannah PIKE (-1689); 9 Mar 1660/1?, 19 Mar 1660/1; Haverhill/Woodridge, NJ/Newbury

AYER, Peter (ca 1632-1699) & Hannah ALLEN (1642-1729); 1 Nov 1659; Haverhill/Boston

AYRES, Richard & Mary _?_ (-1716), Stamford; b 1680?; Stamford, CT

AYER, Robert (-1711) & Elizabeth PALMER (ca 1627-1705); 27 Feb 1650; Haverhill
AYARS, Robert & Hester BOWEN; ca 1673?, b 1673; Westerly, RI/Cohansey, NJ
ÅYRES, Samuel (-1697) & __?__ ; b 1658, ca 1656; Ipswich/Salisbury
AYRES, Samuel (ca 1650-) & 1/wf Abigail FELLOWS (-1723); 16 Apr 1677; Ipswich/Newbury
AYER, Samuel (1654-1708) & Mary/Sarah? (prob error) JOHNSON (1663-); 14 Dec 1681;
   Haverhill
AYER, Samuel & Elizabeth TUTTLE (1670-1752); 21 Nov 1693; Haverhill
AYRES/EYRES, Simon/Simeon?/Davis? (-1695) & Elizabeth STARR; 22 Jul 1679; New Haven
AYER, Thomas (ca 1628-1686) & Elizabeth HUTCHINS (-1710); 1 Apr 1656; Haverhill/Newbury
AYRES, Thomas & Hannah ERINGTON/ERRINGTON; 21 Mar 1677, 1677/8; Ipswich/Newbury
AHHAYRES/AYRES?/EYRES?, Thomas & Mary [WILLIAMS]; b 1690; Manchester
AYER, Thomas & 1/wf Ruth WILFORD; 12 Jun 1694; Haverhill
AIRS, Thomas & Sarah [REYNOLDS]; b 1696; N. Kingston, RI
AYERS, Thomas & 2/wf Elizabeth [HALE?]; b 5 May 1700; Ipswich/Portsmouth, NH
AYERS, Timothy & Ruth JOHNSON (1666-), m/2 Samuel DOW 1691; 24 Nov 1682, 4 Nov;
   Haverhill
EARSE, William & __?__ ; b 1654; Hartford
AYER, William & Sarah [WOOLRYCH/WOOLRICH]; b 1658; Charlestown
EIRES/AYERS, Zachariah & Elizabeth CHASE, m/2 Daniel FAVOR; 27 Jun 1678; Andover
AYLETT, John (1628-) & Mary HAWKINS; 21 Nov 1654; Boston
ALYSWORTH/AYLSWORTH, Arthur (1653-1726) & Mary [BROWN]; ca 1680/2, b 1685;
   Providence
AYRAULT, Nicholas (?1661, ?1656-1706) & 2/w? Marian [BRETOUN], ?m William GOODRICH
   1714; b 1693?, b 1699, b 1696; Wethersfield, CT
AYRAULT, Pierre/Peter (-1711) & Francoise/Frances __?__ (1640-1712); in France, b 1676; Kings
   Town, RI/ E. Greenwich, RI

BABB, Peter & Sarah [CATE]; ca 1698; ?Greenland, NH
BABB, Philip (-1671) & __?__ ; b 1668; Isles of Shoals
BABB, Philip & Lydia [BRAGDON], m/2 Samuel NORTON; ca 1692; York, ME
BABB, Thomas (-1751) & Bathsheba [HUSSEY] (1671); ?Hampton, NH
BABB, William (-1691) & Deborah __?__ ; Essex Co., MA
BABBIDGE/BABADGE, Christopher (1631-1706+) & 1/wf Agnes [TRIGGS] (-1667); Totnes, Eng,
   b 1663, 31 Dec 1655; Salem
BABADGE, Christopher (1631-1706+) & 2/wf Hana/Hannah (JEWETT) CARLETON (1641-1706+),
   w John; 5 Oct 1674; Salem
BABAGE, James & Elizabeth DAVISE; 9 Oct 1693; Boston
BOBBET, Edward (-1675) & Sarah TARNE, dau Miles; 7 Sept 1654; Boston/Taunton
BOBET, Edward (1655-) & Abigail TISDALE; 1 Feb 1683; Taunton
BOBET, Edward (1655-) & Elizabeth THAYER; 22 Dec 1698; Taunton
BOBET, Elkanah (1665-1735) & Elizabeth BRIGGS (1671, 1666?-); 25 Jun 1689; Taunton
BABBITT, Erasmus & 1/wf __?__ ; b 1681; ?Westerly, RI
BABBITT, Erasmus & 2/wf Mary (LAWTON) BABCOCK (-8 Nov 1711), w John; 21 Apr 1698;
   Stonington, CT/Westerly, RI
BABBITT, Erasmus & Thomasin (ELSEN/ELSON) HARRIS (1644-1721), w David; 18 Nov 1700;
   Boston
BADCOCK, Benjamin (ca 1650-1690) & Hannah DANIELL (-1690?); 11 Feb 1673, 1674;
   Milton/Dorchester
BADCOCK, Ebenezer (1662-1717) & Hannah [BARBOUR] (1654-); b 1686(7?); Sherborn
BADCOCK, Enoch (-1695) & Susannah [GREGORY]?; b 1678; Milton
BADCOCK, George (-1671/2) & [Mary] __?__ ; ca 1649?; Dorchester
BADCOCK, George (1665-1695) & Ruth RUGGLES, m/2 John DOWN 1696; 19 Nov 1691; Boston
BABCOCK, George & Elizabeth HALL (-1762); 28 Nov 1694; Westerly, RI/N. Kingston, RI

BADCOCK, James (1612-1679) Stonington, CT & 1/wf Sarah __?__ (-1665?); b 1641; Portsmouth, RI/Westerly, RI

BADCOCK, James (1641-1698±) & Jane [BROWN] (-1719); ca 1665?; Westerly, RI

BADCOCK, James (1612-1679) Stonington, CT & 2/wf Elizabeth __?__, m/2 William JOHNSON 1678; betw 1665 & 1670; Portsmouth, RI/Westerly, RI

BABCOCK, James & 1/wf Elizabeth [SAUNDERS?]/[BABBITT?] (?1663-1731); b 1687?; Westerly, RI

BADCOCK, Job (?1646-1718, 1715?) & Jane [CRANDALL] (-1715, 1718?); ca 1666-1670; Westerly, RI

BABCOCK, Job (?1671-) & Deborah [REYNOLDS]; b 1695?; Westerly, RI

BADCOCK, John (1644-1685) & Mary [LAWTON?] (-1711), m/2 Erasmus BABBITT 1698; ca 1662; Westerly, RI

BABCOCK, John (?1669-1746) & Mary [CHAMPLIN] (-1746+); b 1701; Westerly, RI

BADCOCK, Jonathan (-1731) & 1/wf Mary CURTIS (1655-); 1 Aug 1676; Milton/Scituate/Falmouth

BABCOCK, Joseph & 1/wf Dorothy KEY/KAY? (-1727); 3 Apr 1696, 13 Apr; Stonington, CT

BADCOCK, Nathaniel (-1719) & Hannah __?__; b 1684; Milton

BADCOCK, Nicholas & [?Ann COLE]; ca 8 Oct 1686; Portsmouth, NH

BADCOCK, Return & Sarah DENISON; 1 Dec 1681; Milton/Dorchester/Dartmouth

BADCOCK, Robert (ca 1625-1694) & Isana?/Joanna? __?__ (-1700, ae 71); b 1650?, b 1654?, b 1658?; Dorchester/Roxbury/Milton

BADCOCK, Samuel (?1650-1690) & Hannah EMES; 1 Jul 1674; Milton

BABEL, Hugh & Susanna __?__; b 1680(1?); Boston (related to Dutch fam)

BABSON, James (?1633, ?1623-1683) & Elner HIL/Eleanor HILL (-1714, ae 84); 16 Nov 1647; Gloucester

BABSON, John (-1737) & Dorcas ELWELL (-1737); 8 Nov 1686; Gloucester

BABSON, Philip (1654-1708) & Hannah BAKER (1662-); 22 Oct 1689; Beverly/Salem

BABSON, Richard (1663-) & 1/wf Mary [DOLLIVER] (-1718); b 1687; Gloucester

BABSON, __?__ & Isabella __?__ (?1577, ?1580-1661, ae 84?); in Eng; Salem/Gloucester

BACKHOUSE/BACKUS, Francis & 1/wf Elizabeth [CROSS]; [1672]; ?Wells, ME/Saco, ME

BACKHOUSE, Francis & Dorcas (SEELEY) [GIBBINS], w James; ca 1683?; ?Saco

BACKUS, John (1661/2-1744) & Mary BINGHAM (1672-1747); 17 Feb 1691/2, 17 Feb 1692, 1683; Norwich, CT/Windham

BACKUS, Joseph (1667-1740) & Elizabeth HUNTINGTON (1669-1762); 9 Apr 1690; Norwich, CT

BACKUS, Nathaniel[3] (1669-1728) & 1/wf Lydia EDGERTON (1675-); 22 Mar 1693/4; Norwich, CT

BACKUS, Stephen (ca 1642-1694+, 1695) & Sarah SPENCER; Dec 1666, b 16 Apr 1700; Norwich, CT/Canterbury, NH

BACKUS, William[1] (-1664, 1661?) & 1/wf __?__; b 1635; ?Norwich, CT

BACKUS, William[2] (?1635-1720, 1721) & 1/wf Sarah [CHARLES] (1637-1663?, 1664?); ca 1655, by 1660; New Haven

BACKUS, William[1] (-1664) & 2/wf Anne (STENTON/STETSON?) BINGHAM (-1670), w Thomas; ca 1659/60; Norwich, CT/Saybrook, CT

BACKUS, William[2] (?1635-1720, 1721) & 2/wf Elizabeth PRATT (1641-1730, 1729); (prob 1664) 11 May 1660; Saybrook

BACKUS, William[3] (1660-1706) & Elizabeth [ROYCE] (1662-1688); 3 Nov 1681; Norwich

BACKUS, William (1660-) & 2/wf Mary BENTON/DUNTON? (1662-1757); 31 Aug 1692; Windham, CT

BACON, Andrew & Mary [SHERMAN] (1599-); in Eng, aft May 1619; Hartford?

BACON, Andrew (-1669) & Elizabeth (?MORRICE) [STANLEY] (-1679, ae 76), w Timothy; ca Apr 1648, b 1669; Hadley/Northhampton

BACON, Andrew (1666-1723) & Mehitable WETMORE (1669-1732); 12 Feb 1692, 1689/90; Middletown, CT

BACON, Daniel (?1615-1791) & Mary [REED] (ca 1620-1691) Colchester,Eng; b 1641; Woburn/Bridgewater

BACON, Danyell/Daneil (1641-1719, 1720) & Susan/Susanna SPENCER (1643-1728+); 1 Aug 1664; Salem

BACON, Daniel & Elizabeth MARTIN; 21 Apr 1685; Dedham

BACON, Daniel (-1650+) & Sarah (?LAMBERT) FRUDE (-1721), w Henery or James?; ?7 Sep 1688, ?12 Sep 1688; Salem
BACON, Ephriam (1675-) & Elizabeth GRIGS/GRIGGS; 28 Aug 1700; Dedham
BACON, George (1592-1642) & [?Margaret] _?_ (-1683), m/2 Edward GOLD b 1644; in Eng, b 1623; Hingham
BACON, George (1675-1715) & Mary DAVIS (1676-); 4 May 1699; Roxbury
BACON, Isaac (1650-1684) & Abigail _?_ (-1715); b 1684, ca 1672/78?; Cambridge?/Newton
BACON, Jacob (1654-1709) & Elizabeth [KNIGHT] (1656-1713); b 1677; Cambridge/Charlestown
BACON, Jacob & Dorothy BRADHURST; 24 Dec 1700; Roxbury
BACON, Jeremiah (1657-1706) & Elizabeth HOWES (-1706+); 10 Dec 1686; Barnstable
BACON, John (1624?, 1628?-1683) & Rebecca HALL (-1694); 17 Feb 1651/2, ?17 Dec 1651; Dedham
BACON, John (-1678) & Susanna DRAPER (-1678); 2 Sep 1668; Charlestown
BACON, John (1656-1732) & Lydia DUEIN/DEWING (1660/1-); 15 Dec 1683; Dedham
BACON, John (1661-) & 1/wf Mary HAWES (1664-); 17 Jun 1686; Barnstable
BACON, John (-1723) & Abigail _?_ (-1715?); b 1687, b 1685?; Watertown
BACON, John & Sarah WETMORE (-169[8]); 26 Nov 1689; Middletown, CT
BACON/BEACON?, John (1670-) & Abiel/Abigail CURTIS; 21 Nov 1693; Roxbury
BAKEN/BACON, Jonathan (1672-) & 1/wf Elizabeth GILES (-1738); 3 Jun 1694, 3 Jan 1694; Billerica
BACON, Joseph & _?_ ; b Jan 1687?; Farmington, CT
BACON, Joseph & Margaret BOWEN; 6 Nov 1688; Roxbury
BACON, Michael[1] (?1579-1648) & Alice _?_ (-1647); in Eng, [b 1608] Dedham
BACON, Michael[2] (?1608-1688) & 1/wf Mary [?JOBS] (-26 Aug 1655); b 1639/40, ca 1635, 31 Aug 1624?; Woburn
BACON, Michael[2] (?1608-1688) & Mary (_?_) RICHARDSON (-1670), w Thomas; 26 Oct 1655; Woburn
BACON, Michael[3] (-1701) Billerica & Sarah RICHARD (1640-15 Aug 1694); 22 Mar 1660; Woburn/Billerica
BACON, Michael[2] (?1608-1688) & 3/wf Mary (HAYNES) NOYES, w Thomas; 28 Nov 1670; Woburn
BACON, Michael & Johanna WELLS; 20 Nov 1694; Salem
BACON, Nathaniel (-1673) & Hannah MAYO (-1691+); 4 Dec 1642; Barnstable
BACON, Nathaniel/Thomas? (-1706) & 1/wf Ann [MILLER] (-1680); in Eng?, b 1654; Middletown, CT
BACON, Nathaniel (1645/6-1691) & 1/wf Sarah HINCKLEY (1646-1687); 27 Mar 1673; Barnstable
BACON, Nathaniel (-1706) & 2/wf Elizabeth PIERPONT; 17 Apr 1681; Middletown, CT
BACON, Nathaniel (-1692?) & Hannah [LAMBERT]?, m John DAVIS 1699; ca 1687/8; Barnstable
BACON, Nathaniel (?1674-) & Ruth DOGGET; 11 Nov 1696; Barnstable
BACON, Nathaniel & Judith [WYMAN] (1679-1715+); b 1699/(1700?); Billerica
BACON, Peter (-1694) & 1/wf Sarah [JENKINS] (-1677); 25 May 1670; Hingham
BACON, Peter (-1694) & Martha (HOWLAND) DAMON (-1732, ae 94, Hingham), w John; 16 Feb, 19 Feb 1679/80; Hingham/Taunton
BACON, Samuel & Martha FOXWELL (1638-); 9 May 1659; Barnstable
BACON, Samuel & Mary JACOB, m/2 Elisha BISBEE 1685; 17 Dec 1675; Hingham
BACON/BAKER, Thomas & Mary GAMBLIN (1642-); 27 May 1663; Roxbury
BACON, Thomas & Abigail MESKELL; 12 Mar 1684/5; Simmsbury, CT
BACON, Thomas, New Roxbury & Rebecca BUGBEY/BUGBEE, New Roxbury; 2 Nov 1688; Milton
BACON, Thomas (1667-) & 1/wf Hannah FALES (-1711); 22 Jan 1691; Wrentham
BACON, William (-1653) & Rebecca [POTTER], Coventry (-1655); b 1639(40?), by 1639; Salem
BADGER, Giles (-1647) & Elizabeth [GREENLEAF] (1622-1688+), m/2 Richard BROWNE 1648?; b 1643; Newbury
BADGER, John (1643-1691) & 1/wf Elizabeth [HAYDEN] (-1669); 16 Jun 1663; Charlestown/Newbury
BADGER, John (1643-1691) & 2/wf Hannah SWET/SWETT (-1691); 23 Feb 1670, 1670/1; Newbury/Portsmouth, NH
BADGER, John (1665-) & Rebecca BROWNE; 5 Oct 1691; Newbury

BADGER, Nathaniel (doubtful) & Hannah __?__ ; ca 1650?; Newbury
BADGER, Nathaniel (1676-) & Mary **LUNT** (1677-1763); 27 Mar 1693; Newbury/Norwich, CT
BADGER, Stephen (1671-) & Mercy [**KETTELL**] (1679-); b 1697; Charlestown
BADLAM, William & 1/wf Joan __?__ ; b 1687(8?); Boston
BADLAM, William & Mary [**FRENCH**] (1662-); b 1693, b 1690?, ca 1688; Weymouth
BADMAN, John & Sarah __?__ ; b 1656; Boston
BAGG, Daniel (1670-) & Hannah [**PHELPS**]; 18 Jan 1693/4; Westfield
BAGGS, Henry & Anne __?__ ; b 1695; Portsmouth, RI
BAGG, John (-1683) & Hannah **BURT** (1641-1680); 24 Dec 1657; Springfield
BAGG, John (1665-) & Mercy **THOMAS** (1671-); 30 Mar 1689; W. Springfield
BAGG, Jonathan (1670-) & Mary **WELLER** (1672-1740); 7 Jan 1696/7; Deerfield
BAGGERLEY, Richard (was in Eng ca 1636) & Alice [**DANIEL**], m/2 John **GREEN**; b 1630; Salem
BAGLEY, John (1668-) & Mary (**JACKSON**) [**LYON**], w Joseph; b 1700; Fairfield, CT
BAGLEY, Orlando (ca 1620-) & Sarah **COLEBY/COLBY** (1637-); 6 Mar 1653, 1653/4; Salisbury/Boston
BAGLEY, Orlando & 1/wf Sarah **SARGENT** (1652-1701); 22 Dec 1681; Amesbury
BAGLEY, Samuel & Mary __?__ ; b 1658; Weymouth
BAGLEY, Samuel & Mary **THAYER** (1663-), Braintree; 17 May 1686; Taunton/Weymouth/Braintree
BAGWORTH, Benjamin (-1658) & Jane [**TALBOT**], m/2 William **HABBERFIELD**; Boston
BALE, Benjamin & Bathsheba [**LOTHROP**] (1642-1728), m/2 Alexander **MARSH** 1687+; b 1674; Dorchester
BAILEY, Benjamin (1665-) & __?__ ; b 1700?; ?Haddam, CT
BAILEY, Edward & Frances __?__ ; b 1695, ca 1680/90?; Newport/Tiverton, RI
BAILEY, Elias (-1662) & Sarah __?__, m/2 Henry [**SATTE**]; by 1655?, by 1645?; Stamford, CT
BAILEY, Guydo & 1/wf Elizabeth __?__/[?**MARSTON**]; b 1642; Salem
BAILEY, Guydo & 2/wf Ruth [**GURNEY**] (-1703+), w John of Mendon; by 25 Nov 1693; Bridgewater
BAILEY, Henry & Rebecca __?__ ; b 1640; Salisbury
BAILEY, Henry & Dorothy **BOND**; 20 Sep 1665; Beverly
BALLY, Henry (-1717) & Mary [**PENLEY**] (-1734+); b 1685; Dorchester/Falmouth, ME
BAILEY, Hugh & 1/wf Anna __?__ ; b 1696; Newport/E. Greenwich, RI
BAILEY, Isaac (1654-1740) & 1/wf Sarah **EMERY** (1660-1694); 13 Jun 1683; Newbury
BAILEY, Isaac (1654-1740) & 2/wf Rebecca **BARTLET** (1661-1723); 5 Sep 1700; Newbury
BAILEY, James (?1612-1677) & Lydia __?__ (-1704); b 1643, ca 1640; Rowley
BAILEY, James (1650-1707) & 1/wf Mary **CARR** (1652-1688); 17 Sep 1672; Newbury/Salem/Killingworth, CT
BAILEY, James (1651-1715) & Elizabeth **JOHNSON** (-1743); 12 May 1680; Rowley
BAILEY, James (1650-1707) & 2/wf Mary (**LAMB**) [**SWAN**] (1644-1717), w Thomas; aft 28 Oct 1688; ?Killingworth, CT
BAYLEY, James & Elizabeth [**RUGGLES**] (1677-); ?3 Jun 1697; ?Roxbury
BAILEY, John (-1651) & __?__ ; in Eng, b 1613; Salisbury/Newbury
BAILEY, John (?1613-1691) & Eleanor [**EMERY**] (1624-1700); ca 1640; Newbury/Salisbury
BAILEY, John (?1617-) & __?__ ; by 1645?; Southold, LI/?Westchester Co., NY
BAILEY, John & __?__ ; b 1646; Isles of Shoals
BAILEY, John (-1696) & [Lydia **BACKUS**, not **SMITH**] (ca 1637); b 1661; Hartford/Haddam, CT
BAILEY, John (ca 1640-1686?) & Hannah/Ann [**BOURNE**?] (see below); ca 1666/7?, b 1677, 9 May 1677?, Marshfield; Weymouth
BALLEY, John (-1690) & Mary **MIGHELL** (-1693/4); 17 Jun 1668; Rowley/Salem
BAYLIE, John & Sarah **WHITTE/WHITE**; 25 Jan 1672; Scituate
BAILEY, John (1644-1697) & 1/wf Lydia __?__ (-1691 in 39th y); ca 1675; Watertown
BAILEY, John & Mary **GOODRICH**; 16 Aug 1676; Guilford, CT
BAYLEY, John (-1686?) & 2/wf? Ann **BOURNE** (1651-); 9 May 1677; Marshfield/?Freetown
BAILEY, John & __?__ ; b 1681, Salem; Salem
BAILEY, John (-1736) & Sutton __?__ ; b 1681(2?); Portsmouth, RI/Newport
BAILY, John & Charity __?__ ; b 1682; Boston
BAYLEY, John & Rachel __?__ ; b 1685; Bristol, RI

BAILEY, John (1661-) & Elizabeth [BATES], prob GERARD; b Oct 1688, b 1691; ?New London
BAILEY, John & Elizabeth __?__; b 1692; Westchester, NY
BAILEY, John & Elizabeth [GERARD] (1671-); b 1688; Haddam, CT
BAYLEY, John (-1697) & 2/wf Susanna WILKINS, w John, m/3 Peter THACHER 1699; m int 26 Dec 1695; Boston
BAILY, John & Ruth CLOTHIER; 9 Dec 1699; Scituate
BAYLIE, John & Abigail CLAP (1679-); 19 Feb 1700, 1699/1700, 14 Feb 1700; Scituate
BAYLEY, John & 1/wf Mary BARTLETT; 2 Jul 1700; Newbury
BAILEY, Jonas (1607-1663/4) & 1/wf Elizabeth [DEERING], w George; aft 30 Jun 1695; Scarborough, ME
BALEY, Jonas (1607-1663/4) & 2/wf Eleanor [JACKSON], w John, m/3 Giles BARGE by 1673; b 11 Nov 1663; Scarborough, ME
BAYLEY, Jonathan & 1/wf Hannah WALKER (-1702); 7 Mar 1693/4; Salisbury
BAILEY, Joseph & Alice __?__; b 1653; Huntington, LI
BAILEY, Joseph (-1712) & Abigail [TRUMBULL] (1651-1735); b 1671(2?); Bradford
BAILEY, Joseph (1648-1723) & 1/wf Pricilla [PUTNAM] (1657-1704); b 1675; Newbury
BAILEY, Joseph & __?__; b 1686, b 1682?; Newport
BAILEY, Joshua (1657-1722) & Elizabeth [PUTNAM] (1659-1727+), ca 1680/5?, no issue; Newbury
BAILEY, Nathan/?Nathaniel & Mary SQUIRE, m cont 8 Mar 1687/8; Fairfield, CT/Westchester Co., NY
BAYLY, Nicholas & Margeret __?__; b 20 Jan 1684, b 1663?; Westchester, NY
BAILEY, Richard (-1648) (?related to Thomas PARKER) & Edna [HALSTED], m/2 Ezekiel NORTHEND 1648; b 1647; Rowley
BAYLEY, Samuel & Deliverance [SMITH] (1660-); b 1698; Boston
BAILEY, Samuel & [Elizabeth ROGERS]; Newport
BAYLEY, Stephen (-1715) & Abigail HOOPER?; 8 Aug 1673?; Southold, LI
BAYLEY, Stephen & 2/wf Mary __?__; 15 Nov 1688; Southold, LI
BAILEY, Stephen (1665-1724) & Susanna __?__ (1673-1723); b 1701?; Newport, RI
BAILEY, Theophilus (-1694) & Ruth [IVORY]; b 11 Sep 1649; Lynn
BAYLEY, Thomas (-1681) & __?__; ca 1629/35?; ?Boston
BAYLEY, Thomas & Lydia REDFIN/REDFIELD, m/2 William THORN 1676; 10 Jan 1655/6, 20? Jan 1655; New London
BAYLEY, Thomas (-1690) & 1/wf Ruth PORTER (1639-); 19 Sep 1660; Weymouth
BAILEY, Thomas (1659-1709) & Ruth __?__; ca 1684?; New London
BAILEY, Thomas (-1735) & Elizabeth [WILKINS]; ca 1685; Salem
BAILEY, Thomas (-1689, ae 35) & Rebecca [FRIEND], m/2 William BROWN 1694; b 1686; Boston
BAYLEY, Thomas (-1690) & 2/wf Hannah (ROGERS) [PRATT] (-1721, ae 77), w Samuel; b 1687; Weymouth
BAYLEY, Thomas & Elizabeth __?__; b 11 Feb 1688/9; Gravesend, LI
BAYLEY, Thomas (-1704) & Mary __?__; b 1700; Glouchester
BAILEY, Thomas & Eunice WALKER; 8 Dec 1700; Bradford
BAILY, William & __?__; b 14 Nov 1647; Wenham
BAILEY, William & Grace [PARSONS] (-1677+), m/2 Thomas LAWTON ca 1674?; b 26 Jun 1655; Portsmouth, RI/Newport
BAILEY, William (1664) & __?__; New London, CT
BAINBRIDGE/BANBRIDGE, Guy (-1645) & Justice/Jusha __?__ (1598, 1600?-1668); in Eng, b 1624; Cambridge
BAKER, Alexander (1607-1685) & Elizabeth __?__ (1612-); b 1632; Glouchester/Boston
BAKER, Baysey (-1723) & Hannah WILLET, m/2 Joseph WEBSTER; 1 Apr 1697?, 1696?; Hartford
BAKER, Cornelius (-1716) & Hannah WOODBURY (1636-); 26 Apr 1658; Salem
BAKER, Cornelius (1667-) & Abigail [SALLOWS]; b 1692; Beverly
BAKER, Daniel (1650-) & Elizabeth CHASE (ca 1656-); 27 May 1674; Yarmouth
BAKER, Edward (-1687) & Joan/Jane? __?__ (-1693); b 1641; Lynn/Northampton
BAKER, Edward & Mary MARSHALL (1665-); 7 Apr 1685; Lynn

BAKER, Francis (1611-1696) & Isabel TWINING (-1706), Yarmouth; 17 Jun 1641; ?Yarmouth/
   Plymouth/Boston/Eastham
BAKER, Jeffrey (-1655) & Joan/Jane ROCKWELL (1625-1683), m/2 Richard INGRAM/?INGRA-
   HAM 1668; 25 Nov 1642; Windsor, CT
BAKER, John (1595, 1598?-1680+) & Elizabeth _?_ (1600-1679±); b 1633; Ipswich/Roxbury
BAKER, John & Charity _?_; b 1635; Boston/York/Dover, NH
BAKER, John (-1651+) & ?Sarah/?Rebecca _?_; b 1640; Charlestown
BAKER, John & 1/wf Joan/Jane SWIFT (-1663); error 5 Nov 1657, 1657?, prob 1647; Boston
BAKER, John & Susanna MARTIN; 28 May 1654; Woburn
BAKER, John (-1666) (called William IRELAND "cousin") & 2/wf Thankful FOSTER (-1698, ae
   58 y); 8 Jan 1663/4; Dorchester/Boston
BAKER, John & Lydia [BAYSEY] (-1700, 1702), Hartford; ca 1665?; Hartford
BAKER, John (1634-1718) & Catherine PERKINS (1648-); 13 May 1667; Ipswich
BAKER, John (1643-1690) & Preserved TROTT (1646-1711); 11 Jul 1667; Dorchester
BAKER, John (1645-1719) & Abigail FISHER (1646-1723); 17 Dec 1668; Dedham
BAKER, John & Ruth (LONG) WALLEY (1639-), w William; 7 Mar 1670; Charlestown
BAKER, John (-1712) & Alice [PIERCE] (1650-1712+); b 1672; Yarmouth
BAKER, John[2] (1644/5-1732) & Mary _?_; b 1676; Roxbury
BAKER, John & Elizabeth [WATERHOUSE], dau Jacob, m/2 Peter HACKLEY 1699; ?ca
   1676/90?; New London, CT
BAKER, John & Sarah (WELL) [DEW], w Thomas; ca 1680, ca 1679; Portsmouth, NH
BAKER, John & Hannah POLLY; 18 Oct 1682; Woburn
BAKER, John (-1697) & Mary _?_; b 1691; Hartford, CT
BAKER, John & Tabitha PICKMAN; m int 9 Mar 1695/6; Boston
BAKER, John (1672-) & Anna ANNABLE (1676-); 14 Oct 1696; Barnstable/Windham, CT
BAKER, John (1672-1760) & 1/wf Hannah JONES; 13 Apr 1699; Yarmouth
BAKER, John & Ann _?_; b 1700; Charlestown
BAKER, John & Mary BLIGH; 17 Jan 1700; Marblehead/Salem
BAKER, John (1678-) & Deborah [MORGAN]; b 1701, 28 Dec 16--; Beverly
BACON, Jonathan (1674-) & Elizabeth GILES; 3 Jan 1694, 1693/4, 3 Jun 1694; Woburn
BAKER, Jonathan (1669-) & Mary [COLBURN], m/2 Samuel BALCH; b 1698; Beverly
BAKER, Joseph (-1675) & Ruth HOLTON, m/2 Thomas LYMAN 1678; 5 Feb 1662, 1662/3;
   Northampton
BAKER, Joseph (1655-1691) & Hannah (COOKE) BUCKLAND (1655-), w Thomas, m/3 John
   LOOMIS?; 30 Jan 1676, 1676/7; Windsor, CT
BAKER, Joseph & Hannah BANK?/BAUK?; 4 Oct 1686; Chelmsford/Woburn/?Bristol, RI
BAKER, Joshua (1642-1717) & Hannah (TONGUE) MINTER (1654-), w Tristram; 13 Sep 1674;
   New London, CT
BAKER, Josiah & Mary [?CROSS]/[?PENNIMAN]; b 1680; Boston
BAKER, Kenelm ([1657/8], 1659-1713) & Sarah [BRADFORD] (?1671-); b 1688; Marshfield
BAKER, Launcelot & Judith _?_; b 1644; Boston/New Haven
BAKER, Nathaniel (?1611-1682) & Sarah [LANE] (-1695); b 1639; Hingham
BAKER, Nathaniel (1642-1691) & Mary [PIERCE?] (-1691); b 1670; Yarmouth
BAKER, Nathaniel (1655-1739 in 84th y) & 1/wf Catharine [SCHELLINGER] (1656-1722 in 66th
   y); b 1686, b 1679; East Hampton, LI
BAKER, Nathaniel & Mary _?_; b 1686(7?); Boston
BAKER, Nicholas (1610/11-1678) (ae 53 in 1663) & 1/wf _?_ [?RICHARDS] (-1661); b 1638;
   Hingham/Hull/Scituate
BAKER, Nicholas (-1678, ae 67) & Grace DIPPLE (-1697), wid, Barnstable; 29 Apr 1662;
   Hingham
BAKER, Nicholas & Experience [COLLIER]; b 1686; Hingham
BAKER, Nicholas & Elizabeth (SPURWINK) BARTLETT, wid; m int 14 Jul 1696; Boston/Marble-
   head
BAKER, Richard (ca 1614-1689) & Faith [WITHINGTON] (1616-1689); ?b 4 Nov 1639, ca 1639;
   Dorchester
BAKER, Robert (-1641?) & _?_; b 1637?; Salem
BAKER, Robert (-1720) & Mary _?_; b 1673; Roxbury
BAKER, Roger & Mary _?_, m/2 Richard HARRIS by 1704; Shelter Island, NY

BAKER, Samuel & 1/wf Ellen/Eleanor WINSLOW (?1637-1676); 29 Dec 1656, 20 Dec; Marshfield
BAKER, Samuel (1638-1715?) & 1/wf Fear [ROBINSON] (1644/5-1704+); b 20 Dec 1664, 30 Sep 1664; ?Barnstable
BAKER, Samuel (1644-) & Sara/Sarah COOK (1650-); 30 Jun 1670; Wethersfield, CT/Windsor, CT
BAKER, Samuel & Patience (?BARSTOW) SIMMONS, w Moses; 21 Feb 1677; Marshfield
BAKER, Samuel & Mary (GRANT) GOODFELLOW, w Thomas; 19 May 1687; Wethersfield, CT
BAKER, Samuel & Hannah WINN; 26 Nov 1691; Woburn
BAKER, Samuel & Sarah SNOW; 27 Feb 1699; Marshfield
BAKER, Samuel & Phebe (HOLMAN) EGLINGTON/?EGGLESTON, w Edward; 19 Dec 1699; Boston
BAKER, Thomas (-1683/4) & Elizabeth _?_ (-1685); ca 1640; Roxbury
BAKER, Thomas (?1618-1700) & Alice DAYTON (1620-1709); 20 Jun 1643; ?Milford, CT/East Hampton, LI
BAKER, Thomas & Leah [CLARK]; b 1654; Boston
BAKER, Thomas & Sarah _?_; ?ca 1654/70; Newport, RI/Kingston, RI
BAKER, Thomas (1636-1718) & Prisilla SYMONDS (1648-1734); 26 Mar 1672, ?Apr; Topsfield
BAKER, Thomas & Chistian BEAL (1654-1677); 6 Nov 1674; Hingham/Boston
BAKER, Thomas & Sarah [CARR]; b 1678; Boston
BAKER, Thomas (-1735 in 82nd y) & Elizabeth (EDWARDS) [STRATTON] (-1753 in 84th y), w Richard; 1678?; East Hampton, LI
BAKER, Thomas & Hannah POLAND; 13 Apr 1678; Beverly/Wenham
BAKER, Thomas (-1719) & Mary [HAUGH] (1655-); b 1680; Boston
BAKER, Thomas & _?_; ca 1680/2?; ?Falmouth, ME/?Scarborough
BAKER, Thomas (1654-1735), East Hampton & 1/wf Ann TOPPING (-bef 1711); 24 Apr 1686, 29 Apr; Southampton, LI/East Hampton
BAKER, Thomas (1653-1730+) (ae 77 in 1730) & Mary LEWIS; 10 Jul 1689; Lynn
BAKER, Thomas (-1735) & 2/wf Elizabeth WESTOVER (-1753); 1 May 1695; East Hampton, LI
BAKER, Thomas & Mary _?_; b 1698; Newport/N. Kingston, RI
BAKER, Thomas & Hannah ADAMS, 5 May 1698; York, ME
BAKER, Thomas (1655-) & Bathsheba _?_ ?(LEWIS)/O'KELLEY, w John; b 1701; Yarmouth
BAKER, Timothy (-1729) & 1/wf Grace MARSH (-1676); 26 Jan 1672, ?16 Jan; Northampton
BAKER, Timothy (-1729) & 2/wf Sarah (HOLLISTER) ATHERTON (-1691), w Hope; m cont 24 Mar 1679/80; ?Northampton
BAKER, William (1599-1658) & Joan _?_ (-1669); b 1638; Charlestown/Watertown/Billerica
BAKER, William & Mary _?_; by 1638?; Portsmouth, RI/Warwick, RI
BAKER, William & 1/wf Mary EDINGTON/EDDENDEN (-1653); 23 Sep 1651; Boston
BAKER, William (-1679) & Mary _?_, m/2 Henry JEFTS 1681; in Eng, b 1656; Concord
BAKER, William (-1676) & Pilgrim EDDY, m/2 Isaac STEDMAN 1678?, m/3 Sylvester EVELOTH 1678/9?; 22 Apr 1656; Boston
BAKER, William & Eleanor _?_; b 1669; Boston
BAKER, William (1649-) & Sarah [PARKER]; ca 1671?; Kennebec, ME
BAKER, William & Elizabeth _?_; b 1672; Boston
BAKER, William & Susanna _?_; b 1681; Boston
BAKER, William (-1702) & 1/wf Elizabeth DUTTON (1659-1698); 5 May 1681; Concord
BAKER, William & Sarah FITTS (1661-); 30 Dec 1686; Ipswich
BAKER, William (-1727) & Mercy [LAWRENCE] (1671-1753); b 1692(3?); Yarmouth
BAKER, William (-1702) & 2/wf Abigail _?_, m/2 Samuel WHEAT; aft 7 Apr 1698, bef 8 Jun 1702; Concord
BAKER, William & Sarah CRACKBONE; 17 Oct 1698; Cambridge
BAKER, _?_ & Joan LATIMER; b 8 Nov 1688; ?Marblehead
BALAAM, _?_ & Abigail _?_; b 1690; Beverly
BALCH, Benjamin (1629-1706?, 1715+) & 1/wf Sarah [GARDINER] (1631-1686), dau Thomas; ca 1650; Beverly
BALCH, Benjamin (?1653-1698) & Elizabeth WOODBURY (1654-); 11? Oct 1674, ?4 Oct, b 1677; ?Beverly
BALCH, Benjamin (?1629-1715+) & 2/wf Abigail (MAVERICK) CLARKE (1637-1690), w Matthew; 5 Feb 1688/9; Marblehead
BALCH, Benjamin & 3/wf Grace MALLOTT, w Hosea; 15 Mar 1691/2; Beverly

BALCH, Freeborn (1660-1729) & 1/wf Miriam (MOULTON) BATCHELDER, w Joseph; aft 13 Nov 1682, b 30 Nov 1683; Beverly

BALCH, Freeborn (1660-1729) & 2/wf Mallis _?_ (-1689, 1690); 20 Feb 1688/9; Beverly

BALCH, Freeborn (1660-1729) & 2/w? 3/wf Elizabeth FAIRFIELD; 30 Apr 1690; Beverly

BALCH, John (?1579-1648) & 1/wf Margaret [?LOVETT] (-163-?); b 1628/9, ca 1627; Salem

BALCH, John (-1648) & 2/wf Agnes/Amis [PATCH?] (-1637); Salem/Cape Ann

BALCH, John (-1662, drowned) & Mary [CONANT], m/2 William DODGE 1663?; b 1662, b 1661; Beverly/Kingsley

BALCH, John (1654?, 1657?-1738) & Hannah VERING/VEREN; 23 Dec 1674; Beverly

BALCH, John & Elizabeth OBER; m int 5 Oct 1700; Beverly

BALCH, Joseph & Sarah HART, m/2 William MELLOWES 1716; m int 21 Mar 1697/8; Beverly

BALCH, Samuel (1651-1723) & 1/wf Martha NEWMARTH/NEWMARCH (-1720); 27 Oct 1675; Ipswich/Beverly

BALCOM, Alexander[1] (-1711) & Jane [HOLBROOK], dau Wm.; b 1672, by 1664?; Portsmouth, RI/Providence

BALCOM, Alexander[2] (-1728), Providence & Sarah [WOODCOCK] (1667-1728+); b 1692; Rehoboth/Providence/Attleboro

BALCOM, Henry[1] (-1683) & 1/wf _?_ ; b 1665; Charlestown

BALCOM/RALCOME, Henry[1] (-1683) & 2/wf Elizabeth HAINES/HAYNES (1644-1713+, 1715?); 12 Aug 1666; Charlestown

BALDWIN, Barnabas (1665-1741) & 1/wf Sarah [BUCKINGHAM] (1665-1692?, bef 1692); Milford, CT

BALDWIN, Barnabas (1665-1741) & 2/wf Mary _?_/[?BOTSFORD]; b 1695; Milford, CT

BALDWIN, Benjamin (1642-1726?) & Hannah [SARGENT] (-1721?); ca 1668?; Branford, CT/Deerfield/Newark, NJ

BALDWIN, Benjamin (1673-1736) & Hannah [KNOWLTON] (-1736); b 1697; Woburn/Canterbury, CT

BALDWIN, Daniel (1644-) & Elizabeth BOTSFORD; 27 Jun 1665, 25? Jun; Milford, CT

BALDWIN, Daniel & Hannah RICHARDSON; 6 Jan 1684/5; Woburn

BALDWIN, Daniel (1668-1725) & Sarah [CAMP] (1668-1710); ca 1689; Milford, CT?

BALDWIN, David (1651-1689) & Mary STREAM; 11 Nov 1674; Milford, CT

BALDWIN, George & Anna/Ann?/Hannah? _?_, m/2 Richard BRADLEY by 1648; b 1639; Boston

BALDWIN, George & Mary [EMBREE], w Robert; aft 1656; Stamford, CT/Westchester, NY

BALDWIN, George (1665-1728) & Deborah [ROSE/ROSS?] (1671-1754); b 1690/[1?]; Branford, CT

BALDWIN, Henry (-1698) & Phebe RICHARDSON (-1716); 1 Nov 1649; Woburn

BALDWIN, Henry & Abigail FISK; 4 May 1692; Woburn

BALDWIN, James & 2/wf? Hannah? (Elizabeth wife in 1703) _?_ ; b 1697; Milford, CT/Durham, CT

BALDEN, John (-1639±) & Joanna _?_, m/2 John GAY; b 1635; Dedham

BALDWIN, John (see Josiah) & 1/wf Mary [CAMP?], sister Nicholas; in Eng?, b 1640?, b 1648; Milford, CT/Deerfield

BALDWIN, John & Hannah BIRCHARD; 12 Apr 1653; Guilford, CT/Norwich, CT

BALDWIN, John (-1682) & 2/w? Mary [BRUEN] (1634-1670); b 1653, b 1654, 15 Aug?; Milford, CT/Deerfield

BALDWIN, John (?1622-1687) & Mary RICHARDSON (1638-); 15 May 1655; Billerica/Woburn

BALDWIN, John (-1683) & 1/wf _?_ ; b 1657; Stonington, CT

BALDWIN, John (1640-1700) & 1/wf Hannah BRUEN/BREWER/BROWEN (1643/4-1670, 1680+), New London; 30 Oct 1663, ?3 Oct; Milford, CT/New London, CT

BALDWIN, John (-1688±) & Hannah OSBORNE; 19 Nov 1663; Milford, CT/Fairfield, CT

BALDEN, John (-1673, 1674?) & Arrabella/Arabella/Hannah? NORMAN (1644-1681), m/2? Samuel LEACH b 1678; - Sep 1664; Salem

BALDWIN, John (1635-1683), New London & 2/wf? Rebecca (PALMER) CHESEBROUGH (-1713-), w Elisha; 24 Jul 1672; Stonington, CT

BALDWIN, John (-1705) & Experience ABELL (1654-); 1680, b 1684; Norwich, CT/Lebanon, CT

BALDWIN, John & 2/wf Ruth [BOTSFORD] (1649-); b 1686; Milford, CT/Newark, NJ

BALDWIN, John & Sarah HEYWOOD?/HAYWOOD, Concord; 5 Feb 1689/90, 12 Feb 1689/90; Billerica

BALDWIN, Jonathan (?1649/50-) & 1/wf Hannah WARD; 9 Jun 1693, Milford, 2 Nov 1677; Milford, CT/Deerfield

BALDWIN, Jonathan (1649/50-1739) & 2/wf Thankful [STRONG] (1663-); [1693, 1694]; Milford, CT/Windsor, CT

BALDWIN, Jonathan & Mary FRENCH (1677-); 13 Dec 1695; Billerica

BALDWIN, Jonathan, Milford & Susannah KITCHELL; b 1699; ?Milford, CT/NJ

BALDWIN, Joseph (?1610-1684) & 1/wf Hannah/?Mary [?WHITLOCK]; High Wycombe, Suffolk, 10 Nov 1636, b 1640, ca 1637?; Milford, CT/Hadley/Deerfield

BALDWIN, Joseph (1640-1681) & 1/wf Elizabeth _?_; b 1663; Hadley

BALDWIN, Joseph (?1610-1684) & Isabel ?(WARD) (CATLIN) [?NORTHAM] (-1676), w John, w James; aft 27 Feb 1661; Milford, CT/Wethersfield, CT/Hadley/Deerfield

BALDWIN, Joseph (?1610-1684) & 3/wf Elizabeth (GIBBONS) (HITCHCOCK) [WARRINER] (-25 Apr 1696), w William, w Luke; aft 2 Jun 1676, b 17 Sept 1678; Hadley/Deerfield

BALDWIN, Joseph (1640-1681) & 2/wf Sarah [COLEY?] (1648-); b 1679, b 1670; Hadley/Fairfield, CT

BALDWIN, Joseph (1651-) & Elizabeth [BOTSFORD] (1665-); b 1691; Milford, CT/New Haven/Deerfield

BALDWIN, Joseph (1663-1714) & Elizabeth GROVER; 16 Jun 1691, 26? Jun, 20 Jun; Malden

BALDWIN, Josiah (see John) (-1683) & Mercy? (LANE), m/2 _?_ HINE; 25 Jun 1666; Medford, CT

BALDWIN, Josiah & Mary PIERSON/PERSON; 19 Sep 1700; Derby, CT

BALDWIN, Miles? & _?_

BALDWIN, Nathaniel & 1/wf Abigail [CAMP] (-1648); b 1644, b 1640?; Milford, CT

BALDWIN, Nathaniel (-1658?) & 2/wf Joanna (_?_) WESTCOTT, w Richard, m Thomas SKIDMORE; aft 22 Nov 1645, b 1650?; Milford, CT/Fairfield, CT

BALDWIN, Nathaniel (1645-) & 1/wf Hannah BOTSFORD (1645-); 12 Mar 1670/1; Milford, CT

BALDWIN, Nathaniel (1648-) & Sarah [PHIFFEN/PHIPPENY]; b 1676; Milford, CT/Deerfield

BALDWIN, Nathaniel/Nathan? & 2/wf Martha MITCHELL (-1691); b 1688, ca 1685; Milford, CT/Stratford, CT

BALDWIN, Obadiah (1660-) & Abigail BEAMAN; 15 May 1694, 16 May; Springfield/Milford, CT

BALDIN/BOWDOIN/BAUDOUIN, Peter/Pierre & Rachel DELLOCLOCE, wid; 27 May 1672; Salem

BALDWIN, Peter & _?_ ; b 1680; Milford, CT

BALDWIN, Richard & [Phillipa] _?_ ; b 1637?, b 1611?; Braintree

BALDWIN, Richard (1622-1665) & Elizabeth ALSOP, m/2 William FOWLER 1670; aft 5 Feb 1643?; New Haven/Milford

BALDWIN, Richard (1665-1698) & Anne _?_/Amy? OVIATT? (1668, 1667/8-1728); b 1690; Milford, CT

BALDWIN, Samuel (1645-1674?, 1672) & Rebecca? [PHIPPEN], m/2? Job PRINCE, m/3 George CLARK by 1697; Milford, CT?/Fairfield, CT

BALDWIN, Samuel (1655-1696?) & Abigail [BALDWIN] (1658-1739), m/2 John WADHAMS 1697; b 1678, b 1676?; Guilford, CT/Deerfield

BALDWIN, Samuel (1675-1757/8) & Rebecca [WILKINSON] (1676-1752), m/2 Samuel EELLS; b 1701; Milford, CT

BALDWIN, Sylvanus (1646-1727) & Mildred PRUDDEN (1653-1712); 20 Sept 1671, 19 Sep, 12 Sep; Milford, CT/Fairfield

BALDWIN, Sylvester (-1638 on ship) & Sarah [BRYAN?/BRUEN?] (1606-1669), m/2 John ASTWOOD 1640?; in Eng, ca 1620; Milford, CT

BALDWIN, Theophilus (1659-1698) & Elizabeth CAMFIELD/CANFIELD?, m/2 John MERWIN 1705; 8 Feb 1682/3, 1682; Milford, CT

BALDWIN, Thomas & 1/wf Sarah CAULKINS (-1685); 3 Nov 1684; Norwich, CT

BALDWIN, Thomas & 2/wf Abigail LAY (1673-1753); 20 Sep 1692; Norwich, CT

BALDWIN, Thomas & Sarah [FRENCH] (1681-); b 1699; Billerica

BALDWIN, Timothy (-1665) & 1/wf Mary [WELLS] (-1647); b 5 Mar 1642/3; Milford, CT

BALDWIN, Timothy (-1665) & Mary MEPHAM/MAPPAM?/MAPHAM, w John, m/2 Thomas TOPPING; 5 Mar 1645, 1649?, 1646?, 1648/50, aft 21 Jul 1649; Guilford, CT

BALDWIN, Timothy (1658-1708) & Mary [BEARD] (1658-1703?); b 1682, b 1682(3?); Milford, CT

BALDWIN, Timothy (1661-1734), Woburn & 1/wf Elizabeth **HILL** (-1704), Billerica; 2 Jun 1687; Billerica/Woburn/Stoneham

BALDWIN, William & Ruth **BROOKS**; 2 Jul 1688; New Haven/Milford, CT

BALDWIN, Zachariah (?1660-) & 1/wf Mary **STRINSON** (1652-), b 1680, b 1675?; Milford, CT

BALDWIN, Zachariah (1660-1722) & Elizabeth (**RATCLIFF/RATLEFF/RATLIFE**) [**SANFORD**], w Ezekiel; 1687 or bef 11 Jan 1686; Milford, CT

BALDWIN, _?_ & Elizabeth **HUSTED**, dau Angell

BALDWIN, _?_ & Mary [**ELLISON**]; b 7 Apr 1697; ?Hampstead, LI

BALL, Alling (-1689) & Dorothy [?**FUGILL**] (-1690); b 1649, New Haven, CT

BALL, Alling (1656-1710) & Sarah **THOMPSON** (1654-1716); 24 Nov 1678; New Haven, CT

BALL, David & _?_ ; b 1687; Watertown

BALL, Edward & _?_ ; b 1660

BALL, Edward (-1714) & Mary [**GEORGE**] (1645-1714+); ca 1670?; ?Block Island, RI/New Shoreham, RI

BALL, Edward (-1722) & [Abigail [**BLACHLEY**]; b 1673?; Bramford, CT

BALL, Edward & Hannah _?_ ; b 1695; Boston

BALL, Eleazer (1650-) & 1/wf Priscilla **WOOD/WOODWARD**; 25 Sep 1675; Concord

BALL, Eleazer & 2/wf Sarah **MERRIAM**, m/2 Samuel **FLETCHER** 1699; 14 Jun 1688; Cambridge/Concord

BALL, Eliphalet (-1673) & Hannah **NASH** (1655-1708), m/2 Thomas **TROMBRIDGE** 1689; 13 Feb 1672; New Haven, CT

BALL, Francis (-1648) & Abigail **BURT** (1628-1709), m/2 Benjamin **MUNN** 1649, m/3 Thomas **STEBBINS** 1696; 3 Oct 1644; Springfield

BALL, Francis & Abigail **SALTER**; 27 Jan 1663/4; Dorchester

BALL, Francis (-1700) & Martha **BLACKMAN**, m/2 Benjamin **STEBBINS**; 30 Sep 1699; Springfield

BALL, George & Katharine **TURFREY**, m/2 John **BRIGGS**; 29 Oct 1700; Boston

BALL, Isaac & Jane **BARNES**; 20 Nov 1689; Marbleheadd

BALL, James (1670-1730) & Elizabeth **FISK**; 16 Jan 1693/4; Watertown

BALL, John$_2$ (-1655) & [?Elizabeth **WEBB**]/?Joanne **KING**; b 1620; Concord/Watertown

BALL, John^2 (-1673) & 1/wf Elizabeth [**PIERCE**] (became insane); ca 1640/44; Watertown

BALL, John^2 (-1675) & 2/wf Elizabeth **FOX**; 3 Oct 1665; Watertown/Lancaster

BALL, John (1636) & Joanna _?_ (?1646-); ca 1665/70; Kittery, ME

BALL, John (1644-1732) & 1/wf Sarah **BULLARD**; 17 Oct 1665; Watertown

BALL, John (1649-1711) & Sarah **GLOVER** (1655-1730, 1731); 11 Dec 1678; New Haven

BALL, John & Martha **BIGNALL**; 29 Nov 1682; Concord

BALL, John (1660-1703) & Hannah **RUGG**, m/2 John **WHITTAKER**; 16 Oct 1690; Concord/Lancaster

BALL, John & Bethiah **MEDUP**; 27 Sep 1699; Watertown

BALL, Jonathan (1645-1741) & 1/wf Sarah **MILLER**; 13 Mar 1673, 1672/3; Springfield

BALL, Jonathan & Susannah (?**PIERSON**, no) [**WORTHINGTON**] (1652-), w Nicholas; aft 6 Sep 1683; Springfield

BALL, Nathaniel (-1706) (called cousin by Ralph **MOUSALL**) & 1/wf Mary [?**WAYNE**]/**MOUSALL**? (-1669); b 1649; Concord

BALL, Nathaniel (-1706) & 2/wf Margery (_?_) (**KNIGHT**) **BATEMAN** (-1709), w Philip, w Thomas; 7 Feb 1670; Concord

BALL, Nathaniel (1663-) & Mary **BROOKES** (1666-); 19 Apr 1688; Concord

BALL, Peter (1645-) & _?_ [**JACKSON**]; Portsmouth, NH

BALL, Samuel (1648-1689) & Mary **GRAVES**, Hadley, m/2 Benjamin **STEBBINS** 1690, m/3 James **WARRINER**; 15 Jan 1671, 15 Jun; Springfield/Northampton/Hatfield

BALL, William (-1695) & Mary [**ROBERTS**]; 14 Sept 1687; Kittery, ME

BALL, William & Elizabeth _?_ ; b 1694; Watertown

BALLANTINE, John (-1734) & 1/wf Lydia [**BARRETT**] (1657-1682+); b 1675; Boston

BALLANTINE, John (-1734) & 2/wf Mary (**WOODWARD**) **SAXTON** (-1740), w Thomas; Boston

BALLANTINE, William (-1669, 1667?) & Hannah **HOLLARD**, m/2 William **LONG** b 1671; 23 Jul 1652; Boston

BALLARD, Daniel & Sarah _?_ ; b 1684; Boston

BALLARD, Isaac & Dorothy **HARDING**/?**HEARNDON**; Jun 1699; Providence, RI

BALLARD, Jarvis & _?_ ; b 1658; Boston

BALLARD, Jarvis, Boston & Martha (KNIGHT) GYLLAM/GILLAM, Boston, w Joseph, m/3 John
    BALSTON 1703; b 1688, m bond 20 Sept 1687; Boston
BALLARD, John (1634-) (ae 25 in 1659) & 1/wf? [Susanna STORY]; b 1667 (?doubtful); Lynn
BALLARD, John (called cousin, 1687, by Nathaniel HANDFORD) & Rebecca _?_; b 1673; Lynn
BALLARD, John (1653-1715) & Rebecca HOOPER (1656-1715); 16 Nov 1681; Andover/Boston
BALLARD, John & Hannah SNELL, m/2 Dependence LITTLEFIELD; Portsmouth, NH
BALLARD, Joseph (-1722) & 1/wf Elizabeth PHILLIPS/PHELPS? (-1692); 28 Feb 1665, 1664/5?,
    1666; Andover
BALLARD, Joseph (-1722) & Rebecca (REA) (STEVENS) ORNE?/HORN (-1740), w Samon?, w
    Simon/Simond; 15 Nov 1692; Andover
BALLARD, Joseph & Rebecca JOHNSON; 17 Aug 1698; Andover
BALLARD, Nathaniel (-1722) & Rebecca HUTSON/HUDSON? (-1724); 16 Dec 1662; Lynn
BALLARD, Samuel & 1/wf Lydia [WISWALL] (1645-1678); b 1670; Charlestown
BALLARD, Samuel (-1708, ae 70) & 2/wf Hannah/Anna? BELCHER, 2 Sept 1678, 1? Sep, 1?
    May; Cambridge
BALLARD, William (1603-1639/41) & 2/wf? Elizabeth [LEE] (1609-) (1/wf Mary?), m/2 William
    KNIGHT, m/3 Allen BREED 1656; b 1632; Lynn
BALLARD, William (1617/21-1689) & Grace [?BERWICK] (-1694); b 1641?, b 1653;
    Lynn/Andover
BALLARD, William & Hannah HOOPER (1662-); 20 Apr 1682; Andover
BALLARD, William & Rebecca _?_? (doubtful); b 1668; Lynn
BALLETT/BALLATT, John (1672-1702) & Mary _?_; b 1700?; Charlestown
BALLATT, Samuel (-1708, ae 71) & 1/wf Lydia [WISWALL] (-1678); b 1665; Charlestown
BALLATT, Samuel & 2/wf Hannah BELCHER (-1691); 1 Sep 1678; Charlestown
BALLATT, Samuel & Lydia (MAYNARD) (HALE) MARSHALL, w Samuel, w William; 4 Sep 1691,
    4th 7br 1691; Charlestown
BALLOU, James (1652-1741±, 1744+) & Susanna WHITMAN (1658-1734±); cert 25 Jul 1683;
    Providence
BALLOU, John (-1714±) & 1/wf Hannah [LARKIN]; div 2 May 1676; ?Providence
BALLOU, John (-1714±) & 2/wf Hannah [GARRET/?JARRET]; 4 Jan 1678/9, b 1683; Providence
BALLOU, Maturin (-1662±) & Hannah [PIKE] (-1714±); ca 1646/8; Providence
BALLOU, Peter (1663-1731) & Barbara _?_ (1672-1740); b 1696; Providence
BALLOU, Robert (-1668) & Susanna _?_ (-1668+); ca 1643/7?; Portsmouth, RI/Boston
BALSTON, James & Sarah [ROOT]; b 1653; Boston
BALSTON, James (1657-) & Sarah _?_; b 1688; Boston
BALSTON, John & Lydia _?_ (-25 Apr 1664 a wid); b 27 Aug 1647; Boston
BALSTON, John (1650?-) & Anne _?_; b 1677; Boston
BALSTON, John & Sarah [MARION], dau John; b 1680; Boston
BALSTON, John (-1706, ae 86) & Judith (RAINSBOROUGH) WINTHROP, w Stephen, m cont 31
    May 1687; Boston
BALSTON, John & 2/wf Martha _?_ (-1736?); b 1701; Boston
BAULSTON, Jonathan & Mary [OWFIELD]; b 1645; Boston
BALSTON, Jonathan & Elizabeth _?_; b 1679; Boston
BALSTON, Jonathan & Susanna _?_; b 1687; Boston
BALSTON, Nathaniel & Rebecca _?_; b 1691; Boston
BAULSTON, William (-1679?, ae 78) & 1/wf Elizabeth _?_; b 1630; Boston/Portsmouth, RI
BALSTON, William & 2/wf Elizabeth _?_ (-1683, ae 86); b 1633; Boston
BANCROFT, Ebinezer (1667-1717) & Abigail EATON (-1758); 19 May 1692; Lynn
BANCROFT, Ephraim (1656-) & Sarah STILES, m/2 Thomas PHILLIPS; 5 May 1681; Windsor, CT
BANCROFT, John (-1637) & Jane/Joan _?_, m/2 Thomas BARBER 1640; b 1627?; Lynn
BANCROFT, John (-1662) & Hannah DUPER, m/2 John LUNDON/LONDON; 3 Dec 1650;
    Windsor, CT
BANCROFT, John (1656-1740) & Elizabeth EATON (1662-1705); 24 Sep 1678; Lynn
BANCROFT, Joseph & Mary _?_; b 1698; Reading/Lynn
BANCROFT, Nathaniel (1653-1724) & Hannah WILLIAMS (-1728); 26 Dec 1677; Westfield/Wind-
    sor, CT
BANCROFT, Roger (-1653) & Elizabeth _?_, m/2 Martin SAUNDERS 1654, m/3 John BRIDGE
    1658, m/4 Edward TAYLOR 1673; b 1653, no issue; Cambridge

BANCROFT, Samuel (1667-1742) & Hannah [GRANT] (1670-), w Tahan, Jr.; b 1698; Windsor, CT

BANCROFT, Thomas (1622-1691) (called cousin by William HOOPER) & 1/wf Alice BACON (-1648); 31 Mar 1647; Dedham

BANCROFT, Thomas (1622-1691) & 2/wf Elizabeth METCALFE (1626-1711); 15 Sep 1648; Dedham/Reading/Lynn

BANCROFT, Thomas & 1/wf Margaret WRIGHT (-1689); 8 Dec 1653; Springfield

BANCROFT, Thomas (?1621-1684), Enfield & Hannah GARDNER? (very doubtful), m/2 John BARBER 1689; b 1667, b 1670; Springfield/Westfield/Enfield, CT

BANCROFT, Thomas (1649-1718) & Sarah POOLE (1656-1723); 10 Apr 1673; Reading

BANCROFT, Thomas (1673-1731) & Mary WEBSTER (1679-); 1 Aug 1694; Reading

BANCROFT, Thomas (1659-) & _?_ ; Windsor, CT

BANFIELD, Christopher (?1636-1707) & 1/wf _?_ ; Kittery, ME

BANFIELD, Christopher (?1636-1707) & Grace (ROGERS?) [MILLER], w Richard; b 22 Oct 1694, 15 Mar 1695; Kittery, ME

BANFIELD, Hugh (1673-) & 1/wf Abigail [JONES]; 1698; Portsmouth, NH

BANFIELD, John (1642-1707) & Mary [PICKERING] (1642-1707); b 1673; Portsmouth, NH

BANFIELD, Thomas (-1676) & Elizabeth [LONG] (-1689); 2 Jun 1670; Charlestown

BANGS, Edward (1591, 1592-1678) (86 in 1677) & 1/wf _?_ ; in Eng, b 1623; Plymouth

BANGS, Edward (1591/2-1678) & 2/wf Lydia [HICKS] (-ca 1632/4?); aft 1627, bef 1630?; Plymouth/Eastham

BANGS, Edward (1591/2-1678) & 3/wf Rebecca [HOBART]; b 1636; Plymouth/Eastham

BANGS, Edward (1665-1746) & 1/wf Ruth [ALLEN] (1670-1738); b 1691; Eastham

BANGS, John (-1708) & Hannah SMALLY/SMALY/SMALLEY (1641-1708+); 23 Jan 1660, 1660/1, no issue; Eastham

BANGS, Jonathan (1640-1728) & 1/wf Mary MAYS (-1711, in 66th y); 16 Jul 1664; Eastham

BANGS, Jonathan (1673-) & 1/wf Elizabeth _?_ ; b 1696; Harwich

BANGS, Joshua (-1716) & Hannah SKUDER/SCUDDER (1681-1739?), m/2 Moses HATCH 1712; 1 Dec 1669, had 1 ch who d y; Eastham

BANISTER, Christopher (-1678) & Jane [GOODENOW], m/2 Nathaniel BILLING 1679; b 1670; Marlborough

BANISTER, Edward? (-1649) & _?_ (-1684)

BANISTER, John (1670-1730) & Ruth EAGER (1677-1768); 11 Nov 1695; Marlborough

BANISTER, Nathan & Mary _?_ ; b 1669; Charlestown

BANISTER, Thomas (-1709) & Sarah _?_ (-1711); in Eng, ca 1680; Boston

BANKS, Benjamin (1654-1692) & Elizabeth LYON, m/2 William ROWLANDSON ca 1693/4; 29 Jun 1679, 29? Jan, 27? Jan; Fairfield, CT

BANKS, John (-1685) & 1/wf _?_ TAINTOR, dau Charles; b 1650?; Wethersfield, CT/Windsor, CT/Fairfield, CT/Rye, NY

BANKS, John (-1685) & 2/wf Mary (?FITCH, no) SHERWOOD (?1629-1693/4), w Thomas; b 18 Jan 1658/9; Fairfield, CT/Rye, NY

BANK?/BAUK/BACK?/etc., John (-1683) & Hannah [JENKINS?] (-1716), m/2 Joseph PARKER 1683, m/3 Robert BLOOD 1696; b 1666; Chelmsford

BANKS, John (-1699) & Abigail LYON; 3 Apr 1672; Stamford, CT/Greenwich, CT

BANKS, John (1657-) & 1/wf _?_ ; ca 1680?; York, ME

BANKS, John (1657-) & 2/wf Elizabeth [TURBAT/TARBOT]; ca 1685/90?; York, ME

BANKS, John & Mahitable MATTOX, m/2 Thomas WEBBER; 29 Aug 1694; Boston

BANKS, John & Elizabeth _?_ ; b 1698; Boston

BANKS, Joseph (1667?-1745) & Elizabeth HARMON; 28 Feb 1694, 1694/5; York, ME

BANKS, Joseph (1674?-1712?) & Hannah _?_ ; b 1704, b 1701?; Fairfield, CT/Greenwich, CT

BANKS, Richard (-1692) & 1/w? Joan HARRISON; in Eng, m lic 25 Oct 1631; York, ME

BANKS, Richard (-1692) & 2/w? Elizabeth [CURTIS] (?1624-); ca 1644/6?; Scituate/York, ME

BANKS, Richard (-1692) & 3/wf Elizabeth [ALCOCK] (-1692+); ca 1655?; York, ME

BANKS, Samuel (-1719?) & _?_ ; Rye, NY

BANKS, Samuel (-1693?) & Sarah [?DONNELL]/?STOVER, m/2 John LANCASTER; b 1679?; Portsmouth, NH

BANKS, _?_ & Lydia [JOHNSON], went to London; b 1642?, b 1636?; Salem?

BANOE, John & _?_ ; b 1667; Lynn/?Salem

BANT, Gilbert (1658-) & Mercy **WHITWELL**; 13 Oct 1687; Boston

BARBER, George (?1615-1685) (brother-in-law of Ralph **WHEELOCK**) & 1/wf Elizabeth **CLARKE**; 24 Nov 1642; Dedham/Medfield

BARBER, George (-1685) & 2/wf Joan/Joanna **(FAXON) FISHER**, w Anthony; aft 22 Dec 1683; Medfield

BARBER, James (-1732, ae 80) (son John & Hannah) & Elizabeth **HIDE** (-1739, ae 81); 23 Jun 1680; Dorchester/Bridgewater

BARBER, John & [?Faith] _?_ ; b 1640; Salem

BARBER, John & Hannah _?_ ; ca 1651? Dorchester, Eng; Dorchester

BARBER, John (1642-1712), Windsor, CT/Suffield, CT & 1/wf Bathsheba **COGGIN** (-1688); 2 Dec 1663; Springfield

BARBER, John & Sissily/?Cicely _?_ ; b 1670; Amesbury

BARBER, John (-1688), Medfield & Abigail **BABCOCK**, Milton, m/2 Samuel **MORSE** by 1693; 17 Dec 1674; Dorchester/Milton

BARBER, John (-1690) & Joanna **MILLER**, m/2 James **STEVENSON** 1691; 27 Jan 1677/8; Suffield, CT

BARBER, John (prob son of John & Hannah) & Mary _?_ ; b 1686; Boston

BARBER, John & Hannah (_?_) **BANCROFT**, w Thomas; 1 May 1689; Springfield/Suffield, CT

BARBER, Josiah, Simsbury, CT & 1/wf Abigail **LOOMIS** (-1701); 22 Nov 1677; Wethersfield, CT/Simsbury, CT

BARBER, Moses (1652-1733) & 1/wf _?_ ; ca 1681/[2?]; ?Kingston, RI

BARBER, Moses (1652-1733) & 2/wf Susannah **WEST** (-1758); 24 Mar 1692; N. Kingston, RI

BARBER, Peter, Boston & Sarah **WILLIS/WILLY** (-1742), Boston; 22 Nov 1687, 16 Nov 1687; Charlestown

BARBER, Robert (-1706) & _?_ ; b 1699; Newfields

BARBER, Samuel (1648-1709) & 1/wf Mary **COGGINS/COZZENS**? (-19 May 1676); 1 Dec 1670; Windsor, CT

BARBER, Samuel (1646-1736) & Mary **HARDING** (1653-1731); 22 Dec 1670; Medfield

BARBER, Samuel (1646-1736) & Sarah **MILLES/MILLENS**? (?1654-); 7 Aug 1676; Dedham

BARBER, Samuel (1648-1709) & 2/wf Ruth **DRAKE** (1657-1731); 25 Jan 1676/[7]; Windsor, CT

BARBER, Samuel & Mary _?_ ; b 1698; Bridgehampton, LI

BARBER, Thomas (?1613-1662) & Jane **[BANCROFT]** (1573-1662), w John?; 7 Oct 1640; Windsor, CT

BARBER, Thomas (1644-1713) & Mary/Mercy **PHELPS** (1644-1687); 17 Dec 1661, b 1662?, 1665; Windsor, CT/Simsbury, CT

BARBER, Thomas (-1725) & 1/wf Hannah **ROPER** (1642-1691); 25 Jun 1667; Charlestown

BARBER, Thomas (-1689) & Anne/Anna? **CHASE** (-1691); 27 Apr 1671; Newbury/Suffield, CT

BARBER, Thomas (son of John & Hannah) & Mary **(MUNT)**, Kingston; b 1680; Boston

BARBER, Thomas (-1725) & 2/wf Hannah **(OSBORN) STEDMAN**, w George; 12 Jan 1692/3, 12 Jan 1692; Charlestown

BARBER, Thomas (-1714), Simsbury & Abigail **BUELL** (-1727); 25 May 1699; Windsor, CT/Simsbury

BARBER, William (-1677?) & _?_ ; b 1639; Salem/Dorchester/Charlestown

BARBER, William (-1707) & Ruth [**PECK**?/**PARKER**?] (?1643-); ca 1663, b 1666; Killingworth, CT

BARBER, William & Elizabeth **BRICKFORD**; 2 Dec 1666; Charlestown

BARBER, William (-1677?) & Elizabeth **RUCK**?/**REICH**?/**KIRK**/**RUSH**, dau Jasper, m/2 Jabez **BEERS** 1694; 4 May 1673, 4 Mar; Lynn

BARBER, William (-1704) & Esther **BROWN**; 5 Nov 1700; Windsor, CT/Poquonock, CT

BARBER, Zechariah (1656-1705) & Abiel **ELLIS**; 30 Aug 1683; Medfield

BARCLAY/BARKLY, William & Mary **MIRIOUR**; 13 Jan 1697; Boston

BARD, John & _?_ ; b 1677; Lynn

BARDEN, Abraham (1674-) & Mary **BOOTH**, wid; 20 Oct 1697; Scituate/Middletown

BARDING, Nathaniel & 1/wf _?_ ; b 1625; Hartford

BARDING, Nathaniel (1591-1674) & 2/wf? Abigail [**ANDREWS**] (-1683), w William; Hartford

BARDEN/BURDEN, Stephen (1669-) & Abigail **WILLIAMSON**; 22 Mar 1692; Taunton/Middleborough

BARDEN, Thomas (1592-) & Hannah [**WITTER**]; Lynn/Hartford

BARDEN, Willian (-1693), Middleboro? & Deborah BARKER; - Feb 1660, [1660/1]; Concord/
Barnstable
BARDWELL/BARDALL & Mary GULL; 29 Nov 1676, 21 Nov; Hatfield/Hadley/Deerfield
BARDWELL/BURDWELL?, Thomas, Barbados & Mary [WIARD/WARD] (1647-); b 1666
BAREFOOT, Walter & _?_; b 1662
BEARDING, Nathaniel (-1674) & 1/wf _?_; b 1627?; Hartford
BEARDING, Nathaniel & 2/wf Abigail [ANDREWS], w William; Hartford
BARGE, Giles & Eleanor _?_ (JACKSON) BAILEY/BULLY (-1691), w John, w Jonas; by 1673;
Gloucester/Scarboro, ME/Dorchester
BARGER/BARCHER, Phillip (-1703) & Margaret _?_; b 1686; Boston/Falmouth, ME
BARKER, Barzilla (-1694) & Anna JEWETT (-1712+, 1721?); 5 Dec 1666; Rowley
BARKER, Benjamin (-1750, ae 83) & Hannah MARSTON (1667-); 2 Jan 1688, 1688/9?; Andover
BARKER, Ebenezer (-1747, ae 95) & Abigail WHEELER; 25 May 1686; Andover
BARKER, Edward (-1678) & Jane _?_; b 1650; Boston
BARKER, Edward (-1703) & Elizabeth _?_ (-1705); b 1668; New Haven/Branford, CT
BARKER, Edward (-1721, ae 59) & Mary [PAPILLON] (1674-1728); [1700]; Branford, CT
BARKER, Francis & Mary LINCOLN; 5 Jan 1674, 1674/5?; Duxbury/Hingham
BARKER, Henry & Sarah (TAYLOR) EVERTON, w John; 31 Mar 1699; Charlestown
BARKER, Isaac & Judith PRINCE, m/2 William TUBBS; 28 Dec 1665; Plymouth/Duxbury
BARKER, James (-1634 on ship) & _?_; b 1623, b 1617
BARKER, James (-1678) & 1/wf Grace _?_ (-1666); b 1635?, b 1642; Rowley
BARKER, James (1623-1702) & Barbara [DUNGAN]; b 1644; Newport
BARKER, James (-1678) & 2/wf Mary WIATT/WYATT (-1684), w John; 22 May 1666; Rowley
BARKER, James & 1/wf Mary STICKNEY (1637-); 10 May 1667; Rowley/Suffield, CT
BARKER, James (-1723) & Mercy JOHNS/JONES; 5 Jan 1673, 6 Jan 1675, 5 Jan 1675/6; Suffield,
CT
BARKER, James (1648-) & 2/wf? Sarah [JEFFERAY/JEFFRAY/JEFFERAZ]; 1673; Newport
BARKER, James & Mary [COOK] (1679-1758); 1699; Middletown, RI
BARKER, John (-1652) & Hannah/Ann/Anna? [WILLIAMS], m/2 Abraham BLISH by 1654; b
1632?, b 1639; Barnstable/Duxbury/Marshfield
BARKER, John & 1/wf Judda/Judith SIMONDS; 9 Dec 1668; Concord
BARKER, John (-1722) & 1/wf Mary STEVENS (-1703); 6 Jul 1670; Andover
BARKER, John (-1729, ae 79), Scituate in 32nd y & 1/wf Desire ANNABLE (-1706, ae 53),
Scituate; 18 Jan 1676, [1676/7]; Barnstable
BARKER, Jonathan (1659?-) & _?_; b 1676?
BARKER, Jonathan (-1690) & Jane _?_; b 1690; Middleborough
BARKER, Jonathan (1674-1728) & Mary WARDELL (1677-); 13 Jun 1700; Branford, CT
BARKER, Joseph & Ruth [?HUNT]; b 1652, bef Jan 1652; Weymouth
BARKER, Joseph (?1650-1725+) & Sarah [READ?]; Newport
BARKER, Nathaniel & Mary _?_; b 1672; Rowley
BARKER, Nicholas & _?_; b 1635; Boston
BARKER, Peter (see Jeremiah MEACHAM) & 1/wf Susannah/Susanna SAUNDERS/Freelove
[BLISS?] (1672-1718, 1708+, 1712-) (maiden name PICKHAM? doubtful); b 1692, b 1712;
Westerly, RI
BARKER, Richard (-1693) & Joanna _?_ (-1687); b 1644; Andover
BARKER, Richard & Hannah KEMBALL/KIMBALL; 21 Apr 1682; Andover
BARKER, Robert & Lucy [WILLIAMS]; b 1640; Hingham/Duxbury/Marshfield/Nantucket
BARKER, Robert & 1/w Alice [SNOW?] (1657-); b 1682; Scituate/Duxbury
BARKER, Robert (-1729, 1726?) & Hannah [WANTON] (1677-1726); 1 Apr 1697; Scituate
BARKER, Samuel (-1683/4) & Naomi _?_; ca 1655/65?; Jamaica, LI/Southampton, LI
BARKER, Stephen & Mary ABBOTT; 13 May 1687; Andover/Haverhill
BARKER, Thomas (-1650) & Mary _?_ (sister of Thomas LAMBERT or his wf), m/2 Rev. Ezekiel
ROGERS 1651, (she called Thomas LAMBERT, nephew 1669, Ann NELSON, niece); b 1638;
Rowley
BARKER, Thomas & Leah _?_; b 1657; Boston
BARKER, William (-1718, ae 71) & Mary DIX (1655-1744); 20 Feb 1676, 1676/7; Andover
BARKER, William & _?_; b 1684; Scituate

BARKER, William (1662-1741) & 1/wf [Elizabeth EASTMAN] (1666-1715, ae 50); b 1688, ?1
Oct 1687, 10-1-1687, ?10 Mar 1687; Newport
BARKER, William (?1667-1741) & Elizabeth [HARRISON] (1667/8-); b 1691, 1689?; Branford,
CT/Southampton, LI
BARKER, Willian & Dorothy HAYWARD, m/2 Edward SPAULDING 1705; 12 Mar 1695/6;
Concord
BARKER, _?_ & Dorothy _?_ (-1652), m/2 Enoch HUNT by 1640, m/3 John KING by 1652, ?ca
1647; b 1639; Dorchester
BARLOW, Aaron (-1614 in 89th y) & Beulah [WING] (1659-); b 1684; Rochester
BARLOW, Barthalomew (-1657) & _?_ ; b 1637; Boston
BARLOW, Edmund/Edward? (-1697) & Mary [PEMBERTON] (1636-); b 1661; Charlestown
BARLOW, George (-bef 1665) & Cicely _?_, m/2 Henry WATTS; Exeter, NH
BARLOW, George (-1684) & Jane [BESSE] (-1693), w Anthony d 1657; bef 4 Mar 1661/2, aft
1657, b 1669; Exeter, NH/Sandwich
BARLOW/BARLEY?, George (-1706) & Mary [STILSON]; b 1688; Fairfield, CT/Milford, CT
BARLOW, James (-16 Mar 1690) & Sarah HEALEY changed to HUXLEY, m/2 Ebenezer SMITH;
10 Jan 1688, 1687/8; Suffield, CT
BARLOW, John (-1674?) & Ann/Anna? _?_ (-1685); in Eng, b 1630; Fairfield, CT
BARLOW, John (-1691?) & Abigail [LOCKWOOD]; ca 1667; Fairfield, CT
BARLOW, John (1669?-) & [Elizabeth DILLINGHAM] (-1759); 1692; Sandwich
BARLOW, John[3] & Ruth (SHERWOOD) [DRAKE], w Samuel; b 1695, ca 1692; Fairfield, CT
BARLOW, Joseph (-1697) & Sarah [READ], m/2 Zachariah FERRIS 1699?; Fairfield, CT
BARLOW, Moses & Mary [DEXTER] (1654-); b 1692, 1684?; Rochester
BARLOW, Moses & 2/wf Hannah [WING]; b 1699; Rochester
BARLOW, Nathan & Mary _?_ ; b 1691; Sandwich
BARLOW, Thomas (-1658?) & Rose (SHERWOOD) [RUMBALL], w Thomas, m/3 Edward NASH
by 1673; b 1650/1?, b 1653?, aft 1653?; Fairfield, CT
BARLOW, Thomas (-1661) & Elizabeth ?ROYALL/[BENSON], m/2 John COOMBES 1662, m/3
John WARREN; b 1657; Boston
BARLOW, Thomas (-1691?) & Elizabeth MELLINS, m/2 Samuel TOWNSEND 1693; 29 Oct 1681;
Charlestown
BARNABY, James (-1677?) & Lydia [BARTLETT] (1647-1691), m/2 John NELSON 1677?; ca
1673, b 1670?; Plymouth?
BANEBE, James (ca 1670-1726) & Joanna [HARLOW] (1669-1725); b 1698(9?); Plymouth/Free-
town
BARNABE, Stephen & 1/wf Ruth MORTON (1676-1709); 10 Dec 1696; Plymouth
BARNARD, Bartholomew[1] & 1/wf Alice WEEDEN (-1663); 13 Aug 1626; York, ME/Agamenticus,
ME/Boston
BARNARD, Bartholomew (1627-1698) & Sarah BURCHARD/BURCHWOOD; 25 Oct 1647;
Hartford
BARNARD, Bartholomew & 2/wf Jane [LAXTON] (-1698); ca 1664; Boston/York, ME/Saco, ME
BARNARD, Benjamin (1650-1694) & Sarah _?_/[WENTWORTH?], m/2 Samuel WINCH 1699,
(_?_ PIKE son of Jeremiah PIKE of Reading called "cousin" in 1694); by 1687; Watertown
BARNARD, Charles & _?_ ; b 1688; Hartford
BARNARD, Francis (-1698, ae 81) & 1/wf Hannah MERRILL (-1676); 15 Aug 1644; Hartford
BARNARD, Francis (-1698, ae 81) & 2/wf Frances (FOOTE) DICKINSON; 21 Aug 1677, m cont;
Hadley/Hartford/Deerfield
BARNARD, James (-1720) & 1/wf Abiell PHILLIPS; 8 Oct 1666, no issue; Watertown/Sudbury
BARNARD, James (-1720) & 2/wf Sarah _?_ ; aft 1672, no issue; Watertown
BARNARD, James (-1726) & Judith JENNISON, m/2 John BEMIS 1726; 16 Dec 1692; Watertown
BARNARD, John (1604-1646) & Phebe [WHITING]; b 1631 in Eng; Watertown
BARNARD, John (-1664) (kinsman of Henry HAYWARD of Wethersfield) & Mary [STACY]
(-1665); b 1634, no issue; Cambridge/Hadley
BARNARD, John (1631-) & Sarah FLEMING (1639-); 15 Nov 1654; Watertown
BARNARD, Joseph & Lydia HAYWARD (1661-); b 1691
BARNARD, Massachiel/?Methusiah/Musachiel (1611-) & Mary _?_ (1607-); b 1631; Weymouth
BARNARD, Matthew (1628-) (cousin of Nicholas DAVIS) & 1/wf Sarah _?_ (-1659); b 1654;
Boston

BERNARD, Matthew (-1679, ae 54) & Mary? [DAVIS?], dau Nicholas?; b 1663; Boston
BARNARD, Nathaniel (-1659, Boston) & Mary LUGG (1642-), m/2 James INGLIS?; 11 Feb 1658/9; Boston
BARNARD, Nathaniel (1643-1718) & [Mary/Martha? BARNARD] (?1658, ?1648-); b 1667(8?); Salisbury/Nantucket
BARNARD, Richard (-bef 1706, bef 9 Dec 1695) & Elizabeth NEGUS, dau Benjamin; 2 Mar 1659; Boston
BARNARD, Richard (-1683) & Sarah CLARK, m/2 Richard WAITE 1686; 13 Feb 1670/1; Springfield
BARNARD, Richard & Katherine WILSON (1669-); 3 Apr 1690; Boston
BARNARD, Robert (see Wm.) (-1682) & Joanne [KINGMAN?/HARVEY?] (-1705); b 1642(3?); Salisbury/Andover/Nantucket
BARNARD, Robert & _?_; b 1645; Andover
BARNARD, Samuel (-1728) & Mary COLTON; 5 Nov 1678, 30 Oct 1678; Hadley/Deerfield
BARNARD, Samuel & Ann/Anne? CURRIER; 22 Oct 1696; Amesbury
BARNARD, Samuel (1664-) & Mercy/Mary SHEARMAN; 4 Apr 1700; Watertown
BARNARD, Stephen (?1649-) & Rebecca HOW (-1725); 1 May 1671; Andover
BARNARD, Stephen & Damaris [GARDNER] (1674-); b 1701?; Nantucket
BARNARD, Thomas (-1677±) & Helen?/Eleanor? _?_ (-1694), m/2 George LITTLE 1681; b 1641; Salisbury/Nantucket
BARNARD, Thomas (1641-) & Sarah [PEASLEY]; b 1664; Amesbury/Salisbury
BARNARD, Thomas & Elizabeth _?_; b 1681; Boston
BARNARD, Thomas (-1715, ae 60) & 1/wf Elizabeth PRICE (1671-1693); 14 Dec 1686; Andover
BARNARD, Thomas & Judith _?_; b 1694; Boston
BARNARD, Thomas (-1715, ae 60) & 2/wf Abigail BULL (-1702); 28 Apr 1696, 28 May; Andover/Salem
BARNARD, Thomas & Elizabeth _?_; b 1699; Amesbury
BARNARD, William (see Robert) & Alice [KINGMAN?] (1613?-1663, Boston?); b 1645, b 1634?, aft 1635/6; Charlestown/Weymouth
BARNELL, John & Esther _?_; b 1679; Boston
BARNELL, Thomas & Esther _?_; b 1682; Boston
BARNES, Benjamin (1653-1731) & 1/wf Sarah [?INGERSOLL] (?1660-1732); b 1684; Farmington, CT/Waterbury, CT
BARNES, Benjamin (-1740) & Abigail [?LINSLEY]; b 1700; Branford, CT
BARNES, Bonadventure & _?_; b 27 Oct 1668; ME
BARNES, Charles & Mary [HAND]; b 1655, b 1657; Easthampton, LI
BARNES, Daniel (1659-1731) & Mary TAPPEN (-1740); 13 Jan 1686; New Haven
BARNES, Ebenezer (1675-1756) & Deborah ORVIS (1681-); 8 Apr 1699; Framington, CT
BARNES, Henry (-1669) & Rebecca [WILSON], m/2 Henry BODGE by 1672; Kittery, ME/Spruce Creek
BARNES, Henry (-1705) & Abishag [BEALE], m/2 Frances CARMAN; by 1698; Kittery, ME/Spruce Creek
BARNES, James & 1/wf Hopestill _?_ (-1676); b 1673; Boston
BARNES, James & 2/wf Temperance _?_; b 1680; Boston
BARNES, John (-1671) (calls Henry SAMPSON's wife "cousin" in will 1668) & 1/wf Mary PLUMER (-1651); 12 Sept 1633; Plymouth
BARNES, John (-1671) & 2/wf Jane _?_; aft 2 Jun 1651; Plymouth
BARNES/BARRONS, John (-1715, ae 78) & Johannah [JOHNSON] (1641-1712, ae 69), Weston; 1664?, no issue; Marlborough
BARNES, John & Elizabeth EATON; 29 Jul 1668; Hingham
BARNES, John (?1648-1712) & Mercy BETTS; 16 Nov 1669; New Haven
BARNES, John, Stonington & Hannah LINSLEY, Stonington, CT; 18 Jun 1674, no issue?; Stonington, CT
BARNES, John (-1676) & Deborah RIGHT/WRIGHT, m/2 Eleazer FLACK/FLAGG 1676; 10 Dec 1674; Concord
BARNES, John (1669-) & Mary BARTLETT; 6 Jul 1693; Plymouth
BARNES, John & Hannah [HOWE?] (1677-); b 1695; Marlborough/Framingham
BARNES, John & Rachel _?_; b 1700; Boston

BARNES, John (-1712?) & Dorothy STENT, m/2 Thomas CARNES; 28 Aug 1700; Branford, CT
BARNES, Jonathan (1643-1714) & Elizabeth HEDGE (?1646, 1647-1731); 4 Jan 1665, 1665/6; Plymouth
BAINES, Joseph (?1655-) & Abigail GIBBS; 5 Jul 1684, 8? Jul; Farmington, CT
BARNES, Joshua (-1692) & 1/wf Prudence _?_ (no), 2/wf Amy _?_ (-1692+); b 1649; East Hampton, LI
BARNES, Joshua & Esther (WALDRON) (ELKINS) (LEE) [JOSE], w Henry, w Abraham, w John; b 1699, b Sep 1695; Boston
BARNES, Matthew & 1/wf Rebecca _?_ (-1657); b 1644; Braintree/Boston
BARNES, Matthew (-1667?) & 2/wf Elizabeth HUNT, w Thomas; 4 Nov 1657; Boston
BARNES, Matthew & 1/wf Experience _?_; 12 Jan 1678; Wethersfield, CT
BARNES, Matthew & Abigail (DESBOROUGH) FLOOD, w Robert; 12 Jan 1692; Wetherfield, CT
BARNES, Maybee (1663-1749) & Elizabeth STOWE (1661-1728); 19 Nov 1691; Middletown, CT
BARNES, Nathaniel & Mary _?_; b 1677; Boston
BARNES, Nathaniel & Elizabeth _?_ (-1692), [w John HARRIS]; b 1683; Boston
BARNES, Peter (1652-) & Anna CANTERBURY; Jul 1679; Hingham
BARNES, Richard (d in Eng) & Agnes BENT (1602-), m/2 Thomas BLANCHARD 1637; Weyhill, Hampshire, Eng, 11 Apr 1630
BARRENCE, Richard (-1708) & 1/wf Deborah DICKS/DIX (-1689), w Edward?; 16 Dec 1667; Marlborough
BARNES, Samuel (-1693) & Patience WILLIAMS (-1706+); 9 Nov 1676?; Southampton, LI
BARNES, Shamgar (-1750?) & 1/wf _?_ (-1704); b 1701(2?), b 1694?; East Hampton, LI/Elizabeth, NJ
BARNES, Stephen & Mary (LINSLEY) [BARNES]; b 1700, b 1699; East Hampton, LI/Bramford, CT
BARNES, Thomas (-1672, ae 70) & Ann/Anna _?_ (-1691); b 1641?; Hingham
BARNES, Thomas (-1691) & 1/wf Mary _?_ (-1676, 1662?); ca 1643 (investigate), b 1648; ?Hartford/New Haven/Middletown, CT
BARNES, Thomas (-1663) (ae ca 28 in 1660) & Mary _?_, m/2 James POWLLEN/POLAND 1670; b 1655; Salem
BARENCE, Thomas (-1679) & Abigail GOODENOW; 2 Jul 1662; Marlboro/Concord
BARNES, Thomas & 2/wf Mary ANDREWS (1643-), m/2 Jacob BRONSON b 1679?; m cont 23 Mar 1662/3; Farmington, CT
BARNS, Thomas (-1706) & 1/wf Prudence ALBIE; 16 May 1666; Medfield/Swansea
BARNES, Thomas (1653-1712) & 1/wf Mary HUBBARD; 26 Jun 1675; New Haven
BARNES, Thomas (-1691) & 2/wf Elizabeth _?_ (-1690); aft Apr 1676; New Haven
BARNES, Thomas & Sarah _?_; b 1680; Boston
BARNES, Thomas (1663-) & Mary HOW; 14 Apr 1685; Marlborough
BARNES, Thomas & Joanna/Joan _?_; b 1686; Boston
BARNES, Thomas & 1/wf Mary [RAND]; by 1689; Hog Island
BARNES, Thomas & 2/wf Abigail [FROST], m/2 Samuel TUTTLE; b 1690; New Haven
BARNES, Thomas & Mary JONES; Jun 1690; Farmington, CT/Southington, CT
BARNES, Thomas & 1/wf (?Sarah (TALMAGE) [BEE]), w Thomas; b 3 Mar 1692; East Hampton, LI
BARNES, Rev. Thomas & Elizabeth (BAKER?) KING, w Clemont; 12 Nov 1694; Swansea
BARNES, Thomas & Lydia NOWELL; m int 18 Dec 1695; Boston
BARNES, Thomas & 2/wf Joanna [STEVENES], w Thomas; by 1696; Hog Island
BARNES, Thomas (1670-1706) & Sarah STONE; 25 Mar 1697; Providence
BARNES, William (1620-) & Sarah [WILSHIRE] (-1648), m/2 John TINKER; ca 1640/2, div 6 Apr 1648; Salem
BARNES, William (called "brother" by William FITTS) & Rachel [?FITTS]/[?LORD]; b 1643; Salisbury
BARNES, William & Hannah [PALMER] (ca 1643-); b 1681, 1660-65?
BARNES, William (-1699, 1698?) & Elizabeth _?_ (-1723?, 1624 nr 80); b 1670?; East Hampton, LI
BARNES, William & 1/wf Martha [?HORTON]; b 1677
BARNES, William & Hannah [UNDERHILL] (-1713), m/2 Daniel CLARK; b 1693, b 1692; Westchester, NY

BARNES, William (-1716) & Mary **SMITH** (1673-); 20 Aug 1696; Hadley/East Haddam, CT

BARNES, William (-1706) & Mary [**ROGERS**] (1675-1705); b 1700; East Hampton, LI/Southampton, LI

BARNETT/alias **BARBANT,** John & Mary **BISHOP,** m/2 John **DARLING;** 14 Oct 1661; Salem

BARNET, John & Susanna __?__ ; b 1673; Boston

BARNETT, Thomas & __?__ ; b 1679; New London, CT

BARNY, Daniel & Anne __?__ ; b 1698; Concord

BARNEY, Israel (1675-) & Elizabeth **BARRETT**/?**BARRAS**/**BONNETT**/?**BARROWS;** 18 Nov 1696, int 27 Oct 1696; Rehoboth

BARNEY, Jacob (?1601-1673) & Elizabeth/?Anna __?__ (-1673+); ?ca 1632, b 1639; Salem

BARNEY, Jacob (ca 1635, ca 1632-1692) & 1/wf Hannah **JOHNSON** (-1659); 18 Aug 1657; Salem

BARNY, Jacob (ca 1635, ca 1632-1692?) & 2/wf Ann **WITT** (ca 1642-1701); 26 Apr 1660; Salem/Rehoboth

BARNEY, John (1665-1728) & Mary **THROOP** (1667-1728+); 4 Nov 1686; Bristol, RI

BARNEY, Joseph (1673-1730) & Constance **DAVIS** (1674-); 4 Sept 1692; Rehoboth/Swansea

BARNY, Thomas & Hannah __?__ ; b 1691; Concord

BARNSDALE/BARNSDELL?, William & Mary __?__ ; b 1688/(9?); Boston

BARNUM, Francis (?1671-1736/41) & 1/wf Deborah [**HOYT**] (1679-); b 1694; Woodbury, CT

BARNAM, Richard & Elizabeth __?__ ; b 1667; Boston

BARNUM, Richard (?1675-1739?) & Mary [**HURD**] (?1673-); b 1701?; Danbury, CT

BARNUM, Thomas (?1625-1695) & 1/wf Hannah [?**HURD**]; b 1663; Norwalk, CT/Fairfield, CT/Danbury, CT

BARNUM, Thomas (ca 1625-1695) & 2/wf Sarah (**THOMPSON**) [**HURD**] (1642-1718), Statford, w John; aft 1682; Fairfield

BARNUM, Thomas (1663-1731) & Sarah [?**BEARDSLEY**]; ca 1684/90; Stratford, CT

BARRILL, George (-1648) & Ann __?__ (-1659); in Eng, b 1618, 1644?; Boston

BARREL, John (1618-1658) & Mary [**COLBRON**] (1625-1697), dau William and Margaret, m/2 Daniel **TURRELL** 1659; b 1645; Boston

BARRILL, John (1657-) & 1/wf Elizabeth __?__ ; b 1677; Boston

BARREL, John & 2/wf Sabella/Isabella **LEGG** (1672-1698); 14 Sep 1693; Boston

BARREL, John & Deborah __?__ (-1699)

BARRELL, William (1654-1689) & Lydah/Lydia (**TURNER**) **JAMES** (1652-1714), w John; 20 Apr 1680; Scituate/(?Boston)

BARRETT, Benjamin (-1690) & Sarah **GRAVES;** 27 Apr 1677; Hatfield/Deerfield

BARRETT, Benjamin (-1690) & 2/wf Mary [**ALEXANDER**], m/2 Henry **WHITE** 1691/2; b 1690; Deerfield

BARRETT, Charles/Christopher? & Catharine __?__ ; b 1665; Barbados/Newport

BARRETT, Christopher (-17 Oct 1694) & __?__ ; b 1694; Charlestown

BARRETT, Daniel & Elizabeth [**BARBER**] (1666-); CT

BARRETT, Humphrey (1592-) & Mary __?__ (1590-1663); in Eng, b 1630; Concord

BARRETT, Humphrey & Elizabeth **PAINE;** 17 Jul 1661; Concord (did he have 1/wf __?__ **HAWES?**)

BARIT, Humphrey (?1630-1716) & Mary **POTTER** (1656-1713); 23 Mar 1674/5; Concord

BARRETT, James (1615/19-1672-) & Anna/Hannah (**FOSDICK**) **TINGLEY** (-1681), w Palmer; b 1642; Charlestown

BARRETT, James (-1678?) & Dorcas **GREENE** (1653-1682); 11 Jan 1671/2; Malden

BARRETT, James (1672-1740) & Anna **BRYANT** (-1741); 30 May 1694; Reading/Charlestown

BARRETT, John & Mary __?__ (1617-), m/2 Thomas **LADBROOK** ca 1670; York, ME

BARRETT, John (-1664) & Mary [**LITTLEFIELD?,** prob not] (1607-), m/2 Thomas **PAGE?;** b 1632; Wells, ME/Salisbury

BARRETT, John (-1711) & Mary **POND** (-1711); 19 Sep 1656; Sudbury

BARRETT, John (-1706) & Sarah __?__ ; b 1659, b 1656?; Chelmsford

BARRETT, John & 2/wf? Elizabeth **COUSONS;** 6 Jun 1664; Charlestown/Wells, ME

BERAT, John & Mary [?**BARRETT**]; b 1673, b 1661?; Gloucester

BARRETT, John (-1694) & Dorothy **PROCTOR,** m/2 Samuel **ROBBINS** 1689?; 18 Dec 1679, 16? Dec; Chelmsford

BARRETT, John (-1687) & Ann [?**PEDRICK**], m/2 Pentecost **BLACKINGTON** 1689; b 1682, b 1685; Marblehead

BARRETT, John (1663-1715), Marlboro & Deborah HOW (1667-1743), Marlboro; 27 Sep 1688; Marlborough

BARRETT, John & Mary __?__ ; b 1690; Sudbury (see John BERAT)

BARRETT, John & Mary __?__ ; ca 1692?; Fordham, NY

BARRETT, John & Sabella LEGG; 14 Sep 1693; Watertown

BARRETT, John & Sarah EUSTACE/EUSTIS; 28 Sep 1699; Boston

BARRETT, Jonathan & 1/wf Sarah STEVENS?/LARNED? (1653-1695); b 1676, b 1687; Chelmsford

BARRETT, Jonathan & 2/wf Abigail (EAMES) WESTON/WESSON (-1706), w Samuel; 26 Jun 1696; Woburn/Chelmsford

BARRETT, Jonathan (1678-1749) & 1/wf Abigail TUTTLE (-1715); 8 Dec 1698; Boston/Reading

BARETT, Joseph (-1711) & 1/wf Martha GOOLE/GOULD? (1654-1698); 17 Sep 1672; Chelmsford

BARIT, Joseph (-1742) & Abigail HILDRITH (1672-1729); 15 Dec 1696; Chelmsford

BARRETT, Moses (1662-1742) & Anna/Ann?/?Hannah SMITH (1664-1745), Dorchester; 10 Sep 1684; Chelmsford

BARRETT, Richard (-1651) & Elizabeth __?__ ; ?Lynn

BARRETT, Richard & Mary __?__ ; b 1658, b 1642?; Boston/Southampton, LI

BARRETT, Robert & __?__ ; in Eng, b 1613?; Wells, ME

BARRETT, Robert (-1675) & Hannah [CARTER] (1640-1691); b 1663; Charlestown

BARRETT, Samuel (1661-1736) & Sarah BUTTRIK (1662-1736); 21 Feb 1683; Chelmsford

BARRETT, Samuel & 2/wf Leah __?__ ; b 28 Dec 1691; Yonkers Plantation

BARRETT, Samuel (1670-1733) & Sarah MANNING (-1742); 8 Mar 1694; Boston

BARRETT, Samuel & [Sarah THORNTON]; b 1701?, b 1702; Boston

BARRETT, Stephen (-1689) & Elizabeth (DEXTER) MELLINS (-1693), w James; 14 May 1680; Charlestown

BARRETT, Thomas[1] (-1668) & Margaret __?__ (-1681); in Eng, b 1632?; Braintree/Chelmsford

BARRETT, Thomas (-1652) & Elizabeth [MELLOWES] (1625-1691), m/2 Edward WRIGHT; b 1648; Concord

BARRETT, Thomas (-1702) & 1/wf Frances WOOLDERSON (-1694); 14 Sep 1655; Braintree/Chelmsford

BARRETT, Thomas & Thomasin __?__ ; b 1664; Boston

BARRETT, Thomas (-1673) & Lydia __?__ , m/2 Arthur COLE 1673, m/3 William EAGER 1680, m/4 Reuben LUXFORD, m/5 Nathaniel NOLLINGS 1709; b 1668; Marlborough

BARRET, Thomas (-1702), Chelmsford & 2/wf Mary DIKE; 22 Jan 1694/5; Milton/Chelmsford/Dunstable

BARRAT, William (?1629-1689) & 1/wf Sarah CHAMPNEY (-1661); 19 Aug 1656; Cambridge

BARRETT, William (?1629-1689) & 2/wf Mary BARNARD (1639-1673); 16 Jun 1662; Cambridge

BARRETT, William (?1629-1689, ae 60) & 3/wf Mary SPARHAWK (?1652-1673?); 8 Oct 1673; Cambridge

BARRETT, William (?1629-1689) & 4/wf Margaret [POOLE?]/[BARTLETT?] (-1689+); b 1676; Cambridge

BARRETT, William (1665-1730±) & Hannah [CHEEVER]; b 1695?; Cambridge

BARRETT, __?__ & Agnes/?Annis DENNEN, m/2 Richard DOLLIVER 1697; ?Gloucester

BARRON, Ellis[1] (-1676) & 1/wf Grace __?__ ; in Eng?, ca 1630/2; Watertown

BARRON, Ellis[1] (-1676) & 2/wf Hannah (?HAMMOND) [HAWKINS] (-1685), w Timothy d 1631; aft 1651, ?14 Dec 1653, 4 Dec; Watertown

BARRON, Ellis[2] (ca 1633-1712) & 1/wf Hannah HAWKINS (1637-1674); ?14 Dec 1653, b 1655; Watertown/Groton

BARRON, Ellis[2] (ca 1633-1712) & 2/wf Lydia (PRESCOTT) [FAIRBANKS] (1641-1712+), w Jonas; ca 1678; Watertown/Groton

BARRON, Ellis[3] (1655-1711+) & 1/wf Mary SHERMAN (-1685+), dau Rev. John, 2/wf? Sarah ?INGERSOLL (no); 27 May 1679; Watertown

BARRON/(BARNES wrong), Isaac (1671-1739) & Sarah GOODWIN; 6 Dec 1694; Kittery, ME/Chelmsford

BARRON, John[2] ([ca 1639]-1693) & Elizabeth HUNT (-1704, Concord); 1 Apr 1664; Marlboro/Concord/Groton

BARRON, Moses[2] (1643-1699) & Mary [LEARNED] (1647-); b 1669; Chelmsford

BARON, Moses (-1719, 1720) & Mary (BUNKER) RICHARDSON (-1741), w Ezekiel, m/3 Thomas HOWE of Marlboro; 2 Feb 1697/8; Chelmsford

BARRON, Timothy (1673-1718) & Rachel JENISON (1671-), m/2 John KING 28 Sep 1720; 10 Mar 1699; Watertown

BARROWS, George & Patience SIMMONS (-1723, Plympton); 14 Feb 1694/5; Plymouth

BARROWS/BARRY?, James & _?_, m/2 Niven AGNEW b 1676; b 1662?

BARROWS, John (1609-1692) & Ann _?_; b 1637; Salem/Middleboro

BARROWS, John (-1692) & Deborah _?_; b 1666; Plymouth

BAROW, John & Hannah BRIGGS (-1710?); 13 - 1698; Rochester

BARROWS, John & Sarah _?_; b 1700(1?); Plymouth

BARROW, Robert & 1/wf Ruth BONUM/BONHAM; 28 Nov 1666; Plymouth

BARROW, Robert & 2/wf Lydia [DUNHAM] (1666?-1717); b 1686; Plymouth

BARROWS, Samuel (1672-) & 1/wf Mercy COMBS (-1718); b 1701; Middleboro

BARRUS/BARROWS?, Joshaue & Mary CHAMBERLING; 24 Jul 1696; Chelmsford

BARSHAM, John (?1635, ?1641-1698) & Mahitable _?_; b 1670; Exeter, NH/Portsmouth, NH

BARSHAM, Nathaniel (-1716) & Elizabeth BOND (-1729); 13 Mar 1678, 1678/9, no issue; Watertown

BARSHAM, Philip (-1675) & Sarah _?_; Deerfield

BARSHAM, William (-1684) & Annabelle [BLAND]?, alias SMITH (-1681); ca 1634; Watertown

BASTOW, George (1614-1654) & Susanna [MARRETT] (-1654); b 1650; Boston/Scituate/Cambridge

BEARSTOW, George (1652-1726) & Mercy [CLARK] (1660-1726), dau James; b 1684; Roxbury/Boston/Rehoboth

BARSTOW, Jeremiah (-1676) & Lydia [HATCH] (1633?-), dau Thomas, m/2 Richard STANDLAKE ca 1677; b 1676; Scituate

BARSTOW, John (-1658, ae 33) & Hannah _?_; b 1653; Watertown/Cambridge

BARSTOW, John & Lydia HATCH, dau William; 16 Jan 1678; Scituate

BERSTOW, Joseph (?1639-1712) & Susanna LINKHORNE/LINCOLN (-1730), Hingham; 16 May 1666; Scituate

BEARSTOW, Joseph (1675-1728) & Mary [RANDELL]; b 1699; Scituate

BARSTOW, Michael/Miles? (1600-1676, 1674?) & Grace HALSTEAD; 16 Feb 1625, b 1635, 16 Feb 1624, 15 Feb 1624, no issue; Charlestown

BAIRSTOW, Michael/Mihel/etc. & Rachel THAINE/TRAIN/TRAYNE; 12 Jan 1676, 1676/7, 12 Dec 1676; Watertown

BAIRSTOW, William (1612-1668) & Ann HUBBARD, m/2 John PRINCE ca 1670; 8 Jul 1638; Dedham/Scituate

BERSTOW, William (1652-) & Sarah/?Martha _?_; b 1676(7?); Scituate

BARTER, Henry (-1747) & 1/wf Sarah [CROCKET]; Kittery, ME

BARTER, Peter & ?Margaret _?_; Star Island

BARTHOLOMEW, Andrew (1670-1755?) & Hannah [FRISBIE] (1682-); ca 1698?, b 1699; Branford, CT/Wallingford, CT

BARTHOLOMEW, Henry (-1622) (see Samuel LOTHROP) & Elizabeth [SCUDDER]? (-1682), dau Thomas; b 1641; Salem/Boston

BARTHOLOMEW, Henry (1657-1698) & Katherine [HUTCHINSON] (1653-), m/2 Richard JANVERON/?CHAMBERLAIN 1699; no issue; Salem

BARTHOLOMEW, Isaac (1664-1727) & Rebecca [?FRISBIE] (?1679, ?1676-1738, ae 62); ca 1694; Woodstock, CT/Branford, CT

BARTHOLOMEW, William (-1681, ae 78) & Anne/Mary? [LORD?] (-1683); b 1640, Woodstock, CT; Boston/Charlestown

BARTHOLOMEW, William (1640-) & Mary JOHNSON (1642-); 17 Dec 1663; Roxbury/Branford, CT

BARTLETT, Abijah & Captivity [JENNINGS] (1678-); b 1701?; Hadley

BARTLETT, Abraham (1666-) & Elizabeth [JONES], w James; by 1686; Portsmouth, NH

BARTLETT, Abraham (-1731) & Mary WARNER (1664-1738) Middletown; 11 Jun 1693; Guilford, CT

BARTLETT, Alexander & Sarah _?_; b 1676; Northampton

BARTLETT, Benjamin (1632-1691) & 1/wf Susanna [JENNEY]; ca 1655; Duxbury

BARTLETT, Benjamin (1632-1691) & 2/wf Sarah [BREWSTER]; ca 1656; Duxbury

BARTLETT, Benjamin (1643-1678) & Deborah BARNARD (1640-); Jul 1664, 16 Feb 1664, 8 Jun 1665; Windsor, CT
BARTLETT, Benjamin (1632-1691) & 3/wf Cecilia _?_ (aunt of Sarah COOCK; by 1678; Duxbury
BARTLETT, Benjamin (-1724) & Ruth PABODIE (1658-1725); Nov 1678?, Dec 1678? (prob); Duxbury
BARTLETT, Benjamin & Mary [CLESSON] (1679-); b 1701; Brookfield
BARTLETT, Christopher (-1670) & 1/wf [Mary] _?_ (-1660); 17 Apr 1645, 16 Apr; Newbury
BARTLETT, Christopher (-1670) & 2/wf Mary HOYT, m/2 Richard MARTIN; 17 Dec 1663; 19 Dec 1663; Newbury/Salisbury
BARTLETT, Christopher (-1711) & Deborah WEED, m/2 John KIMBALL; 29 Nov 1677; Haverhill/Newbury
BARTLETT, Daniel (1665-1747) & 1/wf Sarah MEIGS (1667-1688); 11 Jan 1686; Guilford, CT
BARTLETT, Daniel (1665-1747) & 2/wf Concurrence CRANE/EVANS (-1703) Killingworth; 11 Feb 1690/1; Guilford, CT
BARTLETT, Ebenezer (-b 1697) & Hannah [WARREN], m/2 Thomas DELANO 1699; b 1694; Duxbury
BARTLETT, Esaya & _?_
BARTLETT, Faithful & Margaret [_?_]; b 1671; Boston
BARTLETT, George (-1669) & Mary CRESTTENDEN (-1669); 14 Sep 1650; Guilford, CT
BARTLETT, George (-1674?) & Mary _?_ ; b 1674?. b 1680?; Scarborough, ME
BARTLET, Henry & Mary BUSH; 6 Dec 1682; Marlborough
BARTLETT, Ichabod (-1716) & 1/wf Elizabeth WATERMAN (1679-1708); 28 Dec 1699; Marshfield
BARTLETT, Isaiah/Ezayah? (1641-1665) & Abia GIBLET, m/2 John SLAUGHTER 1669; 3 Dec 1663; Windsor, CT
BARTLETT, Jacob & Sarah [?ALBEE]; ca 1700?
BARTLETT, Jehoggada?/Jehoiada/Jehojada?/Jehoidad? (-1718) & Sarah HILLIER; 10 Jul 1673; Windsor, CT/Hartford
BARTLETT, John (1613-1679) & Joan/Joanna _?_ (-1678); b 1639, b 1636?; Salisbury
BARTLETT, John (1607-1670) & [Martha?] _?_, m/2 James RISING 1673; b 1641; Windsor, CT
BARTLETT, John (?1639-) & Sarah KNIGHT; 6 Mar 1659/60; Newbury
BARTLETT, John (-1684) & Sarah [ALDRICH] (-living in 1682); b 1666(?7), b 11 Feb 1666; Weymouth
BARTLETT, John (1645-) & Bethia [DEVEREUX] (1649-); [ca 1680]; Salem
BARTLETT, John (-1736) & 1/wf Mary RUST/RUSH? (1664-); 29 Sep 1680, 29 Oct; Newbury
BARTLETT, John (1666-1732) & Alice _?_ ; 29 Oct 1680, b 1684(5?), b 1688; Rehoboth/Attleboro
BARTLETT, John & Mercy/Mary (WRIGHT) [CHAMBERLAIN] (1666-), w Benjamin; 1692, Hull; Plymouth Co.
BARTLETT, John & _?_ ; b 1693; Portsmouth, NH/Salisbury
BARTLETT, John & Mary [MUNN], wid; aft 1690, b 1713; Woodbury, CT
BARTLETT, Joseph (?1629-1711/12) & Hannah [POPE] (ca 1639-1710); b 1665, b 1663; Plymouth
BARTLETT, Joseph (-1707, 1702?) & Mary WAYTE/WATTE (1646-[721); 27 Oct 1668; Cambridge/Newton
BARTLETT, Joseph, Jr. (1665-1703) & Lydia GRIZWEL/GRISWOLD (1672-1752), m/2 Joseph HOLMES, Jr. 1705; 6 Jun 1692; Plymouth
BARTLETT, Joseph (-1750) & 1/wf Hannah _?_ (-1730); b 1695, b 1697; Sherborn/Newton
BARTLETT, Moses & Deborah HARDING, w Abraham; 5 Mar 1695/6, bef 3 Mar 1695/6; Providence/Smithfield, RI
BARTLETT, Nathaniel & Rebecca [?NICK]; b 1698, b 1699; Marblehead
BARTLETT, Nicholas (1620±-1706+) (ae 86 in 1706) & Elizabeth _?_ ; b 1651?; Scarborough, ME/Salem/Kennebunk, ME
BARTLETT, Richard[1] (-1647) & Johan _?_ ; in Eng, b 1610(11?), b 1621; Salisbury
BARTLETT, Richard[2] (1621-1698, ae 76) & Abigail _?_ (-1687); b 1645(6?), b 1649; Newbury
BARTLETT, Richard (1648-1724) & Hannah EMERY (1654-1705); 18 Nov 1673; Newbury
BARTLETT, Richard & 1/wf Margaret WOODMAN (1676-1718); 12 Apr 1699; Newbury
BARTLETT, Robert (?1603-1676) & Mary [WARREN] (-1683); 1629?, 1628; Plymouth
BARTLETT, Robert (-1676) & Anne/Anna? _?_ (-1676); b 1637?, b 1641; Hartford/Hatfield

BARTLETT, Robert (-1673) & Sarah __?__; ca 1650/8?; New London, CT
BARTLETT, Robert & 1/wf Mary [WALTON] (1644-); b 1664, b 1669; Salem
BARTLETT, Robert (?1663-1718) & 1/wf Sarah BARTLETT (-1688); 28 Dec 1687; Duxbury/Plymouth
BARTLETT, Robert (?1663-1718) & 2/wf Sarah COOKE (ca 1671-1744/5); 1 Apr 1691; Plymouth
BARTLET, Samuel (-1732) & Elizabeth TITCOMB (-1690); 23 May 1671; Newbury
BARTLETT, Samuel (1639-1712) & 1/wf Mary BRIDGMAN/BRIDGHAM (-1674); 29 Apr 1672; Northampton
BARTLETT, Samuel (1639-1712) & 2/wf Sarah [BALDWIN] (1653, 1650?-); b 1677; Northampton/Deerfield
BARTLETT, Samuel (-1713?) & Hannah PABODIE (1662-1714+); 2 Aug 1683; Duxbury
BARTLETT, Samuel, Attleboro & Mary INMAN, Providence; 19 Dec 1695; Rehoboth/Attleboro
BARTLETT, Thomas (1594-1654) & Hannah __?__ (-1676); b 1637, b 1639; Watertown
BARTLET, Thomas (-1689) & Tirza/Tirzah? TITCOMB, m/2 James ORDWAY b 1691; 24 Nov 1685; Newbury
BARTLETT, William (-1658) & Susanna __?__; ca 1647/57; New London, CT
BARTLETT, William & Sarah PURCHASE?; 27 Dec 1688; Marblehead
BARTLETT, William (1674-) & Hannah EVARTS, ?m/2 Thomas DELANO; 21 Apr 1696; Guilford, CT
BURTLES/BARTELLS/BARTLES/BERTLES Edward & Mary __?__; b 1684(5?); Boston
BARTLES/?BARTOL, Edward & Elizabeth BROWN; m int 5 Feb 1696/7; Boston
BARTOLL, John (-1664) & Parnell [HODDER] (1602-); 12 Jun 1628, b 1629, b 1643; Salem/Marblehead
BARTOL, John & 1/wf ?Christian __?__; b 1682, b 1685; Marblehead
BARTOLL, Robert & Sarah BECKETT; 16 Mar 1680/1; Marblehead
BARTOLL, William (1629-1690) & Mary __?__ (-1708); b 1666, b 1662?; Lynn/Salem/Marblehead
BARTOLL, William & Susanna [WOODBURY]; b 1680, no date; Salem
BARTOLL, William & Margaret __?__; b 1682(3?); Salem
BARTON, Benjamin (-1720) & Susanna GORTON; 8 Jun 1669, 18 Jun 1672, 10 Jun; Warwick, RI
BARTON, Edward[1] (-1671) & Elizabeth __?__; ca 1639; Marblehead/Salem/Exeter, NH
BARTON, Elisha (?1655-) & Mary [CROCKET]; ca 1678/87?; Kittery, ME
BARTON, Isaac & Hannah __?__; b 1683; Topsfield
BARTON, James (1643-1729) & Margaret [?OTIS] (1647-1731); b 1680, b 1670?; Newton/Boston
BARTON, John (-1694) & Lidia [ROBERTS] (-1713); ?26 Apr 1676, 7 Jun 1675, b 1677; ?Salem
BARTON, Matthew (1640, 1642?-1724+) & 1/wf Martha __?__ (-1675+); ca 1660?; Salem
BARTON, Matthew (1640-1729) & 2/wf Sarah __?__ (-1687+); b 1680; Salem
BARTON, Matthew & 3/wf Elizabeth (TAPLEY) DICKINSON; 20 Dec 1694; Salem
BARTON, Rufus (1628-), Westchester, NY, & Mary __?__
BARTON, Roger & Bridget [PALMER?]; b 1638; Westchester, NY
BARTON, Rufus (-1648/9) & Margaret __?__, m/2 Walter TODD; b 1637; Portsmouth
BARTON, Samuel (?1664-1732) & Hannah [BRIDGES] (1669-); b 1691; Watertown/Framingham/Oxford
BARTON, William[2] & Anne [GREEN], m/2 Walter PENNEL/PENWELL 1700; 24 Oct 1673; ?Cape Porpoise
BASCOM, John (1672-) & Thankful WEST?/WEBSTER?; 12 Dec 1700; Deerfield/?Lebanon, CT
BASCOM, Thomas (ca 1606-1682) & Avis __?__ (-1676); b 1634; Dorchester/Windsor, CT/etc.
BASCOM, Thomas (1642-1689) & Mary NEWELL (-); 20 Mar 1667; Northampton
BASCOM, Thomas (1668-1714) & Hannah [CATLIN]; ca 1691; Northampton
BASHFORD/BASFORD, Jacob & 1/wf Elizabeth [CLIFFORD] (1659-bef 27 Mar 1708); b 1687, b 1686; Hampton, NH
BASS, John[2] (1633, ?1632-1716, ae 83, in 84th y) & 1/wf Ruth ALDEN (?1640, ?1634/5-1674); 3 Feb 1657/8; Braintree
BASS, John[2] (1633-1716) & 2/wf Hannah/Anne STERTEVANT, Plymouth, w of Samuel?; 21 Sep 1675; Braintree
BASS, John[3] (1658-) & 1/wf Abigail [ADAMS] (1654-1696), dau Joseph; b 1688; Braintree
BASS, John[3] (1675-) & Elizabeth NEALE (1675-); 7 Mar 1694/5, 1695, 7 Apr 1694/5?, 7-2-1694/5; Braintree/Windham, CT
BASS, John[3] (1658-1724) & 2/wf Rebecca SAVIL; 17 May 1698, 17 Mar; Braintree

BASS, Joseph² (-1714) & 1/wf Mary __?__ (-15 Mar 1678); b 1678, no issue; Braintree
BASS, Joseph & Hannah **BRACHETT** (1662-)?
BASS, Joseph³ (1665-1733) & 1/wf Mary **BELCHER** (-1707); 5 Jun 1688; Braintree
BASS, Joseph² (-1714?) & 2/wf Deborah __?__; b 1700; Braintree
BASS, Peter & __?__ [**PARKER?**]/[**JOHNSON?**]; Wells, ME
BASS, Philip & Sarah [**KEMBLE**] (-1746, ae 86); b 1682; Boston/Charlestown
BASS, Samuel¹ (1600-1694) & Ann/Anne [**SAVELL**] (1600-1693); 25 Apr 1625, in Eng, Aug ca 1625/9; Roxbury/Braintree
BASS, Samuel² (-1653?) & Mary [**HOWARD?/HAYWARD?**] (-1691, ae 62), m/2 Isaac **JONES** 1659; b 1653; Braintree
BASS, Samuel³ & Rebecca **FAXON**; 30 Jul 1678; Braintree
BASS, Samuel³ (1660-) & 1/wf Ann __?__ (Elizabeth **KERTLAND** of Lynn was possibly the first & hetherto unknown wife); ca 1687, b 4 Jun 1688, by 1685
BASS, Samuel³ (1660-1751) & 2/wf Mercy **MARSH**; 29 Nov 1689; Braintree
BASS, Samuel³ (1660-1751) & 3/wf Mary [**ADAMS**] (1668-1706), dau Joseph (4/wf Bethiah **NIGHTINGALE** 1706 wrong); b 18 Jul 1694; Braintree/Sherborn
BASS, Thomas² (?1635-1720) & 1/wf Sarah **WOOD** (1642-1678), dau Nicholas; 4 Oct 1660; Medfield/Braintree
BASS, Thomas² (-1720) & Susannah (**BATES**) **BLANCHARD**, w Nathaniel; last of Nov 1680; Braintree
BASSETT, David (in 1694 name is Daniel, wrong) & Mary __?__; b 1684, b 1697; Boston/Charlestown
BASSETT, Elisha & Elizabeth [**COLLINS**] (1666-); b 1689; Lynn/Salem Co., NJ
BASSETT, John (-1653) & Margary __?__ (-1656); in Eng, b 1624; New Haven
BASSETT, John (1652-1714) & Mercy [**TODD**] (1645-1717); [ca 1675], b 1676; New Haven
BASSETT, John (1653?-1736) & Mary __?__ (-1736+); [ca 1675/85?]; ?Lynn
BASSETT, Jonathan & Mary __?__; b 1683; Barnstable
BASSETT, Joseph (1635?-1712) & 1/wf [Mary **LAPHAM**] (-1676, ae ca 35) (?see William); [ca 1658]; Bridgewater
BASSETT, Joseph (?1635-1712) & 2/wf Martha **HOBART** (1647-); 16 Oct 1677; Hingham/Bridgewater
BASSETT, Joseph (ca 1664-) & Bethiah **EATON**; 5 Nov 1691; Taunton
BASSETT, Nathan (1667-1736) & Mary **HUCKINS** (1673-); b 1690; Martha's Vineyard
BASSETT, Nathaniel (?1628-1710/11) & 1/wf Dorcas/Mary? [**JOYCE**]; b 1672?; Yarmouth/Chatham
BASSETT, Nathaniel & Joanna **BORDEN**; 16 Dec 1695, 10 Dec 1695; Windham, CT/Mansfield, CT
BASSETT, Robert & Mary __?__; b 1638; New Haven/Stanford, CT
BASSETT, Robert (-1710) & Elizabeth **RIGGS** (1668-); [ca 1687], b 1689; Fairfield, CT/Stanford, CT
BASSETT, Samuel (1655, 1654-1716) & Mary **DICKERMAN** (1659-1723); 21 Jun 1677; New Haven
BASSETT, Samuel & Elizabeth [**JONES**]; b 1700; Kingston/Greenwich, RI
BASSETT, Thomas (1598-1668) & 1/wf __?__ (-1651); b 1646; Dorchester/Windsor, CT
BASSETT, Thomas (1598-1668) & 2/wf Joanna (__?__) **BEARDSLEY** (1634-), w Thomas; aft 5 Jul 1656, bef 1661; Fairfield, CT
BASSETT, Thomas & Sarah [**BALDWIN**] (1668-); b 1680; Milford, CT
BASSETT, William & 1/wf Margaret **OLDHAM**
BASSETT, William (1595/1600-1667) & 2/wf? Elizabeth __?__ (not **TILDEN**); b 1624, [b 1621?]; Plymouth/Duxbury/Bridgewater
BASSETT, William (1624/6-1703) & __?__ (-1701+); b 1648; Lynn
BASSETT, William (-1684) & Hannah **DICKERMAN**?/Hannah **IVES**, w William; 7 Nov 1648; New Haven
BASSETT, William (-1667) & 2/wf Mary **BURT?**/Mary (**TILDON**) **LAPHAM**, w Thomas; aft 1648, aft 1651; Plymouth/Bridgewater
BASSETT, William² (1624-1670) & Mary **RAYNESFORD** (1632-1664), m/2 James **PERCIVAL**; ca 1652; Sandwich
BASSETT, William (1656-1721) & Rachel **WILLASON/WITTESTON?**, Taunton; 9 Oct 1675; Sandwich
BASSETT, William & Sarah **HOOD** (1657-); 25 Oct 1675; Lynn

BASSETT, William (ca 1667-), Bridgewater & 1/wf Sarah SWEETLAND (-1703), Bridgewater; 14 Jun 1693; Milton

BASSON, Richard (1625-1716) & Elizabeth _?_ (-1728+); Portsmouth, NH/Boston

BASSON/?BOSSON, Samuel (1677-) & Mary PICKWORTH; 25 Jun 1700; Boston

BASTER, John (1657-1691) & Susanna [LANGDON] (1677-), m/2 Samuel GRAY 1695, m/3 Vincent STILSON 1696, m/4 Joseph VYOLL 1702; b 1690; Boston

BASTER, Joseph & Mary _?_ ; b 1643; Cambridge/Boston

BASTER, Joseph (1647-1697) & 1/wf Elizabeth WINCHESTER; b 1673; Boston

BASTARD, Joseph (1647-1697) & 2/wf Hannah (JORDAN) WAKEMAN (ca 1648-1696/7), w Esbon/Ezbon?; ca Sep 1684; Fairfield

BASTER, Roger (-1687) & _?_ ; Newport, RI

BASTON, Thomas & Hannah _?_ (1652-); b 1675; Wells, ME

BATCHELDER, Alexander (-1660) & Anne _?_ (-1661); b 1630(?); Portsmouth, NH

BATCHELDER, Benjamin (1673-) & Susanna PAGE, m/2 John CRAM; 25 Dec 1696; Hampton, NH

BACHILLER, David (1643-) & Hannah PLUMMER (1656-); 30 Dec 1679; Reading

BATCHELOUR, Ebenezer & Sarah TARBOX (Ruth wrong); 29 Sep 1699; 15 Dec 1699; Salem

BATCHELDER, Henry (-1678), Canterbury & Martha WILSON (-1686); m lic 15 Apr 1637; Ipswich

BACHELOR, John (-1676) (?bro of Abigail (BACHELOR) DOMAN wf of John EATON) & Rebecca _?_ (-1662); b 1635; Watertown/Dedham/Reading

BATCHELDER, John (ca 1610-1675) & 1/wf Mary _?_ ; b 1639; Salem

BATCHELDER, John (ca 1610-1675) & 2/wf Elizabeth [HERRICK]; aft 8 May 1653; Salem

BATCHELDER, John & _?_ ; ?b 1661; ?Portsmouth, NH

BACHELOR, John (-1698) & 1/wf Marah/Mary DENNIS (-1665); 12 Jul 1661; Wenham

BACHELLER, John (1634±-1705) & 1/wf Sarah [LUNT] (1639-1685); 7 Jan 1662; Reading

BATCHELDER, John (1631-1698) & 2/wf Sarah GOODALE (1640/1-1730); 4 May 1666; Wenham

BACHELER, John (1650-1684) & Mary HERRICK (-1684); 14 Aug 1673; Salem

BACHELLER, John (1634±-1705?) & 2/wf Hannah (BOYNTON) [WARNER] (1654-1693), w Nathaniel; 10 May 1687; Reading

BACHELLER, John (-1705) & 3/wf Hannah _?_ (-1705+); 12 Jun 1694; Reading

BACHELDER, John (1675-1748) & 1/wf Bethiah WOODBERY (-1708?); 22 Apr 1696; Beverly

BACHELLER, John (-1732) & Sarah POORE; 10 Nov 1696; Reading

BATCHELDER, Joseph (1603/4-1647?) & Elizabeth DICKINSON (1614-); Thenington, Eng, m lic 22 Dec 1628; Salem/Wenham

BACHELDER, Joseph (1644-1688) & Agnes (WADLAND) GILLINGHAM (-1693, ae 50), w William; 22 Dec 1670, 20 Dec; Charlestown

BACHELOR, Joseph (-1681?, 1682?) & Meriam/Miriam MOULTON (1659-), m/2 Freeborn BALCH 1683?; 8 Oct 1677; Salem

BATCHELDER, Joseph (1662-1720) & Sarah _?_ (-1720); b 1687; Wenham

BATCHELDER, Joseph & Mary RAYMENT/RAYMOND; 18 Dec 1700, m int 24 Nov 1700; Salem/Beverly

BATCHELDER, Nathaniel (?1630-1710) & 1/wf Deborah SMITH (?1640-1676); 10 Dec 1656; Hampton, NH

BATCHELDER, Nathaniel (1630-1710) & 2/wf Mary (CARTER) WYMAN (1648-), w John; 31 Oct 1676; Woburn/Hampton, NH

BATCHELDER, Nathaniel (1659-) & Elizabeth [FOSS?] (1666-); b 1686; Hampton, NH

BACHELDER, Nathaniel (1630-1710) & 3/wf Elizabeth KNILL, w John; 23 Oct 1689; Charlestown/Hampton

BACHELLER, Samuel & 1/wf Mary PROCTER; 25 Jun 1694; Reading

BACHELER, Stephen (?1561-1660?) & 1/wf _?_ BATE?; in Eng, b 1589; Lynn/Hampton, NH

BATCHELDER, Stephen (-1660) & 2/wf Christian WEARE, wid; 3 Mar 1623/4

BACHELER, Stephen[1] (-1660) & 3/wf Helena [MASON] (-1635, ae 60?) (ae 48 in 1631?); in Eng, 26 Mar 1627; Hampton, NH

BACHELOR, Stephen[1] (-1660) & 4/wf 5/wf? Mary [BEEDLE], w Robert, div, m/3 Thomas TURNER; b 1650, ca 1648; Hampton, NH

BATCHELDER, Stephen (1676-) & Mary DEARBORN (1678-); 25 Aug 1698; Hampton, NH

BACHELDER, William (-1670, ae 72) & 1/wf Jane COWPER; Standford Dingley, Eng, Oct 1632; Charlestown

BATCHELDER, William (1597-1670) & 2/wf Rachel __?__ (1603-1676); b 1644, b 1640?; Charlestown

BATEMAN, Eleazer & Elizabeth WRIGHT (1664-); 2 Nov 1686; Woburn

BAITMAN, Henry & Abial SHAPLEY; 15 Aug 1688; ?Billerica

BATEMAN, John & Hannah __?__ ; b 1645; Boston/?Woburn/Hingham

BATEMAN, John & Abigail RICHARDSON (1662-); 30 Jun 1681, ?1680; Woburn

BATEMAN, Thomas (1615-1669) & 1/wf Martha [BROOKS], dau Henry; b 1638?, b 1645; Concord

BATEMAN, Thomas & 2/wf Margaret KNIGHT, w Philip, m/3 Nathaniel BALL 1670/1; 27 Jan 1668; Concord

BATEMAN, Thomas & 1/wf Abigail MERRIAM (1647-1684); 25 Apr 1672;' Concord

BATEMAN, Thomas & 2/wf Ruth (WRIGHT) [KNIGHT], w Jonathan; b 1688; Concord/Salem

BATEMAN, William (-1658) & __?__ ; b 1615; Concord/Milford, CT/Fairfield, CT

BATES, Benjamin (1633-1678/9) & Jane [WEEKS], m/2 Moses PAINE 1679; ca 1655/60?, no issue; Hingham

BATES, Benjamin (1665-at Dorchester) & Mary LEAVITT; 10 Oct 1682 at New London; Hingham/Lexington

BATES, Caleb (1666-1747) & 1/wf Ruth __?__ (-1690); 26 Aug 1689; Hingham

BATES, Caleb (1666-1747) & 2/wf Mary LANE (1671-1715); 14 Apr 1691; Hingham

BATES, Clement (1595-1671) & Anna __?__ (1595-1669); ca 1620; Hingham

BATE, Edward (1606-) (ae 63 in 1669) & ?Susan/?Susanna/?Anne __?__ ; b 1639; Weymouth

BATES, Edward & Lydia __?__, m/2 William FLETCHER 1645; b 1642; Boston

BATES, Edward (1655-) & Elizabeth [?EDSELL]; b 1679/[80?]; Weymouth

BATES, Francis & Ann OLDHAM (1634-); - Jul 1657; Salisbury/Topsfield

BATES, Increase (1641-1717) & Mary [WHITMARSH] (1663-1715); b 1681/[2?]; Weymouth

BATES, James (1582-1655) & Alice GLOVER (1583-1657), Saltwood, Eng; 13 Sep 1603, m lic in Eng; Dorchester

BATES, James (-1689) & Ruth LYFORD; 19 Apr 1643, 1642?; Hingham/Scituate

BATES, James (1624-1692) & Ann/Anna/Hannah [WETHINGTON] (ca 1625-1700); b 1648; Dorchester/Haddam, CT/Saybrook, CT

BATES, James (?1647-1719, 1718?, Haddam) & Elizabeth/Hannah? [CARL/KARL]/[CAR-ROLL?]; ?Hempstead, LI/Haddam, CT

BATES, James (1662-1732) & Mary [LORD] (1679-); ca 1697; Haddam, CT

BATES, John & Susan __?__ ; b 1655; ?Weymouth/Chelmsford

BATES, John & __?__ ; b 1663?; Hempstead, LI

BATES, John (?1642-1716) & Mary FARNOLL; 22 Dec 1665; Chelmsford

BATES, John & Martha __?__ ; by 1674; Wells, ME

BATES, John (1641-) & Sarah [CROSS] (-1712); b 1674; Stamford, CT

BATES, John (-1719) & Elizabeth (BECKWICH) [GERARD], (div) wf Robert; by 1677, b 1678; Haddam, CT/Stamford, CT

BATES, John (1666-) & Hannah __?__ ; b 1694; Haddam, CT

BATES, John (1668-1722) & Deborah [SPALDING?] (1670-); b 1694; Chelmsford

BATES, John & 1/wf Elizabeth LOCKWOOD (-1702); 18 Jan 1693/4; Stamford, CT

BATES, John (1678-1740) & 1/wf Elizabeth [MARKHAM]; b 1700; Middletown, CT/E. Haddam, CT

BATES, Joseph (1628-1706) & Esther HILLIARD (1642-1709); 9 Jan 1667/8; Hingham

BATES, Joseph (1660-) & Mary LINCOLN (1662-); 3 Jan 1683/4, at Hull?; Hingham

BATES, Joseph & Anna/Anne [SYLVESTER] (1669-), dau Joseph; b 1689, 1688?; Scituate/Hanover

BATES, Joshua & Rachel TOWER; 15 Jan 1695/6; Hingham

BATES, Robert (-1675) & 1/wf __?__ ; b 1641; Wethersfield, CT/Stamford, CT

BATES, Robert (-1675) & 2/wf Margaret (OAKES)? CROSS, w William; 26 Jun 1657, 1657, 26 Jan 16--; Stamford, CT

BATES, Robert(?) (-1675) & ?3/wf Susanna (SMITH?) [HOYT], w Simon; aft 1657, bef 1 Feb 1674; Stamford, CT

BATES, Robert & Sarah __?__ ; b 1672, b 1673; Lynn

BATES, Samuel & Lydia LAPHAM; 20 Feb 1666/7; Hingham

BATES, Samuel (-1699) & Mary CHAPMAN; 2 May 1676; Saybrook, CT

BATES, Solomon (1671-) & Abigail __?_ ; 1690; Hempstead, LI
BATES, Thomas, Rye, NY & Mary BUTCHER; 21 Feb 1669; Stamford, CT
BATES, __?__ & Mary POTTER?/ROSE?
BATHRICK, Thomas (-1683) & 1/wf Elizabeth WELLS (-1674); 5 Apr 1673; Charlestown
BAVRICK, Thomas (-1683) & 2/wf Ruth [BUCK] (1653-); b 1675, ca 1670; Charlestown/Cambridge
BATSON, John & Elizabeth [SANDERS] (-1728+), m/2 __?__ WALDEN, m/3 John GOVE 1700; ca 1660, Jun 166-; Cape Porpoise/Salisbury
BATSON, John (-1703) & Mary [ODIORNE], m/2 James STILSON; b 1697; Newcastle/Cape Porpoise
BATSON, Robert & Ann WINTER, m/2 __?__ MATTALL; 13 Jul 1676; Marshfield
BATSON, Stephen (-1676) & Elizabeth/Mary? __?_ ; 1636?; Saco, ME/Wells, ME
BATT, Christopher (1601-) (ae 53 in 1654, 37 in 1638) & Ann BAINTON/BAYNTON (not THACHER) (1606-); 12 Oct 1629; Newbury/Boston
BATT, Nicholas (-1677) & Lucy __?__ (-1679); b 1635; Newbury
BATT, Paul (-1678) & Sarah [WILSON] (1650-), m/2 Josiah TORREY 1680; b 1674; Boston
BATT, Paul & Elizabeth MIGHELL, m/2 David HITCHCOCK; 13 Feb 1700, prob 1700-1701; Boston
BATT, Thomas & Lydia [BENJAMIN] (1653-); b 1674; Boston
BATT, Timothy & Abigail [BAYES?]; b 1672; Boston
BATT, Timothy & Sarah TUDMAN; 3 Aug 1699; Boston
BATTELEE, John (1652-1713) & Hannah HOLBROOK; 18 Nov 1678; Dedham
BATTELLE, Jonathan (1658-) & Mary ONION; 15 Apr 1690; Dedham
BATTALY, Thomas (-1706) & Mary FISHER (-1691); 5 Sept 1648; Dedham
BATTELL, __?__ & Experience PRATT
BATTEN, Arthur & Abigail [SPURWELL]; 8 Sep 1664; Saco, ME/Cape Porpoise
BATTEN, Benjamin & Elizabeth [CULLICK]; ?- Oct 1671; Boston
BATTEN, Hugh (-1659) & Ursula [GREENWAY] (1603-1683); betw 1650 & 1659?; Dorchester
BATTEN, John & Sarah [MAINS]; b 1671; Lynn
BATTEN, William & Joan [MOORE]; b 1667, 12 Oct 1655; Saco, ME
BATTER, Edmond (1609-1685) (brother-in-law of Hilliard VEREN) & 1/wf Sarah [ALWOOD?] (-1669); b 1635; Salem
BATTER, Edmond (1609-1685) & 2/wf Mary GOOKIN (?1642-1702); 8 Jun 1670; Salem
BATTER, Edmund (1674-) & Martha PICKMAN; 26 Oct 1699; Salem
BATTEY, James (-1690) & __?_ ; Hog Island, RI
BATTEY, Samson & Dinah [?HAVENS] (-1698); b 1682; Jamestown, RI
BATTIS, John & Mary KELLEY; 15 Jun 1693; Boston
BACKSTER, Daniel & Elizabeth __?_ ; b 1644; Salem
BAXTER, Edward & Deborah TRAFFICK; m int 6 Dec 1695; Boston
BAXTER, Gregory (-1659) & Margaret [PADDY] (-1662) (sister of William); b 1632; Roxbury/Braintree
BAXTER, John (1639-1719) & Anna/Hannah? WHITE; 24 Nov 1659; Braintree
BAXTER, John (-1687, ae 60) & Hannah TRUMBULL (1642-1719, 1703?); 2 Mar 1659, 1658/9, 2-1-1659, 2 Mar 1658/9; Charlestown
BAXTER, John & 1/wf Abigail WHITERIG/WHITTRIDGE?/WHITING?/WHITNEY (-1676); 24 Nov 1667, 25 Nov; Salem
BAXTER, John & 2/wf Elizabeth (?) MACKMALLEN, w Allester; 1 Nov 1679, 4? Nov; Salem
BAXTER, John, Braintree & Huldah HOWARD/HAYWARD, Braintree; 2 Jan 1693, 24 Jan 1692/3; Braintree
BAXTER, John & Rebecca (MAYER) [NOSSITER], w Peter; aft 1696; York, ME
BAXTER, Joseph & Elizabeth WINCHESTER (1640-), dau Alexander; ca 1660?, b 1682
BAXTER, Joseph (1676-1745) & 1/wf Mary FISKE (1673-1711); 16 Sep 1697; Braintree/Medfield
BAXTER, Nicholas (will 1680) & Anne __?_ ; b 1639, b 1640; Boston
BAXTER, Samuel & 1/wf Mary BEALS; 3 Jun 1697; Braintree
BAXTER, Thomas & Bridget [CLARK], m/2 John PALMER; b 1652, div 15 May 1662; Westchester, NY
BAXTER, Thomas (1654-) & Rebecca [?ADAMS]; b 1675; Westchester Co., NY

BAXTER, Thomas (-1713) & Temperance (GORHAM) STURGES (1646-1715), w Edward; 27 Jan 1679, 16 Jan 1679/80, 27 Jan 1679/80; Yarmouth
BAXTER, Thomas (1675-) & Abigail [LOCKWOOD]; b 1699, b 1698
BAYES, Thomas (-1680?) & Ann/Anna? BAKER; 29 Dec 1639; Dedham
BAYLIES, John[1] (-1682) (will 18 Oct 1682, proved 3 Dec 1682) & Rebecca __?__, m William HALLETT 1684; b 1642; Jamaica, LI
BAYLIES, John[2] (1642-) & Ruth RUSCO; 12 Mar 1665; Jamaica, LI
BAYSE, John (1616-1671) & Elizabeth __?__; b 1645, b 1636; Hartford
BAYSEY, __?__ & Elizabeth SLAMY? (1585-1657+); Hartford
BEACH, Azariah (1646-1696) & Martha [IVES]; b 1676; Wallingford, CT/Killingworth, CT
BEACH, Benjamin (1644-1713) & 1/wf Mary [PEACOCK] (-1677?); ca 1670/1, ca 1670; Stratford, CT
BEACH, Benjamin (-1713) & 2/wf Sarah WELLS; 1 Feb 1677/8; Stratford, CT
BEACH, Benjamin (1674-) & Mary [HITCHCOCK] (1676-); b 1696; Wallingford, CT/Stratford, CT
BEACH, Isaac (1645-1735) & Mary __?__ (-1724); ca 1670?, no issue; Newton
BEACH, Isaac (1669-1741) & Hannah BIRDSEY (1671-1750); 3 May 1693; Stratford, CT
BEACH, John (see Richard) & 2/wf Martha __?__; b 1646; Watertown
BEACH, John (-1677) & Mary __?__ (-bef 1677); b 1652; New Haven, CT/Stratford, CT
BEACH, John & Mary ROYCE, m/2 John ATWATER 1718; Dec 1678; Wallingford, CT
BEACH, John (1654-1711) & 1/wf Hannah STAPLES of Fairfield; 18 Dec 1679; Stratford, CT
BEACH, John (1654-1711) & 2/wf Phebe (WILCOXSON) [BIRDSEY] (1651-1743), w John; aft 9 Jan 1697/8, bef 6 Nov 1705; Stratford, CT
BEACH, Joseph (1671-1737) & Abiah [BOOTH] (1674-1741); b 1697; Stratford, CT
BEACH, Nathaniel (1662-1747) & Sarah PORTER (-1738); 29 Apr 1686; Stratford, CT
BEACH, Richard (-1674) & 1/wf Mary __?__; b 1639, b 1636?; Watertown
BEACH, Richard & [Catharine] (?COOK) [HULL], w Andrew; 1640, b 1642, ?1641; New Haven/New London
BEACH, Richard (see John BEACH) & 2/wf Martha __?__; bef 1646
BEACH, Samuel (-1728) (no issue) & Abigail __?__, m/2 Samuel ANDREW; ?ca 1690; Milford, CT
BEACH, Thomas (-1662) & Sarah [PLATT] (-1670), m/2 Miles MERWIN ca 1665; b 1654; New Haven/Milford, CT
BEACH, Thomas (1659-1741) & 1/wf Ruth PECK (-1686); 12 May 1680; Wallingford, CT
BEACH, Thomas & 2/wf Phebe [WILCOXSON] (1668-); ca 1688, aft 1690?; New Haven/Wallingford, CT
BEACH, Zophar (1662-) & [Martha PRATT/PLATT?]; Newark, NJ
BEACHAMP, Edward[1] & 1/wf Mary __?__ (-1668); b 9 Sep 1640; Salem/Lynn
BEACHUM, Edward (-1684) & 2/wf Elizabeth MEDCALF, wid; 8 Nov 1670; Salem
BEAUCHAMP, John (-1740, ae 88 y) & Marguerite __?__ (-1727, ae 59); b 1687; Boston/Hartford
BEAUCHAMP, Robert (-1691) & 1/wf Isabel __?__ (-1659+); b 1642?; Ipswich
BEACHAM, Robert (-1691) & 2/wf Elizabeth (?BRIDGES) JESSUP, w Edward; m lic 4 Nov 1668; Westchester Co., NY
BEALE, Aaron (-1711) & Elizabeth NICHOLSON; 29 Jun 1693, 1692?; Marblehead
BEALE, Arthur & Agnes/Anne [HILTON]; by 1667; York, ME
BALE, Benjamin (-1680) (called cousin in 1672 by Nathaniel PATTEN) & Bathsheba/Bathshua [LATHROP], m/2 Alexander MARSH; b 1669, ca 1668; Boston/Dorchester
BEALE/[BALE] Benjamin (-1753?) & Hannah HOLMAN; 27 Jun 1700; Milton
BEAL, Caleb (1636-1716, ae 79) & Elizabeth HURT (?1645-1721); 30 Dec 1664; Hingham
BEAL, Caleb & __?__; b 1670
BEAL, Caleb & Ruth HERSEY; 4 Feb 1695/6; Hingham
BEAL, Ebenezer & Mary BARTLETT; 3 May 1694; Marblehead
BEALE, Edward & Ann __?__
BEALE, Edward (-1707) & Sarah [COTTON]; b 1684?; New Castle, NH
BEAL, Edward & Elizabeth [LITTLEFIELD]/?MANWARING (-1747+); b 1699, 1694; Charlestown
BEALE, Jacob (1642-1718) & Mary BISBEE (1640-1718); 15 Jan 1678/9; Hingham
BEELS, Jeremiah (1631-1716, ae 85) & Sarah RIPLEY (1627-1715); ?26 Oct 1653, ?18 Nov 1652; Boston/Hingham
BEAL, Jeremiah & Hannah LANE; 22 May 1677; Hingham
BEAL, John[1] (1589-1688) & 1/wf Frances RIPLEY; Wymondham, Eng, 11 Jun 1616; Hingham

BEAL, John[1] (1589-1688) & 2/wf Nazareth (HOBART) TURNER (1601-1658), w Robert; Hingham, Eng, 13 Jul 1630; Hingham
BEAL, John[2] (1627-1694) & 1/wf Elizabeth _?_ (-1660); 6 Jan 1658/9; Hingham
BEAL, John[1] (1589-1688) & 3/wf Mary (GILMAN) JACOB (-1681), w Nicholas; 10 Mar 1659; Hingham
BEAL, John[2] (?1627-1694) & 2/wf Mary GILL (1644-1701); 14 Nov 1660; Hingham
BEALES, John & Susanna _?_ ; b 1683; Boston
BEAL, John (1657-1735) & Hannah _?_ (1669-1762); b 1687; Hingham
BEAL, John & Martha _?_ , m/2 Albert LaCROIX/CROSS, m/3 John WALDRON; b 1688; Marblehead
BEAL, John & Elizabeth HERSEY (-1718); 18 May 1695; Hingham
BEAL, Joseph (1672-1737) & Patience (NICHOLS) ANDREWS (1660-1709), w John; 12 Feb 1695/6; Hingham
BEAL, Joshua (ca 1633-1716) & 1/wf Elizabeth _?_ (-1689); b 1661; Hingham
BEAL, Joshua (ca 1633-1716) & 2/wf Mary (FARROW) STOWELL (-1708); w Samuel; 10 Oct 1689, 10 Apr; Hingham
BEAL, Lazarus (1661-1723) & Susanna LEWIS (1669-1739), m/2 Benjamin EATON; 18 Feb 1689/90; Barnstable
BEAL, Nathaniel (?1629-1708) & Martha _?_ (-1697) (perhaps her mother's name was Christian _?_); b 1646, b 1648?; Hingham
BEAL, Nathaniel (1648-1708+) & Elizabeth JOY (1654-); 15 Mar 1676/7; Hingham
BEALL, Samuel (1654-1699) & Patience LOVILL/LOVEWELL (1662/3-); 28 Mar 1682; Lynn
BEALE, Thomas (1598, 1599-1661) & Sarah _?_ ; ca 1620-30?, (no issue), b 1634; Cambridge
BEAL, Thomas (Did he marry?) & _?_ ; b 1648?, b 1631?; Lynn
BEALE, William[1] (1631, 1632?-) & 1/wf Martha [BRADSTREET] (1632-); b 1654; Marblehead
BEALE, William[1] & 2/wf Elizabeth (PITTINGTON) JACKSON (-1683), w Edward; 16 Dec 1676; Marblehead
BEAL, William[2] (1659-) & Elizabeth [LOVEWELL]; b 1684, b 1680?; Marblehead
BEALE, William[1] & 3/wf Mary HARTT, w Samuel; 5 Mar 1684, 5 Mar 1683/4; Lynn/Marblehead
BEALE, William (1664-) & Jane [TRAFTON] (1672-1737+); ca 1690?
BEALE, _?_ & Hannah _?_ ; b 1670; Salem
BEMENT, Edmond & Prudence MORGAN; 1 Nov 1699; Enfield, CT
BEMAN, Gamaliel (1623-1678) & Sarah _?_ ; b 1649; Dorchester/Lancaster/Westminster/Marlborough/Princeton
BEAMON, George & Mary JACKSON/WEED?; Aug 1679, 28 Aug 1679; New Haven
BEAMAN, John (-bef 1647) & _?_ ; ca 1629/35?; Salem
BEAMAN, John (-1685) & Martha [DENNIS] (1644-1685+); b 1667; Wenham/Dorchester/Enfield, CT
BEAMAN, John (1649-1739?, 1745?) & Priscilla [THORNTON] (1656-1729); ca 1674, b 1681(2?); Lancaster/Taunton/Sterling
BEAMAN, John & Abigail EGGLESTON; 29 Oct 1696; Springfield/Enfield, CT
BEAMON, Josiah/Josias? (1662-) & 1/wf Martha _?_ (-1691); Brookfield
BEAMAN, Josiah/Josias? & 2/wf Lydia WARNER; 29 Apr 1646; Springfield/Brookfield/Deerfield
BEAMAN, Noah (1661-) & Patience TRESCOTE/TRESCOTT; 1 Jan 1684, 1685; Dorchester
BEAMAN, Samuel & Esther [BUCKINGHAM] (1668-); ca 1688-90?; Saybrook, CT
BEAMAN, Samuel & Margaret CHAPMAN (1672-); 10 May 1695; Wenham, CT
BEAMAN, Simon (-1676) & Alice YOUNG (-1708); 15 Dec 1654; Springfield
BEAMAN, Simon (-1712) & Hannah (BARNARD) WESTCARR (-1739 in 99th y), w John; 9 Oct 1680; Deerfield/Hadley
BEMAN/BEMOND, Thomas (1649-1731) & Elizabeth WILLIAMS; 26 Jul 1678; Marlborough
BEAMONT?/BEAUMOUNT, Thomas (-1686) & [Elizabeth STENT], w Eleazer; aft 1646?; New Haven
BEAMON, William (-1699) & Lydia DANFORTH (1627-1686); 9 Dec 1643; Saybrook, CT/Watertown/Cambridge
BEAMAN, Thomas (1652-) & Deborah _?_
BEAMSLEY, William (-1658) & 1/wf Anne/Hannah? _?_ ; b 1633; Boston
BEAMSLEY, William (-1658) & 2/wf Martha (HALLOR) [BUSHNELL] (-1658+, 1663+), w Edmund; b 1646; Boston

BEAMSLEY, _?_ & _?_ ; b 1676; Roxbury/Lancaster

BEAN, Daniel (1666, 1663?-) & Mary (GILES) [FIFIELD?]; b 1690, ca 1685?; ?Exeter, NH

BEAN, James (1672-1753) & 1/wf _?_ [COLEMAN]; ca 1692?; Exeter, NH

BEAN, James (1672-1753) & 2/wf Sarah BRADLEY (1637-1768), m/2? Jonathan ROBINSON; - Dec 1697; Haverhill

BEAN, John[1] & 1/wf [Hannah LISSON]; b 1655; Exeter, NH

BEAN, John[1] & 2/wf Margaret _?_ ; b 1661; Exeter, NH

BEAN, John[2] (1668-1719) & Sarah [BRADLEY], m/2 _?_ ROBINSON; ca 1698; Exeter, NH

BEAN, Lewis & Mary [MILLS], m/2 Charles BRISSON ca 1686?; ca 1668; York, ME

BEAN/BANE, Lewis (1671-) & Mary (AUSTIN) [SEYWOOD/SEYWARD?], w Jonathan; b 1692; York, ME

BEAN, William (-1715) & Sarah [BUFFUM] (-1715+); b 1679; b 1669; Salem

BEANS, William & 1/wf Hannah VERRY (1667-); 6 Feb 1695, 1695/6; Salem

BEARD, Aaron (-1695) & Hannah [GLOVER] (1659-); aft 18 Apr 1677, b 1681; Boston

BEARD, Andrew (-1712+) & [Mary WILLIAMS] (1672-); b 1696, b 1702; Charlestown

BEARD, George & Elizabeth _?_ ; b 1688; Boston

BEARD, George & Abiel/?Abigail/?Abiah (SANDERS) BUTTOLPH, w Thomas; 17 Dec 1691; Boston

BEARD, [James?] & Martha _?_ (-1647/8); in Eng, ca 1620?; Boston/New Haven/Milford, CT

BEARD, Jeremiah (-1681) & _?_ ; no issue; Milford, CT

BEARD, Jeremiah & ?Martha/?Mercy/Mary (Mary wf in 1698) PETTIT; 26 May 1697; Milford, CT

BEARD, Capt. John (-1690) & Anna/Hannah (HAWLEY) UFFORD/OVIATTE (-1698), div wf; aft 1657, b 1654; Milford, CT

BEARD, John & _?_

BEARD, John (1659-) & 1/wf Sarah _?_ (-1703); b 1661; Milford, CT

BEARD, Joseph (1655, 1657?-1704) & Esther [PHILBRICK] (1657-1716+), 2/m Sylvanus NOCK/KNOX; b 1682, b 1680; Dover, NH

BEARD, Samuel (1670-1754) & Sarah CLARK (1678, 1671-1732); 8 Jul 1696; Milford, CT

BEARD, Thomas (1608-1678?) & 1/wf Mary/?Elizabeth _?_, m/2 William WILLIAMS by 1680; by 1650; Dover, NH

BEARD, Thomas & Mary [ANDREWS?]; b 1664, b 1650?; Boston/Hingham

BEARD, William (-killed 1675) & Elizabeth [HUCKINS], w Robert; b 1655, no issue; Dover, NH

BEARDSLEY, Daniel (1644-1730) & Ruth [GOODWIN]/[WHEALER]; b 1681; Stratford, CT

BEARDSLEY, Daniel & Rebecca JACKSON (1674-) (called Deborah as mother); 3 Dec 1695; Stratford, CT

BEARDSLEY, John (1633-1718) & Hannah _?_ ; no issue; Stratford, CT

BEARDSLEY, John (1668-1735) & Abigail [WAKELEE?/DAYTON?] (?1665-1753); b 1692; Stratford, CT

BEARDSLEY, Joseph (1634-1712) & Phebe [DAYTON], Brookhaven; 1665, b 1666; Stratford, CT/Brookhaven

BEARDSLEY, Samuel (1638-) & Abigail [CLARK] (1641-1726); 1663; Stratford, CT/Bridgeport

BEARDSLEY, Samuel (1666-1690/1) & Sarah _?_ ; Stratford, CT

BEARDSLEY, Samuel & Sarah SHERWOOD; 2 Jul 1691; Stratford, CT

BEARDSLEY, Thomas (-1656) & Joanna _?_ (1634?-), m/2 Thomas BASSETT; b 1647?; Stratford, CT

BEARDSLEY?/BEAZLEY, Thomas & Elizabeth HERUEY/HARVEY; 20 Mar 1649, at Milford, CT 1649/50, 20 May 1649/50; New Haven

BEARDSLEY, Thomas (-1667) & Elizabeth _?_, m/2 Samuel DAYTON b 1669(70?); ?7 Feb 1661; Stratford, CT

BEARDSLEY, William (1605-1661) & Mary LAWRENE?; in Eng, b 1631; Hartford/Stratford, CT

BEARDSLEY, William & Elizabeth BROWN (1679-); 5 Jul 1699, 1697, 1699?; Stratford, CT/Newtown, LI

BEIRSE, Austin/Augustine & Mary [?WILDER]; b 1640; Barnstable

BEARSE, James (1660-) & Experience [HOWLAND?] (1668-), dau John, Jr.; ca 1683/87?; ?Plympton/Barnstable

BEARSE, Joseph (1651/2-) & Martha TAYLOR (1650-1728); 3 Dec 1676, 1675; Barnstable

BEAVERLY/BEVERLY?, George & Ann _?_ ; b 1688(?9); Boston

BECK, Alexander (-1674) & 1/wf Mary _?_ (-1639); b 1639; Boston

BECK, Alexander (-1674) & 2/wf Elizabeth [HINDS]; [1639]; Boston/Roxbury

BECK, Caleb (-1695) & Hannah [BOLLES/BOWLES], m/2 Nathaniel WRIGHT; ?by 1661; Portsmouth, NH

BECK, Henry (1617-1699+) & Ann/Anna? [?FROST]; ca 1645; Dover, NH

BECK, Henry (-1686) & Elizabeth _?_, m/2 Richard ESTES 1687; ?ca 1675/80; Great Island

BECK, Manasah (1645-1688) & Mary _?_; b 1668; Boston

BECK, Thomas (±1657-1734, ae 77) & Mary [?FROST] (-1753, ae 94); b 1683; Portsmouth, NH

BECKET/BECKETT, John[1] (1626, 1627?-1683, ae 57) & Margaret _?_ (1627-), m/2 Philip CROMWELL; ca 1655?; Salem

BECKETT, John[2] (-1711+) & Elizabeth [LOCKER]; Salem

BECKETT, William[2] (-1723) & Hannah SIBLEY (-1734+); 18 May 1683; Marblehead

BECKLEY, Benjamin (1649/50-1736) & 1/wf Rebecca _?_ (Indian woman); 7 Oct 1685; Wethersfield, CT

BECKLEY, John (-1696) & Hannah [DEMING]; b 1670(1?); Wethersfield, CT

BECKLEY, Nathaniel (1652-1697) & Comfort DEMING (1668-), m/2 Thomas MORTON 1698?; 18 May 1693; Wethersfield, CT

BECKLEY, Richard (-1690) & 2/wf Frances _?_; b 1640, b 1641; New Haven/Wethersfield, CT

BECKLEY, Richard & Elizabeth DEMING; 23 Nov 1699; Wethersfield, CT

BECKWITH, James & Sarah MARVIN; 18 Feb 1693, 1692; Lyme, CT

BECKWITH, John[2] (1639-) & _?_; b 1665; New London, CT

BECKWITH, John (1665-1757) & Prudence [MANWARING] (1668-1740); ca 1688; New London, CT

BECKWITH, Jonah/Jonathan (-1721) & Rebecca _?_; 26 Apr 1696; Lyme, CT

BECKWITH, Joseph (1653-1718?) & Susanna [?TALLMAN] (ca 1662-), m/2 ?George WAY?/?Joseph WAR; b 1677; Lyme, CT

BECKWITH, Joseph (1679-) & Marah/Mary? [LEE] (1679-), m/2 Daniel STERLING, m/3 Capt. John RIGGS; 18 May 1699; Lyme, CT

BECKWITH, Matthew[1] (?1610-1680) & 1/wf ?Mary/?Elizabeth [?LYNDE] (-1682+), m/2 Samuel BUCKLEND; b 1637, b 1643; Hartford/Lyme, CT

BECKWITH, Matthew[2] (1637, 1645?-1727) & 1/wf ?Sarah/?Elizabeth _?_; b 1667; Guilford, CT/Lyme, CT

BECKWITH, Matthew[2] (1637-1727) & 2/wf Elizabeth (GRISWOLD) (ROGERS) PRATT, div from John ROGERS, w Peter; aft 1688, bef 1691; Lyme, CT

BECKWITH, Nathaniel (1642-1690+) & Martha _?_; b 1671; Lyme, CT

BECKWITH, Thomas & _?_; div 1655; Roxbury/Fairfield, CT

BEDELL, Daniel (1646-) & [Ann POWLE/POWELL/POOLE]; b 1692, aft 22 Nov 1679; Hempstead, LI

BEADLE, Christopher (-1703?) & _?_; Kittery, ME

BEADLE, Christopher (-1708?) & Sarah [LOCKWOOD], m/2 Thomas PHINNEY? 1696; 1686; ME

BEDELL, John & Sarah [SOUTHARD]; 7 Oct 1690; Hampstead, NY

BEADLE, Joseph (-1672) & Rachel DEANE, wid; 28 Oct 1636

BEADLE, Nathaniel & Mary HICKS; 20 Apr 1671, 1670; Salem

BEEDLE, Nathaniel & Elizabeth SHARP, m/2 Samuel COOKE, m/3 Daniel HARRIS; 30 Jan 1694; Boston/Salem

BEADLE, Robert & Mary _?_, m/2 Stephen BATCHELDER (div), m/3 Thomas TURNER; b 1642; Wethersfield, CT/New London, CT/Newbury

BEDELL, Robert (-1702) & Blanche _?_; b 1644, b 1682; Hampstead, NY

BEDLE, Robert (?1642-) & Martha _?_; b 1665, b 1666; Salisbury/Newbury/Amesbury

BEADLE, Samuel (-1664) & Susanna [GRAY]? (-1662); b 1648, b 1643; Charlestown/Salem

BEADLE, Samuel (-1706) & Hannah LEMON (1650-); 10 Jun 1668, 20? Jun; Salem

BEADLE, Thomas (-1700) & Elizabeth DRAKE (1660-) Hampton, NH, m/2 Thomas DEAN; 18 Sep 1679; Salem

BEDELL (see BRIDLE), Thomas & Mary _?_; b 1689, b 1681?; Boston

BEDLE, Thomas & Mary HARINGTON; 20 Sep 1698; Boston

BEDELL, Thomas (-1735) & Elizabeth [GOULD] (1664-); b 1699; Roxbury

BEDFORD, Nathan (1640-1681) & Anne [MUNDEN], m/2 Richard KELLY/CALLEY 1682?; ca 1667?; Scarborough, ME/etc.

BEDFORD, Stephen & Naomi GAGE; 15 Feb 1693; Bristol, RI

BEDFORD, William & Hannah BRIANT/BRYANT; 22 Feb 1697, 1697/8?; Boston

BEDFORD, ? & Margart PERRE, m/2 Nicholas JENNINGS

BEDIENT, Morgan/Mordecai? (d in Eng) & Mary [BARNARD], m/2 Roger TOWNSEND, m/3 Richard OSBORN by 1677; in Eng, b 1651; Hadley

BEDIENT, Thomas (-1699) & Mary [OSBORN]; ca 1676; Fairfield, CT/Woodbury, CT

BEDORTHA, Joseph (1649-) & 1/wf Mary DUMBLETON (-1676); 30 Jan 1671, 1672; Springfield

BEDORTHA, Joseph (1649-1707+) & 2/wf Lydia (LEONARD) DUMBLETON (1650-1683), w John; 2 Oct 1678; Springfield

BEDORTHA, Joseph (1649-) & 3/wf Hannah [MARSHFIELD] (1661-1711); 24 Jul 1684; Springfield

BEDORTHA, Reice/Reese? (-1683, 1682?) & Blanch/Blanche [LEWIS]; 1646?, 1645?; Springfield

BEDORTHA, Samuel (1651-) & 1/wf Mercy DUMBLETON (-1689); 28 Apr 1681; Springfield

BEDORTHA, Samuel (1651-1728) & 2/wf Mary (REMINGTON) LEONARD (1666-1747), w Abel; 30 Jul 1691; Springfield

BEE, Thomas & (?Sarah [TALMAGE]), m/2 Thomas BARNES bef 3 Mar 1692; by 1687; Easthampton, LI

BEEBE, Benjamin (1663-1752) & Hannah [WHEELER?]; b 4 Aug 1695, b 1694?; New London, CT

BEEBE, James & 1/wf Mary BOLTWOOD (-1676); 24 Oct 1667; Hadley

BEEBE, James & 2/wf Sarah BENEDICT; 19 Dec 1679; Hadley/Stratford, CT/Norwalk, CT

BEEBE, John (-on ship 1650) & Rebecca [LADD] (d in Eng?); in Eng, ca 1627; Hartford

BEEBE, John (1628-1708?, 1714?) & Abigail [YORK] (1638/9-1725); ca 1660; New London

BEEBE, Jonathan (1673-1761) & 2/wf? Bridget [BROCKWAY] (1671/2-); b 1694?, ca 1694, ca 1692?; New London/East Haddam/Mollington, CT

BEEBE, Nathaniel & Elizabeth WHEELER, 2 Jul 1697; New London

BEEBE, Samuel (1633, 1631-1712) & 1/wf [Agnes KEENEY?] (-bef 1662); b 1657; New London, CT

BEEBE, Samuel (-1712, ae 91) & 2/wf Mary KEENEY (1640-); aft 1662; New London

BEEBE, Samuel & Elizabeth ROGERS (1658-1716); 9 Feb 1681, 1681/2; New London/Orient, LI

BEEBE, Samuel (1672-) & Hannah ? ; b 1699; Littlefield, CT

BEEBE, Thomas & Millicent (ADDIS) (SOUTHMAYD) ASH, w William, w William; b 1663; New London

BEEBE, William & 1/wf ? ; b 1686; New London, CT

BEEBE, ? & Rebecca BEARDSLEY

BEECHER, Eleazer/Ebenezer & Phebe PRINDLE; 5 Nov 1677; New Haven

BEECHER, Isaac (-1690, ae ca 67) & Mary [?POTTER]; b 1646, b 1645?; New Haven

BEECHER, Isaac (1650-1738?) & Joanna [ROBERTS] (1657-1732); b 1680; New Haven

BEECHER, [?John] & Hannah POTTER (1600-1658), wid; in Eng, b 1625; New Haven

BEECHER, John (?1646-1712) & Elizabeth [ROBERTS]; b 1671; New Haven

BEECHER, Joseph & Lydia [ROBERTS] (1672-); b 1695; New Haven

BEECHER, Samuel (1652-) & Sarah (HARD) SHERWOOD (1666-), w John; 2 Jul 1691; New Haven/Stratford, CT

BEECHER, Thomas (-1637) & Christian/Christiana? (?BARKER) [COPPER/COOPER?], w Thomas, m/3 Nicholas EASTON ca 1638; b 1632; Charlestown

BEEDE, James & Sarah [ELLET/ELLIOT; aft 14 Sep 1660, b 27 Nov 1662, 1660?; Salem

BEEDON/BEADON, Richard & Margaret ? ; b 1687; Boston

BEEFORD, Richard (1608-) & Mary ? ; ca 1643; Gloucester

BEERS, Anthony (see Richard) (-1679) & 1/wf Elizabeth [FIRMIN]; b 1647, b 1639?; Watertown/Roxbury/Fairfield

BEERS, Anthony (-1679) & 2/wf Mary (?) [ADAMS], w Edward; aft 1671, bef 5 Oct 1677; Fairfield, CT

BEERS, Barnabas (1658-1714) & 1/wf Elizabeth WILCOXSON (1666-1694); 4 Apr 1688; Stratford, CT

BEERS, Barnabas & 2/wf [Mary] [HODGKIN] (1672-); aft 11 Oct 1694, prob ca 1698; Fairfield, CT/?Stratford, CT

BEER, Champet & Jane ? ; b 1687; Boston

BEAR, Edward & Mary HALE; 19 May 1693; Boston

BEERES, Eliezer (-1691) & Susanna (HARRINGTON) CUTTING, w John, m/3 Peter CLOYSE 1705; 21 Apr 1690; Watertown

BEERES, Elnathan & Sarah [TAINTER] (1657-); b 1681(2?); Watertown
BEERS, Ephraim (1648-) & Mary GARDNER; 9 Sep 1680; Hadley/Hatfield
BEERS/BEERE?, Henry (-1691) & Patience SCOTT (1648-1717); 28 Sep 1663, 1668?; Providence, RI/?Newport
BEERS, Jabez & Elizabeth (RUSH) BARBER, dau Jasper RUSH, w William; 17 May 1694; Boston/Watertown
BEERS, James & Martha _?_ (-1647)
BEERS, James (-1694) & Martha [BARLOW]; ca 1650; Milford/Fairfield, CT
BEERES, James², Jr. (-1691, 1694?) & _?_ ; b 1677; Fairfield, CT
BEARE, John (1630-1671) & Patience CLIFTON, m/2 William ALLEN 1677; 4 Sep 1664; ?Newport
BEAR, John & Mary FOWLER; 20 Jan 1672, 1672/3; Gloucester
BEERS, John (1652-1683) & Mary _?_ ; b 1679; Stratford, CT
BEAR/BARE?, John & Hannah _?_ ; b 1687, b 1686?; Wenham
BEER, John & Mary EADES; 21 Sep 1694; Boston
BEERS, Joseph (-1696, 1697?) & Abigail [NORTON], m/2 John DUNBAR 1697, 1698; b 1689; Fairfield, CT
BEERS, Richard (see Anthony) (-1675) & Elizabeth [FIRMIN] (1614-1706); b 1639; Watertown/Stratford, CT
BEERE, Robert (-1676) & Elizabeth (BILLINGTON) BULLUCK (1635-), w Richard, m/3 Thomas PATEY/PATTE; 25 Jun 1673; Rehoboth
BEERS, Samuel & _?_ ; b 1655; Milford, CT
BEGAR, Francis & Elizabeth LYNN, m/2 Thomas BATHERICK 1701; 15 Feb 1697/8; Cambridge
BEHONEY, Peter & Sarah _?_ ; b 1688; Watertown
BEIGHTON, Samuel (-1692) & Anne _?_ ; b 1684; Boston
BELCHER, Andrew (?1615-1673) & 2/wf? Elizabeth DANFORTH (-1680, ae 62); 1 Oct 1639; ?Cambridge/Sudbury
BELCHER, Andrew (1648-?31 Oct 1717, 13? Oct) & 1/wf Sarah GILBERT (1651-1689); 1 Jul 1670; Hartford
BELCHER, Andrew (?1648-1717) & 2/wf Hannah (FRARY) WALKER, w Isaac; 13 Feb 1689/90; Boston
BELCHER, David (1662-) & _?_ ; b 1685; ?Ipswich
BELCHER, Edward (1595-) & 1/wf _?_ ; in Eng, b 1627; Boston
BELCHER, Edward (1595-) & 2/wf Christian (TALMAGE) [WORMWOOD?/WORMAN?/WORMLUM?], w Wm.; ca 1650; Boston
BELCHER, Edward & 1/wf Mary WORMWOOD (-1693); 8 Jan 1655/6; Boston
BELCHER, Edward & Mary [CLIFFORD?] (see Jeremiah) (1675-1752); b 1701; Boston/Lynn/etc.
BELCHER, Gregory¹ (1606-1674) & Catherine _?_ (-1680); in Eng, b 1631; Braintree
BELCHER, Gregory (1665-1727), Braintree & Elizabeth RUGGLES (1669-1748), Braintree; 25 Mar 1690, 1689/90, 1690; Braintree
BELCHER, Jeremy/Jeremiah? & 1/wf [?Mary CLIFFORD] (1612-); b 1639; Ipswich
BELCHER, Jeremy/Jeremiah (1613?-1692/3) & 2/wf Mary LOCKWOOD (-1670) Ipswich; m cert 30 Sep 1652; Ipswich
BELCHER, Jeremiah (1641-1723) & Sarah (WEEDEN) [SENTER], w John; b 1668, ca 1667; Boston
BELCHER, John (-1693) & Sarah _?_ (-1693+); b 1656, ca 1655; Braintree
BELCHER, John (1659-) & Theodora _?_, m/2 Simon LEE 1698, m/3 William DARNTON 1700, m/4 Francis POMEROY; b 1689; Boston/Kittery, ME
BELCHER, Rev. Joseph (1641-1678?) & Rebecca GILL (1650-); b [1665], b 1664?; Milton
BELCHER, Joseph (1661-) & _?_ ; [ca 1685/90?]; ?Braintree
BELCHER, Joseph (1669-1723), Dedham & Abigail THOMPSON/TOMPSON (1670-); 8 Mar 1693/4; Braintree
BELCHER, Joseph (1673-) & Hannah BILL, m/2 Richard HUNNEWELL; 7 Jan 1697, 1697/8; Boston
BELCHER, Josiah (-1683, ae 52) & Ranis RAINSFORD (1638-1691); 3 Mar 1654/5; Boston
BELCHER, Josiah (1669-1734+) & Margaret [HAYDEN] (1670-), dau Jonathan; b 1694; Braintree/Boston/Marblehead/etc.
BELCHER, Moses (-1691) & Mary NASH (-1707+); 23 May 1666; Braintree

BELCHER, Moses (1672-1728?), Milton & Hannah LYON (1673-1745), Milton; 19 Dec 1694; Milton/Preston, CT

BELCHER, Richard (1665-) & 1/wf Mary SIMPSON (1664-1703?); 20 Mar 1688/9; Ipswich

BELCHER, Samuel (1637-1679?) & Mary BILLINGS, m/2 Samuel NILES 1680; 15 Dec 1663; Braintree

BELCHER, Samuel (-1715) & 1/wf Mary [COBBOTT] (-ca 1679); ca 1668; ?Lynn/Kittery, ME

BELCHER, Samuel (-1715, in 70th y) & 2/wf Mary (WIGGLESWORTH) [BRACKENBURY] (1655/6-1728, 1723), w Samuel; aft 1679?; Charlestown

BELCHER, Samuel (1666-1714) & Comfort [HARBOUR] (1666-1745), m/2 Stephen CRANE 1723; ca 1688; Braintree

BELCONGER (afterward CONGER in NJ), John & 1/wf Mary KELLY; 12 Apr 1666; Newbury/Woodbridge, NJ

BELDING, Daniel (1648-1732) & 1/wf Elizabeth FOOTE (ca 1654-1696); 10 Nov 1670; Hatfield/Wethersfield, CT/Deerfield

BELDING, Daniel (1648-1732) & 2/wf Hepzibah (BUELL) WELLS (1649-1704), w Thomas; 17 Feb 1698/9; Deerfield

BELDING, Ebenezer (1667-1739) (son Samuel) & Martha __?__ ; Hadley

BELDEN, Ebenezer (?1672-) (son John) & Abigail GROVES?/GRAVES? (1669-); ca 1696; Wethersfield, CT

BELDEN, John (1631-1677) & Lydia [RILEY?]; 24 Apr 1657; Wethersfield, CT

BELDEN, John & 1/wf __?__ [HALE]; b 12 Dec 1676; Norwalk, CT

BELDEN, John (1658-1714) & Dorothy WILLARD (?1663-1754); 15 Jun 1682; Wethersfield, CT

BELDEN, John (1650-1713) & 2/wf? Ruth __?__, m/2 John COPP; b 1694; Norwalk, CT

BELDING, John (?1669-) & Sarah [WAITE] (1674±, 1675-), m/2 Ichabod ALLIS; b 1694; Hadley/Hatfield/Wethersfield

BELDING, Jonathan (1661-1734) & Mary WRIGHT (1664-1741); 10 Dec 1685; Wethersfield, CT

BELDIN, Joseph (1663-1724) & Mary/Mercy? [MEAKIN]/WILLARD? (-1740); 27 Oct 1693; Wethersfield, CT

BELDING, Richard (?1591-1655) & __?__ ; in Eng, b 1622; Wethersfield, CT

BELDING, Samuel[2] (1632, ?1629-1713) & 1/wf Mary __?__ (-1677); b 1655; Wethersfield, CT

BELDING, Samuel[2] (1632, ?1629-1713) & 2/wf Mary (BEARDSLEY) WELLS (-Sep 1691), w Thomas; 25 June 1678; Hadley

BELDING, Samuel[3] (1657-1737±) & 1/wf Sarah (FELLOWES) BILLINGS (-1713), w Samuel; 9 Oct 1678; Hadley/Wethersfield, CT/Hatfield

BELDEN, Samuel & Hannah [HANDY?] (not [EDERKIN]), dau Richard; 14 Jan 1685/6; Wethersfield, CT/New London

BELDING, Samuel[2] (1632, ?1629-1713), Hatfield & 3/wf Mary (MESKIN) (CLARK) [ALLIS], w Nathaniel, w John; 1691, 1692; Hadley/Hatfield/Deerfield/Wethersfield, CT

BELDING, Stephen (1658-1720) & Mary WELLS (-1751), m/2 Joseph FIELD 1723; 16 Aug 1682; Hatfield/Hadley/Wethersfield, CT

BELDING, William (?1622-1655) & [?Thomasine] [?SHERWOOD]; b 1647; Wethersfield, CT/Deerfield

BELDING, William & Margaret ARMS (1683-); 2 May 1700; Deerfield/Norwalk, CT

BELDING, __?__ & Margaret BLIN (1681-); b 1701?; ?Wethersfield, CT

BELKNAP, Abraham (1590-1643/4) & Mary __?__, m/2 Francis INGALLS; in Eng, b 1620; Lynn/Salem

BELKNAP, Abraham (1660-) & Elizabeth AYER; 14 Jan 1690/1, 14 Jun 1690/1, 14 Jan; Haverhill/?Reading

BELKNAP, Ebenezer & Hannah AYER (1672-1779, ae 106 y 11 mo); 25 Feb 1690/1; Haverhill/Reading/Framingham

BELKNAP, Joseph (-1712, ae 82) & 1/wf Ruth [WILLIAMS] (1639, 1638-); b 1659, b 1657/8; Boston/Hatfield

BELKNAP, Joseph & 2/wf Lydia [INGALLS]; b 1668; Boston

BELKNAP, Joseph & 3/wf Hannah [MEAKINS] (-1688); b 1670; Boston

BELKNAP, Joseph (1658-1716) & 1/wf Deborah FITCH (1665-1687, ae 22); b 1684; Boston

BELKNAP, Joseph (1658-1716) & Abigail BUTTOLPH (-1734); 1 Apr 1690; Boston

BELKNAP, Samuel & Sarah [JONES] (-1689); b 1653; Salem/Haverhill/Malden

BELKNAP, Thomas (1670-1755), Woburn & Jane CHEENEY/CHENEY; 6 Mar 1694, 1693/4; Boston/Cambridge/(at Boston)

BELL, _?_ & Anna [CLEVELAND] (1677-1734+); aft 1699; Newport

BELL, Abraham (-1663) & Katherine (BULFINCH) [WAFFE] (-1692, ae 69?, 68?), w John; b 1652; Charlestown

BELL, Francis (-1690) & Rebecca _?_ (-1684); b 1641; Stamford, CT/Wethersfield

BELL, James (-1676) & Esther [LUGG], m/2 Richard MARSHALL 1677; b 1658; Taunton

BELL, James? (see Robert) (1662) & Hannah PRAY; Taunton

BELL, John (-1676?, 1700?) & _?_ ; ca 1640/2; Yarmouth

BELL, Jonathan (1641-1699) & 1/wf Mary/?Mercy CRANE (-26 Oct 1671); 22 Oct 1662, 1662, 4 Nov 1662 Branford, CT; Stamford, CT

BELL, Jonathan (1641-1699) & 2/wf Susanna PIERSON (1652-1707); 31 Oct 1672; Stamford, CT

BELL, Jonathan (1663-) & 1/wf Grace KITCHELL (-1694); 22 Mar 1693, 1692/3?; Stamford, CT

BELL, Robert?, Hartford & [Ruth KING], Windsor, CT; b 1678; Windham, CT?/Hartford

BELL, Robert (see James) & Jonna/Hannah [PRAY] (1665, 1663?-); b 1686; Boston

BELL, Shadrach & Rachel _?_ ; b 1685; Portsmouth, NH

BELL, Thomas (-1655) & 1/wf Anne/Anna? _?_, m/2 William MULLINS 1656; b 1638; Boston/Stonington, CT

BELL, Thomas (-1672), London & _?_ ; b 1640; Roxbury

BELL, Thomas & Rebecca EBBORNE/(ABORNE), Salem; 10 Dec 1680; Salem

BELLAMY?, Jeremiah & _?_ ; b 1661?; Hingham

BELLAMY, Matthew & Bethya FORD (-1692); 1671; New Haven/Guilford, CT

BELLAMY, Lodwell & _?_ (see Nathaniel BOSWORTH)

BELLFLOUR/BELFLOURE, Benjamin (-1661) & Abigall MOULTON (1642-1665+); 3 Feb 1658, 1658/9; Reading

BELFLOURE/BELLFLOWER?, Henry & [Ann] _?_ ; b 1656, b 1657; Reading

BELLINGHAM, Richard (?1585-1672, ae 80?) & 1/wf Elizabeth [BACKHOUSE/BACKUS]; ca 1620?; Manton/Branby/Bath, Eng/Boston

BELLINGHAM, Richard (-1672, ae 80) & 2/wf Penelope [PELHAM] (1619-1702); 9 (9) 1641; ?Cambridge/Boston/Rowley

BELLINGHAM, William (-1650) (d unm? or widower?) & _?_ ; Ipswich

BELLINGHAM, Samuel & Lucy _?_ ; b 1650; Rowley

BELLOWS, Eleazer & Easter/Esther BARRETT; 11 Oct 1692; Marlborough

BELLOWS, Isaac (1663-) & Elizabeth [HOWE] (1673-); b 1695; Marlborough

BELOUSE, John (-1683) & Mary WOOD (-1707); 9 May 1655; Concord/Marlborough

BELLOWS, John (1666-) & Hannah [NEWTON] (1673-1719); b 1695; Marlborough

BELLOW, Robert (-1668) & Susannah _?_ ; Portsmouth, RI/Boston

BELVILLE/BELVELE, Christian, ?Charlestown & Francis HOPKINS; 9 Jun 1656; Boston

BEMIS, Ephraim (1656-1738+) & Elizabeth _?_ ; ca 1681/3; Watertown/Wendham, CT

BEMIS, James (-1665) & Sarah _?_, m/2 Edward GRISWOLD ca 1672; ca 1650/3; New London, CT

BEMISH/BEMIS, John (1659-1732) & 1/wf Mary [HARRINGTON] (1663/4-1716), Waltham; b 1681; Watertown/Waltham

BEMIS, Joseph (?1619-1684) & Sarah _?_ (?1622-); b 1643; Watertown

BEMIS, Joseph (1651-1684) & Anna _?_ ; b 1700?; Westminster

BENDALL, Edward (1608-) & Anne _?_ (-1637); b 1635; Boston

BENDALL, Edward (1608-1682) & Marah _?_ ; b 1639; Boston

BENDALL, Freegrace (1635-1676) & Mary [LYALL] (-1676); b 1664; Boston

BENEDICT, Daniel & Mary [MARVIN] (1658?-); ca 1680; Norwalk, CT/Danbury, CT

BENEDICT, James (1650-1717+) & 1/wf Sarah GREGORY (1652-1696+); 10 May 1676; Norwalk, CT/Danbury, CT

BENEDICT, John & Phebe GREGORY (ca 1650-); 11 Nov 1670; Norwalk, CT

BEDICT, John (1676-1766) & 1/wf [Anna St.JOHN] (1674-) (?Mary HARTE, 2/wf); aft 1693, bef 1701; Norwalk, CT

BENEDICT, Samuel (-1719) & 1/wf [Miss BEEBE]; b 1673; Norwalk, CT

BENEDICT, Samuel (-1719) & 2/wf Rebecca ANDREWS; 4 Jul 1678, 8 Jul 1678, 7? Jul 1678; Norwalk/Danbury

BENEDICT, Thomas[1] (1617-1690) & Mary [BRIDGUM]?; ca 1641; Southold, LI/Norwalk, CT

BENEDICT, Thomas (ca 1642-1688) & Mary MESENGER; - Jan 1665, 1664/5; Jamaica, LI/Norwalk, CT
BENEDICT, Thomas (1670-) & Rachel SMITH (?1677-1737); 13 May 1697, 169-; Norwalk, CT
BENFIELD, William & 1/wf Elizabeth [COULSON]; div 6 Dec 1662; Wethersfield, CT
BENFIELD, William & 2/wf Mary _?_ ; b 1665; Fairfield, CT
BENHAM, John[1] (-1661) & 1/wf _?_ ; b 1634; Dorchester/New Haven
BENHAM, John[2] & 1/wf Sarah (HURST) WILSON (-1667), w Richard; 8 Feb 1654, 1654/5; New Haven
BENHAM, John[1] (-1661) & 2/wf Margery ALCOCK/ALCOTT, w Thomas, m/3 Richard PRITCHARD 1667; 16 Nov 1660, 1659?; Boston
BENHAM, John[2] (-1691) & 2/wf Mercy SMITH (1645-); 3 Mar 1668/9; New Haven
BENHAM, John (1664-1744) & [Comfort MANSFIELD] (1668-); ca 1691; New Haven
BENHAM, Joseph & Winifred KING; 15 Jan 1656/7; Boston/New Haven/Wallingford, CT
BENHAM, Joseph & Hannah (MERRIMAN) IVES, w John; 17 Aug 1682; Wallingford, CT
BENHAM, Nathan (1679-1757) & Sarah [BEECHER] (-1712); b 1700; New Haven
BENJAMIN, Abel (-1710) & Amathia/Amantha/Amithy MERRICKE/MYRICK? (-1713); 6 Nov 1671; Charlestown/Watertown
BENJAMIN, Abel (1668-1720) & Abigail [STIMPSON] (1671-); b 1695; Watertown
BENJAMIN, Caleb (-1684) & Mary [HALE] (1649-1700?), m/2 Walter HARRIS; b 1671; Wethersfield, CT/Glastonbury, CT/Watertown
BENJAMIN, Daniel (1660-1719) & Elizabeth BROWN (1664-1740); 25 Mar 1687; Watertown
BENJAMIN, John (-1645) & Abigail [EDDY] (1601-1687); in Eng, b 1620; Cambridge/Watertown
BENJAMIN, John (1620-1706) & Lydia [ALLEN?] (-1709); b 1651; Watertown
BENJAMIN, John (1651-1687?) & 1/wf Mehitable _?_ ; b 1679; Boston/Watertown
BENJAMIN, John[1] (1651-1687) (see John SHAW & Hannah BRACKETT) & 2/wf Sarah (BRACKETT) SHAW, w John, Jr./?Joseph, m/3 _?_ JENMERSON; b 1686; Boston
BENJAMIN, John (1677-1753) & 1/wf Ann LATIMER (1681-); 26 Jul 1699; Wethersfield, CT
BENJAMIN, Joseph (?1633-1704-) & 1/wf Jemima LUMBARD/LOMBARD (living in 1663); 10 Jun 1661; Boston/Barnstable
BENJAMIN, Joseph (-1704) & Sarah [CLARK?] (-1704+); b 1666?; ?Yarmouth
BENJAMIN, Joseph (?1673-1738?) & Elizabeth COOKE (1678-); 25 Aug 1698; Preston, CT/Stonington, CT
BENJAMIN, Joshua (1642-1684, ae 42) & Thankful STOW (1660-1691), m/2 Ebenezer AUSTIN 1685; 24 Aug 1682; Charlestown
BENJAMIN, Richard & Anna?/Ann _?_, b 1643; Watertown/Southold, LI
BENJAMIN, Richard (1646-1730) & Elizabeth _?_ ; b 1681; Southold, LI
BENJAMIN, Samuel (1628-1669) & Mary _?_ (-1669+); b 1666, b 1660; Watertown/Hartford, CT
BENJAMIN, Simeon & Waite _?_ (-1703); b 1679; Southold, LI
BENJAMIN, _?_ & Sarah [RALPH] (1661-); b 1682
BENMORE, Charles & Elizabeth _?_ ; b 1671?, b 1677; Boston
BENMORE, John & 1/wf Elizabeth _?_ ; b 1692(3?); Boston
BENMORE, John & 2/wf Mary RICHARDS; 16 Nov 1693; Boston
BENMORE, Philip (-1676) & Rebecca (TIBBETTS) KNOX/NOCK? (-1680), w Thomas; 28 Sep 1669; Dover, NH
BENNETT, Aaron (-1708) & 1/wf Hannah _?_ (-1685+); b 1665; Manchester
BENNETT, Aaron (1677-) & 1/wf Ann PICKWORTH; 20 Nov 1700; Manchester
BENNETT, Abraham & Hannah [CHESLEY]; ca 1697?; Dover, NH
BENNETT, Ambrose & Mary SIMONS; 15 Apr 1653; Boston
BENNETT, Anthony & 1/wf Elizabeth [GOODWIN]; b 2 May 1665; ?Gloucester
BENNETT, Anthony (-1690, 1714) & 2/wf Abigail _?_ (-1734, ae 68); ?b 1679; Gloucester/Beverly/Rowley
BENNETT, Anthony (-1697) & Elizabeth (PALMER) WALLINGFORD, w Nicholas, m/3 Henry RILEY 1700; 15 Feb 1686, 1686/7?; Rowley
BENNETT/BENNICKE, Arthur & Mary [GODDARD], m/2 Joseph/John FIELD, m/3 Hans MEDFORD; ca 1664?; Dover, NH
BENNETT, Benjamin & Abial/Abihall _?_ ; b 1700; Ipswich
BENNETT, David (-1719, ae 93) & 1/wf _?_ ; by 1662?, b 1666; ?Rowley

BENNETT, David (-1719, ae 93) & 2/wf Mary (PLUMER) CHENEY (-1682), w John; 29 Apr
1672; Rowley

BENNETT, David (-1719, ae 93) & 3/wf Rebecca (SPENCER) BULLER (-1712), w John
BULLEY; 14 Feb 1682, 1682/3; Ipswich/Rowley

BENNETT, Edward & Susanna [OAKMAN], m/2 Peter KING 1723; ca 1682?; Marblehead

BENNETT, Edward & Esther __?__; b 1686; Boston

BENNETT, Elisha & Dorothy __?__; b 1690; Boston

BENNETT, Francis (1623-1655) & Alice __?__, m/2 Ralph HUTCHINSON 1656; b 1650; Boston

BENNETT, George (-1652) & 1/wf Faith [NEWELL] (ca 1620-bef 1650); b 1648; Boston

BENNETT, George (-1652) & 2/wf ?Adera/?Adey/?Andrey [?RUSCOE], m/2 Francis BROWN by
1656; b 1652; Boston

BENNETT, George (-1675) & Lydia KIBBY (ca 1637-), gr dau Richard LINDON, m/2 George
HEWES 1679; 18 Jun 1655; Lancaster

BENNETT, Henry (1629-1707) & 1/wf Lydia [PERKINS] (1632-1672) (ae 36 in 1669); ca 1651;
Ipswich

BENNETT, Henry (-1726) & Sarah CHAMPION (ca 1646-1727); 25 Dec 1673, 9? Dec; Lyme, CT

BENNETT, Henry (1629-1707) & 2/wf Elizabeth (GOODELL) SMITH/Mary (SMITH) (KELP)
[BURR] (-1708), w Philip, w John; aft 1673, b 18 Feb 1678/9; Ipswich

BENNETT, Henry (1664-1739) & 1/wf Frances BURR; 30 May 1685; Ipswich

BENNETT, Henry & Sarah __?__; b 1687; Boston

BENNETT, Henry (1664-1739) & 2/wf Margaret __?__; b 1694; Ipswich

BENNETT, Isaac (1650-1720) & Elizabeth ROSE (1659-); 2 Jun 1683; Stratford, CT

BENNETT, Jacob (1651-1685/6) & Sarah __?__ (-1705+); b 1676; Ipswich

BENNETT, James (-1659) & Hannah [WHEELER], m/2 Joseph MIDDLEBROOK; b 1640;
Concord/Fairfield, CT

BENNETT, James (1645-1736) & 1/wf [Mary] [JOY]; b 1668; Fairfield, CT

BENNETT, James (-1676) & Mary BROUGHTON, m/2 Benoni STEBBINS 1676?; 18 Feb 1674;
Northampton

BENNETT, James & Elizabeth TARBELL (1657-1684); 4 Feb 1680/1; Charlestown

BENNETT, James (?1645-1736) & 2/wf Mary (OSBORN) [BOOTH], w Ephraim; ca 1684;
Fairfield, CT

BENNETT, James (-1707) & Sarah [LEWIS], m/2 John TAYLOR; b 1691; Stratford, CT

BENNETT, James & Mary (COUCH) [GRIMMAN], w Thomas, m/3 Samuel JENNINGS; ca 1692,
div in 1703; Stratford, CT

BENNETT, James (1666-1730) & 1/wf Ruth ROGERS (1675-1725); 12 Jul 1694, 13? Jul; Bristol,
RI/Roxbury/Taunton/Little Compton, RI

BENNETT, James (1675-1725) & Deborah [ADAMS] (1678±-1748+); b 1701; Fairfield,
CT/Ridgefield, CT

BENNETT, John (-1663) & Margaret __?__; b 1638; Salem

BENNETT, John (-1691) & __?__; b 1658; Stonington, CT

BENNETT, John (1632-1674) & Mary [COBHAM] (-1729), m/2 Richard MEAD 1678; ca 1658-9;
Charlestown

BENNETT, John & Susanna [HEATH] (1652-); b 1671; Roxbury/Boston

BENNETT, John (-1718, ae 76), Middleboro & Deborah [GROVER/GRAVER] (-1718, ae 70); ca
1671; Beverly

BENNETT, John & 2/wf Apphia/Aphra [ADAMS]; b 1677; Boston

BENNETT, John (1648-) & Mary [THOMPSON] (1649-); ca 1678?; Stratford, CT

BENNETT, John (1652-1718+) & [Ursula WHITE]; ca 1679?, by 1673; Newport

BENNETT, John & Ruth BRADSHAW; 3 Jan 1683/4; Charlestown

BENNETT, John & Joanna __?__; b 1687; Boston

BENNETT, John & __?__; b 1687; Durham, NH

BENNETT, John (?1666-) & Elizabeth PARKE; 8 Mar 1687; Stonington, CT

BENNETT, John, Hingham & Frances HOBART, Hingham, w Moses; m bond 26 Jun 1688

BENNETT, John (-1761) & Patience [COBB] (1668-1759); b 1689; Middleboro

BENNETT, John & Agnes __?__; b 1690; Gloucester

BENNETT, John & 2/wf __?__; 22 Oct 1691 (seems doubtful); Stoningham, CT

BENNETT, John (see William BENNETT) & Mary [?PARMENTER] (1670-); b 1693; Boston

BENNETT, John (?1670-1713) & Phebe __?__, m/2 Gideon ALDEN; b 1695; Fairfield, CT

BENNETT, John & Sarah HARRIS (1677-1705); 25 Oct 1699; Boston
BENNETT, Jonathan (1659-1708) & Ann/Anna [WILLIAMS] (1674-1758); b 1694; Newport
BENNETT, Joseph (1644-1708) & Margaret _?_ ; b 1674; Newport
BENNETT, Josiah & Rebecca [CUTLER] (1666-), m/2 William CHARTERIS 1704; b 1694; Charlestown
BENNETT, Nicholas (-1696) & Mary [FLETCHER] (1674-); b 1694; Portsmouth, NH
BENNETT, Peter & Mary [PORTER]; b 1676; Boston
BENNETT/CORNET?, Peter (?1674, 1678-1749) & Priscilla HOWLAND (1681-1746); 30 Oct 1700; Bridgewater/Middleboro
BENNETT, Richard (-1677) & 1/wf Sibil [HOOKER] (-1653) (sister of Ralph); b 1649; Boston
BENNETT, Richard (-1677) & 2/wf Margaret (?DAVIS) GURGSFIELD (sister of Robert DAVIS); 11 Jul 1654/5; Boston
BENNETT, Robert & Rebecca _?_ ; b 1644; Newport
BENNETT, Robert (1650-1722) & Anne [CORY]; ca 1672, ca 1684?; by 1683; Newport/Portsmouth, RI
BENNETT, Robert (1650-1722) & 2/wf Joanna
BENNETT, Samuel (1605/11-) & Sarah/?Mary _?_ ; ca 1633/40, b 1634?; Lyme/Boston
BENNETT, Samuel (-1684) & Anna [?EVERDIN], m/2 Moses FORMAN ca 1684/88; ca 1656?, ca 1664?; Providence/E. Greenwich, RI
BENNETT, Samuel & Sarah [HARGREVE]; b 1665; Chelsea
BENNETT, Samuel (-1745) & 1/wf Sarah FORMAN; 2 Jan 1688/9; E. Greenwich, RI/Coventry
BENNETT, Samuel (1665-1742) & Mary _?_ ; b 1690; Groton/Lancaster/Shrewsbury
BENNETT, Samuel (-1745) & 2/wf Desire BERRY (-1714); Apr 1699, 25 Apr; E. Greenwich
BENNETT, Thomas (1642-1704) & Elizabeth [THOMPSON] (?1644-); b 1665; Fairfield, CT
BENNETT, Thomas (-1700) & Elizabeth GILLINGHAM/GINININGHAM, m/2 Benjamin LAWRENCE 1719; 9 Dec 1686; Charlestown
BENNETT, Thomas & Sarah [HUBBARD]; b 1688; Fairfield, CT
BENNETT, Thomas (-1722?) & Sarah [CODNER]; b 1692?; New London, CT
BENNETT, Thomas (?1669-1739) & Mary BOOTH; 12 Apr 1692; Stratford, CT/Newtown, CT
BENNETT, Thomas & Dorothy _?_ ; b 1695; Boston
BENNETT, William (?1604-1682) & Jane _?_ (1619-); ca 1637; Salem
BENNETT, William & Elizabeth (GOODALE) SMITH, w John; 6 Mar 1674/3, - Mar 1674; Salem
BENNETT, William (1660?-) & Susannah BRIGHT; 30 Oct 1676; Stonington, CT
BENNETT, William (-1753, ae 80) & Rachel (ANDREW) [WEAVER], w Clement; ca 1693; E. Greenwich, RI
BENNETT, William & Mary [?PARMENTER], Sudbury (did she marry William or John?), dau John; b 1694; Boston
BENNETT, _?_ & Eleanor _?_ , m/2 Richard WINDOW; Gloucester
BENNING, Harry (?1661-1688?) & _?_ [BISSETT]; ?Boston
BINNING, Ralph & Ann _?_ , m/2 Henry DEERING 1664; b 1661; Boston
BENSON, Henry & Mary (WATERS)/JONES, dau John, w Cornelius, m/2 _?_ JONES?; Kittery, ME
BENSON, Isaac, Rochester & Mary BRAMPOS/BRAMPAS, Rochester; 17 Mar 1698/9; Sandwich/Rochester
BENSON, John (1608-1678) & Mary _?_ (-1681); b 1634; Hingham/Hull
BENSON, John (?1635-) & _?_ ; ?ca 1660; Hull/Rochester
BENSON, John (ca 1665-1725) & Elizabeth [BRIGGS?] (-1725); b 1688; Rochester
BENSON, Joseph & Sarah _?_ ; b 1684(5?), b 1683?; Hull
BENSON, Joseph (-1737) & Charity CLAPP (1677-1698); 20 Aug 1695, 20 Aug 1696, 1696; Rochester/Sandwich
BENSON, Joseph (-1737) & Deborah SMITH (-1710/11); 17 Apr 1699, 17 Apr 1689; Taunton/Rochester
BENT, Hopestill & Elizabeth BROWN; 27 Nov 1768; Sudbury
BENT, John (1596-1672) & Martha _?_ /[BAKER?] (-1679); in Eng, b 1625; Sudbury
BENT, John (1637-1717) & 1/wf Hannah STONE (1640-ca 1684/7); 7 Jul 1658; Sudbury
BENT, John (1637-1717) & 2/wf Martha [RICE] (1657-1717+); b 1689; Sudbury/Framingham
BENT, Joseph (Josiah is wrong) (-1675) & Elizabeth BOURNE (1646-); last of Jun 1666; Marshfield

BENT, Joseph (1675-1728) & Rachel FULLER (-1725, ae 51); 27 Oct 1698; Milton/Dedham
BENT, Peter (1629-1678) & Elizabeth _?_ (-1679+, 1704+); b 1653; Sudbury/Marlboro
BENT, Robert (1566-1631 in Eng) & Annis/[Agnes] GOSLING (-1634); 13 Oct 1589, Weyhill, Hants; Sudbury
BENTLEY, Richard & Margaret _?_ ; b 1687; Charlestown
BENTLEY, William & Mary HOUGHTON (1653-); 20 Jan 1675; Dorchester
BENTLEY, William (-1720) & Sarah [?LEITHFIELD] (-1720+); ca 1676/80?; Kings Town, RI
BENTON, Andrew¹ (1620-1683) & 1/wf Hannah [STOCKING]; ca 1644; Hartford/Milford, CT
BENTON, Andrew & Elizabeth RELPH?/RALPH? (-1713); 16 Feb 1664; Guilford, CT
BENTON, Andrew¹ (1620-1683) & 2/wf Anne [COLE] (-1686); b 1674; Hartford
BENTON, Andrew (1653-1704) & Martha [SPENCER] (1s657, 1658-); b 1677; Hartford
BENTON, Daniel (-1672) & Rachel GOODRICH; 23 Dec 1658; Guilford, CT
BENTON, Ebenezer & Abigail GRAVE/GRAVES (-1753); 14 Jun 1694; Guilford, CT
BENTON, Edward (1600-1680) & 1/wf Alice PURDEN; in Eng 15 Jan 1626, Epping, Eng; Guilford, CT
BENTON, Edward (1600-1680) & 2/wf Anna/Anne _?_ (-1671); b 1640; Guilford, CT
BENTON, Edward (/1636, ?1638-1698) & Mary [HALE]? (1643-1702, ae 60); ca 1662/66?; Wethersfield, CT
BENTON, James & Hannah (BUCKNELL), wid; ca 1680; Guilford, CT
BENTON, Joseph (ca 1660-1753) & 1/wf [?Martha PECK]/?Mary WOODRUFF (-1680), dau Paul; ca 1680; Hartford/?Tollmoth, CT
BENTON, Joseph (ca 1660-1753) & 2/wf Sarah WATERS; 10 Feb 1697; Hartford
BENTON, Nicholas & Mary AHDEL; 10 Oct 1700 (doubtful); Roxbury
BENTON, Samuel (1658-) & Sarah [CHATTERTON]/[POMEROY?] (1661-); b 1680(1?), ca 1679; New Haven/Milford/Hartford
BERNARD/BERNARDS, William & [Maria BULLOCK], wid?; 1 June 1642; Newtown, LI
BERNON, Gabriel (1644-1736) & 1/wf Esther LeROY (1652-1710), Newport; in France, m cont 23 Aug 1673; ?Oxford, MA/Providence/etc.
BERRIEN, Cornelius Jensen (-1689) & Jannster [STYKER], m/2 Samuel EDSALL ca 1689; Flatbush, LI/Newtown, LI
BERRIEN, John (-1711) & Ruth [EDSALL], m/2 Samuel FISK; 5 Apr 1687; Newtown, LI
BERRY, Ambrose (-1661) & Ann [BULLY], m/2 William SCUTHOCK 1661, m/3 John CARTER 1665; Jul 1653; Saco, ME/Boston
BERRY, Ambrose (-1697) & Hannah _?_ ; b 1686; Boston
BERRY, Anthony & Elizabeth [TRUSONS]?, dau Henry; b 1665?; Yarmouth/Gloucester
BERRY, Benjamin, Kittery & Elizabeth WITHERS, Kittery, ME, m/2 Dodavah CURTIS by 1700; 27 Nov 1689, 1688, 27 Nov 1688; Kittery, ME
BERRY, Daniel & Mary MAYER, Boston; 8 Jul 1697; Boston/Chelsea
BERRY, Daniel & Sarah [?NEWMARCH] (1659-); b 1700; Boston
BERRY, Edward¹ & 1/wf _?_ ; in Eng, b; Salem
BERRY, Edward¹/Edmund? (-1693?) & 2/wf Elizabeth (HARDY) [HASKELL] (-1676), w Roger; ca 1668; Beverly
BERRY, Edward² & Beatrice (BURT) CANTERBURY [PLUMER] (-1684), w William, w Francis; aft 1673, bef Jun 1676; Salem
BERRY, Elisha & 1/wf Elizabeth _?_ ; b 1690; E. Greenwich, RI
BERRY, Elisha (see BARRY) & 2/wf Sarah _?_ ; b 1697; E. Greenwich, RI
BERRY, James & Eleanor JANNESS; 4 Jul 1700; Hamdton, NH
BERRY, James & Eleanor [WALLIS]; b 1674; Newcastle
BERRY, James (-1716+) & Rachel (ATKINS) [DRAKE] (-1716+), w John; b 1689, by 1687; Boston
BERRY, John & Susannah _?_ ; b 1658, b 1659; Hampton, NH
BERRY, John (1642?-) & 1/wf Hannah HODGKINS (-1676); 17 Jan 1670, 1670/1; Ipswich
BERRY, John & 2/wf Mary CHAPMAN; 24 Jan 1676, [1676/7]; Ipswich
BERRY, John (1652-1745), Yarmouth & [Susanna CROWELL]/_?_ ; b 1678; Scituate
BERRY, John & Mary [SOUTHER] (1668-); b 1693, b 1685; Hampton, NH
BERRY, John/James? & Rachel _?_ ; b 1696, ca 1694, b 1688?; Weyham
BERRY, Joseph & Rachel [?GATCH]; b 1683?, b 1671; Kittery, ME
BERRY, Joseph & [?Elizabeth] _?_

BERRY, Nathaniel (-1718) & Elizabeth **PHILBRICK**; 2 Jul 1691; Dover, NH/Mansfield, CT
BERRY, Oliver & Gantrig/Gartbright/Gertrude _?_; b 1678; Boston
BERRY, Richard & Alice _?_; b 1652; Barnstable/Yarmouth
BERRY, Samuel (-1704) & Elizabeth [**BELL**]; b 1682(3?); Yarmouth
BERRY, Trague & _?_
BERRY/BARRY?, Thaddeus (-1718) & Hannah [**FARRAR**] (-1720+); b 1665, ca 1664; Boston/?Lynn
BERRY, Thomas (-1693) & _?_; b 1655?; Ipswich
BERRY, Thomas & Grace [**HAYMAN**] (-1695, ae 58); b 1665, b 1663; Boston/Charlestown
BERRY, Thomas (1663-1696) & Margaret **ROGERS** (1664-1720), m/2 John **LEVERETT** 1697; 28 Dec 1686, 1682?; Ipswich
BERRY, Thomas (1670-1736) & Elizabeth [**DIVAN**]; b 1695; Lynn/Meriden, CT
BERRY, William[1] (-1654) & Jane _?_ (1619-), m/2 Nathaniel **DRAKE** by 1657; b 1636, b 1637; Portsmouth, NH/Newbury
BERRY, William, New Castle & Judith **LOCKE**, m/2 Nathaniel **HUGGINS** 1708; 8 Jul 1678; Newcastle, NH
BERRY, William & Sabina **LOCKE**, m/2 Abraham **LEWIS**; 19 Dec 1689; Dover, NH
BERRY/BURY, _?_ & Mercy [**GARFIELD**] (1674-), dau Samuel; b 1701?; Watertown
BERRY, ?Daniel & Sarah [**NEWMARCH**] (1659-); b 1699-1700
BERTEAU/?BARSTOW, Francis & _?_; b 1660?
BERTRAM/BARTRAM, John (-1675) & Sarah _?_, m/2 Jacob **GRAY** b 1677; b Oct 1658; Stratford, CT
BARTRAM, John (-1740) & Sarah _?_; b 1691; Fairfield, CT
BARTRAM, Thomas & Elizabeth _?_ (-1673); b 1673; Charlestown
BARTRAM, William (-1690) & Sarah [**BURT**?]; ca 1653?, b 1658; Lynn/Swansea
BESHEAU, John & Margaret _?_; b 1687; Boston
BESSE, Anthony[1] (1609±-1657) & Jane _?_ (-1693), m/2 George **BARLOW** bef 4 Mar 1661/2; ca 1640?, ca 1638; Lynn/Sandwich
BESSE, Nehemiah[2] (1643-1699+) & Mary [**RANSOM**]; b 1684, b 1680; Sandwich
BEST, John (-1711) & 1/wf Susana **DURIN**; 10 Oct 1670; Salem
BEST, John (-1711) & 2/wf Edeth **HULL** (-1748); 1 Feb 1692/3; Salem
BEST, John, Jr. & _?_; b 1701; Salem
BETHUNE, Robert & Abigail [**VERMAIS**], m/2 Edward **HUTCHINSON**, Jr. 1650?; b 1642; Boston
BETSCOME, Richard & _?_ [**STRONG**?] (-1646); b 1639; Hingham
BETTS, Daniel (1657-1758) & Deborah **TAYLOR** (1671-1750, 1751?); - Dec 1692; Norwalk, CT
BETTS, James & Elizabeth _?_; b 30 Sep 1690
BETTS, James (1663-1753) & Hannah [**BORSTON**] (?1675-); b 1701?, bef 25 Dec 1706
BETTS, [John?] (d in Eng?) & Mary _?_ (-bef 19 Jul 1647, Hartford); b 1623, [1621], ?Clandon, Eng, b 1627; Hartford
BETTS, John (594-1663) & Elizabeth [**BRIDGE**] (John **BRIDGE** mentions sister **BETTS** in his will); ca 1624?, no issue; Cambridge
BETTS, John (?1627-1690) & 1/wf Abigail [**ELDERKIN**] (1641-); ca 1660/65, 24 Oct, div 1672; Wethersfield, CT
BETTS, John (1642-1684) & 1/wf Mary **HAWS** (-1678 or 1679); 17 Mar 1669/70; Charlestown
BETTS, John (1627-1690) & 2/wf Abigail (**SMITH**) **ADAMS**, w John; 13 Mar 1672/3; Huntington, LI/CT
BETTS, John (-1684) & 2/wf Elizabeth (**THOMAS**) **LISLEY**, w Robert, m/2 John **FOSDICK** 1634?; 17 Jun 1679; Charlestown
BETTS, John (1650-) & 1/wf [Hannah **BELL**] (1665-); ?b 24 May 1689, b 1681; Guilford, CT/b 1692, Norwalk, CT
BETTS, ?Jonathan & Marcie **WARD**; 4 Nov 1662
BETTS, Richard[1] (1613-1713) & Joanna [**CHAMBERLYNE**]; b 1652; Cambridge/Ipswich/Newtown, LI
BETTS, Richard[2] (-1711) & Sarah [**?HUNT**]; b 1680?; Newtown, LI
BETTS, Roger (-1658) & Ann [**BURR**?], m/2 John **CABLE**; ca 1645, Branford; Milford, CT
BETTS, Samuel (1660-1734) & Judith **RENNOLDS/REYNOLDS**; 10 Dec 1692, 16 Dec; Norwalk, CT
BETTS, Samuel & Ruth _?_; Sep 1693?, Fordham, NY

BETTS, Thomas (1615-1688) & 2/wf? Mary __?__ (-1724+), wid?; b 1644, b 1646; Guilford, CT/Norwalk, CT/Milford, CT

BETTS, Thomas (?1648, ?1640-1717) & Sarah MARVIN (1662-); 13 Jan 1680; Norwalk, CT

BETTS, Thomas² (-1709) & Mary?/Mercy [WHITEHEAD] (1663-), m/2 Joseph SACKETT; ca 1683; Newtown, LI

BETTS, Thomas & Mary DIKE; 3 Apr 1696; Ipswich/Topsfield/Wenham

BETTS, William (-1675) & Alice __?__; 23 Nov 1638; Branstable

BETTS, __?__ & Susanna __?__; 27/28 Feb 1638, [1639], b 1695; Fordham, NY

BETTY, James & Sara __?__; b 1661; Salem/Wenham

BEUFORD, Charles & Hannah BICKNER; 10 Feb 1692/3, 1692; Boston

BEWFORD, John & Abigail COLE, m/2 John BABBETT; 31 May 1696; Charlestown

BEVIL, John & Jone __?__ (a wid in 1657); ?Isles of Shoals

BEVINS, Arthur (-1697) & Mary __?__; b 1676; Martha's Vineyard

BEVANS, Benjamin & __?__; b 1689; Framingham, CT

BEVIN, John & Susanna __?__; b 1699; Middletown, CT

BEVANS, Thomas & __?__; b 1671?; Middletown, CT

BERVERS/?BUERS, John & Susanna __?__; b 1674; Boston

BIBBELL, John (-1633) & Sybil/Sibell TINCKNELL (1688-), m/2 Jules NUTT 1657?, 1659, m/3 John DOOLITTLE 1674 (had Grandmother Sarah BROWNE 1683); 7 May 1629, b 1636; Malden/Hull

BICK, James & Elizabeth (HALBROOK) SPRAGUE, w John; b 1689, betw 1684/5 & 9 Sep 1696; Mendon/Scituate

BICKFORD, Benjamin (-1725) & Sarah? __?__; b 1691; Durham, NH

BICKFORD, Benjamin (1672-) & Sarah [BASSUM?/BARSHAM], m/2 Jotham ODIORNE ca 1700; Durham, NH

BICKFORD, Edward & Mary? __?__; by 1670?, b 1655?; Portsmouth, NH

BICKFORD, George (-1678) & Christian __?__ (1649-); 1666; Marblehead

BICKFORD, John (1609/15-1685?) & Temperance [HULL] (1626-), m/2 William HEDGE; b 1641?, b 1640?; Dover, NH

BICKFORD, John & Elizabeth [CATE]; b 1653?

BICKFORD, John (-1715) & Susanna [FURBER], dau Wm.; b 1685, ca 1684,?5 May 1664; Dover, NH

BICKFORD, John (-1690±) (gr son of Richard CATOR) & Jane __?__, m/2 John DOCKUM; Durham, NH

BICKFORD, John (son Thomas?) & 1/wf Elizabeth TIBBETS, dau Jeremy; 1 Dec 1692; Dover, NH

BICKFORD, John & Rebecca PINSON/PYNSON?/PRUSENT?; 8 Feb 1697/8; Marblehead/Salem/Reading

BICKFORD, Samuel (?1642-bef 1701) & Mary [COTTLE] (1653-1706+), m/2 Stephen SNOW 1701; b 1668; Salisbury/Amesbury/Nantucket

BIGFORD, Samuel (-1706) & Sarah __?__; b 1701(2?), ca 1700?; Yarmouth

BICKFORD, Thomas (1640-) & Joanna [LIBBY] (?1640-); ca 1660/2?; Scarborough, ME/Black

BICKFORD, Thomas (1660-) & Bridget [FURBER]; ca 1687?, near 1690; Dover, NH

BICKLEY, William (-1707) & Bethia [BEACH], m/2 John GLOVER; Stratford, CT

BICKNELL/BRICKNELL, Edward & Mary [KEMBLE], m/2 William HOUGH 1693; b 1682; Boston

BICKNELL, John (1624-1678, 1679) & 1/wf Mary [SHAW?] (?1626-1658), wid?; b 1648?; Weymouth

BICKNELL, John (1624-1678, 1679) & 2/wf Mary PORTER; 2 Dec 1658; Weymouth

BICKNELL, John (-1679) (BIGELOW is wrong) & Sarah WHEAT, m/2 Isaac HILL 1680; 27 May 1675; Charlestown

BICKNELL, John (1653/4-1737) & Sarah __?__; b 1682; Weymouth

BIGNELL, Richard & Abigail LAWRANCE; 2 Nov 1699; Boston

BICKNEL/BICKNER, Samuel (-1729), Boston & Hannah BELL; 2 Dec 1669; Charlestown

BICKNELL, Thomas (1670-) & Anna TURNER (1679-); 16 Dec 1696, 16 Feb 1696, 1696/7; Hingham/Weymouth/Middletown

BICKNER, William & 1/wf __?__; b 1646; Charlestown

BICKNOF/BAGNELL/BRIGNELL, William & 2/wf Martha (METCALF) SMYTH (1628-), w Christopher?, m/2 Nathaniel STOW 1662; b 1654; Charlestown

BICKNELL, Zachariah (1668-1748), Ashford, CT & Hannah SMITH (1670-1737+); 24 Nov 1692; Boston/Weymouth/Rehoboth
BICKNELL, Zachary (1590-1636) & Agnes [LOVELL?] (-1645), m/2 Richard ROCHETT/ROCK-WOOD 1637?; in Eng, ca 1623; Weymouth
BIDDLE/BIDWELL, John & Sarah [WILCOX]; b 1658, b 24 Jul 1651, b 1641; Hartford
BIDDLE/?BIDWELL, John & Sarah WELLS; 7 Nov 1678; Hartford
BIDDLE/?BIDWELL, Joseph (-1672) & Rachel DEANE, wid; 28 Oct 1636; Marshfield
BIDDLE/?BIDWELL, Samuel & 1/wf Elizabeth STOW; 14 Nov 1672; Middletown/Hartford
BIDDLE/?BIDWELL, Samuel & 2/wf Sarah [HARRIS]; b 1695; Hartford
BIDGOOD, Richard & _?_; b 28 Sep 1647; Boston/Ipswich
BIDLAKE/?BIDLOACK, Christopher & 1/wf _?_ (-1692); Ipswich
BIDLAKE, Christopher (-1741, ae ca 80), Windham, CT & 2/wf Sarah (FULLER) [HOVEY] (-1739), Windham, CT, w Nathaniel; b 1694?; Ipswich/Hampton, NH
BIDWELL, Daniel (1655-1719) & 1/wf Elizabeth _?_; b 1682; Hartford
BIDWELL, Daniel (1655-1719) & 2/wf Dorothy (BENTON); b 1692; Hartford
BIDWELL, John (-1687) & Sarah [WILCOX] (1618-1690); b 1647, b 1641; Hartford
BIDWELL, John (ca 1648-1692) & Sarah WELLES (1659-1708, ca 1707); 7 Nov 1678; Hartford
BIDWELL/?BIDDLE, Joseph (-1672) & Rachel DEANE, wid; 28 Oct 1636, no issue; Plymouth Colony
BIDWELL, Joseph (ca 1650-1692) & Mary [COLEFAX] (1656-); 18? May 1675, 8? May 1675; Wethersfield, CT
BIDWELL, Richard (-1647) & Anna? _?_, m/2 James ENO 1648; b 1644, b 1620?; Windsor, CT
BEDWELL, Samuel & Mary HODGKINSON; 2 Feb 1653/4, 1653?; Boston
BIDWELL, Samuel (ca 1651-1715) & 1/wf Elizabeth STOW; 14 Nov 1672; Middletown, CT
BIDWELL, Samuel (ca 1651-1715) & 2/wf Sarah [HARRIS] (1663-1696); b 1695; Middletown, CT
BIDWELL, Samuel (ca 1651-1715) & 3/wf Abigail _?_ (-1723); b 1699, (1700?), b 1698; Middletown, CT
BIGELOW, Daniel (1650-1715) & Abial/?Abigail [PRATT]; b 1689; Watertown/Sherborn
BIGELOW, James (-1728) & 1/wf Patience BROWN; 25 Mar 1687; Watertown
BIGULA, James (-1728) & 2/wf Elizabeth CHILDS (1670-1707); 3 Jul 1693; Watertown
BIGULAH, John (1617-1703) & 1/wf Mary WARIN/WARREN; 30 Oct 1642; Watertown
BIGELOW, John (1643-1722, 1721?) & 1/wf Rebecca [OLMSTED] (1648-); b 1670, b 1684, b 1667/8, no issue; Watertown/Hartford
BIGELOW, John (1617-1703) & 2/wf Sarah BEMIS (1642-bef 1712); 2 Oct 1694; Watertown
BIGELOW, John & Jeruska GEARFIELD/GARFIELD; 2 Jan 1695/6, ?12 Jun; Watertown
BIGELAH, Jonathan (1646-1711) & 1/wf [Rebecca SHEPARD] (?1650-1685?); b 1673, 1671?; Watertown/Hartford
BIGELOW, Jonathan (-1711) & 2/wf Mary [OLCOTT] (-1697); b 1686; Hartford
BIGELOW, Jonathan (-1711) & 3/wf Mary [BENTON] COLE, w Nathaniel, m John SHEPARD; aft 17 - 1697; Hartford
BIGELOW, Jonathan (1673-1749) & Mabel EDWARDS (13 Dec 1685-1765); 14 Dec 1699; Hartford
BIGULAH, Joshua (1655-1745) & Elizabeth FLEG/FLAGG (-1729); 20 Oct 1676; Watertown
BIGULAH, Samuel (1653-1731) & Mary FLEGG/FLAGG (1657/8-1728); 3 Jun 1674; Watertown
BIGG, John (-in Eng, 1642?) & Rachel MARTIN (1565-1647); 14 Sep 1583; Dorchester
BIGGS, John (-1666) & 1/wf Mary _?_ (-10 Jan 1649/50); b 1633?; Ipswich/?Boston
BIGGS, John (-1666) & 2/wf Mary [DASSERT/DASSETT] (-1676), m/2 John MINOT 1667+; 1650; Boston
BIGG, John, London & Hannah [LYNDE] (1670-), m/2 Jonathan MITCHELL ca 1692/4?, m/3 Edward GOFF 1696; ?Boston/London
BIGGS, Thomas (-1704(5?) & Hester _?_; b 1695; Exeter, NH/Brookhaven, LI
BIGGS, Thomas & [?Elizabeth MATTHEWS], dau Wm.?; b 1701(2?); New Haven
BIGGS/BRIGS, William (-1681) & Mary YELLING; 10 Jan 1664/5, 1664; Charlestown
BIGGS, _?_ & Mary [WILLIAMS]
BIGGS, John & Elizabeth _?_ (-1694+), m/2 Ralph DAYTON ca 1694; Brookhaven, LI
BILL, Jacob (1669-1705?) & Theodosia _?_, m/2 John ELIOT; b 1693; Boston
BILL, James (1615-) & Mary _?_ (1613-1688); b 1645; Boston

BILL, James (1651-) & Mehitable _?_ ; b 1672; Boston
BILL, John (-1638?) & Dorothy [?TUTTLE]; in Eng, b 1615; Boston
BILL, John & 1/wf Mercy [FOWLER] (1669-); b 1696; New London, CT/Lebanon, CT
BILL, Jonathan (-1729, ae 77) & Frances _?_ ; b 1676; Boston
BILL, Joseph & 1/wf Lydia [MERRILL] (1661-); b 1687, b 1685?; Boston
BILL, Joseph (-1718) & 2/wf Deliverance [WAKEFIELD] (1664-1713); betw 1687 & 1689; Boston
BILL, Joshua & Mary _?_ ; by 1698, Fordham, NY
BILL, Joshua (1675-1735) & 1/wf Joanna POTTS (-1718), New London; 1 Nov 1699; Groton, CT
BILL, Phillip² (-1689), New London & Hannah _?_ /Anne WAITE? (-1709), m/2 Samuel BUCKNELL/BUCKLAND 1696?; b 1658; Boston/Ipswich/New London, CT
BILL, Phillip³ (-1759) & Elizabeth LESTER; b 1691, b 1689?; ?New London, CT/?Groton, CT
BILLS, Richard & _?_ ; b 1675
BILLS, Robert & _?_
BILL, Samuel & Elizabeth [WILSTED?], m/2 Eleazer PHILLIPS 1705; b 1683, b 1682; Boston
BILL, Samuel & 1/wf Mercy [HAUGHTON] (-1693+); ca 1687?; New London, CT/Groton, CT
BILL, Thomas (-1696) & 1/wf Elizabeth (SARGENT) NICHOLS (-5 Mar 1657/8), w David; 14 Jan 1652/3, 14 Jun; Malden/Boston
BILL, Thomas (-1696) & 2/wf Abigail WILLIS [LEADER] (1633-1646), w John, ?dau Michael WILLIS?; aft 5 Mar 1657/8; Boston
BILLE, Thomas (-1721), Shrewsbury, NJ, & 1/wf Anna TWINING (-1675), Eastham; 3 Oct 1672; Barnstable
BILLS, Thomas (-1721), Shrewsbury, NJ, & 2/wf Joanna TWINING; 2 May 1676; Eastham
BILL, Thomas (1664-) & Mary [HOLMAN] (1667-1703+), m/3 Benjamin BLASKLEDGE/BLACK-HEALTH 1693, m/2 Samuel BUCKNELL 1692; b 1686, ca 1685; Boston
BILL, Thomas & Agnes BATCHELDER; 23 Nov 1699; Boston
BILLING, Ebenezer (1656?-) & Hannah [WALES] (-1732); b 1675; Dorchester
BILLING, Ebenezer & Anne COMSTOCK; 1 Mar 1680, last of Feb, 1 Mar; Stonington, CT
BILLINGS, Ebenezer (ca 1669, Hatfield-1745, Sunderland) & Hannah CHURCH (?1672-1756, Sunderland), Maine?; ca 1691, b 1693; Hadley/Hatfield/Sunderland, MA
BILLING, John (-1646) & _?_ , m/2 Rice THOMAS 1647?; ca 1635/39, b 1640; Kittery, ME
BILLINGS, John (?1640-1704) & 1/wf Elizabeth HASTINGS (1643-); 11 Nov 1661; Concord
BILLINGS, John & 1/wf Ann ANDREWS; b 23 May 1674; Kittery, ME/Braveboat Harbor, ME
BILLINGS, John (-1704) & 2/wf Elizabeth (RICE) LAMSON (1641-), w Joseph; 31 Dec 1685; Concord
BILLINGS, [John] (-1696) & Rebecca SCAMMON; b 1690; Kittery, ME/Saco, ME
BILLING, Joseph (-1679?) & Elizabeth _?_ (-1706), m/2 Samuel THOMPSONS 4 Oct 1680; b 1672, b 1666; Boston
BILLING, Joseph (-bef 1683) & _?_ (see above); b 1683; Deerfield
BILLINGS, Joseph (1668/9?-1748) & Hannah _?_ (1656/7-) (see Wm. BILLINGS); b 1691; Boston/Braintree
BILLINGS, Nathaniel (-1673) & _?_ ; b 1640; Concord
BILLENS, Nathaniel (-1714) & 1/wf Jane (GOODENOW) BANISTER (-1708), w Christopher; 19 May 1679; Concord
BILLINGS, Richard (-1679, Hartford) & Margery _?_ (-1679, Hatfield); b 1649; Dorchester/Roxbury/Hartford/Hadley/Hatfield
BILLINGS, Roger¹ (1618-1683, ae 65) & 1/wf Mary _?_ ; b 1643; Dorchester/Braintree
BILLINGS, Roger¹ (-1683, ae 65) & 2/wf Hannah _?_ (-25 May 1662); ca 1644?; Dorchester
BILLINGS, Roger¹ (-1683) & 3/wf Elizabeth [PRATT] (1642-); aft 25 May 1662; Dorchester?
BILLINGS, Roger² (1657-1718) & Sarah PAINE (1657-1742); 22 Jan 1678; Dorchester/?Stoughton
BILLINGS, Samuel & Seaborn TEW (1640-), m/2 Owen HIGGINS aft 1662; 5 Jan 1657[8]; Newport
BILLINGS, Samuel (-1678, Hatfield) & Sarah [FELLOWES] (-1713, Hatfield), m/2 Samuel BELDING 1678; ca 1661, b 1665/6; Hadley/Hatfield
BILLINGS, Samuel (1665-) & 1/wf Hannah WRIGHT (-1687); 18 Nov 1686; Hadley
BILLINGS, Samuel, Hatfield & Rebecca (LEONARD) [MILLER] (1661-), w Thomas; 20 Dec 1690, 30 Dec 1691; Springfield
BILLING, Samuel (1667-1749) & Mary BARRON (ca 1681-1747); 13 Jan 1698/9; Concord

BILLING, William (-1713) & Mary [?ATHERTON] (-1718); 12 Feb 1657/8; Dorchester/Stonington, CT
BILLING, William & Hannah [CROCUM] (probably) (1657-); b 1684; Boston
BILLING, William (1660-1738) & Hannah [STERRY] (1672-1751); b 1689; Stonington, CT/Preston, CT
BILLINGTON, Francis[2] (?1606-1684, ae 80) (ae 68 in 1674) & Christian (PENN) EATON (-1684±?), w Francis; Jul 1634; Plymouth/Yarmouth
BILLINGTON, Francis[3] & _?_ ; Plymouth/Middleboro?
BILLINGTON, Isaac[2] (ca 1644-1704, ae 65 or 66) & Hannah [GLASS] (1651-); ca 1670/4; Plymouth/Middleboro
BILLINGTON, John[1] (-1630) & Helen?/Eleanor _?_ (-1643+), m/2 Gregory ARMSTRONG 1638; in Eng, b 1604; Plymouth
BILLINGTON, Joseph[3] & Grace _?_ ; 26 Sep 1672 (not 1692); New Shoreham, RI
BINGHAM, Abel (1669-1745) & Elizabeth ODELL; 16 May 1694; Fairfield, CT/Stratford, CT/Windham, CT
BINGHAM, Jonathan (1674-1751) & Anne/Ann HUNTINGTON (1675-1756); 28 Oct 1697; Norwich, CT
BINGHAM, Thomas[1] & Anna/Anne STENTON (-1670), m/2 William BACKUS ca 1659/60; Sheffield, Eng, 6 Jul 1631; New London
BINGHAM, Thomas[2] (1642-1730, ae 88) & Mary RUDD (1648-1726, ae 78); 12 Dec 1666; Norwich, CT/Windham, CT
BINGHAM, Thomas[3] (1667-1710) & Hannah BACKUS (?1676-1752), m/2 Daniel TRACY 1712, m/3 Samuel GRISWOLD 1729; 17 Feb 1691/2; Norwich, CT
BINGHAM, Thomas & Elizabeth _?_ ; b 1697; Newport
BINGLEY, Thomas (-1685) & 1/wf Susanna _?_ ; b 1672; Boston
BINGLEY, Thomas (-1683) & 2/wf Abigail (BUTTOLPH) [SAYWELL], w David; aft 1672; Wethersfield, CT/Boston
BINGLEY, William & Elizabeth PRESTON; 27 Feb 1659, 1659/60; Newbury/Woodbridge, NJ
BINEY, John (-1698) & Marsey/Mercy _?_ (-1709); b 1678, b 1687; Hull
BIRCHARD, James (1665-1745+) & Elizabeth BECKWITH (1678-); 17 Mar 1695/6; Norwich, CT
BURCHARD, John (-1702) & 1/wf Christyan/Christian ANDREWS; 22 Jul 1653; Norwich, CT
BURCHARD, John (-1702) & 2/wf Jane (LEE) [HYDE] (1645-1723), w Samuel; aft 1677; Norwich, CT
BIRCHARD, Samuel (1663-1712/13?) & Ann [CAULKINS] (1676-), m/2 Josiah ROCKWELL 1721; b 1697, ca 1695; ?New London, CT/?Coventry
BIRCHARD, Thomas (1595-) & 1/wf Mary _?_ (1597, ?1602-1655); in Eng, b 1622; Roxbury/Edgartown/Saybrook, CT/Norwich, CT
BIRCHARD, Thomas (1595-) & 2/wf Katerin/Catherine [ANDREWS] (-1674+); b 23 Sep 1659; Edgartown
BIRCHARD/BURCHAM, Thomas (1595-) & 3/wf Deborah _?_ (-1680); Charlestown
BIRD, Edward & Dorothy _?_ ; b 1668; Boston
BIRD, James (-1708) & 1/wf Lydia STEELE (-1659/61); 31 Mar 1657, 1656?; Farmington, CT
BIRD, James & 2/wf [Rebecca?] _?_ ; ca 1669; Farmington, CT
BIRD, James (ca 1647-1733, 1723?) & 1/wf Mary GEORGE (1645-1673); 6 Apr 1669; Dorchester
BIRD, James (1644-1733, 1723?, 1725?) & 2/wf Ann WITHINGTON (1656-1723); 13 Nov 1679; Dorchester
BIRD, James (1671-1728) & 1/wf Miriam _?_ (-1723, ae 53); b 1696; Dorchester
BIRD, Jathnell & Hester [FOWLER], m/2 Ezra ROLFE by 1652, m/3 Robert COLLINS bef 1657; b 1641?, b 1650, b 1652; Salisbury
BIRD, John (1641-1732) (blind) & [Elizabeth WILLIAMS] (1647-1724), Taunton; b 1670; Dorchester
BIRD, John (1670-1745) & Mary RYALL/ROYAL (-1751); 20 Nov 1696; Dorchester
BIRD, Joseph (-1695?/6) & [Mary CLARK]; b 1670?, b Mar 1660/1, aft 1 Dec 1659; Farmington, CT
BIRD, Joseph (-1712) & 1/wf Miriam _?_ ; b 1690; Dorchester
BIRD, Joseph (-1712) & 2/wf [Johannah LEEDS] (-1738 in 72nd y); b 1698; Dorchester
BIRD, Joseph (-1708) & Mary [STEELE] (-1729+); b 1700; Farmington, CT

BIRD, Nathaniel (-1704) & Sarah [WOODFORD]; b 10 Dec 1691?, b 10 Dec 1701; Farmington, CT

BIRD, Samuel (-1699) & Esther WOODWARD; 2 Jan 1695/6; Farmington, CT

BIRD, Simon (1615-1666) & Mary _?_ (-1680), m/2 Henry JEFTS 1666; ca 1640/45?, no issue; Billerica

BIRD, Thomas (-1664) & Anne _?_ ; b 1630; Scituate

BIRD, Thomas (-bef 1653, 1662?) & Mary _?_ (-ca 1660, 1664+?); b 1635?, b 1637; Hartford/Farmington, CT

BIRD, Thomas[1] (?1613-1667) & Anne _?_ (-1673); b 1640; Dorchester

BIRD, Thomas (-1662?) & 2/wf _?_ [BELDEN?]; ?Hartford

BIRD, Thomas[2] (1640-1716) & Thankful ATHERTON (1644-1719); 2 Feb 1665/6, 2 Apr 1665; Dorchester

BIRD, Thomas & Mary _?_ ; b 6 Dec 1691; Farmington

BIRD, Thomas (-1725) & 2/wf Mary WOODFORD; 3 Jul 1693; Farmington, CT

BIRDSALL, Benjamin & Mercy/Mary? [FORMAN]; ca 1682; Oyster Bay, LI

BIRDSALE, Henry (-1651) & _?_ ; b 1623; Salem

BIRDSALL, Nathan & [Temperance BALDWIN]; ca 1645?; East Hampton, LI/Oyster Bay, LI

BIRDSALL, Samuel & Jane [LANGDON]; b 5 Mar 1690; Oyster Bay, LI

BIRDSEY, Edward (seems doubtful) & _?_ ; by 1630?; Wethersfield, CT

BIRDSEY, John[1] (1614-1690) & 1/wf Philippa [SMITH]? (ca 1622-by 1687); b 1640, b 1641, b 23 Aug 1640; Wethersfield, CT

BIRDSEY, John[2] (1641-1697/8) & Phebe WILCOXSON (ca 1651-1743), m/2 John BENAH; 11 Dec 1669; Stratford, CT

BIRDSEY, John (1614-1690) & 2/wf Alice TOMLINSON (-1698), w Henry; m cont 8 Oct 1688

BIRGE, Daniel (1644-1698) & 1/wf Deborah HOLCOMB (1650-1686); 5 Nov 1668, at Hartford; Windsor, CT

BIRGE, Daniel (-1698) & 2/wf Abigail [GILLETTE] (1663-), m/2 Joseph LOOMIS 1703; aft 26 May 1686, b 1689; Windsor, CT

BIRGE, John (-1697) & Hannah WATSON (-1690); 28 Mar 1678, 18 Mar 1678; Windsor, CT

BIRGE, John (-1733, in 85th y) & Sarah _?_ (-1717, in 63rd y); b 1683; Boston/Bristol, RI/Yarmouth, MA

BIRGE, Joseph (1651-1705) & Mary (OWEN) [BISSELL] (-1690), w Daniel; ca 1685, b 1686; Windsor, CT

BIRGE, Richard (-1651) & Elizabeth GAYLORD, m/2 Thomas HOSKINS 1653; 5 Oct 1641; Windsor, CT

BISBEE, Elisha[2] (1616-1690) & Joanna _?_ ; b 1645; Scituate/?Duxbury

BISBEE, Elisha[3] (1654-1715) & Mary (JACOB) BACON, w Samuel; 25 Mar 1685; Hingham

BISBEE, Hopestill[3] (1645-1695) & Sarah [KING] (1650-), m/2 Joseph LINCOLN 1696; ca 1680; Hingham

BISBE, John[3] (1647-) & Joanna BROOKS; 13 Sep 1687; Marshfield/Pembroke

BISBEE, Thomas[1] (1590-1674) & 1/wf 2/wf? Anne BAREDEN; in Eng, b 1614, 14 Jan 1618/19; Scituate/Duxbury/Marshfield/Sudbury

BISBEE, _?_ & ?Alice _?_ ; 1634

BISCON, Isaac & Ann/Hannah? BROOKS; 20 Nov 1690; Boston

BISHOP, Benjamin & Susanna PIERSON; 24 Aug 1696; Stamford, CT

BISHOP, Caleb (1660-) & Lydia EVARTS; 19 Aug 1692, 18 Aug; Guilford, CT

BISHOP, Daniel (1663-1751) & 1/wf Hannah [BRADLEY] (-1692); 1688?, b 1689; Guilford, CT

BISHOP, Daniel (1663-1751) & 2/wf Mary HALL (1672-); 16 Jul 1693; Guilford, CT

BISHOP, Ebenezer & Ann LATIMER; 30 Nov 1699; Guilford, CT

BISHOP, Ebenezer (1666-) & Sarah SLAWSON/SLASON? (1667-1734); 2 Oct 1700; Stamford, CT

BISHOP, Edward[1] (-1705) & 1/wf Hannah/?Mary/?Sarah _?_ ; b 1646; Salem

BISHOP, Edward[2] (1648, 1646?-1711) & Sarah [WILDER] (called Mary in Church rec); ca 1670?; Salem/Beverly/Rehoboth

BISHOP, Edward[1] (-1705) & 2/wf Bridget (WARSILBE) [OLIVER] (-1692), w Thomas; ca 1679-80; Salem

BISHOP, Edward[1] (-1705) & 3/wf Elizabeth (LAMBERT) CASH, w William; 9 Mar 1692/3; Salem

BISHOP, Edward[3] & Susannah [PUTNAM] (1670-); b 1699, b 1692; Salem

BISHOP, Henry (-1664) & 1/wf Patience [LAMBERTON] (?1630-1655); b 1655; New Haven/Boston

BISHOP, Henry (-1664) & 2/wf Elizabeth (LECHFORD) WILBORE/WILBUR, w Thomas, w Samuel; 20 Feb 1656/7; Boston

BISHOP, James (-1691) & 1/wf Mary (?) [CURTIS] (-1664), w Thomas; b 1651, betw 1 Dec 1648 & 29 May 1651; New Haven

BISHOP, James (-1691) & 2/wf Elizabeth TOMPKINS/TOMLINS/TOMLINSON (bp 1644-1703); 12 Dec 1665; New Haven

BISHOP, James & Mary [HUDSON] (?1654-1740); ca 1672; Duxbury/Pembroke

BISHOP, James & Joanna (BOICE/BOYSE) [PRUDDEN] (WILLETT) (-1686), w Rev. Peter, w Thomas; winter of 1683; Milford, CT

BISHOP, James & Elizabeth MORSLY/MOSELEY, Dorchester; 16 Nov 1692; ?Marlborough

BISHOP, James & Abigail BENNETT; 11 Dec 1695; New Haven

BISHOP, James (1678-1739) & Thankful [POND]; b 1701?; Guilford, CT

BISHOP, Job & 1/wf Elizabeth [PHILLIPS] (-1652?); b 17 May 1651, ?Dec 1650; Ipswich/Boston

BISHOP, Job & 2/wf Mary [?WILLIAMS] (had sister _?_ SMITH); b 1654?, b 1657; Ipswich

BISHOP, Job & Joanna [TUTTLE] (1664-), m/2 John PICKARD 1691, m/3 Edmund POTTER 1701, m/4 John WHIPPLE 1703; b 1687, ca 1684?; Ipswich

BISHOP, John (?1604-1661) & Anne _?_ (-1676); b 1624?, b 1629; Guilford, CT

BISHOP, John (-1684) & Rebecca (KENT) SCULLARD, w Samuel; 3 Oct 1647; Newbury/Nantucket/Woodbridge, NJ

BISHOP, John (-1683) & Susannah GOLHAM?/GOLDHAM (-1703); 13 Dec 1650; Guilford, CT

BISHOP, John (-1695) & 1/wf Rebecca [GOODYEAR] (probably), dau Stephen; ?ca 1650/2?; Taunton/Boston 1644/Stamford, CT

BISHOP, John & _?_ ; b 1660?, b 1669; Southampton, LI

BISHOP, John (James is wrong) (-1695) & 2/wf Joanna (BOYES) (PRUDDEN) [WILLETT], w Peter, w Thomas; b 8 Nov 1681, aft Aug 1674, 1683; Stamford, CT

BISHOP, John (-1678) & Sarah ?WELLES; - Jan 1675; Wethersfield, CT

BISHOP, John & Lydia _?_ ; b 1682; Southampton

BISHOP, John & 1/wf Elizabeth HITCHCOCK; 3 Jul 1689; Guilford, CT

BISHOP, John (1662-1710) & Abigail [WILLETT]; b 1691, 1689?; New Haven

BISHOP, John (-1733) & Anna/Ann _?_ ; b 1695; Manchester

BISHOP, John (1677-1756) & Elizabeth [KEEN] (1683-1745); ca 1700/1702; Pembroke

BISHOP, Jonathan & Abigail AVERY/AVERILL?; m int 6 Jul 1699, m int 9 Jul 1699; Topsfield/Rehoboth/Beverly

BISHOP, Joseph & Elizabeth KNOWLES; 3 Nov 1691; Stamford, CT

BISHOP, Nathaniel (-1687) & Alice _?_ (not Alice MATTOCKS) (-1674+) (see last of BISHOP's marriages); b 1634; Boston

BISHOP, Nathaniel (-1685?) & _?_ ; ca 1655/62?; Southampton/Easthampton, LI

BISHOP, Nathaniel & Sarah GRANNIS (1671-); 28 Apr 1690; New Haven

BISHOP, Nathaniel & Mary HALL; Jul 1692; Guilford, CT

BISHOP, Nathaniel & Mary/Mercy HUGHES (1676-); 9 Feb 1692/3; Guilford, CT

BISHOP, Richard (-1674) & 1/wf Dulzebella/Dulcebella [KING] (-1658), w Richard; ?1635; Salem

BISHOP, Richard (-1673+) & Alice (MARTIN) CLARK (-1648), w George; 5 Dec 1644; Plymouth

BISHOP, Richard (-1674) & 2/wf Mary GAULT, w William, m/3 Thomas ROBBINS 1675; 22 Jul 1660; Salem

BISHOP, Samuel (1645-1687) & Hester COGSWELL (ca 1656-), m/2 Thomas BURNHAM 1689; 10 Aug 1675, 24? Aug; Ipswich

BISHOP, Samuel & Mary JONES; 13 May 1695; Salem/Attleboro

BISHOP, Samuel & Hannah (YALE) TALMAGE (-1744), w Enos; 14 Nov 1695; New Haven

BISHOP, Samuel & Abigail WETMORE; 20 Apr 1697; Guilford, CT

BISHOP, Samuel & Elizabeth _?_ ; b 1701?, [aft 1698]; Southampton, LI

BISHOP, Stephen (-1690) & Tabitha WILKINSON (-1692); 4 May 1654; Guilford, CT

BISHOP, Stephen (1655-) & Hannah [BARTLETT] (1658-); b 1682, b 1680; Guilford, CT

BISHOP, Stephen & Mercy PIERSON?; b 1682; Stamford, CT

BISHOP, Thomas (ca 1618-1671, 1674?) & Margaret _?_ (-1680, 1681); ca 1635/40?; Ipswich

BISHOP, Thomas (-1694) & Lydia [NORMAN] (1640-1704+); b 1661(2?); Manchester

BISHOP, Thomas & Mary __?__ ; b 1676; Boston
BISHOP, Thomas (-1727, in 82nd y) & 1/wf Prudence __?__ (-11 Oct 1680); b 1680; Roxbury
BISHOP, Thomas (-1727) & 2/wf Elizabeth __?__ (-Dec 1681); aft 11 Oct 1680; Roxbury
BISHOP, Thomas (-1727) & 3/wf Ann (DOUGLAS) GARY (-1691), w Nathaniel; 7 Jun 1683; Roxbury
BISHOP, Thomas & Martha/Rehromy? [GARRETSON]; b 26 Jan 1692; Westchester, NY
BISHOP, Thomas & Esther __?__ ; b 1697; ?Windham, CT/?Lebanon, CT
BISHOP, Townsend & __?__ ; b 1634; Salem
BISHOP, William & 1/wf Dorothy HOOPER; 5 Oct 1700, 15 Oct 1700; Beverly/Salem/Attleboro
BISHOP, Nathaniel & Alice [MATTOCKS?], m/2 John LEWIS 1659, m/3 Abraham HOWE by 1680, m/4 John HARRIS aft 1683; b 1634 (no)
BISHOP, __?__ & Sarah [TOMLINSON] (?1665-); b 27 Apr 1685
BISPHAM?/BISBORN, Robert (-1687) & Susanna [HENDRICK], m/2 Philip PRICE/Philip John PRICE by 1691; b 1680?, b 1685; Fairfield, CT
BISS, James & Jemima __?__ ; b 1665; Boston
BISS, __?__ & Lydia __?__ , m/2 Samuel LARRABEE 1695; b 1695
BISSELL, Benjamin (?1669-5 May 1698, Windsor) & Abigail [ALLYN] (1672-1734), m/2 Rev. John WILLIAMS?; Hartford
BISSELL, Daniel (1663-1738) & 1/wf Margaret DEWEY (1674-1712); ?27 Nov 1692, 27 Oct 1692; Windsor, CT
BISSELL, Jacob (1664-1694) & Mary [GILLETTE], m/2 Peter BUELL 1699, 1698?; b 1689; Windsor, CT/Simsbury
BISSELL, John¹ (1591-1677) & 1/wf ?Mary DRAKE (no)/?Elizabeth THOMPSON (-1/21 May 1641); in Eng, ca 1625/30?; Windsor, CT
BISSELL, John¹ (1591-1677) & 2/wf __?__ (1589-1665); aft 1641; Windsor, CT
BISSELL, John² (-1693) & 1/wf Isabel MASON (-29 Mar 1665, ae 25), Saybrook; 17 Jun 1658; Windsor, CT/Lebanon
BISSELL, John² & 2/wf [?Izrell] __?__ ; ca 1669; Windsor, CT
BISSELL, John (1659-1685) & Abigail FILLY/FILLEY (1658-1708), m/2 Samuel TUDOR 1685; 20? Aug, 26 Aug 1680; Windsor, CT
BISSELL, John & Sarah (WHITE) LOOMIS (?1662-), Hatfield, w Thomas; 12 Nov 1689; Windsor, CT
BISSELL, Joseph (1663-1689) & Sarah STRONG (1666, 1664?-1739), Northampton, m/2 John HIGLEY aft 1694, bef 1697; 7 Jul 1687; Windsor, CT
BISSELL, Nathaniel (1640-1714) & 1/wf Mindwell MOORE (1643-1682); 25 Sep 1662; Windsor, CT
BISSELL, Nathaniel (-1714) & 2/wf Dorothy FITCH (1658-1691); 4 Jul 1683, ?25 Sep 1683; Windsor, CT
BISSELL, Samuel (1636-1700, 1698?) & 1/wf Abigail HOLCOMB (1638-1688); 11 Jun 1658; Windsor, CT
BISSELL, Samuel (1636-1700) & Mary (BUELL) [?MILLS], w Simon; aft 17 Aug 1688, bef 23 Apr 1698; Windsor, CT
BISSELL, Samuel, Jr. (1668/9?-1698) & Mary __?__ ; b 1698; Windsor, CT
BISSELL, Thomas (-1689) & Abigail MOORE (-1688); 11 Oct 1655; Windsor, CT
BISSELL, Thomas (1656-1738) & Esther/?Hester STRONG (1661-1727, Windsor, CT); 15 Oct 1678; Northampton
BITFIELD/?BIDFIELD, Samuel (-1660, Boston) & Elizabeth __?__ (-1669); b 1630; Boston
BITNER, William & Sarah [INGALLS] (1626/8-); b 23 Aug 1648; Lynn
BITTLESTONE, Thomas (-1640) & Elizabeth __?__ (-1672); b 1640; Cambridge
BIGSBEE, Benjamin & Mary [KIMBALL] (2 wfs Mary?); b 1676?, b 1678; Topsfield
BIGSBE, Daniel (-1717) & Hannah CHANDLER; 2 Dec 1674; Andover
BIXBE, George & Rebecca [PORTER?]; b 1693; Boxford
BIXBEE, Jonathan & Sarah SMITH (1674?-); ?1 Feb 1691-2, ?2 Feb 1691-2, 2 Feb 1692-3; Boxford/Topsfield
BIGSBYE, Joseph & Sarah (WYATT) HEARD, w Luke; m cont 15 Dec 1647; Ipswich
BIGGISBY, Joseph & Sarah GOLD/GOULD (1664-1723); 29 Mar 1682; Boxford
BIGSBY, __?__ & Mary __?__ ; b 20 Jun 1640; Boston
BIXBY, __?__ & Mary [HANCOCK]? (1666-1686?); b ?5 Jan 1717/18; Cambridge

BLABOUR/BLABER, Robert & Mary [PEARSON?/PARSON?], dau George, m/2 John BUTT 1700, m/3 Samuel HARE 1709; b 1694; Boston

BLACK, Daniel & [Faith BRIDGES]; b 1664, b 1665; Boxford/Topsfield

BLACK, Daniel & 1/wf Mary COMMINGS (1672-169-); 14 Jul [169?], 1691?; Topsfield/Boxford

BLACK, Daniel & 2/wf Sarah ADAMS; 19 Jul 1695; Boxford/Topsfield

BLACK, George see George BLAKE, 1641

BLACK, John (1591-1645, 1635?) & Susanna _?_, m/2 Robert PLOTT; b 1635; Charlestown/Salem

BLACK, John, Jr. & Freeborne (WOLF) SALLOWS (?1635-1681, ae 46), w Robert; 29 Jul 1664; Salem/Beverly

BLACK, John & 2/wf Deborah _?_ ; b 1686; Beverly

BLACK, John & Mary MORGAN; m int 18 Aug 1700; Beverly

BLACK, [?Josiah] & Mary _?_ (1676-); b 1697; York, ME

BLACK, William (slave) & _?_

BLACKBURN, James & Frances _?_ ; b 1680; Boston

BLACKBURN, Walter & Elizabeth _?_ ; b 1639; Roxbury/Boston

BLACKDEN, Samuel & Mary _?_ ; b 1696; Boston

BLACKINTON, Pentecost & 1/wf Ann (PEDRICK)? BARRETT, w John; 30 Jan 1688/9; Marblehead/Attleboro

BLACKLEECH, Benjamin & Dorcas [BOWMAN], dau Nathaniel, m/2 Hugh MARCH 1676; b 1666; Cambridge/Watertown, CT

BLACKLEECH, Benjamin & Mary (HOLMAN) (BILL) BUCKNELL, w Thomas, w Samuel BUCKNER/BUCKNELL; 18 Sep 1693; Boston

BLACKLEACH, John[1] (-1683) & ?1/wf ?2/wf Elizabeth [BACON] (-1683); in Eng, b 1626; Salem/Boston/Hartford/Wethersfield, CT

BLACKLEACH, John[2] (1626-1703) & Elizabeth [WEBB]?; b 1655?, b 1660; Boston/Hartford

BLACKLEDGE, John[2] (1626-1703) & 2/wf Elizabeth [HARBERT?/HERBERT] (-1708, ae 74); b 1667; Hartford/Wethersfield, CT

BLACKLEDGE, John[3] (-1700) & Susanna (FENN) [HOOKER], w William; aft 1689, bef 1693; Farmington, CT

BLACKLEDGE, Nathaniel & Mary (MILBURY) [FREETHY], w James; by 1695; York, ME

BLACKLEY, Phillip & Ann _?_ ; b 1687(8?); Boston

BLACKLEACH, Richard (1654/5-1731) & 1/wf Abigail HUDSON/HODSON/HODSHON (1654-1713), New Haven; 8 Dec 1680; Stratford, CT

BLACKLEACH, Richard (?1681-) & Sarah [WHEELER] (1678-); b 1700?; ?Stratford, CT

BLACKALER, Philip (-1708/9) & Mary PUFFER; 26 Nov 1700; Boston

BLACKLER, William & Jane [CODNER] (-1701); b 1684, b 1680?; Marblehead

BLACKMAN, Benjamin (1665-1716+) & Jemima [BRICK] (1672-); b 1693, [ca 1690]; Dorchester

BLACKMAN, John (ca 1625-1675) & 1/wf Mary [POND] (-ca 1667?), dau Robert; b 1656 (see below); Dorchester

BLACKMAN, John (ca 1625-1675) & 2/wf Sarah _?_ (-1712, Little Compton), m/2 _?_ JONES; b 1656, b 1670; Dorchester

BLACKEMAN, John (1656-1742) & Jane WEEKES (ca 1659, ?1662-1735); 26 Mar 1685; Dorchester

BLACKMAN, Jonathan (1659-1716, 1690?) & Leah _?_ (1667-1741); 1687; Little Compton, RI

BLACKMAN, Joseph (1661-1720) & Elizabeth CHURCH (1664-); 12 Nov 1685; Dorchester/Little Compton, RI/Freetown

BLACKMAN, Peter & _?_ ; North Yarmouth, ME

BLACKMORE, Henry & Mary TRUMBULL/THRUMBALL (-1671, ae 24); 25 Aug 1663; Charlestown

BLACKMORE, James (-1709, 1710?) & Mary [HAWKINS] (-1724); ca 1682, b 1678?; Providence

BLACKMER, John (1669-1751) & 1/wf Anna BRANCH; 18 Sep 1700; ?19 Sep 1700; Rochester/Marshfield

BLACKMER, Peter (1667-1717) & 1/wf Elizabeth _?_ (-1711); b 1690; Rochester

BLACKMER, William (-1676) & Elizabeth BANKES, m/2 Jacob BUMPUS 1677; 17 Jul 1666; Scituate

BLACKSTONE, John & Catherine _?_ ; b 1692?, b 1694?, b 1700; Rehoboth/Providence/Attleboro/Branford, CT

BLACKSTONE, William (-1675) & Sarah STEPHSON/STEVENSON (-1673), w John; 4 Jul 1659;
Boston/Rehoboth/Providence
BLACKSTONE, William & Abigail [VARNEY] (1669-); b 1696; Dover, NH
BLACKWELL, John (-1688) & Sarah [WARREN] (1644-); ca 1673, b 1675; Sandwich
BLACKWELL, John (1675-) & Lydia [SKIFFE] (1675-); b 1701?; Martha's Vineyard
BLACKWELL, Joshua & Mercy _?_; b 1682(3?); Sandwich
BLACKWELL, Michael/?Miles & _?_; b 1648; Sandwich
BLACKWELL, Robert & _?_; Newtown, LI/NJ
BLAGDON, James (1638±-) & 1/wf Martha _?_; ca 1664?; Isles of Shoals
BLAGDEN, James (1638±-) & 2/wf Joan (_?_) (DIAMOND) [CARTER], w Edward, w William;
aft 22 Dec 1691, by 25 Apr 1693; Isles of Shoals
BLAGDEN, Samuel & Mary (SEWARD) [HULL] (1660, ?1658-1735), w Dodavah; by 1688, aft
1682; Portsmouth, NH/Boston
BLAGROVE, Nathaniel (-1742) & Elizabeth (ALLEN) HAYMAN, w Nathan; 18 Jun 1690; Bristol,
RI
BLAGUE, Henry (-1662) & Elizabeth _?_; b 1643; Braintree/Boston
BLAGUE, Joseph (son Henry) (1660-) & Martha KIRTLAND (1667-), m/2 William SOUTH-
WORTH; 10 Feb 1685; Saybrook, CT
BLAGUE, Nathaniel (-1678) & Judith _?_ (-living 1678); b 1670; Boston
BLAGUE, Newcomb, m/2 Abigail MATHER & Mary _?_ (-ae 38), m/2 Rev. John WHITE; b 1697;
Boston
BLAGUE, Philip (1647-) & Susannah [NEWCOMB], m/2 Benjamin PRICHARD ca 1679/80; b 1671;
Boston
BLAGGE, Samuel (-1713) & Mary [?BONTEL] (tradition); b 1677; Stratford, CT
BLAISDELL, Ebenezer (1657-1710) & Sarah [COLBY]; b 1682, ca 1681; Amesbury
BLAISDELL, Henry (1632-1702/7) & 1/wf Mary [HADDEN] (-1691); b 1657; Salisbury/Amesbury
BLAISDELL, Henry (1663-1703/5) & 1/wf Mary _?_ (-1691); b 1686; Amesbury
BLAISDELL, Henry (1663-) & 2/wf Hannah (ROWELL) [COLBY], w Thomas; ca 1691; Amesbury
BLAISDELL, Henry (1632-1702/5) & 2/wf Elizabeth _?_; aft 1691; Salisbury/Amesbury
BLAISDELL, John (-1732) & Elizabeth (CHALLIS) HOYT, w John; 6 Jan 1692/3; Amesbury
BLAISDELL, Jonathan (1676-) & Hannah [JAMESON]; b 1699; Amesbury
BLAISDELL, Ralph (-1650) & Elizabeth _?_ (-1667); b 1632; Salisbury/York, ME
BLAKE, Andrew (-1755, ae 94) & Sarah STEVENS; 14 Aug 1696; Sherborn/Wrentham
BLAKE, Edward (-1692) & Patience [POPE] (-1690); b 1658, ca 1653?; Boston/Dorchester
BLAKE, Edward (1662-1737) & Elizabeth MORY (-1711), Milton; 26 Jun 1696; Milton
BLACK?/BLAKE, George (1611-1698/9, 1697/8) & Dorothy _?_ (-1702, Boxford); b 1641;
Glouchester/Andover/Boxford
BLAKE, James (1624-1700) & 1/wf Elizabeth CLAPP (1634-1694, 1695?); ca 1651, ca Jan 1652?;
Dorchester
BLAKE, James (1652-1732) & 1/wf Hannah MACY (-1 Jun 1683, 1682?); 6 Feb 1681, 1682/3,
1682; Dorchester
BLAKE, James (1652-1732) & 2/wf Ruth BATCHELDER (1662-1752); 8 Jul 1684; Dorchester
BLAKE, James (1624-1700) & 2/wf Elizabeth (SMITH) HUNT, w Peter; 17 Sep 1695; Rehoboth
BLAKE, Jasper (-1673/4) & Deborah [DALTON]? (-1678); b 1649; Hampton, NH
BLAKE?, John (1618-1685) & 1/wf? _?_ [BRECK] (1622?-); ca 164-, 1640?; Dorchester
BLAKE, John (1618-1688) & 2/wf? Mary (SOUTHER) SHAW (-1693), w Joseph; 16 Aug 1654;
Boston
BLAKE, John (-1700) & Bridget _?_ (-1706); b 1665, ca 1660; Sandwich/Wrentham
BLAKE, John (-1690?/1, 1690) & Sarah HALL (1654-1726), m/2 Edward TURNER by 1694; Mar
1673; ?Middletown, CT
BLAKE, John (-1692?) & Sarah _?_, m/2 Matthew POOLE 1694, m/3 James MYRICK 1711; b
1684, Dec 1682; Boston
BLAKE, John & Deborah KNOWLTON; 8 Jun 1685; Marblehead
BLAKE, John (1657-1718) & 1/wf Mary/?Hannah _?_; b 1687; Boston/Dorchester
BLAKE, John (1656-1716) & Frances _?_; b 1689, b 1686; Hampton, NH
BLAKE, John & Joanna WHITING (-1739); 6 Feb 1689, prob 1688/9; Wrentham
BLAKE, John (1657-1718) & 1/wf? 2/wf Hannah _?_ (1662-6 May 1729, in 67th y, 1722?,
1731?), m/2 Hopestill HUMPHREYS 1719; b 1687, b 1693; Dorchester

BLAKE, Jonathan & Elizabeth **CANDAGE**; 16 Feb 1699, prob 1698/9, ?16 Mar 1699; Boston/Wrentham

BLAKE, Joseph (1667-1739) & Mehitable [**BIRD**] (1674-1751); b 1691, b 5 Apr 1691; Dorchester

BLAKE, Nathaniel (?1659-1720), Milton & Martha **MORY/MOORE**, Milton; 9 Oct 1695; Milton

BLAKE, Philemon (1671-1743) & Sarah **DEARBORN** (1675-); 20 Jan 1698; Hampton, NH

BLAKE, Samuel (1650-1719) & Sarah [**MACY**]; ca 1678?; Taunton

BLAKE, Timothy (1659-1718) & Naomi **SLEEPER** (1655-); 20 Dec 1677; Hampton, NH

BLAKE, William (1594-1663) & Agnes (?**THORNE**) **BAND/BOND**? (-1678), wid; Pitminster, Eng, 27 Sep, 23 Sep 1617; Dorchester

BLAKE, William (1620-1703) & 1/wf Ann/Anna? _?_ ; b 1650; Dorchester

BLAKE, William (1620-1703), Milton & 2/wf Hannah (**TULMAN**) **LYON** (1639-1729), w George; 22 Nov 1693, 12 Nov; Milton

BLAKE, _?_ & Elizabeth _?_ , m/2 George **DURANT** ca 1653 in Eng; Malden, Eng, ca 1651

BLAKE, _?_ (should be BLAGUE, Philip **BLAGUE** m Susanna **NEWCOMB**) (had son Newcomb **BLAKE** of Boston 1696, he was of age in 1697) & _?_ **NEWCOMB**

BLAKEMAN, Adam (1598-1665) & Jane [**HAWLEY**?] (-1673/4); b 1635; Stratford, CT

BLAKEMAN/BLACKMAN?, Benjamin & Rebecca **SCOTTOW** (1655-1715); 1 Apr 1675; Malden/ Boston/Scarboro, ME

BLAKEMAN, Deliverance (-1702) & Hannah _?_ ; b 1687; Stratford, CT

BLAKEMAN, Ebinezer & 1/wf Patience **WILLCOXSON** (1663/4-); 24 Oct 1681, 4 Oct; Stratford, CT

BLAKEMAN, Ebinezer & 2/wf Abigail **CURTIS** (1671-); 3 Nov 1692; Stratford, CT

BLAKEMAN/BLACKMAN?, James (-1689) & 1/wf Miriam [**STILES**], dau Francis; b 1658; Stratford, CT

BLAKEMAN, James (-1689) & 2/wf Miriam [**WHEELER**] (1647-1705), m/2 Edward **GROOM**; [ca 1666], betw 1665 & 1668, ca 1667; Stratford, CT

BLAKEMAN, John (-1662) & Dorothy [**SMITH**] (1636?-), dau Rev. Henry, m/2 Francis **HALL** 1665, m/3 Mark **St.JOHN** 1693, m/4 Isaac **MOORE**; ca 1653; Stratford, CT/Fairfield, CT

BLAKEMAN, John (-1706) & Mary [**KIMBERLY**] (1668-); b 1694; Stratford, CT

BLAKEMAN, Joseph & Hannah **HALL**; 14 Jul 1674; Stratford, CT

BLAKEMAN, Joseph (1675-) & Elizabeth **SEELEY**; 14 Sep 1697; Stratford, CT

BLAKEMAN, Samuel (-1668) & Elizabeth **WHEELER** (1642-), m/2 Jacob **WALKER** 1670; end of Nov 1660; Stratford, CT

BLAKESLEY, Ebenezer (1664-1735) & Hannah [**LUPTON**] (1665-1749); b 1685(6?); New Haven/North Haven/Waterbury

BLAKSLEY, Edward (-Nov 1637) & _?_ ; b 1620; Roxbury

BLAKESLEY, John (1651-) & Grace [**VENTRUS**], m/2 John **DOOLITTLE** 1717; b 1676; New Haven

BLAKESLEE, John (1676-) & 1/wf Lydia _?_ (-1723); ca 1696, b 1696; New Haven

BLAKESLEY/BLACKLY/?BLAKELEY, Moses & Sarah **BENTON**; - Jan 1671, 1 Jan 1701/2?; Guilford, CT

BLACKLEY, Philip & Ann _?_ ; b 1688; Boston/NJ?

BLAKESLEY, Samuel (-1672) & Hannah **POTTER** (-1723), m/2 Henry **BROOKS** 1676; 3 Dec 1650; New Haven/Guilford, CT

BLAKESLEY, Samuel (1662-1732) & Sarah **KIMBERLEY** (ca 1663-); 20 Nov 1684; New Haven/Woodbury, CT

BLAKESLEE, _?_ & _?_ [**PARKER**]; b 1657; CT

BLANCH, Richard & Elizabeth **TAYNOUR**; 5 Nov 1693; Marblehead

BLANCHANT, Richard & Elizabeth **HUNSEY**, m/2 Richard **RANDALL** 1705; 12 Jul 1686; Cape Porpoise/Kittery, ME?

BLANCHARD, Abraham, Malden & Sarah **WHITMARSH**, Weymouth; 25 Jul 1690; Braintree

BLANCHARD, George (see John) & 1/wf ?Mary _?_ ; b 1653; Charlestown

BLANCHARD, George & Sarah **BASSETT**; 15 Dec 1687; Charlestown

BLANCHARD, George (-1700) & 2/wf Mary _?_ ; b 1653?, b 1689, b 1667?; Charlestown

BLANCHARD, James (-bef 9 Mar 1702/3) & Anna [**BLOOD**] (1671-); b 1694; Charlestown

BLANCHARD, John (see George) & Elizabeth [**HILLS**] (1627-); ca 1657/8; Charlestown

BLANCHARD, John (-1694) & Hannah (**BRACHETT**) [**KINGSLEY**] (1634, 1634/5-1706), w Samuel; aft 21 May 1662; ?Charlestown

BLANCHER, John & Abigail [PHILLIPS]; b 1686; Weymouth

BLANCHARD, John & Anna _?_ ; b 1694; Groton

BLANCHETT, Jonathan & 1/wf Anne/Ann LOVEJOY (-1724); 26 May 1685; Andover

BLANCHARD, Joseph (1653-1694) & Hannah SHEPARD; 13 Apr 1681; Charlestown

BLANCHARD, Joseph (-1727) & Abiah HASSELL (-1746); 25 May 1696; Dunstable

BLANCHARD, Joshua & 1/wf Elizabeth _?_ (-1688, ae 21, Malden); b 1688; Charlestown

BLANCHARD, Joshua & 2/wf Mehitable _?_ (1666-1742, ae 76); b 1693; Charlestown

BLANCHARD, Nathaniel & Mehitable NOWELL; 16 Dec 1658 (prob wrong)

BLANCHER, Nathaniel & Susannah BATES, m/2 Thomas BASS 1680; 16 Dec 1658; Charlestown

BLANCHER, Nathaniel (1665-) & Dorothy [CAPEN] (1673-); b 1696; Weymouth/Braintree

BLANCHER, Richard & _?_ ; b 1673; Hartford

BLANCHARD/BLANCHART?, Richard & Elizabeth HUSSEY, m/2 Richard RANDALL 1705; 12 Jul 1686; York Co., ME

BLANCHARD, Samuel (1629-1707) & 1/wf Mary SWEETSER (-1669); 3 Jan 1654/5; Charlestown/ Andover

BLANCHARD, Samuel (1629-1707) & 2/wf Hannah DOGGETT (-1725); 23 Jun 1673, 24 Jun; Charlestown

BLANCHARD, Thomas (-1654) & 1/wf _?_ ; in Eng, b 1618; Charlestown

BLANCHARD, Thomas (-1654) & 2/wf Ann?/Agnes (BENT) BARNES (-1639), w Richard; in Eng, 15 May 1637; Charlestown/Sudbury/Braintree

BLANCHARD, Thomas (-1654) & 3/wf Mary _?_ (-1676); aft 1639; Charlestown

BLANCHARD, Thomas (-1651) & Ann [ROLFE] (1626-), dau Henry & Honour, m/2 Richard GARDENER 1651; ca 1645/7; Charlestown

BLANCHER, Thomas, Dunstable & 1/wf Tabitha LESSINGWELL (1661-1696), Woburn; 13 Feb 1689, 1688/9; Woburn

BLANCHARD, Thomas & 2/wf Ruth ADAMS (1673-); 4 Oct 1698; Dunstable

BLANCHARD, Thomas (-1759) & 1/wf Rose HOLMES (-1714, ae 40); 22 Mar 1698/9; Andover

BLANCHARD, William (-1652) & Ann/Hannah [EVERELL], m/2 George MANNING 1655; b 1645; Boston

BLANCHARD, _?_ & Ann _?_ (-1662, Chelmsford); b 1620; Salem

BLANCHARD, William & Jane [STEERE]; b 1701?

BLAND, John (alias SMITH) (-1667±) & 1/wf Isabel? _?_ & 2/wf? Joanna _?_ ; in Eng, b 1628; Edgartown

BLANDFORD, John (1611-1687) & 1/wf Mary _?_ (-Dec 1641); Sudbury

BLANDFORD, John (1611-1687) & 2/wf Dorothy WRIGHT, wid; 10 Mar 1642, 1641/2?; Sudbury

BLANDFORD, Stephen (1649-) & Susannah LONG; 9 Jun 1682; Sudbury

BLAYNFORD, Thomas & Elizabeth EAMES; 18 Dec 1673; Watertown/Framingham

BLANO, John & 1/wf Hanna KING; 11 Jul 1660; Lynn

BLANEY, John & Sarah (SALLIE) POWELL (-1694, ae 51), w John; 26 Jun 1672; Charlestown

BLANO/BLANEY, John & 2/wf Elizabeth (ANDREWS) (PIKE) PURCHIS/PURCHASE, w Richard, w Thomas; - Nov 1678; Lynn

BLANEY, John, Jr. (1661-) & Elizabeth (WILLIAMS)? PURCHASE, w Thomas?; 20 Dec 1683; Marblehead

BLANY, Joseph (1670-) & Abigail ANDREWS (1670-1765); 16 Jan 1693/4; Hingham/Lynn

BLANTON, William (-1662) & Phoebe _?_ ; b 1642; Boston

BLANDING, William & Bethia WHEATON (-1709); 4 Sep 1674; Rehoboth

BLASHFIELD/?BLASHFORD, Thomas (?1648-1714) & Abigail HIBERD/?HIBBARD/?HIBBERT (1655-1725); 28 Mar 1676; Beverly/North Yarmouth, ME

BLATCHFORD, Peter (?1625-1671) & Hannah (WILLEY) HUNGERFORD, w Thomas, m/3 Samuel SPENCER ca 1673; ca 1663?; New London, CT/Haddam, CT

BLATCHLEY, Aaron (-1699) & 1/wf Mary/Mercy DODD; Feb 1665; Guilford, CT

BLACHLEY, Aaron (-1699) & 2/wf Sarah (POTTER) [FOOTE], w Robert; ca 1686; Branford, CT/Newark, NJ

BLATCHLEY, Daniel (1676-) & Mehitable [EVARTS] (1678-); 10 Feb 1700; Guilford, CT

BLATCHLEY, Moses (1650-1693) & Susanna [BISHOP] (?1657-1729); b 1676, b 1678, b 1677[8?]; Guilford, CT

BLACHLEY, Samuel & Abigail FINCH; 6 Apr 1699; Stamford, CT

BLACHLEY, Thomas (-1674) & Susanna [BALL], m/2 Richard BRISTOW/?BRISTOL; b 1652? or 1653?, b 1650; New Haven/Branford, CT/Guilford, CT

BLETHEN/BLEVIN?, John (-1704/5) (ae 68 in 1692) & 1/wf Jane LEMARCOM/Jane MARKES; 10 May 1676, 10 May 1674; Salem

BLETSOE, Thomas & _?_ ; b 12 Jun 1696; Bristol, RI

BLIN, James & Margaret DENNISON; 6 Dec 1698; Boston

BLIN, Peter (1641-1725) & 1/wf Joanna _?_ ; b 1675; Wethersfield, CT

BLIN, Peter (1641-1725) & 2/wf Mary _?_ ; b 1686; Wethersfield, CT

BLINCO, Charles & Mary _?_ ; b 1680; Boston

BLINMAN, Richard (-Bristol, Eng) & Mary [TOMPSON] (wrong) (1619-) (Mary prob m Henry WISE 1641, Roxbury); b 1642 (doubtful); Glouchester/New London, CT/New Haven

BLISH, Abraham[1] (-1683) & 1/wf Anne [PRATT], dau of John; b 1641; Barnstable

BLISH, Abraham[1] (-1683) & 2/wf Hannah (WILLIAMS) [BARKER] (-1657/8), w John; b 1654; Barnstable

BLISH, Abraham[1] (-1683) & 3/wf Alice DERBEY, w John; 4 Jan 1658, 1658/9; Barnstable

BLISH, Abraham[2] (1654-) & 1/wf Martha [SHAW] (1655-1706); b 1683; Boston

BLISH, Joseph (1648-1730) & Hannah HULL (1657-1732); 15 Sep 1674; Barnstable

BLISS, Ephriam (1649-) & _?_ ; b 1673; Braintree/Quincy/Scituate/Rehoboth/Providence

BLISS, George (1591-1667) & _?_ ; b 1645; Lynn/Sandwich/Newport

BLISS, Isaac & _?_ ; ca 1695?

BLISS, John & Damaris ARNOLD (1648-1715); 24 Jan 1666; Newport

BLISS, John (-1702) & Patience BURT (1645-1732); 7 Oct 1667; Springfield/Northampton

BLISS, John (1669-) & Ann/Anna TERRY; 11 Jan 1693; Springfield

BLISS, Jonathan & Miriam (-1706); b 1649; Rehoboth

BLISS, Jonathan (-1719) & 1/wf Miriam CARPENTER (1674-); 23 Jun 1691; Rehoboth

BLISS, Lawrence & Lydia WRIGHT, m/2 John NORTON, m/3 John LAMB, m/4 George COLTON; 25 Oct 1654; Springfield

BLISS, Nathaniel (ca 1625-1654) & Catherine CHAPIN (1626-1712, 1712/13?), m/2 Thomas GILBERT, m/3 Samuel MARSHFIELD; 20 Nov 1646; Springfield

BLISS, Nathaniel (-1736) & Dorothy COLTON (-1733); 28 Dec 1676, no issue; Longmeadow

BLISS, Nathaniel (1671-1751?) & Mary WRIGHT (1676-); 3 Feb 1697; Springfield

BLISS, Pelatiah (1674-1747/8) & Elizabeth HITCHCOCK (1680-1756); 21 Apr 1698; Springfield

BLISS, Samuel (-1720) & Mary LENARD (1647-1724); 10 Nov 1665; Springfield

BLISS, Samuel (1647-1749) & Sarah STEBBINS (1654-1721); 2 Jan 1671; Springfield

BLISS, Samuel (-1729?) & Anne [ELDERKIN] (-1748); 8 Dec 1681; Norwich, CT

BLISS, Samuel (1660-1720) & Mary KENDRICK (1659-); 15 Apr 1685; Rehoboth

BLISS, Samuel & 1/wf Hannah STILES (-1704); 21 Jan 1687, 1686/7; Springfield

BLISS, Thomas (-1647) & 1/wf Dorothy WHEATLY; 22 Nov 1614, Daventry, Eng; Braintree/Rehoboth

BLISS, Thomas (-1651) & 1/wf _?_ ; Hartford

BLISS, Thomas (-1651) & 2/wf Margaret _?_ (-1684); Hartford

BLISS, Thomas (-1647) & 2/wf Ide _?_ ; ca 1645; Rehoboth

BLISS, Thomas & Elizabeth [?BIRCHARD]; latter end of Oct 1644; Norwich, CT/Saybrook

BLISS, Thomas & Hannah [CADWELL] (1677-); b 1699; Springfield

BLIVEN, Edward (-1718) & Isabella MACOONE (-1753); 2 Oct 1691; Westerly, RI

BLOGGETT, Benjamin (?1658-) & Mary PELLOT, Concord; 14 Feb 1683; Chelmsford

BLOGED, Daniel (1631-1672) & 1/wf Mary BUTTERFIELD (-1666); 15 Sep 1653; Chelmsford

BLOGGETT, Daniel (-1672) & 2/wf Sarah UNDERWOD/UNDERWOOD (?1642-); 10 Mar 1669; Chelmsford

BLODGHEAD, Jonathan & Mary ROWLANDSON; 7 Feb 1687/8; Amesbury

BLOCKED, Jonathan & Mary ROLENDSON, m/2 Samuel PRESTON; 7 Feb 1689; Salisbury

BLODGET, Nathaniel & Elizabeth WARREN; 17 Jul 1695; Chelmsford

BLODGETT, Samuel (1633-1693?, 1720) & Ruth EGGLESTON?/EGGLETON/IGGLEDON? (?1631-1703); 13 Dec 1655; Woburn

BLODGETT, Samuel (1658-1743) & Huldah SIMONDS (-1746); 30 Apr 1683; Woburn

BLOGGET, Thomas[1] (1604, 1605-1642, 1643, 1639?) & Susanna _?_ (-1666), m/2 James THOMPSON 1643/4; in Eng, b 1631; Cambridge

BLOGGETT, Thomas (1654-) & 1/wf Mary PERKIN/PARKHYRST (1657-); 29 Jun 1683; Chelmsford
BLODGETT, Thomas (1661-1740) & Rebecca TIDD (ca 1665-1750); 11 Nov 1685; Woburn
BLADGET, Thomas & 2/wf Mary DRUSE; 8 Jul 1696; Chelmsford
BLADGET, William & Mary WORIN/WARREN; 14 Jun 1696; Chelmsford
BLOOD, _?_ & Mercy BUTTERWORTH (1664-1711+); doubtful, see SLADE
BLOOD, James (?1605-1683) & Ellen/Eleanor _?_ (-1674); in Eng, ca 1626/30?; Concord
BLOD, James (-1692) & Hannah PURCHES/PURCHIS (-1677), Lynn; 26 Oct 1657; Concord
BLOOD, James & 1/wf Elizabeth LONGLEY (-Dec 1676); 7 Sep 1669; Groton/Lynn
BLOUD, James & ?2/wf Isabel ([FARMER]) WYMAN, w David, m/3 William GREEN 1695; 19 Nov 1679; Concord
BLOOD, James (-1692), Groton & 2/wf Abigail KEMP (1665-), Groton; 20 Dec 1686; Groton
BLOOD, Josiah (?1664-) & 1/wf Mary BARRET; 21 Mar 1687/8; Concord
BLOOD, Josiah & Mary TORY [THOMAS?]; 3 Feb 1690/1; Concord
BLOOD, Nathaniel (1650-) & Hannah [PARKER] (1647-1728); 13 Jun 1670; Chelmsford/Groton
BLOOD, Richard (-1683) & Isabel _?_ ; b 1648; Lynn/Groton
BLOD, Robert (-1701) & 1/wf Elizabeth WILLARD (ca 1633-1690); 8 Apr 1653; Concord
BLOOD, Robert (1660-) & Dorcas WHEELER; 12 May 1690; Concord
BLOOD, Robert, Sr. & 2/wf Hannah ?(JENKINS) (BALKE/BAUK?) PARKER (-1716), w Joseph; 8 Jun 1696, 8 Jan 1690; Concord/Chelmsford
BLOOMFIELD, John (-1640?) & _?_ ; b 1620?; Newbury
BLOOMFIELD/BLUMFORD, Robert & 1/wf Pricilla _?_ ; b 1669(70?); Boston
BLUMFORD/BLOOMFIELD?, Robert & 2/wf Elizabeth _?_ ; b 1674; Boston
BLOOMFIELD, Thomas (-1686) & Mary _?_ ; b 1642; Newbury/Woodbridge, NJ
BLOMFIELD, William (1604-) & 1/wf Sarah _?_ ; b 1633?; Cambridge/Hartford/etc.
BLOOMFIELD, William & 2/wf Isabel (_?_) [SACKETT], w Simon; aft 8 Feb 1636, bef 1645; Hartford/New London/etc.
BLOSS, Edmund (1587-) & 1/wf Mary _?_ (1599-1675); b 1623; Watertown
BLOSS/BLOYCE, Edmund & 2/wf Ruth PARSONS (-1711); 27 Sep 1675; Cambridge
BLOYCE, Francis/Frances?, wid? (-1646) & _?_ ; Cambridge
BLOSS/BLOIS?/BLOYCE, Richard (?1623-1665) & Michael/Mychall/Micael JENISON (-1713), m/2 John WARREN 1667; 10 Feb 1657, 1657/8; Watertown
BLOSSE, Richard (1659-), Watertown & Anne CUTLER (1669-), Cambridge; 26 Sep 1688; Cambridge/Watertown
BLOSSOM, Joseph (1673-) & 1/wf Mary PICHON (-1706); 17 Jun 1696; Barnstable
BLOSSOM, Peter (-1706) & Sarah BODFISH; 21 Jun 1663 (4 Jun is wrong); Barnstable
BLOSSOM, Thomas (-1632, 1633?) & Ann [HEJLSDON?/?EISDON] [?PALMER], m/2 Henry ROWLEY 1633; ca 1615?, ca 1620?, 10 Nov 1605; Leyden?/Plymouth
BLOSSOM, Thomas (-1650) & Sarah EWER (1629-); 18 Jun 1645; Barnstable
BLOSSOM, Thomas (1667-) & Fear ROBINSON; 3 Dec 1695; Sandwich
BLOTE/BLOTT, Robert (ca 1585-1665, 1665/6) & 1/wf _?_ ; ca 1617? & 2/wf? Susanna (_?_) BLACK (-1660), w John BLACK; in Eng, ca 1625/28?, aft 1635; Roxbury/Boston
BLOUNT/BLUNT, Samuel (1647-) & Anna FOSDICK (1653-1715, ae 62); 9 Jun 1680; Charlestown
BLUNT, William (?1643-1709) & 1/wf Elizabeth BALLARD (-1689); 11 Nov 1668; Andover/Chelmsford
BLUNT, William (?1643-1709) & 2/wf Sarah _?_ (-1701); aft 11 Jul 1689; Andover
BLUNT, William (1671-1738) & Sarah [?FOSTER] (1676-1760); b 1699; Andover
BLOWER, John (-1675) & Tabitha _?_ ; b 1654(5?); Boston
BLOWER, Pyam (-1709, ae 71) & Elizabeth BELCHER (1640-1709, ae 69); 31 Mar 1668; Cambridge
BLOWER, Thomas (1665-1699) & Elizabeth GRIDLEY, m/2 James TALBOT 1699, m/3 Thomas JEPSON 1708; 21 Sep 1693; Boston/Beverly
BLOWER, _?_ & _?_ BLOWER, Boston, m/2 John TILLY; 1640
BLOWER, Thomas (at Boston 1640) & Alice [FROST]; 1612
BLY, John (?1637-1709+) & Rebecka GOLT/GAULT (1643-); 11 Nov 1663; Salem
BLIGH, John, Jr. & _?_ ; b 1700; Boston/Salem

BLY, Samuel (?1659-1693) & Lois **IVERY/IVORY,** m/2 Ezekiel **ROGERS** 1694, m/3 Joseph **BASS** 1708; 19 Dec 1678; Lynn/Boston

BLIGH, Thomas & Dorothy _?_ ; b 1656; Boston

BLIGH, Thomas[2] (-1682?) & Sarah [**REYNOLDS**] (-1718), m/2 John **FOSDICK** ca 1683; ca 1680?, b 1684; Charlestown

BLIGH, Thomas & Elizabeth (**CLARK**) [**STEVENS**], w Erasmus; b 14 May 1687; Boston

BLIGH, Thomas (-1696) & Sarah **EVERTON,** w William; 10 Sep 1691; Charlestown

BLIGH, _?_ & Priscilla [**GERMAN**]; by 1692

BOAG/BOGUE?/BOOGE?, John & Rebecca [**WALKER/WAKELEE**]; b 4 Aug 1692; Haddam, CT

BOARDMAN, Aaron (1649-1703) & Mary [**HILLS**] (-1717+), dau Abraham; b 1674, b 1673?; Cambridge

BORDMAN, Andrew (-1687) & Ruth **BULL** (-1690); 15 Oct 1669; Cambridge

BORDMAN/BONDMAN, Andrew & Elizabeth **TRUESDELL/TRUESDALE;** 16 Dec 1697; Cambridge/Boston

BORMAN, Daniel & Hannah **HUTCHINSON** (1639-); 12 Apr 1662; Ipswich

BOARDMAN, Daniel (1658-1724/5) & Hannah **WRIGHT** (1664-1741), m/2 James **TREAT;** 8 Jun 1683; Wethersfield, CT

BOREMAN, Isaac (1643-1719) & Abiah [**KIMBERLY**] (1641-1723); b 1666; Wethersfield, CT

BOREMAN, Isaac (1666-1722) & Rebecca **BENTON;** 7 Dec 1699; Wethersfield, CT

BOARDMAN, Jacob (1671-) & 1/wf Martha (**SMITH**) **ROGERS** (1670-1740), w John; m int? 18 May 1699; Ipswich

BOREMAN, Jonathan (1661-1712) & Mercy **HUBBARD** (1664-); 12? Oct 1685, 22 Oct; Wethersfield, CT

BORMAN, Joseph & Prudence **FOSTER** (1675-); 17 Feb 1696/7; Topsfield

BOARDMAN, Joseph & Naomy **CHURCH;** May 1687; Hatfield

BORDMAN, Moses & Abigail **HASTINGS;** 25 Jul 1700, 25 Jun; Cambridge

BOREMAN/BOWMAN, Nathaniel (see **BOWMAN**) & Rebecca (**SMITH**) **SMITH,** div wf of Samuel; b 1669; Wethersfield

BOARDMAN, Affin & 1/wf Sarah **HEARD** (-1738); 28 Feb 1698, 1697/8; Ipswich

BOARDMAN, Samuel (1615-1673) & Mary [**BETTS**] (1623, 1621-1684); b 1642(3?); Ipswich/Wethersfield, CT

BOARDMAN, Samuel (1648-1720) & Sarah **STEELE** (1656-1723); 8 Feb 1682, [prob 1682/3]; Wethersfield, CT

BOARDMAN, Samuel (1668+-1732) & Mehitable **CADWELL** (1680-); 9 Nov 1696, 5? Nov; Wethersfield, CT

BOREMAN, Thomas (1601-1673) & Margaret [**OFFIN**] (-1679); London, 17 Aug 1630; Ipswich

BOARDMAN, Thomas & 1/wf Lucy _?_ (-1676); in Eng, b 1634; Yarmouth/Sandwich

BOWERMAN/BOURMAN, Thomas (-1679) (see **BOWERMAN**) & Hannah **ANNABLE** (?1622-); 10 Mar 1645, 3 Mar 1644, 1 Mar 1645, 1644/5; Barnstable

BORMAN, Thomas (1643-1719) & Elizabeth **PERKINS** (1649-); 1 Jan 1667, prob 1667/8; Ipswich

BOURMAN, Thomas (-1689) & 2/wf Elizabeth (**RYDER**) [**COLE**], w John; aft 20 Dec 1676, aft 1677; ?Yarmouth

BOARDMAN, Thomas & Mary **HARPER;** 9 Apr 1678; Barnstable

BOARDMAN, Thomas (1669-) & 1/wf Sarah [**LANGLEY**]; b 1698, b 1697?; Rowley/Ipswich

BOREMAN, Thomas (1671-) & Mary **CHITTENDEN** (1675-); May 1699, toward the latter end of the month; Wethersfield, CT

BORDMAN, William (1616-1685) & Frances _?_ (-1688+); [b 1640]; Cambridge/Watertown

BOARDMAN, William (1657-1696, Chelsea) & Sarah [**DEXTER**], w John, ?m/2 Daniel **HITCHINS** 1697; b 2 Apr 1684; Malden

BOARDMAN, _?_ (d in Eng) & Rebecca [?**WRIGHT**], m/2 Stephen **DAY** bef 1638; in Eng, b 1614; Cambridge

BOCKFORD, Elnathan & Elizabeth [**FLETCHER**]; Wethersfield, CT/Milford, CT

BODE, Henry (-1657) & Anne _?_ , m/2 Samuel **WINSLEY** 1657; b 1640?; Wells, ME

BODEE, John & Sarah **FREIND;** 16 Mar 1688/9; Marblehead

BODERITT, John & Jane _?_ ; b 1686; Boston

BODFISH, Joseph (1651-1744) & Elizabeth **BESSE** (1651/4-); - - 1674, ?Jun 1674; Barnstable

BODFISH, Robert (-1651) & Bridget _?_ , m/2 Samuel **HINKLEY** 1657; ca 1642?; Lynn/Sandwich

BODGE, Henry (-1694) & 1/wf Elizabeth _?_ (-by 1682?); b 1672, ca 1667; Kittery, ME

BODGE, Henry & 2/wf Rebecca (WILSON)? [BARNES], w Henry; by 1672?; Kittery, ME

BODGE, Henry (ca 1668-ca 1739) & Hannah [SWAIN] (-1765); ca 1700; Charlestown

BODINGTON/?BUDINGTON, Walter (-1713), Groton, CT & Johanne _?_; b 1704, b 1701?; Groton, CT/New London, CT

BODKYN, William & Mary _?_; b 1680; Boston

BODMAN, John & Sarah _?_; b 1645; Boston

BODMAN, Joseph (1653-1711) & 1/wf Hepzibah _?_ (-Jan 1685/6); Westfield

BODMAN, Joseph (1653-1711) & 2/wf Naomi CHURCH (1666-); 4 May 1687, 11 May; Hadley

BODMAN, Samuel & Mary _?_; b 1682; Boston

BODWELL, Henry (ca 1652-1745) & Bethia EMERY (1658-1725+, 1726+); 4 May 1681; Newbury/Andover/Haverhill

BOGLE, Alexander & 1/wf Margaret _?_ (-1662); b 1659; Boston

BOGLE, Alexander & 2/wf Sarah KING; 16 Jul 1662; Weymouth/Boston/Roxbury

BOWHONNO, John & Mary _?_; b 1658; Boston

BOLITHAR, Thomas & Mary RICHARDSON; 27 Jun 1698; Lynn

BOLLARD, Isaac & Sarah JONES, dau Thomas; 3 Jan 1654/5, 3 Jan 1659; Boston

BOLLS, Christopher (-1731) & Elizabeth _?_; b 1687; Ipswich

BOLLES, John (1677-1767) & 1/wf Sarah EDGECOMB (1678-); 3 Jul 1699; New London

BOLLES, Joseph (1608-1678) & Mary [HOWELLS?] (1624-); b 1641; Wells, ME

BOLLES, Joseph[2] (1654-1683) & Mary [CALL], m/2 Nathaniel LORD 1685; b 1674; Ipswich/Wells, ME

BOLLES, Samuel (1646-1723+) & Mary [DYER]; Sheepscot/Saco, ME/Rochester/Bridgewater

BOLLES, Thomas (1644-1727) & 1/wf Zapporah WHEELER (-1678); 1 Jul 1669, 13? Jul; ?New London

BOLLES, Thomas (1644-1727) & 2/wf Rebecca (WALLER) COLLINS (-1712); aft 6 Jun 1687, no issue; ?New London

BOLT, Francis (-1649) & Sarah _?_; Boston/Milford, CT

BOLT, John & Elizabeth CLEMMONS/CLEMENTS; 20 Nov 1694, 23 Nov 1694; Norwalk, CT/Stamford, CT

BOULTER, John (1672-) & Martha [JACKSON], m/2 Bryan DOOR, m/3 Philip TOWLE; b 1700; Hampton, NH

BOLTER, Nathaniel (1625-1693, 1695?) & Grace [SWAINE]; b 1648; Hampton, NH

BOLTER, Nathaniel (1653/4-1689) & Mary [DRAKE] (1658-), m/2 Richard SANBORN 1693; b 1688; Hampton, NH

BOLTER, Richard (-1679) & _?_; b 1640; Weymouth

BOLTER, Thomas (-1690) & 1/wf Experience ALDRIDGE/ALDRICH?; 16 Oct 1660; Weymouth

BOLTER, Thomas (-1690) & 2/wf Hannah/Joanna _?_ (-1715); b 1671(2?); Weymouth

BOLTEN, John (1660-) & Sarah CHESEBROUGH; 8 Mar 1683, 1682/3; Stonington, CT

BOLTON, Nicholas (-1683) & Elizabeth [LEMON?] (-1683+); b 1649; Dorchester

BOLTON, William (-1697) & 1/wf Jane BARTLETT (-1659); 16 Jan 1654, 1654/5; Newbury

BOLTON, William (-1697) & 2/wf Mary DENISON; 22 Nov 1659; Newbury

BOLTWOOD, Robert (-1684) & Mary _?_/Gernow RICE? (-1687); b 1650; Hartford/Hadley

BOLTWOOD, Samuel (-1704) & Sarah [LEWIS] (1652-1722); b 1672; Hadley/Farmington, CT/Deerfield

BONAMIE, Peter & Mary JOHNSON; 16 Aug 1700; Boston

BOND/BOWDE?, Grimstone & Elizabeth _?_; b 1683; Boston

BONDE, John (-1675) & Hester/Esther BLAKELY, m/2 John WILLIAMS 1675; 15 Aug 1649, 5 Aug; Newbury/Rowley/Haverhill

BOND, John (1652-1691) & Hannah COOLEDGE; 6 Aug 1679; Watertown

BOND, John (-1694) & Emma GRAVES/Amy? GROVES?, m/2 Benjamin HASKELL 1698; 23 Nov 1681; Beverly

BOND, Jonas[2] (1664-1727) & 1/wf Grace COOLIDGE (1664-11 Apr 1699); 1688/9, 29 Jan 1688, prob 1688-9; Watertown

BOND, Jonas (Joseph is wrong) (1664-1727) & 2/wf Elizabeth (JACKSON) PRENTICE (1658-1741), w John; 13 Nov 1699; Boston/Watertown

BOND, Joseph (1653-1725) & Sarah WILLIAMS (1662-1700+); 26 Nov 1679; Haverhill

BOND, Nathaniel (1660-1700) & Bethiah FULLER (1661-); 27 Feb 1684, 1684/5; Watertown

BOND, Nicholas (1619±-) & Jane (NORTON) [SIMPSON], w Henry; b 31 May 1650; ?York Co., ME
BOND, Nicholas (-1703) & Sarah ROWLANSON/ROWLANDSON, m/2 Abraham MERRELL; 5 Dec 1684; Salisbury
BOND, Robert (-1677) & Jan/Hannah [PLOMER?]; ca 1639-50?, b 1642, at East Hampton, 1658; Lynn/E. Hampton/Southampton, LI/Elizabeth, NJ
BOND, Thomas (1654-1704) & Sarah WOOLSON (ca 1661-1704+); 30 Sep 1680; Watertown
BOND, Thomas & Mary _?_; b 1687; Watertown
BOND, William[1] & 1/wf Sarah BISCOE (-1693); 7 Feb 1649, 1649/50, 1649-50; Watertown, CT
BOND, William (1650-) & Hepzibah HASTINGS (1664-); 2 Jun 1680; Watertown
BOND, William[1] (-1695) & 2/wf Elizabeth NEVINSON, w John; ca May 1695; Watertown
BOND, _?_ & Margaret _?_ (1631-1715+); York, ME/Portsmouth, NH
BONDFEILD, George & 1/wf Rebecca [BRADSTREET] (-1687); b 1665; Rowley/Marblehead
BONFIELD, George & 2/wf Ann FREED/FROED; 28 Sep 1690; Salem/Marblehead
BONHAM, George (-1704, ae 86 or 95) & ?2/wf Sarah MORTON (1618-1691); 20 Dec 1644; Plymouth
BONHAM, George (1657-1748) & Elizabeth JENNEY (1664-); 27 Apr 1681; Plymouth
BONHAM, Nicholas & Hannah FULLER; 1 Jan 1658, 1658/9; Barnstable/Piscataway, NJ
BONHAM/BENHAM, John & Margery _?_ (ALCOCK/ALCOTT), w Thomas, m Richard PRICHARD 1666/7; 1660?, 1659?; Charlestown
BONNELL, Nathaniel & Susanna WHITEHEAD; 3 Jan 1666; New Haven/Elizabeth, NJ
BONNELL, William & Ann [WILMOT]; New Haven
BONNER, John (-1726, ae 83) & 1/wf Rebecca [GREEN], w Richard; b 30 Jul 1672; Boston
BONNER, John (-1726) (went back to Eng?) & 2/wf Mary [CLARK] (-1697), dau Jonas; b 1686; Boston/Cambridge
BONNER, John & 3/wf Persis WENTON; 28 Sep 1699; Boston
BONEY, James (1672?-1724), m/2 Desire BILLINGTON & 1/wf Abigail BISHOP (1675-1714); 12 Jun 1695, 14 Jun 1695; Duxbury/Pembroke
BONNEY, John (1664-1745) & Elizabeth [?BISHOP] (?1673-1745); b 1690, 1689; Pembroke
BONNEY, Thomas (1604-1693) & 1/wf Mary [TERRY]?; ca 1643?; Duxbury
BONNEY, Thomas (1604-1693) & 2/wf Mary [HUNT]?; ca 1654?; Charlestown/Duxbury
BONNEY, Thomas (-1735) & 1/wf Dorcas SAMPSON; b 1684; Duxbury
BONEY, Thomas (-1735) & 2/wf Sarah STUDLEY; 18 Jul 1695; Duxbury
BONNEY, William (1667-) & 1/wf Anne/Ann [MAY]; b 1694; Plympton
BONNEY, William & 2/wf Mehitable KING; 11 Jul 1700; Plymouth
BONYOT, Peter & Elizabeth _?_; b 1686; Boston
BONYTHON, John (-1680) & Agnes _?_; b 1647; Saco, ME
BONYTHON, John (1647-) & [?Patience CRUCY]; b 1680; Saco, ME
BONYTHON, Richard (-bef 1653) & Lucretia [LEIGH]; in Eng, b 1610; Scarborough, ME/Saco, ME
BOOBYER, Christopher & Margaret PALMER, m/2 _?_ ANDREWS; 11 Aug 1700; Marblehead
BUBIER, Joseph & Joane [CODNER] (1655-); ca 1673?; ?Marblehead
BOOBIER, Joseph & 1/wf Rebecca PINSON, w William; 1 Jan 1697, 1696/7; Marblehead
BOODY/BOWDEY/BOWDEN/VOWDEN/BOWDOIN/BOODEY/BODEN?, Moses & Ruth WILTUM; 29 Nov 1697; Newbury/Dover, NH
BOOMER, Matthew (-1679+) & Eleanor _?_ (-1671+); b 1660?, b 1662; Newport
BOOMER, Matthew (-1744) & Hannah [CHURCH] (1668-); Freetown
BOMER, Thomas & Margaret _?_; b 1693; Boston
BOONE, Matthew & Anna _?_; b 1664; Cambridge
BOONE, Nicholas & Elizabeth [LINSFORD]; b 1678, b 1665?; Boston
BOONE, Robert (should be BEERES) & Elizabeth BULLOCK; 25 Jun 1673; Rehoboth
BOOSEY, James (-1649) & Alice _?_ (-1683), m/2 James WAKELEY; b 1630, b 1635; Wethersfield, CT
BOOSEY, Joseph (1634-1655) & Esther WARD?, m/2 Jehu[2] BURR (not John) b 24 May 1667, b 1660; b 24 Jul 1655; Wethersfield, CT
BOOTH, Abraham (1671-) & Abigail HOWLAND; m int 6-11-1700
BOOTH, Benjamin (1667-) & _?_; b 1693; Scituate

BOOTH, Charles & Abigail MAPHAM (HORTON adopted dau crossed out); ca 1690, ca 1688; Southold, LI

BOOTH, Ebenezer (1651-1732) & 1/wf ?Hannah _?_ ; ca 1673; Stratford, CT

BOOTH, Ebenezer (1651-1732) & 2/wf Elizabeth [JONES] (1665-1709); b 1686?, b 1687; Stratford, CT

BOOTH, Ephriam (1648-1683) & Mary OSBORNE (1653-1726), m/2 James BENNETT ca 1684; 9 Jun 1675; New Haven

BOOTH, George (-1682) & Alice [TEMPLE?] (1640?-), m/2 Michael SHAFFLIN; b 1674, b 1671; Lynn/Salem

BOOTH, George (-1694/5) & Elizabeth _?_ ; last of - Jun 1692; Salem

BOOTH, Humphrey & Rebecca SYMMES (1634-); b 9 Mar 1655/6, ?9 Jan 1656; Charlestown

BOOTH, James & Mary _?_ ; b 4 Mar 1696/7

BOOTH, John (-1689) & _?_ [GILES?]; b 1656?; Southold, LI

BOOTH, John & _?_ ; b 1657, b 1659; Scituate

BOOTH, John (1653-1717+) & Dorothy HAWLEY (1658-1710); Jun 1678, 14 Jun; Stratford, CT

BOOTH, John, Jr. (1661-) & Mary DODSON, m/2 Abraham BARDIN/BARDEN 1697; 12 Dec 1687; Scituate

BOOTH, John (-1707) & Hannah [HORTON]; b 1690; Southold, LI

BOOTH, Joseph (1656-1703) & 1/wf Hannah [WILCOXSON] (1665-1701); ca 1685, ca 1686; Stratford, CT

BOOTH, Joseph (1659-) & Mary [SUTTON], dau John; ca 1687; Scituate

BOOTH, Richard (1607-1688+) & Elizabeth [HAWLEY?]; b 1641; Stratford, CT

BOOTH, Robert (1602/5-1673, 1682?) & 1/wf _?_ ; in Eng, b 1627; Exeter, NH/Wells, ME

BOOTH, Robert (-1673) & 2/wf Deborah _?_ , m/2 Thomas LADBROOK ?1682; b 1655, b 1650; Exeter, ME/Saco, ME

BOOTH, Simon/Simeon (1641-1703) & 1/wf Rebecca FROST (-1688); 5 Jan 1663/4, 1663; Saco, ME/Enfield, CT/Hartford

BOOTH, Simon?/Simeon (-1703, Hartford) & Elizabeth (_?_) ELMER, w Samuel; 8 Dec 1693, 8 Sep; Enfield, CT

BOOTH, Thomas & Mary _?_ ; b 1698, b 1686; Southold, LI

BOOTH, Thomas & 1/wf Elizabeth JUDSON (-1702); 22 Jan 1700, 22 Jan 1700/1, 1700; Stratford, CT

BOOTH, Thomas & Elizabeth CONEY (1672-); b 1701?; Boston

BOOTH, Capt. William (1659-1723) & Hannah [KING] (1666-1742); 1688; Southold, LI/Sterling, LI/Orient, LI/Greenport

BOOTH, William (1664-1753) & Hannah (_?_) BURROUGHS (1658-1729), w John; 30 Aug 1693; Enfield, CT

BOOTH, Zachariah (ca 1666-1741) & 1/wf Mary WARRINER (1669-1692); 15 Jul 1692; ?Enfield, CT/Springfield

BOOTH, Zachariah (ca 1666-1741) & 2/wf Mary HARMON (1671-); 26 May 1696, 28 May; ?Enfield, CT/Springfield

BORDEN, Benjamin (1649-1718?) & Abigail GROVER; 22 Sep 1676; ?Gravesend/?Portsmouth, RI/Shrewsbury, NJ

BORDEN/BREEDEN, Bryant, Malden? & Elizabeth [LEWIS] (1642-); b 1668; Malden/Charlestown

BORDEN, Francis (1628-1703±) & Jane VICARS (-1703), Yorkshire; 12 Feb 1677, 12 4 mo-1677; Portsmouth, RI/Flushing, LI/Shrewsbury, NJ

BORDEN, John (1606?, 1608?-) & Joan _?_ (1612-); in Eng, b 1630; Boston/Stonington, CT/Lyme, CT

BORDEN, John (-1684) & Hannah HOUGH (1646-); 11 Feb 1662, 1661, 11 Jul 1661; New London, CT/Lyme, CT

BORDEN, John² (1640-1716) & Mary EARLE (1655-1734); 25 Dec 1670; Portsmouth, RI/Newport

BORDEN, John (-1709) & Marah/Mary _?_ ; 13 Mar 1689; Lyme, CT

BORDEN, John (1675-1719) & Sarah [?BROWNELL] (1681-), dau George; b 1700?; Swansea?

BORDEN, Joseph (1643-) & Hope _?_ ; b 1664; Portsmouth, RI/Bradford

BORDEN, Matthew (1638-1708) & Sarah CLAYTON (-1735, ae 81); 4 Mar 1674, [1673/4]; Portsmouth, RI

BORDEN, Matthew & Ann _?_ /[?Peace BRIGGS]; 1 Dec 1699; Newport

BORDEN, Richard[1] (1601?, 1596-1671) & Joan FOWLE (1609-1688); Headcorn/Hedcorn, Kent, 28 Sep 1625; Portsmouth, RI/Providence

BORDEN, Richard (1663-1724) & _?_ ; b 1687; Providence, RI

BORDEN, Richard (1671-) & Innocent [?CORNELL/WARDELL?/WODELL?] (1673-); b 1694, ca 1692?; Portsmouth, RI/Tiverton, RI

BORDEN, Samuel (1645-1716), Westchester, NY & Elizabeth CROSSE; 1 Jun 1679; Portsmouth,. RI/Westchester, NY/Monmouth, NJ

BORDEN, Thomas (1627-1676) & Mary HARRIS (-1718); 20 Jun 1664, 1663/4, ?20 Jan 1664, 20 Jan 1663/4; Providence

BORLAND, John (?1661-1727) & Sarah [NEAL]; b 1686, 23 Oct 1683; Boston

BOSS, Edward (-1724) & Susanna [WILKINSON] (1662-); b 1685(6?); Newport

BOSSINGER, Thomas & Mary _?_ ; b 1686; Boston

BASON, Joshua (1652-) & 1/wf Martha [BLACK]; b 1688, ca 1682?; Beverly

BASON/BASSON, Richard (-1716) & Elizabeth _?_ ; b 1675?; Boston

BASON/BASSON, Samuel (-1705) & Mary PICKWORTH; 25 Jun 1700, b 1640; Boston/Windsor, CT

BOASON, Walter (-1674) & Anne [DEVEREUX] (?1647-), m/2 _?_ NICHOLS; ?1667; Beverly

BOSSON, William & Dorothy [HOLBROOK?]; b 1695?; Boston/Roxbury, (dau Dorothy m Elias MONK, Jr. 15 Aug 1714)

BOSSON, _?_ & Mary [BRONSDON] (sister of Robert); Boston

BOSTON, Gideon & _?_ ; b 1689; Lynn

BOSTON, William, London & Cathrin/Catharine CROW, London; 3 Aug 1657; New London

BOSTWICK, Arthur (1603-ca 1680) & 1/wf Jane WHITTEL (1602-); St. Holger's Church Tarporley, Eng, 8 Jan 1627/8; Stratford, CT

BOSTWICK, Arthur (1603-) & 2/wf Ellen [TOMLINSON] (-1677), w Henry?; b 1658; Stratford, CT

BOSTWICK, John (1638-1689) & Mary [BRINSMEAD] (1640-1704?), m/2 John/Wm.? REED 1688+; ca 1665, ca 1666; Stratford, CT

BOSTWICK, John & Abigail [WALKER] (1672/3-); 1687; Stratford, CT/Derby, CT/New Milford, CT

BOSTWICK, Joseph & Ann BUSS (not BURR) (1675-), Concord; 14 Jun 1698; Stratford, CT/Derby, CT/New Milford, CT

BOSTWICK, Zachariah & 1/wf Elizabeth _?_ ; b 1692; Stratford, CT

BOSWORTH, Bellamy (1654-1718), Bristol, RI & Mary SMITH (1666-1740), Roxbury; 11 Nov 1685; Rehoboth/Bristol, RI

BOSWORTH, Benjamin (1615-) & 1/wf [?Mehitable] _?_ ; b 1638; Hingham/Hull

BOSWORTH, Benjamin (1647-1682) & Hannah MORTON; 27 Nov 1666; Plymouth

BOSWORTH, Benjamin (1615-) & 2/wf Beatrice (HAMPSON)? JOSLIN (-1712, ae 89), w Abraham; 16 Nov 1671; Lancaster/Stow

BOSWORTH, David (?1670, 1669-1747) & 1/wf Mercy STURTEVANT (1676-1707); 18 Aug 1698; Plymouth

BOSWORTH, Edward (-1634 on passage to N.E.) & Mary _?_ (-1648); in Eng, b 1611; Hingham

BOSWORTH, Edward (1659-1743) & 1/wf Mary _?_ ; b 1696(7?); Bristol, RI

BOSWORTH, Haniel/Hananiel (1615-1683) & Abigail [SCOTT] (1626-1698+, 1700+); ca 1648-52; Ipswich/Haverhill

BOSWORTH, Jabez (1673-1747) & Susanna _?_ (-1758); b 1701; Rehoboth

BOSWORTH, John (?1656-1725) & Sarah _?_ (1656-1735); b 1682/3; Hull/Bristol, RI

BOSWORTH, Jonathan & Elizabeth _?_ ; b 1632; Hingham/Cambridge

BOSWORTH, Jonathan (?1635-) & Hannah HOWLAND; 6 Jul 1661; Swansea

BOSWORTH, Joseph (-1694) & Esther SMITH (1661/2, 1661-); 10 Feb 1680, 1680/1?; Rehoboth

BOSWORTH, Joseph & Elizabeth (DORBY) [MILLER], w Paul; ca 1698; Hull

BOSWORTH, Nathaniel (1617-1690) & Bridget [BELLAMY], ?w _?_ LODNELL?; b 1647; Hingham/Bristol, RI

BOSWORTH, Nathaniel (1649-1693), Hull & 1/wf Elizabeth MORTON (1652-1673); 7 Dec 1670; Plymouth/Hull

BOSWORTH, Nathaniel (1649-1693) & 2/wf Mary [MORTON]; aft 6 Apr 1673, b 1676; Hull

BOSWORTH, Samuel & Mercy [BUMSTEAD] (1650-) ?m/2 John RALSTON/ROWLESTON; b 1670; Boston

BOSWORTH, Zaccheus/Zachariah (-1655) & Anne __?__ (-1681), m/2 Thomas **COOPER** 1656; b 1638; Boston
BOTSFORD, Elnathan (1641-1691) & 1/wf Elizabeth **FLETCHER** (1645-); 12 Dec 1665, 1664, 1666; Milford, CT
BOTSFORD, Elnathan (1641-1691) & 2/wf Hannah **BALDWIN** (-1706); 12 Dec 1667; Milford, CT
BOTSFORD, Henry (-1686) & Elizabeth __?__ ; b 4 Oct 1640; Milford, CT
BOTSFORD, Henry (1676-) & Christian **GUNN**, m/2 John **SMITH**, m/3 Solomon **FERRY**; 12 Nov 1700; Milford, CT
BOTSFORD, Samuel (1670-1745) & Hannah [**SMITH**] (-1732); b 1701?, 27 Jul; Milford, CT
BOTTS, Isaac (-1675) & Elizabeth [**FREETHY?**], m/2 Moses **SPENCER** 1679; b 1673; Kittery, ME/S. Berwick, ME
BUCHER, Alwin & Edith **BARNARD**; 15 Dec 1698; Boston
BOUCHER, Michael & Mary __?__ ; b 1693; Salem
BOUDESART/BUDESANT/BUDEZERT, John (-1672) & Agnes [**GRIFFIN**] (-1682), w Philip; b 1669; Salisbury
BOUGHTON/BOUTON, John[1] (1615-bef 1647) & [Alice] __?__ (1610-1680), m/2 Matthew **MARVIN** ca 1647; b 1636; Boston/Watertown/Hartford
BOUTON, John[2] (1636-1703) & 1/wf Abigail **MARVIN** (1640-1672, 1686+); 1 Jan 1656, 1656/7; Norwalk, CT
BOUTON, John[3] (1659-1705) & Mary [**HAYES**] (1667?-); b 1684?, b 1683, ca 1682?; Norwalk, CT/Danbury, CT
BOUTON, John[2] & Mary (_?_) (**ALLEN**) [**STEVENSON**], w Thomas, w Jonathan; aft Nov 1689; Fairfield, CT
BOUTON, Joseph[3] (1674-1747) & Mary [**GREGORY**]/**STEVENSON?** (1669-); b 1698?, b 1701?, 1685?; Norwalk, CT
BOUTON, Matthew[3] (1661-) (did he marry?) & __?__ ; b 1701?; Norwalk, CT/Danbury, CT
BOUTON, Richard[2] (?1639-1665) & Ruth [**TURNEY**] (1644-1666); b 1665; Fairfield, CT
BOULDERSON, James & Joanna **GREY**; 19 May 1698; Boston
BOULDERSON, William & Joanna __?__ ; b 1685; Boston
BOUNDS, Richard & Abigail **PRESCOTT**; 2 Nov 1699; Hampton, NH/Portsmouth, NH
BOUND, William & 1/wf Ann __?__ ; b 1636; Salem
BOUND, William & 2/wf Mary **HAVERLAD**; 12 Jul 1669; Lynn
BOURNE, Eleazer (1676-) & [Mercy] [**HATCH**]; b 1701?
BOURNE, Elisha (1641-1706) & Patience **SKIFFE** (-1718); 26 Oct 1675; Sandwich
BOURNE, Ezra (1676-1764) & Martha **PRINCE** (1678-); 27 Dec 1698; Sandwich
BOURNE, Henry (cousin of Thomas **RICHARD**) & Sarah __?__ ; b 1638; Scituate?/Barnstable?
BOURNE, Hezekiah (1675-) & Elizabeth [**TROWBRIDGE**]; b 1701?
BORNE, James & Mary **PROCTOR** (1650-); 3 Apr 1685; Chelmsford
BOURNE, Jared[1]/Garrett & 1/wf [Mary]/[Ann?] __?__ (-1644); b 1643; Boston/Roxbury/Portsmouth, RI
BOURNE, Jared[1] & 2/wf Frances __?__ ; b 1651; Boston/Swansea
BOURNE, Jared[2] (1651±-1718) & Elizabeth [**BRAYTON**] (-1718+); ca 1680?
BOURNE, Job & Ruhamah **HALLETT/HALLET** (-1722), m/2 William **HERSEY** b 1689; 14 Dec 1664; Sandwich
BOURNE, John & Mary [**CUMMINGS?**]; b 1645, 2 ch in 1644; Salem/Gloucester
BOURNE, John (-1684, Marshfield) & Alice/Ales/Allis **BESBEGE/BISBEE** (-1686); 18 Jul 1645; Marshfield
BORNE, John (-1707) & Hanna **BACON**; Oct 1677; Middletown, CT
BURNE, John & Deborah **WHITE**; 13 Jul 1695; Boston
BOARNE, John & Joanna (**DORE**) **CANE/KEEN**, m/3 Stephen **KNOWLES**; Portsmouth, NH
BOURNE, Meletiah (1673/4-1742) & 1/wf Desire **CHIPMAN** (1673/4-1705); 23 Feb 1692/3; Sandwich
BOURNE, Nathan (1676-1749) & Mary **BASSET** (1676-); 3 Feb 1698; Sandwich
BOURNE, Nehemiah & Hannah __?__ ; by 1638?, b 1639; Charlestown/Boston/Dorches ter
BOURNE, Richard & 1/wf ?Bathsheba [?**BARTLETT**]/[?**HALLETT**]; b 1636; Lynn/Sandwich
BOURNE, Richard (-1682) & 2/wf Ruth (**SARGENT**) **WINSLOW** (1642-1715), w Jonathan, m/3 John **CHIPMAN** 1684; 2 Jul 1677; Sandwich
BOURNE, Shearjashub (1643-1719) & Bathsheba [**SHIFF**] (1648-); b 1667?, 1673?; Sandwich

BOURNE, Shearjashub & _?_ ; b 1698; Sandwich
BOURNE, Thomas (1581-1664) & Elizabeth _?_ (1590-18 Jul 1660, ae 70); in Eng, b 1614?, 1613?, ca 1615?; Marshfield
BOURNE, Thomas (1581-1664, ae 83) & 2/wf Martha _?_ ; aft 18 Jul 1660, bef 2 May 1664; Marshfield
BOURNE, Thomas (?1647-) & 1/wf Elizabeth ROWSE/ROUSE (-1701); 18 Apr 1681; Marshfield
BOURNE, Timothy (1666-1744) & Temperance [SWIFT] (ca 1666-); b 1690?; Sandwich
BOUTWELL/BOUTELLE?/BOWTELL, Henry & Elizabeth (WORTHINGTON) BOWERS, w George; 25 Jun 1657; Cambridge
BOUTWELL, James[1] (-1651) & 1/wf? ?Mary/Alice _?_ (-1651+), ?m/2 William COWDREY 1666 ?or Peter PALFREY?; b 1638?, b 1640?; Charlestown/Lynn
BOUTELL/BOUTWELL, James[2] (1642-1716) & Rebecca KENDELL (1645-1713, ae 68); 15 Jun 1665, ?15 Jul; Reading
BOUTWELL, James (1666-1714) & Elizabeth [FROTHINGHAM] (1674-), m/2 Benjamin SWAIN; 20 Jan 1690/1; Reading
BOUTELL, James (1677-) & Abigail STIMSON (1673-1733+); 13 Mar 1699; Reading
BOUTELL, John (-1676, ae 60) & Margaret _?_ ; b 1646; Cambridge
BOUTWELL, John[2] (-1719) & Hannah [DAVIS], dau George; 10 May 1669; Reading
BOUTELL, John & Sarah BURNAP, Reading; 9 Feb 1692/3; Reading
BOUTWELL, John (1671-1713) & Grace EATON (1677-1756), m/2 Josiah HODGMAN 1724; 8 Oct 1695; Reading
BOUTELL, Thomas (1669-) & Abigail [EDWARDS]; 11 Nov 1691; Reading
BOW, Alexander (-1678) & 1/wf Sarah _?_ (-1665); b 1659; Charlestown/Hartford/Middletown, CT
BOW, Alexander (-1678) & 2/wf Rebecca HUGHS/HOUSE/HUSE (-1684), m/2 Thomas FORMAN 1679; 26 Nov 1673; Middletown, CT
BOW, Samuel (1659-1742) & Mary TURNER (-1747); 9 May 1683; Middletown, CT
BOWD, Joseph & Elizabeth _?_ ; b 1657; Boston
BOWDE/BOND?, Grimstone & Elizabeth _?_ ; b 1683; Boston
BOWDITCH, John (-1718) & Temperance [FRENCH] (1651-1720); b 1683; Braintree
BOWDITCH, Nathaniel (1643-) & _?_ ; ?Newport, RI
BOWDISH/BOWDITCH, William[1] (-1681) & Sarah _?_ ; b 1641, ?1631; Salem
BOWDITCH, William[2?] (-1681) & Sarah [BEAR]; 15 Sep 1663, b 1663, in Eng; Salem
BOWDIGE, William[3] (1663, 1665?-1728) & Mary GARDNER; 30 Aug 1688; Salem
BOADEN, Ambrose (1589-1675) & Marie LETHEBRIDGE; Holberton, Devon., 28 Jan 1624/5; Scarboro, ME
BOADIN, Ambrose (?1632-) & Mary _?_ ; ca 1652?; Scarboro, ME
BODEN, Ambrose (1666-) & Lydia SHELDON (1666?-1746); 14 Dec 1693; Salem
BOWDEN, Benjamin & _?_ ; b 1677; New Haven
BOWDEN, John (-1697, Boston) & Grace BULLY (-1710, ae 74 y); 6 Aug 1656; Saco, ME/Boston
BOWDEN, John & Agnes _?_ ; b 1670; Boston
BOWDEN, John (1655-) & 1/wf _?_ [SIMPSON]; b 1699, b 1685; Scarboro, ME
BODIN, Jonathan & Susanna NICHOLSON; 21 Oct 1697; Marblehead
BAUDEN, Michael & Sarah NURSE (1632-); 15 Dec 1669; Topsfield
BOWDEN, Mychall & Sarah DAVES/DAVIS; m int 20 Nov 1697; Lynn
BOWDOIN/BAUDOUIN, Pierre/Peter (-1706, 1719?) (see BALDWIN) & Elizabeth _?_ (1643-1720); in France, b 1676, b 1666?; Casco Bay, ME
BOUDEN, Peter & Mary _?_ ; b 1694; Boston
BOWDEN, Richard & Martha [BLAISDELL], m/2 [Thomas?] SELLEY/John? RICHARD, m/3 John CLOUGH 1686; b 1661; Boston/Isles of Shoals
BOWEN, Daniel & _?_ ; b 1699; RI
BOWEN, Griffin[1]/Griffith? & ?1/wf Mary [?RIFEL]; Wales
BOWEN, Griffin[1] (-1675) & ?2/wf Margaret [FLEMING]; Wales, ca 1627?, ca 1633?; Boston/Roxbury/London
BOWEN, Henry (1633-) & Elizabeth JOHNSON (-1701); 20 Dec 1658; Roxbury/Woodstock, CT
BOWEN, Henry & Susannah (KING)/BARKER? HEATH, w Peleg; 14 Apr 1686, 1684; Roxbury
BOWEN, Isaac (1676-) & 1/wf Hannah [WINCHESTER]; ca 1698, ca 1699; Roxbury/Framingham
BOWEN, John & Hannah DIXCY; 2 Dec 1680; Marblehead

BOWEN, John (1662-1718) & Hannah [BREWER] (1665-1721+); ca 1695; ?Springfield/Roxbury
BOWEN, John & Elizabeth BUCKETT/BRACKETT (1671-); 12 Sep 1700; Rehoboth
BOWEN, John & Elizabeth [ROUNDS?]; b 1689; Rehoboth
BOWEN, Josiah (-1703) & Susannah CLARKE, m/2 Samuel CURTIS; 9 Nov 1694; Wethersfield, CT
BOWEN, Obidiah (1627-1710) & Mary CLIFTON (-1697); b 1651; Rehoboth
BOWEN, Obidiah & Abigail BULLOCK; 25 Jul 1677; Swansea
BOWEN, Richard¹ (-1674/5) & 1/wf Ann [?BORN]; Eng or Wales, b 1627, b 1622; Rehoboth
BOWEN, Richard¹ (-1675) & 2/wf Elizabeth MARSH (-1675+, 1675?), w George; Weymouth, Nov 1648; Hingham
BOWEN, Richard² & 1/wf Ester SUTTON (ca 1626-); 4 Mar 1656, 1646, 1656; Rehoboth
BOWEN, Richard & Mercy/Mary TITUS (1665-); 9 Jan 1683; Rehoboth
BOWEN, Richard & 2/wf Martha (ALLEN) SABIN/SABEN, w William; 20 Jan 1689/90; Rehoboth
BOWEN, Richard & Patience PECK (1669-); 28 Feb 1690/1; Rehoboth
BOWEN, Samuel & Elizabeth [?WHEATON], w Samuel; 26 May 1684; Swansea/Rehoboth/Bristol, RI
BOWEN, Thomas (1622-1674+) & Elizabeth ? (1628?-); ca 1646/52?, b 10 Dec 1646; Salem/Marblehead
BOWEN, Thomas (-1663) & Elizabeth [NICHOLS] (-1713), m/2 Samuel FULLER b 1669, ca 1665, (see John PRENTICE & Hester ?); b 1660, ca 1656?; New London, CT/Rehoboth
BOWEN, Thomas & Sarah ? ; b 1685; Roxbury
BOWEN, Thomas (-1743) & Thankful MASON (1672-); 17 Jun 1689; Swansea/Rehoboth
BOWEN, William & Mary ? ; b 1699; Boston
BOURMAN, Thomas & Hannah ANNABLE; 10 Mar 1645; Barnstable
BOWERMAN, Tristum (1661-) & Ann HOOPER; 28 Jul 1685; Britol, RI
BOWERS, Benanuel (-1698) & Elizabeth DUNSTER (1632, 1637-); 9 Dec 1653, 1654; Cambridge
BOWERS, George (-1656) & 1/wf Barbara SMITH (-1644); Braithwell, Eng, 9 Feb 1614/15; Scituate/Plymouth/Cambridge
BOWERS, George (-1656) & 2/wf Elizabeth WORTHINGTON, m/2 Henry BOUTWELL 1657; 15 Apr 1649; Cambridge
BOWERS, George (1654-1689) & Priscilla KITCHEN [HUNN] (1647-), m/3 John CURTIS 1689, m/4 John GILBERT; b 1686; Charlestown/Kent Co., RI/Groton
BOWERS, Jerathmeel (1650-1721) & Elizabeth ? ; b 1674; Billerica/Chelmsford/Groton
BOWERS, John & Mary ? ; ca 1650, b 1654; Medfield
BOWERS, Rev. John (-1687) & ?1/wf Rebecca [GRIGSON]; b 1657; New Haven/Derby, CT
BOWERS, John & Sarah [DOWD], dau Henry; ?; ?Guilford, CT
BOWERS, Rev. John (-1687) & ?2/wf Bridget [THOMPSON] (1636-1720), ?m/2 William HOADLEY; ca 1660/2?, b 1667; New Haven/Guilford, CT/Derby, CT
BOWERS, John & Judith (FESKE) (PALMER) FERRES, w William, w Jeffery; aft 31 May 1666, bef 9 Mar 1666/7; ?Greenwich, CT
BOWERS, John (-1676) & Sarah CLARKE (1651-), m/2 Samuel SMITH 1677; 7 Jan 1673/4; Medfield
BOWERS, John & Susanna ? ; b 1676, had Robert; Boston
BOWERS, John (-1695?, 1690) & Hannah (CLOSE) KNAPP (ca 1632-1696, 1694?), w Joshua; aft 27 Oct 1684; Stamford, CT/Greenwich, CT
BOWER, Jonas (-1671) & 2/wf Hannah [HILDRETH], w Thomas; aft 1657; Southampton, LI
BOWER, Jonah & Ruth HOWELL; 12 Apr 1686; Southampton, LI
BOWERS, Jonathan (1673-) & Anne/Anna? SYLVESTER; m int 11 Feb 1695/6; Boston/Charlestown/Taunton
BOWERS, Jonathan & Hannah BARETT/BARRETT (1686-1763); 17 May 1699; Chelmsford
BOWER, Nathaniel (-1712) & Deborah ? (-1712, Derby, CT); ca 1696/1700?; Rye, NY/Greenwich, CT/Derby, CT/Newark, NJ
BOWERS, Samuel (1665-1744) & 1/wf Ruth WOOSTER (1668-); [1687]; Derby, CT
BOWER, Samuel & 2/wf Lydia FRENCH (1670-); 4 Nov 1691; Derby, CT
BOWES, Nicholas (1656-1721) & 1/wf Sarah HUBBARD (1662-1688); 26 Jun 1684; Cambridge
BOWES, Nicholas (1656-1721) & 2/wf Dorcas CHAMPNEY; 6 May 1690; Cambridge/Boston
BOWES, Thomas & Sarah BOWES; 21 Jun 1697; Boston

BOWKER, Edmund[1] (1619-1666) & 1/wf? 2/wf Margaret _?_/Elizabeth SMITH?/Mary POTTER?, ?m/2 Thomas HOLBROOK 1669?; b 1647; Dorchester/Sudbury

BOWKER, Edmund (?1661-1706) & Sarah PARMENTER; 29 Mar 1688; Sudbury

BOWKER, James (see SMALL)

BOWKER, James[2] (-1724) & [Mary] _?_ (1665-1733+); b 1684; Scituate

BUNKER/BOWKER, John (-1721, ae 74) & Mary HOWE (1659-1723); 8 Jan 1678; Marlborough

BOWLES, John[1] (-1680) & 1/wf Dorothy [BIDLE] (-Nov 1649); Roxbury

BOWLES, John[1] & 2/wf Elizabeth HEATH (-6 Jul 1655); 2 Apr 1649, [1650]; Roxbury

BOWLES, John[1] (-1680) & 3/wf Sarah (?HOWE) (SIBLEY) [CHICKERING] (-1686), w John, w Francis; aft 2 Oct 1658; Charlestown

BOWLES, John[2] (1653-1691) & Sarah ELLIOT (1662-1687); 16 Nov 1681; Roxbury

BOWMAN, Francis (-1687) & Martha SHERMAN (1641-); 26 Sep 1661; Watertown, CT

BOWMAN, Francis (1662-1744) (had dau Lydia b 4 Apr 1685) & Lydia STONE; 26 Jun 1684, 26 Jul 1684; Watertown

BOMAN, Henry & Mary [TILTON] (1654-); ?Gravesend, LI

BOWMAN, John & _?_; b 1676; Portsmouth, NH

BOWMAN, Joseph (1674-1762) & Phebe [BARNARD] (1673-1757); b 1697; Cambridge

BOWMAN, Nathaniel[1] (-1682) & Anna/Anne _?_; b 1630; Watertown

BOWMAN, Nathaniel (1669-1748) & Anna/Anne? BARNARD (1670-1757); 16 Dec 1692; Cambridge

BOWMAN, Samuel (1679-) & Rebecca ANDREWS (-1713); 21 Nov 1700; Cambridge/Lexington/ Charlestown

BOWMAN/BOARDMAN/BOREMAN, ?Nathaniel (1641-1707) & Rebecca (SMITH) [SMITH] (ca 1631-), div; by 1669; Wethersfield, CT

BOWNE, Andrew (1638-1708) (brother-in-law of John HAYNE) & Elizabeth [HAYNE]?; ?Gravesend, LI/NY/Middletown, NJ

BOWNE, James & Mary STOUT; 26 Dec 1665, ?NJ; Gravesend/NY/Middletown, NJ

BOWNE, John (1627-20 Dec 1695) & 1/wf Hannah FEAHE (?1637-31 Jan 1677/8, funeral 2 Feb 1677/8); 7 May 1656; Flushing, LI

BOWNE, John (-1684), Middletown, NJ, & Lydia [HOLMES]; ca 1663; ?Newport/Gravesend, LI

BOWNE, John (1627-) & 2/wf Hannah BICKERSTAFF (-7 Jun 1690); 2 Feb 1679/80; Flushing, LI

BOWNE, John (1627-) & 3/wf Mary COCKE (1656-); 26 Jun 1693; Flushing, LI

BOWEN, Philip (1640) & _?_; (doubtful); Flushing, LI

BOWEN, Samuel (1667-) & 1/wf Mary BECKET (-1707); 4 Aug 1691; Flushing, LI

BOWNE, Thomas (1595-1677) & _?_; ?Matlock, Eng, b 1627; Boston/Flushing, LI

BOWNE, William & ?Ann _?_; b 1631; Salem/?Gravesend, LI/NJ

BOWRY/BOWREY, Jacob & Sarah _?_; 1670; Boston

BOYCE, Antipas (-1669) & Hannah HILL; 24 Jan 1659/60, returned to Eng 1659/60; Boston

BOYCE, Benjamin[3] (?1674-1767) & 1/wf Mary ALLEN (-1703); 20 Oct 1699; Lynn

BOYES, John & Mary _?_; b 1686; Boston

BOYCE, Joseph[1] (1608-1695) & Eleanor _?_ (-1694+); ca 1637; Salem

BOYCE, Joseph[2] (1644-1716+) & Sarah MEACHUM/MEACHAM (?1646-); 4 Feb 1667/8; Salem

BOYCE, Joseph[3] (1673-1723) & Rebecca (TRASK) POTTER (1674-1739+), w Samuel, m/3 Benjamin VERY; b 1695, b 1695(6?); Salem

BOYS, Matthew (1611-) & Elizabeth _?_; b 1640, returned to Eng; Roxbury/Rowley

BOYES, Richard (-1678) & _?_; b 1674

BOYES, Samuel (-1700) & _?_; b 1666(7?); Milford, CT

BOYES, Samuel (1635-1683) & Lydia BEAMAN (1644-1734), m/2 Alexander PYGAN 1684; 3 Feb 1667, 1667/8; Saybrook, CT

BOYDEN, Jonathan (1652-1732) & 1/wf Marie/Mary CLARK (1649-); 26 Sep 1673; Medfield

BOYDEN, Jonathan & Rachel FISHER; 17 Nov 1698; Medfield

BOYDEN, Jonathan (1675-1749) & 1/wf Elizabeth [LAKIN]; b 1701; Groton

BOYDEN, Thomas[1] (?1613, 1614-1682+) & 1/wf Frances _?_ (-17 Mar 1658, [1657/8]); b 1639; Watertown/Boston/Medfield/etc.

BOYDEN, Thomas[1] (-1682+) & 2/wf Hannah/Anne? (PHILLIPS) MORSE (1616-1676), w Joseph; 3 Nov 1658; Boston

BOYDEN, Thomas[2] (1639-1719) & Martha [HOLDEN] (1646-1687); b 1667; Woburn/Groton/etc.

BOYEN, Henry & Frances GILL; 17 Oct 1656; Boston

BOYER, Simon & Johanna __?__, m/2 George MUNNINGS by 1657, m/3 John LAUGHTON 1659; Boston

BOYKIM, Jarvis & Isabel __?__ (-1673); ?Charington, Eng, b 1641; New Haven

BOYLE/BOYLES, Samuel & Sarah __?__ ; b 1695; Boston

BOYLSTON, Edward & Mary [DASSET], m/2 Josiah FLINT; 27 May 1695; Boston/Watertown

BOYLSTON, Richard (1670±-1752) & Mary (FOSTER) [SMITH] (1678-1764), w James; b 1699; Charlestown

BOYLSTON, Thomas[1] (1615-1653) & Sarah __?__ (-1704), m/2 John CHINERY 1655/[6], 1654/5?; b 1640; Watertown

BOYLSTON, Thomas[2] (1645-1696) & Mary GARDNER (1648-1722); 13 Dec 1665; Charlestown/Roxbury

BOYNTON, Caleb & Mary MOORES (1648-); 24 Jun 1672; Newbury/Ipswich/Salisbury

BOYNTON, Caleb (-1708) & Hannah HARRIMAN; 26 May 1674; Rowley

BOYNTON, John (1614-1671) & Ellen/Eleanor [PELL], Boston, m/2 Maxmilian JEWETT 1671, m/3 Daniel WARNER 1686; b 1644; Rowley/Salisbury

BOYNTON, John & 1/wf Hannah KEIES/KEYES (-1717); 8 Mar 1675; Rowley

BOYNTON, Joseph (1645-1730) & 1/wf Sarah SWAN (1646-1718); 13 May 1669; Rowley/Groton

BOYNTON, Joseph (1675-1755) & Bridget HARRIS (1672-1757); 30 Jan 1692/3; Rowley

BOYNTON, Joshua & 1/wf Hannah BURNET/BARNETT?/BARNEY? (-1722); 9 Apr 1678; Newbury

BOYNTON, Samuel & Hannah SWITCHER (-1718); 17 Feb 1686; Rowley

BOYNTON, William & Elizabeth [JACKSON?] (-1687); b 1640; Rowley

BRABROOK, John (-1654) (nephew of Henry SHORT) & Elizabeth [?SHORT]; b 1640; Watertown

BRABROOK, Joseph & Sarah GRAVES/LEWIS; 23 Apr 1672; Concord

BRABROOK, Joseph (-1719) & Sarah (PARLIN) TEMPLE (1668-), w Richard; 29 Aug 1698; Concord

BRABROOK, Richard (?1613-1681) (uncle of John BAYER/BADGER 1669) & Joanna __?__, m/2 Thomas PENNY 1682; b 1653; Ipswich

BRABROOK, Samuel (-1722) (had son-in-law Jeremiah WATTS 1680) & Mary [WATTS]?, ?wid?_; ?1680; Salem

BRABROOK, Thomas (1643-1692) & Abigail TEMPEL/TEMPLE; 3 Mar 1669, 1668/9; Concord

BRABROOK, __?__ & Ann __?__ (-1648); Roxbury

BRACKENBURY, John & Emma/Amy? ANDERSON (-1703), m/2 Joseph LYNDE 1679?; 17 Jul 1655; Charlestown/Boston

BRACKENBURY, John (1657-) & Dorcas GREENE (1665-1682); 10 Aug 1681; Charlestown

BRACKENBURY, Richard (1600, 1602?-1685) & Ellen __?__ ; b 1632; Salem/Beverly

BRACKENBURY, Samuel (1646-1677/8) & Mercy [WIGGLESWORTH] (1655-1728), m/2 Samuel BELCHER; b 1674, b 1673; Charlestown/Boston/Malden

BRACKENBURY, Samuel (1673-1702) & Ann CHICKERING (1671-1702); 22 Oct 1694; Charlestown

BRACKENBURY, William (1602-1668) & 1/wf ?2/wf ?Ann/Alice __?__ (-1670 or 1671, ?ae 70); ca 1630, b 1629; Charlestown/Malden

BRACKETT, Anthony[1] (1613±-) & __?__ ; b 1638; Portsmouth, NH/Exeter, NH/Casco?

BRACKETT, Anthony[2] (1638, 1636±-1689) & 1/wf Anne [MILTEN] (-ca 1677); b 1668; Hampton, NH

BRACKETT, Anthony[2] (1638-1689) & 2/wf Susanna DRAKE (?1652-1719), m/2 John TAYLOR 1700; 9 Nov 1678, ?Sep 1679, 19? Nov; Hampton/Falmouth, ME?

BRACKETT, Anthony[3] (1669-1716) & Mary __?__, m/2 Richard PEIRCE; 1699; Hampton, NH

BRACKETT, James (1646-1718) & Sarah [MARSH] (1649-1727); b 1669; Boston/Braintree

BRACKET, John (1637-1686) & 1/wf Hannah FRENCH (1643-1674); 6 Sep 1661, 7 Sep 1661, 6-7-1661 at Braintree; Billerica, CT/Braintree

BRACKETT, John (-1667) (son Peter) & Sarah STEDMAN (1644-1730), m/2 Samuel ALCOCK 1668, m/3 Thomas GRAVES 1682, m/4 John PHILLIPS 1701; 23 Aug 1662; Cambridge

BRACKETT, John (?1645-) & 1/wf Martha [PHILBROOK/PHILBRACK] (1651-); ca 1670?; Portsmouth, NH/Greenland, NH/Rye

BRACKETT, John (-1686) & 2/wf Ruth (MORSE) ELLICE/[ELLIS] (1637-), w Joseph; 31 Mar 1675, 3 Mar?; Billerica

BRACKETT, John (?1645-), Rye, NH & 2/wf Dinah (SANBORN) [MARSTON], w James; 24 Nov 1698; NH
BRACKETT, Joshua (?1671-1749) & Mary [WEEKS] (1676-); b 1700; ?13 Oct 1726; Portland/?Greenland, NH
BRACKET, Josiah & Elizabeth WALDO; 4 Feb 1672, 1672/3; Billerica/Chelmsford
BRACKETT, Peter[1] (1609-) & 1/wf? 2/wf? Priscilla _?_; ca 1634?; Braintree
BRACKETT, Peter (1637-) (son Richard) & 1/wf Elizabeth BOSWORTH (1638-1686); 6 Sep 1661; Braintree
BRACKETT, Peter[1] (1609-) & 2/wf Mary [WILLIAMS], w Nathaniel d 1662; bef 30 Jan 1667, b 1663; ?Braintree
BRACKET, Peter (1637-), Billerica (son Richard) & 2/wf Sarah (PARKER) FOSTER (-1718), w Thomas; 16 Mar 1686/7, 30 Mar 1687; Billerica/Cambridge
BRACHETT, Richard[1] (1611-1691, ae 80, 1690/1, 1690) (ae 56 in 1668) & Alice _?_ (1614-1690, ae 76); in Eng, ca 1633; Boston/Braintree
BRACKETT, Samuel (1672-), Berwick & Elizabeth BOTTS (1673-1753); 20 Nov 1694, 25? Nov; Kittery, ME
BRACKETT, Thomas & 2/wf? [Alice] [?WARD] (-1690); b 1645; Salem
BRACHETT, Thomas (?1636-1676) & Mary [MILTON]; b 1671; Falmouth, ME/Casco Bay
BRACY, John (?1659, 1647-1709) & Anne (GRANT?)/(PEARCE) [CARMICHAEL], w John; ca 1677; York, ME
BRACY/BRACE?, Stephen (-1692) & Elizabeth _?_; ca 1666; Swansea/Hartford
BRACY, Thomas (1601-) & 1/wf Hannah HART; in Eng, m lic 30 Jan 1626/7; New Haven
BRACY, Thomas (1601-) & 2/wf Phebe BISBY, m Samuel MARTIN bef 1646; in Eng, 4 Aug 1631; New Haven
BRACY, Thomas & Mary [OSBORN]; 20 Mar 1672, 1672/3; Hatfield
BRACY, William & 1/wf Mary MARSTON; 30 Oct 1699; Hampton, NH
BRADBURY, Jacob (1677-1718) & Elizabeth STOCKMAN, m/2 John STEVENS; 6 Jul 1698; Salisbury
BRADBURY, Thomas[1] (1610-1695) & Mary [PERKINS] (1615?, 1620-1700); b 1637, ?May 1636; Salisbury
BRADBURY, Thomas (1674-) & 1/wf Jemima TRUE (-1700); 30 Oct 1700; Salisbury
BRADBURY, William (1649-1678) & Rebecca (WHEELWRIGHT) MAVERICK (-1678, 1679?), w Samuel; 12 Mar 1671/2; Salisbury
BRADBURY, William (1672-) & Sarah COTTON (1670-); m int 16 Mar 1695/6; Salisbury
BRADBURY, Wymond & Sarah PIKE (1641/2-), m/2 John STOCKMAN 1671; 7 May 1661; Salisbury
BRADBURY, Wymond (1669-1734) & Maria [COTTON] (1672-), m/2 John HEARD; b 1693; Salisbury/York, ME
BRADDICK/BRADDOCK, John & Mary _?_; in Eng, b 1700 (not in 1698 Census); Southold, LI
BRADFIELD, Lesly (-1655) & Mary _?_, m/2 George ADAMS 1657; b 1645; Wethersfield, CT/Branford, CT
BRADFIELD, Samuel & Sarah GRAVES (1656-); 27 Jun 1677; Branford, CT
BRADFORD, Alexander & Sarah [MERRY?]; Dorchester
BRADFORD, Elisha (1669-) & 1/wf Hannah [COLE] (-1718); b 1701?, b 28 Jan 1702/3; Duxbury
BRADFORD, John (-1678, 1676) & Martha [BOURNE] (-1689), m/2 Thomas TRACY; ca 1640?, ca 1653?, no issue; Duxbury/Marshfield/Norwich, CT
BRADFORD, John (1653-1736) & Mercy WARREN (1653-1747, ae 94); 6 Jan 1674, ?5 Feb; Plymouth
BRADFORD, Joseph (?1630-1715) & Jael HOBART (1643-1730, ae 88); 25 May 1664; Hingham/Jones River, Kingston
BRADFORD, Joseph (?1674-1747(8?), in 73rd y) & 1/wf Ann FITCH (1675-1715, Lebanon); 5 Oct 1698; Norwich, CT/Lebanon, CT/New London, CT
BRADFORD, Moses (-1692) & Elizabeth _?_; b 1668; Boston
BRADFORD, Moses & Elizabeth ALLEN, m/2 Richard HUNNEWELL; 8 Dec 1692; Boston
BRADFORD, Robert & 1/wf Martha _?_; b 1644; Boston
BRADFORD, Robert & Hannah _?_; b 1672; Beverly
BRADFORD, Robert & 2/wf Margaret _?_ (-1697, ae 92 y); b 16 Nov 1677; Boston

BRADFORD, Samuel (1667, 1668-1714), Duxbury & Hannah ROGERS (1668-1733+); 31 Jul 1689; Plymouth
BRADFORD, Thomas (-1708, 1731?) & 1/wf Anne RAYMOND (1664-), dau Nehemiah; b 1682; Norwich, CT/Lyme, CT
BRADFORD, William (1588?, 1590-1657) & 1/wf Dorothy MAY (-1620); Amsterdam, 9 Dec 1613, 10? Dec, 30 Nov?; Plymouth
BRADFORD, William (1590-1657) & Alice (CARPENTER) SOUTHWORTH (ca 1590-1670), w Edward; 14 Aug 1623; Plymouth
BRADFORD, William² (1624-1704) & 1/wf Alice [RICHARDS] (1627-1671, ca 44); b 1653, 1652?, 1650 or 1651, m agreement ?23 Apr 1650; Plymouth/Kingston?/Duxbury/Winchester
BRADFORD, William² (1624-1704) & 2/wf __?__ [WISWELL?], wid; b 1674, no evidence?; Duxbury
BRADFORD, William² (1624-1704) & 3/wf Mary (WOOD/ATWOOD) [HOLMES] (-1715, 1714?), w Rev. John; aft 24 Dec 1675; Duxbury/Marshfield
BRADFORD, William & 1/wf Rachel RAYMENT/RAYMOND (1659-); 14 Nov 1676; Beverly
BRADFORD, William (1655-1689), Kingston & Rebecca [BARTLETT], m/2 Robert STANFORD; b 1680, 1679?; Duxbury/Bridgewater
BRADHERSE/?BRODHURST, Ralph & Hannah GORE (-1685, ae 42 y, 1686); 13 Jun 1677; Roxbury
BRADHURST, Ralph & 2/wf Martha __?__ (-1693); Roxbury
BRADHURST, Ralph & 3/wf Hannah [DENISON] (-1710); Roxbury
BRADING, James & Hannah ROCK; 9 Oct 1657, 11 Oct 1657; Boston/Newbury
BRAIDEN, James (1662-), Boston & Priscilla BADG; 5 Jan 1692/3; Lynn
BRADISH, John (1645-1696) & Susanna __?__ ; b 1674; Boston
BROADISH, Joseph (1638-) & Mary [?FROST]; b 1665; Sudbury/Framingham
BRADISH, Robert (-1659) & 1/wf Mary __?__ (-1638); by 1635?; Cambridge
BRADISH, Robert (-1659?) & 2/wf Vashti [MORRILL], wid; 1639?; Cambridge
BRADISH, __?__ & Katrina __?__ ; b 1665; Newtown, LI
BRADLEY, __?__ & Elizabeth __?__ (-1683), m/2 John PARMALEE 1653, m/3 John EVARTS; in Eng, b 1633?; New Haven/Guilford, CT
BRADLEY, Abraham (1650-1718) & Hannah THOMPSON (1654-1718); 25 Dec 1673; New Haven
BRADLEY, Abraham, Guilford & 1/wf Jane LEMING, LI; 13 Jul 1697; Guilford, CT
BRADLEY, Benjamin (1657-1728) & Elizabeth THOMPSON (1659-1718); 29 Oct 1677; New Haven
BRADLEY, Christopher (1679-) & Mehitable [HORTON] (1679-), m/2 Daniel TUTHILL; aft 24 Aug 1700, b 1701?; Southold, LI
BRADLEY, Daniel (-1689) & Mary WILLIAMS (1641-1714); 21 May 1662; Haverhill
BROADLEY/BRADLEY, Daniel (-1697) & Hannah DOW; 5 Jan 1686/7; Amesbury
BRADLEY, Daniel (-1713) & Abigail [JACKSON]; ca 1697; Fairfield, CT
BRADLEY, Francis (-1689) & Ruth [BARLOW]; ca 1660/5; Fairfield, CT/Branford, CT/Hartford
BRADLEY, Francis (?1670-1716) & Sarah [JACKSON], m/2 John BARTRAM; ca 1698; Fairfield, CT
BRADLEY, George (-1694) & Margaret WARD; Newport
BRADLEY, Henry & Judith (BROWN) DAVIS (-1728), w Zachary; 7 Jan 1695/6; Newbury
BRADLEY, Isaac (1647-1713) & Elizabeth __?__ (1656-1713); ca 1675/8; Branford, CT/E. Haven, CT
BRADLEY, John (-1642) (called William ALLEN "brother-in-law") & Mary __?__ ; b 1642; Salem
BRADLEY, John & Catherine __?__ ; b 1641; Dorchester
BRADLEY, John (-1676, at Liverpool) & Mary __?__ ; b 1676; ?Boston
BRADLEY, John (-1703) & Hannah [SHERWOOD], m/2 Cornelius JONES; b 1693; Fairfield, CT
BRADLEY, John & Sarah HOLT; 22 Sep 1699?, 1698?; New Haven
BRADLEY, Joseph (-1705) & Silence BROCKETT/BRACKETT (1648-); 25 Oct 1667; New Haven
BRADLEY, Joseph & Hannah HEATH; 14 Apr 1691; Haverhill
BRADLEY, Joseph (1678-) & Anna [HEATON] (1682-); b 1701?, b 1701/[2]; New Haven
BRADLEY, Joseph & Ellen __?__ ; b 1701?; Fairfield, CT
BRADLEY, Joshua & Judith LUME/LUMBE?; 26 May 1663; Rowley/New Haven?
BRADLEY, Nathan & Mary EVANS (1640-1711); 17 Jul 1666; Dorchester/Roxbury

BRADLEY, Nathan (1638-1710, 1713?) & 1/wf Esther/Hester [GRISWOLD] (1648-); b 1669; Guilford, CT/?New Haven/Wethersfield, CT

BRADLEY, Nathan (1638-1710, 1713?) & 2/wf Hannah (MUNSON) TUTTLE (-1695), w Joseph; 21 Aug 1694; Guilford, CT

BRADLEY, Nathan & Mary _?_ ; aft 1695, aft 1698; Guilford, CT

BRADLEY, Nathan & 1/wf Ruth [HAUSE/HAWES]; 2 Jan 1695/6; Dorchester

BRADLEY, Nathan (-1710?) & 3/wf Rachel (HALTON) STRONG, w Thomas; 16 May 1698; ?Northampton/E. Guilford, CT

BRADLEY, Nathaniel (1661-1743) & Ruth [DICKERMAN] (1668-); ca 1687/8, ?Jan 1687/8; New Haven

BRADLEY, Peter (-1662) & Elizabeth BREWSTER (1638-), m/2 Christopher CHRISTOPHERS; 7 Sep 1653; New London, CT

BRADLEY, Peter (-1687, ae 28) & Mary CHRISTOPHERS (1657-1724), m/2 Thomas YOUNGS, m/3 Nathaniel LYNDE; 9 May 1678; New London, CT

BRADLEY, Peter & Mehitable [HORTON] (1679±-) (no, see Christopher BRADLEY); b 1701?; Southold, LI

BRADLEY, Richard & Hannah [BALDWIN/BALDIN/BELDEN?], ?w George; b 14 May 1648, b 1651; Boston

BRADLEY, Samuel & Phebe [SHERWOOD]; aft 14 Mar 1700, b 1712; Stratford, CT

BRADLEY, Stephen (1642-1702?) & 1/wf Hannah SMITH (1644-); - Nov 1663, 9 Nov, ?1 Nov; New Haven/Guilford, CT

BRADLEY, Stephen & Mary (FENN) [LEETE], w William; aft 1 Jun 1687; Guilford, CT

BRADLEY, Stephen (1668-) & Sarah WARD, m/2 _?_ STONE; ca 15 Nov 1693; Guilford, CT

BRADLEY, William (-1691) & Alice PRICHARD (-1692); 16 Feb 1644/5, 18 Feb; Springfield

BRADLEY, William & Mary (COREY) _?_, wid; betw 1698 & 19 May 1702; Southold, LI

BRADSHAW, Humphrey (-1682) & 1/wf Patience [BOWERS]; b 1653; Cambridge

BRADSHAW, Humphrey (-1682) & 2/wf Martha RUSSELL, w William, m/3 Thomas HALL 1683; 24 Mar 1665; Cambridge

BRADSHAW, John (1655-1745) & Mary [HALL] (1668-1758); b 1687; Medford

BRADSHAW, Peter & Sarah [SKEATH/SCATE] (1662-); b 1687; Boston

BRADSTREET, Dudley (1648-1706) & Ann (WHITE?/WOOD) PRICE, in Salem, w Theodore; 12 Nov 1673; Andover

BRADSTREET, Humphrey (1594-1655) & Bridget _?_ (1604-1660, 1665?); in Eng, b 1625; Rowley

BRADSTREET, Humphrey (1670-1717, ae 49) & Sarah [PIERCE] (1669-), m/2 Edward SARGENT 1719; b 1692; Rowley/Newbury

BRADSTREET, John (1632-1660) & Hannah [PEACH], m/2 William WATERS; b 1660; Marblehead

BRADSTREET, John (1653-1719, 1718) & Sarah PERKINS (1657-1745); 11 Jun 1677, ?17 Jun 1679; Topsfield

BRADSTREET, John (-1699) & Hannah DUMMER, m/2 Nathaniel ELITHORP 1700; 29 Jan 1690/1; Rowley

BRADSTREET, John & Mercy WADE (1678-); 9 Oct 1699; Medford

BRADSTREET, Moses (-1690) & 1/wf Elizabeth HARRIS; 11 Mar 1661, prob 1661/2; Ipswich

BRADSTREET, Moses (-1690) & 2/wf Sarah (PLATTS) [PRIME] (-1697+), w Samuel; aft 8 Mar 1683/4, b 1687; Rowley

BRADSTREET, Moses & 1/wf Hannah PICKARD (-1737); 19 Jul 1686; Rowley

BRADSTREET, Nathaniel & Priscilla [CARRELL]; 16 Oct 1688; Rowley

BRADSTREET, Samuel (-1682) & 1/wf Mercy [TYNG] (1642/3-1669?, ?Sep 1670); b 1664, 1662?; Boston/Charlestown/Cambridge

BRADSTREET, Samuel (-1682) & 2/wf Martha/?Margery _?_ ; aft 1670, bef 1676, b 3 Jul 1674; Cambridge?/Jamaica, WI

BRADSTREET, Simon (1603/4-1697) & 1/wf Ann [DUDLEY] (1612-16 Sep 1672, Andover); ca 1628; Cambridge/Salisbury

BRADSTREET, Simon (1638, 1640-1683) & Lucy WOODBRIDGE (1642-1714), m/2 Daniel EPPS aft 7 May 1685; 2 Oct 1667; New London, CT

BRADSTREET, Simon (1603-1697) & 2/wf Anne (DOWNING) GARDINER?/?GARDNER (1634-1713, ae 79), w Joseph; m cont 2 May 1676, m 6 Jun 1676, ?16 Jun; ?Salem

BRADSTREET, Simon (1671-1741) & Mary LONG (-1725); 7 May 1700; Charlestown

BRAGDON, Arthur (1597/8-1678) & Mary _?_ ; b 1640; York, ME
BRAGDON, Arthur (-1690) & Lydia [TWISDEN] (ca 1640-); ca 1667-8; York, ME
BRAGDON, Arthur (1670) & 1/wf Sarah (not Lydia) [MASTERSON] (-1703)
BRAGDON, Arthur (1666-) & Sarah [CAME], dau Arthur; b 1692; York, ME
BRAGDON, Benoni & Joanna [ALLEN]; b 1700?, Jan 1701/2; York, ME
BRAGDON, Samuel & Mary (MOULTON) [HILTON], w Mainwaring HILTON; b 1673?, ca Dec 1686?; York, ME/?Marblehead
BRAGDON, Samuel, Jr. (1673-1746) & 1/wf Isabella [AUSTIN] (-1722); 25 Dec 1694; York/Saco, ME
BRAGDON, Thomas (?1640-1690) & _?_ ; b 1670; York, ME
BRAGG, Edward & 1/wf Elizabeth (?ROBERTS) [WHITTRIDGE?]/[WHITRED?] (-1691); b 1649?, b 1658?; Ipswich
BRAGG, Edward & 2/wf Sarah (_?_) REDDINGTON, w John; 28 Oct 1691; Ipswich
BRAGG, Henry & Elizabeth MACKMOLLEN; 17 Dec 1677; Salem/Bristol, RI
BRAGG, John & Elizabeth MILLER/MILLARD?, dau Robert; 12 Oct 1684, 12? Dec; Rehoboth/Bristol, RI
BRAGG, Thomas (-2 Sep 1675) & Phebe REDDINGTON (1655-), m/2 Samuel FISKE 1679; 24 Aug 1675; Ipswich
BRAGG, Timothy (-1707?) & Lydia GOTT, ?m/2 Jacob BENNETT 1709; 24 Feb 1685; Ipswich
BRAGG?/BARKER, _?_ & Hannah [ARCHER] (1682-), dau John; b 1707, b 1701?; Salem
BRAINERD, Daniel (1641-1715, ae 74) & 1/wf Hannah [SPENCER] (ca 1640-ca 1691); b 1665?; Lynn/Hartford/Haddam, CT
BRAINERD, Daniel (1666-1743) & Susannah [VENTRES]/[VENTRUS] (1668-1754); ca 1688; Haddam, CT
BRAINERD, Daniel (1641-1715) & 2/wf Elizabeth (WAKEMAN) ARNOLD, w Joseph; 30 Mar 1693; Haddam, CT
BRAINERD, Daniel (1641-1715) & 3/wf Hannah (SPENCER?) SEXTON, w George; 29 Nov 1698; Haddam, CT
BRAINERD, Elijah (1678-1740) & 1/wf Mary [BUSHNELL] (-1735); 28 Sep 1699; Haddam, CT
BRAINERD, James (1669-1743) & 1/wf Deborah DUDLEY (1670-1709); 1 Apr 1696; Saybrook, CT/Haddam, CT
BRAINARD, William (1673-aft 11 Sep 1742) & Sarah BIDWELL (1674-); 13 Dec 1698, 3 Dec 1698; Haddam, CT
BRALEY, Roger & Alice _?_ ; b 1697; Portsmouth, RI
BRAMAN, John & _?_ ; b 1676; Wenham
BRAYMAN/BROOMAN, Joseph & Sarah (BOWEN) SAVAGE, w John; 29 Sep 1681; Rehoboth/S. Kingston, RI
BRAMAN, Thomas & _?_ ; b 1650?, b 1653; Taunton
BRAMAN, Thomas (-1709) & Hannah FISHER (-1714); 20 Jan 1685/6, 1685; Taunton
BRAMAN, _?_ & Jane [BABCOCK]; b 6 Mar 1715, b 1701?; ?Westerly, RI
BRAMHALL, George (-1689) & Martha [BEARD], m/2 Gershom HALL 1698; b 1676, b Dec 1678; Dover, NH/Boston/Portsmouth, NH/Falmouth, ME
BRAMHALL, ?Thomas & Ann _?_ (1612-); b 1677, b 1650?; Boston
BRAN, Thaddeus (-1677) & Sarah _?_ (-1675); b 1670; Lynn
BRANCH, Experience (1666-1697) & Lydia [FORD] (?1668, 1669-1697); ca 1691, b 1691; Marshfield
BRANCH, John (?1628-1711) & Mary SPEED; 6 Dec 1652; Marshfield
BRANCH, Peter[1] (-1638, d on ship) & 1/wf Elizabeth GILLAME (-1632); Halden, Eng, 14 Jan 1623/4, 13? Jan; Stonington, CT
BRANCH, Peter[1] (-1638) & 2/wf Mildred _?_ (-1637); in Eng, ca 1633
BRANCH, Peter (1659-1704) & Hannah [LINCOLN] (1663-1732, Preston, CT); ca 1684; Taunton/Preston, CT
BRANCH, William (-1683) & 1/wf Joanna FARNAM (-1675); at Windsor, CT, 11 Jan 1644, 7 Sep 1643; Springfield
BRANCH, William (-1683) & 2/wf Katherine (_?_) (CARTER) WILLIAMS (-1683), w Joshua, w Arthur; 12 Feb 1677; Springfield
BRAND, George (-1669) & Mathew/Martha HEATH (-1686); 24 Jul 1643; Roxbury
BRAND, Thomas, Stonington & Sarah LARKIN, Stonington; 29 Oct 1672; Stonington, CT

BRAND, Thaddeus (-1677) & Sarah __?__ (-1675); Lynn
BRAND, __?__ & Elizabeth [BADCOCK]; b 26 Mar 1715?, b 1701?; Stonington, CT
BRANDON, William (-1646) & Mary (_?_), m/2 George FRY b 1650; ca 1630?; Weymouth
BRANCKER/BRANKE?, John (-1662) & Abigail __?__ (-1684), m/2 Rev. John WARHAM 1662; no
      issue; Dorchester/Windsor, CT
BRANCUM/BRANSCOMB, Arthur & Deborah __?__ (1652-) (ae 59 in 1711); b 1676; Boston
BRANSON, __?__ & Anna SHAPLEIGH, m/2 John FOSDICK; b 1653; Charlestown
BRANSON, George (1610-1657) & __?__; Dover, NH/York, ME
BRATLE, Edward (1670-1719) & Mary LEGG, m/2 Nathaniel NORDEN; 23 Mar 1692/3;
      Marblehead/Boston
BRATTLE, Thomas (-1683) & Elizaabeth [TYNG] (1638-1682); b 1657; Boston
BRATTLE, William (1662-1717) & 1/wf Elizabeth HAYMAN (1677-1715, in 39th y); 3 Nov 1697;
      Boston/Cambridge
BRAWN, George & 1/wf Mary __?__; by 1678; Dover, NH
BRAWN, George & 2/wf Sarah (WITTUM) SANDERS/SAUNDERS, w William; 1 Apr 1700; Dover,
      NH
BRAWN, Michael, Sr. & __?__; by 1675, by 1655?, b 1643; Dover, NH
BRAWN, John & Ann [DIXON]; b 1640?; York, ME
BRAWN, John, Jr. & Hannah/Anna LANGLEY; Jan 1694/5; Kittery, ME
BRAWN, Richard & Mary __?__; by 1666; York, ME
BRAY, John (1620?-1693/4) & Joan __?__ (1630±-1694+); b 1659, ca 1653; Kittery, ME/etc.
BRAY, John & Ann [LANE]; b 1677?; Billerica
BRAY, John (-1714) & Margaret LAMBERT (-1725); 10 Nov 1679, no issue; Glouchester
BRAY, Nathaniel (1656-) & Marthew/Martha WADIN/WEEDEN?/WARDIN?/WOODEN?; 22 Jan
      1684; Glouchester
BRAY, Richard (-1665, Lynn) & Mary __?__, m/2 __?__ WHITLOCK bef 1689; ca 1645/50?; Exeter,
      NH
BRAY, Richard & Isabella/?Rebecca/?Rebella/?Sabella __?__; b Feb 1650/1, ca 1646; North
      Yarmouth, ME
BRAY, Richard (-1718) & Mary (SAYWARD) [YOUNG], w Robert; by Oct 1691; York, ME
BRAY, Robert[1] (-1692±) & Thomasin __?__; b 1665?; Salem
BRAY, Robert[2] & Christian/[Christiana COLLINS] (-1724+); 5 Nov 1685; Salem
BRAY, Samuel (-1679) & Jane __?__; b 1679; Casco Bay
BRAY, Thomas (?1604-1691) & Marie/Mary WILSON (-1707); 3 May 1646; Glouchester
BRAY/BRAG, Thomas (1658/9-1743) & Mary EMERSON (-1722+); 23 Dec 1686; Ipswich/
      Glouchester
BRAY, Thomas (-1742) & Elizabeth RYDER (-1755); 22 Aug 1700; Yarmouth
BRAYTON, Francis[1] (1612-1692) & Mary __?__ (-1692+); Portsmouth, RI
BRAYTON, Francis[2] (-1718) & Mary FISH (-1747); 18 Mar 1671, 1671/2?; Portsmouth, RI
BRAYTON, Stephen (-1692±) & Ann TALLMAN, ?m/2 William POTTER; 5 Mar 1678, 8 Mar 1679,
      1678/9; Portsmouth, RI
BRAZER, Edward (1603-1689, 1687?) & Magdalen __?__; b 1656; Charlestown
BRAZIER, Henry & __?__; ?b 1649; ?Gravesend, LI
BRASIER, Thomas (1660-) & Elizabeth __?__; b 1691; Charlestown
BRACER, William & Mary MARSTON (1677-); 30 Oct 1699; ?Hampton, NH/Scarboro, ME/York,
      ME
BREEME, Benjamin[1] (-1693) & Hannah/Anna [BARNES] (1647-), dau Thomas, m/2 Robert
      BRONSDON 1694; b 1668; Hingham/Boston
BREAM, Benjamin (1670-) & Elizabeth (INGLES/ENGLISH) CLEMY/CLOMY, w Alexander; 24
      May 1694, 28 May 1694; Boston
BRICK, Arnold & 1/wf Hannah __?__; b 1694; Greenland, NH
BRECK, Edward (?1595-1662) & 1/wf __?__ (-ca 1646?, 1653?); ca 1617?; Dorchester
BRECK, Edward (?1595-1662) & Isabel [RIGBY] (1610-1673), w John, m/3 Anthony FISHER
      1663; ca 1647, aft 1653; Dorchester
BRECK, Edward (1674-1713) & Susannah WEZELL/WISWALL (1672-); 1 Apr 1698; Dorchester/
      Roxbury
BRECK, John[1] (-1660) & __?__; b 1630; Sherborn
BRECK, John (-1691, ae 40) & Susanna __?__ (1648-1711/12); b 1672; Dorchester

BRECK, John & Mehitable MORSE (1681-); 9 Mar 1697?
BRECK/BRICK, Robert (?1620-1662) & 1/wf Margery __?__ (-1652?); ca 1642; Boston
BRECK, Robert & 2/wf Sarah HAWKINS, m/2 ?Rev. James ALLEN 1673; 4 Jan 1653/4; Boston
BRECK, Robert (1658-1684) & Joanna [MASON], m/2 Michael PERRY 1694; b 1681; Boston
BRECK, Thomas² (?1630-1703) & Mary HILL (?1636-1726); 12 Feb 1656/7; Dorchester/Medfield/ Sherborn
BRECKETT, William & Hannah SIBLY; 19 May 1683; Salem
BREED, Allen¹ (1601-1692) & 1/wf Elizabeth WHEELER; Pulloxhill, 14 Nov 1622; Lynn
BREAD, Allen (1601-1692) & 2/wf Elizabeth (_?_) (BELLARD) KNIGHT, w William, w William; 28 Mar 1656; Lynn
BREED, Allen² (1630/1-1707) & Mary [SARGENT] (1637-1671), dau William; b 1656, ca 1654?; Lynn
BREAD, Allen³ (1660-) & Elizabeth BALLARD; 22 May 1684; Charlestown/Lynn
BREAD, John² (1634-1678) & 1/wf Sarah HATHORNE (1644-1676); 28 Dec 1663; Lynn
BREAD, John² (1634-1678) & 2/wf Sarah HART; 4 Mar 1677/8; Lynn
BREAD, John³ (1664-1728) & Mary KERTLAND/KIRTLAND/KIRKLAND/KIRTLIND (1667-1743+); 28 Apr 1686; Lynn
BREED, John³ (-1751) & Mercy PALMER (1668-1752); 17 Apr 1689, 8 Jun 1690?, 11 Apr 1689?, 8 Jan 1690/1?, 11 Mar 1689; Stonington, CT
BREAD, Joseph³ (1658-1713) & Sarah FARRINGTON (1664-1752); 27 Sep 1683; Lynn
BREAD, Samuel³ (1669-) & Anna/Anne? HOOD (1672-); 5 Feb 1691/2; Lynn
BREAD, Timothy³ & 1/wf Sarah NEWHALL (-1693); 3 Mar 1679/80; Lynn
BREAD, Timothy³ & 2/wf Sarah BRAN; - Feb 1693/4; Lynn
BREEDEN, Bryan/Bryant (-1720) & [Elizabeth LEWIS?]; b 1668; Malden/Chelsea
BREDING, James & Hannah ROCKE; 9 Oct 1657; Boston
BRAIDEN, James (?1662-), Boston & Priscilla BODGE; 5 Jan 1692/3; Lynn/Kittery, ME
BRADDEN, John & Prudence [MITCHELL], m/2 Robert TAPLEY, m/3 __?__ SPOOR; Star Island
BREDEAN, Samuel (1671-) & Martha STOCKER; m int 10 Mar 1695/6; Lynn
BREDEN, Thomas (returned to Eng) & Mary __?__ ; b 1661; Boston/Charlestown
BRENTON, Ebenezer (-1708) & Priscilla (BYFIELD) [WALDRON] (-1705); w Isaac; b 1687?, ?Nov 1687; Swansea/Bristol, RI
BRENTON, John & Phebe __?__ ; b 1697; Boston
BRENTON, Richard & __?__ ; b 1635; Boston
BRENTON, William (-1674) & Martha/Dorothy [BURTON]?; aft 1635/50; Boston/Portsmouth, RI/Newport, RI/Taunton
BRENTON, William² (-1697) & Hannah [DAVIS] (1661-1693); b 1678?, b 1680, 1680±; Bristol, RI
BRETT, Elihu & Ann/Hannah [TURNER]; b 1678, b 15 May 1679; Bridgewater
BRETT, Nathaniel (1661-1740) & Sarah HAYWARD (1663-1737); 21 Nov 1683; Bridgewater
BRITT/BRETT?, [?Robert] & Rebecca __?__ ; b 1654; Salem
BRETT, William (?1618-1681) & Margaret [?FORD]; b 1648; Duxbury
BRETT, William (?1648-1713) & Elizabeth [CARY] (1649-); ca 1671?, b 1684; Bridgewater
BREWER, Chrispus/Christover (-1756/7) & Mary __?__ (-1693); b 1659, b 1650?; Boston/Lynn
BREWER, Daniel¹ (1596-1646) & Joanna [MORRILL?] (-1689, ae 87?); in Eng, b 1624; Roxbury
BREWER, Daniel (1624-1708) & Hannah MORRILL (1636-1717); 5 Nov 1652; Roxbury
BREWER, Daniel (1668, 1669-1733) & Katherine CHAUNCEY (1676-1754); 23 Aug 1691; Hadley/Springfield
BREWER, John & Anne/Hannah? __?__ , m/2 Henry LOKER 1647; b 1642; ?Cambridge/Sudbury
BREWER, John (-1684) & Mary WHITMORE/?WHITMAN (-1684); 23 Oct 1647; Ipswich
BREWER, John (1642-1691) & Elizabeth [RICE] (1648-1740); b 1669; Sudbury/Framingham
BREWER, John (-1697) & 1/wf Susanna WARNER (-1688); - Jan 1674; Ipswich
BREWER, John (-1697) & 2/wf Martha PERKINS, m/2 __?__ INGALLS b 8 Oct 1701; 3 Jun 1689; Ipswich
BREWER, John & Mary (PICKMAN/PITMAN?) HODGE, w Robert; 18 Aug 1689; Salem
BREWER, John (1669-1709) & Mary (Hannah is wrong) JONES (1672-); 5 Jul 1693; Sudbury/Watertown
BREWER, Nathaniel (1635-) & 1/wf Elizabeth ?MORRILL/[KINSBURY] (1638-Jun 1661); b 7 Apr 1661; Roxbury

BREWER, Nathaniel (-1692?, 1694?) & 2/wf Elizabeth RAND (1640-); 6 Dec 1661; Roxbury
BREWER, Nathaniel & 1/wf Margaret WELD (1669-); 17 Mar 1692; Roxbury
BREWER, Peter (-1708) & Elizabeth LINFURTH (-1727+); 25 Nov 1669; Haverhill
BREWER, Thomas (-23 Mar 1690) & _?_ ; ca 1626/35?; ?Roxbury/Hampton, NH
BREUER/BREWER, Thomas & Elizabeth GRAVES; 4 Dec 1682; Lynn
BREWER, Thomas & Sarah [KEENEY] (1664-), of Topsfield; b 1685(6?), 13 Jan 1682, 18 Jan;
    Wethersfield, CT/Glastonbury, CT
BREWER, Thomas & Elizabeth [NICHOLS] (1680-); b 1701?; Salisbury
BREWSTER, Benjamin (1633-1710) & Ann (ADDIS) DARTE (-1709), w Ambrose; 28 Feb
    1659/60; Norwich, CT/Preston, CT
BREWSTER, Benjamin (1673-1744) & Mary SMITH; 17 Dec 1696; ?Norwich, CT/Lebanon, CT
BREWSTER, Daniel (1666/7-1735) & 1/wf Hannah GAGER (1666-1727); 23 Dec 1686; Norwich,
    CT/Preston, CT
BREWSTER, Daniel (1662-) & Anna/Anne JAYNE (1676-); ca 1693; Setauket, LI
BREWSTER, Francis & Lucy _?_, m/2 Thomas PELL; in Eng, ca 1617; New Haven, CT
BRUSTER, John & Mary [?KNIGHT]/[?SHERBURNE]; 6 Jul 1652; ?Portsmouth, NH
BREWSTER, John & Mary [SLOPER]; b 1690; Portsmouth, NH
BREWSTER, Jonathan (1593-1659) & 1/wf _?_ (-1619); b 1610; Leyden/Holland
BREWSTER, Jonathan (1593-1659) & 2/wf Lucretia OLDHAM (-1679); 10 Apr 1624;
    Plymouth/Duxbury
BREWSTER, Jonathan (1664-1704) & Judith STEVENS, m/2 Christopher HUNTINGTON 1706; 18
    Dec 1690; Norwich, CT/Preston, CT
BREWSTER, Love (-1650) & Sarah COLLIER (-1691), m/2 Richard PARK; 15 May 1634;
    Plymouth
BREWSTER, Nathaniel (-1690) & 1/wf Abigail [REYNES]; in Eng, ca 1644; New Haven, CT
BREWSTER, Nathaniel (-1690) & 2/wf Sarah [LUDLOW]; in Ireland, ca 1656; Boston/New
    Haven/etc.
BREWSTER, Nathaniel (-1676) & Sarah _?_, m/2 Robert HIXON; ca 1660/65; ?Duxbury
BREWSTER, Timothy & Mary [HAWKINS]; ca 1685; Brookhaven, LI
BREWSTER, William (?1567-1644) & Mary [WENTWORTH?] (-1627); in Eng, b 1593; Plymouth
BREWSTER, William (1625-) & Mary PEAME/PERME; 15 Oct 1651; London
BREWSTER, William (-1723) & Lydia PARTRIDGE (-1743); 2 Jan 1672; Duxbury
BREWSTER, William (1669-1728) & 1/wf Elizabeth READ (-1692); 8 Jan 1692, 1691/2; Norwich,
    CT
BREWSTER, William (1669-1728) & 2/wf Patience _?_ (-ca 1740, Coventry, CT); ca 1694;
    Norwich, CT/Lebanon, CT
BREWSTER, Wrestling (-1 Jan 1696/7) & Mary _?_ (1661-1742), Kingston, m/2 John
    PARTRIDGE; b 1679; Duxbury/Kingston
BRICKENTON/BRICKENDEN?/?BRICKINDINE, Robert & Mary/(should be Sarah) (KIND)
    TYER, w William, m William ROUSE bef 1676 (had Sarah b 3 Sep 1669, m/1 Noah GENTLE
    1701, m/2 John PARKER); b 1669; Boston
BRICKET/BRICKETT, Nathaniel & _?_ ; b 1673; Newbury
BRICKNALL, Edward & Mary [KIMBALL?/KEMBLE], ?m/2 William HOUGH 1693; b 1689, b
    1682; Boston/Charlestown
BRIDGES, Benjamin (1665-1725) & Elizabeth _?_, ?m/2 Moses HAVEN; b 1690(1?); Framingham
BRIDGES, Caleb & Sarah BREWER; 26 Nov 1700; Framingham
BRIDGES, Charles (-1682) & Sarah (CORNELL) WILLETT, w Thomas, m/3 John LAWRENCE
    1682; 3 Nov 1647, 2? Nov; New York/Flushing, LI
BRIDGES, Edward (1612-1684/5) & 1/wf Alice ?MILLINTON (-1641+) (perhaps Alice and
    Elizabeth were the same); b 1637; Ipswich/Topsfield/Salem/Rowley
BRIDGES, Edmund (-1684/5, Ipswich) & Elizabeth _?_ (-1664); Ipswich/Lynn/etc.
BRIDGES, Edmond (ca 1637-1682, by Aug 1682) & Sarah TOWNE (-1703), m/2 Peter CLOYSE;
    11 Jan 1659, 1659/60; Topsfield/Salem
BRIDGES, Edmond (-1684/5) & 3/wf Mary (LANGTON) LITTLEHALE (-1691), w Richard; 6 Apr
    1665; Ipswich
BRIDGES, Edmund (1664-24 Jun 1682) & Elizabeth [CROADE] (1664-), m/2 Daniel LAMBERT
    1693+, m/3 Moses GILMAN 1713; b 1682; Salem
BRIDGE, Edward (1601-1683) & Mary _?_ (-bef 1677); b 1637, b 1635?; Roxbury

BRIDGE, Edward (1668-1724+) & Mary **BROOKS**, dau Gershom; 27 May 1690; Roxbury

BRIDGES, James & Sarah **MARSTON/MARSTONE** (-1736); 24 May 1692; Andover

BRIDGE, John (-1665) & __?__ ; in Eng, b 1615; Cambridge

BRIDGE, John (-1665) & 2/wf Elizabeth (__?__) (**BANCROFT) SANDERS** (-1680), w Roger, w Martin, m/4 Edward **TAYLOR** 1673; m cont 29 Nov 1658; Cambridge

BRIDGE, John (?1635-1674) & Prudence [**ROBINSON**] (1643-); b 1661; Roxbury

BRIDGES, John & 1/wf Sarah **HOW**; 5 Dec 1666; Ipswich/Mendon

BRIDGES, John & 2/wf Mary (**TYLER) POST**, w Richard; 1 Mar 1677/8; Andover

BRIDGES, Josiah (ca 1650-1715) & 1/wf Elizabeth **NORTON** (-1677); 13 Nov 1676; Ipswich

BRIDGES, Josiah (ca 1650-1715) & 2/wf Ruth **GREENSLADE**; 19 Sep 1677; Ipswich/Wenham

BRIDGE, Matthew (1615-1700) & Anne/Anna [**DANFORTH**] (1622-1704); ca 1644, ?19 Jan 1643; Cambridge

BRIDGE, Matthew (1650-1738) & Abigail [**RUSSELL**] (1668-1727); b 1688, 1687?; Cambridge/Lexington

BRIDGES, Obadiah (ca 1646-1677) & 1/wf Mary **SMITH**; 25 Oct 1671; Ipswich

BRIDGES, Obidiah (-1677) & 2/wf Elizabeth __?__ , m/2 Joseph **PARKER** 1680, m/3 Samuel **HUTCHINSON** 1686?; ?25 Oct 1676, b 1677; Ipswich

BRIDGES, Robert (-1656) & ?Mary [**WOODCOCK?/WOODBURN?**]; b 31 Dec 1644; ?Lynn

BRIDGE, Samuel (1647-) & 1/wf Hannah [**BAYES**]? (-1690); b 1672; Boston

BRIDGE, Samuel (1647-) & 2/wf Christian **PIERCE**; 3 Dec 1690; Boston

BRIDGE, Samuel (1672-) & Sarah **SMITH**; 24 Dec 1696; Boston

BRIDG, Thomas (-1656/7) & Dorcas __?__ ; b 1648(9?); Cambridge

BRIDGE, Thomas (-1715) & Amy __?__ ; b 1677; Boston

BRIDGE, William (-1648?) & 1/wf Mary [**OLDHAM**]; b 1644, b 1623?; Charlestown

BRIDGE, William (-1648?) & 2/wf Persis [**PIERCE**], m/2 John **HARRISON** b 1652; b 1647; Charlestown

BRIDGEWATER/BIDGWATER, Thomas & Elizabeth **MACKARTA**; m int 7 Apr 1696; Boston

BRIDGHAM, Henry (ca 1617, 1613-1671) (called bro. by Thomas **BUTTOLPH**) & Elizabeth [**HARDING**] (1623-1672); b 1645; Boston

BRIDGHAM, Henry (-1720) & 1/wf Lydia **ALLEN**; 12 Dec 1700; Boston

BRIDGHAM, Jonathan (-1690) & Elizabeth [**POWNING**] (?1650-1691); b 1675; Boston

BRIDGHAM, Joseph (1652-1709) & 1/wf Sarah [**CLARK**?] (-1696); b 1676; Boston

BRIDGHAM, Joseph (1652-1709) & 2/wf Susanna [?**COX**] (-1696); Boston

BRIDGHAM, Joseph (1652-1709) & 3/wf Mercy **WENSLEY** (1668-), m/2 Thomas **CUSHING** 1712; 17 Apr 1700; Boston

BRIDGMAN, Isaac & Dorothy **CURTIS**; 11 Apr 1700; Wethersfield, CT

BRIDGMAN, James (-1676) & Sarah [?**LYMAN**] (?1620-1668); b 1643; Hartford/Springfield/Northampton

BRIDGMAN, John (-1655) & Elizabeth __?__ ; b 1650; Salem

BRIDGMAN, John (1645-1712) & Mary **SHELDON**; 11 Jan 1670/1; Northampton?/Deerfield

BRIER/BRYER/BRIARD, Elisha (-1718, ae 57) & Abigail **DREW**; 4 Oct 1689; Portsmouth, NH

BRIERS, John & Elizabeth **JACKSON** (-1722, ae 93, Beverly); 25 Mar 1651-2?; Gloucester

BRYER, Joseph (1645-1704, ae 59) & 1/wf Mary **GOULD** (1653-1690/1); 22 Jun 1672; Newport

BRYER, Joseph (-1704) & 2/wf Mary **PALMER**, Westchester, PA?; 5 Feb 1691, 1691/2, 1 Feb 1692

BRYER, Richard & 1/wf Ellinar/Eleanor **WRIGHT** (-1672); 21 Dec 1665; Newbury

BRYER, Richard & 2/wf Mary (**WOOD**) [**FRINK**], w John; b 1679(80?); Ipswich

BRIAR, Richard & 3/wf Mary (**CUTT**) [**CHURCHWOOD**], w Humphrey; aft 16 Nov 1686, bef 16 Dec 1693; Kittery, ME

BRIGDEN, Elias (1673-1717) & Mary **HALE**; 24 Mar 1697/8; Charlestown

BRIGDEN, John (1661-) & Sarah **BARRETT** (1667-1690); 15 Oct 1684; Charlestown

BRIGDEN, Michael (1664-1709) & Joanna **WILSON** (1667-1735, ae 68); 11 Jan 1687/8; Charlestown

BRIGDEN, Nathaniel (1666-) & Elizabeth **WAFFE/WHAFF**, m/2 John **CARY** 1706; 13 Dec 1688; Charlestown

BRIGHAM, Thomas[1] (-1668) & Thomasine __?__ (-1669); in Eng, ca 1631; Charlestown

BRIGDEN, Thomas (-1683) & Mildred [**CARTHRICK**] (-1726, ae 96); b 1656; Charlestown

BRIGDEN, Thomas & Anna __?__ ; b 1680; Charlestown

BRIGGS, Clement (-1648) & 1/wf Joan [ALLEN] (-1638+); b 1 Mar 1630/1; Dorchester
BRIGGS, Clement (-1648) & 2/wf Elizabeth _?_ (-1691); b 1640; Weymouth
BRIGGS, Clement (1642-1669?) & Hannah [PACKARD], m/2 Thomas RANDALL ca 1671; b 1669; Weymouth
BRIGGS, Clement & Elizabeth FIELD; 3 Nov 1697; Bridgewater/Easton
BRIGGS, Cornelius (1649-1694) & 1/wf Mary (DOUGHTY) [RUSSELL], w Samuel; 20 Mar 1677; Scituate
BRIGGS, Cornelius & 2/wf Mehitable (ALLYN) ANNABLE, w Samuel; 6 May 1683; Barnstable
BRIGGS, Daniel (1665-1730) & Lydia _?_
BRIGGS, David (1640-) & Mary BARBER; m lic 26 Oct 1676; Southampton, LI
BRIGGS, David (1669) & Mary _?_; Berkley
BRIGGS, Edward (1665-1718) & Sarah [WILCOX] (-1751); b 1693(4?); Tiverton, RI
BRIGGS, Enoch (-1734) & Hannah (COOKE) WILLCOX, dau John, w Daniel; ca 1692, aft 1689; Portsmouth, RI
BRIGGS, George & Mary _?_; b 1678; Boston
BRIGGS, George & Sarah _?_; b 1679; Boston
BRIGGS, Hugh, Taunton & Martha EVERSON, Plymouth; 1 Mar 1682/3, 1683/4?, 1 Mar 1683; Taunton
BRIGGS, James & Rebecca TILDEN (1654-); 8 Jul 1673; Scituate
BRIGGS, John (1615-1641) & Katherine _?_; ca 1637?; Sandwich
BRIGGS, John & _?_; b 1646; Taunton
BRIGGS, John (1609-1690) & 1/wf _?_/?Sarah CORNELL?; b 1642; Newport/Warwick, RI/Portsmouth, RI
BRIGGS, John (-1690) & 2/wf? Constant (MITCHELL) [FOBES]/[FORBES], w John 1660; 1662; Bridgewater/Portsmouth, RI
BRIGGS, John (-1697+, 1708) & Frances _?_ (-1697+); ca 1662?; Kings Town, RI
BRIGGS, John (1642-1713) & Hannah [FISHER] (-1727+); ca 1664, b 19 Sep 1665; Portsmouth, RI/Tiverton, RI
BRIGGS, John & Mary _?_ (-1697); b 1668(9?); Boston
BRIGGS, John & Mary _?_; b 1673, b 1670; Lyme, CT
BRIGGS, John & Ann _?_; b 1678; Lyme, CT
BRIGGS, John (1645-) & Deborah [HAWKE] (1652-1711), m/2 Thomas KING 1699; b 1684; Scituate
BRIGGS, John & Martha/Matthew WILKINS; m lic 5 Dec 1684; LI?
BRIGGS, John & Hannah HALLOWAY; ca 1696
BRIGGS, John & Sarah CURTIS; 11 Jan 1697; Boston
BRIGGS, John (1672) & Abigail [?HATCH]; Berkeley
BRIGGS, John & Elizabeth ALLEN; 27 Apr 1697; Boston
BRIGGS, Jonathan (1635-1689) & 1/wf Elizabeth _?_ (doubtful); b 1668(9?); Taunton
BRIGGS, Jonathan (1635-1689) & 2/wf (prob 1st & only wf) Experience [?BABBITT] (-aft 8 Feb 1698/9); b 2 Sep 1682, by 1662?; Taunton
BRIGGS, Matthew/Matthias & 1/wf _?_; in Eng, b 1648; Hingham
BRIGGS, Matthias (-1697) & 2/wf Deborah CUSHING (-1700); 9 May 1648; Hingham
BRIGGS, Nathaniel & Barbara _?_; b 1683; New Shoreham, RI
BRIGGS, Peter & Ruth (PINION) [MOORE], w James (she deserted her husband 1665); b 1664; Killingsworth, CT
BRIGGS, Remember (-1696) & Mary _?_, m/2 Jacob STAPLES 1696; b 1686; Weymouth
BRIGGS, Richard (1640-1692) & Rebecca HASKINS/HOSKINS? (-1719+, 1724+), of Lakenham; 15 Aug 1662; Taunton
BRIGGS, Richard (1675-1733) & 1/wf Susanna SPENCER (1681-); 23 Dec 1700, 23 Sep 1700; Bristol, RI/E. Greenwich, RI/Kings Town, RI
BRIGGS, Samuel & [?Bennett ELLIS] (1648/9-1677); b 1665; Sandwich/Rochester
BRIGGS, Samuel (-1706+) & Mary HALL (1672-); ?m/2 Benjamin CASWELL 1707; 27 Jul 1692; Taunton
BRIGGS, Thomas (-1720) & Mary/?Martha [FISHER] (-1717+); b 1671; Portsmouth, RI/Dartmouth
BRIGGS, Thomas (1633-1691?) & Mary _?_; b 1671, b 1665; Boston/?Taunton/Weymouth
BRIGGS, Thomas (1633-1691?) & 2/wf? Ann _?_ (-1696+); Taunton

BRIGGS, Thomas (1609-1740) & Abigail THAYER (-1746+); 24 Oct 1689; Taunton
BRIGGS, Walter & Mary _?_ (-1 Mar 1658+); b 1645; Duxbury
BRIGGS, Walter (-1684?) & Frances (?WATSON) [ROGERS] (-1687), w John; ca 1661?; Scituate
BRIGGS, William & Mary _?_ (-1695+); b 1642; Boston/Lyme, CT
BRIGGS/BIGGS?, William (-1681) & Mary YELLING; b 1666, 10 Jan 1664/5; Middletown, CT
BRIGGS, William (1646, 1644-1728) & Sarah MACOMBER (-1680/1), Marshfield; 6 Nov 1666; Taunton
BRIGGS, William & Abigail MASON; 7 Apr 1680; Dedham
BRIGGS, William (1650-1716) & Elizabeth [COOKE]/Elizabeth (COOKE) BORDEN? (1653-1716+); b 1681; Portsmouth, RI/Little Compton, RI
BRIGGS, William (1663-) & 1/wf Constance LINCOLN; 13 Jul 1687; Taunton
BRIGGS, William (1667/8-) & Elizabeth LINCOLN; 13 Oct 1693; Taunton
BRIGGS, William & Rebecca DYER; 10 Jun 1695; Boston/Watertown
BRIGGS, William, Jr. (1667/8-1731), Taunton & 2/wf Mehitable BLAKE (1673-1732), Milton; 16 Jun 1696; Milton/Taunton
BRIGGS, William (1663-1725) & 2/wf Elizabeth [KINGSBURY] (1670/1-1729); b 1701?; Taunton
BRIGHAM, John (1645-1728) & 1/wf Sarah [DAVIS] (1646-); b 1667?; Sudbury
BRIGHAM, John (1645-1728) & 2/wf Deborah (HAYNES) [BROWN] (-1777), w Jabez; aft 1698?; Sudbury
BRIGHAM, Jonathan (1675-) & Mary [FAY] (1675-1751); 26 Mar 1696; Marlboro
BRIGHAM, Nathan (1671-) & Elizabeth [MAYNARD] (1664-1733); b 1693; Marlboro
BRIDGAM, Samuel (1653-1713) & Elizabeth HOWE (?1665, 1664-1739); 1683; Marlboro
BRIGGAM, Sebastian (?1609-) & Mary _?_ ; b 1640, returned to Eng; Rowley
BRIGHAM, Thomas[1] (1603-1653) & Mercy [?HURD] (-1643), m/2 Edmund RICE 1655, m/3 William HUNT 1664; b 1641, 1637?; Cambridge/Sudbury
BRIGHAM, Thomas (?1640-1717) & 1/wf Mary RICE (1646-); 27 Dec 1665; Marlboro
BRIGHAM, Thomas (-1717) & Susanna (SHATTUCK) (MORSE) FAY, w Joseph, w John; 30 Jul 1695; Marlboro
BRIGHT, Rev. Francis (1603-) (returned to Eng) & _?_ ; b 1627; Salem
BRIGHT, Henry (1602-1686) & Anne [GOLDSTONE] (1615-); b 1635; Watertown
BRIGHT, John (1641-1691) & Mary BARSHAM (1648-1736), m/2 Hananiah PARKER 1700; 7 May 1675, no issue; Watertown
BRIGHT, Nathaniel & Mary COOLEDG/COOLIDGE (1660-1717); 21 Jul 1681; Watertown
BRIGHTMAN, Henry (-1728) & Joan _?_ (-1700+, 1716-); b 1674; Portsmouth, RI/Newport/Freetown
BRIGHTMAN, Henry (1667-1705) & Abiel SHEPLEY (1670-); 15 Aug 1688; Charlestown/Boston
BRIGHTMAN, Henry (-1716) & Elizabeth LAWTON; - Aug 1694; Portsmouth, RI
BRIGNALL, William & Martha [METCALF] (1628-); m/2 Nathaniel STOW 1662; ?Dedham
BRIMBLECOMBE, John (-1678) & 1/wf Barbara (_?_) DAVIS, w George, m/3 Thomas CHADWELL?; 14 Jan 1655/6; Boston/Marblehead
BRIMBLECOME, John (-1678) & 2/wf Tabitha _?_ ; Marblehead
BRIMBLECOM, Philip (-1692) & Sarah FLUENT, m/2 David FURNACE/FURNESS? 1692; 8 Feb 1680; Marblehead
BRINK, _?_ & Alse ARTHUR; 14 Oct 1680; Jamestown, RI
BRINLEY, Francis (1632-1719/21) & Hannah [CARR] (-1719+); 1656; Newport/Boston
BRINLEY, Thomas (-1693) & Catherine [PAGE] (1663-1755), m/2 Edward LYDE; at London, ca 1685?; Boston/London
BRINLEY, William (-1704) & 1/wf _?_ [REAPE], dau William; Newport
BRINLEY, William (-1704) & 2/wf Mary [SANFORD] (1674-1721), m/2 Josiah ARNOLD 1705/1704?; b 1701?; Newport
BRINSMADE, Daniel (-1702) & Sarah [KELLOGG] (1659/60-), m/2 John BETTS; by 1683; Stratford, CT
BRINSMEAD, John (-1673) & 2/wf Mary [CARTER]; b 1640, b 1639; Charlestown/Stratford, CT
BRINSMADE, Paul (-1696) & Elizabeth HOWKINS (1659-bef 1696); 30 Oct 1678; Stratford, CT/Derby, CT
BRINSMEAD, William (-1648) & _?_ ; Dorchester
BRITNALL, Henery (-1690) & Sarah PEDRICKE, m/2 David OLIVER; 15 Sep 1682; Marblehead

BRINTNALL, John & Mary WALDRON (-1688); 13 Mar 1687/8; Marblehead
BRINTNALL, John (-1731) & Phebe [SMITH] (1673-1753), dau John?; b 1691; Boston/Marble-
head/Chelsea
BRENTNALL, Samuel (1665-1735/6) & Hester CARPENTER (-1730); 19 Mar 1687; Swansea
BRENTNALL, Thomas (-1692) & Esther _?_ ; b 1665; Boston
BRENTNALL, Thomas (1669-1733) & Hannah WILLARD (1666-); 23 May 1693; Sudbury
BRISCO, Benjamin & Sarah [LONG]; b 1656; Boston/Lynn
BRISCO, Ezekiel & Rebecca _?_ ; b 1671, b 1670; Boston
BRISCO, James (1649-) & Sarah WHEELER; 6 Dec 1676, 6 Nov; Milford, CT
BRISCO, James (1679-) & Elizabeth ADAMS (?1679-); 1 Jun 1699; Milford, CT
BRISCOE/BISCOE, John (?1622-1690) & Elizabeth BITTLESTONE (-1685); 13 Dec 1650;
Watertown
BRISCO, Joseph (-1658) & Abigail COMPTON, m/2 Abraham BUSBY 1659; 30 Jan 1651/2; Boston
BRISCO, Joseph & Rebecca _?_ ; b 1679; Boston
BRISCOE, Nathaniel[1] (returned to Eng) & Elizabeth _?_ (-1642); in Eng, b 1622; Watertown
BRISCO, Nathaniel & Sarah BEARD; b 1646
BRICOE, Nathaniel (-1683) & [?Mehitable] (GUNN) FENN? (1641-), m/3 Nicholas CAMP aft
1689; aft 28 Mar 1667, b 1646?; Watertown/Wethersfield, CT/Milford, CT
BRISCOE/BISCOE, Nathaniel (-1691) & Mary CAMP, m/2 Joseph GUERNSEY; 29 Nov 1672;
Milford, CT
BRISCO, Robert & 1/wf? Abigail [STONE] (1672-1724, ae 59); b 1691; Beverly
BRISCOE, Thomas (-1692) & Hannah STERNS, ?m/2 Samuel GOOKIN; 24 Dec 1684; Watertown
BRISCO, William & Cecile _?_ ; b 1642; Boston
BRISSON, Charles & Mary (MILLS) [BEAN], w Lewis; b 1686, b 9 Jun 1689; York, ME
BRISTOL, Bezaleel & Hester [STONE] (1676-); b 1701?; Guilford, CT
BRISTOL, Daniel (1671-1728) & 1/wf Esther [SPERRY]; b 1697(8?); New Haven
BRISTOL, Elephalet & Esther [PECK] (1679-); b 1701; New Haven
BRISTOL, Henry (-1695), w? & 1/wf _?_ ; b 1649(50?); New Haven
BRISTOL, Henry (-1695) & Lydia BROWN (?1637/8-1719); 29 Jan 1656, 1656/7?; New Haven
BRISTOL, John (1659-1735±) & [Mercy] [MANSFIELD] (1662-); b 1686; New Haven/Newtown
BRISTOW/BRISTOL?, Richard & 1/wf Eleanor _?_ (-1658); Guilford, CT
BRISTOW, Richard (-1683) & 2/wf ?Susanna (BALL) [BLATCHLEY] (-1677), w Thomas; aft
1674, no ch; Guilford, CT
BRISTOL, Samuel (1651-1692) & Phebe _?_ ; Guilford, CT
BRISTOW, _?_ & _?_ , a wid in 1640; Hampton, NH
BRISTOW, _?_ & Hannah FLACK (1659-), m/2 Robert CLAPP 1703; ?Boston
BRITTON, Edward (-1742) & Mary CODNER (-1757); ?25 Dec 1692, ?1 Jan 1692, 1692/3;
Marblehead/Salem
LeBRETTON/BRITTON, Francis & Elizabeth _?_ ; Falmouth, ME
BRITTAIN, Francis & Hannah _?_ ; b 1695; Newbury
BRITTAINE, James & _?_
BRITTEN, James (1608-1655) & Jane/Joanna [EGGLETON] (1600-), wid?, m/3 Isaac COLE
1658/9; b 1655; Woburn
LeBRETTON, Peter & _?_ ; b 1681
BRITTON, Philip & Elizabeth _?_ ; b 1701; Dorchester
BRITTON/BREEDEN?, William & Mary [PENDLETON] (1652?-), m/2 Joseph CROSS ca 1680?,
m/3 Nicholas MOREY ca 1684
BRITTEN, William (-1726) & Lydia LEONARD (1679-1752+); 26 Oct 1698; Taunton
BROAD, William (-1678) & 1/wf Abigail [GLAMFIELD] (-9 Jun 1670+); b 1664; Isles of
Shoal/etc.
BROAD, William (-1678) & 2/wf Judith _?_ , m/2 Stephen WEBSTER 1678; b 1678; Portsmouth,
NH
BROADBENT, Joshua & Sarah OSBORNE, w Thomas; 6 Apr 1685; Woburn/Boston/Charlestown
BROADBROOK/BROADBROOKS, Beriah (1680-1759+) & Abigail [SEVERANCE] (1676?-); b
1701?, 5 ch in 1710; Harwick
BROADRIDGE, Richard (-1718+) & Constance [WITHINGTON] (1661-1718+); Falmouth, ME
BROCK, Andrew & Anna [GERRISH] (1671-), m/2 James JAFFREY; b 1698; Portsmouth, NH
BROCK, Francis (-1700) & Mary BUTLER (1683-); 29 Jul 1698; Boston

BROCK, Francis & Sarah [HOBART] (1670-1705), dau Israel; b 1699; Hingham

BROCK, Henry (-1652) & Elizabeth [?BARBER]; in Eng, b 1620; Dedham

BROCK, John (1620-1688) & Sarah (SYMMES) HAUGH/HOUGH (-1681), w Samuel; 13 Nov 1662; Reading, CT

BROCKETT, Benjamin (1645-1679) & Elizabeth BARNES, m/2 John AUSTIN (-1684/5); 24 Mar 1668/9; New Haven

BROCKETT, Jabez (1654-) & Dorothy LYMAN, Northampton; 20 Nov 1691; Wallingford, CT

BROCKETT, John[1] (?1613, 1610-1690, Wallingford) & _?_ ; b 1642?, b 1643?; New Haven/Wallingford, CT

BROCKETT, John (1642/3-1720) & Elizabeth [DOOLITTLE] (1652-1731); b 1674/5, b 1673; New Haven/North Haven

BROCKETT, Samuel (1652-1742) & 1/wf Sarah BRADLEY; 23 May 1682, 21 May; New Haven

BROCKETT, Samuel & 1/wf Rachel BROWN (1677-); 15 Apr 1699; Wallingford, CT

BROCKLEBANK, John (-1666) & Sarah WOODMAN, m/2 John ADAMS 1667?; 26 Sep 1657; Rowley

BROCKLEBANK, Capt. Samuel (-1676) & Hannah _?_ , m/2 Richard DOLE 1678/9; 18 May 1652; Rowley

BROCKLEBANK, Samuel & Elizabeth PLATS/PLATTS; 23 Nov 1681; Rowley

BROCKLEBANK _?_ (d in Eng) & Jane _?_ (-1668) (sister-in-law of George ABBOTT of Rowley); in Eng, ca 1627; Rowley

BROCKWAY, Richard (1673-1718) & 1/wf Rachel _?_ (-1718); 25 Oct 1697; Lyme, CT

BROCKWAY, William (1666-1755) & Elizabeth _?_ ; 8 Mar 1692, 1692/3; Lyme, CT

BROCKWAY, Wolston[1] (-1717) (ae ca 70 in 1714) & 1/wf Hannah (BRIGGS) [HARRIS] (1642-1687), w John; b 1664; Lyme, CT

BROCKWAY, Wolston[1] (-1717) & 2/wf Hannah BRIGGS (1666-1739); aft 6 Feb 1686/7; Lyme, CT

BROCKWAY, Wolston[2] (1667-1707) & Margaret [JONES?], m/2 Thomas ENNIS 1711; 4 Dec 1688; Lyme, CT

BROCKWAY, _?_ & _?_ ; 4 Oct 1668; Lyme, CT

BRODGE, Samuel & Sarah _?_ ; b 1699; Boston

BROMFIELD, Edward (1649-) & 1/wf Elizabeth [BRADING], dau James; ca 1678; Boston

BROMFIELD, Edward (-1734) & 2/wf Mary [DANFORTH] (1663-1734); 4 Jun 1683; ?Cambridge/Boston

BROMEFIELD, John & Hannah PARKER, dau Ralph, m/2 Richard WYATT 1704?; 16 Jan 1698/9; New London

BROMLEY, Luke[1] & Hannah [STAFFORD] (-1692(-)); b 1665; Warwick, RI

BROMLEY, Luke[2] (-1697) & Tamsen/Tamzon/Thomasine [PARKER/PACKER] (-1762), m/2 Robert PARK 1698; aft 1692, b 1692?, 1691?; Stonington, CT

BROMLEY, William (-1701) & Lydia [BILLINGS], m/2 Samuel COYE 1704; b 1689; Stonington, CT/New London, CT

BRONSDON/BRINSDON, Robert (-1701) & 1/wf Bathsheba RICHARDS; 15 Apr 1667; Lynn/Boston

BRONSDON, Robert (-1701) & 2/wf Rebecca (HETT?) [COOLEY] (-1689), w Henry; b 1679, ?-Jan 1678, bef 8 Sep 1678, aft 17 Dec 1677; Boston

BRONSDON, Robert (-1701) & 3/wf Hannah/Anna? (BARNES) BREAM (-1730), w Benjamin; 12 Apr 1694; Boston

BRONSON, Abraham (1647-1747) & Hannah/Ann/Anna? BRONSON/(GRISWOLD, dau Matthew)/SCOTT?; 2 Sep 1674; Lyme, CT/Waterbury, CT

BRONSON, Benjamin & Sarah _?_ ; b 1690; Waterbury, CT

BRONSON, Cornalius (ca 1649-1732) & [Abigail WELTON] (-1742+); 1691, b 1692; Woodbury, CT

BRONSON, Isaac (1645-1720) & Mary [ROOT] (ca 1650-); [1669]; Farmington, CT/Woodbury, CT

BRONSON, Jacob (1640/1-1708/9) & 1/wf Mary _?_ ; b 1675

BRONSON, Jacob (1640/1-1708/9) & 2/wf? Mary (ANDREWS) [BARNES] (1643-), w Thomas; b 1689; Farmington, CT

BRONSON, John (?1600-1680) & [?Frances] _?_ ; b 1631, b 1646; Hartford/Farmington, CT/Attleboro, CT

BROMSON/BRONSON?, John & Hannah __?__ [SCOTT]; 25 Oct 1664; Wethersfield, CT

BRONSON, John (?1643-1696?) & Sarah [VENTRUS/VENTRIS] (1649-1712); b 1670, b 1689, b 1698, ?ca 1668; Farmington, CT

BRONSON, John (ca 1670-1749) & 1/wf Rachel BUCK (1678-1708); Jun 1697; Farmington, CT

BRONSON, John (1673-) & Mary HICKOX; 9 Nov 1697; Waterbury, CT

BRONSON, Richard (-ca 1640, Hartford) & __?__

BRONSON, Richard (-1687) & 1/wf Abigail WILBOURNE; 25 Nov 1619, b 1643; Hartford/Farmington, CT

BRONSON, Richard (-1687) & 2/wf Elizabeth (WILBOURNE) (CARPENTER) [ORVIS] (-1694), ?Weyburn, w David, w George (see William PANTRY); aft 27 Apr 1664; Farmington, CT

BRONSON, Samuel & __?__ ; b 1680; Braintree

BRONSON, Samuel & Sarah GIBBS, Windsor; 4 May 1687; Farmington, CT

BRONSON, Samuel (-1733), New Milford & Lydia [WARNER] (1681-), m/2 Jonathan LUM; b 1701?, b 1697; Farmington, CT/Waterbury, CT

BRONSON, Samuel (1676-1725?) & Ruth __?__ ; b 1701?, b 1710; Waterbury, CT

BROOKER, John, Cambridge & Mary SMITH (1668-), Charlestown; 1 Nov 1694; Charlestown/Cambridge/Guilford, CT

BROOKER, Francis & Sarah HUBBERT; 9 Nov 1693; Boston

BROOKHOUSE, John & Anna TUFTS (1676-); 24 Jun 1700; Charlestown/Medford

BROCKUS, William & Mary (BATSON) [CLAY], w Jonas; b 1670; Barbados

BROOKING, Godfrey (1649?-1681) & Hannah [DREW]?, m/2 Nicholas FELLETT, m/3 Abraham HESELTINE/HAZELTON; by 1671; Isles of Shoals

BROOKINGS, Henry & __?__ ; b 1629?, b 1641; Isles of Shoals

BROOKING, Henry (?1641-) & 2/wf? Eleanor [KNIGHT], w George; by 1672, by 10 Oct 1672; Isles of Shoals

BROOKINGS, Henry & 3/wf? Sarah __?__ , m/2 John LINSCOTT, m/3 John DONNELL; b 1686; Spruce Creek/Kittery

BROOKIN, John (-1683) & Elizabeth [HOLLARD] (1638-), m/2 Edward GROVE; b 1659; Boston

BROOKINGS, John & Abigail __?__ ; b 1687; Boston

BROOKINGS, William (?1629-1694) & Mary [WALFORD] (1635-), m/2 William WALKER 1695; by 1660?; Portsmouth, NH

BROOKS, Benjamin (1671-) & Mary __?__ ; b 1693; Springfield

BROOKS, Beriah & Mary YORK; 8 Apr 1698; Stonington, CT

BROOKS, Caleb (-1696) & 1/wf Susannah/Susan ATKINSON (1641-1669/70, 1668/9?); 10 Apr 1660; Concord

BROOKS, Caleb (-1696) & 2/wf Hannah [?ATKINSON] (1642-1709, 1702?); b 1670/[1?]; Medford

BROOKS, Daniel (1663-1733) & Anne/Anna? MERRIAM (1669-1733); 9 Aug 1692; Concord

BROOKS, Ebenezer (1666-) & Martha WILDER; 14 Jun 1687; Woburn/Killingby, CT

BROOKS, Ebenezer (1671-1742/3) & Abigail [BOYLSTON] (1674-1756); ca 1693; Charlestown/Medford

BROOKS, Ebenezer (1662-) & Elizabeth [BELDING]; b 1695, ?8 Oct 1693; Deerfield

BROOKE?/BROCK, Francis & Sarah [HOBART] (1670-19 Jan 1704/5); b 1699; Scituate

BROOKS, Gershom (?1634-1686) & Hannah ECCLES (-1716, 1717?), dau Richard; 12 Mar 1665/6; Concord

BROOKS, Gilbert (1621-1695) & Elizabeth [SIMMONS/SYMONS]? (-1687); b 1645; Scituate/Rehoboth/Marshfield

BROOKS, Gilbert (1621-1695) & 2/wf Sarah (READAWAY) CARPENTER, w Samuel; 18 Jan 1687, 1687/8; Rehoboth

BROOKS, Henry[1] (?1592-1683) & 1/wf __?__ ; in Eng, b 1623?; Woburn/Concord

BROOKS, Henry[1] (?1592-1683) & 2/wf Susanna (?BRADFORD) [RICHARDSON] (-1681), w Ezekiel; aft 21 Oct 1647, ca 1648, by 1651; Concord/Woburn

BROOKS, Henry & Hannah (POTTER) BLAKELY/BLAKESLEY (-1723), w Samuel; 21 Dec 1676; Wallingford, CT/New Haven

BROOKS, Henry[1] (?1592-1683) & 3/wf Annes (JORDAN) JAQUITH, w Abraham; 12 Jul 1682; Woburn

BROOKS, Henry (1671-) & Mary GRAVES, Sudbury; 9 Dec 1692; Woburn

BROOKS, Isaac (1643-1686) & Miriam DANIELS; 10 Jan 1666, 1665/6; Woburn

BROOKS, Isaac (1669-) & Anna/Hannah [TRASK] (1668-), m/2 Timothy WRIGHT; b 1689; Woburn

BROOKS, Jabez (1673-1747) & 1/wf Rachel BUCK (-1697/8); 18 Dec 1694; Woburn

BROOKS, Jabez (1673-1747) & 2/wf Hepzibah CUTTER (-1746, ae 75); 7 Jun 1698; Woburn

BROOKS, James & Jane WERDIN; m int 7 Sep 1696; Boston

BROOKS, John (-1691) & 1/wf Eunice MOUSALL (-1684); 1 Nov 1649; Woburn

BROOKS, John (-1682) & Susanna HANMORE (1632-1676); 25 May 1652; Windsor, CT/Simsbury, CT

BROOKS, John & [?Mary GRIGGS?], ?dau George; b 1654; New Haven/Wallingford, CT

BROOKS, John (1657-1697) & Deborah GARFIELD (1665-); 8 Nov 1682; Watertown

BROOKS, John & _?_; b 1683; Easthampton, LI

BROOKS, ?John & Martha [COLE]? (1662-); ?ca 1683 (doubtful); ?Swansea

BROOKS, John (-1691) & 2/wf Mary (CHAMPNEY) RICHARDSON (-1704), w Theophilus; 25 Feb 1684, 1683/4; Woburn

BROOKS, John (1664-1733) & Mary (BRUCE) CRANSTON, w Walter, m/3 Peter HAY; 30 Jan 1685, 1684/5, 30 Dec 1684; Woburn

BROOKS, John (-1695) & Sarah (OSBORN) PEAT, w John; 25 Mar 1685; Stratford, CT

BROOKS, John (-1712) & Eleanor [FRYE] (?1668-), m/2 John BISHOP; by 1692; Kittery, ME

BROOKS, John, Cambridge & Mary SMITH, Charlestown; 1 Nov 1694; ?Woburn

BROOKS, Joseph (1667-1743) & Lydia WARNER; 8 Dec 1698, 29? Dec; Deerfield/Northfield

BROOKS, Joshua (-1697?) & Hannah MASON (1636-1692); 17 Oct 1653; Watertown/Concord

BROOKS, Nathaniel (1646-) & Elizabeth CURTIS; 24 Dec 1678, 25 Dec 1678; Scituate

BROOKS, Nathaniel (1664-) & 1/wf Mary [WILLIAMS] (1673-1704); b 1696; Deerfield

BROOKS, Noah (1656-1738/9) & Dorothy POTTER (-1752, in 90th y), dau Luke POTTER; b 1686; Watertown

BROOKS, Richard (1611-1687) & _?_; Lynn/Southampton, LI/Easthampton, LI

BROOKS, ?Richard (?1638-1707?) & 1/wf? ?Hannah [HUBBARD] (1641-); Boston

BROOKS, Richard & Mary (?BLANCHARD) [COOPER], ?w Josiah; ca 1679?, b 14 May 1691; Boston

BROOKS, Robert (1596-) & Ann/Anne [DERRICK] (1596-), w William; Canterbury, Eng, m lic 20 Apr 1621, b 1621?; ?New London, CT

BROOKS, Robert & Elizabeth [WINSLOW], m/2 George CORWIN 1669; b 1656?; Plymouth

BROOKS, Samuel (son Richard) & _?_; b 1675; Easthampton, LI

BROOKS, Samuel & Sarah _?_; b 1690; Simsbury

BROOKS, Samuel (1672-1735) & Sarah [BOYLSTON] (1680-1736); b 1701?; Charlestown

BROOKS, Thomas (-1667) & Grace [?WHEELER] (-1664); ca 1624/27?; Watertown/Concord

BROOKS, Thomas (-1668) & 1/wf Lucy _?_; b 1661; Haddam, CT

BROOKS, Thomas (-1668) & 2/wf ?Marah [SPENCER], m/2 Thomas SHALER bef 11 Apr 1670; 1662?; Haddam, CT

BROOKS, Thomas & Hannah _?_; b 1672; Portsmouth, RI/Newport

BROOKS, Thomas (-1704) & _?_; ca 1675; Canterbury, CT

BROOKS, Thomas & Hannah BISBEE; 6 Jun 1687; Scituate

BROOKS, Thomas (1664-1734) & Susannah [ARNOLD] (1675-); 16 Nov 1695/6; Haddam, CT

BROOKS, Timothy (-1712) & 1/wf Mary RUSSELL (-1680); 2 Dec 1659; Woburn/Billerica/Swansea

BROOKS, Timothy (-1712) & 2/wf Mehitable (MOWRY) [KINSLEY], w Eldad; 1680; Swansea

BROOKS, Timothy (1661-1716) & Hannah BOWEN; 10 Nov 1685; Swansea/Conaway, NJ

BROOKS, Titus & Elizabeth NOAKS; 20 Nov 1694; Boston

BROOKS, William (-1684) & 1/wf Bridget _?_ (-1663?); b 8 Sep 1644; Milford, CT

BROOKS, William (1615-) & 1/wf _?_; b 1645; Scituate

BROOKS, William (-1688, Deerfield) & Mary BURT (1635-1689); 18 Oct 1654; Springfield

BROOKS, William (1615-) & 2/wf Susanna (HANFORD) [WISTON/WHISTON], w John; b 6 Mar 1665/6; Scituate

BROOKS, William (-1684) & 2/wf Sarah (?DELL) [WHEELER] (-?1703, 1709?), w William; [1666]; Milford, CT

BROOKS, _?_ & Mary GRIGGS, dau George of Boston; b 4 Jul 1655

BROOM/BROOME, George (-1660/1, 1662?, Boston) & Hannah _?_, m/2 Thomas ASHLEY 1662; b 1660; Boston

BROUGH, Edmund/Edward & Mary __?__ (-1658); Boston
BURPH, Stephen & Elizabeth PERRY (-1689); 29 May 1674; Rehoboth
BRUFF, Stephen & Damores __?__; b 1701; Boston
BROUGHTON, George & Perne [RAWSON] (1646-); b 1668, b 1667; Boston
BROUGHTON, John (-1662) & Hannah BASCOM, m/2 William JANES 1662; 15 Nov 1650; Windsor, CT/Northampton
BROUGHTON, John (-1689) & Abigail [REYNER] (-1716), m/2 Thomas KENDALL 1696; b 1677; Boston
BROUGHTON, John (-1731), Northampton & 1/wf Elizabeth WOODRUFF (?1651-); 29 Oct 1678; ?Farmington, CT/?Northampton/Windham, CT
BROUGHTON, John (-1731, Windham, CT) & 2/wf Hannah ALLICE/ALLIS/ALLEN?; 16 Nov 1691, 19 Nov; Deerfield/Windham, CT
BROUGHTON, Randol & Sarah __?__; b 1699; Boston
BROUGHTON, Thomas (ca 1614, ca 1613-1700, ae 87) & Mary [BRISCOE/BISCOE]; ca 1640, b 1643; Watertown/Boston
BROUGHTON, Thomas (1661-1693) & Hester [COLTON?/COTTON?/WELLS?]; 19 Nov 1684; Deerfield/Hatfield
BROUGHTON, __?__ & Hannah SCOTT (1679-); b 1701?; Deerfield
BROWN, Abraham (-1650, ae 55) & Lydia __?__ (-1686), m/2 Andrew HODGES 1659; in Eng, ca 1624?; Watertown
BROWN, Abraham/Abram (-1690+) & Jane SKIPPER (1635-living in 1682); 19 Aug 1653; Boston
BROWN, Abraham & Rebecca USHER, dau Hezekiah; 1 May 1660; Boston
BROWN, Abraham (-1667) & Mary DIX (-1675), m/2 Samuel RICE 1668; 5 Feb 1662/3, 5 Feb 1662; Watertown
BROWN, Abraham (-1733) & Elizabeth SHEPHERD; 15 Jun 1675; Salisbury
BROWN, Abraham (1671-1729) & Mary [HYDE] (1673-1723); 1691?, b 7 Nov 1692; Watertown
BROWN, Abraham & Mary (WATERS) OAKLEY, w Miles; b Apr 1693
BROWN, Andrew & __?__; b 1651?, 5 sons in 1663; Scarboro, ME/Boston
BROWN, Andrew (1658-1723) & 1/wf Ann [ALLISON]; ca 1686?, b 1691; Scarboro, ME
BROWN, Bartholomew (-1717) & Susannah MAUL, m/2 William MULHUISH/McEHRICH; 1 May 1693; Salem
BROWN, Benjamin (-1736) & Sarah [BROWN] (1658-1730); ca 1679; Hampton, NH/Salisbury
BROWN, Benjamin & Mary [HICKS]; b 1686; Salem
BROWN, Beriah & Sarah HARRIS; 6 Jan 1673, 1673/4; Rowley
BROWN, Beriah (-1717) & Abigail [PHENIX?/PHOENIX]; b 1685?, b 1687; Kingston, RI
BROWN, Boaz (1642-1724) & 1/wf Mary WINSHIP; 8 Nov 1664; Concord/Stow
BROWN, Boaz (1665-) & Abial __?__; b 1686; Stow
BROWN, Boaz & Mary (FULLER) RICHARDS, w John; 30 Sep 1695; Stow/Dedham
BROWN, Chad & Elizabeth SHARPAROWE; in Eng, 11 Sep 1626, High Wycombe; Boston/Providence
BROWN, Charles (-1687) & Mary [ACY/ACIE]; 14 Oct 1647; Rowley
BROWN, Christopher & Grace WEBSTER, ?w Benjamin; 13 Dec 1700; Beverly/Salem
BROWN, Cornelius (?1638-1701) & 1/wf Sarah LAMSON (-1683); 6 Mar 1664/5; Reading
BROWN, Cornelius (?1638-1701) & 2/wf Sarah (BURNETT?/BURNASS) (SOUTHERICK/SOUTH-WICK) COOPER, w John, div wf Thomas COOPER; 20 Nov 1684; Reading
BROWN, Cornelius (?1667-1743) & Susannah (STORY) [CLARK] (-1734, ae 74), w John; b 1689/90; Lynn/Boxford/Reading
BROWN, Cornelius (?1638-1701) & 3/wf Mary (DUSTIN) COLSON, w Adam; 26 Sep 1698; Reading
BROWN, Daniel (-1710) & Alice HEARNDON (1652-1718+); 25 Dec 1669; Providence
BROWN, Daniel (?1666-1733) & Abigail __?__; Newark, NJ
BROWN, Daniel (1668-1722) & Mary [HOWE] (1674-1761); b 1698; New Haven
BROWN, Deliverance & Mary [PURDY]; b 1676; New Haven
BROWN, Ebenezer (1647?-) & Hannah VINCENT (1639-); 28 Mar 1667; New Haven
BROWN, Ebenezer & Mary __?__; b 1692; Cambridge
BROWN, Ebenezer & Eleanor LANE, m/2 Samuel BLAKESLEE; 11 Feb 1695/6; New Haven
BROWN, Ebenezer & 1/wf Mary JEWETT; 29 Jul 1698; Rowley

BROWN, Edmund (-1678) & Ann (?BARNARD) LOVERINE, w John; aft 24 Nov 1638, 1644?, ?19 Jun 1639, no issue; Sudbury

BROWN, Edmund (-1682?) & Elizabeth OAKLEY; 14 Feb 1653/4; Boston/Dorchester

BROWN, Edmund & Martha [SHERMAN]; b 1658, b 1652?; Dorchester

BROWN, Edmund (1653-1695) & Elizabeth (PAYSON) [FOSTER] (1645-), w Hopestill; b 1685; Boston

BROWN, Edward (-1659/60) & Faith [LORD?]/WATSON? (-1679), m/2 Daniel WARNER 1660; Ipswich

BROWN, Edward (1640-1685) & Sarah DIX (1653-1726), m/2 Thomas LAUGHTON 1685; 21 Jul 1679; Reading

BROWN, Edward (1672/3-1711) & Elizabeth [HAPGOOD?]; b 1696; Stow

BROWN, Edward & Mary [MARTINE]; ca 1700; Southold, LI

BROWN, Eleazer (1642-1714) & Sarah [BULKELEY] (1640-1723); ca 1662, b 1633(4?); New Haven

BROWN, Eleazer & 1/wf Dinah SPAULDING (-1707); 9 Feb 1674, 1674/5; Chelmsford/Canterbury, CT

BROWN, Eleazer (1670-1734) & Ann PENDLETON (1667-); 18 Oct 1693; Stonington, CT

BROWN, Eleazer & Abigail [?CHANDLER] (?1681-1766?); b 1700; Chelmsford

BROWN, Ephraim (-1693) & Sarah _?_, m/2 Samuel CARTER, m/3 Benjamin EASTMAN 1719; b 1680; Salisbury

BROWN, Francis (1610-1668) & Mary [EDWARDS] (-1693), m/2 William PAYNE 1668+; in Eng, b 1636; New Haven

BROWN, Francis & 1/wf Mary JOHNSON (-1679); 21 Nov 1653; Newbury

BROWN, Francis & 1/wf Adera/Audery (?RUSCOE) [BENNETT], w George; b 14 Oct 1656; Farmington, CT

BROWN, Francis & 2/wf Martha (_?_) (LAWRENCE) CHAPMAN, w Thomas, w John; 17 Dec 1657; Stamford, CT

BROWN, Francis & 2/wf Mary (WOODHOUSE) (PIERCE) MORSE, w George, w Thomas; 31 Dec 1679; Newbury

BROWN, Francis (-1686) & 3/wf Judith (BUDD) [OGDEN], w John; b 1683; Stamford, CT/Rye, NY

BROWN, George (-1633, in Eng) & Christian HIBBERT (-1641); Salisbury, Eng, 30 Sep 1611; Salisbury

BROWNE, George (-1643) & _?_ ; by 1641?; Newbury

BROWN, George (1622-) & 1/wf Ann EATON (-1683); 25 Jun 1645; Salisbury

BROWN, George (1651/2-1721) & Mehitable [KNOWLES] (1653-1721+); ca 1674?; Eastham

BROWN, George (1622-1699, ae 76) & 2/wf Hannah (GRANT) HAZEN (-1716), w Edward; 17 Mar 1683/4; Haverhill

BROWN, George, Chelmsford & Sarah KIDDER (1667-), Chelmsford; 30 Jan 1689/90; Billerica.

BROWN, George & [?Charity CRANDALL]; b 9 Mar 1692; Westerly, RI

BROWN, George & Mary [BABCOCK]; b 1701?; Stonington, CT

BROWN, Gershom & Hannah [MANSFIELD]; b 1697; New Haven

BROWN, Hachaliah (1646, 1645?-) & Mary [?HOYTE]; b 1670?; Rye, NY

BROWN, Henry (-1701) & Abigail _?_ (-1702); b 1642; Salisbury

BROWN, Henry (?1625, 1626-1703) & 1/wf Wait/Wade [WATERMAN]; ca 1655/65; Salem

BROWN, Henry (1659-1708) & Hannah PUTNAM (1663-); 17 May 1682; Salisbury

BROWN, Henry (?1625-1703) & 2/wf Hannah (FIELD) [MATTHEWSON] (-1703+), w James; aft 1 Sep 1687; Providence

BROWN, Hopestill & 1/wf Abigail HAYNES; 26 Nov 1685; Sudbury

BROWN, Hugh (-1669?) & Sarah _?_ ; b 1641, b 1651, Boston; Salem

BROWN, Ichabod, Cambridge & Martha WOODBURY (1677-); 31 May 1693; Beverly/Cambridge

BROWN, Isaac (?1638-1674, ae 36) & Rebecca BAILEY (1641-1730), m/2 John DOGGETT 1697; 22 Aug 1661; Newbury

BROWN, Jabez (-1692, Stow) & 1/wf Hannah BLANFORD; 23 Dec 1667; Sudbury

BROWN, Jabez (-1692, Stow) & 2/wf Deborah [HAYNES] (1659-1717), m/2 John BRIGHAM; b 1680; Sudbury

BROWN, Jabez (1668, 1667-1747) & 1/wf Jane _?_ ; b 1696; Swansea

BROWN, Jacob & Mary TAPLEASE/TAPLEY?; in Boston, 16 Oct 1661; Billerica

BROWN, Jacob (?1653-1740) & Sarah [BROOKINGS]; b 1684; Hampton, NH
BROWN, James & Elizabeth _?_; b 1634; Charlestown
BROWN, James (?1605-1676) & 1/wf [Judith] [CUTTING]; b 1638; Charlestown
BROWN, James (-1651) & Grace _?_; b 1645; Boston
BROWN, James (?1605-1676) & Sarah [CUTTING] (-1699) (ae 50 in 1679), m/2 William HEALEY 1677, m/3 Hugh MARCH 1685; b 1652; Charlestown/Newbury/Salem
BROWN, James (ca 1623-1710, 11 Jan 1710/11+) (Uncle of William PARKER) & Lydia [HOWLAND] (-1710/11+, 29 Oct 1710); b 1655; Rehoboth/Swansea/Taunton
BROWN, James (-1675) & Hannah BARTHOLOMEW (-1713), m/2 John SWINNERTON 1680; 5 Sep 1664; Salem
BROWN, James (ca 1639-1708) & Hannah HOWES?/HOUSE/HUSE? (-1713); 16 Mar 1669/70, 16-1-1670; Charlestown/Salem/Newbury
BROWN, James (-1683(-)) & Elizabeth [CARR] (-1697+), m/2 Samuel GARDINER 1684?; b 1671; Newport
BROWN, James (ca 1647/8, 1645?-1704) & Remembrance BROOKS (-1713+); 7 Jan 1674, 1673/4?; Hatfield/Colchester, CT
BROWN, James (1655-1718) & Margaret DENISON (?1658, ?1657, 1656?-1741, in 85th y); 5 Jun 1678; Swansea/Barrington, RI
BROWN, James & 1/wf _?_; b 1682; Norwalk, CT
BROWN, James (1666-1732) & Mary HARRIS (1671-1736); 17 Dec 1691; Providence
BROWN, James (-1718) & Deborah _?_ (-1718+); b 1694; Eastham
BROWN, James (1671-) & 1/wf Mary EDWARDS (-1700); 28 Apr 1694, 8? Apr; Newbury/Norwalk, CT
BROWN, James & Elizabeth (PICKERING) NICHOLS (1674-), w Samuel; 22 Feb 1698/9; Salem
BROWN, James & 2/wf Rebecca (REYNOLDS/RUSCOE) (not CLAPHAM, w Peter); b 1700; Norwalk, CT
BROWN, James (-1756) & 1/wf Ann [CLARK]; ca 1700?, b 1700; Newport
BROWN, James & Rebecca [KELLY] (1675-1734+); b 1701, 2 Jan 1701; Newbury
BROWN, Jermiah & 1/wf Mary [?GARDINER]; b 1672; Newport
BROWN, Jeremiah & 2/wf Mary (_?_) [COOK], w Thomas; b 1680; Newport
BROWN, Job (-?1684) & Sarah _?_; b 1681; Boston
BROWN, John (1590, 1579?-1662, Rehoboth) & Dorothy _?_ (1584-1674, in 90th y); in Eng, b 1614; Plymouth/Swansea/etc.
BROWN, John & Margaret [HAYWARD]; in Eng, b 1625; Pemaquid
BROWN, John (1661-1637) & Dorthy _?_; b 1634; Watertown
BROWN, John & Phebe HARDING; 26 Mar 1634; ?Duxbury
BROWN, John (-1685?) & ?Mary/Alice _?_; b 1638, by 1636?; Salem
BROWN, John (-1687) & Sarah [?WALKER] (?1618-1672); ca 1638/42?; Hampton, NH
BROWN, John (-1677) & Mary _?_; b 1643; Ipswich
BROWN, John (-1690) & Mary [BURWELL] (1623-); ca 1643?; Milford, CT/Newark, NJ
BROWN, John (-1662) (called John TISDALE "cousin") & 1/wf [?Ann DENNIS] (-1652?); ca 1645/9?, b 1650; Taunton/Rehoboth
BROWN, John (1631-) & Esther MAKEPEACE (-1694+); 24 Apr 1655; Boston/Marlboro/Watertown/Falmouth, ME
BROWN, John (-1662) & 2/wf Lydia [BUCKLAND], m/2 William LORD 1664, m/3 Thomas DUNK, m/4 Abraham POST; b 1656?; Rehoboth
BROWN, John (1630-1706±) & Mary [HOLMES] (-1690+); ca 1658?; Providence
BROWN, John, Jr. (-1677) & Hannah HOBART/HUBBARD (1638-1691), m/2 John ROGERS 1679; 2 Jun 1658; Salem
BROWN, John (1638-) & Mary WOODMAN (ca 1638-); 20 Feb 1659, 1659/60?; Newbury
BROWN, John (-1714) & 1/wf Elizabeth OSGOOD (-1673); 12 Oct 1659, 18 Oct 1659; Andover/Reading
BROWN, John (1640-) & Mary WALKER, m/2 John CLARK 1675; 1 Jan 1660/1, div 1674; New Haven
BROWN, John & _?_; b 1664; Ipswich
BROWN, John & Elizabeth _?_; b 1665; Boston
BROWN, John ([?1646]-) & 1/wf Rebecca [CLARK] (1646-ca 1693); ca 1665?; ?Milford, CT/Newark, NJ

BROWN, John & Mary [BURWELL]?, w John?; aft 13 Apr 1665; Milford, CT
BROWN, John & Hannah COLLINS; 27 Jan 1668; Salem
BROWN, John (1650-1709) & Anne MASON (1650-); 8 Nov 1672; Swansea/?Saybrook, CT
BROWN, Capt. John (?1634-1717), Reading & 1/wf Anna/Hannah FISKE (1646-1681); 30 May 1677; Chelmsford/Reading
BROWN, John (?1640-1727) & Hannah [DENISON] (1652-1727); b 1678; Ipswich
BROWN, John & 1/wf Dorcas _?_ (-29 Feb 1678); Dorchester
BROWN, John & 2/wf Mary _?_ ; b 1681; Dorchester
BROWN, John (-1714, ae 86) & 2/wf Sarah [BARSHAM]?; 14 Nov 1681; Reading
BROWN, John (-1695) & Rebecca [BOADEN] (-1725); ca 1682?, 6 ch living 1695; ?Marblehead/etc.
BROWN, Capt. John (?1634-1717) & 2/wf Elizabeth (BULKELEY) EMERSON (?1643, ?1638-1693, in 56th y), w Joseph; 29 Mar 1682; Reading
BROWN, John & Elizabeth POLLY; 22 Apr 1682; Billerica/Woburn
BROWN, John (-1707) & Elizabeth _?_ (-1768?); b 1683; Colchester, CT
BROWN, John & Ruth HUSE; 27 Aug 1683; Newbury
BROWN, John (1657-1719?) & ?Hannah/Ann PORTER (1668-); 1 Apr 1685; Middletown, CT
BROWN, John (1653-) & Abigail BROWN (1665-); 31 Aug 1685; Rowley
BROWN, John & Mary [AMBLER] (1664-); ?Bedford, NY
BROWN, John & Elizabeth LEGG; 28 May 1686; Salem/Marblehead/Wenham
BROWN, John (1666-) & Rachel GARDNER (1662-), m/2 James GARDNER; 31 Aug 1686; Salem
BROWN, John & _?_ ; b 1690; Ipswich
BROWN, John & _?_ ; b 1690; Eastham
BROWN, John (1668, 1668/9-1728/9) & Elizabeth LOOMIS (1671-1723); 4 Feb 1691/2; Windsor, CT
BROWN, John & Elizabeth MINER (1674-); - Oct 1692; Stonington, CT
BROWN, John (1671-1731) & Elizabeth [CRANSTON] (1671-1756), m/2 Rev. James HONEYMAN; b 1693, b 1696, ca 1695; Stonington, CT
BROWN, John, Jr. & Elizabeth FITCH (1672-1696); 29 May 1694; Reading
BROWN, John (-1732) & 1/wf Rebecca _?_ (-1711); b 1695; Glouchester
BROWN, John & Elizabeth [SAFFORD] (1670-); ca 1696; Ipswich/Wenham/Preston, CT
BROWN, John (1662-1719) & Isabel/Isabella? MATHEWSON (-1719+); 9 Jun 1696; Providence
BROWN, John (1675-1752) & 1/wf Abigail COLE; 2 Jul 1696; Swansea/?Newport
BROWN, John (1678-) & 1/wf Mary (FELLOWS) [HOVEY] (1676-), w Nathaniel; ca 1697, aft 31 Mar 1696, b 1698; Newbury/Salisbury
BROWN, John & Sarah DEXTER; 19 May 1697; Malden/Reading
BROWN, John (?1634-1717) & 2/wf Rebecca (CRAWFORD) SPRAGUE (1634-1710), w Samuel; 24 Jun 1697; Malden/Reading
BROWN, John & Sarah [HOWE] (1676-); b 1698; Roxbury
BROWN, John & Sarah (RUCK) (HAWTHORNE) BURROUGHS, w William, w George; 21 Apr 1698; Boston
BROWN, John & [Hannah (NORTON) WILLIAMS], w Augustine; b 1700, ca 1693; Killingworth, CT
BROWN, Jonathan (-1691) & Mary SHATTUCK (1645-1732); 11 Feb 1661/2, 11 Feb 1661; Watertown
BROWN, Jonathan (-1667) & Abiel BURR?/BURRILL, m/2 Samuel SHRIMPTON 1668; 28 Jun 1664; Salem
BROWN, Jonathan & 1/wf _?_ ; b 1686; Southold, LI
BROWN, Jonathan & 2/wf Eliza SILVESTER; aft Mar 1695/6; Southold, LI
BROWN, Jonathan (1668-) & Lydia KENDRICK; 6 Apr 1694; Ipswich
BROWN, Jonathan (1670-) & Mindwell LOOMIS; 1 Oct 1696; Windsor, CT
BROWN, Joseph (?1639, 1641-1694) & Hannah/Anna? (called Abigail in 1684, error) ASSELBIE/ASLETT?; 27 Feb 1671; Ipswich
BROWN, Joseph (1647-1708) & Elizabeth BANCROFT (1653-1708+); 26 May 1674; Reading
BROWN, Joseph (1652-1694) & Hannah FREEMAN (1656-)
BROWN, Joseph (?1646-1678) & [Mehitable] [BRENTON] (1652-1676); b 3 Oct 1675; Charlestown
BROWN, Joseph (1658-1731) & Hannah FITCH (-1739); 10 Nov 1680; Rehoboth

BROWN, Joseph & Sarah JONES; 22 Dec 1680; Lynn
BROWN, Joseph & [Mary] _?_ ; b 1686; Stamford, CT
BROWN, Joseph (-1732) & Sarah [TREADWELL] (-1736+); ca 1694; Salisbury/Newbury
BROWN, Joseph & Lydia EMERY (1674-); m int 23 May 1696; Newbury
BROWNE, Joseph (ca 1675-) & Margaret JOHNSON (ca 1672-); b 1701?; Newark, NJ
BROWN, Joseph (1677-1766) & Ruhamah WELLINGTON (1680-1772); 15 Nov 1699; Watertown
BROWN, Joshua & Sarah SAWYER (1651-); 15 Jan 1668, 1668/9?; Newbury
BROWN, Joshua & Rebecca [LIBBY] (1651-); ca 1670/75?; Scarboro, ME
BROWN, Joshua & Elizabeth [BARTLETT] (1672-); b 1693; Newbury
BROWN, Josiah (?1636-1691) & Mary FELLOWS (-bef 1699); 23 Feb 1666/7; Reading/Marblehead
BROWN, Josiah (1675-1754) & Susanna GOODWIN (1681-); 19 Dec 1700; Reading
BROWN, Moses & _?_ ; b 1675; Flushing, LI
BROWN, Nathaniel (-1658) & Eleanor WATTS (ca 1625-1703), m/2 Jasper CLEMENTS, m/3
    Nathaniel WILLET; 23 Dec 1647; Hartford/Middletown, CT/Springfield
BROWN, Nathaniel & _?_ ; b 1653; ?New Haven
BROWN, Nathaniel (1645-1723) & Hannah FELLOWS (-1727); 18 Oct 1666, 16 Nov; Salisbury
BROWN, Nathaniel (1644-) & Hannah _?_ (-1672?); b 1668, had Sarah; Ipswich
BROWN, Nathaniel (?1652-1717) & Judith PERKINS (1655-); 16 Dec 1673; Ipswich
BROWN, Nathaniel (1654-1712) & Martha HUGHES/HUSE (1655-1729); 2 Jul 1677; Middletown,
    CT
BROWN, Nathaniel (1660-1731) & Mary WHEELER (1670-); 4 Jun 1685; Rowley
BROWN, Nathaniel (1661-1739) & 1/wf Sarah [JENCKS] (1660-1708); b 1688; Rehoboth
BROWN, Nathaniel & Elizabeth [FISKE] (1677-); b 1699; Ipswich
BROWN, Nicholas (-1673) & Elizabeth _?_ (-1674); b 1634; Lynn/Reading
BROWN, Nicholas (-1694) & 1/wf _?_ ; ca 1638; Portsmouth, RI
BROWN, Nicholas & 2/wf Frances [PARKER], w George; aft 1656; Portsmouth, RI
BROWN, Nicholas & Mary LINFURTH; 27 Jan 1669; Haverhill
BROWN, Nicholas (-1713) & Rebecca NICHOLS (1684-1765), m/3 Jonathan BARRETT 1716; 22
    May 1700; Reading
BROWN, Obadiah & _?_ ; b 1647; New London, CT
BROWN, Peter (-1633) & 1/wf Martha [FORD] (1634+-), wid; ca 1624; Plymouth
BROWN, Peter (-1633) & 2/wf Mary _?_ (-1634+); betw 1637 & 1641, 1627-1631?; Plymouth
BROWN, Peter (-1658) & 1/wf Elizabeth _?_ (-21 Sep 1657); b 1638, b 1632?; New
    Haven/Stamford, CT
BROWN, Peter (ca 1632, ca 1631-1692) & Mary GILLETT (ca 1635, ca 1638, aft 1692-1719?);
    15 Jul 1658; Windsor, CT
BROWN, Peter (-1658) & 2/wf Unity (_?_) BUXTON, w Clement, m/3 Nicholas KNAPP 1659; 22
    Jul 1658; Stamford, CT
BROWN, Peter & Rebecca [?DISBROW]; 20 Aug 1694; Rye, NY
BROWN, Peter (-1722) & Mary BARBER; 22 Jul 1696; Windsor, CT
BROWN, Philip (-1729) & Mary BUSWELL (-1683); 24 Jun 1669; Salisbury
BROWN, Richard & 1/wf _?_ ; ca 1600/1610; Watertown
BROWN, Richard (-1661) (ae 81 or 82 in 1657) & Elizabeth (_?_) MARCH, w George, m/3
    Richard JACKSON 1662?; Watertown
BROWN, Richard & 1/wf Edith _?_ (-1647); b 1642; Newbury
BROWN, Richard (-1661) & 2/wf Elizabeth (GREENLEAF) [BADGER] (1622-), w Giles; ?16
    Feb 1647/8, aft 10 Jul 1647; Newbury/Salisbury
BROWN, Richard & Hannah [KING] (?1629-); ca 1650?; ?Southold, LI
BROWN, Richard & Mary JAQUES; 7 May 1674; Salisbury/Newbury
BROWN, Richard & Dorothy KING, m/2 Samuel DAYTON 1705; 8 May 1683; Southold, LI
BROWN, Richard & Mary _?_ ; b 1689; Boston
BROWN, Richard (1676-1774) & Mary [RHODES]; 25 Nov 1697; ?Providence
BROWN, Robert (-1690) & Barbara EDEN (-1693); 8 May 1649; Cambridge
BROWN, Samuel & Mary MATTOCKE, m/2 Thomas BISHOP?; 9 Jul 1661; Boston
BROWN, Samuel (1645-) & Mercy TUTTLE (1650-1695+); 2 May 1667; New Haven/Wallingford,
    CT
BROWN, Samuel (?1656, ?1660-1691) (had Samuel & Bethiah) & Martha HARDING (-1692+); 19
    Feb 1682; Eastham

BROWN, Samuel & 1/wf Eunice **TURNER** (1676-1706); 19 Mar 1695/6; Salem
BROWN, Samuel & Anna [**TAYLOR**] (1680-); b 1699; New Haven
BROWN, Stephen & Sarah _?_ ; b 1640; Newbury
BROWN, Thomas (1607-1687) & Mary [?**EMERY**] (-1654, 1655); Malford, Eng, b 1633?; Newbury
BROWN, Thomas (-1688) & Bridget _?_ ; b 1642; Concord/Cambridge
BROWN, Thomas (1628-1693) & Mary [**NEWHALL**] (1637-1701+); b 1653?; Lynn
BROWN, Thomas (-1690, 1691) & Martha (**EATON**) **OLDHAM** (1630-), w Richard; 7 Oct 1656; Cambridge
BROWN, Thomas (?1628-) & Hannah (**CARTER/KENDALL?**) [**GREEN**] (-1658, 1657), ?w William; b 1658; Charlestown
BROWN, Thomas (-1709) & 1/wf Patience **FOSTER** (1646-1703); 29 Sep 1667; Sudbury
BROWN, Thomas & Hannah **COLLINS** (1659/60-); 8 Jan 1677, 1677/8; Lynn/Stonington, CT
BROWN, Thomas (1651-1718) & Ruth (**WHEELER**) **JONES** (-1740), w Ephraim, m/3 Jonathan **PRESCOTT**; 12 Nov 1677; Concord
BROWN, Thomas (1655-1711?) & Mary **FREEMAN** (1658-); Newark, NJ
BROWN, Thomas & Abigail _?_ ; b 1680(1?); Lexington
BROWN, Thomas & Mary **HALL**; 23 May 1681; Cambridge
BROWN, Thomas (1657-1744) & Abial [**SHAW**] (1662-1739); b 1686; Hampton, NH
BROWN, Thomas (-1717, Colchester) & Hannah **LEE**; 8 Mar 1687, 1687/8?; Springfield/Westfield
BROWN, Thomas (1667-1739) & Rachel [**POULTER**]; b 1692; Concord
BROWN, Thomas (-1723) & Sarah [**DICKENS**] (-1723), w Nathaniel; aft 1692; New Shoreham, RI
BROWN, Thomas & Elizabeth **BERRY**; m int 31 Aug 1695; Newbury
BROWN, Thomas & Mary **PILLSBURY**; 6 Oct 1697; Haverhill/Newbury
BROWN, Thomas & Elizabeth **MacDOWELL**; 25 Nov 1700; Boston
BROWN, Thomas & Elizabeth [**MASON**] (1678-); b 1701?; Cambridge/Boston/Watertown
BROWN, Walter (1659+-1712?) & 1/wf _?_ ; ca 1685/94, 2 ch in 1698; Southold, LI
BROWN, Walter & 2/wf Jane **CONKLIN**, m/2 Daniel **EDWARDS** 1712; 15 May 1700; Easthampton, LI/Southold
BROWN, William (1585-1650) & Jane **BURGIS/BURGESS**; Rusper, Sussex, 20 Jun 1617; Hampstead, LI/Saybrook, CT/Southampton, LI
BROWN, William & Thomasine _?_ ; b 1634; Boston
BROWN, William (1609-) & 1/wf Mary [**YOUNGS**] (1609-1636, 1638); b 1635; Salem
BROWN, William (1609-) & 2/wf Sarah [**SMITH**] (-1668); ca 1637?, aft 1636, bef 1639; Salem
BROWN, William (-1676) (Mrs. Ann **HARVEY** his aunt) & Mary **BISBY/BISBEE/BESBOTH?**; 15 Nov 1641; Sudbury
BROWN, William & Elizabeth **MUNFORD?/MURFORD**; ?25 Jun 1645, betw 25 Jun 1645 & 11 Aug 1646; Salisbury
BROWN, William (-1662) & 1/wf or 2/wf Mary (_?_) **ROBINSON**, w Abraham, m/3 Henry **WALKER** 1662; 15 Jul 1646; Gloucester
BROWN, William (-1694) & Mary **MURCOCK/MURDOCK?** (-1694+); 16 Jul 1649; Plymouth/Eastham
BROWN, William & _?_ ; b 1650; Reading, had Sarah
BROWN, William (-1662?) & Hannah _?_ ; b 1653; Boston
BROWN, William & Elizabeth **RUGGLES**, m/2 John **ROGERS** 1669; 24 Apr 1655; Boston
BROWN, William (-1689) & [Lydia] **PARCHMENT** (-1680, ae ca 46); 11 Apr 1656; Boston/Bristol, RI
BROWN, William & Mary [?**CHINN**], m/2 Richard **GROSS** 1684; b 1664; Marblehead
BROWN, William & Persis _?_ ; b 1664; Boston
BROWN, William & 1/wf Hannah **CORWIN** (1646-1692); 29 Dec 1664; Salem
BROWN, William (1638?-1678) (ae 35 in 1673) & Elizabeth **DOWNE**; 5 Jan 1664/5, 1664; Charlestown/Boston
BROWN, William & Sarah [?**BARSHAM**]; b 1669; Salem/Marblehead
BROWN, William (-1724, ae 78) & 1/wf Mary **GOODWIN** (?1656-1678, ae 22); 29 Feb 1671/2, 29 Feb 1672; Charlestown
BROWN, William (-1686+, 1695, 1697?, will 1689) & ?Jemima/Jennings?/Jinnus? [**WILLIAMS**]; b 1673; ?Portsmouth, RI/Bristol, RI

BROWN, William (?1650-1705) & Margaret STONE (1653-1718), m/2 Joseph FOSTER 1714; 11 Jan 1675, 1675/6?; Sudbury

BROWN, William (-1724, ae 78) & 2/wf Mary LATHROP (?1660-1713); 21 May 1679; Charlestown

BROWN, William & Catherine _?_ ; ca 1683; Southold, LI

BROWN, William & Secunda _?_ ; b 1684; Boston

BROWN, William & Mary _?_ (-1741+); b 1688, b 1686; Boston

BROWN, William (-1716) & Rebecca (FRIEND) BAILEY, w Thomas; 26 Apr 1694; Salem/Boston/Watertown

BROWN, William & 2/wf Mary JACKLIN; 29 Oct 1694; Boston

BROWN, William & Hannah JOY; 6 Sep 1695, 23 Sep 1695; Salem/Marblehead

BROWN, William & Mary _?_ ; bef, b 1695/6, b 1696; Hadley

BROWN, William & Mary BAKER; at Lynn, 4 Nov 1696; Salem

BROWN, William & Ann FROST; m int 14 Dec 1696; Boston

BROWN, William & Sarah _?_ ; b 1697; Bristol, RI/Swansea

BROWN, William & Rebecca _?_ ; b 1697; Sherborn

BROWN, William & Joanna TAYNOUR; 11 Nov 1697; Marblehead

BROWN, William & Susannah [HARDING], w John; 27 Oct 1699; Eastham

BROWN, (?John) & Martha (MATTHEWS) [SNELL], wid; b 1678; Dover, NH

BROWN, _?_ & Elizabeth NICHOLSON (1616-), w Edward/Edmund

BROWNELL, George (1646-1718) & Susanna PEARCE (1652-1743); 4 Dec 1673; Portsmouth, RI/Tiverton, RI

BROWNELL, Robert (1652-1728) & Mary _?_ (-1728+); b 1687, b 1677?; Portsmouth, RI

BROWNELL, Thomas¹ (-1665±) & Ann [BOURNE?] (-1665+); 20 May 1637, ca 1638/44; Portsmouth, RI/Little Compton, RI

BROWNELL, Thomas (1650-1732) & Mary [PEARCE] (1654-1736); 1678?; Portsmouth, RI/Tiverton, RI/Little Compton, RI

BROWNELL, Thomas³ & Esther TABER; May 1698, 15 Nov 1698; Tiverton, RI/Little Compton, RI

BROWNELL, William² (ca 1648-1715+) & Sarah [SMITON] (1654-1715+); b 1674, 1672?; Portsmouth, RI/Little Compton, RI

BROWNING, Henry & Mary _?_ ; b 1640; New Haven

BROWNING/BRUNNING, Joseph (-1691) & Marah/Mary COBHAM (-1739?), m/2 John ROGERS 1693?; b 1690; Boston

BROWNING, Malachi (-1653) & Mary [COLLIER] (-1672); b 1636; Boston

BROWNING, Nathaniel & Sarah [FREEBORN] (1632-1670); b 1650; Portsmouth, RI

BROWNING, Thomas (-1671, ae 83) & Mary _?_ (-1682+); b 1637(8?), b 1628?; Salem/Topsfield

BROWNING, William (-1730) & 1/wf Rebecca [WILBUR]; ca 1687; Portsmouth, RI/South Kingston, RI

BROUCE, David (-1708), Marlboro & Mary BIGELOW/BEGELOW (1677-1708), m/2 Thomas READ, Jr. 1701; 26 Jan 1699, 1699/1702; Watertown

BRUCE, George (-1692) & Elizabeth CLARK (1642-1710); 20 Dec 1659, 28 Dec; Woburn

BRUCE, John & [Elizabeth] _?_ ; b 1671, b 1672; Marlboro

BRUCE, John (1670-) & 1/wf Rose WATTLE; 31 Jan 1693, 1692/3, 1693/4; Woburn

BRUCE, John & Elizabeth _?_ (1674-1739); b 1695; Framingham

BRUCE, Roger (-1733) & Elizabeth (?ANGIN); b 1691(2?), b 1691; Marlboro/Framingham

BRUCE, Thomas & Magdalen _?_ ; b 1665; Marlboro

BRUCE/BRUSH?, William (1667-) & Elizabeth GOULD, ?w John; 15 Mar 1693, 1692/3; Woburn/Charlestown

BRUCKEN, John & Elizabeth [HOLLARD]; b 1671; Boston

BRUEN, Obadiah (1606-1681±) & Sarah _?_ ; ca 1633/36; Gloucester/New London, CT/Newark, NJ

BRUEN, John (1645) & 1/wf Hannah LAWRENCE

BRUEN, John (1645) & 2/wf Esther SMITH

BRUGGE, Samuel & _?_ ; b 1672; Boston

BRUMIDGE, Edward (-1699) & Hannah (FARNUM) TYLER?/WHITE?, w Abraham TYLER; aft 1673; Haverhill

BRUNDISH, John (-1639) & Rachel [?HUBBARD], m/2 Anthony WILSON; b 1629; Watertown/ Wethersfield, CT

BRUNDISH, John (1635/6-1697) & Hannah _?_ ; ca 1660/5?; Fairfield/Rye, NY

BRUNO, Francis & Sarah VRINGE; 26 Jan 1699; Boston

BRUSH, Edward & Hester BRUSH (1670-); 10 May 1688, 10 Jan 1688?; Huntington, LI

BRUSH, Jacob & Mary [ROGERS]; b 4 Oct 1700; Huntington, LI

BRUSH, John & 1/wf Sarah ADAMS/Elizabeth [PLATT]/GRIFFIN (1665-1740+); by 1682, ca 1685?; Huntington, LI

BRUSH, John & Elizabeth _?_ ; b 18 Dec 1700; Huntington, LI

BRUSH, Richard & ?Joanna/?Johanah SAMMIS?; b 1670; Huntington, LI

BRUSH, Richard & Deborah _?_ ; b 1698; Huntington, LI

BRUSH, Thomas (-1675?) & Rebecca [CONKLING] (-1670); b 1650, ?ca 1650; Southold, LI/Huntington, LI/Flushing

BRUSH, Thomas (-1698?) & Sarah [WICKES?/WEEKES?], m/2 Nathaniel WILLIAMS; b 1681; Huntington, LI

BRYAN, Alexander (1602-1679, 1670?) & 1/wf Ann BALDWIN (1605/6-1661); ca 1631; Milford, CT

BRYAN, Alexander (1602-1679) & 2/wf Susanna (_?_) WHITING) FITCH (-1673), w Wm., w Samuel; m cont 27 Jun 1662; Milford, CT

BRYAN, Alexander (?1651-1701, 1700?) & Sybil [WHITING] (1655-), m/2 Hugh GRAY; b 30 Aug 1674, b 1674; Milford, CT

BRYAN, Richard (-1689) & 1/wf Mary [PANTRY] (1629-); b 1649, b 16 Nov 1649; Milford, CT/Huntington, LI

BRYAN, Richard (-1689) & 2/wf Mercy/Mary? WILMOT; 15 Jul 1679; Milford, CT

BRYAN, Richard (-1689) & 3/wf Elizabeth (POWELL?) [HOLLINGWORTH] (1646-1698), w Richard, m/3 Robert TREAT 1705; aft 29 Nov 1685; Milford, CT

BRYAN, Richard & Sarah [PLATT] (1673, 1674?-); b 13 Aug 1699?, 1696?

BRYAN, Samuel (1661-1698) & Martha WHITING (?1662-1701), m/2 Samuel EELLS 1700, 1701; 25 Dec 1683; Milford, CT

BRYAN, _?_ & Joan _?_, m/2 Owen MORGAN 1650; b 1650; New Haven/Norwalk, CT

BRYANT, Abraham (-1720) & 1/wf Mary KENDALL (1647-8 Mar 1687/8, ae 40); 2 Feb 1664; Reading

BRYANT, Abraham (-1720) & 2/wf Ruth (GEORGE) FROTHINGHAM (-1693), w Samuel; 7 Jun 1688; Charlestown

BRYANT, Abraham (1671-1714) & Sarah BANCROFT (1676, 1675?-); 29 Nov 1693; Reading

BRYANT, Abraham, Sr. (-1720) & ?3/wf Dorcas (?GREEN) EATON, w John; 28 Dec 1693; Reading

BRYANT, Daniel[2] (1660-) & [Dorothy] _?_ ; b 1688; Scituate

BRYANT, John[1] (-1638) & _?_ [?SCADDING] (see John[2] BRYANT); b 1633?; Taunton

BRYANT, John[1] (-1684) & 1/wf Mary LEWIS (-2 Jul 1655), Barnstable; 14 Nov 1643; Scituate

BRYANT, John[1] (-1684) & 2/wf Elizabeth WETHERELL (living in 1662); 22 Dec 1657; Scituate

BRYANT, John[2] (-1693) & [Elizabeth?] [?SCADDING] (see John[1] BRYANT); ca 1657?; Taunton

BRYANT, John[1] (-1684) & 3/wf Mary HILAND (1632-), m/2 Robert STETSON; Apr 1664; Scituate

BRYANT, John[1] & Abigail BRYANT (-1715, Plympton); 23 Nov 1665; Plymouth

BRYANT, John[2] (1644-1708), Scituate & Mary BATTELLE (1650-); 20 Mar 1677, [1676/77]; Dedham

BRYANT, John[2] (1650-1736) (son Stephen) & Sarah [BONHAM] (1653-1742, in 89th y); b 1678; Plymouth/?Plympton

BRYANT, John[3] (son John[2] of Taunton) & Hannah _?_ ; b 1691; Rochester

BRYANT, John[3] (1678-) & Mary WEST; 11 Jul 1700; Plymouth

BRYANT, Jonathan & 1/wf Margaret WEST (1678-); 27 Feb 1700, 1700/1701?; Plymouth

BRYANT, Joseph (1671-) & [Elizabeth BARKER?] (1677-); b 1694+; Scituate/Hingham

BRYANT, Samuel[2] (1673-1750) & Joanna _?_ /COLE? (-1736, in 65th y); b 1699; Plymouth/ Plympton

BRYANT, Simon (1664-1748, Killingly, CT) & Hannah SPEAR (1671-1747); 28 Dec 1694; Braintree/Killingby

BRYANT, Stephen[1] & Abigail SHAW (-1694); ca 1646, b 1650; Plymouth
BRYANT, Stephen[2] (1658-) & Mehitable [?PACKARD]/?STANDISH; b 1684; Plymouth
BRYANT, Thomas (1674-1738?, Sudbury) & Mary FITCH; 10 Dec 1696; Reading
BRYANT, William (-1679) & Hannah [GILLETTE]; b 1683, ca 1681; Boston
BRYANT, William (-1697) & Hannah DISITER/?DISSATER, ?w Edward; 9 Jun 1692; Boston
BUCHANAN, John & Elizabeth [CLARK], dau Percival; b 1694; Boston
BUCHER/BUKER?/BEUKER?, Alwin & Elizabeth BARNARD; 15 Dec 1698; Boston
BUCK, David (1667-1738) & Elizabeth HURLBUT?/HUBBARD (?1669, 1666-1733, 1735?); 14 Jun 1690; Guilford, CT/Wethersfield, CT
BUCK, Emanuel/Enoch (1623, 1621-1706?) & 1/wf Sarah [RILEY?]/ARNOLD?; b 1650(1?); Wethersfield
BUCK, Emanuel/Enoch (-1706?) & 2/wf Mary [KIRBY] (1645-1712); 17 Apr 1658; Wethersfield, CT
BUCK, Ephraim & Sarah BROOKS (1652-); 1 Jan 1670, 2670/1; Woburn
BUCK, Ephraim (1676-) & Esther WAGET/WAGGETT?; 1 Dec 1696; Woburn
BUCK, Ezekiel (-1713, 1712?) & Rachel [ANDREWS]/BEEBE? (1654-1713); 18 Mar 1675, 1675/6; Wetherfield, CT
BUCK, Ezekiel (1677-1715) & Sarah BRONSON (1672-); 13 Jan 1698, 1697/8; Wethersfield, CT/New London
BUCK, Henry (1626-1712) & Elizabeth CHURCHILL (1642-); 31 Oct 1660; Wethersfield, CT
BUCK, Henry (1662?-) & Rachel __?__ ; b 1692?; Wethersfield, CT
BUCK, Isaac[1] (?1601-1695) & Frances [MARSH/MARCH?] (1615-); ca 1645/50?; Charlestown/Scituate
BUCK, Isaac, Jr. (-1689) & Eunice TURNER (1662-), m/2 Jonas DEANE, m/3 James TORREY 1701; 24 Oct 1684; Scituate/Hanover
BUCK, James & Lydia? __?__ ; at Dorchester, 4 Jun 1639; Hingham
BUCK, James (1665-) & Abigail [CHURCH] (1666-1727), m/2 Nathaniel HARLOW 1691/2?; ca 1685/8?; Scituate
BUCK, John (-1697) & 1/wf Susan? __?__ (not Elizabeth HOLBROOK); b 1653; Scituate
BUCK, John, Wethersfield & Deborah HEWS; 10 Oct 1665; Wethersfield, CT/?Guilford, CT
BUCK, John (-1697) & 2/wf Susan/?Sarah (FAUNCE) DOTEN/DOTY (-1695), w Edward; 26 Apr 1693; Scituate/Plymouth
BUCK, Jonathan (1653/5, 1655-) & 1/wf __?__ ; ca 1675/90?; Wethersfield, CT
BUCK, Jonathan (1653/5, 1655-) & 2/wf Margery (INGERSOLL) GOFF?, w Jacob; aft 12 Nov 1697
BUCK, Jonathan, Jr. & Mary ANDREWS/ANDRUS; 4 Mar 1700, 1700/1; Wethersfield, CT/New Medford
BUCK, Joseph & 1/wf Rose NEWLAND (-25 Nov 1683); 2 Feb 1682; Sandwich
BUCK, Joseph & 2/wf Remembrance/Remember? JENNING/JENNEY (1668-), m/2 John GOODSPEED 1697; 20 Sep 168[6?], [1685]; Sandwich
BUCK, Roger (1617, ?1616-1693) & Susan/Susanna __?__ (-1685); b 1644, b 1638; Cambridge/Woburn
BUCK, Samuel (-1690) & Rachel LEVEN (-1694); 16 Mar 1669/70; Cambridge
BUCK, Samuel (-1709) & Sarah BUTLER; 23 Jan 1690; Wethersfield, CT
BUCK, Thomas[2] (1655-) & Mary [TURNER] (1658-); b 1682; Boston/Scituate
BUCK, Thomas (1665-) & Susannah __?__ ; ca 1690-2; Middletown, CT
BUCK, William (1585-1658) & __?__ ; b 1617; Cambridge
BUCK/BRICK, __?__ & Abigail BULL, dau Thomas; aft 1684; Deerfield
BUCK, __?__ & __?__ ARNOLD, gr dau John ARNOLD
BUCKINGHAM, Daniel (1636-1711, 1712?) & 1/wf Hannah/?Sarah FOWLER; 21 Nov 1661; Milford, CT
BUCKINGHAM, Daniel (1636-1711, 1712?) & 2/wf Alice [NEWTON] (1664?, 1674-1741/2); ?1689; Milford, CT
BUCKINGHAM, Daniel (-1725) & Sarah LEE (1675-), Lyme, m/2 Nathaniel LYNDE; 24 May 1693; Saybrook, CT
BUCKINGHAM, John (1673-) & Sarah [BEARD] (1675-); b 1698/9; Milford, CT
BUCKINGHAM, Samuel (1641-1700) (he called Anthony HOWKINS "uncle") & Sarah BALDWIN (1645-); 12 Dec 1663, 14 Dec; Milford, CT

BUCKINGHAM, Samuel (1668-1708) & Sarah [ROGERS] (1665-), m/2 Abraham NICHOLS; b 1693; Milford, CT
BUCKINGHAM, Stephen (1675-1746, Norwalk) & Sarah [HOOKER] (1681-1759); b 1701?
BUCKINGHAM, Thomas[1] (-1657, Boston) & 1/wf Hannah _?_ (-1646); in Eng, b 1632; New Haven/Milford, CT
BUCKINGHAM, Thomas[1] (-1657, Boston) & 2/wf Ann [?FOWLER] (-1659/1662); aft 28 Jun 1646, bef 1649; Milford, CT
BUCKINGHAM, Thomas (1646-1709) & 1/wf Hester/?Esther HOSMER (-1702); 20 Sep 1666; Hartford/Saybrook, CT
BUCKINGHAM, Thomas (-1739) & Margaret GRISWOLD (1668-); 16 Dec 1691; Saybrook, CT
BUCKINGHAM, Thomas (1671-1731, ae 62, in 62nd y) & Ann FOSTER; 29 Nov 1699; Hartford
BUCKINGHAM, Thomas (-1703) & Mary [BISCOE]; b 1700; Milford, CT/?Hartford
BUCKITT, Francis & Frances _?_ ; b 1688; Boston
BUKLIN, Barak & Ellis/Alice WOODCOK/WOODCOCK (1669-1732); 9 Apr 1689; Rehoboth
BUCKLAND, Benjamin (1640-1676) & Rachel [WHEATLAND?/WHEATLEY] (1643-1713), m/2 John LORING 1679; b 1663; Braintree/Rehoboth/Attleboro?
BUCKLEN, Isaac & ?Mary/?Martha MARCH; 3 Jan 1698; Rehoboth
BUKLIN, Joseph (-1718) & Deborah ALLEN (-1690); 5 Nov 1659; Rehoboth
BUCKLAND, Joseph (1663-1729) & Mehitable SABEN (1673-1751); ?30 Jul 1691, 30 Jun; Rehoboth
BUCLAND, Joseph & Deborah BARROW; 17 Oct 1693; Plymouth
BUCKLAND, Nicholas (1647-1728) & 1/wf Martha WAKEFIELD (1650-1684), New Haven; 14 Apr 1668, 21 Oct 1668; Windsor, CT
BUCKLAND, Nicholas (1647-1728) & 2/wf Elizabeth DRAKE (-1697/8); 3 Mar 1685/6; Windsor, CT
BUCKLAND, Nicholas (-1728) & 3/wf Hannah (SMITH) (TRUMBULL) STRONG (-1714), w Joseph, w John STRONG; 16 Jun 1698; Windsor, CT
BUCKLAND?/BUCKNELL?, (should be BUCKNELL) Samuel (-1700) & 1/wf ?Mary/[?Elizabeth BECKWITH?], w Matthew; aft 1680; New London
BUCKLAND?/BUCKNELL?, Samuel (-1700) & Hannah (?WAITE) BILL (-1709), w Philip; ca 1690?, (see BUCKNELL); New London
BUCKLAND, Thomas (-1662) & Temperance [DENSLOW]/WILLIAMS? (ca 1623, ?1619-1681); b 1639; Windsor, CT
BUCKLAND, Thomas (1650-1676) & Hannah COOKE (1655-), m/2 Joseph BAKER 1676/7, m/3 John LOOMIS; 21 Oct 1675, 1675?; Windsor, CT
BUCKLAND, Thomas & Abigail HANNUM; 25 Jan 1693; Windsor, CT
BUCKLAND, Timothy (1638-1689) & Abigail VORE (-1727); 27 Mar 1662, 7 Mar 1662; Windsor, CT
BUCKLAND, William[1] (-1683) & Mary [BOSWORTH] (1611-1687); in Eng, b 1633?, ?1626; Hingham/Rehoboth
BUCKLAND, William (-1691) & _?_ ; b 1679; Windsor, CT
BUCKLAND, William (-1724) & Elizabeth [?HILL/?HILLS/?WELLS] (1666-); b 1699, b 1691?; Hartford
BUCKLEY, David & Hannah TALLY (1680-); 3 Jun 1697; Boston
BUCKLEY, Joseph (1659-) & Joanna (SHUTE) NICHOLS, w Nathaniel; b 1691, m bond 16 Nov 1687; Charlestown/Boston
BUCKLEY, Richard & Sarah [BINDING]; b 1659; Boston
BUCKLEY, William (-1702, ae 80) & Sarah [SMITH]; b 1657, b 1643; Ipswich
BUCKLEY, William & Abigell CAVES; 21 Dec 1697; Salem/Topsfield
BUCKMINSTER, Jabez (-1686) & Martha (VOSE) [SHARP], w John; aft 21 Apr 1676, bef 10 Sep 1683; Dorchester
BUCKMINSTER, Joseph (-1668) & Elizabeth [CLARKE] (1648-), dau Hugh, m/2 Abiel LAMB by 1675; b 1666; Boston
BUCKMINSTER, Joseph (1666-1747, Framingham) & 1/wf Martha SHARP (1667-1716+); 12 May 1686; Roxbury/Framingham
BUCKMINSTER, Thomas[1] (-1656) & ?Hannah/Joanna _?_, m/2 Edward GARFIELD 1661; in Eng, b 1624; Boston
BUCKMINSTER, Thomas[2] (-1659) & Mary _?_ ; Boston

BUCKMASTER, Zachariah (-1691+, bef 1704) & Sarah WEBB (-1704, Roxbury); 7 May 1654/5; Boston

BUCKMASTER, Zechariah & Mary __?__; Sherborn

BUCKMAN, John & Hannah/Ann [KNOWER?]; b 1653; Boston

BUCKMAN, John (-1681) & Sarah __?__ (-bef 1681); b 1663(4?); Boston

BUCKNAM, Joses[2] (1641-1694) & 1/wf __?__ [?KNOWER], dau George; b 1666(7?); Malden

BUCKNAM, Joses[2] (1641-1694) & 2/wf Judith WORTH, m/2 John LYNDE by 1700; 1 May 1673; Malden

BUCKNAM, Joses[3]/Jorse (1666/7-1741), Boxford & Hannah PEABODY, Boxford; 24 Feb 1690/1, 1690; Charlestown/Malden/Topsfield

BUCKMAN, Richard & Eliza/Elizabeth __?__; b 1665; Boston

BUCKNAM, Samuel & Martha (BARNARD) [HAYES], w Thomas; b 1687; Amesbury/Newbury

BUCKNAM, Samuel (1674-1751) & Deborah (SPRAGUE) MELLEN (1670-1731), w William; 22 Sep 1697; Malden

BUCKNAM, William[1] (-1679) & 1/wf [Sarah] WILKINSON, dau Prudence WILKINSON, wid; b 1635?; Malden

BUCKNAM, William[1] (-1679) & 2/wf [Sarah?] [KNOWER?] (?1622-) (ae 34 in 1656); b 1641; Malden

BUCKNAM, William (1652-1693, Malden) & Hannah WAITE (1656-), m/2 Joseph HASEY 1694; 11 Oct 1676, no issue; Malden/Charlestown

BUCKNELL, George (1620-) & Elizabeth __?__

BUCKNELL, Roger & __?__; b 1635?; Richmond Island

BUCKNELL, Samuel & Sarah BISHOP; 18 Sep 1654; Boston

BUCKNELL/BUCKLAND?, Samuel & __?__ BECKWITH, w Matthew; ?aft 1680; New London, CT

BUCKNELL/?BUCKLAND, Samuel (-1700) & Anne/?Hannah (WAITE?) [BILL] (-1709), w Philip; aft 8 Jul 1689; New London, CT

BUCKNER/BUCKNELL, Samuel (-1693) & Mary (HOLMAN) BILLE, w Thomas, m/3 Benjamin BLACKLEACH 1693; 27 Oct 1692; Boston

BUCKNELL, Thomas & Esther __?__; b 1677; Boston

BUCKNER, Charles (-1684) & Mary (HUNTING) [JAY], w William; b 1668; Dover, NH/Boston

BUDD, Edward (-1710) & Dorothy __?__ (-aft 8 Sep 1705); b 1665; Boston

BUDD, John[1] (-1673, bef 8 Feb 1673(4?)) (had John, Joseph?) & Katherine [BROWN?]; in Eng, b 1620; Stamford, CT

BUDD, John[2] (1620-1684) (had John, Joseph) & Mary [HORTON], dau Barnabas; b 1653?; Rye, NY/Southold, LI

BUDD, John[3] (1659-bef 1727) (son John[2]) (had John, Joseph, Joshua) & Esther/Hester __?__; b 1688, b 1687; Southold, LI

BUDD, Joseph[3] (?1669-1722) (son John[2]) (had John, Joseph, Elisha, Underhill, Gilbert) (Joseph a minor 6 Dec 1689) & Sarah UNDERHILL, ?m/2 Samuel PURDY; m lic 11 Oct 1695; Southill, LI

BUDLONG, Francis (-1675) & Rebecca (LIPPITT) HOWARD (-1675), w Joseph HOWARD; 19 Mar 1668/9; Warwick, RI

BUDLONG, John (1672-1744) & Isabel [POTTER] (1674-1731(-)); b 1698; Warwick, RI

BOULL/[BUEL], John & Elizabeth CLEMENTS; 23 Nov 1694; Stamford, CT

BUEL, John (1672-1746) & Mary LOOMIS (-1768); 20 Nov 1695, 12? Nov, 13? Nov; Windsor, CT/Killingly, CT/Litchfield

BUELL, Peter[2] (1644-1729) & 1/wf Martha COGGENS/COGAN? (-1686, Simsbury), Simsbury; 31 Mar 1670; Windsor, CT

BUELL, Peter[2] (1644-) & 2/wf Mercy/Mary [?STRONG] (-1688, ae 22); ca 1687; Windsor, CT

BUELL, Peter[2] (1644-1729) & 3/wf Mary (GILLETTE) BISSELL (-1734), w Jacob; 30 Jun 1699; Simsbury

BUELL, Samuel[2] (1641-1720) & Deborah GRISWOLD (1646-1719, 1718?); 13 Nov 1662; Windsor, CT/Killingly, CT

BUEL, Samuel[3] (1663-1732) & Juliett STEVINS (1668-1732); 16 Aug 1686; Killingly, CT

BUEL, William[1] (1610-1681) & Mary [POST?/THOMAS?] (-1684); 18 Nov 1640; Windsor, CT/Hadley

BUEL, ?William & __?__ (-Dec 1639); b 1639; Windsor, CT

BUERLY, Lanix & Mary FARROW (1665-); b 1689; Hingham

BUFF, Daniel & Mary EMBLEN; 12 May 1698; Boston
BUFFET?, ?John & Hannah [TITUS] (1669-); 1696; ?Hempstead, LI
BUFFINGTON, Benjamin (1675-) & Hannah _?_ (1677-); b 1699, ?Aug 1697; Salem/Swansea
BOUENTON, Thomas (1644-1728) & Sara/Sarah SOTHWICK/SOUTHWICK (1644-1733+); 30 Dec 1671, ?1670; Salem
BUFFINGTON, Thomas (1672-1705?) & Hannah ROSS (-1705+); 28 Feb 1699; Salem
BUFFUM, Caleb (1650-1731) & Hanna POPE (1648-); 26 Mar 1672; Salem
BUFFUM, Joshua (1635-) & Damaris [POPE] (1643-); b 1663, no date; Salem
BUFFAM, Robert (-1669) & 2/wf Thomasin (WARD) THOMPSON (-1688), w John; 11 Aug 1634, b 1635; Salem
BUFFUM, Robert (1675-) & Elizabeth FAIRER/FARRAR; 13 May 1700; Lynn
BUGBEE, Edward (?1594-1669) & Rebecca _?_ (1602-); b 1630; Roxbury
BUGBEE, Edward (1669-) & Abigail [HALL] (1674-1729); b 1694; Roxbury
BUGBEE, John (-1704) & Joanna _?_ (-1690); b 1665; Roxbury
BUGBEE, John & Abigail/?Abiah CORBETT/CORBIT?, w Robert; 10 Jul 1696; Woodstock, CT
BUGBEE, Joseph (1640-1735) & Experience [PITCHER] (1642-1721); b 1664; Roxbury
BUGBEE, Joseph (1664-) & Mehitable _?_ ; b 1699; Woodstock, CT/Voluntown, CT
BUGBY, Richard (-1635) & Judith _?_ (?1600-), m/2 Robert PARKER 1635; ca 1629?; Roxbury
BULFINCH, Adoni/Adino/Adinah & Abigail _?_ ; b 1694; Charlestown
BULFINCH, John & _?_ ; b 1640/3?; Salem
BULGAR, Richard (1608-1679+) & [Lettice UNDERHILL]; b 1634; Boston/?Portsmouth, NH/Roxbury/Exeter, NH/Dover, NH
BULKLEY see Jonathan WADE
BULKLEY, Dr. Charles (1663-) & Hannah [RAYMOND] (1668-1742), m/2 Thomas AVERY 1693; b 1693; New London, CT
BULKLEY, Edward (1614-1696) & Lucian/Lucyan _?_, wid, (she had dau Lucy who m John LAKE); b 1640; Concord/Chelmsford
BULKLEY, Gershom (1636?, 1635?-1713) & Sarah CHAUNCEY (1631-1699); 6 Oct 1659, ?26 Oct; Concord/Cambridge/New London, CT/Wethersfield, CT
BULKLEY, Gershom (?1676-1753) & 1/wf Eunice [HANFORD] (1676-1702?); ca 1700; ?Norwalk, CT/Fairfield, CT
BULKLEY, John (see Thomas) & Esther [BURR/BOWERS?] (?1633-); b 1682?; Fairfield, CT
BULKLEY, Joseph (1648-1719) & 2/wf? Martha [BEERS]/Elizabeth KNOWLES; b 1682, b 1680; Fairfield, CT
BULKLEY, Capt. Joseph (1670-1748) & 1/wf Rebecca (JONES) MINOT (-1712), w James; 19 Mar 1695?, 1696?; Concord
BULKLEY, Peter (1583-1659) & 1/wf Jane ALLEN (-1626); Goldington, Eng, 12 Apr 1613; Concord/Wethersfield, CT
BULKLEY, Peter (1583-1659) & 2/wf Grace CHETWOOD (1602-1669); in Eng, ca Apr 1635, bef 8 May 1635; Concord
BULKLEY, Peter (1643-1686) & Rebecca WHEELER, m/2 Jonathan PRESCOTT 1689; 16 Apr 1667; Concord
BULKLEY, Peter (1643-1691) & Margaret _?_ ; b 1672; Fairfield, CT
BULKLEY, Peter (1664-1701) & Rachel TALCOTT (1676-), m/2 Henry WOLCOTT; 21 Mar 1700, 1699/1700; Wethersfield, CT
BULKLEY, Thomas (1617-1658) & Sarah [JONES] (?1620-1683), m/2 Anthony WILSON; b 1640, ca 1638; Concord
BULKLEY, Thomas (see John) (son of Rev John) & Esther [BOWERS?]; b 1685; Boston
BULL, Daniel (1677-) & Mary [MYGATT]; b 1701?; Hartford
BULL, David & Hannah CHAPMAN; 27 Dec 1677; Saybrook, CT
BULL, Elisha (1657-1722) & Deborah WILSON (1666-); 7 Jun 1689, 2? May; Cambridge
BULL, Ephraim (1669-1721) & 1/wf Mary COGGESHALL (1662-1699); 27 Oct 1692; N. Kingston, RI
BULL, Ephraim & 2/wf Hannah HOLWAY; 20 Jun 1700, 20 Jan 1700; N. Kingston, RI
BULL, Ezekiel (1671-1727) & Elizabeth SAGE (1666-1720), Middletown, CT; 11 Jan 1694; Boston/?Portsmouth, RI
BULL, Henry (1610-1694) & 1/wf Elizabeth _?_ (-1 Oct 1665); b 1638, b 1633?; Roxbury/Newport

BULL, Henry & 2/wf Esther/Hester **ALLEN** (1648-1676); [14 Feb 1664/5?], 1665/6?; Sandwich/Providence

BULL, Henry (1610-1694) & 3/wf Ann (**CLAYTON?**) **EASTON** (-1708, ae 80), w Nicholas; 28 Mar 1677; Portsmouth, RI

BULL, Henry (-1691±) & Anne [COLE] (1661-1704); b 1687; N. Kingston, RI

BULL, Isaac & Sarah **PARKER**; 22 Jun 1653; Boston?/Worcester

BULL, Isaac (-1716) & 1/wf _?_ ; b 1682; Newport

BULL, Jirah (1638-1684±) & ?Elizabeth _?_ ; b 1659, Newport/Kingston, RI

BULL, Jirah (1659-1709) & 1/wf Godsgift [**ARNOLD**] (1658-23 Apr 1691); b 1682; Newport

BULL, Jirah & 2/wf Sarah [**BOWDITCH**]; aft 23 Apr 1691; Newport

BULL, John & Mary [**BAXTER?**] (1640-1728); b 1663, 1658?; Boston

BULL, John (-1721) & 1/wf Mary **PITTS** (-1696); 21 Nov 1672; Hingham

BULL, John (1653-1703?) & Sarah _?_ , ?m/2 William **BUSHNELL** 1705; in Eng?, b 1679(80?); Saybrook

BULL, John & Mary **WOODWARD**; 21 Apr 1692; Boston

BULL, John (-1720) & 2/wf Margaret **DAMON** (1676-); 4 Mar 1696/7; Hingham

BULL, John (-1705) & Esther **ROYCE**, Hartford, CT; 23 Nov 1698; Farmington, CT/Deerfield

BULL, John (-1700) & Mary **CLAY** (1671-), m/2 Nicholas **MASON** 1701; b 1700; Guilford, CT/Saybrook, CT

BULL, Jonathan (-1702, ae 53) & Sarah **WHITING**, m/2 John **HAMLIN**; 19 Mar 1684/5; Hartford

BULL, Joseph & 1/wf Sarah **MANNING** (1646-), m/2 John **HAMLIN**; 11 Apr 1671; Hartford

BULL, Joseph (-1712) & 2/wf Hannah/Anna [**HUMPHREY**] (1669-), m/2 Joseph **COLLIER**; ca 1691?, ca 1697?, bef 14 Apr 1697; Windsor, CT/Hartford/Deerfield

BULL, Joseph & Sarah **SEARLE**; 26 Nov 1699; Marblehead

BULL, Robert & Phebe **JOSE?**; ca 15 Dec 1649; Saybrook, CT

BULL, Robert & 2/wf Sarah (**RUSCO**) [**COLE**], w Henry; b 1679; ?Wallingford, CT

BULL, Samuel & Elizabeth **GODDIN**; 23 Jan 1700, 1699/1700; Cambridge

BULL, Samuel & Elizabeth [**WALKER**] (1674-); b 1701?; Woodbury

BULL, Thomas (1610-1684) & Susanna _?_ (1610-1680); in Eng, b 1635, b 1644; Hartford/Deerfield

BULL, Thomas (-1708) & 1/wf Esther **COWLES** (-1691, ae 42); 29 Apr 1669, ?20 Apr; Farmington, CT

BULL, Thomas (-1708) & 2/wf Mary (**CHEEVER**) **LEWIS** (1640-1728), w William; ?4 Dec 1692, 13 Jan 1691/2, 13 Jan 1691; Farmington, CT

BULL, William (-1688) & Blithe/Blythe _?_ (1618-1690); b 1644; Cambridge

BULL, William & 1/wf Abiah **PERRY**; 3 Jan 1673, [1673/4]; Watertown

BULL, William & 2/wf Elizabeth **UNDERWOOD**, w Joseph; 13 Sep 1693, 13 Nov; Watertown

BULLARD, Richard & Elizabeth **INGRAHAM**; 4 Aug 1647

BULLARD, Augustine & Hannah (**RIDDEN**) **DYER**, w Henry; 12 Oct 1693; Dover, NH

BULLARD, Benjamin (?1634-1689) & 1/wf Martha **PIDGE**; 5 Apr 1659; Dedham/Sherborn/Medfield

BULLARD, Benjamin (?1634-1689), Medfield (m/3? Sarah _?_) & 2/wf Elizabeth **ELLIS/ELLICE**, m/2 John **HILL** 1698?; 1 May 1677 (15 Apr 1690 wid Eliz son Samuel) (7 Apr 1691 wid Sarah, son Samuel); Billerica/Sherborn

BULLARD, George[1] (1608-1689) & 1/wf Margaret _?_ (-Feb 1640); ca 1630/39?; Watertown

BULLARD, George[1] (1608-1689) & 2/wf Beatrice [**HALL**] (-1652); aft Feb 1640, b 1642?, b 20 Jun 1640; Watertown/Dedham

BULLARD, George[1] (1608-1689) & 3/wf Mary (?**RICHARDS**) **MAPLEHEAD** (-1684+), wid; Apr 1655, 18 Apr, 20 Apr, 30? Apr; Watertown

BULLARD, George (1608-1689) & 4/wf Jane (**LISHAM**) **ELLIS/ELSE**, w Roger; 2 May 1672; Charlestown

BULLARD, Isaac (-1676) & Ann (**BURNAP**) **WIGHT**, w John, m/3 David **JONES**, Sr. 1685; 11 Apr 1655; Dedham

BULLARD, John (1601-1678) & 1/wf Magdalen _?_ (-1661); b 1639, b 1634; Dedham

BULLARD, John (1601-1678) & 2/wf Ellen [**DICKERMAN**], w Thomas; aft 29 Nov 1661; Medfield

BULLARD, John[2] (-1668) & [Hannah **JONES**]; b 1664; Dedham

BULLARD, John (1669-) & 1/wf Margaret _?_ ; ca 1692/1700?; Dedham

BULLARD, Jonathan (1647-1684+, 1696+) & Hester/Esther MORSE (1646-); 9 Dec 1669; Watertown

BULLARD, Jonathan (1672-1719) & Anna RICE (1678-), m/2 Edward HARRINGTON 1727; b 1700; Watertown

BULLARD, Joseph (1643-) & Sarah __?__ (-1722); b 1665; Medfield

BULLARD, Joseph (1675-) & Margaret CHENEY (1670-); 25 Jun 1691; Medfield

BULLARD, Nathaniel (1634-1705) & Mary RICHARDS (1639-); 15 Dec 1658; Dedham

BULLARD, Richard (-1678) & __?__ (-1683); Greenwich, CT

BULLARD, Robert (1599-1639) & Anne __?__, m/2 Henry THORP 1639; b 1634, b 1630?; Watertown/Charlestown

BULLARD, Samuel (?1634-) & Hannah THORP; 14 Jan 1682/3; Dedham/Dorchester

BULLARD, Samuel & Deborah ATHERTON; - Jun 1691, 1690; Sherborn

BULLARD, William (1594-1687, 1686?) & 1/wf [Mary?] __?__ ; bef 1630; Cambridge

BULLARD, William (1594-1687, 1686?) & 2/wf Mary (?POST) GRISWOLD (-1685), w Francis; ca Jan 1653/4, aft 4 Nov 1652, ?4 Jan 1653, ca 1653; Charlestown

BULLARD, William (1673-1747) & Elizabeth AVERY; 6 Aug 1697; Dedham

BULLINE/BULLEN, Elisha & Hannah MEDCALFE/METCALF; 31 May 1683; Medfield/Sherborn

BULLIN, Ephraim (1653-1694) & Grace __?__ (-1689); b 1681; Sherborn

BULLIN, John (1648-1703) & 1/wf Judith FISHER (1663-); 3 Jan 1683/4; Medfield

BULLIN, Joseph (-1704) & Abigaill SABIN (1653-1721); 15 Mar 1673/4, no issue; Medfield

BULLEN, Samuel (-1692) & Mary MORSE (1620-1692); 10 Aug 1641; Dedham/Medfield

BALLINE, Samuel & Experience SABIN (-1728); 20 Aug 1672, no issue; Rehoboth/Medfield

BULLIER, Jullian (-1677) & Elizabeth BROOKS, m/2 James FITZGERALD 1678; 15 Jan 1665, 1665/6; Saybrook, CT

BULLIS, Philip & Judith (HART) (RATCHELL) REAP, w Robert, w Thomas; 3 Dec 1663; Charlestown

BULLIVANT, Benjamin & __?__ ; b 1686; Boston

BULLOCK, Ebenezer & Sarah MOULTON; 29 Mar 1698; Rehoboth

BULLOCK, Edward (1603-will 1649) & __?__ (returned to Eng) (had dau-in-law Hannah JOHNSON); Dorchester

BULLOCK, Henry[1] (1595-1663) & 1/wf Susan __?__ (1593-1644); in Eng, b 1627; Charlestown/Salem

BULLOCK, Henry[1] (1595-1663) & 2/wf Elizabeth __?__ (-1663+); betw 1644 & 1663; Salem

BULLOCK, Henry[2] (1627-1656, 1657?) & Alice [FLINT] (1636-), m/2 John PICKERING; b 1654, 1650?; Salem

BULLOCK, John (1654-1694) & Mary/Elizabeth? MAVERICK; 3 Aug 1681; Salem

BULLOCK, John & Elizabeth BARNES; 29 Jan 1695; Swansea

BULUK, Richard (1622-1667) (ae 25 in 1647) & 1/wf Elizabeth INGRAHAM (-1660); 4 Aug 1647; Rehoboth

BULLUK, Richard (-1667) & 2/wf Elizabeth BILLINGTON, dau Francis?, m/2 Robert BEERS 1673, m/3 Thomas PATEY/PATTY; 21 Sep 1660, (21 May is worong); Rehoboth

BULLUCKE, Samuel (1648-1718) & 1/wf Mary THURBER (-1674); 12 Nov 1673; Swansea

BULLUK, Samuel (-1718) & 2/wf Thankful ROUSE/ROUNDS?/RENEFF?/BONET?/BARRETT?; 26 May 1675; Rehoboth

BULLY/BULLER?, John (-1679, 1678?) & Rebecca [?SPENCER] (-1712), dau Roger, m/2 Dr. David BENNETT 1682/3; b 1677; Boston

BULLY, Nicholas (-1678) & __?__ ; b 1632; Saco, ME/Boston

BULLY, Nicholas (-1664) & Ellen BOOTH (1684-), m/2 John HENDERSON 1669; Jul 1652; Saco, ME

BULLEY, Samuel & Elizabeth WEBBER; 22 Feb [1693]; Ipswich

BULMAN, Alexander & Margaret TAYLOR; 22 Dec 1690; Boston/Watertown

BUMPAS, Edward (-1693) & Hannah __?__ (-1693); b 1631; Duxbury/Marshfield/Middleboro

BUMPAS, Jacob (1644-) & Elizabeth (BANKS) BLACKMOR, w William; 24 Jan 1677; Scituate

BUMPUS, John (1636-1715, Rochester) & __?__ ; b 1671; Scituate/Middleboro/Rochester

BUMPUS, John (1673-) & 1/wf Hannah [MOWRY]; b 1695; Rochester

BUMPAS, Joseph (1639-1765, Middleboro) & Wybra [GLASS] (-1711, Middleboro); b 1669; Plymouth

BUMPAS, Philip (-1726) & Sarah [EATON]; b 1687(8?); Bristol, RI/Plainfield, CT

BUMPAS, Thomas & Phebe LOVEL (1656-); - Nov 1679; Barnstable
BUMSTEED, Jeremiah (1637-1709, ae 72) & Anna/Anne/Hannah ODLIN (1643-); b 1664; Boston
BUMSTEED, Jeremiah (1637-1709, ae 72) & Sarah __?__; b 1674; Boston
BUMSTED, Jeremiah (1670-) & Sarah ABRAHAM; 16 Jun 1700; Boston
BUMSTEAD, Thomas (ca 1610-1677) & Susanna? __?__ (-1688); ca 1636; Roxbury/Boston
BUNCE, John² (-1734) & Mary [BARNARD] (ca 1659-); b 23 Apr 1685, b 1683; Hartford
BUNCE/BURR?, Thomas¹ (ca 1612-1683) & Sarah __?__ (-1694); b 1645; Hartford
BUNCE, Thomas² (-1712) & 1/wf Susannah [BULL] (-1684); ca 1675/78?, 1669?; Hartford
BUNCE, Thomas² (-1712) & 2/wf __?__; 1684, 1685?; Hartford
BUNDY, John (-1681) & Martha [?CHANDLER] (-1674); b 1649; Boston/Taunton
BUNDEY, John & 2/wf Ruth (?RATCHELL) GURNEY, Mendon, w John, m/3 Guydo BAILEY; 9 Jan 1676, 1676/7; Taunton
BUNKER, Benjamin (-1670) & Mary __?__ (-1677+); Malden
BUNKER, Benjamin (-1735) & Abigail FOWLE (1674-), m/2 Benjamin GERRISH 1738; 17 May 1698; Charlestown
BUNKER, George¹ (-1664, Malden) & 1/wf Judith [TOPSFIELD?] (-1646, 1648?); b 1631?, b 1635; Charlestown
BUNKER, George (-1658) & Jane [GODFREY] (-1662), m/2 Richard SWAIN/SWAINE; ca 1644?; Ipswich/Topsfield
BUNKER, George¹ (-1664) & 2/wf Margaret (WELLS) [HOW] (-1660), w Edward; 1647; Charlestown/Malden
BUNKER, George (1671-) & Deborah COFFIN; 10 Oct 1695; Nantucket
BUNKER, James¹ (1628-1698) & [Sarah NUTE]; ca 1650/70?; Dover, NH
BUNKER, James² & 1/wf [Anne THOMAS]; b 1701?, b 1689?
BUNKER, John (1631-1672) & Hannah MELLOWES (MILLER is wrong); Sep 1655; Malden
BUNKER, John (1662-) & Rebecca EATON; 28 Apr 1690; Cambridge
BUNKER, John (-1707) & Dorcas [FIELD]; near 1695; Dover, NH
BUNKER, Jonathan (1638-1677/8) & Mary HAYWARD?/HOWARD, m/2 James LOWDEN 1679; 30 Jan 1662/3; Charlestown
BUNKER, Jonathan (1675-1721) & Elizabeth [COFFIN], m/2 Thomas CLARK; b 1703, b 1701?; Nantucket
BUNKER, Joseph & [Mary] __?__ (1674-), m/2 Richard DENBO; near 1692; Dover, NH
BUNKER, Peleg (1676-1730) & Susanna COFFIN (-1740); 9 Jan 1700; Nantucket
BUNKER, William (-1658) & __?__
BUNKER, William (1648-1712) & Mary MACY (1648-1729); 11 Apr 1669; Nantucket
BUNN, Edward (-1673) & 2/wf Elizabeth MASON, m/2 Joseph HOWE 1673; 20 Aug 1657; Boston
BUNN, Matthew & Esther __?__; b 1659; Boston
BUNN, Nathaniel (1664-) & Hannah WILLIAMS (-1708); 28 Nov 1688; Taunton
BUNNELL, Benjamin (-1696?) & 1/wf Rebecca [MALLORY]? (1649-1691); b 1667(8?); New Haven
BUNNELL, Benjamin (-1696?) & 2/wf Elizabeth (POST) [SPERRY] (1655-1715), w John, m/3 Edmund DORMAN 1700; b 1695, aft 12 Mar 1691; New Haven
BUNNELL, Nathaniel & Susannah WHITEHEAD; 3 Jan 1665; New Haven/Elizabeth, NJ
BUNNELL, William (-1654) & Ann [WILMOT]; b 1645, 1640?; New Haven
BUNNELL, Samuel (should be BURWELL) & __?__; b 1663; Milford
BURBANK, Caleb (1646-1690) & Martha SMITH, m/2 John HARDY 1695; 6 May 1669; Rowley
BURBANK, Caleb & 1/wf Lydia GARFIELD (-1698); 2 Jan 1693, 1693/4; Watertown
BURBANK, Caleb & 2/wf Hannah ACCEE/ACY/ACIE; 31 Aug 1698; Rowley
BURBANK, Ebenezer & Rebecca (TAYLOR) PRICHARD, w William; 9 Oct 1699; Suffield, CT
BURBANK, John (?1611-1681, 1682/3?) & 1/wf Ann [?JORDAN] (?1619-ca 1641/2); b 1641, b 1640?; Rowley
BURBANK, John (-1681) & 2/wf Jemima __?__; b 1644; Rowley
BURBANK, John (?1640-1709) & 1/wf Susanna MERRILL (-1690, Suffield, CT); 15 Oct 1663; Newbury/Haverhill/Suffield, CT
BURBANK, John (-1709) & 2/wf Sarah (HUNT) SCONE (-1692), w John; 15 Jul 1692; Springfield/Suffield, CT
BURBANK, John (-1709) & 3/wf Mehitable (BARTLETT) SAUNDERS/SANDERS (-1728), w George; 9 Jan 1694, 1693/4; Springfield

BURBANK, John (1670-1729) & Mary GRANGER, m/2 John AUSTIN 1734; 21 Dec 1699; Suffield, CT
BURBANK, Timothy (1668-) & Rebecca DARLING; 3 Jul 1695; Salem/Boston
BURBEEN, James (1668-1729) & Mary (LOWDEN) GEORGE (-1724), w John; aft 3 Sep 1692, bef 1 May 1693; Charlestown
BURBEEN, John (-1714) & Sarah GOULD (1637-1670); 16 Apr 1660; Woburn
BURCH, George (-1672) & Elizabeth [FOOTE], m/2 _?_ COLE; b 1659; Salem
BURCH, Jeremiah?/Jonathan? & _?_ ; b 1671; Stonington, CT
BURCH, Jeremiah & Elizabeth WHEELER; Jun 1696; Woodbridge, CT/Stratford, CT
BIRCH, Joseph (1643-) & Mary [WALES]; b 1672; Dorchester
BIRCH, Joseph & Elizabeth EDWARDS; 2 Aug 1700; Boston
BIRCH, Thomas[1] (-1657) & _?_ ; b 1643; Dorchester
BIRCH, Thomas & Bathsheba SANFORD; 24 Jan 1683, 1683/4; Swansea/Bristol, RI
BIRCH, _?_ & 2/wf Elizabeth? _?_
BIRCH, Jonathan (see Jeremiah) (-1704) & _?_ ; b 1684; Stonington, CT
BURCHAM, Edward (returned to Eng) & [?Elizabeth ALLEN]; b 1634; Plymouth/Lynn/Salem
BURCHAM, Thomas & Deborah _?_ (-1680); b 1680; Charlestown
BUSTED/BURCHSTED, John Hennery (-1721, ae 64) & Mary (RAND) KERTLAND, w Nathaniel; 24 Apr 1690; Lynn
BUSTED/BURCHSTED, John Hennery (-1721, ae 64) & ?2/wf Mary WHITING (1667-1740)
BURDEN, George (1615-1657) (returned to Eng) & Anne [SOULSBY?]; b 6 Nov 1636; Boston/Charlestown
BURDEN, Robert & Susannah [WHITTER], m/2 Edmund CHAMBERLAIN 1670; b 5 Jul 1659; ?Marblehead
BURDEN, Samuel, NY, & Elizabeth CROSS; 1 Jun 1679; Westchester, LI
BURDEN, William see William BARDEN
BURDETT, George & _?_
BURDITT/BURDEN, Robert (-1667) & Hannah WITTER?/WINTER?/WALTER (-1696), m/2 Edmund CHAMBERLAIN 1670; - Nov 1653; Malden
BURDITT, Thomas (1655-1729) & 2/wf? Elizabeth _?_ (-1718, ae ca 65); b 1682; Malden/Chelmsford
BURDICK, Benjamin (-1741) & 1/wf Mary [REYNOLDS]? (-1716); b 1699; Westerly, RI
BURDICK, Robert (-1692) & Ruth HUBBARD (1640-1691+); 2 Nov 1655; Westerly, RI
BURDICK, Robert & Dorcas LEWIS?/?Rebecca FOSTER/FORSTER?, New London; ?4 Jan 1700; Westerly, RI
BURDICK, Samuel (1673-1756) & Mary FORSTER/FOSTER (1675-1752+, 1768), New London, dau Thomas; ca 1695; Westerly, RI
BURDICK, Thomas (-1732) & 1/wf Martha _?_ ; b 1694; Westerly, RI
BURFE, Thomas & Mary _?_ (-1658); Boston
BURGE, John (-1678) & 1/wf 2/wf? Rebecca _?_ (-1 May 1661); ca 1643-48; Weymouth
BURGE, John (-1678) & 2/wf Mary (STEARNS) LARNED (1626-1663), w Isaac LEARNED; 9 Jun 1662, ?10 Nov; Chelmsford
BURGE, John (-1678) & 3/wf Grisell (FLETCHER) (JEWELL) GRIGGS GURNEY (-1669), w Thomas, w Henry, w John, (maiden name FLETCHER, her 5th mar); 3 Jul 1667; Chelmsford
BURGE, John (-22 Oct 1678) & 4/wf Jane GURNELLIN/GURNE/GORNELL? (-4 Apr 1678), w John; 6 Sep 1677; Chelmsford
BURGE, John (-1704) & Trail/Triall THARE/THAYER (1655, 1656-1737), Braintree; 14 Sep 1677; Chelmsford
BURGESS, Abraham & Sarah _?_ ; b 1684; Newport
BURGESS, Ebinezer (1673-1750) & Mercy LOMBARD (1673-); ca 1696?; Sandwich/Wareham
BURGESS, Francis & Joyce _?_ ; b 1654; Boston
BORG/BURGESS, Jacob (-1719) & Mary NYE (-1706); 1 Jun 1660, 1670; Sandwich
BURGESSE, James (-1690) & Lydia MEED/MEADE; 19 Oct 1652; Boston
BURGIS, James & Sarah _?_ ; b 1681; Boston
BURGIS, James & Elizabeth _?_ ; b 1688; Boston
BORG/BURGESS, John & Mary WORDDEN/WORDEN (-1723), dau Peter LEARNED?; 8 Dec 1657; Yarmouth
BURGESS, John & Sarah NICKERSON (1674-1723), dau Nicholas; b 1695; Yarmouth

BURGESS, Joseph (-1695) & Patience [FREEMAN]; b 1667(8?); Sandwich/Rochester
BURGESS, Joseph & Thomasine BANGS (1678-); b 1701(2?); Yarmouth
BURGESS, Richard & _?_; b 1653; York, ME
BURGES, Richard & Anne _?_; b 1672; Boston/Fairfield, CT
BURGESS, Richard (-1685) & 2/wf Phebe PEACOCK (-1686+); m cont 20 Oct 1677, 6 Oct; Stratford, CT
BURGES, Robert (1621?-) & 1/wf Sarah _?_ (-1669); b 1669; Lynn
BURGIS, Robert & Elizabeth _?_; b 1670; Boston
BURGESS, Robert & Sarah HULL/HALL; 13 Apr 1671, 12 Apr; Lynn
BURGES, Roger & Sarah (GRIGGS) KING? (-1664), w William; b 1659; Boston
BURGES, Roger & Elizabeth _?_; b 1667; Boston
BURGES, Roger & Sarah _?_; b 1685; Boston
BURGES, Roger & Esther PALMER (-1709, Roxbury?); 3 Aug 1698; Boston
BURGESS, Thomas (1603-1685) & Dorothy _?_ (-1687); in Eng, b 1627; Lynn/Duxbury/Sandwich
BURGESS, Thomas (-1687+) & 1/wf Elizabeth BASSETT (1626?-); 8 Nov 1648, div 10 Jun 1661; ?Sandwich
BURGESS, Thomas (-1662) & Sarah _?_ (1643-); b 1662; Boston
BURGESS, Thomas (-1687+) & 2/wf Lydia GAUNT, dau Peter/Zackariah?; b 1668?; Newport?
BURGESS, Thomas & _?_; b 1688; Lynn
BURGESS, Thomas (1668-1743) & 1/wf Esther [RICHMOND] (1669-1706); b 1691, b 1692; Newport/Little Compton, RI
BURGESS, Thomas (-1720?) & Sarah STORRS; 26 Feb 1696, [1695/6], 1696/7; Yarmouth/Windham Co., CT
BURGESS, William & Hannah STEEVINSON/STIMSON; 20 May 1684; Cambridge/Ipswich
BURKE/BUCK/BURT, John & Rebecca [GROUT] (1670-); b 1690; Sudbury/Groton
BURKE, Richard (-1694) & Mary PARMENTER (-1727), m/2 _?_ ALLEN; 24 Jun 1670; Sudbury
BURKE, Richard & Sarah (WOODFORD) ALLEN (1649-1712), w Nehemiah, m/3 Judah WRIGHT 1706; 1 Sep 1687; Northampton
BURKE, Richard (1671-) & Abigail [SAWTELLE] (1672-); ca 1691; Stow/Sudbury/Brookfield
BURKE, Thomas & Deborah HEWES/HOUS; 10 Oct 1665; Middletown, CT
BURLEIGH/BIRDLY, Andrew (1657-1718/19?) & Mary CONNANT/CONANT (1662-), m/2 Caleb KIMBALL; 14 Mar 1681, 1681/2; Ipswich
BIRDLY, Gyles[1] (-1668) (called cousin of Andrew HODGES) & Rebecca/Elizabeth _?_, m/2 Abraham FITTS 1668/9; b 1657; Ipswich
BARLY, James (1659/60-) & 1/wf Rebecka STACY (1657-1686); 25 May 1685; Ipswich
BIRDLEY, James & 2/wf Elizabeth [WHEELER] (1663-); b 1693; Ipswich
BURLING, Edward (-1697) & Grace _?_; b 1674; Flushing, LI
BURLING, Edward (1674-) & Phebe FERRIS; 11 Jun 1700; Westchester, NY
BURLINGAME, John (1664-) & Mary [LIPPETT]; ca 1685?; Providence
BURLINGAME, Roger (-1718) & Mary _?_ (-1718+); b 1664; Stonington, CT/Warwick, RI/Providence
BURLINGAME, Roger & Eleanor _?_; b 1701?; Providence/Warwich, RI/Coventry
BURLINGAME, Thomas (1667-1758) & 1/wf Martha [LIPPETT] (-1723); b 1688; Providence/Cranston, RI
BURLISON, Edward (-1690, Suffield, CT) & Sarah _?_ (-1707); b 1677; Suffield, CT/Windsor, CT
BURLISON, John (1677-) & Sarah HALLADAY; 16 Nov 1698; Suffield, CT
BURNAP, Benjamin & Elizabeth NEWHALL; 19 Jun 1700, 18 Jun 1700; Reading/Malden
BURNAP, Isaac (1630-1667) & Hannah ANTRUM; 8 Nov 1658; Salem
BURNAP/BURNET, John & Mary RICE/ROYCE?; 7 Apr 1684; Charlestown/Reading
BURNAP, Joseph & Tabitha [EATON]; int? 23 Dec 1690, 31 Jan 1690/1; Reading
BURNAP, Robert[1] (-1688) & Ann/Agnes/Annis [MILLER] (1600-1681); in Eng, ca 1625; Reading/Roxbury
BURNAP, Robert[2] (1627-1695) & 1/wf Ann _?_ (-1661); b 1653; Reading
BURNAP, Robert[2], Jr. (1627-1695) & 2/wf Sarah [BROWNE]; 28 May 1662; Reading
BURNAP/BURNETT, Thomas (-1691) & Mary PEERSON; 3 Dec 1663; Reading/Lynn
BURNAP, Thomas, Reading & Sarah WALTON, Reading; 28 May 1688; ?Reading/?Concord
BURNELL, Robert (-1700) & 1/wf Catherine _?_ (-9 Sep 1693); Lynn
BURNELL, Robert & 2/wf Sarah CHILLSON; 2 Feb 1693, 1693/4; Lynn

BURNELL, Samuel & Anne/Amy MOORE; 9 Oct 1674; Charlestown/Boston
BORNELL, William (-1660) & 1/wf Mary _?_ (-16 Nov 1645); b 1644; Boston
BURNELL, William (-1660) & 2/wf Sarah _?_ (-1687+); aft 16 Nov 1645; Charlestown
BURNETT, Aaron (1655-1755) & Elizabeth _?_ ; ca 1680; Southampton
BURNETT, Dan & Abigail _?_ (-1698); Southampton
BURNETT, Dan/Daniel? & 2/wf Elizabeth [BARBER] (?1657-1707+); aft 1698; Killingworth, CT
BURNET, John & Deborah [ROGERS] (1678-), dau William, wid?; b 1697, int 13 Jul 1695; Boston
BURNETT, Lot (-1702) & Phebe MILLS; 20 Oct 1675; Southampton
BURNETT, Matthias & Elizabeth _?_ ; b 1 May 1700; Southampton, LI
BURNETT, Thomas & 1/wf Mary _?_ ; b 1655; ?Lynn
BURNETT, _?_ & Sarah _?_ (-1694, ae 80); Charlestown
BURNHAM, Aaron (1676-1727) & Hester [BISHOP] (1684-); b 1701?; ?Lisbon, CT
BURNUM, James (1651, ?1650-1729) & Mary [?COGSWELL]; b 1677; Ipswich
BURNHAM, Jeremiah (-1718) & 1/wf [Temperance BICKFORD]/?Catharine SHERBURNE; b 1690; Durham, NH
BURNAM, Job (1673-) & [Abigail] [HARRIS]; b 1698; Ipswich
BURNHAM, John[1] (-1694) (nephew of Robert ANDREWS) & Mary _?_ (1635-); [ca 1655?]; Ipswich
BURNHAM, John (1648-1704) & Elizabeth WELLS; 9 Jun 1669, 6 Jun 1668, 13 Jun 1668; Ipswich
BURNHAM, John/Joseph (-1712) & Sarah _?_ (1661-1708+); ca 1684?; Ipswich
BURNHAM, John (-1721?) & Mary OLCOTT; 12 Nov 1684; Windsor, CT
BURNHAM, John & Sarah CHOATE; 18 Apr 1693, 13 Apr; Ipswich
BURNAM, Josiah (1662-1692) & Abigail VARNEY (-1692); 12 Jul 1687; Ipswich
BURNAM, Moses (1670-) & Ann [BELCHER] (?1668-); b 1699; Ipswich
BURNAM, Nathaniel (?1662-) & Eunice [KINSMAN] (1670-1750); b 1700; ?Ipswich/?Boxford
BURNAM, Richard & Sarah HUMPHRES/HUMPHREY?; 11 Jun 1686; ?Hartford/?Windsor, CT
BURNHAM, Robert (1624-1691) (nephew of Robert ANDREWS) & Frances [HILL]/Mary? ANDREWS?; nr 1647, b 1647; Boston/Ipswich/Dover, NH
BURNHAM, Robert (1664-1759) & Elizabeth [SMITH] (1667-); b 1697, b 1716; Dover, NH
BURNHAM, Samuel (1649-1719, 1695/6?) & ?[Mary _?_]; ca 1670/84?, b 1675; Dover, NH
BURNHAM, Samuel (-1728) & Mary CADWELL/FITCH; 8 Oct 1684; Windsor, CT
BURNHAM, Thomas[1] & Mary [LAWRENCE]/TUTTLE?; 1645?; Ipswich
BURNHAM, Thomas (1617-1688) & Anna ?WRIGHT/WIGHT (1622-1703); b 1640; Hartford/Windsor, CT
BURNHAM, Thomas (1623-1694) & Mary (TUTTLE)? LAWRENCE? (1625?-1705) (ae 35 in 1659); ca 1645
BURNHAM, Thomas (1646-1728) (nephew of Robert ALLEN) & 1/wf Lydia PENGRY (-1684); 13 Feb 1665, 1665(6?); Ipswich
BURNHAM, Thomas (1646-1726) & Naomi HULL (1657-1726); 4 Jan 1676, 16? Jan at Killingworth, 1670/7; Windsor, CT
BURNHAM, Thomas (-1694) & 2/wf Esther/?Hester (COGSWELL) BISHOP, w Samuel; 16 Dec 1689, (1685 is wrong); Ipswich
BURNHAM, Thomas (1673-1748) & Susannah _?_ (-1748); bef 1700?, bef 1693?
BURNHAM, William & _?_ ; b 1657; Malden
BURNHAM, William & 1/wf Elizabeth LOOMIS (1655-1717); 28 Jun 1681, 28 Jun 1671; Wethersfield, CT
BURNS, Samuel & Hannah [WILLIAMS] (1670±-); Taunton
BURPEE, Thomas[1] (-1701) & 1/wf Martha (CHANEY) [SADLER] (?1629-1658), w Anthony; b 14 Jun 1653; Rowley
BURPBE, Thomas[1] (-1701) & 2/wf Sarah KELLE/KELLEY (1644-1713); 15 Apr 1659; Rowley
BURKBEE, Thomas[2] (1663-1709) & Hester HOPKINSON (1667-1722); 3 Dec 1690; Rowley
BURPH, Stephen & Elizabeth PERRY; 29 May 1674; Rehoboth/Boston
BURR, Benjamin (-1681) & Ann/Anne/Hannah _?_ (1617-); in Eng, b 1637; Roxbury/Hartford
BURR, Daniel (-1695) & 1/wf Abigail BREWSTER (-bef 1678); Feb 166[8/9?]; Stamford, CT
BURR, Daniel (?1642-1695) & 2/wf Abigail GLOVER (1652-1720); 11 Dec 1678; New Haven
BURR, Daniel[3] (1660±-1727) & 1/wf Hannah [BANKS]; b 1681; Fairfield, CT
BURR, Daniel[3] (1660±-1727) & 2/wf Mary [SHERWOOD]; b [1687?]; Fairfield, CT

BURR, Daniel[3] (1660±-1727) & 3/wf Elizabeth [PINCKNEY] (1673-1722); b 1696; Fairfield, CT
BURR, Daniel[3] (1670-1748) & 1/wf Esther [PERRY] (1678?-); prob ca 1698; Fairfield, CT
BURR, Jehu[1] & _?_ ; in Eng, b 1625; Roxbury/Springfield
BURR, Jehu[2] (?1625-1692) & 1/wf Esther (?WARD) BOOSEY, w Joseph; b 1656, aft 1655, bef 1660; Fairfield, CT
BURR, Jehu[2] (?1625-1692) & 2/wf Elizabeth PRUDDEN (1643-living in 1681); by 1666; Fairfield, CT
BURR, Jehu[2] (?1625-1692) & 3/wf _?_ ; ca 168-; Fairfield, CT
BURR, John (?1633-1694) & 1/wf Mary WARD (-1635?); b 1657; Fairfield, CT
BURR, John (-1673) & Mary (SMITH) [CALL] (1631±-), w Philip, m/3 Henry BENNETT bef 1679; b 1665; Ipswich
BURR, John (1633-1694) & 3/wf Sarah [FITCH] (-1696?); b 1673; Fairfield, CT
BURR, John (-1716) & Mary WARREN (-1742); 24 Dec 1685; Hingham
BURR, John (1673-1705) & Elizabeth [HANFORD] (1667-); b 1694; Fairfield, CT
BURR, John (1673-1750) & 1/wf Deborah [BARLOW] (1674, 1675-1726); b 3 Nov 1698; Fairfield, CT
BURR, Jonathan (1604/5-1641) & Frances _?_ (1612-1682), m/2 Richard DUMMER ca 1643; in Eng, ca 1630?; Dorchester
BURR, Nathaniel[2] (1640±, 1637?-1712) & 1/wf Sarah [WARD] (1637?-); aft Jun 1659, ca 1660; Fairfield, CT
BURR, Nathaniel[3] (1664±-1700/1) & Susannah [LOCKWOOD], m/2 Benjamin RUMSEY; b 1694, b 1691?; Fairfield, CT
BURR, Nathaniel[2] (?1637/40±-1712) & Hannah/Ann (GOODYEAR) [WAKEMAN] (- 1721), w Samuel; aft Sep 1692, bef 1712; Fairfield, CT
BURR, Peter (1668-1724) & 1/wf Abigail _?_ ; b 1700; Fairfield, CT
BURR, Samuel (1638-1682) & Mary [BAYSEY/BAISIE?]; b 1663; Hartford
BURR, Samuel (1663-1698) & Mercy [?BAYSEY] (-1714); b 1691, b 1690; Hartford
BURR, Samuel (1679-1719) & 1/wf Dorothy (THOMPSON) SHOVE (SHORE is wrong) (-1702, ae 30), w Samuel; 16 Dec 1700; Cambridge
BURR, Simion (?1618-1692) & 1/wf Rose? _?_ ; b 1644; Hingham
BURR, Simion (-1692) & 2/wf Hester _?_ (-1693); 28 Nov 1648; Hingham
BURR, Simon (1655-1722) & Mary LASELL (1664-); Aug 1690, 29? Aug; Hingham/?Rehoboth
BURR, Thomas (1645-1731) & Sarah _?_ ; b 1681; Hartford
BURRAGE, John (1616-1685) & 1/wf Mary _?_ ; b 1641, ca 1639; Charlestown
BURRAGE, John (-1663) & Avis?/Agnes? _?_ , m/2 Thomas HAMMETT; b 1642; Scarborough, ME
BURRAGE, John (1617-1685) & 2/wf Joanna [STOWER] (-1689, ae 65); b 1657, 1654, 1655; Charlestown
BURRAGE, John (1646-1678?) & Susanna CUTLER (1654-), m/2 Alexander LOGAN 1679, 1679/80?; 15 Jun 1675; Charlestown
BURRAGE, Thomas (1663-1717+) & 1/wf Elizabeth BREAD/BREED (-1709); 16 Nov 1687; Lynn
BURRAGE, William (1657-1720) & Sarah _?_ (-1745); b 1686; Boston/Newton
BURREN/BUSSY, George & Sarah _?_ ; b Jul 1674; ?Kittery, ME
BURRILL, Abraham & Sarah _?_ ; b 1695; Lynn
BURRILL, Ephraim (uncle of Susannah COLLINS 1696) & Lydia [ROGERS]; b 1689; Weymouth
BURRILL, Francis (1628-1704) & Elizabeth _?_ (1634-1716); b 18 Oct 1653; Lynn
BURRILL, George (1592-1653) & 2/wf Mary COOPER (1607-1653), Appley; m lic 12 Jan 1626, [1626/7]; Lynn
BURRILL, George (1621-1698) & Deborah [SIMPKINS]; b 1654; Boston
BURREL, George & Mary _?_ ; b 1691; Boston
BURRILL, Jacob & Mary ELWILL, m/2 _?_ NICHOLS; m int 1 Jul 1699; Lynn
BURRILL, James (-1712) & Dinah [NICHOLSON] (1660-); b 1685; Bristol, RI
BURRILL, John (-1657) & Sarah _?_ ; b 1634; Roxbury
BURRILL, John (1631-1703) & Lois IVORY (1640-1720); 10 May 1656; Lynn
BURRILL, John & Rebecca _?_ ; b 1658; Weymouth
BURRELL, John & Sarah _?_ , m/2 Robert SEAVER
BURRILL, John (-1721) & Mary STOWERS (-1728, in 74th y), Charlestown; 28 Jul 1680, no issue; Lynn/Charlestown
BURRILL, John & Anne _?_ ; b 1686; Chelsea

BURRILL, John (1658-1731) & Mercy ALDEN; 26 Jun 1688; Taunton
BURRILL, John & Hannah (PREBLE) MILBURY, w William; 28 Sep 1694; ?York, ME
BURRILL, Joseph & Dorcas NEWBURY/NEWBERRY; 28 Oct 1686; Salem
BURRILL, Moses (-1698, Salem, NJ) & Dorcas _?_, m/2 Daniel SMITH; b 1693; Lynn
BURRELL, Samuel (1656-) & Martha [CLARK]; b 1686; Boston
BURRELL, Samuel & Hannah _?_; b 1693; Boston
BURRILL, Samuel & Margaret (RUCK) JARVIS, w Elias, m/3 Daniel MANSFIELD; 14 Sep 1697, 17? Sep; Boston
BURRELL, Theophilus & 1/wf Lydia GATHERCOLE/GETHERCOLE (1666-1726); 5 Jul 1694, no issue; Boston/Lynn
BURRILL, _?_ & Anne _?_ (-3 Aug 1659), wid; Boston
BURRINGTON, Bartholomew (1635-) & _?_; b 1670, b 1666?; Isles of Shoals
BURRINGTON, Thomas & Lydia _?_; b 1687; Boston
BURRINGTON, William¹ (1637-1729) & Jane _?_ (-1725+); ca 1667/74?; Portsmouth, RI
BENNINGTON, William² (-1740) & 1/wf Sarah PHETTEPLACE; 10 Sep 1700; Portsmouth, RI
BURRITT, John & 1/wf Deborah BARLOW; 1 May 1684; Fairfield, CT
BURRITT, Stephen (1641-1697) & Sarah NICHOLS (1649-); 8 Jan 1673/4, 28 Jan; Stratford, CT
BURRITT, William (-1651) & Elizabeth _?_ (-1683); b 1641; Stratford, CT
BURROUGHS, [William?] & Hannah FISHER (1653-), dau Joshua; Dedham
BURROWS, Edward (-1705) & Mary [HIGBY], m/2 Thomas OAKLEY; ca 1676; ?Jamaica, LI
BURROWS, Francis & _?_; London, Eng, ca 1680?; Boston
BURROUGHS, George (?1650-1692) & 1/wf Hannah _?_ (-1681); b 1674; Roxbury/Falmouth, ME/etc.
BURROUGHS, George (?1650-1692) & 2/wf Sarah (RUCK) [HATHORNE], w William, m/3 John BROWN 1698; 1681; Salem
BURROUGHS, James & 1/wf Sarah CHURCH; 8 Dec 1674; Hingham/Boston/Bristol, RI
BURROUGHS, James & 2/wf Ann _?_; b 1694; Bristol, RI
BURROUGHS, Jeremiah (-1660) & _?_, dau John HEWES?/HEWETT?; - May 1651; Marshfield
BURROUGHS, Jeremiah (1651/2-) & _?_; ?Marshfield
BURROUGHS, Jeremiah (1651-1698) & Martha (FURMAN) [REEDER], w Jacob; Newtown, CT
BURROWS, John (1609-) & Ann _?_ (1597-); b 1637; Salem
BURROUGHS, John (1617-1678) & 1/wf Joanna [JESSUP]; b 1641; Newtown, LI
BURROUGHS, John (1617-1678) & 2/wf Elizabeth [READ], wid; b 1665?; Newtown, LI
BURROWS, John (-1716) & _?_ (Mary is wrong) CULVER; 14 Dec 1670; New London, CT/Groton, CT
BURROWS, John (1651-1693) & Hannah _?_ (1658-1729), m/2 William BOOTH 1693; ca 1681; Enfield, CT
BURROUGHS, John (1665-) & _?_ [WOODWARD], dau Lambert WOODWARD; ca 1690?; Newtown, LI
BURROUGHS, John (-1713) & Patience HINMAN; 10 Jan 1694/5; Stratford, CT
BURROWS, John & Lydia HUBBARD; 14 Oct 1700; Groton, CT
BURROUGHS, Richard & Mary [CLOYES] (1657-)
BURROUGHS, Robert (-1682) & 1/wf Mary [IRELAND] (-Dec 1672), w Samuel; b 1642; Wethersfield, CT
BURROWS, Robert & 2/wf _?_; 17 Jun 1673; Wethersfield, CT
BURROWS, [Samuel] & Mercy [CHESTER] (1673-); b 1701?; ?New London, CT
BURROUGHS, Thomas & Mary [VIALL?]; b 1684, b 3 Jan 1681; Boston
BURROUGHS, Thomas (-bef 13 Nov 1703) & Mary (WHITEHEAD) [TAYLOR], w John, m/3 Rev. William URGUHART (-1709); aft 1695, b 1701?; Jamaica, LI
BURROWES, William (1616-1664) & _?_; b 1640; Providence
BURROUGHS, [?Nathaniel] (had son Rev. George BURROUGHS) & Rebecca _?_; b 1654?; VA/Roxbury
BURSELL, James (-1676) & Emott _?_ (-living in 1676); Yarmouth
BURSLEY, John (-1660) & Joanna HULL, m/2 Dolor DAVIS; ca 28 Nov 1639; Sandwich/Barnstable
BURSLEY, John (ca 1651, 1652-1726) (m/2 Elizabeth _?_) & Elizabeth HOWLAND (1655-1686+); - Dec 1673; Barnstable
BURSLEY, John & Susanna WYETH; b 1654; Hampton, NH/Exeter, NH

BURT, Abel (-1711) & Grace ANDREWS (-1709, ae 43); 26 Jun 1685; Taunton

BURT, David (1629-1690) & Mary HOLTON (ca 1626-1713), m/2 Joseph ROOT by 1692; 18 Nov 1655; Northampton

BURT, Edward (1627-) (ae 28 in 1655) & Elizabeth [BUNKER] (-1703); b 1656; Charlestown

BURT, Ephraim (1674-1704) & _?_ ; b 1701?; Taunton

BURT, Henry (ca 1595-1662) & Eulalia MARCHE (-1690); 28 Dec 1619, lic 23 Dec; Roxbury/Springfield

BURT, Henry (?1660-1735) & 1/wf Elizabeth ALVORD (1655-1687); 12 Dec 1684; Northampton

BURT, Henry (?1660-1735) & 2/wf Hannah DENSLOW (1662-1689); 9 Dec 1687; Northampton

BURT, Henry (1663-1748) & 1/wf Elizabeth WARRINER; 16 Jan 1688, 1688/9, 16 Jun 1689; Springfield

BURT, Henry (-1735) & 3/wf Mary [?DYER]; [?22 Aug 1690]; Northampton

BURT, Hugh[1] (?1691-1660) (70 in 1661) (53 in 1635?) & 1/wf Lusellah _?_ (-1628); b 1620, London; Lynn

BURT, Hugh[1] & Ann (HOLLAND) [BASSETT] (1603-), w Roger (d in Eng); aft 3 Oct 1628, b 1635; Lynn

BURT, Hugh[2] (1620-1650) & Sarah _?_ ; b 1647, ca 1645?; Lynn

BURT, James & Anna _?_ (-17 Aug 1665), ?w Humphrey GALLUP; b 1655; Taunton

BURT, James (-1743, ae 84?) & Mary THAYER; 2 Sep 1685; Taunton

BURT, John (1658-1712) & Sarah DAY (1664-1716); 21 Feb 1683, 1683; Springfield

BURT, John (-1704) & Mary LOMBARD, m/2 Deliverance BROOKS 1708; 23 Dec 1697; Springfield/Longmeadow

BURT, John & _?_ ; b 1701; ?Taunton

BURT, Jonathan (1625-1715) & 1/wf Elizabeth LOBDELL (-1684); 20 Oct 1651 in Boston, 30 Oct; Springfield

BURT, Jonathan (1654-1707) & Lydia DUMBLETON (1661-1739), m/2 Daniel COOLEY 1709; 8 Dec 1681; Springfield

BURT, Jonathan (1625-1715) & 2/wf Deliverance (LANGTON) HANCHETT (-1718), w Thomas; 14 Dec 1686; Springfield

BURT, Jonathan (-1745) & Mindwell TAYLOR; 2 Jun 1696; Northampton

BURT, Nathaniel (?1638-1720) & Rebecca SIKES (1641-1712); 15 Jan 1662, 1662/3; Springfield

BURT, Nathaniel & 1/wf Elizabeth DUMBLETON (-1692); 21 Jan 1691; Springfield/Longmeadow

BURT, Nathaniel & 2/wf Mary FERRY (1671-1739); 18 Jan 1699, 1699/1700; ?Springfield/Longmeadow

BURT, Richard (-1647?) & _?_ ; b 1629, in Eng; Taunton

BURT, Richard (1629-1685) & Charity (?HALL) [GALLUP] (1634/5-1711), dau George?, w John; b 1657; Taunton

BURT, Richard (1663-) & 1/wf Eunice LEONARD (1668-); 18 Feb 1685/6; Taunton/Newtown, LI

BURT, Roger & Susan _?_ ; b 1643; Cambridge

BURT, Thomas (-1735) & Mary SOUTHWICK; 18 Nov 1672; Salem/Reading

BURT, Thomas & [Jemima PHILLIPS]; b 1690?, b 1701?; Taunton/Swansea/Dighton

BURT, William & Elizabeth _?_ ; b 1686; Boston

BURTON, Boniface (-1669, ae 113, 115, Boston) & Frances _?_ ; Lynn/Reading/?Boston

BURTON, Edward & Margaret [OTIS] (-1670); b 1633, b 1641; Charlestown/?Hingham

BURTON, Isaac (?1645-1706) & Hannah _?_ , m/2 John KIMBALL; b 1685, ca 1675-80; Topsfield

BURTON, John[1] (1608-1684) & _?_ ; b 1641; Salem

BURTON, John (1667-1740) & Mary _?_ (-1768), m/2 Benjamin SEARLE

BURTON, Solomon & Mercy JUDSIN (1665-); 1 Aug 1687; Stratford, CT

BURTON, Stephen (-1693) & 1/wf Abigail [BRENTON] (-1684); b 1677; Boston

BURTON, Stephen (-1693) & 2/wf Elizabeth WINSLOW (1664-1735); 4 Sep 1684; Marshfield/Bristol, RI

BURTON, Thomas & _?_ (see Edward BURTON); b 1641; Hingham

BURTON, Thomas & Elizabeth _?_ ; b 1687; Boston

BURTON, William (-1714) & 1/wf Hannah [WICKES] (1634-); ca 1652; Warwick, RI/Providence

BURWELL, Ephraim & Sarah STREAME (1667/8-1729); 27 May 1698; Milford, CT

BURWELL, John & Ether/Hester WINCHESTER; Hitchen, Eng, 25 Nov 1624

BURWELL, John (1602-1649) & 2/wf 3/wf Alice HEATH (-1666), m/2 Joseph PECK 1650; b 1640, 24 Jun 1635 Minsden Chapel, Hitchins, Hertfordshire; Milford, CT

BURWELL, John (-1665) & [?Mary] _?_, ?m/2 John BROWNE; b 1653, b 1659; Milford, CT
BURWELL, John (-1690, 1698?) & Hannah [LOCKWOOD], m/2 Thomas HANFORD 1692; ca 1686; Greewich, CT
BURWELL, Nathan & Temperance BALDWIN/FOWLER? (1650-); 14 Jan 1673, 14 Jun 1673, 15 Jun 1673/4, 14 Jan 1675; Milford, CT/Newark, NJ
BURWELL, Samuel (BUNNELL is wrong) (1640-1715) & 1/wf Sarah [FENN] (1645-); b 1663; Milford, CT
BURWELL, Samuel (ca 1660-1719) & Rebecca BUNNELL (1669-1738); 27 Nov 1684; Milford, CT
BURWELL, Samuel (1640-) & 2/wf Susannah (NEWTON) [STONE] (1654-1703), w John; 1687; Milford, CT
BURWELL, Samuel & Deborah [MERWIN] (1670-1706); Milford, CT
BURWELL, Zechariah (ca 1639-) & Elizabeth BALDWIN (1644-); 18 Nov 1663; Milford, CT/Newark, NJ
BUSBY, Abraham (1618-1687) & 2/wf? Abigail (COMPTON) BRISCO, w Joseph; 23 Sep 1659; Boston
BUSBYE, Nicholas (-1657) & Bridgett COCK (-1660) 24 Jun 1605; Watertown/Boston
BUSBY, Nicholas (-bef 1657) & _?_ ; b 1657; Boston
BUSECOT, Peter (-1692±) & 2/wf Mary [BISHOP]? (1664-1692+, 1702+); Boston/Warwick, RI
BUSH, Abiel/Abia (1661-), Marlboro & Grace BARRETT, Marlboro; 27 Jun 1688; Marlboro
BUSH, Edward (-1710/11) & 1/wf Mary HIDE; 16 Oct 1665, 17? Oct; Salem
BUSH, Edward (-1711) & 2/wf Elizabeth (ESTWICK) PITMAN/PICKMAN?, w William; 1 Aug 1678; Salem
BUSH, John (-1663) & Elizabeth _?_, m/2 Robert MANN 1671?; b 1654, b 1652?; Cambridge
BUSH, John (-1670) & Grace [SANDERS], m/2 Richard PALMER 1670, 1671; b 1660; Cape Porpoise?, ME
BUSH, John (-1688) & Hannah PENDLETON (1655-1703+, 1741), m/2 John RUTTER, m/3 James SMITH 1693, m/4 Joseph WATERS, m/5 Zechariah MAYNARD 1721; 13 Jan 1679; Sudbury/[Lancaster]
BUSH, John & Mary HARRIS; 4 Sep 1684; Marblehead
BUSH, Jonathan & Sarah LAMB (1660-); 22 Jul 1679; Springfield/Enfield, CT
BUSH, Joseph (1654-) & Hannah _?_ (-1736); 22 Dec 1691; Newton
BUSH, Randall/Renold/Randolph & 1/wf Elizabeth _?_ ; b 1632; Cambridge
BUSH, Randoll & 2/wf Susanna LOVETT/LOVILL?/LOWELL, m/2 Thomas HALL b 1686; m cont 2 Sep 1678; Cambridge
BUSH, Samuel (?1642-1733) & 1/wf Mary [GOODWIN] (-1687), dau John; b 1677, ca Jul 1677?, b 1678; Sudbury/Suffield/Springfield/Medfield, CT
BUSH, Samuel & 2/wf Abigail LEE; 11 May 1688
BUSH, Samuel & 3/wf? Mary TAYLOR; 16 Apr 1699; Springfield
BUSHELL, Henry & Rebecca _?_ ; b 1687; Boston/Charlestown
BUSHNELL, Caleb & Ann LEFFINGWILL; 9 Jan 1699/1700; Norwich, CT
BUSHNELL, Ephraim & Mary LONG; 9 Nov 1697; Saybrook, CT
BUSHNELL, Francis[1] (-1646) & 1/wf Ferris QUYNELL (1587-1628); 13 May 1605, Horsham, Eng; Guilford, CT
BUSHNELL, Frances[1] (-1646) & 2/wf Joan KINWARD; 2 Jun 1629, Horsham, Eng; Guilford, CT
BUSHNELL, Francis[2] (1609-) & 1/wf Mary GROMBRIDGE; 27 Jun 1631, Horsham, Eng; Salem/Guilford, CT/Saybrook, CT
BUSHNELL, Frances[2] (1609-) & (2/wf) Grace (WELLS) [NORTON]; b 1660; Guilford, CT/Saybrook, CT
BUSHNELL, Frances (1650-1697) & Hannah SEYMOUR (1654-); 12 Oct 1675; Norwalk, CT/Danbury, CT
BUSHNELL, Isaac & Anne [ORDWAY] (1670-); [1690]; Salem
BUSHNELL, John (-1667) & Jane _?_, m/2 John HILLS 1670; b 1641; Boston
BUSHNELL, John & Sarah SCRANTON (1645-); May 1665, ca middle 1665; Saybrook, CT
BUSHNELL, John (1664-) & Sarah (LOVERING) [PLACE], w John; b 1687; Boston
BUSHNELL, John & Rebecca COLE, Hartford; 10 May 1692; Saybrook, CT
BUSHNELL, Joseph & Mary LEFFINGWELL; 28 Nov 1673; Norwich, CT
BUSHNELL, Joshua (1644-1710) & Mary SEYMOUR (1655-); May 1682; Saybrook, CT

BUSHNELL, Richard & Mary MARVIN, m/2 Thomas ADGATE; 11 Oct 1648; Hartford/Saybrook, CT
BUSHNELL, Richard (1652-1727) & Elizabeth ADGATE (1651-); 7 Dec 1672; Norwich, CT
BUSHNELL, Robert & Hannah TYLER; 9 Dec 1697; Preston, CT
BUSHNELL, Samuel (1645-1727) & 1/wf Patience RUDD; 7 Oct 1675; Saybrook, CT
BUSHNELL, Samuel (-1689) & 2/wf Ruth SANFORD; 19 Apr 1684, 17 Apr, no issue; Saybrook, CT
BUSHNELL, Samuel (1645-1727) & 2/wf Priscilla PRATT; 19 Apr 1700, 17 Apr; Saybrook, CT
BUSHNELL, William (?1610, 1611-1683) & [Rebecca CHAPMAN?] (-1703); b 1644; Saybrook, CT
BUSHNELL, William (1648-1711) & 1/wf Rebecca [STRATTON] (-1703); 7 Oct 1673; ?Saybrook
BUSHNELL, Samuel & 1/wf Susannah WADHAMS/WADDAMES (-1683), w John/William; aft 1676?; Wethersfield, CT
BUSHNELL, ?Edmund/?Edward?/?John (-1636, Boston) & __?__/?Martha [HALLOR] (-1636+), ?m/2 William BEAMSLEY; b 1632; Boston
BUSHROD, Peter & Elizabeth [HANNUM] (1645-); b 1680; Northampton
BUSS, John (?1640-) & 1/wf Elizabeth BRADBURY (1651-); 12 May 1673; Salisbury/Durham, NH
BUSS, John (?1640-) & 2/wf Mary [HILL] (1649-1716); Durham, NH
BUSS, Joseph (1649-) & Elizabeth JONES, m/2 John WILCOXSON 1683; 21 Dec 1671, 23? Dec; Concord
BUSSE, Nathaniel (1647-1717) & Mary HAES/HAVEN?; 16 Dec 1668; Concord
BUSSE, William (-1698) & 1/wf Ann [?MERRIAM] (-1674); b 1640?; Concord
BUSS, William (-1698) & 2/wf Dorcus JONES (-1709), w John; 24 Dec 1674; Concord
BUSSEY, John (1654?-) & Sarah __?__; ca 1685?; Oyster River, NH/Durham, NH
BUSSY, Simon & Margaret [WOODWARD/WORMWOOD?]; 1658, 4 Jul 1659; ?Cape Porpoise, ME
BUZELL, Arister & __?__; b 1665; Lynn
BUSWELL, Isaac (1592-1683) & 1/wf Margaret __?__ (-29 Sep 1642); in Eng, b 1626, b 1624?; Salisbury
BUSWELL, Isaac (1592-1683) & 2/wf Susanna __?__ (-1677); b 1645; Salisbury
BUSWELL, Isaac (1650-1679) & 1/wf Mary EASTE/?ESTY; 11 Oct 1671, Oct 1672, 12 - 1671; Salisbury
BUSWELL, Isaac (1650-1679) & 2/wf Susannah PERKINS, m/2 William FULLER 1680; 19 May 1673, 12 May 1673; Salisbury/Hampton, NH
BUSWELL, Isaac (-1709) & Anna [ORDWAY], m/2 William BAKER; betw 1689 & 1691; Salisbury
BUSSELL, John & Elizabeth STILES; 8 Jul 1700; Boxford/Topsfield/?Dover, NH
BUSWELL, Robert & Hannah TYLER; 9 Dec 1697; Andover/Preston, CT
BUSWELL, Samuel (-1704) & Sarah KEIES/KEYES/WINSLEY?; 8 Jul 1656, Jul 1656; Salisbury/Rowley/Topsfield
BOSWELL, Samuel & Mary __?__; b 1678; Boston
BOSWELL/BUSWELL, Samuel (1662-) & Jane [SIMMONS]; b 1690; Bradford
BUSSELL, Stephen (-1683) & Mary __?__; b 1683, b 1674?; Charlestown
BUSWELL, William (-1699?, in 73rd y) & Sarah [STACEY?] (-1709); b 1650?, b 1655?; Salisbury/Ipswich
BUSWELL, William & Ruth STILEMAN, ?m/2 Richard TARLTON; 5 Sep 1687; ?Portsmouth, NH
BUTCHER, John & Mary DEANE; 30 Jan 1661/2; Boston
BUTCHER, John (-1699) & Sarah __?__; b 1695; Roxbury
BUTCHER, Robert & Elizabeth __?__; b 1670; Boston
BUTLAND, John & Sarah [STOVER]? (see John BANKS/John LANCHESTER); by 1670; ?
BUTLAND, William & __?__; by 1635?; ?Boston
BUTLER, Benjamin/John? & Susanna [GALLUP]; ?7 Mar 1676; ?Boston
BUTLER, Daniel (-1712) & Hannah/?Elizabeth [HOWES?]; ca 1667?; Falmouth/Sandwich
BUTLER, Daniel (1650-1692) & Mabel [OLMSTED], m/2 Michael TAINTOR 1697; ca 1679; Hartford/Wethersfield
BUTLER, Rev. Henry (went to Eng) & 2/wf? Ann (BISHOP?) [HOLMAN], w John; b 1651, prob aft 18 Mar 1652/3, 9 Mar 1654/5?; Dorchester
BUTLER, Henry (1672-) & 1/wf Sarah __?__; b 1701; Martha's Vineyard
BUTLER, Isaac (1667-) & Tabitha [SEWALL]; 1687; Boston
BUTLER, James (-1681, Billerica) & Mary __?__, m/2 John HINDS 1682; b 1677; Woburn/Billerica

BUTLER, James (-1689) & Grace [NEWCOMB] (1664-), m/2 Andrew RANKIN 1692; b 1684; Boston/Oxford
BUTLER, James² & 1/wf Lydia [SNOW] (1676-1723); ca 1700?
BUTLER, John (1625-) & Mary [LYNDE] (1629-), m/2 William WEEKS; ca 1648, b 1656; Martha's Vineyard
BUTLER, John (-1679?, 1680?) & 1/wf _?_; ca 1660; Boston/Branford, CT
BUTLER, John & Elizabeth MORRELL; 3 Jan 1665; New Haven
BUTLER, John/Benjamin? & Susanna [GALLUP?]; ?7 Mar 1676, b 1678; Boston
BUTLER, John (-1679?, 1680) & 2/wf Benedicta _?_ (1657-); ca 1670?, b 1667; Branford, CT
BUTLER, John (1651-) & Priscilla NORTON; ca 1671; Martha's Vineyard
BUTLER, John & Katherine [HAUGHTON] (-1729, ae 67); ca 1677; New London, CT
BUTLER, John (-1691) & Hannah POTTER; 17 Nov 1684; Branford, CT
BUTLER, John (-1696) & Mary _?_, m Robert LOCKWOOD; Stratford, CT
BUTLER, John & Mary CLEMMONS/CLEMENTS; 23 Nov 1694, 23-9-1694; Stamford, CT
BUTLER, John & Eleanor _?_; b 1700(01?); Boston
BUTLER, Jonathan & Lydia _?_; b 1694; Branford, CT
BUTLER, Joseph (1648-1732) & 1/wf Mary [GOODRICH]? (1651-1705?); b 30 Jan 1677; Wethersfield, CT
BUTLER, Joseph & Esther HUBBARD; b 1695; Hartford
BUTLER, Judah & _?_ (2 wfs named Mary?)
BUTLER, Nathaniel (1641-1697) & Sarah _?_, m/2 Philip ALCOTT 1699; ca 1665; Wethersfield, CT
BUTLER, Nicholas & 1/wf Mary COTTERELL (-1623); St. George's, Canterbury, 18 Jul 1613; Martha's Vineyard
BUTLER, Nicholas (-1671) & 2/wf Joyce BAKER; 22 Jan 1623/4; Dorchester/Martha's Vineyard
BUTLER, Peter (1616) & Mary ALFORD, Charlestown, m/2 Hezekiah USHER, m/3 Samuel NOWELL; b 1655; Boston/Salem
BUTLER, Peter (-1694) & Elizabeth [BROWN] (1664-), m/2 Ephraim SAVAGE; b 1683; Boston
BUTLER, Richard (-1684) & 1/wf _?_ [BANBURY?]; b 1635; Hartford/Wethersfield
BUTLER, Richard (-1684) & 2/wf Elizabeth [BIGELOW] (-1694, 1691?); b 1639?, b 1643?, b 1647; Hartford/Wethersfield
BUTLER, Richard (-1676) & _?_; b 1645?; Stratford, CT
BUTLER, Richard (-1713) & Elizabeth [CHURCHILL?] (1679-); ca 1695?; Branford, CT
BUTLER, Samuel (1639-1692) & Mary [OLMSTEAD] (1646-17 Oct 1681, Wethersfield), Haddam, CT; b 1665; Hartford/Wethersfield
BUTLER, Samuel & Sarah [MOSES] (1662, 1663-); ca 1682?, b 1687; ?Windsor, CT/Southampton
BUTLER, Samuel (1665-1711) & Mary KILBURNE (ca 1670-1752); 26 Nov 1696; Wethersfield, CT
BUTLER, Samuel & _?_; b 1700?; Southold, LI
BUTLER, Samuel (-1712?) & Hannah [ALLIS] (1673-); b 1701?; Deerfield/?Hartford
BUTLER, Stephen (1620?-) & 1/wf Jane _?_ (-1667?); b 1653; Boston
BUTLER, Stephen (1620?-) & 2/wf Mary _?_; b 1671; Boston
BUTLER, Stephen & Tabitha [BLOWER] (1654-); b 1681; Boston
BUTLER, Thomas & Dorothy _?_; b 1650(1?), b 1648; Sandwich
BUTLER, Thomas (1637-1688) & Sarah (?MAYNARD)/(STONE?) (1639?-); ?ca 1657, b 1670; Hartford/Wethersfield
BUTLER, Thomas & Elizabeth STONE, adopted by Richard WEBB; b 5 Oct 1665, b 1661?; Norwalk, CT
BUTLER, Thomas & Jemima DAGGETT (1666-); 27 Nov 1682, b 1685; Martha's Vineyard
BUTLER, Thomas (1661-1725, ae 64) & Abigail SHEPARD; 6 Aug 1691; Hartford/Bloomfield, CT
BUTLER, Thomas & Elizabeth [ABBOTT] (-1728); ca 1697; Kittery, ME
BUTLER, Walter (-1693) & Rebecca [REYNOLDS]; b 1672?, b 1684; Greenwich, CT
BUTLER, William (-1648) & Eunice [COFFIN] (1618-); aft 1642; Salisbury/Hartford
BUTLER, William (?1653-) & 1/wf Sarah [CROSS] (1655-bef 2 Jul 1703); b 1675, b 1676, b 1677, 1675; Ipswich
BUTLER, William (-1714) & Hannah HILLS (1672-1743); 23 May 1695; Wethersfield, CT
BUTLER, William (?1653-) & 2/wf Mary [INGALLS] (1668-); ?b 1701; Ipswich
BUTLER, William & Mary [GREENLEAF]; b 1701?; Boston

BUTLER/CUTLER, _?_ & Lydia MERCER, m/2 John STANWOOD 1680
BOOTEMAN, Jeremiah (-1694, ae ca 62) & 1/wf Hester/Esther? LAMBERT; 8 Oct 1659; Salem
BUTMAN, Jeremiah & Mehitable (GILES) [COLLINS], w John; aft 1677, b 1679; Gloucester
BUTMAN, John & Sarah ROBINSON; 30 Jun 1690; Gloucester
BUTMAN, Joseph & Rebekah (STONE) HARRIS, w Joseph; m int 18 Sep 1698; Beverly
BUTMAN, Matthew (1665-1718) & Elizabeth HOOPER; 28 Apr 1690; Beverly
BUTTELS, Leonard (1613-1654+) (ae 41 in 1654) & Judith _?_; b 23 May 1641; Boston
BUTTALL, Thomas (-1667, ae 64) & [Ann/Hannah BRIDGHAM] (-1680, ae 69); in Eng, b 1639; Boston
BUTTELL, _?_ & Jane [ROOT]; ?b Feb 1666; Boston
BUTTERFIELD, Benjamin[1] (-1688) & 1/wf Ann _?_ (-1660, 1661?); b 1636?; Charlestown/Woburn/Chelmsford
BUTTERFIELD, Benjamin[1] (-1688) & 2/wf Hannah (CHAWKLEY) WHITTMORE, w Thomas; 3 Jun 1663; Chelmsford
BUTERFILD, Benjamin (-1715) & Sarah BATS/BATES, m/2 David CARVER, m/3 Richard HILDRETH; 16 Feb 1697; Chelmsford/Woburn
BUTTERFIELD, Henry & Jane _?_; b 1691; Boston
BUTTERFEILD, Jonathan (-1673) & Mary DICSON/DIXON (1650-); 12 Jun 1667, 16? Jun; Chelmsford
BUTTERFIELD, Jonathan (?1672-1744, in 72nd y) & Ruth WRIGHT (-1754, ae 80); 20 Mar 1693/4; Charlestown/Cambridge/Woburn?
BUTTERFIELD, Joseph (1649-1720) & Lydia BALLARD (1657-1728+), Andover; 12 Apr 1674; Andover/Chelmsford
BUTERFILD, Joseph & Eunes/Eunice HALE/HEALD; 21 Jan 1697/8, 1696/7; Chelmsford
BUTTERFEILD, Nathaniel (1643-1719+) & Deborah UNDERWOOD (?1653-1691); 31 Dec 1668; Chelmsford
BUTERFILD, Nathaniel & Sarah FLATCHER; 18 Jan 1697/8; Chelmsford
BUTTERFIELD, Samuel (1647-1715) & Mary (not Ann) [BALLARD]; b 1670; Chelmsford
BUTTERS, William (-1692) & ?Mary/?Sarah _?_; b 1665; Woburn
BUTTERS, William & Rebecca [JONES]; b 1689; Woburn
BUTTERWORTH, Abraham (?1622-) & _?_; b 1684; RI
BUTTERWORTH, Benjamin (1672-1711) & Huldah HAYWARD; 6 Jan 1692; Swansea
BUTTERWORTH, Henry & Mary _?_, m Thomas CLIFTON 1641; ca 1626; Weymouth
BUTTERWORTH, John[1] (1630, 1624-1708) & Sarah _?_; b 1651; Rehoboth/Bristol, RI
BUTTERWORTH, John (1651-1731) & Hannah WHEATON (1654-1724); 4 Sep 1674; Rehoboth
BUTTERWORTH, Joseph (1657-1746) & Elizabeth BOOMER; 22 Jul 1691; Swansea
BUTTOLPH, David (?1669, 1670-1717) & Mary [?GOODRICH]; b 1692(3?); Wethersfield, CT
BUTTOLPH, George (1667-1693) & _?_ BUCK? (1672-1752), m/2 Robert LATIMER? aft 1696; b 1690; Wethersfield, CT
BUTTOPTH, John[1] (1640-1693) & 1/wf Hannah GARDNER (1644-1681); 16 Aug 1663, 16 Oct 1663; Salem/Boston/Wethersfield, CT
BUTTOLPH, John[1] (-1692?) & 2/wf Abigail (?BLAKE/CLARK) [SANFORD] (-1687), w Nathaniel; 27 Jun 1682; Wethersfield, CT
BUTTOLPH, John (-1693) & Mary/Susanna? (KELLY) [SANFORD], w Nathaniel; bef 20 Mar 1692, aft 14 Oct 1687; Hartford?/Wethersfield, CT
BUTTOLPH, John (1664-1713) & 1/wf Sarah [PICKERING] (1668-); b 1688; Salem
BUTTOLPH, John (1664-1713) & 2/wf Priscilla [GIBSON] (-1731), m/2 Simon WILLARD; b 1692; Salem
BUTTOLPH, Nicholas (1668-1727) & Mary GUTTRIDGE; 28 Jun 1699, 21? Jun; Boston
BUTTOLPH, Thomas (1603-1667) (called Henry BRIDGHAM "brother") & Ann/Hannah/Anna [HARDING] (1611-1680); in Eng, b 1635; Boston/Wethersfield, CT
BUTTOLPH, Thomas (1637-1669) & Mary BAXTER, m/2 Joseph SWETT b 1673; 5 Sep 1660; Boston
BUTTOLPH, Thomas (1663-1690) & Abiel/Abiah? SANDERSON/SAUDERS, m/2 George BEARD 1691; 3 Dec 1689; Boston
BUTTON, Benjamin & Elizabeth _?_; b 1674, b 1670?; Boston
BUTTON, John (1594-1681?) & 1/wf Grace _?_ (-1639); b 1638; Boston
BUTTON, John (see Matthias) & 2/wf Joan [?THORNTON]; b 25 Oct 1640; Boston

BUTTON, John & 3/wf [Mary] [SIMMONS]; b 22 May 1670; Boston
BUTTON, Matthias (-1672) (see John) (m/2 Joane THORNTON; bef 16 Nov 1639) & 1/wf [Lettyse] _?_ (-1652); b 1633?, b 1634; Salem/Boston/Ipswich/Haverhill
BUTTON, Matthias (-1672) & 3/wf Teagle _?_ (-1662/3); 1652?, 1653?; Haverhill
BUTTON, Matthias (-1672) & 4/wf Elizabeth (?WHEELER) DUSTON (-1690), w Thomas; 9 Jun 1663, no issue; Haverhill
BUTTON, Matthias[2] (1658-) & Mary NEFFE; 24 Nov 1686; Haverhill/Chelmsford, CT
BUTTON, Peter (1660-1726), New London & Mary [LAMPHERE] (-1727+); ca 1687, b 1689, Stonington; ?Westerly, RI/Stonington, CT
BUTTON, Robert (-1651?) (see BETHUEN) & [Abigail VERMAES], m/2 Edward HUTCHINSON, Jr. 1651; b 1642; Salem/Boston
BUTTON, Samuel (1649-) & Elizabeth (BOSWELL) MORSE, w John; 1682+, bef 20 Dec 1688
BUTTRICE, Nicholas & Martha _?_, m/2 Miles IVES by 1639; b 1633; Cambridge
BUTTRICK, John (1653-) & Mary BLOOD (1655-); 8 Apr 1679; Stow
BUTREKE, Samuel (1655-1726) & Elizabeth BLOOD (1653-1734); 21 Jun 1677; Concord
BUTTRICK, William (-1698) & 1/wf Mary [HASTINGS]?; b 1648; Concord
BUTTRICK, William (-1698) & 2/wf Sarah [BATEMAN]? (-1664); b 1653; Concord
BUTTRICK, William (1616-1698) & 3/wf Jane GOODNOW, w Thomas; 21 Feb 1667; Concord
BUTTERY/BUTTERS?, John & ?Elizabeth KNAPP (1635-), widow in Eng in 1662; b 1660; Reading/Watertown
BUTT, John & Mary (PEARSON) BLABER, w Robert, dau George PEARSON, m/3 Samuel HARE 1709; 21 Mar 1700
BUTTS, Moses (1673-1734) & [Alice LAKE] (1677-); ca 1699, ca 1695; Little Compton, RI
BUTT, Nathaniel (1670-1721) & Elizabeth BRECK (-1743); 16 Sep 1698; Dorchester
BUTT, Richard & Deliverance (HOPPIN) WOODWARD (1648-1699) (had son Smith WOODWARD); b 1670; Dorchester
BUTT, Sherbiah (1675-) & Silence RIGBY; 19 Nov 1697; Dorchester
BUTTS, Thomas & Elizabeth [LAKE], dau Henry; b 1667, b 1660; Portsmouth, RI/Little Compton, RI/?Dartmouth
BUTTS, Zaccheus (?1665, 1667-1718?) & Sarah [CONKLIN], m/2 John COLE; ca 1690?
BUXTON, Anthony[1] (?1601-1684) (cousin of William VINCENT/VINSON) & Elizabeth _?_ (-1713, in 90th y)?; b 1643?; Salem/Lancaster
BUXTON, Clement (-1657) & Unity _?_, m/2 Peter BROWN 1658, m/3 Nicholas KNAPP 1659; ca 1650?; Stamford, CT
BUXTON, Clement & [Judith] _?_; b 1678; Stamford, CT
BUXTON, John[2] (-1715, ca 71) & 1/wf Mary SMALL (-1676); 30 Mar 1668; Salem
BUXTON, John (-1715) & 2/wf Elizabeth HOLTON; 7 Oct 1677; Salem
BUXTON, John (1675-1749) & 1/wf Priscilla LYNN; 26 Nov 1700; Salem/Middleton
BUXTON, Joseph (-1752) & Esther [SOUTHWICK]; b 1689, ca 1683?; Salem
BUXTON, Thomas (-1654) & _?_; Salem
BIAM, Abraham (1644-1732) & Experience ADVERD (-1683), Scituate; 18 Jun 1672; Chelmsford/Scituate
BYAM, Abraham & Sarah ONG (-1718), wid; 22 Jan 1689/90; Chelmsford
BYAM, George (-1680) & Abigail _?_; b 1644; Salem/Wenham/Chelmsford
BYFIELD, Nathaniel (-1733, in 80th y) & 1/wf Deborah [CLARK] (-1717); b 1677, by 1675?, b 1675, bef 25 Apr 1676; Boston/Bristol, RI
BYINGTON, John & _?_; b 1678; Ipswich/Branford, CT
BYINGTON, John & Jane (WESTOVER) [SWAYNE] (-1720+), w John; b 1699; Branford, CT
BILES, Jonathan & 1/wf Sarah GOULDSMITH (1650-1674); 29 Sep 1668; Wenham/Beverly
BOILES, Jonathan & 2/wf Elizabeth PATCH; 15 Nov 1674; Beverly
BYLES, Joseph & Rebecca [FORBUSH] (1672-1768); Marlborough
BYLES, Josias (1656-1708) & 1/wf Sarah [AUBER]; in Eng, b 1682; Boston
BYLES, Josias & 2/wf Sarah [DAVIS] (-1703); b 1701; Boston
BILES, Richard & Mary DAVICE/DAVIS; m int 22 Jan 1695/6; Beverly
BYLES, _?_ & _?_ BRACHEMBURY; ?Salem
BYLEY/BILEY, Henry (1612-1638+) & Rebecca SWAYNE (-1695), m/2 John HALL 1641, m/3 Rev. William WORCHESTER 1650, m/4 Samuel SYMONDS 1663; St. Edward, Salisbury, Eng, 21 Jan 1632/3; Salisbury

BYRAM/BYRUM, Nicholas (-1688, Bridgewater) (m/1 Grace SHAW?) & 2/wf [Susannah SHAW]; b Oct 1638; Weymouth
BYRUM, Nicholas (-1727) & Mary EDSON (?1647-1727); 20 Sep 1676; Bridgewater

CABLE, John (-1682) & 1/wf [Sarah] [?BURR]; b 1641, b 1631?; Springfield/Fairfield, CT
CABLE, John (-1682) & 2/wf Ann [BETTS], w Roger BETTS d 31 Aug 1658, 1660?; b 1652?; Fairfield, CT
CABLE, John (1641-1673) & Elizabeth _?_, m/2 Thomas SHERWOOD; ca 1661; Fairfield, CT
CABLE, John & Abigail [SHERWOOD]; b 1701; Fairfield, CT
CABLE, Joseph & Abigail [ADAMS], m/2 Elijah CRANE; b 1701?; Fairfield, CT
CADMAN, George (-1718, Dartmouth) & Hannah [HATHAWAY] (-1749, 1718+); by 1676?; Portsmouth, RI/Dartmouth
CADMAN, Richard (-1695(-)) & Sarah [ALMY] (1662-1708(-)), m/2 Jonathan MERIHEW (1662-1701) 1695?; ca 1682; Portsmouth, RI
CADMAN, William (-1684±) & Elizabeth _?_ (-1688+); ca 1650?, ca 1652/55; Portsmouth, RI
CADWELL, Edward (1660-1716, 1719) & Elizabeth [BUTLER]; b 1681; Hartford
CADWELL, Matthew (1668-1719) & Abigail BECKLEY, m/2 Caleb LEETE 1721; 25 Mar 1695; Hartford
CADWELL, Thomas (-1694) & Elizabeth (STEBBINS) [WILSON], w Robert; b 1659(60?), b 1660, 1658?; Hartford
CADWELL, Thomas (1662-) & Hannah BUTLER; 23 Sep 1687; Hartford
CADYE, Daniel (1659-1736) & Mary GREENE (ca 1663-1736); 6 Jul 1683; Chelmsford/Brooklyn, CT/Canterbury, CT
CADE/KADE, James & Margaret BROWNE; in Eng, 21 Aug 1633; Boston/Yarmouth
CADY, James (1655-1690) & Hannah BARRON (1658-); 14 Jun 1678, 14 Jan 1678; Watertown/Groton/Windsor, CT
CADY, John (1651-) & Joanna _?_; ca 1675?, ca 1677?; Watertown/Groton/Canterbury, CT
CADY, John (1678?-1751) & 1/wf Elizabeth [GREEN]; b 1699; Groton/Windsor, CT
CADY, Joseph (1666-) & Sarah [DAVIS] (1667-); b 1690; Groton/Canterbury, CT/Killingly, CT
CADE, Nicholas & Judith [KNAPP], ca 1650?; Watertown/Groton
CADY, Nicholas, Groton & Patience RIDLAND/REDLAND?, Groton; 20 Mar 1685; Chelmsford/Preston, CT
CADY, _?_ & Sarah KING; LI
CAFFINCH, John & Mary [FOWLER]; b 1651; Guilford, CT/Milford, CT
CAFFINCH, Samuel & Ann [ATWATER]; b 1649?, b 1651; New Haven
CAHOONE, Joseph & 1/wf Hannah [KENT] (1667-); b 1690; Charlestown/Swansea/Bristol, RI/E. Greenwich, RI
CAHOONE, Joseph & 2/wf Elizabeth _?_; b 1701; E. Greenwich
CAHOON, Nathaniel (1675, 1674/5-) & Jane [JONES]; b 1702, b 1701?, 25 Feb 1702, 1701/2; Warwick, RI
COHOUN, William[1] (-1675) & _?_; b 1670(1?), b 1665?; Swansea
CAHOON, William (-1702) & Elizabeth [NICKERSON]; aft 1690; Chatham
CAIN/CANE, Arthur & Sarah GOLD (-1732); 29 Nov 1675; Hingham
CANE, Charles (-1686) & Catherine [TAYLOR]; b 1682; Boston/etc.
CANE, Christopher (-1653) & Margaret _?_ (-1687, ae 70); b [1640]; Cambridge
CANE, David & Joanna [DORE], m/2 John BOURNE, m/3 Stephen KNOWLES; Portsmouth, NH
CANE, Jonathan (1640-1695) & Deborah WELCH (-1689, ae 36); 14 May 1674; Cambridge/Charlestown
CANE, Nathaniel & Elizabeth _?_; b 1678; Boston
CAINE, Philip & Thomasin BULLOCK; 27 Jun 1700; Marblehead
CANE, Samuel & Jane _?_; b 1667; Boston
CANE, _?_ & Elizabeth _?_ (-1662), wid; Boston

CANE, _?_ & Mercy WARD; Charlestown
CAKEBREAD, Isaac (-1698) & 1/wf Hepzibah JONES (-1685, Suffield, CT); 20 Dec 1677; Springfield/Suffield, CT/Hartford
CAKEBREAD, Isaac & 2/wf Mary (LILLY) [ANDREWS], w John; b 1693/4; Hartford
CAKEBREAD/KAKEBREAD, Thomas (-1642?, [1642/3], Sudbury) & Sarah _?_, m/2 Philemon WHALE 1649; Watertown/Dedham/Sudbury
CALDWELL, Dillingham (1667-1745) & 1/wf Mary [LORD]; b 1695; Ipswich
CALDWELL, Dillingham (1667-1745) & 2/wf Mary [HART] (1665-); aft 21 Oct 1698, bef 1700; Ipswich
CALDWELL, John (-1692) & Sarah [DILLINGHAM] (1634-1722); b 1658, ca 1654?; Ipswich
CALDWELL, John & Sarah FOSTER (1665-1721); 1 May 1689; Ipswich
CALDWELL, Robert & Margaret [WHITE], m/2 Thomas WALLEN/[WALLING] 1669, m/3 Daniel ABBOTT 1678; ca 1660, div 1667; Providence/LI
CALDWELL, Robert (1662-1748) & Amy [DOWNING]; b 1699; Bristol, RI
CALEF, Joseph (?1671, 1672-1707) & Mary AYER (1666-1732+), m/2 Thomas CHOATE; 24 Mar 1693, 1692/3; Boston/Ipswich/Salisbury
CALEF, Robert¹ (1648-1719) & Mary _?_ ; ca 1670; Boston/Roxbury
CALFE, Robert (-1722/3) & Margaret BARTON; 23 Dec 1699; Boston
CALL, Caleb (1670-1748) & Ann WAFFE/WHAFF (-1737, ae 60+); 3 Mar 1697/8; Charlestown
CALL, John (see COLE) (1635-1697) & Hannah KETTELL (1637-1708, ae 71); 21 Jun 1656, 22 Jan; Charlestown
CALL, John (-1713, ae 55) & Martha LOWDEN (1659-1729, ae 70); 20 Jul 1681, 29 Jul; Charlestown
CALL, Nathaniel (1666-) & Temperance HURRY (1666-); 15 May 1690; Charlestown
CALL, Philip (-1662) & Mary [SMITH] (-1708), dau Richard, m/2 John BURR b 1665, m/3 Henry BENNETT; ca 1658?, b 1660; Ipswich
CALL, Thomas (ca 1597/8-1676) & 1/wf Bennett _?_ ; ca 1630; Malden
CALL, Thomas (-1676, ae 79) & 2/wf Joanna [SHEPARDSON] (-1661), w Daniel; aft 26 Jul 1644; Charlestown/Malden
CALL, Thomas (ca 1633, 1635-1678, ae 43, Malden) & Lydia SHEPARDSON (1637-1723), m/2 Thomas SPINNER 1678?, aft 1679; 22 Jul 1657; Malden
CALL, Thomas (1662-) & Elizabeth CROSSWELL (1666-1725, ae 59+); 23 May 1683; Charlestown
CALLENDER, Ellis (-1728, ae 87) & 1/wf Mary _?_ (-1719); b 1675, b 1674/5; Boston
CALLENDER, George (-1695) & Sarah _?_, m/2 William EVERDEN 1696; b 1687; Boston
CALLENDER, John & Elizabeth _?_ ; Rehoboth/Attleboro
CALLENDER, Philip & Mary [?EATON]; b 1705, b 1701?; Newport
CALLEY, James (-1734) & Martha _?_ (1667-1727); b 1701?; Marblehead
CALLEY, John (?1630-) & _?_ ; ca 1656; Salem
CAULEY, John & Susanna STACY; 29 Jun 1685; Marblehead
CALLEY, Joseph & Hannah [KIRTLAND]; b 1671; Boston
CALLEY, Peter & Ruth _?_ ; b 1670; Medfield
CALLEY, Richard & Anne (MUNDEN) [BEDFORD], w Nathan; by 1682
CALLEY, Robert (-1703) & Mary _?_, m/2 Leonard DROWN; b 1700, b 1688?; Charlestown/Malden
CAULY, Thomas (-1672) & Mary [PARMENTER]; b 1660; Marblehead
CALLO, Nathaniel & Anne _?_ ; b 1688; Boston
CALLOWE/CALLOW/CALLOWAY, Oliver (-1675) & Judith CLOCKE (-1684), w; 29 Feb, - Feb 1655/6, last of Feb; Boston
CALLUM/?McCALLUM, John & Elizabeth GUTTERSON, w William; 17 Nov 1670; Haberhill
CALLUM, John & Elizabeth BEANS/DYNN?, m/2 Richard COMAN?/COMER? 1693; 30 Nov 1685; Salem
CALLUM, Mackum & Martha _?_ ; b 1659; Lynn
CAMDEN, Edward & Ruth PASCO; 25 Sep 1694; Boston
CAME, Arthur & Violet _?_ ; ca 1670?; York, ME
CAME, Samuel (1676, 1673?-1768) & 1/wf Patience BRAGDON (1678-1753, ae 77); 22 Nov 1699; York, ME
CAMER, Edward (1626-) & Mary _?_ ; b 1677, ca 1650; Kinnebec, ME
CAMLER, Henry & Elizabeth _?_ ; b 1699; Boston

CAMMOCK, Thomas (1593-1643) & Margaret _?_, m/2 Henry JOCELYN/JOSLIN; Scarboro, ME/West Indies

CAMP, Edward (-1659) & Mary [CRANE?/CANFIELD?], m/2 John LANE 1660; b 1650; New Haven

CAMP, Edward (1650-1721?) & 1/wf Mehitable SMITH (1655-); 15 Jan 1673, 1673/4; Milford, CT

CAMP, John (-1711) & Mary [SANFORD] (1650-1727); b 1672; Hartford

CAMP, John & 1/wf Hannah [BENTON]; b 1672; Milford, CT

CAMP, John & 2/wf _?_ ; 1675; Milford, CT

CAMP, John (1662-1769) & Sarah SARGEANT

CAMP, John (1662-1731) & Mary [NORTHROP] (?1670-); ?ca 1690?; Milford, CT

CAMP, John (?1675-1711) & Lydia _?_ ; b 1692?, b 1699; Hartford

CAMP, Joseph (1657-1750) & Hannah [ROGERS] (1664-1740?), ?dau Eleazer; b 1690; ?Milford, CT

CAMP, Nicholas[1] & 1/wf [?Sarah _?_] (-1645); b 1630, b 1622?; Wethersfield, CT/Guilford, CT

CAMP, Nicholas[1] & 2/wf Edith [TILLEY], w John; 1646; Milford, CT

CAMP, Nicholas[1] & 3/wf Catherine (_?_) THOMPSON, w Anthony; 14 Jul 1652; New Haven/Milford, CT

CAMP, Nicholas[2] (1630-1706) & 1/wf Sarah [BEARD] BRISCOE (-1689), w Nathaniel; ca 1652; Milford, CT

CAMP, Nicholas[2] (1630-1706) & 2/wf ?Mehitable (?GUNN) (?FENN) [BRISCOE], w Benjamin, w Nathaniel; aft Aug 1689; Milford, CT

CAMP, Samuel (?1648-1744) & 1/wf Hannah BOTTS (1652-1680/1); 13 Nov 1672; Milford, CT

CAMP, Samuel & Mercy SEWARD?/SCOVILL? (1657-); 6 Jan 1681/2, 6 Jan 1681; Milford, CT

CAMP, Samuel & 1/wf 2/wf Mary CAMP (1664-); 10 Oct 1682; Milford, CT

CAMP, Samuel (1675-) & Mary [BALDWIN]; b 1691?, ca 1700?; ?Milford, CT

CAMP, Samuel & 2/wf 3/wf? Rebecca (ADKINSON) CANFIELD (1660-1711), w Thomas; 28 Apr 1695, 1696; Milford, CT

CAMP, Samuel (ca 1669-1744) & 1/wf Mary BALDWIN (-1733); bef 1697, ca 1700

CAMP, Samuel (-1733) & Martha (AFFORD) [CARR/CAROW?/CARROW] (-1739), dau John, w Peter; b 1699; Stratford, CT

CAMP, William (ca 1633-1694+) & Mary SMITH (1642-), New Haven; 29 Jan 1661/2, ?New Haven, 29 Jan 1661; Milford, CT/Newark, NJ

CAMP, William (-1713) & Elizabeth SMITH, dau Richard; ca 1683?, ca 1688?; New London, CT

CAMPBELL, Duncan & Susanna [PORTER]; b 1687; Boston

CAMBALL, Ebenezer & Hannah PRAT; 29 Mar 1694; Taunton

CAMPBELL, John & Sarah (ROGERS) HACKLETON, w William; 9 Mar 1686/7; Southampton/Easthampton

CAMBALL, John (-1728, ae 75) & Mary _?_ ; b 1696; Boston

CAMPBELL, Sylvanus (-1718) & Mary _?_ (-1724); b 1692(3); Norton

CAMPENALL, Daniel & Elizabeth SHELTIN; m int 1 Apr 1696; Boston

CANNEDY, Alexander & Elizabeth ANNABLE; b 1678; Plymouth

CANNADY, Daniel (-1695) & Hannah COOKE; 10 Nov 1681; Salem

CANNADIE, James & Grace BARKER; 3 Nov 1680; Rowley

CANDAGE, John (-1700+) & 1/wf Mary _?_ (-1677/8); b 1662; Charlestown

CANDAGE, John (-1700+) & 2/wf Mary (MOORE) [SWAIN], w John; 1678?, b 2 Oct 1677; Charlestown/Boston

CANDAGE, Thomas (-1713) & Sarah [JONES] (-1737); b 1693; Marblehead

CANDIDGE/CANDIGE, William (1666-) & Mary BACON (-1719+); - Nov 1689; Salem

CANDEE, Zaccheus (1640-1720) & Rebecca BRISTOL (1650-); Dec 1670, 5 Dec 1670; New Haven

CAMFIELD, Ebinezer & Mary HENNERY; 24 Mar 1693/4; Norwalk, CT

CANFIELD, Ebenezer (-1716) & Sarah _?_ ; b 1695; Norwalk, CT

CANFIELD, Jeremiah (1662-1740) & Alice [HINE] (1667-1740); ca 1687; Milford, CT/New Milford, CT

CANFIELD, Matthew[1] (-1673) & Sarah [TREAT] (1625, 1620-); ca 1643; New Haven/Norwalk, CT

CANFIELD, Samuel (1645-1690) & Sarah [WILLOUGHBY] (living 1677), left widow Elizabeth; ca 1668; Norwalk, CT

CANFIELD, Samuel & Elizabeth [MERWIN?/WILLOUGHBY?] (see above); ?; Norwalk, CT
CANFIELD, Thomas & Phebe [CRANE]; b 1654, ca 1650; Milford, CT
CANFIELD, Thomas (1654-1689) & Rebecca ADKINSON (-1711), m/2 Samuel CAMP 1695; 26 Feb 1679; Milford, CT
CANN, John & Esther READ; 30 Jul 1661; Boston
CANNEY, Joseph (-1690) & 1/wf Mary _?_; by 1669; Dover, NH
CANNY, Joseph (-1690) & 2/wf Mary CLEMENT (1651-); 25 Dec 1670; Salisbury
CANNEY, Joseph & 3/wf Mary [DAM], m/2 William HARFORD 1701; ca 1673; Dover, NH
CANNEY, Joseph (1674-) & Leah ALLEN; 1 Dec 1699; Dover, NH
CANNEY/KENNEY, Richard & Deborah STOKES; 15 Aug 1687; Dover, NH
CANNEY/KENNEY?, Samuel (1677-) & Sarah (HACKETT) RANKIN, w Joseph; 15 Mar 1698/9; Dover, NH
CANNEY, Thomas & 1/wf _?_; b 1645, b 1635?; Dover, NH
CANNEY, Thomas & 2/wf Jane _?_; b 1661?; Dover, NH/York, ME
CANNEY, Thomas (?1644-1678) & Sarah [TAYLOR], m/2 John WINGATE, m/3 Richard PAINE; by 1663?; Dover, NH
CANNEY, Thomas & Grace _?_; by 4 May 1696?, by 1696; Dover, NH
CANNON, John & Katherine THORNTON; 24 Oct 1700; Boston
CANON, Robert (-bef 30 Dec 1701) & Sarah [ANDREWS]; b 1674; Boston/?New London, CT
CANNON, _?_ & Joanna _?_; by 1680?, 5 ch bpt 19 Apr 1691; Barnstable
CANNOWAY, George & Anna WILSON (-1692, ae 58); 3 Apr 1671; Charlestown
CANTERBURY, Cornelius (-1672) & Anna _?_; b 1652; Hingham
CANTERBURY/CANTLEBURY, William (-1663) & Beatrice [BURT], m/2 Francis PLUMER 1665, m/3 Edward BERRY 1673/76; b 1636; Lynn/Salem
CAPEN, Barnard/Bernard (1568-1638) & Joan PURCHASE (1578-1653, 1652); ?Dorchester, Eng, 31 May 1596, Mar/Apr; Dorchester
CAPEN, Bernard (1650-1691) & Sarah TROT (1653-1724); 2 Jun 1675; Dorchester
CAPEN, James (1654-1718) & Hannah LAWRENCE (?1658-) (ae 23 in 1683); 21 Sep 1682; Charlestown
CAPAN, John (1612-1692) & 1/wf Radigon CLAPP (-1645); 20 Oct 1637; Dorchester
CAPEN, John (1612-1692) (ae 51 in 1604/5) & 2/wf Mary BASS (1631-1704); 20 Sep 1647; Dorchester
CAPEN, John (1639-1707?) & Susanna BARSHAM (1642-); 19 Nov 1663, 1662?; Dorchester/Roxbury
CAPEN, Rev. Joseph (1658-1725) & Priscilla [APPLETON] (1657-1743?); b 1685; Topsfield
CAPEN, Preserved (1656/7-1708) & Mary PASON/PAYSON (1665-), m/2 Samuel WILLIAMS; 16 May 1682; Dorchester
CAPEN, Samuel (1648-1733) & Susanna PAYSON (1655-1738, 1707?); 9 Apr 1673; Dorchester
CAPEN, Samuel (1667-1720) & Ann STONE (1668-); 16 Nov 1693; Boston/Watertown
CAPRIL/CAPRILL, Christopher & Tamazin _?_; b 1692; Boston
CAPRON, Benfield/Banfield (-1735) & [Elizabeth] [CALENDER] (1663-); 1682; Rehoboth/Attleboro/Newport
CARD, Francis & _?_; b 1676; ME?
CARD, James (see Richard CARD) & 1/wf _?_/Ruth? HAVENS?; b 1684; Newport/Kings Town, RI
CARD, Job & 1/wf Martha [ACRES] (1668-); - Nov 1689; New Shoreham, RI/Charlestown, RI
CARD, John & 1/wf Mary _?_; bef 1643; Dover, NH
CARD, John (-1705) & 1/wf Martha _?_ (-bef 1667); Portsmouth, RI/Kings Town, RI
CARD, John (-1705) & 2/wf Martha _?_; Portsmouth, RI/Kings Town, RI
CARD, John (1643-living 1674) & _?_; by 1670?
CARD, John & 2/wf Elizabeth WINCHESTER, w Robert; 16 Jan 1683/4
CARD, John & Anne [RANDALL]; by 1699?; Newcastle, NH
CARD, Joseph (1648-1729, 1708+) & Jane _?_ (-1717?); b 1678; Newport, RI
CARD, Richard (see James CARD) (-1674?) & Rebecca _?_, m/2 George HASSELL b 1692; b 1648; Newport
CARD, Thomas & Martha WINCHESTER; 26 Jul 1694; York, ME
CARD, William & Hannah (ELLERY?/HAYWARD?) [COITE], w John; 10 Jan 1692/3; Gloucester
CARDER, James (1655-1714) & Mary WHIPPLE (1665-1740); 6 Jan 1686/7; Warwick, RI

CARDER, John (-1700) & 1/wf Mary HOLDEN (1654-); 1 Dec 1671; Warwick, RI
CARDER, John (-1700) & 2/wf Hannah _?_ (-1700+); Warwick, RI
CARDER, John (1673-1749) & Elizabeth [WILLIS] (1677-1720+); by 1697?; Boston/Warwick, RI
CARDER, Joseph (1659-1694) & Bethiah _?_; b 1693; Warwick, RI
CARDER, Joseph & Elizabeth CLARKE; 5 Jun 1698; Marblehead
CARDER, Richard (-1676±) & 1/wf _?_; b 1637; Boston/Portsmouth, RI/Warwick, RI
CARDER, Richard (-1676±) & 2/wf Mary _?_ (-1691); b 1651?; Warwick, RI/Newport
CARDER, Richard (-1707±) & Mary RICHARDSON, m/2 _?_ LAKE; - Jan 1700, Jun 1700; New London
CARDER/CHARDER?, ?Helling & Rebecca _?_; 20 Jul; Salem/?Marblehead
CARDIS, Isaac & _?_; b 1674; Roxbury
CAREW, Thomas & Anna _?_; b 1701; Boston
CARY, David (1658/9-), Bristol & Elizabeth BRACKETT, Billerica, m/2 Ephraim KIDDER; 10 Dec 1687; Billerica/Bristol, RI/Providence
CAREY, Francis (164--) & Hannah BRETT; ca 1676; Bridgewater
CAREY, James (-1681, ae 81) & Eleanor _?_ (-1697, ae 80); b 1640; Charlestown
CARY, James (1652-1706) & [Mary STANDISH/SHAW] (1660-1735); 4 Jan 1681; Bridgewater
CAREW, John (-1680, 1681?) & Elizabeth GODFREY (-1680); Jun 1644; Duxbury/Braintree?
CARY, John (1645-1721) & [Abigail] [PENNIMAN/ALLEN?] (1651-) (PENNIMAN prob cousin Mrs. BARDAY); 7 Dec 1670, ?6 Dec 1670; Bridgewater/Bristol, RI
CAREY, John & Sarah _?_; b 1692; Boston
CAREY, Jonathan (1647-1737) & Hannah WINDSOR (-1715, ae 59); 30 Sep 1675; Charlestown
CARY, Jonathan & Elizabeth _?_; Boston
CAREY, Jonathan (1656-1695) & Sarah [ALLEN] (1667-), m/2 Benjamin SNOW 1705; ca 1687/95; Bridgewater
CAREY, Jonathan & Margaret PARKER, wid; 19 Apr 1699; Charlestown
CARY, Joseph (1663-1722, Windham, CT) & 1/wf Hannah _?_ (-1691, ?living 1700); b 1689; Norwich, CT/Preston, CT
CARY, Joseph (1663-1722, Windham, CT) & 2/wf Mercy (BUSHNELL) [RUDD] (1657-1731), w Jonathan; b 1693; ?Norwich, CT/Preston, CT
CAREY, Matthew (-1706) & Mary SYLVESTER (-1707); 1 Aug 1693; Bristol, RI/Boston
CAREY, Nathaniel (1645-) & Elizabeth [WALKER]; b 1676, 9 Jul 1674, Lancaster, Eng; Charlestown
CARKEET, William (-1662) & [?Margaret WADDOCK]; Saco, ME
CURKEET, William & Lydia GLAVEFEILD/GLANFIELD (1666-); 10 May 1686; Salem
CARLE/?KARLE, Abiel & _?_; b 1701; East Hampton, LI
CARLE, Richard (±1627-1697+) & Em?/Amie? [WYETH?]; Kittery, ME
CARLE, Thomas & Sarah HALSTEAD; 27 Feb 1656; ?Hempstead, LI
CARLE, Timothy (?1659-) & _?_; Great Island
CARLL, Timothy & Mary [PLATT]; 1697; Hempstead, LI/Huntington
CARROLL/?CARL, _?_ & Martha [CLARK]; b 1686; Suffolk Co., NY
CARLE, Thomas (-1709) & Elizabeth _?_; Hempstead, LI
CARLTON, Edward (returned to Eng) & Ellen NEWTON (1614-); York, St. Martin, 3 Nov 1636; Rowley
CARLETON, Edward (1665-1708) & Elizabeth [KIMBALL] (1669-); b 1691, ca 1689; Bradford/Haverhill
CARLETON, John (ca 1637-1668) & Hannah [JEWETT] (1641-), m/2 Christopher BABBAGE 1674; b 1658?, ca 1660; Rowley/Haverhill
CARLTON, John & Katharine _?_; b 1688; Boston
CARLETON, John (1663-1745) & Hannah OSGOOD (1673-1754); 27 Aug 1688; Andover
CARLETON, Joseph & Abigail OSGOOD (1673-); 2 Aug 1694; Andover/Bradford
CARLETON, Thomas (1667-1734) & Elizabeth HAZELTON/HAZELTINE (1677-1738, 1758); 16 Feb 1694/5; ?Bradford
KERLY, William (1633-1719) & Jane _?_ (1650-1720); b 1667; (?Sudbury)/Cambridge
CARLISLE, Bartholomew & Hannah _?_; b 1686; Sudbury
CARLILE, Francis & Sarah _?_; b 1682; Boston
CERLILE, John & Hannah [MOORE] (1662-), dau Thomas; b 1692; Boston
CARLISLE, Joseph & 1/wf Elizabeth [BEAN]; York, ME

CARLISLE, Joseph & Rachel (MAINS) PREBLE (?1665-1749+), w Stephen; 29 Mar 1695, 28? Mar; York, ME
CARMAN, Caleb (1645-) & Elizabeth _?_ ; b 1666?;Jamaica, LI/Cape May, NJ
CARMAN, John (-1653) & Florence [?FORDHAM] (probably not) (-1656), m/2 John HICKS by 1661; b 1631?, b 1633; Lynn/Sandwich/Roxbury/Stamford, CT/Hempstead, LI
CARMEN, John (1633-1684) & Hannah _?_ ; ca 1660?; Hempstead, LI
CARMAN, John & Hannah [SEAMAN]?; b 1683; Hempstead, LI
CARMAN, John & 1/wf Elizabeth SUDHAM, [dau William]; m lic 20 Jan 1683
CARMAN, Samuel & Sarah _?_ ; b 1698; Hempstead, LI
CARMICHAEL, John (-1677) & Anne [PIERCE?], m/2 John BRACY ca 1677; York, ME
CAIRNESS, John & Elizabeth MORTIMOR, m/2 Nathaniel KENNY; 24 Jun 1697; Boston
CARNES, Thomas & 1/wf Anna _?_ ; b 1684; New Haven
CARPENTER, Abiah (1643-) & [Mary REDWAY?] (1646-); b 1667?, b 1665; Pawtuxet, RI?
CARPENTER, Abiah (1665/6-) & Mehitable REED; 30 May 1690; Rehoboth
CARPENTER, Benjamin (1658-1727) & 1/wf Renew [WEEKS] (1660-1703); b 1680[1?]; Swansea
CARPENTER, Benjamin (1653-1711) & Mary [TILLINGHAST] (1661-1711+); ca 1680-87; Pawtuxet, RI
CARPENTER, Benjamin (1663-1738) & Hannah STRONG (1671-1762); 4 Mar 1691; Northampton/Coventry, CT
CARPENTER, Daniel (Samuel is wrong) (1669-1721) & 1/wf Bethiah BLISS (-1702); 15 Apr 1695; Rehoboth/Coventry, CT
CARPENTER, David (-1651?) & Elizabeth _?_ (-1694), m/2 George ORVIS, m/3 Richard BRONSON; b 1644; Farmington, CT
CARPENTER, David (-1700) & Sarah [HOUGH] (1651-), m/2 William STEVENS 1703; b 1677; New London
CARPENTER, David (-1701, 1702) & Rebecca (_?_) HUNT, w Ephraim; 22 Nov 1697; Rehoboth
CARPENTER, Ephraim (-1703±) & 1/wf Susannah [HARRIS] (-bef 3 Dec 1677); ca 1661; Pawtuxet, RI/Oyster Bay, LI
CARPENTER, Ephraim (-1703±) & 2/wf Susannah ENGLAND (-1684); 3 Dec 1677; Oyster Bay, LI
CARPENTER, Ephraim (-1703±) & 3/wf Lydia [DICKENSON] (1662-); b 1 Jul 1693; Oyster Bay, LI
CARPENTER, Hope (-1713) & Mary [MILLS?/ASHMAN?] (had son Ashman); b 1685; Jamaica, LI
CARPENTER, James & 1/wf Dorothy BLISS (1668-); 26 Jun 1690; Rehoboth
CARPENTER, James (1668-) & 2/wf Grace PALMER (1668-); 15 Apr 1695; Rehoboth
CARPENTER, John (?1628-1695?) & Hannah [SMITH?]/[HOPE?]; b 1658, Huntington, LI/Hempstead, LI/Jamaica, LI
CARPENTER, John (1652-) & 1/wf Rebecca [REDWAY/READAWAY] (1654-) b 1677; Rehoboth/Swansea/Woodstock, CT
CARPENTER, John (-1695) & Dorothy [?RHODES], dau John; 9 Feb 1680; Jamaica, LI/Weymouth?/Attleboro
CARPENTER, John (1658±-1732) & Mary [RHODES?]; b 1685; Jamaica, LI
CARPENTER, John (1652-) & 2/wf Sarah (FULLER) DAY, w Ralph, m/3 Samuel WARD/[?WEARE]; aft 21 Oct 1694; Woodstock, CT
CARPENTER, John & Mary COLESON; 4 Jun 1700; Boston
CARPENTER, Jonathan (1672-1716) & Hannah FRENCH (1679-); 13 Mar 1699; Rehoboth
CARPENTER, Joseph (1633±-1675) & Margaret SUTTON (-1700, ae 65); 25 Nov 1655, 25 May 1655; Rehoboth
CARPENTER, Joseph (-1684), ?Swansea & 1/wf Hannah CARPENTER (-1670±, 1673?); 21 Apr 1659; Rehoboth/Musketa Cove, LI
CARPENTER, Joseph (1635-1687) & 2/wf Ann/Anna WEEKS/SIMKINS (1651-); b 1674; Oyster Bay, LI
CARPENTER, Joseph (1650, ?1656-1713, 1717?) & Mary _?_ (-1713, ae ca 59); 23 Feb 1681; Swansea/Warren, RI
CARPENTER, Joseph (1666-1690) & Anne THORNEYCRAFT?, ?dau Thomas; b 1685; Oyster Bay, LI
CARPENTER, Josiah (1664-1728) & Elizabeth READ (1669-1739); 24 Nov 1692, 24 May 1692; Rehoboth

CARPENTER, Lawrence (-1677) & _?_ ; b 1674
CARPENTER, Nathaniel & Tamar COLES (1673-); 5 Nov 1690; Musketa Cove, LI
CARPENTER, Nathaniel (1667-) & 1/wf Rachel COOPER (-1694, ae 23); 19 Sep 1692, 18 Sep 1693, 19 Sep 169-, 19 Sep 1693; Rehoboth
CARPENTER, Nathaniel (1667-) & 2/wf Mary PRESTON (1675-1706); 13 Dec 1695, 17 Nov 1695; Dorchester/Rehoboth
CARPENTER, Noah (1672-1753, Attleboro) & 1/wf Sarah JONSON/JOHNSON of Dorchester (-1726); 3 Dec 1700; Rehoboth/Attleboro/Dorchester
CARPENTER, Oliver (1675±-) & Sarah _?_ ; b 1704, b 1701, b 1695?; Pawtuxet, RI
CARPENTER, Philip & _?_ ; b 1701?, b 1698; Cape Elizabeth, ME/Kittery
CARPENTER, Samuel (-1683) & Sarah REDAWAY, m/2 Gilbert BROOKS 1687/8; 25 May 1660; Rehoboth
CARPENTER, Samuel (?1661-1737) & Patience IDE (1664-1732); 8 Jan 1683; Rehoboth
CARPENTER, Samuel (1666±-) & _?_ ; b 1692; Jamaica, LI
CARPENTER, Samuel & _?_ ; b 1695; ?Pawtuxet, RI
CARPENTER, Silas (1650-1695) & Sarah ARNOLD (1665-1701+, 1727); [ca 1680?]; Pawtuxet, RI
CARPENTER, Solomon (1670±-) & _?_ ; b 1690; Jamaica, LI
CARPENTER, Solomon (1677-) & Elizabeth TEFFT; 1696, ca 1702?, 1st ch b 1703; South Kingston, RI
CARPENTER, Timothy (?1648-1726) & Hannah BURTON (-1726(-)); b 1665; Providence
CARPENTER, William[1] (1576-) & ?_?_ ; in Eng, b 1605; Weymouth
CARPENTER, William[2] (1605-1659) & Abigail _?_ (1606-1687); in Eng, b 1628; Weymouth/Rehoboth
CARPENTER, William (-1685) & Elizabeth ARNOLD (1611-1683+); in Eng, b 1635; Providence/Pawtuxet, RI
CARPENTER, William[3] (?1641-) & 1/wf Priscilla BENET/BONNETT (-1663); 5 Oct 1651; Rehoboth
CARPENTER, William[3] (-1704) & 2/wf Miriam SALE (-1722, ae 76, ae 93?); 10 Feb 1663/4, 10 Dec -, 10 Dec 1663; Rehoboth
CARPENTER, William (1659-1719, Attleboro) & Elizabeth ROBENSON/ROBINSON; 8 Apr 1685; Rehoboth/Attleboro
CARPENTER, William (1662±, 1666?-) & 1/wf ?Sarah _?_ & 2/wf ?Elizabeth MUDGE (1675-); b 1687, b 1688; Hempstead, LI/Jamaica, LI
CARPENTER, William (1662-1749) & 2/wf Elizabeth _?_ ; b?; Hempstead, LI
CARR, Caleb[1] (?1624-1695) & 1/wf ?Ann/Mercy [EASTON?]/[VAUGHN?] (1630/1-1675); b 1650?, b 1654; ?Newport/Jamestown RI
CARR, Caleb (-1690) & Phillippa?/Phillip/Phillis [GREENE?] (1650-1703(-)), m/2 ?Charles/?John DICKERSON/DICKINSON 1706?; ca 1675, b 1678; Portsmouth, RI?/Jamestown, RI
CARR, Caleb[1] (-1695) & 2/wf Sarah (CLARKE) [PINNER] (1651-1706+), w John; ca 1677; Newport
CARR, ?Caleb[1] (-1695) & 2/wf [Mercy VAUGHAN] (1630-1675)
CARR, Caleb (1657-1700) & Deborah [SAYLES?] (-1700+); b 1681; Jamestown, RI
CARR, Edward (1667-1711) & Hannah STANTON (1670-1712); 6 Oct 1686; ?Jamestown, RI/?Newport
CARR, Esek (1650-1744) & Susanna _?_ ; b 1685; Little Compton, RI/Tiverton, RI
CARR, Francis (ca 1678-1717) & Damaris ARNOLD (1684-); 18 Jun 1700; Newport
CARR, George (-1682) (bro-in-law of Capt. James OLIVER) & Elizabeth [?HAZARD/?DEXTER]/[OLIVER?]/[CARTER?] (-1691); b 1642; Salisbury
CARR, George & Marian GOLDTHWAIT?; 8 Jun 1645; Bristol, RI
CARR, George (-1697+?) & Anne COTTON (1661-1702), m/2 William JOHNSON 1688?, betw 1697, 1702; 8 Nov 1677; Salisbury
CARR, James (1650-1740) & Mary SEARS (1657-); 14 Nov 1677; Newbury
CARR, John (?1664-) & Waite [EASTON] (1667/8-1725); ca 1686/7?; Newport
CARR, Nicholas (1654-1709) & Rebecca NICHOLSON (1656-1703); b 1689, b 1678, b 1679; Jamestown, RI
CARRE, Richard (-1689) & 1/wf? Elizabeth _?_ ; Hampton, NH/Ipswich
CARR, Richard of Amesbury, MA, & Dorothy BOYCE; b 10 Feb 1684, b 1694; Killingworth, CT

CARR, Robert (1614-1681) & _?_ ; b 1640; Portsmouth, RI/Newport
CARR, Robert (-1704) & Elizabeth [LAWTON] (-1724); b 1689, b 1679?; Jamestown, RI/?Portsmouth, RI
CARR, Samuel (1659-1694) & _?_ ; b 1689; Newport
CARR, William (-1672) & Susan ROTHCHILD (-1671); in London, Eng, 16 May 1699; Plymouth/Bristol, RI
CARR, William & Elizabeth PIKE (-1715); 20 Aug 1672; Salisbury
CARR, William (1648-) & Rosannah CARR of NC (1650-); 9 May 1675; RI
CARR, _?_ & Christian (HARRIS) WILLIAMS, w Samuel, w Lewis, m/4 John WYATT; by 1698
CARRIER, Richard (-1749) & 1/wf Elizabeth SESSIONS (-1704?, Colchester, CT); 18 Jul 1694; Andover/Colchester
CARRIER alias MORGAN, Thomas (-1735, ca 108/109) & Martha ALLEN (-1692); 7 May 1674; Billerica/Andover/Colchester, CT
CARRINGTON, Edward (1613-1684) & Elizabeth _?_ (-1684); b 1639; Charlestown/Malden
CARRINGTON, John (1602-) & Mary _?_ (1602-); came in 1635
CARRINGTON, John (-1651, 1653?) & Joan _?_ (-1651); b 1643?; Wethersfield, CT
CARRINGTON, John (-1670) (had son Clark) & _?_ [CLARK?] (-1690?); b 1666; Farmington, CT/Waterbury, CT
CARRINGTON, Peter (-1727) & Anna (WILMOT) [LINES], w Benjamin; b 1692; New Haven
CARROLL, Anthony & [Katherine] _?_ ; b 1658; Topsfield
CARYLL, John (-1691) & Remember _?_ ; Easthampton, LI; -, LI
CARROLL, Joseph & Priscilla (MAIMS) PREBBLE/PREBLE, w Nathaniel; - Jul 1695; Salem
CARROL, Nathaniel & Mary [PEACE] (probably); b 1661, b 1662; Salem
CARROLL, Nathaniel & Priscilla DOWNING; 1683; Salem/Boxford
CARROW, Peter & Martha [UFFORD] (1659-1739, Durham, CT), m/2 Samuel CAMP bef 1699; Milford, CT
CARSLEY, John & Alice _?_ ; b 1642, b 1 Mar 1641/2; Barnstable
CARSLEY, John (-1693) & Sarah _?_ , m/2 Samuel NORMAN 1697; Barnstable
CASELY/CARSELEY, William & _?_ (sister of Mrs. Marmaduke MATTHEWS of Yarmouth); ca 28 Nov 1639; Sandwich
CARTE, Phillips & Elizabeth YORKE, dau Richard; 23 Sep 1668; Exeter, NH
CARTER, Abraham & Elizabeth _?_ ; b 1693; Newton
CARTER, Caleb (1642-1694) & Mary TUTTLE (1653-1728, in 74th y); in Eng, 4 Dec 1678, 14? Dec; Charlestown
CARTER, Edward (-1691) & Joan [DIAMOND], w William, m/3 James BLAGDON 1691/3
CARTER, Edward & Elizabeth SHERIFF/SHREVE (-1719); ca 1685/90?, no issue; RI
CARTER, Isaac (-1687) & Prudence _?_ ; b 1687; Charlestown
CARTER, John (-1692, ae 76) & Elizabeth ?KINDALL (1613-1691); b 1643; Woburn
CARTER, John & Anne (BULLY) (BERRY) SCADLOCK, w Ambrose, w William; 27 Dec 1665; Boston?/Saco, ME
CARTER, John (1653-1727) & Ruth BURNHAM (1658-1724); 20 Jun 1678; Woburn/Charlestown
CARTER, John & Sarah STOWERS (1656-), m/2 John EMERSON b 1695?; 21 Apr 1680, no issue; Charlestown
CARTER, John (1650-) & Martha [BROWN?] (1654-); b 1681; Salisbury
CARTER, John & Sarah _?_ ; b 1682; Boston
CARTER, John & Sarah [HILLIARD] (1662-), ?m/2 Paul MANSFIELD 1693; 28 Dec 1682; Salem
CARTER, John & Eleanor BRIARS; 19 Apr 1687; Marblehead
CARTER, John (-1692) & 2/wf Elizabeth [GROSE]; 1691 [aft 7 May]; Woburn
CARTER, John & 1/wf _?_ ; in Eng; Star Island
CARTER, John & 2/wf Ruth [WELCOME]; ?ca 1693; Star Island
CARTER, John & [Phillipe/Philippa] WHITE, m/2 Samuel GREENWOOD 1710; 6 Nov 1699; Boston
CARTER/(CARTERET?), John & Ann _?_ ; b 1701?; Southold, LI
CARTER, Joseph (-1676) & Susanna [CHAMBERLAIN?] (1615-), ?m/2 Richard ECCLES 1677; b 1650; Charlestown
CARTER, Joseph (-1692) & Bethiah [PEARSON?]; b 1671, b 1663?; Woburn/Charlestown
CARTER, Joshua (-1647) & Catherine _?_ , m/2 Arthur WILLIAMS 1647, m/3 William BRANCH 1677; b 1638; Dorchester/Windsor, CT/Hartford/Deerfield

CARTER, Joshua (1638-1675) & Mary FIELD, wid; 2 Oct 1663, 22 Oct 1663, 6? Oct, 2/4 Oct; Northampton/Deerfield
CARTER, Joshua & Mary SKINNER; 21 May 1691; Hartford/Deerfield
CARTER, Obed (-1685) & Mary _?_
CARTER, Obed (-1720) & Elizabeth CHINN (-1726+); 18 Feb 1696/7; Marblehead
CARTER, Ralph & Susanna _?_ ; b 1666; Boston
CARTER, Richard (-1667) & Anna/Anne [ORGRAVE], m/2 John HUNT 1671; b 1641; Boston/Charlestown
CARTER, Richard & Agnes _?_ (-1650), m/2 Michael MADEVER?; b 1645; N. Yarmouth, ME
CARTER, Robert & _?_ ; b 1669; Malden
CARTER, Robert & Hannah LUCAS; 19 Apr 1694; Bristol, RI
CARTER, Robert & Mary WILMARTH; 17 Sep 1696; Rehoboth/Swansea
CARTER, Samuel (1616-1681) & Winifred [HARROD?/HARWOOD?] (-1675), w Henry?; b 1640; Charlestown
CARTER, Samuel (1642-1678) & 1/wf Bethiah COWDREY (1643-1673); 18 Sep 1667; Charlestown
CARTER, Samuel (1640-1693) & Eunice BROOKS (1655-), m/2 James PARKER 1693+, m/3 John KENDALL; b 1673, 1672; Woburn/Lancaster?
CARTER, Samuel, Jr. (1642-1678) & 2/wf Abigail BAMON (1654-1695), m/2 Nathaniel RAND 1679?; 9 Sep 1676 (9 Jul is wrong); Charlestown
CARTER, Samuel & 1/wf Mercy BROOKS (1669-1701); 4 Dec 1690; Deerfield/Norwalk
CARTER/CATER?, Samuel (1668-1691) & Elizabeth _?_/THOMAS, m/2 John BENJAMIN 1702; b 1691; Charlestown/?York, ME
CARTER, Sebrean (-1703, Concord) & Elizabeth [ALLEN?], dau Daniel, m/2 Joseph FLETCHER; b 1696, b 1693; Newton/Concord
CARTER, Thomas (-ca 1652) & Mary _?_ (-1664/5); in Eng, b 1616, b 1607?; Charlestown
CARTER, Thomas (1610-1684) & Mary PARKHURST (?1614-1687); b 1640, b 1638?; Woburn/Charlestown/Watertown/Sulisbury
CARTER, Thomas[2] (-1694, ae 87) & Anna/Ann [?WILLIAMS] (-1679, ae 71/72); b 1640; Charlestown
CARTER, Thomas (-1669) & Mary _?_ ; b 1641; Sudbury
CARTER, Thomas (1654-1721) & Esther MARLOW from London (-1709, ae 62); b 1677, b 12 Mar 1675/6?; Charlestown
CARTER, Thomas (-1694, ae 84) & Elizabeth (JEFTS?)/(STORY?) JOHNSON (-1684), w William; 24 Oct 1679; Charlestown
CARTER, Thomas (1655-) & Margery/Margaret? WHITMORE/?WHITMAN (1668-1734); 1682; Woburn/Charlestown
CARTER, Thomas (-1700), Sudbury & Elizabeth (GOBLE) WHITE, w John; 7 Jun 1682; Sudbury/Charlestown
CARTER, Thomas & Ruth MOUNTFORD; 2 May 1693; Boston
CARTER, Timothy (1653-1727) & Anna/?Hannah FISK (-1713); 3 May 1680; Woburn
CARTERET, Philip & Elizabeth (SMITH) LAWRENCE, w William, m/3 Richard TOWNLEY, Elizabeth, NJ; Apr 1681, aft 1680, aft 30 Mar 1681; (see John CATER & Ann)
CARTHEW, John & Joanna _?_ ; b 1670; Boston
CARTHRICK, Michael (-1647) & Sarah _?_ ; in Eng, b 1633; Charlestown
CARTWRIGHT, Arthur & Jone/Joan _?_ (-1671); by 1664; Dorchester
CARTWRIGHT, Edward (-1671) & Elizabeth [MORRIS] (-1673); ca 1668?, by 1663; Boston
CARTWRIGHT, Edward (-1705) & 1/wf Mary _?_ ; by 1672?; Nantucket
CARTWRIGHT/CARTER?, Edward & Elizabeth _?_ ; b 1673; Isles of Shoal
CARTWRIGHT, Edward (-1705) & 2/wf Elizabeth [TROTT] (-1729); Nantucket
CARTRITH, John & Anna [RACKET], wid; 17 Dec 1686; Southold, NY
CARTWRIGHT, Nicholas (-1706) & Orange [ROGERS] (1671-); b 1695; Nantucket
CARTWRIGHT, Sampson (1677/8-) & Bethiah PRATT (1680-1741); b 1702, by 1700?; Nantucket
CARTWRIGHT, _?_ & _?_ ; b 1683; Flushing, LI
CARVER, David & 1/wf Ruth WHITMARSH; 14 Dec 1696, 16? Dec; Hingham/Canterbury, CT
CARVER, Eleazer (-1744), Taunton & Experience (BLAKE) SUMNER (1665-), w Samuel; 11 Jun 1695; Milton/Taunton/Canterbury, CT

CARVER, John (-1621) & Kathrine (WHITE) [LIGETT] (-1621), ?w George; in Eng, b 1617, b 1609; Plymouth
CARVER, John (?1635/7-1679, ae 41/42?) & Millicent FORD, m/2 Thomas DRAKE 1681; 4 Nov 1658; Marshfield
CARVER, John & Mary BARNES; 24 Oct 1689; Plymouth
CARVER, Richard (1577-1641) & Grace _?_ (1597-); in Eng, b 1618?; Watertown
CARVER, Robert (?1594-1680, ae 86) & Christian _?_ (-1658); in Eng, ca 1619?, b 1637?; Marshfield/Boston
CARVER, Robert & Dorothy/Dorcas? GARDNER; 19 Jun 1688; Salem
CARVER, William (1659-1760) & 1/wf Elizabeth FOSTER (1664-1715); 18 Jan 1682, 1682/3; Marshfield
CARVER, _?_ & Martha _?_, m/2 Matthew ALGER
CARWITHEN/CORWITH?, Caleb & [?Grace LUDLAM]; Huntington, LI
CARWITHEN, David (-1665) & (Grace?) [?ALCOCK]; b 1638, b 1632?; Salem/Boston
CARWITHEN, David & Frances OLDAM, wid; 22 Sep 1660; Boston
CARWITHEN, David & Elizabeth (CARRINGTON) [PAINE] (-1711, ae 73), w Stephen; b 1688(9?), ca 1693; Boston
CARWITHY, Edward & Rebecca [SLOPER] (1673-); Portsmouth, NH
CORWITH, John & _?_ ; b 1682?; Southampton/Cape May, NJ
CARWITHY, Joshua (-1663) & Elizabeth FARNAM, m/2 Edmund MUMFORD 1663, 1664; 6 Aug 1657; Boston
CASE, Bartholomew (-1725) & Mary HUMPHREY; 7 Dec 1699; Simsbury, CT
CASE, Edward & _?_ ; b 1640; Watertown
CASE, Henry & Martha CORWIN, m/2 Thomas HUTCHINSON 1666; - Nov 1658, last week in Nov; Southold, LI
CASE, Henry & Martha [PAINE]; b 1701?; Southold, LI
CASE, Humphrey & _?_ [BALDWIN]; ca 1665/70?; Salem/Saco, ME
CASE, Humphrey & 1/wf Rachel NICHOLS; 11 Jan 1698/9; Salem/Topsfield
CASE, James & Anna/?Hannah _?_ ; b 1685; Portsmouth, RI/Little Compton, RI
CASE, John (-1704, Simsbury) & 1/wf Sarah [SPENCER] (1636-1691, ae 55); by 1656; Windsor, CT/Simsbury, CT
CASE, John & Desire [MANTER]; ca 1683; Martha's Vineyard
CASE, John (1662-1733) & 1/wf Mary OLCOTT, Hartford; 12 Sep 1684; Simsbury, CT
CASE, John (-1704) & 2/wf Elizabeth (MOORE) [LOOMIS] (-1728, ae 90), w Nathaniel; aft 3 Nov 1691; Windsor, CT/Simsbury, CT
KASE/CASE?, John & Joanna JOHNSON; 27 Apr 1692; Dover, NH
CASE, John (1662-1733) & 2/wf Sarah [HOLCOMB] (1668-); ca 1693; Simsbury, CT
CASE, Joseph (1654-1741) & Hannah [SMITH] (-1712); b 1678; Portsmouth, RI/S. Kingston, RI
CASE, Joseph (1674-1748) & Ann ENNO/ENO (-1760); 6 Apr 1699; Simsbury, CT
CASE, Richard (-1694) & Elizabeth [PURCHASE]; b 17 Dec 1663; E. Hartford, CT/Simsbury, CT
CASE, Samuel (-1725) & 1/wf Mary [WESTOVER] (-27 Sep 1713); b 1696, b 1695(6?); Simsbury, CT
CASE, Thomas (-1692), Newtown, LI, & Mary [MACOCK/McCOCK], w? Peter; ca 1659-1662
CASE, Theophilus & Hannah _?_ ; -bef 1686; Southold
CASE, William[1] (-1676(-)) & Mary _?_ (-1680+); b 1654; Newport, RI
CASE, William[2] (-1713) & 1/wf _?_ ; ca 1675/85?; E. Greenwich, RI
CASE, William & Mary STARKEY; 28 Jan 1685/6; Charlestown
CASE, William (1665-1700) & Elizabeth HOLCOMB (1670-1762), m/2 John SLATER 1704, m/3 Thomas MARSHALL; 1688, b 1689; Windsor, CT/Simsbury, CT
CASE, William[2] (-1713) & 2/wf Abigail _?_ (-1736); ca 1693?; E. Greenwich, RI
CASE, _?_ /?Samuel & Hannah [BUTLER], dau Nathaniel; b 9 Feb 1697/8; Wethersfield, CT
CASEY, Thomas (1636±-1719±) & Sarah _?_ (-1706+); b 1663; Newport
CASEY, Thomas (1663-1719(-)) & Rebecca _?_ (-1719+); b 1695; Newport
CASH, William (-1717+) & Elizabeth LAMBERT, m/2 Edward BISHOP 1693; - Oct 1667; Salem
CASH, William & 1/wf Sarah FLINDER; - May 1698; Salem
CASELEY, William & _?_ MATTHEWS; - Nov 1639; Sandwich
CASS, Ebenezer (1671-) (see CASE) & Patience DRAPER (1668-); 13 Mar 1689, 1689/90; Roxbury/Lebanon, CT/etc.

CASS, John (-1675) & Martha [PHILBRICK], m/2 William LYON 1676; ca 1648?; Hampton, NH
CASS, Jonathan (1663-1693) & Ann _?_ (-1694); b 1687; Roxbury
CASS, Joseph (1656-) & 1/wf Mary HOBBS (1657-1692); 4 Jan 1677; Hampton, NH
CASS, Joseph (1656-) & 2/wf Elizabeth (GREEN) [CHASE] (1656-), w James; aft 1692, b 1698?;
    Hampton, NH
CASS, Samuel (1659-) & Mercy SANBORN (1660-); 7 Dec 1681; Hampton, NH
CASTLE/CASTEL, Henry (-1698) & Abigail [?DICKERSON] (-1725); ca 1665?; Woodbury, CT
CASTLE, Henry (-1745) & 1/wf Hannah SQUIRE (-1714); 12 Apr 1699, 20? Apr, 12? Aug;
    Woodbury, CT
CASTLE, Isaac (?1672-1727) & 1/wf Sarah [ADAMS] (1680-1708); b 1701?; Woodbury, CT
CASTLE, Samuel (?1668-1707) & Susanna (_?_) (FAIRCHILD) [NICHOLS], w Thomas, w
    Samuel; b 1693; Woodbury, CT/Stratford, CT
CANSTINE, William & 1/wf Isabel _?_ (-25 Jan 1653/4); Boston
CASTINE, William & 2/wf Mary _?_ ; b 1655; Boston
CASWELL, Francis (1671-) & Priscilla TAPRIL/TAPRILL; 18 Aug 1699; Boston
CASWELL, John[2] (1656-) & Elizabeth HALL; 26 Nov 1689; Taunton/Newton, MA
CASWELL/CASTLE, Matthew & Mary STOWERS (-1705, ae 44); 4 Aug 1687; Charlestown
CASWELL, Peter[2] (1652-) & Hannah _?_/RICHMOND?; b 7 Aug 1691; Taunton
CASWELL, Samuel[2] (1663-) & Ruth [BABBITT] (1671-); b 1701?; ?Taunton
CASWELL, Stephen[2] (1649-1711/14) & Hannah THRASHER; 29 Dec 1672, 24 Dec; Taunton
CASWELL, Thomas[1] (-1697) & Mary _?_ ; b 1648(9?); Taunton
CASWELL, Thomas[2] (1651-) & Mary [SANDERSON?]/JONES?/KINGSWILL; b 1675; Taunton
CASWELL, Thomas & Mary RANSDEN; 2 Dec 1691; Taunton
CASWELL/CASTLE, William & Mary [HUDSON], m/2 John NEVIL by 1679; b 1669; Boston
CASWELL, William[2] (1660-) & Mercy [LINCOLN] (1670-), dau Thomas; b 4 May 1694;
    Hingham/Taunton
CATE, Edward & Elizabeth [TUCKER]; b 1693; Portsmouth, NH
CATE, James (-1677) & Alice _?_ , m/2 John WESTBROOK; b 1665?; Portsmouth, NH
CAYTE, John & Mary _?_ ; b 1653; Gloucester
CATES, John & _?_ ; in Eng, b 1686; Windham, CT
CATE, John (-1748) & 1/wf Joanna JOHNSON/Elizabeth SHERBURNE; 27 Apr 1692; ?Greenland,
    NH
CATER, Richard & 1/wf _?_ ; by 1650; Portsmouth, NH
CATER, Richard & 2/wf Mary RICORD; m cont 16 Apr 1672; Portsmouth, NH
CATER, Richard[2] & _?_ ; b 1675; Kittery, ME
CATER, Richard[3] & Elizabeth _?_ ; b 1696; ?Portsmouth, NH/Newington
CATHCART, Robert (-1719, Boston) & Phebe [COLEMAN] (1674-), m/2 Samuel ATHEARN; ca
    1691; Martha's Vineyard
CATLIN/CALTIL, John (-1644?) & Isabella [WARD?] (-1672), m/2 James NORTHAM 1644+,
    m/3 Joseph BALDWIN aft 1661; b 1642?; Hartford
CATLIN, John (-1704) (son John) & Mary [BALDWIN]; 23 Sep 1662; Hartford
CATLIN, John (?1643-) (son Thomas) & Mary MARSHALL (-1716); 27 Jul 1665, 1663?; Hartford
CATLIN, Joseph & Lydia [ALLEN]; b 1701? (?doubtful); Kittery, ME/Dover, NH
CATLIN, Thomas (1612-1690) & 1/wf [Mary] _?_ (-bef 1675); b 1644; Hartford
CATLIN, Thomas & Mary [ELMER/ELMORE], w Edward; aft Mar 1676; Hartford
CATON, Daniel & Mary LISCOMB; - Jul 1681; Salem
CAULKINS, David (-1717) & 1/wf Mary [BLISS] (1649-); ca 1673; New London, CT
CALKINS, Hugh (1600-1690) & Ann _?_ ; ca 1625?; Gloucester/New London/etc.
CAULKINS, Hugh (1659-1722) & 1/wf Sarah SLUMAN (1669-1703); - May 1689; Norwich, CT
CAULKINS, John (1634-1703) & Sarah [ROYCE] (-1717, ae 77); b 1659; New London,
    CT/Norwich, CT
CALKINS, John & Abigail BURCHARD; 23 Oct 1690; Norwich, CT/Lebanon, CT
CALKINS, Jonathan (1679-) & Sarah TURNER; 11 Dec 1700; New London
CALKINS, Samuel (-1720) & Hannah GIFFORD; - Nov 1691, 16? Nov; Norwich, CT/Lebanon, CT
CAVE, Thomas & Mary [NICHOLS]; b 1674; Topsfield/Salisbury
CAVERLY, Philip & _?_ ; b 1687, b 1677?; Portsmouth, NH
CAVERLY, William & Mary (ABBOTT) [GUPTILL], w Thomas; by 1696; Portsmouth, NH
SENTER, John (-1667) & 1/wf Mary MUZZY (-1658); 27 Mar 1656; Boston

CENTER, John (-1667) & 2/wf Sarah [WEEDON], m/2 Jeremiah BELCHER 1667?; b 1666, b 1663?; Boston

CENTER, John (1660-1706) & Ruth [HUNT] (-1717, ca 60), m/2 Josiah WRIGHT; b 1687, b 10 Apr 1682; Boston/Chelsea

CENTER/SENTER?, William (1654-) & Mary [MATTHEWS] (1654-), dau Walter; b 1678; Isles of Shoals, NH

CHADBOURNE, Humphrey (?1626, ?1600-1667) & Lucy [TREWORGY] (1632-), m/2 Thomas WILLS, m/3 Elias STILEMAN; b 1653; Kittery, ME

CHADBOURNE, Humphrey (1653±-1695) & Sarah [BOLLES] (1657-); b 1678; Kittery, ME

CHADBOURNE, James (-1685?, 1686?) & Elizabeth [HEARD], m/2 Samuel SMALL by ±1688; b 1681; Kittery, ME

CHADBOURNE, William & _?_ ; in Eng, b 1610; Kittery, ME

CHADBOURNE, William (1610-) & Mary _?_ ; b 1644; Boston

CHADWELL, Benjamin (-1679) & Elizabeth HAWES/HOWE, m/2 John JEWETT by 1686, m/3 Ezekiel JEWETT 1716, m/4 Andrew STICKNEY; 20 Dec 1636; Charlestown/Lynn

CHADWELL, Moses (1637-1684?) & Sarah IVORY; - Feb 1660/1; Lynn/?Bristol, RI

CHADWELL, Richard (-1681) & Katherine PRESBERRY/PRESBURY, w John; 22 Jul 1649; Sandwich/?Dover, NH

CHADWELL, Samuel (1676-) & Mary _?_ ; b 1700; Ipswich

CHADWELL, Thomas (1611-1683) & 1/wf Margaret _?_ (-1658); b 1637; Lynn

CHADWELL, Thomas (1611-1683) & 2/wf Barbara (_?_) (DAVIS) [BRIMBLECOME] (-1665), w George, w John; aft 1658; Lynn/Boston

CHADWELL, Thomas (1611-1683) & 3/wf Abigail (WYETH) [JONES] (-1683), w Thomas; b 1679; Charlestown

CHADWELL, Thomas & Hannah [SMITH]; b 1687; Ipswich

CHADWICK, Charles (1596-1682) (called bro. by Jeremiah NORCROSS 1657) & Elizabeth [?NORCROSS], m/2 Thomas FOX 1683; ca 1625/30?; Watertown

CHADWICK, Charles (1674-) & Sarah WHITNEY (1679-); 11 Apr 1699; Watertown

CHADWICK, James & Hannah BUTLER (living 1693); Feb 1676/7; Malden

CHADWICK, John (-1681) & Joan _?_ (-1674); ca 1646?; Malden

CHADWICK, John (-1711, 1710?) & Sarah _?_ ; ca 1670; Watertown

CHADWICK, John (1651-1707) & Mary BARLOW (-1722+, ?Bradford); 30 Oct 1674; Cambridge

CHADWICK, John & Priscilla _?_ ; b 1693; Boston

CHADWICK, Samuel (-1690) & Mary STOCKER; 22 Jan 1685, 22 Dec 1684; Woburn/Reading

CHADDOCK/CHADWICK, Thomas & Sarah WOOLCUTT (1657-); 6 Apr 1674; Newbury

CHADWICK, Thomas (1677-) & Mary [BOSS?]; ca 1700

CHAFFEE, John & Sarah HILLS, Malden; 17 Jul 1700; Swansea

CHAFFEE, Joseph (-1694); & Agnes/Anne/Annis MARTIN (?1649-); 8 Dec 1670; Rehoboth/Swansea

CHAFEY, Matthew & Sarah _?_ ; b 1641; Boston/Middleboro, Eng

CHAFFEE, Nathaniel & Experience BLESS; 19 Aug 1669; Swansea/Rehoboth

CHAFFEE, Thomas (-1683) & [?Dorothy] _?_ ; b 1638?; Hingham/Rehoboth/Swansea

CHAFFEE, Thomas (1672-) & Margaret CARPENTER; 4 Jun 1695; Rehoboth

CHALKER, Abraham & 1/wf Hannah SANFORD (-1683); 16 Jan 1679, 1679/80; Saybrook, CT

CHALKER, Abraham & 2/wf Sarah INGHAM (1658-1687); 23 Sep 1686; Saybrook, CT

CHALKER, Abraham & 3/wf Deborah BARBER; 19 Nov 1691; Killingworth, CT

CHALKER, Alexander & Catharine POST, m/2 John HILL 1673; 29 Sep 1649; Saybrook, CT

CHALKER, Samuel & Phebe BULL (1670-); ?31 Oct 1676, 7 Nov 1676; Saybrook, CT

CHALKLEY, Robert (-1672) & Elizabeth _?_ (-1678); b 1672, b 1647?, no issue, adopted 3 ch; Charlestown

CHALIS, John (1655-) & Sarah FRAME; 26 Jan 1698/9; Amesbury

CHALLIS/WATSON, Philip (1617-ca 1681) & Mary [SARGENT] (-1716); b 1653; Salisbury

CHALLIS, Thomas & Mary [COLBY]; b 3 Sep 1696; Amesbury

CHALLIE, William (1663-) & Margaret FOWLER; 2 Jan 1698/9; Amesbury

CHAMBERLAIN, Abraham (1665-1728+) & 1/wf Elizabeth _?_ ; 9 Mar 1691/2; Newton

CHAMBERLAIN, Abraham, Muddy River & 2/wf Mary RANDALL (1662-), Watertown; 24 Feb 1697/8; Watertown

CHAMBERLIN, Alexander & Sarah (ADKINS) TINNEY/TENNEY, w John; 20 Apr 1699; Boston

CHAMBERLINE, Benjamin & Sarah BALL (?1655-); 5 Jun 1677; Sudbury
CHAMBERLING, Benjamin (bpt 1662-) (son William of Hull?) (prob son of Henry) & Mary/Mercy WRIGHT (1666-), m/2 John BARTLETT 1692?; 13 Oct 16o5; Hingham/Hull
CHAMBERLAIN, Clement (1669-) & Mary __?__, m/2 Roger TOOTHAKER; b 1692(3?); Billerica
CHAMBERLAIN, Daniel (1671-1725+) & Mary __?__; b 1695; Billerica
CHAMBERLIN, Edmund & 1/wf Mary TURNER (-1669); 4 Jan 1646; Roxbury/Chelmsford
CHAMBERLAIN, Edmund & 2/wf Hannah (?WINTER/WITTER) BURDEN?/BURDETT (-1696?), Malden, w Robert; 22 Jun 1670; Chelmsford/Woodstock, CT/Malden
CHAMBERLIN, Edmund & 1/wf Mercy ABBOTT (-1698), Woburn, w John; 26 Aug 1690, 26 Aug 1691; Billerica/Woburn/Middlesex
CHAMBERLAIN, Edmund & Elizabeth BARTHOLOMEW; 21 Nov 1699; Woodstock, CT
CHAMBERLAIN, Henry (-1694) & Jane/Joan? __?__; in Eng, ca 1616/25; Hingham
CHAMBERLAIN, Henry (returned to Eng) & Grace __?__; Hingham, Eng, ca 1634; Hingham
CHAMBERLAIN, Henry[2] ([1618/26]-1678) (son Henry?) & Sarah [JONES] (-1710, ae 75), dau Thomas (see Wm. CHAMBERLAIN); b 1652; Hull
CHAMBERLAIN, Henry[3] (?1654-1706) & Jane __?__; b 1683, b 1672?; Hull
CHAMBERLAIN, Henry (?1658-) & Ann [?LAFFETRA]/[?WEST]; b 1684?; Sandwich/Shrewsbury, NJ
CHAMBERLAIN, Jacob (1658-1721) & 1/wf Mary CHILD (1660-1718?); 24 Jan 1684, 1683?, 1683/4; Roxbury/Boston/Brookline
CHAMBERLAIN, Jacob (1658-1712, Newton) & Experience __?__ (?1666-1749), ?m/2 Jonathan DYKE; b 1692?; Medford
CHAMBERLINE, Jacob & Susannah __?__; b 1701, b 1699; Rowley/Cambridge
CHAMBERLAIN, Job (son William of Hull) & Joanna [WAY]; b 1685; Boston/Dorchester
CHAMBERLINE, John & 1/wf Anne/Anna BROWNE; 19 May 1653; Boston/Newport
CHAMBERLIN, John (-1667?, 1666?) & 2/wf Catherine [CHATHAM]; ca 1663; Newport
CHAMBERLIN, John (1654-1690, ae 36) (son William of Hull) & Deborah [TEMPLAR] (1667-), m/2 Abraham MILLER 1691; b 1679; Charlestown
CHAMBERLAIN, John (-1712) & 1/wf Deborah JACO/JANCO? (-1704); 6 Dec 1681; Billerica
CHAMBERLAIN, John & Hannah [?HOREY/?BURDETT/?BERDET]; b 1681, b 1686, b 1677, b 1683; Charlestown/Malden
CHAMBERLAIN, Joseph & Hannah GILBERT; 28 Oct 1682; Sudbury/Oxford
CHAMBERLAIN, Joseph (1665-1752, ae 87) (son William of Hull) & Mercy DICKINSON (?1668-1735); 6 Jun 1688, 8 Jun; Deerfield/Colchester, CT
CHAMBERLING, Nathaniel (1659-1716) (son William of Hull) & Abigail ROGERS (6 Nov 1663-); 19 Sep 1681 (9 Sep is wrong); Scituate/?Duxbury/Pembroke
CHAMBERLINE, Peleg (1666-) & Susannah __?__ (1668-1722); Newport
CHAMBERLINE, Richard & 1/wf __?__; b 1642; Braintree/Roxbury
CHAMBERLAIN, Richard & __?__; Great Island
CHAMBERLINE, Richard & 2/wf Sarah [BUGBEE] (1630-); b 1665, ca 1653?, ca 1652?; Roxbury/Braintree/Sherborn/Sudbury
CHAMBERLYN, Richard (-1673) & 3/wf Elizabeth JAQUES; 30 Mar 1672; Sudbury
CHAMBERLIN, Samuel (1645-1722) & Elizabeth [EMERSON?] (?1660-1722); b 1685; Chelmsford
CHAMBERLAIN, Thomas & Mary [NEWTON?]; b 1636; Woburn/Chelmsford
CHAMBERLINE, Thomas & Sarah PROCTOR; 10 Aug 1666; Chelmsford
CHAMBERLAIN, Thomas, Sr. & 2/wf Mary (__?__) (POULTER) PARKER (1604-1692), w __?__, w John; 16 Apr 1674, 17 Apr 1674; Billerica/Chelmsford
CHAMBERLAIN, Thomas & Elizabeth HAMMOND (1664-); 18 Apr 1681, 1682; Cambridge
CHAMBERLAIN, Thomas (1667-1709±, 1710?) & 1/wf Elizabeth HALL/HEALD (-1699); 9 Jan 1690; Chelmsford
CHAMBERLAIN, Thomas & 2/wf Abigail NUTTING; 16 Aug 1699; Concord/Groton
CHAMBERLAIN, William/Henry (-1678) & ?1/wf 2/wf __?__ (not Sarah JONES, see Henry)
CHAMBERLAIN, William (?1604, ?1621-1706, ae 85) & 2/wf? Rebecca [SHELLEY?] (-1692?); b 1655, b 1649?; Concord/Billerica
CHAMBERLING, William (-1709) (son William) & Eunice EWALL; 9 Sep 1678, 9 Nov; Scituate/Hull
CHAMBERLAIN, William (ca 1659-1717) & __?__; ca 1695?; Newport/Shrewsbury, NJ
CHAMBERLIN, William (-1734) & Deliverance FERGUSON; 20 Dec 1698; Watertown/Cambridge

CHAMBERLAIN, _?_ & _?_ (1647); ?Ipswich
CHAMBERLAIN, _?_ & [Christian STOUGHTON] (-1659, ae 81); ?Hingham, Eng, ca 1595/98?;
Hingham
CHAMBERS, Charles (1660-1743) & 1/wf Rebecca PATEFIELD (-1735); 30 Jan 1687/8, 31? Jan;
Charlestown
CHAMBERS, Edward (1640±-1676) & _?_; Kittery, ME
CHAMBERS, Thomas & Richarden CURTIS (-1673), w Thomas; Sandwich, Eng, 25 May 1632;
Scituate
CHAMBERS, Thomas, Jamaica, LI, & _?_ [CUTLER], dau James; 1695; Charlestown
CHAMBLETT, Morris/Maurice & Margaret (BROWN) GOULD, w Alexander; ME/Marblehead
CHAMPNEYS/CHAMBLET?, Maurice/Morris? & Elizabeth TAYNOUR; 20 Oct 1692; Marblehead
CHAMBLET, Samuel & Margaret (BROWN) [GOULD], w Alexander
CHAMPANELL, Daniel & Elizabeth _?_; b 1696; Boston
CHAMPERNOWNE, Francis (1614-1681) & Mary (HOLE/HOEL) CUTT, w Robert; by 1682, aft
Jul 1674, no issue; ME
CHAMPION, Henry[1] (-1708) & 1/wf [Sarah?] _?_; Aug 1647; Saybrook, CT/Lyme, CT
CHAMPION, Henry (1654-1704) & Susanna DeWOLF, m/2 John HAUTLEY ca 1708; 1 Apr 1684;
Lyme, CT
CHAMPION, Henry (-1709, 1708?, ae 98) & 2/wf Deborah JONES, m/2 Henry CRANE; m cont 21
Mar 1697/8; Saybrook, CT/Lyme, CT
CHAMPION, Robert (-1657) & Elizabeth _?_; Piscataqua, NH
CHAMPION, Thomas (1656-1705) & Hannah BROCKWAY (1664-1750), m/2 John WADE; 23 Aug
1682; Lyme, CT
CHAMPION, John[2] (?1647-1727) & Sarah [WILLIAMS] (-1718); b 14 Feb 1692/3, ca 1672?;
Jericho, LI
CHAMPION, Thomas[1] & Frances _?_; b 1642; Hempstead, LI
CHAMPION, Thomas[2] & _?_ [JECOCKS]
CHAMPLIN, Christopher (1656±-1732) & 1/wf _?_; ca 1682; Westerly, RI
CHAMPLIN, Christopher (1656±-1732) & 2/wf ?Elizabeth DANELL, wid
CHAMPLIN, Jeffrey[1] (-1695(-)) & _?_; ca 1640/50, b 1652; Newport, RI/Westerly, RI
CHAMPLIN, Jeffrey (1652±-1715±) & _?_; ca 1671; Westerly, RI/Kings Town, RI
CHAMPLIN, Jeffrey (-1718) & 1/wf Susanna [ELDRED]; ca 1700, ca 1701, b 1702; Kings Town,
RI
CHAMPLIN, William (1654-1715) & Mary [BADCOCK/BABCOCK] (?1648-1747); ca 1674;
Westerly, RI
CHAMPLIN, William (-1747) & Mary CLARK (1680-1760+); 18 Jan 1700, 1699/1700; Westerly, RI
CHAMPNEY, Christopher & Margaret _?_; b 1645; Cambridge
CHAMPNEY, Daniel (1645-1691) & 1/wf Dorcas BRIDGE (1649-1684); 3 Jan 1665, prob 1665/6;
Cambridge
CHAMPNEY, Daniel (1645-1691) & 2/wf Hepzibah (CORLET) MINOTT, w James; 9 Jun 1684, 4
Jun; Cambridge/Billerica
CHAMPNEY, Daniel (1669-1754) & Bethiah [PHIPPS?] (-1754); ?2 Apr 1695; Charlestown/Cam-
bridge
CHAMPNEY, John (-bef 1642) & Joanna/Joan _?_, m/2 Golden MOORE; ca 1634/8; Cambridge
CHAMPNEY, Joseph (-1656) & Sarah _?_; Cambridge/Billerica
CHAMPNEY, Joseph (1669-1729) & Sarah _?_ (1672-1730); b 1697; Cambridge
CHAMPNEY, Richard (-1669) & Jane _?_; in Eng, b 1629; Cambridge
CHAMPNEY, Samuel & 1/wf Sarah HUBBARD; 13 Oct 1657; Billerica/Cambridge
CHAMPNEY, Samuel & 2/wf Ruth (MITCHELSON) [GREEN] (-1728, ae 88), w John; aft 3 Mar
1691, b 1695; Charlestown/Cambridge
CHAMPNEY, Samuel (1667-) & Hannah SMEDLEY (1671-1748); m int 1 Oct 1695; Boston/Cam-
bridge
CHAMPNOIS, Henry (-1679?) & _?_; ca 1639/50?; East Boothbay
CHAMPNOIS/CHAMPNEY, Henry & Elizabeth WORTHYLAKE; 8 Dec 1693; Boston
CHAMPNOIS, James & _?_; ca 1682/4?; Boston?
CHANDLER, Benjamin (-1691) & Elizabeth [BUCK] (1653-1732?); b 1672; Scituate/Duxbury
CHANDLER, Edmund[1] (-1662) & 1/wf _?_; b 1619?, b 1626?, b 1635; Duxbury
CHANDLER, Edmund (-1662) & 2/wf _?_; ?; Duxbury

CHANDLER, Edmund[3] (-1720) & Elizabeth [ALDEN], m/2 Peletiah WEST 1722; b 1698; Duxbury
CHANDLER, Henry (1669-1737) & Lydia ABBOTT (1675-1748); 28 Nov 1695; Andover/Enfield, CT
CHANDLER, John (-1647+) & _?_ ; b 1640, b 1630?, b 1624?; Concord/Boston
CHANDLER, John (-1703, ae 68) & Elizabeth DOUGLAS (1641-1705); 16 Feb 1658; Roxbury
CHANDLER, John (1665-1740) & Hannah ABBOTT (1650-1741); 20 Dec 1676; Andover
CHANDLER, John (1665-1740) & 1/wf Mary RAYMOND (1672-1711); 10 Nov 1692; Woodstock, CT
CHANDLER, Joseph (-1666) & Hannah _?_ ; b 1662; Boston
CHANDLER, Joseph (?1638-1731) & Mercy _?_ (-1727?); b 1670; Duxbury
CHANDLER, Joseph & Sarah ABBOTT; 26 Nov 1691; Andover
CHANDLER, Joseph & Mary HALE; 10 Feb 1699/1700; Newbury
CHANDLER, Philemon (1671-1752) & 1/wf Hannah CHEANY/CLARY? (?1672-1735); 18 Apr 1700; Cambridge/Pomfret, CT
CHANDLER, Roger (had dau Sarah before 1622, had dau Martha m John BUNDY) & Isabella CHILTON (1587-); Leydon, 21 Jul 1615; ?Duxbury
CHANDLER, Roger (1637-1717) & Mary SIMONDS (1647-); 25 Apr 1671; Concord
CHANDLER, Samuel[2] (-1683) & _?_ ; b 1655, no issue known; Duxbury
CHANDLER, Samuel & Sarah (BURRILL) DAVIS (-1665), w Richard; 21 Dec 1664; Dorchester
CHANDLER, Samuel & Esther _?_ ; b 1669, b 1675, b 1678; Dorchester
CHANDLER, Samuel & Abigail PALMER; 10 Apr 1684; Dorchester
CHANDLER, Samuel (-1748), Amesbury? & Mercy PERKINS (1671-); 12 Jul 1694; Hampton, NH/?Newbury/Bridgewater
CHANDLER, Samuel (1674-1759) & Dorcas BUSS; 11 Dec 1695; Concord
CHANDLER, Thomas (1626-1703, ae 73) & Ann/Hannah/Joanna [BREWER]? (1630-1717); 1650, b 1652; Andover/Reading
CHANDLER, Thomas (-1737, ae 72) & Mary PETERS; 22 May 1686; Andover
CHANDLER, William & Alice THOROGOOD; Bishop-Stodford, Eng, 29 Jan 1621/2
CHANDLER, William (-1641, 1642) & 2/wf? Ann?/Annis?/Anmer?/Hannah [ALCOCK?] (1603-1683?, 1642?), m/2 John DANE 1643, m/3 John PARMENTER; 6 Nov 1625; Roxbury
CHANDLER, William & 1/wf Mary [FOWLER]; b 1648; Newbury
CHANDLER, William & 1/wf Mary DANE (1638-1679), Ipswich; 24 Aug 1658; Andover
CHANDLER, William[1] & 2/wf Mary LORD (-1676); 26 Feb 1666, 1666/7; Newbury
CHANDLER, William (-1701, ae 84) & 3/wf Mary CARTER; 16 Apr 1677; Newbury
CHANDLER, William, Andover & 2/wf Bridget (HENCHMAN) RICHARDSON, w James; m cont 6 Sep 1679, 8 Oct 1679, - Oct 1679; Andover/Chelmsford
CHANDLER, William (1661-1727) & Sarah BUCKMASTER/BUCKMAN (1661-1735); 28 Dec 1682; Andover
CHANDLER, William & Eleanor PHELPS; 21 Apr 1687; Andover
CHANDLER, William & Hannah HUNTINGTON; 29 Nov 1692; Newbury
CHANDLER, _?_ & [Hester BRIGHTMAN]; b 1701?, b 1716; Newport, RI
CHANTERELL, John & Mary [MELLOWS] (?1651-); b 1671; Boston
CHANTRILL, Joseph (?1672, 1673-) & Amie GARDNER; 13 Dec 1697; Boston (John CHANTRELL deposed 14 Jan 1689, 1690? (18 yrs))
CHAPIN, Caleb & Sarah _?_ ; b 1682; Boston
CHAPIN, David (?1624/5-1672) & Lydia CRUMP; 29 Aug 1654; Springfield/Boston
CHAPIN, Ebenezer & Elizabeth [ADAMS] (1667-); b 1690; Boston
CHAPIN, Henry (1631-1718) & Bethia COOLEY (1644-1711); 15 Dec 1664; Springfield
CHAPIN, Japhet (1642-1712) & 1/wf Abilena COLEY (1643-1710); 22 Jul 1664; Milford, CT/Springfield
CHAPIN, Josiah (?1634-1726) & 1/wf Mary KING (1639-1676); 30 Nov 1658; Weymouth/Braintree/Mendon?/Milford, CT
CHAPIN, Josiah (-1726) & 2/wf Lydia (?BROWN) PRATT, w Thomas; 26 Sep 1676, 20? Sep; Braintree/Mendon
CHAPIN, Samuel (1598-1674) & Cicely PENNY (1602-1683); Paignton, Eng, 9 Feb 1623; Roxbury/Springfield
CHAPIN, Samuel (-1692) & Mary HOBART (1663-), m/2 Mordecai LINCOLN; 9 May 1688; Milton/Braintree

CHAPIN, Samuel (1665-1729) & Hannah SHELDON (1670-), Northampton; 24 Dec 1690; Springfield

CHAPIN, Seth (1668-1746) & 1/wf Mary READ; 20 May 1689; Mendon

CHAPIN, Seth (1668-1746) & 2/wf Bethiah THURSTON (1671-1744)

CHAPIN, Shem & Deborah _?_; b 1665; Boston

CHAPIN, Thomas (1671-1755) & Sarah WRIGHT (1673-); 15 Feb 1694, 1693/4; ?Lebanon, CT

CHAPLIMAN/CHAPLEMAN, Michael (-1722) & Rebecca NEEDHAM (1656-); - Jan 1675; Salem

CHAPLIN, Clement (1587-1656) & Sarah [HINDS]; in Eng, returned to Eng; Cambridge

CHAPLIN, Hugh (-1653) & Elizabeth _?_ (-1694), m/2 Nicholas JACKSON 1656; in Eng, b 1643; Rowley

CHAPLIN, John & Mary [HUTCHINSON]; b 1679; Salem/Woodbridge, NJ

CHAPLINE, Joseph (1647-1705) & Elizabeth WEST (-1702); 21 Feb 1671, 1671/2; Rowley

CHAPLIN, Joseph (1673-1754) & 2/wf? Mehitable _?_; b 1696; Rowley/Attleboro

CHAPLIN/CHAPLEY, William (-1697) & _?_ (-1705+); b 1661?; Dorchester/Swansea

CHAPLIN, William (1642-) & _?_; b 1679; Isles of Shoals

CHAPMAN, Edward (?1612-1678) & 1/wf Mary SYMONDS (?1614-1658); ca 1639; Ipswich

CHAPMAN, Edward/Edmund? (-1664?) & Joan [BARTOLL]; b 1651; Marblehead

CHAPMAN, Edward (?1612-1678) & 2/wf Dorothy (SWAN) ABBOTT (-1710), w Thomas, m/3 Archelaus WOODMAN 1678; aft 10 Jun 1658, aft 1659?; Ipswich

CHAPMAN, Edward (-1675/6) & Elizabeth [FOX?], m/2 Samuel CROSS 1687; b 1663, by 1660?; Windsor, CT/Simsbury, CT

CHAPMAN, Edward (1669-) & Mary _?_; ca 1698?; Ipswich

CHAPMAN, Henry (1663-1713) & Hannah GRANT (1668-1718?); 11 May 1692; Windsor, CT

CHAPMAN alias FEVERSHAM, Hope (1654-1698) & Martha QUINBY; 13 May 1683; Westerly, RI/Stratford, CT

CHAPMAN, Isaac (1647-1737) & Rebecca LEONARD; 2 Sep 1678; Barnstable

CHAPMAN, Jeremiah (?1670-1755, ae 88?) & Hannah [POST]; b 1696; New London, CT

CHAPMAN, John & Martha (_?_) LAWRENCE, w Thomas, m Francis BROWN 1657; aft 1648, ca 1650; New Haven/Fairfield, CT/Stamford, CT

CHAPMAN, John (-1711) & 1/wf Elizabeth HALLY/HAWLEY (-1676), Stratford; 7 Jun 1670; Saybrook, CT/E. Haddam, CT

CHAPMAN, John (-1677) & Rebecca SMITH, m/2 Francis YOUNG 1678; 30 Sep 1675; Ipswich

CHAPMAN, John (-1711) & 2/wf Elizabeth BEAMAN (1649-1694); 26 Mar 1677; Saybrook, CT/Haddam, CT

CHAPMAN, John (1653-) & Sarah _?_; ca 1677?; Deerfield/Colchester, CT

CHAPMAN, John (-1744) & 1/wf Hannah (BECKET) STEARNS (-1700), w ?Isaac; 7 Dec 1694, 7 Jan 1694/5; Salem/Beverly

CHAPMAN, John & 3/wf Lydia (GILBERT) RICHARDSON, w Stephen; aft 10 Aug 1696, bef 23 May 1700; ?Stonington, CT

CHAPMAN, Joseph (1673-1732) & Sarah [SPENCER] (ca 1679-); b 1701(2?), ca 1700; Saybrook, CT

CHAPMAN, Nathaniel & Mary WILBORN (?1649, 1657-); 30 Dec 1674; Ipswich/Kittery, ME

CHAPMAN, Nathaniel (1653-) & 1/wf Mary COLLINS, Guilford; 29 Jun 1681; Saybrook, CT/?Guilford, CT

CHAPMAN, Nathaniel & Ruth DAVIS; - Jun [1697?], 1696, 1 Jan 1696/7; Ipswich

CHAPMAN, Nathaniel (1653-1726) & 2/wf Hannah BATES (-1750, ae 83); 26 Jul 1698; Saybrook, CT

CHAPMAN, Ralph (1615?, 1618-1671) & Lydia WILLS/WELLS? (probably WILLS); 23 Nov 1642; ?Marshfield

CHAPMAN, Ralph (-1711(-)) & 1/wf Mary _?_ (-1688); b 1680; Newport/Marshfield/Salem

CHAPMAN, Ralph & 2/wf Abigail _?_ (-1694); b 1691; Newport

CHAPMAN, Ralph & 3/wf Mary (CLARK) GOULD (1661-1711), w Daniel _?_; aft 1694; Newport

CHAPMAN, Richard (-1669) & Mary _?_ (2/wf? ?Joan); b 1647; Braintree/Stratford, CT

CHAPMAN, Robert (1617-1687) & Ann BLISS/BLITH (-1685); 29 Apr 1642; Saybrook, CT/Hartford

CHAPMAN, Robert & Elizabeth [STEVENSON]; b 1664; ?Portsmouth, NH/Dover, NH

CHAPMAN, Robert & 1/wf Sarah GRISWOLD (1653-1692), Norwich; 27 Jun 1671; Saybrook, CT/Windsor, CT

CHAPMAN, Robert (-1711) & 2/wf Mary (?DURANT) SHEATHER/SHETHER, Killingworth, w Samuel; 29 Oct 1694; Saybrook, CT

CHAPMAN, Robert (1675-1760) & Mary [STEVENS] (1674-1767); b 1698, [1696?]; East Haddam, CT/Haddam, CT

CHAPMAN, Samuel & 1/wf Ruth INGALLS (-1700); 20 May 1678; Ipswich/Hampton, NH

CHAPMAN, Samuel (1655?, 1665?-) & Bethiah _?_; b 1689; Deerfield/New London, CT

CHAPMAN, Samuel (not Robert) & Margaret GRISWOLD; 6 Dec 1693; Saybrook, CT/Windsor, CT

CHAPMAN, Simon & Mary BREWER (1648-); 21 Mar 1666; Rowley

CHAPMAN, Simon (1669-1749) & Sarah _?_ (1675-1735); b 1696; Windsor, CT

CHAPMAN, Thomas (-1687) & Sarah MIRICK (1657-1694+); 8 Sep 1675; Charlestown

CHAPMAN, Willliam & _?_; in Eng, b 1623; Hingham

CHAPMAN, William (-1699/1700) & Sarah _?_; b 1653; Deerfield/New London, CT

CHAPMAN, William/Thomas? & Elizabeth (PALMER) SLOAN, w Thomas; 26 Oct 1677; Stonington, CT

CHAPMAN, William & Elizabeth SMITH; 30 Mar 1682; Ipswich

CHAPMAN, William & Hannah LESTER; 27 Mar 1690, b 1690, b 1691; Deerfield/Groton, CT/New London, CT

CHAPMAN, _?_ & Elizabeth [BILL]; aft 1694, bef 1707; Groton, CT

CHAPPELL, Caleb (1671-1733) & Ruth ROICE/ROYCE (1669-); 4 Jun 1694; Norwalk, CT/Lebanon, CT

CHAPPELL, Francis & 1/wf Martha (SMITH) RUSHMORE, w Thomas; b 22 Feb 1688/[9], Hempstead, LI

CHAPPELL, George (1615-1709) & 1/wf Christian _?_; b 1644, b 1642?; Wethersfield, CT/New London

CHAPPELL, George (1615-1709) & 2/wf Margaret _?_; b 1653/4; New London, CT

CHAPPELL, George (1654-1712) & 1/wf Alice [WAY]; ?3 Oct 1676; New London, CT

CHAPPEL, John & Elizabeth (CARPENTER) [JONES], w Richard? (see Ebenezer HILL); b 1674; Haddam, CT/?Lyme, CT/Flushing, LI

CHAPELL, John (1672-) & Sarah LEWIS; 26 Aug 1698; New London, CT

CHAPPELL, Nathaniel (1668-) & HOPESTILL _?_ (?1663-1753), m/2 Thomas BOLLES; b 1694; New London

CHAPPELL, William (-1690) & Christian [?BELL], m/2 Edward STALLION 1693; b 1669; New London, CT

CHARD, ?Allen & Hannah GRAY? (1659-); 28 Dec 1671; Salem

CHARD, Caleb & Eleanor WATERS; 23 Apr 1700; Bridgewater

CHARD, Samuel (1665-) & Mary [LOVELL] (1674-); b 1698; Weymouth

CHARD, William & 1/wf Grace [SMITH] (-1655/6), w Thomas of Charlestown; Weymouth

CHARD, William & 2/wf Elizabeth PRATT (-1726); 22 Nov 1656; Weymouth

CHARDER, Helling & ?Rebecca _?_ (1651-1736); 20 Jul 168[0?], b 1675?; Marblehead/Salem (ch under CARDER, 5 ch bpt 1683 Salem)

CHARDON, Peter & Mary _?_; b 1697; Boston

CHARLES, John (-1673) & [?Sarah] [MOSS?]; ca 1633?; Charlestown/New Haven, CT/Branford, CT/Saybrook, CT

CHARLES, John (1649-1690) & 1/wf _?_; b 1677; Branford, CT

CHARLES, John (1649-1690) & 2/wf Abigail WELLS; 3 Nov 1684; Stratford, CT

CHARLES, John (1649-1690) & 3/wf Hannah _?_; b 1690; New Haven

CHARLES/CHEARLS, John & Alina _?_; Fordham, NY, ca 1692

CHARLES, Jonathan & Rebecca _?_; b 1686; Boston

CHARLES, William (1595-1673) & Sarah _?_; Salem/?Marblehead

CHARLET, Nicholas & Katherine/Catherine _?_ (-1670), m/2 Richard HAUGHTON; b 1645; Boston

CHANNECK/CHARNOCK, John (1673-) & Mary KING; m int 16 May 1700; Lynn/Boston

CHASE, Abraham (-1738) & Elizabeth _?_; b 1693; Dartmouth/Tiverton, RI

CHASE, Aquila (1618-1670) & Ann [WHEELER] (1621-1689), m/2 Daniel MUSSILOWAY/(SILLOWAY) 1672; ca 1644?, ca 1639; Hampton, NH/Newbury

CHASE, Aquila (1652-) & Esther [BOND] (1655-); ca 1673; Newbury

CHASE, Benjamin (1639-1731) & Phillip/Phillopa [SHERMAN] (1652-); ca 1672?; Portsmouth, RI/Freetown

CHASE, Benjamin & Amy BORDEN (1678-); 21 Sep 1696; Portsmouth, RI/Tiverton, RI

CHASE, Daniel (1661-1707) & Martha KIMBLE/KIMBALL (1664-), m/2 Josiah HEATH?; 25 Aug 1683; Newbury

CHASE, Isaac (?1650-1727) & 1/wf Mary PERKINS (1658-); 20 Feb 1673; Salisbury

CHASE, Isaac (-1727) & 2/wf Mary TILTON (ca 1658-1746); Martha's Vineyard, 5 Oct 1675; Salisbury

CHASE, Jacob (?1647-1734) & Mary [HALL]; ca 1674?; Yarmouth/Swansea

CHASE, James & Elizabeth GREEN (1656-), m/2 Joseph CASS; 2 Nov 1675; Salisbury

CHASE, John (?1649-) & Elizabeth [BAKER]; b 1668; ?Yarmouth

CHASE, John (1655-) & 1/wf Elizabeth BINGLEY; 23 May 1677; Newbury

CHASE, John (1655-) & 2/wf Lydia CHALICE/CHALLIS (1665-); 21 Dec 1687; Salisbury

CHASE, John & Abigail [CHASE] (1681-); b 1698; Hampton, NH

CHASE, John & Sarah HILLS; 17 Jul 1700; Swansea

CHASE, John & Mercy [HALL]; b 1701?; ?Harwich

CHASE, Joseph (-1718) & Rachel PARTRIDGE (-1718); 31 Jan 1671/2; Hampton, NH

CHASE, Joseph (-1724/5) & Sarah SHERMAN (?1677,1667-1748); 28 Feb 1693/4; Portsmouth, RI/Swansea

CHASE, Joseph & Abigail THURSTON; 8 Nov 1699; Newbury

CHASE, Moses (1663-) & 1/wf Anne FOLLANSBEE (1668-1708); 10 Nov 1684; Newbury

CHASE, Samuel & Sarah [SHERMAN] (1682-); ca 1699; Portsmouth, RI/Swansea

CHASE, Thomas (-1652) & Elizabeth [PHILBRICK], m/2 John GARLAND 1654, m/3 Henry ROBY 1674; b 1643; Hampton, NH

CHASE, Thomas (1654-) & 1/wf Rebecca FOLLANSBEE (-1711); 22 Nov 1677; Newbury

CHASE, Thomas (1680-) & Sarah [STEVENS] (?1680-); b 1700, ca 1699; Newbury

CHASE, William[1] (1595±-1659) & Mary __?__ (-1659); in Eng, b 1625?, b 1622?; Roxbury/Scituate/Yarmouth

CHASE, William[2] (?1625±, 1622±-1685) & 1/wf __?__ ; ca 1645?; Yarmouth/Swansea

CHASE, William[2] (?1625±, 1622?-1685) & 2/wf __?__ ; ca 1670; Swansea

CHASE, William (?1646±-1737) & 1/wf Hannah [SHERMAN] (1647-); ca 1673; Portsmouth, RI/Dartmouth/Freetown/Swansea

CHEATER/CHATER, John (?1618-1671?) & Alice EMERY; b 1644; Newbury/Wells, ME

CHATFIELD, George (-1671) & 1/wf Sarah [BISHOP] (-Sep 1657); b 1657; Guilford, CT

CHATFIELD, George (-1671) & 2/wf Isabel NETTLETON (ca 1643-); 29 Mar 1659; Guilford, CT/Killingworth, CT

CHATFIELD, George (1668-1720) & Esther HULL (1672-1716); 10 Feb 1692, [1691/2]; Killingworth, CT

CHATFIELD, John (1661-1748) & Anna HARGER; 5 Feb 1684, [1684/5]; Derby, CT

CHATFIELD, John (?1655-), Easthampton? & Mary __?__ ; Southampton, LI

CHATFIELD, Thomas (1621±-1687) & Anna/?Ann [HIGGINSON] (1626-); b 1649; Guilford, CT/New Haven/Easthampton, LI

CHATFIELD, Thomas (?1652-1713) & __?__ ; b 1686; Easthampton, LI

CHATFIELD, __?__ & Mary [FOSTER] (?1669-); b 1705, b 1701?; Southampton, LI

CHATTERTON, John (1668-) & 1/wf Mary CLEMENT; last of Apr 1690; New Haven

CHATTERTON, John (1668-) & 2/wf Mary [PECK], m/2 John BRONSON 1709; b 1696; New Haven

CHATTERTON, Samuel (1671-1733) & Elizabeth [WARNER]; b 1696; New Haven

CHATTERTON, William (-1700) & Mary/Sarah? [CLARK]; b 1661, ca 1660; New Haven

CHATTERTON, __?__ & Jane __?__ ; b 1642; Piscataqua

CHATWELL, Nicholas (-1700, ae 54) & Sarah (YOUNG) MARCH (-1718) (ae 72 in 1710), w John; 15 Feb 1671/2; Salem

CHAUNCEY, Charles (1592-1672) & Catharine EYRE (1602-1668); in Eng, 17 Mar 1630; Cambridge/Plymouth

CHANUCEY, Charles (1668-1714) & 1/wf Sarah BURR (1675-1697); 29 Jun 1692; Stratford

CHAUNCEY, Charles (1668-1714) & 2/wf Sarah WOLCOTT (-1704); 16 Mar 1698; Stratford, CT/Windsor, CT

CHANCY, Charles (-1711) & Sarah WALLY/WALLEY?; 19 Oct 1699; Boston

CHAUNCEY, Elnathan (?1639/41-1683, 1684? Barbados) & Thomasine __?__ (-1686); b 1681, no issue; Boston
CHAUNCEY, Isaac (1670-1745) & 1/wf Sarah BLACKLEDGE/BLACKLEATH?; b 1698; Stratford, CT
CHAUNCEY, Israel (1644-) & 1/wf Mary NICHOLS (1648-); 8 Jan 1667, [1667/8], 1666/7; Stratford, CT
CHAUNCEY, Israel (1644-) & 2/wf Sarah HODSON/HUDSON?/HODSHON (1657-); 11 Nov 1684; New Haven
CHAUNCEY, Nathaniel (?1639-1685) & Abigail STRONG (?1645-1704), m/2 Medad POMEROY 1686; 12 Nov 1673, at Northampton; ?Northampton/?Hadley
CHECKLEY, Anthony (1636-1708, ae 72) & 1/wf Hannah [WHEELWRIGHT]; b 1664, by 1664; Boston
CHECKLEY, Anthony (-1708) & 2/wf Lydia (SCOTTOW) [GIBBS], w Benjamin, m/3 William COLEMAN; 1678?, no issue; Boston
CHECKLEY, John & 1/wf __?__; b 1636; Boston
CHEECKLEY, John (-1685, ae 75) & 2/wf Ann EIRES/EYRES? (-1714); 5 Mar 1651/2; Boston
CHECKLEY, John (1653-) & __?__; b 1680; Boston
CHICHLEY/CHECKLEY?, Richard & __?__; b 1642; Boston
CHECKLEY, Samuel (1653-1739) & Mary [SCOTTOW] (1656-1721); 1680, b 1683; Boston/Roxbury
CHECKLEY, Samuel (1661-1712) & Elizabeth __?__ (-1719); b 1687; Boston
CHEESEHOLME, Thomas (1604-1671) & Isabel __?__; - - 16--, ca 1636?; Cambridge
CHEEVER, Bartholomew (1617, ?1607-1693) (called cousin by John PARMENTER 1671), St. Alphage, Canterbury, & Lydia [BARRETT] (-1701); ca 1642/50?, no issue; Boston
CHEAVERS, Daniel (1621-1704) & Esther __?__; b 1645(6?); Cambridge/Sudbury
CHEEVER, Ezekiel (?1614-1708) & 1/wf [Mary] __?__ (-1649(50?)); b 1638, 1638?; Charlestown/New Haven/Ipswich/Boston
CHEEVER, Ezekiel (?1614-1708) & 2/wf Ellen LOTHROP (-1706); 18 Nov 1652; Charlestown/Ipswich
CHEEVERS, Ezekiel (1655-1731) & Abigail LEFFINGWELL (-1724+); 17 Jun 1680; Salem/Danvers
CHEEVERS, Israel (1662-) & Bridget WOODHEAD (1669-); 10 Jun 1690; Cambridge
CHEEVERS, Peter (ca 1642-1699) & 1/wf Lydia HALY; 19 Apr 1669; Salem
CHEVERS, Peter (-1699) & 2/wf Mary MACKMILLAN (-1707+); 29 Jun 1685?, 1695; Salem
CHEEVERS, Peter & Lydia ELKINS, m/2 John STEVENS; 10 Dec 1700; Salem
CHEEVER, Richard (1660-1709) & Abigail __?__ (1660-1733); 7 Oct 1680; Boston
CHEEVER, Richard & Mary __?__; b 1692; Boston
CHEEVER, Richard & Abigail __?__ (see Abigail above); b 1696, m 1686; Boston
CHEEVER, Samuel (1639-1724) (ae 37 in 1676) & Ruth ANGIER (-1742, ae 95), Cambridge; 28 Jun 1671; Salem/Marblehead
CHEEVER, Thomas (1658-1749) & 1/wf Sarah [BILL] (1658-1705); b 1681; Boston/Lexington
CHEAVERS, William & Sarah __?__; b 1662; Sudbury
CHELSTON, Robert & Anne __?__; b 1674; Boston
CHENEY, Benjamin & Martha RYALL/RYAL (1679-); 2 Feb 1698/9, 22 Feb; Dorchester
CHENEY, Benjamin & Mercy PAGE; b 1698; Charlestown
CHENEY, Benjamin (1675-) & 1/wf Mary CHENEY (1683-1705); b 1701; Cambridge
CHENEY, Daniel (?1634-1694) & Sarah BAILEY (1644-1714); 8 Oct 1665; Newbury
CHENEY, Daniel (1670-1755) & Hannah DUSTIN (1678-1754+); b 1699, ca 1698; Newbury
CHENEY, John (?1600-1666) & Martha __?__/?SMITHE (-3 Mar 1631?); in Eng, b 1627, ca 1625; Roxbury/Newbury
CHENEY, John (?1631-1671/2) & Mary PLUMER (1634-1682), m/2 David BENNETT 1672; 20 Apr 1660; Newbury
CHENEY, John, Sr. (-1675 Watertown?) & 2/wf Girzell KIDBEE; 12 Nov 1661; Braintree
CHENEY, John & Mary CHUTE (1674-); 7 May 1693/4; Newbury
CHENEY, Joseph[2] & 1/wf Hannah THURSTON (-1690); 12 Mar 1667/8, 1667/8; Medfield
CHENEY, Joseph & Mehitable (PLYMPTON) HINSDALE, w Ephraim, m/3 Jonathan ADAMS; 21 Jul 1691; Medfield
CHENEY, Joseph (1670-) & Rebecca [ROBBINS] (1672-); b 1694; Cambridge

CHENEY, Peter (?1638-1695/7) & Hannah NOYES (1645-1705), m/2 John ATKINSON 1700; 14 May 1663; Newbury

CHENEY, Peter & Mary HOLMES (1655-1746), wid; 7 Oct 1691; Watertown/Newbury

CHENEY, Thomas (-1693?) & Jane ADKINSON/ATKINSON (-1724); 11 Jan 1655; Roxbury

CHENEY, Thomas & Hannah WOODDIS/WOODEY? (1657-1720); 24 Sep 1684; Roxbury

CHENEY, William[1] (?1604-1667) & Margaret _?_, m/2 _?_ BURGE/BURGESS b 1679/80; in Eng, ca 1626; Roxbury

CHENEY, William (-1704) & 1/wf _?_ ; ca 1655/60?; Middletown, CT

CHENEY, William (-1681) & Deborah WISWALL; b 1661; Medfield/Dorchester

CHENEY, William (-1704) & 2/wf Hope (LAMBERTON) (AMBROSE) [HERBERT], w Samuel, ?w Wm.?; aft 1685, b 1698; Middletown, CT

CHENEY, William (1666-1696) & Rebecca NEWELL, m/2 Josiah SABIN; 24 May 1686; Roxbury

CHENEY, William & Margaret _?_ (-1740); b 1695; Mendon

CHERRY, John & Sarah [WICKHAM], dau Thomas, m/2 Jonathan HUDSON 1686; 26 Jun 1669, b 1679; Wethersfield, CT

CHESEBROUGH, Elihu (1668-1750) & Hannah MINER (1677-1751); 4 Jul 1698; Stonington, CT

CHESEBROUGH, Elisha (1637-1670) & Rebecca PALMER (-1713), m/2 John BALDWIN 1672; 20 Apr 1665; Stonington, CT

CHESEBROUGH, Elisha (1667-) & 1/wf Mary MINER (1671-1704); 27 Jan 1692, 1691/2, 27 Jan 1691; Stonington, CT

CHESEBROUGH, Nathaniel (1630-1678) & Hannah DENISON (1643-), m/2 Joseph SAXTON 1680; b 1660; Stonington,CT

CHESEBROUGH, Nathaniel (1666-1732) & Sarah STANTON (1674-); 13 Jan 1692, 13 Jan 1691/2; Stonington, CT

CHESEBROUGH, Samuel (1627-1673) & Abigail [?INGRAHAM], m/2 Joshua HOLMES 1675, m/3 James AVERY 1698; 30 Nov 1655; Stonington, CT

CHESEBROUGH, Samuel (1660-) & Mary INGRAHAM (1666-); 8 Dec 1687; Swansea

CHESEBROUGH/CHEESEBROOK, Samuel (1674-1736) & Priscilla ALDEN (?1679-1736+), Duxbury; 4 Jan 1699, 1699/1700; Duxbury

CHEESEBROUGH, William (-1667) & Anna/?Anne STEVENSON (-1673); Boston, Eng, 15 Dec 1620; Stonington, CT

CHEESBROUGH, William (1662-) & 2/wf? Mary McDOWELL (?1677-); 13 Dec 1698; Stonington, CT

CHESLEY, George (1671-1710) & Deliverance [RICE?], m/2 Moses DAVIS; b 1701?, by 1699?; Durham, NH

CHESLEY, Philip (1606/8-1685+) & 1/wf Elizabeth _?_ (-1661); b 1642?, b 1646; Dover, NH

CHESLEY, Philip & 2/wf Joanna _?_ (-1685+); by 1673, b Jun 1671; Dover, NH

CHESLEY, Philip[2] (?1646-) & Sarah [ROLLINS?]; by 1680; Dover, NH

CHESLEY, Samuel & Elizabeth [SMITH], m/2 Amos PINKHAM; b 1701?; Dover, NH

CHESLEY, Thomas (-1697) & Elizabeth THOMAS; 22 Aug 1663; Dover, NH

CHESLEY, Thomas (1664-1700) & Ann [HUNTRESS], m/2 Joseph DANIELS ca 1700; b 1688; Dover, NH

CHESTER, John (-1628, in Eng) & Dorothy [HOOKER] (came to N.E.); b 1610; Wethersfield, CT

CHESTER, John (1635-1698) & Sarah WELLES?/WELLS (?1631, ?1633-1698); Feb 1653/4; Charlestown

CHESTER, John & Elizabeth PITMAN; 30 Jun 1663; Charlestown

CHESTER, John (1656-1711) & Hannah TALCOTT (?1665-1741); 25 Nov 1686; Wethersfield, CT

CHESTER, Leonard (1610-1648, ae 38/39) & Mary SHARPE?/WADE? (-1688), m/2 Richard RUSSELL 1655?, 1656; b 1633; Charlestown/Wethersfield, CT

CHESTER, Samuel (-1710) & 1/wf Mary [?CONDY]; b 1663?; New London, CT

CHESTER, Samuel (-1710), Groton, CT, & 2/wf Hannah _?_ ; b 1695; New London, CT/Groton, CT

CHESTER, Stephen (1659, 1660-1697) & Jemima TREAT (1668-1755); 17 Dec 1691; Wethersfield, CT

CHESTER, Thomas (1662-1712) & Mary TREAT (1666-1748); 10 Dec 1684; Wethersfield, CT

CHEVARLY/CHEVERLEY, _?_ & _?_ ; b 1692; Salem

CHEW, ?John (-1672) & _?_ ; Hempstead, LI

CHEW, Nathaniel & _?_?; b 1647

CHEW, Richard & Frances [WOODWARD]; [b 1683]; Flushing, LI
CHICHESTER, David & Alice _?_; b 5 Jul 1699; ?Huntington, LI
CHICHESTER, James & Eunice [PORTER]; b 1643?; Taunton/Salem
CHICHESTER, James, Jr. (1654-) & _?_; b 1686; Huntington, LI
CHICHESTER, William (-1658+) & Mary [CORWITHEY] (-1663+); b 1648; Salem
CHICK, Richard (-1686, ae 48 y) & Alice _?_ (-1699); b 1678; Roxbury
CHICK, Thomas & 2/wf? Elizabeth [SPENCER], m/2 Nicholas TURBET; ca 12 May 1674; S. Berwick, ME
CHICKERING, Francis (-1658) & 1/wf Anne [FISK] (1610-1649); in Eng, b 1630; Dedham
CHICKERING, Francis (-1658) & 2/wf Sarah (?HOWE) SIBLEY (-1686), m/3 John BOWLES; 11 Jun 1650; Charlestown/Dedham
CHICKERING, Henry² (1589-1671) & 1/wf Elizabeth SMYTHE (-1626), w Benjamin; in Eng, lic bond 4 May 1622; Dedham
CHICKERING, Henry² (1589-1671) & 2/wf Ann GROSSE (-1675); in Eng, 10 May 1628, lic bond; Dedham
CHICKERING, John (1634-1676) & Elizabeth [HACKBURNE/HAGBOURNE] (1635-1679), m/2 Thomas GRAVES 1677; b 1662; Charlestown
CHICKERING, John & Susanna [SYMMES] (1670-), m/2 Benjamin STEVENS 1715; b 1693; Charlestown
CHICKERING, Nathaniel (1647-1699) & 1/wf Mary JUDSON (-27 Jan 1668/9); 30 Dec 1668; Dedham
CHICKERING, Nathaniel (-1699) & 2/wf Lydia FISHER (-1737); 3 Dec 1674; Dedham
CHICKERING, Nathaniel & 1/wf Mary THORP; 14 Aug 1700; Dedham
CHIDSEY, Caleb & 1/wf Anne THOMPSON (-1692); 10 May 1688; New Haven/East Haven
CHIDSEY, Caleb & 2/wf Hannah DICKERMAN (-1703); 6 Jul 1693; New Haven/East Haven
CHIDSEY, Ebenezer (1666-) & Priscilla [THOMPSON] (1671-); b 1689; New Haven
CHIDSEY, John (1621-1688) & Elizabeth _?_ (-1688); b 1650; New Haven
CHIDSEY, Joseph (1655-) & [Sarah HULL] (1675-); b 1696(7?); New Haven/Guilford
CHILD, Benjamin (?1620-1678) & Mary [BOWEN] (-1707); ca 1652?, 3 ch bpt 1658; Boston/Roxbury
CHILD, Benjamin (1656-1724) & Grace MORRIS (1661-1723); 7 Mar 1683, 1682/3; Roxbury
CHILD, Ephraim (1593-1663) & Elizabeth (BOND) PALMER (-1667); 8 Feb 1625, no ch; Watertown
CHILD, Henry (-1691) & Sarah [NASON], m/2 John HOYT 1695; b 1680; ?Berwick, ME
CHILD, Jeremiah & Martha _?_; b 1672, b 1683; Swansea
CHILD, Jeremiah & 2/wf Elizabeth (THURBER) [ESTEBROOK], w Thomas (probably wrong); aft 1689; Swansea
CHILD, John (1636-1676) & 1/wf Mary _?_; b 1664; Watertown
CHILD, John (1636-1676) & 2/wf Mary WARREN (1651-), m/2 Nathaniel FISKE 1677; 29 May 1668; Watertown
CHILD, John (-1683, 1685?) & Ann [WAKEFIELD], w John; aft 1667; Boston
CHILD, John & Hannah FRENCH (1676-); 5 Oct 1693, 5 Sep 1693; Watertown
CHILD, John, Roxbury & Elizabeth WILES; 17 Jun 1694; Braintree
CHILD, John & Margery HOWARD/HAYWARD (1673-1766, Warren, RI); 30 Jan 1695/6, 13 Jan 1695/6; Rehoboth/Swansea
CHILD, Joseph (-1698) & Sarah PLATTS; 3 Jul 1664; Watertown
CHILD, Joseph (1659-1711) & 1/wf Sarah NORCROSS; 23 Sep 1680; Watertown
CHILDS, Joseph (-1718) & Elizabeth [SEABURY]; b 1691; Marshfield
CHILD, Joshua (1657-1730) & Elizabeth MORRISS (1666-1754, 1752?); 9 Mar 1685; Roxbury
CHILD, Richard (?1624-) & Mary LINNELL; 15 Oct 1649; ?Barnstable/Deerfield
CHILD, Richard (?1631-1694) & 1/wf Mehitable DIMICK (-1676) (kinswoman of Magdalen UNDERWOOD); 30 Mar 1662, 17 Apr 1662; Watertown
CHILD, Richard (-1691) & Mary TREUANT/TRUANT; 24 Jan 1664, 1664/5; Marshfield
CHILDS, Richard (-1683) & 2/wf Elizabeth CROCKER (1660-1696, 1716?); 1678, (b 1679); Barnstable
CHILD, Richard (?1631-1694) & 2/wf Hannah TRAINE (1657-); 16 Jan 1678/9, 1678; Watertown
CHILD, Richard (1663-1691) & Mary FLAGG; 30 Dec 1686; Watertown
CHILD, Richard & 2/wf Hannah [HAMLIN?], dau James?; ca 1698; Yarmouth

CHILD, Samuel & _?_; b 1629?
CHILD, Shubael (1665-1694) & Abigail SAUNDERS; 27 Oct 1687, 16 Oct; Watertown
CHILD, Thomas & Katherine MASTERS, Boston; m bond 14 Apr 1688
CHILD, William & _?_; in Eng, b 1629; Watertown
CHILLINGWORTH, Thomas (-1653) & Joanna/Jane? _?_ (-1684), m/2 Thomas DOGGETT 1654; b 1645; Lynn/Marshfield
CHILSON, John & Sarah JENKES/JENKS; 28 Jul 1667; Lynn
CHILSON, Walsingham (-1655+) & Mary _?_ (-1674); b 1642; Salem/Saco, ME
CHILSON, William (-1676) & Grace [BRIER?/BRIERS/BRIAR] (1635-), m/2 Samuel OAKMAN 1676, 1677; 167-; Saco, ME/?Scarborough, ME
CHILSON, William & Jane RHOADS; m int 23 May 1696; Lynn/Mendon
CHILTON, James (-1620) & _?_; in Eng, ca 1584, Canterbury; Plymouth
CHINERY, Isaac & Elizabeth GAMLINE/GAMLIN (1634-); 16 Nov 1654; Medfield
CHINARY, John (-1675) & Sarah BOYLSONN/BOYLSTON, w Thomas; 12 Mar 1655, 1655/6; Watertown
CHINREY, John (1657-) & Elizabeth STRATTON; 4 Jun 1685; Watertown
CHENERY, Lambert (1593-1674) & 1/wf _?_ [ELLIS], wid; ca 1615/32; Watertown/Dedham
GENERY, Lambert (1593-1674) & 2/wf Tamazin HEWS (-1669/70); 14 May 1658; Dedham
CHINN, George & Elizabeth _?_; b 1653; Marblehead
CHINN, [?John] & Rebecca [MERRETT] (-1717?); b 1681; Salem/Marblehead
CHIPMAN, John[1] (1614?, 1620, ca 1621-1708) (had uncle Christopher DERBY and cousin John DERBY) & 1/wf Hope [HOWLAND] (?1629-1683/4); ca 1646, ca 1645; Plymouth/Barnstable
CHIPMAN, John[1] (-1708) & 2/wf Ruth (SARGENT) (WINSLOW) [BOURNE] (1642-1713), w Jonathan, w Richard (mentions sister FELCH (not FINCH) at Reading in will 1710); 1684; Barnstable/?Sandwich
CHIPMAN, John (1670/1-1756) & 1/wf Mary [SKIFF] (1671-1711); b 1691; Barnstable/Newport
CHIPMAN, Samuel (1661-1723) & Sarah COBB (1663, 1662/3-1742/3); 27 Dec 1686; Barnstable
CHESEMORE/CHISHOLM/CHISEMORE/CHEESEMORE/CHISIMORE?, Daniel (1671-) & Cyprian [SAMPSON] (1672-); b 1694; Newbury
CHISHOLM, Duncan & _?_; b 1671
CHITTENDEN, Benjamin (-1676) & _?_; b 26 Mar 1676; Scituate
CHITTENDEN, Henry (-1713) & _?_; b 1657; Scituate
CHITTENDEN, Isaac & Martha VINALL; - Apr 1646; Scituate
CHITTENDEN, Isaac & _?_?; b 1682; Scituate
CHITTENDEN, Israel (1651-) & Deborah BACKER/BAKER (?1652-); 25 Apr 1678; Scituate
CHITTENDEN/CINTTENDEN, John (-1717, 1716?) & Hannah FLETCHER (1643-); 12 Dec 1665; Guilford, CT
CHITTENDEN, Joseph & _?_; b 1684; Scituate
CHITTENDEN, Joseph (1672-1727) & Mary KIMBERLY (ca 1671-1742), New Haven; 26 Aug 1692; Guilford, CT
CHITTENDEN, Nathaniel (-1690, 1691?) & Sarah _?_; b 1669; Guilford, CT
CHITTENDEN, Nathaniel (1669-) & Elizabeth [STEVENS] (1668-1738); b 1691(2?); Killingworth, CT
CHITTENDEN, Stephen (1654-) & Mehitable BUCKE/BUSH; 6 Nov 1679, 5 Nov 1679; Scituate
CHITTENDEN, Thomas (1584-1668) & Rebecca _?_ (1596-); b 1621?; Scituate
CHITTENDEN, Thomas (-1683) & Joanna [?PRUDDEN] (1640-); b 1664; Guilford, CT
CHITTENDEN, Thomas & Abigail [HULL] (1669-1710); 1690; Killingworth, CT
CHITTENDEN, William (?1594-1661) & Joanna [SHEAFE] (?1608-1668), m/2 Abraham CRUTTENDEN? 1665; in Eng, b 1637?, ca 1629; Boston/New Haven/Guilford, CT
CHITTENDEN, William (1666-1738) & Hannah _?_ (-1702); b 1699; Guilford, CT/Stratford, CT
CHOATE, John[1] (1624-1695) (ae 58 in 1683) (ae ca 30 in 1660) (ae ca 32 in 1660) & Ann/Anne _?_ (1637-1727, 1729?); b 1660; Ipswich
CHOTE, John (1661-1733) & 1/wf Elizabeth GRAVES (1667-); 7 Jul 1684; Ipswich
CHOTE, John (1661-1733) & 2/wf Elizabeth (_?_) GIDDINGS, w Thomas; 19 May [1690?]; Ipswich
CHOTE, Samuel (-1713) & Mary WILLIAMS (1669-), m/2 Samuel STORY; 23 Nov 1688; Ipswich
CHOATE, Thomas & 1/wf Mary [VARNEY] (1669-1733); b 1691; Ipswich
CHRISTEN, Abise & Sarah TYLESTONE; 18 Jan 1699; Boston

CHRISMAS/CHRISTMAS, John & Mary __?__; b 1673; Boston
CHRISTOPHERS, Abraham & Mary [FOX]; b 1693/4?; Boston
CHRISTOPHERS, Christopher (1632, ?1634-1687 in 56th y) & 1/wf Mary BERRY (1621-1676); 16 Aug 1654; New London
CHRISTOPHERS, Christopher (1631-1687) & 2/wf Elizabeth (BREWSTER) [BRADLEY] (-1708, ae 70), w Peter; aft 13 Jul 1676; New London, CT
CHRISTOPHERS, Jeffrey (?1621-1706+) & __?__; by 1665?; New London/Southold, LI
CHRISTOPHERS, Jeffrey (-1696) & Jane __?__ (-1690); b 1690, no issue; New London, CT
CHRISTOPHERS, John (1668-1703) (his mother was Elizabeth BREWSTER) & Elizabeth MULFORD (1676?-1720), m/2 John PICKETT (1685-1738) 1706; 28 Jul 1696; New London, CT
CHRISTOPHERS, Richard (1662-1726) & 1/wf Lucretia BRADLEY (1661, 1660?-1691); 26 Jan 1681, [1681/2]; New London
CHRISTOPHERS, Richard & 1/wf Ann/Anna __?__; b 1687, b 1682; Boston
CHRISTOPHERS, Richard (1662-1726) & 2/wf Grace TURNER (1668-1734), Scituate; 3 Sep 1691; New London, CT
CHUBB, Pascoe (-1698) & Hannah FAULKNER (1658-1698); 24 May 1689; Andover
CHUBB, Thomas (-1688, ae 81) & Avis/Annis __?__; b 29 Jun 1641; Salem/Beverly/Manchester
CHUBB, Thomas & Mercy PLUM; 9 May 1672; Beverly/Attleboro
CHUBB, William & __?__; b 1684; Salem
CHUBBUCK, John (1648-1690) & Martha BEAL, m/2 Samuel STODDER 1699; 2 Dec 1668; Hingham
CHUBBUCK, Nathaniel (1635-1703) & Mary GARDNER/GARNET/GANNETT (-1710), w John; 18 Jun 1669, no issue; Hingham
CHUBBUCK, Thomas (-1676) & Alice GILMAN (1607-1675); in Eng, ca 1632, 28 Feb 1631, Hardingham, Eng; Charlestown/Hingham
CHUBBUCK, Thomas & Mary HERSEY; 15 Feb 1698/9; Hingham
CHURCH, Benjamin (-1718) & Alice SOUTHWORTH (1646-1719); 26 Dec 1667; Hingham/Duxbury/Little Compton, RI
CHURCH, Caleb (1647-1722) & 1/wf Joanna SPRAGUE (1645-1678); 16 Dec 1667; Hingham/Dedham
CHURCH, Caleb (1647-1722) & 2/wf Deborah __?__ (-17 Jan 1690/1) (Hannah CUTLER a relative); 6 Jun 1680; Watertown
CHURCH, Caleb (1647-1722) & Rebecca SCOTTOW, ?w John; 6 Nov 1691; Watertown
CHURCH, Cornelius (-1697) & Sarah TARBELL; 14 Jun 1670, 4 Jun 1670; Groton
CHURCH, David (1657-) & Mary __?__; b 16 Jun 1686; Watertown
CHURCH, Edward (?1628-1704) & Mary __?__ (1637-1690, 1691); b 1654; New Haven/Norwalk, CT
CHURCH, Garret (1611-) & Sarah __?__; b 1637; Watertown
CHURCH, John (1636-1691) & Sarah BECKLEY (-1689+); 27 Oct 1657; Hartford
CHURCH, John (-1696) & 1/wf Abigail SEVERANCE (1643-); 29 Nov 1664; Salisbury
CHURCH, John (-1696) & 2/wf Sarah __?__; by 1683; Dover, NH
CHURCH, John & Mary __?__; b 10 Mar 1690; Rye, NY
CHURCH, John (ca 1666-1756) & Rebecca [BLACKMAN] (1668-1748); b 1693; Little Compton, RI
CHURCH, John (1670-1735) & Abigail COLDWELL; - Apr 1699, 1695?; Hartford
CHURCH, John (-1711) & Mercy HANSON, m/2 Nathaniel YOUNG; 1 Dec 1699; Dover, NH
CHURCH, Joseph (ca 1638-1711) & Mary TUCKER (?1640, 1641-1710, ae 67?, 69?); 30 Dec 1660; Hingham/Little Compton, RI
CHURCH, Joseph (1663-1715) & Grace SHAW (1666-1737); b 1688, b 1689; Little Compton, RI
CHURCH, Josiah (1673-) & Thankful BROOKS (1679-); 24 Nov 1699; Hadley/Deerfield
CHURCH, Nathaniel (-1689) & Sarah [BARSTOW]; b 1666; Hingham/Scituate
CHURCH, Nathaniel & Judith BOSWORTH; 7 Jan 1696/7; Hull/Scituate
CHURCH, Richard (-1667) & Anne __?__; ?Braintree, Eng, ?18 May 1627, ca 1625/30? (not in 1627); Hartford/Hadley
CHURCH, Richard (?1608-1668, Hingham) (ae 56 in 1664) & Elizabeth [WARREN] (-1670); ca 1636; Plymouth/Charlestown/Dedham
CHURCH, Richard (1668-1730) & Elizabeth NOBLE (1663, ?1673-1741); 3 Mar 1692, prob 1691/2; Westfield

CHURCH, Richard (1669-1696) & Sarah **BARTLETT**; 24 Jan 1695/6; Hadley
CHURCH, Richard (-1703) & Hannah [**STOVER**], m/2 David **BRYANT**; 2 Feb 1696/7; Scituate
CHURCH, Samuel (ca 1638-1684) & Mary [**CHURCHILL**]? (1639-1690); b 1665/(6?); Hadley
CHURCH, Samuel & Rebecca **SHATTUCK**; 7 Feb 1671/2; Watertown
CHURCH, Samuel (1667-) & 1/wf Abigail **HARRISON** (1673-1717); 7 Jul 1692; Hadley
CHURCH, Samuel (1671-1718) & 1/wf Elizabeth [**STANNARD**] (-1708); b 1697, b 1699; Hartford
CHURCH, Samuel (1663-1718) & [Susannah **HUNGERFORD**]; b 1699; ?Lyme, CT
CHURCH, Samuel & Mary **EDWARDS** (1671-); 27 Nov 1700; Stonington, CT
CHURCH, Thomas (1674-1746) & 1/wf Sarah **HAYMAN** (1679-); 21 Feb 1698, 1698/9?; Little Compton, RI/Bristol, RI/Tiverton, RI
CHURCH, _?_ & Elizabeth [**DAVIS**] (1658-); b 1699; Charlestown
CHURCHILL, Benjamin (1652-) & 1/wf Mary _?_ (-1712, ae 59); 8 Jul 1676; Wethersfield, CT
CHURCHILL, Eleazer (1652-1716) & Mary [**BRYANT**?] (1654-1715); b 1676; Plymouth
CHURCHILL, Henry (1660/1, 1660/3-1715) & Mary (_?_) **DOTY** (1664-), w Thomas; 8 Feb 1687/8, no issue; Plymouth
CHURCHILL, John (-1662, 1662/3) (Abigail **CLARK** called him "kinsman") & Hannah **PONTUS** (-1690, 1691?), m/2 Giles **RICKARD** 1669; 18 Dec 1644; Plymouth
CHURCHILL, John (-1723) & 1/wf Rebecca **DELLENS/DELANS** (-1709); 28 Dec 1686; Plymouth
CHURCHILL, John, Jr. (1678-) & Desire **HOLMES**; 19 Nov 1700; Plymouth
CHURCHILL, Joseph & Sarah **HICKES/HICKS**; 3 Jun 1672; Plymouth
CHURCHILL, Joseph (1649-1699) & Mary [**CATLIN**?]/**TOWZEY**?/**TOWSEY**? (?1649-1738); 13 May 1674; Wethersfield, CT
CHURCHILL, Josiah (1614-1687) & Elizabeth [**FOOTE**] (1616-1700); ca 1638, b 1639(40?); Wethersfield, CT
CHURCHILL/CHURCHER?, Robert & 1/wf Sarah [**CABLE**]; b 1694/5, ca 1690?; Fairfield, CT
CHURCHILL, William (-1722 Plympton) & Lydia **BRIANT/BRYANT** (1662-1736); 17 Jan 1683, 1683/4; Plymouth
CHURCHMAN, Hugh (-1644) & _?_ (left wf in Eng); in Eng; Lynn
CHURCHWELL, Arthur (-1710) & Eleanor [**BONYTHON**]; ca 1692; Kittery, ME
CHURCHWELL, John & _?_
CHURCHWOOD, Humphrey & Mary [**CUTT**], m/2 Richard **BRIAR/BRIER** by 1693; aft 16 Nov 1686; Kittery, ME
CHUTE, James (1614-1691) & Elizabeth [**EPPS**] (1621?, 1622-); ca 1647; Ipswich
CHUTE, James & Mary **WOOD**; 10 Nov 1672, 1673?; Ipswich
CHUTE, Lionel (1580-1645) & Rose [**BARKER**?/**BAKER**?], m/2 Matthew **WHIPPLE** 1646; in Eng, b 1614; Ipswich
CLAGHORN, James & Abigail/Abia **LUMBARD** (-1677); 6 Jan 1654, 1653/4; Barnstable
CLAGHORN, Shubael & Jane [**LOVELL**] (1670-), m/2 John **BUMPAS** 1729; b 1689; Barnstable
CLAPHAM, Peter (-1698) & 1/wf Isabella [**BARLOW**]; b 28 Mar 1674; Fairfield, CT
CLAPHAM, Peter (-1698) & 2/wf Rebecca [**REYNOLDS/RUSCOE**] (-1730, ae 75), m/2 James **BROWN** 1699?; ca 1694; Fairfield, CT
CLAPHAM, _?_ & [?Ann] [**WILSON**?]; b 1640; Fairfield, CT?
CLAP, Desire (1652-1717) & 1/wf Sarah **POND** (-1716, ae 63, [1715/16]); 21 Oct 1679; Dorchester
CLAPP, Ebenezer (1643-1712) & 1/wf Elizabeth [**TUCKER**] (1644-1701), no issue; b 1681, b 7 Oct 1677; Milton
CLAP, Edward (?1605-1664/5) & 1/wf Prudence [**CLAP**?] (-1650?); b 1633?, b 1637, b 1634?; Dorchester
CLAP, Edward (-1664/5) & 2/wf Susanna (**COCKERELL/COCKERILL**) (-1688); ca 1656, b 1656?; Dorchester
CLAPP, Ezra (1640-1717/8) & 1/wf Abigail [**POND**] (1646-1682); b 1667; Milton
CLAPP, Ezra (-1717/18) & 2/wf Experience **HOUGHTON** (1659-1717); 22 May 1684; Dorchester
CLAP, Hopestill (1647-1719) & Susanna **SWIFT** (1652-1732); 18 Apr 1672; Dorchester
CLAP, Increase (-1716) & Elizabeth (**BURSLEY**) **GOODSPEED**, w Nathaniel; Oct 1675; Barnstable/Braintree
CLAPP, John (-1655) & Joan _?_, m/2 John **ELLIS** (no ch); b 1655, ca 1637-40?; Dorchester/Medfield

CLAPP, John & Hannah __?__ ; b 1679; Boston
CLAPP, John (-1726?) & 3/wf Dorothy [RAY] (1669-); b 1690; Flushing, LI
CLAP, John (-1735) & Silence FOSTER; 26 May 1698; Dorchester/Sudbury
CLAPP, John (1676-) & [Dorcas EARL]; b 1701; Rochester
CLAP, Joseph (1668-1747), Scituate & Abigail ALLEN (1674-); 17 Jan 1694/5; Braintree/Scituate?
CLAP, Joshua (1667-1728) & 1/wf Mary BOYDEN (-1718); 22 Dec 1696; Dedham
CLAP, Nathaniel (1640-1707) & Elizabeth SMITH (1648-1722); 31 Mar 1668; Dorchester/Roxbury
CLAP, Nehemiah (?1646-1684) & Sarah LEAVITT (1659-), m/2 Samuel HOWE 1685; 17 Apr 1678; Hingham/Dorchester
CLAP, Nicholas (1612-1679) (ae 52 in 1604/5) & 1/wf Sarah [CLAP] (-ca 1650?); b 1637; Dorchester
CLAP, Nicholas (1612-1679) & 2/wf Anna/Annable (WHIPPLE?), w John; b 1667 b 15 Apr 1667, aft 14 Jul 1666; Dorchester/Roxbury
CLAP, Noah (1657-1753) & 1/wf Mary WRIGHT (1666-1725); 28 Jul 1690; Sudbury
CLAPP, Preserved (1643-1720) & Sarah NEWBERRY (1650-); 4 Jun 1668; Northampton
CLAP, Robert (ae 55 in 1604/5) (?called cousin by Robert MARTIN 1660) (son of Thomas CLAPP?/Roger CLAPP) & Mary __?__ ; b 1687; Boston
CLAP, Roger (1609-1690/1) (cousin Robert MARTIN) & Joanna FORD (1617-1695); 16 Nov 1633; Dorchester
CLAP, Samuel (1634-1708) & Hannah LEEDS (1640-1708); 15 Jan 1668/9; Dorchester
CLAPP, Samuel (1642-1715+) & Hannah GILL (1645-1722); 14 Jun 1666, 13 Jun 1666; Scituate/Hingham
CLAPP, Samuel & 1/wf Sarah [BARTLETT] (-1703); 1697; Northampton
CLAP, Samuel (-1724) & Mary PAUL, m/2 Abiel BIRD; 7 Apr 1698; Dorchester
CLAP, Stephen (1670-1756) & Temperance GORHAM (1678-); 24 Dec 1696; Barnstable/Scituate
CLAPP, Thomas (?1609-1684) & 1/wf [?Jane MARTIN] (2/wf __?__); b 1639; Weymouth/Scituate
CLAP, Thomas (-1684) & 2/wf Abigail (WRIGHT) [SHARPE], w Robert, m/3 William HOLBROOK 1684+; aft Jan 1655, 1656?; Dedham/Weymouth/Scituate
CLAP, Thomas (1639, 1639/40?-1691) & Mary FISHER (1644-); 10 Nov 1662; Dedham
CLAPP, Thomas (1663-1704) & Mary __?__ , m/2 __?__ JENNERY; b 1686; Dedham
CLAP, William & Mary HELMAN; 24 Nov 1685; Marblehead/Boston
CLAPP, __?__ & Dorothy RAY (1664-), dau Daniel; Rye, NY
CLARKE, Aaron & Sarah LANGE; 6 Mar 1687; Swansea
CLARKE, Abraham & __?__ ?; b 1668; Bristol, RI
CLARKE, Abraham (?1650-1694) & ?Deliverance/?Elizabeth DREW; Durham, NH
CLARK, Abraham & Mary MULLEIN; 1 Mar 1698/9; New London, CT
CLARK, Andrew (-1706) & Mehitable [SCOTTO] (1648-); b 1672; Boston/Harwich
CLARKE, Arthur (-1665) & Sarah __?__ ; b 1644; Boston/Salem/Hampton, NH
CLARKE, Benjamin (-1724) & Dorcas MORSE (1645-1725); 19 Nov 1665; Medfield
CLARKE, Benjamin & Mercy/?Mary [SMITH]; b 1693; S. Kings Town, RI
CLARK, Carew (1602/3-1679+) & Datre/?Dorothy __?__ (-1658); b 1658; RI
CLARK, Carew & Ann DYER; 4 Feb 1693/4, ?14 Feb; Newport/N. Kings Town, RI
CLARK, Christopher & Rebecca __?__ ; b 1647; Boston
CLARK, Christopher (-1698) & Mary BOWIGER; 12 Dec 1695; Salem
CLARK, Charles & Experience (__?__) DAWES, w Samuel; Weymouth
CLARK, Capt. Daniel (?ca 1622-1710) & 1/wf Mary NEWBERRY (1622-1688); 13 Jun 1644; Windsor, CT
CLARK, Daniel (-1690) & [Mary] BEANE (1625-); b 1645, 2 Mar 1639/40, 3 Mar; Ipswich/Topsfield
CLARK, Daniel (1654-) & Hannah [PRATT]; ca 1678; Hartford/Colchester, CT
CLARK, Daniel (1658-1704) & ?2/wf Mary __?__ , m/2 Philip BILL; b 1684, b 1683(4?); Killingworth, CT
CLARK, Daniel & ?1/wf Ruth [BARBER] (1664-); ?ca 1684; ?Killingworth, CT
CLARK, Daniel (-1710, ae 87) & Martha (PITKIN) [WOLCOTT] (1639-1719, ae 80), w Simon; aft 29 Aug 1688, 1684?; Windsor, CT
CLARKE, Daniel (1665-1749) & 1/wf Damaris DORMAN (1666-1727); 29 May 1689; Topsfield
CLARK, Daniel (-1725?) & Mary BURR; - Jun 1693; Hartford

CLARK, Daniel & Martha [LITTLE] (1677-); ?ca 1698; New London Co., CT

CLARK, Daniel (1677-) & Hannah [BEECHER] (1679-); b 1701?; New Haven

CLARK, Ebenezer (1651-1721) & 1/wf Sarah PECK (1653-1696); 6 May 1678; Wallingford, CT/New Haven

CLARK, Ebenezer (-1721) & 2/wf Elizabeth (PARKER) ROYCE/ROADS, w Josiah, m/3 Nathaniel ANDREWS; 22 Dec 1696; Wallingford, CT

CLARK, Edmund (-1666/7) & Agnes [?DIKE], ?nee TYBBOT; b 1632 (see Edward CLARK); Gloucester, CT

CLARK, Edmund (-1681/4) & Mary _?_, m/2 Obadiah ROGERS by 1687; ?Southampton, LI

CLARK, Edward (-1661) & Barbara _?_, ?nee TABBOTT, m/2 John SMITH; b 1639; Marblehead/Cape Porpoise

CLAKE, Edward & 1/wf Dorcas [BOSWORTH] (-1681); b 1658?; Haverhill

CLARK, Edward (-1675) & 1/wf Elizabeth [FERNALD]; ca 1660; Portsmouth, NH

CLARK, Edward (-1675) & 2/wf Mary [FARROW], m/2 John SMITH; aft 1663; Portsmouth, NH

CLARK, Edward & 2/wf Mary (JOHNSON) DAVIS, w Ephraim; 1 Nov 1682; Haverhill

CLARK, Edward & Sarah _?_; b 1693; Boston

CLARK, Elisha (1665-) & Sarah [TAYLOR]; b 1691; Kittery, ME

CLARKE, Ephraim & Mary BULLIN; 6 Mar 1668/9; Medfield

CLARK, George, Sr. (1611-18 Jun/Aug? 1690) & ?Mary/Sarah _?_ (-22 Sep 1689); ca 1636?; Milford, CT

CLARKE, George & Alice MARTIN, m/2 Richard BISHOP; 22 Jan 1638, 1638/9?; Barnstable

CLARK, Dea. George, Jr. (-16 Jan/Aug? 1690) (nephew of Mrs. Zachary WHITMAN) (?farmer/?carpenter) & Sarah _?_ (-19 Jul 1689); b 1640, by 1637?; Milford, CT

CLARKE, George & Dorothy _?_; b 1659; Gloucester

CLARKE, George (-1696) & 1/wf Elizabeth _?_; in Eng, b 1675?; Roxbury/Boston

CLARK, George (1648-1734) & 1/wf Deborah [GOLD] (?1660-1697); b 1678; Fairfield, CT/Milford, CT

CLARK, George (-1696) & 2/wf Ann LUTTERELL; 3 Feb 1690; Boston

CLARK, George & Mary [?WHITINGHAM] (?1665-); b 1691; Boston/Charlestown

CLARK, George (1648-) & 2/wf Rebecca (PHIPPEN) (BALDWIN) [PRINCE] (1657-1712), w Samuel, w Job; b 13 Oct 1697; Boston/Milford, CT

CLARK, George, 3rd (?1682-) & 3/wf [?Mary] [COLEY] (1685-); b 1701; Milford, CT

CLARKE, Hanniel (?1650-1718) & Mary GUTTERSON; 20 Aug 1678; Haverhill

CLARKE, Henry (-1675) & Jane _?_ (-1672); b 1640; Windsor, CT/Hadley

CLARK, Henry & Katherine [BULL] (-26 Feb 1691); Boston

CLARKE, Henry (1673-) & 1/wf Elizabeth GREENLEAF; 7 Nov 1695; Newbury

CLARKE, Henry & Judith [PECKHAM]; b 1701?; RI

CLARK, Hugh (1613-1693, 1692?) & Elizabeth _?_ (-1692); b 1641; Watertown/Roxbury

CLARK, Isaac (1666-1768) & Sarah [STOW] (not STONE) (-1761, ae 88), dau Samuel b 1674, Concord; b 1691; Framingham

CLARKE, Jacob (1668-1754) (son of Abraham) & Ethalannah [BURTON] (1672-1757); ca 1695?, b 1710; Providence/Cranston, RI

CLARK, Jacob (-1722) & Alice [DAVIE/DAVIS]; ca 1699?; Portsmouth, NH

CLARK, James (-1674) & 1/wf _?_; b 1643; New Haven/Stratford, CT

CLARK, James (-1674) & Elizabeth/?Eleanor [WRIGHT] (1621-); b 1646?; Boston/Roxbury

CLARK, James & Abigail LAYTHROP (1639-); 7 Oct 1657; Plymouth

CLARKE, James (-1674) & 2/wf Ann WAKEFIELD, w John; 17 Oct 1661; New Haven

CLARKE, James (-1713) & 1/wf Deborah [PEACOCK] (-1705, ae 61); b 1664; New Haven

CLARK, James (1649-1736) & Hope/Hopestill [POWER] (1650-1718); b 1673; Newport

CLARK, James & 1/wf Hannah HEATH (-1 Apr 1683); 27 Apr 1681; Roxbury

CLARK, James & 2/wf Sarah CHAMPNEY; 24 Sep 1685; Cambridge

CLARK, James & Elizabeth POWSLAND; 19 Jul 1694; Marblehead

CLARK, James (1665-1712) & Jane (BLAKEMAN) (RUSSELL) GRIFFIN, w Joseph, w Thomas, m/4 Nathan ADAMS; 24 May 1698?, 1695, b 1696?; Stratford, CT

CLARK, James & Elizabeth [WHITTEMORE] (1679-1723); b 1701?; Charlestown

CLARK, Jeremiah/Jeremy? (1605-1652) & Frances (LATHAM) [DUNGAN] (1610-1677), w William, m/3 William VAUGHAN; b 1638; Newport

CLARKE, Jeremiah (1643-1729) & Ann [AUDLEY/ODLYN?] (-1732); b 1667?; Portsmouth, RI/Newport
CLARKE, Jeremiah (?1667-) & Elizabeth [SISSON] (1669-1752); Newport/S. Kings Town, RI
CLARK, John (-1673/4), Milford, CT & 1/wf Mary/Elizabeth [?COLEY]; ?b 1624, b 1621?; Cambridge/Hartford/Saybrook, CT/Milford, CT
CLARK, John (1598-1666?, 1664) & Martha [?SALTONSTALL/?KAYE] (1595-1680) (wf called Martha in will, Elizabeth in probate); ca 1627/30?; Newbury/Boston
CLARK, John (1609-1676) & 1/wf Elizabeth [HARGES?/HARRIS]; ca 1635?, no issue; Newport
CLARK, John (1612-1649, 1648) & ?Mary __?__ (-1648?); b 1637; New Haven
CLARK, John (-1684) & Elizabeth STEBBINS (1628-1700); 2 Mar 1646/7; Springfield
CLARKE, John (-1677) & Rebecca PORTER (printed as PARKER corrected) (1630-1682/3), m/2 __?__/?Jared/Gerard SPINSER; 16 Oct 1650; Saybrook, CT
CLARK, John (?1620-1700) & ?Elizabeth __?__ (?1640-); ?ca 1660; Kittery, ME
CLARK, John & __?__; b 1661; Wenham
CLARK, John (1637-1719) & 1/wf Sarah SMITH (1642-1674); 1 Feb 1661, [1661/2]; New Haven
CLARK, John (-1673/4, Milford, CT) & 2/wf Mary (WARD) [FLETCHER] (?1607-1679), w John; aft 18 Apr 1662; Milford, CT
CLARK, John (-1712/13) & Rebecca [MARVIN] (?1639-); b 1663; Hartford/Farmington, CT
CLARKE, John (-1690) & 1/wf Martha [WITTINGHAM?]; b 1667; Boston
CLARK, John & Sarah __?__; b 1668; Boston
CLARK, John (1609-1676) & 2/wf Jane FLETCHER (-19 Apr 1672), w Nicholas?; 1 Feb 1671; Newport
CLARK, John (1641-1695) & Abigail __?__; b 1672; Roxbury
CLARK, John (1650-1736) & Mary POOR (1654-1726); 10 Jan 1672; Rowley
CLARK, John (?1640, ?1639-1709) & Mary BURNHAM (ca 1652-1708); 9 Oct 1672; Ipswich/Norwich, CT
CLARK, John (1609-1676) & 3/wf Sarah [DAVIS] (-1692+), w Nicholas; aft 2 Sep 1673; Newport
CLARK, John (-1731) & Elizabeth [WHITE] (1655-1711); by 1675, b 1676; Middletown, CT
CLARK, John (1637-1719) & 2/wf Mary (WALKER) BROWN, div w John BROWN; 28 Nov 1675; New Haven
CLARK, John[2] (?1651-1704) & 1/wf Rebecca COOPER (1657-8 May 1678); 12 Jul 1677; Northampton
CLARK, John[2] (1651-1704) & 2/wf Mary STRONG (1654-1738); 20 Mar 1679, 1678/9, ?16 Mar, 1679/80?; Northampton
CLARKE, John & Mary SHEFFIELD; 9 Jan 1679/80; Medfield
CLARK, John & 2/wf Lydia BUCKMINSTER; 18 Nov 1680; Roxbury
CLARK, John (-1709) & Mary __?__; ca 1680?; New London, CT/Norwich, CT
CLARK, Capt. John & Mary [ATWATER] (1660-1726), m/2 John CONEY 1694; b 1681; Boston
CLARK, John (-1685) & Susannah STORY (1660-1734), m/2 Cornelius BROWN b 1689/90; 13 Jul 1681; Lynn
CLARK, John & Sarah [SMITH]; b 1683; Beverly/Rochester, MA
CLARK, Dr. John (-1690) & 2/wf Elizabeth (WILLIAMS) [SANFORD] (1640-), w Thomas; aft 7 Aug 1683; Boston
CLARK, John (1655-1736) & Rebecca BEAUMONT/BEAMAN (1659-); 17 Dec 1684; Saybrook, CT
CLARK, John & Elizabeth MORMAN/NORMAN; 18 Dec 1684; Newton
CLARKE, John (1656-1715) & Mary [CROWE], m/2 William RANDALL; ca 1685; Windsor, CT
CLARK, John & Barbara [SQUIRE], w William; aft 7 Oct 1686, aft 11 Aug 1680; ?Westchester Co., NY
CLARK, John (-1694, ae 29) & Mary __?__ (-1725?); ca 1687?; Portsmouth, NH
CLARK, John & Sarah POWER; 6 Dec 1687; Newbury
CLARK, John (-1703?) & Hannah STANLEY (-1704); 20 Sep 1689; Topsfield
CLARK, John & 2/wf Hannah (ASHWOOD) FREEMAN, w Samuel; aft 1689
CLARK, John (1663-1701) & Abigail [AMBROSE], m/2 John WILLIAMS; b 1690; Middletown, CT
CLARK, John (1667-1728) & 1/wf Sarah SHRIMPTON (1669-1717); 30 Apr 1691, 25? Apr; Boston
CLARK, John & Sarah TITHERTON (1673-); 11 Aug 1692; Stratford, CT

CLARK, John (1670-1705) & Elizabeth WOODBRIDGE (1673-), m/2 John ODLIN; 19 Jun 1694; ?New Castle, NH/Exeter, NH

CLARK, John (-1709) & Sarah [WARNER] (1670-), ?m/2 Job ELLSWORTH; ca 1694?; Farmington, CT

CLARK, John (-1712) & Rebecca LINCOLN, m/2 Israel NICHOLS; 14 May 1695; Hingham/Plymouth

CLARK, John (?1645-1705) & Mary BENJAMIN (1670-); 16 Aug 1695; Barnstable/Yarmouth

CLARK, John & Susanna GIDDINGS; 17 Dec 1695; Ipswich

CLARK, John (1672-, Roxbury) & Anne BIRD (1671-); 16 Apr 1697; Dorchester/Norwich

CLARK, John & Anna [SHAYLOR/SHALER]; b 1701?; Haddam, CT/Hartford

CLARK, John (1673-1708+) & Deborah [PARKE] (1680-); b 1701?; ?Preston, CT

CLARKE, John & Lydia [KELLOGG] (1676-), m/2 Thomas OVIATT 1705; b 1703, b 1701?; Milford, CT

CLARK, Jonas (1620-1700) & 1/wf Sarah __?__ (-Feb 1649/50); b 1642; Cambridge

CLARK, Jonas & 2/wf Elizabeth CLARK (-1673, ae 41); 30 Jul 1650; Cambridge

CLARK, Jonas & 3/wf Elizabeth COOK; 19 Aug 1673; Cambridge

CLARK, Jonas (-1738) & Susanna [BENNETT] (1651-); ca 1677?; Boston

CLARK, Jonathan & Lydia TITCOMB; 15 May 1683; Newbury

CLARK, Jonathan (ca 1661-2-) & Mary MAGOON; 6 Sep 1686; Dover, NH

CLARK, Jonathan & Elizabeth CHURCH (1674-); b 1701? (seems doubtful); Wethersfield, CT

CLARK, Joseph (-1641, Windsor, CT) & __?__ (-1639); b 1638, b 1634?; Dorchester/Windsor, CT

CLARK, Joseph (-1684) & 2/wf Alice [PEPPER]? (1628-1710); in Eng, b 1641; Dedham

CLARK, Joseph (1618-1694) & 1/wf __?__ ; 1642±; Newport/Westerly, RI

CLARK, Joseph (-1663?) & __?__ ; b 27 Aug 1658; Saybrook, CT

CLARKE, Joseph (-1702) & Mary ALLEN (1641-1702); 25 Jun 1663; Medfield

CLARK, Joseph (?1643-1727) & 1/wf Bethiah HUBBARD (1646-1707); 16 Nov 1664; Westerly, RI

CLARK, Joseph & Damaris FRANCIS; 19 Aug 1675; Braintree

CLARK, Joseph (-1723) & Ruth [SPENCER] (?1658-1744); ?ca 1676/81?; Haddam, CT

CLARK, Joseph (1650-1696) & Hannah DAVIS; 27 Mar 1682; Gloucester

CLARKE, Joseph (1653-) & Mary DAVIS; 18 Aug 1685; Haverhill

CLARK, Joseph (1618-1694) & 2/wf Margaret __?__ (-1694); b 25 Sep 1685; Westerly, RI

CLARK, Joseph & Mary WIGHT; 8 Apr 1686; Medfield

CLARKE, Joseph (1670-1718) & 1/wf Dorothy MAXSON; 5 Jan 1692; Westerly, RI

CLARK, Joseph & Elizabeth LANE; - May 1693; New Haven

CLARK, Joseph & Sarah WELLS; 11 Dec 1693; Boston

CLARKE, Joshua (-1702+) & Alice [PHILLIPS] (-1702+); b 17 Aug 1686; Providence/Newport

CLARKE, Josiah (-1691) & Mercy BOYNTON, m/2 Joseph GOODHUE 1692, m/3 John HOVEY 1712; 14 Dec 1670; Ipswich

CLARK, Josiah & Sarah (?) [SAMPSON], w Richard; b 1677; Portsmouth, NH

CLARKE, Josiah (1648-) & Mary (BURR) CROWE, w Christopher; b 1682(3?); Windsor, CT

CLARKE, Josiah (1671-1738) & Elizabeth __?__ (-1735); b 1695; Ipswich

CLARKE, Latham (1645-1719) & 1/wf Hannah [WILBUR]; b 1666?; Portsmouth, RI

CLARK, Latham (1666-1691, ae 25) & Hope __?__ (1668-1690, ae 22); b 1689(90?); Newport

CLARKE, Latham (1645-1719) & 2/wf Anne (COLLINS) NEWBERRY, w Walter; 20 Sep 1698; ?Portsmouth, RI

CLARK, Matthew (1627-1684) & Abigail MAVERICK (1637-1690), m/2 Benjamin BALCH 1689; 4 Jun 1655; Boston

CLARK, Matthew & Mary (DOW) WILFORD, w Gilbert; 2 Apr 1679; Haverhill

CLARK, Matthias & Ann BARTON; 25 Dec 1699; Boston

CLARK, Nathan (1662-) & __?__ ; b 1698; Bedford, NY

CLARK, Nathaniel[2] (1641-1669) & Mary MEEKING (-1704?), m/2 John ALLIS 1669, m/3 Samuel BALDEN 1691, 1692; 8 May 1663, 18 May; Northampton

CLARK, Nathaniel (1642-1690) & Elizabeth SOMERBY (-1716), m/2 Rev. John HALE 1698; 23 Nov 1663; Newbury

CLARK, Nathaniel (1643-1717) & Dorothy (LETTICE) GRAY (1648-1728), w Edward; aft Jun 1681; Plymouth

CLARKE, Nathaniel (-1690) & Elizabeth TAPPAN (1665-); 15 Dec 1685; Newbury

CLARK, Nathaniel & Patience [WELLS]; b 1692; Salisbury
CLARK, Nathaniel (1672-) & Sarah (LAY) DeWOLF (1665-), w Simon; 3 Dec 1696; ?Lyme, CT
CLARK, Nicholas (-1680) & _?_ ; ca 1632/4?, b 1640; Cambridge/Hartford
CLARK, Percival (-1716) & Elizabeth _?_ ; b 1665; Boston
CLARK, Perley/?Thomas & _?_ ; b 1669(70?) (seems doubtful); Reading
CLARKE, Peter & Penelope [FAIRWEATHER], m/2 Jonathan EVERETT 1697; b 1687; Boston
CLARK, Richard & Alice _?_ ; - Aug 1643; Rowley
CLARK, Richard (-1697) & Elizabeth _?_ ; b 1662, b 1661?; Southold, LI/Elizabeth, NJ
CLARK, Richard & Hannah _?_ ; b 1693; Boston/Newport
CLARK, Richard (-1725) & Mary _?_ ; ca 1695/99?, b 8 Jan 1699; Brookhaven, LI
CLARK, Robert (-1694) & 1/wf Sarah [STILES] (-1683), w Francis; b 1665; Stratford, CT
CLARK, Robert & 2/wf Hannah _?_ (Woodbury, CT), m/2 John BOOTH; 1683; Stratford, CT
CLARK, Rowland (-1639) & Mary _?_ (-1642); in Eng, b 1620; Dedham
CLARK, Samuel (-1679, 1677?, 1708?) (called brother-in-law by Thurston RAYNER 1667) &
    [Hannah/Susannah FORDHAM] (bpt 1616-), dau Rev. Robert; ca 1654?, b 1640?, by 1674;
    Stamford, CT/Southampton, LI
CLARK, Samuel (1645-1691) & [Sarah/Anna? LEADER]; b 10 Feb 1667; Portsmouth, NH
CLARKE, Samuel (-1730) & 1/wf Hannah TUTTLE (1655-1708); 7 Nov 1672; New Haven
CLARK, Samuel (1645-1719) (son George) & 1/wf Mary CLARK (1651-), dau George, farmer; 21
    Dec 1673, 26 Dec; Milford, CT
CLARKE, Samuel & Bethiah _?_ ; b 1674; Boston
CLARK, Samuel (-1699) & Sarah _?_ ; ca 1675?; Southampton, LI
CLARK, Samuel (1646-1730) & Rachel [NICHOLS] (-1722, ae 58 y 3 m); b 1676;
    Boston/Concord
CLARK, Samuel (-1709) & 1/wf Hester/Esther WHITE; 11 Jul 1678; Southampton, LI
CLARK, Samuel[2] (1653-1729) & Elizabeth EDWARDS (1660-1740/[1]); 1 Mar 1682; ?Northamp-
    ton
CLARK, Samuel & Anne [ATKINS]; b 1686; Marblehead
CLARK, Capt. Samuel (1661-1725, 1720?, 1728) & Mehitable [THRALL] (1664-1723, 1721?); ca
    1687; Windsor, CT/Milford, CT
CLARK, Samuel & Rebecca BROWN (1672-); 23 Feb 1691/2; New Haven
CLARK, Samuel & Sarah AVIS; 8 Sep 1692; Boston
CLARK, Samuel (1654-) & Elizabeth CRAFTS (1665-); 5 May 1696; Boston
CLARKE, Samuel (1666-1725) & Mehitable (PHIPPEN/PHIPPENY) [FORD] (1668-1721), w
    Thomas; b 1698; Milford, CT
CLARK, Samuel & Hannah (?HUDSON/PAINE?) FAIRWEATHER, w Thomas; 23 Jun 1698;
    Boston
CLARK, Samuel (1673-) & Mary BROWN (1674-1747); 15 Nov 1698; New Haven
CLARK, Samuel (1672-1719±) & Ann CHAMPLAIN/CHAMPLIN; 19 Jan 1698/9; Westerly, RI
CLARK, Samuel (1675-) & Mary [KIRKLAND/KIRTLAND]?; 14 Dec 1699; Saybrook,
    CT/?Milford, CT
CLARKE, Samuel & Hannah [WILCOX]; b 1701?; ?Newport, RI
CLARK, Solomon (1678-1747) & Mary WHITE (1675-1740); 24 Oct 1698; Dedham/Medfield
CLARK, Thaddeus (-1690) & Elizabeth [MITTON] (1644-1736, Boston); ca 1662; Falmouth, ME
CLARK, Theophilus (1670-) & Rachel [PARTRIDGE] (1669-); b 1692; Medfield/Medway
CLARK, Thomas (1605-1694) & Jane _?_ (-1663+); ca 1628/33?, no issue; Newport
CLARK, Thomas (1599, ?1605-1697, ae 98) (ae 59 in 1664) (called brother by Gov. Thomas
    PRINCE) & 1/wf Susanna [RING] (1609, 1610?-); ca 1634; Plymouth/Boston/Harwich
CLARK, Thomas (-1691), tanner & Mary/?Sarah _?_ ; ca 1637?; Ipswich/etc.
CLARK, Thomas (-1690), cooper & Mary/Sarah _?_ ; ca 1638?; Ipswich/etc.
CLARK, Thomas (-1678) & 1/wf Elizabeth _?_ ; b 1639; Boston
CLARK, Major Thomas (1607-1683) (Capt. STOUGHTON, a relative) & 1/wf Mary _?_ ; b 1640;
    Dorchester/Boston
CLARK, Thomas (1618-1693) & 1/wf Else/Alice _?_ (-1658); ca 1641/46?; Lynn/Reading
CLARK, Thomas (-1668?) & Anne (BISHOP)? JORDAN (-1672), w John; 1 May 1652, May 1652;
    Guilford, CT
CLARK, Thomas (1618-1693) & 2/wf Mary (_?_) SWAYNE (-1688), w Jeremy; 31 Aug 1658;
    Reading

CLARK, Thomas (1638-1719) & 1/wf Hannah GIBBARD (GILBERT wrong) (1641-1703); 20 May 1663; Milford, CT

CLARK, Thomas (-1697) & 2/wf Alice (HALLETT) NICHOLS, w Mordecai; m cont 20 Jan 1664; ?Boston/Plymouth

CLARK, Thomas (1638-1682) (?ae 34 in 1676), tailor & Abigail [COGSWELL] (-1728, ae 87); b 1664, b 1666; Boston/Ipswich

CLARK, Thomas & ? ; b 1672; Ipswich

CLARK, Thomas (1640-1695) & ? [LESTER]; b 1666; Hartford

CLARKE, Thomas & Hannah ? ; b 1674(5?); Boston

CLARKE, Thomas & Jane ? ; b 1674(5?); Boston

CLEARK, Thomas & Mary VOAKER; 4 Mar 1675; Salem

CLARKE, Thomas & Martha CURTICE/CURTIS (1657-); 11 Jan 1676, ?2 Jan; Scituate

CLARK, Thomas (-1683) & 2/wf Ann ? ; b 1678; Boston

CLARKE, Rev. Thomas (1653-1704) & 1/wf Mary [BULKELEY] (-1700); b 1679; Chelmsford

CLARK, Thomas & 1/wf Rebecca MILLER (-1688); 15 Feb 1681; Yarmouth/Plymouth

CLARK, Thomas & ? ; b 1683; Brookhaven, LI

CLARK, Thomas & Sarah LYNDE (1665-), m/2 Seth SWEETSER 1692; 15 Oct 1684; Charlestown

CLARK, Thomas (-1719?) & Grace (JUDSON) [PRUDDEN] (1651/2-), w Samuel; aft 1685; Milford, CT

CLARK, Thomas (1668-) & 1/wf Sarah [NOYES] (1670-); b 1690; Newbury

CLARK, Thomas, Sr. (-1697) & 2/wf Elizabeth CROW (-1695); 12 Feb 1689/90; Plymouth

CLARK, Thomas & Rebecca (GLOVER) SMITH (1655-), w Thomas; 30 Apr 1691; Boston

CLARK, Thomas (-1705+) & Elizabeth [?BAKER] (-1705+); b 1695; Newport, RI

CLARK, Thomas & Elizabeth [BAILEY]?; b 17 Jun 1696; ?Haddam, CT

CLARK, Thomas (-1703) & Elizabeth BURR; 6 Apr 1698; Hartford

CLARK, Thomas & 3/wf Susannah [MILLER]; b 1700; Plymouth

CLARK, Thomas (1672-1759) & 1/wf Sarah [GRAY]; b 1700; Harwich

CLARK, Thomas & Sarah (BURNHAM) [FARLOS/FARLEY], w Meshech; b 26 Mar 1700; Ipswich

CLARK, Thomas & Mary CHURCH; 13 Dec 1700; Nantucket

CLARK, Thomas & Elizabeth [ROWLAND]; b 1701?; Fairfield, CT

CLARK, Thurston/?Tristram (1590-1661) & Faith ? (-1663); in Eng, b 1619, b 1618?; Duxbury

CLARK, Timothy (-1737, ae 80) & Sarah [RICHARDSON/SPRAGUE?]; b 11 Sep 1679; Boston/Charlestown/Bristol, RI

CLARK, Timothy (1677-1725) & 1/wf Elizabeth [PRATT] (1682-1702); 1700?; Medfield

CLARKE, Uriah & 1/wf Joanna/Hannah [HOLBROOK] (-28 Feb 1681/2, 1678?, Roxbury); ?Oct 1674, b 1677; Boston

CLARK, Uriah & 2/wf Mary (TWELLS) [?KING] (-1700), w Ebenezer?; b 1683; Roxbury/Watertown

CLARK, Uriah, Jr. & Martha PEASE, Cambridge; 21 Nov 1700; Watertown

CLARK, Walter (1640-1714) & 1/wf Content [GREENMAN] (1636-1666); ca 1660; Newport

CLARK, Walter (1640-1714) & 2/wf Hannah SCOTT (1642-1681); Feb 1666/7; ?Newport

CLARK, Walter (-1714) & 3/wf Freeborn (WILLIAMS) HART (1635-1709, 1710?), w Thomas; 6 Mar 1683, 1682/3; Newport

CLARK, Weston (1648-) & 1/wf Mary EASTON (1648-1690); 25 Dec 1668; Newport/Portsmith, RI

CLARK, Weston & 2/wf Rebecca (THURSTON) EASTON, Newport, w Peter; 21 Nov 1691, 25 Nov 1691; ?Newport

CLARK, William & 1/wf Elizabeth [QUICK]; b 1630; Salem

CLARK, William (-1682, ae 87) (ae 27 in 1635) & Margaret ? (1599, 1614?-1694, ae 95) (ae 21 in 1635); b 1635, b 1634?; Watertown/Woburn

CLARK, Lt. William (1609-1690) & 1/wf Sarah ? (-1675); b 1638; Dorchester/Northampton

CLARK, William (-1647) & 2/wf Catharine ? , m/2 John GEDNEY; b 1638; Salem

CLARK, William (-1683) (called brother by George DAVIS, 1666) & Mary? ? (-1693); b 1641; Lynn

CLARK, William (-1681) & [?Catherine BUNCE]; ca 1644?; Hartford/Haddam, CT

CLARK, William (-1668) (did he marry?) & ? ; ca 1646?; Yarmouth

CLARK, William (-1684, 1687) & Martha [NASH], dau Samuel; ca 1648/50?, no issue; Duxbury

CLARK, William & Elizabeth __?__ (1633-), m/2 Mordecai LARCUM by 1656; ca 1653/4?, b 25 Mar 1656, b 1650?; Ipswich

CLARK, William & Anne [?HOWARD], dau Robert; b 1659; Boston

CLARK, William (1636, ?1634-) & 1/wf Sarah WOOLCOTT (-12 Mar 1675/6); 1 Mar 1659, 1659/60; Plymouth

CLARK, William, Boston & Martha FARR, Lynn; 18 Sep 1661; Boston

CLARK, William (-1711) & Susannah [?TREAT]; b 1669; Wethersfield, CT

CLARK, William & Eleanor DEARSEFORD/DEARNFORD; 23 Aug 1669; Lynn/Boston

CLARKE, William (-1697) & __?__ ; ca 1674?; Bedford, NY

CLARK, Lt. William[1] (1609-1690) & 2/wf Sarah (SLYE) COOPER (-1688), w Thomas; 15 Nov 1676; Springfield/Northampton

CLARKE, William & Sarah __?__ /[?CRAWFORD]; b 1677(8?), ?b 28 Feb 1675(6?); Boston

CLARK, William & Elizabeth [STONE] (1659-); b 1678; Beverly

CLARK, William (1636-) & 2/wf Hannah GRISWELL/GRISWOLD (1658-1687/8); 7 Mar 1677, 1677/8; Saybrook/Plymouth

CLARKE, William & Rachel __?__ ; b 1679; Boston

CLARK, William (-30 Sep 1683) & Hannah [WEEDEN], m/2 Thomas PECKHAM, m/3 Joseph CLARK; ca 1680; Jamestown, RI

CLARK, Capt. William[2] (1656-1725) & 1/wf Hannah STRONG (1659-1694); 15 Jul 1680; Northampton

CLARKE, William & Rebecca __?__ ; b 1681; Boston

CLARKE, William (-1710) & [Mary WHITTINGHAM] (1665-1730), m/2 Gurdon SALTONSTALL 1712; 1683, no issue; Boston

CLARK, William & 3/wf Abia WILDER (-1725, ae 69); 3 Aug 1692; Plymouth

CLARK, William (1670-) & Hannah __?__ (1673-); Bedford, NY, b 1695

CLARK, William[2] (1656-1725) & 2/wf Mary SMITH (1662-1748), dau Benjamin of Milford, CT; 31 Jan 1694/5, 31 Jan 1695; Northampton/Lebanon, CT

CLARK, William & Mary [DAY]; 14 Nov 1699; Haddam, CT

CLARK, William (1673-) & Hannah KNIGHT (1680-); 11 Apr 1700, 15 Apr; Newport/Charlestown, RI

CLARK, William & __?__ ; b 1701; Stamford, CT

CLARK, William (1673/4-1708) & Margaret [BLINN] (1684-), m/2 Daniel BELDEN; b 1701?; Wethersfield, CT

CLARK, __?__ & Frances __?__ , m/2 Thomas DEWEY, m/3 George PHELPS; Dorchester

CLARK, __?__ & Hannah EDDY

CLARK, __?__ & Mary ARNOLD (1678-)

CLARK, __?__ & Mary HINMAN; ?Woodbury, CT

CLARY, John (1612-1691) & Sarah CASSELL; 5 Feb 1643/4; Watertown/Hadley

CLARY, John (-1688) & Ann/Hannah DICKINSON, m/2 Enos KINGSLEY 1692; ?16 Jan 1670, ?16 Jun 1670; Hatfield/Northampton

CLASON, [?David] (1662-) & 1/wf Priscilla [ABBOTT]; b 1689; ?Norwalk/Stamford, CT

CLASON, [?David] (1662-1721) & ?2/wf Mary HOLMES (1662-1716); 12 Jan 1692, ?1 Dec 1692; Stamford, CT

CLASON, Jonathan (1656-1686) & Sarah ROBERTS (1661-1684); 16 Dec 1680; Stamford, CT

CLASON, Samuel (-1723) & Hannah DENHAM/DUNHAM (-1721); 7 Dec 1693; Stamford, CT

CLASON, Stephen & Elizabeth PERIMENT (-1714); 11 Jan 1654/5; Stamford, CT

CLASON, [Stephen?] (1657/8-) & Rebecca (DRAKE) (JONES) [ROGERS] (1658-), w Joseph, w __?__ ; b 1699, b 1698; Stamford, CT/Bedford, NY

CLATTERY, Richard & Mary __?__ ; b 1684; Marblehead

CLAY, Humphrey & Katharine __?__ ; b 1664; New London, CT

CLAY, John & Anna/Ann [PLATTS], dau Thomas, m/2 Samuel SARSON 1694, m/3 John WORTH; b 1690; Boston

CLAY, Jonas & Mary [BATSON], m/2 William BROCKUS b 1670; Wenham/Dorchester

CLAY, Jonas (-1704) & Mary ALLEN; 22 Oct 1678; Salem/Boston

CLAY, Joseph (-1695) & Mary [BOW?/LOVE] (-1692); 18 Apr 1670; Guilford, CT

CLAYTON, David (-1730) & Amy/?Ann [COOKE] (1670-1729+); b 1689; Newport

CLAYDON, Richard (1595-) (returned to England) & __?__ ; b 1629; Salem

CLEASBY, Ezekiel (1663-) & Sarah __?__ ; b 1689; Boston/Chesebourgh

CLEASBY, John (-1695, ae 62) (called brother by Edward **GOODWIN**) & Hannah [**EDENDEN**] (-1724, ae 86/88); ca 1656/60?; Charlestown

CLEABEY, William & Amy **GILBERT** (1663-); 19 Aug 1694, at Hartford, 1684?; Stonington

CLEEVE, George (1586-) & Joan [**PRICE**] (1585-); Shrewsbury, Eng, 1617; Falmouth, ME

CLEAVES, John & 1/wf Mercy **EATON**; 26 Jun 1699; Beverly

CLEAVES, William (-1676) & Sarah **CHANDLER** (-1618+, Sandwich), m/2 _?_ **STEVENS** by 1681, m/3 John **PARKER** by 1684, m/4 _?_ **ALLEN** by 1691; 4 Nov 1659, 1681; Roxbury (Margaret **CLEAVES** dau of William and Sarah, m/1 Thomas **PARKER** of Newton, m/2 James **ATKENS** of Roxbury)

CLEAVES, William & Martha [**COREY**]; b 1676; Beverly

CLEAVES, William & 2/wf Margaret [**COREY**], m/2 Jonathan **BYLES**; b 1686; Beverly

CLEAVES, William & Hannah **LOVELL** (1668-); 28 Jan 1699/1700; Sandwich

CLEMENCE, Richard (-1723) & Sarah **SMITH** (-1725); b 1688; Providence

CLEMENCE, Thomas (-1688) & Elizabeth _?_ (-1721+); b 1673, ca 1650/55?; Providence

CLEMENS, John & Mehitable **MILLER** (1669-); 20 Apr 1688; Springfield

CLEMENS, _?_ & _?_ ; ?Boston

CLEMENS/CLEMENT, Abraham (1657-) & Hannah **GOVE** (1664-); 10 May 1683; Newbury/Bristol Co./PA

CLEMENTS, Austin/Augustine (-1674) & Elizabeth _?_ ; b 1635, b 1633?; Dorchester

CLEMENTS, Faun/Fawne (1662-) & 1/wf Sarah **HOYT** (-1712); 21 Nov 1688; Amesbury/Salisbury

CLEMENT, James (-1724) & 1/wf Jane _?_ ; in Eng, b 1670; Flushing, LI/etc.

CLEMENT, James (-Feb 1674/5) & Martha **DEANE**, m/2 Ralph **POWELL** 1676; 28 Dec 1674; Marshfield

CLEMENT, James (-1724) & 2/wf Sarah [**FIELD**] (-1724); b 1701?; Flushing, LI

CLEMENT, James (1670-) & Sarah [**HENCHMAN**]; b 1701?, m lic 2 Jul 1696; Flushing, LI/Gloucester, NJ

CLEMENT, James & 2/wf Abigail **FARRINGTON**; int 3 Oct 1700

CLEMENT, Jasper (1614-1678) & 2/wf Eleanor (**WATTS**) **BROWN**, w Nathaniel, m/3 Nathaniel **WILLOTT**; aft 1 Jan 1659/60?; Middletown, CT

CLEMENT, Job (1615-) & 1/wf Margaret **DUMMER** (-1653±); 25 Dec 1644; Haverhill/Dover, NH

CLEMENT, Job (1615-) & 2/wf Lydia _?_ ; b 1657; Haverhill/Dover, NH

CLEMENT, Job (1615-1683) & Joanna (?SOLSBY) **LAUGHTON** (1617/18-1704), w Thomas; 16 Jul 1673; ?Dover, NH

CLEMENT, Job & Abigail **HEARD** (-1734); 28 Feb 1688/9; Dover, NH

CLEMENT, John & Sarah **OSGOOD**; 1 Jun 1648, 4 Jun 1648; Haverhill

CLEMENCE, John & Apphia _?_ ; b 27 Feb 1649; Marblehead

CLEMENT, John (1653-1692) & Elizabeth **AYRES/AYER**, m/2 Samuel **WATTS** alias **MERCER** 1697; 22 Feb 1676, 1675; Haverhill

CLEMENT, Jonathan (?1659-) & Elizabeth _?_ ; b 1694; Haverhill/Woodbridge, NJ/Durham, CT

CLEMENT, Joseph & Mary _?_ ; b 1677; Boston

CLEMENT, Joseph & Mary [**DALTON**] (1675-); b 1701?; Hampton, NH

CLEMENT, Robert (-1658) & 1/wf [Lydia] _?_ (-1642); in Eng, b 1624, b 1618?; Salisbury

CLEMENT, Robert (1634-) & Elizabeth **FAWNE**; 8 Dec 1652; Haverhill

CLEMENT, Robert (-1658) & 2/wf Judith _?_, m/2 John **WHITNEY** 1659; b 1657; Haverhill

CLEMENT, Robert (-1673) & Joanna **CARR**; 2 Apr 1667; Salisbury

CLEMENT, Robert & Deliverance **ODDIHORN/ODIORNE**; 18 Dec 1690; Haverhill

CLEMENT, Samuel & 1/wf Hannah **INGS/ENGLISH/INGLISH** (-1658); 2 Jul 1657; Boston

CLEMENT, Samuel (-1679) & 2/wf Deborah _?_ ; b 1669; Boston

CLEMONS?/CLEMENTS?, Samuel & Sarah _?_ ; b 1689; Salem

CLEMANCE, William & Susan _?_ ; b 1646?, pet for divorce, 12 May 1656; Cambridge

CLEMANCE, William (-1672+) & Ann **TAYLOR** (-1672+); 3 Apr 1660; Cambridge

CLEMENTS, William & Mary [**ROCH**], dau Joseph; b 16 Aug 1664; Boston

CLEMMONS/CLEMENTS?, William (-1702) & Elizabeth _?_ (-1727/8); b 1678; Stamford, CT

CLEMENTS, William & Mary **CORY**; 18 May 1683; Beverly/Marblehead

CLEMENTS, _?_ & Margaret _?_, m/2 John **LENERUS/LUNERNS**? 1652; Boston

CLEARE, George & Abigail **MILNER**; 20 Sep 1638; Newport

CLEARE, George & Martha **WARD**; 26 Jan 1648/9; Dedham

CLERE, John[1] (-1678) & Ann _?_ ; ca 1650?; Boston

CLEARE, John[2] (-1678) & Elizabeth [PAINE] (1648-), dau Moses; b 1674; Boston
CLEARE, Richard (-1679) & Jane __?__; b 1673(4?); Boston
CLEAR, William (1674-) & Bethiah GREENLEAF; 21 Dec 1699; Boston
CLISSON, Matthew (-1715, Deerfield) & Mary PHELPS (1651-1687); 22 Dec 1670; Northampton
CLEVELAND, Aaron (1655-) & 1/wf Dorcas WILSON (1657-1714); 26 Sep 1675; Woburn/Cambridge
CLEVELAND, Edward (1664-) & 1/wf Deliverance [PALMER] (-1717); ca 1683; ?Kingston, RI/N. Kings Town/Canterbury, CT
CLEAFLAND, Enoch (1671-1729) & 1/wf Elizabeth COUNTS (-1719); 9 Oct 1695; Charlestown/Concord
CLEVELAND, Isaac (1669-1714) & Elizabeth (PIERCE) CURTICE (1666-), w John, m/3 Clement STRATFORD; 17 Jul 1699, 18 Jul 1699; Norwich, CT/Charlestown
CLEVELAND, Josiah (1667-1709) & Mary [BATES] (1667-), m/2 Robert BUSWELL; ca 1689, Chelmsford/Plainfield, CT/Canterbury, CT
CLEVELAND, Moses[1] (-1702) & Ann WINN; 26 Sep 1648; Woburn/Charlestown
CLEVELAND, Moses & Ruth [NORTON]; 4 Oct 1676; Woburn/Southold, LI/Martha's Vineyard
CLEVELAND, Samuel (1657-), Woburn & 1/wf Jane KEYES/KEIES (1660-1681); 17 May 1680; Chelmsford/Woburn
CLEVELAND, Samuel (1657-) & 2/wf Perses HILDRETH (1660-1698, Plainfield, CT); 23 May 1682; Chelmsford/Canterbury, CT
CLEVELAND, Samuel (1657-) & 3/wf Margaret (?FREEMAN) FISH (?1652-), w John; 25 Jul 1699; Canterbury, CT
CLEVERLY, John[1] (-1703, ae 68) & 1/wf Sarah STEVENS (1641-1692, 1694?); 18 Mar 1663/4, 13? Mar; Braintree
CLEVERLY, John[2] & Hannah SAVIL (1674-); 24 Jun 1695; Braintree
CLEVERLY, John (-1703) & 2/wf Sarah (HOBART) COWELL (1644-1696), w Edward; 17 Oct 1695; Boston
CLEVERLY, John (-1703) & 3/wf Elizabeth ?(FRANKLIN) GLOVER (?1638-1705), w John, m/3 James MOSMAN 1703; 5 Nov 1696; Boston
CLIFFORD, George & __?__; b 1646, b 1614?; Boston (doubtful)
CLIFFORD, Henry & Rebecca ADAMS (1661-); 29 May 1686; Flushing, LI
CLIFFORD, Isaac (1664-1694) & Elizabeth PULSIFER/PULCEFER (-1755), m/2 Jonathan PRESCOTT 1696?; 13 Aug 1693; Newbury
CLIFFORD, Israel & Ann SMITH; 15 Mar 1680, 1678/9, 1679/80; Hampton, NH
CLIFFORD, Jacob (-1665) & Elizabeth [MAYHEW] (1677-), m/2 Ichobod ALLEN 1728; b 1701; Martha's Vineyard
CLIFFORD, John[1] (1614-1680?, 1694) & 1/wf Sarah __?__; b 1645; Hampton, NH
CLIFFORD, John (-17 Jun 1698 in 68 y) (ae 63 in 1692) & __?__; ?; Lynn/Salem
CLIFFORD, John[1] (-1664?, 1694) & 2/wf Elizabeth (WISEMAN) RICHARDSON (-1667), w William; 28 Sep 1658; Hampton, NH
CLIFFORD, John[2] (1646-) & Sarah GODFREY (1642-1694); 18 Aug 1670; Hampton, NH
CLIFFORD, John[1] (-1694) & 3/wf Bridget HUGGINES (-1686), w John; 6 Apr 1671 (6 Feb 1672 is wrong); Hampton, NH
CLIFFORD, Philip & __?__ (doubtful); b 1688; Lynn
CLIFFORD, Stephen & Margaret __?__; b 1688; Boston
CLIFFT/CLIFT, William (-1722), Marshfield & Lydia WILLS (1676-), dau Samuel; 25 Nov 1691 (1671 is wrong); Scituate
CLIFTON, Henry & Rebecca ADAMS; 22 Aug 1686; Flushing, LI
CLIFTON, Savery & Dorothy [BURGESS] (1670-); b 1690; Rochester
CLIFTON, Thomas (1606-1681) & Mary [BUTTERWORTH] (1600, 1606-1681, 1687), w Henry; aft 18 Jan 1640/1; Rehoboth/Newport
CLINTON, Lawrence (-1704+) & 1/wf Rachel HALSELD/HALFIELD/HAFFIELD; - Dec 1665, div 1681?; Ipswich
CLINTON, Lawrence (-1704+) & 2/wf Mary WOODEN (1653-1690); 9 Feb 1680/1; Providence
CLINTON, Lawrence & 3/wf Margaret (PAINTER) [MORRIS], wid, m/3 Jeremiah MOTT; Newport
CLISBY, Ezekiel & [Prudence RANGER] (1672-); b 1701?
CLISBY, James & Elizabeth [BURWELL]; b 1695; NJ?

CLOAD, Andrew (-1664) & Elizabeth **BUGBY**; 29 Sep 1653; Boston

CLOCKE, _?_ & Judith _?_ (-1684), m/2 Olive **CALLOWE** 1656; Boston

CLOMY/CLEEMY?/CLEMY?, Alexander (-1693) & Elizabeth [ENGLISH/INGLES], m/2 Benjamin **BREAM/BRAME**? 1694; b 1693; Boston

CLOSE, Thomas (-1709) & Sarah [HARDY]; b 1670; Greenwich, CT

CLOSE, _?_ /Joseph? & Elizabeth _?_ (-1656), m/2 George **STUCKEY**; b 1641, b 1637, b 1632; Fairfield, CT

CLOSSON, Josiah (1655-1699) & Mary **WILLIAMSON**; 10 May 1678/9; Wethersfield, CT/Little Compton, RI/Tiverton, RI

CLOSSON/CLESSON?, Matthew & Mary **PHELPS** (1651-1687); 22 Dec 1670, 12 Dec 1670; Northampton

CLOUGH, Benoni (1675-) & Hannah _?_ ; b 1694; Salisbury/Kingston, NH

CLOW, Ebenezer & 1/wf Martha **GOODWIN** (1675-); 28 Mar 1693; Boston

CLOUGH, John & Susanna _?_ ; ca 1630/40; Watertown

CLOUGH, John (1614-1691) & 1/wf Jane/Joan _?_ (-1680); b 1642; Salisbury

CLOW, John (-1668) & Elizabeth _?_ ; b 1655; Boston

CLOUGH, John & Mary _?_ ; b 1669; Boston

CLOUGH, John & Mercy **PAGE**; 13 Nov 1674; Salisbury

CLOUGH, John & Martha _?_ ; b 1684; Boston

CLOUGH, John (1614-1691) & 2/wf Martha **CILLEY?/SIBLEY?/SEALEY?/SILLEY/?SEELEY**, w John?/Richard?; 15 Jan 1686; Salisbury

CLOUGH, John & Margaret _?_ ; b 1693; Boston

CLOUGH, John (1664-) & Mary **BEARD**; 12 Apr 1693; Boston

CLOUGH, John & Priscilla _?_ ; b 1694; Boston

CLOW, John & Elizabeth _?_ ; b 1696; Boston

CLOUGH, Samuel & Elizabeth **BROWN**; 3 Aug 1679; Salisbury

CLOUGH, Samuel & Ruth _?_ ; b 1689; Boston

CLOUGH, Thomas & 1/wf Hannah **GILE** (-1683); 10 Mar 1679/80; Salisbury

CLOUGH, Thomas & 2/wf Ruth [CONNER]; b 1688; Salisbury

CLOUGH, William (1633-1684) (ae 45 in 1678) & Mary [ADAMS] (-1688); b 1657, b 1656; Charlestown/?Boston

CLOUGH, William & 1/wf Lydia _?_ ; b 1686; Boston

CLOUTMAN/CLOUDMAN?, Edward & Sarah **TUTTLE**; 22 Apr 1698; ?Exeter, NH

CLOUTEMAN, Thomas & Elizabeth **STORY**; 26 Jul 1672; Salem

CLOYSE, John (ca 1610-1676) & 1/wf Abigail _?_ ; b 1638; Watertown

CLOISE, John (ca 1610-1676) & 2/wf Jane _?_ (-ca 1666?); b 3 May 1656; Charlestown

CLOISE, John (-1676) & 3/wf Julian [SPURWELL?] (ca 1620-1679+), ?w Christopher; by 1667, b 1669

CLOYES, John (1638-) & 2/wf? Mary [MILLS]; by 1688, by 1665/70?, 1681; Wells, ME

CLOISE, Nathaniel (1642/3-) & Sarah [MILLS]; by 1684; Charlestown/Wells, ME

CLOIS, Peter (1640-1708, Framingham) & 1/wf Hannah [LITTLEFIELD] (1633-ca 1680); ca 1662; Wells, ME/Salem

CLOYES, Peter (1643-1708) & 2/wf Sarah (TOWNE) [BRIDGES] (?1638, bpt 1643-1703), w Edmund; ca 1683?; Salem

CLOYCE, Peter & Mary **PRESTON**; 13 Dec 1693; Salem

CLOYES, Thomas (-1690) & Susanna [LEWIS]; b 1677, 1670?; Salem/Saco, ME/Falmouth, ME

CLUGSTON, Michael & Mary [WAKEMAN]; by 1694; Fairfield, CT

CLUNGEN/CLUNGER?, Thomas & Eliza[beth] _?_ ; b 1670; Salem

CLUTTERBUCK, William & Elizabeth _?_ ; b 1680; Charlestown/Boston

COARS/COARES?, Micah/?Michael & Rachel **SHORT**; 7 Jul 1699; Boston

COATES, John & _?_ ; Hempstead, LI

COOTS, John[2] (-1727) & 1/wf Mary **WITHERDIN** (-1682); 14 Apr 1681; Lynn

COOTS, John[2] (-1727) & 2/wf Naomi _?_ (-1687); aft 18 Jun 1682; Lynn

COOTS, John[2] (-1727) & 3/wf Alice **HENLEY**; 3 Nov 1690; Lynn

COATES, Robert[1] (1627/8-) & Jane [SUMNER] (1641-); b 1663, b 1660?; Lynn

COOTS, Robert[2] (-1724, Stonington, CT) & Mary **HODGKIN**; 29 Dec 1682; Lynn/Ipswich/Stonington, CT

COATS, Thomas & _?_ [FLOOD?]; b 1646; Lynn

COOTS, Thomas & Martha GAY/GEE; 29 Dec 1685; Lynn/Newbury
COBB, Austin?/Augustine? & Bethia _?_; b 1670(1?); Taunton
COBB, Ebenezer & 1/wf Mercy HOLMES/Mary FREEMAN?; 1 Jun 1693; Plymouth
COBB, Edward (1633-1675) & Mary HOSKINS/HASKINS (ca 1640-), m/2 Samuel PHIPPS/PHIL-
     LIPS 1676; 28 Nov 1660; Plymouth
COBB, Edward & Sarah HACKETT; 18 Dec 1689; Taunton
COBB, Henry (-1679) & 1/wf Patience HURST (-1648); b 1632; Plymouth/Barnstable/Scituate
COBB, Henry (-1679) & 2/wf Sarah HINCKLEY (1629-); 12 Dec 1649; Plymouth
COBB, Henry (1665-1725, 1722?, Stonington, CT) & Lois HALLET; 10 Apr 1690; Barnstable
COBB, James (1634, 1633-1696, 1695?) & Sarah LEWIS (1644-1735), m/2 Jonathan SPARROW,
     1698; 26 Dec 1663; Barnstable
COBB, James (1673-) & Elizabeth HALLET; 15 Sep 1695; Barnstable
COBB, John & Martha NELSON; 28 Apr 1658; Plymouth
COBB, John & 1/wf Martha _?_, Taunton
COBB, John & 2/wf Jane (GODFREY) WOODWARD (-1736), w Israel; 13 Jun 1676; Taunton
COBB, John, Jr. (1662-1727) & Rachel SOULE (-1727); 7 Sep 1688, 5 Sep 1688; Plymouth/Middle-
     town
COBB, John & Susanna _?_; b 1691; Providence
COBB, John & Mary FARRINGTON; 20 Dec 1700; Dedham
COBB, Jonathan (1660-1728) & Hope (CHIPMAN) HUCKINS (1652-1728), w John; 1 Mar 1682/3;
     Barnstable
COBB, Richard (1666-1709) & Esther BATES (1663-); 16 Sep 1691; Hingham/Boston
COBB, Samuel (1654-1727) & Elizabeth TAYLOR (ca 1655-1721); 20 Dec 1680; Barnstable
COBB, Thomas & Dorothy HOBBY?; in Eng, 24 Jul 1656; Boston/Hingham
COBB, Thomas & _?_ [BANISTER?]; in Eng, b 1666; Boston/Hingham
COBB, William & Mary NEWLAND; 11 Feb 1684/5; Taunton
COBBETT, John & Elizabeth [COOPER] (1663-), dau Josiah; b 1685; Ipswich/Charlestown
COBBETT, Josiah & Mary [HAFFIELD]; Boston
COBBETT, Samuel (-1713) & Sarah _?_; b 1676; Lynn/Bristol, RI
COBBETT, Thomas (?1608-1685) & Elizabeth _?_ (-1686); b 1645?, b 1653; Lynn/Ipswich
COBBETT, Thomas & Mary [LEWIS], m/2 John HINCKIS; b 2 Oct 1682; ?Portsmouth, NH
COBHAM, Joshua (1648-1688) & Elizabeth [AUSTIN], m/2 Samuel HILL b 1690; b 1682; Boston
COBHAM, Josiah (-1705, Boston) & Mary [HALFIELD/HARFFIELD?/HAFFIELD] (?1618-); b
     1640; Salisbury/Boston/Ipswich
COBHAM, Josiah² & Deborah _?_; b 1672?, b 1676; Boston
COBLEIGH/COBLEY, John & Mary [BOSWORTH] (1647-); b 1672(3?); Swansea
COCHRANE/COCKRANE/COCKERUN, William (returned to Eng) & [Christian] [IBROOK]; b
     1635; Hingham
COCKCROFT, Jonathan & Joanna _?_; b 1687; Boston
COCKER, Robert & _?_; b 12 Jul 1642
COCKER, Thomas & Sarah WALDREN; 3 Apr 1697; Boston
COCKERILL, William (-1661), fisherman & Elizabeth _?_ (prob not IBROOK) (-1664) (had daus
     Mary, Susanna, Elizabeth); b 1630 in Salem by 1651; Hingham/Marblehead/Salem
COCKSHOTT, James (-1693) & Elizabeth _?_ (-1700); Haddam, CT
CODDINGTON, John (-1655) & Emma _?_; m/2 John JEPSON/JEPHSON 1656; b 1651, b 1649?;
     Boston
CODDINGTON, John (1654-), Boston & 1/wf Anne/Hannah [GARDNER] (-1690), dau Richard;
     ca 1675/80?; Charlestown/Woodbridge, NJ
CODDINGTON, Nathaniel (1653-1724) & Susanna [HUTCHINSON] (1649-); b 1677; Newport
CODDINGTON/CUDDINGTON?, Stockdale (-1650) & Hannah _?_ (-1644, "aged"); Roxbury/
     Hampton, NH
CODDINGTON, Thomas (1655-1694?) & 1/wf Priscilla [JEFFERAY] (1654-1688); b 1684, b 18
     Sep 1682; Newport
CODDINGTON, Thomas (-1693?), RI & 2/wf Mary HOWARD, NY, m/2 Anthony MORRIS 1695,
     1694; 22 Jan 1689, 22 Feb 1689; ?Newport
CODDINGTON, William¹ (1601, 1602, 1603?-1678) & 1/wf Mary [BURT] (-1630) (see below); in
     Eng, b 1627, 1625?; Boston/Newport

CODDINGTON, William[1] (1601-1678) & 2/wf Mary [MOSELEY] (-1647); in Eng, 1631±; Boston/Newport

CODDINGTON, William (1601-1678) & 3/wf Ann [BRINLEY]/VASE?/WASE? (1628-1708); 12 Jan 1649-50, ca 1648/50, ca 1650; Newport, RI

CODDINGTON, William & 1/wf Content ARNOLD (1681-); 12 Nov 1700; Newport

CODLE/CODDALE, John & Jane [WILLIAMS]; b 1684; RI

CODMAN, Robert (-1678) (called "brother" by John STEVENS 1646) & _?_ ; b 1641, b 1637?; Salem/Salisbury/Hartford/Saybrook/Edgartown

CODMAN, Stephen (-1706, ae 55) & Elizabeth RANDALL (-1708, ae 54, 53); 19 Nov 1674; Charlestown

CODMAN, _?_ & Hannah HATHAWAY, dau Arthur; b 9 Feb 1709/10, b 1701?; Dartmouth?

CODNER, Christopher (-1660) & Mary [BENNETT] (1638-), m/2 Elias WHITE 1661 (div), m/3 Richard DOWNING; b 1655; Marblehead

CODNER, Edward (-1670) & 1/wf Priscilla _?_ ; ca 1640; Saybrook, CT

CODNER, Edward (-1670) & 2/wf Alice (CRANSDEN) [HAND], w John; aft 1660, 1663?; New London, CT/East Hampton, LI

CODNER, Gregory & Lucy (BAND) ROWLAND, w Richard; 5 Dec 1692; Marblehead

CODNER, John & 1/wf? Elizabeth _?_ ; b 1659; Marblehead

CODNER, John (1625-1710) & Joan (BARTOL) [CHAPMAN], w Edward/Edmond; b 1664; ?Marblehead

CODNER, Lawrence & Sarah _?_ ; b 1664?; New London, CT

CODNER, Peter & Rachel [NEIGHBORS], m/2 _?_ /John? PASCO; b 1674; Boston

CODNER, Richard, Swansea & Phebe BARTON; 23 May 1671; Warwick, RI/Newport

CODNER, Robert & Susanna ASHTON; 14 Oct 1684; Marblehead

CODNER, William & Sarah/Susanna YOUNG; 21 Nov 1697; Boston

COE, Andrew & Deborah [LYON], m/2 William PROBY; ca 1685; Rye, NY

COE, Benjamin (1629?-) & Abigail [CARMAN] (1625-), m/2 Daniel WHITEHEAD; b 1660; Hempstead, LI/?Jamaica, LI

COE, Benjamin (1660?-) & 1/wf _?_ [?WHITEHEAD]; b 1685; Jamaica, LI

COE, Benjamin (1660?-) & 2/wf Mary [EVERETT] (ca 1679-1763), m/2 James WHEELER; ca 1700; Jamaica, LI

COE, John (?1626-) & _?_ ; b 1655; Stamford, CT/Stratford, CT/Greenwich, CT

COE, John & ?Mary/?Margaret [?MEACOCK]; b 1657; Newtown, LI

COE, John (1649-1728) & Sarah PABODIE (1656-1740), m/2 Caesar CHURCH; 10 Nov 1681; Duxbury/Little Compton, RI

COE, John (1656-1741), Rye, NY, & Mary HAWLEY (1663-1731); 20 Dec 1682; Stratford, CT

COE, Jonathan & Esther _?_ (-1758); ca 1700; Newtown, LI

COE, Matthew & Elizabeth WAKLY/WAKELEY; 15 Jun 1647; Glouchester/Falmouth, ME

COE, Robert (1596-1672+) (?brother-in-law of Richard CRABB) & 1/wf Mary _?_ ; in Eng, ca 1623; Watertown

COE, Robert (1596-) & 2/wf Anna/Hannah DEARSLAY (1591-); Assington, Eng, 29 Apr 1630; Watertown/Wethersfield, CT

COE, Robert (1626-1659) & Hannah [MITCHELL]? (1631-1702), m/2 Nicholas ELSEY; ca 1650; Stratford, CT

COE, Robert (1596-) & 3/wf Jane (_?_) (SMITH) ROUSE, w John, w Edward; m lic 15 Feb 1674/5; LI

COE, Robert (-1734, ae 75) & [Elizabeth?] _?_ (-1733?); b 1701; Newtown, LI

COFFIN, Ebenezer (1678-1730) & Eleanor BARNARD; 12 Dec 1700; Nantucket

COFFIN, Edward (1669-) & Ann [GARDNER]; b 1701, no issue; Salem

COFFIN, Enoch (1678-1761) & Beulah [EDDY] (ca 1684-); ca 1700, bef 1702; Nantucket

COFFIN, James (1639-) & Mary SEVERANCE; 3 Dec 1663; Salisbury/Nantucket

COFFIN, James (1659-) & Florence HOOKE; 16 Nov 1685; Newbury

COFFIN, James (-1741) & 1/wf Love [GARDNER] (1672-1691); ?ca 1691; Nantucket

COFFIN, James (-1741) & Ruth GARDNER (1676/7-1748); 19 Mar 1692, 14 May; Nantucket

COFFIN, Jethro (1663-1726) & Mary [GARDNER] (1670-1727?); [ca] 1686; Nantucket/Salisbury

COFFIN, John (1647-1711), Edgarton & Deborah [AUSTIN] (-1718); [1668]; Nantucket

COFFIN, John (-1717) & Hope [GARDNER] (1669-1750); [1692]; Nantucket

COFFIN, Nathaniel (1671-1721) & Damaris GAYER (1673-1764); 17 Oct 1692; Charlestown/Nantucket
COFFIN, Nathaniel (?1669-1749) & Sarah (BROCKLEBANK) DOLE (-1750), w Henry; 29 Mar 1693; Newbury
COFFIN, Peter (-1627/8, in Eng) & Joan [KEMBER] (1584-1661); in Eng, b 1600; Salisbury
COFFIN, Peter (1630-1715) & Abigail [STARBUCK]; ca 1655, near 1657, b 1657; Dover, NH/Salisbury/Exeter, NH
COFFIN, Peter (1666-1699) & Elizabeth STARBUCK (1665-), m/2 Nathaniel BARNARD, Jr.; 15 Aug 1682; Nantucket
COFFIN, Peter (1667-1746) & Apphia [DOLE] (1668-); b 1688(9?), b 1688; Gloucester
COFFIN, Peter (1673, 1671-) & 1/wf Christian (GARD) CONDY, w William; m int 18 Jul 1695; Boston/Nantucket
COFFIN, Robert (1667-1710) & Joanna GILMAN (1679-1720), m/2 Henry DYER aft 1710; b 1701?, no issue; Exeter, NH
COFFIN, Seaborn & _?_ ; b 1656; Windsor, CT
COFFIN, Stephen (1652-1734) & Mary [BUNKER] (-1724); ca 1668/9, 1669, [b 1671]; Nantucket
COFFIN, Stephen (1664-1725) & Sarah ATKINSON; 8 Oct 1685; Newbury/Haverhill/Nantucket
COFFIN, Stephen (1676-1725) & Experience LOOK; 21 Sep 1693, 21 Nov; Nantucket/Martha's Vineyard
COFFIN, Tristram (1605, 1609?-1681) & Dionis STEVENS (1616-1681(2?)); in Eng, ca 1629; Salisbury/Newbury/Nantucket
COFFIN, Tristram (1632-1704) & Judith (GREENLEAF) SOMERBY (1626-1705), w Henry; 2 Mar 1652/[3]; Newbury
COFFIN, Tristram (1665-) & Deborah COLCORD (1664-); ca 1684
COFFIN, William (-1709) & Sarah [ABORNE]; b 1691; Salem
COGGIN, Henry (-1649) & Abigail [BISHOP], m/2 John PHINNEY/FINNEY 1650; b 1637; Barnstable
COGGAN, John[1] (-1658) & 1/wf Anne _?_ ; b 1636; Boston
COGGAN, John[1] (-1658) & 2/wf Mary _?_ (-24 Jan 1651/2); Boston
COGGAN, John[1] (-1658) & 3/wf Martha (RAINSBOROUGH) (COYTMORE) WINTHROP (-1660, suicide), w Thomas, w John; 10-1-1651, 10 Mar 1651/2; Boston
COGGAN, John (1643-) & Mary LONG (-1681); 22 Dec 1664; Charlestown
COGGIN, John (1666-) & Elizabeth RICHARDSON; 12 Apr 1692; Woburn
COGGAN, Thomas (-1653) & Joanna _?_ , m/2 Obadiah MILLER/MILLARD; Barnstable/Taunton
COGGESHALL, Daniel (1665-) & Mary MOWRY/MOREY; 23 Oct 1689, ?23 Aug; Jamestown, RI
COGGESHALL, Freegift (1657-) & Elizabeth MATTHEWS (1664-1748); 31 Dec 1684, ?Yarmouth; Newport
COGGESHALL, James (1660-1712) & Mary [BULL] (1661/3-1754), dau Henry; ca 1685?; Newport
COGGESHALL, John (1601-1647) & Mary [?HOLMES] (1604-1684); in Eng, b 1620; Roxbury/Boston/Portsmouth, RI/Newport
COGGESHALL, John (?1618, ?1620-1708) & 1/wf Elizabeth BAULSTONE, m/2 Thomas GOULD 1655?; 17 Jun 1647, div 25 May 1655; Portsmouth, RI
COGGESHALL, John (?1618, ?1620-1708) & 2/wf Patience THROCKMORTON (?1640-7 Sep 1676); Dec 1655; ?Newport
COGGESHALL, John (1649-) & Elizabeth TIMBERLAKE; 24 Dec 1669, 1670?; Portsmouth, RI
COCKSHALL, John (?1620-1708), RI & 3/wf Mary (HEDGE) STURGES (1648-), w Samuel; 1 Oct 1679; Yarmouth
COGGESHALL, John (1659-1727) & Mary [STANTON] (1668-1747); b 1687; Portsmouth, RI
COGGESHALL, John (1673-) & Mary SLOCUM? (1675/6-); Mar 1696/7, 18? Mar; Portsmouth, RI
COGGESHALL, Joshua (-1688) & 1/wf Joan WEST (1635-1676); 22 Dec 1652; Portsmouth, RI
COGGESHALL, Joshua (-1688) & 2/wf Rebecca RUSSELL, m/2 Thomas HARFORD; 21 Jul 1677, 22? Jan; Portsmouth, RI
COGGESHALL, Joshua & 1/wf Sarah (GEORGE) GRIFFIN (-20 Mar 1697), w Benjamin (doubtful); ?13 May 1681, 1st ch b same day; Portsmouth, RI
COGGESHALL, Joshua & 2/wf Sarah _?_ ; 1st ch b 1698, 20 Aug 1697, 26 Aug 1697; Portsmouth, RI

COGGESHALL, William (1654±-) & Rachel __?_; b 1671?, b 1677?; Portsmouth, RI
COGSWELL, Adam (1666/7-1749) & [Abigail] __?_; b 1687; Ipswich
COGSWELL, John (1592-1669) & Elizabeth THOMPSON (-1676); in Eng, 10 Sep 1615; Ipswich
COGSWELL, John (1622-1653) & __?_ (-1652); b 1648; Ipswich
COGSWELL, John & Margaret GIFFORD; 22 Jul 1674; Ipswich
COGSWELL, John (1665-) & Hannah [GOODHUE] (1673-), m/2 Thomas PERLEY; b 1693; Ipswich
COGSWELL, Jonathan (1661-1717) & Elizabeth WAINWRIGHT (1667-1723); 24 May 1686; Ipswich
COGSWELL, Samuel & Susannah HAVEN/HEARN?; 27 Oct 1668; Saybrook, CT
COGSWELL, Wastall/Westall (1674-1709) & 1/wf Hannah __?_, m/2 __?_ BECKWITH?; b 1697?; Saybrook, CT
COGSWELL, Westall (1674-) & 2/wf Martha __?_ (-1705); 24 May 1697; Lyme, CT/Saybrook, CT
COGSWELL, William (1619-1700) & Susannah/Elizabeth? [HAWKES] (1633-); b 1650; Ipswich
COGSWELL, William & Martha EMERSON; 9 Oct 1685; Ipswich
COIT, Job (1661-1690) & Hannah HAYWARD?/ELLERY? (1666, 1667?, 1661-1710+?), m/2 William CARD 1693; b 1689; Gloucester
COIT, John (-1659) & Mary GANNERS?/JENNERS? (-1676, ae 80); b 1632; Gloucester
COIT, John (-1663) & Mary STEVENS, m/2 John FITCH 1667; 21 Sep 1652; Gloucester
COIT, John (1670-1744) & Mehitable CHANDLER (1673-1758), m/2 John GARDNER?; 25 Jun 1695, 5? Jun; Woodstock, CT/New London
COIT, Joseph (1643-1704) & Martha HARRIS (-1710), Wethersfield; 17 Jul 1667, 13? Jul, 15? Jul; New London
COIT, Nathaniel (1659-) & 1/wf Elizabeth DAVIS (-1700); 16 Feb 1686/7; Gloucester
COIT, William (-1703) & Sarah CHANDLER (-1711), m/2 John GARDINER; 9 Jun 1697; Woodstock, CT/New London, CT
COITMORE, Rowland (-1626, in Eng) & 2/wf Katherine (MILES/MYLES) GRAY (-1659), w Thomas; in Eng, Harwich, 23 Dec 1610; Charlestown
COITMORE, Thomas (-1644) & Martha RAINSBOROUGH (-1666), m/2 John WINTHROP 1647, m/3 John COGGAN 1652; Wapping, Eng, 14 Jun 1635, 24 Jun?; Charlestown
COKER, Benjamin (1650-1705) & Martha PEARLY/PERLEY; 31 May 1678; Newbury
COKER, Benjamin (1671-) & Anne PRICE; 24 Nov 1692; Newbury
COKER, Joseph (1640-) & 1/wf Sarah (HATHORNE) HELWISE (-1688) (div wf of Edward HELWISE); 13 Apr 1665; Newbury
COKER, Joseph & 2/wf Mary (JONES) [WOODBRIDGE] (-1714), w Thomas; b 1701?, ca 1695?; Newbury
COKER, Robert (1606-1680) & Catherine __?_ (-1678); b 1640; Newbury
COLBURN, Benjamin & 1/wf Abiah/Abiel? [FISHER] (1656-1688); 5 Mar 1684, 5 Mar 1684/5; Dedham/Medfield
COLBURN, Benjamin & Bethia [BULLEN] (1664-), m/2 __?_ DREW; b 1689; Dedham
COBORN, Daniel (1654-) & Sarah BLOOD (1658-1741); 18 Jun 1685; Chelmsford/Concord
COLBOURN, Daniel & Elizabeth CONANT; m int 21 Sep 1700; Beverly
COBORN, Edward (1618-) & Hannah [ROLFE?]; b 1642; Ipswich
COLEBOURNE, Edward & Katherin [FORBUSH]; 20 Feb 1686/7; Westchester, NY
COBURN, Edward & 1/wf Sarah HAWARD/HAYWARD; 12 Jan 1692/3, 29 Mar 1694; Marblehead/Beverly
COBORN, Ezra (1658-1739) & Hannah VARNAM (1661-), Ipswich; 22 Nov 1681; Chelmsford/Dracut
COLEBORNE, Henry & Sarah GOLT/GAULT; Dec 1665; Salem
COBORN, John (-1695) & 1/wf Susannah READ, Salem; ?10 Mar 1671, ?18 Mar 1671, 1670/1; Chelmsford/Salem
COLBORN, John (1648-1706) & Experience LEALAND/LELAND (?1654, 1656-1708); 25 Jun 1674; Medfield/Dedham
COBORN, John (-1695) & 2/wf Elizabeth __?_/[?RICHARDSON] (-1740); b 1679; Chelmsford
COBURN, John (-1737) & Johanna [DUNKEN], Billerica; b 1701; Dracut
COBORN, Joseph (1661-1733) & 1/wf Hannah __?_ (-1721); b 1684; Chelmsford
COALBURN, Joseph & Mary [HOLBROOK]; b 1687; Dedham
COLEBORNE, Nathaniel (-1691) & Priscilla CLARKE (-1692); 25 Jul 1639; Dedham

COLEBURNE, Nathaniel & 1/wf Mary BROOKS (1649-1708); 19 Nov 1669; Dedham

COBURN, Robert (1608-1685(-)) & Alice _?_ (1608-); Ipswich

COLBURN, Robert (?1647-1701, Concord) & Mary BISHOP (1651-), m/2 Eliphalet FOX, m/3 Joseph LEE, m/4 Daniel HOAR; 16 Mar 1669; Beverly/Chelmsford

COALBURNE, Samuel (1655-1694) & Mary/?Mercy PATERIDG/PARTRIDGE, m/2 Cornelius FISHER; 12 March 1682/3; Dedham

COBORN, Thomas (1648±-1728), Dracut & 1/wf Hannah ROUF/ROLFE; 6 Aug 1672; ?26 Aug; Chelmsford

COBORN, Thomas (1648-1728) & 2/wf Mary RICHARDSON (1662-); 17 Nov 1681; Chelmsford

COBORN, Thomas & Mary [FARWELL] (?1680-1739); b 1700; Dunstable

COLEBORNE/?COLBRON, William (-1662) & [Margery] _?_ (-1662+); b 1628; Boston

COLBY, Anthony (-1661) & Susanna ?NUTTING/?SARGENT/?HADDON [WATERMAN], wid; m/3 William WHITRIDGE 1669?; b 1633; Boston/Salisbury

COLBY, Isaac (1640-1684) & Martha [PARRAT] (1649-1730); b 1669(70?); Haverhill/Rowley

COLEBY, John & Frances HOYT, m/2 John BARNARD 1676; 14 Jan 1655, 1655/6; Salisbury/Amesbury

COLBY, John & Sarah (OSGOOD?) ELDRIDGE; 25 Dec 1675; Amesbury

COLBY, Samuel (ae 53 in 1693) & Elizabeth [SARGENT]; b 1670, b 1668?; Amesbury/Haverhill

COLBEY, Samuel & Dorothy [AMBROSE]; b 1694; Amesbury

COLBY, Thomas (1651-) & Hannah ROWELL (1653-), m/2 Henry BLAISDELL ca 1691; 16 Sep 1674; Amesbury

COLBY, Thomas & Mary ROWELL; 21 Nov 1688; Amesbury

COLBEY, Thomas & Frances _?_ ; b 1699; Amesbury

COLCORD, Edward (-1682) (ae 43 in 1659, ae 56 in 1673) & Ann [WADD?]/[NUDD?]; b 1640, b 1656; Salem/Dover, NH

COLCORD, Samuel (1656-1736) & Mary [AYER] (1660/1-1739); ca 1681, b 1682; Hampton, NH/Kingston, NH

COLDHAM, Clement & _?_ ; b 1622?; Lynn

COLDOM, Clement (1623-1703, ae 80) & Mary [PEIRCE] (-1705); b 1647; Gloucester

COULDUM, Thomas (-1675, ae 86) & Joanna _?_ ; b 1623; Lynn

COLE, Abraham & Mary EDGEWOOD; 15 Mar 1666/7, 15 Jan 1666/7; Hampton, NH

COLE, Abraham & Sarah DAVIS; 11 Jun 1670; Salem

COLE, Abraham & Ann TOWNSEND, w Peter; 30 Sep 1697; Boston

COAL, Alexander & Bethia (PITMAN) SELSBY/SILSBEE, w Henry; 15 Sep 1680; Marblehead

COLE, Alexander & Bethiall HILL; b 1688; Salem

COLE, Ambrose & Silence _?_ ; b 1693; Scituate

COLE, Arthur (-1676) & Lydia (_?_) BARRETT, w Thomas, m/3 William EAGER 1680, m/4 Reuben LUXFORD, m/5 Nathaniel BILLINGS 1709; 27 Nov 1673; Cambridge

COLE, Daniel (1614-1694, ae 80) & Ruth [COLLIER]? (1627-1694, ae 67); b 1644; Eastham

COLE, Daniel (-1692) & Mahershallalhashbaz [GORTON]; ca 1662; Providence/Pawtucket, RI

COLE, Daniel, Jr. (1664-1736) & Mercy [FREEMAN] (1673-1735), dau Samuel; no issue; Eastham

COLE, Daniel, Jr. (-1713) (son Job?) & Mercy [FULLER] (-1712+); by 1 Oct 1695; Eastham

COLE, Dennis (-1688) & Marie LINDLE; 5 Jul 1672; Stonington, CT

COLE, Ebenezer (1671-1719) & Mehitable [LUTHER]; b 1699, 1697?; Swansea/Warren, RI

COLE, Ephraim & Rebecca GRAY; 3 Jan 1687; Plymouth

COLE, Francis & Sarah _?_ ; b 1689; Boston

COLE, George (-1653) & Mary _?_ ; Lynn

COLE/COLESWORTHY, Gilbert & Frances _?_ ; b 1678, b 1672?, b 1666; Boston

COLE, Henry (-1676) & Sarah RUSCO, m/2 Robert BULL b 1679; 10 Dec 1646; Hartford

COLE, Henry (1647-) & Mary _?_ ; b 1673?; Middletown, CT

COLE, Henry (-1716) & Mary _?_ ; b 1687; Boston

COLE, Hugh (-1699/1700) & 1/wf Mary FOXWELL (1635-); 8 Jan 1654; Plymouth/Swansea

COLE, Hugh (1658-1738, Warren, RI) & Deborah BUCKLAND (1660-1724); 6 May 1681; Swansea

COLE, Hugh (-1699/1700) & 2/wf Elizabeth (LETTICE) (SHURTLEFF) COOK (-1693), w William, w Jacob; 1 Jan 1688/9; Plymouth

COLE, Hugh (-1699/1700) & 3/wf Mary (SHELLEY) (HARLOW) MORTON (1669-), w William, w Ephraim; 30 Jan 1693/4; Plymouth

COLE, Isaac (-1674) & Joane?/Joanna _?_ (1600?-), wid?, w James **BRITTON**; b 1631; Boston/Charlestown

COLE, Isaac (-1674) (ae 58 in 1664) & Jane _?_ **EGGLETON BRITTON** (-1687) (ae 74 in 1674), w _?_, w James; 1 Feb 1659, 1658/9, no issue, 1 Feb 1658; Woburn

COLE, Israel (1653-1724) & Mary **(PAINE) ROGERS** (-1710+), w James; 24 Apr 1679; Eastham

COLE, Jacob (-1678) & Sarah **TRAINE** (-ca 1712); 12 Oct 1669; Charlestown

COLE, James & Mary [LOVEL/deLOVEL?/**LOBEL**?] (-1660); ca 1623/25?, b 1628, Plymouth/Duxbury/Middleboro/Swansea

COLE, James & 1/wf ?Frances **MUNTER**/_?_ (d in Eng); in Eng, b 1638, b 1636?, b 1635, 9 Nov 1623, St. Botloph's, Bishopsgate; Hartford

COLE, James & 2/wf? Damaris **SEABROOK**

COLE, James (-1652) & 2/wf 3/wf Ann/?Agnes [**EDWARDS**] (-1679), w Richard; in Eng, b 1639, 6 Dec 1625, St. Dunstan's, Stefney; Hartford

COLE, James, Jr. (?1625-1709) & Mary **TILSON** (-1660); 23 Dec 1652; Plymouth

COLE, James (London in 1654) & Ruth _?_, m/2 Henry **MUDD** 1655+; ca 1653?; Charlestown

COLE, James (1655-) & Mary _?_; ca 1676; Swansea

COLE, James & 2/wf Abigail **DAVENPORT** (-1710?); b 1679, 1654, b 1660; Plymouth

COLE, James & Susanna _?_; b 1680, b 1689; Swansea

COLE, James (1655-) & Hannah **CHILDS**; 10 Jan 1683/4; Eastham/Harwich

COLE, Job (-1670+) & Rebecca **COLLIER** (1610-1698 ae 88); 15 May 1634, 16? May; Plymouth?/Duxbury/Yarmouth/Eastham

COLE, John & Joan _?_; b 1641/2, [ca 1640]; Boston

COLE, John (-1686, 1685) & Mary _?_; in Eng, b 1645, b 1647, b 1646(7?); Hartford/Farmington

COLE, John & _?_; b 1651; Wells, ME/Cape Porpoise

COLE, John (1625-1707) & Susanna **HUTCHINSON** (1633-); 30 Dec 1651; Boston/Kingston, RI

COLES, John (-1665, 1675?) (ae 42 in 1663) & Ann _?_; ca 1654?; ?Oyster Bay, LI

COLE, John & Ursula **CHAMBERLAIN** (1633-prob 1656/7); b 1658, ca 1655; Charlestown

COLE/CALL, John, Charlestown & Hannah **KETTLE**; 22 Jan 1656

COLE, John (-1661) & Mary **CHILSON**; 23 Dec 1658; Saco, ME

COLE, John & _?_; b 1664; Milford, CT

COLE, John (-1689) & Rachel _?_; b 1665; Farmington, CT/Hartford

COLE, John (1644-1725/6) (ae 27 in 1671) & Ruth **SNOW** (?1646-1717); 12 Dec 1666, 10 Dec 1666; Eastham/Duxbury/Yarmouth

COLE, John (-1703) & Mary **KNIGHT**; 28 May 1667; Salem

COLE, John (-1677) & Elizabeth **RYDER**, m/2 Thomas **BOARDMAN** (had John & Eliz. COLE); 21 Nov 1667; Plymouth

COLE, John & Mehitable _?_/[**HART**?] (see John, Jr.); b 1669, b 1688; Gloucester

COLE, John & _?_ (-1678); b 1672; Groton

COLE, John & _?_; b 1675; Charlestown (from Groton)

COLES, John & Ann _?_, m/2 William **LINES** b 1693?; b 1672?, b 1683; Oyster Bay, LI

COLE, John & Mary [**GALLOP**]; b 1684; Boston

COLE, John (1660-1724, Plympton) & 1/wf Patience [**BARBER**]?; ca 1685, b 1697; Plymouth

COLE, John & Sarah **ASLETT**?/**ALBREE**?/**ALSBEE**? (1662-1728+); ca 1675, b 1687, b 1675 & 1686; Malden/Lynn/Salem/Boxford

COLE, John (1660-1748) & 1/2/wf Susannah [**GRAY**] (1668-1727); b 1689, b 1697, 1688? (mix up about two Johns); Swansea/Warren, RI/Plympton

COLE, John (1668-1737) & Mary [**EATON**?] (?1669-1746); 24 Dec 1691; Reading/Boxford

COLE, John, Jr. & Mehitable [**LOOMIS**]; Jun 1691, 5 Jan 1691?, 1692; Farmington, CT

COLE, John & Mary **LEWIS** (1677-); 10 Jun 1693; Rehoboth/Swansea

COLE, John (1670-1746) & Mary [**ROGERS**] (1675-1732), dau James; b 1694; Eastham

COLE, John & Elizabeth **ALLEN**; 23 Sep 1700; Kittery, ME

COLE, Joseph & Sarah [**RANDALL**] (1666-), m/2 Thomas **WEST**; b 1698; ?Beverly

COLE, Joseph & Abigail **ROYCE**; 13 Jul 1699; Wallingford, CT

COLES, Joseph (1675-1767), ?Musketa Cove & Elizabeth [**WRIGHT**]; b 1701, ?ca 1704; Oyster Bay, LI

COLE, Matthew (-1665) & Susanna **CUNLIFF/CANLIFF** (1645-), m/2 John **WEBB**, Jr. 1665; 16 Jul 1663; Northampton

COLES, Nathan & Rachel [?**HOPKINS**]; 21 Feb 1690/1

COLES, Nathaniel (1640-1712±), Oyster Bay & 1/wf Martha JACKSON (-1668), dau Robert; 30 Aug 1667; Warwick, RI

COLES, Nathaniel (1640-1712±) & 2/wf Deborah [WRIGHT]; aft 17 Dec 1668; Oyster Bay, LI

COLE, Nathaniel (-1708) & 1/wf Lydia DAVIS (-1683, Hartford); Nov 1676; Hartford, CT

COLE, Nathaniel & Sarah [?BOUNEY]/[?THOMAS]; b 1680; Duxbury

COLES, Nathaniel (1668-1705) & Rose [WRIGHT] (-1712), m/2 John TOWNSEND 1709, m/3 Samuel BIRDSALL; ?ca 1687/90

COLE, Nathaniel (-1708/9) & 2/wf Mary BENTON, m/2 Jonathan BIGELOW; 23 Oct 1684; Wethersfield, CT/Hartford

COLES, Nathaniel (1640-1712) & 3/wf Sarah [?HARCURT], m/2 John ROGERS 1714; b 1696; Oyster Bay, LI

COLE, Nicholas (1626-1678+) & Jane _?_ (-1668+); b 1656; Wells, ME

COLE, Nicholas (1656-1729+) & Mary _?_ ; b 1701?; Wells, ME

COLE, Philip & Mary _?_ ; b 1698/9; Amesbury

COLE, Rice & Arrold _?_ (-1661); b 1621; Charlestown

COLE, Richard & Dorcas _?_ ; b 1696; Boston

COLE, Robert & Mary [HAWXHURST], m/2 Matthias HARVEY; ca 1630; Roxbury/Providence/Warwick, RI

COLE, Robert & Phillip _?_, m/2 William MORRIS; b 1629; Charlestown

COLES, Robert (-1676) & Ann _?_ ; ca 1654

COLES, Robert (-1715) & Mercy WRIGHT (-1708); 1 Jan 1670; Oyster Bay, LI

COLE, Robert & Anne [?STAINES]; b 1680; Boston

COLE, Sampson & Elizabeth [WEEDEN]; b 1674; Boston

COLE, Samuel (-1667) & 1/wf Ann _?_ ; in Eng, b 1625; Boston

COLE, Samuel (-1667) & 2/wf Margaret [GREENE] (-31 Sep 1658+); b 30 Sep 1647; Boston

COLE, Samuel (-1667) & 3/wf Ann/Anna?/Anne (MANSFIELD) KEAYNE; 16 Oct 1660, prob 1659; Boston

COLE, Samuel (-1694) & Mary _?_ ; b 1673; Hartford

COLE, Samuel (-1718) & Lydia [SMITH]; 25 Sep 1679; Wethersfield, CT

COLE, Samuel (-1717) & _?_ ; Harwich

COLE, Samuel, Jr. (-1766) & Mary _?_ ; Harwich

COLE, Samuel & Mary KINGSBURY, Plainfield; 2 Jan 1693, [1692/3]; Hartford

COLES, Samuel & Elizabeth [ALBERTSON]; b 1700; ?Oyster Bay, LI

COLE, Solomon & Mary [WEEDEN?] (1660?-); b 1681, b 1678?; Beverly

COLE, Thomas (-1679) & Ann _?_ (-1680); in Eng, b 1635; Salem

COLE, Thomas (-1696) & Abigail _?_ (-1696); b 1688?, b 1684-5?; Wells, ME

COLE, Thomas & Lydia [REMICK] (1676-); b 1701; Eastham

COLE, Timothy (1642-) & _?_ (had Timothy & Daniel); Eastham

COLE/COLLES, Tobiah (-1664?) & _?_ ; b 1661; Woburn

COLE, William & Elizabeth [DOUGHTY]; b 1625; Taunton

COLE, William & _?_ ; b 1626

COLE, William (-1644) & Elizabeth [DOUGHTY]; ca 1637?

COLE, William & Ann _?_ ; b 1653; Boston

COLE, William (1574-1662) & Eunice _?_ (-1680); b 1656, b 1647; Wells, ME, Hampton, NH

COLE, William (1663?-) & Hannah SNOW (1666-1737); 2 Dec 1686; Eastham

COLE, William & Martha _?_ ; b 1687; Boston

COLE/COOK, William & Sarah [CONGER], m/2 Jeremiah SMITH; 27 Jul 1688; 27 Jul 16[--]; Wallingford, CT

COLE, William & Mary _?_ ; b 1700; Boston

COLE, William (1671-1734) & [Ann PINDER]; b 1701?; Kings Town, RI

COLE, _?_ & Elizabeth [BURCH], w George; aft 22 Nov 1672, b 1719

COLE, _?_ & Margaret [JENKINS]; b 5 Jul 1703

COLE, _?_ & Willmet _?_, m/2 Jerwin ROOTES

COLE, _?_ & Alice [ALBAN]

COLEBROOK, _?_ & _?_ ; b 1675; Salem

COLEMAN, Benjamin & 1/wf Jane CLARK; at London?, 8 Jun 1700; Boston

COLEMAN, Edward (-1691), Boston & Margaret LOMBARD (-1691+); 27 Oct 1648; Eastham

COLEMAN, Edward & Katherin FOOREBUSH; 20 Feb 1687/8; Newtown, LI

COLEMAN, Ephraim & Susannah __?__ ; b 1701; Newbury
COLEMAN, Henry & Mary MEADS; m lic Dec 1691
COLEMAN, Henry & Eleanor HUNT; m lic 27 Jul 1698
COLEMAN, Isaac (1672-1752) & 1/wf Ann [REYNOLDS]; b 1701?, no issue; Nantucket
COLEMAN, Jabez (1669-) & Mary PRESCOTT (1677-), m/2 Thomas CROSBY, m/3 James BEAN; 2 Nov 1699; Hampton, NH/Kingston, NH
COLEMAN, James & Mehitable [HINSDALE], wid; b 1672; ?Medfield
COLEMAN, James & Sarah __?__ ; b 1672(3?); Ipswich
COLEMAN, James (-1714) & Patience [COBB] (1668-), m/2 Thomas LOMBARD; b 1695; Barnstable
COLEMAN, John (-1711) & 1/wf Hannah PORTER (1642-1677); 29 May 1663; Hadley
COLEMAN, John (1644-1716, 1715?) & Joanna [FOLGER] (-1719); b 1667; Nantucket
COLEMAN, John (1635-1711) & 2/wf Mehitable (JOHNSON) (HINSDALE) ROOT (1644-), w Samuel, w John; 16 Mar 1678/9, 11 Mar 1679; Hatfield/Northampton
COLEMAN, John & Judith HABBEY/HOBBEY (1674-); 19 Jul 1694; Boston
COLEMAN, John (1667-1762) & Priscilla [STARBUCK] (?1626-1762); b 1695, b 1705; Nantucket
COLEMAN, John (-1703) & Hannah WRIGHT; 24 Apr 1695; Wethersfield, CT
COLEMAN, John (1635-1711) & 3/wf Mary (DAY) (ELY) STEBBINS (1641-1725), w Samuel, w Thomas; 11 Dec 1696; Springfield/Hadley/Deerfield/Longmeadow/Wethersfield, CT
COLEMAN, Joseph (-1674/5) & Sarah __?__ ; in Eng, b 1629; Charlestown/Hingham/Scituate/Norwich, CT
COLEMAN, Joseph (-1690) & Ann [BUNKER]; b 1673; Nantucket
COLEMAN, Noah (-1676) & Mary CROW, m/2 Peter MONTAGUE 1680; 27 Dec 1666; Hadley/Wethersfield, CT
COLEMAN, Noah (1671-1711) & Hannah __?__ (-1765); b 1701(2?), b 1703; Hatfield/Colchester, CT/Wethersfield, CT
COLEMAN, Thomas (1598-1674) & 1/wf __?__ (-1640, 1641); b 1635?; Wethersfield, CT
COLEMAN, Thomas (1602-1685) & [Susannah] __?__ (-1650); b 1635, b 1638; Newbury/Hampton, NH/Rowley
COLEMAN, Thomas (1598-1674) & 2/wf Frances [WELLS] (-1678), w Hugh; aft 1645; Wethersfield, CT/Hadley/Hartford
COLEMAN, Thomas & 2/wf Mary (__?__) JOHNSON (-1663), w Edmund; 11 Jul 1651, 16? Jul; Newbury/Nantucket
COLEMAN, Thomas (-1682) & Margaret/Margery (FOWLER) (OSGOOD) [ROWELL], w Christopher, w Thomas, m/4 Thomas OSBORN 1682; b 1670; Salisbury/Nantucket
COLEMAN, Thomas & __?__ ; b 1681; Scituate
COLEMAN, Thomas (1669-1753) & Jane CHALLINGE, w John; b 1701?; Nantucket
COLEMAN, Tobias (?1638-) & Lydia JACKSON; 16 Apr 1668; Rowley
COLEMAN, William (1619-1680) & 1/wf __?__ (doubtful); b 1650; ?Gloucester
COLEMAN, William (1619-1680?) & 2/wf? Bridget (?JEGGLES) ROE/ROWE (-1681), w John; 14 Nov 1662, no issue; Gloucester
COLEMAN, William (1643-) & Elizabeth __?__ ; in Eng, b 1671; Boston
COLEMAN, William (?1650-1705?) & 2/wf Sarah/Mary [MAPES] (?1662-1707?); b 1680; Southold, LI
COLEMAN, William & Hannah __?__ ; b 1685; Boston
COLEMAN, William & Margaret HAYWOOD; 30 Jun 1692; Boston
COLEMAN, William^2 (1650?-) & 2/wf? Mary __?__ ; b 1698; Southold, LI
COLEMAN, Zachariah & Joanna CUDWORTH; 16 Sep 1696; Scituate
COLESWORTHY, Gilbert (-1710, ae 66) & Francis __?__ (-1702); b 1666; Boston
COLEWORTHY, John & Mary __?__ ; b 1696; Boston
COLEY, Jarbis & Mary __?__ (-22 Jan 1697, 1697/8?); Boston
COLEY, Peter (?1641-1690) & Sarah [HIDE], m/2 Thomas SHERWOOD 1695; b 1664; Fairfield, CT
COLEY, Peter (1671-) & Hannah [COUCH], m/2 Joshua HOYT; b 1700; Fairfield, CT
COLEY, Samuel (-1684) & Anne/Ann [PRUDDEN] (1618-1689, 1659); ca 1640; Milford, CT/Fairfield, CT
COLEY, Samuel (1641, bpt ?1646-) & Mary CARTES/CURTIS/CURLOS, Milford; 25 Oct 1669; Milford, CT/Fairfield, CT

COLEY, Samuel (ca 1664-1713) & 1/wf Esther [FROST] ca 1685; Fairfield
COLEY, Samuel (ca 1664-1713) & 2/wf Mary __?_; by 1702
COLEY, Thomas (1637-) & Martha [STREAME] (1654-); Milford, CT
COLFAX, Jonathan (1659/60-1711) & Sarah [EDWARDS] (1671-), m/2 Robert WEBSTER; 28 May 1696; Wethersfield, CT
COLFAX, Richard & __?_; ?1656; Newtown, LI
COLFAX, William (-1660) & Alse __?_, m/2 Alexander KEENEY; b 1653; Wethersfield, CT
COLDFAX, Zemis & Mary DAYE; 20 Aug 1666; Salem/Boston
COLGROVE/COLEGROVE, Francis (-1698) & __?_ (-1698); b 1689; ?Newport/Warwick, RI
COLLAMER, Anthony (-1693) & Sarah CHITTENDEN; 14 Jun 1666; Scituate
COLLAMORE/CULLAMORE?, Isaac & 1/wf Margaret __?_ (-13 Dec 1651; b 1638?, b 1643; Braintree/Boston
COLLAMORE/CULLAMORE?, Isaac & 2/wf Margery PAGE; 22 Jun 1651/2; Boston
COLLAMORE, Peter (1613-1684) & Mary __?_; ca 1640/50?; Scituate
COLAMER, Peter & Abigail DAVIS, Roxbury; 8 Nov 1694; Scituate/Roxbury
COLLER, James (-1749) & Elizabeth __?_; b 1696; Framingham
COLLER, John (1633-1705+) & Hannah [CUTLER]? (1638-) (doubtful); b 1661(2?); Cambridge/Boston
COLLER, John (1633-1705+) & 2/wf? Mary [?CUTLER] (1644-); b 25 Nov 1684; Watertown/Natick
COLLER, John (1661-1718) & Elizabeth __?_; b 1699; Framingham/Natick
COLOR/COLLAR/COHAR, Nathaniel (-1711), Sudbury & Mary BARRETT (1663-), Chelmsford; 10 Oct 1693; Chelmsford/Oxford
COLLICOTT, Edward (1615-) (did he marry?) & __?_; Hampton, NH
COLLICOT, Preserved (1649-) & Deborah [DOWSE] (1651-); b 1672; Boston
COLLICOT, Richard (1604-1686) & 1/wf Joan/Joanna THORNE (-5 Aug 1640); b 1640, 25 Sep 1627, Barnstaple, Eng; Dorchester/Boston/etc.
COLLICOTT, Richard (1604-1686, Boston) & 2/wf Thomasin __?_; [1640]; Dorchester/Boston/Milton/etc.
COLICUTT, Richard & Ann [PALMER?]; b 1696; Boston
COLLIER, Edward (ae 56 in 1704) & Mary __?_; b 2 Mar 1695; ?Westchester, NY
COLER, Gershom (-1753 in 80th y) & Elizabeth POOL (1678-1723); 25 Jan 1696/7; Hull
COLYER, John (-1713) & Mercy __?_ (-1748, in 82nd y); b 1693; Hull
COLLIER, Joseph (-1691) & Elizabeth [SANFORD] (1645-1695); b 1662?, b 1668, 1667, b 1667; Simsbury/Salisbury/Hartford, CT
COLLIER, Joseph (1668-) & Sarah FORBES; 15 Apr 1695; Hartford
COLLIER, Moses & 1/wf Elizabeth JONES (-10 Apr 1657); 29 Mar 1655; Hingham
COLLIER, Moses & 2/wf Elizabeth [BULLARD]; 1657, ?17 Dec 1657; Hingham/Woodbridge, NJ
COLLIER, Richard & Mary JARVIS; 25 Jan 1699; Boston
COLLIER, Thomas (-1647) & Susanna __?_ (-1667); in Eng, b 1622; Hingham
COLLIER, Thomas (-1691) & 1/wf Jane CURTIS, step dau Robert JONES; 30 Dec 1647; Hingham
COLLIER, William (-1670) & 1/wf __?_; in Eng; Duxbury
COLLIER, William (-1670) & 2/wf Jane [WALKER?/COLLINS?]; b 1635; Duxbury
COLLINS, Abraham & Phebe [FARROW] (1650-); aft 1676; Wells, ME
COLLINS, Arnold (-1735) & 1/wf Sarah __?_; b 1688; Newport
COLLINS, Arnold (-1735) & 2/wf Amy (?SMITH)/(BILLINGS) WARD (1658-), w Thomas; 16 Mar 1691/2; Newport
COLLINS, Benjamin (-1683) & Martha EATON, m/2 Philip FLANDERS 1686; 5 Nov 1668; Salisbury
COLLINS, Benjamin (-ca 1711) & 1/wf Priscilla KIRTLAND (-1676); 25 Sep 1673; Lynn/Colchester, CT
COLLINS, Benjamin & Elizabeth (LEACH) PUTNAM (1653-1730), w Samuel; 5 Sep 1677; Lynn/Colchester, CT
COLLINS, Christopher (-1666) & Jane __?_; b 1640; Boston/Braintree/Lynn
COLLINS, Daniel (1641-1690) & [Sarah] [TIBBALS], m/2 Joseph WARRINER 1691, m/3 Obadiah ABBE; 3 Jun 1677; Enfield, CT/?Derby, CT
COLLINS, Daniel (-1704) & Mary HOBARD/HIBBARD; 12 May 1691, 1692; Beverly/Salem
COLLINS, Daniel & Rebecca CLEMANS/CLEMENT; 13 Dec 1693; Boston/Watertown

COLLINS, Daniel & Ruth WILKINSON/WILKISON; 7 Dec 1694; Milford, CT
COLLINS, Daniel/David? (1677-) & Abigail THOMPSON; 8 Sep 1698; New Haven, CT
COLLINS, Ebenezer & Ann (LEATE) TROWBRIDGE (1661-1747), w John; 9 May 1696; New Haven
COLLINS, Ebenezer & Ann _?_ ; b 1696; Gloucester
COLLINS, Edward (1603-1689) & Martha _?_ (1609-1700); b 1629, b 1630?, b 1629?; Cambridge
COLLINS, Edward & Sarah BELL (1659-1678, ae 19); 1677; Boston
COLLINS, Edward & Sarah _?_ ; b 1687; Boston
COLLINS, Eleazer & Rebecca NEWHALL (1670-); m int 23 Dec 1699, ?16 Dec; Lynn
COLLINS, Elizur (1622-1683) & Sarah [WRIGHT]? (-1700±), m/2 John POTTER 1685; b 1664; Warwick, RI
COLLINS, Ezekiel & Elizabeth RIGGS; 28 Apr 1692; Gloucester
COLLINS, Francis & Elizabeth [COCKERILL]; b 1653; Medford
COLLINS, Francis (-1689) & Hannah [COCKERELL]; b 1660; Salem
COLLINS, Henry (1606-1689) & Ann _?_ (1605-1691); b 1630; Lynn/Eastham
COLLINS, Henry & [Mary] _?_ ; b 1651; Lynn
COLLINS, Henry & 1/wf Hannah LAMSON; 3 Jan 1681, 1681/2; Lynn
COLLINS, Henry & 2/wf Sarah HEIRES/EYRE?/AYRES (?1661-); 24 Jun 1685; Lynn
COLLINS, James & 1/wf Hannah _?_ ; b 1674 (see below); Gloucester
COLLINGS, James & 2/wf Hannah DUTCH; 22 Dec 1674; Ipswich/Salem
COLLINS, James & Elizabeth _?_ ; b 8 Apr 1695, b 4 Sep 1694; Boston
COLLINS, John & Joan/Joanna _?_ ; b 1636; Gloucester
COLLINS, John (ca 1610-1670) & Susan/Susannah _?_ ; b 1645, b 1644, b 1640?; Boston
COLLINS, John (-1670) & Catherine [ALLEN], w George; ca 1648, aft 2 May 1648; Boston
COLLINS, John & _?_ ; bef 1654; Milford, CT
COLLINS, John (?1632-) & Abigail [JOHNSON], dau Richard; b 1656; Lynn
COLLINS, John & Mehitable GILES (1637-), m/2 Jeremiah BUTMAN; 9 Mar 1658/9; Salem/Gloucester
COLLINS, John (?1640-1704) & 1/wf Mary [TROWBRIDGE]? (-1667?); b 1664; Boston
COLLINS, John (?1640-1704, Guilford), Branford & 2/wf Mary (STEVENS) KINGSNOTH/KINGS-NORTH, w Henry; 2 Jun 1669; Boston/Guilford, CT/Middletown, CT/Saybrook/Branford
COLLINS/COLLRIM, John (see CALLUM) & Elizabeth GUTTERSON, w William; 17 Nov 1670; Hampton, NH
COLLINS, John & Anne/Hannah _?_ (-1688); b 1677; Boston
COLLINS, John (-1732) & Mary BURCHE (1667-); 3 Dec 1688; Salem
COLLINS, John (1665-1751, ae 86) & Ann LEETE (1671-1724); 23 Jul 1691; Guilford, CT
COLLINS, John & Elizabeth [BARNARD]; b 1695; Amesbury
COLLINS, John & Jane LOYD/LLOYD; 22 Apr 1697; Boston
COLLINS, John (1673-) & Mary _?_ , m/2 James STEVENS 1701
COLLINS, John (?1640-1704) & 3/wf Dorcas (SWAIN) TAINTOR (-1704), w John; 6 Mar 1699, 1699/1700; Branford, CT
COLLINS, Joseph (1642-) & Sarah [?SILSBEE]; b 1669; Lynn
COLLINS, Joseph (-1723/4) & 1/wf Ruth KNOWLES (-1714); 20 Mar 1671/2; Eastham
COLLINS, Joseph & Sarah SILSBEE; 25 Feb 1682; Lynn
COLLINS, Joseph & Mariah SMITH; 15 Oct 1684; Lynn
COLLINGS, Joseph & Margaret DOWNING; 9 Jun 1686; Salem
COLLINS, Matthew & Naomi [DOWSE] (1653-); b 1676, b 1688 same?; Boston
COLLINS, Rev. Nathaniel (1641-1684) & Mary WHITING (1640, 1643?-1709); 3 Aug 1664; Middletown, CT
COLLINS, Nathaniel & Mary SILSBE; m int 27 Mar 1699; Lynn
COLLINGS, Paul & Mary [TOHNAN?] (1651-); b 1688; Boston
COLLINS, Richard & Mary _?_ ; b 1660; Boston
COLLINGS, Robert & Elizabeth (FOWLER) (BIRD) ROLF/Hester BIRD?, w Jathnell, w Ezra; aft 28 Sep 1652, b 1657?; Ipswich
COLLINS, Robert & 1/wf Lois BURNETT (-1704), Southampton; 24 Dec 1689; Guilford, CT
COLLINS, Samuel (ca 1636-1696) & [Mary] [MARVIN/DIXWELL] (1636-1714); ca 1662?, ca 1658; Cambridge/Middletown, CT
COLLINS, Samuel (1659-) & 1/wf Hannah _?_ (-1694); b 1682; Lynn

COLLINS, Samuel & Sarah WHITE; 16 Mar 1689, 1698, 1699; Salisbury
COLLINS, Samuel (1668-) & Susan/Susanna HENCHMAN (1667-1748, ae 80), dau Daniel, m/2 John HARRIS 1702/3; b 1693; Boston
COLLINS, Samuel (-1721+) & 2/wf Rebecca (HASSEY) HOWLAND (1662-1739?), w Joseph; 20 Aug 1695, 16 Aug 1695, 6 Aug; Lynn/Duxbury
COLLINS, Thomas (1664-1726) & 1/wf Abigail HOUSE (-1700/1707); 17 Feb 1692; Warwick, RI
COLLINS, William (-1643) & Anne? HUTCHINSON (1626-1643); 1643?, 1641?
COLLINS, William & Sarah MARETT/MORELL/MORRILL (1650-); 1 Jan 1667; New Haven
COLLINS, William & Rebecca WALLER, m/2 Thomas BOLLES
COLLINS, William (-1712) & Sarah WHITMAN, m/2 _?_ PETERSON; Apr 1697; Newport
COLLINS, _?_ & Ann _?_, m/2 John SMYTH; ?Warwick, RI
COLLINS, _?_ & Mary _?_, m/2 John SHALOTE 1696
COLLIS, John & Anna _?_ (1678-); b 1701?; Cambridge
COLLISHAWE/COWLISHHAWE, William & Ann [MORRIS]; in Eng, b 1617; Boston
COLON, Samuel & Lydia _?_; b 1696; Charlestown
COLSTON, Adam (-1687) & Mary DUSTIN/DASTIN, m/2 Cornelius BROWN 1698; 7 Sep 1668; Reading
COLSON, Nathaniel & Sarah _?_; b 1678; Newport
COLT, Abraham, Sr. & ?Dorothy _?_
COLT, Abraham & Hannah LOOMIS (1663-), Windsor; 1 Jan 1690, 1 Jul 1690; ?Windsor, CT/Glastenbury
COLT, Jabez & Mary [MORTON]; b 1701; Windsor, CT
COLT, John & Ann [SKINNER] (1636-); by 1658?, b 1655? Windsor, CT/Hartford, CT
COLT, John & Hester _?_ (living in 1666); b 1666; Pondunk, CT
COLT, John (?1655-1751, ae 90) & 1/wf [?Mary FITCH] (1658±-); ca 1678/83?; Hartford
COLT, John (?1658, 1661-1751, ae 90) & 2/wf [Sarah LORD] (-bef 2 Dec 1746); ca 1690/2, b 13 Nov 1695; Lyme, CT
COLT, Joseph (-1719?, 1721?) & Ruth LOOMIS; 29 Oct 1691; Windsor, CT
COLTON, Ephraim (1648-1713) & 1/wf Mary DRAKE (1649-1681, 1682), Windsor, CT; 17 Nov 1670; Springfield
COLTON, Ephraim (1648-1713) & 2/wf Esther MARSHFIELD (1667-1714); 26 Mar 1685; Springfield
COLTON, Ephraim & Mary NOBLE (1680-); 1 Feb 1699/1700, m int 24 Dec 1699; Longmeadow
COLTON, George[1] (-1699) & 1/wf Deborah [GARDNER]? (-1689, 1688?); ca 1644; Springfield
COLTON, George (-1699) & 2/wf Lydia (WRIGHT) (BLISS) (NORTON) LAMB (-1699), w Lawrence, w John, w John; 1 Mar 1692, 1691/2; Springfield
COLTON, Isaac (1646-1700) & Mary COOPER (1657-1742/3, 1742), m/2 Edward STEBBINS 1701; 20 Jun 1670, 30 Jun 1670; Springfield
COLTON, John (1659-1727) & 1/wf Abigail PARSONS (1666, 1667?-1689); 19 Feb 1684, 1684/5; Springfield
COLTON, John (1659-1727) & 2/wf Joanna WOLCOTT (1668-1755), Windsor, CT; 2 Sep 1690; Springfield
COLTON, Thomas (1651-1738) & 1/wf Sarah GRISWOLD (?1653-1690), Lyme, CT; 11 Sep 1677; Springfield/Lyme, CT
COLTON, Thomas (1651-1738) & 2/wf Hannah BLISS (1665-); 17 Dec 1691; Longmeadow
COLVIN, John & 1/wf Dorothy ALLAN _?_; ca 1676/7, b 1679; Sandwich/Providence/Dartmouth
COMAN/COMER?, Richard & Martha REWE; 25 Oct 1683; Marblehead
COMAN/COMER?, Richard & Elizabeth (DYNE) KALLUM/CALLUM/McCALLUM, w John; 4 Feb 1692/3; Salem
COMAN, _?_ & Mary TILTON; ?Gravesend, LI
COMAR, John & Sarah _?_; b 1662; Weymouth
COMER, John & Eleanor _?_; b 1674; Boston
COMER, John (1674-) & Mary PITTOM; 9 Feb 1698; Boston
COOMER/COMAN?, Richard (-1716, Providence) & 1/wf Martha GILBERT/Martha REWE; 23 Oct 1663, 1683, 25 Oct 1683; Salem/Marblehead
COMER/COMAN?, Richard (-1716, Providence) & 2/wf Elizabeth (DYNN/DYNE/BRANS) KALLUM/CALLUM/McCALLUM, w John; 4 Feb 1692/3; Salem/Providence
COMER, William?, Ipswich (doubtful?) & Mary STACY (1661-1701+), dau Thomas

COMY, David (-1676) & 1/wf Elizabeth _?_ (-1671, 1670/71); b 1661; Woburn/Concord
MACOMEY, David (-1676) & 2/wf Hester/Esther HARVEY, m/2 Samuel PARRY 1682; 6 Sep 1671; Charlestown
COMY, John (1665-), Concord & Martha ROE/MUNROE, Cambridge; 21 Jun 1688; Cambridge/Concord
COMPTON, John & Susanna _?_ (-1664); b 1636; Roxbury
CUMPTON, William & Mary MARTIN; 21 Apr 1663; Haverhill
COMSTOCK, Christopher (-1702) & Hannah PLATT (1643-1701+); 6 Oct 1663; ?Milford, CT/?Norwalk, CT/Fairfield, CT
COMSTOCK, Daniel (1633-1683) & Paltiah [ELDERKIN] (-1713); ca 1654?; Norwich, CT/New London, CT
COMSTOCK, Daniel/John (-1725) & 1/wf [Alea/Alice DeWOLF?]; b 1685; Lyme, CT
COMSTOCK, Daniel & 2/wf Mary (BALDWIN) NICHOLS (1653-), w Isaac; aft 1690, bef 1711; ?Lyme, CT
COMSTOCK, Daniel (1664-1694) & Elizabeth WHEELER (1667-), m/2 Samuel WELLES; 13 Jun 1692, 30 Jun 1692; ?Norwalk, CT
COMSTOCK, Daniel (1671-) & [Elizabeth] PRENTICE; 23 May 1700; New London, CT
COMSTOCK, John (-ca 1680) & Abigail [CHAPPELL] (1644-), m/2 Moses HUNTLEY 1680, 1680/1?; b 1662; Lyme/Saybrook
COMSTOCK, Kingsland (1673-) & Mary [ATWELL]; b 1697; New London, CT
COMSTOCK, Samuel (-1660(-)) & Ann _?_/TUCKER? (John SMITH); b 1654; Providence, RI
COMSTOCK, Samuel (1654-1727) & Elizabeth ARNOLD (-1747); 22 Nov 1678; Providence
COMSTOCK, Samuel & 1/wf Sarah DOUGLAS (-1704); 22 Jun 1699; ?New London, CT
COMSTOCK, William[1] & 1/wf [?Elizabeth DANIEL]; b 1621?, b 1625?; Milford, CT/New London
COMSTOCK, William[1] & 2/wf? Elizabeth _?_ (1608-); b 1659; New London, CT
COMSTOCK, William (1669-1728) & Naomi [NYLES/NILES]; 10 Sep 1695; Lyme, CT
CONANT, Exercise (1637-1722) & Sarah [ANDREWS?] (?1645-1718), gr dau Robert, dau John, niece of Thomas; ca 1663; Beverly/Boston/Mansfield/Windham, CT
CONANT, John (1650-1738) & Elizabeth _?_ (1652-1711); ca 1676?; Marblehead
CONNANT, John (1652-) & Bethia MANSFIELD (1658-1720); 7 May 1678; Beverly
CONANT, Joshua (-1659) & Seith [GARDNER?/BALCH?] (1636-1659?, 1707?), m/2 John GRAFTON 1659; b 1657; Salem
CONANT, Joshua & 1/wf Christian MORE/MOWER (1652-1680); 31 Aug 1676; Salem
CONNANT, Joshua & 2/wf Sarah NEWCOME (1670-), m/2 William ELDRIDGE 1707; 9 Jan 1690/1; Salem/Eastham/Truro
CONANT, Lot (1624-1674?) & Elizabeth [WALTON] (1629-), m/2 Andrew MANSFIELD 1681; ca 1649; Salem/Beverly/Marblehead
CONANT, Lot (1657-) & 1/wf Abigail _?_; b 1687; Beverly
CONANT, Lot & Martha CLEAVES; 16 May 1698, 15? May; Beverly
CONANT, Lot & Elizabeth PRIDE; 14 Jun 1698; Beverly
CONANT, Nathaniel (1650-1732) & Hannah [MANSFIELD] (?1655-1732+); b 1677; Beverly/Bridgewater
CONANT, Roger (1593-1679) & Sarah HORTON (-1667); 11 Nov 1618; Salem
CONANT, Roger (-1672) & Elizabeth [WESTON]; ca 1650/60?; Salem/Marblehead
CONANT, Roger (1669-1745) & Mary RAIMENT/RAYMOND; 25 Apr 1698; Beverly/Salem
CONANT, William & Mary [WOODBURY], dau John; b 1694; Beverly
CONDY, Samuel (-1678) & 1/wf Rebecca _?_; Marblehead
CONDY, Samuel (-1678) & 2/wf Ann _?_; b 1645?; Marblehead
CONDY, William (1638-1685) & 1/wf Mary [PARKER] (1643-); ca 1663; New London/Boston
CONDY, William (-1685) & 2/wf Elizabeth [WILKEY/WILKIE] (1653-1713), m/2 Andrew DOLBERRY 1689, m/3 Nathaniel THOMAS 1698; 22 Sep 1675, b 1683; Hingham/Boston
CONDEY, William & Christian [GUARD/GARD] (1670-), m/2 Peter COFFIN 1695; b 1689; Boston
CONE, Daniel (ca 1627-1706) & 1/wf Mehitable [SPENCER] (ca 1638-1691); ca 1662, b 1662(?3); Hartford/Haddam, CT
CONE, Daniel (-1706) & 2/wf Rebecca [WALKLEY], w Richard; b 4 Aug 1692; Haddam, CT
CONE, Daniel (1666-1725) & Mary GATES (1675-1742); 14 Feb 1693, 1693/4; Haddam, CT
CONE, Ebenezer (1673-1719) & Sarah [OLMSTED]; by 1696; Haddam, CT

CONE, Jared (1668-1718) & Elizabeth __?_ ; ca 1693; E. Haddam, CT
CONE, Nathaniel (1675-1731/2) & Sarah [HUNGERFORD] (1679-); b 1698, b 1699; E. Haddam, CT/Haddam
CONEY, John (-1630) & Elizabeth HAWKREDD (1605-1670+), m/2 Oliver MELLOWS 1 Jan 1633/4, m/3 Thomas MAKEPEACE 1641; 16 Dec 1624; Boston, Eng
CONNEY, John (1628-1690) & Elizabeth NASH; 20 Jun 1654; Boston
CONEY, John (1655-1722) & Sarah [BLAKEMAN] (-17 Apr 1694); ca 1677; Boston
CONEY, John (1655-1722) & 2/wf Mary (ATWATER) CLARK, w John; 8 Nov 1694; Boston
CONEY, Nathaniel & Elizabeth GREENLAND (1679-); 11 Oct 1699; Hingham
CONGDON, Benjamin (1650±-1718) & Elizabeth [ALBRO] (-1720); ca 1670/2; Portsmouth, RI/Kings Town, RI
CONGDON, John & Mary [SMITH]; b 1701?; Kings Town, RI
CONGDIL/CONGDON?, William & 1/wf Mary BROWNELL (-1718(-)); 3 Mar 1698, 1697/8?, 1693?; Little Compton, RI/Tiverton, RI/Kings Town, RI
CONKLIN, Ananias (-1657) & 1/wf Mary LAUDER/LANDER; St. Peter's, Nottingham, 23 Feb 1630, 1630/1; Salem/Southold, LI/E. Hampton, LI
CONKLIN, Ananias (-1657) & 2/wf Susan __?_ ; b 1650?, b 1643; Salem/Southold, LI/E. Hampton, LI
CONKLING, Ananias (-1657) & 3/wf Dorothy (_?_) [ROSE], w Robert; b 1654; East Hampton, LI
CONKLIN, Ananias (1672-1740) & [Hannah LUDLOW?]/Martha STRATTON; b 1698?, b 1700?; East Hampton, LI/Huntington, LI
CONKLIN, Benjamin (-1709) & Hannah [MULFORD] (-1712); ca 1668; East Hampton, LI/Elizabeth, NJ
CONKLIN, Benjamin & Sarah [BUDD] (?1670-); aft 1684, ca 1688?; Southold, LI/East Hampton, LI
CONKLIN, Cornelius (-1668) & Mary [?ODIORNE/?ABORN], m/2 Robert STARR 1669, m/3 William NICK 1680, m/4 George JACKSON 1690; Salem
CONKLIN, Cornelius (-1748 in 84th y) & Mary __?_ ; b 1700, b 1698?; East Hampton, LI
CONKLIN, David & __?_ ; b 1700; East Hampton, LI
CONKLIN, Edmund & __?_ ; b 1694
CONKLIN, Jacob (-1715) & Mary [YOUNGS]; b 1668; Southold, LI
CONKLIN, Jacob & Hannah [PLATT] (1679-); b 1701?; Huntington, LI
CONKLIN, Jeremiah (1634-1712/13) & Mary [GARDINER] (1638-1727, ae 89); b 1658; East Hampton, LI
CONKLIN, Jeremiah (-1734, ae 73) & Jane [LUDLAM?] (-1741, ae 76); no issue?, St. Peter's, Nottingham
CONKLIN, John (-1684) & Elizabeth ALLSAEBROOK; 24 Jan 1624, 1624/5; Salem/Southold, LI
CONKLIN, John (1631-1694) & Sarah (HORTON) SALMON, w William; 2 Dec 1657, 1656?; Southold, LI
CONKLIN, John & Helena __?_ ; bef 1661; Flushing/etc.
CONKLIN, John & Sarah [SCUDDER] (?1663-1753); b 1686; Southold
CONKLIN, John & Mehitable (TIPPETT) [HALDEY], w Joseph; 1694?, ?ca 1687/90?; Fordham, NY/Rye, NY
CONKLIN, John (1669-1746) & __?_ (1665-1735, ae 70); b 1694, b 1692; Easthampton, LI
CONKLIN, John (1673-1751) (son Timothy) & Mary [EDWARDS]?/[BRUSH?] (?1679, 1674-1749 in 71st y); b 1701?, b 1697; Huntington, LI
CONKLIN, Joseph & Sarah [CURTIS?/HORTON] SALMON, dau Barnabas, w William; ca 1670?; Southold, LI
CONKLIN, Joseph (-1698) & Abigail TUTHILL (1670-1705), m/2 John PARKER 1698+; Nov 1690; Southold, LI
CONKLIN, Joseph & Mary EDWARDS; by 1699
CONKLIN, Lewis & ?Mary/?Mirah __?_ ; b 1700; Easthampton, LI
CONKLIN, Nicholas (1661-1751, Orange Co., NY) & Sarah HUNT; b 1691; Eastchester, NY
CONKLIN, Timothy (-1708+) & Martha [WICKES]/?Sarah SCUDDER; b 1668; Huntington, LI
CONKLIN, Timothy & Abigail __?_ ; b 1697(8?); Huntington, LI
CONLEY, Abraham & 1/wf Elizabeth __?_ ; Kittery, ME
CONLEY, Abraham & 2/wf Margaret (?WATHEN) (EVERETT) [NASH], w William, w Isaac

CONLEY, _?_ & Mary HAMLIN (1663), dau Ezekiel, ch: Ezekiel, Elizabeth; ?Boston
CONNER, Cornelius (1637-1687) & Sarah [?BROWN] (1634-1709+); b 1659; Salisbury
CONNIARS/CONNER?, James & Naomi HARMON; m int 15 Aug 1696; Boston
CONNOR, Jeremiah (1672-) & Ann GOVE (1677-); 3 Jul 1696; Salisbury/Exeter, NH
CONNER, John & Elizabeth PODINGTON/PURINGTON; 15 May 1691; Salisbury
CONNER, _?_ & _?_ MARDEN
CONNETT, James & Mehitable BLANCHARD? (1647?-), dau Richard; b 1690; Charlestown/Wood-
   bridge, NJ
CONNETT, John & [Mehitable GARDNER]?; b 1690; Charlestown
CONNOWAY/CONWAY, George & Anna WILSON (-1692), w Benjamin; 3 Apr 1671; Charlestown
CONOWAY, Robert & Mary _?_ ; b 1687; Ipswich
CONNAWAY, _?_, Boston & Sarah HILLIARD; b 9 May 1701, b 1674; Salem
CONSTABLE, Thomas (-ca 1650) & Ann _?_, m/2 Philip LONG by 1652; Boston
CONSTABLE, _?_ & Katharine [?MOORE] (-1683, ae 95), m/2 Richard MILES aft 1644?
CONVERSE, Allen (-1679) & Elizabeth _?_ (1618-1691); b 1642; Woburn
CONVERSE/CONYERS, Edward[1] (1590-1663) (John PARKER, a kinsman) & 1/wf? Jane
   [CLARK?] (-1617?); in Eng, b 1617?; Charlestown/Woburn
CONVERSE, Edward[1] (1590-1663) & ?2/wf Sarah _?_ (-14 Jan 1662, 1661/2); in Eng, ca 1618;
   Charlestown/Woburn
CONVERSE, Edward[1] (1590-1663) & 3/wf Joanna (WARREN) SPRAGUE (-1680), w Ralph; 9
   Sep 1662; Malden/Woburn
CONVERSE, Edward (-1692) & Sarah STONE, m/2 Ebenezer HILLS 1697; 5 Nov 1684; Woburn
CONVERS, Jacob & Mary _?_ ; b 1686; Billerica
CONVERSE, James (1620-1715) & 1/wf Ann/Anna? LONG (1623-1691); 24 Oct 1643; Woburn
CONVERSE, James (1645-1706) & Hannah CARTER (1651, 1650/1-); 1 Jan 1668, 1668/9; Woburn
CONVERSE, James & Anna (SPARHAWK) [COOPER] (-1717/18?, 1712+), w John; aft 22 Aug
   1691, 1692, bef 20 Mar 1692/3; Cambridge
CONVERSE, John (1673-) & Abigail SAWYER, m/2 John VINTON; ?22 May 1699; Woburn
CONVERSE, Josiah (1617-1689/90) & Esther CHAMPNEY, m/2 Jonathan DANFORTH 1690; 26
   Mar 1657; Woburn
CONVERSE, Josiah & 1/wf Ruth MARSHALL; 8 Oct 1685; Woburn
CONVERSE, Robert & Mary SAWYER; 19 Dec 1698; Woburn
CONVERSE, Samuel (-1669) & Judith CARTER (-1676), m/2 Giles FIFIELD 1672; 8 Jun 1660;
   Woburn
CONVERSE, Samuel (1653-1699) & Sarah _?_ ; b 1684; Woburn
CONVERSE, Samuel & Dorcas [PAINE?], had son Pain 1706; b 1694; Woburn
CONVERSE, Zachariah (1642-1679) & Hannah BATEMAN (-1679); 12 Jun 1667; Woburn
COOKE, Aaron[1] (1614-1690) & 1/wf _?_ ; ca 1636; Dorchester/Windsor, CT/Northampton
COOKE, Aaron[1]2 (1614-1690) & 2/wf Joan [DENSLOW] (-1676); aft Nov 1645; Windsor, CT
COOKE, Aaron[2] (1641-1716) & Sarah WESTWOOD (-1730); ?20 May 1661, ?30 May; Hadley
COOKE, Aaron[1] (1614-1690) & 3/wf Elizabeth NASH (1647-1687); 2 Dec 1676; New Haven
COOKE, Aaron[3] (1664-1725) & Martha ALLYN (1667-1732); 3 Jan 1683; Hartford
COOKE, Aaron[1] (1614-1690) & 4/wf Rebecca (FOOTE) SMITH (ca 1630-1701), w Philip; 2 Oct
   1688; ?Hadley/Northampton
COOK, Abiel & _?_ ; ca 1683; Southampton, NY
COOKE, Andrew (-1718) & Phebe [LOVEN/LOVEWELL]; 24 Jul 1685; Chelmsford/Dunstable
COOK, Arthur & Margaret _?_ ; b 1679 Portsmouth, RI/Philedelphia
COOKE, Barnabas & Mary GOODWIN, m/2 Stephen WEBSTER 1700; 3 Dec 1689, 4 Dec 1689;
   Cambridge
COOKE, Caleb (1651-1722) & Jane _?_ ; ca 1681; Plymouth
COOK, Caleb & Mary PARMENTER; 31 Jul 1685; Watertown
COOK, Caleb & Joanna PEDERICK; 27 Mar 1698; Marblehead
COOKE, Elisha (1637-1715) & Elizabeth LEVERETT (1651-1715); 9? Jun 1668; ?Boston
COOK, Ellis (-1679) & Martha [COOPER] (1630-1690+); ca 1646-7; Southampton, NY
COOK, Ellis & _?_ ; Southampton, NY
COOKE, Francis[1] (-1663) & Hester MAHIEN (-1666+); betrothed Leyden, Holland, 30 Jun 1603;
   Plymouth
COOKE, Francis & Mary _?_ ; b 1677; Boston

COOK, Francis (1663-1746) & Elizabeth LAYTHUM/LATHAM (ca 1664-1730); 2 Aug 1687; Plymouth

COOKE, George (-1652) & ?Anne/?Alice _?_; b 1640; Cambridge

COOK, George (-1704) & Sarah [PLACE], m/2 Daniel MACOONE 1705; RI

COOK, Gregory (Robert BURRAGE, Seething, Norfolk Co., Eng, was his "brother-in-law") & 1/wf Mary [CONSTABLE]; b 1647; Watertown

COOK, Gregory & Susanna (STOWERS) (WHEELER) GOODWIN, w George, w Edward, m/4 Henry SPRING 1691; 1 Nov 1681; Watertown

COOKE, Henry (?1615-1661) & Judith BIRDSALE (-1689); - Jun 1639, ?29 Jun; Salem

COOKE, Henry (1652-1705) & Mary HALL (ca 1654-1718); last of Sep 1678; Salem/Wallingford, CT

COOKE, Isaac (1640/2-1692) & Elizabeth BUXSTONE/BUXTON (-1713+); 3 May 1664; Salem

COOKE, Jacob (ca 1618-1675) & 1/wf Damaris HOPKINS (-1666+); ca 10 Jun 1646, 20 Jun 1646; Plymouth

COOKE, Jacob (-1675) & 2/wf Elizabeth (LETTICE) SHURTLEFF (-1692), w William, m/3 Hugh COLE 1689; 8 Nov 1669; Plymouth

COOKE, Jacob (-1747) & Lydia MILLER; 29 Dec 1681; Plymouth/Kingston

COOK, John[2] (1607-1695) & Sarah WARREN (-1696+); 28 Mar 1634; Plymouth/Dartmouth

COOK, John (-1655+) & Mary _?_ (-1682+), m/2 Thomas ROLFE 1656; Rehoboth/Warwick, RI

COOK, John & _?_; b 1640; Salem

COOK, John (?1631-1691) & Mary [BORDEN] (1633-bef 1691); b 1653; Portsmouth, RI/Providence

COOK, John & Phebe _?_; div 1684; Warwick, RI/New Providence/Tiverton/CT

COOK, John (?1646-1716) & Mary BUXTON (-1716+); 28 Dec 1671; Salem/Lancaster

COOK, John (-1727) & Mary _?_ (-1754); b 1678?; Portsmouth, RI/Tiverton, RI

COOK, John & Mary (COLLINS) ELWELL, w Josiah, m/3 James DAVIS 1697; 2 Feb 1679/80; Gloucester

COOKE, John & Lydia [CURTIS]; by 1680; ?York, ME/Kittery,ME

COOK, John & Naomi THAYER; 16 Apr 1684; Mendon/Uxbridge

COOK, John & Ruth [SHAW]; by 1684?; Tiverton, RI

COOKE, John & Mary DOWNS; 25 Nov 1686; Hampton, NH

COOK, John (?1650-1719) & Elizabeth _?_; b 1687; Southampton

COOKE, John (1662-1712) & Sarah FISKE (1664-1714+), Wenham; 14 Sep 1688; Topsfield/Hartford

COOK, John & Ruth GREENLIEFE/GREENLEAF; 16 Dec 1689; Boston

COOK, John (-1705) (who was 1/wf?) & 2/wf Hannah [HARRIS] (1670-), m/2 Jonathan SPRAGUE; b 1691, b 1685; Middletown, CT

COOK, John & Hannah THORP; 8 Dec 1697, 3 Dec; Wallingford, CT

COOK, Joseph & Elizabeth _?_; b 1643; Cambridge

COOKE, Joseph (1643-) & Martha STEDMAN; 4 Dec 1665; Cambridge

COOKE, Joseph (-1746) & Susanna BRIGGS; 19 Apr 1692; Portsmouth, RI

COOKE, Joseph & Ann _?_; b 1694; Boston

COOKE, Joseph & Abigail _?_; b 1700; Wallingford, CT

COOKE, Josiah (ca 1610-1673) & Elizabeth (RING) DEAN (-1687), w Stephen; 16 Sep 1635; Plymouth/Eastham

COOK, Josiah (-1732) & Deborah HOPKINS (1648-); 27 Jul 1668; Eastham?

COOK, Josiah (1664-) & Ruth _?_ (-1697); b 1690; Windsor, CT

COOKE, Josiah (1670-1727) & Mary [GODFREY]; b 1694; Eastham/Provincetown

COOK, Moses (1645-1676) & Elizabeth CLARK, m/2 Job DRAKE 1677; 27 Sep 1669, 25 Nov 1669; Westfield/Windsor, CT

COOK, Moses (1675-1758) & Mary BURNARD/BARNARD (1681-1753); 4 Jul 1698; Hadley

COOK, Nathaniel (-1688) & Lydia VORE (-1698); 29 Jun 1649; Windsor, CT

COOK, Nathaniel & Sarah KELLUM/KILLAM/KILHAM (1661-); 21 Jun 1687; Ipswich/Deerfield?

COOKE, Nathaniel (1658-1725) & Lydia [?BROOKS]; b 1689; Windsor, CT

COOK, Nicholas (?1659, 1660-1730?) & 1/wf Johannah/Joanna ROCKET/ROCKWOOD (1647-1710±); 4 Nov 1684; Mendon/Blackstone

COOK, Nicholas & Elizabeth CARWITHEN; 28 Jun 1700; Boston

COOK, Noah (1657-1699) & Sarah [NASH]? (-1720+); ca 1679; Hartford/Northampton

COOK, Philip (-1667) & Mary [LAMSON] (-1715); b 1652; Cambridge
COOK, Philip & Sarah READ; 18 Mar 1698; Cambridge
COOKE, Richard (-1673) & Elizabeth _?_ (-1690, in 75th y); b 1636; Boston
COOKE, Richard (1610?-1658) & Frances [WHEELER]? (1608-), w Isaac, m/3 Thomas GREEN 1659; b 1649; Malden/Charlestown
COOK, Richard & [Grace] _?_ ; b 1681, 1681(2?); Preston, CT/Norwich, CT
COOKE, Richard (1672-1754) & Hannah _?_ ; b 1697; Eastham/Plainfield, CT
COOK, Robert & Sarah _?_?; b 1643; Charlestown
COOKE, Robert & Penelope _?_ ; b 1669; Boston
COOKE, Robert & Sarah _?_ ; b 1670; Boston
COOKE, Robert & Mary [ATKINSON], nee JENKINS? (see Marmaduke ATKINSON); aft 1674; Scituate/Abington
COOK, Robert & Tamar TYLER; 5 Dec 1678; Portsmouth,RI
COOK, Robert & _?_ ; b 1680; Dorchester
COOK, Robert & Submit WEEKS (1671-); 26 Oct 1693; Boston/Dorchester/Dedham/Needham
COOK, Samuel (-1652?) & _?_ ; b 1640?; Dedham
COOK, Samuel (1641-1702) & 1/wf Hope PARKER (1650-1686/91); 2 May 1667; New Haven/Wallingford, CT
COOKE, Samuel (-1752) & Lydia WIGHT/WHITE? (prob WHITE); 27 Apr 1681; Medfield/Mendon
COOKE, Samuel (-1731, ae 76) & Abigail GRIGGS (-1714); 14 Nov 1681; Cambridge/Charlestown
COOK, Samuel (1641-) & 2/wf Mary _?_ (-1695, ae 39); ca 1691; Wallingford, CT
COOK, Samuel & 1/wf Hannah IVES (?1672-1715); 3 Mar 1692; Wallingford, CT
COOK, Samuel (1641-1703) & 3/wf Mary (MALLORY) ROBERTS (1656-1752), w Eli, m/3 Jeremiah HOW 1705; 14 Jul 1696; Wallingford, CT
COOK, Samuel (1672-1745) & Ann MARSH (1680-); 21 Jun 1698; Hadley
COOKE, Stephen & Rebecca FLEGG/FLAGG (1660-1721); 19 Nov 1679; Watertown
COOKE, Thomas² (-1669/70?) & ?Thomasin _?_ ; b 1627; Taunton/Boston
COOKE, Thomas (-1674) & 1/wf _?_
COOKE, Thomas (-1674) & 2/wf Mary [?SLOCUM/?HAVENS], m/2 Jeremiah BROWN 1680± (see below); aft 1631; Portsmouth, RI
COOKE, Thomas (-1692+) & 1/wf [Elizabeth] _?_ , m/2 Joseph LANGTON; b 1646?; Guilford, CT
COOK, Thomas (-1650) & Rachel VARNEY?, did she m/2 William VINSON/VENSEY?; b 1650, div 1661; Ipswich/Gloucester, CT
COOKE, Thomas (1628-1670(-)) & Thomisen _?_/Mary HAVENS (see above)
COOK, Thomas (-1692) & 1/wf Hannah LINDON (1650-1676); 30 Mar 1668, 13 Mar, 1667/8?; Guilford, CT
COOKE, Thomas (-1701) & 2/wf Sarah WESSON (-1701); 15 Apr 1677; Guilford, CT
COOKE, Thomas & Anne _?_ ; b 1678; Boston
COOK, Thomas & Mary _?_ , m/2 Jeremiah BROWN b 1680 (see above); RI
COOKE, ?Thomas & Lydia [?WHITE]; ca 1682; Braintree?
COOKE, Thomas (-1724) & [Alice] _?_ (-1705, Windsor, CT); b 1683; Windsor, CT
COOKE, Thomas (1668-1726) & Mary [COREY] (-1726); b 1701?; Tiverton, RI
COOKE, Thomas (-1699) & Elizabeth [PEARCE?] (-1699+); b 1696, b 1692?; Portsmouth, RI/Monmouth, NJ
COOK, Walter¹ (-1696) & 1/wf Experience _?_ (-1662+); b 1648?, b 1654; Weymouth/Mendon
COOKE, Walter (-1696) & ?1/wf Catherine [ALDRICH] (-1696) (doubtful); aft 1 Mar 1682/3, b 1695, 3 Feb 1685?; Weymouth/Mendon
COOK, Westwood (1670-) & Sarah [COLEMAN]; 1692; Hadley
COOKE, William & Sarah _?_ ; b 1678; Boston
COOKE, _?_ & Ruth [BARTON], dau James; b 1701?
COOKE, _?_ & Mary [MOTT] (1666-1711+), dau Jacob
COOKERY/COOKEY, Henry (-1662?) & Hannah LONG (1637-1710), m/2 Luke PERKINS 1663; 22 Oct 1657; Charlestown
COOKERY, Henry (-1704, ae 46) & 1/wf Mary MASSON (-1687); 21 Jan 1685; Charlestown
COOKERY, Henry (-1704,ae 46) & Mary BEMAN/BEAMAN (1656-); 23 Jan 1689; Charlestown
COOLEY, Benjamin (1617-1684) & Sarah _?_/?COLTON/?TREMAINE (-1684); b 1643?, b 1644; Springfield
COOLEY, Benjamin (1656-1731) & Abigail BAGG (1673-1739); 7 Feb 1695, 1694/5; Springfield

COQLE/COULLY, Charles & Mary _?_ ; b 1684, b 1688; Boston

COOLEY, Daniel (1651-1727) & 1/wf Elizabeth WOLCOTT (1662-1708); 8 Dec 1680, 10 Dec; Springfield

COOLEY, Eliakim (1649-1711) & Hannah [TIBBALS] (1657-1711); 12 Mar 1678, [1678/9]; Springfield

COOLEY/COWLEY?, Henry (-1677) & Rebecca [HETT?], m/2 Robert BRONSDON 1678; b 1669; Boston

COOLEY, John (-1654) & Elizabeth _?_, ?m/2 Gilbert CRACKBONE 1656, m/3 Richard ROBBINS 1676; ca 163-?; Ipswich

COOLEY, Joseph (1662-1740) & Mary GRISWOLD (1663-1739); 22 Jan 1684; Springfield/Somers, CT

COOLEY, Obadiah (1647-1690) & Rebecca WILLIAMS (1649-1715?), m/2 John WARNER; 9 Nov 1670; Springfield

COOLIDGE, John[1] (?1664-1691) & Mary _?_ (1603-1691); in Eng, ca 1627, ca 1628; Watertown

COOLIDGE, John[2] (-1691) & 1/wf Hannah LIVERMORE (-1678, ae 45); 14 Nov 1655; Watertown

COOLEDGE, John (-1691) & 2/wf Mary (WELLINGTON) MATTOCK/MADDOCK, w Henry; 16 Sep 1679, ?13 Sep; Watertown, CT

COOLEDGE, John (1662-1714) & Mary _?_ (1662-13 Sep 1724, ae 62 y 9 m); b 1685, ca 1683; Sherborn

COOLLIDGE, John (-1755) & Margaret BOND; 16 Jan 1699/1700; Watertown

COOLEDGE, Jonathan (1647-1714) & Martha RICE (1662-1695); 3 Dec 1679; Watertown

COOLLEDGE, Jonathan (?1672-1729) & Mercy/Mary? _?_ (-1724); b 1701; Newton

COOLIDGE, Joseph & Rebecca [FROST] (1669-1750); b 1697, "ca 1695"; Cambridge/Watertown

COOLEDGE, Nathaniel (-1711) & Mary BRIGHT (-1712); 15 Oct 1659; Watertown

COOLIDGE, Nathaniel (1660-1733), Charlestown & Lydia JONES (1669-1718), Charlestown; 2 Jan 1687/8; Watertown

COOLEDGE, Obadiah (1663-1707, 1706), Sudbury & Elizabeth ROOSE/ROUSE?/ROSE?, Hartford, m/2 John CUNNINGHAM 1715; 28 Feb 1686, 1686/7, 1685/6?; Sudbury/Watertown

COOLIDGE, Richard (-1732) & 1/wf Mary BOND (-1700); 21 Jun 1693, 22 Jun, 21 Jun; Watertown

COOLEDGE, Simon (-1693) & 1/wf Hannah BARRON (1635, ?1637-1680); 17 Nov 1658; Watertown

COOLEDGE, Simon (-1693) & 2/wf Priscilla ROGERS (-1694); 14 Jan 1681/2, 1681; Watertown

COLLEDGE, Stephen (1639-1711) & Rebecca _?_ (-1702); ca 1660/5?, no issue; Watertown

COOLLEDGE, Thomas (1670-1737) & 1/wf Sarah EDDY (-1711); 15 Nov 1699, ?16 Nov; Watertown

COOMBS, Anthony & Dorcas WOODEN (1671-); 5 Sep 1688; Wells, ME/York Co., ME

COOMBS, Francis (-1682) & 1/wf Deborah [MORTON]; b 29 Oct 1673; Plymouth

COMBS, Francis (-1682) & 2/wf Mary (BARKER) PRATT, w Samuel, m/3 David WOOD 1685; ca 1678?, 1676?; Plymouth/Middleboro

COMES, Francis (-1700) & Mary _?_ ; Newtown, LI

COOMBS, Henry (-1669) & Elizabeth _?_ (-1709), m/2 Stephen GRIGGS; b 1635; Salem/Marblehead

COOMBS, Henry (1645-1725) & ?Sarah (PREBLE) PARKER (1659-1724), w Abraham; ca 1675?, ca 1680/5?; Salem?

COOMES, Humphrey & Bathsheba RAYMOND/RAYMENT (1637-); 29 Jul 1659; Salem

COOMBS, John (-1646/8) & Sarah PRIEST; ca 1630; Plymouth/Middleboro

COOMBS, John (1664-) & Elizabeth (BALLENTINE) YELLING, sister of Benjamin, w Roger; b 1689; Boston

COOMES, John (-1668) & Elizabeth (ROYALL?) BARLOW, w? Benson, w Thomas, m/3 John WARREN 1669±; 24 Feb 1661, at Boston, 1662?; Hingham

COMBS, John & 1/wf Mary _?_ ; b 1695; Northampton

COOMBS, John & Elizabeth [HOBART?]; b 1696; Northampton

COOMES, Michael (1638-) & Jane/Joanna _?_ ; b 1669; Salem

COOMS, Michael & Ruth ROADS/RHODES; 12 Jul 1698; Marblehead

COOMES, Philip & Naomy _?_ ; b 11 Nov 1687; Westchester, NY

COOMES, Richard & Margaret _?_, m/2 John HARRIS; b 1689; Marblehead

COOMS, Robert & Mary [BENSON] (1637-); b 16 Apr 1678, b 1663?; Hull
COOMS, Thomas & Elizabeth [PHIPPEN/PHIPPENY] (-1724), dau George; b 1695; Hull
COMES, Timothy & Jane __?__; b 1687; Glouchester
COMES, __?__ & Abigail __?__, m/2 Thomas AVERY 1697
COOPER, Alexander (-1684) & __?__; b 1667; Berwick, ME
COOPER, Anthony (-1636) & 1/wf Margaret CLARK (-1617 in Eng); Hingham, Eng, 25 Jul 1609; Hingham, MA
COOPER, Anthony (-1636) & 2/wf Frances __?__; Hingham
COOPER, Benjamin (?1587-1637, 1638) & Elizabeth __?__ (?1589-); in Eng, b 1616?; Salem
COOPER, Benjamin & Eleanor/Helena WILKINS, dau William; m lic 7 Apr 1694; Southampton, NY
COOPER, James & ?[Elizabeth SHIPPEE]; b 1688; Warwick, RI
COOPER, James (-1722±) & __?__; b 1695; Southampton, NY
COOPER, John (1594/6-1662) & Wibroe __?__ (1594-); ?Olney, Eng, b 1618?; Lynn/Southampton, NY
COOPER, John¹ (-1689) & 1/wf __?__; in Eng, b 1636?; New Haven
COOPER, John (-1683), Scituate, Barnstable & Priscilla (CARPENTER) WRIGHT (1598-1689), w William; 27 Nov 1634, no issue; ?Plymouth/Barnstable
COOPER, John (1618-1691) & Anne/Anna [SPARHAWK] (-1717/18), m/2 James CONVERSE 1692?; b 1643; Cambridge
COOPER, John (?1625-1677) & Sarah [MEW] (niece of Benjamin LING); ca 1650?; Southampton, LI
COOPER, John (1642-1714) & Mary THOMPSON (1652-); 27 Dec 1666; New Haven
COOPER, John (-1689) & 2/wf Jane (WOOLEN) HALL, w John; 1678, 1679; New Haven
COOPER, John (1656-1736) & 1/wf Elizabeth BOARDMAN (-1713); 28 Apr 1686; Cambridge
COOPER, John & Sarah LORD; 13 Dec 1691; Berwick, ME
COOPER, John (1671-) & Sarah (THOMAS) DORMAN, div wf of John DORMAN; ?1693, ?1694; New Haven
COOPER, John (1675-) & Elizabeth WINTER (1678-); 1 Feb 1697/8; Concord/Killingly, CT
COOPER, Josiah (-1678) & Waitawhile MAKEPEACE (1641-), m/2 __?__ DENNIS; 13 Sep 1661; Boston
COOPER, Josiah & Mary BLANCHARD?, m/2 Richard BROOK b 1691, ca 1679; ?Boston
COOPER, Nathaniel & Judith HUNT (1648-1724), m/2 Isaac WILLIAMS 1677; 17 May 1667; Rehoboth
COOPER, Nathaniel & Mary SABIN (1675-1712), m/2 Nathaniel CARPENTER 1707; 8 Dec 1696; Rehoboth
COOPER, Peter (1607-1668) & Emm/Ame __?__ (-1689); b 1642; Rowley
COOPER, Philip & Sarah WRIGHT; 29 Oct 1700; Boston
COOPER, Richard (-1724) & Hannah WOOD/?ATWOOD; 1 Feb 1692/3; Plymouth
COOPER, Samuel (-1714) & Mary __?__; ca 1680/82?; Southampton
COOPER, Samuel (1653, 1654-1718) & Hannah HASTINGS (1666-1732); 4 Dec 1682; Cambridge
COOPER, Samuel (1647-1727) & Mary HERIMAN/HARRIMAN; 25 Jun 1691; Rowley
COOPER, Samuel (1673-1725) & 1/wf Dorothy [WARD] (1672-1697); b 1697; Springfield
COOPER, Samuel & Ruth WILLMARTH/WILMARTH; 16 Feb 1697; Rehoboth
COOPER, Samuel & Elizabeth SMITH; 15 Nov 1699; New Haven
COOPER, Simon (-1690/1) & Mary TUCKER (-1710); 20 Jan 1663/[4]; ?Newport
COOPER, Simon (1672-) & Martha PRYOR (1672-); 24 Jul 1693; Oyster Bay, NY
COOPER, Thomas (d in Eng) & Christiana [BARKER], m/2 Thomas BEECHER 1629, m/3 Nicholas EASTON 1639; ?Wapping, Eng; Charlestown
COOPER, Thomas (-1690) (called brother by Henry SMITH 1647, called brother by Joseph PECK, mentioned in will of Margaret KINGSBURY 1660) & 1/wf Rachel __?__; in Eng, ca 1627; Hingham/Rehoboth
COOPER, Thomas (1617-1675) & Sarah [SLYE] (-1688), m/2 William CLARK 1676; ca 1641; Springfield
COOPER, Thomas (1628-1687) & Mary [RAYNER?]; ca 1649, 1648?; Southold, LI
COOPER, Thomas (-1690) & 2/wf Ann BOSWORTH (-1680/1), w Zaccheus; 17 Oct 1656; Boston/Rehoboth
COOPER, Thomas (-1712, Rehoboth) & Mary [KINGSBURY] (1637-1700); b 1658; Rehoboth

COOPER, Thomas (-1676+), plasteter (Matthew SMITH called son-in-law, drowned, did he m _?_
COOPER, dau Thomas, plasterer) & Mary [SMITH]? (-1676+); b 1658; Boston
COOPER, Thomas (1646-1722, Middletown) & Desire LAMBERTON (1642/3-1708+); Aug 1667, 1669?; Springfield
COOPER, Thomas (1654-1712) & 1/wf Sarah (BURNAP) SOUTHWICK, w John, m/2 Cornelius BROWN 1684; 12 Jun 1674, div 1684; Salem
COOPER, Thomas & Deliverance MARSTON; 27 Dec 1680; Salem
COOPER, Thomas (-1712) & 2/wf Abigail [SIBLEY]; b Jun 1684, aft 15 Mar 1679/[80]; Newport
COOPER, Thomas (-1705) & Mehitable MINOT (1668-), m/2 Peter SARGENT 1706, m/3 Simeon STODDARD 1715; 6 Mar 1683; ?Boston
COOPER, Thomas (-1691, 1692?) & Joanna _?_, m/2 Joseph PIERSON aft 3 Oct 1692; ?; Southampton, NY
COOPER, Thomas & Susanna BULLARD; 20 Aug 1690; Rehoboth
COOPER, Timothy (-1659) & Elizabeth _?_ (-1659+); b 1641; Lynn/Reading
COOPER, Timothy (1644-bef 1680, by 1679) & Elizabeth MUNSON (-1706), m/2 Richard HIGGINBOTHAM 1681±; 19 Oct 1664; Springfield
COOPER, Timothy (-1676) & Sarah MORSE (?1648-1709), m/2 Nathaniel PATTEN 1678; 2 Jun 1669; Groton/Watertown
COOPER, Timothy (?1670-1726) & 1/wf Elizabeth [WHITMAN] (1673-); b 1695; Charlestown
COOPER, ?Simon (d in Eng, ca 1618) & Lydia _?_, m/2 Gregory STONE
COOPER, _?_ & [Mary ADAMS] (1664, ?1643, ?1654-), Chelmsford
COOTSAY/COOKSAY?, _?_ & Sarah [RICE], dau Richard; Cambridge
COPELAND, John (1659-1714) & Ruth [?NEWCOMB]; b 1683; Braintree
COPELAND, Lawrence (-1699, ae 100) & Lydia TOWNSEND (-1688); 12 Dec 1651; Braintree
COPELAND, Thomas (-1706) & 1/wf Mehitable ATWOOD (-1695, ae 30), wid; 3 Feb 1691/2; Braintree
COPELAND, Thomas (-1706) & 2/wf Mercy _?_ (-20 Feb 1698/99); Braintree
COPELAND, Thomas (-1706) & 3/wf Mary ARNOLD (1681-), w Ephraim, m/3 _?_ NEWCOMB; 17 May 1699; Braintree/Boston
COPELAND, William (1656-1716) & Mary (BASS) WEBB (1669/70-), w Christopher; 31 Aug 1694, 13 Apr 1694; Braintree
COPLEY, Thomas (-1712) & Ruth DENSLOW (1653-1692, Suffield, CT); 13 Nov 1672, ?15 Nov; Westfield/Springfield/Suffield, CT
COPLEY, Thomas (-1712) & Ruth (COGAN) TAYLOR (-1724), w Samuel; 25 May 1693; Suffield, CT
COPLEY, _?_ & Elizabeth _?_ (1627-1792), m/2 Nathaniel PHELPS 1650; b 1650; Springfield/ Windsor, CT
COPS, Aaron (?1676-1729?) & Mary HEATH (1672-); 30 Dec 1698; Haverhill
COPE, David (1635-1713) & 1/wf Obedience TOPLIFFE (1642-30 May 1678); 20 Feb 1659, at Dorchester; Boston
COPP, David (1635-1713) & 2/wf Amy _?_ (-1718, ae 82 y); aft 30 May 1678; Boston
COPP, David, Jr. (1663-) & Patience SHORT (-1736, in 60th y); 27 Dec 1694; Boston
COPP, John & Mary (JAGGERS) PHELPS, w Ephraim; 16 Mar 1698, 15 Mar 1697/8; Stamford, CT/?New London, CT
COPP, Jonathan (1640-) & Margaret _?_ ; b 1670; Boston
COPP, Jonathan (1665-1746, Montville, CT) & Catherine LAYE (1672-); 18 Aug 1690; Stonington, CT
COPP, Samuel (1671-) & Hannah [SALE] (-1722); b 1697; Boston
COPP, William[1] (1589-1670) & 1/wf Ann ROGERS (-1633); Hatton, Eng, 24 Nov 1614; Boston
COPP, William[1] (1589-1670) & 2/wf Goodith/Judith ITCHENOR (?1605-1670); Hatton, Eng, 21 Jul 1634; Boston
COPP, William (1667-) & Ann RUCK (-1699); 24 May 1692; Boston
CORAM, Thomas, Taunton? & Eunice WAIT/WAITE (1677-); 27 Jun 1700; Boston
CORBET/CORBETT, Clement & Dorcas BUCKMASTER; 1 Mar 1654/5; Boston
CORBET, Robert & Priscilla ROCKETT; 26 Feb 1682/3; Medfield/Mendon
CORBET, Robert (-1695) & Abigail/Abiah _?_, m/2 John BUGBEE 1696; b 1692; Woodstock, CT
CORBET, William (d at Providence) & 1/wf Eleanor BATRAP; 19 Sep 1683; Bristol, RI/Swansea (he m/2 Hannah BAKER 1710, Swansea)

CORBIN, Clement (1626-) & Dorcas BUCKMASTER (1629-1722); 7 Mar 1654/5; Boston/?Dorchester/Roxbury/Woodstock, CT

CORBIN, Jabez (1668-) & Mary [MORSE] (1672-1728); 1692; Woodstock, CT

CORBIN, James (1668-) & Hannah EASTMAN (1679-); 7 Apr 1697; Woodstock, CT/Dudley, MA/Boxford, CT

CORBIN, John & _?_; b 1691

CORBIN, Robert (-1676) & Lydia [?MARTIN]/[ATWELL?]; Casco Bay, ME

CORBEE, Samuel (1665-1694) & Mary CRIPPEN, Haddam, m/2 Moses ROWLEY; 28 Jan 1691/2; Haddam, CT

CORBE, William (-1674) & _?_ [LANGDON?]; b 1656; Haddam, CT

CURRIER/CORDEY/CORDAY?/CARDER, Gilbert & Joanna _?_; b 1683; Boston

CORLET, Elijah & Barbara [CUTTER]; b 1629, b 1644; Cambridge

CORLET, Elijah & 2/wf Esther [?MUSE/?MUST/?HUME]; Wethersfield, CT

CORLIS, George (-1686) & Joanna DAVIS, m/2 James ORDWAY 1687; 26 Oct 1645; Haverhill

CORLIS, John (1648-) & Mary WILFORD, m/2 William WHITTAKER; 17 Dec 1684; Haverhill

CORNELIUS, Aaron (-1695) & 1/wf _?_/?Anne (_?_) GRIDLEY, w Believe; b 1675; Flushing, LI

CORNELIUS, Aaron (-1695) & 2/wf Patience _?_; Flushing, LI

CORNELIUS, John & Mary YATES; 7 Aug 1682, ?2 Aug, 8-7-1682; Flushing, LI

CORNELL, Edward (-1708) & Mary _?_; Hempstead, LI

CORNELL, George (1676-1752) & 1/wf Philadelphia ESTES (1679-1698), Salem; 19 Mar 1695/6, 19 Mar 1696; Salem/Newport

CORNELL, George (1676-1752) & 2/wf Deliverance CLARK (1678-1732); 18 Jan 1699; Portsmouth, RI

CORNELL, John (?1637-1704) & Mary [RUSSELL] (?1645-); ca 1669?; Dartmouth/Hempstead, LI

CORNELL, John (1652-1753?) & Hannah [?SMITH]; b 1684; Hempstead, LI

CORNELL, John (-1716+) & Sarah [THORNE]; ?b 1696; Hempstead, LI

CORNEAL, Peter & Joanna MARSHALL; 9 Aug 1695; Billerica

CORNELL, Richard (-1694) & Elizabeth _?_ (-1694+); ca 1655; Flushing, LI/Rockaway, LI

CORNELL, Richard (-1725) & Sarah _?_; b 1685?; Flushing, LI/Success, LI/?Hempstead, LI

CORNELL, Samuel (-1715) & [?Deborah] [?CODMAN]; b 1685; Dartmouth

CORNELL, Stephen (?1656-) & Hannah [MOSHER]; ca 1686?; Portsmouth, RI/Swansea

CORNELL, Thomas (?1595-1655±) & Rebecca [BRIGGS] (1600-1673) (?wid), (?Ireane of John BRIGGS); b 1620?, b 1625; Boston/Portsmouth, RI

CORNELL, Thomas & 1/wf Elizabeth FISCOCK; New York, 2 Nov 1642; Portsmouth, RI/Swansea

CORNELL, Thomas[2] (-1673) & 2/wf Sarah [EARLE] (-1690+), m/2 David LAKE; ca 1660/65; Portsmouth, RI

CORNELL, Thomas (?1653-1714±) & Susannah [LAWTON] (-1712); b 1674; Portsmouth, RI

CORNELL, Thomas (1674-1728) & Martha FREEBORN (1671-1748); 26 Mar 1696; Portsmouth, RI

CORNELL, Thomas & _?_ [?SMITH]; b 1700; Rockaway, LI

CORNELL, William (?1667-1743) & [?Elizabeth ?SMITH]; ?ca 1692; Rockaway, LI

CORNING, John (1675-1734) & Elizabeth _?_ (-1753); b 1699; Beverly

CORNING, Samuel (-1695) & Elizabeth [HUNTLEY] (-1688); b 1640; Salem

CORNING, Samuel (1641-1714) & Hannah [BATCHELDER] (1645-1718); b 1670; Beverly

CORNING, Samuel & Elizabeth (ALLEN) KETTLE, w John; 13 Nov 1688; Beverly

CORNING, Samuel & Susanna KNOWLTON; 27 May 1690; Beverly/Ipswich

CORNISH, Benjamin (1652-1736) & Rebecca _?_ (-1737); ca 1684?; Newtown, LI

CORNISH, Gabriel (-1702), Westfield & Elizabeth WOLCOTT (1650-), m/2 Philip MINOT; 15 Dec 1686; Windsor, CT

CORNISH, James (-1698, Simsbury, CT) & 1/wf _?_; b 1658?; Saybrook, CT/Northampton/etc.

CORNISH, James (-1698) & 2/wf Phebe (BROWN) (LEE) [LARRABEE] (-1664), w Thomas, w Greenfield; ca 1661?, by 5 Dec 1661; Simsbury, CT

CORNISH, James & Mary KAY; 25 May 1687; Watertown/Boston

CORNISH, James, Westfield & 1/wf Elizabeth THRALL (-1714); 10 Nov 1693; Windsor, CT

CORNISH, John (-1696) & Martha _?_; b 1686; Boston

CORNISH, Joshua & Susanna BENNET; 8 Nov 1692; Boston/Watertown

CORNISH, Richard (-1644) & Katherine _?_; b 1634; Weymouth/York, ME

CORNISH, Richard (-1693(4)) & [Sarah?] _?_; ca 1674?; Boston
CORNISH, Samuel (1670-) & Susannah CLARKE; 27 Oct 1692; Plymouth
CORNISH, Thomas (-1662) & Mary STONE; 4 Sep 1641; Gloucester/Exeter, NH/Newtown, LI/Middleboro, LI
CORNISH, Thomas (?1649-1724) & Martha _?_ (-1725); Boston
CORNWALL, Jacob (1646-1708) & Mary WHITE (1659-), m/2 John BACON; 18 Jun 1678, 16 Jan 1677, 16 Jan 1678; Middletown, CT
CORNWELL/CORNWALL, John (1640-1707) & Martha PECK (1641-1708); 8 Jun 1665; Middletown, CT
CORNWALL, John (1671-) & 1/wf Elizabeth HINSDALE (-1698); 15 Sep 1695; Middletown, CT
CORNWALL, John (1671-) & 2/wf Mary HILTON (1671-); 23 Mar 1698/9; Middletown, CT
CORNWELL, Samuel (1642-1728) & Rebecca BULL (1644-); 15 Jan 1667; Middletown
CORNWELL, Thomas (1648-1702) & Sarah CLARKE, Saybrook; 14 Nov 1672; Middletown, CT
CORNWELL, William (-1678) & 1/wf Joan/Jean _?_ (-ca 1634/5); ca 1630?; Roxbury/Hartford/Middletown, CT
CORNWELL, William (-1678) & 2/wf Mary _?_; ca 1639; Roxbury/Middletown, CT
CORNWELL, William (1641-1691) & Mary BULL/BELL (1649-1717); 30 Nov 1670; Middletown, CT
CORNWALL, William (1671-1747) & Esther WARD (1669-1734); 22 Jan 1692, [1691/2]; Middletown, CT
CORNWALL, William & Mary THOMPSON; Dec 1699; Middletown, CT/Wethersfield, CT
CORNWALL, William (-1704) & Esther _?_; b 1700; Middletown, CT
CORP/CORPS, John (-1691) & Deliverance [?BRADLEY/?BROWN], m/2 John GEREARAY; b 1679, b 1680; Boston/Bristol, RI
CORRELL, James & Elizabeth _?_; b 1686; Boston
CORRELL, James & Mary _?_; b 1688; Boston
CORSE, James & Elizabeth [CATLIN]; ca 1690, b 1692; Deerfield
CORWIN, Daniel (-by 1719) & Mary [RAMSEY] (-1719+, 1725?), dau Simon; aft 1698, b 1701?; Southold, LI
CORWIN/CURWEN?, George (1610-1685) & 1/wf Elizabeth/Alice? (HERBERT) [WHITE] (1611-1668), w John; b 1637; Salem
CORWIN, George (1610-1685) & 2/wf Elizabeth (WINSLOW) BROOKES, w Robert; 22 Sep 1669; Salem
CORWIN, George (1666-1696) & 1/wf Susanna GEDNEY; 23 Apr 1688, no issue; Salem
CURWIN, George (1666-1696) & 2/wf Lydia [GEDNEY] (1669-1706); b 1693; Salem
CORWIN, John (?1630-1702) & Mary GLOVER (-1690); 4 Feb 1658; Southold, LI
CORWIN, John (1638-1683) & Margaret WINTHROP (-1697); - May 1665; Salem
CORWIN, John & Elizabeth _?_; b 1678; Boston
CORWIN, John (1663-1729) & Sarah _?_; b 1690; Southold, LI
CORWIN, Jonathan (1640-1718) & Elizabeth (SHEAFE) GIBBS (-1718), w Robert; 20 Mar 1675/6, 1670; Salem
CORWIN, Matthias (-1658, 1661?) & Margaret [SHATSWELL?/MORTON?]; b 1630, b 1626; Ipswich/Southold, LI
CORWIN, Matthias (1676-1769) & Mary [ROE?] (-1725?); aft 1698, b 1701?, ca 1708?, b 1710; Southold, LI
CORWIN, Samuel (-8 Dec 1705) & Anne? _?_; aft 1698, b 1701?; Southold, LI
CORWIN, Theophilus (?1634-bef 1692) & Mary _?_; b 1658; Southold, LI
CORWIN, Theophilus (1678-1762) & Hannah [RAMSAY] (1684-1760), dau Simon; b 1701?; Southold, LI
COREY, Abraham (?1641-1702) & Margaret [CHRISTOPHERS], m/2 John PARKER/PACKER; ca 1665/72, b 1680, 7 in fam 1686 or 3?; Southold, LI
COREY, Caleb (-1704) & Sarah _?_; b 1704, b 1701?; Dartmouth
COREE, Giles (±1619-1692) & Margaret _?_; b 1658; Salem
COREE, Giles (-1692) & 2/wf Mary BRITE/BRITZ (-1684, ae 63), from England; 11 Apr 1664, 11 Apr 1673; Salem
COREY, Giles (-1692) & 3/wf Martha [RICH?] (-1692); ca 1684, b 27 Apr 1690; Salem
COREY, Isaac (-1702) & Sarah LINDE?/LUDLE?/LINDLEY?/LUDLAM?, w Anthony; 1682; Southold, LI/Southampton, LI

COREY, Jacob (-1706) & Ann [TUTHILL?] (-1739); by 1672; Southold, LI
COREY, John (-1685) & 2/wf? Ann/?Margaret [?SALMON] (b 1686); ca 1638?, b 1649, ca 1638?; ?Southold, LI/?Southampton, LI
COREY, John & Mary CORNISH, m/2 John SAMMIS betw 1686 & 1693; 15 Dec 1667; Huntington, LI
COREY, John (-1712) & Elizabeth _?_ (-1713+); b 1679?; Portsmouth, RI
COREY, John & Elizabeth _?_ ; b 1691; Chelmsford
CORY, Jonathan & Sarah RUSSELL; 12 Dec 1699; Chelmsford/Concord
CORY, Roger (-1754) & 1/wf _?_ ; b 1699; Tiverton, RI/Richmond, RI
COREY, Thomas & Abigail [GOOLE]; 19 Sep 1665; Chelmsford
CORY, Thomas & Hannah [PAGE]; b 1695; Chelmsford
CORY, Thomas (-1738) & 1/wf Elizabeth [WICKES/WEEKS?]; b 1701?; Tiverton, RI
COREY, William (-1682) & [Mary EARLE] (-1718), m/2 Joseph TIMBERLAKE ±1683; ca 1660/3; ?Portsmouth, RI
CORY, William (-1764) & Martha [COOK] (1664-1704(-)); b 1688; Portsmouth, RI
COSIER/COZIER?, Richard & Abigail [STEWART]; b 5 Dec 1688; Norwalk, CT
COSTIE/COSTA, _?_ & Hester AUGUR (?1624-1691, New Haven); in Eng, b 20 Sep 1669; New Haven
COSTIN/COSTONE, William, Lynn? & _?_ ; b 1642, b 1655; Concord/Boston
COTTA, John (1646-1723) & Mary [MOORE] (1650-); b 1668; Boston
COTTA, John & Elizabeth _?_ ; b 1681; Boston
COTTA, John & Mary _?_ ; b 1693; Boston
COTTA, John & Sarah WHARTON (1671-); 4 May 1698; Boston
COTTER, Robert & Joan/Jane _?_ ; b 1638; Salem
COTTER, William & Eleanor _?_ ; 12 May 1659; New Haven/?New London
COTTLE, Edward (?1627-1710+, Nantucket) & Judith _?_ ; b 1651(2?); Salisbury
COTTLE, Edward (1666-1751?) & 1/wf Esther [DAGGETT] (-bef 1708); b 1700, 1690/98; Martha's Vineyard
COTTLE, Ezra & Mary WOODBRIDGE; 6 Jul 1695; Newbury
COTTLE, James (1668?-1750?) & Elizabeth [LOOK] (1675-1742+); b 1693; Martha's Vineyard
COTTLE, William (1626-1668) & Sarah [BING] (-1699), m/2 John HALE 1673?; b 1662; Newbury
COTTON, Benjamin (-1724) & Elizabeth _?_ ; b 1689; Portsmouth, NH
COTTON, Ephraim & Mary NOBLE; 1 Feb 1697; Medfield
COTTON, John (1585-1652) & 1/wf Elizabeth HORROCKS (d in Eng); in Eng, 3 Jul 1613; Boston
COTTON, John (1585-1652) & 2/wf Sarah (HAWKRIDGE) STORY (-1676), w William, m/3 Richard MATHER 1656; Boston, Eng, 25 Apr 1632; Boston
COTTON, John (1634-) & Joanna/Hannah? ROSSITER (1642-1702); 7 Nov 1660; Wethersfield, CT/Guilford, CT
COTTON, John & Mary _?_ /[?STOW] (?1639-), m/2 Samuel FLETCHER, Sr. 1684, m/3 John SPAULDING 1700; b 1666; ?Boston/Concord
COTTON, John (?1650-1714) & Sarah [EARL?/HEARL?]; ca 1675?; Portsmouth, NH
COTTON, John & Mary STONE (1643-), m/2 John SPAULDING 1705; 12 Aug 1682; ?Middletown, CT
COTTON, John (1658-1710) & Ann/Anne/Anna? LAKE (1663-), m/2 Increase MATHER 1715; 17 Aug 1686; Salisbury/Boston/Hampton, NH
COTTON, John (1661-1706) & Sarah HUBBARD (1659-1706); b 1691; ?Yarmouth
COTTON, Richard (-1722, ae 55) & Elizabeth (SALTONSTALL) DENISON (-1736), w John; aft 12 Sep 1689, ?Sep 1692?, 1690?; ?Ipswich/Sandwich
COTTON, Samuel & 1/wf Lydia BATES (-1713); 22 Jul 1695; Chelmsford/Milton, CT
COTTON, Seaborn (1633-1688) & 1/wf Dorothy BRADSTREET (-1672); 14 Jun 1654; Andover
COTTON, Seaborn (1633-1688) & 2/wf Prudence (WADE) CROSBY, w Anthony, m/3 John HAMMOND ca 1689?; 9 Jul 1673; Salisbury
COTTON, Thomas, London & Bridget HOARE (1673-); London, 21 Jun 1689, in Eng
COTTON, William & Anne _?_ ; b 1642, b 1641; Boston
COTTON, William (-1678) & Elizabeth HAM (-1678+); b 1650?; Portsmouth, NH
COTTON, William (-1737) & Abigail [PICKERING]; b 1679; Portsmouth, NH
COTTON, William & Ama/Anna?/Anne? CARTER; 6 Nov 1699; Boston

COTTRELL, Gershom (-1711) & Bethiah WILCOX (-1711+); 15 Feb 1677; Stonington, CT/Westerly, RI/Kingstown, RI
COTTRELL, Jabesh/Jabez & Ann/Anna? [PEABODY]; b 22 Mar 1686/7; Stonington, CT/Newport
COTTRELL, John (-1721) & Elizabeth/Penelope _?_; b 1679; Kingstown, RI
COTTRELL, Nicholas[1] (-1680) & 2/wf Martha _?_ (ae 36 in 1681), ?m/2 Walter MOREY/MOWRY?; ca 1645?; Newport/Westerly, RI
COTTRELL, Nicholas[2] & Ann PEABODY
COTTRELL, Nicholas[3] & Dorothy PENDLETON
COTTRELL, Nicholas (-1715?, 1716?) & 1/wf _?_; ca 1658/70?; Westerly, RI
COTTRELL, _?_ & [Dorothy PENDLETON]
COUCH, David & Mary _?_; b 1686, b 1685/6; Boston
COUCH, James (-1720, drowned at Cape Cod) & Rebecca [DOWNE?]; b 1701?; Boston
COUCH, Joseph & 1/wf Joanna DEERING (-living 1699); b 1677; Kittery, ME
COUCH, Joseph & Anne [ADAMS], m/2 David HILL, m/3 Nicholas WEEKS; b 1696?; Kittery, ME
COUCH, Joseph & 2/wf Catherine _?_; aft 1699, by 1712; ?Kittery, ME
COUCH, Robert & Elizabeth _?_; b 1663; Boston
COUCH, Samuel & 1/wf Pity (_?_) DEAL (Indian woman), wid; aft 1672; Milford, CT
COUCH, Samuel & 2/wf Mary [STILLSON], w Vincent; 1691; Milford, CT
COUCH, Samuel (-1741) & Edna (HURLBUT) [GILBERT] (1674-1737), w Benjamin; b 1695; Fairfield, CT
COUCH, Simon (1634-1689) & Mary [ANDREWS?] (-1691); b 1663, ca Jan 1662/3?; Fairfield, CT
COUCH, Simon (1669-1713) & Abigail [HARGES] (-1730, ae 57), m/2 John ANDREWS; b 1694; Fairfield, CT
COUCH, Thomas (-1687) & 1/wf Rebecca _?_ (-1672); 22 Nov 1666; Wethersfield, CT
COUCH, Thomas (-1687) & 2/wf Hannah _?_; b 1674
COULTMAN, John (-1688) & Mary _?_, m/2 Theophilus SHERMAN; Sep 1667, ca 24 Sep 1667; Wethersfield, CT
COUNTS, Edward & Sarah ADAMS (1637-); 25 Feb 1662, 1662/3; Malden
COUNCE, Roger & Elizabeth _?_; b 1681?; Charlestown
COUNCE, Samuel (1671-1715?) & Hannah PIERCE (1671-); 29 Jan 1695/6, 1695; Charlestown
COURSER/CORSER, Archelaus (-1680) & Rachel ROPER; 1661; Lancaster
COURSER, John (?1642-1713?) & Margaret _?_ (1640-1713); b 1668; Boston
COURSER, William (1609-1673) & Joanna _?_; b 1638; Boston
COURTNEY, George & Dorcas SELLY/SELLEY; 2 Jun 1698; Boston
COUSENS, Abraham & Mary EAMES (1661-); 19 Nov 1684; Woburn
COUSSINS, Edmond & Margaret BIRD; 1656, 1657, prob Jan 1656/7; Boston
COUSINS, Isaac (1613-1702) & 1/wf Elizabeth _?_ (-14 Oct 1656); ca 1643/6?; Rowley/Boston/etc.
COUSSINS, Isaac (1613-1702) & 2/wf Ann (?EDWARDS) HUNT, w John; 1657; Boston
COUSINS, Isaac (1613-1702) & 3/wf Martha (STANBURY)? PRIEST; by 1677
COUSINS, Isaac[2] (-1675) & Susannah [MILLS], m/2 Peter FOLSOM 1678; Wells, ME
COZENS, Richard & Bethia OSBOURNE; 8 Apr 1673/4; Stonington, CT
COOZENS, Richard & Mary CHALKER; 7 Mar 1677/8; Saybrook, CT/New Shoreham, RI
COUSINS, Thomas (1649-1690?); & _?_ (-1690/76?; Wells, ME
COVELL, Ephraim (1677?-1753?) & 1/wf Mercy _?_ (-1728); ca 1700; Chatham
COUVEY/COVEE/COVEL?, James & Mary _?_; b 1639; Braintree
COVEL, James & Abigail [?SMITH]; b 1685; Martha's Vineyard
COVELL, Joseph (1675-1732+) & 1/wf Lydia [STEWART]; ca 1700; Chatham
COVELL, Nathaniel & Sarah [NICKERSON]; ca 1662; Chatham
COVEL, Nathaniel (ca 1670-1747) & Judith NICKERSON (-1746+); 5 Mar 1696/7; Eastham
COVEL, Philip & Elizabeth ATWOOD; 16 Nov 1688, 26 Nov; Malden
COVEL, Richard & Sarah [BUSHNELL] (1655-); b 1678; Boston
COVEL, William (?1673-1760) & Sarah _?_; ca 1700; Chatham/Harwick/etc.
COWDALL, John & Mary (MEAYS) [DAVIS], w William; 1655; Boston/Newport/New London, CT
COWDRY, Matthias[3] (1679-1724+) & 1/wf Sarah _?_; ca 1700?, b 1701, b 30 Oct 1701; Boston
COWDRY, Nathaniel[2] (1630±-1690) & 1/wf Elizabeth [GOULD?] (-1659); 21 Nov 1654; Reading
COWDRY, Nathaniel[2] (1630±-1690) & Mary BACHELDER/BATCHELDER (?1636-1729); 22 Nov 1660; Reading

CODRY, Nathaniel[3] (1661-1690) & Elizabeth PARKER, m/2 Jeremiah SWAIN; 17 Nov 1685; Reading

COWDRY, Samuel[3] (1657-) & Elizabeth _?_ ; 28 Apr 1685; Reading/Charlestown

COWDRY, William[1] (1698/1702-1687) & 1/wf Joanna LICENCE (-1666); High Wycombe, Bucks, 17 Apr 1626, ca 69 or 70 in 1672; Lynn/Reading

COWDRY, William[1] (1698/1702-1687) & Alse/Alice [BOUTWELL]?, w James?; 5 Dec 1666; Reading

COWDRY, William[3] (1666-) & 1/wf Esther [BURRILL] (1674-1698); b 1695(6?); Reading

COWELL, Edward (1614-1691) & Margaret _?_ ; b 1644; Boston

COWELL, Edward & Sarah [WILSON?]; b 1660; Boston/?Great Islands, NH

COWELL, Edward (-1677) & Agnes [HARVEY?], m/2 George SNELL; Portsmouth, NH

COWELL, Edward & 2/wf Sarah HOBART (1644-1696), m/2 John CLEVERLY 1695; 26 Jun 1668; Hingham

COWELL, John (-1693, ae ca 49) & Hannah [HURD] (-1713, ae 73); b 1668; Boston

COWELL, Joseph (-1709) & Mary (CARTER) [HUNTER?/HUNT?] (-1702), w William; b 1673; Boston

COVWELL/COVILL?, Joseph & Alice PALMER; 27 Feb 1685; Woburn

COWEL, Joseph (1673-1708) & Elizabeth WILLIAMS; 6 Aug 1696; Boston

COWELL, Samuel & Hannah [MILLER]; ca 1698?; Portsmouth, NH

COWELL, Thomas & Elizabeth (?GUNNISON/LYNN) [SEELEY], w William; ca 1674-5; Kittery, ME

COWELL, ?Joseph/Richard & Hannah TOWER (1652-), dau John, m/2 David WHIPPLE 1677; b 1673, no marriage; Hingham

COWES, Anthony & Dorcas WOODEN; 5 Sep 1688; York Co., ME

COWES, Gyles (1642-1696) & 1/wf Mary DUTCH (-1672); 29 Jul 1668; Ipswich

COWES, Gyles (1642-1696) & 2/wf Agnes BERRYE (-1731); 27 Feb 1672, 1672/3; Ipswich

COWES, Henry & Charity _?_ ; b 29 Nov 1655

COWES/COES, [Michael] (1639-1715) & Grace [STACEY] (1659-1736), dau Grace m Thomas POWSLAND 1699; b 1684, ca 1677; Marblehead

COWES, _?_ & Rachel _?_ ; b 1702?, b 1700; Marblehead

COWING, Israel (1664-1717/18, 1717) & Hannah [LITCHFIELD] (1672-1747/49); b 1699, b 1691; Scituate

COWEN, John & Rebecca MAN, w Richard; last of Mar 1656, 31 Mar; Scituate

COWEN, John & Sarah _?_ ; b 1688; Scituate

COWEN, _?_ & Elizabeth _?_ (-1653); ?Boston

COWIN, _?_ & Hannah [NILES?] (1637-); Braintree?

COWLAND, Ralph (-1679+) & 1/wf Alice [SHOTTON] (-1666), w Samson; Portsmouth, RI

COWLAND, Ralph & 2/wf Eleanor (_?_) WAIT, w Thomas; ca 1668

COWLAN, Ralph (-1679+) & 2/wf Joan HIDE; 25 Jun 1677; Portsmouth, RI

COWLES, Isaac (1675-1756) & 1/wf Mary ANDREWS (1674-1708); 3 Jan 1694, 2 Jan 1694; Farmington

COWLES, John (1598-1675) & Hannah _?_ (1613-1683, 1684); b 1639; Hartford/Farmington, CT/Hatfield

COWLES, John (-1689?, Farmington) & Deborah BARTLETT (1647-1711); 22 Nov 1668; Northampton/Hatfield?

COWLES, John (1671-1748) & Experience [CHAPPELL]; b 1701?, no issue; Farmington, CT

COWLES, Jonathan (1671-1756) & Prudence FRARY (1671-1756); 21 Jan 1697, 1696/7; Hadley

COWLES, Joseph & 1/wf Abigail ROYCE; 13 Jul 1699; Wallingford, CT/Meriden, CT

COWLES, Nathaniel (-1672/3) & 1/wf Phebe WOODRUFF; 11 Feb 1696/7; Farmington, CT

COWLES, Samuel (?1639-1691) & Abigail STANLEY (-1734?, 1736?); 14 Jun 1660; Farmington, CT

COWLES, Samuel (1662-1748) & Rachel PORTER (1658-1743); 12 May 1685, ?13 May, ?17 Nov; Farmington, CT

COWLES, Samuel (-1750) & Sarah [HUBBARD] (1672-); b 1698; Hadley

COWLES, Timothy & Hannah PITKIN (1666-); 1 Jan 1690, 1689/90; Farmington, CT

COPPERTHWAITE, Hugh[1] (1648-1730, ae 82, 20 May 1720) & 1/wf Elizabeth _?_ (-25 Nov 1697, 15 Dec 1697); Flushing, LI

COPPERTHWAITE, Hugh[2] & Elizabeth ROGERS (1669-1707); 10 May 1699; Marshfield?/Flushing, LI

COWPERTHWAITE, John & Sarah ADAMS; 1-1-1690, Jan 1690/1; Flushing, LI

COCKE, Clement & Elizabeth _?_; b 1687; Braintree

COX, Edward/?Edmond & Agnes [CARD], m/2 _?_ KALLY/CELLEY of NY; b 1670?, by 1680; York, ME

COX, Edward (-1675) & Margaret _?_; b 1672; Boston

COX, Edward (-1737) & Mary SWACY/SWASEY/SAWYER? (-1737), wid; 28 Nov 1695, 1694; Salem

COX, Edward & Mary [PARSONS]; m int 8 Mar 1696/7; Boston

COCKES, George (-1706) & Mary MASON (-1706+); 23 Feb 1667; Salem

COX, George (1668-) & Mary INGERSOLL (1671-); bef 1695; Salem/Boston

COX, Gowen & Mary [?SHERBURNE], m/2 Peter MATTHEWS by 1697; b 1697?; Portsmouth, NH

COCK, Henry (1678-1733) & 1/wf Mary FIKE (1678-30 Dec 1715); 28 Aug 1699; Matinecock, LI

COCK, James & Sarah [?CLARK]; b 1656; Southold, LI/Setauket, LI/Oyster Bay, LI/Killingworth, LI

COCKES, James & Mary ROW; m int 11 Dec 1695; Boston

COCK, James (1674-1728) & Hannah FEKE; 1 Dec 1698; Matinecock, LI

COX, John (living 1689) & _?_ [LAMBERT] (-1686); b 1658?, b 1661?; Pemaquid, ME

COX, John (-1690) & Mary (KIRTLAND) THOMAS? [SHERMAN] (1640-), w Nathaniel, m/3 Thomas ROOT (her mother Alice m/2 Evan/Ewins THOMAS); b 1672; Boston

COCK, John (-1736+) & 1/wf Susanna [POPE] (-1702+); ca 1680, 5 ch bpt, 5 Mar 1692/3; Dorchester/etc.

COCK, John (1666-1717) & 1/wf _?_; b 1689; ?Matinecock, LI

COX, John & Hannah (ROBERTS) HILL (-1720+), w William; 22 May 1694; Oyster River, NH

COCK, John (1666-1717) & 2/wf Dorothy [HARCOURT] (-1739?); b 1698; ?Matinecock, LI

COX, John & Joanna BROWN; 18 Nov 1698; Boston

COCKE, Joseph (-1679) & Susanna UPSHALL (1639-), dau Nicholas, m/2 Joseph BRIDGEMAN; 10 Nov 1659; Boston

COX, Joseph & Martha _?_; b 1669(70?); Boston

COX, Moses (-1687) & 1/wf Alice _?_ (-1657); b 1640?; Hampton, NH

COX, Moses (-1687) & 2/wf Prudence (MARSTON) SWAIN, w William; 16 Jun 1658; Hampton, NH

COCKE, Nicholas & Sarah [?WHITMAN] (-1740), m/2 Robert GOULD; b 1693; Boston

COX, Philip & Remember _?_, m/2 Bartholomew _?_; b 1686; Salem

COX, Richard & _?_; b 1685; Boston

COX, Robert & 1/wf Martha _?_; b 1671; Boston

COX, Robert (-1684) & 2/wf Hester/Esther _?_; b 8 Feb 1683; Boston

COCKE, Robert (-1731) & 1/wf Mary [POPE?] (-1702?); b 1693; Scituate/Boston

COX, Thomas & _?_; b 1654; Pemaquid

COX, Thomas & Martha _?_; b 1671; Pemaquid/Boston

COCK, Thomas (1658-1685) & [Esther]/[Hester] [WILLIAMS]; ca 1680; Lusum, LI/Jericho, LI

COX, Thomas (1664-1711, 1710?) & Hannah [?WOODBURY], (see William COX); ca 1686/8, 2 ch bpt, 1690; Beverly

COX, Thomas & Sarah _?_; b 1697(8?); Boston

COX, William & Mary _?_; ca 1660/70?; Salem/etc.

COX, William & Mary (JENKINS) [ATKINSON] (?1652-), div wf of Marmaduke; b 1676; Scituate

COXE, William (-bef 1708) & Hannah [WOODBURY] (1664-1721+); b 1688; Salem

COCK, William & Elizabeth SANDERS; 23 Aug 1688; Marblehead

COY, John & Elizabeth EDWARDS; 23 Jun 1679; Beverly/Wenham

COY, Matthew (1633-) & Elizabeth ROBERTS; 29 Aug 1654; Boston

COY, Matthew (1656-) & Ann [BREWSTER] (1662-); b 1685; Norwich, CT/Preston, CT

COY, Richard (1625-1675) & Martha [HAYFIELD]; b 8 Apr 1652, b 1649?; Salisbury/Wenham/Brookfield

COY, Richard & Sarah KENT; 1 Dec 1674; Springfield

CRABB, Henry & Hannah EMMONS; 1 Jan 1657/8; Boston

CRABB, Richard (see Robert COE) & 1/wf _?_; b 1640; Wethersfield, CT/Stamford, CT/Greenwich, CT

CRABB, Richard (-1680) & 2/wf Alice [WRIGHT] (-1685), w Peter; b 1675, b 14 Sep 1663; Oyster Bay, LI
CRABTREE, John & Alice _?_, m/2 Joshua HEWES 1657; b 1639; Boston
CRABTREE, John & 1/wf Mary _?_ (-31 May 1683); b 1673; Swansea
CRABTREE, John & 2/wf Mary _?_; 1 Nov 1683; Swansea
CRACKBONE, Benjamin (-1675) & Elizabeth DUTTON; 6 Nov 1657; Cambridge
CRACKBONE, Gilbert (1612-1672) & 1/wf _?_; b 1637; Cambridge
CRACKBONE, Gilbert (1612-1672) & Elizabeth COOLIDGE/COOLEY, w John of Ipswich, m/3 Richard ROBBINS 1673; 17 Jun 1656, no issue; Cambridge
CRACKBONE, Joseph & Abigail RICE; 11 May 1698; Cambridge
CRACKSTON, John & _?_ [SMITH?]; b 1620?; Plymouth
CRADDICK, Matthew & 1/wf Damares [WINN]; b 1623; Charlestown
CRADOCK, Matthew & 2/wf Rebecca [JORDAN], m/2 Richard GLOVER bef 1650, w Benjamin WHITSHCOCK/WICKOTT; Salem
CRAFORD, Mordecai (1624-) & Edith _?_; b 1649; Salem
CRAFFORD, Mungo (-1712) & 1/wf Mary [ROBERTS?]; b 1681; Boston
CRAFFORD/CRAWFORD, Mungo (-1712) & Susanna (BILL) KENNET (1666-1713), w Richard; 29 Jan 1694; Boston
CRAFFORD/CRAWFORD, Stephen (-bef 1642?) & Margaret _?_, m/2 Thomas WILLEY; Kittery/Isles of Shoals
CRAFT, Ebenezer & Elizabeth WELD; 14 Nov 1700; Roxbury
CRAFT, Ephraim (1677-) & Hannah READ; 15 May 1699; Chelmsford
CRAFTS, Griffin¹ (-1689) & 1/wf Alice _?_ (-1673, ae 73); in Eng, b 1629; Roxbury
CRAFTS, Griffin¹ (1600-1689) & 2/wf Ursula ROBINSON (-1679), w William; 15 Jul 1673; Charlestown
CRAFTS, Griffin¹ (-1689) & 3/wf Dorcas (FRENCH) PEAKE (-1697), w Christopher; aft 1676, aft 1679
CRAFTS, John (1630-1685) & 1/wf Rebecca WHEELOCK (ca 1632-1667); 7 Jun 1654; Roxbury
CRAFTS, John (1630-1685) & 2/wf Mary HUDSON (-1724), Lynn; 30 Mar 1669; Roxbury
CRUFFS/?CRAFTS, John & Eleanor BROWN; 29 Nov 1689; Marblehead
CRAFTS, Moses (1641-1718) & Rebecca GARDNER (1647-1699+); 25 Jun 1667, ?24 Jan; Roxbury/Deerfield
CRAFT, Richard & Elizabeth (WOOD) NICHOLSON, w Thomas; 15 Jan 1693/4; Marblehead
CRAFT, Samuel² (1665-1693) & Elizabeth SEAVER (1643-1731); 16 Oct 1661; Roxbury/Woodstock, CT
CRAFT, Samuel (1667-1709) & Elizabeth SHARP (1642-), m/2 James SHED ?1718; 25 Dec 1693; Roxbury
CRAFT, Thomas (-1692/3) & Abigail DICKINSON, m/2 Samuel CROWFOOT 1704; 6 Dec 1683; Hadley
CRAFT, William (-1689) & Ann (SOUTH) [IVORY] (-1689), w Thomas; aft 1664, 1667, b Sep 1660; Lynn
CRAFTS, William (-ca 1694) & Joan (PALMER) [DEERING], w Roger; aft 26 Jun 1676, bef 23 Feb 1691; ME
CRAFT, William & _?_; b 1683?; Hempstead, LI
CRAGGENE/CRAGIN, John & Sarah DAWES; 4 Nov 1661; Woburn
CRAGGEN, John (1677-) & Deborah SKELTON; m int ?13 Apr 170^; Woburn
CRAGE/CRAIGIE?/CRAIG, David & Deborah MAN; 3 Jul 1698; Boston
CRAGG, John & Sarah [PARKMAN] (1662-), dau Elias; b 1681; Boston
CRAM, Benjamin (1638-1711) & Argentine CROMWELL (-1708+); 28 Nov 1662, ?25 Nov; Hampton, NH
CRAM, Benjamin (1666-) & Sarah [SHAW] (1676-); b 1697?; Hampton, NH/Hampton Falls, NH
CRAM, John (1597-1682) & Hester/Esther WHITE (-1677); Bilsby, Eng, 7 Jun 1624, ?8 Jun; Boston/Exeter, NH/Hampton, NH
CRAM, John (1665-1740) & 1/wf Mary WADLEIGH; b 1693; Hampton, NH
CRAM, Joseph (1671-) & Jane PHILBRICK; 17 May 1700; Hampton, NH
CRAM, Thomas (1644-1751) & Elizabeth WEARE (1658-); 20 Dec 1681; Hampton, NH
CROMPTON/CRAMPTON, Dence/Dennis (-1690) & 1/wf Mary PARMELEE (-1667); Sep 1660, 16 Sep; Guilford, CT

CRAMPTON, Dennis (-1690) & 2/wf Sarah (HULL/HALL?) MUNGER, w Nicholas; b 1669, 1669?; Guilford, CT/Killingworth, CT
CRAMPTON, Dennis (-1690) & 3/wf Frances _?_; Guilford, CT
CRAMPTON, John & 1/wf Hannah [ANDREWS]; b 6 Jun 1662; Norwalk, CT
CRAMPTON, John & 2/wf Sarah ROCKWELL; 8 Oct 1676; Norwalk, CT
CRANDALL, Eber (1676-1727) & 1/wf Mary _?_; b 1701?; Newport/Westerly, RI
CRANDALL, Jeremiah (-1718) & Priscilla [WARNER] (-1750), m/2 Abraham LOCKWOOD; ?ca 1695, ?b 1701, b 1702; Newport/Westerly, RI
CRANDALL, John[1] (-1676) & 1/wf ?Sarah _?_ (-1670); Newport/Westerly, RI
CRANDALL, John (-1676) & 2/wf Hannah [?GAYLORD] (1646-1678+), ?dau William; b 6 Dec 1677; Providence/Newport/etc.
CRANDALL, John[2], Jr. (-1704) & Elizabeth GORTON (-1704); 18 Jun 1672, 1673?; Warwick, RI/Newport
CRANDILL, Joseph (ca 1661-1737) & [Deborah BURDICK]; ?by 11 Apr 1685, ?ca 1687; Westerly, RI/Kingston, RI
CRANDALL, Peter (-1734) & Mary [?BABCOCK/ELDER]; by 1674?; Westerly, RI
CRANDALL, Samuel (1662, 1663-1736) & Sarah ?CILLEY/?CELLEY/?CERLEY/?COLBY; ca 1685; Little Compton, RI/Tiverton, RI
CRANE, Abraham (-1713) & Hannah _?_; b 1697(8?); Wethersfield, CT
CRANE, Azariah (1649, ?1651-) & Mary [TREAT] (1647-1704); ca 1672?; ?Newark, NJ
CRANE, Benjamin (ca 1630-1691) & Mary BACKUS (ca 1633-1717); 23 Apr 1655; Wethersfield, CT
CRANE, Benjamin (-1694+) & Eleanor BRICK (-1694+); 12 Sep 1656; Medfield/Marlborough/etc.
CRANE, Benjamin (1656-1693) & 1/wf Mary CHAPMAN (-1687); 12 May 1686; Wethersfield, CT
CRANE, Benjamin (1656-1693) & 2/wf Martha [BOREMAN/BOARDMAN] (1666-), m/2 Samuel TERRY 1698; aft 28 Apr 1687, aft 5 Apr 1687, b 1690, ca 1689; Wethersfield, CT
CRANE, Benjamin & Elizabeth _?_; b 1688; Milton/Farmington
CRANE, Ebenezer (1665-), Milton & Mary TOLMAN (1671-), Dorchester; 13 Dec 1689, 13 Nov; Milton/Dorchester
CRANE, Elijah (1665-) & 1/wf Mary SHERMAN (1666-1716); b 1698; Stratford, CT/Wethersfield, CT
CRANE, Henry (1625-1710) & 1/wf Tabitha KINSLEY (ca 1626-23 Oct 1682); b 1656, b 1654?; Dorchester/Milton
CRANE, Henry (?1635-1711) & 1/wf Concurrence [MEIGS] (1643-1708); aft 1663, b 1667; Milford, CT/Killingworth
CRANE, Henry[1] (1625-1710) & 2/wf [Elizabeth] _?_; 2 Apr 1683; Milton
CRANE, Henry, Jr. & Elizabeth VOSE (1661-), dau Thomas; 18 Oct 1683; Milton
CRANE, Israel & Lydia WRIGHT (1672-); 13 Sep 1695; Wethersfield, CT
CRANE, Jasper (1600-) & Alice _?_; b 1635?, b 1642; New Haven/Branford, CT
CRANE, Jasper (1651-) & Joanna [SWAYNE] (1651-1720); b 1686; ?Newark, NJ
CRANE, John (?1635-) & Elizabeth [FOOTE]; b 1671; Branford, CT/Newark, NJ
CRANE, John (1659-1718) & Hannah LEONARD (1671-1760); 13 Dec 1686; Taunton
CRANE, John (1663-1694) & Abigail BUTLER, m/2 Samuel WALKER 1697, m/3 Samuel WRIGHT; 27 Oct 1692; Wethersfield, CT
CRANE, John (ca 1664-) & Martha DAGGETT (1672-); 25 May 1694, 28 May 1694, 25 May 1695; Windsor, CT/Killingworth, CT
CRAIN, John & Mary [CURTIS] (1675-); b 1701?; Wallingford, CT?
CRANE, Jonathan (1658-1735) & Deborah GRISWOLD (1661-); 19 Dec 1678; Norwich, CT/?Windham, CT
CRANE, Jonathan & Mary HIBBARD (1674-); 31 Jul 1700; ?Windham, CT
CRANE, Joseph (1661-1707) & Sarah KILBORNE (ca 1663-), m/2 Joseph LEONARD, m/3 Benjamin ANDREWS; 10 Dec 1684, ?16 Dec; Wethersfield, CT
CRANE, Nathaniel & Mary _?_; b 1686(7?); Newton
CRANE, Stephen (?1657-1738) & 1/wf Mary DENISON (1661-1721); 2 Jul 1676; Milton
CRANE, Theophilus (1674-) & Margaret LANE; 5 Dec 1699; Killingworth, CT
CRANNEVER/CRANIVER, Richard (-1677) & Elizabeth WOOLLAND; 7 Apr 1665; Salem
CRANMER, John & Elizabeth _?_; b 1688; Boston
CRANSTON, Benjamin & Sarah [GODFREY], m/2 Samuel SWEET; ca 1700/1701; Newport

CRANSTON, Caleb (?1662-1694?) & Judith [PARROTT] (-1737), m/1 Samuel CRANSTON 1711, m/2 William PEASE; b 1685?; Newport

CRANSTON, John (1626-1680) & Mary [CLARKE] (1641-1711), m/2 Philip JONES of NY, m/3 John STANTON aft 29 Oct 1685, bef 1 Nov 1688; 1658, 3 Jun 1658; Newport

CRANSTON, Samuel (1659-1727) & 1/wf Mary [HART] (1663-1710); ca 1681?, b 1684; Newport

CRANSTON, Walter & Mary BRUCE (1665-), m/2 John BROOKS 1685, m/3 Peter HAY; 4 Jun 1683; Woburn/Lynn

CRANSTON, William & Mary/Mercy STANTON/_?_ (1668-), m/2 Samuel GIBBS 1696±?; b 1690?; Newport

CRARY, John & Esther _?_ ; b 1671(2?); Boston

CRARY, John & Mary _?_ ; b 1678; Boston

CRARY, Nicholas & Esther _?_ ; b 1677; Boston

CRARY, Peter (-1708) & Christobel GALLUP; 31 Dec 1677, - Dec 1677; New London, CT

CRAVATH/CORNETH, Ezekiel & Mercy (SANDYS) [MEARS], w John; b 1669; Boston

CRAVATH, Ezekiel (1671-1717) & Elizabeth HOOK; 14 Jun 1698; Boston

CRAW, Richard & Jane _?_ ; bef 10 Oct 1697

CRAW, Robert & _?_ ; Newport

CRAWFORD, Gideon (1651-1707) & Freelove FENNER (1656-1712); 13 Apr 1687; Providence

CRAWFORD, John, Liverpool, Eng, & Mary ALFORD, wid; 22 Nov 1692; Charlestown

CRAFFORD, John & Elizabeth _?_ ; b 1676; Portsmouth, NH/(?NJ)

CRAWFORD, [?John] (-1634) & Winifred _?_ (-1701), m/2 John WOLCOTT, m/3 Thomas ALLYN; b 1633; Watertown

CRAWLEY, Thomas (-1677+) (ae 36 in 1654) & 1/wf _?_ ; b 1660; Exeter, NH

CRAWLEY, Thomas & Joanna [SAYERS/SAYWARD]/[SEWARD], w Robert

CRAY, George & Mary _?_ ; b 1678; Boston

CREATTY, Andrew (-1695, ae 44) & Mary _?_ , m/2 William DODGE 1698; b 1681; Marblehead

CREDIFORD, Joseph (-1713, 1714) & Rachel [BUSSY]; ca 1691, by 1692; Wells, ME

CREBER/CREEBER, Thomas & 1/wf _?_ [MOSES]; by 1666?, by 1668, bef 1664/5; Portsmouth, NH

CREBER, Thomas & 2/wf Mary [PEASE], w John; b 3 Jun 1689; Portsmouth, NH

CREED, William (-1717) & Sarah [?WIGGINS]; by 1670?; Jamaica, LI

CREED, William[2] (-1710) & Mary [CORNELL] (1675±-), m/2 Richard BETTS; ca 1695-1700?; Jamaica, LI

CREHORE, Teague (-1696) & Mary [SPURR], m/2 Matthias PUFFER 1697; b 1666; Milton

CREHORE, Timothy (?1667-1739), Milton & Ruth RIOL/ROYAL? (1668-), Dorchester; 10 Feb 1688, 1688/9; Milton

CRESEY, John & _?_ ; in Eng, b 1676; Boston

CREESY, John (1659-1735) & Sarah [GAINES] (1665-1751); b 1686; Beverly/Salem

CRESSY, John & 1/wf Abigail KNAPP (ca 1671/2-1706); 1 Dec 1692, 12 Jan 1692; Stamford, CT

CREESEY, John & Mary GREEN; betw 1694 & 1698 at Salem; Ipswich

CRESSEY, Michael/Mighill (1628-1670) & 1/wf Mary [BATCHELDER] (1640-1659); ca 1658; Salem

CRESIE, Michael/Mighill (1628-1670) & 2/wf Mary QUILTER (1640-), m/2 John HORSLEY 1671; 6 Apr 1660; Ipswich

CRESEE, Michael/Mighill (1661-1740) & Sarah [HIDDEN] (1661-1751); 20 Aug 1686; Rowley

CRESE, Robert & _?_ ; b 1658(9?); Ipswich

CREESE, Thomas & Rooksby GREENLEAF; 30 Jun 1697, int?; Boston

CREESY, William (?1636-1685) & _?_ ; b 1658?; Stamford, CT

CRESSEE, William (1663-1718) & Anne HIDDEN (-1748); 23 Jan 1688, b 1688, 1687, 1686-7, 1685/6; Rowley

CRESSY, William & _?_ ; b 1695; Stamford, CT

CREASSON/CRESSONS, Thomas (-1717) & Sarah [WILSON] (1668-1716); b 1698; Woburn

CREW, Francis & Dorothy POUSLY/POWSLAND, w Richard?; 19 Dec 1700; Boston

CRIPPEN, Thomas[1] (-1709/10) & [?Frances _?_]; b 1676; Falmouth/E. Haddam, CT

CRIPPEN, Thomas[2] & Mary [ACKLEY]; ca 1695; East Haddam, CT

CRISP, Benjamin (ca 1610, 1611-1683) & 1/wf Bridget _?_ (-1666+, 1676?); b 1637; Watertown/Groton

CRISP, Benjamin (1611-1683) & 2/wf Joanna (?GOFF) [LONGLEY] (-1698, ae 78, ae 79), w William; ca 1683, ca 1681; Watertown

CRISP, George (-1682) & 1/wf Mary __?__ (-20 Feb 1676, 1676/7?); Eastham

CRISPE, George (-1682) & Hepzibah COLE (1649-), m/2 Daniel DOANE; 24 May 1677; Eastham

CRISPE, Jonathan (1640-1680) & Deliverance [?PEASE], m/2 William LONGLEY, Jr. by 1686; no ch recorded; Groton

CRISP, Richard & 1/wf Hannah (HUDSON) RICHARDS, w Benjamin; ca 18 Oct 1666; Boston

CRISP, Richard & 2/wf Sarah [WHEELWRIGHT], m/2 Nathaniel WILLIAMS 21 Feb 1700/[1701]; b 1671; Boston

CRITCHET/CRITCHETT, Elias (?1646-) & 1/wf __?__; ca 1670-90?; Portsmouth, NH

CRITCHFIELD, William & Susanna/Susan __?__; b 1686; Boston

CROYCHLEY, Richard & Alice DINELY (-1645), w William; Aug 1639, b 1640; Boston

CRITCHLEY, Richard & Jane __?__; b 1647; Boston

CRITCHLEY, Richard & Elizabeth __?__; b 1675; Boston

CROAD, John (-1670) & Elizabeth PRICE, m/2 John RUCK 1672; 17:1 mo. 1658, ?17 Mar 1659; Salem

CROAD, John (1663-) & 1/wf Deborah THOMAS; 1 Dec 1692 at Marshfield; Salem/Berwick, ME

CROAD, Richard (-1689, ae 61) & Frances HERSEY; 29 Apr 1656, ?29 May; Hingham/Salem

CROCKER, Daniel (-1681?) & Sarah BALDEN; 30 Nov 1660; Boston

CROCKER/CROOKER?, Daniel (-1692) & Mary BUMPUS; 2 Jan 1682, ?20 Jan; Marshfield

CROCKER, Eleazer (1650-1723) & 1/wf Ruth CHIPMAN (1663-1698); 7 Apr 1682; Barnstable

CROCKER, Francis & Mary GRANT (-1693?); b 1641?, b 1647?, m lic 2 Mar 1646/7; Barnstable/Scituate

CROKER, Francis & __?__ [?MEADALL] (-Mar 1692/3); Marshfield

CROCKER, Job (1645-1719) & 1/wf Mary WALLEY; beginning of Nov 1668; Barnstable

CROCKER, Job (1645-1719) & 2/wf Hannah TAYLOR (ca 1658-1743); 19 Jul 1680; Barnstable

CROCKER, John (-1669) & Jane/Joan? __?__; b 1636?, no issue; Scituate/Barnstable

CROCKER, John (1637-1711) & 1/wf Mary BODFISH (-1662); - Nov 1659; Barnstable

CROCKER, John (1637-1711) & 2/wf Mary BURSLEY (1643-); 25 Apr 1663; Barnstable

CROCKER, John (1672-) & Mary TUBBS; b 1701?, b 1706; New London, CT

CROCKER, Jonathan (1662-1740, 1746?) & Hannah HOWLAND (1661-bef Feb 1710/11; 20 May 1686; Barnstable

CROCKER, Joseph (1654-) & Temperance BURSLEY; beginning of Dec 1677; Barnstable

CROCKER, Joseph (1667/8-bef 11 Feb 1741) & Anne HOWLAND (1670-); 18 Sep 1691; Barnstable

CROCKER, Josiah (1647-1698/9) & Meletiah/Melatiah HINCKLEY (1648-1714); 23 Oct 1668; Barnstable

CROCKER, Richard & Elizabeth GROVER; m int 1 Oct 1695; Boston

CROCKER, Samuel (1671-1718) & 1/wf Sarah PARKER; 10 Dec 1696; Barnstable

CROCKER, Samuel (?1676-1756, 1754?) & Hannah WOLCOTT; 30 Dec 1697; Norwich, CT

CROCKER, Thomas (1633-1716) & Rachel CHAPPEL (1649-); b 1669, ca 1667?; New London, CT

CROCKER, Thomas (1671-1728) & Hannah GREEN (-1729); 25 Mar 1696; Barnstable

CROCKER, Thomas & Mary CARPENTER; 8 Apr 1697; New London?

CROCKER, Thomas (1670-) & Ann BEEBE; 23 Apr 1700; New London, CT

CROCKER, William (?1608-1692) (ae 65 in 1673) & 1/wf Alice __?__ (-1683+); b 1636; Barnstable/Scituate

CROCKER, William (-1692) & 2/wf Patience (COBB) [PARKER] (1642-), w Robert; aft 4 May 1684, bef 1692, 1686?; Barnstable

CROCKER, __?__ & Anne __?__, wid; b 1650; Scituate

CROCKETT, Elihu & 1/wf Mary [WINNOCK]; b 1684; Kittery, ME

CROCKETT, Ephraim (-1688) & Ann [EDGE?] (-1695+); by 1667; Kittery, ME

CROCKETT, Hugh & Margaret __?__; by 1697; Kittery, ME

CROCKETT, Joseph & Hannah [CLEMENTS]; b 1679; Kittery, ME

CROCKETT, Joseph & Mary BALL; 12 Oct 1700; Kittery, ME

CROCKETT, Joshua & Sarah [TRISKEY]; 1683, ?b 19 May 1682; Kittery, ME/Newington

CROCKETT, Thomas[1] (1611-1679) & Ann __?__ (1617-1701+), m/2 Digory JEFFREY by 1683; b 1641; Kittery, ME

CROCKFORD, James & Elizabeth __?__; b 1693(4?); Boston

CROCUM/?CROAKUM/?CROWKHAM, Francis (-1669) & Joan [WALLER], w Thomas; b 1656(7?); Boston

CROAKHAM, John (-1679, 1678) & Rebecca [JOSSELYN] (-1713), m/2 Thomas HARRIS 1679, m/3 Edward STEVENS 1700; no issue; Boston

CROMLONE alias CROMWELL, Gyles & Alice WISEMAN; 10 Sep 1648; Newbury

CROMLONE, Thomas (-1635) & _?_ (-1635); Newbury

CROMWELL, Giles (-1673) & 1/wf [Alice] WEEKE (-14 Jun 1648); Erling?/Eling, Hampshire, 8 Feb 1629/30; Newbury

CROMLON alias CROMWELL, Giles (-1673) & 2/wf Alice WISEMAN (-1669); 10 Sep 1648; Newbury

CRUMWELL, John (-1661) & Rebecca/Seaborn [BACHELDER] (1635, 1634?-1664), m/2 Robert PARRIS 1663; b 1654; Boston/Charlestown

CROMWELL, John (1636-) & Joan BUTLER; 2 Nov 1662; Newbury

CROMWELL, John (-1700) & Hannah [BARNEY] (-1712+?, 1699/1700); b 1673; Salem

CROMWELL, John (1666-) & 1/wf Elizabeth THOMAS; 13 Jan 1691/2; Dover, NH

CROMWELL/CROMMETT?, John & Mary OAKLEY, w Miles; b 1668, b 1696, b 1688; Westchester Co., NY

CROMWELL, Philip (1614, ?1610-1693) & 1/wf _?_ /?Elizabeth TUTTLE; b 1635; Salem

CROMWELL, Philip (1610/1614-) (ae ca 48 in 1660) & 2/wf Dorothy KENISTON (-1673, ae 72), w Allen; m cont 10 Apr 1669; Salem

CROMWELL, Philip (?1634-1708) & _?_ [TUTTLE], dau John; by 1663; ?Dover, NH

CROMWELL, Philip (?1634-1708) & 2/wf Elizabeth [LEIGHTON] (-1708+); by 26 Sep 1671, ?20 Sep; ?Dover, NH

CROMWELL, Philip (-1693) & 3/wf Mary LEMON (-1683, ae 72), w Robert; 19 Nov 1674; Salem

CROMWELL, Philip (-1643) & 4/wf Margaret [BECKETT], w John; b 1687; Salem

CROMWELL, Thomas (?1617-1649) (ae ca 43 in 1660?) & Ann _?_, m/2 Robert KNIGHT by 1652, m/3 John JOYLEFFE 1657; b 1643?; ?Hampton/Boston/etc.

CROMWELL, Thomas (1625-1687) & Anna _?_ ; b 9 Sep 1655; Salem

CROOKER, Daniel (-1692) & Mary BUMPUS; 2 Jan 1682; Marshfield

CROOKER, Francis (-1700?) & Mary GAUNT (-1693); m lic 2 Mar 1646/7; Scituate/Marshfield

CROOKER, Jonathan (?1650-1745) & Mary [?BURROUGHS] (1656-1728); b 1679(80?); Marshfield

CROOKER, William[1] (-bef 1660) & Ann [GREGORY], m/2 John ROGERS ca 1608-9; b 1648, b 1647?, by 1647; New Haven, CT/Stratford, CT/Oyster Bay, LI

CROOKER, William[2] & [?Sarah ?HAWXHURST]; Oyster Bay, LI

CROOKSON, John & Tabitha HILL; m int 12 Aug 1695; Boston

CROSBY, Anthony (1632-) & Prudence WADE, m/2 Seaborn COTTON 1673, m/3 John HAMMOND ca 1689?; 28 Dec 1659; Rowley

CROSBY, Ebenezer (1675/6-) & [Ann]/Hannah _?_ ; b 1701; Harwich

CROSBY, Henry & Deliverance COREY; 5 Jun 1683; Salem

CROSBY, Joseph (1639-1695, ae 56) & 1/wf Sarah BRACKETT (-1690); 1 Jun 1673; Braintree

CROSBY, Joseph & Sarah FRENCH (1671-); 6 May 1691; Billerica

CROSBY, Joseph (1668?-1723), Yarmouth/Eastham & Mehitable MILLER; 16 Feb 1692/3; Yarmouth

CROSBY, Joseph (1639-1695) & 2/wf Ellen/Eleanor (VERSEY) PAYNE/RAINE, w Stephen; 5 Oct 1693; Braintree

CROSBY, Nathaniel (-1700) & Elizabeth BENNETT (1672-), m/2 John SCOTT; 13 Dec 1693; Rowley

CROSBY, Robert (1596-in Eng, 1640?) & Constance [BRIGHAM] (-1639) (came to New Eng); ca 1622; Rowley

CROSBY, Simon (-1639) & Anna/Anne BRIGHAM (-1675, ae 69), m/2 Rev. William THOMPSON ca 1641; in Eng, 21 Apr 1734; Cambridge

CROSBY, Simon (1637-) & Rachel BRACKETT (-1735, ae 96); 15 Jul 1659); Billerica

CROSBY, Simon & Hannah [EVERETT] (-1702); b 1689; Billerica

CROSBY, Simon (1665-1718) & Mary NICKERSON (1668-1746); 27 Aug 1691; Eastham

CROSBY, Thomas (1575-1661) & Jane SOTHERON (-1662); in Eng, 19 Oct 1600; Cambridge/Rowley

CROSBY, Thomas (1635?-1702, Harwich) & Sarah _?_, m/2 John MILLER 1703; b 1663; Eastham

CROSBY, Thomas (-1735) & 1/wf Deborah **FYFIELD**; 29 Oct 1685; Hampton, NH
CROSBY, Thomas (1663-1731) & Hannah __?__ (1673-1729, ae 57); b 1701?; Harwich
CROSBY, William (ae 56 in 1676) & __?__ ; in Eng; Isles of Shoals
CROSBY, ?Eleazer & Mary **BARKER** (1678-1772?), dau Isaac of Duxbury, (1) Patience **FREEMAN** 1706; b 1701
CROSS, Abraham & Martha **BEALE**; 20 Sep 1700; Marblehead
CROSS, Edmund & Martha **DAMMON**; 21 Apr 1699; Boston
CROSS, George & [?Martha **BONFIELD**]; b 1689; Ipswich
CROSS, John (1584-1651) & Anne __?__ (1596-1669); b 1634; Ipswich/Watertown/Hampton, NH
CROSS, John (-Sep 1640) & Mary __?__, m/2 Robert **SAUNDERSON/SANDERSON**; b 1640; Watertown
CROSS, John (-1676) & Francis/Joan? __?__ ; b 1642; Wells, ME
CROSSE, John & Susanna __?__ ; b 1665; Boston
CROSSE, John & Susanna **GOOSE** (1667-); 28 Nov 1682; Charlestown
CROSS, John (-1721) & Mary (**HULL**) **GRANT** (1648-1720, 1726?), w John; 3 Nov 1686; Windsor, CT
CROSS, John & Esther [**MANSON**], m/2 Alexander **DENNETT**; b 1688
CROSS, Joseph (-1684) & Mary (**PENDLETON**) **BRITTON**, w William, m/3 Nicholas **MOREY**; b Apr 1683, 1680?; Wells, ME
CROSS, Nathaniel & 1/wf __?__ ; b 1687(8?); Stamford
CROSS, Nathaniel (-1714) & Hannah **KNAPP**, m/2 Samuel **PALMER**; 6 Nov 1696; Stamford
CROSS, Peter (-1737, ae 84) & 1/wf Mary [**CRANE**]? (-1695?); b 1679; Windham, CT
CROSS, Peter & 2/wf Mary [**WADE**], wid Robert; b 1698; Windham, CT/Mansfield, CT
CROSS, Phinias & Deborah __?__
CROSS, Ralph (1658-1711) & Mary __?__ ; Ipswich
CROSS, Richard & Jane **PUDESTER**; 24 Nov 1670; Salem
CROSS, Robert (1612-) & Anna/Hannah [**JORDAN**] (-1677); 20 Aug 1635; Ipswich
CROSS, Robert (1642-1713) & Martha **TREADWELL** (-1738, 1738/9, ae 95); 19 Feb 1664; Ipswich
CROSS, Robert (1612-1689+) & 2/wf Mary __?__ (-1694+); aft 29 Oct 1677
CROSS, Samuel (-1707) & Elizabeth (**FOX**)? **CHAPMAN**, w Edward; 12 Jul 1677; Windsor, CT
CROSS, Stephen (1648±-1704?) & Elizabeth [**CHENEY**] (1647-1694+); b 1674, b 1672?, ca 1665?; Ipswich
CROSS, Stephen & Mary (**PHILLIPS**) (**MUNJOY**) **LAWRENCE**, w George, w Robert; 23 Jan 1692, 1692/3; Boston
CROSS, Thomas (1667-) & Esther __?__, m/2 William **STONE/OAKES**? 1689; ca 1690; Ipswich
CROSS, William (-1656, 1655) & [Margaret] ?**WEECHE**, m/2 Robert **BATES**; ?11 Nov 1630; Windsor, CT/Wethersfield, CT/Fairfield, CT
CROSS, __?__ & [Faith **BELCHER**] (1663-), m/2 Mark **PILKINGTON** 1691; ?Boston
CROSS, __?__ & [Margaret **NORTHEND**], m/2 John **PALMER** 1650; b 1638; Boston
CROSSMAN, Bartholomew & Anna (**STREET**) [**MERRIMAN**], w Samuel; aft 1694?, b 1701?; Wallingford, CT
CROSSMAN, John (1588-1688) & __?__
CROSMAN, John (1654-1731) & Joanna **THAYER**; 7 Jan 1689, 1689/90?; Taunton
CROSMAN, Joseph (1659-) & Sarah **ALDIN**; 24 Nov 1685; Taunton
CROSSMAN, Robert[1] (ca 1621-1692) & 1/wf Sarah **KINGSBURY**; 25 May 1652; Dedham/Taunton
CROSMAN, Robert (1657-1738) & Hannah **BROOKS**; 21 Jul 1679; Taunton
CROSSMAN, Robert[1] (ca 1621-1692) & 2/wf Martha (**BALLINGTON**) **EATON** (-1695), Bristol, w Samuel; ca 1688?, m cont 7 Dec 1687; Taunton
CROSMAN, Samuel (1667-1755) & 1/wf Elizabeth **BELL** (1668-1695); 19 Dec 1689; Taunton
CROSMAN, Samuel (1667-1755) & 2/wf Mary **SAWYER**; 22 Dec 1696; Taunton
CROSTHWAITE, Charles & Judith [**DAWSON**], dau George; b 1671; Boston
CROSSWELL, Caleb (1678-1713) & Abigail **STIMPSON** (1679-1738?); 14 Oct 1700; Charlestown
CROSSWELL, Thomas (-1708, ae 75) & Priscilla [**UPHAM**] (1642-1717); b 1663; Charlestown
CROUCH, Arthur & Elizabeth (?**HERRICK**) **UNDERWOOD**, Watertown; 21 May 1682; Chelmsford
CROUCH, David (1659-) & Mary __?__ ; b 1687; Boston
CROUCH, Jonathan (1657-1714) & 1/wf Sarah __?__ ; Charlestown
CROUCH, Jonathan (1657-1714) & 2/wf Elizabeth **FOSKETT** (1665-); 16 Dec 1684; Charlestown

CROUCH, William (1625-1678, ae 36 in 1663) & Sarah [LAMSON] (-1717, above 90); b 1653; Charlestown

CROUCH, William (1654-) & Elizabeth BRADSHAW; 20 Jun 1675; Charlestown

CROW, Christopher (-1680) & Mary BURR, m/2 Josiah CLARK; 15 Jan 1656, prob 1656/7; Hartford

CROE, Christopher & Deliverance BENNETT; 8 Oct 1657; Salem

CROW, Christopher & Abigail KNOWLTON; m int 17 Feb 1699/1700; Wenham

CROW, Daniel (-1693) & _?_ (-1693+); no issue; Hartford

CROW, Ely & Susannah DOLBERRY; m int 2 Aug 1695; Boston

CROW, John (1606-1685/6) & 1/wf _?_ (-ca 1644?); in Eng, b 1628? (doubtful); Hartford, CT

CROW, John (1606-1686) & 2/wf (1/wf?) Elizabeth [GOODWIN] (-1686+); ca 1645?, b 1628?; Hartford/Hadley

CROW, Nathaniel (-1695) & Deborah [LEFFINGWELL], m/2 Andrew WARNER; b 1685; Hartford/Hadley

CROW, Samuel (-1676) & Hannah LEWIS, m/2 Daniel MARCH 1676; 17 May 1671; Hadley

CROW, Samuel (1662-) & 1/wf Martha [MOSES] (1672-); 30 Jan 1689; Windsor, CT

CROW, Samuel & 2/wf Ruth _?_ (-1698); Windsor, CT

CROW, William (1629-1684?) (kinsman of John ATWOOD) & Hannah WINSLOW (1644-), m/2 John STURTEVANT; 1 Apr 1664, 5 Apr 1664; Plymouth

CROW/CROWELL?, William & Elizabeth SARGENT; 10 Dec 1691; Boston

CROWEL, Edward (-1689) & Mary LATHROP (1654-), m/2 James DENNIS 1690?; 16 Jan 1673, 1673/4; (d in Cape May, NJ) Barnstable

CROWE, John (-1672?) & Elishua _?_ (-1688); b 1635; Charlestown/Yarmouth

CROW, John (?1639, ?1638-1689) & Mehitable [MILLER] (1638-1715); b 1662, b 1654?; Yarmouth

CROW, John (1642, 1641/2-1732) & Hannah _?_ (-1753); b 1682; Yarmouth

CROW, John (1662-1728) & Bethia SEARES (-1724, Chatham); 27 May 1684; Yarmouth

CROWELL, John & Margaret _?_ ; b 1686; Manchester

CROWELL, John (-1715) & Sarah [?O'KELLEY] (not FULLER, see Samuel), ?dau David, wid? (her dau Jane O'KELLEY was living in 1714, b bef 1691); ca 1682, b 1691, ch b 1691-1711; Yarmouth

CROWELL, Samuel & 1/wf? Hannah?/Sarah _?_ ; b 1675?, b 1674?; Yarmouth

CROWELL, [Samuel?] (-1723) & Sarah [FULLER] (1654-); b 1674/5, b 29 Oct 1683; Yarmouth

CROW, Thomas (1645-1690) & Agnes _?_ (-1690+); b 1668; ?Yarmouth

CROWELL, Thomas (1649-) & Deborah _?_ (-1722); b 1685; Yarmouth

CROWELL, Thomas (-1733) & Elizabeth [JONES]; ca 1690; Yarmouth

CROW, Yelverton (-1683/4) & Elizabeth _?_ (-1703); b 1642; Yarmouth

CROWFOOT, James (1667-) & ?[Perses/Percy GREGORY] (1671-); b 1701?; Danbury, CT

CROWFOOT, John (1663-) & Sarah [KENT] (1657-); 7 Apr 1692; Springfield

CROWFOOT, Joseph (-1678) & Mary HILLIARD/HELLIER, m/2 John MATTHEWS 1680; 15 Apr 1658; Springfield

CROWFOOT, Joseph (1660-1722) & Margaret _?_ (-1733); 30 Dec 1686; Wethersfield, CT

CROWFOOT, Samuel (-1733, ae 71) & 1/wf Mary [WARNER] (1672-1702); b 1694; Springfield

CROWN, Henry (1648±-1696) & Alice ROGERS (-1719+); 1 May 1676; Portsmouth, NH

CROWN, William & Agnes [MACWORTH]; in Eng, ca 1640; Mendon/etc.

CROWINSHEL/CROWNINSHIELD, John Kasper Richter & Seaborn _?_ ; b 1659; Charlestown

CROWNSHIELD, John & Elizabeth ALLEN (1673-), m/2 Thomas POMFRET 1712; 5 Dec 1694; Lynn/Boston

CRUFF, John & Eleanor BROWNE; 29 Nov 1689; Marblehead

CRUFF/CRUFT, Edward & Sarah [EDMONDS]; b 1690; Boston

CROMBE, Daniel (-1713) & 2/wf Alice [HAUGHTON] (-1716), w Richard; aft 1682; Westerly, RI

CRUMB, William & Mercy [SAUNDERS]; b 1701?; RI

CROMPTON, Francis & Hannah [WARDWELL] (1667-); b 1694; Ipswich

CRUMPTON, Samuel & Jane _?_ , m/2 Capt. Richard MOORE; b 1675

CRUTTENDEN, Abraham[1] (-1683) & 1/wf Mary _?_/HICKSON? (-1664); ca 1630/5?; Guilford, CT

CRUTTENDEN, Abraham[2] (-1694) & Susanna GRIGSON/GREGSON; 13 May 1661; New Haven

CRUTTENDEN, Abraham[1] & 2/wf Joanna/Jane (SHEAFE) CHITTENDEN (-1668), w William; 1 May 1665; Guilford, CT
CRUTTENDEN, Abraham & Susanna KIRBY (1664-); 6 May 1686; Middletown, CT/Guilford, CT
CRUTTENDEN, Isaac (-1685) & Lydia THOMPSON (-1729), m/2 John MEIGS [1691+?]; 20 Sep 1665; Guilford, CT
CRUTTENDEN, Joseph & Mary/Mercy HOYT; 2 May 1700; Guilford, CT
CRUTTENDEN, Thomas & 1/wf Abigail HULL (1669-1710), Killingworth; 11 Sep 1690; Guilford, CT
CUDWORTH, Israel[2] (1641-) & _?_ ; b 1678; Scituate/Freetown
CUDWORTH, James (-1682, London) (cousin of Rev. Zechariah SYMMES) (called Rev. Zechariah SYMES "cousin") & _?_ (widow Martha's dau called Mary WILDER in 1638, Mary WILDER m Joseph UNDERWOOD); b 18 Jan 1634, 1634/5; Scituate
CUDWORTH, James[2] (1635-1697) & Mary [HOWLAND] (-1699); b 1665; Scituate
CUDWORTH, James &[2] [Betty HATCH]; b 1697; Freetown
CUDWORTH, Jonathan[2] & Sarah JACKSUN, dau Jonathan; 31 May 1661, 1667, 1669; Scituate
CUE, Robert (1655-) & 1/wf Mary (REDINGTON) HERRICK (?1651-), w John; 13 Mar 1681/2; Beverly/Salem
CUE, Robert & Elizabeth [KIMBALL] (sister of Thomas KIMBALL), m/2 John DAY 1704; Beverly
CULLICK, John (-1663) & 1/wf _?_ ; by 1639?; Charlestown/Hartford
CULLICK, John (-1663) & 2/wf Elizabeth FENWICK (-1683), m/2 Richard ELY 1664?; 20 May 1648; Hartford/Boston
COLVER, Edward (-1685) & Ann ELLICE/ELLIS; 19 Sep 1638; Dedham/Roxbury/New London
COLVER, Edward & Sarah BACKUS (1668-); 15 Jan 1681, 1681/2; Norwich, CT/Lebanon, CT
COLVER, Ephraim & Mary _?_ /[PACKER]; b 1692; Groton, CT?
COLVER, Gershom (1646-1716) & Mary _?_ ; b 1674?, b 1675; Southampton, LI
COLVER, Jeremiah & 1/wf Mary PIERSON (1680-1707); 28 Dec 1700, 5 Dec 1700; Southampton, LI
COLVER, John (1640-) & Mary/Mercy CLARK (1644-); b 1676, b 1672?, b 8 Aug 1665; New Haven/New London
COLVER, Joseph & Margaret [GALLUP/WINTHROP?]; b 1679, b 1680?; Groton, CT
COLVER, Joshua (1642-1713) & Elizabeth FORD, m/2 Ebenezer PECK; 23 Dec 1672; New Haven/Wallingford, CT
COLVER, Samuel & Martha ?ELAND [FISH] (wf of John FISH); eloped 1674?, 1672?/8? (did they marry); ?Warwick, RI
CULVER, John (1670-) & Sarah _?_ ; b 1700; New London, CT
CUMBY, Humphrey & Sarah _?_ ; b 1651(2?); Boston
COMBEY, Robert (1654/5-) & Rebecca [CROMWELL] (1654-); b 1679; Boston
CUMMINGS, Abraham, Dunstable & Sarah [WRIGHT] (1670-), m/2 Aaron PRATT 1707; 28 Feb 1686/7; Woburn/Dunstable
CUMMINGS, David (-1690) & Elizabeth [BRABROOK] (-1689?); b 1667; Boston/?Ddorchester
CUMMINGS, Isaac (1601/3-1677) & _?_ ; b 1630; Ipswich/Topsfield
COMINGS, Isaac (1633?-) & Mary ANDREWS (ca 1638-); 27 Nov 1659; Topsfield
CUMMINS, Isaac & 1/wf Alice HOWLET/HOWLETT; 25 Dec 1688; Topsfield
COMINGS, Isaac & 2/wf Frances SHERWIN (1682?-); 23 Nov 1696; Ipswich/Topsfield
COMMINGS, John (?1630-1700) & Sarah [HOWLETT] (-1688); ca 1655; Boxford/etc.
CUMMINGS, John & Elizabeth KINSLEY (1657-1706); 13 Sep 1680?, 1681?; Dunstable
CUMMINGS, John & Susanna TOWNE; 23 Jan 1688/9; Topsfield
CUMMINGS, John & Mary [?LEE]; b 1692; Woburn
CUMMINS, Nathaniel (1659-ca 1728) & Abigail PARKHURST; 14 Apr 1697; Chelmsford/Dunstable
CUMMINGS, Philip & Elizabeth _?_ ; b 1686(7?); Dunstable
CUMMINGS, Richard (1601/3-1679) & Jane _?_ (-1677); Portsmouth, NH?
CUMMINGS, Richard (-1676) & Elizabeth [BONYTHON]; ca 14 Jul 1647; Saco, ME/York, ME/Isles of Shoals
CUMMINGS, Thomas (1658-1723) & Priscilla WARNER (1666-); 19 Dec 1688; Dunstable
CUMMINS, Timothy & Susannah _?_ ; ca 1690/93?; Marblehead
CUMMINGS, _?_ & Joan _?_ (-1644); Salem

CUNLITH/?CONLIFFE/?CUNLIFFE, Henry (-1673) & Susanna _?_; b 1644/5; Dorchester/ Northampton
CUNNABELL, John[1] (1650-1724) & 1/wf _?_ (-ca 1687); ca 1672; Boston
CANIBALL, John & 2/wf Sarah CLOISE/CLOYSE (1667, 1668?-); 13 Mar 1688, 1688/9; Salem/Boston
CUNNIBILL, John[2] (?1673-1705) & Lydia BEIGHTON; 2 Nov 1694, no issue; Boston
CUNNABELL, John (1650-1724) & 3/wf Martha HELY/HEALY (-1735); 10 Dec 1700; Boston
CRUNMELL, Timothy & Phillippe _?_; b 1666; Boston
CUNNELL, Timothy (-1697) & Phillippee _?_; b 1663; Boston
CUNNINGHAM, Andrew & Sarah [GIBSON] (-1713+); b 1686; Boston
CUNNINGHAM, ?John & _?_; b 1699; Watertown
CUNNINGHAM, Timothy (-1712, ae 46, Exeter, NH) & Ruth (WEARE) EDWARDS (-1745), w George, dau Peter WEARE; ca 1688; Boston
CURNEY/CORNEY, Elisha (1672-1753+) & Rebecca SMITH; 16 Dec 1697; Gloucester
CURNEY, John & Abigail SKILLING/SKILLINS? (1652-); 18 Nov 1670; Gloucester
CURRIER, Jeffrey (1635?-) & _?_; b 1669?; Isles of Shoals/etc.
CURRIER, John (?1673-1709) & Ann _?_; ?b 1701; Hog Island
CURRIER, Richard (1616-1689) & 1/wf Ann _?_; ca 1636/8?, b 1643; Salisbury
CURRIER, Richard (1616-1689, 1687?) & 2/wf Joanna (PINDOR) (ROWELL) SARGENT, w Valentine, w William; 26 Oct 1676; Amesbury
CURRIER, Richard (?1669-1707) & Elizabeth [WAYMOTH], m/2 Nathaniel LORD; ca 1690?, betw 1688 & 1703; Salisbury
CURRIER, Richard & Dorothy BARNED/BARNARD; 29 Aug 1695; Salisbury
CURRIER, Samuel (?1636-1713) & Mary [HARDY]; ca 1665?; Salisbury
CURRIER, Samuel & Dorothy FOOT; m int 14 Dec 1700; Amesbury
CURRIER, Thomas & Mary OSGOOD (1650-1705); 9 Dec 1668; Amesbury
CURRIER, Thomas & Sarah BARNARD (1677-); 19 Sep 1700; Amesbury
CURRY, Thomas & _?_; b 1674; ?New Haven
CURTES, Benjamin & Sarah _?_; b 1679; Stratford, CT
CURTIS, Benjamin (1652-1733) & 1/wf Esther JUDSON (1660-1713); 23 Mar 1680/1, 1681; Stratford, CT
CURTIS, Benjamin (-1703) & Martha [FARROW]; ca 1681 (no issue); York, ME/etc.
CURTIS, Benjamin & Mary SILVESTER (1666-); 1689; Scituate
CURTICE, Benjamin (-?1727, Plympton) & Mary BESSEE (1680-1753?, Plympton) Sandwich; 24 Dec 1700, 23 Dec 1700; Plymouth/Sandwich
CURTICE, Caleb (1646-1730) & Elizabeth RIDER (-1711), dau Thomas; 1 Dec 1670; Southold, LI
CURTIS, Daniel (1652-1719) & 1/wf Mary [?JENNINGS] (1668-1698); b 1695; Stratford, CT
CURTIS, Diodatus & Rebecca _?_, m/2 Joseph ARNOLD 1648; b 1643; Braintree
CURTIS, Dodovah & Elizabeth (WITHERS) [BERRY], w Benjamin; by 1700; ?York, ME
CURTIS, Ebenezer (?1657, 1659-1751) & Ruth PORTER (1669-); b 1691, ca 1690; Stratford, CT
CURTIS, Ephraim & Elizabeth KILBOURNE (1663-); 6 Sep 1693; Reading
CURTICE, Francis (-1717, Plympton) & Hannah SMITH, bur Plympton; 28 Dec 1671; Plymouth
CURTICE, Francis & Hannah BOSWORTH; 5 Nov 1700; Plymouth
CURTIS, Henry (-1678) & Mary?/Mercy? [GREY?/GAY?] PARKER?, dau Nicholas; ca 1640; Sudbury/Watertown
CURTIS, Henry (-1661) & Elizabeth ABELL, m/2 Richard WELLER 1662; 13 May 1645; Windsor, CT/Wethersfield, CT/Stratford
CURTIS, Henry & Jane _?_; b 1653; Boston/Sheepscote, ME
CURTIS, Henry & Elizabeth _?_ (1671?-); b 1695
CURTIS, Holland (1671, Roxbury-) & Elizabeth [LAWTON], m/2 Robert CARR; 1694; Newport
CURTIS, Isaac (1642-1695) & Hannah POLLY (-1720, Roxbury); 10 May 1670; Roxbury
CURTIS, Isaac (1658-1712) & Sarah FOOT/FOOTE (1662-), Branford, m/2 Nathaniel HOWE; 13 Aug 1682; Wallingford, CT
CURTICE, Isaac (-1725) & _?_; b 1691; Stonington, CT
CURTIS, Israel (1644-1704) & Rebecca [BEARDSLEY]/WISWALL?, m/2 James BEEBE; b 1667; Stratford, CT
CURTIS, Israel (1668-) & Mary MOREHOUSE?; b 1695, b 1687?, b 1696, ca 1693; Woodbury
CURTIS, James (-1690) & Abigail _?_, m/2 Andrew ROBY 1691; 8 Jul 1686; Wethersfield, CT

CURTIS, John (d at CT) & Elizabeth HUTCHINS (-1658); in Eng, 19 Apr 1610, Nazing, Eng; Stratford, CT/Roxbury

CURTIS, John (1615-1707) & 1/wf Elizabeth __?__ (-1682); b 1642; Stratford, CT

CURTIS, John (1629-) & 1/wf Rebecca WHEELER (1643-1675); 26 Dec 1661; Boston

CURTIS, John (1639-1715) & Lydia __?__ ; 20 Nov 1666; Wethersfield, CT

CURTIS, John (-1718) & [Mary]/Sarah [LOOKE]/LOCKE?/LOOK (1654-1745); 4 Dec 1672; Topsfield

CURTIS, John (1642-) & Hannah (?PRESTON) [KIMBERLY], w Abraham; aft 4 Mar 1674/5, aft 1680; Stratford/Newark, NJ

CURTIS, John & Miriam BROOKS; 4 Apr 1678; Scituate

CURTIS, John & Agnes NOSTER/NORSITER?; 12 Oct 1680; Marblehead

CURTIS, John & Dorcas PEAK; b 1682, aft 1676, b 1668; Roxbury

CURTIS, John & Mary __?__ ; b 1687; Boston

CURTICE, John & Elizabeth PIERCE (1666-), m/2 Isaac CLEVELAND 1699, m/3 Clement STRATFORD; 3 Jan 1689/90; Charlestown

CURTIS, John (1667-1712) & Elizabeth WRIGHT (1667-); 3 Apr 1690; Wethersfield, CT

CURTICE, John (1673-) & 1/wf Priscilla GOULD (1674-1715); 15 Apr 1695, 25 Apr; Topsfield

CURTICE, John (1673-) & __?__ ; b 1696; Plymouth

CURTISS, John (1670-1749) & Johannah/Hannah [BURR] (-1754); ca 1696, b 1700/1; Woodbury, CT/Stratford, CT

CURTIS, Jonathan (-1681) & Abigail THOMPSON (1646-1731), m/2 Nicholas HUGHS, m/3 Samuel SHERMAN; ca 1669, 1679?, b 1671, ca 1670; Stratford, CT

CURTIS, Jonathan (1672-1717) & Sarah LYON (1673-); ca 1700, b 1708, b 1698?; Roxbury

CURTIS, Jonathan (1679-) & 1/wf Hannah __?__ ; b 1701, b 1702; Stratford, CT

CURTIS, Joseph (-1683) & Mercy [DEMING], m/2 Joseph WRIGHT 1685; 8 Feb 1674, 1673/4; Wethersfield, CT

CURTIS, Joseph (1650-1742) & Bethia BOOTHE (1658-1699+, 1699); 9 Nov 1676; Stratford, CT

CURTICE, Joseph & Abigail GROUT; 5 Feb 1677, 1677/8; Sudbury

CURTIS, Joseph & Sarah FOXWELL; ca 1677, Sep 1678; York, ME

CORTAS, Joseph & Mary ELLINE; 18 Nov 1687; Milton

CURTIS, Joseph & Rebecca __?__ ; b 1692; Scituate

CURTIS, Joshua (1646-1706) & Mercy __?__ ; b 1680, ca 1665?; Stratford, CT/Cohansey, NJ

CURTICE, Joshua & Mary YOUNGS (1676-); 8 Sep 1698; Southold, LI

CURTIS, Josiah (1662-1745) & 1/wf Abigail JUDSON (1669-1697); Jul 1692, 21 Nov 1697; Stratford, CT

CURTIS, Josiah (1662-1745) & 2/wf Mary BEACH (1676-); ca 1698; Stratford, CT

CURTIS, Nathaniel (1677-) & 1/wf Sarah HALL (-1700); 6 Apr 1697; Wallingford, CT

CURTIS, Philip (1632-1675) & Obedience HOLLAND (1642-), m/2 Benjamin GAMLIN 1678; 30 Oct 1658; Roxbury

CURTIS, Richard (1611-1681, Wallingford, CT) & 1/wf Elizabeth __?__ (-1687); b 1643; Dorchester/Wallingford, CT

CURTICE, Richard (-1671) & Sarah [?CARWITHEN]; b 1646; Salem/Southold, LI

CURTIS, Richard (-1693) & 1/wf Ann [HALLET]; ca 1649, b 1649, b 1648; Marblehead/Scituate

CURTIS, Richard (1611-1681) & 2/wf Sarah (HOWE)? [STRANGE?], w John; 25 Sep 1657, ?25 Jul 1657; Dorchester/Wallingford, CT

CURTIS, Richard (-1671) (did he marry?) & __?__

CURTIS, Richard (-1693) & 2/wf Lydia __?__ ; b 1692?, b 26 Dec 1692; Scituate

CURTICE, Samuel & Sarah ALEXANDER; 6 Jul 1678, 23 Jul 1678?; Deerfield

CURTIS, Samuel (-1688) & Sarah __?__ (-1707+); 20 Feb 1683; Wethersfield, CT

CURTIS, Samuel & Elizabeth __?__ ; b 1684, b 1686; Marblehead/Beverly

CURTIS, Samuel & Elizabeth [TILDEN] (1665-); b 1694, 1690?; Scituate

CURTIS, Solomon (-1711, ae 69) & Prudence GATLIVE (-1727, ae 76); 11 Jun 1673; Braintree/Bristol, RI

CURTIS, Stephen (1673-1723) & Sarah MINOR (1678-); 2 Nov 1699; Stratford, CT

CURTIS, Theophilus (-1710) & Hannah PAINE (1656-1742); 31 Dec 1673, 30 Dec 1673, 7 Jan 1673, 27 Jan 1673, 21 Jan 1673; Braintree/Dorchester

CURTIS, Thomas (d in Eng) & Richardene/Richardine __?__, m/2 Thomas CHAMBERS 1632; b 1624, b 1619

CURTIS, Thomas (-1681) & Elizabeth __?__; b 1639/40; Wethersfield/Wallingford
CURTIS, Thomas (1619-1706?) & 1/wf Elizabeth __?__; b 1644; Scituate/York, ME
CURTIS, Thomas (1619-1706?) & 2/wf Abigail __?__
CURTIS, Thomas (-1648) & Mary __?__ (-1664), m/2 James BISHOP; by 1648?; Stratford, CT
CURTIS, Thomas (1648-1706) & Mary MERRIMAN (1657-); 9 Jun 1674; Wallingford, CT
CURTIS, Thomas & Sarah __?__; b 1694; Boston
CURTICE, Thomas & 1/wf Mary COOK; 6 Mar 1694/5; Scituate
CURTIS, William[1] (1592-1672, ae 80) & Sarah ELLIOT (1599-1673); in Nazing, Eng, 6 Aug 1618; Roxbury
CURTIS, William (1618-1702) & 1/wf Mary __?__; b 1642; Stratford, CT
CURTIS, William & Alice [RUMBALL]; b 1658; Salem
CURTIS, William & [?Deborah] __?__; b 1664, ca 1660; Scituate
CURTIS, William (1618-1702) & 2/wf Sarah (MARVIN?/MORRIS) [GOODRICH] (1631-1702), w William; ca 1680; Stratford, CT
CURTIS, William & Judith NEEDHAM; 22 Mar 1687; Salem
CURTICE, William & Lydia [HILL]/[NEALE?]; b 1688; Salem
CURTICE, William & Anna SMITH; 31 Dec 1692; Salem
CURTIS, William & __?__, b 1696; Scituate
CURTIS, Winlock & [Ann BOWERS]; b 1690
CURTIS, Zaccheus (?1619-1682) & Jane?/Joan?/Joanne? __?__ (see Richard CURTIS); b 1659, b 1652, b 1646; Charlestown/Gloucester
CURTIS, Zaccheus & 1/wf Mary BLEAKE; 4 Dec 1673; Topsfield/Boxford
CURTIS, Zachariah (1659-1748) & Hannah [PORTER] (1665-1738); b 1691, b 1690?; Stratford, CT
CURTIS, __?__ & Sarah [TOWER] (1650)
CURTIS, __?__ & Jane __?__ (-1694?), m/2 Robert JONES b 1631; (see Thomas COLLIER)
CUSHING, Caleb (1673-1752) & Elizabeth (COTTON) ALIN/ALLING (-1743), w James; 14 Mar 1698/9; Salisbury
CUSHING, Daniel (1619-1700) & 1/wf Lydia GIBMAN (-1689); 19 Jun 1645, Jun 1645, 19 Jan; Hingham
CUSHING, Daniel (1648-1716) & Elizabeth THAXTER (1661-1727); 8 Dec 1680; Hingham
CUSHING, Daniel (1619-1700) & 2/wf Elizabeth (JACOB) THAXTER (1632-1725), w John; 23 Mar 1690/1, 6? Mar; Hingham
CUSHING, Jeremiah (-1622) (ae ca 40 in 1665) & Elizabeth [WILKIE], w John; b 11 Mar 1661; Boston
CUSHING, Jeremiah (1654-1706, ae 52) & Hannah LORING (-1710), m/2 John BARKER; 5 Jun 1685; Hingham/Provincetown
CUSHING, Jeremiah (-1710, ae 46) & Judith PARMINTER/PARMENTER; 29 Mar 1693, 12 Apr; Boston/Scituate
CUSHING, John (1627-1708) & Sarah HAWKE (1641-1679); 20 Jan 1658, prob 1657/8; Hingham/Scituate
CUSHING, John, Jr. (1662-) & 1/wf Deborah LORING (1668-1713); 20 May 1688; Scituate
CUSHING, Joshua & Mary BACON; 31 May 1699; Scituate
CUSHING, Matthew (1589-1660) & Nazareth PITCHER (-1681, ae 95); 5 Aug 1613; Hingham
CUSHING, Matthew (1623-1701) & Sarah JACOB (-1701); 25 Feb 1652/3, no issue; Hingham
CUSHING, Matthew (-1715) & Jael JACOB (-1708); 31 Dec 1684; Hingham
CUSHING, Matthew & Deborah JACOB; 27 Dec 1694; Hingham
CUSHING, Peter & Hannah HAWKE; 4 Jun 1685; Hingham
CUSHING, Theophilus (1657-1718) & Mary THAXTER, m/2 Joseph HERRICK; 28 Nov 1688; Hingham
CUSHING, Thomas (1663-) & 1/wf Deborah THAXTER (-1712); 17 Oct 1687; Boston/Hingham
CUSHMAN, Eleazer (1657-) & Elizabeth COOMBS; 12 Jan 1687, 1686/7?; Plymouth
CUSHMAN, Elkanah (1651-1727) & 1/wf Elizabeth COLE (-1682); 10 Feb 1677, 1676/7?; Plymouth
CUSHMAN, Elkanah (1651-1727) & 2/wf Martha COOKE (1660-1722); 2 Mar 1683, 1682/3; Plymouth
CUSHMAN, Isaac (1648-1732) & Rebecca HARLOW (1654-1727); ca 1675; Plymouth

CUSHMAN, Robert (1577/8-1625) & 1/wf Sarah REDER (-1616, Leyden); 31 Jul 1606, St. Alphage, Canterbury; Plymouth

CUSHMAN, Robert (1577/8-1625) & Mary (CLARK) SINGLETON, w Thomas; 5 Jun 1617, Leyden, Holland; Plymouth

CUSHMAN, Robert (1664-1757) & 1/wf Persis __?__ (try PRATT) (-1744, in 73rd y); ca 1697; Plymouth

CUSHMAN, Thomas (1607/8-1691) & Mary ALLERTON (1616-1699); 163-, ca 1636?; Plymouth

CUSHMAN, Thomas (1637-1726) & 1/wf Ruth HOWLAND; 17 Nov 1664; Plymouth

CUSHMAN, Thomas (1637-1726) & 2/wf Abigail FULLER (1653, ca 1652-1734); 16 Oct 1679; Rehoboth

CUSHMAN, Thomas (1670-1727) & Sarah STRONG (-1726); b 1703; Duxbury/Lebenon, CT

CUTLER, David & Abigail FLAGG, m/2 Henry CANNER/?Stephen WRIGHT; 12 Dec 1700; Woburn/?Boston

CUTLER, Ebenezer & Mary MARCH?/MARSH; 11 Mar 1689; Salem

CUTLER, James (1606-) & 1/wf Anna/Anne [?GROUT]/?CAKEBREAD (-1644?) (sister of or wf of John GROUT); in Eng, b 1635; Watertown

CUTLER, James & 2/wf Mary (__?__) KING (-1654), w Thomas; 9 Mar 1644/5; Watertown

CUTLER, James & 3/wf Phebe [PAGE]; ca 1662?, ca 1659/60?; Cambridge/Lexington

CUTLER, James (1635-1685) & Lydia (MOORE) WRIGHT (1643-1723), w Samuel; 15 Jun 1665; Sudbury

CUTLER, John (?1600-1638?) (7 ch) & Mary __?__, m/2 Thomas HEWETT 1649+; in Eng, ca 1634,?Sprowston, Norfolk; Hingham

CUTLER, John (ca 1625-1678, 1679-) & 1/wf Olive THOMPSON; 3 Sep 1650; Woburn

CUTLER, John (1629-1694) & 1/wf Ann/Anna [WOODMANSEY] (?1627-1683, 1681?); b 1652; Charlestown

CUTLER, John (-1678, 1679) & 2/wf Mary (BROWNE) [LEWIS], w John; betw 1657 & 1667, b 1663; Woburn

CUTLER, John (ca 1650-1708) & Martha WISWALL; 23 Apr 1674; Charlestown

CUTLER, John & Mary COWELL, Boston; 4 Jan 1674/5, 1674; Hingham

CUTLER, John & 1/wf Hannah/Anna BELFLOURE (-1681); 25 Mar 1678; Reading

CUTLER, John & 2/wf Susanna BAKER; 22 May 1682; Woburn

CUTLER, John (-1694, in 66th y) & Mehitable (NOWELL) HILTON (-1711, ae 73) w William; 29 Oct 1684; Charlestown

CUTLER, John & 3/wf Elizabeth REED (-1710), wid; 14 Oct 1692; Woburn

CUTLER, John & Mary STEARNS (1663-); 19 Jul 1693, 1 Jan 1693/4?; Cambridge

CUTLER, John & Hannah SNOW (1677-), Woburn; 6 Feb 1700, 6 Feb 1701, 1700/01?; Cambridge/Killingly, CT/Woburn

CUTLER, Joseph (1672-1715) & Hannah __?__; b 1701?, prob ca 1708, 4 ch bpt 1737; Waltham

CUTLER, Nathaniel (1630-1716, ae 86?, 1724) & 1/wf Mary __?__ (-1708); 29 Sep 1655; Reading

CUTLER, Nathaniel (1640-1678) & Elizabeth CARTER (1647-1694); 2 Sep 1668; Charlestown

CUTLER, Nathaniel & 1/wf Elizabeth UNDERWOOD; 23 May 1700, 24 May; Reading

CUTLER, Robert (-1665) & Rebecca __?__ (-1677); in Eng, b 1629; Charlestown

CUTTLER, Robert & Sarah DOWNHAM/DUNHAM; 31 Jul 1689; Plymouth

CUTLER, Samuel (1629-1700) & 1/wf Elizabeth __?__ (-1693); b 1655; Salem/Marblehead/Topsfield/etc.

CUTLER, Samuel (ca 1658-1688) & Dorothy BELL, m/2 Josiah TREADWAY 1698; 20 Jun 1681, 30 Jun; Charlestown

CUTLER, Samuel & Sarah SATLE/SAWTELLE; 20 Jan 1691; Salem

CUTLER, Samuel & 2/wf Sarah CHURCH; 7 Jul 1698; Salem

CUTLER, Thomas (ca 1635-1683) & Mary [GILES?/VERY], m/2 Matthew SMITH, Sr. 1684; 19 Mar 1659/60; Reading/Charlestown

CUTLER, Thomas (?1648-1722) & Abigail __?__ (-1711); b 1674; Cambridge/Lexington

CUTLER, Thomas & 1/wf Elizabeth FELTCH (-1699+); 30 Dec 1686, 1685; Reading/Charlestown

CUTLER, Timothy (-1694) & Elizabeth HILTON (1650-); 22 Dec 1673; Charlestown

CUTLER/BUTLER, __?__ & Lydia [MERCER], m/2 John STANWOOD 1684

CUTT, John (-1681) & 2/wf? Hannah STARR (1632-1674); 30 Jul 1662; ?Portsmouth, NH/Boston

CUTT, John & Sarah MARTYN (1657-); 15 Jun 1672; ?Portsmouth, NH

CUTTS, John (-1681) & 3/wf? Ursula __?__; aft - 1674; Portsmouth, NH

CUTTS, Joseph & Sarah [RAYNES], m/2 Joseph HADLEY?; b 1671
CUTTS, Richard (1615-) & 2/wf? Eleanor [?ALDERSEY]; b 1650; Portsmouth, NH
CUTTS, Richard (1660-) & Joanna [WILLS] (-1738+); ca 1686; Portsmouth, NH
CUTTS, Robert (-1674) & 1/wf _?_; Kittery, ME
CUTTS, Robert (-1674) & 2/wf Mary [HOLE/HOEL], m/2 Francis CHAMPERNOWNE; ?Portsmouth, NH/Isles of Shoals
CUTTS, Robert (-1759, 1735?) & Dorcas HAMMOND (1674-1757); 18 Apr 1698; ?Portsmouth, NH/?Wells, ME
CUTTS, Samuel (1669-1698) & Eleanor [HARVEY], m/2 Thomas PHIPPS 1699, m/3 John PRAY; b 1694; Portsmouth, NH
CUTTER, Ephraim (1651-) & Bethia WOOD (-1731); 11 Feb 1678, 1678/9; Cambridge/Charlestown/Watertown
CUTTER, Gershom (-1738) & Lydia HALL; 6 Mar 1677/8; Cambridge
CUTTER, Nathaniel (1663-1713), Cambridge & 1/wf Mary FILLABROWN (1662-1714), Charlestown; 8 Oct 1688; Cambridge
CUTTER, Richard (1611-1693) & 1/wf Elizabeth [WILLIAMS]? (1620-1662); b 1645; Cambridge
CUTTER, Richard (1611-1693) & 2/wf Frances (PERRIMAN) EMSDEN/AMSDEN, w Isaac; 14 Feb 1662; Cambridge
CUTTER, William (1650-1723) & Rebecca [ROLFE] (1662-1751), m/2 John WHITMORE 1724; b 1681; Cambridge
CUTTER, [?Samuel] (d in Eng) & Elizabeth _?_ (-1664, ae 87?); in Eng, b 1611; Cambridge
CUTTING, James & Hannah COTLER/COLLER?; 16 Jun 1679; Watertown/Framingham
CUTTING, John (-1659) & Mary [?WARD] (-1663), m/2 John MILLER; b 1620; Charlestown
CUTTING, John, Jr. & _?_ (had dau Mary); bef 1642
CUTTING, John (-1689) & ?Susanna/Susan HARRINGTON, m/2 Eleazer BEALS 1690, m/3 Peter CLOYSE 1705; 9 Feb 1671/2; Watertown
CUTTING, Richard (1621/2-1696) & Sarah _?_ (1625-1685); b 1648; Watertown
CUTTING, Zechariah (-1732) & Sarah _?_; b 1681; Watertown

DADEY, Nathaniel (1637-1665) & Hannah MILLER (-1707), m/2 John EDMUNDS 1667, m/3 Aaron LUDKEIN 1684; 17 Jun 1663; Charlestown
DADEY, William (-1682, ae 77) & Dorothy _?_ (-1671); b 1633; Charlestown
DADEY, William² & Martha (_?_) MARCH (-1709), w Nicholas; 29 Jun 1670; Charlestown
DADEY, William (1671-) & Sarah BRACKETT; 28 Jan 1694 at Bristol, RI; Charlestown
DAFFORN, John & Mary [WOODY/WOODIE] (1650-); b 1667; Boston
DAGAN, Richard & _?_; b 1693; Scituate
DAKIN, John (1661-1711, prob) & Sarah [WOODIS] (1664-1700); b 1686; Concord
DAKIN, Joseph (ca 1669-1744) & Dorothy WOOSTER (1675-); 16 Jul 1696; Concord
DAKIN, Simon (ca 1663-1739/40) & Elizabeth [BROOKS] (1672-); b 1694; Concord
DAKIN, Thomas (1624-1708) & 1/wf Sarah _?_ (-1659); b 1659; Concord
DAKEN, Thomas (1624-1708) & Susan (_?_) STRATON/STRATTON (-1698), w Richard; 11 Jun 1660; Concord
DALE, Robert (-1700) & Joanna FARRAR (1661-1733); 30 Nov 1680; Woburn
DALE, _?_ & Mary [WILLIAMS]; b 14 Feb 1692/3; Jericho, LI
DALLISON, Gilbert & Margaret STORY; 24 Oct 1661; Boston
DALLY, Peter & Esther [LATOMIE]; b 1696; Boston
DALTIN, John & Sarah HACKER (1681-); 24 Feb 1700, 1700/01?; Salem
DALTON, Philemon (1595-1662) & 1/wf Hannah _?_ (1605-); in Eng, b 1629; Dedham/Hampton, NH
DALTON, Philemon (1595-1662) & 2/wf Dorothy _?_, m/2 Godfrey DEARBORN 1662; Hampton, NH

DALTON, Philemon (1664-1721) & Abigail GOVE (1670-), m/2 Benjamin SANBORN 1724, m/3 James PRESCOTT 1746; 25 Sep 1690; Hampton, NH

DALTON, Samuel (1629-1681) & Mehitable PALMER (ca 1630-), m/2 Zachariah SYMMES 1683; 6 Feb 1650; Hampton, NH

DALTON, Samuel (1656-) & 1/wf Dorothy SWAN (1666-1700); 23 Nov 1683; Haverhill

DALTON, Rev. Timothy (-1661) & Ruth [?PARKHURST] (-1666); in Eng, b 1618; Hampton, NH

DAYLY, John & Elizabeth _?_ ; b 1679, b 1666; Mendon/Providence

DALEY/DALY, Thomas & Elizabeth _?_ ; b 1682; Salem

DAM, John (1610-1690) & 1/wf _?_ ; b 1638, b 1637?, b 1636/7; Dover, NH

DAM, John (1610-1690) & 2/wf Elizabeth [POMFRET/POMPHRET]; b 1649; Dover, NH

DAM, John (1638-1706) & 1/wf Sarah [HALL] (-1663); ca 1660/2; Dover, NH

DAM, John (1638-1706) & 2/wf Elizabeth FURBER; 9 Nov 1664; Dover, NH

DAM, John (1668-) & 1/wf Jane [ROWE]; ca 1690?; Dover, NH

DAME, Richard & _?_ ; b 1676; Ipswich

DAM, William (1653-1718) & Martha [NUTE/POMFRET?] (-1718); ca 1680?, b 1682?; Dover, NH

DAMON, Ebenezer (1665-) & _?_ [BACON]; Scituate

DAMON, Experience (1662-) & 1/wf Patience [?RAWLINS] (?1658-); b 1687; Scituate

DAMEN, John (-1677) & 1/wf Katherine MERRIT (-1655); Jun 1644, ?16 Jun; Scituate

DAMON, John (-1708) & Abigail [SHERMAN] (-1713), dau Richard; ca 1650?; Reading

DAMEN, John (-1677) & 2/wf Martha HOWLAND (1638-1732), m/2 Peter BACON 1680; 15 Jan 1659; Scituate

DAMON, John (1652-1697, 1691) & Susan/Susannah WILEY (-1729, ae 74); 15 May 1678; Reading/Charlestown

DAMON, Joseph (1661-) & Elizabeth KINGSBURY/KINGSBERY (1668-); 12 Dec 1686; ?Dedham

DAMON, Samuel (1656-1724?) & Mary (DAVIS) GROVER (1658, 1669?-1727?), w Matthew; b 1681; Reading/Charlestown

DAMON, Thomas & _?_ (had Thomas 31 Jan 1658?); b 1658(9?); Reading (prob error for John)

DAMMOND, Thomas (1659-1723) & Lucian/?Lucy Ann EMMERSON (1667-); 15 May 1683; Reading

DAMEN, Zachariah/Zachary (1654-1730, ae 76) & Martha WOODWORTH (-1721+), dau Walter; - Jun 1679; Scituate

DAN, Francis & Elizabeth CLASON; 19 Nov 1685; Stamford, CT

DANA, Benjamin (1660-1738), Cambridge & Mary BUCKMASTER/BUCKMINSTER (ca 1665-1756+), Muddy River, m/2 Joshua FULLER 1742; 24 May 1688; Cambridge

DANA, Daniel (1663-1749) & Naomi [CROSWELL] (1670-1750/1); b 1694; Charlestown

DANA, Jacob (1655, 1654?-) & Patience [SABIN?]/[WHITE?] (-1711); b 1679; Cambridge

DANEY, Joseph (1656-1700) & Mary GOBLE, m/2 David MEADS; 17 Jan 1682/3; Concord

DANA, Richard (1617-1690) & Ann [BULLARD] (-1711); ca 1648; Cambridge

DAINES/DAYNE/DEAN, Abram/Abraham & Sarah [PIKE], m/2 Micah ROWE 1691; b 1681, 22 Dec 1671; Norwich, CT

DAIN, Daniel & _?_

DANE, Francis (1616-1697) & 1/wf Elizabeth [INGALLS] (1622-1676); b 1645; Andover

DANE, Francis (1616-1697) & 2/wf Mary THOMAS (-1689), wid?; 22 Nov 1677; Andover

DANE, Francis (1656-1738, ae 81) & Hannah POOR; 16 Nov 1681; Andover

DANE, Francis (1616-1697) & 3/wf Hannah (CHANDLER) [ABBOTT] (-1711), w George; aft 18 Feb 1688/9, ca 1690; Andover

DANE, John[1] (-1658) & 1/wf [Frances BOWYER]? (-ca 1642); in Eng, b 1612?; Roxbury

DANE, John[2] (1612/13-1684) & 1/wf Eleanor [CLARK?]; b 1638?, b 1640

DANE, John[1] (-1658) & 2/wf Agnes/Annis/Ann/Hannah (BAYFORD) CHANDLER, w William, m/3 John PARMENTER 1660; 2 Jul 1643; Roxbury

DANE, John[2] (-1684) & 2/wf Alice [DUTCH] (NEWMAN), w John, m/3 Jeremiah MEACHAM 1684; Ipswich

DANE, John (ca 1643, 1644-) & Abigail WARNER; 27 Dec 1671; Ipswich

DAINS, John & 1/wf Abigail [PAINE] (?1676-); ca 1698?; Southold, LI

DEANE, Nathaniel (?1645-1725) & Deliverance HASELTINE (?1654-1735); 12 Dec 1672; Andover

DANE, Philemon (?1646-1716) & 1/wf Mary THOMPSON; 7 Oct 1685; Ipswich

DANE, Philemon (-1716) & 2/wf Ruth CONVERSE (1665-); 25 Dec 1690; Ipswich

DANE, Thomas & Jane ? ; b 1698; Boston
DANFORTH, John (1660-1730) & Elizabeth MINOTT/MINOT (1663-1722); 21 Nov 1682; Dorchester
DANFORTH, Jonathan (1628-1712) & 1/wf Elizabeth [ROWTER]/[POULTER] (-1689); 22 Nov 1654; Billerica/Cambridge/Boston
DANFORTH, Jonathan (-1711), Billerica & Rebecca PARKER (1661-1754), m/2 Joseph FOSTER 1718; 27 Jun 1682; Billerica/Cambridge/?Boston
DANFORTH, Jonathan (1628-1712) & 2/wf Esther (CHAMPNEY) CONVERSE, Woburn, w Josiah; 17 Nov 1690; Billerica/Woburn/Cambridge
DANFORTH, Nicholas (1589-1638) & Elizabeth [SYMMES?] (-1629); in Eng, b 1619; Cambridge
DANFORTH, Samuel (1626-1674) & Mary WILSON (-1713), Boston, m/2 Joseph ROCK 1674+; 5 Nov 1651; Boston
DANFORTH, Samuel (1666-1727), Taunton & Hannah ALLEN (1668-1761); 4 Oct 1688; Boston/Taunton
DANFORTH, Samuel (-1742) & Hannah CROSBY (1672-), m/2 Enoch KIDDER; 8 Jan 1694/5; Billerica
DANFORTH, Thomas (?1623, 1622-1699) & Mary WITHINGTON (ca 1623-1697); 23 Feb 1643, 1643/4, ?2 Feb; Cambridge
DAMFORD/DANFORTH?, William & 1/wf Hannah KINSMAN (-1678); 20 Mar 1670, no issue; Ipswich/Newbury
DAMFARD, William & ? ; b 1675; Flushing, LI/Nantucket
DANFORD/DANFORTH?, William & 2/wf Sarah [THURLOW]; b 1680; Newbury
DANIELS, Davy & 2/wf? Naomi [HILL] (1640-); b 1655; Durham, NH
DANIELS, John (-1709, 1710) & Mary CHAPPELL; 19 Jan 1664, 1664/5; New London
DANIELL, John (1648-1718) & Dorothy BADCOCK; 29 Mar 1672; Milton
DANIELS, John (1666-1756) & Agnes BEEBE (1667-); 3 Dec 1685; New London
DANIELL, John (1648-1718), Milton & Abigail SCOTT (-1717); 3 Jul 1694; Braintree/Milton
DANIELL, John & Sarah DURHAM; 5 Apr 1699; Sherborn
DANIELLS, Joseph² (1640?-1715, Medway) & 1/wf Mary/Marie FAYRBANKS (1647-1682); 16 Nov 1665; Medfield
DANIEL, Joseph (-1715) & 2/wf Rachel [SHEFFIELD] (1660-1687, 1689?); b 1684; Medfield
DANIEL, Joseph (1666-1740) & 1/wf Rachel [PARTRIDGE] (1660-) (did not m Theophilus CLARK?); b 1689 (doubtful); Medfield
DANIEL, Joseph (1666-1740) (son Joseph) & 2/wf 1/wf? Bethia [BRECK/?PARTRIDGE] (1673-1754); b 1693; Medfield
DANIEL, Joseph (-1715, Medway) & 3/wf Lydia (ADAMS) [ALLEN] (1653-1731), w James; 1697; Medfield/Needham
DANIELS, Joseph (-1720) (son Samuel) & Lydia ADAMS; 27 Jan 1696/7; Dedham
DANIEL, Joseph & 1/wf Ann (HUNTRESS) [CHESLEY], w Thomas; ca 1700; Dover, NH
DANIEL, Robert (1590±-1655) & Elizabeth [MORSE] (1606-1640); b 1630; Medfield/Cambridge/Watertown
DANIEL, Robert & Bridget [LOKER/DRAPER]; aft 1643;Salem/Providence
DANIEL, Robert (-1655) & 2/wf Reana (?) (JAMES) ANDREWS, w Edmund, w William, m/4 Edmund FROST by 1669; 2 May 1654; Cambridge
DANIELS, Robert (1672-) & Hester ? ; b 1696; Sherborn
DANILL, Samuel (-1695) & Mary/Mercy? (BECKWITH) GRANT; 10 May 1671; Watertown
DANIEL, Samuel & Deborah (WALDO) FORD (1661-), w Joseph; 15 Mar 1694; Boston
DANIELL, Stephen & Anna [GREGSON] (-1709); [1651?]; New Haven/?Saybrook
DANIELL, Stephen (-1687) & 1/wf Mary PRINCE (-1679); 26 Jul 1666; Salem
DANIELL, Stephen (-1687) & 2/wf Susanna (BAXTER) HIDE, w Isaac 1680, m/2 ?Samuel GARDNER 1690?; 3 Dec 1680; Salem
DANIEL, Stephen & Mary MARSTON; 1 Jan 1692, ?1 Jun, 1692/3; Salem
DANIEL, Thomas (-1683) & Bridget [CUTTS], m/2 Thomas GRAFFORT 1684; b 1675; Portsmouth, NH
DANIEL, William¹ (-1678) & Catherine/Katharine [GREENWAY] (-1680); b 10 Aug 1650, b 1657; Milton
DANIEL, William & Dorothy [BUD?]; 17 Sep 1699; Boston
DANIEL, ? & Alice BEGGARLY, wid, m/3 John GREEN 1638+; by 1638

DANIEL, _?_ & Elizabeth [CHAMBERLAIN]; b 15 Apr 1673; ?Sudbury
DANIELSON, James (1649-1728) & Hannah (GEORGE) ROSE (1648-1692±), w Tourmet/Four-
mot/etc.; 11 Mar 1685, ?11 Jan, ?11 Jun; ?New Shoreham, RI
DONELSON, James & 2/wf Mary TOSH, w William; 22 Jan 1700; New Shoreham, RI
DANKS, Robert & Elizabeth (SWIFT) [WEBB] (1640-1691); b 1680, aft 26 Mar 1672;
Northampton
DARBYSHIRE, John & Mary [BLANCHARD], m/2 Nathaniel WOODS; b 1698; Dunstable/Groton
DARE, John & Elizabeth _?_ ; b 1677; Boston
DARLING, Benjamin (1672-1709), Salem (son of George) & Mary RICHARDS (1675-), m/2
Jonathan SHAW 1715; m int 29 Oct 1698; Lynn/Plympton
DARLING, Cornelious (1675-) & 1/wf Mary [FREBRAY?]; b 1695, b 1698, aft 1700;
Mendon/Attleboro/Rehoboth
DARLING, Cornelious (1678-) & 2/wf Sarah MITCHELL
DARLING/DARLEY, Denice/Dennis (-1718, ae 77, Mendon) & Hannah FRANCIS; 3 Jan 1662, 3
Jan 1662/3; Braintree/Mendon
DARELING, Ebenezer & Mary (WHEATON) MAN/MANN, w Thomas; 30 Mar 1698, ?3 Mar;
Rehoboth
DARLING, George (-1693) & Katherine [GRIDLEY]; b 1667, b 1660?, b 31 Mar 1657;
Lynn/Marblehead
DARLING, Henry & Joanna MITCHELL; 24 Feb 1697/8; Marblehead
DARLING, James & 1/wf Hannah (?LEWIS) MAINE/MAINS; 16 May 1683; Marblehead
DARLING, John & Elizabeth DOWNAM/DOWNHAM; 13 May 1664; Braintree/Mendon
DARLING, John & Mary (BISHOP) [BARNEY] (BARNETT/BARNET alias BARBANT) (1635-); b
1680; Salem
DARLING, John & Elizabeth MUZZEY; 4 Feb 1680; Marblehead
DARLING, John (1664-1753) & 1/wf Elizabeth [THOMPSON] (-3 Apr 1687); ca 1686;
Mendon/Bellingham
DARLING, John & 2/wf Ann/Anna/Anne/Joane ROCKET/ROCKWOOD (-1690); 2 Jan 1687/8;
Boston
DARLING, John (-1719) & Elizabeth [BEERS]; b 1689; Fairfield, CT
DARLING, John & 3/wf Elizabeth [MORSE] (1668-); b 1692; Mendon
DARLING, Richard & [?Abigail] [MESSENGER], m/2 Zachariah MILLS b 1686; b 11 Apr 1662,
div 1674; ?Jamaica, LI/?New Haven
DARLING, Thomas & 1/wf Joanna _?_ ; b 1691; Salem/Middleboro?
DARLING, _?_ & _?_ ?[BURROWS]; b 1695; ?Jamaica, LI
DARLING, _?_ & _?_ ; (Naomi FLANDERS had son John DARLING)
DARNTON, William & Thedow/Theodora (_?_) BELCHER LEE, w John, w Simon, m/4 Francis
POMEROY; 20 Nov 1700; Boston
DARROW, Christopher (1678-) & Elizabeth BAKER; b 1701?, 27 Jun 1701; New London, CT
DARROW, George (-1706) & Elizabeth/?Mary SHARSWOOD, w George; b 1675?; New London,
CT
DARROW, _?_ & Elizabeth [MARSHALL]; b 8 Sep 1702, b 1701?
DARROW?, ?Nicholas & _?_
DART, Ambrose & Anne ADDIS (-1709), m/2 Benjamin BREWSTER 1666; 24 Jun 1653;
Gloucester/Boston
DART, Daniel & Elizabeth DOUGLAS (-1714); 4 Aug 1686; New London
DART, Richard (1635-1724) & 1/wf Bethia _?_ ; ca 1663, b 1664/5; New London, CT
DART, Richard (1667-1741) & Elizabeth STRICKLAND (bpt 1675-1749); 22 Jun 1699; New
London
DARVILL/DARVALL, Robert & Esther/Hester _?_ ; b 1642; Sudbury
DARWIN/DURRUM, Ephraim & Elizabeth GOODRICH (1653-); 10 Jun 1678, 16 Jun; Guilford, CT
DASSETT, John[1] (-1677) & _?_ ; by 1639?; Braintree/Boston
DASSITT, John[2] (-1699) & 1/wf Hannah/Anna? FLINT (1643-); 15 Nov 1662; Braintree
DASSETT, John[2] (-1699) & 2/wf Martha _?_ (-1723, ae 70); b 1685?; Boston
DAVENPORT, Addington (1670-1736) & Elizabeth WAINWRIGHT (1679-1756); 10 Nov 1698;
Ipswich
DAVENPORT, Charles (1652-1720) & Waitstill [SMITH] (?1658, 1659-1747); b 1679; Dorchester

DAVENPORT, Ebenezer (1661-1738) & 1/wf Dorcas [ANDREWS] (-1723), Falmouth; b 1683; Boston/Falmouth/Dorchester

DAVENPORT, Eleazer (-1678) & Rebecca [ADDINGTON] (1648-); ca 1668, b 1670; Boston

DAVENPORT, Francis, Boston & Anne/Ann SNELLING; in Eng, ca 1672?; Boston

DAVENPORT, Humphrey & 1/wf Rachel [HOLMES]; b 1664; Dorchester/Hartford

DAVENPORT, Humphrey & 2/wf Johanna ROSECRANS; 18 Apr 1684; Kingstown, NY

DAVENPORT, Rev. John (1597-1670) & Elizabeth [?WOOLEY/?WOLLEY] (1603-1676); b 1635; Boston

DAVENPORT, John (?1635-1687, [1677?]) & Abigail PIERSON (?1643-1717); 27 Nov 1662, Branford; Branford, CT/New Haven/Boston

DAVENPORT, John, Boston & Bridget WATKINS; 1 Nov 1667; Dorchester/Boston

DAVENPORT, John & Abial?/Abigail? _?_; b 1669; Boston

DAVENPORT, John & Mary _?_; b 15 Jan 1682/3

DAVENPORT, John[2] (1664-1725) & Naomi [FOSTER]? (?1668-?May 1739); b 1695; Dorchester

DAVENPORT, Rev. John (?1668/9-1731) & 1/wf Martha (GOLD) SALLECK (-1712), w John; 18 Apr 1695; ?Stamford, CT

DAVENPORT, Jonathan (1659-1729) & Hannah MANER/MAYNARD (?1660-1729), dau John; Dec 1680; Dorchester/Little Compton, RI

DAVENPORT, Nathaniel (-1675) & Elizabeth [THATCHER/THACHER], m/2 Samuel DAVIS 1677?; no issue; Boston?/Salem

DAVENPORT, Richard (1606-1665?, 1678) & Elizabeth [HAWTHORNE]?; b 1634; Salem/Boston

DAVENPORT, Richard & 1/wf Abigail SHAW, dau John; b 1699(1700?); Weymouth/Bridgewater

DAVENPORT, Thomas[1] (-1685) (?cousin of Christopher GIBSON) & Mary ?NEWMAN (-1691); b 1643; Dorchester/Cambridge?

DAVENPORT, William & 1/wf Elizabeth _?_ (1670-1697); Hartford

DAVENPORT, William (-1698?, 1709+) & Mary [HITCHCOCK], w John; b 30 May 1681; Westchester, NY

DAVENPORT, _?_ & Jane [HIRST]?

DAVIDS, James & 2/wf Joanna (_?_) LING (-1673), w Benjamin; 3 Nov 1673; New Haven

DAVIDS/DIXWELL, James & Bathshua HOW; 23 Oct 1667; New Haven

DIXWELL, John & _?_; (see John DIXWELL)

DAVIS, Aaron (-1713+) & Mary _?_; ca 1668; Newport, RI/Dartmouth

DAVIS, Aaron (1670-1730) & Mary _?_ (1675-1731); b 1697(8?), b 1694?; Little Compton, RI

DAVIS, Andrew (?1650-1719) & Mary [BAILEY] (1657-); b 1684; New London, CT/Groton, CT

DAVIS, Anthony (-1674) & Elizabeth _?_; b 1666; Boston

DAVIS, Barnabas (1599-1685) & Patience _?_ (?1603-1690); b 1638; Charlestown

DAVIS, Benjamin (1649-) & 1/wf Sarah [RICHARDS] (1661/2?-); b 1680; Boston/Roxbury

DAVIS, Benjamin & Rebecca (?RIDER) [REEVE] (1644-), w Thomas; aft 28 Aug 1685; Southampton

DAVIS, Benjamin (1649-) & 2/wf Mary TIPPET; m int 15 Jan 1696/7; Boston

DAVIS, Benjamin (?1680-1761) & _?_; ca 1699?; Brookhaven, LI

DAVIS, Cornelius (1653-) & 1/wf Sarah _?_ (-1696); b 1689; Newbury

DAVIS, Cornelius (1653-) & 2/wf Sarah (JEWETT) HEDDEN, w John HIDDEN; 24 Aug 1696, 29 Aug 1696; Rowley/Newbury

DAVIS, Daniel & Mary HUBBARD (?1682-1741?); 27 Apr 1699; Concord

DAVIS, David (-1696) & Susanna _?_, m/2 James DURGIN; b 1687; Oyster River, NH

DAVIS, Dolor (-1673) & 1/wf Margery WILLARD (1602-); E. Farleigh, Eng, 29 Mar 1624; Cambridge/Duxbury/Barnstable/Concord

DAVIS, Dolor (-1673) & 2/wf Joanna (HULL) [BURSLEY] (-1688+, 1686+), w John; 1671?, aft 1660; Barnstable

DAVIS, Dolor (1660-1710) & Hannah LINNELL; 3 Aug 1681; Barnstable

DAVIS, Ebenezer & Dinah BROWNE; 14 Feb 1700; Chelmsford

DAVIS, Ebenezer (1678-1712) & Hannah WHITE (1673-), m/2 Nathaniel CRAFT; 18 Apr 1700; Roxbury

DAVIS, Edward & Hannah GRIDLEY; 16 Sep 1657; Boston

DAVIS, Elisha (1670-) & Grace SHAW; 19 Jun 1694; Haverhill/Rehoboth/Scituate

DAVIS, Emanuel & Mary (?KENDALL) [TARBOT/TURBET], w John; b 1687; Wells, ME

DAVIS, Ephraim, Haverhill & Mary JOHNSON, Andover, m/2 Edward CLARK 1682; 31 Dec 1659, 29 Dec 1660, 11 Feb 1659; Haverhill/Andover

DAVIS, Ephraim & Elizabeth KINGSBURY; 9 Jun 1687; Newbu. y

DAVIS, Ephraim (1665-) & Mary EIRES/AYRES; 19 Mar 1687/8; Andover/Norwich, CT/Canterbury, CT

DAVIS, Evan & Hannah __?__; b 1687; Hartford

DAVIS, Evan & Mary [ROGERS] (1674±); Southold, LI

DAVIS, Francis & Mary TAYLOR; 20 Jan 1673; Amesbury

DAVIS, Fulk & 1/wf __?__; b 1642?; Southampton, LI/Easthampton/Jamaica

DAVIS, Fulk & 2/wf Mary (_?_) (HAINES) [DAYTON], w James, w Ralph; b 11 Mar 1660; Easthampton, LI

DAVIS, George (-1667) (calls William CLARK of Lynn "brother") & 1/wf __?__ AUDLEY?/ODLIN?, wid?; b 1642, b 1640?, b 1626?; Lynn

DAVIS, George (-1667) & 2/wf Sarah [CLARK]/COLT? (-1698) (had son Joseph COULT), m/2 Nicholas REST/RESSE? (see RICE); b 1642, b 27 Oct 1642; Lynn/Reading/Charlestown

DAVIE, George (-living in 1680) & __?__; ca 1645?; Wiscasset, ME

DAVIS, George (-1655) & Barbara __?__, m/2 John BRIMBLECOME 1656, m/3 Thomas CHADWELL?; b 1647; Boston

DAVIS, Gershom (ca 1644-1717/18) & Sarah __?__ (1658-1713); b 1681; Boston/Cambridge

DAVIS, Hopewell (-1712, ae 68) & 1/wf Sarah BOYNTON (-1704, ae 47); 18 Sep 1682; Charlestown

DAVIS, Hopkin & Ruth [ROBERTS]; in Wales?, b 1670, b 1651; Portsmouth, NH

DAVIS, Ichabod & Bethia [PEPPER?]/[HOPKINS?] (-1768); b 1701?; Roxbury

DAVIS, Isaac & __?__; in Eng, b 1636 (doubtful, went back); Salem

DAVIS, Isaac & Lydia BLACK; 28 Sep 1659; Beverly/Casco?

DAVIS, Jabez (-1710) & Experience LINNEL/LINNELL (-1712+), m/2 Benjamin HATCH 1712; 20 Aug 1689; Barnstable

DAVIS, Jacob (ca 1640-) & Elizabeth BENNETT; 20 Jan 1661, 1661/2?; Gloucester

DAVIS, Jacob (1662-1718) & Mary HASKELL (1668-), m/2 Ezekiel WOODWARD 1719; 14 Sep 1687; Gloucester

DAVIS, Jacob (-1701) & Susanna [DAWES] (1666-); b 1688; Boston

DAVIS, James (-1679) & Cicely THAYER (-1673); Thornbury, Eng, 11 Jun 1618; Gloucester/Haverhill

DAVIES, James (-1661) & Joanna __?__; b 1639; Boston

DAVIS, James & Barbara __?__; b 1640; Boston

DAVIS, James & Mary __?__; b 1647; Braintree

DAVIS, James & Elizabeth EATON (-1684); 1 Dec 1648; Haverhill

DAVIS, James (?1636-1715) & 1/2f Mehitable __?__ (-1666); b 1659(60?); Gloucester

DAVIS, James (ca 1636-1715) & 2/wf Elizabeth BATCHELLER (-1697); 6 Dec 1666; Gloucester

DAVIS, James & Elizabeth [RANDALL] (1652-); b 1673; Scituate/Charlestown

DAVIS, James (-1694) & 2/wf Mary __?__; ca 1685?; Salisbury

DAVIS, James (1663-1743) & 1/wf Bethiah LEACH (-1733); 7 May 1685; Gloucester

DAVIS, James (1662-1749) & Elizabeth CHESLEY; 1 Oct 1688; Dover, NH

DAVIS, James & Sarah (?WINNOCK) WIGGINS, w James; 16 Aug 1693; Haverhill

DAVIS, James (ca 1636-1715) & 3/wf Mary (COLLINS) (ELWELL) COOK (1646-1725), w Josiah, w John; 3 Aug 1697; Gloucester

DAVIS, Jenkin (-1662) & Mary __?__ (-1682+); b 1635?, b 1643; Lynn

DAVIES, Jeremiah (1648-) & Mary (HUNTINGTON) JOYE, w Abraham; 5 Mar 1688/9; Amesbury/Newbury

DAVIS, John & ?Alice/?Frances [?NEWMAN]; b 1639, b 1636; Gloucester

DAVIS, John (1613-) (ae ca 70 in 1683) & Mary __?__; b 1641; York, ME

DAVIS, John (-1675) & Eleanor __?__; b 1642; Newbury

DAVIES, John & Mary [SPRING] (-1656); b 1642; Watertown

DAVIS, John & Jane PEASLEY; 10 Dec 1646; Haverhill/Oyster River, NH

DAVIS, John (-1703) & Hannah LINNELL/LYNNETT?; 15 Mar 1648, 1648/9?; Barnstable

DAVIS, John & Katherine __?__; b 1654; Cape Porpoise/Portsmouth, NH

DAVIS, John & Return GRIDLEY (1638-); 9 Apr 1656; Boston/Block Island

DAVIS, John & Mary (POOKE) [PURINGTON], w George; b 1661, b 15 Mar 1661/2; Salisbury

DAVIS, John & Elizabeth __?_ ; b 1661?; Southampton, LI
DAVIS, John & Sarah KIRTLAND (1646-), m/2 Thomas LEE by 1670?; 5 Oct 1664; Lynn
DAVIS, John (1643-1705, Roxbury) & Mary DEVOTION (-1683, Roxbury); 5 Feb 1667; Roxbury
DAVIS, John (-1712) & Lydia (_?_) WALLER, w Joseph; m cont 26 Dec 1672; Fairfield, CT/Woodbury, CT
DAVIS, John (1651-1717) & Mary TORREY (1654-1717); 14 Jan 1673; Dorchester/Roxbury
DAVIS, John, Jr. (1650-) & 1/wf Ruth GOODSPEED; 2 Feb 1674, 1674/5; Barnstable/Falmouth, MA
DAVIS, John (-1705) & Mary LEEKE (-1696); 9 Mar 1674/5; New Haven/East Hampton, LI
DAVIS, John & Mary __?_ ; ?b 1676; Boston/Watertown
DAVIS, John & Hannah [LATTIN/LATTING] (-1687?); b Nov 1676; Brookhaven, LI
DAVIS, John & Sarah __?_ ; b 1679; Beverly
DAVIS, John & Sarah CARTER; 8 Apr 1681; Newbury/Amesbury
DAVIS, John & 1/wf __?_ ; b 1682?; Derby, CT
DAVIS, John & Elizabeth __?_ ; b 1682; Boston
DAVIS, John & Elizabeth [BOADEN/CILLEY?]; ca 1683; Amesbury
DAVIS, John & Sarah __?_ ; b 17 Oct 1683; Boston/Westfield
DAVIS, John (1651-1694) & 1/wf Mary __?_ (-12 Jan 1684); Dover, NH?
DAVIS, John (-1694) & 2/wf Elizabeth [BURNHAM] (1651-1694); aft 12 Jan 1684; Oyster River, NH
DAVIS, John (1660-1742+) & __?_ ; b 1686; Falmouth, ME/Gloucester
DAVIS, John (1660-1729) & Ann HARRADEN (1661-1729); 6 Jan 1685/6; Gloucester
DAVIS, John (-1687, nr 57) & Sarah __?_ (-1688); b 1687 (prob 1660-70?), no ch mentioned; Charlestown
DAVIS, John & Hannah __?_ ; b 1687; Boston
DAVIS, John & Mary [SHORTRIDGE]; b 1689; Portsmouth, NH
DAVIS, John & 2/wf Mary (SMITH) GUNN, w Abel; 12 May 1691; Derby, CT
DAVIS, John & 3/wf Abigail [HARGER/TIBBELLS?]; 1691?, by 1692; Derby, CT?
DAVIS, John, Jr. (1650-) & 2/wf Mary HAMLIN (-1698); 22 Feb 1692; Barnstable
DAVIS, John & Mehitable [?SHEDD]; b 1693; Groton
DAVIE, John & Elizabeth [RICHARDS]; b 1693, b 29 Sep 1691; Groton, CT
DAVIS, John (-1728) & Elizabeth __?_ (-1728+); b 1696; N. Kingstown, RI/Westerly, RI
DAVIS, John & Dorothy __?_ (doubtful); b 1698; LI
DAVIS, John & Puah [PARSONS] (-1747, in 74th y); LI
DAVIS, John & 3/wf Hannah (?LUMBERT) BACON, w Nathaniel; 8 May 1699; Falmouth, MA
DAVIS, John, Enfield, CT, & Hannah [ROOT] (1677-), Farmington, CT; b 1701?
DAVIS, Jonathan (-1674) & Sarah __?_ ; b 1674; Jamaica, LI
DAVIS, Jonathan (1665-) & Ann/Anna? __?_ ; b 1695/[6?]; Roxbury
DAVIS, Joseph & Elizabeth SAYWELL; 7 May 1662; Boston
DAVIS, Joseph (-1676?) & [?Hannah] __?_ ; b 1669; Reading
DAVIS, Joseph (1647-) & Sarah CHAMBERLAIN; 28 Oct 1697; Roxbury
DAVIS, Joseph (-1691) & Elizabeth __?_ ; ca 1670?; Southampton, LI/Brookhaven, LI
DAVIS, Joseph (-1690) & Mary CLAGHORN (1655-1706); 28 Mar 1682; Barnstable
DAVIS, Joseph, Reading & Rebecca PATTEN (1675-); 18 Jun 1691; Billerica/Reading
DAVIS, Joseph & Mary [STEVENS]; b 1693; Oyster River, NH
DAVIS, Joseph (1665-1735) & Hannah COBB (1671-1739); - Mar 1695; Barnstable
DAVIS, Joseph (1672-1717) & 1/wf Sarah __?_ ; b 1697; Roxbury
DAVIS, Joseph & Jemima EASTMAN (1677-); 14 Jun 1698; Amesbury/Salisbury
DAVIS, Joshua (-1736) & Mary [SCOTT] (1666-1734+); ca 1690?; Newport/E. Greenwich, RI
DAVIS, Joshua & Rebecca PIERCE/PEIRCE; 24 May 1699; Reading/Boston
DAVIS, Josiah[2] (1656-1709) & Ann TAYLOR (?1659-bef 1709); 25 Jun 1679; Barnstable
DAVIS, Lawrence (?1625-1711) & ?2/wf Elizabeth [ATKINS] (1645-), m/2 George NICHOLSON; b 1663; Falmouth, ME/Ipswich/Beverly, MA
DAVIS, Matthew (1664-) & Margaret CORBIN; 27 Feb 1690/1; Woodstock, CT/Pomfret, CT
DAVIS, Moses (1657-1724) & Ruhamah DOW; 16 Jan 1681; Haverhill/Oyster River, LI
DAVIS, Nathaniel & 1/wf Mary CONVERSE (-1690, ae 36); 31 Mar 1675; Woburn
DAVIS, Nathaniel & 2/wf Mary EDMUNDS (-1721, ae 65); 15 Jul 1692; Charlestown

DAVIS/DAVIES, Nicholas (1595-1670) (had cousin William LOCKE) & 1/wf Sarah _?_ (1595, 1587-1643); b 1622; Charlestown/Woburn
DAVIS, Nicholas (1595-1670) & 2/wf Elizabeth ISAAC/ISAACS, w Joseph; 12 Jul 1643; Woburn
DAVIS, Nicholas (-1672) & Sarah _?_ (-1692+), m/2 John CLARK; b 1652; Barnstable/Newport
DAVIS, Nicholas & Rebecca _?_ ; b 1687; Boston
DAVIS/DAVIES?, Philip (1626-1689) & Esther [COLEMAN] (1637-); ca 1655?; Hartford
DAVIS, Richard (-1663) & Sarah [BURRILL], m/2 Samuel CHANDLER 1664; ca 1654?, b 1657; Dorchester/Roxbury
DAVIS, Robert[1] (-1693) & 1/wf _?_ ; b 1645(6?); Yarmouth
DAVIS, Robert (1608-1655) & Bridget [LOKER?/LOOKER?] (ca 1613-1685), m/2 Thomas KING 1655; b 1646, ca 1644; Sudbury
DAVIS, Robert & _?_ ; b 1648; Sagamore Creek
DAVIS, Robert[1] (-1693) & 2/wf Ann _?_ (-1701); b 1656; Barnstable
DAVIS, Robert[2] (?1654-) & _?_ ; b 1688; Rehoboth
DAVIS, Robert & Jane (ANDREWS) ALGER (1663-1732), w Andrew; 19 Feb 1693; Boston
DAVIS, Roger & _?_ ; b 1690; Isles of Shoals
DAVIS, Samuel (-1672) & Anna NORCROSS; ?30 Nov 1631; Boston
DAVIS, Samuel & Sarah THAYER; 20 Jul 1651; Boston/Braintree
DAVIS, Samuel (-1699) & Mary WATERS (1638-1713); 1656; Lancaster/Groton
DAVIS, Samuel (-1696) & Deborah BARNES (1646-1719); 17 Dec 1663, 19 Dec 1663; Haverhill/Salisbury
DAVIS, Samuel & 1/wf Mary MEDDOWES/MEADS? (-1710); 11 Jan 1665, 11 Jan 1665/6; Concord/Lynn
DAVIS, Samuel (?1650-) & 1/wf Hannah EDWARDS (1644-1680); 4 Mar 1668, 1668/9; Northampton/Deerfield/Northfield
DAVIS, Samuel (1642+-1692) & Mary _?_ ; ca 1670-1672?; Southampton/Jamaica, LI
DAVIS, Samuel & 1/wf? Deborah _?_ (-20 Nov 1673); b 28 Jul 1673; Boston
DAVIS, Samuel & Elizabeth (THATCHER) [DAVENPORT], w Nathaniel; 1677; Weymouth
DAVIS/(not JANES?), Samuel (-1690) & 2/wf Elizabeth SMEAD (1662-1682); 23 Feb 1680/1; Northampton
DAVIS, Samuel (-1690) & Hannah (?HULL) [ALEXANDER], m/- Nathaniel PRITCHARD 1691; aft 26 Aug 1682; Northampton
DAVIS, Samuel (-1699) & Anna _?_ ; b 1694; Groton
DAVIS, Samuel & Hannah _?_ ; b 1695; Chelmsford
DAVIS, Samuel (1673-) & Thankful CLESSON (1673-); 28 Oct 1695; Deerfield/Brookfield
DAVIS, Samuel & Abigail READ (1675-1709, 1709/10); 2 Mar 1697/8; Concord
DAVIS, Samuel & Katherine HASTINGS; 20 Apr 1699; Haverhill
DAVIS, Samuel & _?_ ; b 1701; Brookhaven, LI
DAVIS, Simon (?1636-1713, ae 77) & Mary BLOOD (1640-); 12 Dec 1660; Concord
DAVIS, Simon & Ann LOW; 24 Sep 1685; Bristol, RI
DAVIS, Simon (1661-) & 1/wf Elizabeth WOODIS/WOODHOUSE (-1711); 14 Feb 1688/9; Concord
DAVIS, Stephen & Sarah _?_ ; b 1673; Boston
DAVIS, Stephen & Mary TUCKER (1666-), m/2 Joseph PEASLEY; 23 Dec 1685; Haverhill
DAVIS, Sylvanus (?1635-1703) & 2/wf? Elizabeth _?_ ; Sheepscot, ME/Hull
DAVIS, Thomas (1603-) & Christian _?_ (-1668, Haverhill); ca 1626?; Salisbury
DAVIS, Thomas & Elizabeth _?_ ; b 28 Oct 1678; Medfield
DAVIS, Thomas & Mary _?_ (-1681); b 1680; Boston
DAVIS, Thomas & _?_ ; b 1683; Flushing, LI
DAVIS, Thomas & Martha [LORD]; b 1687; Boston/Dover, NH
DAVIS, Thomas & Hannah (LAVERETT) ALLEN (1661-1732), w Eleazer; 12 Sep 1689; Boston
DAVIS, Thomas & Abigail WADSWORTH, Milton; 25 Nov 1689; Milton
DAVIS, Thomas & Susanna SOWDIN; 8 Nov 1692; Marblehead
DAVIS, Thomas & Grace HULT (called Jane in Sep 1698); 27 Jan 1697; Boston
DAVIS, Thomas & Hannah HARTSHORN (1679-); 27 Dec 1698; Reading/Cambridge
DAVIS, Thomas & _?_ ; b 1699; Rehoboth
DAVIS, Thomas & Mary SHEPHERD; 22 May 1700; Haverhill
DAVIS, Timothy (1651-) & 1/wf Joanna [MOSES]; b 1680; Portsmouth, NH

DAVIS, Timothy (1651-) & 2/wf Constant __?__ ; ca 1684?; Portsmouth, NH
DAVIS, Timothy & Sarah PERRY; 7 Mar 1690
DAVIS, Tobias (-1690) & 1/wf Sarah [MORRILL] (-1648); b 1647; Roxbury
DAVIS, Tobias (-1690) & 2/wf Bridget KINMAN/KINGMAN; 13 Dec 1649; Roxbury
DAVIS, Tristram (1666-) & Sarah (?HOLBROOK) ARCHER, Braintree, wid; 19 Mar 1694/5;
   Scituate
DAVIS, Walter & Mary DAVIS; 19 Oct 1674; Cambridge
DAVIS, William (-1659) & Martha WAKEMAN (1596-1663?, 1664?); Bewdley, Eng, 30 Nov 1621;
   New Haven
DAVIS, William (-1644), locksmith & 1/wf __?__ ; b 1624; Boston
DAVIS, William (-1644), locksmith & 2/wf Mary [MEANS], m/2 John COWDALL 1655±; b 1635;
   Boston
DAVIS, William (1617-1683, ae 66) & 1/wf Elizabeth __?__ (-1658); b 1643; Roxbury
DAVIS, Capt. William (-1676) & 1/wf Margaret PYNSHON (-1653); 6 Dec 1644; ?Boston
DAVIS, William (-1653) (perhaps not a resident of Boston) & __?__ ; ca 1645?; Boston
DAVIS, William & Margaret __?__ , m/2 Richard POTTS; by 1653?
DAVIS, William & Mary [PARKER] (-1678+); b 1655; Boston/Barbados
DAVIS, Capt. William (-1676) & 2/wf Huldah [SYMMES] (1631-1674?); b 1656, ca 1655; Boston
DAVIS, William (-1683, ae 66?) & 2/wf Alice THORPE (-1667/8); 21 Oct 1658; Roxbury
DAVIS, William (-1683, ae 66) & 3/wf Jane __?__ (-1714, Watertown); aft Feb 1667/8
DAVIS, Capt. William (-1676) & 3/wf Dorothy __?__ (-8 Apr 1670); b 1670; Charlestown
DAVIS/DAVIE?, Capt. William (-1676?) & Rebecca __?__ (1656-), m/2 Simon HINKSON; ca
   1673?
DAVIS, William (1646-1707) & Elizabeth [HILL], m/2 John AVERY; ca 1673?; Greenland
DAVIS, William (-1676, ae 59) & 4/wf Sarah [FARMER], m/2 Edward PALMES 1677; aft 16 Aug
   1674; Charlestown
DAVIS, William (1653-1685) & Abigail [ELIOT]; b 1680; Boston
DAVIS/DAVIES?, William (-1701) & Mary __?__ ; b 1682; Boston
DAVIS, William & Martha/?Mary __?__ ; b 1685 (doubtful); Boston
DAVIS, William & Mary MAKEPEASE; 1 Mar 1685/6; Taunton/Freetown
DAVIS, William & Frances __?__ ; b 1693/5?; Newport/E. Greenwich, LI
DAVIS, William & __?__ ; b 1696; Westerly, RI
DAVIS, William & Mary CALEE/?KELLY (1678-); 31 Dec 1700; Haverhill/Newbury
DAVIS, William (1673-1706) & Charity [HOLMES]; b 1701; Roxbury
DAVIS, Zachariah & Sarah __?__ ; b 1686/7?; Boston
DAVIS, Zachary & Judith BROWN (1660-1728), m/2 Henry BRADLEY 1696; 4 Feb 1680/1;
   Newbury
DAVIS, __?__ & Elizabeth [SCOTT]; by 1689, b 11 Jun 1690; ?CT
DAVIS, __?__ & Margery __?__ , m/2 Charles GRIST/GRICE; b 15 (1) 1645; ?Boston
DAVIS, __?__ & Mary (COOKE) [TABOR], w Philip; aft 4 Mar 1693, bef Aug 1693; ?Dartmouth
DAVIS, __?__ & Sarah [WOODRUFF] (1660-), dau John; b 1703; Southampton, LI
DAVISON, Daniel (1639-) & Margaret LOW; 8 Apr 1657; Ipswich
DAVISON, Daniel (1601-) & Abigail COFFIN (1657-); 16 Dec 1673; Charlestown/Newbury
DAVISON, Daniel (-1704) & Sarah DODG/DODGE; 28 Jun 1685; Ipswich/Stonington, CT/New
   London, CT
DAVISON, John (-1735), Ipswich & Martha [DODGE] (1674-1736); b 1705, b 1701?
DAVISON, Nicholas (1611-1664) & Joanna [MILLER alias HODGES] (1621-), m/2 Richard
   KENT, Jr. 1674, 1674/5?; b 1639; Charlestown
DAVISON, Peter & Ann MORGAN, ?m/2 Jeremiah RIPLEY; 6 Jan 1695/6; ?Preston,
   CT/Norwich/Mansfield, CT
DAVISON, Samuel & Hannah [EDWARDS]; 1669; Northampton
DAVISON, Thomas (-1724) & Hannah TRACY (1677-); 28 Nov 1695; ?Preston, CT
DAVISON, William & Mary [NOWELL] (1669-); b 1693; Ipswich
DAVOL, Benjamin & Elizabeth [PEABODY]; b 22 Mar 1686/7; Newport/Monmouth, NJ
DAVOL, Jonathan (-1709+) & Hannah __?__ (1643-) (she m Peter BUMSTEAD, had Hannah 21
   Nov 1664); b 1665?; Newport/Dartmouth
DEVOL, Jonathan & Hannah __?__ ; b 1698; Dartmouth

DAVOL, Joseph (-1716) & 1/wf Mary [BRAYTON]; b 6 Jan 1671; Portsmouth, RI/Newport/Dartmouth

DAVOL, Joseph (-1716) & 2/wf Elizabeth _?_ (-1716+); b 27 Mar 1702, b 1701?; Newport/Westerly, RI

DEVEL, Joseph (-1726) & Mary [SOULE] (-1726+); b 1700; Dartmouth

DAVOL, William (-1680+) & _?_; b 1643; Duxbury/Braintree/Rehoboth/Newport

DAVOL, William (-1719) & Elizabeth _?_, m/2 Christopher CHAMPLIN; b 1698; Westerly, RI

DAVIE, George (-1680) & _?_; Portsmouth, NH

DAVY, Humphrey (-1689) & 1/wf Mary [WHITE?/DAVIE?]; b 1662; Boston

DAVIE, Humphrey (-1689) & 2/wf Sarah (GIBBONS) [RICHARDS], w James; b 1686; Boston

DAVIE, John (-1727, in Eng) & Elizabeth [RICHARDS] (-1713); b 1693; New London, CT/Groton, CT

DAVIE, William & Rebecca DENHAM (?1656-), m/2 Simon HINKSON; ca 1673; ?Portsmouth, NH

DAVOY?/DAVIE?, _?_ & Mary MIRICK (-1711+); b 1676; Charlestown

DAWES, Ambrose (1642-1705) & Mary [BUMSTEAD] (1642-1706); b 1664; Boston

DAWES, James & Frances _?_; b 1668; Boston

DAWES, John (-1684) & Mary _?_; b 1655; Boston

DAWES, Samuel (1664-) & Experience _?_, m/2 Charles CLARK; b 1700; Weymouth

DAWES, Jonathan (1661-1690) & Hannah [MORSE] (1665-), m/2 Richard GRIDLEY 1694, [1694/5?]; b 1683(4?); Boston

DAWES, William[1] (?1620-1703/4) & Susanna [MILLS] (-living 1687); b 1642; Braintree/Boston

DAWSON/DANSON, George (-1692?) & Elizabeth _?_, m/2 _?_; Boston/Plymouth/etc.

DAWSON, Henry & _?_; b 1641; Boston

DAWSON, Henry & Abigail _?_; b 1678; Boston

DAWSON, Richard & Mary DAYTON; 10 Dec 1698; Stratford, CT

DAWSON, Robert & 1/wf _?_; b 1677; East Haven, CT

DAWSON, Robert & Elizabeth _?_; b 1687; Boston

DAWSON, Robert (-1717/18) & 2/wf Hannah [RUSSELL] (-1713/14), w John; b 1687; East Haven, CT

DAWSON, Thomas & _?_; b 1699; Newport/New Haven

DAY, Anthony (1616, 1614?, ?1624/27-1707) & Susannah RING?/[probably MACHETT?] (1624-1717); b 1650, aft 11 Sep 1649; Gloucester

DAY, Ebenezer (1677-1763) & Mercy HITCHCOCK (1681-1761); 18 Apr 1700, 10 Apr; W. Springfield

DAY, Emanuel/Manuel/Manning? & Hannah [BISHOP] (1661-); b 1688; Manchester

DAY, Ezekiel & Mary ROWE; 27 Jan 1690; Gloucester

DAY, George & _?_; LI

DAY, Isaac & Susanna [MERRIAM]?; b 1686; Cambridge

DAY, James & Susanna [AYRES?], dau John; b 1684(5?); Ipswich

DAY, John (1645-) & 1/wf 2/wf Mary GAYLORD/?Mary MAYNARD/?Sarah STONE?/?Sarah BUTLER (1651-); by 1670, b 1663; Springfield

DAY, John & Sarah PENGRY; 20 Apr 1664; Ipswich

DAYE, John (-1680) & Ann COLEMAN; 16 Jul 1668; Salem

DAY, John (-1730) & Sarah [MAYNARD?] (see above); b 1675?; Hartford

DAY, John (1654-1727) & Abigail POND (1652-); 22 May 1678; Dedham/Wrentham

DAY, John & Abigail LEACH; 12 Dec 1681, 1682; Gloucester

DAY, John & Sarah WELLS (1671-); 27 Jan 1691; Ipswich

DAY, John (ca 1676-1752) & 1/wf Grace SPENCER (1676-1714); 21 Jan 1696, 1696/7; Hartford/Colchester, CT

DAY, John (1673-1752) & 1/wf Marah/Mary? SMITH (1677-1742); 10 Mar 1696, 1696/7, 1697; Hadley/Hatfield

DAY, John & Mary [HALES]?/[KIMBERLY?] (1675-1749); b 1701?, b 1719, aft 20 Feb 1708/9; Colchester, CT

DAY, Joseph & Hannah _?_; b 1694; Boston

DAY, Joseph & Elizabeth GAUGE?/GOUGE?; 15 Aug 1695; Gloucester

DAY, Joseph & Abigail [CROEL/CROWELL?]; 17 Oct 1700; Gloucester

DAY, Mark & Mary _?_, ?m/2 John SQUIRE bef 1687; b 1675; Boston

DAY, Nathaniel (1665-1735) & Ruth ROW (1671-1736); 13 Feb 1689/90; Gloucester/Attleboro

DAY, Ralph (-1677) & 1/wf Susan FAIRBANKS (-1659); 12 Oct 1647; Dedham

DAY, Ralph (-1677) & 2/wf Abigail (CRAFTS) RUGGLES, w John, m/3 Edward ADAMS 1678; 15 Nov 1659; Dedham

DAY, Ralph & Sarah FULLER (1659-1736), m/2 John CARPENTER aft 1694, m/3 Samuel WARD/WARE?; 6 Dec 1682; Dedham

DAY, Robert (1605-1648) & 1/wf Mary __?__ (1607-); b 1635; Cambridge/Hartford

DAY, Robert, Ipswich & Mary __?__; bef 1637

DAY, Robert (-1648) & 2/wf Editha [STEBBINS] (-1688), m/2 John MAYNARD ca 1648, m/3 Elizur HOLYOKE ca 1658; betw 1636 & 1644, b 1648, ca 1667; Springfield

DAY, Robert (-1683) & 2/wf [Hannah PENGRY]; b 1644, ca 1637; Ipswich

DAY, Samuel & 1/wf Rachel ROE/ROWE; 9 Aug 169-, 1692; Gloucester

DAY, Samuel (1671-1729) & Marah/Mary DUMBLETON (ca 1675-1759); 22 Jul 1697; W. Springfield

DAY, Stephen (-1668) & Rebecca (WRIGHT) [BOARDMAN] (-1659), wid; b 1638, aft 18 Feb 1616/17; Cambridge

DAY, Thomas (?1638-1711) & Sarah COOPER (ca 1642-1726); 27 Oct 1659; Springfield

DAY, Thomas & Mary [COOK?/LANGTON?], m/2 Thomas MEADE 1672; b 1667, b 28 Jun 1653; Salem

DAY, Thomas & Ann/Anna/Anne WOODWARD (1651-); 20 Oct 1672, 2 Oct; Ipswich

DAY, Thomas & Mary LAUGHTON/LANGTON?; 30 Dec 1673; Gloucester

DAY, Thomas (1662-1729) & Elizabeth MERRICK (1661-1743); 28 Jan 1685, 1684/5; Springfield/Colcester, CT

DAY, Thomas & __?__; b 1698; Haverhill

DAY, Thomas (ca 1672-1725?) & Hannah WILSON, m/2 Nathaniel DICKINSON; 21 Sep 1698; Hartford

DAY, Thomas & Mary DENNING, m/2 Ebenezer STEVENS; 7 Mar 1700; Gloucester

DAY, Timothy (1653-1723) & Phebe WILES/WILDE?/WILDES (ca 1653, 1657-1727); 24 Jul 1679; Gloucester/Topsfield

DAY, Wentworth & [Elizabeth STORY] (1622-); b 1641; Boston

DAY, William & Elizabeth __?__; b 1683; Boston

DAY, Manning/Emanuel & Hannah BISHOP (1661-); [b 1688], b 1702, b 1701

DAYTON, Abraham & 1/wf Mary [BEARDSLEY]; ca 1686; Brookhaven, LI

DAYTON, Abraham & 2/wf Catherine __?__; b 22 Jul 1693; Brookhaven, LI/Southampton, LI

DAYTON, Beriah (1674-1746) & Jane __?__ (-1754, ae 79); b 1700; East Hampton, LI

DAYTON, Isaac (-1688) & Rebecca [TUTTLE]? (1664-); b 1684; Southold, LI

DAYTON, Ralph (1588-1658) & 1/wf Alice (GOLDHATCH) TRITTON; Ashford, Kent, 16 Jun 1617, 16 Jun 1616; New Haven/etc.

DAYTON, Ralph (-1658) & 2/wf Mary (__?__) HAYNES, w James, m/3 Fulk DAVIS by 1660; Jun 1656; Southold, LI

DAYTON, Ralph & Elizabeth BIGG, w John; ca 19 Nov 1694; Brookhaven, LI

DAYTON, Robert (bpt 1629, 1626-1712) & Elizabeth [WOODRUFF]; b 1665; ?Easthampton, LI

DAYTON, Robert (-1722) & Hannah __?__; b 1696; Easthampton, LI/Southampton

DAYTON, Samuel (1624-1690) & 1/wf Medlen/Wilhelmina __?__; b 12 Dec 1656, b 12 Sep 1653; Southampton

DAYTON, Samuel & 2/wf Mary DINGLE; 14 May 1666

DAYTON, Samuel & 3/wf Elizabeth [BEARDSLEY], w Thomas; b 1669(70?); Stratford, CT/Brookhaven, LI

DAYTON, Samuel (-1716) & ?Dorothy __?__ (-1750, in 86th y); b 1692, b 1701 East Hampton, LI; Easthampton/Brookhaven, LI

DAYTON?, [Samuel] & Ruth DIMON/DEMMING; b 1682; Southampton

DEACON, John (1610-) & 1/wf Alice __?__ (1605-1657); b 1635; Lynn

DEACON, John & 2/wf Elizabeth PICKERING (-1662), w John; 25 Dec 1657; Lynn/Boston

DEACON, John & 3/wf Ann __?__; aft 1662, bef 5 Apr 1670; Boston

DEACON, Joseph (-1670/71) & Rachel [ALLEN], dau Hope, m/2 William SHUTE; b 31 May 1670 at Lynn; Boston

DEAL, Charles (-1686, 1685?) & Pity ?BOTS/BETTS? (Indian woman); 3 Jul 1672, no issue; Milford, CT

DEALE, Charles & Rachel __?__; b 1687(8?); Boston

DEALE/DALE?, John & Elizabeth [KINNEY/KINNE]; b 1685; Salem
DEALE/DALE?, William (-1664) & Mary SHATSWELL/SATCHWELL?, m/2 Nicholas SMITH of
   Exeter, m/3 Charles RUNLETT 1676; 30 Jun 1662; Haverhill
DEAN, Benjamin & Sarah WILLIAMS (1666-); 6 Jan 1680, 1680/1; Taunton/Enfield, CT
DEAN, Daniel (-1625, Sudbury) & 1/wf Mary [GOBLE]; b 1675; Charlestown/Sudbury
DEAN, Daniel & Mary __?_ ; b 2 Mar 1699; Jamaica, LI
DEAN, Ezra & Bethia EDSON, Bridgewater; 17 Dec 1676; Taunton/Bridgewater
DEAN, George (1639-1696) & Elizabeth __?_ (-1696+); b 1660[1?]; Salem
DEAN, Isaac & Hannah LEONARD; 24 Jan 1677; Taunton
DEAN, James (-1725) & Sarah [TISDALE]; ca 1671; Taunton/Stonington, CT/Plainfield, CT
DEAN, James (1674-) & Sarah PACKER (-1734, ae 62); 2 Jun 1677; Stonington, CT
DEAN, John & Alice __?_ ; ca 1630-7?; Dorchester/Taunton
DEAN, John (-1716/17) & Sarah EDSON (ca 1640-), Bridgewater; 7 Nov 1663; Taunton
DEAN, John & Sarah __?_ ; b 1677; Dedham
DEAN, John & Mary __?_ ; ca 1679; Jamaica, LI
DEAN, John (-1694) & __?_ ; by 1685; Dover, NH
DEAN, John (1659-) & Abigail __?_ ; [prob by 1690], b 1700; Stamford, CT
DEAN, John (1674-1724) & Hannah BIRD (1677-1748); 21 Sep 1699; Dorchester/Taunton
DEAN, John & Mary __?_ ; ca 1700; Jamaica
DEAN, Jonas & Eunice (TURNER) [BUCK], w Isaac, m/3 James TORREY 1701; b 1691; Scituate
DEAN, Jonathan & Margaret __?_ ; ca 1682?; Jamaica, LI
DANE/DEAN, Joseph (-1718) & Elizabeth FULLER (1645-); 26 Nov 1662; Concord
DEAN, Joseph (-1729) & Mary __?_ ; b 1681; Taunton/Dighton
DEAN, Joseph & Rebecca/Deborah? [ALLEN] (1664-); b 1696; Sudbury
DEAN, Joseph & Elizabeth FLINT; 16 Mar 1697, 1696, 1696/7?; Salem
DEAN, Samuel & [Ann HOLMES]; b 1659, b 1639?; Stamford, CT
DEAN, Samuel & Elizabeth __?_ ; ca 1656, ca 1657; Jamaica, LI
DEAN, Samuel & Anna [HOLMES] (1634±-1703); b 1672, b 1659; Taunton/Jamaica, LI
DEAN, Samuel (1660±-) & Ann/?Hannah RUSTORP; Jamaica, LI
DEAN, Samuel (1667-1731) & Sarah ROBINSON (?1667-1741); 15 Dec 1692; Taunton
DEAN, Stephen (-1634) & Elizabeth [RING?], m/2 Josiah COOKE 1635; aft 1627; Plymouth
DANE, Thomas (ca 1603-1676) & Elizabeth __?_ ; b 1638; Concord
DEAN, Thomas & 1/wf Sarah [BROWN] (1649-); b 1666; Boston/Salem
DEAN, Thomas & Elizabeth BURRAGE, m/2 John POOR 1680; 15 Sep 1668; Charlestown
DEAN, Thomas (-1697) & Katherine STEVENS (-1727); 5 Jan 1669; Taunton
DEAN, Thomas & Mildred __?_ ; b 1673; Concord
DEAN, Thomas & 2/wf Ann [FARR?/TARR?]; b 1674, b 1673?; Boston
DEAN, Thomas (1664-), Concord & 1/wf Sarah BLANCHARD, Charlestown; 27 Aug, 22 Aug
   1687, 29 Nov 1687; Cambridge/Concord/Charlestown
DEAN, Thomas (-1735) & Jane [SCAMMON/SKETMAN] (1667-1726), dau Richard, w Thomas; b
   1692, 12 Oct 1691; by 1691; Boston
DEAN, Thomas & 1/wf Mary [PRINCE] (1670-1701); b 1692; Salem
DEAN, Thomas, Taunton & Mary KINSLEY/KENSLEY (-1750), Milton; 7 Jan 1696, 1696/7;
   Milton/Taunton/Raynham
DANE, Thomas (1664-) & 2/wf Susanna DAVIS, Boston; 9 Feb 1676/7; Concord/?Pembroke
DEAN, Walter (1612-) & Eleanor [COGAN/COZAN] (-1693+) (William COGAN's wf?); in Eng, b
   1634?; Dorchester/Taunton
DEAN, William & Martha BATEMAN; 1 Sep 1670, 1669?, 1 Jul; Billerica/Woburn
DEAN, William & Mehitable WOOD; 13 Dec 1677; Dedham
DEAN, William & Jane __?_ ; b 1679; Boston
DEAN, __?_ & Miriam COOKE
DEAN, __?_ & Rachel __?_ (had dau Martha), m/2 Joseph BIDDLE/BEADLE 1636; ?Marshfield
DEARBORN, Godfrey (?1603-1686) & 1/wf __?_ (-living 1650); in Eng, b 1632; Exeter, NH
DEARBORN, Godfrey (-1686) & 2/wf Dorothy DALTON (?1600-), w Philemon; 25 Nov 1662;
   Hampton, NH
DEARBORN, Henry (1634, 1633?-1725) & Elizabeth MARION/MARRIAN (1644±-1716, ae 72);
   10 Jan 1665/6; Hampton, NH
DEARBORN, John (1642±-1731) & Mary WARD (1652±-1725); 12 Dec 1672; Hampton, NH

DEARBORN, John (1666-1750) & Abigail BATCHELDER (1667-1736); 4 Nov 1689; Hampton, NH
DEARBORN, John (1673-1746) & Hannah DOW (1676-1733); 10 Jan 1695; Hampton, NH
DEARBORN, Samuel (1670-) & Mercy BATCHELDER (1677-); 12 Jul 1694; Hampton, NH
DEARBORN, Samuel (1676-) & Sarah GOVE; 16 Dec 1698; Hampton, NH
DEARBORN, Thomas (1632, ?1634-1710) & Hannah COLCORD (1645-1720); 28 Dec 1665 (1675 is wrong); Hampton, NH
DEARBORN, Walter & _?_ ; b 1664; Springfield
DEARLOVE, Peter & Jone MULIKIN; 27 Oct 1697; Boston
DEASE/DEAS, Joseph & Anna _?_ ; b 1687; Boston
DEATH, John & Mary [PEABODY]? (?1656-), m/2 Samuel EAMES; b 1670; Topsfield
DEATH, John (1677-1754) & 1/wf Elizabeth BARBER; 17 Jan 1698/9; Sherborn
DEATH, Oliver (1670-1705) & Martha FAIRBANK; 17 Apr 1697; Sherborn/Framingham
DECKER, John (-1694) & Mary SCOTT (1652-1700); 18 Jun 1680; Rowley/Haverhill
DECOSTER/DeCOSTA, Isaac & Mary TEMPLE; 2 Nov 1699; Boston
DECROW/DECRO, Valentine & Martha BOURNE (-1724, ae 72); 26 Feb 1678, 27 Feb 1678; Marshfield/Braintree
DEDICOT, Henry & Hannah _?_ ; b 1672; Boston
DEE, Henry & Hannah HILLARD; 30 Sep 1697; Boston
DEARE/DEERE, Edward/Edmund & Elizabeth GRIFFEN; 3 Mar 1660, 1659/60; Ipswich
DEAR, Edward/Thomas? & Hannah _?_ ; Ipswich
DEERING, Clement (1654-) & Joan [BRAY] (1658?-); b 1680; Kittery, ME
DEERING, George & Elizabeth _?_ , m/2 Jonas BAILEY; ca 1634?; Kittery, ME/Scarboro, ME
DEARING, Henry & Ann BENNING, w Ralph; 8 Jun 1664; Salisbury
DERING, Henry (-1717) & Elizabeth (MITCHELSON) ATKINSON (-1717), w Theodore; 15 Nov 1676; ?Boston
DEERING, Joseph & Mary [BRAY]; b 1698; Kittery, ME
DEERING, Roger (-1676) & Joan PALMER, m/2 William CRAFTS; Dartmouth, Eng, 30 Aug 1647; Kittery, ME
DEERING, Roger (1648-) & Mary _?_ (1649-); ca 1670/4; Kittery, ME
DEERING, Samuel (-1671) & 1/wf Bethia BAXTER (-1651, 1650); 1647; Braintree
DEERING, Samuel (-1671) & 2/wf Mary RAY (1636-1657); 5 Nov 1651; Braintree
DEERING, Samuel (-1671) & 3/wf Mary NEWCOMB, m/2 George SPEAR 1675; 10 Nov 1657; Braintree
DEARING, Samuel (-1653), Dedham & 1/wf Hannah FAREBANKS/FAIRBANKS (-1707), Dedham; 26 Jun 1688; Milton/Wrentham
DEERING, Thomas & 1/wf Hannah VINE; 29 Jun 1682; Dartmouth
DEERING, Thomas (1659-) & Elizabeth _?_ (1669-); - Mar 1688; Kittery, ME
DeFOREST, David & Martha BLAGGE, m/2 John THOMPSON; ca 1696; Stratford, CT
DeFOREST, Henricus & Frainettia (Phebe) VanFLAISBEEN; New York
DeFOREST, Isaac & Sarah duTRIEUX; 9 Jun, 9 Jul 1641; New York
DeFOREST, Isaac & Lysbeth VanderSPIGEL; New York
DeFOREST, John & Susannah VERLET; New York
DeFOREST, Philip & Tryntie KIP; New York
DEGRISHA/DECREECHY, Thomas & Agnes CRACKER; 16 Mar 1699; Boston/Malden
DeKAY, Jacobus/James? & Sarah WILLETT; 9 May 1694; ?Newtown, LI
DELAND, Benjamin (-1691) & Katherine HODGES/HODG (1664-1713); 7 Dec 1681; Beverly
DELAND, John (-1700) & Elizabeth [STERLING] (1662-); b 1685; Beverly/Newbury
DELANE, Philip & 1/wf Margery/Margaret _?_ (-1694); Portsmouth, NH/Newbury
DELANE, Philip & 2/wf Jane ATKINSON; m int 26 Oct 1695; Newbury
DELANO, Benoni (1667-1738) & Elizabeth [DREW] (1673-); b 1697; Duxbury
DELANO, Ebenezer (-1706?) & Martha SIMMONS, m/2 Samuel WEST 1709; 29 Dec 1699; Duxbury
DELANO, John (?1644-1690+) & Mary [WESTON]; b 1679?, b 1686; Duxbury
DELANO, Jonathan (?1648-1720) & Mercy WARREN; 28 Feb 1677/8; Dartmouth
DELANO, Jonathan (ca 1676, 1674-1765) & Hannah DOTEN/DOTY (1675-1764); 12 Jan 1698, 1698/9, 1698; Duxbury
DELANOE, Philip (1603?, 1605-1682) & 1/wf Hester/Esther DEWSBURY; 19 Dec 1634; ?Duxbury/?Plymouth

DELANO, Philip & 2/wf Mary (PONTUS) [GLASS], w James; 1657?, b 17 Jan 1653, b Jan 1653/4; Duxbury
DELANO, Philip (-1708) & Elizabeth [SAMPSON], dau Abraham; b 1670?, b 1675, 1668?; Duxbury
DELANO, Samuel (?1659-1728) & Elizabeth [STANDISH]; ca 1682?, ca 1679?; Duxbury/?Newbury
DELANO, Thomas (?1642-1722, 1723) & 1/wf [Rebecca] [ALDEN]; b 1667; Duxbury
DELANO, Thomas (1669?-) & [Hannah] _?_; b 1694; Duxbury
DELANO, Thomas & Hannah (WARREN) BARTLETT, w Ebenezer; 24 Oct 1699, 1698; Duxbury
DELAROCK/DILLOROCK, Philip & Elizabeth _?_; b 1695; Boston
DELL/DILL, George & Abigail [HANDS?], m/2 John HANNIFORD 1655; b 1645; Boston
DELL/DILL, Joseph & Elizabeth [HANNIFORD?]; b 1674
DELLOCLOCE, _?_ & Rachel _?_, m/2 Pierre BANDOUIN/Peter BALDWIN 1672; b 1672; Salem
DELVER, Matthew & Elizabeth HARRISON; m int 20 May 1696; Boston
DEMANZADAY/DEMONSEDAY, Philip & Margaret GLANSHA; 22 Nov 1682; Dorchester
DEMERITT/DEMERIT, Eli & Hopestill/Hope? [REYNOLDS?/RUNNELLS?], gr dau of William REYNOLDS; b 1696(7?); Dover, NH
DEMERRETT, Thomas & Mary BROCK; 22 Oct 1685; Marblehead/Salem
DUMERY/DEMERRY?, Charles & 1/wf Mary _?_; b 1682; Boston
DAMEERE, Charles & 2/wf Sarah _?_; b 1688; Boston
DEMING, David (1652-1725) & Mary [?BELDING] (-1724, ae 72); 14 Aug 1678; Wethersfield, CT
DEMING, Ebenezer (-1705) & Sarah [?GRANT]; 16 Jul 1677, 1677; Wethersfield, CT
DEMING, Hezekiah & Lois WYARD; 22 Nov 1700; Wethersfield, CT/Farmington, CT
DEMING, Jacob (1670-bef 1712) & Elizabeth EDWARDS (1675-), m/2 Jonathan HINCKLEY; 14 Mar 1695; Hartford
DEMING, John (?1615-1705?, ca 1694?) & 2/wf? Honor [TREAT] (1616-); b 1632?, b 1637; Wethersfield, CT
DEMING, John (-1711/12) & Mary [MYGATT/MYGATE] (-1714); 12 Sep 1657, ?20 Sep, 12 Dec 1657; Wethersfield, CT
DEMING, John (1658-1729) & Mary GRAVES; 5 Jun 1684; Wethersfield, CT
DEMING, Jonathan (?1634-1700) & 1/wf Sarah GRAVES (-1668); 21 Nov 1660, ?11 Nov; Wethersfield, CT
DEMING, Jonathan (?1639-1700) & 2/wf Elizabeth GILBERT (1654-1714); 25 Dec 1673; Wethersfield, CT
DEMING, Jonathan (1661-) & 1/wf? Sarah [BOW?] (1662-); ca 1684?; Wethersfield, CT
DEMING, Jonathan (1663-) & Mary?/Martha BUCK (1667-); 27 Oct 1687; Wethersfield, CT
DEMING, Joseph (1661-) & [Mary BOWEN] (1666-); b 1693; Woodstock, CT
DEMING, Nicholas & Emma [BROWN]; Pemequid, ME
DEMING, Samuel (1668-1709) & Sarah [BUCK] (1669-1754), m/2 Benjamin CHURCHILL; 29 Mar 1684; Wethersfield, CT
DEMEN, Thomas & Mary [SHAFF/SHEAFE?]; 24 Jul 1645; Hartford
DEMING, Thomas (1679-1741) & Mary WILLIAMS; 2 Jun 1698; Wethersfield, CT
DEMSDALL, William & Martha _?_; b 1651; Boston
DENBOW, Salathiel (1642-) (ae 38 1680) & _?_ (ROBERTS) SIAS, m/3 William GRAVES; by 1674; Dover, NH
DENBO, Salathiel[2] & 1/wf? _?_; b 1701?, b 1714
DENHAM, Alexander (ae 26 in 1667) & Elizabeth (SLEEPER) PERKINS, w Abraham, m/3 Richard SMITH; 24 Dec 1677; Salisbury
DENHAM, Isaac & 1/wf Mary [PIERCE], w Jacob; ca Dec 1694; Westchester Co., NY
DENHAM, Thomas (1621-1688/9) & Sarah [_?_], m/2 John HENDRICKSON by 1691; Mar 1659, ca 1660?; Marshfield/Bedford, NY
DENNISON, Alexander & Elizabeth _?_; b 1680; Hampton, NH
DENISON, Daniel (1612-1682) & Patience DUDLEY (-1690); 18 Oct 1632; ?Cambridge/Ipswich
DENISON, Edward (1616-1668) & Elizabeth WELD (-1717); 30 Mar 1641; Roxbury
DENISON, Edward (?1678-1726) & 1/wf Mercy _?_ (-1715?); b 1699; Westerly, RI
DENISON, George (1626-1694) & 1/wf Bridget THOMSON (1622-1643); Mar 1640; Roxbury
DENISON, George (1620-) & 2/wf Ann [BORODELL] (-1712); ca 1644; Stonington, CT

DENISON, George & Mercy [GORHAM]; ca 1677; Westerlv, RI

DENISON, George (1671-) & Mary (WETHERELL) [HARRIS], w Thomas; ca 1694; New London, CT

DENISON, James & Bethiah BOYKIN (1643-); 25 Nov 1662; New Haven

DENISON, John (-1683) & Priscilla ? (-1692/3); b 1648; Ipswich

DENISON, John (1641-1671) & Martha SYMONDS, m/2 Richard MARTYN; 2 Feb 1663, 3 Feb 1663; ?Ipswich

DENISON, John (1646-1698) & Phebe LAY (1650/1-1699); 26 Nov 1667; ?Saybrook, CT

DENISON, John (ca 1650-1723) & 1/wf Ruth [AYER] (1660-1695); b 1684; Ipswich

DENISON, Rev. John (1665-1689) & Elizabeth [SALTONSTALL] (1668-1726), m/2 Rowland/Roland COTTON 1692?, 1689, 1690?; b 1684; Cambridge/Ipswich

DENISON, John (1669-1699) & Ann [MASON], m/2 Samuel COGSWELL; [1690?], [b 1692]; Saybrook, CT

DENESON, John (-1725) & Elizabeth (GIDDINGS) [HASKELL], w Mark; aft 8 Sep 1691, bef 1700; Ipswich

DENISON, Robert (d in Newark, NJ) & 1/wf ? ; b 1641, b 1656; Milford, CT

DENISON, Robert (-1672) & 2/wf Esther [BURWELL] (1625-); b 1654; Milford, CT/NJ

DENISON, Robert (1673-1737) & 1/wf Joanna STANTON (-1715); [ca 1694]; New London/Montville

DENISON, William (1571-1654) & Margaret (CHANDLER) MONCK (1577-1646), w Henry; Bishop's Stortford, Eng, 7 Nov 1603; Roxbury

DENISON, William & Mary PARKER; 27 Oct 1659; Boston

DENESON, William (-1691) & ? ; b 1668; Milton

DENISON, Lt./Capt.? William (?1655-1715) & Sarah (STANTON) PRENTICE (?1655, 1656?-1713), w Thomas; ?May 1686; ?Stonington, CT

DENISON, William (1664-1718) & Dorothy WELD (1664-), m/2 Samuel WILLIAMS; 12 May 1686; Roxbury

DENISON, William (1677-1730) & Mary AVERY (1680-1762), m/2 Daniel PALMER 1732; Mar 1698; Stonington, CT

DENISON, ? & Mary (BOARDMAN) ROBBINS (1645-1721), w John; aft 7 Mar 1698/9

DENMAN, John (ca 1623 in Eng) & Judith [STOUGHTON] (-1639), m/2 William SMEAD bef 1635; b 1620?; Dorchester

DENMAN, John (1621-) & ? ; b 1643; ?Southampton, LI

DENMAN, John (1643-1714) & Mary [GANNUGH/GANO/GENNUNG?]; b 1700; Newtown, LI

DENMAN, Philip (-1698) & Hasadiah [SLOUGH?/PRUDDEN?]; Apr 1677; Derby, CT

DENMARK, James (1666-) & 2/wf? Elizabeth (BARRETT) LITTLEFIELD, w Nathan; 1 Apr 1694; Wells, ME

DENMARK, Patrick & Hannah?/Anna ? ; by 1663; Saco, ME/Dover, NH

DENNETT, Alexander (-1698) & ? ; b 1660?; Portsmouth, NH/Newcastle, NH

DENNETT, Alexander (-1733) & 1/wf Mehitable [TETHERLY] (1663-); b 1693; Portsmouth, NH

DENNETT, John & ? ; b 1646

DENNETT, John (-1709, ae 63) & Amy ? ; b 1675; Kittery, ME/Portsmouth, NH

DENNING, Nicholas[1] (1645-1725) & 1/wf Emma/Eme/?Nem [BROWN]; New Harbor/etc.

DENNING, Nicholas[1] (1645-1725) & 2/wf Sarah PAINE; 25 Nov 1697; Gloucester

DENNING, Nicholas[2] & Elizabeth DAVIS; 7 Dec 1699; Gloucester

DENING, William (-1654, Boston) & Ann ? ; Boston

DENNIS, Amos & Elizabeth RUSSELL; 15 Mar 1691/2; Marblehead

DENNIS, Ebenezer & Damaris ROBINSON; 3 May 1699; Boston

DENNIS, Edmund/Edward & Sarah ? , m/2 Abner ORDWAY 1656; b 1640, b 1639?; Boston

DENNIS, George & 1/wf ? ; b 1656?; Oyster Bay, LI

DENNIS, George, LI & 2/wf Elizabeth (SMITH) RAYMOND, w Joshua; 26 Jan 1681, prob 1681/2, 1680/1; New London

DENNIS, James & Mary [CONEY]; b 1654, b 1653?; Boston

DENNIS, James (-1730, ae 96) (ae 92 in 1684) & Mary [CHARLES]; ca 1654?; Marblehead

DENNIS, James & Sarah PITMAN; 25 Mar 1682; Marblehead

DENNIS, [James] & Mary (LATHROP) CROWELL (1654-), w Edward; aft 1689, aft 6 Jun 1685, b 1691; Boston

DENNIS, James & Mary ? (see above); b 1699; Marblehead

DENNIS, John & Ruth WHITE; 12 Jun 1679; Wenham
DENNIS, John (1672-1757) & 1/wf Lydia WHITE (1673-1712); 31 Aug 1699; Ipswich
DENNIS, Josiah (1648-) & Sarah BAKER; 22 Feb 1671
DENNIS, Lawrence (m twice?) & _?_ [MORGAN]; b 1658; Arrousic/Beverly
DENNIS, Robert & Mary _?_; b 1645?, b 1649; Yarmouth/Tiverton, RI/NJ
DENNIS, Robert (-1691), Portsmouth & Sarah HOWLAND (?1645-1712, ae 67), Duxbury; 19 Nov 1672; ?Portsmouth, RI
DENNIS, Robert (1677-1730) & Susanna BRIGGS (1681-); 22 Jan 1700, prob 1700/1; Little Compton, RI/Tiverton, RI
DENNIS, Samuel & Sarah [SCULLARD]; b 1670; prob in Nantucket
DENNIS, Thomas & _?_; in Eng, b 1630; Boston/Woodbridge, NJ
DENNIS, Thomas & Mary (BUSHNELL) ROBISON/ROBINSON, dau Wm. (no), w George; ca 1657?, aft 1657, b Nov 1668; Boston
DENNIS, Thomas (?1638-1706) & Grace (_?_) SEARLE (?1636-1686), w William; 26 Oct 1668; Ipswich
DENNIS, Thomas & 2/wf Sarah _?_, m/2 John HOWE; aft 1686; Ipswich
DENNIS, Thomas (1669-1703) & Elizabeth _?_; b 1700
DENNIS, William (-1649/56?) & _?_; b 1620, b 1615; Scituate
DENNIS, William & Susanna _?_; b 1684; Boston
DENNIS, _?_ & Waitawhile (MAKEPEACE) COOPER (bpt 1642-), w Josiah; aft 1678; Dorchester
DENNY, Albert (-1708) & Elizabeth [WAKEMAN]; b 1694; Fairfield, CT
DENSLOW, Henry (-1676) & Susannah _?_ (-1683); b 1646; Winsor, CT
DENSLOW, John (-1689) & Mary EGGLESTON (1641-1684); 7 Jun 1655 (7 Jan 1653 is prob wrong); Windsor, CT
DENSLOW, Nicholas (1573, 1577-1667, 1666?) & Elizabeth [DOLING?] (1584/5-1669, ae 84); in Eng, b 1620?, 24 Jan 1608; Dorchester
DENSLOW, Samuel (1659-1743) & Patience GIBBS (1666-1736); 2 Dec 1686; Windsor, CT
DENTON, Daniel (1628-) & 1/wf Abigail [STEVENSON] (-1717), m/2 Daniel WHITEHEAD; b 1661, div 1672; ?Jamaica, LI
DENTON, Daniel (ca 1628-) & 2/wf Hannah LEONARD (1660-by 1718); 24 Apr 1676, 1675?); Springfield/Jamaica, LI
DENTON, Daniel (1661-1690) & Deborah [LEONARD] (1663-), m/2 Gabriel LUFFE?/LASSEE; b 1681, by 1681
DENTON, James & Jane [TITUS] (1670-); ?Hempstead, LI
DENTON, Josiah & _?_
DENTON, Nathaniel (1629-) & Sarah _?_; ca 1650; Jamaica, LI
DENTON, Nathaniel, Jr. & 1/wf [Deborah ASHMAN]
DENTON, Nathaniel, Jr. & 2/wf Elizabeth ASHMAN; by 1695, ca 1693
DENTON, Richard (1586-1663?, ae 76) & _?_; in Eng, b 1628; Wethersfield, CT/Stamford, CT/Hempstead, LI
DENTON, Richard (-1658) & Ruth TILESTONE (1641-1677), m/2 Timothy FOSTER 1663; 11 Dec 1657; Dorchester
DENTON, Samuel (1645-1699) & Mary [?SMITH] (-1698+); b 1671, by 18 Apr 1665; Hempstead, LI
DENTON, Samuel & 2/wf Abigail (BARLOW) [ROWLAND], w Jonathan; aft 1691, b Nov 1697; Fairfield, CT/Hempstead, LI
DARBY, Abraham & Hannah [LOMBARD] (ae 32 in 1674); b 1673; Boston
DARBY, Edward & Susanna HOOKE; 25 Jan 1659/60; Boston
DERBY, Edward (-1724) & 1/wf Ruth [WHITMARSH?]; b 1688, b 1687?; Weymouth/Braintree
DARBY, Eleazer & Mary _?_; b 1688; Boston
DERBY, Francis (-1663) & Ann _?_, m/2 John READ b 1669; b 1660; Warwick, RI
DERBY, ?Francis & _?_; Warwick, RI/Southold, LI
DARBY, John (-1652?, 1655/6?) & Alice _?_, m/2 Abraham BLACK 1658; b 1647(8?); Yarmouth
DARBY, John (-1690?) & Alice _?_, m/2 John WOODBURY 1690; b 1679; Marblehead
DARBEY, John & Rachel CODNER, m/2? Andrew SAMPSON 1695, m/3 John SHORES; 9 Oct 1690; Boston
DAWBY/DARBY, Joseph & Jane PLIMPTON (-1728); 14 Jan 1676; Sudbury
DARBEY, Robert & Sarah [SANDERSON] (1651-); b 1679; Boston

DARBY, Robert & Martha [WORMSTALL]; Lancaster
DERBY, Roger (-1698) & 1/wf Lucretia HILLMAN/?KILHAM (1643-1689); Topsham, Eng, 23 Aug 1668; Ipswich/Salem
DARBY, Roger (-1698) & 2/wf Elizabeth (HASKETT) [DYNN] (-1740), w William; b 1692; Salem
DARBEY, Samuel (1673-) & Hannah YOUNGS, m/2 Daniel CLARK 1729; b 1698; Southold, LI
DERBY/DARLEY/DABY, Thomas & Mary [BROWN] (1662-); b 1683; Salem
DERBY, [Robert?] & Marie/Mary (HOADLEY) FRISBIE, w Jonathan, m/3 Nathaniel FINCH b 1699; b May 1696; ?Branford, CT
DERICH/DERRICK, John & Martha FOSTER (1674-); 25 Oct [1697?], 1698?, 1698/9?; Salem
DERICH, Michael & Mary [BASSETT?/HOOD?], m/2 _?_ RICH; b 1690; Lynn
DERRY, James & Elizabeth _?_, m/2 Ezekiel PITMAN by 1695, m/3 John PINDER; Oyster River, NH
DERRY, John & Deliverance _?_, m/2 Nathaniel PITMAN 1697?; b 1694; Oyster River, NH
DESCHAMPS, Isaac & _?_; b 1674; Boston
DESPARD/DEEPAR, Lambert & ?Hannah [NEWELL?]; b 1692; Braintree/Salisbury
DEUCE, Richard & Jane _?_; b 1657; Boston
DEUSBERRY/DUSEBERRY, Daniel & Dorothy _?_; b 1695; Boston
DEVAULX, Peter & Susanna _?_; b 1692; Boston
DEVENISH/DAVENISH, Thomas & Mary _?_; b 1641; Salem
DEVEREAUX, Humphrey (1655/6-1690) & Elizabeth _?_; b 1676?, b 1680; Salem
DEVEREAUX, John (1615-1695) (ae ca 70 in 1685) (ae ca 80 in 1694) & Ann _?_ (±1620-1708) (ae ca 62 in 1685); b 1641; Salem/Marblehead
DEVEREUX, John & Susanna [HARTSHORN] (1650-1718), m/2 Stephen PARKER 1695; b 1683; Marblehead
DEVEREAUX, Robert & Hannah [BLANY] (1667-); b 1693; Marblehead
DEVERSON, Thomas (-1704) & Sarah [CLARK] (1663-), m/2 _?_ WARD; b 1684; Portsmouth, NH
DEVON, John & Ruth BADCOCK; m int 20 Aug 1696; Boston
DEVOTION, Edward[1] (1621-1685) & Mary [CURTIS?] (1621-1685, 1713?); ca 1648; Boston/Roxbury
DEVOTION, John (1659-1783) & Hannah [POND]? (1660-); ca 1679; Roxbury/Suffield, CT
DUE, Ambrose & Ester BARKER; 10 Feb 1651/2; Boston
DEW, Thomas & Sarah [WALL], m/2 John BAKER ca 1679; b 1670, 1663?
DUE, _?_ & Mercy [VAUGHAN], dau George; b 30 Jun 1694; Middlebourgh
DEWEY, Adijah?/Abijah (1666-1741) & Sarah ROOT (1670-); b 1689; Westfield
DEWEY, David (1675-) & Sarah _?_ (1682-); ca 1699; Westfield
DEWEY, Israel[2] (1645-1678) & Abigail DRAKE (1648-1682), m/2 Andrew HILLYER 1687; 23 Aug 1668, 20 Aug 1668, 28 Aug; Northampton/Windsor, CT/Westfield
DEWEY, Israel (1673-1730?) & Lydia (QUIMBY) [HOLDRIDGE]?, w William; b 23 Feb 1696/7, by 1693; Stonington, CT
DEWEY, Ens. Jedediah[2] (1647-1718) & Sarah [ORTON] (1652-1711); b 1672; Windsor, CT/Westfield, MA
DEWEY, Josiah[2] (1641-1732) & Hepzibah LYMAN (?1644-1732); 6 Nov 1662; Northampton/Westfield
DEWEY, Josiah[3] (1666-1729+, ca 1750?); & Mehitable MILLER (1666-1729+); 15 Jan 1690/1; Westfield
DEWEY, Nathaniel[3] (1673-) & Margaret BURROUGHS (1677-); 24 Jan 1700, 24 Jan 1699, [1699/1700]; New London, CT/Lebanon, CT
DEWEY, Samuel (1670-) & Sarah WELLER (1677-1709); 19 Dec 1695; Westfield
DEWEY, Thomas[1] (-1648) & 1/wf _?_; ca 1633/5, b 1633?; Dorchester
DEWEY, Cornet Thomas[1] (-1648) & 2/wf? Frances (_?_) CLARK (-1690), wid, m/3 George PHELPS 1648; 22 Mar 1638, 1638/9; Windsor, CT
DEWEY, Thomas[2] (1640-1690) & Constance HAWES (1642-1703, 1702); 1 Jun 1663; Dorchester
DEWEY, Thomas (1665-1690) & Hannah SACKETT (1669-1749), m/2 Benjamin NEWBERRY 1692, m/3 John MERRIMAN; ca 1688; Westfield
DUING, Andrew (-1677) & 1/wf Lydia [GOODNOW] (-13 Oct 1651); ca 1649; Dedham
DEUING, Andrew & 2/wf Ann DONSTALL; 10 Nov 1652; Dedham/Needham

DUEING, Andrew (1656-1718) & Dorothy HIDE; 27 Dec 1682; Dedham/Needham
DUEIN, Jonathan (1663-) & Susannah BACON; 7 Jan 1692, 1691/2; Dedham/Needham
DEWING, ?Henry & Deliverance [STEVENS]? (1649, 1650)
DeWOLF, Balthazer (-1696) & Alice _?_ (-1687+); b 1646; Wethersfield, CT/Lyme, CT
DeWOLF, Charles (1673-1731) & Prudence [WHITE]; b 1695; Middletown, CT/Glastenbury, CT
DeWOLF, Edward (1646-1712, 1710?) & Rebecca _?_ (-1710+); b 1671; Lyme, CT
DeWOLF, Simon (-1695) & Sarah LAY (1665-), m/2 Nathaniel CLARK 1696; 12 Nov 1682; Lyme, CT
DeWOLF, Simon & Alice BOLT; 19 Jan 1693; Boston
DeWOLF, Stephen (1650-1702) & 1/wf _?_ ; b 1686; Lyme, CT
DeWOLF, Stephen (1650-1702) & 2/wf Hannah _?_ ; b 1690; Lyme, CT
DEXTER, Benjamin (1670-) & Sarah ARNOLD; 17 Jul 1695; Rochester
DEXTER, Gregory (1690-1700) & Abigail [FULLER?/FULLERTON] (-1706+); in Eng, b 1647; Provincetown
DEXTER, James (1650-1676) & Esther [ARNOLD] (1647-1688+), m/2 William ANDREWS 1680, m/3 Edward HAWKINS 1684?; b 1673; Providence
DEXTER, James (1662-1697) & Elizabeth/Ealse/[Alice?] [TOBEY], m/2 Nathan HAMMOND b 1699; b 1692; Rochester
DEXTER, John (1639-1677) & Sarah _?_, m/2 William BOARDMAN by 1684; b 1671; Charlestown
DEXTER, John (-1717+) & Mehitable HALLETT; 10 Nov 1682; Sandwich
DEXTER, John[1] (1652-1706) & Alice SMITH (1665-1736), m/2 Joseph JENCKES 1727; 16 Feb 1688; Providence
DEXTER, John (1671-1722) & Winifred [SPRAGUE] (1673-1702); b 1696(7?); Malden
DEXTER, John (1673-1734) & 1/wf Mary [FIELD] (1673-1727); b 1698; Providence/Smithfield, RI
DEXTER, Philip (1659-1741) & [Alice] [ALLEN]; b 1701; Falmouth
DEXTER, Richard (1598-1680) & Bridget _?_ (1612±-); ca 1634-39?; Charlestown/Malden
DEXTER, Richard (1678-) & Sarah BUCKNAM; 23 Feb 1697/8; Malden
DEXTER, Stephen (1647-1679) & Mary ARNOLD?/Abigail [WHIPPLE]?, m/2 William HOPKINS 1682; b 1673, b 1670?; Providence
DEXTER, Stephen (1657-) & Anna SANDERS/SAUNDERS?; 27 Apr 1696; Barnstable
DEXTER, Thomas (-1677, Boston) & _?_ ; in Eng?, b 1623?; Lynn/Sandwich/Barnstable/Boston
DEXTER, Thomas, Jr. (-1686) & Elizabeth VINCENT (-1714); 8 Nov 1648; Sandwich
DEXTER, Thomas & 1/wf Mary MILLER; 17 Jul 1695; Rochester
DEXTER, William (-1694) & Sarah VINSEN/VINCENT (-1694+); Jul 1653; Barnstable
DEXTER, _?_ & Hannah DAVIS (1658); Barnstable
DIAMOND, Aholiab & Elizabeth NORMAN, m/2 William HINE 1688; 8 Jan 1684/5, 1685/6; Marblehead
DIAMOND, Andrew (?1642-1707) & 1/wf Joan (_?_) [GRANT] (?1629-); w Roger; ca 1668; Smuttynose
DIAMOND, Andrew & Elizabeth [ELLIOT], m/2 Theophilus COTTON 1708; b 1700; Ipswich
DIAMOND, Edward (1640/2-1732) & Rebecca [NORMAN] (1650±-); b 1671; Marblehead
DIAMOND, Israel & Abiell/?Abihail/Abigail PROWSE; 5 Jan 1690, 1690/1; Amesbury
DYMONT/DIAMOND?, James (1646-1721) & 1/wf Hannah JAMES (-1706); m cont 21 Aug 1677; East Hampton, LI
DIAMOND, John (-ca 1667) & Grace SAMMON; St. Petrox, Dartmouth, Eng, 2 Jun 1635; Kittery, ME
DIAMOND, John (?1639-1693) & _?_ RAYNES, dau Francis; ca 1665/73?; ?Star Island
DIMON, John & Rebecca (BEMIS) MINTER, w Tobias, m/3 Benedict SATTERLEE 1682; 16 Jun 1674, 17 Jun 1674; Killingworth, CT
DIMON, Moses (-1684) & Abigail WARD (1647?-), m/2 Edward HOWARD 1685; 2 May 1670; Fairfield, CT
DIMON, Moses (1672-1748) & 1/wf Jane [PINCKNEY] (1675-); ca 1697; Fairfield, CT
DIMON, Thomas (-1658) & _?_ ; b 1638; Fairfield, CT
DYMONT/DEMEN/etc., Thomas (see DEMING) (-1682?) & Mary SHAFF/SHEAFE (-1706); 24 Jul 1645; Southampton; Hartford/Wethersfield, CT/Farmington/Southampton, LI/East Hampton, LI
DIMON, Thomas (-1687) & Elizabeth BRADLEY (1664/5-); 22 Sep 1670; New London

DIAMOND, Thomas (1641-1708) & 1/wf Mary [WEYMOUTH], w James; aft 25 Jun 1678, no issue; Salisbury/Star Island

DYMONT, Thomas & _?_ ; b 28 Jul 1682; East Hampton, LI

DIAMOND, William (-1679) & Joan _?_ (1643-), m/2 Edward CARTER, m/3 James BLAGDON 1691/3; ca 1668/70; Kittery, ME

DEEBLE, Abraham (-1690, Suffield, CT) & Lydia [TEFFT]; b 1648; Boston/Windsor, CT?/Haddam, CT/?Suffield, CT

DIBBLE, Benjamin & Mary [BENJAMIN] (1671-); 169-, b 1700; Gloucester, CT/Salisbury

DEBBLE, Ebenezer (1641-1675) & Mary WAKEFIELD, m/2 James HILLIER 1677; at New Haven, 27 Oct 1663, Nov 1663; Windsor, CT/New Haven

DIBBLE, Ebenezer & 1/wf Mary LOOMIS (-1703); 16 Jul 1696; Windsor, CT/Colchester

DEBLE, Israel (1637-1697) & Elizabeth HULL (-1689); 28 Nov 1661; Windsor, CT

DIBBLE, John (-1646) & [Sarah] _?_ , m/2 William GRAVES 1647; ca 1641; Springfield/Stamford, CT

DIBOL, John & Mary SEVERANCE; 26 Nov 1697; Deerfield

DIBELL, Josiah & Hannah COGSWELL; 20 Jan 1691/2; Saybrook, CT

DEEDBLE, Robert[1] (-1652+) & _?_ ; in Eng, b 1613?; Dorchester/Windsor, CT

DEBBLE, Samuel (1643-1709) & 1/wf _?_ ; b 1666; Windsor, CT

DEBBLE, Samuel (1643-1709) & 2/wf Hepzibah BARTLETT (1646-1701); 21 Jan 1668; Windsor, CT/Simsbury

DEBLE, Thomas[2] (1613-1700) & 1/wf ?Meriam/Miriam _?_ (-1681); b 1637; Windsor, CT

DEBELL, Thomas (1647-) & Mary TUCKER (1653-); 10 Oct 1676; Windsor, CT

DIBBLE, Thomas (-1700) & 2/wf Elizabeth (_?_) (HAWKS) HINSDALE (-1689), w John, w Robert; 25 Jun 1683; Windsor, CT

DIBBLE, Thomas & Rachel MULFORD; 2 Apr 1700; Easthampton, LI

DIBBLE, Wakefield (1667-) & 1/wf Sarah LOOMIS (-1693); 27 Dec 1692; Windsor, CT/Simsbury, CT

DIBBLE, Wakefield & 2/wf Jane FILER (1671-); 20 Sep 1694; Windsor, CT

DIBBLE, Zachariah & Sarah WATERBURY, m/2 Nicholas WEBSTER, m/3 Edward TREHERNE; 10 May 1666, div 1672; Stamford, CT

DIBBLE, Zachariah & Sarah CLEMENTS; 13 Aug 1698; Stamford, CT

DIBBS, John & Hepsibah MORRILL (1664-); 1688, 1689, b 1690; Salisbury/Norfolk, VA

DICKENS, John & Jane/Joanna? [BALL]; b 1701?; New Shoreham, RI

DICKENS, Nathaniel (-1692) & 1/wf Joan [TILER/TYLER], wid; b 1664?, b 24 Aug 1648; Providence/Newport/New Shoreham

DICKENS, Nathaniel (-1692) & 2/wf _?_

DICKENS, Nathaniel (-1692) & 3/wf Sarah _?_ , m/2 Thomas BROWN; b 3 Sep 1680; Newport

DICKENS, Richard (doubtful) & _?_ ; b 1697; Tiverton, RI

DICKENS, Thomas (-1718) & Sarah [DODGE] (1675-1733); 25 Dec 1693; New Shoreham, RI

DICKERMAN, Abraham (1634-1711) & Mary COOPER (1640-1706); 2 Dec 1658; Dorchester

DICKERMAN, Abraham (1673-) & 1/wf Elizabeth GLOVER; 6 Jan 1697/8; New Haven

DICKERMAN, Isaac & Bethia _?_ (27 Apr 1687-); Westchester, NY, b 1698;

DICKERMAN, John (1666-) & Sarah [EDWARDS] (1673-); 11 Nov 1691; Reading/Milton

DICKERMAN, Thomas (-1658) & Ellen _?_ , m/2 John BULLARD; b 1623?; Dorchester

DICKERMAN, Thomas (1623-) & 1/wf Elizabeth [?SMITH] (-1671); b 1653; Malden

DICKERMAN, Thomas (1623-) & 2/wf Anna _?_ ; b 1674; Malden

DICKESON/?DICKSON/?DICKENSON, Henry & Elizabeth CASTLE/CASWELL; 25 Oct 1693; Boston

DICKARSON, John (see DICKINSON) & Elizabeth (HOWLAND) [HICKS], w Ephraim; 10 Jul 1651; Plymouth

DICKERSON, Peter (1648-1721/2) & 1/wf? _?_ REEVE

DICKERSON, Peter (1648-1721/2) & 2/wf? Naomi [MAPES] (1648, ?1667-1725); b 1672, 1687?; Southold, LI

DICKINSON?/DICKERSON, Philemon (?1598-1672) & Mary [PAYNE] (1611-1677, 1697/8?); b 1642; Salem/Southold, LI

DICKERSON, Thomas[1] (-1658) & Mary _?_ , m/2 Daniel FINCH by 1660, m/3 Nicholas PINNION; b 1637; Fairfield

DICKERSON, Thomas[2] (?1652-1699/1700) & 1/wf Hannah [HENDRICK] (-living 1691); b 1685

DICKERSON, Thomas^2 (-1699/1700) & 2/wf Lydia [MILLS], m/2 Thomas SHARPE; b 1693; Stratford, CT
DICKERSON, Thomas (?1643-1704) & _?_ ; Southold, LI/NJ
DICKERSON, [?Charles]/?DICKINSON, [?John] & Phillip (GREENE) [CARR] (1658-bef 1706), w Caleb; aft 1690; RI
DICKINSON, Azariah (1648-1675) & Dorcas _?_, m/2 Jonathan MARSH 1676; b 1675; Deerfield/Hatfield
DICKINSON, Azariah, Hadley & 1/wf Hannah [SPENCER] (ca 1681-ca 1705), dau Timothy; b 1701?, b 1705; Hadley/?Haddam, CT
DICKINSON, Charles & Esther/Hester [GILBERT]; b 1688; Hartford
DICKINSON, Daniel & Elizabeth CROW; b 1695
DICKINSON, Eliphalet (-1733) & Rebecca BRONSON (1679-1755); 24 Nov 1697; Farmington, CT
DICKESON/DICKERSON/DICKSON?, Henry & Elizabeth [CASTLE/CASWELL]; 25 Oct 1693; Boston
DICKINSON, Hezekiah (1645-1707, Springfield) & Abigail BLACKMAN/BLAKEMAN, m/2 Thomas INGERSOLL 1708; 4 Dec 1679, 8 Dec 1679-80, 24 Dec ?; Stratford/Haldley/Hatfield
DICKINSON, James (1640-) & Rebecca _?_, m/2 John DRESSER 1702; b 1664; Rowley
DICKINSON, James (1675-) & _?_ ; b 1701?; Oyster Bay, LI/?Smithtown
DICKINSON, John & Mary _?_ (-1647); b 1639; Salisbury
DICKINSON, John (-1680) & 1/wf Frances FOOTE; b 1648; ?Boston
DICKINSON, John (1630-1676) & Frances [FOOTE] (1629-), m/2 Frances BARNARD 1677; b 1648?; Wethersfield, CT/Hadley
DICKINSON/DICKERSON?, John (-1680) & 2/wf Elizabeth (HOWLAND) HICKS (-1691, Oyster Bay), w Ephraim; 10 Jul 1651; Plymouth
DICKINSON/DICKISON, John & Hannah GOUGH/Ann GOUGE? (-1679); 17 May 1671, betw 1647 & 1662?; Salisbury
DICKINSON, John & Hannah (JACKSON) [ANDREWS], w John; aft 1679, bef 1696; Boston
DICKINSON/DICKISON, John (-1683) & Alice ROPER, w John of Dedham?, m/3 William ALLEN 1684?; 14 Apr 1681; Salisbury
DICKINSON, John (1652-) & Susanna [SMITH] (1667-); 31 Jan 1688; Hatfield/Wethersfield, CT/Deerfield/Hadley
DICKINSON, John (1667-) & Sarah _?_ (-1707?); 13 Jun 1688; Hatfield/Hadley
DICKINSON, Joseph (-1675) & Phebe [BRACEY/BRACE], dau of Mrs. MARTIN, m/2 John ROSE 1670, m/3 Samuel HALE 1676?; b 1666, 1657?; Wethersfield, CT/Hadley/Northfield/Northampton
DICKINSON, Joseph (?1654-) & Rose [TOWNSEND] (?1658, 1652?-); ca 1680?, 1675, b 1668; Oyster Bay, LI
DICKINSON, Joseph (1676-) & _?_ [CARPENTER]; b 1697; Musketa Cove, LI
DICKINSON, Nathaniel (-1676) & Ann (_?_) (_?_) [GULL], w William; E. Bergholt?, Suffolk, 16 Jan 1630; Watertown/Wethersfield, CT/Hadley/Whately
DICKINSON, Nathaniel (?1643-1710) & 1/wf Hannah [BEARDSLEY] (-1679); 1662, b 1663; Wethersfield, CT/Hadley/Fairfield/Stratford, CT/Dedham
DICKINSON, Nathaniel (?1643-1710) & 2/wf Elizabeth (HAWKES) GILLETT, w Joseph; 16 Dec 1680; Deerfield/Hatfield/Hadley
DICKINSON, Nathaniel (?1643-1710) & 3/wf Elizabeth (BURT) WRIGHT, w Samuel; 26 Sep 1684; Hadley
DICKINSON, Nathaniel & Hepzibah [GIBBS] (1664-); b 1685(6?); Hadley/Hatfield/Deerfield/Windsor, CT
DICKINSON, Nathaniel (1670-1745) & Hannah [WHITE] (1679-); b 1699; Hatfield
DICKINSON, Nehemiah (1645-1723) & Mary/Sarah? [COWLES]?; 1670; Hadley/Hatfield/Deerfield
DICKINSON, Nehemiah (?1672-) & Mehitable [CHURCH] (1672-); b 1701?; Hadley
DICKINSON, Obadiah (?1641-1698) & 1/wf Sarah BEARDSLEY; 8 Jan 1669, [1668/9], 8 Jun 1668; Hatfield/Hadley/Deerfield/Northampton/Fairfield/Stratford, CT/Wethersfield, CT
DICKINSON, Obadiah (-1698) & Mehitable HINSDALE (1663-), m/2 Joseph HILLS ca 1699; 1692, 1690?; Wethersfield, CT/Hatfield/Hadley
DICKINSON/DICKERSON?, Philemon (-1668) & [Mary PAYNE] (1671-); b 1642; Salem/Southold, LI

DICKINSON, Samuel (1638-1711), Hatfield & Martha BRIDGMAN (1649-1711); 4 Jun 1668, 4 Jan 1668; Northampton/?Springfield/Hadley/Deerfield

DICKINSON, Samuel (1665-1733, Cedar Swamp) & Lydia _?_ ; ca 1685-92?; Oyster Bay, LI

DICKINSON, Samuel (1669-) & Sarah [BILLINGS] (1676-); b 1699; Hatfield

DICANSON, Thomas (-1662) & Janet/Jennet/Jeanette _?_ (-1686), m/2 John WHIPPLE; in Eng, b 1640; Rowley

DICKINSON, Thomas (-1716, 1713?) & Hannah/Anna? CROW (1649-); 7 Mar 1667, 1667/8?; Hadley/Wethersfield, CT

DICKINSON, Thomas (1666-) & 1/wf Elizabeth PLATTS (-1716); 3 Jun 1691; Rowley

DICKINSON, Thomas (1668-1717) & Mary LOVELAND (-1744+), m/2 Bennizer HALE; 1 Jun 1693, Glastonbury; Wethersfield, CT

DICKINSON, Thomas (-1723) & Mehitable [MEEKINS] (1675-); b 3 Nov 1693, 1694, b 1695; Hadley/Hartford

DICKINSON, _?_ & Elizabeth [TAPLEY] (1664-), m/2 Matthew BARTON 1694

DICKINSON, _?_ & Dorothy [NORTON] (1699-), Branford; ?Farmington, CT

DIGGER, _?_ & Elizabeth _?_ , m/2 John KEITH; b 1683; Salem

DIGGENS/DIGGINS, Jeremiah & Mary [CALDWELL?] (1659-); b 1678, b 18 Apr 1677; Windsor, CT

DIGGENS, John & Rebecca MAN; 19 Jan 1696; Boston

DILL, Daniel & Dorothy [MOORE]; b 1679, by 1678; York, ME

DILL, Daniel & Elizabeth FOOT, m/2 Henry BEEDLE; 8 Nov 1698; York, ME

DILL, George (-1715/16) & Elizabeth _?_ ; ca 1680?; Watertown

DELL, Peter (-1692) & Thankes SHEPERD/SHEPARD (1651-), Concord; 13 Dec 1669; Chelmsford/Concord

DILLINGHAM, Edward (1595-1667) & Ursula CARTER (-1656); 14 Feb 1614; Lynn/Sandwich

DILLINGHAM, Edward (1665-) & Abigail NYE (1678-); 26 Sep 1695; Sandwich

DILLINGHAM, Henry (1624-1705) & Hannah PERRY (-1673); ?15 Dec 1651, ?24 Jun 1652, 1659; Sandwich

DILLINGHAM, John (1606-1636) & Sarah [CALY]; in Eng, b 1630; Ipswich

DILLINGHAM, John (1630-1715) & 1/wf Elizabeth FEAKE; 24 Mar 1650, ?1650/1; Sandwich/Harwich

DILLINGHAM, John (1658-1733) & Lydia [HATCH/CHAPMAN?] (1669, 1679-1760?); b 1695; Harwich

DILLINGHAM, John (1630-1715) & 2/wf Elizabeth _?_ (1647-1720); b 1701?; Harwich

DIMOCK, John (1666-) & Elizabeth LUMBER/LUMBERT; - Nov 1689; Barnstable

DIMOCK, Joseph (1675-) & Lydia FULLER (-1755, ae 80); 12 May 1699, 17 May 1699, 1694?; Sandwich/Barnstable/E. Haddam, CT

DIMOCK, Shobal/Shubael (1644-1732) & Joanna BURSLEY (1646, 1653-1727, ae 83 y); Apr 1663; Barnstable/Mansfield, CT

DIMOCK, Shobal/Shubael (1673-1728) & Tabitha LOTHROP (-1727); 4 May 1699; Barnstable

DIMOCK, Shubael[2] did not m/1 Bethia CHIPMAN (numerous refences that he m Bethia CHIPMAN are all wrong)

DIMOCK, Thomas (-1657) & Ann [?HAMMOND] (1616-); b 1640; Dorchester/Barnstable/Scituate/Hingham

DIMOCK, Thomas (1664-1697) & Desire [STURGES] (1665-1749), m/2 John THACHER 1698; b 1686; Barnstable

DIMOCK, Timothy (1668-1718, Ashford, CT) & 1/wf Bethia (CHIPMAN) GALE, dau of John CHIPMAN, ?w _?_ GALE; ca 169-; Barnstable

DIMOCK, Timothy (1668-1718, Ashford, CT) & 2/wf _?_ (had dau Silence); ca 1700

DIMOCK, Timothy (1668-1718, Ashford, CT) & 3/wf Abigail DOANE

DINELY/DINGLEY, John & Sarah (POLLARD) QUILLINGTON, w Abraham; b 1695; Boston

DINELY, Fathergone (-1675) & Hannah [PORTER]; Apr 1663, b 1666; Boston

DINELEY, William (-1638) & Alice _?_ , m/2 Richard CRITCHLEY 1639±; b 1636; Boston

DINGE, Christopher & Mary _?_ ; Hempstead, LI

DINGE, Robert & _?_ ; Hempstead, LI

DINGE, Robert & Rebecca _?_ ; ca 1685/90; Hempstead, LI

DINGHAM, Henry (-1645) & Elizabeth (_?_) ALCOCK, w George; Apr 1647; Roxbury

DINGLEY, Jacob (1642-1691) & Elizabeth [NEWTON] (-1718); b 1667; Marshfield

DINGLY, John (-1690?) & Sarah [?CHILLINGWORTH]; b 1638; Marshfield
DINGLEY, John & Sarah [POLLARD] (1659-); Boston
DINSDALL, Adam (son-in-law of Miles TARNE) & Hannah (TARNE) [MANNING], wid; b 1671; Boston
DINSDALL, John (1644-1689) & Anne _?_ ; b 1670; Boston
DINSDALE, John (-1726?) & Hannah BANFORD; 19 Sep 1694; Boston
DINSDALE, William (1616-1675?) & Martha _?_ (-1696); b 1644; Boston
DINSDALL, William & Mary _?_ ; b 1678; Boston
DINSDALL, William & Sarah (_?_) [LUX], w John; b 1686; Boston
DIONS, Anthony & Anna _?_ ; b 1678; Boston
DIONS, Joseph & Hannah/Ann? _?_ ; b 1680; Boston
DIPPLE, _?_ & Grace _?_, m/2 Nicholas BAKER 1662; b 1650; Scituate
DISBROW, Nicholas (1612-1683) & 2/wf? Mary [BRONSON]; b 1640, b 1648?; Hartford/Killingworth, CT
DISBOROUGH, Nicholas (1612-1683) & Elizabeth (?SHEPARD) STRICKLAND, w Thwaite; bef? Jun 30 1674; Hartford
DISBROW, Peter (1631-1688?) & Sarah/(Femy 2/wf?) KNAPP (-1681?); 6 Apr 1657; Stamford, CT/Rye, NY
DISBROW, Thomas & Mercy ?[HOLLINGWORTH/?NICHOLS] (John NICHOLS deserted his wf); ca 1679?; Fairfield, CT
DISBOROUGH, Walter & Phebe _?_ ; ca 1630?; Roxbury
DISBROW, Henry & _?_ ; b 1664; Mamaroneck, NY
DISBROW, _?_, Jr. & [Mary GRIFFIN] (1679/81?-); ca 1700?, b 1698, ca 1696; ?Flushing, LI
DISBROW, Henry (ae 39 in 1705) & Margaret/Mary _?_ (ae 33 in 1705); Mamaroneck, NY
DISBROW, Samuel & _?_ ; b 1680; Lynn
DICER/DISER, William & 1/wf Elizabeth AUSTIN (-1704); 20 Nov 1664; Salem
DISPAW/DISPAU, Edward[2] & _?_ ; b 1691; Lynn
DISSPAW, Henry[1] (-1676) & _?_ ; in Eng, b 1660; Lynn
DISPAW, Henry[2] & _?_ ; b 1680; Lynn
DISSATER, Edward & Hannah _?_, ?m/2 William BRYANT 1692; b 1689; Boston
DUTCHFIELD/DITCHFIELD, Thomas (-1645) & Anne _?_ ; b 1644; Boston
DITSON, Hugh & Sarah ROSS; 31 Aug 1694; Billerica
DIVEN, John (-1684) & _?_ ; b 1647; Lynn
DIVEN, John, Jr. (1650±-1707) & Elizabeth _?_ (-1674); b 1672; Lynn
DIVEN, John & Hannah (NEEDHAM) [ARMITAGE] (-1683+), w Eleazer; b 1675; Lynn
DEUALL/DIVOL, John (-1676) & Hannah WHITE (-1709, ae 63), m/2 Samuel LUMAS 1678±; 23 Dec 1663; Lancaster
DIVOLL, William (1672-1731) & Ruth [WHITCOMB] (1672-); b 1695; Lancaster
DIKE/DIX, Anthony (-1638) & Tabitha _?_, m/2 Nathaniel PITMAN/PICKMAN; Salem
DIKE, Anthony (-1679) & Margery _?_, m/2 John POLAND/POLEN 1680; ca 1660?; Salem
DIKE, Anthony (-1702+) & Sarah [DAVISON]; 26 Nov 1688; Salem/Topsfield/Ipswich
DIX, Edward (-1660) & 1/wf Jane [?WILKINSON]; b 1637; Watertown
DIX, Edward (-1660) & 2/wf Susanna _?_ (-1661+); Watertown
DIX, John (-1714) & Elizabeth BARNARD; 7 Jan 1670/1; Watertown
DIX, John & Mary [BIDWELL]; ca 1672/79; Hartford
DIX, John (1661-1711) & Rebecca _?_ ; b 1684(5?), b 1685/6?; Wethersfield, CT
DIX, John (?1658-) & 1/wf Lydia [BURNAP] (-1699); 30 Jun 1692; Reading
DIX, John (-1722?) & Sarah [BARNES] (1669-); ca 1692/5?; Hartford, CT
DEEX, John & Martha LAWRENCE; 29 Nov 1697; Watertown
DIX, John (-1745) & 2/wf Anna/Ann? (KIBBEY) FITCH (-1750, ae 80); w Joseph; 28 May 1700; Reading
DIX, Leonard (-1696, 1697) & Sarah _?_ (-1709); b 1658; Wethersfield, CT
DIX, Ralph (-1688) & Esther _?_ ; b 1653; Ipswich/Reading
DIX, Samuel & Joan _?_ ; came 1637
DIX, Samuel & Mary (?MOORE) CATLIN/COLLINS/MOORE?, ?dau Richard; 19 Jun 1684; Wethersfield, CT
DIX, Samuel (1661-) & 1/wf Lydia [BURRELL] (1663-25 Mar 1693); b 1689, b 1692; Reading

DIX, Samuel (1661-), Redding & 2/wf Hannah SMITH (-1696), Charlestown; 10 Jul 1693; Reading

DIX, _?_ & 3/wf Sarah (DUTTON) [LEWIS], w Samuel; bef 1706; Charlestown

DIX, Edward? & Deborah _?_, m/2 Richard BARNES 1667

DIXY, John (1639-1673) & Elizabeth [ALLEN] (1651-), m/2 John FAYERWEATHER 1674?; b 1676, 6 Nov 1668; Beverly

DIXEY, John (1657-) & Sarah COLLINS (-1737); 9 Dec 1679; Beverly

DIXI, Samuel (1663-) & Margaret PARKER; 23 Oct 1684; Marblehead

DIXY, Thomas (-1680?, 1686?) & Mary _?_ ; b 1645, b 1643; Salem/Marblehead

DIXY, Thomas (1654-1691) & Elizabeth [MERRITT], m/2 John HARWOOD 1695; b 1683; Salem

DIXY, William (?1667-1690 ae 82) (ae 73 1680) & Anna/Hannah _?_ (-1685); b 1636; Salem/Beverly

DIXON, George (d in Eng) & Anne [WATTS]; b 1665; Scarborough, ME

DIXON, John (1656-1738, 1737?, ae 81) & Margery WINSHIP (-1734, ae 71); 12 May 1687; Cambridge/Lexington

DIXON, Peter & Mary [REMICK] (1658-); b 1679; Kittery, ME

DIXON, William (-1666) & Joan _?_, wid?; ca 1636; York, ME

DICKSON, William (ca 1614-1692, ae 78) & Jane _?_ (ca 1616-1689, ae 73); b 1644; Cambridge

DIXWELL, John (1607-1689) & _?_ ; New Haven

DIXWELL, John & Joanna LING, w Benjamin; 3 Nov 1673; New Haven

DIXWELL, John (-1688/9) (see David DAVIDS) & Bathsheba HOW; 23 Oct 1677; New Haven

DOAK, Michael & Deliverance [?ASHTON]; b 1687; Marblehead

DOANE, Daniel (1636/7-1712) & 1/wf _?_ ; Eastham

DOANE, Daniel (1636/7-1712) & 2/wf Hepzibah (COLE) CRISP (1649-), w George; aft 28 Jul 1682; Eastham

DOANE, Daniel (?1666-1743) & 1/wf Mehitable [TWINING?]; b 1687(8?); Eastham/Bucks Co., PA

DOANE, Ephraim (1645-1700) & 1/wf Mary KNOWLES; 5 Feb 1667; Eastham

DOANE, Ephraim (-1700) & 2/wf Mary (SMALEY) SNOW (1647-1703), w John; aft 1692, b 1695?; Eastham

DOANE, Hezekiah (1672-1732) & 1/wf Hannah [SNOW?]; b 1692; Eastham/Barnstable

DOANE, Isaac (1670-) & Margaret [WOOD/ATWOOD?]; 2 Dec 1700; Eastham

DOAN, Israel (ca 1672-) & 1/wf Ruth [FREEMAN] (1680?-1728); b 1701; Eastham

DOANE, John (-1686, 1 Jan 1685, [1685/6]) (ae 88 in 1675) & 1/wf Ann [PERKINS?] (-4 Dec 1648+); b 1632, b 1627?; Plymouth/Eastham

DOANE, John (-1686) & 2/wf Lydia _?_ ; b 1 Apr 1659; Eastham

DOANE, John (1635-1707/8) & 1/wf Hannah BANGES (?1644-1677+); last of Apr 1662; Eastham

DOANE, John (1635-1707/8) & 2/wf Rebecca PETTE/PETTEE; 14 Jan 1684; Eastham

DOANE, John (1664-) & 1/wf Mehitable SCUDER/SCUDDER; 30 Jun 1686; Eastham

DOAN, John & 2/wf Hannah (HOBART) [SNELL] (1666-1731), w Samuel; b 1696, b 6 Mar 1694/5; Boston/Wellfleet

DOANE, Joseph (1669, 1668-1757) & 1/wf Mary GODFREY (1672-1725); 8 Jan 1690; Eastham

DOANE, Samuel (1673-) & Martha HAMBLEN (1673-), Barnstable; 30 Dec 1696; Barnstable

DOBSON, George & Mary BOSTWICKE? (1629-); 24 Nov 1653; Boston

DOBYSON/DOBSON?, _?_ & Sarah MASTERS, dau John; b 1639; Cambridge

DODD, Daniel (-1666) & Mary [WHEELER] (-1657); ca 1646, b 1651; Branford, CT

DODD, Daniel & Phebe BROWNE (1660)

DODD, George (-1663?) & Mary [DAVIS] (-1713+), m/2 Matthew AUSTIN, m/3 William WRIGHT; b 1647; Boston

DOD, John & Mary GALE; 14 Sep 1696; Marblehead

DODD, Joseph & Mary (BARTOLL) KNIGHT, w John; 14 Jul 1700; Marblehead

DODD, Stephen (-1691) & Mary/?Sarah STEVENS; 18 May 1678, 18 Apr 1678; Guilford, CT

DODD, [?Thomas] & Sarah [PITMAN], dau Thomas; ?by 1664?; Salem

DOD, Thomas & Mary GRANT; 12 Nov 1688; Marblehead

DOD, Thomas & Abigail PICKWORTH; 5 Jun 1693; Marblehead

DODGE, Andrew (1676-1718) & 1/wf Hannah FISKE; m int 4 Apr 1696, m 26 May 1696?; Beverly/Wenham

DODGE, Antipas & Johanna/Joanna? LOW, m/2 Joseph HALE 1708; 24 Jan 1699, 1699/1700?; Ipswich
DODGE, Ebenezer (1670-1718) & Lydia NOWELL (1674-); 12 Jan 1696, 1696/7; Salem
DODGE, Edward (-1727) & Mary HASKELL (1660-1737); Apr 1673, 30 Apr; Beverly
DODGE, Israel (1647-1733) & Hannah __?__ ; b 1689; New London/Montville, CT
DODGE, John (ca 1636-) (son William) & 1/wf Sarah PROCTOR; 10 Apr 1659; Beverly
DODGE, John (1631-1711) (son Richard) & Sarah __?__ (-1706, ae 60); b 1661; Beverly/Wenham
DODGE, John (-1729) & Mary __?__ ; b 1680(1?), 4 Oct 1676; New Shoreham, RI
DODGE, John & 2/wf Elizabeth (_?_) [WOODBURY], w John; aft 1682?, ca 1675?; Beverly
DODGE, John (1662-1704) & 1/wf Martha FISKE (1667-1697); b 1688; Wenham
DODGE, John (1661-1700) & 1/wf Sarah [HASKELL]?; b 1690; ?Wenham
DODGE, John (1661-1700) & Mary [BRIDGES] (1667-); b 1694, b 1684, ca 1688; Beverly
DODGE, John & __?__ ; 4 Feb 1696, bef 1681; New Shoreham, RI
DODGE, John (1662-1704) & 2/wf Ruth GROVER; 11 Apr 1698; Beverly/Wenham
DODGE, Joseph (ca 1651-1716) & Sarah EATON (-1714, ae 64); 21 Feb 1671; Beverly/Salem/Reading
DODGE, Joseph & 1/wf Rebecca BALCH (-1704); 28 Nov 1695, ?20 Nov; Beverly
DODGE, Joseph (1670-) & Martha [WHITE]; b 1696; Ipswich
DODGE, Joshua (1669-1694) & Joanna [LARKIN] (1676-), m/2 John THORNDIKE 1696; b 1694; Beverly
DODGE, Josiah (1665-1715) & Sarah [FISK] (1672-1730); b 1696, b 1693; Beverly
DODGE, Richard (1602-1671/2?) & Edith __?__ (1603-1678); b 1631, b 1628; Ipswich/Beverly/Wenham
DODGE, Richard (1643-1705) & Mary/Marah EATON (?1643-1716), dau Wm.?; 23 Feb 1667; Wenham
DODGE, Richard & Martha LOW (1669-); 16 Nov 1694; Ipswich
DODGE, Samuel (1645-1705) & Mary [PARKER]? (1647-1717, ae 73?); b 1668(9?); Ipswich
DODGE, Tristram (?1628-1720) & __?__ ; b 1640?; New Shoreham, RI
DODGE, Tristram & Dorcas DICKENS (1664?-); 7 Jan 1680, 1679/80, 30 Jan; Block Island, RI
DODGE, William (-1685/1692) & Elizabeth __?__ ; b 1636; Salem
DODGE, William (1640-1720) & 1/wf Mary (CONANT) [BALCH], w John; ca 1663; Beverly
DODGE, William & Elizabeth HASKELL; 10 Jul 1665; Beverly
DODGE, William (1642-) & Sarah [GEORGE] (1658-); b 1680(1?), b 1674/5; New Shoreham, RI
DODGE, William (1640-1720) & 2/wf Joanna (HALE) LARKIN (-1693, ae ca 47), w John; 26 May; 1685; Beverly
DODGE, William & Mary PORTER; 12 Dec 1689, 9 Dec 1710, 1689; Beverly/Salem
DODGE, William (1665-) & Hannah [WOODBURY]; b 1693; Beverly
DODGE, William & 2/wf? __?__ ; 24 Apr 1694 (doubtful); New Shoreham, RI
DODGE, William (1640-1720) & 3/wf Mary CREATTY (-1702?), w Andrew; 26 Apr 1698, 27 Oct 1698; Marblehead/Charlestown
DODGE, William (1678-) & Prudence FAIRFIELD; m int 27 Jul 1699; Wenham
DODSON, Anthony & Mary WILLIAMS (-1695, 1696) (sister of John); 12 Nov 1651; Scituate
DODSON, Jonathan (1659-) & 1/wf? Abigail [GANNETT/GARNETT?] (-1695?, ae 44 y); b 1694; Scituate
DOE, John (1669-1742) & Elizabeth __?__ ; by 1690?; Dover, NH
DOE, Nicholas (1631-1691) & Martha [?THOMAS]; b 1669; Dover, NH
DOE, Sampson (1670-) & 1/wf Temperance __?__ ; by 1700?; Dover, NH
DOGGETT, John (-1673) & __?__ [?BROTHERTON]; in Eng, b 1626; Watertown/Rehoboth/Martha's Vineyard
DOGGET, John (1626?-) & Anna/Anne? SUTTON (ca 1629-1673+); 23 Nov 1651; Rehoboth
DOGED, John (-1673) & 2/wf Bathsheba (_?_) PRATT, w Joshua; 24 Aug 1667; Plymouth
DOGGETT, John & 1/wf Persis [SPRAGUE] (1643-1684); b 1674, 1673; Hingham/Marshfield
DOGGETT, John (-1724) & Sarah [PEASE/?SKIFF/NORTON?], m/2 Banfield CAPRON; b 1686; Tisbury?/Attleboro
DOGGETT, John & 2/wf Mehitable TREWANT/TRUANT; 23 Sep 1691, 3 Sep; Marshfield
DOGGETT, John & 3/wf Rebecca (BAILEY) BROWNE, w Isaac; 22 Jun 1697; Newbury
DAGGETT, Joseph & Alice SISSETON (Indian woman); b 1668; Martha's Vineyard

DAGGETT, Joseph & Amy [EDDY] ([MANTOR?] is wrong) (-1712+); ca 1685, b 1693; Martha's Vineyard

DAGGETT, Joseph (1657-) & Mary PALMER; 14 Feb 1688/9; Rehoboth

DAGGETT, Joshua (1664?-) & Hannah [NORTON]; b 1686; Martha's Vineyard

DAGGETT, Nathaniel (1661-1708) & Rebecca MILLER (-1711); 24 Jun 1686; Rehoboth

DOGGED/DOGGETT, Samuel & 1/wf Mary ROGGERS/ROGERS (1668-1690); 24 Jan 16--, 24 Jan 1682, 1682/3?; Marshfield

DOGGETT, Samuel & 2/wf Bathsheba HOLMES; 21 Jan 1691; 1691/2; Marshfield

DOGGETT, Thomas (-1692) & ? (-23 Aug 1642); b 1642; Concord/Weymouth

DOGGETT, Thomas (-1692) & 2/wf Elizabeth (HUMPHREY)? [FRYE] (-1653), w William; ca 1643; Weymouth

DOGGED, Thomas (-1692) & 3/wf ?Jane/Joane CHILLINGWORTH (-1684, Marshfield), w Thomas; 17 May 1654, (17 Aug wrong); Marshfield

DAGGETT, Thomas (?1630-1691?) & Hannah [MAYHEW] (1635-1722), m/2 Samuel SMITH; ca 1657; Martha's Vineyard

DAGGETT, Thomas (?1658-1720) & Elizabeth HAWES (1662-1732); 22 Jan 1683; Bristol, RI

DOGETT, Thomas (-1737) & 1/wf Experience FORD (1676-1728); 18 Jan 1698, 1698/9; Marshfield

DAGGETT, William (1661-1694?) & Rebecca [WORMSTALL] (-1727+); b 1685, ca 1681; Saco, ME

DOGOOD/?DOGGETT, Thomas & Elizabeth POW; 2 Aug 1690; Marblehead

DOLBERY, Andrew (-1694) & Elizabeth (WILKEN) CONDEY, w William, m/3 Nathaniel THOMAS 1696; 31 Dec 1689; Boston

DOLEBEAR/DOLBEARE, Edmund & 1/wf ? (-1681); in Eng, b 1664; Boston

DOLEBEAR, Edmund & 2/wf Sarah ? ; b 1684; Boston/Salem

DOLBEAR, John (1669-1740) & Sarah COMER (1675-1745?); 9 Jun 1698; Boston

DOLBEAR, Joseph & Hannah HEWES; m int 26 Sep 1695; Boston

DOLBERRY, Thomas & Sarah ? ; b 1677; Boston

DOLE, Abner (1672-1740) & 1/wf Mary JEWETT/JEWIT (-1695); 1 Nov 1694; Newbury

DOLE, Abner (1672-1740) & 2/wf Sarah BELCHER (-1730), Boston; 5 Jan 1698, prob 1698/9; Boston/Newbury

DOLE, Benjamin & Elizabeth [HARVEY], m/2 Robert JORDAN b 1685; b 4 Sep 1678; ?Portsmouth, NH

DOLE, Benjamin (1679-1707) & Frances SHERBURNE (1676-1744), m/2 William/Joseph? STANFORD; 11 Dec 1700; Hampton, NH

DOLE, Henry (1663-1690) & Sarah BROCKLEBANK, m/2 Nathaniel COFFIN 1693; 3 Nov 1686; Newbury

DOLE, John (1648-1699?) & Mary GERRISH (1658-); 23 Oct 1676; Newbury

DOLE, John & Mary JESSUP; 26 Mar 1688; Lusum, LI

DOLE, Richard (1622-1705) & 1/wf Hannah ROFE/RULFE (-1678); 3 May 1647; Newbury/Salisbury

DOLE, Richard (1650-1723) & Sarah GREENLEFE/GREENLEAF (1655-1718, ae 62 y); 7 Jun 1677; Newbury

DOLE, Richard (1622-1705) & 2/wf Hannah (?) BROKLEBANK (-1690), w Samuel; 4 Mar 1678, 1678/9; Newbury

DOLE, Richard (1622-1705) & Patience (JEWETT) WALKER, w Shubael; m cont 29 Oct 1690; Newbury

DOLE, William (1660-) & Mary BROCKLBANCK; 13 Oct 1684; Newbury

DOLLIVER, John (1671-) & Susanna MARINER; 1 Nov 1700; Gloucester

DOLLIVER, Joseph (1629-1688) & ?Margaret [PEACH?] (sister of John); b 1667; Marblehead

DOLOVER, Joseph & 1/wf ? ; b 1670?; E. Greenwich, RI

DOLLABER, Joseph & Mary POWSLAND/SALMON?; 16 Jan 1689/90; Marblehead

DOLLIVER, Joseph & 2/wf Rachel (RICE?) EVERETT, w Jedediah; aft 18 May 1699; Kings Town, RI/E. Greenwich, RI

DOLOVER, Peter (-1698) & Mary [WARD] (1669-), m/2 William WATERS 1699; b 1684; Charlestown

DOLEVER, Richard (1665-) & Agnes/?Annis (DENNEN/DENNING?) BARRET, wid; 25 Nov 1697; Gloucester

DOLLIVER, Samuel (1608-1683) & 2/wf? Mary ELWELL, m/2 James GARDNER 1684; 15 Aug 1654; Gloucester

DALLEBAR, Tristram (1598-1664?) & 1/wf Mary _?_ (-3 Jul 1644)

DALLEBAR, Tristram (1598-1664?) & 2/wf Sarah PEAVIS; 31 Aug 1657

DOLLIVER, William (1656-) & Ann HIGGENSON; [4 Oct 1682]; Gloucester

DOLLOFF/DOLLOF, Christian (1639-1708) & 1/wf [Rachel MOULTON]; b 11 Mar 1666/7; Exeter, NH

DOLLOFF, Christian (1639-1708) & 2/wf Sarah SCAMMON; 10 Dec 1674; Exeter, NH

DOLLOFF, Richard & Catherine [BEAN] (1680±-1750+); 1700, b 1702(3?); Exeter, NH

DONNELL, Henry (1602/8-) & Francis [GOOCH?]; b 1636; York, ME

DONELL, Joseph & Ruth [REDDING], m/2 Thomas FAVOR 1697; b 1680, aft Apr 1675; Casco Bay, ME

DONNELL, Samuel (1645-1718, 1717/18) & Alice [CHADBOURNE] (-1744), m/2 Jeremiah MOULTON 1723; b 1682; York, ME

DONNELL, Thomas (±1636-1699) & Elizabeth [WEARE]; b 1660; York, ME

DOOLITTLE, Abraham[1] (ca 1620-1690) & 1/wf Joan ALLEN/ALLING (1617-); b 1642; Boston/New Haven/Wallingford, CT

DOOLITTLE, Abraham[1] (ca 1620-1690, ae 70, Wallingford) & 2/wf Abigail MOSS (1642-1710, Wallingford, CT); 2 Jul 1663; New Haven

DOOLITTLE, Abraham[2] (1650-1732) & 1/wf Mercy HOLT (1649-1688); 9 Nov 1680; Wallingford, CT

DOOLITTLE, Abraham[2] (1650-1732) & 2/wf Ruth (ROYCE) LATHROPE, w John; 12 Feb 1689; Wallingford, CT

DOOLITTLE, Abraham[2] (1650-1732) & 3/wf Elizabeth THORP (1668-); 5 Jun 1695; Wallingford, CT

DOOLITTLE, Daniel (1675-1755) & Hannah CORNWALL/CONNELL (1677-); 3 May 1698; Wallingford, CT/Middletown, CT

DOOLITTLE, Ebenezer (1672-1711) & Hannah HALL; 6 Apr 1697; Wallingford, CT

DOLITTLE, John (-1680) & 2/wf Sibella/Sybil (BIBBLE) NUTT (-1690), w John, w Miles; 30 Oct 1674; Cambridge/Charlestown

DOOLITTLE, John (1655-) & 1/wf Mary PECK (1666-1710); 13 Feb 1682; Wallingford, CT

DOOLITTLE, Joseph (1667-1733) & Sarah BROWN (1672-); 24 Apr 1690; Wallingford, CT

DOOLITTLE, Samuel (1665-1714) & Mary [CORNWALL] (1666-1742); b 1689; ?Wallingford, CT/Middletown, CT

DOOLITTLE, Theophilus (1678-) & Thankful HALL (-1715); 5 Jan 1698/9, 1698/9; Wallingford, CT

DORCHESTER, Anthony (-1683?) & 1/wf Sarah _?_ (-1649); b 1644; Windsor, CT/Springfield

DORCHESTER, Anthony (-1683?) & 2/wf Martha (CHAPMAN) KRITCHWELL/KITCHERELL (-1662), w Samuel; 2 Jan 1650, ?1650/1; Hartford, CT/Springfield

DORCHESTER, Anthony (-1683?) & 3/wf Elizabeth [HARMON], w John; bef Dec 1664, aft 1662; Springfield

DORCHESTER, Benjamin (-1676) & Sarah BURT (1656-1746), m/2 Luke HITCHCOCK 1676/7; 22 Apr 1675; Springfield

DORCHESTER, James & Sarah PARSONS (1656-); 1 Mar 1676/7; Springfield

DORCHESTER, John (1644-1705) & Mary HARMON (1651-); 20 Apr 1671; Springfield

DOREY?, Joseph & Sarah [WOODIN] (1657-); Rochester

DORE, Richard (-1716) & Tamsen [JACKSON]; b 1673; Portsmouth, NH

DORIFIELD, Barnabas (-ca 1650) (had nephew Samuel SPENCER of Braintree, his chief heir) & Elizabeth _?_ (-1679); b 1679, b 1640?; Boston/Braintree

DORMAN, Benjamin & Ruth JOHNSON; 10 Oct 1698; New Haven

DORMAN, Edmund & 1/wf Hannah HULL (1642-); 25 Dec 1662; New Haven

DORMAN, Edmund & 2/wf Elizabeth (POST) (SPERRY) BUNNELL (1655-), w John, w Benjamin; 19 Sep 1700; New Haven

DORMAN, Ephraim (?1645-1721) & Mary _?_ (-1705); b 1674; Topsfield

DORMAN, John (-1662) & Mary COOPER (1642-1677, [1676/7]), m/2 John HOWE bef 1665; 21 Nov 1660; Topsfield

DORMAN, John (-1712) & Sarah THOMAS (1672-), m/2 John COOPER; 4 Jan 1693, div 1693; Hartford

DORMAN, Joseph & Mary WILMOTH/WILMOT (1676/7-), m/2 Benjamin WOODING/WOODEN?; 24 Aug 1693; New Haven

DORMAN, Thomas (1600-1670) (calls Daniel BRADLEY "cousin" in 1670) & Ellen [?BRADLEY/ ?HADLEY] (-1668); b 1640; Topsfield/Ipswich

DORMAN, Thomas (nephew of George HADLEY) & Judith WOOD; 16 Mar 1662, 6 Nov 1662; Boxford/Topsfield

DORMAN, Timothy (1663-1743) & Elizabeth KNOWLTON (-1738); 15 Nov 1688; Boxford/Topsfield

DORMAN, _?_ & _?_ (wid in 1661); b 26 Aug 1661; Salem

DORR, Edward (1648-1734) & 1/wf Elizabeth [HAWLEY] (1656-1719); b 1680, ca 1679; Roxbury

DORRELL/?DARRELL, Benjamin & Rebecca _?_ ; b 1680; Braintree

DORRELL, John & Palti _?_ ; b 1680; Boston

DORY, Joseph & Sarah [WOODIN] (1657-); Rochester, MA

DORY, Philip & Mary _?_ ; b 1686; Salem

DOTTERIDGE/?DODDRIDGE, _?_ & Sarah JOY (1667); Salem

DOUGHTY, ?Charles/?Isaac (1667-) & Elizabeth [JACKSON] (1668-); 1688±, ca 1690; ?Oyster Bay, LI

DOTY, Edward¹ (-1655) & 1/wf _?_ ; Plymouth

DOTY/DOTEN, Edward¹ (-1655, Plymouth) & 2/wf Faith CLARK (1619-1675), m/2 John PHILLIPS 1667; 6 Jan 1634, [1634/5]; Plymouth/Yarmouth

DOTY, Edward (?1643-1690) & Sarah/?Susan FAUNCE, ?m/2 John BUCK 1693; 25 Feb 1662, 26 Feb 1662; Plymouth

DOUGHTY, Elias (1632±-1696+) & Sarah [?ONEAL] (-1726); ca 1658; Flushing, LI

DOUGHTY, Elias, Jr. (1664-) & _?_ ; ca 1686/8

DOUGHTY, Francis & 1/wf Bridget [STONE?]; in Eng, b 1632; Taunton/Newtown, LI

DOUGHTY, Francis & Margaret (HOWELL) [MOORE], w John; ?1660, aft Sep 1665, b 1661/2?; ?Southampton, LI

DOUGHTY, Francis & Mary PALMER (ca 1666-); ca 1685; Fairfield, CT

DOTY, Isaac (?1647/8, 1649-) & Elizabeth [ENGLAND]; ca 1673; Oyster Bay, LI

DOTY, ?Isaac/Charles (1673±-) & Elizabeth [JACKSON]; betw 1696 & 1703; Oyster Bay, LI

DOUGHTY, Jacob (1672-) & Amy [WHITEHEAD] (1679-), Newtown; b 1697; Flushing, LI

DOUGHTEY, James & Lydia TURNER; 15 Aug 1649; Scituate/CT

DOTY, John (1639/40-1701) & 1/wf Elizabeth [COOKE] (1649-1692); ca 1667; Plymouth

DOTY, John (1668-) & 1/wf Mehitable NELSON (1670-); 2 Feb 1692/3; Plymouth

DOTY, John, Sr. (-1701) & 2/wf Sarah JONES (1671-), m/2 Joseph PETERSON; 22 Nov 1694; Plymouth

DOTY, Joseph (?1651-ca 1732) & 1/wf _?_ , m/2 William GREEN; b 1674/5; Sandwich

DOTY, Joseph & Deborah ELLIS? (1662-1711), dau Walter; ca 1680/2?; Sandwich/?Rochester

DOTY, Samuel (-1715) & Jane HARMAN (-1717+); m lic NJ, 1678, ?15 Nov; Piscataway, NJ

DOTY, Theophilus & Ruth [MENDALL] (1675-); b 1697; Rochester

DOUGHTY, Thomas & Elizabeth BULLY; 24 Jan 1669/70; Saco, ME

DOTY, Thomas (?1642, 1641-1678/9, Dec 1678) & Mary [CHURCHILL?] (1654-); ca 1672-4; Plymouth

DOTY, Thomas & 2/wf Mary _?_ , m/2 Henry CHURCHILL 1688; 1678

DOUTY, _?_ & Elizabeth NURSE (1678-), dau John; b 1701?; Salem

DUBLEDEE, Elijah (1677-) & 1/wf Abigail _?_ (-1696); b 1696; Wenham

DUBBLEDEE, Elijah (1677-) & Sarah PAIN; 23 Jan 1697, 1697/8; Boston

DOUBLEDAY, Elisha (1672-1715) & Mary [WOODHEAD]; b 1693; Charlestown

DOUBLEDAY, Roger (-1690) & Ann _?_ (-1711, above 80); b 1672; Boston

DOUGLAS, Alexander (-1688) & _?_ [CLARK]; b 28 Jan 1679/80; Hartford

DOUGLAS, Alexander & Abigail SHARP; 3 May 1700; Lynn/Salem

DOUGLAS, Henry (-1667) & Judith/Judea? _?_ (-1680); b 1644?; Boston

DOUGLAS, John & Shuah (COLARD) NASON, w Richard; 16 Sep 1687; South Berwick, ME

DOUGLAS, Joseph & 1/wf Mary _?_ ; b 1694; Salem/Malden

DOUGLAS, Robert (?1639-1716) & Mary HEMPSTEAD (1647-1711); 28 Sep 1665; New London

DUGLAS, Thomas & _?_ ; b 1676; Boston

DOUGLAS, William (1610-1682) & Ann MATTLE/MATLAT?/MOLTEY?/MABLE? (1610-1685); in
	Eng, ca 1636; Gloucester/Boston/New London
DOUGLAS, William (1645-1725) & 1/wf Abiah HOUGH (1648-1715); 18 Dec 1667; New London,
	CT/Voluntown, CT
DOUGLAS, William (1672/3-1719) & Sarah [PROCTOR]; b 1696; New London, CT/Plainfield, CT
DOUGLAS, William (1666-) & Hannah __?__; b 1701; New London, CT
DOVE, Francis (returned to Eng) & Alice THATCHER; Salisbury, Eng, 19 Oct 1641; Salisbury
DOVE, Matthew & Hannah [ARCHER] (1632-); b 1652; Salem
DOW, Daniel (1641-1718) & Elizabeth LAMPREY; 13 Nov 1673; Hampton, NH
DOW, Henry[1] (1608-1659) & 1/wf Joan NUDD (-Jun 1640), w Roger; St. Michael, Ormsby, Eng,
	6 Feb 1630/1; Watertown/Salisbury/Hampton, NH
DOW, Henry[1] (1608-1659) & 2/wf Margaret [COLE], Dedham, m/2 Richard KIMBALL 1661; aft
	Jun 1640, b 1643; Watertown/Salisbury/Hampton, NH
DOW, Henry (1634-1707) & 1/wf Hannah PAGE (1641-1704); 17 Jun 1659; Hampton, NH
DOW, Henry & Elizabeth COLBY; 11 Apr 1692; Haverhill
DOWN, Henry (-1739) & Mary MUSSEY (1677±-1739); 7 Dec 1694; Hampton, NH/Salisbury
DOWN, Jabez & Esther SHOW (1666-); 24 Mar 1693, 1692/3; Hampton, NH
DOW, Jeremiah (1657-1723) & [Elizabeth/?Susanna DEAR] (-aft 1700); ca 1670-80?; Ipswich
DOW, Jeremiah (-1735+) & Elizabeth PERKINS (1676-); 5 Apr 1697; Hampton, NH
DOW, John (-1673) & Mary PAGE, m/2 Samuel SHEPARD 1673; 23 Oct 1665; Haverhill
DOW, John & Sarah BROWN; 23 May 1696; Haverhill/Salisbury
DOW, John & Hannah PAGE; 27 Nov 1696; Hampton, NH
DOW, Joseph (1638?, 1639-1703) & Mary SANBORN (-1733); 17 Dec 1662; Hampton, NH
DOW, Joseph & Mary CHALLIS (1668-1697); 25 May 1687; Amesbury
DOW, Joseph & Hannah (?CHALLIS) (Indian girl); ca 1699, betw 1698 & 1703; Salisbury
DOW, Samuel & Mary GRAVES (-1673); 12 Dec 1665; Hartford, CT
DOW, Samuel & 1/wf Abigail HOBBS (1664-); 12 Dec 1683; Hampton, NH
DOW, Samuel & Ruth (JOHNSON) AYER, w Timothy; 5 May 1691; Haverhill
DOW, Simon & 1/wf Sarah MARSTON (1665-1698); 5 Nov 1685; Hampton, NH
DOW, Simon & 2/wf Mehitable GREEN, m/2 Onesiphorus PAGE; 29 May 1700; Hampton, NH
DOW, Stephen (1642-) & 1/wf Ann/Anne STORIE?/STACY?/STAY?/STORCE?/STONE?; 16 Sep
	1663; Haverhill
DOW, Stephen, Jr. & 2/wf Mary HUTCHINS (1678-); 14 Dec 1697; Haverhill
DOW, Thomas (-1656) & Phebe __?__, m/2 John EATON 1661; ca 1635/41?; Newbury/Haverhill/
	Salisbury
DOW, Thomas (1653-) & Sarah [WALL] (-1682, 1681?); [by 1675], ?b 25 Jun 1668; Ipswich
DOW, Thomas & Dorcas KIMBALL (ca 1648-); 17 Dec 1668; Bradford/Haverhill
DOW, Thomas & 2/wf Susanna __?__ (-1724); b 1685; Ipswich
DOWD, Henry (-1668) & Elizabeth __?__ (-1713); b 1639?, b 1648; Guilford, CT
DOWD, John (-1712) & 1/wf Hannah SELLMAN/SALMON/SALLMAN/TALLMAN (-1687); 14 Jun
	1679; Guilford, CT
DOWD, John (-1712) & 2/wf Mary [BARTLETT]; ca middle of Jan 1687; Guilford, CT
DOWD, Thomas (-1713) & Ruth [JOHNSON] (-1713); 11 Dec 1679; Guilford, CT
DOWDING, Joseph (-1715) & Ann SANDS/SANDYS?; 21 Sep 1694; Boston
DOWDING, Leonard (-1682) & Mercy [PADDY] (-1694); b 1667; Boston
DOWELL, Francis (1671-1704) & Prudence RUSSELL (1675-1727+); 26 Jul 1698; Charlestown
DOWELL, James & Frances __?__; b 1665; Boston
DOWELL, James & Elizabeth WING; 27 Apr 1683; Boston
DOWNS, Deliverance (1669-) & Rebecca [LOBDELL]; b 1700; Medford, CT
DOWNES, Ebenezer & Mary (UMBERFEILD) MALLORY, w Thomas, m/3 Thomas CARNES; 28
	Nov 1694; New Haven
DOWNS, Edmund (-1669) & Mehitable [CLARK], m/2 Humphrey WARREN; Boston/etc.
DOWNES, John & Dorothy __?__; b 1657; Boston
DOWNES, John & ?Mary __?__; b 1659; New Haven
DOWNS, John & Hannah ROCKWELL; 1 Mar 1693/4; Norwich, CT
DOWN, John & Ruth (RUGGLES) BADCOCK, w George; 30 Aug 1696; Boston
DOWNS, John (1672-1753) & 1/wf Mary [PERRY]; b 1698; Fairfield, CT
DOWNE alias FORD, Richard (1635) & Rebecca __?__; Kittery, ME/Isles of Shoals

DOWNE, Samuel (1662-) & Christian PINION; 1 Jul 1692, 1 Jul 1691?; New Haven
DOWNES, Thomas (1612-1697) & Catherine _?_ (-1702); b 1652; Boston/Dover, NH
DOWNES, Thomas & Susanna (ELIOT) [HOBART] (-1688), w Peter; aft 1665; Hingham?
DOWNS, Thomas (1654-) & 1/wf [Martha] _?_ ; b 1680/1; Dover, NH
DOWN, Thomas & Mary _?_ ; b 1689; Boston
DOWNS, Thomas & 2/wf Mary [LORD] (-1696); b 1691; Dover, NH
DOWNS, Thomas (-1711) & 3/wf Abigail (ROBERTS) HALL, w John; 24 Oct 1698; Dover, NH
DOWNES, William (-1693) & 1/wf Hannah [APPLETON] (1652-); b 1676, b 29 Dec 1674; Boston
DOWNE, William & 2/wf Mary [TORREY]; b 1682; Boston
DOWNS, _?_ & Elizabeth [LAKEMAN]; b 11 Dec 1706, b 1701?
DOWNS, William & Elizabeth [?LAKEMAN]; b 1701; Bristol, RI
DOWNES, William & Abigail [RIDER]; b 1699; Southold, LI
DOWNER, Andrew (1672-) & Susannah HUNTINGDON; 20 Dec 1699; Newbury
DOWNER, Joseph & Mary KNIGHT (1634-); 9 Jul 1660; Newbury
DOWNER, Joseph (1666-) & Hannah [GRAFTON] (-1741); ca 1692; Newbury/Norwich, CT
DOWNER, Moses (-1699) & Sarah _?_ (1670?-); b 1694; Newbury
DOWNER, Robert (-1721) & Sarah EATON (1654-); 6 May 1675; Salisbury
DOWNAM, Deerman/DUNNING, Dorman (-1672/3) & Elizabeth _?_ ; b 1645; Braintree
DOWNHAM, John & 1/wf Dorothy _?_ (-1662); b 1644, 14 Mar 1643; Braintree (see John DUNHAM)
DOWNHAM, John & 2/wf Sarah _?_ ; b 1673; Braintree
DOWNING, Benjamin & Sarah [HUNTER?] (1662-); 29 Oct 1679; Hatfield?
DOWNING, Dennis (-1697?) & Anne DAINES, wid; Stepney, Eng, 17 Nov 1634; Kittery, ME
DOWNING, Emanuel (1585-1657?) & 1/wf [Anne] WARE (ca 1592-ca 1622); 7 Jun 1614, 7 Jan 1614?; Salem
DOWNING, Emanuel (1585-1656+) (returned to Eng) & 2/wf Lucy WINTHROP (1601-1656+, 1679); in Eng, 10 Apr 1622; Salem
DOWNING, George & 1/wf Mary [COLES]; ca 1692/3; Oyster Bay, LI
DOWNING, John (-1662/3) & Joanna _?_ , m/2 Richard HOLLEY 1663; b 1659; Charlestown
DOWNING, John (-bef 1702) & _?_ ; ca 1660/6?; Chatham/?Wells, ME
DOWNING, John & _?_
DOWNING, John & Mehitable BRABROOK (ca 1653-); 2 Nov 1669, ?29 Oct 1669; Ipswich
DOWNING, John & Mary (BUNCE) MEEKINS, w Thomas; 20 Jul 1676; Hatfield/Hadley
DOWNING, John & 1/wf Susannah [MILLER]; by May 1684, ?b 1684; ?Dover, NH
DOWNING, John (1675-) & Hannah RIDGAWAY/?SHEPARD; 27 Sep 1698, int 27 Dec 1697, Lynn; Boston
DOWNING, Joseph & _?_ ; b 1701?; Chatham
DOWNING, Joshua & ?1/wf Patience [HATCH]; by 1673, b 1669?, b 15 Jan 1676; Kittery, ME/Wells, ME?
DOWNING, Joshua & ?2/wf Rebecca (ROGERS) TRICKEY, w Joseph
DOWNING, Machum/Malcolm? (-1683), Scotchman & Margaret SULEAVAN/?SULLIVAN; - Jun 1653, 4 Mar 1653; Lynn
DOWNING, Moses & Sarah SAMSON/SCARBOROUGH; 23 Dec 1686; York Co., ME
DOWNING, Richard (1637-) & Mary/Joane? (BENNETT) (CODNER) WHITE (1638-), w Christopher (see Elias WHITE); ca 1662/5, 1667?; Salem/Marblehead/Ipswich
DOWNING/DUNNING?, Theophilus & Ellen _?_ ; b 1642; Salem
DUNNING, Thomas & Mary CHADWELL/CHATWELL (1673-); 15 Apr 1698; Salem
DOWNTON, William (-1696) & 1/wf Rebecca _?_ (-21 Apr 1691+); b 1658; Salem
DOWNTON, William (-1696) & 2/wf Joanna _?_ (-1702+); aft 21 Apr 1691; Salem
DOWNTON, William² (1665-) & Mary [LOVELL]; b 1695; Ipswich
DOWSE, Benjamin (1656-1723) & 1/wf Mary HEWINS; 7 Apr 1680; Charlestown
DOWSE, Eleazer (1669-1726, 1725) & Mary EDMANDS (1673-); 21 Sep 1693; Charlestown
DOUSE, Francis (-1680) & Katherine _?_ (-1698); b 1642; Boston/Charlestown
DOWSE, John (1644-1677) & Relief HOLLAND (-1743), m/2 Timothy FOSTER 1681, m/3 Henry LEADBETTER 1692; 31 Oct 1672; Charlestown
DOWSE, Jonathan (ca 1661-1745) & 1/wf Elizabeth BALLATT (1674-1701); 18 Nov 1694; Charlestown
DOWSE, Joseph (ca 1654-1694) & Mary GEORGE; 11 Jul 1678; Charlestown

DOUSE/DOWSE, Lawrence (1614-1692) & 1/wf Martha __?__ (-1644); ca 1642; Boston/Charlestown
DOUSE, Lawrence (1614-1692) & 2/wf Margaret [RAND] (-1714, ae 90); ca 1645; Charlestown
DOWSE, Lodowick/DOWSO, Lewis & Elizabeth WHITE; 9 Jan 1676, 1670/7; Sudbury/Sherborn
DOUSE, Nathaniel (1658-1719) & Dorothy EDMANDS (1668-); 7 Sep 1685; Charlestown
DOWSE, Samuel (ca 1642-) & 1/wf Hannah/?Anna LUDKIN (-1676); 8 Aug 1670; Charlestown
DOWSE, Samuel & 2/wf Faith JEWETT (1652-1738, 1737?); 7 Mar 1676/7; Charlestown
DOWSE, Samuel (?1665-), Portsmouth, NH, & Sarah BERRY, Newcastle; 1 Mar 1689, 1688/9; NH
DOXEY, Thomas (-1652) & Katherine [WESCOTT?], w Thomas, m/2 Daniel LANE 1652+, m/3 Thomas MOORE by 1680; New London, CT
DOYLE, William & Elizabeth __?__; b 1698; Westerly, RI
DRAGHADY, Stiles & Rebecca [GREEN] (1665-); b 22 Apr 1682; Boston
DRAKE, Abraham (?1628, 1621-1712+) & Jane __?__ (-1676); b 1652; Exeter, NH/Hampton, NH
DRAKE, Abraham (1654-1714) & Sarah [HOBBS]; b 1686; Hampton, NH
DRAKE, Benjamin & Sarah [POOL]; b 1700; Weymouth/Taunton
DRAKE, Enoch (1655-1698) & Sarah PORTER, m/2 Josiah BARBER; 11 Nov 1680; Windsor, CT
DRAKE, Francis (-1687) & Mary [WALKER]?; b 1657; Portsmouth, NH/Dover, NH/Piscataway, NJ
DRAKE, Jacob (-1689) & Mary BISSELL (-1689); 12 Apr 1649, no issue; Windsor, CT
DRAKE, Job (-1689) & Mary WOLCOTT (-1689); 25 Jun 1646; Windsor, CT
DRAKE, Job, Westfield & Elizabeth ALVORD; 20 Mar 1671, 1671/2; Windsor, CT
DRAKE, Job & Elizabeth (CLARK) COOKE, w Moses; 13 Sep 1677; Windsor, CT
DRAKE, John (1585-1659) & Elizabeth [ROGERS]? (-1681 in 100th y); in Eng, b 1625?; Dorchester/Windsor, CT/Windham, CT/Taunton
DRAKE, John (-1689, Simsbury, CT) & Hannah MOORE (-1686, 1686/7?); 30 Nov 1648; Windsor, CT/Simsbury, CT
DRAKE, John (1649-1689) & Mary [WATSON/WESTON?] (1651-1693); 20 Mar 1671, b 1674; Windsor, CT/Simsbury, CT
DRAKE, John & Rachel [ATKINS], m/2 James BERRY/BARRY by 1687; b 1680; Boston
DRAKE, John (-1717), Weymouth, Easton, & Sarah KING, Weymouth (not 2/wf); 12 Dec 1687; Milton/Weymouth
DRAKE, John & Sarah __?__; b 1695; Eastchester, NY
DRAKE, Joseph (ca 1663-) & Mary SHUTE; 31 Dec 1685; ?Eastchester, NY
DRAKE, Joseph & 1/wf Elishama __?__ (-1718); b 1687; Weymouth
DRAKE, Joseph & 1/wf Ann [MORTON] (-1717, 1716), Hartford; [1696]; Windsor, CT
DRAKE, Nathaniel (1612-) & 1/wf __?__; ?; Hampton, NH
DRAKE, Nathaniel (1612-) & 1/wf? 2/wf? Jane [BERRY] (1619-), w Wm.; betw 1654 & 1669, by 1637; Hampton, NH
DRAKE, Robert (?1580-1668) & __?__; in Eng, b 1612; Hampton, NH
DRAKE, Samuel (-1686) & Ann BARLOW; 13 Sep 1650; Fairfield, CT/Eastchester, NY
DRAKE, Samuel (-1692, 1690/1?) & Ruth SHERWOOD, m/2 John BARLOW; b 1688; ?Fairfield, CT/?Stratford, CT
DRAKE, Simon (-1712) & Hannah MILLS; 15 Dec 1687; Windsor, CT/Torrington, CT
DRAKE, Thomas (-1692+) & 1/wf Jane [HOLBROOK]; b 1657; Weymouth/Scituate
DRAKE, Thomas & Millicent (FORD) CARVER, w John; 9 Mar 1680/1; Marshfield
DRAKE, Thomas (1657±-1725) & Hannah __?__ (-1728); ca 1685/90?, no issue; Weymouth
DRAKE, William (1661-1727) & Sarah [NASH] (1669-1735+); b 1687; Weymouth
DRAKE, __?__ & Joan __?__ (-1637); in Eng, b 3 Aug 1634; Boston
DRAKELY, Thomas & Lydia __?__; b 1697; Woodbury, CT
DRAPER, Adam & Rebecca BRABROOK, m/2 Thomas BUTTON 1678, 1679; 15 Sep 1666; Concord
DRAPER, Daniel & 1/wf Elizabeth BRACKET (1664-12 Sep 1692?); 16 Nov 1691; Dedham
DRAPER, Daniel & 2/wf Elizabeth (ASPINWALL) [STEVENS] (1671-), Salem, w Robert; b 1695; Dedham
DRAPER, James (1618?, 1622/3-1697, ae ca 73) (ae 54 in 1676) & Miriam STANSFIELD (1625-1697, 1700/1?); Hopstonstall, Eng, 21 Apr 1646; Roxbury/Dedham
DRAPER, James (1654-1698) & Abigail WHITING (1663-1721); 18 Feb 1680, prob 1680/1; Roxbury

DRAPER, John & 1/wf Abigail MASON; 3 Sep 1686; Dedham
DRAPER, John & Rachel _?_ ; b 1689; Boston
DRAPER, Moses (-1693) & 1/wf Hannah CHANDLER (1669-1692, Roxbury); 7 Jul 1685; Roxbury
DRAPER, Moses (-1693) & 2/wf Mary THATCHER, m/2 Joseph GRANT; 3 Nov 1692; Boston
DRAPER, Nathaniel & 2/wf? _?_ [MERCER], m/2 Robert SCOTT by 1680; Sherborn
DRAPER, Nathaniel (1669?-) & 1/wf Elizabeth _?_ ; b 1699; Boston
DRAPER, Richard (ae 25 in 1694) & Sarah KILBEY; 22 Oct 1689; Boston
DRAPER, Roger & 1/wf _?_ ; b 1641; Concord
DRAPER, Roger (-bef 1668) & 2/wf Mary [HADLOCK] (-1683), w Nathaniel; aft 1648; Charlestown
DRAPER, Stephen & Mercy _?_ ; b 1700; Boston
DRESSER, John (1607-1672) & Mary _?_ (-1672+); b 1640; Rowley
DRESSER, John (?1640-1725) & 1/wf Martha THORLEY/THORLA (-1700); 27 Nov 1662; Rowley/Newbury
DRESSER, John & Mercy DICKINSON; 7 Jun 1688; Rowley
DRESSER, Jonathan (1674-1744, Pomfret, CT) & Sarah LEAVER (-1756); 31 Oct 1699; Rowley/Pomfret, CT
DRESSER, Samuel (1643-1704) & Mary LEAVER (1649-1714); 9 Dec 1668; Rowley
DRESSER, Samuel (1673-1752) & 1/wf Mary BURKBEE/BURPEE (1675-1732); 13 May 1700; Rowley
DREW/DRUCE?, ?Erzomand/?Erozomand/?Rosemund & Mary (WINCHESTER) DRUCE?; aft 1675, 1677
DREW, Francis (1648-1694) & [Lydia BICKFORD]; ca 1672, ca 1673; Dover, NH
DREW, James (-1674) & Mary [JONES]; b 1667, by 1663; Portsmouth, NH
DREW, John (1642-1721) & Hannah [CHURCHILL] (?1649-); b 1673(4?); Plymouth
DREW, John (1651-1723) & 1/wf Sarah [FIELD] (1651-); ca 1675; Dover, NH
DREW, John (-1706) & _?_ ; b 1701?, b 1695?; Dover, NH
DREW, John (1676-1745) & Sarah [DELANO] (-1746+); b 1701?; Halifax
DREW, John & _?_ ; Portsmouth, NH
DREW, Richard & Mary [?DRUSE]; b 1679; Boston
DRUE, Robert & Jemima CLARKE; 6 Nov 1656; Boston
DREW/DRUCE?, ?Rosemund/?Erasomund (ae 22 in 1673) & Mary (WINCHESTER) DRUCE/DRUSE (-1719), w John (see ?Erzomand DREW); 18 Feb 1677; Roxbury
DREW, Samuel (-1669?) & Abigail _?_ , m/2 Anthony ELLINS 1669?, m/3 John JACKSON 1691; Great Island
DREW, Samuel & Ann L'-?; b 169-; Boston
DREW, Thomas (1632-1694) & Mary (?BROWN) [PARKER?], m/2 Richard ELIOT; NH
DREW, Thomas (1665-) & Mary [BUNKER]; b 1692, b 1683/4, b 1687; Dover, NH
DREW, Thomas & Tamsen _?_ ; ca 1694; Little Bay
DREW, William (1627-1669) & Elizabeth [MATTHEWS?] (1628-), m/2 William FOLLETT 1671?/1672?; b 1648?; Isles of Shoals
DREW, _?_ & Elizabeth [LARKIN], w Thomas (see John DYER); Charlestown/Boston
DRING, Thomas (1666-) & Mary [BARTLETT?/BUTLER?] (1670-); 21 May 1696; Little Compton, RI
DRINKER, Edward (?1622-1700) & 1/wf Hannah [DUFFY?] (-1693); ca 1650?, no ch in will, b 1647?; Charlestown/Boston
DRINKER, Edward (?1622-1700) & 2/wf Mary EMMONS; 6 Mar 1694; Boston
DRINKER, John (1627-) & Elizabeth _?_ (ca 1625-); b 1653; Charlestown/Beverly
DRINKER, Joseph (?1653-) & Ruth [BALCH] (1665-1731+); b 1684; Beverly
DRINKER, Philip (1596-1647) & Elizabeth _?_ (1603-1647+); in Eng, b 1622; Charlestown
DRINKWATER, Thomas & Elizabeth [HASKELL] (1672-); ca 1700?, 1695; Newport
DRISCO, John (-1697) & _?_ [EMERSON?]; b 1690; Wells, ME
DRISCO, Lawrence & Elizabeth _?_ ; b 1689; Boston
DRISCO, Timothy alias Teague & Sarah [PITMAN]?, m/2 Benjamin JONES 1696?; by 1682; Dover, NH
DRISCOLL, Florence/Flurance? (-1678) & Mary WEBSTER; 24 Apr 1674; Windsor, CT
DRIVER, John & 1/wf Elizabeth _?_ (-1674); b 1673; Lynn
DRIVER, John & 2/wf _?_ ; b 1678; Lynn/Boston

DRIVER, Robert[1] (1592-1680) & Phebe _?_ (-1683); b 1631?, b 1628?; Lynn
DRIVER, Robert[2] & 1/wf _?_ ; ca 1652?; Lynn
DRIVER, Robert/Richard & 2/wf Sarah SALMON; 6 Jan 1663/4; Lynn
DRIVER, Salmon/Solomon (1670-) & Sarah _?_ ; b 1694; Lynn
DRIVER, William (-1691) & Mary [GLOVER] (1666-), m/2 Daniel GRANT 1693; b 1681?; Salem
DROWN, Leonard (1647-1729) & 1/wf Elizabeth [ABBOTT] (-1706); b 1677; Portsmouth, NH/Boston
DROWN, Samuel (-1721, Eliot, ME) & Elizabeth MORRELL (-1740+); 3 Feb 1698; Boston
DRUMMOND, John & Lydia HALLET, wid; 27 Nov 1661; Boston
DRURY, Hugh (ca 1616-1689) & 1/wf Lydia [RICE] (1626-1675); b 1646; Boston
DRURY, Hugh (ca 1616-1689) & 2/wf Mary [FLETCHER] (-1680), w Edward; ?Oct 1676, in 1675, 1676, by 23 May 1676; Boston
DRURY, John (1646-1678) & Mary [WEARE]; b 1668; Boston
DRURY, Thomas (1668-1723) & Rachel RICE (1664-); 15 Dec 1687; Sudbury
DRUCE, John (1641-1675) & Mary [WINCHESTER] (1648-), m/2 Erzoman/Rosemund DRUE/DREW? 1677; ca 1668; Newton/Roxbury
DRUCE, John & Elizabeth BISHOP; 23 May 1700; Roxbury
DRUSE, Richard & Jane _?_ ; b 1660; Boston
DRUCE, Vincent[1] & _?_ ; b 1641; Hingham
DRUSE, Vincent (-1683) & Elizabeth _?_ (not Mehitable); b 1668; Cambridge
DRY, Moses & Ann _?_ ; b 1695; Boston
DUDGEON, Patrick & Elizabeth _?_ ; b 1700; Boston
DUDLEY, Biley (1647-1728), Exeter, NH, & Elizabeth GILMAN (1663-), m/2 Samuel THING; 25 Oct 1682, no issue; Salisbury/Exeter, NH
DUDLEY, Caleb (1673-1730) & Elizabeth BUCK (1676-1738), Wethersfield, CT; 23 Jun 1700; Guilford, CT/Wethersfield, CT
DUDLEY, Francis & Sarah WHEELER (1640-1713); 26 Oct 1665; Concord
DUDLEY, Hugh & Mary [COPLEY?/COPSEY?]; 1656, 30 Oct 1656; Springfield
DUDLEY, James (1663-1720), Exeter, NH & Elizabeth [LEAVITT], m/2 Robert BRISCO, m/3 Rev. John ODLIN; ca 1685/92?, no issue; Salisbury/Exeter, NH
DUDLEY, John (-1690) & [Martha FRENCH] (1654-); ca 1673, b 1678; Guilford, CT
DUDLEY, John & Hannah POULTER (-1707); 19 May 169-, 9 May 1697, 16 May; Concord/Medford
DUDLEY, Joseph (1647-1720) & Rebecca [TYNG] (1651-1722); b 1668?, b 1670, 1669?; Roxbury/Boston
DUDLEY, Joseph (1645-1712) & Ann/?Anna ROBINSON; 16 Oct 1670, 6 Oct 1670; Guilford, CT
DUDLEY, Joseph & Abigail GOBLE (1669-); 25 Feb 1690/1; Concord
DUDLEY, Joseph (1674-1744) & Sarah PRATT (1680-); 10 Dec 1697; Saybrook
DUDLEY, Paul (1650-1681) & Mary LEVERETT (1656-1699), m/2 Penn TOWNSEND; ?15 Dec 1675, ca 1676; Cambridge/Boston
DUDLEY, Samuel (?1610, 1608-1683) & 1/wf Mary [WINTHROP] (1612-12 Apr 1643); ca 1632; Boston/?Cambridge
DUDLEY, Samuel (?1610-1683), Exeter, NH, & 2/wf Mary [BILEY] (1615-); aft 12 Apr 1643; Cambridge
DUDLEY, Samuel (?1610-1683), Exeter, NH, & 3/wf Elizabeth [?LEGAT] (1628?-); b 1652; Cambridge/?Salisbury/Exeter, NH
DUDLEY, Samuel (-1732), Exeter, NH, & Elizabeth THING (1664-); ca 1697; Salisbury
DUDLEY, Samuel (1672-1713) & Elizabeth [HILL] (1679-), m/2 Jared SPENCER; b 30 Sep 1702, b 1701?, ca 1698?; Saybrook, CT
DUDLEY, Stephen, Exeter, NH, & 1/wf Sarah GILMAN (1667-1713); 24 Dec 1684; Salisbury
DUDLEY, Thomas (1576-1653) & 1/wf Dorothy YORKE (1582-1643); Hardingstone, in Eng, 25 Apr 1603; Roxbury/Cambridge
DUDLEY, Thomas (-1653) & Catharine (DIGHTON) HAGBURNE/HACKBURNE? (1618-1671), w Samuel, m/3 Rev. John ALLIN 1653; 14 Apr 1644, ?4 Apr; Roxbury
DUDLEY, Thomas (-1713) & 1/wf Mary _?_ ; b 1697, no issue; Salisbury
DUDLEY, William (-1684) & Jane LUTMAN (-1674); ?Oksley, Eng, 24 Aug 1636, 4 Aug, ?21 Aug; Guilford, CT/Saybrook, CT
DUDLEY, William (1639-1701) & Mary ROE, m/2 Richard DART; 4 Nov 1661; Saybrook, CT

DUDLEY, William (1665-1717) & Mary HILL (ca 1676-); 18 Apr 1695; Saybrook, CT
DUDSON, Francis & Martha _?_; b 1675; Boston
DUDSON, Joseph & Abigail [BUTTON], m/2 Barnabas LOTHROP 1698 (called "sister" by Henry BARTHOLOMEW); b 1669; Boston
DUGGELL, Alexander & Abigail _?_; b 1701; Lynn
DUGGALL, Alister & Hannah _?_; b 1660; Lynn
DULEY, Philip & Grace [ROBERTS], m/2 Timothy MOSES; ca 1682, 1683?; Dover, NH
DUMBLETON, John (-1702) & Mercy _?_ (-1704); b 1650; Springfield
DUMBLETON, John (1650-1675) & Lydia LEONARD (-1683), m/2 Joseph BEDORTHA 1678; 18 Mar 1674, 18 Mar 1674/5; Springfield
DUMBLETON, Nathan/Nathaniel (1664-1737) & Hannah ALLEN (ca 1675-ca 1745); 29 Dec 1696; Springfield/Northampton/Deerfield
DUMMER, Jeremiah & Ann ATWATER; m cont 3 Sep 1672; Boston
DUMMER, Richard (?1599±-) & 1/wf Jane/Mary? [MASON]; in Eng, b 1635; Newbury
DUMMER, Richard (-1679, ae 88) & 2/wf Frances [BURR] (1612-1682), w Jonathan; ca 1643; Newbury
DUMER, Richard (1650-1689) & Elizabeth APLETON; 2 Nov 1673; Rowley
DUMMER, Shubael (1636, 1635-1692) & Lydia [ALCOCK]/?Mary RICHWORTH; 1656; Salisbury/York, ME
DUMMER, Stephen (?1609-1670) (returned to Eng) & Alice [ARCHER] (-1661); b 1628, b 1622; Ipswich
DUMMER, Thomas (returned to Eng) & _?_; b 1619; Salisbury
DUNBAR, James (1664-1690) & Jane [HARRIS], m/2 Pelatiah SMITH 1691?; b 1689; Bridgewater
DUNBAR, John (1657-) & 1/wf ?Martha/Mattithia ALDRIDGE; 4 Jul 1679; Hingham/Mendon
DUNBAR, John (-1733) & Anne/?Anna _?_, ?Malden, ?m Thomas DUNBAR; b 1689; Salem/Fairfield, CT
DUNBAR, John (-1733) & Abigail (NORTON) BEERS, w Joseph; aft 24 Mar 1696/7, b 1 Nov 1698; Fairfield, CT
DUNBAR, John (-1733) & 2/wf Elizabeth BECKER; 24 Jul 1700; New Haven
DUNBAR, Joseph (1662-) & Christian [GARNET] (1668-); b 1692; Hingham
DUNBAR, Joshua (1670-1736) & Hannah HATCH (1673-1743); 21 Sep 1699; Hingham
DUNBAR, Peter (1668-1719) & Sarah THAXTER (1668-); 25 Mar 1691; Hingham/Bridgewater
DUNBAR, Robert & Rose _?_; b 1657; Hingham
DUNCAN, Alexander (-1713) & Elizabeth TURNEER; 6 Jul 1698; Boston
DUNKIN, John & Joanna JEFTS, m/2 Benjamin DUTTON 1690; 23 Feb 1674/5; Billerica
DUNCAN, Nathaniel (-1668) & Elizabeth JOMDAINE; St. Mary Arches, Exeter, Eng, Jan 1616; Dorchester/Boston
DUNCAN, Peter (1630-1716) & Mary [EPPES] (1629-1692); b 1655; Boston/Gloucester
DUNKIN, Peter (1665-) & Jemima _?_; b 1688; Hingham
DUNKIN, Samuel (-1693) & Mary _?_; b 1647?, b 1651; Boston
DUNKIN, Samuel (?1647-) & Deliverance [?CURTIS]; b 1669(70?); Roxbury
DUNCAN, _?_ & Mercy ALLEN (1656-); RI
DUNCKLEY, Elnathan (-1670) & Silence BOWERS, m/2 Nicholas ROCKETT 1675; 14 Dec 1656; Dedham
DUNKLEE, Nathaniel (1669-, Dedham) & Mary (FRENCH) SHARP (1670-), w Robert; 23 Mar 1693, 1695/6?; Watertown/Woburn
DUNGAN, Thomas (?1634-1688) & Elizabeth [WEAVER] (?1647-1697); ca 1663; Newport, RI/Cold Spring, PA
DUNGAN, William (-1636, in Eng) & Frances [LATHAM] (1609-1670), m/2 Jeremiah CLARKE ?1637, m/3 William VAUGHAN; in Eng, ca 1627, 27 Aug 1629, St. Martin's in-the-Fields, London; Newport
DUNHAM, Benaiah/Benajah/Benjamin (-1686) & Elizabeth TILSON; 25 Oct 1660; Eastham/Plymouth/Piscataway, NJ
DUNHAM, Daniel (1639-1681?, 1677) & Mehitable/Hannah [HAYWARD?] (1643?-); b 1670; Plymouth/Dorchester/Bridgewater
DUNHAM, Daniel (?1675-) & Elizabeth _?_; b 1696; RI

DUNHAM, Eleazer (1659-) & Bathsheba [WHEATON/WISTON] (1660-), dau John; b 1682, b 1683; Plymouth/Scituate

DUNHAM, Gershom & Mary ? /CLARK?; b 1694; Martha's Vineyard

DONHAM, Isaac P.? (-1723) & Mary PIERCE, w Jacob; 1695; ?Rye, NY

DUNHAM, John (-1669) & 1/wf Susan KENNEY; in Eng or Holland, ca 1615, by 1614?, 17 Oct 1619?; Plymouth/Martha's Vineyard

DUNHAM, John (-1669, ae ca 80) & 2/wf Abigail [BARLOW]; Leydon, 22 Oct 1622; Leyden/Plymouth

DUNHAM, John (-1692, Eastham/Plymouth) & 2/wf? Mary? ? (in 1641?), Boston; ca 1642 (see John DOWNHAM); Plymouth/Barnstable

DUNHAM, John & ? ; b 1645; Woburn

DUNHAM, John (1649-1697, Barnstable) & Mary SMITH (-1697+); 1 Mar 1679/80, Barnstable?; Barnstable/Plymouth

DUNHAM, Jonathan & 1/wf Mary DELANO/DELANOY; 29 Nov 1655; Plymouth

DUNHAM, Jonathan (-1717), Barnstable & 2/wf Mary COBB (1637-); 15 Oct 1657; Plymouth/Edgartown/Middleboro

DUNHAM alias SINGLETARY, Jonathan & ?

DUNHAM/DENHAM, Jonathan & Mary [BLOOMFIELD] (-1705), Hartford?; b 1667; Plymouth/Hartford/New Haven/Woodbridge, NJ

DUNHAM, Jonathan (1661-) & 1/wf ? ; ca 1681; ?Falmouth

DUNHAM, Jonathan (1658-1745?) & 2/wf Esther (NORTON) [HUXFORD] (ca 1662-), w Samuel; ca 1691; Martha's Vineyard

DUNHAM, Joseph (-1703) & 1/wf Mercy MORTON (-1666, [1666/7]); 18 Nov 1657; Plymouth

DUNHAM, Joseph (-1703) & 2/wf Hester/Esther WORMALL (1648-1715+), Rowley; 20 Aug 1669; Plymouth

DUNHAM, Micajah & Elizabeth ? ; b 1701; Plymouth

DUNHAM, Nathaniel & Mary ? ; b 1689; Wrentham

DUNHAM, Nathaniel (not same as Wrentham Nathaniel) & Mary TILSON (-1714), Plympton; 21 Jan 1691; Plymouth

DUNHAM, Samuel (-1712) & 1/wf Martha (BEAL) FOLLOWAY/FALLOWELL (-1690), w William; 29 Jun 1649; Plymouth

DUNHAM, Samuel & 2/wf Mrs. Mary [WATSON]?, wid; ?19 May 1659

DUNHAM, Samuel & Elizabeth [MARTIN]?; 1680?

DUNHAM, Samuel, Jr. (1651-1768) & Mary HARLOW (1659-1743); 30 Jun 1680; Plymouth

DUNHAM, Samuel (-1712) & 2/wf Sarah WATSON (-1706), wid; 15 Jan 1693/4; Plymouth

DUNHAM, Thomas (-bef 15 May 1677) & [Martha KNOTT?], dau George, m Thomas TOBY; 1646?, b 2 May 1648?, aft 1 May 1648 (see Thomas DENHAM); Plymouth/Hartford

DUNHAM/DINHAM/DURRAM?, Thomas (?1647/8-1688) & Sarah [?BUMPHIS]; b 1668; New Haven/Rye, NY/Bedford, NY/White Plains, NY

DUNK, Thomas[1] (-9 Aug 1683) & 1/wf Mary (PRICE) (PITTSFIELD) [NORTH], w Philip of Englan, w Thomas; b 1670, by 1668; Guilford/Saybrook/Lyme, CT

DUNK, Thomas[1] (-1683) & 2/wf Elizabeth STEDMAN (-1 Oct 1678); 10 Jul 1677; Saybrook, CT

DUNK, Thomas[1] (-1683) & 3/wf Lydia (BUCKLAND) BROWN [LORD], w John, w William, m/4 Abraham POST aft 1683; aft 1 Oct 1678; Saybrook, CT

DUNK, Thomas[2] (1678-) & Hannah [BULL] (1679/81-1711); b 1702; Saybrook, CT

DUNKLIN, Nathan & Hannah WYER (1665?-); 15 Dec 1686; Charlestown

DUNN, Nathaniel (1671-1735) & Elizabeth [LAWTON] (1674-1741); b 1698; New Shoreham, RI

DUNN, Nicholas & Elizabeth [ROBERTS], m/2 Thomas ALLEN ca 1700; ca 1682/86; Oyster River, NH

DUNN, Richard[1] (-1690+) & ? [BOWDITCH]; b 1670; Newport

DUNN, Richard[2] & Hannah ? (1675-1734); b 1692; Newport

DUNN, Thomas & Margaret ? (-1659); Weymouth

DUNNELL/DWINELL?, Michael & Mary ? ; b 1668/9; Topsfield

DUNWILL, Michael[2] (1670-1761) & 1/wf Hannah/Elizabeth CAVE; 5 Feb 1692/3; Salem/Topsfield

DUNNELL, Thomas & Mary ? ; b 1687; Malden

DUNNELL, Thomas & Rebecca ? ; b 1695; Malden

DUNNELL, ? & Sarah [DOWSE] (1657-); b 13 Dec 1680; ?Boston

DUNNING, Andrew & ? [GOODENOW?]; b 2 Mar 1653/4

DUNNING, Benjamin & Mary _?_; b 1679(80?); Boston/_?_, LI
DUNNING, Benjamin & Mary [SEELEY]; ca 1700, b 1707; Stratford, CT
DUNNING/DUNHAM?/DENHAM?, Hicks & Sarah JOY; 7 Dec 1669; Hingham
DUNNING, Jonathan & _?_; b 1666; Killingworth, CT
DUNNING, Theophilus & Ellen _?_; b 1642; Salem
DUNSTER, Henry (1609-1659) & 1/wf Elizabeth (HARRIS) GLOVER (-1643), w Jesse; 22 Jun 1641, ?21 Jun, ca 1 Jul; Cambridge
DUNSTER, Henry (1609-1659) & 2/wf Elizabeth [ATKINSON?] (?1630-1690); 1644?; Cambridge
DUNSTER, Jonathan (1653-1725) & 1/wf Abigail ELYOTT/ELIOT (-1682); 5 Dec 1678; Cambridge
DUNSTER, Jonathan (1653-1725) & 2/wf Deborah WADE (1667-bef 25 Nov 1719); 5 Apr 1692; Charlestown/Cambridge
DUNTLIN, Nathaniel, Woburn & Mary SHARP, Billerica; 23 Mar 1693/4; Billerica/Woburn
DUNTON, John & Ruth _?_; b 1686; Reading
DUNTON, Nathaniel (1656-) & 1/wf Sarah _?_; b 1688; Reading/Needham/Sudbury?
DUNTON, Robert & _?_; Salem/Lynn/Reading
DUNTON, Samuel (-1685) & Anna/Hannah [FELCH] (-1689); b 1647; Reading
DUNTON, Samuel (1647-1683) & Sarah KENDALL, m/2 Thomas PATTEN 1686, m/3 Thomas RICHARDSON; 17 Jun 1673; Reading
DUNTON, Samuel (1674-1705) & Anna DAVIS, m/2 Benjamin FARLEY 1707, Cambridge/Billerica; 23 Feb 1697/8; Cambridge/Reading
DUPERY, Moses & Lydia _?_; b 1696; Watertown
DURANT, Edward (1661-) & Ann/Hannah? [HALL?] (1661-); b 1692; Boston
DURANT, George (-1687, 1691?) & Elizabeth [BLAKE], wid; in Eng, ca 1653?; Middletown, CT
DURANT, John & Susanna/Susan? DUTTON (1654-), m/2 Justinian HOLDEN 1693; 16 Nov 1670, 1669?; Billerica
DURANT, John & Margaret _?_ (gr dau Miles CLAY), Braintree, Eng; 14 Jan 1679; Wethersfield, CT
DURANT, John & Elizabeth JAQUITH; 10 Aug 1695; Billerica
DURANT, John & Elizabeth BRYAN (1680-); NY m lic 10 Nov 1698, b 27 Feb 1698/9; Stratford, CT/Derby, CT
DURE, Thomas & Anne _?_; b 1652; Boston
DEWER, Sampson & Sarah _?_; b 1674; Boston
DEWER, Davis & Jannet NEAL; 29 Jul 1697; Boston
DURRELL, Moses & Sarah SAMPSON (1668-), Scarborough; 23 Dec 1686; Scarborough, ME
DURRELL/DUDLEY?, Philip & _?_; Arundel
DURFEE, Benjamin (1674-1755±) & Prudence [EARLE] (1681-1733); b 1699?; Portsmouth, RI/Newport
DURFEE, Richard (-1700) & Ann [ALMY] (1667-), m/2 Benjamin JEFFERSON; ca 1685?; Portsmouth, RI
DURFEY, Robert (1665-1718) & Mary [SANFORD] (1664-1748), m/2 Jeremiah THOMAS; ca 1687?, b 1690; Freetown, MA
DURFEE, Thomas (1643-1712) & 1/wf _?_; b 1605?; Portsmouth, RI
DURFEY, Thomas (1643-1712) & 2/wf Deliverance (HALL) TRIPP (-1721), w Abiel; betw 1684 & 1689?; Portsmouth, RI
DURFEY, Thomas (-1729) & [Ann FREEBORN] (1669-1729-); b 1691; Portsmouth, RI
DURFEE, William (-1727) & 1/wf Ann _?_; b 14 Jan 1697; Tiverton, RI
DURGIN/DURGEN, James & Susanna [DAVIS], w David; aft 27 Aug 1696, 1697?, by 16 Jan 1699/1700; Durham, NH
DURGIN, William (1643-1703) & 1/wf _?_
DURGIN, William (1643-1703) & 2/wf Katherine (MATTHEWS) FOOTMAN, w Thomas; 25 Jun 1672; Durham, NH
DURHAM, Humphrey (1638-) & _?_; ?; Portland, ME/etc.
DURHAM, Samuel & Elizabeth REED; 6 Jul 1691; Boston
DURRAM/DENHAM?, Thomas & Sarah BUMPUS (1631-); last of Mar 1659; Marshfield
DURGEE/DURKEE, John (1665-) & 1/wf Elizabeth [PARSONS] (1669-1711); b 1689; Ipswich
DIRGEY, Thomas & 1/wf Elizabeth FORD/LORD?; 5 Mar 1700; Ipswich

DIRKYE, William (1634, 1632?-1712) & Martha CROSE/CROSS, dau Robert; 20 Dec 1664; Ipswich
DUSTIN, Josiah (-1672, 1671?) & Lydia _?_; b 1645; Reading
DUSTIN, Thomas (1610, 1606?-) & Elizabeth [WHEELER]? (-1690), m/2 Matthias BUTTON 1663; Dover, NH/Kittery, ME/Portsmouth, NH
DUSTIN, Thomas (-1703) & Hannah EMERSON (1657-); 3 Dec 1677; Haverhill
DUTCH, Benjamin (1665-1695) & Elizabeth BAKER, m/2 John APPLETON 1700;· 30 Jun 1690; Ipswich
DUTCH, Hezekiah (1647-) & Martha _?_, m/2 William JEWELL; ca 1670/80; ?Ipswich
DUTCH, John (1646-1685) & Elizabeth [ROPER] (-1692); b 1673, b 1671(2?); Ipswich
DUTCH, Osman (-1684) & 1/wf Margaret HAYWELL (1592-1628)
DUTCH, Osman (-1684) & 2/wf Grace PRATT (-1694); 20 Mar 1628/9; Gloucester
DUTCH, Robert (1623±, 1621?-1686) & Mary [KIMBALL] (?1625, ?1629-1686); ca 1644, b 1646; Gloucester
DUTCH, Robert (1647-) & Hannah LOVELL, m/2 Joseph AYRES 1710 int; - Dec 1677, ?26 Dec; Ipswich/Bristol, RI
DUTCH, Samuel (1650-1712) & Abigail GIDDING (-1713); 12 Feb 1673, 1673/4; Ipswich
DUTCH, Samuel (-1695±, 1693/4) & Susanna [MORE] (1650-), m/2 Richard HUTTON 1694?, m/3 John KNOWLTON 1714; b 1677, 1675?; Salem
DUTTON, Benjamin (1669-) & 1/wf Joanna (JEFFTS) DUNKIN/DUNCAN (-1690), w John; 1 Jul 1690; Billerica
DUTTON, Benjamin & Susanna (SHED)? [HOOPER], w William; aft 8 Aug 1692, b 1694; Billerica
DUTTON, James (1665-) & Mary ROBBINS; 9 Dec 1690; Groton
DUTTON, John (1656-1735) & 1/wf Sarah SHED; 20 Sep 1681; Billerica
DUTTON, Joseph (1661-) & 1/wf Rebecca (MERRIAM) FITCH, w Samuel; 19 Aug 1685; Reading
DUTTON, Joseph (1661-), Reading & 2/wf Mary (CUTLER) SMITH, Charlestown, w Matthew SMITH; 7 Dec 1693, ?27 Dec; Charlestown/Lyme, CT/E. Haddam
DUTTON, Thomas[1] (1621-) & 1/wf Susanna/Susan _?_ (1626-1684); b 1648; Reading/Woburn/Billerica
DUTTON, Thomas & 1/wf Rebecca (BRABROOK) DRAPER, Concord, w Adam; 1 Jan 1678/9, 31 Dec 1678; Billerica/Concord
DUTTON, Thomas[1] (1621-) & 2/wf Ruth (?MARSHALL) HOOPER, w William?; 10 Nov 1684; Billerica/Reading
DUTY, William & Elizabeth HIDEN/HIDDEN; 1 May 1684; Rowley
DWELLY, ?John & ?1/wf Mary [GLASS]; b 2 Sep 1690; Scituate
DWELLY, John (1660-1718) & ?2/wf Rachel BUCK; 4 Jan 1692/3; Scituate
DWELLEY, Richard[1] (-1692) & Dinah _?_; b 1660; Hingham/Scituate
DWELLY, Richard (-1708) & 1/wf Eame/Amy GLASS, Duxbury; 4 Apr 1682; Scituate
DWELLEY, Richard (-1708) & 2/wf Elizabeth [SIMMONS]; b 17 Jun 1689; Scituate
DWIGHT, John (-1661) & 1/wf Hannah [CLOSE?] (-1656); in Eng, b 1625; Watertown/Dedham
DWIGHT, John (-1661) & 2/wf Elizabeth (THAXTER) RIPLEY (-1660), w Thomas, w William; 20 Jan 1657/8; Dedham
DWIGHT, John (1675-1751) & Elizabeth HARDING (1678-1758); 3 Dec 1696; Dedham
DWIGHT, John (1675-) & Elizabeth _?_; ca 1696/7; Medfield/Sturbridge
DWIGHT, Josiah (1671-1748) & Mary PARTRIDGE (1677/8-), Hatfield; 4 Dec 1695; Hatfield/Woodstock, CT
DWIGHT, Nathaniel (1666-1711) & Mehitable PARTRIDGE (1675-1756, ae 82), Hatfield; 9 Dec 1693, 29 Dec 1693; Hadley
DWIGHT, Seth (1673-1732?) & Abigail DAVIS (-1719); m int 8 Oct 1696; Boston
DWIGHT, Timothy (1629-1718) & 1/wf Sarah (?SIBLEY) PERMAN?/PENNAN (-1652); 11 Nov 1651; Dedham
DWIGHT, Timothy (1629-1718) & 2/wf Sarah POWELL (-1664); 3 May 1653; Dedham
DWIGHT, Timothy (1610-) & 1/wf Mary _?_ (-1669?, 1668?); ca 1652?; Medfield
DWIGHT, Timothy (1629-1718) & 3/wf Anna FLINT (1643-1685/6); 9 Jan 1664/5; Dedham
DWIGHT, Timothy (?1613, 1610-1677) & 2/wf Dorcas WATSON (-1707), ?m/2 John ADAMS 1677; 8 Jul 1669; Medfield
DWIGHT, Timothy (1654-1692) & Elizabeth [ALCOCK] (1659-1711), m/2 Joseph GALLOP 1694; ca 1676/80?; Dedham

DWIGHT, Timothy (1629-1718) & 4/wf Mary (POOLE) EDWIND/EDWARDS (-1688), w Matthew; 7 Jan 1686/7, 1685/6?; Dedham
DWIGHT, Timothy (1629-1718) & 5/wf Easter/Esther (HUNTING) FISHER (-1691), w Nathaniel; 31 Jul 1690; Dedham
DWIGHT, Timothy (1629-1718) & 6/wf Bethia MORSE (1651-1718); 1 Feb 1691/2; Dedham
DYE, William (1654-) & Sarah [HOWARDS] (1660-); 1681, b 1682; Little Compton, RI
DYER, Barrett (-1753) & 1/wf Hannah STEWART (?1672-1729); 29 Jun 1699; Boston
DYER, Benjamin & Hannah AVERY (1660-); 22 May 1677, 1676?; Dedham
DYER, Benjamin (1653-) & 1/wf Mary NANNY (1661-15 Mar 1690); b 1690, 10 Mar 1679/80; Boston
DYER, Benjamin (1653-) & 2/wf Hannah ODLIN; 10 Dec 1691; Boston
DYER, Charles (1650-1709) & 1/wf Mary [?LIPPET]; ca 1672/5?; Newport
DYER, Charles (1650-1709) & 2/wf Martha (BROWNELL) [WAIT] (1643-1744), w Jeremiah; aft 8 Mar 1690, 1690/1, no issue; Newport/Providence
DYER, Christopher (1640±, 1646±-1689) & 1/wf _?_ ; b 1663, 1664; Sheepscot, ME
DYER, Christopher (1640±, 1646±-1692) & 2/wf Ruth _?_ (1642-), m/2 John HATHAWAY 1692; b 1682, b 1679?; Braintree
DYER, Christopher & Hannah NASH; b 1699 (wrong); Weymouth
DYER/DEAR?, Edward & _?_ [MORGAN]; by 1693; Ipswich/etc.
DYER, Edward (1670-) & Mary [GREENE] (1677-); b 1701(2?); N. Kingston, RI
DYER, George (-1672) & ?Abigail/?Elizabeth _?_ ; b 1630, b 1625 (called bro. by Bernard CAPAN); Dorchester
DYER, George & Mary WISE; 5 Jul 1692; Marblehead
DIER, Giles (-1713) & Hannah _?_ ; b 1674; Boston
DYER, Henry (1647-1690) & Elizabeth [SANFORD] (1655-1718), m/2 _?_ /?Daniel REMINGTON, m/3 _?_ SIMPSON; RI/?Newport
DYER, Henry (-bef 25 Apr 1692) & Hannah RIDDAN (1662-), m/2 Augustus BULLARD 1693; ca 1680/2?; Portsmouth, NH
DYER, Henry & 1/wf Mary _?_ ; b 1697; Newport/Lebanon, CT/Boston
DYER, James (1669-) & 1/wf _?_ ; b 1697(8?); Tiverton, RI/Little Compton, RI/Middletown, RI
DYER, John (1643-1696) & 1/wf Mary [BICKNELL] (-1677/8, ae 28 y); b 1671(2?); Weymouth/Boston
DYER, John (1648-1733), from Sheepscot, ME, & 1/wf Sarah (DOWSE) [LARKIN] (1647-1683+) (see below); b 1678; Braintree
DYER, John (1643-1696) & 2/wf Elizabeth (DOUSE) [LARKIN], w Thomas (see above); b 1679; Boston
DEER, John & Abigail [BALL?]; b 1691; Dorchester
DYER, John (1671/2-) & Hannah MORTON; 6 Jun 1694; Boston
DYER, John (1648-1733) & 2/wf or 3/wf Anna/?Hannah ADAMS, m/1 Samuel HOLBROOK, Jr., m/2 Henry DYER; b 1696, b 1693; Weymouth
DYER, John (1671-) & _?_ ; b 1701; Plymouth
DYER, Joseph (1653-1704) & 1/wf Hannah FRARY (1660-1678, 1682?); 9 Feb, b 1676; Weymouth
DYER, Joseph (1653-1704) & 2/wf Hannah [BAXTER] (1661-1727), m/2 Joseph MORSE 1713; b 1682, b 1683; Weymouth
DYER, Mahershallalhashbaz (see Charles) (1643-bef 1670) & Martha PEARCE/BROWNELL? (1645-1744); Portsmouth, RI
DYER, Nathaniel (1667-1729) & Elizabeth PARROTT; 9 Aug 1688; Newport
DYER, Samuel (?1636, 1635-1678±) & Anne [HUTCHINSON] (1643-1717), m/2 Daniel VERNON 1679; b 1664; Boston/Newport/Kingston, RI
DYER, Samuel (1655, 1665?-) & 1/wf Lydia [WILLIAMS] (1671-); b 1689; Boston
DYER, Samuel (1655-) & 2/wf Mary (COTTA) SAMPSON (1668-), w Hugh; b 1695, b 1701; Boston/Bristol, RI
DYER, Thomas (1612-1676) & ?Agnes/?Mary/?Alice REED? (-1667); b 1641; Weymouth
DYER, Thomas (-1676) & Elizabeth (?ADAMS) (HARDING) FRARY (-1678), w Abraham, w John, m _?_ aft 1675; aft 1670, bef 1673; Medfield/Weymouth
DYER, William (-1672, in 93rd y) (did he have issue?) & _?_ ; ?in Eng, ?b 1610; Dorchester

DYER, William (?1587, ?1600-1676?, 1677±) & 1/wf Mary BARRETT (-1 Jun 1660); 27 Oct 1633 London, St. Martin-in-the-Field, London, b 1635; Boston/Newport/?Portsmouth, RI

DYER, William (-1676, 1689) & _?_; b 1646, b 1640?; Saco, ME/Sheepscot, ME

DYER, William (?1587-1676?, 1677±) & 2/wf Catharine _?_; aft 1 Jun 1660, bef 25 Jul 1670, ca 1662?; Boston/Newport/etc.

DYER, Major William (-1688?) & Mary [WALKER] (-1688+); ca 1660/8?; Newport/NY/PA/DE/ ?Boston/Lynn

DIER, Dr. William (ca 1653-1738, ae ca 85) & Mary TAYLOR (ca 1658-1738, ae ca 80); Dec 1686; Barnstable

DYER, William (?1663±-) & 1/wf Joanna [CHARD] (1667-); b 22 Mar 1693; Weymouth

DIKE/DIX?, Anthony & Tabitha _?_, m/2 Nathaniel PICKMAN; ca 1636?; Salem

DIKE, Anthony (-1679?) & Margaret _?_, m/2 John POLAND/POLIN 1680; b 1666; Salem

DIKE, Anthony & Sarah DAVISON; 26 Nov 1688; Topsfield/Ipswich

DYKE, Jonathan (1673-1750) & Bethiah BAKER (1677-1716, Newton); 8 Dec 1698; Salem/Bever- ly/Newton

DIKE, Richard & Rebecca DOLEVER/DOLLIVER; 7 Aug 1667; Gloucester

DYKE, _?_ & ?[Agnes TIBBETS], dau Walter, had Richard & Elizabeth, m/2 Edmund CLARK; b 1636; Ipswich/Gloucester

EAGER, Abraham[2] (?1667, ?1670-1734) & Lydia WOODS (1672-1739); 15 Nov 1692; ?Marlboro/?Worcester/Shrewsbury

AUGER/EAGER, William[1] (?1629-1690) & 1/wf Ruth HILL (1640-1680, ae 39); 7 Dec 1659; Malden, CT

EAGER, William[1] (-1690) & 2/wf Lydia (BARRETT) COLE (Hester is wrong), w Thomas w Arthur, m Reuben LUXFORD; 13 Apr 1680; Cambridge/Marlboro

EAGER, Zechariah[2]/Zachary? (1667-1742) & Elizabeth [NEWTON] (1672-1756); b 1694; Marlboro/Framingham

EAGER, Zerubbabel[2] (1672-1747) & Hannah KERLEY (1675-1745+), dau Henry; 23 Mar 1698; Marlboro

EAMES, Anthony & Margery [PIERCE?/PRISSE?]; b 1616; Charlestown/Hingham

EAMES, Anthony (ca 1656-1729, 1739?) & Mercy SAWYER (1668-1729); 2 Dec 1686; Marshfield

EAMES, Anthony (1664-1739) & Elizabeth _?_ (-1711); b 1700, prob b 1695; Marshfield

EAMES, David & Mehitable _?_; b 1691; Dedham

EAMES, Gershom (-1676) & Hannah [BRIGHAM/JOHNSON?] (1650-1719), m/2 William WARD 1679; b 1671; Cambridge

EMES, Henry & Elizabeth [?ANDREWS]; b 1674; Boston

EMMS/AMES?, Jacob & Mary VAUGHAN; 4 Jun 1700; Boston

EAMS, John (1642-) & 1/wf Mary [ADAMS] (1652-1681); b 1676, ca 1671?; Watertown/Framing- ham/Sherborn

EAMES, John (1642-1733) & 2/wf Elizabeth EAMES (1659-1727); 11 May 1682; Sherborn

EAMES, Jonathan (-1724, in 69th y) & Hannah TRUANT; 11 Jan 1682; Marshfield

EAMES, Joseph & Mary EVERETT; 20 May 1697; Woburn

EAMES, Justus & Mehitable CHILLINGWORTH; 2 May 1661; Marshfield

EAMES, Mark (-1693) & Elizabeth [ANDREWS?] (-1693); ?20 May, 26 May 1648; Hingham/ Charlestown/Marshfield

EAMES, Nathaniel (1668-) & Anna/Anne [PATTEN] (1674-); b 1694; Cambridge

EAMES, Robert (-1712) & Elizabeth _?_ (-1710); b 1653; Charlestown/Woburn

EAMES, Samuel (1664-1747) & 1/wf Mary DEATH, w John?; 6 Jan 1689/90; Sherborn/Woburn

EAMES, Samuel & 2/wf Patience TWITCHELL; 21 Apr 1698; Sherborn

EAMES, Thomas (?1618-1680/1) (ae 34 In 1652) & 1/wf Margaret _?_; b 1641; Dedham/Cam- bridge

EAMES, Thomas & 2/wf Mary (BLANFORD) [PADDLEFORD/PADDLEFOOT?], w Jonathan; ca 1661; Dedham/Sudbury/Cambridge

EAME, William, LI/?Boston & Mary BALSTON; 12 Jul 1693; Boston

EARLE, Caleb & Mary _?_, m/2 Joseph HICKS 1693+, by 1698; ?Warwick, RI

EARLE, John (1639-) & 1/wf Mary WEBB (-1676); 24 Mar 1663, 1662/3; Northampton

EARLL, John & 2/wf Mary RAYNOR; Nov 1678; Southampton, LI

EARLE, John (1664-) & Mary _?_; b 1687; Boston

EARLL, John (-1728) & Mary [WILCOX] (-1735); b 1687; Dartmouth/Tiverton, RI

EARLE, John, Boston & Mary LAWRENCE (1671-), m/2 Michael FLAGG 1704; 5 Apr 1689; Watertown/Boston

EARLE, John (-1759) & Mary WAIT (-1759+); 27 Feb 1700, 1700/1; Portsmouth, RI/Tiverton, RI

EARLE, Ralph[1] (1606-1678) & Joan SAVAGE (-1699+); in Eng, 29 Jun 1631; Portsmouth, RI

EARLE, Ralph (1632-1716) & Dorcas [SPRAGUE]; ca 1658, b 26 Oct 1659; Plymouth/Taunton/Dartmouth

EARLE, Ralph (1660-1757) & Mary (CARR) [HICKS], w John; b 1690; Dartmouth/Freetown/Portsmouth, RI/Lancaster, MA

EARLE, Ralph (-1718) & Dorcas [DILLINGHAM] (1662-1742); b 1693; Dartmouth

EARLE, Robert & Hannah [RUST]; b 1664; Boston

EARLE, Robert (1673-) & Sarah CANNON; m int 2 Jul 1696; Boston

EARL, Roger (1673-) & Lydia TRAVISE (-1722, ae 47); 25 Oct 1694; Boston

EARL, Samuel & 1/wf Lydia FLOOD (-1696); 20 Apr 1694; Boston

EARLE, Samuel & 2/wf Mary CONDAGE/CANDAGE; 13 Dec 1698; Boston

EARLE, Thomas (-1727) & Mary [TABER] (-1759); b Nov 1693; Dartmouth/Portsmouth, RI/Swansea/Warwick, RI

EARLE, William[1] (1634-1715) & 1/wf Mary [WALKER]; ca 1654?; Portsmouth, RI/Dartmouth, MA

EARL/?HEARL, William (1634-1715) & 2/wf Prudence _?_; b 1680; Portsmouth, RI

EARL, William & Elizabeth _?_; b 1695; Wenham

EARLE, William & Elizabeth _?_; Freetown/?Dartmouth/Springfield/NJ

EARLE, William (1672-) & Hepzibah BUTTS; 26 Dec 1695; Little Compton, RI/Tiverton, RI

EARLY, George (-1671) & Abigail FOOT; 15 Oct 1670; Salem

EARTHY, John & 2/wf? Mary [SALOS/GARDNER?/ATTY?]; b 1687, b 1674?; Boston

EASDELL/?ESDELL, James & Rebecca _?_; Plymouth

EAST, David (?1647-1685) & Abigail (PHILLIPS) WOODBURY, w Jonathan, m/3 Thomas WALTER 1687; aft 1677; Boston

EAST, Francis & Mary _?_; b 1640; Boston

EAST, Samuel (1640-) & Mary/[Mercy] [WOODWARD]; b 1673; Boston

EAST, William (-1681) (called "brother" by John LANE of Milford 1669) & 1/wf _?_; b 1643?; Milford, CT

EAST, William (-1681, 1661 (wrong), 1781) & 2/wf Mary (BALDWIN) PLUM (-1708), w Robert; 16 Mar 1675/6; Milford, CT

EASTCOURT, Richard & Alice _?_; b 1700; Ipswich

ESTABROOK, Benjmain (1671-1697) & Abigail WILLARD (1665-1746), m/2 Rev. Samuel TREAT 1700; 29 Nov 1694; Boston

ESTABROOKS, John (1669, 1668?-1728) & Mehitable _?_; b 1697; Swansea/Warren, RI

ESTERBROOK, Joseph (?1640-1711), Concord & Mary MASON (1640-); 20 May 1668; Watertown

ESTABROOK, Joseph (1669-) & 1/wf Millicent WOODDIS/WOODHOUSE; 31 Dec 1689; Concord/Lexington

ESTABROOK, Joseph (1669-1733) & 2/wf Hannah (LEAVITT) LORING (1663-), w Joseph; 25 Aug 1693; Hingham/Lexington

EASTERBROOK, Thomas (-1713, ae 64?) & Sarah [WOODCOCK]; b 1668; Rehoboth/Swansea/Warren, RI

ESTABROOK, Thomas (-1721) & Sarah TEMPLE (-1726); 11 May 1683; Concord/Swansea

ESTABROOK, Thomas (1670-1724) & Mary [LUTHER] (1668-); b 1693(4?), no marriage, had Thomas; Swansea

EASMAN, Benjamin (1653-) & 1/wf Anne (PITTS) JOY, w Samuel; 5 Apr 1678; Salisbury

EASTMAN, Benjamin (1653-) & 2/wf Naomi FLANDERS (1656-); 4 Apr 1699; Salisbury

EASMAN, John (1640-1720) & 1/wf Hannah HELIE/HEALEY (1644-); 27 Oct 1665; Salisbury

EASMAN, John (1640-1720) & 2/wf Mary BOYNTON (1648-); 5 Nov 1670; Salisbury
EASTMAN, John & Huldah KINGSBURY; m int 31 Jul 1697; Salisbury
EASTMAN, Joseph (?1650, 1651-1692) & Mary TILTON (1644-), m/2 James GUERNSEY 1693; b 1683; Hadley/Suffield, CT
EASTMAN, Nathaniel (1643-1709) & Elizabeth HUDSON (-1716); 30 Apr 167[2]; Salisbury
EASTMAN, Philip (1644-) & 1/wf [?Susanna PUSEY]; b 1673; Salisbury
EASTMAN, Philip (1644-) & 2/wf Mary (BARNARD) MASSE/MORSE (1645-), w Anthony; 22 Aug 1678; Haverhill/Newbury/Woodstock, CT
EASTMAN, Philip (1644-) & 3/wf Margaret [DAVIS]; aft 1695, b 1701?; Woodstock, CT
EASMAN, Robert & _?_ ; b 1687; Kittery, ME
EASTMAN, Roger (1610-1694) & Sarah [SMITH?] (1621-1698); b 1640(1?); Salisbury
EASMAN, Samuel (1657-) & Elizabeth SCRIBNER/SCREVEN (1658-); 4 Nov 1686; Salisbury/ Kingston
EASTMAN, Thomas (1646-1688) & Deborah CORLIS (1655-), m/2 Thomas KINGSBURY 1691; 20 Jan 1679; Haverhill
EASTMAN, Timothy (1648-1733) & Lydia MARKHAM; 16 May 1682; Hadley/Suffield, CT
EASTMEAD, Arthur & Mary HIX; 4 Aug 1693; Boston
EASTON, James (1662-1697) & Miriam [ALLEN] (1661-1731); b 1682; Newport
EASTON, John (1621, 1624-1705) & 1/wf Mehitable GAUNT/GAUT?/GAULT? (-1673); 4 Jan 1660/1; Newport
EASTON, John (1646-1716, 1718?) & Elizabeth _?_ (-1710, Hartford); b 1670; Hartford
EASTON, John (1624-1705) & 2/wf Alice _?_ (1621-1689); aft 11 Nov 1673; Newport
EASTON, John (1647-1739) & Dorcas PERRY (1661-); 23 Aug 1679; Newport/?Saybrook
EASTON, Joseph (?1602-1688) & _?_ ; b 1645; Cambridge/Hartford
EASTON, Joseph (1646-1711) & Hannah [ENSIGN]; b 1669; Hartford
EASTON, Joseph (1669-1735) & Sarah [SPENCER] (ca 1671-); b 1694; Hartford
EASTON, Joshua (1662-1690) & Rose _?_ (1665-1690); Newport/Jamaica, West Indies
EASTON, Nicholas[1] (1593, 1592?-1675) & 1/wf _?_ ; in Eng, b 1621; Charlestown/Ipswich/etc.
EASTON, Nicholas[1] (-1675, ae 82) & 2/wf Christian (BARKER) (COOPER?/COPPER?) [BEECHER] (-1665), w Thomas, w Thomas; ca 1638; Charlestown/Ipswich/Newbury
EASTON, Nicholas (-1677) & Elizabeth [BARKER?] (-1676); 30 Nov 1666; Newport
EASTON, Nicholas[1] (-1675) & 3/wf Ann CLAYTON (-1708), m/2 Henry BULL 1677; 2 Mar 1671; Newport
EASTON, Nicholas (1668-) & Mary [HOLMES] (1664-1741), dau Jonathan; b 1694; Scituate, RI
EASTON, Peter (1622-1693/4) & Ann COGGESHALL (1626-1689); 15 Nov 1643; Newport/Ports-mouth, RI
EASTON, Peter (1659-1690) & Rebecca [THURSTON] (1662-1737), m/2 Weston CLARK 1691; b 1684; Newport
EASTON, Thomas & Jerusha _?_ (doubtful); b 1686; Portsmouth, RI
EATON/EDSON?, Benjamin (-1712, Plympton) & Sarah HOSKINS/HODGKINS?; 4 Dec 1660; Plymouth
EATON, Benjamin (ca 1664-) & 1/wf Mary COOMBS (-1728); 18 Dec 1689; Plymouth
EATON, Benoni (?1639-1690) & Rebecca _?_, m/2 John HASTINGS 1691; b 1667; Cambridge
EATON, Daniel (1639-1708+) & Mary [INGALLS?] (-1706+), m _?_ KING; 21 Dec 1664; Reading
EATON, Daniel (-1704) & Rebecca (EMERY) [SADLER], Weymouth, w Robert, w Thomas; aft 9 Mar 1680/1; Little Compton, RI
EATON, Ephraim & Mary TRUE; 5 Feb 1688; Salisbury
EATON, Francis (-1633) & 1/wf Sarah _?_ (-1621); in Eng?, b 1620; Plymouth
EATON, Francis (-1633) & 2/wf _?_ (-died soon); ca 1621; Plymouth
EATON, Francis (-1633) & 3/wf Christian [PENN], m/2 Francis BILLINGTON 1634; ca 1623/5; Plymouth
EATON, Jabez (see HEATON) & Experience MEDE/MEADE; 4 Dec 1663; Dorchester
EATON, Job & Mary SIMONS; 10 Jan 1678/9, 25 Jun 1695, 10 Jan 1698; Haverhill
EATON, John & 1/wf _?_ ; in Eng, b 1618; Salisbury
EATON, John & 2/wf? Ann/Anna _?_ ; m lic 26 Dec 1621; Salisbury
EATON, John (-1658, Dedham) (called Edward HODSMAN "kinsman") & Abigail (BACHELOR) DAMON, w Henry; 5 Apr 1630; Staple, Eng/Dedham/Watertown

EATON, John (1619-) & Martha [ROWLANDSON]; b 1645; Salisbury
EATON, John (1635-1695) & Elizabeth [KENDELL] (1643-); 8 Mar 1658, 1658/9, 8 Jan 1658/9; Reading
EATON, John, Sr. (-1668) & Phebe DOW (-1673), w Thomas; 20 Nov 1661; Haverhill
EATON, John (1636?-1694) & Alice/Elle __?_; b 1665; Dedham
EATON, John (1645-1691) & Dorcas PEARSON (1650-) (dau John & Dorcas), m/2 Abraham BRYANT 1693; 26 Nov 1674; Reading/Charlestown
EATON, John (1646-1718) & Mary __?_; b 1685; Salisbury
EATON, John (1667-) & Hannah [PRATT] (1670?-), Medfield; 23 Mar 1690/1; Reading/Medfield
EATON, John (1671-1694) & Ann/Anna? [WHITING] (1672-), m/2 John LEWIS 1700, m/3 James HERRING/HENRY?; b 1694; Dedham
EATON, John (1664-) & Mary SINGLETERY; 25 Jun 1700; Haverhill
EATON, Jonas (1618-1673/4?) & Grace __?_, m/2 Henry SILSBEE 1680; b 1643(4?); Watertown/Reading
EATON, Jonas & Hannah MASON; 25 Sep 1677; Reading
EATON, Jonathan (1655-1743) & 1/wf Elizabeth BURNAP (-1688); 15 Aug 1683; Reading
EATON, Jonathan (1655-1743) & 2/wf Mary COWDRY?/BROWNE (-1727+); 2 Apr 1691; Reading
EATON, Jonathan & 1/wf Sarah SANDERS; 17 Mar 1695/6, 1695; Haverhill/Salisbury
EATON, Jonathan & 2/wf Ruth PAGE; 20 Jan 1699/1700, 1699; Haverhill
EATON, Joseph & Hannah __?_/Sarah GROVER/?Mary PEARSON; b 1682, 1680?, b 1681; Beverly
EATON, Joseph & Mary FRENCH; 14 Dec 1683; Salisbury
EATON, Joshua (1653-1717) & 1/wf Rebecca KINDELL (1657-1690); 25 Apr 1678; Reading
EATON, Joshua (1653-1717) & 2/wf Ruth (PIERCE) [KIRTLAND] (-1748), w Philip, m/3 Jonathan DUNSTER 1719, m/4 Amos MARRETT 1722, m/5 Peter HAY 1742; 18 Dec 1690; Reading/Charlestown
EATON, Nathaniel (see HEATON) & Elizabeth __?_, m/2 Joseph PELL d 1650, m/3 John MINOR/[MAYNARD] by 1658; b 1636; Boston
EATON, Nathaniel (1609-1640+, 1660+) & ?Mary __?_; b 1643; Charlestown/Cambridge/VA
EATON, Samuel (-1684) & 1/wf Elizabeth __?_ (-1652+); b 20 Mar 1647; Plymouth
EATON, Samuel (?1630-1655) & Mabel (HARLAKENDEN) HAINES (-1655), w John; 17 Nov 1654; New Haven
EATON, Samuel (-1684) & 2/wf Martha BILLINGTON, ?m/2 Robert CROSSMAN 1687; 10 Jan 1661, 10 Jan 1660, 10 Jan 1660/1; Plymouth
EATON, Samuel (-1724) & Elizabeth FULLER (1666?-); 24 May 1694; Middleborough
EATON, Samuel & Ruth [FAIRFIELD]; Weymouth
EATON, Theophilus (1591-1658) & 1/wf Grace HILLER; in Eng, London?, 3 Dec 1622, St. Mary Woolchurch, London
EATON, Theophilus (1591-1658, 1657?, New Haven) & 2/wf Ann (LLOYD) YALE (-1659), w Thomas
EATON, Thomas & 1/wf Martha KENT (-1657); 14 Aug 1656; Haverhill
EATON, Thomas (-1698) & Unity/Eunice? SINGLETARY; 6 Jan 1658, Dec 1678, 2 Jan 1659, 6 Jan 1659; Andover/Haverhill
EATON, Thomas & Hannah HUBBARD (1647?-); 14 Nov 1679; Salisbury
EATON, Thomas & Hannah WEBSTER; 5 May 1684; Haverhill
EATTON, Thomas (-1688) & Jerusha (MAYHEW) WING, w Joseph; 12 Dec 1684; Yarmouth/Portsmouth, RI/etc.
EATON, Thomas & Lydia GAY (1679-); 5 Oct 1697; Dedham
EATON, Timothy (1674-1763) & Ruth [CHAPMAN]; b 1701?; Salisbury
EATON, William (-1673) & Martha [JENKINS]; in Eng, 28 Jan 1627/8; Watertown
EATON, William, Lynn & Mary BURNET/BURNAP, Reading; 12 Jan 1692, 11 Jan 1692/3; Lynn/Tolland, CT
EATON, William & Mary [SWAIN], dau Jeremiah; 29 Apr 1695; Reading
EBERAL, Job & Mary PREBBLE; 26 Apr 1700; Boston
ECKLES/ECCLES, Richard (1614-) & Mary [PLATTS] (-23 Aug 1665) (kinswomen of Richard JACKSON); b 1644(5?); Cambridge
ECLES, Richard & 2/wf Susanna (?CHAMERLAIN) CARTER/CARLEY?/KERLEY?, w Joseph CARTER; 4 Jun 1677; Charlestown
EDDENDEN, Edmund & 1/wf Elizabeth WELLER; Cranbrook, 12 Jul 1625

EDDENDEN, Edmund & 2/wf Elizabeth WHITMAN/WIGHTMAN/WHITEMAN, m/2 Samuel SKIFT; 4 Jul 1631/2; Scituate/Boston/Charlestown

EDDY, Caleb (-1713, ae 69) & Elizabeth BULLOCK; 6 Dec 1671, 6 Dec 1670, 6 Nov 1670; Swansea/Warren, RI/Rehoboth

EDDY, Caleb & Sarah BUTCHER; m int 5 Jun 1696, m 5 Jun; Boston

EDDY, Jabez & Mary [RICKARD] (1677-); b 1700; Plympton

EDDY, John (1597-1684) & 1/wf Amy [DOGGETT] (1597-); in Eng, ca 1620, aft 22 May 1619, bef 1622; Plymouth/Watertown

EDDY, John (1637-) & Hepzibah [DAGGETT]; ca 1658; Martha's Vineyard

EDDY, John (ca 1640-1695) & 1/wf Susannah PADDUCK (-1670, 1671), Dartmouth; 12 Nov 1665, last of Nov 1665; Taunton

EDDY, John (1597-1684) & 2/wf Joanna (?BATES) [MEADE?] (1603-1683), w Gabriel; aft 1666; Watertown

EDDY, John (ca 1640-1695) & 2/wf Deliverance OWEN (1654/5-1717), Braintree; 1 May 1672; Taunton

EDDY, John (1666-1726) & 1/wf Mary [HATCH] (1658-aft 8 Jul 1700); b 1690; Swansea

EDDY, John (?1666-1694) & Sarah WOODWARD (1674-), m/2 Isaiah WHITNEY 1695?, 1696?; 6 Jul 1693; Cambridge

EDDY, Obadiah (1645-1727) & Bennett [ELLIS?] (1649-1702+); b 1669(70?); Plymouth

EDDY, Samuel[1] (1608-1688) & Elizabeth [SAVORY?] (-1689?, 1682, ae 81?); b 1637; Plymouth/Middleboro

EDDY, Samuel (1640-1711), Cambridge & Sarah MEADE; 31 Nov 1664 [sic], 30 Nov; Dorchester

EDDY, Samuel (1668-1746) & Elizabeth WOODWARD (1664-1753); 7 Dec 1693; Watertown

EDDY/ADY, William & Hannah SMITH; 19 Jul 1697; Bristol, RI

EDDY, Zachariah[2] (1639-1718) & 1/wf Alice PADDOCK (1640-1692); 7 May 1663; Plymouth/Middleboro

EDDY, Zachariah, Jr. & Mercy BAKER (-aft Oct 1703); 13 Feb 1683; Swansea/Providence

EDDY, Zachariah[2] (1639-1718) & 2/wf Abigail [SMITH], w Dermit/Jeremiah; aft 1692, aft 1707; Swansea/Middleboro

EDES, John (1651-) & Mary TUFTS (1655-); 15 Oct 1674; Charlestown

EADES, John & Catherine __?_; b 1680; Boston

EDES, John (-1721) & Grace LAWRENCE (1680-1758); 13 Apr 1698; Charlestown

EDES, Nicholas (-1685) & Mary ?FURMAN, w John; Newtown, LI

EDES, Philip & Ann/Anna? HOMANS; 12 Dec 1691; Charlestown

EDEES, William & Elizabeth __?_; b 1687; Boston

EDGARTON, John (1662-) & Mary REYNOLDS (1664-1728), m/2 Samuel LOTHROP 1697; 20 Mar 1689/90; Norwich, CT

EDGERTON, Peter & Clemence __?_ ; b 1671; Boston

EDGERTON, Richard & Mary SYLVESTER; 8 Apr 1653, 7 Apr 1653; Saybrook, CT/Norwich, CT

EDGERTON, Richard (1665-) & Elizabeth SCUDDER; 4 Jan 1691; Norwich, CT

EDGECOMB, John & 1/wf Sarah STALLION; 9 Feb 1673, 1673/4; New London, CT

EDGECOMB, John & 2/wf? Susanna [BOADEN]; by 1680; Saco, ME

EDGECOMB, John (1675-) & Hannah HEMPSTEAD (1680-); 28 Feb 1699/1700, 1699; New London, CT

EDGECOMB, John & 2/wf Elizabeth (LARRABEE) HEMPSTEAD (1653-), w Joshua; b 1701?, b 1 Apr 1704, 28 Jan 1699; New London, CT

EDGECOMB, Michael & Joan CROCKER, ?m/2 John GASKIN?; Sep 1687

EDGECOMB, Nicholas (-1681) & Wilmot [RANDELL] (-1685+); ca 1642; Scarborough, ME/Saco, ME

EDGECOMB, Robert (-1730, ae 73) & Rachel [GIBBINS] (1660-1724); b 30 May 1682; Marblehead

EDGERLY, John (1670-1750) & Elizabeth [?RAWLINGS]; 1700, 1697±; Oyster River, NH

EDGERLY, Samuel (1668-) & Elizabeth [TUTTLE], m/2 John AMBLER; 1695; Oyster River, NH

EDGERLY, Thomas & Rebecca (AULT) HALLOWELL, w Henry; 28 Sep 1665; Oyster River, NH

EDGERLY, Thomas (1666-1719) & 1/wf Jane WHEDON/WHIDDON; 3 Dec 1691; Oyster River, NH/Exeter, NH

EDLIN/EDLING, David Ludecas (-1660) & Elizabeth __?_ (-1663); b 1659; Dover, NH

EDMESTER, James & Anne MAKEPEACE; 19 Apr 1689; Taunton/Freetown

EDMINSTER, John (?1638, ?1633-) & 1/wf Hannah __?__ (?1642-); b 1663; Charlestown
EDMINSTER, John & 2/wf Sarah TOMPSON (?1639-), ?w George; 17 Jun 1679; Charlestown
EDMONDS, Andrew (-1695) & Mary HEARNDEN; 14 Oct 1675; Providence/Swansea
EDMANDS, Daniel (?1630-1688, ae 59 near 60) & Mary [SPRAGUE] (1634-1717); b 1664; Charlestown
EDMUNDS, John/Jonathan & 1/wf Sarah HUDSON (-1682); 16 Dec 1662; Lynn
EDMANDS, John (-1677) & Hannah (MILLER) DADY, w Nathaniel, m/3 Aaron LUDKIN 1684; 4 Oct 1667; Charlestown
EDMONDS, John (calls Joshua BLANCHARD "brother-in-law") & Mary (_?_) GEORG, wid; 17 Sep 1683; Marblehead
EDMANDS, John (1671-) & 1/wf Sarah BLANY (1675-1713); 1 Nov 1693; Charlestown
EDMUNDS, John (-1696) & Mary __?__ ; Portsmouth, NH
EDMANDS, Jonathan (1669-1732) & Ruth FROTHINGHAM (1670-); 26 Nov 1691; Charlestown
EDMUNDS, Joseph (1643-) & 1/wf Susanna __?__ ; b 1670; Lynn
EDMUNDS, Joseph & 2/wf __?__ ; b 1673; Lynn
EDMUNDS, Joseph & 3/wf Elizabeth BURGESS; 27 Jan 1685; Lynn
EDMANDS, Joshua (1624-1683) & 1/wf Mary [WILLARD] (ca 1631-); ca 1647?; Concord/ Charlestown
EDMANDS, Joshua (1624-1683) & 2/wf Elizabeth __?__ (1643-) (ae 39 in 1682), m/2 Richard MARTIN; b 1664; Charlestown
EDMUNDS, Robert (1628?-) & 1/wf __?__ ; ?Kennebec/etc.
EDMUNDS, Robert (1628?-) & 2/wf Rebecca PASMORE, w William; 26 Mar 1695; Boston
EDMONDS, Samuel & Elizabeth MERRIAM; 11 Aug 1675; Lynn
EDMUNDS, Thomas (-1696) & __?__ ; Portsmouth, NH
EDMANDS, Walter (-1667) & Dorothy __?__ (-1671); in Eng, b 1624; Concord/Charlestown
EDMUNDS, William (1610/11, 1616?-1693) & 1/wf Mary __?__ (-1657); ca 1638; Lynn
EDMUNDS, William & 2/wf Ann MARTINE, wid; 1 Sep 1657; Boston
EDMUNDS, __?__ & Mary WISWALL (see EMMONS) (Benjamin & Obadiah)
EDSALL, Samuel & 1/wf Jannetie WESSELS; 29 May 1655; New York/Newtown, LI
EDSALL, Samuel & 2/wf Naomi [MOORE] (-1677), w Samuel; Newtown, LI
EDSALL, Samuel & 3/wf Ruth [WOODHULL]; ca 1678; Newtown, LI
EDSALL, Samuel & 4/wf Jannetie/Jannetye (STRYKER) [BERRIEN], w Cornelius J.; ca 1689; Newtown, LI
EDZALL, Thomas (-1676) & 1/wf Elizabeth FERMAN/FARMAN?; 16 Sep 1652; Boston
EDSELL, Thomas (-1676) & 2/wf Jane __?__ (-1663); b 1662; Boston
EDSON, Joseph (-1711) & 1/wf Experience [HOLBROOK/?FIELD] (1661-1685); 1678; Bridgewater
EDSON, Joseph (-1711) & 2/wf Mary TURNER; 2 Nov 1686; Bridgewater
EDSON, Josiah (-1734) & ?Abigail/Elizabeth [DEAN?/HAYWORTH?] (-1734); ca 1675?, no issue; Bridgewater
EDSON, Samuel (1612/13-1692) (Thomas SNELL his nephew) & Susanna [ORCUTT] (1618-1700); in Eng, ca 1638; Salem/Bridgewater
EDSON, Samuel (1645-1719) & Susanna [BYRAM] (ca 1648-1742); b 1679(80?); Bridgewater
EDWARDS, Alexandar (-1690) & Sarah (BALDWIN) SEARLE (1621-), w John; 28 Apr 1642; Springfield/Northampton
EDWARDS, Benjamin (1652-1724) & Thankful SHELDON (1662-); 23 Feb 1680, 20 Feb 1680/1; Northampton/Deerfield
EDWARDS, Benjamin (-1723) & Martha GAMES/GAINES; 14 Jul 1681; Wenham
EDWARDS, Benjamin (-1723) & Mary __?__ (-1723); b 1695; Wenham
EDWARDS, Daniel & Elizabeth MORE; 27 Feb 1700; Windham, CT
EDWARDS, Daniel & Martha __?__ ; b 1701; Boston
EDWARDS, David & Mary [SWEET]; b 1676; Boston
EDWARDS, Ephraim (-1716) & Sarah __?__ ; b 1699; East Hampton, LI
EDWARDS, George (-1688, adm 2 Apr 1688) & Ruth [WEARE?], m/2 Timothy CUNNINGHAM 1688?, b 1680; Boston
EDWARDS, Griffin & Elizabeth [MYLES?], dau Rev. John & Ann; b 1681; Boston
EDWARDS, Henry & Ursula HEWSON/HUSON; 7 Nov 1667; Charlestown/Boston
EDWARDS, John & 1/wf __?__ ; b 1635?, b 1637?, b 1621?; Watertown

EDWARDS, John & Elizabeth [PALGRAVE] (-1707); b 8/4/1651
EDWARDS, John & Ann _?_ (-bef 1660?), ?m/2 _?_ HUNT, m/3 Isaac COUSINS ?1657; b 1656; ?Boston/Sherborn
EDWARDS, John (-1664) & 2/wf Dorothy (MOULTON) FINCH?, w Abraham, m/3 Richard TOWSLEY 1677; b 1638, b 20 Feb 1664/5; Glastenbury, CT/Wethersfield, CT
EDWARDS, John & Mary SAMS; 24 Nov 1658; Ipswich
EDWARDS, John & 1/wf Mary SOLART/SOLARRE?/SOLARE?; 20 May 1666, 21 May 1666; Beverly
EDWARDS, John² (-1693) & Mary [STANBOROUGH]; 1666, b 1668, b 1670; East Hampton, LI
EDWARDS, John (-1690) & Elizabeth [WALKER] (-1694); b 1676, b 1687; Charlestown
EDWARDS, John (1639-1700) & Elizabeth _?_, Salem
EDWARDS, John, Sr. & 2/wf Sarah [WOODIN], m/2 Joseph DOTY of Rochester, MA; b 1687, b 1696, aft 1671; Wenham
EDWARDS, John & Martha _?_ ; b 1689; Boston
EDWARDS, John (1662-1744) & 1/wf [Mary HANFORD] (1663-); b 1695, 2 children bpt ca 1690; Fairfield, CT/Stratford, CT
EDWARDS, John & Hannah _?_ ; b 1691; Boston
EDWARDS, John & Amy WARREN; 2 Mar 1693; Boston
EDWARDS, John (1639-1723) & Margaret [LOVELL]? (-1731), dau Thomas; ca 11 Apr 1693; Ipswich, b 1694
EDWARDS, John & Sibella NEWMAN; 29 Oct 1694; Boston
EDWARDS, John & Anna DODGE (1674-); m int 1 Apr 1698; Wenham
EDWARDS, John (1678-1728) & Anna _?_ ; b 1701?, b 1707; East Hampton, LI
EDWARDS, Joseph (1648-10 Dec 1681) & Sarah _?_ (-1687); 12 Nov 1670; Wethersfield, CT/Glastenbury, CT
EDWARDS, Joseph & 1/wf Elizabeth ELMORE (?1659-1673); 2 Jan 1672; Northampton
EDWARDS, Joseph (1647-1690) & [Hannah] ATKINSON (1653-1735), m/2 Benoni STEBBINS 1691?, m/3 Thomas FRENCH 1709; 27 Nov 1674, 17 Nov 1674; Northampton/Hadley
EDWARDS, Josiah (1670±-1713) & Mary CHURCHILL (1675-); Apr 1699; East Hampton, LI
EDWARDS, Matthew (-1683, ae 52) (called "cousin" by John FAIRFIELD 1646) & Mary POOLL, m/2 Timothy DWIGHT 1687; 2 Dec 1657; Reading
EDWARDS, Nathaniel (1657-) & 1/wf Hepzibah JANES (1665-9 Nov 1690); ?17 May 1687; Northampton
EDWARDS, Nathaniel (1657-1731) & 2/wf Elizabeth _?_ ; aft 9 Nov 1690, b 1694; Northampton
EDWARDS, Oads (-1651) & _?_ ; Isles of Shoals
EDWARDS, Rice & 1/wf Eleanor _?_ (deposed 1680, ae 40); b 1680; Boston/Salem
EDWARDS, Rice & 2/wf Joan _?_ (1620-adm 1647, Boston); b 1647, b 26 Dec 1643
EDWARDS, Richard (d in Eng) & Anne _?_, m/2 James COLE 1625; in Eng, b 1620
EDWARDS, Richard (1647-1718, ae 71) & 1/wf Elizabeth TUTHILL?/TUTTLE (1645-); 19 Nov 1667, div ca 1692, 1691; New Haven/Hartford
EDWARDS, Richard (-1718) & 2/wf Mary TALCOTT (1661-1723); ca 1692; Hartford
EDWARDS, Robert (-1646) & Christian _?_ ; b 1640; Concord
EDWARDS, Roger & Sarah _?_ (-1668); Hampton, NH
EDWARDS, Samuel (1643-1713) & Sarah BOYKIN/BAYCON? (CORLIN wrong) (1646-1724?), dau Jarvis; 15 May 1675, May 1675; Northampton
EDWARDS, Stephen (-bef 1 Mar 1669) & Elizabeth [BEADLEY]?, m/2 Peter STAPLES; b 1669; Kittery, ME
EDWARDS, Thomas & Elizabeth _?_ ; [b 1630]; Salem
EDWARDS, Thomas (1621?, 1623?-) & _?_ (wid LOVENOW/?LOVELAND); b 1652; Wethersfield, CT
EDWARDS, Thomas & Sarah [STONE] (1645-); ca 1663, b 1663(4?); Boston
EDWARDS, Thomas & Mary BIRCH; 10 Mar 1670/1; Dorchester
EDWARDS, Thomas² (-1698) & Abigail _?_ ; ca 1670/2?; East Hampton, LI
EDWARDS, Thomas (-1712), Boston & Mary HOW, Milford; 25 Nov 1679; Stratford, CT
EDWARDS, Thomas & 1/wf Sarah _?_ (-1716); Beverly/Wenham
EDWARDS, Thomas (1668-1736, 1737?) & Mary _?_ ; ca 1690/5?, b 1697; East Hampton, LI
EDWARDS, Timothy (1669-1758) & Esther STODDARD (1672-1770, 1771); 6 Nov 1694; Northampton/E. Windsor, CT/Windsor, CT

EDWARDS, William & _?_ (see below); b 27 Dec 1643; Lynn/Windsor, CT
EDWARDS, William (1605-1685?) & Ann _?_ ; ca 1630?; Southampton, LI/East Hampton, LI
EDWARDS, William (1618-) & Agnes (?) SPENCER, w William; 1645, b 11 Dec 1645; Hartford/Windsor, CT
EDWARDS, William & Mercy [NEWLAND?]; b 1694, prob bef 1685; Weymouth
EDWARDS, William³ & Alice [DAYTON]; b 1705, b 1701, b 1700; East Hampton, LI
EDWARDS, ?Matthew & ?Frances ?FAIRFIELD (-1645), m/2 Robert HAWES by 1641
EELLS/ELLES, John (returned to Eng) & _?_ [JOHNSON?]
EELLS, John (1670-1698) & Frances [OVIATT?] (1669-1738); b 1693; Milford, CT
EELLS, Samuel (1640-1709) & 1/wf Anna LEUTHAL (-1687); 1 Aug 1663, 5 Aug 1663, at Lynn; Milford, CT
EELLS, Samuel (1640-1709) & 2/wf Sarah (BATEMAN) NORTH (-1717), w Edward; 22 Aug 1689; Hingham
EELLS, Samuel (-1725) & 1/wf Esther [OVIATT?] (1665-1700); b 1698; Milford, CT
EELLS, Samuel (1666-1725) & Martha (WHITING) BRYAN (?1662-1741, 1743?), w Samuel; betw 6 Dec 1700 & 14 Jan 1700/1; Milford, CT
EGBEER/EGBEAR?, John & Elizabeth _?_ ; b 1690; Boston
EGGINGTON, Jeremiah & Elizabeth COTTON (1637-1656); 12 Oct 1655; Boston
EGLETON, John (?1611-1659) & Peaceable _?_ , m/2 Daniel SILLIMAN 1661; Fairfield, CT
EGLETON, _?_ & Joanna/Jane (?1600-1687), m/2 James BRETTON b 1655, m/3 Isaac COLE 1658/9; Woburn
EGLESFIELD/EGGLESFIELD, Emanuel (d in Eng) & Susanna GRAY (1593-); London, Eng?
EGLESTON, Bagot/Baggot (1587-1674) & 1/wf _?_ ; in Eng, ca 1616/18?; Dorchester/Windsor, CT
EGLESTON, Bagot (1587-1674) & 2/wf Mary [TALCOTT/AYLETT?] (?1610-1657); ca 1630/5, b 1638; Dorchester/Windsor, CT
EGGLESTON, Benjamin (1653-) & Hannah (OSBORN) SHADDOCK (1657-1713), w Elias; 6 Mar 1678; Windsor, CT
EDLINGTON/EGGLESTON?, Edward (-1696) & Phebe HOLMAN, m/2 Samuel BAKER 1699; 27 Jul 1693; Boston
EGGLESTON, Isaac (1669-1735±) & Mary STILES (1669-1764); 21 Mar 1694/5; Windsor, CT
EGGLESTON, James? (?1620-1679) & Hester [_?_] (-1720), m/2 James ENNO 1681, m/3 John WILLIAMS 1686?; b 1656; Windsor, CT
EGGLESTON, John & Esther/Hester MILLS; 1 Jun 1682; Windsor, CT
EGGLESTON, Joseph (1651-) & _?_ ; ?N. Stonington, CT
EGGLESTON, Nathaniel (1666-) & Hannah ASHLEY (1675-), Westfield; 13 Sep 1694; Windsor, CT/Westfield
EGGLESTON, Samuel (?1620-1691) & Sarah [DISBROW], Wethersfield; b 1663; Windsor, CT/Middletown, CT
EGGLESTON, Stephen (-1638, on ship) & Elizabeth BENNETT; in Eng, 30 Nov 1628; Fairfield, CT
EGGLESTON, Thomas (1661-1732) & Grace [HOSKINS?/HASKINS] (1666-1739); b 1687; Windsor, CT
EAGLESTON, William & Dorcas (WELCH) GRETIAN, w Anthony; 28 Sep 1699; Charlestown/Boston
EGLIN, William & Phoebe [WILLIAMS] (1643-); b 1667; Boston
ELA, Daniel (?1630-1710) & 1/wf Elizabeth _?_ (-7 Jul 1698); Haverhill/Boston
ELA, Daniel & 2/wf Eleanor _?_ ; aft 7 Jul 1698
ELA, Daniel & Elizabeth BASTAR; 29 Aug 1698 (illegally m); Haverhill
ELA, Israel (?1638-1700) & Abigail BOSWORTH (-1717); 11 Nov 1680; Haverhill
ELY?/ELA?, John & Mary _?_ ; b 1674; Boston
ELA, John & Jane _?_ ; b 1701; Boston
ELLA, _?_ & Dorothy SPALDING (1664-bef 1702)
ELATSON, Jonathan & 1/wf _?_ (-bur 6 Mar 1694/5); Boston
ELATSON, Jonathan & 2/wf ?Sarah/Elizabeth (PEMBERTON) (PURKIS) WESSENDANK, w Warner, w George; b 12 Feb 1695/[6]; Boston
ELBRIDGE, John & Abigail [LITTLEFIELD] (1662)
ELBRIDGE, Thomas (-1682) & Rebecca _?_ (-1684); b 1652; Pemaquid, ME

ELCOCK, Anthony (-1672) & __?__ ; b 1661; New Haven
ELCOCK, Thomas (1666-) & Martha [MUNSON] (1667-); b 1693; New Haven
ELDING, Read & Hannah PEMBERTON; 13 Feb 1695/6; Watertown/Boston
ELDER, Daniel (-1692) & Lydia HOMES (1635-1687); 1 Mar 1666/7, 12 Mar 1666/7; Dorchester
ELDER, John & Abigail [WHITMORE]; b 1701?; Cambridge
ELDERKIN, John (-1687, ae 71) & 1/wf Abigail KINGSLANE?; b 1641; Lynn
ELDERKIN, John (-1687), New London & 2/wf Elizabeth (DRAKE) GAYLORD (-1716, ae 95),
     w Wm.; 1 Mar 1660; Windsor, CT/Norwich
ELDERKIN, John (1664-) & 1/wf Abigail FOWLER; 8 Feb 1685; Norwich, CT/Milford, CT
ELDRED, David (-1726) & Mary [PHILLIPS?/ROUSE?] (-1750) (had gr-son Rouse NORTHRUP);
     b 1688; Kings Town, RI/Stonington, CT/North Kingstown, RI
ELDRED, Elisha (1653-1739) & __?__ ; b 1690; Eastham/Wellfleet
ELDRIDGE, Jehoshaphat (ca 1658-1732) & Elizabeth [COVELL?]; ca 1690?; Chatham
ELDRIDGE, John & Abigail __?__ ; ca 1680; Salisbury
ELDRED, John & Abigail [LITTLEFIELD]; b 1681; Wells, ME
ELDRED, John (1659-1724) & Margaret [HOLDEN] (1663-1740); ca 1683?; N. Kingstown, RI
ELDRIDGE, Joseph & Elizabeth __?__ ; b 1678; Boston
ELDRED, Joseph (-1735) & Elizabeth [JONES?]; ca 1685/90?; Chatham
ELDRIDGE, Joseph (-1735) & 2/wf Elizabeth (PHILLIPS) GROSSE, w Thomas, m Elias HEATH,
     m Francis BURROUGHS; m int 9 Oct 1695; Boston
ELDRED, Nicholas (1650-1702) & Elizabeth __?__ ; ca 1675/80?; Yarmouth/Chatham
ELDRED, Robert (-1683) & Elizabeth NICARSON/NICKERSON (-1706); last week of Oct 1649;
     Yarmouth
ELDRED, Samuel & Elizabeth __?__ ; b 1642; Cambridge/Stonington, CT/Kings Town, RI
ELDRED, Samuel (-1765/6) & Kerziah/Keziah TAYLER (1656-1734); 6 Feb 1680, prob 1680/1;
     Yarmouth
ELDRED, Samuel & Elizabeth [HEDGES] (-1711+); b 14 Sep 1694; Chatham
ELDRED, Samuel (1644-1720, 1721?) & Martha [KNOWLES] (1651?-1728); b 1695, b 1685?;
     Kings Town, RI
ELDRIDGE, Thomas & Mary [KEENE]?; b 1668; Boston
ELDRED, Thomas (1648-1726) & Susannah [COLE]; ca 1670/2?; Kings Town, RI
ELDRIDGE, Thomas & Ruhama __?__ ; b 1684; Boston
ELDRED, William (-1679) & Ann/Anne [LUMPKIN] (-1676); b 3 Mar 1645/6; Yarmouth
ELDRIDGE, William (-1749) & 1/wf __?__ ; ca 1696; Chatham
ELIOT, Andrew (-1704, ae 76) & 1/wf Grace WOODIN?/WOODIER (-1652, in Eng); East Coker,
     Eng, 23 Apr 1649; Beverly
ELIOT, Andrew (-1704, ae 76) & Mary VIVION; in Eng?, 2 Feb 1654; Beverly
ELIOTT, Andrew (1651-1688) & Mercy/Mary? SHATTUCK (1655-), m/2 Benjamin TRASK; 9 Dec
     1680; Beverly
ELIOTT, Andrew & Sarah __?__ ; b 1683; Boston
ELIOTT, Asaph (1651-1685) & 1/wf Elizabeth [DAVENPORT] (1652-1680/1); b 1679(80?);
     Boston
ELIOTT, Asaph (1651-1685) & 2/wf Hannah [PAINE]; b 1683; Boston
ELLIOTT, Daniel & Hannah [CLOYES] (?1665, ?1670-); b 1687; Framingham/Salem
ELIOTT, Edmund (1629-1683±) & Sarah [HADDON], m/2 Samuel YOUNGLOVE 1685?; b 1660;
     Salisbury
ELLIOTT, Francis (1615-1677) & Mary [SANDERS?/SAUNDERS] (1619-1697); b 1640;
     Braintree/Lexington
ELIOT, Francis[1]/John & Abigail/Anna NICHOLS? (1665-); 14 Jun 1686, 6? Jun; Salem
ELIOT, Francis & Abigail __?__ ; b 1690; Salem/Boxford
ELLIOT, Henry & Deborah (BELL) YORK, w James; 12 Mar 1679; Stonington
ELLIOTT, Humphrey & 2/wf? Elizabeth CUTTS, m/2 Thomas/?Robert WITHERICK; b 13 Jul
     1685; aft 1684, betw 1684 & 1686; Portsmouth, NH
ELYOTT, Jacob (1602-1657) & Margery/Margaret __?__ (-1661); b 1632; Boston
ELLIOTT, Jacob (1632-1693) & Mary (POWELL) WILCOX, w William; 9 Jan 1654/5; Boston
ELIOT, John (1604-1690, Roxbury) & Anne/Ann MOUNTFORD/MUNEFORD (1604-1684);
     ?Sep/Oct 1632, aft 16 Sep 1632; Roxbury
ELLETT, John & Margaret/Mary? __?__ (-1658); b 1634; Watertown/Stamford, CT

ELIOT, John[2] (1636-1668) & 1/wf Sarah [WILLET] (1643-1664); b 1662; Newton/Cambridge
ELYOTT, John[2] (1636-1668) & 2/wf Elizabeth GOOKIN (-1700), m/2 Edmund QUINCY 1680; 23 May 1666; Cambridge/Newton
ELLIOT, John (1660-) & Naomi [TUXBURY] (1667-); b 1686; Amesbury
ELIOT, John (1667-1719) & 1/wf Elizabeth (STOUGHTON) MACKMAN (1664-1702), w James; 31 Oct 1699, no issue; Windsor, CT
ELIOT, Joseph & Mercy _?_ ; b 1674; Boston
ELLIOT, Joseph (1638-1694) & 1/wf [Sarah BRENTON]; b 1676; New London, CT/Guilford, CT
ELIOT, Joseph (1638-1694) & 2/wf Mary [WYLLYS] (1656-1729, ae 73); ca 1684; ?Hartford/ Guilford, CT?
ELIOT, Joseph (1664-1700) & Silence [BAKER] (1666-); b 1689; Boston
ELIOT, Joseph & Sarah COLLINS; 29 Jul 1697; Boston
ELIOTT, Nathaniel & Mary CRATEY; 24 Aug 1699; Marblehead
ELLIOTT, Philip (1602-1657) & Elizabeth SYBTHORPE (1605, 1601-); m lic London, 20 Oct 1624; Roxbury/Dedham
ELIOT, Richard? & Mary DREW, w Thomas
ELLIOTT, Robert (1643-1724, 1720?) & 1/wf _?_ PEPPERELL?; ca 1663?; Strawbery Bank, NH/Portsmouth, NH/Gerish's Island/Scarborough, ME/Kittery, ME
ELLIOTT, Robert (1643, 1631-172-) & Margery (BATSON) (KENDALL) YOUNG, w Richard; b 1670?, b 29 May 1683, aft 1673; NH/Kittery, ME
ELLIOTT, Robert (1643-172-) & 3/wf Sarah FRYER (1656-); aft 7 Jun 1692, bef 10 May 1702; Kittery, ME
ELLIOTT, Thomas & Hannah GOULD (1641-); 10 Jun 1675; Charlestown
ELIOT, Thomas (-1700) & Jane [?BELL] (-1689, Taunton); b 1678/9?; Boston/Taunton/Rehoboth
ELIOT, Thomas & Hannah _?_ ; b 1680(1?); Boston
ELLET, William (-1660) & Sarah _?_ ; b 1660, b 1659; Salem
ELLIOTT, William & Mary (BROWN) PARKER (1657-), w Nathan; 10 Jun 1681; Beverly
ELATHORP, John (1643-1719) & Mary [?TODD] (-1724); b 1678; Newbury/Beverly/Manchester/ Rowley
ELITHORP, Nathaniel (1631-1709) & Mary BATT (-1710); 16 Dec 1657; Rowley/Ipswich
ELITHORP, Nathaniel & Hannah (DUMMER) BRADSTREET, w John; 3 Dec 1700; Rowley
ELETHORPE, Thomas & 1/wf ?Margaret _?_ (-1635)
ELITHORP, Thomas & 2/wf Abigail SUMMER, w Thomas, m/3 Thomas JONES 1657; b 1637; Rowley
ELKINS, Eleazer (-1694?), Exeter & Deborah BLAKE (1652-); 31 Dec 1673; Hampton, NH/Andover
ELKINS, Gershom (1641-1718) & Mary SLEEPER; 15 May 1667; Hampton, NH
ELKIN, Henry (-1668) & Mary _?_ (-1659); b 1638?, b 1641; Boston/Hampton, NH
ELKINS, Henry & Joanna EDGECOMB, m/2 William PRUNCHIN/PYNCHON?/PINCHEON 1693; by 1671
ELKINS, Henry/Nathaniel (-1678) & Esther/Hester [WALDRON] (1660-), m/2 Abraham LEE 1686, m/3 John JOSE 1691?, m/4 Joshua BAINES by 1695; by 1685; Dover, NH
ELKINS, Oliver (-1722) & Jane _?_ (-1716, ae 53); b 1687, by 1684; Salem
ELKINS, Robert & Patience (FERNALD) EVANS, w Ebenezer; 9 Nov 1686; Dover, NH
ELKINS, Samuel (1677-) & Mercy [TILTON] (1679-); b 1701?; Hampton, NH
ELKINS, Thomas (-1705) & Sarah [GUTCH] (1654-1732+); b 1674; Salem
ELLEN, Daniel & Mary [BADCOCK]; b 1667(8?); Dorchester
ELLEN, Nicholas (-1667) & 1/wf Sarah _?_ ; b 1647; Dorchester
ELLEN, Nicholas (-1667) & Mary (BALL/BULL) POND, w Robert, m/3 Daniel HENSHAW b 1671; 3 Jul 1663; Dorchester/Milton
ELLERY, Benjamin (1669-1746) & Abigail WILKINS; 30 Jul 1696; Gloucester/Bristol, RI
ELLAIRE, William (ca 1643-1696) & 1/wf Hannah VINSON (-1675); 8 Oct 1663; Gloucester
ELERY, William (ca 1643-1696) & 2/wf Mary COYT/COIT (1655-); 13 Jun 1676; Gloucester
ELENWOOD, Benjamin (1668-) & Mary _?_ ; b 1688; Beverly/Salem
ELLINGWOOD, John (1659-) & Elizabeth ROWLANDSON (1660-); 8 Jan 1684/5, 13 Jan 1684; Marblehead/Salisbury/Beverly
ELENWOOD, John & Sarah MORRELL; 30 Mar 1698; Beverly
ELENWOOD, Ralph & 1/wf _?_ ; b 1644; Salem

ELLENWOOD, Ralph (-1674) & 2/wf Ellen/?Eleanor LYN; 14 Mar 1655; Salem
ELLINWOOD, Ralph (1657-) & Martha ROWLANDSON (1665-); 19 Aug 1691; Beverly/Marble-
head/Salem
ELLINS, Anthony & 1/wf _?_ ; ca 1648?; Portsmouth, NH
ELLINS, Anthony (-1681) & 2/wf Abigail [DREW], w Samuel, m/3 John JACKSON; b 3 Jul 1669;
Portsmouth, NH
ELLINS, Lawrence & _?_ ; b 1631; Portsmouth, NH
ELLIS, Edward (-1695, ae 74) & Sarah BLOTT (ca 1628, 1631-1665+); 6 Oct 1652; Boston
ELLIS, Edward & Lydia _?_ ; b 1669(70?); Boston
ELLIS, Eleazer & Marie/Mary MEDCALFE/METCALFE; 26 Oct 1687; Medfield
ELLIS, Eleazer & Mehitable THURSTON; 27 May 1690; Dedham
ELLIS, Francis & Sarah _?_ ; b 1681(2?); Boston
ELLIS, Francis (-1708) & Sarah [WILLARD] (-living in 1712); b 1692; Salem
ELLIS, Freeman (see Matthias ELLIS) & Mercy [?NYE] (?1652-) (had child in 1705); b 1687;
Rochester
ELLIS, Henry & Joanna [WILLIS] (1651-); b 1670; Boston
ELLIS, James & _?_ ; b 1663; Wenham
ELLIS, James & Frances _?_ ; b 1665; Boston
ELLIS, James & Susanna [CHAPMAN]; b 1670; Boston/?Stonington, CT (see John & Richard
ELLIS)
ELLIS, John & 1/wf Susan/Susanna LUMBER (-1654); 10 Nov 1641; Dedham
ELLIS, John (-1677) & Elizabeth [FREEMAN] (1624-); ?bef 20 Aug 1644; Sandwich
ELLIS, John (-1697) & 2/wf Joan (_?_) CLAPP (-1706), w John; ?4 Jun 1655, ?16 Jun 1655, aft
24 Jul 1655, ?16 Jun 1656; Medfield
ELLICE, John & Mary HERRING; 1 Feb 1677/8; Medfield
ELLIS, John & Susanna [?CHAPMAN] (see James ELLIS, see Richard ELLIS); b 1678(9?); Boston
ELLIS, John, ?Muddy River & Sarah [BACON] (-1713, in 51st y); ca 1680/4; Boston/Brookline/
Muddy River
ELLIS, John (1656-) & Elizabeth FISHER (1662-); 10 Mar 1685/6; Medfield
ELLIS, John (-19 Oct 1712) & Martha _?_ ; b 1700?; Chatham
ELLIS, John (1646-1716) & 2/wf Mary HILL (1662-1729); 7 Apr 1698; Boston/Medfield/Medway
ELLIS, John & _?_ ; nr 1700; Dover, NH
ELLIS, John & Sarah HOLMES (1680-); 7 Nov 1700; Plymouth
ELLICE, Joseph & Ruth [MORSE], m/2 John BRACKETT 1675; b 1662; Dedham
ELLIS, Joseph (1666-) & Mary GRAVES; 25 Oct 1688; Dedham
ELLIS, Joseph & Lydia LOVELL; 23 Nov 1688; Medfield
ELLIS, Joseph & Dorothy SPALDING (1664-); 18 May 1690; Dedham
ELLIS, Joseph & Elizabeth [METCALF]; b 1697; Medfield
ELLIS, Matthias (1657-1748) (see Freeman ELLIS) & ?Mercy NYE/?Mary BURGESS (1656-); aft
1678/9, b 1679(80?); Sandwich/Yarmouth
ELLIS, Mordicai (1651-1710) & Sarah _?_ (-25 Oct 171-, 1717?); ca 1676?; Sandwich
ELLIS, Richard (-1694) & Elizabeth FRENCH (1629-); 19 Sep 1650; Dedham
ELLIS, ?Richard (see James ELLIS, see John ELLIS) & Susannah [CHAPMAN] (1649, 1648-); b
1668; Stratford, CT
ELLIS, Richard & Mary [LANE?] (1653-); b 1685; Boston
ELLIS, Robert & _?_ ; b 1671; Boston
ELLIS, Robert/Ruben & Elizabeth PEMBERTON (1678-); 4 Jun 1698, b 1698(9?); Boston
ELLIS, Roger (-1668) & Jane LISHAM, m/2 George BULLARD 1672; b 1648, b 1647?, lic 12 (9)
1644, 12 Nov 1644 lic; Yarmouth
ELLIS, Samuel & _?_ ; b 1690; very doubtful
ELLIS, Samuel, Medfield & Deborah LOVELL, Medfield; 20 Dec 1693; Medfield/Middlesex Co.
ELLIS, Thomas (-1696) & Mary WIGHT (-1693); 21 May 1657, 21 May 1659; Medfield
ELLIS, William & _?_ ; b 1661; Boston
ELLIS, William & Mary MITCHELL; 5 Jul, 5/5/1675; Middlesex Co.
ELLIS, William & Susanna _?_ ; b 1689; Boston
ELLIS, William & Lydia _?_ ; ca 1694?; ?Sandwich/Middleboro
ELLIS, _?_ & Esther NICHOLS (1650-), dau Adam; b 1682; ?Hartford
ELLIS, _?_ & Sarah _?_ ; b 1639; Lynn

ELLISON, John (-1685+, 1687+) & _?_; Hempstead, LI
ELLISON, ?John & [Preserved LYMAN] (1676-); ?Newark, NJ
ELLISON, Lawrence (-1665?) & _?_; b 1620?; Windsor, CT/Hempstead, LI
ELLISON, Richard (-1683) & Thomasine/Tomasine _?_; b 1646; Braintree/Hempstead, LI
ELLISON, Richard (1660-1732) & Alice/Elace/Elishaba? _?_; ca 1685?; Hempstead, LI/Monmouth Co., NJ
ELLISON, Richard & Elizabeth GRAVES; ca 1690?; Hempstead/Mansfield, NJ
ELLISON, Thomas (-1697) & Martha CHAMPION (?1642-); [ca 1650?], ca 1660?; Hempstead, LI
ELLISON, William (-1707) & Mary [SINGLETARY] (1663/4-); ca 1688?; Salisbury/Woodbridge, NJ
ELLISTON, George & Lydia [MORTON]; b 1671; Boston
ELLISTON, John & Lucy CORWIN (1670-), m/2 Thomas GWIN; m int 24 Sep 1696; Boston
ELASSON, Jonathan & 1/wf Priscilla _?_ (-1695); Boston
ELLISTON, Jonathan & 2/wf Elizabeth WESENDOCK; 27 Jun 1695; Boston
ELLSWORTH, Jeremiah (-1704) & 1/wf Mary SMITH (-May 1687), w Hugh; 2 Dec 1657; Rowley
ELLSWORTH, Jeremiah (-1704) & 2/wf Sarah JEWETT (1663-); 13 May 1689; Rowley
ELLSWORTH, Job & 1/wf Mary TRUMBULL (-1710); 19 Dec 1695; Windsor, CT
ELLSWORTH, John (1671-) & Esther WHITE (?1671-1766); 7 Dec 1696, 9 Dec 1696; Hatfield
ELLSWORTH, Jonathan (-1749) & Sarah GRANT (1675-1755); 26 Oct 1693; Windsor, CT
ELLSWORTH, Josiah/Josias? (?1629-1689) & Elizabeth HOLCOMB (ca 1634-1712); 16 Nov 1654; Windsor, CT
ELLSWORTH, Josiah/Josias? (1655-1706) & Martha GAYLORD (1660-1721); 30 Oct 1679; Windsor, CT
ELLSWORTH, Thomas (1665-) & Sarah [MILLS] (1670-); aft 24 Jul 1691, b 1696; Windsor, CT
ELMER, Edward (-1676) & Mary _?_, m/2 Thomas CATLIN; ca 1644; Hartford/Northampton
ELMER, Edward (1654-1725) & Rebecca _?_ (-1710); b 1684; Windsor, CT
ELMER, John (-1712?) & Rosamund GINNUARIE?/GENIVERE?; ca Oct 1669; Windsor, CT
ELMER, John (?1670-1722) & Mary [ADKINS]; ca 1695?; Windsor, CT
ELMER, Joseph (?1678-1758) & Jane ADKINS (1678-1766); 4 Apr 1700; Windsor, CT
ELMER, Samuel (1647-1691) & Elizabeth _?_ (1654-), m/2 Simeon/?Simon BOOTH 1693; b 1677; Hartford
ELMES, Jonathan (1663-), Scituate & Patience SPUR, Dorchester; 24 May 1693; Milton/Scituate
ELMES, Rodolphus (1620-1696/99?) & Catharine WHITCOMBE; 25 Dec 1644; Scituate
ELMES, Rodolphus (1668-1749) & Bethiah DODSON (-1746); 20 Feb 1695/6; Scituate/Middleborough
ELSEY/?ELSON, Nicholas & 1/wf _?_; Salem
ELSEY, Nicholas (-1690) & 2/wf Hannah (MITCHELL)? COE (1631-1702), w Robert; aft 1659, ca 1665, b 1668; New Haven
ELSON, Abraham (-1648) & Rebecca _?_, m/2 Jarvis MUDGE 1648, 1649; b 1644; Wethersfield, CT
ELSON, James (1643-) & Sarah HAYMAN (-1680, ae 38); 13 Oct 1668; Charlestown
ELSON, John (-1648?) & Margaret [HILLIARD], w Benjamin?, m/3 Thomas WRIGHT; no issue; Wethersfield, CT
ELSON, John (-1684) & Joanna/Joan WADDOCK (-1684+); b 1664, 3 Nov 1658; Wells, ME/Salem
ELSON, Samuel & Mary [POTTER] (1663-); b 1686; Salem
ELSON, William & 1/wf _?_; b 1643; Charlestown
ELSON, William & 2/wf Elizabeth _?_; Charlestown
ELSON, _?_ & Hannah REED (1670), Woburn; Cambridge
ELTHAN, William & _?_; b 1690; Woburn
ELTON, John & Anne (_?_) [HILLS], w Philip, m/3 Capt. HUDSON
ELTON, John (-1675) & Anne (WINES) [NICHOLS], w Francis, m/3 John TOOKER, m/4 John YOUNGS 1690; aft 1650; Stratford, CT/Southold, LI
ELTON, John (-1686/7?) & Jane [HALL] (1652/3-), m/2 Thomas STEVENS; ca 1672, b 1672; Middletown, CT
ELVES, John & Jane BROCK; 6 Oct 1698; Boston
ELVE, William (-1694) & Margaret _?_ (-1694); b 1650; Newton
ELWELL, Ebenezer (1671-) & Jean/Jane ELWELL (1671-); 2 Jan 1694/5; Gloucester
ELWELL, Eleazer & Em DA--/DENNING/DENNEN; 21 Jan 1696/7; Gloucester

ELWELL, Elias (1668-1737) & Dorcas LOW (1674-); 12 Nov 1690; Gloucester
ELWELL, Hezekiah & Elizabeth [ENDLE?/PHOENIX?/FENNIX?]; b 1693; Kittery, ME
ELWELL, Isaac (1642-1715) & Mehitable [MILLET] (1642-1699); b 1666; Gloucester
ELWELL, Isaac (1642-1715) & 2/wf Mary (PRINCE) ROWE (-1723, ae 65), w Hugh; ?aft 28 Sep 1699; Gloucester
ELWELL, Jacob (1657-1710) & Abigail VINSON/VINCENT; 5 Jul 1686; Gloucester
ELWELL, John (1640-1712) & Jane DURIN; 1 Oct 1667; Salem
ELWELL, John (1668-) & Mary [ROBINSON?] (1669-); b 1690; Gloucester
ELWELL, Joseph & Mary DUTCH (-1680?); 22 Jun 1669; Gloucester
ELWELL, Joseph (-1701) & Margaret __?__ ; Newport
ELWELL, Josiah (-1679?) & Mary COLLINS (1646-1725), m/2 John COOK 1680, 1679, m/3 James DAVIS 1697; 15 Jun 1666, 1665?; Gloucester
ELLWELL, Robert (-1683) & Jane/Joan __?__ (-1675); ?b 1636; Dorchester/Gloucester
ELWELL, Robert (-1683) & 2/wf Alice LEACH (-1691), w Robert; 29 May 1676; Gloucester
ELWELL, Robert & Sarah GARDNER/GARDENER; 12 Oct 1687; Gloucester/?Kittery, ME
ELWELL, Samuel (ca 1636-) & Hester/?Esther DUTCH (-1721, ae ca 82); 7 Jun 1658; Gloucester
ELWELL, Samuel (1660-1726) & Sarah [WHEADON] (1666-); b 1690; Branford, CT
ELWELL, Thomas & Sarah BASSETT; 23 Nov 1675; Gloucester/Salem Co., NJ
ELY, Joseph (1663-1755) & Mary [RILEY] (1665-1736); b 1686, 9 Jul 1685; Springfield
ELY, Nathaniel (1605, 1607/9-1675) & [Martha] __?__ (-1688, 1683?); in Eng?, b 1639; Cambridge/Hartford/Norwalk/Springfield
ELY, Richard (-1684) & 1/wf Joane?/Jane? [?PHIPPS] (-1660); Plymouth, Eng, b 1647; Lyme, CT
ELY, Richard (-1684) & 2/wf Elizabeth (FENWICK) [CULLICK] (-1683), w John; 1664; Boston/Saybrook
ELY, Richard (1657-) & Mary [MARVIN] (1666-), m/2 Daniel STARLING/STERLING 1699; ca 1685; Lyme, CT
ELY, Samuel (-1692) & Mary DAY (ca 1641-1721), m/2 Thomas STEBBINS 1694, m/3 John COLEMAN 1696; 28 Oct 1659; Springfield
ELY, Samuel (1668-1732) & 1/wf Martha BLISS (1674-1702); 10 Nov 1697; Longmeadow
ELY, William (1647-1717) & Elizabeth [SMITH] (?1662-1750); 24 May 1681; Lyme, CT
EMBREE, John & Sarah [PARCELL]; ca 1666; Flushing, LI
EMBREE, Robert (-1656) & Mary __?__, m/2 George BALDWIN; b 1646; New Haven
EMBREE, Robert & [?Sarah] __?__ (-1729?); ca 1694; Flushing, LI
EMBRY, ?Moses & __?__
EMERSON, Edward & Rebecca WALDO (1662/3-1752); 27 Jan 1697/8; Chelmsford/Newburyport/Boston
EMERSON, Ephraim (1672-1706, ae 34) & Elizabeth WALKER, m/2 Elisha MAY; 7 Jan 1695/6; Taunton
EMERSON, James[3] & Sarah [INGERSOLL?] (1663-1732, Mendon); b 1680(1?); Marshfield/Ipswich/Mendon
EMERSON, John & Barbara LOTHROP (1619-); 19 Jul 1638; Duxbury/?Scituate
EMERSON, John (-1700) & Ruth [SYMONDS?]; b 1660?, 1662?; Gloucester
EMERSON, John & Anne [RICHBELL?], w John (dau Ann RICHBELL by 1st husband); b 10 Sep 1686; Mamaroneck, NY/MD
EMERSON, John (1652-1745) & 1/wf Judith [CHENEY] (1668-1709?); ca 1689; Newbury
EMERSON, John & Elizabeth LEECH, wid?; 27 Dec 1693; Bridgewater
EMERSON, Rev. John (?1654-1712) & Sarah (STOWERS) [CARTER], w John; b 1695?; Charlestown/Salem/etc.
EMERSON, John (1670-1732) & Mary BATTER/BATTERS; 14 May 1696; Salem/New Castle, NH/Portsmouth, NH
EMERSON, Jonathan & Hannah DAY; 15 Jun 1699; Haverhill
EMERSON, Joseph[2] (1620-1680) & 1/wf Elizabeth [WOODMANSEY] (-bef 7 Dec 1665); b 1645?; Ipswich/Wells/Mendon/Concord?
EMERSON, Rev. Joseph (1620-1680) & 2/wf Elizabeth BULKELEY (1643?, 1638-1693), m/2 Capt. John BROWN 1682; 7 Dec 1665; Concord/Milton/Mendon/York, ME
EMERSON, Joseph & Mary __?__, ?gr-dau John EMERY?; b 1677; Boston/?York, ME
EMERSON, Joseph & 1/wf Martha TOOTHAKER (1668-); 16 Jul 1690; Haverhill
EMERSON, Michael (?1627-1715±) & Hannah WEBSTER (-living 1709); 1 Apr 1657; Haverhill

EMERSON, Nathaniel (1630-1712) & 1/wf Sarah __?__ (-1670); b 1657; Ipswich
EMERSON, Nathaniel & 2/wf Lydia (THURLOW) [WELLS] (1638-1716), w Nathaniel; betw 1681 & 1694; Salisbury
EMERSON, Nathaniel (1657-1738) & Martha WOODWARD (1662-); [1 Feb 1685]; Ipswich
EMMERSON, Peter & Anna BROWN; 11 Nov 1696; Reading
EMERSON, Robert (1629-1694) & Ann GRANT (1637-1718); 4 Jan 1658/9; Rowley/Haverhill
EMMERSON, Samuel & Judith DAVIS; 14 Dec 1687; Haverhill
EMERSON, Stephen & Elizabeth DUSTON; 27 Dec 1698; Haverhill
EMERSON, Thomas[1] (1584-1666) & Elizabeth BREWSTER (-1666+); Bishop's Stratford, Eng, 1 Jul 1611; Ipswich/Salisbury
EMERSON, Thomas (-1738?) & Phillipa/Phillis? PERKINS (1670-1738); 20 Nov 168[5?], 1683, 1685; Ipswich
EMMERSON, Thomas (-1697) & Elizabeth GOARDIN/GORDON (-1697); 26 May 1686; Haverhill
EMERSON, __?__ & Hannah SMITH; b 1699; Providence
EMERY, Anthony (1601-1680+) & 2/wf? Frances __?__; ?b 1630; Newbury/Kittery/etc.
EMERY, Daniel (1667-) & Margaret GOWEN alias SMITH; 17 Mar 1695; ?Kittery, ME
EMERY, George (1609-1687) & Mary __?__ (-1673); no ch mentioned; Salem
EMERY, James (?1632-) & 1/wf Elizabeth __?__; b 1658; Kittery, ME/Berwick, ME
EMERY, James (1658-1724) & 1/wf Margaret HITCHCOCK; 18 Dec 1685; ?Saco, ME
EMERY, James (1658-) & 2/wf Elizabeth (NEWCOMB) PIDGE, w John PIGG; 28 Dec 1695; Newbury
EMERY, Job (1670-), Berwick & Charity NASON, Berwick; 6 Apr 1696; ?Berwick, ME
EMERY, John[1] (1596, 1599-1683) & 1/wf [?Alice GRANTAM?]; 26 Jun 1620?, in Eng, 1620, b 1628, b 1624; Newbury
EMERY, John (1599-1683) & Mary (SHATSWELL) WEBSTER (-1694), w John (see m of Thomas PLUMER 1649, really 1647?); 29 Oct (wrong), [1647]; Newbury
EMERY, John (1629-1693) & Mary __?__/Mary WHIPPLE (-1705); b 1652, b 10 Oct 1650
EMERY, John & Maria [BASSETT]; b Jun 1653; Stratford, CT/?Hempstead, LI
EMERY, John (1656-1730) & 1/wf Mary SAWYER (1660-1699); 13 Jun 1683; Newbury
EMERY, John & 2/wf Abigail BARTLETT (1653-); 27 May 1700; Newbury
EMERY, Jonathan[2] (1652-1723) & Mary WOODMAN (1654-1723); 29 Nov 1676; Newbury
AMORY, Joseph (-1712) & Elizabeth [WASHBURN]; b 1682; Little Compton, RI
EMERIE, Joseph (1663-1721) & Elizabeth MERRILL (1669-); 2 Oct 1693; Andover/Newbury
EMERY, Samuel (1670-1724) & Tabitha [LITTLEFIELD] (-1736); b 1698; Wells, ME
EMRY, Simon & Mary __?__; b 1674; Boston
EMERY, Stephen (1666-1747) & Ruth JAQUES (1672-1764); 29 Nov 1692; Newbury
EMERY, Zachariah/Zachary (1660-) & Elizabeth GOODWIN, m/2 Philip HUBBARD 1692; 9 Dec 1686; Topsfield
EMOTT, James & Mary [LAWRENCE]; 1682, 1683; LI
EMETT, John & Elizabeth __?__; b 1679; Boston
EMMONS, Abraham & Rebecca STILWELL (1675-); 20 Oct 1693; Gravesend, LI
EMANS, Andrew & Rebecca VanCLEEFE; 14 Nov 1693; Gravesend, LI
EMONS, Benjamin (see Obadiah) & 1/wf Mary [WISWALL?] (1649-1690); b 1668; Boston
EMONS, Benjamin (-1710) & Elizabeth [COLLIER] (-1738); b 1693; Boston
EMMONS, Benjamin & Mary AMORY (-8 Oct 1740, ae 67), dau Capt. AMORY of Barnstable, Eng; Barnstable, Eng?, 10 Sep 1694; Boston
EMMONS, Edward & __?__
EMMONS, Henry & Mary __?__; b 1690; Boston
EMANS, Jacobus & Geertye ROMEYN; 10 May 1700; Gravesend, LI
EMMONS, Jacob (rather doubtful) & Elizabeth __?__; b 1701; Boston
EMMONS, Joseph (?1647, ?1651-) & Elizabeth __?__; b 1670; Boston
EMMONS, Joseph (1647/51-) & 2/wf 1/wf Mary (WEBSTER) SWAINE (1658-), w William; 12 Jun 1694 cont; Hampton, NH
EMONS, Nathaniel (-1721) & Mary WARMAL/WARMALL; 15 Sep 1698; Boston
EMMONS, Obadiah (1635-1705) & Alice SHARP; b 1658/9, 16 Oct 1656; London/Boston
EMMONS, Obadiah (see Benjamin) & 2/wf Mary [WISWALL?] (1649-); b 1675; ?Boston
EMMONS, Obadiah & Judith HUBBERD; 7 Nov 1699; Boston/?Southold, LI
EMONS, Peter & 1/wf Martha KILLUM/KILHAM; 8 Nov 1692; Ipswich

EMMONS, Peter, Ipswich & 2/wf Martha EATON (1673-); m int 19 Nov 1698; Lynn/Reading
EMONS, Robert & Bethiah _?_; b 1675(6?); Boston
EMMONS, Samuel (-1685?) & Mary SCOTT; 16 Aug 1660; Boston
EMMONS, Samuel (1671-1767) & Elizabeth [BUTLER] (1667-); ca 1692; Wethersfield, CT/East Haddam, CT
EMANS, Thomas (-1664) & Martha _?_ (-1666); b 1635; Newport, RI/Boston
EMMONS, Thomas & Mary [HANCOCK]; b 1683; Cambridge
ENDLE/ENDALL, Michael (1620, 1621-) & Wilmot [BAILEY]; by 1662; Kittery, ME/Isles of Shoals
ENDLE, Richard (1632-) & Agnes [TURPIN]; ca 1661; Kittery, ME/Isles of Shoals
ENDLE, Richard (1662±-1716) & Jane _?_ (-1707+); ?Spruce Creek
ENDICOTT, Benjamin (1667-1735) & 1/wf Abigail/Elizabeth? _?_; no issue; Boxford
ENDICOTT, Benjamin (1667-1735) & 2/wf? Hannah _?_; b 1701?, no issue; ?Boxford
INDICUT, Gilbert (?1658-1715, Canton) & Hannah GOWGE, m/2 John MINOT; 28 Apr 1686; York Co., ME/Reading
ENDICOTT, John & 1/wf Anna [GOWER] (-1629); in Eng, b 1628; Salem
ENDICOTT, John (-1665) & 2/wf Elizabeth (COGAN) GIBSON (1611-1676); 18 Aug 1630; Boston/Salem
ENDICOTT, John (1632-1668) & Elizabeth HOUCHIN/HOWCHIN (1638-1673), m/2 Rev. James ALLEN 1668; 9 Nov 1653, no issue; Boston/Salem
INDICOT, John & Elizabeth _?_; b 1677; Boston
ENDICOTT, Dr. John (1657-1694±) & Anna/Anne?/[Hannah] [EDWARDS] (-1720), dau John; in London?, ca 1688; Salem
INDICOT, John (-1711, ae 70) & Mary [TALBOT] (1655-1718); b 1691; Boston
ENDICOTT, Joseph (1672-1747) & Hannah _?_; b 1701?; ?North Hampton, NJ
ENDICOTT, Samuel (-1694) & Hannah [FELTON] (1663-1737), m/2 Thorndike PROCTOR 1697; ca 1684; Salem
ENDICOT, William (-1709+) & Elizabeth _?_; b 1686; Boston
ENDICOT, William (-1709+) & 2/wf Joanna? BELL?
ENDICOT, Zerubbabel (?1635-1684) & 1/wf Mary [SMITH] (1636-20 Jun 1677); ca 1654; Salem
ENDICOTT, Zerubbabel (-1684) & 2/wf Elizabeth (WINTHROP) [NEWMAN] (1636-1716), w Antipas; 1677; Salem
ENDICOTE, Zerubbabel (1665-1706) & Grace SIMONS/SYMONDS? (1667-); Jul 16[89?], 16[90?]; Topsfield
ENGELL/INGALL?, Benjamin & Mary (PAINE) TRAPP (-1687), w John; 4 Apr 1682; Portsmouth, RI
ENGLAND, John (-1655) & Frances _?_, m/2 Edward HITCHCOCK 1656, m/3 Thomas JOHNSON 1663; New Haven/Branford, CT
ENGLAND, Stephen & ?Hannah/?Martha [THOMPSON]; b 1701?, b 1707; ?Stratham, NH
ENGLAND, William & Elizabeth _?_ (1613-1684+), m/2 Hugh PARSONS; b 1641, ?ca 1631; Portsmouth, RI
ENGLISH, Benjamin (1676-) & 1/wf Sarah WARD?/PHIPPEN (1676-1700?); 8 Jun 1699; Salem
ENGLES, Bernard & Elizabeth _?_; b 1662; Boston
ENGLISH, Clement (-1682) & Mary WATERS, m/2 John STEVENS bef 1685; 27 Aug 1667; Salem
ENGLISH/INGLES/INGLISH (see INGALLS), James & Joanna FARNUM; 7 Jan 1657/8; Boston
ENGLISH (see INGALLS), James & Love [PROUT] (1677-1743?), m/2 John RAWLINGS; b 1698; Boston
ENGLISH, Joseph (1673-) & Mary (PHIPPEN) SEARL, w John; ?- Dec 1693, ?20 Dec 1694?; Salem
ENGLISH/ENGS/ENGLES/INGS/ENGLYS/etc., Maudit & Jane _?_; b 1639; Boston
ENGLISH, Philip (1651-) & 1/wf Mary HOLLINGWORTH (-1694); 1 Sep 1675; Salem
ENGLISH, Philip & 2/wf Sarah (HASKETT) INGERSOLL, w Samuel; 20 Sep 1698; Salem
ENGLISH, Richard (-1734?) & Jane [BUSHNELL] (1655-); b 1681(2?); Boston
INGGS/ENGS, Samuel (-1708) & Mary BEAL; 21 Feb 1672/3; Hingham/Boston
ENGLISH/INGLISH, William (-1682) & Sarah/Mary? _?_; b 15 Mar 1663; Boston/Ipswich/Hampton, NH
ENGS, Samuel & Ann REED; 2 Jan 1700; Boston
INGS/ENGS, Samuel & Mary BEAL, m/2 Joshua LIE 1688?; 21 Feb 1682/3; Hingham

ENGS, Maudit & Joan _?_ ; b 1639; Boston (had son Samuel, mentions gr-ch Madet, Samuel & Mary)

ENO, James[1] (-1682) & 1/wf Ann BIDWELL (-1657), w Richard; 18 Aug 1648; Windsor, CT

ENO, James[1] (-1682) & 2/wf Elizabeth HOLCOMB (-1679), w Thomas; 5 Aug 1658; Windsor, CT

ENO, James[2] (1651-1714) & Abigail BISSELL (1661-1728); 26 Dec 1678; Windsor, CT

ENO, James[1] (-1682) & 3/wf Hester (WILLIAMS) EGLESTON (-1720), w James, m/3 John WILLIAMS 1686?; 29 Apr 1680; Windsor, CT

ENO, John & Mary DIBBLE (?1664-); 10 May 1681, b 1680?; Windsor, CT

ENSIGN, David (1644-1727) & Mehitable GUNN (1644-1720), m/2 Isaac SHELDON 1685?, 1686?; 22 Oct 1663, div Oct 1682; Hartford

ENSIGN, David (1644-1727) & 2/wf Sarah [WILCOX] (1648-1717/18), div wf of Thomas; long aft 1688; Windsor, CT

ENSIGN, James (-1671, 1670) & Sarah _?_ (-1676); b 1635?; Cambridgge/Hartford

ENSIGN, James (1666-) & 1/wf Lydia BAKER (-1701); 20 Mar 1689/90; Hartford

ENSIGN, John (-1676) & _?_ ; b 1669; Scituate

ENSIGN, Thomas (-1663, Scituate) & Elizabeth WILDER (-1676+); 17 Jan 1638, 1638/9; Hingham/Scituate/Duxbury

ENSIGN, Thomas (1668-) & Hannah SHEPARD; 1 Dec 1692; Hartford, CT

EPES, Daniel (called "cousin" by Mrs. Lydia BANKS) & Martha [READ] (1602-), m/2 Samuel SYMONDS; in Eng, ca 1621; Salisbury

EPPS, Daniel (1623-1693) & 1/wf Elizabeth SYMONDS (1624-1685); 20 May 1644; Salisbury

EPES, Daniel (1649-1722) & 1/wf Martha BOARDMAN (-1692); 17 Apr 1672; Salem

EPES, Daniel (1623-1693) & 2/wf Lucy (WOODBRIDGE) [BRADSTREET] (1642-), w Simon; aft 7 May 1685; Cambridge/Ipswich

EPES, Daniel (1649-1722) & 2/wf Hannah [WANWRIGHT], w Francis; aft 1692, 1693; Salem

EPES, Symonds & _?_ ; b 1699; Ipswich

ERRINGTON, Abraham (1622-1677) & Rebecca CUTLER (-ca 1697); no date, [1649, 1650]; Cambridge/Charlestown

ERRINGTON, _?_ & Ann _?_ (1576-1653, ae 77); ca 1600-1610, [b 1622]; Cambridge/Charlestown

EZGATE, Eleazer & Joyce GOODWIN; 24 Jun 1675; Braintree

ESGATE, Eliazer & Rachel PUFFER; 7 Jan 1694/5; Braintree

ESLAND/ERLAND, John & Elizabeth GENNEY/JENNEY (-1702); 17 Oct 1700; Plymouth

ESTEN, Henry (1651-1711) & 1/wf Elizabeth [MANTON]; b 1683; Providence

ESTEN, Henry (1651-) & 2/wf Sarah [HARDING] (-1731); b 1695; Providence

ESTEN, Thomas (1612-1691+) & Ann _?_ (-1686+); in Eng, 23 Apr 1640; Providence

ESTEN, Thomas (1647-1708) & Priscilla [HARDING] (-1708(-)); b 1687; Providence

ESTES, Matthew (1645-1723) & Philadelphia (JENKINS) HAYES (1645-1721), w Edward; 14 Jun 1676; Lynn

ESTES, Richard (1647-1737) & Elizabeth BECK, w Henry; 23 Jun 1687, at Dover, NH, 24? Jun; Salem

ESTOWE/ESTOW, William (-1655) & Mary MOULTON, wid; Ormesby, St. Margaret, Co. Norfolk, Eng, 15 Jul 1623; Newbury/Hampton, NH

EASTWICK, Edward (-1665) & Hester/Esther [VERMAYE/MASON?] (-1708); b 1656, b 1659, aft 1650; Salem

ESTWICK, Pheasant & Sarah [BARRON] (1640-); b 1671; Boston/Cambridge

ESTYE, Isaac (1627-1712) & Mary [TOWN] (1634-1692); b 1656; Salem/Topsfield

ESTIE, Isaac (-1714) & Abigail KYMBALL/KIMBALL (1667-), m/2 William POOLE; 14 Oct 1689; Topsfield

ESTY, Jeffrey (-1657) & Margaret POTE?/PETT?; Freston, Eng, 29 May 1606; Salem/Southold, LI/Huntington, LI

ESTIE, John & 1/wf Mary DORMAN; ?31 May 1688, ?20 Jul 1668; Topsfield

EASTY, John & 2/wf Hannah _?_ ; b 1695; Topsfield/Middleton

EASTY, Joseph & Jane STEWARD; 2 Jun 1682; Topsfield/Dorchester/Stonington

ETHERIDGE, Nathaniel & Susanna [WYATT]; b 1701(2?), 13 Mar 1700, 7 Mar 1700/01; Milton

ETHERINGTON, Thomas (-1664) & Mary SPENCER (?1634-1664); ca 1656; Kittery, ME/S. Berwick, ME

EUSTISS, David (1670-) & Rachel _?_ ; b 1693(4?); Boston

EUSTIS, John (1654-1722) & 1/wf Elizabeth [MORSE] (1661-1714?); b 1685(6?); Boston
EUSTACE, Jonathan (1675-) & Sarah SCOLLEY; 16 Nov 1699; Boston
EUSTIS, Joseph (1662-1690) & Abigail _?_; b 1689; Boston
EUSTIS, William (-1694) & Sarah [JACKSON] (1637-1713); b 1659; Charlestown
EUSTACE, William (1661-1737) & Sarah CUTLER/CURTIS (?1666-1748); 29 Oct 1688; Charlestown/Boston
EVANS, Benjamin & _?_; b 1680?; Hampton, NH
EVANS, David (-1663) & Mary [CLARK?]; b 1653; Boston
EUINS, David & Sarah [BAILEY]; b 1701; Freetown
EVANS, Ebenezer (-1686) & Patience [FERNOLD] (1664-), m/2 Robert ATKINS/ELKINS 1686; ca 1684?; ?Durham, ME/NH?
EVANS, Edward (-1767, ae 100) & Dorcas [BUSEY]; b 1700; Dover, NH
EVANS, Henry (-1667) & 1/wf Amy _?_; b 1644; Boston
EVANS, Henry (-1667) & 2/wf Hester [MORRIS], w Rice; b 1650; Boston
EVANCE, John & Susanna [NORTON] (-1667), m/2 Henry HATSELL; b 1646; New Haven
EVANS, John (1632-1689) & [?Eleanor] _?_; b 1663; Dover, NH
EVENS, John & 1/wf Mary _?_; b 1671; Roxbury/Hadley
EVENS, John & 2/wf Mary (HAWKS) HINSDALE, w Experience; 22 Jul 1677?; Hadley
EVANS, John & Mary CLAP; 7 Jan 1694?; Boston
EVANS, Jonathan (-1728) & Mary BRONSDON (1670-); 4 Oct 1688; Boston
EVENS, Matthias (-1684) & Patience MEADE (-1670); 28 Apr 1669; Dorchester
EVANS, Matthias (-1684) & 2/wf Susanna [ELLIS]; b 1682, b 1673; Dorchester/Medfield
EVANS, Nathaniel (-1710, Malden) & Elizabeth [DUNTON] (1658-); b 1680; Reading
EVENS, Nicholas (-1689, Simsbury) & Mary PARSONS, m/2 Robert WESTLAND by 1701; 17 Nov 1670, (7 Nov prob wrong); Windsor, CT/Simsbury, CT
EVANS, Peter & _?_; Plymouth, Eng?, b 1673; Isles of Shoals
EVENS, Philip (-1693) & Deborah [PILLSBURY?]; b 1687; Newbury/Ipswich
EVANS, Richard (-1662) & Mary _?_; b 1641; Dorchester
EVANS, Richard & Rebecca _?_; b 1670; Dorchester
EVENS, Richard & Mary _?_; b 1679(80?); Rehoboth/Providence
EVANS, Richard (-1727, ae 81) & Patience ALLEN; 10 Jun 1686; Sandwich/Newport
EVANS, Robert & 1/wf Elizabeth [COLCORD] (-by 1675); b 1675; Dover, NH
EVANS, Robert & 2/wf Ann (THOMPSON) [HODSDON], w Israel; ca 1675, b 1682?, ?aft 1696; Dover
EVANS, Robert (1665-) & ?Ann/?Mary (HEARD) [HANSON], w Isaac; b 1700, b 1690?; Kittery, ME
EVANS, Samuel & _?_; b 1699; Windsor, CT
EVANS, Thomas (-1634) & _?_; Plymouth
EVENS, Thomas & Hannah GLOVER (1665-1759); 10 Mar 1686; Dorchester
EVENS, Thomas & Hannah BROWN; 30 Sep 1686; Salisbury
EVANS, William & Agnes _?_; b 1640; Dorchester
EVANS, William (-1671) & Ann [HAILSTONE] (-1672+); ca 1647/53?; Gloucester/Topsfield
EVARTS, Daniel (1638-1692) & 1/wf Mary [?MEIGS] (-1663); Guilford, CT
EVARTS, Daniel (-1692) & 2/wf Rebecca DOWD (-1703); Mar 1664, 1 Mar 1664, 1663/4, ?4 Mar, 22 May 1663, 1st Wed Mar 1664, 2 Mar 1663/4; Guilford, CT
EVARTS, Daniel & Sarah HAYDEN; 9 May 1690; Guilford, CT
EVARTS, Daniel & Mary WEST; 1 Oct 1700; Guilford, CT
EVARTS, James (-1684) & Lydia [GOODRICH/GUTRIDGE], dau Richard; b 1662; Guilford, CT/?Eastchester, NY
EVERTS, James & Mary CASTER, m ?Samuel DOWD; 7 Mar 1694, 169[-]; Guilford, CT
EVARTS, James & ?Elizabeth/?Anna BOW; ?1699; Guilford, CT
EVARTS, John (-1669) & 1/wf ?Elizabeth _?_; ca 1632/5?, b 1631?; Concord/Guilford, CT
EVARTS, John (-1669) & Elizabeth (_?_) (BRADLEY) PARMELEE (-1683), w _?_, w John; 27 May 1664; New Haven/Guilford, CT
EVARTS, John (1640-) & 1/wf Mary FRENCH (-1668?, 1673?); 14 Sep 1665; Guilford, CT
EVARTS, John (1640-1692) & 2/wf Mary BOW (-1700); 5 Dec 1676; Guilford, CT
EVARTS, John (1664-) & 2/wf Sarah SCRANTON; 23 Oct 1688; Guilford, CT
EVARTS, John & Sarah FREEMAN; 24 Dec 1694; ?Killingworth, CT

EVARTS, Joseph (1642-1696), Guilford & Mary HAYDEN (1648-), Kenilworth; 3 Aug 1670; Guilford, CT/Windsor, CT
EVE, Adam & Elizabeth BARSHAM (1659-); 5 Jul 1694; Watertown/Boston
EVELETH, Isaac & Abigail COYT, m/2 Thomas MILLETT b 1689; 18 Nov 1677; Gloucester
EVELETH, Isaac (1679/80-) & Sarah __?__ (1679-); b 1701; Gloucester
EVELETH, John (1670-1734, S. Berwick, ME) & Mary BOWMAN (-1747, Stow); 2 Dec 1692; Cambridge/Lexington/Manchester/Stow
EVELETH, Joseph & Mary BRAGGE; 1 Jan 1667/8, 1 Jan 1669; Gloucester/Ipswich
EVELETH, Sylvester (-1689) & 1/wf Susan/Susanna __?__ (1607-); in Eng, ca 1637; Boston/Gloucester
EVELETH, Silvester (-1689) & 2/wf Bridget PARKMAN, w Elias; 6 Sep 1662, 1672?; Gloucester
EVELETH, Sylvester (-1689) & 3/wf Pilgrim (EDDY) (BAKER) [STEDMAN], w William, w Isaac; aft 11 Jan 1677, bef 13 Jun 1681, 1678/9?; Boston
EVERDEN, Anthony & __?__ ; Providence
EVERDEN, Richard & __?__
EVERDEN, William & Abigail __?__ ; b 1684(5?); Boston
EVERDEN, William & Sarah CALENDAR, w George; m int 12 Dec 1696; Boston
EVERILL, Abiel (-1660?, 1659?) & Elizabeth PHILLIPS, m/2 John ALDEN 1659, 1660; 6 Jul 1655; Boston
EVERELL, James (ae 79 in 1682) & 1/wf Elizabeth __?__ ; b 1636, b 20 Jul 1634; Boston
EVERELL, James (-1683) & 2/wf Mary __?__ (had gr-dau Elizabeth ADKINS); b 1682; Boston
EVERINDEN, John & Rachel MARCH/MEROH; 26 Sep 1700; Dorchester
EVERENDEN/EVERDEN?, Walter & Ruth __?__ ; b 1685(6?); Dorchester
EVEREST, Andrew & Barbara __?__ ; ca 1644; York, ME
EVEREST, Isaac & Joanna __?__ (-1703); b 1675; York, ME/Guilford, CT
EVERETT, Edward & Sarah __?__ ; b 1686(7?); Boston
EVERITT, Francis & Mary EDWARDS, m/2 John POLLY 1681; 8 Dec 1675, 7 Dec 1675; Reading/Cambridge
EVERED, Israel (1651-1678) & Abigail [MORSE] (1646-), m/2 William JONES 1687; b 1676; Dedham/Springfield
EVARED, Jedediah (1656-1699) & Rachel [RICE?], m/2 Joseph DOLLIVER; b 1681; Dedham
EVERID, John (-1714, 1715?) & Elizabeth PEPPER (1645-1715); 13 May 1662; Dedham/?Roxbury
EVERETT, John (-1689/91) & Elizabeth [STEVENSON]; b 31 Dec 1670; Jamaica, LI
EVERETT, John (1676-1751) & 1/wf Mercy BROWNE (-1748, 1758?, 1749?); 3 Jan 1699/1700; Dedham
EVERITT, John (-1729) & Sarah [WELLES] (1674-); b 1704, b 1701?; Jamaica, LI
EVERRARD/EVERETT?, Jonathan & Penelope (FAIRWEATHER) CLARK, w Peter; 9 Aug 1697; Boston
EVERITT, Nicholas & __?__ ; b 1679; Jamaica, LI
EVERARD, Richard (-1682) & 1/wf Mary __?__ ; b 1637?; Dedham/Springfield
EVERETT, Richard (-1682) & 2/wf Mary WINCH; 20 Jun, 29 Jun 1643; Springfield
EVERETT, Richard (-by 1666) & __?__ ; b 1650?; Jamaica, LI
EVERED, Samuel (1639-1718) & Mary PEPPER (1651-); 28 Oct 1669; Dedham
EVERITT, William (-1652/3) & Margaret [?WATHEM], m/2 Isaac NASH b 1656, m/3 Abraham CONLEY; b 1640; Kittery, ME
EVERED, William & Sarah FILLEBROWN; 30 Jan 1658/9; Charlestown
EVERSON, John & __?__ ; b 1669
EAVERSON, Richard & Elizabeth __?__ (-1716, Plympton); b 1700; Plymouth/Plympton
EVERTON, Fownell (1666-) & Mary [SPRAGUE]; ca 1686; Charlestown
EVERTON, John (1663-) & Sarah TAYLOR (1663-), m/2 Henry BARKER 1699; 15 Dec 1686; Charlestown
EVERTON, Joseph (1676-) & Katharine TUCK; 23 Sep 1697; Charlestown
EVERTON, Samuel & Joanna LYNDE (1676-), m/2 Henry PHILLIPS 1708; 14 Apr 1700, 19 Apr, 19 Apr 1700; Charlestown
EVERTON, William (-1668, 1669) & Sarah __?__, m/2 Thomas BLIGH 1691; b 1663; Manchester/Charlestown
EVERTON, William & Ruth WALLY (1666-); 19 Nov 1684; Charlestown
EWELL, Gershom (1650-1718) & 1/wf Mary __?__ ; b 1683; Scituate

EWELL, Henry (-1681) & Sarah ANNABLE (1622-1687); 22 Nov 1638, 23? Nov, 23 Nov 1638; Scituate

EWELL, Ichabod (1659-1717) & Mehitable GWINNE; 1 May 1689; Scituate

EWELL, John (1640-1686) & Mary [GOODALE] (calls Richard HUBBELL "cousin"); b 1666; Boston/Newbury

EWER, John (1628-1652) & Mary __?__, m/2 John JENKINS 1652/3; b 1652; Barnstable

EWER, Thomas (1593-) & 1/wf Bridget HIPSLEY; 13 Sep 1614

EWER, Thomas (1593-1638) & 2/wf Sarah LEARNAD/?LINWELL (1607-), m/2 Thomas LOTHROP 1639; 13 Jan 1623/4; Charlestown

EWER, Thomas (1634-1667?) & Hannah/Anna __?__, m/2 Daniel WING 1666?; b 1667; Sandwich/Barnstable

EWER, Thomas (1663-1722) & 1/wf Mercy [MANTER]; b 1689; Barnstable

EWER, Thomas (1663-1722) & 2/wf Elizabeth LOVELL (1660-1713); - Oct 168[9]; Barnstable

EXELL, Richard (-1714) & Hannah (ROWE) REEVES, w Thomas; 4 Jun 1651; Springfield

EYRE, John (1654-1700) & Catharine BRATTLE, m/2 Waitstill WINTHROP 1707; 20 May 1680; Boston

EYRE, Simon (1587-1658, Boston) & 1/wf Dorothy [PAIN] (1597-1650); ca 1615; Wethersfield, CT

EYRE, Simon (1587-1658, Boston) & 2/wf Martha (HUBBARD) WHATTINGHAM (-1687), w John; ca 1651; Boston

EYRE, Simon, Jr. (1624-1653) & Lydia [STARR] (1634/5-1653); ca 1651; Boston

EYRE, Simon (1652-1695) & Elizabeth (ALLERTON) STARR (1653-1740), w Benjamin; 22 Jul 1679; New Haven

EYRE, Simon & Elizabeth __?__; b 1691; Boston

EYRE, Thomas & Ann __?__; b 1691; Boston

FABES, John (1625/28-1698) & Elizabeth (?SMITH) [?GILMAN] (-1711), w Edward[2]?; b 1655; Stratford/Isles of Shoals

FABIAN James & Joanna BARNES (1667-); 15 Oct 1687; Marblehead

FABYAN, George (-1693) & Elizabeth __?__; b 15 Sep 1668; Portsmouth, NH

FABYAN, John & Sarah [HALL]; b 1681; Portsmouth, NH

FAIRBANKS, Benjamin (1662-1694) & Mary [RICHARDS] (1675-), dau John, m/2 Richard TRUESDALE 1697, m/3 Samuel GATES 1710; b 1693; Dedham

FAIRBANK, Eleazer (1655-) & Martha [LOVETT/BABBERT?] (1654-1749?); b 1678; Medfield

FAIREBANCK, George[2] (1619-1682) & Mary ADDAMS/ADAMS (-1711); 26 Oct 1646; Dedham

FAYRBANKS, George[3] & 1/wf Rachel ADAMS (1651-1678); 1 Dec 1678; Medfield

FAIRBANK, George[3] & 2/wf Susannah __?__; b 1681, b 1680; Medfield

FAIRBANKS, George[3] & 3/wf Sarah [?DEAN/?MERRIFIELD], m/2 Abraham HARDING b 1696?; b 1688; ?Medfield

FAIRBANKS, Jabez (1671-1758) & 1/wf Mary [WILDER?] (1675-1718, ae 43); b 1694, b 1693; Lancaster

FAIRBANKS, Jeremiah, Bristol, RI, & Mary PENFIELD; 14 Apr 1698, 19 apr 1698, b 1698?; Taunton/Bristol, RI

FAIRBANKS, John & __?__?; in Eng, b 1628?; Dedham

FAIREBANCK, John (1617/18-) & Sarah FISKE/?FISHER (prob wrong); 16 Mar 1640/1; Dedham

FAIRBANK, John & Hannah [WHITING]; b 1672; Dedham/Windham, CT

FAIREBANCK, John & Mary WHITEING (1652-1740); b 1 Mar 1671/2; Dedham/Windham, CT

FAIRBANKS, Jonas (1623?, 1625?-1676) & Lydia PRESCOTT (1641-), m/2 Elias BARRON ca 1678; 28 May 1658, 28 Mar; Lancaster

FAIRBANKS, Jonathan[1] (1629-1665) & Grace SMITH; ?Wartey, in Eng, 20 May 1617; Halifax, Eng; Dedham

FAIRBANKS, Jonathan & Deborah [SHEPARD] (?1639-1705); b 1654; Dedham

FAIRBANK, Jonathan & Sarah _?_ ; b 1685; Sherborn

FAIRBANK, Jonathan (1666-1697), Lancaster & Mary HAYWARD, Concord, m/2 David WHITCOMB 1700; 24 Aug 1688; Watertown/Lancaster

FAYERBANK, Joseph (-1737) & Dorcas _?_ (-1738); b 1682, b 1683; Dedham

FAIRBANKS, Richard & Elizabeth [DAULTON]; Boston, Eng, b 1636, b 1633, 17 Sep 1618; Boston, ?dau Lydia, m/1 Edward BATES, m/2 William FLETCHER

FAIRCHILD, Joseph (1664-1713) & Johannah [WILCOXSON] (1667-1713); b 1687; Stratford, CT

FAIRCHILD, Samuel (1640-1705) & Mary [WHEELER] (1655-), m/2 Benjamin BEACH 1705, m/3 Thomas YALE; b 1681; Stratford, CT

FAIRCHILD, Samuel (1677-) & Mary LEWIS (1674-); 22 Nov 1699; Stratford, CT

FAIRCHILD, Thomas (-1670) & 1/wf ?Emma/?Sarah SEABROOK; b 1640; Stratford, CT

FAIRCHILD, Thomas (-1670) & 2/wf Katharine CRAIGG/CRAIG/CRAGG, m/2 Jeremiah JUDSON 1675; m cont 22 Dec 1662; Stratford, CT

FAIRCHILD, Thomas (1645/6-1686) & ?Sarah PRESTON/Susanna _?_, m/2 Samuel NICHOLS 1686?, 1696?, m/3 Samuel CASTLE 1692?, 1705?; b 1672; Stratford, CT

FAIRCHILD, Zechariah (1651-1703) & Hannah BEACH (1665-), m/2 John BURRITT; 3 Nov 1681; Stratford, CT

FAIRFIELD, Daniel (?1601-) & Elizabeth _?_ ; b 1639; Boston/Salem

FAIRFIELD, Daniel & 1/wf Sarah LUDDEN; 4 Jan 1659; Weymouth/Boston

FAIRFIELD, Daniel & 2/wf Ruth (HAWKINS) [MARSHALL], w John; b 1680; Boston

FEREFEILD, John (-1646, 1647?) & 1/wf? 2/wf [Elizabeth] [KNIGHT?], m/2 Peter PALFREY 1646+; b 1632, ?7 Jun 1632; Charlestown/Salem

FAIRFIELD, John (-1689+) & Anphillis _?_ (-1689+); by 1655?; Newport/Westerly, RI

FAIREFIELD, John (1639-1672) & Sarah GRAVE, m/2 Daniel KILHAM 1673; 26 Mar 1666; Wenham

FAIRFIELD, John (1660-1690) & Mary [MARSHALL] (1662-); b 1683; Boston

FAIRFIELD, John & Elizabeth BADSON/BATSON; 18 Apr 1643; Boston/Ipswich

FAIREFIELD, Walter (1633-1723, ae 91, Wenham) & Sarah SHIPPEN/SKIPPEN/SKIPPERARY; 28 Dec 1654; Reading/Wenham

FAIRFIELD, Walter & 1/wf Sarah [ADAMS] (1675-); b 1696; Ipswich

FAIRFEILD, William (1662-1741) & Esther [BATCHELDER] (1668-1723, ae 55); b 1696, b 1690; Wenham

FAIREWEATHER, John (1634-1712) & 1/wf Sarah TURNER (1641-); 15 Nov 1660; Boston

FAIRIWEATHER, John (1634-1712) & 2/wf Elizabeth (ALLEN) [DIXCY/DICKSEY], w John; 1674?, b 1677; Swansea

FAIRWEATHER, John (1634-1712) & 3/wf Mary HEWES; 17 Nov 1692; Boston

FAIREWETHER, Thomas (-1638) & Mary [?OSBORN], m/2 John WEBB alias EVERELL, m/3 William GOODHUE 1669; b 1634; Boston

FAIRWEATHER, Thomas (1661-) & Hannah ?HUDSON/PAINE, m/2 Samuel CLARK 1698; b 1690; Boston

VALES, James (-1708) & Ann BROCK (-1712); 28 May 1655; Dedham

FALES, James (1656-1742) & Deborah FISHER (1661-); 20 Oct 1674; Dedham/Walpole

FALE, John (1658-1706) & Abigail HAWES; 20 Jun 1684; Wrentham

FALES, Peter (-1725) & Abigail [ROBBINS]; b 1690; Dedham

FALLOWELL, Gabriel[1] (-1667, ae 80 or 83) & Catharine [FINNEY] (-1673); in Eng, b 1618?; Boston/Plymouth

FALLOWELL, John[3] (-1675) & Sarah WOOD/ATWOOD; 13 Feb 1667, 1667/8; ?Plymouth

FALLOWELL, William[2] & Martha BEALE (?1620-1690), m/2 Samuel DUNHAM 1649; 16 Mar 1648; Hingham

FANNING, Edmund (?1620-1683, Stonington, CT) & Ellen _?_ ; ca 1649?; Stonington, CT/New London, CT

FANNING, Edmund & Margaret BILLINGS; 13 Aug 1678, 31 Aug; Stonington, CT

FANNING, John & Margaret [CULVER]; ca 1684; New London, CT

FANNIN, John & Rebecca _?_ ; b 1697; Swansea/Bristol, RI

FANNING, Joseph & Elizabeth BOULTER (1669-); 6 May 1689; Hampton, NH

FANNING, Thomas (-1685) & Elizabeth DANIEL (1630-1722); 17 May 1655; Cambridge/Watertown

FANNING, Thomas & Frances ELLIS; 19 Oct 1684; Stonington, CT

FANNING, William & Elizabeth ALLEN; 24 Mar 1667/8; Newbury
FANTON, Jonathan (?1655-1713/14) & 1/wf Mehitable [STAPLES] (1651±-); aft 1688; Fairfield, CT
FANTON, Jonathan (-1713/14) & 2/wf Sarah [HIDE] (1670-1760), m/2 William HILL; b 1694; Fairfield, CT
FARGO, Moses & Sarah __?__; b 1680; New London, CT
FRARLOW/[FARLEY?], Ambrose & Mary MARTIN; 2 Dec 1668; Chelmsford
FARLEY, Caleb (1645-1712) & 1/wf Rebecca HILL (-1669); 5 Jul 1666, 1667?; Billerica
FARLEY, Caleb (1645-1712) & 2/wf Lydia MORE/MOORE (1645-1715); ?3 Nov 1669, ?9 Nov; Billerica/Roxbury
FARLEY, Caleb (1667-) & 1/wf Sarah GODFREY (-1704); 8 Apr 1686; Billerica
FARLEY, George (-1693) & Christian/Bietnes BIRTHS (-1702); 9 Apr 1641, 9 Feb 1641/2; Woburn/Billerica
FARLEY, George & Rebecca (CHAMBERLAIN) STEARNS (1663-), w Thomas; 14 Jul 1699; Billerica
FARLEY, Meshack/Mesheck (-1696, 1698?) & Sarah BURNAM (1664-), m/2 Thomas CLARK 1699?; 6 Aug 1684; Ipswich
FARLEY, Michael & __?__; b 1660; Ipswich
FARLEY, Samuel (1654-1691+) & Elizabeth SHED; 11 Apr 167-, 1677; Billerica
FARMER, Edward (-1727) & Mary __?__ (-1716); b 1669; Billerica/Woburn
FARMER, John (d in Eng) & Isabella [?BARBAGE]/[MUSTON] (-1686), m/2 Thomas WISWALL; b 1640; Billerica
FARMER, John (1671-1736) & Abigail [SHED?] (-1754); b 1700; Billerica
FARNEY, Thomas & Mary __?__; b 1679; Boston
FARNAM, David & Dorothy [?LACY]; b 1687; Boston
FARNHAM, Edward & Mary __?__; b 1667; Boston
FARNUM, Ephraim & Priscilla HOULT/HOLT; Mar 1699/1700, 20 Mar 1699/1700; Andover
FARNHAM, Henry (-1700) & Joanna [PUCKE] (-1689, Killingworth, CT), w __?__, m/1 __?__ KALSOE?, m/1 Henry SWAN?; b 3 Dec 1662; Roxbury/LI/Killingworth, CT
FARNHAM, John (-1670+) & Elizabeth __?__; b 1636?, b 1639(40?); Dorchester/?Dedham
FARNHAM, John & 1/wf __?__; b 1642; Boston
FARNUM, John & ?2/wf Susanna ARNOLD; 7 Apr 1654; Boston
FARNUM, John (-1723) & Rebecca KENT (1650-1729); 12 Nov 1667; Andover
FARNUM, John & Elizabeth PARKER; 10 Apr 1684; Andover
FARNHAM, John & Dorothy/Deborah MEAN; 16 Sep 1687; Boston/Charlestown
FARNUM, John & Mary TYLER; 30 Jun 1693; Andover
FARNUM, John & Mary __?__; b 1701; Mendon
FARNUM, Jonathan & Martha [COE]; ca 1684?; Boston
FARNHAM, Joseph & Mary __?__; b 1674; Boston
FARNHAM, Peter (-1704) & Hannah WILCOXSON (1666-1708), m/2 Nathaniel ROYCE; 8 Dec 1686; Killingworth, CT
FARNHAM, Ralph (?1603-) & Alice __?__ (1607-), m/2 Solomon MARTIN 1648; in Eng, b 1628; Boston/Ipswich/Andover
FARNUM, Ralph (?1633-1692) & Elizabeth HOLT; 26 Oct 1658; Andover
FARNUM, Ralph (1662-) & Sarah STERLING; 9 Oct 1685; Andover
FARNUM, Samuel & Hannah HOLT; 4 Jan 1697/8; Andover
FARNUM, Thomas (-1686) & Elizabeth SIBBORNS/SIBBORN?/SEABORN?/SEAVERN? (-1683); 8 Jul 1660; Andover
FARNUM, Thomas & Hannah HUTCHINSON; 14 May 1693; Andover
FARNHAM, Thomas & Johannah JEWETT; 10 Nov 1697; Rowley
FARNSWORTH, Benjamin (?1677, ?1667-1733) & Mary [PRESCOTT] (1644-1735); ca 1695; Groton
FARNSWORTH, John (-1729), Groton & Hannah ALDIS (1666-), Dedham; 8 Dec 1686; Groton
FARNSWORTH, Jonathan (-1748) & Ruth [SHATTUCK]; b 1698; Groton
FARNSWORTH, Joseph[1] (-1659/60) & 1/wf Elizabeth __?__; b 1635, b 1628?; Dorchester
FARNSWORTH, Joseph[1] (-1659/60) (called "brother" by William LANE) & 2/wf Mary (LANE) LONG (-1690+), w John/Joseph, m/3 John WILCOX 1660?; aft 28 Feb 1650/1, ca 1654?; Dorchester

FARNSWORTH, Matthias[1] (1612-1689) & Mary [FARR] (-1717; b 1647?, b 1657; Lynn/Groton
FARNSWORTH, Matthias (1649-1693?) & Sarah [NUTTING] (1663-), m/2 John STONE 1698; b 1681; Groton
FARNSWORTH, Samuel, Dorchester & 1/wf Mary STOUGHTON (-1684); 3 Jun 1677; Windsor, CT
FARNSWORTH, Samuel & 2/wf Mary MOSES (1661-); Nov 1685; Windsor, CT
FAR/FARR, Benjamin & Elizabeth BURILL/BURRELL; 28 Jul 1680; Lynn
FARR, George (1594-1662) & Elizabeth [STOWER] (1607-1687); ca 1630?, by 1646; Lynn
FARR, Joseph (1647-1737) & 1/wf Hannah WALDEN (-1691); 22 Sep 1680; Lynn
FARR, Joseph (1647-1737) & 2/wf Rebecca KNIGHT (-1727); 15 Sep 1696; Lynn
FARR, Robert (-1657) & _?_ [STOWER]; Charlestown
FARR, Stephen & Mary TAILER/TAYLOR (1650-); 25 May 1674; Concord/Billerica/Stow?
FARRAND, Nathaniel & _?_ ; Milford, CT/Fairfield, CT
FARRAND, Nathaniel (1645-1724) & [Mary COBB]; b 1676; Milford, CT
FARRAR, George[3] (1670-1760) & Mary HOW/HOWE (-1761); 9 Sep 1692; Concord
FARRAR, Isaac[3] (see Isaac FAWER) (1671-) & Mary WALCOTT (1675-); 29 Apr 1696; Woburn/Ashford, CT
FARRAR, Jacob (1614-) & 1/wf Grace DEAN; 21 Nov 1640, Halifax, Eng
FARRAR, Jacob (1614-1677, 1675?) & 2/wf Ann _?_ , m/2 John SEARS 1680; in Eng; Lancaster/Woburn
FARRER, Jacob[2], Jr. (1641-1675) & Hannah HAYWARD (1647-), dau George, m/2 Adam HALLOWAY 5 Mar 1680/1; 11 Nov 1668; Lancaster
FARRAR, Jacob[3] (1669-1732) & Susannah REDDIT/REDIATE (-1737/8); 26 Dec 1692; Concord/Worcester
FARRAR, John (?1611-1690) & 2/wf [Johanna] _?_ (-1687+, 1701+); b 1656; Woburn
FARRER, John (-1670, ?3 Nov 1669) (son Jacob) & Mary/Hannah HILLARD (no) (see John FARROW & Mary), did she m/2 John WHITCOMB 1671; 30 Jun 1667, 11 Nov 1668; Lancaster
FARRAR, John[3] (?1672-1707) & Elizabeth MERRIAM (1673-1755), m/2 Isaac GATES ca 1710?, aft 16 Jun 1708; 6 Dec 1699; Concord
FARRER, Thomas (1615-1693/4) & Elizabeth _?_ (-1680/1); ca 1645?; ?Roxbury/Lynn
FARRAR, Thomas (-1734) & 1/wf Abigail COLLINS; 3 Mar 1680/1; Lynn
FARRER, Thomas (-1734) & 2/wf Elizabeth HOOD; 6 Dec 1682, no issue?; Lynn
FARRETT, William & Mary DAILIE; 8 Dec 1681; Medfield
FARRINGTON, Benjamin & _?_ ; b 1697; Branford, CT
FARINGTON, Daniel (1664-) & Abigail FISHER (1674-); 5 Oct 169-, 1691; Wrentham
FARRINGTON, Edmund (1588-1671) & Elizabeth _?_ (1586-); b 1621; Lynn/LI
FARINGTON, Edward/Edmund? (-bef 1695) & 2/wf Dorothy [BOWNE]; ca 1650; Flushing, LI
FARINGTON, Edward (1662-) & Martha BROWNE (-1738), Reading, dau John; 9 Apr 1690; Andover
FARRINGTON, John & Mary BULLARD, m/2 William HOADLEY 1686?; 23 Apr 1649; Dedham/Charlestown
FARINGTON, John (?1624-) & Elizabeth [KNIGHT]?, m/2 Mark GRAVES 1667; b 1662, earlier?; Lynn
FARRINGTON, John (1654-) & Mary JANES; 24 Sep 1677; Dedham
FARRINGTON, John & Lydia HUDSON; 7 Oct 1679; Lynn
FARRINGTON, John (-1715) & _?_ ; b 1683; Flushing, LI
FARRINGTON, John & Sarah FRANKLIN; 18 Oct 1698; Marblehead
FARRINGTON, Matthew (?1623-1700/1) & _?_ ; b 1658, b 1649; Lynn
FARRINGTON, Matthew (1649-1727) & Sarah POTTER (-1687), ?Newhall; 28 Apr 1675; Charlestown/Lynn
FARRINGTON, Matthew (1649-1727, 1728?) & Mary/Hannah _?_ ; b 1689; Flushing, LI
FARRINGTON, Nathaniel (1656-) & Sarah [WHITING] (1660-1723); b 1683?; Dedham
FARRINGTON, Thomas (-1704±?, 1697?, 1699) & Abigail [PALMER] (ca 1668-); b 30 Nov 1692, ca 1685?, b 1683?, b 1677; Newtown, LI/Flushing, LI
FARRINGTON, William & Lydia [MANSFIELD] (1662-1726); b 1683?, b 1684; Lynn
FARRINGTON, _?_ & 2/wf Mary JOHNSON, dau Samuel; b 1693; Lynn
FARRINGTON, _?_ & _?_ [PONTON]; b 11 Nov 1695, b 1690?, b 1674?; Westchester, NY
FAROUGH, George & Ann WHITMORE; 16 Jan 1643/4; Ipswich

FARROW, John[1] (-1687) & Frances __?__ (-1689); in Eng, b 1632; Hingham
FARROW, John (1639-1716) & 1/wf Mary HILLIARD; 14 Aug 1664; Hingham
FARROW, John (1639-1716) & 2/wf Frances __?__ ; 16 Nov 1691; Hingham
FAROW, John (1670-), Hingham & Persis HOLEBROKE/HOLBROOK, Scituate; 30 Apr 1696; Scituate
FARROW, Nathan (1654-) & 1/wf Mary GARNET/GARDNER; 5 Dec 1683; Hingham
FARWELL, Henry (-1670) & Olive WELBIE (-1692); Boston, Eng, 16 Apr 1629; Concord
FARWELL, Henry (1674-) & Susannah RICHARDSON; 23 Jan 1695/6; Chelmsford
FARWELL, John & 1/wf Sarah WHEELER (-1662); 4 Nov 1658; Concord
FARWELL, John & 2/wf Sarah [FISKE]; aft 23 May 1662, no issue; Concord
FARWELL, Joseph (1641-) & Hannah LEARNED/LARNED (1649-); 25 Dec 1666; Chelmsford
FARWELL, Joseph (1670-) & Hannah COLBORN/COLBURN; 23 Jan 1695/6; Chelmsford
FARWELL, Thomas & Sarah [POOLE?], m/2 George SHOVE 1686; Taunton
FASSIT, John & Mary HILL; 31 Mar 1697; Billerica
FASSETT, Joseph (1672-) & Mary [MUNROE] (1678-); b 1701; Lexington/Cambridge
FASSET, Patrick (-1713, 1711?) & Sarah [?REYLEY]; b 1670?, b 1672; Malden/Billerica/Concord
FATHOM, Thomas & Elizabeth __?__ ; b 1686; Boston
FAULKNER, David (1620-) & Mary __?__ ; b 1653; Boston
FAULKNER, David & Elizabeth __?__ ; b 1687; Malden
FAWKNER, Edmund[1] (-1687) & Dorothy (_?_) ROBINSON (-2 Dec 1668), wid; Salem, 4 Feb 1647; Andover
FAUKNER, Francis[2] (?1651, ?1652-1732) & Abigail DANE (1652-1730); 12 Oct 1675; Andover
FAULKNER, John[2] (1654-1706) & Sarah ABBOTT (1660-1723); 19 Oct 1682; Andover
FALCONER, Patrick (-1692) & Hannah JONES, m/2 James CLARK, m/3 John BOOTH 1715; 2 Oct 1689; New Haven
FAUNCE, John (-1653) & Patience [MORTON] (1615?-1691), m/2 Thomas WHITNEY; ca 1633; Plymouth
FAUNCE, Joseph (1653-1687) & Judith RICKARD; 3 Jan 1677, 1677/8; Plymouth
FAUNCE, Thomas (-1741) & Jean/?Jane NELSON (1651-1717); 12 Dec 1672, 13 Dec; Plymouth
FAVOR, Philip & Mary [OSGOOD] (1669-); ca 1688; Salisbury
FAVOR, Thomas & Ruth (REDDING) DONNELL, w Joseph; 9 Jul 1697; York, ME
FAWER, Barnabas (-1654) & 1/wf Dinah __?__ (-1642); Dorchester
FAWER, Barnabas (-1654) & 2/wf Grace NEGOOSE (-1671), m/2 John JOHNSON 1656+; 10 Mar 1642/3; Dorchester
FAWRE, Eleazer (1642-1665?) & Mary PRESTON (?1645-), m/2 Samuel JENKINS 1670; 28 May 1662; Boston
FAWER/FARR, Gibson (1666-1726) & Rebecca [ELLERTON] (-1720); b 1688(9?); Boston
FAWER, Isaac, Woburn (see [FARRAR]) & Mary WALCOTT (1675-); 29 Apr 1696; Danvers
FAWNE/?FANE, John & Elizabeth __?__ ; ?in Eng, b 1636; Ipswich/Haverhill/Salisbury
FAXON, Josiah (1660-1731) & Mehitable [ADAMS] (1665-1753); b 1690; Braintree
FAXON, Richard (-1674) & Elizabeth [SHEPARD?] (-1704), m/2 Caleb HOBART 1676; b 1655; Braintree
FAXON, Thomas[1] (ca 1601-1680) & 1/wf Joane __?__ (-?1665/1670); in Eng, ca 1625; Braintree
FAXON, Thomas[2] (1629-1662) & Deborah THAYER (1630, 1634?-1662); 11 Apr 1653; Braintree
FAXON, Thomas[1] (-1680) & 2/wf Sarah (MULLINS) (GANNETT) SAVILL (1621-1697), w Thomas, w William; 5 Sep 1670; Braintree
FAXON, Thomas (1662-1690) & Mary [BLANCHARD] (1662-); b 1686; Braintree
FAY, David (1679-1738) & Sarah LARKIN (1677-); 1 May 1699; Marlborough/Charlestown/Southborough
FAY, John (-1690) & 1/wf Mary [BRIGHAM] (-1676); ca 1667; Marlboro/Cambridge
FAY, John (-1690) & 2/wf Susannah (SHATTUCK) MOSS/MORSE (1643-), w Joseph, m/3 Thomas BRIGHAM 1695; 5 Jul 1678; Watertown, CT
FAY, John (1669-1747) & 1/wf Elizabeth WELLINGTON (1673-1729); ?1 Dec 1690; Watertown/Cambridge/?Marlboro
FAY, Samuel & Tabitha WARD; 16 May 1699; Marlborough
FAY, Josiah & [Mary THORNTON]; b 1707, b 1701?
FEAKE, Henry (-1657) & 1/wf Jane WOOLSTONE; St. Saviour's, Southwark, Eng, 23 Jan 1615, 1615/16; Sandwich/Newtown, LI

FEAKE, Henry (-1657) & 2/wf 4/wf? Joanna [WHEELER], wid?; 1654; Newtown, LI
FEAKE, James (-1727) & Mary [PATRICK]; b 1660; Flushing, LI?
FEAKE, John (-May 1724) & Elizabeth PRIOR/PRYER (1656-25 Jan 1701/2); 15 Sep 1673; Killingworth, LI
FEAKE, Robert (-1662) & Elizabeth (FONES) WINTHROP, w Henry, ?m/3 William HALLETT; 1630, 1631; Boston
FEAKE, Tobias & 1/wf Anneke (VanBEYEREN) [PATRICK] (-1656), w Daniel; 1644/49; Flushing, LI
FEAKE, Tobias & 2/wf Mary [?PATRICK] (-1692), [wid]; Flushing, LI?
FEARING, Israel (1644-) & Elizabeth WILDER; 22 Jan 1673; Hingham
FEARING, John (-1665) & Margaret [?HAWKS] (-1690), m/2 Robert WILLIAMS 1675; b 1642; Hingham
FEARING, John & Hannah BEAL (?1656-1717); Boston, 15 Dec 1676; Hingham
FERN, John & Susanna _?_; b 1695; Lynn
FELCH, Henry[1] (-1670) & 1/wf Margaret _?_ (-1655, Boston); in Eng, b 1625; Gloucester/Reading/?Boston/?Watertown
FELCH/FITCH, Henry[2] (-1699) & Hannah [SARGENT] (1629-1717); b 1649, 1640?; Reading/Boston
FELCH, Henry[1] (-1670) & 2/wf Elizabeth [WIBORNE], w Thomas; ca 1657; Boston
FELTCH, John (1660-1746) & Elizabeth GOING; 25 May 1685; Reading/Weston
FELCH, Joseph (-1727) & Mary _?_ (-1731); b 1689; Reading
FELLOWS, Ephraim (1639-1702+) & 1/wf Mary _?_ (-1671); b 1668, b 1666; Salisbury/Plainfield, CT
FELLOWS, Ephraim (1639-1702+) & 2/wf Anne (CROSS) MARSHALL (ca 1651-1710+), w Thomas; b 1685; Ipswich/Plainfield, CT
FELLOWS, Isaac (1635-1721) & Joanna BORN/BOREMAN?/BOARDMAN (?1646-1732); 29 Jan 1672, 1671/2; Ipswich
FELLOWS, John (?1668, 1673?-) & Rachel VARNEY; 14 Oct 1692; Ipswich/Plainfield, CT
FELLOWS, Joseph (-1693) & Ruth FRAILE (-1729); 19 Apr 1675; Ipswich
FILLOW/FELLOWS?, Lewis & Mary HARRIS; 24 Oct 1700; Boston
FELLOWS, Richard (-1663, Hatfield) & Ursula _?_ (-1690, Hatfield); b 1642?, b 1646; Hartford/Springfield/etc.
FELLOES, Samuel (-1698) & Ann _?_ (-1684); b 1647, ca 1640?; Salisbury
FELLOES, Samuel (1647-1730) & Abigail BARNERD/BARNARD; 2 Jun 1681; Salisbury
FELLOWS, Samuel & Deborah SANBORN (1681-), m/2 Benjamin SHAW; 15 Nov 1698; Hampton, NH
FELLOWS, William[1] (?1609-1677) (ae ca 50 in 1659) & [Mary] [?AYERS]; b 1635?; Ipswich
FELLOWS, William (1666-1737) & Elizabeth RUST; 7 Dec 1693; Ipswich
FELT, George (-1693, ae 92) & Elizabeth [?WILKINSON], dau wid Prudence; ca 1633?, bef 1639; Charlestown
FELT, George & Philippa ANDREWS, m/2 Samuel PLATTS 1682, m/3 Thomas NELSON 1690; 25 Nov 1662; Falmouth, ME
FELT, George & 1/wf Hannah [HOLMES] (1667-1693), wid?; b 1687; Salem/Watertown/Cambridge/Falmouth, ME
FELT, George & 2/wf Jemima (BONFIELD) LUCKEIS/LUCKES (see LUCAS), w Oliver; 27 Feb 1695/6; Marblehead
FELT, Jonathan (-1702) & 1/wf Elizabeth PURCHAS/PURCHASE; 3 Jan 1694/5; Salem/Falmouth, ME
FELT, Jonathan (-1702) & 2/wf Elizabeth [BLANEY], m/2 John TAYLOR; (see Thomas PURCHASE)
FELT, Joseph & Sarah MILLS (1675-); m int 12 Oct 1700; Lynn/N. Yarmouth, ME
FELT, Moses (?1651-) & Lydia [MAINS] (1657±-), dau of John; Casco Bay, ME/Chelsea
FELT, Samuel & Elizabeth _?_, m/2 Benjamin PLUMER; b 1691?, b 1696; Salem
FELTON, Benjamin & Mary _?_; b 1639; Salem
FELTON, Henry & _?_; b 1699, Salem; Salem
FELTON, John & 1/wf Mary TOMPKINS (1649-1688); 29 Nov 1670; Salem
FELTON, John & 2/wf Hannah _?_; b 1693; Salem

FELTON, Nathaniel (-1705, in 90th y) (ae 78 in 1695) & Mary [SKELTON] (1627-1701); ca 1643; Salem
FELTON, Nathaniel & Ann ORNE/HORNE (1657-); b 1680; Salem
FELTON, Nathaniel & Elizabeth FOOT; 29 Jun 1698; Salem
FELTON, _?_ & Ellen/Eleanor _?_ (-1652+); b 1613; Salem
FENN, Benjamin (-1672) & 1/wf Sarah [BALDWIN] (1621-1663); ca 1658; Milford, CT
FENN, Benjamin (1640-1689) & Mehitable GUNN (1641-living 1706), ?m/2 Nicholas CAMP, Jr. aft 1689 (see Nathaniel BRISCOE); 21 Dec 1660, 20 Dec; Milford, CT
FENN, Benjamin, Sr. (-1672) & 2/wf Susanna WARD/WOOD/WORD; 12 Mar 1663, 1663/4, 10 Mar 1663/4; Milford, CT/Boston/New Haven
FENN, Benjamin (1662, bpt 1667-1732) & Sarah [CLARK] (1664-1727); b 1693; Milford, CT
FENN, Edward (-1732) & Mary THORPE (1666-); 15 Nov 1688; Wallingford, CT
FENN, George (-1669) & _?_ (-1676); b 1669; Charlestown
FENN, James (1672-) & Joanna [PRUDDEN] (1676-); b 1697; Milford, CT
FENN, Joseph & Esther HATCH
FENN, Robert & 1/wf Deborah [TOOGOOD?]; b 1641; Salem/Boston
FEN, Robert & 2/wf Mary (_?_) HAWKINS, w Thomas, m/3 Henry SHRIMPTON 1661; 26 Jun 1654; Boston
FENNER, Arthur[1] (?1619, 1622?-1703) & 1/wf Mehitable [WATERMAN] (-1684(-)); b 1652, ca 1642?, ca 1649; Salem/Providence
FENNER, Arthur[1] (?1619, ?1622-1703) & 2/wf Howlong HARRIS (-1708); 16 Dec 1684, 1686?; Providence
FENNER, Arthur[2] (-1725) & Mary [SMITH] (-1737); ca 1694/1700; Providence
FENNER, John (1631-1709) & Sarah [CLARK], dau William of Haddam, CT; b 1673; Saybrook, CT
FENNER, Thomas (1652-1718) & 1/wf Alice [ROLPH/RALPH] (1657-1682(-)); ca 1675; Providence
FENNER, Thomas (1652-1718) & 2/wf Dinah BORDEN (1664-1761); 26 Jul 1682; Providence
FENNO, Benjamin[2] (1673-), Milton & Mary BELSHER/BELCHER (1676-1758?), Milton; 23 Sep 1696; Milton
FENNO, John[1] (ca 1629-1708) & Rebecca [TUCKER] (-1690); b 1662; Milton
FENNO, John, Jr. (1665-1741), Milton & Rachel NEWCOME/NEWCOMB (-1750), Braintree; b 1692, on or aft 25 Jun 1690; Milton/Stonington/Canton
FENSUM/FENSEM?/FENECUM?, Isaac & Hannah DICKERMAN (-1706); 15 Mar 1685/6, 15 Mar 1685; Malden/Charlestown
FENTON, Robert & Dorothy (Deborah is wrong) FARRAR; 27 Feb 1688, 1687/8; Woburn/Windham, CT
FENTON, Thomas, Boston & Elizabeth BASSETT, Boston; 17 Aug 1687; Watertown/Boston/Cambridge/Bridgewater
FENWICK, Jeremiah & Elizabeth STEADFORD/STRATFORD; 3 Jan 1699, 3 Jan 1700; Boston
FENWICK, George (1603-1656/7) (returned to Eng) & 1/wf Alice (APSLEY) BOTELER (-1645?), w John; in Eng; Saybrook, CT
FENWICK, George (1603-1656/7) & 2/wf Katherine HESILRIGE; 1652
FERGUSON, Alexander (-1731) & Elizabeth GOING/GOWEN?/SMITH alias GOWEN (1673±-); 11 Feb 1694, 1694/5; Kittery, ME
FERGUSON, Archibald (ae 37 in 1685) & Mary [MAVERICK?] (1637?-1695); b 1684; Marblehead
FERGUSON, Daniel (-1676) & Mary _?_ (-1708+); b 1655; Kittery, ME
FERGUSON, James & _?_ ; b 1660; Stratford, CT/?Westchester, NY
FERGUSON, James (-1707) & Elizabeth [HODSDON] (-1707); ca 1699; Kittery, ME/Berwick, ME
FERGUSON, John (1655-) & Mary _?_ ; by 1679
FORGASON, John & Mary [TURNER], sister of David; b 1684, b 28 Feb 1681; Westchester, NY
FORGINSON, Richard (-1701) & Sarah HURLEY, m/2 John LAICORE; 30 Jul 1690, 31 Jul; Cambridge
FORGASON, John, Sr. & Sarah _?_ ; Westchester, NY
FORGASON, Thomas & Mary [FARRINGTON?]/[PONTON?]; b 1 Jul 1697; Westchester, NY
FERNALD, John (1642-1687, 1697?) & Mary [NORMAN]; b 1673; Wells, ME
FERNALD, John (1673-1754) & Sarah _?_ ; b 1698; Kittery, ME

FERNALD, Renald (1595-1656) & Joanna (?WARBURTON) (1603-1660); b 1633, b 1620; Kittery, ME

FERNALD, Samuel (ca 1644-1698) & Hannah [SPINNEY]?/?NORMAN (?1650, 1657?-); b 1676, ?9 Feb 1670, ca 1674; Portsmouth, NH/Eliot, ME

FERNALD, Samuel & 1/wf Susanna PAUL; 12 Oct 1699; Kittery, ME

FERNALD, Thomas (1633-1697) & 2/wf? Temperance [HUNKING]/WASHINGTON? (-1714+); b 1659?, ca 1666?, ca 1660, 1639?; Kittery, ME

FERNALD, Thomas (1668-1709?) & Elizabeth [HUNKING], m/2 Samuel WINKLEY; no issue; Kittery, ME

FERNALD, Thomas & Mary THOMPSON; 28 Nov 1700; Kittery, ME

FERNALD, William (1646/7-) & Elizabeth LANGDON; 16 Nov 1671; Kittery, ME

FERNSIDE, John (?1611-1693) (?cousin of James CUSHMAN) & Elizabeth [STARR] (1621-1704); b 1642; Duxbury/Boston

FERNES, John (1666-bef 1693?) & __?__, m/3 Robert SMALL of Norwalk, CT?; Woodbury, CT

FERNES, John (1666-bef 1693?) & 2/wf? __?__, wid of Robert SMALL

FERNES, Samuel (-1704) & __?__ (-1701, ae 58); b 1663; New Haven

FERRIS, Aaron & Grace __?__; Isles of Shoals/etc.

FERRYES/FARRIS?, James & Mary __?__; b 1686(7?); Boston

FERRIS, James² & __?__; b 1670; Greenwich, CT

FERRIS, James² (1662/1674-1726) & Mary __?__; ca 1698; Greenwich, CT

FERRIS, Jeffrey¹ (-1666) & 1/wf ?Mary/[--]ne __?__ (-1658); ca 1634?; Watertown/Wethersfield, CT/Stamford, CT/Greenwich, CT

FERRIS, Jeffrey¹ (-1666) & 2/wf Susanna (NORMAN) LOCKWOOD (-23 Dec 1660, Greenwich), w Robert; bef 20 Oct 1658?; Fairfield, CT

FERRIS, Jeffrey¹ (-1666) & 3/wf Judith (FESKE) PALMER, w Willaim, m/3 John BOWERS 1666?, 1667; b 6 Jan 1664; Stamford, CT

FERRIS, John² (1639-1715) & 1/wf Mary [JACKSON] (-1704); ca 1685; Stamford, CT/Westchester Co., NY

FERRIS, John³ & Abigail HAIGHT/[HOYT], Norwalk; 13 Feb 1695, Greenwich, CT; ?Norwalk, CT

FERRIS, Joseph² (-1699) & Ruth KNAPP, m/2 John CLAPP?; 20 Nov 1657; Stamford, CT

FERRIS, Joseph³ (1658-1740) & Mary [HOYT?]/[SMITH?]; ?12 Dec 1686, b 1688; Stamford, CT

FERRIS, Peter² (-1706) & 1/wf Elizabeth REYNOLDS; 5 Jul 1654, ?15 Feb 1654; Stamford, CT

FERRIS, Samuel³ & Sarah PINCKNEY; 1699, ca 11 Dec 1699; Greenwich, CT

FERIS, William & Abigail EVERED; 18 Oct 1687; Watertown

FERRIS, Zechariah (-1711) & Sarah (BLONDS?)/BLOUDS?; 17 Nov 1673, 12 Nov 1673; Charlestown

FERRIS, Zachariah (1674-) & Sarah (READ) [BARLOW], w Joseph; ca 1699?, aft 3 Nov 1698; Fairfield, CT

FERRIS, __?__ & Elizabeth [HALL] (1678-)

FERRY, Charles (-1690, 1699) & Sarah HARMON (1644-1740); 29 Mar 1661; Springfield

FERRY, Charles (1665-1720) & 1/wf Rebecca BURT (1665-); 29 Jan 1690, 1690/1; Deerfield/Springfield

FERRY, Charles (1665-1720) & 2/wf Abigail WARNER (1675-), m/2 Thomas HALE; 4 May 1693; Springfield

FARRY, Henry (-1702) & Susanna __?__; b 1694(5?); Boston

FERRY, John (1662-1745) & 1/wf Martha MILLER (1665-1691); 11 Nov 1686; Springfield

FERRY, John (1662-1745) & 2/wf Mary MUDGE (-1694); 17 Nov 1692; Springfield

FERRY, John (1662-1745) & 3/wf Mary COOLEY (1675-1708); 28 May 1696; Springfield

FESSENDEN, John (-1666) & Jane __?__ (-1682, ae 80); b 1658, [ca 1625/30?]; Cambridge/Lexington

FESINDEN, Nicholas (ca 1650-1719) & [Margaret] [CHENEY] (1656-1717); b 1674; Cambridge-/Lexington

FEVERYEAR, Edmund (-1710) & Mary (GRAFTON) HARDY (-1705), w Joseph; 6 Jun 1688; Salem

FEVERYEARE, Edward & Tabitha PITMAN/PICKMAN?; 30 Aug 1664; Salem

FICKETT, Peter & Mary BONDFEILD/BONFIELD?, m/2 Pentecost BLACKINTON 1689; 9 Dec 1681; Marblehead

FICKETT, John (1645-) & Abigail [LIBBY]; ca 1670/5?; Scarborough, ME

FIELD, Alexander (-1666) & 1/wf _?_; b 1642, b 1640?; Charlestown/Salem

FIELD, Alexander (-1666) & 2/wf Gillian (DRAKE) [MANSFIELD] (-1669), w Richard; 1657; New Haven

FIELD, Ambrose & _?_; b 1701?; Newtown, LI

FIELD, Anthony (?1638-1689) & Sarah [HEDGES] (-1691+); b 1663; Flushing, LI

FIELD, Benjamin (1640-1732) & 1/wf _?_; b 1674; Flushing, LI

FIELD, Benjamin (son of Robert) & 1/wf Hannah BOWNE (1665-1707); 30 Nov 1691; Flushing, LI

FIELD, Benjamin & Experience ALLEN; ?29 May 1692, ?m int 26 Aug 1692; Newtown, LI?/Flushing, LI

FIELD, Benjamin & Sarah _?_; b 1701?; Flushing, LI

FIELD, Darby (-1651) & Agnes _?_, m/2 William WILLIAMS; b 1645; Dover, NH

FIELD, Ebenezer & Mary DUDLEY (1678-); 14 Jan 1697, 1696/7; Deerfield/E. Deerfield/Guilford, CT

FIELD, Elnathan (-1754?) & Elizabth _?_; b 1696, ca 1690?; Newtown, LI

FIELDS, George (-1693) & Margery [LEWIS] (-1694+); b 1691; Sandwich

FIELD, John (-1686) & [?Ruth] _?_ (-1686+); in Eng, b 1640?; Providence

FIELD, John (-1717, ?Coventry, Hatfield) & Mary EDWARDS (1650-); 17 Dec 1670, 15 Dec; Hatfield/Northampton

FIELD, John (-1698) & Elizabeth [EVERDEN]; b 1671(2?); Bridgewater

FIELD, John & Mary (GODDARD) BENNETT, w Arthur, m/3 Hans WALFORD (see Joseph); aft 20 Jan 1682/3

FIELD, John (1659-) & Margaret GAMING; b 1689, ca 1683?; Flushing/Piscataway, NJ/Bound Brook, NJ

FEILD, John, Boston & Sarah (SMITH) STEVENS FRANKLIN (1646-), w James, w Jonathan?; 30 Aug 1694; Haverhill/Newbury

FIELD, John (1673-) & Mary BENNETT, Northampton; 9 Nov 1696; Deerfield

FEILDS, John (1671-) & Elizabeth AMES (1680-); - Nov 1697; Bridgewater/Providence

FIELD, John (1672-), Hatfield & Sarah COLEMAN (1673-), Hatfield; 1698?, b 1700?; Hatfield/Deerfield/Hadley

FIELD, John (-1718) & Elizabeth TREWORGY; b 1701?; Portsmouth, NH

FIELD, Joseph (1658-1736, ae 78), Hatfield & Joanna WYATT (-1722), Hartford; 28 Jun 1683; Hatfield/Sunderland

FIELD, Joseph & Mary (GODDARD) BENNETT, w Arthur?, m/3 Henry WOFFORD (see John FIELD)

FIELD, Robert (1602-) & 1/wf Ruth FAIRBANK; Halifax, Eng, 23 Nov 1624; Newport, RI/Flushing, LI

FIELD, Robert & 2/wf Elizabeth TAYLOR; Bradford, Eng, 18 May 1630; Newport, RI/Flushing, LI

FIELD, Robert (-1673?) & 3/wf Charity _?_; b 1638; Newport/Flushing, LI

FIELD, Robert (-1677) & Mary [PHILLIPS]/STANLEY?; b 1644; Boston

FIELD, Robert (?1636-1701) & Susannah [STEVENSON]; b 1660?; Flushing, LI/Newtown, LI

FIELD, Robert (1653-1710?) & Mary JENNERY/CHINERY (1659-), dau Lambert; 11 Oct 1680; Braintree

FIELD, Robert (-1735) & Phebe (TITUS) SCUDDER (1660-1742), w Samuel d 1685; 24 Feb 1698/90; Westbury, LI/Newtown, LI

FIELD, Samuel (1651-1697), Hatfield & Sarah GILBERT (1655-1712), Springfield, m/2 Ebenezer CHAPIN 1702; 9 Aug 1676; Hatfield/Springfield?/Deerfield/Hadley

FIELD, Thomas/Wm.? (1648±-1717) & Martha HARRIS (-1717(-)); b 1670; Providence/Braintree

FEILD, Thomas & Mary LEACHE (1654-); 22 Mar 1680; Salem

FIELD, Thomas (1670-1752) & 1/wf Abigail [DEXTER]/[HOPKINS]; ca 1693?; Providence

FIELD, Thomas & Anne BISHOP; m int 28 Jun 1695; Boston/?Bridgewater

FIELD, Thomas (1674-) & Hannah _?_ (1680-1761); b 1701; Flushing, LI

FIELD, William (-1665) & Deborah _?_ (-1679); no issue; Providence

FIELD, William (1650-) & 1/wf Martha [TWELVES/TUELL]; b 1684; Braintree

FIELD, William (1650-) & 2/wf Rebecca _?_

FIELD, Zachariah (-1666) & Mary [?STANLEY] (-1670); b 1643, ca 1641; Deerfield/Northampton/Hatfield/Hadley

FIELD, Zachariah (-1674, Deerfield) & Sarah WEBB (1646-1704), Northampton, m/2 Robert PRICE; 17 Dec 1668; Northampton/Deerfield/Hadley/Hatfield

FIELD, Zachariah/Zacharias? (1648-1711+) & Sarah ROBERTS, dau John; by 1677; Dover, NH

FIELD, Zachariah (-1693) & Sarah [THORNTON] (-1716), m/2 John GURNEY b 1706; b 1685(6?); Providence

FIELD, _?_ & Mary _?_, m/2 Joshua CARTER 1663

FIELD, _?_ & Mary (BISHOP) (HODGKINS) [JOHNSON], w _?_, w Isaac; aft 1687; ?CT

FIELD, _?_ & Mary [MILLER] (1664-); Charlestown

FIELDER, Stephen (-1686±) & Mary [GRIGGS] (1659-), m/2 John SEARLE 1713; ca 1682, b 1685; Roxbury/Boston

FIFIELD, Benjamin (?1648-1706) & Mary COLCORD (1649-1741); 28 Dec 1673; Hampton, NH/Hampton Falls

FIFIELD, Giles (?1624-) (called Henry GREEN "uncle" in 1660) & 1/wf Mary PERKINS (bpt 1639-); 7 Jun 1652, ?17 Jun; Charlestown/Hampton, NH

FIFIELD, Giles (-1676) & 2/wf Judith (CARTER) CONVERSE (-1678, 1676?, 1677?), w Samuel; 2 May 1672; Charlestown

FIFIELD, Giles (1658-1718) & Elizabeth [RAINSFORD] (-1743, ae 84); b 1683(4?); Boston

FIFIELD, John (1671-) & Abigail _?_/[?BEAN]/[?SLEEPER]; b 1698; Hampton, NH

FIFIELD, Richard (1665-) & 1/wf Mary THURSTON (-1701); 6 Aug 1688; Boston/Hampton, NH

FIFIELD, William (-1700) (ae 80 in 1696) & Mary _?_ (-1711, in 93rd y) (ae 76 in 1696); b 1646; Hampton, NH

FIFIELD, William (1652-1715) & Hannah CRAM (1673-); 26 Oct 1693; Hampton, NH

FIGG, John & Anne/Amey _?_ ; b 1684; Boston

FILER, George & _?_ ; b 1664; Northampton/Westfield

FILER, John (1642-1723) & 1/wf Elizabeth DOLMAN (-1684), England; 17 Oct 1672; Windsor, CT

FILER, John (1642-1723) & 2/wf Bethesda POLE/POOLE (-1716); 21 Oct 1686; Windsor, CT

FILER, Samuel & _?_ ; b 1700, b 1698?; East Hampton, LI

FILER, Walter (-1683) & Jane _?_ (-1690); b 1642; Windsor, CT

FILER, Zerubbabel (1644-1714, 1715?) & Experience STRONG (1650-1716+); 27 May 1669; Windsor, CT/Suffield

FILLEBROWN, John & Sarah [WYER] (1678-1716); b 1698, b 1697; Cambridge

FILLEBROWN, Thomas (ca 1632-1713, ae 82) & Anna/Anne _?_ (1632-1714); b 1658?, b 1662; Cambridge

FILLEBROWN, Thomas, Charlestown & Sarah/Rebecca CUTTER, Cambridge; 19 Dec 1688; Cambridge

FILLEY, John (1645-1690) & Abigail DYBLE/DIBBLE, m/2 Thomas ELGAR 1691; 1 Feb 1681; Suffield, CT

FILLEY, Jonathan (1672-) & Deborah LOOMIS; 5 Jun 1700, ?5 Sep; Windsor, CT

FILLEY, Samuel (1643-1711/12) & Ann/?Anna GILLET (1639-1711); 29 Oct 1663; Windsor, CT

FILLEY, William (?1620-) & Margaret _?_ ; 2 Sep 1642, 164-; Windsor, CT

FILMINGHAM/FILLINGHAM?/FELMINGHAM?, Francis & _?_ [COOPER]; b 1637; Salem

FINCH, Abraham[2] (-1637, inv 1640) & Dorothy [MOULTON], dau Robert, m/2 John EDWARDS 1637, m/3 Richard TOWSLEY 1669; Watertown/Wethersfield, CT

FINCH, Abraham & _?_ ; b 1681

FINCH, Abraham & [Martha COUCH]; aft 22 Dec 1687, b 1696; Fairfield, CT

FINCH, Daniel (-1667) & 1/wf _?_ ; b 1615; Watertown/Wethersfield, CT/Stamford/Fairfield, CT

FINCH, Daniel (-1667) & 2/wf Elizabeth THOMPSON, w John; m cont 25 Dec 1657, ?25 Jun; ?Stamford, CT

FINCH, Daniel & Mary DICKERSON, w Thomas, w _?_, m/3 Nicholas PINNION; by 4 Apr 1660

FINCH, Humphrey & Rebecca BONDFIELD; 16 Oct 1684; Marblehead

FINCH, Isaac & 1/wf Elizabeth BASSETT; - Oct 1658, 8 Oct 1658; Stamford, CT

FINCH, Isaac & 2/wf Anna/Ann _?_ (-1703); b 1683; Stamford, CT

FINCH, Israel & Sarah GOLD; 1 Dec 1692; Stamford, CT

FINCH, John (-1657) & Martha _?_, m/2 John GREEN 1658; b 1650; Stamford, CT

FINCH, John (-1685?) & Hannah (MARSH) [FULLER], w Launcelot; aft 8 Nov 1652; New Haven

FINCH, John & 1/wf Hannah [PETTIT] (1666)

FINCH, John (1659-will 1703) & ?2/wf Hannah (SCOFIELD) [WEBB] (-1710, Stamford, CT), w Joseph

FINCH, Joseph & Elizabeth AUSTIN; 23 Nov 1670; Stamford, CT

FINCH, Nathaniel & 1/wf Mary HEMINGWAY (1668-1692?, 1691?); by 1691; New Haven/Branford, CT

FINCH, Nathaniel & 2/wf Elizabeth [HEMINGWAY] (1672-), m/2 Zachariah HOW, m/3 Samuel BROCKETT; b 1694, 1693?, denounced by both parties; New Haven/Branford, CT

FINCH, Nathaniel & Mary (HOADLEY) (FRISBIE) DARBY, w Jonathan, w Robert; b 1699; ?Branford, CT

FINCH, Samuel (-1674) & 1/wf Katherine __?__; b 1638; Roxbury

FINCH, Samuel (-1674) & Judith POTTER (-1683?); 13 Dec 1654; Roxbury/Wethersfield, CT

FINCH, Samuel (-1698) & [Sarah?] HOYT (-1713), dau Simon; b 1658?; Stamford, CT

FINCH, Samuel & Sarah GOLD; 1 Dec 1692; Stamford, CT

FINSON, Thomas (d at sea) & [Esther?] [?HARWOOD]; b 1644; Boston

FIRMIN, David & Mary [MORRELL]; ?Hempstead, LI/?Newtown, LI

FIRMIN, Giles¹ (-1634) & Martha [DOGGETT]; Ipswich

FIRMIN, Giles (?1614-1697, in Eng) & Susan [WARD]; Boston/Ipswich/Haverhill

FURMAN, John (-bef 16 Jan 1648/9) (ae 46 in 1634) & __?__; Watertown

FURMAN, John (1631-1677, ae 46) & Mary __?__, m/2 Nicholas EADS/EDES; by 1656?; Hempstead, LI

FURMAN, John (-1684) & Elizabeth __?__; b 1674/5; Salem/Newbury/Enfield, CT

FURMAN, John (1650, ?1656-1726) & ?Margaret/Mary [LYNCH] (1660-1742); Newtown, LI

FURMAN, John & Margaret __?__; b 1693; Hempstead, LI/Newton, LI

FURMAN, Joseph (1655-) & __?__ [BULL]?, w John; Newtown, LI

FURMAN, Josiah (1625-) & ?Alice [?BEERS] (-1688+); b 1650; Watertown/Hempstead, LI

FURMAN, Josiah (1652, 1654-1703+) & 1/wf Sarah [STRICKLAND] ROBERTS (1644/5-1742, ae 97), w Thomas; b 1685, ca 1680; Newtown, LI

FERMIN/FORMAN, Josiah & 2/wf Mary (?FURMAN) [WAITE] (-1714), w John; aft 12 Mar 1689/90; Fairfield, CT/Taunton, CT

FURMAN, Samuel (-1732) & Elizabeth [ROBERTS]; by 1675?; Newtown, LI

FURMAN, Thomas (-1648) & Sarah __?__; b 1648, ca 1635?; Ipswich/Salisbury

FIRMAN, Thomas & Rebecca (HUSE/HUGHES) BOW (1657-1683), w Alexander; 8 Oct 1679; Middletown, CT

FISH, Ambrose (-1691) & Hannah [SWIFT?] (-1721), m/2 Thomas TOBEY; b 1676; Sandwich

FISH, Daniel (-1723) & Abigail MUMFORD (-1717); 1 May 1682; Portsmouth, RI

FISH, Daniel & Mercy ACKERS; 19 Oct 1685; New Shoreham, RI

FISH, Gabriel & Elizabeth __?__; b 1642; Boston/Exeter, NH

FISH, John (1619-) & 1/wf ?Martha [?ELAND]; ca 1650/55?, div 1680; Lynn/Sandwich/New London, CT/Stratford, CT

FISH, John (-1663) & Cecilia [RALLOCK?]; b 1663; Sandwich

FISH, John & 2/wf Martha [STARK] (eloped with Samuel CULVER ca 1673/4); b 1674

FISH, John (-1730, ae 76) & Margaret [FREEMAN?] (?1652-), ?m/2 Samuel CLEVELAND 1737; b 1679; Sandwich

FISH, John (-1742) & Joanna __?__ (-1744); ca 1680?; Portsmouth, RI/Dartmouth

FISH, John & 2/wf Hannah (PALMER) (HEWETT) STERRY (1639-), w Thomas, w Roger; 25 Aug 1681; Stonington, CT

FISH, John & Margaret __?__, ?m/2 Samuel CLEVELAND 1699 (see above); ca 1687; Canterbury, CT

FISH, Jonathan (1616-1663+) & [Mary] __?__, m/2 Gershom MOORE; b 1650, b 1644; Lynn/Sandwich/Newton, CT

FISH, Nathan (1650-1734) & 1/wf __?__

FISH, Nathan & __?__; b 1680; Newtown, LI

FISH, Nathan (1650-1734) & 2/wf Judith __?__; b 1701?, b 1696?, b 4 Jul 1705, b 1689; Falmouth, MA

FISH, Nathan & Deborah BARROWS; 20 Dec 1689, 25 Dec 1686; Plymouth

FISH, Nathaniel (1619-1694) & 1/wf __?__; b 1648; Lynn/Sandwich
FISH, Nathaniel (-1694) & 2/wf Lydia [MILLER] (1640-1694+); Charlestown/Sandwich
FISH, Preserved (1679-1745) & Ruth COOKE (1683-); 30 May 1699?, 1690; Portsmouth,
   RI/Tiverton, RI
FISH, Robert & Mary HALL; 16 Sep 1686; Portsmouth, RI
FISH, Samuel (1656-1733) & Sarah STARK?/CLARK? (-1622, ae 62); b 1684, b 1682, b 1676?;
   Stonington, CT/Groton
FISH, Stephen & Mary MICRIST; 22 Nov 1680; Salem/Reading
FISH, Thomas[1] (1619-1687) & Mary [?SHERMAN] (-1699); b 1648; Portsmouth, RI
FISH, Thomas[2] (-1684) & Grizzel STRANGE; 10 Dec 1668; Portsmouth, RI
FISH, Thomas & Margaret WOODWORTH; 10 Jan 1697; Marshfield/Duxbury
FISH, __?__ & Phebe REDINGTON (1656-)
FISH, __?__ & Mary TURNER (1679-), Scituate, dau Daniel; b 1701?; Scituate
FISHER, Amos & 1/wf Mary ELLICE/ELLIS (-1691); 12 Mar 1678/9, 1680; Dedham
FISHER, Amos & 2/wf Ruth ADAMS; 22 Dec 1691; Dedham/Boston
FISHER, Anthony (1591-1671) & 1/wf ?Mary [FISKE]?; in Eng, b 1620; Dorchester/Dedham
FISHER, Anthony (?1620-1670) & Joan/?Joanna FAXIN/FAXON (-1694), m/2 George BARBER;
   7 Sept 1647; Dedham
FISHER, Anthony (?1591-1671) & 2/wf Isabel (__?__) (RIGBY) BRECK (1610-1673), w John, w
   Edward; 14 Nov 1663; Dorchester
FISHER, Cornelius & 1/wf Leah HEATON/EATON?; 22 Feb 1652/3; Dedham/Wrentham
FISHER, Cornelius & 2/wf Sarah EUERITT/EVERITT (-1676); 25 Jul 1665, 24 Jul; Dedham
FISHER, Cornelius (1660-1743) & 1/wf Hannah/Anna [WHITNEY/?WHITING] (1660-1701); b
   1691; Wrentham/Watertown
FISHER, Daniel (ca 1618-1683) & Abigail MERRIOTT/MARRETT/MORSE (-1683); 17 Nov 1641,
   16 Nov; Dedham
FISHER, Daniel & Hannah [HILL] (1641-); b 1663; Dorchester/Taunton/Norwich
FISHER, Daniel (1650-1713) & Mary FULLER (1655-1726); 19 Jan 1674/5; Dedham
FISHER, Daniel & Mercy EDDY (1673-); 7 Feb 1694/5; Taunton
FISHER, Ebenezer & Abigail ELLES/ELLIS (1669-); 7 Feb 1695, prob 1694/5; Wrentham
FISHER, Edward (-1677) & Judith __?__ (-1682±); b 1648; Portsmouth, RI
FISHER, Eleazer & 1/wf Hannah [LEONARD?/LORAN/LORANSE]; 21 Mar 1688, prob 1687/8;
   Wrentham
FISHER, Eleazer & Hannah EDDY; 24 Dec 1696; Taunton
FISHER, Eleazer (1669-1722) & Mary AVERY (1673-1749); 13 Oct 1698; Dedham
FISHER, John (-1668) & 1/wf Elizabeth BOYLSTON (1640-); 6 Apr 1658, 1656; Medfield
FISHER, John (-1668) & 2/wf Mary TREDAWAY/TREADWAY (1642-), m/2 Timothy HAWKINS
   1675; 12 Sep 1665, b 1666, 12 Sep, Sudbury; Dedham
FISHER, John (1652-1727) & 1/wf Judith __?__; b 1673; Dedham
FISHER, John (1652-1727) & 2/wf Hannah ADAMS, m/2 Joseph METCALF; 6 Mar 1673/4;
   Medfield
FISHER, John & Rebecca ELLIS; 15 Jun 1681; Dedham
FISHER, John & Marie/Mary MEDCALFE/METCALF (-1727), dau Thomas; 8 Jun 1683; Medfield
FISHER, Jonathan & Rachel [FAIRBANKS] (1672-); b 1692; Medfield
FISHER, Joshua (1585-1674) & 1/wf ?Elizabeth __?__; in Eng, b 1619; Dedham
FISHER, Joshua (1585-1674) & 2/wf Anne LUSON; Eng, 7 Feb 1638; Dedham
FISHER, Joshua (1621-1672) & 1/wf Mary ALDIS (-1653); 15 Mar 1642/3; Dedham
FISHER, Joshua (1621-1672) & 2/wf Lydia OLIVER [OLIVER] (-1683), w Samuel; 16 Feb
   1653/4; Dedham
FISHER, Joshua (1651-1709) & Esther WISWALL (1654-1710/11); 23 Apr 1674; Medfield
FISHER, Joshua & Hannah FULLER (1675-); ca 1695, [b 1700]; Dedham
FISHER, Josiah (1654-1736) & 1/wf Meletiah BULLING/BULLEN (1655-1693); 27 Jan 1679/80;
   Dedham
FISHER, Josiah (1654-1736) & 2/wf Joanna MORSE (1674?-); 1 Sep 1693; Dedham
FISHER, Josiah (1654-1736) & 3/wf Abigail GREENWOOD (-1708); 15 Feb 1696/7; Newton
FISHER, Nathaniel (-1676) & Esther HUNTING (-1671), m/2 Timothy DWIGHT 1690; 26 Dec
   1649; Dedham
FISHER, Noah & Martha __?__; b 1694(5?); Dedham

FISHER, Samuel (-1704) & Melatiah/Meletiah/Milcha SNOW (1638-); 22 Mar 1658/9, 1659?; Dedham/Warwick

FISHER, Samuel & Abigail HEATH; 9 Apr 1684; Wrentham

FISHER, Samuel (1669-) & Lydia __?__; b 1701?; Taunton?/Newton

FISHER, Thomas (-1638) & Elizabeth __?__ (-1652); in Eng, b 1638, ca 1632; Dedham

FISHER, Thomas (-1707) & Rebecca WOODWARD (1647-1727); 11 Dec 1666; Dedham

FISHER, Vigilance & 1/wf Rebecca PARTRIDGE (-1694, ?aft 1702); 27 Nov 1678; Dedham

FISHER, Vigilance & 2/wf Hannah (HEWINS) LYON (1665-), w Israel; 14 Jun 1696, 14 Apr; Dorchester

FISHER, William & Elizabeth [PECK]; b 1678; Boston

FISHER, William & [Lydia] WALKER/HOULTON/HOLTEN; 17 Mar 168-, 17 Mar 1684; Marshfield

FISHER, __?__ & Mary (HATCH) PRIOR, w Daniel; aft 1656; ?Scituate

FISHLOCK/FITCHLOCK?, Gabriel & Catharine __?__; b 1686; Boston

FISKE, Benjamin & Bethshua MORSE (1653-); 6 Nov 1674; Medfield

FISKE, Benjamin (1674-) & Mary QUARLES (1678-); m int 31 Dec 1698, m 7 Mar 1699; Wenham

FISKE, David (-1660, 1661) & Sarah [SMITH]; in Eng, b 1624, b 1623; Watertown/Cambridge

FISKE, David (?1624-1710/11) & 1/wf Lydia [COOPER] (-1654); b 1647; Cambridge/Lexington

FISKE, David (-1710) & 2/wf Seaborne/Seaborn WILSON (-1721); 6 Sep 1655; Cambridge/Lexington

FISKE, David & Sarah DAY (1650-1729); 17 Jun 1674; Ipswich

FISK, David (-1694) & Elizabeth REED (1653-1718, Watham); 15 Dec 1674; Watertown

FISKE, James (?1620-1689) & Hannah?/[Anna PIKE]; b 1646?, b 1649; Salem?/Haverhill/Chelmsford/Groton

FISKE, James, Groton & Tabitha BUTTERICK, Groton; 2 Feb 1686/7, 1686; Groton?

FISKE, John (-1637, on ship) & Anna [LANTERSEE/LAUTERSEE?]; in Eng, b 1601

FISKE, John & 1/wf Ann [GIPPS/GIBBS?/GIPPES] (-1672); b 1635; Salem

FISK, John (-1683) & Remember [GOTT] (-1702), dau Charles, m/2 William GOODHUE 1689?; 10 Dec 1651; Ipswich

FISK, John (John CLARK, Newport, d ca 1684, was uncle of the ch of John & Sarah (WYATH) FISKE) & Sarah WYETH; 11 Dec 1651; Watertown

FISKE, John & Lydia FLETCHER (1647-), m/2 __?__ HILL; 27 Mar 1666, 5 Mar 1649; Chelmsford

FISKE, John & 2/wf Elizabeth HENCHMAN/HINCHMAN/HINCKSMAN, w Edmund; 1 Aug 1672, 18? Aug; Chelmsford

FISK, John (1655-1718/19?) & 1/wf Abigail PARKS/PARK (1658-); 9 Dec 1679, 1 Dec; Watertown

FISK, John & Hannah BALDWIN (1663-); 17 Jan 1681/2; Milford, CT/Wenham

FISKE, John & Hannah RICHARDS; 19 Jan 1699, 7 Jan; Watertown

FISK, Joseph & Elizabeth HAMMAN/HAMMONDE?; 22 May 1677; Lynn/Rehoboth/Swansea

FISK, Joseph & 1/wf Susanna/Susan [WARNER] (-1742); b 1696; Wenham/Ipswich

FISK, Moses (-1708, in 66th y) & 1/wf Sarah SYMMES (1652-1692), Charlestown; 7 Nov 1672, 7 Nov 1671, 9 Sep 1671; Braintree/Charlestown

FISK, Moses (-1708) & 2/wf Ann (SHEPARD) QUINSEY (-1708), w Daniel; 8 Jan 1700, 7 Jan 1700, 7 Jan 1700/01, 7 Jan 1701; Boston/Braintree

FISK, Nathan (?1615, 1592?-1676) & Susan/Susanna [BROWN?]; b 1642; Watertown

FISKE, Nathan & Elizabeth FRY (1639-); 26 Apr 1665; Dorchester/Watertown

FISK, Nathan & 1/wf Sarah COOLIDGE; 14 Oct 1696; Watertown

FISKE, Nathaniel & Mary (WARREN) CHILD, w John; 13 Apr 1677, 3 Apr; Watertown

FISK, Noah & Mercy GOOLD/GOOLE?; 16 Jun 1686; Chelmsford

FISKE, Phinehas/Phineas (1610, 1606-1673) & 1/wf Sarah [FRANCIS] (-1659); b 1630?, in Eng, 1638, 2 Oct 1617; Wenham

FISKE, Phinehas/Phineas (-1673) & 2/wf Elizabeth EASTWICK; 4 Apr 1660, 4 Jun; Wenham

FISKE, Samuel & Phebe (REDINGTON) BRAGG (1655-), w Thomas; 6 Nov 1679; Wenham

FISKE, Samuel (1660-) & Elizabeth [WHIPPLE]; ca 1683, 1682?, ca Nov 1682?; Wenham/Ipswich

FISKE, Samuel & 2/wf Hannah ALLEN (1662-), w William; m int 26 Apr 1697, m 24 May 1697; Wenham

FISK (FISH is wrong), Samuel (1672-), Wenham & Elizabeth BROWN (?1671-), dau Josiah; 5 Dec 1699; Wenham/Rehoboth/Reading

FISK, Theophilus & Phebe **LAMSON** (1573-); m int 18 Jul 1700, m int 19 Jul 1700, m Aug?; Ipswich/Wenham

FISKE, Thomas (?1630-1707) & 1/wf Joanna [**WHITE**]/Peggy? _?_ (1638?-); b 1652, 1650?; Wenham

FISKE, Thomas (-1723) & Rebecca **PERKINS** (1662-); 3 Nov 1678, 14 Jun 1676; Salisbury

FISKE, Thomas & Rebecca **PICKRING/PICKERING/?PERKINS**; 4 Jun 1679; Wenham

FISKE, Thomas (-1707), Wenham & Martha (**FISKE**) **FITCH**, Boston, w Thomas; 14 May 1695; Charlestown

FISKE, William (-1654) & Bridget [**MUSKETT/MATCHET**], m/2 Thomas **REX** 1661; ca 1640, b 1637?; Salem

FISKE, William (1643-1727/8) & Sarah **KILLIM/KILLHAM** (1641/2-1736/7); 15 Jan 1662, 1662/3; Wenham/Windsor, CT

FISK, William & Hannah **SMITH**; 25 Oct 1693; Watertown

FISKE, William & Marah/?Mary _?_ ; b 1695; Wenham/Andover

FITCH, Benjamin (-1713) & 1/wf Elizabeth **SKERRY** (-17 Aug 1697); 27 Feb 1665/6; Reading

FITCH, Benjamin (-1739, ae 73) & Mary **HETT**; 2 Mar 1693, 1692/3; Boston

FITCH, Benjamin (-1713) & 2/wf Mary (**ECCLES**) [**WATSON**] (-1718), w John; aft 17 Aug 1697; Reading

FITCH, Daniel (1665-) & Mary **SHERWOOD**, m/2 James **BRADFORD** ca 1716; 4 Mar 1698; Preston, CT

FITCH, James (1605-) & Elizabeth/Abigail _?_ ; b 1635; Boston

FITCH, James (1622-1702, Lebanon, CT) & 1/wf Abigail **WHITFIELD** (-1659); Oct 1648; Norwich, CT/Saybrook, CT

FITCH, James (1622-1702, Lebanon, CT) & 2/wf Priscilla **MASON** (1641-1714); Oct 1664; Norwich, CT

FITCH, James (1649-1727) & 1/wf Elizabeth **MASON** (-1684); Jan 1670; Norwich, CT/Canterbury, CT

FITCH, James (1649-1727, Canterbury) & Alice (**BRADFORD**) **ADAMS** (-1745), w William; 8 May 1687; Norwich, CT

FITCH, Jeremiah (1622-1692) & 1/wf Esther _?_ (-14 Sep 1656); b 1652/[3?]; Boston

FITCH, Jeremiah (1622-1692) & 2/wf Sarah **CHUBBUCK** (1638-); 25 Sep 1657, Boston; Hingham/Boston/Rehoboth

FITCH, Jeremiah (1622-1692) & 3/wf Martha **MESSENGER**, w John; 5 Sep 1689; Boston

FITCH, Jeremiah (1670-) & Ruth [**GIFFORD**] (1676-); b 1699; Lebanon, CT/Coventry, CT

FITCH, John (-1698) & Mary [**SUTTON**]; b 1651; Rehoboth

FITCH, John (-1676) & Ann (_?_) **HILLIER** (-1673), w John; 9 Dec 1656, ?16 Jul 1656; Windsor, CT

FITCH, John (-1715) & Mary (**STEVENS**) **COIT**, w John; 3 Oct 1667; Gloucester

FITCH, John & Rebecca **LINDALL** (1653-); 3 Dec 1674; Norwalk, CT

FITCH, John (1668-1743) & Elizabeth **WATERMAN** (1675-1751); 10 Jul 1695; Windham, CT/Norwich, CT

FITCH, Joseph (-1727) & Mary [**STONE**]; b 1654; Norwalk, CT/Northampton/Hartford/Windsor, CT

FITCH, Joseph (-1694) & Hannah **SWEETSER** (1639-1671); 2 Jul 1661; Reading

FITCH, Joseph (1662-1695) & Anna **KIBBE** (-1750), m/2 John **DIX**; 29 Jun 1688; Reading

FITCH, Joseph & Ann _?_ ; b 1697; Windsor, CT

FITCH, Samuel & Susanna (_?_) [**WHITING**], w William, m/3 Alexander **BRYAN** 1662; b 1650; Hartford

FITCH, Samuel (-1684) & 1/wf Sarah **LANE** (-1679); 28 Apr 1673; Reading

FITCH, Samuel & Sarah **BRYAN**, m/2 Mungo **NESBETT** ca 1696?; 23 Oct 1678; Milford, CT

FITCH, Samuel (1655-) & Mary **BREWSTER**; 28 Nov 1678; New London, CT/Norwich, CT

FITCH, Samuel (-1684) & (2/wf) Rebecca **MERRIAM**, m/2 Joseph **DUTTON** 1685; 26 Jul 1681; Reading

FITCH, Samuel (-1742) & (1/wf) Elizabeth **WALKER** (-1716); 20 Mar 1695/6; Billerica

FITCH, Thomas & Anne **REEVE** (-1669+?, Hartford); 8 Aug 1611, Bocking, Eng

FITCH, Thomas (?1612-1704?) & Anna **STACIA/STACEY**; 1 Nov 1632, Bocking, Eng; Norwalk, CT

FITCH, Thomas (-1678) & Martha **FISKE**, m/2 Thomas **FISKE** 1695; ca 1654/5; Boston/Cambridge

FITCH, Thomas (-1684) & Ruth [CLARK] (1642-), m/2 Robert PLUMB, m/3 John WHEELER; ca 1662; Norwalk, CT

FITCH, Thomas (1652-1704) & (1/wf) Abigail GOODRICH (1662-1684); 15 Sep 1680; Wethersfield, CT

FITCH, Thomas (ca 1652-1704) & (2/wf) Sarah [BOARDMAN] (1655/6-1746); aft 7 Nov 1684; Wethersfield, CT

FITCH, Thomas (-1736) & Abiel DANFORTH (1675-), m/2 John OSBORN; 12 Apr 1694; Boston

FITCH, Thomas (1668-1731) & (1/wf) Elizabeth [LANE] (1677/8-) (dau Robert); ca 1695/9?; ?Norwalk, CT

FITCH, Zachariah (-1662) & Mary __?__ ; b 1622; Lynn/Reading

FITCH, __?__ & Mary (MOORE) STACY; b 13 Feb 1681/2, aft 1676

FITCHUE/FITZHUE/?FITCHEW/?FITZHUGH, Robert & Hannah MANN/MAN; 4 Apr 1695; Boston/Watertown

FITTS, Abraham (-1692) & 1/wf Sarah TOMSON/THOMPSON (-1664); 16 May 1655; Salisbury

FITT, Abraham (-1692) & 2/wf Rebecca [BURLEIGH/BIRDLEY], w Gyles; 7 Jan 1668, ?23 Feb 1669; Ipswich

FITTS, Abraham (-1714) & 1/wf Margaret [CHOATE] (-1692); b 1685; Ipswich

FITTS, Abraham (-1714) & 2/wf Mary ROSS; 9 Jan 1693, [1693/4]; Ipswich

FITS (FITCH is wrong), Isaac (1675-) & Bethia [HACKER] (1676-1722); b 1698, 29 Jan 1696/7; Salem

FITTS, Richard (-1672) & Sarah ORDWAY (-1667?); 8 Oct 1654, no issue; Newbury

FITTS, Richard (1672-1745) & Sarah THORNE (-1773); 18 Mar 1694/5; Ipswich

FITT, Robert[1] (1600-1665) & ?2/wf Grace [LORD]? (-1684); by 1632?, b 1629?; Cambridge

FITZGERALD/FITZFARRALD, James & Elizabeth (BROOKS) BULLIER, w Julian; 28 Apr 1678; Saybrook, CT

FitzRANDOLPH/FittsRANDLES, Edward (1607-) & Elizabeth BLOSSOM (?1620±-1713), m/2 John PIKE; 10 May 1637; Scituate/Barnstable/Piscataway, NJ

FITTSRANDLE, Nathaniel (1642-1713) & Mary HOLLEY (-1703); - Nov 1662; Barnstable/Piscataway, NJ/Woodbridge, NJ

FIZE, Daniel & Sarah LAMBERT; 6 Nov 1699; Boston

FLACK, Cotton (1597-) & Dorothy WRIGHT (-1623); Saffron, Walden, Eng, 1 Jul 1611

FLACK, Cotton (-1658) & Jane __?__ ; b 1633; Boston

FLACK, John (1653-) & Mary VARNEY; 23 Dec 1693; Boston

FLACK, Samuel (1621-1699) & 1/wf Mary __?__ (-1656); b 1653; Boston

FLACK, Samuel (-1699) & 2/wf Ann [WORMWOOD?]/[WORNAL?]/[WORNAN?]/[WORMBUM?]; b 1659; Boston

FLEG, Allen (1665-1711) & Sarah BALL (1666-); 12 Mar 1684, 1684/5, 12 Mar 1684; Watertown

FLEGE, Benjamin (1662-1741) & Experience CHILD (1669-); 26 Sep 1690; Watertown/Worcester

FLEGG, Christopher & Elizabeth __?__ ; b 1696; Boston

FLAGG, Ebenezer & Elizabeth CARTER (1680-); 25 Dec 1700; Woburn

FLACKE, Eleazer (1653-1722) & Deborah (WRIGHT) BARNES, w John; 10 Oct 1676; Concord

FLAGG, Eleazer (-1726) & Esther GREEN (1674-); 17 Jan 1694, 17 Jan 1695, 1694/5; Woburn/Malden

FLAGG, Gershom (1641-1690) & Hannah LEPINGWELL/LEFFINGWELL (1646-1724), m/2 Israel WALKER 1696; 15 Apr 1668; Woburn

FLAGG, Gershom (1669-1755) & Hannah __?__ ; b 1693; Woburn

FLEG, John (1643-1697) & Mary GALE; 30 Mar 1670; Watertown

FLEGE, John & Anna [EAMES]; b 1698; Watertown

FLAGG, John & [Abiah KORNIE]; b 1698; Boston

FLEGG, Michael (1651-1711) & 1/wf Mary BIGELOW/BIGULAH (1644-1704); 3 Jun 1674; Watertown

FLAGG, Thomas (1615-1698) & Mary __?__ (1619-1703); b 1641; Watertown

FLEGG, Thomas (1646-) & Rebecca DIKES/DIX (1641/2-); 18 Feb 1667, 1667/8; Watertown

FLANDERS, John (1659-1745) & Elizabeth SARGENT (-1716); 18 Jan 1687/8; Amesbury/Salisbury

FLANDERS, Joseph (1677-) & 1/wf Hester CASH (-1702); 5 Aug 1700; Salem

FLANDERS, Philip (1652-) & Martha (EATON) COLLINS (1648-), w Benjamin; 4 Nov 1686; Salisbury

FLANDERS, Stephen[1] (-1684) & Jane __?__ (-1683); b 1646; Salisbury
FLANDERS, Stephen (1646-1744) & Abigail CARTER (1653-1718); 28 Dec 1670; Salisbury
FLAVELL, Thomas & [Ann] __?__; b 1621; Plymouth
FLEMINGE, John (-1657) & Ann(a?)/Hannah? __?__ (-1657); in Eng, b 1639, ca 1631?; Watertown
FLEMMING, Robert (-1681?) & Joanna [ROSE], wid, m/3 __?__ OLMSTED bef 1687; b 8 Dec 1674; Stonington, CT
FLETCHER, Edward (-1667?) (called "bro." by Henry SHRIMPTON) & Mary __?__, m/2 Hugh DRURY (1675?); b 1642; Boston
FLETCHER, Francis (1636-1704+) & Elizabeth WHEELER/WHELER (-1704); 11 Oct 1656; Concord
FLETCHER, John (1602-1662), Wethersfield & [Mary WARD] (1607-1679, at Farmington), dau wid Joice, m/2 John CLARK; b 1634; Milford, CT
FLETCHER, John (-1695) & Joane __?__; b 1674, b 1661, 12 Jul 1660; Portsmouth, NH
FLETCHER, John (1665-) & Hannah HUNT (1670-); 18 Feb 1689/90; Concord
FLETCHER, Jonathan (-1685) & Catherine __?__; Eliot, ME?
FLETCHER, Joseph (-1700) & ?Isadel/Ja-- (PIKE) TRUE (-1700), w Henry; 18 Jun 1660; Salisbury
FLETCHER, Joseph (1661-1705+) & 1/wf Mary DUDLEY; 7 Jun 1688 (not Jun 17); Concord
FLETCHER, Joshua (1648-1713) & 1/wf Grissell JEWELL (1651-1682); 4 May 1668; Chelmsford
FLETCHER, Joshua (1648-1713) & 2/wf Sarah WILY/WILLEY/WOOLLEY? of Reading? (1658-); 18 Jul 1682; Chelmsford
FLETCHER, Moses & 1/wf Maria/Mary [EVANS]; in Eng or Leyden, b 1663; Plymouth
FLETCHER, Moses & Sarah DINGLEY; Leyden, 21 Dec 1613; Plymouth
FLETCHER, Nicholas (1669-) & ?Abigail/Agnes BANFIELD, m/2 Richard PARSLEY 1713; 15 Feb 1695/6, 5 Dec 1695; Portsmouth, NH
FLETCHER, Pendleton (?1655-1698, 1699?) & Sarah [HILL] (1661-), m/2 William PRIEST, m/3 Andrew BROWN 1710; ca 1680/2; ?Saco, ME/Biddeford, ME
FLETCHER, Robert (1592-1677) & [?Sarah] __?__; in Eng, b 1620?; Concord
FLETCHER, Robert & Susanna WORTHILEG; 13 Jan 1697; Boston
FLETCHER, Samuel (1632-1697) & Margaret HAILSTONE, 1st at Taunton?; 14 Oct 1659; Chelmsford
FLETCHER, Samuel (1652-) & 1/wf Hannah WHEELER (-1697); 5 Jul 1673; Chelmsford
FLETCHER, Samuel (1632-1697) & 2/wf Hannah FOSTER (-1683); 16 - 1677?; Chelmsford
FLETCHER, Samuel (1657-1744) & Elizabeth WHEELER (1664-1744); 15 Jun 1682; Concord
FLETCHER, Samuel (1632-1697) & 2/wf Mary COTTEN/COTTON, Concord, w John, m John SPAULDING 1700?; 3 Sep 1684; Chelmsford
FLETCHER, Samuel (1664-1706) & Maria COTON/COTTON (1678-1706, ae 28); 7 Jun 1692; Chelmsford
FLETCHER, Samuel (1652-) & 1/wf Sarah (MERRIAM) BALL (1634-1703), w Elazer/Eleazer; 7 Jun 1699; Chelmsford/Concord
FLETCHER, Seth (-1682, Elizabeth, NJ) & 1/wf Mary [PENDLETON]; b 1652; Watertown/Hampton, NH
FLETCHER, Seth (-1682) & 2/wf Mary (COOPER) PIERSON, w Henry; m cont 30 May 1681; ?Southampton
FLETCHER, Rev. William (-1668) & __?__; ca 1625; Oyster River, NH/Saco, ME
FLETCHER, William[1] (-1677/8?) & 1/wf Rachel __?__; b 1645; Concord
FLETCHER, William[1] (ca 1622-1677/8) & 2/wf Lydia (?FAIRBANKS) BATES (?1622-1704, Chelmsford), w Edward; 7 Nov 1645; Concord/Chelmsford
FLETCHER, William[2], Jr. (1657-1713) & Sarah RICHARDSON (1660-1748); 19 Sep 1677; Chelmsford
FLETCHER, ?Nicholas & Jane __?__, m/2 John CLARK 1671
FLINDER, Richard & 1/wf Jane __?__ (kinswoman of Henry HARROD); 12 Jul 1663; Salem
FLINDER, Richard & 2/wf Mary __?__; Salem
FLINT, Benoni & ?2/wf Mary BROWNE (-1724, ae 70); 10 Jun 1675; Southampton
FLINT, David & 1/wf [Hannah/Mary] SANDERS; 4 Feb 1694/5; Lynn
FLINT, David (-1736) & 2/wf Ruth FLINT (1679-); 4 Jan 1699; Salem
FLINT, Edward (?1638-1711) (ae 57 in 1695) & Elizabeth HART; 20 Oct 1659; Salem

FLINT, Ephraim (1642-1723) & Jane BULKELEY (-1706, ae 61); 20 Mar 1683/4, no issue; Concord
FLINT, George (1652-1720) & 1/wf Elizabeth [PUTNAM] (1662-1697); b 1685; Reading/Salem
FLINT, George & 2/wf Susannah GARDNER; 2 Mar 1698/9; Salem
FLINT, George (1672-1749+) & Sarah _?_ ; b 1701?; Salem
FLINT, Henry (-1668) & Margery (HOAR) [MATTHEWS] (-1687, 1675?), w John; b 1642; Briantree
FLINT, John (-1687, 1686?) & Mary OAKES (-1690); 12 Nov 1667; Concord
FLINT, John (1655-1730) & Elizabeth _?_ ; b 1679; Salem
FLINT, Joseph (1662-1710) & Abigail HOWARD/HAYWARD (1667-); 6 Aug 1685; Salem
FLINT, Joseph & Experience DARBY/DERBY (1671-); 23 Jun 1698?; Salem
FLINT, Josiah (1645-1680) & [Esther WILLARD?/WILLETT] (?1648, 1647-1737); 24 Jan 1671/2; Dorchester
FLINTT, Samuel & Susannah PITTMAN/PICKMAN; 18 Dec 1694; Salem
FLINT, Thomas (1603-1653, ?ae 50, 1651), Matlock, Eng (calls William WOOD of Concord "uncle") & Abigail _?_ (1607-1689); in Eng?, b 1642; Concord
FLINT, Thomas (-1663) & ?Hannah/Ann _?_ (-1672), m/2 John SOUTHWICK; b 1645; Salem
FLINT, Thomas (1645-1721) & 1/wf Hannah MOULTON (-1673); 22 May 1666; Salem
FLINT, Thomas & 2/wf Mary [DOUNTON]/[DOUGHTON?]; 15 Nov 1674; Salem
FLINT, Thomas (-1719) & Elizabeth JOHNSON (1659-); 12 Aug 167[8], 1677?; Salem
FLINT, William (-1673) & 1/wf _?_ /?[Alice] [BOSWORTH?] (?1607-1700?); in Eng, b 1636, 5 Sep 1635?; Salem
FLINT, William (-1673) & 2/wf? [Alice WILLIAMS?] (-1700?); 1644?; Salem
FLOOD, Benjamin & Mary _?_ ; b 1701; Boston
FLOOD, James (-1699) & Hannah [?MORSE] (1641-); ca 1667; Boston/Medfield
FLOOD, John & Sarah [BARKER] (1655-); ca 1675?; b 1687; Boston
FLOOD, Joseph & Joanna MITCHELL; 10 Mar 1698; Boston
FLOOD, Philip & Mary _?_ ; b 1684; Newbury (from NJ)
FLOOD, Richard & Elizabeth HARMON; 1 Dec 1691; Boston
FLOOD, Richard (-1654?) & Lydia _?_ , m/2 Joseph GRIDLEY 1654; b 1643; Boston
FLOOD, Robert (-1689) & Abigail [DISBOROUGH] (1646-), m/2 Matthew BARNES 1692; b 9 Nov 1670; Wethersfield, CT
FLOWER, Sherman (-1695) & Elizabeth _?_ ; ca 1680/88?; Hempstead, LI
FLOWER, Lamarock (-1716) & Lydia [SMITH]; 1686?, b 1686(7?); Hartford, CT
FLOYD, Daniel (1675-) & Mary HALLOWELL; 18 Jan 1697; Boston
FLOYD, Henry & Mary _?_ ; b 1666; Boston
FLOYD, Hugh (-1730) & Eleanor _?_ ; b 1686; Boston/Chelsea
FLOYD, John (returned to England) & Ann _?_ ; ca 1625/30?; Boston/Scituate
FLOYD, John (?1637-1702) & Sarah [DOOLITTLE]; ca 1661; Lynn/Malden/Boston
FLOYD, John (-1724) & Rachel [PARKER] (1665-); b 1687; Malden
FLOYD, Joseph (1590-1666+) & Anne/?Jane _?_ ; in Eng, b 1626; Dorchester/Lynn/Chelsea
FLOYD, Joseph (1667-) & Elizabeth [POTTER] (1670-), m/2 _?_ JENKS; b 1689; Malden/Reading
FLOYD, Richard (1626-1706) & Susanna _?_ ; b 1665; Brookhaven, LI
FLOYD, Richard (1665-1738?) & Margaret [NICOLLS] (-1718, in 57th y); b 1688, ?10 Sep 1686, ?May; Brookhaven, LI
FOBES/FORBES?, Caleb (-1710, Preston) & 1/wf Sarah GAGER (1651-); 30 Jun 1681; Norwich, CT
FOBES/FORBES?, Caleb (-1710) & Mary/Marah [HUNTINGTON?] (1657-1710+); b 1699; Preston, CT
FOBES, Edward (1651-1732?) & Elizabeth [HOWARD]; b 1677; Bridgewater
FOBES, John[1] (-1662, 1660?, Sandwich) & Constant [MITCHELL], m/2 John BRIGGS (1662?); ca 1640?; Duxbury/Bridgewater
FOBES, William (1649/50-1712) & 1/wf ?Eliz. SOUTHWORTH (no)
FOBES, William (1649/50-1712) & Martha (PABODIE) [SEABURY] (1651-1712), w Samuel; aft 5 Aug 1681, 1682?; Little Compton, RI
FOGG, Daniel (1660-1755) & Hannah [LIBBY]; ca 1684; Scarboro, ME/Kittery, ME/Hampton, NH
FOGG, David (1640-) & Susanna _?_ ; b 1676; Salem
FOGG, James (1668-1760) & Mary BURREN; 9 Jan 1695; Hampton, NH

FOGG, Ralph & Susanna __?__ ; b 1638; Salem
FOGG, Samuel[1] (-1672) & 1/wf Anne SHAW (1636-); 12 Dec 1652; Hampton, NH
FOGG, Samuel[1] (-1672) & Mary PAGE (-1700); 28 Dec 1665; Hampton, NH
FOGG, Samuel (1653-) & Hannah MARSTON (1656-); 19 Dec 1676; Hampton, NH
FOGG, Seth & Sarah [?SHAW] (1669-); 1693, 1694, ca 1688; Hampton, NH
FOLGER, Eleazer (1648-1716) & Sarah [GARDNER] (-1729); ca 1671; Nantucket
FOLGER, John & Meribah [?GIBBS]/Merible SWIFT (-1664+); in Eng, b 1617; Watertown/Martha's Vineyard
FOLGER, John (1659-) & Mary [BARNARD]/[?BROWN]; b 1689; Nantucket
FOLGER, Nathan (1678-1747) & Sarah CHURCH; 29 Dec 1699; Dover, NH/Nantucket
FOLGER, Peter (1617-1690) & Mary [MORRILL] (-1704); ca 1644; Salisbury/Martha's Vineyard/Nantucket
FOLGER, Peter (1674-1707) & Judith [COFFIN] (-1760), m/2 Nathaniel BARNARD, m/3 Stephen WILCOX; b 1700, b 1699; Nantucket
FOLINSBEE, Thomas (1637-1713+, 1717+) & 1/wf Mary __?__ (1639-1673+); b 1660; Portsmouth, NH/Newbury
FOLLANSBEE, Thomas & 2/wf Sarah __?__ ; Salisbury
FOLLINGSBY, Thomas & 1/wf Abigail (BOND) ROAFE/ROLFE, w Ezra; 19 Jun 1694; Haverhill/Newbury
FALLAND, Thomas (-1686, 1687) & __?__ ; Yarmouth
FOLLEN, William & Elizabeth __?__ ; b 1677; Yarmouth
FOLLET, Abraham (1671-) & 1/wf Sarah CALLAM/CALLUM (-1714); 30 Mar 1697; Salem/?Attleboro
FOLLET, Isaac (1674-) & Hannah STARR (1673-); 13 Apr 1699; Salem
FOLLETT, John & __?__ ; b 1640?; Dover, NH
FOLLETT, John (1669-1719) & Martha CALLUM/KALLUM (1670-1706); 10 Jul 1694; Lynn/Attleborough
FOLLET, John & Sarah GULLISON/GUNNISON?; 14 Mar 1700; Boston
FOLLET, Nicholas (-1663?) & Abigail __?__ (1626-), m/2 Richard NASON 1663+; by 1657, b 1649?; Dover, NH
FOLLET, Nicholas, Jr. (-1700) & 1/wf Hannah __?__ ; b 1677; Dover, NH
FOLLETT, Nicholas, Jr. (-1700) & 2/wf Hannah (DREW?) BROOKING/MEADER, w Godfrey, m/3 Abraham HASELTINE?; aft 1681; Dover, NH
FOLLETT, Nicholas (1677-1722) & Mary HULL; 12 Sep 1700; ?York, ME/?Portsmouth, NH
FOLLETT, Robert & Persis BLACK (bpt 1640-); 29 Nov 1655; Salem
FOLET, Robert (1659-) & __?__ ; b 1687; Salem
FOLLETT, William & 1/wf? [?Jane THOMPPSONS]; [b 1654]; Dover, NH
FOLLETT, William (-1690) & 2/wf? Elizabeth (MATTHEWS?) DREW (1628-), w William; 23 Jul 1671?, 1672?; Dover, NH
FOLSOM, Ebenezer (?1666-) & Hannah [SMITH]; Exeter, NH
FOLSOM, Ephraim (1655-1709) & Pholiel/?Phaltial [HULL]; b 1678?; ?New Market, NH
FOLSOM, Ephraim & __?__ [TAYLOR], dau Edw.; b 1700; NH
FOLSOM, John (1665-1681) & Mary GILMAN (1615-); Hingham, Eng, 4 Oct 1636; Hingham, ME/Exeter, NH
FOLSOM, John (1641, ?1638-1715) & Abigail PERKINS (1655-), Hampton; 16 Nov 1675; Hampton, NH/Exeter, NH
FOLSOM, Nathaniel (1644-) & 1/wf Hannah FARROW; 4 Jun 1674; Hingham/Exeter, NH
FOLSOM, Nathaniel & Mary (JONES) [ROBERTS], w George, m/3 Nicholas NORRIS; by 1696; ?Exeter, NH
FOLSOM, Peter (1649-1717) & Susanna (MILLS) COUSINS, w Isaac; 6 May 1678; ?Exeter, NH
FOLSOM, Samuel (1641-1700?) & Mary ROBEY; 22 Dec 1663, 1664, 1663; Hampton, NH/Greenland
FONES, Jeremiah & 1/wf Elizabeth __?__ (-1709); 30 May 1694; Kingstown/N. Kingstown, RI
FONES, John[1] (-1703) & Margaret __?__ (-1709+); b 1663; Newport/Jamestown, RI/Kingstown, RI
FONES, John (1663-1738) & Lydia [SMITH] (1668-1741); ca 1692?; North Kingstown, RI
FONES, Samuel (1666-1757) & 1/wf Ann [TIBBITTS] (-1702); b 1689; N. Kingstown, RI
FOOTE, Daniel (1652±-) & 1/wf Sarah __?__ (-1704, ae 48); b 1680?; Stratford, CT
FOOTE, Gooring & Patience GARY; 7 Sep 1696, m int; Boston
FOOT, Isaac & Abigail JEGLES; 2 Dec 1668; Salem

FOOT, John & Sarah BLISS; 20 Jul 1659
FOOTE, John (1660-1737) & Bathsheba _?_ (-1727); ca 1680?, b 1692; Amesbury
FOOTE, John & Mary [TRUESDALE] (1673-); b 1694(5?); Newton/?Watertown
FOOT, John (1670-1713) & Mary [?PALMER] (1673-); b 1696, 1697; Branford, CT
FOOTE, Joseph & Abigail JOHNSON; ?b 20 Jun 1691; Branford, CT
FOOTE, Nathaniel (1593-1644) & Elizabeth [DEMING] (1595-1683), m/2 Thomas WELLES; in Eng, b 1616; Watertown
FOOTE, Nathaniel (?1620-1655) & Elizabeth [SMITH] (?1627-), m/2 William GULL; ca 1646; Wethersfield, CT
FOOT, Nathaniel (1647-1703) & Margaret BLISS (1649-1745); 2 May 1672; Springfield/Wethersfield, CT
FOOTE, Nathaniel (1660-1709) & 1/wf Margaret _?_ ; ca 1682; ?Branford, CT
FOOTE, Nathaniel (1660-) & 2/wf Tabitha [BISHOP] (1657-1715); b 1696; Branford, CT/Guilford, CT
FOOT, Pasco (-1670) & _?_ ; ca 1635?, 8 ch bpt 6 Feb 1653; Salem
FOOTE, Pasco & 1/wf Martha WARDE (1650-); 2 Dec 1668; Salem/Newfoundland
FOOT, Pasco (-1685±) & 2/wf Margaret STALLION, m/2 James HAYNES 1688?; 30 Dec 1678; Killingworth, CT
FOOTE, Robert (ca 1627-1681) & Sarah [POTTER], m/2 Aaron BLACHLEY ca 1686; b 1660; New Haven/Branford, CT
FOOTT, Samuel & 1/wf Hannah CURIER; 23 Jun 1659; Salisbury
FOOT, Samuel (1649-1689), Hatfield & Mary [MERRICK] (1647-1690); b 1671, b 1672, ?30 May 1671; Springfield
FOOT, Samuel (1668-1696) & Abigail [BARKER], m/2 Jonathan ROSE 1699; b 1694?; Branford, CT
FOOTE, Samuel & Mary PALMER (1673-); 12 Nov 1696; Salem
FOOTMAN, John & 1/wf Sarah CROMWELL/CROMMETH; 18 Dec 1691; Dover, NH
FOOTMAN, Thomas (-1667, 1668?) & Catharine [MATTHEWS], m/2 William DURGIN 1672; b 1663; York, ME/Dover, NH
FORBEE/FORBY?, John & Penelope LEIGH; 4 Dec 1699; Boston
FORBES, Alexander (-1675) & Kat ROBINSON; 29 Oct 1674; Charlestown
FORBES/FOBES?, Caleb & 1/wf Sarah GAGER (1651-); 30 Jun 1681; Norwich, CT
FORBES, David (1671-) & Sarah [TREAT] (?1674-); b 5 Jan 1707/8, b 1701?; Wethersfield, CT/?Hartford
FORBES, James (-1692) & Catharine _?_ ; ca 1645?; Wethersfield, CT/Hartford
FORBES, James & 1/wf Sarah [WILLIAMS]; b 1701?; Wethersfield, CT
FORBES, John (-1713) & Mary [GRIFFIN]; b 1695; Wethersfield, CT
FORBES, _?_ & [Jane KING] (1679-); b 1701?; Boston
FORBES, Caleb (see FOBES) & 2/wf Mary HUNTINGTON (1657-), dau Simon; b 1706, b 1699; Preston, CT/?Saybrook, CT
FORBES/FORBUSH, Alexander (-1675) & Catharine ROBINSON; 29 Oct 1674 (see FORBES); Charlestown/Boston
FARRABAS, Daniel (-1687) & 1/wf Rebecca [?PENNIMAN/PERRIMAN] (-1677); 27 Mar 1660; Cambridge/Concord/Marlboro
FORBUSH/FARRABAS, Daniel (-1687) & 2/wf Deborah RIDIATT (1652-), m/2 Alexander STEWART 1688; 22 May 1679; Cambridge
FORBASH, Daniel (1664, 1665?-) & Dorothy [PRAY] (1668-); b 1689?, b 1680(1?); Kittery, ME
FURBOSH, John & _?_ ; b 1675; Flushing, LI
FORBUSH, Samuel & Abigail RICE (1671-); 8 Mar 1698/9; Marlboro
FORBUSH, Thomas & Margaret _?_ ; b 1666(7?); Boston
FORBUSH, Thomas (1667-living 1724) & Dorcas [RICE] (1664-); b 1693; Marlboro
FURBISH, William & [Rebecca] _?_ ; b 1669; Kittery, ME
FURBUSH, William & 2/wf? Christian _?_ (?1652-); b 1686?; Kittery, ME
FORCE, Benjamin (ca 1668-) & Elizabeth _?_ ; b 1690(1?); Wrentham/Providence, RI
FORCE, Mark & Deborah MACCAME; 13 Oct 1698; Wrentham
FORCE, Matthew & Elizabeth [PALMER]; b 1669, Apr 1667; Gravesend, LI
FORCE, Thomas (ca 1676-) & Hannah _?_ ; Westchester Co., NY/Woodbridge, NJ
FORD, Andrew (-1693) & Ellen/Eleanor LOVELL (?1629, ?1633-); b 1650; Weymouth
FORD, Andrew (?1650-1725) & Abiah _?_ ; b 1682; Weymouth

FORD, Israel (1670-1736) & Sara [PRATT] (-1718); ca 1695?; Weymouth
FORD, James & ? ; b 1675
FORD, James (1675-1735) & Hannah DINGLEY (1675-1746); 28 Feb 1698, 1698/9; Marshfield
FORD, James & Lydia ROSS; 26 Dec 1699, 25 Dec; Haverhill
FORD, John & Joanna (ANDREWS) [SEARLE], w John; b 1679; Scarboro/Braveboat Harbor/etc.
FORD, John (1659-1693) & Hannah [SHERMAN]?; b 1684; Marshfield
FORD, John (1654-1711) & Sarah [FITCH]; b 1693; Milford, CT
FORD, Joseph & Deborah WALDO, m/2 Samuel DANIEL 1694?; 6 Dec 1683; Bristol, RI
FORD, Joseph (1661-) & 1/wf Lois [STETSON] (1672-1735); b 1694; Marshfield
FORD, Josiah (1664-1721) & Sarah [BAKER?/PRATT?] (her husband called Isaac?) (see Samuel
   FORD); b 1688; Marshfield
FORD, Martin/?Matthew & Lydia GRIFFING/GRIFFIN, m/2 William KNOWLTON; 25 Mar 1684;
   Bradford
FORD, Matthew (-1694) & Mary BROOKS; 12 Jan 1674, ?12 Jul 1674; New Haven
FORD, Matthew & Elizabeth [BRADLEY]; b 1699; New Haven
FORD, Michael (ca 1640-1729) & 1/wf Abigail SNOW (-1682); 12 Dec 1667; Marshfield
FORD, Michael (ca 1640-1729) & 2/wf Bethiah HATCH (1661-); 29 Mar 1683; Marshfield
FORD, Nathaniel (1658-1703) & Joanna [?BICKNELL]; b 1683(4?); Weymouth
FORD, Nicholas & Elizabeth ELLIS; 23 Mar 1684/5; Marblehead
FOORD, Oswald & ? ; b 1693; Brookhaven, LI/Staten Island, NY
FORD, Robert & Mary KENT; 20 Mar 1666/7; Haverhill
FORD, Samuel & Elizabeth HIPKINS; 27 Jan 1673; New Haven
FORD, Samuel (1656-1711) (see Josiah FORD) & ?[Sarah PRATT]; b 1681?; Weymouth
FORD, Stephen & Joanna/Joan ? ; b 1665; Smuttynose Island
FORD, Stephen & Jane FOWLER, ?m/2 Richard KIMBALL; 24 Nov 1681; Haverhill
FORD, Thomas (-1676) & 1/wf Joan WAY (d in Eng); 13 Dec 1610, Powerstock, Eng
FORD, Thomas (-9 Nov 1676) & 2/wf Elizabeth (CHARD) COOKE (-1643), w Aaron; Bridport,
   Eng, 19 Jun 1616; Dorchester/Windsor, CT/Northampton, MA
FORD, Thomas (-1676) & 3/wf Ann (?) SCOTT (1587-1675, Northampton), w Thomas; 7 Nov
   1644; Hartford
FORD, Thomas (?1624-) & Elizabeth [KNOWLES], m/2 Eleazer ROGERS; ca 1650; Milford,
   CT/Fairfield, CT
FORD, Thomas (-1697) & [?Esther] [NOBLE] (-1723?); b 1675; Flushing, LI
FORD, Thomas (1656-1693) & Mehitable [PHIPPEN] (1668-), m/2 Samuel CLARK 1697?; b 1687;
   Boston
FORD, Thomas & ?Sarah/?Eliza [BOWNE] (1681/2-1699?); Flushing, LI
FORD, Timothy & ? ; b 1640; Charlestown/New Haven
FORD, William (1604-1676) (ae 67 in 1671) & Anna [?EAMES], dau Anthony; b 1633;
   Marshfield/Duxbury
FORD, William & Mary [HADLOCK] (1641-1708); b 1664; Charlestown
FORD, William, Jr. (-1721, ae 88) & Sarah DINGLEY (?1639-1727, ae 78); 4 Nov 1658;
   Marshfield
FORD, William (?1672-) & Erlenia/?Eleanor/Elizabeth ? (-1745?); b 1696; Marshfield
FORD, ? & Martha ? , m/2 Peter BROWN ca 1624; Plymouth
FORDHAM, Jonah (-1713±) & 1/wf Martha ? (-4 Oct 1688); Hempstead, LI/Southampton/
   Brookhaven, LI
FORDHAM, Jonah (-1713±) & 2/wf Hester [TOPPING] (1671-); b 29 Jan 1696, 1696/7, aft 7 Apr
   1691; Southampton, LI
FORDHAM, Joseph (?1645-1688) & Mary [?CLARK], ?m/2 Daniel SAYRE; b 1669; Southampton,
   LI
FORDHAM, Joseph (1669-) & Mary MALTBY (1673, 1671-1719); 5 Dec 1689; Southampton, LI
FORDHAM, Nathan (-1712?) & Charity ? ; b 1701?; ?Southampton, LI
FORDHAM, Robert (1603-1674) & 1/wf ? ; Stamford, CT/Hempstead, LI/Southampton, LI
FORDHAM, Robert (1603-1674) & 2/wf Elizabeth [BENNING]; aft 18 Jul 1641; Stamford,
   CT/Hempstead, LI/Southampton, LI
FORMAN, Aaron (1633/35?-1697+) & Dorothy ? ; Hempstead, LI/Jamaica, LI/Oyster Bay,
   LI/Monmouth Co., NJ
FORMAN, Aaron, Jr. & Susannah [TOWNSEND] (?1662-); ?Matinecock, LI/Oyster Bay, LI
FORMAN, Alexander & Rachel ? ; b 9 Mar 1693; Oyster Bay/NJ

FORMAN, Moses & 1/wf Hannah [CROOKER], m/2 Joseph WEEKS; by 1666?, b 15 May 1674, he deserted wf Hannah; Oyster Bay, LI

FORMAN, Moses & 2/wf Anna (?EVERDEN) [BENNETT], w Samuel d 1684; b 10 Feb 1687/8, aft 4 Sep 1684; E. Greenwich, RI

FORMAN, Moses, Jr. (-1727) & Jude?/Judith _?_ ; b 1699; Oyster Bay, LI

FORMAN, Robert (-1671) & Johanna _?_ ; ca 1625?; Flushing, LI/Hempstead, LI/Oyster Bay, LI/Monmouth Co., NJ

FORMAN, Samuel & 1/wf _?_ (sister of Thomas HOUS wf); ca 1646/8, b 1650; Fairfield, CT

FORMAN, Samuel (-1682) & 2/wf Miriam [HOYT], m/2 Richard HARCURT ca 1683; 25 Mar 1662; Fairfield, CT

FORMAN, Samuel (1663-1740, in 78th y) & Mary [WILBUR] (1667-1728, in 62nd y); b 1688; ?Portsmouth, RI/Providence/Freehold, NJ/Springfield, NJ

FORMAN, Thomas & Rebecca (HUSE/HUGHES?/HOASE) BOW/ROW, w Alexander; 8 Oct 1679; Middletown, CT

FORSYTH, John & Hannah [COMSTOCK]; CT

FORTUNE, Elias & Mary [PITMAN], dau Thomas; b 1670; Salem/Marblehead

FORWARD, Joseph (1674-1704) & Lydia [GREGORY] (1677-), m/2 Thomas WILDMAN; b 1698; Danbury, CT

FORWARD, Samuel & 1/wf [Miriam HOYT]?

FORWARD, Samuel (-1684) & Anne _?_ (-1685, Windsor, CT); b 1671; Windsor, CT

FORWARD, Samuel (1671-1738) & Deborah [MORE] (1677-1734); b 1703, b 1701?; Windsor, CT/Belchertown, MA

FOSDICK, James (1649-1696) & Hannah _?_ , m/2 John PRICE; b 1689; Charlestown

FOSDICK, John (?1629, 1626?-1716) & 1/wf Ann/Anna (SHAPLEIGH) [BRANSON] (-1679, ae 52), w Henry; aft 26 Sep 1653?; Charlestown/?Malden

FOSDICK, John (-1716, ae 90) & 2/wf Elizabeth (?THOMAS) (LISLEY) BETTS (-1716, ae 60), w Robert, w John; aft 15 Oct 1679, ca 17 Jun 1684, aft 22 May 1684; Charlestown

FOSDICK, John (1657-), Boston & Sarah (REYNOLDS) [BLIGH] (1659-), w Thomas; ca 1683; Charlestown/Boston

FOSDICK, Jonathan (1669-) & Sarah [SPRAGUE] (1672/3-); b 31 May 1692?, b 1693; Charlestown

FOSDICK, Samuel (1655-1701) & Mercy/Mary PICKET (1661-1725), m/2 John ARNOLD 1703 (New London); 1 Nov 1682; Charlestown/New London, CT

FOSDICK, Stephen (1583-1664) & 1/wf _?_ ; in Eng, b 1615, ca 1610?, 6 ch; Charlestown

FOSDICK, Stephen (1583-1664) & 2/wf Sarah [WETHERELL] (?1589-); ca 1624; Charlestown

FOSDICK, Stephen & Margaret [MARTIN] (1667-); b 1687; Charlestown

FOSDICK, Thomas (?1616-1650), Watertown & Damaris _?_ , m/2 James HADLOCK b 1682; Charlestown

FOSDICK, Thomas & Mary MARTIN (1677-); 16 May 1695; Charlestown

FOSKET/FOSKETT, John[1] (-1689) & 1/wf Elizabeth [POWELL] (-1683); ca 1659; Charlestown

FOSKET, John[1] (-1689) & 2/wf Hannah [?LEACH]; aft 31 Jan 1682/3; Charlestown

FOSKET, Robert (1672-) & 1/wf Mercy GOODWIN (-1714); 27 Mar 1700; Charlestown

FOSKET, Thomas (-1694) & Miriam CLEVELAND (-1745, ae 80); 13 Dec 1683; Charlestown

FOST/FOSS, John (1636±-) & Mary [BERRY]/?CHADBURNE; b 1660; Rye Beach

FOSS, John (1660-) & 1/wf Mary _?_ ; b 1700, by 1695?; Greenland

FOSS, Samuel & Mary _?_ ; by 1682?, by 1700?; ?Portsmouth, NH

FOSS, Thomas & Abigail COLE, m/2 Samuel FOLSOM bef 1710; 5 Feb 1696; Hampton, NH

FOSS, William & Sarah BUSWELL (1676-); 29 Nov 1700; Hampton, NH

FOSSECAR/FOSECAR, John & Elizabeth [JOHNSON], w Peter; b 1661; Fairfield, CT

FOSSET/FOSSETT, William & Rebecca _?_ ; b 1699; Charlestown

FOSSY/FOSSEY, Thomas & Elizabeth RAYNER; 4 Feb 168[5?], [1685]; Ipswich

FOST/FOSS?, John (-1700) & 1/wf Mary [CHADBOURNE]? (1644-1673+); b 1667; Dover, NH

FOST/FOSS?, John (-1700, 1699) & 2/wf Elizabeth [GOSS]/GOFFE, w James, m/3 James EMERY; 25 Jan 1686/7, 25 Jan 1686; Dover, NH

FOST, William & 1/wf Margery [LORD]; ca 1692, (?Nov 1692); Kittery, ME

FOSTER, Abraham (1622-1711) & 1/wf? 2/wf Lydia [BURBANK]? (?1644-); b 1657?; Ipswich/Rowley/Andover

FOSTER, Abraham (-1723) & Esther FOSTER (-1734); 13 Jul 1681; Andover

FOSTER, Abraham (1659-) & Mary [ROBINSON?] (?1665-); 15 Nov 1693?; Ipswich

FOSTER, Abraham (1667-1720) & Abigail [**PARSONS?**] (1678-1732); 2 Jul 1699; Gloucester/Ip-
swich
FOSTER, Andrew (-1685) & 2/wf? Ann _?_ (-1692); ca 1635/39; Andover
FOSTER, Andrew (1640-1697) & Mary **RUSE/RUSS** (-1721); 7 Jun 1662; Andover
FOSTER, Anthony & Sarah **HAMBLETON**; 23 Jan 1700, 1700/1?; Boston
FOSTER, Bartholomew (-1689) & Hannah **VERY** (1652-), m/2 Thomas **SAWYER** 1691; 9 Nov
1664; Gloucester
FOSTER, Bartholomew & Mary _?_; b 1694; Wethersfield, CT
FOSTER, Benjamin (-1705) & Lydia _?_; b 1668; Southampton, LI
FOSTER, Benjamin & Martha **POST** (-1741); 28 Apr 1691; Southampton, LI
FOSTER, Benjamin (?1665-) & _?_; b 1699; Ipswich
FOSTER, Benjamin (1670-1735) & Anne _?_; b 1700; Ipswich/Topsfield/Lunenberg
FOSTER, Christopher (1603-1670+) & Frances [**STEVENS**]; b 1630; Lynn/Southampton, LI
FOSTER, Christopher & Deborah **WILSON**; 6 Sep 1681; Salem
FOSTER, Christopher & 1/wf Hannah **PIERSON/PARSONS** (-1697); 26 Nov 1691; Southampton,
LI
FOSTER, Christopher & 2/wf Abigail (**LUPTON**) **TOPPING**, ?w James; 19 Aug 1697; Southampton,
LI
FOSTER, Daniel (1670-) & 1/wf Catharine **FREESE** (1671-1695); 2 Mar 1693; Topsfield
FOSTER, Daniel (1670-1753) & 2/wf Mary **DRESSER** (1670-); 4 Dec 1696, 1695?; Rowley/Ip-
swich/Lebanon, CT
FOSTER, David (1665-1748) & Hannah **BUXTON** (1666-); 13 Jan 1687, 1686/7; Salem
FOSTER, Ebenezer (1677-) & Anna **WILKINS** (1681-), m/2 Isaac **WILKINS**; 19 Dec 1700; Salem
FOSTER, Edward (-1644) & Lettice **HANFORD** (1617-1684), m/2 Edward **JENKINS** bef 1650; 8
Apr 1635; Scituate
FOSTER, Edward (-1720) & 1/wf Hester **BLISS** (1640-1683); 26 Dec 1661; Springfield
FOSTER, Edward (-1712) & 1/wf Elizabeth **HARRIS** (-1684); 20 Jun 1670; Middletown, CT
FOSTER, Edward (-1720) & 2/wf Sarah (**MARSHFIELD**) **MILLER** (-1709), w Thomas; 17 Jan
1684, 1683/4; Springfield
FOSTER, Edward (1657-) & Rebecca _?_; b 1690; Chelmsford
FOSTER, Eli (-1717) & Judith **KEIES/KEYES**; 17 Oct 1680; Chelmsford
FOSTER, Elisha (-1682, ae 29) & Sarah **PAYSON**, m/2 Ebenezer **WISWALL** 1685; 10 Apr 1678;
Dorchester
FOSTER, Ephraim (1657-) & 1/wf Hannah [**AMES**]?/[**EAMES**]? (1661-1731), dau Robert; b 1678;
Andover
FOSTER, George & _?_; b 1675; ?Plymouth/Lynn
FOSTER, George (1675-) & ?2/wf Mary [**WEAVER**]; b 11 May 1699; Newport/E. Greenwich, RI
FOSTER, Hatherly (-1751) & Bathshua [**TURNER**] (-1744); 1 Dec 1698; Scituate
FOSTER, Henry (-1683/4) & Jane _?_; Jamaica, LI
FOSTER, Hopestill (1620, 1617?-1676) & Mary [**BATES**] (-1703, in 84th y, 1702/3); b 1640;
Dorchester
FOSTER, Hopestill & Elizabeth **PAYSON**, m/2 Edmund **BROWN** by 1685; 15 Feb 1666/7;
Dorchester
FOSTER, Hopestill (1648-1679) & Elizabeth (**PIERCE**) **WHITTEMORE** (-1692), w Thomas, m/3
Nathaniel **PIERCE** 1680/1; 15 Oct 1670; Woburn
FOSTER, Isaac (-1692) & 1/wf Mary **JACKSON** (-1677); 5 May 1658; Ipswich
FOSTER, Isaac (-1692) & 2/wf Hannah **DOWNING**; 25 Nov 1678; Ipswich
FOSTER, Isaac & Mehitable (**WYLLES**) **RUSSELL**, w Daniel, m/2 Timothy **WOODBRIDGE** 1685;
m cont 27 Jan 1679, 1679/80?; Charlestown/Hartford
FOSTER, Isaac (-1692, ae 62) & 3/wf Martha **HALE** (-1692+); m cont 27 Jan 1679, 16 Mar 1679,
1679/80; Ipswich
FOSTER, Jacob (?1635-) & 1/wf Martha **KINSMAN** (-15 Oct 1666); 12 Jan 1658; Ipswich
FOSTER, Jacob (1635-1710) & 2/wf Abigail **LORD** (-1729); 26 Feb 1666, 1666/7; Ipswich
FOSTER, Jacob (1662-) & 1/wf Sarah **WOOD** (-1697); 12 Sep 1688; Topsfield/Ipswich?
FOSTER, Jacob (1670-) & 1/wf Mary **CALDWELL** (1672-1709); 5 Mar 1697; Ipswich
FOSTER, Jacob (1662-) & 2/wf Mary **EDWARDS**; 20 May 1700; Ipswich/Topsfield/Lebanon, CT
FOSTER, James (1651-1732) & 1/wf Mary **CAPEN** (1652-1678); 22 Sep 1674; Dorchester
FOSTER, James (-1732) & 2/wf Anna **LANE** (-1732); 7 Oct 1680; Dorchester
FOSTER, Jeremiah (?1671-1757) & Hannah [**MEIGS**] (1678-); b 1701?; Southampton, LI

FOSTER, John (-1688) & [Martha TOMPKINS], m/2 Richard ADAMS 1688; ca 1645/7; Salem
FOSTER, John (1634-1687) & Emden [SHAW], dau Edmund; b 1662(3?), ca 1655?; Southampton, LI
FOSTER, John (1642-1732) & 1/wf Mary [CHILLINGWORTH] (-1702); ca 1663; Marshfield
FOSTER, John & Elizabeth _?_; b 1668; Boston
FOSTER, John (1655-) & 1/wf Mary STUARD; 18 Mar 1672, 1672/3?; Salem
FOSTER, John (1648-1691?, 1711) & 1/wf Lydia [TURELL] (1660-); b 1678(9?); Boston
FOSTER, John (1648-1691, 1711?) & 2/wf Abigail (HAWKINS) (MOORE) KELLOND, w Samuel, w Thomas; 28 Nov 1689; Boston
FOSTER, John (1662-) & Hannah ABBOTT; 5 Dec 1689; Southampton, LI
FOSTER, John & Mary _?_; b 1691; Ipswich
FOSTER, John (1666-1723) & 1/wf Sarah RICHARDSON; 31 May 1692; Newbury
FOSTER, John (1655-) & 2/wf Mary (COWES) PUMMERY/POMEROY, w John; 12 Jul 1692; Salem
FOSTER, John (1666-1741) & Hannah STUDSON/STETSON (-1747); 16 Nov 1692; Plymouth
FOSTER, John (1678-) & Margaret JACOBS (1675-); 30 Nov 1699; Salem
FOSTER, John & Sarah [?BALSTON], m/2 John THOMAS?; b 1701; Boston/[?Marshfield]/?Stow/ ?Chelmsford
FOSTER, Jonathan & Abigail KIMBALL (1677-); 14 Dec 169[2?], 1693?; Boxford/Billerica
FOSTER, Jonathan (1671-1740+) & Abigail _?_ (-1759); b 1698; Stow/Chelmsford
FOSTER, Joseph (1638-1708) & _?_; b 1665; Southampton
FOSTER, Joseph & Experience _?_; b 1670; Billerica
FOSTER, Joseph (1650-) & 1/wf Alice GORTON (-1712); 11 Dec 1672; Billerica
FOSTER, Joseph & Anna/?Ann (TRASK) WILSON (1654-), w Robert; 21 Nov 1683; Salem/Dorchester
FOSTER, Joseph (ca 1674-) & Rachel BASSETT (1679-1744); 8 Sep 1696; Barnstable/Sandwich
FOSTER, Joseph & _?_; b 1698?, b 1701; Southampton, LI
FOSTER, Josiah (1669-1757) & 1/wf Sarah [SHERMAN] (1676-1713); b 1696; Pembroke
FOSTER, Nathaniel (1633-1687) & _?_; Huntington, LI
FOSTER, Reginald/Renold & 1/wf Judith [WIGNOL] (-1684); 1619; Ipswich, MA/London Garden, Essex, Eng
FOSTER, Reginald (-1707) & Elizabeth [DANE]; b 1653?; Ipswich
FOSTER, Reginald[1]/Randall (-1681) & 2/wf Sarah (?LARRIFORD) MARTIN (-1683), w? John, m/3 William WHITE 1682; - Sep 1665, 19 Oct 1665; Ipswich/Charlestown
FOSTER, Richard (1595-1630, in Eng) & Patience [BIGG] (1595, ?1588-); in Eng, ?Biddenden, ca 1616?; Dorchester
FOSTER, Richard (-1658?) & Mary BARTLETT, m/2 Jonathan MOWRY/MOREY 1659; 16 Sep 1651; Plymouth
FOSTER, Richard (1663-1745) & Parnell WINSLOW (1667-1751); 4 May 1686; Charlestown
FOSTER, Samuel (-1702, ae 82) & Esther KEMP; 15 Nov 1648; Dedham/Windham/Chelmsford
FOSTER, Samuel & 1/wf Sarah STEWARD; 14 May 1676; Salem
FOSTER, Samuel (1650-) & Sarah KEIES/KEYES; 28 May 1678; Chelmsford
FOSTER, Samuel & 2/wf Mary [MARJERY] (1673-); b 1692; Salem
FOSTER, Samuel (-1702) & Rebecca [BRISCO], m/2 Thomas MORRIS, m/3 William SCORCH; b 1699; Boston
FOSTER, Samuel & Elizabeth [MILLET]; b 31 Dec 1700; Gloucester
FOSTER, Standfast (1660-1727), Dorchester & 1/wf Abigail HOLMAN (-1713), Milton; 3 Oct 1688; Milton/Dorchester
FOSTER, Thomas & [Abigail WIMES]; Boston
FOSTER, Thomas (-1682) & Elizabeth _?_ (-1695); b 1640; Weymouth/Braintree/Billerica
FOSTER, Thomas (1640-1679) & Sarah PARKER (1640-1718), m/2 Peter BRACKETT 1687; 15 Oct 1662; Roxbury/Cambridge
FOSTER, Thomas (-1685) & Susannah PARKER, m/2 John FOX ca 1707; 27 Mar 1666, 1665; New London, CT
FOSTER, Thomas (1663-) & Experience PARKER, m/2 Jonathan GEER 1719?; 30 Nov 1686?; Cambridge/Stow
FOSTER, Timothy (1640, ?1638-1688) & 1/wf Ruth (TELESTON) DENTON (1641-1677), w Richard; 13 Oct 1663; Dorchester
FOSTER, Timothy (-1688, ca 51) & Relief (HOLLAND) DOUSE/DOWSE, w John, m/3 Henry LEADBETTER 1692; 9 Mar 1680/1; Dorchester

FOSTER, Timothy (1672-) & Mary DORMAN (1674-); 2 Oct 1699; Topsfield
FOSTER, William (1618-1698) (see Christopher HOBBS) & Anne/Susanna [BRACKENBURY]
   (1629-1714); b 1645?, b 1652; Charlestown/Boston
FOSTER, William (-1690) & _?_ ; Newport
FOSTER, William² (?1633-1713) & Mary JACKSON (1639-); 15 May 1661; Rowley
FOSTER, William (-1687/8) & ?Anne/Hannah _?_ ; ca 1668?; Jamaica, LI
FOSTER, William (1670?-) & Sarah KIMBALL (1669-1729); 6 Jul 16[92?]; Boxford
FOSTER, _?_ & Ann _?_ (-1721); b 1679?; ?Hartford
FOTHERGILL, Robert & Elizabeth _?_ ; b 1682(3?); Boston
FOLKE/FOULKE, John & _?_ ; b 1661; Scituate
FOUNELL/?FOWNELL, John (-1673) & Mary _?_ (-1696), m/2 William HUDSON 1677; b 1636;
   Charlestown
FOUNTAIN, Aaron & 1/wf Mary [BEEBE]; b Dec 1681; New London
FOUNTAIN, Aaron & 2/wf Hannah [WINTON], w Andrew?; prob by 1690; Fairfield, CT
FOUNTAIN, Peter (-1704?) & Mehitable [MASCOLL] (1655-1704+); b 1682; Salem
FOWLE, Abraham & Hannah HARRIS (1663-); 14 Jul 1679; Charlestown
FOWLE, Edward & Sarah _?_ ; b 1678; Boston
FOWLE, George (-1682, ae 72) & Mary _?_ (-1677, ae 68); b 1637; Concord/Charlestown
FOWLE, Isaac (?1648-1718) & Beriah BRIGHT (1651-1735, 1734?), Watertown; 30 Nov 1671;
   Charlestown
FOWLE, Isaac (-1724) & Rebecca BURROUGHS, m/2 Ebenezer TOLMAN; 1 Dec 1698;
   Charlestown
FOWLE, Jacob (-1766) & Susanna NICK; 31 Oct 1700; Marblehead/Charlestown
FOWLE, James (1642-1690, Woburn) & Abigail [CARTER] (1648-), dau John, m/2 Samuel
   WALKER 1692, m/3 Samuel STONE; b 1667(8?); Charlestown
FOWLE, James & Margaret? _?_ ; b 1671?; Boston
FOWLE, James & Mary RICHARDSON, m/2 Samuel WALKER 1692; 2 Oct 1688; Woburn
FOWLE, John (1637/8-1711) & Anna CARTER (1640-1709, in 70th y); 25 Jan 1658/9;
   Charlestown
FOWLE, Rev. John (-1701) & Love (GIBBONS) [PROUT], w William; aft 1675; Bermuda
FOWLE, John (-1725) & Katharine GUTRIDGE, Boston; 18 Feb 1689/90; Charlestown/Boston
FOWLE, John & Elizabeth PRESCOTT (1678-); 1 Jul 1696; Woburn
FOWLE, Peter & Mary [CARTER] (1646-1714), dau John; b 1666; Charlestown/Woburn
FOWLE, Peter & Sarah WINN (1672-); 30 Oct 1691; Woburn/Charlestown
FOWLE/COVELL, Philip & Elizabeth ATWOOD; 26 Nov 1688; Malden
FOWLE, Samuel & Susanna [BLANEY] (1673-), m/2 Thomas COOK 1704; b 1696; Charlestown
FOWLE, Thomas (returned to Eng) & Margaret _?_ ; b 1640; Boston
FOWLE, Zachariah (-1678) & Mary PAYNE (-1678); 24 Dec 1675; Charlestown
FOWLES, Zachariah (1676-1718) & Ruth INGERSOLL; 21 Nov 1700; Salem/Charlestown
FOWLER, Abraham (1652-1720, 1719?) & Elizabeth BARTLETT (1653-1742); 29 Aug 1677;
   Guilford, CT/Branford, CT
FOWLER, Ambrose (-1704) & Joanna/Jane?/Joan ALVORD (1623-1684); 6 May 1646; Windsor,
   CT/Westfield
FOWLER, Ambrose (1658-1712) & Mary BAKER; 11 Sep 1693; Westfield
FOWLER, Christopher (1655?-) & _?_ ; ?ca 1680/2; Southampton, LI
FOWLER, George (1662-) & Abigail/?Eunice [SOUTHARD]; b 1690; Providence/Hempstead, LI
FOWLER, Henry¹ (-1687) & Rebecca [NEWELL] (1636-); b 4 Jun 1655; Providence/E.
   Fairfield/Mamaroneck/East Chester, NY/Sandwich?
FOWLER, Henry (1657, 1658-1730/33) & 1/wf Abigail [HOYT]; b 1679?; Eastchester, NY
FOWLER, Henry (1658-) & Rose [BURTON] (see John FOWLER); ca 1680; Eastchester, NY
FOWLER, Henry (1679-) & 1/wf _?_ ; ca 1700; Eastchester, NY
FOWLER, ?John/Jeremiah (1673-1723) & Elizabeth DRAKE?/[BARLOW] (1677-), m/2 Miles
   OAKLEY; b 1703, b 3 Aug 1689, b 1696, ca 1692?; Fairfield, CT
FOWLER, John (-1676) & Mary [HUBBARD] (-1683); ca 1646?, b 1648, Guilford, CT; Plymouth
FOWLER, John & 1/wf Anne (DODD?)/(NORTON) [JOHNSTON] (-1702), wid?; 1680, 1682;
   Guilford, CT (see below)
FOWLER, John & 1/wf Sarah _?_ ; b 1683; Salisbury
FOWLER, John (1648-1738) & Mercy [MILLER] (1662-); 29 Nov 1688, 1687, b 1689;
   Springfield/Westfield

FOWLER, John (1651-1693) & Sarah [WELCH] (1660-), m/2 Samuel NEWTON ca 1697?; b 1688?; ?New Haven/?Milford
FOWLER, John & Hannah (DODD?) JOHNSTON [NORTON], w _?_, w John; b 1691, 1680?; Guilford, CT (see above)
FOWLER, John & 2/wf? Hannah [BUCK] (1671-); ca 1690/2?; Wethersfield, CT
FOWLER, John (-1749+) & 2/wf Hannah SCOTT (1668-); 31 Oct 1695; Springfield
FOWLER, John/?Henry (?1668-ca 1753?) & Rose [BURTON]; b 1703, b 1701?, b 1693?
FOWLER, Jonathan (1657?-) & _?_ ; ?White Plains, NY
FOWLER alias SMITH, Jonathan (-1696) & 2/wf? Elizabeth REYNOLDS (1666-), m/2 Samuel LYMAN 1699; 3 Aug 1687; Norwich, CT
FOWLER, Joseph (bef 1610-) & Sarah [BETTS]; ca 1630/5?; RI?/Newtown, LI
FOWLER, Joseph (1622-1676) & Martha [KIMBALL] (1629-); b 1647; Salisbury
FOWLER, Joseph (1647-1711) & [Elizabeth] [HUTTON]; b 1678; Wenham
FOWLER, Mark (-1686) & Mary _?_ ; b 1681, b 1687; New Haven
FOWLER, Philip (159(-)-1678, 1679, ae 88) (see Samuel) & Mary/Martha? [WINSLEY/WINS-LOW?] (-1694, 30 Aug 1659); Marlborough, Eng, b 1615; Salisbury, MA
FOWLER, Philip & 2/wf Mary (?MACHIAS) NORTON, w George; 27 Feb 1659, m cont 1659/60; Ipswich
FOWLER/FOWER, Philip (1648-1715) & Elizabeth HERRICK (-1727); 28 Jan 1672/3, 1672, 20 Jan 1672, 20 Jan 1673; Salisbury, MA/Ipswich
FOWLER, Richard & _?_ [FOSTER?]; b 1655, b 1662?; RI?/Rye, NY
FOWLER, Samuel[2] (1618-) & _?_ [WINSLEY?] (see Philip FOWLER); ca 1641?; Salisbury
FOWLER, Samuel (1618-1711) & 2/wf Margaret (NORMAN) [MORGAN], w Robert; aft 1673?, ca 1673?; Salisbury
FOWLER, Samuel (1652-), Westfield & Abigail BROWN (-Nov 1683), Windsor, CT; 6 Nov 1683?, Nov 1683?; Windsor, CT/Westfield
FOWLER, Samuel (-1737) & Hannah WATHEN/WORTHEN (1663-1737+); 5 Dec 1684; Salem
FOWLER, Thomas & Hannah JORDAN/JORDON (1638-); 23 Apr 1660; Ipswich
FOWLER, Thomas & Sarah [BARRETT], m/2 William HALL; b 28 Sep 1688, b 29 Nov 1687; Boston
FOWLER, William (-25 Jun 1660/1, 21 Jun) & [Sarah?] _?_ ; in Eng, b 1627; Milford, CT
FOWLER, William (-1683) & 1/wf Mary [TAPP]; 1645 or before; Milford, CT
FOWLER, William (-1683) & 2/wf Elizabeth (ALSOP) BALDWIN, w Richard; 1 Nov 1670; Milford, CT
FOWLER, William (-1707) & Elizabeth _?_ ; ca 1675/80?; Portsmouth, NH
FOWLER, William (-1714) & Mary [THORNE] (-1714+); no date, b 1690; Flushing, LI
FOWLER, William (1660-1713) & [Mary DRAKE?]; b 1687; Eastchester, NY
FOWLER, William (1660-1713) & 2/wf "Judy" _?_
FOWLER, William (1664-) & Anna [BEARD] (1664-); b 1691; Milford, CT
FOWLER, William (1668-1745) & Hannah [DOW] (1672-); b 1692; Amesbury/Salisbury, MA
FOWLER, William & Judith [FEAKE]; b 1698; Flushing
FOX, David & 1/wf Lydia JAQUITH; 10 Jan 1678; Woburn
FOX, David & 2/wf Mary [HAYWOOD] (1654-), dau Samuel; b 1694; Woburn/Charlestown
FOX, Edward & Mary [ALLEN]; ca 1680/85?; Hampton, NH
FOX, Eliphalet (-1711) & 1/wf Mary WHEELER (1645-1678/9); 26 Oct 1665; Concord
FOX, Eliphalet (-1711) & 2/wf Mary (STONE) HUNT (-bef 15 Apr 1702), w Isaac; 30 Nov 1681; Concord
FOKES/FOWKES? (see FOULKE), Henry (-1640) & Jane _?_, m/2 William HOSFORD b 1655; 1642?; Windsor, CT
FOX, Isaac & Abigail OSBORN; 18 Jul 1678; Billerica/Medford/New London, CT
FOX, Jabez (1647-1703) & Judith [RAYNER] (1658-1756, ae 98), m/2 Jonathan TYNG; b 1678; Cambridge
FOX, John, Concord, MA, & 1/wf Sarah LARRABEE; 28 Jun 1678; New London, CT
FOX, John & 2/wf Hannah (ISBOLL) [STEDMAN], w Thomas; ca 1690; New London, CT
FOX, Nathaniel (-1689) & 1/wf Mary [ROGERS]; b 1674; Boston
FOX, Nathaniel (-1689) & Mary STILEMAN (1658-); Jun 1682; Salem
FOX, Nicholas (-1677) & Elizabeth _?_ ; b 1670?; ?Marblehead
FOX, Richard[1] (ca 1642-1709, ca 67, Glastonbury) & Beriah [SMITH] (ca 1657-); ca 1676; Wethersfield, CT

FOX, Samuel (1651-1727) & 1/wf Mary LESTER (1647-); 30 Mar 1675/6, 1676?, 31 Mar 1675;
New London, CT

FOX, Samuel & 2/wf Joanna [?WAY] (-1689); ca 1684?, New London; ?Providence

FOX, Samuel (-1727) & 3/wf Bathshua (ROGERS) [SMITH] (1650-), w Richard; ca 1690, aft
1689; New London, CT

FOX, Samuel, Concord & Ruth KNIGHT, Concord; 13 Jun 1693; Woburn

FOX, Thomas[1] (-1658) & 1/wf Rebecca [?WHEAT] (-11 May 1647); b 1642; Concord

FOX, Thomas[1] (-1683, 1693) & 1/wf _?_ ; b 1647; Cambridge

FOX, Thomas[1] (-1658) & 2/wf ?Ann/Hannah BROOKS, m/2 Andrew LESTER ca 1661, m/3 Isaac
WILLEY 1670/72?; 13 Dec 1647; Concord

FOX, Thomas[1] (-1683, 1693) & 2/wf Ellen (_?_) GREEN (-27 May 1682, ae 82), w Percival; m
cont 24 May 1650; Cambridge

FOX, Thomas & _?_ ; in Eng, aft 1670?, b 1673

FOX, Thomas (-1692) & Elizabeth _?_ ; b 1683; Boston

FOX, Thomas (-1693, ae 85) & 3/wf Elizabeth (?NORCROSS) CHADWICK (1615-1685), w
Charles; 24 Apr 1683; Watertown

FOX, Thomas & 4/wf Rebecca (_?_) (ANDREWS) WITH/WYETH (-1698), w Thomas, w
Nicholas; 16 Dec 1685; Cambridge

FOX, Thomas & Esther JARVISE; 21 Mar 1690; Boston

FOX, William & Elizabeth _?_ ; b 1694; Boston

FOX, _?_ & Margaret CLARKE (-1673) (ae ca 80, 1669) (sister of Henry CLARK); in Eng;
Windsor, CT

FOX, _?_ & Mary [EELLS?]; b 6 Jun 1690

FOX, [John] & 3/wf Susannah (PARKER) FOSTER, w Thomas FORSTER; aft 1685, ca 1707;
?New London, CT

FOXCROFT, Francis (?1657-1727) & Elizabeth DANFORTH (-1721); 3 Oct 1682, ?4 Oct;
Cambridge/Boston

FOXALLS/FOXHALL, John & _?_ ; b 1632; Boston

FOXWELL, John (1639-1677) & Deborah [JOHNSON], m/2 John HARMON by 1680; b 1673;
York, ME

FOXWELL, Nathaniel (1676-1703) & Margaret [BOWDOIN?]; b 1701?

FOXWELL, Philip (1651-1690) & Eleanor [BRACKETT] (1662-1740), m/2 Elisha ANDREWS b
1698, m/3 Richard PULLEN (see Richard ROGERS); by 1680; Kittery, ME

FOXWELL, Richard (-1668) & 1/wf _?_ ; in Eng, b 1627; Roxbury

FOXWELL, Richard (-1668) & 2/wf Ann [SHELLEY]; ca 1632; Roxbury/Scituate/Barnstable

FOXWELL, Richard (?1606, 1604-1676) & Susannah/Sarah? [BONYTHON]; ca 1636?

FOYE, James (ca 1657±-) & Grace _?_ ; ca 1687?; Kittery, ME

FOY, Jeffrey (-1677/8) & Rochard _?_ ; no issue; Boston

FOYE, John & Dorothy [CLEARE], dau John; b 1672; Boston

FOYE, John (1674-) & 1/wf Sarah (BELCHER) LYNDE (1674-), w Joseph; 16 Nov 1699;
Boston/Charlestown

FRAILE/FRAYLE, George (-1663) & Elizabeth _?_ (-1669); b 1641; Lynn

FRAYE/FRAYLE, Samuel (1645/6-1736+) & 1/wf Mary CARRELL (1661-1682); 1678; Salem

FRAYE/FRAYLE, Samuel (1645/6-1736+) & Ann UPTON; 4 Apr 1684; Salem

FRARY, Eliezer (1639, 1639/40-1709) & 1/wf Mary GRAVES (1647-betw 1710 & 28); 28 Jan
1666, 1665/6; Hatfield/Hadley/Northampton/Deerfield

FRARY, John (-1675) & Prudence _?_ (-1691, above 90); in Eng, b 1630; Dedham/Medfield

FRAIRY, John (-1670) & Elizabeth ?(ADAMS)/(?HASTINGS)/?THURSTON HARDING, w
Abraham, m/3 Thomas DYER 1670/73; 25 Dec 1656; Medfield

FRAIRY, Samson (-1704) & Mary DANIELL/DANIEL (1642-1704); 14 Jun 1660; Medfield/Had-
ley/Hatfield/Deerfield

FRARY, Samuel (1674-1762) & 1/wf Sarah [BOARDMAN] (ca 1673-1733/4, 1733); b 1696;
Hadley/Deerfield

FRARY, Theophilus (-1700, near 72) & 1/wf Hannah ELLIOTT/ELIOT (1637-); 4 Jun 1653;
Boston

FRAREY, Theophilus (-1700) & 2/wf Mary (ALLEN) GREENWOOD (-1709), w Nathaniel; 12 Jun
1690; Boston

FRAME/FREAM, Thomas & Mary ROWELL; 18 Sep 1673; Amesbury

FRAMPTON, William & Elizabeth PORTER; 27 Jul 1680; RI

FRANCIS, Abraham & Mary [MANNING], m/2 Thomas HUNT; b 1684; Boston
FRANCIS, John (1598-1653+) & _?_ ; ca 1630/35?; Lynn
FRANCIS, John & Rose _?_ (-1659); b 1657; Braintree
FRANCIS, John & Frances _?_ ; b 1680(1?); Boston
FRANCIS, John (1658-1711) & 1/wf Sarah DIX (-3 Apr 1682); 16 Jan 1680, 10 Feb 1680; Wethersfield, CT
FRANCIS, John (1658-1711) & 2/wf Mercy/Mary [CHATTERTON/?CHITTENDEN] (1664-1745); 16 Jan 1683; Wethersfield, CT
FRANCIS, John (1650-1728) & Lydia COOPER (1662-1725); 5 Jan 1687/8; Cambridge/Charlestown/Medford
FRANCIS, Richard (1606-1687) & Alice [WILCOX?] (?1611-1687+); b 1644(5?); Cambridge/Medford?
FRANCIS, Robert (1668/9-1712) & Joan [?SIPPERANCE/SIBBERANCE] (1629/30-1705); b 1651; Wethersfield, CT
FRANCIS, Stephen & _?_ ; b 1656(7?); Reading
FRANCIS, Stephen (1645-1719) & 1/wf Hannah HALL (1648-1683); 27 Dec 1670; Cambridge/Reading/Charlestown/Medford
FRANCIS, Stephen (1645-1719) & 2/wf Hannah DICKSON/DIXON, m/2 Isaac AMSDEN 1725; 16 Sep 1683; Cambridge/Charlestown
FRANCIS, William & Triphena YELLING; 29 Apr 1699; Boston
FRANK, John (1637-1676) & Sarah WELD (1640-1694); 23 Jul 1663; Roxbury/Boston/Essex Co., MA
FRANCKLIN, Benjamin (1643-) & Katharine _?_ ; b 1672; Boston
FRANKLIN, Benjamin & Phebe _?_ ; b 1690; Marlboro
FRANKLIN, Henry & 1/wf Dorothy BOWNE (1669-1690); 27 May 1689; Flushing, LI
FRANKLIN, Henry & Sarah [JOHNSON] (1665-); b 1692; Boston
FRANKLIN, Henry & Sarah COCK; 26 Feb 1697/8; ?Matinecock, LI/Flushing, LI
FRANKLIN, James & 1/wf _?_ ; b 1682; Dartmouth?
FRANKLIN, James & 2/wf Elizabeth HAMMOND (1673-1760), m/2 Jonathan HOWARD 1722, m/3 John CHAFFER 1735; 17 Apr 1695; Swansea
FRANKLIN, Jonathan (-1693) & Sarah (SMITH) [STEVENS?] (-1694), w James, m/2 John FIELD of Boston 1694; 1 Feb 1686/7, b 1687; Hingham/Boston/Haverhill
FRANKLIN, John & _?_ ; b 1692, 1666?; Southold, LI
FRANKLIN, Josiah (1657-1745?) & 1/wf Ann [CHILD] (-1689); Ecton, Eng, ca 1677; Boston
FRANKLIN, Josiah (1657-1745?) & 2/wf Abiah FOULGAR/FOLGER (1667-); 25 Nov 1689; Boston
FRANKLIN, Matthew & _?_ ; b 1669; ?Flushing, LI
FRANKLIN, Richard & Abigail STAMBURY; 29 Sep 1697; Boston
FRANCKLIN, William (1607-1658) & 1/wf Alice [ANDREWS]; b 1638?; Ipswich/Newbury/Boston
FRANCKLIN, William (-1641) & Joanna/Jane? _?_ (-1659?); b 1642; Boston
FRANCKLIN, William (-1658) & 2/wf Phebe _?_ (-1658), m/2 Augustine LINTON; b 1644, b 2 Apr 1641; Boston
FRANCECO, Francis & Mary _?_ ; b 1665(6?); Boston
FRAZER, Colin & 1/wf Anna/?Hannah STUARD/STUART; 10 Nov 1685; Newbury
FRAZER, Colin & 2/wf Ann [WICOM] (1674-); m cont 17 Dec 1691; Rowley
FREAKE, John (-1675) & Elizabeth CLARKE, m/2 Elisha HUTCHINSON [1677]; 28 May 1661; Boston
FREETHE/FREATHY, James (-1690) & Mary [MILBURY], m/2 Nathaniel BLACKLEDGE by 1695; ca 1678; York, ME
FREETHE, John (1650±-) & Hannah [BRAY] (1660-1729), m/2 Robert HAZELTON 1709; ca 1678?; York, ME
FREETHE, William & Elizabeth BARKER; 15 Sep 1640, Plymouth, Eng; Richmond Is., ME/York, ME
FREDERICK, Christopher & Mary [?PALMER]; b 1701?; Great Island
FREDERICK, William & 1/wf Mary [TUTTLE] (1666-); b 1685; Wallingford, CT/Woodbury, CT
FREDERICK, William & 2/wf Abigail [DOOLITTLE]; b 1696; New Haven/Wallingford,CT
FREEBORN, Gideon² (-1720) & 1/wf Sarah BROWNELL (1641-1676); 1 Jun 1658; Portsmouth, RI

FREEBORN, Gideon² (-1720) & 2/wf Mary (BOOMER) LAWTON (-1716), w John; 3 Jun 1678; Portsmouth, RI

FREEBORN, William¹ (1594-1670) & Mary _?_ (?1601-1670, ae 80?, 70?); b 1627; Boston/Portsmouth, RI

FREEMAN, William³ (-1705) & Mary HALL, m/2 Clement WEAVER; 21 Dec 1698, 13 Sep 1698; Portsmouth, RI

FREELOVE, Morris & Elizabeth WILBUR; 9 Feb 1680/1; Portsmouth, RI

FREEMAN, Constant (1669-1745, Truro) & Jane TREAT (1675-1729); 11 Oct 1694; Eastham/Truro

FREEMAN, David (-1733, in 75th y, Attleboro), Rehoboth & Margaret INGRAHAM (-1689), Swansea; 4 Apr 1683; Rehoboth

FREEMAN, David (-1733) & 2/wf Mary?/Mercy?/?Elizabeth _?_ (-1723, in 57th y, Attleborough); 1698+; Attleboro

FREEMAN, Edmund¹ (1596, 1590?-1682, ae 92?) & 1/wf Bennett HODSOLL (-1630); Gravel cum Chesfield?, 16 Jun 1617, Cowfold; Lynn/Sandwich

FREEMAN, Edmund¹ (1596, 1590?-1682) & 2/wf Elizabeth GOURNEY (-1676, 1675), wid; aft 1630; Sandwich

FREEMAN, Edmund² (1620-1703) & 1/wf Rebecca PRENCE (-1650?); 22 Apr 1646; Eastham/Sandwich

FREEMAN, Edmund², Jr. (1620-1703) & 2/wf Margaret PERRY (-1703+); 18 Jul 1651; Sandwich

FREEMAN, Edmund³ (1657-1717, 1718?) (not 1719) & 1/wf Ruth MERRICK (1653-1680); Jan 1677/8, Jan 1677; Eastham

FREEMAN, Edmund (1657-1717/18, 1718, 1717?) & 2/wf Sarah [MAYO] (1660-1746); ca 1681; Eastham

FREEMAN, Edmund (1655-1720) & Sarah [?SHIFF] (-1742?, ae 90?); ca 1682; Sandwich

FREEMAN, Henry/Samuel (-1672) & 1/wf Hannah STEARNS (1628-1656); 25 Dec 1650; Watertown

FREEMAN, Henry (ca 1625-1672) & 2/wf Mary SHERMAN (1639-1703), m/2 Lewis ALLEN by 1677; 27 Nov 1656; Watertown

FREEMAN, James & Rachel BOND; 17 Oct 1700; Boston

FREEMAN, John (1600-) & 1/wf Mary _?_ ; in Eng, b 1626; Sudbury

FREEMAN, John (?1600-1648) & 2/wf Elizabeth [NOYES], m/2 Josiah HAYNES 1649; ca 1643; Sudbury

FREEMAN, John (1627-1719, in 98th y) & Mercy PRENCE (?1631-1711); 14 Feb 1649/50, 14 Feb 1649, 13 Feb 1649; Sandwich/Eastham

FREEMAN, John (1651-1721) & 1/wf Sarah MERRICK (1654-1696); 18 Dec 1672; Eastham

FREEMAN, John (1651-1721) & 2/wf Mercy (HEDGE?) [WATSON] (-1721, ae 57, ae 62), w Elkanah; ca 1697-8?, ca 1701?, aft 21 Apr 1696; Eastham/Harwich

FREEMAN, Jonathan (1674-1713) & Mary WOODCOCK; 1 Jul 1689; Rehoboth/Attleboro

FREEMAN, Joseph (1645-1688) & Dorothy HAYNES (?1652-1698); 6 May 1680; Sudbury/Stow/Preston, CT

FREEMAN, Joshua & _?_ ; b 1680(1?); Hingham

FREEMAN, Nathaniel (1669-1760) & Mary [?HOWLAND] (?1666-1743, ae 76); ca 1690; Eastham

FREEMAN, Nathaniel & Alice PENUEL/PENNELL?/PENWELL?; 18 Jan 1699; Boston

FREEMAN, Ralph (-1718) & Katharine LYON; 21 Dec 1652; Dedham/Attleborough

FREEMAN, Ralph & Sarah _?_ ; b 1689; Dedham/Attleboro

FREEMAN, Samuel & Apphia QUICK, m/2 Thomas PRENCE; St. Anne, Blackfriar, London, 14 Jul 1624; Watertown

FREEMAN, Samuel (1638-1712) & Mercy SOUTHERNE/?SOUTHWORTH; 12 May 1658; Eastham

FREEMAN, Samuel (-1655) & Sarah _?_ ; b 1683; Eastham

FREEMAN, Samuel (?1662-1743) & 1/wf Elizabeth SPARROW; 5 Feb 1684; Eastham

FREEMAN, Samuel (?1668-) & Elizabeth BROWN (-1732)

FREEMAN, Samuel (1662-1743) & 2/wf Bathshua (LOTHROP) SMITH (1673-), w Samuel, Jr.; ca 1693; Eastham

FREEMAN, Stephen (-1675) & Hannah ASTWOOD, m/2 Robert PORTER aft 1675, m/3 ?[John] CLARK; b 1653; Milford, CT/Newark, NJ

FREEMAN, Thomas (1653-1715/6) & Rebecca SPARROW (1655-1740); 31 Dec 1673; Eastham/Harwich

FREEMAN, Thomas & Mary MEEK; 11 Nov 1697; Marblehead

FREEMAN, Thomas & Alice TEWELL; 23 Nov 1700; Boston
FREEMAN, William (ca 1660-1686) & Lydia [SPARROW] (-1709+), m/2 Jonathan HIGGINS; ca 1683, 1667+; Eastham
FREEZE, James (1641-) & Elizabeth __?__, m/2 Thomas RIGGS 1695; b 1667; Salisbury
FREEZE, James & Mary MERRILL; 2 Jun 1697; Newbury
FREEZE, John & Dorothy CARR, m/2 Fawne CLEMENT, m/3 Archelaus ADAMS; m int 25 Jul 1696; Salisbury/Newbury
FRENCH, Dependence (-1732) & 1/wf Mary [MARSH]; b 1684; Braintree/Brockton
FRENCH, Dependence (-1732), Braintree & Rebecca FENNS (1662-1741), Milton; 27 Apr 1688; Milton
FRENCH, Ebenezer (1658-1736) & Susannah BLATCHLEY (-1728); 8 Oct 1684; Guilford, CT
FRENCH, Edward (1590-1674) (called "bro." by William WORCESTER) & Ann [SWAYNE?]; b 1632; Salisbury
FRENCH, Edward & Mary WINSLEY; 17 Sep 1695, m int; Salisbury
FRENCH, Francis, Derby & Lydia BUNNELL (-1708); 10 Apr 1661; Derby, CT/Milford, CT
FRENCH, Henry & Elizabeth COLLINS; 7 Nov 1695; Salisbury
FRENCH, Humphrey (-1712) & Abigail __?__ (-1712+); b 1693; Salem
FRENCH, Jacob (1640-1713) & 1/wf Mary CHAMPNEY (-1681); 20 Sep 1667; Billerica
FRENCH, Jacob (1640-1713) & 2/wf Mary CONVERSE (1655-1686); 30 Jun 1685; Billerica/Woburn
FRENCH, Jacob (1640-1713) & 3/wf Mary __?__; aft 1686; Billerica
FRENCH, James & __?__; b 1695/[6?]
FRENCH, John & 1/wf 2/wf? Sarah?/[Joan] __?__ (-1646); b 1635, b 1633?; Cambridge
FRENCH, John (?1612-1692) & 1/wf Grace __?__ (1621-1680); b 1641; Dorchester/Braintree
FRENCH, John (1622-1697) (son of Thomas) & Freedom [KINGSLEY] (?1630-1689); b 1655, ca 1654; Ipswich/Rehoboth/Northampton/Attleboro
FRENCH, John & Mary NOYCE/NOYES (1641-); 23 Mar 1659; Salisbury
FRENCH, John (1635-1712) & 1/wf Abigail COGGIN (ca 1637-1682); 21 Jun 1659, at Barnstable; Billerica
FRENCH, John (1635-) & 2/wf Hannah BURRIDGE (1643-1667); 3 Jul 1662, 3 Jul 1663; Charlestown/Billerica/Cambridge
FRENCH, John (1642-) & [Phebe KEYES?] (1639-1761); b 1663, b 1665; Topsfield
FRENCH, John (1635-1712) & 3/wf Mary ROGERS (-1677); 14 Jan 1667, 1667/8, 14 Nov 1667; Billerica
FRENCH, John (1635-1712) & 4/wf Mary (LITTLEFIELD) KITTREDGE, w John; 16 Jan 1677/8; Billerica
FRENCH, John & Mary SHEADER/SHEATHA; 31 Jul 1675
FRENCH, John (1655, ?1657-1709, 1725) & Hannah PALMER (Mary PALMER is wrong) (1657-); 27 Nov 1678; Rehoboth
FRENCH, John (1612-1692) & 2/wf Eleanor (THOMPSON) VEAZIE (-1717, ae 85), w William; m cont 8 Jul 1683; Braintree
FRENCH, John (1641-) & Experience [THAYER] (1658-1719); b 1686; Braintree
FRENCH, John & 1/wf Lydia __?__ (-1709); b 1694; Hampton, NH
FRENCH, John (1671-) & Elizabeth __?__; b 1696; Topsfield/Norwich, CT
FRENCH, John & Elizabeth __?__; b 1699; Taunton
FRENCH, Jonathan (-1714) & Sarah [WARNER?] (1668-); [b 1692]; Northampton/Hadley/Guilford
FRENCH, Joseph (-1710) & Susanna [STACEY?] (-1687); 1654; Salisbury/Ipswich
FRENCH, Joseph (1640-1694) & Experience FOSTER; 4 Nov 1663; Billerica/Taunton
FRENCH, Joseph (-1732, Bedford) & Elizabeth KNIGHT (-1742, Monson); 2 Jan 1672; Charlestown/Concord
FRENCH, Joseph (1654-1684, 1683?) & Sarah EASTMAN (1655-1748), m/2 Solomon SHEPARD 1684; 13 Jun 1678; Salisbury
FRENCH, Joseph & __?__; b 1680; Taunton
FRENCH, Joseph (?1676-) & Hannah __?__; b 1698; Salisbury
FRENCH, Joseph & Abigail BROWN; 20 Dec 1699; Salisbury
FRENCH, Michael & __?__; by 1674?; Lamprett River
FRENCH, Nathaniel & Mary TISDALE (1658-1751); 9 Jan 1676, 1675/6; Taunton
FRENCH, Philip & __?__; b 1695; NH

FRENCH, Richard (1625-1688) & [Martha] _?_ ; b 1653; Cambridge/Marshfield
FRENCH, Richard (1676-) & Elizabeth _?_ ; b 1700; Enfield, CT
FRENCH, Samuel & 1/wf Abigail BROWN (1644-1680); 1 Jun 1664; Salisbury
FRENCH, Samuel (-1718?) & Ann/Anna/Hannah MARSH (-1712); b 1680; Braintree
FRENCH, Samuel (-1718?) & 2/wf Hannah (MORTON) (FULLER) LATHROP
FRENCH, Samuel (1653-) & Sarah CUMMINGS; 28 Dec 1682, 24 Dec, 26 Dec, 2 Apr 1679; Chelmsford
FRENCH, Samuel & 2/wf Esther _?_ ; bef 1683; Salisbury
FRENCH, Samuel (1672-) & Abigail [HUBBELL]; b 1694, ca 1693; Fairfield, CT
FRENCH, Simeon & Abigail [NOYES] (1659-); 1707
FRENCH, Simon & 1/wf Joanna [JACKMAN] (-1704); b 1686; Salisbury
FRENCH, Stephen (-1680) & Mary _?_ (-1655); ca 1635, b 1612?; Dorchester/Weymouth
FRENCH, Stephen & Hannah WHITMAN; 19 Sep 1660, ?6 Sep; Weymouth
FRENCH, Stephen & (2/wf) Hannah (JACOB?) [LORING] (-1720, in 84th y, Plympton), w Thomas; ca 1679, b 1701?, b 1692?; Weymouth
FRENCH, Stephen (1664-1742) & Abigail BEAL; 24 Sep 1691, 26 Sep; Hingham/Weymouth
FRENCH, Thomas (-1639?) & Susan RIDDLESDALE (-1658); 5 Sep 1608, Hasington, Eng; Ipswich
FRENCH, Thomas (-1639) & Alice _?_ /Mary ?SCUDEMORE/MORTON?, m/2 Thomas HOWLETT?; b 1632, b 1640; Boston
FRENCH, Thomas & 1/wf Mary/Elizabeth? [BUTTON]; b 1652, b 1649?; Charlestown/Guilford, CT
FRENCH, Thomas[2] & Mary ADAMS; 29 Feb 1659, 1659/60; Ipswich
FRENCH, Thomas & 2/wf Deborah (WALTHAM) [JOY], w Walter; b 1667; Guilford, CT
FRENCH, Thomas (1657-) & 1/wf Mary CATLIN (-1704); 18 Oct 1683; Deerfield
FRENCH, Thomas (-1717) & Elizabeth [BELCHER] (1677-1718); b 1696; Braintree
FRENCH, William (1603-1681) & 1/wf Elizabeth GODFREY?/[SYMMES?] (1603-1668); in Eng, b 1625?, b 1634?, b 1639; Cambridge/Billerica
FRENCH, William (1603-1681, ae 78) & 2/wf Mary (LOTHROP) STEARNS (1640-1735+), w John, m Isaac MIXOR 1687; 6 May 1669; Billerica
FRENCH, William (-1691) & Rachel TWELVE/TWELLS (-1691); 25 Sep 1689; Braintree
FRENCH, William (1668-1723) & Sarah DANFORTH (1670-), m/2 Ebenezer DAVIS 1729; 22 May 1695; Billerica
FRENCH, William, Stratham, NH, & Abigail WIGGIN (1678-); b 1701?, ca 1698, Sep 1698; Exeter, NH/Stratham, NH
FREIND/FRIEND, James & Mary MOULTON; 12 Dec 1662; Wenham
FREIND, John (-1656) & _?_ ; ca 1632; Salem
FREND, John & Mary DEXTER, m/2 James OLIVER; Oct 1639; Barnstable
FREIND, Richard (-1706, 1681?) & Anna/Hannah? CURTES/CURTICE (1656-); 19 Apr 1677; Salem
FRIERSON, Randall & Mary JAMES; 16 Mar 1687/8; Beverly
FRINK, John & Grace [STEVENS] (-1717); b 1658; Stonington, CT
FRINK, John (-1675) & Mary [WOOD], m/2 Richard BRIAR/BRIER 1679?; b 1664; Ipswich
FRINK, John (1671-1718) & Hannah PRENTICE (1672-); 15 Feb 1694, 1693/4; Stonington, CT
FRINK, John & 1/wf Hannah MORGRAGE; 10 Apr 1700; Kittery, ME
FRINK, Samuel & Hannah MINOR; 6 Jan 1692, 1691/2; Stonington, CT
FRINCKS, Thomas (1674-) & Sarah [NOYES]; b 1699; Sudbury
FRISBIE, Benoni (1654-1700) & Hannah [ROSE]; b 1679(80?); Branford, CT
FRISBIE, Caleb & Hannah [ROSE] (1676-); b 1696?, b 1698; Branford, CT
FRISBIE, Ebenezer (1673-1714) & Mary [HARRINGTON], m/2 John BARTHOLOMEW; b 1701; Branford, CT
FRISBIE, Edward & Hannah [?CULPEPPER]; b 1644?, b 1650; Branford, CT
FRISBIE, John (1650-1694) & Ruth BOWERS (1657-1736), m/2 William HOADLEY; 2 Dec 1674; Branford, CT
FRISBIE, Jonathan (1659-1695) & Mary [HOADLEY], m/2 Robert? DARBY, m/3 Nathaniel FINCH b 1699; b 1685(6?); Branford, CT
FRISBIE, Nathaniel (-1711) & Mary _?_ ; b 1699; Branford, CT
FRISBIE, Samuel (1655, 1654?-1681) & Rebecca [POTTER] (1662-), m/2 Charles TYLER; ?b 1675, no issue; Branford, CT

FRISSELL/FRIZZELL, James (-1717, ae 90) & Sarah [?BUSKETH] (-1713); b 1656; Roxbury
FRISSEL, John & Dorothy PARNEL, m/2 _?_ SALTONSTALL; 22 Jul 1698; Boston
FRIZELL, Joseph (-1704) & Abigail BARTHOLOMEW (1673-1752), m/2 Samuel PARNE 1709; 11 Jan 1691/2; Woodstock, CT
FRISSIL, Samuel & Martha [ALEXANDER] (1668-); b 1695; Roxbury
FRISSEL, William (-1685) & Hannah CLARKE (1646-), m/2 Peter TALBOT 1687; 28 Nov 1667; Concord
FROE/FRO, David (-1710) & Priscilla (CORISH) HUNTER (-1725), w William; 7 Feb 1677/8, 7 Feb 1677; Springfield/Suffield
FROST, Abraham & _?_ ; Fairfield, CT/Hempstead, LI
FROST, Benjamin & Mary [DAVIS?] (1656-) (see John & Thomas); b 1696; Boston/Watertown
FROST, Charles (1631-1697) (ae 52 in 1683) & Mary BOLLES (?1641-1704); 27 Dec 1665?, 1675?, by 1664; Kittery, ME
FROST, Charles & 1/wf Sarah WAINWRIGHT (1682-1714); 7 Feb 1698/9; Kittery, ME
FROST, Daniel/Wm.? (-1675, 1663) & 1/wf _?_ ; Fairfield, CT
FROST, Daniel (-1684/5) & 2/wf Elizabeth [BARLOW] (-1686); [ca] (1639); Fairfield, CT
FROST, Daniel (-1708) & Mary [ROWLAND], m/2 Moses JACKSON; b 12 Dec 1691, b 30 Dec 1690; Fairfield, CT
FROST, Edmund (-1672) & 1/wf Thomasine _?_ (-1650); in Eng, b 1632; Cambridge
FROST, Edmund (-1672) & 2/wf Mary _?_ ; ca 1650?, 1642?; Cambridge
FROST, Edmund (-1672) & 3/wf Reana (_?_) (JAMES) (ANDREW?) DANIEL, w Edmund, w William, w Robert; b 1669, b 12 Apr 1669; Cambridge
FROST, Ephraim (-1718, ae 70) & Hepzibah [PRATT] (1655-1719); b 1678; Cambridge/Weymouth
FROST, George/Daniel? & _?_ ; ca 1630/40?; Winter Harbor, ME
FROST, Isaac (1666-1757) & Mary BARBER (1677-1758); 3 Dec 1696, b 1696/7; W. Springfield
FROST, James (-1711) & 1/wf Rebecca HAMLET (-1666); 7 Dec 1664, 17 Dec 1665; Billerica
FROST, James (-1711) & 2/wf Elizabeth FOSTER; 22 Jan 1666/7; Billerica
FROST, James, Jr. & 1/wf Hannah TRULL (1671-); 22 Nov 1693; Billerica
FROST/TURFS?, James & 1/wf Hannah WOODEN (1669-); 1 Jul 1696; Wells, ME/S. Berwick, ME
FROST, Jasper/Joseph? & Elizabeth WAKEFIELD; 20 Aug 1660; Boston
FROST, John[1] & _?_ ; b 1622?; Boston/Southold, LI
FROST, John[2] (-1679+) & Abigail _?_ ; b 1642; Southold, LI/Oyster Bay, LI
FROST, John (-1677) & Rose _?_ ; b 1656?, b 1652; York, ME
FROST, John (1642-1700) & Mercy PAINE; 9 Jun 1664, 1665; New Haven
FROST, John (-1672) & Rebecca ANDREWS, ?m/2 George JACOBS 1675; 26 Jun 1666; Cambridge
FROST, John & 1/wf Mehitable _?_ (1651-); b 1669(70?); Boston
FROST, John (-1718) & Sarah [KELLY]; ca 1673; Isles of Shoals/Star Island, ME?
FROST, John (see Benjamin & Thomas) & 2/wf Mary [DAVIS?] (1656?-); b 1681; Boston
FROST, John (1668-) & Abigail BARNES (1656/7-); 20 Aug 1691, 1692 (no); New Haven/Newark, NJ
FROST, Joseph & Mary BROADISH; 10 Apr 1664; Sudbury
FROST, Joseph (-1692) & Hannah MILLER (1649-); 22 May 1666; Charlestown/Billerica
FROST, Joseph (-1698) & Elizabeth [HUBBELL] (1659-1712), m/2 Samuel HULL by 1700; b 1692, b 1680?; Fairfield, CT
FROST, Nicholas (?1585-1663, ae 74?) & Bertha CADWALLES? (1610?-); in Eng, b 1632, Jan 1629/30, Tiverton, Eng?; Kittery, ME
FROST, Nicholas & Mary [SMALL] (?1656-1712±); b 23 Mar 1674; Kittery, ME
FROST, Philip & Martha (MERRY) [RANKIN] (1647-), w Andrew; ca 1677?, b 1677?, aft 15 Jan 1677/8; Martha's Vineyard
FROST, Samuel & Mary COALE/COLE; 12 Oct 1663; Cambridge/Billerica
FROST, Samuel (1638-1718) & Elizabeth [MILLER] (1649-); b 1674; Cambridge
FROST, Samuel (1664-) & 1/wf Margaret _?_ (-1689); Springfield
FROST, Samuel (1664-) & Experience MILLER; 22 Oct 1691; Springfield/Wallingford, CT
FROST, Stephen & Elizabeth WOODWARD; 1 Feb 1699/1700; Charlestown/Cambridge
FROST, Thomas (1647-1724) & 1/wf Mary (GIBBS) GOODRIDGE (-1691), w John; 12 Nov 1678; Sudbury
FROST, Thomas & Hannah (CRAFT?/GROSS?/?GREFTE) JOHNSON (-1712), w Solomon; 9 Jul 1691; Sudbury

FROST, Thomas/Benjamin & Mary [DAVIS?]; b 1694; Boston
FROST, Thomas & Sarah DUNTON (1677-); 31 May 1694; Woburn/Billerica
FROST, Thomas (1667-1742) & Rebecca FARLEY (1668/9-1705); 12 Dec 1695; Billerica
FROST, William (-1645) & _?_ ; in Eng, ca 1598/1605?, 1610; Fairfield, CT
FROST, William (-1690) & Mary [WAKEFIELD], m/2 Israel HARDING 1691?; b 1670, b 1659?;
  Salem
FROST, William (-1719) & 1/wf Rebecca (WRIGHT) [LEVERICH], div from Eleazer
  LEVERICH; b 20 May 1673, aft 24 Feb 1670/1, ca 1672/3, 1672; Brookhaven, LI/Oyster Bay,
  LI
FROST, William & Esther LEE; 6 Aug 1688; Charlestown
FROST, William (-1721) & 1/wf Rachel [LITTLEFIELD]; 6 Dec 1694; Wells, ME/Salem
FROST, William (1675-1728) & Hannah [PRIER/PRIOR] (1681-); ca 1700, b 1702; Matinecock,
  LI
FROST, William & Rebecca [WRIGHT]; b 1676, ca 1672
FROST, Wright & Mary UNDERHILL (1677-); 9 May 1698
FROST, _?_ & Rebecca _?_, ?m/2 George JACOBS 1675; b 1674; Salem
FROST, _?_ & Susannah DIXON, dau William; Kittery, ME
FROTHINGHAM, John & 1/wf Anna BLANEY (1677-); 19 Nov 1699; Charlestown/Boston
FROTHINGHAM, Nathaniel (1646-) & Mary SLETT (1649-), m/2 Samuel KETTELL 1694; 6 Feb
  1667/8, 6 Dec 1667; Charlestown
FROTHINGHAM, Nathaniel (1671-1730) & Hannah RAND (1672-1760, in 88th y); 12 Apr 1694;
  Charlestown
FROTHINGHAM, Peter (1636-1688) & Mary LOWDEN (1645-1703, ae 58); 14 Mar 1665;
  Charlestown
FROTHINGHAM, Samuel (-1683) & Ruth GEORGE, m/2 Abraham BRYANT 1688; 4 Dec 1668;
  Charlestown/Reading
FROTHINGHAM, Samuel & 1/wf Hepzabeth EATON/ORTON (-1703), dau John; 6 Dec 1697;
  Charlestown
FROTHINGHAM, Thomas & 1/wf Esther [CALL] (1676-1708); b 1694; Charlestown
FROTHINGHAM, William (-1651) & Anna _?_ (-1674, ae 67); by 1630; Charlestown
FROTHINGHAM, William & Esther [GREEN] (1675-1727); b 1693; Charlestown/Boston
FRUDE, ?Henry/?James (-by 1695) & [Sarah LAMBERT] (1660-), m/2 Daniel BACON 1688; b
  1688; Salem
FRY, Adrain & ?Hannah/Sarah [WHITE] (-1709); b 1668; Kittery, ME
FRY, Anthony & Hannah _?_ ; b 1671; Yarmouth/Bristol, RI
FRIE, Benjamin (-1696±) & Mary PARKER (-1725); 23 May 1678; Andover
FRY, Francis & _?_ ; b 1686; Lusum, LI
FRYE, George (?1618-1676) & 2/wf? Mary (_?_) [BRANDON], w William; b 1650, aft 16 Nov
  1647; Weymouth
FRIE, James (1652/3-1734) & Lydia OSGOOD (1660-1741); 20 Jan 1679, 1679/80?; Andover
FRY, John (?1601-1693) & Ann [?STRATTON] (-1680); ?Basing, Eng, b 1633?; Andover/New-
  bury
FRY, John (-1692) & Eunice POTTER (-1708); 4 Oct 1660, no issue; Andover
FRY, John & Mary WILLETS (1663-1688); 7 Mar 1686/7; Jericho, LI
FRIE, John (1672-1737) & Tabitha FARNUM (1678-); 1 Nov 1694; Andover
FRY, John & Deliverance _?_ ; b 1695; Bristol, RI
FRY, John & Elizabeth HUMMERY; 18 Jun 1695; Bristol, RI
FRY, Joseph & Mary CLARKE; 12 Dec 1700; Newport
FRY, Samuel (-1725) & Mary ASLETT (-1747); 20 Nov 1671; Andover
FRY, Thomas (1632-1704) & Mary [GRIFFIN] (1649-1717); b 1666; Newport
FRY, Thomas (1666-1748) & Weltham/Welthyan GREENE (1670-); 1 Feb 1688; East Greenwich,
  RI
FRY, William (-1643) & Elizabeth [HUMPHEY?], m/2 Thomas DOGGETT ca 1643; b 1639;
  Weymouth
FRY, William & Thomasin _?_ ; b 1691; Oyster Bay, LI
FRY, William & Hannah [HILL]; nr 1694, b 1694(5?); Dover, NH
FRYERS, James & Katharine _?_ (-1640); Cambridge
FRYER, James (-1676) & Jane [SCARLET] (1653-); b 1673(4?); Boston

FRYER, Joshua & Abigail [FROST] (-1723), m/2 William MOODY; b 1690/1?, by 1690; Kittery, ME

FRYER, Nathaniel/Emanuel (-1703) & 1/wf Christian [ALLISON], w James; b 1653; Boston

FRYER, Nathaniel (-1703) & 2/wf Dorothy WOODBRIDG/WOODBRIDGE; 29 Oct 1679; Newbury

FRYER, Nathaniel & _?_

FRYER, Thomas & Elizabeth _?_ ; ca 1639-42?; Gloucester/Salem

FUGILL, Thomas (returned to Eng) & _?_ [BALL?]; b 1640; New Haven

FULFORD, Abraham & Phebe [CLARKE] (1675-); b 1693?, b 1700; Stratford, CT

FULFORD, Richard & Elizabeth [PIERCE]; b 1676?; ?Misconcus, ME

FULLAM/FULHAM, Francis (ca 1669/70-1758) & 1/wf Sarah [LIVERMORE] (1672, 1672/3?-1723/4); b 1692, ca 1691; Watertown/N. Brookfield

FULLER, Barnabas & Elizabeth YOUNG; 25 Feb 1680, 1680/1; Barnstable

FULLER, Benjamin (1660-1724+) & Sarah BACON (-1724+); 15 Dec 1685; Salem/Ashford, CT

FULLER, Benjamin (?1657-1712) & 1/wf Mary _?_ ; ca 1678, b 1685?, b 1689?; Salem/Rehoboth

FULLER, Benjamin & Susanna BALLARD (1673-); 5 Nov 1690; Lynn

FULLER, Benjamin (?1657-1712) & 2/wf Judith SMITH; 13 Jan 1698/9, 3 Jan 1698/9, 23 Jan 1698; Rehoboth/Attleboro

FULLER, Daniel & Mary _?_ ; b 1690, b 1689?; ?Salem/Rehoboth

FULLER, David & Mary ORMSBY; 15 Jul 1691; Rehoboth/Attleboro

FULLER, Edward (-1621) & Ann? _?_ (-1621); Eng or Leyden?, b 1612?, b 1608?, b 1602?; Plymouth

FULLER, Edward & Hannah LEWIS; 12 May 1686; Lynn

FULLER, Elisha & Elizabeth WALDEN; 10 Sep 1690; Lynn

FULLER, Giles (-1676) & _?_ ; ca 1650; Dedham/Hampton, NH

FULLER, Jabez (-1720, 1721) & Mary [HALLETT]; b 1687(8?), ca 1686; Barnstable

FULLER, Jacob (1655-1731) & Mary BACON (1660-1741); 14 Jun 1683; Salem/Middleton

FULLER, James & Mary RING/KING? (-1732, ae 85); 20 Oct 1672; Ipswich

FULLER, James & Phebe _?_ (-1746); b 1700; Ipswich

FULLER, Jeremiah (1658-1743) & 1/wf Mary [BASS?] (?1673-1689); ca 1688?; Cambridge/Newton

FULLER, Jeremiah (1658-1743) & 2/wf Elizabeth BLAKE (1658-1700); b 1694; Newton

FULLER, Jeremiah (1658-1743) & 3/wf Thankful [BIRD] (1667/8-); b 1701, 1700; Newton

FULLER, John (-1698) & Elizabeth _?_ /FULLER? (-1723?); in Eng, b 1626; Boston

FULLER, John[1] (ca 1611-1698) & Elizabeth _?_ (-1700); b 1645; Cambridge/Newton

FULLER, John (-1695) & Elizabeth [FARRINGTON] (1627-); 1646; Lynn

FULLER, John (-1666) (ae ca 39 in 1660) & Elizabeth EMERSON, m/2 Thomas PERRIN; in Eng?, b 1648, b 1643?; Salisbury/?Ipswich

FULLER, John & Judith GAY (1649-); 8 Jan 1672, 8 Nov (8 Feb is wrong); Dedham

FULLER, John (1653-1675) & Rebecca PUTNAM (1653-), m/2 John SHEPARD 1677; 22 Apr 1672; Salem

FULLER, John & Abigail TITUS; 25 Apr 1673; Rehoboth

FULLER, Dr. John (-1690) & 1/wf ?2/wf Bethiah [?SKIFF]; b 1675; Barnstable

FULLER, John & Rachel BRABROOK/BRABRICK (1655-1715); 19 Mar 1677; Hampton, NH

FULLER, John & Sarah MILLS; 27 Aug 1678 (27 Jun); Dedham

FULLER, John (ca 1656-1726) & Mehitable ROWLEY (1660/1-ca 1732); b 1679?, b 1683?, ca 1676?, ca 1678?; Barnstable/East Haddam, CT

FULLER, John (1645-1721, 1720?) & 1/wf Abigail BALSTONE/BOYLSTON? (1662-); 30 Jun 1682; Cambridge/Newton

FULLER, John & Mehitable [JONES] (1651-), Rowley?; b 1684? (b 1688 is wrong); Barnstable/E. Haddam, CT

FULLER, Dr. John (-1691) & 2/wf Hannah [MORTON] (-1736), m/2 John LOTHROP 1695; 24 Mar 1687; Plymouth/Barnstable

FULLER, John & Mercy [NELSON]; ca 1686 (b 1693); Middleboro

FULLER, Jonathan & Elizabeth WILLMARTH/WILLMOT; 14 Dec 1664; Rehoboth

FULLER, Jonathan & Mary _?_ (-1701); b 1673; Dedham

FULLER, Jonathan (1648-1722, ae 74) & Mindwell TROWBRIDGE (1662-1758); 2 May 1684, no issue; Cambridge/Newton

FULLER, Jonathan & Mary SHOVE/SHAW/STEVENS; 15 Feb 1687, 15 Feb 168-, b 1696; Rehoboth

FULLER, Jonathan & Susanna/Susan TRASK; 3 Jan 1694; Salem

FULLER, Joseph² (1652-1740) & Lydia JACKSON (1655?-1726); 13 Feb 1678/9, 1680/1, 1681, 13 Dec 1680; Cambridge/Newton/Watertown

FULLER, Joseph & Mary HOWARD/HAYWARD/---WORD/WOOD; 17 Oct 1685, Oct 1685, Oct [1686?], 1 Oct 1685; Ipswich

FULLER, Joseph/Jasper & Rebecca BELCHER; 3 Nov 1687, 30 Nov 1687; Lynn

FULLER, Joseph (1661?-) & Thankful BLOSSOM (1675-); b 1701, ca 1700; Barnstable

FULLER, Joshua (1654-1752) & (1/wf) Elizabeth WOOD?/WARD (1660-1691?); 7 May 1679, 7 Jun; Cambridge/Newton

FULLER, Joshua (1654-1752) & 2/wf? Hannah (GRIGGS) [RAINSFORD] (-1739), w David; aft 28 Nov 1691, b 1695; Newton

FULLER, Joshua & Abigail?/Hannah? _?_ (see above); b 1697?, b 1700; Watertown/Cambridge

FULLER, Launcelot & Hannah [MARSH], m/2 John FINCH; b 1652; Fairfield, CT

FULLER, Matthew (1603-1678) & 1/wf ?2/wf Frances _?_ (-living 25 Jul 1678) (mentioned in will); in Eng?, b 1625; Plymouth/Barnstable

FULLER, Matthew & 2/wf Hannah _?_ ; b 1678; Falmouth

FULLER, Matthew (1663?-1744?) & Patience YOUNG (1673-1746); 25 Feb 1692/3, 25 Feb 1692; Scituate/Barnstable

FULLER, Nathaniel (1675-1730+) & Anne [BUTTERWORTH] (1677-1737), dau Abraham; b 1698, 1697; Rehoboth/Mansfield, CT

FULLER, Robert & 1/wf Ann? _?_ (-1646); b 1643; Dorchester/Dedham

FULLER, Robert & (2/wf) Sarah _?_ ; b 1648, 1646, 1647; Dorchester/Dedham

FULLER, Robert (ca 1620-1706) & 1/wf Sarah [BOWEN] (-1676) (dau Richard); ca 1639/44?; Salem/Rehoboth/Attleboro

FULLER, Robert (-1706) & 2/wf Margaret [WALLER] (-1700), Salem, MA, w Christopher; aft 1676, ca 1678; Rehoboth

FULLER, Robert & 1/wf Elizabeth SHEPARDSON (-1701); 19 Jan 1698, 4 Jan 1699, 19 Jan 1699; Rehoboth

FULLER, Samuel (?1580-1633?) & (1/wf) Alice/Elsie [GLASCOCK] (-1613); in Eng?, b 1613; Plymouth

FULLER, Samuel (?1580-1633?) & (2/wf) Agnes CARPENTER (-1615); Leyden, Holland, 24 Apr 1613, 30 Apr 1613; Plymouth

FULLER, Samuel (?1580-1633?) & 3/wf Bridget LEE (-1667+); Leyden, Holland, 27 May 1617; Plymouth

FULLER, Samuel (-1683) & Jane LATHROP (1614-); 8 Apr 1635; Scituate

FULLER, Samuel (1625-1695) & (1/wf) _?_ ; b 1656; Plymouth/Middleboro

FULLER, Samuel (1638-1691) & Anna/Ann? FULLER (not Elizabeth BREWSTER?); b 1659; Barnstable/Falmouth

FULLER, Samuel (?1635-) & Mary _?_ ; b 1660, b 1661; Barnstable

FULLER, Samuel (-1695) & Elizabeth [BOWEN] (-11 Nov 1713, Plympton), w Thomas; aft 11 Apr 1664, ca 1665, b 1669; Plymouth/Plympton/Middleboro?

FULLER, Samuel (-1676) & Mary IYDE/IDE (1649-), m/2 John REDAWAY 1677; 12 Dec 1673; Rehoboth

FULLER, Samuel (1659-1728) & Mercy EATON; 7 Jan 1685; Plymouth

FULLER, Samuel (1676-1716) & Elizabeth THATCHER, m/2 _?_ STANDISH; 3 Oct 1700; Mansfield, CT/Preston, CT

FULLER, Thomas (1618-1698) & 1/wf Elizabeth TIDD; 13 Jun 1643; Woburn/Salem

FULLER, Thomas (1690-) & Hannah FLOWER (neice of Margaret KINGSBURY); 22 Nov 1643; Dedham

FULLER, Thomas & _?_ ; b 1650; Salem

FULLER, Thomas (-1718) & (1/wf) Ruth [RICHARDSON]; b 1671, ca 1670; Salem/Windham, CT

FULLER, Thomas (-1718) & Elizabeth LOTHROP (1659-); 29 Dec 1680; Barnstable

FULLER, Thomas (?1618-1698) & 2/wf Sarah (NUTT) WYMAN (-1688), w John; 25 Aug 1684; Woburn

FULLER, Thomas, Jr. (1662-1734), Dedham & Esther FISHER (1667-1747), Dedham; 25 Apr 1688; Dedham

FULLER, Thomas (?1618-1698) & 3/wf Hannah/Harnet? (?JAMES) WILSON, w John WILSON; aft 25 Aug 1688; Woburn
FULLER, Thomas & Elizabeth COBLEY/COBLEIGH?/COOLEY; 8 Jan 1693, 8 Jun 1693?; Rehoboth
FULLER, Thomas & Elizabeth ANDREWS, ?wid; 3 May 1693?, 1694?; Salem/Middleton
FULLER, Thomas (-1718) & 2/wf Martha DURGY?/DURKEE?; 19 Jul 1699; Salem/Windham, CT
FULLER, Thomas & Anne [WOODCOCK] (1672-, Hingham); b 1701; Attleboro
FULLER, Timothy & Sarah GATES (1670-); b 1695; East Haddam, CT
FULLER, William (?1610-) & Elizabeth _?_ (-1642); b 1641; Concord/Ipswich
FULLER, William (1610, 1608?-1693) & Frances _?_ (-1699, ae "above" 80); b 1678, b 9 Jan 1671/2; Hampton, NH
FULLER, William & Susanna (PERKINS) BUSWELL/BUZZELL/BOSWELL (1652-), w Isaac; 29 Jun 1680, 22 Jun 1680; Hampton, NH/Ipswich/Salisbury
FULLER, William & Bethiah MAPLESDAME; 17 Oct 1696, m int; Lynn
FULLER, William & Ruth (BISHOP) [PIERCE], w John; b 1701?, aft 1684, 27 Feb 1683; Watertown/Lexington
FULLER, _?_ & Ann _?_ (1583-1662); Salem
FULLER, _?_ & Elizabeth [BUXTON] (1672-); b 1715, b 1701?; Salem
FULERTON/FULLERTON, Alexander & Mary _?_ ; b 1694; Boston
FURBER, Jethro (-1682?, 1686?) & Amy (COWELL) SHERBURNE, w Joseph?, m/3 Nathaniel AYRES b 1692; 19 Oct 1678 (m/1 Joseph SHERBURNE on this date?); Portsmouth, NH
FURBER, William[1] (1610/14, 1614-) (ae 62 in 1676) & Elizabeth [CLARK] (1629?-); by 1646, b 1645?; Dover, NH
FURBER, William[2] (1646-1707) & 1/wf Esther [STARBUCK?]; by 1672; Dover, NH
FURBER, William (1646-1707) & 2/wf Elizabeth (HEARD) NUTE (1653-1705), w James; 13 Aug 1694; Dover, NH
FURBER, William (1673-1757) & Sarah [NUTE] (1676-1762)
FURBER, ?Moses & Amy _?_ , ?m/2 Samuel WINSLOW b 1692?
FURNELL, John & Olive _?_ ; b 1677(8?); Boston
FURNELL, Strong & Eleanor _?_ , m/2 Michael LAMBERT 1659; b 1643; Boston
FURNELL, William & Eleanor/?Ellen/?Helen _?_ ; b 1652; Boston
FURNESS/FURNACE, David & Sarah (FLUENT) BRIMBELCOMB, w Philip; 2 Jun 1692; Marblehead
FURNESS/FERRIS?, George & [Abigail TITUS]; b 1701?; Newtown, LI
FURNACE, William (-1689) & Christian _?_ ; b 1682, ca 1680?; Marblehead
FURS/FURSE, John & Jane WILSON; 21 Sep 1698; Boston
FUSSELF, John (ca 1575-1675/6) & Edith (SQUIRE) [ADAMS] (1587-1673), w Henry; b 1650?, b 1651?; Medfield

GAGE, Adam & _?_ ; b 1691; Yarmouth/Harwich
GAGE, Benjamin & 1/wf Mary KEYES (1645-); 16 Feb 1663; Andover
GAGE, Benjamin (-1672) & 2/wf Prudence LEVAR/LEAVER (1644-), m/2 Samuel STICKNEY 1674; 11 Oct 1671; Bradford
GAGE, Benjamin (-1706) & Elizabeth LUMBARD (1663-); 20 Mar 1683/4; Yarmouth
GAGE, Daniel (-1705) & Sarah KIMBALL (ca 1654-); 3 May 1675, 1674?; Bradford
GAGE, Daniel & 1/wf Martha BURBANK; 9 Mar 1697/8; Bradford
GAGE, Edmund & Joanna _?_ ; b 1681; Boston
GAGE, John (1609-) (ae ca 50 in 1659) & 1/wf Amy/Anna? [?WILFORD/?KINGSBURY] (-1658); b 1638; Ipswich/Salisbury
GAGE, John (1609-1673) & 2/wf Sarah (_?_) KEYES (-1681), w Robert; 7 Nov 1658; Ipswich
GAGE, John & 1/wf Sarah _?_ ; b 1695, ?13 Jun 1694?; Bradford
GADG, Jonathan (-1675), Rowley & Hester CHANDLER, m/2 John WILSON; 12 Nov 1667; Andover

GAGE, Josiah (1647-1717) & 1/wf Lydia LAD/LADD (1645-1696); 15 May 1669, no issue; Bradford

GAGE, Josiah (1647-1717) & 2/wf Martha DOW (1673-1717); 17 May 1697; Haverhill

GRAGE, Moses (1668-1740?) & Sarah [DODGE] (1668-1747); b 1692, ca 1690; Beverly

GAGE, Nathaniel (-1728) & Mary (WEEKS) [GREENE], w Thomas, m/3 Joseph JEWETT; b 1696; Bradford

GAGE, Samuel (1638-1676) (ae 25 in 1663) & Faith STICKNEY (1641-); 10 Jun 1674; Bradford

GAGE, Thomas (-1695) & Joanna [KNIGHT]; b 1648; Yarmouth/Harwick

GAGE, Thomas (1656-1707) & Sarah _?_ (1654-1694, ae 40); b 1680, b 1678); Beverly

GAGE, Thomas (1656-1707) & Elizabeth (NORTHEND) (HOBSON) MIGHILL (1656-1737), w Humphrey, w Ezekiel; 11 Jun 1695; Salisbury

GAGE, Thomas (1680, 1678?-) & Mary SMITH; 10 Dec 1697; Rowley

GAGER, John (-10 Dec 1703, Norwich) & Elizabeth [GORE] (-1703+); b 1647; New London, CT

GAGER, John (1647-1691) & Deborah [ALLYN]; aft 1683, no issue; Norwich, CT

GAGER, Samuel (1654-1740) & Rebecca (LAY) [RAYMOND] (1665, 1666-), w Daniel; Apr 1695, ?aft 1696; Norwich, CT

GAGER, William (-1630) & _?_ (-1630); Salem/Charlestown

GAINES, Benoni & Abigail FERMAN; 29 Nov 1700; Enfield, CT

GAINES, Daniel & 1/wf Mary [FORBES]; b 1701?; Wethersfield, CT

GAINES, Henry & Jane _?_ (-1644); b 1632; Lynn

GAINES, John (1636-1689, 1688?) & Mary [TREADWELL/TREDWILL] (1636-1695+); b 1659; Ipswich

GAINS, John & Naomi [HALE] (1680-); b 1701?, ca 1699; Glastonbury, CT

GAINS, Samuel (?1643-1700) & 1/wf Ann WRIGHT; 7 Apr 1665; Lynn

GAINS, Samuel (-1700) & 2/wf Anna [BURNHAM] (1644-1722); b 1 May 1668; Glastonbury

GAINES, Samuel & [?Rebecca COUCH]; ca 1694?, b 1697; Wethersfield, CT

GAINES, Thomas & 1/wf _?_; b 1697; Hartford, CT

GALE, Abel & Dinah _?_ (-living 1724); ca 1665, ca 1667; Jamaica, LI

GALLE, Abraham (ca 1643-1718, Waltham) & Sarah FISH (-1728, ae ca 72); 3 Sep 1673; Watertown

GALE, Abraham (1666-) & Lydia ROUPES/ROPES (1672-), m/2 Thomas ROLLS; 31 Mar 1695/6, 19 Mar 1695/6, Mar 1695; Salem/Beverly

GALL, Abraham (1674-) & Rachel PARKHURST (1678-1767); 6 Dec 1699; Watertown

GALE, Ambrose (?1631-1708?) & 1/wf Mary [WARD] (-5 Feb 1694/5, ae 63 y); b 1663; Salem

GALE, Ambrose (?1665-1717) & 1/wf Sarah _?_; b 1690; Marblehead

GALE, Ambrose (-1708?) & 2/wf Deborah GIRDLER, w Francis; 19 Aug 1695; Marblehead

GALE, Azor & Mary ROOTS; 9 May 1698; Marblehead

GALE, Bartholomew (ca 1641-1678+) & 1/wf Martha LEMON (-23 Dec 1662); 25 Jul 1660; Salem

GALE, Bartholomew (-1678+) & 2/wf Mary [BACON] (-1678+), dau of Daniel; 1 Feb 166-, betw 1662 & 1666, had Abraham 18 Nov 1666; Salem

GALE, Benjamin & 1/wf Lydia _?_; b 1677; Marblehead

GALE, Benjamin & 2/wf Deliverance [CODNER] aft 3 Oct 1699, b 1701?; Marblehead

GALE, Daniel (1676-) & Rebecca SWETT; m int 9 Dec 1700; Newbury

GALE, Edmund (-1642) & _?_ [BARTHOLOMEW?]; b 1630?; Boston

GALE, Edmund (-by 1718) & Sarah [DIXEY] (1643-1718+); b 1666; Salem/Falmouth, ME

GAAL, John & Elizabeth SPRING, m/2 John MELLEN?; 27 Sep 1677; Watertown

GALE, John (-1688) & Sarah _?_; Great Island

GALE, John (-1650) & ?Mary _?_ (-1750+); ca 1696; Jamaica, LI/Goshen, NY

GALE, Richard (-1679) & Mary CASTLE; certificate 16 Sep 1640; Watertown

GALE, Samuel (1666?-) & Mary _?_; 1690(1?); Salem

GALE, Thomas & _?_; b 1655; New Haven

GALE, _?_ & Bethia CHIPMAN (1666-1702+), m/2 Timothy DIMMOCK; ca 1690?, ca 1682?; ?Barnstable (had daughter Mary GALE)

GALLISON, Joseph & Jean/Jane MITCHELL; 18 Sep 1698; Marblehead

GALLOWAY, Benjamin & Elizabeth HODGDON, m/2 Benjamin RICHARDS; 31 Jan 1699; Kittery, ME

GOLLOWAY, Hugh & Anne _?_; b 1694; Star Island

GILLOWAY, John & Sara KEASER; 7 Apr 1666; Salem

GALLUP, Adam/Benadam (1655-1727) & Esther/Hesther PRENTICE (1660-1751); b 1683; Stonington, CT/New London, CT

GALLOP, Benjamin & Hannah SHARP; 1 Nov 1694; Boston

GALLOP, Humphrey & Anne _?_, ?m/2 James BURT; b 1633; Dorchester

GALLUP, John (?1590-1649/50) & Christobel BRUSKETT (-1655, Boston); in Eng, 19 Jan 1617, ca 1616/21?; Boston

GALLUP, John (1618-1675) & Hannah [LAKE] (1621-); ca 1643; Boston/New London, CT

GALLOP, John (-1656) & Charity [HALL?] (-1711, ae 76), dau George?, m/2 Richard BURT 1656?; b 1653; Taunton

GALLOP, John (1646-) & Elizabeth [HARRIS] (1654-); ca 1674; Ipswich

GALLOP, Joseph (1661-) & Hannah _?_; b 1686(7?); Boston

GALLOP, Joseph & Elizabeth (ALCOCK) DWIGHT, w Timothy; 1 Mar 1694; Boston

GALLUP, Nathaniel & Margaret EUELEY/EVELEY/EVELEIGH; 11 Jun 1682; Boston

GALLOP, Samuel & Mary PHILLIPS; 20 Jan 1650/1; Boston

GALLUP, Samuel (?1657-) & Elizabeth SOUTHWORTH (-1709); 12 May 1685; Bristol, RI

GALLUP, William (1658-) & Sarah CHESEBROUGH (1662-); 4 Jan 1687, 4 Jan 1687/8?; Stonington, CT

GALLEY/GALLY, John (1605-1783) & Florence _?_; b 6 Oct 1635, b 1635, b 1641; Salem/Ipswich

GALPIN, Benjamin (-1731) & Rebecca [BROWN]; by 1682; Woodbury, CT

GALPIN, John (-1706) & Mary [MORGAN] (-1710+, 1711+); b 1680; Rye, NY

GALPIN, Joseph & Elizabeth _?_; b 16 Sep 1691; Rye, NY

GALPIN, Philip (-1684) & 1/wf Elizabeth [SMITH]; aft Jun 1646, b 1650; New Haven/Fairfield, CT/Rye, NY

GALPIN, Philip (-1684) & 2/wf Hannah [JACKSON], m/2 Stephen SHERWOOD; ca 1672/4; Stratford, CT/Rye, NY?

GALPIN, Samuel (1650-1698) & 1/wf Esther THOMPSON (-1678); 22 Mar 1677, 1676/7; Stratford, CT

GALPIN, Samuel (1650-1698) & 2/wf Elizabeth [St.JOHN] (1656-), m/2 Edward CAMP; ca 1679; Stratford, CT

GALUSIAH/GALUSHA, Daniel & Hannah GOOLD/GOULD; 10 Oct 1676; Chelmsford

GAMAGE, John & Mary [PERKINS?]/[KNIGHT?]; b 1676(7?); Ipswich

GAMBLIN, Benjamin & Obedience (HOLLAND) CURTIS (1642-), w Philip; 11 Feb 1677/8, 1677/8; Boxbury

GAMLIN, Robert[1] (-1642) & _?_; b 1600?; Roxbury/Concord

GAMLIN, Robert (-1663) & Elizabeth [MAYO] (-1681), w Thomas?; in Eng, b 1632; Roxbury

GANNETT, Joseph (-1714, in 66th y), Scituate & Ruth _?_; 17 Jan 1676/7; Rehoboth

GANNETT, Joseph (-1693) & Deborah COMBS/(SHARPE?) (-1722, 1728), dau Henry, m/2 Joseph HOUSE 1703 (she is called widow SHARPE); 15 Aug 1682; Marblehead/Scituate

GANNETT, Matthew[1] (1618-1694, 1695, Scituate) & Hannah [ANDREWS] (1622-1700, Scituate), dau Joseph; ca 1646/49; Hingham/Scituate

GANNETT, Matthew (-1703, ae 51), Scituate & _?_; b 1685; Hingham/Piscataway, NJ

GANNETT, Rehoboth & 1/wf [Sarah SCADLOCK]; by 1671; Scituate/Piscataway, NJ

GANNETT, Thomas (-1655), Duxbury/Bridgewater & Sarah [MULLINS], m/2 William SAVILL 1655, m/3 Thomas FAXON 1670; no issue; Duxbury/Bridgewater

GANSON, Benajamin & 1/wf Elizabeth _?_; b 1670; Salem

GANSON, Benjamin & Bethiah (WILLIAMS) PICK, w Obadiah; b 1682; Salem

GARDE, John (1618-) & _?_ [TETHERLY]; Bideford, Devon; Boston/Portsmouth, RI

GARDE, John (1604-1665, ae 61) & Harte _?_ (-1660, ae 55); Newport

GARDE, John & Martha [BRENTON]; Newport

GARDE, Roger & Phillipa GIST; Bideford, Devon, 4 Jul 1610; York, ME

GUARD, William & Mary [?JAMESON]/GIMSON (1647-), m/2 William GAYER 1690; 30 Jul 1666; Charlestown/Boston

GARDINER, Benoni (-1731±) & Mary [DYER?] (1645-1730, 1729); b 1667, b 1671; Newport/Kingstown, RI/Wickford, RI

GARDINER, Christopher (sent home) & _?_ (two wfs in Eng & Mary GROVE); in Eng

GARDINER, David (1636-1689) & Mary HARRINGMAN, w Aaron; St. Margaret's, Westminster, Eng, 4 Jun 1657; Gardiner's Isl./Southold, LI

GARDINER, David (1662-1733) & Martha [YOUNGS] (1664-1737); b 1685; Southold, LI

GARDINER, George (-1677±) & 1/wf Sarah **SLAUGHTER?**; St. James, Clerkenwell, London, 29 Mar 1680

GARDINER, George (-1677±) & 2/wf Herodias (**LONG**) **HICKS**, m/3 John **PORTER** by 1673 (see John **HICKS**); ca 1645/6, common law marriage, div 1665, petition 5 May; Kingstown, RI/Newport

GARDINER, George (-1677±) & 3/wf Lydia [**BALLOU**], m/2 William **HAWKINS** 1678; ca 1665/8; Swansea

GARDINER, George (-1724) & Tabitha **TEFFT** (1653-1722+); 13 Feb 1670, 17 Feb 1670; Kingstown, RI

GARDINER, Henry (1645-1744) & 1/wf Joan _?_ (-1715+?); ca 1666/72?; Kingston, RI

GARDINER, Henry (1645-1744) (see William **GARDINER**) & 2/wf Abigail (**RICHMOND**) [**REMINGTON**] (1656-1749), w John; aft 12 Dec 1688, aft 1715; N. Kingston, RI/Newport

GARDINER, John (1661-1738?) & 1/wf Mary [**KING**] (1670-1707); b 1691; Southold, LI/Easthampton, LI

GARDINER, Joseph (1669-1726) & Katharine **HOLMES** (1673-1758), m/2 Daniel **WIGHTMAN**; 30 Nov 1693; Newport/Wickford, RI

GARDINER, Lion (1599-1673?, 1663?) & Mary [**WILAMSON/DEURCANT?**] (1601-1655); Worden, Holland, b 1635?; Saybrook, CT/Gardiner's Isl./East Hampton, LI

GARDINER, Lion (1665-1723) & [Desire **HAVENS**] (1668-1723); b 1688; East Hampton, LI

GARDINER, Nicholas (1654-1712) & Hannah [**PALMER**]; ca 1681; Kings Town, RI/Wickford, RI

GARDINER, Samuel (1662-1696) & Elizabeth (**CARR**) [**BROWN**] (-1697+), w James; b 1685?, b 1684 (1683); Freetown/Swansea/Stonington, CT/Wroporton

GARDINER, Stephen (-1744) & Amy [**SHERMAN**] (1681-1752); 1700?; Portsmouth, RI/Kingston, RI

GARDINER, William (-1711) & Elizabeth _?_ (-1737); by 1679; Swansea/Kings Town, RI

GARDINER, William (1671-1732) (see Henry **GARDINER**) & Abigail [**REMINGTON**] (1651-1763), m/2 Job **ALMY**; b 1696

GARDINER, _?_ & Mary **WARREN**

GARDNER, Abel & Sarah [**PORTER**] (1675-); b 1696; Salem

GARDNER, Andrew (1642-) & Sarah **MASON** (1651-); 20 May 1668; Watertown/Boston/Reading/Brookline

GARDNER, Benjamin (1663-1714) & Margaret [?**BULKLEY**]; 21 Jun 1688; Wethersfield, CT

GARDNER, Benjamin (see Benjamin **GARNETT**) & Sarah **DUNBAR**; 13 Jan 1695/6; Hingham

GARDNER, Ebenezer (-1685) & Sarah **BARTHOLOMEW** (-1682); 7 Nov 1681; Salem

GARDNER, Ezekiel & Ruth [**EDDY**]; b 1671; Boston

GARDNER, Francis (-1689) (see Francis **GARNETT**) & Joanna **MAY**, m/2 Thomas **WHITON**, m/3 Nathan **FARROW**; 5 Jan 1680/1, ?14 Jan; Hingham

GARDNER, George (-1679) & 1/wf Hannah [?**SHATTUCK**]; b 1644; Salem/Hartford

GARDNER, George & 2/wf Elizabeth (**FREESTONE**) **TURNER**; aft 1650; Salem

GARDNER, George (1602-1679) & 3/wf Elizabeth (**ALLEN**) [**STONE**], w Samuel; ca 1673; Hartford

GARDNER, George (-1750) & Eunice [**STARBUCK**] (1674-1766); b 1698, ca 1695?; Nantucket/Salem

GARDNER, Habbakkuk & Ruth **GEDNEY** (1672-); 22 Mar 1696/7; Salem

GARDNER, Henry & Elizabeth [**CROMWELL**]; b 1665, Westchester, NY

GARDNER, Henry (1658-) & Elizabeth [**LANE**] (1663-1703); b 1695; Woburn/Charlestown

GARDNER/GARNER?, Jacob & Hannah [**GILLETT?**] (?1654-), dau John; b 1676, b 1674?; Hadley/Boston

GARDINER, James & Elizabeth **VINCEN/VINSON**; 19 Jun 1661, 16 Jun 1661, 19 Jan 1662; Gloucester

GARDNER, James & Mary (**ELWELL**) **DOLEVER**, w Samuel; 16 Dec 1684, 8? Dec; Gloucester

GARDNER/GARNETT, James & Elizabeth **WARD**; 18 Jun 1685; Hingham

GARDNER, James & 1/wf Mary [**STARBUCK**] (1663-1696); b 1695, aft 1689?, ca 1686?, b 1686?, b 1687; Nantucket/Salem

GARDNER, James & 2/wf Rachel (**GARDNER**) [**BROWNE**] (1662-), w John; b 1701?, b 1704; Nantuckest/Salem

GARDNER/GARNETT, John & Mary _?_, m/2 Nathaniel **CHUBBUCK** 1669; 10 Apr 1651; Hingham

GARDNER, John (ca 1624-1706) & Priscilla [GRAFTON]; b 1654, 20 Feb 1654 (20 Feb 1652 and 20 Feb 1653/4 are wrong); Salem/Nantucket
GARDNER, John & Susanna [GREEN]; b 1681; Boston/Salem
GARDNER, John (-1684) & Mehitable [HINSDALE]; b 1681; Hadley
GARDNER/GARNETT/GARNET, John & Mary STOWELL; 25 Feb 1682/3, 25 Feb 1681; Hingham
GARDNER, Joseph (-1675, 1676?) & Ann DOWNING (1634-1713), m/2 Simon BRADSTREET; bef 8 Aug 1656, Aug 1656, no issue, b 8 Aug 1658; Salem
GARDNER, Joseph & Bethia MACY (1650-); 30 Mar 1670; Nantucket/Salisbury
GARDNER, Joseph/Josiah? (see Joshua) & Mary [CORBIN?] (1658?-1721, ae 61); b 1679; Hadley/Roxbury
GARDNER, Joseph/James? & Hannah ELWELL (1674-); 2 Jan 1694/5; Gloucester
GARDNER, Joshua (see Joseph) (-1700) & Mary WELD?/GARDNER; 22 Mar 1681/2, 23 Mar 1681, 22 Mar 1681; Roxbury
GARDNER, Nathaniel (1669-1713) & Abigail [COFFIN] (-1709); b 1686; Nantucket
GARDNER, Nicholas & _?_; b 1649
GARDNER, Peter (1617-1698) & Rebecca CROOKE (-1675, ae 45); 9 May 1646; Roxbury
GARDNER, Richard (1626-1638) & Sarah [SHATTUCK?] (1632-1724); ca 1645, 1652; early settler of Nantucket/Salem/Martha's Vineyard
GARDNER, Richard (-1698, ae 79) & Ann/Anna BLANCHARD, w Thomas; 18 Oct 1651; Woburn/Charlestown
GARDNER, Richard (1653-1728) & Mary AUSTIN (-1721); 17 May 1674; Nantucket/Martha's Vineyard
GARDNER, Samuel (-1696) & 2/wf Elizabeth _?_ (-1676); b 1648; Hartford/Wethersfield, CT/Hadley
GARDINER, Samuel (1629-1689) & 1/wf Mary [WHITE] (-1675); b 1658; Salem
GARDNER, Samuel (1648-) & (1/wf) Elizabeth (BROWN) GRAFTON, w Joseph; 24 Apr 1673, 24 Jun; Salem
GARDNER, Samuel (ca 1627/8-1689) & 2/wf Elizabeth PAINE, w John; 2 Aug 1680; Salem
GOARDINER/GARNER/GARDINER? (-1690, 1695?) & Susannah SHELLEY; 20 Dec 1682; Plymouth
GARDNER, Samuel & Susanna (BAXTER)? ?HYDE/DANIEL, w Stephen; 1690 or bef, ?3 Dec 1680?; Salem
GARDENER/GARDINER?, Samuel & Elizabeth GOODWIN; 11 May 1693; Boston
GARDNER/GARNET, Stephen & Sarah WARREN; 22 Dec 1687; Hingham
GARDNER/GARDINER, Stephen (1667-1743) & Amy [SHERMAN] (1681-); b 1700
GARDNER, Thomas[1] (-1638) & _?_ (-1658); in Eng, b 1614; Roxbury/Cambridge
GARDENER, Thomas (1592-1674) & 1/wf ?Margaret [FRYER] (-1659) (doubtful); b 1620; Salem
GARDNER, Thomas (1615/16-1689) & Lucy SMITH (-1687); 4 Jul 1641; Charlestown/?Roxbury/Cambridge
GARDENER, Thomas (-1682) & 1/wf ?Hannah HOPSCOTT?/HAPSCOTT? (-1644+); b 1643; Salem
GARDNER, Thomas & _?_; b 1654?; Pemaquid
GARDNER, Thomas[1] (ca 1592-1674) & 2/wf Damaris [SHATTUCK] (-1674), wid; b 1668, ca 1659; Salem
GARDNER, Thomas (-1682) & 2/wf Elizabeth [HORNE/ORNE]; b 1668; Salem
GARDNER, Thomas (-1695) & Mary PORTER (1645-); 22 Apr 1669, 24 Jun 1669, 22 Jun; Salem
GARDNER, Thomas[3] (ca 1645-) & Mary BOWLES (1655-); 17 Nov 1673, 19 Nov; Roxbury
GARDNER, Thomas (-1696) & Mary HIGGINSON, m/2 Edward WELD 1689, m/3 James LINDALL; 4 Apr 1695, 4 Jun 1695, no issue; Salem
GARFFEILD, Benjamin (1643-1717, Waltham) & 1/wf Mehitable [HAWKINS] (1656-1675); b 1 Apr 1673; Watertown
GARFEILD, Benjamin (1643-1717) & 2/wf Elizabeth BRIDGE, m/2 Daniel HARRINGTON 1720; 17 Jan 1677; Watertown
GARFIELD, Benjamin (1674-) & Bethia [HOWE?]; b 1701?; Watertown
GEARFFIELD, Edward (1575-1672, ae 97?) & 1/wf Rebecca _?_ (?1606-1661); ca 1622; Watertown
GERFILD, Edward (1595-1672) & 2/wf Joanna/Hannah (_?_) BUCKMASTER/BUCKMINSTER, w Thomas; 1 Sep 1661; Watertown
GARFFEILD, Edward & Mehitable CHILD; 8 Jul 1691; Watertown

GARFIELD, Robert?/John (1654-) (son Samuel) & Deborah HOLMAN, dau Jeremiah; 3 Nov 1687; Watertown

GARFIELD, Jonathan (1672-) & Elizabeth [PARMENTER] (1672-), dau John; b 1701?; Sudbury

GEARFFEILD, Joseph (1637-1692), Watertown/Sudbury & Sarah/Sary GALE (1641-); 3 Apr 1663; Watertown

GARFIELD, Robert (see John)

GERFFIELD, Samuel (-1684) & 1/wf Susan/Susanna? _?_ (-1652); b 1645(6?); Watertown

GEARFFIELD, Samuel (-1684) & 2/wf Mary BENFFIELD/BENFIELD; 28 Sep 1652; Watertown

GARFORD, Jarvis/Gervase & _?_ ; b 1649

GARLAND, George & 1/wf _?_ ; in Eng, by 1660

GARLAND, George & [Sarah MILLS]/Lucretia HITCHCOCK, w Richard; 1668?, 1672?

GARLAND, Jabez (-1710) & Dorcas [HEARD/HURD] (1665-); b 1693(4?); Dover, NH

GARLAND, Jacob & Rebecca SEARS; 17 Jan 1681; Newbury/Hampton, NH

GARLAND, John & 1/wf Elizabeth CHAPMAN; 26 Oct 1652; Hampton, NH

GARLAND, John (1621-1672) & 2/wf Elizabeth (PHILBRICK) CHASE (1621-1677), w Thomas, m/3 Henry ROBY 1674; 26 Oct 1654; Salisbury

GARLAND, John & 1/wf Elizabeth ROBINSON (1653, 1651?-1715); 24 Dec 1673; Hampton, NH

GARLAND, Peter & Elizabeth _?_ (1599-1687); by 1637?; Charlestown

GARLAND, Peter & Joan _?_ ; b 1654; Boston

GARLAND, Peter (1659-) & 1/wf Elizabeth _?_ (-1688); b 1686; Hampton, NH

GARLAND, Peter (1659-) & 2/wf Sarah [TAYLOR], m/2 Samuel DOW; b 1689; Hampton, NH

GARLICK, Joshua (-1678) & [Elizabeth] _?_ ; b 1658; East Hampton/Southampton, LI

GARLICK, Joshua & Abigail _?_ ; b 16 Jun 1700; East Hampton, LI

GARLICK, _?_ & _?_ BLANCHARD; b 1652

GARNET, Benjamin (1666-1700) & Sarah DUNBAR; 13 Jan 1695/6; Hingham

GARNET/GARDNER?, Francis (1653-1689) & Joanna MAY (1665-), m/2 Thomas WHITON 1690, m/3 Nathan FARROW; 5 Jan 1680/1; Hingham

GARNET/GARDNER, James & Elizabeth WARD; 18 Jun 1685; Hingham

GARNET/GARDNER?, John (-1668) & Mary _?_, m/2 Nathaniel CHUBBUCK 1669; 10 Apr 1651, at Boston; Hingham

GARNET/GARDNER?, John (1652-1700) & Mary STOWELL; 25 Feb 1682/3; Hingham

GARNETT/GARDNER?, Stephen (1662-1715) & Sarah WARREN, m/2 John PRATT; 22 Dec 1687; Hingham

GARNOCK/GARNICK, Duncan & Margaret _?_ ; b 1686; Woodbury, CT

GARROD/GARRETT?/GARRAD, Daniel & _?_ ; b 1646(7?); Hartford

GARRELL/GERALD, James & Deborah MILLER (1662-); 9 Jun 1692; Springfield

GARRETSON/GARRESON, Edward & Joane/Joan PULLEN; 29 Aug 1660; Boston

GARRETSON, John & Alice WILLEY; 5 Dec 1659; Boston

GARRETSON, Richard & Mary _?_ ; b 1696; Westchester, NY

GARRETT/GARRAD?, Daniel (1612-1687+) & _?_ ; b 1646/7; Hartford

GARRETT, Erasmus & _?_ ; b 1676; Boston

GARRETT, James (-1657) & Deborah _?_ (returned to Eng); b 1638; Charlestown

GARRETT, John (1651-) & Susanna [BUCK] (1664-), dau John; ca 1684/7?; Scituate/Boston

GARRETT, Joseph (1648-) & Ruth BUCK; 17 Jan 1676; Scituate

GARRETT/GARRARD/GARWOOD, Joseph & Mary [ELMER] (1658); Hartford/Glastonbury

GARRETT, Richard (-1631) & _?_ ; Charlestown

GARRETT, Richard (-1662) & Lydia [TILDEN] (1625-); b 1648; Scituate/Boston

GARRETT, Richard & Persis PEIRCE; 3 Dec 1695; Scituate

GARRET alias BOUCHER, Robert (-1660, 1668?) & Mary [OAKLEY], ?wid; b 1642; Boston

GARRET, Thomas & Bethia [HARRISON]; b 1686; Salisbury

GARVEN/GARVIN, John & _?_ ; b 1662; Salem

GARY/GERRY?, Arthur (1599-1666) & Francis WARMAN (1601-1672); Bishops Stortford, Herts., 18 Apr 1625; Roxbury

GAREY/GERRY?, Benjamin, Lynn & Abigail GOOLD (1672-); 15 May 1693; Charlestown

GARY/GERRY?, Nathaniel (?1631-1679, 1678?) & Ann/Anne DOUGLAS, ?m/2 Thomas BISHOP 1683; 14 Oct 1658; Roxbury/?Lynn

GARY, Nathaniel (1663-) & Ann RICE (1661-); 12 Nov 1685; Roxbury/Woodstock, CT

GARY, Samuel (1638-) & 1/wf Elizabeth PARKER (1645-living in 1700), dau James; 6 Dec 1669; Roxbury

GARY, Samuel & 2/wf Martha CLARK (no) (called Samuel HEATH a "kinsman"); 19 Jun 1677
GARY, Samuel (-1757) & Sarah LOVELL/LOVEL (-1750); 29 May 1700; Dedham/?Pomfret, CT
GARY, Stephen (-1692) & 1/wf Mary MANUELL; 14 Aug 1673; Charlestown
GARY, Stephen & 2/wf Patience _?_; b 1692; Charlestown
GAREY, Thomas (1638-1690) & Sarah [LEFFINGWELL/LEPINGWELL] (1647-); b 1668; Reading/Charlestown
GARY, William (1628-1712) & Hannah CURTIS; 25 Aug 1651; Roxbury
GARY, William & Elizabeth [PARKER] (1645-); b 1677; Roxbury
GARY, William (1667-) & Susanna _?_; b 1698; Woodstock, CT/Pomfret, CT
GASKALL, Edward[1] (?1603-1690?) & Sarah _?_ (-1690+); ca 1634; Salem
GASCOYNE, Edward (1667-) & Hannah ENDICOTT (1676?-); 10 Apr 1693; Salem
GASKIN, John (-1690) & Joanna (EDGECOMB) [CROCKER], w Michael; Kittery
GASKELL/GASKILL, Samuel[2] (ae 60 in 1695) & Provided SOTHWICKE/SOUTHWICK (1641-1728?) (ae 56 in 1695); 30 Dec 1662; Salem
GASKALL, Samuel (1650-1706) & 1/wf Elizabeth _?_ (-1686, Cambridge); Watertown/Cambridge/New Haven
GASKELL, Samuel[3] (1663-1725) & Bethiah [WOODIN]; b 1686; Salem
GASKIN/GASKELL, Samuel (1650-1706, ae 56), Charlestown & 2/wf Elizabeth SHERMAN (1651-1736), Watertown; 20 Jul 1687, m bond 26 Jul 1687; Sudbury/Boston/Charlestown/New Haven
GAISHET/GASSETT, Henry & Sarah HASKINS; 2 Sep 1697; Taunton
GATCH, Edmund & Hannah/?Joanna _?_ (1647-); b 1677, b 14 Apr 1676, b 1670?; Boston
GATES, George (1635-1724) & Sarah [OLMSTEAD] (1641-1709); ca 1661; Haddam, CT
GATES, Isaac (1673-1748) & 1/wf Mercy/Mary BENJAMIN (1675-ca 1709?); 2 Jul 1695; Concord
GATES, John (1668-1742) & _?_; b 1701?; Haddam, CT
GATES, Joseph (1662-1712) & Elizabeth [HUNGERFORD] (-1759, in 89th y); b 1695; Haddam, CT
GATES, Nathaniel (?1675-1731) & Mary GIBSON; 17 Oct 1700; Concord/Stow
GATES, Samuel, Mashamunghet, CT/Pomfret, CT, & Mary (RICHARDS) FAIRBANKS, w Benjamin, m/2 Richard TRUESDALE 1697; m 1710, b 1701?, b 1711, aft 1701; Woodstock
GATES, Simon (?1643-1692) & Margaret [BARSTOW] (1650-1707); b 1671; Cambridge/Lancaster/Boston
GATES, Simon (1667-1752), Stow & Hannah BENJAMIN (1669-1752+), Stow; 4 May 1688; Stow/Marlborough
GATES, Stephen[1] (-1662) & Ann VEARE (1603-1683), m/2 Richard WOODWARD 1663; Hingham, Eng, 5 May 1628; Hingham/Cambridge/Lancaster
GATES, Stephen[2] (1634-1707) & Sarah [WOODWARD] (1643-1707+); ca 1665; Cambridge/Boston/Marlboro/Stow/?Charlestown
GATES, Stephen[3] (1665-1732), Stow & Jemima BENJAMIN (?1664-), Plymouth Colony; 8 Nov 1686; Stow/Preston, CT
GATES, Thomas (?1642-1726) & Elizabeth FREEMAN (1648-); 6 Jul 1670; Sudbury/Preston, CT/etc.
GATES, Thomas (1664/5-) & Hannah BRAINERD (1667-1750); 3 Oct 1692; Haddam, CT
GATES, Thomas (1669-1732) & Margaret GEER (1669-); Dec 1695; Preston, CT
GATLIFFE/GATLINE, Jonathan (-1675) & Mary RICHARDSON; - Jun 1663; Boston/Braintree
GATLIVE, Thomas (-1663) & 1/wf _?_; b 1643; Braintree
GATLIVE, Thomas (-1663) & 2/wf Prudence _?_ (-1663+); b 1651?, b 1655(6?); Braintree
GATTINSBY, John (-1671) & Susanna [SPENCER], m/2 Ephraim JOY; ca 1657; Kittery, ME/Berwick, ME
GATTENSBY, Moses & _?_; b 1697; Berwick, ME
GAUD, John & Elizabeth _?_; b 1693(4?); Boston
GAULT, William (?1608-1659) & Mary _?_, m/2 Richard BISHOP 1660, m/3 Thomas ROBBINS 1675; b 1641; Salem
GAUNT, Israel (-1698) & Hannah _?_; no children; Sandwich
GAUNT, Peter & [?Lydia] _?_ (-1691, 1692); b 1666?, b 1645; Sandwich
GANT, Zachariah & Hannah _?_ (-1674); Newport
GAVETT, John & 1/wf Elizabeth _?_; b 1699; Newport
GAVETT, Philip & Hannah MACCHONE (1659-); 6 Sep 1681 Mablehead/Salem
GAWDREN, _?_ & ?Mary COLE, wid, m/2 Edmund JACKSON [1653]; 7 Jan 1652/3, b Jan 1652/3; Boston

GAY, Archibald & Margaret __?__ ; b 1695; Newton
GAY, Edward (1666-1730) & Rebecca FISHER; 25 Mar 1688; Wrentham
GAY, Eleazer (1647-1777) & Lydia [HAWES] (1649-); b 1679; Dedham/Wrentham
GAY, John (-1688) & Joanna [?BALDEN/?BALDWICKE] (-1691), w John; b 1639; Watertown/
Dedham
GAY/GUY?, John (-1678) & Hannah __?__ ; b 1668; Watertown
GAY, John (1651-1731) & Rebecca BACON (-1732); 13 Feb 1678/9; Dedham
GAY, John (1668-1758) & Mary FISHER (-1748); 24 May 1692; Dedham
GAY, Jonathan (1653-1713) & Mary BULLARD (-1725+); 29 Aug 1682; Dedham
GAY, Nathaniel (1643-1713) & Lydia [STARR] (1652-1744); b 1675; Dedham
GAY, Samuel (1639-1718) & Mary BRIDGE (1637-1718), Roxbury; 23 Nov 1661; Dedham
GAY, Samuel & Abigail __?__ ; b 1687(8?); Roxbury/Swansea
GAY, Timothy (1674-1719) & Patience [LEWIS] (1668-); b 1698; Dedham
GAYER, William (-1710) & 1/wf Dorcas [STARBUCK]; b 1673; Nantucket
GAYER, William & 2/wf Maria (?JAMESON/?GIMSON) GAURD/GUARD/GARD (?1647-), w
William; 4 Jul 1690; Boston
GAYLORD, Benjamin (1655-1691) & ?Ruth WILLIAMS; ?Windsor, CT
GAYLORD, Daniel & __?__ ; b 1701; Windsor, CT
GAYLORD, Eleazer (1662-1714) & Martha THOMPSON; 11 Aug 1686, ?18 Aug; Windsor, CT
GAYLOR/GAYER?, Jeremiah & __?__ ; had lands, 1668; Stamford, CT
GAYLORD, John (-1689) & Mary DRAKE (-1682); 17 Nov 1653, 1655?; Windsor, CT
GAYLORD, John (1649-1699) & Mary CLARK, m/2 Jedediah WATSON 1700?; 13 Dec 1683;
Windsor, CT
GAYLORD, Joseph (1649-1777) & Sarah STANLEY (1652-), Farmington; 14 Jul 1670; Windsor,
CT
GAYLORD, Joseph (1673-) & Mary HICKOX (1678-), Waterbury, CT; 8 Feb 1699, 1699/1700;
Windsor, CT
GAYLORD, Nathaniel (1656-1720) & Abigail BISSELL; 17 Oct 1678; Windsor, CT
GAYLORD, Samuel (1619-1689) & 1/wf Elizabeth HULL (1625-1680); 4 Dec 1646; Windsor, CT
GAYLORD, Samuel (1619-1689) & 2/wf Mary (BROMSON) (WYATTS) (GRAVES) ALLES, w
John, w John, w William; 16 Mar 1681, 1681/2?; Windsor, CT
GAYLORD, Samuel (1657-1690) & Mary __?__ ; b 1670; Windsor, CT
GAYLORD, Thomas & __?__ ; b 1682; Windsor, CT
GAYLORD, Walter (ca 1626-1689) & 1/wf? Mary STEBBINS (-1657, Apr 1648); Apr 1648, 29
Apr 1648, ?16 Apr, ?22 Apr 1648, ?29 Apr; Hartford/Windsor, CT
GAYLORD, Walter (-1689) & 2/wf Sarah ROCKWELL (1638-1683); 22 Mar 1659, 1657/8, 1658?;
Windsor, CT
GAYLORD, William, Sr. (1585-1673) & [?Ann] __?__ (-1657); in Eng, b 1617?; Dorchester/Wind-
sor, CT
GAYLORD, William, Jr. (1616-1656) & 1/wf ?Ann/?Anna/Anne PORTER (1621-1653); 1641, 24
Feb 1644, 1641/2, 1641?; Windsor, CT
GAYLORD, William, Jr. (1616-1656) & 2/wf Elizabeth DRAKE (1621-1716), m/2 John
ELDERKIN 1660; 9 Feb 1653; Windsor, CT
GAYLORD, William (1651-1680) & Ruth CROW, m/2 John HALEY; 21 Dec 1671; Windsor, CT
GEAFFALLS, Aaron & Mary __?__ ; b 1689; Boston
GEDNEY, Barthelomew (1640-1698) & 1/wf Hannah CLEARK (-4 Jan 1696); 22 Dec 1662; Salem
GEDNEY, Barthelomew & 2/wf Anne [STEWART], ?w William; 1697; Salem
GIDNEY, Eleazer (1642-1683) & 1/wf Elizabeth TURNER; 6 Jun 1665; Salem
GIDNEY, Eleazer (1642-1683) & 2/wf Mary PATTASHALL/PATESHALL (-1716); 6 Jun 1678, ?2
Jun; Salem
GEDNEY, Eleazer (1666-1722) & Anna [?METT] (?1670-1750?); b 1697; Mamaroneck, NY
GEDNEY, John[1] (1603-) & 1/wf ?Sarah __?__ ; in Eng, ca 1632
GEDNEY, John[1] (1603-) & 2/wf ?Mary PRINCE (perhaps Mary is wrong name, see below), wid;
Salem
GEDNEY, John[1] (1603-) & 2/wf Catherine [CLARK], w William; ca 1646/50?, aft 1647;
Salem/Ipswich
GEDNEY, John[2] (1637-1684) & Susanna CLEARKE, m/2 Deliverance PARKMAN 1689+; 4 May
1659; Salem
GEDNEY, John[1] (1603-) & 3/wf Mary [PRINCE], wid; (see above); Salem

GEDNEY, Nathaniel (ca 1670-1701) & Mary [LINDALL], m/2 Thomas PHIPPEN; b 1697; Salem
GIDNEY, William (1668-1730) & 1/wf Hannah GARDNER; 9 Jun 1690, ?7 May, ?7 Jan; Salem
GIE, Hugh & Elizabeth PREDY; 18 Sep 1682; Marblehead
GEE, John (-1669) & Hazelpaneh [WILLIX] (1636-1714), m/2 Obadiah WOODS; b 1662; Boston
GEE, John (-1693) & Joan __?__ (-1693); b 1678; Boston
GEE, John & Mary __?__; b 8 Mar 1688/9; Eastchester, NY
GEE, Joshua (-1723) & 1/wf Elizabeth HARRISE (-25 Jan 1693/4+); 25 Sep 1688; Boston
GEE, Joshua (-1723) & 2/wf Elizabeth [THATCHER], m/2 Peter THACHER 1727; b 1697; Boston
GEE, Peter & Grace __?__; b 1648?; ?Boston/?Isles of Shoals
GEER, Daniel (1673-1749) & __?__; b 1700; Preston, CT
GEERE, Dennis (1605-1637) & Elizabeth __?__ (1613-); ca 1631?; Lynn
GEER/GRAVES, George (?1621-1726) & Sarah ALLYN (1642-1723+); 17 Feb 1658, 1658/9; New London, CT
GERE, John & Sarah [WILLS]; b 1701?, b 1689; Kittery, ME
GEER, Jonathan (1662-1742) & 1/wf Mary __?__ (-1718); ?ca 1686; Preston, CT
GEER, Joseph (1664-1743) & Sarah HOWARD (1668-); 7 Jan 1692, 1691/2; Preston, CT
GERE, Robert (1676-1742) & Martha TYLER (1676-1741); 3 Apr 1700; ?Preston, CT
GEARE, Thomas (-1722, ae 99?) & Deborah [DAVIS] (1645/6-1736); ca 1666?; Barnstable/Enfield, CT/Beverly
GEERE, William (-1672) & Tryphena __?__ (-1676+); b 1641(2?); Salem
GELGRIS, Robert & Elizabeth __?__; b 1687; Boston
GUINON/GENUNG/GUENON/GANUNG, Jean & Margarita/Margareta/Gretie SNEDEN; 13 Aug 1662; Brooklyn, LI/Flushing
GAMNUNG, Jeremiah & Martha __?__; b 1690; (see DENMAN, Jeremiah GANNUGH)
GEORGE, Francis & Sarah [HALLOCK]; b 1701; Amesbury/Salisbury
GEORGE, James?/George & Elizabeth __?__; b 1691?, b 1700; Boston
GEORGE, James & Sarah [JORDAN] (1636-); b 1659; Salisbury
GEORGE, James (1660-1717?) & Sarah __?__; ca 1685/90?; Salisbury/Portsmouth, NH
GEORGE, James (see George) & Elizabeth __?__; b 1697(8?); Boston
GEORGE, John[1] (-1647) & 1/wf __?__; b 1630?; Watertown/Boston
GEORGE, John[1] (-1647) & 2/wf Anne/Hannah (_?_) GOLDSTONE (-1670, ae 79), w Henry; aft 25 Jul 1638, b 1647; Watertown/Sudbury
GEORGE, John (-1666) & Elizabeth __?__, m/2 Henry HERBERT 1668; b 1648; Charlestown
GEORGE, John & __?__; b 1655?; Boston
GEORGE, John (-1691/2) & 1/wf Elizabeth MARSH (-1683); 25 Mar 1679; Charlestown
GEORGE, John & Mary __?__; b 1680; Dorchester
GEORGE, John (-1691/2) & 2/wf Mary LOWDEN (1670-), m/2 James BUSBEEM 1693?; 11 Sep 1688; Charlestown
GEORGE, John (1665-1716) & Ann [SWADLOCK]; b 1690
GEORGE, John & Lydia [LEE], m/2 Cotton MATHER 1715; b 1692; Boston
GEORGE, John & Hannah GROVER; 22 Aug 1699; Boston
GEORGE, Joshua (-1690) & Elizabeth __?__ (-1676); b 1671; Dorchester
GEORGE, Joshua (-1690) & 2/wf Mary __?__ (-1689); ca 1676, b 1689; Dorchester
GEORGE, Nicholas (-1675) & Elizabeth __?__ (1602-1699); b 1620; Dorchester/Charlestown
GEORGE, Nicholas & Abigail __?__; b 1663(4?); Charlestown/Boston
GEORGE, Nicholas & Mary WALES (1658-), m/2 Ebenezer HOLMES 1697; 4 Jun 1684; Dorchester
GEORGE, Peter (-1693) & Mary (ROWNING) [RAY] (1613-), w Simeon; b 1643; Braintree/New Shoreham, RI
GEORGE, Richard & Mary PELL; 1 Nov 1655; Boston
GEORGE, Richard & Elizabeth __?__; b 1682; Dorchester
GEORGE, Samuel (1651-) & Sarah RATHBONE (1659-), ?m/2 John MITCHELL b 1684; 20 Dec 1678; Block Island, RI
GEORGE, Samuel & Elizabeth FREAM/FRAME; 15 Jan 1693/4; Amesbury
GEORGE, Thomas & Hannah [FISHER] (1665, 1670?-); b 1688; Wrentham/Dedham
GERRARD, Isaac & Mary __?__; b 1686(7?); Boston
GERARD, Robert & Elizabeth [BECKWITH], div, m/2 John BATES by 1677; b 1671, 1665?; ?Haddam, CT
GEREARDY, John (-1681+) & Renewed [SWEET] (-1681+); b 1654; Warwick, RI/Providence

GEREARDY, John & 1/wf _?_
GEREARDY, John & Deliverance (?BRADLEY/BROWN) [CORP], w John; aft 1 Nov 1691, b 1696; Warwick, RI/Bristol, RI
GERMAN, John & Hester/Esther WERLIDGE; m int 6 Nov 1695; Boston
GERMAINE, Jean & _?_ ; b 1680
GARMAN, Thomas & ?Dorothy _?_ ; b 1676, [ca 1670?]; Isles of Shoals
GERRISH, Benjamin (1652-1713) & 1/wf Hannah RUCK (-1685); 24 Oct 1676; Salem
GERRISH, Benjamin (-1713) & 2/wf Anna PAINE (-1695); 12 Nov 1685; Salem
GERRISH, Benjamin & 3/wf Elizabeth TURNER (1673-1734); 24 Sep 1696; Salem
GERRISH, James (?1648-1692?) & (Agnes?) _?_
GERRISH, John (1646-1714) & Elizabeth WALDRON (-1724, in 79th y); 19 Aug 1667; Salem
GERRISH, John & 1/wf Lydia WATTS (-1698, ae 27±); 19 Apr 1692; Boston
GERRISH, John & 2/wf Sarah [HOBBES/NOYES?] (1676-); by 28 Apr 1699; Boston
GERRISH, Joseph (1649-1720) & Anna/Ann? [WALDRON]; ca 1670; Salem
GERRISH, Moses (1656-1694) & Jane SEWALL (1659-); 24 Sep 1677; Newbury
GERRISH, Nathaniel (1672-1729) & Bridget [VAUGHN] (1678-); b 1701?; Portsmouth, NH/Berwick, ME
GERRISH, Richard & Jane [JOSE] (1670-); b 30 May 1695; Kitterty, ME
GERRISH, William[1] (-1687) & 1/wf Joanna LOWELL OLLIVER (-Jun 1677, ae 58 y), w John; 17 Apr 1645; Newbury/Boston/Salem
GERRISH, William[2] (1648-1683) & Ann _?_ , m/2 Lawrence HAMMOND 1685; b 1673(4?); Newbury/Boston/Charlestown
GERRISH, William[1] (-1687) & 2/wf Ann (PARKER) [MANNING], w John; aft Jun 1677; Boston
GATCHELL, Jeremiah & Hannah SAITH, Salem/Malden; 3 Feb 1662, 1672; Charlestown
GETCHELL, Jeremiah (1646-) & Elizabeth _?_ ; b 1679?; Mablehead/Salem
GATCHELL, John (ca 1610/12-) & Wibera/?Waybrough/Wilborough _?_ (1619-1684); b 1642?, b 1639; Marblehead/Salem
GATCHELL, Jonathan (?1646-) & Mary (TRIPP) WODELL (-1716), w Gershom; 5 Mar 1682, 1682/3?; Portsmouth, RI
GATCHELL, Joseph (1652) & Bethiah _?_ ; Marblehead
GETCHELL, Samuel (-1697) & Dorcas _?_ (-1685); b 1639?, b 1646?; Salem/Hampton, NH
GETCHELL, Samuel (1639-) & Bethiah _?_ ; b 1669; Salem/Marblehead
GETCHELL, Samuel (1657/8-1710) & Elizabeth JONES (1666?-); 27 Nov 1679; Amesbury
GATCHEL, Thomas & [Sarah BRAYTON]; b 1680; Dartmouth
GIBBARD, Timothy (1655-1685) & Sarah [COE] (1656-), m/2 Jeremiah OSBORN 1687±; b 1682; ca 1680?; New Haven
GIBBARD/GILBERT, William (-1663) & Anna [TAPP] (-1701), m/2 William ANDREWS 1665; b 1641; New Haven
GIBBONS, Ambrose (-1656) & Elizabeth/Rebecca POTTER?/_?_ (-1655); 23 Aug 1612?, by 1620; Dover, NH
GIBBONS, Edward (-1654) & Margaret _?_ ; b 1631; Cambridge/Boston
GIBBINS, James & Judith [LEWIS] (1626-); ca 1646?; Lynn/Saco, ME
GIBBINS, James (1648-1683) & Dorcas SEALY/GITTEY, m/2 Frances BACKUS ca 1683; Dec 1668, 166-; Isles of Shoals/Saco, ME
GIBBONS, Jotham (-1658) & ?Susanna _?_ ; Bermuda/Boston
GIBBONS, William (-1689) (ae 58 in 1670) & _?_ (-1679); New Haven
GIBBONS, William (-1654) & Ursula _?_ ; b 1645; Hartford
GIBBINS, William & Anne [ADAMS?]; b 1687(8?); Boston
GIBBONS, William & Patience _?_ ; b 1692; Boston
GIBB, Andrew & Mrs. Hannah SMITH; m bond 13 Apr 1696; ?Brookhaven, LI
GIBBS, Benjamin & Lydia [SCOTTOW], m/2 Anthony CHICKLEY 1678?, m/3 William COLMAN; b 1665; Boston
GIBBS, Benjamin & Ann TUPPER (1679-); 4 - 1698/9, ?4 Feb; Sandwich
GIBBS, Giles (-1641) & 2/wf Katherine _?_ (-1660, Windsor, CT); ca 1633; Dorchester/Windsor, CT
GIBBS, Gregory (-1707, Suffield, CT) & Joyce (SMITH) [OSBORN] (-1684+), w James; aft 1676, no issue; Windsor/Springfield/Suffield, CT
GIBBS, Henry & Marah/Mary _?_ ; b 1664; Boston
GIBBS, Henry & Sarah _?_ ; b 1688(9?); Boston

GIBBS, Henry (1668-1723) & Mercy GREENOUGH (-1717); 9 Jun 1692; Boston?/Cambridge/Watertown
GIBBS, Henry & Mary MIDDLECOTT, m/2 Othniel HAGGETT; m int 21 Nov 1695; Boston
GIBBS, Isaac & Hannah DICKINSON (1671-); 22 Oct 1696; Flushing, LI
GIBBS, Jacob (-1709) & 1/wf Elizabeth ANDROSS/ANDRUS?/ANDROS? (-1696), Hartford; 4 Dec 1657; Windsor, CT
GIBBS, Jacob (1666-1711/12) & Abigail OSBORN; 16 May 1689; Windsor, CT
GIBBS, James (-1731) & Sarah _?_ (?1674-1756); b 1691; Bristol, RI
GIBBS, Job (1655-) & Judith BATES; 28 Apr 1697; Sandwich
GIBBS, John (-1690) & 1/wf _?_ (-1668); b 1647; New Haven
GIBBS, John (1634-1725?) & Elizabeth _?_ /?Jane BLACKWELL, dau Michael; ca 1665-8?; ?Sandwich
GIBBS, John (-1690) & 2/wf Hannah PUNDERSON (1642-), m/2 John SLAWSON of Stamford 1690+; 27 Oct 1670; New Haven
GIBBS, John (?1662-1718), Sudbury & 1/wf Anne/Ann/Anna GLEASON (-1692), Sherborn; 27 Apr 1688; Sudbury
GIBBS, John, Jr. & Hester [SWIFT]; b 1690; Plymouth
GIBS, John (?1662-1718), Sudbury & 2/wf Sarah CUTLER (1665-1725), Reading; 31 May 1694; Reading/?Sudbury
GIBBS, John & Mary _?_ ; b 1701; Boston
GIBBS, Matthew & Mary [BRADISH?]; ca 1650?, b 1656; Sudbury/Charlestown/Cambridge
GIBS, Matthew (1656-1732) & 1/wf Mary MOORE (1655-1705); 12 Nov 1678; Sudbury
GIBS, Matthew & Elizabeth [MOORE] (1657-); b 1680(1?); Sudbury
GIBBS, John & [Jane BLACKWELL]; ca 1666?; Barnstable Co.
GIBBS, Richard & Elizabeth _?_ ; b 1669; Boston
GIBBS, Robert (1636-1674?, 1673, ae 37) & Elizabeth SHIAFFE, m/2 Jonathan CORWIN 1676; 7 Sep 1660; Boston
GIBBS, Robert (1630-1718) & Elizabeth _?_ ; b 1670; [Swansea]/Somerset
GIBBS, Robert (1665-1702) & Mary SHRIMPTON, m/2 Samuel SEWALL 1722; 19 May 1692; Boston
GIBBS, Samuel (-1720) & Hepzibah DEBLE/DIBBLE (-1701, 1698?); 15 Apr 1664; Windsor, CT/Deerfield
GIBBS, Samuel (1639-) & 1/wf _?_ ; b 1676?; Sandwich
GIBBS, Samuel & 2/wf Patience BUTLER; 5 Mar 1676; Sandwich
GIBBS, Samuel & ?Mary/?Mercy (STANTON) CRANSTON, w William; b 1697; Jamestown, RI
GIBBS, Thomas (-1685, ae 80) & _?_ (-1693+); b 1634?, b 1636/7, b 1655; Sandwich
GIBBS, Thomas, Jr. (1636-1733) & Ellis/Alice WARREN (1656-by 1725), dau Nathaniel; 23 Dec 1674; Sandwich
GIBBS, Thomas & Elizabeth _?_ ; div 17 Sep 1681; NY
GIBBS, Warren & _?_ GRAY?
GIBSON, Benjamin (-1751, ae 73) & Mehitable (WELSTED) AUSTIN (-24 Jan 1743/4, ae 70), sister of William, w Richard; 4 Jan 1699, 1699/1700; Boston/Charlestown
GIBSON, Charles & Mercy GROS; m int 29 Oct 1696; Boston
GIBSON, Christopher (-1674) & 1/wf [Sarah SALE]; Dorchester
GIBSON, Christopher (-1674) & 2/wf Margaret [BATES] (1621-), dau James; Dorchester/Boston
GIPSON, Edward & Ruth COMER; 11 Jan 1699; Boston
GIPSON, Jeremiah & Mary HUNTER; 13 Apr 1698; Boston
GIBSON, John (-1694, ae 93) & 1/wf Rebecca _?_ (-1661); b 1635, b 1631?; Cambridge
GIBSON, John (-1694, ae 93) & 2/wf Joanna/Joan (_?_) PRENTICE, w Henry; 24 Jul 1662; Cambridge
GIBSON, John (?1631, 1641?-1679) & Rebecca ERRINGTON; 4 Dec 1668; Cambridge
GYPSON, John & Emm _?_ ; b 1673; Boston
GIBSON, John & Hannah UNDERWOOD/VNDERWOOD; 14 Oct 1680; Watertown
GIBSON, Rev. Richard & Mary [LEWIS] (1619-); b 14 Jan 1638/9, ca 1637; Saco, ME
GIPSON, Roger (-1680) & Martha [MORRIS], m/2 Thomas ALLYN 1681?; ca 1670?; ?Saybrook, CT/?New London, CT
GIBSON, Samuel (1644-1710) & 1/wf Sarah PEMBERTON (1638-1676); 30 Oct 1668; Cambridge
GIBSON, Samuel (1644-1710) & 2/wf Elizabeth (REMINGTON) STEDMAN (-1680), w John; 19 Jun 1679; Cambridge

GIBSON, Samuel (1644-1710) & 3/wf Abigail __?_ ; b 1690; Cambridge
GIBSON, (GILSON is wrong), Timothy (?1679-1757) & 1/wf Rebecca GATES (1682-1754); 17 Nov 1700; Concord
GIBSON, William (-1701), Scotchman & 1/wf Sarah [PURCHASE]; b 1663; Boston/Lynn
GIBSON, William (-1701) & 2/wf Hannah [PHIPPEN] (1653-1705+); b 1673; Boston
GIBSON, William & Hannah HAZEN?, dau Edward (very doubtful)
GIBSON, William & 1/wf __?_ ; ca 1670?; London/New London, CT/Kings Town, RI
GIBSON, William & 2/wf __?_ WEEDEN
GIBSON, __?_ & Elizabeth [COGAN], m/2 John ENDICOTT 1630; in Eng, b 1630
GIDDINGS, George[1] (1610-1676) & Jane [LAWRENCE] (bpt 18 Dec 1614-); lic 20 Feb 1634, b 1635; Ipswich
GIDDINGS, George & 1/wf Mary SCAMP/SKAMP (-1706); 19 May 1690; Gloucester
GIDINGS, James (1641-) & Elizabeth [ANDREWS] (1652-1709+); ca 1668/72?; Ipswich
GIDDINGS, James & Mary [HUTCHINSON]; 1693
GIDDINGS, Job (1677-1708) & Sarah [BUTLER], m/2 John BAILEY; b 1701; ?Ipswich
GIDDING, John (1639, 1638?-1691) & Sarah [ALCOCK], m/2 Henry HERRICK ca 1692; ca 1663; Ipswich
GIDDINGS, Joseph[2] (-1691) & Susanna RINGE/RINDGE; 20 Jul 1671; Ipswich
GIDDINGS, Samuel (1645-) & 1/wf Hannah MARTIN; 4 Oct 1671; Ipswich
GIDDINGS, Samuel (1645-) & 2/wf Elizabeth SAMPLE; 8 Nov 1699; Ipswich/Boston
GIDDING, Thomas (1638-1681) & 1/wf Mary GOODHUE; 23 Feb 1658; Ipswich
GIDDINGS, Thomas (1638-1681) & 2/wf Elizabeth __?_ , m/2 John CHOATE 1690?; b 1674?; Ipswich
GIDDENS, William & Sarah ?HUTCHINGS/HITCHINGS (-1766); m int 19 Sep 1698; Lynn
GIDLEY, Henry & Joan __?_ ; b 1663; Boston
GIDLEY, Henry & Mary __?_ ; b 1670; Boston
GIDLEY, Hezekiah (1664/5-) & Annis __?_ ; b 1692; Boston
GIFFORD, Christopher[2] (1658-1748) & Deborah [PERRY] (1665-1724); b 1685, b 1687; Sandwich
GIFFORD, Hananiah & Elizabeth __?_ (doubtful); ?Sandwich
GIFFORD, John (1625-1693) & Margaret [TEMPLE]; ca 1651; Lynn
GIFART, John (-1708) & [Elishua CROWELL]; b 1665; Sandwich
GIFFORD, John & Desire SPRAGUE; 24 Nov 1696; Falmouth/Sandwich
GIFFORD, Peter & Eleanor CARTER; 1 Dec 1692; Lynn
GIFFORD, Philip (-1690) & Mary DAVIS (1668-); last of Jun 1684; Lynn
GIFFORD, Robert (1660-1730) & 1/wf Sarah [WING] (1658-1724); ca 1680?, ?Jul 1680; Sandwich
GIFFORD, Robert & Mary __?_ ; b 1693; Marblehead
GIFFORD, Samuel (1668-1714) & Mary CALKINS/COLLINS; 1 Nov 1693; Windsor, CT/Norwich, CT/Lebanon, CT
GIFFORD, Samuel & Joan?/Jane LORING (1663-); 2 Nov 1699; Sandwich/Hingham/Falmouth
GIFFORD, Stephen (?1641-1724) & 1/wf Hannah GORE (1645-1670/1); - May 1667; Norwich, CT
GIFFORD, Stephen (-1724), Norwich & Hannah GALLOP (1644-1721); 18 Jun, 12 May 1672; Stonington, CT
GIFFORD, William[1] (-1681) & __?_ ; b 1646?, b 1658?; Sandwich/Falmouth
GIFFORD, William & [?Deborah PERRY]; b 1676; Falmouth
GIFFORD, William (-1687?) & 2/wf Mary/Leady? MILLS (-bef 1701); 16 Jul 1683; Sandwich
GIFFORD, [Gideon] & Mehitable JENNEY (1673-), dau John; b 1727, b 1701?; Dartmouth?
GILBERT, Benjamin[3] (1652-1711) & Mary RILEY; 25 Nov 1680; Wethersfield, CT
GILBERT, Benjamin (-1693) & Adry/Edree [HURLBURT], m/2 Samuel COUCH 1694±; b 1 Jul 1693; Fairfield, CT
GILBERT, Caleb (1668-1736+) & Elizabeth __?_ ; b 1694; Southampton, LI
GILBERT, Ebenezer (?ca 1669-1736) & Esther/Hester ALLYN (1677-1750); b 1694; Hartford/Windsor, CT/Farmington, CT
GILBERT, Eleazer (-1701) & Elizabeth CRANE (1663-), m/2 George TOWNSENDS 1705; 23 May 1682; Milton
GILBERT, Eleazer (1663-1704) & Mary __?_ ; ca 1690/5?; Wethersfield, CT/St. Mary Magdelen, Bermondsey, Suffolk Co., Eng

GILBERT, Gyles (ca 1624, 1627-1717/8, 1718) & 1/wf Sarah PARKER (-aft 17 Feb 1681/2), w John; aft 26 Feb 1667, b 17 Feb 1681/2, ca 1670; Taunton
GILBERT, Gyles (-1718) & Mary (WILMOUTH) ROCKETT, w Joseph, ?m/3 Jeremiah WHEATON 1723; 28 Oct 1686; Taunton
GILBERT, Henry (1662-1740) & 1/wf Elizabeth BALDEN (?1663-1735); 31 Jan 1692/3; Springfield
GILBERT, Humphrey (1606-1658) & 1/wf _?_ ; ca 1645/8; Ipswich
GILBERT, Humphrey (1606-1658) & 2/wf Elizabeth [BLACK?/BLANCH], m/2 William RAYNER 1658, m/3 Henry KIMBALL 1673+, m/4 Daniel KILLAM 1678?; 1656?; Ipswich
GILBERT, John (1580-1657) & 1/wf Mary STREET (1578/9-); Bridgewater, Eng, 17 Jan 1602, 1602/3; Dorchester/Tauton
GILBERT, John & Alice HOPKINS (-1688); ?Bristol, Sep 1606
GILBERT, John (-1657) & 3/wf 2/wf Winifred (ROSSITER) COMBE (-1663+); in Eng, b 1619; Dorchester/Taunton
GILBERT, John[2] (ca 1626-1690) & Amy LORD (1626-1691/2); 6 May 1647; Hartford
GILBERT, John & Mary EATON; 5 May 1653; Boston
GILBERT, John (-1673) & Sarah GREGSON/GREYSON, m/2 Samuel WHITEHEAD 1676; 12 Dec 1667; New Haven
GILBERT, John & Elizabeth KILLAM/KILHAM (1657?-); 27 Sep 1677, ?12 Sep; Ipswich
GILBERT, John (1657-1709) & 1/wf Hannah [BLACKMAN/BLAKEMAN] (1664, 1665-); b 1688, ca 1687; Stratford, CT
GILBERT, John & 1/wf Mary IVES/JONES (-1712); 21 Jan 1691/2, 20 Jan; New Haven
GILBERT, John (1657-1709) & 2/wf Hannah CANFIELD (1667-), m/2 John OSBORN 1710/11; 2 Jul 1695; Stratford, CT
GILBERT, John & Martha DODGE (1673-); m int 23 Dec 1699; Ipswich
GILBERT, Jonathan (ca 1618-1682) & 1/wf Mary WHITE (?1626-1649); 29 Jan 1645/6, 1645; Hartford
GILBERT, Jonathan (ca 1618-1682) & 2/wf Mary WELLS (-1700, ae 74); ca 1650; Hartford/Deerfield
GILBERT, Jonathan (1648-1698) & Dorothy STOW (1659-); 22 Jun 1679, [167-]; Middletown, CT
GILBERT, Joseph (1629-) & _?_ SLOCUM
GILBERT, Joseph & Mary _?_ , m Joseph GILLETTE; Hartford/Fairfield, CT
GILBERT, Joseph (1666-1751) & Elizabeth SMITH (1672-1756); 7 May 1695; Hartford
GILBERT, Josiah[2] (ca 1628-1688) & 1/wf Elizabeth [BELCHER] (1632-1682); b 1652; Braintree/Wethersfield, CT/Westchester, NY
GILBERT, Josiah[2] (ca 1628-1688) & 2/wf Mary (HARRIS) WARD (1645-1721?), w John; - Jan 1687/8, m cont prob 18 Oct 1689; Wethersfield, CT
GILBERT, Matthew & Jane [BLACK?/BAKER?]; b 1644; New Haven
GILBERT, Matthew (1655-1711) & Sarah PECK (1663-), m/2 Joseph MOSS; 2 May 1684; Lyme, CT
GILBERT, Moses (1666-1715, 1713) & Jane DIRCKS/FLUNT, m/2 Moses DIMON; 4 Apr 1694; New York/Fairfield, CT
GILBERT, Nathaniel (1676/7-) & Elizabeth ENDICOT (1675-); 14 Oct 1700; Boston/Salem
GILBERT, Obadiah[2] (ca 1630-1674/5) & Elizabeth (BURR) OLMSTEAD, w Nehemiah, m/3 Nathaniel SEELEY; ca 1660/2; Fairfield, CT
GILBERT, Obadiah[3] (1662-1726?) & Abigail [?BRADLEY]; ca 1694?; Fairfield, CT
GILBERT, Roger & Sarah _?_ ; b 1682; Boston
GILBERT, Samuel (1663-1733) & Mary ROGERS (1662-1756); 2 Oct 1684?; Hartford/Colcester
GILBERT, Samuel (-1721) & Hannah LITTLE (1671-); b 1697, ca 1695; New Haven, CT
GILBERT, Thomas[1] (?1582-1659, ae 77?) & Lydia _?_ ; in Eng, b 1618; Braintree/Windsor, CT/Wethersfield, CT/Stamford, CT
GILBERT, Rev. Thomas (1610-1673) & Sarah/Elizabeth [SHARPE]; ca 1632/43?; Charlestown
GILBERT, Thomas (-1676, 1677) & Jane (COMBE) ROSSITER (-1691), Taunton, ?w Hugh?; 23 Mar 1639, 1639/40 (no); Taunton
GILBERT, Thomas[2] (?1620-1662) & Catherine (CHAPIN) BLISS (1626-1712), w Nathaniel, m/3 Samuel MARSHFIELD 1664; 31 Jun 1655, 30 Jun 1655, ?31 Jul; Springfield
GILBERT, Thomas (1643-1725, ae 82 y), ?Boston & Anna BLAKEY/BLACKE of Milton (1653-1722); 18 Dec 1676; Taunton

GILBERT, Thomas (1659-1698) & 1/wf Abilene MARSHFIELD (1664-1689); 4 Aug 1680, 15 Aug 1680; Springfield
GILBERT, Thomas (1658-1706) & 1/wf Deborah BEAMONT (-1683); 27 Sep 1681; Saybrook, CT
GILBERT, Thomas (-1706) & 2/wf Bethia [YOUNGS] (-1684, ae 22); 1683?; Southold
GILBERT, Thomas (1659-1698) & 2/wf Anna BANCROFT (1663-1726), m/2 James SEXTON 1702; 9 Apr 1690; Springfield
GILBERT, Thomas (-1719, in 64th y) & 1/wf Lydia BALLOTT (1670-1708); 26 Nov 1690, 26 Nov 1689, 1692; Charlestown
GILBERT, Thomas (-1711) & Sarah PECK (1673-), m/2 Joseph MOSS; 31 Mar 1698; New Haven
GILBERT, William (-1693) & Rebecca [TINESDALE]; b 1672, b 1674, 16 Mar 1669/70; Cambridge/Boston
GILDERSLEEVE, Richard (1601-1681) & ?Experience _?_ (1601-1679+); ca 1625; Watertown/ Wethersfield, CT/Stamford, CT/Hempstead, LI/Newtown, LI
GILDERSLEEVE, Richard (ca 1626-1691) & Dorcas [WILLIAMS]? (1634-1704+), m/2 Henry PEARSALL; Newtown, LI/Hempstead, LI
GILDERSLEEVE, Richard (ca 1655-1717) & Experience [ELLISON]; Hempstead, LI/Huntington, LI
GILDERSLEEVE, Robert? & _?_ ; Stamford, CT
GILDERSLEEVE, Thomas (1661-1740) & Mary _?_ ; 1684; Hempstead, LI
GILES, Edward (?see Thomas) & 1/wf _?_
GILES, Edward_2 (-1650±) & 2/wf Bridget [VERY] (1600-1680), wid; b 6 Oct 1635; Salem
GILES, Eleazer^2 (1640-1726) & 1/wf Sarah MORE (-1676); 25 Jan 1664/5; Beverly/?Salem/?Lynn
GILES, Eleazer^2 (-1726?) & 2/wf Elizabeth BISHOP (1657-1732/3), New Haven; 25 Sep 1677, ?12 Sep; Salem
GILES, James (1616-1690) & 2/wf? Elizabeth _?_ ; b 1668; Braintree/Pemaquid/Piscataway, NJ
GILES, John (1645-1730, ae 77?) & 1/wf Elizabeth [TIDD] (May 1642-), dau Samuel; b 1671; Salem
GYELLS, John (1645-) & 2/wf Elizabeth (GALLEY) TRASK, w Osmund; 5 May 1679; Salem
GILES, John (-1730, ae 77) & Mary _?_ (-1736+); b 1686; Pemaquid/Salem
GILES, John & Abigail RAYMOND; 26 Apr 1698; Beverly
GILES, Mark (-1704) & 1/wf _?_ ; by 1666?; Dover, NH
GILES, Mark (-1704) & 2/wf Frances PERKINS, w Thomas; ?2 Sep 1680; Dover, NH
GILES, Mark & Sarah [?TWOMBLEY]; nr 1698, b 1698; Dover, NH
GILES, Matthew (-1667) & [Elizabeth] _?_ ; by 1643?; Dover, NH
GYLES, Robert & Margaret BARRET; 17 Feb 1692, prob 1692/3; Boston
GILES, Thomas/[?Edward] & _?_ ; b 1634; Gloucester/?Salem
GYLES, Thomas & Margaret _?_ ; b 1670; ?Kennebeck, ME/Pemaquid?
GYLES, Thomas & Martha BILL; 18 Jan 1699, prob 1699/1700; Boston
GILES, Valentine & Mary _?_ ; b 1680; Boston
GILL, Arthur (1608-1654?) & Agnes _?_ ; b 1635, b 1639; Dorchester/Boston
GILL, John (-1678) & 2/wf Ann [BILLINGS] (-1683) (sister of Roger); b 1630; Dorchester
GILL, John (-1690) & Phoebe BUSWELL (1626, 1634?-); 2 May 1645; Salisbury
GILL, John & 1/wf Elizabeth [WARE/WEARE]; b 1647, b 1656; Boston/Dorchester
GILL, John (1647-1712) & Martha [GOODALE]; b 1674; Salisbury/Middletown, CT
GILL, John, Dedham & Mary CARWITHY, Dedham; 31 Dec 1686; ?Dedham
GILL, John & Elizabeth PARSONS; 1 Jun 1698; Boston
GILL, Michael (-1720) & Relief DOWSE (1676-1759); 26 May 1696; Charlestown
GILL, Moses (1656-) & 1/wf Sarah [ESTY] (1660-), ?m/2 _?_ IRELAND; b 1685; Salisbury/Canton
GILL, Obadiah & Elizabeth [SMITH?]; b 1675; Boston
GILL, Samuel (1651-) & Sarah WORTH; 5 Nov 1678; Salisbury
GILL, Samuel (-1729) & Ruth LINCOLN (-1751); 13 Jan 1684/5; Hingham
GILL, Thomas (1616-1678) & Hannah [OTIS] (1618-1676); b 1644; Hingham
GILL, Thomas (1649-1725) & Susanna WILSON (-1725); 31 Dec 1673; Hingham
GILL, William (-bef 1696?) & Hannah MEACHUM, m/2 John PRIEST 1700; 6 Feb 1677; Salem
GILL, William & Elizabeth SCARLET; 3 May 1692; Boston
GILL, _?_ & Lydia _?_ ; b 1695; Boston
GILLAM, Benjamin^1 (-1670) & Anne _?_ (1607-1674); b 1634; Boston

GILLAM, Benjamin[2] (-1685) & Hannah SAVAGE, m/2 Giles SYLVESTER 1685; 26 Oct 1660; Boston

GILLAM, Benjamin (1663/4-1706) & Abigail __?_ ; b 1684(5?); Boston

GILLAM, Joseph[2] (1644-1681) & Martha [KNIGHT], m/2 Jarvis BALLARD 1687; b 1673; Boston

GILLAM, Zachary?/Zechariah[2] (1636-) & Phebe PHILLIPS (1640-), 26 Jul 1659; Boston

GILLETT, Cornelius (ca 1636-1711) & [Priscilla KELSEY] (-1723); b 1658, b 1659(60?); Windsor, CT

GILLETT, Cornelius (1665-1711) (m/2 __?_ ROWELL prob 1711/12) & 1/wf [?Elizabeth] [BIRGE] (1674-), dau Daniel; b 1693?, ca 1702?; Windsor, CT

GILLETT, Elias (1649-) & 1/wf Sarah GRIFFIN; 29 Oct 1676; Simsbury

GILLET, Elias & Rebecca [KELSEY]; b 1700; Simsbury

GILLETT, Elephal (1673±-1747) & 1/wf Mary [WHEELER] (1677/8-1730, 1732, ae ca 65); b 1695; Milford, CT

GILLETT, Elephal & 2/wf Elizabeth __?_ (-1732)

GILLETT, Jeremiah (1647-1693) & Deborah BARTLETT (1666-), m/2 Samuel ADAMS 1694; 15 Oct 1685; Windsor, CT

GILLETT, John (-1663) & Elizabeth (_?_) PERRY, w Arthur, m/3 William WARDELL 1656, 1657?; 22 Dec 1653; Boston

GILLETT, John (-1682) & Mary/Mercy BARBER (1651-), m/2 George NORTON 1683; 8 Jul 1669; Windsor, CT

GILLETT, John & __?_ ; b 1692(3?); Windsor, CT

GILLETT, John & Sarah TRYON/TRYAN (?1675-); 7 Apr 1697; Wethersfield, CT

GILLET, John (1671-) & Experience DEWEY (1682-); 3 Jan 1699/1700, 3 Jan 1700; Lebanon/Windsor, CT

GILLETT, Jonathan (-1677) & Mary [DOLBERSON/DOLBISON] (1601-1685, 1685/6?); Colyton, Eng, 29 Mar 1634; Dorchester/Windsor, CT

GILLETT, Jonathan (-1698) & 1/wf Mary KELSEY (-1676); 23 Apr 1661, 22 Apr; Windsor, CT/?Hartford

GILLETT, Jonathan (?1634-1698) & 2/wf Miriam DIBBLE (1645-1710+, 1703+), m/2 Timothy PALMER; 14 Dec 1676; Windsor, CT

GILLETT, Joseph (1641-1675) & Elizabeth HAWKS (1640/1-1682), m/2 Nathaniel DICKINSON 1680; 1664?, 1663, ?24 Nov; Windsor, CT

GILLETT, Joseph (1664-1746?) & 1/wf Esther GULL (1665-); 3 Nov 1687; Hadley

GILLETT, Joseph (1664-1746) & 2/wf Mary GRISWOULD/GRISWOLD (1671-1719), dau Joseph; 17 May 1692; Hartford

GILLETT, Josiah (1650-1736) & Joanna TAINTOR (1657-1735); 30 Jun 1676; Branford, CT?/Windsor, CT

GILLET, Nathan (-1689) & __?_ (-1670/1); b 1639; Windsor, CT

GILLET, Nathan & 1/wf Rebecca OWEN (1666-); 30 Jun 1692; Windsor, CT

GILLET, Samuel (1642-1676), Hatfield & Hannah DICKINSON (1648?, 1646-), m/2 Stephen JENNINGS 1677; 23 Sep 1668; Hadley

GILLETT, Samuel (1672-1769) & Hannah [HASTINGS] (1677-); b 1698; Hadley

GILLETT, Thomas (1676-) & 1/wf Martha MILLS; 21 Nov 1700; Windsor, CT

GILLET, William (1673-1719) & Mary SAXTON (1673-), m/2 Jonathan HOLCOMB 1721; 14 Sep 1699; Simsbury, CT

GILLETT, __?_ & Rebecca [BANCROFT] (1685-), dau Thomas; b 1701?; Windsor, CT

GILLING, Edward & Mary THORTES/THWAITE/THOITS; 25 Dec 1696; Boston

GILLINGHAM, James (-1719) & Rebecca BLY (1670-); 22 May 1692; Salem

GILLINGHAM, William & Agnes WADLEN/WADLAND, m/2 Joseph BATCHELDER 1670; 31 Oct 1664, 13 Oct 1664; Charlestown

GILLOW, John & Rose __?_ ; b 1646; Lynn

GILLOW/?GILLOWAY, John (-1672) & Sarah KEASER, m/2 John JOHNSON 1675; 7 Apr 1666; Lynn

GILMAN, Daniel (1652-1683) & Alice [CARTIE], m/2 Nehemiah LEAVETT ca 1684; ca 1673?, b 2 Jul 1680; Exeter, NH

GILMAN, Edward (1587-1655) & Mary CLARK (-1681); Hingham, Eng, 3 Jun 1614; Hingham/Rehoboth/Ipswich/Exeter, NH

GILMAN, Edward (1617-1653?) & Elizabeth SMITH, ?m/2 John FABES?; [Sep] 1647, b 28 Sep 1647, b 26 Sep; Ipswich

GILMAN, Edward (ca 1649-1692) & Abigail MAVERICK (-20 Dec 1674); 20 Dec 1674?; Exeter, NH

GILMAN, Edward (1675-) & [Abigail FOLSOM] (1676-); b 1705, b 1701?, Sep 1701; Exeter, NH

GILMAN, James (1665-) & Mary [DOLLOFF] (1667-); ca 1686; Exeter, NH

GILMAN, Jeremiah (1660-) & Mary [WIGGIN] (1668-), dau Andrew; ca 1688?, b 1690, 30 Jul 1685; Exeter, NH

GILMAN, John (1626-1708) & Elizabeth TRUEWORTHY/TREWORGY (ca 1638-1719); 30 Jun 1657, ?3 Jun; Exeter, NH

GILMAN, John (1639-) & 1/wf Elizabeth GODDARD; ca 1663; Dover, NH

GILMAN, John (ca 1650-) & Grace YORK; 3 May; Exeter, NH

GILMAN, John (1668-1753) & 1/wf Dorothy WIGGIN (1680-1704+); 19 Nov 1695; Hampton, NH/Exeter, NH

GILMAN, John (1676-) & 1/wf Elizabeth COFFIN (1680-1720); 5 Jun 1698; ?Exeter, NH

GILMAN, Moses (1630-1702) & Elizabeth [HERSEY], dau William; bef 1660, 1659, ca 1658; Hingham/Exeter, NH

GILMAN, Moses (1659-1746) & 1/wf Ann [HEARD]; b 1693; ?Exeter, NH

GILMAN, Nicholas (1672-1749) & 1/wf Sarah CLARK (1678-1741); 9 Jun 1697, 10? Jun; Newbury/Exeter, NH

GILMAN/GILSMAN, Richard & Elizabeth [ADKINS]; b 1 Sep 1690, b 1676; Hartford, CT

GILMORE, Briant & Mercy _?_; b 1701; Boston

GILSON, James[1] (-1712) & Mary _?_ (-1712); b 1674(5?); Rehoboth

GILSON, John (1674-1707) & Sarah [BLOOD] (1675-), m/2 Richard WARNER; b 1697(8?); Groton

GILLSON, Joseph & Mary COOPER/CAPER (1641-), dau Timothy of Lynn; 10 Nov 1661, 18 Nov 1661?, 18 Nov; Chelmsford

GILSON, Joseph (1667-1739) & Elizabeth/Hephzebah? [LAWRENCE] (?1669-), ?dau Peleg; b 1690, b 1694? (no); Groton

GILSON, William (-1639) (uncle of John DAMON) & Frances _?_ (-1649); b 1634; Scituate

GILVIN, Thomas (-bef 1 Jun 1639) & Katheren _?_; ?Ipswich

GIRDLER, Benjamin (-1729) & Sarah BONDFEILD; 1 Nov 1692; Marblehead

GIRDLER, Francis (-1692) & Deborah _?_, m/2 Ambrose GALE 1695; b 1667; Salem

GIRDLER, George & [Deborah] _?_; b 1687; Marblehead

GIRLING, Richard & _?_; b 1637; Cambridge

GISBORNE, Francis, Portsmouth, RI, & Mary WICKES; 8 Jan 1671, 8 Jun 1671, 9 Jun 1671; Warwick, RI/Portsmouth, RI

GLADING, John & Elizabeth ROGERS; 17 Jul 1667; Newbury/Bristol, RI

GLADDING, John (1670-) & Alice WARDELL; 31 Oct 1693; Bristol, RI

GLADDING, William (1673-) & Mary _?_; b 1700; Bristol, RI

GLANFIELD/GLANVILLE?, Daniel & Mary MOORE; 4 Jul 1676, by Jul 1676; Scarborough

GLANFEILD, Robert (1643-1702) & Lydia WARDE; 12 Jul 1665; Salem

GLANFIELD, Peter & Margaret _?_; b 1643; Dover, NH/Salem/etc.

GLASSE, James (-1652) & Mary PONTUS, m/2 Philip DELANO 1653?; 31 Oct 1645; ?Plymouth

GLASS, James & Elizabeth _?_; b 1687(8?); Boston

GLASS, Richard & Elizabeth _?_; ca 1673; Salem/Manchester

GLASS, Roger (-1692) & Mary _?_ (-1692+); ca 1650/60?; Duxbury

GLAZER, John (-1691) & Elizabeth [GEORGE/SAGE?], m/2 _?_ POPE 1691/95; b 1663; Woburn/Lancaster

GLAZIER, George (1676-) & Sarah BARRETT; 17 Dec 1700; Chelmsford/Lancaster

GLASIOR, Zechariah (1666-) & Hannah EMERSON, m/2 Beamsley PERKINS 1697?, 1698?; 20 Apr 168[6?], 1685; Ipswich

GLEALING, Joseph & Martha _?_; b 1668; Sudbury

GLEASON, Isaac (1654-1698) & Hester EGGLESTON (1663-); 26 Jun 1684, at Enfield/Windsor, CT/Enfield, CT

GLEASON, Isaac & Deborah LEALAND/LELAND (1679-); 11 Dec 1700; Sherborn

GLEISON, John & Mary ROSS; 15 Jan 1678; Sudbury

GLEASON, Joseph & 1/wf Martha [RUSSELL] (-1684); b 1668; Sudbury

GLEASON, Joseph (-1711), Sudbury & 2/wf Abigail GARFIELD (1646-), Watertown; 22 Dec 1686; Sudbury

GLEASON, Thomas (1607-1686) & Susanna [PAGE] (-1691); in Eng?, b 1631; Cambridge

GLEASON, Thomas (1637-1705) & 1/wf Sarah _?_ (-1703); b 1665(6?); Sudbury/Framingham
GLEASON, Thomas (1671-) & Mary MILLINS/MELLON (-1727); 6 Dec 1695; Sherborn
GLEASON, William (-1691) & Abiah _?_ (not BARTLETT), m Jonathan SANDERSON; b 1679; Cambridge
GLEDEN, Charles (ca 1632-1707+) & Eunice SHORE (ca 1640-1707+); Bideford, Eng, 7 Apr 1658, in Eng; Boston/Portsmouth, NH/Exeter, NH
GLIDDEN, John (ca 1670-1718) & Elizabeth [LADD] (1681-); ca 1697?, ca 1695; Exeter, NH
GLIDEN, Joseph (1668-1700) & Jane [BUDD] (1673-), m/2 Christopher MARVIN 1708; b 1695; Boston
GLIDDEN, Richard (-1728) & Sarah _?_ /?GILMAN; ca 1686; Portsmouth, NH
GLIDE, John & Mary _?_ ; b 1679; Salem
GLOVER, Charles (-1665) & 1/wf [Elizabeth] _?_ (-1648?); b 1640?, b 1644; Salem/Gloucester/Southold, LI
GLOVER, Charles (-1665) & 2/wf 3/wf? Esther/Hester (ROLFE) SAUNDERS, w John; 12 Feb 1649/50; Gloucester
GLOVER, Charles & Martha _?_ (-1713, in 36th y); b 1701?; Orient, LI
GLOVER, Habakkuk (-1693) & Hannah/(Ann) ELIOTT (1633-); 4 May 1653; Boston/Roxbury
GLOVER, Henry (1603-1653?, 1655?) & Abigail _?_ ; ca 1630/5?; Medfield
GLOVER, Henry (1610-1689) & Ellen/Helena [RUSSELL/DAVIS]/WAKEMAN?/COOPER? (-1698); ca 1640; New Haven
GLOVER, Henry (1642-1714) & Hannah _?_ (1641-1720); b 1663; Boston/Milton
GLOVER, Henry (1670-), Milton & Mary CREHORE (1677-), Milton; 31 Mar 1696, 1 Mar; Milton/Bristol, RI/Lebanon, CT
GLOVER, John (-1654) & 1/wf Anna/Anne _?_ ; in Eng, ca 1625; Dorchester/Springfield/Milton
GLOVER, John & Mary _?_ ; b 1659, b 1661; Boston
GLOVER, John (1633?-1695) & Mary GUPPY (-1700+); 2 Jan 1660, 1660/1; Salem
GLOVER, John (1648-1679) & Joanna DANIEL, m/2 William THOMPSON 1682; 7 Dec 1671; New Haven
GLOVER, John (1654-1690) & 1/wf Mary [PROCTOR?] (-1687); ca 1672; Dorchester
GLOVER, John (1629-1696) & Elizabeth MAY (?1638-1705), m/2 John CLEVERLY 1696, m/3 James MOSMAN 1703; ca 1680; ?Ipswich/Swansea
GLOVER, John & Hannah _?_ ; 29 May 1682; Norwich, CT
GLOVER, John & 2/wf Miriam SMITH (-1720); b 1689, b 24 Mar 1688/9; Dorchester
GLOVER, John (1674-) & 1/wf Margaret/Margery prob HUBBARD; 27 Nov 1700; New Haven
GLOVER, Jonathan (-1736) & Abigail HENDERSON (-1738+); 31 Mar 1697?; Salem
GLOVER, Jorse/etc. (-1638, on ocean) & 1/wf Sarah [OWFIELD] (-1628); in Eng, b 1623; Cambridge
GLOVER, Jorse/Joseph/etc. (-1638) & 2/wf Elizabeth HARRIS (-164[-]), m/2 Henry DUNSTER 1641; in Eng, ca 1629-30; Cambridge
GLOVER, Joseph (-1692?) & Elizabeth [NORRIS], m/2 Samuel MOULTON 1700; b 1683?; Salem
GLOVER, Nathaniel (-1657) & Mary [SMITH] (ca 1630-1703), m/2 Thomas HINCKLEY 1660; ca 1647/52; Dorchester
GLOVER, Nathaniel (?1653-1724) & Hannah [HINCKLEY] (1651-1730); b 1674(5?); Milton/Roxbury/Dorchester
GLOVER, Pelatiah (-1692) & Hannah CULLICK (?1640-1689); 20 May 1660?; Dorchester
GLOVER, Pelatiah (-1737) & Hannah PARSONS (1663-1739); 7 Jan 1686, 1686/7, 6 Jan; Northampton
GLOVER, Richard & Rebecca (JORDAN) [CRADOCK], w Matthew; b 1650, b 1644; Salem
GLOVER, Robert (1673-) & _?_ ; b 1697?; Boston
GLOVER, Samuel (1644-) & Sarah [MOORE]; b 1691, prob 1670/90; Southold, LI
GLOVER, Stephen (-1686) & Ruth STEVENS (1642-1664); 7 Oct 1663; Gloucester
GLOVER, Thomas (1663-) & Susanna BRADLEY (1670-); 1 Jan 1700, prob 1700/1701; Milton
GORD, Joseph & Ann CHAPLIN; 23 Mar 1680/1; Roxbury
GOURD, Richard (1618-1683) & Phebe [HOWES?/HEWES?] (-1679); 30 Nov 1639; Roxbury
GOBLE, Daniel (1641-1676) & Hannah BREWER (1645-1697), m/2 Ephraim ROPER 1677; 25 Feb 1663, 1664; Sudbury/Concord/Charlestown
GOBLE, Daniel (1669-) & Sarah [HOUGHTON] (1672-); ?Lancaster/Hanover, NJ
GOBLE, John, Concord & Abigail ROGERS (1671?-), dau William?; 23 May 1693; Charlestown
GOBLE, Thomas (-1657) & Alice _?_ ; b 1631; Charlestown/Concord

GOBLE, Thomas (prob did not m/1 Ruth _?_, 3 ch in 1657) & Mary [MOUSELL]; b 1653; Concord

GOBLE, Thomas & Sarah SHEPARD, m/2 _?_ WHITNEY; 4 Jan 1686, prob 1686/7, 4 Jul 1686/7; Concord

GODBERTSON/?CUTHBERTSON, Godbert (-1633) & 2/wf Sarah (ALLERTON) PRIEST (-1633), w Degory; Leyden, Holland, 13 Nov 1621; Plymouth

GODDARD, Benjamin (1668-1748) & 1/wf Martha PALFREY (1670-1737); 30 May 1689; Cambridge/Charlestown

GODDARD, Daniel & _?_

GODDARD, Edward (-1754) & Susannah STONE (1675-1754); - Jun 1697; Watertown/Boston/Farmingham

GODDARD, Giles & 1/wf Mary _?_; b 1678; Boston

GODDARD, Henry & Mary HOWLAND; 12 Aug 1693; Jamestown, RI

GODDARD, John (1608-1660) & Welthean _?_ (1621-1703+), m/2 John SYMONDS; nr 1640, came 1634; Dover, NH

GODDARD, John & 1/wf Sarah FARINGTON (1677-1732); m int 19 Jun 1697; Lynn/Roxbury

GODDARD, Joseph (1655-1728) & 1/wf Deborah TREADAWAY/TREADWAY (1657-1714, Roxbury); 25 Mar 1680; Watertown

GODDARD, Josiah (1672-1720) & Rachel DAUICE/DAVIS (1672-1740); 28 Jan 1695/6; Watertown

GODDARD, Nicholas (see GOSARD)

GODDARD, William (1627-1691) & Elizabeth [MILES] (-1698); ca 1662?; Watertown/Cambridge

GODDARD, William (-1708) & Leah FISHER (1657-1720, Roxbury); 10 Dec 1685; Sherborn

GODDARD, William & Elizabeth FAYREFIELD/FAIRFIELD (1674-); 29 Oct 1697; Boston

GOODDIN/GODDING, Henry & Elizabeth PEERY/BEERS/PERRY; 7 Apr 1663; Watertown

GODFREY, Christopher (-1715, Stratford) & [Anne] _?_ (1667-); b 1685/6; Fairfield, CT

GODFREY, Edward (1584-) & 1/wf Elizabeth OLIVER

GODFREY, Edward (1584-) & 2/wf Anne (?BURDETT) MESSANT; aft 1640; ME

GODFREY, Francis (-1669) & [Elizabeth] _?_; in Eng, ca 1626/9?; Duxbury/Bridgewater

GODFREY, George & _?_; b 1662(3?); Eastham

GODFREY, Isaac (1639-1717) & Hannah MARRIAN/MARION; 15 Jul 1670; Hampton, NH

GODFREY, James & Hannah KIMBALL; 10 Feb 1700; Newbury

GODFREY, John (?1632-1697) & Mary COX; 6 May 1659; Hampton, NH

GODFREY, John (son Richard) & Martha [JOYCE], dau Hosea; ca 1675/81?, bef 1692?; Yarmouth

GODFREY, John & Sarah _?_ (no) (-1702+); b 1681; ?Newport, RI

GODFREY, Moses (1667-1743) & Deborah [COOKE/COOK] (1678-1745); b 1707, b 1701?; Eastham?

GODFREY, Peter (1630-1697) & Mary BROWNE (1635-1716); 13 May 1656; Newbury

GODFREY, Richard[1] (-1691) & 1/wf _?_ (perhaps Jane _?_), dau John; b 1654, b 1651?; Taunton

GODFREY, Richard (?1651-1724?) & Mary RICHMOND (1654-1732); 1 Jan 1679, 1679/80; Taunton

GODFREY, Richard[1] (-1691) & 2/wf Mary PHILLIPS, w James; 26 Mar 1684; Taunton

GODFREY, Robert & Hannah HACKET; 14 Jan 1684/5; Taunton

GODFREY, Thomas & Mary _?_; b 1701; Boston

GODFREY, William (-1671) & 1/wf Sarah _?_; b 1632; Dedham/Watertown/Hampton, NH

GODFREY, William (-1671) & 2/wf Margaret (_?_) [WEBSTER] (-1637, ae 78), w Thomas, m/3 John MARION 1671; ca 1635?, b 1639, ca 1638; Hampton, NH

GODFREY, William & Priscilla ANNIS (1677-1708); 17 Jul 1700, 17 Jan 1700/01?; Hampton, NH

GODSOE, William (1644/8?-) & Elizabeth LORD; 17 Apr 1680, 17 Feb; Salem

GODSOE, William & Jane [WITHERS], w Thomas; 1694, betw 1 Apr & 13 Jun 1691; Kittery, ME

GOFF, Aaron (-1772) & Hannah COLE; 19 Jan 1681, [1681/2]; Wethersfield, CT

GOFF, Anthony, Billerica & Sarah POLLEY, Woburn; 29 Sep 1685; Billerica/Woburn

GOFFE, Christopher & Abigail [PHILLIPS], m/2 Samuel WENTWORTH 1699; b 1688(9?); Boston

GOFFE, Edmund (1670-1740) & Hannah (LYNDE) (BIGG) MITCHELL, w John, w Jonathan; m int 7 May 1696, b 26 May 1697, no issue; Boston

GOFFE, Edward (-1658) & 1/wf Joyce [CUTTER?] (-Nov 1638); in Eng, ca 1624/29; Cambridge

GOFFE, Edward (-1658, ae 64) & Margaret [WILKINSON?], m/2 John WITCHFIELD 1662; ca Feb 1638/9; Cambridge

GOFFE, Edward (1658-1691) & Mary [BISCOE] (1658-), Watertown; b 1687; Cambridge

GOFFE, Edward & Elizabeth _?_ ; b 1694; Boston

GOFF, Jacob (1649-1697) & Margery INGERSOLL, Westfield, m/2 Jonathan BUCK; 5 Dec 1679; Wethersfield, CT

GOFFE/GOSS?, James & Sarah/Elizabeth? _?_ , m/2 John FOST 1687, m/3 James EMERY; b 1680; Boston

GOFF, John (-1641) & Amy _?_ ; Newbury

GOFF, John (-1716) & Hannah [SUMNER] (1659-); b 1678; Boston

GOFFE, John (-1748) & Hannah [PARRISH]; [1699?]; Chelmsford/Londonderry, NH

GOFF, Moses (1656-1717) & Mercy [DIX] (-1711); ?1687; Wethersfield, CT/?Branford, CT

GOFF, Philip (-1674) & Rebecca _?_ (-1674+); b 1649; Wethersfield, CT/Middletown, CT

GOFF, Philip (1654?-1725) & Naomi (LATIMER) [REYNOLDS], w John; ca 1683; Wethersfield, CT

GOFF, Samuel (?1630-1706) & 1/wf Hannah/Anna? BARNARD (1635-1679); 25 Jun 1656; Cambridge

GOFF, Samuel (-1706, ae 76) & 2/wf Mary (_?_) SAXTON, w Thomas; 9 Nov 1682; Cambridge

GOFFE, Gen.? William (-1679±) (Regicide) & [Francis WHALLEY]; Wethersfield, CT

GOFF, _?_ & Elizabeth _?_ , ?m/2 John PEMBERTON

GOYTE/GOIT, John, Sr. & [?Mary] _?_ ; b 1643; Dorchester/Salem/Marblehead

GOLD, John (-1712) & Hannah SLAWSON, m/2 Samuel HOYT 1714; b 1673; Stamford, CT

GOLD, Nathan[1] (-1694) & 1/wf Martha (_?_) [HARVEY] (-1657+), w Edmund; betw 1648 & 1655; ?Milford, CT/Medford, CT

GOLD, Nathan (-1694) & 2/wf Sarah (PHIPPEN), w Thomas; b 1665; Fairfield, CT

GOLD, Nathan[2] (1663-1723) & 1/wf Hannah TALCOTT (1663-1696); 8 Feb 1683; Fairfield, CT

GOLD, Nathan[2] (1663-1723) & 2/wf Sarah [BURR?/COOKE?] (-1711); 1696+; Fairfield, CT/Hartford, CT

GOLDING, Ephraim & Rebecca GIBBS; 26 Jun 1689, Barbados; Hempstead, LI

GOULDING, Jacob & Elizabeth _?_ ; b 1699(1700?); Boston

GOLDING, John & Grace [SKIDMORE]; b 1674?, b 1683/4; Huntington, LI

GOLDING, Joseph & Eleanor _?_ ; b 1664; Gravesend, LI

GOLDING, Peter (1635, 1630?-1703) & 1/wf Jane _?_ ; b 1665(6?); Boston/Sudbury

GOLDING, Peter (1635-1703) & 2/wf Sarah [PALMER?]/[SMITH?]; b 1673; Boston/Sudbury/Marlboro/Hadley

GOULDING, Roger (-1694/5) & Penelope ARNOLD, m/2 _?_ CUTLER; 1 Jan 1672, 1 Jan 1673, 1672/3; Newport

GOLDING, William (1613-) & _?_ ; Gravesend, LI/Cape May, Co., NJ

GOLDING, William & Margaret LAKE; 7 Apr 1676, 2 Apr; Gravesend, LI

GOULDING, William, Gravesend & Deborah QUIMBY, Westchester Co.; 18 Jun 1689, 1689; Gravesend, LI

GOLDEN, Winsor (1675-) & Elizabeth INGOLSBY; 14 May 1698; Boston

GOLDSMITH, John & 1/wf Prudence [WINES]; - Nov 1679; Southold, LI

GOLDSMITH, John & 2/wf Anne WELLS; - May 1683; Southold, LI

GOLDSMITH, John & Elizabeth (TUTHILL) WELLS, w William; 2 Feb 1696/7; Southold, LI

GOLDSMITH, Joshua & Mary HUNTINGTON; 14 Aug 1667; Salisbury

GOLDSMITH, Richard & Mary [?PERKINS]; b 1648; Wenham/Chelmsford

GOLDSMITH, Thomas & 1/wf _?_ ; Salem/Southampton, LI/Southold, LI/Killingworth, CT

GOLDSMITH, Thomas & 2/wf Susanna [SHRATHER], w John; aft 1 May 1677; ?Guilford, CT

GOLDSMITH, Thomas & Bethiah TERRY (-1739), m/2 Thomas MAPES, m/3 Richard STEER; 7 Jun 1693; Southold, LI

GOLDSMITH, Zaccheus & Martha [HOUTTON] (1662-); b 1696, b 1686?; Wenham

GOLDSMITH, Zaccheus (1674-1707) & Mary [?HORTON], dau Jonathan?; b 1701?; Southold, LI

GOLDSMITH, _?_ & Rebecca _?_ ; b 1701; Newport

GOLDSTONE, Henry (1591-1638) & Anne/Anna/Hannah _?_ (1589-1670, ae 79?), m/2 John GEORGE by 1647; b 1615; Watertown

GOLTHITE, Ezekiel (1674-1761) & Esther BOYCE (?1676-); 20 Mar 1695/6; Salem

GOLTHWRITE, Samuel & Elizabeth CHEEVER (1645-); 8 Sep 1666, 6 Sep 1666, 6 Sep; Salem/Charlestown

GOLTHRITE, Samuel & Mary THOMAS (1671-); 2 Dec 1697; Salem
GOLDTHWAITE, Thomas[1] (-1683) & 1/wf Elizabeth _?_ ; b 1637; Salem
GOLDTHWAIT, Thomas (-1683) & 2/wf Rachel (LEACH) [SIBLEY] (-1683+), w John; b 1671; Salem
GOLDWYER/GOLDWIER, George & Martha MOYCE (?1619-), m/2 Robert PIKE 1684; ca 1674; Salisbury
GOOCH/GOOGE/etc., Edward (-1705) & [?Frances] _?_ ; b 1697/[8?]; Boston
GOOCH, James (-1676) & _?_ HAMMOND (-1676); ca 1665?; Wells, ME
GOOCH, James (-1738) & 1/wf Hannah [EMMONS]; 10 Feb 1691/2; Charlestown/Boston/Wells, ME
GOOCH, James (-1738) & 2/wf Elizabeth PECK (-1702); m int 15 Aug 1695; Boston
GOOCH, John (-1667) & Ruth _?_ ; in Eng, ca 1623; Wells, ME/York, ME
GOOCH, John (1623-1672) & Lydia [?HAMMOND], m/2 Israel HARDING; ?ca 1650; Wells, ME/York, ME
GOOCH, William (-1645) & Ann _?_ ; b 1640; Lynn
GOOD, William & 2/wf? Elizabeth DRINKER; 7 Jun 1693; Ipswich
GOOD, William & 1/wf Sarah [SNOW?] (-1692); b 29 Feb 1691/2, b 1690, b 1685?; Salem
GOODELL, Isaac (1634-1679) & Patience COOKE, m/2 James STIMSON bef 1684; 25 Jan 1668/9; Salem
GOODALE, Isaac & Mary [ABLE?]; 31 Dec 1692; Salem
GOODALE, John (-1625, in Eng) & Elizabeth [TAYLOR] (-1647) (mother of Richard?); by 1600?; Salisbury/Newbury
GOODALE, John & Mary [MODESLEY]; b 1687; Dorchester
GOODALE, Joseph, Boston & Sarah (BLIGHE/BLITHE) RICKS/RIX, w Thomas; b 1681; Charlestown.
GOODALL, Joseph & Elizabeth _?_ ; ca 1685; Southampton, LI
GOODALL, Joseph (1672-) & Mary [SAMP]/[SAMPSON?] (1670-); 6 Apr 1694; Salem
GOODALL, Nehemiah (calls Richard HUBBARD, "kinsman") & Hannah HAVEN (1646-1726, Framingham); 30 Jul 1673; Charlestown/Lynn
GOODALE, Richard (1594-1666) & Dorothy _?_ (-1665); in Eng, b 1623; Newbury/Salisbury
GOODALE, Richard & Mary _?_ ; b 1653; Salisbury/Boston
GOODALE, Richard (1655-) & Mary [COLE] (1658-); b 1678; Middletown, CT
GOODALE, Richard (1679-) & Joanna [CLARK]; 23 Jan 1699/1700; Middletown
GOODELL, Robert[1] (1604-) & 1/wf Katherine [?KILHAM] (1606-); ?Dennington, Suffolk, b 1630; Salem
GOODALE, Robert (-1683) & 2/wf Margaret LAZENBY; m cont 30 Aug 1669; Salem
GOODALE, Samuel[3] (1669-1719?) & Mary BUXTON (1669-1723?); 25 Dec 1697; Salem
GOODALE, Thomas (-1756) & Sarah HORREL/HORRELL (-1750); 2 Dec 1698; Beverly/Woodstock, CT/Pomfret, CT
GOODALL, Zachariah[2] (?1640-) & Elizabeth BEACHUM/BEAUCHAMP; last of Dec 1666; Salem
GOODALE, Zachariah & Sarah [WHIPPLE] (1670-); b 1693, ca 1690?; Salem
GOODALE, Zachariah & 1/wf Elizabeth COUSINS; 22 May 1700; Wells, ME
GOODENHOUSE, Samuel & _?_ [TURNER]; aft 1646; New Haven
GOODENHOUS, Samuel & Bethia _?_ ; b 1691; Boston
GOODFELLOW, Thomas & _?_ ; Hartford
GOODFELOW, Thomas (-1685) & Mary [GRANT], dau Peter, m/2 Samuel BAKER 1687; b 1683, ca 1681, b 5 Oct 1681; Wethersfield, CT
GOODHUE, Joseph (1640-1697) & 1/wf Sarah WHIPPLE (1641-1681, 1683); 13 Jul 1661; Ipswich
GOODHUE, Joseph (1640-1697) & 2/wf Rachel TODD (-1691); 15 Oct 1684; Ipswich
GOODHUE, Joseph (1640-1697) & 3/wf Mercy (BOYNTON) CLARKE (-1730), w Josiah, m/3 John HOVEY 1712; 4 Jul 1792; Ipswich
GOODHUE, Nathaniel (1670-) & Mercy HAWKS (1675-); m int 25 Nov 1696; Lynn
GOODHUE, Nicholas (1575-) & Jane _?_ (1577-); came 1635
GOODHUE, William[1] (1615-1699/1700) & 1/wf Margery [WATSON] (-28 Aug 1668); b 1639; Ipswich
GOODHUE, William (1645-1712) & Hannah DANE, Andover; 14 Nov 1666; Ipswich
GOODHUE, William[1] (1615-) & 2/wf Mary (?OSBORN) (FAIRWEATHER) WEBB (-7 Sep 1680), w Thomas, w John; 7 Sep 1669; Ipswich

GOODHUE, William[1] (1615-) & 3/wf Bethia (REA)/(LATHROP) [GRAFTON], w Joseph; ca 1683, ?26 Jul 1682, ?24 Jul; Ipswich

GOODHUE, William[1] (-1699, ae 86?) & 4/wf Remember FISK (-1702), w John; 3 Dec 1689?; Ipswich

GOODHUE, William[3] (1666-1722) & Mary [LOWDEN?/OSBORNE?] (1667-1729); ca 1686; Ipswich

GOODHUE, _?_ & ?Elizabeth _?_ (gr dau Alice ROPER)

GOODMAN, John (1661-1725) & Hannah [NOBLE] (1663-), m/2 Nathaniel EDWARDS, m/3 Samuel PARTRIDGE; b 1686; Hadley

GOODMAN, Richard (1609-1676), Cambridge/Hartford & Mary TERRY, (1635, ?1633-1692); 8 Dec 1659, at Hartford?; Hadley/Windsor, CT

GOODMAN, Samuel & Grace _?_ ; b 1687; Boston

GOODMAN, Thomas (1673-1748) & Grace [MARSH] (1677-1756); b 1699, ca 1701?; Hadley

GOODENOUGH, David (-1698) & _?_ ; b 1682(3?); Ipswich

GOODENOW, Edmund[1] (1611-1688) & Anne/Hannah? _?_ (-1675); in Eng, ca 1634; Sudbury

GOODENOW, Edmund[2] & 1/wf Dorothy MAN/MANN (-1689); 6 Jun 1686; Sudbury

GOODENOW, Edmund[3] & 2/wf Sarah _?_ (-1691); ca 1690; Sudbury

GOODNEW, Edmund[3] (1661-1727?) & 3/wf Rebecca _?_ (-1720); b 1696; Sudbury

GOODNOW, John[2] (1596-1654) & Jane _?_ (-1666); in Eng, ca 1626/32; Sudbury

GOODENOW, John (?1635-1721) & 1/wf Mary AXDELL (?1639-1704); 19 Sep 1656; Sudbury

GOODENOW, John, Jr. & 1/wf Ruth WILLIS, dau Roger; 28 Feb 1689/90; Sudbury

GOODENOW, John & 2/wf Sarah _?_ (-1723); b 1701; Sudbury

GOODENOW, Joseph (1674-1732+) & Patience _?_ ; b 1701; Sudbury

GOODENOW, Samuel (?1646-1717) & Mary _?_ ; b 1672; Marlboro

GOODNOW, Samuel & Sarah [BRIGHAM] (?1674-); b 1701?, b 1709; ?Marlboro

GOODENOW, Thomas (1608-1666) & Jane _?_ , m/2 William BUTTRICK 1667; b 1637; Sudbury/Marlboro

GOODENOW, Thomas, Jr. (-1663) & Joanna _?_ , ?m/2 William BUTTRICK 1667; 18 Dec 1652; Marlboro

GOODRICH, Bartholomew (1647 (no)-1696) & Mary BARTHOLOMEW (1668-); (no) 1684?; Guilford, CT/Branford, CT

GOODRIDGE, Benjamin (1642-) & 1/wf Deborah (Mary is wrong) JORDAN (-1676); 8 Sep 1663; Newbury

GOODRIDGE, Benjamin (1642-) & 2/wf Sarah CROAD; 16 Nov 1678; Newbury/Rowley

GOODRIDGE, Daniel & Mary ORDWAY; m int 16 Nov 1698; Newbury

GOODRICH, David (1667-1755) & 1/wf Hannah WRIGHT (1671-1698); 7 Mar 1688, 1688/9; Wethersfield, CT

GOODRICH, David (1667-) & 2/wf Prudence CHURCHILL (1678-); 1 Dec 1698; Wethersfield, CT

GOODRICH, Ephraim (1663-1739) & 1/wf Sarah TREAT (1664-1712); 20 May 1689; Wethersfield, CT

GOODRIDGE, Jeremiah (1636±-1707) & Mary ADAMS (1642-); 15 Nov 1660; Newbury

GUTTRIDGE, John & Prudence _?_ ; b 1642; Boston

GOODRICH, John (-1680) & 1/wf Elizabeth _?_ (?sister of Katherine, wf of Thomas REDD); b 1645; Wethersfield, CT

GOODRIDGE, John (1643-1676) & Mary GIBBS (1652-), m/2 Thomas FROST 1678; 23 Mar 1674, 1674/5; Sudbury/Wethersfield, CT

GOODRICH, John (-1680) & 2/wf Mary (FOOTE) STODDARD (-1685), w John, m/3 Thomas TRACEY; m cont 4 Apr 1674; Wethersfield, CT

GOODRICH, John (1653-1730) & Rebecca ALLEN (1660-); 28 Mar 1678; Charlestown

GOODRICH, John (-1728) & Mary [ALLING/ALLEN] (1662-); ca 1682?, no issue; Guilford, CT

GOODRICH, Jonathan (ca 1665-1742+) & Abigail CRAFTS (ca 1676-); 3 Dec 1691; Wethersfield, CT

GOODRIDGE, Joseph (1639-1716) & Martha MOORES (1643-); 28 Aug 1664; Newbury

GOODRIDGE, Philip (1669-1729) & Mehitable WOODMAN (1677-1755); 16 Apr 1700; Newbury/Lunenburg

GUTTERIDGE, Richard (-1676) & 1/wf _?_ ; b 1644, b 1642?; Guilford, CT

GUTTERIDGE, Richard (-1676) & 2/wf Dinah _?_ ; 7 Jun 1646; Guilford, CT

GUTRIDGE, Robert (see under **GUTTRIDGE** & **GUTHRIE**) & 1/wf Margaret **IRELAND** (1623-1687); 25 Dec 1656; Braintree

GUTTERIDGE, Robert (see Thomas **GOODRIDGE**) & Mary [?**ALLING**] (1661-); b 1677?, b 1682; Boston

GUTTRIDGE/GUTTERY, Robert (-1692) (see **GUTTRIDGE**) & 2/wf Ann (**ALCOCK**) **WILLIAMS** (1650-1723), w John; 5 Jun 1689; New Shoreham, RI

GOODRIDGE, Thomas & Catherine __?__, ?m/2 Richard **SHUTE**?; b 1666; Boston

GOODRIDGE, Thomas (-1691) (see Robert **GUTTERIDGE**) & Mary [?**ALLING**]; b 1682; Boston

GUTTRIDGE, Walter & Anna **GROSS**; 12 Nov 1696; Charlestown/Boston

GUTTERIG, William (1608-1647, 1645?) & Margaret (**BUTTERFIELD**)/__?__ (1599-1682), m/2 John **HULL**; ?12 Aug, ?19 Aug 1631, ca 1632; Watertown

GOODRICH, William (1622-1676) & Sarah **MARVIN** (1631-1702), m/2 William **CURTIS**; 4 Oct 1648; Hartford

GOODRICH, William (1661-1737) & 1/wf Grace **RILEY** (1661-1712); 22 Nov 1680; Wethersfield, CT

GOODSELL, Thomas (1646-) & Ruth [**BUTLER**], m/2 Joseph **WOODWARD**; div 1683; New Haven

GOODSELL, Thomas & Sarah **HEMINGWAY** (1663-); 4 Jun 1684

GOODSPEED, Benjamin (1649-) & Mary [**DAVIS**] (1654-), m/2 John **HINCKLEY** 1697; ca 1676 (doubtful); Barnstable

GOODSPEED, Ebenezer (1655-) & Lydia **CROW/CROWELL**; 15 Feb 1677, - Feb 1677, 1677/8; Yarmouth/Barnstable

GOODSPEED, John (1645-1719) & Experience **HOLLEY** (-1719+); 9 Jan 1668, 1668/9; Barnstable

GOODSPEED, John (1673-1721) & Remembrance/Remember (**JENNING/JENNEY**) **BUCK** (1668-), w Joseph; 16 Feb 1697, 1696/7; Barnstable/Sandwich

GOODSPEED, Nathaniel (1642-1670) & Elizabeth **BURSLEY** (1649-), m/2 Increase **CLAPP** 1675; - Nov 1666; Barnstable

GOODSPEED, Roger & Alice **LAYTON** (-1689); - Dec 1641; Barnstable

GOODWIN, Adam (1617-) & Margaret __?__; b Jul 1650; Providence

GOODWIN, Christopher[1] (-1692+) & Mary __?__ (1617/18-1682/3, ae 65); b 1642; Charlestown

GOODWIN, Christopher[2] (?1649-1703) (ae 35 in 1682) & 1/wf Mercy **CROUCH** (-1678, ae 25); 11 May 1672, 1671; Charlestown

GOODWIN, Christopher[2] (?1649-1703) & 2/wf Joanna (**LONG**) **JOHNSON** (?1646-), w Nathaniel; 10 Dec 1678; Charlestown

GOODWIN, Daniel & 1/wf Margaret [**SPENCER**]; b 1656, b 1654?, m cont, b 1654-55; Kittery, ME

GOODWIN, Daniel & Sarah (**SANDERS/SAUNDERS**) [**TURBET**], w Peter; ca Mar 1670, aft Jul 1672; Kittery, ME

GOODWIN, Daniel & Amy **THOMPSON**; 17 Oct 1682; Kittery, ME

GOODWIN, Edward & 1/wf __?__; b 1657, b 1655?; ?Newbury/Salisbury

GOODWIN, Edward & 2/wf Susanna (**STOWERS**) **WHEELER**, w George, ?m/3 Gregory **COOKE** 1681, m/4 Henry **SPRING** 1691; 5 Jun 1668; Newbury

GOODIN, Edward (-1694) (calls John **CLEASBY** of Boston "brother") & Elizabeth __?__; b 1676; Boston

GODWIN, George (-1658) & [Ellen **SMITH**]; ?21 Feb 1651, b 1650?, 1651/2; Hartford/Fairfield, CT

GOODWIN/GOODING?, George & Deborah **WALKER**; 9 Feb 1685/6; Taunton

GOODIN/GODDIN?/GODDEN?/GIDDING?/GOODING?, Henry & Elizabeth **BEERS**, ?m/2 __?__ **PECK**?; 7 Apr 1663; Watertown/Fairfield, CT

GOODING/GOODWIN, James & Mehitable [**GOULD**]; prob b 1675; Charlestown

GOODWIN, James (-1697) & Sarah **THOMPSON**, m/2 William **HEARL**; 9 Dec 1686, 11 Dec 1686; Berwick, ME

GOODWIN/GOODING, James & Margaret **DAVENPORT**; m int 23 Jan 1695/6; Boston

GOODWIN, John[2] (?1647-1712) & Martha **LATHROP** (1652-1728), m/2 Dea. John **PEARSON** 1714; 2 Dec 1669; Charlestown/Boston

GOODWIN, John (-1712, ae 65) & Hannah __?__; b 1682; Boston

GOODWIN, John[3] (1675-1757) & Tabitha **PEIRSON** (1680-1769); 25 May 1696; Reading

GOODWIN, John (1672-1757) & 1/wf Sarah [**SKINNER**?] (-1735); ca 1698; Hartford/E. Hartford

GODWIN, John & __?__; b 1700; Eastchester, NY/Fairfield

GOODWYN, John & Mary HOPKINS; 23 May 1700; Boston
GOODWIN, Joseph (-1711) & Margaret [TROWBRIDGE] (1666-); b 1695; New Haven
GOODWIN, Moses (-1726) & Abigail TAYLOR (-1730+); 7 Sep 1694; Kittery, ME
GOODWIN, Nathaniel (1637-1714) & 1/wf Sarah [COWLES/COLES?] (1644-1676); b 1665, 1664; Hartford/Hadley/Hatfield
GOODWIN, Ens. Nathaniel² (?1642-1693) & 1/wf Mary _?_ (-1675) (see below); 18 Oct 1665; Reading
GOODWIN, Nathaniel² (?1642-1693) & 1/wf Mary LUNT (1648-1675) (see above); 19 Dec 1665, 18 Oct 1665; Reading
GOODWIN, Nathaniel² (?1642-1693) & 2/wf Susanna [KENDALL] (1658-1732), m/2 Timothy WILEY 1696?; 25 Oct 1676; Reading
GOODWIN, Nathaniel (1637-1714) & 2/wf Elizabeth [PRATT]; aft 1676, b 1682; Hartford/Hadley
GOODWIN, Nathaniel (1660-1747) & Mehitable [PORTER] (1673-1726); ca 1688/9; Hartford/Hadley
GOODWIN, Nathaniel (1665-) & 1/wf Lois [PORTER] (1670-1697); b 1691, b 1689?; Hartford
GOODWIN, Nathaniel & 1/wf Elizabeth EMES; m int 9 Jan 1695/6; Boston
GOODWIN, Nathaniel (1665-) & 2/wf Sarah EASTON (1675-); 14 Sep 1699; Hartford
GOODWIN, Ozias (1596-1683) & Mary [WOODWARD]; in Eng, b 1629; Hartford
GOODWIN, Philip & Elizabeth LUXFORD; 14 Jun 1694; Cambridge/Boston
GOODWIN, Richard & Bridget [FITTS?], m/2 Henry TRAVERS/TRAVIS, m/3 Richard WINDOW 1659; b 1640, in Eng; Gloucester
GODINGE, Richard & Hannah JONS/JONES (ca 1645-1725); 20 Nov 1666; Gloucester
GOODWIN, Richard² & Mary FOWLER; 14 Nov 1677; Amesbury
GOODWIN, Richard & Hannah MAJOR (1673-); 26 Mar 1692; Newbury
GOODWING, Robert & Margaret (FLINT) NORMAN (-1705), dau Wm.; 15 Oct 1685; Marblehead
GODWIN, Samuel & 1/wf _?_ GRAY; b 1677; Eastchester, NY/Fairfield
GOODWIN/GODEN, Robert/Samuel & 2/wf? Sarah [FOWLER], m/2 Edward HANCOCK 1692?; b 1682?; Fairfield/Eastchester, NY
GOODWIN, Thomas & Ruth ROGERS, m/2 Obadiah WHEELER, m/3 Ephraim STILES 1669; 9 Nov 1661; Milford, CT
GOODWIN, Thomas & Mehitable [PLAISTED] (1670-); ca 1685, b 1697, b 1690; Kittery, ME
GOODWIN, Timothy² (1662-1701) & 1/wf Elizabeth [BARTLETT] (-1688, ae 18 y 11 m), dau Robert; ca 1687; Marblehead
GOODIN, Timothy² (1662-1701) & Sarah (WALDRON) LEACH (1668-), w John; 7 Feb 1688/9; Marblehead
GOODWIN, William, Bocking & Elizabeth WHITE (1591/2-); Eng, 7 Nov 1616
GOODWIN, William (-1673, 1689?, Farmington) & Susanna (GARBRAND) [HOOKER] (1616-1676, (not 1698)), m/3 John SHEPARD (no); aft 7 Jul 1647, bef 1658; Cambridge/Hartford
GOODWIN, William (1658?-1733) & Elizabeth [SHEPARD] (1660-1742); ?Jul 1680, 1684?; Hartford
GOODWIN, William & Deliverance [TAYLOR] (1670±-); b 1687, Oct 1687; Kittery, ME
GOODWIN, William & Susanna FEUENS, m/2 John SHEPARD; b 1658
GOODWIN, _?_ & Bethiah SMITH, m/2 Caleb STODDARD 1684
GOODYEAR, John (1650-1702) & Abigail GIBBARD (1660-betw 1716 & 1719); 26 Jun 1683; New Haven
GOODYEAR, Stephen (-1658) & 1/wf Mary _?_ (-1646); ca 1632?, in Eng, b 1628; New Haven
GOODYEAR, Stephen (-1658) (returned to Eng) & 2/wf Margaret (LEWEN) [LAMBERTON] (ae 56 in 1670), w George; ca 1648, 1647; New Haven
GOOKIN, Daniel¹ (?1612-1687) & 2/wf? Mary [?DOLLING/DOLLENGER?] (-1683); London, ?m lic 11 Nov 1639; Cambridge/Roxbury
GOOKIN, Daniel² (-1718) & 1/wf Elizabeth [QUINCY] (-1691); 1681?, 4 Oct 1682 (no); Cambridge/Sherborn
GOOKIN, Daniel¹ (1612-1687) & 1/wf? Hannah (TYNG) [SAVAGE] (-1688, 1689, ae 48), w Habyah; b 10 Apr 1685, 1684?, betw 28 Jun & 13 Aug 1685; Cambridge
GOOKIN, Daniel (-1718) & 2/wf Bethiah COLLICUT (-1729); 21 Jul 1692; Sherborn
GOOKIN, Nathaniel (1656-1692) & Hannah SAVAGE (1667-1702); 3 Aug 1685?, aft ?13 Aug; Cambridge
GOOKIN, Samuel (1652-1730) & 1/wf Mary [?LARKIN]; b 1679; Cambridge

GOOSS, John & 1/wf Mary ROBISSON (1643-1665); 18 Jun 1665; Salem
GOOSE, John & 2/wf Sarah TRERICE (-1686); 10 Aug 1666; Charlestown
GOOSE, Joseph (-1685?) & Mary _?_; b 1683; Charlestown
GOOSE, William (-1645) & Mary _?_, m/2 John JACKSON bef 1655; b 1643; Salem
GOOSE, William & 1/wf Susanna [JONES] (-1674, ae 34); b 1658?, b 1664; Charlestown
GOOSE, William & 2/wf Mary KING, m/2 Solomon GREEN 1679; 21 Sep 1677; Charlestown
GOURDING, Abraham & Elizabeth [BURRILL]; b 1685(6?); Boston
GOURDEN, Abraham/Abram & Abigail TOWERS; 5 Jan 1692; Boston
GOURDEN, Abraham & Sarah HODDER; 12 May 1698; Boston
GORDON, Alexander (-1697) & [Mary LISSON/?LYSSON]; b 1664(5?), b 10 Oct 1664, b 1663?; Exeter, NH
GORDEN, Alexander (1675-) & 1/wf Sarah SEWALL (1676-); 14 Sep 1699
GORDON, James (1673-) & Abial/Abiel REDMAN (1681-), m/2 Moses KIMMIN; 7 Aug 1700; Hampton, NH/Exeter
GOORDING, John (1670?-) & Sarah ALLEN; 23 Dec 1697; Salisbury
GORDEN, Lott & Elizabeth _?_; b 1675; Boston
GORDEN, Miles & Elizabeth SMITH; 16 Oct 1693; Taunton
GORDEN, Nicholas (1666-) & 1/wf Sarah (HALE) SEWALL, w Edward; aft 20 Jun 1656; Exeter, NH
GORDON, Thomas (1678-1762), Exeter & 1/wf Elizabeth HERRIMAN/HARRIMAN; 22 Nov 1699; Haverhill
GORDON, _?_ & _?_ SUNDERLAND
GORDON, _?_ & Joanna?/Hannah? _?_, m/2 Moses PHILLIPS; b 1691
GORE, John (-1657) & Rhoda _?_, m/2 John REMINGTON 1657+, by 1659, m/3 Edward PORTER?; in Eng, b 1634; Roxbury
GORE, John (1634-1705) & Sarah GARDNER (1662-); 31 May 1683; Roxbury
GORE, Samuel (1638-1692) & Elizabeth WELD, m/2 _?_ TUCKER; 28 Aug 1672; Roxbury
GOREN/GORIN/GOING/GORHAM?, Henry & _?_; b 1679; Windsor, CT
GOROM, Jabez (1656-1725) & Hannah (STURGIS) GRAY (-1736), w John; b 1677; Yarmouth/Bristol, RI
GORHAM, James (1650-1707) & Hannah HUCKENS/HUCKINS (1653-1727/8); 24 Feb 1665, prob 1674/5; Barnstable
GORHAM, John (?1621-1676) & Desire [HOWLAND] (?1624-1683); ca 1643; Plymouth/Marshfield/Yarmouth/Barnstable
GORHAM, John (1652, 1651/2-1716) & Mary/?Mercy OTIS (1653-1738); 24 Feb 1674, prob 1674/5; Barnstable
GORHAM, John & Desire HOWLAND
GORHAM, Joseph (1654-1726) & Sarah [STURGES] (?1656-1739); b 1678(9?); Yarmouth
GORHAM, Ralph (?1575-1643?) & Margaret STEPHENSON; Oundle, Eng, 23 May 1610; Duxbury
GORHAM, Shubael (1667-bef 7 Aug 1750) & Priscilla HUSSEY (-bef 23 Sep 1748); - May 1695; Barnstable
GOWAN, Henry & _?_; b 1679; Windsor, CT
GORING/GOING, William (1679-1715?) & Sarah BUELL, m/2 Elias SLATER; 11 Sep 1700; Windsor, CT/Simsbury
GURNELL/GORNELL, John (1611-1675) & Jane _?_ (-1678, ae 78), m/2 John BURGE 1677; b 1643?; Dorchester/Weymouth
GORTON, Abraham & Mary SUMNER (1664-) 31 May 1683; Roxbury/Billerica
GORTON, Benjamin (-1699) & Sarah CARDER (-1724); 5 Dec 1672; Warwick, RI
GORTON, Benjamin (-1734, 1737) & Ann [LANCASTER?] (-1737+) (had son Lancaster); b 1701?; Warwick, RI/E. Greenwich, RI/Norwich, CT
GORTON, John (-1676) & Mary _?_; b 1636; Roxbury
GORTON, John (-1714) & Margaret WHEATON/WEEDEN?/WOOTEN?; 28 Jun 1668, ?20 Jan 1668; Warwick, RI
GORTON, John & Patience HOPKINS, Providence; 2 Feb 1699, 1699/1700; Warwick, RI
GORTON, Othniel (1669-1733) & 1/wf Mercy [BURLINGAME]; b 1693; Warwick, RI
GORTON, Samuel (1692-) & Mary MAPLET/MAYPLETT (1609-); in Eng, b 1630?, b 11 Jan 1629/30; Plymouth/Providence
GORTON, Samuel (?1630-1724) & Susannah BURTON (1665-1739), m/2 Richard HARRIS; 11 Dec 1684; Warwick, RI

GORTON, Samuel (1672-1721) & Elizabeth COLLINS (1672-1724); 9 May 1695; Warwick, RI

GORTON, Thomas & Agnes GRIMSHAW; Manschester, Eng, 14 Sep 1612; Portsmouth, RI

GOSARD/GODARD, Nicholas & Elizabeth _?_ ; b 1672/3; Simsbury, CT

GAZEAU/GEFFEERE/GOSIER/?GEFFREY, Bastian & Elizabeth _?_ ; b 1686, b 1687, b 1689, b 1690; Boston

GOSLING/GOSLEE/GOSLINE/?GORSLINE, Henry (-1724) & Mary FOX, Glastonbury; 25 Feb 1694/5; Glastenbury, CT

GOSMER, John & Elizabeth WOODRUFF; St. Mary, Northgate, Eng, 24 Oct 1611; Southampton, LI

GOSS, James & Elizabeth _?_ , m/2 John FOST/FOSS 1687, m/3 James EMERY; b 1687 (see James GOFFE); NH

GOSS, John (-1644, 1645?) & Sarah _?_ , m/2 Robert NICHOLS 1644+; b 1631; Watertown

GOSS, Philip (-1698) & 1/wf Hannah [HOPKINS] (1657-), dau William, m/2 John MURRAY; b 1677, div 1690; Boston

GOSS, Philip (-1698) & 2/wf Mary PRESCOT (1669-), m/2 John HOUGHTON, Jr. 1698; 29 Mar 1690; Concord/Lancaster

GOSS, Philip (1677-1747) & Judith HAYWARD (1675-1745); 30 Aug 1699; Concord/Lancaster/Brookfield

GOSS, Richard & 1/wf _?_ ; b 1662

GOSS, Richard & Jane (WILFORD) [PIVERLY], w Thomas; aft 30 Jun 1670; Portsmouth, NH

GOSS, Richard (1662-1715) & [Martha FOSS]; ca 1695/1700?, by Dec 1693; Gloucester

GOSS, Robert & Jane BERRY; 5 Jan 1692/3; Dover, NH

GOSSWELL, Adam & Abigail WISE; 19 Nov 1686; Ipswich

GOSWELL, Jonathan & _?_ ; b 1687; Ipswich

GOSWELL, William & _?_ ; b 1688; Ipswich

GOTT, Charles[1] (-1668) (called cousin of Andrew[2] MANSFIELD) & Gift PALMER (-1668+) (?m/2 Mary _?_ (no)); St. Andrew the Great, Cambridge, 30 Oct 1625; Salem

GOTT, Charles[2] (1639-1708) & 1/wf Sarah DENNIS (-1665); 12 Nov 1659; Wenham

GOTT, Charles[2] (1639-1708) & 2/wf Lydia CLEARKE/CLARK (-1717/18); 25 Dec 1665; Lynn/Wenham

GOTT, Charles[3] (1662-1708) & Elizabeth [WARNER] (1666-); b 1696, b 1686; Wenham

GOTT, Daniel[2] (1646-1715+) & Elizabeth MORRIS (1643-), dau of Thos. MORRIS (relation of John MANSFIELD's wf); 2 Jan 1665/6; Lynn/Wenham

GOTT, John[3] (1668-1723) & Rebecca TARBOX (1672-), m/2 William FAIRFIELD; 19 Jul 1693; Salem

GOTT, Samuel[3] & Margaret ANDROSS/ANDREWS (-1716); m int 26 Jun 1697; Wenham

GOUGE, James, Wells & Hannah EMMONS; 10 Feb 1691/2; Charlestown/Wells, ME

GOOG, William (-1646) & Ann _?_ ; b 1640? Lynn

GOULD, Adam (-1748?) & Rebecca COOPER; ?15 Sep 1677, ?16 Sep 1677, ?17 Sep 1677, 15 Aug; Salem/Groton/Woburn

GOULD, Adam, Groton & Hannah KNIGHT, Woburn; 28 Sep 1687; Woborn/Groton

GOULD, Alexander & Margaret [BROWN], m/2 Morris CHAMBLET; b 1659; Pemaquid, ME

GOULD, Benjamin & Elizabeth [ROBINSON] (1662-1745); ca 1680/4?; Guilford, CT

GOULD, Benjamin (1669-) & Elizabeth _?_ (1664-1745); [ca 1690?]

GOULD/GOLD, Benjamin & Mary DINLEY/DINSLY; 5 May 1698, 16 Apr 1698; Boston

GOULD, Benjamin & Elizabeth _?_ ; b 1701; Martha's Vineyard

GOULD, Daniel/David (1665-1716, ae 90) & Wait COGGESHALL (1636-1718, ae 84); 18 Aug 1651, 18 Dec 1651; Portsmouth, RI/Newport

GOULD, Daniel (1656-1694) & Mary [CLARKE] (1661-1711), m/2 Ralph CHAPMAN; ca 1680, b 1681(2?); Newport

GOLD, Daniel (-1697) & Dorcas BELCHER (1656-1730(9) in Stoneham); b 1685; Reading/Charlestown

GOLD, Edward (1607-) & Margaret [BACON?], w George; b 1644; Hingham/Boston

GOULD, Edward (1651-) & _?_ ; ca 1670/80?; Star Island

GOLE/GOOLE?/GOLD?, Francis & Rose/?Mary _?_ ; b 1649(50?); Braintree/Dunstable

GOLD, Henry & Sarah WARR/WARD; 20 Sep 1675, 24 Sep 1675; Ipswich

GOULD, James (1666-) & Catharine [CLARKE] (1671-1752), m/2 Nathaniel SHEFFIELD; b 1696; Newport

GOULD, James & 1/wf Deborah _?_ ; b 1691(2?); Salem

GOOLD, Jarvis (1605-1656) & Mary _?_ ; b 1646; Boston/Hingham
GOULD, Jeremiah/Jeremy? & Priscilla GROVER; in Eng, 27 Nov 1604; Weymouth/Newport
GOULD, John (1610-) & 1/wf Grace _?_ (1610-); in Eng, b 1635; Charlestown
GOULD, John (1610-1690/1) & 2/wf? Mary _?_ (-1642); b 1636?, b 1637; Charlestown
GOULD, John (1610-1690/1) & Joanna _?_ (1608-1697); b 1644; Charlestown
GOULD, John (1635-1710) & Sarah BAKER (1641-1709); 14 Oct 1660, 12 Oct, 14 Oct; Ipswich
GOULD, John (-1712) & Abigail [BELCHER] (1653±-1657); b 1671; Reading/Charlestown
GOULD, John (-1680+) & Margaret [HAST] (-1671+), w Edward; b 1671
GOULD, John (1646-1711) & Mary CROSSMAN (1655-); 24 Aug 1673, 21 Aug, 24 Aug; Taunton
GOULD, John & Sarah [EXTELL]; b 1680; CT/LI/Elizabeth, NJ
GOULD, John (1662-1724) & Phebe FRENCH (1667-1718); 10 Nov 1684; Topsfield
GOULD, John (1659-1704) & Sarah PRIOR (1664-1714+), m/2 Walter CLARK 31 Aug 1711; 25 Jan 1685/6, 30 Aug 1686; Matinecock, LI
GOULD/GOOLL, John (-1689) & Elizabeth CUMMINGS, ?m/2 William BRUCE 1693; 2 Jul 1686; Dunstable
GOULD/GOLD, John (-1712) & 2/wf Martha REDINGTON (1655-); b 1691; Reading/Charlestown
GOULD, John (1671-) & Sarah _?_ ; b 1695; Charlestown
GOULD/GOOLD, John (1672-1762) & Lydia JACOB (19 Apr 1687-1742); 17 Jan 1698/9; Hingham/Hull
GOULD, Joseph (-1710) & Bethia RAYE (1662-), m/2 Joseph HUTCHINSON 1710; 12 May 1685, 22 May; Salem
GOLD, Nathan (-1693) & Elizabeth _?_ (-1692+); b 1650, b 1659?; Salisbury
GOULD, Richard (1662-) & Cruft _?_ ; in Eng, b 1693; Branford
GOOLD, Robert & 1/wf ?Mehitable/Experience/Elizabeth? [BOSWORTH] (bpt 1638, 1647 (no)-1681); b 1667, ca 1666; Hull/Hingham
GOULD, Robert & 2/wf Judith [HARVY/HERVEY] (1 Sep 1650-1734), w Wm.?, aft 7 Jun 1689, ca 1687, by 1695; Hull/Reading
GOULD, Robert (1667?-) & Jane (HARRIS) [SMITH], w John; b 1692; Hull
GOULD/GOOLE, Samuel, Dunstable & Mehitable BARRETT (1668-); 17 Mar 1680; Chelmsford/Dunstable
GOLD, Samuel & Sarah ROWELL; 6 Apr 1693; Amesbury
GOLD, Samuel & Elizabeth [THORNDIKE] (1670-); b 1695; Beverly/Hopkinton
GOULD, Samuel (1670-1724) & Margaret STONE (1678-); 20 Apr 1697; Topsfield
GOLD, Samuel & Mary CRISP (1678-); 1 Dec 1700; Eastham?/Topsfield?
GOULD, Thomas (1607-) & Mary _?_ ; b 1639; Cambridge
GOULD, Thomas & Hannah [MILLER?] (-1647); b 1641; Charlestown
GOULD, Thomas & ?Hannah _?_ ; ?b 1652, ca 1667?; Charlestown
GOULD, Thomas (-1674) & 2/wf Mary (?HARRIS) [HAYWARD?/HOWARD?]; b 1654; Charlestown
GOULD, Thomas (-1693) & Elizabeth (BALSTON) [COGGESHALL] (-1696+), div wf of John; 1655?; South Kingston, RI/Wishford, RI
GOOLD, Thomas (-1662) & Francis ROBINSON (-1671?, Guilford, CT); 10 Sep 1656; Boston
GOULD, Thomas (-1690) & Elizabeth _?_ ; b 1662/3; Salem
GOLD, Thomas & Experience [SUMNER] (1664-), m/2 Eleazer CARVER 1695; b 1687; Boston
GOULD, Thomas & Frances _?_ ; b 1685, b 1687; Boston
GOULD, Thomas (1655-1734) & Elizabeth MOTT (1672-1749); 13 Mar 1689/90; ?Newport, RI
GOULD, Thomas & Abigail [NEEDHAM] (1671-); b 1692; Salem
GOLD, Thomas (1667-1752) & 1/wf Mercy/Marcy YATES (?1675-); 2 Dec 1700; Eastham
GOULD, Thomas & [?Mercy SUMNER]; b 1701; Topsfield
GOLD, William & Mercy HARRIS; 16 Apr 1699; Boston
GOULD, Zaccheus (1589-1668, 1670?) & Phebe [DEACON] (-1663); in Eng, b 1620; Ipswich/Plymouth
GOULD, Zaccheus & _?_ ; b 1650; Lynn
GOULDER, Frances (-1664) & _?_ ; b 1650(1?); Plymouth
GOVE, Ebenezer (1670-) & Judith SANBORN (1675-); 20 Dec 1692; Hampton, NH
GOVE, Edward (-1691) (called "brother" of Nehemiah PARTRIDGE) & Hannah [PARTRIDGE/TITCOMB?] (-1712); b 1661; Hampton
GOVE, John (-1648) & 1/wf [Sarah MOTT?] (1601-); in Eng, ca 1625; Charlestown

GOVE, John (-1648) & 2/wf [Mary SHARD] (?1604-1681), m/2 John MANSFIELD 1648?; b 1627?,⁴ b 1645, 6 Feb 1630/1; Salisbury

GOAVE, John (1632-1704) & 1/wf Mary ASPINWALL (-1667); 6 Oct 1658; Cambridge

GOVE, John (-1704) & 2/wf Sarah (MERRIAM) [HALL] (1639-1676), w William; aft 10 Mar 1667, b 8 Oct 1675; Cambridge

GOVE, John (-1704) & 3/wf Mary (BROWN) WOODHEAD/WOODWARD? (1664-1700), w William, div?; 15 Mar 1677; Cambridge

GOVE, John (1661-1737) & Sarah [?RUSSELL], w William; b 1686?, b 1687?; Salisbury

GOVE, John (-1704) & 4/wf Elizabeth (SANDER) (BATSON) WALDEN/WALDON/WALDRON? (-1704?, 1725+), w ?John, w John; 2 Dec 1700; Cambridge

GOVE, Nathaniel (1667-1752) & 1/wf Mary _?_ ; b 1690; Watertown/Lebanon, CT

GOWELL, Richard & 1/wf _?_

GOWELL, Richard & 2/wf? Hannah [REMICK] THOMPSON? (1656-), ?w John; b 1678, b 1685, aft 17 Jun 1684; Kittery, ME

GOWING, Daniel & 1/wf Sarah STREETER/STREETTER; 15 Oct 1691; Lynn

GOWING, Daniel & 2/wf Mary WILLIAMS; m int 23 May 1698; Lynn

GOWEN alias SMITH, James (1675-) & Mary _?_/WHEELWRIGHT; b 1701?, 1701; Kittery, ME/Wells, ME

GOWINGE, John (1645-) & Johanna/Joanna _?_ ; b 1683; Lynn

GOWEN, John (1668-1733) & Mercy [HAMMOND] (?1670-); ca 1690, ?12 Oct 1691, 3 Oct 1693?, b 1692?; Kittery, ME

GOWING, Nathaniel & Martha PROCTER; 22 Jul 1686; Reading

GOWEN, Nicholas (?1668-1752) & Abigail HODSDON/[HODGDON]/COOK?; 1694; Kittery, ME

GOWING, Robert (1618-1698) & Elizabeth BROCK; 31 Oct 1644; Dedham

GOWEN alias SMITH, William (1634±-) & Elizabeth FROST (1645/6-); 14 May 1667; Kittery, ME

GOWEN, _?_ & Rebecca TARBOX; b 1670

GRAFFORT, Thomas (-1697, Boston) & Bridget (CUTTS) DANIEL, w Thomas; 11 Dec 1684; ?Portsmouth, NH

GRAFTON, John (1639-1715) & Seeth (GARDNER/GARDINER?) CONANT/?BALCH (1636-1707), w Joshua; 1 Dec 1659; Salem

GRAFTON, Joseph¹ & 1/wf Mary [MOORE] (-1674); in Eng, b 1622; Salem

GRAFTON, Joseph (1637-1670/1) & 1/wf Hannah HUBBARD/HOBART, dau Joshua; 29 Oct 1657, 30 Oct 1657; Salem/Hingham

GRAFTON, Joseph (1637-1670/1) & 2/wf Elizabeth BROWNE, m/2 Samuel GARDNER 1673; 30 Jun 1664; Salem/Hingham/Charlestown

GRAFTON, Joseph¹ (-1683) & 2/wf Bethiah (REA/RAY) [LOTHROP], w Thomas, m/3 William GOODHUE 1683?; aft 1675, b 11 Jun 1680; Salem

GRAFTON, Joseph (1658-) & Mary [BELKNAP] (1660-); b 1682; Salem/Boston

GRAFTON, Joshua (-1699) & Hannah GEDNY (1667-); 2 Aug 1686; Salem

GRAFTON, Nathaniel (1642-1671) & Elizabeth MAVERICK (1649-), m/2 Thomas SKINNER 1676?; 6 Apr 1665; Salem

GRAFTON/GRAFFAM, Stephen & Mary _?_, m/2 Richard ABBOTT

GRAHAM, Benjamin (-1725) & 1/wf Abigail HUMPHREY (-1696); 12 Feb 168[4?], prob 1684/5, 1687; Hartford/Windsor, CT

GRAHAM/GRIMES?, Benjamin (-1725) & 2/wf Sarah (MYGATT) WEBSTER, w John; 20 Nov 1698, 28? Nov; Hartford

GRAHAM, John & _?_ ; b 1692; Windsor, CT

GRAMES, Nathaniel & Martha _?_ (-1701, ae 75?); 16 Jan 1655, 1654/5; Wethersfield, CT

GRAMES, Samuel & Frances _?_ ; b 1639; Boston

GRANGER, George (1658-) & Lydia YOUNGLOVE; 26 Apr 1693, 29? Apr; Suffield, CT

GRANGER, John & Grace _?_ (-1648), wid; Scituate

GRANGER, John (-1725) & Martha POOR (1654-1723); 9 Feb 1679; Andover

GRANGER, Lanncelot (-1689, Suffield, CT) & Joanna ADAMS (1634-1701+); 4 Jan 1653, 1653/4?; Newbury/Suffield, CT

GRANGER, Samuel (1668-1721) & [?Ellen/?Esther HANCHETT] (1679-1715); 16 Mar 1700?, 16 May 1700?; Suffield, CT

GRANGER, Thomas (-1730) & Mindwell TAYLOR (1663-); 14 Nov 1683; Suffield, CT

GRANIS/GRANNIS, Edward (-1719) & 1/wf Elizabeth ANDREWS; 3 May 1655; Hartford

GRANIS, Edward (-1719) & Hannah [WAKEFIELD] (1644-1711); 1662; Hadley

GRANT, Benjamin & Mary BECKWITH, m/2 Samuel DANIELS 1681; ca 1664; New London, CT/Lyme, CT

GRANT, Benjamin & Priscilla MORSE; 14 Sep 1692; Medfield/Wrentham

GRANT, Benjamin & Elizabeth [PANTON]/Elizabeth FARRINGTON 1697; Westchester, NY, b 1694

GRANT, Caleb (1639-1694) & Mary _?_ (-1684); b 1671; Watertown

GRANT, Christopher (1608/10-1685) & Mary _?_ ; b 1635; Watertown

GRANT, Christopher & Martha (MILLS) [SMITH], w James; aft 10 Aug 1681; Kittery, ME

GRANT, Daniel (-1718) & Mary (GLOVER) DRIVER (-1707?, 1737+), w William; 6 Mar 1692/3; Salem

GRANT, Edward (-1682) & Sarah [WEARE] (-1682+); b 1658; Boston

GRANT, Francis & Susanna COMBS; 22 Oct 1668; Marblehead

GRANT, Francis (1673-1712) & Priscilla _?_ ; b 1705, 2 ch bpt, b 1701?; Marblehead

GRANT, Israel, Sandwich & Hannah COLEMAN, Scituate; 16 Jun 1690; RI

GRANT, James (-1683) & Elizabeth [EVERELL] (1641-), m/2 Edward TOOGOOD; ca 1660?; Kittery, ME?/York, ME?

GRANT, James, Scotchman (-ca 1663?) & Joan _?_ , m Peter GRANT 1664; ca 1661?, ca 1654?; Kittery, ME

GRANT, James (-aft 14 Apr 1693) & Hannah _?_ , m/2 Samuel JOHNSON 1693?; ca 1660/70?, 1694?; ?York, ME

GRANT, James & Sarah OTHEA (-1674/5); 28 Jan 1664; Dedham

GRANT, James (-1698) & Margaret WOOD; 5 Dec 1676; Dedham

GRANT, James & Joanna [INGLES]; b 1687; Boston

GRANT, James (1671±-) & 1/wf Mary NASON; 6 Oct 1693; Kittery, ME?

GRANT, John (1628-1697) & Mary _?_ (-1698) (sister of Ann, wf of Thomas WOOD); ca 1650-60?, no issue; Rowley

GRANT, John (1642-1684) & Mary HULL (1648-), m/2 John CROSS 1686; 2 Aug 1666; Windsor, CT

GRANT, John (1664-1695) & Elizabeth SKINNER, m/2 Joshua WELLES 1697; 3 Jun 1690, 5 Jun? (wrong); Windsor, CT

GRANT, John & Sarah [GOODRIDGE]; b 1691, ca 1690; Newbury

GRANT, Joseph & Mary GRAFTON/GRAFFAM? (1664-); 24 Dec 1684; Watertown

GRANT, Joseph & Hannah [DASSETT], dau John; b 1691; Boston

GRANT, Joshua (1637-1676) & _?_ /Sarah [BECKWITH]?; ca 1660/5?; Kennebec River, ME

GRANT, Josiah (1668-1732) & Rebecca MINOR (1672-1747); 8 Jul 1696; Stonington, CT/Windsor, CT

GRANT, Matthew (1601-1681) & 1/wf Priscilla _?_ (1601-1644, ae 43); in Eng, 16 Nov 1625; Dorchester/Windsor, CT

GRANT, Matthew (1601-1681) & 2/wf Susanna (CAPEN) ROCKWELL (1602-1666), w William; 29 May 1645; Windsor, CT

GRANT, Matthew (1666-1735) & Hannah CHAPMAN (1671-1752); Oct 1690, 1? Oct, 29 Oct; Windsor, CT

GRANT, Nathaniel (1672-) & Bethia WARNER; 12 Oct 1699, 16 May 1699; Windsor, CT

GRANT, Peter (1631-) & 1/wf _?_ ; b 1661; Kittery, ME

GRANT, Peter (-1681) & Mary _?_ , m/2 William RANDALL 1681+; b 1663; ?Boston/Hartford/Windsor, CT

GRANT, Peter (1631-1712) & 2/wf Joan [GRANT], w James?; ca 1664, 28 Nov 1664; Kittery, ME

GRANT, Peter & Sarah (ADAMS) (WACUM) SCARLET, w _?_ , w _?_ ; 25 Jul 1694; Boston

GRANT, Peter & Mary [THOMAS]; b 1701?; Newcastle, NH

GRANT, Robert & Mary FOSTER (1669-); 27 Feb 168[6?]; Ipswich

GRANT, Roger & Joan _?_ (1628?-), m/2 Andrew DIAMOND ca 1668; ca 1648?; Isles of Shoals

GRANT, Samuel (1631-1718) & Mary PORTER; 27 May 1658; Windsor, CT

GRANT, Samuel, Jr. (1659-1710) & 1/wf Anna/Hannah FILLEY (-1686); 6 Dec 1683; Windsor, CT

GRANT, Samuel (1659-1710) & 2/wf Grace MINOR (1669/70-1753); 11 Apr 1688, ?Stonington, CT; Windsor, CT

GRANT, Seth (-1646) & _?_ ; Hartford

GRANT, Tahan (1633-1693) & 1/wf Hannah/?Anna PALMER; 22 Jan 1663, 1662/3; Windsor, CT

GRANT, Tahan (1665-) & Hannah [BISSELL] (1670/1-), m/2 Samuel BANCROFT b 1698; ca 1690; Windsor, CT
GRANT, Thomas (160[-]+-bef 1643?) & Jane HABURNE (-1696?, 1698?); 21 Sep 1624, b 1634?, b 1628, b 1631?; Rowley
GRANT, Thomas (-1690) & [Sarah BROOKS], m/2 Samuel LYON 1692; b 1668; Rehoboth
GRANT, Thomas (1670-) & Sarah PINNEY; 13 Feb 1695/6; Windsor, CT
GRANT, William & Sarah BROWN; 29 Mar 1634; Braintree
GRANT, William & 1/wf Jane WARREN; 4 Aug 1690; ?Kittery, ME
GRANT, William, Berwick & Martha NELSON; 26 Dec 1695; ?Kittery, ME/York Co., ME
GRANT, _?_ (had Matthew) & _?_ ; in Eng, b 1601; Windsor, CT
GRANTHAM, John & Martha BANT; 8 Dec 1690; Boston
GRAVENER/?GROSVENOR, Richard & Sarah SMITH, ?m/2 Richard ALLEN 1711; 28 Dec 1699; Charlestown
GRAVES, Abraham & Anne/Ann HEAWARD/HAYWARD; 28 Jun 1677; Concord/Andover
GRAUES, Benjamin & Mary HOARE; 21 Oct 1668; Concord/Sudbury, MA/Saybrook, CT
GRAVES, Daniel & Mary [COLTON] (1671-); ca 1688/91?
GRAVES, Daniel (1664-) & Hannah WARRINER (1675-); b 1698(9?), int 27 Nov 1696, 25 Jan 1696, 1696/7; Springfield
GRAVES, Ebenezer (1666-) & Mary [COLTON] (1671-); 22 Mar 1693/4; Springfield/Bromfield
GRAVES, Francis (nephew of Samuel HALL) & Amy (ONION)/(DAVIS?) PUDDINGTON/ PURINGTON, w Robert; 27 Aug 1689; Dover, NH
GRAVES, George[1] (?1605-1673) & _?_ (-bef 1629?); in Eng; Hartford/Middletown, CT
GRAVES, George[1] (-1673) & 2/wf Sarah [ANDREWS?]; b 1640, b 12 Feb 1669/70; Hartford
GRAVE, George[2] (-1692) & Elizabeth VENTRES/VENTRISS?; 2 Apr 1651; Hartford/Middletown, CT
GRAVES, Isaac (ca 1620-1677) & Mary [CHURCH]; b 1697; Hartford/Deerfield/Wethersfield, CT/Hatfield
GRAVES, Isaac (?1656-) & 1/wf Sarah WYATT (-1690); 1 Apr 1679, 5 Apr; Hadley
GRAVES, Isaac & 2/wf Abigail _?_ (-1697); b 1691?; Hadley
GRAVES, Isaac & 3/wf Deliverance (_?_) GRAVES, w Samuel; aft 13 Jul 1697, b 1701?; Hadley
GRAVES/CRANE?, James, Hartford & Rebecca STILWELL; 23 Mar 1644; NY?
GRAVES, John (-1644) & 1/wf Mary _?_ (-1633, 1634); in Eng, b 1623?; Roxbury
GRAVES, John (-1644) & 2/wf Judith ALWARD/ALLARD?, m/2 William POTTER 1646; Dec 1635; Roxbury
GRAVES, John & _?_ ; b 1645; Concord
GRAVES, John (ca 1622-1677) & 1/wf Mary [SMITH] (?1630-1660, 1668?); b 1653; Wethersfield, CT/Hadley/Hatfield/Deerfield
GRAVES, John (?1633-1695?) & 1/wf Elizabeth STILLWELL (-1669); 26 Nov 1657; Guilford, CT
GRAVES, John (-1677) (see below) & Mary (BRONSON) WYATT, w John, m/3 William ALLES 1678, m/4 Samuel GAYLORD 1681/[2?]; 20 Jul, ?25 Jul 1671, ca 1668, 20 Jul 1671?; Hadley
GRAVES, John (?1633-1695) & 2/wf Elizabeth [CRUTTENDEN] (1639±-), m/2 John SPERRY, m/3 Benjamin BENNETT/BURNETT/BURNELL?; 1669?; Hartford/Guilford, CT
GRAVES, John & Mary CHAMBERLING/CHAMBERLAIN; 1 Dec 1671; Concord
GRAVE, John (-1702) & 1/wf Susannah [WEBSTER] (1658-); ca 1675/80?, 11 May 1681; ?Hartford
GRAVES, John (see above) & Mary (BRONSON) [WYATT], w John, m William ALLES/Samuel GAYLORD; b 1678, 20 Jul 1671; Haddam, CT/Deerfield/Hatfield
GRAVES, John (bef 1654-) & _?_
GRAVES, John (ca 1652-1730) & Sarah WHITE (1661-1741); 12 Feb 1677/8, 12 Feb 1678; Hatfield/Hadley/Deerfield
GRAVES, John (1660-ca 1699) & Martha MITTON (-1700); ca 1681?, ca 1700?; Ipswich/Casco?/ Berwick/?Portsmouth, NH/Kingston, RI/?Portland, ME
GRAVE, John & Elizabeth FOOT (1664-1730); 6 Jan 1685, 1684/5, 1684?, 6 Jan 1684/5, 12 Jan 1684/5; Guilford, CT
GRAVES, John & Sarah BAUKE/BAWKE?/BANKS?; 25 Oct 1686, 26 Oct; Chelmsford/Hatfield
GRAVE, John & 2/wf Hannah DAVIS; 1690; Guilford, CT
GRAVES, Jonathan (1667-1737) & 1/wf Sarah [PARSONS] (1678-1711); b 1700(01?); Hadley/Deerfield

GRAVES, Joseph & 1/wf Elizabeth **MAYNARD** (1649-1676); 15 Jan 1665, 15 Jan 1666, 15 Jan 1661; Sudbury

GRAVES, Joseph & 2/wf Mary [**ROSS**]; b 1678; Sudbury

GRAVE, Joseph & Margaret [**WILCOXSON**] (1673-1763); b 1699; Hartford/Guilford, CT

GRAVES, Mark (1617-) & Amy _?_ (-1665, Andover); b 1652; Lynn/Gloucester/Andover

GRAVES, Mark & Elizabeth (**KNIGHT**)? **FARRINGTON**, w John; 14 Nov 1667, 12 Nov 1667; Andover

GRAVES, Mark & Rebecca _?_ ; b 1690; Lynn

GRAVES, Nathaniel (1632, ?1629-1682) & Martha **BETTS**? (1625?-1701?); 16 Jan 1655; Wethersfield, CT

GRAVES, Nathaniel (-1679) & Elizabeth **RUSSELL** (-1714), m/2 John **HERBERT** 1684; 24 Aug 1664; Charlestown

GRAVE, Nathaniel (1678-) & Elizabeth [**BARNES**]; b 1701?; Hartford

GRAVES, Richard & Dorothy _?_, 3 ch bpt, 14 Mar 1641, b 1640; Salem/Boston

GRAVES, Richard & Dorothy _?_ ; b 1692; RI

GRAVES, Richard (1672-) & Joanna _?_ (-1728); b 1701; Sudbury

GRAVES, Samuel & _?_ ; b 1624; Lynn

GRAVES, Samuel (1628?, 1624, 1622?-) & Grace [**BEAMSLEY**] (1635-1730, ae 95, in 99th y?); b 14 Sep 1658; Ipswich

GRAVES, Samuel & Sarah **BRUER/BREWER**; 12 Mar 1677/8, 12 Mar 1678; Lynn

GRAVES, Samuel (1655-1692) & 1/wf Sarah **COLTON** (1653-1689); 1 Oct 1678, 30 Oct 1678; Hadley/Deerfield

GRAVES, Samuel (1658-) & 1/wf Joanna [**PIERCE**] (1659-); b 1683; Ipswich

GRAVES, Samuel (1657?-) & Sarah _?_ ; b 1688(9?); Hadley/Hatfield

GRAVES, Samuel (1655-1692) & 2/wf Deliverance _?_, m/3 Isaac **GRAVES**; 1 Jan 1690, 1 Jan 1689, 1689/90; Hadley/Hatfield

GRAVES, Samuel (1667-) & Anne [**STONE**] (1671-); ca 1700; Sudbury/Framingham

GRAVES, Thomas & _?_ ; in Eng, b 1620; Dorchester

GRAVES, Thomas (?1585-1662) & Sarah _?_ (-1666); b 1621, b 1620?; Hartford/Hadley/Hatfield

GRAVES, Thomas (1605-1653?) & Katharine [**GRAY**?] (1604, 1606?-1682); b 1632, b 1635, b 1631; Charlestown

GRAVES, Thomas (-1697) & 1/wf Elizabeth (**HAGBOURNE/HACKBURNE**) **CHICKERING/ CHICKEREY** (1635-1679, ae 44), w John; 16 May 1677; Charlestown

GRAVES, Thomas (-1697) & Sarah (**STEDMAN**) (**BENNETT**) **ALCOCK** (1644-1729/30, 1731?), w John, w Samuel, m/4 John **PHILLIPS** 1701; 15 May 1682; Charlestown

GRAVES, William & 2/wf Sarah **DIBBLE** (-1651, 1656), w John; 7 Nov 1647; Springfield

GRAVES, William (-1679) & 3/wf Ann/Anne [**STEVENSON**], w Edward; aft 10 Jul 1662, bef 31 Dec 1670; Newtown, LI

GRAVES, William & 1/wf Elizabeth [**YORK**], w Richard; bef 8 Jun 1681, bef Oct 1680; ?Exeter, NH

GRAVES, William & 2/wf _?_ (**ROBERTS**) (**SIAS**) [**DENBO**?], w Salathiel; York

GRAVES, William & Deliverance _?_ ; b 1695; Newtown, LI

GRAVES, _?_ (-1679) & Hannah **SCUDDER**

GRAY, Arthur & Hannah **HIDE**; 17 Nov 1668; Salem

GRAY, Benjamin (-1716/17) & Mary **BEADLE** (1673-1722+); 31 Mar 1699, ?1 Apr 1700, 1699?; Salem

GRAY, Edward (-1681, ae 52) & 1/wf Mary **WINSLOW** (-1663); 16 Jan 1650, 1650/1; Plymouth

GRAY, Edward (-1681, ae 52) & 2/wf Dorothy **LETTICE** (1648-1726), m/2 Nathaniel **CLARK**; 12 Dec 1665; Plymouth

GRAY, Edward & 1/wf Priscilla [**SPARROW**] (1658, 1658/9-); b 1681; Eastham

GRAY, Edward & 2/wf Melatiah **LEWIS**; 16 Jul 1684; Yarmouth/Eastham

GRAY, Edward (1667-1726) & 1/wf Mary [**SMITH**] (-living 1707); b 1691; Tiverton, RI

GRAY, Edward & Susanna **HARRISON** (1677-); 11 Aug 1699; Boston

GRAY, George (-1643) & Sarah _?_, m/2 Francis **HARLOW** by 1698; Jul 1672; Kittery, ME

GRAY, Henry (-1658) & Lydia **FROST**; 1639?; Fairfield, CT

GRAY, Henry (?1653-1731) & 1/wf _?_ ; b 1685; Fairfield, CT

GRAY, Henry & Mary **BLUNT** (1679-); 3 May 1699, 13 May 1699; Andover/Billerica

GRAY, Henry & 2/wf Hannah (**SANFORD**) **GUNN**, w Samuel; ca 1700, [b 1704], aft 12 Nov 1700; Fairfield, CT

GRAY, Jacob (-1712) & 1/wf Johanna [SMITH] (1649-); b 10 Sep 1669; Fairfield, CT
GRAY, Jacob (-1712) & 2/wf Sarah [BERTRAM/BARTRAM], w John; b 1677; Fairfield, CT
GRAY, Jeoffrey & Abigail (SHUTE) [SOLEY], w John; 1697; Charlestown
GRAY, John & Elizabeth (FROST) [WATSON], wid, m/3 John RAMSDEN; ?ca 1640; Fairfield, CT
GRAY, John (-1674) & [?Hannah LUMPKIN]; b 1648, b 1647? Yarmouth
GRAY, John & Hannah [STURGES?] (1654?-1735, 1736), m/2 Jabez GORHAM b 1677; b 1671; Harwich
GRAY, John (1661-) & Joanna MORTON; 9 Dec 1686; Plymouth
GRAY, John & Susannah [CLARKE] (-1731); b 1691; Harwich
GRAY, Joseph & 1/wf Rebecca HILL (-13 May 1676); 25 Feb 1667; Taunton
GRAY, Joseph (-1690) & Deborah WILLIAMS, m/2 James HOLGRAVE 1690; 10 Aug 1675; Salem
GRAY, Joseph & 2/wf Hester/Esther [THAYER] (1636-); aft 13 May 1676, bef 20 May 1695; Taunton
GRAY, Joseph & Mary _?_; prob bef 1701; Taunton/Boston
GRAY, Robert (-1662) & Elizabeth _?_, m/2 Nicholas MANNING 1663 (relative of Thomas WICKES); b 1651(2?); Salem/Andover
GRAY, Robert (-1679+) & Hannah HOLT; 8 Mar 1668; Salem
GRAY, Robert (-1725) & Sarah GROVER (1666-1728+); 7 Aug 1685; Salem
GRAY, Robert & Dorothy COLLINS; m int 19 Oct 1700; Lynn
GRAY, Samuel (-1672) & Abigail LORD; 28 Dec 1671, ?28 Oct; Salem
GRAY, Samuel (?1657-) & Susanna [LANGDON]; b 1682, b 1685, ca 1686?; Boston
GRAY, Samuel, Salem & Susanna BASTER, w John; 15 Apr 1695; Boston
GRAY, Samuel (-1712) & Deborah CHURCH, m/2 Daniel THROOP/TROOPE; 13 Jul 1699; Little Compton, RI
GRAY, Thomas (1669-1721), Plymouth & 1/wf Anna/Ann/Anne LITTLE (1672-1706), Marshfield; 3 Jul 1694; Boston/Little Compton, RI
GRAY, William (1650-1723) & Rebecca [DILLINGHAM], dau John; ca 1690?; Harwich
GRAY, Thomas (d in Eng) & Katherine [MILES], m Rowland COTYMORE/COITMORE 1610; in Eng, b 1606, by 1592; Charlestown
GRAZILLIER, Ezekiel & Mary _?_; b 1688; Boston
GRELEE, Andrew (1619/20-1697) & Mary [MOYSE] (-1703); b 1644; Salisbury
GRELE, Andrew (1646-) & Sarah BROWN (1654-); 12 Jun 1673; Salisbury
GREELEY, Benjamin (-1690) & Elizabeth SMITH, m/2 Daniel WOODWARD?; 24 Jan 1681; Haverhill
GREELEY, Jonathan (1673-) & Jane WALKER; 21 Mar 1697/8; Salisbury
GREELEY, Joseph & Martha WILLSFORD (1670-); 7 Feb 1694/5; Haverhill
GRELE, Philip (1644-) & Sarah ILSLY (1644-); 17 Feb 1669/70; Salisbury
GREELEY, Thomas & Rebecca _?_; ca 1699?; Portsmouth, NH
GREEN, Abraham & Esther SWETT; 9 Jul 1668; Hampton, NH
GREEN, Bartholomew & Elizabeth _?_ (-1677, ae 88); b 1620; Cambridge
GREEN, Bartholomew (-1713) & Maria MATHER, m Richard FIFIELD 1713; 4 Dec 1688; Charlestown
GREEN, Bartholomew (1666-1732), printer & Mary [SHORT]; b 1690; Cambridge/Boston
GREEN, Benjamin & 1/wf Susanna ROBERTS (-1694); 10 Apr 1683; Stamford, CT
GREEN, Benjamin (-1718) & Humility [COGGESHALL] (1671-); ca 1687; N. Kingston, RI
GREEN, Benjamin (1666-1757) & Susanna HOLDEN (1670-1734); 21 Jan 1689; Warwick, RI
GREEN, Benjamin & Hester CLEMENCE/CLEMENTS; 26 Mar 1696; Stamford, CT
GREEN, Benjamin & Elizabeth LOBDELL; 8 Jun 1699; Cambridge
GREEN, Benjamin (1678-) & Joanna PARNELL; 27 Oct 1699; Salem
GREEN, Charles & Esther [YEO] (1655-); by Jul 1675; Marblehead/Edgartown
GREEN, Daniel (-1730) & Rebecca BARROW (-1724+); 16 Jul 1689; Kingston, RI/N. Kingston
GREEN, David (1677-) & 1/wf Mary SLOCUM (1679-); 7 Jan 1698, 3 Jan 1698/9; Jamestown, RI
GREEN, Edmund (-1668) & Lydia TUCKEY (1650-), m/2 Richard WEBBER by 1674; ?ca 1667; Newcastle, ME
GREEN, Edward (-1711+) & Mary [TIBBETTS]; b 1680; Kings Town, RI/_?_, NY
GREEN, Eleazer (1672-1739) & Elizabeth [PRESCOTT] (1676-1744); ca 1694-5; Groton
GREEN, Henry (1620-1700) (called "uncle" by Giles FIFIELD, 1660) & 1/wf Mary _?_ (-1690); b 1644; Hampton, NH

GREEN, Henry (-1648) & Frances [STONE] (1619-), m/2 John HORNE/ORNE; ca 1645; Watertown/Reading

GREEN, Henry (1638-1717) & Hester HASSE/Esther HASEY? (1649/50-1748); 11 Jan 1671/2; Malden

GREEN, Henry (1620-1700) & 2/wf Mary (HUSSEY) PAGE, w Thomas, m/3 Henry DOW; 10 Mar 1690/1; Hampton, NH

GREEN, Henry & Hannah FLAGG (1675-); 9 Jan 1695/6; Malden/Killingly, CT

GREEN, Isaac & Mary/Mery/Haercy CASS; 18 Feb 1673; Salisbury

GREEN, Isaac (1663-1740) & 1/wf Sarah __?__; b 1694; Charlestown/Falmouth, MA

GREEN, Jabez (1673-) & Mary BARTON (1648-1713); 17 Mar 1697/8; Warwick, RI

GREEN, Jacob & Elizabeth (HOPKINS) [LONG], w Robert; b 1654; Charlestown

GREEN, Jacob & Mary [WHIPPLE], w Matthew; betw 1658 & 1661; Charlestown

GREEN, Jacob (-1702) & Mary ROBINSON (1659-); 8 Jan 1676/7; Charlestown

GREEN, Jacob (-1726) & Sarah __?__ (-1723); b 1693; Hampton, NH

GREEN, James (-1687, ae 77) (uncle of Henry WAY) & Elizabeth [NEWMAN]; ?Stroud, Eng, b 1642; Charlestown/Malden

GREENE, James (1626-1698) & 1/wf Deliverance [POTTER] (1637-1664±); ca 1658; Warwick, RI

GREENE, James & Rebecca JONES (1642-); 9 Nov 1661; Boston

GREEN, James (1626-1638) & 2/wf Elizabeth ANTHONY (1646±-1698?); 3 Aug 1665; Warwick, RI

GREEN, James (1655-1728) & 1/wf Elizabeth __?__; ?ca 1676; N. Kings Town, RI

GREEN, James & Anna/Hannah [GREENWOOD] (1669-1707), m/2 Nathaniel HENCHMAN 1694; b 1688; Boston

GREEN, James, Jr. (1659-1712) & Mary FONES (-1721); 29 Jan 1689; Warwick, RI

GREEN, Job (1656-1745) & Phebe SAYLES, Providence; 22 Jan 1684/5; Warwick, RI

GREEN, John (1590-1658) & 1/wf Joan TATTERSALL (-1633+); Salisbury, Eng, 4 Nov 1619; Salem/Warwick, RI

GREEN, John & 1/wf Perseverance [JOHNSON]; in Eng, b 1625; Charlestown

GREEN, John & __?__; in Eng, b 1625; Kittery, ME

GREEN, John & Elizabeth __?__ (-1681, ae 63), m/2 Jacob LEAZER 1637; Hadley, Eng, ?ca 1634; Dorchester

GREEN, John (-1638/9) & Mary __?__, m/2 Thomas GRIGGS 1640, m/3 Jasper RAWLINS; ?ca 1637; Roxbury

GREEN, John (?1590-1659) & 2/wf Alice [DANIEL] (-1643), wid; aft 1638, no issue; Salem

GREEN, John (1590-1659) & 3/wf Phillippa __?__ (1601-1633); in London, ca 1644?

GREEN, John (1620-1708) & Ann [ALMY] (1627-1709); ca 1647-8; Warwick, RI

GREEN, John (-by 1683) & Julia/Juliana __?__; b 1650; Kittery, ME

GREEN, John (-1695+) & Joan __?__ (-1682); b 1651; Kings Town, RI

GREEN, John & 1/wf? Ann/Mary __?__ (-1657); Stamford, CT

GREEN, John & 2/wf Joanna [SHATSWELL], w John; b 1656; Charlestown

GREEN, John (1636-1691) & Ruth MICHELSON/MITCHELSON; 20 Oct 1656; Cambridge

GREEN, John & Martha [FINCH], w John; Sep 1658; Stamford, CT

GREEN, John (-1691) & Mary WARREN (-1706+); 7 Dec 1659; Salem

GREEN, John (-1707) & Sarah WHEELER (1643-1717); 18 Dec 1660; Malden/Charlestown/Portsmouth, RI

GREEN, John (1640?-) & Mary [JEFFRIES/GORTON?] (1642-) (see Peter GREEN); ca 1661/5?; Newport, RI

GREEN, John (-1693) & Mary JENKINS, m/2 Humphrey AXALL aft 1693; 12 Sep 1666; Dover, NH/Portsmouth, NH?

GREEN, John (-1709) & Mary __?__ (see below); b 1668; Malden

GREEN, John (1649-) & Sarah BATEMAN (1649-); 3 Jul 1671; Woburn

GREEN, John & Mary __?__ (see above); b 1672; Boston

GREEN, John & Priscilla [?DAVIS]; b 1672; Boston

GREEN, John & __?__; b 1675; Huntington, LI

GREEN, John/?Samuel & Hannah [?GALLOP]; b 1680; Boston

GREEN, John & Sarah [REMICK], m/2 Barnabas WIXAM; b 1683; Kittery, ME

GREEN, John (?1651-) & Abigail [WARDWELL]/Nabbie WODDLE (1665-); 1684, b 1685; Ipswich?/Kingston, RI

GREEN, John & Mary BRADISH; b 1694, 22 Nov 1684; Stamford, CT/Cambridge

GREEN, John of Groton & Mary PIERCE (1634-), ?Watertown, m/2 Samuel SCRIPTON 1700; 25 Dec 1688; Concord

GREEN, John & Hannah BUTLER?/HOBBY, m/2 Cornelius BRINKHAM aft 1702; b 1690; Fairfield

GREEN, John & Sarah PICKHAM; b 1690; to NJ

GREEN, John (-1753) & 1/wf Sarah __?__; b 1690; Newport

GREEN, John & Bethiah MESSINGER (1668-); 17 Jan 1692; Boston

GREEN, John (-1697) & Hannah DODGE (1671-), m/2 John FROST; 24 Jan 1692, 4 Jan 1693; Beverly

GREEN, John (1661-) & Patience [DAVIS] (1674-); 1692; Charlestown/Weymouth

GREEN, John & Mary [WEEKS]; b 1695; Salisbury

GREEN, John & Sarah SIMES/SYMMES (1675-); m int 30 Oct 1695; Boston/Charlestown

GREEN, John & Abial/Abiel MARSTON (1677-); 23 Dec 1695; Hampton, NH

GREEN, John (1674-) & Mary GREEN; 23 Feb 1697/8; Malden

GREEN, John (-1736) & Isabel [WYMAN] (1677-1765); 1700, b 1700?; Malden/Charlestown

GREEN, John & Rebecca __?__; b 1701; Bradford

GREEN, John & Annie/Abigail? [NORMAN] (1677-); b 1701?; Salem

GREEN, Jonas & Jane PYGAN (1671-); 29 Mar 1694; New London, CT

GREEN, Jonathan & Mary ESTABROOK; 30 Apr 1700; Concord

GREEN, Joseph (-1700) & Elizabeth WHITMAN (-1720); - May 1657; Weymouth

GREEN, Joseph (-1672) & __?__; 1672; Boston

GREEN, Joseph (-1710) & [Elizabeth]/Mary? __?__; b 1681; Stamford, CT

GREEN, Joseph (1658-) & Ann [TURNER] (1652-1711); b 1686, 1695; Plymouth/Weymouth

GREEN, Joseph & Elizabeth MATTEN; 24 Mar 1696/7; Hull

GREEN, Joseph & Mary BECK; 30 Jul 1698; Boston

GREEN, Rev. Joseph (1675-1715) & Elizabeth GERRISH, m/2 William BRATTLE; 16 Mar 1698/9; Salem/Cambridge

GREEN, Joseph & Hannah GREEN (-1765); 24 Dec 1700; Malden

GREEN, Mark & Elizabeth FARRINGTON?; 14 Nov 1667; Andover

GREENE, Nathaniel & Mary HOUCHIN (1640-); 22 Jun 1657; Boston

GREEN, Nathaniel & Elizabeth __?__; b 1692(3?); Boston

GREEN, Nathaniel & __?__

GREEN, Nathaniel & __?__

GREEN, Nicholas[1] (-1663) & Susanna __?__, m/2 Jeremiah SHEARES 1663?; ca 1645/8?; York, ME

GREEN, Nicholas & Rebecca CLAY; 22 Mar 1697; Boston

GREEN, Percival (?1603-1639) & Ellen __?__ (1610-), m/2 Thomas FOX 1650; b 1635; Cambridge

GREEN, Peter (1622-1659) & Mary [GORTON], m/2 John SANFORD 1663; ca 1657, no issue; Providence/Warwick, RI

GREEN, Peter & 1/wf Elizabeth (DUSTIN) KINGSBURY, w John; 11 Dec 1672; Haverhill

GREEN, Peter & 2/wf Mary GREEN; 4 Nov 1678; Haverhill

GREEN, Peter (?1654, 1654/5-1723) & Elizabeth ARNOLD (1659-1728); 16 Dec 1680, 6 Dec 1680; ?Warwick, RI

GREEN, Peter (1666-) & Elizabeth SLOCUM (1678-); 12 Feb 1695/6; Warwick, RI

GREEN, Ralph & [Elizabeth] [JEGGLES]?, m/2 Richard TOZIER/_?_ ?BLOTT (see William GREEN); b 1642; Boston/Malden

GREENE, Richard & __?__; b 30 Jun 1653

GREEN, Richard/James? (-1672) & Rebecca __?__, m/2 John BONNER 1672; b 1665; Boston

GREEN, Richard & 1/wf Katherine __?__; b 1669, b 1666?

GREEN, Richard & 2/wf Susanna __?__; b 1687; Kittery, ME

GREEN, Richard (1667-) & Mary CARDER; 1691?, 1700; RI/Warwick, RI

GREEN, Richard & Hannah SHERRAR; 1 Jun 1692; Boston

GREEN, Richard (1660-1724) & Ellen/Eleanor SAYLES (1671-); 16 Feb 1692/3; Warwick, RI

GREENE, Richard (-1724) & [Mary CARDER]

GREEN, Robert & Elizabeth NICHOLS; 18 Oct 1666; Hingham

GREEN, Robert & Ruth [BACKUS] (1674-); b 1701?; Canterbury, CT

GREEN, Samuel (1615-1702) & 1/wf Jane [BAINBRIDGE?/BANBRIDGE] (-1657); b 16 Apr 1640; Cambridge

GREEN, Samuel (-1702) & 2/wf Sarah CLARKE; 23 Feb 1662, 1662/3, 1662; Cambridge

GREEN, Samuel (1645-1724) & 1/wf Mary [COOK] (-1715); ca 1666; Malden/Charlestown
GREENE, Samuel & Elizabeth SILL (1668-); 18 Nov 1685; Cambridge/Boston
GREEN, Samuel & Elizabeth UPHAM; 28 Oct 1691; Malden/Leicester
GREEN, Samuel, Malden & Mary WHEELER (-1730), Malden; 4 May 1694; Malden/Charlestown
GREEN, Samuel (1670, 1671-1720) & Mary GORTON (1671, 1673-1732); 24 Jan 1694/5; Warwick, RI
GREEN, Solomon & Mary (KING) GOOSE (-1689), w William; 19 Dec 1679; Charlestown
GREENE, Thomas (?1606-1667) & 1/wf Elizabeth _?_ (-1658); 1628?; Charlestown
GREEN, Thomas (-1674) & 1/wf Margaret [CALL] (-1667); b 1653; Malden
GREEN, Thomas (-1672) & Rebecca [HILLS] (1634-1674); ca 1653; Malden
GREEN, Thomas (1628-1717, in 88th y) & Elizabeth BARTON/GREENE (ca 1637-1693); last of Jun, 30 Jun 1659; Warwick, RI
GREEN, Thomas, Sr. (-1667) & 2/wf Frances (WHEELER) COOKE (1608-), w Isaac, w Richard; 5 Sep 1659, 5 Jul; Malden/Charlestown
GREEN, Thomas (-1674) & 2/wf Elizabeth WEBB; 19 Aug 1667; Malden/Charlestown
GREEN, Thomas (-1705) & Mary NEWBERRY (-1705+); 16 Nov 1671; Salem
GREEN, Thomas (1653-1694, Malden) & Mary WEEKS, m/2 Nathaniel GAGE 1695?, m/3 Joseph JEWETT; 22 Mar 167[5/6?], 1675, 1676; Malden
GREENE, Thomas (1662-1698/9) & Anne GREENE (1663-1713); 27 May 1686; Warwick, RI
GREEN, Thomas & Hannah VINTON; 10 May 1698; Malden/Woburn
GREEN, Thomas & Hannah HASELTINE (1681-); 7 Aug 1700; Bradford
GREEN, Tobiah & Mary _?_ ; b 1695; Hull
GREEN, Tobias & _?_ /Mary _?_ ; Glastonbury, CT?
GREEN, Tobias & Mary GENT, m/2 Matthew NEGRO; 17 Nov 1699; Boston
GREEN, William (?1591, 1620-1654) & Hannah [CARTER] (1625-1658), m/2 Thomas BROWN/ LINDELL?; b 1645, b 1644; Woburn/Charlestown
GREEN, William (-1705, Malden) & 1/wf Elizabeth WHEELER; 13 Sep 1659, 13 Mar 1659; Malden/Charlestown
GREENE, William (-1713) & Mary [?CRISPE] (1638-1713+); b 1661, b 1665; Cambridge/Groton?
GREEN, William (1652/3-1679) & Mary SAYLES (1652-), m/2 John HOLMES 1680; 17 Dec 1674; Warwick, RI/?Providence
GREEN, William (1651-1717) & 1/wf Mary/Hannah FELCH (1653?-1676); b 1675, ca 1674; Woburn
GREEN, William (1651-1717) & 2/wf Hannah [KENDALL] (1655-1719?); aft 1676, b 1678; Woburn
GREEN, William & Sarah _?_ ; b 1678(9?); Boston
GREEN, William (-1691) & Elizabeth HILLS (-1699), m/2 John LYNDE 1691; ca 1682, b 1686; Malden
GREEN, William (-1685) & Elizabeth WARREN (1654-); b 1684; Plymouth
GREEN, William (-1705, ae 70) & Isabel (FARMER) (WYMAN) BLOOD (1652-1737), w David, w James; m cont 6 Feb 1694/5; Charlestown
GREEN, William & Katherine READ, ?w Christopher; m int 19 Nov 1696; Boston/Groton
GREEN, William & _?_ ; b 1700; Stonington, CT
GREEN, William & [Elizabeth JEGGLES]; b 1675; Malden
GREEN, [?John] & [Hannah BUTLER], dau Richard; b 2 Apr 1677; Wethersfield, CT
GREEN, William & Mary (_?_) LIBBY, w John
GREEN, _?_ & _?_ BLOTT
GREEN, _?_ & Abigail HAMMON; b 1692
GREENFIELD, Peter (1635-1672) & Hannah [DEVEREAUX], m/2 Richard KNOTT ca 1672, m/3 John SWETT; b 1668; Salem
GREENFIELD, Samuel (1608, 1610-) & 1/wf Barbara _?_ (?1602, 1612-); in Eng, ca 1633?; Salem/Ipswich
GREENFIELD, Samuel & Susan [WYATH?/WISE], w Humphrey; b 4 Mar 1638(9?); Salem/Hampton, NH/Exeter, NH
GREENHALGH/GREENHALGE, William & _?_ ; b 1676; Boston
GREENHILL, Samuel & Rebecca _?_ , m/2 Jeremy ADAMS ca 1636?; b 1634
GREENLAND, Daniel & Elizabeth [BALLANTINE] (1660-); b 1678; Boston
GREENLAND, Henry & Mary _?_ ; in Eng, b 1663; Kittery, ME/Piscataway, NJ
GREENLAND, John (1602-) & Lydia _?_ ; b 1644; Charlestown

GREENLAND, John (1644-1728) & Lydia SPRAGUE (-1705, ae 51); 5 Jul 1670; Charlestown
GREENLEAF, Edmund (-1671) & 1/wf Sarah [DOLE?]; in Eng, b 1626, b 1612; Newbury/Boston/ Salisbury
GREENLEAF, Edmund (-1671) & 2/wf Sarah (JOURDAN) [HILL] (1599-1671, Boston), w William; aft 1663; Salisbury
GREENLEAF, Edmund (1671-) & Abigail SOMERLY; ?2 Jul 1691, 2 Jun; Newbury
GREENLEAF, Enoch (1617/18-1683+) & Mary _?_ (-1683+); b 1647; Salisbury/Malden/Boston
GREENLEAF, Enoch (1647-1705) & 1/wf Bethia WOODMAN (-1678); 20 Oct 1675; Salisbury
GREENLEAF, Enoch (1647-1705) & 2/wf Kate/Catherine TRUESDALE (1653-1712); 29 Aug 1679; ?Boston/Cambridge/Salisbury
GREENLEAF, John (ca 1632-1712), Boston (kinsman Mrs. Richard SHERMAN) & Hannah/Anna VEAZIE; 26 Sep 1665; Braintree
GREENLEAF, John (1662-) & 1/wf Elizabeth HILLS; 12 Oct 1685; Newbury
GREENLEAF, Joseph & Sarah [BEAL] (1667-1690); b 1683(4?); Boston
GREENLEAF, Samuel (1665-1694) & Sarah KENT (1667-), m/2? Peter TOPPANS 1696; 1 Mar 1685/6; Newbury
GREENLEAF, Stephen (1628-1690) & 1/wf Elizabeth COFFIN (1634-1678); 13 Nov 1651; Newbury
GREENLEAF, Stephen (1652-1743) & 1/wf Elizabeth GERRISH (1654-1712); 23 Oct 1676; Newbury
GREENLEAF, Stephen (1628-1690) & 2/wf Esther (WEARE) SWETT (-1718, ae 89), w Benjamin; 31 Mar 1678, 1679?; Hampton, NH
GREENLEAF, Tristram (1668-1742) & Margaret PIPER (1668-); 12 Nov 1689; Newbury
GREENMAN, Edward (-1688+) & Mary _?_ ; b 1663?; Newport
GREENMAN, Edward (1663-1749) & Margaret _?_ (-1739+); b 1692, b 1689?; Stonington, CT/Kingstown, RI/Charlestown, RI
GREENMAN, John & _?_ ; in Eng, b 1627; Newport
GREENMAN, John (1666-1727) & Elizabeth _?_ ; ca 1690; Newport
GREENMAN, Thomas (1669-1728) & Mary [WEEDIN] (-1728+); b 1701?; South Kingston, RI
GREENMAN, William & Anne [CLARK] (1675-); b 1701?; Kingstown, RI/Westerly, RI/Newport
GREENOUGH, John (1672-1732) & Elizabeth GROSS; 18 Oct 1693; Boston
GREENOUGH, Luke (1667-), Boston & Abigail HAMMOND, m/2 James WHIPPO 1692; 30 Jan 1689/90; Charlestown
GREENOW, Robert (-1718) & 1/wf Martha [EPPS] (1654-); b 1679?; Rowley
GREENOUGH, Robert (-1718) & 2/wf Sarah (PHILLIPS) MIGHELL (-1707), w Stephen; 6 Mar 1687, 1688?, 1687/8; Rowley
GREENOUGH, William (?1627-1678) & Elizabeth UPSHALL (1637-), m/2 Timothy PROUT 1685+; 4 Jul 1652; Boston
GREENOUGH, William (?1639-1693) & 1/wf Ruth SWIFT; 10 Oct 1660; Boston
GREENOUGH, William (?1639-1693) & 2/wf Elizabeth [RAINSFORD] (-1688); b 3 Aug 1680; Boston
GREENOUGH, William (-1693, ae 52), Boston & 3/wf Mrs. Sarah SHOVE?/SHOW?, Chelmsford; 29 Nov 1688; Chelmsford/Braintree
GREENOUGH, William (1670-) & Elizabeth MATHER (1666-), m/2 Josiah BYLES 1703; m int 23 Jun 1696, in Jul?, Jul 1696; Boston
GREENSLETT/GREENSLADE, John (-1690) & Abigail [CURTICE/CURTIS], m/2 Thomas MASON 1693; b 1692; Salem/Casco Bay
GREENSLAD, Thomas (-1674) & Ann _?_ (-1692), m/2 Jacob PUDESTOR/PUDEATER 1677+; b 1651; Falmouth, ME/Scarboro, ME
GREENSMITH, Nathaniel & Rebecca _?_ ; b 1662, by 1658?; CT
GRENAWAY/GREENWAY/GRINAWAY/GRINOWAY/GRINNOWAY, John[1] (-1664) & Mary _?_ (-1659); b 1591?, b 1624, b 1606, b 1603; Dorchester
GREENEWEY, John & Elinora BRAYLIE; m lic 15 Jan 1615
GREENWOOD, Isaac (ca 1665-1701), Boston & Anna LYDE/LYNDE (1674-), Charlestown, m/2 John PHILLIPS 1702; 6 Sep 1694; Reading
GREENWOOD, John (-1737) & 1/wf Hannah [TROWBRIDGE] (1672-1728); b 1696; Newton
GREENWOOD, Nathaniel (1631-1684) & Mary ALLEN (-1704), m/2 Theophilus FRAIRY 1690; 23 Jan 1654/5, 24 Jan 1655, 1655/6; Weymouth

GREENWOOD, Samuel (ca 1646-1711) & Mary [THORNTON], w _?_ WRIGHT; b 1673, b 12 Dec 1670; Boston
GREENWOOD, Samuel (1662-1721) & Elizabeth [BRONSDON] (?1670-1721); b 1687; Boston
GREENWOOD, Thomas (-1693) & 1/wf Hannah WARD (-168[-]); 8 Jun 1670 Cambridge/Newton
GREENWOOD, Thomas (-1693) & 2/wf Abigail _?_ ; b 1687; Cambridge/Newton
GREENWOOD, Thomas (1673-1720) & Elizabeth WISWALL (1668-1736); 28 Dec 1693; Newton/Rehoboth
GREET, John & _?_ HART; b 1670(1?); Westfield
GREGORY, George & _?_ ; in Eng, b 1666; Kittery, ME
GREGORY, Henry (1570-1656?) & _?_ (-1641?, 1642?); in Eng; Springfield/Stratford, CT
GREGORY, Jackin & Mary _?_ ; b 1669; Norwalk, CT
GREGORY, John (-1689+) & Sarah _?_ (-1689); b 1636?, b 1644?; New Haven/Norwalk, CT
GREGORY, John & Elizabeth MOULTHORP; 18 Oct 1663; New Haven/Norwalk
GREGORY, John & Hannah _?_ ; b 1669; Weymouth
GREGORY, Jonas (1641-) (ae 42 in 1683) & 1/wf Hannah [DOW] (-Feb 1672); 1670; Ipswich
GREGORY, Jonas & 2/wf Elizabeth HELY/HEALY (1647-); - May 1672, 10 May 1672; Ipswich
GREGORY, Judah (-1648?) & Sarah BURT (1621-), m/2 Henry WAKELEE/WAKELY 1649; 20 Jun 1643; Springfield
GREGORY, Judah & Hannah HOYT/HOITE (?1648-); 20 Oct 1664; Norwalk, CT/Duxbury, CT
GREGORY, Samuel (-1702) & Rebecca [WHEELER]; ca 1670/2; Fairfield, CT
GREGORY, Samuel & Mary SILLAVAN/SWILLAWAY; 28 Dec 1699; Fairfield, CT
GREGORY, Thomas (-1693) & Elizabeth PARDEE (1660-), New Haven, m/2 John OLMSTED by 1696; 25 Dec 1679; Norwalk
GREGORY, _?_ & Sarah (MESSENGER) [PALMER], w Ephraim; b 1701?, aft 1684; Jamaica, LI?/Greenwich, CT?
GRETIAN, Anthony & Dorcas [WELCH] (1663-), m/2 William EAGLESTON 1699; b 1693; Charlestown
GRECIAN, Thomas (-1699) & Dorothy _?_ ; b 1668(9?); Boston
GRICE, Samuel & Priscilla GREEN; 14 Jul 1691; Boston
GRICE, Charles (-1663) (calls William OWEN son-in-law 1661) & Margery DAVIS (-1669), wid; Braintree
GRICE?, Robert, Boston & Hannah CHANLER, Boston; 16 Apr 1688; Middlesex
GRIDLEY, Believe (1640-1672) & Anne/Anna _?_ , m/2 _?_ CORNELIUS; b 1664; Boston
GRIDLEY, Joseph (1629-1687) & 1/wf Elizabeth _?_ ; ca 1650/2?; Boston
GRIDLEY, Joseph (1629-1687) & 2/wf Lydia FLOOD/FLOYD?, w Richard FLOOD; 9 Jun 1654; Boston
GRIDLEY, Joseph (1629-1687) & Elizabeth (EMMONS) HICKMAN/HINCKMAN, w John; 24 Jun 1675; Dorchester
GRIDLEY, Richard (1600, 1602?-1674) (ae 65 in 1667) & Grace SURREY (-1674+, 1675); 25 Jul 1628, b 1628?, b 1632; Boston
GRIDLEY, Richard & Anna _?_ ; b 1658; Boston
GRIDLEY, Richard & Abigail _?_ ; b 1684; Boston
GRIDLEY, Richard & Hannah (MORSE) DAWES, w Jonathan; 27 Feb 1694, 1694/5; Boston
GRIDLEY, Samuel (1647-1712) & [Esther THOMPSON?] (1655, 1656-1696); b 19 Oct 1680; Farmington, CT
GRIDLEY, Samuel (1647-1712) & [Mary HUMPHREYS], ?m/2 _?_ /[John] WADSWORTH in 1714; b 1694? (see above), 1 Dec 1698; Farmington, CT
GRIDLEY, Thomas (-1655) & Mary SEAMORE/SEYMOUR, m/2 John LANGDON 1655+; 29 Sep 1644; Hartford/Farmington, CT
GRIDLEY, Thomas (1650-) & Elizabeth CLARK (-1696); 25 Dec 1673?, 1674?; Farmington, CT
GRIDLEY, Tremble (1642-1675) & Elizabeth (?WEEDEN/?BATEMAN) [GROSS?] (1647-), dau John, w Isaac, m Joseph ARNOLD; b 1671; Boston
GRIFFIN, David & Catherine HOWARD; 14 Jun 1697; Boston
GRIFFIN, Ebenezer & Mary (HARRIS) [HUBBELL], w Ebenezer; aft 1698, b 1701?, 9 Feb 1702/3; New London, CT
GRIFFIN, Edward & Mary _?_ ; b 1658, b 1656?; Flushing, LI
GRIFFIN, Edward & Deborah BARNES; 4 Jan 1678; Flushing, LI
GRIFFIN, Francis & 1/wf Sarah CURTISS (-1707); 25 Nov 1697; Stratford, CT
GRIFFIN, Hugh (-1656) & Elizabeth [UPSON], wid, m/3 Philemon WHALE 1657; b 1640; Sudbury

GRIFFIN, Hugh (-1691) & 1/wf Dorothy SKIDMORE (-1670); 20 Jul 1652, b 1686; Stratford, CT
GRIFFIN, Hugh (-1691) & Mary (ANDREWS)? [NORTON], w Peter; ca 1670; Stratford, CT
GRIFFIN, Humphrey (1605-1661/2) & Elizabeth [?ANDREWS] (-1670), m/2 Hugh SHERRAT/
  SHARRATT 1662/3; ca 1639/40?; Ipswich/Gloucester
GRIFFIN, Humphrey (-1661/2) & Joanna __?_ (-1657); b 1657; Gloucester
GRIFFIN, Isaac & Sarah __?_ ; b 1685; Boston
GRIFFIN, Jasper (1640, 1646?-1718) & Hannah __?_ (1650, 1652?-1699); b 1674, ca 1675?;
  Southold, LI
GRIFFIN, Jasper & Ruth PECK (1676-); 29 Apr 1696; Lyme, CT/N. Lyme
GRIFFIN, John (-1681) & Anna/Hannah? BANCROFT; 13 May 1647; Windsor, CT/?Simsbury, CT
GRIFFINE, John & Susannah PRICE; 27 Apr 1655; Boston
GRIFFINGS/GRIFFYN, John (-1688) & Lydia (SATCHWELL/SHATSWELL) (-1729); 17 Sep
  1663; Haverhill
GRIFFIN, John (-1742) & Elizabeth __?_ ; ca 1685?, b 1683?; Flushing, LI
GRIFFIN, John & Sarah __?_ ; b 1681, b 1692; Westchester, NY
GRIFFEN, John & Elizabeth __?_ ; b 1694; Concord
GRIFFIN, John (1671-) & 1/wf Mary __?_ (-1728); b 1695; Bradford
GRIFFINE, John & Susannah BROWN; m int 17 Sep 1695; Salisbury
GRIFFIN, John & Sarah __?_ ; b 1698; Stratford, CT
GRIFFIN, Jonathan (1647-1685?) & Mary LONG; 25 Oct 1676; Sudbury
GRIFFIN, Jonathan & Susanna CARTER; 28 Nov 1698, 29 Nov; Charlestown
GRIFFIN, Joseph (-1714) & Sarah DEVOTION (1666-1732); b 1686; Roxbury
GRIFFIN, Joseph & Lydia __?_ ; b 1687; Boston
GRIFFIN, Joseph & Sarah BASSETT (1676-), m/2 __?_ NEWFOLD?/HAWKES?; 13 Jun 1696;
  Lynn/Ipswich
GRIFFIN, Joshua & Priscilla __?_ ; Scarboro, ME
GRIFFIN, Matthew[1] & 1/wf Joan __?_ ; b 1654; Charlestown
GRIFFIN, Matthew[1] & 2/wf Hannah CUTTER/CUTLER (-1656+, 1678(-)); 29 Aug 1654;
  Charlestown
GRIFFIN, Matthew[1] & 3/wf Deborah (NORTON) [HILL], w Zechary; aft 1672, bef 1678, bef
  1686; Charlestown
GRIFFIN, Matthew[2] (1656-1691) & Eleanor __?_ , m/2 John ASBURY 1699; b 1684; Charlestown
GRIFFIN, Nathaniel & Elizabeth RING; 26 Aug 1671; Andover
GRIFFINE, Oliver & Ann __?_ ; b 1663; Boston
GRIFFIN, Philip (-1657) & Ann/Agnes __?_ , m/2 John BUDEZERT by 1659, 1660?; b 1653;
  Salisbury/Portsmouth, ME
GRIFFIN, Philip (-1668) & __?_ ; Scarborough, ME
GRIFFIN, Richard (-1667) & Mary __?_ ; b 1650; Roxbury
GRIFFIN, Richard (-1661, ae 70) & 2/wf or 3/wf? Mary HAWARD/HAYWARD?/HARROD?,
  wid; 10 Dec 1660; Concord
GRIFFIN, Richard & __?_ ; Flushing, LI
GRIFFIN, Richard[2]/Robert, Newport, RI, & Susanna HAIGHT; ca 1690/2?, b 1712; Flushing, LI
GRIFFIN, Robert & Mary RUDDOCK; 1 Feb 1693; Boston
GRIFFIN, Samuel & Lydia [?YOUNGLOVE], m/2 Henry WITHAM 1691; b 1680; Ipswich/
  Gloucester
GRIFFIN, Samuel (1659-1706) & Priscilla [CROSSWELL/CROSWELL] (1664-); b 1682;
  Charlestown
GRIFFIN, Samuel (-1691?) & Elizabeth PLATT, ?m/2 John BRUSH?; m lic 7 Jan 1684, m 14 Jan
  1684/5; Huntington, NY
GRIFFIN, Samuel & Elizabeth __?_ ; b 1685; Stratford, CT
GRIFFIN, Thomas (-1661) & __?_ ; New London, CT/Stonington, CT
GRIFFIN, Thomas (1662-1703?), Simsbury & Jane/Joan (BLADEMAN/BLACKMAN) RUSSELL
  (1668-), w Joseph, m/3 James CLARK, Jr., m/4 Nathan ADAMS; aft 17 Nov 1688; Stratford,
  CT
GRIFFIN, Thomas (1658-1719) & Elizabeth [WILSON?/WELTON?]; b 1695(6?); Simsbury, CT
GRIFETH, Stephen & Rebecca RYDER; 13 Apr 1699; Yarmouth/Chatham/Harwich
GRIFFITH, William & __?_ ; [ca 1660-70]; Sandwich/Chatham
GRIFFITH, Phillip & __?_
GRIFFETH, William & __?_

GRIGGS, George (1593-1660) & Alice __?__ (1593-1662); in Eng, b 1620; Boston
GRIGGS, Humphrey (-1657) & Grizell (FLETCHER) JEWELL/JUELL, w Thomas, m/3 Henry
    KIBBY 1657, m/4 John GURNEY 1661, m/5 John BURGE 1667; 1 Nov 1655; Braintree
GRIGGS, Isaac (-1686) & Sarah __?__; b 1684; Boston
GRIGGS, Jacob (1658-1733) & Eleanor HASKELL (1663-); 12 Nov 1685; Gloucester/Beverly
GRIGGS, John (?1622-1692) & Mary PATTEN (ca 1634-1674+, bef 1692); 11 Nov 1652; Roxbury
GRIGGS, John & Elizabeth [CASS] (1666-); [?Jun] 1682, 6 Jun 1682; Roxbury
GRIGGS, Joseph (?1625-1714/15, ae 90) & 1/wf Mary [CRAFTS] (1632-1653); ca 1652; Roxbury
GRIGGS, Joseph (?1625-1714/15, ae 90) & 2/wf Hannah DAVIS (ca 1635-1684); 8 Nov 1654;
    Roxbury
GRIGGS, Thomas (-1646) & 1/wf Mary __?__ (-1639); in Eng, b 1622; Roxbury
GRIGGS, Thomas (-1646) & 2/wf Mary (_?_) GREEN, w John, m/3 Jasper RAWLINS 1651; 26
    Aug 1640; Roxbury
GRIGGS, William (-1693) & Rachel [HUBBARD]; b 1640; Boston
GRIGGS, William (1640-) & 1/wf Hannah [HANNAFORD] (-1679); b 1676; Boston
GRIGGS, William (1640-) & 2/wf Thankful [BAKER] (1646/7-1729); b 1682; Boston
GRIGSON, Thomas (-1647) & Jane __?__ (-1702); b 1635; New Haven
GRIMES?/GRAHAM?, Benjamin & 1/wf Abigail HUMPHREY (-1687); 12 Feb 1684; ?Hartford
GRIMES?/GRAHAM?, Benjamin & 2/wf Sarah (WYGETT) [WEBSTER], w John; 20 Nov 1698, 28
    Nov
GRIMES, George (1649-1710+) & Elizabeth BLANCHARD; 15 Apr 1675; Charlestown/Billerica/
    etc.
GRIMES/GRAHAM, Henry (-1684) & Mary __?__ (-1685); b 1662; Hartford
GRIMES/GRAHAM, John & Priscilla [GILLETTE] (1661-); b 1701?, by 1711, b 1692; ?Windsor,
    CT
GRIMES, John & Joanna __?__; b 1700; Newton
GRIMES/GRAHAM, Joseph (-1734) & Deborah STEBBINS (-1712); 20 Nov 1686; Wethersfield,
    CT
GREAMES, Samuel & 1/wf Frances __?__; b 1639; Boston/Plymouth/?Braintree
GRIMES, Samuel & 2/wf Ann __?__; b 1657; Plymouth
GRIMES, ?John & Mary HARVEY (1669-1698+); b 1691; Fairfield, CT
GRIMSTED, __?__ & Margaret __?__ (-1650); b 1650; Boston
GRINNELL, Daniel (1636±-1703) & Mary [WODELL] (1640-); b 1663; Portsmouth, RI/Little
    Compton
GRINNELL, Daniel (1668-1740) & Lydia [PABODIE] (1667-1745); ca 1683?, b 31 Jul 1694;
    Little Compton, RI/Saybrook, CT
GRINNELL, Daniel & Sarah [CHASE] (1676?-); b 1696; Freetown
GRINNELL, Jonathan (?1670-) & 1/wf Rebecca [IRISH]; b 1698, b 16 Apr 1697; Little
    Compton, RI
GRINNELL, Jonathan (?1670-) & 2/wf Abigail FORD; 8 Dec 1698; Little Compton, RI
GRINNELL, Matthew[1] (-1643(-)) & Rose __?__, m/2 Anthony PAINE 1643, m/3 James WEEDEN
    1650; ca 1633?; Newport
GRINNELL, Matthew[2] (-1705+) & __?__ (-1705+); ca 1660/5?; Portsmouth, RI/East Greenwich, RI
GRISSELL, Francis (-1652) & Mary __?__; b 1639; Charlestown
GRISSELL?, __?__ & Hannah [BILL], m/2 John KENT 1662; Charlestown
GRISWOLD, Benjamin & Elizabeth COOKE (1673-); 4 Jan 1693; Windsor, CT
GRISWOLD, Daniel & Mindwell BISSELL (-1728); 3 Feb 1680; Windsor, CT
GRISWOLD, Edward (1607-1691), Kenilworth, Warwickshire & 1/wf Margaret [HICKS?] (-1670);
    in Eng, b 1629; Windsor, CT
GRISWOLD, Edward (-1691) & 2/wf Sarah? [BEMAS], w James; ca 1672, in 1672-3;
    Killingworth, CT
GRISSWOLD, Edward (-1688) & Abigail WILLIAMS (-1690); 3 Nov 1681; Windsor, CT
GRISWOLD/GRISSELL, Francis & Mary [?POST], m/2 William BULLARD 1653?; b 1639;
    Cambridge
GRISWOLD, Francis (1632?, ?1629-1671, Norwich) & [?Mary/?Sarah POST?]; b 1653; Saybrook,
    CT
GRISWOLD, George (1633?-1704) & Mary HOLCOMB (ca 1636-1708); 3 Oct 1655; Windsor, CT
GRISWOLD, Isaac (1658-) & Elizabeth [BRADLEY] (?1671-1732), m/2 William WELLMAN; b
    1690; Guilford, CT/Killingworth, CT

GRISWOLD, Jacob & Mary [WRIGHT] (1665-1735); 10 Dec 1685; Wethersfield, CT
GRISWOLD, Jacob & Abigail HAND; 30 Nov 1696; Wethersfield, CT
GRISWOLD, John & 1/wf Mary/?Mercy BEMIS (-1679); 28 Nov 1672; Killingworth, CT
GRISWOLD, John & 2/wf Bathsheba [SMITH?/NORTH?] (-1736); aft 27 Oct 1679, bef 4 May 1681; Windsor, CT/Killingworth, CT
GRISWOLD, Joseph (1648-1716) & Mary GAYLORD (1649-); 16 Jul 1670, ?11 Jul; Windsor, CT
GRISWOLD, Joseph (1677-) & Deborah _?_; b 1700; Windsor, CT
GRISWOLD, Matthew (1618-1698) & Ann/Anna WOLCOTT (1621, ?1620-1700/1); ?16 Oct 1646; Windsor, CT
GRISWOLD, Matthew (1653-1716) & 1/wf Phebe HYDE (-1704); 21 May 1683, ?21 Jul 1683; ?Lyme, CT
GRISWOLD, Michael (-1684) & Anne/Anna? [ADAMS?]; b 1646?; Wethersfield, CT
GRISWOLD, Michael & Elizabeth BURNHAM (1674-); 12 May 1692; Wethersfield, CT
GRISWOLD, Samuel (1665-1740) & 1/wf Susannah HUNTINGTON (1668-1727); 10 Dec 1685; Norwich, CT
GRISWOLD, Thomas (1646-) & Mary HOWARD?/HAYWARD? (1647, 1649-1718); 28 Nov 1672; Wethersfield, CT
GRISWOLD, Thomas (1658-) & ?Esther/Hester DRAKE (-1692); 11 Aug 1681, 16 Aug; Windsor, CT
GRISWOLD, Thomas, Wethersfield & Sarah BRADLEY (-1729); 9 May 1697; ?Guilford, CT
GRONSLEY, _?_ & Susanna POTTER (1659-1688); 1679; Portsmouth, RI
GROOM, Edward & Miriam (WHEELER) [BLACKMAN/BLAKEMAN] (1647-1693), w James; b 1690, aft 7 Nov 1689; Stratford, CT
GROSS, Clement² & 1/wf Mary _?_; b 1649; Boston
GROSS, Clement², & 2/wf Anna/Ann _?_; b 1669; Boston
GROSSE, Edmund² (-1655) & 1/wf Catharine _?_; b 1642; Boston
GROSS, Edmund² (-1655) & 2/wf Ann [COLE], m/2 Samuel SHEARS in 1655, 1656; b 1652; Boston
GROSS, Edmund & Dorothy BELCHER (1673-1694?); 14 Feb 1693, 1693/4; Boston
GROCE, Edmund (1669-1728) & Martha [BACON]; b 1700; Hingham
GROSS, Harrison & Mary EDES; 12 Jul 1700; Boston
GROCE, Isaac¹ (-1649) & Anne _?_ (-1653); in Eng, b 1620; Boston/Exeter, NH
GROSS, Isaac (1642-1666) & Elizabeth [BATEMAN?/WEEDEN?], m/2 ?Tremble GRIDLEY bef 1666; b 1666; Boston
GROSS, Isaac & _?_; b 1688; Boston
GROASS, Isaac (?1670-) & Elizabeth ATHERTON; 28 Aug 1691; Milton
GROSSE, Matthew (-1694) & 1/wf Mary TROTT; 5 Oct 1652; Boston
GROSS, Matthew (-1694) & 2/wf Eleanor _?_; b 1670; Boston
GROSS, Richard & Mary (?CHINN) BROWN, w William; 20 Mar 1684; Marblehead
GROSS, Richard & Miriam REDERICK, w John; 4 Dec 1688; Marblehead
GROCE, Simon (-1696) & Mary BOND (1657-), Boston; 23 Oct 1675; Hingham
GROSS, Thomas & Elizabeth [PHILLIPS] (-1725+), m/2 Joseph ELDREDGE 1695, m/3 Elias HEATH 1699, m/4 Francis BURROUGHS; b 1672; Boston
GROSS, Thomas & Hannah MERRIT; 2 Jun 1696; Marblehead
GROSS, William (?1666-1694) & Maria Catharine [SMITH], m/2 Samuel MEARS 1697; Boston
GROSS, _?_ & [?Mary] KINSLEY, dau Stephen (had Isaac, b 1670); b 1670, by 1666?; Milton
GRAVEENOR/GROSVENOR, John (-1691, in 49th y) (ae 53 in 1679) & Esther/Hester [CLARK] (1652-1738, Pomfret, CT); b 1672; Roxbury
GROUT, John¹ (1615-1697) & 1/wf Mary [?CAKEBREAD], dau Thomas; b 1641; Watertown
GROUT, John¹ (1615-1697) & 2/wf Sarah [BUSBY] (1619-1699); b 1649; Watertown
GROUT, John² (1641-1707) & Rebecca TOLL (1643-); 15 Apr 1667; Sudbury
GROUT, Joseph (1649-) & Susanna [HAGER]; b 1681; Watertown
GROVE, Edward (-1686) & 1/wf Mary _?_ (-1683, ae 73); Salem
GROVE, Edward (-1686) & Elizabeth (HOLLARD) [BROOKING], w John; aft 1683; Salem
GROVE, John & Martha [MITTON]; Kittery, ME/Little Compton, RI
GROUE/GROVES/LaGROVES/etc., Nicholas & Hannah [?SALLOWS]; b 1672; Beverly
GROVES, Philip (-1676) (see GROW) & Ann [?HAWLEY/?SMITH]; b 1644; Stratford, CT
GROVER, Andrew (-1674) & Hannah HILLS (1657-1674); 7 Feb 1673, 7 Feb 1673/4; Cambridge/Malden

GROVER, Andrew (1673-1751?) (another Andrew at Norton) & Mary [FREETHY]; b 1698; Malden/York, ME

GROVER, Edmund (?1600-1682) & ?Margaret _?_ ; in Eng, b 1628; Salem

GROVER, Edmund & Mary LOW; 10 Jan 1698/9; Beverly

GROVER, Ephraim (ca 1675-1766) & Mary PRATT; 1700; Malden/Norton

GROVER, John (-1686, ae 80) & Elizabeth _?_ ; b 1641; Charlestown/Boston?/Chelsea

GROVER, John (?1628-1716) & 1/wf Sarah BARNEY (-by 1673); 13 May 1656; Salem

GROVER, John & Hannah _?_ ; b 1664; Boston

GROVEER, John & 2/wf Sarah _?_ ; ca 1677/8

GROVER, John & 1/wf Sarah LOW (-1692); 23 Jun 1687; Ipswich/Beverly

GROVER, John & 2/wf Margaret _?_ ; b 1695; Beverly

GROVER, Jotham (had son Dean GROVER) & Margaret [WINTHROP?/?DEAN] (-1695, ae 35); b 1687; Boston/Chelsea

GROVER, Lazarus (1642-1715) & Ruth [ADAMS] (1642-1674); b 1665; Malden

GROVER, Lazarus (-1715) & Elizabeth _?_ (-1688); Malden

GROVER, Lazarus (-1715) & 3/wf Mercy [MUDGE] (-1725+); b 1694; Malden

GROVER, Matthew (-1679) & Mary [DAVIS], m/2 Samuel DAMON 1680±; b 1674(5?); Boston/Malden/Reading

GROVER, Nehemiah (?ca 1640-1694) & Ruth HASCOLL/HASKELL (ca 1654-1714); 2 Dec 1674; Beverly

GROVER, Peltiel & Lydia _?_ ; b 1669(70?); Boston

GROVER, Simon[1] (-1705) & Elizabeth [MOORE] (1647-1720); b 1672; Southold, LI

GROVER, Simon (?1654-1717, ae 63/73) & Sarah [BARRETT] (-1726); b 1687(8?); Malden/Charlestown

GROVER, Stephen (-1694) & Sarah _?_ ; b 1685(6?); Malden

GROVER, Thomas (-1661) & Elizabeth _?_ (-1676), m/2 Philip ATWOOD 1675; b 1642; Charlestown/Malden

GROVER, Thomas (1643-1710) & Sarah CHADWICK; 23 May 1668; Malden/?N. Charlestown

GROVER, Thomas & Sarah BUCK (1674-); 27 Feb 1694; Woburn

GROVER, Thomas & Bethia BURNAP; 24 May 1696; Reading/?Cambridge

GROVER, Thomas (1671-1728) & Mary COX; 29 Jul 1697; Malden

GROW, John & Hannah LORD; 15 Dec 1669; Ipswich

GROW, Samuel (1671-) & Ruth FOSTER (1674-); 25 Apr 1694; Topsfield/Ipswich

GROTH/GROWTH, John & Elizabeth EATON, m/2 William HUTCHINS 1685; 7 Jan 1673; Salisbury

GRUBB, Gabriel & Frances _?_ ; b 1666, b 1664?; Isles of Shoals

GRUBBE, Thomas & Anne [?SALTER]; b 1637; Boston/Medford

GRUMMAN, John[1] (?1627-1685) & Sarah [TRY] (ca 1632-1691); b 1652, by 1655; Fairfield, CT

GRUMMAN, John[2] (ca 1652-1695±) & 1/wf Esther [THOMPSON] (1654±-1690±); b 1680, ca 1678; Fairfield, CT

GRUMMAN, John[2] (ca 1652-1695±) & 2/wf Esther (LYON) PERRY (?1658-1699, 1695+), w Nathaniel; ca 1691, b 1694; Fairfield, CT

GRUMMAN, Samuel (ca 1654-1691) & Mary [HUBBARD], m/2 Jacob PATCHEN by 1692; by 1689; Fairfield, CT

GRUMMAN, Thomas (?1656-1691) & Mary [COUCH], m/2 James BENNETT 1692?, m/3 Samuel JENNINGS 1727; aft 1690, 1691; Fairfield, CT

GRUNDY, Robert & Mary [PARKER], dau Edward; b 1676; Roxbury

GARNSEY, Henry (-1692) & 1/wf Hannah [MUNNING] (?1629-); b 1648?, b 1660; Dorchester

GARNSEY, Henry (-1692) & 2/wf Elizabeth (LANE) [RIDER], w Thomas; Dorchester

GARNSEY, Henry (-1759, ae 80) & Sarah WHEELOCK; 7 Nov 1700; Dedham/Medfield

GUERNSEY, James & Mary (TILTON) EASTMAN (1643-), w Joseph; 17 Feb 1693, 17 Feb 1692; Hadley/NJ

GARNSEY, John (1648-) & 1/wf Elizabeth _?_ (-1714, Rehoboth); b 1673; Milton/Dorchester/Swansea/Rehoboth

GARNSEY, Joseph (-1688) & Rose (LOCKWOOD) WATERBURY, w John; 11 May 1659; Stamford, CT

GARNSEY, Joseph (1650-1730) & 1/wf Hannah COLEY (1654-); 10 Apr 1673; Milford, CT

GARNSEY, Joseph (-1709) & Mary LOCKWOOD; 2 Mar 1692/3; Stamford, CT

GUERNSEY, William & Elizabeth _?_ ; in Eng, b 1652?; York, ME

GILD/GUILE/GILES?, Ephraim & Martha BRADLEY/BROADLEY; 5 Jan 1686, 5 Jan 1686/7; Haverhill/Amesbury
GILE, James & Ruth PARKER (-1708+); 21 Feb 1688, 21 Feb 1688/9; Andover/Haverhill
GUILD, John & Elizabeth CROOKE; 24 Jun 1645; Dedham
GUILD, John (1649-1723) & Sarah FISHER (1658-); 22 May 1677; Dedham/Wrentham
GILD, John & Sarah (GARFIELD) SUTTON (1655-), Newbury, w William (called Mary in m to Wm. SUTTON 1679); 3 Jan 1680, 1680/1; Haverhill
GILD, Samuel & Judith DAVIS; 1 Sep 1647; Haverhill
GUILD/GUELL, Samuel (1647-1730) & Mary WOODCOCK/WODCOKE; 29 Nov 1676, 28 Nov; Dedham/Rehoboth
GULE?/GUILD, John & _?_ ; b 1701; Preston, CT
GILFORD/GUILDFORD, John (-1660) & Susanna [NORTON?]; ca 1650; Hingham
GILFORD, Paul (1653-1690) & Susannah PULLEN (-1690); 20 Feb 1676/7; Hingham
GILFORD, William & Mary _?_ ; b 1653; Boston
GILFORD, _?_ & Mary _?_ (-1660); b 1630?; Hingham
GUIRE, Luke & Mary ADAMS, m/2 _?_ MERWIN, m/3 Stephen SHERWOOD; 23 Feb 1663, ?25 Feb; Fairfield, CT
GUIRE, Luke (-1699) & Rebecca [ODELL], m/2 Robert TURNEY; ca 1686?; Fairfield, CT
GULL, Richard & Rebecca HILL; 24 Jan 1694; Boston
GULL, William (d in Eng) & Ann/Anna _?_, m/2 Nathaniel DICKINSON 1630/1; in Eng, b 1628?; Deerfield
GULL, William & Elizabeth (SMITH) [FOOTE], w Nathaniel d 1655; aft 1655; Wethersfield, CT
GULLY/GULLEY, Jacob & Mercy/Mary _?_ ; b 1677; Boston
GULLIVER, Anthony[1] (1619-1706) & 1/wf Lydia [KINGSLEY] (-1682); b 1650; Dorchester/Milton
GULLIVER, Anthony[1] (1619-1706) & 2/wf Eleanor (_?_) VEERING, w John; aft Jan 1689/90, aft 1682, bef 10 Jan 1691/2; Milton
GOULIVER, Jonathan[2] (1659-1737) & Mary ROBERNSON/ROBINSON (1668-1703), Dorchester; 17 Jan 1686; Milton
GULLIVER, Nathaniel[2] (1675-1743),Milton & Hannah BILLING (-1760, ae 80), Dorchester; 1 Jul 1698; Milton
GULLIFER/GULLIVER, Samuel[2] (1653-1676?) & Jan/Jane GILBORD/GILBERT; 15 Nov 1675; Milton
GUMAR/?GUMMER/?GUMAER, Francis & Ruth GROSSE; m int 3 Jun 1696; Boston
GUNN, Abel (1643-1688) & Mary SMITH (1648-1691), m/2 John DAVIS 1691; 29 Oct 1666, 1669?; Milton, CT/Derby
GUNN, Daniel & Deborah [COLEMAN] (1645-1703), Hatfield; ca 1672, no issue; Hadley/Milford, CT
GUNN, Jasper (1606-1670) & 3/wf? Christian _?_ (-1690); b 1633; Roxbury/Milford, CT
GUNN, Jobamah (-1715) & 1/wf Sarah LANE; 30 Oct 1663; Milford, CT/Derby, CT
GUNN, Jobamah & 2/wf Mary [BRISTOL] (1661-); ca 1681; Milford, CT
GUNN, John (-1726, ae 82) & Mary WILLIAMS (1652-1711); 22 Jan 1678, 1678/9?; Westfield
GUNN, Nathaniel & Sarah DAY (ca 1640-1677), m/2 Samuel KELLOGG 1669; Sep 1658, 17 Nov 1658; ?Branford, CT
GUNN, Samuel (-1755) & Elizabeth WYATT; 22 Jan 1684; Hatfield/Sunderland
GUNN, Samuel (-1699) & Hannah [SANFORD], m/2 Henry GRAY ca 1700; ca 1692?; Milford, CT
GUNN, Ens. Samuel (1669-1749) & Mercy SMITH (?1674-1750); 11 Nov 1697; Milford, CT
GUNN, Thomas (-1681) & _?_ (-1678); b 1640, b 1639; Windsor, CT/Westfield
GUNNISON, Elihu & Martha TRICKEE/TRICKEY; 10 Nov 1674; Dover, NH
GUNNISON, Elihu & Elizabeth (INGERSOLD) [SKILLINGS], w John; by 1690; Kittery, ME
GUNNISON, Hugh & 1/wf Elizabeth _?_ (-1645/6); b 1638, b 1636?; Boston
GUNNISON, Hugh & Sarah (TILLEY) LYNN, w Henry, m/3 John MITCHELL ca 1660, m/4 Francis MORGAN 1664, 1665; 23 May 1647; Boston
GUNNISON/GALLISON?/GULLISON?, Philip (-1676) & Mary _?_ ; by 1 Jul 1673; Kittery, ME
GUPPY, John (1618-1694) & Elizabeth _?_ (1606-1693); Weymouth/Charlestown
GUPPY, John (1648-) & 1/wf Abigail KITCHIN; 3 Jun 1669; Salem
GUPPY, John (1648-) & 2/wf Susannah (BATTEN) STARKEY, w John; 26 Jan 1699/1700; Salem
GUPPY, Reuben (1605-1684+) & Ellen/Eleanor _?_ ; b 1640; Salem

GUPTILL, Thomas & Mary [ABBOTT], m/2 William CAVERLY by 1696; by 1674; Portsmouth, NH
GURCHFIELD/GURGEFIELD, _?_ & Margaret [DAVIS] (1612-), m/2 Richard BENNETT 1653; b 1653; Framingham
GURLEY, William (-1689) & Esther [INGERSOLL], m/2 Benjamin JONES 1689; 1684; Northampton
GURNEY, John[1] (-1663) & 1/wf _?_ (-1661); b 1628; Weymouth
GURNEY, John[1] (1603-1663) & 2/wf Grezell (FLETCHER) (JEWELL) (GRIGGS) KIBBEE (-1669), w Thomas , w Humphrey, w Henry, m/5 John BURGE 1667; 12 Nov 1661; Braintree
GURNEY, John[2] (-1675?) & Ruth ?RETCHELL, m/2 John BUNDY 1676, m/3 Guydo BAILEY; b 1671(2?); Menden (had John, Samuel, Mary)
GURNEY, John[3] & Elizabeth [GREEN] (1664-); b 1689; Weymouth
GURNEY, John[3] (-1723) & Sarah (THORNTON) [FIELDS] (-1714), w Zachariah; b 1701?, b 1706, aft 4 Feb 1696, b 1714; Providence
GURNEY, Richard[2] (-1691) & Rebecca [TAYLOR]; b 1656(7?), b 1654; Weymouth
GURNEY, Samuel[3] (1671-) & Sarah ATKINS? STAPLES/SHAPLEY, dau Thomas, w _?_ ; 26 Oct 1693; Boston/Little Compton, RI
GURNEY, Zachariah[3] & Mary [BENSON] of Hull, MA; b 1695; Weymouth
GUSTIN, John (1647-) & Elizabeth BROWNE (1657-); 10 Jan 1676/7; Salem/Lynn
GUTCH, Robert (1617-) & Lydia [?HOLGRAVE/?HOLLINGWORTH]; b 1641; Salem/Salisbury/Kennebunk, ME
GUTTERSON, John (1662-) & Abigail BUCKMASTER; 14 Jan 1688/9; Andover
GUTTERSON, William (-1666) & Elizabeth _?_ , ?m/2 John CALLUM/COLLINS?/KILHAMS? 1670; b 1658; Ipswich
GUTTRIDGE/GUTHRIE, Robert (-1692) & 1/wf Margaret IRELAND (1623-1687); 25 Dec 1656; Block Island, RI
GUTTRIDGE/GUTHRIE, Robert (-1692) & Ann (ALCOCK) WILLIAMS (1658-), w John; 5 Jun 1689; New Shoreham, RI
GAY/GUY?, Nicholas (1588-1649) & 2/wf? Jane _?_ (1608-1669); b 1626; Watertown
GUY, John & _?_ ; b 1688; Purpooduck
GWIN, David (-1711) & Martha _?_ ; b 1691; Boston
GWIN, John & Mary [BUNKER], m/2 Eleazer LUSHER 1662; b 1647; Charlestown
GWINN, John & Ruth _?_ ; b 1666; Boston
GWIN, Thomas (-1669) & Elizabeth [GILLAM]; b 1661; Boston
GWIN, Thomas & Joanna ARMITAGE; 21 Nov 1689; Boston
GWIN, Thomas & Sarah DIXEY (1672-); - Nov 1691; Boston

HABBERFIELD, William & Mary _?_ (-1697); b 1697, b 1676?; Boston
HABBERFIELD, William & (2) Jane [BAGWORTH], w Benjamin; 1698+?
HACK, William (returned to Eng) & Mary [LINCOLN], m/2 Richard STEVENS ca 1666, 1667?; ca 1660?; Taunton
HACK, William (?1663-), Taunton & Hannah/Susannah? KINGSLEY, Milton; 13 Nov 1694; Milton
HACKER, George (-1702) & Bethiah MEACHUM, m/2 John DARLING 1717+, 1709; last week of Sep 1672; Salem
HACKETT, Jabez (-1686) (ae 45 in 1669) & Frances _?_ (ae 54 in 1686); b 1654; Taunton
HACKET, John (1654-) & Eleanor GARDNER; 10 Sep 1688; Taunton
HACKETT, Samuel (1664-) & Mary CRANE (1666-); 28 Mar 1690; Taunton
HACKETT, William & 1/wf _?_ ; Dover/etc.
HACKETT, William & 2/wf Mary [ATKINS]; by 1666
HACKETT, William & 3/wf Margaret _?_ , m/2 _?_ SMITH; Dover, NH/Exeter, NH
HACKETT, William & Sarah BARNARD (1647-); 31 Jan 1666/7; Salisbury
HACKLETON, Francis & Joanna/Hannah? [WAKEMAN] (ca 1636/7-); b 1662, b 6 Sep 1662; ?Hartford/Northampton

HACKELTON, William (-6 Sep 1685) & Sarah [ROGERS] (-1688?), dau Obadiah, m/2 John
   CAMPBELL 9 Mar 1686/7; Southampton, LI
HADDON/HAYDEN?, Ferinan & Elizabeth _?_, m/2 Thomas WATTS; 5 May 1657; Boston
HADON, Jared (1608-1663+) & Margaret _?_ (-1673); b 1640; Cambridge
HODON/?HAYDEN, William & Patience _?_ ; b 1685; Boston
HADDEM, John & Elizabeth _?_ ; b 6 May 1689, b 1688; Westchester, NY
HADDON, _?_ & Catherine _?_ ; b 1640; Cambridge
HADE, [John] & Joan/Joanna [GREEN] (1630-); RI
HADLEY, George (uncle of Thomas DORMAN, Jr. 1663)
HADLEY, George (-1686) & 1/wf 2/wf? Martha [PROCTOR]; b 1655, b 1651?; Ipswich/Topsfield
HADLEY, George (-1686) & 2/wf Deborah SKILLING (1622-), w Thomas; 29 Jun 1668; Ipswich
HADLEY, John (-1711) & Susanna PITTIS, m/2 Peter PETTIS; 3 Sep 1682; Ipswich/Gloucester
HADLEY, Joseph (-1695?) & 1/wf Mary [RICHARDSON]; by 1673?; Yonkers, NY/Westchester
   Co., NY
HADLEY, Joseph & [?Sarah (RAYNES) CUTT], w Joseph
HADLEY, Joseph (-1694?) & 2/wf Mehitable/Hiltabell [TIPPETTS], m John CONKLIN 1694; aft
   1679; Westchester Co., NY/Yonkers Plantation
HADLEY?/HADLY, Richard & Mary _?_ ; Mamaroneck
HADLEY, Samuel (1652?-) & Jane [MARTIN?/NORTH?] (1656-); ca 1676; Amesbury
HADLOCK, James & Damaris [FOSDICK], w Thomas; b 1652; Charlestown/Wenham
HADLOCK, James (-1687) & Rebecca HUTHESON/HUTCHINSON (1632-1687); May 1658; Salem
HADLOCK, James & 1/wf Sarah DRAPER (-1675); 19 May 1669; Roxbury
HADLOCK, James & 2/wf Abigail MARTIN?; 3 Dec 1679; Salisbury
HADLOCK, James & _?_ (had John, James?); b 1679
HADLOCK, John (-1676) & Elizabeth STOW (-1675); 13 May 1673; Concord
HADLOCK, John & _?_ ; b 1681; Haddam, CT
HADLOCK, John & Sarah PASQUE/PASCO (1671-); 16 Jan 1694, 1694/5; Salisbury
HADLOCK, Nathaniel (-1653) & Mary _?_, m/2 Roger DRAPER aft 1648, aft 1653; b 1641;
   Charlestown
HADLOCK, Nathaniel (?1643-) & Remember JONES (-1718); 1 May 1673; Gloucester
HAGER, Samuel[2] (1647-1705) & Sarah [MIXER] (1657-); b 1691; Watertown
HAGAR, William[1] (-1684) & Mary BEMIS (-1695); 20 Mar 1645, 1644/5; Watertown
HAGER, William[2] (1658/9-1731) & Sarah BENJAMIN (-1745); 31 Mar 1687, ?30 Mar, 31 Mar;
   Watertown
HAGBORNE/HAGBOURNE, Abraham & Elizabeth _?_ ; b 1639; Boston
HAGBORNE, Samuel (-1643) & Catherine [DIGHTON], m/2 Thomas DUDLEY 1644, m/3 John
   ALLEN 1653; b 1635; Roxbury
HAGGETT, Henry (?1594-1678) & Ann _?_ ; Salem/Wenham
HAGGETT, Henry & Elizabeth _?_ (-1705); b 1695; Wenham
HAGGET, John & Rebecca _?_ ; b 1676; Boston
HAGGETT, Moses & Joanna JOHNSON/JOHNSTON?, dau John & Susanna; 23 Oct 1671, 20 Nov;
   Andover
HAGGET, Moses, Jr. & Martha GRANGIER; 21 Feb 1699/1700; Andover
HAIGHT, Nicholas (see HOYT) & [?Susanna JOYCE]; b 1647, ca 1660?; Flushing, LI
HAIGHT, Nicholas & Patience TITUS (1679-); b 1701?, 5 Jul 1704; Westbury, LI/?Flushing, LI
HAIGHT, Samuel (1647-1712) (see HOYT) & Sarah _?_ /?Charity [FIELD] (-1712+); b 1683, b
   1667?, b 1679?; Flushing, LI
HAILSTONE, William & _?_ ; b 1643; Taunton
HALBIDGE, Arthur (-1648) & _?_ /Susanna _?_, m/2 Rev. John JONES; New Haven
HALE, Arthur & Mary _?_ ; b 1687/[8?]; Boston
HALE, Bennezer (1661-) & 1/wf Mary _?_ ; b 1690; Wethersfield, CT
HALE, Henry (-1724) & Sarah KELLY (1670-1741); 11 Sep 1695; Newbury
HALE, John (1635-1707) & 1/wf Rebecca LOWLE/LOWELL (1642-1662); 5 Dec 1660; Newbury
HALE, John (1635-1707) & 2/wf Sarah SOMERBY (1645-1672); 8 Dec 1663; Newbury
HALE, John (1636-1700) & 1/wf Rebecca BYLEY/BILEY (1636-1683); 15 Dec 1664; Ipswich
HALE, John (1647-1709) & Hannah [NOLT] (1649-); 8 May 1668; Wethersfield, CT
HALE, John (1635-1707) & 3/wf Sarah (RING) [COTTLE] (?1636-1699), w William; aft 19 Jun
   1672; Newbury
HALE, John (1661-1726) & Sarah JAQUES (1664-); 10 Oct 1683; Newbury

HALE, John (1636-1700) & 2/wf Sarah NOYES (1656-1697); 31 Mar 1684; Newbury
HALE, John (1668-) & Mary [BEVIN] (?1678-); b 1697; Wethersfield, CT
HALE, John (1636-1700) & 3/wf Elizabeth (SOMERBY) CLARK (1646-1716), w Nathaniel; 8 Aug 1698; Newbury/Beverly
HALE, Joseph & ? JENKES?; b 1668; Concord
HAIELL/HALE, Joseph (1671-1761) & 1/wf Mary WATSON (1671±-1708); 15 Dec 1693, 15 Nov; Beverly
HALE, Joseph (1674-1755) & Mary MOODEY (1678-1753); m int 25 Dec 1699; Newbury
HALE, Richard (-1720) & Mary [BULLOCK] (1652-1730); b 1677; Swansea/Warren, RI
HALE, Richard & ? ; b 1700; Newcastle
HALE, Robert (?1610-1659) & Joanna [?CUTTER] (1603-1679/81?), m/2 Richard JACOB 1662; b 14 Oct 1632, b 1630, in Eng; Charlestown/Ipswich
HALE, Robert (1668-1719) & Elizabeth CLARK (?1684-), m/2 John GILMAN 1720; m int 4 Feb 1699/1700; Beverly
HALE, Samuel (ca 1615-1693) & Mary [?SMITH] (ca 1624-1712); b 1643; Wethersfield, CT
HALE, Samuel (-1679) & Lydia MAYNARD (?1648-), m/2 William MARSHALL 1687, m/3 Samuel BALLATT 1691; 19 Mar 1668/[9]; Charlestown
HALE, Samuel (1645-1711) & 1/wf Ruth EDWARDS (-1682, ae ca 30); 20 Jun 1670; Wethersfield, CT
HALE, Samuel & Sarah ILSLY/OLSLEY (1655-); 21 Jul 1673; Newbury
HALE, Samuel (1645-1711) & 2/wf Mary WELLES (1666-1715); b 1695; Wethersfield, CT
HALE, Samuel (1674-1745) & 1/wf Martha PALMER (1677-1723); 3 Nov 1698; Rowley/Bradford
HALE/HALL, Thomas (1606-1682) (ae ca 50 in 1660) & Thomasin DOWSETT (-1682); St. Hellen's Bishopsgate, London, 11 Dec 1632; Newbury/Salem
HALE, Thomas[1] (-1679) & 1/wf Jane [LORD]; ca Feb 1639/40; Roxbury/Hartford
HALE, Thomas (1633-1688) & Mary HUTCHINSON (1630-1713), m/2 William WATSON 1695; 26 May 1657; Newbury
HALE, Thomas[1] (-1678, 1679?) & 2/wf Mary NASH (-1696+); 14 Dec 1659; Charlestown/Norwalk, CT
HALE, Thomas[2] (1651-1725, Norwalk, CT) & 1/wf Priscilla MARKHAM (1654-1712); 18 Nov 1675; Hadley/Enfield, CT
HALE, Thomas (1653-1723) & Naomi KILBOURN (1656-1735); 30 Oct 1679; Wethersfield, CT
HALE, Thomas (1659-1730) & Sarah NORTHENDS (1661-1730, 1732); 16 May 1682; Newbury
HALE, Thomas (1675?-) & 1/wf? Mary [HOWSE] (1677-1751); b 1701?, 1697
HALE, Timothy (1641±-1689, Suffield, CT) & Sarah BARBER (1646-); 26 Nov 1663; Windsor, CT/Suffield, CT
HAELL, William (-1668, Billerica) & Anna CASE, Billerica; 30 Oct 1663; Billerica/Charlestown
HALE, Zechary & Mary WILLIAMS; b 1676; Charlestown
HALEY, Andrew (-1697) & Deborah [WILSON]; ca 1665?; Kittery, ME
HALEY, Andrew (-1725) & Elizabeth SCAMMON, m/2 Nicholas WEEKS 1742; 25 Jul 1697, ?15 Jul; Kittery, ME
HALEY, James & Dinah ? ; b 1682; Boston
HALEY, John (-1688) & 1/wf Ruth (CROW) [GAYLORD], w William; aft 1680; Hadley
HALEY, John (-1688) & 2/wf Hannah [BLISS] (1666-), m/2 Simeon/Simon? SMITH 1689; ca 1687?; Hadley
HALEY, Thomas & 1/wf Mary [WEST] (-1658); ca 1649?; Saco, ME
HALEY, Thomas & 2/wf Sarah ? ; b 1672; Saco, ME
HALEY, Thomas (-1695) & Sarah [MAYER] (1661-1727), m/2 Richard CARR; ca 1683; Saco, ME
HALEY, William & Mary ? ; b 1689; New London, CT
HALEY, William & Sarah [INGERSOLL] (1677?-); ?b 1699, b 1707; Kittery, ME/Boston
HALL, Andrew & Ann [RATCHELL]; 1677; Boston
HALL, Andrew (1665-) & 1/wf Susannah/Susan [CAPEN] (1664-1736); b 1691; Medford/Newton
HALL, Benjamin (1650-1730) & Frances PARKER; 27 Jul 1676; Portsmouth, RI
HALL, Benjamin (1653-1727) (?son of John) & Mehitable MATTHEWS (?1653-1741, in 90th y); 7 Feb 1677; Yarmouth/Harwich
HALL, Benjamin & Sarah FISHER; 9 Jan 169-, 1691/2, 1692; Wrentham
HALL, Christopher & Sarah ? ; b 1670; Chelmsford/Groton/Concord
HALL, Christopher, Groton & Ruth GARFIELD, Watertown; 2 Feb 1687/8; Watertown?
HALL, Christopher & Mary HOMER, ?w Michael; 5 Feb 1699/1700; Cambridge

HALL, Daniel (-1675) & Mary RUTHERFORD, m/2 John PROUT 1681; 11 Nov 1670, b 1668?; New Haven/?Middletown/Barbados?

HALL, Daniel & Thankful LYMAN (1672-); 15 Mar 1693, prob 692/3; Wallingford, CT

HALL, David & Sarah ROCKWELL (1653-); 24 Dec 1676; Wallingford, CT

HALL, Ebenezer (1678-1724, 1723?) & Deborah HILAND (-1758); 11 Apr 1700; Guilford, CT

HALL, Edward (1608-) & Margaret _?_ (-1676); [ca 1630/35]; Cambridge

HALL, Edward (-1657) & Sarah _?_ ; b 1646; Lynn

HALL, Edward (-1670) & Esther/Hester _?_ , m/2? Thomas JORDAN 1674; b 1651; Braintree/Duxbury

HALL, Edward & Mary REYNAR; 18 Jun 1677; Cambridge

HALL, Edward (-1719) & Mary [BALL] (-1719+); [ca 1678/85?], ca 1694; Westerly, RI

HALL, Edward (-1682) & Ann/Anna/Hannah _?_ , m/2 Nicholas MASON; b 1680; Wethersfield, CT

HALL, Elisha & Lydia _?_ (-1724); b 1681, b 1680; Yarmouth

HALL, Ephraim & Sarah RAND; 1 Jul 1674; Lynn/Boston

HALL, Francis (?1608-1690, 1689) & 1/wf Elizabeth [THOMPSON] (-1665); b 1629?, b 1635; Fairfield, CT/Stratford, CT

HALL, Francis (-1689, 1690) & 2/wf Dorothy (SMITH) BLAKEMAN, w John, m/3 Mark St.JOHN 1692/3, m/4 Isaac MOORE; last of Oct 1665; Stratford, CT

HALL, George (-1669) & Mary _?_ ; b 1640; Taunton

HALL, Gershom (1648-1732) & 1/wf Bethia [BANGS] (1650-15 Oct 1696, 1693?, ae 54); b 1669; Yarmouth/Harwich

HALL, Gershom & Martha (BEARD) BRANHALL (-1724, ae 69), w George; 9 Dec 1698, 7 Dec 1698; Hingham

HALL, Henry (-1705) & _?_ ; b 1652?, b 1658; Newport/Westerly, RI

HALL, Henry[2] (?1658-1717) & Constant _?_ (-1719); b 1672, ca 1680; Westerly, RI

HALL, Hugh (-1732, Boston) & 1/wf Lydia [GIBBS] (1670-1699); b 1693; Boston/Barbados

HALL, Isaac (-1714, ae 84?) & 2/wf? Lydia KNAPP (1647?-1716); 16 Jan 1666, 1665?, 1666/7; Fairfield, CT

HALL, Isaac (1667-) & Jane BURGIS; 24 Jan 1689; Fairfield, CT/Redding, CT

HALL/HALLET, Isaac (ca 1675-1738) & Sarah REED; 24 Apr 1700; Windham, CT/Mansfield, CT?

HALL, James (1635?) & Margaret _?_ ; Newport, RI

HALL, James & Mary (ASH) [HOYT], w Thomas; b 1693, ca 1692; Salisbury

HALL, James (-1745) & Sarah [BADCOCK] (-1734+); b 1693; Westerly, RI

HALL, John (-1677) & Mary _?_ ; b 1617; Dover, NH

HALL, John (-1673, ae 89, Middletown, CT) & _?_ ; in Eng, b 1619; Roxbury/Hartford/Middletown, CT

HALL, John & _?_ ; b 1635; Portsmouth/Newport

HALL, John (-1696) & Bethia [?FARMER] (-1683); [b 1636]; Charlestown/Barnstable

HALL, John & Rebecca (SMYNE) BYLEY, w Henry, m/3 William WORCESTER 1650, m/4 Samuel SYMONES 1663; 3 Apr 1641; Salisbury

HALL, John (1619/21-1694, 1694/5) & 1/wf Ann/Anna [WILCOX] (-1673, ca 57, Middletown, CT); ca 1643?, b 24 Jul 1651; ?Roxbury/Hartford/Middletown, CT

HALL, John (1605, 1610?-1676) & Jeane/Jane [WOOLEN/WOOTEN?] (-1690), m/2 John COOPER ca 1678; b 1644, b 1641?; Roxbury/Hartford/Wallingford, CT

HALL, John (-1693) & Elizabeth [LEARNED?] (1621-); b 1645; Charlestown/Dover, NH

HALL, John (?1617-1677) & Elizabeth [LAYTON]?; b 1649, b 1645, as early as 1641; Dover, NH

HALL/HALE, John (1627-1701) & Elizabeth GREENE (1639-1714); 4 Apr 1656; Concord/Medford

HALL, John, Jr. (1637/8-1710) & Priscilla [BEARSE] (1644-1712); b 1663, b 1660; Yarmouth

HALL, John & Mary PARKER (1647-1725); 6 Dec 1666; New Haven

HALL, John (1640-1693) & Hannah PENIMAN (1648-), m/2 Samuel HOSKINS 4 Jun 1702; 4 Feb 1667, 1671; Taunton

HALL, John (?1648-1704), Guilford & Elizabeth SMITH (1649-), New Haven; 17 Nov 1669, 13 Nov 1669; New Haven

HALL, John (1648-1711) & 1/wf Elizabeth [CORNELL/CORNWELL] (1651-); b 1670, b 1680; Middletown, CT/Guilford, CT

HALL, John (?1645-1697) & Abigail ROBERTS, m/2 Thomas DOWNS 1698; 8 Nov 1671; Dover, NH

HALL, John & Elizabeth RAND; 3 Mar 1673/4; Lynn

HALL, John (-1695) & 2/wf Mary (CURTICE) HUBBARD (-1709), w Thomas; 1 Oct 1674; Middletown, CT
HALL, John & Mary NEWELL; 18 Nov 1684; Rehoboth
HALL, John (-1720), Medford & Jemimah SILL (-1712), Cambridge; 21 Dec 1687, 2 Dec 1687; Cambridge
HALL, John (-1692) & Rebina _?_; b 1691; Wethersfield, CT
HALL, John (1670-1730) & Mary LYMAN; 8 Dec 1692; Wallingford, CT
HALL, John & Esther BELL (1672-); 14 Dec 1692; Taunton/Norton
HALL, John (-1712) & Elizabeth [BALL] (ca 1693); Westerly/Charletown, RI
HALL, John & Frances ALLEN (1676-) (see John below); 16 Dec 1690, b 1701?; Middletown, CT/Fairfield, CT
HALL, John & Frances ALLYN, m/2 William WARD; 24 Feb 1692/3; Middletown, CT
HALL, John (?1666-1735) & Margaret MILLER (-1724); 30 Apr 1694; Yarmouth
HALL, John (1673-) & Elizabeth _?_, m/2 Benjamin PIERCE; b 1696; Dover, NH
HALL, John & Esther CHESLEY; 3 Jul 1699; Dover, NH
HALL, John & Elizabeth KING, m/2 Samuel RICHARDSON; 17 Dec 1696; Taunton
HALL, John & Abigail [SUMMERS]; b 1701; Fairfield/Stratford
HALL, Jonathan & Hannah _?_; b 1677; New London, CT
HALL, Jonathan (1659-1718) & 1/wf Elizabeth [WITHINGTON] (1666-1700); b 1692; Dorchester
HALL, Jonathan & Margaret SEWARD, ?m/2 Thomas FOSTER 1703, Middletown, CT; 21 Jun 1698; Boston/Middletown, CT
HALL, Joseph (1642-1716) & Mary _?_ (1648-1718); ca 1670/2?; Mansfield, CT
HALL, Joseph & Joanna [SMALLIDGE]?
HALL, Joseph & Elizabeth RAND; 3 Mar 1674, ?1673/4; Lynn
HALL, Joseph & Elizabeth [SMITH] (-1717, ae 62), m/2 Thomas PACKER 1687; "by 1676"; Dover, NH/Greenland, NH
HALL, Joseph & Jane/Mary [HILTON?] (-1737), m/2 Richard MATTOON 1699?; 18 Feb 1689; Dover, NH
HALL, Joseph (1663-) & 1/wf Hannah MILLER (1666-1710); 12 Feb 1689, 1690; Yarmouth
HALL, Joseph & Sarah [HALL] (1668/9-); ca 1690?; Fairfield, CT/Hempstead, LI
HALL, Joseph & Silence [CROSWELL] (1673-); ca 1690; Charlestown/Dorchester
HALL, Joseph & Mary BALL? (1669-); 13 Jul 1693; Boston
HALL, Joseph (1674-) & Blanche _?_; b 1700(01?); Dorchester
HALL, Joseph & Mary [MOODY]; 1700
HALL, Kinsley & 1/wf Elizabeth DUDLEY (1652-); 25 Sep 1674; Dover, NH
HALL, Kinsley (1652-1736), Exeter, NH, & 2/wf Mary (ELIOT) [WOODBURY], w Nicholas; 29 May, 1687, 1702; Beverly, MA
HALL, Martin (1620+-) & 1/wf? _?_; Portsmouth, NH
HALL, Martin & Susanna CHUBB; 2 Nov 1676; ?Beverly
HALL, Nathaniel (1646-) & Ann [THORNTON]; b 1675; Hingham/Delaware River
HALL, Nathaniel (1666-1725) & Elizabeth CUTTER (1669-1742); 16 Apr 1690; Medford/Cambridge
HALL, Nathaniel & Hannah [SWETT] (1664-); b 1696; Dover, NH
HALL, Nathaniel & Elizabeth CURTIS (-1735); 11 May 1699; Wallingford, CT
HALL, Nathaniel (1678-) & Jane MOORE; 29 Aug 1700; ?Yarmouth/Lewistown, PA
HAUL, Nicholas & Mary _?_; b 1678; Boston
HALL, Paul & _?_; b 1671, b 1670
HALL, Percival (-1752) & Jane WILLIS/WILLOWES? (1677-); 2 Feb 1696; Woburn/Cambridge
HALL, Preserved (1663-1740) & 1/wf Lydia (JACKSON) LEAVITT (1658-), w Israel; 25 Jan 1698/9; Hingham
HALL, Ralph & Mary _?_ (2 Ralphs)
HALL, ?Rodolphus/Ralph (1619-1690+, 1701) & Mary _?_; b 1647(8?); Charlestown/Hempstead, LI
HALL, Ralph & 1/wf Elizabeth [DODGE]; ca 1676
HALL, Ralph (-1706) & 2/wf Mary CHESLEY; m 26 May 1701, b 1680?, by 1685; Dover, NH
HALL, Ralph & 1/wf _?_ [PHILBROOK?]; Dover, NH
HALL, Richard (1620-1691) & Mary _?_ (-1691); b 1646, b 1648; Middletown, CT
HALL, Richard (-1691) & Elizabeth [COLLICOT] (-1693); b 1648; Dorchester
HALL, Richard & Martha _?_; b 1672(3?); Bradford

HALL, Richard (1656-1727, Roxbury) & Elizabeth (HEMANWAY) HOLBROOK (1645?, 1655-), w
John; 22 May 1679; Roxbury
HALL, Richard (1676-1730) & Abigail DALTON (1673-); 24 Apr 1699; Bradford
HALL, Richard (1672-1726) & Hannah [MILES] (1681-); b 1700; New Haven
HALL, Samuel (-1679/80) (returned to Eng) & Sarah __?__; b 1633?; Salisbury
HALL, Samuel (-1640?) & Joanna/Joan [KNOT]?; b 1638, b 1637, m lic 15 Jul 1629; Charlestown
HALL, Samuel (?1636-1694) & Elizabeth [FOLLAND], Yarmouth, m/2 Jeremiah JONES 1699 (no
ch mentioned in will); ca 1662?; Barnstable/Yarmouth
HALL, Samuel (-1691) & Elizabeth [COOKE] (1640?-); [1662], b 3 Feb 1663; ?New London,
CT/Middletown, CT
HALL, Samuel (1644-1690) & [Elizabeth] [WHITE] (-1707), m/2 Jonathan PRATT; b 1664;
Taunton
HALL, Samuel (1648-) & Hannah WALKER (1646-1728); - May 1668; New Haven
HALL, Samuel (1650-1733) & Elizabeth JOHNSON (1652-); 22 Dec 1674; Guilford, CT
HALL, Samuel & Bashua/Bathsheba HINCKLEY; 6 Jun 1681; Dorchester
HALL, Samuel (-1694) & 1/wf Mary __?__; 26 Mar 1682, 20 Mar 1682/3; Fairfield, CT
HALL, Samuel (1664-) & Abigail PRATT (1665-); 3 Jan 1683; Taunton
HALL, Samuel & Phebe WARD; 6 Dec 1683; Middletown, CT
HALL, Samuel & Elizabeth BOURNE; 17 Apr 1686, 7 Apr 1686; Taunton
HALL, Samuel (-1694, in 59th y) & 2/wf Hannah __?__ (-1687); 16 Mar 1686/7; Fairfield, CT
HALL, Samuel (-1694) & 3/wf Susannah __?__; [say 1688/9]; Fairfield, CT
HALL, Samuel (1664-1740) & Sarah HINSDALE/HINSDEL/HEWSDELL (ca 1670-); 8 Jan 1690/1,
8 Jan 1691; Middletown, CT/Hadley/Deerfield
HALL, Samuel & Patience RIDER; 2 Feb 1696/7, 7 Feb 1696/7; ?Yarmouth
HALL, Samuel (1665-) & Hannah [SAWTELLE]; b 1698; Stow/Groton
HALL, Samuel/Stephen (-1724, in 87th y) & Ruth DAVIS (1644-1715); 3 Dec 1663;
Concord/Charlestown/Stow/Medford/Plainfield, CT
HALL, Stephen (1667-) & 1/wf Grace [WILLIS] (-1721); b 1693; Medford/Charlestown
HALL, Stephen (1670-) & 1/wf Elizabeth WILLIS/WILLOWES? (-1714); 18 Oct 1697, no issue;
Woburn/Cambridge
HALL, Thomas & 1/wf Isabel?/Elizabeth __?__ (-1682); b 1648; Cambridge/Charlestown
HALL, Thomas & Hannah __?__; b 1664; Boston
HALL, Thomas & 1/wf Sarah [COOK]; ca 1670/75?; Guilford, CT
HALL, Thomas (1649-1711) & Grace WATSON (1653-1731); ca 5 Jun 1673, m 5 Jun 1673;
Wallingford, CT
HALL, Thomas & Elizabeth (DOWSE) MILES, w Samuel; 24 Dec 1673; Charlestown/Woburn
HALL, Thomas & Martha (__?__) (RUSSELL) BRADSHAW (-1694±), w William, w Humphrey; 24
May 1683; Cambridge/Charlestown
HALL, Thomas & 2/wf Hannah [SHEATHER]; 1685; Guilford, CT
HALL, Thomas & Susannah (LOVETT/LOWELL) [BUSH], w Reynold; b 1686, b 1688;
Worcester/Norwich, CT
HALL, Thomas & Abigail MARTIN; 25 Feb 1690; Dedham
HALL, Thomas (1671-) & 1/wf Mary HILAND (1672-1738); 1 Feb 1692; Guilford, CT
HALL, Thomas & Hannah PAINE; 15 Feb 1694, 14 Feb 1695; Boston
HALL, Thomas (1675-1732) & Mary __?__; "by 1700", b 1707; Dover, NH
HALL/HALE?, Timothy & Sarah BARBER; 26 Nov 1663; Windsor, CT
HALL, William (1613-1675) & Mary __?__ (-1680+); ca 1640?; Portsmouth, RI
HALL, William (-1669) & Esther __?__ (-1683); b 1648; Guilford, CT
HALL, William (-1667) & Sarah MERRIAM, m/2 John GOVE; 14 Oct 1658, no issue; Concord
HALL, William (-1698) & Alice TRIPP (1650-); 26 Jan 1670, 1671?; Portsmouth, RI/E. Greenwich
HALL, William (1651-1727) & Esther __?__ (-1726, ae 70); b 1680; Mansfield, CT
HALL, William & Elizabeth __?__; b 1688; Boston
HALL, William & Sarah (BARRETT) [FOWLER], w Thomas; aft 28 Sep 1688, bef 18 Aug 1691;
Boston
HALL, William (1672-) & Sarah [TIBBETTS]?; b 1698, b 1698/9; N. Kingston, RI/Portsmouth, RI
HALL, Zuriel (-1691) & Elizabeth [TRIPP] (?1648±-1701+); ca 1665?
HALL, Zuriel & Susanna SHEFFIELD; 1 Sep 1697; Medford/Sherborn/Hingham/Dover, NH
HALL, __?__ & Elizabeth __?__, m/2 Thomas PARKER by 1637
HALL, __?__ & [Mary STEELE]; b 14 Feb 1684/5

HALL, _?_ & Mary [WILCOX]; b 1636, b 1627?; Concord
HALLOM, Isaac & Hannah (CLOYES) [HONNSELL], w Edward; b 1685(6?); Boston
HALLAM, John (1661-1700) & Prudence RICHARDSON (1662-), m/2 Elnathan MINER 1703; 15 Mar 1683, 1682/3; Stonington, CT
HALLAM, Nicholas (-1714) & 1/wf Sarah PYGAN (1670-1700); 8 Jul 1686; New London, CT
HALLAM, _?_ & Alice _?_ (-1698), m/2 John LIVEEN; b 1661; Barbados
HALLOCK/HALLECK, John (?1658-1737) & Abigail [SWAZEY/SWEEZY?] (-1737?); ca 1678?, 1679?; Southold, LI/Setauket, LI/Westbury, LI/Brookhaven
HALLOCK, John (?1679-1765) & Hannah _?_; ca 1700?; Brookhaven, LI
HALLOCK, Peter & 2/wf? _?_ ?[HOWELL], wid?; in Eng, b 1640?; Southold, LI
HALLOCK, Peter & 1/wf Elizabeth _?_; by 1686?, b 1690, 5 ch in 1698; Southold, LI
HALLOCK, Thomas (-1718) & Hope [COMSTOCK] (-1732/3); by 1680?; Southold, LI
HALLOCK, William (-1684) & Margaret [HOWELL?/YOUNGS?]; by 1655?; Southold, LI
HALLOCK, William (?1667-1736) & Mary _?_ (1667-1752); ca 1688; Southold, LI
HALLET, Andrew & Mary _?_; in Eng, b 1608?, b 1615?; Yarmouth
HALLETT, Andrew (-1684) & 2/wf? Ann/Anna/Anne [BERSE/BEESE/BESSIE?] (ca 1641-1694); b 1646; Sandwich/Yarmouth
HALLET, Isaac & Sarah READ (see Isaac HALL); 24 Apr 1700; Windham, CT
HALLETT, John (-1674) & Ann _?_; b 1633; Scituate
HALLETT, John (1650-1726) & Mary HOWES (-1733); 16 Feb 1681, 1681/2; Yarmouth
HALLET, Jonathan (1647-1717) & Abigail DEXTER (-1715); 30 Jan 1683, 10 Jan; Yarmouth
HALLETT, Joseph & Elizabeth [GORHAM] (1648-); 1666; Sandwich
HALLETT, Joseph & Abigail ROADS; 25 Dec 1682; Marblehead
HALLETT, Richard & ?Lydia _?_, m/2 John DRUMMOND 1661; b 1636?; Boston
HALLETT, Samuel (1649±, 1657-1724, ae 73) & _?_
HALLETT, William[1] (1616-1706) & 1/wf Elizabeth (FONES) (WINTHROP) FEAKE (1610-) (see Robert FEAKE); ?LI
HALLETT, Capt. William[2] (?1648-1729, ae 71) & 1/wf Sarah [WOOLSEY] (1650-1691+); ca 1669/73; ?Newtown, LI
HALLETT, William[1] (1616-1706) & 2/wf Susannah THORN, w William; b 25 Apr 1674, div/seperated, by Jun 1669; LI
HALLETT, William[1] & 3/wf Katherine _?_; b 9 Apr 1684
HALLETT, William[1] & 4/wf Rebecca BRADLY; b 5 Oct 1693, aft 1682, b 30 Nov 1686; Suffield Co., NY
HALLETT, William[3] (1670-1798?) (killed by slaves 24 Jan 1707, 1707/8) & Ruth _?_ (-1708); Newtown, LI
HALLETT, _?_ & Lydia _?_, m/2 John DRUMMOND 1661; Boston
HALLYDAY/HALLIDAY, John & Ann SADIE; 21 Mar 1670; Charlestown
HALLADAY, Walter (-1709, Suffield, CT) & Katherine HUNTER; 22 Apr 1673; Springfield/Suffield, CT
HALLAWELL, Benjamin (1656-) & Mary STOCKER; 12 May 1692; Boston
HALLOWELL, Henry (-1663) & Rebecca [AULT] (?1641-), m/2 Thomas EDGERLY 1665; b 1661; Oyster River, NH
HALLWELL/HOLLOWAY?, (?William) & Anne (BLAKE) LEAGAR (1618-1681), w Jacob; by 1679?; Boston
HALSALL, George & Elizabeth _?_; b 1642; Boston
HALSALL, George & Joan [RUCK?]; b 1652; Boston/New London, CT
HALSEY, Daniel (-1682) & Joanna/Jemima? _?_; b 1669; Southampton, LI
HALSEY, Daniel (1669-1734) & Amy [LARISON] (1679-1734); b 1699; Southampton, LI
HALSEY, David (1663-1731/2) & Hannah _?_; ca 1696?; Southampton, LI
HALSEY, George & Rebecca _?_ (1624-1700); Newport
HALSEY, Isaac (?1632-1703) & Mary [BARNES]; b 1665; Southampton, LI
HALSEY, Isaac (1660-1757, 1759?) & 1/wf Abigail HOWELL; 28 Nov 1689; Southampton, LI
HALSEY, Isaac (1664/5-1752) & Phebe [HOWELL] (-1750+); ca 1690?, b 4 Aug 1697; Southampton, LI
HALSEY, Isaac (1660-) & 2/wf Hannah (REEVES) STRATTON (-1732, ae 62), w Stephen; 19 Dec 1699; East Hampton, LI/Southampton, LI
HALSEY, James & Dinah _?_; b 1669(70?); Boston
HALSEY, Jeremiah (1667-1732) & 1/wf Ruth _?_ (1668-1717); ca 1689; Bridgehampton, LI

HALSEY, John & Jane TALY/TALLEY; 10 Dec 1700; Boston
HALSEY, Joseph (1668-1725) & Elizabeth [HALSEY]?; ca 1690/3?; Southampton, LI/Elizabeth, NJ
HALSEY, _?_ & Rebecca BENTON (1671-)
HALSEY, Joseph & Elizabeth ELDRIDGE; 29 Jan 1697; Boston
HALSEY, Josiah (1656/7-1732) & 1/wf Sarah TOPPING; 12 Sep 1678; Southampton, LI
HALSEY, Nathaniel (-1705) & Hannah GROSS; 22 Jun 1693; Boston
HALSEY, Nathaniel & Ann STARBOROUGH; 15 Dec 1697; Southampton, LI
HALSEY, Thomas[1] (1592-1678) & 1/wf Phebe _?_ (-1649); in Eng, b 1626; Lynn/Hempstead, NH
HALSEY, Thomas[2] (1626-1688) & Mary _?_ (-1699); b 1654; Southampton, LI
HALSEY, Thomas[1] (-1678) & 2/wf Ann JONES/JOHNES, w Edward?/Rice?; ca 25 Jul 1660; Southampton, LI
HALSEY, _?_ & Margaret [PHIPPS], m/2 James ANDREWS 1696
HALSTED, Jonas (1611-1683) & [Sarah] _?_ ; by 1635?; Hempstead, LI
HALSTEAD, Joseph (1642-1679) & Susannah [HARCUTT], m/2 Peter STRINGHAM 1680?; ca 1670
HALSTED, Joseph & Sarah [FERRIS] (1676-); b 1701?, b 1712; Stratford, CT/Hempstead, LI
HALSTED, Nathan/Nathaniel? (-1644) & Isabelle _?_ (-1641); b 1625?, b 1622?; Concord
HALSTED, Timothy (1636-1703) & Hannah [WILLIAMS]; b 1657?, 1657; Hempstead, LI
HALSTED, Timothy (-1703) & Abigail [WILLIAMS/?CARMEN/?CARMAN]; ca 1685?, b 28 Jul 1667?; Hempstead, LI/Elizabeth, NJ
HALSTEAD, William & Martha _?_ ; b 1667; Boston
HAM, John[3] (-1727) & Mary HEARD (1649-1706); 6 May 1668; Dover, NH
HAM, John (?1671-1754) & Elizabeth KNIGHT; 14 Mar 1697/8; Dover, NH/Portsmouth, NH
HAM, John & _?_ [LYDSTON]; ?ca 1690/5?; Portsmouth, NH
HAM, Matthew[2] (-bef 1665) & [Sarah] _?_ , m/2 Tobias TAYLOR by 1667; ca 1643?; Portsmouth, NH
HAM, Samuel & ?Elizabeth [SLOPER]; b 1700, b 1710; Dover, NH
HAM, William (-1692) & Honour STEPHENS; St. Andrew's, Plymouth, Eng, 20 Nov 1622; Exeter, NH/Portsmouth, NH
HAM, William (-1695) & Sarah [?DENNATT], m/2 John GILDEN 1698+; ca 1680/4?; Portsmouth, NH
HAM, _?_ & Mary SHATTUCK; Boston
HAMANT, Francis (-1692) & Sarah _?_ (-1708); b 1651; Medfield
HAMANT, Timothy & Meletiah CLARK, m/2 William PARTRIDGE; 19 Jan 1696, 1696/7; Boston
HAMARY/HOMARY?, John & Sarah _?_ ; b 1695; Tiverton, RI
HAMILTON, Daniel (-1739, 1738) & 1/wf Mary [SMITH] (1669-), dau Samuel; b 1694; Eastham
HAMILTON, David (-1692) & Anna JACKSON; 14 Jul 1662, 166-?; Dover, NH
HAMILTON, John & Christian _?_ ; b 1668; Concord
HAMILTON, John (1668-1747) & Hannah _?_ (perhaps had 1/wf Sarah); b 1697; Concord
HAMILTON, Nathaniel (see Nathaniel HAMLIN/HAMBLIN, Suffield, CT) & Mary PEIRCE; 10 Apr 1695; Manchester/Marblehead
HAMBLETON/?HAMILTON, Thomas & Lydia [WING] (1647-), dau Daniel; b 1671(2?); Sandwich
HAMBLETON, William & Mary RICHARDSON; 7 Aug 1654; Boston
HAMILTON, William (1647-1749) & Mercy [BERRY/BRACY?]; ca 1668/75?; N. Kings Town, RI/Danbury, CT
HAMLET, Jacob[2] (-1703) & 1/wf Hannah PARKER (-1669); 22 Jul 1668; Billerica
HAMLET, Jacob[2] (?1641-1703) & 2/wf Mary DUTTON (-1678); 21 Dec 1669; Billerica
HAMLET, Jacob[2] (?1641-1703) & 3/wf Mary (ADFORD) [JAQUITH] (1651-), w Abraham; 1679?; Billerica/Woburn
HAMLET, William[1] (?1614-1679+) & Sarah (?IVES) [HUBBARD] (-1689), w James; aft Jan 1639; Cambridge/Billerica
HAMLIN/HAMBLIN, Bartholomew (1642-1704) & Susannah DUNHAM; 20 Jan 1673; Barnstable
HAMLIN, Ebenezer (1674-) & Sarah LEWIS (-1755, Sharon, CT); 4 Apr 1698; Barnstable
HAMLIN, Eleazer (1649-) & Mehitable JENKINS (1655-); ca the middle of Oct 1675; Barnstable
HAMBLEN, Eleazer (1668-1698) & Lydia [SEARS?] (1666-), m/2 Thomas SNOW 1706; b 1698; Yarmouth/Ipswich
HAMLIN, Ezekiel & Elizabeth DRAKE; 8 Aug 1654; Boston

HAMLIN, Giles (1622-1689), Middletown & Esther [CROW] (?1628-1700), Hartford; ca 1654; Middletown, CT/Hadley?

HAMLIN, Isaac (1676-1710) & Elizabeth HOWLAND (-1729+), m/2 Timothy CARINON 1711; 14 Sep 1698; Barnstable

HAMLIN, Israel (1652-) & 1/wf [Abigail] [LUMBARD?] (-1700?); b 1687; Barnstable

HAMLIN, James (-1690) & Ann/Anne __?__ (-1690+); in Eng, b 1630?; Barnstable

HAMLIN, James (1636?-1718) & Mary DUNHAM (-1715); 20 Nov 1662; Barnstable

HAMLIN, James (1669-) & Ruth LEWIS; 8 Oct 1690; Barnstable

HAMLIN, John (1644-) & Sarah BIERSE/BEARSE (1646-); Aug 1667; Barnstable

HAMLIN, John (1658-1733) & Mary COLLINS (1666-1722); Jan 1684, 11 Jan 1684, 1684/5; Middletown, CT

HAMLIN, Nathaniel (1671-) (see Nathaniel HAMILTON) & Mary [PIERCE?]; 10 Apr 1695, Manchester/Marblehead; Suffield, CT

HAMBLEN, Thomas & Lydia [WING]; b 1671(2?); Sandwich

HAMLEN, Thomas & Esther (CRABTREE) [PLATTS], w Thomas; b 1688(9?); Boston

HAMLIN, William & Mary [RICHARDSON]; b 1666, [1654]; Boston

HAMLIN, William (-1733, in 66th y) & Susanna COLLINS (1669-1722); 26 May 1692; Middletown, CT

HAMMOND, Benjamin (1621-1703) & Mary VINCENT (1633-1705); 8 Nov 1648; Sandwich/Rochester

HAMMOND, Benjamin (1673-1747) & Elizabeth [HANNEWALL]; b 1702, b 1701?; Dorchester

HAMMONS, Edmond[1] & Mary __?__; Kittery, ME

HAMMONS, Edmond[2] & Jane [MONTISSE]; b 1684, b 1681; Kittery, ME

HAMMON, Edward & Susannah BRADLEY/BROWN?; 5 Jan 1684; Bristol, RI

HAMMONS, Edward & Elizabeth BALLS, m/2 Francis PETTIGREW; 20 Oct 1700; Kittery, ME

HAMMOND, Isaac & Ann/Hannah? KENRICK (1670-); 7 Dec 1692; Newton

HAMMOND, John & 1/wf Abigail [SALTER] (?1623-1663?); ca 1652; Watertown/Lexington

HAMMONS, John & Mary SOMES (1642-); 17 Oct 1660; Gloucester

HAMMOND, John & 2/wf Sarah [NICHOLS] (1643-1688/9); ca 1664?, 2 Mar 1663; Watertown/Charlestown

HAMMONS, John & Ruth STANWOOD; 7 Jul 1686; Gloucester

HAMMOND, John & Prudence (WADE) (CROSBY) [COTTON] (-1711, ae 74), w Anthony, w Seaborn; ca 1689?; Watertown

HAMMONS, John (-1718, ae 54) & Annis/Agnes TENNY; 20 Jan 1691, ?2 Jan 1691; Gloucester

HAMMOND, John (1663-1749) & Mary [ARNOLD] (1672-1749+); b 1693, [ca 1692], 1691; Rochester

HAMMOND, Jonathan (1644, 1641-1709?, 1704?, 1717) & 1/wf? Mary [GOUCH?]; ca 1665/70?; Wells, ME

HAMMOND, Joseph (-1710, 1709) & Katherine (FROST) LEIGHTON (-1715), w William; 5 Jul 1670; Kittery, ME

HAMMOND, Joseph (1677-1753) & Hannah STORER (1680-), Wells; 14 Sep 1699; Wells, ME?

HAMMOND, Lawrence (-1699) & 1/wf Audrey EATON (-1663); 30 Sep 1662; Charlestown

HAMMOND, Lawrence (-1699) & 2/wf Abigail (COLLINS) WILLETT (-1674), w John; 12 May 1665; Charlestown

HAMMOND, Lawrence (-1699) & 3/wf Margaret WILLOUGHBY (-1683), w Francis; 8 Feb 1674/5; Charlestown

HAMMOND, Lawrence (-1699) & 4/wf Ann GERRISH/GEARISH, w William; 14 Jan 1684/5; Charlestown

HAMMOND, Nathan (1670-) & Alice [POPE?]/?Elizabeth (TOBEY) DEXTER, w James DEXTER; b 1699; Rochester

HAMMOND, Nathaniel (1642/3-1691) & Mary [GRIFFIN], m/2 Isaac WILLIAMS; b 1666; Cambridge/Watertown

HAMMOND, Richard (-1676) & Elizabeth [SMITH], w James, m/3 John ROWDEN 1676+; aft 29 May 1660, b 1667; Salem

HAMMOND, Samuel (1655-1728+) & Mary [HATHAWAY], dau Arthur; ca 1680; Rochester/?Yarmouth

HAMMOND, Thomas (1603-1675) & Elizabeth CASON/CARSON?; Lavenham, Eng, 12 Nov 1623; Hingham/Cambridge

HAMMOND, Thomas (-1655) & Hannah [CROSS] (1636-1657); ca 1654; Watertown

HAMMOND, Thomas (-1677, 1678) & Elizabeth STEDMAN (-1715); 17 Dec 1662; Cambridge/ Newtown/Watertown

HAMMOND, Thomas & 1/wf Elizabeth NOYES (-1679); 21 Aug 1678; Watertown

HAMMOND, Thomas & 2/wf Sarah PICKARD (1657-1713); 6 Dec 1679; Watertown/Rowley

HAMMOND, Thomas & Mehitable VERAY/VERY? (-1704); 15 Jun 1693; Boston/Newton

HAMMOND, William (1575-1662?) & Elizabeth PAYNE?/PENN? (-1640); in Eng, London?, 9 Jun 1605, Lavenham, Eng; Watertown/Boston

HAMMOND, William (-1637, 1638?) & Elizabeth _?_; b 1630?; Lynn

HAMMOND, William (1597-1702?) & Benedict [GOUCH]; b 1644; Wells, ME

HAMMOND, William & Elizabeth _?_; b 1659?; Watertown/?Swansea

HAMMOND, William (-1675) & ?Mary _?_; b 1661; Rehoboth

HAMMOND, William (-1709) & Elizabeth BALTICOME; 9 Jul 1672; Rehoboth

HAMMOND, William (?1659-) & [Elizabeth] _?_; b 1690

HAMMOND, William & Elizabeth COLE (-1705); 10 Jan 1695, 10 Jun 1695; Swansea

HAMMOND, _?_ & Phillippa _?_, m/2 Robert HARDING

HAMOR/HAMES?/[HAYNES?], _?_ (-1665) & Mary SHATTUCK (sister of Samuel); b 1658?; Salem (see Mark HAYNES)

HAMPTON, Henry & Sarah [BARNEY] (1662-); b 1683; Salem/Bristol, RI

HAMPTON, James & Jane _?_; b 1650?; Salem/Southampton, LI

HANBURY, William (-1649) & Hannah SOWTHER/SOUTHER?, m/2 Francis JOHNSON 1656; 28 Sep 1641; Plymouth/Duxbury/Boston

HANCE, John (-1710) & Elizabeth [HANSON] (1645-1732); 1669; Dover, NH (went Shrewsbury, NJ)

HANCOCK, Anthony & Sarah WILSON; 17 Apr 1678; Dorchester/Wrentham

HANCOCK, Edward/Edwin? & Sarah (FOWLER) [GODWIN/GOODWIN], w Samuel; b 1693?; Eastchester, NY

HANCOCK, John (1671-1752) & Elizabeth CLARK; 11 Nov 1700, 11 Dec 1700, at Chelmsford; Cambridge/Chelmsford

HANCOCK, Nathaniel (-1652) & Joanna/Joan?/Jane? _?_; b 1634; Cambridge

HANCOCK, Nathaniel[2] (1638-1719) & 1/wf Mary PRENTICE (-1699); 8 Mar 1663/4; Cambridge

HANCOCK, Nathaniel (1668-1755) & Prudence [RUSSELL] (1670-1742); b 1690; Cambridge

HANCOCK, Nathaniel[2] (-1719) & 2/wf Sarah GREEN, m/2 John COOPER 1720; 26 Dec 1699; Cambridge

HANCOCK, Samuel (1674-1735) & Dorothy _?_ (-1756); b 1697; Cambridge/Charlestown

HANCOCK, Thomas (ca 1645-1734), Farmington, CT, & Rachel LEONARD (1665-); 14 Mar 1684/5; Springfield

HAND, Benjamin & Elizabeth [WHITTLER]; 27 Feb 1669, b 1672; Southampton, LI/Cape May Co., NJ

HANDS, Benjamin (-1740) & Sarah WARD (-1744); 14 Jun 1688; Middletown, CT

HAND, Benjamin, Guilford & 1/wf Mary WILCOX, Middletown; 10 Jul 1695; ?Middletown, CT

HAND, James (1651, 1647?-1733) & 1/wf _?_ [BISHOP] (-1704); Southampton, LI

HAND, James & 2/wf _?_ (-1710); East Hampton, LI

HAND, John (-1660) & Alice _?_ (1613-), m/2 Edward CODNER/CODNOR 1663?; ca 1634?, b 1633?; Southampton, LI/East Hampton, LI

HAND, John & Rebecca [BUSHNELL] (1646-); Guilford, CT

HANDS, John & Mary [BELL]; b 1678; Boston

HAND, Joseph (1638-1724) & Jane [WRIGHT] (1644-1724?); 1662?, 1664; E. Guilford, CT/Killingworth, CT

HAND, Joseph (1671-1699), Guilford & 1/wf Esther WILCOX (1673-1698); 16 May 1692, ?14 May, 10 May 1692; Middletown, CT/Guilford, CT

HAND, Joseph (1671-1699) & 2/wf Hannah [SEWARD] (1678-), m/2 John TUSTIN; 1699; ?Guilford, CT

HANDS, Mark (-1664) & 1/wf Avery _?_; b 1646; Boston

HANDS, Mark (-1664) & 2/wf Mary _?_; by 1647; Boston

HAND, Samuel & Elizabeth _?_; b 1693; Southampton, LI

HAND, Shamgar & _?_ [?PIERSON]; b 1671?; Southampton, LI/Cape May Co., NJ

HAND, Stephen (-1693) & 2/wf? Rebecca [STRATTON?/BUSHNELL?]; b 1680, b 1661?; Guilford, CT/Easthampton, LI

HAND, Stephen (1661, ?1674-1740) & 1/wf Sarah [WRIGHT] (1674-bef 14 Feb 1711/12), Wethersfield; 6 Nov 1700; Southampton, LI/Guilford, CT

HAND, Thomas & Mary [TALMAGE]; Easthampton, LI/Cape May Co., NJ

HENDY, Owen & Martha CLARK; 25 Aug 1670; Charlestown

HENDEE, Richard (-1670) & [Hannah ELDERKIN]; ca 1664?; Wethersfield, CT/Norwich, CT

HANDY, Richard (-1719) & Hannah _?_ (-1732, ae 89); b 1672; Sandwich

HENDEE, Richard & Sarah SMITH (-1694); 1 Mar 1693; Windham, CT/Norwich, CT/Killingworth, CT

HENDEE, Richard & 2/wf Elizabeth CONANT; 17 Oct 1695; Norwich, CT

HANDY, Richard (1672-) & Patience RANDALL (1678/9-); 21 Feb 1699/1700; Sandwich/Scituate

HANFORD, Elnathan (1672-1702) & 1/wf Sarah [WILSON]; b ?5 Nov 1694; Fairfield, CT

HANFORD, Elnathan (1672-1702) & 2/wf Abigail (BURR) LOCKWOOD (-1731), w Daniel, m/3 Nathaniel SHERMAN 1707; 26 Jun 1700; Fairfield, CT

HANFORD, Jeffrey (-in Eng, 1626) & Eglin (HATHERLY) DOWNE (1588-), wid, m/3 Richard SEALIS 1637; Framington, Eng, 31 Mar 1611; Scituate

HANDFORD, Nathaniel (1609/15-1687) & Sarah _?_ ; Lynn

HANFORD, Samuel (?1674-1751) & Isabel [HAYNES]; b 1701; Norwalk, CT

HANFORD, Thomas[1] (?1623-1693) & 1/wf Hannah [NEWBERRY] (ca 1633-); ca 1653; Norwalk, CT

HANFORD, Thomas[1] (-1693) & 2/wf Mary (MILES) INCE (-1730), w Jonathan; 22 Oct 1661; Norwalk, CT

HANFORD, Thomas (1668-1743) & Hannah (LOCKWOOD) [BURWELL], w John; 1692; Norwalk, CT/?Greenwich, CT

HANKS, Benjamin (?1665-1755) & 1/wf Abigail HEIFORD/HAYFORD (-1726); 8 May 1700; Pembroke/Easton

HANMER, Isaac[2] & _?_ ; Scituate

HANMER, John[1] (-1677) & Hannah _?_ ; b 1639?; Scituate

HANMORE, John[2] & _?_ [SAMPSON], dau Henry; b 24 Dec 1684

HANMORE, Joseph[2] & Bethiah TUBS; 24 Jun [1674?]; Marshfield

HANNAH, Robert (-1706) & Mary [WILSON] (1663-1737), m/2 George WEBB 1708; ca 1681; Portsmouth, RI/Kings Town, RI

HANNAH, Robert & Hannah MATSON/MAESON; 2 May 1695; Boston/Watertown

HANNAH, Williamm & Martha CLARK, Roxbury; 9 Apr 1696; Watertown/Boston

HANNIFORD, John (-1661) & 1/wf Hannah [BUTTON] (-1653); b 1645; Boston

HANNIFORD, John (-1661) & 2/wf Abigail (HANDS) DILL/DELL, w George; 8 Nov 1655; Boston

HANNIFORD, Richard (-1709) & Miriam [RUSSELL]; b 1669; Marblehead

HANNUM, John (-1712, ae 76) & 1/wf Sarah WELLER (1643-1673); 20 Nov 1662; Northampton

HANNUM, John (-1712) & 2/wf Elizabeth LAUGHTON/?Esther LANGDON/LANGTON; 20 Apr 1675; Northampton

HANNUM, John (1676-) & 1/wf Elizabeth CLESSON (1677-); 30 Nov 1698; Deerfield

HANNUM, William (?1600-1677) & Honour [CAPEN] (?1615-1680, Westfield); b 1636; Dorchester/Windsor, CT/Northampton/Deerfield

HANSCOM/HANSCOMB, Thomas & Ann _?_ , m/2 James TOBEY; 16 May 1664; Kittery, ME

HANSCOM, Thomas (1666-1713) & 1/wf Alice [ROGERS] (1665?-); b 1690; Kittery, ME

HANSCOM, Thomas (1666-1713) & Tamsin (GOWELL) [SHEARS], w Robert; by 1698; Kittery, ME

HANSETT, John (-1684) & 1/wf _?_ ; b 1641; Braintree

HANSET, John (-1684) & 2/wf Elizabeth PERRY; 2 Apr 1644; Roxbury

HANCHETT, John (1649-1744) & Hester/?Esther [PRITCHETT] (-1711, Suffield, CT); 6 Sep 1677; Westfield/Suffield, CT

HANCHETT, Peter & Mary [PARKER] (1648-); b 1680; Cambridge/Roxbury

HANCHETT, Thomas (-1686, Suffield, CT) & Deliverance [LANGTON], m/2 Jonathan BURT 1686; b 1649; Wethersfield, CT/New London/etc.

HANCHET, Thomas & Elizabeth LOOMIS; 18 Nov 1673; Windsor, CT/Westfield

HANSON, Isaac (-1683) & ?Ann/?Mary [HEARD], m/2 Robert EVANS 1690?; b 1679; Dover, NH/Portsmouth, NH

HANSON, Thomas (-1666) & Mary _?_ (-1689); b 1641; Dover, NH

HANSON, Thomas (1643-1710) & Mary (KITCHEN) ROBISON/ROBINSON, w Timothy; 3 Jun 1669; Salem
HANSON, Timothy & [Barbara BOWERS] (-1718); b 1679; Lynn
HANSON, Tobias[2] (1641-1693) & Elizabeth [BOYCE] (1642-1689?); Salem/Dover, NH
HANSON, Tobias[3] & 1/wf Lydia [CANNE/CANNEY]; ca 1694; Dover, NH
HANSON, Tobias[3] & 2/wf Anne LORD; 28 Aug 1698; Kittery, ME
HAPGOOD, Nathaniel & Elizabeth WARD; 14 Aug 1695, ?6 Sep; Marlborough/Stow
HABGOOD, Shardrack (1642-1675) (kinsman of Peter NOYES) & Elizabeth TREADAWAY, m/2 Joseph HAYWARD 1677; 21 Oct 1664; Sudbury
HAPGOOD, Thomas (1670-1764) & Judith [BARKER] (1671-1759); b 1694; Marlborough
HARRADEN, Benjamin (1671-1725) & Deborah NORWOOD; 15 Jan 1695/6; Gloucester
HARRADAINE, Edward (-1683) & Sarah ? (1630-1699); ca 1650, ca 1648?; Gloucester
HARRADEN, Edward (ca 1650-1737) (see Richard WOODBURY) & 1/wf Sarah HASKELL (1666-1692); 5 Feb 1684; Gloucester
HARADEN, Edward (ca 1650-1727) & 2/wf Hannah YORK; 31 Oct 1693; Gloucester
HARRADAN, John (1665-1724) & Sarah GIDDINGS (-1722); 7 Feb 1693/4; Gloucester
HARRIDON, John & Mildred [PAGE]; b 1700; Watertown
HARRADAN, Joseph (1668-1716) & 1/wf Jean GIDDINGS (-6 Sep 1700); 26 Nov 1691; Gloucester
HARADEN, Joseph (-1716) & Hannah STEVENS; 1 Feb 1700, prob 1700/01; Gloucester
HARBOR/HARBERT?/HERBERT?, Benjamin & 1/wf Christian NETHERCOOLL/NETHERCOOLE/ ?NETHERCOTT (-1667); ca 22 Aug 1644; Hartford
HARBOR/HARBERT?, Benjamin & 2/wf Jane ? ; Hartford
HARBOUR, John[1] (-1675) & 1/wf ? ; b 1634; Braintree
HARBOUR, John[1] (-1675) & 2/wf Hannah (?) SCOTT (-1677?), w Benjamin; 21 Sep 1647; Braintree
HARBOUR, John[2] (-1680) & Jael THAYER (1633-1701); ?17 Mar 1653/4, 17 (1) 1654; Braintree/Mendon
HARBER/HERBERT?, William (-1670) & ?
HARBOR, John (John HERBERT of Salem) & ? ; b 1683/4; Reading?
HARCURT/HARCOOT?, Benjamin (1659-) & Elizabeth/Mercy [DICKINSON]?; b 1680, 1680
HARCURT, Daniel (1658?-) & Sarah [?FORMAN]; b 1696, 1680?; Oyster Bay, LI
HARCUT, John? & ? ; Huntington, LI
HARCURT, Richard (1623±-1696±) & 1/wf Elizabeth [POTTER]/?Isabel DICKINSON?; b 1680, ca 1663?, ca 1651?; Warwick, RI/Jamaica, LI/Oyster Bay, LI
HARCUT, Richard (-1696) & 2/wf Miriam (HOYT) [FORMAN], w Samuel; ca 1683; Oyster Bay, LI
HARD, James & Elizabeth [TOMLINSON]; b 1695?, b 1696?; Derby, CT/Newtown, CT
HARDING?/HARDIER/?HARDEN, John & Hannah ? ; b 1679; Braintree
HARDIER, Richard (-1657) & Elizabeth ? ; Braintree
HARDING, Abraham (-1655) & Elizabeth [?HARDING], m/2 John ADAMS?/FRACY? 1656, m/3 Thomas DYER 1670/73; b 1644; Braintree/Dedham/Medfield/Medway
HARDING, Abraham (1655-) & 1/wf Mary MASON; 26 Apr 1677; Medfield
HARDING, Abraham[2] (-1694?) & Deborah ? , m/2 Moses BARTLETT 1696; by 1677?; Providence
HARDING, Abraham (-1734) & Sarah (?MERRIFIELD/DEAN?) [FAIRBANK] (?1678-1741), dau John of Dorchester, w George; b 1698, b 1698?; Medfield
HARDING, Henry (1673-1764) & 1/wf Mary ALINE/ALLEN (-1723); 7 Jul 1698; Dedham
HARDING, Ichabod (1675-1729/30) & 1/wf Abigail BARBER (1679-); 15 Nov 1699; Dedham/Milton/Medfield
HARDING, Israel & 1/wf Lydia [GOOCH], w John; b 7 Oct 1673; Wells, ME
HARDING, Israel & 2/wf Mary (WAKEFIELD) [FROST], w William; ca 1691, b 25 Feb 1690/1; Wells, ME
HARDIN, Israel & Sarah [MEDBURY?], w John?; b 1697; Swansea/Warwick, RI/Newport
HARDING, John (-1682) & ? ; ca 1636; Weymouth
HARDING, John & ? ; b 1647; Hingham
HARDING, John & Mary TYBBOT, w Walter; 22 Apr 1652; Gloucester
HARDING, John (1644-1720) & 1/wf Hannah WOOD (-1668); 28 Nov 1665; Medfield
HARDING, John (1644-1720) & 2/wf Elizabeth ADAMS (1649-1727); 16 Dec 1668; Medfield

HARDIN, Rev. John (1644-1700) & Sarah [BUTCHER?], m/2 Hugh MOSHER; ca 1670?; Providence

HARDING/HARDEN?/?HARDIER, John (-1718, 1719) & Hannah/Anna? _?_; b 1679; Briantree/ Bridgewater

HARDING, John (1673-1697) & Susanna _?_, m/2 Williamm BROWN 1699; b 1697; Eastham

HARDING, Joseph (-1630) & Martha DOANE (-1633); 1624

HARDING, Joseph & Bethiah COOK; 4 Apr 1660; Eastham

HARDING, Joseph (1667-1745) & Dinah [?HEDGES] (1673-1739, ae 76); ca 1690?; Chatham

HARDING, Josiah (1669-1752+) & Hannah [WELCH]; b 1693; Eastham/Provincetown

HARDING, Maziah/Amaziah (1671-) & Hannah [ROGERS] (1669-), dau Thomas; b 1694(5?); Eastham

HARDING, Nathaniel & Hannah COLLINS

HARDING, Nathaniel & Hannah LONG; m bond 5 Mar 1687

HARDING, Nehemiah & Hannah [NEAL]; b 1679; Briantree

HARDING alias HARDY, Philip (-1674) & Susannah HAVILAND, w Edward?; 23 Aug 1659; Boston/Marblehead

HARDING, Richard (-1657) & 1/wf _?_; in Eng, b 1620; Braintree

HARDING/HARDIER, Richard (-1657) & Elizabeth [ADAMS?] (-1664) (related to John KENT); b 1635; Braintree

HARDING, Capt. Robert (returned to Eng) & 1/wf Philippa [HAMMOND], wid; Boston/Newport

HARDING, Capt. Robert (returned to Eng) & 2/wf Hester/Esther WILLYS; 17 Oct 1645; Hartford

HARDING, Stephen¹ (-1698) & Bridget [?ESTANCE], dau Thomas (doubtful); ca 1642?; Providence

HARDING, Stephen (-1680) & Mercy WINSOR (-1680); 28 Jan 1678/9, 1672?; Providence

HARDING, Stephen³ (?1677-) & 1/wf _?_; ca 1700; Providence

HARDING, Thomas & Jane _?_; b 1667(8?); Boston

HARDING, [?Joseph] & Martha [?DOANE] (-1633); ca 1620/3, b 1618?, 1624?; Duxbury

HARDING?/HARDEN?, _?_ & Ann _?_ (-1722, ae 80?)

HARDISON, Stephen (-1697) & Mary [TAYLOR] (1662±-), m/2 _?_/George? COSS, m/3 John LEGROW; b 1691; Kittery, ME

HARDMAN, John & Sarah _?_; b 1652; Lynn/Braintree/Fairfield, CT

HARDMAN, John (?1654-) & Hannah _?_; b 1673?; Braintree

HARDY, George (-1694) & Mary FOGG (1662-), m/2 Benjamin POOR 1696; 24 Nov 1686; Newbury

HARDY, Jacob & Lydia [EATON]; b 1691; Bradford

HARDY, James (-1703) & Ruth MARSH (1668-), m/2 Elizabeth UPTON; 20 Jun 1687; Salem

HARDY, John (-1652) & 2/wf? Elizabeth [TYBBOT]? (-1654); in Eng, b 1621; Salem

HARDAY, John & 1/wf Mary JACKMAN (-1689?); 2 Apr 1667; Rowley

HARDY, John & 2/wf Martha (SMITH) BURBANK (-1716), w Caleb; 3 Jul 1695; Rowley/Bradford

HARDY, Joseph (-1688) & Martha _?_; b 1648; Salem

HARDY, Joseph (-1687) & Mary GRAFTON, m/2 Edmund FEVERYEAR 1688; 25 Jul 1678; Salem

HARDY, Joseph & Mary BURBANK; 6 Apr 1698; Bradford

HARDY, Richard & Ann [HUESTED] (1623±-1707); b 1654; Stamford, CT

HARDIE, Samuel & Mary DUDLEY (1650-); 24 Jan 1675, 1675/6; Beverly

HARDY, Samuel & 1/wf Rebecca HOBBY (-bef 1693); 18 Nov 1686; Stamford, CT

HARDY, Samuel (1656-) & 2/wf Rebecca FURBUSH (1674-); 12 May 1693, 1692; Stamford, CT/Bedford, NY

HARDY, Samuel & Hannah/Anna? HARDY; 5 Jul 1700; Bradford

HARDY, Thomas (-1678, ae 72) & 2/wf? ?Lydia/?Ann/?Anna _?_ (-1689); b 1644, b 1635?; Rowley/Bradford

HARDY, Thomas (1644-) & Mercy TENY/TENNEY (-1716); 22 Nov 1664; Rowley/Bradford

HARDY, William (-1728) & 1/wf Ruth TENNEY/TENNY (-1689); 3 May 1678; Bradford

HARDY, William & 2/wf Sarah _?_; b 1690, [1689]; Bradford

HARDY, William & Priscilla _?_; b 1690; Concord

HARE, George & Mary _?_; b 1677; Boston

HARE, John & Joanna _?_; b 1669(70?); Boston

HARGER, Ebenezer (1674-) & Abigail TIBBALS; 15 Sep 1698; Derby, CT

HARGER, Jabez[1] (-1678) & Margaret TOMLINSON (1642-1698), m/2 John TIBBALS; 5 Nov 1662; Stratford, CT/Derby, CT
HARGER, Samuel & Hannah (ROSE) STILES, w Isaac, m/3 John TIBBALS 1700; 9 May 1693; Derby, CT
HARKER, Anthony (1609-1675) & Mary _?_ ; b 1639; Boston
HARKER, John & Dorothy [MILLS], w Robert; b 1647; York, ME
HARKER, John & Patience FOLGER/FOWLER, m/2 James GARDNER (wrong); 14 Dec 1680; Boston
HARKER, William (1594-1662?) & Elizabeth _?_ ; Lynn?
HARLAKENDEN, Roger (1611-1638) & 1/wf Emlen _?_ (-bur 18 Aug 1634); in Eng; Cambridge
HARLAKENDEN, Roger (-1638) & Elizabeth BOSVILLE, m/2 Herbert PELHAM; in Eng, 4 Jun 1635; Cambridge
HARLOCK, Thomas & Bethia [MAYHEW] (1636-); b 1659; Martha's Vineyard
HARLOCK, Thomas (1659-) & 1/wf _?_ ; b 1692; Martha's Vineyard
HARLOCK, Thomas (-1744) & Sarah (MARCHANT) AREY, w Richard; 16 Nov 1696; Edgartown
HARLOW, Benjamin (?1662-aft 1664) & _?_ ; Little Compton, RI/Southold, LI/Orange Co., NY
HARLOW, Francis & [Sarah GRAY], w George; aft 30 Aug 1693, b 1698; Kittery, ME
HARLOW, Nathaniel (1664-1721, Plympton), Plymouth/Plympton & Abigail (CHURCH) BUCK (1666-1727), w James; 17 Mar 1691; Plymouth
HARLOW, Samuel (1652/3-1727?, 1734?) & 1/wf Priscilla _?_ ; b 1678(9?); Plymouth
HARLOW, Samuel (1652/3-1727?, 1734?) & 2/wf Hannah _?_ (-1734); b 1685, b 1683; Plymouth
HARLOW, William (ca 1624-1691) & 1/wf Rebecca BARTLETT (-1657/8); 20 Dec 1649; Plymouth
HARLOW, William (ca 1624-1691) & 2/wf Mary FAUNCE (-1664); 15 Jul 1658; Plymouth
HARLOW, William (ca 1624-1691) & 3/wf Mary SHELLEY (1628-), m/2 Ephraim MORTON 1692, m/3 Hugh COLE 1694; 25 Jan 1665, 1665/6; Plymouth
HARLOW, William (1657-1711/12) & Lydia [CUSHMAN] ([1659/61]-1717, 1718/19?); b 1683(4?); Plymouth
HARMON, Francis (1592-) & _?_ ; in Eng, b 1623; Plymouth
HARMON, James & Sarah CLARK; 6 May 1658?, 1650?, 1659; Saco, ME
HARMON, John (-1661) & Elizabeth _?_ (-1699), m/2 Anthony DORCHESTER ca 1662/4; b 1641; Springfield
HARMON, John & Mary DORCHESTER; 7 Jan 1668, 1668/9, [1668/9]; Springfield
HARMON, John & 1/wf Elizabeth [CUMMINGS]; b 1 Jul 1673; York, ME
HARMON, John & Sarah [ROBERTS], Oyster River, NH; b 1679?, b 1681; Wells, ME
HARMON, John & 2/wf Deborah (JOHNSON) [FOXWELL], w John; by 21 Jan 1680?; Saco, ME?/York, ME
HARMON, Joseph (1646-1729) & Hannah PHILLEY/FILLEY (1653-); 22 Jan 1673; Springfield/Suffield, CT/?Simsbury, CT
HARMON, Nathaniel & Mary [BLISS] (1616-); b 1641; Braintree
HARMON, Nathaniel (-1712) & Mary SKINNER, m/2 John HANCHETT at Suffield; 19 Nov 1685, Suffield; Springfield/Suffield, CT
HARMON, Samuel & _?_ ; b 1692; Boston
HARNDEN, Benjamin (1671-) & Mary _?_ ; 10 Feb 1690/1; Reading
HARNDEN, Ebenezer (-1741, 1738?, ae 63) & Rebecca ALLEN (-1764); 1700; Malden
HARNDEL, John (-1687) & _?_ ; b 1646; Newport
HARNDELL/HARNDEN, John (1668-) & 1/wf Susanna _?_ (-1707); 16 Apr 1690; Reading
HARNDEN, Richard (-1695) & Mary _?_ ; 24 Oct 1666; Reading
HARNETT, Edward[1] & ?Cicely/?Priscilla _?_ ; b 1630; Salem
HARNETT, Edward[2] & Eunice [PORTER]; b 1650; Salem
HORNETT, Edward & 2/wf Mary [MART/MARCH]; b 1685, 11 Dec 1671; Westchester, NY
HARNY, George & Sarah _?_ ; b 1687; Salem
HARPER, Joseph & Kithtina _?_ ; b 1666; Braintree
HARPER, Robert & 1/wf Deborah PERRY (-1665); 9 May 1654; Sandwich
HARPER, Robert & 2/wf Prudence BUTLER; 22 Jun 1666; Sandwich
HARRIMAN, John (-1683) & Elizabeth _?_ (-1680); b 1646, 1647?; New Haven
HARRIMAN, John (?1646-1705), New Haven & Hannah BRYAN (1654-1705+); 20 Nov 1672; Milford, CT/Elizabeth, NJ/etc.
HARRIMAN, Jonathan & 1/wf Sarah [PALMER] (1661-1688); b 1686; Rowley

HERRIMAN, Jonathan (1657-1742) & 2/wf Margaret (ELITHORP) WOOD, w Samuel; 19 Aug 1691; Rowley

HARRIMAN, Leonard (-1691) & Margaret __?__ (-1676); b 1650; Rowley

HERRIMAN, Matthew (1652-) & 1/wf Elizabeth SWAN (1653-); 22 Dec 1673; Haverhill

HERRIMAN, Matthew & Martha PAGE; 19 Dec 1700; Haverhill

HERRINGTON, Benjamin (1652-1724) & Abigail BIGELOW (-1754); 10 Dec 1684; Watertown

HERRINGTON, Daniel (1657-1729) & 1/wf Sarah WHETNY/WHITNEY (1654-1720); 18 Oct 1681; Watertown

HERRINGTON, David (1669-) & 1/wf Mary OCINGTON/OCKINGTON; 30 Mar 1692; Watertown

HARRINGTON, James & Mary __?__; b 1673; Boston

HERRINGTON, John (1651-1741) & Hannah WINTER (-1741); 17 Nov 1681; Watertown/Waltham

HARRINGTON, Joseph (1659-1690) & Joanna MIXER (1666-), m/2 Obadiah WARD 1693; 7 Nov 1688; Watertown

HARRINGTON/ARRINGTON?, Richard (-1659) & Elizabeth __?__; b 1643; Charlestown

HERINGTON, Robert (1616-1707) & Susan/?Susanna GEORGE (ca 1632-1694); 1 Oct 1649, prob 1648; Watertown

HARRINGTON, Samuel & Hannah (PLYMPTON) SUTLEFF, w Nathaniel; 24 Jan 1676; Hatfield

HERRINGTON, Samuel (1666-1712) & 1/wf Grace LEVERMORE/LIVERMORE (-1703, Waltham); 6 Oct 1691; Watertown

HARRINGTON, Samuel & Hannah BARNES; 27 Jul 1693; Branfield, CT

HERRINGTON, Thomas (1665-1712, Waltham) & Rebecca (BEMIS) WHITE (1654-), w John; 1 Apr 1686; Watertown

HARRIS, Andrew (1635-1686) & Mary TEW (1647-1688+); 8 Dec 1670; Providence/Newport, RI

HARRIS, Anthony (-1651) & Elizabeth __?__; b 1651, no issue; Ipswich/Boston

HARRIS, Arthur (-1674) & Martha [?LAKE/WINSLOW?]; b 1630?, b 1640?; Roxbury/Boston/Duxbury/Bridgewater

HARRIS, Bernard/Barnard? & Mary __?__; b 1666; Boston

HARRIS, Daniel (?1618-1701) & Mary [WELD] (1627-1711); ca 1646/8; Rowley/Cambridge/Middletown, CT/Wethersfield, CT

HARRIS, Daniel (1653-1735) & 1/wf Abigail BARNES (1657-1723); 11 Dec 1680, 14 Dec 1680; Middletown, CT

HARRIS, Daniel & Joanna BREWER/[BROWN?]; 14 Nov 1682, ?14 Jun; Roxbury

HARRIS, Daniel & Sarah __?__; b 1687; Boston

HARRIS, David & Tamazin [ELSON], m/2 Erasmus BABBITT 1700; b 1676?, b 1679; Charlestown

HARRIS, Ebenezer & 1/wf Rebecca CLARKE (-1699); 15 Sep 1690; Ipswich/Plainfield, CT

ORRIS, Experience & Abigail __?__; b 1676; Boston

HARRIS, Gabriel (-1684) & Mary?/Elizabeth ABBOTT (-1702); 3 Mar 1653/4, 1653; Guilford, CT/New London

HARRIS, George & __?__; b 1630; Salem

HARRIS, George & __?__; b 1660?

HARRIS, George & __?__; b 1670; Southampton, LI

HARRIS, George & 1/wf Lydia GROSE; 21 Nov 1671; Concord/Lancaster

HARRIS, George (-ca 1686) & Joanna __?__; b 1686, b 1682; Boston

HARRIS, George & 2/wf Sarah VINTON; 5 Dec 1688; Concord

HARRIS, George & ?Sarah __?__; b 1698; Southampton, LI

HARRIS, Henry (-1672) & __?__; b 1652

HARRIS, Isaac (-1707) & 1/wf Mercy [LATHAM] (1650-); b 1671, ca 1668; Bridgewater

HARRIS, Isaac & 2/wf? Mary DUNBAR (1660-); b 1680, 28 Jun 1698

HARRIS, James (-1715) & Sarah [DENISON]; b 1667(8?), 1666; Boston

HARRIS, James & Elizabeth BAILEY; 14 Feb 1692/3, 1692?; Bridgewater

HARRIS, James & Elizabeth FRY/IRISH; 11 Mar 1695/6; Bridgewater

HARRIS, James (1673-1757) & Sarah [ROGERS] (1676-1748); b 1696, 1696; New London, CT?/Boston

HARRIS, John (1607-1695) & 1/wf Bridget [ANGIER]? (-1672); b 1643; Rowley

HARRIS, John & Amy [HILLS]; b 1656; Charlestown

HARRIS, John & Hannah BRIGGS (ca 1643-1688), m/2 Wolston BROCKWAY 1664; 10 Sep 1657; Boston

HARRIS, John (-1680/2) & Elizabeth __?__, m/2 __?__ BARNES; b 1669; Boston

HARRIS, John (-1690) & Mary SAUGER; 20 Sep 1670, 2 Sep 1670; Watertown/Roxbury

HARRIS, John & Joanna __?__; b 1671; Boston
HARRIS, John & Sarah __?__; b 1673; Marblehead
HARRIS, John & Esther __?__; b 1673; Ipswich
HARRIS, John, Boston & Susanna BRECK; 20 Mar 1673/4; Dorchester/Roxbury
HARRIS, John & 2/wf Elizabeth (ROWLANDSON) WELLS (-1679), wid; 24 Oct 1677; Rowley
HARRIS, John (-1695) & 3/wf Alice (__?__) (LEWIS) [HOWE?], w Bishop John, w Abraham; aft 29 Dec 1679, b 1692, aft 20 Nov 1683; Rowley
HARRIS, John & Grace SEARLE; 8 Jan 1685, 1686, 1685; Ipswich
HARRIS, John & Mary [SPARKS]; b 1690, m bond 24 Jun 1687; Ipswich
HARRIS, John & Hannah [STACKPOLE?]; b 1690, b 1677?; Marblehead/Portsmouth, RI
HARRIS, John (ca 1663-1740) & Hannah [MANNING] (bpt 1671-1732); ca 1693, b 1686, b 1689; New London, CT
HARRIS, John & Margaret COOMS/COOMBS; 19 Jan 1693/4; Marblehead/Ipswich
HARRIS, John (1675-) & Margaret ELSON; 22 May 1695; Salem
HARRIS, John & Mary STEPHENS; 6 Dec 1696; New London
HARRIS, John (-1739) & 1/wf Mary HOUGHTON (1666-); 6.23.1698
HARRIS, John & 2/wf Susannah (ELLERY) WARDWELL (1673-1705); 19 Nov 1700; Ipswich
HARRIS, John & Mehitable DANKS, dau Robert; b 1701?
HARRIS, Jonathan & __?__; b 1677; Newbury
HARRIS, Joseph (1648-) & Mary __?__ (1648-1710?); b 1672; Charlestown
HARRIS, Joseph & Dorcas __?__; b 1680; Beverly
HARRIS, Joseph (1665-1732) & Naomi [STEVENS] (?1665-1710); b 1689; Charlestown/Casco Bay, ME
HARRIS, Joseph (1673-) & Mary STEVENS (1677-); 1 Dec 1696; New London, CT
HARRIS, Joseph & [Rebecca STONE] (1676-), m/2 Joseph BUTMAN 1698; b 1698; Beverly
HARRIS, Leonard & Mary __?__; b 1693; Bridgehampton, LI
HARRIS, Nathaniel (ca 1647-1732) & Elizabeth HAZEN (1651-); 1 Apr 1670, 5 Apr 1670, 1 Apr, 5 Apr; Rowley
HARRIS, Nathaniel & Mary __?__; b 1697(8?); Ipswich
HARRIS, Nicholas (1671-1746) & Ann [?HOPKINS]; b 1691; Providence
HARRIS, Peter (1660-1718) & Elizabeth MANWARING (?1638-1720); 7 Jul 1686; New London
HARRIS, Richard & Margaret __?__; b 1663(4?); Braintree
HARRIS, Richard (-1714) & Hannah DOVE (1654-); 10 Mar 1670; Salem/Boston
HARRIS, Richard (-1697) & Elizabeth BLACKLEDGE (-1710+); b 1680; Boston
HARRIS, Richard & Hannah __?__; b 1682, b 1693; Charlestown
HARRIS, Richard (1668-1750) & 1/wf [?Elizabeth] KING; b 1697; Providence
HARRIS, Robert (-1701?) & Elizabeth BOFFEE/BOUGHEY; 24 Jan 1642, [1642/3]; Roxbury/Brookline
HARRIS, Samuel (-1682?) & Mary HOARE; 30 Jun 1671; Beverly
HARRIS, Samuel (-1678) & Hannah __?__; Boston
HARRIS, Samuel & Christian __?__ (1656±-), m/2 Lewis WILLIAMS 1681?, m/3 __?__ CARR, m/4 John WYATT; Portsmouth, NH
HARRIS, Samuel (-1679) & Agnes WAY, m/2 Thomas PEMBER ca 1686?; 14 May 1679; New London, CT
HARRIS, Samuel (1665-) (see William) & Elizabeth [GIBSON/GIPSON]; b 1690, 5 Aug 1687; New London, CT
HARRIS, Thomas (-1661?, 1632?) & Elizabeth [WILLIAMS?] (1577-1670), wid, m/2 William STETSON; in Eng, ca 1600/05; Charlestown
HARRIS, Thomas (1600-1686) & Elizabeth [LEATHERLAND] (-1687+); ?20 Apr 1632, b 1639; Providence
HARRIS, Thomas (?1618-1687) & Martha LAKE; 15 Nov 1647; Ipswich
HARRIS, Thomas & __?__; b 1658/60; Hingham
HARRIS, Thomas (-1681) & Joanna __?__; b 1650; Shelter Island, NY
HARRIS, Thomas (-1711) & Elnathan TEW; 3 Nov 1664; Providence/Newport
HARRIS, Thomas (1637-1698) & 1/wf __?__; b 1667?; Boston/?Hull
HARRIS, Thomas (1648-beyond the sea, bef 1687) & __?__; ca 1672
HARRIS, Thomas & 1/wf __?__; b 1675; Boston
HARRIS, Thomas & Sarah __?__; b 1677; Boston
HARRIS, Thomas (-1696/99) & Ruth [JAMES], m/2 Joseph MOORE 1704; ?Easthampton, LI

HARRIS, Thomas (-1698) & 1/wf Jane _?_
HARRIS, Thomas (-1698) & 2/wf Rebecca (JOSLIN)| [CROAKHAM] (-1713), w John, m/3 Edward STEVENS 1700; b 1680, 1679; Boston/Lancaster
HARRIS, Thomas & _?_ ; b May 1685; York, ME
HARRIS, Thomas (1664-1747) & 1/wf Hepzibah CROSSWELL (1668-1718); 25 Feb 1685/6; Charlestown
HARRIS, Thomas & Mary SHEPHERD; 17 Sep 1688; Concord/Stow
HARRIS, Thomas (1637-1700) & 1/wf Zipporah _?_ (-8 Jan 1688/9); b 1689; Middletown, CT
HARRIS, Thomas (-1691) & Mary [WETHERELL] (1658-1711), m/2 George DENISON 1694?; b 1690; New London, CT
HARRIS, Thomas (1665-1741) & Phebe [BROWN] (-1723); b 1694, b 1690?; Providence
HARRIS, Thomas (-1700) & 2/wf Tabitha _?_ (-1712); b 1695; Middletown, CT
HARRIS, Thomas & Jane EDWARDS; 5 Mar 1700; Windham, CT
HARRIS, Timothy & Phebe PEARSON; 24 Aug 1682; Rowley
HARRIS, Timothy (1650-) & Abigail MOREY/MOWREY; 9 Apr 1697, 20 Apr, 2 Apr; Brookline
HARRIS, Walter (-1654, New London) & Mary [FRYE?] (-1655/6, New London) (sister of William); in Eng, b 1622; Dorchester/Weymouth/New London, CT
HARRIS, Walter (-1716) & Mary (HALE) [BENJAMIN], w Caleb; aft 8 May 1684; Glastonbury, CT
HARRIS, Walter (-1716) & Mary [HOLLISTER]; ca 1696?, b 1701?, by 1701; Wethersfield, CT
HARRIS, Walter & Mercy [RANNEY] (1682-1714); b 1701?; Middletown, CT
HARRIS, William (?1610-1681, 1682?) & Susanna _?_ (-1682+); b 1634, b 1635; Salem/Providence
HARRIS, William (-1717) & Edith _?_ (-1685); b 1642; Charlestown/Rowley/Middletown, CT
HARRIS, William & Hannah _?_ ; b 1663; Charlestown/?Boston
HARRIS, William & [?Rebecca] [GRANT]; b 1667; Smuttynose
HARRIS, William & Hannah _?_ ; b 1672; Boston
HARRIS, William & Elizabeth [ENOS?], m/2 Richard SMITH, m/3 Roger ALGER; 24 Jul 1672; New Shoreham, RI
HARRIS, William (-1684) & 1/wf Sarah _?_ ; b 1675?; Boston
HARRIS, William (-1684) & 2/wf Susan _?_ (no) (-1702); b 1684; Boston
HARRIS, William (-1714, 1717?) & 2/wf Lydia (WRIGHT) [SMITH], w Joseph; aft 5 Aug 1685, bef 3 May 1687; ?Wethersfield, CT/?Middletown, CT
HARRIS, William (1665-1718?) & Martha COLLINS (1666-); 8 Jan 1689/90; Middletown, CT
HARRIS, William & Elizabeth BRONSON (-1733); b 1695; Hartford
HARRIS, William (-1721) & Sarah CRISP (1672-1744), m/2 _?_ LEVERETT 1722, m/3 John CLARK 1725, m/4 Benjamin COLEMAN 1731; 11 Apr 1695; Boston
HARRIS, William & Mary MERRETT; 29 Jul 1695; Marblehead
HARRIS, William (1661-) & Sarah [NEWMAN?]; b 1696, ca 1685?; Ipswich
HARRIS, William/Samuel? (see Samuel) & Elizabeth [GIBSON]?/[ROGERS?]; b 1697; New London, CT/?Lyme, CT
HARRIS, William & Elizabeth BACK/BROCK/BROCKWAY? (1676-); 30 Nov 1697; New Shoreham, RI
HARRIS, William (1673-1726) & Abigail _?_ (1679-); b 1700; Providence
HARRIS, [Thomas] & Sarah (NETTLETON) MILLER, w Thomas; aft 1680
HARRISON, Abraham & Elizabeth _?_ ; b 1685; Boston
HARRISON, Edward & Eleanor _?_ ; b 1646; Boston
HARRISON, Erasmus & Mary ROUSE, dau William, m/2 William FASSETT bef 18 Aug 1705; 3 Jun 1694; Boston
HARRISON, Henry & Katherine [?MARTIN]; b 1687; Rehoboth
HARRISON, Isaac (-1676) & Martha MONTAGUE (-1691), m/2 Henry WHITE 1677; 1 Dec 1671; Hadley
HARRISON, Isaiah & Elizabeth [WRIGHT]; 1688
HARRISON, John & 1/wf Grace _?_ ; b 1642; Salisbury
HARRISON, John (-1684, ae 77) & 2/wf Perses (PIERCE) [BRIDGE] (-1683), w William; b 1652; Charlestown/Boston
HARRISON, John (-1666), Watertown/Wethersfield, CT, & Katharine [?GILBERT]; 4 May 1653; Wethersfield, CT
HARRISON, John & Susanna _?_ ; b 1677; Boston

HARRISON, John & 1/wf _?_; b 1683; Flushing, LI/_?_, NJ
HARRISON, Nathaniel (1658-1728) & Hannah [FRISBIE] (?1669-1723); b 1690; New Haven/Branford
HARRISON, Nicholas & Mary [BICKFORD]; b 13 May 1677; Durham, NH
HARRISON, Richard (?1585-1653) & [?Sarah] _?_; b 1623; New Haven/Branford, CT
HARRISON, Richard (-1683/4) & Sarah [HUBBARD] (?1634-); ca 1643/50?, ca 1650?; Branford, CT/Newark, NJ
HARRISON, Samuel (-1705) & Sarah [JOHNSON]; no issue; ?Branford, CT/Newark, NJ
HARRYSON, Thomas (went to Eng) & [Dorothy SYMONDS] (1619-); b 1649; Boston
HARRISON, Thomas (?1630, 1627-1704) & 1/wf Dorothy [THOMPSON], w John; ca 1656, ?Feb 1655/6; New Haven
HARRISON, Thomas (?1630-1704) & 2/wf Elizabeth (_?_) STENT?, w Eleazer; 29 Mar 1666; New Haven/?Branford
HARRISON, Thomas (1657-1726) & Margaret [?STENT] (-1731); ca 1689, b 1690; Branford, CT
HARRISON, William (-1686?, 1681?) & Prudence _?_; b 1677; Boston
HARRISON, William & Sarah _?_; b 1698(9?); Boston
HARRISON, _?_ & Hannah RING, dau Robert; Salisbury
HART, Dennis & Mary SMITH (?1667-); 28 Mar 1684; Huntington, LI
HART, Edmund & _?_; b 1640; Weymouth/?Westfield
HART, Edward & Margaret _?_ (-1671+), m/2 John GOULD; b 1635?; Providence, RI/Flushing, LI
HART, George & 1/wf Elizabeth WELLS; 5 May 1698; Ipswich
HART, Isaac (1615-1700) & Elizabeth [HUTCHINS?/HUTCHINSON] (-1700); ca 1650?; Lynn/Reading
HART, James (1666-1693) & 1/wf Mary [CLARKE] (1670-1690); ca 1689; Newport
HART, James (1666-1693) & 2/wf Frances [CLARKE] (1674-1693); ca 1692; Newport
HART, John (-1667) & Ann _?_ (1615-), m/2 William LUCUMB; b 1634?; Boston/Portsmouth, NH
HART, John (1595-1656) & 1/wf Mary _?_ (1604-living 1637); b 1635; Salem/Marblehead
HART, John (-1666) & Sarah _?_; b 1653; Farmington, CT
HART, John (?1595-1656) & 2/wf Florence [NORMAN], m/2 Thomas WHITTRIDGE 1656?; ca 1638?; Salem
HART, John (1655-1714/15) & Mary [MOORE] (1664-); b 1686, b 1684, ca 1682; Farmington, CT
HART, John & Priscilla [GOULD] (1661-1689); ca 1686/7?; Newport
HART, John & _?_; Newtown, LI
HART, John & Mary _?_; b 1678?, b 1690; Newtown, LI
HART, John & Hannah (STEELE) TREAT (1668-1738), wid; 12 Apr 1694; Wetherfield, CT
HART, Jonathan & 1/wf _?_; b 1658; Marblehead
HART, Jonathan (1650±-1711+) & Hannah [BUDD] (1657±-); ca 1670/75?, ca 1685?; ?Southold, LI
HART, Jonathan (-1707+, 1721?) & 2/wf Lydia NEALE (1650-); - Nov 1671; Salem
HART, Joseph (1659-) & Ruth CHADWELL; 24 Jun 1685, 1684; Lynn
HART, Lawrence & Dorothy JONES; 12 Feb 1678; Newbury
HART, Nicholas (-1654±) & Jane/Joan [ROSSITER] (1616, ?1615-1685±, 1691); b 1635?; Taunton/Warwick, RI/Portsmouth, RI/Plymouth
HART, Nicholas & [Alice PEARCE?]; b 1699; Little Compton, RI
HART, Richard[2] (-1696(-)) & Hannah [?KEEN] (-1696+); b 1664; Taunton/Portsmouth, RI
HART, Richard (1667-1745) & Hannah [WILLIAMS?]; b 1693; Tiverton, RI/Little Compton, RI
HART, Samuel (1622-1683) & 1/wf Mary (NEEDHAM) [HOWE] (-1671), w Joseph; b 1656, [ca 1653?]; Lynn
HART, Samuel (-1683) & 2/wf Mary WITTERIGE/WHITTRIDGE?/WHITING; 29 Jan 1673; Lynn
HART, Samuel (-1723) & Sarah NORTON; - Feb 1678, 2 Feb 1678; Ipswich
HART, Samuel & 1/wf Elizabeth INGALLS (-1681); 4 Jan 1680, 1680/1; Lynn
HART, Samuel (-1730?) & 2/wf Abigail LAMBERT; 9 Jun 1684; Lynn
HART, Samuel (1656-1730) & Sarah [ENDICOTT?] (1673?-); b 1686; Lynn
HART, Samuel (1672-1697) & Anna _?_; b 1697; Farmington, CT
HART, Samuel (-1714) & Mary EVANS (1676-); 2 May 1699; Dover, NH
HART, Stephen[1] (?1603, 1605-1683) & 1/wf _?_; in Eng, b 1628?, b 1626?; Boston/Hartford/Farmington

HART, Stephen[2] (-1689?) & [Ann FITCH], m/2 John THOMPSON by 1696; b 1662; Farmington, CT

HART, Stephen[1] (-1683) & 2/wf Margaret (_?_) NASH, w Joseph, w Arthur SMITH; aft 3 Sep 1678?, ca 1679; Hartford/Farmington, CT

HART, Stephen (1657?-) & Sarah COWLES; 18 Dec 1689; Farmington, CT

HART, Thomas (1607-1674) & Alice _?_; b 1640; Ipswich

HART, Thomas (-1671) & Freeborn [WILLIAMS] (1635-1710), m/2 Walter CLARKE 1683; b 1660?; Newport, RI

HART, Thomas & Mary NORTON (1643-1689); 14 Oct 1664, 12 Oct; Ipswich

HART, Thomas (1644-1726) & 1/wf _?_ NASH; by 1666

HART, Thomas (1644-1726) & 2/wf? 1/wf? Ruth [HAWKINS] (1649-1724); ca 1677, b 1667; Framington, CT/Wethersfield, CT

HART, Thomas (-1728) & Elizabeth JUDD (1670-); 18 Dec 1689; Farmington, CT

HART, Thomas (1667-) & Elizabeth _?_ (wf Mary 1697); b 1701?; Portsmouth, NH

HARTFORD/HARFORD, Nicholas & Elizabeth _?_; by 1700; Dover, NH

HARTSHORNE, Benjamin (1654-1694) & 1/wf Mary TOMSON/THOMPSON; 28 Feb 1681, 1681/2; Reading

HARTSHORN, Benjamin (1654-1694) & 2/wf Elizabeth BROWN (1660-), m/2 Nathaniel HAZELTON; 26 Nov 1684, 20 Nov 1684; Reading

HARTSHORN, David (1657-1738) & Rebecca [BATCHELDER] (1663-); 15 Mar 1683; Reading/Norwich, CT

HARTSHORN, John & Ruth SWAN (-1690); 19 Sep 1672; Haverhill

HARTSHORNE, John (-1708) & Hannah FRAME, m/2 William SMITH; 16 Mar 1695/6; Haverhill

HARTSHORN, John & Abigail [BROWN] (1675-); b 20 Nov 1697

HARTSHORNE, Jonathan (1672-1751) & Mary BURCKARD; 15 Aug 1700; Norwich, CT

HARTSHORNE, Joseph (1652-1727) & Sarah _?_ (-1727); b 1677; Reading/Dedham/Walpole

HARTSHORNE, Richard (1641-1722) & Margaret CARR; in Eng?, 27 Nov 1670; ?RI/Middletown, NJ

HARTSHORN, Thomas (-1683) & 1/wf Susannah [BUCK]; b 1646; Reading

HARTSHORNE, Thomas (-1683) & 2/wf Sarah (?AYRES) LAMSON, w William; 10 Apr 1661; Reading

HARTSHORNE, Thomas (1648-) & 1/wf Hannah GOODWIN (-1673); 10 May 1671; Reading

HARTSHORNE, Thomas (1648-) & 2/wf Sarah SWAN (1655-); 21 Oct 1674; Haverhill/Windham, CT

HARTSHORNE, Timothy & Martha EATON; 26 Dec 1685; Reading

HARTWED, Thomas & Katharine _?_; b 1671; Boston

HARTWELL, Ebenezer (1666-1724) & Sarah SMEDLEY (1670-1715); 27 Mar 1690; Concord

HARTWELL, John (1641-1703) & 1/wf Priscilla WRIGHT (-1681), ?Woburn; 1 Jun 1664; Concord

HARTWELL, John (1641-1703) & 2/wf Elizabeth WRIGHT (?1655-1704); 23 Oct 1682; Concord

HARTWELL, John & Sarah SHEPHERD; 1 Jun 1697; Concord/Lebanon, CT

HARTWELL, John (1673-) & 1/wf Deborah [EAGER?] (1676-1744); b 1701?; ?Concord/Bedford

HEARTWELL, Samuel (1645-) & Ruth WHEELER (ca 1641-1703); 26 Oct 1665; Concord

HARTWELL, Samuel (1666-) & Abigail STEARNS (-1709); 23 Nov 1692; Concord

HARTWELL, William[1] (?1600-1690) & Jazen _?_ (-1695); b 1638; Concord

HARVARD, John (1607-1638) & Ann SADLER (1614-), m/2 Rev. Thomas ALLEN; South Melling, 19 Apr 1629, b 1638, 1637, b Feb 1637, [1637/8?], b 5 May 1637; Charlestown

HARVEY, Edmund[1] (-1648) & 1/wf _?_; in Eng, b 1626; Milford, CT/Fairfield, CT

HARVEY, Edmund (-1648) & 2/wf Martha _?_, m/2 Nathan GOLD; b 1640; Milford, CT/Fairfield, CT

HARVEY, Francis, Frenchman & Ann [SMALL], m/2 Thomas WHEDON 1661; ca 1658, Jan 1660?; New Haven?

HARVEY, George (1647-) & Sarah HOWARD (1658-); 19 May 1677; Beverly/Gloucester

HARVEY, Henry (1650-) & ?2/wf Sarah (BROWN) ADAMS, w John; 12 Dec 1700; Salem

HARVEY, Joachim (1631-) & Char _?_; Great Island

HARVEY, John (-1705, Lyme, CT) & Elizabeth _?_ (-1705, Lyme, CT); b 1676; Taunton/New London, CT/Lyme, CT

HARVEY, John (1655-1706) (see Thomas HARVEY) & Sarah (BARNES) [ROWELL], w Thomas, m/3 Daniel HOYT 1706+; ca 1685-6; Amesbury

HARVEY, Joseph (1645-1680/1) & Esther/Hester [STACEY]; [1680]; Taunton

HARVEY, Josiah (1640-1698) & 2/wf? Mary [STAPLES] (1646±-); b 1669; Fairfield, CT
HARVEY, Matthias & Mary (HAMBLEHURST) [COLE/COLES] (-1682), w Robert; ca 1655/6, aft
   Oct 1655; Oyster Bay, LI
HARVEY, Matthew & 2/wf Margaret [FURBUSH]; m lic 17 Dec 1682
HARVEY, Nathaniel (1673-) & Susannah _?_ ; b 1701?; Taunton
HARVEY, Peter (-1671?) & Elizabeth (CLEEVES) [MILTON], w Michael; ca 1663; Falmouth, ME
HARVEY, Peter & Hannah GILBERT (ca 1646-); Jan 1670, [1670/1]; Salem
HARVEY, Peter & Sarah _?_ ; b 1691, b 1696, ca 1684/5; Beverly/Weymouth
HARVEY, ?Richard (1613-1689) & 1/wf? Ann _?_ ; in Eng?, b 1635?; ?Concord/etc.
HARVEY, Richard (1613-1689) & ?2/wf Margaret _?_ (-1639); b 1639; Concord/Stratford, CT
HARVEY, Richard (1613-1689) & ?3/wf _?_ ; b 1644; Concord/Hartford, CT
HARVEY, Richard & Jehoidan [HORNE]/[ORNE]; b 1659; Salem
HARVEE, Richard & _?_ [HOWES?]; b 1668; Southold, LI
HARVEY, Thomas (-1651) & Elizabeth [ANDREWS], m/2 Francis STREET, m/3 Thomas
   LINCOLN 1665; ca 1642; Taunton
HARVEY, Thomas & Elizabeth [WALL]; b 1663?, b 20 Aug 1663; Hampton, NH
HARVEY, Thomas & Experience [HARVEY] (1644-); 1668; Taunton
HARVEY, Thomas & Sarah ROWELL; 26 Oct 1676; Amesbury
HARVEY, Thomas (1643, ?1641-1728) & Elizabeth WILLIS (-ca 1719), dau John; 10 Dec 1679;
   Taunton
HARVEY, Thomas & Elizabeth [KELLY]; b 7 Nov 1681; ?Boston
HARVEY, Thomas & Joanna LIGHTFOOT; 10 Nov 1683; Marblehead
HARVEY, Thomas (1669?-1748) & Mary [HUCKINS] (-1756); ca 1694; Taunton
HARVEY, William (-1691) & Joane HUCKER/?HOSKIN; 2 Apr 1639; Taunton/Boston
HARVEY, William (-1658) & Martha [COPP], m/2 Henry TEWKESBURY [1659]; b 1651; Boston
HARVEY, William (1645-) & _?_ ; b 1674; Taunton?
HARWOOD, Benjamin (1663-) & Mehitable [PHILLIPS] (1667-1737), m/2 Thomas SAVAGE 1690;
   b 1687; Boston
HARWOOD, George & Jane _?_ ; b 1639; Boston/New London
HARDWOOD, Henry (-1635?) & [Winifred?/?Elizabeth] _?_ (-1632+); b 1630?; Charlestown/
   Boston
HARDWOOD, Henry (-1664) & [Elizabeth] _?_, wid; Salem
HARDWOOD, Henry & Elizabeth _?_ ; b 1665; Boston/Casco Bay, ME
HARWOOD, James (1655-) & Lydia BARRETT (1659-); 11 Apr 1678; Chelmsford
HARWOOD/HARROD?, John (?1626-) & Elizabeth [USHER?]; b 1650?, b 1653?, returned to
   Eng; Boston/Cambridge
HARROD/HARWOOD?, John (-1690) & Em/Emma _?_ ; 11 Jul 1659; Salem
HARWOOD, John (1639-) & _?_ ; ca 1665?; New London?
HARRUDE, John (same as above John b 1639?) & Elizabeth COOKE; 24 Dec 1666; Warwick, RI
HARWOD, John & Hannah _?_ ; b 1677; Boston
HARWOOD, John, Boston & Martha BARTON, Boston; 20 Nov 1679; Chelmsford
HARROD, John (same as John & Hannah?) & Susannah [SNELL]; b 1687, b 1677; Boston
HARROD, John & Mary [PARKER]; ca 1688/92?; Marblehead
HARWOOD, John & Elizabeth (MERRITT) DIXEY, w Thomas; 29 Oct 1695, ?28 Oct; Salem
HARWOOD, Jonathan (1666-) & Rebecca [?TWISS]; b 1701?; Salem/Sutton
HARWOOD, Nathaniel (1626-1716) & Elizabeth _?_ (-1715); b 1665; Boston/Concord
HARWOOD, Nathaniel (1669-1751) & Mary [BARRON] (1673-1708); b 1696; Concord/Chelms-
   ford
HARWOOD, Peter (1671-1740) & Mary FOX (1673-1742); 7 Nov 1700; Concord/Littleton
HARWOOD, Philip & Content [CLARK]; RI
HARWOD, Richard & Williamse _?_ ; b 1680?; Southold, LI
HARWOOD, Robert (-1678?) & Joanna _?_ (-1696) (member Roxbury church); ca 1671?, b
   1673(4?); Boston
HARWOOD, Thomas (-1706) & Rachel (SMITH) WOODWARD, w Robert; 7 Jul 1654; Boston
HARWOOD, William (1665-1740) & Esther PERRY (1674-1747); 11 May 1692; Concord/Dunstable
HARRUD, _?_ & Elizabeth HALLOCK; b 1675
HARWOOD/HASWOOD, William & Phebe CARINTON; 10 Sep 1700; Boston
HASEY, Joseph (1657-1707) & 1/wf Hannah _?_ (-18 Aug 1693); b 1681; Boston

HASIE, Joseph (1657-1707) & 2/wf Hannah (WAITE) BUCKMAN/BUCKNAM (1656-), w William; 12 Jan 1693, 1693/4; Boston
HASEY, William[1] (1619-1689) & 1/wf Sarah __?__ (-1682); b 1654, b 1650; Boston
HASEY, William[2] (1652-1695) & Judith [JACOB] of Ipswich (1650-1718); b 1679, by 1672, b 12 Nov 1675; Boston
HASEY, William[1] (1619-30 May 1689) & Judith (_?_) POOLL, w Jonathan, m/3 Robert GOULD b 20 Sep 1695; 16 May 1689; Reading
HASKELL, Benjamin (ca 1648-1740/1) & 1/wf Mary RIGGS (1659-1698); 21 Nov 1677; Gloucester
HASKELL, Benjamin & 2/wf Emma (GRAVES) BOND, w John; 10 Jun 1698; Beverly/Gloucester
HASKELL, John (?1640, ?1639-1706 in 67th y, Middleboro) & Patience [SOLE/SOULE] (-1706, Middleboro); - Jan 1666; Middleboro
HASKELL, John (ca 1649-1718) & Mary BAKER (1665-1723); 20 May 1685; Gloucester
HASCALL, John (1670-1727+, 1728, prob) & Mary SQUIRE (1681-); 2 Mar 1699, 2 Mar 1698/9; Middleboro/Cambridge
HASKELL, Joseph (1646-1727) & Mary GRAVES (1653-1733); 2 Dec 1674, 1675; Gloucester
HASKELL, Joseph (1673-1718) & Rachel ELWELL, m/2 Ezekiel WOODWORTH 1719; 19 Mar 1695/6; Gloucester
HASKALL, Josiah (-1684) & Sarah GRIGGS; 22 Nov 1682; Beverly/Gloucester
HASKELL, Mark (?1621-1669?) & Hannah (WOODBURY) [PATCH] (-1703), w James; Beverly
HASKELL, Mark (-1699, Rochester) & Mary SMITH; 20 Mar 1677/8; Beverly/Rochester
HASKELL, Mark (1658-1691) & Elizabeth GIDINS/GIDDINGS, m/2 John DENNISON; 16 Dec 1685; Gloucester
HASKELL, Mark & Charity (GALE) PITMAN, w John; 7 Jan 1696/7; Marblehead
HASKELL, Roger (1614-1667) & 1/wf? __?__ (-1650?, 1648?); Salem
HASKELL, Roger (1614-1667) & Elizabeth [HARDY], m/2 Edward BERRY ca 1668; b 1639?; Salem
HASKALL, Roger & Hannah WOODBERRIE/WOODBURY; 21 Dec 1680; Beverly
HASKELL, William (-1630), in Eng & Elinor __?__, m/2 John STONE (came to N. E.); b 1614 in Eng
HASKELL, William (1618-1693) & Mary TYBBOT/TIBBETTS (-1693); 6 Nov 1643, ?16 Nov; Gloucester
HASKELL, William (1644-1708) & Mary BROWNE (?1649-1715), step-dau Henry WALKER; 3 Jul 1667; Gloucester
HASKELL, William & Miriam HILL (1658-); 1 May 1679; Salem
HASKELL, William & Ruth WEST; 29 Mar 1688; Beverly
HASKELL, William (1670-1731) & Abigail DAVIS (1672-1730); 8 Sep 1692; Gloucester
HASKET/HASKETT, Stephen ([1634/6]-1709) & Elizabeth [HILL] (-1740); Exeter, Eng, 2 Aug 1659; Salem
HASSAM, William & Sarah ALLIN; 4 Dec 1684; Marblehead
HERSOME, __?__ & Mary __?__ (-1646); Wenham
HASSELL, George & Joan __?__; b 1664 (div); Boston
HASSELL, George & Rebecca [CARD], w Richard; b 20 Nov 1692; Newport
HASSELL, John & Margaret __?__ (-1660(1?)); Ipswich
HASSALL, Joseph (1645-1691) & Anna (Mary is wrong) PERRY; 21 Aug 1667; Cambridge/Watertown/Concord/Dunstable
HASSALL, Joseph & Hannah __?__; b 1701; Dunstable
HASSELL, Richard (1622-) & Joane __?__; b 1643; Cambridge
HASTINGS, Benjamin (1659-1711) & 1/wf Elizabeth [GRAVES] (1662-1695?); ca 1683; Northampton/Deerfield/Hatfield
HASTINGS, Benjamin (1659-1711) & 2/wf Mary (CLARK) [PARSONS], w Jonathan; ca 1696; Northampton
HASTINGS, George & Dorothy __?__; b 1692; Newport
HASTINGS, John (-1657) & 1/wf [Elizabeth?] __?__; in Eng, b 1631; Braintree/Cambridge
HASTINGS, John (-1657) & 2/wf Anne [MEAN/MEANS] (-1666, ae 60), w John; [aft 1646]; Cambridge
HASTINGS, John & 1/wf Hannah MOORE (1643-1667); 1 Mar 1665/6; Cambridge
HASTINGS, John & 2/wf Lydia CHAMPNEY (-1691); 20 May 1668; Cambridge
HASTINGS, John (-1718, Waltham) & Abigail HAMMOND (1659-1718); 18 Jun 1679; Watertown

HASTINGS, John & 3/wf Rebecca EATON, w Benoni; 28 Sep 1691; Cambridge
HASTINGS, Joseph & 1/wf Ruth RICE (1662-1683); 21 Nov 1682, 31 Nov 1682; Watertown
HASTINGS, Joseph (-1695) & 2/wf Martha SHEPHEARD; 8 Jan 1684, 1684/5; Watertown
HASTINGS, Joseph & Elizabeth EDWARDS; 17 Jan 1699; Cambridge/Reading
HASTINGS, Nathaniel (1661-1694) & Mary [NEVINSON] (1668-1700); ca 1685/90?; Watertown
HASTINGS, Robert & Elizabeth DAVIS (1654-); 31 Oct 1676; Haverhill
HASTINGS, Samuel & Mary MEANE/MEANS; 12 Nov 1661; Cambridge
HASTINGS, Samuel & 1/wf Lydia CHURCH (-1691); 4 Jan 1686/7, ?1 Jan, ?14 Jan; Watertown
HASTINGS, Samuel & Elizabeth NEVINSON; 24 Apr 1694; Watertown
HASTINGS, Samuel (1668-1699) & Hannah [MARRETT] (1668-); b 1699; Cambridge
HASTINGS, Thomas (1605-1685) & 1/wf Susan/Susanna __?__ (1600-1651); b 1634, no issue; Watertown
HASTINGS, Thomas (1605-1685) & 2/wf Margaret [CHENEY] (-1685); ca Apr 1651, 10 Apr 1651; Watertown
HASTINGS, Thomas (1652-1712) & 1/wf Anne HAWKES (-1705); 10 Oct 1672; ?Hadley/Hatfield
HASTINGS, Thomas (1671-) & Sarah TARBOT/TURBET/TARBALL, Newton; ?31 May 1693, ?31 Aug 1693; Watertown/Newton
HASTINGS, Walter (?1632, 1631-1705) & 1/wf Sarah ?MELINE/MEEN/MEANS (1638-1672, 1673); 10 Apr 1655; Cambridge
HASTINGS, Walter & 2/wf Elizabeth BRIGHT (-1702); 23 Jul 1674, 5 Jul, 25 Jul; Cambridge
HASWOOD/HARWOOD, William & Phebe CARINTON; 10 Sep 1700; Boston
HATCH, Benjamin (1655-) & 1/wf [Mercy HAMLIN?/LUMBERT?] (-1681/2); 17 Jan 1678, 17 Jun; Falmouth, MA
HATCH, Benjamin (1655-) & 2/wf Eles/?Alice/Eliz.? EDDY (1659-); 16 Mar 1682, 1682/3; Falmouth, MA
HATCH, Charles (1613-1655) & __?__ (wf in Eng); b 1639, b 1637; York, ME
HATCH, Israel (-1740, ae 74) & Mercy [DUNHAM] (1662, 1668?-1733, ae 65); 1693; Marshfield
HATCH, Israel (1667-1740) & Elizabeth HATCH (1669-); 27 Jul 1699; Scituate
HATCH, James (1674-) & [Abigail] [SMITH] (1673-), dau Jeremiah; b 1698; Scituate
HATCH, Jeremiah (1626-1713?) & Mary HEWES (-1716); 29 Dec 1657; Scituate
HATCH, Jeremiah (1660-) & Elizabeth __?__ (-1708); b 1690; Scituate
HATCH, John (-1701) & Sarah __?__; b 1693; Portsmouth, NH
HATCH, John (1664-1737) & Mary FOSTER (1671-1750); 30 Dec 1696; Marshfield/Scituate
HATCH, Jonathan (-1710) & Sarah ROWLEY; 11 Apr 1646; Barnstable/Falmouth
HATCH, Jonathan (1652-) & Abigail WEEKS; 4 Dec 1676; Martha's Vineyard
HATCH, Joseph (1654-1736?) & Amey/Anme ALLEN (1663-1710); 7 Dec 1683, 2 Dec; Falmouth, MA
HATCH, Moses (1662/3-) & 1/wf Hepzibah EDDY (-living in 1690/1); 9 May 1686; Martha's Vineyard
HATCH, Moses (1662/3-) & 2/wf __?__ ; Martha's Vineyard
HATCH, Moses (1662-1747) & 3/wf Elizabeth THATCHER (1677-1710); 18 Oct 1699; Falmouth
HATCH, Nathaniel & Elizabeth ESTES; Sea Deal, Eng, 9 Oct 1681; Boston
HATCH, Philip (1616-) & Patience [?EDGE] (-1674+); b 1651, b 1648?; York Co., ME
HATCH, Philip (?1651) & __?__
HATCH, Samuel (1653, 1652?-1735) & Mary DOTY; betw 10 Jul 1677 & 28 Feb 1679/80; Scituate
HATCH, Samuel (1660-) & 1/wf Mary LITTLEFIELD (-bef 1723); b 1685, ca 1684, May 1685; Wells, ME
HATCH, Samuel (1659-1718) & Lydia __?__ ; b 1694; Falmouth
HATCH, Thomas (-1661) & Grace [?LEWIS], ?m/2 Ralph SMITH; b 1624, in Eng; Yarmouth/Barnstable
HATCH, Thomas (-1646?) & Lydia __?__, m/2 John SPRING by 1654; in Eng, b 1624, ca 1622; Dorchester/Scituate
HATCH, Thomas (1628-1684) & Sarah ELMES (1645-); 4 Feb 1662, 1662/3; Scituate
HATCH, Thomas (1649-) & Abigail CODMAN; 22 Jan?/Jun? 1679, 22 Juenye, 22 Jan 1679, 22 Jun; Falmouth, MA
HATCH, Thomas (1670-1760) & Hannah CUDWORTH (1674-1731); 6 Mar 1695/6; Scituate
HATCH, Walter[2] (1623?-1699) & 1/wf Elizabeth HOLBROOKE (1634-); 6 May 1650; Scituate/Swansea?

HATCH, Walter[2] (1623?-1699) & 2/wf Mary BOLES? STABLE/?STAPLES; 1 Aug 1674, 5 Aug; Marshfield
HATCH, William[1] (-1651) & 1/wf _?_; in Eng, ca 1622; Scituate
HATCH, William[1] (-1651) & 2/wf Jane YOUNG (-1654), m/2 Thomas KING 1653; in Eng, 9 Jul 1624, lic; Scituate
HATCH, William[2] (1629-1657?) & Abigail [HEWES], m/2 John KING 1658; b 1652; Scituate
HATCH, William (?1624-1702?) & Susanna ANNIBALL/ANNABLE (?1630-); 13 May 1652; Scituate/Swansea
HATCH, William (1660-) & Mary _?_; b 1687, b 1688; Swansea
HATCH, [?William] & 1/wf [Dinah DARTE] (1664-1711+, living 1711); ca 1690?; ?New London
HATHAWAY, Abraham (1652-1725) & Rebecca WILBUR (1665-); 28 Aug 1684; Taunton/Berkley
HATHAWAY, Arthur, Jr.? (-1711?) & Sarah COOKE (-1709+); 20 Nov 1652; Plymouth/?Marble-head/Dartmouth
HATHAWAY, Ephraim (1661-1716) & Elizabeth [TALBOT?/TABBOT?]; b 1690; Dighton
HATHAWAY, Gideon & Patience BEAUMOND/BEAUMONT, Dorchester; 21 Jan 1697
HATHAWAY, Isaac (1655-1722) & Mary PITTS; 17 Mar 1686/7; Taunton/Berkley
HATHAWAY, Jacob & Phillippa/Philip? CHASE; 28 Jan 1696/7, 1696; Taunton
HATHAWAY, John (1629-1705) (ae 67 in 1697) & 1/wf Martha [SHEPHERD?] (-1683+); b 1650; Taunton
HADEWAY, John (-1697) & Hannah HALLET/HALLETT/HOLLETT, wid; 1 Jul 1656; Barnstable
HATHAWAY, John (-1697) & 2/wf Elizabeth COLEMAN (-1697+); 1 May 1672; Yarmouth
HATHAWAY, John (1650-1730) & 1/wf Hannah [BURT]; [b 1677]; Taunton/Freetown
HATHAWAY, John (1653-) & Joanna POPE (1659?-1695); 5 Mar 1682/3, 15 Mar 1682; Harwich?/?Dartmouth
HATHAWAY, John, Taunton & 2/wf Ruth DYER (1640-1705), Braintree, w Christopher; 25 Dec 1692, 10 Oct 1692; Braintree
HATHAWAY, John & Patience [HUNNEWELL/POPE?]; 29 Sep 1696; Dartmouth
HATHAWAY, Nicholas (-1639+) & _?_; in Eng, b 1629; Braintree
HATHAWAY, Thomas & [Hepzibah STARBUCK] (1680-); b 1697?, b 1698?; Dartmouth
HATHAWAY, Thomas & Sarah BAKER (-1710); 15 Dec 1698; Yarmouth
HATHERLY, Henry & Elizabeth BARLOW; 4 Jul 167[1?]; Saco, ME
HATHERLY, Thomas (called George in 1676) & Abigail _?_; b 1668; Boston
HATHERLY, Thomas (1668-) & Lydia GREEN; 1 Aug 1693; Boston
HATHERLY, Timothy (ca 1586-1666) & 1/wf Alice COLLARD; St. Olaves, Southwark, Eng, 26 Dec 1614; Scituate
HATHERLY, Timothy (-1666) & 2/wf Susan _?_; b 1640; Scituate
HATHERLY, Timothy (-1666) & Lydia (HUCKSTOP) [TILDEN] (1588-), w Nathaniel; 1642?; Scituate
HATHORN, Ebenezer (1656-) & Esther WITT (1664-); 26 Dec 1683; Lynn/Salem
HATHORNE, Eleazer (1637-1680) & Abigail CORWIN (1643-), m/2 James RUSSELL 1684; 28 Aug 1663; Salem
HATHORNE, John (1621-1676) & Sarah _?_ (-1676+); b 1644; Salem/Malden/Lynn
HATHORNE, John (1641-1717) & Ruth GARDNER; 22 Mar 1674/5; Salem
HATHORNE, Nathaniel & Mary [GOTT]; b 1691; Lynn
HATHORNE, Nathaniel (1678-) & Sarah HIGGINSON (1682-1699); 22 Jun 1699; Salem
HATHORN, William (1607-1681) & Ann [JOHNSON] (-1681+) (see Roger MOWRY); b 1635; Dorchester/Salem
HATHORN, William (1645-1678) & Sarah [RUCK], ?m/2 George BURROUGHS 1681?, ?m/3 John BROWN 1698; Salem
HATHORN, William & Joan THISTLE; 19 May 1679; Beverly
HATHORNE, William (1673-1709) & Abigail CUTLER; 23 Dec 1700; Woburn
HAUGHTON, Benoni (see HORTON) & Mary TRUMAN; 15 Apr 1700; Middletown, CT
HAUGHTON/HORTON?, John (-1705) & 1/wf Hannah _?_; b 1686/7?; Boston/?New London
HAUGHTON/HORTON?, John (-1705) & 2/wf Ruth [BROWN]; b 1700; New London
HAUGHTON, Richard (-1681) & 1/wf Sarah _?_; b 1639; Milford, CT/New London, CT
HAUGHTON, Richard (-1681) & 2/wf Katherine [CHARLET] (-1670, New London), w Nicholas; New London, CT
HAUGHTON, Richard & 3/wf Alice _?_, m Daniel CRUMB aft 1682; b 1673?; New London, CT

HAUGHTON/HORTON?, Richard (-1682), Beverly, MA, & 2/wf? Mary _?_; Beverly (d at Wethersfield)
HAUGHTON/HOUGHTON, Robert (-1678) & Sarah PHIPPEN (1648-), m/2 Benjamin SMITH 1682; 8 Sep 1668; Cambridge/Boston/Milford, CT
HAUGHTON, Sampson (?1667-1718) & Sarah _?_; b 1692, b 1687; ?Montville, CT/New London
HAWGHTON, William & _?_; b 1651; Boston
HAWKHURST/HAUXHURST, Christopher & Mary [REDDOCK]; b 1671?, b 1674?, b 1668?, ca 1655?; Oyster Bay, LI
HAWKHURST, Samson (?1671, 1670-1732) & Hannah [TOWNSEND] (1680-1757); b 18 Jan 1698?, ?18 Jan; Oyster Bay, LI
HAVENS, George & 1/wf _?_ [GREEN], dau Edward; b 1675?, much later; RI
HAVENS, George (-1706+, 1724?) & ?2/wf Eleanor [THURSTON] (1655-1724+), m/2 Thomas TERRY; b 1681, 1674?; Jamestown, RI
HAVENS, John (-1687) & Ann _?_ (-1687+); b 1654; Portsmouth, RI
HAVEN, John (-1705) & Hannah HITCHINGS?/HICKINS, m/2 John HOWE; 3 Oct 1686; Lynn/Framingham
HAVENS, Jonathan & Hannah [BROWN]; b 1682; Southold, LI
HAVEN, Moses & 1/wf Mary [BALLARD/?BULLARD] (1666-); b 1689; Lynn/Framingham
HAVEN, Nathaniel (1664-1746) & Elizabeth [TRAVERS]; b 1690; Lynn/Framingham
HAVEN, Richard (1626-1703) (ae 74 in 1690) & Susannah [?WASTALL/NEWHALL] (1624-1682); ca 1647/50; Lynn/Framingham
HAVEN, Richard (1651-) & Susannah _?_; b 1677; Lynn/Framingham
HAVENS, Robert & Elizabeth [EARLE]; b 1686; Portsmouth, RI/Dartmouth
HAVENS, Thomas (-1704) & _?_; ca 1665/70?; Portsmouth, RI/Kings Town, RI
HAVENS, William (-1683) & Dionis _?_ (-1692+); ca 1630?; Portsmouth, RI
HAVILAND, Benjamin (1660-1726?) & Abigail [MOTT] (1660-); Rye, NY
HAVILAND, Edward & Susan _?_; b 1657; Boston
HAVILAND, John & Sarah _?_; b 1698; Flushing, LI
HAVILAND, Joseph & Mary _?_; b 1670?; Flushing, LI/Westchester, NY
HAVILAND, William (1618/25?-1697), Flushing, LI, & Hannah [HICKS?] (-1712); 1638/1645; Newport, RI/Great Neck, LI
HAWES, Daniel & Abiel GAY (1649-); 23 Jan 1677/8; Dedham/Wrentham
HAWS, Ebenezer (1678-) & Sarah NORTON; 23 Feb 1699/1700; Edgartown/Yarmouth/Martha's Vineyard
HAWES, Edmond (1612-1693) & _?_ (-1689); b 1635; Duxbury/Yarmouth
HAWS, Edward (-1686) & Eliony LUMBER/LOMBARD?; 15 Apr 1648; Dedham
HAWES, Eleazer (-1676) & Ruth HAINES/HAYNES (-1672); 23 Feb 1669/70; Dorchester
HAWES, Isaac & Bethiah _?_; b 1701; Yarmouth
HAWES?/DAWES, James (1664-) & Damaris [BIRD] (1675-); b 1694; Dorchester
HAWES, John (-1701) & Desire GORHAM (1644-1700); 7 Oct 1661; Barnstable
HAWSE, John & Sarah DEERING; 27 May 1683; Dedham
HAWES/HOUSE, John (1669-1723) & Mary _?_; ca 1690/95?; Providence
HAWS, Joseph (1664-) & Deborah [?DEWING]; b 1696; Dedham
HAWES, Joseph (1673-1752) & 1/wf Mary [HOWES] (ca 1670?, 1672±-1729); b 1696; Yarmouth
HAWES, Matthew & Mary [COLE]; ca 1654?; Salem
HAWSE, Nathaniel, Dedham & Sarah NEWELL, Roxbury, m/2 Samuel ROCKET/ROCKWOOD; 29 Mar 1688; ?Newton
HAWES, Obadiah (1635-1690) & 1/wf Mary [HUMPHREY] (1645-1676); b 1663; Dorchester
HAWES, Obadiah (1635-1690, ae 56) & 2/wf Sarah (?WISWALL) [HOLMES] (?1643-1717?), w John; aft 1676, b 7 Oct 1678; Dorchester
HAWS, Obadiah (1663-) & Rebecca COWEN/COWING (1666-); 19 Dec 1693; Boston
HAWES, Richard (1606-1656?, 1657?) & Ann [?CLAPP]; in Eng, b 1632; Dorchester
HAWES, Robert (-1666, ae 84) & 1/wf _?_; Salem
HAWES, Robert (-1666) & 2/wf Frances (FAIRFIELD?) [EDWARDS] (-1645), w Matthew?; b 12 Jun 1641; Salem
HAWES, Robert (-1666) & 3/wf Mary [PIERREPONT?]; Dorchester/Roxbury?
HAWES, William & Susanna _?_ (-1651?); b 1652; Boston
HAWKES, Adam (1608-1671/2) & 1/wf Anne [HUTCHINSON] (-1669), wid; b 1634, ca 1631?; Charlestown/Lynn

HAWKES, Adam (-1671/2) & 2/wf Sarah HOOPER, m/2 Samuel WARDLE 1672/3; - Jun 1670; Lynn

HAWKS, Adam (-1694) (see Gershom HAWKS) & Elizabeth _?_ (had son John), ?m/2 George LIBBY 1695?; b 1690; Lynn

HAWKES, Eleizer (1655-1727) & Judith SMEAD (1665-1719), Northampton; 30 Apr 1689; ?Hadley

HAWKES, Gershom (see Adam HAWKES) & Elizabeth [PRATT]?, dau Richard; Charlestown

HAWKE, James (1649-1716) & Sarah JACOB (1652-1694); 9 Jul 1678; Hingham

HAWKE, James & Hannah BEEBE; 16 Jan 1698/9; New London, CT

HAWKES, John (-1662) & Elizabeth _?_, m/2 Robert HINSDALE bef 1668, m/3 Thomas DIBBLE 1683; b 1643; Windsor, CT/Hadley

HAUKES, John/Jonathan (-1694) & 1/wf Rebecca MAVERICK (1639-1659); 3 Jun 1658; Lynn

HAUKES, John (-1694) & 2/wf Sarah CUSHMAN, ?m/2 Daniel HITCHINGS 1695; 11 Apr 1661; Lynn

HAWKES, John (1643-1721+, Waterbury, CT) & 1/wf Mary [BALDWIN?] (-1676); 26 Dec 1667

HAWKS, John & Thankful [SMEAD]; b 1696; Deerfield

HAWKES, John (1643-1721+) & 2/wf Alice (_?_) ALLIS, w Samuel; 20 Nov 1696; Hadley/Waterbury, CT

HAWKS, John & Abigail FLOID/FLOYD, Boston; m int 7 Jan 1698/9; Lynn

HAWKES/HOUGH, John & Hannah [BEEBE]; b 1701?, 1697, ?16 Jan 1698/9?, 88/9?; New London

HAWKE, Matthew (1610-1684) & Margaret [?TOWLE] (-1684); in Eng, ca 1638; Hingham

HAWKES, Moses (1659-1709) & Margaret COGSWELL, Ipswich; 10 May 1698; Lynn

HAWKINS, Abraham (-1648) & Elizabeth _?_; b 1643; Charlestown

HAWKINS, Edward (-1726) & Esther (ARNOLD) (DEXTER) [ANDREWS] (1647-1688±), w James, w Wm.; b 1685; Providence

HAWKINS, Edward (-1726) & 2/wf Anne _?_; b 1690; Providence

HAWKINS, James (ca 1604-1670) & Mary [MILLS] (1616-1692, ae 76?); b 1646, b 1636?; Boston

HAWKINS, James (1654-5 Jan 1709/10, ae ca 56 y) & Lydia/Hannah [RICE] (-1718?, 1688); b 1679(80?); Boston/Framingham

HAWKINS, James (-1727) & Elizabeth HUMPHREYS; 5 Mar 1692/3; Marblehead

HAWKINS, Job (1620?-) (kinsman of Major William HOLMES) & Frances _?_; b 1646/7; Boston/Portsmouth, RI

HAWKINS, John & Sarah DAMARILL, w Humphrey; 15 Sep 1654; Boston

HAWKINS, John (-1726) & Sarah _?_; b 1679?; Providence

HAWKINS, John (-1712) & 1/wf _?_; Hempstead, LI

HAWKINS, John & Abigail SHORE; m int 11 Mar 1698/9; Lynn

HAWKINS, Joseph (1642-) & Abigail HOLBROOK (1648-); 8 Apr 1668; Milford, CT/Derby, CT

HAWKINS, Joseph & [Mercy JOHNSON]; b 1681; ?Derby, CT

HAWKINS, Joseph & Lydia [FRENCH]; 1688; Derby, CT?

HAWKINS, Joseph (1668/9-), Derby & Elizabeth GUNN (1672-), Milford; 9 Aug 1693, at Derby; Milford, CT

HAWKINS, Richard (-1656±) & Jane _?_ (-1656+); in Eng, b 1609, b 1604?; Boston/Portsmouth, RI

HAWKINS, Robert (1610-1682?) & Mary _?_ (1611-); b 1635; Charlestown/?Derby, CT

HAWKINS, Robert & Esther HUGHS; 7 Jun 1694; Boston

HAWKINS, Thomas (1609?-1654?) & Mary _?_, m/2 Robert FENN 1654, m/3 Henry SHRIMPTON 1661, (1661/2?); b 1638, b 1636?; Dorchester/Boston

HAWKINS, Thomas (1609?-1671) & 1/wf Hannah _?_ (-1644); b 1637, b 1636; Boston

HAWKINS, Thomas (?1609-1671) & 2/wf Rebecca _?_; b 1645; Boston

HAWKINS, Timothy (-1651) & Hannah/Anna [HAMMOND?] (1616-), m/2 Ellis BARRON 1653; b 1637; Watertown

HAUKINS, Timothy & 1/wf Mary SHERMAN (1644-1667); 18 Jan 1666/7, 1666; Watertown

HAUKINS, Timothy & 2/wf Grace _?_ (-1675); b 1675; Watertown

HAUKINS, Timothy & Mary (TREADWAY) FISHER (1642-1677), w John; 21 Jul 1675; Watertown

HAUKINS, Timothy & 4/wf Ruhamah JOHNSON, m Daniel SMITH 1700; 13 Jun 1680; Watertown

HAWKINS, William (1609-1699+) & Margaret [HARWOOD?] (1612-); ca 1633/40?; Providence

HAWKINS, William & Sarah/Anna _?_; b 1663; Boston

HAWKINS, William & Dorothy __?_; b 1668; Boston
HAWKINS, William (-1723) & Lydia (BALLOU) [GARDINER/GARDNER?], w George; 14 Jun 1678; Providence
HAWKINS, William & [Hannah/Anna BIRCHAM], dau Edward; b 1684; ?Reading
HAWKINS, Zechariah/Zachary (?1639-1698) & Mary [BIGGS] (-1696+); b 1664?; Brookhaven, LI
HAWKINS, [?Thomas] & Agnes __?_; ca 1673, 5 ch bpt 1685; Marblehead
HOXWORTH/HAWKSWORTH, Peter & Elizabeth (WEBSTER) STEPHENS, w David; 27 Feb 1699, 1699/1700?; Boston
HAUXWORTH, Thomas & Mary __?_; b 1641; Salisbury
HAWLEY, Ebenezer (1654-1681) & Esther/Hester WARD, dau Wm., m/2 Ephraim NICHOLS 1682, m/3 Eliphalet HILL 1691, m/4 Robert LORD by 1696; m cont 19 Apr 1678; ?Fairfield, CT/Stratford, CT
HAWLEY, Ephraim (1659-1690) & Sarah WELLS (1664-1694), m/2 Ayer TOMLINSON 1692; 4 Dec 1683; ?Stratford, CT
HAWLEY, John (1661-1729) & Deborah PIERSON (1666-1739) & 23 Apr 1686; Stratford, CT
HAWLEY, Joseph (?1603-1690) & Catherine [BOOTH/BIRDSEY?] (-1692); ca 1646; Wethersfield, CT/Hartford, CT
HAWLEY, Joseph (1654-1711) & Lydia MARSHALL (?1655, 1657-1732), Windsor; 24 Sep 1676; ?Northampton
HAWLEY, Joseph (1675-) & Elizabeth WILCOXSON (1673-); 7 Jun 1697; Stratford, CT/Farmington, CT?
HAWLEY, [Richard] (-1698, ae 63) & Johanna __?_; ca 1670, 6 ch bpt 1684; Marblehead
HAWLEY, Samuel (ca 1647/8-1734) & 1/wf Mary THOMPSON (bpt 1653-1691, 1690?), Farmington; 20 May 1673; Stratford, CT
HAWLEY, Samuel (-1734) & 2/wf Patience (NICHOLS) [HUBBELL] (1660-1734), w John; 1691?; Stratford, CT
HAWLEY, Thomas (-1676) & 1/wf Emm/Emma/Amy __?_ (-Nov 1651); Roxbury
HAWLEY, Thomas (-1676) & 2/wf Dorothy (HARBOTTLE) LAMB (-1698), w Thomas; 2 Feb 1651, 1651/2; Roxbury
HAYE, Patrick/Peter (1658-1748, in 91st y) & 1/wf Mary KIBBEE (-1694); 26 Mar 1685; Reading/Charlestown/Lynn
HAY, Patrick/Peter (-1748) & Sarah __?_ (-1729, in 69th y); b 1696; Charlestown/Shoreham
HAY, Samuel & __?_; b 1683(4?); Ipswich
HAY/HAYES?, Thomas & Bridget __?_; b 1687; Boston
HAYDEN, Daniel (1640-1713) & Hannah WILCOXSON (-1722); 17 Mar 1664, 1694/5; Windsor, CT
HAYDEN, Ebenezer (1645-1718, ae 73) & Ann?/Hannah __?_; b 1673(4?); Milton/Braintree
HAYDEN, Edward & Hannah __?_; b 5 Feb 1696; Westchester, NY
HAYDEN, Ferman & [Elizabeth] __?_, m/2 Thomas WATTS; 5 May 1657; Boston
HAYDEN, James (1609-1675) & Elizabeth __?_ (-1680, ae 76); b 1638; Charlestown
HAYDEN, John (-1682) & Susan/Susanna __?_ (-1695+); ca 1634; Braintree
HAYDEN, John (1635-1718) & Hannah AMES (1641-1689); 6 Apr 1660; Braintree
HAYDEN, John (1639-1675) & Hannah MAYNARD (1653-1675); 14 Oct 1669; Charlestown
HADEN, John & Elizabeth/(Abigail in 1694(5?)) __?_; b 1680?; Westchester, NY
HAYDEN, John & [Mary] WATERHOUSE, w John; aft 1687; Saybrook, CT
HAYDEN, John & Elizabeth __?_ (-1694); Braintree
HAYDEN, Jonathan (1640-) & Elizabeth LADD/LEE; 20 Apr 1669; Braintree
HAYDEN, Jonathan & Hannah/Sarah? [HOBART] (1668-), dau Caleb; 1692; Bridgewater
HAYDEN, Joseph & Elizabeth __?_; b 1697; Braintree
HAYDEN, Josiah (1669-), Braintree & Elizabeth GOODENOW (1672-); 6 Mar 1691; Sudbury
HAYDEN, Nathaniel (1644-1706) & Sarah (FRENCH) PARMELEE (-1717), Guilford, w Nathaniel; 17 Jan 1667/8, 1677; Killingworth, CT
HOIDEN, Nehemiah (1648-1718) & Hannah NEALE (1663-1720); Mar 1678; Braintree
HAYDEN, Samuel (-1676) & Hannah THAYER, m/2 Jonathan PADDLEFORD 1679?; 28 Oct 1664; Braintree
HAYDEN, William (-1669, Killingworth, CT) & 1/wf __?_ (-1655) (sister of Sarah, wf of Francis STILES); b 1640; Dorchester/Hartford/Windsor, CT/etc.
HAYDEN, William (-1669) & 2/wf Margaret [WILCOXSON] (-1668+, 1676), w William; aft 1655; Windsor, CT

HAYDEN, William & _?_ [TOMPKINS], w John; b 1661; Fairfield, CT/Eastchester, NY
HAYDEN, William & Hannah _?_/[?THOMPSON]; b 1666; Braintree
HEYDEN, William & Patience _?_; b 1685; Boston
HEYDEN, William & Experience _?_; b 1688(9?); Boston
HAIES, Christopher & Sarah KING; 2 Dec 1669; Charlestown
HAYES, Edward (-1676?, 1675) & Philadelphia [JENKINS] (1645-), m/2 Matthew ESTES 1676;
    ca 1665/70?; Kittery, ME
HAYES, George (?1655-1725) & 1/wf Sarah _?_ (-1683); ca 1680, 1681; Windsor, CT
HAYES, George (?1655-1725) & 2/wf Abigail DIBBLE (166(-)1-); 29 Aug 1685; Windsor,
    CT/Simsbury
HAYES, John (-1708) & Mary HORNE; 28 Jun 1686; Dover, NH
HAYES, Luke & 1/wf Elizabeth [LANGTON] (-1703); by Dec 1692; Hartford
HAYES, Nathaniel (-bef 12 Mar 1706/7) & Mary [KIMBERLY]; ca 1658/64?; Norwalk, CT
HAYES, Nathaniel (-1748) & Sarah _?_; b 1701?
HAYES, Samuel (?1641-1712), Norwalk & 1/wf [?Ruth] MORE, Farmington; b 1673, b 1666;
    Norwalk, CT
HAYES, Samuel (?1641-1712) & 2/wf Elizabeth (KEELER) [PICKETT?] (-1729?) (see below); b
    1701?; Norwalk, CT
HAYES, Samuel & 1/wf Elizabeth [PICKETT?] (1680-), dau James; b 1701?; Danbury, CT
HAYES/THAYER, Thomas & Elizabeth PECK (1651-); 29 Dec 1677; Milford, CT/Newark, NJ
HAYES/HAY?, Thomas & Bridget _?_; b 1687; Boston
HYES, _?_ & Mary BARNES
HAFFIELD/HAYFIELD, Richard (1581-1639) & 1/wf Judith _?_; in Eng, b 1618; Ipswich
HAFFIELD, Richard (1581-1639) & 2/wf Martha _?_ (1593-1667); in Eng, b 1627, b 1629;
    Ipswich
HERFORD/HEIFORD, John & Abigail ALLBINS/ATKINS, m/2 Thomas WASHBURN 1711; 8 Apr
    1678, 8 Apr 1679; Braintree
HAFFATT, William (1620-) & _?_; Essex Co./Old Norfolk Co.
HAYMAN, John (1611-1686) & Grace _?_ (-1683, ae 70); b 1650, ca 1640?; Charlestown
HAYMAN, Nathan/?Nathaniel (-1689) & Elizabeth ALLEN, m/2 Nathan/Nathaniel? BLAGROVE
    1690; 11 Mar 1673/4; Charlestown/Bristol, RI
HAYMAN, Nathaniel/Nathan? & Priscilla [WALDRON] (1661-), m/2 John SPARHAWK; b 18 Dec
    1699; Bristol, RI
HAYMAN, Samuel (-1712) & 1/wf Hannah TRUMBALL (-1684, ae 39); 18 Aug 1670; Charlestown
HAYMAN, Samuel (-1712) & 2/wf Mary (ANDERSON) (LYNDE) SHEPHERD (-1717), w Thomas,
    w Thomas; 16 Jun 1686; Charlestown
HAINES, Abraham & Abigail _?_; b 1685; Braintree
HAYNES, Benjamin (1643-1687) & 1/wf Hannah CLARK; b 1698, b 1690?, b 1665; Southampton,
    LI
HAYNES, Benjamin (1643-1687) & 2/wf Johannah JENNINGS
HAYNES, Benjamin (-1714) & Lydia _?_; Southampton, LI
HAYNES, Charles (-1685) & Mary _?_; b 1664(5?); New London, CT
HAYNES, Charles (?1669-) & Frances _?_; b 1699; Bristol, RI
HAYNES, David (1670, 1671?-1755) & Tabitha [STONE] (1673-); ca 1700; Sudbury
HAYNES, Edmund (-1646) & [Hannah] _?_, m/2 George LANGTON 1648; b 1642?, b 1646;
    Springfield
HAYNES, Francis (-1717) & Elizabeth HOOPER; 25 Dec 1695; Marblehead
HINDS?/HAINES, James (-1653, 1655) & [Mary] _?_, ?dau of Mrs. Anne KNIGHT?, m/2 Ralph
    DAYTON 1656, m/3 Fulk DAVIS by 1660; b 1639; Salem/Southold, LI
HAYNES, James & Margaret (STALLION) [FOOT], w Pasco; ca 1688; New London, CT
HAYNES, James (1660-1732) & Sarah NOYES (1669-); 21 Nov 1689/90, 21 Dec 1689; Sudbury
HAYNES, John & 1/wf [?Mary THORNTON]; in Eng, b 1625?; Cambridge
HAYNES, John (?1594-1654) & 2/wf Mabel HARLAKENDEN (1614-1655), ?m/2 Samuel EATON
    1654; ca 1636; Cambridge/Hartford
HAINE, John (1621-1697) & Dorothy NOYES (1626-1715); 13 Oct 1642; Sudbury
HAYNES, John (1649-1710) & Ruth ROPER (1655-); 19 Jun 1683; Sudbury
HAYNES, John (1669-1713) & Mary GLOVER (1672-); 7 Nov 1693, 31 Oct 1693?;
    Hartford/Springfield
HAYNE, Jonathan & 1/wf Mary MOULTON (-1674)

HAYNES, Jonathan (bpt 1648, ?1646-1698) & Sarah MOULTON (1656-); 30 Dec 1674, 1 Jan 1674/[5]; Hampton, NH/Newbury (wrong)

HAYNES, Jonathan (1674-) & Sarah [ROGERS] (1682-); b 1699; ?New London

HAYNES, Joseph (-1679, ae 38) & Sarah [LORD] (?1638-1705); b 1669; Hartford

HAINE, Josiah (1623-) & Elizabeth (NOYES) FREEMAN, w John; 13 Nov 16[49], 13 Nov 1646; Sudbury

HAYNES, Josiah (1655?-) & Elizabeth (STARK) LAMBERT, w Micah/Michael; 3 Mar 1693; Groton, CT/Preston, CT

HAINES/HAMES?, Mark (-1665) (see HAMOR) & Mary [SHATTUCK?]; b 1647; Boston

HAINES, Matthias (?1650-1689) & Jane BRACKETT, wid, m/2 Isaac MARSTON 1697; 28 Dec 1671; [?Portsmouth], NH

HAYNES, Peter (1654-) & Elizabeth RICE (1656-1727); 2 Jan 1677; Sudbury

HAYNES, Richard (-1681) & Mary (?FRENCH) [PEASE], w Robert; aft 1694; Beverly

HAINES, Robert (1611?-) & _?_ ; ca 1640

HAINES, Robert & [Rachel DAVIS], m/2 Jonathan WEDGEWOOD 1700; b 1685/90; Falmouth, ME

HAINES, Samuel (1611-1686) & Ellenor NEATE (-1682+); in Eng, 1 Apr 1638; Portsmouth, NH

HAINES, Samuel (1646-1688±) & Mary FIFIELD (-1723/5); 9 Jan 1672, 9 Jan 1673, 1672/3?; ?Portsmouth, NH

HAINES, Samuel (1674-) & [Alice] [WHIDDEN], m/2 William JENKINS; b 1700?, by 1701; Greenland, NH

HAYNES, Thomas & Martha BARNARD (1645-), m/2 Samuel BUCKNAM b 1687; 26 Dec 1667; Salisbury

HAINES, Thomas & Sarah RAY/REA; 15 Dec 1676; Salem/Salem, NJ

HAYNES, Thomas & Joyce _?_ ; b 1678; Salisbury

HAINES, Thomas (1670-) & Lydia [YOUNG], m/2 Samuel BRAGDON; b 1698; Amesbury

HAYNE, Thomas & Rebecca GREEN; 9 Jan 1699, 9 Jan 1700; Boston

HAINES, Walter & 1/wf Susan _?_

HAINES, Walter (?1583-1664) & Elizabeth _?_ (-1659); in Eng, b 1621; Sudbury

HAINES, William & Sarah [INGERSOLL], m/2 Joseph HOLTON 1651; ca 1644; Salem

HAYNES, William (1648?-1712) & 1/wf Elizabeth [HUSSEY?]; ?ca 1670/2?; Norwalk, CT

HAYNES, William (-1702) & Margery [WHITE], w Nicholas; b 1674, betw 25 Nov 1667 & 20 Aug 1672; Falmouth, ME/etc.

HAYNES/HINDS?, William² & Abigail [WARD]; b 1684; Charlestown

HAYNES, William & 2/wf Mercy [MATTHEWS] (1660-1711); ca 1698; Norwalk, CT

HAINES, _?_ & Rachel _?_ (-9 Nov 1749, ae 88 y); b 1685; Hampton, NH

HAINES, _?_ & Sarah RISLEY

HEITER/HAYTER?, _?_ & Hannah _?_ ; b 1688; Marblehead

HAYWARD/HOWARD?, Anthony (?1639-1689) & Margaret [POWELL], dau Michael; b 1674; Boston

HAYWARD, Benjamin & Sarah [ALDRICH?]; b 1701; Bridgewater

HOWARD, Benjamin (1675-) & Mary [AMOS] (1671-), dau Hugh; b 1697; Windham/Norwich, CT/Preston, CT

HOWARD, Daniel (-1675) & Deborah PITTS (1651-), m/2 Matthew WHETON/WHEATON; 13 May 1672; Hingham

HOWARD, Edward & Hannah/Esther HAWKINS, dau Thomas; 7 Jun 1661; Boston

HOWARD, Edward & Abigail (WARD) DIMOND (?1667-), w Moses; m cont 2 Jun 1685; Fairfield, CT/?Roxbury, MA

HOWARD, Edward & Martha ROW; 22 Aug 1689; Dover, NH/Lynn

HOWARD, Ephraim (1657-1690) & Abigail NEWBURY; 8 Jan 1684/5; Windsor, CT

HOWARD, Ephraim (-1704?, Dorchester), Bridgewater & Mary [KEITH]; b 1689, m bond 24 Oct 1688; Bridgewater

HAYWARD, George (-1671) & Mary _?_ (-1693); b 1640; Concord

HAYWARD, George (?1673, 1654-) & Hannah CHADWICK; 17 Jan 1695/6; Concord

HOWARD/HAYWARD, Henry (-1769) (kinsman of John BARNARD of Cambridge) & Sarah STONE (-living in 1716); 28 Sep 1648; Hartford

HAYWARD, James (1613-1642) & Judith [PHIPPEN], m/2 William SIMONDS; aft 22 Mar 1635; Woburn

HOWARD, James & Elizabeth _?_ ; b 1677(8?); Boston

HOWARD, James & Abigail __?__ ; b 1680; Boston
HOWARD, James (-1690) & Elizabeth [WASHBURN], m/2 Edward SEALEY/SEELEY 1692?; ca 1685; Bridgewater
HOWARD, James & __?__ [?SHORTRIDGE]/[?PITMAN]; b 1697; Portsmouth, NH
HOWARD, Jeremiah & Mehitable __?__, m/2 Peter WELCOME; b 1677; Boston
HAYWARD, John (-1672, ae 79) & 1/wf __?__ ?[PHILLIPS]/[?SARGENT]; ca 1630/5?, no issue; Watertown/Dedham
HEWARD, John & __?__ ; b 1648, b 1647; Plymouth
HOWARD, John (-1701) & Martha [HAYWARD]; b 1656; Bridgewater
HAWARD/HEYWOOD, John² (-1672) & 1/wf Rebecca ATKINSON (-1665); 17 Aug 1656; Concord
HAYWARD, John (-1672) & 2/wf Mary (ALDRICH) [JUDSON] (-1684), w Henry, w Samuel; aft 1657; Charlestown
HAYWARD, John (ca 1642-1710) & Sarah [MITCHELL] (ca 1645-); b 1662; Bridgewater
HEYWOOD, John² (1640-1701) & 2/wf Sarah SIMONDS (-1692); 30 Nov 1665; Concord
HOWARD, John & Sarah [?CHEEVER]; b 1667; Boston
HEAWARD/HAYWARD, John (1640-1700, 1701) & Anna WHITE (1649-1714, ae 64); 2 Jun 1671; Concord
HAYWARD, John & Mary __?__ ; b 1672; Boston
HAYWARD, John (1650-1695) & 1/wf Silence [TORREY]; b 1677; Boston
HOWARD, John & 1/wf Susannah ?LATHAM
HOWARD, John & 2/wf Sarah __?__ ; 1678; Bridgewater
HOWARD/HAYWARD, John (1650-1695) & 2/wf Experience PIERPONT; 12 Nov 1678; Roxbury/Boston
HOWARD, John, Jr. & Dorothy __?__ ; b 19 Dec 1684; Dartmouth
HAYWARD, John (-1687) & 2/wf Elizabeth (COOMBS) (WARREN) [SENDALL], w John, w Samuel, m/4 Phineas WILSON; aft 1684; Boston
HEYWOOD/HAYWARD, John (1662-1718), Concord & Sarah BLODGETT (1668-1692), Woburn; 7 Jan 1686/7; Woburn/Concord
HOWARD/HAYWARD, John (1661-1721) & 1/wf Mary __?__ (-1698); 1 Jun 1687; Wethersfield, CT
HAWOOD, John & Elizabeth DIXCY; 28 Oct 1695; Marblehead
HAYWARD, John (1667-1705) & Susanna [EDSON] (1679-), m/2 Elihu BRETT 1706?; b 1699; Bridgewater
HAYWARD, Jonathan (?1640-1690, ae 49) & Sarah THAYER; 6 May 1663; Braintree
HAWARD, Jonathan & 1/wf Susanna KEITH; 8 Jan 1688/9; Taunton
HAYWARD, Jonathan (ca 1667-1702) & Elizabeth LEE, m/2 John WILSON; 24 May 1690, 14 May 1690, 24 May; Charlestown/Malden
HOWARD/HAWARD, Jonathan (1660-) & Sarah DEAN (1668-); 8 Oct 1691; Taunton
HAYWARD, Jonathan & 1/wf Hannah HOBARTE; 17 Feb 1691/2; Braintree
HAYWARD, Jonathan (1672-) & 1/wf Trial [ROCKWOOD] (1678-1701/4); b 1694; Swansea/Mendon
HOWARD/HAYWARD, Jonathan & Mary FLINT; 29 Dec 1698; Salem
HOWARD, Joseph & Rebecca LIPPITT (-1675), m/2 Francis BUDLONG 1669; 2 Feb 1664, 1664/5?; Warwick, RI
HEAWARD/HAYWARD, Joseph (1643-1714) & 1/wf Hannah HOSMER (1644-1675); 26 Oct 1665; Concord
HAYWARD, Joseph & 1/wf Alice [BRETT]; b 1673; Bridgewater
HAYWARD, Joseph & 2/wf __?__ ; aft 15 Dec 1673; Bridgewater
HEAWARD, Joseph (1643-1714) & Elizabeth (TREADWAY) HAPGOOD, w Shadrack; 23 Mar 1676/7; Concord
HAYWARD, Joseph (-1718) & 3/wf Hannah [MITCHELL] (-1702+); b 1683; Bridgewater
HAYWARD, Joseph (1669-) & Mehitable DUNHAM; 30 May 1700; Bridgewater
HOWARD/HAYWARD?, Nathan & Abigail PEASE (1682-); 8 Jan 1699/1700; Enfield, CT
HAYWARD, Nathaniel (ca 1640-) & Hannah [WILLIS], dau John; b 1664; Bridgewater
HAWARD/HAYWARD, Nathaniel (1642-1720) & Elizabeth [CORNING] (1643-1719+); b 1666; Salem/Beverly
HOWARD, Nathaniel & 1/wf Sarah WILLARD (1642-1678); 2 Jul 1666; Charlestown/Chelmsford
HOWARD, Nathaniel (1643-1709/10) & 2/wf Sarah PARKER (1654-1739); 1 Jul 1678; Charlestown/Chelmsford

HAYWARD, Nathaniel (1664-) & Elizabeth [CROSMAN] (FOBES no) (1665-); b 1688(9?); Bridgewater
HOWARD/HAYWARD, Nathaniel (1669-) & Hannah RAIEMENT/RAYMOND (1673-), m/2 _?_ HUTCHINSON; 17 Apr 1689; Beverly
HOWARD, Nathaniel (1671-1720) & Elizabeth BUNKER; m int 29 Feb 1695/6; Boston
HAWARD, Nathaniel & Deborah _?_; b 1699; Beverly
HOWARD, Nehemiah (-1665) & Ann DIXY (1638-), m/2 Thomas JUDKINS 1665; 11 Aug 1657; Salem/Ipswich
HOWARD, Nehemiah (1670-) & Ruth CLARKE; 12 Jan 1692/3; Marblehead/Beverly
HAYWARD, Nicholas (-1683) & _?_; b 1642; Salem
HOWARD, Nicholas & Elizabeth _?_; b 1665; Boston
HOWARD/HAYWARD?, Nicholas (-1748) & Jemima RAE (1680-); 3 Sep 1700; Salem
AWARDS, Richard & _?_; b 1615?, b 1629; Salem
HOWARD, Robert (-1683) & Mary _?_ (-1683); b 1640; Dorchester/Boston
HOWARD, Robert (1613-1684) & Lydia [KILBOURNE] (1616-), m/2 Samuel HAYES?; ca 1642?; Dorchester/Windsor, CT
HEYWOOD, Robert & Elizabeth [LEWIS] (1623-1682); ca 1642-44?; Saco, ME/Barbados
HOWARD, Robert & Elizabeth _?_; b 1681; Boston
HAIEWARD, Samuel & [Isabel?] FELCH; 2 Mar 1641; Gloucester/Boston
HAYWARD, Samuel (1613-1681) & 1/wf Sarah/?Martha [STOWERS] (-1662); b 1646; Charlestown/Malden
HAYWARD, Samuel (?1613-1681) & 2/wf Elizabeth (_?_) (OAKES) [SWEETSER] (-1686), w Thomas, w Seth; aft 1 May 1662; Charlestown
HOWARD, Samuel[2] (ca 1643-1713) & Mehitable TOMSON; 28 Nov 1666; Medfield/Mendon
HAWARD, Samuel (1646-1697) & Susanna WILKINSON (-1720); 10 Mar 1670/1, 10 Mar 1670; Charlestown/Malden
HAYWARD, Samuel & Sarah _?_; b 1677; Braintree
HAYWARD, Samuel (-1716) & Susanna BUNCE (-living in 1716); 18 Feb 1696/7; Hartford
HAYWARD, Samuel & Mary HARDIE/HARDY; 15 Jun 1699; Beverly
HOWARD/HAYWARD, Samuel & Elizabeth BARBOR; 27 Dec 1699; Dorchester/Bridgewater
HOWARD, Samuel (1671-) & Sibyl LEWIS (1674-); 1700; Malden
HAYWARD, Simon/Simeon/Thomas (1649-), Concord & Elizabeth DANFORTH, Billerica; 7 Mar 1686/7; Billerica
HAYWARD, Thomas (-1681) & Susanna [TOWNE/TOWN] (aunt of Peter TOWNE?); by 1632?, b 1627?, ch in 1634; Duxbury/Bridgewater
HOWARD, Thomas (-1686) & _?_; b 1635, b 1632?; Ipswich
HAYWARD, Thomas & Sarah [AMES]; ca 1660?, no issue; Bridgewater
HOWARD, Thomas (-1676) & Mary WOOLMAN/WELLMAN?, m/2 William MOORE 1677; - Jan 1666, 1666/7; Norwich, CT
HOWARD, Thomas & Ruth JONES (1645-); 15 Nov 1667 (1677 is wrong); Lynn/Enfield, CT/Salem
HAYWARD, Thomas & Mary HINSDALE; 29 Jun 1699; Deerfield
HAYWARD, William[1] (ca 1604-1659) & Margery [?THAYER]/[?BARRON] (-1676); ca 1633, ca 1657?; Weymouth/Braintree
HOWARD, William (1609-1674) & Alice _?_; by 1638?; Portsmouth, NH/Boston
HOWARD, William & Rose _?_; b 1640, 1640; Salem
HOWARD/HAYWARD, William & Tabitha [KINSMAN]?; b 1667; Ipswich
HAYWARD, William & Anna STRATON/STRATTON; 14 Apr 1671; Concord
HOWARD/HAYWARD, William (?1650-1717) & 1/wf Sarah [BUTTERWORTH] (1653-1702/4); b 1672; Swansea/Mendon
HAYWARD, William (1669-) & Esther/Hester [HARBOR] (1663-); 1691; Mendon
HAYWARD, William & Hannah NEWCOMB, ?m/2 William THAYER 1699; 22 Nov 1693; Briantree
HAYWARD, William & Martha HODGKINS; 7 Jan 1695; Ipswich
HOWARD, William & Elizabeth GUARD; 28 Jul 1699; E. Greenwich, RI
HAYWARD, _?_ & Hannah CHADWICK
HOWARD, _?_ & Mary [HARRIS?], m/2 Thomas GOULD bef 1654; Charlestown
HOWARD, _?_ & Sarah FROST (1678-), dau James; b 1701?; Cambridge/Billerica
HAZARD, George (-1743) & Penelope ARNOLD/?WILBUR (1669-); b 1690(1?); N. Kingston, RI
HAZARD, Jeremiah/John (1675-1768) & Sarah [SMITH] (1678-1765); b 1699; N. Kingston, RI

HAZARD, Jonathan (-1711) (ae 72 in 1710) & Hannah [LAURENSON/LAURONSON], dau James (wf Sarah in 1707); b 1682; Newtown, LI
HAZARD, Robert (?1635-1700+) & Mary [BROWNELL] (1639-1739); b 1660, b 1658?; Portsmouth, RI/Kingston, RI
HAZARD, Robert (-1718) & Amy [CHAMPLIN] (-1718+); b 1698; N. Kingston, RI/Kings Town
HAZARD, Stephen (-1727) & Elizabeth HELME (-1727(-)); b 1695; N. Kingston, RI/S. Kings Town
HAZARD, Thomas (1610-1680+) & 1/wf Martha __?__ (-1669+); b 1635; Boston/Portsmouth, RI/Newtown, LI
HAZARD, Thomas (1610-1680) & Martha [SHERIFF/SHREVE] (-1691), w Thomas; aft 29 May 1675; Portsmouth, RI
HAZARD, Thomas (1659, ?1660-1741) & Susanna [NICHOLS] (1662-); b 1683; N. Kingston, RI
HASELTINE, Abraham² (1648-1711) & 1/wf Elizabeth LANGHORNE/LONGHORNE (1649-1704); 7 Oct 1669; Rowley
HAZLETON, Charles¹ & 1/wf __?__ ; b 1658; Kingston, RI
HAZELTON, Charles² (-1712) & 1/wf Catherine WESTCOTT (1664-1692±); 25 Mar 1688; E. Greenwich, RI
HAZELTON, Charles¹ & 2/wf Hannah (PARSONS?/BAILEY) MATTESON, w Henry; 9 Aug 1693; East Greenwich, RI
HAZLETON, Charles² (-1712) & 2/wf Elizabeth [WHALEY] (-1752); b 1694(5?); East, Greenwich, RI
HASELTINE, David² (ca 1644-1717) & Mary JEWETT (1647-1728?); 26 Nov 1668; Bradford
HASLETON, Gershom² (1661-1711) & Abiah DALTON (1670-1746), m/2 Andrew MITCHELL; 23 Jun 1690; Bradford
HAZELTON, James, Kingston & Catherine RATHBOURN? WESTCOTT, w Robert; 10 Apr 1678, 10 Aug; Warwick, RI
HASELTINE, John (-1690, ae 70?) & Hannah?/Joan/Jane [ANTER?/AUTER] (-1698) (servant of Mr. HOLMAN, Bideford, Eng); b 8 Mar 1646, b 1646; Rowley/Newbury/Salisbury
HASELTINE, John (-1733) & Mary NELSON; 17 Jul 1682; Haverhill
HASELTINE, Nathaniel (1656-) & 1/wf Deliverance ROBEE/ROBEY (1657-1686), Hampton; 28 Dec 1680; Haverhill
HASSELTONE, Nathaniel (1656-) & 2/wf Ruth (PLUMER) JAQUISH/JAQUES, w Richard; 18 Jul 1688, 20 Jul 1688; Andover/Haverhill
HASELTON, Robert¹ (-1674), Lincolnshire/?Bideford, Eng/Devonshire & Ann/Anna? __?__ (-1684); 23 Dec 1639; Rowley/Bradford
HASELTINE, Robert² (1657-1729) & 1/wf Elizabeth JEWETT (1650-1708); 21 Jul 1680; Bradford
HASELTINE, Samuel (1645-1717) & Deborah COOPER (1650-); 28 Dec 1670; Haverhill/Hampton, NH
HAZEN, Edward (1614-1683) & 1/wf Elizabeth __?__ (-1649); by 1649; Rowley
HAZEN, Edward (1614-1683) & 2/wf Hannah GRANT (1631-1715/16), m/2 George BROWNE 1684; Mar 1650; Rowley
HAZEN, Edward (1660-1748) & Jane PICKARD (1666-1745+); 6 Nov 1684; Rowley
HAZEN, Richard (1669-1733) & 1/wf Mary PEABODY (1672-1731); 5 Dec 1694; Haverhill
HAZEN, Thomas (1658-1735) & Mary HOWLET/HOWLETT (ca 1664-1727); 1 Jan 1683, 1683/4?, 1682/3?; Rowley/Boxford/Weymouth, CT
HASELWOOD/HAZLEWOOD, Francis & Sarah __?__ ; b 1672; Boston
HEAD, Arthur & 1/wf Ann __?__ ; b 1683?; Great Island
HEAD, Arthur & 2/wf Sarah __?__ ; by 1694
HEAD, Henry (1647-1716) & Elizabeth __?__ (1654-1748); b 1677; Little Compton, RI
HEAD, John & Judith CAMPENALL; m int 9 Sep 1695; Boston
HEADLY, Dennis (-1742) & Joanna BULLARD; 22 Mar 1680; Watertown/Sudbury
HEDLEY, John & Mary __?__ (-1694, ae 51); b 1674; Newport
HEDLEY, John (1677-1729) & 1/wf Mary SLOCUM (-1705); 24 Aug 1699; Newport
HEADLEY, Richard (1642-) & Hannah [DRAKE]; Eastchester, NY
HEADLEY, Richard & Mary __?__ ; b 20 Jan 1691/2; Eastchester, NY
HELD, Gershom (1647-1721+) & Ann VINTON (1656-1698); 6 May 1673; Concord/Springfield
HEALD, Gershom² (1647-) & Hannah PARLING/PARLIN; 19 Feb 1689/90; Concord
HEALES, Isaac (ca 1656-1717) & Elizabeth __?__ (-1717+); b 1682; Stow
HEALD, Israel (1660-1738) & Martha [WRIGHT] (1659-1746); b 1686; Stow

HEALD, John[1] (-1662) & Dorothy ROYLE (-1694?); 3 Dec 1636, in Eng; Concord
HELD, John[2] (1637-1689) & Sarah DANE (-1689); 10 Jun 1661; Concord
HEALD, John & Mary CHANDLER (1672-); 18 Dec 1690; Concord
HEALY, Nathaniel (1659-1734) & Rebecca HAGAR (-1733); 14 Jul 1681; Watertown/Newton
HEALEY/HOLLEY, Paul (1664-1718) & Elizabeth _?_ ; b 1696; Rehoboth
HELE, Samuel (1662-) & 1/wf Hannah SMITH; 26 May 1685; Salisbury
HEALEY, Samuel (1667-) & 2/wf Judith ROBY (-1725); 15 Sep 1693; Salisbury
HEALY, William[1] (-1683) & 1/wf _?_ ?ROGERS (no) (-1649); b 1644; Lynn/Roxbury/Cambridge
HEALY, William[1] (-1683) & 2/wf _?_ ?ROGERS (no) (-1653); Roxbury
HEALE, William[1] (-1683) & 3/wf Grace BUTTERICE/BUTTRICE; 14 Oct 1653; Cambridge
HEALEY, William[1] (-1683) & 4/wf Phebe GREENE; 15 Aug 1661; Cambridge/Newton
HEALEY, William[1] (-1683) & 5/wf Sarah (CUTTING) [BROWN], w James, m/3 Hugh MARCH
    1685; 29 Nov 1677; Cambridge/Newton
HEALEY, William[2] & ?Sarah/?Mary BROWN; bef 29 Jan 1674/5; Charlestown
HELE, William[2] (1652-) & Mary _?_ /[BROWN?]; b 1689/90; Salisbury
HEARD, Benjamin (1644-1703?) & 1/wf Elizabeth [ROBERTS]; b 1673; Dover, NH
HEARD, Benjamin (-1710) & 2/wf Ruth EASTMAN (1662-), m/2 John TAPPAN 1717; 23 May
    1690; Salisbury
HEARD, Edmond/Edward & Elizabeth WARNER (ca 1648-1724); 26 Sep 1672; Ipswich
HEARD, James (-bef 1676) & Shuah [STARBUCK], m/2 Richard OTIS 1676?; b 1658; Kittery,
    ME
HEARD, James & Elizabeth _?_ ; b 1695; Derby, CT
HEARD, John (-1677) & Isabel _?_ (-1677+); b 1630?; Great Island/Sturgeon Creek
HEARD, John (-1688) & Elizabeth [HULL] (1627/8?-1706); b 1644; Dover, NH
HERD, John & Mary [CURTIS] (1659-), m/2 Jonathan LOOK 1678; div - Jul 1678
HEARD, John (1659-1752) & 1/wf Phebe LITTLEFIELD (-1697, 1696?); 27 Apr 1690; Salisbury
HEARD, John (-1752) & Jane (COLE) LITTLEFIELD, w Joseph; 2 Jul 1698; Kittery, ME
HEARD, Luke (-1647) & Sarah [WYATT], Assington, Eng, m/2 Joseph BIXBY 1647; b 1644, b
    1643?, 2 ch in 1647; Ipswich/Salisbury
HEARD, Nathaniel (1668-1700) & Sarah [FERNSIDE], m/2 William POST 1703; ca 1688/94;
    Salisbury
HEARD, Samuel (1663-) & Experience OTIS (?1666-), m/2 Rowland/Joseph? JENKINS 1699; ca
    20 Mar 1685/6; Salisbury
HEARD, Tristram (1667-1734, 1735) & Abigail _?_ (-1734+); nr 1692; Salisbury
HEARL/HEARLS, William (1614-1691) & 3/wf Patience [ETHERINGTON] (-1697); aft 29 Feb
    1675/6, b 1688, b 1689; Kittery, ME/Berwick, ME
HEARL, William (1614-1691) & 2/wf Beaton [HUNKING], w Hercules; aft 8 Nov 1659, by 1679,
    by 1677; Portsmouth, NH
HEARNES/HEARN?, Nathaniel & Mary _?_ ; b 1666; Dedham
HEARNDEN, Benjamin (-1687) & Elizabeth [WHITE], m/2 Richard PRAY 1688±; b 9 Jul 1647;
    Lynn/Providence
HEARNDEN, Benjamin (-1694) & Lydia _?_ (-1710); ca 1675/79?; Providence
HEARNDEN, Isaac (1668-1727) & Sarah _?_ (-1728+); b 10 Feb 1689; Providence/Norwich, CT
HEARNDEN, John & [?Esther] _?_ ; b 1701; Providence/Scituate, RI
HEARNDEN, Joseph (?1652-1694) & Sarah _?_ ; b 1675; Providence
HEARNDEN, William (1660-1727) & 1/wf Esther _?_ ; b 1687; Providence
HEARNDEN, _?_ & 2/wf Deliverance _?_ ; b 1701?
HURST, Edward & ?Margaret _?_ ; b 1642?; Charlestown
HURST/HIRST, Grove (1675-1717) & Elizabeth SEWAL (1681-1716); 17 Oct 1700; Boston
HURST, James (-1657) & ?Catharine _?_ (-1670) (wf Gertrude in 1657); by 1616?; Plymouth
HURST, John & Alice _?_ ; b 1688; Boston
HURST, Thomas (-1702), Hadley/Deerfield & Mary [JEFFREYS]; b 1685; Deerfield
HURST, William (-1641), Sandwich & Katherine THICKSTON/THURSTON? (-1670?); 17 Mar
    1639; ?Sandwich/?Plymouth
HERST, William (-1717) & Mary GROVE (-1717); 30 Jul 1674; Salem
HEATH, Bartholomew (?1616-1681) & Hannah [MOYCE] (?1616-1677); b 1643; Newbury
HEATH, Bartholomew & Mary BROADLY/BRADLEY?; 23 Jan 1690/1; Haverhill
HEATH, Charles & Mary _?_ ; b 1683; Boston

HEATH, Elias (-1706, ae 55) & Elizabeth (PHILLIPS) (GROSS) ELDRIDGE, w Thomas, w Joseph, m/3 Francis BURROUGHS; 13 May 1699; Boston
HEATH, Isaac (1585-1661) & Elizabeth [MILLER] (1595-1665); in Eng, b 1630, ca 1628; Roxbury
HEATH, Isaac (-1694) (relative of Roger MOWRY's wf) & Mary DAVIS; 16 Dec 1650; Roxbury
HEATH, Isaac (-1684) & Ann/Anna? FISHER, m/2 Francis YOUNGMAN 1685; 2 Feb 1680, prob 1680/1; Roxbury
HEATH, John (-1712+) & Elizabeth _?_ (1627-1711); ca 1650/60?; E. Greenwich, RI
HEATH, John & Sarah PARTRIDGE (1647-1708, Hampton, NH); 14 Nov 1666; Haverhill
HEATH, John & Frances HUTCHINS; 12 Jan 1696/7; Haverhill
HEATH, John & Hannah HAINES; 16 Dec 1697; Haverhill/Norwich, CT
HEATH, Joseph (-1673?, 1672?) & Martha DOW, m/2 Joseph PAGE 1673, m/3 Samuel PARKER 1689; 27 Jun 1672; Haverhill
HEATH, Joseph (-1714) & Mary _?_ ; ca 1690; Charlestown/Boston
HEATH, Joseph & Hannah [BRADLEY] (1677-); b 1698; Haverhill
HEATH, Josiah & 1/wf Mary DAVIS; 19 Jul 1671; Amesbury/Haverhill
HEATH, Josiah (1674-1721) & Hannah STERLING/STARLING (1667-); 5 Apr 1694; Haverhill
HEATH, Peleg (1625-1671) (called "cousin" by Clement TOPLEFF) & Susanna [BARKER?] KING? (dau widow Dorothy HUNT KING, w Enoch, w John); b 1652; Roxbury
HEATH, Richard & Mercy _?_ ; b 1686; Swansea
HEATH, Thomas & Mary _?_ ; b 1676; Boston
HEATH, William (-1652) & 1/wf _?_ ; ca 1622?, 5 ch in 1632; Roxbury
HEATH, William (-1652) & 2/wf Mary (CRAMPHORNE) [SPEAR?] (1592-), wid?; ca 1632?, b 1625?, ca 1622?; Roxbury
HEATH, William & 1/wf Hannah WELD (-1697); 11 Nov 1685, ?11 Mar; Roxbury
HEATH, William & 2/wf Anna/Ann [RUGGLES]? (1672-1758); ca 1698/9; Roxbury
EATON/HEATON, Jabez & Experience MEDE/MEADE; 4 Dec 1663; Dorchester/Boston
HEATON, James (ca 1640-1712) & Sarah STREET; 20 Nov 1662; New Haven
HEATON/EATON, Nathaniel & Elizabeth? _?_ , m/2 Joseph PELL, m/3 John MAYNARD?, m/4 John MINOR; b 1636; Boston
HEATON/EATON, Nathaniel & Mary _?_ ; b 1687, b 1676?; Wrentham
HEATON, Nathaniel (1664-1725) & Mary [TODD] (1675-), m/2 Samuel FRARY 1734; b 1695; New Haven
HEATON, Nathaniel (-1733, ae 60) & Susanna SIMPSON (1675-); m int 15 Apr 1696/7 [sic], 1697; Boston/Charlestown
HEATON, _?_ & Elizabeth _?_ , m/2 Benjamin WILMOT ca 1644, m/3 William JUDSON 1660; b 1642; New Haven
HEDGE, Elisha (1642-1713, 1732?) & Mary [?STURGES] (1646-1713); b 1666; Yarmouth
HEDGE, Henry? (see HEDGER)
HEDGES, Isaac (1636±-1676) & Joanna [BARNES], dau Joshua; b 1664; Southampton, LI
HEDGES, Isaac, Jr. (?1664-1726) & _?_ (-1706); b 1685; Southampton, LI
HEDGES, John (1670-1737) & Ruth [STRATTON]; b 1699; East Hampton, LI
HEDGE, John (1673-) & Thankful LOTHROP; 25 Jan 1699/1700; Barnstable
HEDGE, Samuel (1675-1714) & Grace SNOW, m/2 George LEWIS 1716; 8 Dec 1698; Eastham
HEDGES, Samuel & Lois _?_ (1680-1718); b 1701?; East Hampton, LI
HEDGES, Stephen (1635-1734?) & _?_ [STRATTON]; b 1670; Southampton
HEDGES, Tristram & Ann NICKERSON; 20 Dec 1657; Boston
HEDGES, William (-1674) & Rose _?_ (-1674+); b 1635; Southampton, LI
HEDGE, William (-1670) (had sister BROOKS) & 1/wf _?_ ; ca 1638?; Lynn/Sandwich/Yarmouth
HEDGE, William (-1670) & 2/wf Blanche [HULL], w Tristram; aft 12 Mar 1666/7; Yarmouth
HEDGE, William, Jr. & Elizabeth [STURGES] (1648-); b 1682/3; Bristol, RI
HEDGER?/HEDGE?, Henry & _?_ ; b 1689; Pemaquid, ME
HEDGER, Joseph (-1713) & Hannah/?Susanna [GENUNG/GANONG] (1664-); Flushing, LI
HEDGER, Thomas¹ (called "Sr." in 1663) & _?_ ; b 1640, 1639?; Warwick, RI
HEDGER, Thomas² (-1707) & Elizabeth BURTON; 30 Oct 1674; Warwick, RI/Flushing, LI
HEDGER, _?_ & Elizabeth _?_ ; b 1692; Westchester, NY
HEDGER, Henry? & _?_ ; by 1677?
HEFFERLAND, John & Abigail [MOTT] (1666-1712+); Portsmouth, RI
HEFFERLAND, John & Mary BUCKAWAY?/BACKAWAY?; 2 Feb 1697; Portsmouth, RI

HELME, Christopher (-1650) & Margaret _?_ (-1650+); Exeter, NH/Warwick, RI
HELME, Rouse (-1712) & Mary [ELDRED/ELDREDGE] (1646-1712); b 1671?, b 1676?; Kings Town, RI
HELME, Samuel (-1728) & Dorcas _?_ ; b 1700; S. Kingston, RI
HELME, Thomas & Mary (MILLS) [NORTON], w Nathaniel; b 1688?, b 1691?, b 1701?; Brookhaven, LI
HELWISE, Edmund & Sarah [HATHORNE] (1634/5-), div 1664, m/2 Joseph COOKER 1665; b 1666; Salem
HEMENWAY, John & Mary TRESCOTT (1649-); 6 Oct 1665; Dorchester/Roxbury
HEMINGWAY, John (1675-1737) & Mary [MORRIS] (1673-1743); b 1700; New Haven/East Haven
HEMENWAY, Joshua^2 (1643-) & 1/wf Joanna EVANS; 16 Jan 1667; Roxbury
HEMENWAY, Joshua^2 (1643-) & 2/wf Mary _?_ (-1703); b 1681?
HEMINGWAY, Joshua (1668-) & 1/wf Margaret [KENRICK] (-1694); b 1691; Roxbury
HEMENWAY, Joshua (1668-) & 2/wf Rebecca _?_ ; b 1697; Framingham
HEMENWAY, Ralph^1 & Elizabeth HEWES; 5 Jul 1634; Roxbury
HEMENWAY, Ralph (1673-) & Sarah _?_, m/2 Joseph ELLIS; b 1699; Dedham
HEMENWAY, Samuel & Sarah COOPER; 23 Mar 1661/2; New Haven
HEMPSTEAD, Joshua (1649-1700) & Elizabeth [LARRABEE] (1656-), m/2 John EDGECOMB 1700?; b 1672, b 1670; New London, CT
HEMPSTEAD, Robert (-1655?) & 2/wf Joanna [WILLEY?] (-1655, 1660?), m/2 Andrew LESTER ?1655+; b 1647; New London, CT
HEMPSTEAD, Joshua & Abigail [BAILEY]; b 1698?, b 1699; New London
HEMPSTEAD, Robert (1664-1728) & Elizabeth [DYMOND]
HENBERY, Arthur (1646-1697) & 1/wf Lidia HILL; 5 May 1670; Simsbury/Hartford
HENBURY, Arthur (-1697) & 2/wf Martha BEAMAN/BEMENT, m John SHEPARD 1698; Feb 1687/8; Windsor, CT/Hartford
HENCHMAN, Daniel (-1685, Worcester) & 1/wf Sarah [WOODWARD]; b 1662?, b 1667, ca 1654?; Boston/Worchester
HENCHMAN, Daniel (-1685, Worchester) & 2/wf Mary POLE/POOLE; 26 Apr 1672; Dorchester
HENCHMAN, Edmund (-1668) & Elizabeth _?_ (-1667), m/2 Rev. John FISKE 1672; ca 1634?; Chelmsford/Marshfield
HENCHMAN, Hezekiah (-1694, ae 35?) & Abigail [RUCK]?, m/2 William THOMAS 1701; b 1688(9?); Boston
HINCKSMAN, John & Elizabeth EMMONS, m/2 Joseph GRIDLEY 1675; 10 Aug 1660; Boston
HINCKMAN, John & Sarah [HARRISON]; b 1675?; Flushing, LI/Gloucester Co., NJ
HENCHMAN, John & Mary _?_ ; b 1683; Charlestown
HENCHMAN, Joseph & Mary _?_ ; b 1685; Scituate
HENCHMAN, Nathaniel (ca 1661-) & Hannah/Anna/Ann (GREENWOOD) GREEN (-1706, ae 37 y), w James; 11 Jan 1693, 1693/4; Boston
HENCHMAN, Richard (-1725) (-1725, ae 70, Copp's Hill Cem) & Esther WEBSTER (-1731, ae 75), w Henry; 24 Dec 1697; Boston
HENCHMAN, Thomas (-1703) & Elizabeth [MERRIAM]? (-1704); Concord/Chelmsford
HINCHMAN, Thomas & _?_ ; b 1670; LI
HINCHMAN, Thomas & Miriam _?_ /?Sarah CLEMENT; b 1698, by 1695?; Flushing, LI
HINCKESMAN, William & Mary PHILBERD; 20 Jan 1652/3; Boston/Marshfield
HINKSMAN, _?_ & Sarah _?_ ; b 1698; Salem
HENDERSON, John & Ellen (BOOTH) BULLY, w Nicholas; 25 Sep 1664, ?29 Jun 1664, ?26 Sep, ?26 Dec, 24 Sep; Saco, ME
HANDERSON/HANNISON/etc., John & Martha [?STEELE] (-1712); b 1671; Hartford, CT
HENDERSON, John (1666-) & Abigail _?_ ; 6 May 1687; Salem
HENDERSON, John & _?_ ; b 1688; Woodbury, CT
HENDERSON, John & Aniball _?_ ; b 1694; Boston
HENDERSON, John & Susanna GRANT; m int 9 Feb 1700; Ipswich
HENDERSON, Peter & Abigail BULLY (1634-); 29 Dec 1670, 16--; Saco, ME
HENDERSON, Peter (1667-1722) & Hannah GLOVER (1670-); 2 Apr 1687; Salem
HENDERSON, Richard & Elizabeth _?_ ; b 1694; Boston
HENDERSON, William & [?Sarah] [HOWARD]; ca 1670?; Dover, NH
HENDERSON, William & Sarah FERNALD; 16 Jul 1700; Kittery, ME

HENDRICK, Daniel & 1/wf Dorothy [PIKE]; b 1645; Haverhill
HENDRICK, Daniel & 2/wf Mary (HATCH?) (SONE) STOCKBRIDGE, w Robert, w John; 8 Apr 1660; Boston
HENDREKES, Gerret & _?_ ; b 1675; Flushing, LI
HENDRICK, Henry (-1684) & Hannah _?_ , m/2 Daniel SILLIMAN; b 1672; Fairfield, CT
HENDRICK, Henry (-1741) & Elizabeth [BENNETT] (?1672-1755); b 1695; Fairfield, CT
HENDRICK, Israel & Sarah GUTTERSON (1665-1701+); 8 Nov 1688; Haverhill
HENDRICK, John (-1692) & Abigail [MORSE], m/2 Moses PINGRY 1692+; b 1678; Newbury
HENDRICKSON, Harmon (-1701) & Margaret [SODDER]; b 1678; Hempstead, LI
HENDRICKSON, Isaac & Rebecca [DUNHAM] (1671±)
HENDRICKSON, John & Sarah [DENHAM], w Thomas; b 15 May 1691; Westchester Co., NY
HENDRICKSON, Peter & Margaret _?_ ; b 1639; Boston
HENFIELD, Joseph & Mary [GARDNER] (1662-); b 1687; Salem
HENFIELD, William (-ca 1692/4) & Elizabeth PRESTON (-1698+); 12 Jul 1671; Salem
HENNING, Richard & _?_ ; b 1671; Newbury
HENLEY, Benjamin & Miriam (PEDERICK) WALDRON/WALERNE?, w Samuel, m/3 Abraham LASHERE; 12 Apr 1694; Marblehead
HENLY, Elias (-1699) & Sarah THOMPSON; 4 Nov 1657; Boston/Marblehead
HENLY, Elias (-1713) & Margaret GREENFIELD, m/2 John GIRDLER; 27 Jul 1686; Marblehead
HENLEY, George (John is wrong) & Hannah [BURTON]; b 1668; Boston
HENLEY, John (1671-) & _?_ ; b 1701?
HENLY, Joseph (-1699) & Sarah HANNIFORD (1671-); 9 Jun 1692; Marblehead
HENLEY, Terrence & Elizabeth WEEKS (1653-); 2 Apr 1694; Boston
HANDLEY, Capt. Thomas & Rebecca [YOUNG]; b 1680; Boston
HENLEY, Thomas & Sarah CURTIS, m/2 John WESCOAT/WESTCOTT?; 15 Jul 1687; Marblehead
HENRYSON/HENNYSON?, John (-1687) & Martha STEEL; b 1662(3?); Springfield/Hartford
HENSHAW, Daniel (1644-1732) & Mary/Ellen? (BALL/BULL) (POND) [ALLEN] (-1719, in 83rd y), w Robert, w Nicholas; b 1671; Milton
HENSHAW, Joshua (1642-1719) & Elizabeth [SUMNER] (1652-); b 1671; Dorchester
HOUSHA, Joshua (1672-) & Mary WEBSTER; 7 Nov 1700; Boston
HENSHAW, Thomas (-1700) & Hannah CLEVELAND, m/2 Thomas LEFFINGWELL 1706; 24 Sep 1677; Woburn
HEPBURNE, George (-1666) & Hannah _?_ ; b 1638; Charlestown
HEBBOURN, William & Sarah SOUTHWICK; 24 Jun 1693; Lynn
HEPPE, William & Margaret _?_ ; b 1699(1700?); Boston
HEPWORTH, William & Mary LOCK; 3 Jan 1697; Boston
HARBERT, Benjamin (see HARBOUR)
HARBARD, Henry (1607-1677) & 1/wf Eleanor [MILLER] (1602-1667), w Richard; ca 1662; Charlestown
HARBARD/HARBOUR, Henry (1607-1677) & 2/wf Elizabeth GEORGE (-1691, ae 70), w John; 9 Jun 1668; Charlestown
HERBERT, Jaques & Katharine WINSLOW; m int 16 Jul 1695; Boston
HERBERT, John & 1/wf Mary? _?_ ; b 1640; Salem/Southold, LI
HERBERT, John & Mary FOLLETT (1656-); 15 Apr 1672; Salem
HERBERT, John from Southold, LI, & 2/wf Elizabeth [HAUGH]; b 1678 (see HARBOR); Boston
HERBERT, John (-1712), Reading & Elizabeth (RUSSELL) GRAVES (-1714, ae 70), w Nathaniel; 15 Oct 1684; Charlestown
HERBERT, Sylvester & 1/wf _?_
HARBERT, Sylvester (-1683) & 2/wf? Lucy ADAMS; 21 Sep 1652; Boston/Kittery, ME
HERBERT, [Wm.?] & Hope (LAMBERTON) AMBROSE, w Samuel, m/3 William CHENEY by 1698 (called Hope HERBERT 1687); New Haven
HEROD, John & Susanna _?_ ; b 1687; Boston
HERRICK, Ephraim (1638-1693) & Mary CROSS (1640-1710+); 3 Jul 1661; 10 Jul 1661; Beverly/Salem
HERRICK, Ephraim (1664-) & Judah?/Judith? WOODBERRY (1667-); 2 Jan 1688/9; Beverly/Preston, CT
HERRICK, George (-1696, 1695?) & Martha [HOWETT?]; b 1687; Beverly
HERRICK, Henry (-1671) & Edith [LASKIN] (1612?-); b 1632, by 1629; Salem
HERRICK, Henry (1640-1720, 1702?) & 1/wf Lydia [WOODBURY?]; ca 1660/3; Beverly/Salem

HERRICK, Henry & 2/wf Sarah (ALCOCK) GIDDINGS, w John; 1690?, aft 3 Mar 1691, bef 29
Mar 1692, betw 1672 & 1690; Beverly/Ipswich/Salem
HERRICK, Henry (-1747) & Susanna BEADLE/BEEDEL?; 23 Jul 1694; Salem
HERRICK, Isaac & Sarah [RAND] (-1732); by 1681; Portsmouth, NH/Rye, NH
HERRICK, James (-1687) & Martha [TOPPING/TAPPAN?]; b 1654; Newtown, LI/Southampton,
LI
HERRICK, James (-1707) & Sarah [STANBROUGH] (-1626); Southampton
HERRICK, John & Sarah KIMBALL; 26 Dec 1646, m 1 Dec 1646; Wenham/Beverly
HERRICK, John (1650-1680) & Mary REDDINGTON, m/2 Robert CUE 1682; 25 May 1674, ?25
Mar, ?20 May; Beverly
HERRICK, John & Bethiah SALAIT/SOLART?; 21 Apr 1684; Beverly/Salem/Wenham
HERRICK, John & Anna WOODBURY (1674-); 29 Nov 1694; Beverly
HERRICK, Jonathan & Elizabeth DODGE (1673-1713); 28 Oct 1696; Beverly/Concord
HERRICK, Joseph (1645-1718) & 1/wf Sarah LEACH (1648-1674?); 7 Feb 1665; Beverly
HERRICK, Joseph & 2/wf Mary [ENDICOTT?]/REDINGTON?; ca 1675/9, b 1680, ca 1677-8;
Beverly/Salem
HERRICK, Joseph (-1726) & Mary DODGE (1666-1719); ca 1685; Beverly
HERRICK, Joseph & Elizabeth [WOODBURY] (1676-); b 1696; Wenham
HERRICK, Samuel & Sarah LEACH (1673-); 25 Mar 1690/91, 15 May 1690, ?25 May 1601;
Beverly/Salem
HERRICK, Samuel & Mehitable WOODWARD; m int 23 Oct 1698; Beverly/Preston, CT
HERRICK, Stephen (1670-) & Elizabeth TRASK; 3 Dec 1691, 1692?; Beverly
HERRICK, Thomas (m dissolved) & Hannah ORDWAY; b Nov 1673; Salem
HERRICK, William & _?_ ; b 1640?; Southampton
HERRICK, William (?1654-1708) & Mehitable _?_ (-1736); ca 1680/90?; Southampton
HERRICK, Zachary/Zachariah? (-1695) & Mary DODGE (?1632-1710); b 1650?, b 1653?, b 1654;
Beverly/Salem
HERRICK, _?_ & Phebe [?FORDHAM]; b 1688; Southampton
HERRIDGE, John & Christian _?_ ; b 1683; Boston
HERRING, James (1656-) & Sarah STEADMAN; 16 Apr 1685; Dedham
HEARING, Thomas (-1684) & Mary PEARCE/PIERCE; 15 Apr 1650; Dedham
HERING, Thomas (1670-) & Mehitable _?_ ; b 1695; Dedham
HERSEY, James (1643-1684) & Mary FEARING (1647-1705); 15 Dec 1665; Hingham
HERSEY, John (1640-1726) & Sarah [RICHARDS] (1650-1732), dau Edward; 18 May 1669, at
Dedham; Hingham
HERSEY, John (1659-1725) & Elizabeth _?_ ; b 1694; Hingham/Milton
HERSEY, William[1] (-1658) & Elizabeth _?_ (-1671); b 1631; Hingham
HERSEY, William[2] & 1/wf Rebecca CHUBBOCK (1641-1686); 1 Sep 1656; Hingham
HERSEY, William[3] (1657-) & 1/wf Mary _?_ (-1690); 12 Jun 1683; Hingham
HERSEY, William[2] & 2/wf Ruhamah (HALLETT) [BOURNE] (-1722), w Job; b 1689; Hingham
HERSEY, William[3] (1657-) & 2/wf Sarah (LANGLEE) MAY, w Jonathan; 2 Oct 1691;
Hingham/Abington
HETHRINGTON/HETHERINGTON, Andrew & Hannah BRIGGS; 11 Apr 1695; Boston
HETHERSEY/HETHERSAY, Robert & [?Mary SMITH]; b 1643; Lynn/Concord/Charlestown
HETT/HITT, Eliphalet (1639-) & Ann DOUGLAS (-1678, ae 38); 1 Sep 1660; Charlestown/Boston
HETT, Thomas (1613-1668) & Ann [NEEDHAM] (-1688, ae 75); b 1639; Charlestown/Boston
HETT, Thomas (1644-1692, ae 48) & Dorothy EDMUNDS, m/2 Joseph KETTELL 1694, 1693?; 8
Jan 1666/7, 8 Jan 1666; Charlestown
HEWES/HOWES, Solomon & Martha CALEF; m int 19 Jun 1700, m int 28 Sep 1700, m 28 Sep
1700; Newbury/Boston
HEWES, George & Mary ALLEN (1644-); b 1672; Salisbury
HEWES, John (-1700+) & Ruth SAWTELL (ca 1650-1721); 9 Mar 1676; Watertown (Scituate)
HEWES, Joshua (-1676) & 1/wf Mary GOLDSTON/GOLDSTONE; 8 Oct 1634; Roxbury
HEWES, Joshua & 2/wf Alice CRABTREE (1625-), w John; 11 Feb 1656/7; Boston
HEWES, Joshua & Hannah [NORDEN]; b 1667; Boston
HEWES, James & Elizabeth _?_ ; b 1668(9?); Boston/Gloucester
HEWES, John & Mary SMITH? (1661?-), b 1671?, b 1685(6?); Boston
HEWES/HUGHES, William & Elizabeth [MAVERICK/GRAFTON?] (1667-1734); b 1685, 21 Nov
1684?, 25 Nov 168-9?; Boston

HEWES, James & Bethiah SWETMAN/SWEETMAN (1661-); 12 Dec 1692; Cambridge
HEWES, Joshua & Elizabeth _?_; b 1697(8?), b 1695; Boston
HEWES, Samuel & Hannah JOHNSON (1678-); 11 Dec 1700; Boston
HEWES, Richard (call Richard HUGHES) & Anne _?_; b 1637; Dorchester/Guilford, CT
HEWES, George & Lydia (KIBBEY) BENNETT (1637-), w George; 3 Jul 1679; Lancaster/Concord
[HUSE, James]? & Hannah WOODIN?; 1 Jul 1696; Salisbury
HEWES, William & Parnell _?_; b 1624?; Lynn/Weymouth
HEWES, John & Mary _?_ (-1655, Boston); b 1641; Scituate/Plymouth
HEWES, John (-1674) & Jone/Joanna? _?_; 1633; Scituate
HEWES, Thomas (-1697) & Abigail _?_; b 1670?, b 1697; Plymouth
HEWES, Joshua & Mary GOLDSTONE (1620-); 8 Oct 1634; Roxbury
HEWES, William & Mary _?_; b 1700; Boston
HEWES, _?_ & Mary SMITH; b 1697; Charlestown
HEWES, Ralph (-1692) & Esther _?_; b 9 Dec 1692; Boston
HEWES, Zechariah & _?_; b 1701; Boston
HUGHES, Richard & Mary _?_; Guilford, CT
HEWITT, Benjamin (1662-1723) & Mary FANNING; 24 Sep 1683; Stonington, CT
HEWETT, Ephraim (-1644) & Isabel/?Elizabeth _?_ (-1661); ca 1630/34?; Windsor, CT
HEWETT, Ephraim (1639-1678) & Elizabeth FOSTER (1644-1682/3), m/2 James RAY 1682; 4 Nov 1665; Scituate
HUIT/HUNT, Ephraim (1676-) & Catherine/Katharine ACRES (1675-); m int 8 Oct 1698; Newbury/Easton
HEWITT, Herculus/Archelaus? & Jane _?_; b 1693; Boston
HUET, John (1641-) & Martha WINTER (-1691), dau Christopher; 4 - 1668; Marshfield
HUET, Nicholes & _?_; b 1645; Boston
HEWITT, Solomon (-1715, ae 45) & Sarah [WATERMAN] (1674-); b 1700; Marshfield
HUET, Thomas (-1670) & 1/wf Elizabeth [CHAPMAN] (-1649); b 1639; Hingham
HUET, Thomas (-1670) & Mary [CUTLER], w John; aft 22 May 1649; Hingham
HEWITT, Thomas & Hannah PALMER (1634-), m/2 Roger STERRY 1671, m/3 John FISH 1681; 26 Apr 1659, 1663?; Stonington, CT
HEWITT, Thomas (1660-1686) & Lydia UTLEY, ?m/2 Jonas PICKLES 1690; Jun 1683, Feb 1684; Stonington, CT
HUET, Timothy (1647-) & Susanna _?_ (1667-1753); b 1690; Hingham
HEWINS, Jacob (-1711) & Mary/?Mercy _?_ (-1716); ca 1655; Boston/Dorchester
HEWENS, Jacob (-1691) & Martha TRESCOTT (1661-), m/2 Henry ADAMS 1694; 24 Feb 1680, 1680/1; Dorchester/Boston/Roxbury
HEWINS, Joseph (1668-1755) & Mehitable LYON (1669-1733); 29 Jan 1690; Dorchester
HEWINS, _?_ & Susan _?_; b 1650; Charlestown
HULETT, Cornelius & Elizabeth [DUE]; b 30 Jun 1654?, b 2 Dec 1654
HULATE, George & Mary [TAYLOR]; 1664
HEWLETT, George & Mary BAYLESS, Jamaica; 14 May 1680; Gravesend, LI/Jamaica, LI
HEWSON, John & Susanna NORDEN; 17 Aug 1693; Boston
HEYLETT, Edwund & Lydia [PALGRAVE] (1635-); b 1669; Charlestown
HIBBERT, John & Ruth WALDERNE, dau Edward WALDIN/WALDRON; 16 Nov 1679; Wenham/Beverly
HIBBARD, Joseph (-1701) & Elizabeth/Abigail GRAVES; 20 Oct 1670; Beverly
HIBBARD, Joseph (1678-1755) & Abigail KENDALL/LINDALL/LYNDON; 20 Apr 1698; Windham, CT
HEBARD/HIBBERT?, Robert (1613-1684) & Joan/Joanna? [LUFF?/LOVE?] (-1696); b 1641; Salem/Beverly
HEBBART, Robert (1648-1710) & Mary [WALDEN] (ca 1655-1736), dau Edward?; b 1674; Wenham/Windham, CT
HIBBARD, Samuel (1658-1702) & Mary BOND; 16 Nov 1679; Salem
HIBBARD, William (1673-) & Ruth [ROSE] (bpt Feb 1675/6-); b 1701?, b 18 Feb 1707; Salem/Portsmouth, NH
HIBBERT, _?_ & Hannah [GIBBINS], m/2 Robert MACE 1729; , b 1689, ?ca 1690; ME?
HIBBINS, Giles (-1693) & [Mary PENNELL]; 20 Jul 1674, 21 Jul; Saco, ME/Charlestown
HIBBINS, William & 2/wf Anne [BELLINGHAM] (-1656); b 1654; Boston
HIBBINS, William & 1/wf Hester BELLINGHAM; 4 Mar 1632/3, Boston, Eng

HITCHBORNE, David & Catherine _?_ (-1661); b 1654; Boston
HITCHBORN, Thomas & Ruth _?_; b 1672; Boston
HICHBORN, Thomas & Mary _?_; b 1682; Boston
HICKOCKS, Benjamin (-1745) & Hannah SKEEL (-1746); 3 Nov 1697, 3 Mar 1697; Woodbury, CT
HICKOCKS, Joseph (-1687) & Mary [CARPENTER] (1650-), Farmington, m/2 Samuel HINMAN b 1694, aft 1687; b 1673; Woodbury, CT
HICKOCKS, Joseph (1673-1717) & Ruth FAIRCHILD (1679-1728); 3 Nov 1697; Woodbury, CT
HICKOK, Joseph (1678-) & Elizabeth GAYLORD; 8 Feb 1699/1700; Waterbury, CT
HICKOCKS, Samuel (1648-1695) & [Hannah UPSON], Farmington; b 1668; Farmington, CT/Waterbury, CT
HICKOX, Samuel (-1713) & Elizabeth PLUMB, (-1749), Milford; 16 Apr 1690; Milford, CT/Waterbury, CT
HICKCOCKS, Samuel (see Samuel HITCHCOCK) & Mehitable _?_; b 1696; Fordham, NY
HICKOX, Thomas (1675-) & Mary BRONSON (1680-); 27 Mar 1700; Waterbury, CT
HICKOX, William (-1737) & Rebecca [ANDREWS] (1672-); b 1699(1700?); Waterbury, CT
HICKOCK/HEACOCK, William? & Elizabeth _?_, m/2 William ADAMS b 1649; b 1643; Farmington, CT
HICKE/HICKS, Daniel & Rebecca HANMOR/HANMORE; 19 Sep 1659; Scituate
HIX, Daniel (1660-) & Sarah EDMONDS (1679-); 11 Feb 1695; Swansea
HICKS, Dennis (-bef 15 Nov 1725) & Sarah [DEERING] (1657-); ca 1680/5; Durham, NH
HICKS, Ephraim (-12 Dec 1649, 2 Dec?) & Elizabeth HOWLAND, m/2 John DICKINSON 10 Jul 1651; 13 Sep 1649; Plymouth
HICKS, Ephraim & 1/wf _?_; ca 1686?; Swansea
HICKS, George & Mary [GOULD] (-1706); b 1701; Newport
HICKS, Isaac (1678-1745) & Elizabeth [MOORE]; b 1701?; Flushing, LI/Hempstead, LI
HICKS, Jacob (?1669-1753) & Hannah [CARPENTER]; ca 1690-5?; Glencove, LI
HICKS, John (-1672) & 1/wf Herodias [LONG], m/2 George GARDINER, m/3 John PORTER; ca 1636, div? 3 Dec 1644, 1655?; Flushing, LI/Hempstead, LI
HICKS, John (-1672) & Florence [CARMAN], w John; aft 1653; Hempstead, LI
HICKS, John & Rachel STARR?, w Thomas; m cont 22 Jan 1662?; Charlestown/Oyster Bay, LI/Hempstead, LI
HICKS, John (-1688) & Mary [CARR], m/2 Ralph EARLE bef 1691; ca 1678?; Portsmouth, RI
HICKS, Joseph (1662-1746) & Bethia [GREEN] (?1673-1708); ca 1693; Cambridge/Easthampton, LI
HICKS, Joseph & Mary [EARLE], w Caleb; aft 1693; ?Dartmouth
HICKS, Michael (-1688) & Lucy [CHADBOURNE], m/2 Peter LEWIS; Kittery, ME
HICKS, Michael (-by 1697) & Sarah [WALFORD], m/2 _?_ SAVAGE; ?ca 1685; Kittery, ME
HICKS, Peter (1662-) & Sarah [MATHER], wid; aft 1690, bef 9 May 1695; Dorchester/Dorchester, SC
HICKS, Richard & Mary _?_; b 1649; Boston
HICKS, Richard & Susanna _?_; ?by 1660, bef 12 Oct 1669; Cape Porpoise
HICKS, Robert (?1580-1647) & 1/wf [?Elizabeth MORGAN]; Plymouth/Duxbury
HICKS, Robert (?1580-1647) & 2/wf Margaret [?WINSLOW] (-1666); Plymouth
HICKS, Robert & Isabel (SAYLES) TILLINGHAST (?1658-); aft 16 Dec 1690
HICKS, Samuel (-1677) & Lydia DOANE; ?11 Sep 1645; Eastham/Dartmouth
HICKS, Samuel & Hannah EVANS; 27 Sep 1665; Dorchester/Roxbury/Swansea
HICKS, Thomas (-1653) & Margaret [WEST], dau Zachariah of London; b 1625?; Scituate/Marblehead
HICKS, Thomas & 1/wf Mary (BUTLER) [WASHBURN] (-1713), w John; aft 30 Oct 1658, b 1660; Weymouth/Hempstead, LI/Flushing, LI/Newport, RI/Stratford, CT
HICKS, Thomas (-1698) & Mary [ALBRO] (-1710+); b 1677; Dartmouth/Portsmouth, RI
HICKS, Thomas & 2/wf Mary DOUGHTY; m lic Jul 1677; ?Flushing, LI
HICKS, Thomas (1661?-1712) & Deborah [WHITEHEAD], dau Daniel; ca 1695; Flushing, LI
HICKS, Timothy (1649-) & Dorcas VEREN (-1673); 21 Feb 1671/2; Salem
HICKS, William & Christian HARPER; 27 Nov 1699; Boston
HICKS, Zachariah (1628-1707) & Elizabeth SCELL/SILL/SILLS (1666-1730); 28 Oct 1652; Cambridge
HICKS, Zachariah (1657-) & Ruth GREENE (-1704); 18 Nov 1685; Cambridge
HICKS, _?_ & _?_ GAUNT; b 1691

HEADEN, Andrew & Sarah HOSETIN/HOUSTIN; 7 Jun 1654; Rowley
HIDDEN, John (-1695) & Elizabeth JEWETT (-1728), m/2 Cornelius DAVIS 1696; 16 May 1687; Rowley
HIDDEN, Samuel (-1717) & Mary CRESSEY (?1667-); 20 Apr 1698; Rowley
HIGBY, Edward[1] (-1699) & 1/wf Jedidah [SKIDMORE]; b 1649; New London, CT/Jamaica, LI/etc.
HIGBY, Edward[1] (-1699) & 2/wf Lydia [SMITH] (?1643-); ca 1661
HIGBY, Edward[2] & Abigail [ADAMS] (1660-); b 29 Mar 1684; Huntington, LI
HIGBY, Edward & Mary _?_; b 1695; Huntington, LI
HIGBY, John (1658-1685) & Rebecca TREADWELL; 1 May 1679; Middletown, CT
HIGBY, Nathaniel & Elizabeth _?_; b 1696?; Jamaica, LI
HIGBY, Thomas & 1/wf Mary TAYLOR; 4 Jul 1682; ?Huntington, LI/?Hempstead, LI
HIGBY, Thomas & 2/wf Elizabeth _?_; 1697; ?Huntington, LI/?Hempstead, LI
HIGGINBOTTOM, Richard (-1713+) & 1/wf Elizabeth (MUNSON) [COOPER] (-1706), w Timothy; b 1682; New Haven
HIGGINS, Abraham & Sarah [MIDDLEBROOK] (1675-); b 28 Feb 1694/5; Fairfield, CT
HIGGINS, Benjamin (1640-1691) & Lydia BANGS; 24 Dec 1661; Eastham
HIGGINS, Beriah (1661-1699) & _?_; Portsmouth, NH
HIGGINS, Ichabod (1662-1728) & Melatiah [HAMLIN?] (1668-); b 1692; Eastham
HIGGINS, Isaac (1672-1760) & Lydia [COLLINS] (1676-); b 1697(8?); Eastham
HIGGINS/EAGINS, John & Elizabeth _?_ (1650-), m/2 _?_ WELDEN; b 1675; Boston
HIGGINS, John & Mary [BRADLEY]; b 1701?, prob aft 1701; Westchester Co., NY
HIGGENS, Jonathan (1637-) & 1/wf Elizabeth ROGERS (-1678, 1679); - Jan 1660, 9 Jan 1660; Eastham
HIGGINS, Jonathan (1637-) & 2/wf [?Hannah ROGERS]; ca 1680; Eastham
HIGGINS, Jonathan (1664-1753/4) & Lydia (SPARROW) [FREEMAN], w William; ?aft 3 May 1687; Eastham
HIGGINS, Joseph (1667-) & Ruth _?_; b 1690, b 1692; Eastham
HIGGINS, Joshua (1668-living in 1757) & 1/wf Elizabeth [SMITH] (1668-); b 26 Oct 1696
HIGGINS, Owen & Seaborn (TEW) [BILLINGS] (1640-), w Samuel; aft 1662; Newport, RI
HIGINSE, Richard & 1/wf Lydia CHANDLER; 11 Dec 1634, 23 Nov 1634; ?Plymouth/Eastham
HIGGENS, Richard & Mary YATES, w John, m/3 Isaac WHITEHEAD; Oct 1651; Eastham
HIGGINS, Richard (1664-1732) & Sarah [HAMLIN?/HAMBLEN?], m/2 John COLE; b 1695; Eastham
HIGGINS, Richard & Elizabeth [HISCOX]; b 1699; Newport, RI
HIGGINS, Robert (-1665) & Susanna WESTOE; 2 Nov 1654; Boston
HIGGINS/EAGINS, Thomas & _?_; Middlesex Co., MA
HIGGINSON, Francis (1586-1630) & Ann HERBERT (-1640); St. Peter's, Nottingham, in Eng, ?8 Jan 1615, 1615/16; Charlestown
HIGGINSON, John (1616-1798) (see John WILSON) & 1/wf Sarah [WHITFIELD] (-1675); b 1646, ?Guilford, CT, 1652?; Salem
HIGGINSON, John (1646-1720) & Sarah SAVAGE (1653-1713); 9 Oct 1672; Salem
HIGGINSON, John & 2/wf Mary (BLACKMAN?/BLAKEMAN) [ATWATER] (1636-1709), w Joshua; aft 16 May 1676, 1676; Stratford, CT
HIGGINSON, John (1675-1718) & 1/wf Hannah GARDNER (1676-1713); 11 Sep 1695; Salem
HIGGINSON, Theophilus (-1657, ae 37) & Elizabeth _?_; b 1648; New Haven
HIGGINSON?/HIGGISON, William (-1720) & Sarah [WARNER] (1657-); ca 1685?, b 14 Mar 1678/9; Farmington, CT
HIGGS, John & Elizabeth _?_, m/2 Francis THRASHER 1694; b 1687; Boston
HIGLEY, John (1649-1714) & 1/wf Hannah DRAKE (1653-1694, Simsbury); 9 Nov 1671; Windsor, CT
HIGLEY, John (1649-1714) & 2/wf Sarah (STRONG) [BISSELL] (1665-1739), w Joseph; b 1697, aft 1696, ca 1696; Simsbury, CT
HELDRETH, Ephraim (ca 1655, ca 1654-1731) & 1/wf Dorothy BARNES (-1686); 11 Jun 1685; Stow
HILDRETH, Ephraim (-1731) & 2/wf Anna MOOR/MOORE (1666-1760, ae 95), Sudbury; 8 Oct 1686; Stow
HILDRETH, Isaac (1663-) & Elizabeth WILLSON/WILSON; 24 Jul 1685, 12 Nov 1685; Chelmsford/Woburn

HELDERETH, James (ca 1631-1695) & Margaret **WARD** (ca 1636-1693); 1 Jun 1659; Chelmsford
HILDRETH, James & [Deborah] _?_ ; ca 1677/90?; Southampton
HILDRETH, Joseph & Hannah **JESSUP**; 11 Sep 1678; Southampton, LI
HILDRETH, Joseph (1658-1706) & Abigail **WILLSON/WILSON** (1666-(170-)), ?m/2 Jonathan **BARRETT** 1708±; 25 Feb 1683/4, at Woburn; Chelmsford
HILDRETH, Richard (?1604-1688, ae 83) & 1/wf Sarah _?_ (-1644); in Eng, b 1628?; Cambridge
HILDRETH, Richard (-1688, ae 83) & 2/wf Elizabeth _?_ /**HINCHMAN?** (1625-1693, Malden); b 1646; Cambridge/Chelmsford
HILDRETH, Richard (-1760, ae 83) & 1/wf Dorcas **WILSON** (-1727); 6 Feb 1699/1700; Billerica/Concord
HILDRETH, Thomas (-1657) & Hannah _?_ , m/2 Jonas **BOWERS**; ca 1649?; Southampton, LI
HILDETH, Thomas (1662-) & Mary _?_ ; b 1686; Chelmsford
HILL, Abraham (1615-1670) & Sarah [**LONG**] (1616-living 1679); b 1640; Charlestown/Cambridge/Malden
HILL, Abraham (1643-1713) & Hannah **STOWER** (-1738, in 89th y); - Oct 1666; Malden/Charlestown
HILL, Abraham (-1720), Cambridge & 1/wf Sarah **LONG** (?1672-1695), Charlestown; 29 Jun 1694; Charlestown
HILL, Abraham (1670-) & Sarah [**COOPER**] (-1752, ae 79); b 1695; Charlestown/Cambridge
HILL, Abraham (-1720) & 2/wf Martha **CARY** (1678-), m/2 Stephen **HALL**; 1 Jul 1697; Charlestown
HILL, Ambrose & _?_ ; b - Jul 1675
HILL, Charles (-1684) & 1/wf Ruth (**BREWSTER**) **PICKET** (-1677), w John; 2 Jul 1668; New London, CT
HILL, Charles (-1684) & 2/wf Rachel **MASON** (1648-1679); 12 Jun 1678; New London
HILL, Ebenezer & 1/wf Mercy **BROOKS**, m/2 Edward **SCOTT** ca 1693; 24 Oct 1677, div 1692; New Haven
HILL, Ebenezer (-1696) & 1/wf Ruth [**BAILEY**]; ca 1683; Bridgewater
HILL, Ebenezer & [Elizabeth **CARPENTER?**]/Elizabeth (**CARPENTER**) **JONES**, w Richard?; ca 1685?; Farmington, CT
HILL, Ebenezer (-1696) & 2/wf Sarah [?**BAILEY**]; ca 1692; Bridgewater
HILL, Ebenezer & Mary [**WHITE**]; b 1692(3?); Sherborn
HILL, Ebenezer & 2/wf Abigail **WOODING**; - Jun 1692; New Haven
HILL, Edward & [Deborah **PENSE**]; b 1695; Boston
HILL, Edward & Mary **ARCHER**; 15 Feb 1699; Boston
HILL, Eleazer (-1725?) & Sarah **GILLET**; 29 Dec 1679; Simsbury, CT
HILL, Eleazer[3] & 1/wf Sarah [**BRECK**]; ca 1687; Sherborn
HILL, Eliphalet & Ann _?_ ; b 1670; Boston
HILL, Eliphalet (-1695) & Esther (**WARD**) (**HAWLEY**) **NICHOLS**, w Ebenezer, w Ephraim, m/4 Robert **LORD**; - Nov 1691, ?16 Nov; Fairfield, CT
HILL, Francis & Hannah _?_ ; b 1663/[4?]; Boston
HILL, Henry & Sarah **BASSETT**; 8 Nov 1673; ?Woodbury, CT
HILL, Henry (1661-) & Elizabeth _?_ ; ?ca 1687; Kings Town, RI/E. Greenwich, RI
HILL, Henry (-1726, ae 70) & Mary _?_ ; b 1691(2?); Boston
HILL, Isaac (1641-) & 1/wf Hannah **HAWARD/HAYWARD/HAYWOOD/HOWARD?** (-1679); - Jun 1666; Malden/Charlestown
HILL, Isaac & 2/wf Sarah (**WHEAT**) **BICKNELL**, w John; 12 Jan 1679/[80]; Cambridge
HILL, Jacob (-1690) & Sarah [**STONE**] (1657-1717), m/2 Samuel **JONES** 1705; b ca 1679; Cambridge
HILL, James & Hannah **HINCKSMAN/HENCHMAN** (1638-); 10 Apr 1662; Boston
HILL, James (?1646-1707) & Sarah [?**GRISWOLD**] (-1729); b 1683; Guilford, CT
HILL, John[1] (-1664) & Frances _?_ , m/2 Jonas **AUSTIN** 1667 (sister of Robert **TURNER**'s wf?); in Eng, ca 1629; Dorchester
HILL, John & Margaret _?_ ; b 1641; Boston
HILL, John & 1/wf Frances _?_ (-1673); ca 1648?; Guilford, CT
HILL, John & 1/wf Hannah [?**JOHNSON**/?**HOLBROOK**] (-1690) (had son **JOHNSON**); ca 1653; Medfield
HILL, John & Elizabeth **STRONG**; 16 Jan 1656/7; Boston/Portsmouth, NH
HILL, John & Abigail **WOODBURY** (1637-); 12 Oct 1657

HILL, John (-1680) & 1/wf Miriam [GARDNER]; b 1658; Salem

HILL, John (-1680) & 2/wf Lydia BUFFUM (1644-), m/2 George LOCKER 1680+; 26 Aug 1664; Salem

HILL, John & Mary _?_ ; b 1668; Boston

HILL/HILLS, John (see HILLS) & Jane BUSHNELL, w John; 14 Apr 1670; Saybrook

HILL, John (-1690) & Thankful [STOWE] (1646-1711); b 1671; Guilford, CT

HILL, John (-1689) & Catharine (POST) CHALKER, w Alexander; 3 Sep 1673, 25 Dec 1673, ?22 Sep 1673; Saybrook, CT/Guilford, CT

HILL, John (1650-1710) & 1/wf Hannah GRANNIS (-1692); 13 Jan 1680/1; New Haven

HILL, John (-1690/1) & Priscilla [SHATTUCK] (1658-), m/2 Hugh NICHOLS 1694; ?ca 1686; Salem

HILL, John (ca 1630-1718) & 2/wf Elizabeth (ELLIS) [BULLARD] (-1719), w Benjamin; ca 1693; Medfield/Sherborn

HILL, John (1661-1738) & Hannah [ROCKWOOD] (1673-1730); ca 1693; Medfield

HILL, John (1650-1710) & 2/wf Hannah [?PARMELEE] (?1667-1702); - Jul 1693; New Haven

HILL, John (1672-1740) & Hannah [HILAND] (1669-1752); ca 1694; Guilford, CT

HILL, John (1666-1713) & Mary FROST; 12 Dec 1694; York Co., ME

HILL, John & Elizabeth OAKES; 27 Apr 1696; Salem

HILL, John & Sarah [BRACKETT]; ca 1695; Greenland

HILL, John & Ruhamah WYER (1670-); m int 14 Oct 1696; Boston/Charlestown

HILL, John & Sarah [PHELPS] (1672-); ca 1696; Simsbury, CT

HILL, John (?1669-) & _?_ ; b 1699; Westerly, RI

HILL, John (-1727) & Jane _?_ (-1774, ae 98?), m/2 Moses DIMOND 1738, m/3 Gideon ALLEN 1749; ca 1700; Fairfield, CT

HILL, Jonathan (1638-) & Mary _?_ ; b 1657; Warwick, RI

HILL, Jonathan & Mary HARTWELL; 11 Dec 1666; Billerica

HILL, Jonathan (1640-1709+) & Mary _?_ (-1718+); b 1676; Dorchester/Bridgewater

HILL, Jonathan (1657-1731) & _?_ ; ca 1680; Warwick, RI/Portsmouth, RI

HILL, Jonathan (1674-) & Mary [SHARSWOOD] (1672-); b 1702, ca 1700?; New London, CT

HILL, Joseph & Ellen _?_ ; b 1663(4?); Boston

HILL, Joseph (1657-1714) & 1/wf Catherine KNIGHT; Dec 1688; Kittery, ME

HILL, Joseph & Mabel _?_ ; b 1690; Boston

HILL, Joseph & Hannah LITTLEFIELD (1673-1738); 24 Jan 1694; Wells, ME

HILL, Joseph (1657-1714) & 2/wf Susanna [BEEDLE]; ca 1696; Durham, NH

HILL, Joseph & Elizabeth PECK; 22 Dec 1698; Boston

HILL, Joseph (-1743?) & Hannah/?Sarah [BOLLES/BOWLES]; b 1701?; ME

HILL, Luke (-1690, Simsbury) & Mary HOUT/HOYT/HART; 6 May 1651; Windsor, CT

HILL, Luke, Jr. & 1/wf Anna/Hannah [BUTLER]; b 1687; Simsbury, CT

HILL, Nathaniel & Elizabeth HOLMES; 21 Jun 1667; Billerica

HILL, Nathaniel (1660-) & Sarah [NUTTER] (1659-); ca 1690?; Oyster River, NH/Durham, NH

HILL, Peter (-1667) & _?_ ; b 1638, b 1631; Saco, ME/Biddleford, ME

HILL, Philip (-1649(+or-?)) & Ann _?_?, m/2 John ELTEN, m/3 "Capt." HUDSON; b 1633; Barbados?

HILL, Philip & Sarah CROAD/CROADE? (1666-); 23 Dec 1689; Salem

HILL, Ralph & 1/wf _?_ ; b 1630

HILL, Ralph (-1663) & 2/wf? Margaret TOOTHAKER, w Roger; 21 Dec 1638; Plymouth

HILL, Ralph & Martha TOOTHAKER (1636?-); 15 Nov 1660, 5 Nov; Billerica

HILL, Richard & Mehitable WAITE; in Eng, b 1613

HILL, Robert (1615-1662, 1663) & 1/wf _?_ ; b 1648, b 1652(3?); New Haven

HILL, Robert (-1690+) & Mary PEARCE (1662?-), m/2 James SWEET 1690+; b 1684?; Warwick, RI/Prudence Isl., RI

HILL, Robert (-1662, 1663?) & 2/wf Adeline (_?_) JOHNSON, w Robert, m/3 John SCRANTON 1666; Jan 1662, 22 May; New Haven, CT

HILL, Robert & _?_ ; b 1701; Salem

HILL, Roger (1635-1702, 1696?, 1693) & Mary CROSS (-1720?, 1696); Nov 1658, 1 Nov 1658, 1658; Wells, ME?/Salem

HILL, Roger & Elizabeth _?_ ; b 1699; Beverly

HILL, Samuel & Martha _?_ (-1715); b 1667; Dorchester

HILL, Samuel[3] (?1656-1723) & Hannah TWICHELL/TWITCHILL (ca 1661-1690); 4 Nov 1679; Medfield

HILL, Samuel & Elizabeth WILLIAMS/WILLYAMS (1655-); 28 Oct 1680; Dover, NH/Portsmouth, NH

HILL, Samuel & 1/wf Elizabeth (AUSTIN) COBHAM, w Joshua; b 1690; Charlestown

HILL, Samuel & Sarah PAGE; 7 Jan 1698/9; Billerica

HILL, Tahay (1659-1692) & Hannah PARMELEE (1667-), m/2 Thomas MERRILL 1693, m/3 Josiah STEVENS; Nov 1688; Guilford, CT

HILL, Thomas & Eleanor MUNT, w Thomas; b Mar 1668, b 28 Apr 1666; Boston

HILL/HILLS, Thomas (-1704) & Mary _?_ (-1704+), ?m/2 John RUE; b 1678, b 1676; Middletown, CT

HILL, Thomas & Anne/Annis _?_ ; b 1681

HILL, Thomas & Sarah _?_ ; b 1689; Boston

HILL, Thomas & Abigail WAKEMAN; aft 9 Nov 1685, 1685, b 1695; Fairfield, CT

HILL, Valentine & 1/wf Frances [FREESTONE] (1610-1646); b 1638, by 1637; Boston/Durham, NH

HILL, Valentine (-1661) & 2/wf Mary [EATON] (-1708), wid, m/3 Ezekiel KNIGHT ca 1675; b 1647, in 1647; Boston?

HILL, William[1] (-1659) & Sarah JOURDAIN, m/2 Edmund GREENLEAF aft 1663; in Eng, 28 Oct 1619; Dorchester/Wethersfield, CT

HILL, William[2] (-1684) & [Elizabeth JONES] (1635?-); ca 1650?, ca 1643?; Dorchester/Windsor, CT

HILL, William & Judith _?_ ; b 1657, b 1646; Oyster River, NH/Durham

HILL, William & Hannah [ROBERTS], m/2 John COX 1694; b 1669; Oyster River, NH

HILL, William[2] (see William above) & Sarah (JOURDAN?) [WILSON (no)] (-1671), m/3 Edmund GREENLEAF aft 1683; b 1664?; Windsor, CT/Fairfield, CT

HILL, William & Rebecca CHARLES; 19 Jun 1691; Milton

HILL, William & 1/wf Abigail OSBORN (-1712?); 7 Oct 1691; Fairfield, CT

HILL, William & Judith _?_ (see William above, m bef 1646); Mar 1698/9; ?Oyster River, NH

HILL, Zachariah/Zechary? & Judith [BUCKNAM]; 1700; Malden/Charlestown

HILL, Zebulon (-1699/1700) (ae 64 in 1691) & Elizabeth DIKE (-1690+); 16 Nov 1651; Gloucester/Salem

HILL, Zechary (ca 1645-1672) & Deborah NORTON, m/2 Matthew GRIFFIN; 24 Sep 1668; Charlestown

HILL, [John?] & Mary [DOWSE] (1659-); ?Boston

HILL, _?_ & Sarah _?_ , m/2 Nathaniel SOUTHER 1654

HILLIER, Andrew (1646-1698) & 1/wf Hannah BURR (-1684); Sep 1681; Simsbury, CT

HILLIER, Andrew (1646-1698) & 2/wf Abigail (DRAKE) DUCE/DEWEY (1648-1689+, 1692(-)), w Israel; 17 Nov 1687; Simsbury, CT

HILLIARD, Benjamin & ?[Elizabeth WANTEN], wid (had dau Margaret); b 1670; Wethersfield, CT

HILLIARD, Clemens & Hannah BATES; 1 Jul 1700; Boston

HILLIARD, David (-1702) & Priscilla BRAY; 15 Aug 1689; Salem

HILLIARD, David (1678-) & 1/wf Joanna ANDREWS/ANDROS (-1716); 13 Jul 1699; Little Compton, RI

HILLIARD, Edward (-1706) & Martha _?_ ; b 1658; Salem

HILLIARD, Edward & Lydia [MORRILL] (1661-1705), m/2 Daniel WEAR 1698; b 1684; Boston

HILLIARD, Emanuel (-1657) (kinsman of Timothy DALTON) (-1657) & Elizabeth [PARK-HURST] (1628-), m/2 Joseph MERRY 1659; b 1655; Hampton, NH

HILLIER, Hugh (-1647?, 1648) & Rose [TILLYE?] (1616-1687), m/2 Thomas HUCKINS 1648; b 1643; Barnstable/Yarmouth

HILLIER, James (1644-1720?, Simsbury?) & 1/wf Mary (WAKEFIELD) DIBBLE, w Ebenezer; ?28 Jun 1677; Windsor, CT/Danbury, CT

HILLIER, James (1644-) & 2/wf Mary (CASE) ALDERMAN, w William; 30 Mar 1699; Simsbury, CT

HILLIARD, Job (-1670) & 1/wf Sarah _?_ (-14 Oct 1660); b 1656; Salem

HILLIARD, Job (-1670) & 2/wf Mary OLIVER, ?dau Thomas, m/2 William WEST 1672; 1 Apr 1661; Salem

HILLIARD, Job & Mary FOWL (1669-); 4 Jul 1693; Boston

HILLIER, John (-1655) & Ann ? , m/2 John FITCH 1656; b 1637/[8?]; Windsor, CT
HILLIER, John (1637/8-1729) & Anne BAXTER (-1728); 30 Sep 1664; Hadley
HILLIER, John & ? ; b 1680; Windsor, CT
HILLER, Joseph & Susanna [DENNIS]; b 1685; Boston
HILLIARD, Joseph (-1746) & Rachel ALLEN (1675-1746+); 10 Oct 1694; Lynn
HELYAR, Roger & Experience [HALL] (1662-), m/2 Walter WRIGHT 1704; b 1689; Charlestown
HILLER, Samuel (1646-) (son Hugh) & Mary ? ; b 1692; ?Sandwich
HILLIARD, Timothy (ca 1645-1723) & 1/wf Apphia PHILBRICK (1655-); 3 Dec 1674; Hampton, NH
HILLIARD, William (?1614-) & Ester/Hester ? ; prob 1640; ?Duxbury/Boston/Hingham
HILLIARD, William (?1650-1714) & Deborah WARREN (1652-1718); 12 Jun 1671; Hingham/Little Compton, RI
HILLIARD, [?Hugh/?Benjamin] & Margaret ?   (-1671), m/2 John ELSON 1648?, m/3 Thomas WRIGHT
HILLYARD/HILLIER, ? & Mary [KING], dau Edward; b 1701?, b 8 Sep 1702; ?Hartford/LI
HILLMAN, John & Hannah [COTTLE] (?1661-); b 1682; Martha's Vineyard
HILLMAN, Josiah & Hannah ? ; b 1676; Boston/Hingham
HILLMAN, [?Thomas] & Elizabeth (ALCOCK) [SOPER], w Joseph; b 23 Jun 1685; ?Boston
HILLS, Benjamin (ca 1653-1728?) & Mary BRONSON (1668-); 11 Jan 1688; ?Hartford
HILLS, Ebenezer (1660-1727) & 1/wf Sarah (STONE) CONVERSE (1661-1703), w Edward; 14 Jan 1697, 1696/7; Woburn/?Sherborn
HILLS, Ebenezer & Abigail BENJAMIN (1673-1755); b 1706?, b 1702; Wethersfield, CT/Glastonbury, CT
HILLS, Gershom (1639-) & Elizabeth CHADWICK (1648-); 11 Nov 1667; Malden/Charlestown
HILLS, John (1615-) & Jane BUSHNELL, w John; 14 Apr 1670; Saybrook, CT
HILLS, John (-1692) & Mary ? , m/2 Thomas ADKINS
HILLS, John & Susanna ? b 1685; Boston
HILLS, Jonathan (?1665-1727) & Dorothy [HALE] (1667-1733?); b 1696(7?), b 1688?; Hartford
HILLS, Joseph[1] (1602-1688) (ae 36 in 1638) & 1/wf Rose CLARKE (-1650); Great Burstead, Eng, 22 Jul 1624; Malden
HILLS, Joseph[1] (1602-1688) & 2/wf Hannah (SMITH) MELLOWS, w Edward; 24 Jun 1651; Malden
HILLS, Joseph[2], Jr. (1639-1674) & Hannah SMITH (1633-1674); - Nov 1653; Malden
HILLS, Joseph[1] (1602-1688) & 3/wf Helen ATKINSON; Jan 1655/6; Malden/Newbury
HILLS, Joseph[1] (1602-1688) & 4/wf Ann LUNT (-1688+), w Henry; 8 Mar 1664, 1664/5; Newbury
HILLS, Joseph[3] (1655-1679) & Hannah ? ; b 1674; Malden
HILLS, Joseph (1650-1713) & 1/wf [Elizabeth?] ? ; b 1680, b 1677; Glastonbury
HILLS, Joseph & 2/wf Mehitabel (HURSDALE) DICKENSON (1663-), w Obadiah; ca 1699
HILLS, Joseph & 3/wf Elizabeth ? ; ca 1702
HILLS, Samuel (1652-1732) & Abigail WHEELER (1656-1742); 20 May 1679; Newbury
HILLS/HILL, Samuel & Phebe LEONARD; 6 Nov 1694; Duxbury/Lebanon, CT
HILLS, Samuel (1669-) & Sarah [PAGE?]; b 1695, 1699?; Malden
HILLS, William[1] (-1683) & 1/wf Phillis [LYMAN] (1611-); ca 1632, bef 22 Apr 1640?; Roxbury/Hartford
HILLS, William[1] (-1683) & 2/wf [?Mary]/ ? RESLEY/RISELY, w ?Richard; aft 17 Oct 1648, bef 7 Dec 1648?; Hartford
HILLS, William[1] (-1683) & 3/wf Mary (WARNER) [STEELE], w John; bef 1658, aft 1653, bef 25 Jan 1669; Hartford/Hadley
HILLS, William[2] (±1646, 1640-1693) & Sarah ? ; b 1667; Hartford
HILTON, Dudley (-1710?) & Mercy [HALL]; b 1701?; Exeter, NH
HILTON, Edward[1] (1596-1676, ?1669/70) & 1/wf ? ; b 1626?, b 1630; Exeter, NH/Dover, NH
HILTON, Edward[1] (1596-1676, ?1669/70) & 2/wf Catherine (SHEPLEIGH) [TREWORGIE] (-1676), w James; ca 1654?, soon aft 1654; ?Dover, NH
HILTON, Edward[2] (?1626, ?1630, ?1629-1699) & Anne [DUDLEY] (1641-); ca 1660?; Exeter, NH
HILTON, John & ? ; Dover, NH/Exeter, NH
HILTON, John (-1687), Middletown & ? ; b 1672; Wethersfield, CT
HILTON, John & Abigail SNELLING; 12 Oct 1694; Marblehead/Boston
HILTON, John (1668-) & Sarah [PARRUCK]; 1701?; Charlestown
HILTON, Jonathan & [Sobriety HILTON]; b 1701?; ?Kittery, ME

HILTON, Mainwaring (-1671, 1670?) & [Mary MOULTON], m/2 Samuel BRAGDON ca Dec 1686?; by 1670, 1671; York, ME

HILTON, Richard & Anna __?__; b 1632

HILTON, Richard & [Anne HILTON]

HILTON, William[1] (?1581-1655/6) & 1/wf __?__ (-1635(+or-?)); in Eng, ca 1618?, b 1610?; Plymouth/Exeter, NH/Dover, NH/York, ME

HILTON, William[1] (-1655/6) & Frances __?__ (?1617-), m/2 Richard WHITE; ca 1640?, ca 1651; Dover, NH

HILTON, William[2] (-1675) & 1/wf [Sarah GREENLEAF] (1620-1655?); b 1641; Newbury/ Charlestown

HILTON, William (?1620-1675) & 2/wf Mehitable NOWELL (-1711), m/2 John CUTLER 1684; 16 Sep 1659; Charlestown

HILTON, William (ca 1631-1690±) & Rebecca [SIMMONS?/SYMMONS/SYMONDS?]; b 18 Apr 1667, ca 1660; Kittery, ME?

HILTON, William (-1700?) & Anne [PARSONS?/BEALE?/WILSON?] (1657-); b 1678, ca 1675; York, ME

HILTON, William (-1723) & Margaret STILSON, m/2 John ALLEN 1727; 2 Jun 1699; Marblehead

HILTON, Winthrop (-1710) & Anne [WILSON] (-1744), m/2 Jonathan WADLEIGH; b 1701?; Exeter, NH

HIMS, David & Joan __?__; 28 Apr 1659; Dorchester/Milton

HINKLEY, Benjamin & Sarah COBB (1666-); 27 Dec 1686; Barnstable

HINKLEY, John (1644-1709) & 1/wf Bethiah LOTHROP (-1694?); - Jul 1668; Barnstable

HINKLEY, John (1667-1706) & Thankful TROT/TROTT (1667-), Dorchester, ?m/2 __?__ CROCKER; 1 May 1691; Barnstable

HINKLEY, John (1644-1709) & 2/wf Mary (DAVIS) GOODSPEED, w Benjamin; 24 Nov 1697; Barnstable

HINKLEY, Joseph (1671-1753) & Mary GORHAM (1679-1748); 21 Sep 1699; Barnstable

HINCKLEY, Samuel (1589-1662) & 1/wf Sarah SOULE/SOOLE (1600-1656); Hawkhurst, Kent, 7 May 1617; Scituate/Barnstable

HINCKLEY, Samuel (1589-1662) & 2/wf Bridget (_?_) [BODFISH], w Robert; ca 15 Dec 1657; Barnstable

HINKLEY, Samuel (1642-1727) & 1/wf Mary GOODSPEED (-1666); 14 Dec 1664; Barnstable

HINKLEY, Samuel (1642-1727) & 2/wf Mary FITTRANDE/FitzRANDOLPH (1650-1738); 15 Jan 1668, 1668/9?; Barnstable

HINKLEY, Samuel (1653-1697) & Sarah POPE (1652-1727), m/2 Thomas HUCKINS 1698; 13 Nov 1676; Barnstable

HINKLEY, Samuel & Martha LATHROP (-1737, Stonington, CT); 29 Sep 1699; Boston/Stonington, CT

HINCKLEY, Thomas (1619-1705) & Mary RICHARDS (-1659); 7 Dec 1641; Barnstable

HINCKLEY, Thomas (1619-1705) & 2/wf Mary (SMITH) GLOVER (?1650-1703), w Nathaniel; 16 Mar 1659/60; Barnstable

HINKS, Samuel & __?__; b 1687; Lynn

HINCKS, John (1650-) & 1/wf Elizabeth [FRYER] (1657-); b 1680/5?, by 1686; New Castle, NH

HINCKSON, Peter & ?Elizabeth/_?__?_; b 1653; Scarboro, ME

HINKSON, Peter (1666?-) & Elizabeth PARSONS, w John; 12 Jul 1698; York, ME

HINKSON, Philip (1616?) & Margaret __?__, m/2 George TAYLOR; Saco, ME

HINKSON, Robert & Sarah BREWSTER; 26 Sep 1679; Greenland

HINKSON, Simon (1653-) & Rebecca (DENHAM) [DAVIE] (?1656-), w William; Great Island/Scarboro, ME

HINKSON, Thomas (-1664) & Martha [WALFORD] (1645-), m/2 John WESTBROOK b 1666; by 1662; Portsmouth, NH

HINDS, Francis & Elizabeth __?__; b 1655; Casco Bay, ME/Marblehead

HINDS, Francis & Esther [CANE?]; Boston

HINDES, John & Mary (_?_) BUTLER, w James; 9 Feb 1681/2, 9-12-1682, 1682/3?; Lancaster/Billerica/Brookfield

HINE, John (1656-1739) & Mary FENN (1667-); 4 Jul 1684; Milford, CT

HINE, John & Constance BENNETT; 25 Nov 1700; Marblehead

HINE, Samuel (1660-) & Abigail [MILES] (1669/70-); ca 1686, ca 1688; Milford, CT

HINE, Stephen (1663-1719+) & Sarah [BRISTOL] (1668-1719+); by 1690?, b 1693; Milford, CT

HINE, Thomas (-1698) & Elizabeth __?__; b 1653; Milford, CT
HINE, Thomas (1653-1742) & 1/wf Rebecca HIET/HYATT; 13 Nov 1678; Milford, CT
HINE, Thomas (1653-1742) & 2/wf Hannah BRISTOL (1663-); 9 Nov 1684, 10 Nov 1684; Milford, CT/New Haven
HINE, William & 1/wf Abigail [WARD] (-1688); b 1682; Marblehead
HINES, William & 2/wf Elizabeth (NORMAN) DIMON (-1716), w Aholiab DIAMOND; 13 Nov 1688; Marblehead
HINES, __?__ & Hannah [PRATT]; b 1701?, aft 1706 (prob); Weymouth
HINDS, __?__ & __?__; ME
HINMAN, Benjamin (-1727) & Elizabeth LUMM/LUM; 12 Jul 1684; Woodbury, CT
HINMAN, Edward (-1681) & Hannah [STILES]; b 1653; Stamford, CT
HINMAN, Edward (1672-) & Hannah [BURROUGHS] (1678-1777?); b 1700; Stratford, CT
HINMAN, Samuel (1658-1713) & ?Mary (CARPENTER) [HICKOCK], w Joseph; b 6 Apr 1694, aft 1687; Woodbury, CT
HINMAN, Titus (1655/6-1736) & Hannah [COE] (-1703), Rye, NY; b 1685; ?Stratford, CT
HINSDALE, Barnabas (1639-1675) & Sarah (WHITE) TAYLOR, w Stephen, m/3 Walter HICKSON 1678/9; 15 Oct 1666
HINSDALE, Barnabas (1668-1725) & Martha SMITH (-1738); 9 Nov 1693
HINSDELL, Ephraim (1650-1681) & Mehitable PLIMPTON, m/2 Joseph CHENEY 1691, m/3 Jonathan ADAMS; 28 Sep 1676; Medfield
HINSDALE, Experience (1646-1676) & Mary HAWKS, m/2 John EVANS 1677; 10 Oct 1672
HINSDELL, Gamaliel (1642-1689) & Rachel MARTIN (-1679); 7 Nov 1672; Medfield
HINSDALE, John (-1705?, 1675?) & __?__; ca 1670?
HINSDALE, Mehuman & Mary [RIDER] (1680-), m/2 George BEAL; b 1699
HINSDELL, Robert (?1617-1676) & 1/wf Ann __?__ (-1666), dau Peter?; b 1639; Dedham/Medfield
HINSDALE, Robert (-1676, 1675?) & 2/wf Elizabeth (_?_) [HAWKES], w John, m/3 Thomas DIBBLE 1683; aft 30 Jun 1662, b 1668, parted b 30 Mar 1674
HINSDELL, Samuel (-1675) & Mehitable JONSON/JOHNSON (1644-), m/2 John ROOT 1676?, m/3 John COLEMAN 1679; 31 Oct 1660; Medfield
HINSDELL, Samuel (-1694), Sherborn & Susanna ROCKWOOD, Medfield, m/2 Ebenezer THOMPSON 1698?; 20 Dec 1693; Medfield
HINTON, John (-1687) & Jane NYLES; 20 Mar 1683, 20 Nov 1683; Bristol, RI
HIRES, Patrick & Sarah [STEVENSON]; b 1670; Newtown, LI
HISCOX/HISCOCK, William (1638-1704) & Rebecca __?__/?Agnes POIGNES?; b 1686, b 1683; Newport
HISKET, George & Sarah CLARKE; 11 Jun 1662; Boston
HISCOT/HISKETT, John (1665-) & Dorcas __?__; b 1693(4?); Boston
HITCHCOCK, Edward (-1658) & 1/wf Mary __?__; b 1638, b 1639(40?), b 1638(9?); New Haven
HITCHCOCK, Edward & 2/wf Frances (_?_) ENGLAND, w John, m/3 Thomas JOHNSON 1663; 20 May 1656; Branford, CT
HITCHCOCK, Eliakim & Sarah MERRICK (1643-); 4 Nov 1667; New Haven
HITCHCOCK, John (1642-1712) & Hannah CHAPIN (1644-1719); 27 Sep 1666; Springfield
HITCHCOCK, John (1650-1716) & 1/wf Abigail MERRIMAN (1654-1675); 18 Jan 1670, 1670/1; New Haven/Wallingford
HITCHCOCK, John & Mary __?__, m/2 William DAVENPORT; b 1677; Westchester, NY
HITCHCOCK, John (1670-1751) & Mary BALL (1673-1760); 24 Sep 1691; Springfield
HITCHCOCK, John (1650-1716) & 2/wf Mary (THOMPSON) LINES, w Samuel, m/3 Samuel CLARK 1716; aft 1692, b 1701?; Wallingford, CT?
HITCHCOCK, Luke (-1659) & Elizabeth [GIBBONS] (-1696), m/2 William WARRINER 1661, m/3 Joseph BALDWIN ca 1676; b 1642; New Haven/Wethersfield, CT
HITCHCOCK, Luke (1655-1727) & Sarah (BURT) DORCHESTER (1656-1746), w Benjamin; 14 Feb 1676, 1676/7; Springfield
HITCHCOCK, Luke (1675-1752) & Elizabeth WALKER (1676-1765); 23 Nov 1699, 3 Nov; Springfield
HITCHCOCK, Matthias (?1610-1669) & Elizabeth [?ROGERS] (?1621-1676); b 1651, b 1640?; Watertown/New Haven
HITCHCOCK, Nathaniel & Elizabeth MOSS (1652-); 18 Jan 1670, 1670/1?; New Haven/Wallingford, CT
HITCHCOCK, Richard (-1671) & 1/wf __?__; b 1653; Saco, ME

HITCHCOCK, Richard (-1671) & 2/wf Lucretia [WILLIAMS] (-1675?); b 1665, b 1659?; Saco, ME
HITCHCOCK, Samuel (1672-1727) & Sarah WELLER (1678-1761); 17 Nov 1698, int 15 Oct; Northampton
HITCHCOCK/HICKOCK?, Samuel & Elizabeth PLUMB?/_?_; b 1697; Waterbury, CT
HITCHCOCK/HICKCOCKS, Samuel & Mehitabel (BETTS) TIBBETTS VITREY, w Louis?, w George; b 18 Oct 1681, b 12 Mar 1677
HITCHESON, Thomas (-1684?) & Agnes _?_, m/2 _?_ SUTTON; New Haven
HICHENS/HITCHINS, Daniel[1] (1632-1731) & 1/wf Eleanor _?_ (-1691); b 1668; Lynn/Reading
HUCHINGS, Daniel[1] (-1731) & 2/wf Sarah (CUSHMAN)? HAWKS, ?w John; m int 7 Nov 1695; Lynn
HICHINGS, Daniel[2] (-1735) & 1/wf Sarah BORDMAN? (-1708, ae 57, Malden), ?w William; m int 16 Feb 1696/7; Lynn
HICHEN/HUTCHINGS/etc., Joseph (-1693) & Mary EDMUNDS; 1 Sep 1657; Lynn/Boston
HITFIELD, Matthias & Mariah (MELYN) PARDIE/PARDICE; 25 Aug 1664; New Haven
HITT, Henry & Sarah BASSETT, m/2 Simon LOBDELL; 5 Jan 1673/4; Stratford, CT
HIXSON, Richard (-1718) & Margaret WADKINS/WATKINS; 14 Sep 1686; Milton
HICKSON, Walter (-1696) & Sarah (WHITE) (TAYLOR) HINSDALE, w Barnabas, w Stephen; Feb 1678, 1678/9; Hatfield
HICKSON, Robert, Eastham & Sarah BREWSTER, w Nathaniel; 26 Sep 1678; Exeter, NH
HOADLEY, Abraham (-1748) & Elizabeth MALTBY; 14 Mar 1698, 1697/8; Branford, CT
HOADLEY, John (returned to Eng) & Sarah BUSHNELL (1625-); 14 Jul 1642; Guilford, CT
HOADLEY, Richard & _?_ [DRAKE]; b 1681; Eastchester, NY
HOADLEY, Samuel & Abigail FARRINGTON; 6 Mar 1689; Branford, CT
HOADLEY, William (1630±-1709) & 1/wf _?_; ca 1660/2; Saybrook, CT/Branford, CT
HOADLEY, William (-1709) & 2/wf Mary (BULLARD) [FARRINGTON] (-1703), w John; aft 1681, ca 1686?; Branford, CT
HOADLEY, William & 1/wf Abigail [FRISBIE] (1657-1696); b 1691; Branford, CT
HOOG, John[1] (1643, 3-4-1643/4-1728+) (bpt 10 Mar 1643/4 ae ca 7 d?) & Ebenezer EMERY (1648-1724+); 21 Apr 1669; Newbury/Amesbury
HOAG, Benjamin (?1671-) & 1/wf Sarah NORRIS (1678-), dau Nicholas; b 1701?, 23 Jun 1702; Newbury
HOAR, Benjamin (1680-) & Rebecca SMITH; 10 Apr 1699; Bristol, RI
HOARE, Charles (-1638, in Eng) & Joanna [HENCHMAN?/HINCHAMAN] (-1651); in Eng, b 1612; Braintree
HOAR, Daniel & 1/wf Mary STRATEN/STRATTON; 19 Jul 1677; Concord
HOAR, Hezekiah (cousin of Rev. Samuel NEWMAN) & Rebecca _?_; b 1654(5?); Taunton
HOAR, John (-1704) & Alice _?_ (-1696); b 1650; Scituate/Concord
HOAR, Leonard (1630-1675) & Bridget [LISLE] (-1723), m/2 Hezekiah USHER 1676; b 1673; Cambridge
HOARE, Nathaniel (1656-) & Sarah WILBORE; 2 Feb 1681; Taunton
HOARE, Richard & Elizabeth _?_ (-1680); b 1641?; ?Yarmouth
HOAR, Thomas & Mary ELSON; 21 Jun 1692; Marblehead
HOAR, William & Dorcas [GALLEY?]; ca 1669?, ca 1664?; Beverly
HOARE, William (-1698) & Hannah [WRIGHT]; b 1670(1?); Boston/Bristol, RI
HOARE, William & Sarah ROSS; 3 Jun 1685; Beverly
HUBBERT, Aaron (1661-1705), Hingham & Rebecca SUMNER (1671-), m/2 Edward DERBY 1705, m/3 Samuel PAINE; 27 Jan 1696/7; Milton
HOBART, Benjamin (1677-) & Susannah NEWCOMB (1673-1725); 5 Apr 1699; Braintree/Boston
HOBART, Caleb (?1630-1711) & 1/wf Elizabeth CHURCH (-1659); 20 Jan 1657/8; Hingham
HOBART, Caleb (?1630-1711) & 2/wf Mary ELIOT (-1675); 17 Apr 1662; Braintree
HOBART, Caleb (-1711) & 3/wf Elizabeth (?SHEPARD) FAXON (-1704, ae 71), w Richard; 15 Jan 1675/6; Braintree/Hingham
HUBERD, Caleb & Rachel LORING (1674-); 23 Sep 1700; Hull
HOBART, Daniel (1650-) & 1/wf Elizabeth WARREN (-1696); 11 Oct 1677; Boston
HOBART, David (1651-1717) & 1/wf Joanna QUINCY (1654-1695); Jun 1680; Hingham
HOBART, David (1651-1717) & 2/wf Sarah (CLEVERLY) JOYCE (1665-1729), w William; 4 Dec 1695; Hingham
HOBART, Edmund[1] (-1646) & 1/wf Margaret DEWEY; Hingham, Eng, 7 Sep 1600; Hingham

HOBART, Edmund[2] (1602/3-1686) & Elizabeth **ELMER** (-1675); Hingham, Eng, 18 Oct 1632; Hingham

HOBART, Edmund[1] (-1646) & 2/wf Sarah (?**OAKLEY**) **LYFORD** (-1649), w Rev. John; 10 Oct 1634; Charlestown

HOBART, Enoch (1654-) & Hannah **HARRIS**; 7 Aug 1676; Hingham/Boston

HOBART, Gershom (1645-1707) & Sarah **ALDIS** (1652-1712); 26 Apr 1675, 25 Apr; Dedham

HOBART, Israel (1647-1731) & Sarah **WETHERELL** (1645-); 30 Dec 1668; Hingham/Scituate

HOBART, Jeremiah (1631-1715, Haddam, CT) & Elizabeth **WHITING** (-1717+, Hartford); 6 Apr 1659; Topsfield/Hempstead, LI/Jamaica, LI

HOBART, John (1642-1675) & Hannah **BURR**, m/2 John **RECORD** 1677; 2 Apr 1674; Hingham

HOBART, Joshua (1614-1682) & Ellen **IBROOK** (1622-1700); Mar 1638, at Cambridge; Hingham

HOBART, Joshua (1629-1717) & 1/wf Margaret **VASSALL**; 16 Apr 1656, 25 Apr; Barbados/Southold, LI

HOBART, Joshua (1629-1717) & 2/wf Mary (**SUNDERLAND**) **RAINSFORD** (-1698), w Jonathan; 16 Jan 1671/2; Hingham

HOBART, Joshua (1650-) & Faith __?__ ; b 1684; Bridgewater

HOBART, Josiah (1634-1711) & 1/wf Priscilla [**ALLEN**] (?1634-1705), dau Bogan; b 1672; Hingham/Easthampton, NY

HOBART, Josiah (1670-) & Mary **CLEVERLY** (1669-); 21 Mar 1694/5; Braintree

HOBART, Nathaniel (1665-1734) & Mary (**BEAL**) **STOWELL** (-1748), w John; 31 May 1695; Boston

HOBART, Nehemiah (1648-1712) & Sarah **JACKSON** (?1650-1711/12); 21 Mar 1676/7; Cambridge

HOBART, Peter (1604-1679) & 1/wf Elizabeth [**IBROOK**] (1608-1645?); b 1628, in Eng; Hingham

HOBART, Peter (1604-1679) & 2/wf Rebecca [**PECK**] (1620-1693); ?1646; Hingham

HOBART, Peter (-1664/5, Barbados) & Susanna **ELLIOTT**, m/2 Thomas **DOWN/DOWNES**; 18 Dec 1662; Boston

HOBART, Peter & Deborah **HAYWARD**; 17 May 1700; Braintree

HOBART, Peter (1676-) & Elizabeth [?**CASE**]; b 1701; Southold, LI

HOBART, Samuel (1645-1718) & Hannah **GOLD/GOULD** (1644-1722); 26 Feb 1673/4; Hingham

HOBART, Solomon (1652-) & ?Frances __?__, m/2 John **BENNETT** 1688; b 1680; Hingham

HOBART, Thomas (1606-1689) & 1/wf Anne **PLOMER**; 2 Jun 1629, Wymondham, Eng; Hingham

HOBART, Thomas (1606-1689) & 2/wf Jane __?__ ; b 1649; Hingham

HOBBS, Christopher[1] (-1677) (had brother-in-law William **FOSTER**) & __?__ (-living 1666); ca 1650/2?; Saco, ME

HOBBS, Christopher[2] (-1690?) & __?__ ; ca 1670/4?; Saco, ME

HOBBS, Henry (-1698) & Hannah [**CANNEY**] (1641-); b 1661; Dover, NH

HOBBS, Henry (1670-1724) & Mary [**HOBBS**?], m/2 Jacob **REMICK**; b 1701?, b 1704, Mar 1698/9; Dover, NH

HOBBS, James (-1679) & Sarah **FIFIELD**; 31 Jul 1673; Hampton, NH

HOBBS, John (-1718) & Sarah **COLCORD**; 30 Dec 1668; Hampton, NH

HOBBS, Jonathan & Rebecca __?__ ; b 1677; Ipswich/Topsfield

HOBBS, Josiah (1649?-) & 1/wf Mary __?__ ; b 1684?, b 1685; Woburn/Lexington

HOBBS, Josiah (1649-1741) & 2/wf Tabitha __?__ ; aft 1688, bef 1699; Lexington

HOBBS, Morris/Maurice (?1615-1706) & Sarah [**ESTOW**] (?1625-1686?); b 1642; Newbury

HOBBS, Morris & Sarah **SWETT**; 13 Jun 1678; Hampton, NH

HOBBS, Morris (-1735) & Joanna [**CROMWELL**]; b 1700; Dover, NH

HOBBS, Nehemiah (-1730) & Mary **HOLMES** (-1706); Sep 1693; Hampton, NH

HOBBS, Robert & __?__ ; b 1674; Stonington, CT

HOBBS, Robert & Elizabeth **MOTT**, w Adam 1686+

HOBBS, Thomas (-1691) & __?__ ; b 20 Feb 1648/9; Topsfield/Wenham

HOBBS, William (?1642-) & Avis __?__ ; b 1671; Topsfield

HOBBS, William & Deliverance __?__ ; b 1692; Topsfield

HOBS, William & Mary **KNIGHT**; 1 Aug 1700; Topsfield

HOBBY, Sir Charles (-1715) & Elizabeth [**COLMAN**] (-1716); Boston

HOBBY, John (?1632-1707) & __?__ ; b 1657; Greenwich, CT

HOBBY, John (1661-1711, Boston) & 1/wf Hannah __?__ (-1690, ae 27); b 1685; Dorchester/Boston

HOBBY, John & 2/wf Ann [**WENSLEY**]; b 1693; Boston

HOBBY, Thomas (?1660-1742) & Rebecca [?REYNOLDS]; b 1693; Greenwich, CT
HOBBY, William & Anne _?_; b 1661; Boston
HOBSON, Henry & Mary _?_ (-1668+); Newport
HOBSON, Humphrey (1655-1684) & Elizabeth NORTHEND, m/2 Ezekiel MIGHILL 1686, m/3 Thomas GAGE 1695; 25 Jul 1683; Rowley
HOBSON, James & Elizabeth [LILLIE] (1666-); b 1687(8?); Boston
HOBSON, John (1653-1684?) & Sarah VARNUM, m/2 Philip NELSON b 1686; 4 Dec 1679; Chelmsford/Rowley
HOBSON, John & Dorcas PEARSON; 7 Sep 1699; Rowley
HOBSON, William & Ann REYNER; 12 Nov 1652; Rowley
HOBSON, William (1659-1725) & Sarah JEWETT (-1733); 9 Jun 1692; Rowley
HOCKINGTON, Thomas & Rebecca _?_; b 1686; Dedham
HODGES, Andrew (-1666, 1665?) (calls Giles BIRDLEY/BURLEY "cousin") & 1/wf Ann _?_ (-1658); b 1658; Ipswich
HODGES, Andrew (-1666) & 2/wf Lydia BROWNE (-1686), w Abraham; 27 Nov 1659; Ipswich
HODGES, Charles & Ann _?_; 1 Jul 1686; Lyme, CT
HODGES, George & 1/wf Mary HUTSON/HUDSON? (-1665); 16 Sep 1663; Salem
HODGES, George & 2/wf Sarah PHIPPEN (1645-1709+); 24 Sep 166-, betw 1665 & 1669; Salem
HODGES, Henry (1652-1717) & Hester/Esther? GALLOP (1653-); 17 Dec 1674; Taunton
HODGES, Humphrey & Mary _?_; b 1665; Charlestown/Boston
HODGES, John & Mary [MILLER?/DAVISON?], m/2 John ANDERSON 1655; ca 1633/40; Charlestown
HODGE, John (ca 1643-1692) & Susanna DENSLOW (1646-1698); 12 Aug 1666, 9 Aug; Windsor, CT/Suffield, CT
HODGES, John (?1650-1719) & Elizabeth MACY; 15 May 1672; Taunton
HODGE, John (1667-1737+) & Margaret _?_; b 1694; Windsor, CT/Killingworth, CT
HODGES, John (1673-1744) & Mercy TISDALE (1675-1749); b 1698; Taunton
HODGES, Joseph & Hannah TRUMBULL; b 1700; Guilford, CT
HODGE, Joseph (1672-1707+) & Ann _?_ (1681-); b 1701?; ?Springfield
HODGE, Nicholas & ?Seaborn [REYNOLDS/THACHER?]; b 1680; Rye, NH
HODGE/HODGES?, Robert (-1695) & Mary [PICKMAN/PITMAN], m/2 John BREWER 1689; 22 Jun 1665; Salem
HODGES, Samuel (1678-) & Experience LEONARD; 31 Dec 1700; Taunton
HODGES, Thomas & Exercise (BLACKLEACH) RAZOR/RASER (1638-), w Richard; 23 Mar 1663; Charlestown/Boston
HODGE, Thomas (1669-1712) & Judith [BUNNELL] (1672-1746), m/2 Daniel BRISTOL; b 1693?, b 1694; New Haven
HODGES/HEDGES, William (-1654) & Mary ANDREWS, m/2 Peter PITTS 1654?; ca 1648; Taunton
HODGES, _?_ (-bef 1687) & Jane _?_; b 1675; Charlestown
HODGES, _?_ & Dorcas _?_, m/2 Thomas KIRKHAM 1687+; Wethersfield, CT
HODGKINS, Christopher (-1724) & Tabitha HAYWARD/HOWARD; 29 Jan 1689; Ipswich
HODGKIN, John (-1682) & Mary BISHOP (1652-), m/2 Isaac JOHNSON 1682, m/3 _?_ FIELD; 4 Apr 1670; Guilford, CT
HODGKINS, John (-1690) & Elizabeth _?_; b 1684/[5?]; Ipswich
HODGKIN/HOTCHKIN, John & Mary HULL (-1750); 16 Mar 1696/7, no issue; Guilford, CT
HODGKINS, Samuel (1658-) & Hannah/Anna [GEE]; b 1684; Gloucester
HODGKINS, Thomas (1668-1719) & Abigail HOVEY; 12 Dec 1689; Ipswich
HODGKINS, William & [?Grace DUTCH]; b 1658; Ipswich
HODGKIN, William & Elizabeth BROWNE (?1664-); 11 Nov 1687; Newbury
HODGMAN, Josiah (-1749) (born Josiah WEBBER) & 1/wf Elizabeth _?_ (-1712); 18 May 1691; Reading
HODGMAN, Thomas & Katherin MORE; - Oct 1661; Salem
HODGMAN, Thomas (-1729) (called Joseph UNDERWOOD of Charlestown "cousin" in 1719) & Mary [MORRELL] (-1735 in 96th y), wid; 12 Aug; 1663; Reading
HODSDON/HODGDON, Alexander & 1/wf Jane [SHACKFORD]; ca 1699; Dover, NH/Newington, NH
HODSDON, Benoni (1647-1718) & Abigail [CURTIS]; ca 1670/75?; Boston/Kittery, ME

HODSDON, Israel (1646-1696) & Ann [THOMPSON], m/2 Robert EVANS; aft 4 Jul 1671; Kittery, ME

HODSDON, Israel (1674-1750/1) & Ann [WINGATE] (1667-); ca 1696; Kittery, ME

HODSDON, Jeremiah (1643, 1636?-) & Anne [THWAITS] (1650-); ca 1666/7; Dover, NH/Portsmouth, NH

HODSDON, John (±1654-1734) & Rebecca __?_ ; no ch; ?Kittery, ME/?Boston

HODSDON, Joseph (1656-bef 1691) & Tabitha [RAYNES]; ?ca 1674/8?; ?Falmouth, ME/York, ME

HODSDON, Joseph (-1764) & Margaret [GOODWIN]; Oct 1700; Kittery, ME

HODSDON, Nicholas & 1/wf Esther [WINES] (-1647); ca 1639; Charlestown/Hingham

HODSDON, Nicholas & 2/wf Elizabeth ?NEEDHAM/?WINCOLL, w John; aft 25 May 1648, b 2 Oct 1650; Kittery, ME

HODSDON, Timothy (?1652-1719) & Hannah __?_, ?m/2 __?_ SMITH; ca 1680/90; York, ME

HODSON, Daniel & Sarah SHERMAN; 20 Oct 1696; Boston

HODSHON, John (-1690) & Abigail TURNER (-1693); 2 Sep 1651; New Haven

HODSHON, John & Elizabeth TROWBRIDGE; 5 Apr 1691; New Haven

HODSHON, Nathaniel & Abigail [CHAUNCEY] (1677-), m/2 Samuel GASKELL, m/3 Edward BURROUGHS; Stratford, CT

HODGSON, Robert (-1696) & Rachel SHOTTEN; 3 Aug 1665; NY/Portsmouth, RI

HODGSON, Robert & Sarah [BORDEN]; b 1697/[8?]; Portsmouth, RI

HOGGE/HOGG/HOAG?, Richard & Joan __?_ ; b 1637; Boston

HOG, John, mariner & Eliza/Elizabeth LEWIS; 22 Feb 1699; Boston

HOLBROOK, Abel (-1747, in 94th y, Derby) & 1/wf Hannah MERWIN/MARWIN; 20 Dec 1683; Milford, CT/Derby, CT

HOLBROOK, Cornelius (1662-1742) & 1/wf Margery [EAMES?/LOWELL?]; b 1687(8?); Weymouth

HOLBROOK, Cornelius (1662-1742) & 2/wf Experience __?_ ; b 1695; Weymouth

HOLBROOK, Daniel (-1673) (son Richard) & Miriam [DRAPER], m/2 Edward JOHNSON 1675; b 1667; Dedham/Roxbury

HOLBROOK, Daniel (1671-) (Sr. in 1717/18) (son of Daniel, calls him son of John, b 1676), blacksmith & Elizabeth SEAVER (1675-); 29 May 1696; Roxbury/Lebanon, CT

HOLBROOK, Daniel³ (1676-1719) (son of John), coalminer & farmer & 1/wf Abigail CRAFT (1675-1702); 29 May 1698; Roxbury

HOLBROOK, Eleazer (1660-), Sherborn & Sarah POND (1679-); 14 Jun 1698; Dedham

HOLBROOK, Ichabod (1662-1718) & Sarah [TURNER] (1665-1739), dau John; b 1689; Weymouth/Scituate

HOLBROOK, Israel & Mary WELSH, m/2 John MERWIN 1683; 20 Dec 1677, 1680; Milford, CT

HOLBROOK, John (1618-1699) & 1/wf Sarah [FRENCH?] (-1644, 1643); ca 1640?; Weymouth

HOLBROOK, John (1618-1699, ae 82) & 2/wf Elizabeth STREAM (1624-1688, ae 64); ca 1646?; Weymouth

HOLBROOK, John² (?1639-1678, Roxbury) (son Richard) & Elizabeth HEMINGWAY (1645-), m/2 Richard HALL; 24 Nov 1663; Dorchester

HOLBROOK, John (1650-1731) & Abigail [PIERCE] (-1723, ae 77), dau Michael; b 1671?, ca 1670; Weymouth/Scituate

HOLBROOK, John (1664-1735) & Mary CHEENEY (1665-1751); 24 Sep 1684; Roxbury/Boston

HOLBROOK, John (1618-1699) & 3/wf Mary (JACOB) [OTIS], w John; aft 25 Jun 1688; Weymouth

HOLBROOK, John² (?1667-1740) & Silence [WOOD] (1676-1756); 6 Mar 1692/3; Sherborn

HOLBROOK, Nathaniel (1677-) & 1/wf Mary MORSE (1670-); b 1701; Marlboro

HOLBROOK, Pelatiah, Milford & Martha SANFORD (bpt 1671-); b 1701, ca 1692?, b 4 Apr 1704; Milford, CT

HOLBROOK, Peter³ (1655-1712) & 1/wf Alice [GODFREY] (-1705), dau Richard; b 1679; Weymouth/Mendon?

HOLBROOK, Richard (-will 1670) & 2/wf? [Agnes]/_?_ __?_, wid; b 1648?, b 1655?, b 1640?; Dorchester?/Milford, CT/Huntington, LI

HOLBROOK, Samuel (?1644, 1643-1712, ae 69) & Mary PIERCE (-1735); 23 Jun 1675, had Persis 1676, at Weymouth; Medfield/Hingham/Scituate/?Weymouth

HOLBROOK, Samuel (?1654-1695) & Lydia [FORD?] (-1745), m/2 Joseph ALLEN 1704; b 1680?, b 1684; Weymouth

HOLBROOK, Thomas[1] (ca 1589-1677) & 1/wf Jane POWYES/POWYS? (-1677+); St. John's Glastonbury, Eng, 12 Sep 1616; Weymouth

HOLBROOK, Thomas[2] (-1697) & ?Joane/?Anne [KINGMAN] (1624-1697+), Wales?; b 1653, b 1651?; Braintree/Weymouth

HOLBROOK, Thomas[1] (-1705) & 1/wf Hannah SHEPPARD (?1639-1668); 28 May 1656; Medfield

HOLBROOK, Thomas (-1728) & 1/wf Deborah __?__ ; b 1666; Weymouth

HOLBROOK, Thomas (-1705) & 2/wf Margaret (_?_) BONKER (-1690), w Edmund; 26 Jan 1668/9; Medfield/Sherborn

HOLBROOK, Thomas (?1659-) & Margaret/Mary BOWKER (-1692), wid; 20 Jan 1684; Sherborn

HOLBROOK, Thomas (?1624-1705) & 2/wf, 4/wf Mary ROGERS/WHITE? (1669?-1738), Weymouth, dau Thomas?; 21 Oct 1683, 31 Oct; Braintree

HOLBROOK, William[2] (1620-1699) & Elizabeth [PITTS] (-1701); ca 1643, b 1658, b 1655; Hingham/Weymouth/Scituate/Mendon

HOLBROOK, William (?1620-1699) & 2/wf Abigail (WRIGHT) (SHARP) [CLAPP] (-1707), w Robert, w Thomas?; aft 1679, aft 1684; Weymouth

HOLBROOK, William (1687-1714) & Margaret FAIRBANKS, m/2 Josiah THAYER 1719; 23 Jan 1683; Sherborn/Mendon

HOLBROOK, __?__ & Patience RISE, m/2 Ebenezer LELAND?; b 1691; ?Sherborn

HOLCOMB, Benajah (1644-1736/7) & Sarah ENO/ENNOS (1649-1732); 11 Apr 1667; Windsor, CT

HOLCOMB, John & __?__ ; b 1673; Springfield

HOLCOMB, Jonathan & Mary [SILLYAR]; b 1701; Simsbury, CT

HOLCOMB, Joshua (1640-1690, Simsbury) & Ruth SHERWOOD (ca 1646-1699, Simsbury); 4 Jun 1663; Windsor, CT/Simsbury

HOLCOMB, Joshua (1672-1728) & 1/wf ?Hannah CARRINGTON (no) (1675-1708?); b 1694; Simsbury, CT

HOLCOMB, Nathaniel (1648-1741) & 1/wf Mary BLISS (1651-1722?); b 1722?, 27 Feb 1670; Windsor, CT/Simsbury

HOLCOMB, Nathaniel (1673-1766) & Martha BUELL (1675-1760); 1 Nov 1695; Simsbury, CT

HOLCOMB, Thomas (-1657) & Elizabeth [?FERGUSON] (-1679?), m/2 James ENNO 1658; ca 1633?; Dorchester/Windsor, CT

HOLCOMB, Thomas (1666-1731) & 1/wf Elizabeth TERRY (-1699); 1 Jan 1689/90; Simsbury

HOLCOMB, Thomas (1666-1731) & 2/wf Rebecca PETTIBONE (1675-); 5 Dec 1700; Simsbury

HOLDEN, Charles (1666-1717) & Catharine [GREENE] (1665-); ca 1688, b 1690; Warwick, RI

HOLDEN, John & 1/wf Abigail __?__ (-1685); b 1685; Woburn

HOLDEN, John & 2/wf Sarah PIERCE (ca 1669-1717); 19 Jun 1690; Woburn

HOLDEN, John (1675-ca 1767) & Grace JENNISON (1679-); 7 Nov 1699; Watertown/?Concord

HOLDEN, John & Deborah [FABES]; by 1700, aft 14 May 1696; Dover, NH

HOLDEN, Justinian (1611-1691) & 1/wf Elizabeth __?__ (-1673); ca 1641/4, no issue; Cambridge/Billerica

HOLDEN, Justinian (1611-1691) & 2/wf Mary [RUTTER] (1647-1714+, 1716+); 1673; Cambridge/Groton

HOLDEN, Justinian (1644-) & 1/wf Mary [FREEMAN?] (-1691); b 1680; Groton/Woburn

HOLDEN, Justinian (1644-) & 2/wf Susannah (DUTTON) DURANT, w John; 6 Dec 1693; Billerica/?Cambridge

HOLDEN, Randall (1612-1692) & Frances DANGAN (?1630-1697); b 1649; RI

HOLDEN, Randall (1660-1726) & Bethiah WATERMAN (1664±-1746, 1742); 27 Jan 1687, 1686/7?; ?Warwick, RI

HOLDEN, Richard (1609-) & Martha [FOSDICK] (-1681); b 1642; Watertown/Woburn/etc.

HOLDEN, Samuel & Anna __?__ (-1731, ae 72) (grave stone in Stoneham); b 1682(3?); Groton

HOLDEN, Samuel (1674-1726) & Susanna [SHATTUCK]; b 1699; Watertown/Cambridge

HOLDEN, Stephen (1642-) & [Hannah LAWRENCE] (1664-); b 1685; Groton

HOLDER, Christopher (1631-1688, in Eng) & 1/wf Mary SCOTT (-1665); in Eng?, 12 Aug 1660; Newport

HOLDER, Christopher (1631-1688) & 2/wf Hope CLIFTON (-1680); 30 Dec 1665; Newport

HOLDER, Christopher & 3/wf Grace [BEATON]

HOLDRIDGE, John & Elizabeth PERRY; 16 Sep 1663; Dedham/Roxbury

HOLDRIDGE, Samuel & Mehitable __?__ ; b 1701; Pomfret, CT

HOLDRED, William (1610-) & Isabella __?__ (-1689); b 1640; Ipswich/Salisbury/Haverhill

HOULDREDG, William (1647-), Exeter, NH, & Lydia QUEMBY/QUINBY (1658-), ?Israel DEWEY by 1693; 10 Apr 1674; Amesbury
HOULDRIDGE, William & Deborah ELLIOT; 4 Nov 1696; Stonington, CT
HOLSWORTH/HOLDSWORTH, Joshua & Sarah ROWLINS, m/2 John KNIGHT 1683; 10 May 1669; Lynn/Boston
HOLE, John (1636?-) & Elizabeth [LEADER] (-1705); b 1668; Kittery, ME
HOLGRAVE, James & Deborah (WILLIAMS) GRAYE, w Joseph; 14 Jun 1690; Salem
HOLGRAVE, John (-1666) (had dau Lydia) & ?Elizabeth/?Lydia/?Alice __?__ (-1653+); b 1614; Salem/Gloucester
HOLGRAVE, Joshua & Jane __?__ (1611-1661), niece of Roger CONANT, m/2 Elias MASON b 1647; b 1640; Salem
HOLKINS, George & Susanna __?__; b 1698; Preston, CT
HOLLAND, Adam & Rebecca [BISHOP] (1652-); b 1687
HOLLAND, Christopher (-1704, ae 91) & Anne __?__ (1618-1714); b 1647(8?); Boston
HOLLAND, Edward & Elizabeth __?__; b 1701; Ipswich
HOLLAND, Francis & Joanna __?__; b 1686; Boston
HOLLAND, John (-1652) & Judith __?__, m/2 John KENDRICK by 1652?; b 1634, b 1637, b 1638; Dorchester
HOLLAND, John (1648-) & Sarah __?__; b 1674, b 1671; Boston
HOLLAND, John (1674-) & Elizabeth [PARK] (1674-1723); b 1699; Newton/Marlboro
HOLLAND, Joseph (1659-) & Elizabeth __?__; b 1688; Watertown
HOLLAND, Nathaniel (1631-1709+) & 1/wf Mary __?__; b 1659; Charlestown
HOLLAND, Nathaniel (1631-1709+) & 2/wf Sarah [STREETER] (1643-); b 1662; Watertown
HOLLAND, Nathaniel, Jr. (1668-1716±) & Mary [WHITE] (1670-), m/2 __?__/?Joseph ESTY; b 1692; Brookline
HOLLAND, Samuel & Mary COLLER; 9 Jan 1695, 9 Oct 1695; Marlboro/Framingham
HOLLAND, Thomas (-1687) & __?__; b 1641; Yarmouth
HOLLAND, Thomas (1670?-) & Elizabeth [?VARY]; Southampton, Eng, 1692; Newcastle
HOLLARD, Angel (-1670) & Catherine RICHARDS, m/2 John UPHAM 1671; Beaminster, Eng, 12 Aug 1634; Weymouth/Boston
HOLLARD, George & Sarah __?__; b 1664(5?); Boston
HOLLARD, George & Anne [?PHIPPS]/Anne (HARRIS) THORNTON, w William; b 1687(8?); Boston
HOLLY, Elisha (1659-1719) & Martha HOLMES (-1721); 2 Dec 1686; Stamford, CT
HOLLEY, Increase (?1646-1732, 1726/7?) & Elizabeth NEWMAN (?1654-); 2 Apr 1679; Stamford, CT
HOLLY, John (1618-1681) & Mary __?__; b 1641; Stamford, CT
HOLLEY, John (-1716) & Hannah NEWMAN (-1712); 2 Apr 1679; Stamford, CT
HOLLEY, John (-1722) & Mary CRESSY; 10 Mar 1697, prob 1696/7; Stamford, CT
HOLLY, Jonathan (1663-1712) & Sarah FINCH (1662-1751); 2 Dec 1686; Stamford, CT
HOLLEY, Richard & Joanna DOWNING, w John; 29 Oct 1663
HOLLEY, Samuel (-1643) (son John of age in ?) & Elizabeth __?__, m/2 John KENDALL 1644?; b 1618?/20?; Cambridge
HOLLY, Samuel (1641-1709) & Mary CLOSE (-1725+); 25 Jun 1668; Stamford, CT
HOLLIMAN, Ezekiel (-1659) & 1/wf Susanna OXSTON alias FOXE; in Eng; Dedham/Salem/Warwick, RI
HOLLIMAN, Ezekiel (-1659) & 2/wf Mary [SWEET], w John; ca 1638; Providence, RI/Warwick, RI
HOLLINGSHEAD, John & Grace __?__; in Eng, b 1675; Salem/Burlington, NJ
HOLLINGSWORTH, Richard (1595-1654) & Susan [WOODBURY]/HUNTER? (1605-); b 1628; Salem
HOLLINGSWORTH, Richard & Elizabeth POWELL, dau Michael, m/2 Robert BRYAN 1685+, m/3 Robert TREAT 1705; 23 Aug 1659; Salem/Boston/Milford, CT
HOLLINGSWORTH, William (1628-1677, 1689?) & Ellen/Eleanor [?STORY] (-1690); b 1655; Salem
HOLLINGSWORTH, __?__ & Sarah HILLIARD, m/2 __?__ CONNOWAY of Boston; b 22 Feb 1674/5
HOLLIS, John (-1700) & Elizabeth [PRIEST]; b 1664; Weymouth
HOLLIS, John (1664-) & Mary [?YARDLEY]; b 1691; Weymouth/Braintree
HOLLIS, William (-1695) & Kertland [PELUD]; b 1672; Salem

HOLLISTER, John[1] (?1612-1665) & ?Joanna TREAT (1618-1694); say 1639, b 1640?, Apr 1641?; Wethersfield, CT

HOLLISTER, John (1642, 1644-1711), Glastonbury & Sarah GOODRICH (1649-1700); 20 Nov 1667; Wethersfield, CT

HOLLISTER, John (1669-1741) & 1/wf Abiah HOLLISTER (1672-1719), Wethersfield; 7 Jun 1693; Wethersfield, CT

HOLLISTER, Jonathan (ca 1676-1712) & Elizabeth WILLIAMS (1677-1724+); 22 Sep 1698; Wethersfield, CT

HOLLISTER, Joseph (1674-1746) & 1/wf Ann [BURNHAM] (ca 1679-1712, in 34th y); 27 Nov 1694, Wethersfield, CT

HOLLISTER, Stephen (1658-1709) & 1/wf Abigail [TREAT] (1659-1702?, ca 1704); b 1684(5?); Wethersfield, CT

HOLLISTER, Thomas (1645-1701) & 1/wf Elizabeth LATIMER (1652-); b 1672, ca 1669; Wethersfield, CT

HOLLISTER, Thomas & 2/wf Elizabeth [WILLIAMS], w Amos; ca 1690, aft 1683; Wethersfield, CT

HOLLISTER, Thomas (1672-1741) & Dorothy HILLS (ca 1678-1741); Josiah b ?7 Jun 1696, b 1696, ch b Glastonbury, no date of m, ca 1695; Wethersfield, CT

HOLLOWAY, Adam (-1733, ae 80) & Hannah (HAYWARD) FARRAR (1647-), w Jacob; 5 Mar 1680-1; Concord

HALLAWELL, Benjamin & Mary STOCKER; 12 May 1691; Boston

HALLOWAY, Elisha (bpt 7 Apr 1650-1678) & Mary _?_ ; b 23 Aug 1679; Taunton

HOLLOWAY, Jacob (-1711) (had son Curtis H-) & Mary [CURTIS]?; b 1694; Boston/Watertown/New London, CT

HALLOWAY, John (-1684) & Mary _?_ ; 1663, ?div 1667; Hartford

HALLAWAY, John & Mary GRANT; 2 Feb 1692; Boston

HOLLOWAY, Joseph (1605-1647) & Rose [ALLEN] (sister George?), m/2 William NEWLAND 1648; b 1641; Dorchester/Sandwich

HOLLOWAY, Joseph (-1693) & _?_ ; b 1653, by 1650?; Lynn

HOLLOWAY/HOLLEY, Joseph & Mary [HULL]; 1661?, b 1664; Sandwich

HOLLOWAY, Joseph & Mary _?_ ; b 1673; Lynn

HOLWAY/HOLLOWAY, Joseph & Ann _?_ ; b 1694; Sandwich

HOLLAWAY, Joseph & Bethiah WITT; m int 7 Oct 1699; Lynn

HOLLOWAY, Michael/Malachi & Elizabeth [SHOVE]; b 1692?; Taunton

HOLLOWAY, Nathaniel (1670-) & Deliverance [BABBITT/BOBBETT] (1673-); b 1701?, 13 Mar 1699/1700; Taunton

HOLLOWAY, Samuel (-1702/7) (son William) & Jane BRAYMAN; 26 Mar 1666; Taunton

HOLLOWAY, William (1586-1653) & Grace _?_, m/2 John PHILLIPS 1654; by 1650?, ca 1645?; Plymouth/Marshfield

HOLLOWAY, William (?1586-1665, Boston) & 1/wf Elizabeth/Hannah _?_, dau Benjamin?; 4 ch bpt 1650, by 1627; Taunton?/Dorchester/Boston

HALEWELL, William (1625-1702, ae 77 y) & 1/wf Mary WARD (-1658, 1656+, 24 Jan 1657/8); ca 1652; Dorchester/Boston

HOLLOWAY, William (-1702) & 2/wf Elizabeth _?_ (-1680?); b 1659; Boston

HOLLOWAY, William & Decline _?_ ; b 1673; Boston/Roxbury

HOLMAN, Abraham (-1711, Stow) & Sarah PITTS (1639-1714+), dau Edmund; 21 Feb 1662/3; Hingham/Stow/Cambridge

HOLMAN, Abraham & Susanna [TARBELL?], d Thomas; b 1697; Cambridge

HOLMAN, Edward & Amy (GLASSE) [WILLIS], w Richard; b 1645; Plymouth

HOLMAN, Edward (1647?-) & Richard [sic] [HOOPER]/BRIMBLECOME? (1646-); ca 1665?, ca 1670?; Marblehead

HOMAN, Edward & Elizabeth GOLD; 27 Oct 1692; Marblehead

HOLLIMAN/HOLYMAN, Ezekiel (-1659) & 1/wf Susanna [OXSTON] alias FOXE; in Eng, b 1638; Dedham/Salem/Providence

HOLLIMAN/HOLYMAN, Ezekiel (-1659) & 2/wf Mary [SWEET], w John; 1638?; Providence

HOLMAN, Gabriel (-1691) & Mary [DIXEY] (1645-1680+); ?Marblehead

HOLMAN, Jeremiah (1629-1709) & 1/wf Mercy [PRATT], dau Phineas; b 1663?, b 1667; Cambridge

HOLMAN, Jeremiah (1670-1739) & Abigail _?_ (1672-1746); b 1695; Sudbury/Stow

HOLMAN, Jeremiah (1629-1709) & 2/wf Susanna _?_; b 6 May 1703, prob aft 1700; Cambridge
HOLMAN, John (-1652/3) & 1/wf Anne [?BISHOP] (-1639); b 1637(8?); Dorchester
HOLMAN, John (1603-1652/3) & 1/wf? 2/wf Anne [BISHOP?] (1616-1673), m/2 Rev. Henry
    BUTLER 1655?; b 1641; Dorchester
HOLMAN, John (-1700+) & Mary [BLANTON] (1645-), dau of Wm. & Phebe; b 1667; Boston
HOLMAN/HOMAN?, John & Mary BEAL; 5 Dec 1695; Marblehead
HOLMAN, Joseph & Hannah _?_; b 1671; Boston
HOLMAN, Samuel (1646-1689) & Rachel [BATEMAN] (1651-); b 1671; Boston
HOLMAN, Samuel & Sarah TREBY?; 5 Nov 1696; Marblehead
HOMAN, Solamon/Solomon (1671/2-1753) & 1/wf Mary [BARTON] (-1736, ae 63); b 1695, b
    1694?; Newbury
HOLMAN, Thomas (1641-1704) & Abigail RIGBY (1645-1703); 19 Feb 1663/4, 19 Dec 1663;
    Dorchester/Milton
HOLMAN, William (1595-1653) & Winifred _?_ (-1671, ae 74); in Eng, b 1626, ?Northampton,
    Eng; Cambridge
HOMAN, John? & Anna [BARTLETT?]; b 1684, 3 ch bpt 1688; Marblehead
HOLMES, Abraham (1641-1722) & 1/wf [Elizabeth] [ARNOLD] (-1690, 1692); b 1666;
    Marshfield/Rochester
HOLMES, Abraham & 2/wf Abigail NICHOLS; 19 Apr 1695; Hingham
HOLMES/HIMS, David (-1666) & Joan _?_, m/2 John McINTOSH 1668?; 18 Apr 1659;
    Dorchester/Milton
HOLMES, David (1668-) & Ruth _?_; b 1693
HOLMES, Ebenezer (1669-1746) & 1/wf Sarah (LEADBETTER) WITHINGTON (1659-1696), w
    Henry; 2 Feb 1692, 1692/3; Boston/Dorchester
HOLMES, Ebenezer & Phebe BLACKMUR/BLACKMER?/BLACKMORE? (1672-); 26 Dec 1695;
    Plymouth
HOLMES, Ebenezer (1669-1746) & 2/wf Mary (WALES) GEORGE, w Nicholas; 5 Aug 1697;
    Dorchester
HOLMES, Elisha & Sarah BARTLET/BARTLETT; 2 Sep 1695; Plymouth
HOLMES, Ephraim & Mary [HARLOW]; 1692; Plymouth
HOLMES, Francis (1600-1675) & Ann _?_; b 1634; Stamford, CT
HOLMES, Francis & Rebecca WHARFE; 15 Feb 1693, 1693/4; Boston
HOLMES, George (1594-1645?, 1646?) & 1/wf? 2/wf? [Deborah] _?_ (-1663?, 1641?); b 1635?,
    b 1640?; Roxbury
HOLMES, George & _?_; b 1687; CT
HOLMES, Isaac (Israel is wrong) (1644-) & Anna ROWSE/ROUSE; - Apr 1677, 1678?; Marshfield
HOLMES, Isaac (1674-) & Mary [ALLERTON]; b 1701?; Kingston
HOLMES, Israel (-1685) & Desire (DOTY) SHERMAN (1645-), w William, m/3 Alexander
    STANDISH 1686?; 24 Nov 1681; Marshfield
HOLMES, Israel & Elizabeth [TURNER]; b 1701?; Scituate
HOLMES, James (1663?-), Worcester (son David) & Jane STEPHENS, Worcester; 26 Jan 1687/8,
    ca 1689; Marlboro/Woodstock, CT
HOLMES, James & Martha WHIGHT/WHITE; 1 Feb 1692; Ipswich
HOLMES, Jeremiah & Sarah WALKER; 22 Sep 1689; Dover, NH
HOLMES, John (-1667) & Sarah _?_ (-1650, Plymouth?); ca 1633?; Plymouth
HOLMES, John (?1639-1729) & Rachel WATERBURY (1639-1642); 11 May 1659, 12 May 1659;
    Stamford, CT
HOLMES, John (-1697) & Patience FAUNCE; 20 Nov 1661; Plymouth/Duxbury
HOLMES, John (-1675) & Mary ATWOOD?/WOOD? (-1715), m/2 William BRADFORD; 11 Dec
    1661; Plymouth
HOLMES, John (1639-) & Hannah THATCHER; 13 Sep 1664; Watertown/Cambridge
HOMES, John (see Nathaniel) (-1676) & Sarah [WISWALL?] (?1643-1676+, 1717?), m/2 Obadiah
    HAWES ca 1677; b 1665; Dorchester/Roxbury
HOLMES, John (1635-1710+) & _?_; b 1675, b 1660; Bedford, NY
HOLMES, John (1637-) & Martha [WALFORD]; b 1666; Portsmouth, NH
HOLMES, John & Mary [BEVERLY] (1645?, 1643-); b 1666
HOLMES, John (1649-1712) & 1/wf Frances HOLDEN (1649-1679); 1 Dec 1671; Warwick,
    RI/Newport

HOLMES, John (-1718) & Sarah (FARR?) KENE/KEENEY/KENNEY, w John; 21 Apr 167-, 1672; Salem

HOLMES, John & Sarah [BROUGHTON] (1658-); b 1678; Deerfield

HOLMES, John (1649-1712, ae 63), Newport & Mary (SAYLES) GREEN (1652-), w William; 12 Oct 1680; Warwick, RI/Newport

HOLMES, John (-1728), Middletown & 1/wf Sarah [THOMAS] (-1700); b 1690, 13 Feb [1686/90]; Plymouth

HOLMES, John (1664-1713) & Hannah NEWEL (1671-1743); 9 Apr 1690; Roxbury/Woodstock, CT

HOLMES, John & Elizabeth [GATES] (1671-1726); ca 1690; Stow/Preston, CT/Colchester, CT

HOLMES, John & Margett/Margaret? _?_; b 1694; Boston

HOLMES, John (1660-) & Sarah [CHURCH?] (1674-); b 1697; Bedford, NY

HOLMES, John & Mary [ABBOT?]; b 1700(1701?); Kittery, ME

HOLMES, John (1672-1748) & Mary [TAYER?]/[THAYER?]; b 1701?, Jul 1701; RI

HOLMES, Jonas & Sarah _?_; 11 May 1692; Wethersfield, CT

HOLMES, Jonathan (-1713) & Sarah [BORDEN] (1644-1705, 1708?); ?20 Dec 1667, May 1664?, 1664/5; RI?/Middletown, NJ/Newport

HOLMES, Jonathan & Dorothy _?_ (bef 1688)

HOLMES, Joseph & [Elizabeth CLAPP] (1638-1711); b 1661, ca 1660; Dorchester

HOLMES, Joseph (see Thomas HOLMES) & Joane [FREETHE]; b 1671; York, ME

HOLMES, Joseph (1665-1733) & 1/wf [Sarah] [SPRAGUE] (1666-); ca 1687/93?; Kingston, RI

HOLMES, Joseph (1665-1733) & 2/wf Mary [BREWSTER] (1679-1717); b 1697, b 1696; Plymouth

HOLMES, Joseph (-1704) & Ann [GOLDING]; b 1697?, b 1690; ?Staten Is., NY/Gravesend?

HOLMES, Joshua (-1694) & Abigail (INGRAHAM) CHESEBROUGH, w Samuel, m/3 James AVERY 1698; 5 Jun 1675, 15 Jun 1675, 16 Jun?; Stonington, CT

HOLMES, Joshua (1678-1729) & Fear STURGIS (1681-1753); 21 Nov 1698; Stonington, CT

HOLMES, Josiah[2] & Hannah SAMSON; 20 Mar 1665, 1665/6; Duxbury

HOLMES, Josiah (1672-) & _?_; b 1701?; Rochester

HOLMES, Nathaniel (see John) & 1/wf Sarah [WISWALL?] (1643-); b [1666]; Plymouth

HOLMES, Nathaniel (1639-1713) & 2/wf Patience TOPLIFF (1644-1697); 27 Mar 1667; Dorchester/Roxbury

HOLMES, Nathaniel (-1727, ae 84) & Mercy FAUNCE (1651-1732); 29 Dec 1667; Plymouth

HOLMES, Nathaniel (1664-1711) & Sarah THAXTER, m/2 John CUSHING; 1 Oct 1691; Boston/Hingham

HOLMES, Nathaniel & Joanna CLARK; 21 Dec 1698; Plymouth

HOLMES, Nathaniel & Eleanor BACOR/BAKER?/RACER; 13 Mar 1700, 1700/1701?; Plymouth

HOLMES, Obadiah (?1607, ?1610-1682) & Katherine HYDE (-1682+); in Eng, Manchester, 20 Nov 1630; Salem/Rehoboth/Newport

HOLMES, Obadiah (1644-) & Elizabeth [COOKE?]/[COLE?]; b 1668/9?; Gravesend, LI/Middletown, NJ

HOLMES, Richard & Alice [NORTHEND?]; 23 Aug 1647; Rowley

HOLMES, Richard (ca 1637?-1704) & Sarah [GRANT] (-1706); b 1672, (b 1654?); Norwalk, CT

HOLMES, Richard & Mary _?_ (1671-); b 1694; Bedford, NY

HOLMES, Robert (-1663) & Jane _?_ (-1653); b 1638; Cambridge

HOLMES, Robert (did he come to N. E.?) & _?_; b 1655; Stonington, CT

HOMES, Robert (-1673) & Esther/Hester? MORSE (1651-), m/2 Thomas SMITH; 26 Feb 1668, 1668/9; Newbury/Ipswich

HOLMES, Samuel (-1679) & Ales/Alice/Abigail STILWELL (1645-), m/2 William OSBORN, m/3 Daniel LAKE 1684?; 26 Oct 1665; Gravesend, LI

HOLMES, Samuel & _?_; b 1674; Rehoboth

HOLMES, Samuel & Lydia _?_; b 1677; Boston

HOLMES, Samuel & Mary _?_; b 1682; Boston

HOLMES, Samuel (-1690?) & Mary _?_; b 1686; Marshfield

HOLMES, Samuel & 1/wf Mary BULLARD; 26 Dec 1696; Dedham

HOLMES, Stephen (-1710) & _?_ (-1728); b 1670; Stamford, CT

HOLMES, Stephen (-1710) & Mary HOBBY; 18 Nov 1686; Stamford, CT/Greenwich

HOLMES, Thomas (-1724) & Lucretia/Lucia DUDLEY (-1689); b 1686(7?); New London

HOLMES, Thomas (-1691) & Joanna [FREATHY]; b 1671?, by 1671; Kittery, ME

HOLMES, Thomas & Joanna MORTON; 6 Jan 1696/7; Plymouth

HOLMES, Thomas & Elizabeth (DAWES) [POLL/POOLE] (1661-), w Edward POLL; b 1798(9?); Boston

HOLMES, William[1] (1592, 1600?-1678, ae 86) & Elizabeth __?__ (1603/4-1689, in 86th y, 1698?); ca 1634/6?; Scituate/Duxbury

HOLMES, __?__ & Patience (BONUM) [WELLES], w Richard; b 6 Aug 1699

HOLT, Eleazer & 1/wf Tabitha THOMAS (1653-1725); 5 Nov 1674; New Haven

HOLT, George (1677-1748) & 1/wf Elizabeth FARNUM; 10 May 1698; Andover

HOLT, Henry (1644-1719) & Sarah BALLERD/BALLARD (-1733); 24 Feb 1669, 1669/70; Andover

HOLT, Henry (1673-1751) & Martha [MARSTON] (-1754, ae 76); ca 1700; Andover

HOLT, James (1651-1690) & Hannah ALLEN (-1698); 12 Oct 1675; Andover

HOLT, John & Elizabeth THOMAS (1648-); Jan 1673; New Haven

HOLT, John (-1687) & Sarah GEERY/[GARY], m/2 John PRESTON 1687; 3 Jul 1685; Andover

HOLT, Joseph (1655-1697) & Elizabeth FRENCH (1664-1739); 20 Nov 1684; Wallingford, CT

HOLT, Nathaniel (1647-1723) & 1/wf Rebecca BEEBE (-1689); 5 Apr 1680; New London/Newport

HOLT, Nathaniel & 2/wf __?__ ; aft Mar 1689; ?Newport

HOLT, Nicholas (?1602-1685) & 1/wf Elizabeth [SHORT] (-1656); b 1636, b 1632; Boston/Newbury/Andover

HOLT, Nicholas (-1685) & 2/wf Hannah (BRADSTREET) ROFE/ROLFE (1625-1665), w Daniel; at Ipswich, 12 Jun 1658, 20 Jun; Andover

HOLT, Nicholas (-1685) & 3/wf [Martha] (__?__) PRESTON (1623-1703), w Roger; 21 Mar 1666; Andover

HOLT, Nicholas (1647-1715) & Mary RUSSELL (-1717); 8 Jan 1679; Andover

HOLT, Oliver (1672-1747) & 1/wf Hannah RUSSELL (1679-1715); 9 Mar 1697/8; Andover

HOLT, Richard & Lydia WORMWOOD; 10 May 1693; Bridgewater

HOLT, Samuel (1641-1703) & Sarah [ALLEN] (1646-1716); b 1670; Andover

HOLT, Samuel & Hannah FARNUM/FARNHAM?; 28 Mar 1693; Andover

HOLT, William (1610-1683) & Sarah __?__ (-1717), m/2 William PECK; b 1645; New Haven

HOLTON, Benjamin (-1689) & [Sarah] __?__ , m/2 Benjamin PUTNAM 1706; b 1689; Salem

HOLTON, Henry & Abigail FLINT (1668-); 4 Mar 1688?, 1689?, 1688/9; Salem

HOLTON, James (1665-) & 1/wf Ruth [FELTON]; b 1685; Salem

HOULTON, John (1640-1712) (born HORTON son of Thomas, Springfield) & Abigail FISHER (1649-1718+); 1 Mar 1666/7; Dedham

HOLTON, John & Mary STAR/[STARR], m/2 John REA; 16 Jan 1688; Salem

HOLTON, Joseph & Sarah (INGERSOLL) HAYNES, w William; 13 Nov 1651; Newbury

HOLTON, Joseph & Hannah [ABORNE/EBORNE]; b 1678; Salem

HOLTON, Joseph (1673-1708) & Susanna __?__ ; b 1701?, b 1708; Boston

HOULTON, Robert & Ann __?__ , m/2 Richard WALKER; b 1634; Boston

HOLTON, Samuel (1646-1730), Northampton & Mary (GILBERT) ROSSITER, w John (div in 1681); Hartford, 21 Jun 1673, 24 Jun 1673, no issue; Northampton

HOLTON, Samuel (1646-1730), Northampton & 2/wf Abigail __?__ (-1732)

HOLTON, William (1610-1691) & Mary __?__ (-1691?, 1708); b 1639, 1636, 1638?; Hartford/Northampton

HOLTON, William (-1711) & Sarah MARSHFIELD (1656-1711), Springfield; 22 Nov 1676; ?Springfield/Northampton

HOLYOKE, Rev. Edward (-1660) (returned to Eng?) & 1/wf Prudence STOCKTON, Kinholt, Eng; Tamworth, 18 Jun 1612; Lynn

HOLYOKE, Elizur/Eleazer (ca 1616-1676) & 1/wf Mary PYNCHON (-1657); 20 Nov 1640; Springfield

HOLYOKE, Elizur/Eleazer (ca 1616-) & 2/wf Editha (STEBBINS) (DAY) [MAYNARD], w Robert, w John; ca 1658; Springfield

HOLYOKE, Elizur/Eleazer (1651-1711) & Mary ELIOT (1655-1721); ?2 Jan 1677/8, 1677; ?Boston

HOLYOKE, Edward (relative of Thomas MORRIS and Mary, wife of John MANSFIELD) & 2/wf Ann (TAYLOR) [TUTTLE], w Richard; b 1648

HOMAN, John & __?__ ; b 1693; LI

HOMAN, Mordecai & Esther __?__ , ?m/2 Caleb HORTON; b 1681, b 1669; Southold, LI

HOMAN, John? & Anna BARTLETT; Marblehead

HOMER, John (-1717, ae 70?) & Margery STEPHENS (-1762); 13 Jul 1693; Boston
HOMER, Michael & Hannah [DOWSE]? (-28 Apr 1693); b 1693; Boston
HOMER, Michael & Mary BURROUGHS, ?m/2 Christopher HALL 1700; 13 Jul 1693; Boston/Cambridge
HOMES, William (-1746) & Katharine CRAIGHEAD/CRAGHEAD? (-1754); in Ireland, 26 Sep 1693, 21 Sep; Martha's Vineyard
HOOD, John & Elizabeth _?_ ; in Eng, b 1625?; Lynn
HOOD, John (1664-) & Sarah [BREED] (1667-1744+); b 1694; Lynn
HOOD, Joseph (1674-1729, Copp's Hill Cem) & Mary [WATERS?]; b 1699; Boston
HOOD, Richard (ca 1625-1695) & Mary [NEWHALL]; ca 1652?; Lynn
HOOD, Richard (1655-1696) & Hannah [BERRY] (1668-), m/2 Edmund NEEDHAM; b 1690; Lynn
HOOD, Samuel (1667-) & Deborah THWING; 17 Jul 1692; Boston
HOOKE, Francis (-1695) & Mary (MAVERICK) PALSGRAVE (-1706), w John; 20 Sep 1660, no issue; Boston/Kittery, ME
HOOKE, Humphrey (1676-1741) & Judith MARCH (1682-); 10 Jul 1700; Newbury
HOOKE, William (1601-1677) (returned to Eng) & Jane [WHALLEY]; in Eng, ca 1624/30?; Taunton/New Haven
HOOKE, William (-1654) & Eleanor (?KNIGHT) [NORTON], w Walter; b 1636; York Co., ME
HOOK, William (-1721) & Elizabeth [DYER] (-1717); in Eng, b 1668; Salisbury
HOOKE, William & 1/wf Mary (FOLLANSBEE) [PIKE], w Robert; b 1693, ca 1691; Salisbury
HOOKER, James (1666-1740?) & Mary LEETE; 1 Aug 1691; Guilford, CT/Farmington, CT
HOOKER, John (1665-1746) & Abigail STANDLEY/STANLEY (1669-1743); 24 Nov 1687; Farmington, CT
HOOKER, Joseph & Anna _?_ ; b 1692, Wenham
HOOKER, Joseph & Mary DYER; 28 Dec 1699; Marblehead
HOOKER, Matthew & Rachel _?_ ; b 1678; Ipswich
HOOKER, Nathaniel (1671-1711) & Mary STANLEY (1677-), m/2 John AUSTIN; 22 Dec 1698, 28 Dec 1698, 23 Dec 1698; Farmington, CT/Windsor, CT
HOOKER, Samuel (1633-1697) & Mary WILLETT (?1637, 1643-1712), m/2 Thomas BUCKINGHAM 1703; 22 Sep 1658; Plymouth/Farmington, CT
HOOKER, Samuel (1661-1730) & Mehitable HAMLIN (1664-), Middletown; 28 Jun 1687; ?Middletown, CT/Farmington, CT
HOOKER, Thomas (?1586-1647) (called "uncle" by Leonard CHESTER 1648) & Susan/Susanna GARBRAND, m/2 William GOODWIN, m/3 John SHEPARD; Amersham, Bucks, Eng, 3 Apr 1621; Hartford
HOOKER, Thomas (1659-1720) & Mary (SMITH) [LORD] (-1702), w Richard; aft 5 Nov 1685, 1686?; Hartford
HOOKER, William (1663-1689) & Susanna [FENN] (1669-), m/2 John BLACKLEACH by 1693; b 1689; Farmington, CT
HOOKIE, Nicholas & Mary BREDSHAW (-1678); 17 Dec 1673; Charlestown
HOOKEY, Stephen (1674-) & Sarah _?_ ; b 1701; Newport
HOOPER, Benjamin (1656/7-1718) & Eleanor CLARK; 20 Jul 1681, ?21 Jul; Salem
HOOPER, Edward (1678-) & Susanna [HASKINS]; b 1701?
HOOPER, Francis & Julian HOLWAYE?; in Eng, Nov 1642?
HOOPER, George & Mary [PRECIOUS]; b 1673; Boston
HOOPER, Henry & Mary (COLLINS) NORMAN, w Joseph; 15 Mar 1691/2; Marblehead
HOOPER, John (1641-) & Christian [CONDY?] (1645-); ca 1663; Marblehead
HOOPER/HOPPER?, John (-1669) & Elizabeth _?_ ; b 1666/(7?); Boston
HOOPER, John & Mary LITCHFIELD; 27 Jan 1690; Boston
HOOPER, John & Abigail [HILLIARD] (1662-); b 1694(5?), b 1690(1?); Marblehead
HOOPER, John (-1709) & Sarah HARDEN/(VARDEN?), m/2 Francis WOOD; b 1697; Bridgewater
HOOPER, John & Charity [KAY]; b 1701(2?); Kittery, ME
HOOPER, Richard (-1690) & Elizabeth _?_ ; b 1683; Hampton, NH/Watertown
HOOPER, Robert & Elizabeth [?FLETCHER]; b 1641; Marblehead
HOUPER, Robert & Anna GREENFIELD/GRINFIELD, m/2 William POTE 1689; 4 Dec 1684; Marblehead
HOOPER, Samuel & Elizabeth _?_ ; b 1683; Boston
HOOPER, Samuel (-1710?) & Mary (HEWES) WHITE (1667-), w Richard, m/3 John PERKINS; 16 Feb 1693; Boston/Marblehead

HOOPER, Thomas (1660-) & Elizabeth [SMALL]; b 1694; Kittery, ME/York, ME
HOOPER, Thomas (1668-) & Elizabeth [RICHARDS]; b 1708, b 1701?; Medfield
HOOPER, William & 1/wf Elizabeth [MARSHALL?] (Thomas BANCROFT, a relative called Capt.
Thomas MARSHALL (brother) "cousin"); b 1647; Reading
HOOPER, William & 2/wf Ruth [?MARSHALL], m/2 Thomas DUTTON 1684; b 14 Dec 1664,
prob b 1658; Reading
HOOPER, William (-1679, ae 30) & Elizabeth _?_; b 1672, ca 1668; Beverly
HOOPER, William (-1692) & Susannah [SHEDD?] (1662-), m/2 Benjamin DUTTON 1693?; b
1687; Reading
HOOPER, William & Abigail MANSFIELD (1668-); 9 Dec 1697; Marblehead?/Salem?
HOOPER, William & Priscilla BAKER; 5 Apr 1698; Beverly
HOPKINS, Benjamin (1671-) & Mehitable _?_; b 1693/[4?]; Boston
HOPKINS, Caleb (1651-1728) & Mary [WILLIAMS]; ca 1683; Eastham/Truro
HOPKINS, Charles & Margaret [HENCHMAN]; b 1663; Boston
HOPKINS, Ebenezer (?1668-1711) & Mary BUTLER (?1670-1744); 21 Jan 1691, 1691/2?;
Hartford, CT/Wethersfield, CT
HOPKINS, Edward (1600-1657, in Eng) & Ann [YALE] (?1615-1698); b 1648; Hartford/Boston
HOPKINS, Giles (-1690) & Katharine WHELDON (-1689+); 9 Oct 1639; Plymouth/Yarmouth
HOPKINS, Ichabod (1669-1730) & Sarah [COLES] (-1723); b 12 Sep 1693; Oyster Bay, LI
HOPKINS, John (-1654) & Jane _?_, m/2 Nathaniel WARD, m/3 Gregory WOLTERTON; b 1634;
Cambridge/Hartford, CT
HOPKINS, John (?1662-1732) & Hannah [STRONG?] (1660-1730); b 1689; Waterbury, CT
HOPKINS, John & Sarah _?_; b 1690; Newcastle
HOPKINS, Joseph (?1650-1674) & Elizabeth [?ARNOLD], m/2 Richard KIRBY; b 1668;
Providence
HOPKINS, Joseph (-1690), Boston & Ruth LONG (-1719); 1 Dec 1686; Charlestown
HOPKINS, Joseph & 1/wf Phebe _?_; b 1696/[7?]; E. Greenwich, RI
HOPKINS, Joseph (-1712) & Hannah PECK, m/2 John PORTER; 27 Apr 1699; Hartford
HOPKINS, Joseph & 2/wf Martha [WHALEY] (1680-1773); ?ca 1699, b 1704; E. Greenwich,
RI/Kingston, RI
HOPKINS, Joshua (1657-1738±) & Mary COLE (1658-1734); 26 May 1681; Eastham
HOPKINS, Samuel (returned to Eng) & Hannah TURNER; 5 Dec 1667; New Haven/Milford, CT
HOPKINS, Samuel (-1738) & Susanna _?_ (-1732+); ca 1697; Kingston, RI
HOPKINS, Stephen (-1644) & 1/wf _?_; in Eng, ca 1605?; Plymouth
HOPKINS, Stephen (-1644) & 2/wf Elizabeth FISHER (-by 1651); London, 19 Feb 1617/18;
Plymouth
HOPKINS, Stephen (?1634-1689) & Dorcas [BRONSON] (ca 1639-1697); ?ca 1657; Hartford
HOPKINS, Stephen (1642-1718) & 1/wf Mary MERRICK (1650-bef 1701); 23 May 1667; Eastham
HOPKINS, Stephen (1663-1703) & 1/wf Sarah JUDD (1665-1693); 17 Nov 1686; Hartford/Water-
bury, CT
HOPKINS, Stephen (1670-1723) & Sarah HOWES (1673-), m/2 Joseph HAWES; 19 May 1692;
Eastham/Harwich
HOPKINS, Stephen (see John HOPKINS) (-1703) & Hannah [?STRONG] (1660-1745); aft 11 May
1693; Windsor, CT
HOPKINS, Thomas (?1616-1684) & Elizabeth [?ARNOLD] (1611-); b 1648; Providence/Oyster
Bay, LI
HOPKINS, Thomas (-1698) & Sarah _?_ (-1699+); ?b 1666; Providence
HOPKINS, Thomas (-1718) & Mary SMITH (-1718+); m int 1 Apr 1678; Providence
HOPKINS, William (-1644) & Mary _?_, m/2 Richard WHITEHEAD; in Eng, ca 1623; Stratford,
CT/Hadley/?Farmington
HOPKINS, William (-1688) & Hannah/Susannah [ANDREWS] (-1679); ca 1655; Roxbury
HOPKINS, William (1647-1723) (kinsman of Abraham MANN) & Abigail (WHIPPLE) DEXTER, w
Stephen; Jan 1681; Providence
HOPKINS, William & Sarah HARRIS; 31 Dec 1685; Marblehead
HOBKINS, William & Deborah _?_; b 1695; Reading/Billerica
HOPKINSON, Caleb (1649-) & 1/wf Sarah WALLINGFORD (-1682); 25 Nov 1679; Bradford
HOPKINSON, John (1647-) & Elizabeth PEARSON; 8 Jun 1670; Rowley
HOPKINSON, Jonathan (1643-) & 1/wf Hester CLARKE; 11 May 1666; Rowley
HOPKINSON, Jonathan (1643-) & 2/wf Elizabeth DRESSER; 10 Jun 1680; Rowley

HOPKINSON, Michael (1610-1649) & Ann [?GOTT], m/2 John TRUMBLE 1650, m/3 Richard SWAN 1659; b 1641; Rowley

HOPKINSON, Michael/?Mighill (1674-) & 1/wf Sarah COLLMAN/COLEMAN (1670-); 16 Jun 1696; Rowley

HOPPER, John & Elizabeth __?__; b 1669; Boston

HOPPER, William & Mary __?__; b 1685(6?); Boston

HOPPER, John & __?__; b 1698; Flushington, LI

HOPPER, Christopher & __?__; b 1698; Flushington, LI

HOPPIN, Stephen & Hannah [MAKEPEACE]; ca 1647, 1650?; Roxbury

HOPPIN, Matthias & Mary DIAMENT; 20 Jun 1700, ?20 Aug 1699; East Hampton, LI

HOPPIN, Nicholas & Susanna [JACKLIN]; b 1700; Charlestown

HOPPIN, John & Rebecca [SMITH] (-1715, ca 75), w Roger; ca 1673; East Hampton, LI

HOPSON, John & 1/wf Sarah __?__ (-1669); b 1666, b 1665; Guilford, CT

HOPSON/HOBSON?, John & 2/wf Elizabeth SHIPTON/SHIPMAN (-1683); 3 Dec 1672, ?9 Dec 1672; Saybrook, CT/Guilford, CT

HOPSON, John (-1701) & 3/wf Elizabeth [ALLING]; b 1684; ?New Haven/Guilford, CT

HOBSON, John (1665-1730), Guilford & 1/wf Dorothy LORD (-1705), Saybrook; 28 Feb 1699/1700; Guilford, CT

HORNE (now ORNE), Benjamin (1636-1702) & Sarah [ABORNE]; b 1684, ?27 Jan 1680/1; Salem/Lynn

HORNE, Humphrey & __?__; in Eng, b 25 Feb 1650/1

HORNE, John[1] & 1/wf Ann/Anna? __?__; b 1636; Salem

HORNE, John[1] (-1684) & 2/wf Frances (STONE) [GREENE], w Henry; ca Dec 1648; Salem

HORNE/ORNE, John & 1/wf Mary CLARKE (1645-); 30 Oct 1667; Salem

HORNE, John (-1697) & Mary HAM (1668-), m/2 John WALDRON 1698; 30 Jun 1686; Dover, NH

HORNE, John & Naomi __?__; b 1693, aft 19 Jun 1690; Lynn

HORN, John & Mary HARMAN; 20 Dec 1700; Boston

HORNE, Joseph & Anna TOMSON/THOMPSON; 18 Jun 1677; Salem

HORNE, Joseph & __?__

HORNE, Simond/Simon? (-1687) & Rebecca (REA) STEVENS, w Samuel, m/3 Joseph BALLARD 1692; 28 Feb 1675, 1675/6; Salem

HORNE, Thomas & 1/wf Judith RICKER (1681-); 14 Apr 1699; Dover, NH

HORNE, William & Elizabeth [CLOUGH?]; b 1662; Dover, NH/Salisbury

HORNE, William (1674-1697) & __?__; ca 1694; Dover, NH

HORNER, Isaac & Lydia WRIGHT, dau Peter; m int 1682, 17 Mar 1683/4; Oyster Bay, LI/Mansfield/NJ

HORRELL, Humphrey & __?__; b 1650; ?Isles of Shoals

HORRELL, Humphrey & Elizabeth SMITH, m/2 Samuel STURTEVANT; 10 Jan 1687/8; Beverly

HORRELL, Humphrey (1650±-) & Sarah __?__; b 1673; Boston/Beverly

HORSSLEY/HORSELEY, John & Mary (QUILTER) CREASEE/CRESSEY, w Mighill; 6 Apr 1671; Rowley

HORSWELL, Francis & Mary [CANTLEBURY]; b 1690; Hingham

HORSWELL, Peter (-1733) & Elizabeth __?__ (-1733+); b 1693; Little Compton, RI

HORTMAN, Timothy & Katharine __?__; b 1673; Boston

HORTON, Barnabas[1] (1600-1680) & 1/wf [?Ann SMITH] (fake record); ca 1624; Hampton, NH/Southold, LI

HORTON, Barnabas[1] (1600-1680) & 2/wf Mary [?LANGTON] (-1691+) (fake record); b 1690; Hampton, NH/Southold, LI

HORTON, Barnabas (1666-1696) & Sarah HINDS/HAYNES, dau Benjamin; ca 1686; Southold, LI

HORTON, Barnabas (1675±-1705) & Elizabeth [?BURNETT], ?dau Aaron; b 1701?; Southold, LI

HORTON, Benjamin[2] (1627-1690) & 1/wf Ann/Anna TOOKER?/TUCKER (sister of Christopher YOUNGS' wf), w John?; 22 Feb 1659, no issue; Southold, LI

HORTON, Benjamin[3], Jr. (-1723, Southold) & Ann [BUDD] (1666-); aft 1684, 18 Jun 1686, bef 28 Dec 1688; Southold, LI/Rye, NY

HORTON, Benjamin[2] (1627-1690) & 2/wf Mary [MAPHAM], w John; 1686; Southold, LI

HORTON, Caleb (1640-1702) & 1/wf __?__; Southold, LI/Cutchogue

HORTON, Caleb[3] (1676-1706, ae 30-1-14) & Abigail HALLOCK (-1697?); 23 Dec 1696; Southold, LI

HORTON, Caleb (1640-1702) & 2/wf Esther/Hester [MAPES?] (suggest Esther HOMAN, w Mordecai); ca 26 Apr 1699 (his will); Southold, LI/Cutchogue, LI
HORTON, David & Hannah [CANDEE] (1673-), dau Zaccheus; prob ca 1690/5; Rye, NY
HORTON, Jeremiah/Jeremy (-1682) & 1/wf Ruth ELY (-1662); 3 Oct 1661; Springfield, MA
HORTON, Jeremiah/Jeremy (-1682) & 2/wf Mary GIBBARD; 5 May 1664; New Haven, CT
HORTON, Jeremy/Jeremiah & Mary TERRY; 5 Nov 1690; Springfield, MA
HORTON, John & Hannah _?_ ; b 1672; Guilford, CT
HORTON, John (?1647-1707) & Rachel [HOIT/HOYT]; Rye, NY
HORTON, John (1672-) & Mehitable [GARNSEY] (-1742); ca 1698; Rehoboth
HORTON, Jonathan[2] (1648-1708, ae 60) & Bethia [WELLS] (1654-1733); ca 1672-4?; Southold, LI
HORTON, Jonathan[3] (-1697) & Bethia [?WINES/?CONKLIN]; ?ca 1693; Southold, LI/Cutchogue, LI
HORTON, Jonathan & _?_ ; b 1694; Rye, NY
HORTON, Joseph (?1623-1696) & Jane [BUDD]; ca 1646?; Southold, LI/Rye, NY
HORTON, Joseph (?1649-) & 1/wf Mary [HALLOCK]; ca 1678; Rye, NY
HORTON, Joseph (-1704+) & Sophia (CLAES) [PARK], w Roger, m/3 Jonathan VOWLES by 1707; b 1696; Rye, NY
HORTON, Lt. Joshua[2] (?1643-1729, ae 86 y) & Mary [WHEELER?]/[TUTTLE?] (-1718); ca 1667; Southold, LI
HORTON, Ens. Joshua[3] (?1669-1749, Elizabeth, NJ) (had 4 daughters in 1698) & 1/wf Elizabeth [GROVER] (?1672-1713), dau Simon; ca 1690; Southold, LI
HORTON, Nathaniel (1662-) & Sarah BURT (1675-); 8 Feb 1693, 1693/4; Deerfield/Somers, CT
HORTON, Samuel (1667-) (son Jeremy/Jeremiah) & Sarah [JOHNSON] (1676-); b 1700; New Haven
HORTON, Thomas (-1640) & Mary _?_, m/2 Robert ASHLEY 1641; b 1638; Springfield
HORTON, Thomas & 1/wf Sarah _?_ ; b 1669; Milton/Rehoboth
HORTON, Thomas & 2/wf Susannah KENEY/KENNEY, w John; 25 Dec 1693; Milton
HORTON, Thomas & 3/wf Katherine HARRISON, ?w Henry; 6 Jun 1700; Rehoboth
HORTON, Thomas (1677-) & Hannah GARNSEY (1676-); 7 Jun 1700; Rehoboth
HORTON, William (1677±-) & Christiana (YOUNGS); b 1701?; Southold, LI/Orange Co., NY
HOSFORD, John[2] (-1698) & Phillipa THRALL (-1683); 5 Nov 1657; Windsor, CT
HOSFORD, John (-1698) & Deborah BROWN (1678-); 9 Apr 1696; Windsor, CT
HOSFORD, Nathaniel (1671-) & Mary PHELPS (1674-); 19 Apr 1700; Windsor, CT
HOSFORD, Samuel (1669-) & 1/wf Mary PALMER (-1715); 4 Apr 1690; Windsor, CT
HOSFORD, Thomas & _?_ ; b 1657; Windsor, CT
HOSFORD, Timothy (1662-) & 1/wf Hannah PALMER (1666-1702); 5 Dec 1689; Windsor, CT
HOSFORD, William[1] & 1/wf _?_ (-1641); b 1626?; Dorchester/Windsor, CT
HOSFORD, William[1] (returned to Eng) & 2/wf Jane [FOOKES] (-1671+), w Henry; b 23 Jul 1655; Windsor, CT
HOSIER, Samuel (1614-1665) & Ursula (ADAMS) STREETER (1619-), w Stephen, m/3 William ROBINSON ca 1666, m/4 Griffin CRAFTS 1673; 13 Oct 1657; Charlestown
HOSKINS, Anthony (1632-1707) & Isabel BROWN (-1698); 16 Jul 1656; Windsor, CT
HOSKINS, Anthony (1632-1707) & 2/wf Mary WILSON (-1715), w Samuel; ?Oct
HOSKINS, Anthony, Jr. (1664-) & _?_ ; b 1686; Windsor, CT
HOSKINS, John (-1648, Windsor) & Ann [FILER?] (-1662, 1663?), wid?; ca 1620/30?; Dorchester/Windsor, CT
HOSKINS, John (-1707+, 1715) & Elizabeth (_?_) KNAPP (-1707+); w Aaron; by 1675?; Taunton/Dighton
HOSKINS, John (1654-1734) & 1/wf Deborah DENSLOW (1655-); 29 Jan 1677; Windsor, CT
HOSKINS, John & Hannah _?_ (-1751); 1681/2; Windsor, CT
HASKINS, John & Ruth [ATKINS]; b 1699; Scituate/Rochester
HOSKINS, John (1654-) & 2/wf Ruth (ATKINS?) PECK, w Joseph; 14 Dec 1699; Windsor, CT
HOSKINS, Joseph (1675-) & _?_ ; b 1699; Windsor, CT
HASKINS, Richard (-1717, 1718), Portsmouth & Jane FEUSTER?/FLUSTER?/PENSTER?, Taunton; 2 Aug 1686; Taunton
HASKINS, Richard (-1718, 1717), Taunton & Mary [TISDALL] (?1672-1718+), dau James; ca 1689?; Taunton/Norwich, CT
HASKINS, Robert (1662-) & Mary GILLETTE; 27 Oct 1686; Windsor, CT/Simsbury, CT

HASKINS, Roger & 1/wf Susanna [ROOTES], dau Josiah; b 1666; Beverly/Salem?
HASKINS, Roger & 2/wf Ruth [STACKHOUSE]; b 1683, b 1672?; Beverly/Salem
HASKINS, Samuel² & 1/wf Abigail [STACEY]; Taunton
HOSKINS, Samuel² (1654-1726/27?) & 2/wf Mary AUSTIN (-1718/19); 5 Feb 1684, 1684/5?;
    Taunton
HOSKINS, Samuel² (1654-) & 3/wf Rebecca BROOKS (1657-); 12 May 1692; Taunton
HOSKINS, Thomas (-1666) & Elizabeth (GAYLORD) BIRGE (-1675), w Richard; 20 Apr 1653;
    Windsor, CT
HASKINS, Thomas (1673-) & Elizabeth MILLS; 23 Feb 1698/9; Windsor, CT
HOSKINS/HODGEKINS, William¹ (-7 Sep 1695) & 1/wf Sarah CUSHMAN; 2 Nov 1636; Plymouth
HOSKINS/HODGEKINS, William¹ (-1695) & 2/wf Ann HYNES/HAYNES?/HANDS; 21 Dec 1638;
    Plymouth
HOSKINS, William² (1647-1730) & Sarah CASEWELL/CASWELL (1658-1726+); 3 Jul 1677;
    Taunton
HASKINS, William (-1712) & Christian _?_ , m/2 Henry WILLIAMS; b 1701?, b 1678?; Hampton,
    NH
HOSLEY, James (-1677?) & Martha PARKER (1649-), dau John & Joanna; 13 Dec 1674;
    Dorchester
HOSLEY, James (1676-1728) & Mariah _?_ ; b 1700; Billerica
HOSMAN, John & Hester CRAFORD; 23 Dec 1669; Salem
HOSMER, James¹ (1605-) & 1/wf Ann/Anna _?_ (1608-); in Eng, b 1633; Concord
HOSMER, James¹ (1605-) & 2/wf Mary _?_ (-1641); b 1637?; Concord
HOSMER, James¹ (1605-1685) & 3/wf Alice/Ellen _?_ (-1665); [1641] (prob); Concord
HOSMER, James² (1637?-1676) & Sarah WHITE, m/2 Samuel RICE 1676; 13 Oct 1658; Concord
HOSMER, James (1660-), Marlborough & Elizabeth SAWYER (1663-), Lancaster; 6 Feb 1687/8;
    Concord/Marlboro
HOSMER, John (1671-) & Mary BILLING/BILLINGS (1680-); 12 May 1699; Concord
HOSMER, Stephen (1642-1714) & Abigail WOOD (1642-1717); 24 May 1667; Concord
HOSMER, Stephen (1645±-1693) & Hannah [BUSHNELL]; ca 1670; Hartford
HOSMER, Thomas (1603-1687) & 1/wf Frances _?_ (?1602-1675); b 1642, b 1639?;
    Cambridge/Hartford/etc.
HOSMER, Thomas (1603-1687) & 2/wf Catherine (HOSKINS) WILTON, w David; ca 6 May 1679;
    Hartford
HOSMER, Thomas (1672-) & Hannah HARTWELL (1675-); 18 Feb 1695/6; Concord
HOSMER, Thomas (1675-) & Ann PRENTISS (1679-); 24 Dec 1700; Hartford
HOTCHKISS, Daniel & Esther SPERRY, m/2 Stephen PIERSON; 21 Jun 1683; New Haven
HOTCHKISS, John & Mary BISHOP; 4 Apr 1670; Guilford, CT
HOTCHKISS, John (-1689) & Elizabeth PECK (1649-1732); 4 Dec 1672; New Haven
HOTCHKISS, John (1673-) & Mary [CHATTERTON] (1673-); b 1694; New Haven/Wallingford,
    CT
HOTCHKISS, Joseph & Hannah CRUTTENDEN; Apr 1699; New Haven
HOTCHKISS, Joshua & 1/wf Mary PARDEE (-1684?); 29 Nov 1677; New Haven
HOTCHKISS, Joshua & 2/wf Hannah [TUTTLE] (1662-1719); ca 1685; New Haven
HOTCHKISS, Joshua & Susanna [CHATTERTON] (1678-), m/2 Abraham DICKERMAN; b 1701;
    New Haven
HOTCHKISS, Samuel (-1663) & Elizabeth CLEVERLY (-1681); 7 Sep 1642; New Haven
HOTCHKISS, Samuel (HODGKINS is wrong) (ca 1645-1705) & 1/wf Sarah TALMAGE; 18 Mar
    1678/9; New Haven
HOTCHKISS, Samuel (1645-1705) & 2/wf Hannah (THOMPSON) [MOULTHORP] (-1712/13), w
    Matthew?; b 1701?, aft 1 Feb 1690/1; New Haven
HOTCHKISS, Thomas (-1711) & Sarah WILMOT (1663-1731), m/2 Daniel SPERRY; 27 Nov 1677;
    New Haven
HAUGH, Atherton (-1650) & 1/wf Elizabeth (BULKELEY) WHITTINGHAM (-1643), w Richard;
    Boston, Eng, 9 Jan 1617/18; Boston
HAUGH, Atherton (-1650) & 2/wf Susanna _?_ (-1651); b 4 Apr 1646; Boston
HAUGH, Atherton (1678-) & Mercy WINTHROP (-1702, ca 29); 11 Jul 1699; Boston
HOUGH, Edward (d in Eng) & Ann _?_ (-1672, ae ca 85, 88?); in Eng, b 1619; Gloucester
HOUGH, John (1655-1715) & Sarah POST (1659-); 27 Jan 1680, 1679/80; Norwich, CT/New
    London

HOUGH, Jonathan & Margaret [?ORVIS] (1661-); b 1681; Woodbury, CT/Farmington, CT
HAUGH, Samuel (1621-1662) & Sarah [SYMMES] (-1684), m/2 Rev. John BROCK 1662; b 1650; Reading/Charlestown
HAUGH, Samuel (1651-1679) & Anna/Ann [RAINSFORD] (1652-); b 1675(6?); Boston
HOUGH, Samuel (1653-1718) & 1/wf Susanna WROTHAM (-1684, Wallingford, CT); 25 Nov 1679; Farmington, CT/Wallingford, CT/Saybrook, CT
HOUGH, Samuel (1653-1718) & 2/wf Mary BATES (1654-); 18 Aug 1685; Saybrook, CT
HAUGH, Samuel (1676-) & Margaret (COWELL) JOHNSON, w John; 30 Sep 1697; Boston
HOUGH, William (-1683) & Sarah CALKIN/CAULKINS; 28 Oct 1645; Gloucester/New London, CT
HOUGH, William & ?Lydia/Mary _?_; b 1680?, b 1685; Boston
HOUGH, William & Elizabeth BATES; 6 Aug 1685
HOUGH, William (1657-1705) & Ann [LOTHROP] (1667-1745, Norwich); New London, CT
HOUGH, William & Mary (KEMBLE) BRICKNELL/BICKNELL, w Edward; 24 Mar 1693; Boston
HOUGHTON, Henry (1676-1756, Bolton) & 1/wf Abigail BARRON (1680-1711); 2 Jan 1699/1700; Watertown/Lancaster
HOUGHTON, Jacob (1674-1750) & Rebecca [WHITCOMB] (1671-1750, 1752); b 1696 (m 1704 is wrong); Lancaster
HOUGHTON, James & Mary _?_ (-will 1686)
HOUGHTON, James (1650-1719) & Mary _?_ (-1724+), m Nathaniel WILDER; b 1690, b 1680?; Lancaster/Harvard
HOUGHTON, John (?1624-1684) & Beatrix _?_; b 1650; Dedham/Lancaster
HOUGHTON, John (1650-1737) & 1/wf Mary FARRAR (1648-1724); 22 Jan 1671/2; Lancaster
HOUGHTON, John (?1672-1724) & 1/wf Mary (PRESCOTT) GOSS (1669-), w Philip; 20 Nov 1698; Concord/Lancaster
HOUGHTON, Jonas/Jonah (-1723) & Mary BERBEANE/BURBEEN (1661-1720, in 60th y); 16 Feb 1681, 1680/1; Woburn/Lancaster
HAUGHTON, Joseph (?1657-1737), Lancaster & 1/wf Jane VOSE (1668-1707), Milton; 31 Oct 1693; Milton/Lancaster
HOUGHTON, Ralph (-1705, Milton) & Jane [STOWE?] (1626-1701, Milton); ca 1650?, b 1653; Lancaster
HOUGHTON, Ralph (-1692) & Mary [BLACKBURN?]; b 1692; Dorchester
HOUGHTON, Robert (1659-1723) & Esther [LEPPINGWELL?] (1658-1741); b 1682; Woburn/Lancaster
HOUSE, ?Joseph & _?_
HOUSE, Samuel (1610-1681, 1661?) & Elizabeth [HAMMOND] (1619-), dau William; b 1636; Watertown/Cambridge/Scituate
HOUSE, Samuel & Rebecca NICKOLLES/NICHOLS; 15 Mar 1664, [1664/5]; Scituate
HOUSE, Samuel (1665-) & Sarah PINSON; 25 Feb 1691/2; Scituate
HOUSE, Thomas & _?_ (sister of Samuel FORMAN's 1/wf); b 1660; ?Fairfield, CT
HOUSE, Walter (-1670) & Mary _?_ (-1670+); b 1663?; Kings Town, RI
HOUSE, William & Mary _?_; b 1660; Boston
HOUSE, William (-1704) & Sarah [BIDWELL] (ca 1653-); b 1674, ca 1670; Hartford
HOUSE, _?_ & Elizabeth [PECK] (1643); Wallingford, CT
HOUSING, Peter (-1673) & Sarah [CLOYES] (1653±-); bef Oct 1667; Falmouth, ME/Framingham
HOUSTON, James & Mary DORR/DORE; 23 Dec 1692; Dover, NH
HOVEY, Daniel[1] (1618-1692, 1695?) (ae ca 42 in 1660) & Abigail [ANDREWS]; b 1642; Ipswich/Brookfield/Hadley
HOVEY, Daniel[2] (?1641-1695) (ae ca 18 in 1660) & 1/wf Rebecca [DANE?] (-1665); b 1665; Ipswich
HOVEY, Daniel[2] (-1695) & 2/wf Hester/Esther TREADWELL (1641-1730); 8 Oct 1666; Ipswich
HOVEY, Daniel (1672-) & Mercy HOWARD?/[HAYWARD?] (1673-1742); b 1695; Ipswich
HOVEY, James (-1675) & Priscilla WARNER; b 1670, 2 Nov 1670; Ipswich/Brookfield
HOVEY, James & Jane/?Deborah [BARLOW]; b 1695; Malden/Mansfield, CT
HOVEY, John (-1718) & 1/wf Dorcas IVORYE (-1711); 3 Aug 1665; Ipswich
HOVEY, John & 1/wf Mary DUNWELL/DWINELL?; 11 Jan 1691, 1691/2; Topsfield
HOVEY, Joseph (-1690) & Hannah PRATT; 31 May 1677; Hadley/Milton
HOVEY, Luke & Susannah PILSBURY; 25 Oct 1698; Newbury

HOVEY, Nathaniel (-1696?, 1693?) & 1/wf Sarah FULLER, m/2 Christopher BIDLAKE b 1684?;
- Nov 1679; Ipswich
HOVEY, Nathaniel (-1696) & 2/wf Mary [FELLOWS] (1671-), m/2 John BROWN 1697?; b 1693?;
Ipswich
HOVEY, Thomas (?1648-1739) & Sarah COOK (1662-1734+, 1739+, 1752); ?1 Nov 1677, Nov
1677; Hadley
HOVEY, Thomas & Martha [BALCH] (1676-); ca 1698; Ipswich
HOUTCHIN/HOWCHIN, Jeremy/?Jeremiah & Esther __?__; b 1640, 10 Mar 1643/4?; Boston
HOWDE/HOWD, Anthony (-1676) & Elizabeth HITCHCOCK, m/2 John NASH 1677; Jan 1672, 22
Aug; New Haven
HOWE, Abraham[1] (-1676) & 1/wf [Elizabeth? __?__] (-1645); b 1631; Boston/Roxbury
HOWE, Abraham[2] (-1676) & 2/wf Sarah __?__ (-1675); aft 1645; Boston/Roxbury
HOWE, Abraham[2] (-1683) & 1/wf __?__; b 1653; Roxbury
HOWE, Abraham & Hannah WARD; 26 Mar 1657, 6? May; Marlboro/Watertown
HOWE, Abraham (-1683) & 2/wf Alice (BISHOP) LEWIS, w John, m/3 John HARRIS of Rowley
aft 1683; aft 1667, bef 2 Jan 1680; Roxbury
HOWE, Abraham[3] (1653-1684) & Sarah __?__, m/2 Samuel KNIGHT 1685; b 1676; Roxbury
HOWE, Abraham & Sarah PEABODY (1650-); 26 Mar 1678; Ipswich
HOW, Abraham (-1704) & Mary HOW; 14 Nov 1695, 9 Nov; Marlboro
HOWE, Daniel & __?__; b 1630?; Lynn/New Haven/Southampton
HOW, Daniel (1658-1718) & Elizabeth KERLEY (1660?-1735); 12 Oct 1686, 6 Oct; Marlboro
HOWE, Daniel & 1/wf Margery [ANDREWS] (1681-); b 1700; Waterbury/Wallingford, CT
HOWE, David (1674-) & Hepzibah DEATH (1680-); 25 Dec 170[0?]; Sudbury
HOW, Edward (-1644) & Margaret WELLS (-1660), m/2 George BUNKER 1647?; in Eng, 16 Aug
1610; Watertown
HOW, Edward (1575-1639) & Elizabeth __?__ (1585-); in Eng, b 1613; Lynn/?Topsfield/?Framing-
ham
HOW, Eleazer & Hannah HOW (1664-); - Nov 1684; Marlboro
HOW, Ephraim (1621-1680) & [Anne/Ann HOUGH]; b 1653; New Haven
HOWE, Isaac (1628±-) & __?__; b 1649; Lynn/Greenwich, CT
HOW, Isaac (1648-1724) & Francis/Frances WOODS (-1718); 17 Jan 1671, 17 Jun 1671;
Marlboro/Dorchester
HOWE, Isaac (-1718) & Hannah [ROBIOHN]?; b 1678; Dorchester
HOWE, Isaac (1656-1718) & Deborah HOWE (-1734+); 11 May 1685; Roxbury/Charlestown
HOWE, Israel (1644-1715) & 1/wf Anne __?__; b 1668; Boston/Dorchester
HOWE, Israel (1644-1715) & 2/wf Tabitha [MILLER?]; b 1695
HOWE, James (-1702) & Elizabeth DANE (-1693); Bishop's Stortford, Eng, 27 Jun 1628;
Roxbury/Ipswich
HOWE, James & Elizabeth JACKSON (-1692); 13 Apr 1658, 5 May 1658; Ipswich
HOWE, Jeremiah/Jeremy? (1614?-1690) & Elizabeth __?__ (-1696); b 1645; New Haven
HOWE, Jeremiah (-1740) & Elizabeth [PECK] (1643-1703); 29 Oct 1674; Wallingford, CT
HOW, John[1] (1602-1680) & Mary __?__ (-1698); b 1638?, b 1640; Sudbury/Marlboro
HOW, John (1640-1676) & Elizabeth [WARD], m/2 Henry KERLEY 1678?, 1676?, 1677; 22 Jan
1662; Marlboro
HOW, John & 1/wf Mary [COOPER] DORMAN (1642-1677), w John; b 1665; Topsfield
HOW, John & 2/wf Sarah [TOWNE] (1657-); ca 1678, bef 20 Dec 1686, b 19 Jul 1685; Topsfield
HOW, John (1664-), Sudbury & 1/wf Elizabeth WOOLSON (1668-), Watertown; 3 Nov 1686;
Sudbury
HOW, John (-1697) & Hannah [BROWN?], m/2 Ephraim ROBERTS; b 1691; Ipswich
HOWE, John & Hannah [HEMENWAY] (1670-); b 1693; New Haven
HOW, John (1671-) & 1/wf Rebecca [JOSLIN] (1672-1731); b 1695; Marlboro
HOW, John & Sarah CAVES/CAVE?; 27 Sep 1697; Topsfield/Boxford
HOW, Joseph (-1651) & Mary [NEEDHAM], m/2 Samuel HART ca 1653; b 1650; Lynn
HOWE, Joseph & 1/wf Frances WILLEY; 16 Jul 1652; Boston
HOW, Joseph & Elizabeth (MASON) [BUNN], w Edward; b 1674, m cont 2 Oct 1673; Boston
HOW, Joseph (-1700) & Dorothy MARTIN; 29 Dec 1687; Marlboro/Charlestown
HOWE, Joseph (1653-1703) & Esther [BOTSFORD] (1668-), m/2 Thomas HUMISTON; ca 1690/4?
HOW, Josiah (-1687) & Mary HAYNES (?1647-1718), m/2 John PRESCOTT 1710; 18 May 1671
(not 8, 18 Mar); Sudbury

HOW, Nathaniel (-1723) & Elizabeth [CURTIS] (1644-1713); b 1666; New Haven
HOW, Nathaniel & _?_ [BOWERS]; b 1669/72?, b 1679; Greenwich, CT
HOW, Nicholas & Mary SUMNER (-1706, Newport), m/2 John TROW bef 1678; 19 Jan 1671/2; Dorchester
HOW, Nicholas & Ellen DYE; 17 Feb 1697; Little Compton, RI
HOW, Samuel (1642-) & 1/wf Martha BENT (1643-1680); 5 Jun 1663; Sudbury
HOW, Samuel & 1/wf Mary WOOLIE/WOOLEY (-1677); 27 Mar 1673; Concord
HOW, Samuel & 2/wf Mary NUTTEN/NUTTING; 26 Mar 1678; Concord/Plainfield, CT
HOW, Samuel (1642-1713) & 2/wf Sarah (LEAVITT) CLAPP, w Nehemiah; 18 Sep 1685; Sudbury
HOW, Samuel & 1/wf Abigail MIXTER/MIXER, Watertown; 11 Dec 1690; Sudbury
HOWE, Thomas (1654-) & 1/wf Sarah OSMER/HOSMER (-1724); 21 Jun 1681, 8 Jun; Marlboro
HOW, William & Mary _?_ ; b 1654, b 1657; Concord
HOW, Zachariah (-1703) & Sarah GILBERT (-1713); 22 Mar 1666/7; New Haven/Wallingford, CT
HOWELL, Abraham (1653-1712) & 1/wf Abigail WHITE (-1688, ae 27); 19 Oct 1682; Southampton, LI
HOWELL, Abraham & Anne (WAKEMAN) JAMES, w Nathaniel; 2 Oct 1690; Fairfield, CT
HOWELL, Arthur (1632-1683) & 1/wf Elizabeth [GARDINER] (1641-1658); b 23 Feb 1657; Southampton, LI
HOWELL, Arthur (1632-1683) & 2/wf Hannah [RAYNOR], m/2 Job Sayee 1685; b 1661, Southampton; Southampton
HOWELL, ?David & Mary _?_ , m/2 John LARRISON 20 Dec 1686; doubtful, bef 15 Jul 1680; Southampton
HOWELL, Edmund (1635-1706) & _?_ [SAYRE]; ca 1657?; Southampton
HOWELL, Edmund (-1706) & 2/wf Sarah JUDSON (1645/6-1688); 11 Nov 1664, ?11 Oct; Stratford, CT
HOWELL, Edward (1584-1656) & 1/wf Frances _?_ (-bur 2 Jul 1630); in Eng, b 1618; Boston/Lynn/Southampton
HOWELL, Edward (1584-1656, 1655?, b 6 Oct 1655) & 2/wf Eleanor _?_ ; in Eng, 1630, 1631, Southampton; Boston/Lynn/Southampton
HOWELL, Edward (1626-1699) & Mary [FORDHAM] (-1699+, 1717); b 1651; Southampton, NY
HOWELL, Elisha (1674-1750) & Damaris [SAYRE] (1669-1757); b 14 Jan 1697; Southampton, LI
HOWELL, Ephraim (1646±-) & Hannah COE; 10 Nov 1684; Southampton, LI
HOWELL, John (1624-1696) (called "cousin" by Thurston RAYNER 1667) & Susanna [MITCHELL] (1627-1711, ae 83); b 1648; Southampton, LI
HOWELL, John & Prudence _?_ ; by 1666; Scarborough, ME
HOWELL, John (1648-1692) & 1/wf Martha WHITE (-7 Jun 1688); 12 Jun 1673; Southampton, LI
HOWELL, John (1648-1692) & 2/wf Mary (BRYAN) (MALTBY) TAYLOR (1654?-), w John, w Joseph; 30 Jan 1690, 1689/90; Southampton, LI
HOWELL, Jonah (see Richard) (-1727) & Elizabeth [HALSEY?] (-1727+); b 1701?, b 1708; Southampton, LI
HOWELL, Joseph (1651-1734?) & Lydia [STOCKING] (1662, 1663-); ca 1682/6?, b 1694; Southampton/?Bridgehampton, LI
HOWELL, Josiah (1675-1752) & 2/wf? (1/wf?) ?Mary/?Phebe JONES (1681-1766); b 1699; Southampton, LI
HOWELL, Matthew (1651-1706) & Mary HALSEY (1654-); 8 Nov 1677; Southampton, LI
HOWELL, Nathaniel (1664-1725/6) & Hannah [HALSEY] (1665-1725+); b 3 Aug 1688; Southampton, LI
HOWELL, Richard (1629-) & 1/wf Elizabeth [HALSEY] (-1677+); ca 1660-68?, b 1669; Southampton, LI
HOWELL, Richard (-1709) & Elizabeth [HALLOCK] (-1709+); b 1676?; Southold, LI
HOWELL, Richard (1629-) & 2/wf _?_/?Eleanor [RAYNOR], dau Joseph; aft 1677; Southampton, LI
HOWELL, Richard (?1670-1740) & Sarah BARTTEY?/?BANTHY/[DUNHAM?]; b 1701; Southampton, LI
HOWELL, Theophilus (1662-1739) & Abigail [HALSEY?] (1673-1739+, 1750); b 1697; Southampton/Bridgehampton, LI/Sag Harbor, LI
HOWELL, _?_ & _?_ HOWELL, m/2 Peter HALLOCK? 1643?
HOWELL, Thomas (-1647) (uncle of Job LANE) & _?_ ; Marshfield
HOWELL, _?_ & Sarah [ROYAL] (1665/6); ?Boston

HOWEN, Israel & Ann __?__ ; b 1665; Boston
HOWEN, Jacob & Martha __?__ ; b 1684; Boston
HOWEN, John & Joanna __?__ ; b 1665; Boston
HOWEN, John & Elizabeth __?__ ; b 1685; Boston
HOWEN, Robert & Elizabeth __?__ (-1653, Boston); b 1640; Boston
HOWES, Ebenezer (-1727) & 1/wf Sarah **GORHAM** (1678-1705); 20 Apr 1699, 24? Apr; Yarmouth
HOWES, Jeremy/Jeremiah (1637-1708) & Sarah [**PRENCE**] (1648, 1643/46?-1706, ae 60?); ca 1668; Yarmouth
HOWES, Jeremiah (-1708?, 1706) & Mary [**DAGGETT**]; aft 18 Oct 1693; Martha's Vineyard
HOWES, John (1666-1736) & 1/wf Elizabeth **PADDOCK** (1666-); 28 Nov 1689; Yarmouth
HOWES, John (1666-1736) & 2/wf Mary **MATHUES/MATTHEWS** (ca 1670-); 8 Jul 1691; Yarmouth
HOWES, Jonathan (1669?, 1670?-1751) & Sarah [**?VINCENT**]; b 1695; Yarmouth
HOWES, Joseph (ca 1634-1695), Yarmouth & Elizabeth [**MAYO**] (-1700/01); b 1657; Yarmouth
HOWES, Joseph, Jr. (-1736) & 1/wf Mary **VINSENTT/VINCENT**; 28 Nov 1689; Yarmouth
HOWES, Joseph & Hannah (**SNOW**) [**RICHARDS**], w Giles; b 1701?
HOWES, Prince/?Prence (1659-1753, in 84th y) & Dorcas **JOYCE** (1674-1740+); 8 Aug 1695; Yarmouth
HOWES, Samuel (-1723) & Rebecca __?__ ; ca 1678?, b 1685?, b 1690?; Yarmouth
HOWES, Thomas (-1665) & Mary [**BURR?**] (-1695), m/2 Thomas **PRENCE** 1667?; ca 1628/32?, b 1631?; Lynn/Yarmouth
HOWES, Thomas (-1676) & Sarah [**BANGS**] (?1638-1683); b 1656?, b 1657?; Eastham/Yarmouth
HOWES, Thomas (1663-1698, 1737) & Sarah **HEDGE** (1679?-1716); 23 Jun 1698; Yarmouth
HOUSE, Thomas (1663-1700) & Abigail **HUSSEY**, m/2 Joseph **MARSHALL**; 5 Apr 1700; Nantucket/Yarmouth
HOWES, Thomas & Rebecca [**HOWES**] (no)/Content **SMITH** 11 Dec 1701; b 1701?; Yarmouth
HAWKENS/HOWKINS, Anthony (-1674) (called "uncle" by Samuel **BUCKINGHAM**) & 1/wf ?Mary __?__/(?Isabel **BROWN** error) (-1655); b 1644; Windsor, CT/Farmington, CT
HOWKINS, Anthony (-1674) & Anne (**WELLS**) **THOMPSON** (-1680), w Thomas; ?aft 25 Apr 1655, b 6 May 1656, by May 1656; ?Farmington, CT
HOWKINS, John (-1676) & ?Elizabeth/__?__ [**BUNKHEAD**]
HOWLAND, Abraham (1675-1747) & Ann/Anne [**?ROUSE**]/?**COLSON** (1678-); ca 1700; Pembroke/Hanson/?Newport
HOWLAND, Arthur (-1675) & 1/wf __?__ ; by 1636?
HOWLAND, Arthur (-1675) & 2/wf Margaret [**WALKER**] (-1683), wid; b 6 Jun 1643; Marshfield
HOWLAND, Arthur (-1711+) & Elizabeth **PRENCE** (-1711+); 9 Dec 1667; Marshfield
HOWLAND, Arthur (?1674/5-) & Deborah __?__ ; ca 1700; Marshfield
HOWLAND, Benjamin (1659-1727) & Judith **SAMSON**; 3 Apr 1684; Dartmouth
HOWLAND, Daniel (1661-) & Mary __?__ (not **SAMPSON**); b 1689; Tiverton, RI
HOWLAND, Henry (-1671) & Mary __?__ (not **NEWLAND**) (-1674); in Eng, ca 1628; Duxbury/Plymouth
HOWLAND, Henry (1672-1729) & Deborah **BRIGGS** (1674-1712); 3 Jun 1698; Dartmouth
HOWLAND, Isaac (ca 1650-1724) & Elizabeth [**VAUGHAN**] (1653-1727); b 1677; Middlebury
HOWLAND, Isaac (1659-) & Ann **TAYLOR** (1664-); 27 Dec 1686; Barnstable
HOWLAND, Jabez (1644-1711, 1712) & Bethiah [**THATCHER/THATHER**] (-1725, 1712+); b 1669; ?Plymouth/Duxbury/Bristol, RI
HOWLAND, Jabez (1669-1732) & Patience [**STAFFORD**] (1669-1721, ae 52); ca 1697?; Bristol, RI
HOWLAND, James & 1/wf Mary **LOTHROP** (1675-); 8 Sep 1697; Barnstable
HOWLAND, John (-1692/3) & Elizabeth [**TILLEY**] (1607-1687, Swansea); ca 14 Aug 1623; Plymouth
HOWLAND, John (1626-1702) & Mary **LEE** (-1691+); 26 Oct 1651; Plymouth/?Barnstable
HOWLAND, John & Mary **WALKER**; 29 Jan 1684/5; Duxbury
HOWLAND, Joseph (-1743/4) & 1/wf Elizabeth **SOUTHWORTH** (-1717); 7 Dec 1664; Plymouth
HOWLAND, Joseph (-1692) & Rebecca **HUSSEY**, m/2 Samuel **COLLINS**; 4 May 1683, at Hampton; Lynn/Duxbury
HOWLAND, Nathaniel (1657-1723/4) & Rose [**ALLEN**] (1665-); b 1685; Dartmouth

HOWLAND, Nathaniel (-1746) & Martha COOLE/COLE (1669, ca 1672-1718); 16 Mar 1696/7; Plymouth

HOWLAND, Nicholas & Hannah WOODMAN; 26 Oct 1697; Little Compton, RI

HOWLAND, Samuel (-1716) & Mary [SAMPSON], dau Abraham, gr-dau Samuel NASH; b 1675; Freetown

HOWLAND, Shubael (1672-1737) & Mercy BLOSSOM (1678-bef 6 Mar 1759); 13 Dec 1700; Barnstable

HOWLAND, Thomas (1672-) & 1/wf Mary __?__; b 1698; Marshfield

HOWLAND, Thomas (-1739) & Hannah/?Joanna [COLE] (-1760); b 1700; Plymouth

HOWLAND, Zoeth (-1676) & Abigail __?__, m/2 Richard KIRBY; Dec 1656

HOWLET, John (1643/4-1675) & Susanna [HUDSON], m/2 Edmund PERKINS, m/3 Christopher SLEG 1696; b 1670(1?); Boston

HOWLETT, John & Abigail [POWELL?]; b 1679, b 1672/3; Boston

HOWLET, John (1677-1735) & Barsheba/Bathsheba HOYTE (-1740); 26 Dec 1699; Topsfield

HOWLET, Samuel (?1646-1720) & Sarah CLARK (1651-1717); 3 Jan 1670; Topsfield

HOWLETT, Thomas (?1606-1677/8, Sep 1678) & 1/wf Alice [FRENCH] (1610-1666), w Thomas; ca 1634?; Ipswich

HOWLETT, Thomas (?1638-1667) & Lydia [PEABODY] (1640-1715), m/2 Thomas PERLEY bef 1677, 1668; ca 1662; Ipswich

HOWLETT, Thomas (ca 1606-1678) & 2/wf Rebecca [SMITH] (-1680), w Thomas; aft 26 Jun 1666; Newbury

HOWLET, Thomas (-1713) & Rebecca CUMINGS/CUMMINGS, m/2 Michael WHIDDEN; 13 Jan 1695/6; Topsfield

HOWLETT, William (1650-1718) & Mary PERKINS (?1651-1728); 27 Oct 1671, no issue; Topsfield

HOXIE, Gideon (1670-) & Grace [GIFFORD] (1671-); b 1696; Sandwich

HOXIE, John (1669-1767) & Mary [HULL] (1677-); b 1701?, prob ca 1704, b 4 Oct 1706; Stonington, CT

HAUKSIE, Joseph (1667-) & Sarah/Mary [TUCKER] (1674-); b 1695; Sandwich

HOXIE, Lodowick & Mary PRESBURY (1644-); ?Jun 1664; Sandwich/Stonington, CT

HOYLE, John & Anna [?KNIGHT]; b 1669; Marblehead

HOYLE, Samuel & Mary FORTUNE; 16 Nov 1699; Marblehead

HOYT, Benjamin (1645-1736) & 1/wf Hannah WEED (ca 1650-1711); 5 Jan 1670; Stamford, CT/Windsor, CT

HAIT, Benjamin, Jr. (1671-1747, 1749?) & Elizabeth JAGGER (ca 1679-); 10 Jun 1697; Stamford, CT

HOYT, [Daniel?] & Elizabeth KEELER (1678/9-), dau John; b 1701?, b 17 Feb 1718/19; Norwich, CT

HOYT, David (-1704?) & 1/wf Sarah WELLS? (1655-1676?); 3 Apr 1673; Hadley

HOYT, David (-1704?) & 2/wf Mary [WILSON]; ?ca 1676/7, b 1684; Hadley

HOYT, David (-1704) & 3/wf Abigail (COOKE) POMEROY, w Joshua, m/3 Nathaniel ROYCE; b 1691; Hadley/Deerfield

HOYT, David (-1703) & Mary EDWARDS (1675-); 14 Apr 1699, 14 Aug; Hadley/Deerfield

HAIGHT, David (1670-) & Phebe __?__; b 1701; Rye, NY

HOYT, Ephraim & 1/wf Hannah GODFREY (1670-); 25 Apr 1695; Hampton, NH

HOYT, John & 1/wf Frances [TUXBERRY?] (-1643); ca 1635; Salisbury

HOYT, John & 2/wf Frances __?__; 1643, 1644; Salisbury

HOYT, John (?1614-1684) & 1/wf __?__; ca 1640/50?; Fairfield, CT/Rye, NY

HOYT, John (1614-1684) & 2/wf Mary (BRUNDISH) [PURDY], w Francis __?__; aft 20 Oct 1658, ca 1659; Rye, NY/Eastchester, NY

HOYT, John & Mary BARNES; 23 Jun 16[59]; Salisbury

HOYT, John³ (1644-ca 1711) & 1/wf Mary LINDALL, New Haven; 14 Sep 1666; Norwalk, CT/Danbury, CT

HOYT, John (-1691) & Elizabeth [CHALLIS], m/2 John BLAISDELL 1693; ca 1685; Amesbury

HOYT, John (-1723/26) & Elizabeth [?SHERWOOD]; aft 1684, 1685?, ca 1687/9?; Rye, NY

HOYT/HAYTE, John & Sarah (NASON) CHILD, w Henry; 10 Nov 1695; Kittery, ME/Dover, NH

HOYT, John (1644-1711?) & 2/wf Hannah __?__; aft 1686, bef 28 Feb 1712, b 1701?; Norwalk, CT/Danbury, CT

HOYT, John (1669-1746) & Hannah [DRAKE], dau John of Simsbury; b 1701?, b 10 May 1699; Norwalk, CT/Danbury, CT

HOYT, Jonathan (1649-1698) & 1/wf Sarah POND (1652-16 Oct 1676); 6 Mar 1671/2, 1671; ?Guilford, CT/Stamford, CT

HOYT, Jonathan (1649-1697/8) & 2/wf Mary [BELL?/BILL?]; aft 16 Oct 1676; Stamford, CT/Guilford, CT

HOYT, Jonathan (1673±-1752±) & Rebecca __?_ ; b 1701?; Rye, NY

HOYT, Joseph (1678-1730/1) & Sarah [PICKET] (1678-), dau James; b 1701?; Norwalk, CT

HOIT, Joshua (1641-1690) & Mary [BELL] (-1724), m Joseph TURNEY; b 1664; Stamford, CT

HOYT, Joshua (1670-1745) & Mary PICKETT; 16 Mar 1698, prob 1697/8; Stratford, CT/Stamford, CT

HOYT, Moses (?1636-) & ?Elizabeth __?_ ; b 1660?, b 1659, b 1658; Fairfield, CT/Eastchester, NY

HOYT/HAIGHT, Moses (1662-1712) & Elizabeth __?_ ; b 1692; Eastchester, NY

HOYT, Nicholas (1622-1655) & Susanna (_?_) JOYCE (-1655), ?w William; 12 Jul 1646, 12 Jun?, 1 Jun; Windsor, CT

HAIGHT, Samuel (1647-1712) & Sarah __?__ (1650-1740?) (see HAIGHT); b 1667?; Flushing, LI/Eastchester, NY

HOYT, Samuel (1643-1720) & 1/wf Hannah HOLLY (-1710); 16 Nov 1671, 16 Nov 167-, 167[0]; Stamford, CT

HOYT, Samuel (1667-1712) & Charity [?FIELD]; b 1692 (see HAIGHT); Flushing, LI/Westchester, NY

HOYT, Samuel & 1/wf Susanna (_?_) SLAWSON/SLASON (-1707), w Eleazer (see SLAWSON); 24 Oct 1700; Stamford, CT

HOYT, Samuel & Mary SCOFIELD, ?Norwalk, ?Danbury; b 1701?, 31 Dec 1700?, Upway, Eng

HOYT, Simon (1590-1657) & 1/wf Deborah STOWERS (1593-); 2 Dec 1612, Dec 1612, 1? Dec; Salem/Dorchester/Scituate

HOYT, Simon (1590-1657) & 2/wf Susanna [SMITH] (-1674), m/2 Robert BATES; bef Apr 1635; Dorchester/Windsor, CT

HYATT, Thomas (1618-1656) & Elizabeth [RUSSELL?], m/2 Cornelius JONES 1657; b 26 Aug 1633; Dorchester/Stamford, CT

HOYT, Thomas (1641-) & 1/wf Mary [BROWN], dau Wm.; ca 1667; Amesbury

HYATT, Thomas & Mary St.JOHN; ca 10 Nov 1677; Stamford, CT/Norwalk, CT

HOYT, Thomas, Jr. & 1/wf Elizabeth HUNTINGTON; 22 May 1689, 1690?; Amesbury

HOYT, Thomas (1641-) & 2/wf Mary ASH, m/2 James HALL, ca 1692; 29 Nov 1689, 1690; Amesbury

HOYT, Thomas (1674/5-) & __?_ ; b 1701?; ?Norwalk

HOYT, Walter (1616-1698) & 1/wf __?_/?Elizabeth St.JOHN?; b 1644; Windsor, CT

HOYT, Walter (1616, 1624?-1698, 1699?) & 2/wf Rhoda (_?_) [TAYLOR], w John; b 1652; Windsor, CT/Deerfield

HOYT, William & Dorothy COLBY; 12 Jan 1687/8; Amesbury

HOYT, Zerubbabel (1654?, 1652?-1727/8?) & 1/wf [?Hannah KNAPP]; b 1675?, b 1676, 1673?; Norwalk, CT

HUBBARD, Anthony & (1/wf) Sarah BACON (ca 1626-1652); 14 Apr 1648; Dedham

HUBBARD, Anthony & (2/wf) Jane ELY; 5 Jan 1652/3; Dedham

HUBBARD, Benjamin (returned to Eng) & Alice [WARD]; b 1633; Charlestown

HUBBARD, Benjamin & __?_, ?m/2 John RHODES; Jamaica, LI

HUBBARD, Daniel (1644-1720) & Elizabeth JORDAN (ca 1642-1731+); 17 Nov 1664; Guilford, CT

HUBBARD, Daniel (1645-1704) & 1/wf Mary CLARKE (-1673); 24 Feb 1669/70; Middletown, CT/Haddam, CT

HUBBARD, Daniel (1645-1704) & 2/wf Sarah CORNWELL (1647-); 16 Oct 1675; Middletown, CT

HUBBARD, Daniel (1661-1744) & Esther/Hester RICE (1665-); 1 Nov 1683; Hadley

HUBBARD, Daniel (1666-1702) & Elizabeth CRUTTENDEN (1670-), m/2 William SMITH; 5 Dec 1691; Guilford, CT

HUBBARD, Daniel (1673-) & Susannah [BAILEY]; 8 Dec 1697; Haddam, CT

HUBBARD, Ebenezer (1664-1743) & Mary WARNER (1665-1739); 5 May 1690; Middletown, CT

HUBBARD, Edward (1643-1688+) & Martha TURNER, w Laurence; 2 Mar 1670, E. A., NY; Westchester, NY

HUBBARD, Elias (1673-) & Jaunetie VanDRIEST, w John BARENSZ; 15 Dec 1699; Gravesend, LI

HUBBARD, George (?1594-1683) & Mary __?__ (-1676); b 1628; Watertown/Wethersfield, CT/Milford, CT/Guilford, CT?

HUBBARD, George (1601-1684/5) & Elizabeth [WATTS] (1616, ?1622-1702?); b 1640, b 1641/2?; Hartford/Middletown, CT/Wethersfield

HUBBARD, George (-1688) & Abigail __?__; b 1688; Greenwich, CT/Hartford/Middletown, CT

HUBBARD, George & Mehitable [MILLER] (1680/1-); b 1701?; Middletown, CT

HUBBARD, Hugh (-1685) & Jane (LATHAM) (1648-1739), m/2 John WILLIAMS; 18 Mar 1672/3; New London, CT

HUBBARD, Isaac (1667-1750) & Ann/Anna?/Anne [WARNER] (1669-1750); b 1693; Hadley/Hatfield/Sunderland

HUBBARD, Isaac (1679-) & Hannah [DICKINSON], m/2 Benjamin CHURCH 1714; b 1701; Glastonbury, CT

HUBBARD, James (1608-1639) & Sarah [IVES]?, ?m/2 William HAMLET; ca 1630, [b 1635]; Watertown/?Cambridge

HUBBARD, James & 1/wf Martha __?__; b 1655; Charlestown/Lynn/Gravesend, LI

HUBBARD, James (1631-1693) & 1/wf Sarah WINSHIP (-1665); 29 Sep 1659; Cambridge/Lexington/Watertown

HUBBARD, James & 2/wf Elizabeth BALIES/BAILES (-1693); 31 Dec 1664; Gravesend, LI

HUBBARD, James (1631-1693) & 2/wf Hannah IVE/IVES (1643-1690); 8 Jan 1667; Cambridge

HUBBARD, James (1665-) & Rachel BERGEN; b 1686; Gravesend, LI/Middleton, NJ

HUBBARD, John (-1706) & Mary SHEAFE?/MERRIAM?/MORRISON (1625-); b 1650/1?; Wethersfield, CT/Hadley/Hatfield

HUBBARD/HUBBERD?, John & Mary BAKER (1649-); 1 Mar 1670; Northampton

HUBBARD, John (1648-1710) & Ann [LEVERETT] (1652-1717); b 1673, 1671, 12 Nov 1672; Boston

HUBERT, John & [Rebecca?] [WELLS?]; b 1674; Roxbury/Boston?

HUBBARD, John (1655+-) & Mary __?__; 1676 ca?; Hadley/Glastonbury, CT

HUBBARD/HUBERT, John & Sarah __?__; b 1683; Boston

HUBBARD, John (1669-) & Jane FOLLANSBEE; 1688; Kingston, NH/Salisbury

HUBBARD, John (1677, 1678?-1712) & Sarah TYRRELL; b 1701?; Guilford, CT

HUBBARD, Jonathan (1659-1728) & Hannah RICE (1650, 1658?-1749); 15 Mar 1681; Concord

HUBBARD, Joseph (1643-1686) & Mary PORTER/PARFFER (1650-1707); 29 Dec 1670; Middletown, CT

HUBBERT, Joseph & Thankful BROWN; 4 Aug 1698; Sudbury/Boston

HUBBARD, Nathaniel (1652-1738) & Mary EARLE [1663-1732]; 29 May 1682, 168[-]; Middletown, CT

HUBBARD, Philip (-1713) & Elizabeth (GOODWIN) EMERY, w Zachary; 22 Dec 1692; Topsfield/Berwick?

HUBBARD, Philip & Wilmott __?__; b 1699; Marblehead

HUBBARD, Richard (1631-1681) & Sarah BRADSTREET, m/2 Samuel WARD; ca 1658; Cambridge/Ipswich

HUBBARD, Richard (-1719, ae 88) & [Martha] [ALLEN] (1646-1718); b 8 Jun 1666; Salisbury

HUBBARD, Richard (1655-1732) & Martha CORNWELL/CORNELL (1669-); 31 Mar 1692; Middletown, CT

HUBBARD, Richard (-1699) & Elizabeth CLARK, m/2 Rev. Cotton MATHER 1703; 9 Nov 1697; Ipswich/Boston

HUBBARD, Robert & Margaret ALLEN, wid; 2 Jun 1654; Boston/Dover, NH?

HUBBARD, Samuel (1610-1689) & Tacy/Tase COOPER (1608-1697±); 4 Jan 1636; Windsor, CT/Newport/Springfield/Fairfield, CT/Wethersfield, CT

HUBBARD, Samuel (1648-1732) & Sarah KIRBY (1653-); 9 Aug 1673; Middletown, CT/Wethersfield, CT/Hartford, CT

HUBBARD, Samuel (1678-1745) & Martha PECK (1679-1752); 1 Nov 170[0], 1701?; Wallingford, CT?

HUBBARD, Thomas (-1671) & Mary [CURTIS], m/2 John HALL 1674; b 1656(7?); Middletown, CT

HUBBARD, Thomas (-Nov 1662) & Elizabeth HUIT/HEWETT; 15 Oct 1662; Billerica

HUBBARD, Thomas (1653-1717) & Mary [TUTHELD] (1669-1726, 1720?); ca 1690; Boston

HUBBARD, William (1594-1670) & __?__; in Eng, b 1613; ?Ipswich

HUBBARD, William (1594-1670) & 2/wf? Judith [KNAPP] (1610?-); in Eng, b 1620; Ipswich/Boston/Salisbury
HUBBARD, William (1621-1704) & [Mary?/?Margaret ROG..RS?] (1628-1685+); b 1647; Lynn/Wethersfield/Hartford/Salisbury
HUBBARD, William (1640/2-1684, 1702) & (Abigail DUDLEY)/?Catherine AUSTIN, w John?; b 1670, aft 24 Aug 1657, b 1663, aft 13 May 1658; Greenwich, CT/Stamford, CT
HUBBARD, William (1670?-1723) & Hannah [MEAD]; b 1694; Stamford, CT
HUBBARD, William (-1704) & 2/wf Mary (GIDDINGS) PEARCE (-1711, ae 53), w Samuel PEARCE; m cont 15 Mar 1694; Salisbury
HUBBERT/HOBBERT, _?_ & Elizabeth _?_ (-1644); Boston
HUBBELL, Ebenezer (-1698) & Mary [HARRIS] (1667-), m/2 Ebenezer GRIFFING 1703; b 1693; New London, CT
HUBBELL, John (1652±-1690) & Patience [NICHOLS] (1660-), m/2 Samuel HAWLEY 1691?; b 1681; Stratford, CT
HUBBELL, Richard[1] (-1699) & 1/wf Elizabeth [MEIGS] (-1664); ca 1651; New Haven/Guilford, CT/Fairfield/Stratford, CT
HUBBELL, Richard[1] (-1699) & 2/wf Elizabeth [GAYLORD] (1647-1688), Windsor; ca 1669; Windsor, CT
HUBBELL, Richard[2] (1654±-1738) & 1/wf Rebecca MOREHOUSE (-1692); 5 Nov 1685, Fairfield; Stratfield, CT
HUBBELL, Richard[1] (1617-1699) & 3/wf Abigail (PRUDDEN) WALKER (1648-1717), w Joseph; m cont 16 Apr 1688; Stratford, CT
HUBBELL, Richard[2] (-1738) & 2/wf Hannah SILLOWAY/SWILLOWAY (1666-); 12 Oct 1692; Fairfield, CT
HUBBELL, Samuel (-1714) & 1/wf Elizabeth WILSON (-1688); 4 Apr 1687; Fairfield, CT
HUBBELL, Samuel (-1714) & 2/wf Temperance (NICHOLS?) PRESTON, w Jehiel; 17 Apr 1688; ?Stratfield, CT
HUBBELL, Samuel & Elizabeth [BURR?]; b 1695; Fairfield, CT
HUBBEY, Joseph & _?_ ; 1689; Milton
HUBBS, John (1646-1697) & Susannah [LININGTON]; NY
HUBS, Robert & Ann (?REDMAN)/[(RICHBELL)] MOTT (-1698+); w Adam; b 5 Nov 1691; Mamaroneck, LI
HUCKINS, James (-1689) & Sarah [BURNHAM/BARNHAM] (1654-), m/2 John WOODMAN 1700; ca 1671; Dover, NH
HUCKENS, John (1649-1678) & Hope CHIPMAN (1652-1728), m/2 Jonathan COBB 1683; 10 Aug 1670; Barnstable
HUCKINS, Robert & Elizabeth _?_, m/2 William BEARD b 1655; b 1644?, b 1654; Dover, NH
HUCKINS, Robert (1672-1720) & Welthean [THOMAS], m/2 John GRAY; ca 1692; Dover, NH
HUCKENS, Thomas (?1617-1679) & 1/wf Mary [WELLS] (-1648); 1642; Barnstable
HUCKINS, Thomas (?1617-1679) & 2/wf Rose (_?_) HYLLIER/TILLYE (1616-1687), w Hugh; 3 Nov 1648; Barnstable
HUCKINS, Thomas (1651-1714) & 1/wf Hannah CHIPMAN (1658/9-1696); 1 May 1680; Barnstable
HUCKINS, Thomas (1651-1714) & 2/wf Sarah (POPE) HINKLEY (1652-1714+, 1727), w Samuel; 17 Aug 1698; Barnstable
HUKLY/HUCKLEY, William (-1731) & Sarah CARR (1681-); 30 Dec 1700; Salisbury
HUDELSTON/HUDLESTON, Valentine (-1727, ae 99, Dartmouth) & Katharine _?_ ; b 1673; Newport
HUDSON, Daniel (?1617-1697) & Joanna [WHITE?] (-1697), dau John; b 1648(9?); Lancaster/Watertown/Cambridge/Framingham
HUDSON, Daniel (1651-) & Mary MAYNARD (1651-1677); 21 Jul 1675; Sudbury/Concord
HUTSON, Daniel & Mary ORCUTT (bpt 11 Apr 1675-, Scituate); 19 May 1697; Bridgewater
HUDSON, Francis (1618-1700) & 1/wf Mary _?_ ; b 1640; Boston
HUDSON, Francis (1618-1700) & 2/wf Elizabeth WATKINS; m int 20 Aug 1695; Boston
HUDSON, Francis & Mary GOODWYN; 1 May 1700; Boston/Charlestownn
HUDSON/HUTCHINGS?, George & Jane _?_ ; b 1639; Cambridge
HUDSON, James & 1/wf Anne _?_ (-1652); b 1643; Boston
HUDSON, James & 2/wf Rebecca BROWNE (-Nov 1653, Boston); 3 Feb 1652/3; Boston
HUDSON, James & 3/wf Mary _?_ ; b 1654(5?); Boston

HUDSON/HODSHON, John (see HODSHON) (-1690, ca 1688) & Abigail TURNER; 2 Sep 1651; New Haven

HUDSON, John (-1688) & 2/wf? Ann (ROGERS) [RUSSELL], dau John, w George; b 1656?, b 1660(1?), b 1664?; Duxbury

HUDSON, John & Abigail HOUGHTON (1664-); ?14 May 1688; Milton

HUDSON, John & 2/wf? Mary BEARD; Jul 1689, 25 Jul; Dover, NH

HUDSON/HODSHON/HODSON, John & Elizabeth TROWBRIDGE; 5 Apr 1691; New Haven

HUDSON, John & Susanna NORDEN; 17 Aug 1693; Boston

HUDSON, Jonathan & 1/wf Elizabeth _?_ (-1698); b 1658, b 1656?; Lynn

HUDSON, Jonathan & Sarah (WICKHAM) CHERRY, w John; 13 Jun 1686, 17 Jun; Lyme

HUDSON, Jonathan & 2/wf Elinor WATTS, w Jeremiah; 21 Jun 1698; Salem

HUDSON, Moses & Sarah COLLINS; 12 Nov 1685; Lynn

HUDSON, Nathaniel[1] & Elizabeth ALFORD, dau William; 1 Dec 1659; Boston

HUDSON, Nathaniel (1671-1697) & Rebecca [RUGG]; 1692?, 1693?; Lancaster

HUDSON, Nathaniel (-1701) & Rachel [SCOVILLE], w Arthur, m/3 James SMITH; b 1696; Lyme, CT

HUDSON/HODSHON, Nathaniel (1671-1701) & Abigail [CHAUNSEY] (1677-), m/2 Samuel GASKELL, m/3 Edward BURROUGHS; b 1698 (see HUDSON); Stratford, CT

HUDSON, Ralph (1692-1651) & Mary [THWING?]/?FITCH (1592-); in Eng, b 1621; Boston

HUDSON, Robert (1673-1724) & Mary MILLER? (1668-), m/2 Isaac HALSEY; b 1701; Easthampton, LI

HUDSON, Samuel (1650-) & Abigail [SHORE] (1653-), m/2 William CLOUGH; b 1673, Dec 1674; Boston

HUDSON, Thomas & ?Mary/_?_ _?_; b 1638, b 1617?; Lynn

HUDSON, Thomas & Sarah CROCKER; 24 Oct 1697; Boston

HUDSON, William & Susan _?_; b 1630?, b 1634; Charlestown/Boston (returned to Eng)

HUDSON, William (-1681) (ae 57 in 1670) & 1/wf Anne _?_; 1641?; Boston

HUDSON, William & _?_ LATTING, dau Richard; ca 1670/5?; Stratford, CT

HUDSON, William (-1681) & 2/wf Mary FOWNELL (-1696, in 85th y), w John; 23 Feb 1676/7, ?23 Jan; Charlestown

HUDSON, William (1664/5-1729+) & Experience [WILLIS]; ca 1690/1700?, no issue; Bridgewater

HUDSON, _?_ & Hannah _?_; b 1685; Hempstead, LI

HUSTED/HUESTED, Angel (?1620-1706) & Rebecca [?SHERWOOD] (-1706+); b 1656, b 1645?; Greenwich, CT

HUSTED, Angel (-1727) & Mary _?_/?MEAD; b 1690; Greenwich, CT

HUSTED, John (1662±-) & Mary _?_; b 1701?; Greenwich, CT

HUSTED, Jonathan (-1706) & Mary [LOCKWOOD], m/2 Joseph KNAPP; by 1681, no issue; Greenwich, CT

HUSTED, Joseph & _?_; b 1685; Greenwich, CT

HUSTED, Robert (?1596-1652) & Elizabeth [MILLER?] (-1654); b 1620?; Boston/Braintree/Greenwich/Stamford, CT

HUSTED, Robert (-1704) & Elizabeth BUXTON; 9 Jan 1655; ?Stamford, CT/Westchester, NY

HUSTED, Samuel (1665, 1675?-1741) & Sarah _?_/KNAPP?; b 1698?; Greenwich, CT

HUFF, Ferdinando & Mary [MOSES]; b 1 Mar 1664/5; Portsmouth, NH

HUFF, Thomas & Grace FERRIS; 2 Jan 1700, 1700/01; Kittery, ME

HUFF, William & Lydia _?_; b 1673; Boston

HOUGH, William & Mary _?_; b 1685; Boston

HUGGINS, John (1609-1670) & Bridget _?_ (1616?, 1605-1695), m/2 John CLIFFORD 1671; b 1636, b 1640; Hampton, NH

HUGGINS, John (1652-1704, Suffield, CT) & 1/wf Hannah BURPEE (1655-1683); 19 Oct 1681, 1682 (HIGGINS is wrong); Suffield/Hampton, NH

HUGGINS, John (1652-1704) (HIGGINS is wrong) & Experience JONES (1662-1714); 4 Feb 1684; Suffield, CT/Springfield

HUGGINS, Nathaniel (1660-) & 1/wf Sarah [HAINES] (1673-1714+); Greenland, NH

HUGGINS, Thomas & Sarah _?_; b 1700; Boston

HUSE, Abel (1602-1690) & 1/wf Eleanor _?_ (-1663); no issue; Newbury

HUSE, Abel (1602-1690) & 2/wf Mary (HILTON) SEARS, w Thomas; 25 May 1663; Newbury

HUSE, Abel (1664-1757) & Judith [EMERY] (1672-1753); b 1696, b 1694; Newbury

HEWES, Arthur & 1/wf Dunie STEVENS; 30 Jun 1660-63; Saco, ME/Salem

HEWES, Arthur & 2/wf Sarah [ANGIER], w Sampson; b 20 Jan 1693/4; Saco, ME/Portsmouth, NH
HEWES/HUGHES, Arthur & Ruth BOLTON/BOULTON (1667-); 15 Aug 1698; Boston
HEWES, George & Mary [ALLEN] (1644-); b 1672; Salisbury
HEWES, George (-?1712, Sudbury) & Lydia (KIBBY) BENNETT (1637-), w George; 3 Jul 1679; Lancaster/Concord
HUGHES, James & Elizabeth _?_; b 1670, b 1680; Gloucester/Boston
HEWS, James & Bethiah SWETMAN; 12 Dec 1692; Cambridge
HUGHES/HUES, Robert, Stow & Mary [CRANE], Stow; b 1688(89?), 21 Sep 1688; Stow/Marlboro
HUGHS, John & Mary HOBART (-1674); 9 Dec 1664; Hingham
HUGHES/HEWES?, John & Deliverance PALLARD; 15 Sep 1698; Boston
HUGHS, William (see HEWES) & Elizabeth [GRAFTON?] (1667-); b 1699, 25 Nov 1689?, 1684; Boston
HUGHS, William & Mary [?SMITH]; b 1699(1700?); Boston
HUGHES, Samuel (-1693) & Mary DOWD; 26 Apr 1666; Guilford, CT
HUGHES, Lewis, Lyme, CT, & Sarah HUNGERFORD (1654?, 1659?-); Haddam, CT?/Lyme, CT
HUGHES/HUSE, Nicholas (-1692) (see HUSE) & Abigail THOMPSON CURTIS (1646-1731), wid; ca 1692, aft 1681; Guilford, CT
HUSE, Lewis & Martha HAZARD (1630?-), wid; b 22 Mar 1691, ca 1690; Portsmouth, RI
HUGHS, Robert & Elizabeth BUXTON; 6 Jan 1655; Stamford, CT
HEWES/HUGHES, Richard & 1/wf Anne _?_; b 1637; Dorchester/Guilford, CT
HUGHES/HUES, Richard (-1658) & 2/wf Mary _?_, m/2 William STONE; b 1651; Guilford, CT
HUGHS, Humphrey & Martha _?_; b 1669; Southampton/Bridgehampton, LI
HUKE, Richard & Hannah [BEARDSLEY?]; b 1686
HULING, Alexander (1665-1725) & Elizabeth WIGHTMAN (1664-1756); b 1695?; Newport/N. Kingstown, RI
HULING, Josiah & Amy _?_; b 1674+; New Shoreham, RI
HULLING, Josiah/Jesse? & Mary [DOLOVER]; 22 Jan, 11 Jan 1675; New Shoreham, RI
HULING, James (1635-1687) & Margaret _?_ (1632-1707); b 1658; Newport
HULING, John (1658±-1708+) & Sarah _?_ (1668-1708); Newport
HULING, Walter (-1710±) & Martha _?_ (-1718+); b 1701?; Newport, RI
HULL, Andrew (1606-1640) & Catherine/Katharine [COOK?] (1612-), m/2 Richard BEACH 1641?; b 1635; New Haven
HULL, Benjamin & Mary [FERNSIDE] (1646-); ca 1664; ?Portsmouth, NH/Portland, ME
HULL, Benjamin (1639-) & Rachel [YORK]; b 1668; Oyster River, NH/Piscataway, NJ
HULL, Benjamin (1672-1741) & Elizabeth ANDREWS (1674-1731); 14 Dec 1693, 14 Sep 1693; Stratford, CT/Wallingford, CT
HULL, Cornelius (1626, 1628-1695) & Rebecca JONES (?1633-), ?m/2 Joseph THRALE; 19 Nov 1652; Fairfield, CT
HULL, Cornelius (1654-1740) & Sarah [SANFORD] (1656-1744+, 1753?); ca 1685?; Fairfield, CT
HULL, Dodivah (-1682) & Mary [SEWARD] (1658-), m/2 Samuel BLAGDON by 1688; York, ME/Portsmouth, NH
HULL, Edward & Eleanor NEWMAN; 20 Jan 1652/3; Boston
HULL, George (1590?-) & [Tamsen/Thomasine? MITCHELL] "of Stocklande"; in Eng, 27 Aug 1614, 17 Aug 1614, 27 Sep 1614; Dorchester/Windsor, CT/Fairfield, CT
HULL, George (-1659?) & 2/wf Sarah (_?_) [PHIPPEN] (-1659), w David; ?ca 31 Oct 1650, ca Jun 1654, 1654; Stratford, CT
HULL, George & Elizabeth WELLMAN (-1740, ae 80); 20 Aug 1674; Beverley/Salem
HULL, Hopewell & Mary Martin in NJ; Durham, NH
HULL, Isaac (-1706) & _?_; b 1655
HULL, Isaac (-1708, Wenham) & Sarah (COCK) SOLART (1654/5-1739, in 84th y), w John; 1 Sep 1675, in Eng; Salem/Beverly
HULL, Jeremiah & Hannah BALDWIN (1642-); 6 May 1658; New Haven/Milford, CT
HULL, Jeremiah & Mehitable [SMEAD] (1668-1704), m/2 Godfrey NIMS 1692; 1688; Deerfield
HULL, John (1624-1683) & Judith QUINCY (1626-1695); 11 May 1647; ?Boston
HULL, John (-1670) & Margaret [CUTHERIDGE] (-1683); ca 1650?, aft 3 Apr 1647; Watertown/Newbury
HULL, John (1644-1728) & Abigail KELSEY; 3 Dec 1668; Killingworth, CT
HULL, John & 2/wf Mary JONES; 19 Oct 1671, 1672?; ?Stratford

HULL, John (-1673) & Mary [SPENCER], m/2 William PHIPS, m/3 Peter SARGEANT 1701; b 1673, no issue; Boston/Saco, ME?

HULL, John (-1711) & 1/wf Mary BEACH?/ANDREWS? (1642-); b 1661(2?); Stratford, CT/Derby, CT/Wallingford, CT

HULL, John (-1711) & 2/wf Mary JONES; 19 Oct 1671, 1672; New Haven/Derby, CT

HULL, John (?1654-1732, ae 80?) & Alice TEDDEMAN (-1734, ae 75); Harsloadown, Southwark, Eng, 23 Oct 1684; Barnstable, MA/Newport/Jamestown

HULL, John & 2/wf Tabitha (TOMLINSON) [WOOSTER] (-1691), w Edward; 1690; New Haven/Fairfield

HULL, John (1662-1714) & Mary [MERWIN]/Hannah PRINDLE? (1666-); ca 1690, b 1691; Stratford, CT/Derby, CT

HULL, John of Wallingford (Derby) & 3/wf Mary (MESSENGER) [BENEDICT]; aft 22 Feb 1688/9, b 13 May 1693

HULL, John (1668-) & Mary?/Mercy? JACOBS; 1 Jan 1695; New Haven

HULL, John & 3/wf, 4/wf Rebecca (KESLER) TURNEY, w Benjamin; 21 Sep 1699, 20 Sep 1699; Wallingford, CT/Fairfield, CT

HULL, Rev. Joseph (1595-1665) & 1/wf [Joane?] _?_ (-1632+?); in Eng, b 1620; Weymouth/Hingham/etc.

HULL, Rev. Joseph (1595-1665) & 2/wf Agnes _?_ (1610-); in Eng, b 1630, ?aft 1632?, b 1631; Weymouth

HULL, Joseph (1622-) & _?_ ; b 1642; York, ME

HULL, Joseph (1652-1709+) & Experience HARPER (1657-); Oct 1676; Barnstable/Kings Town, RI

HULL, Joseph & Mary _?_ ; b 1678, 1676; Killingworth, CT

HULL, Joseph & Mary [MERWIN] (1666-) (no)

HULL, Joseph (1669-1744) & 1/wf Mary NICHOLS (1674-1733); 20 Jan 1691, 1691/2; Stratford, CT/Derby, CT

HULL, Joseph & _?_ ; b 1700; Falmouth, ME

HULL, Joseph & Elizabeth [?FARNHAM]/[?RUCKE]; b 13 Feb 1699/1700; ?Killingworth, CT

HULL, Joseph & Ann [GARDINER]; 1700, b 23 May 1701; Kingston, RI/etc.

HULL, Josiah/Josias (1612?, 1620-1675) & Elizabeth LOOMIS (-1665+); 20 May 1641, 1640?; Windsor, CT/Killingworth, CT

HULL, Josias (1642-1670) & Elizabeth _?_, m/2 _?_ TALMAGE?; b 1665; Killingworth, CT

HULL, Phineas (1648-) & 1/wf Jerusha [HITCHCOCK]; b 1671?; Kittery, ME

HULL, Phineas & 2/wf Mary (RISHWORTH) WHITE (aft 21 Dec 1654-), m/3 James PLAISTED; b 1690, aft 28 Mar 1673/4, betw Nov 1673 & Jun 1679

HULL, Reuben (1644?-1689) & Hannah (ALCOCK)? [FERNSIDE] (1650-), m/3 George SNELL; ca 1672, 1673, 1670; Portsmouth, NH

HULL, Richard (1599-1662) & _?_ ; b 1633?; New Haven

HULL, Robert & Elizabeth [STORER?] (-1646), w? Paul; b 1624; Boston

HULL, Robert (-1666, ae 73) & 2/wf Judith (PARES) QUINCY [PAINE], w Edmund, w Moses; aft 7 May 1646, b 1654; Boston

HULL, Samuel & 1/wf Mary [MANNING]; 1677, NJ?; Durham, NH

HULL, Samuel (?1663-1720) & 1/wf Deborah [BEERS]; b 14 Nov 1694, b 1685; Fairfield, CT

HULL, Samuel (?1663-1720) & 2/wf Elizabeth (HUBBELL) [FROST] (-1712), w Joseph; ca 1699?, b 1700; Fairfield, CT

HULL, Theophilus (-1710) & Mary [SANFORD] (1670-1712); ca 1690/93, 2 ch bpt 1694, ca 1690; Fairfield, CT

HULL, Thomas (-1670) & Hannah TOWNSEND, m/2 Hope ALLEN 1671?, m/3 Richard KNIGHT 1674?, m/4 Richard WAY 1689; 3 Apr 1657; Boston

HULL, Thomas (1665-) & Hannah SHEATHER; 10 Dec 1685; Killingworth, CT

HULL, Tristram (1624-1667) & Blanche _?_, m/2 William HEDGE; b 1645; Barnstable

HULL, Tristram & Elizabeth DYER; 9 Feb 1698, 19 Dec 1698; ?Newport/Jamestown?

HULSE, Richard & Hannah [BEARDSLEY?], m/2 Samuel SWEZEY; b 1665/70; Brookhaven, LI

HUMBER, Edward & _?_ ; b 1664; Weymouth/Salem

HUMMERSTON/HUMBERSTON, Henry (-1663) & Joan WALKER, m/2 Richard LITTLE 1664; 28 Aug 1651; New Haven

HUMISTON, John (1659-) & Sarah TUTTLE, m/2 Roger TYLER 1698; 10 Sep 1685; New Haven

HUMMERSON, Samuel (1653-1691) & Hannah JOHNSON; 21 Jun 1677; New Haven

HUMRSTON, Thomas (1656-) & 1/wf Elizabeth SAMFORD/SANFORD; 31 May 1694, at Wallingford; New Haven
HUMPHREY, Arthur (-1752, in 89th y, Ashford, CT) & Rachel _?_ (-1744, in 77th y); b 1690; Woodstock, CT
HUMPHRIS, Benhemoth & Elizabeth WHITEMORE; 11 Mar 1699/1700; Dedham
HUMPHREY, Edward (had son Combs) & Elizabeth [COMBS?], dau Henry?; b 1674; Marblehead
HUMPHREY, Edward & Naomi COLLINS; 27 Jun 1700; Marblehead
HUMPHREY, George (-1732) & Elizabeth CARVER (-1748, ae 84); 16 Feb 1686/7; Hingham
HUMPHREYS, Henry & Sarah BROWNE; 18 Jul 1700; Marblehead
HUMPHREY, Hopestill (1649-1731) & 1/wf Elizabeth BAKER (1660-1714); 21 Nov 1677; Dorchester
HUMPHREY, Isaac (1651-1735) & 1/wf Patience ATHERTON (1654-1691); 7 Jul 1685; Dorchester
HUMPHREY, Isaac (1651-1735) & 2/wf Ruth LEADBETTER (1669-1752); 6 Oct 1692; Dorchester
HUMPHREY, James (1608-1686, in 78th y) & Mary _?_ (-1677); b 1635; Dorchester
HUMPHREY, James (1665-1718) & 1/wf Thankful WHITE (1668-1699, Weymouth); 4 Nov 1697; Boston/Weymouth
HUMPHREY, John (ca 1595-1661) (returned to Eng) & 2/wf Susan [LINCOLN?]/CLINTON?; ca 1625, b 1620?, 1628+, ca 1630; Salem
HUMPHREY, John (1650-1698, Simsbury) & Hannah [GRIFFIN] (1649-); b 1671; Windsor, CT/Simsbury, CT
HUMPHREY, John & Kate JOHNSON; 2 Jun 1698; Boston
HUMPHREY, John (1671-) & Sarah (PETTIBONE) MILLS, w John; 6 Jul 1699; Simsbury, CT
HUMPHREYS, John & Elizabeth _?_; b 1699(1700?); Boston
HUMPHREY, Jonas[1] (-1662) & 1/wf Frances COLEY/COOLEY?; Wendover, Bucks, 11 Jun 1607; Weymouth
HUMPHREY, Jonas (?1621-1699) & Martha _?_ (-1712); b 1649; Weymouth
HUMPHRY, Jonas (-1662) & 2/wf Jane (CLAPP) WEEKS (-1660), w George; Dorchester
HUMPHREY, Jonas & Mary [PHILLIPS] (1661-), m/2 Peter NEWCOMB 1689+; ca 1678; Weymouth
HUMPHRY, Joseph & Sarah SMITH; 28 Oct 1697; Boston
HUMPHREY, Joseph (-1766) & 1/wf Mary _?_ (1673-1742); b 1698; Hingham
HUMPHREY, Michael (-1697) & Priscilla GRANT (1626-); 14 Oct 1647; Windsor, CT
HUMPHREY, Nathaniel (-1701, ca 48) & Elizabeth _?_; b 1685; Weymouth
HUMPHREY, Samuel (?1649, 1650-) & Mary [TORREY] (1656-1714+); b 1679; Weymouth/RI
HUMPHREY, Samuel (1656-1736) & Mary [MILLS] (1662-1730); b 1681; Windsor, CT/Simsbury, CT
HUMPHREY, Thomas & Hannah LANE (1639-); 23 Dec 1665; Hingham/Dover, NH
HUNGERFORD, Thomas (-1663) & 1/wf _?_; b 1648; Hartford/New London, CT
HUNGERFORD, Thomas (-1663) & 2/wf Hannah [WILLEY], m/2 Peter BLATCHFORD 1663?, m/3 Samuel SPENCER 1673?; ca 1658; New London, CT
HUNGERFORD, Thomas (1648-1714) & Mary [GREEN?/GRAY?] (had son Green); b 1670?, b 6 Jun 1671; New London, CT/Haddam, CT
HUNGERFORD, Thomas (1672-) & Elizabeth [SMITH]; ca 1699; E. Haddam, CT
HUNKINGS, Hercules (-1659) & Beaton _?_, m/2 William HEARL; ca 1630; Star Island
HUNKINGS, John (-1682) & 1/wf Ann/Agnes [HUNKINGS] (ca 1630-); b 1651; Portsmouth, NH
HUNKINGS, John & Sarah [LEIGH]; ?b 1672, b 1677; Ipswich/Portsmouth, NH
HUNKINGS, John (-1682) & 2/wf Richord _?_, m/2 George SNELL; by 1679, ?aft Oct 1681; Star Island/Portsmouth, NH
HUNKINS, John (1660-1715) & Mary [LEIGHTON] (1657-); by 23 Sep 1682; Kittery, ME/?Boston
HUNKINGS, Mark (-1667) & Ann _?_ (-1667+); Portsmouth, NH
HUNKING, Mark (-1728) & Sarah [SHERBURNE] (1651-1720+); ca 1671
HUNKING, Mark (1670-) & Mary HARVEY, m/2 John NEWMARCH 1699; 29 Jun 1697; Kittery, ME/NH
HUNKINS, William (1668-) & Sarah PARTRIDGE (1668-); 12 May 1692; Durham, NH
HUNLOCK, Edward & Margaret _?_; b 1682; Boston/Burlington, NJ
HUNLOCK, John (-1717) & Joanna [SENDALL] (1651-1706); b 1667; Boston

HUNN, George (-1640?) & Ann _?_, m/2 William PHILPOT 1651; in Eng, b 1626; Boston
HUNN, Nathaniel (ca 1627-1704, 1702) & 1/wf Sarah (KIENE); b 1652, b 1650?, 1649; Boston
HUNN, Nathaniel (-1679) & Priscilla KITCHIN (1647-), m/2 George BOWERS; - Oct 1672; Salem
HUNN, Nathaniel (ca 1650-bef 1711) & Rebecca [HALE] (1651-); b 1682, b 1672; Wethersfield, CT
HUNN, Samuel (ca 1672-1738) & Sarah DIKES/DIX (-1753); 18 Aug 1696; Wethersfield, CT
HUNNEWELL, Ambrose & Jane? HOMES?; Plymouth, Eng, 1 Nov 1659; ME
HONYWELL, Ambrose (?1657-1731+) & Hannah _?_; b 1685(6?); Boston
HUNNEWELL, Charles (-1737) & Elizabeth DAVIS (-1763, ae 91); 17 Nov 1698; Charlestown
HONEYWELL, Israel (1655-1719) & Mary [SPOFFORD] (1656-1729?), m/2 Josiah HUNT; ca 1686?; ?Essex Co., MA/Westchester Co., NY
HUNNEWELL, John & 1/wf Lydia _?_ (-1683); 1 Jan 1680, 1679/80; Wethersfield, CT/Middletown, CT
HUNNEWELL, John & 2/wf Elizabeth [HARRIS] (1660-), Middletown; aft 1683, b 1689; Wethersfield, CT
HUNNEWELL, Richard (-1703) & Elizabeth [STOVER]/[MOORE], m/2 Jeremiah WALFORD, m/3 John DOWNING; 31 Mar 1674; Scarboro, ME
HUNNEWELL, Richard (-1703) & Sarah [ADAMS] (1657-1723); b 1690, no issue; Boston/Scarboro, ME
HUNNEWELL, Roger (-1654) & Bridget _?_, m/2 Richard MOORE; ca 1644; Saco, ME
HUNNEWELL, Roger & Mary MOORE; 2 Oct 1700; York, ME
HUNNEWELL, Stephen & Mary [SHAPLEY]; b 1693, aft 1687; Charlestown
HUNNIBORN, George & Elizabeth (SMITH) [SANFORD], w James; b 1664(5?); Boston
HUNNIBORN, John & Elizabeth _?_; b 1663; Boston
HUNT, Bartholomew (-1687) & Ann _?_ (-1687+); b 1654; Dover, NH/Newport, RI
HUNT, Bartholomew (1654-1718) & Martha _?_ (-1718); ca 1675/80?; Newport/Tiverton, RI
HUNT, Benjamin & Mary PECK (1662-); 4 Feb 1690/1; Rehoboth
HUNT, Ebenezer (1676-1743) & Hannah CLARK (?1681-1758), m/2 Thomas LOOMIS 1743; 27 May 1698; Northampton/Lebanon, CT
HUNT, Edward & 1/wf Sarah [BETTS]; Newtown, LI
HUNT, Edward[1] (-1727) & Ann WEED; 10 Feb 1674, 19 Feb; Amesbury
HUNT, Edward (perhaps his sister witnesses) & ?Cicely _?_; b 9 Apr 1691; Westchester Co., NY
HUNT, Edward & 2/wf Elizabeth [HAZARD]; b 1698; Newtown, LI
HUNT, Enoch & 1/wf _?_; b 1610; Weymouth
HUNT, Enoch & 2/wf Dorothy [BARKER], wid, m/3 John KING; b 1640; Weymouth
HUNT, Enoch & Mary PAINE (1660-); 29 Oct 1678; Rehoboth
HUNT, Ephraim (1610-1687) & 1/wf Ann/Anne/Anna _?_ (-1650?); ca 1645; Weymouth
HUNT, Ephraim (1610-1687) & 2/wf Ebbett [BRINSMEAD] (-1712); b 1655; Weymouth
HUNT, Ephraim (1650-1713) & Joanna [ALCOCK] (1659-1746, ae 87); b 1679; Weymouth/Acushnet
HUNT, Ephraim (1661-1694) & Rebecca _?_, ?m/2 David CARPENTER 1697; b 1687; Rehoboth
HUNT, Ezekiel (1663-1748) & Sarah _?_; ca 1680/85?, b 20 Nov 1693; Freetown/Newport, RI/E. Greenwich, RI
HUNT, George & Mary [NATT]; b 1698, 1695 or bef; Newington, NH
HUNT, Isaac (?1647-1680) & Mary STONE (1649?-1701?, 1706?), m/2 Eliphalet FOX 1681; 14 May 1667; Concord
HUNT, Isaac (1675-1717), Braintree & Mary WILLARD, Braintree, m/2 _?_ LILAND; 26 Apr 1698; Weymouth/Braintree
HUNT, John & Ann (ORGRAVE) CARTER, w Richard; 2 Jan 1671; Charlestown
HUNT, John & [Alice/Elsje BAXTER] (1652-)
HUNT, John & Martha [NEIGHBORS], dau James; b 1674; Boston/Stonington, CT?
HUNT, John & 2/wf? Grace [FOWLER]; ca 1681; Eastchester, NY/Westchester, NY
HUNT, John (1656-1712) & 1/wf Martha [WILLIAMS] (1663-1701); b 1683(4?), b 1679?; Rehoboth/Swansea
HUNT, John (1654-1724) & Ruth QUINCY (1658-1748); 19 Oct 1686, 9 Oct, 13 Oct; Weymouth
HUNT, John (-1691) & Mehitable _?_; b 1690/1; ?Boston
HUNT, Jonathan (1637-1691) & Clemence HOSMER (1642±-1698, 1695?), m/2 John SMITH of Milford, CT, prob 1695; 2 Sep 1662; Hartford/Deerfield

HUNT, Jonathan (1666-1738) & Martha [WILLIAMS] (1671-1751), Pomfret, CT; b 1694; Northampton/Deerfield/Northfield/Stonington, CT
HUNT, Jonathan & Phebe [TITUS]; b 1701?; ?Newtown, LI
HUNT, Joseph (1670-) & Margaret [KEITH?] (-1750); b 1694; Milton/Bridgewater
HUNT, Joseph & [?Elizabeth SEELEY]; b 1694; Westchester Co., NY
HUNT, Joseph, Jr. & Bethiah _?_; b 1694; Westchester, NY
HUNT, Joseph & Lydia (POST) [MOON] (1655-), w Abel; b 1701?; CT
HUNT, Josiah (?1652-) & 1/wf Rebecca [HARRISON] (1654-); b 1672?, b 1674; ?Westchester Co., NY
HUNT, Josiah (?1652-) & 2/wf Martha _?_; b 16 Aug 1688, b 1680; Westchester, NY
HUNT, Josiah, Jr. & Abigail HUSTIS/HUESTED/HUSTED; m bond 24 Dec 1695; Westchester/Westchester Co., NY?
HUNT, Josiah, Jr. & ?Bethia FERGUSEN; m bond 20 Dec 1697; Westchester Co., NY
HUNT, Lewis & 1/wf Mary LAKE (1669-1695); 27 Nov 1684; Salem
HUNT, Lewis & 2/wf Elizabeth PALFRAY; 30 Nov 1696, 25 Nov 1696; Salem
HUNT, Nehemiah (?1631-1717/18) & Mary TOWLE/TOOLL/TOLL/TODD?; 1 Jun 1663; Concord
HUNT, Peter (1615-1692) & Elizabeth SMITH, m/2 James BLAKE 1695; 14 Dec 1646; Rehoboth
HUNT, Peter (1650-1676) & Rebecca PAINE (1656-), m/2 Samuel PECK 1677; 24 Dec 1673; Rehoboth
HUNT, Ralph (-1677) & _?_; b 1656; Newtown, LI
HUNT, Ralph & Susannah (_?_) SMITH?; Jamaica, LI/Maidenhead, NJ
HUNT, Richard (-1682) & Mary _?_; b 1676; Boston
HUNT, Robert (-1640) & Susanna _?_ (-1642); b 1635?, b 1630?; Charlestown/Sudbury
HUNT, Samuel (1633, 1635?-) & Elizabeth [REDDING] (1635?-); b 1657; Ipswich/Concord?
HUNT, Samuel (1640-1707) & Mary _?_ (-1712); ca 1665/70?; Duxbury
HUNT, Samuel (1657-1742) & Mary TOD; 1 May 1678; Ipswich/Concord/Billerica
HUNT, Samuel & 2/wf Mary _?_; b 1689; Billerica/Tewksbury
HUNT, Samuel (1672-1695) & Eleanor DAVIS (1672-1739), m/2 Nehemiah HUNT 1705; 14 May 1695; Concord
HUNT, Samuel & Mary [UNDERHILL]; [b 1694]?, b 20 Jun 1704, b 1701?; ?Lebanon, CT
HUNT, Thomas & [Cicely] [PASBEY]/CLARK; b 1645?, b 1646; Westchester, NY
HUNT, Thomas (-1657) & Elizabeth _?_, m/2 Matthew BARNES 1657; b 1654; Boston
HUNT, Thomas (-1694) & Elizabeth [JESSUP]; bef 6 Aug 1666; Westchester, NY/Stamford, CT/Fairfield, CT
HUNT, Thomas (1648-1722) & 1/wf Judith [TORREY] (1655-1693) (his wf called Joanna in 1677 prob wrong); b 1674; Boston
HUNT, Thomas & 1/wf Mary [FITCH] (1658-1703); b 1681; Boston
HUNT, Thomas (1663-) & Mary _?_; b 1690(1?); Deerfield/Lebanon, CT
HUNT, Thomas (1648-1722) & 2/wf Susanna (ADAMS) SAXTON (1648-), w Samuel; 21 Jun 1694; Boston
HUNT, Thomas (1666-) & Elizabeth [GARDNER] (1666-1724/1672-1729?); b 1697, b 1698?; ?Westchester, NY
HUNT, William (1605-1667) & Elizabeth _?_ (-1661); b 1631; Concord/Sudbury
HUNT, William (-1667) & 2/wf Mercy ?(HURD) (BRIGHAM) [RICE] (-1693), w Thomas, w Edmund; Oct/Nov 1663, May 1663; Cambridge
HUNT, William & Sarah _?_; b 1681, b 1682; Boston
HUNT, William & 1/wf Sarah NEWMAN; 9 Jun 1684; Ipswich
HUNT, William & Mary [BRADFORD] (-1720); b 1687(8?); Weymouth/Chilmark
HUNT, _?_ & Ann EDWARDS, w John, m/3 Isaac COUSENS 1657
HUNTER, Robert (-1647) & Mary _?_; Rowley
HUNTER, Thomas (-1728) & Sarah BASTER (1674±-); 17 Dec 1691; ?Newport
HUNTER, Thomas & Elizabeth [WINES]; b 1695; Southold, LI
HUNTER, William (-1676) & Scissilla/Priscilla CORISH, m/2 David FROW/FROE/THROW? 1678; 30 Jan 1656/7; Boston/Springfield
HUNTER, William & Mary [CARTER], m/2 Joseph COWELL by 1673; b 1659; Boston
HUNTER, William & Rebecca BESSE (1657, 1659?-); 17 Feb 1670, 1670/1; Barnstable/Sandwich
HUNTING, John (1597-1696) & Esther/Hester [SEABORN?]; in Eng, ca 1619/20; Dedham/Southampton, LI
HUNTING, John (-1718) & Elizabeth PAINE (1648-); 18 Apr 1671; Dedham

HUNTING, John & Mary FISHER; 23 Feb 1697/8; Dedham
HUNTING, Samuel (1640-1701) & Hannah HACKBURN/HACKBORNE (1642-); 24 Dec 1662; Dedham
HUNTING, Samuel (1666-) & Mary _?_; b 1695; Boston
HUNTINGTON, Christopher (ca 1626-1691) & Ruth ROCKWELL (1633-); 7 Oct 1652; Windsor, CT/Saybrook/Norwich
HUNTINGTON, Christopher (1659-1735) & 1/wf Sarah ADGATE (1664-1705); 20 May 1681; Norwich, CT
HUNTINGTON, John & 1/wf Elizabeth HUNT; 25 Dec 1665; Salisbury
HUNTINGTON, John & Elizabeth [BLAISDELL]; ca 1686; Amesbury
HUNTINGTON, John (1666-1695+) & Abigail LOTHROP, m/2 Samuel BAKER aft 1704; 9 Dec 1686; Norwich, CT
HUNTINGTON, Joseph (1661-1747, Windham), Norwich & Rebecca ADGATE (1666-1748, Windham), Norwich; 28 Nov 1687; Norwich, CT/Windham
HUNTINGTON, Samuel (1665-1717, in 52nd y) & Mary CLARK (-1743, in 77th y); 29 Oct 1686; Norwich, CT/Lebanon, CT
HUNTINGTON, Simon (-1633, on ship) & 2/wf Margaret [BARRET], m/2 Thomas STOUGHTON; in Eng, 2 May 1627?, ca 1627; Roxbury
HUNTINGTON, Simon (1629-1706) & Sarah CLARK (1633-1721, ae 88), Saybrook; Oct 1653; Norwich, CT
HUNTINGTON, Simon (1659-1736) & Lydia GAGER (1663-1737); 8 Oct 1683; Norwich, CT
HUNTINGTON, Thomas (1631-1685) & 1/wf _?_ [SWAIN], dau William; Branford, CT/Newark, NJ
HUNTINGTON, Thomas & 2/wf [Hannah CRANE], dau Jasper; bef 1660; Branford, CT/Newark, NJ
HUNTINGTON, Thomas (1664-1732) & Elizabeth BACKUS (ca 1670-1728); 10 Feb 1686, 1686/7; Norwich, CT/Widham, CT
HUNTINGTON, William & Joanna [BAILEY?]; b 1643; Hampton, NH/Salisbury
HUNTLEY, Aaron (1654-1745) & Mary CHAMPION (1651-1732); 22 Feb 1676, 1676/7?; Lyme, CT
HUNTLEY, John (-1676) & 1/wf Jane _?_; b 1652; Boston/Roxbury/Lyme, CT
HUNTLEY, John (-1676) & 2/wf Mary [BARNES]; 1669, ?3 Jun 1669; ?Lyme, CT
HUNTLEY, John (1677-) & Elizabeth _?_; 2 Feb 1699, 1698/9; Lyme, CT
HUNTLEY, Moses (1652-) & Abigail (CHAPELL) COMSTOCK (1644-), w John; 18 Jan 1680; Lyme, CT/New London
HUNTON/HUNTOON, Philip & 1/wf Betsey [HALL]; b 1689; Hampton, NH
HUNTRESS, George (-1715?) & Mary [NATT/NOTT] (ae 27 in 1675), m/2 _?_ DARLING/DAL-LING; ca 1670; Dover, NH
HURD, Adam & Hannah [?BARBRAUM]; b 1640; Stratford, CT
HORD, Benjamin (-1679) & Elizabeth [FIELD?] (-1679); b 1676(7?); Boston
HURD, Benjamin (1667-1754) & Sarah [KIMBERLY] (1672-1749); b 1691; Stratford, CT/Woodbury, CT
HURD, Ebenezer & Sarah [LANE] (1667-); b 1694; Woodbury, CT
HURD, Jacob (1655-1694) (ae 39 in 1694) & Anna WILSON (1655-1728); 21 Dec 1675; Charlestown
HURD, Jacob (1676-1749) & Elizabeth [TUFTS] (1673-); b 1699; Charlestown
HURDE, John (-1690) & Mary _?_; b 1639; Boston
HURD, John & Mary _?_; Stratford, CT
HURD, John & _?_; ca 1639?; Windsor, CT/Stratford, CT
HURD, John (-1682) & Sarah THOMPSON (-1718), m/2 Thomas BARNUM; 1 Dec 1662; Stratford, CT
HURD, John & Ann (TUTTLE) JUDSON, w Joshua; 10 Dec 1662; Stratford, CT
HURD, John & Deborah (KENDRICK) YATES (1646-), w John; b 1685(6?); Boston/Eastham
HURD, John & Elizabeth WEBB; 16 Mar 1691, 1690/1; Boston
HURD, John (1664-1732) & Abigail WALLIS (1670-1728); 5 Jan 1692, 1692/3; Stratford, CT
HURD, Joseph & Sarah [LONG]; b 1667; Boston
HURD, Joseph (1665-1751) & Jane [MUNN]; b 1696; Stratford, CT
HURLBURT, Cornelius & Rebecca [BUTLER]; b 1686(7?); Wethersfield, CT
HURLBUT, John (1642-1690) & Mary DEMAN/DEMING; 15 Dec 1670; Middletown, CT

HURLBURT, John (1671-) & Rebecca **WARNER** (1675-); 8 Jul 1698; Middletown, CT
HURLBUT, Jonathan & Sarah **WEBB**; 27 Jul 1699; Wethersfield, CT
HURLBURT, Joseph (?1652-1732) & Rebecca _?_ (-1712); ca 1675?; Woodbury, CT
HURLBUT, Joseph & Mary **CASTLE** (-1712); 17 May 1698; Woodbury, CT
HURLBURT, Nathan & Mary **BLIN/BLINN** (1677-); ?9 Jul 1699, ?30 Dec 1699; Wethersfield, CT
HURLBUT, Samuel (?1644-1712) & Mary _?_; b 1668; Wethersfield, CT
HURLBURT, Stephen & 1/wf Phebe [**DICKENSON**]; 12 Dec 1678; Wethersfield, CT
HURLBURT, Stephen (1668-1712) & [Hannah] [**DOUGLAS**] (1673-); b 1693; ?New London/Norwalk, CT
HURLBUT, Thomas[1] (-1689) & 1/wf [Sarah] _?_; b 1642; Wethersfield, CT
HURLBURT, Thomas[2] (?1651-1697) & Mary [**BROWN**] (1655±-); b 1674; Woodbury, CT/Fairfield, CT
HURLBUT, Thomas[1] (-1689) & 2/wf Elizabeth _?_; b 1680; Wethersfield, CT
HURLBUT, William (-1694) & Ann [**ALLEN**] (-1687), w Samuel; aft 28 Apr 1648?; Dorchester/Windsor, CT
HULBURD/HURLBART/HURLBERT, William[2] & 2/wf Mary **HOWARD**; 1643; Enfield, CT
HULBURD, William[2] & 1/wf Ruth **SALMON**; Enfield, CT
HULBERD, John & Mary **BAKER**; 1671; Northampton
HURRY, William (-1689, ae 55) & Hannah [**HETT**] (1635-), m/2 _?_ **RAND**; b 1662; Charlestown
HURRY, William (1664-) & Hannah **CALL** (1673-1747); 13 Mar 1689/90, 30? Mar; Charlestown
HUSE, Abel (1602-) & 1/wf Eleanor _?_ (-1663); Newbury/Salisbury
HUSE, Abel (-1690) & 2/wf Mary **HILTON SEARS**, w Thomas; 25 May 1663; Newbury
HUSE, Abel & Judith [**EMERY**] (1622/3-); b 1694; Newbury/Salisbury
HUSE, Albert & Mary **HUBBARD** (1653-); Salisbury
HUSE, Nicholas & Abigail **THOMPSON CURTISS**, w Jonathan; 1692; Stratford, CT
HUSE, Thomas & Hannah [**WEBSTER**]; b 1691; Newbury/Salisbury
HUSE, William & Anne **RUSSELL**; m int 22 Jul 1699, 17 Aug 1699; Newbury/Boston
HUSSEY, Christopher (1599-1686) & 1/wf Theodate [**BACHILER**] (1596, ?1588-1649, 1648?); in Eng, b 1629; Lynn/Newbury/Hampton, NH
HUSSEY, Christophey (-1686) & 2/wf Ann **MINGAY** (-1680), w Jeffery; 9 Dec 1658; Hampton, NH
HUSSEY, John[1] (d in Eng) & Mary **WOOD/MOOR**? (-1660); Dorking, Eng, Surrey, 5 Dec 1593, ?7 Dec; Hampton, NH
HUSSEY, John[2] (?1635-1707) & Rebecca **PERKINS**; 21 Sep 1659, 1 Sep; Hampton, NH/Newcastle, LI
HUSSEY, Richard & Jane _?_; b 1691; Dover, NH
HUSSEY, Stephen (?1630-1718) & Martha **BUNKER** (1656±-1744); 8 Oct 1676; Nantucket
HUTCHINS, Benjamin & Sarah **LAMPRY**; 5 Jun 1694; Haverhill
HUTCHINS, David (-1708) & Mary [**LEWIS**] (1659-); ca 1682/90?; Kittery, ME
HUTCHINS, Enoch (-1698), Kittery & Mary **STEVENSON** (1651±-); 5 Apr 1667; Durham, NH
HUTCHINS, Enoch (-1706) & Hopewell **FURBISH**, m/2 William **WILSON** 1711; 12 May 1693, ?13 May; Kittery, ME
HUTCHINS, John (1604-1685/6) & Frances _?_ (-1694); ca 1637; Newbury/Haverhill
HUTCHINS, John (-1681) & _?_; b 1677; Wethersfield, CT
HUTCHINS, John (1668-) & Abigail [**WHITNEY**]; b 1693; Groton/Framingham
HUTCHINS, John (1673-) & Elizabeth **HASELTINE** (1674-); 25 Dec 1693; Haverhill
HUTCHINS, John & Sarah **PAGE**; 11 Nov 1695; Haverhill
HUTCHINS, Joseph & Mary **EDMUNDS**, Lynn; 1 Sep 1657; Boston/Lynn
HUTCHINS, Joseph (1640-) & Johana **CORLISS** (1650-); 29 Dec 1669; Haverhill
HUCHIN, Nicholas (-1693) & 1/wf Elizabeth **FAR/FARR**; 4 Apr 1666; Lynn/Groton
HUTCHINS, Nicholas (-1693) & 2/wf Mary _?_; Groton
HUTCHINS, Samuel & Hannah **JOHNSON**; 24 Jun 1662; Andover/Haverhill?
HUTCHINS, Thomas & Mary _?_; b 1669; Boston
HUTCHINS, Thomas & Sarah **ELLIS**; 26 Aug 1697; Marblehead
HUTCHINS, Thomas (-1698) & Susanna _?_; Hempstead, LI
HUTCHINS, William & Sarah **HARDEY**; 1 Jul 1661; Haverhill
HUTCHINS, William & Elizabeth (**EATON**) **GRATH/GROTH/GROWTH**, ?w John; 30 Apr 1685; Bradford

HUTCHINSON, Benjamin (1666-1733) & (1/wf) Jane PHILLIPS (-1711); 14 Nov 1689; Salem

HUTCHINSON, Edward (-1631, 1632, in Eng) & Susanna ? (d Wells, ME); Boston/Wells, ME

HUTCHINSON, Edward (1613-1675) & 1/wf Catherine HAMBY (-1650±); 13 Oct 1636, Ipswich, Eng; Boston/Portsmouth, RI

HUTCHINSON, Edward (1613-1675) & 2/wf Abigail (VERMAES) [BUTTON] (-1689), w Robert; b 1651?; Boston/Marlborough

HUTCHINSON, Edward (-1694) & 1/wf [?Mary CUSHMAN]; b 1654; Lynn

HUTCHINSON, Edward & 2/wf ? ; Lynn

HUTCHINSON, Eliakim (-1718) & Sarah [SHRIMPTON]; b 1668/[9?]; Boston

HUTCHINSON, Elisha (1641-1717) & 1/wf Hannah [HAWKINS] (1644-1676); 19 Nov 1665; Boston

HUTCHINSON, Elisha? & Frances [SANFORD]; b 1674

HUTCHINSON, Elisha & Susan [?CLARK]; b 1674/[5?]; Boston

HUTCHINSON, Elisha (-1717) & 2/wf Elizabeth (CLARK) FREKE, w John; 12 Sep 1677; Dorchester

HUTCHINSON, Francis (1636-1702) & 1/wf Sarah LEIGHTON (-1661); 11 Dec 1661; Lynn

HUTCHINSON, Francis (1636-1702) & 2/wf Martha [STEARNS] (-1708); b 1679; Lynn/Reading

HUTCHINSON, George (-1660) & Margaret ? ; b 1633; Charlestown

HUTCHINSON, George & Margaret ? ; b 1680?; New London, CT

HUCHASON, Hananiah (see Francis) & Martha [STEARNS?], m Frances HUTCHINSON; b 1690; Lynn/Lexington

HUCHENSON, John (1643-1676) & Sarah PUTNAM (1654-1676); - Jul 1673, 1672?; Salem

HUTCHINSON, John & Hannah ROOT (1662-); 27 Dec 1682; Deerfield/Lebanon, CT

HUTCHINSON, John (1666-1746) & 1/wf Mary GOLD/GOULD/GOOLD; 7 May 1694; Salem

HUTCHINSON, Joseph (1633-) & 1/wf (Bethiah) PRINCE/GEDNEY?; ca 1656; Salem/Boxford

HUTCHINSON, Joseph (ae 48 in 1684) (ae ca 27 in 1660) & 1/wf 2/wf Lydia (BUXTON) SMALL, w Joseph; - Feb 1678, 28 Feb 1678/9?, 1677/8, 28 Feb 1678; Salem

HUTCHINSON, Joseph (bpt 1666-1751) & 1/wf Elizabeth [SWINNERTON] (1663-1699, 1700); b 1689?, b 1684?, b 1690; Salem

HUTCHINSON, Joseph & 1/wf Elizabeth ? (-1700); b 1691; Salem

HUTCHINSON, Joshua & Mary GOBLE; 6 Jun 1692; Concord

HUTCHINSON, Judah & Mary BRIDGMAN (1672-); Jan 1692; Northampton

HUTCHINSON, Matthias (1668-1724) & Mary ? (1674-1721/2); b 1701?, aft 1698; Southold, LI

HUTCHINSON, Moses (1671-1704) & Mary CLARY, m/2 Samuel KINGSLEY 23 Dec 1703?; ca 1692/1700?; Northampton

HUTCHINSON, Nathaniel (1633-1693) & Sarah BAKER (bpt 1638-1710, ae 76); 16 Mar 1658/9, 16-1-1659, 16 Mar 1660; Charlestown

HUTCHINSON, Ralph & Alice BENNETT, w Francis; 8 Aug 1656; Boston/Northampton

HUCHESON, Richard (-1682) (ae ca 58 in 1660) & 1/wf Alice BOSWORTH (1630-1668); Cotgrave, Eng, 7 Dec 1627, not in Nottingham; Salem

HUCHINSON, Richard (-1682) & 2/wf Susanna (?) ARCHER (-1674), w Samuel; 2? Oct, Oct 1668; Salem

HUTCHINSON, Richard (-1682) & 3/wf Sarah [STANDISH], w James, m/3 Thomas ROOT 1682?; aft 26 Nov 1674; Salem

HUTCHINSON, Samuel (1624-1675+) & ? ; ca 1645/52?; ?Portsmouth, NH

HUTCHINSON, Samuel & Hannah ? ; b 14 May 1670; Reading

HUTCHINSON, Samuel & Elizabeth (?) BRIDGES PARKER/BARKER, w Obadiah, w Joseph; ?26 Feb 1686, 19 Feb 1687, 26 Apr, 1686; Andover/Salisbury

HUTCHINSON, Samuel & Sarah ROOT; May 1691, ?Northampton; Deerfield/Lebanon, CT

HUTCHINSON, Samuel (1672-1737) & Elizabeth COREY (1681-1751), m/2 John BUDD; b 1698; Southold, LI

HUTCHINSON, Thomas (-1676) (late of Lynn, 1660) & Martha (CORWIN) CASE, w Henry (wid in 1698); 11 Jan 1665/6; Southold, LI

HUTCHINSON, Thomas & Mary ? ; b 1672; Boston

HUTCHINSON, Thomas (-1749, in 83rd y) & ? ; Southold, LI

HUTCHINSON, William (1586-1642) & Anne MARBURY (1591-1643); St. Mary, Woodnoth, London, 9 Aug 1612; Boston

HUTCHINSON, ? & Ann ? , m/2 Adam HAWKES; ca 1631?; Lynn

HUTCHINSON, Edward (-bur 14 Sep 1631) & Mary ? (-164-, in NH); b 1586

HUTHWITT, John & Judith _?_ ; b 1689; Woodbury, CT
HUTTON, Richard (?1618-1713) (ae 59 in 1680) & Elizabeth [KILHAM]; ca 1650; Salem/Wenham
HUTTON, Richard & Susanna (MORE) [DUTCH], w Samuel, m/3 John KNOWLTON 1714; b 1694, b 3 Dec 1693, b 13 Dec 1694; Wenham
HUXFORD, Samuel & Esther [NORTON], m/2 Jonathan DUNHAM ca 1691; b 1683; Boston
HUXLEY, John (?1670-) & 1/wf Elizabeth KING (-1705); 23 Jun 1698; Suffield, CT
HUXLEY, Thomas (-1721) & 1/wf Sarah [SPENCER] (1647-1712, Suffield); b 1668; Hartford/Suffield, CT
HUXLEY, Thomas (-1712) & _?_ ; ca 1689; Suffield, CT
HYATT, Abraham & Hannah [TOMPKINS]; b 16 Apr 1702, b 1701?; Eastchester, NY
HYATT, Caleb (1640?-) & _?_ ; Rye, NY
HYATT, John (1647 or bef) & Mary [?JONES] (1648); Stamford, CT/Rye, NY/Yonkers, NY
HYATT, Simon (1590-) & Deborah STOWERS; Upway, 2 Dec 1612; Salem/Charlestown/Dorchester/Scituate/Windsor, Ct/Stamford, CT
HYATT, Thomas (1618-1656) (called "bro." by John RUSSELL of Dorchester 1633) & Elizabeth _?_ , m/2 Cornelius JONES 1657; b 1641; Stamford, CT
HYATT, Thomas (-1698) & Mary SENSION/St.JOHN; ca 10 Nov 1677; Norwalk, CT
HYDE, Daniel? (-1736) & Sarah HYDE (-1754); 2 Feb 1696/7; Newton
HYDE, Eleazer (-1732) & 1/wf Hannah [HYDE] (1680-1720); b 1701; Newton
HYDE, George (-1645) & Anne _?_ , m/2 Daniel WELD 1647; b 1642; Boston
HIDE, Humphrey (-1684) & Ann _?_ ; b 1642, b 1640?; Windsor, CT/Fairfield, CT
HYDE, Ichabod (1668-1700) & Hannah [WILLIAMS] (1671-); b 1695; Newton
HYDE, Isaac (1642-1680) & Susanna BAXTER, m/2 Stephen DANIEL, m/3 Samuel GARDNER; 12 Jul 1665; Salem
HYDE, Job (1643, ?1640-1685) & Elizabeth [FULLER] (1647±-1685); b 1664; Cambridge/Watertown
HIDE, John (1642-) & Elizabeth [HARVEY] (1644-1701); b 1668; Fairfield, CT/Stratford, CT
HYDE, John (1656-1738) & Hannah (Mary is wrong) (JACKSON) KENDRICK, w Elijah; 20 Jan 1682, prob 1681/2; Cambridge/Newton
HIDE, John (1668-) & Rachel RUMSEY (1671-1738); ?1 Jan 1692, ?1691/2, 15 Jan 1691/2; Fairfield, CT
HYDE, John (1667-1727) & Experience ABELL (1674-1763); 3 Mar 1697/8; Norwich, CT
HIDE, Jonathan (?1626-1711) & 1/wf Mary [FRENCH] (1633-1672); b 1651; Cambridge/Roxbury
HYDE, Jonathan (-1711) & 2/wf Mary REDIAT; 8 Jan 1673, 1673/4; Cambridge/Newton
HYDE, Jonathan (-1731) & 1/wf Dorothy KIDDER; 6 May 1673; Billerica/Newton
HYDE, Jonathan & Elizabeth WILLIAMS; 3 Jan 1698/9; Newton/?Canterbury, CT
HYDE/IDE?, Nicholas & Jane (DAMON?) PLIMPTON, w ?John; 16 Mar 1679/80; Medfield
HYDE, Richard (-1687) & _?_ ; b 1642; Salem
HYDE, Samuel (1610-1689) (ae 42 in 1652) & Temperance _?_ (-ca 1694); b 1642, b 1640, b 1639?; Cambridge
HYDE, Samuel (ca 1637-1677) & Jane LEE (1640-1723), m/2 John BURCHARD; 4? Jun, - Jun 1659; Norwich, CT
HYDE, Samuel (-1725) & Hannah STEDMAN (-1727); 20 Jan 1673, 11 Jan 1673, m cont 3 Jan 1673/4, 20 Jan 1673/4; Cambridge/Newton
HYDE, Samuel (1667-1741) & Deliverance [DANA] (1667-1741); b 1689; Cambridge/Watertown
HYDE, Samuel (1665-1755) & Elizabeth CAULKINS (-1752); 10 Dec 1690, 16? Dec 1690; Norwich, CT
HYDE, Thomas (1672-1735) & [Mary] BACKUS (ca 1677-1752); - Dec 1697; Norwich, CT
HYDE, Timothy & Elizabeth OLCOTT (1643-1678+); aft 7 Feb 1674; ?Hartford
HYDE, William (-1681) & 1/wf _?_ ; b 1637, b 1634?; Hartford/Saybrook/Norwich, CT
HYDE, William & 2/wf? Joanna ABALL, w Robert; 4 Jun 1667; Rehoboth
HYDE, William (1662-1699) & Elizabeth HYDE (1664-1743); 3 Jan 1687; Newton
HYDE, William (1669-) & Ann/Anne BUSHNELL (1674-); 2 Jan 1694, ?6 Jan 1695, Lyme?; Norwich, CT
HILAND, George (-1692) & Hannah [CRUTTENDEN]; Jul 1665, b 1666; Guilford, CT
HILAND, John (1669-) & Elizabeth JAMES; 3 Jan 1694/5; Scituate
HILAND, Samuel & Isabel _?_ , m/2 Samuel WETHERELL 1677?, m/3 Josiah TORREY 1684; Scituate

HYLAND, Thomas[1] (1604-1683) & Deborah __?__; in Eng, b 1629; Scituate
HILLAND, Thomas (1629-) & Elizabeth STOCKBRIDGE (1642-); 1 Jan 1661, 1660/1?, 1661/2?;
Scituate

IBROOK, Richard (-1651) & Margaret __?__ (-1664); Southold, in Eng, b 1606, b 1607; Hingham
IYDE, Nicholas (-1690) & Martha [BLISS?] (-Nov 1676); b 1647; Rehoboth
IYDE, Nicholas, Jr. (1654-1723, Attleborough) & 1/wf Mary (PERRIN) ORMSBEY (-1690), w
Jacob; 27 Dec 1677; Rehoboth
IDE, Nicholas, Jr. & Elizabeth [HEWINS], m/2 Daniel FREEMAN; b 1693; Rehoboth
IDE, Timothy (1666-1735) & Elizabeth COOPER (1662-1745); 20 Oct 1687; Rehoboth
IGGLEDEN, Richard (-1667) & Ann PRINCE; 19 Jul 1660; Boston
IGGLEDEN, Stephen (d in Eng) & Elizabeth BENNETT, m/2 Joseph PATCHEN 1642; in Eng, 30
Nov 1628; Roxbury
ILSLEY/ILLSLEY, Elisha (-1691) & Hannah POORE; 14 Mar 1667, 1667/8?; Newbury
ILSLEY, Elisha (1668-) & Elizabeth (HARVEN) PLANTER, w Elisha, m/3 Robert RUTHER-
FORD; aft 1 Jul 1683
ILSLEY, Isaac (1652-) & Abigail [POOR]; b 1683; Newbury
ILSLEY, John (1616-1683) & Sarah [HAFFIELD] (-1673); b 1642; Salisbury
ILSLY, Joseph (-1704, in 76th y) & Sarah LITTLE; 3 Mar 1681/2, 1? Mar; Newbury
ILSLEY, William (1612-1681) & Barbara __?__ (1618-1681+); in Eng, b 1638; Newbury
INCE, Jonathan & __?__; Boston/Hartford
INCE, Jonathan[2] & Mary MILES, m/2 Thomas HANFORD 1661; 12 Dec 1654; New Haven
INGALLS/ENGELL, Benjamin & Mary TRIPP; 4 Apr 1682; Portsmouth, RI
INGELL, Benjamin (-1690) & Waitstill __?__ (-1728), m/2 Gershom MARBLE 1697; b 1690; Bristol,
RI
INGALLS, Edmund (ca 1598-1688) & Ann/Anna? __?__; ca 1618, b 1622; Lynn
INGALLS, Eleazer & Mary [HENLEY] (1666-); b 1684; Marshfield
INGALLS, Francis (1602-1672) & Mary [BELKNAP], w Abraham; 1644+; Lynn
INGALLS, Henry (1627-) & 1/wf Mary OSGOOD (-1686); 6 Jul 1653; Andover
INGALLS, Henry (-1699) & Abigail EMERY (1668-1718+); 6 Jun 1688; Andover
INGALLS, Henry (1627-) & 2/wf Sarah (FARNHAM) ABBOTT, w George; 1 Aug 1689; Andover
INGLES, James & 1/wf Joanna [FARNHAM/FARNUM] (living in 1678); b 1660; Boston
INGLES, James & 2/wf Mary __?__; b 1702
INGALLS, James & Hannah ABBOTT; 16 Apr 1695; Andover/Pomfret, CT
INGLES, James (1679-) & Love [PROUT], m/2 John RAWLINGS 1746; b 1698; Boston
INGOLLS, John (1665-1721) & Elizabeth BARRETT, Salem; 26 May 1667; Lynn
INGALLS, John & 1/wf __?__; ca 1686?
INGALLS, John & Phebe __?__; b 1693(4?); Swansea
INGALLS, John (1661-) & 2/wf Sarah RUSSELL; 10 Jun 1696; Andover
INGALLS, Nathaniel (-1739) & Anna/Anne [INGALLS/COLLINS] (1673-); b 1692; Lynn
INGALLS, Robert & 1/wf Sarah [HARKER]; b 1647; Lynn
INGALLS, Robert & 2/wf Sarah __?__
INGALLS, Robert (-1689) & Rebecca LAUGHTON/LEIGHTON (-1680); 10 Jun 1675; Lynn
INGALLS, Samuel & Ruth EATON; 9 Dec 1656; Ipswich
INGALLS, Samuel & Hannah BRUER; 2 Feb 1681, prob 1680/1; Lynn
INGALLS, Samuel (1654-1733) & Sarah HENDRICK; 4 Jun 1682; Andover
INGOLLS, Stephen & Dinah ELSON; 2 Jan 1690/1; Salem
INGLLS, __?__ & Martha (PERKINS) BREWER, w John; b 8 Oct 1701
INGELLS, __?__ & Mary SARGENT (-1697), w Andrew; betw 1691 & 1697; Gloucester
INGERSOLL, Elisha & Mary __?__; b 1697(8?); Kittery, ME
INGERSOLL, George (1618-1694) & Elizabeth __?__; b 1643; Salem/Gloucester/Cambridge
INGERSOLL, George (1646-1721) & Catherine [NICHOLSON/NICHOLS] (-1721, ae 78),
Scarboro; b 1675; Charlestown/Salem

INGERSOLL, John (1620±-1683) (ae 55 in 1678) & Judith [FELTON], dau wid Eleanor; b 1644; Salem
INGERSOLL, John (ca 1615-1684) & 1/wf Dorothy [LORD] (1629-1656/7, 1656(7?)); ca 1651; Haverhill/Northampton/Weymouth
INGERSOLL, John (1615-1684) & 2/wf Abigail BASCOM (1640-1666?); 12 Dec 1657, 21 Dec, 17 Sep, 12 Sep 1657; Northampton
INGERSOLL, John (1645?-1710) & Deborah [SKILLINGS?/GUNNISON] (1642, 1645-); b 1666, 2 Dec 1666; Kittery, ME
INGERSOLL, John (1615-1684) & 3/wf Mary HUNT (-1690); 1667, ca 1668; ?Westfield
INGERSOLL, John (-1694) & Mary COOMES; 17 May 16[70?]; Salem
INGERSOLL, John & Jane (SKIDMORE) [WHITEHEAD], w Adam?; ca 1673; Huntington
INGERSON, John & Elizabeth (?SIMONDS) NEWHALL, w Nathaniel; m int 8 Jan 1696/7; Lynn
INGERSOLL, John & Isabella BROWN (1677-); 12 Apr 1699; Springfield
INGERSOLL, Joseph (1646-1718) & Sarah [COE]; b 1670; Falmouth, ME/Charlestown
INGERSON, Nathaniel (1647-1683) (ae 45 in 1678) & Mary PRESTON (-1684); 8 Oct 1670; Salem
INGERSON, Nathaniel, Sr. (1672-1719) & Hannah COLLINS; 25 Mar 16--; Salem
INGERSOLL, Richard (-1644) & Ann/Agnes LANGLEY (-1677), m/2 John KNIGHT 1645+; Sandy, Eng, Bedfordshire, 20 Oct 1676; Salem
INGERSOLL, Richard (1651-1684) & Sarah __?__, m/2 Joseph PROCTER 1684; b 1684, b 20 Nov 1683; Salem
INGERSOLL, Richard (-1708) & Ruth DODGE; 28 Apr 1698; Beverly/Salem
INGERSOLL, Samuel (1646-) & Judith [MADDIVER]; ca 1683; Charlestown
INGERSOLL, Samuel (1658-1696) & Sarah [HASKETT] (1665-), m/2 Philip ENGLISH 1698; 28 Apr 1684; Salem
INGERSOLL, Samuel & Elizabeth WAKEFIELD (-1702), Boston; 5 Sep 1700; Salem
INGERSOLL, Stephen & __?__; ca 1694, 5 ch bapt 1703; Salem
INGERSOLL, Thomas (1668-1732) & 1/wf Sarah ASHLEY (1673-); 22 Jul 1692, 1691; Westfield/Springfield
INGHAM, Joseph (-1716) & Sarah BUSHNELL (?1639-); 20 Jun 1655; Saybrook, CT
INGHAM, Joseph & Mary [ATWELL], w Benjamin b 1686; aft 1683; Saybrook, CT
INGHAM, Samuel & Rebecca WILLIAMS; 3 Nov 1686; Saybrook, CT
INGHAM, Thomas & [Mary] __?__; b 1647(8?); Scituate
INGLESFEELD/INGLEFIELD, William & Fortune __?__; b 1692; Boston
INGOLSBY/INGOLDSBY, John (-1684) & Ruth __?__; b 1649; Boston
INGLESBY, Nicholas & Ruhamah __?__; b 1689; Boston
INGLESBY, Thomas & Mildred __?__; b 1685, b 1680; Boston
INGRAM, Henry & Lydia [DOWSE] (1655-); b 1672; Boston
INGRAM, Jarrett/Jared? (-1718) & 1/wf Rebecca SEARLES/SALE?/SAYLES (-1690, 1691); 28 May 1662; Boston/Swansea/Rehoboth?
INGRAHAM, Jarrett/Judith (-1718) & Waitstill (_?_) SABIN (-1718), w Joseph; 22 Apr 1692; ?Rehoboth
INGRAM, Job & Hannah __?__; b 1687; Boston
INGRAM, John (-1722) & Elizabeth GARDNER (-1684); 20 Nov 1664, 21? Nov; Hadley
INGRAM, John (1666-1742+) & Mehitable DICKINSON; 26 Jun 1684; Hadley/Amherst
INGRAM, Joseph & Sarah [BUSHNELL] (1668?-); ?Saybrook, CT
INGRAHAM, Joseph (1678-1753) & Mary SHEPARDSON; 11 Apr 1700; Rehoboth
INGRAM, Nathaniel (1674-) & Esther SMITH (1674-); 20 Oct 1696, 20 Nov; Hadley
INGRAHAM, Philip & Grace __?__; b 1691; Ipswich
INGRAHAM, Richard (-1683) & 1/wf [?Elizabeth WIGNALL]; b 1631, ?4 Apr 1628, doubtful; Rehoboth/Northampton
INGRAHAM, Richard (-1683) & Joan (ROCKWELL) BAKER, w Jeffrey/Geoffery; 11 Dec 1668; Northampton
INGRAM, Samuel (1670-) & Hannah WARNER (1675-); 14 Oct 1696; Hadley
INGRAM, Samuel & Sarah (BROOKS) LORD, w William; aft 4 Feb 1696, b 2 Mar 1702/3, 25 Feb 1702/3, Haddam; ?E. Haddam, CT
INGRAM, Thomas & Mary __?__; 1699
INGRAHAM, Timothy & Sarah [COWELL] (?1660, ?1669-); b 1691(2?); Boston/Bristol, RI
INGRAM, William & Elizabeth __?__; b 1653; Boston

INGRAM, William (-1721) & 1/wf Mary BAIRSTOW/BARSTOW (1641-1708); 14 May 1656; Boston

INGRAHAM, William & Elizabeth [CHESEBROUGH] (1669-); b 1690(1?); Bristol, RI/Stonington, CT

INGS, Samuel & Mary BEAL, m/2 Joshua LEE; 21 Feb 1672/3; Hingham

INGS/ENGS, Madit & Joan __?__; b 1641; Boston

INMAN, Edward (-1706) & 1/wf __?__; b 1648; Braintree/Warwick, RI/Providence

INMAN, Edward (-1706) & 2/wf Barbara [PHILLIPS], w Michael; b 17 Aug 1686; Warwick, RI/Providence

INMAN, Edward (1654-1735) & Elizabeth [BENNETT] (-1721+); b 1689; Providence/Smithfield, RI

INMAN, John (1648-1712) & Mary [WHITMAN] (1652-1720); aft 20 Jan 1669/70, ca 1671/74; Providence

IRONS?/IJONS/INES/INGLES?/INGLISH?/IYONS/etc., Matthew (Michael is error) (-1681) & Anne __?__; b 1631, b 1651; Boston

IRELAND, Abraham (1673-1753) & Abigail DURRANT/DURANT; 9 Aug 1697; Cambridge/Charlestown

IRELAND, David & __?__; b 1640; Ipswich

IRELAND, John & Grace HEALY (-1730, ae77); 15 Jul 1680; Charlestown/Boston

IRELAND, John & Mary [BLOWERS?] (1657-), dau John; b 1683; Boston

IRELAND, Philip & Grace [IVES?] (-13 May 1692); b 1691(2?); Ipswich

IRELAND, Philip & 2/wf Joanna [RANDALL], w Walter; b 28 Oct 1692; Ipswich?

IRELAND, Robert & Martha __?__; b 1688; Boston

IRELAND, Samuel (1603-1639) & Mary __?__ (1605-1672), m/2 Robert BURROWS/BURROUGHS by 1692; b 1635, b 1633; Wethersfield, CT

IRELAND, Thomas (-1668) & Joan __?__, m/2 Richard LATTIN 1670; ca 1647/50?; Hempstead, LI

IRELAND, Thomas & Mary __?__ (-1723, Southold); ca 1680?; Hempstead, LI

IRELAND, William (called "cousin" by John BAKER 1666) & 1/wf __?__; b 1649; Dorchester/Boston

IRELAND, William (1655-) & Elizabeth __?__; b 1682; Boston

IRELAND, William & 2/wf Abigail [GREENSLAND] (?1641-1715); 1 May 1685; Boston

IRESTON, Benjamin & Mary LEACH (1654-); 1 Aug 1680; Lynn

IRESON, Edward (1600-1675/6) & Alice __?__ (-1681, Charlestown); b 1637; Lynn

IRISH, David (1673-1748) & Martha NELSON (-1760); 4 Jan 1699, 1698/9; Little Compton, RI

IRISH, Elias (-ca 1684) & Dorothy WITHERELL, m/2 William WOOD 1686; 26 Aug 1674; Taunton

IRISH, John[1] (-1677) & Elizabeth __?__ (-1687); b 1645; Duxbury/Middleboro

IRISH, John[2] (1641, 1645-1717) & 1/wf Elizabeth __?__ (1654-1707); 1672; Middleboro/Little Compton, RI

IRONS, John & Elizabeth __?__; b 1674(5?); Boston

IRONS, Matthew (-1681) & Anne __?__; b 1631; Boston

IRONS, Samuel & Sarah BELCHER; 13 Nov 1677; Braintree

ISAAC, Joseph & Elizabeth __?__, m/2 Nicholas DAVIS 1643; b 1642; Cambridge

ISBELL, Eleazer (1640-1677) & Elizabeth FRENCH; 11 Nov 1668; Killingworth, CT/New London

ISBELL, Robert (-1655) & Ann [KINGMAN] (-1689), m/2 William NICHOLS; b 1640; Salem/New London

ISBELL, Robert (1676-) & 1/wf Elizabeth [HALL]; b 1696?; Guilford, CT?

ISBELL, Robert & Miriam CARTER; 16 Jun 1698, 15 Jun; Killingworth, CT

ISGATE/ESGATE, Eleazer & Joyce GOODWIN; 24 Jun 1675; Braintree

ISGATE, Eleaser & Rachel PUFFER (1667-); 7 Jan 1695, 17 Jan 1694/5, 7 Jan 1694/5; Braintree

ISSUM/ISHAM, John (-1713) & Jane PARKER (?1664-1713+, 1720?); - Dec 1677 (should be 1687), 16 Dec 1677; Barnstable

IVES, John (1644-1682) & Hannah MERRIMAN (1651-), m/2 Joseph BENHAM 1682; 12 Nov 1668; New Haven

IVES, John (1669-) & Mary GILLETTE; 6 Dec 1693; Wallingford, CT

IVES, Joseph (1647-1694) & Mary YALE (1650-1704); 2 Jan 1672; New Haven/Wallingford, CT

IVES, Joseph (1674-1755) & Esther BENEDICT (1679-1752), Norwalk; 11 May 1697; Wallingford, CT

IVES, Joseph (1673-) & Sarah BALL; 7 Jan 1700, prob 1700/1701; New Haven

IVES, Miles (-1684, ae 86) & Martha [BUTTRICE] (-1683), w Nicholas; b 1639; Watertown
IVES, Nathaniel (1677-1711) & Mary COOK (1675-), m/2 Jonathan PENFIELD; 5 Apr 1699; Wallingford, CT
IVES, Thomas (1648-1695) & 1/wf Martha WITHE/WYETH; 1 Apr 1672; Salem
IVES, Thomas (1648-1695) & 2/wf Elizabeth [METCALF], m/2 John WHITE 1695/6; ca 1679; Salem
IVES, William (-1647/8) & Hannah [?DICKERMAN], m/2 William BESSETT 1648; by 1641; New Haven
IVIE, John & ? ; b 1643; Newbury
IVEY, John (-1698?) & Mercy BARTLETT; 25 Dec 1668; Plymouth
IVORY, John (1669-1719) & Ruth POTTER; m int 2 Jul 1698; Lynn
IVORY, Theophilus (1670-1748) & Katharine ? (-1745, ae 70); b 1695; Charlestown
IVORY, Thomas & Mary DAVICE/DAVIS (-1732); ca 17 May 1660; Lynn
IVORY, William (1607-1652) & Ann [SOUTH], m/2 William CROFT/CRAFTS?; b 1640, ca 1632; Lynn

JACKLIN, Edmund (-1681) & Susan/?Susanna [PEASE] (-1687); b 1640; Boston
JACKLIN, John & Elizabeth ? ; b 1674(5?); Boston
JACKLIN, Samuel (1640-1681) & Mercy ? ; b 1673; Boston
JACKMAN, James (-1694, ae 83) (had nephew Henry SHORT) & Joanna ? ; b 1644; Newbury
JACKMAN, James & Rachel [NOYES] (1661-1718+); b 1683; Newbury
JACKMAN, Richard & Elizabeth PLUMER; 26 Jun 1682; Newbury
JACKSON, Abraham & Remember MORTON (-1707); 18 Nov 1657; Plymouth
JACKSON, Abraham (1655-1740) & Elizabeth BISCOE (-1737); 20 Nov 1679; Watertown
JACKSON, Abraham, Jr. & Margaret HIXAT/HIX/HICKS; 7 Jan 1685; Plymouth
JACKSON, Caleb (1652-1718) & Elizabeth HOW (1661-1701); ca 1682; Rowley
JACKSON, Clement (-1708) & Sarah HALL, m/2 Joseph HUBBARD 1717+; 17 Oct 1700; Portsmouth, NH
JACKSON, Daniel & Elizabeth JOHNSON; 2 Apr 1697; Boston/Portsmouth, NH
JACKSON, Daniel & Mary [PRESTON] (-1734); b 1701?; Stratfield, CT/Newton, CT
JACKSON, Edmund (-1675) & 1/wf Martha ? (-1652); Boston
JACKSON, Edmund (-1675) & 2/wf Mary (COLE) GAWDREN (-1660, ?11 Mar 1659, 18 Jan 1659, 1658/9), wid (had son Elisha b 12 Feb 1658/9, bapt 20 Feb 1658/9); 7 Jan 1652/3; Boston
JACKSON, Edmund (-1675) & 3/wf Elizabeth PILKENTON/(PILKINGTON), m/2 William BEALE 1676; 27 Oct 1660, 1659 (dau Sarah b 24 Sep 1660, Mary bapt 30 Sep 1660); Boston
JACKSON, Edmund (-1724) & Mary WHITMARSH (1674-1737); 19 Mar 1690/1; Hingham/Braintree/Weymouth/Abington
JACKSON, Edward (-1681) & 1/wf Frances ? (-1648?); in Eng, b 1631(2?); Cambridge/Newton
JACKSON, Edward (-1681) & 2/wf Elizabeth (NEWDIGATE) OLIVER (-1709), w John; 14 Mar 1648/9; Cambridge
JACKSON, Edward (1652-1727) & 1/wf Grace ? (1655-1685); b 1681; Newton
JACKSON, Edward (1652-1727) & 2/wf Abigail [WILSON] (1664-1746); ca 1686; Newton
JACKSON, Edward & Mary [?THAYER] (not NEWTON); b 1696; Newton
JACKSON, Ephraim & 1/wf Mary [CURRIER]; ca 1700
JACKSON, Eleazer (1669-) & Hannah RANSON (?1670-); 29 Jan 1690/1; Plymouth
JACKSON, George & 1/wf ? ; by 1684; Marblehead
JACKSON, George & 2/wf Mary (ABORN) NICK, w William; 8 Dec 1690; Marblehead
JACKSON, Henry (?1606-1686) (cousin of John TEY) & ? ; b 1635?; Watertown/Fairfield, CT
JACKSON, Henry (-1718, Stratfield) & Mary [ABBOTT?], dau Geo.; ca 1680-90?; Stamford, CT/Stratford, CT
JACKSON, James & ? [SMITH]; b 10 Oct 1666; Cape Neddick
JACKSON, James & Rachel [NOYES]; 1682
JACKSON, James (-1705) & Rebecca [HALLETT] (?1675-1730); 1694; Flushing, LI

JACKSON, James (-1718) & Sarah [?RICE]; ca 1700; Dover, NH
JACKSON, Jeremiah & Faith [PECK] (1658-), m/2 Cornelius WALDO; b 1677; Boston
JACKSON, John & Eleanor _?_ (?1601, 1602-1673+), m/2 Jonas BAILEY, m/3 Gyles BARGE; b 1630; Gloucester/Scarboro
JACKSON, John & Margaret [?MACHIAS] (1599-1643+); b 1633, in Eng; Salem
JACKSON, John (-1648) & Catherine _?_ ; b 1635?; Ipswich
JACKSON, John (-1667) & Joanna _?_ (-1675+); ?by 1635; Portsmouth, NH
JACKSON, John (-1675) & 1/wf _?_ ; b 1639; Cambridge/Newton
JACKSON, John (1610-1670, 1673) & Abigail _?_ (1610-1672+); b 1639; Boston
JACKSON, John (-1675) & 2/wf Margaret _?_ (1624-1684); b 1643?; Cambridge
JACKSON, John (-1656) & 2/wf Mary [GOOSE] (-1664+), w William; aft 1650, bef 1655; Salem
JACKSON, John (-1683) & Mary HULL (-1665); 1 Mar 1653/4; New Haven/Derby, CT
JACKSON, John & Jane THOMAS; 14 Nov 1657; Boston
JACKSON, John & Susanna JONES (1639-1662); 12 Jul 1659, 22 Jul; Gloucester
JACKSON, John (1640-1689) & Elizabeth [SMITH], dau Giles; ?1662; Stamford, CT
JACKSON, John & (2/wf) Margaret _?_ ; aft 1662
JACKSON, John (-1683) & Sarah (_?_) SMITH (-1686+), w George; 2 Jul 1668; New Haven
JACKSON, John (-1725) & Elizabeth [SEAMAN] (1647-); ?ca 1668; Hempstead, LI
JACKSON, John & Elizabeth POORE; 27 Apr 1669; Rowley
JACKSON, John & Elizabeth _?_ ; b 1671; Boston
JACKSON, John (1645-1709) & Sarah _?_ (Feb 1650-1700); ca 1671?; Cambridge
JACKSON, John & Sarah [PALMER]; bef 1672; Portsmouth, NH
JACKSON, John & _?_ ; b 1674; Eastchester, NY
JACKSON, John & (?3/wf) Hannah HOPPAN; 16 Jul 1679; Dorchester
JACKSON, John & Sarah _?_ ; b 1682; Bradford
JACKSON, John & Abigail (_?_) (DREW) ELLINS, w Samuel, w Anthony; m cont 7 Oct; 1685
JACKSON, John (-1691) & Margaret [CLARK], m/2 Philip WHITE 1693±, m/3 Roger SWAN by 1701; by 1688; Portsmouth, NH
JACKSON, John (1673-), Plymouth & Abigail WOODWORTH (ca 1664-); 24 Dec 1695, 25 Dec 1695; Scituate/Plymouth
JACKSON, John & Susanna HAYDEN; 19 May 1699; Boston
JACKSON, John (1675-) & 1/wf Mary [CURTIS]; b 1701; Newton
JACKSON, Jonathan (-1693) & Elizabeth [BAKER] (1641-1681); ca 1668; Newton/Boston
JACKSON, Jonathan & Hannah/Anna/Ann GARFIELD; 6 Dec 1681; Rowley
JACKSON, Jonathan (1647-) & _?_ ; b 1685; Scituate
JACKSON, Jonathan (1672-) & Mary SALTER; 26 Jun 1700; Boston/Newton
JACKSON, Joseph (-1681) & Mary [GODWIN], m/2 Joseph SEELEY by 1684; ca 1670?; Fairfield, CT
JACKSON, Joseph & Elizabeth _?_ ; b 1683; Boston
JACKSON, Joseph & Mary [SARGENT] (1673-); ca 1691; Newcastle
JACKSON, Joseph (-1714, Stratford) & Elizabeth (SANFORD) JACKSON, w Joshua, m/3 Thomas CHAMBERS; 23 Nov 1699; Fairfield, CT
JACKSON, Joshua (-1698) & Elizabeth [SANFORD] (1679-), m/2 Joseph JACKSON 1699, m/3 Thomas CHAMBERS; prob 1697, Nov or Dec; Stratfield, CT
JACKSON, Manus & Rebecca _?_ ; b 1643; Charlestown
JACKSON, Moses (-1712) & (1/wf) Deborah HYATT; 24 Oct 1672; Fairfield, CT
JACKSON, Moses (-1712) & 2/wf Esther (?STEVENS) [SEELEY], w Obadiah; ca 1682 (prob); Stratfield, CT
JACKSON, Moses (?1665-1746) & 1/wf Hannah [TROWBRIDGE] (1668-); b 1689
JACKSON, Nathaniel & Ruth JENNEY; 20 Dec 1686; Plymouth
JACKSON, Nathaniel & Margaret ELLINS; 14 May 1694
JACKSON, Nicholas (-1698) & 1/wf Sarah RILEY (-1655); - Jul 1646; Rowley
JACKSON, Nicholas (-1698) & 2/wf Elizabeth (_?_) CHAPLIN (-1694); 9 Dec 1656; Rowley
JACKSON, Richard (-1672, ae 90) & 1/wf Isabel _?_ (-1661/2); Cambridge
JACKSON, Richard & [?Joan ?SEWARD]; ca 1657; Portsmouth, NH
JACKSON, Richard (-1672, ae 90) & Elizabeth MARSH BROWN (-1677), w George, w Richard; 12 May 1662; Cambridge
JACKSON, Robert (1620-1685) & Agnes [PUDDINGTON?/WASHBURNE]; b 1645; Stamford, CT/Hempstead, LI/Jamaica, LI

JACKSON, Samuel & 1/wf _?_ (-1638); ca 1634; Scituate
JACKSON, Samuel & Hester SILLIS/SEALIS (1619-); 20 Nov 1639; ?Scituate
JACKSON, Samuel (-1715) & (1/wf) ?[Jedidah HIGBEE]; b 167[?1]; Fairfield, CT
JACKSON, Samuel & _?_; b 1676; Boston
JACKSON, Samuel & Mary MELCHER; 12 Oct 1693; Dover, NH
JACKSON, Samuel & _?_; b 1695; Stratfield, CT
JACKSON, Samuel & Hannah MARE; 7 Dec 1698; Boston
JACKSON, Sebas (-1690) & Sarah BAKER (1651-1725), Roxbury; 19 Apr 1671; Cambridge
JACKSON, Thomas (1640-) & Hannah [JOHNSON]; b 1663; Portsmouth, NH
JACKSON, Thomas & Hannah TAYLOR (-1689); 2 Jul 1685; Reading
JACKSON, Thomas & Temperance _?_; b 1687; Boston
JACKSON, Thomas (Bro-in-law of William HUGHS) & Priscilla GRAFTON (1671-1698+); 15 Oct 1690; Boston
JACKSON, Walter (-1683) & Jane _?_, m/2 Henry RICE; b 1669; Dover, NH
JACKSON, William (-1688) & Joan _?_; b 1639; Rowley
JACKSON, William (?1670-) & Mary _?_; b 1700; Dover, NH
JACKSON, _?_ & Mary FERRIS, m/2 John STURTEVANT 1709; Fairfield, CT
JACOBS, Bartholomew (-1693) & Mercy BARNES, m/2 Joseph THOMPSON 1694; 20 Dec 1666, at Branford, CT; New Haven
JACOBS, Daniel & Abigail FIELD; 24 Oct 1697; Durham, NH
JACOB, David (1664-1748) & Sarah CUSHING (1671-1723); 20 Dec 1689; Scituate
JACOBS, George[1] (1612-1692) & Mary _?_, m/2 John WILD 1693; b 1649; Salem
JACOBS, George (ca 1649-) & Rebecca (ANDREWS) FROST, w John; 9 Feb 1674/5; Salem
JACOB, John (1629-1693) & 1/wf Margery EAMES (1630-1659); 20 Oct 1653; Hingham
JACOB, John (1629-1693) & 2/wf Mary RUSSEL (1641-1691); 3 Oct 1661; Hingham
JACOB, John (-1689/90?) & Jane _?_ (-1687); b 1680; Boston
JACOBS, John (-1689/90?) & Susannah (HASEY) LINDER/LINDELL, ?w James; 7 Oct 1687; Lynn
JACOB, Joseph (1646-1708) & Hannah [BOSWORTH] (1650-); ca 1670; Hingham/Bristol, RI
JACOB, Joseph (ca 1655-1697) & Susanna SYMONDS (1668-); 18 Dec 1690; Ipswich
JACOBS, Joseph (1672-1764) & Sarah LYNZEY/LINDSAY; 18 Dec 1693; Lynn/Mansfield, CT
JACOB, Nicholas[1] (-1657) & 1/wf _?_; Norwich, Eng; Hingham
JACOB, Nicholas (-1657) & 2/wf Mary [GILMAN] (-1684), m/2 John BEAL 1659; in Eng, b 1629; Hingham
JACOB, Peter (1668-) & Hannah ALLEN; 7 Dec 1693; Hingham
JACOBS, Richard (-1672?) & 1/wf Martha [APPLETON] (1620-1659); ca 1638?, ca 1636?; Ipswich
JACOB, Richard (-1672) & 2/wf Joanna (CULLER?/CUTTER?) HALE (-1688), w Robert; 24 Sep 1662, m cont 6 Oct; Charlestown
JACOB, Richard & Mary WHIPPLE (-1674/5); 15 Jan 1673; Ipswich
JACOB, Samuel (ca 1639-1672) & Anna/Ann _?_, m/2 Joshua MOODY; Ipswich
JACOB, Samuel (1671-1695) & Elizabeth _?_ (not Hannah); Hingham
JACOB, Thomas (ca 1641-1707) & 1/wf Sarah BROWNE (ca 1648-1679/80); 21 Dec 1671; Ipswich
JACOB, Thomas (ca 1641-1706, 1707) & 2/wf Mary [?WHIPPLE] (1667-); b 1682; Ipswich
JACOBS, Thomas & Mary DINNIS/DENNIS; 21 Mar 1695; Boston
JAGGER/GAGER?, Jeremiah (-1744) & Hannah _?_; ca 1685/90?; Southampton, LI
JAGGER, Jeremy (-1658) & Elizabeth _?_, m/2 Robert USHER 1659; b 1646; Wethersfield, CT
JAGGER, Jeremy (?1646-1690) & _?_ [FERRIS], dau Peter, Jr.; b 1677; Stamford, CT
JAGGER, John (-1699) & Hannah _?_; ca 1650/60; Southampton, LI
JAGGER, John (-1684) & Hannah [CROSS] (-1675/82); b 1666; Stamford, CT
JAGGER, Jonathan (1675-) & Rebecca HOLMES (-1749); 22 Aug 1700; Stamford, CT
JAMES, Benjamin & Sarah LINSSEY/LINDSAY; 10 Apr 1690; Lynn
JAMES, Benjamin & Deliverance GALE; 24 Nov 1692; Marblehead
JAMES, Charles & Anna COLLINS; 17 Jul 1673; Gloucester
JAMES, Edmund & Reana _?_, m/2 William ANDREW 1640, m/3 Robert DANIEL 1654, m/4 Edmund FROST by 1669; b 1640; Watertown
JAMES, Edmund (-1682?) & Mary MICHELL/MITCHELL?; 23 Jun 1669; Bradford/Newbury?
JAMES, Erasmus (1605-1666?) & Jane _?_ (1601?-1665+); b 1635; Marblehead

JAMES, Erasmus & 1/wf __?__ ; b 1667?
JAMES, Erasmus & 2/wf Mary [ROWLAND]; b 1673; Marblehead
JAMES, Erastus & Johannah (BRIGHAM) NEWMARSH, w John; 1692, m cont 31 Mar 1692; Ipswich
JAMES, Francis (-1647) (no issue) & __?__ ; in Eng, b 1638; Hingham
JAMES, Francis (-1684) & Elizabeth [HILAND] (1632-); b 1660, b 1657?; Hingham
JAMES, Gawdy (1624-) & Anna __?__ (no issue); b 1642, b 1641; Charlestown
JAMES, John (-1676) & Lydia TURNER (1652-1714), m/2 William BARRELL 1680; 1675; Scituate
JAMES, John & Deliverance (CHARLES) [ROSE], w Jonathan; aft 21 Aug 1684; ?Branford, CT
JAMES, John & Mary __?__ ; b 1698; Derby, CT
JAMES, John (-1761) & 1/wf Eunice STETSON (1683-1717); 18 Mar 1700; Scituate
JAMES, Joseph (-1687) & [Mary] [DICKERSON]; b 5 Mar 1616, b 1665?; Fairfield, CT
JAMES, Nathaniel & Ann [WAKEMAN], m/2 Abraham HOWELL 1690; ca 1685?, no issue; Fairfield, CT
JAMES, Philip (-1639?) & Jane __?__ (1606-), m/2 George RUSSELL 1640; in Eng, b 1630?; Hingham
JAMES, Rev. Thomas (1595-) & 2/wf Elizabeth __?__ /Olive INGOLDSBY (20 Apr 1620-); b 1632, b 1624?; Charlestown
JAMES, Thomas (returned to England) & __?__ ; b 1637?; Salem
JAMES, Thomas (1636-1660) (cousin of Christopher LEWIS) & __?__ (wf in Eng); Lancaster
JAMES, Thomas & 1/wf [Ruth JONES] (1627-1664+); b 1648, ca 1646; Fairfield, CT/Easthampton, LI
JAMES, Thomas (?1624-1696) & 2/wf Katharine BLUX, wid? Return; 2 Sep 1669; ?East Hampton, LI
JAMES, William & Elizabeth __?__ ; b 27 Sep 1636; ?Salem
JAMES, William & Jane __?__ ; b 1638; Salem
JAMES, William & Rebecca __?__ ; b 1665; Boston
JAMES, William & Mehitable __?__ ; ?ca 1673; Scituate
JAMES, William & Susannah MARTIN (-1726?), m/2 Benjamin TAYER/THAYER?; 10 Dec 1677; Newport
JAMES, William & Honor DICER; 26 Dec 1700; Wells, ME
JAMES, __?__ & Anna __?__ ; Hingham
JAMES, __?__ & Sarah [HAYDEN]
JAMES, __?__ & Ann JENNINGS
JAMESON, James (-1661/2) & Sarah __?__ (-1696); b 1647; Boston
JIMSON, John (-1713+) & Hester/Esther MARTYN (1653-1696+); 15 Mar 1669/70; Amesbury
JAMESON, William (-1714) & 1/wf Sarah PRISE (-1691, ae 38); 18 Oct 1677; Salem/Charlestown
JAMISON, William (-1714) & 2/wf Sarah/Mary? [PHILLIPS] (1649-1710); aft 1691; Charlestown
JAMISON, William (1679-) & Elizabeth GOLDING, Sudbury; 20 Jun 1700; Charlestown
JANES, Abel (-1718, Lebanon, CT) & Mary JUDD (1655-1735, Lebanon, CT); 4 Nov 1679, ?14 Nov; Northampton
JANES, Benjamin (1672-) & Hannah [EDWARDS?] (1675-); b 1696; Northampton/Coventry, CT
JANES, Samuel (1663-) & Sarah [HINSDALE]; 1692?; ?Northampton
JANES, William (-1690) & 1/wf Mary __?__ (-1662); b 1631?; New Haven/Northampton/Northfield
JANES, William (-1690) & 2/wf Hannah (BASSON) BROUGHTON (-1681), w John; 20 Nov 1662; Northampton/Deerfield
JANES, William (-1726) & Sarah CLARKE (1666/7-1739); 26 Nov 1685; Stratford, CT
JANSE, Hendrick & Elizabeth [LAKE]; b 1677; Gravesend, LI
JANVERIN/CHAMVERLAIN?/JANVRIN, Richard & Catherine (HUTCHINSON) BARTHOLO-MEW, w Henry; 30 Oct 1699; Salem
JAQUES, Daniel (1667-) & Susanna WILLIAMS (1672-1725); 20 Mar 1692/3; Newbury
JAQUES, Henry (ca 1619-1687) & Anne/Anna KNIGHT (-1705); 8 Oct 1648; Newbury
JAQUES, Henry (1649-1679) & ?Ann/Hannah [?TRUEMAN], m/2 Samuel MOORE; ca 1670/2?; Newbury/Woodbridge, NJ
JAQUES, Richard (1658-1683) & Ruth PLUMER, m/2 Nathaniel HASELTON 1688; 18 Jan 1681, 1681/2?; Newbury
JAQUES, Stephen (1661-1744) & Deborah PLUMER; 13 May 1684; Newbury
JAQUITH, Abraham (-1676) & Ann/Annis/?Anne/?Anna [JORDAN], m/2 Henry BROOKS 1682; b 1643; Charlestown

JAQUITH, Abraham (1644-) & Mary ADFORD/ADVERD (1651-), m/2 Jacob HAMLET ca 1679?; 13 Mar 1671; Woburn
JAQUITH, Abraham (1673-) & Sarah JONES; 26 Dec 1700; Woburn
JARRAT/JARRATT, John (-1648) & Susannah __?_/?Ann RUSSELL, ?m/2 John SCALES 1649?; b 1648; Rowley
JARVIS, Elias (1663-) & Margaret [RUCK], m/2 Samuel BUSSILL 1697, m/3 Daniel MANSFIELD; b 1691; Boston
JARVIS, Isaac & Abigail (KEMBLE) VOWDEN/?VOLDEN, w Philip; 19 Jan 1698; Boston
JARVIS, James & Penelope WATERS; 18 Jul 1694; Boston
JARVIS, John & Rebecca PARKMAN; 18 Sep 1661; Boston
JARVIS, John & Mary [WATERS]; b 1687; Boston
JARVIS, Jonathan & __?_; b 1685; Huntington, LI
JERVISE, Martyn, Phila & Mary CHAMPIAN, Westbury; 1 Sep 1698; Jericho, LI
JARVIS, Nathaniel & __?_, wid?; b 1641; Boston
JAVISE, Nathaniel & Elizabeth SALTER; 28 Sep 1691; Boston
JARVIS, Stephen[1] & Mary [PORTER]
JARVIS, Stephen[2] & __?_; b 1683; Huntington, LI
JARVIS, Thomas & __?_; b 1669; Huntington, LI
JARVIS, Thomas[2] (1669-) & 1/wf [?Hulda] __?_; b 1701?; Huntington, LI
JARVIS, William & 1/wf Mary __?_; b 1686; Boston
JARVIS, William & 2/wf Elizabeth [STRATTON] (1665-), ?m/2 Solomon TOWNSEND 1698; b 1694; Boston
JARVIS, William & Esther __?_; b 1696; Huntington, LI
JAYE, John & Mercy __?_; b 1672; Boston
JAY, William & Mary [HUNTING], m/2 Charles BUCKNER b 1668; b 1653?; Boston
JAYNE, William (-1714) & 1/wf Annie/Anna BIGGS; 10 Jun 1675; New Haven
JAYNE, William (-1714) & 2/wf Mehitable [JENKINS]; 1694; Setauket, LI
JEFFORDS, Aaron & Mary __?_; b 1673; Boston
JAFFORD, Francis & __?_; b 1700, ca 1680/?4; Casco Bay
JEFFORDS/(JEFFREY?), John & Joanna __?_; b 1690; Lynn
JEFFORD, Robert & Mary WATERS; 2 Oct 1685; Marblehead
JEFFARD, Roger & __?_; in Eng, b Aug 1668; Portsmouth, NH
JEFFORDS, Simon & Elizabeth [COLE]; b 1701?; Salem
JEFFERY, Barnaby & __?_
JEFFRIES, David (1688-1742) & Elizabeth USHER (1669-1698); 15 Sep 1686; Charlestown/Boston
JEFFREYS, Digory/Digery? (see Gregory) (1604-) & 1/wf __?_; b 1631
JEFFREYS, Digory/Digery? (see Gregory) (1604-) & 2/wf Mary (MUSSELL) [ROWE] (-1669+), w Michael, m/3 John LUX ca 1663; b 1662; Kittery, ME
JEFFREY, Digory & 2/wf Ann [CROCKETT] (1617-1701+), w Thomas; b 1683; Kittery, ME
JEFFRY, George (-1707) & 1/wf Elizabeth WALKER; 7 Dec 1665; Newbury/Boston/New Castle, NH/?Suffield, CT
JEFFRY, George (-1683, Suffield, CT) & Mary [BLACKLEACH/BLACKLEDGE], dau John; b 1668; Windsor, CT/Suffield, CT
JEFFREY, George (-1707) & 1/wf 2/wf Anna/Agnes? __?_ (-1682, ae 18); Portsmouth, NH
JEFFEREYS, George (-1707) & 3/wf Hannah/Anna? PORTER (-1736), m/2 Penn TOWNSEND; 28 Nov 1694; Boston
JEFFREY, Gregory (see Digory) (-1662) & 2/wf Mary [?ROWE/?MUSSELL], m/2 John LUX ca 1663; b 1651?; Cape Porpoise/Wells, ME
JEFFREYS/JEFFERAYS, Jethro (1638-1739) & Mehitable __?_; b 1679; Newport/Portsmouth, RI
JEFFREY?/JEFFORDS?, John (see JEFFORDS) & Joanna __?_; b 1690; Lynn
JEFFRIES, John & Margaret SWEATMAN; 3 Jan 1700; Boston
JEFFRIES, Nicholas & Hannah ARCHER (1677-); 30 Aug 1697; Salem
JEFFEREYES, Robert (1605-) & Mary __?_ (1608-); in Eng, b 1628?, b 17 Apr 1636; Charlestown/Newport
JEFFREY, Thomas (-1690) & Mary HARVEY (1647-); 1 May 1674; Fairfield, CT
JEFFERAYS, Thomas (1679-1761) & Sarah TIMBERLAKE (-1769); 13 Dec 1699; Portsmouth, RI
JEFFERAY, William (1591-1675) & Mary [GOULD] (-1675+); b 1642(3?), 1640±; Weymouth/Newport
JEFFERY, William & Lydia __?_; b 1680; Boston

JEFTS, Henry (-1700) & 1/wf Anna/Ann STOWERS; 13 Sep 1647; Woburn
JEFTS, Henry (-1700) & 2/wf Hannah BIRTHS (-1662); 21 May 1649; Woburn
JEFTS, Henry (-1700) & 3/wf Mary BIRD (-1679), w Simon; 3 Oct 1666; Billerica
JEFTS, Henry[2] (1659-) & Mary BALDWIN (1663-); 13 Apr 1681; Billerica
JEFTS, Henry & 4/wf Mary BAKER, Concord, w William; 5 May 1681; Billerica
JEFFES, John & Sarah _?_ ; b 1655(6?); Boston
JEFTS, John (1651-), Billerica & Lydia FISH, Sandwich; 6 Apr 1688; Billerica
[JEFTS, ?Peter] & [Mary PIERCE?]
JEGGLES, Thomas[2] & Abigail SHARP (?1630-1686+); 27 Oct 1647; Salem
JEGGLES, Thomas[3] & Mary WESTON; - Mar 1683; Salem
JEGGLES, William[1] (?1591-1659) & ?2/wf Elizabeth _?_ ; Salem
JEGGLES, William[1] (?1591-1659) & 1/wf ?Mary _?_ (-1636+); m 1614±?
JELLISON, Nicholas & Barbara [GREEN]; b 1680, by 1671?; Berwick, ME
JENKINS, David & Grace LEAVENWORTH, w Thomas; aft 1683, bef 1688; Woodbury, CT
JENKINS, Edward (-1699) & 1/wf Lettice (HANFORD) FOSTERS (1618, 1617-), w Edward; b
    1654, b 1651?, b 1650; ?Scituate
JENKINS, Edward (-1699) & 2/wf Mary (FARNSWORTH) RIPLEY (1657-1705), w Abraham; 17
    Jun 1684, in Hingham; Scituate
JENKINS, Ezekial (1649-1705) & Sarah [GOING], dau Robert of Lynn; b ca 1670/80?; Malden
JENKINS, Jabez (1655-1699) & Hannah CURTIS (1664-1737+?), York; b 19 Apr 1680, betw 1678
    & 1680, 9 Dec 1678+, 19 Apr 1680; Kittery, ME
JENKINS, Job, Exeter & Elizabeth YORK, Dover; ca 1676; Dover, NH
JENKINS, Job & [Hannah TAYLOR] (1661-); 26 Aug 1682; ?Yarmouth
JENKINS, Joel (-1688) & Sarah [GILBERT] (-bef 1688); 1640, m int Jun 1640; Braitree/Boston
JENKINS, John (-1684) & [?Susanna] _?_ ; b 1649; Sandwich
JENKINS, John & Mary (_?_) EWER, w John; 2 Feb 1652, 1652/3; Barnstable
JENKINS, John & Sarah [?HAWKINS] (1657-); b 1684; Boston
JENKINS, John & Deborah BUTTERWORTH (1659-); 24 Nov 1685; Swansea/Rehoboth
JENKINS, John (1659-1736) & 1/wf Mary PARKER (1658-1704); b 1687; Barnstable
JENKINS, John & Mary [HUTCHINS] (1669-), dau Thomas & Mary; b 1690; Boston
JENKINS, Joseph (?1669-1734) & Lydia HOWLAND (1663-1734+), dau Joseph; Oct 1694;
    Barnstable
JENKINS, Joseph (-1700) (see Rowland JENKINS) & Experience (OTIS) HEARD?, w Israel; ca
    1697, aft 20 Feb 1696/7; ?Dover, NH
JENKINS, Joseph & Hannah [MERROW/MERRY] (1668/9-); b 1704; Durham, NH
JENKINS, Lemuel & 1/wf Elizabeth OAKES (1650-); 12 Jul 1670; Malden
JENKINS, Lemuel, Malden & 2/wf Mercy (TUFTS) WAITE (-1736), Malden, w Joseph; 11 Jun
    1694; Malden/?Rumney Marsh
JENKINS, Lemuel & Mercy CHADWICK; 30 May 1699; Charlestown
JENKINS, Obadiah (1650-1720) & Mary (JONES) LEWIS, w Joseph; 11 Jan 1676/7; Malden
JENKINS, Peter (-bef 1707) & Sarah [JONES?], m/2 Jonathan PEASE; b 1675; Martha's Vineyard
JENKINS, Reginald/Reynold? (1608-) & Ann [GALE?] (-1661+); 28 Jun 1635, b 1644(5?); Dover,
    NH/Lynn?
JENKINS, Richard & Sarah _?_ ; b 1692; Boston
JENKINS, Rowland (see Joseph JENKINS) & 1/wf Experience (OTIS) HEARD (-1700), w Samuel;
    Mar 1698/9; Dover, NH
JENKINS, Samuel & Mary (PRESTON) FARR/[FAWER], w Eleazer; 6 Jul 1670; Scituate/Dover,
    NH
JENKINS, Stephen (1653-1694) & 1/wf Elizabeth PITMAN (-1687, suicide); bef 1682; Dover, NH
JENKINS, Stephen (1653-1694) & 2/wf Ann/Anne [TOZIER], m/2 David KINCAID/KINCADE,
    m/3 Thomas POTTS; aft 1687; Dover, NH
JENKINS, Thomas (-1739, ae 88) & Martha _?_ ; b 1679; Scituate
JENKINS, Thomas (1666-1746) & 1/wf Experience HAMLIN; 24 Aug 1687; Barnstable
JENKINS, Thomas & Anna _?_ ; b 1696/7; Scituate
JENKINS, Zachariah (-1696, Sandwich?) & [Abiah ALLEN] (1666-); ?11 Dec 1686; ?Sandwich
JENKINS, _?_ & Sarah _?_ (1617-); ca 1640/50; Rowley
JENKINS, _?_ & Mehitable _?_ ; b 1694; ?Setauket, LI
JENKS, Daniel (1663-) & Katharine (BALCOM) ALLEN, w Isaac; b 1694, b 1692?; Rehoboth

JENCKS, Ebenezer (1664-1726) & Mary BUTTERWORTH (1677-1726+); 4 Mar 1695/6, 1695; Rehoboth/Providence

JENKS, John (1660-1698) & Sarah MERRIAM (1660-), m/2 John LEWIS; 11 Jul 1681; Lynn

JENKS, Joseph[1] (1606-1683, 1679) & 1/wf [?Ann]/Ellen HORTON; in Eng, b 1632, 5 Nov 1627, Horton, Eng; Lynn

JENCKES, Joseph[1] (-1679?, 1683?) & 2/wf Elizabeth _?_ (-1679?); b 1648; Lynn

JENCKS, Joseph (1632-1717) & Esther [BALLARD] (1632-1717+); b 30 Nov 1652; Lynn?/Providence/Warwich, RI/Pawtucket, RI

JENCKS, Joseph (1656-1740) & 1/wf Martha [BROWN] (-1727?); Providence

JENCKES, Nathaniel (1663-1723) & Hannah BOSWORTH (1663-1720); 4 Nov 1686; Swansea/Providence

JYNKS, Samuel (-1738, ae 84) & 1/wf Elizabeth [DARLING]; Lynn

JENKS, William (?1675-1765) & 1/wf Patience [SPRAGUE]; b 1699, ca 1696?; Providence

JENKS, _?_ & Elizabeth [GROVER] (1642), dau John; Charlestown

JENNER, David (1663-1709) & Mabel RUSSELL (1669-); 14 Jun 1688; Charlestown

JENNER, John (-1679) & Alice [PIGG], dau Robert; b 1648; Stratford, CT/Brookhaven, LI

JENNER, Samuel (-1738) & Hannah [BEARDSLEY]/HINMAN? (1671-1743, 1736); b 1689; Woodbury, CT

JENNER, Thomas (-by 1649) & [?Esther] _?_ ; b 1605; Weymouth

JENNER, Thomas (1605-1676, Dublin) & Ellen/Esther _?_ , m/2 _?_ WINSLEY/WENSLEY; b 1628; Charlestown

JENNER, Thomas (1628, ?1630-1686) & Rebecca TRERICE (1636-1722); 22 May 1655; Charlestown

JENNER, Thomas (1658-) & Marah MARCH; 9 Jul 1685; Charlestown/Brookhaven, LI

JENNESS, Francis (-1716) & 1/wf Hannah SWAIN (-1700); 15 Feb 1669/70; Hampton, NH/Rye, NH

JENNESS, Hezekiah & Ann FOLSOM; 13 May 1697; Hampton, NH/Rye, NH

JENNEY, John (-1644) & Sarah CAREY (-1655); Leyden, Holland, 1 Nov 1614; Plymouth

JENNEY, John (1648-1727) & 1/wf _?_ ; b 1672; Dartmouth

JENNEY, John (1648-1727) & 2/wf Mary (MITCHELL) [SHAW], w James; b 17 Nov 1699; Dartmouth

JENNEY, Lettice (-1752) & Desire [BLACKWELL] (1679-1773); b 1697; Dartmouth

JENNEY, Mark & Elizabeth _?_ ; b 1701; Dartmouth

JENNEY, Samuel & 1/wf _?_ WOOD (-1654)

JENNEY, Samuel (1616-1692) & 2/wf? Anne/Anna? [LETTICE]; b 1648?, ca 1656?; Plymouth/Dartmouth

JENNE, Samuel (1659-1716) & Hannah [HICKS?/HIX?] (1669-1749), ?dau Samuel (had son Hix JENNEY); b 1697; Dartmouth

JENNINGS, Francis & Hannah [COX?], dau Moses?; Hampton, NH/Rye, NH

JENNINGS, Gabriel & Sarah [BLAIDS], wid; 11 Jan 1698; Portsmouth, RI

JENNINGS, Isaac (1677-) & 1/wf Rose GOODSPEED (-1720?); 10 Jul 1700; Sandwich

JENNINGS, John (-1698?, 1687) & Anne _?_ ; ca 1655/60?; Hartford/Southampton, LI

JENNINGS, John & (2/wf?) Ruhamah _?_ ; b 1668, ?29 Jun 1667; Sandwich

JENNINGS, John & Mary [PARKER?]; b 1690, 1698/9?; Westchester, NY

JENNINGS, John, Jr. & Rachel TURNER; b 1698; Westchester, NY

JENNINGS, Jonathan (-1733, in 79th y) & 1/wf Susanna _?_ ; b 1680; Norwich, CT/Windham, CT

JENNINGS, Joseph & 1/wf Abigail [TURNEY] (1661-); ca 1681/6; Fairfield, CT

JENNINGS, Joseph & Mary _?_ ; b 1691; Tiverton, RI

JENNINGS, Joshua (-1675) & Mary WILLIAMS, m/2 George SLAWSON 1682; 23 Dec 1647; Hartford

JENNINGS, Joshua & Hannah [LYON] (1661-1743); b 1686; Fairfield, CT

JENNINGS, Matthew (-1737) & Mary _?_ ; b 1695; Fairfield, CT

JENNINGS, Nicholas (1612-) & Margaret (PIERE?/PERRE?) [BEDFORD]; b 2 Aug 1643; Saybrook, CT?

JENNINGS, Richard & _?_ ; b 1666?; ?Plymouth/Bridgewater

JENNINGS, Richard, Barbados & Elizabeth REYNOLDS; beginning Jun 1678; New London, CT

JENNINGS, Richard (-1751) & Mary [BASSETT] (ca 1659-1734); b 1694; Bridgewater

JENNINGS, Samuel & _?_ [WOOD?]; b 1655; Portsmouth, RI

JENNINGS, Samuel (-1732) & 1/wf Sarah **GRUMAN** (-bef 24 Oct 1727); ca 1691?, by 14 Apr 1691; Fairfield, CT
JENNINGS, Stephen, Hatfield & Hannah **(DICKINSON) GILLETT**, w Samuel; 15 May 1677; Hadley/Brookfield
JENNINGS, Stephen & Hannah **STANHOP/STANHOPE** (?1660-); 1 Apr 1686; Sudbury
GENING, Thomas (-1674+) & Ann __?__ (-1684+); ca 1644; Portsmouth, RI
JENNINGS, Thomas (-1691) & Dorothy __?__ (-1691+); b 1686(7?); Boston/Portsmouth, RI
JENNINGS, William & Rebecca **HITCHENS**; 30 Aug 1686; Lynn/Marblehead
JENNINGS, William (-1746) & Mary __?__ ; ca 1690?; Southampton, LI
JENNISON, Robert (-1690) & 1/wf Elizabeth __?__ (-1638, ae 30); b 1637; Watertown
JENNISON, Robert (-1690) & 2/wf Grace __?__ (-1686); b 1640; Watertown
JEMISON, Samuel (?1645, 1642-1700, 1701?) & Judith **NEWCOMB** (1646-1723); 30 Oct 1666; Watertown
JENISON, Samuel (1673-1730) & Mary **STEARNS** (1679-1732); 2 Nov 1699; Watertown
JENNISON, William (1676-1744) & Elizabeth **GOLDING** (1673-); 20 Jun 1700, at Charlestown; Sudbury/Worcester
JEPSON, John[1] (1610-1687) & 1/wf __?__ ; b 1639; Boston/Mendon
JEPSON, John[1] (1610-1687, 1688?) & 2/wf Emm/Emma **CODDINGTON** (-1702), w John; 7 May 1656; Boston
JEPSON, John[2] (1661-1722) & 1/wf Ruth [**GARDNER**] (1661-1695); b 1682; Boston/Charlestown
JEPSON, John[2] (1661-1722) & 2/wf Apphia **ROLFE** (1667-1713); 1 Apr 1696; Newbury/Boston/Woodbridge, NJ
JEPSON, Thomas (1663-1702) & 1/wf Hannah __?__ (-1703); ca 1690; Boston
JEPSON, William (1667-1746) & Anna [**COOPER**] (?1676-1720, 1724), dau Josiah; Boston
JESSE, David & Mary [**WILSON**], dau Phineas of Hartford; b 1700, 18 Aug 1698; Boston
JESS/JESSE, William & __?__ ; b 1645, b 1645(6?); Springfield
JESSON/JESSONS, Jacob & Elizabeth __?__ ; b 1670; Boston
JESSUP, Edward[2] (-1666) & 1/wf __?__ ; b 1650; Stamford, CT/Newtown, LI/Westchester, NY
JESSUP, Edward[2] & 2/wf Elizabeth [?**BRIDGES**], m/2 Robert **BEACHAM** 1668; Fairfield
JESSUP, Edward[2] (1663-) & 1/wf __?__ [?**HUSTED**]; b 1690?; Fairfield
JESSUP, Edward[3] (1663-) & 2/wf Elizabeth [**HYDE/HIDE**] (?1668, ?1669-1747); ca 1691-2, 1693?; Fairfield
JESSUP, Isaac (1673-1753/4) & Abigail __?__ ; b 1698; Southampton, LI
JESSUP, John[1] (-1637/8) & Joanna __?__, m/2 John **WHITMORE**; ca 1623; Hartford/etc./Wethersfield, CT
JESSUP, John[2] & __?__ ; ca 1645; Southampton, LI
JESSUP, John (-1710) & [?Elizabeth] __?__ ; 16 Jun 1669; Southampton, LI
JESSUP, Thomas & Mary **WILLIAMS**; 23 Nov 1683; Southampton, LI
JESSUP, [?John] (?1671-) & Hannah **STRATTON**; b 1701?; Easthampton, LI
JEWELL, Joseph (1642?-) & 1/wf Martha __?__ ; ca 1670, b 1673; Watertown
JEWELL, Joseph (1642-) & 2/wf Isabel/Isabella [**CATE**]; b 8 Aug 1682, m cont 5 Jun 1681; Portsmouth, NH/Newbury/Simsbury
JUELL, Nathaniel (-1712) & 1/wf Mary **(SMEDLEY) SHEPARD**, w Issac; 9 Jan 1676, 1676/7; Concord/Plainfield, CT
JEWELL, Nathaniel (-1695) & 1/wf Eleanor (__?__) [**PHIPPEN**], w Benjamin; b 1685; Boston
JEWELL, Nathaniel (-1695) & 2/wf Hannah [**WEARE**], m/2 Michael **SHALER/SHULLER**? 1697; b 7 Nov 1694; Boston
JEWELL, Nathaniel & 2/wf Margaret __?__ ; b 1699; Plainfield, CT
JEWELL, Samuel (-1657) & Mary __?__ ; York/etc./Boston
JEWELL, Thomas (-1654) & 1/wf __?__ ; b 1640; Braintree
JEWELL, Thomas (?1608-1654) & 2/wf Grisell [**FLETCHER**] (?1618-1669), m/2 Humphrey **GRIGGS** 1655, m/3 Henry **KIBBY** 1657, m/4 John **GURNEY** 1661, m/5 John **BURGE** 1667; ca 1640?, b 1642; Braintree
JEWELL, Thomas & Susanna **GILFORD/GUILFORD**; 18 Oct 1672; Hingham
JEWELL, William & Martha (__?__) **DUTCH** (1653-), w Hezekiah
JEWELL, __?__ & __?__ (-1699, wid)
JEWIT, Abraham (?1639-) & Ann **ALLEN/ALIN** (1645-), dau Bozoan; 2 Apr 1661; Rowley
JEWETT, Eleazer (1673-) & 1/wf Mary/Sarah **(ARMSTRONG) LAMB**, w Ebenezer; 1 Apr 1700; Norwich, CT

JEWIT, Ezekiel (1643-) & 1/wf Faith PARROT (1642-1715); 26 Feb 1663, 1663/4; Rowley
JEWET, Francis (1665-) & Sarah HARDIE/HARDY; 20 Jun 1693; Bradford
JEWET, Isaac & Dorcas HOVEY (1669-); 12 Jun 1695; Topsfield/Killingly, CT
JEWET, Jeremiah (1637-1714) & Sarah DICKINSON; 1 May 1661; Rowley
JEWETT, Jeremiah & 1/wf Elizabeth KEMBALL/KIMBALL (1666-); 4 Jan 1687/8; Ipswich/Topsfield
JEWET, John (?1639-1708+) & 1/wf Elizabeth CUMMINGS (-1679); 2 Apr 1661; Rowley
JEWETT, John & 2/wf Elizabeth (HOWE) CHADWELL, w Benjamin, m/3 Ezekiel JEWETT 1710, m/4 Andrew STICKNEY; b 1681; Charlestown
JEWETT, John & Elizabeth REYNER/RAYNER; 28 Nov 1700; Rowley
JEWETT, Jonathan & Mary WICOM; 24 Jul 1699/1700; Rowley
JEWETT, Joseph (-1661) & 1/wf Mary MALLINSON?/MELLINSON (1606-1652); Bradford, Eng, 1 Oct 1659; Rowley
JEWETT, Joseph (-1661) & 2/wf Ann (?) ALLEN, w Bozoan; 13 May 1653; Boston
JEWET, Joseph & Rebecca LAW (?1655-); 2 Mar 1676, 1676/7; Rowley
JEWETT, Joseph (1656-1694) & Ruth [WOOD] (1662-1754), m/2 John LUNT 1696; 16 Jan 1680/1; Rowley
JEWET, Maxmilion (1607-1684) & 1/wf Ann [COLE?/PARRATT?] (-1667); b 1643; Rowley
JEWET, Maxmilion (1607-1684) & Eleanor (PELL) BOYNTON (-1689), w John, m/3 Daniel WARNER 1686; 30 Aug 1671; Rowley
JEWETT, Maxmilion (1672-) & Sarah ? , m/2 Samuel PICKARD; b 1699; Rowley
JEWET, Nehemiah (1643-1720), Ipswich & Exercise PIERCE/PEARCE (?1647-1731); 19 Oct 1668; Lynn
JEWETT, Thomas (1666-1731) & 1/wf Hannah (STORY) SWAN (1662-), w Richard; 18 May 1692; Rowley
JOHNSON, Benjamin (1657-) & Rebecca HERSEY; 11 Jun 1683; Hingham
JOHNSON, Benjamin & Sarah WALKER; 22 Nov 1699; Billerica/Woburn
JOHNSON, Caleb & Agnes BENT (1661-); 9 Jul 1684; Sudbury
JOHNSON, Daniel (-1696?) & Martha TARBOX (-1691); 2 Mar 1673/4; Lynn
JOHNSON, Daniel & Dorothy LAMB, Framingham; 23 Dec 1697, ?22 Dec; Marlborough
JOHNSON, David & Priscilla ? ; b 1687; Boston
JOHNSON, Ebenezer & 1/wf Elizabeth WOOSTER; 16 Nov 1671; Stratford, CT/Derby, CT
JOHNSON, Ebenezer & 2/wf Hannah [HOLBROOK]; 23 Nov 1676; Derby, CT
JOHNSON, Ebenezer & Sarah WINN; 13 Apr 1691; Woburn
JOHNSON, Edmund & Mary ? , m/2 Thomas COLEMAN 1651; b 1639; Hampton, NH
JOHNSON, Edmund & Abigail GREEN (1669-); ?25 Sep 1693; Hampton, NH
JOHNSON, Edward (1598-1672) & Susan/Susannah MUNTER (-1690); in Eng, ca 1620; Charlestown/Woburn
JOHNSON, Edward & Priscilla ? (1617-1682+); ca 1639?; York, ME
JOHNSON, Edward (1621-1692) & Catherine/?Katherine BAKER (-1701); 10 Jan 1649/50, 10 Jun 1650?; Woburn
JOHNSON, Edward (-1717) & Miriam (DRAPER) HOLBROOK, w Daniel; 24 May 1675; Charlestown/Southold, LI
JOHNSON, Edward (1653-1725) & 1/wf Sarah WALKER (1670-1704); 12 Jan 1686/7; Woburn
JOHNSON, Edward & Esther [WHEATON?/WHEADEN] (1667/8-); b 1690; Branford, CT
JOHNSON, Eleazer & Susanna JOHNSON; 8 Nov 1698; Charlestown
JOHNSON, Eliphalet (ca 1668-1718) & 1/wf Deborah WARD
JOHNSON, Francis (ae 60 in 1658) (ae 80 in 1674?) & 1/wf Joan ? ; b 1638; Salem/Marblehead
JOHNSON, Francis & 2/wf Hannah (SOUTHER) HANBURY, w William; 24 Oct 1656; Boston
JOHNSON, Francis & ? ; b 1670?; Pemaquid
JOHNSON, Francis & 1/wf Sarah HAWKES; 1 Feb 1693, 1693/4; Andover
JOHNSON, George & Hannah DORMAN; 4 Jan 1695, 1694/5; Stratford, CT
JOHNSON, Humphrey (?1618/20-) & 1/wf Ellen CHENEY (ca 1620-1678); 20 Mar 1642; Roxbury/Scituate
JOHNSON, Humphrey & 2/wf Abigail (STANSFIELD) MAY, ?w Samuel; 6 Dec 1678; Roxbury/Hingham
JOHNSON, Isaac (?1600-1629/31) & Lady Arabella CLINTON/FYNES (-1630); in Eng, 5 Apr 1623?; Charlestown
JOHNSON, Isaac (ca 1615-1675) & Elizabeth PORTER (-1683); 20 Jan 1636, 1636/7; Roxbury

JOHNSON, Isaac (1644-1720) & Mary HARRIS (-1740, by 1714); 26 Oct 1669; Roxbury/Middletown, CT

JOHNSON, Isaac (1649-1711) & Mary STONE (-ca 1732); 22 Nov 1671; Charlestown

JOHNSON, Isaac (-1687) & Mary (not Sarah) (BISHOP) HODGKIN, w John, m/3 _?_ FIELD; 16 Jul 1682; Guilford, CT

JOHNSON, Isaac (1668-), Hingham/Bridgewater & Abiah (LEAWITH) [LASELLE], w Isaac; b 1692; Hingham

JOHNSON, Isaac (1676-) & Margaret [MILLER] (1676-); 12 Sep 1695; Middletown, CT

JOHNSON, Isaac & Alice [TAYLOR] (1676-); 1696?, b 1699; Charlestown

JOHNSON, Isaac & Abigail COOPER; 25 Apr 1699; New Haven

JOHNSON, Jacob (1669-) & Abigail HITCHCOCK (1674-); 14 Dec 1693; Wallingford, CT

JOHNSON, Jacob (1672-) & Sarah [BENHAM] (1676-); b 1701?; Staten Isl., NY

JOHNSON, Jacob & Mary _?_ ; b 20 Mar 1700/01; Westchester, NY

JOHNSON, James (-1678) & Mary _?_ (1613-); ca 1638?; Portsmouth, NH

JOHNSON, James & 1/wf Margaret _?_ (-28 Mar 1643); Boston

JOHNSON, James & 2/wf ?Abigail OLIVER; 1643?, 1644; Boston

JOHNSON, James (1643-) & Ann FURNELL; 28 Jun 1667; Charlestown/Boston

JOHNSON, James & Sarah DANIELS; 26 Mar 1675; Hampton, NH

JOHNSON, James & Elizabeth (FARNHAM) PEETERS/PETERS, w Andrew; 26 Apr 1692; Andover

JOHNSON, James & Elizabeth MASON (1674-); 10 Nov 1698; Hampton, NH

JOHNSON, Jeremiah (ca 1638-1712) & Sarah [HOTCHKINS]; b 1664; New Haven, CT

JOHNSON, Jeremiah & Elizabeth [JOHNSON] (1672-); b 1692; Derby, CT

JOHNSON, John (ca 1590-1659) & Margaret _?_ /[?SCUDDER]/?HEATH (-1655); in Eng, b 1616; Roxbury

JOHNSON, John (1609-) & Susan _?_ (1611-1683); in Eng, b 1633; Ipswich/Andover

JOHNSON, John¹ (-1640?, 1639?), from Kingston upon Hull & _?_ ; by 1634?; New Haven/Rowley

JOHNSON, John & Dorothy _?_ (-1651); b 1651; Guilford, CT

JOHNSON, John (-1687) & Hannah PARMELEE (-1693+); last Sep, 30 Sep 1651; Guilford, CT/New Haven

JOHNSON, John (-1681) & Elizabeth (DESBROUGH) [RALPH] (-1669), div wf of Thomas RALPH; 1 Oct 1651; Guilford, CT

JOHNSON, John (-1659) & 2/wf Grace (NEGUS) [FAWER] (-1671), w Barnabas; aft 9 Apr 1656; Roxbury

JOHNSON, John² (ca 1630-1686) & Hannah CROSBIE/[CROSBY] (1634-1717); 6 Dec 1655; Rowley

JOHNSON, John (-1708, ae 79) & 1/wf Elizabeth MAVERICK (1639-1674); 15 Oct 1656; Charlestown/Haverhill

JOHNSON, John (1635-1720?) & Bethiah REED (?1637/8-1718?, 1717?); 28 Apr 1657; Woburn/Canterbury, CT

JOHNSON, John (1629±-1713) & Deborah WARD (ca 1637-1697, ae 60); 19 - 1657, 19 Nov; Sudbury, CT

JOHNSON, John & Mary KINGE; 19 Oct 1659; Watertown/Lancaster

JOHNSON, John & Eleanor BRACKETT; 26 Dec 1661; ?Portsmouth, NH

JOHNSON, John & Jane _?_ ; b 1664; Boston

WORRELL alias JOHNSON, John & Mary DOWNE/Mary Ann DOWNE?; 7 Dec 1668, 15 Dec 1667?; Warwick, RI

JOHNSON, John & Sarah [NEIGHBORS]; b 1672; Boston

JOHNSON, John (-1702) & Mary _?_ ; b 1673; Rehoboth/Westerly, RI

JOHNSON, John & Hannah [CHAMPION] (ca 1650-); ?Hempstead, LI

JOHNSON, John (-1708) & 2/wf Sarah (KEASER) GILLO/GILLOW (-1676), w John; 3 Mar 1674/5; Haverhill/Charlestown

JOHNSON, John & Hester BEERES/?Esther BEERS; 23 Feb 1677/8; Salem

JOHNSON, John (-1708, in 76th y) & 3/wf Catherine (SKIPPER/SKEPER) MAVERICK (-1708, in 70th y), w John; 8 Sep 1680; Haverhill/Charlestown

JOHNSON, John, Jr. & 1/wf Mary MOUSALL (-1688); 8 Sep 1680; Haverhill

JOHNSON, John & Hannah [LEWIS]; ?ca 1682, aft Sep 1673; Dover, NH

JOHNSON, John & Susanna _?_ ; b 1683; Norwich, CT

JOHNSON, John & Mabel/?Mehitabel GRANNIS; 2 Mar 1684/5; New Haven

JOHNSON, John/Jean, Huguenot (-1696) & Susan [SIGOURNEY], m/2 Daniel JOHONNOT 1700; b 1686?; Oxford
JOHNSON, John (1658?-1747, Willington, CT?) (see Jonathan JOHNSON) & Mary [CARLEY] (1667-), dau William CARLEY; b 1687; Cambridge/Lexington/Woodstock, CT
JOHNSON, John & 2/wf Lydia CLEMENT (-1696); 19 Feb 1688/9; Haverhill
JOHNSON, John & Margaret MORRIS; 4 Apr 1689; Roxbury/Woodstock, CT
JOHNSON, John & 2/wf Eleanor BALLARD; 13 Sep 1689; Andover
JOHNSON, John & Margaret COWELL, m/2 Samuel HAUGH 1697; 2 Aug 1693; Boston
JOHNSON, John (1667-1744) & Abigail [SHERMAN] (1665-1739); b 1694; New Haven
JOHNSON, John (1668-) & Mary WASHBURN (1675-); 24 Sep 1694; Derby, CT/Waterbury, CT
JOHNSON, John & Mary JOHNSON (1677-); 17 May 1697; Haverhill
JOHNSON, John & Sarah [TISDALE] (1677-); b 1701?; ?Taunton/Lebanon, CT
JOHNSON, Jonas & Elizabeth HOARE; 13 Nov 1676; Beverly
JOHNSON, Jonathan (1641-1712) & Mary NEWTON (1644-1728); 14 Oct 1663; Marlborough
JOHNSON, Jonathan (1668-1708) & Mary [?KEELEY] (1666-1741, ae 75) (see John JOHNSON); m 1689, b 1690, ?26 Dec 1689; Marlborough
JOHNSON, Joseph (1637-1714) & 1/wf Mary SOATLIE (-1665); 19 Apr 1664, no issue; Charlestown
JOHNSON, Joseph (1637-1714) & 2/wf Hannah [TENNEY] (1643-1714+); b 1667; Haverhill
JOHNSON, Joseph (-1668) & Susannah _?_; 19 Nov 1667; Marlborough
JOHNSON, Joseph (1659-1733) & Rebecca PEARSON (1654-1732)
JOHNSON, Joseph & Elizabeth (TRAFTON) [RACKLIFF], w John; aft 5 Nov 1691; York, ME
JOHNSON, Joseph & Hannah BARKER; 30 Jun 1693; Haverhill
JOHNSON, Joseph & Anna BELCHER (1672-); m int 26 Jan 1696/7; Boston
JOHNSON, Joseph (?1666, 1671-1755?) & Elizabeth BLAKE (1679-1720/1, 1724?); 25 Jan 1698, 1698(9?); Middletown, CT/Plainsfield, CT/Canterbury, CT
JOHNSON, Joseph & Elizabeth _?_; b 1699; Plainfield, CT/Canterbury, CT
JOHNSON, Lambert & Sarah BARNE; 30 Jun 1673; Gravesend, LI
JOHNSON, Lambert & Anna [BENHAM] (?1669-); b 1701?; Staten Isl., NY
JOHNSON, Marmaluke (-1676) & Ruth CANE; 28 Apr 1670; Cambridge/Lexington
JOHNSON, Matthew (1633-1696) & 1/wf Hannah PALFREY (-1662); 12 Nov 1656; Woburn
JOHNSON, Matthew & 2/wf Rebecca WISWALL (1638-); 23 Oct 1662; Woburn
JOHNSON, Matthew & Mary REED; 12 Dec 1695; Woburn
JOHNSON, Moses & Mary [ROSE] (1655-); ca 1676; Hartford, CT/Newbury, CT
JOHNSON, Myndert & Hannah [HUBBARD]; b 1701?; Gravesend, LI
JOHNSON, Nathaniel (1642-1698) & Mary SMITH (1642-1713+); 29 Apr 1667; Roxbury/Woodstock, CT
JOHNSON, Nathaniel (?1643-) & Joanna LONG, m/2 Christopher GOODWIN 1678; 24 Nov 1668; Charlestown
JOHNSON, Nathaniel (1638-1718) & Mary PLIMPTON (1648-1737); ?16 Nov 1671, 14 Nov 1671; Marlborough/Medfield
JOHNSON, Nathaniel (1666-1755?, Pomfret, CT) & 1/wf Abigail MAY (1659-1745), dau Samuel; b 1685; Hingham/Sherborn
JOHNSON, Nathaniel (1670-) & Hannah HADLEY/HOADLEY, Branford; - Nov 1690; Woodstock
JOHNSON, Nathaniel (1678-1704?, 1705?) & Mary BLAKE (1677-1740); - Feb 1699; Middletown, CT
JOHNSON, Nicholas & Mary [COLEY] (1677-); b 15 Mar 1694(5?); Fairfield, CT
JOHNSON, Obadiah (1664-1740) & Rebecca [BROOKS] (-1752); 7 Sep 1696; ?Canterbury, CT/Plainfield, CT
JOHNSON, Peter & Elizabeth _?_, m/2 John FOSSECAR b 1661; b 1641, b 1635?; Boston/Fairfield, CT
JOHNSON, Peter (-1674) & Ruth MOULTON (?1641-1718); 3 Apr 1660; Hampton, NH
JOHNSON, Peter & Mehitable FARNUM; 29 Nov 1693; Andover
JOHNSON, Return & Mary JOHNSON; 7 Sep 1673; Andover/Hampton, NH/Medfield
JOHNSON, Richard (1612-1666) & Alice _?_; b 1640; Lynn/Charlestown/Watertown
JOHNSON, Richard & Elizabeth _?_; b 1680; Swansea
JOHNSON, Robert (-1661) & 1/wf _?_; in Eng, ca 1625?; New Haven
JOHNSON, Robert (-1661) & 2/wf Ada/Adaline/Adlin _?_, m/2 Robert HALL 1662, m/3 John SCRANTON 1666; New Haven

JOHNSON, Samuel (-1654) & Mary __?__; b 1653; Boston
JOHNSON, Samuel (1641-1723) & Mary COLLINS (-1682); 22 Jan 1663/4; Lynn
JOHNSON, Samuel & Phebe [BURTON]; b 1670; Boston
JOHNSON, Samuel & Hannah __?__/?Anna COLE (sister of Henry); b 1670(1?); Boston
JOHNSON, Samuel & Elizabeth MARTIN (1663-); 2 Sep 1679; Charlestown
JOHNSON, Samuel (1653-) & __?__; b 1687; New Haven
JOHNSON, Samuel (1656-1711) & Elizabeth [ADAMS]; by 1690?; York, ME
JOHNSON, Samuel (1670-) & 1/wf Hannah [GRANT], w James; aft 1693, b 11 Jan 1693/4; York, ME
JOHNSON, Samuel & 2/wf Francis WICOME; 31 May 1694; Rowley
JOHNSON, Samuel (1670-) & Mary SAGE; 7 Nov 1694; Guilford, CT/Middletown, CT
JOHNSON, Samuel & 2/wf Abigail [WITTAM]; ca 1697; Kittery, ME
JOHNSON, Samuel & Mary STEVENS; 20 Dec 1698; Boston
JOHNSON, Samuel (1671, ?1670-1727) & Abigail __?__; b 1701?, b 1696; ?New Haven/Cape May Co., NJ
JOHNSON, Smith (1672-) & Sarah [MILLS/MILLER] (1678, 1665-1766); b 1701; Woodstock, CT
JOHNSON, Solomon[1] & Eleanor __?__; in Eng, b 1627; Watertown/Marlborough/Su dbury
JOHNSON, Solomon[2] (1627-1690) & 1/wf Hannah [HOLOMAN] (-4 Jun 1685); b 1654; Sudbury
JOHNSON, Solomon[2] (1627-1690) & 2/wf Hannah GREFTE/CRAFTS?/GROSS?/GROSE (-1712), m/2 Thomas FROST 1691; 1 Feb 1686/7; Watertown
JOHNSON, Stephen (-1690) & Elizabeth DANE; 5 Nov 1661; Andover
JOHNSON, Thomas (-1640) & __?__; in Eng, by 1630?; New Haven
JOHNSON, Thomas (1610-1656) & Margaret __?__ (-1660); ca 1636?; Hingham
JOHNSON, Thomas (?1637, ?1630-1696?) & Ellen [BOSTWICK] (1633-1694); b 1651; New Haven
JOHNSON, Thomas (-1661) & __?__; ca 1654?; Dover, NH
JOHNSON, Thomas & Priscilla GOZNEE; 5 Jan 1656, 1656(7?); Sandwich/Falmouth
JOHNSON, Thomas & Mary HOLT (-1700); 5 Jul 1657; Andover
JOHNSON, Thomas (-1695) & Frances (__?__) (ENGLAND) HITCHCOCK, w John, w Edward; Sep 1663; New Haven
JOHNSON, Thomas (-1679) & Sarah [CROUCH], m/2 Thomas STAMFORD; 1670; Charlestown
JOHNSON, Thomas & Elizabeth GREEN; 8 Jan 1682/3; Cambridge/Boston
JOHNSON, Thomas (1664-1732) & 1/wf Sarah SWAINE
JOHNSON, Thomas & Elizabeth PAGE; 1 May 1700; Haverhill
JOHNSON, Thomas (1673-) & Margaret PAGE/Margaret (PAGE) RULE, w John, m/3 Benjamin SNELLING ; 23 Sep 1700; Boston
JOHNSON, Timothy (-1688) & Rebecca ASLETT (1652-); 15 Dec 1674; Andover
JOHNSON, Timothy (1672-1696) & Anne/Ann/Anna? MAVERICK; 25 Oct 1695; Haverhill
JOHNSON, Walter & 1/wf Joanna [ROYCE] (1670-1688); b 1688; Wallingford, CT
JOHNSON, Walter & 2/wf Tryntie HENERIG, w William EDWARDS; 5 Jul 1689; Flatbush, LI
JOHNSON, William (1603-1677) & Elizabeth [JEFTS?/STORY?], m/2 Thomas CARTER 1679; b 1632; Charlestown
JOHNSON, William & Judith __?__; b 1643; Charlestown
JOHNSON, William (1630-1702) & Elizabeth BUSHNELL (-1702, 1672); 3 Jul 1651, ?2 Jul; Saybrook, CT/Guilford, CT
JOHNSON, William (1629-1704) & Hester/Esther WISWALL (1635-); 16 May 1655; Woburn
JOHNSON, William & Hannah __?__, prob m/2 George PARKER; b 1660?; York, ME
JOHNSON, William & Elizabeth [TUTTLE]; b 22 Feb 1660/[1]; Southold, LI
JOHNSON, William/Wingle? & Sarah HALL; Dec 1664; New Haven
JOHNSON, William (-1677?) & Temperance [RATCHELL] (1658-); ca 1676; Boston
JOHNSON, William & Sarah LOVEJOY (1654-); 23 May 1678; Andover
JOHNSON, William (-1696) & Elizabeth BABCOCK/BADCOCK, w James; 22 Sep 1679; Portsmouth, RI/Stonington, CT
JOHNSON, William & Sarah BURRAGE (1658-); 5 Apr 1682; Charlestown/Boston
JOHNSON, William (-1712) & Hester TAYLOR; 21 Dec 1682; Charlestown
JOHNSON, William (1665-1754) & 1/wf Hannah (not Mary) LARKIN (1667-1696); 27 Jan 1684; Marlborough
JOHNSON, William & Mary __?__; b 1685; Falmouth, MA
JOHNSON, William (-1730) & Esther [GARDNER] (1659-1706); b 1686; Woburn

JOHNSON, William & Anne (COTTON) CARR (-1702), w George?; ?Jun 1688, ?betw 1697 & 1702; York, ME

JOHNSON, William (1662-1713) & Mary COOK, m/2 Thomas STEVENS; 18 Feb 1690/1; Cambridge/Canterbury, CT

JOHNSON, William/Wingle? (1665-1742) & 1/wf Elizabeth [MANSFIELD] (1666-); b 1692; New Haven

JOHNSON, William (1665-1754) & 2/wf Hannah RIDER (1678-1757); 7 Nov 1699; Sherborn/Marlboro

JOHNSON, Zechariah (?1646-) & Elizabeth [JEFFS/JEFTS?] (-1717); b 1673; Charlestown

JOHNSON, _?_ & Elizabeth (TREAT) [WOLCOTT]/Joanna TREAT THOMPSON; b 13 Feb 1668(9?); Wethersfield, CT?

JOHNSON, _?_ & Susanna _?_ (1671-1738+)

JOHNSON, _?_ & Sarah [BROUGHTON]; wid in 1701; ?Boston

JOHNSON, ?John & Dorothy [JOSLIN?] (1662), ?dau Nathaniel; (doubtful)

JOHNSON, _?_ & Katherine (WAYT) [THOMPSON], w William

JOHNSTON, _?_ & Anne [?DODD]/?NORTON, m/2 John FOWLER ca 1680; ?Guilford, CT

JOHNSON, _?_ & Mary _?_ (-1669/70); ?Boston

JOHANNOT/JOHONNOT, Daniel (1668±-) & Susanna (SIGOURNEY) JOHNSON, w Jean/John; 18 Apr 1700; Boston

JOYLIFFE, John & Ann (_?_) (CROMWELL) KNIGHT, w Thomas, w Robert/Richard; 28 Jan 1656/7; Boston

JOLLS, Thomas & 1/wf Abigail _?_; b 1672; Boston

JOLLS, Thomas & 2/wf Susanna _?_; b 1677; Boston

JOLLS, Thomas (-1686) & Hannah (BRIGGS) [WINSLOW] (-1714+), w Samuel; b 1681?; Boston

JONES, Abraham (?1629-1717/18) & Sarah [WHITMAN] (-1718); ca 1653; Hull

JONES, Abraham (?1659-1735) & Naomi [?FOSTER] (1669-1732+); b 1690; Hull/Raynham

JONES, Adam & Mary BAKER; 26 Oct 1699; Barnstable

JONES, Alexander[1] (-bef 1665) & ?Catherine _?_ (-1660); Great Island

JONES, Alexander (?1616-) & Hannah [WALFORD]; ca 1649; Great Island

JONES, Andrew & Mary _?_; b 1697; Charlestown

JONES, Benjamin (1630-1692) & Hannah SPENCER; 2 May 1661; Milford, CT

JONES, Benjamin (-1718) & Elizabeth WILDES (-1718+); 22 Jan 1678/9; Gloucester/Enfield, CT

JONES, Benjamin (1638-1718) & Bathsheba [BOSWORTH] (?1654-1740); ?ca 1684, no issue; Bristol, RI

JONES, Benjamin (-1663) & 1/wf Susanna BEAL (1665-1689); 14 Dec 1686; Hingham

JONES, Benjamin & Hannah BROWN, m/2 Benjamin WOODING 1694; 30 Nov 1687; New Haven

JONES, Benjamin & [?Sarah SINCLEAR] (1664-); ca 1689?, b 1686?, Exeter, NH; Stratham, NH

JONES, Benjamin (1666-1704) & Patience _?_ (-1747), m/2 Daniel HOBART 1704, m/3 Ibrook TOWER 1712; b 1694; Hingham

JONES, Benjamin (?1668-1748) & Elizabeth [DERRING] (-1748); b 1695; Hull

JONES, Benjamin (?1663-) & 2/wf Hannah WALKER; 8 Apr 1695; Taunton

JONES, Benjamin (1668-1748) & Elizabeth BORDEN (-1748); 18 Sep 1696; Bristol, RI/Swansea

JONES, Benjamin & Sarah (PITMAN) DRISCO, w Timothy; 1696

JONES, Benoni (-1704) & Esther (INGERSOLL) GURLEY, w William; 23 Jan 1689; Northampton/Springfield

JONES, Benoni & Abigail [FAIRMAN]; b 1698?, 1700?; Northampton/Enfield, CT

JONES, Caleb & [Rachel CLARK]; b 1701?; Hebron, CT

JONES, Cornelius & (1/wf) _?_; b 1646; Stamford, CT

JONES, Cornelius (-1691) & (2/wf) Elizabeth (?INGERSOLL) HYATT, w Thomas; 6 Oct 1657; Stamford, CT

JONES, Cornelius & Mary [WATERS], m/2 Henry BENSON; Feb 1687/8; Kittery, ME

JONES, Cornelius & Mercy [COREY], m/2 Charles GONZALES 1704; b 1693; Bristol, RI

JONES, Daniel & Sarah _?_; b 1701?; Newcastle/Spruce Creek

JONES, David (-1694) & 1/wf Sarah TOPLIFF (1639-1683); 11 May 1659; Dorchester

JONES, David (-1694) & 2/wf Anne (BURNAP) (WRIGHT) BULLARD, w John, w Isaac; 18 Mar 1685; Dorchester

JONES, David & Elizabeth [CHATFIELD]; b 22 Jun 1686; LI

JONES, David (-1691, ae 26) & Ann [BALLARD]; b 1689; Dorchester

JONES, Ebenezer (1646-1720+) & _?_; Westchester Co., NY

JONES, Ebenezer & Mercy **BAGG** (1660-1738); 26 Jun 1679; Springfield/Northampton
JONES, Ebenezer & Barbara **CHAPLIN**; 2 Jun 1685; Dorchester
JONES, Ebenezer & Lydia **NORCOT/NORTHCOTT**; 17 May 1694; Boston
JONES, Edward & Elizabeth _?_ ; b 1664; Boston
JOHNES, Edward & _?_ ; b 1678; East Hampton, LI
JONES, Elephalet (1641-1731?) & Martha [**LAWRENCE**] (1646-); no issue; Stamford, CT
JONES, Ephraim (1650-1677) & Ruth **WHEELER**, m/2 Thomas **BROWN**, m/3 Jonathan **PRESCOTT** 1718; 7 May 1673; Concord
JONES, Ephraim (-1717+) & Mary _?_ ; b 1682; Manchester
JONES, Francis (-1718) (ae 57 in 1695) & Susannah [?**WILLIX**]; b 27 Apr 1669; Portsmouth, NH
JONES, Geoffrey & Elizabeth [**GLOVER**]; ?LI
JONES, George (1630-) & Mary _?_ (1628, 1631-); b 1651?; Sagamore Hill/Exeter, NH
JONES, George (1654-) & Sarah [**PEARCE**], m/2 Hubertus **MATTOON** (div bef 1682), m/3 Henry **SEAVEY** by 1682; by 1673, ?1673
JONES, George & Mary _?_ ; b 1683; Boston
JONES, Griffith (-1676) & 1/wf Margaret _?_ (-1665?); b 1645?; Springfield
JONES, Griffith (-1676) & 2/wf Sarah _?_ (-1665?); Springfield
JOANES, Hugh (?1637-1688) & 1/wf Hannah **TOMPKINS** (1641-1672); 26 Jun 1660; Salem
JONES, Hugh (?1637-1688) & 2/wf Mary **FOSTER** (1651-); 31 Dec 1672; Salem
JONES, Isaac & 1/wf Hannah [**HEATH**] (1629-); b 1655; Dorchester
JONES, Isaac (-1731) & Mary (**HOWARD/HAYWARD**) [**BASS**] (-1691, ae 62), dau Robert, w Samuel; 7 Apr 1659; Dorchester/Roxbury
JONES, Isaac (1635-1710) & Sarah _?_ ; ca 1660?; ?Hingham
JONES, Isaac (-1701) & Mary [**BATEMAN**] (1660-); b 1687; Charlestown
JONES, Isaac (-1761) & Ann _?_ ; aft 23 Oct 1691; Dorchester
JONES, Isaac (1671-1741) & 1/wf Deborah **CLARK** (1672-1735?, 1733?), Stratford, CT; 21 Nov 1692, m at Stratford; New Haven
JONES, James & Elizabeth _?_ , m/2 Abraham **BARTLETT** by 1686; bef 1679; Portsmouth, NH
JONES, James & Joanna **WILLIAMS**; 2 Apr 1697; Boston
JONES, Jedediah (1656-) & Hannah **DAVIS**; 18 Mar 1681, 1682; Plymouth/Barnstable
JONES, Jenkin & Abigail [**HEARD?/HURD**] (1651-); ca 1678?, ca 1671/5?, bef 24 Jan 1688/9, b 2 Apr 1687; Dover, NH
JONES, Jeremiah (-1705) & 1/wf _?_/Sarah **DILLINGHAM**; b 1691; Yarmouth
JONES, Jeremiah (-1705) & 2/wf? _?_ ; b 1685?, ca 1678
JONES, Jeremiah & 3/wf Elizabeth (**FOLLAND/?POLLAND**) **HALL**, w Thomas; 27 Apr 1699; Chatham
JONES, John (1593-1665) & 1/wf Sarah _?_ (1601-); in Eng, bef 1620; Concord/Fairfield, CT
JONES, John (1614?-) & Ann _?_ , m/2 John **MOSES** ca 1667?; ca 1640?; Portsmouth, NH
JONES, John (-1673) & Dorcas _?_ (-1709), m/2 William **BUSS** 1674; b 1648; Cambridge/Concord
JONES, John (1624-bef 1673, 1665+) & Mary/?Miriam _?_ , m/2 John **OSBORN**?; b 1649?; ?Fairfield, CT/Nevis/Bermuda
JONES, John (-1684) & [Mary] _?_ ; ca 1650/2?, [b 1673], b 17 Aug 1669; Providence
JONES, John (-1657) & Joan _?_ (-1675); b 1657; New Haven
JONES, John (-1665) & 2/wf Susanna [**HOLLINGSWORTH**? (doubtful)]/**HOLDSWORTH**?/**HOLBRIDGE** (1605-), w Arthur; b 1665, b 1663, aft 1654; Fairfield, CT
JONES, John & Elizabeth _?_ ; b 1665; Boston
JONES, John (-1690) & Rebecca **SALLY**; 10 Sep 1666; Charlestown
JONES, John & Hannah [**CUDWORTH**]; b 1680, b 1681; Boston/Scituate
JONES, John (1656-1753) & Sarah **FAREWELL/FARWELL**; 5 May 1681; Concord
JONES, John (1669-) & Sarah [**LOBDELL?/FORD?**] (1666?-1750) (see **BOSWORTH**) (see Joseph); b 1694, b 1705; Hull/Mendon/Milford, CT
JONES, John & Marrah/Mary **KNOWLTON**; 7 Jan 1695/6; Reading/Salem/Framingham
JONES, John & Eleanor **WINSLOW**; 17 Feb 1697, 17 Feb 1698; Marshfield
JONES, John & Margaret **BULL/BALL**?; 17 Feb 1695, 1697, 29 May 1699; Boston
JONES, John & Ann _?_ ; b 1701?; Dover, NH
JONES, Jonathan, Dorchester & Rebecca **RUGGLES** (-1707), Braintree; 17 Jan 1694/5; Braintree
JONES, Joseph & Patience **LITTLE**; 16 Nov 1657; Weymouth/Hingham
JONES, Joseph (?1652-1686+) & Rebecca [**DRAKE**], m/2 _?_ **ROGERS** of Eastchester, NY; b 1676, b 1677; New Haven

JONS, Joseph (1664-1689) & Mary GOULD (-1714+); 23 Oct 1684; Amesbury
JONES, Joseph & Sarah [?FORD] (see John); b 1690; Hingham
JONES, Joseph (-1740) & Lydia [NEALS] (1672-bef 1720), Braintree; b 1696, ?24 Jul 1695; Hull
JONES, Joseph (?s Thomas) & Abigail CASWEL (1666-); 6 Apr 1696; Taunton
JONES, Joseph & Mary DRAKE; b 1701; E. Chester, NY
JONES, Josiah (?1643-1714) & Lydia TREADWAY (1650-1743); 2 Oct 1667; Watertown
JONES, Josiah (-1742/3, E. Greenwich, RI) & Elizabeth BERRY (1656-); 28 Nov 1677; Yarmouth
JONES, Josiah & _?_ ; b 1690; Bedford, NY
JONES, Josiah (1670-1734) & Abigail [BARNES] (1671-1749); b 1693; Watertown
JONES, Lewis (-1684) & Anna BULLARD/[STONE?] (-1680); prob m dau Simon STONE, b 1638, b 1636?; Roxbury/Watertown
JONES, Lewis & Deborah [PALMER], dau Henry, m/2 Henry CHAMPION 1698; 4 Dec 1660, b 1667; Wethersfield, CT/Saybrook, CT
JONES/GONES/INES, Matthew (see Rice JONES) (see Edward JONES) & Ann _?_ ; b 1631?; Boston/New London, CT
JONES, Matthew (1654-) & Susanna [WALKER] (1662-), dau Thomas; b 1684(5?); Boston
JONES, Matthew & Mercy GOODSPEED (1669-); 14 Jan 1694, 1684?, had Benj. 1690, 1688; Plymouth
JONES, Nathaniel & Abigail ATWATER (1660-); 7 Oct 1684; New Haven
JONES, Nathaniel & Mary REDDIT; 1 Sep 1696; Concord
JONES, Nathaniel & Elizabeth (POLLARD) HALL; 27 Apr 1699; ?Yarmouth or Barnstable?
JONES, Nicholas & _?_
JONES, Pelatiah (1664-) & Sarah MEEKINS (1666-1739); b 1701; Springfield
JONES (JAMES is wrong), Ralph (-1691/2) & Mary FULLER; 17 Apr 1650 (1655 is wrong); Plymouth/Barnstable
JONES, Ralph & [Deborah COOMBS]; b 1696; Plymouth
JONES, Rice (-1662) & Ann [GRIGGS], m/2 Robert LATTIMER 1662?; b 1651; Boston
JONES, Richard (-1641) & Alice _?_ (-1642/3?, 1673?), ?m/2 John KINGSLEY 1642; b 1634?; Dorchester
JONES, Richard (-1670) & [Elizabeth CARPENTER], m/2 Ebenezer BOOTH, m/3 John CHAPPELL; b 1663; Haddam, CT/?Farmington, CT
JONES, Robert[1] (-1692, 1691) & 1/wf Elizabeth SOANE/Jane CURTIS, wid (had Elizabeth CURTIS, Jane CURTIS, m Thomas COLLIER); b 1625, b 1631; Hingham/?Scituate
JONES, Robert[2] (-1675) & Anna [BIBBLE] (ca 1630-); b 1653, aft 28 Oct 1651, b 1 Jul 1683; Hingham/Rehoboth
JONES, Robert (-1710+) & Joanna/Jone [OSGOOD] (-1700+); b 1659, ca 1658; Salisbury
JONES, Robert[1] (-1692) & 2/wf Elizabeth _?_ (-1712); b 1662; Hingham
JONES, Robert & _?_ ; b 1674; Swansea
JONES, Robert & [Ann SANDS]; ca 26 Mar 1679; Boston
JONES, Roland & Bethiah CARTER; 13 Feb 1691; Woburn
JONES, Samuel (-1704) & Mary BUSHNELL; 1 Jan 1663, 1666?; Saybrook, CT
JOHNES, Samuel (-1693) & Sarah [FOSTER] (-1692); b 1672; Southampton
JONES, Samuel (1648-1717) & Elizabeth POTTER (-1696); 16 Jan 1672, 1673; Concord/Cambridge
JONES, Samuel & Ann DANFORTH; 5 Sep 1679; Roxbury
JONES, Samuel & 1/wf Sarah [DAVENPORT] (1643-1680); b 1680; Dorchester
JOANES, Samuel & 2/wf Mary TUCKER; 25 Jul 1681; Dorchester
JONES, Samuel & Deborah SANFORD; 12 Jun 1690; Saybrook, CT
JONES, Samuel (1672-1753) & Abigail [SNOW] (1677-); b 1696; Woburn
JONES, Samuel (1671-) & Marah LAY, Lyme/Saybrook, CT; 2 Dec 1697; Lyme
JONES, Samuel (1674-1755) & Ruth BROWN (1679-1755); 10 Nov 1698; Concord
JONES, Samuel (1677-1718) & Mary WOOLSON (1673-1757), m/2 Frances FULHAM 1724; 9 May 1700, 2 May 1700, 19 May 1700; Watertown
JOHNES, Samuel (1672-) & Esther [STEPHENS] (1679-); b 1700; Southampton, LI
JONES, Stephen & Elizabeth FIELD; 28 Jan 1663, 1663/4, ?29 Jan; Dover, NH
JONES, Teague & _?_ ; b 1650; Chatham
JONES, Thomas (1695-1667) & Ellen/Helen (1599-1678); b 1627; Dorchester
JONES, Thomas (1602-1681) & 1/wf [?Ann] _?_ ; b 1634, b 1629?; Hingham/Scituate/Hull
JONES, Thomas (1598-1671) & Mary [NORTH]; ca 1637; Gloucester/Manchester
JONES, Thomas & Ann _?_, m/2 Paul WHITE 1665; b 1638; Salisbury/Newbury/Charlestown

JONES, Thomas (-1654?) & 1/wf Mary _?_ (-1650); ca 1640; Guilford, CT
JONES, Thomas (ca 1608-1666) & Abigail [WYETH?/WISE], m/2 Thomas CHADWELL b 1679; b 1640; Charlestown
JONES, Thomas & Margaret _?_ (-1648); Charlestown
JONES, Thomas & 1/wf _?_ ; b 1651; Fairfield, CT/Huntington, LI
JONES, Thomas & Ann [?CUDWORTH]; b 1654; Boston/?Hingham/?Hull
JONES, Thomas (see below) & Lydia SANDERSON; 13 Dec 1654; Boston
JONES, Thomas (see above) & _?_ ; b 1657?, b 1659; Taunton
JONES, Thomas (-1651) & Abigail (SUMNER) ELITHORP, w Thomas, w Thomas; 25 Jun 1657; Boston/Manchester
JONES, Thomas (-1669) & 2/wf Catharine (ESTY) [SCUDDER], w Henry; aft 1661; Huntington, LI
JONES, Thomas & Sarah [CROUCH], m/2 Thomas SANFORD bef 1681; ca 1670, ca 1669; Charlestown
JONES, Thomas (-1724) & Abigail ROWLAND; 5 Mar 1670/1; Fairfield, CT
JONES, Thomas (1640-1719) & Elizabeth PITTS (?1648-1739); 29 Dec 1673; Hingham/Hull
JONES, Thomas & Katherine GAMMON; 25 Jun 1677, New London; New London
JONES, Thomas (-1686) & Abigail [WAITE], m/2 Thomas ATKINS 1689; b 1681; Charlestown
JONES, Thomas & Elizabeth GRAVES (1662-); 31 Aug 1682; Springfield
JONES, Thomas (1662-1724) & Mary [PAUL] (1667-); ca 1687; Taunton
JONES, Thomas & Catherine GAMMON, dau Thomas of Newfoundland; 26 Jun 1677; New London, CT
JONES, Thomas (1656/7-) & Mary [LORING] (1668-1757); b 1693; Hingham
JONES, Thomas (?1665-1713) & Freelove [TOWNSEND] (1674-1726), m/2 Timothy BAGLEY; b 1695; Oyster Bay, LI
JONES, Thomas (-1729, ae 56) & Elizabeth _?_ ; b 1701; Sherborn
JONES, Timothy (step-son of John KINSLEY) & _?_ ; b 1655; Dorchester
JONES, Timothy & Elizabeth _?_ ; b 1680; Gloucester
JONES, William & _?_ ; in Eng, b 1640; Dover, NH
JONES, William (1587?-) & [?Margaret] _?_ ; b 1644, b 1634?; Charlestown
JONES, William (1624-1706) & 1/wf _?_ ; London?, ca 1646/52?; New Haven
JONES, William (1624-1706) & 2/wf Hannah EATON (1632-1707); London, m cont 4 Jul 1659; New Haven
JOAN, William & Dorothy _?_ ; b 1668; Scituate
JONES, William & _?_ ; b 1687; Wenham
JONES, William (-1700), Watertown & Abigail (MORSE) AVERAD/EVERETT, Dedham, w Israel; 18 Oct 1687, b 1688; Watertown/Guilford, CT
JONES, William & Mary _?_ ; b 1688; Amesbury
JONES, William & Mehitable _?_ ; b 1697; Rehoboth
JONES, William & 1/wf Mary [MARDEN]; b 1701; Newcastle
JONES, William & Mary [CHESLEY]; b 1701, by 1698?; Dover, NH
JONES, _?_ & Sarah [HAYDEN]; b 1701
JONES, Jeremiah & Sarah [DILLINGHAM] (-bef 1707)
JONES, _?_ & Mary [JUDD] (1658-); CT
JORDAN, Baruch (1654-1699) & Mary WILDER; 3 Aug 1692; Plymouth
JORDAN, Dominicus (?1654-1703) & Hannah [TRISTRAM], dau Ralph, m/2 Stephen GREEN-LEAF; 1681, b 1683; Bidleford, ME
JORDAN, Francis & Jane WILSON; 6 Nov 1635; Ipswich
JORDAN, James (-1655) & _?_ ; in Eng, ?b 1627; Dedham
JORDAN, Jedediah (-1735) & _?_ ; b 1684; ?Kittery, ME
JORDAN, Jeremiah & Deborah BICKFORD, m/2 William JONES; 10 Mar 1685/6, 1686/7; York Co., ME/Newcastle
JORDAN, Jeremiah & Katherine _?_ ; ca 1688?; ?New Castle, ME
JORDAN, John (-1650) & Anne/Anna [BISHOP] (-1672), wid, m/3 Thomas CLARK 1652, by 1654; b 1640; Guilford, CT
JORDAN, John (-1691?) & [?Esther] _?_ (-1702); b 1650(1?), b 1648?; Plymouth
JORDAN, John & _?_ ; b 1673; Milton
JORDAN, John (?1650-1725) & Elizabeth [STILEMAN/STYLEMAN] (?1663-); 1677(8?), m cont 25 Jan 1677/8; Salem

JORDAN, John (1645-) & Deborah [JOY/?ROSE] (?1648-1667); b 1677; Guilford, CT

JORDAN, John & 2/wf Katherine [CHATHER] (1657-); ?Saybrook, CT

JORDAN, John & Mary FRIZELL; 4 Oct 1699; Boston

JORDAN, Robert (1611-1679) & Sarah [WINTER/WINTERS] (ca 1620?-); ca Jan 1643/4; 1642?, b 1645; Cape Elizabeth, ME/Portsmouth, NH

JORDAN, Robert (?1651-) & Eliza/Elizabeth (HARVEY) [DALE], w Benjamin; ca 1675?, by 12 Nov 1685; Portsmouth, NH

JORDAN, Samuel & Mary _?_ (1671-); b 1690; Kittery, ME

JORDAN, Stephen & 1/wf _?_ ; b 1619?; Newbury

JORDAN, Stephen (-1669) & Susanna (WILTERTON) [MERRILL] (-1673), w Nathaniel; ca 1655?, b 1677, b 1661; Salisbury

JORDAN, Thomas & Frances _?_ ; b 1640, 1641; Dedham

JORDAN, Thomas & Dorothy [WHITFIELD]; b 1653, b 1652, returned to Eng; Guilford, CT

JORDAINE, Thomas & Esther/Easter HALL, w Edward?; 24 Dec 1674; Rehoboth

JORDAN, _?_ & Sarah _?_ ; b 1647; Wethersfield, CT

JORDAN, _?_ & [Margaret MARTIN], m/2 Thomas LYNDE 1634

JOSE, Christopher (-1676) & Jane [CUMMINGS]; b 1660; Portsmouth, NH

JOSE, John & Esther (WALDRON) (ELKINS) LEE, w Henry?, w Abraham, m/4 Joshua BARNES by 1695; aft 19 Jan 1690/1, b 1692; Boston

JOSE, Richard (1660-1707) & Hannah MARTYN (1664-), m/2 Edward AYRES; 16 Oct 1683; Portsmouth, NH

JOSELYN, Abraham (1619-1670) & 2/wf? Beatrice [HAMPSON] (-1712, ae 88 y), m/2 Benjamin BOSWORTH 1671; b 1649, b 1646?; Hingham/Lancaster

JOSLYN, Abraham (1649-1676) & Ann/Anna? [HUDSON] (-1676); 29 Nov 1672; Lancaster

JOSSELYN, Henry (-1683) & Margaret CAMMOCK, w Thomas; ca 1641/3, aft 1643?; Black Point, ME

JOSLINE, Henry (-1730) & Abigail STOCKBRIDGE (1660-1743); 4 Nov 1676; Scituate/Hanover

JOSLEN, Henry & Bridget DAY; 4 Jun 1678; Gloucester

JOSELIN, Henry & Mary LAMBERT; 9 Nov 1685; Gloucester

JOSSELYN, Joseph (1663-1726), Bridgewater & 1/wf Hannah FARROW (1667-); 17 Mar 1686/7; Hingham

JOSLIN, Nathaniel (1627-1694) & Sarah KING (ca 1632-1706) (wf called Mary in 1662); 1656; Lancaster/Marlboro

JOSLIN, Nathaniel, Jr. (1658-1727) & Esther MOSS/MORSE (-1725); 8 Feb 1682; Marlboro/Watertown

JOSLIN, Peter (1661-1759) & 1/wf Sarah HOWE (-1692); b 1686; Lancaster

JOSLIN, Peter (1666-1759) & 2/wf Joanna [WHITCOMB] (1674-1717); bef 1698, ca 1693-4?; Lancaster

JOSSELYN, Thomas (1592-1661) & Rebecca [MARLOWE?] (1592-1673); London, Jan 1614?; Hingham

JOSLIN, Thomas & Mary (_?_) VAUGHAN, w David; b 14 Dec 1681; Portsmouth, RI

JOYE, Abraham (-12 Aug 1657) & Mary HUNTINGTON, m/2 Jeremiah DAVID 1689; 24 Mar 1687, 1686/7; Amesbury

JOY, Ephraim (1646-1697?) & Susanna (SPENCER) [GATTENSBY], w John; b 1 Jul 1673; Hingham/Kittery, ME

JOY, Jacob (-1691, 1690) & Elizabeth (SPENCER) WELLMAN, w William; 23 May 1671; Killingworth, CT

JOY, Joseph (1646-1697) & Mary PRINCE; 29 Aug 1667; Hingham

JOY, Joseph & Elizabeth ANDREWS; 22 May 1690; Hingham

JOY, Peter & Sarah GASKIN/GASKELL?; 24 May 1661; Salem

JOEY, Richard & _?_ ; in Eng, b 1625; Richmond Isl., ME

JOY, Samuel (-1671) & Ann PITTS, m/2 Benjamin EASTMAN 1678; 13 Nov 1668; Hingham/Boston

JOY, Samuel & Marah EASTMAN; 9 May 1696; Salisbury

JOY, Samuel & Lydia HANMER; 31 Oct 1699; Sandwich/?Dartmouth

JOY, Thomas (-1678, in 69th y) & Joan [GALLOP] (-1691); ca 1637; Boston/Hingham

JOY, [Thomas?] & Dorothy _?_ (-1676, Newport); Kings Town, RI

JOY, Thomas & Elizabeth STODDER/STODDARD; 6 Mar 1695, 1694/5; Boston/Hingham

JOY, Walter & Deborah [WATKEN] (1625-), m/2 Thomas FRENCH; b 1632; ?Guilford, CT

JOYCE, Hosea & 1/wf Martha _?_ (-1670); ca 1666; Yarmouth

JOYCE, Hosea (-1712) & 2/wf Elizabeth [CHIPMAN] (1647, 1648-living 1712/13); b 1674; Yarmouth

JOYCE, John (-1666) & Dorothy [COCHET]; ca 1653?, b 5 Sep 1657; Lynn/Sandwich/Yarmouth

JOYCE, Walter & Elizabeth _?_ ; b 1676; Wethersfield

JOYCE, William & 1/wf Sarah _?_ ; b 1686; Boston

JOYCE, William & 2/wf Sarah CLEVERLY (1666-1729), m/2 David HOBART 1695; 24 Sep 1691; Boston

JOYCE, William (-1648) & _?_ (wf in London)

JOYCE, William & Susanna _?_ , m/2 Nicholas HOYT 1646; b 1644; Windsor, CT

JUDD, Benjamin (-1689) & Mary [LEWIS] (1645-1691); 1667?, b 1668; Farmington, CT

JUDD, Benjamin (1671-) & Susannah NORTH; 18 Jan 1694, 1693/4

JUDD, John (?1640-1715) & Mary [HOWKINS] (1644-); b 1670; Farmington,CT

JUDD, John (1667-1717?) & Hannah [HICKOX] (-1750); 16 Apr 1696; Waterbury, CT

JUDD, John (-1710) & Rachel [St.JOHN] (-1717); b 1698 or 1699; Farmington, CT

JUDD, Philip (?1649-1689) & Hannah [LOOMIS] (1658-1690+); b 1681; Farmington, CT/Waterbury, CT

JUDD, Roger & Elizabeth _?_ (-1720, ae 69); b 1673(4?); Boston

JUDD, Samuel (?1651/3-1721) & Maria [STRONG] (1663-1751); ca 1682/3?, b 1682; Farmington, CT/Northampton

JUDD, Thomas[1] (1608-1688, Northampton) & 1/wf Elizabeth _?_ (-1678); b 1633?, b 1628; Cambridge/Bradford, CT

JUDD, Thomas (?1638-1703, Waterbury, CT) & Sarah [STEELE] (-1695, in 57th y); aft 12 Aug 1657, bef 30 Jan 1663; Farmington, CT

JUDD, Thomas[1] (1608-1688) & 2/wf Clemence (_?_) MASON (-1696), w Thomas; 2 Dec 1679; Northampton

JUDD, Thomas (1622-1647) & Sarah FREEMAN (1670-1738); 9 Feb 1687, 1687/8; Waterbury, CT

JUDD, Thomas (1662-1724) & Sarah GAYLORD (1671-1738); 11 Apr 1688; Waterbury/Farmington, CT

JUDD, William (-1690) & Mary STEELE (-1718), Farmington; 31 Mar 1657, 31 Mar 1658; Farmington, CT

JUDKINS, Job & Sarah _?_ (-1657, Boston); b 1637; Boston

JUDKINS, Job (1675-) & Elizabeth _?_ ; b 1701?; Exeter, NH

JUDKINS, Joel (1643-) & Mary BEAN, m/2 David ROBINSON by 1721; 25 Jun 1674; Exeter, NH

JUDKIN, Samuel (-1676) & Elizabeth LEAVITT (1644-1688?); 25 Mar 1667; Hingham/Boston

JUDKIN, Thomas (-1695, ae 66) & Anna/?Hannah (DIXCY) HOWARD (-1706), w Nehemiah; 25 Nov 1665; Gloucester

JUDSON, Andrew & Martha _?_ ; b 1676; Boston

JUDSON, Isaac (1654-1687) & Mary HICKS; 5 Dec 1678; Stratford, CT

JUDSON, James (1650-1721) & 1/wf Rebecca WELLES (1655-1717, 13 Aug); 18 Aug 1686; Stratford, CT

JUDSON, Jeremiah (1621-1700) & 1/wf Sarah [FOOTE] (1632-1673); aft 1652; Stratford, CT

JUDSON, Jeremiah & 2/wf Catharine (CRAIG/CRAGG) FAIRCHILD (-1706), w Thomas; 8 Nov 1675; Stratford, CT

JUDSON, Jeremiah (1671-1734) & Mary WELLS (1673-); 24 Apr 1695; Stratford, CT

JUDSON, John (1647-1709?) & 1/wf Elizabeth CHAPMAN; 12 Mar 1673, 1673/4; Stratford, CT

JUDSON, John (1647-1709/10?) & 2/wf Hannah (HAWKINS) (NICHOLS) WARD (-1698), w Jonathan, w Samuel; ca 1693; Stratford, CT

JUDSON, John & Sarah BEERS; Sep 1698, 28 Sep 1698; Fairfield, CT

JUDSON, John (1647-1709) & 3/wf Mary (TUDOR) ORTON, w John; 5 Jul 1699; Farmington, CT

JUDSON, Joseph (1649-1690), Milford, CT, & Sarah PORTER (1625-1696); 24 Oct 1644; Windsor, CT/Guilford, CT

JUDSON, Joshua (-1661) & Ann [PANTRY (1643 (doubtful)-), m/2 John HURD 1662; b 1656, b 1658; Stratford, CT

JUDSON, Samuel & 1/wf Bridget WARNE; 2 Apr 1644; Dedham

JUDSON, Samuel (-1657) & Mary ALDRICH/ALDRIDGE, w Henry, m/3 John HAYWORTH 1659+; 6 Oct 1646; Dedham

JUDSON, Samuel (1660-) & Mary [BOSTICK]; b 1695; Stratford, CT

JUDSON, William (-1662) & 1/wf Grace _?_ (-1659); in Eng, b 1619; Concord/Hartford/Stratford, CT

JUDSON, William (-1662) & 2/wf Elizabeth (?) **(HESTON) WILLMOTT** (-1685?), w _?_, w Benjamin; 8 Feb 1659, [1659/60]; New Haven/Stratford, CT
JUKIN, John (son Job Cooke JUKIN, b 14 Apr 1655) & _?_ ; b 1655; Sandwich
JUNE, Peter (-1707) & Sarah _?_ ; b 1680(1?); Stamford, CT
JUNKINS, Alexander & Catherine [**STACKPOLE**]; b 1701; ?Kittery, ME/?York, ME
JUNKINS, Robert & Sarah [**SMITH**] (1646-); ca 1664/6; York, ME/Dover, NH

KADE, James & Margaret [**BROWN**], m 1633; b 1640; Boston
KAY, John & _?_ ; Kittery, ME
KAY, Thomas & _?_ ; b 1671; ?Boston/Watertown
KEECH/KEACH, George & Mary _?_ ; b 1672; RI
KEETCH, John & Hannah _?_ ; b 1656; Boston
KEECH, John & Abigail [**STONE**] **(TAYLOR)** (1653-1730), m/3 Thomas **CLARK** 1713; b 1684; Boston
KETCH, _?_ & Mary _?_ ; b 1658; Stratford, CT
KEAYNE/KAINE, Benjamin (1619-1662) & Sarah [**DUDLEY**] (1620-1659), m/2 Thomas **PACEY**; b 9 Jun 1639, ?div 1647, ?1648; Boston/Cambridge
KEAYNE, Robert (1595-1656, Boston) & Ann/Anna [?**MANSFIELD**], m/2 Samuel **COLE** 1660; in Eng, b 1619, m lic 17 Jun 1617, 18 Jun; Boston
KEELER, John & Mehitable **ROCKWELL**, m/2 Zerubbabel **HOYT**; 18 Jun 1679?, 1678?; Norwalk, CT
KEELER, Ralph[1] (1613-1672) & 1/wf _?_ ; b 1650(1?), ca 1645?; Hartford/Fairfield/Norwalk, CT
KEELER, Ralph[1] & 2/wf Sarah (?) **(TREADWELL) [WHELPLEY]**, w Edward, w Henry, m/4 Thomas **SKIDMORE**; aft 6 Jun 1662; Fairfield, CT/Norwalk, CT
KEELER, Ralph & Grace [**LINDALL/LINDON?**] (1656-), New Haven; ca 1674; Norwalk, CT
KEELER, Samuel (1655/6-1713) & Sarah **SENTION/St.JOHN** (1660-); 10 Mar 1681/2; Norwalk, CT/Ridgefield, CT
KEELING, Samuel (-1730?) & Elizabeth **OLIVER** (1680-); 14 Sep 1699; Boston
KEEN, Arthur (-1687) & Jane _?_ ; b 1650; Boston
KEEN, Christopher & _?_ ; b 1642; Cambridge
KEEN, John (-1650) & Jane _?_ ; b 1621; Hingham
KEEN, John & Hannah _?_ ; b 1660; Boston
KEEN, John (1660-) & Mehitable _?_ ; b 1689; Boston
KEEN, John[2] & Rebecca [**BARKER**]; b 1694/[5?]; Pembroke/Duxbury
KEEN, Josiah[1] (-1710) & 1/wf Abigail [**LITTLE**]; ca 1654/8; Duxbury
KEEN, Josiah[1] (-1710) & 2/wf Hannah [**DINGLEY**]; b 1661; Duxbury
KEEN, Josiah[2], Jr. (-1732) & Lydia [**BAKER**]; b 1682; Duxbury/Scituate
KEENE, Matthew & _?_ ; b 1630, in Eng
KEEN, Matthew & Martha **MACOMBS/McFARLAND** (1672-); 20 Dec 1698; Hingham/Duxbury/Pembroke
KEENE, Nathaniel (1642-), Kittery, ME, & Sarah **GREENE**, Kittery, ME; 2 Nov 1688; York Co., ME
KEEN, Patrick & _?_ ; b 1689; Salem/Newport
KEEN, William & Jane _?_ ; b 1686, b 1683?; Boston/?Concord
KEEN, _?_ & Martha _?_ (ae 60 in 1638)
KEENEY, Alexander (-1680) & Alice [**COLLOX**] (-1683), w William; b 1662; Wethersfield, CT
KEENEY, John (-1716) & 1/wf Sarah **DOUGLAS** (1643-1669); Oct 1661; New London
KEENEY, John (-1716) & 2/wf Elizabeth [**LATHAM**]; 1690?; New London
KEENY, Joseph (1666-1753) & Hannah [**HILLS**] (ca 1676-); b 1693; Hartford
KEENEY, Richard (1674-) & Eunice _?_/Mary **MILES** (1670-); b 1704, b 1701?, ca 1700; Glastonbury, CT
KEENEY, William (?1601-) & Agnes _?_ (1599-); b 1628, b 1638, Boston; Gloucester/New London, CT

KEENEY, Richard & [Mary **MILES**] (1670-)
KEENEY, John & [Sarah **FARR**], m/2 John **HOLMES** 1672; b 1657; Salem
KEEP, John[1] (-1676) & Sarah **LEONARD** (1645-1676); Dec 1663, 31 Dec 1663; Springfield
KEEP, Samuel (1670-1755) & Sarah **COLTON** (1678-1754); 27 Feb 1695, 1695/6?; Springfield
KEET, Francis & Hannah **FRENCH** (1661, ?1664-); b 1690; ?Northampton
KEHOE, Christopher & Elizabeth _?_ ; b 1695; Dorchester
KEIGWIN/KEGWIN, John & Hannah **BROWN** (1680-); 10 Oct 1700; Stonington, CT
KEITH, James (ca 1643-1719) & 1/wf Susanna [**EDSON**] (?1638-1705); ?3 May 1668, 1665?; Bridgewater
KEITH, James (1669-) & Mary [**THAYER**?]/[**HODGES**?]; ?3 Sep 1695; Bridgewater/Mendon
KEITH, Joseph (1675-) & Elizabeth [**FOBES**] (1677-); b 1695; Bridgewater
KELLEN, James & Hannah (**LYNDE**) TRERICE (-1690, ae 48), w John; 12 Dec 1679; Charlestown
KELLOGG, Daniel (?1630-1688) & 2/wf? Bridget [**BOUTON**] (-1689); 1655; Norwalk, CT
KELLOGG, Daniel (1671-1709) & Elizabeth/?Hannah **PRESTON** (1676-); b 1698; Norwalk, CT
KELLOGG, Edward (1660-), Hadley & Dorothy _?_ ; b 1692; Hadley/Brookfield
KELLOGG, John (1656-) & Sarah **MOODY** (1660-1689); 23 Dec 1680; Hadley
KELLOGG, John & 2/wf Ruth [**WARNER**]; b 1693; Hadley
KELLOGG, Joseph[1] (1626-1707) & 1/wf Joanna _?_ (-1666, Hadley); b 1651(2?); Farmington/Boston/Hadley
KELLOGG, Joseph (1626-1707) & 2/wf Abigail **TERRY** (1646?-1715+); 9 May 1667, 9 Mar 1667; Hadley
KELLOGG, Martin (1658?, Boston-), Hatfield & 1/wf Anna **HINSDALE** (1666-1689), Deerfield; 10 Dec 1684; Hadley/?Suffield
KELLOGG, Martin (1658-) & 2/wf Sarah (**DICKINSON**) LANE (-1722), w Samuel; 27 Feb 1691, 1690/1, 27 Feb 1690; Hadley/Suffield, CT
KELLOGG, Nathaniel (-1659) & Elizabeth _?_ ; ca 1650?, no issue; Farmington, CT
KELLOGG, Nathaniel (1669-1750) & Sarah **BOLTWOOD** (1672-), Hadley; 28 Jun 1692; Hadley/Andover
KELLOGG, Nathaniel (1671-1757) & Margaret [**BELDEN**] (1628-1747, ae 71); b 1697; Hadley/Colchester, NY
KELLOGG, Samuel (ca 1630-1711) & 1/wf Sarah (**DAY**) GUNN (-1677), Hartford, w Nathaniel; 24 Nov 1669; Hatfield
KELLOGG, Samuel (-1711) & 2/wf Sarah **ROOT** (1660-1719), Westfield; 22 Mar 1678/9, 22 Mar, ?30 Mar; Hatfield/Hadley/Deerfield
KELLOGG, Samuel (1662-1717) & Sarah **MERRILL** (1664-1717, 1718?); 22 Sep 1687; Hartford
KELLOGG, Samuel (1669-1708), Hatfield & Hannah [**DICKINSON**] (1666-1745); b 1694, 1690?; Hadley/Colchester
KELLOGG, Stephen (1668-1722), Westfield & Lydia **BELDING** (1675-); 8 May 1695, 1694; Hadley
KELLOND, Thomas & Abigail (**HAWKINS**) (**MOORE**), w Samuel, m/2 John **FOSTER** 1689; b 1665; Boston
KELLON, Thomas & Susanna _?_ ; b 1673; Boston
KELLON, Thomas & Elizabeth _?_ ; b 1689; Boston
KELLY, Abiel (1672-) & Rebecca **DAVIS**; 5 Jan 1696, 1696/7; Newbury/Methuen
KELLEY, Charles & Joanna **FERNOLD**; 25 May 1698; ?York Co., ME/Kittery, ME
KELLEY, David (-1662) & Elizabeth _?_ , m/2 Robert **SMITH** 1663; b 1647; Boston
KELLY, Duncan (-1742, ae 98) & Patience _?_ (-1750, ae 96); b 1691; Barrington, RI
KELLEY, Edward & Elizabeth [**YEOMANS**]; b 1664; Boston
KELLY, James & Susan [**CLARK**] (1652), m/2 Nathaniel **SANFORD**; ?Hartford
KELLY, John[1] (-1644) & _?_ ; b 1640(1?); Newbury
KELLY, John & _?_ ; b 1652; Southampton
KELLY, John[2] (1642-1718) & 1/wf Sarah **KNIGHT** (1648-1714+, ca 1715); 20 May 1663; Newbury
KELLEY, John, Hartford & [Grace?] [**WAKEMAN**] (ca 1638/9-); b 10 Jun 1663
KELLY, John (-1700) & Emma [**TABSON**] (1656-), m/2 Silvanna **PLUMER** 1700; b 1684; Boston
KELLY, John & 1/wf Grace **WOODS**; 16 Oct 1684; Marblehead
KELLY, John (-1718) & 2/wf Rose _?_ ; b 1694; Marblehead
KELLY, John (1668-1736?) & Elizabeth **EMERY** (1679-1735+); - Nov 1696; Newbury

KELLY, Michael (-1680) & Isabel _?_, m/2 _?_ 1681; Jamestown, RI
KELLY, Reynold & Joanna [DOLLEN], m/2 James MANDER by 1689; Mooheqan
KELLY, Richard (1666-) & 1/wf Sarah [SMITH] (1668-1725); Salisbury
KELLY, Roger (1650-) & Mary _?_ ; by 1660?, by 1653; Isles of Shoals
KELLY, Roger & Mary HOLDRED/(HOLDRIDGE); 29 Sep 1681; Exeter, NH/Newcastle
KELSEY, Daniel (1630-1727) & 1/wf Mary STEVENS; 24 Mar 1672; Killinqworth, CT
KELSEY, Daniel & 2/wf Jane CHALKER (1662-1742); betw 1683 & 1693, b 1702; ?Killinqworth, CT
KELSEY, John (-1709) (left wid Hannah) & [Hannah?/Phebe? DESBOROUGH]; b 1668, b 1670; Wethersfield, CT/Hartford/Killinqworth
KELSEY, John & 1/wf Phebe CRANE (-1728); 22 Jun 1697; Killinqworth, CT
KELSEY, Joseph & Mercy [EVANS]; b 1693(4?); Salisbury
KELSEY, Joseph & Hannah HAYDEN (1681-); 23 Mar 1699, 1698/9; Killinqworth, CT
KELSEY, Mark & 1/wf Rebecca HOSKINS (-1683); 8 Mar 1658/9, prob 1658; Windsor, CT
KELSEY, Mark & 2/wf Abigail ATWOOD (-1713), w Thomas; 26 Dec 1683; Windsor, CT
KELSEY, Stephen (1647-1710) & Hannah INGERSOLL/HINGESON, Westfield; 15 Nov 1672; Hartford/?Wethersfield, CT
KELSEY, Stephen (-1745) & Dorothy BRONSON (1675?-); 11 Jan 1699/1700; Wethersfield, CT
KELSEY, Thomas (1663-1715), Windsor & Elizabeth _?_ (-1726); ca 1686/8; Windsor, CT
KELSEY, Timothy & _?_ ; b 1667?; Huntinqton, LI
KELSEY, William & Bethia [?HOPKINS]; b 1635; Cambridqe/Hartford/Killinqworth
KELSEY, William (1670-1698) & Abigail WHITCOMB (1674-), m/2 Ebenezer WATSON 1703; 23 Mar 1695, 1694?, 1694/5, Abigail b 1694?; Windsor, CT
KELSEY, William (1674-) & Elizabeth SHEATHER (1679-), m/2 Thomas SPENCER; 26 Auq 1696; Killingworth, CT
KELTON, John & Lydia [HALSEY?]; b 1691; Boston
KELTON/KILTON?, Robert & Bethiah [FENNER]; b 1690; Providence
KELTON, Thomas & Susanna _?_ ; b 1661; Boston/Reading
KELTON, Thomas & Jane BLAKE (1658-); 25 Mar 1685; Milton
KEMBLE, Henry & 1/wf Sarah FOUNALL (-1657); 13 Nov 1656; Charlestown
KEMBLE, Henry & 2/wf Mary [BRIGDEN] (-1696); b 1663; Charlestown
KEMBLE, John (1656-1702) & Elizabeth _?_ ; b 1695; Charlestown/New York
KEMBLE/KIMBALL?, Joseph & Elizabeth RICHARDS; m int 7 Sep 1696; Boston
KEMBLE, Thomas (1622-1688/9, Boston) & Elizabeth [TRERICE] (-1717, 1712?); b 1656; Charlestown/Boston
KEMBLE/KIMBALL, Timothy (1672-) & Catharine/Katharine FOWLE (1668-); 18 Auq 1698; Boston
KEMP, Edward (-1668) & Ann _?_ ; b 1632; Dedham/Wenham/Chelmsford
KEMP, Jonathan (1668-) & Mary _?_ ; b 1699; Groton
KEMP, Samuel & Sarah FOSTER; 23 May 1662; Billerica/Andover/Groton
KEMP, Samuel (1663-1707+) & Susanna [LAWRENCE]; [ca 1683-90?]; Groton?
KEMP, William (-1641) & Elizabeth [PARTRIDGE], m/2 Rev. Thomas THATCHER 1643; ca 1635/8, 7 Jan 1638/9; Duxbury
KEMPSTER, Daniel (he calls Thomas MOULTON "cousin" & Samuel ANDREW "kinsman") & Abigail _?_ ; ?b 1620, b 1627?; Cambridqe
KEMPTHORN/KEMPTHORNE, Simon (-ca 1657) & Mary [LONG] (1627-1675); b 1657; Charlestown
KEMPTON, Ephraim (-1645) & _?_ ; b 1624; Scituate
KEMPTON, Ephraim (-1655) & Joan/Joanna/Hannah RAWLINGS (-1656); 28 Jan 1645, 1644/5, 23 Jan; Scituate
KEMPTON, Ephraim (1649-1716) & Mary [REEVE]; b 1674; Salem
KEMPTON, Manasseh (-1662, [1662/3]) & Juliana (CARPENTER) MORTON (-1665, ae 81, 1664, [1664/5]), w George; betw 1624 & 1627, no issue; Plymouth
KENDALL, Francis alias MILES (1620-1708) (65 in 1684) & Mary TIDD (-1705); 24 Dec 1644; Woburn/Charlestown
KENDALL, Jacob (1661-) & 1/wf Persis HAYWARD/HAYWOOD? (-Oct 1694); 2 Jan 1683, 1683/4, prob 1682/3; Woburn
KENDALL, Jacob (1661-) & 2/wf Alice (HASSELL) TEMPLE, w Christopher; 10 Jan 1694, 1694/5; Woburn

KENDALL, John (-1661) & 1/wf _?_ ; b 1630?; Gloucester/Cambridge
KENDALL, John (-1661) & 2/wf Elizabeth (_?_) [HOLLEY], w Samuel; aft 1643, ca 1644; Cambridge
KENDALL, John (1646-1732) & 1/wf _?_, m John KIMBALL; 29 Jan 1668, b 1671; Woburn
KENDALL, John (1646-1732) & 2/wf Elizabeth COMEY (1661-1701); 29 Mar 1681; Woburn
KENDALL, Samuel (1659-1749?) & 1/wf Rebecca MIXER (-1691); 13 Nov 1683; Woburn
KENDALL, Samuel (1659-1749?) & 2/wf Mary LOCKE (-1742+); 30 Mar 1692; Woburn/Lancaster
KENDALL, Thomas (-1681, ae 63) & Rebecca [?PAINE] (?1616-1703, ae 85?); b 1639?, ca 1641?; ?Lynn/Roxbury
KENDALL, Thomas (1649-1730) & 1/wf Ruth [BLODGETT] (1656-1695); b 1675; Woburn
KENDALL, Thomas (1649-1730) & 2/wf Abigail (RAYNER) BROUGHTON (-1718), w John; 30 Mar 1696; Woburn
KINDRICK, Elijah (1644/5-1680) & Hannah [JACKSON], m/2 John HYDE 1682; b 1668(9?); Cambridge/Newton
KENERICK, George & Jane _?_ ; b 1639, b 1646, Scituate/Boston
KENDRICK, George & 1/wf Ruth BOWEN (-1688); 23 Apr 1647; Rehoboth
KENDRICK, George & 2/wf Jane IDE (-1694); 1 Apr 1691; Rehoboth
KENRICK, John (?1605-1686) & 1/wf Anna [SMITH] (-1656) (sister Robert); b 1640?, b 1638?, ca 1635?; Boston/Newton
KIMRIGHT/KENDRICK/KENRICK, John (1605-1686) & 2/wf Judith [HOLLAND/HOTTON] (should be HOLLAND) (-1687, Roxbury), w John; aft 15 Nov 1656; Farmingham/Guilford, CT/Newton
KENRICKE, John (-1716) & Lydia CHENY (ca 1640-1708+); 12 Nov 1657; Newbury/Ipswich
KINDRICK, John (1641-1721) & Esther [HALL?] (1654-1723), Rehoboth?; b 1673, ?23 Oct 1672; Cambridge
KENRICKE, Thomas & Mary PERREY; 17 Jun 1681; Rehoboth
KENEL/KENELINE?, John & _?_ ; b 1674; Wenham
KENNARD, Edward & Elizabeth [MARTYN] (1662-), m/2 William FURBER, m/3 Benjamin NASON; ca 1680; Portsmouth, NH
KENNARD, John (-1689, 1688?) & Rebecca [SPENCER] (ca 1660-), m/2 John TANNER 1689; 1682?; Haddam, CT
KENNEDY, William (-1728) & _?_ ; b 1692; Preston, CT
KENNET, Richard & Susanna [BILL] (1666-), m/2 Mungo CRAFFORD 1694; b 1689; Boston
KENNY, Andrew & Elizabeth _?_ ; b 1690; Malden
KENNY, Daniel & Elizabeth BURGES; m int 30 Jul 1696; Boston
KENNE, Henry (ae 60 in 1684) & Ann [HOWARD?]; b 1651(2?), ?3 May 1650; Salem
KENNY, Henry (1669-) & 1/wf Priscilla LEWIS; 14 May 1691; Salem/Sutton
KENNEY/KEENEY, John (-1670) & Sarah [FARR], m/2 John HOLMES 1672; b 1657; Salem
KENEY, John (-1693) & Susannah _?_, m/2 Thomas HORTON 1693; b 1667; Milton
KENNE, John & Elizabeth LOOKE; 17 Jun 1675; Salem/Topsfield/Newbury
KENNEY, John & Lydia [TABOR] (1673-); b 1696; Dartmouth
KENNY, John & Mary [CURTIS] (1677-); b 1701; Topsfield/Newbury?/Salem
KENNEY, Joseph & Leah ALLIN; 1 Dec 1699; NH
KENNY, Moses (1668-) & Margaret LEATHERLAND; 24 Jul 1691; Boston
KENNEY/[CANNEY?], Richard & Deborah STOKES; 15 Aug 1687; NH
KENNEY/CANNEY?, Samuel & Sarah (HASKET) RANKIN, w Joseph; 15 Mar 1698/9; ?Dover, NH
KENNE, Thomas (1656-1691) & Elizabeth KNIGHT; 23 May 1677; Salem
KENNICUT, John (-1722, in 53rd y) & Elizabeth LUTHER (1671-1754, in 83rd y); 14 Apr 1699; Taunton/Warwick, RI
KENICOTT, Roger & Joanna SHEPARDSON/SHEPERSON (1642-); - Nov 1661; Malden/Charlestown/Swansea
KENNING, Henry & Magdalen (HILTON) WIGGINS, w James; m int 14 May 1698; Newbury
KENNING, _?_ /[John] (-1654) & Jane _?_ (-1653); Ipswich
KENNISTON, Allen (-1648) & Dorothy _?_, m/2 Philip CROMWELL 1649; b 1636; Salem
KENNISTON, Christopher (1655-) & Mary MUSHAMORE/MUCHEMORE; 4 Dec 1677; Exeter, NH
KENISTON, George & Bridget _?_ ; b 1701?, b 1680?; Brentwood, NH/Greenland
KENNISTON, James (-1747) & [?Dorcas] _?_ ; b 1693(4?); Stratham, NH
KENNISTON, John (-1677) & Agnes _?_, m/2 Henry MAGOON; b 1655; Dover, NH

KENT, Cornelius & Mary _?_ ; b 1671; Ipswich
KENT, James (-1681) & _?_ ; b 1641; Newbury
KENT, John & Hannah GRIZOLD/GRISWALD?/GRISSELL? (?1645-1691) (see William KENT); 21 May 1662; Dedham/Charlestown
KENT, John (1641-1718) & Mary HOBBS (1643-1725, ae 82); 24 Feb 1664; Newbury
KENT, John (1645-1718) & Sarah WOODMAN (1642, 1640/1?-); 13 Mar 1665, 1665/6?; Newbury
KENT, John (1666-1721) & 1/wf Abigail DUDLEY (1667-1707); 9 May 1686; Suffield, CT
KENT, John, Charlestown & Sarah SMITH, Charlestown; 22 Dec 1692; Scituate/Marshfield/ Charlestown
KENT, John & Rebecca [SOMERBY] (1672-); b 1696; Newbury
KENT, Joseph (-1704+or-) & Susanna [GEORGE?] (1643-); b 1665; Rehoboth
KENT, Joseph, Jr. (-1734/5) & 1/wf Dorothy BROWN (1666-1727); 12 Nov 1690; Swansea
KENT, Joseph (1660-1727) & Jane _?_ ; ca 1690/97?; Durham, NH
KENT, Joshua (-1664) & Mary [CUMBERS?/TUMBERS?] (-1664+), wid; b 1647; Dedham
KENT, Joshua (1673-) & Agnes OAKMAN, m/2 Robert COX?; 4 Nov 1697; Boston
KENT, Josiah & Mary LUFKIN (-1725); 17 Apr 1689; Gloucester
KENT, Oliver (-1670+, 1669?) & Dorothy [HULL?] (1631-), m/2 Benjamin MATTHEWS 1670?; b 1660; Oyster River/Dover, NH
KENT, Richard (-1654) & Emma _?_ (-1676); b 1626; Newbury
KENT, Richard (-1689) & 1/wf Jane _?_ (-26 Jun 1674); b 1634; Newbury
KENT, Richard (-1689) & 2/wf Joanna [?HODGES/?MILLER] DAVISON (-1699), w Nicholas; 6 Jan 1674, 1674/5; Newbury
KENT, Richard & Amee/Amy _?_ ; b 1699; Braintree
KENT, Samuel (-1691) & 1/wf Frances WOODALL (-1683, Suffield, CT); 17 Jan 1654; Gloucester/Suffield, CT
KENT, Samuel (-1691) & 2/wf Mary _?_ ; aft 10 Aug 1683; Suffield, CT/Springfield, MA
KENT, Samuel & 1/wf Priscilla HUNTER/HUNT (1665-1695); ?22 Oct 1683, ?1 Nov 1683; Suffield CT
KENT, Samuel & 2/wf Martha ALLEN (-1698); 28 Jul 1696; Suffield, CT/Deerfield
KENT, Samuel (-1740) & 3/wf Esther/Hester (HOSFORD) PHELPS (-1760), w Joseph; 1 May 1700; Suffield, CT
KENT, Stephen (1607-) & 1/wf Margery [NORRIS?]; in Eng, b 1638, ?10 Aug 1637; Newbury/Haverhill/Woodbury, NJ
KENT, Stephen & 2/wf Ann _?_ (-1660); b 1653; Haverhill
KENT, Stephen & 3/wf Eleanor (?) SCADLOCK, w William; 29 May 1663, 9 May, 9 May 1662; Haverhill/Woodbridge, NJ
KENT, Thomas (-1658) & _?_ [?NOYES] (-1671); b 1634; Gloucester
KENT, Thomas (-1692) & Jane/Joane? PENNY; 28 Mar 1658; Gloucester/Brookfield
KENT, Thomas & [Ann] [CORNELL?]; b 1659
KENT, William (-1691, ae 57) & 1/wf _?_, ?m Ezekiel CRAWITH bef 1669; 1662?, 1664?; Boston
KENT, William (-1691) & 2/wf Hannah [BILL?]
KENYON, James (-1724) & Ruth [WELLS] (-1720+); b 1693; Kings Town, RI
KENYON, John[1] & _?_ ; b 1657; Kings Town, RI
KENYON, John (1657-1732) & 2/wf Anna _?_ ; b 1682; Kings Town, RI/Westerly, RI
KENYON, Roger & Mary RAY (1667-1714), m/2 Samuel SANDS; 11 Oct 1683; New Shoreham, RI
KENYON, _?_ & Mary PECKHAM (1674-); b 1701?; ?Newport, RI
KERLY, Henry (1632-1713) & 1/wf Elizabeth WHITE (1635-10 Feb 1676); 2 Nov 1654; Sudbury/Lancaster
KERLEY, Henry (1632-1713) & 2/wf Elizabeth (WARD) HOWE (1643-1710), w John; 18 Apr 1676?, 18 Feb 1678?; Charlestown/Lancaster/Marlboro
KERLEY, William[1] (-1670) & 1/wf Ann _?_ (-1658); b 1632; Hingham/Sudbury/Lancaster
KERLY, William[2] (-1683/4) & Hannah KING (?1625-1698); 6 Oct 1646; Sudbury/Lancaster/Marlboro
KERLY, William[1] (-1670) & 2/wf Bridget (?BRADSTREET) (MUSSEY/MUZZEY) ROWLANDSON (-1662), w Robert, w Thomas; 31 May 1659; Lancaster
KERLY, William[1] (-1670) & 3/wf Rebecca (MARLOWE?) JOSELIN, w Thomas; 16 May 1664, 6 May 1664; Lancaster

KERLEY/CARLEY, William (1633-1719) & Jane __?__ (1650-1720); b 1667; Sudbury/Marlboro/ Cambridge
KER/KEN?/KEYNE?/CAN/CANN/CARR/KERR, Robert & Mary __?__; b 1682; Reading/Salem
KESKEYS, Henry & Ruth GRAVES (had Henry b 3 May 1656, 1657, had Diniana 31 Oct 1658); 7 Aug 1656, 1655?; Boston
KETCHAM, Edward[1] (-1655) & 1/wf Mary [HALL]; Cambridge, Eng, 22 Aug 1619
KETCHUM, Edward[1] (-1655) & ?Sarah __?__, m/2 Henry WHITNEY by 1660; b 1630?; Ipswich/Southold, LI/Stratford, CT
KETCHAM, Edward[2] (-1678?) & Mary __?__; b 1672?; Huntington, LI
KETCHAM, [?Edward] & Mercy [HARCURT/HARCOURT] (had son Daniel); Huntington, LI
KETCHAM, John[2] (-1697) & 1/wf Susan/Mary? __?__; b 1650?; Southold, LI/Setauket/Huntington, LI
KETCHAM, John & __?__ (see above); by 1655?; Newtown, LI
KETCHAM, John (-1714+) & Elizabeth [WICKS]; b 1674; Huntington, LI
KETCHAM, John (-1697) & 2/wf Bethia RICHARDSON; m lic 26 Feb 1676/7; Newtown, LI
KETCHAM, Joseph (-1730) & Mercy LINDALL (1655-); 3 Apr 1679; Norwalk, CT
KETCHAM, Philip & [Martha BETTS]; Newtown, LI
KETCHAM, Samuel (1651-) & Mary [TITUS]?; b 1672, ca 1675?; Newton/Brookhaven, LI/Huntington
KETCHAM, __?__ & [Sarah JAGGER] (1670±-), dau John
CETILL, Edward & Susannah GODFREY, dau Richard; 13 Jul 1682; Taunton
KETTLE, James & Elizabeth [HAYWARD] (1666-1735); b 1689; Salem
KETTELL, John (1621-1685) & Elizabeth [ALLEN] (1634-), m/2 Samuel CORNING 1688; b 1654; Gloucester/Salem
KETTLE, John (1639-) & 1/wf Sarah [GOODNOW] (1642/3-); b 1660; Lancaster/Sudbury
KETTELL, John (1639-1685) & 2/wf Elizabeth [WARD]; b 1670?; Lancaster
KETTELL, John (-1691) & Abigail AUSTIN (1664-1703+); 13 Sep 1688; Charlestown
KETTELL, Jonathan (-1720, ae 74) & Abigail CONVERSE (1658-1691); 30 Mar 1676; Charlestown
KETTELL, Joseph (1641-) & 1/wf Hannah FROTHINGHAM (1642-1693); 5 Jul 1665; Charlestown
KETTELL, Joseph (1641-1711) & 2/wf Dorothy (EDMUNDS) HETT (-1710), w Thomas; 15 Mar 1693/4, 20 Dec 1693; Charlestown
KETTELL, Nathaniel (-1723) & 1/wf Hannah EVILLE (-1670); 13 Jan 1669/70; Charlestown
KETTELL, Nathaniel (-1723) & 2/wf Hannah KIDDER; 30 Oct 1672; Charlestown
KETTLE, Nathaniel (1670-) & Joanna ELLISE; 5 Oct 1692; Boston
KETTELL, Richard (-1680) & Esther/Hester [WARD] (-1679); b 1637; Charlestown
KETTELL, Samuel (-1694) & 1/wf Mercy HAYDEN (-1692); 11 Jul 1665; Charlestown
KETTELL, Samuel (-1694) & 2/wf Mary (HETT) FROTHINGHAM (-1710), w Nathaniel; 3 May 1694; Charlestown
KETTOW, Edward (-1701) & Mercy BELCHER; 4 Dec 1691; Boston
KEY, John & 1/wf __?__; by 1673; Dover, NH/Kittery, ME
KEY, John & 2/wf Sarah (JENKINS) [MASON], w Jonathan; aft 1691; Kittery, ME
KEY, John (-1737) & Grizzel [GRANT]; b 1697; Kittery, ME
KEIES, Elias (1643-) & Sarah BLANFORD, m/2 John MAYNARD 1679?; 11 Sep 1665; Sudbury
KEYES, James (1670-1746) & Hannah [DIVOLL] (-1712, ae 73 y 9 m); b 1694; Marlboro/Bolton
KEESE, John & Ann MANTON; 18 Sep 1682; Portsmouth, RI
KEYES, John (1675-) & Mary EAMES; 11 Mar 1695/6; Marlboro/Lancaster/Shrewsbury
KEYES, Joseph & Joanna CLEVELAND; 28 May 1690, ?21 May; Chelmsford
KEYSE, Moses (1671-1747) & Mehitable KEMP (-1768); 27 Jun 1693; Chelmsford
KEYES, Peter & Elizabeth __?__; b 1667(8?), b 1664?; Sudbury
KEYES, Robert (-1647) & Sarah __?__ (1605-1681), m/2 John GAGE 1658; b 1633; Watertown/Newbury
KAIAS/KEYES, Samuel & Mary (RIDDON) HODDY, w John; 4 Feb 1695/6
KEYES, Solomon (-1702) & Frances GRANT (1634-1708); 2 Oct 1653; Newbury/Wethersfield
KEYES, Solomon (1665-) & 1/wf Mary __?__; b 1688; Chelmsford
KEYES, Thomas (1675-1742) & Elizabeth HOW (-1764); 23 Jan 1698/9; Marlboro
KEASER, Eleazer & 1/wf Mary COLLINS; 9 Dec 1679; Salem
KEASER, Eleazer & 2/wf Hannah (FLINT) [WARD], w Joshua; 1680+; Salem

KEYSER, George (1618, ?1614-1690) & 1/wf Elizabeth [**HOLYOKE**] (-1659); ca 1645?, b 1650; Lynn/Salem

KEYSER, George (1614-1690) & 2/wf Rebecca (**AYERS/AYER**) [**ASLET/ALSBEE?**] (-1667+), w John; aft 1659, 1671; Salem

KEYZAR, John (-1697) & Hannah **DAVIS**, m/2 Samuel **DALTON** 1701; 28 Sep 1677; Haverhill

KEISAR, Thomas & Mary __?__; b 1640; Lynn/Boston

KIBBEY/KIBBEN, Arthur (-1685) (see **KIPPEN**) & Abigail [**AGER**]; b 29 Jun 1654; Salem

KIBBY, Edward (1611, 1607?-1694?) & Mary [**PARTRIDGE**]; b 1640; Boston/Roxbury/Reading

KIBBE, Edward (1670-) & 1/wf Rebecca **HADLOCK** (-1692); 15 Feb 1691, 1691/2, 11 Feb 1691/2; Enfield, CT

KIBBE, Edward (1670-), Enfield, CT, & 2/wf Dorothy **PHELPS** (1675-); 13 Nov 1693, 30 Nov

KIBBE, Elisha (1644-1735) & Rachel **COOKE** (-1740); 12 Dec 1667, 7 May 1667; Salem

KIBBY, Henry (-1661) & 1/wf Rachel [**LINDON**] (ca 1612-1657), dau Richard; b 1637; Dorchester

KIBBY, Henry (-1661) & 2/wf Grizel (**FLETCHER**) (**JEWELL**) **GRIGGS**, w Thomas, w __?__, m/2 John **GURNEY** 1661, m/4 John **BURGE** 1667; 8 Oct 1657; Dorchester/Weymouth

KIBBY, James (1641/2-) & Anna/Hannah? [**CARY?**/[**FLETCHER**]/[**?EDSON**] (had grandson Edson **DIX**); b 1668(9?); Concord

KIBBY, James (1641/2-1681+, 17 Feb 1731/2, Reading) & 2/wf Sarah (**STIMPSON**) **LOWDEN** (1640-1720), w John; 23 Oct 1679; Charlestown

KIBBY, John & Mary **BROWN** (1677-); 12 Oct 1695; Enfield, CT

KIBBE, John (1668-) & Hannah **PHELPS** (1677-); 18 Aug 1698; Enfield, CT

KIBBY, Joshua (-1731) & Mary **COMEY** (1663-1712), Woburn; 24 May 1688; Woburn

KIBBY, Sheribiah & Elizabeth **PARLING**; 12 Dec 1691; Concord/Lexington

KIDDER, Enoch (1664-1752) & 1/wf Mary [**HAYWARD/HAYWOOD?**] (?1669-1742); b 1693; Billerica

KIDDER, Ephraim & Rachel **CROSBEY**; 4 Aug 1685, 1 Aug; Billerica/Medfield

KIDDER, James (?1626-1676) & Anne?/Anna [**MOORE**]; b 1651; Cambridge/Billerica

KIDDER, James & Elizabeth **BROWN** (-1691); 23 Sep 1678; Billerica

KIDDER, John & Lydia **PARKER** (1665-); ?3 Dec 1684, ? Sep; Chelmsford

KIDDER, Samuel (1666-1724) & Sarah **GRIGGS** (-1738, ae 72); 23 Oct 1689; Cambridge/Charlestown

KIDDER, Stephen (1662-1748) & Mary [**JOHNSON**] (-1722, in 50th y); b 1694; Charlestown

KILBORNE, Abraham (ca 1675-1713) & Sarah **GOODRICH** (-1719), m/2 Thomas **BOARDMAN** 1718; 26 Oct 1699; Wethersfield, CT

KILBOURN, Ebenezer (?1665-1711) & Grace **BULKELEY** (ca 1670-); 20 Sep 1692; Wethersfield, CT

KILBOURN, Ebenezer (1679-1732) & 1/wf Sarah **FOX** (-1714); 1 Jun 1698, 1696?; Glastonbury, CT/Morris Co., NJ

KILBORNE, George (-1685) (called "bro." by James **BARKER**, by Mary **BARKER** wid James) & Elizabeth [**?BARKER**] (-1698); b 1649; Rowley

KILBURN, George (ca 1668-1741) & Abigail **ATTWOOD** (1668-1740); 16 May 1689; Wethersfield, CT

KILBORNE, Isaac (1659-1713) & Mary **CHENEY**; 24 Jul 1684; Rowley

KILBOURNE, John (1624-1703) & 1/wf Naomi __?__ (-1 Oct 1659); ca 1650, b 1651(2?); Wethersfield, CT

KILBORNE, John (1624-1703) & 2/wf Sarah **BRONSON?** (ca 1669-1711, ae 70+); aft 1 Oct 1659, b 1665; Weathersfield, CT

KILBOURNE, John (1651/2-1711) & 1/wf Susanna/?Hannah [**HILLS**] (ca 1651-1701, ae 50); 4 Mar 1673; Wethersfield, CT

KILBOURN, John (1677-) & 1/wf Sarah **KIMBERLY** (-1703); 25 Jan 1699/1700; Glastonbury, CT/Springfield

KILBURNE, Joseph (1652-1723) & Mary **TRUMBLE/TRUMBULL** (1654-); 30 May 1678; Rowley

KILBOURN, Joseph (1672-1744) & 1/wf Dorothy **BUTLER** (-1709); 4 Jun 1696; Wethersfield, CT/Litchfield, CT

KILBURNE, Samuel & Mary **FOSTER** (1662-); 20 Nov 1682; Rowley

KILBOURNE, Thomas (1678-1640, bef 1639) & Frances **MOODY** (1585-1650); Moulton, Eng, 5 Sep 1604; Wethersfield, CT/Windsor, CT/Hartford

KILBOURNE, Thomas (1602-) (returned to Eng?) & Elizabeth _?_ (1614-); b 1635; Wethersfield, CT

KILBOURNE, Thomas (1653-1712) & 1/wf Hannah HILLS (ca 1654-), m/2 Nathaniel FITCH aft 1726?; b 1677; Hartford

KILBOURNE, Thomas (ca 1677-1712) & Hannah/?Susannah HILLS (ca 1680-1749), m/2 Nathaniel FITCH aft 1726; 1 Feb 1699, prob 1699/1700; Hartford

KILBEY, Christopher (1666-) & Sarah SIMKINS (1668-); 20 Mar 1691, 1691/2; Boston

KILBY, John (-1710) & Elizabeth (JOSLIN/JOSSOLYN) YEOMANS (1628-), w Edward; 9 May 1662; Boston

KILBY, John (1664-) & 1/wf Elizabeth [BUCKMINSTER] (1665-); b 1686; Boston

KILBY, John (1664-) & 2/wf Rebecca [SIMPKINS] (1665, 1665/6?-); b 1688, ca 1690; Boston

KILCUP, Ralph & Mary ARNOLD; m int 9 Dec 1696; Boston

KILKUP, Roger & Anne _?_ ; b 1685; Boston

KILCUP, Roger (-1702, ae 52) & Abigail DUDSON, m/2 Ezekiel LEWIS 1704; 4 Jul 1695; Boston

KILCUP, William (-1689, ae 87) & Grace _?_ (-1679, ae 80); Lynn/Boston

KILHAM, Augustine?/Austin (1595-1667) & Alice _?_ (1597-) (?relation of Charles GOTT?); in Eng, ca 1618; Salem/Dedham/Wenham

KILLAM, Daniel[2] (1620-1699/1700) & 1/wf Mary [SAFFORD] (-bef 1678); Oct 1648; ?Wenham/Ipswich

KILLAM, Daniel[3] (1649-1734) & Sarah (GRACE) FAIREFIELD (-1716, ae 70), w John; 13 Apr 1673; Wenham

KILLAM, Daniel[2] (1620-1699/1700) & 2/wf Elizabeth (BLACK) (GILBERT) (REYNER) KIMBALL, w Humphrey, w William, w Henry; ca 1678, aft 16 Jun 1676, bef 25 Dec 1679; ?Wenham

KILLUM, Daniel[2] (1620-1699/1700) & 3/wf Rebecca/?Mary SMITH (-1696, Wenham); 29 Mar 1693; Topsfield

KILLAM, Daniel[2] (1620-1699/1700) & 4/wf Mary (ABBY) MAXCY/MAXEY (-1726), w Alexander; ca 1697; Salem/Wenham

KILHAM, John (?1627-) & Hannah [PICKWORTH/PICKWITH] (1638-); ca 1659; Wenham

KILLUM, John (-1706) & Susanna _?_ (-1731); b 1689; Springfield

KILLUM, Lott (1640-) & Hannah GOODELL/GOODALE (1645-), dau Robert; 22 May 1666, 21 May 1666; Salem/Wenham/Enfield, CT

KELLUM, Samuel (1662-1745) & Deborah _?_ (-1746); b 1696, ca 1689; Wenham

KELLUM, Thomas (-1725) & Martha [SOLART]; b 1682; Wenham/Boston

KILLIOWE, Christopher & Elizabeth FOSTER (1669-); 28 May 1694; Boston

KIMBALL, Abraham & Mary GREEN; 8 May 1700; Bradford

KIMBALL, Benjamin (±1637-1696) & Mercy HASELTON (1642-1707/8); 16 Apr 1661; Salisbury

KIMBALL, Benjamin (1670-1716) & Mary KIMBALL (1671-); 16 Jan 1694/5; Topsfield

KIMBALL, Caleb (-1682) & Anna/Ann/Anne/Hannah HASELTINE (1641-1688); 7 Nov 1660; Ipswich

KIMBALL, Caleb & 1/wf Lucy EDWARDS (1667-1714); 23 Nov 1685; Ipswich

KIMBALL, Caleb (1665-1731) & Sarah [SAFFORD] (1667-); b 1694; Wenham

KIMBALL, David (1671-1743) & Elizabeth [GAGE] (1674-); b 1695; Bradford

KIMBALL, Ephraim & Mary [FRIEND] (1666-1741); [24 Nov 1685]

KIMBALL, Henry (-1648) & Susanna (STONE) CUTTING, m/3 Thomas LOWE 1648+; in Eng, 27 Nov 1628; Watertown

KIMBALL, Henry (1615-1676) & 1/wf Mary [WYATT] (-1672, Wenham); b 1641; Watertown/Boston/Wenham

KIMBALL, Henry (-1676) & 2/wf Elizabeth (BLACK) (GILBERT) [REYNER], w Humphrey, w William, m Daniel KILLAM ca 1678; 167-; Ipswich

KIMBALL, Henry & Hannah MARSH; 14 Dec 1677; Haverhill

KIMBALL, John (1631-1698) & Mary [BRADSTREET] (1633-1665); b 1657; Rowley

KIMBALL, John & Hannah _?_ ; ca 1660?; Salisbury

KIMBALL, John (1645-1726) & Mary JORDAN (1641-); 8 Oct 1666; Ipswich

KIMBALL, John & Hannah BARTLETT; 19 Jan 1667/8; Watertown

KIMBALL, John (1649/50-1721) & (1/wf) Sarah _?_ (-1706); b 1669; Boxford

KIMBALL, John, Ipswich & Sarah GOODHUE, Ipswich; 2 Dec 1692, at Watertown; Middleboro, CT

KIMBALL, John & Hannah [GOULD]; b 1699; Amesbury

KIMBALL, Jonathan (1673-1749) & (1/wf) Lydia DAY (1676-1739); 15 Jul 1696; Bradford

KIMBALL, Joseph (1675-) & Sarah [WARNER] (1678-); aft 26 Sep 1699, bef 26 Dec 1699; Ipswich

KIMBALL, Joseph (1662-1713) & Elizabeth [NEEDHAM] (1674-1708); b 1701; Boston

KIMBALL, Moses (-1750) & Susanna [GOODHUE]; b 28 Mar 1696; Ipswich

KIMBALL, Richard (?1595-1675) & 1/wf Ursula [SCOTT] (1597-1661); Rattlesden, Eng, ca 1614-15; Ipswich

KIMBALL, Richard (1623-1676) & 1/wf Mary [SMITH?] (-1672), dau John; ca 1697?; Ipswich/Wenham

KIMBALL, Richard (?1595-1675) & 2/wf Margaret (COLE) DOW, w Henry; 23 Oct 1661

KIMBALL, Richard (1643-) & 1/wf Rebecca ABBYE/ABBE (-1704); 13 May 1667; Wenham

KIMBALL, Richard (1623-1676) & 2/wf Mary (MORRIS) [MANSFIELD], w John (sister of Thomas); aft 1672; Beverly/Wenham

KIMBALL, Richard & Sarah __?__; b 1678; Bradford

KIMBALL, Richard (1659-1733) & 1/wf Sarah SPOFFORD (1661-1713/[14?]; 17 Sep 1682, 19 Sep; Bradford

KIMBALL, Richard & Lydia WELLS; 13 Jan 1685/6; Ipswich

KIMBALL, Richard & Mehitable DAY, m/2 Capt. Richard KIMBALL 1714; 6 Sep 1692; Bradford

KEMBALL, Richard & Hannah DORMAN (1680-); 22 Feb 1698/9; Boxfield/Topsfield

KIMBALL, Robert & Alice NORTON; 25 Oct 1699; Ipswich

KIMBALL, Samuel & Marah/Marey/Mary WITT; 20 Sep 1676; Wenham

KEMBALL, Samuel & Elizabeth FOWLER (1678-1736); m int 23 Dec 1698, m or m int 25 Jan 1698/9; Wenham

KIMBALL, Thomas (1633-1676) & Mary [SMITH] (-1686+), dau Thomas; ca 1655?, b 1658; Bradford/Ipswich/Wenham

KIMBALL, Thomas (1657-1732) & Elizabeth [POTTER] (1661-); b 1683, ca 1681; Wenham

KIMBAL, Thomas, Bradford & 1/wf Deborah PEMBERTON, Malden; 22 Dec 1686; Malden

KIMBERLY, Abraham[2] (-bef 1680, 1674?) & Hannah [?PRESTON], m/2 John CURTIS; b 1655/6; Stratford, CT

KIMBERLY, Abraham (1675-1727) & Abigail FITCH (ca 1681-); 11 May 1696; Stratford, CT

KIMBERLY, Eleazer (1639, 1638?-1709, Glastonbury) & 1/wf Mary [ROBBINS] (1642-1680); ca 1660?, ca 1662?, no issue; Wethersfield, CT

KIMBERLY, Eleazer (-1708/9) & 2/wf Ruth [CURTIS] (-1683); by 1680, bef 10 Feb 1679/80, prob ca 1674; Wethersfield, CT

KIMBERLY, Nathaniel (1636-1705) & Mary/Miriam __?__; b 1667(8?); New Haven

KIMBERLY, Nathaniel (ca 1688-1720) & Hannah DOWNES (1670/1-); 22 Sep 1692; New Haven

KIMBERLY, Thomas[1] (1604-1672) & 1/wf Alice AWOOD/ATWOOD (-1659); b 1638, 28 Aug 1628; New Haven

KIMBERLY, Thomas (1604-1672) & 2/wf Mary (SEABROOK?) PRESTON, w William; aft 1659, ca 1660; New Haven/Stratford

KIMBERLY, Thomas (1622/3-1708) & Hannah [RUSSELL] (-1714); b 1669?, no issue; New Haven

KINCAID/KINCADE?, David & 1/wf __?__; b 1680?; Cambridge/Boston/etc.

KINCAID, David (-1722) & 2/wf Anne (TOZIER) JENKINS, w Stephen, m/3 Thomas POTTS; b 1701?, aft 18 Jul 1694; Derham, NH

KINCUM, Andrew & Elizabeth [NICHOLS]; b 1701?; Malden?

KYNDE/KIND, Arthur & Jane __?__; b 1646; Boston

KINDE, John & Rachel __?__; b 1672; Boston

KING, Benjmin & Mary JANES (1680-), m/2 Jonathan GRAVES; 16 May 1700; Northampton

KING, Clement (see Edward KING) & 1/wf Susanna __?__ (-1699?); b 1655; Marshfield

KING, Clement & 2/wf Elizabeth [?BAKER] (-1708), m/2 Rev. Thomas BARNES 1694; Providence, RI

KING, Daniel (ca 1602-1672) & Elizabeth GUY (-1677); in Eng, 4 Oct 1624; Lynn

KING, Daniel (?1632-1695) & Tabitha WALKER (1647-); 11 Mar 1662; Lynn

KING, Daniel (1669-) & 2/wf Elizabeth PICKERING (1677-), m/2 Nathaniel BEADLE, m/3 Richard PALMER; 28 Mar 1695; Salem

KING, Daniel & Mary [VAUGHN] (1671-); ca 1697, b 31 Jan 1693/4; Salem/Portsmouth, NH?

KING, Ebenezer (-1677) & Mary TWELLS (1656-), m/2 [Arich] CLARK by 1623; 4 Sep 1676, 4 Nov 1676; Braintree

KING, Ebenezer (1677-) & Hannah MANNING; 7 Dec 1699; Billerica/Cambridge
KING, Edward (error for Clement?) & _?_ ; b 1670; Marshfield
KING, Edward (-1702) & _?_ ; b 1672?; Windsor, CT
KING, Fearnot (1655-1702) & Mary FOWLER (1659-); 14 May 1677; Westfield
KING, Harmanus & _?_ ; b 1683; Flushing, LI
KING, Hezekiah & Mary [?SHAW]; b 1679; Weymouth
KING, Isaac (-1728, ae 77) & Mehitable BRYANT (-1725, ae ca 52); 13 Aug 1689, no issue;
     Plymouth/Plympton
KING, James & Elizabeth FULLER (1652-); 23 Mar 1674; Ipswich
KING, James (?1647-1722) & 1/wf Elizabeth [EMERSON] (-1715); b 1675; Suffield, CT
KING, James (1675-) & Elizabeth HUXLEY; 23 Jun 1698; Suffield, CT
KING, John[1] (?1600-1669+) & 1/wf [?Mary] _?_ ; b 1626; Weymouth
KING, John[2] (-1691) & Esther [BAYLEY] (-1701); b 1647; Weymouth
KING, John[1] (-1669+) & 2/wf Dorothy (_?_)/(BARKER) [HUNT] (-1652), w Enoch; ca 1647;
     Weymouth
KING, John (1628-1703) & 1/wf Sarah HOLTON (ca 1628-1638); 10 Nov, 18 Nov 1656;
     Northampton
KING, John[1] (-1669+) & 3/wf Abigail (HEWES) HATCH, w William; 14 Oct 1658; Weymouth
KING, John[2] & Elizabeth GOLDTHWAITE; Sep 1660; Salem
KING, John & Mary _?_ ; b 1665; Boston
KING, John (-1703) & 2/wf Sarah (WHITING) [MYGATE], w Jacob; [1683]; Northampton
KING, John (1657-1722) & Mehitable POMEROY (1666-1755); 4 Nov 1686; Northampton
KING, John & Annis/Annie? HOAR; 10 Sep 1688; Salem
KING, John & [Bashua] [SNOW] (1664-1706/8); b 1690?, b 1695, b 1698; Harwich
KING, John (-1723) & 1/wf Hannah _?_ ; b 1701?; Providence
KING, John (-1741) & Alice DEANE (1678-1746); 1 Feb 1699/1700; Taunton/Raynham
KING, John (1674-1719) & Sarah _?_ ; b 1701?; Salem
KING, Joseph & Elizabeth BRYANT (1665-); 15 Jan 1689/90; Plymouth
KING, Joseph (1673-1734) & 1/wf Mindwell POMEROY (1677-1732); 3 Jun 1696; Northampton
KING, Mark (?1632-1679, ae 28 in 1660) & Mary _?_ (-1681+); b 1659; Charlestown
KING, Peter (-1704, ae 72 in 1699) & Sarah [?RICE]; no issue; Sudbury
KING, Peter & Mary _?_ (1658-); b 1676; Boston/Berwick, ME
KING, Philip & Judith [WHITMAN]; b 1668; Weymouth/Braintree/Taunton
KING, Ralph (ca 1639-1690) & Elizabeth WALKER, m/2 John LEWIS 1699, m/3 Joseph RENDLE
     1709; 2 Mar 1663; Lynn
KING, Richard (-1635) & Dulzabella/Dulsabell _?_ (1607±-1658), m/2 Richard BISHOP 1635?;
     Salem
KING, Richard (-1653) & Susanna _?_ (1629-), m/2 Gabriel TETHERLY 1653+; ca 1651;
     Kittery, ME
KING, Richard & _?_ ; b 1672(3?); Boston
KING, Richard (1653?-1723) & Mary [LIDDEN], m/2 Samuel JOHNSON; b 1687; Kittery, ME
KING, Richard & Elizabeth [GEDNEY] (1669-); b 1695; Salem
KING, Richard & Abigail ROGERS (1681-), m/2 Samuel DUDLEY; 18 Apr 1699; Concord/Boston
KING, Samuel (1619-1705, upwards of 90) & Ann [FINNEY?] (-1688) (Giles R. called "father-
     in-law"); b 1639?, b 1649; Plymouth
KING, Samuel (1649-) & Experience PHILLIPS (1641-); 17 Sep 1658; Weymouth
KING, Samuel (-1721?) & Frances LUDLAM (-1692(3?), ae 53+); 10 Oct 1660; Southampton, LI
KING, Samuel & Hannah _?_ ; b 1668; Boston
KING, Samuel (1649-) & Sarah DUNHAM (-1738, in 88th y); b 1670; Plymouth
KING, Samuel & Jane [CHAMBERLAIN] (1667-1702); Providence
KING, Samuel (1665-1701) & Joanna (TAYLOR) [ALVORD] (1665-1741), w Thomas, m/3
     Deliverance BRIDGMAN 1702; ca 1690; Northampton
KING, Samuel alias RICE (1667-), Sudbury & Abigail CLAP (1675-1713), Milton; 30 Oct 1693;
     Milton
KING, Samuel & 1/wf Elizabeth MARSH; 15 Dec 1696; Salem
KING, Samuel, Jr. (1674-) & Bethia _?_ ; b 1697; Plymouth
KING, Samuel (1675-) & Hannah _?_ (1674?-1712); 1 Jan 1697, [1696/7]; Southold, NY
KING, Thomas[1] (ca 1600-1676) & 1/wf Ann [?COLLINS] (-1642); ca 1626?; Sudbury
KING, Thomas & 1/wf Susan _?_ ; b 1635

KING, Thomas (1613, 1604-1692) & 1/wf Sarah [?BROWN/?PIKE] (-1652); b 1639, ca 1637?; Scituate

KING, Thomas (-1644) & Mary _?_, m/2 James CUTLER 1645; b 1640/[1]; Watertown

KING, Thomas (-1667?) & Miriam [MOULTON]; b Dec 1641; Exeter, NH/Hampton, NH

KING, Thomas (1604-1691) & 2/wf Jane (YOUNG) HATCH (-Oct 1653), w William; 31 Mar 1653, 3 Mar; Scituate

KING, Thomas (-1691) & 3/wf Anne/Anna? [?SUTLEFFE]; aft 1653; Scituate

KING, Thomas[1] (ca 1600-1676) & 2/wf Bridget (LOKER) DAVIS (?1613-1685), w Robert; 26 Dec 1655; Sudbury/Marlborough

KING, Thomas (1645-1711) & Elizabeth CLAPP (-1698); 20 Apr 1669; Weymouth/Scituate

KING, Thomas (-1713, ae 70?) & Mary [SPRAGUE] (1652-); b 1670; Weymouth/Hingham

KING, Thomas (1662-1711) & 1/wf Abigail STRONG (1666-1689); 17 Nov 1683; Hadley/Hatfield/Hartford

KING, Thomas & _?_ ; b 1686; Dighton

KING, Thomas (-1711) & 2/wf Mary WEBSTER (-1706?); 7 Nov 1690, Nov 1690; Hatfield/Hartford/Hadley

KING, Thomas (1645-1711) & Deborah [HAWKE] BRIGGS (1652-1711), w John; 15 Jun 1699; Scituate

KING, William[1] (1595-1650?) & Dorothy [HAYNE?] (1601-); Sherborne, Dorset, in Eng, 17 Feb 1616/17; Salem

KING, William (1607-) & _?_ ; b 1636; Salem/Lynn

KING, William (-1669) & ?Susanna _?_ ; ca 1644?, b 1646; Isles of Shoals

KING, William (1627-1684) & Katherine SHAFFLIN (-1719); b 1652, 1642?; Salem

KING, William & Sarah MEAD?/GRIGGS? (1637-), m/2 Roger BURGESS b 1659; b 1655; Boston

KING, William & Sarah [PALMER]; ca 1669; Kittery, ME

KING, William (-1690, Boston) & Deborah PRINCE (1657-); 11 Jul 1678; Hingham/Boston

KING, William & Sarah ALLISON; 12 Nov 1684; Hadley/Hatfield

KING, William (1660-1728) & Elizabeth [DENSLOW] (1665-1746); b 1686; Northampton/CT

KING, William & 1/wf Abigail BROWNE (-1716, ae 49); 17 Jan 1686/7; Southold, LI

KING, William & 1/wf Hannah COOK; 4 Jun 1695; Salem/Sutton

KING, William & Rebecca [LITTLEFIELD?/WAKEFIELD?]; b 1701?; Salisbury

KING, Ralph? & [Mary INGALLS]; b 21 Mar 1663, 1662/3

KING, ?Thomas & [Mary SPENCER] (-bef 2 Jun 1712, living in 22 Jun 1709), dau Obadiah; b 1701?; ?Hartford

KINGMAN, Henry (-1667) (ae 74 in 1667) & Joane/Joanna _?_ (1596-1659); in Eng, b 1619; Weymouth

KINGMAN, Henry (1668-1738, ae 74) & Bethiah [HOWARD] (-1755); b 1693; Bridgewater

KINGMAN, John (1633/4-1690) & Elizabeth [?EDSON/?BYRAM], m/2 Richard PHILLIPS; ca 1662, b 1664; Weymouth/Bridgewater

KINGMAN, John (1664-1755) & 1/wf Desire [HARRIS] (-1698); b 1690; Bridgewater

KINGMAN, John (1664-) & 2/wf Bethiah NEWCOMB (1694-); 1 Dec 1698; Bridgewater

KINGMAN, Samuel (1670-ca 1742) & Mary MICHELL/MITCHELL (-bef 1740); 1 Jan 1695/6; Bridgewater

KINGMAN, Thomas (1628-1705) & Rebecca _?_ ; b 1664; Weymouth

KINGMAN, Thomas (1670/1-1742) & 1/wf Mercy [RANDALL] (-1737); b 1698; Weymouth

KINGSBURY, Eleazer (1645-) & Esther JUDSON (-1717); 30 Oct 1676; Dedham

KINGSBURY, Eleazer (1673-) & Sarah MACCANE; 4 Apr 1696; Wrentham

KINGSBURY, Henry & Margaret (BLYTH) ALABASTER, w Thomas; Assington, Eng, 18 May 1631; Boston/Ipswich

KINGSBURY, Henry (ca 1615-1687) & Susannah [GAGE?] (-1679); b 1645?; Ipswich/Haverhill/Windsor, CT

KINGSBERY, James & Sarah BURTON?; 6 Jan 1673; Haverhill/Needham/Plainfield, CT

KINGSBURY, John (-1660) & Margaret [WHISSON/FLOWER] (-1662); 8 Mar 1618, b 1639; Watertown/Dedham

KINGSBURY, John (-1671) & Elizabeth DUSTON (-1667), m/2 Peter GREEN 1672; b 1664; Haverhill/Rowley

KINGSBURY, John (1643-1669) & Elizabeth FULLER (-1732), m/2 Michael METCALF 1672; 29 Nov 1666; Dedham

KINGSBURY, John (1667-) & Hannah _?_ ; b 1689; Newbury

KINGSBURY, Joseph (-1676) & Millicent [AMES?/EAMES?] (-1676+); b 1637; Dedham
KINSBURY, Joseph (1641-) & 1/wf Mary _?_ (-1680); b 1665; Dedham/Watertown
KINGSBERY, Joseph (1658-1741) & Love AYERS (1663-1735); 2 Apr 1679; Haverhill/Franklin, CT
KINGSBURY, Joseph & 2/wf Mary DONICE?/DONIER?/DENNIS?; 7 Sep 1681; Wrentham
KINGSBURY, Nathaniel (1650-1694) & Mary BACON; 14 Oct 1673; Dedham
KINGSBURY, Nathaniel & Sarah _?_ ; b 1681; Haverhill
KINGSBERY, Nathaniel (1674-1725) & Abigail BAKER (-1764); 5 Dec 1695; Dedham
KINGSBERY, Samuel (-1698) & Huldah CORLIS/CORLISS; 5 Nov 1679; Haverhill
KINGSBERY, Thomas & 1/wf Deborah (CORLISS) EASTMAN, w Thomas; 29 Jun 1691, 2 ch; Haverhill
KINGSBURY, William (-1645) & [Sarah?] _?_ ; b 18 Dec 1643; Dedham
KINSLEY, Eldad (1638-1679), Rehoboth & Mehitable MOWRY, m/2 Timothy BROOKS 1680?; m int 9 May 1662; Providence
KINGSLEY, Enos (?1640-1708?) & Sarah HAINES/HAYNES (-1691); 15 Jun 1662; Northampton
KINGSLEY, Enos, Northampton & Hannah/Anna (DICKINSON) [CLARY] (1636-), w John; 30 Nov 1692; Deerfield
KINGSLEY, John[1] (-1678) & 1/wf Elizabeth _?_ ; b 1636; Dorchester
KINGSLEY, John[1] (-1678) & 2/wf Alice [JONES] (-1673), w Richard; b 1642, 1642; Dorchester/Rehoboth
KINSLEY, John (?1636-1698) & 1/wf Susanna DANIEL (-1670); 25 Jun 1669; Milton
KINSLEY, John (?1636-1698) & 2/wf Abigail LEONARD; b 1672; Milton
KINSLEY, John[1] (-1678, 1678/9) & 3/wf Mary (JOHNSON) MAURY/MOWRY, w Roger MOWRY; 16 Mar 1673/4, 1674; Rehoboth
KINGSLEY, John (1665-1733, Windham) & Sarah SABIN (1667-1709); 1 Jul 1686; Rehoboth/Windham, CT
KINGSLEY, Jonathan & Mary COLE; 24 Nov 1697, 1698; Rehoboth/Swansea
KINGSLEY/KINSLEY, Samuel[2] (-1662) & Hannah BRACHETT (1645-1706), m/2 John BLANCHARD 1662+; b 1656, b 1662; Braintree
KINGSLEY/KINSLEY, Samuel[3] (1662-1713, Easton) & Mary [WASHBURN] (1669-1740?); aft 30 Oct 1686, bef 28 Jul 1690; Boston
KINSLEY, Stephen[1] (1598-1673) (deposed 29 Apr 1653, aged 55 y or thereabouts) & [Mary SPALDING]? (-1668); Boston, Eng, 29 Apr 1624; Boston/Braintree/Milton
KINGSTON, Thomas & Mary [MUNT]; b 1667, b 28 Apr 1666; Boston
KINGSWORTH/KINGSNOTH, Henry (1618-1668) & Mary [STEVENS], m/2 John COLLINS 1669; Wolcow, Eng?; Guilford, CT
KINNE, Henry[1] (1624-) & Ann HOWARD (1632?-1680+); b 1651(2?), 3 May 1650; Salem?
KINNE, Henry & Anne [LANE], w James; aft 13 Sep 1688?
KINNEY, Henry (see KENNEY) & Priscella LEWIS; b 1696, 14 May 1691; Salem
KINNEY, John & Lydia [TABOR] (1673-); b 1696
KINNE, Thomas (1656-) & Elizabeth KNIGHT; 23 May 1677; Salem
KINNEY, _?_ & Jane KNOWLTON
KINSMAN, Joseph (1673-) & 1/wf Susanna [DUTCH] (1675-1734); b 1700; Ipswich
KINSMAN, Robert[1] (-1664/5) & _?_ ; in Eng, b 1629; Ipswich
KINSMAN, Robert (1629-1712) & Mary [BOREMAN]; b 1657; Ipswich
KINSMAN, Robert & 1/wf Lydia MOORE; 3 Apr 1700, 4 Apr, at Boston; Ipswich
KINSMAN, Thomas (1662-1696) & Elizabeth BURNHAM/BURNUM, m/2 Isaac RINDGE 1700; 12 Jul 1687; Ipswich
KIPPEN, Arthur (-1685) & Abigail [AGER]; b 30 Nov 1652; Lynn
KERBEY, Henry & Elizabeth [ADAMS?]; b 1680; Boston
KIRBY, John (-1677) & Elizabeth [BOOTH?/HINDS?], m/2 Abraham RANDALLS? 1681; ca 1644, b 1646; Wethersfield/Middletown, CT
KIRBY, John & _?_ ; b 1695; Dartmouth
KIRBY, Joseph (-1711, in 56th y) & 1/wf Sarah MARKHAM; 10 Dec 1681, ?10 Nov 1681; Wethersfield, CT/Middleboro, CT
KIRBY, Joseph (1656-1711) & 2/wf Abiah [KIMBERLY[(?ca 1673-1704); b 1700; New Haven
KERBEY, Richard (-1688) & Jane _?_ (-1649); ca 1638/40?; Lynn/Sandwich
KIRBY, Richard (-1720) & 1/wf Patience GIFFORD; 9 Oct 1665; Sandwich/Dartmouth
KIRBY, Richard & Elizabeth (?ARNOLD) [HOPKINS], w Joseph; aft 1674; Oyster Bay, LI

KIRBY, Richard (-1720), Dartmouth & 2/wf? Abigail (_?_) HOWLAND (-1708), Dartmouth, w Zooth; 2 Nov 1678, 2 Dec?
KIRBY, Robert (?1674-1767) & Rebecca [POTTER] (-1773), Portsmouth, RI; b 1701?, b 1704; Dartmouth
KIRBY, Thomas & Ann [HOPKINS]; b 1701?; LI
KIRBY, William & Elizabeth _?_; b 1640; Boston
KIRBY, William & Annis/Hannah _?_; b 1 Apr 1652; Boston
KIRK, David & Mary _?_; b 1694; Charlestown
KIRKE, Henry (1638?-) & 1/wf _?_; b 1664?; Boston
KIRKE, Henry (1638?-) & Ruth (GLANFIELD) [STEVENS], w Caleb; aft 1675; Portsmouth, NH/Ipswich
KIRKE, John & Deborah [SEAMAN]; b 5 Aug 1694; Hempstead, LI
KIRKE, Thomas & Mary _?_; b 1687; Boston
KIRK, Zachary & Abigail RAWLINS; Oct 1686; ?Boston
KIRKHAM, Thomas & _?_; b 1648; Wethersfield, CT
KIRKOM, Thomas & Jane _?_; 24 Mar 1684, 1683/4; Wethersfield, CT
KIRKHAM, Thomas & Dorcas [HODGE/HODGES], wid; aft 12 Jul 1687; Wethersfield, CT
KIRTLAND, John (1607-) & Barbara _?_; Easthampton, LI/?Saybrook, CT
KIRKLAND, John (1659-1716) & Lydia PRATT; 18 Nov 1679, 8 Nov; Saybrook, CT
KIRTLAND, Jonathan & Sarah _?_; b 1665; Lynn
KERTLAND, Nathaniel (1616-1686) & Parnell _?_, m/2 John LAITON/LEIGHTON/LAUGHTON 1687; b 1652?, b 1658, ca 1642-5; Southold, LI/Lynn
KERTLAND, Nathaniel (-1690) & Mary RAND/WHITING?, m/2 J. H. BURCHSTED/John BURLEA 1698; 20 Jun 1675; Lynn/Southold, LI
KERTLAND, Philip[1] & _?_; in Eng, b 1607; Lynn
KERTLAND, Philip (?1614-1659?) & Alice _?_, m/2 Evan THOMAS 1659; b 1640; Lynn
KERTLAND, Philip (-1688, 1690?) & Ruth PEARSE/PIERCE (?1662-1748), m/2 Joshua EATON 18 Dec 1690, m/3 Jonathan DUNSTER 25 Dec 1717, m/4 Amos MARRETT 22 Nov 1732, m/5 Peter HAY 29 Oct 1742; 14 Oct 1679; Lynn
KISSAM/OCKESON/OKESON, John & Susannah THORNE; 16 Jul 1667; Flushing, LI
KISSAM, Danail (1669-1752) & Elizabeth COOMBS (1673-1736); b 1753; Great Neck, LI/Hempstead, LI
OKESON, John & Elizabeth [MOTT]; b 1701?, b 1703; Hempstead, LI?
KITCHELL, Robert & 1/wf _?_; ?Rolvendon, Eng
KITCHELL, Robert (1604-1672) & 2/wf Margaret SHEAFE (1601-1681, 1682); m lic 21 Jun 1631, m 21 Jul 1632, Canterbury, Eng, ?9 Jan 1632; Guilford, CT
KITCHELL, Samuel (1635-1690) & 1/wf Elizabeth WAKEMAN; 11 Mar 1656/7, 11th 1st mo, 1656; New Haven/Guilford, CT/Newark, NJ
KITCHELL, Samuel (1635-1690) & 2/wf Grace [PIERSON] (1650-); b 1679, 1666?; ?Newark, NJ
KITCHEN, John (1619-1676) & 1/wf [?Elizabeth] _?_; ca 1640?; Salem
KITCHEN, John (1619-1676) & Elizabeth (GRAFTON) [SAUNDERS] (1625-), w John; b 1643?, b 1655?, aft 10-28-1643; Salem
KITCHEN, Robert (1655-1712) & 1/wf Mary [BOARDMAN] (1655/6-); ca 1680-1?; Salem
KITCHEN, Robert (1655-1712) & 2/wf Bethia [WELD] (1668-); b 1689, b 17 Jul 1688, 1687?; Salem
KITCHERELL/DORCHESTER, Benjamin & Sarah BURT 22 Apr 1675; Springfield
KITCHERELL/KEDGERER, Joseph & _?_; Salem
KITCHERELL, Samuel (-1650?) & Martha [CHAPMAN], m/2 Anthony DORCHESTER 1650/(1); b 1645(6?); Hartford
KITT, John & Margaret MURREL/MORRELL; 23 Sep 1697; Boston
KITTREDGE, Daniel (1670-) & Elizabeth FOSTER; 19 Dec 1694; Billerica
KITTRIDGE, James (1668-) & Sarah [FOWLE]; b 1699; Roxbury/Charlestown
KITTREDGE, John & Mary LITTLEFIELD, m/2 John FRENCH 1678; 2 Nov 1664, 1665?; Billerica
KITTERIDGE, John (-1714) & Hannah FRENCH (1664-); 3 Aug 1685; Billerica
KLINE, _?_ & Catherine BRACKENBURY; b 1684
KNAPP, Aaron (-1674) & Elizabeth _?_, m/2 _?_ HOSKINS?; b 1659, b 1654?; Taunton/Roxbury
KNAP, Aaron & Rachel BURT; 8 Dec 1686; Taunton
KNAPP, Benjamin (1673-1716) & Elizabeth BUTLER, m/2 _?_ SEAGER; 18 Apr 1700, 13 Apr 1700, 28 Feb 1700, 18 Apr 1700, 28 Feb 1700/1; Greenwich, CT

KNAPP. Caleb (1637-1674, 1675) & Hannah [SMITH], m/2 Thomas LAWRENCE by 1687, ca 1674?; b 1661; Stamford, CT
KNAPP, Caleb (1661-) & Hannah CLEMENTS; 23 Nov 1694; Stamford, CT
KNAPP, Caleb (1677-1750) & Sarah RUNDELL; 1 Apr 1697; Stamford, CT
KNAPP, Isaac (1672-1744) & Anna/Ann [EATON]; b 1695; Cambridge
KNAP, James (?1625-1698+) & Elizabeth WARREN (1629-); b 1655; Watertown/Groton
KNAPE, John (1624-1696) & Sarah YOUNGE/YOUNG; 21 May 1660, 25 May 1660; Watertown
KNAPP, John & Sarah [HULL], m/2 Robert SALLIMAN by 1691
KNAP, John & Sarah AUSTIN; 7 Oct 1685; Taunton
KNAPP, John (1662-1733) & Sarah [PARKS/PARK] (1666-1727); 4 Aug 1686; Newton/Cambridge
KNAPP, John (1662, ?1664-1749) & 1/wf Hannah FERRIS; 10 Jun 1692; Greenwich, CT
KNAPP, Joseph (1664-) & Mary (LOCKWOOD) HUESTED? (-aft 1706?)
KNAPP, Joshua (1635-1684) & Hannah CLOSE (ca 1632-1696), m/2 John BOWERS 1684+; 9 Jun 1657; Stamford, CT/Greenwich, CT
KNAPP, Joshua (1663-) (did he m/2 Abigail BUTLER 1691) & 1/wf Elizabeth REYNOLDS (1667-); 16 Mar 1687, 1684?; Greenwich, CT
KNAPP, Josiah & [Sybil DICKERSON], m/2 James NICHOLSON; b 1677; Fairfield, CT
KNAPP, Moses (ca 1645/6-1756?) & Abigail WESTCOTT (ca 1647-); ca 1669?, b 4 Jan 1669, b 16 Jun 1667?, by 1669; Stamford, CT
KNAPP, Moses (ca 1666-1753) & Elizabeth CRISSY; 30 Oct 1689, 31 Oct 168-; Greenwich, CT
KNAPP, Nicholas (-1670) & 1/wf Eleanor [?LOCKWOOD] (-1658); b 1631; Watertown/Wethers-field, CT
KNAPP, Nicholas (-1670) & 2/wf Unity (?) (BUXTON) BROWN, w Clement, w Peter; 9 Mar 1659, 1658/9; Stamford, CT
KNAPP, Roger & 1/wf _?_ (1653); New Haven/Fairfield, CT
KNAPP, Roger (-1673, 1675) & 2/wf Elizabeth DICKERSON (1637-); ca 1654/5?; New Haven/Fairfield, CT
KNAP, Samuel (-1715/1719) & Elizabeth COB/COBB (1670-); 26 May 1687; Taunton
KNAP, Samuel (1668-1739) & Hannah [BUSHNELL] (1676-); b 1701?, 1696 prob; ?Stamford, CT/Danbury, CT
KNAPP, Thomas (-1697) & Mary GROUT; 19 Sep 1688; Sudbury
KNAPP, Timothy (1622-) & Bethia BRANDISH/BRUNDISH (1637-) (see Joseph TAYLOR); ca 1658; Greenwich, CT/Rye, NY
KNAPP, Timothy (1668-1733) & 1/wf Elizabeth SEAMORE/SEYMOURE (1673-); 16 Mar 1699; Greenwich, CT
KNAPP, William[1] (1578-1658) & 1/wf ?Meye/Meze/_?_ _?_ (-?1654); b 1610?; Watertown
KNAPP, William[2] (-1676) & 1/wf Mary _?_; b 1642; Watertown
KNAPP, William[2] (-1676) & 2/wf Margaret _?_; b 1652(3?), ca 1631; Watertown
KNAPP, William[1] (1578-1658) & 2/wf Priscilla [AKERS], w Thomas; betw 1655 & 1658; Watertown
NELAND, Edward (?1643-1711) (called Joseph FOWLER "brother" in his will) & Martha [FOWLER?]; b 1670?, b 1673; Ipswich
NELAND, Edward (1677-1745) & Mary _?_ (-1753); by 1697?; Ipswich
KNEELAND, John (1632-1691, Roxbury) & Mary [HAWKINS], dau James; b 1659; Boston
KNEELAND, John & Mary [GREEN]; b 1692; Boston
KNEELAND, Samuel & Mary POLLARD; m int 26 Mar 1696; Boston
KNELL, Isaac (1655-1708) & Phebe NICHOLS (1671-), m/2 George CLARK; 28 Dec 1697; Woodbury, CT
KNILL, John & Elizabeth _?_, m/2 Nathaniel BACHELDER 1689; b 1679; Charlestown
KNELL, Nicholas (-1675) & Elizabeth (NEWMAN) [KNOWLES], w Thomas; ca 1650; Stratford, CT
KNELL, Nicholas & Sarah _?_; b 1678; Boston
KNILL, Philip (1637-1695) (ae 38 in 1675) & Ruth ALLIN, w Richard; 5 Oct 1666; Charlestown
KNIFFEN, Ebenezer (-1723) & Anna _?_; Rye, NY
KNIFFEN, George (1632-1694) & Mary (_?_) [WHELPLEY]; Stratford, CT
KNIFFEN, Nathan (-1732+) & _?_; Rye, NY
KNIFFEN, Samuel (-1707/8) & Mary [PURDY]; Rye, NY
KNIGHT, Alexander (-1664) & Anne/Hannah [TUTTY], m/2 Robert WHITMAN 1664; b 10 Oct 1640; Ipswich

KNIGHT, Benjamin & Abigail [JAQUES?] (1674-); b 1693; Newbury
KNITE, Charles (ca 1642-1693) & Sarah LEMON (-1693+); 9 May 1667; Salem/Manchester
KNIGHT, David (-1744) & Sarah BACKUS (1668-); 17 Mar 1691/2; Norwich, CT
KNIGHT, Edward & Joanna WINN; 13 Jul 1699; Woburn
KNIGHTS, Ezekiel[1] (-1687) & Elizabeth _?_ (-1642); b 1632?; Salem/Braintree
KNIGHT, Ezekiel[1] (-1687) & 1/wf 2/wf Anne _?_ ; b 20 Aug 1645; Dover, NH/Wells, ME
KNIGHT, Ezekiel[1] (-1687) & 2/wf 3/wf Esther [LOVERING] (-1675), w John; ca 1668, b 4 Apr 1672; Dover, NH
KNIGHT, Ezekiel[1] (-1687) & 3/wf 4/wf Mary (EATON) [HILLS] (-1708), w Valentine; aft 1675, b 1680; Dover, NH/Wells, ME
KNIGHT, Ezekiel[2] (1680-) & Sarah [LITTLEFIELD], w Thomas; ca 1696?
KNIGHT, George & _?_ ; in Eng, b 1638; Hingham
KNIGHT, George (-1671, 1672) & Eleanor _?_, m/2 Henry BROOKINGS 1672; b 1671; Black Point/Scarborough, ME
KNIGHT, George (-1699) & Sarah [CHURCH] (1658-), m/2 Samuel HUBBARD; b 1680, b 1682?; Hartford
KNIGHT, Jacob & 1/wf Sarah BURTT/BURT (-1682); 25 Dec 1668; Lynn
KNIGHT/KING?, Jacob & Hannah RAND (-1683); 18 Sep 1682; Lynn
KNIGHT, Jacob & Elizabeth (PITMAN) RUSSELL, w Henry; 18 Dec 1684; Marblehead
KNIGHT, Jacob & Rebecca STEPHENS; 12 Oct 1693; Marblehead
KNIGHT, John (1595/6-1670) & Mary _?_ (-1676); in Eng, b 1620, b 1625; Charlestown/Watertown
KNIGHT, John & 1/wf Elizabeth _?_ (-1645); in Eng, b 1622, b 1625; Newbury
KNIGHT, John[1] (1595/6-1670) & 2/wf Ann/Agnes (LANGLEY) [INGERSOLL] (-1677), w Richard; aft 20 Mar 1644/5, bef 1652; Salem
KNIGHT, John (1622?, 1626-1677) & Bathshua [INGERSOLL] (-1705); [1647]; Newbury
KNIGHT, John (ca 1632-1714) & 1/wf Ruhamah JOHNSON (1635-1659?); 25 Apr 1654; Charlestown
KNIGHT, John & _?_ (had Martha); b 1657; Lynn
KNIGHT, John (-by 1683) & Sarah _?_ ; by 1660-1663, 1655?; ?Newport/?E. Greenwich
KNIGHT, John (ca 1632-1714) & 2/wf Abigail [STOWERS] (1636-1668); aft 29 Apr 1660, b 23 Oct 1667; Charlestown
KNIGHT, John (ca 1632-1714) & 3/wf Mary BRIDGE (-1678); 22 Jun 1668; Charlestown
KNIGHT, John (1648-) & Rebecca NOYES (1651-); 1 Jan 1671; Newbury
LIGHT?, John & 2/wf Dorothy (PIKE) [PIERCE], w Joshua (see John LIGHT); aft 14 Jan 1670/1, 11 Sep 1674; Newbury
KNIGHT, John (-1710±) & Ann _?_ ; b 1675; E. Greenwich, RI/Norwich, CT
KNIGHT, John & 4/wf Mary (_?_) CLEMENTS (-1682), wid; 19 Dec 1678; Charlestown
KNIGHT, John & Abigail CRAGGEN/CRAGEN; 2 Mar 1681, 1680/1; Woburn
KNIGHT, John & Mary BARTOLL, m/2 ?Joseph DODD 1700; 12 Oct 1681; Marblehead
KNIGHT, John & Mary [WHITTIER], w Abraham; aft 1674, bef 1682
KNIGHT, John (-1714) & 5/wf Sarah (RAWLINS) HOLSWORTH/HOLLWORTH (-1713), w Joshua; 24 May 1683; Charlestown
KNIGHT, John (-1720) & Bridget SLOPER (1659-); 29 Mar 1684; ?Dover, NH/Newington
KNIGHT, John (-1710±) & Ann _?_ (see above); b 1685, b 1675; E. Greenwich, RI
KNIGHT, John & Elizabeth _?_ ; b 1686; Beverly
KNIGHT, John (-1694) & Leah [NUTE], m/2 Benedictus TORR/TARR 1704; b 1694; Dover, NH
KNIGHT, John & Dorcas CLEEVELAND/CLEVELAND; 12 Mar 1699/1700; 1699; Cambridge
KNIGHT, Jonathan (-1683) & Ruth WRIGHT (1646-1714), m/2 Thomas BATEMAN by 1688; 31 Mar 1663; Woburn/Salem
KNIGHT, Jonathan (-1693) & Bethia [JOHNSON] (1660-), m/2 Joseph WOLCOTT; ca 1678?; Lexington/Cambridge/Concord?
KNIGHT, Jonathan (-1717), Warwick/Providence & Hannah _?_ ; b 1680, ca 1676; Newport/Charlestown, RI
KNIGHT, Joseph (ca 1624-1687) & Hannah [RUSSELL?] (-1695); b 10 Dec 1649; Watertown/Woburn
KNIGHT, Joseph & Mary [SPAULE]; b 1664(5?); Boston
KNIGHT, Joseph (1652-) & Deborah COFFIN (1655-); 31 Oct 1677; Newbury
KNIGHT, Joseph (1665-) & Ruth _?_ ; b 1687; Woburn

KNIGHT, Joseph (1673-) & Martha (GIBSON) LILLEY, w Reuben; 4 Apr 1699; Woburn
KNIGHT, Lawrence (-1728) & Elizabeth INGERSOLL, m/2 John BATTEN 1729; 2 Nov 1696; Salem
KNIGHT, Macklin?/Mautlyn?/Matting? & Dorothy _?_; b 1643; Boston
KNIGHT, Michael & Mary BULLARD; 20 Oct 1657; Woburn
KNIGHT, Nathan & Mary [WESTBROOK]; b Mar 1693/4; Portsmouth/Scarboro
KNIGHT, Philip (-1668) & Margery _?_, ?m/2 Thomas BATEMAN, m/3 Nathaniel BALL 1670/1; b 1647; Charlestown/Topsfield
KNIGHT, Philip & Margaret [WILKINS]; b 1669; Topsfield
KNITE, Philip (1669-1696) & Rebecca [TOWNE] (1668-); b 20 Aug 1693; Topsfield
KNIGHT, Richard (1602-1683) & Agnes [COFFLEY?] (-1679); b 1632; Newbury
KNIGHT, Richard & 1/wf _?_; Hampton, NH
KNIGHT, Richard & Dinah _?_; b 15 May 1642; Boston
KNIGHT, Richard (-1680) & 2/wf? [Sarah ROGERS] (-1685+); b 16 Jan 1648(9?), b 1647?, 1648±; Newport, RI
KNIGHT, Richard & Joanna _?_ (not Ann CROMWELL, w Thomas, m/3 John JOYLIFFE/JO-LIFFE, see Robert KNIGHT); b 1652?; Boston
KNIGHT, Richard & Julian _?_; b 1664; Boston
KNIGHT, Richard & Hannah (TOWNSEND) HULL [ALLEN], w Thomas, w Hope, m/4 Richard WAY 1687; b 1680; Boston/Dover, NH?
KNIGHT, Richard & Remember GRAFFTON/GRAFTON; 10 Apr 1685; Marblehead/Boston
KNIGHT, Richard & Sarah [KEMBALL] (-1727, New London); b 1689; Charlestown
KNIGHT, Richard & _?_; b 1690; RI
KNIGHT, Richard (1666-) & Elizabeth [JAQUES] (1669-); b 1697; Newbury
KNIGHT, Robert (1585, 1590-1676) & _?_; b 1631, ca 1620?; York, ME
KNIGHT, Robert (ae 51 in 1666) & 1/wf _?_; b 1640; Boston/Salem/Marblehead/Manchester
KNIGHT, Robert (-1655) & 2/wf Ann CROMWELL, w Thomas, m/3 John JOYLIFFE 1656/7; b 1652; Boston
KNIGHT, Robert (1667-1739+) & 1/wf Abigail WILLSON/WILSON; 3 Feb 1686; Ipswich/Manchester
KNIGHT, Roger (1596-1673) & [Anne] _?_; b 1636, b 13 Jul 1633; ?Portsmouth, NH
KNIGHT, Samuel (1649-) & Amy [CARLE]; ca 1670, bef 27 Jul 1676; Kittery, ME
KNIGHT, Samuel (-by 1715) & Sarah (_?_) HOW, w Abraham; 16 Oct 1685; Roxbury
KNIGHT, Samuel (1675-1721) & Rachel CHASE, m/2 S. MUNKLEY; 19 Jul 1700; Tisbury/Charlestown/Sudbury
KNIGHT, Walter & Elizabeth _?_ (-1634?); b 1610?
KNIGHT, Walter (1587-) & ?2/wf [?Ruth GRAY]; b 1642, b 1620?, 1635?; Salem
KNIGHT, William (-1655/6) & 1/wf [?Emma POTTER]; b 1638, b 1635?; Salem/Lynn
KNIGHT, William (-1655/6) & 2/wf Elizabeth (?LEE) BALLARD/[BULLARD], w William, m/3 Allen BREAD; aft 1639; Salem
KNIGHT, _?_ & Sarah _?_ (1665-1727); New London
KNIGHT, _?_ & Sarah _?_; Boston
KNIGHT, Walter & _?_; b 1651; Braveboat Harbor
KNOTT, Andrew & Susanna _?_; b 1689; Boston
KNOTT, George (-1648) & Martha _?_ (-1673/4); b 1630?, b 1634; Sandwich
KNOTT, Richard (-1684) & Hannah (DEVEREUX) [GREENFIELD], w Peter, m/3 Joseph SOUTH by 1689; ca 1674?, aft 1672, ca 1672; Marblehead
KNOWER/KNOWES, George (1617, 1697?-1675) & Elizabeth _?_; b 1650; Charlestown
KNOWER, Jonathan & Sarah [WINSLOW]; b 1685, b 1680; Malden/Charlestown
KNOWLES, Alexander (-1663) & _?_; b 1634?; Fairfield, CT
KNOWLES, Edward (1671-1740) & 1/wf Ann RIDLEY; 27 Feb 1699/1700; Eastham
KNOWLES, Eleazer (?1645-1731) & Mary _?_ (-1732); ca 1681?, b 1683; Woodbury, CT
KNOLLYS, Rev. Hanser (1598-1691, in Eng) & Anne? ...ENEY (-1671, in 63rd y); Dover, NH/Eng
KNOWLES, Henry (?1609-1670) & _?_ [POTTER?] (-1670+); b 1645; Warwick, RI
KNOWLES, Henry & _?_
KNOLLES, John (-1685) & Elizabeth [WILLIS?/BILLS?], w Ephraim DAVIS?; b 1641; Watertown/Eng
KNOWLES, John (-1705) & Jemima ASTEN/AUSTIN (1641-); 10 Jul 1660; Hampton, NH

KNOWLES, John & Rebecca [CABLE]; ca 1661?; Fairfield, CT
KNOWLES, John (-1675) & Apphia BANGS (1651-167-), m/2 Stephen ATWOOD/WOOD b 1677; 28 Dec 1670; Eastham
KNOWLES, John (1661-) & Susanna _?_ (-1745, ae 82); b 1686; Hampton, NH
KNOWLES, John (1673-1757) & Mary [?SEARS]? (1672-1745); b 1696, 1693?; Eastham
KNOWLES, Joshua (-1712) & ?Judanna [WHEELER] (?1661-); b 1690, no issue; Fairfield, CT
KNOWLES, Richard & Ruth BOWERS/BOWER; 15 Aug 1639; ?Plymouth
KNOWLES, Robert (-2 Apr 1703?) & Katharine GRAVES, Charlestown, m/2 Calvin GALPIN 1702?, 1703; 27 Dec 1693; Charlestown
KNOWLES, Samuel (1651-1737) & Mercy FREEMAN (1659-1744); Dec 1679, ?16 Dec; Eastham
KNOWLES, Simon (1667-) & 1/wf Rachel _?_ (-1696); b 1696; Hampton, NH
KNOWLES, Simon (1667-) & Rachel JOY; 23 Aug 1700, - Aug 1700; Hampton, NH
KNOWLES, Thomas & Elizabeth [NEWMAN], m/2 Nicholas KNILL/KNELL ca 1650; ca 1643; New Haven
KNOWLES, Thomas (1648-1705) & Mary _?_ ; ca 1670/75?, no issue; Stratford, CT
KNOWLES, William (?1645-1727) & Alice [FISH] (-1734); b 1675; ?Kingston, RI
KNOWLMAN, John & _?_ ; b 1669?; Taunton
KNOWLMAN, John & Eleanor EVINS/EVANS; 5 Feb 1688/9; Taunton
KNOWLTON, Benjamin (-1690) & Hannah MERRICK/MIRICK; 30 Nov 1676; Springfield
KNOWLTON, Ebenezer & Sarah LOWELL/TOWLE; 14 Feb 1698, 1699; Newbury
KNOWLTON, Ezekiel (-1706) & Sarah LEACH; 29 Jan 1698/9; Marshfield
KNOWLTON, John (-1654?) & Margery [WILSON?/KENNING?] (sister of Mrs. Jane KENNING); b 1629, b 1633; Ipswich
KNOWLTON, John (-1684) & 1/wf Deborah [GRANT?] (-living 10 Sep 1666); b 1656; ?Ipswich
KNOWLTON, John (-1684) & 2/wf Sarah _?_ ; 1661?
KNOWLTON, John & 1/wf Bethia EDWARDS/EDMANDS; b 1670; Ipswich/Manchester
KNOWLTON, John & Abigail BATCHELDER; 20 Dec 1697; Manchester
KNOWLTON, Joseph/Jonathan (1650-) & Mary WILSON (1657-) (see above); 14 Aug 1677; Ipswich
KNOWLTON, Joseph & Deborah _?_ (-1704, Newport); b 1698; Lebanon, CT
KNOWLTON, Nathaniel (1658-) & Deborah JEWETT (1664-); 3 May 1682; Ipswich
KNOWLTON, Rice & Mary DODGE (1680-); m int 5 Nov 1698, m 2 Jan 1699; Windsor
KNOWLTON, Robert & _?_ ; b 1701?
KNOWLTON, Samuel & Elizabeth WITT/WAITT; Apr 1669; Ipswich
KNOWLTON, Thomas (1622?-1692?) & 1/wf Susannah _?_ (-1680); b 1655/6?, b 14 Jan 1655; Ipswich
KNOWLTON, Thomas (?1641-1692, 1711?, Norwich, CT) & Hannah GREENE (1647-1708, Norwich, CT); 24 Nov 1668; Ipswich/Charlestown
KNOWLTON, Thomas (-1692) & 2/wf Mary/Mercy KIMBALL; 17 May 1682; Ipswich
KNOWLTON, Thomas & Margaret GOODHUE; 2 Dec 1692, at Watertown; Ipswich/Watertown
KNOWLTON, Thomas (1673-1730) & 1/wf Mercy/Mary? _?_ (-1694?); b 1694; Norwich, CT/E. Haddam, CT
KNOWLTON, Thomas (-1730) & Susannah _?_ ; b 1698; Norwich, CT/E. Haddam, CT
KNOWLTON, William (1615-1655?) & Elizabeth [BALCH] (-living in 1655); b 1641, 10 Jan 1640/1?; Ipswich
KNOWLTON, William (1642-) & 1/wf Susannah [?WHITRIDGE]; b 1667, ?28 Oct 1667; Ipswich
NOCK, Henry (1667-1714) & Sarah ADAMS, m/2 Eleazer WYER; 10 Jan 1691/2; Dover, NH
KNOX, John & Hannah _?_ ; b 1686; Watertown
NOCK, Sylvanus (ca 1657-1716, 1717) & 1/wf Elizabeth EMERY (-1704); 20 Apr 1677; Dover, NH/Kittery, ME
NOCK, Thomas (-1666) & Rebecca [TIBBETTS], m/2 Philip BENMORE 1669; by 1654, ca 1653; Dover, NH
KNOX, _?_ & Sarah MELLOWES, w John; Boston

LABORIE, James & 1/wf Jane RESSEGUIE; in Eng, b 1692; New Oxford, MA/NY
LABROS, Charles & Sarah (LAWRENCE) WINSLOW, w Joseph; aft 1679; LI
LACKEY, Richard, Boston & Anne GRANDFIELD/?GREENFIELD, Plymouth; m bond 11 Jul 1637
LACKEY, William & Mary _?_; b 1684; Boston
LACY, Edward & Sarah _?_; b 1682?; Stratford, CT
LACY, Lawrence & Mary FOSTER (1652-1707); 5 Aug 1673; Andover
LACY, Morgan & _?_, ?m/2 Ralph TRISTRAM; b 1642; Saco, ME
LADBROOKE, Thomas & Mary BARRETT, w John; b 13 Jul 1671, 1670; Wells, ME
LADBROOK, Thomas & Deborah BOOTH, w Robert; ca 21 Feb 1682
LADD, Daniel (-1693) & Ann _?_ (-1694); b 1640; Ipswich/Salisbury
LADD, Daniel[2] (1642-) & Lydia SINGLETERY (1648-); 24 Nov 1668, no issue; Haverhill
LAD, Ezekiel (1654-) & Mary FOULSHAM/FOLSOM (1664-); 30 Nov 1687; Haverhill
LADD, Joseph (-1683) & Joanna _?_ (-1669+); b 1655; Portsmouth, RI
LADD, Joseph & Rachel _?_; b 1686; Little Compton, RI
LADD, Nathaniel (1651, ?1652-1691) Exeter, NH, & Elizabeth GILMAN (1661-), m/2 Henry
  WADLEIGH 1693; 12 Jun 1678, 12? Jul; Salisbury
LADD, Richard & Martha _?_; b 1689, b 1686; Boston
LADD, Robert & Bridget [STRATTON] (1664-1743); b 1694; Boston
LAD, Samuel (1649-1698) & Martha CORLES/CORLISS; 1 Dec 1674; Haverhill/Boston
LADD, William (1665-1729) & Elizabeth TOMPKINS (-1729+); 17 Feb 1696, 1695/6; Little
  Compton, RI
LAHORNE/LAHERNE, Rowland (-1648+, 1654+) & Flower/Flora _?_ (-1654+); 14 Jan 1635;
  [Plymouth]
LAKE, Daniel & 1/wf _?_; ca 1675?; Gravesend, LI/Staten Island, NY
LAKE, Daniel & 2/wf Alice (STILLWELL) (HOLMES) OSBORNE, w Samuel, w William; aft 1680,
  1684; Gravesend, LI?/Staten Island, NY
LAKE, David (-1696, 1709+) & Sarah (EARLE) CORNELL (-1690+), w Thomas; b 1678, ca
  1673?, by 1667?, ca 1677; Portsmouth, RI/Tiverton, RI/Little Compton, RI
LAKE, David (-ca 1700?, Portsmouth, RI) & Mary WILCOX; ca 1700
LAKE, Henry & Alice _?_ (-1650?); b 1642; Dorchester, etc.
LAKE, Henry (-1733) & Priscilla WILES/WILDES (1658-1688/9); 9 May 1681; Topsfield
LAKE, John (d in Eng) & Margaret [REED] (1598-1672); in Eng, b 1631, ca 1616; Ipswich
LAKE, John (-6 Aug 1677) (ae 5 in 1610) & 1/wf Mary [COY] (1612-1654+); b 1645; Boston
LAKE, John (-1696?, 1694) & Anne [SPICER]; ca 1646/50?; Gravesend, LI
LAKE, John (-1677) & 2/wf Lucy [BISHOP?] (-1678) (dau of Lucian, wf of Rev. Edward
  BULKELEY); aft 1654; Boston
LAKE, John & Nealtje [CLAESSEN]; b 1688; Flatlands/Gravesend, LI
LAKE, Thomas (1615-1676) (called "cousin" by Humphrey MILAM) & Mary [GOODYEAR]
  (1630-); b 1650; London/New Haven/Boston
LAKE, Thomas (1618, ?1608-1678, ae 70) & Alice/Els _?_ (1608, ?1598-1678); Dorchester
LAKE, Thomas (?1644-) & _?_; b 1677; Dartmouth
LAKE, Thomas (-1628) & Sarah [PEET/PEAT] (1665-); b 1688; Stratford, CT
LAKE, William (-1679) & Ann STRATTON/?SHARP (-1680); ca Aug 1661; Salem
LAKEMAN, William & Margery _?_; Ipswich/ Isles of Shoals
LAKIN, Abraham (1667-) & Abigail [SNOW]; b 1701?; Groton
LAKIN, John (1627-1697) & Mercy?/Mary [BACON] (?1640-1701+), dau Michael; b 1657?;
  Groton
LAKIN, John (?1659-1697) & Sarah [WHEELER] (1666-1742+), dau Richard, m/2 William
  TAYLOR 1699; b Mar 1646/7; Groton
LAKIN, Jonathan (1664-1740/46) & _?_; b 1701?; Groton
LAKIN, Joseph (1670-1747) & Abigail [LAKIN] (1674-); b 1691, ?15 May 1695; Groton
LAKIN, William[1] (-1672, ae ca 91 y) & _?_; in Eng, ca 1602; Reading/Groton
LAKIN, William[2] (d in Eng) (Reading, Eng) & Mary _?_ (-1669), m/2 William MARTIN bef 1648;
  in Eng, b 1624; Reading
LAKIN, William[3] (1624-1700) & Lydia [BROWN] (1633-1686+); b 1649; Reading/Groton

LEAKING, William, Groton & Elizabeth ROBINSON/ROBERTSON? (1668-), Groton; 4 Jan 1685; Chelmsford

LAMB, Abiel (1646-) & Elizabeth (CLARK) [BUCKMINSTER], w Joseph; b 1675; Roxbury

LAMB, Abiel & Hannah TAILOR/TAYLOR; 4 Dec 1699; Marlboro/Framingham

LAMB, Caleb (1641-) & Mary WISE; 30 Jun 1669; Roxbury

LAMB, Daniel (-1692) & Elizabeth ATCHINSON/ATCHISON? (1672-), m/2 Robert OLD 1697; 12 Jun 1690; Springfield

LAMB, Ebenezer (-1694) & Mary ARMSTRONG, m/2 Eleazer JEWETT 1700; 6 May 1690; Norwich, CT

LAMB, Ebenezer & Sarah __?_ ; b 1700; Norwich, CT

LAMB, Edward (-1649?) & Margaret [FRENCH], m/2 Samuel ALLEN ca 1650?; b 1633; Watertown/Boston

LAMB, Isaac (-1723) & Elizabeth __?_ ; b 1695, prob b 1692; New London, CT/ Groton

LAMB, John & 1/wf Joanna __?_ (-1683); b 1651; Springfield

LAMB, John & __?_ ; New London, CT

LAMB, John & 1/wf Mary (FRENCH) [POOLE], w Samuel; b 1677; Braintree/Stonington, CT

LAMB, John (-1690) & Lydia (WRIGHT) (BLISS) NORTON (-1699), w Lawrence, w John, m/4 George COTTON 1692; 26 Jan 1687/8, 27 Jan; Springfield

LAMB, John (-1704) & 2/wf __?_ ; b 1690; Braintree/Stonington, CT

LAMB, Joshua (1642-1690) & Mary [ALCOCK] (1652-1700); b 1675; Roxbury

LAMB, Samuel (-1729) & Rebecca BIRD, m/2 William WARRINER; 1 Dec 1687; Springfield/Farmington, CT

LAMB, Thomas (-1646) & 1/wf Elizabeth __?_ (-1639); in Eng, ca 1626; Roxbury

LAMB, Thomas (-1646) & 2/wf Dorothy HARBITTLE/HARBOTTLE, m/2 Thomas HAWLEY 1651/2; 16 Jul 1640; Roxbury

LAMB, Thomas, Dorchester & Thankful HILL, Dorchester; 10 Feb 1688, 1688/9; Milton/Dorchester

LAMB, William (-1690) & Mary [HEWES] (1641-1710); b 14 Apr 1680; Boston

LAMBERT/LOMBARD?, Caleb & __?_ (-1682); b 1682; Bristol, RI

LAMBERT, Daniel (-1695) & 1/wf Mary GRAY (1661-29 Aug 1693); 5 Jun 1682 Salem

LAMBERT, Daniel (-1695) & 2/wf Elizabeth (CROADE) [BRIDGES] (1661-1724), w Edmund, m/3 Moses GILMAN int 6 Jun 1713; aft 29 Aug 1693; Salem

LAMBERT, Ebenezer (1674-1728) & Mary [HARDY]; b 1696; Salem

LAMBERT, Francis (-1647, 1648?) & Jane [BARKER] (-1659) (sister of Thomas); ca 1635?; Rowley/Ipswich

LAMBERT, Gershom & Deborah [FRINK]; 1686; Stonington, CT

LAMBERT, Jesse (-1718?) & 1/wf Deborah FOWLER; 10 May 1685, 1683; ?Milford, CT

LAMBERT, John (-1684) & __?_ ; in Eng, b 1629; Salem/Beverly

LAMBERT, John (1629-1710?) & Preserved [GASKELL] (1639-); b 1658; Salem

LAMBERT, John (-1667) & Abigail HUTCHINSON (1636-), m/2 Anthony ASHBY by 1670; 14 May 1662; Rowley

LAMBERT, John & Mary LEWS/LEWIS; 15 Jan 1667; Saybrook, CT

LAMBERT, John & Sarah __?_ ; b 1686; Salem

LAMBERT, John & Sarah KILSON; 12 Jul 1687; Ipswich

LAMBERT, John[2] (son of Thomas) & [Anna?] __?_/Hannah HOLMES? (1667-), dau Josiah?; b 1693, b 1687?; Scituate (from Hingham?)

LAMBERT, John & Abigail WOODBURY; 9 Aug 1694; Beverly

LAMBERT, John & Margaret __?_ ; b 1695; ?Salem

LAMBERT, Jonathan (1669-1710, Boston) & Elizabeth [DEAN], m/2 John BUCANAN; b 1697(8?); Boston

LAMBERT, Michael (-1676) & 1/wf Elizabeth __?_ (-Oct 1657); b 1647; Lynn

LAMBERT, Michael & 2/wf Eleanor FURNELL, w Strong; 1659; Boston

LAMBERT, Michael, Boston, Lynn & ?3/wf __?_ ; b 1673; Boston

LAMBERT, Michael/Micah? & Elizabeth STARK/STRATTON, m/2 Josiah HAYNES 1693; 19 Apr 1688; Stonington, CT

LAMBERT, Philip & Susanna [LEAR]; 14 Oct 1697; Dover, NH

LAMBERT, Richard (-ca 1657) & ?Ann/?Sarah __?_ ; b 1643?; Salem

LAMBERT, Samuel (-1732) & Margaret [BROWNE] (1671-) dau John; b 1690(1?); Salem

LAMBERT, Thomas[1] & Mary __?_ ; b 1659; Boston/Scituate

LAMBERT, Thomas (-1685) (Nephew of Mrs. Mary (?) (BARKER) (ROGERS), wf of Rev. Ezekiel) & Edna NORTHEND (-1722), m/2 Andrew STICKNEY 1689; 4 Nov 1669; Rowley

LAMBIRD, Thomas & Sarah HAMMOND; 19 Dec 1699; Watertown/Rowley

LAMBERT, William & _?_ ; b 1658; Ipswich

LAMBERT, Thomas, Jr./John?; & _?_ HOLMES, dau Josiah; b 1693?

LAMBERT, _?_ & Alice _?_ ; see John COX

LAMBERTON, George (-1646) & Margaret LEWEN, m/2 Stephen GOODYEAR ca 1648, 1647; St. Nicholas, Acons, London, in Eng, 6 Jan 1629, 1628/9; New Haven

LAMERE, Thomas & Hannah HODGE; 11 Aug 1699; Boston/Plymouth

LANDFEAR, George (-1731) & _?_ ; b 1675; Westerly, RI

LANDFEAR, Shadrach & Experience REED, m/2 Samuel LINCOLN; 15 Jun 1696, 15 Jun 1697; Westerly, Stonington/Norwich, CT

LAMPREY, Benjamin (1660-) & 1/wf Jane BATCHELDER (1670-); 10 Nov 1687; Hampton, NH

LAMPREY, Daniel & _?_ ; b 1662?; Hampton, NH

LAMPREY, Henry (1616-1700) & Julian _?_ (-1670?); b 1641; Boston

LAMPREY, Henry & Elizabeth MITCHELL; 24 Jul 1686; Hampton, NH

LAMSON, Barnabas (-1640) & Mary _?_ (aunt of Peter LIDGETT); Cambridge

LAMSON, Ebenezer & Sarah HARTWELL; 19 Apr 1698; Concord

LAMPSON, John (1642-1717) & Martha PERKINS (1649-1728+); 17 Dec 1668, 1669?; Ipswich

LAMSON, John (1669-1760) & Abigail [WOODBURY] (1671-1753); b 1695; Ipswich

LAMSON, Joseph (1638-1679) & _?_ /?Elizabeth RICE (1641-), dau Richard, m/3 John BILLING 1685; ca 1663?; Cambridge/Concord/Reading

LAMSON, Joseph (1658-) & 1/wf Elizabeth MITCHELL (-1703, ae 45); 12 Dec 1679; Charlestown

LAMSON, Joseph (-1743) & Elizabeth ADAMS; 18 Aug 1686; Concord

LAMSON, Samuel (1642-1692) & Mary NICHOLS/NICKELS; 18 May 1676; Reading

LAMSON, Samuel & Elizabeth EATON (1681-); 11 Apr 1700; Reading

LAMPSON, Thomas (-1663) & 1/wf _?_ ; b 1645; New Haven

LAMPSON, Thomas (-1663) & 2/wf _?_ WILLIAMSON, w Paul; Feb 1650; New Haven

LAMPSON, Thomas (-1663) & 3/wf Elizabeth (HARRISON) LINES, w Henry, m/3 John MORRIS 1666; 6 Nov 1663; New Haven

LAMPSON, William (-1659) & Sarah [AYRES?], m/2 Thomas HASPTORN, 1661; b 1642; Ipswich

LANCASTER, Daniel & _?_ ; b 1657

LANCASTER, Henry (-1705) & _?_ ; b 1638; Salisbury

LANKESTER/LANGSTAFF, Joseph & 1/wf Mary [CARTER] (1641-); b 1666; Salisbury

LANCASTER/LANGSTAFF, Joseph & 2/wf Hannah _?_ ; aft 1676; Salisbury

LANKESTER, Joseph (1666-) & Elizabeth HOYT; 31 Mar 1687; Amesbury

LANKESTER, Thomas (-1703) & Mercy GREEN (1675-); 3 Mar 1696, 1695/6; Hampton, NH

LANCASTER, William & Jane [WEATLEY] (1655-); b 1677; Boston

LANDER/LAUNDERS, James & Elizabeth GRANT, m/2 John TURNER, 1694, m/3 William HEARLE; Salem Falls

LANDERS, John (1653-1705) & Rachel [FREEMAN] (1659-1705+); b 1687; Sandwich

LANDERS, John (-1698/9) & Sarah [WILLIAMS] (bpt 1664-1718+); b 1688, ?int 4 Oct 1677; Salem

LANDERS, Richard & Sarah FREEMAN (1662-1733); 6 Jan 1695/6, 18 Jan 1697; Sandwich/Falmouth

LANDER, Thomas (-1675) & Jane KERBIE/KERBY; 2 Jul 1651; Sandwich

LANDER, Thomas & Deborah [FREEMAN] (1665-); b 1687; Sandwich

LANDMAN, Samuel & Mary _?_ ; b 1690; Boston

LANDMAN, Thomas & Lucy [ELTON?]; in Eng, b 1694; Watertown

LANDON, Daniel & Ann/Anna [?LOBDELL]; b 1682; Charlestown/Bristol, RI

LANDON, James (-1692) & Elizabeth _?_ ; b 1667?; Boston/Suffolk Co., MA

LANDON, Nathan (1664-1718) & Hannah [BISHOP] (1671-1701); ca 1692; Southold, LI

LANE, Ambrose (-1656) & 1/wf ?Mary LACKINGTON; 1631, in Eng; Strawberry Bank

LANE, Ambrose (-1656) & 2/wf Christian _?_ ; Strawberry Bank

LANE, Andrew (-1675) & Tryphena _?_ (1612-1707); ca 1639; Hingham

LANE, Andrew (-1717) & Elizabeth EAMES -1727); 5 Dec 1672; Hingham

LANE, Charles & Elizabeth [KNAPP]; b 1691; Fairfield, CT

LANE, Daniel & Katherine [DOXEY], w Thomas, m/3 Thomas MOORE bef 1680; 1652; New London/Southold/Brookhaven, NY

LANE, Ebenezer (1650-1726) & Hannah HERSEY (1669-); 27 Dec 1688; Hingham
LANE, Edward & Hannah/Ann?/Anna? KEAYNE, m/2 Nicholas PAIGE; 11 Dec 1657; Boston
LANE, George (-1689) & Sarah [HARRIS] (-1696); ca 1634/6; Hingham/Weymouth
LANE, George (-1709+) & Mercy [?HINE] (-1709+); b 1666?; Rye, NY
LANE, George & Elizabeth STOWELL (1673-1746); 14 Dec 1699; Hingham
LANE, Isaac (1639-1711) & Hannah BROWN; 5 Nov 1669; Middletown, CT
LANE, James (-1662) & Dousabella __?__ (-in Eng 1662); Boston
LANE, James (-1688) & ?1/wf ?2/wf Ann?/Sarah WHITE?, ?m/2 Henry KINNE; b 1651?, b
    1652?; Malden/Casco Bay, ME
LANE, Job (?1620-1697) (nephew of Thomas HOWELL) & 1/wf Sarah [BOYER] (-1659); 1647;
    Malden/Billerica
LANE, Job (?1620-1697) & Anna/Hannah? REYNER (-1704?); Sep 1660, 2 Sep 1660, July 1660;
    Malden/Dover, NH
LANE, John (-1669) & 1/wf [Sarah] __?__ (-bef 1660); b 1639; Milford, CT
LANE, John (-1669) & 2/wf Mary [CRANE?/CRANFIELD?] CAMP (-1680), w Edward; 4 Apr
    1660; Milford, CT
LANE, John & 1/wf Mehitable HOBART (1651-1690); 18 Jun 1674; Hingham
LANE, John & __?__ ; b 1677; Topsfield
LANE, John (-1730) & 1/wf Sarah BEAL (-1693), m/2 __?__ ; 21 Jan 1679/80; Hingham
LANE, John (1652-1738) & Dorcas [WALLIS] (1659-1751); b 1682, ca 1680; Glouster/Falmouth,
    ME
LANE, John (1661-1714/15 & Susanna WHIPPLE (1661±-1713); 20 Mar 1681/2, 20 Dec 1683;
    Billerica
LANE, John & __?__ ; b 1687; Boston
LANE, John & Sarah (BEALL)/ORMSBY/[BRIGGS?] (-1727, ae 83?); ca 1690, b 1694;
    Norton/Hingham
LANE, John & Joanna __?__ (1672-), m/2 Nicholas MYGOOD; Nov 1693, 1692; Newbury/Hampton,
    NH/York Co, ME
LANE, John & [?Sarah ORMSBY], dau John 1665; b 1694; Rehoboth
LANE, John & Tabitha STODDER/STODDARD (1672-); 18 Nov 1697; Hingham
LANE, John (1674-1759) & 1/wf Lydia KELSEY (-1710); 31 Dec 1700; Killingworth, CT
LANE, Joshua (1654-1710) & Elizabeth __?__ (-1710+); b 1678, b 1677?; Hingham
LANE, Joshua (-1710) & 1/wf Sarah [WHITE]; b 1684; Boston
LANE, Josiah (1641-1714) & 1/wf Mary [BACON] (-1671); b 1671; Hingham
LANE, Josiah (1641-) & 2/wf Deborah GILL; 9 May 1672, May 1671?; Hingham
LANE, Robert (1638-1718) & Sarah PICKETT (1648-1725); 19 Dec 1665; Stratford, CT
LANE, Samuel (1651-1690) & Sarah DICKINSON (1656-), m/2 Martin KELLOGG 1691; 11 Dec
    1677, 4 Dec; Deerfield/Hadley/Suffield
LANE, Samuel (-1724) & Abigail __?__ ; [b 1690?], b 1692; Salem
LANE, Samuel & __?__
LANE, Samuel & Elizabeth HALL (1672-); b 1701?; Fairfield, CT
LANE, Thomas & __?__ ; b 1679(80?); Dorchester
LANE, Thomas & Susanna __?__ ; b 1687; Boston
LANE, Thomas & Opportunity [HOPPIN]; b 1687; Boston
LANE, William (-1654) & 2/wf? [Agnes?] [?FARNSWORTH]; in Eng, b 1618; Hingham/Dor-
    chester
LANES, William & __?__ ; b 1648; Hartford
LANE, William & 1/wf Mary [KELWAY] (-1656); b 1652, b 1651(2?), b 1650; Boston
LANE, William & Mary BREWER; 21 Aug 1656; Boston
LANE, William (1659-1749) & Sarah WEBSTER (1661-1745); 21 Jun 1680; Hampton, NH/Boston
LANE, William (-1702) & Mary [BOYLSTON?]; b 1694; Charlestown
LANE, __?__ & Elizabeth RAYNOR; Southampton, LI
LANG, John & __?__ ; b 1689; Kennebec
LANG, John & 1/wf Grace BROOKINS; Mar 1694/5; Portsmouth, NH
LANG, Nathaniel & Elizabeth [?CURRIER]; b 1697?; Isles of Shoals
LANG, Nicholas & Anne PALMER/PALMES?; 10 Jan 1687/8; Swansea
LANG, Robert & Ann WILLIAMS; 19 Aug 1668; Portsmouth, NH
LANG, Stephen & Jane [?WALLIS]; b 1699; Portsmouth, NH
LANG, __?__ & Mary __?__ ; ?Boston

LANGBURY/LANGBURRO, John & Elizabeth __?__; b 1688; Boston
LANGDON, Andrew (-1655?) & Margaret __?__ (-1667+); no issue; Wethersfield, CT
LANGDON, Benjamin & Phoebe __?__; b 1678; Boston
LANGDON/LANDON?, David (1650-1723) & Martha __?__; b 1685; Boston
LANGDON, John (-1677, Essex Co.) & Sarah [VERMAES], dau wid Alice; b 1648?; Boston
LANGDON, John (see John LANGTON) & Mary (SEYMOUR) [GRIDLEY], w Thomas; aft 1655; Farmington, CT
LANGDON, John (1660-1732) & Elizabeth __?__; b 1686; Boston/Cambridge
LANGDON, Philip (-1697) & Mary __?__ (-1717); b 1675?, b 1677; Boston
LANGDON, Thomas (-1666?) (called brother by Edward WOOSTER of Derby) & __?__ [OSBORN?], wid (had son William OSBORN); b 1649/50?; Lynn, NH/Derby, CT/Hempstead, LI
LANGDON, Tobias (-1664) & Elizabeth [SHERBURNE] (1638-), m/2 Tobias LEAR 1667, m/3 Richard MARTYN, 1684, ca 1681?; 10 Jun 1656; Portsmouth, NH
LANGDON, Tobias & Mary HUBBARD; 17 Nov 1686; Salisbury
LANGER, Richard (-1661) & __?__; b 1640, b 1627?; Hingham
LANGFORD, Thomas (-1670) & Mary [COOKE]; b 1670; Newport
LANGFORD, Thomas (1670±-1709) & 1/wf Comfort __?__ (-1699±); Newport/E. Greenwich, RI
LANGSFORD, __?__ & Ruth [MANSFIELD] (1662, 1663?-); b 1696; ?Salem
LONGHORNE/LONGHORN?, Richard (ca 1617-1689) & Mary CROSBY (1629-1667; 16 Jan 1647/8; Rowley
LANGHORNE, Thomas (ca 1622-) (ae 48 in 1669) & Sarah [GREEN]; b 1647; Cambridge
LANGLEY, Abel & 1/wf Sarah [MAKEPEACE] (-16 May 1666); Rowley
LANGLEY, Abel & 2/wf Mary DICKINSON (-1673); 21 Dec 1666; Rowley
LANGLEY, Abel (-1687) & 3/wf Sarah [QUILTER] (-1683); b 1675; Rowley
LANGLEY, George (-1703) & Rebecca __?__; Flushing, LI
LANGLEY, James & Mary [RUNNELS]; nr 1700, prob aft 1700; Durham, NH
LANGLEE, John & Sarah GILL; 13 Jan 1665/6; Hingham
LANGLEY, John & Mary ADAMS; m int 10 Sep 1695; Boston
LANGLEY, Stephen (had son Simes) & [?Frances SYMMES/SIMES?]; b 1674; Milton
LANGLEY, Thomas & Elizabeth __?__; b 1662?; Portsmouth, NH
LANGMAND, Richard (-1660) & Ellen __?__; b 1660; Charlestown
LANGSTAFF, Bethuel & Hannah [BUCKINGHAM] (1663-); b 1699; ?Milford, CT
LANGSTAFF, Henry (?1645/62?-1705) & __?__; Dover, NH
LANGTON, George (-1676) & 1/wf __?__; in Eng, b 1629; Wethersfield, CT
LANGTON, George (-1676) & 2/wf Hannah (__?__) HAYNES, w Edmund; 29 Jun 1648, 28 Jun; Springfield/Northampton
LANGTON, John & 1/wf __?__
LANGTON, John (-1689) (see John LANGDON) & 2/wf Mary (SEYMOUR) [GRIDLEY], w Thomas; 1655+, by 20 Oct 1655; Hartford/?Farmington
LANGTON, John (-1683) & Mary [SALMON], Northampton; ca 1681; Farmington, CT
LANGTON, Joseph & Rachel (PARSONS) [COOK] (-1692), Varney, w Thomas, m/3 William VINSON, 1661; 26 Jul 1652, div 1661?; Ipswich
LANGTON, Joseph (1660-) & Susannah ROOT (-1712?); 1 Oct 1683; Farmington, CT
LANGTON, Roger (-1669/2) & Joan/Jane? __?__ (-1683?); b 1630?; Ipswich/Haverhill
LANGTON, Samuel (1653-1683) & Elizabeth (COPLEY/COOLEY) TURNER, w Praisever, m/3 David ALEXANDER 1683+; 1 Dec 1676; Northampton
LANGTON, Samuel (1672-) & Hannah KINGSLEY; 10 Jun 1699/1700; Northampton
LANGWORTHY, Andrew (-1680+) & Rachel HUBBARD (1642-); 3 Nov 1658; Newport
LANGWORTHY, John (ca 1661-1700) & Elizabeth [WITTER] (1662-), m/2 __?__ CRANDALL
LANGWORTHY, Samuel & Rachel __?__; 21 Jul 1680
LANPHERE, George & __?__; ?ca 1669; Westerly, RI
LANPHERE, John (-1757) & Ruth __?__ (-1730+); b 1701(?); Westerly, RI
LANPHERE, Shadrack & Experience READ, m/2 Samuel LINCOLN; 15 Jun 1696; Stonington, CT
LAPHAM, John & __?__ HOLLIS; Aug 1671; Malden
LAPHAM, John (1635-1710) & Mary MANN (-1710+); 6 Apr 1673; Providence/Newport/Dartmouth
LAPHAM, John (1677-) & Mary RUSSELL (1683-); 3 Apr 1700; Dartmouth/Smithfield, RI
LAPHAM, Thomas[1] (-1648, 1644) & Mary TILDEN (1610-), m/2 William BASSETT 1651+; 13 Mar 1636/7; Scituate/Hingham

LAPHAM, Thomas (1643-1720) & 1/wf Mary [BROOKS?]; b 1670; Scituate/Marshfield
LARKUM/LARCOM, Cornelius (-1747, ae ca 94) & 1/wf Abigail BALCH (-1736); 8 Feb 1681; Beverly
LARCUM, Daniel (-1745?) & Phebe STONE (1672-); 29 May 1693; Ipswich
LARCKUM, Mordecai & Elizabeth [CLARK], w William; b 25 Mar 1656; Ipswich
LARKUM, Mordecai (1658-1717) & Abigail SOLART; 10 Nov 1681; Beverly/Wenham
LARKHAM, Thomas (1601-) (ret'd to Eng) & _?_ ; b 1632, b 1630; Dover, NH
LARCUM, Thomas & 1/wf Hannah [KETTLE?] (-1697); b 1695, ?10 Jul 1674; Manchester
LARCUM, Thomas & Abigail (?LOVETT) [WOODBURY], w Thomas; b 26 Mar 1700, Feb 1699/1700?
LARGE, John & Phebe/Sarah? LEE (1642-1664?); 1 Nov 1659; Saybrook/?Lyme, CT/Killingworth, CT
LARGE, John (-1691) & ?Hannah/?Abigail [BUSHNELL/SHAPMAN/SHIPMAN], m/2 John WHITTLERAY; b 1691; Haddam, CT
LARGE, Joseph & Elizabeth _?_ ; b 1673; Amesbury/Bucks Co, PA
LARGE, Simon (-1702) & Hannah LONG, m/2 Jonathan MOORE 1706; 24 Jan 1699/1700; Saybrook, CT
LARGE, William & _?_ ; b 1635; Hingham
LARGE, John? & Hannah [BUSHNELL] (1670-), m/2 James BENTON 1694; b 1686
LARGIN, Henry & Anna _?_ ; b 1646; Boston
LARGIN, Henry & Alice [MOORE], w Jeremiah; b 1653; Charlestown
LARIFORD, Thomas & Sarah _?_ ; b 1695; Reading
LARKIN, Edward (-1652) & Joanna [HALE?] (1616-1686), sister of Robert, m/2 John PENTICOST; b 1639; Charlestown
LARKIN, Edward & _?_ ; ca 1655?; Newport/Westerly, RI
LARKIN, Edward & Mary WALKER; 1 Nov 1688; Charlestown
LARKIN, Edward (-1741) & 1/wf Elizabeth [HALL]; ca 1698; Westerly, RI
LARKIN/LACKIN, Hugh (-1659) & Alice _?_ (-1658); in Eng, b 1614; Salem
LARKIN, John² (1640-1678) & Joanna HALE (1647±-), m/2 William DODGE 1685; 9 Nov 1664; Charlestown
LARKIN, John & Sarah _?_ ; b 1676; Boston
LARKIN, John (-1705) & Rebecca _?_ ; b 1701; Westerly, RI
LARKIN, Roger (1671-) & 1/wf Hannah [BADCOCK], dau James; b 1706, b 1701?; Stonington, CT
LARKIN, Thomas (1643, 1643/4?-1677) & 1/wf Hannah REMINGTON (1643-1673); 13 Sep 1666; Charlestown
LARKIN, Thomas (1643-1677) & 2/wf Elizabeth DOWSE (1647-1732+), m/2 _?_ DREW?/John DYER by 1679; 18 Jun 1674; Charlestown
LARKIN, Thomas & Jane _?_ ; b 1687; Boston
LARKIN, Thomas & Sarah ROW; 5 Sep 1700; Boston
LARKIN/LACKIN?, Timothy (-bef 1659) & Damaris [MAYNARD?]/STEBMAN?, m/2 Paul MANSFIELD 1659?; ca 1655?; Salem
LARKIN, Timothy (-1700) & 1/wf _?_ ; Salem
LARKIN, Timothy (-1700) & 2/wf Elizabeth _?_ (-1702+); Salem
LARRABEE, Benjamin (1666/7-1733/4), N. Yarmouth & Deborah INGERSOLL, Falmouth; 1 Dec 1686; Falmouth, ME/etc.
LARRABEE, Greenfield & Phebe (BROWN) LEE (-1664), w Thomas, m/3 James CORNISH by 1661; b 1648; Saybrook, CT/Preston, CT
LARRABEE, Greenfield (1648-1739) & Alice PARK, New London; - Mar 1672/3, 16? Mar; Norwich, CT
LARRABEE, Isaac (1664-1745) (left wid Eleanor) & 1/wf _?_ [TOWN?];b 1692, 1690 Salem?; N. Yarmouth, ME/Lyme
LARRABEE, John & Sarah MORGAN; 15 Apr 1684; Windham, CT
LARRABEE, John (1677-) & Rebecca [PARKE]; b 1701?; CT
LETHERBEE/LARRABEE?, Samuel & Lydia BISS/BLISH?/BLISS?/BUSH?, wid; 15 Nov 1695; Boston
LARRABEE, Stephen (1625-1676) & _?_ [MAINS?]; 1652; N. Yarmouth, ME
LARRABEE, Stephen (1652-1718) & Isabelle _?_ ; b 1682; Malden/N. Yarmouth, ME
LARRABEE, Thomas (1660-1723) & Elizabeth [ROE/ROWE]; ca 1683; N. Yarmouth, ME/ etc.

LARRABEE, Thomas (1675-) & Mary WILLETT; 19 Jul 1697; Norwich, CT
LARRABEE, William (-1692) & Elizabeth FELT; Nov 1655, ?Jun; Malden
LARRABEE, William (1658-) & 1/wf Joanna [MELLNEY] (1662-); b 1678; N. Yarmouth, ME/Wells, ME
LARRABEE, William (1678-1703) & Mary CAME; 14 Mar 1699, 1699/1700; York, ME
LARRIMORE, Thomas & Abigail (TRASK) [ROWLAND], w John, m/3 William JACOBS; b 1696; Salem
LARRISON/LARISON, John & 1/wf Jemima HALSEY; 22 May 1683, 23? May; Southampton
LARISON, John & 2/wf Mary (?) HOWELL, ?w David; 20 Dec 1686; Southampton
LARY, Cornelius & __?__; Exeter, NH
LARY, John (see John LAY) & __?__; 1 Nov 1659; Saybrook, CT/?Lyme
LARY, John (-by Jul 1698) & Sarah [LYDSTON/LITTEN?], m/2 Robert ALLEN 1700; Kittery, ME
LASELL, Isaac (1660-1690) & Abial LEAVITT (1667-), m/2 Isaac JOHNSON by 1692; 20 Jan 1685/6; Hingham
LASELL, Israel (1671-) & Rachel LINCOLN; 6 Jul 1698; Hingham
LASOLL, John (-1700, ae 81) & Elizabeth GATES (?1630-1704); 29 Nov 1649; Hingham
LASELL, John & Deborah LINCOLN; 26 Mar 1696; Hingham
LASELL, Joshua (1634-1689) & Mary __?__, m/2 Benajah PRATT by 1695; - Jan 1680/1; Hingham
LASELL, Stephen (1656-1718) & Sarah __?__ [?STEVENS] (-1733+) (Sarah m someone on 1 Feb 1686/7?); b 1688; Hingham
LAZELL, Thomas (1652-) & Mary ALLEN (1665-); 22 Apr 1685, 26 Apr; Duxbury
LASENBY/LESENBY, Thomas & ?Mary/?Mercy __?__; b 1688(9?); Boston
LASH, Nicholas & Gertrude __?__; b 1659?, b 1672; Boston
LASH, Robert (-1712, ae 53) & 1/wf Mary __?__; b 1695; Boston
LASH, William (-1693) & Joanna __?__, m/2 John MANNING 1698; Boston
LASKEY, Robert & __?__; b 1694; Marblehead
LASSEE, Gabriel & Deborah [?WHITEHEAD] [?DENTON], w Daniel DENTON?; b 13 Nov 1703, b 1701?
LATHAM, Cary (1613-1685) & Elizabeth (MASTERS) LOCKWOOD, w Edmund; b 1639; Cambridge/New London, CT
LATHAM, Cary (1668-) & Susanna FORSTER; b 1690; Groton, CT
LATHAM, Chilton & Susanna KINGMAN (1679-); 6 Dec 1699; Bridgewater
LATHAM, James & Deliverance [ALGER?], ?dau Thomas; b 1693; Bridgewater
LATHAM, John & __?__; ca 1685
LATHAM, Joseph (?1642-1706), New London & Mary __?__; b 1668; Newfoundland/New London, CT
LATHAM, Joseph & Phebe [FENNER] b 1688?; Providence/Saybrook
LATHAM, Robert & 1/wf Susannah WINSLOW (-bef 3 Oct 1683; b 1649; Plymouth/Marshfield
LATHAM, Robert & 2/wf Susanna __?__; b 6 Mar 1685; Plymouth/Marshfield
LATHAM, Samuel & Lydia?/Mary? __?__; b 1701?; New London, CT
LATHAM, Thomas (1639-1677) & (Rebecca) WELLS, (1652-), Wethersfield, m/2 John PACKER 1698, m/3 __?__ WATSON?; 11 Oct 1673, 15? Oct; New London, CT
LATHAM, William & Hannah MORGAN (1674-); b 1699; Groton, CT
LATHLEY, Philip (-1718) & Mary [BISHOP]; ca 1697?, 1700?; Duxbury/Marshfield/Plymouth
LATIMER, Bezaleel (1657-1688) & Saint ROBINSON (1656-1717), m/2 William TRYON 1688?; 18 Aug 1680; Wethersfield, CT
LATIMER, Christopher[1] (1620-1690) & Mary [PITT/PITTS] (1632-1687); b 1659, b 2 Feb 1659; Marblehead
LATTAMORE, John[1] (-1662) & Ann __?__, ?m/2 Robert MORRIS; b 1646; Wethersfield, CT
LATIMER, John (1650-) & Mary ROBINSON (1654-1727); 29 Apr 1680; Wethersfield, CT/Windsor, CT
LATIMER, Robert (-1671) & Ann (GRIGGS?) JONES, w Edward/Matthew?/Rice?; 1 Sep 1662; Charlestown/New London, CT
LATTAMORE, Robert (1664-1728) (see George BUTTOLPH) & Elizabeth [DIMOND] [BUTTOLPH] (1672-), w George; ca 1693, ?ca 1692, aft 1696; New London, CT
LATTEN, Josiah/Josias (?1641-1720) & Sarah [WRIGHT]; aft 22 Oct 1667; Stratford, CT/Hempstead, LI/Huntington, LI/Oyster Bay, LI
LATTING, Josias, Jr. & Susanna [COLES]; b 12 Sep 1693; Oyster Bay, LI/Matinecock

LATTIN, Richard (-1673) & 1/wf Christian __?__ (-1667); b 1641(2?); Concord/Stratford, CT/Hempstead, LI/Oyster Bay, LI

LATTIN, Richard & Joan/Jean [IRELAND], w Thomas; ?1668 prob, 24 Aug 1670; Stratford, CT/?Hempstead, LI

LATTIN, Thomas (1643-1713) & 1/wf Abigail [GRISWOLD] (1655-); b 1678, b 1672?; Wethersfield, CT

LATTEN?, Thomas (1643-1713) & 2/wf Mary/Mercy? [WAKELEE], m/2 Moses **WHEELER;** b 1687; Stratford, CT

LAUGHTON/LEIGHTON?/LAYTON, John & Joanna (__?__) **BOYER MULLINGS/MUNNINGS,** w Simon, w George; 21 Sep 1659; Boston

LAITON/LAWTON, John & Parnall **KERTLAND** (-1694), w Nathaniel; 31 Oct 1687; Lynn

LAUGHTON, John (-1688) & Sarah [CONKLING]; 28 Jul 1680; Southampton, LI

LORTON/LAUGHTON?, John & Mary [LONGLEY] (1674-); b 1691(2?); Cambridge/Concord

LAUGHTON, Samuel (-1730) & Sarah **GRAVS;** 14 Feb 1680; Lynn

LAUGHTON, Thomas (1612-1697) & Sarah [LENTHALL] (-1691); Weymouth

LAUGHTON, Thomas (-1713) & 1/wf Sarah **REDNAP** (-1679); 28 Dec 1670; Lynn

LAUGHTON, Thomas (-1713) & 2/wf Hannah **SILSBEE** (-1682); 2 Dec 1680; Lynn

LAUGHTON, Thomas (-1713) & 3/wf Sarah (DIX) **BROWN** (1653-1726, ae 73), w Edward; 24 Nov 1685; Lynn

LAURENSON, James & __?__ [?SAWTELLE]; ?Newtown, LI

LAVENUCK/LAVENUKE, Stephen & Mary **DIVALL;** 25 Sep 1672; Newbury

LAVISE, William & Elizabeth __?__ ; b 1692; Boston

LAWES, Francis (1595-1665/6) & Lydia __?__ (1588-); ?Norwich, in Eng, ca 1615/20; Salem

LAW, John & Lydia **DRAPER** (1641-); 5 Mar 1659/60; Concord

LAW, Jonathan (ca 1636-1712 in 75th y) Stamford & 1/wf Sarah **CLARK** (-1726, 1727), Milford, dau George, Sr.; 1 Jun 1664; Milford, CT

LAW, Jonathan (1674-1750) & 1 wf Ann **ELIOT** (1677-1703); 20 Dec 1698; Milford, CT

LAW, Lyman & __?__ ; ca 1650?; Gravesend, LI

LAW, Richard & Margaret [KILBOURNE] (1607-); ca 1635, ca 1636?; Wethersfield, CT

LAW, Stephen (1665-1733) & Deborah __?__ ; no ch recorded; Concord

LAWES, Thomas & Mary __?__ ; b 1664(5?); Sudbury

LAW, William (-1668) & 1/wf Mary **CHENEY** (?1627-1664/5; 3 Sep 1645; Rowley

LAW, William (-1668) & Faith (PARRATT) **SMITH** (-1705), w John; 2 May 1666; Rowley

LAWRENCE, Benjamin (1666-1737), Watertown & 1/wf Mary **CLOUGH** (1673-1695); 4 Jul 1689; Boston?

LAWRENCE, Benjamin (1666-1737); & 2/wf Ann/Anna **PHILLIPS** (-1716), w Benjamin; 3 Feb 1695/6; Charlestown

LAWRENCE, Daniel (1666-1743) & 1/wf Sarah **COUNTS** (-1694); 19 Jun 1689; Charlestown

LAWRENCE, Daniel (1666-1743) & 2/wf Hannah **MASON** (-1721); - Nov 1695; Charlestown

LAWRENCE, David (-1710) & Mary [?TAYLOR] (1667-); Exeter, NH

LAWRENCE, Eleazer (1674-1754) & Mary [SCRIPTURE] (?1679, ?1680-1761); b 1699 (1700?), b 1697; Groton

LAWRENCE, Enoch (1649-1744) & Ruth (WHITNEY) **SHATTUCK** (1645-), w John; 6 Mar 1676/7; Groton

LAWRENCE, George (-1709) & 1/wf Elizabeth **CRISP** (1637-1681); 29 Sep 1657; Watertown

LAWRENCE, George (-1709) & 2/wf Elizabeth **HOLLAND;** 16 Aug 1691; Watertown

LAWRENCE, George (1668-1736) & Mary __?__ ; b 1696(7?); Watertown

LAWRENCE, Henry (-bef 1646) & Christian __?__ (-1647/8); 1618±; Charlestown

LAWRENCE, Isaac (-1731, ae 73) & Abigail **BELLOWS** (1661-1726 in 64th y); 19 Apr 1682; Cambridge/Lexington/Norwich, CT

LAWRENCE, John (-1667) & 1/wf Elizabeth [COOKE] (-1663, Groton); b 1635; Watertown/Groton

LAWRENCE, John (-1699) & Susannah __?__ ; b 1642; Hempstead, LI/Flushing, LI

LAWRENCE, John (?1618-1672) (ae 36 in 1654, ae 35 in 1655) & Susanna __?__ , m/2 Thomas **TARBALL** 1676; b 1642; Charlestown

LAWRENCE, John & Elizabeth **ADKINSON/ATKINSON;** 8 Feb 1653/4; Boston

LAURANCE, John (1636-1712) & 1/wf Sarah **BUCKMASTER** (-1690); 30 Sep 1657; Boston/Wrentham

LAWRENCE, John (1609-1667) & 2/wf Susannah **BATCHELDER** (-1668); 2 Nov 1664; Groton

LAWRENCE, John & Ursula _?_ ; b 1667; Boston
LAWRENCE, John (-1714/15) & Elizabeth [CORNELL] (1662-); b 1679; Flushing, LI
LAWRENCE, John & Sarah (CORNELL) (WILLETT) BRIDGES, w Thomas, w Charles; m lic 20 Nov 1682; ?NY/LI?
LAWRENCE, John (-1694) & Sarah SMITH, m/2 Ebenezer WELLS 1705; 16 Oct 1684; Hadley/Brookfield
LAWRENCE, John (-1747), Groton & Anna/Hannah TARBELL (-1732, ae 62); 9 Nov 1687; Groton
LAWRENCE, John (-1729) & Deborah [WOODHULL] (1654-1740); b 1695; Newtown, LI
LAWRENCE, John & Janetie STEVENSON; m lic, 6 Apr 1696; LI?/NY?
LAWRENCE, John (1636-1712, Natick) & 2/wf Susanna _?_ ; b 1698, aft 1690; Sherborn/Natick
WHEELER, Jonathan (-1725) & Rebecca RUTTER (1647-1724); 5 Nov 1677; Cambridge
LAWRENCE, Joseph (1643-) & Rebecca/Lydia DAVIS; 13 Mar 1670/1; Charlestown/Boston
LAWRENCE, Joseph (son of William) & _?_ ; b 1691; Flushing, LI
LAWRENCE, Joseph (son of John) & _?_ ; b 1698; Flushing, LI
LAWRENCE, Joseph, Sandwich & Hannah CHADDACK, Falmouth; 25 Jan 1699/1700; Sandwich
LAWRENCE, Nathaniel (1639-1724) & 1/wf Sarah MOSS/MORSE (1643-1683, Groton); 13 Mar 1660/1, 13 Mar 1660; Groton/Sudbury
LAWRENCE, Nathaniel (1661-1737) & 1/wf Hannah [RUTTER]; ca 1682/4; Sudbury
LAWRENCE, Nathaniel (1661-1737) & 2/wf Anna/Hannah [FISKE]; ca 1689; Groton/Sudbury
LAWRENCE, Nathaniel (1639-1724) & Sarah _?_ (-1717); b 31 Oct 1695, [aft 1683]; Charlestown
LAWRENCE, Nicholas (-1685) & Mary [HARRIS] (-1685+); b 19 Jan 1655; Dorchester
LAWRENCE, Nicholas (-1711) & 1/wf Mary HARRIS; 3 Nov 1681; Dorchester
LAWRENCE, Nicholas (-1711) & 2/wf Abigail (LAWRENCE) WYER, w Edward, m/3 Edward CLIFFORD; 25 Dec 1689; Charlestown
LAWRENCE, Peleg (1648-1692, 1693) & Elizabeth MORSE (1647-); 22 Dec 1668; Medfield/Groton
LAWRENCE, Richard & Sarah _?_ ; b 1651(2?); New Haven/Branford, CT
LAWRENCE, Richard & Charity CLARK, m bond, 24 Sep 1699; Flushing, LI
LAWRENCE, Robert? (see William) (will at Plymouth) & _?_ SPRAGUE?; b 1644; Marblehead
LAWRENCE, Robert & _?_ ; b 1676(7?); Sandwich
LAWRENCE, Robert (-1690) & Mary PHILLIPS) MUNJOY, w George, m/3 Stephen CROSS 1692/3; ca 1686/7; b 7 Mar 1683/4, b Apr 1684; Falmouth, ME/Charlestown
LAWRENCE, Robert & Susanna _?_ ; b 1685(6?); Marblehead
LAWRENCE, Samuel & Rebecca LEWYN/LUEN, w John; 14 Sep 1682; Charlestown/CT?
LAWRENCE, Samuel (1671-1712) & Abigail _?_ ; b 1701; Watertown/Killingly, CT
LAWRENCE, Thomas & Joan SUTROBUS (1592-); 1609; St. Albans, Eng
LAWRENCE, Thomas (-1655) & Elizabeth [BATES] (-1679, Dorchester); ca 1635; Wenham/Dorchester
LAWRENCE, Thomas (-1648) & Martha/Deborah WOMBREY, m/2 John CHAPMAN, m/3 Francis BROWN; b 1646; Milford, CT/Stamford, CT
LAWRENCE, Thomas (-1703) & Mary _?_ , m/2 _?_ WHITE; ca 1650; Newtown, LI
LAWRENCE, Thomas (1648-1691) & Hannah (SMITH) [KNAPP], w Caleb; b 1687, ca 1674(?), b 4 Jul 1687, aft 1674; Stamford, CT
LAWRENCE, Thomas (-1703) & Mary FERGUSON; m lic 9 Nov 1692; Fluhing, LI?
LAWRENCE, William (see Robert) & [Ann]/Mary SPRAGUE; b 1 Apr 1644; Plymouth/Springfield
LAWRENCE, William (1623-1680) & 1/wf [Elizabeth?] _?_ (1629-aft 20 Feb 1664); ca 1647, ca 1650?, b 1657 Milford?; Newtown, LI
LAWRENCE, William (1623-1680) & 2/wf Elizabeth SMITH, m/2 Philip CARTERET 1681?, m/3 Richard TOWNSLEY; m lic 4 Mar 1664/5; ?Smithtown, LI/Flushing, LI
LAWRENCE, William & Annetje/Anna EDSALL; 1672; Newtown, LI/Bergen Co., NJ
LAWRENCE, William (-1719/20) & Deborah SMITH; 1 Jun 1680; Flushing, LI
LAWRENCE, William (-1732) & 2/wf Elizabeth (SCUDDER) ALBURTES, w John; by 1701?; Newtown, LI
LAWRENCE, _?_ & Abial/Abiel (THORNTON) PAGE (-1710), w Edward; b 1707, b 1701, aft 1693; ?Boston
LAWRENCE, _?_ & Rebecca DAVIS (1658-)
LAWRISON, John (-1717) & Mary _?_ ; Newtown, LI

LAWRESON, Thomas & Eleanor LOE/LOWE; 26 Aug 1691; Boston
LAWSON, Christopher & Elizabeth [JAMES]; ca 1639, b 1643; Boston/ME
LAWSON, Deodat & 1/wf Jane _?_ ; b 1682; Boston/Salem
LAWSON, Deodat/Theodat & 2/wf Deborah ALLEN (1674-); 6 May 1690; Boston/Scituate
LAWSON, John & Ann EYERS/AYRES; 28 Dec 1699; Boston
LAWSON, George & Martha _?_ ; b 1686; Boston
LAWTON, Daniel (-1719) & Rebecca _?_ ; ca 1662?; Portsmouth, RI
LAWTON, George (-1693) & Elizabeth [HAZARD]; b 1639?; Portsmouth, RI
LAWTON, George (-1697) & Naomi HUNT (1658-1721), m/2 Isaac LAWTON 1701; 17 Jan 1677, prob 1677/8; Portsmouth, RI
LAWTON, George & Mary [DENNIS] (1673-); b 1694; Tiverton, RI
LAWTON, Isaac (1650-1732) & 1/wf Mary [SISSON] (-1674); Portsmouth, RI
LAWTON, Isaac (1650-1732) & 2/wf Elizabeth TALLMAN (ca 1654-1701); 3 Mar 1673/4; Portsmouth, RI
LAWTON, James & Abigail LAMB (1670-1696); 9 Nov 1693, 3 Nov 1693; Suffield, CT
LAWTON, James & Faith NEWELL; 3 Apr 1699; Suffield, CT
LAWTON/LEIGHTON, John (see John LEIGHTON/LAYTON) & Joanna (_?_) BOYER MUN-NINGS, w Simon, w George; 21 Sep 1659; Boston
LAWTON, John (-1690, Suffield, CT) & Benedicta _?_ (-1692, ae 57); b 1662, ca 1660?; Ipswich/Suffield, CT
LAWTON, John (-1678) & Mary [BOOMER], m/2 Gideon FREEBORN 1678; ca 1670/5; Portsmouth, RI
LAWTON, John/Josiah & Sarah CONKLIN; 28 Jul 1680, b 1681; Southampton
LAWTON, Robert (-1706) & Mary WODELL/WADDELL/WARDELL (-1731, [1732]); 16 Feb 1680/1; Portsmouth, RI
LAWTON, Thomas (-1681) & 1/wf _?_ ; ca 1637; Portsmouth, RI
LAWTON, Thomas (-1681) & 2/wf Grace (PARSONS) [BAILEY], w William; b 1674?, b 20 Apr 1677; Portsmouth, RI
LAWTON, _?_ & Sarah (DIX) BROWN, w Edward; aft 25 Apr 1655; Portsmouth, RI
LAY, Edward (1608-1692) & Martha _?_ (-1682+); Portsmouth, RI/etc.
LAY, Edward (?1666-1758) & Marah/Mary _?_ (?1679-1761); b 1702, b 1701?, ca 1695; Lyme, CT
LAY, John[1] (-1695) & 1/wf _?_ ; in Eng, b 1633; Lyme, CT
LAY/LARY, John, Jr. (1633-1696) & Sarah _?_ (-1702); ?6Nov 1659, b 1664(5?); Lyme, CT/ Killingworth, CT
LAY, John[1] (-1695) & 2/wf Abigail _?_ (-1686); b 1670?; Lyme, CT
LAY, John[2] (1655-1712) & Joanna [SMITH/QUARLES?], m/2 John COLT; 26 May 1686; Lyme, CT
LAY/LEE?, Lewis & Jane JERMAN; 19 Dec 1700; Boston
LAY, Robert (1617-1682) & Sarah (FENNER) TULLY (1615-1676, ae ca 59), w John; Dec 1647; Saybrook, CT
LAY, Robert (1654-) & Mary STANTON (1660-); 22 Jan 1679, 1679/80; Saybrook, CT
LAY, William & Mary HOWEN; 11 Jan 1689; Boston
LAY?/LEE?, _?_ & Mary _?_ ; b 1661; Salem
LAYDON, James & Elizabeth _?_ ; b 1668(9?); Boston
LITON/LEIGHTON?, Ezekiel & Rebecca WOODMAN (1663-); 23 Mar 1686, 1685/6; Rowley
LEIGHTON, John & _?_ ; b 1643?; Kittery, ME
LEIGHTON, John & Joanna (_?_) BOYER MULLINGS/MUNNINGS, w Simon, w George; 1 Sep 1659; Kittery, ME
LEIGHTON, John & Martha BOOTH (1645-); 2 Oct 1663; Saco, ME/Kittery, ME
LAYTON, John & _?_ ; b 1677; Windsor, CT
LEIGHTON, John (1661-1724), Kittery & Oner/Honor LANGTON (-1737, ae 73), Portsmouth; 13 Jun 1686; Portsmouth, NH
LAITON, John (see LAUGHTON) & Parnall KERTLAND/KIRKLAND/KIRTLAND, w Nathaniel; 31 Oct 1687; Lynn/Ipswich
LIGHTON, John & Martha CHENEY, m/2 John ROGERS 1702; 4 Jun 1691; Rowley
LEIGHTON, John & Sarah [? CROMWELL]; by 1697?; Dover, NH
LEIGHTON/LIGHTON, Richard (-1682) & Mary _?_ ; 14 Nov 1650; Rowley

LEIGHTON, Thomas (1604, 1605?, 1602?-1672) & Joanna/[?Hannah **SILSBY**] (-1704, ae 86), m/2 Job **CLEMENTS** 1673); b 1643; Dover, NH

LAYTON, Thomas (-1677?) & Elizabeth [**NUTTER**] (-1674?); Dover, NH

LAYTON, Thomas (-1677?) & 2/wf Elizabeth **KIRTLAND**; 31 Oct 1687

LEIGHTON, William (-1666) & Catherine [**FROST**] (1637-1715), m/2 Joseph **HAMMOND** ?1670; ca 1655, 1656?; Kittery, ME

LEIGHTON, _?_ & Mary _?_, m/2 John **HUNDING**; by 23 Sep 1682

LEACH, David (-1657) & Hannah [**WHITMAN**]; b 1693; Bridgewater

LEACH, Giles (-1705+) & Anne **MOAKES**/[**NOKES**]; 30 Jan 1656, prob 1656/7; Weymouth

LEACH, James (-1697) & 1/wf Jane [**TURPIN**] **MUCHMORE**, w Walter (see below); b 1652; Portsmouth, NH

LEACH, James (-1697) & 2/wf Jane (**TURBIN**) **MINCHMORE/MUCHEMORE**, w Walter (see above); ca 1654?; Portsmouth, NH

LEACH, James (1654-1726, Windham, CT) & ?2/wf Mary _?_/?Sarah **CHURCHWELL?** (-1795); b 1709, b 1701?; Portsmouth/Windham, CT

LEACH, John, Sr. (1655)

LEACH, John (-1662?) & 1/wf [Sarah **FULLER?**] (wrong) (?1629-1681±); b 1648, 1643, b 1643?; Salem

LEACH, John (-1698) & 2/wf Sarah [**WALDRON**] (1662-), m/2 Timothy **GOODWIN** 1689; 15 Dec 1683 Marblehead; Salem

LEACH, John (1647?, bpt 1648-) & Elizabeth **FLINT** (1650-); 22 May 1667, 20 May; Salem

LEACH, John & Mary [?**EDWARDS**]; b 1680?, b 1690?; Salem

LEACH, John & Elizabeth _?_; b 1687; Boston

LEACH, John & Mary [**CROCUM**]; b 1687; Boston

LEACH, John (1665-1743?) & Alice _?_; b 1695; Bridgewater

LEACH, Lawrence (?1580, ?1577-1662, ae 85) & Elizabeth _?_ (-1674); in Eng, b 1605; Salem

LEACH, Peter & Hannah _?_; b 1694; Boston

LEACH, Richard (-1687) & [Sarah **FULLER**]; b 1645; Salem

LEACH, Robert (1605-1688) & 1/wf Mary _?_ (-1673); b 1639; Charlestown

LEACH, Robert (-1674) & 2/wf Alice _?_ (-1691), m/2 Robert **ELWELL** 1676; b 1665, b 1655?; Gloucester/Manchester

LECH, Robert & Sarah _?_; 1678; Manchester

LEACH, Robert & Hannah _?_; b 1685; Manchester

LECH, Samuel (1655-) & 1/wf Arabella [**NORMAN**] (-1681), w John **BALDEN**; b 1678; Manchester

LEACH, Samuel & Hannah (**NORMAN**) **BALDWIN** (no); b 1682; Manchester

LEACH, Samuel (1677-1731/2); & 1/wf Ginger **PORTER** (1679-1706); 25 Sep 1699; Salem

LEACH, Samuel (1662-) & Mary [**BYRAM**]; b 1704, b 1701?; Bridgewater

LEACH, Seth & Mary [**WHITMAN**]; b 1701?; Bridgewater

LEACH, Thomas (1652-1732) & Abigail **HAUGHTON**] (-1684); b 1679?; New London, CT

LEACH, Thomas & 2/wf Mary [**MINOR**] (1664-); ca 1688?, 2 ch bpt 1692; New London, CT

LEADBETTER, Henry (1635-1722) & 1/wf Sarah [**TOLMAN**] (-1688+); 18 Mar 1658/9; Dorchester

LEADBITTER, Henry (1635-1722) & 2/wf Relief (**HOLLAND**) (**DOWSE**) **FOSTER** (1650-1743), w John, w Timothy; 9 Mar 1691/2; Dorchester

LEADER, George & _?_; b 1651?; Berwick, ME

LEADER, John & Abigail [**WILLIS?**] (1633?-), m/2 Thomas **BILL** 1658+; b 1652; Boston

LEADER, Richard (1609-1661) & _?_ [?**ALDERSEY**]; by 1640?; Lynn

LEADER, Thomas (-1663) & 1/wf Rebecca _?_ (-16 Dec 1653); b 1631); Dedham/Boston

LEADER, Thomas (-1663) & 2/wf Susanna [**HABORNE/HEYBORNE**] (-1657), w George; Boston

LEADER, Thomas (-1663) & 3/wf Alice _?_ (-1663+); Boston

LEADER, _?_ & 2/wf _?_; b May 1658

LEAGER, Jacob (1603-1663) & 1/wf Elizabeth **GLAMFIELD** (-living 20 Mar 1635/6); Belstead, Eng, 15 Oct 1628

LEAGER, Jacob (1603-1663) & 2/wf Elizabeth **GREENE**, w John; m lic 30 Sep 1637 in Eng; Dorchester

LEAGER, Jacob (1603-1663) & 3/wf Ann [**BLAKE**] (1618-1681), m/2 [?William] **HALLOWELL** bef 5 Sep 1699; ca 1650; Dorchester/Boston

LEAR, Hugh & Mary [**SAVAGE**], m/2 Peter **WELLS** by 1694; Portsmouth, NH

LEAR, Tobias (1632-1677?) & Elizabeth (SHIRBURNE) LANGDON (1635-), w Tobias, m/3 Richard MARTAIN 1684?; aft 27 Jul 1664; Portsmouth, NH?

LEARNED, Benoni (1657-1738) & 1/wf Mary FANNING (1662-1688); 10 Jun 1680; Sherborn

LEARNED, Benoni (1657-1738) & 2/wf Sarah [WRIGHT] (1664-1737); b 1690; Sherborn

LEARNED, Isaac (?1624-1657) & Mary STEARNS (1626-1663), m/2 John BURGE 1662; 9 Jul 1646; Woburn/Chelmsford

LEARNED, Isaac (1655-1737) & Sarah BIGALOW/BIGELOW (1659-1702+); 23 Jul 1679; Sherborn

LEARNED, William[1] (-1646) & 1/wf Judith _?_ ; b 1607?; Charlestown/Woburn

LEARNED, William[1] (-1646) & 2/wf Jane/Sarah _?_ (-1661 Malden, 24 Jan 1600); aft 1632; Charlestown/Woburn

LEATH/HEATH, Francis (-1733) & Mary _?_ (-1737?, Woburn?); b 1686; Beverly/?Woburn

LEETH, John & Hannah _?_ ; b 1654; Boston

LETHERLAND, William (-1684+) & [Margaret?] _?_ ; Boston

LETHERLAND, Zebulon/Zebron & Rachel _?_ (-1692); b 1670; Boston

LEATHERS, Benjamin & Deborah INGERSOLL; 1 Dec 1686; ?N. Yarmouth, ME

LEATHERS, Edward[1] (1639-) & _?_ [HEARD]/[JONES/NUTE?]; by 1675; Durham, NH

LEATHERS, Edward & 2/wf Mary _?_ (1660?-); aft 1694; Oyster River, NH

LEATHERS, Edward & Christian [?RAND]

LEATHERS, Richard & Susanna _?_ ; b 1690, b 1687; Manchester/Boston

LEATHERS, William[2] & Abigail [WILLEY]; b 1701, bef 24 Jun 1701, by 1702; Oyster River, NH

LEAVENS, James (1679-) & Mary CHAMBERLAIN (1676-); 21 Nov 1699; Woodstock, CT

LEAVENS, John & 1/wf Elizabeth _?_ (-1638); in Eng?, b 9 Mar 1632; Roxbury

LEVINS, John (-1648?) & 2/wf Rachel WRIGHT; 5 Jul 1639; Roxbury

LEAVINS, John (1640-1696) & 1/wf Hannah/?Sarah WOODS (-1666?); 7 Jun 1665; Roxbury

LEAVENS, John (1640-1696) & 2/wf Elizabeth PRESTON, m/2 Peter ASPINWALL 1699; 23 Nov 1674; New Haven, CT/Roxbury, MA/Woodstock, CT

LEAVENSWORTH, John (-1702) & Mary BROWN; 21 Aug 1694; Boston

LEAVENWORTH, Thomas (-1683) & Grace _?_ (-ca 1715?), m/2 David JENKINS bef 1688; b 1673; Stratford, CT/Boston/Woodbury, CT

LEAVENWORTH, Thomas (1673-1754) & Mary [DORMAN] (1680-1768); ca 1698; Stratford, CT

LEAVER, Thomas (-1683) & Mary BRADLEY (-1684), ?w John; 1 Sep 1643; Rowley

LEAVER, Thomas (1641-) & Damaris BALLEY/BAILEY (1648-); 8 May 1672; Rowley

LEVET, Aretas/Aratus (1646-1739) & Ruth SLEEPER (1650-1726); Aug 1678, 1 Aug 1678; Hampton, NH

LEVET, Hezron (-1712) & Martha TAYLOR (1647±-); 25 Sep 1667; Hampton, NH

LEAVITT, Israel (1648-1696) & Lydia JACKSON (1658-), m/2 Preserved HALL 1699; Plymouth, 10 Jan 1676/7, 10? Jun; Hingham

LEVET, James (1652-1718) & Sarah (ELLINS) PARTRIDGE, w Nehemiah; ca 1692, aft 18 Feb 1690/1, bef 4 Jan 1691/2, no issue; Hampton, NH/Portsmouth, NH

LAVITT, John (-1691, ae 83) & 1/wf Mary? _?_ (-4 Jul 1646); b 1637; Dorchester/Hingham

LEAVITT, John (1608-10 Nov 1691) & 2/wf Sarah GILMAN (1622-1700); 16 Dec 1646, 15 Dec 1646, 6? Dec; Hingham/Dorchester

LEAVITT, John (1637?-1673?) & Bathsheba HOBART (1640-1724, m/2 Joseph TURNER 1674; 27 Jun 1664; Hingham

LEAVITT, John (1670-) & Sarah HOBBS (1669-1701); 30 Dec 1691; Hampton, NH

LEAVITT, Josiah (1653-1708) & Margaret JOHNSON (1659-1739?); 20 Oct 1676; Hingham

LEAVITT, Moses (1650-1730) & Dorothy DUDLEY; 26 Oct 1681; Exeter, NH

LEAVITT, Moses (1674-) & Mary CARR; 11 Dec 1700; Hampton, NH

LEAVITT, Nehemiah (1656, 1655/6-1715) & Alice (CARTEE) GILMAN, w Daniel; ca 1684?, b 1693; Hingham

LEAVITT, Samuel (1641-1707) & [Mary ROBINSON]; b 1665; Exeter, NH

LEVET, Thomas (1616-1696) & Isabella (BLAND) ASTON/AUSTIN (±1612-1699/1700, 1698/9?), w Francis; b 1644; Hampton, NH

LEBARON/LeBARON, Francis (1668-1704) & Mary WILDER (1668-), m/2 Return WAITE, Jr. 1707; 6 Sep 1695; Plymouth

LeBLOND/LeBLOUD, James & Ann [WINSLOW?]/Anna [GRAY]?; b 1690; Boston

LECHFORD, Thomas (-1648?, 1645?) & Elizabeth _?_ , m/2 Samuel WILBUR 1645, m/3 Henry BISHOP 1657; b 1645?; Boston

LECOCKE?/LECOCK/?LEACOCK, _?_ & Abigail MOULTON (1666-1705); Exeter, NH/Hampton, NH

LECODY/LeCODY, Philip & Martha _?_; b 1695; Beverly

LEE, Abraham (-1689) & Esther (WALDRON) ELKINS, w Nathaniel, m/3 John JOSE 1691?, m/4 Joshua BARNES by 1695; 21 Jun 1686; Dover, NH

LEE, David (1674-) & 1/wf Lydia STRONG (1675-1718); 5 Sep 1695; Northampton/Coventry, CT

LEE/LEES, Edward (-1727) & 1/wf Elizabeth WRIGHT (1653-1685±); 7 Nov 1676; Saybrook, CT/Guilford, CT

LEE, Edward (-1727) & 2/wf Abigail [STEVENS] (1666-1727); b 1689; Guilford, CT

LEE, Henry (-1675) & Mary _?_ (-1690, 1691), m/2 John WEST 1675; b 1657; Boston/Manchester

LEE, John (-1671) & [Anna/Joanna HUNGERFORD]; b 1639; Ipswich

LEE, John (1620-1690) & Mary [HART] (?1631-1710), m/2 Jedediah STRONG 1692; 1658; Hartford/Farmington, CT

LEE, John & _?_ [WHITE?]; b 1676; Sheepscot, ME/Scituate

LEIGH, John (-1692?) & Rebecca [LONG], m/2 Henry POWNELL 1692?; b 1679; Charlestown

LEE, John (1657-1711) & 1/wf Sarah PIXLEY (1665-15 Jul 1683); 9 Dec 1680; Westfield

LEE, John (1659-) & Elizabeth LOOMIS (1664-); 27 Dec 1682; Farmington, CT/Guilford, CT

LEE, John (1661-1744) & 1/wf Sarah [PARSONS] (1663-14 Jan 1687/8); b 1685; Manchester

LEE, John (1657-1711) & 2/wf Sarah _?_; b 1687; Westfield

LEE, John & Elizabeth [CRAMPTON/SCRANTON?]; b 1688; Killingworth, CT/E. Guilford, CT

LEE, John (1661-1744) & 2/wf Sarah [?WARREN]; 1690?; Manchester

LEE, John (1670-) & Elizabeth SMITH, m/2 John BAILEY; 8 Feb 1692; Lyme, CT

LEE, John & ?Johanna/?Mary _?_, m/2 _?_ GREEN; b 1697(8?); Ipswich

LEE, Joseph (-1716) & 1/wf Mary WOODIES/WOODHOUSE; 27 Nov 1678; Concord/Ipswich

LEE, Joseph (-1716) & 2/wf Mary (MILES) WIGLEY, (-1708), w Edmund; 15 Nov 1697; Concord

LEE, Joshua, Boston & Mary (BEAL) ENGS/(?INGS), Boston, w Samuel; 14 Dec 1688; Charlestown

LEE, Lewis & _?_

LEE, Nathaniel (1663-) & Abigail [WARNER] (ca 1673-); b 1698; Westfield

LEE, Richard (1643-) & [Sarah] [?COY]; b 1671; Ipswich

LEE, Richard & Joanna MANNING, m/2 Thomas TUCKER 1698; 18 Jul 1691; Marblehead

LEE, Robert (related to John ATWOOD who m Ann) & Mary [ATWOOD] (-1681); b 1635; Plymouth

LEE/LEIGH?, Rev. Samuel (1623-1691) & Martha? _?_; in Eng, ca 1648?; Boston/Bristol, RI

LEE, Samuel, Virginia & Elizabeth BOWLAND/?ROWLAND; 2 Aug 1655; Boston

LEE, Samuel (1640-1676, ae 36, Malden) & Mercy CALL, m/2 John ALLEN 1677; 4 Nov 1662, 4 Dec 1662; Malden

LEE, Samuel & 1/wf Rebecca MASTERS (?1675-1723?); 8 Feb 1692; Manchester

LEE, Samuel & Mary _?_; b 1696; Watertown/Killingly, CT

LEE, Simon & Theodora (_?_) BELCHER, w John, m/3 William DARNTON 1700, m/4 Francis POMEROY; 9 Dec 1698; Boston

LEE, Stephen (1669-1753) & Elizabeth ROYCE, Wallingford, CT; 1 Oct 1690; Farmington, CT

LEE, Stephen & Elizabeth WOODWARD; 23 Dec 1691; Westfield/Lebanon, CT

LEE, Thomas (1579-1662) & Alice _?_; Ipswich

LEE, Thomas (-1645 at sea) & Phebe [BROWN] (1620-1664), m/2 Greenfield LARRABEE by 1648; m/3 James CORNISH by 1661; in Eng, ca 1632/4, ca 1639; Saybrook, CT/Lyme, CT

LEE, Thomas (1644-1705) & 1/wf Sarah (KIRTLAND/KIRKLAND) (not DAVIS, w John) (-1676); b 1670, b 1672, b 1674; Lyme, CT

LEE, Thomas & Ann _?_ (-1676); Lyme?

LEE, Thomas (-1705) & 2/wf Mary DeWOLF (1656-1724), m/2 Matthew GRISWOLD; 13 Jul 1676?; Lyme, CT

LEE, Thomas (1672-) & Elizabeth GRAHAM; 24 Jan 1695; Lyme, CT

LEE, Thomas & Anna/Hannah _?_; b 1698; Ipswich

LEE, Thomas (1671-) & 1/wf Lydia [BENTON] (-1700±); ca 1699; ?Hartford/?Farmington

LEE, Thomas (1673-1766) & Deborah [FLINT] (1672-1763); b 1701; Boston

LEE, Thomas (1672-) & Elizabeth [GRAHAM], Hartford; b 1701?; ?Hartford

LEE, Walter (-1718, 1719?) & 1/wf Mary _?_ (-1695/6); b 1657; Windsor, CT/Northampton/Westfield

LEE, William & _?_ [MARVIN]; Hempstead, LI

LEE/LEES, William & Margaret [RUSCO]; b 1682; Norwalk, CT
LEE, _?_ & Martha MELLOWES (1653/4-); Boston
LEEDS, Benjamin (-1718, ae 80) & 1/wf Mary BRINSMADE (-1692); 17 Sep 1667; Dorchester
LEEDS, Benjamin (-1718, ae 80) & 2/wf Abigail KNIGHT (-1712); 11 Aug 1696; Dorchester
LEEDS, John & Abigail _?_ ; ca 1669?, b 1676; Ipswich
LEEDS, John (1641-1697?) & Elizabeth LATHAM; 25 Jun 1678; New London
LEEDS, John (-1702+) & Mary _?_ ; b 1693; Stamford, CT
LEEDS, Joseph (1637-1715) & Miriam COOK (1642-1720); 8 Nov 1661; Dorchester/Roxbury
LEEDS, Joseph (1665-1747) & Mary [WEEKS] (1668-); b 1694, ca 1689; Dorchester
LEEDS, Richard (1605-1693, ca 1698?, ae 88) & Joan _?_ (1614-1682/3); in Eng, b 1637; Dorchester
LEEKE, Ebenezer (1647-1734) & Hannah [BAKER] (1650-); b 1674; New Haven/Easthampton, LI
LEEKE, Philip (-1676) & Joanna _?_ ; b 1646; New Haven
LEEK, Thomas (1648-1719) & Sarah [HITCHESON] (-1729); b 1679; New Haven
LEEK, [Philip] (1646-) & [Elizabeth DAYTON]; Southampton
LEEKEY/LECKY/LACKEY, Richard, Boston & Ann/Anne GREENFIELD/GRANDFIELD, Boston; 4 Jul 1687; Watertown/Boston
LEETE, Andrew (1643-1702) & Elizabeth JORDAN (-1701); 1 Jun 1669; Guilford, CT
LEETE, Caleb (?1673-1760) & Mary HUBBARD (1676-); 4 Nov 1697; Guilford, CT
LEETE, John (1639-1692) & Mary CHITTENDEN (1647-1712); 4 Oct 1670; Guilford, CT
LEETE, John (1674-1730) & 1/wf Sarah [ALLEN] (1676-1712); b 1698/9; Guilford, CT
LEETE, William[1] (?1611-1683) & 1/wf Anne/?Anna PAINE (1621-1668); Hail Weston, Huntingdon, Eng, 1 Aug 1636; Guilford, CT
LEETE, William[1] (-1683) & 2/wf Sarah (_?_) [ROTHERFORD] (-1673), w Henry; 7 Apr 1670; New Haven
LEETE, William (-1687) & Mary [FENN], m/2 Stephen BRADLEY 1687+; b 1672; Milford, CT/Guilford, CT
LEETE, William[1] (-1683) & 3/wf Mary (_?_) (NEWMAN) STREET (-1683), w Francis, w Nicholas; aft 22 Apr 1674; New Haven
LEETE, William & Hannah STONE (1678-); 12 Feb 1699; ?Guilford, CT
LEAPINGWELL/LAPPINWALL, Michael (?1603-1687) & Isabel _?_ (-1671); b 1638; Cambridge/Woburn
LEFFINGWELL, Nathaniel (?1656, ?1646-1697) & Mary SMITH (-1714+); 8 Jun 1682; Norwich, CT
LEFFINGWELL, Samuel (-1691) & Hannah DICKINSON (1670-1691); 16 Nov 1687; Norwich, CT
LEFFINGWELL, Thomas[1] (?1622/4-1714) & Mary [WHITE]? (-1711); b 1648?; Saybrook, CT
LEFFINGWELL, Thomas[2] (1649-1732) & Mary BUSHNELL (1654/5-1745; Sep 1672; Norwich, CT
LEPINGWELL, Thomas (1649-1752) & 1/wf Sarah KNIGHT (-Aug 1691); 11 May 1675; Woburn
LEPINGWELL, Thomas (1649-1752) & 2/wf Hannah DUNTLIN (-1703); 15 Jan 1691/[2]; Woburn
LEFFINGWELL, Thomas (1674-1733) & Lydia TRACEY (1677-1757); 31 Mar 1698; Norwich, CT
LEGARE, Francis (ca 1636-1711) & 1/wf Anne [LANCOIS] (-living in 1682); b 1674
LEGARE, Francis (ca 1636-1711) & 2/wf Elizabeth [KIRTLAND] (1664-); ca 1688; Hingham
LEGARE, Solomon (1674-1760) & 1/wf Sarah _?_ ; b 1693; Boston
LEGG, John (-1674) & Elizabeth _?_ ; b 31 Dec 1639; Salem/Marblehead
LEGG, John (ae 64 in 1709) & Elizabeth [PEACH?]; b 1678; Salem/Marblehead
LEGG, Samuel & Deliverance _?_ ; b 1669(70?); Boston
LEGROE, John (-1735+) & Martha DUTCH (-1735+); 13 Apr 1699; Salem
LeGROS/LAGRO/LAGROE/GROVE/GROVES, Nicholas & Hannah [BLACK/SALLOWS]; b 1672, 16 May 1671; Beverly
LEALAND, Ebenezer (1657-1742) & 1/wf Deborah _?_ (-1691/2); b 1679; Sherborn
LEALAND, Ebenezer (1657-1742) & 2/wf Patience [RICE] (1671-1720); b 1695; Sherborn
LELAND, Eleazer (1660-1703) & Sarah _?_, m/2 Eleazer BULLARD 1705; 13 Jul [1690?], no issue, bef 4 Oct 1691; Sherborn/Medfield
LEALAND, Henry (?1625-1680) & Margaret [?BABCOCK] (sis of Robert); b 1653; Dorchester/Medfield
LEALAND, Hopestill (1655-1729) & 1/wf Abigail HILL (-1689); 5 Nov 1678; Medfield
LEALAND, Hopestill (1655-1729) & 2/wf Patience HOLBROOK (-1740), dau Thomas; 2 Feb 1691; Sherborn

LELLOCK/KELLOGG, Joseph & Joanna __?_; b 1658; Boston
LEMMON/LEMON, Joseph (?1662-1709) & Mary BRADLEY, m/2 Samuel PHIPPS ca 1717; 12 Jun 1690; Charlestown
LEMAN, Nathaniel (1677-) & 1/wf Thankful HENSHA/HENSHAW; 27 Jan 1699/1700; Dorchester
LEMMON, Robert (-1667) & Mary __?_, m/2 Philip CROMWELL 1674; b 1639; Salem
LEMAN, Samuel (-1699?) & Mary LONGLEY (-1714); 30 Jul 1666; Charlestown/Groton
LEAMAN, Samuel (1667-) & Margaret HUTCHINSON (1670-), m/2 John WOODWARD 1700; 20 Feb 1689/90; Charlestown/Reading
LENTHAL/LENTHALL, Robert & Cicely __?_ (-1650?); 1636?, by 1636; Weymouth/Hingham
LENTHAL, Robert & 2/wf Margaret __?_; aft 1650; Weymouth
LEONARD, Abel (1656-1690) & Mary REMINGTON, m/2 Samuel BEDORTHA 1691; 4 Mar 1686/7; Springfield
LEONARD, Benjamin & Sarah THRESHER; 15 Jan 1678/9; Taunton
LEONARD, Benjamin (1654-1724) & Sarah SCOTT (1663-1751); 9 Feb 1679/80; Springfield
LEONARD, George (1671-1716) & Anna TISDALE (-1733), m/2 Nathaniel THOMAS; 4 Jul 1695; Taunton
LEONARD, Henry (ae 37 in 1655, ae 40 in 1660) & Mary __?_; b 1645; Lynn/Topsfield/Boxford/Monmouth Co., NJ
LEONARD, Isaac (ca 1650-ca 1717) & Deliverance __?_; b 1680; Bridgewater
LEONARD, Isaac & Mary BAILEY; b 1701?, 16 Apr 1701; Bridgewater?
LEONARD, Jacob (1647-1717) & 1/wf Phoebe ?CHANDLER (-1678); b 1670; Weymouth?
LEONARD, Jacob (1647-1717) & 2/wf Susanna [KING] (1659-); b 1680; Weymouth/Bridgewater
LEONARD, James (?1621-1691) & 1/wf __?_ MARTIN; ca 1640; Lynn/Braintree/Taunton
LEONARD, James (-1691) & 2/wf Margaret __?_ (-1701?); b 1662? or later?; Taunton
LEONARD, James, Jr. (1643-1726) & 1/wf Hannah __?_ (-1674); b 1668; Braintree/Taunton
LEONARD, James, Jr. (1643-1726) & 2/wf Lydia CULIPHER/GULLIVER (1657-1705), Milton; 29 Oct 1675; Taunton
LEONARD, James & Hannah (WALLEY) STONE (1666-1725); 28 Feb 1698/9; Taunton
LEONARD, John (-1676) & Sarah HEALD, m/2 Benjamin PARSONS 1677, m/3 Peter TILTON 1690; 12 Nov 1640; Springfield
LEONARD, John (1643-1699) & Sarah __?_ (not CHANDLER); ca 1676; Bridgewater
LEONARD, John (1668-) & Mary [KING] (1668-); ca 1690-3?; Taunton
LEONARD, John & Elizabeth (ALMY) [MORRIS], w John; b 1701?; Boxford
LEONARD, Joseph (1644-1716) & 1/wf Mary FELLOWS (-1680/1); 24 Mar 1671, 1671/2; Springfield
LEONARD, Joseph (1655-1692) & Mary BLAKE, m/2 Joseph WILLIS by 1699; 15 Dec 1679; Milton/Taunton
LEONARD, Joseph (1644-1716) & 2/wf Elizabeth LYNIAN (-1689); 29 Mar 1683; Springfield
LEONARD, Joseph (1644-1716) & 3/wf Ann (FORD) NEWBERRY (-1690/1), w Thomas; 16 Jan 1689/90; Springfield
LEONARD, Joseph (1644-1716) & 4/wf Rebecca DUMBLETON (-1693/4); 2 Mar 1693, 1692/3; Springfield
LEONARD, Joseph (1644-1716) & 5/wf Margaret [THOMPSON] (-1711), w John; 1695; Springfield
LEONARD, Joseph & Martha [ORCUTT]; b 1696; Bridgewater
LEONARD, Josiah (1658-1688/9) & Sarah DUMBLETON (1655-), m/2 Thomas ROOT 1692/3; 19 Dec 1678; Springfield
LEONARD, Josiah & 1/wf Marjoram WASHBURN; 1 Nov 1699, 2 Nov 1699; Bridgewater
LEONARD, Philip (-1708) & Lydia __?_ (-1707); b 1678; Marshfield/Duxbury
LEONARD, Rice (Richard wrong) (-1700, Taunton) & [Mary?] __?_ (-1700); 27 Oct 1651; Rehoboth
LEONARD, Samuel (1645-) & Sarah BROOKS; b 1668; Boxford/NJ
LEONARD, Samuel (1643-1720) & 1/wf Abigail [WOOD?/ATWOOD?] (-1698±); b 1676; Plymouth
LEONARD, Samuel & Phebe __?_; b 1682; Bridgewater
LEONARD, Samuel & Mary FREEMAN (1655-), m/2 Richard WEEKS 1724 Attleboro; 4 Aug 1690, 7 Aug; Rehoboth
LEONARD, Samuel (1643-1720) & 2/wf Deborah __?_; b 1703, b 1701?; Preston, CT

LEONARD, Solomon (?1610-1686) & Mary [CHANDLER] (-bef 1 May 1671); b 1640, b 1643?; Duxbury/Bridgewater
LEONARD, Solomon[2] & Mary _?_ ; b 1680; Bridgewater
LEONARD, Thomas (1641-1713) & Mary WATSON (ca 1642-1723, ae 81); 21 Aug 1662; Plymouth
LEONARD, Thomas (1666-) & Johanah/Joanna PITCHER, of Milton; 1 Dec 1699; Taunton
LEONARD, Uriah (1662-) & Elizabeth CASWELL (1665-); 1 Jun 1685; Taunton
LERVEY/LERVAY, Peter & Mary _?_ ; b 1684; Wenham
LESTER, Andrew[1] (-1669) & 1/wf Barbara _?_ (-1653/[4]); b 1642; Gloucester/New London
LESTER, Andrew[1] (-1669) & 2/wf Joanna [WILLEY?] [HEMPSTEAD], w Robert; ?ca Jun 1653, ?aft Jun 1653; New London, CT
LESTER, Andrew[1] (-1669) & 3/wf Ann/Anna/Hannah (?BROOKS) [FOX] (-1692), w Thomas, m/3 Isaac WILLEY? 1670/72?; ca 1661; New London, CT
LESTER, Andrew[2] (1644-1708) & 1/wf _?_ [CLARK], dau Nicholas; ?Groton, CT/Hartford, CT
LESTER, Andrew[2] (1644-1708?) & 2/wf Hannah [BRADLEY]; ca 1676; ?New London, CT/Groton, CT
LESTER, Andrew (1674-) & 1/wf Lydia [BAILEY] (1673-), dau Thomas; ?ca 1695; New London, CT
LESTER, Benjamin (1666-) & Ann [STEDMAN] (1671/2-1712); ca Dec 1689; New London, CT
LESTER, Daniel (1642-1717) & Hannah FOX; 1 Oct 1668, 11 Aug 1669; New London, CT
LESTER, Joseph (1664-) & Katharine _?_ ; b 1693; New London, CT
LESTER, Thomas & Dorcas [GILDERSLEEVE] (ca 1663-), dau Richard, Jr.; b 1691; Hempstead, LI
LESTER, Timothy (1662-) & _?_ ; b 1693; ?Preston, CT
LETTICE/LETTIS, Thomas (-1682) & Anna/Anne _?_ (-1687); b 1671, b 1650, b 1639, b 1636; Plymouth
LEVERETT, Hudson (1640-1694) & 1/wf Sarah PAYTON (1643-7 Jun 1679); 20 Aug 1661; Boston
LEVERETT, Hudson (-1694) & 2/wf Elizabeth [GANNETT] TAY (-1714, Roxbury), Scituate, dau Matthew, w John; aft 7 Jun 1679; Boston?
LEVERIT, John (1616-1679) & 1/wf Hannah [HUDSON] (-1646, 1643+); ?18 Jun 1639, b Sep 1639; Boston
LEVERETT, John (1616-1679) & 2/wf Sarah [HOUGHTON] [SEDGWICK] (1629/31-1705), w William; 7 Sep 1647, 9? Sep, 1645?; Boston
LEVERET, John (1662-1724) & Margaret (ROGERS) BERRY (1664-1720), w Thomas; 25 Nov 1697; Boston/Cambridge
LEVERETT, Thomas (-1650) & Anne FITCH (-1656); Boston, Eng, 29 Oct 1610; Boston
LEVERICH, Caleb (-1717, ae 79) & Martha [SWAIN], w Francis; by 1663; Newtown, LI?
LEVERICH, Eleazer & Rebecca [WRIGHT], m/2 William FROST 1671?; 1662, div 22 Oct 1670; Huntington, LI/Oyster Bay, LI
LEVERICH, John (-bef 1705) & Hannah _?_ ; b 1696; Newtown, LI
LEVERICH, William (±1603-1677) & _?_ ; b 1638; Dover, NH/Sandwich, MA/Oyster Bay/etc.
LEVESTON/LEVESTONE/LAVISTONE/LEVISTONE?/LIVINGSTON?, John & Margaret ROSS (-1705); 12 Sep 1681; Billerica
LEWIS, Abraham & Rachel [BERRY]; ca 1700?; Portsmouth, NH
LEWIS, Barachiah (-1710) & Judith [WHITING/?WHITNEY] (1670-1747), m/2 Joseph ELLIS; b 1689; Roxbury/Dedham
LEWIS, Benjamin & Hannah [CURTIS] (1654/5-); ca 1671; Stratford, CT
LEWIS, Benjamin (1675-1726) & Margaret FOLLAND; 10 Feb 1696/7; Barnstable
LEWIS, Christopher & Grace _?_ ; b 1695; Malden
LEWIS, Daniel (-1718, ae 50) & Mary [MAXSON] (-1721+); b 1701; Westerly, RI
LEWIS, David & _?_ ; b 1683; Falmouth, MA
LEWIS, David (-1718, ae 50) & Elizabeth [BABCOCK] (-1716); b 1699; Westerly, RI
LEWIS, Ebenezer (-1709) & Elizabeth MERRIMAN (1660-), m/2 William FREDERICK; 2 Dec 1685; Wallingford, CT
LEWIS, Ebenezer & 1/wf Anna LOTHROP (1673-1715); - Apr 1691; Barnstable
LEWIS, Edward (?1601-1651) & Mary _?_ (1602-1658); b 1631, in Eng; Watertown
LEWIS, Edward (-1703) & Hannah COBB; 9 May 1661; Barnstable
LEWIS, Eleazer (1664?-) & Hannah [FULLER] (1668-); aft 27 Jul 1696; Plymouth
LEWIS, George[1] (-1663) & 1/wf Sarah [?JENKINS] (?sis of Edward); b 1623, in Eng; Lynn/Scituate/Hingham/?Plymouth/Barnstable

LEWIS, George (-1682) & _?_ ; b 1635?; Casco Bay/Falmouth, ME

LEWIS, George[2] (-1710) & Mary LUMBART (1637-); - Dec 1654, beginning of Dec; Barnstable

LEWIS, George[1] (-1663) & 2/wf Mary _?_ ; b 1663, b 1654?; Barnstable

LEWIS, George (1655-1683) & Elizabeth _?_ ; ca 1678; Barnstable

LEWIS, George & Elizabeth _?_ ; b 1685; Watertown

LEWIS, Isaac (?1644-1691) & Mary DAVIS (1663-), m/2 Thomas PRATT [1691?]; 25 Mar 1680; Charlestown/Boston/Malden/Lynn

LEWIS, Isaac (-1701) & Hannah _?_ ; 3 Dec 1700; Rehoboth

LEWIS, Israel (-1719, ae 49) & Jane/?Joanna [BABCOCK] (-1717, ae 50); b 1695; Westerly, RI/Exeter, RI

LEWIS, Jabez (1670-) & Experience HAMLIN (1668-); 20 Feb 1695; Barnstable

LEWIS, James (1631±-1713) & Sarah LANE (1637-); last of Oct 1655; Barnstable

LEWIS, James & Eleanor/Mary JOHNSON; 27 Mar 1679; Falmouth

LEWIS, James & Mary [MEEKINS] (1670-); b 1694; Farmington, CT/Hartford

LEWIS, James (1664-1748) & 1/wf Elizabeth LOTHROP; - Nov 1698; Barnstable

LEWIS, James (-1745) & Sarah [BABCOCK] (-1790+); by 1699; Westerly, RI

LEWIS, John & 1/wf Sarah MEAD/MEED (-1657); Tenterden, Kent, 21 Feb 1631/2; Scituate/Boston

LEWIS, John (-1657) & 1/wf Margaret _?_ (-1649); b 1638; Charlestown/Malden

LEWIS, John (-1676) & _?_ ; b 1645(?); New London, CT

LEWIS, John (-1659) & 2/wf Mary BROWN, m/2 John CUTLER; 10 Apr 1650; Malden

LEWIS, John & _?_ ; ca 1658?; Westerly, RI

LEWIS, John (1631-) & 1/wf Hannah MARSHALL; 17 Jun 1659; Lynn

LEWIS, John & Alice (MATTOCKS? no?) BISHOP, m/2 Abraham HOWE bef 1680, m/3 John HARRIS 1683+; 22 Nov 1659; Boston

LEWIS, John (1635-1685) & Hannah [?WHITCOMB] (-1714); b 1663; Lancaster/Dorchester

LEWIS, John (?1617-1701) & Elizabeth _?_ ; ca 1663?; Newcastle

LEWIS, John (-1677) & Eleanor [?REDDING]; b 20 Mar 1674; Casco Bay, ME

LEWIS, John (-1713) & Mary HUMPHREY; 16 Jun 1675; Hartford

LEWIS, John (1638-1676) & Margaret _?_ ; b 1676; Barnstable

LEWIS, John (-1717) & Elizabeth HUNTLEY; 24 May 1677; New London, CT/Waterbury, CT

LEWIS, John (1656-1715) & Hannah LINCOLN (-1715); 17 Nov 1682; Hingham

LEWIS, John (-1735) & Ann/?Anna _?_ (-1748); b 1683; Westerly, RI

LEWIS, John (1660-1711) & Elizabeth BREWER/BRUER; 18 Apr 1683; Lynn

LEWIS, John (1666-) & Elizabeth HUCHINS (1671-1741); 4 Jun 1695; Barnstable

LEWIS, John (1674-1708) & Martha (BROOKINGS) WAKEHAM, w John, m/3 Joseph RENDLE 1709; Jun 1699; Portsmouth, NH

LEWIS, John & Elizabeth (WALKER) KING, w Ralph, m/3 Joseph RENDLE 1709; m int 2 Sep 1699; Lynn

LEWIS, John & Ann (WHITING) EATON, w John, m/3 James HERRING; 4 Apr 1700; Dedham

LEWIS, Jonathan (?1658-1709) & 1/wf Jemima [WHITEHEAD]; ca 1683?, b 31 Dec 1683; Oyster Bay, LI/Huntington, LI

LEWIS, Jonathan (?1658-1709) & 2/wf Deliverance; b 1700?

LEWIS, Joseph (-1674) & Mary JONES, m/2 Obadiah JENKINS 1677; 13 Jun 1671; Swansea

LEWIS, Joseph (-1680) & Elizabeth CASE (?1658-1718), m/2 John TULLER 1684?; 30 Apr 1674; Windsor, CT

LEWIS, Joseph (1672-) & Hannah [JONES?] (-1760); 1700; Malden/Woburn/Wilmington

LEWIS, Jotham & ?Mary (LEWIS) [SKILLINGS] (-1732+), w Thomas, m/3 Henry WILKINS; aft 1676, b 1701?, ca 1719?, b 1682?, aft 1676, bef 1685; Portsmouth, NH

LEWIS, Nathaniel (1639, 1645?-1683) & Mary _?_ (-1674/5?); b 1673; Swansea

LEWIS, Nathaniel (1676-) & 1/wf Abigail ASHLEY (1681-); 25 Nov 1699; Farmington, CT/Hadley

LEWIS, Peter (ca 1644-) & [Grace DIAMOND]?; b 1669?; Kittery, ME/Salisbury, MA

LEWIS, Peter (?1669-1701) & 1/wf Lucy (CHADBOURNE) HICKS, w Michael; ca 1700?, aft 13 Jun 1688; Kittery, ME

LEWIS, Philip (1623-bef 1701) (cousin of John TUCK) & ?Mary/?Hannah [PHILBRICK?]/Mary? CASS?; ca 1654?, ca 1650/60?, ?2 Apr 1671; Dover, NH/Portsmouth, NH

LEWIS, Philip & _?_ ; Casco Bay

LEWIS, Philip (1646-) & [Sarah] ASHLEY (1648-); [ca 1670]; Farmington/Hartford

LEWIS, Philip & 2/wf Elizabeth _?_ ; b 1694; Fairfield

LEWIS, Richard & _?_ ; b 1673; Portsmouth, NH
LEWIS, Robert (1607-1643) & Elizabeth _?_ (1613-); in Eng, b 1635; Salem/Newbury
LEWIS/LUIST, Robert & Rebecca (JENNER) LYNDE, w Samuel; 6 Apr 1682; Charlestown/Boston
LEWIS, Samuel & Sarah DUTTON, m/2 Samuel DIX 1706; 3 Apr 1683; Billerica
LEWIS, Samuel (?1648-) & Elizabeth/Hannah? [JUDD?]/[ORTON] (1654-); b 1688; Farmington, CT
LEWIS, Samuel (1659-) & Prudence LEONARD (1670-); 10 Dec 1690; Barnstable
LEWIS, Samuel (-1739) & Joanna [?CRANDALL] (-1734+); ca 1695/1700?; Westerly, RI
LEWIS, Samuel (-1726) & Mary _?_ ; b 1701; Farmintqon, CT
LEWIS, Thomas (-1637/40) & 1/wf Elizabeth MARSHALL (survived her husb, living 1640); St. Shads, 29 Aug 1618; Saco, ME
LEWIS, Thomas (-1637/40) & Elizabeth _?_ (no); b 1624; Saco, ME
LEWIS, Thomas (-1709?) & 1/wf Mary DAVIS (-1687); 15 Jun 1653; Barnstable
LEWIS, Thomas (1633-1709, ae 76) & Hannah BAKER (-1717); 11 Nov 1659; Lynn/Bristol, RI/Swansea
LEWIS, Thomas & _?_ (not Mary JUDD), m/2 Thomas LOOMIS; b 1663; Northampton
LEWIS, Thomas (1656-) & Sarah BASSETT (1662-); ca 1686?, b 19 Jan 1691/2; Falmouth
LEWIS, Thomas (1663-1714) & Mary BREED/BREAD, of Lynn (1664-1737); 25 Oct 1686; in Middlesex Co., MA
LEWIS, Thomas & Sarah [PERCIVAL]; b 1687; ?Middleton, CT?/E. Haddam
LEWIS, Thomas & Elizabeth BROOKS; 10 Apr 1689; Swansea/Bristol, RI?
LEWIS, Thomas (ca 1654-1718) & Joan/Jane?/Joanna? _?_ (-1720?); b 1691, b 1686; Eastham/?Falmouth/?b 1689 Marblehead
LEWIS, Thomas & Experience HUCKINS/HUCKENS/HOPKINS (1675-); 28 Sep 1698, 1699; Barnstable
LEWIS, William (-1683) & Felix (COLLINS) (no) (-1681?, 1671?); Cardiff, Wales, 7 Feb 1618; Braintree/Cambridge/Hartford
LEWIS, William (-1671) & Amy/Anne [WELLD?/WELLS]; in Eng, b 1635; Lynn/Roxbury
LEWIS, William (-1690) & 1/wf Mary [HOPKINS]; ca 1644; Farmington, CT/Hadley
LEWIS, William (-1690) & 2/wf Mary CHEEVER (1640-1728), m/2 Thomas BULL 1692; 22 Nov 1671; Farmington, CT/Hadley
LEWIS, William (1656-1737) & Phebe [MORE/MOORE] (1669-); b 1697; Farmington/Hadley
LEWIS, _?_ & Sarah MOORE?; ca 1678?
LEWIS, _?_ & Sarah ERRINGTON; Cambridge
LEWYN/LUEN/LEWIN, John & Rebecca _?_, m/2 Samuel LAWRENCE 1682; b 1682; Charlewtown
L'HOMMEDIEN, Benjamin (-1748) & Patience SYLVESTER (-1749); b 1694; Shelter Isl., NY/Southold, LI
LIBBY, Anthony (?1649-1717/18) & Sarah [DRAKE] (1656-1716, aft 1723/4), ca 1682; Scarboro, ME/Portsmouth, NH/Falmouth, ME
LIBBY, Daniel (?1665,?1666-1735, 1736?) & Mary ASHTON (-1735+); 23 Feb 1687; ?Scarboro, ME/York Co, ME
LIBBY, Daniel (1678±-) & Elizabeth [KIRKE], m/2 or m/3 John MEADER; ca 1700?; Portsmouth, NH
LIBBY, David (?1657-1736?) & Eleanor _?_ (-1725+); ca 1680/3?; Scarboro, ME/Portsmouth, NH/Kittery, ME
LIBBY, Henry (1647, ca 1648-1732) & Honor [HINKSON] (-1724, ae 60); ?ca 1687; Scarboro, ME
LIBBY, James & Mary HANSON; 9 Jun 1698; Portsmouth, NH
LIBBY, John[1] (-1683) & 1/wf [?Judith] _?_ ; 27 Apr 1635, in Eng, b 1636, b 1637; Scarboro, ME
LIBBY, John[1] (-1683) & 2/wf Mary _?_ (-1686+), ?m/2 William GREEN; b 1663; Scarboro, ME
LIBBY, John[2] (1636-living 1719/20) & Agnes _?_ (-living 1717); b 1668, b 1669; Scarboro, ME/Portsmouth, NH
LIBBY, John (1665±-) & Eleanor KIRKE; 29 Dec 1692; ?Portsmouth, NH
LIBBY, Joseph (1670±-) & Rebecca _?_, ?m/2 Thomas MUZEET 1700; b 1693; Portsmouth, NH
LIBBY, Matthew (1663-) & Elizabeth [BROWN]; ca 1689; Scarboro, ME/Portsmouth, NH/Kittery, ME
LIBBY, Samuel & Sarah [WELLS] (no), m/2 Samuel WATERHOUSE; b 1697; Portsmouth, NH

LIDDEN, Edward (-1691) & Katherine [CHADBOURNE], m/2 James WEYMOUTH; by 1685?; Kittery, ME
LIDDEN, George (-1693) & Sarah _?_ (1640-); b 1660?; Kittery, ME
LIDGETT, Charles (1650-1698?) & 1/wf Bethia [SHRIMPTON]; ca 1676, ca 29 Apr 1676; Charlestown/Boston
LIDGETT, Charles (-1698?) & 2/wf Mary [HESTER] (-1719); b 1684(5?); Boston/London
LIDGETT, Peter (-1676) & Elizabeth [SCAMMON], m/2 John SAFFIN 1680; ca 1648; Boston
LIGHT, John & Dorothy (PIKE) PIERCE (-1714), w Joshua; 11 Sep 1674; Salisbury/NH
LIGHTFOOT, Francis (-1646) & Anne _?_ (-1646+), ?m/2 Daniel THURSTON 1648; b 1640; Lynn
LIGHTFOOT, John & Elizabeth SWASEY (1655-); - May 1680; Salem
LIGHTFOOT, John & Elizabeth FORTUNE; 17 Nov 1692; Marblehead
LIGHTFOOT, William (1632-) & [Mary?] [BARTOLL] (1642-); b 1669?; Marblehead
LIGHTFOOT, _?_ & Mary _?_ ; b 1699; Marblehead
LILLIBRIDGE, Thomas & 1/wf Mary [HOBSON]; ca 1695?; Newport, RI
LILLIBRIDGE, Thomas & 2/wf Sarah LEWIS; b 1703, b 1701?
LILLY, Edward (-1688/9) & Elizabeth _?_ (-1693+); b 1663; Boston
LILLY, George (-1691) & 1/wf Hannah SMITH (-1666); 15 Nov 1659; Reading
LILLIE, George (-1691) & 2/wf Jane _?_ ; 6 May 1667; Reading
LILLY, George (1667-) & Elizabeth (PRATT?) HAWKES (-1707, Lynn), w Adam; 15 Oct 1695, ?int 5 Sep 1696; Lynn/Salem
LILLY, Henry & Anne _?_ ; b 1680 in Eng
LILLEY, John & Ruth _?_ ; b 1647(8?); Wethersfield, CT
LILLEY, John (1662-) & Hannah [BASSETT] (1660-); b 1691; Woburn
LILLEY, Reuben (1669-) & Martha [GIBSON], m/2 Joseph KNIGHT 1699; b 1697(8?); Woburn
LILLIE, Samuel (1663-1730) & Mehitable FRARY (1665-); 4 Jun 1683; Boston
LILLY, Samuel (1665-) & Hannah BOUTELLE (1672-); 23 Dec 1692; Reading
LILLY, Thomas (1667/8-) & Elizabeth HOBBY, m/2 Oxenbridge THACHER 1714; 2 Jun 1698; Boston
LINCOLN, Benjamin (-1700) & Sarah FEARING; ?6 Feb 1666/7, ?6 Jan 1667, Feb 1667; Hingham
LINCOLN, Benjamin & Mary LEWIS, 18 Jan 1694/5, 17 Jan 1694; Hingham
LINCOLN, Caleb & 1/wf Rachel BATES/BATE (-1696); 8 May 1684; Hingham
LINCOLN, Caleb & 2/wf Hannah JACKSON; 2 Sep 1698; Hingham
LINCOLN, Daniel (?1621-1699) & Susanna _?_ (-1704); b 1654; Hingham
LINCOLN, Daniel & Elizabeth LINCOLN (1664-); 23 Jan 1677/8; Hingham
LINCOLN, Daniel & Sarah NICHOLS; 16 Apr 1687; Hingham
LINCOLN, David (-1714) & Margaret LINCOLN (-1716); 4 Jan 1692/3; Hingham
LINCOLN, John & Edith MAYCUMBER/MACOMBER; - Nov 1664; Marshfield
LINCOLN, John (1665-) & Martha CHUBBUCK (1670-1699); b 1688, m bond, 9 Feb 1687/[8]; Hingham/Taunton
LINCOLN, Jonah (1660-1712) & _?_ ; no ch
LINCOLN, Joseph (-1715) & Prudence FORD (1663-1695); 14 Jun 1682; Hingham
LINCOLN, Joseph (-1716) & Sarah (KING) BISBEE/BESBYE, w Hopestill; 24 Feb 1695/6, 27? Feb; Hingham
LINCOLN, Joshua (-1694) & Deborah HOBART (-1684); 20 Apr 1666; Hingham
LINCOLN, Joshua & 1/wf Mary _?_ (-9 Aug 1693); 27 Jun 1692; Hingham
LINCOLN, Joshua & 2/wf Hannah PALMER; 12 Feb 1693, [1693/4]; Boston/Hingham
LINCOLN, Josiah (1677?-) & Jane _?_ ; b 1701?; Taunton?/Hingham
LINCOLN, Mordecai (1657-1727) & 1/wf Sarah [JONES]; b 1686; Hingham/Scituate
LINCOLN, Robert (-1663) & Ann/Anne _?_ (-1663+); b 9 May 1647; Boston
LINCOLN, Samuel (1622-1690) & Martha [LYFORD]? (-1693); b 1650; Salem/Hingham
LINCOLN, Samuel (?1638-) & ?Catherine/?Jane _?_ (-1698+); b 1664+, b 1661; Taunton/Hingham
LINCOLN, Samuel (1664-1734) & Experience [BRIGGS] (-1763); b 1685; Taunton
LINCOLN, Samuel (1658-1707+) & 1/wf [Sarah ROYCE] (1665-); ca 1684; Taunton/Windham, CT
LINCOLN, Samuel & Deborah HERSEY; 29 Apr 1687; Hingham
LINCOLN, Samuel (1658-) & 2/wf Elizabeth JACOBS; 2 Jun 1692, 20 Jun 1692; Windham, CT
LINCOLN, Stephen (-1658) & Margaret _?_ (-1649); Wymondham?, in Eng, b 1638; Hingham
LINCOLN, Stephen (-1692) & Elizabeth HAWKE (1639-1713); Feb 1659/60; Hingham
LINCOLN, Thomas (1603-1684), miller & 1/wf Elizabeth _?_ ; in Eng, b 1628; Hingham

LINCOLN, Thomas (-1691), cooper & Annis/Avith? LANE (-1683); in Eng, ca 1630; Hingham/Taunton
LINCOLN, Thomas (-1675?), weaver & 1/wf Susanna _?_ (-Mar 1641); aft 1633; Hingham
LINCOLN, Thomas (-1675?), weaver & ?Mary _?_ ; aft Mar 1641; Hingham
LINCOLN, Thomas (-1692), husbandman & Margaret [LANGER]; b 1643; Hingham
LINCOLN, Thomas (?1628-1694) & 1/wf Mary [AUSTIN]; b 1652; Taunton
LINCOLN, Thomas (1638-1708) & 1/wf Mary CHUBBOCK (-1690); 18 Feb 1662/3, no issue; Hingham
LINCOLN, Thomas (1603-1684), miller & Elizabeth (ANDREWS) (HARVEY) STREET, w Thomas, ?w Francis; 10 Dec 1665; Taunton
LINCOLN, Thomas (1656-) & 1/wf Mary STACEY (-1689?); 1679; Taunton/Hingham
LINCOLN, Thomas (1652-) & Sarah LEWIS, m/2 Robert WATERMAN 1699; Dec 1684?, 6 Jan 1684, 6 Jan 1684/5, 1684; Hingham/Barnstable
LINCOLN, Thomas (1664-1715) & 1/wf Mary _?_ ; b 1686; Boston
LINCOLN, Thomas (1664-1728) & 2/wf Mehitable FROST (1671-); 3 Aug 1689; Boston/Hingham
LINCOLN, Thomas (1667-) & Susannah SMITH; 14 Nov 1689; Taunton
LINCOLN, Thomas (1638-1708) & 2/wf Lydia HOBART (1659-1732); 12 Nov 1690; Hingham
LINCOLN, Thomas (1674-), Hingham & Rachel HOLMES/HOLMAN, Braintree; 7 Nov 1695, 21 Nov 1695; Hingham
LINCOLN, William & Elizabeth _?_ ; b 1669; Gloucester/Lancester
LINCOLN, William (-1675/6) & 2/wf? Prudence _?_ , m/2 Samuel PAYSON 1677, m/3 Benjamin THOMPSON 1698
LINCOLN, _?_ & Joan _?_ (mother of Stephen); in Eng, b 1615?; Hingham
LINDALL, Henry (see Henry LENDON) & 2/wf Rosamond [STREET], m/2 _?_ RICHARDS; b 1644?, b 1646; Norwalk, CT?
LINDALL, James (-1652) & Mary _?_ (-1652); b 1641; Duxbury
LINDALL, James (-1684) & Susanna [?HASEY], ?m/2 John JACOBS 1687; b 1680; Boston
LINDALL, Timothy (1642-1699?) & Mary VEREN (1648-1732); - Feb 1672/3, 7? Feb; Salem
LYNDON, Augustine/Augustus? & 1/wf Jane _?_ (-1653); b 1653; Charlestown/Boston
LYNDON, Augustine/Augustus? & 2/wf Elizabeth _?_ (-1657); Charlestown
LYNDON, Augustus & 3/wf Phebe FRANKLIN, w William; Dec 1658; Charlestown
LINDON, Augustus & 4/wf Mary [SANDERSON], w Joseph, m/3 William ARDELL 1682; div 1679; Charlestown?/Boston?
LINDON/LINDALL?, Henry (-1661) & Rosamond ?STREET, m/2 Nathaniel RICHARDS 1664 (see Henry LINDALL); b 1640; New Haven
LINDON, Joshua & _?_ ; b 1683; Newport
LINDEN, Josiah (1647-1709, Newport) & Abigail PEARCE; 27 Dec 1671; Ipswich/Newport
LINDSEY, Christopher (-1669) & Margaret _?_ (-1668); b 1644?, b 1647; Lynn
LINSY, Eleazer (1645-1716) & Sarah ALLY (1651-1731); - Aug 1668; Lynn
LYNSSY, Eleazer (1671-) & Elizabeth [MAULE] (1673-); b 1695; Lynn
LINSY, John (-ca 1705) & 1/wf Mary ALLEY (1642-1681); 6 Jun 1667; Lynn
LINZY, John & 2/wf Amy (GRAVES) RICHARDSON, w Richard; - Jul 1682; Lynn
LINDSEY, John & Elizabeth MUNRO; 29 Aug 1694; Bristol, RI
LINSLEY, Benjamin (1660-) & Mary _?_ ; b 1699, b 1698(9?); Branford, CT
LINDSLEY, Benjamin & Dorcas _?_ ; b 1701?; Orange Co., NY
LINDSLEY, Ebenezer (1635-) & Eleanor _?_ ; Branford, CT
LINDSLEY, Francis & _?_ ; b 1656
LINSLY, Francis (moved to NJ) & Susanna CULLPEPER; 24 Jun 1655; Branford, CT
LINDSLEY, Gabriel & _?_ ; b 1659/60?; Branford, CT
LINDSLEY, John (-1650) & _?_ ; in Eng, b 1600; Guilford, CT
LINDLSEY, John & Ellen _?_ (-1654); b 1654; Branford, CT/Guilford
LINSLEY, John & Sarah (HALL, no) POND, w Samuel; 9 Jul 1655, 6 Jul 1655; Windsor, CT/Branford, CT
LINSLEY, John (-1684) & Hannah (GRIFFIN) [POND?] (-1737); Branford, CT
LINDSLEY/LINSLEY, John & 1/wf [Mary HARRISON?] (1668-); b 1694, 6 Jun 1699; Guilford, CT/Branford
LINSLEY, John & Mary HARRISON (1669-); 6 Jun 1699; Branford, CT
LINDSLEY, John & Elizabeth FORD (1681-); b 1700?
LINDSLEY, John & _?_ ; E. Hampton, LI

LINERSON, Isaac & Deliverance __?__; b 1693; Mendon

LINES, Benjamin (-1689) & Anna [WILMOT], m/2 Peter CARRINGTON ca 1691; b 1689; New Haven

LINES, Henry (-1663) & Elizabeth HARRISON, m/2 Thomas LAMPSON 1663, m/3 John MORRIS 1666; b 1656; New Haven

LINES, John & Hannah COOPER; 27 Dec 1700; New Haven

LINES, Joseph & Abigail JOHNSON; 30 Mar 1692, 30-31 Mar, 30? May; New Haven

LINES, Ralph (-1689) & [Alice] [BUDD?]; b 1649; New Haven

LOINES, Ralph & Abiah BASSETT (1658-); 27 Apr 1681; New Haven

LINES, Samuel (1649-1692) & Mary [THOMPSON] (1652-), m/2 John HITCHCOCK 1692+, m/3 Samuel CLARK 1716+; - Nov 1674; New Haven

LINES, William & Ann [COLES], w John; b 1693, 1683?; Matinecock, LI

LINFIELD, William & Abigail __?__; b 1694; Braintree

LINFURTH, Thomas (1615-1692) & Elizabeth EMERSON; [b 1648]; Haverhill

LING, Benjamin (-1673) & Joanna __?__, m/2 John DIXWELL 1673; no issue; New Haven (Sarah (MEW) COOPER niece of Benjamin LING, Ellis MEW nephew)

LIVINGTON, Henry (-1691/2) & Catharine [ELLISON]; Hempstead, LI

LINNEL/LINNETT?, David (-1689) & Hannah SHEALY/SHELLEY/SHIRLEY? (1637-1709); 9 Mar 1652, ca 15 Mar 1652/3, 9? Mar; Barnstable

LINNEL, John (1671-1747) & Ruth [DAVIS]; b 1696; Barnstable

LINNELL, Jonathan (1668-1726) & 1/wf Elizabeth __?__ (1667-1723, 1725); b 1694; Eastham

LINNELL, Robert (-1663, 1662/3) & ?Jemima/?Peninah/Pininna [HOUSE]; b 1627?, aft 1632, b 16 Sep 1638; Scituate

LINSCOTT, John (-1712) & 1/wf Lydia [MILBURY]; ca 1691?; York, ME

LINSFORD/LINCFORD, Edward & Hannah PLUMLY, dau Alexander; 16 May 1667; Braintree

LINSFORD, Francis & Ann __?__; 30 Dec 1647

LINSFORD, Thomas (-ca 1652) & Elizabeth __?__; Boston

LINTON, Richard (-1665) & Elizabeth __?__ (-1663+, ca 1674?); in Eng, b 1612?, b 1615; Lancester/Watertown/Concord (his dau Ann m Lawrence WATERS b 1634)

LIPPINCOTT, Bartholomew & Elizabeth SQUYRE; Plymouth, Eng, 1 Nov 1636; Dover, NH/etc.

LIPPINCOTT, Richard & Abigail __?__; b 1639; Dorchester/Boston/Shrewsbury, NJ

LIPPITT, John[1] (-1669+) & __?__; b 1640?, b 1644?; Providence/Warwick, RI

LIPPITT, John[2] (-1670±) & Ann (GREEN?)/GROVE?, m/2 Edward SEARLE 1671; 9 Feb 1664, 1664/5; Warwick, RI

LIPPITT, John (1665-1723) & Rebecca [LIPPITT] (-1723+); Warwick, RI

LIPPITT, Moses (-1703) & Mary KNOWLES (-1719); 19 Nov 1668, 1667?; Warwick, RI

LIPPETT, Moses & Sarah THROCKMORTON; 8 Dec 1697; Warwick, RI/Middletown, NJ

LIPSEY, Elias & Elizabeth __?__; b 1689; Boston

LISCOMB, Ebenezer (1676-) & Mehitable CURTICE; 18 Oct 1694; Boston

LISCOMB, John (-1680) & Hannah [JOHNSON]; b 1667; Boston

LYSEUM/LISCOMB, John & Ann/Anne JONES; 2 Aug 1692; Bristol, RI

LISLEY, Robert & Sarah [FRANE]; Charlestown

LISLEY, Robert & Elizabeth [THOMAS], m/2 John BETTS 1679, m/3 John FOSDICK 1684; b 1679, div 1679; Charlestown

LISSEN/LISSON, Nicholas & 1/wf Alice __?__; b 1644, b 1638; Exeter, NH

LISSEN, Nicholas & 2/wf Jane __?__; 14 Dec 1682; Exeter, NH

LITCHFIELD, Josiah (?1647-) & Sarah BACKER/BAKER; 22 Feb 1671; Scituate

LITCHFIELD, Lawrence (-ca 1649) & [Judith DENNIS] (-1693), m/2 William PARKS ca Oct 1649, 1650; ca 1640; Barnstable/Scituate

LEICHFIELD, Thomas & __?__; b 1678; Dorchester/Boston

LITCHFIELD, Thomas & Sarah DAVIS; 2 May 1693; Amesbury

LITTLE, Ephraim (1650-1717) & Mary STURDEVANT/STURTEVANT; 22 Nov 1672; Scituate-/Marshfield

LITTLE, Ephraim (1626-1723) & Sarah CLARKE (-1731+); 29 Nov 1698, no issue; Plymouth/Scituate

LITTLE, George (-1694) & 1/wf Alice __?__ (-1680, ae 63); b 1652; Newbury

LITTLE, George (-1694) & 2/wf Eleanor BARNARD (-1694), w Thomas; 19 Jul 1681; Newbury

LITTLE, Isaac (1646-1699) & Bethiah [THOMAS] (-1718); b 1674; Marshfield

LITTLE, Joseph & Mary COFFIN (1657-); 31 Oct 1677; Newbury

LITTLE, Moses (1657-1691) & Lydia [COFFIN] (1662-), m/2 John PIKE 1695; b 1679/[80?]; Newbury

LITTLE, Richard (-1689) & Jane (WALKER) HUMISTON, w Henry; 15 Dec 1669; New Haven

LITTLE, Samuel (1655-1707) & Sarah GRAY (1659-1737); 18 May 1682; Marshfield/Bristol, RI

LITTLE, Thomas (1610-1671/2) & Ann WARREN (1612-); 19 Apr 1633; Plymouth/Marshfield

LITTLE, Thomas (1674-1712) & Mary MAYHEW; 5 Dec 1678; Marshfield

LITTLEFIELD, Anthony (1621-1661/2), Wells & Mary [PAGE]; b 1653?, b 1656; ?Wells, ME

LITTLEFIELD, Caleb & Lydia [MOTT] (1666-); b 1692; Braintree/Weymouth/Kingston, RI

LITTLEFIELD, Daniel (-1718), Wells & Mehitable [DODD?] (1660-), dau George, gr-dau Nicholas DAVIS; b 1701?, b 1702?; ?Wells, ME

LITTLEFIELD, David (-1751?), Wells & 1/wf ?Mary/?Mercy [HILL] (1672-); 14 Nov 1694, 15 Nov 1694; ?Wells, ME

LITTLEFIELD, Dependence (?1671-), Wells & 1/wf Hannah (SNELL) BALLARD; ca 1700, b Feb 1706/7; ?Wells, ME

LITTLEFIELD, Ebenezer (1669-) & Lydia [PARKER] (-1717); b 1697; Newton

LITTLEFIELD, Edmund[1] (-1661) & 1/wf _?_; in Eng, b 1614; Exeter, NH/Wells, ME

LITTLEFIELD, Edmund[1] (1592-1661) & 1/wf? 2/wf [Annis/Agnes AUSTIN] (-1677, 1678); Tichfield, Hunts, 16 Oct 1614; Exeter, NH/Wells, ME

LITTLEFIELD, Edmund (?1653-) & 1/wf _?_; b 1686?; Cape Porpoise, ME

LITTLEFIELD, Edmund & 2/wf Elizabeth MOTT (1671-); 30 Dec 1690; Braintree/Wells, ME

LITTLEFIELD, Eliab, Wells, ME, Manchester, MA, & Rachel SIBLEY; 29 Oct 1696; Manchester

LITTLEFIELD, Francis (1619?-1713), Wells, ME, Woburn, MA, Dover, NH, & 1/wf Jane [HILL?] (-1646), dau Ralph; b 1646; Charlestown/Woburn

LITTLEFIELD, Francis (1619-1713) & 2/wf Rebecca _?_ (1630-1683+); ca 1648-9; Wells, ME/Woburn/Dover, NH/Ipswich

LITTLEFIELD, Francis, Jr. (?1631-1675) & Meribah [WARDELL/WARDWELL?] (1637-1677+); b 1654; Wells, ME

LITTLEFIELD, Francis (see Samuel) (1619-)& Mary (WADE) SIMONDS, w William; by 1689

LITTLEFIELD, James (-1687+, 1690) & Katharine [HEARD] (-1687+), m/2 John WOODEN by 1691; b 1687; Wells, ME

LITTLEFIELD, John (?1624-1697) & Patience _?_ (-1701+); ca 1649/55?; Wells, ME

LITTLEFIELD, John & Mary MERE (-1675); 9 May 1650; Dedham/Wrentham?

LITTLEFIELD, John[3] (-1689) & Mehitable _?_; aft 1668?, bef 1685?

LITTLEFIELD, Jonathan (-1734/5) & Abigail [SIMPSON]; ca 1692?, by 1695; Wells, ME

LITTLEFIELD, Joseph (-1698?) & Jane [COLE], dau Nicholas, m/2 John HEARD 1698; b 1689; Wells, ME

LITTLEFIELD, Josiah & Lydia [MASTERS] (-1707); b 1698?, 6 ch b bef 28 Jun 1702; Wells, ME

LITTLEFIELD, Moses & Martha [LORD], m/2 John ABBOTT, m/3 Alex TAYLOR; Dec 1687; Wells, ME

LITTLEFIELD, Nathan (-1689) & Elizabeth [BARRETT], m/2 James DENMARK 1694; b 1689; Wells, ME

LITTLEFIELD, Samuel (-1688) (son Anthony) & Mary COALE/COALT; 4 Dec 1686; York Co., ME

LITTLEFIELD, Thomas (-ca 1689), Dover, Wells & 1/wf Ruth _?_; b 1663, b 1650?; Wells, ME

LITTLEFIELD, Thomas & 2/wf Sarah _?_ (-1720+), m/2 Ezekiel KNIGHT ca 1691; Wells, ME

LITTLEFIELD, Dependence & Hannah (SNELL) [BALLARD], w John; b 1707, b 1701?; Wells, ME/NH

LITTLEFIELD, Samuel & Joanna _?_; b 1701

LITTLEFIELD, [Francis]/Samuel & Mary SYMONDS (1633-1695), w Wm. (Wm. d 1679); aft 1679

LITTLEHALE, Isaac (1660-) & Elizabeth DAVIS; 13 Oct 1686; Ipswich

LITTLEHALE, Richard (-1663) & Mary LANCTON/LANGTON (-1691), m/2 Edmund BRIDGES 1665; 15 Nov 1647; Haverhill

LITTLEHALE, Richard (1655-) & Sarah COLLINGS/COLLINS; 23 Oct 1676, 1675?; Ipswich

LIVEEN, John (-1689) & [Alice HALLAM] (-1698), wid; aft 1664; Barbados, West Indies/New London

LIVERMORE, Daniel & Mary COOLIDGE; 28 May 1697; Watertown

LIVERMORE, John (?1606, ?1604-1684) & Grace [SHERMAN] (1616?-1691); in Eng, b 1633; Wethersfield/New Haven/Watertown

LIVERMORE, John (ca 1638-1719) & 1/wf only wife Hannah/Anne __?__/GROUT (1646-1680); b 1668(9?); Watertown

LIVERMORE, John (ca 1638-1719) & 2/wf Elizabeth (GROUT) ALLEN (1666-1732), w Samuel; b 1695, b 24 Jan 1697; Watertown

LIVERMORE, Jonathan & Rebecca BARNES (1680-1765); 23 Nov 1699; Watertown

LIVERMORE, Joseph (1675-1770) & Elizabeth [STONE] (1678-1764); b 1699; Watertown

LIVERMORE, Samuel (1641, ?1640-1690) & Hannah/Anna? BRIDGE (-1727), m/2 Oliver WELLINGTON 1690+; 4 Jun 1668; Watertown

LIVERMORE, Samuel (1673-) & 1/wf Hannah __?__ (-1698, ae 19); b 1697; Watertown

LIVERMORE, Samuel (1673-) & 2/wf Elizabeth PARKER (1679-1716); 15 Nov 1699; Cambridge

LIVERMORE, Thomas & Mary [POTTER], m/2 John RUSSELL 1691; b 1687; Charlestown

LIVERMORE, William (-1691) & Elizabeth __?__ ; ca 1658; Beverly

LIVINGSTONE, Daniel & Joanna (DOWMAN) [PRAY], w John; aft 31 Oct 1676, bef 1680; Kittery, ME

LOYD, Benjamin & Mary DINSDELL; 17 Jan 1699; Boston

LLOYD, Edward (-1709?) & 1/wf Hannah [GRIFFIN] (1657-1699); b 1682; Charlestown

LLOYD, James (-1693) & 1/wf Grizzell/Griselda SYLVESTER; 13 Jul 1676; Boston?

LOYD, James (-1693) & 2/wf Rebecca LEVERETT (1664-1739?); 3 Nov 1691; Boston

LOADER, John & Elizabeth [CURTIS]; 6 Apr 1687, b 1689, b 1691; Charlestown/Salem

LOADER, __?__ & Susanna [BARNES]; b 1687

LOBDELL, Isaac (-1718) & Martha [WARD] (-1708); b 1657; Hingham

LOBDELL, Isaac (1657-) & 1/wf Sarah BRYANT/[KING] (1656-1697); b 1680(1?); Plymouth

LOBDELL, Isaac & 2/wf Hannah BISHOP, ?dau Thomas; 12 Aug 1697; Boston

LOBDELL, John (1638-1673) & 1/wf Hannah LEAVITT (1639-1662, ae 23); 19 Jul 1659, ?20 Jul; Hingham

LOBDELL, John (1638-1673) & 2/wf ?Hannah/?Sarah BOSWORTH (-bef 1673); 21 Feb 1664/5; Hingham

LOBDALE, Joseph & Elizabeth (PRICE) TOWNSEND, w James; 1 Sep 1692, ?1 Dec; Boston

LOBDELL, Joshua (1671-1713+) & Mary BURWELL; 11 Aug 1695; Milford, CT

LOBDELL, Nicholas & 2/wf [?Bridget PIERCE?] (-1641); b 1641, had grant 1636; Hingham

LOBDELL, Nicholas (1663-1698) & Elizabeth PERKINS (1669-); 18 Aug 1687; Charlestown

LOBDELL, Simon & 1/wf Persis [PIERCE?]; b 1669; Milford/Hartford/Springfield

LOBDELL, Simon & 2/wf Sarah (BARRETT) [HITT], w Henry; 4 Mar 1698/9, aft 30 Mar 1689/90; ?Milford, CT

LOCKARD, John & Rachel [HAYNES] (1655-); Sudbury, no ch

LOCKE, Ebenezer & 1/wf Susanna WALKER (-1700); 18 Oct 1697; Woburn

LOCKE, Edward & Hannah [JENNESS] (1673-); b 1694; Hampton, NH

LOCKE, James & 1/wf __?__ ; b 1699; Hampton, NH

LOCK, James (1677-) & Sarah CUTTER; 5 Dec 1700; Cambridge/Woburn

LOCKE, John (?1626-1696) & Elizabeth [BERRY]; ca 1652; Hampton, NH/Rye, NH

LOCKE, John/Philip? & Elizabeth [BOLLES/BOWLES], m/2 William PITMAN; b 1683; Hampton, NH

LOCKE, John (-1756) & 1/wf Elizabeth PLYMPTON (1658-1720); 31 May 1683; Woburn

LOCKE, Joseph (1664-1754) & 1/wf Mary [?SMITH] (-1710); b 1696, ca 1690?; Lexington

LOCKE, Nathaniel & Judith/Sabina? [HERMINS/HEMINS, ?m/2 William MARSTON, ?m/3 John REDMAN; b 1656; Newcastle, NH

LOCKE, Nathaniel (1661-1734) & Dorothy BLAKE (1665-1737); 22 Jan 1688/9; Hampton, NH

LOCKE, Samuel (1669-) & 1/wf Ruth [CARLY] (1678-1714); b 1698?; Lexington

LOCKE, William (?1628, ?1631-1720) (cousin of Nichoas DAVIS) & Mary CLARK (1630-1715); 27 Nov 1655, 27 Dec; Woburn

LOCKE, William & 1/wf Sarah WHITMORE (1662-); 29 May 1683; Woburn

LOCKE, William & 2/wf Abigail HAYWARD; 8 Jun 1698; Woburn

LOCKE, William, Portsmouth/Rye & Hannah KNOWLES (1678-); 23 Nov 1689; Hampton, NH/Rye, NH

LOCKER/LOKER?, George (1658-) & Lydia (BUFFUM) HILL, w John; 1680+; Salem

LOCKERSON, John & Susannah [THORNE]; 1667; ?Flushing, LI

LOCKWOOD, Abraham (1669/70-1747) & 1/wf Sarah [WESTCOTT] (1673-1706+); ca 1693; Warwick, RI

LOCKWOOD, Daniel[2] (1640-1691) & Abigail [SHERWOOD] (-1692, 1693); b 1669, ca 1668; Fairfield, CT
LOCKWOOD, Daniel[3] (1664-1697/8) & Abigail [BURR] (1671/2-1631), m/2 Elnathan HANFORD 1700, m/3 Nathaniel SHERMAN 1707; ca 1692; Fairfield, CT
LOCKWOOD Daniel[3] (1668-1712) & Sarah [BENEDICT] (1677-); ca 1699
LOCKWOOD, Edmund[1] (?1599-) & 1/wf __?_; b 1632, b 1629, b 1627, b 1630; Cambridge
LOCKWOOD, Edmund[1] (?1599-) & 2/wf Elizabeth [MASTERS], m/2 Cary LOTHAM bef 1639; b 1632, b 1635; Cambridge
LOCKWOOD, Edmund[2] (1627-1692/3) & Hannah SCOTT (?1636-1706); 7 Jan 1655/6, 1655/6; Stamford, CT
LOCKWOOD, Eliphalet & Mary GOLD; 11 Oct 1699; Stamford, CT
LOCKWOOD, Ephraim[2] (1641-1685) & Mercy St.JOHN (-1694/5); 8 Jun 1665; Norwalk
LOCKWOOD, Gershom[2] (1643-1719) & 1/wf [?Ann MILLINGTON?]; ca 1664; Fairfield, CT
LOCKWOOD, Gershom[2] (1643-1719) & Elizabeth (TOWNSEND) WRIGHT (-1719+), w Gideon; 3 Aug 1697; Oyster Bay, LI/Greenwich, CT
LOCKWOOD, Jonathan (1634-1688) & Mary FERRIS (-1708), m/2 Thomas MERRITT 1696; 6 Jan 1664; Stamford, CT/Greenwich, CT
LOCKWOOD, Joseph (1638-1717) & 1/wf __?_ BEACHAM?/[JESSUP?]; aft 1666; Stamford CT
LOCKWOOD, Joseph (1638-1717) & 2/wf Mary (COLEY) (SIMPSON) [STREAM] (-1705), w Peter, w John; aft 1689?
LOCKWOOD Joseph & 1/wf Elizabeth AYERS (-1715); 19 May 1698; Stamford, CT
LOCKWOOD, Richard (?1632-) & Deborah [GUNNISON?]; b 1669, b 1653?, 1649?; Kittery, ME/Wells, ME/Virginia
LOCKWOOD, Robert[1]/Trent (-1658) & Susanna [NORMAN] (-1660), m/2 Jeffrey FERRIS 1658; b 1634; Watertown/Stratford, CT/Fairfield, CT
LOCKWOOD, Robert[2] (-1733) & 2/wf (who was 1/wf?) Mary [BUTLER], w John; b 1693(4?), aft 1696; Greenwich, CT
LUFF, John & [Bridget?] __?_; b 1625?, b 1620?, b 1648; Salem
LUFF, John & __?_; b 1663; Salem
LUFF, Gabriel & Deborah (LEONARD) DENTON (1663-), w Daniel; b 13 Nov 1703, ca 1699?; LI?
LOFT, Richard & Elizabeth __?_; b 1667(8?); Boston
LOGAN, Alexander (ae 44 in 1691) & Susanna (CUTLER) BURRAGE (1669-), w John; 5 Jan 1679, 1679/80; Charlestown
LOGIN, Robert & Lydia [COFFIN] (1669-), m/2 Thomas TRAXTER 1696; b 1692(3?); Boston
LOKER, Henry (alias RIDDLESDALE) (1577-1631, in Eng) & Elizabeth __?_ (-1648, Sudbury); ca 1604?; Sudbury
LOKER, Henry (-1688) & Hannah BREWER (-1679), ?w John; 24 Mar 1647; Sudbury
LOKER, John (?1613-1653) & Mary [DRAPER?] (-1697+); b 1650, ca 1640?; Sudbury
LOKER, John (1650-1719) & 1/wf Sarah [RICE] (1655-1702); ca 1673/5?, b 1676; Sudbury
LUMBART, Benjamin[2] (1642-1725) & 1/wf Jane WARREN (-1682/3); 19 Sep 1672; Barnstable
LUMBART, Benjamin[2] (1642-1725) & 2/wf Sarah WALKER (-1693); 19 Nov 1685; Barnstable
LUMBART, Benjamin (1642-1725) & 3/wf Hannah (LUMBERT) WHETSTONE/WHISTON (?1663-1754), w John; 24 May 1694; Barnstable
LUMBART, Barnard/Bernard? (1607/8-) (ae 60 in 1668) & [?Mary __?_]; b 19 Apr 1635, b 1632?; Scituate/Barnstable
LUMBART, Barnard/Bernard? & 1/wf [Susanna] __?_ (-1734); b 1692; Barnstable
LOMBARD, Caleb & [?Mary PROUT]; ca 1660-70?; Barnstable/Yarmouth
LOMBARD, David (1650-1716) & Margaret FILLEY?/PHILLY? (1651-1714); 17 Apr 1675; Springfield
LUMBART, Jabez[3] (bpt 1641-) & Sarah DERBY; 1 Dec 1660; Barnstable
LUMBER, Jedediah[2] (1640-) & Hannah WING (1642-1682); 20 May 1668; Barnstable
LUMBART, Jedediah (1669-1739, 1743?) & Hannah LEWES (1674, 1676?-); 8 Nov 1699; Barnstable
LOMBARD/LAMBERT, John (ca 1624-1672, 1662?) & Jane/Joanna/Joan PRITCHARD/PRICHARD (-1680); 1 Sep 1647; Springfield
LUMBART, Jonathan (1657-) & Elizabeth EDEY/EDDY; 16 Dec 1688; Barnstable/Tisbury
LUMBARD, Joshua[2] (-1690?) & Abigail LINNEL/LINNETT? (-1690+); end of May, 27 May 1651, - May 1650; Barnstable

LUMBART, Joshua (1660-1724) & Hopestill BULLOCK; 6 Nov 1682; Barnstable
LUMBERT, Thomas[1] (-1664) & 1/wf _?_ ; in Eng, b 1607; Dorchester/Scituate/Barnstable
LUMBART, Thomas[1] (-1664) & 2/wf Joyce _?_ ; b 1630?; Dorchester/Barnstable
LUMBARD, Thomas[3] & Elizabeth DARBY/DERBY; 23 Dec 1665; Barnstable
LUMBART, Thomas, Jr. & 1/wf Hannah [PARKER?]; b 1690; Barnstable
LUMBER, Thomas (1671-1736) & Mary NEWCOM/NEWCOMB; 4 Oct 1694; Barnstable
LONDON/LUNDEN?, John & Hannah (_?_) BANCROFT, w John; aft 1 Dec 1664; Windsor, CT
LONG, Abiel & Hannah HILLS; 27 Oct 1682; Newbury
LONG, John (1629-) & 1/wf Abigail [NORTON] (-1674); b 1655(6?); Charlestown
LONG, John & 2/wf Mary (NOWELL) WINSLOW (-1683?), w Isaac; 10 Sep 1674, 10 Sep, 16 Sep;
    Charlestown
LONG, John (1656-1678) & Elizabeth _?_ (-1678); b 1678; Charlestown
LONG, [Joseph]/John? (d in Eng) & Mary LANE, dau Wm., m/2 Joseph FARNSWORTH, m/3 John
    WILCOX 1660?; b 1635?; Dorchester
LONG, Joseph (-1676) & Mary _?_ ; 3 Feb 1661/2; Dorchester
LONG, Joseph (1668-) & [Martha SMITH] (1674-); b 1701?
LONG, Michael (1615-1689) & Joanna/Joan _?_ (-1691?, 1698?); b 1646; Charlestown
LONG, Nathaniel & Elizabeth [HAWKINS], m/2 Adam WINTHROP, m/3 John RICHARDS 1654;
    b 17 Oct 1649 (see Robert LONG); Boston/Barbados?
LONG, Norton & Sarah FOWLE (1672-); 31 May 1692; Charlestown
LONG, Philip (ae 40 in 1654) & 1/wf _?_ ; b 1640; Ipswich/Boston/Edgartown
LONG, Philip (-1658/9) & Anne [CONSTABLE], w Thomas; b 1652; Boston
LONG, Philip (-1726) & Hannah _?_ (-1726+); Newport/E. Greenwich
LONG, Richard (-1694) & Ann?/Anna FRENCH, m/2 Thomas MUDGETT ca 1695, m/3 Alexander
    MAGOON; 21 Jul 1680; Salisbury
LONG, Robert (1590-1664, 1663/4) & 1/wf Sarah TAYLOR (1595-1630); 3 Oct 1619;
    Charlestown
LONG, Robert (1590-1663/4) & 2/wf Elizabeth [ROBERTS?/ROSS?] (1605-1687); in Eng, ca
    1633; Charlestown
LONG, Robert (1621-) & Alice [SHORT?/STEVENS?]; b 1647; Newbury
LONG, Robert[2] (1619-) & Elizabeth (HOPKINS)/[HAWKINS]?, m/2 Jacob GREEN; b 1647;
    Charlestown
LONG, Robert (1669-) & Sarah [SKIFFE] (1678-); b 1695; Martha's Vineyard/Nantucket
LONG, Samuel (1647-1671) & Elizabeth PINKHAM, ?m/2 John WYATT 1674: 23 Jan 1668/9, 20
    Jan 1668; Charlestown
LONG, Shubael & Hannah MERRILL (1671-); 26 Aug 1695; Newbury
LONG, Thomas & 1/wf Sarah [WILCOX] (1648-), m/2 David ENSIGN aft 1688; b 1668, div 1681;
    Hartford
LONG, Thomas & 2/wf [Sarah ELMER] (1664-); b 1688; Windsor, CT/Hartford?/Roxbury
LONG, William & Hannah (HOLLAND?/BROOKING?) [BALLANTINE] (-1718), w William; b
    1671; Boston
LONG, William (1674-) & Mary [HENBURY]; b 1697
LONG, Zechariah (1630-1688) & 1/wf Sarah TIDD (1636, ?1638-1674); 29 Sep 1656; Charlestown
LONG, Zechariah (1630-1688) & 2/wf Mary [BURR] (1639-1681); b 1676; Charlestown
LONG, Zechariah (1630-1688) & 3/wf Sarah (FOSTER) MOORE, w Benjamin, m/3 Caleb
    [STANLEY] 1690; 9 Aug 1682; Charlestown
LONG, Zechariah (1662-) & Elizabeth [CHECKLEY] (1672-); b 1690; Boston/Charlestown
LONG, _?_ & Bridget ELDREDGE; Cape Cod
LONG, [Thomas] (-1712) & 2/wf Sarah ELMER/ELMORE (1664-1741); ?Hartford
LONG, _?_ & Hannah UPHAM (1635-1679), dau John; Watertown
LONG, _?_ & Margaret PIERCE (-1688), m/2 Thomas POPE 1681; ?Suffield, CT
LONGBOTTOM/LONGBOTTUM, Daniel & Elizabeth LAMB; 15 Feb 1692; Norwich, CT
LONGFELLOW, William (1650-1690) & Anne SEWALL (1660-), m/2 Henry SHORT 1692; 10 Nov
    1678; Newbury
LONGLEY, John[2] & Scicilia/Siseliah?/?Hannah [ELVIE], m/2 _?_ HONOREL; b 1669(70?);
    Groton/Lynn/Salem
LONGLEY, John, mariner & Mary [?WISWALL]; b 1697; Charlestown
LONGLEY, Nathaniel[3] (1676-1732) & Anna/Ann [SHEPHERD] (-1758), m/2 Thomas HAMMOND;
    b 13 Sep 1699; Newton

LONGLEY, William[1] (1610-1680) & Joanna [GOFF?] (1619-1698), m/2 Benjamin CRISPE; b 1640?; Lynn/Groton

LONGLEY, William[2] (-1694) & 1/wf Lydia __?__ ; 15 May 1672; Groton

LONGLEY, William[2] (-1694) & 2/wf Deliverance [CRISPE]?/PEACE? (-1694), w Jonathan; b 1687, b 1686?; Groton

LONGLEY, William[3] (1669/70-1755) & Deborah BUTTERFIELD (-1761, ae 92 or 93; 12 Feb 1697, prob 1696/7; Chelmsford

LONGWORTH, Thomas & Deborah [YOUNG] (?1660-1711/12); b 1682; Southold, LI

LOOK, Jonathan (1651-1736) & 1/wf Mary CURTIS (1659-), m/1 John HEARD, div Jul 1678; 19 Nov 1678; Topsfield

LOOK, Jonathan (1651-1736) & 2/wf Elizabeth WALLINGFORD (-1736); 29 Dec 1693; Haverhill/Rowley

LOOKE, Thomas (1622-) & Sarah?/Mary __?__ (-1666); b 1646; Lynn

LOOK, Thomas (1646-) & Elizabeth [BUNKER]; b 1672; Nantucket

LOOMER/?LUME, Stephen (-1700) & Mary [MILLER], m/2 Caleb ABELL 1701; b 1684; New London

LOOMAN, __?__ & Anne __?__ (-1659); Weymouth

LOOMIS, Daniel (1657-1740) & Mary ELLSWORTH (1660-1713); 23 Dec 1680; Windsor, CT

LOOMIS, David (1668-) & Lydia MARSH (1667-); 8 Dec 1692; Windsor, CT/Hadley/Hatfield

LOOMIS, Ebenezer (-1708) & Jemima WHITCOMB (1678-1712); 15 Apr 1697; Windsor, CT

LOOMIS, Hezekiah & Mary PORTER; 30 Apr 1690; Windsor, CT

LOOMIS, James & Mindwell [DRAKE] (1671-1736); 1696; Windsor, CT

LOOMIS, John (ca 1622, 1620-1688) & Elizabeth SCOTT (ca 1622-1696); 6? Feb 1648, 3 Feb, 1648/9; Windsor, CT

LOOMIS, John & Mary [TRASK] (1632-); b 1669; Salem

LOOMIS, John & 1/wf Mary __?__, gr-dau of Miles CLAY; b 1670; Hadley

LOOMIS, John & __?__ ; b 1673; Windsor, CT

LUMIS, John & 2/wf Sarah (BOLTWOOD) WARNER, w Isaac; 30 Dec 1696, 26 Dec 1696; Deerfield

LOOMIS, Jonathan (-1707) & Sarah GRAVES (-1699), dau George; 27 Dec 1688; Windsor, CT

LOOMIS, Joseph[1] (ca 1590-1658) & Mary WHITE (1590-1652); Shalford, Eng, 30 Jun 1614; Windsor, CT

LOOMIS, Joseph (1615-1687) & 1/wf Sarah HILL (-1653); 17 Sep 1646; Windsor, CT

LOOMIS, Joseph & 2/wf Mary [SHARWOOD] (-1681); 28 Jun 1659; Windsor, CT

LOOMIS, Joseph (-1699) & Hannah MARSH; 28 Jan 1675, 1675/6; Hadley

LOOMIS, Joseph & 1/wf Lydia DRAKE (-1702); 10 Apr 1681; Windsor, CT

LOOMIS, Josiah & Mary ROCKWELL (1663-1738); 23 Oct 1683; Windsor, CT

LOOMIS, Matthew (-1688) & Mary GAYLORD (1664-); 6 Jan 1686, 1686/7; Windsor, CT

LOOMIS, Moses[3] & Joanna GIBBS (1671-); 27 Apr 1694; Windsor, CT

LOOMIS, Nathaniel[2] (?1626-1688) & Elizabeth MOORE (1638-1728), m/2 John CASE 1689 bpt; 1 Nov 1653, 27 Nov 1654, 4 Nov 1654, 24 Nov 1653; Windsor, CT

LOOMIS, Nathaniel (1657-) & Elizabeth ELLSWORTH; 23 Dec 1680; Windsor, CT

LOOMIS, Nathaniel & Ruth PORTER (1671-); 28 Nov 1689; Windsor, CT

LOOMIS, Nathaniel (1670-1730) & Elizabeth __?__ (doubtful); b 1701?, no ch mentioned; Windsor, CT

LOOMIS, Nehemiah (1670-1740) & Thankful WELLER (1674-1748); 3 Jan 1694, 1694/5; Westfield

LOOMIS, Samuel (?1628-1689) & Elizabeth JUDD; 27 Dec 1653, 29? Dec; Farmington/Windsor, CT

LOOMIS, Samuel (-1711) & Hannah HANCHET, m/2 James KING 1786; 4 Apr 1678, 14 Apr; Windsor, CT/Westfield

LOOMIS, Samuel, Windsor & 1/wf Elizabeth WHITE (-1736), Hatfield; 2 Jul 1688; Windsor, CT/Hadley/Colchester, CT

LOOMIS, Stephen (1668-) & Esther COLT (-1714); 1 Jan 1690, prob 1690/1; Windsor, CT

LOOMIS, Thomas (?1624-1689) & 1/wf Hannah FOWKES/FOX (-1662); 1 Nov 1653; Windsor, CT

LOOMIS, Thomas, Sr. (?1624-1689) & 2/wf Mary JUDD (-1684), Farmington; 1 Jan 1663, 1662, 1662/3; Windsor, CT

LOOMIS, Thomas (-1688) & Sarah WHITE (1662-), Hatfield, m/2 John BISSELL 1689; 31 Mar 1680, 30 Mar 1680; Hadley/Hatfield

LOOMIS, Thomas (1656-1746) & Hannah PORTER (1662-1739?); 17 Dec 1682, ?2 Jan 1680, 17 Dec 1683?; Windsor, CT

LOOMIS, Timothy (1661-1710) & Rebecca PORTER (1666-); 20 Mar 1689/90; Windsor, CT

LOOMIS, Joseph? & Hannah SHERWOOD (?1620-); b 1694; Fairfield

LOOMIS, John & Hannah (BUCKLAND) BAKER (doubtful); aft 1691?, aft 1695?; Windsor, CT

LOPER, Jacob, NY, & Magdalene [MELYN]/Cornelia MELYN, Staten Isl., m/2 Jacob SCHELLINGER; banns, 30 Jun 1647

LOPER, James & Elizabeth __?_/[HOWELL]?; b 1688, 1674, ca 6 Dec 1674; East Hampton/Boston/Southampton

LORD, Abraham (?1658-1706?) & Susanna __?_, m/2 Robert KNIGHT 1714; b 11 May 1695; Kittery, ME

LORD, Benjamin[3] (1666-1713) & Elizabeth PRATT (1673-); 13 Apr 1693; Saybrook, CT

LORD, James[3] (1668-1731) & Elizabeth HILL (1674-1742); 13 Dec 1693; Saybrook, CT

LORD, John[2] (1624-1677+) & 1/wf Rebecca [BUSHNELL] (1621-bef 1647); ca 1645; Hartford, CT

LORD, John[2] (1624-1677+) & 2/wf Adrian BAYSEY; 15 May 1648; Hartford, CT

LORD, John (1640-) & Nam-a-tam-a-hansett, Indian?; Hingham

LORD, John & Elizabeth CLARKE; 9 Dec 1695; Ipswich

LORD, Joseph (1672?-1748) & 1/wf Abigail HINCKLEY (1669-1725); 2 Jun 1698; Barnstable

LORD, Joseph & Abigail (?WILMOT) ADAMS, ?w Abraham; 23 Jul 1700; Boston

LORD, Nathan (?1603-1690) & 1/wf __?_ [CONLY]; ca 1653-4; Kittery, ME/Berwick, ME

LORD, Nathan (?1603-1690) & 2/wf Martha [EVERETT] (1640-1723+); b 20 Jun 1656; Kittery, ME/Cold Harbor

LORD, Nathan (1657-1733) & Martha TOZIER; 22 Nov 1678; Kittery, ME

LORD, Nathaniel & Mary (CALL) BOALS, w Joseph BOLLES; 31 Dec 1685; Ipswich

LORD, Nathaniel (1666-1707) & Anna FROTHINGHAM (1671-1708); 4 Aug 1698; Charlestown

LORD, Richard[2] (1611-1662) & Sarah [?GRAVES/BRACKETT?] (-1676); b 1636; Hartford

LORD, Richard (1636-1685) & Mary SMITH (1643-1702), m/2 Thomas HOOKER 1685+; 25 Apr 1665; Springfield/Hartford

LORD, Richard (1647-1727) & Elizabeth [HYDE] (1660-173-); 1682?, b 1683; Lyme, CT

LORD, Richard (1669-1712) & Abigail WARREN (1676-1754), m/2 Timothy WOODBRIDGE 1716; 14 Jan 1691/2; Hartford

LORD, Robert (1602?, 1604-1683, ae 79) (ae 57 in 1660) & Mary WAITE?; Finchingfield, Co. Essex, Eng, 11 Nov 1630; Ipswich

LORD, Robert[2] (1620-1675+) & Rebecca [STANLEY (crossed out)/PHILLIPS]; b 1651; Boston/London, Eng

LORD, Robert (-1696) & Hannah [DAY]; b 1657; Ipswich

LORD, Robert & Abigail AYRES; 7 Jun 1683; Ipswich

LORD, Robert[3] (1651-) & Esther (WARD) (HAWLEY) (NICHOLS) [HILL] (-1732), w Ephraim, w Ebenezer, w Eliphalet; 25 Apr 1696; ; Fairfield, CT

LORD, Samuel (-1696) & 1/wf Elizabeth TIDD/TED (-1684); 15 Oct 1667; Charlestown

LORD, Samuel (-1696) & 2/wf Rebecca EDDINGTON, m/2 Edward WILSON 1696; 16 Dec 1684; Charlestown

LORD, Samuel (?1670-1701?) & Susanna [COLLINS]? (1674-), m/2 Daniel BARTLETT 1707; Saybrook, CT

LORD, Thomas[1] (?1585-1639+) & Dorothy BIRD (1588-1675); Towcester, Eng, ?lic 10 Feb 1610/11, m 20 Feb, 23? Feb; Hartford

LORD, Thomas[2] (1616-1662) (called bro. by John TAYLOR, Windsor 1648) & Hannah THURSTON, m/2 Gregory WOLLESTON; 23 Sep 1652; Boston/Hartford

LORD, Thomas (1713, ae 80) & Alice RAND (-1721, ae 87); 26 Jun 1660; Ipswich

LORD, Thomas & Mary BROWNE, m/2 John CLARK 1702; 24 May 1686; Ipswich

LORD, Thomas[3] (1645-1730) & Mary __?_ (not LEE) (-1735, ae 63?, 65); 22 Dec 1693; Lyme, CT

LORD, William (-1673, ae 97) & Abigail __?_ (-1682), m/2 Resolved WHITE 1679; no ch; Salem

LORD, William[2] (1618-1678) & 1/wf __?_; b 1643, 18 Jan 1641; Saybrook, CT

LORD, William (-1685) & Jane [?ROWLAND]/[?GRAY] (-1685+) (widow called Eliza); b 1656; Salem

LORD, William[2] (1618-1678) & 2/wf Lydia (BUCKLAND) [BROWN], w John, m/3 Thomas DUNK, m/4 Abraham POST; ca 18 Apr 1664, aft 26 Jun 1663; Rehoboth/Saybrook, CT

LORD, William[3] (1643-1696) & Sarah **[BROOKS]** (1662-), m/2 Samuel **INGRAM/INGHAM** 1703; ca 1676/80; Lyme, CT/E. Haddam, CT
LORD, William & 1/wf Mary **MOULTON** (1661-); 7 Apr 1680; Salem
LORD, William & Dorothy **BEADLE** (1669-), m/2 Jeremiah **NEALE**; 10 Aug 1693; Salem
LORD, _?_ & Katherine _?_, mother of Robert; b 1603
LORD, _?_ & Dorothy _?_, m/2 William **RACKLIFF**; 18 Oct 1681; Kittery, ME
LORESON, Cornelius & Abiel **PAIG**; 4 Nov 1697; Boston
LORING, Benjamin (1644-1716) & Mary **HAWKE** (-1714); 8 Dec 1670; Hingham
LOREIN, Caleb (1674-1732) & Lydia **GREY/GRAY** (-1771, ae 93); 7 Aug 1696; Plymouth/Plympton
LORING, Daniel (1672-) & Priscilla **MAN/MANN** (-1716); 2 Feb 1698; Boston
LORING, David & Elizabeth **(OTIS) ALLYN** (1676-1716), w Thomas; 30 Jan 1699, [1698/9], ?20 Jul; Barnstable
LOUREIN, George & Agnes _?_ ; b 1693; Boston
LOREING, Isaac (1666-1702) & Sarah **YOUNG**; 5 Aug 1691; Boston
LORING, John (1630-1714) & 1/wf Mary **BAKER** (1639-1679); 16 Dec 1657; Hingham/Hull
LORING, John (1630-1714) & 2/wf Rachel **(WHEATLAND?/WHEATLEY) BUCKLAND** (-1713, ae 70), w Benjamin; 22 Sep 1679; Hingham/Hull
LORING, Jonathan & Elizabeth **AUSTIN** (1675-); Feb 1700
LORING, Joseph (-1691) & Hannah **LEAVITT** (1663-1728?), m/2 Joseph **ESTEBROOK** 1693; 25 Oct 1683; Hingham/Lexington
LORING, Josiah (1642-1713) & Elizabeth **[PRINCE]** (1640-1727); b 1663, ?Jul 1662; Hingham
LORING, Nathaniel (**RORING** is wrong) (1670-) & Susanna **BUTLER**; 13 Dec 1699; Boston
LORING, Thomas (-1661) & Jane **[NEWTON]** (-1672); in Eng, b 1626; Dorchester/Hingham
LORING, Thomas (1626-1678/9) & Hannah **JACOB** (1640-1720), m/2 Stephen **FRENCH**; 16 Dec 1657; Hingham
LORING, Thomas (1662-) & Leah **BUCKLAND**; 10 Jan 1686/7, at Hull; Hingham
LOREIN, Thomas (1668-1717, Duxbury), Plymouth & Deborah **CUSHEN/CUSHING**, m/2 Sylvester **RICHMOND**; at Boston, 19 Apr 1699; Boston/Plymouth/Scituate
LORING, _?_ & Mary **[WHITE]**, m/2 _?_ **HOLBROOK**; b 12 Jul 1699
LORTON/?LORTHON/?LORTHOM/?LOTEN, John & Mary **[LONGLEY]** (1673/4?-), dau John; b 1691(2?); Cambridge/Concord
LORTHORN/?LORTON/LAWTON, John & Mary **[LONGLEY]** (1673/4-); b 1696, b 1691(2?); Charlestown/?Cambridge
LOTHROP, Barnabas (1636-1715) & 1/wf Susannah **CLARK** (-1697); 1 Dec 1658, 3 Nov 1658; Barnstable
LOTHROP, Barnabas, Jr. (1662-1732) & Elizabeth **HEDGE** (1666-); 14 Nov 1687; Barnstable
LOTHROP, Barnabas (1636-1715) & 2/wf Abigail **(BUTTON) DUDSON**, w Joseph; 15 Nov 1698; Boston
LOTHROP, Benjamin (1631-1691) & Martha _?_ ; b 1652; Charlestown
LOTHROP, Benjamin (?1660-1690) & Abigail **[EDWARDS]** (1671-), m/2 Thomas **STOUGHTON** 1697; 1689(?); ?Hartford
LOTHROP, Hope & Elizabeth **LOTHROP**; 17 Dec 1696; Barnstable
LATHROP, Isaac & Elizabeth **BARNES** (1677-); 29 Dec 1698; Plymouth
LATHROP, Israel (1659-1733) & Rebecca **BLISS** (1663-1737); 8 Apr 1686; Norwich, CT
LOTHROP, John (1584-1653) & 1/wf Hannah **HOUSE**; m lic, 10 Oct 1610, in Eng; Scituate/Barnstable
LOTHROP, John (1584-1653) & 2/wf ?Ann **HAMMOND**; ca 1635; Scituate/Barnstable
LOTHROP, John (1648-1688) & Ruth **ROYCE**, m/2 Abraham **DOOLITTLE** 1689; 15 Dec 1669; ?Wallingford, CT
LOTHROP, John (1644-1727) & 1/wf Mary **COLE**; 3 Jan 1671, 3 Jan 1671/2; Plymouth/Barnstable
LATHROP, John (1667-1695) & **[Elizabeth GREEN]** (1662-1732), Boston, m/2 Thomas **CROCKER** 1701; b 1692; Barnstable
LOTHROP, John (1644-1727) & 2/wf Hannah **(MORTON) FULLER** (-1714), w John; ca middle of Dec 1695, 9 Dec 1695; Barnstable
LATHROP, John & Joanna **PRINCE**; 21 Jan 1697; Boston
LOTHROP, Joseph & Mary **ANSEL**; 11 Dec 1650; Barnstable
LOTHROP, Joseph (1661-1740) & 1/wf Mercy **SCUDDER** (-1695); 8 Apr 1686; Norwich, CT
LOTHROP, Joseph & Abigail **CHILD** (1672-); 14 Jan 1695; Barnstable

LATHROP, Joseph (1661-1740) & 2/wf Elizabeth WATERHOUSE (1672-1726); 21 Feb 1696/7; Norwich, CT
LATHROP, Mark (-1686), Salem, Duxbury, Bridgewater & _?_ ; b 1663; Bridgewater
LOTHROP, Melatiah (1696-1712) & Sarah FARRAR (-1712); 20 May 1667; Lynn
LOTHROP, Nathaniel (1669-1700) & Bethiah _?_, m/2 Robert CLAGHORN 1701; b 1696; Barnstable
LOTHROP, Samuel & Elizabeth SCUDDER; 28 Nov 1644; Barnstable/New London, CT
LOTHROP, Samuel & 1/wf Hannah ADGATE; - Nov 1675; Norwich, CT
LATHROP, Samuel & Sarah [DOWNER?/DONNER?]; b 1683; Bridgewater
LOTHROP, Samuel (1664-) & Hannah CROCKER (1665-); 1 Jul 1686; Barnstable
LOTHROP, Samuel (-1700, 1701) & 2/wf Abigail DOANE (1633?-1735 7/6) (she was 100, 13 Jan 1733); ca 1690-92, 1690; Norwich, CT
LOTHROP, Samuel (1650-1732) & 2/wf Mary (REYNOLDS) EDGERTON (1664-1728), w John; 30 Dec 1697; Norwich, CT
LAYTHORP, Thomas (1613-) & Sarah (LARNED/LEARNED/LINNELL?) EWER, w Thomas; 11 Dec 1639; Charlestown
LOTHROP, Capt. Thomas (-1675) & Bethia [REA], dau Daniel, m/2 Joseph GRAFTON, m/3 William GOODHUE 1685?; ?ca 1640; Salem
LOTHROP, Thomas & Mehitable [SARSON]; b 1693; Martha's Vineyard
LOTHROP, Thomas³ (1674-) & Experience GORHAM; 23 Apr 1697; Barnstable
LOTT, Lawrence & Catherine _?_ ; b 1687; Boston
LOTT, _?_ & Sarah _?_ , m/2 Adam MOTT; b 1631; Portsmouth, RI
LOUD/LOWD, Francis & Sarah _?_ ; b 1700; Ipswich
LOUGEE/LOJEE, Philip & Mary SNASHER; 17 Sep 1673; Salem
LOUNSBERY, John? & Abigail/Ann? (THOMAS) [PRESTON] (1674-), w Samuel; b 1701?; Rye
LOUNSBERRY, Richard (-1694) & Elizabeth (_?_) (SCOFIELD) [PENNIGER] (±1652-), w Richard, w Robert; ca 1670?, b 1684; Rye, NY
LOVE/LORD, Thomas & Hannah THURSTON; 23 Sep 1652; Boston
LUFF/LOVE?, John (-1667?, 1668) & Bridget _?_ (1587-); Salem
LOVE, John & Susanna BENNETT, [dau Peter]; b 1701?, 1 Jan 1701; Boston
LOVE, William (-1687) & Mary [TAYLOR], m/2 Samuel WYLLYS 1688; Kittery, ME
LOVE _?_ & _?_ ; b 1698; Boston
LOVEJOY, Christopher (1661-1737) & Sarah RUSS; 26 May 1685; Andover
LOVEJOY, Ebenezer & Mary FOSTER (1673-); 11 Jul 1693; Andover
LOVEJOY, John (-1690) & 1/wf Mary OSGOOD (1633-1675, Andover); 1 Jan 1651, Ipswich, ?1 Jun 1651, 1652?; Andover
LOVEJOY, John & Hannah PRICHARD; 12 Jan 1676/7; Andover
LOVEJOY, John & Naomi HOIT/HOYT, m/2 Richard STRATTON 1686/7; 23 Mar 1677/8; Andover
LOVEJOY, Joseph & Sarah PRICHARD; 26 May 1685; Andover
LOVEJOY, Nathaniel & 1/wf Dorothy HOYT; 21 Mar 1693/4; Andover
LOVEJOY, William & Mary FARNUM; 29 Nov 1680; Andover
LOVELAND, John (-1670) & _?_ ; Hartford
LOVELAND, Robert (-1768) & Ruth GILLAM; 19 Aug 1697; Wethersfield, CT
LOVELAND, Thomas (ca 1641-1716+) & _?_ ; b 1677; Wethersfield, CT
LOVELAND, Thomas (-1725) & _?_ ; b 1700; Wethersfield, CT
LOVELL, Alexander (-1709) & 1/wf Lydia ALBY/ALBEE (-1661); 30 Oct 1658; Medfield
LOVELL, Alexander (-1709) & 2/wf Lydia [LELAND]? (-1700); b 1664, 1661; Medfield
LOVELL, Alexander & Elizabeth SAWFORD/SAFFORD?/SANFORD? (1670-); 20 Jul [1692?], 1696?; Ipswich
LOVEL?, Andrew (1668-) (son John) & [Hannah MAGOON]? (1671-); b 1689; Scituate/Barnstable
LOVELL, Enoch (1670-) & Mary REED; 24 Nov 1697; Weymouth
LOVEL, James (1634-1706) & 1/wf Jane _?_ ; b 1664(5?); Weymouth/?Barnstable
LOVEL, James (1662-) (son John) & Mary LUMBART (1666-); - May 1686; Barnstable
LOVELL, James & Elizabeth POOL (1674-); 7 Jun 1694; Weymouth
LOVELL, James (1634-1706) & 2/wf Anna _?_ ; b 1697 prob; Weymouth
LOVELL, John (1627-1709) & Jane [HATCH] (1631-1709+); ca 1648, b 1651, b 6 Nov 1651; Weymouth/Barnstable
LOVEL, John (1658-) (son John) & Susannah LUMBART; - Jun 1688; Barnstable

LOVELL, John & Elizabeth PINDER; 12 Sep 1689; Ipswich
LOVEL, John & Mary WORTHYLAKE; 6 Mar 1699/1700; Sandwich
LOVELL, John (1676-) & Mary [SHAW]; b 1701?; Weymouth/Middleboro
LOVEL, Nathaniel & Elizabeth DAVIS (1679-); 28 Jun 1696; Dedham
LOVELL, Nathaniel & Elizabeth [DAVIS]; b 1698 (see above); Medfield
LOVELL, Robert[1] (1595-1672?, 1651?) & Elizabeth _?_ (1600-); in Eng, b 1619; Weymouth/ Hingham
LOVELL, Splan/Splann & Mary _?_ ; b 1685; ?Portsmouth, NH
LOVELL, Thomas (1621-1710) (ae 74 in 1694) & Ann _?_ ; b 1648; Ipswich
LOVELL, Thomas & Elizabeth WATSON; 28 Dec 1667; Charlestown
LOVELL, Thomas & Mary _?_ ; b 1687; Plymouth?
LOVEL, William (1664-1753) (son John) & Mehitable LUMBART (1674-); 24 Sep 1693; Barnstable
LOVERILL, John, Piscataqua & 1/wf Hannah KELLUM/KILLAM/KILHAM; 1 Mar 1686; Ipswich
LEVERAN, John (-1638) & Anna WHITING?/BARNARD?/Anne WILSON?, m/2 Edmund BROWN 1644?, 1639?; Watertown
LOVERING, John (-1668) & Esther/Hester _?_ , m/2 Ezekiel KNIGHT ca 1668; by 1660; Dover, NH
LOVERING/LOVERELL, John (1663-) & 1/wf Hannah KILHAM; 1 Mar 1681; Ipswich/Piscataqua, NH
LOVERING, John & Jane _?_ , m/2 John PHELPS 1695; b 1689; Boston
LOVERAN, Thomas (1626-1692) & Anna _?_ , m/2 William THOMAS 1695; ca 1663?, no issue; Watertown
LOVERING, William (-1688) & Margaret [GUTCH]; ca 1665?, b 1676(7?); Boston
LOVETT, Daniel (-1691/2) & Joanna [BLOTT] (1620-), dau Robert; betw 7 Sep 1644 & 8 Jun 1645; Braintree/Mendon
LOVETT, James (1648-), Mendon & Hannah TEYLER/TYLER; 17 Feb 1668/9, 20 Jan 1668, 17 Feb; Medfield/Roxbury/Mendon
LOVET, John (1612, ?1610-1686) & Mary _?_ ; b 1637, b 1636?; Salem
LOVETT, John (1636, 1637-1727) & Bethia [ROOTS] (?1639-); b 1659; Beverly
LOVETT, John (?1665-1750) & Mary PRIDE; 5 Mar 1694/5; Beverly
LOVETT, John & Ursula [WOODWARD]; b 1701; Mendon/Attleboro
LOVETT, Joseph & Elizabeth [SOLART]; b 1673; Beverly
LOVET, Joseph & Catherine [SALLOWS]; b 1696; Beverly
LOVET, Samuel (1675-1750) & Prudence DODGE (1680-); 5 Feb 1699/1700; Beverly
LOVITT, Simon (1659-1744) & Agnes/Annis? SWETLAND, w William; 10 Oct 16--, 1682, 1684+; Beverly
LOVET, Thomas (1671-) & Bethia _?_ ; b 1693; Beverly
LOWWELL/LOVELL, John, Boston (-1700+) & Elizabeth SILVESTER (1644-1700+); 24 Jan 1658; Scituate/Boston/Rehoboth/Dunstable
LOVEWELL, John (1660-) & Anna HASSELL; 7 Dec 1686; Dunstable
LOVEWELL, Joseph (1662-1732) & 1/wf Mary _?_ (-1729); b 1691; Dunstable/Watertown
LOWDEN, Anthony & Sarah/?Elizabeth OSBORNE; 16 Sep 1696; Dover
LOWDEN, James (?1648-1740) & Mary (HOWARD) BUNKER (-1706), w Jonathan; 17 Dec 1679; Charlestown
LOWDEN, John (1641-1678) & Sarah STEVENSON, alias STIMPSON, m/2 James KIBBY 1679; 29 May 1662; Cambridge
LOWDEN, John (1663-) & Elizabeth SPENSER, dau Richard?; 5 Jun 1684; Charlestown
LOWDEN, Joseph (1676-) & 1/wf Mary [HORNE/ORNE] (-1706); b 1700; Boston
LOWDEN, Richard (1613, 1612?-1700) & Mary [COLE] (1618-1683, ae 65); b 1641; Charlestown
LOWDEN, Richard (1665-1709) & Mary _?_ , m/2 Timothy HAY bef Jan 1713/14; b 1693(4?); Boston
LOWDER, Henry & Mercy/[Mary POLLARD]; b 1671; Boston
LOW, Ambrose & Ruth ANDREWS (1660-1718); 22 Feb 1687/8; Hingham
LOW, Andrew (-1670) (had son in Eng) & 1/wf _?_ ; [New Haven]
LOWE, Andrew (-1670) & Joan (?ALLEN) [PECK], w Henry; aft 1651; New Haven
LOW, Anthony (-1693, 1692?) & Frances _?_ (1632-1702); [b 1655]; Boston/Warwick, RI/Swansea
LOW, Arthur (1660-1690) & _?_
LOW, David (1667-1746) & Mary LAMB (-1735); 28 Dec 1699; Ipswich

LOW, John (-1653) & Elizabeth __?__ ; b 1632?; Boston
LOW, John (-1697) & Elizabeth STODDER/STODDARD (-1658); 28 Feb 1648/9; Hingham
LOWE, John & Hannah LINCOLN (doubtful); Sep 1659; Hingham
LOW, John (1635, 1633/4?-1695?) & 1/wf Sarah THORNDICK/THORNDIKE (-1672); 10 Dec 1661; Ipswich
LOW, John (-1676) & [Elizabeth HOWLAND], dau Arthur; b 1665?, b 1670; Marshfield
LOW, John & Mary RHODES; 3 Mar 1674/5, 3 Mar 1675, 3 Mar 1674; Warwick, RI
LOW, John & Ruth JOY; 25 Sep 1679; Hingham
LOW, John (-1695?, 1706?) & 2/wf Dorcas __?__ ; b 1685, b 1674; Ipswich
LOW, John, Jr. (1665-) & [Anna BURNHAM]; b 1690[1?], b 1695 (same?); Ipswich
LOW, Jonathan (1665-) & Mary THOMSON; 8 Mar 1692/3, 1692; Ipswich
LOW, Samuel (-1718) & 1/wf Anne __?__ ; b 1701; Swansea/Barrington
LOW, Thomas (1605-1677) & 1/wf Margaret TODD?; Polstead, Eng, 22 Jun 1630; Ipswich
LOW, Thomas (1605-1677) (ae ca 55 in 1660) & 2/wf Susannah (STONE) (CUTTING) [KIMBALL] (?1598-1684?, 1688, ae 86), w __?__ , w Henry; aft 1648?; Ipswich
LOW, Thomas (1631-1712) & 1/wf Martha BOSMAN (-1720, in 79th y); 4 Jul 1660; Ipswich
LOW, Thomas (1631-1712) & 2/wf [Mary BROWN?]; aft 1676?; Ipswich
LOW, Thomas (?1661-1698) & Sarah SYMONDS (1668-1731+); 2 Dec 1687, prob wrong 1681; Ipswich
LOW, ?John & Elizabeth (SPAFFORD) SESSIONS (1647-1724+), w Alexander; aft 1688/9, ca 1692?; Andover
LOW, __?__ & Sarah WADSWORTH (1648-)
LOWLE, Benjamin (1642-1714) & Ruth WOODMAN (1646-1724+); 17 Oct 1666; Newbury
LOWLE, Ebenezer (1675-) & Elizabeth SHOLER, Hingham; 30 Jun 1694; Boston
LOWLE, Gideon (1672-) & 1/wf Mary/Miriam SWETT (1672-1734); 7 Jul 1692; Newbury
LOWLE, John (?1595, ?1605-1647) & 1/wf [Mary?] __?__ ; in Eng, b 1629, ca 1625; Newbury
LOWLE, John (?1595, ?1605-1647) & 2/wf Elizabeth [GOODALE] (-1651); ca 1641; Newbury
LOWLE, John (-1694) & 1/wf Hannah PROCTOR; 3 Mar 1652/3; Boston
LOWELL, John (-1694) & 2/wf Naomi [TORREY] (1641-1694+); b 1669; Boston
LOWELL, John (1660-) & Esther __?__ ; b 1687; Boston
LOWELL, Joseph (1639-1705) & Abigail PROCTOR (1635-1707); 8 Mar 1660, 1659; Boston
LOWELL, Joseph (1665-) & Patience PECK (-1714?); m int, 12 Jul 1685; Boston
LOWLE, Percival (?1571-1664/5) & Rebecca __?__ (-1645); in Eng, b 1595?, b 1602; Newbury
LOWLE, Percival (?ca 1639/40-) & Mary CHANDLER (-1707); 7 Sep 1664; Newbury
LOWELL, Richard & 1/wf Margaret __?__ (1641/2); Newbury
LOWELL, Richard (1602-1682) & 2/wf Margaret __?__ (1604-1686+) (2 wives Margaret); aft 27 Jan 1641/2; Newbury
LOWLE, Richard (1668-) & Sarah BROWNE (1678-); 8 Apr 1695; Newbury
LOWEL, Samuel & Rachel WILLIAMS; 22 Jul 1698; Boston
LOWERY, John & Mary DAVIS; 13 Nov 1699; Boston
LOWTHER/LOADER?, John (-1718?) & Elizabeth CURTICE/CURTIS (-1737+); ?- - 1686, ?6 Apr 1687; Salem
LUCAS, Augustus (1667-) & Bathsheba/Barsheba [ELIOT] (?1682-1716); b 1697, b 1701?; Newport/?Fairfield, CT
LUCAS, Benoni & Repentance [HARLOW]; b 1684; Plymouth
LUCAS, John & Mary __?__ ; b 1684; Middletown, CT
LUCKEIS, Oliver (-1690) & Jemima BONFIELD, m/2 George FELT 1696; 7 Oct 1686; Marblehead
LUCAS, Samuel (1661-1716) & Patience WARREN (1660-); 16 Dec 1686; Plymouth
LUCAS, Thomas & __?__ ; b 1656; Plymouth
LUCAS, William (-1690) & Esther/Hester? CLARK/BLUNT? (-1690); 12 Jul 1666; Middletown, CT
LUCAS, William (1667-1759) & Elizabeth ROWLEY; - Jul 1695, 15 Jul 1695; Middletown, CT
LUCE, Eleazer & Sarah [WINES], dau Barnabas; b 1700; Southold, LI
LUCE, Experience & Elizabeth [MANTER] (1674-1770); ca 1694; Martha's Vineyard
LUCE, Henry & Remember [LITCHFIELD] (1644-); b 1667; Scituate/Rehoboth/Tisbury
LUCE, Henry (-1743) & Sarah [LOOK] (1678-); b 1699; Edgartown
LUCE, Robert & Desire __?__ ; b 1689; Martha's Vineyard
LUCE __?__ & [Sarah ALLEN] (1669-)
LUCY, Thomas (-1698) & Mary [BROOKINGS]; ca 1690?; Portsmouth, RI

LUDDEN, Benjamin (1658-1690, 1691) & Eunice [HOLBROOK] (1658-); b 1679; Weymouth
LUDDEN, James (ca 1611-1693) & Alice/?Mary JOHNSON?; b 1636, 10 Feb 1636?; Weymouth
LUDDEN, Joseph & Elizabeth [SMITH] (1667-), m/2 Samuel ANDREWS 1691; Weymouth
LUDDINGTON, Henry (1679±-) & Sarah COLLINS (1679-1743); 20 Aug 1700; New Haven
LUDDINGTON, William (1608-1661) & Ellen/?Helen [MOULTHORP] (1619-), m/2 John ROSE, Sr. 1663; b 1637; Charlestown/Malden/New Haven
LUDDINGTON, William (1655±-1737) & 1/wf Martha [ROSE]; b 1679; ?Branford, CT
LUDDINGTON, William (1655±-1737) & 2/wf Mercy WHITEHEAD (1668-1743); - Jun 1690; Branford, CT?
LUDKIN, Aaron (1618-1694) & 1/wf Anna?/Hannah? [HEPBURN] (-1682); b Apr 1650?, b 1654; Hingham
LUDKIN, Aaron (1618-1694) & 2/wf Hannah (MILLER) (DADY) EDMANDS (-1717), w Nathaniel, w John; 22 May 1684; Charlestown
LUDKIN, George (-1648, Braintree) & _?_ ; b 1635; Hingham
LUDKIN, William (1604-1652) & Elizabeth _?_ (1603-1652+); b 1637; Hingham/Boston
LUDLAM, Anthony^2 (-1681/2) & Sarah _?_ , m/2 Isaac COREY; ca 1666?; Southampton, LI
LUDLAM, Anthony^3 (1670-1723) & 1/wf Patience [BARNES] (1677-1708); ca 1695; Bridgehampton, LI
LUDLAM, Henry^2 (1638-) & _?_ SHAW; b 27 Apr 1665; Southampton, LI
LUDLAM, Henry^3 (?1669-1737) & Rachel [HALSEY]; b 1698; Southampton
LUDLAM, John^2 (1658-) & Ruth [CARPENTER]; b 1690; Jamaica, LI
LUDLAM, Joseph^2 (1646-1698) & Elizabeth _?_ (-1723); ca 1670-84; Southampton/Oyster Bay, LI
LUDLAM, Joseph^3 (1667-) & _?_ [?CREED]; b 1690; Jamaica, LI
LUDLAM, Joseph^3 (1675-) & Elizabeth [RYDER]; ca 1695; Southampton, LI/NJ
LUDLAM, William^1 & Clemence _?_ (-1646); b 1628; Southampton, LI
LUDLAM, William^2 (1628-1667) & Elizabeth [SMITH], m/2 Nehemiah SMITH; b 1658; Southampton, LI/Jamaica, LI
LUDLAM, William^3 (?1667-1732) & Sarah [HIGBY]; b 1688; Jamaica, LI
LUDLOW, Roger (brother-in-law of John ENDICOTT) & _?_ ENDICOTT?; Dorchester/Windsor, CT
LUDLOW, Roger (1590-) & [Mary COGENS]; in Eng; Dorchester/Fairfield, CT
LOVEKIN, Ebenezer (1676-) & Sarah AVERELL (1666-); 12 Apr 1700; Gloucester
LUFKIN, Jacob & Mercy [LITTLEFIELD], m/3 Richard STEVENSON 1702; b 1696; ?Wells, ME
LOVEKIN, Thomas & _?_ ; b 1669; Gloucester
LOVEKIN, Thomas^2 (1669-1747) & 1/wf Mary MILES (-1690); 22 Jan 1689/90; Gloucester
LOVEKIN, Thomas^2 (1669-1747) & 2/wf Sarah DOWNING (-1724); 22 Dec 1692; Gloucester/Ipswich
LUGG, John (-1644+) & Jane DIGHTON/DEIGHTON (1609-1671+), m/2 Jonathan NEGUS/NEGOOSE 1647; 3 Jan 1627; Boston
LUIST, Robert & Rebecca (JENNER) LYNDE, w Samuel; 6 Apr 1682; Charlestown
LUKE, George & Hannah BAXTER (1663-), m/2 John PRICE 1691; 30 Apr 1685; Charlestown
LULL, Simon & Anna DAY; 13 Jan 1695; Ipswich
LULL, Thomas (-1719, ae 82) & 1/wf Elizabeth [BREWER?]; b 1661, b 1660?; Ipswich
LULL, Thomas (-1714) & Rebecca KIMBOLE/KIMBALL (1664-); 21 Jan 1689; Ipswich
LULL, _?_ & Meribah [SINCLAIR]; by 1700
LUM, John & _?_ (STRICKLAND); b 1642?; Stamford, CT
LUM, Jonathan & 1/wf Sarah RIGGS; 10 Oct 1700; Derby, CT
LUM, Samuel (1644±-1685+) & Hannah [?MEIGS]; b 1672; Southampton, LI
LUM, Samuel & _?_ ; b 1695; Southampton, LI
LUME, _?_ (-1661/2) & Ann (_?_) PICKARD; b 1646; Rowley
LUMAS/LOOMIS, Edward (1611-) & Mary _?_ ; b 1640(1?), ca 1636?; Ipswich
LUMAS, Edward, Jr. (?1645-) & _?_ ; ?Ipswich/Cohansey, NJ
LUMAS, John & Mary [TRASK] (ae 58 in 1695); b 1659; Salem
LUMMUS, Jonathan (1643-1728) & Elizabeth _?_ (-1716); b 1683; Ipswich
LAMOS, Nathaniel & 1/wf _?_ ; b 1690?; Dover, NH
LUMAS, Samuel (1639-) & 1/wf Sarah SMITH; 18 Nov 1664; Ipswich
LUMMIS, Samuel & ?2/wf Hannah (WHITE) DIVOLL (-1709, ae 63), w John; b 1679; Ipswich

LUMPKIN, Richard (1582-1642) & Sarah BAKER, m/2 Simon STONE ca 1655; in Eng, 20 Oct 1614, no issue; Cambridge

LUMPKIN, William (-1671) & Thomasine/Tamsen __?__ (-1671+), ?m/2 Rev. John MAYO; b 1626; Yarmouth

LUNN, Thomas & __?__ ; b 1662, b 1660; Boston

LUND, Thomas & Eleanor __?__; b 1682; Dunstable

LUNERUS, Polus & Margaret CLEMONS, wid; 1 Jul 1652; Boston

LUN, Thomas & Elizabeth BOWKER; 28 Mar 1679; Cambridge

LUNN, __?__ & [Mary MUZZY]; b 1701?

LUNT, Daniel (1641-1689) & 1/wf Hannah COKER (1645-1679); 16 May 1664; Newbury

LUNT, Daniel (1641-1689) & 2/wf Mary (CUTTING) MOODY, w Samuel; 24 Jun 1679; Newbury

LUNT, Henry (-1662) & Ann __?__, m/2 Joseph HILLS 1664; b 1639; Newbury

LUNT, Henry (1653-1709) & Jane BROWN (1657-), m/2 Joseph MAYO; b 1677; Boston/Newbury

LUNT, Henry (1669-1725) & 1/wf Mary __?__ (-1721); b 1695; Newbury

LUNT, John (1643-1678) & Mary SKERRY (1640-), m/2 Thomas NELSON 1680; 19 Nov 1668; Newbury

LUNT, John (1669-1741) & 1/wf Ruth (WARD) JEWETT (1662-1734), w Joseph; 26 Oct 1696; Rowley/Salisbury

LUNT, Thomas & Opportunity HOPPIN (1657-); 17 Jun 1679; Newbury

LUPTON, Christopher (-1686/8) & __?__ (not Abigail) [RAYNOR]; ca 1654?; Southampton, LI

LUPTON, John (-1716) & Hannah [STANBOROUGH] (1674-); Southampton

LUPTON, Joseph & __?__ ; Southampton

LUPTON, Thomas (-1685) & Hannah [MORRIS]; 1662; New Haven/Norwalk

LUPTON, Thomas & Mary [MAPHAM] (-1749); b 26 Jan 1692; Southampton, LI

LUPTON, __?__ & Abigail [DEMING]; b 13 Dec 1721, prob by 1710; Southampton

LUPTON, __?__ & Abigail WHEELER; b 15 Sep 1726; East Hampton, LI

LURVEY, Peter & Mary __?__ ; b 1679; Ipswich

LUSCOMBE, Humphrey (-1688) & Susanna [?KELLOND] (1665?-), dau Thomas?; b 1683; Boston

LYSOM/LUSCOM, John & Abigail [BREWER] (1664-); ca 1691, b 1693; Lynn

LUSCOMB, William & Susannah __?__ ; b 1660; Salem

LUSCOMB, William (-1733/4) & Jane [GARLAND]; b 1700; Salem

LUSHER, Eleazer & 1/wf __?__ ; b 1638; Dedham

LUSHER, Eleazer (-1672) & 2/wf Mary (BUNKER) GWIN, w John; 8 Aug 1662; Charlestown

LUSON, John (-1661) & Martha [?HUBBARD] (-1679); no issue; Dedham

LUTHER, Hezekiah (1640-1723) & 1/wf Elizabeth __?__ ; 30 Jan 1661/2; Dorchester/Milton

LUTHER, Hezekiah[2] (1640-1723) & 2/wf Sarah [BUTTERWORTH (prob wrong)] (?1641-1722); b 1674, ca 1668; Swansea

LUTHER, John (-1644) & ?Elizabeth __?__ ; b 1638; Taunton

LUTHER, John (-1697, ae 34) & Hopestill BUTTERWORTH, m/2 John EDDY; 25 Jan 1697/8; Swansea/Warren, RI

LUTHER, Joseph (-1747, ae 77) & Experience BRAMAN (-1721); 1 Jan 1700; Rehoboth/Warren, RI

LUTHER, Nathaniel (1665-) & Ruth COLE (1666-1710); 28 Jun 1693; Swansea/Warren, RI

LUTHER, Rev. Samuel (1638-1716, ae ca 80) & Mary [ABELL]?; b 1663; Rehoboth/Swansea

LUTHER, Samuel (1663-1714) & Sarah __?__ ; b 1689; Swansea/Warren, RI

LUTHER, Theophilus (1665-) & Lydia KINNECUTT; 24 Nov 1686; Swansea

LUX, John (-1714) & 1/wf __?__ ; b 1646; Damariscove

LUX, John (-1714) & Mary (?MUNSELL) ROWE [JEFFREY], w Michael, w Gregory; ca 1663; Damariscove

LUX, John (-1677) & 1/wf Agnes __?__ ; b 1667/[8?]; Boston

LUX, John (-1677) & 2/wf Sarah __?__, m/2 William DINSDALE bef 1686; aft 1671; Boston

LUX, Richard & Mary __?__ ; b 1694(5?); Boston

LUX, William (-1684) & Audrey [MUSSELL] (1619-1692); b 1638; Richmond Isl.

LUXFORD, James & Elizabeth [ALBONE], m/2 __?__ COLE; b 1637, div 1640; Cambridge

LUXFORD, Reuben (1641-1703) & 1/wf Margaret __?__ (-1691); 22 Jun 1669; Lancaster

LUXFORD, Reuben (-1703) & 2/wf Lydia __?__, w Arthur COLE/William EAGER, m/2 Nathaniel BILLINGS; aft 31 Aug 1691; Cambridge

LUXFORD, Stephen (-1676) & __?__ ; no issue, ?married; Haddam, CT

LYALL/LOYALL, Francis & Alice __?__ ; b 1638, b 1639; Boston

LYDE, Allen (-1672) & Sarah **FERNALD**, m/2 Richard **WATERHOUSE** 1672; 3 Dec 1661; ?Portsmouth, NH

LYDE, Allen (1666-1701?, 1702?) & Eleanor [?**MERCER**]; b 1691; Portsmouth, NH

LYDE/LLOYD, Edward & Mary **WHEELWRIGHT**, m/2 Theodore **ATKINSON** 1667; 4 Dec 1660; Boston

LYDE, Edward & 1/wf Susannah **CORWINE** (1672-); 29 Nov 1694; Salem

LYDE, Edward & 2/wf Deborah **BYFIELD** (-1708); m int, 24 Sep 1696, m 22 Oct 1696; Boston

LYDSTON, John (1673±-) & Mary **(ROBY)** [**TETHERLY**]; b 30 Aug 1693; Kittery, ME

LYDSTON, Weymouth (-1696) & Martha __?__; b 1670; Kittery, Me

LYFORD, Francis & 1/wf Elizabeth [**SMITH**] (1646-); ca Jun 1671, ca 1670; Boston

LYFORD, Francis & 2/wf Rebecca **DUDLEY**; 21 Nov 1681; Exeter, NH

LYFORD, Rev. John (-1632) & Sarah **OAKLEY** (-1649) (ae 53 in 1639), m/2 Edmund **HOBART** 1634; ca 1615/20?; Plymouth/Hingham

LYFORD, Thomas (1672-) & Judith [**GILMAN**]; b 1701?; Exeter, NH

LYMAN, Benjamin (1674-1723) & Thankful **POMEROY** (1679-1773); 27 Oct 1698; Northampton

LYMAN, John (1623-1690) & Dorcas **PLUMB** (1623-1725); 12 Jan 1654, 1654/5; Branford, CT/Northampton

LYMAN, John (1666-1740) & Mindwell **(SHELDON) POMEROY** (1660-), w John; 19 Apr 1687; Northampton

LYMAN, John (-1727) & 1/wf Sarah __?__; b 1688; Northampton

LYMAN, John (1654, 1655-1727) & 2/wf Abigail (?**HOLTON**) (ca 1672-1714); b 1696; Northampton

LYMAN, Moses (1663, ?20 Feb 1662, ?23 Nov 1662-1701) & Ann __?__; b 1686; Northampton

LYMAN, Richard[1] (1580-1640) & Sarah [**OSBORN**]?; b 1611, ca 1608; Hartford

LYMAN, Richard[2] (1618-1662) & Hepzibah [**FORD**] (1625-1683), m/2 John **MARSH** 1664; ca 1641; Windsor, CT/Northampton

LYMAN, Richard (?1647-1708) & Elizabeth **COWLES**; 26 May 1676; Northampton

LYMAN, Richard & Mary **WOODWARD**; 11 Apr 1700; Lebanon, CT

LYMAN, Robert (1629-1690?) & Hepzibah **BASCOMB** (1644-1690); 15 Nov 1662, 1 Nov, 5 Nov; Northampton

LYMAN, Samuel & Elizabeth **(REYNOLDS) FOWLER**, w Jonathan **FOWLER** alias **SMITH**; 9 May 1699; Lebanon, CT

LYMAN, Thomas (-1725) & Ruth **(HOLTON)** [**BAKER**], w Joseph; ca 1678, ?14 Mar 1678; Northampton/Durham, CT

LYMAN, __?__ & Sarah **SAYRE** (1680-); b 1701?

LYNDE, Benjamin (1666-1745) & Mary **BROWNE** (1679-1753); 27 Apr 1699, 22 Apr; Salem/Boston

LYNDE, John (1648-) & 1/wf Mary [**PIERCE**] (1656-1690, ae 34); b 1672?, b 1678; Charlestown

LYNDE, John & 2/wf Elizabeth **(HILLS) GREEN** (-1699), w William; 25 Aug 1691; Malden

LYNDE, John & Judith **(WORTH)** [**BUCKMAN**] (-1735, ae ca 83), w Joses; b 1700; Malden

LYNDE, Joseph (1636-1727) & 1/wf Sarah **DAVISON** (1647-1678); 24 Mar 1665, 29 Mar 1665; Charlestown

LYNDE, Joseph (1636-1727) & 2/wf Emma **(ANDERSON)** [**BRACKENBURY**] (-1703), w John; prob 1679; betw 12 Dec 1678 & 30 Jan 1680; Charlestown

LYNDE, Joseph (1652-1736) & Elizabeth [**TUFTS**] (1660-); b 1684?, b 1686; Malden

LYNDE, Joseph (1671-) & Sarah [**BELCHER**] (1674-), m/2 John **FOY** 1689; b Aug 1694 (lost at sea); Charlestown

LYNDE, Nathaniel (1659-1729) & 1/wf Susanna **WILLOUGHBY** (1664-1710); b 1683; Charlestown/Saybrook, CT

LYNDE, Nicholas (1672-1703) & Dorothy **STANTON**, m/2 John **TRERISE** 1708, m/3 Samuel **FUNK**?, m/4 Robert **DENISON**?; 7 May 1695, 9 May 1696; Stonington, CT/Charlestown

LYNDE, Samuel (1644-) & Rebecca **JENNERS/JENNER**, m/2 Robert **LEWIS/LUIST** 1682; 3 Jun 1673; Charlestown

LYNDE, Samuel (1653-1721) & 1/wf Mary **BALLARD** (1657-1 Feb 1697/8); 20 Oct 1674; ?Boston

LYNDE, Samuel (-1721) & Mary (?**BENDALL**) **(ALLEN) RICHARDSON** (-1727), w Dr. Daniel?, w John?; 15 Sep 1698; Boston

LYNDE, Simon (1624-1687) & Hannah **NEWGATE** (1635-1684); 22 Feb 1652/3; Boston/Saybrook, CT

LYNDE, Thomas (-1671) & 1/wf ?Mary __?__; b 1616?, b 1627?, b 1629; Charlestown
LYNDE, Thomas (-1671) & 2/wf Margaret (MARTIN) JORDAN (-1662), w Henry; b 1634; Malden/Charlestown
LYNDE, Thomas (-1690, ae 81?) & Elizabeth [TUFTS?] (1612-1693?); b 1647; Charlestown
LYNDE, Thomas¹ (-1671) & 3/wf Rebecca TRERICE (-1688), w Nicholas; 6 Dec 1665; Charlestown
LYNDE, Thomas (1647-) & Mary ANDERSON, m/2 Rev. Thomas SHEPARD 1682, m/3 Samuel HAYMAN 1686; b 1677; Charlestown
LYNDE, __?__ & 2/wf Mary BRICK; Salisbury
LINN, Henry & Sarah [TILLY] (1619-), dau Wm., m/2 Hugh GUNNISON 1647, m/3 Capt. John MITCHELL 1660±, m/4 Dr. Francis MORGAN bef 1665; b 1636; Boston
LYNN, Ephraim (1639-), Portsmouth, NH, & Ann [LOCKWOOD]; bef 1667; Kittery, ME
LYNN, __?__ & Rebecca __?__; b 1701; Cambridge
LYON, Andrew & Mary __?__; b 1691; Norwalk, CT
LYON, Ebenezer (1661-1689) & __?__; b 1689; Dorchester
LYON, Ebenezer & Elizabeth TORBET/?TURBET; 15 Jul 1600; Dedham/Roxbury
LION, Elkanon (1652-1690) & Mary __?__; 24 Jan 1682; Milton/?Dorchester/Boston
LYON, George (-1690, 1691?) & Hannah [TOLMAN] (1640, 1641/2-1729), m/2 William BLAKE 1693; 14 Dec 1661; Dorchester
LION, George (-1695), Milton & Thankful BADCOCK, Milton, m/2 Richard SMITH; 14 Feb 1688, 1687/8; Milton
LYON, Henry (-1703) & 1/wf ?Elizabeth/?Mary BATEMAN; b 1653; Milford, CT/Elizabeth, NJ/Newark, NJ
LYON, Israel (-1690) & Hannah HEWENS, m/2 Vigilance FISHER 1696; 25 Mar 1690; Dorchester/Boston
LYON, John (1647-1702/3) & Abigail POLLY (1659-1702/3); 10 May 1670; Roxbury
LYON, John (-1736, Greenwood) & __?__; b 6 Dec 1689; Fairfield, CT/Greenwich, CT
LYON, John (-1736) & ?2/wf Rebecca [HULL]; betw 1695 & 1713; Fairfield
LYON, John (1673-1725) & Elizabeth __?__ (-1762 in 95th y); b 1697; Woodstock, CT/Rehoboth
LYON, Joseph & Mary BRIDGE (1661-); 23 Mar 1680/1; Roxbury
LYON, Joseph & Mary [JACKSON], m/2 John BAGLEY b 1700; b 1695; Fairfield, CT
LYON, Joseph (1677-1761) & Sarah __?__; b 1700?; Rye, NY
LYON, Joshua & __?__; b 1686; Salem
LYON, Moses (-1698) & Mary (MEEKER) ADAMS, w Samuel, m/3 John THORPE; aft Feb 1693/4; Fairfield, CT
LYON, Nathaniel (1654-1705) & __?__ (-1705); b 1681; Concord/Dorchester
LYON, Peter (-1694) & 1/wf? Ann/?Susanna __?__ (-1689); b 1650; Dorchester
LION, Peter (1663-1733) & Jane [VOSE] (1665-); b 1686; Dorchester
LYON, Richard (-1678) (he calls Mary FITCH "cousin") & 2/wf? Margaret __?__ (-1705) (2nd m ca 1668?, ca 1666); b 1653, b 1649?; Fairfield, CT
LYON, Richard (1653-1740) & Mary [FRYE?]; b 1688; Fairfield, CT
LION, Samuel (1650-1713) & 1/wf Deliverance __?__; b 1673; Rowley/Roxbury
LYON, Samuel (1650-) & 1/wf Sarah [BEACH]; [say 1675]; ?Milford, CT/Newark, NJ
LYON, Samuel & Sarah (BROOKS) GRANT, ?dau Gilbert, w Thomas; 5 Dec 1692; Rehoboth
LYON, Samuel & [?Susanna JACKSON] (1680-); ca 1697?; Fairfield, CT
LYON, Samuel (-1707) & 2/wf Hannah [PIERSON]; b 1701; NJ
LYON, Thomas & 1/wf Joanna WINTHROP (1630-); ca 1647, 1649?; Fairfield
LYON, Thomas (-1689) & 2/wf Mary HOYT, m/2 John WILSON b Nov 1691?; ca 1654; Stamford, CT
LYON, Thomas (1648-) & Abigail GOULD/GOLD?; 10 Mar 1669; Roxbury
LYON, Thomas & Joanna PAYSON; 23 Oct 1690; Dorchester
LYON, Thomas & 1/wf Ann CASE/CASS? (-1693?); 1 Nov 1692, 1 Nov 1693; Roxbury/Boston (wrong)
LYON, Thomas (1673-) & Abigail [?OGDEN]; ca 1697?; Stamford, CT/Greenwich, CT
LYON, Thomas & 2/wf Abigail CLARK; 8 Jul 1698; Dedham/Roxbury
LYON, William (1620-1692) & 1/wf Sarah RUGGLES (1628-1689); 17 Jun 1646; Roxbury
LYON, William & 1/wf Sarah DUNKIN/DUNCAN? (-1689); - Sep 1675, 1675; Roxbury
LYON, William (1620-1692) & 2/wf Martha (PHILBRICK) CASS, w John; 30 Nov 1676, 1677?; Rowley

LYON, William & 2/wf Deborah ?FAIRBANKS; ?18 Nov 1690; ?Roxbury/?Woodstock, CT
LYON, William (?1660-1700) & Phebe _?_, m/2 Daniel CROFERT, m/3 Samuel JACKSON, m/4 Zechariah LAWRENCE; b 1694; Fairfield, CT
LYON, William & Deborah COLBURN; 8 Nov 1699; Woodstock, CT
LYON, _?_ & Susanna _?_ (see Peter)

MABER, Richard (ae 40 in 1684-6) & Mary ALLEN; 21 Nov 1670; Salem
McALLS/?McCALL, _?_ & Rachel [TURNER]; b 1701?; Scituate
MUCCALL/McCALL/MACALL, James (-1693) & Anna/Anne? [WINTER]; b 1688, b 1690; Marshfield
MACCANE/MEACKENY, John & Elizabeth _?_; b 1695; Wrentham
MECAINE, William & Ruth [KILHAM]; b 1662; Dedham/Wrentham
McCARTHY/MECCARTY, Florence (-1712, Roxbury) & 1/wf Elizabeth _?_ (-1696); b 1687; Boston
MACARTIE, Florence (-1712) & 2/wf Sarah NEWWORK; 24 Aug 1697; Boston
MACCARTY, Thaddeus (1640-1705) & Elizabeth [JOHNSON] (1642-1723, ae 82); b 1665; Boston/Roxbury
McCARTY, Timothy & Elizabeth WILLIAMS, m/2 Thomas PAINE; 21 Nov 1700; New Shoreham, RI
McCAULEY/MECHALLY, John & Sarah TREVY; 2 Nov 1691; Marblehead
MACOY/COY, Archibald & Margaret [LONGLEY], dau John; 16 Mar 1691/2; Newton
McKAY, Daniel & Sarah _?_; b 1673; Newton/Roxbury
McCOY, Hugh (-1683) & Alice _?_; Wethersfield, CT
McCRANNEY/?MACKRANNEY/MACCRANEY, William & 1/wf Margaret RILEY (1661-); 8 Jul 1685, 9 Jul; Springfield
McDOUGALL/MACKDUGGELL, Allister & Hannah MEADOWES; 1 Feb 1659/60; Lynn
McDOWELL, Fergus & Mary [CLEASBY]; b 1679, b 1677?; Stonington, CT
MACE, Robert & Deborah _?_; b 1665; Sudbury
MACE, Robert & 1/wf _?_; b 1680?; Isles of Shoals, ME
MACE, Robert & 2/wf Hannah (GIBBONS) [HIBBART]; ca 1690; ME
MACE, William & Sarah [GORTON]; b 1677
McEWEN/McKUNE, Robert & Sarah WILCOXSON (1670-); 20 Jun 1695; Stratford, CT
McFARLAND/MACKFARLAND, Duncan & Mary [CHECKLEY] (1673-), m/2 John PERKINS 1697; b 1693(4?); Boston
MACVARLO/MAGVARLOW, Purdy?/Purtie/Purthy & Patience RUSSELL; 3 Jul 1667; Hingham/ Duxbury
McGUINNIS/MACKGINNIS/?MAGINNAH/MACGINNIS, Daniel & Rose NEAL; 10 Feb 1676; Woburn/Billerica
McGREGORY/MAGGRIGE/MAGREGOR/?GREGORY/?McGREGOR, Daniel & Elizabeth ROBIN- SON; 20 Dec 1693; Watertown
MACKINTIRE, Daniel/?Alexander (1669-1730) & Judith [PUDNEY] (1665-1730+); b 1697; Salem
McINTIRE, Micom/Malcolm & Dorothy (PIERCE) MACKONEER, w Alexander; b 4 Sep 1671; Dover
MAKENTIER, Philip (-1719?) & Mary _?_; 6 Sep 1666; Reading
MACKINTIRE, Philip (1667-1724+) & Rebecca WILKINS/WILLIAMS? (-1724+), dau Henry WILKINS; 20 Feb 1694/5, 1695; Salem/Reading
MAKINTIRE, Thomas (?1676, 1668-ca 1756) & Mary [MOULTON] (1673-); b 1701; Salem
McINTOSH/MACKINTOCK, John & 1/wf Rebecca METCALFE (1635-1667); 5 Apr 1659; Dedham
MACKIN[TOSH], John & 2/wf Jane/?Joan [HOLMES], w David; b 1668(9?), ca 1668?; Dedham
MAKINTOSH, William, Dedham & Experience HOLBROOK, Dedham; Sherborn, 28 Feb 1692/3; Dedham/Sherborn
MACK, John (1653-1721) & Sarah BAGLY/BAGLEY (1663-1732); 5 Apr 1681; Salisbury/Concord/ Lyme, CT

MACKANETENE/?MACKENSTINE, Matthew & Grace MITCHELL, wid; 10 Feb 1700; Newbury
MACOY/MAKOE/McCOY, Archibald & Margaret [LONGLEY]; 1692; Cambridge/Newton
MACKEY, Daniel & Sarah _?_ ; b 1663(4?), b 1670; Roxbury
MACKEY, Daniel & Dorothy [BILLINGS]; b 1695; Stonington, CT
McKAY/McKEE/MAKEY, John & Mary THORPE; 7 May 1691, 6 May 1692, 6 May 1691; Wethersfield, CT
MACKENAB/?MACKINAB/MAKINAB, James & Sarah ROPER; 18 Apr 1669; Dedham
McKENNEY, John & _?_ ; ca 1668/72; Black Point, ME
McKENNEY, Robert & [Rebecca (_?_) SPARKS], wid; 1692, 1 Dec 1696; Portsmouth/Dover, NH
MACKENY, William & Ruth [KILLEM/KILHAM]; b 1662; Dedham
McKENZIE/MacKENZIE, Dougal (-1729) & Sarah (KNOWLES) WAKEMAN, w Samuel; 18 Nov 1696; Fairfield, CT
MAKARORY, James & 1/wf Mary EVERITT (1638-13 Jun 1670); - Nov 1662; Dedham
MACKERWITHY, James & 2/wf Patience/(?Experience) CUBBY; 20 Feb 1670, 20 Feb 1671; Dedham
MACROON/MACKROREY, James & Experience _?_ ; b 1673 (see above); Dedham
MAKERWITH, James & Bethiah [LEWIS]; b 1695; Dedham
MACKFASSY/MACKFASSEY, Patrick?/Patriach & Sarah _?_ ; b 1670; Charlestown
MACKGUDY, Archibell & Sarah _?_ ; b 1694; Boston
MACKHUE?/?MACKHOE/MACKHEW, Timothy & Ann DRY; 15 May 1699; Boston
MACKMALLEN/MACKMALLION/?McMILLAN/?CALLUM, Allister (-1679) & Elizabeth _?_, m/2 John BAXTER 1679; 28 Sep 1658; Salem
MAKALLUM, Callum/Malcolm?/Makum? & Martha _?_ ; b 1664, bef 1659; Lynn
MACKMAN, James (-1698) & Elizabeth STOUGHTON (1660-1702), m/2 John ELIOT 1699; 27 Nov 1670, 1680, no issue; Windsor, CT
MACCHONE?/?MACCOON/MACOONE, John & Deborah BUSH; 8 Nov 1656; Cambridge
MACOONE, John & Sarah WOOD; 14 Jun 1665; Cambridge
MACKOON, John & _?_ ; b 1674; Westerly, RI
MACOUNE, Samuel & [Martha COLES]; ca 1700; Oyster Bay, LI/RI
MACKREST/MACREST, Benoni (-1690) & Lydia FIFIELD; 12 Sep 1681; Woburn/Salisbury
MACKWORTH/?MACWORTH, Arthur (-1660) & Jane [ANDREWS]; aft 1637/8; Falmouth, ME/Saco, ME
McLAUGHLIN/(now CLAFLIN)/?CLAFLIN/?MACKCLAFFIN/MACKCLOTHAN/MACLOTHIAN/ MACKCLAFLIN, Robert (-1690) & Joanna WARNER (ca 1643-ca 1685; 14 Oct 1664; Wenham/Brookfield
MACLOUGHLIN, William & Olive _?_ ; b 1689; Boston
McLEOD/MACKLOAD, Mordecai (-1675) & Lydia LEWIS (-1675); 13 Jan 1670/1; Lancaster
McMILLAN/McMILLION/?CALLUM/?MACCALUM/?MACKMALLON/?McMULLEN, Alexander & Rebecca ELDREDGE (at Salem 1728-1734); 15 Dec 1698; ?Wells, ME/Salem
MACKMALLION/MACKMALLIN (see MACKMALLEN), Allister/Alister (1631-1679) & Elizabeth _?_, m/2 John BAXTER 1679; b - Sep 1658; Salem
MACKMILLEN, John & Mary GILSON; 11 Dec 1684; Salem
MACOCK/?MEACOCK, Peter (-?b 1662/3) & Mary (_?_) PERRY, m/3 Thomas CASE ca 1659/62; b 1650?; Greenwich, CT/Fairfield, CT
MACOCK, Thomas (-1707) & Lettice [prob ATRED]; Milford, CT/Guilford, CT
MAYCOME/McCOMB/?MECOME, Duncan & Mary SMITH; 18 Apr 1695; Boston
MAKCUM, Duncan & Mary HORE/HOAR (1669-1711+); 2 Dec 1698; Boston
MACOMB/MACCOMB/MACKOON, John & [Sarah WEEKS] (1666); ?Greenwich, RI
MACOMBER, John[1] & 1/wf _?_ ; b 1652; Taunton
MAYCOMBER, John & Anna EVANS; 16 Jul 1678; Taunton
MACOMBER, John & Hannah [BOBBIT] (1660-); b 1684; Marshfield
MACOMBER, John[1] & 2/wf Mary BADCOCK/BABCOCK; 7 Jan 1685/6; Taunton
MAYCUMBER, Thomas & Sarah CROOKER/CROCKER?; 2- Jan 1676, 20 Jan; Marshfield
MAYCOMBER, William (1615-1670) & Ursula _?_ ; b 1649(50?); Marshfield
MACOMBER, William (1647-1711) & Mary _?_ ; b 1673; Dartmouth
MAYCUMBER, William, Dorchester, Dartmouth & Elizabeth [RANDALL not TURNER] (1673-); 9 Mar 1697/8; Scituate
MacQUEDDY/MACQUARRING/MACQUERRY?, Archibald (-1717, ae 50), Lofin, Scotland, & Sarah LOWDEN (-1737+); 2 Jan 1693/4; Cambridge/Boston/Charlestown

MACY, George (?1630, ?1620-1693) & Susanna [?STREET]; b 1656; Taunton
MACY, John (1655-1691) & Deborah [GARDNER] (1658-1712), m/2 Stephen PEASE by 1694; b 1675; Salisbury
MACY, Thomas[1] (1608-1682) & Sarah [HOPCOTT] (1612-1706); b 1644; Salisbury/Newbury
MADDIVER, Joel & Rebecca __?__; b 1672; ?Scarborough/Boston/Derby
MADDIVER, Michael (-1670) & 1/wf Judith __?__; b 1657/8; Spurwink
MADIVER/MADDIVER, Michael (-1670) & 2/wf Agnes [CARTER] (1600-), w· Richard; Falmouth, ME
MAGOUN, Alexander (1661-) & Sarah [BLAKE] (1661-1701+); 7 Dec 1682; NH
MAGOON, Henry & 1/wf Elizabeth LESSEN (-1675); 8 Oct 1661; Dover, NH/Exeter, NH
MAGOON, Henry & 2/wf Agnes KENNISTON, w John; betw 1 Aug 1677 & 19 Nov 1681
MAGOUN, Isaac (1675-) & Elizabeth __?__; b 1699; Windham, CT
MAGOUN, James (1666-1705) & Sarah [?FORD], m/2 Stephen BRYANT 1710; b 1697; Duxbury
MAGOON, John (-1709) & Rebecca [HOBART] (1637-); 7 Nov 1662; Hingham/Scituate/Pembroke
MAGOON, John, Jr. (bpt 1669-1739, ae 73) & Hannah [TURNER] (1668-); b 1705, b 1701?, 30 Apr 1702; Scituate
MAGOON, John (1658-) & Martha [ASH] (1674-); b 1706, b 1701?; Exeter, NH
MAHOOUNE/MAHONE?, Dorman/?Dermin & Dinah __?__; b 1646; Boston
MAHOONE, Dorman (-1661) & Margaret __?__ (-1655); Boston
MATHUE/MAHOON, ?Dorman & Mary __?__ (-1661+)
MANWARING/MAINWARING, Oliver (-1723 in 89th y) & Hannah [RAYMOND] (1642-1717); ca 1660/3?; Salem/New London, CT
MAGER/MAJOR/?MASURY, George & Susanna [PARY?]; 21 Aug 1672; Newbury
MAJORY, John & [Mary LARCUM]?; 16 Jul 1690, 1693; ?Salem
MAJER, Thomas & Ann ELY; 10 Jan 1700, 1700/01?; Boston
MAKEPEACE, Thomas (1592-1667) & 1/wf __?__; Boston
MAKEPEACE, Thomas (1592-1667) & 2/wf Elizabeth (HAWKREDD) (CONEY) MELLOWES (1605-1670+), w John, w Oliver; aft 1638, b 25 Jul 1641; Boston
MAKEPEACE, Thomas (-1705±) & 1/wf Mary/?Sarah [CHASE]; b 1695
MAKEPEACE, Thomas (-1705±) & 2/wf Mary BURT; 10 Jan 1697/8; Taunton
MAKEPEACE, William (-1681) & Ann JOHNSON; 23 May 1661; Boston/Freetown
MAKEPEACE, William & Abigail TISDALE (1667-), dau John; 2 Dec 1685; Taunton/Freetown
MALAVERY, John (-1712) & Elizabeth __?__ (-1718+); b 1682?, b 1680?; Providence
MALIN/MALINS, Robert (-1679, ae 30) & Patience EASTON, m/2 Thomas RODMAN 1682; 1 Jan 1674, 1674/5; Newport
MALLESIE, John & Izabell/Irabelle WELLS; 4 Oct 1670; Charlestown
MALLETT, Hosea & Grace __?__, m/2 Benjamin BALCH 1692; b 1678; Boston
MALLETT, John (-1722, ae 78) & __?__ (-1721); b 1684; Boston/Charlestown
MALLETT, John & __?__; b 1700?; Stratford, CT/Milford, CT
MALLETT, Thomas (1650-1704, 1705) & Mary (WOOD) [WILCOX] (-1705+), w Samuel, m/3 John SANFORD; b 14 Apr 1697; Newport, RI?
MALLERY, John (1664-1712) & Elizabeth KIMBERLY, m/2 Benjamin BARNES; 30 Dec 1686; New Haven
MALLERY, Joseph (1666-) & 1/wf Mercy [PINION]; b 1690; New Haven
MALLORY, Peter[1] & Mary [PRESTON]? (1629-); b 1649(50?); New Haven
MALLORY, Peter[2] (1653-1720) & 1/wf Elizabeth TROWBRIDGE; 28 May 1678; New Haven
MALLORY, Samuel (1672/3-1711) & Mary [BEACH] (1676-), m/2 __?__ REYNOLDS; b 1701?, no issue
MALLORY, Thomas (1659-1691) & Mary UMBERFIELD/HUMPHREVILLE, m/2 Ebenezer DOWNS 1694, m/3 Thomas EARNES 1713; 26 Mar 1684; New Haven
MALLERY, William (1675-1738) & Anna __?__, m/2 Nathaniel FITCH; b 1699; Fairfield, CT
MALOON/MALONE/MALLOON, Luke & Hannah CLIFFORD (1649-); 20 Nov 1677; Salisbury/Dover, NH
MALTBY, John (-1676) & Mary BRYAN (1650-), m/2 Joseph TAYLOR 1677?, m/3 John HOWELL, Jr. 1690; 28 Feb 1666; Milford, CT
MALTBY, John (?1670-1727) & Hannah LORD (-aft 1727), m/2 Joseph HOEGHIN; 13 Aug 1696; Saybrook, CT
MALTBY, John (1673-1706) & Susanna [CLARK], dau Samuel & Sarah; b 1698; Southampton, LI

MALTBY, William (1645-) & 1/wf _?_; b 1670; New Haven/Bramford, CT
MALTBY, William & 2/wf Hannah (HOSMER) [WILLARD], w Josiah; aft 1674, b 27 Feb 1685(6?); Bramford, CT
MALTBY, William (1645-) & 3/wf Abigail (BISHOP) [TALMAGE] (1659-1716), w John; b 1693; New Haven
MALTBY, William (1673/4-1701) & Elizabeth [MORRIS] (1675-), m/2 John DAVENPORT; b 1701?; Bramford, CT
MANCHESTER, Job (-1713) & Hannah _?_; b 1689; Tiverton, RI/Dartmouth
MANCHESTER, John & [?Mary] _?_; ca 1680?; Portsmouth, RI
MANCHESTER, Stephen & Elizabeth WOODELL/WODELL (-bef 1697); 13 Sep 1684; Portsmouth, RI/Tiverton, RI
MANCHESTER, Stephen & 2/wf Damaris _?_ (-1719+)
MANCHESTER, Thomas[1] (-1691+) & Margaret [WOOD] (-1693±); b 1647; Portsmouth, RI
MANCHESTER, Thomas[2] (-1718+, 1722) & Mary [BROWNING] (-1718+, 1735+); b 30 Dec 1681, b 6 Jan 1677/8; Portsmouth, RI
MANCHESTER, William (1654-1718) & Mary [COOK] (1653-1716+, 1725+); b 1688, b 1678?; Portsmouth, RI/Tiverton, RI
MANDER, James & Joanna (DOLLEN) [KELLY], w Renold; b 1689; Charlestown
MANDER, Walter & [Patience DARLING/(DOLLIN?)]; Martha's Vineyard
MANLEY/MANLY, William (-1717) & 1/wf Rebecca _?_; b 1675, 1676?; Weymouth
MANLY, William & 1/wf Phoebe [BROOKS] (1652-1720); b 1686, 1676?; Boston
MANLY, William & 2/wf Sarah _?_; b 1687, 1687/8?; Weymouth/Easton
MANN, Benjamin & Dorothy _?_; b 1688; Sudbury
MAN, James & _?_; b 2 Oct 1650; Rehoboth/Newport, RI
MANN, John & 1/wf Mary [WILLIS] (1636-1678), [?wid]; b 1657; Boston
MANN, John & Alice BOURNE (1649-); 4 Dec 1672; Braintree/Milton
MANN, John & 2/wf Hannah/Hannah A.? _?_; aft 27 May 1678, b 1681; Boston
MAN, Nathaniel (-1704) & Deborah [PERRY] (1649-1718); b 1671(2?); Boston
MAN, Richard (-1655) & Rebecca _?_, m/2 John COWAN/COWING/CARWIN 1656; b 1646; Scituate
MAN, Richard (1652-) & Elizabeth [SUTTON] (1662-); b 1684, ca 1683; Scituate/Lebanon, CT
MANN, Robert (1636-1719) & 1/wf Deborah DRAPER (-1665); 1 Apr 1664; Sudbury
MANN, Robert (1636-1719) & 2/wf [Elizabeth BUSH] (-1703), w John; ?20 Dec 1671; Sudbury
MAN, Rev. Samuel (1647-1719) & Esther WARE (1655-1734); 13 May 1673, 19? May; Dedham/Wrentham
MAN, Thomas (-1694) (see Thomas MANNING) & 1/wf Rachel BLISS (-Jun 1676); 28 Oct 1674; Rehoboth
MAN, Thomas (1650-1694) & 2/wf Mary WHEATON (1656-), m/2 Ebenezer DARLING 1698?; 9 Apr 1678, 3 Jul 1676 (wrong), 1678; Rehoboth/Providence
MAN, Thomas (1650-1732) & Sarah _?_; b 1679(80?); Scituate
MAN, William (-1662) & Mary [JARRAD]/GERRARD?/IASARD?; b 1643, b 1647?; Cambridge
MAN, William (-1651?) & Frances [HOPKINS] (1614-1700, Dartmouth); b 1650; Providence
MAN, William (-1662) & 2/wf Alice (TEEL) TIDD/?TEEL (-1665), w John; 11 Jun 1661; Cambridge
MANN, William (1671-1736) & Rebecca [BURNHAM]; betw 24 Jun 1688 & 26 Jan 1690, ?5 Apr 1685; Boston/Wethersfield, CT
MANNELL/?MANNEL, John & Sarah THAIUR/THAYER; 7 Oct 1669; Charlestown
MANNING, Dennis & Catherine [INNIS]; b 1679; Nantucket
MANNINGS, Edward & Mary _?_; b 1637; Dorchester
MANNING, George (-1677) & 1/wf Mary HASODEN; 15 Jun 1653; Boston
MANNING, George (-1677) & 2/wf Hannah (EVERALL) BLANCHARD, w William; 18 Mar 1655, 1654/5; Boston
MANNING, George (ca 1644, 1655-) (see George MUNNINGS m Mary MIXTUR/MOXY 1 Nov 1680) & _?_; b 1683?; Boston?
MANNING, Jacob (-1756) & Sarah STONE (1668-); 4 May 1683; Salem
MANNING, Jeffrey (-1693) & Hepzibah [ANDREWS]; ca 1660-70?; Hingham/Piscataway, NJ
MANNING, John & Susan _?_; b 1638(9?); Ipswich
MANNING, John & 1/wf Abigail [MAVERILL] (1614-1644); b 1643; Boston

MANNING, John & 2/wf Ann [PARKER], dau Richard, m/2 William GERRISH 1677+, ?1676; b 1647; Boston
MANNING, John & Sarah [SPALDING]; b 1691; Billerica
MANNING, John (1668-1727) & Joanna LASH, w William; 9 May 1695; Boston
MANNING, Nicholas (1644-) & 1/wf Elizabeth GRAY (-1681+), w Robert; 23 Jun 1663, 166-, div 1683; Salem/Sheepscot, ME
MANNING, Nicholas & 2/wf Mary [MASON]; by 1686; New Dartmouth, ME
MANNING, Richard (1622-d in Eng) & Austice [CALLEY]; in Eng, b 1644; Salem
MANNING, Samuel (1644-1710) & 1/wf Elizabeth STEARNS (-1671); 13 Apr 1664; Watertown
MANNING, Samuel (1644-1710) & 2/wf Abiel WIGHT (1654-); 6 May 1673; Billerica/Medfield/Cambridge
MANNING, Samuel & Deborah [SPALDING]; b 1688(9?); Billerica/Stonington, CT
MANNING, Thomas (?1599-1668) & _?_ ; bef 1645, b 1641?; Ipswich
MANNING, Thomas (see Thomas MANN) & Rachel BLISS (wrong); 28 Oct 1674; Swansea/Rehoboth
MANNING, Thomas (?1664-1737) & Mary [GIDDINGS] (?1669-); b 1695, ?19 Jun 1689; Ipswich?
MANNING, William[1] (-1665/6) & 1/wf _?_ (-ca 1634); in Eng, b 1614; Cambridge
MANNING, William[1] (-1665/6) & 2/wf Susanna _?_ (-1650); in Eng, ca 1635?; Cambridge
MANNING, William[1] (-1665/6) & 3/wf Elizabeth _?_ (-living 1665); aft 1650; Boston
MANNING, William[2] (?1615-1691) & Dorothy _?_ (1612-1692); b 1642; Cambridge/Stonington, CT
MANNING, _?_ & Hannah _?_ (see Adam DINSDALE)
MANSER, John (1670?-) & 1/wf Mary MIRICK; 24 Apr 1695; Boston/Charlestown
MANSER, Robert (-1689?) & Elizabeth BROOKS (?1651-1695); 6 Jun 1670; Charlestown
MANSFIELD, Andrew[1] & Elizabeth _?_ (1593-1673); b 1619; Lynn
MANSFIELD, Andrew[2] (ca 1621-1683) (ae ca 38 in 1661) (cousin of Charles GOTT, Sr.) & 1/wf Bethiah [?TOWNSEND] (ca 1632-1672); b 1652; Lynn
MANSFIELD, Andrew[2] (ca 1621-1683) & 2/wf Mary (LAWES) NEALE (-27 Jun 1681), w John; 4 Jun 1673; Lynn
MANSFIELD, Andrew[2] (ca 1621-1683) & 3/wf Elizabeth (WALTON) CONNATT/CONANT (1629-), w Lot; 10 Jan 1681; Lynn
MANSFIELD, Daniel (1669-1728) & Hannah [JOHNSON] (1670-1714), dau Samuel; b 1688; Lynn
MANSFIELD, Henry & _?_ [LEACH]
MANSFIELD, John (1619-1671) & Mary [MORRIS] (sister of Thomas, kinswoman of Edward HOLYOKE 25 Dec 1658); ca 1640+?; Lynn
MANSFIELD, John (-1674) & Mary (?SALE/SHART) GROVE (-1682), w John; aft 22 Jan 1647/8; Charlestown
MANSFIELD, John (-1689) & Elizabeth [?FARNSWORTH] (-1689+); b 1656; Hingham
MANSFIELD, John (1656-1717) & Sarah NEAL (1661-1736); 5 Jun 1683; Hingham
MANSFIELD, John (-1727) & Sarah (PHELPS) MOORE (1654-1732), w Andrew; 13 Dec 1683; Windsor, CT
MANSFIELD, Joseph (?1637-1692) & Mary [POTTER]; b 1658; New Haven
MANSFIELD, Joseph (-1694) & Elizabeth [NEEDHAM]; ca 1652?; Lynn
MANSFIELD, Joseph (1655/6-1739) & Elizabeth WILLIAMS (1660-1748); 1 Apr 1678; Lynn
MANSFIELD, Joseph (1673-1739) & Elizabeth [THOMAS] (?1677-1763); b 1701; New Haven/North Haven
MANSFIELD, Moses (1640-1701, 1703) & 1/wf Mercy GLOVER (1643-); 5 May 1664; New Haven
MANSFIELD, Moses (1640-1701, 1703) & 2/wf Abigail YALE (1660-1709); aft 15 Feb 1685/6; New Haven
MANSFIELD, Oliver & Patty _?_ ; b 1673(4?); Boston
MANSFIELD, Paul (-1666) & Damaris/Constance? [LASKIN], w Timothy (-1715+); b 1658, 1659?; Salem
MANSFIELD, Paul & Sarah CARTER, w John?; 9 Nov 1693; Marblehead
MANSFIELD, Richard (-1655) & Gillian DRAKE (-1669), m/2 Alexander FIELD 1657; Exeter, Devon, 10 Aug 1636; New Haven
MANSFIELD, Robert (-1666?) & Elizabeth _?_ (1586-1673); in Eng, ?b 1610; Lynn
MANSFIELD, Robert & Joan _?_ ; b 1680; Boston
MANSFIELD, Samuel (ca 1652-1679) & Sarah BARSHAM; 3 Mar 1673/4; Lynn
MANSFIELD, William & Mary _?_ ; Isles of Shoals/Falmouth, ME

MANSFIELD, _?_ & Jane _?_
MANSON, John & Lydia _?_ ; by 1701; Kittery, ME
MANSON, Richard (-1702) & _?_ ; b 1680, b 1660?; Kittery, ME
MANSON, Robert (-1677) & Elizabeth _?_, m/2 Henry PUTT; Isles of Shoals, ME
MANTER, Benjamin (1671-) & Mary WHITNY/WHITTENE (1674-); 4 Apr 1695; Tisbury
MANTON/MANTER, John (-1708) & Martha LUMBART/LOMBARD (1640-1721); 1 Jul 1657; Barnstable
MANTER, John & Hannah [EDDY]; b 1693; Tisbury
MANTON, Edward¹ (-1682(-)) & _?_ ; ca 1635?; Providence
MANTON, Edward³ (1658-1723) & Elizabeth THORNTON; 9 Dec 1680; Providence
MANTON, Shadrack² & Elizabeth [SMITH]; b 1658; Providence
MANERING, Oliver (1634?-1723) & Hannah RAYMENT?/?RAYMOND (1642, 1643-1717); b 1685, by 1668?, 1662?; Salem/New London
MANNERING/MANNING?, Thomas & Elizabeth WINCHESTER, dau John, she was gr-dau of John ANDREWS; no; Kittery, ME/Braveboat Harbor, ME
MANWARING, _?_ & Hannah HARWOOD
MAPES, Jabez² (1664-1732) & 1/wf Mary [CORWIN] (1659-), dau John; b 1686; Southold, LI
MAPES, Jabez² (1664-1732) & 2/wf Elizabeth [ROE] (-1717), dau John; ca 1688; Southold, LI
MAPES, John (-1681+) & Oodee?/Martha _?_ (-1697); Southold, LI
MAPES, Jonathan (1670/1-1747) & 1/wf Esther HORTON (-1709), dau Caleb; 17 Mar 1696, 1696/7?; Southold, LI
MAPES, Joseph (-1707), Quaker & Ruth _?_ (-1711/12); b 1691; Southold, LI
MAPES, Thomas¹ (1628-1687) & Sarah [PURRIER] (1630-1697?), dau William; ca 1648/9; Southold, LI
MAPES, Thomas² (1651-1711/12) & 1/wf Mary [WELLS] (-1709), w William; aft 1671, no issue; Southold, LI
MAPES, William² (1657-1698) & Hannah _?_ ; b 1698, b 1686; Southold, LI
MAPLEHEAD?/MARPLEHEAD, _?_ & ?Mary RICHARDS?, m/2 George BULLARD 1655; b 1655; Watertown
MARBLE, ?Ephraim (wit 1683) & _?_
MARBLE, Gershom² (?1658-1725) & 1/wf Mary _?_ (-1694); b 1694; Charlestown/Hingham
MARBLE, Gershom² (?1658-1725) & 2/wf Waitstill INGLE (-1728), w Benjamin (see Benjamin INGALLS); 29 Dec 1697; Scituate
MARBLE, John¹ (-1695, ae nr 90) & Judith _?_ ; b 1646, b 1644?; Boston/Charlestown
MARRABLE, John² (1646-1730) & Mary (KNOWER) WHITTEMORE, w Nathaniel; 3 May 1673; Charlestown
MARBLE, Joseph (?1650-1728) & Mary FAWKNER/FAULKNER (?1649-1725?); 30 May 1671; Andover/Sudbury/Marlboro
MARBLE, Joseph (1673-1749) & 1/wf Hannah BARNARD (1678-1718+); 23 Apr 1695; Andover
MARBLE, Nicholas (1629-1680+) & Elizabeth? _?_ ; b 1654; Ipswich/Gloucester
MARBLE, Samuel & _?_ ; b 1666; Concord
MARBLE, Samuel² (?1648-1720) & Rebecca ANDREWS; 26 Nov 1675; Andover/Salem
MARBLE/MARVIN?, Samuel & Rebecca WILLIAMS (1666-1698+); 14 Oct 1686; Haverhill/Salem, NH?
MARRABLE, Thomas (?1660-) & Sarah BELL (1665-); 30 Aug 1689; Charlestown
MARRABLE, William (ae 40, 36? in 1642) & Elizabeth _?_ (ae 40 in 1652); b 1642; Charlestown
MARCH, George & Mary FOULSOM/FOLSOM, m/2 Joseph HERRICK; 12 Jun 1672; Newbury
MARCH, Hugh¹ (-1693) & 1/wf Judith _?_ (-1675); b 1646; Newbury
MARCH, Hugh¹ (-1693) & 2/wf Dorcas (BOWMAN) BLACKLEACH (-1683), w Benjamin; 29 May 1676; Newbury/Watertown
MARCH, Hugh (1656-) & Sarah MOODY (1663-); 29 Mar 1683; Newbury
MARCH, Hugh¹ (-1693) & 3/wf Sarah (CUTTING) (BROWN) HEALY (-1699), w James, w William; 3 Dec 1685; Newbury
MARCH, Hugh (1673-1695) & Sarah [COKER], m/2 Archelaus ADAMS 1698; b 1694; Newbury
MARCH, James (-1721?) & Mary [WALKER] (1669-), dau Shubael, m/2 John EMERY; b 1690; Newbury
MARCH, John¹ (-1666) & 1/wf Rebecca _?_ ; b 1638; Charlestown
MARCH, John (-1666) & Anna [?BICKNER]; b 1666; Charlestown
MARCH, John & Jemima TRUE; 1 Oct 1679; Newbury

MARCH, John & Mary **ANGIER**; 11 Dec 1700; Newbury/Reading

MARCH, Nicholas & Martha _?_, m/2 William **DADEY**? 1670; b 1657; Charlestown

MARCH, Stephen & Anna **WILBORN**; 26 Jan 1691/2; Taunton

MARCH/MARSH, Theophilus (-1694) & Elizabeth **HUNT**; 10 Jan 1664/5, 3 Feb 1664/5, 3 Feb 1664; Cambridge/Charlestown

MARCH, _?_ & _?_ **FIELD**; b 1701?; Flushing, LI

MARCY, John (1662-1724) & Sarah/Mary [**HADLOCK**] (1670-1743); prob 1686; Roxbury/Woodstock/Salisbury

MARDEN, James (-1710+) & Abigail **WEBSTER** (1676-1710+), m/2 Samuel **BERRY**; 23 Oct 1695, b 1698; New Castle/Salisbury/Haverhill

MARDEN, John (1671-), Newcastle & Alice **PARKER**, Newcastle; 11 Nov 1699; Hampton NH

MARDEN, John (-1707) & Rachel [**BERRY**]; Rye

MARE/MARES/MAYS/MAYER/MAZE/MOORE/MEARS, Henry & Alice _?_; 14 Sep 1669, b 1670, b 1674; Lancaster/Dorchester/Boston

MARE, Robert & Hannah [**BRACKETT**] (1656-), m/2 John **SHAW**; b 1683; Boston

MARE, Walter & [_?_ **MADDIVER**]; see **MAYER**

MARINER, Andrew & Ruth [**HOLLARD**], dau George; b 1685; Portsmouth, NH/Boston

MARRINER, Charles & Esther **RANSTROPE**; 5 Sep 1700; Boston

MARINER, James (1651-1732) & _?_; ca 1680?; ?Dover, NH/Falmouth, ME/Boston

MARINER, John (-1717) & [?Elizabeth] _?_; b 1680; Gloucester

MARINER, Joshua & Hannah _?_; b 1689?, b 1694; Boston

MAREAN, Dorman (-1703), Muddy River, Boston & Mary _?_; ca 1675?; Boston

MARION, Isaac (1653-1724, ae 72) & Phebe [**WEARE**] (-1724, ae 67); b 1682; Boston

MARION, Isaac, Woburn (very doubtful) & Mary **CUTLER** (1656-); 5 Sep 1682;

MARRIAN, John & 1/wf Sarah _?_ (-1671); b 1640; Watertown/Hampton, NH

MARRIAN, John (-1705, in 86th y) & Sarah [**EDDY**] (1626-1710); b 1651; Boston

MARION, John & 2/wf Margaret (_?_) (**WEBSTER**) **GODFREY** (-1686), w Thomas, w William; 14 Sep 1671; Hampton, NH

MARION, John (1651-1728) & 1/wf Anna [**HARRISON**] (1656-1692); b 1683; Boston

MARION, John (1651-1728) & 2/wf Prudence (**BALSTON**) **TURNER** (1655-), dau Jonathan, wid; 28 Jun 1700; Boston

MARION, Samuel (1655-1726?) & 1/wf Hannah _?_ (-4 Apr 1688); b 1681; Boston/Charlestown

MARION, Samuel (1655-1726?) & Mary [**WILSON**] (1662-1726); b 1689; Charlestown

MARKANDROS, William & Mary _?_; b 1679?; E. Greenwich, RI

MARKHAM, Daniel (-1712/13) & 1/wf Elizabeth **WHITMORE** (1649-); 3 Nov 1669; Cambridge/Middletown, CT

MARKHAM, Daniel (-1712/13) & 2/wf Patience **HARRIS** (-1733); 2 Jan 1677, 21 Jan 1677; Middletown, CT/Hadley

MARKHAM, Israel & Mary **BOOTH**; 10 Dec 1700; Enfield, CT

MARKHAM, James (1675-1731) & Elizabeth **LOCKE** (-1753); 14 Oct 1700, 1699; Woburn/Middletown, CT

MARKHAM, William (1621-1689), kinsman of Nathaniel **WARD** & 1/wf Priscilla [**GRAVES**]; b 1654; Hadley

MARKHAM, William (1621-1689) & 2/wf Elizabeth [**WEBSTER**] (-1688±); b 1658?; Hadley

MARKS, Gregory & Mercy [**DICKENS**]; b 1690; ?Oyster Bay, LI/Block Island, RI

MARKES, Joseph & Mary _?_; b 1694?, b 1696; Dedham/Brookfield

MARK/MARKS, Patrick (1635-) & Sarah _?_; b 1662; Charlestown

MARKS, Roger & Sarah **HOLT**? (-1690); Andover

MARKS, William & _?_; b 1692; Woodbury, CT

MARKS, William & Mary _?_; b 1695; Charlestown

MARLTON, William & Sarah **WHALY**; 1 Jan 1696; Boston

MARRE/MARR, John & Joanna **BRUNSON**; 18 Jul 1682; Salem

MARRETT, Amos (1657/8-1739) & 1/wf Bethia **LONGHORN** (1662-1730); 2 Nov 1681, no issue; Cambridge

MARRETT, Edward (1670-) & Hannah (**BRADISH**) [**STANHOPE**], w Joseph; b 1694; Cambridge

MARRETT, John & Abigail **RICHARDSON**; 20 Jun 1654; Cambridge

MARRETT/MERRETT?, Richard & Mary **SIMMONS**; 12 Jan 1685; Charlestown/Boston

MARRETT, Thomas (1589-1664) & Susan/Susanna [?**CRANNIWELL**] (-1665); b 1625; Cambridge

MARSH, Alexander (1628-1698, ae ca 70) & 1/wf Mary BELCHER (1634-1678/9+); 19 Dec 1655; Braintree

MARSH, Alexander (1628-1697/8) & 2/wf Bathshua/Bathsheba (LOTHROP) [BALE] (1642-1723), w Benjamin; aft 18 Sep 1683, bef 20 Nov 1691; Braintree

MARSH, Daniel (ca 1653-1725), Hadley & Hannah (LEWIS) CROW, w Samuel; 5 Nov 1676; Hadley

MASH/MARSH, Ebenezer (1674-1722) & Alice BOOTH (1678-); 25 Nov 1699?, 25 Nov 1700?, Nov 1699; Salem

MARSH, Ephraim & 1/wf Elizabeth LINCOLN (-1711); 26 Jan 1681/2; Hingham

MARSH, George (-1647) & Elizabeth _?_ (-1677), m/2 Richard BROWN 1648, m/3 Richard JACKSON; in Eng, b 1618; Hingham

MARSH, Henry (1660-1715?), Durham & Elizabeth [JACKSON]; prob by 1695, by - Jul 1701; Dover, NH

MARSH, John (-1674) & 1/wf _?_ ; b 1635, b 1637

MARSH, John (-1674) & 2/wf Susan/Susannah [SKELTON?] (1625-1685), m/2 Thomas RIX 1680+; b 1646; Salem

MARSH, John (1618-1688) & 1/wf Anne [WEBSTER] (1621-1662); ca 1640; Hartford/Hadley

MARSH, John (-1668, Barbados) & Sarah YOUNGE, m/2 Nicholas CHATWELL; 20 Mar 1661, 1662; Salem

MARSH, John (-1688) & 2/wf Hepzibah (FORD) LYMAN (1625-1683), w Richard; 7 Oct 1664; Northampton

MARSH, John, Jr. (?1643-1727) & Sarah LYMAN (-1707?); 28 Nov 1666; Northampton

MARSH, John & Sarah _?_ ; b 1669; Boston/Hatfield

MARSH, John & Margaret _?_ ; b 1674; Boston

MARSH, John (1665-) & Alice _?_ ; b 1687; Lynn/Salem/Killingly, CT

MASH, John & 1/wf Lydia EMERSON (-1719); 16 Nov 1688; Haverhill

MARSH, John (1668-1744) & 1/wf Mabel PRATT (-1696); 12 Dec 1695; ?Hartford/Litchfield, CT

MARSH, John (1668-1744) & 2/wf Elizabeth PITKIN (1677-1748); 6 Jan 1698; ?Hartford

MARSH, John (1672-1744) & Mary _?_ ; b 1701?; ?(Hadley)/Hatfield

MARSH, Jonathan & Mary _?_ ; b 1643?, 4 ch bpt Oct 1653; ?Milford/Norwalk, CT

MARSH, Jonathan (1650-1730) & Dorcas (_?_) DICKINSON (-1723, ae 69), w Azariah; 12 Jul 1676, ?evidence; ?Hadley

MARSH, Jonathan (-1704) & 1/wf Sarah [REAFES] (1664-26 Sep 1687); b 1687; Newport

MASH, Jonathan (1672-) & 1/wf Mary VERRY; 24 May 1697, 20 May; Salem

MARSH, Jonathan (-1704), Newport & 2/wf Phebe (COOKE) [ARNOLD], w Oliver, m/3 Robert BARKER 1705; 1 Jan 1700; Jamestown, RI

MARSH, Joseph & Ann THUROGOOD; 2 Mar 1692; Boston

MARSH, Joseph & Hannah? _?_ ; ca 1696?; Hartford/Lebanon, CT

MARSH, Onesephorus (1630-1713) & 1/wf Hannah CUTLER (-1686); 6 Feb 1654/5; Hingham/Haverhill

MASH, Onesephorus (1655-) & Sarah LADD/LAD (1657-); 8 Dec 1685; Haverhill

MASH, Onesephorus (1630-1713) & 2/wf Elizabeth (PARROTT) WORCESTER (-1690), w Samuel; 29 Oct 1686; Haverhill

MASH, Onesephorus (-1713) & 3/wf Sarah (TRAVERS) WALLINGFORD, w Nicholas; 18 May 1691; Haverhill

MARSH, Samuel & [Comfort] _?_ ; b 1648; New Haven/Elizabeth, NJ

MARSH, Samuel (?1645-1728), Hatfield & Mary ALLISON (-1726); 6 May 1667; Hadley?/Hatfield

MARSH, Samuel & Priscilla TOMPKINS (1653-), m/2 William HAYWARD 1708; 14 Aug 1679; Salem

MARSH, Samuel (1670-) & _?_ ; b 1699?; ?Hatfield

MARSH, Thomas (1618-1658) & Sarah BEAL (?1624-1710), m/2 Edmund SHEFFIELD 1662; 22 Mar 1648/9; Hingham

MARSH, Thomas (-1725) & Sarah LINCOLN (1650-173-); 6 May 1675; Hingham

MARSH, William & Elizabeth _?_ ; b 1683; Stonington, CT/Plainfield, CT

MARSH, Zachariah/Zechary/Zachery (1637-) & Mary SILSBY; 15 Aug 1664; Salem

MARSH, _?_ & Hannah (GLOVER) KENT; aft 9 Jun 1691, b 1702; Boston

MARSHALL, Benjamin (-1715) & Prudence WOODWARD, m/2 John CHOATE; 2 Nov 1677; Ipswich

MARSHALL, Benjamin (1660-1688+) & Rebecca [DAWES] (1666-), m/2 Eleazer MORTON 1693, 1692?; b 1684; Boston

MARSHALL, Christopher & _?_ ; b 1638; Boston

MARSHALL, David (1661-1694) & Abigail PHELPS (1666-), m/2 Stephen WINCHELL 1698; 9 Dec 1686; Windsor, CT

MARSHALL, Edmund (1598-1673) & Millicent _?_ (1601-1668+); b 1636(7?); Salem

MARSHALL, Edmund (1644?-1731/2) & 1/wf Martha/Mercy _?_ (-1697, Windsor, CT, Suffield); b 1677; Newbury/Windsor, CT/Suffield, CT

MARSHALL, Edmund & 2/wf Lydia (MORGAN) PIERCE, Enfield, w John; 18 Jul 1700; ?Suffield, CT

MARSHALL, Edward & Mary _?_ ; b 1658; Warwick, RI

MARSHALL, Edward & Mary [SWAYNES] (?1647), wid; 9 Jun 1665; Reading

MARSHALL, Edward/Edmund & Martha _?_ (-1697); Windsor, CT

MARSHALL, Francis & Martha _?_ (-1697?) (2/wf Mary?); b 1682(3?); Boston

MARSHALL, James (1659-1694?) & Elizabeth [SOPER] (1665-); b 1682; Boston

MARSHALL, John & Mary PARTRIDGE; m cont, Eng, Nov 1631; Duxbury

MARSHALL, John (?1621-1715) & Sarah _?_ (-1689); b 1645; Boston

MARSHALL, John (-1672) & Ruth [HAWKINS?], m/2 Daniel FAIRFIELD; b 1659, b 1661(2?); Boston

MARSHALL, John & 1/wf Hannah ATKINSON (-1665); 19 Nov 1662; Billerica

MARSHALL, John (-1702) & Mary BURRAGE (1641-1680); 27 Nov 1665; Billerica/Charlestown

MARSHALL, John (1646-1712) & Sarah [WEBB]; b 1674, b 1680; Greenwich, CT

MARSHALL, John & Damaris WAITE; 30 Nov 1681; Billerica/Malden

MARSHALL, John & Phebe _?_ ; b 1685; Boston

MARSHALL, John & [?Hannah HARDY] (1663-), dau Joseph; b 1687; Lynn/Boston

MARSHALL, John (1664-) & Mary (SHEFFIELD) MILLS (1663-1718), Boston, dau Edmund SHEFFIELD, w Jonathan; 12 May 1690, 13? May; Braintree

MARSHALL, John & Sarah _?_ ; b 1691; Boston

MARSHALL, John (1672-1699) & Abigail [TROWBRIDGE] (1670-1698); b 1693; Windsor, CT

MARSHALL, John (1645-) & Mary [NORTH] (1674-); b 1 Jan 1693/4, ?Farmington; Wethersfield, CT

MARSHALL, John & Eunice ROGERS; 8 Dec 1695; Billerica

MARSHALL, John & Rachel _?_ ; b 1696(7?); Boston

MARSHALL, John (?1646-1712, 1733?) & 2/wf _?_ [ROCKWELL]; ca 1683; Greenwich, CT

MARSHALL, John (-1712) & 3/wf Elizabeth [LYON] (-1712?); b 2 Jun 1698?, ca 1684; Greenwich, CT

MARSHALL, John, Boston & Jane ALLIN/ALLEN, Scituate; 10 Nov 1697, 16 Nov 1697; Scituate

MARSHALL, John & Sarah WEBB (1664?-); 26 May 1699; Boston

MARSHALL, John (1674-1727) & Abigail BANKS (-1758); b 1700?; Greenwich, CT

MARSHALL, Joseph & Elizabeth [HOWELL]; b 1674, 18 Mar 1673/4; Boston/Southampton, LI

MARSHALL, Joseph & _?_ ; b 1690; Ipswich

MARSHALL, Joseph (1672-) & Mercy/Mary? SHORT (?1676-1712?); 29 Jul 1694; Boston

MARSHALL, Peter & Abigail [BARNEY] (1663-); b 1684, b 1692; Ipswich/Newbury

MARSHALL, Richard & Esther/Easter? (LUGG) BELL (-1714+), w James; 11 Feb 1676, 1676/7; Taunton

MARSHALL, Richard & Agnes _?_ ; b 1701; Wenham

MARSHALL, Robert & Mary [BARNES]; betw 2 Dec 1658 & 25 Oct 1660, 1660?, b 1661(2?); Plymouth

MARSHALL, Samuel (-1675) & Mary WILTON (-1683); 6 May 1652; Windsor, CT

MARSHALL, Samuel (1653-) & Rebecca NEWBERRY (1655-1718); 22 Jun 1675; Windsor, CT

MARSHALL, Samuel (1646±-1742) & Ruth RAWLINS (1655-1714); b 1676; Boston

MARSHALL, Samuel (-1690) & Sarah _?_ (-1690); b 1690; Barnstable

MARSHALL, Thomas (-1664) & 1/wf Alva? _?_ ; b 1632, b 1616?; Boston

MARSHALL, Thomas (-1664) & 2/wf Alice [WILLEY] (-1664), wid; b 1637, b 1631?; Boston

MARSHALL, Thomas (1615, ?1613-1708?) & Joan _?_ (-1708/9, 1663+) (doubtful) (two Thomases at Reading); b 1640; Reading/Lynn

MARSHALL, Thomas (1615-1689) & Rebecca _?_ (1622-1693) (ae 34 in 1656); ca 1663, b 1647?, b 1640; Reading/Lynn

MARSHALL, Thomas (-1692) & [Mary STEBBINS] (1641-); b 1670; Hartford

MARSHALL, Thomas & Anna [CROSS], m/2 Ephraim FELLOWS; b 1678; Ipswich
MARSHALL, Thomas & Abizag (LUX) PALMER, w William; 4 Feb 1686, 1686/7; Dover, NH?/Porstmouth (prob)
MARSHALL, Thomas (-1735) & 1/wf Mary DRAKE (1666-1728); 3 Mar 1685/6; Windsor, CT
MARSHALL, Thomas (1656-) & Dorcas _?_ ; b 1689; Boston
MARSHALL, Thomas & 2/wf Joanna [HOLLY/HAWLEY]; aft Dec 1695; Newcastle, NH
MARSHALL, Thomas (-1700) & Mary CHANTRIL/CHAUNTRELL; 18 Jun 1697; Boston
MARSHALL, Thomas & Mary _?_ ; b 8 Jan 1700/01; Greenwich, CT
MARSHALL, William & 1/wf Mary HILTON (-1678, ae 33); 2 Oct 1666, 1667?, 8 Apr 1666; Charlestown
MARSHALL, William & 2/wf Lydia (MAYNARD?) HALE, w Samuel, m/3 Samuel BALLATT 1691; 14 Jun 1681, Mar 1691; Charlestown
MARSHALL, William (1669-) & Elizabeth _?_ ; b 1691; Charlestown
MARSHFIELD, Josiah/Josias (1665-1712) & Rachel GILBERT (1668-1754); 20 Sep 1686, 22 Sep; Springfield
MARSHFIELD, Samuel (?1626-1692) & 1/wf Hester/Esther WRIGHT (-1664); 18 Feb 1651/2, ?13 Feb; Springfield
MARSHFIELD, Samuel (?1626-1692) & 2/wf Catherine (CHAPIN) (BLISS) GILBERT (- 1711/12), w Nathaniel, w Thomas; 28 Dec 1664; Springfield
MARSHFIELD, Thomas & ?Mercy/?Priscilla _?_ (-1639, Windsor); in Eng, b 1626; Scituate/Windsor, CT/Springfield
MAISHFIELD, _?_ & Hannah [BROWNE], dau John; b 1689; ?Bristol, RI
MARSHFIELD, _?_ & Mercy _?_ (-1634), ?w Thomas; Springfield
MARSTON, Benjamin (1652-1720) & 1/wf Abigail VEREN (1655-1693?); 25 Nov 167[5?]; Salem
MARSTON, Benjamin (-1720, Ireland) & 2/wf Patience ROGERS (1676-1731); 15 Apr 1696; Ipswich
MARSTON, Caleb (1672-) & Anna MOULTON (1679-); 12 Nov 1695; Hampton, NH
MARSTON, Ephraim (1643-) & Elizabeth _?_ ; b 1673; Salem
MARSTON, Ephraim (1655-1742) & Abial/Abiel/Abigail SANBORN (1653-); 19 Feb 1677; Hampton, NH
MARSTON, Isaac & 1/wf Elizabeth BROWN (-1689); 23 Dec 1669; Hampton, NH
MARSTON, Isaac & 2/wf Jane (BRACKETT) HAINES, w Matthias; 19 Apr 1697; Hampton, NH
MARSTONE, Jacob (1658-1727) & Elizabeth POOR (1661-1700); 7 Apr 1686; Andover/Hampton, NH
MARSTON, James (1656-1693) & Dinah SANBORN, m/2 John BRACKETT 1698; 23 Jul 1678; Hampton, NH
MARSTON, James & Elizabeth _?_ ; b 1689; Salem
MARSTON, John (-1681) & Alice?/?Sarah [EDEN]; ?4 Aug 1640; Salem
MARSTON, John (1630-1708) & Martha ?MOULTON/FULTON (-1723, ae 87); 15 Jan 1652/3; Hampton, NH/Andover
MARSTON, John & Ann/Anna [LEGG/?LEG]/Dievertje JANS?; 27 Oct 1650, b 1657; (Dutch) Flushing, LI
MARSTON, John & _?_ ; ?b 1660; Salem
MARSTON, John (1641-) & 1/wf Mary CHICHESTER (-1686, ae 43); 5 Sep 1664; Salem
MARSTON, John (-1699) & Mary WALL (1656-1708); 5 Dec 1677; Hampton, NH
MARSTON, John & Priscilla [?STACY]; ca 1682-3? uncertain; Salem
MARSTON, John & 2/wf Mary (GARDNER) TURNER, w Habakuck; 15 Sep 1686; Salem
MARSTONE, John (ca 1664-1741) & Mary OSGOOD (-1700); 28 May 1689; Andover
MARSTON, John (1667-) & Susannah [STACY] (1667-); b 1691?, b 1693; Salem
MARSTON, Joseph (1663-1738) & Martha _?_ (-1745+); no issue; Andover
MASTONE, Manasseh (-1703/4), nephew of Guido BAILEY & Mercy PEARCE/PIERCE; 23 Aug 1667, 22 Aug 1667; Salem/Charlestown
MARSTON, Nathaniel & ?Mary _?_ (doubtful); b 1630; Flushing, LI
MARSTON, Robert (1608-1643, ca ae 60) (did he marry? no); Hampton, NH
MARSTON, Samuel (1661-1723) & Sarah [SANBORN] (1663?, 1666?, ?1667-1738); ca 1683/4; Hampton, NH
MARSTON, Thomas (1617?, 1621?-1690) & Mary [EASTOW/ESTO] (1628-1708); b 1648?; Newbury
MARSTON, Thomas & Elizabeth [WILLIAMS] (1663-), dau John; Salem

MARSTON, Thomas (-1702) & Elizabeth CULLIVER/GULLIVER?/COLLEVER? (-1702+); 14 Jun 1694, 14 Jun 1695, 4 Jun 1694; Salem/Marblehead

MARSTON, William₂(-1672, ae 80) & 1/wf [?Sarah] _?_; in Eng, ca 1616; Hampton, NH

MARSTON, William² (1622, ?1621-1704) & 1/wf Rebecca PAGE (1636-1673); 15 Oct 1652; Hampton, NH

MARSTON, William & Sarah _?_; b 1653?, b 1655; Salem/Hampton, NH/Newbury

MARSTON, William¹ (-1672, ae 80) & 2/wf Sabina? [LOCKE?/PAGE?], m/2 John REDMAN 1673; ca 1660-2; Hampton, NH

MARSTON, William² (1622-1704) & 2/wf Ann (ROBERTS) PHILBRICK (-1704+), w James; 5 Jul 1675, 8? Jul; Hampton, NH

MARSTON, William & Elizabeth [HILL] (1665-); 24 Sep 1690; Salem

MARSTON, William (1669-) & Susanna [PALMER] (1681-); b 1701?; Hampton, NH

MARTIN, Abraham (?1584-1670?, 1669, Rehoboth) & _?_; no ch recorded; did he marry? Hingham

MARTIN, Abraham & [Hannah] _?_; b 1680; Ipswich

MARTIN, Ambrose & [Joan?] _?_; b 1640; Concord/Dorchester

MARTIN, Anthony (-1673) & Mary HALL, m/2 John PAYNE 1676; 7 Mar 1660/1, 11 Mar; Middletown, CT

MARTIN, Christopher (-1621) & Marie PROWER; Great Burstol, Essex, Eng, 26 Feb 1606/7; Plymouth

MARTIN, Christopher & Hannah/Ann?/Anna [KIMBALL] (1664-); b 1691; Bradford

MARTIN, Edward (1640-) & Gillian _?_; ca 1665/70?; Smuttynose

MARTINE/MARTYN, Capt. Edward & Sarah [WHITE] (1671-), dau John; b 1692(3?); Boston

MARTIN, Ephraim & Thankful BULLOCK (1681-1712); 6 Dec 1699; Rehoboth

MARTIN, Francis (returned to Eng) & [?Prudence DEACON]; 10 Oct 1619, Plymouth, Eng

MARTIN, George & 1/wf Hannah _?_ (-1645?); b 1644; Salisbury

MARTYN, George & 2/wf Susanna NORTH; 11 Aug 1646; Salisbury

MARTIN, George & [Elizabeth] _?_; b 1680, b 1679; Ipswich

MARTIN, George & Abigail _?_; ca 1680-5, b 1686; Edgartown/Newport/Martha's Vineyard

MARTIN, John & Rebecca _?_; b 1639; Charlestown

MARTIN, John & Sarah [LARRIFORD], m/2 Reginald FOSTER 1665, m/3 William WHITE 1682; b 1643; Charlestown

MARTIN, John (-1687) & Hester [ROBERTS] (-1687); 1652?, ca 1650?, b 7 Sep 1647; Dover, NH/Piscataway, NJ

MARTIN, John & Martha LUMBERT/LOMBARD (1639-); 1 Jul 1657; Barnstable

MARTIN, John (1642-) & Mary MUDGE; 14 Apr 1671; Malden/Swansea/Bristol, RI/Lebanon, CT

MARTIN, John (1633-1713) & Joan/Joanna EUSTANCE?/ENSTANCE/ESTEN/ASTIN/etc? (-1733, ae 88); 26 Apr 1671; Swansea

MARTIN, John (1650-) & Mary [WEED]; ca 1678?; Amesbury

MARTIN, John/?Thomas (see Thomas MARTIN) & Sarah [NORTHEY?]; by 1678; ?Marblehead

MARTIN, John (?1652-1687?) & Mercy/Mary? BILLINGTON; 27 Jun 1681; Rehoboth

MARTIN, John & Elizabeth HOWE (1666-); 15 Jan 1684; Wallingford

MARTIN, John (1662-) & Elizabeth _?_ (-1718); b 1685; Middletown, CT

MARTIN, John & Wilmot _?_; b Dec 1685; Newcastle

MARTIN, John & 1/wf Abigail _?_ (-1696); b 1692; Gloucester/Salem?

MARTIN, John & 2/wf Abigail _?_; b 1700

MARTIN, John & Margaret EGLON; 14 Aug 1700; Boston

MARTIN, John & Hannah [DARLING] (1677-); b 1701?

MARTIN, Melatiah (1673-) & Rebecca BROOKS; 6 Nov 1696; Swansea

MARTINE, Michael (-1682, ae 60) & Susanna HOLLIOCKE/HOLYOKE (ca 1630-); 12 Sep 1656; Boston

MARTIN, Michael & Sarah [?RUDKIN]; in Eng, b 1697

MARTIN, Peter & Martha LAWRENCE; 11 May 1695; Marblehead

MARTIN, Richard (-1694?, 1695?) (bro of Abraham) & Elizabeth SALTER (is this reliable?); 9 Jun 1631, b 1633; Rehoboth

MARTIN, Richard (-1673) & Dorothy [ATWELL], w Benjamin; b 1646, b 11 Jan 1672/3; Falmouth, ME/Saco Bay, ME

MARTINE, Richard & 1/wf Sarah TUTTLE (1632-1666); 1 Feb 1653/4, b 1655; Boston

MARTYN, Richard & Sarah _?_; Portsmouth, NH

MARTINE, Richard (-1671) & 2/wf Elizabeth [GAY]; 1660?, 1666+?; Boston
MARTIN, Richard (-1694, ae 62) & 1/wf Elizabeth [TRUMBULL] (1641-1689); b 1663; Charlestown
MARTYN, Richard (1647-) & Mary (HOYT) BARTLETT, (1646-), w Christopher; aft 15 Mar 1669/70, [b 1674], 1678?; Amesbury/Salisbury
MARTYN, Richard & 2/wf Martha (SYMONDS) DENNISON (-1684), w John; ?Apr 1672; Stonington, CT
MARTYN, Richard & Elizabeth (SHERBURNE) (LANGDON) LEAR, w Tobias, w Tobias; aft 1684, ca 1681; Sherburn
MARTIN, Richard (-1694) & 2/wf Elizabeth EDMUNDS (-1726, ae 84), w Joshua; 28 Nov 1689, 29 Nov; Charlestown
MARTYN, Richard (-1694) & 3/wf 4/wf Mary (BENNING) [WENTWORTH], w Samuel; aft 13 Mar 1690/1, by 1691, aft Apr 1691; Portsmouth, NH
MARTIN, Robert (1591-1660) (called Robert/Roger CLAPP "cousin") & Joane UPHAM (1591-1669?) (sis of John); prob bef 1620, bef 1635, 16 Nov 1618; Weymouth/Rehoboth/Swansea
MARTIN, Robert (1616-) & _?_; b 1646; New Haven
MARTIN, Robert & Bethia BARTLETT; 15 Oct 1700; Marblehead
MARTIN, Samuel (-1683) & Phebe BIXBY/BISBIE BRACEY, w Thomas; in Eng, b 1646; Wethersfield, CT
MARTIN, Samuel (-1696) & Abigail NORTON; 30 Mar 1676; Andover
MARTIN, Samuel & Elizabeth FULFORD; 6 Jan 1696/7; Marblehead
MARTEN, Solomon & 1/wf Mary PINDAR (-1648); 21 Mar 1642/3; Gloucester
MARTIN, Solomon & 2/wf Alice VARNHUM/FARNUM/FARNHAM, w Ralph; 18 Jun 1648; Gloucester/?Andover
MARTIN, Thomas & Alice ELLIOT; 1 Jun 1650; Woburn
MARTIN, Thomas & Rachel [FARNHAM]; b 1668; Boston
MARTIN, Thomas & Hannah _?_; b 1680; RI
MARTIN, Thomas (?see John MARTIN) & Sarah [?NORTHEY]; b 1687, b 1675?; Boston
MARTIN, Thomas (-1701) & Jane/Johanna/Joanna _?_; bef 1688, bef 1671?, bef 1675; Marlborough
MARTIN, William (-1673, ae ca 76) & [Mary?] LAKIN (-1669), w William; b 1646; Reading/Groton
MARTIN, William (-1715, Woodbury) & Abigail [NICHOLS?] (1664-1715+); [25 Jun] 1685?; Stratford, CT
MARTIN, William & Mary [STONE?]; b 1697; Amesbury
MARTIN, William & [Hannah PIERCE]; b 1701?; Warwick, RI?
MARTIN, _?_ & _?_ (-1665, a wid); Hingham
MARTIN, _?_ & Ann _?_, m/2 William EDMONDS 1650; ?Boston
MARTIN, _?_ & Mary _?_; Hempstead, LI
MARTINDALE, Isaac & Godsgift [ARNOLD] (1672-); b 1693, ?13 Mar 1695; Newport
MARVIN, John & Hannah [SMITH]; b 1687; Hempstead, LI
MARVIN, John (1664-1711) & Sarah GRAHAM/GRIMES?; 7 May 1691; Lyme, CT
MARVIN, Matthew (1600-1680) & 1/wf Elizabeth [?GREGORY]; b 1623; Hartford/Norwalk
MARVIN, Matthew (1600-1680) & 2/wf Alice [BOUTON] (1610-1680), w John; ca 1647; Hartford/Norwalk, CT
MARVIN, Matthew (1626-1712) & Mary _?_ (-1707+); ca 1650; Norwalk, CT
MARVIN, Matthew (1656-1691) & Rhoda [St.JOHN] (1666-); ca 1688; Norwalk, CT
MARVIN, Reinold (1594-1662) & Marie _?_ (-1661); ca 1617/18; Hartford/Farmington, CT/Lyme, CT/Saybrook, CT
MARVIN, Reinold (1631-1676) & Sarah CLARKE (-1710), m/2 Joseph SILL 1678; 27 Nov 1663; Milford, CT/Saybrook, CT
MARVIN, Reinold/Reynold (1669-1737) & 1/wf Phebe [LEE] (1676-1707); ca 1696; Lyme, CT
MARVIN, Robert & Mary [BROWN] (1622-); ca 1639; Southampton, LI
MARVIN, Samuel (1671-1743) & Susannah GRAHAM (1677-); 5 May 1699; Lyme, CT
MASCROFT/?MARSHCROFT, Daniel & Mary [GORTON]?; b 1669(70?), b 1667; Sudbury/Roxbury
MASCALL, John (-1704+) & Ellen LONG; - Mar 1649; Salem
MASCOLL, John (1650-) & Hester BABBADG/BABBIDGE; 6 Oct 1674; Salem

MASKELL, Thomas (-1671) & Bethia PARSONS, m/2 John WILLIAMS 1672; 10 May 1660; Windsor, CT/Simsbury, CT
MAXELL, Thomas (1657-) & Mary [SWASEY] (1659-); b 1683; Salem
MASKELL, Thomas (1666-) & 1/wf Clemons [SCUDDER]; b 1696; East Hampton, LI
MASON, Arthur (-1708, ae 71) & Joanna PARKER (-1708); 5 Jul 1655; Boston
MASON, Benjamin (1670-1740) & Ruth [ROUND]; b 1696; Swansea
MASON, Daniel (1652-1737) & 1/wf Margaret [DENISON] (1650-); b 8 Feb 1673/4; Roxbury
MASON, Daniel (1652-1737) & 2/wf Rebecca HOBART (1659-1727); 10 Oct 1679; Stonington, CT
MASON, David & Elizabeth CLARK; 12 Dec 1693; Boston
MASON, Ebenezer & Hannah CLARK (1666-); 25 Apr 1691; Medfield
MASON, Edward (-1640) & Mary _?_ (-by 1659); by 1640; Wethersfield, CT
MASON, Elias (-1688) & Jane (CONANT) [HOLGRAVE] (1611-1661), w Joshua; b 1647; Salem
MASON, Elias & 2/wf Elizabeth _?_ ; aft 9 Nov 1661; Salem
MASON, Henry (-1676) & Esther [HOWE], m/2 John SEARS 1677; by 1676; Dorchester/Boston
MASON, Hezekiah (1677-) & 1/wf Ann BINGHAM (1677-1724); 7 Jun 1699; Windham, CT/Lebanon, CT
MASON, Hugh (1605-1678) & Esther WELLS (1612-1692); Jan 1632, in Eng; Watertown
MASON, Issac (1667-1742) & Hannah _?_ ; b 1694(5?); Rehoboth
MASON, Jacob (-1695) & Rebecca _?_ ; b 1674, b 1671; Boston
MASON, James & Mary [MULFORD]; b 1691; East Hampton, LI
MASON, Capt. John (-1635, London) & Ann GREEN; 29 Oct 1606, in Eng; (did not come to N. E., owned land in N. E.)
MASON, Major John (ca 1600-1672) & 1/wf _?_ (-1639); ca 1630/33; Dorchester/Windsor, CT/Saybrook, CT/Stonington, CT
MASON, Major John (-1672, in 72nd y) & 2/wf Ann/Anna/Anne PECK (1619-1671); - Jul 1639; Hingham/Saybrook, CT/Windsor, CT
MASON, John (?1625-1686+) & Hannah _?_ ; ?1650±; Salem
MASON, John & Mary EATON; 5 May 1651; Dedham
MASON/MASSON, John & Annover/Annver COLLIHAN/COLLIHAM/COLLEHAM; 30 Jan 1658/9; Charlestown
MASON, John (-1661) & Hannah RAMESDEN/RAMSDEN?; 11 Dec 1662; Concord
MASON, John & Elizabeth/Mary? [GENT], m/2 John ALLEN; b 1670; New Dartmouth, ME
MASON, John (1648, ?1646-1676) & Abigail [FITCH] (1650-); ca 1670; Norwich, CT
MASON, John (-1696) & Elizabeth WARD (1651-1697); 11 Jul 1672; Hampton, NH
MASON, John & Hannah [HEARD] (1655-); ?1675±; Dover, NH
MASON, John & Hannah HAWES; 5 Jan 1676/7; Dedham
MASON, John & Sarah [PEPPER] (1657-); b 1668?, b 1681; Boston/Framingham
MASON, John (1645-1730) & Elizabeth [HAMMOND]; b 1677; Newton
MASON, John (-1683?) & Constant WALES; 15 Oct 1679; Dorchester
MASON, John & Sarah HARTHORNE/?HAWTHORN/?HARTSHORNE, w Thomas; 30 Mar 1684; Dedham
MASON, John & Elizabeth [CLARK] (1669-), w?; b 1695; Dedham
MASON, John & Hannah [(?ARNOLD)]; b 1696; Hartford
MASON, John & Sarah DRIVER, m int 4 Mar 1696/7; Boston
MASON, John (1677-) & Elizabeth SPRING (1675-); 18 Oct 1699; Lexington
MASON, John (1674-1706) & Mercy [MERRICK] (1674-1754); b 1705, b 1704, b 1701?
MASON, Jonathan/Joseph? & Mary [FISKE]; b 1685; Brighton
MASON, Joseph & _?_ ; b 1661; NH
MASON, Joseph (1646-1702) (see above) & Mary FISKE (1661-1725, 1724?); 5 Feb 1683, 1684, 1683/4; Watertown
MASON, Joseph & 1/wf Anna DAGET/DOGGETT; 12 Mar 1683, 1684; Rehoboth
MASON, Joseph & 2/wf Lydia [BOWEN]; 4 Sep 1686; Swansea
MASON, Nicholas & 1/wf Mary _?_ (-1683); b 1655; Wethersfield, CT/Saybrook, CT?
MASON, Nicholas & 2/wf Ann HILL/HALL (-1711), w Edward; 22 Jan 1683/4; Wethersfield, CT
MASON, Nicholas & Mary DUDLEY (1662-1686?); 11 Mar 1686, 11 Mar 1685/6, 11 May; Saybrook, CT/Guilford, CT
MASON, Noah (ca 1651-) & 1/wf Martha _?_ (-1676); b 1675(6?); Rehoboth
MASON, Noah (ca 1651-1700) & 2/wf Sarah FITCH (-1719); 6 Dec 1677; Rehoboth

MASON, Pelatiah & 1/wf Hepzibah/Hepzibeth BROOKS (1674-1727); 22 May 1694; Swansea
MASON, Peter & Mary _?_; b 19 Dec 1692, b 1687?; Dover, NH
MASON, Ralph (1600-1679) & Anne _?_ (1600-); b 1630; Boston
MASON, Richard & Sarah MESSINGER (1643-); 20 Nov 1660; Boston
MASON, Robert (-1667, Dedham) & 1/wf _?_ (-1637); b 1625; Roxbury/Dedham
MASON, Robert & Abigail _?_ (-1667)
MASON, Robert & Sarah [?REYNOLDS] (?1629-1686/1706); b 1657, ca 1653; Boston
MASON, Robert (-1700) & Abigail EATON; 10 Nov 1659, 9 Oct 1659, 16 Nov; Dedham/Medfield
MASON, Robert (-1688) & _?_; Portsmouth, NH
MASON, Robert (-1691) & [Mary?] [KINSLEY], dau Stephen; b 1671; Milton
MASON, Robert & Elizabeth CHANDLER (-1688); 18 Nov 1680; Roxbury
MASON, Robert Tufton (-1688) & Elizabeth [TAYLOR]; in Eng, b 1659
MASON, Robert Tufton (-1696) & Katherine [WIGGIN], m/2 Simon WIGGIN; ca 1686?; ?Dover, NH
MASON, Robert & Christian _?_; betw 1690 & 1700; Boston
MASON, Robert & Mary?/?Marion/Marya/Maria/Mariah/Marie REDMAN (-1736); 31 Jan 1643?, 30 Jan 1643?, ?31 Jan; Boston
MASON, Sampson (-1676) & Mary [BUTTERWORTH] (ca 1628-1714); b 1651; Rehoboth/Weymouth/Dorchester/Swansea
MASON, Samuel (1632-1691) & Mary HOLEMAN/HOLMAN; 29 May 1662; Boston
MASON, Samuel (1644-1705) & 1/wf Judith SMITH (1650-); 20 Jun 1670; Hingham
MASON, Samuel (1657-1718) & Elizabeth MILLER (-1718); 2 Mar 1681/2, 2 Mar 1682, 28 Mar 1682, 2 Mar, 1681/2; Rehoboth
MASON, Samuel (1644-1705) & 2/wf Elizabeth PECK, m/2 Gershom PALMER; 4 Jul 1694 at Rehoboth; Stonington, CT
MASON, Stephen & Sarah _?_; b 1686; Boston
MASON, Stephen & 2/wf? Rebecca STEPHENS, m/2 Thomas MOSELEY/MANDESLEY 1700 at Milton; m int 27 Dec 1695; Boston
MASON, Thomas (-1678) & Clemence _?_ (-1696?), m/2 Thomas JUDD 1679; b 1650?; Watertown/Hartford?
MASON, Thomas (-1676) & Margery PARTRIDGE (-1711), m/2 _?_ STACY; 23 Apr 1653; Medfield
MASON, Thomas & 1/wf Christian OLIVER; b 1687; Salem
MASON, Thomas & 2/wf Abigail (CURTIS) GREENSLITT/GREENSLADE (1664-), w John, m/3 Thomas HORTON 1717; 1 Nov 1693; Salem
MASON, William & Elizabeth PERRY; 16 Jun 1678?; Portsmouth, NH
MASON, William & Sarah [CLARK?] (-1686); Southampton, LI
MASON, _?_ & Emma [ROOTS] (-1646), wid; b 1636; Salem
MASSEY, Jeffrey & Ellen _?_; b 1631; Salem
MASSEY, Jeffrey & Martha ANGUR; 9 Nov 1700; Salem/Gloucester
MASSY, John (1631-1709±) & Sarah WELLS (-1703+); 27 Apr 1658; Salem
MASSEY, John & Sarah _?_; b 1687; Roxbury
MASSEY, Thomas & Abigail WILLIAMS; 3 Jan 1698; Salem
MASTERS, Abram/Abraham (-1713) & Abigail KILLUM/KILHAM; 18 May 1691; Manchester/Wenham
MASTERS, Francis & _?_; b 1656; Salem
MASTERS, George (-1686), NY & Mary WILLIS (-1702), NY in 1702; 27 Nov 1678; ?Westbury, LI
MASTERS, John[1] (1585-1639) & Jane _?_ (-1639); b 1617; Cambridge
MASTERS, John (ae 62 in 1716) & 1/wf Elizabeth ORMES (1660-); 17 Jul 1678; Salem
MASTERS, John (-1721) & Deborah DOVE (1665-); 18 Oct 1683; Marblehead
MASTERS/?MASTERSON, Nathaniel (1630-) & Ruth [PICKWORTH] (1638-); ca 1654; Salem/Manchester
MASTERS, Samuel & Ann KILLUM/KILHAM; 25 Dec 1698; Manchester
MASTERSON, Nathaniel & Elizabeth COGGSWELL; 31 Jul 1657; Ipswich/York, ME
MASTERSON, Richard (?1590-1633); & Mary GOODALL (1600-); Leyden, Holland, 23 Nov 1619, 26 Nov; Plymouth
MAZURE, Benjamin & Margaret ROW; 23 Oct 1676; Salem
MAZURY, John (-1728) & Mary [LARCOM?] (-1736+); b 1694; Salem

MAZURY, Joseph & Sarah (MARSTON) PICKWORTH, w Samuel; 25 Mar 1679-80; Salem
MARJERY/MAJERY, Joseph & Judah MUNYON, m/2 Joshua MACKMILLION?; 11 Apr 1694; Salem
MAZURE, Lawrence/Laurence & 1/wf Mary KEBBEN; 25 Oct 1670; Salem
MAZURE, Lawrence/Laurence & Susanna MAJORE?, wid; 1 Jul 1683?, 16 Dec 1697?
MAZURY, Martin & [?Sarah LAROKE]?; b 1688, ?20 Sep 1675; Salem
MASURY, William (-bef 1717) & Abigail [SWANSEY] (1661-); b 21 Apr 1688, ?23 Dec 1682; Salem
MATHER, Atherton (1663-1734) & 1/wf Rebecca STOUGHTON (1673-1704); 20 Sep 1694; Suffield, CT/Windsor, CT
MATHER, Benjamin & Mary NEWHALL; 4 Nov 1700; Boston
MATHER, Cotton (1663-1728) (ca 46 in 1680?) & 1/wf Abigail PHILLIPS (1670-1702); 4 May 1686; Charlestown
MATHER, Eleazer (1637-1669), Northampton & Esther WARHAM (1644-1736), m/2 Rev. Solomon STODDARD 1670; 29 Sep 1659; Windsor, CT/Deerfield/Northampton
MATHER, Increase (1639-1723) & 1/wf Maria/Mary? COTTON (1642-1714); 16 Mar 1662, 6 Mar 1662/3?, 6 Mar 1661/2; ?Dorchester
MATHER, Jeremiah & Hannah [GRIGGS]; b 1694; Roxbury
MATHER, Joseph (1661-1691), Dorchester & Sarah CLAP; 20 Jun 1689, 2(?) Jun; Dorchester
MATHER, Richard (1596-1669) & 1/wf Katherine HOLT (-1655), Bury, Lancashire; Bury, Lancashire, 29 Sep 1624; Dorchester
MATHER, Richard (-1669) & 2/wf Sarah (HAWKRIDGE) (STORY) COTTON (1601-1676), w William, w John; 26 Aug 1656; Boston
MATHER, Richard (1653-1688) & Katharine WISE/Elizabeth __?__ (1658-); 1 Jul 1680; Dorchester/Lyme, CT/Windsor, CT
MATHER, Samuel (1651, 1650?-1728) & Hannah [TREAT] (1661-1708), Milford, CT; b 1677; Windsor, CT/Deerfield/Bramford, CT
MATHER, Timothy (1628-1685) & Catherine/Elizabeth [ATHERTON] (1628-1678); b 1650?, b 1651; Dorchester
MATHER, Timothy (1628-1684) & 2/wf Elizabeth (_?_) WEEKS (?1631-1710), w William; 20 Mar 1678, prob 1678/9; Dorchester/Roxbury
MATHER, Warham (1666-1745) & Elizabeth DAVENPORT (1666-1744); Dec 1700; New Haven
MATSON, John (1636-) & Mary COTTON, dau William; 7 Mar 1659/[60]; Boston
MATSON, John & Jane __?__; b 1672(3?); Boston
MATSON, John (1665-1728) & Mary __?__; b 1692; Simsbury, CT
MATSON, Joshua (1640-1686) & Elizabeth __?__; b 1679; Boston
MATSON, Nathaniel (-1686) & __?__ [THOMAS]; b 1684; Lyme, CT
MATSON, Thomas (-1677) & Amy/Ann [?PICKERING] (-1678) (sis of Abigail, wf of Theodore ATKINSON); b 1633; Boston/Braintree
MATSON, Thomas (1633-1690) & Mary READ, w Thomas; 14 Aug 1660; Boston
MATTESON, Francis & Sarah NICHOLS; 12 May 1700, 1702?; E. Greenwich, RI
MATTESON, Henry (1646-1690±) & Hannah [BAILEY?/PARSONS]?, m/2 Charles HAZLETON 1693; ca 1670?; E. Greenwich, RI
MATTESON, Henry (-1752) & Judith WEAVER; 19 Apr 1693; E. Greenwich, RI
MATTESON, Thomas (-1740) & Martha SHIPPEE; 14 Nov 1695; E. Greenwich, RI
MATTHEWS, Benjamin (-1710) & ?Dorothy (HULL)? KENT, w Oliver (doubtful?); ?1670, aft Jun 1670; Dover, NH
MATHUES, Benjamin (ca 1668-) & Hannah RIDER; 16 Jan 1698/9; ?Yarmouth
MATTHEWS, Daniel & Mary (NEIGHBORS) [WINDSOR], w John; bef 1669; Boston/Charlestown
MATTHEWS, Daniel & Elizabeth __?__; b 1692; Marblehead
MATTHEWS, Francis (-1647?, 1648?) & Tamson/Thomasine [CHANNON] (-1704?, 1690+), Ottery, St. Mary, Devonshire, b 1630, b 1628, 22 Nov 1622, ?28 Nov; Dover, NH
MATTHEWS, Francis (-1749+) & Ruth BENNETT; 23 Feb 1691/2; Dover, NH
MATTHEWS, George & Hannah __?__; b 1687; Boston
MATTHEWS, Hugh & Mary EMERSON; 28 Aug 1683; Newbury
MATTHEWS, James (-1668) & Sarah __?__; b 1646; Yarmouth
MATTHEWS, James (-1684) & [?Sarah HEDGES]; b 1668; Yarmouth
MATHEWS, James & Hannah __?__; b 1696; Boston

MATTHEWS, John (d in Eng) & Margaret HOAR, m/2 Henry FLYNT b 1642; Gloucester, Eng, 25 Dec 1633
MATHEWS, John (-1670) & Elizabeth _?_; b 1641; Roxbury/Boston
MATHEWS, John (-1684) & 1/wf Penticost BOND (-1675); 24 Feb 1643, 1643/4; Springfield
MATTHEWS, John (-28 Jun 1659) & Margaret HUNT; 7 Jan 1658/9; Charlestown
MATTHEWS, John & Grace _?_; b 1670(1?); Boston
MATHEWS, John (-1684) & 2/wf Mary (HILLIARD) CROWFOOT (-1681), w Joseph; 11 May 1680; Springfield
MATHEWES, John & Mary JOHNSON (1664-1710); 20 Sep 1686; Marlborough
MATTHEWS, John & Sarah SMITH (1672-); 11 Dec 1690; Huntington, LI
MATTHEWS, John & Lydia _?_; b 1697; Marlborough
MATHEWS, Marmaluke (1607-) (returned to Eng) & Catharine _?_; b 1641; Barnstable/Boston
MATTHEWS, Peter & Mary (_?_) [COX], w Gowen; by 1697; Ipswich/New Castle
MATTHEWS, Samuel & _?_ [?STRICKLAND]; ?b 1656; ?Jamaica, LI
MATHUES, Samuel (1647-) & Elizabeth [CROWELL] (1649-); b 1672(3?), ca 1671; Yarmouth
MATTHEWS, Samuel & _?_ [RAYNES]; betw 1678 & 1680?; Smuttynose
MATTHEWS, Thomas (-1688) & Sarah _?_ (-living in 1688), m/2 Joseph RIDER; b 1664; Yarmouth
MATTHEWS, Thomas & _?_; b 1683; Yarmouth
MATTHEWS, Thomas & Abiah PARKER; 23 May 1700; Wallingford, CT/Cheshire, CT
MATTHEWS, Walter (-1678) & Mary _?_; b 1656, b 1652; Dover, NH
MATTHEWS, William (-1684) & [Jane?/Jean?] _?_; b 1672; New Haven/Guilford, CT
MATHUES, William & Hannah HOWES; 15 Dec 1698; Yarmouth
MATTHEWSON, James (-1682) & Hannah [FIELD], m/2 Henry BROWN 1687+; ca 1660/2; Providence
MATHEWSON, James (1666-1737) & Elizabeth CLEMENCE (1673-1736+); 5 Apr 1696; Providence/Scituate, RI
MATHEWSON, John (-1716) & Deliverance MALAVERY (-1716+); 17 Nov 1698; Providence
MATHEWSON, Thomas (1673-1735) & Martha [FIELD] (-1735+); b 1701?; Providence/Scituate, RI
MATHEWSON, Zachariah (-1749) & 1/wf Sarah _?_; ca 1700?; Providence
MATTOCK, David (-1654) & Sarah _?_, m/2 Thomas RAWLINS 1656; Braintree/Roxbury
MADOCKS, Edmund & Rebecca MUNINGS/MUNNINGS; 14 Jan 1651/2; Boston
MADDOCK, Henry & Mary WELLINGTON (1640-), m/2 John COOLIDGE 1679; 21 May 1662; Watertown
MATTOCK/MADDOCK, Henry & Rachel _?_; b 1673; Saco, ME/Boston
MATTOX, Henry & Diana SOUTHER; 3 Mar 1698; Boston
MATTOCKS, James (-1667) & Mary [SPOORE?]; b 1637; Boston
MADDOCKS, John (-1703) & Ruth CHURCH, m/2 Joseph CHILD, m/3 Thomas INGERSOLL 1720; 23 Jun 1689; Watertown
MATTOCK, John (1669-) & Elizabeth _?_; b 1701?; Boston
MATTOCKE, Richard & Grace TOD (1650-); 2 Mar 1668/9; New Haven
MATTOCKE, Samuel & Constance FAIRBANKS; 30 Mar 1653; Boston
MATTOCKS, Samuel (1659-) & Anna/Ann?/Anne MARCH; 12 Apr 1688; Charlestown/Boston
MATTOON, Hubertus & 1/wf Margaret [?WASHINGTON]; bef 5 Feb 1663, by 1656?; Portsmouth
MATTONE, Hughbert/Hughbrecht & 2/wf Sarah (PEARCE) JONES, m/3 Henry SEAVEY 1682?; Jun 1673, div 1682; Kittery, ME
MATTOON, Hubertus & 3/wf _?_; by 1690
MATTON, John & Dorothy _?_; b 1687; Boston
MATTOON, Philip & _?_; b 1657; Hadley
MATTOON, Philip (-1696) & Sarah HAWKS, m/2 Daniel BILLING 1704+; 10 Sep 1677; Deerfield
MATTOON, Richard & Jane (HILTON) HULL, w Joseph; 1699, aft 1684; Ipswich/Newmarket
MATTONE, _?_ & ?[Martha] HUGGINS, m/2 _?_ MUSHAL; b 1 Sep 1679
MAUD, Daniel (-1655), Wakefield?, Eng, & 1/wf [Anna FAIRBANK] (very doubtful); 9 Oct 1625, b 1635?; Elland, Yorkshire/Boston
MAUD, Daniel (-1655) & 2/wf Mary BONNER, wid?, had 4 ch; betw 1634 & 1644, bef 1 Aug 1642; Boston/Dover, NH
MAULE/MAUL, Thomas & Naomy LYNSEY/LINDSAY; 22 Jul 1670; Salem

MAVERICK, Antipas (?1619-1678) & _?_ ; b 1654, b 1658; Kittery, ME/Exeter, NH/Isles of Shoals

MAVERICK, Elias (?1604-1684?) & Anna/Ann/Anne? HARRIS (-1697), dau wid Elizabeth HARRIS/Thomas HARRIS & Eliz.; b 1636, ca 1633?; ?Charlestown/Falmouth

MAVERICK, Elias (1644-) & Margaret SHERWOOD; 8 Dec 1669; Charlestown/Boston

MAVERICK, Elias (1670-1696) & Sarah SMITH, m/2 George ROBINSON 1698; 3 Feb 1695, 4 Feb 1695/6; Boston/Watertown

MAVERICK, James & Esther [BRENTNALL?], m/2 Benjamin WHITNEY 1705; b 1693; Framingham

MAVERICK, John (1578-1636, 1636/7) & Mary GYE (-1668+, 1666+); Ilsington, Eng, 28 Oct 1600; Dorchester

MAVERICK, John (1621-) & 1/wf Jane _?_ /?ANDREWS; b 1653, 15 Apr 1649?; Boston

MAVERICK, John (1636-bef 1680) & Catherine SKIPPER/?SKEPER (-1708), m/2 John JOHNSON 1680; 9 Apr 1656; Charlestown/Boston

MAVERICK, John (1621-) & 2/wf Rebecca _?_ ; b 1662; Boston

MAVERICK, Jotham (1660-) & Elizabeth HANNIFORD (1669-); 16 Aug 1690; Marblehead

MAVERICK, Moses (1611, ?1610-1685?, 1686, ae 76) & 1/wf Remember ALLERTON (?1614-1652+, 1656?); b 6 May 1635; ?Plymouth/Salem/Marblehead

MAVERICK, Moses (-1686?) & 2/wf Eunice (BROWN, wrong) ?COLE ROBERTS (1628-1698+), w Thomas; 22 Oct 1656; Boston

MAVERICK, Paul (1657-1709+) & Jemima [SMITH] (1665-), m/2 Henry RICHMAN/RICHMOND; b 1680(1?); Boston/Charlestown

MAVERICK, Peter (-1681+, bef 1681) & Martha [BRADFORD]; b 1670(1?); Boston

MAVERICK, Samuel (1602-1670/76) & Amyas/?Amias (COLE) [THOMPSON], w David; ca 1627-8; Boston

MAVERICK, Samuel (-1664) & Rebecca [WHEELWRIGHT] (-1678, 1679), Wells, m/2 William BRADBURY 1672; 1660, 4 Dec 1660; Boston

MAVERICK, Samuel (?1647-) & Martha _?_ ; b 1671(2?); Boston

MAVERICK, _?_ & Abigail [VIALL] (1656-), dau John; b 3 Jan 1681; Swansea

MAXCY, Alexander (-1684) & Mary [ABBE] (-1726), m/2 Daniel KILHAM ca 1697; b 1662; Wenham

MAXE, Alexander & Abigail MILES; 21 Feb 1692/3; Topsfield/Attleboro

MAXEY, David (1662-) & Sarah _?_ ; b 1696; Wenham

MAXEY, William & Sarah KNOWLTON, m int 6 Mar 1696/7; Wenham

MAXFIELD, Clement (-1692) & Mary [DENMAN] (?1621-1707); b 1639: Taunton/Dorchester

MAXFIELD, John (-1703) & Elizabeth HAMONS; 24 Jul 1679; Gloucester/Salisbury

MAXFIELD, Joseph & Mary _?_ ; b 1697; ?Bristol, RI

MAXFIELD, Samuel & 1/wf Mary [DAVENPORT] (1649-1707, 1691?); b 1671; Dorchester

MAXFIELD, Samuel & ?2/wf Christian POOTTER; 11 Dec 1691; Dorchester/Bristol, RI

MAXON/MAXSON, John (1639-1720) & Mary [MOSHER/MOSHIER?] (1641-1718); b 1667; Newport/Westerly, RI

MAXSON, John (1667-1748) & Judith CLARKE (1667-); 19 Jan 1687/8; Westerly, RI

MAXSON, Joseph (1672-1750) & Tacy [BURDICK] (-1747+); b 1692; Westerly, RI

MAXSON, Richard¹ & _?_ ; b 1639; Boston/Portsmouth, RI

MAXWELL, Alexander & 1/wf Agnes/Anne/Annis [FROST]; b 4 Sep 1671, by 1671; Kittery, ME/Beverly

MAXWELL, James & 1/wf Margery/Margaret _?_ ; b 1667; Boston

MAXWELL, James & 2/wf Dorcas _?_ ; b 1677(8?); Boston

MAXWELL, John & Elizabeth CORDENER, m int 5 Nov 1696; Boston

MAY, Edward & Hannah [KING]; b 1673

MAY, Edward (-1691) & Dorcas [BILLINGTON]; b 1685?; Plymouth

MAY, Eleazer (1668-1689) & Sarah [BULLARD]; 1687; Roxbury

MAY, Elisha (1669-1744, ae 76) & Elizabeth [WALKER]; b 1699; Rehoboth/?Taunton/?Bristol, RI

MAY, George & Elizabeth FRANCKLINE/FRANKLIN, m/2 John GLOVER?, m/3 John CLEVERLY, m/4 James MOSMAN; 6 Oct 1656; Boston

MAZE/[MAYS], Henry & Alice _?_ ; 14 Sep 1669; Lancaster

MAY, Israel & Elizabeth BARBER; 5 Feb 1700; Plympton

MAY, John (1590-1670) & 1/wf _?_ (-18 Jun 1651); b 1631; Roxbury

MAY, John (1590-1670) & 2/wf Sarah __?__ (-1671); aft 8 Jun 1651, bef 29 Apr 1660; Roxbury
MAY, John (1631-1671) & Sarah BREWER/BRUCE? (1638-); 19 Nov 1656; Roxbury
MAY, John & Hannah DAMON (1672-), m/2 Preserved HALL; 12 Dec 1695; Hingham
MAY, John (1663-1730) & Prudence BRIDGE (1664-1723); 2 Jun 1684; Roxbury
MAY, Jonathan (-1690) & Sarah LANGLEE/LONGLE, m/2 William HERSEY 1691; - Nov 1686; Hingham
MAY, Joseph & Susannah __?__ ; b 1679; Marlboro
MAY, Samuel (-1677) & Abigail STANFFULL/STAMFIELD (1638-), m/2 Humphrey JOHNSON 1678; 7 Jun 1657, 7 Jan 1657; Roxbury/Boston
MAY, Samuel (1661-) & Mary __?__, had Dinah; b 1693; Roxbury
MAY, __?__ & Hannah [KING], dau Samuel; b 1676
MAYER, Nicholas & Abigail REITH; 3 Nov 1696; Marblehead
MAYER/MOORE/etc. (see MARE), Henry (-bef 7 May 1699) & Hannah __?__ ; b 1697; Boston
MAYER, John & __?__ ; Blackpoint, etc.
MAYER, Walter & __?__ MADDIVER; b 1654; Saco, ME
MAYFIELD, Benjamin & Sarah PITMAN/PICKMAN, m/2 Samuel PHILIPS; 10 Apr 1690; Salem
MAYFIELD, Samuel & Sarah __?__ ; b 1694; Lynn
MAYHEW, Experience (1673-) & Thankful HINCKLY (1671-); 12 Nov 1695; Barnstable
MAYHEW, John (1652-1689) & Elizabeth [HILLIARD] (1655-1746), Hampton, NH; b 1673(4?); Martha's Vineyard
MAYHEW, John, Devonshire, Eng, & Joanna CHRISTOPHERS; 25 Dec 1676, 26 Dec; New London, CT
MAYHEW, John & Mehitable [HIGGINS]; b 1701; Martha's Vineyard
MAYHEW, Matthew[3] (1648-1710) & Mary [SKIFFE] (1650-1690); 1 Mar 1674; Chilmark
MAYHEW, Matthew (1674-1725?) & Anna [NEWCOMB] (1677-); b 1697; Martha's Vineyard
MAYHEW, Paine/Payne? (1677-1761) & Mary RANKIN (1676-1753); 8 Dec 1699; Chilmark
MAYHEW, Thomas[1] (1593-1681) & 1/wf Abigail PARKUS; b 1621; Martha's Vineyard
MAYHEW, Thomas[1] (?1593-1681) & 2/wf Jane (GALLION) [PAINE], w Thomas; b 1635; Watertown
MAYHEW, Thomas[2] (1621-1657) & Jane (GALLION) [PAINE], w Thomas, m/2 Richard SARSON 1667+; b 1648; Martha's Vineyard
MAYHEW, Thomas (?1650-) & Sarah [SKIFFE] (1646-); ca 1673; Martha's Vineyard
MAYHEW, Thomas & Hannah COLE; 22 Apr 1700; Boston
MAYHEW, __?__ & Mary __?__, m/2 Benjamin HORTON
MAYLEM, Joseph, Boston & 1/wf Hannah KING (1666-); 31 Oct 1688; Charlestown/Boston
MAYLESS, __?__ & Hannah HUBBARD; Watertown
MAYNARD, John[1] (-1672) & 1/wf __?__ ; in Eng, ca 1629?; Sudbury
MAYNARD, John[1] (-1658) & 1/wf Mary STARR (1620-bef 2 Jan 1659, living 1648) (left 5 dau); [1640?], ?6 Apr 1640; Duxbury
MAYNARD, John[1] (-1672) & 2/wf Mary AXDELL/AXTELL, w Thomas; 16 Jun 1646; Sudbury
MAYNARD, John (-1658) & Editha (STEBBINS) DAY, w Robert, m/3 Eliza HOLYOKE, ch 1658; ca 1648, no issue; Hartford
MAYNARD, John[2] (1630-1711) & 1/wf Mary GATES (1636-1678?); 5 Apr 1658; Sudbury/Lancaster
MAYNARD, John[2] (1630-1711) & 2/wf Sarah (BLANDFORD) KEYES (1643-), w Elias; b 1680; Sudbury
MAYNARD, John[3] (1661-1731) & Lydia [WARD] (-1740); b 1690; Marlboro
MAINARD, Simon (1668-) & Hannah [NEWTON] (1671-); b 1694; Marlboro
MYNARD, William (-1711) & Lydia RICHARDS; 15 Nov 1678, 15 Oct; New London
MAYNARD, Zachariah (1647-1724) & 1/wf Hannah GOODRIDGE/GOODRICH? (ca 1658, 1659-1719); 15 Jul 1678; Sudbury
MAINOR, Zachariah (?1672-1739) & Mary GEER (1671/2-1739+); 23 Sep 1697; Groton, CT
MAINE, Ezekiel (-1714) & Mary __?__ ; b 1669; Stonington, CT
MAINE, Ezekiel, Jr. & Mary WELLS (-1693); 14 Jan 1689; Stonington, CT
MAIN, Ezekiel (-1715) & Hannah ROSE; 22 Oct 1695; Stonington, CT
MAINE, Henry (-1687) & __?__ ; b 1661?; Isles of Shoals
MAINE, Henry & Joanna ROADS; 4 Nov 1681; Marblehead
MAINE, Jeremiah & Ruth BROWN, wid; 11 Oct 1699; Stonington, CT
MAINE, John (1614±-) & Elizabeth __?__ (1623±-); b 1641; York, ME?

MANE, John & Lydia _?_ ; b 1670; Boston
MAYN, John & Mary PEACOCK; 24 Jul 1690; Boston
MAINE, Josiah & Dorothy [TRAFTON]; b 1700; York, ME
MAIN, _?_ & [Hannah LEWIS], m/2 James DARLING 1683; ?Lynn
MAINS, Thomas & Elizabeth _?_ ; York, ME/N. Yarmouth, ME
MAINS, Thomas (-1726, 1734(-)) & Patience _?_ ; Portsmouth, NH
MAYO, Daniel (1664-1715±) & [Sarah HOWES]; ca 1694/6?; Eastham
MAYO, James (?1656-1708) & 1/wf _?_ (-1697); b 1688; Eastham
MAYO, James (?1656-1708) & 2/wf Sarah [ELKINS] (1674-), dau of Thomas, m/2 Edward KNOWLES; b 1701?, 1702?; Eastham
MAYO, John & 1/wf _?_ (-living in 1670); b 1624; Barnstable/Eastham/Boston/Yarmouth/Oyster Bay, LI
MAYO, John & Hannah LECRAFT/RICRAFT; 1 Jan 1650, 1 Jan 165-; Eastham
MAYO, John (1630-1688) & Hannah GRAVES (1636-1699); 24 May 1654; Roxbury
MAYO, John & 2/wf Thomasin [LUMPKIN], w William; ca 1672-3?; Eastham/etc.
MAYO, John & Hannah FREEMAN (1664-1743/4); 14 Apr 1681; Hingham/Harwich
MAYO, John (-1735) & Sarah BURDEN; 8 Jul 1685; Roxbury
MAYO, Joseph (-1714+) (ae 45 in 1695) & 1/wf Sarah SHORT (-1710); 29 May 1679; Newbury
MAYO, Joseph & Elizabeth HOLBROOK (-1735); 10 Mar 1692, 1691/2; Roxbury
MAYO, Nathaniel (-1662) & Hannah PRINCE, m/2 Jonathan SPARRO; 13 Feb 1649; Eastham
MAYO, Nathaniel (1652-1709) & Elizabeth WIXAM; 28 Jan 1678; Eastham
MAYO, Nathaniel (?1667-1716) & 1/wf [?Mary] _?_ ; b 1697; Eastham
MAYO, Samuel (-1663?, 1664) & Thomasine [LUMPKIN] (1626-1709), Yarmouth, m/2 John SUNDERLAND 1665?; b 1645; Barnstable/Oyster Bay, LI
MAYO, Samuel (1655-29 Oct 1738, ae 83) & [Ruth HOPKINS?] (1658?-) (no evidence); b 1690, ca 15; Eastham
MAYO, Samuel (1658-bef 1732) & [Sarah CANTERBURY] (had Cornelius); b 1693?, ca 1689; Eastham
MAYO, Thomas (1650-1729) & Barbara KNOWLES (1656-1715); 13 Jun 1677; Eastham
MAYO, Thomas (1672-) & [Molly] _?_ ; ca 1693; Eastham
MAYO, Thomas (1673-1750) & Elizabeth DAVIS (1678-); 4 May 1699; Roxbury
MAYO, William (1654-1691) & Elizabeth [RING] (1652-1691?); ca 1680/5; Eastham
MAYO, [?Thomas] & Elizabeth _?_ , m/2 Robert GAMBLIN, Jr., b 1632; in Eng, b 1630; Roxbury
MEACHUM, Isaac[2] (ca 1643-1715) & Deborah (BROWNING) PERKINS (1647-1704+), w John; 28 Dec 1669; Salem/Enfield, CT
MEACHAM, Isaac (1672-1715) & Mary ROOT (1673-), ?m/2 Thomas TERRY 1722; 10 Dec 1700; Enfield, CT
MEACHAM, Jeremiah[1] (1613-1695) & 1/wf Margaret _?_ ; ca 1642; Salem/Southold, LI
MEACHUM, Jeremiah[2] (?1644-1743) & 1/wf Mary TRASK (1652-bef 6 Jul 1683); 3 Jan 1672/3, 5 ch; Salem
MEACHAM, Jeremiah[1] (1613-1695) & 2/wf Alice (DUTCH) (NEWMAN) [DANE] (-1734), w John, w John; aft 29 Sep 1684; Salem
MEACHAM, Jeremiah[2] (1644-1743, ae 99 y, Windham, CT) & 2/wf Deborah [BROWN] (1673-1721, 1731, Windham); ?25 May 1693, b 1694; Salem
MEACHAM, Jeremiah[3] (1673-12 Apr 1715) & Freelove [BLISS]? (1672-22 Mar 1715), dau John; b 1701?, b 1699?, ca 1690; Newport, RI
MEACHAM, John[3] & Mary CASH (1675-); 28 May 1697; Salem
MEAD, Benjamin (1666-1746) & 1/wf Sarah WATERBURY (1677-); 15 May 1700; Stamford, CT/Greenwich, CT
MEAD, David & Hannah WARREN; 26 Sep 1675, 24 Sep; Cambridge/Billerica/Watertown /Woburn
MEAD, Ebenezer (?1663-) & Sarah [KNAPP] (1670-1728); b 1692; Greenwich, CT
MEAD, Gabriel (1589-12 May 1666) & ?2/wf Joanna/Susanna? [BATES?], ?m/2 John EDDY; b 1637; Dorchester
MEAD, Israel (-1714) & Mary HALL (-1692); 26 Feb 1668/9; Charlestown/Cambridge/Lexington
MEAD, James & Judith _?_ (-9 Oct 1694); b 1692; Wrentham
MEEDES, James & Mary WILLIAMS; m int 10 Nov 1696; Boston
MEAD, John (ca 1634-1700) & [Hannah POTTER?]; ca 1657?, b 1662, b 1656; Stamford, CT/Greenwich, CT/Hempstead, LI
MEAD, John (ca 1658-1693) & Ruth HARDY; 27 Oct 1681; Stamford, CT

MEAD, Jonathan (1665?-1727?) & Martha [FINCH]; ca 1688; Greenwich, CT
MEAD, Joseph (1630-1690) & Mary BROWN; 4 Dec 1654; Stamford, CT
MEAD, Joseph (1657-1714) & Sarah [REYNOLDS] (1665-), m/2 _?_ St.JOHN; b 1695; Greenwich, CT/Norwalk, CT
MEAD, Joseph (1660-1725) & Mary _?_; b 1698; Greenwich, CT
MEAD, Nathaniel (?1669-1703) & Rachel _?_, m/2 James FERRIS, Jr.; b 1701?; Greenwich, CT
MEAD, Nicholas & Elizabeth _?_; b 1679; Charlestown/Bristol, RI/Mendon
MEAD, Richard & 1/wf _?_; b 1658; ?Roxbury
MEADES, Richard (-1689) & 2/wf Mary (COBHAM) BENMET/BENNETT, w John; 6 Nov 1678; Roxbury/Charlestown
MEAD, Samuel (-1713) & Hannah _?_; b 1696; Greenwich, CT
MEADE, Thomas & Mary DAY, w Thomas; 31 Jan 1672; Salem
MEAD, Thomas & Hannah SMITH; 31 Jan 1695; Cambridge/Woburn/Lexington
MEAD, William (?1600-1663?) & [?Kilvy] _?_ (-1657, 1658); in Eng, ca 1625/30; Stamford, CT
MEAD, William (-1683) & Rebecca _?_ (-1683); b 1650, b 1655; Charlestown/New London
MEADE, _?_ & Hester _?_; b 169-; Middleboro
MEADER, John (?1630-1715+) & Abigail [?TUTTLE/?FOLLETT]; ca 1653; Dover, NH
MEADER, John (1655±-) & 1/wf Sarah [FOLLETT] (1654-); b 1681; Dover, NH
MEADER, Joseph (1664-1728+) & Elizabeth _?_ (-1723); ca 1690; Dover, NH
MEADER, Nathaniel (1671-1704) & Eleanor [HALL?/MERROW?]; b 1696; Dover, NH
MEADOWS, Philip & Elizabeth INGULDEN/IGGULDON?; - Apr 1641; Roxbury
MEAKIN, John (-1706) & 1/wf _?_; b 1663; Hartford
MEAKINS, John (-1706) & 2/wf Mary [BIDWELL] (1647-1725); by 1665; Hartford
MEEKINS, John (-1754) & Ruth BELKNAP; 24 Apr 1696; Hatfield/Hadley
MEAKINS, Thomas[1] (-1645) & Catherine [BELL] (-1651); b 1619, by 1615?; Boston/Roxbury
MEEKINS, Thomas[2] (-1687) & 1/wf Sarah [BEARDSLEY]? (-1651); b 1639; Boston/Roxbury/etc.
MEAKINS, Thomas[2] (-1687) & 2/wf Elizabeth TULSTON (-1683); 14 Feb 1650, 1650/1; Roxbury
MEEKINS, Thomas[3] (1643-1675) & Mary [BUNCE] (1645-), m/2 John DOWNING 1676; b 1666; Hadley
MEEKINS, Thomas[4] (1673-1723?) & Sarah (CLARK) [MILLS], w Samuel; ca 1693/5?; Hadley/Hartford
MEANE/MEANS, John & Anne _?_, m/2 John HASTINGS aft 1646; b 1638(9?); Cambridge
MEARS, James (1649-1712, ae 69) & Elizabeth [MELLOWES]; b 1666; Charlestown/Boston
MEERES, John (1635-1663) & Mary _?_/[Mercy SANDYS] (dau of a sister of Thomas DINSDALE), m/2 Ezekiel CRAVATH by 1668 (John MEARS whose wf was Mary d by 1661, she m/2 William KENT by 1665); Boston
MEERS, John (-1691?) & Lydia _?_; b 1678; Boston
MEARS, Robert (1592-1667) & Elizabeth [JOHNSON?] (1602?, 1605?-1670+); b 1637, b 1630; Boston
MEARS, Samuel (1641-1676) & Mary [STACY?], m/2 _?_ FITCH?; b 1665; Boston
MEARS, Samuel (1671-1727) & 1/wf Mariah [Catherine] (SMITH) GROSS, w William; 7 Dec 1697; Boston
MEASURE, William (-1688) & Alice (?SMITH) TINKER (-1714, ae 85), w John [1664]; New London, CT/Lyme, CT
MECARTER, John (-1722) & Rebecca MEACHUM/MEACHAM; 27 Jan 1674; Salem/Providence
MEDBERY, John (-1694) & Sarah _?_, ?m/2 Israel HARDING ca 1696?; b 1680; Swansea
MEDBURY, William & Sarah _?_; b 1701?;
MEECH, John & Hannah YEOMAN; 26 Aug 1691, b 1699; Preston, CT/Stonington, CT
MEEK, Richard & Mary PALMER; 12 Jun 1699; Marblehead
MEEK, _?_ & _?_; b 1681
MEEKER, Daniel (-1716) & Elizabeth [OGDEN]; ca 1685?; Fairfield, CT
MEEKER, John (-1727) & Elizabeth SMITH?; ca 1690?; Stratford, CT
MEEKER, Robert (-1685, 1684?) & Susan TURBERFIELD; 16 Sep 1651; New Haven
MEEKER, William & Sarah [PRESTON]; b 1649; Stratford, CT/Newark, NJ
MAGDANIEL/MacDANIEL, Dennis & Alice _?_; b 1671; Boston
MEGDANIELL, John & Elizabeth SMITH; 17 May 1658; Boston
MEIGS, Ebenezer (1675-) & Mercy WEEKS, Falmouth, MA; 7 Oct 1700; Guilford, CT
MEIGS, Janna/Junna? (-1739) & Hannah WILLARD (1674-); 18 May 1698; Wethersfield, CT

MEIGS, John (1612-1671/2) & Tamsen/Tamazine/Thomasin/Tamazin [FRY], sister of William; b 1632; Weymouth/Guilford, CT

MEIGS, John (-1713) & 1/wf Sarah WILCOXSON (-1691), Stratford, CT; 7 Mar 1665/6, 1665; Killingworth, CT/Guilford, CT

MEIGS, John (-1713) & 2/wf Lydia (THOMPSON) [CRITTENDEN], w Isaac; aft 24 Nov 1691; Guilford, CT

MEIGS, John (1670-1718) & Rebecca HAND; 20 Jul 1694; Guilford, CT

MEIGS, Mark (?1614-1673) & Avis __?__ ; ca 1656?; Southampton, LI/Huntington, LI

MEIGS, Vincent (?1583-1658?) & __?__ [CHURCHILL?]; in Eng, ca 1608; Guilford, CT/etc.

MEKUSETT, Mordecai & Sarah __?__ ; b 1690; Braintree

MELCHER, Edward & Elizabeth __?__ ; Portsmouth, NH

MELCHER, Nathaniel (-1724) & [Elizabeth LEAR]; Portsmouth, NH

MELCHER, Samuel & Elizabeth CRAM; 16 May 1700; Hampton, NH

MELYEN, Cornelius (-1674, 1663) & Janneken/Jannetie ARIENS (-1674); ca 1640, 22 Apr 1627; Staten Island, NY

MELYN, Isaac & 1/wf Dorothia SAMSON

MELYN, Isaac (1646-1693) & 2/wf [Temperance LIVERIDGE]; 5 Oct 1679

MELYEN, Jacob (1640-1706?) & Hannah [HUBBARD] (1637-1717); ca 1662; Wethersfield, CT/NY/Boston

MELLENS, James (?1642-1680), Malden & Elizabeth [DEXTER] (-1693), m/2 Stephen BARRETT 1680; b 1659; Charlestown

MELLENS, James (1663-) & Elizabeth __?__ ; b 1695; Charlestown/Boston

MELLENS, John (1666-1695) & Elizabeth [BUCKNAM] (-1729+), m/2 Samuel TOWNSEND 1701; b 1695; Charlestown

MELLEN, Richard & __?__ ; b 1642; Charlestown/Weymouth

MELLEN, Simon (ae 27 in 1663) & Mary __?__ ; b 1665; Boston/Malden/Watertown/Sherborn

MELLENS, Simon (1665-) & Elizabeth FISK; 27 Dec 1688; Sherborn

MELLENS, Thomas (1668-) & Elizabeth __?__ ; b 1691; Sherborn/Framingham

MELLENS, Thomas (1670-) & Mary THREDNEEDLE; 28 Sep 1693; Boston

MELLEN, William (1671-1697) & Deborah [SPRAGUE] (1670-), m/2 Samuel BUCKNAM 1697, b 1695; Malden

MELLISON/MELLESON, John & Sarah __?__ ; b 1681; Boston

MELLOWS, Abraham[1] (?1570-1639) & Martha [BULKELEY] (?1572-); in Eng, ca 1596; Boston, Eng/Charlestown

MELLOWES, Edward (1610-1650) & Hannah [SMITH], w Samuel?, m/2 Joseph HILLS 1651; b 1636; Charlestown

MELLOWES, John (1622-1675?) & Martha __?__ , m/2 Deane WINTHROP by 1678; b 1647; Boston

MELLOWS, John & Sarah __?__ , m/2 __?__ KNOX; b 1680(1?); Boston

MELLOWES, Oliver (?1597, ?1598-1638) & 1/wf Mary JAMES (1597-); 3 Aug 1620); Boston, Eng

MELLOWES, Oliver (?1598-1638) & 2/wf Elizabeth (HAWKREDD) CONEY (1605-1670+), w John, m/3 Thomas MAKEPEACE 1641?; 1 Jan 1633/4; Boston, Eng/Boston

MELLOUS, Thomas & Sarah MUMFORT; 3 Nov 1697; Boston

MELOY/?MEALOY, Dargett & __?__ ; b 1687; Watertown

MELTEN, Robert & Sarah [CHAMBERLAIN]; b 1675; Hull

MELTON, Robert & Hannah WHITCOMB; m int 10 Sep 1695, Boston; Hull

MELVILLE/MELVIN, David & 1/wf Mary WILLARD (1669-1723); m int 25 Jun 1696; Boston/Eastham

MELVIN, John & 1/wf Hannah [LEWIS] (-1696); b 1679; Charlestowwn

MELVIN, John & Margaret SHANESBERG, m int 27 Aug 1696; Charlestown/Boston

MELVINE, Walter & Mary __?__ ; b 1685; Southampton

MEMRY/MEMORY, John & [Mary TRAIN]; b 1642; Dorcester/Watertown

MENDALL, John[1] (-1720) & __?__ OAKMAN?; b 1663; Marshfield

MENDALL, John[2] (1663-1743) & Joanna [STANDLAKE]; b 1688; Rochester

MENDUM, Jonathan[2] & Mary [RAYNES], m/2 John WOODMAN; b 2 Mar 1672, ca 1660/70?; Kittery, ME

MENDUM, Jonathan[3] & Sarah [DOWNING] (1675/6-), m/2 Joseph CUSTIS 1719; ca 1700?, b 20 May 1702; Kittery, ME

MENDUM, Robert[1] (1604-1682) & 1/wf Mary __?__ ; ca 1630/2?; Duxbury/Kittery, ME

MENTOR, Robert (-1720?) & [Hannah COMSTOCK] (1673-); ?Colchester, CT

MEPHAM, John (-1647) & Mary _?_ (-1676), m/2 Timothy BALDWIN by 1650, m/3 Thomas TAPPING/TOPPING 1666; aft 31 Jul 1647; Guilford, CT

MAPHAM, John & [Mary HAMPTON], m/2 Benjamin HORTON 1686?; Southampton, LI

MERCER, Abiel (1670-) & Abigail MASH/MARSH; 3 Jan 1694/5; Haverhill

MERCER, Francis (-1692) & Gertrude [MAIN], m/2 m/3? Edward TOOGOOD by 1695; Portsmouth

MERCER, Richard & Hannah SHATSWELL/SATCHWELL; 18 Mar 1668/9; Haverhill

MERCER, Thomas (-1699) (1/wf Edith?) & Elizabeth [HAWKINS?]; b 1671, b 1662?; Boston

MERCER, _?_ & Ann/Hannah MERRICK, m John WALKER 1672; court case 13 Mar 1669/70, had Mary illegitimate

MARCHANT, Abishai (1651-1712+) & Mary [TAYLOR] (1649-1717/18); ca 1673; Martha's Vineyard

MERCHANT, John[1] (?1600-) & Sarah _?_ (-1638); b 1625; Braintree/Newport/Yarmouth

MERCHANT, John (-bef 1693) & _?_ ; b 1648, b 1647?; Yarmouth

MARCHANT, Joseph (1666-1711+) & Ann _?_ ; Edgartown

MARCHENT, William (-1668) & Mary _?_ (-1680); b 1641(2?); Watertown/Ipswich

MERIER?/MESSENGER?, Thomas & Elizabeth _?_ ; b 1694; Boston (dau Mary died)

MERIAM, George[1] (ca 1603-1675) & Susan/Susanna RAVEN (-1675+); Tunbridge, Eng, 16 Oct 1627; Concord

MARION, John & Sarah _?_ ; b 1655; Boston

MIRRIAM, John (1641-1724) & Mary COOPER (1645-1730/1); 21 Oct 1663; Cambridge/Concord

MIRIAM, John (-1727), Cambridge & Mary WHEELER, Concord; 14 Nov 1688; Concord

MIRIAM, John (1666-1748) & 1/wf Sarah WHEELER (1666-1692); 22 Jul 1691; Concord

MIRIAM, John (1666-1748), Concord & 2/wf Sarah SPALDEN/SPALDING (1669-), Chelmsford; 16 Feb 1692/3; Chelmsford/Littleton

MERRIAM, John & Rebecca SHARP; 23 May 1694; Salem/?Lynn

MERRIAM, Joseph (-1642, 1641?) & Sarah [GOLDSTONE] (-1671), m/2 Joseph WHEELER; in Eng, b 1624; Cambridge/Concord

MERRIAM, Joseph (1629-1671) & Sarah STONE (1633-1704); 12 Jul 1653; Concord

MERRIAM, Joseph (-1702) & Sarah JENKINS; 19 Apr 1675, 19? Aug; Lynn

MIRIAM, Robert (?1613, 1614?-1683) & Mary [SHEAFE] (?1621, 1620-1693); ca 1639/45?, no issue; Concord/Charlestown

MERRIAM, Robert (1667-1718) & Abigail [CUTLER] (1674-1717); b 1697; Lexington

MERRIAM, Samuel (1643?-1713+) & Elizabeth TOWNSEND (-1705); 21 Nov 1669, 22 Dec 1669; Concord/Lynn

MERRIAM, Thomas & Mary HARWOOD; 23 Dec 1696; Concord/Cambridge

MERRIAM, William & 1/wf Elizabeth [BREED], dau Allen; b 1654; Lynn

MERRIAM, William & 2/wf Anna JONUS/JONES? (-1677); 11 Oct 1676; Lynn

MERRIAM, William (1624-1689) & 3/wf Sarah _?_ (-1689+); aft 29 Jul 1677; Lexington

MERRIAM, William & 1/wf Hannah DAGGLE/DUGALD? (-1693); 3 Jun 1690; Lynn

MERRIAM, William & 2/wf Athildred/Ethelred/Aetheldred BERRY; 20 Dec 1695; Lynn/Walling-ford, CT

MERRIAM, _?_ & _?_ SMITH

MIRICK, Benjamin (1644-) & 1/wf Sarah [ORTON] (-1691); b 1674(5?); Charlestown

MIRICK, Benjamin (1644-) & 2/wf Elizabeth [WYER] (1659-1726+); b 1695; Charlestown

MERRICK, Benjamin (1664-) & 1/wf Rebecca [DOANE]; ca 1700?; Eastham

MIRICK, Isaac/Henry MERRICK (1665-) & Mary NEWELL (1669-); 22 Aug 1694, 2 Aug 1694; Charlestown/Newbury

MIRICK, James (?1612, 1613-) & Marjery/Margaret _?_ (-1708); b 1652?, b 1648?, b 1647?, by 1634?; Charlestown/Newbury

MIRICK, James & Hannah _?_ ; b 1683, b 1687-8 Boston; Newbury/Boston

MERRICK, James (1670-1765) & 1/wf Sarah HITCHCOCK (1678-1734); 30 Jul 1696; Springfield

MERRICK, John (-1647) & Elizabeth [FELLOWS] (-1650); ?b 1635, b 1647; Hingham

MIRICK, John (1614-) & Hopestill _?_ (1619-); b 1643; Charlestown

MIRICK, John (?1662-1706) (Thomas WISWALL was a kinsman) & Elizabeth TROWBRIDGE (1660-1734); 9 Feb 1681/2, 9 Feb 1682; Cambridge/Newton

MERRICK, John (1658-1748) & 1/wf Mary DAY (1660-1723); 11 Feb 1687, 10 Feb 1686/7, 1686/7; Springfield

MERRICK, Joseph (1662-1737) & 1/wf Elizabeth [HOWES]; 1 May 1684; Eastham

MIRICK, Joseph (1661-) & Saraj/Sarah [COLE] (1671-1716); b 1691; Charlestown
MERRICK, Nathaniel (1675-1743, Harwich) & Alice [FREEMAN] (-1756?); ca 1699?; Duxbury/Harwich
MERRICK, Stephen (1646-1705) & 1/wf Mercy BANGS (1651-); 28 Dec 1670, Dec 1671; Eastham/Norwalk, CT
MERRICK, Stephen (1646-1705) & 2/wf Anna WILBORE/WILBUR; 25 Jan 1690/1, 26 Jan, 25 Feb 1691/2; Taunton
MERRICK, Thomas (1620-1704) & 1/wf Sarah STEBBINS (ca 1623-1649); 14 Sep 1639; Springfield
MERRICK, Thomas (1620-1704) & 2/wf Elizabeth TILLEY; 21 Oct 1653; Springfield
MERRICK, Thomas (1664-1743) & Hannah DUMBLETON (-1737); 18 Dec 1690; Springfield
MERRICK, Tilley (1667-) & Sarah COOLEY (1673-); 6 Sep 1694; Springfield/Brookfield
MIRICK, Timothy (1666-1719) & Mary LANCHASTER/LANCASTER; m int 9 May 1696; Newbury
MERRICK, William (-1643) & Elizabeth SNOW, w Jabez; aft 1630
MERRICK, William (1600-1689) (ae ca 86 in 1688, 1686) & Rebecca [TRACY?] (-1689+); b 1643; Duxbury/Eastham
MERRICK, William (1643-1732, Harwich) & Abigail HOPKINS (1644-); 23 May 1667; Eastham
MEARIFIELD, Benjamin (1658-) & Prudence __?__; b 1693; Dorchester
MERRIFIELD, Henry & Margaret __?__; b 1645; Dorchester
MERRIFIELD, John (?1645-1678) & __?__ [GOAD], dau Joseph; b 1665(6?); Dorchester
MERYFIELD, John (1665/6-) & Sarah [NEALE]?; b 1690; Boston
MERRIFIELD, Joseph & Mary ROGERS; 6 Apr 1699; Boston
MERIHEW, Jonathan (1662-1701) & Sarah (ALMY) [CADMAN] (1662-), w Richard; b 1695/6; Dartmouth/RI
MEREHOE, Josiah & Hope __?__; b 1695; Dartmouth
MERRIHEW, Samuel & Sarah [KIRBY] (1667-); ?Dartmouth
MERRIHEW, __?__ & Mercy __?__; b 1694; Dartmouth
MERRILL, Abel (1644-1689) & Priscilla CHASE (1649-); 10 Feb 1670, 1670/1; Newbury
MERRILL, Abel (1671-1759) & Abigail STEVENS (1673-1757); 19 Jun 1694; Haverhill/Newbury
MERRILL, Abraham (-1722) & 1/wf Abigail WEBSTER (ca 1642-1712); 18 Jun 1660, 1660/1; Newbury
MERRILL, Abraham & Abigail BARTLETT; m int 7 Oct 1696; Newbury
MERRILL, Abraham & Prudence KELLOGG (1675-); 18 Apr 1699; ?Hartford/Farmington
MERRELLS, Asa & Sarah [REEVE?] (1663); ?Hartford
MERRILL, Daniel (1642-1717) & 1/wf Sarah CLOUGH (1646-1706); 19 May 1667; Newbury
MERRILL, Daniel & Esther [CHASE] (1674-); b 1694; Newbury
MERRILL, Daniel (1673-1750) & 1/wf Susanna PRATT (1680-); 18 Jan 1697/8; Hartford
MERRILL, Jeremiah & Sarah __?__ (-Jul 1658?); b 1652; Boston
MERRILL, John & ?1/wf Annis BISHOP; in Eng, 24 Jan 1628/9
MERRILL, John (-1673) & 2/wf Elizabeth __?__ (-1682); in Eng, b 1631, b 1630?; Newbury
MERRILL, John (-1712) & Sarah WATSON; 23 Sep 1663; Hartford
MERRILL, John & Lucy [WEBSTER] (1664-); b 1687; Newbury
MERRILL, John (1669-) & Sarah MARSH; 29 Sep 1694; Hartford
MERRILL, Nathan & Hannah KENT; 6 Sep 1699; Newbury
MERRILL, Nathaniel (1601-1655) & Susanna WILTERTON?/?WOLLERTON (-1673), m/2 Stephen JORDAN; ca 1630?, in Eng?, 16 Mar 1635?; Newbury
MERRILL, Nathaniel & Joanna NANNY?/NINNY?/NINIAN?/KENNEY?/KINNEY?; 15 Oct 1661; Salisbury
MERRILL, Nathaniel & 1/wf Rebecca [BROWN] (-1689); b 1688; Newbury
MERRILL, Nathaniel & 2/wf Sarah [WOODMAN] (1665-); b 1692; Newbury
MERRILL, Peter (-1697) & Mary [BROWN] (1673-), m/2 John SAWYER 1700; b 1693; Newbury
MERRELLS, Thomas & __?__; b 1646; Hartford
MERRILL, Thomas (?1646-1711) & 1/wf Elizabeth ROE (ca 1665-); b 1685; Saybrook, CT
MERRILL, Thomas & 2/wf Hannah (PARMELEE) HILL, w Tahan; 25 May 1693; Saybrook, CT
MERRIMAN, Caleb (1665-1703) & Mary PRESTON (1674-1755), m/2 Samuel MUNSON; 9 Jul 1690; Wallingford, CT
MERRIMAN, John (1660-1741) & 1/wf Hannah LINES (1665-1688), New Haven; 28 Mar 1683; Wallingford, CT

MERRIMAN, John (1660-1741) & 2/wf Elizabeth PECK (1673-1709+); 20 Nov 1690; Wallingford, CT

MERRIMAN, Nathaniel (1613/14-1694) & Jane/Joan? __?__ (1628-1709 in 82nd y); b 1647; New Haven/Wallingford, CT

MERRIMAN, Samuel (1662-1694) & Anna [STREET] (1665-1705), m/2 Bartholomew CROSSMAN; b 1687; Wallingford, CT

MERRITT, Henry (-1653) & __?__ ; in Eng, ca 1620/22?; Scituate

MERRITT, Henry² (-1667) & Judith __?__ ; ca 1641/3?; Scituate/Boston

MERRITT, Henry (1663/4-1732) & Deborah [BUCK]; b 1687(8?); Scituate

MERRITT, [?James] (1647-1713) & Sarah __?__ (?1658-1740); b 1685; Marblehead

MERRITT/MERICK, John (-1676/7) & Elizabeth WYBORNE; 3 Apr 1655; Boston

MERRET, John (1642-1707) & Mary __?__ ; b 1670; Marblehead

MERRITT, John & Mary [BROWN?]; 1 May 1680; Rye, NY

MERRITT, John (1661-1740) & Elizabeth [HYLAND] (1664-1746); ca 1686; Scituate

MERRITT, John & Sarah GRANT (1675-); 2 Jun 1696; Marblehead

MERRITT, John & __?__ ; ?b 1697; Rye, NY

MERRITT, Joseph (-1754) & Jane __?__ ; b 1695(6?); Rye, NY

MERRITT, Nicholas (?1613-1686) & [Mary SANDIN]; ca 1636?; Salem

MERRITT, Nicholas & __?__ ; ca 1662; Salem

MERRITT, [Nicholas] & Elizabeth __?__ ; b 1690; Marblehead

MERRITT, Philip & Abigail GALE; 27 May 1694; Beverly

MERITT/MARRETT?, Philip (?1671-1741, Boston) & Mary __?__ (?1676-1735); b 1695; Boston, Gloucester

MERRITT/MARRETT?, Richard & Mary SIMMONS; 12 Jan 1685, 21? Jan; Charlestown/Boston

MERRIT, Samuel (-1697?) & Abigail __?__ ; b 1684; Marblehead

MERRITT, Samuel & ?Elizabeth/?Sarah [UNDERHILL]; 1698?; Rye/White Plains, NY

MERRITT, Thomas (?1634-1725?) & 1/wf Jane SHERWOOD (1636-1685); 3 Dec 1656; ?Wethersfield, CT/Rye, NY

MERRITT, Thomas (-1725) & 2/wf Abigail FRANCIS (1660-); ?13 Aug 1688, bef 20 Oct 1688; ?Rye, NY

MERIT, Thomas & Lucy WARD; m int 2 Sep 1695; Boston

MERRITT, Thomas (-1725) & 3/wf Mary (FERRIS) LOCKWOOD (-1708), w Jonathan; m cont 5 Jun 1696, 3? Jun, 18? Jun; ?Greenwich, CT/Rye, NY

MERRITT, Thomas (1670-1719) & Martha [MARSHALL] (?1680); b 1701(?); Rye, NY

MERRITT, __?__ & [Sarah LYON]; b 1701?, b 1713

MERRITT, __?__ & [Ruth SHERWOOD]; b 1701?, b 7 Oct 1704

MERROW, Daniel & Elizabeth STIMPSON; b 1696?, b 1707

MERROW, Henry (-1685) & Jane (LINDES) WALLACE/WALLIS, w Nicholas; 19 Dec 1661, 19 Dec 1660; Woburn/Reading/Charlestown

MERROW, Henry (1662-) & Miriam [BROOKS] (1673-); b 1695, by 1691; Woburn/Reading

MERCY, John (1663-1735) & Deliverance [?BELLFLOWER] (1662?-1733); b 1686; Reading

MERROW, Samuel (1670-) & Mary PAGE; 16 Dec 1695; Haverhill/Reading/Durham, NH/Rochester, NH

MERRY, Cornelius & Rachel BALL/BALLARD; 11 Aug 1663; Northampton

MERRY, John & Constance __?__ ; b 1663; Boston

MERRY, John & Sarah __?__ ; b 1688; Roxbury

MERRY, John & Puah __?__ (1673-1747), m/2 Abraham REEVES, m/3 John DAVIS 1706; b 1701?; East Hampton, LI

MERRY, Joseph (-1710 in 103rd y) (Philip WOOLIDGE was his nephew) & 1/wf Mary __?__ (-1657); b 1647; Hampton, NH

MERRY, Joseph (-1710 in 103rd y) & 2/wf Elizabeth (PARKHURST) HILLIARD (1628-), w Emanuel; 14? Dec, m cont 13 Dec 1659; Hampton, NH

MERRY, Ralph & Lucy [COBB]; b 1673; Plymouth

MERREY, Samuel (1669-) & Remember/Remembrance? [LUCE]; ca 1688; Tisbury

MERRY, Walter (-1657) & 1/wf Rebecca __?__ ; b 29 Dec 1633; Boston

MERRY, Walter (-1657) & 2/wf Mary DOLING/DOLENS?/DOWLING?, m/2 Robert THORNTON 1657; 18 Aug 1653; Boston

MERRY, Walter (1656-) & 1/wf Martha COTTERELL; 17 Feb 1682, prob 1682/3, ?17 Jan 1682; Taunton

MERRY, Walter & 2/wf Elizabeth **CUNNELL**; 21 Jan 1685/6, 24? Jan; Taunton
MERWIN, John (1650-) & 1/wf Mary **(WELCH) HOLBROOK**, w Israel; 12 Apr 1683; Milford, CT
MERWIN, Miles (1623-1697) & 1/wf Elizabeth __?__ (-10 Jul 1664); b 1650; Milford, CT
MERWIN, Miles (1623-1697) & 2/wf Sarah **(PLATT)** [BEACH] (-1670), 1698), w Thomas; ca 1665; Milford, CT
MERWIN, Miles (1623-1697) & 3/wf Sarah (__?__) **SCHOFIELD** (-1698), w Daniel; 30 Nov 1670; Stamford, CT
MERWIN, Miles (1658-) & Hannah **(WILMOT) MILES**, w Samuel; 20 Sep 1681, 21 Sep, 26 Sep; New Haven/Milford, CT
MERWIN, Samuel (1656-1706) & 1/wf Sarah **WOODING** (-1691); 13 Dec 1682; New Haven/Milford, CT
MERWIN, Samuel (1656-1706) & 2/wf Hannah __?__, m/2 Isaac **BEECHER**; aft 9 Mar 1690/1; Milford, CT
MERWIN, Thomas (1654-) & Abigail **CLAPHAM**; Mar 1678/9; Fairfield, CT/Norwalk, CT
MERWIN, __?__ & Mary **(ADAMS)** [GUIRE], m/3 Stephen **SHERWOOD**; b 1680; Milford, CT
MASERVEY, Aaron[2] (-1706) & Susanna **SAWYER**, m/2 John **BATTEN**; 20 Nov 1695; Salem
MESERVE, Clement (?1655-) & Elizabeth __?__; b 1700?, by 1673; Scarborough/Portsmouth, NH
MESERVE, Daniel & Deborah [OTIS] **MERROW**? (1677?-); nr 1700, aft 1 Dec 1701; Dover, NH
MESSENGER, Andrew[1] & __?__ ?MANNING/?SEELEY; b 1639?; New Haven/Greenwich, CT/Jamaica, LI
MESSENGER, Andrew[2] & 1/wf Rebecca **(PICKETT)** [St.JOHN], w James; b 1685?; Norwalk, CT
MESSENGER, Andrew & 2/wf Rachel [HAYES]; b 1701?, b 1705?; ?Norwalk, CT
MESSENGER, Ebenezer (1665-1689+), Boston & Rose **COLLINS**, Boston; 4 Jul 1687; Watertown/Boston
MESSENGER, Edward & __?__; b 1650; Windsor, CT
MESSENGER, Henry (-1681) & Sarah __?__ (-1697); b 27 Jan 1640(1?); Boston
MESSENGER, Henry (-1686) & Mehitable [MINOT] (-1690), m/2 Edward **MILLS** 1687, 1688?; no issue; Boston
MESSENGER, John (1641-) & Martha __?__, m/2 Jeremiah **FITCH** 1689; b 1670(1?); Boston
MESSENGER, John & Susannah [BEST] (1673-); b 1701?, b 1708; ?Salem/LI
MESSENGER, Nathan/Nathaniel? & Rebecca **KELSEY** (1660-); 5 Apr 1678; Windsor, CT
MESSENGER, Samuel (-1685, 1681±?) & Susannah [MILLS?/?ROGERS] (-1686+); m lic 20 Apr 1669; ?Huntington, LI/?Jamaica, LI
MESSENGER, Simeon (1645-) & Bethiah [HOWARD], dau Robert; b 1668; Boston
MESSINGER, Thomas (1661-1697+) & Elizabeth [MELLOWES] (1656-); b 1686(7?); Boston (see MERIER)
MESSINGER, Thomas (1661-1697+) & 2/wf Martha **MELLOWES**
MEDCALF, Eleazer (1653-1704) & Meletiah **FISHER** (1667-); 9 Apr 1684; Wrentham
METCALFE, John (1622-1680) & Mary **CHICKERING** (-1698); 23 Mar 1646/7, 22? Mar; Dedham
MEDCALFE, John & Marie/Mary **BOWERS**; 21 Dec 1676; Medfield
METCALF, Jonathan (1650-1727) & Hannah **KENDRICK/KENRICK**? (-1731); 10 Apr 1674; Dedham/Newton/Cambridge
METCALF, Joseph (1605-1665) & Elizabeth __?__, ?m/2 Edward **BEACHAM**; in Eng?, b 1630; Ipswich
MEDCALF, Joseph (?1661-1714) & Rebecca __?__ (-1723); b 1681; Ipswich
METCALF, Joseph & 1/wf Sarah **BOWERS**; 21 Jan 1685/6; Medfield
METCALF, Michael[1] (1586?, 1592-1664) & 1/wf Sarah **ELLWYN/ELWYN** (1593-1644); Heigham, Eng, 13 Oct 1616; Dedham
METCALFE, Michael[2] (1620-1654) & Mary **FAIRBANKS**, m/2 Christopher **SMITH** 1654; 2 Apr 1654; Dedham
METCALFE, Michael[1] (1592-1664) & 2/wf Mary **(SOTHY) RIDGE** (-aft 1664, 1672/3?, Dedham), w Thomas; 13 Aug 1645, m cont same day; Dedham
METCALF, Michael (1645-1693) & Elizabeth **(FULLER) KINGSBURY** (-1732), w John; 19 Sep 1672; Dedham
MEDCALFE, Michael & Elizabeth **BOWERS**; 21 Dec 1676; Medfield
METCALFE, Thomas (1629-1702) & 1/wf Sarah **PAIGE/[PIDGE]**; 12 Sep 1656; Dedham
METCALF, Thomas & 1/wf [Abigail] __?__ (-6 Dec 1688); b 1654; Ipswich
MEDSELFE/METCALFE, Thomas (1629-1702) & 2/wf Ann **(CHICKERING) PAINE**, w Stephen Jr.; 2 Dec 1679; Rehoboth/Dedham

MEDCALF, Thomas (1630-) & Lydia [DAVIS] (1639-1727); 168[9?]; Ipswich
METCALF, Thomas (-1702), Dedham & 3/wf Mehitable (HAND) SAVIL, Braintree, w John, ?m/3 Josiah CHAPIN 1713?; 22 Jan 1688/9; Braintree
METCALF, Thomas (1671-1704) & Sarah AVERY (-1748), m/2 Joseph WIGHT 1709; 24 Nov 1696; Dedham
METHUP/METTUP/MEDDUP/etc., Daniel (-1717) & Bethiah/Bethuah BECH/BEERS (-1722); 25 Mar 1664, 27 Mar; Watertown/Weston
MEW, Ellis & Ann [GIBBONS] (-1704); New Haven
MEW, Noel (-1692) & Mary __?__, m/2 Thomas COLEMAN 1703; b 1682; Newport
MICALL/?MYCALL, James & Mary FARR; 11 Dec 1657; Braintree
MICO, John (-1718) & Mary BRATTLE; 20 Aug 1689; Boston/Cambridge
MIDDLEBROOK, Joseph[1] (-1686) & 1/wf __?__ [BATEMAN]; b 1650; Fairfield, CT
MIDDLEBROOK, Joseph[1] (-1686) & 2/wf Mary (ODELL) [TURNEY], w Benjamin; aft 1650, b 24 Mar 1656; Fairfield, CT
MIDDLEBROOK, Joseph[1] (-1686) & 3/wf Hannah (WHEELER) [BENNETT] (1618-), w James; aft Aug 1659; Fairfield, CT
MIDDLEBROOK, Joseph (1650-1710+) & 1/wf Sarah __?__; b 1675; Fairfield, CT
MIDDLEBROOK, Joseph (1650-1710+) & 2/wf Bethia __?__ (-1746?); b 1701?; Fairfield, CT
MIDDLECOTT, Richard (-1704) & Sarah (WINSLOW) (STANDISH) PAYEN (1636?-1726, 1728?), m/1 Miles STANDISH 1660, m/2 Tobias PAINE ca 1625-7; 1672, b 1674; [Boston]
MIDLETON, Matthew & Faith [GILLAM], dau Benjamin, m/2 Wentworth PAXTON; b 1696; Boston
MIDDLETON, William (-1699, ae 74) & Elizabeth __?__; b 1672(3?)); Boston
MIDDLETON, William & Dorothy BREWER; 28 May 1694; Haverhill
MIGHILL, Ezekiel (-1694) & Elizabeth (NORTHEND) HOBSON, w Humphrey, m/3 Thomas GAGE 1695; 10 Oct 1686; Rowley
MIGHILL, John (-1702) & Sarah BATT; 6 Jul 1659; Rowley/Dover, NH/Suffield, CT
MIGHELL, John & Elizabeth FERMAN; 27 Sep 1698; Springfield
MIGHILL, Nathaniel (1646-1677) & Mary __?__, m/2 Thomas STEVENS 1681; Rowley
MIGHILL, Samuel (-1699) & Elizabeth TAPPAN (-1704); 26 Mar 1657; Rowley
MIGHILL, Stephen (1651-1687) & Sarah PHILIPS, m/2 Robert GREENOUGH; 3 Nov 1680; Rowley
MIGHILL, Thomas[1] (-1654) & 1/wf Ellen __?__ (-1640); b 1637?; Roxbury/Rowley
MIGHILL, Thomas[1] (-1654) & 2/wf Ann [PARROT] (-1694); b 1642; Rowley
MIGHILL, Thomas (1639-1689) & Bethula/Bethia/Bethulia WELD (-1711); 8 Nov 1669; Roxbury/Milton/Scituate
MIGHEL, Thomas & Abigail McCLAFLIN/McLAFLIN; 12 Dec 1700; Suffield, CT
MILLAM, Humphrey (-1667) (Capt. Thomas LAKE called "cousin") & Mary [GORE]; b 1652; Boston
MILAM, John & Christian/Ann? __?__; b 1636; Boston
MILAM, Joseph (1652-), Boston & 1/wf Hannah KING (1666-); 31 Oct 1688; Charlestown/Boston
MILES, Francis (alias KENDALL) & Mary TODD, 24 Dec 1644; Woburn
MILES, John (-1693) & 1/wf Sarah __?__ (-1678); b 1640; Concord
MYLES, John (-1683) & Anne/Anna (HUMPHREY) PALMES/[PALMER?] (-1693), w William (see below); in Wales?, b 1646; Salem/Swansea
MILES, John (1644-1704) & 1/wf Elizabeth HARRIMAN (1648-1675); 11 Apr 1665; New Haven
MYLES, John, Jr. & Mary? __?__; b 1666; Rehoboth/Swansea
MYLES, John & 2/wf Ann (HUMPHREY) [PALMER] (-1695) (see above); b 15 Jan 1680; Swansea
MILES, John (-1693) & 2/wf Susannah (GOODNOW) REDIAT (1647-), w John, m/3 John WILSON 1698; 10 Apr 1679; Concord
MIALS, John (1644-1704) & 2/wf Mary ALLSUP/ALSOP (1654-1705); 2 Nov 1680; New Haven
MILES, John (1667-1710) & 1/wf [?Hannah PRINDLE]? (1671-); b 1688; East Haven, CT
MILES/MILLS, John (1666-) & Sarah DAVIS; 14 Mar 1689; Bristol, RI/Boston/Newbury
MILES, John (1668-1710) & 2/wf Abigail (THOMPSON) ALSOP (1651-1727), w Joseph; aft 12 Jan 1691; East Haven, CT
MILES, John & __?__ [HILL]; b 1699?; NH?
MILES, John & 1/wf Mary WHELASE/WHELOCKE (?1638-1663); 18 Jan 1661/2, 28 Jan 1662/3; Salem/Medfield
MILES, Joseph (-1693) & 2/wf Exercise FELTON; 7 Nov 1664; Salem

MILES, Richard[1] (?1598-1666, 1667?) & 1/wf __?__ (-ca 1644?); b 1630?; Milford, CT
MILES, Richard[1] (-1666/7) & 2/wf Catharine (ELITHORPE)/(SPOORE?) [CONSTABLE] (-1683?,
    1687, ae 95), w Marmaluke; b 1638?, b 1642; New Haven
MILES, Richard (-1669, 1670) & 1/wf Elizabeth EDMONDS; 8 Sep 1659; Charlestown
MILES, Richard (-1669, 1670) & 2/wf Experience [COLLACOT/COLLICOTT] (1642-1691); b
    1664; Boston
MILES, Richard (1672-) & Hannah [EASTON]; b 1695; New Haven
MILES, Samuel & Elizabeth DOWSE (1642-); 16 Oct 1659; Boston
MILES, Samuel (1640-) & 1/wf __?__; b 1663(4?); New Haven
MILES, Samuel (1640-1678) & 2/wf [Hannah WILMOT] (1648-), m/2 Miles MERWIN, Jr. 1681; 9
    Apr 1667; New Haven
MILES/MILLS/MEULS/WELLS?, Samuel & Mary TWITCHELL/TWICHELL (-1694?); 3 Feb 1684,
    1684/5; Dedham/Medfield
MYLES, Rev. Samuel (-1728) & Ann [DAVEY] (-1731), w Joseph; b Apr 1698; Boston
MILES, Samuel (1672-) & Sarah [GUNN] (1674-); b 1699; Milford, CT
MILES, Stephen & Mary [HOLBROOK]; 1697; Milford, CT
MILES, Theophilus (1676/7-1701) & Bethia [?PETTIT], m/2 Josiah TIBBALS; b 1700; ?Derby, CT
MILK, John (-1689) & Sarah WESTON; 3 Apr 1665; Salem
MILK, John & Elizabeth HEMPFIELD/HEMPFEILD; 20 Aug 1689; Marblehead/Salem
MILLBORNE/MILBOURN/MILBURNE?, Rev. William (-1694) & Hannah/Susannah __?__ (-1687+),
    m/2 __?__ WATSON; b 1680; Boston/Saco, ME
MILLER, Abraham (-1726/28) & 1/wf Deborah (TEMPLAR) CHAMBERLAIN (-1693), w John; 13
    Aug 1691; Charlestown
MILLER, Abraham (1672-1727) & Hannah CLAPP (1681-1758), m/2 John PARSONS 1729; 1 Jan
    1698/9, 1 Jan 1699; Northampton
MILLER, Abraham (-1726/8) & 2/wf Sarah BILTON (-1742); 8 Nov 1699; Charlestown
MILLER, Alexander (-1725, ae 61) & Dorcas __?__ (-1725, ae 66); b 1691; Boston/Portsmouth, NH
MILLER, Andrew (-1717?, 1718?) & [?Sarah/Mary?] __?__; ca 1665/70; Miller's Place, LI
MILLER, Andrew (1648-1708, ae 60) & Margaret __?__ (-1710); ca 1670/80; Enfield, CT
MILLER, Andrew[2] (-1716) & __?__; b 1690; Miller's Place, LI/East Hampton, LI
MILLER, Anthony (?1675-) & Mary __?__; b 1701?; Rye, NY
MILLER, Benjamin & __?__; b 1684; Dedham
MILLER/MILLARD?, Benjamin & Lydia REYNOLDS (1671-1756, Windham, CT); 2 Mar 1693/4;
    Norwich, CT
MILLER, Benjamin (1672-22 Nov 1747) & 1/wf Mary JOHNSON (1674-1709); 18 Sep 1695;
    Woodstock, CT/Middletown, CT
MILLER, Daniel & Elizabeth BUCKLAND/BUCLAN; 11 Dec 1700; East Hampton, LI
MILLER, David & Hannah [JONES] (1680-); b 1701?; Stamford, CT
MILLER, Ebenezer (1664-1737) & Sarah ALLEN (1668-); 9 Feb 1688; Northampton
MILLER, Ebenezer (1667-1754) & Hannah KEEP (1673-bef 1744); 16 Oct 1690; Springfield
MILLER, George (-1668) & ?Mary/?Hester [CONKLING]; by 1654; East Hampton, LI
MILLER, George (-1690) & __?__; ca 1660?; New London, CT/Groton, CT
MILLER/MILLARD, Humphrey (-1684, Reading) & Elizabeth SMITH (1658-); 12 Sep 1677;
    Cambridge/Charlestown/Reading
MILLER, Isaac & Priscilla BALL; 6 Jan 1696/7; Concord?/Sudbury
MILLER, James (-1688, over 70) & Mary __?__ (-1704); by 1660?; Charlestown
MILLER, James & Martha __?__; b 1670; Norwalk, CT/Rye, NY
MILLER, James (-1705) & Hannah GEORGE (-1733); 25 Nov 1673; Charlestown
MILLER, Jeremiah (1655-1723) & Mary [MULFORD] (1654-1748); b 4 Dec 1683, by 1679?; East
    Hampton, LI
MILLER, Rev. John (-1663, Groton) & Lydia __?__ (-1658); b 1632; Dorchester/Roxbury/Rowley/
    Yarmouth/Sandwich/Groton
MILLARD, John (-1685, living 1686?, bef 7 Feb 1689) & 2/wf Elizabeth __?__ (-1680); ca 1652;
    Rehoboth
MILLER, John (-1642) & Mary __?__, ?m/2 Obadiah SEELEY by 1648; b 1636?; Stamford, CT
MILLER, John & __?__; by 1640?; East Hampton, LI
MILLER, John & __?__; b 1647; Yarmouth
MILLER, John (-1676) & Mary __?__; b 1659; Rehoboth

MILLER, John (1632-1711) & 1/wf Margaret WINSLOW (1641-); 24 Dec 1659; Marshfield/Yarmouth

MILLER, John & Mary (?WARD) CUTTING, w John; aft 27 Mar 1660; Newbury

MILLER, John & _?_ ; b 1662; Stamford, CT/Bedford, NY

MILLER, John (1639/40-) & Hannah [CHATER] (1644-); ca 1662; Wells, ME/Cape Porpoise

MILLER, John & Mary/Mercy? _?_ ; b 1669; Middleboro

MILLER, John (-1699) & Mary _?_ ; by 1675?; East Hampton, LI/Cohansey, NJ

MILLER, John (1657-1735) & Mary [BEAMON]; ca 1690/95?; Springfield

MILLER, John (1665-) & Mary _?_ (1662-); b 1696; Bedford, NY

MILLARD, John & [Elizabeth WEST]; b 1701?; Martha's Vineyard

MILLER, John (1674-1745) & Mercy BEVIN; 25 Dec 1700; Middletown, CT

MILLER, John (1669-1727) & Lydia [COOMBS] (1678-1735); b 1701?; Middleboro

MILLER, Jonathan & Mary TEED; 28 Sep 1685; Huntington, LI

MILLER, Jonathan (1667-) & Sarah HOLMES (1672-); 25 Feb 1690/1; Bedford, NY

MILLER, Joseph (-1697), Marlboro & Mary [POPE] (-1711); b 1675, b 1674, ca 1652; Cambridge/Newton

MILLER, Lazarus (1655-1697) & Mary BURBANK, m/2 William McCRANNEY 1702, m/3 James SEXTON 1734; 2 Dec 1685; Springfield

MILLARD, Nathaniel (1672-1741) & 1/wf Susannah GLADDING (1668-1727); 30 Mar 1694?, 30 May 1694?; Rehoboth

MILLARD, Nehemiah (1668-1751) & 1/wf Judith MASON (-1696); 14 Jul 1691; Rehoboth

MILLARD, Nehemiah (1668-1751) & 2/wf Phebe SHORE/SHOVE (1674-1715); 3 Mar 1696/7, int 13 Feb; Rehoboth

MILLER, Obadiah & Joanna [COGGAN] (-1695), w Thomas; b 1655; Springfield

MILLER, Obadiah & Benedicta LAWTON; 15 Jun 1683; Springfield

MILLER, Paul & Elizabeth [DORBY], m/2 Joseph BOSWORTH ca 1698; b 1684; Boston

MILLER, Richard (-1648±) & Eleanor [POPE] (-1667), w Walter, m/2 Henry HARBERD/HERBERT? 1649/50±, ca 1662; ca 1639, b 1620; Charlestown/Cambridge

MILLER, Richard (1649-1692) & Grace [?ROGERS], m/2 Christopher BANFIELD by 1694; b 1672?; Kittery, ME

MILLER, Robert[2] (1632-1699, ae 67) & Elizabeth [SABIN] (1643-1717/18, ae 75), m/2 Samuel HOWARD/HAYWARD; 24 Dec 1662; Rehoboth

MILLER, Robert & Lydia _?_ ; b 1665/[6?]; Boston

MILLER, Robert (-1711) & _?_ ; b 1685; New London, CT

MILLARD, Robert (1666-1709, 1710) & Charity THURBER (-1741), m/2 John WOOD; 14 Feb 1689/90, 12 Feb 1689/90; Rehoboth/Warren, RI

MILLER, Robert & Susannah WAY; m int 25 Aug 1696; Boston

MILLARD, Samuel[2] (1658-1726) & 1/wf Ester/Hester BOWEN (-1699); 20 Jul 1682; Rehoboth

MILLER, Samuel (1655-1727) & Ruth BEAMON (-1704); 9 Apr 1685; Springfield

MILLARD/MILLER, Samuel, Rehoboth & Rebecca BELCHER (1671-), Dorchester; 25 Jun 1690; Rehoboth

MILLER, Samuel & _?_ ; b 1692; Rye, NY

MILLER, Samuel & Mary [NEALE]; Jan 1693/4; Kittery, ME

MILLARD, Samuel[2] (1658-1720) & 2/wf Esther JENCKES (1664-), Providence; m int 1 Jun 1700; Rehoboth

MILLER, Thomas (1610-1680) & 1/wf Isabel _?_ (-1666); b 1637; Rowley/Middletown, CT

MILLER, Thomas (-1653) (see Thomas MILWARD/MILLARD) & Ann [GOODALE/LOWELL?], m/2 Daniel PIERCE 1654; ca 1639; Newbury/Boston

MILLER, Thomas (-1675) & Sarah MARSHFIELD (-1709), m/2 Edward FOSTER 1684; 12 Oct 1649; Springfield

MILLER, Thomas (1610-1680) & 2/wf Sarah NETTLETON (1642-1728), m/2 [Thomas] HARRIS; 6 Jun 1666; Middletown, CT

MILLER, Thomas & _?_ ; b 1678; Newbury

MILLER, Thomas (-1690) & Rebecca LEONARD (1661-), m/2 Samuel BILLINGS 1691; 1 Dec 1681; Springfield

MILLER, Thomas (1666-1727) & 1/wf Elizabeth TURNER (-1695/6); 28 Mar 1688; Middletown, CT

MILLER, Thomas (1626-1727) & 2/wf Mary ROWELL; 25 Dec 1696; Middletown, CT

MILLER, Thomas & Sarah DAY; 8 Jul 1698, 8 Aug 1698; Boston

MILLER, William[1] (-1690) & Patience _?_ (-1716) (no evidence that her name was BACON); ca 1650?; Northampton
MILLER, William (1659-1705) & Mary [BUSHNELL] (1623-1735), m/2 Joseph BUTLER 1710; 19 Apr 1693; Saybrook, CT/Glastonbury
MILLER, _?_ & Elizabeth DEMING; b 1682; Southampton, LI
MILLETT, John & _?_ ; b Aug 1651; Kittery, ME
MILLITE, John (-1678) & Sarah LEECH/LEACH, m/2 Morris SMITH; 3 Jul 1663; Gloucester/Falmouth, ME
MILLETT, Nathaniel (1647/8-1719) & Ann LESTER/LISTER? (1650/1-1682); 3 May 1670; Gloucester
MILLETT, Thomas (1605-1676) & Mary [GREENAWAY] (1606-1682); b 1633; Dorchester
MILLAT, Thomas (1633-) & 1/wf Mary EVELIGH/EVELETH (-1687); 21 May 1655; Gloucester
MILLETT, Thomas (1633-) & 2/wf Abigail (COIT) EVELETH, w Isaac (-1726); b 1689; Gloucester
MILLETT, Thomas & Martha INGERSOLL (1670-); 10 Jan 1694/5; Gloucester
MILLETT, Thomas (1675-) & 1/wf Elizabeth BATCHALER/BATCHELDER; 18 Jun 1696; Gloucester
MILLIKEN, John (-1749) & Elizabeth ALGER (-1754); b 1701, b 1691; Boston
MILLING, Simon & _?_ ; b 1686, ca 1670?; Watertown
MILLINGTON, John (-1720) & Sarah SMITH; 14 Apr 1668; Windsor, CT
MILLS, Benjamin (1651-) & Mary THORNE (?1655-); 1 Jul 1674; Dedham
MILLS, Edward (1665-1732) & 1/wf Mehitable (MINOT) [MESSINGER] (1665-1690), w Henry; aft 5 May 1687; Boston/Dorchester
MILLS, Edward (1665-1732) & 2/wf Elizabeth [CARY] (1676-); b 1696; Boston
MILLS, George (1585-1674) & Rebecca _?_ ; Jamaica, LI
MILLS, Henry (1649-1725) & Jane _?_ (1649-1725); Watertown
MILLS, James & Martha ALLEY (1649-); 1 Apr 1671; Lynn
MILLS, James (1674-) & 1/wf Naomi HINCKSON/?HINKSON; 26 Dec 1700; Lynn
MILLS, John (-1678) & Susanna _?_ (-1675 in 80th y); in Eng, b 1625, b 1620, b 1616?; Boston/Braintree
MILLS, John (1632-1694) & Elizabeth SHOVE (ca 1631-1711); 26 Apr 1653, 6 Apr 1653; Braintree
MILLS, John & 1/wf ?Sarah _?_ ; b 1655?; Scarborough, ME
MILLS, John & 2/wf Mary _?_ ; b 1667
MILLS, John & [?Mary] _?_ ; ca 1670/75?; Milford, CT
MILLS, John & Mary _?_ ; b 1679; Boston
MILLS, John & Joanna (ALGER) [OAKMAN], w Elias; b 1686; Boston
MILLS, John (1660-1722) & Hannah _?_ ; b 1689; Braintree
MILLS, John (1658-1698) & Sarah [PETTIBONE] (1667-1748?), m/2 John HUMPHREY 1699; 4 Nov 1690; Simsbury, CT
MILLS, John & Sarah _?_ ; b 1695(6?); Boston
MILLS, Jonathan (?1636-) & Martha _?_ ; Jamaica, LI
MILLS, Jonathan (-Jul 1688?, Nov 1690?) & Mary [SHEFFIELD] (1663-), m/2 John MARSHALL 1690; ca Jun 1686, b 1687; Braintree
MILLS, Joseph & Martha _?_ ; b 1684
MILLS, Peter[1] (-1702) & 1/wf Dorcas [MESSENGER] (1650-1688); b 1668?, b 1672, b 1666?; Windsor, CT
MILLS, Peter[1] (-1702) & 2/wf Jane THAMSIN?/FANNIN/WARREN, Hartford; 10 Dec 1691; Hartford, CT/Windsor, CT
MILLS, Peter[2], Jr. (?1668-1754) & Joanna PORTER (1671-1756); 21 Jul 1692, 24 Jul; Windsor, CT/Stratford, CT
MILLS, Richard & 1/wf [?Mary] [NICHOLS]; b 1647?; Stratford, CT
MILLS, Richard & 2/wf _?_ , w Vincent, prob m/2 William OLIVER; aft 1653; Stratford, CT
MILLS, Richard & Lydia [KNAPP]; aft 15 Feb 1669/70, bef 23 Nov 1672; ?Greenwich, CT
MILLS, Robert (-1647) & Dorothy _?_ , m/2 John HARKER; b 1639?; Kittery, ME
MILLS, Samuel (-1694/5) (see also MILES) & Frances PIMBROOK (-1684); 11 Mar 1644/5, 1644/5; Dedham
MILLS, Samuel (1632-1727) & Susannah [PALMER]; ca 1659; Jamaica, LI

MILLS, Samuel (-1685, Southampton), Stratford & Mary __?__ ; b 1668?; Stratford CT/Southampton, NY

MILES, Samuel & Mary TWITCHELL (-1699); 3 Feb 1684; Dedham/Medfield

MILLS, Samuel & Sarah [DENTON]; ca 1693; Jamaica, LI

MILLS, Simon & 1/wf Jone __?__ (-bur 5 Jul 1659); 18 Oct 1639; Windsor, CT

MILLS, Simon (-1683) & 2/wf Mary BUEL (?1642-1718), m/2 Samuel BISSELL bef 1697; prob wrong 23 Feb 1656, 23 Feb 1659, [1659/60]; Windsor, CT/Simsbury

MILLS, Thomas & Mary [MEDLEIGH/WADELL?]; b 1652; Salisbury

MILLS, Timothy (?1667-1751) & Sarah [DENTON?] (see record bef 1693 above); b 13 Mar 1698; Jamaica, LI/Smithtown, LI

MILLS, Zechariah (-1696) & Abigail (MESSENGER) DARLING, w Richard; b 1686; Jamaica, LI

MILLS, __?__ (seems doubtful) & Mary [PITCHER] (1644), m Isaac RUSH; Dorchester

MILLS, __?__ & [Lydia WILKINS] (1644-); Dorchester (see John NICHOLS)

MILNER, Paul & Elizabeth __?__ ; b 1694; Boston

MILTON, Edward & 1/wf Mercy [POND]; b 1679; Sandwich

MILTON, Robert (-1702) & Sarah [CHAMBERLAIN] (1652-1719); b 1675?, b 2 Dec 1678; ?Hull

MILTON, Robert & Hannah WHITCOMB/WHETCOMB (-1749); m int, 10 Sep 1695; Boston/Hull

MILWARD/MILLARD, Thomas (1600-1653, Boston) & Ann LOWELL (-1690), m/2 Daniel PEIRCE 26 Dec 1654; b 1642 (see Thomas MILLER); Newbury/Salisbury/Gloucester

MINER, Benjamin (1676-1711) & Mary SAXTON (1681-1750), m/2 Joseph PAGE 1713; 15 Nov 1697; Stonington, CT

MINER, Clement (1638-1700) & 1/wf Frances (BURCHAM) WILLEY (-1672/3, New London), w Isaac; 26 Nov 1662; Stonington, CT/New London?

MINER, Clement (1638-1700) & 2/wf Martha WELLMAN (-1681, New London); 20 Feb 1672/3; Stonington, CT

MINER, Clement (1638-1700) & 3/wf Joanna (-1700, New London); aft 5 Jul 1681; Stonington, CT/New London

MINER, Clement (1668-1740) & Martha MOULD (1674-1743); 4 Aug 1698; Middletown, CT/New London, CT

MINER, Elnathan (1673-1756, 1758?) & 1/wf Rebecca BALDWIN (-1700/1); 21 Mar 1694; Stonington, CT

MINER, Ephraim (1642-) & Hannah AVERY; 20 Jun 1666; Stonington, CT/New London

MINER, Ephraim (1668-) & Mary STEVENS, Taunton; 24 May 1699 at Taunton; Stonington, CT

MINOR/MAYNARD, John (-1658) & Elizabeth (__?__) EATON [PELL], w Nathaniel, w Joseph; Boston; Suffolk Co.

MINER, John (1635-1719) & Elizabeth BOOTH (1641-1732); 19 Oct 1658, 21 Oct, ?14 Oct; Stratford, CT

MINER, John (1659-1731) & Sarah [ROSE] (1664-); b 1686; Woodbury

MINER, Joseph (1694-1712) & 1/wf Mary AVERY (1648-1708); 28 Oct 1668, 28? Oct; Stonington/New London, CT

MINER, Joseph (1666-1752) & 1/wf Elizabeth COMSTOCK (1665-1692); 12 Mar 1689; ?New London

MINER, Joseph (1669-) & Sarah TRACY (1677-); 18 Jun 1700; Stonington, CT

MINER, Manasseh (1647-1728) & 1/wf Lydia MOORE/MORE (1650-1720); 26 Sep 1670; Stonington, CT/New London

MINER, Samuel (1652-1682) & Marie/Mary LORD, Stonington, m/2 Joseph PEMBERTON 1683; 15 Dec 1681; Stonington, CT

MINER, Thomas (1608-1690) & Grace PALMER (1614-1690, Stonington, CT); 23 Apr 1634; Charlestown/Stonington/Hingham/New London

MINER, Thomas (1662-1723) & Hannah [CURTIS] (1675?-); ca 1691/1692?, b 1694; Woodbury, CT

MINER, William (1670-1725) & Anna?/[Sarah BECKWITH]; b 1690; Lyme, CT

MINER, __?__ & Sarah __?__ m/2 John PHILLIPS 1676

MINGAY, Jeffrey (-1658) & Ann __?__, m/2 Christopher HUSSEY 1658; b 1637?; Dedham/Hampton, NH

MINGO, Robert & Eliza/Elizabeth CANE; 27 Sep 1687; Newbury

MINOT, George (1594-1671) & Martha __?__ (1597-1657); in Eng, b 1624; Dorchester

MINOTT, James (1628-1676) & 1/wf Hannah STOUGHTON (1627-1670); 9 Dec 1653; Dorchester

MINOTT, James (1628-1676) & 2/wf Hepzibah CORLETT, m/2 Daniel CHAMPNEY 1684; 21 May 1673; Cambridge
MINOT, Capt. James (1653-1735) & Rebecca [WHEELER] (1666-1734, ae 68); ca 1680?, b 1684(5?); Concord
MINOT, James (1659-) & Rebecca JONES, m/2 Joseph BULKELEY (-169-); 9 Feb 1687/8; Concord
MINOTT, John (1626-1669) & 1/wf Lydia BUTLER (-1667); 19 May 1647; Dorchester
MINOT, John (1626-1669) & 2/wf Mary (DASSETT) [BIGGS] (?1627-1676), w John; aft 25 Jan 1667; ?Boston/Dorchester
MINOT, John (1648-1691) & Elizabeth BRECK (-1690); 11 Mar 1670; Dorchester
MINOT, John (1672-1717/[18]) & 1/wf Mary BAKER (1674-1716); 21 May 1696; Dorchester
MINOTT, Samuel (1665-) & Hannah HOWARD (1644-); 23 Jun 1670; ?Boston
MINOT, Samuel (1665-) & Hannah [JONES]; b 1693; Concord
MINOT, Stephen (1631-1672) & Truecross DAVENPORT (1634-1692); 10 Nov 1654; Dorchester
MINOT, Stephen (-1732) & Mary CLARK (1666-); 1 Dec 1686; ?Boston
MINSHALL, William (d in Eng) & Sarah __?__, m/2 William SARGENT; in Eng; Malden
MINTER, Tobias (-1673) & Rebecca BEMAS/BEMIS, m/2 John DYMOND 1674, m/3 Benedict SATTERLY 1682; 1 Apr 1672, 3 Apr; New London, CT
MINTER, Tristram & Hannah [TONGUE], m/2 Joshua BAKER 1674; New London, CT
MINVIELLE/?MIENVILLE/?MAURELLE, Gabriel (-1702) & Susannah [LAWRENCE], m/2 William SMITH; m lic 25 Jan 1676, 1676/7; Flushing, LI
MITCHELL, Abraham (?1658-) & [Sarah WHEELER] (1663-); ca 1686, b 1678, by 1687; Stratford, CT/Windham, CT
MITCHELL, Abraham & Mary (KNOWLTON) ABBE, w Samuel; 27 Apr 1699; Windham, CT
MITCHELL, Alexander (-1718, ae 52) & Susanna BURRAGE (1676-1706, ae 40, 30); 22 Feb 1694/5; Charlestown
MITCHELL, Andrew (?1656-1736, Haverhill) & 1/wf Abigail ATWOOD (1662-1714, Haverhill); 12 Nov 1686; Charlestown
MITCHELL, Christopher[1] (-1686?, 1688?) & Sarah [ANDREWS] (1641, 1642-1732); ca 1660/65?, 1665?; Kittery, ME
MITCHELL, Christopher[2] & 1/wf Mary [BRACKETT] (1674-); b 1693; Kittery, ME
MITCHELL, Christopher[2] & 2/wf [Sarah] __?__; b 1694 b 1695; Kittery, ME
MITCHELL, Daniel (1666?-) & Susanna [SHERMAN] (1670-); ca 1698, b 1701(2?); Stratford, CT
MITCHELL, David (1619-1686) & 1/wf __?__; ca 1650, (b 1653); Stratford, CT
MITCHELL, David (-1686) & 2/wf Elizabeth [GRAVES] (1651?) (doubtful); ca 1677; Stamford, CT
MITCHELL, Edward & 1/wf Mary HAYWARD; b 1668?, b 1666?; Bridgewater
MITCHELL, Elisha & Hannah __?__; b 1686
MITCHELL, Experience[1] (-1684) & 1/wf Jane [COOK]; 1628?, aft 22 May 1627, ?Jun 1627; Plymouth/Duxbury
MITCHELL, Experience & 2/wf Mary __?__; b 1688, 1680+; Bridgewater
MITCHELL, Experience (1676-) & __?__; b 1701?; Providence/Bridgewater
MICHEL, George & Mary __?__; b 1645; Boston
MITCHELL, George & Barbara __?__; b 1690; Boston
MITCHELL, George & Sarah __?__; b 1694; Salem
MICHELL, Jacob (-1675) & Susanna POPE (ca 1649-1675); 7 Nov 1666; Plymouth
MITCHELL, Jacob & 1/wf Deliverance KINGMAN; 1 Jan 1695/6; Bridgewater
MITCHELL, John (-1683) & Mary __?__; b 1655; Hartford
MITCHELL, John (-1663) & 2/wf? Sarah (TILLEY) (LYNN) GUNNISON, w Henry, w Hugh, m/4 Francis MORGAN 1664?; ca 1660, aft 14 Mar 1658/9; Kittery
MITCHELL, John & __?__; b 1660; Southampton, LI
MICHEL, John & 1/wf Mary BONEY/BONNEY (-1676); 14 Dec 1675; Duxbury
MITCHELL, John (1654-) & Elizabeth [KNELL] (1653-1730); ca 1677, b 1679; Stratford, CT
MICHEL, John & 2/wf Mary LATHROP (-1680); 14 Jan 1679; Duxbury
MITCHELL, John (1651-1731) & 1/wf Hannah SPAFORD/SPAFFORD (1654-); 20 May 1680; Newbury
MICHEL, John & 3/wf Mary/Marry? PRIOR; 24 May 1682; Duxbury/Providence
MITCHELL, John (-1717) & 1/wf Sarah (RATHBONE) [GEORGE], w Samuel; b 1684; Southampton, LI

MITCHELL, John & Sarah _?_/[RATHBONE?]; aft 1688; New Shoreham, RI/?Newport
MITCHELL, John (-1717) & Elizabeth _?_ (-1749, ae 83); b 1691; Charlestown
MITCHELL, John (-1695) & ?Elizabeth GRAVE, m/2 John RAEBOURN; Hartford
MITCHELL, John (1651-1731) & 2/wf Constance (LONGHORNE) MOOERS/MOORES (1652-), w
    Jonathan; 15 Nov 1697, ?1 Nov; Newbury
MICHELL, Jonathan (1624-1668) & Margaret (BORODELL/BORADELL) SHEPARD, w Thomas;
    19 Nov 1650; Cambridge
MITCHELL, Jonathan (?1667-1695) & Hannah (LYNDE) BIGG (-1725), w John, m/3 Edmund
    GOFFE 1695; ca 1692/5?; Cambridge
MITCHELL, Matthew (?1590-1646) & Susan (WOOD) OVENDEN BUTTERFIELD, w Nathaniel?,
    w Thomas; 16 Apr 1616; Charlestown/Concord/Springfield/Stamford, CT
MITCHELL, Matthew (?1653-1736) & Mary THOMPSON (1655-1711); ca 1676, b 1679, ca 1677;
    Stratford, CT
MITCHELL, Michael & Sarah COTLIN; ca 1694; Deerfield/Wallingford, CT
MITCHELL, Paul (-1653) & _?_; b 1639; Kittery, ME
MITCHELL, Richard & Mary [WOOD]; ca 1684?; Nantucket
MITCHELL, Richard & Sarah [COUCH]; b 1700; Kittery, ME
MITCHELL, Robert (1669±-) & Sarah [DEERING]; b 1694; Kittery, ME/Braveboat Harbor
MITCHELL, Samuel (-1693) & Rachel _?_; by 1689; Newcastle
MITCHELL, Thomas (-1677?, Boston) & Anne _?_; b 1636; Charlestown
MITCHELL, Thomas & 1/wf _?_
MITCHELL, Thomas (-1659/60) & 2/wf Elizabeth _?_, m/2 Jeremy WHITNELL; b 1651(2?); New
    Haven
MITCHELL, Thomas (-1709, ae 81) & Mary MOLTON/MOULTON (-1712, ae 76); - Nov 1655;
    Malden
MITCHELL, Thomas (-1687) & _?_; bef 1671?, b 1683; ?Duxbury/Block Island
MICHEL, Thomas & Ann _?_; b 1660, b 1664; Boston
MITCHELL, Thomas² & Margaret [?RATHBONE]; b 1682; New Shorham, RI
MITCHELL, Thomas & Martha TARBALL/TARBELL; 18 May 1685; Salem
MITCHELL, Thomas (-(172-)) & Elizabeth KINGMAN; 1 Jan 1695/6; Bridgewater
MICHILL, William (-1654) & Mary SAYER/SAWYER, m/2 Robert SAVERY 1656; 7 Nov 1648, 8
    Nov 1648; Newbury
MITCHELL, William & 1/wf Honor _?_; 1 Oct 1702, ca 1683-98?; Isles of Shoals
MITCHELL, William & Mercy NICKERSON, m/2 James GRIFFITH bef 1 Nov 1709; ca 1689, b
    1691; Chatham
MITCHELL, _?_ & _?_; Portsmouth, NH
MITCHELL, _?_ & Grace _?_, m/2 Matthew MACHENETINE 10 Feb 1700, Haverhill; Newbury
MICHELSON, Edward (-1681) & Ruth [BUSHELL] (1612-); ca 1636; Cambridge
MITCHELSON, Thomas (1657-) & _?_; b 20 Dec 1682; Cambridge
MICHELSON, William (-1668) & Mary BRADSHAW; 26 Apr 1654; Cambridge
MITTON, Michael (-1660, bef 1662/3) & Elizabeth [CLEEVE] (-1671), m/2 Peter HARVEY ca
    1663?, bef 1666; ca 1637, b 1637; ?Falmouth, ME/Casco Bay, ME/Salisbury/Framingham
MIX, Caleb (1661-1708±) & 1/wf Hannah [CHIDSEY] (1663-1693); b 1685; New Haven
MIX, Caleb (1661-1708±) & 2/wf Mary [BRADLEY] (1672-), m/2 Joshua TUTTLE; b 1695;
    Guilford, CT/New Haven
MIX, Daniel (1653-1720) & Ruth ROCKWELL (1654-); 2 May 1678; Wallingford, CT
MIX, John (1649-1712) & Elizabeth [WILMOT] (1649-1711); b 1676; New Haven
MIX, Nathaniel (1651-1725) & Mary [PANTRY] (1654±-); b 1682; New Haven
MIX, Samuel (1663-1730) & Rebecca PARDEE; 26 Jul 1699; New Haven
MIX, Stephen (1672-1738) & Mary STODDARD (1670/1-1734), Northampton; 1 Dec 1696, ?2 Oct
    1695; Northampton
MIX, Thomas (-1691) & Rebecca [TURNER] (-1731); b 1649; New Haven
MIX, Thomas (-1706) & Hannah FITCH (1655-); 30 Jun 1677; Norwich, CT
MIXER, Daniel (1676-) & Judith _?_; b 1701; Groton/Framingham
MIXER, Isaac (1602-1655) & Sarah THURSTON (1601-); Capel St. Mary, Suffolk, Eng, 11 May
    1629; Watertown
MIXER/MIXTER, Isaac (-1716) & 1/wf Mary COOLEDGE (-1660); 19 Sep 1655; Watertown
MIXER, Isaac (-1716, Waltham) & 2/wf Rebecca GEARFFEILD/GARFIELD (1641-1683); 10 Jan
    1660/1; Watertown

MIXER, Isaac & Elizabeth PEIRCE; 17 Oct 1684; Watertown
MIXER, Isaac & 3/wf Mary (LATHROP) (STEARNS) FRENCH, w John, w William; 29 Jun 1687; Billerica
MIXER, John & Abigail FISKE; 15 Aug 1695; Watertown
MOFFATT/MUFFET, William & Mehitable __?__; b 1693; Newbury/Killingly, CT
MAGGRIGGE/MOGGRIDGE, Daniel & Elizabeth ROBINSON; 20 Dec 1693; Watertown
MOGRIDGE, Robert & Elizabeth __?__; b 1688(9?); Boston
MONY/?MONEY, John & Jane POPE; 2 Apr 1698; Dorchester
MONK, Christopher & Mary [WALKER] (1667-), m/2 Thomas PRANKET 1704; b 1686; Boston
MONK, Elias & Hope __?__; b 1696, b 1691; Dorchester/Roxbury/Stonington
MONK, George & 1/wf Lucy (GARDNER) [TURNER] (1655-), w John; b 1683; Boston
MONK, George & 2/wf Elizabeth (CLARK) [WOODMANCY], w John; aft 17 Aug 1686; Cambridge/Boston
MONROE, David (alias ROE) & Elizabeth TED; 27 May 1690; Huntington, LI/Norwalk, CT
MUNROE, George (1671-1749) & Sarah [MOORE] (1677/8-1752); b 1700; Cambridge/Lexington
MUNROE, George & Mary __?__; b 1701; Bristol, RI
MUNROE, John (1666-1754) & Hannah [MOOER] (1676-1716, ae 42 y); ca 1692?; Cambridge/Lexington
MONROE, John & Mehitable __?__; b 1696; Bristol, RI
MONROW, Thomas & Mary WORMWELL (-1705/6); 13 Oct 1698; Taunton/Bristol, RI
MUNROE, William[1] (?1625-1718, ca 92) & 1/wf Martha [GEORGE], dau John; b 1665/6; Charlestown/Cambridge/Lexington
MUNROE, William[1] (-1718) & 2/wf Mary [BALL] (1651, 1640?-1692, ae 41); b 1673; Charlestown/Cambridge/Lexington
MONROE, William (-1718, ae ca 92) & 3/wf Elizabeth (JOHNSON) [WYER] (-1715, ae 79), w Edward; aft 3 May 1693, b 1697?; Cambridge/Boston
MUNROE/ROE, William[2] (1669-1759) & 1/wf Mary CUTTLER/CUTLER (1681-1713); 3 Oct 1697; Concord
MUNSON, John (1673-) & 1/wf Sarah COOPER (1673-); 10 Nov 1692; New Haven
MUNSON, Joseph (1677-1725) & Margery HITCHCOCK (1681-), m/2 Stephen PECK; 10 Mar 1699, ?1699/1700; Wallingford, CT
MONSON, Richard (-1702) & Esther __?__; b 1680?; Portsmouth, NH
MUNSON, Samuel (1643-1692/3) & Martha BRADLEY (1648-), m/2 Eliaseph PRESTON 1694, m/3 Daniel SHERMAN; 26 Oct 1665; New Haven
MUNSON, Samuel (1669-1741, ae 74) & 1/wf Martha [FARNES] (-1707); ca 1688, b 1690; Wallingford, CT
MUNSON, Theophilus (1675-1747) & Esther [MIX] (1678-1746, ae 68); b 1697; New Haven
MUNSON, Thomas (1612-1685) & Joanna [?MEW] (1610-1678); b 1643; New Haven
MUNSON, Thomas (1671-1746) & Mary WILCOXSON (1676-1755); 15 Sep 1694; New Haven/Cheshire, CT
MONTAGUE, Griffin & Margaret [KELWAY]; b 1650; Cape Porpoise
MONTAGUE, John (1653-1732) & Hannah SMITH (1662-1694); 23 Mar 1681, prob 1680/1; Hadley
MONTAGUE, Peter (1651-1725) & 1/wf Mary (PARTRIDGE) SMITH (-1680), w John; Sep 1679; Hadley
MONTAGUE, Peter (1651-1725) & 2/wf Mary (CROW) COLEMAN (-1720), w Noah; 16 Sep 1680; Hadley
MONTAGUE, Richard (1614-1681) & Abigail [DOWNING]? (-1694); ca 1637?, b 1642; Wells, ME/Boston/etc.
MONUPS/MONUMPS/MONAMPS, George & Roby __?__; b 1695; Rehoboth
MOODY, Caleb & 1/wf Sarah PEIRCE (-1665); 24 Aug 1659; Newbury/Salisbury
MOODY, Caleb (1637-1698) & 2/wf Judith BRADBURY (1638-1700?); 9 Nov 1665, 9 Oct 1665; Newbury/Salisbury
MOODY, Caleb (1666-1741) & Ruth MORSE (1669-1748); 9 Dec 1690; Newbury
MOODY, Clement & 1/wf Sarah [?CLARK]; b 1701?
MOODY, Cutting & Judith LITTLE; 25 Mar 1696; Newbury
MOODY, Daniel & Elizabeth SOMERBY; 29 Mar 1683; Newbury/Gravesend, LI
MOODY, Sir [Henry] (d in Eng in 1632) & Deborah [DUNCK] (-1658+); b 23 Nov 1605; Salem/Lynn

MOODY, John (1593-1655) & Sarah COX (-1671); St. James Bury, St. Edmunds, 8 Sep 1617, b 1633; Roxbury/Hartford

MOODY, John & Hannah DOLE (1665-); 18 May 1692; Newbury

MOODY, John (1661-1732) & Sarah EVETTS/EVARTS; 3 Apr 1700; Hartford

MOODY, Rev. Joshua (1633±-1697) & 1/wf Martha [COLLINS] (1639-1674 (before)), dau Edward; ca 1659, b 1664?; Portsmouth, NH/Boston

MOODY, Joshua (-1697) & 2/wf Ann/Anna [JACOBS], w Samuel d 16 Jun 1672; aft 16 Jun 1672; Portsmouth, NH

MOODY, Joshua & Mary GREENLEAF (1676-); m int 1 May 1696; Newbury

MOODY, Samuel (-1675) & Mary CUTTING, m/2 Daniel LUNT 1679; 30 Nov 1657; Newbury

MOODY, Samuel (-1689) & Sarah [DEMING] (ca 1643-1717); ca 1659; Hadley

MOODEY, Samuel (-1729, ae 61, 59?), New Castle & Esther GREEN; 4 Apr 1695; Boston

MOODEY, Samuel (1676-1747) & Hannah SEWALL (-1728); m int 15 Jul 1698, 15 Nov 1698; Newbury/York, ME

MOODEY, Samuel & Sarah KNIGHT; 16 Apr 1700; Newbury

MOODY, Samuel (1670-) & Sarah LANE; 5 Sep 1700; Hadley

MOODEY, Thomas & Judith HALE (1670-); 24 Nov 1692; Newbury

MOODY, William (-1673) & Sarah __?__ (-1673); in Eng, b 1630?; Ipswich/Newbury

MOODY, William & 1/wf Mehitable SEWALL (-1702); 15 Nov 1684, 18 Nov; Newbury

MOON, Abel & Lydia [POST] (?1655), m/2 Joseph HUNT; ?Norwich, CT

MOON, John & Sarah [SHERIFF/SHREVE] (-1732); b 1685; Portsmouth, RI

MOONE, Robert & Dorothy __?__; b 1645; Boston

MOONE, Robert & 2/wf Hannah __?__; b 1698; Newport

MOON, ?Ebenezer & ?Deborah/?Rebecca PEABODY; b 22 Mar 1686/7; ?Newport

MOON, __?__ & Sarah VIALL (1652-); b 3 Jan 1681(2?); (see Nathaniel MOORE m Sarah VAIL 1665/7)

MOORE, Abel (-1689) & Hannah HEMPSTEAD (1652-), m/2 Samuel WALLER; 22 Sep 1670; New London, CT

MOORE, Abel (1674-) & Lydia [POST] (1674-), m/2 Joseph HARRIS?/HUNT?; b 1705, b 1701?; New London, CT

MOORE, Abraham & Priscilla POOR; 14 Dec 1687; Andover

MOORE, Andrew (-1719) & Sarah PHELPS (1653-1726+, 1732); 15 Feb 1671; Windsor, CT

MOORE, Benjamin (1640-1690) & Anna [HAMPTON] (-1726), m/2 Jeremiah VAIL; b 23 Aug 1671; Southold, LI

MOORE, Benjamin (-1680) & Sarah [FOSTER] (1654-), m/2 Zachariah LONG 1682, m/3 Caleb STANLEY, 1690; b 1674; Charlestown

MOORE, Benjamin (1648-1729) & Dorothy WRIGHT (1662-1717); 11 Nov 1686; Sudbury

MOORE, Benjamin (-1728) & Abigail [HORTON] (1676±-1746); b 1697, b 1699; Southold, LI

MOOR, Benoni & Mehitable ALLIS; 13 Dec 1698; Deerfield/Hatfield/Northfield

MOORE, Ebenezer & 1/wf Joanna DEERING; 25 Nov 1700; Kittery, ME

MOORE, Enoch & Rebecca [CONVERSE] (1651-1733); b 1678(9?); Woburn

MOORE, Francis (-1671, ae 85) & 1/wf Catherine __?__ (-1648); b 1616?, b 1620; Cambridge

MOORE, Francis (-1689, ae 69) & Albee/Alba/Abby EATON (1632-1708); 7 Sep 1650; Cambridge

MOORE, Francis (-1671, ae 85) & 2/wf Elizabeth PERIMAN (?wid); 6 Dec 1653; Cambridge

MOORE, Francis & Elizabeth WOODBURY; last of Aug 1666; Salem

MOORE, Francis & Martha (EATON) (OLDHAM) [BROWN], w Richard OLDHAM, w Thomas BROWN; aft 1691

MOORE, Francis & Jannetye [LAWRENCE]; b 1696; Newtown, LI

MORE, George & __?__; b 1659; Lynn

MOORE, Gershom & Mary [FISH], w Jonathan; aft 1663; Newtown, LI

MOORE, Goulden/?Goldin (1610-1698) & Joanna/Jane/Joan? [CHAMPNEY] (-1675), w John; b 1643; Cambridge/Billerica

MORE/MARE/etc., Henry & [Alice] __?__; b 1670, b 21 Jul 1672, 14 Sep 1669 Lancaster; Dorchester/Boston

MORE, Henry & Elizabeth SHAREL/SHARD, wid?; 11 Mar 1694/5, 1695; Salem/Wenham

MOORE, Isaac & 1/wf Ruth STANLEY (?1629-1691?); 5 Dec 1645; Hartford, CT/Norwalk/Farmington

MOORE, Isaac & Dorothy (SMITH) [SENSION]/(St.JOHN) (-1706), w John BLAKEMAN, w Francis HALL, w Mark St.JOHN; ca 1693?, ca May 1696; Stratford, CT

MOORE, Jacob (1645-1716+) & Elizabeth LOOKER/LOKER; 29 May 1667; Sudbury
MOORE, James & Mary BOTH/BOOTH?; 6 Feb 1656/7; Boston
MORE, James (-1659) & Ruth PINNION/PINION, m/2 Peter BRIGGS ca 1664; 28 Dec 1657; Lynn
MORE, Jeremiah (-1650) & Alice _?_, m/2 Henry LARGIN by 1653; b 1647; Boston
MOORE, John (?-1674) & 1/wf _?_; b 1621?; Sudbury/Lancaster
MOORE, John (-1674) & 2/wf Elizabeth [WHALE] (-1690); b 1627, 1640; Sudbury/Lancaster
MOORE, John & [?Hannah] _?_; b 1636; Salem
MOORE, John, & _?_; b 1638?; Newport, RI/Warwick, RI
MOORE, John[1] (-1677) & Abigail _?_ (-1677+); ?16 Jun 1639; Cambridge?/Dorchester
MOORE, Rev. John (1620-1665) & Margaret [HOWELL] (?1622, ?1628-), m/2 Rev. Francis DOUGHTY; 1640±, ca 1645; Southampton, LI
MOORE, John & Bridget _?_ (-1643); Braintree
MOORE, John (-1679, ae 99, Roxbury) & Elizabeth _?_; by 1644?; Roxbury
MOORE, John "Sen" (-1702?) & Judith _?_ (-1700+); ca 1650?, aft 1671; Lancaster
MOORE, Ens. John (-1702) & 1/wf Ann SMITH (-1671); 16 Nov 1654; Sudbury/Lancaster
MOORE, John & _?_; b 1656?; Newtown, LI
MOORE, John & _?_ (-1661); Braintree
MOOR, John & Elizabeth HART; 26 Jun 1661; Weymouth
MOORE, John (-1718) & 1/wf Hannah GOFFE (-1697); 21 Sep 1664; Windsor, CT
MOORE, John & Margaret _?_; bef - Jun 1665; Star Island/Kittery, ME
MOORE, John (-1677) & Agnes _?_; bef 1666?; Star Island/etc.
MOORE, John (-bef 26 Mar 1636) & Hannah _?_, m/2 Thomas PETTIT; Newtown, LI
MOORE, John, brewer (-1693) & Lydia _?_; b 1671; Boston
MOORE/?MOWER, John & Susannah MARSHALL; 21 Jul 1673; Lynn
MOORE, John & Mary _?_, m/2 Thomas MONSALL 1679; b 1678; Charlestown
MOORE, John & Martha [WALFORD]; b 1679; York, ME
MOORE, John (-1683 in VA) & Mary _?_; b 1683; Boston
MOORE, John & 2/wf Mary WHITCOMB, w John; 23 Aug 1683; Lancaster
MOORE, John & Mary PETTIT; 31 Mar 1692; Flatbush, LI/Newtown, LI
MOORE, John (1665-) & Abigail STRONG (1667-1733); 8 Feb 1693/4; Windsor, CT
MOORE, John & Sarah [CUTT]; b 1696, by 1696; Kittery, ME
MOORE, John & Hagadiah/Habadiah FAIRBANK (1668-); 1 Jan 1697/8, 1 Jan 1698; Concord/Lancaster
MOORE, John & Martha CLARK (-1719+), m/2 John HARVEY; 30 Jul 1700; Boston
MOORE, Jonathan (1669-1741) & Hannah [SAWYER] (1675-1741); b 1700; Boston/[Lancaster]
MOORE, Joseph & Ruth STARR (-1658); 21 May 1656; Boston
MOORE, Joseph & Hannah GELLUME?; 1659; Charlestown
MOORE, Joseph (1647-1726) & 1/wf Lydia [MAYNARD] (-1717) (HAYWARD wrong); b 1669; Sudbury
MOORE, Joseph (1651-) & 1/wf Sarah [HALSEY] (?1661, 1658-); b 3 Aug 1688; Southampton, LI
MOORE, Joseph & Elizabeth _?_; b 1699?, b 1701; Sudbury
MOORE, Miles & Isabel [JOYNER]; b 1644?, b 1647; Milford, CT/New London, CT
MOORE, Miles & Sarah DANIELS; 28 Dec 1698; New London, CT
MOORE, Nathaniel (1642-1698) & Sarah [VAIL] (1647/9-1733); ca 1665/7?; Southold, LI
MORE, Philip (-1698) & Lydia _?_
MORE, Richard (1614-1690+) & 1/wf Christian HUNT (1616-1676); 20 Oct 1636; Plymouth
MOORE, Richard (-1681) & Bridget [HUNNEWELL] (1621-), w Roger; b 1647?, betw 1654 & 1664; Cape Porpoise, ME/now Kennebunk
MORE, Richard (1648-) & Sarah _?_ (-1690+); b 1673; Salem
MORE, Richard (1614-1690+) & 2/wf Jane (HOLLINGWORTH) CRUMPTON (-1686), w Samuel; aft 1676; Salem
MOORE, Richard (1671-) & Mary [COLLINS]; b 1694; Sudbury
MOORE, Robert & Anne [PENWILL/PENNELL]; b 1686; Boston
MOORE, Samson, Boston & Elizabeth MATSON, Boston; 15 Dec 1687; Charlestown
MOORE, Samuel & _?_; b 1636; Salem
MOORE, Samuel & Abigail HAWKINS, m/2 Thomas KILLOM/(?McKELLUM), m/3 John FOSTER; 13 May 1660; Boston
MOORE, Samuel & Mary [REED] (1651-1738); ca 1667/70; Newtown, LI/Southampton, LI

MOORE, Samuel (-1676) & Naomi _?_ ; b 1670; Boston/NY
MORE, Samuel (1642-) & Sarah _?_ ; b 1673; Salem
MORE, Samuel & Elizabeth DANIEL; 9 Jun 1691?, 9 Jun 1697?; Newton, MA
MOORE, Samuel & Mary (PARTRIDE) [BARNWELL], w Richard, m/3 Richard ELLIOT, m/4 John LEACH; aft Sep 1694, b 1696; Durham, NH
MOORE, Theodorius & Joane (GUY) [GENDALL], w Walter; b 1689?, b 27 Nov 1700; Marshfield/Bridgewater
MORE, Thomas (-1636) & Ann _?_ (-1668+); in Eng, b 1610; Salem
MOORE, Thomas[1] (-1645) & _?_ ; in Eng, b 1618; Dorchester/Windsor, CT
MOORE, Thomas (?1615-) & 1/wf Martha [YOUNGS] (1613-1671), sis of Christopher YOUNGS of Salem; b 31 Jul 1636; Salem/Southold, LI
MOORE, Thomas & Sarah HODGES; 9 Nov 1653; Cambridge/Boston
MOORE, Thomas (1615-1691) & 2/wf Katherine (_?_) (DAVY) LANE, w Thomas, w Daniel; aft 1671; Southold, LI
MOORE/(MOWRY), Thomas & Susanna NEWEL; 3 Oct 1673; Dorchester
MOORE, Thomas (-1738 in 76th y) & Jane _?_ (1676-1756); 13 Mar 1694/5; Southold, LI
MOORE, Thomas & Deborah GRISWOLD/BASSETT? (1674-); 12 Dec 1695; Windsor, CT
MOORE, Thomas & Hannah [?HARRIS/?WILLIAMS]; b 17 Feb 1696/7; York, ME
MOORE, William & _?_ ; b 1638; Exeter, NH
MORE, William & _?_ ; b 1644; Ipswich
MOORE, William (-1691) & Dorothy _?_ (dau of Joane, wf of William DIXON); ca 1650/55?; York, ME
MOOR, William, Quamscot & Mary (WIGGIN) VEASEY, Quamscot, w George; 7 Oct 1673; Hampton, NH
MORE, William & 1/wf Mary (WELLMAN) HOWARD (-1700, Windham, CT), w Thomas; - Aug 1677; Norwich, CT
MOORE, William & Ann [WALKER] (1676-1711+); b 1695; Boston
MOORE, William & Mary (_?_) ALLEN, w Joshua; 17 Jul 1700; Windham, CT
MOORE, William & Sarah [WIGGIN] (1682-); ?b 1701; Concord, NH
MOORES/MOORE, Edmund[1] (?1614-1699) & Ann _?_ (-1676); b 1643; Newbury
MOORES, Edmund & Sarah COOPPER/COOPER; 3 Jan 1676, 3 Jan, 2 Jan 1676, 3 Jan 1676/7; Newbury/Rowley
MOORES, Jonathan (1646-1693) & Constance LONGHORNE (1652-), m/2 John MITCHELL 1697; ca 10 May 1670; Newbury/Rowley
MOORE, Matthew & Sarah LAROY/[LARY?]/SAVORY; 27 Mar 1662; Newbury
MOORS, Samuel & 1/wf Hannah PLUMER (-1654); 3 May 1653; Newbury
MOORES, Samuel & 2/wf Mary ILSLY (1638±-1678); 12 Sep 1656; Newbury
MORDOGH?/MORDOE, Patrick/Peter? & Joanna? _?_ (1682-); b 1683(4?), b 1708; Stratford, CT
MORECOCK, Nicholas & _?_ ; b 1699; Boston
MORECOCK, Nicholas & Elizabeth BURNHAM (1640-1720); CT
MOREHOUSE, Daniel (1678-1739) & Hannah [ADAMS]; b 1700; Fairfield, CT
MOREHOUSE, John (-1701) & _?_ ; b 1684; Southampton, LI
MOREHOUSE, John & Ruth [BARLOW]; b 3 Nov 1698; Fairfield, CT
MOREHOUSE, Jonathan & 1/wf Mary [WILSON]; b 1677; Fairfield, CT
MOREHOUSE, Jonathan & 2/wf Rebecca KNOWLES; 16 Apr 1690; Fairfield, CT
MOREHOUSE, Samuel (-1687) & Rebecca [ODELL] (1642-); ca 1662/4; Fairfield, CT
MOREHOUSE, Samuel (-1732) & _?_ ; b 1688; Fairfield, CT/Stratford, CT
MOREHOUSE, Thomas[1] (-1658) & Isabella/Isabel _?_ ; ca 1638?; Wethersfield, CT/Stamford, CT/Fairfield, CT
MOREHOUSE, Thomas[2] & 1/wf _?_ [KEELER], dau Ralph; 5 Nov 1672; Fairfield, CT
MOORHOUSE, Thomas (-1698?) & Mary HILL (1670-), m/2 Joseph STURGES 1701; 3 Apr 1690; Boston
MOREHOUSE, Thomas[2] (-1725) & 2/wf Martha [HOBBY] (1666±-), m/2 Abraham ADAMS, m/3 _?_ MILLER; b 1 Nov 1696; Fairfield, CT
MOREHOUSE, Thomas (-1748) & Mary _?_ (-1758); b 1701; Fairfield, CT/Westport, CT
MORER, William & Ann _?_ ; b 1693; Boston
MOREY, Daniel & Susanna LYON; 8 Nov 1682; Milton/Boston
MOREY, George (-1640) & _?_ ; ca 1631/33?; Plymouth/Duxbury
MOREY, George & Hannah LEWIS (-1717); 22 Jan 1683; Bristol, RI

MOREY, John & Constant [?MARTIN]/Constance BRACEY; b 1661; Wethersfield, CT
MOREY, Nicholas (-1730/1) & Mary (PENDLETON) (BRETTON/BRITTON) CROSS, w William, w Joseph; b 25 May 1685, betw 28 Oct 1684 & 31 Mar 1685; Wells, ME/Taunton/Freetown/Dighton
MOREY, Walter (-1727, 1707?) & Mary [CLARK] (-1727); b 1667/[8?]; Milton
MORGAN, Benjamin & Christian _?_; b 1695; New London
MORGAN, Charles & Elizabeth [?FEAKE]; b 1683; Flushing, LI
MORGAN, David (1648-1721) & Mary CLARK (1654-1755?); 16 Jan 1672, 1672/3; Springfield
MORGAN, Edward & Elizabeth FORD; 3 Feb 1695/6; Marblehead
MORGAN, Francis & Sarah (TILLY) (LYNN) (GUNNISON) MITCHELL (1619?-), w Henry, w Hugh, w John; aft 28 May 1664, bef 22 Apr 1665, aft 5 Jul; Kittery, ME
MORGAN, Isaac (1652-1701) & Abigail GARDNER; 12 Nov 1673; Springfield/Enfield, CT
MORGAN, Isaac (?1670-1725) & 1/wf Mary [SPAULDING]; b 1700, b 1701?, b 1702; Preston, CT
MORGAN, James (ca 1607-1685, 1686?, 1667?) & Margery HILL; 6 Aug 1640; Roxbury/New London, CT/Groton, CT
MORGAN, James (1644-1711, Groton, CT) & 1/wf Mary VINE (1641-1689); - Nov 1666, 3 Nov?; New London, CT
MORGAN, James & Selphina/Salphin _?_; b 1676; Boston
MORGAN, James (1644-1712) & 2/wf Hannah [CROMWELL?] (1640-1711); aft 1689; ?New London, CT/?Groton
MORGAN, James (1667-) & 1/wf Hannah _?_; b 1693; Stonington, CT
MORGAN, John (-1712) & Rachel DEMING/DYMOND; 16 Nov 1665; New London, CT
MORGAN, John (1645-1712) & 2/wf Elizabeth (JONES) WILLIAMS (1664-); b 1690; Preston, CT/New London, CT
MORGAN, John (1667-1746) & Ruth SHAPLEIGH (1672-1744); b 1697; New London, CT
MORGAN, John & Ann DART; Aug 1699; New London
MORGAN, John & Deborah BLAKE; 10 Jul 1700, 19 Jul; Hampton, NH
MORGAN, Jonathan (1646-1730) & Sarah COOLEY (1654-); 5 Jan 1679, 15 Jan 1679/80; Springfield/Longmeadow
MORGAN, Joseph (-1732) & 1/wf Deborah HART; 12 Jul 1669; Lynn/Beverly
MORGAN, Joseph (1646-1704, Preston) & 2/wf Dorothy PARKE (1652-1705+); Apr 1670, 26 Apr; ?New London, CT/Preston, CT
MORGAN, Joseph (-1732) & 2/wf Sarah HILL, wid; 25 Oct 1694; Beverly
MORGAN, Joseph & Sarah EMANS/[EMMONS?]; 14 Oct 1696, Greenwich, CT?; Gravesend, LI, NY/Dorchester
MORGAN, Joseph (-1703) & Elizabeth WALLICE/WALLACE; m int 11 Aug 1700; Beverly
MORGAN, Luke (-1714) & Susanna [CLARK?]; b 1701; Beverly
MORGAN, Miles (?1615-1699) & 1/wf Prudence [GILBERT?] (-1660), Beverly; ca 1643?; Salem/Springfield
MORGAN, Miles (?1615-1699) & 2/wf Elizabeth BLISS (-bef 25 Jun 1684); 15 Feb 1669, 18? Feb 1669/70; Springfield
MORGAN, Nathaniel (1671-1732) & Hannah BIRD (-1751); 19 Jan 1691; Springfield
MORGAN, Owen & Joan BRYAN, wid; 9 Apr 1650; New Haven/Norwalk
MORGAN, Peletiah (1677-1755) & Lydia [BIRD] (ca 1699-1735); bef Jun 1700; Springfield
MORGAN, Ralph & Margaret _?_; b 1688; Charlestown
MORGAN, Richard, Dover, NH, & Rebecca HOULDRIDGE/HOLDRIDGE (1643-); 21 May 1660; Andover/Ipswich/Exeter, NH
MORGAN, Richard & Abigail HARRIS; 17 May 1699; Hampton, NH
MORGAN, Robert (-1672, 1673?) & [Margaret NORMAN], m/2 Samuel FOWLER ca 1673; b 1638, ?27 Jan 1638; Salisbury/Salem (5 ch bpt 1650)
MORGAN, Robert (1670-1762) & 1/wf Ann/Anna OBER (-1702); 4 Jul 1692, 8 Jul; Beverly
MORGAN, Samuel (-1698) & 1/wf Elizabeth DIXY (1641-1690); 15 Dec 1658; Salem/Marblehead
MORGAN, Samuel (1637-1698) & 2/wf Mary _?_; bef 24 Jul 1692, aft 24 Feb 1690; Beverly
MORGAN, Samuel (1666-) & Sarah HERRICK (1662-), m/2 Thomas WHITTREDGE; 22 Dec 1692; Beverly
MORGIN, Thomas & Grete GARETS; 24 Jan 1673, Gravesend, LI
MORGAN, Thomas (-1725) & Rachel _?_, m/2 Abel COLLIER; b 1694; Hartford
MORGAN, William & Abiel/Abigail _?_; b 1689; Wells, ME
MORGAN, William & Margaret AVERY; 7 Jul 1696, 17 Jul 1696; ?New London, CT

MORGAN, _?_ & Hannah SMITH; b 1694
MORGRIDGE/MORGRAGE, John & Sarah [STEVENS]; ca 1678; Kittery, ME
MORLEY, John (-1661) & Constant STARR (1610-1669); 20 Apr 1647; Braintree
MORLEY, Ralph (-1630) & Catharine _?_ (-1630+); Charlestown
MARLOW/MORLEY, Thomas (-1712) & Martha WRIGHT (1662-1740); 8 Dec 1681; Westfield
MORRILL, Abraham (-1662) & Sarah CLEMENT, m/2 Thomas MUDGETT; 10 Jun 1645; Salisbury
MORRILL, Abraham (1652-) & Sarah [BRADBURY] (1662-); ca 1688; Salisbury
MORRELL, Abraham & Elizabeth SARGENT; 2 Jan 1695/6; Salisbury
MORRILL, Ezekiel (-1663) & Mary _?_, m/2 Thomas HODGMAN (see Matthew GIBBS); b 1657; Cambridge
MORRELL, Henry (-1665) & [Blanche] _?_ (-1684); b 1650; New Haven
MORRILL, Isaac (1588-1661, ae 74) & Sarah _?_ (1600-1672, 1673); in Eng, ca 1624/28?; Roxbury
MORRILL, Isaac (1646-) & Phebe GILL; 14 Nov 1670; Salisbury
MORRILL, Isaac (-1737) & Abigail BROWNE; 30 May 1696; Salisbury
MORRILL, Jacob (1648-) & Susanna WHITTIER; 15 Jul 1674; Salisbury
MORRILL/MURRILL?, Jeremiah (-1679) & Sarah [?GROVER] (1632-1709); b 1658(9?), b 1652; Boston
MORRILL, John & Lydia/Lysbell MORRELL; 31 Aug 1659; Boston
MORRILL, John (1640-) & Sarah [HODSDON]; b 1667; Kittery, ME
MORRELL, Jonathan (1670-1726±) & Judith _?_; b 1697; Newtown, LI
MORRELL, Joseph (1667-1742) & Hannah _?_; b 1701?; Newtown, LI
MORREL, Moses (1655-) & 1/wf Rebecca [BARNES] (-1727); b 1686; Amesbury
MORRELL, Nicholas & Margaret LANGDON, Portsmouth, dau Tobias; 4 Aug 1679; Exeter, NH
MORRELL, Nicholas (1667-) & Sarah [FRYE]; 1695, Apr 1695; Kittery, ME
MORRELL, Peter & Mary BUTLER; 27 Sep 1675; Salem
MURRELL, Robert & _?_; b 1690?; Salem
MORRELL, Samuel (?1664-) & Susannah _?_; b 1701?; Newtown, LI
MORRELL, Thomas & Hannah [GLEN]; b 1662; Newtown, LI
MORRELL, Thomas (?1662-) & Martha _?_; b 1686; Newtown, LI
MORRELL, William & Elizabeth _?_; b 1701?; Newtown, LI
MORRILL, _?_ & Vashti _?_, m/2 Robert BRADISH 1639?
MORRIS, Anthony, PA & Mary (HOWARD) CODDINGTON, w Thomas; 18 Jan 1693/4, 18 Jan 1695, 18 Jan 1694; RI
MORRIS, Archibald & Elizabeth _?_; b 1684(5?); Boston
MORRISE, Charles & Esther RAINSTORPE/RANSTOP?; b 1701, 5 Sep 1700; Boston
MORRIS, Dorman & Eleanor _?_; b 1671(2?); Boston
MORRIS, Ebenezer (1664-1718) & Sarah DAVIS; 1 Sep 1692; Woodstock, CT
MORRIS, Edward (1630-1689?, 1692?) & Grace BELT?/BELL?/BURR?/BUTTS? (-1705); 20 Nov 1655; Boston/Roxbury/Woodstock, CT
MORRIS, Edward & Elizabeth BOWEN?/?BROWN; 24 May 1683; Roxbury
MORRIS, Eleazer (1648-1710, 1723?) & Anna [OSBORN] (1663-1726); b 1682; E. Haven, CT/New Haven
MORRIS, Isaac & 1/wf Hannah MAYO (1660-1701, Roxbury); 2 Mar 1680; Roxbury/Woodstock, CT
MORRICE, John & Elizabeth CORNWELL; 9 Sep 1650; Gravesend, LI
MORRIS, John & 1/wf Ann _?_ (-1664); New Haven
MORRIS, John (-1669) & [Martha] _?_; b 1664; Hartford
MORRIS, John & Elizabeth (HARRISON) (LINES) LAMPSON, w Henry, w Thomas; 29 Mar 1666; New Haven/Newark, NJ
MORRIS, John (1646-1711) & Hannah BISHOP (1659-1711, 1710?); 12 Aug 1669; New Haven
MORRIS, John & Sarah [JOHNSON?] (see below); b 1683; York, ME
MORRIS, John & Sarah _?_ (see above); b 1690; Boston
MORRIS, John & Elizabeth [ALMY] (1662); m/2 John LEONARD
MORRIS, John (1666-1749) & Sarah [?CRANE] (1665-1739); b 1701?; CT?/Newark, NJ
MORRIS, Joseph & Esther WINSTON (1662-), m/2 Nathaniel SPERRY; 2 Jun 1680; New Haven
MORRIS, Philip (-1694) & Joanna _?_; ?New Haven/Newark, NJ
MORRIS, Rice (-1647) & Hester _?_, m/2 Henry EVANS by 1650; b 1634; Charlestown

MORRIS, Richard & 1/wf Leonara (PAULEY) [UNDERHILL], w John; ca 1630-2, 28 Nov 1628, The Hague; Boston/Portsmouth, RI/etc.

MORRIS, Richard & 2/wf Mary _?_ (6 Nov 1692 she had gr-ch Mary STOKES); b 18 Dec 1658; Portsmouth, RI

MORRIS, Robert & 1/wf Anna _?_ ; b 1663; Wethersfield, CT

MORRIS, Robert (-1684) & _?_ [LATIMER], w John; (div-no ch); Hartford/Wethersfield, CT

MORRIS, Samuel & Mehitable [MAYO] (-1703); b 1695; Roxbury

MORRIS, Thomas (-1638) & Grissie [?HEWSOME]; Boston

MORRIS, Thomas (-1673) (mentioned in will of Edward HOLYOKE, 25 Dec 1658) & Elizabeth _?_ (-1681); b 1641/2; New Haven

MORRICE, William (?1618-1697) & Dorcas [?HILL]; b 1665; Boston/Wethersfield, CT/Charlestown?

MORRIS, William & Lettice CARTER; 15 Sep 1683; Charlestown

MORRIS, William (1614-) & Phillip [COLE], w Robert; b 1660; Charlestown

MORRIS, _?_ & Margaret PAINTER (1667-), m/2 Lawrence CLINTON, m/3 Jeremiah MOTT; Providence

MORRISH, _?_ & Rose HANNIFORD, sis of John of Boston; b 26 Dec 1657

MORRISON, Andrew & Sarah JONES, m/2 John DUDLEY; 21 Oct 1687; New Haven

MORISON, Daniel (-1737) & 1/wf Hannah GRIFFIN (-1700); b 1691; Newbury/Salisbury

MORSE/MOSS, Anthony[1] (1606-1686) & 1/wf Ann COX (-1680); St. Mary's, Marlborough, Wiltshire, 2 May 1629, in Eng, b 1630; Newbury/Salisbury

MORSE, Anthony & 1/wf Elizabeth KNIGHT (-1667); 8 May 1660; Newbury

MORSE, Anthony & 2/wf Mary BARNARD (1645-), m/2 Philip EASTMAN 1678; 10 Nov 1669, 11 Nov; Newbury

MORSE, Anthony & Sarah/Mary PIKE (1666-); 4 Feb 1685, 1685/6; Newbury

MORSE, Benjamin (1640-1714/16?) & Ruth SAWYER (1648-1715+); 27 Aug 1667, 26 Aug 1667; Newbury

MORSE, Benjamin (1669-) & Susanna _?_ ; b 1691; Newbury

MORSE, Benjamin (1668-) & Susanna MERRILL (1673-); 28 Jan 1691/2; Newbury

MORSE/MOSSE, Christopher & Prudence WOODWARD; [July?] 1661; Boston

MORSE, Daniel (1613-1688) & Lydia [FISHER]; b 1639; Dedham/Medfield/Sherborn

MORSE, Daniel (-1702) & Elizabeth [BARBOUR] (-1700); 21 Jun 1669; Medfield/Sherborn

MORSE, Daniel (1672-1719) & 1/wf Susanna HOLBROOK; 22 May 1696; Sherborn

MORSE, Edmund & _?_ ; b 1678; Newbury

MORSE, Edward & Mary [CLARK] (1667-), dau Percival; b 1689; Boston

MORSE, Ephraim & _?_ ; Newtown, LI

MORSE, Ezra (-1697) & Joanna HOARE (-1691, Braintree); 18 Feb 1670; Dedham

MORSE, Ezra (1671-1760) & Mary [?LOVETT]; b 1694; Dedham

MORSE, Francis & 1/wf Elizabeth _?_ ; b 1667; Boston

MORSS, Francis & Ann/Anna/Anne? _?_ ; b 1669; Boston

MORSE, Isaac & _?_ (-1719); Watertown

MORS/MORSE, James & Abigail MORS/MORSE, m/2 John HOLDEN; 27 Apr 1699; Watertown

MORSE, Jeremiah & _?_ ; b 1647; Boston

MORSE, Jeremiah (1651-1716) & Elizabeth [HAMANT] (-1733); b 1678; Medfield

MOSS, Jeremiah & 1/wf Abigail WOODWARD; 13 Jan 1681, 1682, 1681/2; Watertown/Newtown

MORSE, Jeremiah & 2/wf Sarah [GLEASON]/[WOODWARD? see above] (1665/6?); ca 1682, ca 1683, b 1689; Newtown/Watertown

MORSE, Jeremiah & Mehitable CHANEY/CHENEY; 19 Nov 1699, 1700; Medfield

MORSE, John (1611, 1608-1657) & Annis/Hannah/?Agnes [CHICKERING] (-1691) (called Francis brother; Francis did not have sis Annis); b 1637; Dedham/Watertown

MORSE/MOSS?, John & Mary JUPE; 24 Dec 1652; Boston

MORSE, John & [Dinah] _?_ ; b 1657; Ipswich/Groton/Watertown

MORSE, John (-1702) & 1/wf Anne [SMITH]; b 1660; Watertown/Lancaster

MORSE, John (1639-1679, 1678?) & Elizabeth [BOSWORTH] (1640-), m/2 Samuel BUTTON bef 1688; b 1660(1?); Boston/Mendon?

MORSE, John (-1702) & 2/wf Abigail STEARNS/EDWARDS (-1690); 27 Apr 1666, 27 Apr 1660; Watertown

MORSE, John & Dinah KNIGHT; 5 Mar 1686; Woburn/Watertown

MORSE, John & 1/wf Elizabeth GOODING/GODDING?/GOODWIN (-1701?); 8 Jan 1689/90; Watertown
MORSE, John (-1702) & 3/wf Sarah _?_; aft 16 Oct 1690
MORSE, John (1646-) & Sarah [EASTMAN?]; 1696, b 1700; Salisbury (see John MOSS)
MORSE, John (1670-1721) & Hannah WILLIAMS; 10 May 1697; Woodstock, CT?
MORSE, Jonathan (?1640-1709, Middleboro) & _?_; Middleboro
MORSE, Jonathan (1643-) & Mary BARBOUR (-1700); 8 Jul 1666, 8 Sep 1666; Medfield/Sherborn
MORSE, Jonathan & Mary CLARKE; 3 May 1671; Newbury/Middleboro/Beverly
MORSE, Jonathan (1643-1686) & Abigail SHATTUCK, m/2 Joshua PARKER 1690; 17 Oct 1678; Watertown/Groton
MORSE, Jonathan (1667-), Sherborn & Jane WHITNEY (1669-), Sherborn; 4 Jan 1692/3, 4 Jan 1693/4; Sherborn/Framingham
MORSE, Joseph (1587-1646?) & Dorothy BARBER; in Eng, b 1610; Ipswich
MORSE, Joseph (1610-1691) & Esther/Hester PIERCE; b 1637; Watertown
MORSE, Joseph (1613-1654) & Hannah/Annis/Anne/Ann PHILLIPS (-1676), m/2 Thomas BOYDEN 1658; 1 Sep 1638, 7 Jan 1638, 1 Jul 1638; Dedham
MORSE, Joseph (1637-1677) & Susanna/Susan SHATTUCK (1643-1716), m/2 John FAY 1678, m/3 Thomas BRIGHAM 1690; 11 Feb 1660/1, 11 Feb 1661/2, 12 Apr 1661; Watertown, CT/Groton
MORSE, Joseph & Priscilla COLBURN (1646-); 12 Nov 1668; Dedham
MORSS, Joseph (-1679) & Mary (WOODHOUSE) [PIERCE], w George, m/3 Francis BROWN 1679; b 1669, ca 1665?; Newbury
MORSE, Joseph (1649-) & 1/wf Mehitable WOOD/WYETH (1655?-1681); 17 Oct 1671; Sherborn/Medfield
MORSE, Joseph (1649-) & 2/wf Hannah BADCOCK/BABCOCK (1664/5-1711); 11 Apr 1683; Medfield/Sherborn
MORSE, Joseph (-1689) & 1/wf Lydia PLUMMER (-2 Nov 1689); 4 Jan 1688, 1688/9; Haverhill
MOSE, Joseph & Grace WARREN; 20 Jan 1690, [1690/1], 1691; Cambridge/Framingham/Marlboro
MORSE, Joseph (1671-1709) & Elizabeth SAWTEL, m/2 Benjamin NOURSE; 25 Aug 1691; Watertown
MOSS, Joseph (1673?-) & Elizabeth POOR; 30 Jan 1692/3; Newbury
MORSS, Joseph & Sarah MERRILL (1679-); m int 7 Oct 1696; Newbury/Casco Bay
MORSE, Joseph (1671-1732) & Amity HARRIS (1678-1749); b 1701?, 1698?, b 1706, b 1705; Providence/Watertown
MORSE, Joshua (1653-1691) & 1/wf Joanna/Hannah [KIMBALL] (1661-1690, 1691?); ca 1680; Newbury
MORSE, Joshua & _?_; b 1692; RI
MORSE, Joshua & 2/wf Mary _?_; aft 1691, aft May 1691; Newbury
MORSE, Joshua & Elizabeth DOTY; 12 Dec 1698; Plymouth
MORSE, Joshua & Elizabeth PENNIMAN; 8 Nov 1699, 15 Nov 1699; Braintree/Dedham
MORSE, Nathaniel (1658-1728) & Mary _?_; b 1680; Sherborn
MORSE, Obadiah (1639-1704) & Martha JOHNSON; 27 Mar 1665/6; Medfield
MORSE, Obadiah (1645-) & Elizabeth [ROLLINS]; by 1670; Portsmouth, NH/Salisbury
MORSE, Obadiah & Hannah _?_; b 1694; Portsmouth, NH
MORSE, Peter (1674-1721) & Priscilla CARPENTER (1681-1759); 28 Dec 1698, 22 Dec, ca 1695; Woodstock, CT?/Salisbury
MORSE, Robert & Elizabeth _?_; b 1644; Boston/Elizabeth, NJ
MORSE, Robert (1629-) & Ann LEWIS; 30 Oct 1654; Newbury/Elizabeth, NJ
MORSE, Samuel (1576-1654) & Elizabeth JASPER (1580-1635); Redgrave or Suffolk, b 1611, 29 Jun 1602, ca 1610; Dedham/Medfield
MORSE, Samuel & Mary [BULLEN]; b 1642, b 1641?; Dedham
MORSE, Samuel (1639/[40]-) & 1/wf Elizabeth WOOD/?MOORE (-1682); 10 Feb 1664, 10 Feb 1665; Sudbury/Medfield/Framingham
MORS, Samuel (1639/40-) & 2/wf Sarah THURSTUN/THURSTON; 29 Apr 1684; Medfield
MORSE, Samuel (1661-) & Deborah _?_; b 1687; Sherborn
MORSE, Samuel (1666-) & Abigail (BABCOCK) [BARBER] (1656-1693), w John; b 1693; Medfield
MORSE, Samuel (1676-) & Bethiah [HOLBROOK]; b 1695; Sherborn
MORSE, Samuel (1670-1758) & Grace _?_; b 1696, b 1695?; Watertown
MORSE, Walter & ?Mercy CLARK, dau James; b 1667; Boston

MORSE, William (1614-1683) & Elizabeth _?_ (-1684+); in Eng, b 1635; Newbury
MORSE, William (1674-1749) & Sarah MERRILL (1677-living in 1744); 12 May 1696; Newbury
MORSE, _?_ & Deborah _?_ (1651); Portsmouth, NH
MORTIMORE, Edward (-1709) & Jane _?_, m/2 _?_ HOLLANSBY; b 1674; Boston
MORTIMER, Richard & Ann _?_ ; b 1664; Boston
MORTIMER, Thomas (-1710) & Elizabeth _?_ (-1710); b 1674; New London, CT
MORTON, Charles (-1698) & Joan _?_ (-1693); ca 1656-60? (no issue); Charlestown
MORTON, Eleazer & Rebecca (DAWES) MARSHALL (-1705+, prob 1732), w Benjamin; 11 Apr 1693, 1692?; Boston/Plymouth
MORTON, Ephraim[2] (1623-1693) & 1/wf Ann COOPER (-1 Sep 1691, 6 Sep); 18 Nov 1644; ?Plymouth
MORTON, Ephraim[3] (1648-1732) & Hannah [PHINNEY] (1657-); b 1677; Plymouth
MORTON, Ephraim (1623-1693) & 2/wf Mary (SHELLEY) HARLOW, w William, m/3 Hugh COLE 1694; 18 Oct 1692, m cov 11 Oct; Plymouth
MORTON, Ephraim[4], Jr. (1671-) & Hannah _?_, m/2 John COOKE; b 1699; Plymouth
MORTON, George (-1624) & 2/wf Juliana CARPENTER (ca 1583-1665, 1685?), m/2 Manassah KEMPTON betw 1624 & 1627; Julian calendar 23 Jul 1612, 2 Aug 1612; Plymouth
MORTON, George & 1/wf Phebe _?_ (-22 May 1663; b 1663, b 1640; Plymouth
MORTON, George & 2/wf Joanna KEMPTON (1647-); 22 Dec 1664; Plymouth
MORTON, John (-1673) & Lettice _?_ (-1691), m/2 Andrew RING; b 1649, aft 1642/3?; Plymouth/Middleboro
MORTON, John & Martha _?_ ; b 1678(9?); Boston
MORTON, John (1650-1718, Middleboro) & 1/wf Phebe [SHANE] (-1686), dau Jonathan; ca 1680-1; Plymouth
MORTON, John (ca 1650-1718, Middleboro) & 2/wf Mary RING (-1731, Middleboro); 4 Mar 1687; Plymouth
MORTON, John & Ruth _?_ ; b 1700(1?); Hatfield
MORTON, Joseph & Mary [MARSH?] (1678-); b 1699; Hadley/Hatfield
MORTON, Josiah (-1694) & Susanna WOOD/?WARD, m/2 Dea. _?_ CLARK; 8 Mar 1686, 1685/6; Plymouth
MORTON, Nathaniel (?1613-1685) & 1/wf Lydia COOPER (-1673), sis of John of Scituate; 25 Dec 1635; ?Plymouth
MORTON, Nathaniel (-1685) & 2/wf Anne/Hannah? (PRITCHARD) TEMPLAR (-1690, ae 66), Charlestown, w Richard; 29 Apr 1674; Plymouth
MORTON, Richard (-1710) & Ruth _?_ (-1714); b 1668, b 1666?; Hartford/Hatfield
MORTON, Richard & _?_ ; b 1683(4?); New Shoreham, RI
MORTON, Richard (-1691/2) & Mehitable GRAVES (1671-1742), m/2 William WORTHINGTON; 29 Jan 1690; Hatfield/Hadley
MORTON, Thomas (-1689?) & Rose _?_ (-1685); b 1685; Plymouth
MORTON, Thomas (1667-1748) & Martha DOTEY/DOTY (1671-); 23 Dec 1696; Plymouth
MORTON, Thomas (1661-1741) & Comfort (DEMING) BECKLEY, w Nathaniel; 1698; Wethersfield, CT
MORTON, William (-1712) & Mary BURNHAM (-1720, Windsor, CT); 21 Mar 1670; ?Westfield/Hartford
MORTON, _?_ & _?_ HOWLAND, dau Samuel[2] HENRY; b 1715; (had dau Mary)
MORTON, _?_ (see Thomas MORTON) & Elizabeth WORTHINGTON, dau Nicholas; Hadley
MOSAMY/?MOSEMY, Thomas & Elizabeth _?_ ; b 1692; Boston
MOSELEY/MORELEY, Benjamin (1666-) & Mary SACKETT (-1729); 2 Oct 1689; Westfield/Windsor, CT
MOSLY, Ebenezer (1673-) & 1/wf Elizabeth [TRESCOTT] (-1705); b 1695; Dorchester
MOSELEY, Henry (1611-) & _?_ ; b 1638; Dorchester/Braintree
MODSLEY, Increase (1663-1690) & [Sarah TRESCOTT] (1662-), m/2 John PEABODY 1703; b 1690; Dorchester
MOSELEY, John (-1661) & 2/wf? Cicely _?_ (-1661); ca 1635?; Dorchester
MAUDSLEY, John (1638-1690) & Mary NEWBERRY, m/2 Isaac PHELPS 1690; 14 Dec 1664, 10? Dec; Windsor, CT/Westfield
MAUDSLEY, John (1676-) & Hannah CLARK; 28 Jul 1700; Dorchester
MOSELEY, Joseph (1670-1719) & 1/wf Abigail ROOT; 13 Sep 1696; Westfield/Glastonbury, CT
MOSELEY, Richard & Mary [EYRE] (?1652-); b 1675?; Boston

MOSELEY, Samuel (1641-1680?) & Anne [ADDINGTON] (1647-), m/2 Nehemiah PIERCE 1684+; b 30 May 1665; Boston

MODESLEY, Thomas (1635-1706) & Mary LAWRENCE/Mary COOPER (-1723); 28 Oct 1658; Dorchester/Roxbury

MOADSLIE, Thomas (1667-) & Susannah RIGBIE/RIGBY; 24 Dec 1690; Dorchester

MAUDSLEY, Thomas & Rebecca (STEVENS) MASON, w Stephen?; 11 Jul 1700; Milton

MOSES, Aaron (ca 1650-1713) & 1/wf Ruth SHERBURN (1660-); 1 Jun 1676?

MOSES, Aaron & 2/wf Mary LEACH, m/2 John SHERBURN

MOSISES, Eleazer (1673-) & Hannah WARD; 24 Jun 1697; Salem

MOSES, Henry (-1685) & Remember GILES (1639-); 1 Apr 1659; Salem

MOSES, John & _?_ ; b 1633?, doubtful; Plymouth

MOSES, John (1616-) & 1/wf Alice _?_ ; b 1639?; Portsmouth, NH

MOSES, John (-1683) & Mary BROWN (-1689); 18 May 1653; Windsor, CT/Simsbury, CT

MOSES, John & 2/wf Ann [JONES], w John; ca 1667; Portsmouth, NH

MOSES, John (1654-1714) & Deborah THRALL (-1715); 14 Jul 1680; Simsbury, CT

MOSES/MOGEY, Joseph & Tamosen BEAN; 31 Jul 1699; Salem

MOSES, Samuel & Grace _?_ ; b 1675; Ipswich

MOSES, Thomas & _?_ ; b 1665; Dorchester

MOSES, Timothy & 1/wf Mary [JACKSON]; bef 1700, by Jul 1701; Dover, NH

MOISER, Arthur & Rebecca _?_ ; b 1677(8?); Boston

MOSHER, Hugh (-1666) & _?_ ; b 1640; Falmouth, ME

MOSHER, Hugh (1633-1713) & 1/wf Rebecca [HARNDEL]; b 1666; Newport/Portsmouth, RI/Dartmouth

MOSHER, Hugh (1633-1713) & 2/wf Sarah (?BUTCHER) [HARDIN], w John; b 1701?; Newport/Dartmouth

MOSHER, John (1640-1695+) & Elizabeth _?_ (-1695+); Setauket, LI/Brookhaven, LI

MOSHER, John & Experience KIRBY (1670-1754); 5 Mar 1692; Dartmouth

MOSHER, Joseph (1670-1754) & Lydia [TABER] (1673-1743); b 1695; Dartmouth

MOSHER, Nicholas & Elizabeth _?_ ; b 1690; ?Dartmouth/Tiverton, RI

MOSMAN/MOSEMAN?/MOSTMAN, James & Anna _?_ ; b 1677, b 1675; Dedham/Roxbury/Wrentham

MOSSE/MORSE?, Christopher & Prudence WOODWARD; 1661; Boston

MOSS, John (1604-1707) (John CHARLES "brother-in-law") & _?_ [CHARLES?]; b 1639(40?); New Haven/Wallingford, CT

MOSS, John & Mary JUPE; 24 Dec 1658; Boston

MOSS, John (1650-1717) & Martha LOTHROP (1657-1719); 12 Dec 1676; Wallingford, CT

MOSS/?MORSE, John & Sarah _?_ ; b 1694; Salisbury

MOSS, John (1643-1727) & 1/wf Mary ALLING (1643-1716); 11 Apr 1667; New Haven

MOSS, Joseph & Mary _?_ ; b 1686(7?); Boston

MOSS, Mark & Christian HOYLE, m/2 John BARTOL; 9 Nov 1699; Marblehead

MOSS, Mercy (1649-1685) & Elizabeth [CURTIS], m/2 John ROSE b 1687; b 1677(8?); New Haven

MOSS/?MORSE, Ephraim & Isabel [POTTER], m/2 William BURTON ca 1701; ca 1657/70?

MOSSETT, Thomas & Catherine/Katherine _?_ ; b 1689; Braintree

MOTT, Adam (1596-1661) & 1/wf Elizabeth CREEL; 28 Oct 1616, in Eng, b 1621; Roxbury/Hingham/Portsmouth, RI

MOTT, Adam (1596-1661) & 2/wf Sarah [LOTT] (1604-), wid; in Eng, b 1633, 11 May 1635, ?Oct 1647; Roxbury/Hingham/Portsmouth, RI

MOTT, Adam (1619-1686) & 1/wf Jane/Jenne HEWLET/HALLET/HULET?; 28 Jul 1647; New York/Hempstead, LI/Staten Island

MOTT, Adam (-1673+) & Mary LOTT (1631-1712); Oct 1647; ?Portsmouth, RI

MOTT, Adam (1619-1686) & 2/wf _?_ [BOWNE]; ca 1667?; NY

MOTT, Adam (1619-1686) & 3/wf Elizabeth ?REDMAN, m/2 Robert HUBS/HOBBS bef 1691; b 1670, 22 Nov 1667?; ?Mamaroneck, NY

MOTT, Adam (1649-), Hempstead & Mary STILLWELL, Gravesend; m lic 9 Jul 1678; ?Hempstead, LI

MOTT, Charles (1676-1740) & Elizabeth _?_ ; ca 1694-5; Hempstead, LI/(Cow Neck)

MOTT, Ebenezer (-1713, 1736?), Scituate & Grace VINALL, Scituate; 19 Feb 1700, 1699-1700; Scituate

MOTT, Edward (1673-1735) & Penelope (NILES) TOSH (-1751+), w William; 3 Dec 1695, 9? Dec; New Shoreham, RI
MOTT, Gershom & Sarah CLAYTON?; 4 Mar 1696, m lic 12 Feb 1696; ?Portsmouth, RI
MOTT, Henry (1657-1680) & Hannah _?_; ca 1675?; ?Hempstead, LI
MOTT, Jacob (1633-1711) & Joanne [SLOCUM] (1642-1728); b 1661; Portsmouth, RI
MOTT, Jacob (1661-) & 1/wf Cassandra [SOUTHWICK] (1667-); 1689; Salem/Portsmouth, RI
MOTT, James & Mary REDMAN; m lic 5 Sep 1670; ?Hempstead, LI/Mamaroneck, NY
MOTT, James (-1707) & 2/wf Elizabeth _?_; Mamaroneck, NY
MOTT, John & _?_; b 1596 in Eng; Portsmouth, RI
MOTT, John (1658/9?-) & ?[Sarah SEAMAN]; ca 1680-5?, b 1694
MOTT, John & Marcy/Mercy TOSH/MacINTOSH?; 16 Oct 1683; New Shoreham, RI/Lyme, CT
MOTT, John & Elizabeth _?_; b 1694; N. Kingston, RI/Kingstown
MOTT, John & Elizabeth _?_; ca 1698?; Mamaroneck, NY
MOTT, Joseph (1661-1735) & ?Marian/?Mary [SMITH]; ca 1690?; ?Hempstead, LI/Cow Neck
MOTT, Nathaniel & Hannah SHOOTER, w Peter; 25 Dec 1656; Braintree
MOTT, Nathaniel (1661-) & 1/wf Hepzibah WINSLEY/WINSLOW?; 29 Nov 1682; New Shoreham, RI/Block Island
MOTT, Nathaniel & 2/wf Sarah TOSH/McINTOSH?; 23 Jan 1693/4; New Shoreham, RI
MOTT, Richbell & Elizabeth THORNE; m lic 14 Oct 1696, [1695]; NY
MOTT, Samuel (1669-) & 1/wf Mary [BROCKWAY]; 6 Apr 1692; Lyme, CT
MOTT, Samuel (1678-1727) & Mary WOLTERTON (-1729); b 1709, b 1701?; Dartmouth/Newport, RI
MOTT, _?_ & [Lydia WING]
MOULD, Edward (-1688, ae 58) & Wellmude _?_ (-1684, ae ca 58); Salem
MOULD, Hugh & Martha COIT (1644-1730), m/2 Nathaniel WHITE 1694+; 11 Jun 1662; New London, CT
MOULD, Samuel & Mary SWAINE (-1709); 3 Feb 1686/7; Charlestown
MOULD, Thomas (ca 1648-1690+) & Mary [KEYSER]; b 16 Mar 1677/8; Salem
MOLLES, Thomas & Sarah _?_; b 1700; Boston
MOULDER, Nicholas & Christian _?_; 10 Jun 1653; Barbados/Boston
MOULTHROP, John & Abigail BRADLEY (-1743); 29 Jun 1692; New Haven
MOULTHROP, Matthew (-1668) & Jane _?_ (-1672); in Eng?, b 1638; New Haven
MOULTHROP, Matthew (-1691) & Hannah THOMPSON (-1681), m/2 Samuel HOTCHKISS ?b 1701?; 26 Jun 1662; New Haven
MOLTROOP, Matthew (1670-) & [Mary BROCKETT?] (1675-); b 1694; New Haven
MOULTON, Benjamin & Hannah [WALL] (1658-); b 1680; Hampton, NH
MOULTON, Daniel (-1671) & Hannah [WOODIS?]; Great Island
MOULTON, Daniel & Mary _?_; b 1700; Hampton, NH
MOULTON, Henry (?1623-1701) & [Sobriety] HILTON (1653-1718, 1718/19, ae 85), Dover; 20 Nov 1651; Hampton, NH
MOLTON, Jacob & Ruhamah HAYDEN (1641-); 3 Jul 1663; Charlestown
MOULTON, James (-1678/9) & [Mary] _?_; b 1637; Salem/Wenham
MOULTON, James (1637/8-1696) & Elizabeth ADDAMS/ADAMS; 10 Feb 1662; Wenham
MOULTON, Jeremiah (-1731) & 1/wf Mary [YOUNG] (-24 Jun 1722); aft 12 Aug 1673, bef 27 Jun 1678
MOULTON, John (-1650) & Anne GRENE/GREENE; St. Margaret, Armsby, Eng, 24 Sep 1623; Hampton, NH
MOULTON, John (-1707) & Lydia TAYLOR; 23 Mar 1666, [1665-6], 1665/6; Hampton, NH
MOULTON, John (1639-1741) & Elizabeth CORY; 16 Sep 1684; Marblehead
MOULTON, John & Mary PERKINS (1673-1707); 26 Oct 1692; Hampton, NH
MOULTON, John & Sarah CONANT; 16 Aug 1693; Beverly
MOULTON, Jonathan & Sarah HERRICK; 5 Jan 1699/1700, 1699; Salem
MOULTON, Joseph & Bethiah SWAYNE (1652-); 24 May 1677; Hampton, NH
MOULTON, Joseph (-1691/2?), York, ME, & _?_ [LITTLEFIELD]; ca 1678?;
MOULTON, Joseph & 1/wf Mary [PULMAN]?; ?30 Dec 1697; York, ME
MOULTON, Josiah & 1/wf Lucy [MARSTON] (-1688); b 1686; Hampton, NH
MOULTON, Josiah & 2/wf Elizabeth WORTHINGTON; 25 Apr 1689; Hampton, NH
MOULTON, Robert (-1655) & [?Deborah] _?_/Mary SMITH; in Eng, b 1622, b 1620?, 15 May 1595?; Salem/Charlestown

MOULTON, Robert (-1665) & Abigail [GOODE?]/GOADE/CROADE?/GOAD; ca Feb 1640, b 1642; Salem
MOULTON, Robert (1644-1731±) & Mary COOKE (1650-1732+); 17 Jul 1672; Salem
MOULTON, Robert & Lucy (MARSTON?) SMITH (1665-); 29 May 1689; Hampton, NH
MOULTON, Robert & Hannah GROVE/LaGROVE; 12 Apr 1698; Beverly/Salem/Windham, CT
MOULTON, Samuel & Sarah __?__; 30 Nov 1665, doubtful; Rehoboth
MOULTON, Samuel & Sarah PHELE (-1698); 20 Jun 1678; Wenham/Rehoboth
MOULTON, Samuel (1642-) & Elizabeth (NORRIS) GLOVER, w Joseph; 18 Jul 1700; Salem/Rehoboth
MOLTON, Thomas (-1657) & Jane __?__; b 1633; Charlestown
MOULTON, Thomas (-1684+) & Martha/Mary? __?__; b 1639; Newbury/Hampton, NH/York, ME
MOULTON, William (1617-1664) & Margaret [PAGE] (1629-1699?), m/2 John SANBORN 1671; ca 1645?; Hampton, NH
MOULTON, William (1664-1732) & 1/wf Abigail WEBSTER (1662-1723); 27 May 1685; Newbury
MOULTON, William & 1/wf Mary __?__ (-3 Mar 1694)
MOULTON, William & Jane CONANT; 4 Jul 1695; Beverly/Salem/Wenham/Ipswich/Windham, CT
MOULTON, William & Hannah [MERRILL]; 1695
MOUNTFORD, Edmund (-1691) & Elizabeth [CARWITHY] (ae 57 in 1691), w Joshua; b 1664; Boston
MOUNTFORD, Edmund & Elizabeth __?__; b 1695; Boston
MOUNTFORD, Henry (-1691, ae 54) (ae 19 in 1656) & Ruth [WISWALL] (-1697); b 9 Jul 1687, b 1684?; Boston
MOUNTFORD, Henry & Sarah DASSET; 27 Sep 1694; Boston
MOUNTFORD, John (-1724) & Mary COCK; 17 Jan 1693; Boston
MOUSALL, John[1] (1595-1665) & Joanna [THOMPSON?]; ca 1628; Charlestown/Woburn
MOUSALL, John (-1698) & Sarah BROOKS (-1705); 13 May 1653, no issue; Woburn
MOUSALL, John[2] (-1703) & 1/wf Elizabeth [RICHARDSON] (1635-1685, ae 51); b 1659; Charlestown
MOUSALL, John[2] (-1703) & 2/wf Eleanor HOW (-1694); 26 Mar 1686; Charlestown/Cambridge
MOUSAL, John (1666-1713) & Dorothy HIT/HETT (1673-), m/2 Joseph LAMSON 1715; 1 Jul 1691; Concord/Charlestown
MOUSALL, John[2] (-1703, ae 74) & 3/wf Mercy MIRICK; 24 Apr 1695; Charlestown/Boston
MOUSALL, Ralph[1] (-1657) (mentions cousin Nathaniel BELL) & Alice __?__ (-1674, 1677?); b 1630; Charlestown
MOUSALL, Ralph (-1718) & Anna FOWLE (ca 1661-1742); 6 Aug 1689 at Boston; Charlestown
MOUSALL, Thomas[2] (1633-1713) & 1/wf Mary [RICHARDSON] (1638-1677); b 1655; Charlestown
MOUSALL, Thomas (1633-1713) & Mary MOORE (-1690), w John; 21 Apr 1679; Charlestown
MOWER, John & Susannah MARSHALL; 21 Jul 1673; Lynn
MOWER, Richard (-1689) & 1/wf Alice __?__ (-1661); b 1642; Lynn
MOWER, Richard (-1689) & Elizabeth WILD/WILDES, w William; 6 Nov 1662; Lynn
MOWER, Samuel & Joanna [MARSHALL]?; b 1676; Lynn
MOWRY, Benjamin (1649-1719+) & Martha (HAZARD) POTTER, w Ichabod; ca 1676; Roxbury, MA/Kingston, RI
MOWRY, John (?1645-1690) & Mary __?__ (-1690±); b 1672?; Providence
MOWRY, John (-1730+) & Elizabeth CLARK (?1679); 29 Mar 1699; Providence
MOWRY/MORREY, Jonathan (1637-1708) & 1/wf Mary (BARTLETT) FOSTER (-1692), w Richard; 8 Jul 1659; Plymouth
MOWRY, Jonathan (-1723) & Hannah BOURNE (1667-); 24 Jan 1689/90; Plymouth
MOWRY, Jonathan (-1708) & 2/wf Hannah (PINSON) (YOUNG) WETHERELL/WITHERELL (1642-1720+), w George, w John; b 27 Jun 1694; Plymouth
MOWRY, Joseph (1647-1716) & Mary [WILBUR] (1654-1720); ca 1671?; Little Compton, RI/Kingston, RI/Jamestown, RI
MOWRY, Joseph (-1755) & Alice WHIPPLE (1675-1746+); 3 Jun 1695; Providence/Smithfield, RI
MOWRY, Nathaniel (1644-1718) & Joanna INMAN (-1718+); ?Jul 1666, wit 28 Aug 1666; Providence
MOWRY, Roger (-1668) & 1/wf Elizabeth __?__; b 1637, b 1641; Salem

MOWRY, Roger (-1668, 1666?) & Mary [JOHNSON] (-1670) (sis of Mrs. Lydia BANKS, kinswoman of Isaac HEATH), m/2 John KINSLEY 1674; b 1636?, aft 1641?, ca 1644?; Plymouth/Salem/Providence

MOWRY, Thomas (1652-1717?) & Susanna NEWELL (1656-); 6 Sep 1673; Roxbury

MOXON, George (1600/1602-1687) & _?_; b 1641(2?), b 1642; Dorchester/Springfield

MOYCE, Joseph & Hannah _?_ (-1655); b 1627; Salisbury

MUCHMORE, James? & Sarah [?MENDUM]; b 1667; NH

MUCHMORE, John & Ann/?Amie [WELLCOME/WELCOM/WELCOMB; Isles of Shoals

MUCHMORE, Walter & [Jane] [TURPIN], m/2 James LEACH ca 1654; Isles of Shoals

MUDD, Henry & Ruth [COLE], w James; aft 28 Aug 1655; Charlestown (went to Eng?)

MUDD, Peter & _?_; b 1653?; Charlestown

MUDGE, George (-1685) & Elizabeth SHIPPIE (-1678); 27 May 1673; Charlestown

MUDGE, Gilbert & _?_; b 1661; Hog Island

MUDGE, Jarvis & Rebecca [ELSEN], w Abraham; aft 8 May 1648, b 9 Dec 1649; Wethersfield, CT

MUDGE, Jarvis (1672-1741) & Jane [HAWXHURST]; b 1701?, no issue?; Hempstead, LI

MUDGE, John (1654-1733) & Ruth [BURDITT]; b 1685; Malden

MUDGE, Micah (1650-1729, Hebron) & Mary ALEXANDER; 23 Sep 1670; Northampton

MUDGE, Moses & Elizabeth WEEDEN/WOOD?; 17 Dec 1665, 1 Dec 1668; Warwick, RI

MUDGE, Moses (1652-1729) & Mary _?_; 1671; Oyster Bay, LI

MUDGE, Thomas (1624-) & Mary _?_ (?1628-); b 1648; Malden

MUDGETT, Thomas & Sarah (CLEMENT) MORRILL (-Aug 1694), w Abraham; 8 Oct 1665; Salisbury

MUDGET, Thomas & Ann (FRENCH) [LONG], w Richard, m/3 Alexander MAGOON; b 1696, ca 4 Sep 1694; Salisbury

MULBERRY/MULBERY/?MULLERY, John & Abigail _?_; b 1672; Boston

MULFORD, Benjamin & _?_; b 1699?; East Hampton, LI/Cape May, NJ

MULFORD, John (-1686, ae 80?) & 1/wf _?_; b 1644; East Hampton, LI/Salem/Southampton, LI/

MULFORD, John (-1686, ae 80?) & 2/wf Friediswude OSBORN, w William; - May 1663; New Haven/East Hampton

MULFORD, John (1650-1734) & 1/wf Mary [BLUX] (-1705); b 1683; East Hampton

MULFORD, John & Peace PERRY; 20 Oct 1697; Sandwich/RI

MULFORD, John (1670-1730) & Jemima HIGENS/HIGGINS (-1723); 1 Nov 1699; Eastham

MULFORD, Samuel (1644-1725) & 1/wf Esther/Hester [CONKLIN] (ca 1654, 1653-1717, ae 64); b 1678; Southampton, LI/East Hampton, LI

MULFORD, Thomas (ca 1640-1706) & 1/wf _?_; b 1666; Eastham

MULFORD, Thomas (-1706) & 2/wf Hannah (WILLIAMS) [SMITH] (-1718), dau Thomas WILLIAMS, w John; b 1669, 1673; Eastham

MULFORD, Thomas (?1650, 1655-1727, 1732 in 77th y) & Mary [CONKLING] (1658, 1659?-1743 in 85th y); ca 1678; ?East Hampton, LI

MULFORD, Thomas, Jr. (-1710?) & Mary BASSET/BASSETT, dau Nathaniel; 28 Oct 1690; Eastham

MULFORD, William (1620-1687) & 1/wf [Sarah AKERS], dau Thomas; b 1650; East Hampton, LI

MULFORD, William (1620-1687) & 2/wf Sarah HEDGES, dau Wm.

MULFORD, William & _?_; b 1700; East Hampton, LI

MULLEGIN/MILLIKEN/MULLIKEN, Hugh & Eleanor _?_ (1668-); b 1681; Boston

MULLEGAN, John (-1749, ae 85?) & Elizabeth [ALGER] (1669-1756); b 1691; Boston/Martha's Vineyard

MULLICKEN/MULLICAN, Robert & Rebecca SAVERY/SAVORY; 15 Dec 1687; Newbury

MULIGAN, Thomas & Elizabeth _?_; b 1693; Boston

MULENER/MOLYNEUS, Hosman & Elizabeth _?_; b 1696; Westchester, NY

MULLINER, Thomas[2] & Martha [BROWN]; Debach, Suffolk, Eng, b 1656; New Haven/Westchester, NY

MULLINER, Thomas (-ca 1690) & Elizabeth [HORSEMAN]; 1617; New Haven

MOLLINS, Thomas & Mary _?_; b 1700; Boston

MULLINES, William (-1621) & Alice [PORETIERS]?; ca 1595?; Plymouth

MULLINS, William (-1673) & 1/wf Elizabeth _?_; bef 1642; Duxbury

MULLINGS, William (-1673) & 2/wf Ann BELL (-1667), w Thomas; 7 May 1656; Boston/Braintree

MOLYNES, _?_ & [Hannah HUBBARD], dau George

MUMFORD, Edmund & Elizabeth (FARNHAM) [CARWITHY], w Joshua; 1663, 1663+
MUMFORD, John (-1749) & Peace PERRY (-1740, ae 69); 20 Oct 1697, 1699?; Newport/Kings Town/Exeter, RI
MUMFORD, Peleg (1659-1745) & _?_ ; b 1692/3; S. Kings Town, RI
MUMFORD, Stephen (1639-1701) & Ann _?_ (1635-1698); b 1665; Newport
MUMFORD, Stephen (1666-1731) & 1/wf Mary TIMBERLAKE (1673-1715); 30 Aug 1697; Boston/Newport
MUMFORD, Thomas (-1692±) & Sarah [SHERMAN] (1636-); b 1656; Portsmouth, RI/Kings Town, RI
MUMFORD, Thomas (1656-1726) & 1/wf Abigail _?_ (1670-1707); b 1687; S. Kings Town, RI
MUMFORD, William (-1718) & Ruth [COPP]? (1643-); b 1671; Boston
MUNDAY, Henry (had nephew Philip WOLLIDGE) & _?_ ; b 1654; Salisbury
MUNDAY/MUNDEN?, Stephen & Deborah _?_ (1630/1); Portsmouth, NH
MUNDEN, Abraham (-1645) & Anne MUNSON, m/2 John STEBBINS 1646; 16 May 1644; Springfield
MUNGER, John (1660-1732) & Mary EVERTS/EVARTS (1674-1734); 3 Jun 1684; Guilford, CT
MUNGER, Nicholas (1628-1668) & Sarah [HALL], m/2 Dennis CRAMPTON; 2 Jun 1659; Guilford, CT
MUNGER, Samuel (-1717) & Sarah [HAND] (1665-1751), m/2 Caleb WOODWORTH; b 1689, 1 Oct 1688, 11 Oct 1688; Guilford, CT
MOUNTJOY, Benjamin (-1658, 1659?) & Martha [WALTON] (1632-); b 1655?; Salem/Marblehead
MONTJOY, George (1627-1681) & Mary [PHILLIPS] (1636-), m/2 Robert LAWRENCE ca 1686/7, 1684?, m/3 Stephen CROSS 1692/3; b 1653; Boston/Dorchester/Falmouth, ME
MONJOYE, George (1656-1698) & Mary [NOYES], m/2 John SMITH; b 1687; Sudbury
MUNJOY, John (1653-1676) & ?Temperance _?_ ; Falmouth, ME
MOUNTJOY, Walter (-1684) & Elizabeth OWEN, w Morgan; 18 Jan 167-; Salem
MUNN, Benjamin (-1675) & Abigail (BURT) BALL (1623?-1705), w Francis, m/3 Thomas STEBBINS 1676; 2 Apr 1649, 12 Apr 1649; Springfield
MUNN, James (1657-1743) & Mary (MOODY) PANTHERON?/PANTON?/PANTHERN?/PATTEN?; 27 Jun 1698, 29? Jun; Deerfield/Colchester, CT
MUNN, John (1652-1684) & Abigail PARSONS (1662-), m/2 John RICHARDS 1686; 23 Dec 1680; Westfield
MUNN, Nathaniel (1661-1743) & Sarah CHAPIN (1668-1747); 24 Mar 1689, 1689/90?; Springfield
MUNN, Samuel & Mary _?_ ; b 1678; Woodbury, CT
MUNNINGS, Edmund (1595-1667) (returned to Eng) & 1/wf Mary _?_ ; in Eng, b 1626; Dorchester
MUNNING, Edmund (1595-1667) (returned to Eng) & 2/wf Markiet _?_ ; Dorchester
MUNNINGS, George (1597-1658) & 1/wf Elizabeth GROOME (1593-1651+); Rattlesden, Eng, 12 Jun 1620; Watertown
MUNNING, George (-1674+) & Hannah [BOYER]; b 1655; Boston
MUNNINGS, George (-1658) & 2/wf Johanna [BOYER] (1612-), w Simon, m/3 John LAUGHTON/LAWTON 1659; 23 Jun 1657; Boston
MUNNINGS/MANNING?, George (1655-) (see George MANNING) & Mary MIXTER/MIXER? (1656-); 1 Nov 1680; Charlestown
MUNNINGS, John & Jane POPE; b 1700
MUNNINGS, Mahalaleel (1632-1660) & Hannah [WISWALL] (1636-1694), m/2 William READ 1661?, m/3 Thomas OVERMAN 1672?; b 1655; Dorchester
MUNNINGS, Return (1640-1706) & Sarah HOBART, dau Edmund; 9 Dec 1664; Hingham/Boston
MUNNION, Edward & Sarah PROCTOR/PROCTER; 23 Oct 1700; Lynn/Salem
MANSELL, Samuel & Katharine _?_ ; b 1667; Boston
MANSELL, Samuel & Elizabeth _?_ ; b 1686; Boston
MUNSELL, Thomas (-1712) & Lydia _?_ ; b 1690; Lyme/Windsor, CT
MUNSELL, William & Katherine _?_ ; b 1665; Boston
MANSELL, William & Rebecca JACOBSON; 29 Jun 1694; Boston
MUNCY, Francis (-1675) & Hannah ADAMS, m/2 John RAMSDEN; 6 Dec 1659; Ipswich/Brookhaven, LI
MUNCEY, John (1660-Feb 1690/1) & Hannah [BREWSTER], m/2 Samuel THOMPSON; ca 1685/8?; Brookhaven, LI

MUNSEY, William (-1698) & Margaret [?CLEMENT]; b 1676; Dover, NH/Kittery, ME/Brookhaven, LI
MUNSEY, William & Rosamond JACKLIN; 10 Jan 1698/9; Dover, NH
MUNT, Thomas & 1/wf Dorothy _?_ (-1639/40); b 1639/40; Boston
MUNT, Thomas & 2/wf Faith _?_ ; b 1645; Boston
MUNT, Thomas (-1664) & 3/wf Eleanor _?_, m Thomas HILL by 1668; Boston
MORDOW, John (-1756) & 1/wf Lydia YOUNG (-1701+); 10 Dec 1686; Plymouth
MURDOCK, Robert (-1754) & 1/wf Hannah STEDMAN (1667-1727); 28 Apr 1692; Roxbury
MURPHY/MORFREY, Bryan & Margaret MAYHOONE; 20 Jul 1661; Boston
MURRAY, Jonathan (-1747) & Anna/Ann BRADLEY (1669-1749); 17 Jul 1688; Guilford, CT
MURREY, William & Mary _?_ /[Elizabeth GOULD?] (1677-); b 1691/2, b 1697; Salem
MUSSILOWAY/now SILLOWAY, Daniel (alias Roger WALDRON) & 1/wf Ann (WHEELER) CHASE (-1687), w Aquila; 14 Jan 1672; Salisbury/Newbury
MUSSILOWAY, Daniel & Mary LONG; 7 Sep 1687; Salisbury/Newbury
MUZEET, Thomas & 1/wf Joanna FEYE; ca 1700, Oct 1700; Kittery, ME
MUZEET, Joseph & Mary [WALFORD] (1656-); b 1680, b 8 Mar 1680; Great Isle, NH
MUZZEY, Benjamin & Alice [DEXTER]; b 1651; Malden
MUZZEY, Benjamin (1657-1732) & 1/wf Sarah [LANGHORNE] (1660-1711); b 1683, ca 1681; Cambridge
MUZZEY, ?Edward & Esther _?_, m/2 William ROSCOE 1636?, went to Hartford; b 1633; Cambridge
MUSSEY, Jeremiah & Elizabeth [PERKINS]; b 1699(1700?); Salisbury
MUSSEY, John (-1690) & Lydia _?_ ; b 1635?; Newbury/?Ipswich
MUSSEY, John (-1690) & Elizabeth _?_ ; b 1689?; Salisbury
MUZZY, Joseph (-1680) & Esther JACKMAN; 9 Feb 1670, 1670/1; Newbury
MUZZY, Joseph (1677-) & Joanna PETENGALL/PETTINGILL, m int 2 Nov 1700; Newbury
MUSSEY, Robert (1589-1674) & _?_ ; b 1619; Portsmouth, NH
MUSSEY, Robert (-1644) & 1/wf _?_ ; b 1629; Malden/?Ipswich
MUSSEY, Robert (-1644) & 2/wf? Bridget [BRADSTREET?/DANE?], m/2 Thomas ROWLANDSON ca 1644/5, m/3 William KERLEY 1659; b 1628; Salisbury/Ipswich
MUSSEY, Thomas & _?_ ; ca 1663/75?; Cape Porpoise
MYGATE, Jacob (1633-) & Sarah WHITING (-1704), m/2 John KING 1683?; m cont 27 Nov 1654; Hartford
MYGATE, Joseph (1596-1680) & Ann _?_ (1602-1686); b 1633; Cambridge/Hartford
MYGATE, Joseph (-1698) & Sarah WEBSTER (1655-1740, 1744), m/2 Bevil WATERS; 15 Nov 1677; Hartford
MYNGES/?MYNGS, Christopher & Joyce _?_ ; b 1699(1700?); Boston

NANNEY, Robert (-1663, Boston) & Catherine [WHEELWRIGHT] (1630/2-), m/2 Edward NAYLOR bef 1667; b 1652?, b 1654; Boston
NAPTOLI, _?_ & Rachel _?_ ; b 1695; Newport
NARAMORE/NARRAMORE, Richard & Ann [WATERS]; b 1676; Boston
NARRAMORE, Thomas & Hannah [SMITH]/Hannah (SMITH) SWELL, w John; b 1671; Boston/NH
NASH, Edward (1623-) & 1/wf [?Hannah] _?_ ; b 1650?, b 1651(2?); Stratford, CT/Norwalk
NASH, Edward & Rose (SHERWOOD) (RUMBLE/RUMBULL) BARLOW, w Thomas, w Thomas; aft? 8 Sep 1658, bef 1673; ?Fairfield
NASH, Francis (-1713) & 1/wf Elizabeth _?_ ; b 1677; Braintree
NASH, Francis (-1713) & 2/wf Mary (PURCHASE) NILES, w Increase; 5 Apr 1697, ?2 May, 2 Jul 1697; Braintree
NASH, Gregory (-1631) & _?_ (-1630); b 1630, b 1614?; Charlestown
NASH, Isaac & Margaret (?MATTEN) EVERETT (-1664?), w William, m/3 Abraham CONLEY 1664?; b 1656; Dover, NH
NASH, Isaac (-1662) & Phebe _?_ , m/2 John PIERCE/PEARCE 1663?; bef Jul 1662; Dover

NASH, Isaac & Dorothy **LITTLEFIELD**; 6 Dec 1694; Braintree/Kingston, RI
NASH, Jacob (-1718) & Abigail [**DYER**] (1647-); b 1667, b 1666; Weymouth
NASH, James (-1650) & _?_ ; b 1626?; Weymouth
NASH, James & Sarah [**SIMMONS**]; b 1669; Weymouth
NASH, James & Hannah _?_ ; b 1701; Weymouth
NASH, John (?1615-1687) & Elizabeth [**TAPP**] (-1676); b 1647(8?); New Haven
NASH, John & Mary _?_ ; b 1662; Weymouth
NASH, John (-1712) & Rebecca [**SMITH**] (1644-), ?m/2 Jeremiah **BELCHER**; b 1667; Boston/Weymouth
NASH, John (-1682, 1683?) & Elizabeth (**HITCHCOCK**) **HOWD**, w Anthony; 22 Aug 1677; Bramford, CT
NASH, John (-1713) & Mary [**BARLEY**]/**BARBY/BARLOW/COMBS** (-1711); 1 May 1684; Norwalk, CT
NASH, John (1667-1743) & 1/wf Hannah **PORTER** (1670-1689); 29 Mar 1689; Hadley
NASH, John (1667-1743) & 2/wf Elizabeth **KELLOGG** (1673-1750); 27 Nov 1691; Hadley
NASH, John & Mary _?_ ; b 1695; Weymouth
NASH, Joseph (-1678) & 1/wf Mary [?**MORTON**]; b 1650; New Haven/Hartford
NASH, Joseph (-1678) & 2/wf Margaret [**SMITH**], w Arthur, m/3 Stephen **HART** ca 1679?; b 15 Jun 1665; New Haven/Hartford
NASH, Joseph, Boston & 1/wf Elizabeth [**HOLBROOK**]; b 1674, b 1675; Weymouth
NASH, Joseph & Grace _?_ ; bef 1687; Boston
NASH, Joseph & 1/wf Phebe **MARSH** (1676?-); 17 Mar 1698/9, 17 May 1699; Hingham
NASH, Joseph (-1732, ae 58) & Hannah **CURTIS**; 1 Jan 1700; Scituate
NASH, Joshua (son Thomas b 1660, called son of Joseph) & Elizabeth **PORTER**; 23 Feb 1658; Boston
NASH, Robert (-1661) & [Sarah] [**WHEELER?**] (-1688, ae 89); b 1630?, b 1638; Charlestown/Boston
NASH, Samuel (1602?-) (ae 80 in 1682) & _?_ ; ca 1623?, ca 1620-40?; Plymouth/Duxbury
NASH, Thomas (-1658) & Margery [**BAKER**] (-1656, 1657); in Eng, b 1615; Boston/New Haven
NASH, Thomas (-1728) & Hannah **COLEMAN** (1667-1722); - Aug 1685, 1 Aug; Hadley
NASH, Thomas & Mary **NYLES**; 2 Jul 1697; Braintree
NASH, Timothy (1626-1699) & Rebecca [**STONE**] (-1709); ca 1657, m 1657; New Haven/Hartford
NASH, Timothy & Mary **FOSTER** (1671-); 2 Apr 1694; Boston
NASH, William (-bef 1638) & Mary _?_ (-1674); b 1634; Charlestown
NASH, _?_ & _?_ ; b 1677; Newbury
NASON, Baker & Elizabeth [**HATCH**]; b 1692, by 1692; Berwick, ME
NASON, Benjamin & 1/wf Martha **KENNEY/CANNEY**; 30 Jun 1687; Dover
NASON, John (1640-1719) & 1/wf Hannah **HEARD**; 6 Nov 1674; Dover, NH
NASON, John (1640-1719), Berwick & 2/wf Bridget **WEYMOUTH**, Berwick; 7 Oct 1687, 1687; Kittery, ME
NASON, Jonathan (-1691) & Sarah [**JENKINS**], m/2 John **KEY** 1691+; by 1691, ca 1670?; Kittery, ME
NASON, Joseph & Mary [**SWAIN**] (1661-1714); b 1682; Nantucket
NASON, Richard[1] & 1/wf Sarah [**BAKER?**]; b 1640; Kittery, ME
NASON, Richard[1] & 2/wf Abigail [**FOLLETT**] (1626-), w Nicholas; aft 1663; Dover
NASON, Richard (-1675?) & Shuah [**COLCORD**] (1662-), m/2 John **DOUGLAS** 1687; Kittery, ME
NAYLOR, Edward & Katharine (**WHEELWRIGHT**) **NANNEY** (-1716), w Robert; b 1667; Boston/Charlestown/Salisbury
NAILOR/NAYLOR, James (-1671) (did he marry?)
NEALE, Andrew & Millicent _?_ ; b 1665; Boston
NEAL, Andrew (ca 1665-1739) & Katharine/Catherine [**FURBISH/FURBUSH**] (-1739+); ca 1694; Kittery, ME
NEAL, Arthur, Kennebec & _?_ ; b 21 Oct 1689; Charlestown
NEALE, Benjamin (-1746, in 78th y), Braintree & Lydia **PAYNE** (1670-), Braintree; 20 Jan 1688/9, 22 Jan 1688, 1688/9; Braintree/Milton
NEALE, Edward (-1698) & Martha **HART**; 24 Jan 1662; Weymouth/Hatfield
NEALE, Francis (1626-1696) & Jane **ANDREWS** (dau Samuel & Jane _?_), m/2 _?_ **COLLINS**; Casco, ME/Salem

NEALE, Francis (-1691) & Sarah [PICKWORTH] (-1697+); b 1688; Salem
NEALE, Henry (1607-1678) & 1/wf Martha _?_ (-bur 23 Jul 1653) (called Martha NOLL); b 1643; Braintree
NEALE, Henry (1607-1678, 1691?, 1688?) & 2/wf Hannah PRAY (-1691+); 14 Feb 1655/6; Braintree/Providence
NEAL, Henry & Sarah TEMPLE; 1 Aug 1700; Boston
NEALE, Jeremiah (1695-1722) & 1/wf Sarah HART (-1672); 15 Jun 1668; Salem
NEALE, Jeremiah (-1722) & 2/wf Mary BUFFUM (-1682+); 22 Sep 1675, ?2 Sep; Salem
NEALS, Jeremiah (?doubtful) & Ruth (INGERSOLL) ROSE (1649-), w Richard; aft 1684; ?Salem
NEAL, John (-1672) & Mary [LAWES], dau Francis, m/2 Andrew MANSFIELD 1673; b 1672, b 1656?, b 1666, b 1662, b 1647; Salem
NEALE, John (-1704) & Joanna [SEARL]; ca 1670; Kittery, ME
NEALE, John (-1679) & Ann [NICHOLS], m/2 William STERLING 1683; b 1673; Salem
NEALE, John (1673-1699) & Martha SKERRY (1674-), m/2 _?_ WELLS of Boston; b 1700, b 29 Dec 1694; ?Boston/Salem
NEALE, Joseph (1662-) & Judith [CROAD]; b 1682; Salem
NEALE, Joseph (1660-1737) & Mary _?_ (-1747, ae 83); b 1689; Braintree
NEALE/NEILL, Nathan & Mary _?_ ; b 1663; Hampton, NH
NEALES, Nicholas & _?_ [?MESSENGER]; b 1676; Boston
NEALE, Samuel (1647-) & Abigail BENNIMAN/BENJAMIN?, wid?; 18 Apr 1678; Braintree
NEALE, Samuel & [Abigail COLLINS], ?m/2 Henry ELKINS; b 1689; Salem/Stowe
NEAL, Samuel (1661-1702) & Jane [FOSS]; b 1697, ca 168-; ?Greenland, NH
NEAL, Samuel, Westfield & Elizabeth GOZZARD; 2 Aug 1699; Simsbury
NEALE, Walter (?1633-) & Mary [AYRES?]; b 1661; Dover, NH
NEAL, _?_ (see Nicholas NEALE) & Ann?/Rebecca/Lydia/Priscilla MESSINGER, dau Henry[1]; b 1686; ?Boston
NECK, John & Mary RICHARDS (-1725+); 22 Mar 1675/6; Lynn
NEEDHAM, Anthony (1628-1696+) & Ann POTTER (-1696+); 10 Jan 1655, 1655/6; Salem
NEEDHAM, Anthony (1663-1757/8) & Mary SWINERTON (1670-); 3 Jan 1695; Salem
NEEDHAM, Daniel & Ruth CHADWELL; 24 Feb 1658/9; Lynn
NEEDHAM, Edmund (-1677) & Joan/Jane? _?_ (-1674, ae 65; b 1639; Lynn
NEADOM, Ezekiel & Sarah KING; 27 Oct 1669; Lynn
NEEDHAM, Ezekiel (1670-) & Priscilla HALSEY; m int 10 Mar 1695/6; Boston
NEEDHAM, John & Elizabeth _?_, m/2 Nicholas HODSON/HODSDON?; b 25 May 1648
NEEDHAM, John (-1690) & 1/wf Hannah SAVIL; - May 1669; Braintree
NEEDHAM, John (-1690) & Elizabeth HICKS (-1691); 10 Oct 1679; Cambridge/Boston
NEEDHAM, John & Keziah _?_ ; b 1692; Boston
NEEDHAM, ?Nathaniel (see Daniel) & _?_ ; b 1682, had Ruth; Lynn
NEEDHAM, Nicholas & ?Ann _?_ ; b 1636?; Braintree/Exeter, NH/ME
NEEDHAM, _?_ & [Sarah FAIRFIELD] (1655-), m/2 Thomas ABBE 1683; ca Mar 1680/1
NEEDHAM, ?Anthony & 1/wf Sarah HOLTON (1669), dau Joseph; Salem
NEFF, William (-1689), Newbury & Mary CORLIS/CORLISS (1646-); 23 Jan 1665, 23 Jun 1665; Haverhill
NEGUS, Benjamin (-1696) & Elizabeth _?_ ; b 1640; Boston
NEGUS, Isaac (-1700) & Hannah ANDREWS (?1659, 1643-), m/2 William CORBETT; 7 Apr 1679; Taunton/Swansea
NEGUS, Jabez (1648-1723) & Sarah BROWN; 9 Jan 1693; Boston
NEGOOSE, Jonathan (1607-) & Jane (DIGHTON) [LUGG], w John; b 27 Oct 1647?; Boston
NEGUS, Thomas & Sarah _?_ ; b 1694(5?); Boston
NEGUS, _?_ & [Hannah PHILLIPS] (1643-); Charlestown
NEIGHBOR/NEIGHBOUR, James (-1671?) (ae 46 in 1663) & Lettice _?_ ; b 1657; Boston
NAYBOUR, James & Rachel PASCO?, w John; b 1701?, (1706+); ?Huntington, LI (she had dau Rachel who m John SHORES bef 1707)
NELSON, Charles (-1688) & Mary _?_ (-1716+); b 1665?; Kittery, ME
NELSON, Gershom (1672-1727) & Abigail ELITHORP/ELITHORPE (1678-1765); 17 Jul 1700; Rowley/Menden
NELSON, John (-1697) & 1/wf Sarah WOOD (-1676); 28 Nov 1667; Plymouth
NELSON, John (-1697) & 2/wf Lydia (BARTLETT) [BARNABY] (1647-1691?), w James; ca 1677; Plymouth/Middleboro

NELSON, John & Hendrica __?__; Mamaroneck, NY
NELSON, John (1654-1734) & Elizabeth [TAYLOR] (1667-1734), niece of Gen. STOUGHTON; b 1688; Dorchester
NELSON, John & Hannah/?Hendrica __?__; ca 1691; Mamaroneck
NELSON, John & 3/wf Patience MORTON; 4 May 1693; Plymouth
NELSON, John & Elizabeth HALEY, m/2 William HOYT 1702, m/3 Nicholas HILLIARD 1718, m/4 John DAM; b 1695?, 1 Jan 1694/5, Jan 1694/5; Kittery, ME
NELSON, John & Mary TRUMBLE; 18 Jan 1697/8; Rowley/Boxford
NELSON, Matthew (-1713) & 1/wf [Jane RAWLINGS?]; b 1684
NELSON, Matthew (-1713) & ?2/wf Agnes [HAWKING?] (Rachel his widow); b 1694, 1690/1; ?Portsmouth, NH
NELSON, Philip (?1636, ?1633-1691) & 1/wf Sarah JEWETT (?ca 1639-14 Feb 1665); 24 Jun 1657; Rowley
NELSON, Philip (-1691) & 2/wf Elizabeth LOWELL (1646-); 1 Jan 1666/7, 1 Nov 1666, 1 Jan 1666; Rowley/Newbury
NELSON, Philip (1659-1721) & Sarah (VARNUM) [HOBSON], w John ; b 1686; Rowley
NELSON, Thomas (-1648) & 1/wf __?__; in Eng, ca 1634, ca 1632?; Rowley
NELSON, Thomas (-1648) & 2/wf Joan DUMMER ; m cont 15 Jan 1641/2, 15 Feb; Rowley
NELSON, Thomas (-1712) & 1/wf Ann LAMBERT (-1678), niece of Mrs. Mary (_?_) (BARKER) ROGERS, wf Rev. Ezekiel; 16 Dec 1659, 10 Dec; Rowley
NELSON, Thomas (-1712) & 2/wf Mary (SKERRY) LUNT (1640-1688), w John; 13 May 1680; Rowley
NELSON, Thomas (1661-1719) & 1/wf Hannah [FRENCH] (1669/70-); b 1688; Rowley
NELSON, Thomas (-1712) & 3/wf Phillipp (ANDREWS) (FELT) PLATTS, w George, w Samuel; 9 Apr 1690; Rowley
NELSON, Thomas & Hope HUCKINS (1677-1782, ae 105); 24 Mar 1697/8; Middleboro
NELSON, William & Martha FORDE (-1680+); 29 Oct 1640; ?Plymouth
NELSON, William & [Elizabeth] [CROSS] (1636-1688+); b 1659(60?); Ipswich
NELSON, William (-1718, Middleboro) & Ruth [FOXEL/FOXWELL] (1641-1726, Middleboro); b 1677?, b 1675?, b 1668; Plymouth
NESBIT/NISBET, Mungo & Sarah (BRYAN) [FITCH], w Samuel; b 9 Dec 1698, 1696, aft 1690, ca 1696; Milford, CT/Stratford, CT
NISBIT, William & Hannah WOODMAN; 5 Jun 1690; Newbury/Salisbury
NEST, Joseph (-1711) & [?Sarah BODDINGTON]; New London, CT
NETTLETON, John (ca 1648-1691) & Martha HULL; 29 May 1670; Killingworth, CT
NETTLETON, John (-1715) & Sarah WOODMANSE; 21 Jan 1692, 1691/2; Killingworth, CT
NETTLETON, Samuel (1605/10-1658?) & Mary __?__ (-1658); ca 1636; Wethersfield, CT/Bramford, CT
NETTLETON, Samuel (ca 1655-ca 1713) & Martha BALDWIN (1663-); 8 Feb 1681, 1681/2; Milford, CT
NETTLETON, Samuel (1672-1702) & Hannah [BARBER], dau William; b 1698; Killingworth, CT
NEVERS, Richard & Martha __?__; b 1689; Woburn
NEVIL/NEVILLE, John & Mary (HUDSON) [CASWELL]; b 1679; Boston
NEVINSON/NEVISON, John (-ca 1695) & Elizabeth ?PAYNTON (1640-1720), m/2 William BOND 1695?, b 1672, ca 1668?; Watertown
NEWBERRY, Benjamin (-1689?) & Mary ALLYN (-1703); 11 Jun 1696; Windsor, CT
NEWBURY, Benjamin (1653-1711, ae 58) & Leah __?__ (1662-1740, ae 78); b 1684; Newport, RI
NEWBERRY, Benjamin (1669-1710) & Hannah (SACKETT) DEWEY (1669-1749), w Thomas, m/3 John MERRIMAN; 3 Mar 1691/2, 3 May 1691, 3 Mar?; Menden/Windsor, CT
NEWBERRY, Richard (-1685) & Sarah [ROBINSON?] (-1702+), dau William; b 1655; Weymouth/Malden
NEWBERRY, Thomas (1594-1636) & 1/wf Joane/?Jane [DABINOTT]; in Eng, b 1620?; Dorchester/Windsor, CT
NEWBERRY, Thomas (1594-1636) & 2/wf Jane [DABINOTT?], m/2 Rev. John WARHAM; in Eng, ca 1630; Windsor, CT
NEWBERRY, Thomas (1657-1688) & Ann FORD (-1691), m/2 Joseph LEONARD 1690; 12 Mar 1676, 1676/7; Windsor, CT
NEWBERRY, Trial (-1705) & Priscilla __?__; b 1686; Malden

NEWBURY, Walter (-1697, ae 49), Newport & Anne COLLINS (1652-1732), London, m/2 Latham
  CLARK 1698; 13 Apr 1675; Newport
NEWBY, George & Mary __?__; b 1680; Boston
NEWBY, George & Elizabeth FOX; b 1693(4?), 7 Apr 1693; Boston/Charlestown
NEWCOMB, Andrew[1] (1618-1686) & 1/wf __?__; b 1640; Charlestown
NEWCOMB, Andrew[2] (?1640-) & 1/wf Sarah __?__ (-1674?); b 1662; ?Kittery, ME
NEWCOMB, Andrew[1] (1618-1686) & 2/wf Grace [RICKS/RIX], w William; b 1664; Boston/?Ed-
  gartown
NEWCOMB, Andrew (-1706/1708) & Anne [BAYES]; ca 1676; Martha's Vineyard
NEWCOMB, Francis (?1592, 1605-1692, ae 100) & Rachel __?__ (1615-); in Eng, b 1632;
  Boston/Braintree
NEWCOMB, John (1634-1722) & 1/wf Ruth __?__ (-1697, ae 61); b 1659; Braintree/Spencer, VA
NEWCOMB, John (1659-) & Elizabeth [EVERETT] (1665-1708); b 1689(90?), b 1685?; Braintree
NEWCOMB, John (1634-1722) & 2/wf Elizabeth __?__, from Bridgewater; aft Jun 1697; Braintree
NEWCOMB, Michael & Anna __?__, m/2 William STEVENS 1700; b 1692; Charlestown
NUCOM, Peter (1648-1725) & 1/wf Susan/Susanna CUTTINGE/CUTTING; 26 Jun 1672, 2 Jun;
  Braintree/Watertown
NEWCOMB, Peter & Mary (PHILLIPS) [HUMPHREY] (1661-1738), w Jonas; aft 30 Oct 1689, b
  1701?, b 1704; Braintree
NEWCOMB, Peter (ca 1674-) & Mercy SMITH; 11 Mar 1699/1700; Sandwich
NEWCOMB, Samuel (1661-1708) & Sarah SHEFFIELD, m/2 Joseph PARMENTER; 24 Apr 1689, 16
  Jan 1689/90; Braintree
NEWCOMB, Simeon (1662-) & __?__; b 1683?; Martha's Vineyard
NEWCOMB, Simon[3] (?1665-1745) & Deborah __?__ (1664-1756); ca 1687; Martha's Vineyard/Leba-
  non, CT
NEWCOMB, Thomas (1668-) & Elizabeth COOKE (1674-); first week in Oct 1693; Eastham
NEWELL, Abraham (-1672, ae 91) & Frances __?__ (-1683); in Eng, b 1620; Roxbury
NEWELL, Abraham (1626-1692) & Susanna RAND; 8 Feb 1651; Roxbury/Charlestown
NEWELL, Abraham (1654-1726) & Abigail RHOADES (-1686?); 21 Jul 1681; Roxbury
NEWELL, Andrew & Mary [PITT] (-1684, in 78th y); b 1634?; Charlestown
NEWELL, Ebenezer (1674-1746) & [Mary] __?__; b 1700; Roxbury
NEWEL, George & Elizabeth __?__; b 1700; Boston
NEWELL, Isaac (1632-1707) & Elizabeth CURTIS (1625-1707); 14 Dec 1659; Roxbury
NEWELL, Isaac, Jr. & Sarah __?__; b 1688; Roxbury
NEWELL, Jacob (1634-1678) & Martha GIBSON (1639-); 3 Nov 1657; Roxbury
NEWELL, Jacob & Joice/Joyce GLEZIN/GLEASON, Sudbury; 23 May 1700; Roxbury
NEWELL, James & Mary __?__; b 1691; Scituate
NEWELL, John (1634-1704) & Hannah LARKIN (1645-1704, ae 60); 15 Feb 1664/5; Charlestown
NEWELL, John (1665-1747) & Hannah HURRY (ca 1662-1745); 22 Dec 1687; Charlestown
NEWELL, Joseph (-1709) & Sarah TUTTLE (-1719, ae 63); 11 Nov 1680; Charlestown
NEWELL, Joseph & Hannah __?__; b 1681; Charlestown
NEWELL, Joseph (-1704) & 1/wf Margaret __?__ (-1689, in 23rd y); b 1687; Charlestown
NEWELL, Joseph (-1704) & Elizabeth TUCK (1672-); 7 Apr 1698; Charlestwon
NEWELL, Samuel (1660-) & Mary HART; 20 Dec 1683; Farmington, CT
NEWELL, Samuel (1667-) & Mary [BROWNING?]; b 1697; Roxbury
NEWELL, Thomas (-1689) & Rebecca [OLMSTEAD] (-1698); b 1643(4?); Hartford/Farmington,
  CT
NEWELL, Thomas (1650-1733, 1723?) & Elizabeth WROTHAM (-1740); 5 Nov 1679; Waterbury,
  CT/Farmington
NEWDIGATE, John (?1580-1665) & 1/wf Lydia __?__ (-1620?); in Eng; Boston
NEWDIGATE, John (?1580-1665) & 2/wf Thomasine HAYES (-1625); London, All Hallows,
  London Wall, 1 Nov 1620; Boston
NEWDIGATE, John (?1580-1666) (72 in 1653) & 3/wf Hannah/Anne (__?__) (HUNT) DRAPER
  (1595-1679, ae 84); in Eng, ca 1625; Boston
NEWDIGATE, Joseph (?1630-1658) & Elizabeth __?__; Boston
NEWGATE, Nathaniel & Sarah LYNDE (-1727); 5 Jun 1688; Charlestown
NEWHALL, Anthony (-1657) & __?__; in Eng, ca 1617?; Lynn
NEWHALL, John & Elizabeth NORMINTON/NORMANTON; 31 Dec 1656; Lynn
NEWHALL, John & 1/wf Elizabeth [LEIGHTON/?PATON] (-1677); 3 Feb 1657/8; Lynn

NEWHALL, John & Esther BARTRAM; 18 Jun 1677; Lynn
NEWHALL, John & 2/wf Sarah FLANDERS (1654-); 17 Jul 1674; Lynn
NEWHALL, John (1664-) & Rebecca COLLINS; 28 Mar 1691; Lynn
NEWHALL, Joseph (1658-1706) & Susanna [FARRAR] (1659-), m/2 Benjamin SIMONS; ca 1677; Lynn
NEWHALL, Nathaniel (1658-) & Rest __?__, relative of Nathaniel HANDFORD?; b 1687; Lynn/Boston
NEWHALL, Nathaniel (1660-1691) & Elizabeth [SYMONDS?], m/2 John INGERSOLL 1697; b 1685; Lynn
NEWHALL, Samuel & Mary HALLEWELL; m int 25 Aug 1685; Lynn
NEWHALL, Samuel (1672-) & Abigail LYNSEY/LINDSEY (1677-); m int 31 Dec 1695; Lynn
NEWHALL, Thomas (-1674) & [?Mary] __?__ (-1655?, 1665?); in Eng, b 1624; Lynn
NEWHALL, Thomas (-1687) & Elizabeth POTTER (-1687); 29 Dec 1652; Lynn
NEWHALL, Thomas (1653-1728) & Rebecca GREEN (1654-); b 9 Nov 1674, Nov 1694?, 1674; Malden/Charlestown/etc.
NEWLAND, Anthony (1650-) & Esther AUSTIN; 16 Dec 1682; Taunton/Northampton
NEWLAND, Jeremiah (-1681) & Katherine __?__ ; b 1657; Taunton
NEWLAND, Jeremiah & Susannah HARRIS; 7 Apr 1696; Bridgewater
NULAND, John (-1694+) (bro of William) & Elizabeth __?__ (-1671); ca 1643/50; Sandwich
NEWLAND, Richard & Elizabeth (WILMOT) [RAWLINGS], w Caleb; b 1695; Boston
NEWLAND, William (-1694) (mentions "brother-in-law" William ALLEN) & Rose (ALLEN) HOLLOWAY, w Joseph, sister of William ALLEN, sister of George ALLEN; 19 May 1648, 1647?; Sandwich
NEWMAN, Antipas (-1672) & Elizabeth WINTHROP (1636-), m/2 Zerubbabel ENDICOTT 1677?; b 1659; Wenham
NEWMAN, Daniel (-1695) & Sarah __?__ ; b 1670?; Stamford, CT
NEWMAN, David (1664-1748) & 1/wf Hannah KENRICK; 8 Oct 1696; Newton/Rehoboth
NEWMAN, Francis (-Nov 1660) & Mary __?__ (-1683), m/2 Rev. Nicholas STREET, m/3 Wm. LEETE 1674+; in Eng, ?ca 1620, no issue; New Haven
NEWMAN, Henry & Margaret DOWNING; 16 Dec 1686; Salem
NEWMAN, John (-1672) & Alice [DUTCH] (-1704?), m/2 John DANE by 1676, m/3 Jeremiah MEACHAM 1684+; b 1648, b 1643?; Ipswich
NEWMAN, John & Sarah SMITH; 9 Nov 1664; Ipswich
NEWMAN, John (1660-) & Ruth [EMERSON]; b 1686; Wenham
NEWMAN, John (1665-1712) & Abigail __?__ (-1742); ca 1686-95?, no issue; New Haven
NEWMAN, Noah (-1678) & Joanna FLINT (1649-1678, Dorchester); 30 Dec 1669; Braintree/Rehoboth
NEWMAN, Richard (-1680+) & __?__ ; b 1656; New Haven
NEWMAN, Robert & __?__ ; b 1642, "went home"; New Haven
NEWMAN, Samuel (1602-1663) & Sybel/Sybil FEATLEY (1604-1672); in Eng, 25 Dec 1623, ?10 Jun 1624; Weymouth/?Rehoboth
NEWMAN, Samuel (1625-1711) & 1/wf Bathsheba/Bethia?/Bethshua? CHICKERING (1640-1687); 6 Dec 1659; Rehoboth
NEWMAN, Samuel & 2/wf Elizabeth (SMITH) VIALL (-29 Sep 1693), w John; aft 8 Aug 1687, bef 1688; Swansea
NEWMAN, Samuel (1656-1689) & Elizabeth ROSE (-1690); 15 Feb 1687/8; New Haven
NEWMAN, Samuel, Rehoboth & Hannah BUNKER/BANKER?, Cambridge; 2 May 1689; Cambridge/Rehoboth
NEWMAN, Samuel (1625-1711) & 3/wf Theodosia (JACKSON) WISWALL (-1725), w Noah; aft 29 Sep 1693, b 1703, ca 1694?; Cambridge/Rehoboth
NEWMAN, Thomas (-1676) & [Sarah] __?__ (-19 Nov 1679); b 1634; Ipswich
NEWMAN, Thomas (?1584-1659, 1660?) & Mary [?MOORTON]; [b 1610]?; Stamford, CT
NEWMAN, Thomas (1634±-1702+) & Hannah MORSE (ca 1645-), dau Anthony; 8 Jun 1665; Ipswich
NEWMAN, Thomas, Dorchester & __?__ ; b 1666; Scituate
NEWMAN, Thomas & Joanna __?__ ; b 1677; Boston
NEWMAN, Thomas & Hester PALMER; 26 Aug 1684; Marblehead
NEWMAN, Thomas & Mary __?__ ; Stamford, CT
NEWMAN, Thomas (1670-1715) & Rose SPARK (1673-1743); 1 Jun 1692; Ipswich

NEWMAN, William (-1676?) & Elizabeth [?BOWSTRED/?BOWSTREET]; b 1642?, b 1657; Stamford, CT

NEWMAN, _?_ & Joanna ANDERSON (1655-); b 20 Sep 1677; Charlestown

NEWMARCH, John (-1697) & Martha [GOULD] (1623-1699); b 1651; Ipswich

NEWMARCH, John (-1691) & Joanna BORMAN/BURNHAM, m/2 Erastus JAMES 1692; 22 Nov 1671; Ipswich

NEWMARCH, John (1672-1754) & 1/wf Mary (HARVEY) HUNKING w Mark; 5 Dec 1699; Kittery, ME

NEWMARCH, Zaccheus (1653-1731) & Frances _?_ (-1731); b 1700; Ipswich

NEWPORT, Richard & Ruth _?_ ; b 1668; Boston

NEWSOM/NEWSON/NEWSOME/NEWSHAM/NOWSHOM, Leonard & Experience TITUS; 18 Jul 1693, 12 Jun 1692, 169-; Rehoboth

NEWTON, Anthony (1614-1704) & _?_ ; b 1647, b 1641; Milton

NEWTON, Benoni (-1706, ae 52) & Joanna _?_ (-1710, ae 56); ca 1680?; Southampton

NEWTON, Bryan & Alice/Elsjre _?_ ; b 20 Dec 1680, b 14 Nov 1649; ?NY/Jamaica, LI

NEWTON, Daniel (1655-1739) & Susannah MOSS/[MORSE] (1664, ?1663-1724); 30 Dec 1679; Marlborough

NEWTON, David (1672-1702) & Hannah LENARDSON/LEONARD? (1680-); 11 Mar 1696/7; Marlborough

NEWTON, Edward (1676-1704) & Mary LENNARDSON, m/2 David BRIGHAM 1709; 23 Dec 1700; Marlborough

NEWTON, Ephraim (1647-) & Ruth [PITCHER], dau Andrew; b 1672, 1670; Milton

NEWTON, Isaac (ca 1657-1685) & Rebecca _?_ , ?m/2 Samuel NEWTON 1688; b 1685; Marlborough

NEWTON, James (1654-1739) & Mary [HUBBELL] (1661?-); b 1681(2?); Stratford, CT/?Colchester

NEWTON, John & _?_ ; b 1643; Dorchester/Dedham

NEWTON, John (1641-1723), Marlborough & Elizabeth LARKIN (1641-1719); 5 Jun 1666; Charlestown

NEWTON, John & ?Mehitable/?Sarah _?_ ; b 1677(8?); Boston

NEWTON, John (1656-1699), Milford & Lydia FORD (1661-), dau Thomas; 14 Apr 1680; Milford, CT

NEWTON, John & Hannah MORS/(MORSE); 19 Jun 1690; Marlborough

NEWTON, Joseph (ca 1648-1729) & 1/wf Catherine [WOOD/WOODS] (-1717); b 1671; Marlborough

NEWTON, Joseph (1673-) & Abigail _?_ (-1749); b 1699, b 1698?; Marlborough

NUTON, Moses (1646, ?1645-1736) & 1/wf Joanna LARKIN (?1646, ?1649-1713); 27 Oct 1668, 28 Oct 1668; Marlborough/Charlestown

NEWTON, Moses & Sarah HOW/HOWE; 11 Dec 1695; Marlborough

NEWTON, Richard (-1701) & Anne/Hannah? [LOKER/RIDDLESDALE] (ca 1616-1697); b 1641; Sudbury

NEWTON, Roger (-1683) & Mary [HOOKER] (?1623-1675/6); b 1646; Cambridge/Farmington, CT

NEWTON, Roger (1651, ?1648-1690) & Abigail [FLETCHER] (1652-); b 1685; ?Newtown, LI/?Middlebury, LI

NEWTON, Samuel (1646-1708) & 1/wf Martha FENN (1650-); 14 Mar 1669, 1668/9, 12 Mar; Milford, CT

NEWTON, Samuel (1668-), Marlboro & Rebecca NEWTON, Marlboro, w Isaac?, m/3 Philip PRATT by 1698; 8 Sep 1688; Concord

NEWTON, Samuel (1646-1708) & 2/wf Sarah (WELSH) [FOWLER] (1659-), w John; ca 1697?; ?Milford, CT

NEWTON, Thomas & 1/wf Dorothy _?_ (-bef 1648)); b 1648; Fairfield, CT

NEWTON, Thomas & 2/wf Joan SMITH (-1664), dau Richard; 31 Mar 1648; ?Newtown, LI

NEWTON, Thomas (?1661-aft 28 May 1721) & Christian _?_ ; ca 1690/5?; ?Boston

NEWTON, Thomas (1674-1746) & Record WARD (1677-1746); 17 Aug 1698; Marlborough/Marlboro

NEWTON, Zachariah & Mary AXTELL (1670-); 24 May 1698; Concord/Marlborough

NICCOLET/NICKOLET, Charles & _?_ ; b 1673; Salem

NICHOLS, Abraham (1662-) & 1/wf Rachel KELLOGG; 3 Dec 1684; Stratford, CT

NICHOLS, Abraham (1672-) & Sarah [KNOWLES]; ca 1695/1700?; Fairfield, CT

NICHOLS, Adam (-1682) & Ann [WAKEMAN] (1614-); b 1645; New Haven/Hartford/Hadley
NICHOLS, Allen/Alleyn? & Abigail BERRE (1647-); 12 Apr 1670; Barnstable
NICHOLS, Benjamin (1676-1736) & Mary _?_; b 1698/[9?]; E. Greenwich, RI
NICHOLS, Benjamin (1660-) & 1/wf Abigail _?_; b 1701; Stratford, CT
NICHOLS, Caleb (-1690/1) & Anne [WARD] (?1629-1718); b 1651; Stratford, CT
NICHOLS, Cyprian^1 & _?_; b 1652?; Hartford
NICHOLS, Cyprian^2 (?1642-) & Mary _?_; b 1672, by 1669; Hartford
NICHOLS, Cyprian^3 (1672-1736) & 1/wf Helena [TALCOTT] (1674-1702, 1703); b 1700; Hartford
NICHOLS, David (-1653) & Elizabeth [SARGENT], m/2 Thomas BELL 1653; b 1653; Boston
NICHOLS, Ephraim (1648-1693) & Abigail _?_; 15 Feb 1675; Hingham
NICHOLS, Ephraim (1657-1690?) & Esther (WARD) HAWLEY, w Ebenezer, m/3 Eliphalet HILL, m/4 Robert LORD; 17 Oct 1682; Fairfield, CT
NICHOLS, Francis (?1590-1650, 1655?) & 1/wf _?_; in Eng, b 1630?, ca 1625, ca 1610-12?; Stratford, CT
NICHOLS, Francis (?1590-1650, 1655?) & 2/wf Anne/Hannah [WINES], m/2 John ELTON, m/3 John TOOKER, m/4 John YOUNGS; 1645; Stratford, CT
NICHOLS, Francis & Jane _?_; b 19 Oct 1695; Kittery, ME
NICHOLS, Hugh & Priscilla (SHATTUCK) HILL (1658-), w John; 26 Apr 1694; Salem
NICHOLS, Isaac (-1695) & Margaret WASHBURN?/SHERMAN?/SHUMAN?/FAIRCHILD?; b 1648; Fairfield, CT
NICHOLS, Isaac (-1713?, Derby) & Esther CLARK (-1717?, Derby); 1 Aug 1672, 15 Aug 1672; Stratford, CT
NICHOLS, Isaac (1654-1690) & Mary BALDWIN (1653-), m/2 Daniel COMSTOCK; Sep 1675; Milford, CT/Stratford, CT
NICHOLS, Israel (1650-) & 1/wf Mary _?_ (-1688); 26 Sep 1679; Hingham
NICHOLS, Israel, Hingham & 2/wf Mary SUMNER (-1724, ae 59), Milton; 10 Jan 1688, 1688/9?, 10 Jun; Milton/Hingham
NICHOLS, James (-1694) & Mary FELT; - Apr 1660; Malden
NICHOLLS, James & Mary POOLE (1660-); 9 Nov 1682, 9 Oct 1682; Cambridge/Reading
NICHOLS, James (1662-1726) & 1/wf Hannah WHITTEMORE (ca 1668-1689); 15 Nov 1686; Malden/Woburn/Charletown
NICHOLS, James (1662-1726) & Abigail _?_; b 1691; Malden
NICHOLS, John & 1/wf _?_ (-1650±?); b 1640?, b 1636; Watertown/Wethersfield, CT/Fairfield, CT/Stratford, CT
NICHOLS, John (-1655?) & 2/wf? Grace _?_, m/2 Richard PERRY; Stratford, CT
NICHOLS, John (?1640-1700) & Lydia [WILKINS]?, m _?_ WILLS; b 1663; Salisbury
NICHOLS, John (?1652-1721) & Abigail [KENDALL] (1655-); 18 May 1676; Reading
NICHOLS, John (-1694) & Sarah _?_ (-1678, in 21st y); b 1678; Charlestown
NICHOLS, John & Susanna [DAWES] (1652-1695+); b 1678(9?); Boston
NICHOLS, (John?) & Frances ELLIOT; 14 Jun 1686; Salem
NICHOLS, John (1667-) & 1/wf Hannah FORMAN (-1716, ae 51 y); 8 Jun 1687, 1689, 1687; East Greenwich, RI
NICHOLS, John (1667-) & 1/wf Constant _?_; b 1692; Topsfield
NICHOLS, John & 1/wf? [Abigail] _?_ (-1749); b 1695; Fairfield, CT
NICHOLS, John & Mercy MILLER; m int 18 Dec 1695; Boston/Charlestown
NICHOLS, Jonathan (1655-1689) & Hannah HAWKINS/HOWKINS (ca 1661-1698), m/2 Samuel WARD 1691?, m/3 John JUDSON ca 1693; 21 Dec 1681; Stratford, CT/Derby, CT
NICHOLS, Joseph & Bathsheba PINSEN; 12 Jan 1696/7; Scituate
NICHOLS, Josiah (1652-1691) & Hannah HAWLEY (1657-), m/2 John WOLCOTT 1692, m/3 Samuel PORTER, m/4 Henry WOLCOTT; 13 Dec 1678; Stratford, CT
NICOLL, Matthias (-1687); Brookhaven, NY
NICHOLS, Mordecai (-1663) & Alice [HALLETT], m/2 Thomas CLARK 1664; b 1653; Boston/Barnstable
NICHOLS, Nathaniel (-1687?) & Joanna [SHUTE], m/2 Joseph BUCKLEY 1687; b 1682; Charlestown
NICHOLS, Nathaniel (1653-1731) & Sarah LINCOLN (1664-); Mar 1687, 16 Apr 1687; Hingham
NICHOLS, Nathaniel (1666-1725) & Sarah _?_; b 1692; Malden
NICHOLS, Nicholas & Elizabeth _?_; b 1687; Andover

NICHOLS, Randall & Elizabeth [PIERCE]? (-1692); b 1643; Charlestown
NICHOLS, Randall (1663-) & Sarah _?_ ; b 1701; Charlestown
NICHOLS, Richard & Phebe _?_ ; b 1666; Warwick, RI
NICOLLS, Richard (-1674) & Ann/Annas?/Annis? _?_ (-1692); b 1651; Ipswich/Reading
NICHOLS, Robert & Sarah [GOSSE], w John; aft 1644; Watertown/Southampton, LI
NICHOLS/NICHOLSON, Robert & Anne (DEVEREUX) BOSSON, w Walter; bv 1684
NICHOLS, Robert (1671-) & Mary CASE; Feb 1698; Newport
NICHOLS, Samuel (-1737) & Mary BOWERS (-1736); - May 1682; Stratford, CT/Derby, CT/Fairfield
NICHOLS, Samuel (1658-1691) & Susan/Susanna (_?_) [FAIRCHILD], w Thomas, m/3 Samuel CASTLE 1692?, 1708?; b 1687, b 1691; Stratford, CT/Woodbury/Derby?
NICHOLS, Samuel & Elizabeth [PICKERING] (1674-), m/2 James BROWN 1699; b 1696; Salem
NICHOLS, Thomas (-1696) & 1/wf Rebecca [JOSSELYN] (1618, 1616?-1675); ca 1637/8; Hingham/Scituate
NICHOLS, Thomas & Mary MOULTON; Sep 1655; Charlestown
NICHOLS, Thomas (-1708+) & Hannah [GRIFFIN] (1642-); b 1660; Newport
NICHOLLES, Thomas (?1638-) & Sarah WHISTON (ca 1643-); 25 May 1663; Scituate
NICHOLS, Thomas & Mary _?_ /[?MOULTON]; b 1663; Salisbury
NICKOLS, Thomas & Rebecca EATON; 1 Dec 1680; Reading
NICHOLS, Thomas (-1696) & 2/wf Dorcas (-1694); 23 Sep 1681; Hingham
NICHOLS, Thomas (1660-1745) & Mercy/Mary REYNOLDS (1664-); b 1684(5?); E. Greenwich, RI
NICHOLS, Thomas (1670-1724) & 1/wf Jane JAMESON (-1674); b 1694?, 1695?; Amesbury
NICHOLS, Thomas & Joanna TOWNE (1668-); 12 Dec 1694, 13 Dec 1694; Salem/Topsfield
NICHOLS, Thomas & Martha [WHEATLEY], dau Lionel; b 1699; Boston
NICHOLS, William (1599-1696) (over 100 in 1694?) & 1/wf Margaret/?Mary _?_ ; b 1640?; Salem
NICHOLS, William (-1673, New London) & Ann [ISBELL] (-1684, New London), w Robert; aft 1655; Salem/New London
NICOLL, William (1657-1723) & Anna [VanRENSSELAER]; b 1694; Islip, LI
NICHOLS, William (1599, 1590?-1696) & 2/wf Mary (SOUTHWICK) [TRASK] (1630, 1628?-), w Henry; aft 1689, b 1694; Salem
NICHOLS, _?_ & Ann (DEVEREUX) BOASUM/BASUM (1647±-), w Walter, had son John BASUM/BOSSON
NICHOLS?/NICHOLSON?, _?_ (see John NICHOLSON) & Mercy HOLLINGSWORTH, m/2 Thomas DESBROW; ca 1679?; Fairfield, CT
NICHOLS, ?Samuel & Abigail _?_ ; ca 1685?; Portsmouth, NH
NICHOLS, _?_ & ?Mary/?Mercy [BUDD?], m/2 John YOUNGS, m/3 Christopher YOUNGS; Rye, NY
NICHOLSON, Christopher (1638-) & Hanna REDKNAP; 22 Oct 1662; Lynn
NICHOLSON, Edward/Edmund? (-1660) & Elizabeth [?SIMPSON] (1616-), m/2 _?_ BROWN; b 1638; Salem/Marblehead
NICHOLSON, James (-1709) & Sybil (DICKERSON) [KNAPP], w Josiah; ?Fairfield, CT
NICHOLSON, John (deserted his wf) & Mercy ?HOLLINGSWORTH, m/2 Thomas DISBRO/DESBOROUGH; Fairfield, CT
NICHOLSON, John (?1646-) & Dorothy _?_ ; b 1695; ?Falmouth, ME/Charlestown/Boston
NICHOLSON, Joseph (-1693/4) & Jane _?_ (-1691); in Eng, b 1650; Salem/Portsmouth, RI/Jamestown, RI
NICHOLSON, Joseph (1650-) & _?_ ; ?Portsmouth, RI
NICHOLSON, Robert[1] & _?_ ; b 1650?
NICHOLSON, Robert[2] & ?Winnifret BONYTHON (-1729+); 1 Jul 1673; Falmouth, ME
NICHOLSON, Robert, Jr. (1676-1750) & Martha BARTLETT (-1736); 10 Oct 1700; Marblehead
NICHOLSON, Samuel (1644-) & Judith _?_ ; b 1681; Marblehead
NICHOLSON, Samuel (1671-1724) & Agnes COES/COWES; 25 Apr 1700; Marblehead
NICHOLSON, Thomas (1653/4-1693?) & Elizabeth [WOOD], m/2 Richard CRAFT 1694; ca 1685; Marblehead
NECK, John & Mary RICHARDS (-1725+); 22 Mar 1675/6; Lynn
NICKS, John (-1693) & Urith (WATERS) [WHITWAY], w John; b 1689; Boston/Charlestown
NICK, William (-1683) & Mary (ABORN) (CONKLIN) STARR (1648-), w Cornelius, w Robert, m/4 George JACKSON 1690; 8 Sep 1680; Marblehead

NICKERSON, John (-1735, 1728?) & Sarah [WILLIAMS], ?m/2 John ROGERS 1728; b 1696;
Branstable
NICKERSON, John (1664-) & Elizabeth [BAKER]; 14 Aug 1696, ?19 Aug; Yarmouth
NICKERSON, Joseph (1647-) & Ruhamah [?JONES]; b 1668; Yarmouth
NICKERSON, Nicholas (-1682) & ?2/wf Mary [DERBY] (-1706); b 1656; Yarmouth
NICKERSON, Robert & Sarah [BASSETT] (-1710, ae 82); ca 1664
NICKERSON, Robert & [Rebecca COLE] (1654-1710+); ca 1685
NICKERSON, Samuel (-1719) & Mary [BELL]; ca 1660, b 1682; Yarmouth/Harwich
NICKERSON, Thomas & Mary [BANGS] (1671-); ca 1690; Chatham
NICKERSON, William (1604-1655+) & Ann [BUSBY] (1609-); in Eng, ca 1627; Watertown/Yar-
mouth
NICKERSON, William (1646-1719) & Mercy [WILLIAMS] (-1739); ca 1670?; Chatham
NICKERSON, William (1659-1720, 1721) & Mary SNOW (1661-); 22 Jan 1690, 1690/1;
Eastham/Harwich
NICKERSON, William (-1742) & 1/wf Deliverance [LUMBART?]; b 1701
NIGHTINGALE, William (-1714, ca 77) & Bethiah [DEERING]; b 1670(1?); Braintree
NIGHTINGALE, William, Jr. & Rebecca NEALE; 14 Dec 1691; Braintree
NYLES, Benjamin (1651-1712) & [Ruth] __?__ (-1712+); b 1679; Block Isl, RI/Lyme, CT
NILES/NIEL, Benjamin (1675-1725) & 1/wf Ruth SCANT; 14 May 1698; Braintree
NILES, Increase (1646-1693) & Mary PURCHASE, m/2 Francis NASH 1697; 4 Dec 1677;
Braintree
NILES, John (-1694, ae 91) & 1/wf Jane [REED]? (-15 May 1654); ca 1635?; Braintree
NILES, John (-1694, ae 91) & 2/wf Hannah (_?_) [AMES], w William; 6 Apr 1660?, ca 1656/7;
Braintree
NILES, John & Abigail __?__, m/2 John BANNING; ca 1679; New Shoreham, RI
NILES, John & Catherine __?__; b 1696(7?); Braintree
NILES, Joseph (1640-) & Mary MYCALL; 15 Nov 1661, 2 Nov 1662; Braintree
NILES, Nathaniel (1642-) & Sarah SANDS (?1656-); 14 Feb 1671; New Shoreham, RI
NILES, Nathaniel (1677-1766) & Mary HANNAH (-1765+); 26 Jan 1699; North Kingstown, RI
NILES, Nicholas & __?__ [POTTER] (-living 30 Apr 1639), w George; b 4 Feb 1646; ?Portsmouth,
RI
NILES, Lt. Samuel (1644-1715?, 5 Sep 1724?) & Mary (BILLINGS) BELCHER (1645-1715+), w
Samuel; 20 Apr 1680; Braintree
NIMS, Godfrey (ca 1650-1705) & Mary (MILLER) WILLIAMS (-1688), w Zebediah; 26 Nov 1677,
28 Nov 1677; Deerfield
NIMS, Godfrey (-1705) & 2/wf Mehitable (SMEAD) HULL, w Jeremiah; 27 Jan 1692, 27 Jun;
Deerfield
NIX, John & Urith/Eunice [WATERS] (-1695+, 1704), b 1689; Charlestown
NIXON, Matthew & Elizabeth __?__; 1640 or bef; Salem
NOKES/(OAKES), Robert & 1/wf Mary; b 1665/(6?); Boston
NOKES/NOAKES, Robert & Mary EMERSON; 17 Aug 1699; Boston
NOAKES, Robert & 2/wf Mary [WRIGHT]; b 1683, prob, certainly bef 1700; Boston
NOKES/NOCKS/NOAKS, Walter & __?__; b 1672; Huntington, LI
NOAKES/KNOX?, __?__ & Elizabeth [SCUDDER]; b 1686; Southold, LI
NOKES, __?__ & Rebecca CONKLIN?; Southold?
NOAKES, __?__ & Eunice NIX
NOBLE, [?Christopher] & Martha [PEVERLY] (1647-); 19 Apr 1670, betw 1666 & 1670, perhaps
in or bef 1665; Portsmouth, NH
NOBLE, James (1677-) & 1/wf Ruth __?__ (-1702); ca 1699; Westfield
NOBLE, John (1662-1714) & 1/wf Abigail SACKETT (1663-1683); 13 Sep 1682; Westfield/North-
ampton/Springfield/New Milford, CT
NOBLE, John (-1714, New Milford, CT) & 2/wf Mary [GOODMAN]; 1684; Westfield
NOBLE, Lazarus? & Mary?/Elizabeth?/Ruth?/Lydia? [?GARFIELD], dau Samuel, had John &
Mary; b 1698 b 1709, b 1701?; Watertown
NOBLE, Luke (1675-) & Hannah STEBBINS (1680-1705); 1 Feb 1700, 1699/1700; Springfield
NOBLE, Mark (?1670-1741) & Mary/Mercy [MARSHALL] (-1733); b 1698(9?); Westfield
NOBLE, Matthew & Hannah DEWEY (1672-); 10 Dec 1690; Westfield
NOBLE, Thomas (-1704) & Hannah WARRINER (1643-1709+), m/2 Medad POMEROY 1704,
1704/5; 1 Nov 1660; Springfield/Westfield

NOBLE, Thomas (-1750) & Elizabeth DEWEY (1677-1757); 19 Dec 1695; Westfield
NOBLE, William (-1697) & _?_/Ann? [HAIGHT?] (-1699?); b 1658?; Flushing, LI
NORCROSS, Jeremiah (1595-1657 (in Eng)) (uncle of Stephen PAINE) & 1/wf _?_; b 1618; Watertown
NORCROSS, Jeremiah (1595-1657) (called Charles CHADWICK "brother") & 2/wf [Adrean/ ?Adrian/?Andria] SMITH, wid; b 1640; Watertown
NORCROSS, John (returned to Eng) & _?_; ca 1638?; Cambridge
NORCROSS, Nathaniel (?1618-1662) & Mary [GILBERT]; ca 1657; Dorchester/London/Walsing-ham, Eng
NORCROSS, Nathaniel (-1717) & 1/wf Mehitable HAGAR (-1691); 20 Jun 1687; Watertown
NORCROSS, Nathaniel (-1717) & 2/wf Susannah [SHATTUCK] (1675-); ca 1693, b 1695; Watertown
NORCROSS, Richard (-1709) & 1/wf Mary BROOKES (-1672); 24 Jun 1650; Watertown, CT
NORCROSS, Richard (-1709) & 2/wf Susan/Susanna (_?_) SHATTUCK (-1686), w William; 18 Nov 1673; Watertown, CT
NORCROSS, Richard & 1/wf Rose WOODWARD (1659-); 10 Aug 1686; Watertown
NORCROSS, Richard (-1709) & 3/wf Mary _?_; aft 1686; Watertown
NORCROSS, Richard & 2/wf Hannah SANDERS (-1743); 6 Aug 1695; Watertown
NORDEN, Nathaniel (1653-1728) & Jane/Mary [LATIMER] (-1722); b 8 Nov 1688, b 13 Jun 1687; ?Marblehead
NORDEN, Samuel & 1/wf Joanna [COPP] (1625-29 Jun 1656); b 1647; Boston
NORDEN, Samuel & 2/wf Elizabeth [PORMOTT/PORMORT] (1629-); 1656; Boston
NORGRAVE, _?_ & Anne _?_ (-1660, Boston), wid; Boston
NORMAN, Hugh & Sarah WHITE; 8 Oct 1639; ?Plymouth/Yarmouth
NORMAN, John (1612/13-1672) & Arabella _?_ (-1679); b 1637; Salem/Manchester
NORMAN, John (-1713, ae 76) & Mary ROPES (-1713, ae 67); 17 Nov 1663; Salem
NORMAN, John (1660-1709) & Sarah MAVERICKE (1665, 1660?, 1662-living 1706); 10 Nov 1683; Marblehead
NORMAN, Joseph (1656-1691) & Mary COLLINS, m/2 Henry HOOPER 1692; 24 Jan 1688/9; Marblehead
NORMAN, Nathaniel & Mary [SKINNER]; b 1694 (doubtful); Windsor, CT
NORMAN, Richard & _?_ (-1645+); in Eng, b 1612; Salem/Marblehead
NORMAN, Richard & Elizabeth WHITRIDGE (-1659?); 15 Jul 1654?
NORMAN, Richard (?1622, 1624?, 1623-1683) & 2/wf? Margaret [FLINT] (?1635-1705), m/2 Robert GOODWIN 1685; ?28 Mar 1660; Marblehead
NORMAN, Richard[3] (-1682) & Elizabeth BULLOCK; 13 Jan 1671/2, 1674/5; Salem
NORMAN, Samuel & [Sarah] CASLY/CARSLY, w John; 29 Nov 1697; Barnstable
NORMAN, Timothy (1670-1694/5) & Abigail COALE/COLE, m/2 _?_ ANDREWS 1695; 20 Dec 1693; Salem
NORMAN, William (m 2 wives) & 3/wf Margery RANDALL (div), m/2 Thomas SPINNEY; Kittery, ME
NORMAN, William (1658-1699) & Rebecca _?_ (1657-1729); ca 1680?, b 1681; Salem/Marble-head
NORMAN, William & Huldah MOUNTJOY; m int 25 Mar 1696; Boston
NORRAWAY, James & Elizabeth _?_; b 1698; Dover, NH
NORRIS, Edward (-1659) & Eleanor _?_; b 1615; Roxbury/Salem
NORRICE, Edward (-1684, in 70th y) & Dorothy [JOHNSON]; b 22 Mar 1655/6; Salem
NORRICE, Edward (-1700) & Mary SYMONDS, m/2 _?_ STARR; 3 Dec 1685; Salem
NORRIS, Henry & Abigail [STRATTON]; b 30 Aug 1684; Easthampton, LI
NORRIS, Jonathan (1673-) & Lydia [HEARD], m/2 Joseph ROLLINS; Jun 1696; Exeter, NH
NORRIS, Moses & Ruth FOLSOM; 4 Mar 1692; Exeter, NH
NORRIS, Nicholas & 1/wf Sarah COX; 21 Jan 1663/4, 1664; Hampton, NH/Exeter, NH
NORRIS, Oliver & Margery _?_; b 1696; Sandwich
NORRIS, Peter & [?Sarah] _?_; Southampton
NORRIS, Robert & Hannah _?_; Southampton
NORTH, Edward (-1683) & Sarah [BATEMAN], m/2 Samuel EELLS 1689; b 1677; Boston
NORTH, James (1647-1689) & Sarah [EDWARDS] (1654-); 20 Nov 1677; Northampton
NORTH, John (1615-1692?) & [Hannah]/Mary? [BIRD]/BUEL? (2/wf? Mary BIRD bef 10 Aug 1662); b 1640?, b 1641; Farmington

NORTH, John (1641-1682) & Susannah FRANCIS (1651-), m/2 John STEDMAN 1683; 15 Apr 1671; Wethersfield, CT

NORTH, John (1669-1745) & 1/wf Mary WARNER (1669-1695); 16 May 1692; Farmington, CT

NORTH, John & 2/wf Mary SEYMOUR (-1733); 25 Sep 1700?, 25 Apr 1700; ?Farmington, CT

NORTH, Joseph (1660-) & 1/wf Sarah PORTER (1666-); bef? 3 Jan 1686/7; Farmington, CT

NORTH, Nathaniel (1657-) & _?_ ; b 1680?, b 1687?; CT

NORTH, Richard (-1667) & 1/wf _?_ ; in Eng, b 1624; Salisbury/Salem

NORTH, Richard (-1667) & 2/wf Ursula _?_ (-1670); aft 1630, b 1649; Salisbury/Salem

NORTH, Samuel (1643-1682) & Hannah NORTON (1649-), m/2 John REW 1683?; 3 Jan 1666/7, 3 Jan 1666, 1666; Farmington, CT

NORTH, Thomas & Mary (PRICE) PETERSFIELD (?1626-1676?), w Philip, m/3 Thomas DUNK; ca 1648; New Haven

NORTH, Thomas & 1/wf ?Mary [?BIRD]; ca 1672?, b 1662?; Farmington, CT

NORTH, Thomas (1649-1712) & 2/wf Hannah [NEWELL] (?1658, 1656?-1757); ca 1676/7?; Farmington, CT

NORTH, Thomas (1673-1725) & Martha ROYCE (1679-), Wallingford, m/2 Matthew WOODRUFF; 1 Dec 1698; Farmington, CT

NORTH, Thomas & Hannah WOODFORD; 4 Dec 1699, 14? Dec; Farmington, CT

NORTHAM, James & 1/wf _?_ ; Hartford

NORTHAM, James & ?1/wf ?2/wf Isabella (WARD?) CATLIN, w John, m/3 Joseph BALDWIN aft 1661; aft 1 Jul 1644; Hartford/Wethersfield, CT

NORTHAM, Samuel (-1726) & Mary [DICKINSON] (1650-); b 1675, 1674; Deerfield/Colchester, CT

NORTHCOTT/NORCUT, William (-1693) & Sarah [CHAPMAN] (1645-); 1662(63?); Marshfield

NORCOTT, William & Experience _?_ ; b 1690, b 1696; Marshfield/Boston

NORTHEND, Ezekiel (1622-1698) & Edna (?HALSTEAD) BAILEY (-1706), w Richard; 1 Dec 1648; Rowley

NORTHEND, Ezekiel (1666-1732) & Dorothy SEAWALL/SEWELL, m/2 Moses BRADSTREET 1737; 10 Sep 1691; Rowley

NORTHEND, John (did he marry?) & Jane _?_ ; Wethersfield, CT

NORTHEY, John[1] (1607?-1694) & _?_ ; b 1645?; Marblehead

NORTHEY, John & Sarah [EWELL] (1645-); b 1674/5; Marblehead/Scituate

NORTHRUP, Benjamin (1662-) & Susannah ALMY; 3 Jul 1681 (doubtful); RI

NORTHRUP, Daniel (1664-1728) & Sarah [HAUGHTON] (1672-); b 1691; Milford, CT/Ridgefield, CT

NORTHRUP, David (-1725) & Susanna [CONGDON] (-1725+); b 1701; N. Kingstown, RI

NORTHRUP, Henry (1663-1740) & Mary _?_ (-1746+); ca 1685/90?; N. Kingstown, RI

NORTHRUP, Jeremiah (1653, 1654?-) & Phoebe _?_ ; ca 1688, Milford, CT

NORTHROP, Joseph (-1669) & Mary [NORTON]; ca 1647; Milford, CT

NORTHROP, Joseph (1649-1700?) & Miriam [BLAKEMAN/BLACKMAN] (1670/1-), m/2 John SMITH 1701?; b 1689; Milford, CT

NORTHRUP, Joseph (-bef 1726) & Hopestill [SMITH] (-1720+); N. Kingstown, RI

NORTHROP, Samuel (1651-) & Sarah _?_ , m/2 Samuel CLARK; b 1687; Stratford, CT/Milford, CT

NORTHROP, Stephen (-1687+) & _?_ ; b 1660?, b 1655?; Providence/Kingstown, RI

NORTHROP, Stephen (1660-1733) & Mary THOMAS; Jan 1684/5; Jamestown, RI/N. Kingstown

NORTHROP, William (1666-1728) & Mary [PECK] (1670-); ca 1692; Milford, CT

NORTHRUP, Zophar (1681-1729) & 1/wf Sarah [TIBBALS]; b 1696; Milford, CT

NORTHRUP, _?_ & Mary BROOKS; b 24 Apr 1704, b 1701?; ?Canterbury, CT

NORTHWAY, _?_ & [Susanna BRIGGS]; b 1690, b 1670?; Portsmouth, RI

NORTHWAY, _?_ & [Hannah NORTH]; b 11 Nov 1706

NORTON, Benjamin (1659-) & Hannah [?BOLTER]; b 1685; Edgartown

NORTON, Bonus (-1718, ae 61) & Mary [GOODHUE] (1664-); b 1691; Ipswich/Hingham

NORTON, Caleb & Susanna FRAME; 6 Mar 1699/1700; Amesbury/Salisbury

NORTON, David (1664-1721) & Temperance/Temferance [NORTON/ADAMS]?; b 1687; Boston

NORTON, David & [Phebe TEMPLE]; b 1701?; Boston

NORTON, Francis (?1584-1667) & Mary (HAUGHTON) [PHILLIPS], m/3 William STILSON; b 1640, b 1630?; Charlestown

NORTON, Freegrace & Lydia SPENCER; 3 Aug 16[58-62?], ca 1660; Saco, ME/Ipswich

NORTON, George (-1659) & Mary [?MACHIAS] (sis of Margaret JACKSON & Bethia CARTWRIGHT), m/2 Philip FOWLER; b 1635; Salem/Gloucester/Wenham

NORTON, George (1641-1696) & 1/wf Sarah HART (1647-1682); 7 Oct 1669; Ipswich/Suffield, CT

NORTON, George & Mary [FOXWELL]; 1672; Scarborough, ME/York, ME

NORTON, George & 2/wf Mary/Mercy (BARBER) GILLETTE, w John; 14 Jun 1683, 20 Jun 1683; Windsor, CT/Suffield, CT

NORTON, George & Hannah YOUNGLOVE; 11 Dec 1695; Suffield, CT

NORTON, George & Mary ASHLEY (1681-); 20 May 1698; Charlestown

NORTON, Henry (1618-1659?, 1657?) & Margaret _?_; York, ME

NORTON, Isaac (1641-1723) & Ruth BAYES (1643-); ca 1663; Martha's Vineyard

NORTON, Isaac (1665?-) & Elizabeth _?_; b 1690; Brookhaven, LI

NORTON, Jacob & 1/wf Dinah COFFIN (1671-); b 1690; Martha's Vineyard

NORTON, Rev. John (1606-1663, 1662?) & Mary [?FERNELEY]? (-1678); ca 1630/40?; Ipswich

NORTON, John (1622-1709, 1708) & 1/wf Dorothy _?_ (-1652/3); b 1645; Branford, CT/Hartford/Farmington, CT

NORTON, John (-1708) & 2/wf Elizabeth [WATTS?]/HUBBARD?/ALLEN? (?1638-6 Nov 1657); b 1657; Branford, CT

NORTON, John (-1708, 1709?) & 3/wf Elizabeth [CLARK]?/HUBBARD? (-1702); aft 6 Nov 1657; Branford, CT/Farmington, CT

NORTON, John (1637-) & Mary SHARP; 3 Apr 1660; Salem

NORTON, John (1628, 1638?-1704) & [?Hannah STONE] (1644-1712?); b 1666; Guilford, CT

NORTON, John (1650/1?-1725) & Ruth [MOORE] (1657-); b 1675; Farmington, CT

NORTON, John (-1687) & Lydia (WRIGHT) BLISS (-1699), w Lawrence, m/3 John LAMB 1688, 1687, m/4 George COLTON 1692; 31 Oct 1678, 3? Oct; Springfield

NORTON, John (1653-1716, ae 65) & Mary MASON (-1740); 29 Nov 1678; Hingham

NORTON, John (1668-1712) & Hannah [PECK/BUCK?/BEACH], ?m/2 John FOWLER?; 14 Nov 1694; ?Guilford, CT

NORTON, John (?1674-1730) & Mary [TORREY] (1676-); b 1700; Martha's Vineyard

NORTON, Jonathan & Mary RICHARDSON? (1676-); b 1701?; Newbury

NORTON, Joseph & Susanna GATCHELL; 10 Mar 1661/2, 1662; Salisbury

NORTON, Joseph (1652-1741?) & 1/wf Mary [BAYES]; ca 1673; Martha's Vineyard

NORTON, Joseph (?1676-1734) & _?_/Sarah SWAIN? (1670-); b 1695; Martha's Vineyard

NORTON, Joseph & Elizabeth BROWN; 16 Nov 1699; Salisbury

NORTON, Joseph & [Deborah CRUTTENDEN]; b 1701?; Durham, NH

NORTON, Nathaniel (1639-1685) & Mary [MILLS?/MILES?], dau Richard MILLS, m/2 Thomas HELME; ca 1660/5?; Southampton, LI

NORTON, Nicholas (1610-1690?) & Elizabeth _?_; b 1641; Weymouth/Martha's Vineyard

NORTON, Peter (-1667?, 1670) & Mary [ANDREWS], m/2 Hugh GRIFFIN ca 1670; aft 6 Jun 1662; Fairfield, CT

NORTON, Richard (-1657, 1656?) & Dorothy _?_; b 1650; Boston

NORTON, Samuel/John? & Abigail WARD; 25 Jan 1692/3; Guilford, CT

NORTON, Samuel & Content COGGESHALL/STANTON? (1676, 1675-); b 1708, b 1701?; Newport

NORTON, Solomon & Sarah _?_; b 1695; Salisbury

NORTON, Thomas (1609-1648) & Grace [WELLS], m/2 Francis BUSHNELL; ?5 May 1631; Guilford, CT

NORTON, Thomas (1626-1712) & Elizabeth MASON (-1699); 8 May 1671; Saybrook, CT/Durham, CT

NORTON, Thomas & Anna _?_; b 1678; Boston

NORTON, Thomas & Hepzibah [SKIFFE]; b 1699; Martha's Vineyard

NORTON, Thomas (1660-1729) & Hannah ROSE; 7 Jun 1700, 1 Jul, 7 Jan 1700; Farmington, CT

NORTON, Thomas & Mercy RUST; 14 Nov 1700; Ipswich

NORTON, Walter & 1/wf Jane (REEVE) [REYNOLDS]; b 1627; Weymouth

NORTON, Walter & 2/wf Eleanor KNIGHT, m/2 William HOOKE bef 1636; Weymouth

NORTON, William (?1610-1639) (NOLTON wrong) & Ann _?_ (-1675), m/2 John RUCKER 1649; b 1628; Hingham

NORTON, William (1628, ?1626-1694, ae 68) & Lucy [DOWNING]? (-1698); ca 1649, [b 1650]; Ipswich

NORTON, William (-1690) & Susanna MASON, dau Ralph; 14 Dec 1659; Boston

NORTON, ?John & Ann DODD?, m/2 _?_ JOHNSTON, m/3 John FOWLER

NORWOOD, Francis (-1709) & Elizabeth COLDOM/COLDHAM (-1711); 15 Oct 1663; Gloucester

NORWOOD, Francis & Mary STEVENS; 24 Jan 1692/3; Gloucester

NORWOOD, Thomas & Mary BROWN (1666-); 24 Aug 1685; Lynn

NAZITER/NOSSITER, Michael & Jane HOBBS, m/2 Richard PEARD 1669; 2 Sep 1664; Saco, ME

NOSSITOR, Peter & Rebecca MAYER, m/2 John BAXTER aft 1696; 19 May 1688; Marblehead

NOTT, John (-1682) & Ann _?_ ; b 1646, b 1649; Wethersfield, CT

NOTT, John (1651-1710) & Patience MILLER (-1737+, 1745+?); 28 Mar 1683; Northampton?/We-
thersfield, CT

NOURSE/NURSE, Benjamin (1665-) & Tomasin SMITH/?JAMESON; 21 Feb 1688; Salem/Framing-
ham

NURSE, Francis (-1695, ae 77) & Rebecca [TOWNE] (1621-1692); ca 1645?; Salem

NURSE, Francis (1661-1716) & Sarah CRAGIN, Woburn?; b 1686(7?); Reading

NURSS, John (ca 1645-1719) & 1/wf Elizabeth SMITH (-1673); 1 Nov 1672; Salem

NURSS, John (-1719) & 2/wf Elizabeth VERRY (-1723+); 17 Aug 1677; Salem

NURSE, John (1673-1747) & Elizabeth GALE; 21 Feb 1699/1700; Sherborn/Framingham

NURSE, Salem (ca 1647-1720) & Mary SMITH (-1715+); 5 Apr 1677; Salem

NURSE, Samuel (1678/9-) & Elizabeth _?_ ; b 1699; Salem

NOWELL, George & Lydia [WILLIS]; bef 1659; Boston

NOWELL, George & Elizabeth JOHNSON (1677-); 13 Oct 1693; Boston

NOWELL, Increase (-1655) & Parnell (GRAY) [PARKER] (1602±-1687); b Aug 1629;
Boston/Cambridge

NOWELL, Michael & Lydia _?_ ; b 1686; Boston

NOWELL, Peter & Sarah [WEARE] (-1701+); b 1698; York, ME

NOWELL, Robert (-1691) (ae 34 in 1680) & Mary TATCHELL (-1704+); 1 Jan 1667/8; Salem

NOWELL, Samuel (1634-1688) & Mary (ALFORD) (BUTLER) [USHER] (-1693), w Peter, w
Hezekiah; aft 14 May 1676, in 1683, no issue; Charlestown

NOWELL, Thomas (-1649) & Elizabeth _?_ ; Windsor, CT

NOWELL, Thomas (-1694) & Sarah (WILLIAMS) [SHARPE], w Robert, m/3 Solomon PHIPPS; aft
4 Mar 1690/1; Boston

NOYES, Cutting & Elizabeth KNIGHT (1655-); 25 Feb 1673; Newbury

NOYES, James (1608-1656) & Sarah [BROWN]? (-1691); in Eng, ca 1633; Newbury

NOYES, James & _?_ ; bef 1666

NOYES, James (1640-1719/20) & Dorothy STANTON (1651, 1652?-1743, 1742/3); 12 Sep 1674,
11 Sep; Stonington, CT

NOYES, James & Hannah KNIGHT (1664-); 31 Mar 1684; Newbury

NOYES, John (1645-) & Mary POORE (1651-1716+), m/2 Eliphalet COFFIN?; 23 Nov 1668;
Newbury

NOYES, John (-1678) & Sarah [OLIVER] (1644-); b 1672; Boston/Cambridge

NOYES, John (1674-1749) & Susanna EDWARDS; 16 Mar 1699; Boston

NOYES, John & Mary NOYES; m int 6 Apr 1700; Newbury

NOYES, Joseph (-1661) & Mary NORTON (-1657); 30 Oct 1656; Charlestown

NOYES, Joseph & Sarah LINE; 18 Feb 1656; Charlestown

NOYES, Joseph & 1/wf Mary DARVELL; 12 Nov 1662; Sudbury

NOYES, Joseph (-1717) & Mary (DUNSTER) WILLARD (-1715), w Simon; 14 Jul 1680; Sudbury

NOYES, Joseph & Ruth HAYNES (1668-1727); 20 Dec 1693; Sudbury

NOYES, Moses (1643-1726) & Ruth PICKETT, dau John; b 1676, b 1678; Lyme, CT

NOYES, Nicholas & Mary CUTTING; b 1641; Newbury

NOYES, Nicholas & Sarah LUNT; m int 17 Jul 1695; Newbury/Abington

NOYES, Peter[1] (1591-1657?) & [?Abigail] _?_ ; in Eng, b 1623, b 1618; Sudbury

NOYES, Peter & Elizabeth DARVELL; 30 Nov 1654; Sudbury

NOYES, Thomas (1623-1666) & Mary HAYNES, m/2 Michael BACON 1670; b 1657, no issue;
Sudbury

NOYES, Thomas (1648-) & 1/wf Martha PEIRCE (1649-1674); 28 Dec 1669; Newbury

NOYES, Thomas (1648-) & 2/wf Elizabeth GREENLEAF (1660-); 24 Sep 1677; Newbury

NOYES, Thomas (-1695) & Sarah KNIGHT; 16 Nov 1686; Newbury/Haverhill

NOYES, Timothy (1655-1718) & Mary KNIGHT (1657-); 13 Jan 1680, prob 1680/1; Newbury

NOYES, William (1653-) Sarah COGSALL/COGSWELL; 6 Nov 1685; Newbury

NUDD, [Roger?] (1598-1630) (d in Eng) & [Joan] _?_, m/2 Henry DOW 1631; Ormsby, Eng, b 1629
NUDD, Thomas & Sarah DEARBORN (1641-1714); 9 Dec 1659; Hampton, NH
NUTE, Abraham (1644-) & 1/wf _?_; Dover, NH
NUTE, James[1] & 1/wf _?_; b 1643; Dover, NH
NUTE, James[1] & Sarah _?_; b 1652, b 1644; Dover, NH
NUTE, James[2] (1643-1691) & Elizabeth HEARD (1653-1705), m/2 William FURBER 1694; ca 1671?, by 1675; Salisbury
NUTT, Miles & 1/wf? _?_; b 1627; Watertown/Woburn
NUTT, Miles (1598-1670) & Sybil [BIBBLE] (1618, 1608-1690), w John, m/3 John DOOLITTLE 1674; b 1658?, ?Jan 1658/9; Charlestown/Woburn/Malden
NUTTER, Anthony (?1630-1686) & Sarah [LANGSTAFF]; b 1662; Dover, NH
NUTTER, Hatevil (?1603-1675) & 1/wf [?Mary] _?_; b 1630; Dover, NH
NUTTER, Hatevil & 2/wf Anne [AYRES]; Dover, NH
NUTTER, John & Mehetabel EDINGTON/EDDENDIN; 7 Oct 1674; Charlestown
NUTTER, John & Rosamond [JOHNSON] (1665-); aft 1691; Bloody Point, NH
NUTTING, Ebenezer (1666-) & Lydia _?_; b 1692; Medford/Cambridge
NUTTING, James (1653-) & Lydia LONGLEY; 15 May 1672; ?Groton
NUTTING, John (-1676) & Sarah EGGLETON/EGGLESTON (-1676+); 28 Aug 1650; Woburn/ Chelmsford
NUTTING, John & 1/wf Mary LAKIN; 11 Dec 1674; Groton
NUTTING, Jonathan (1668-) & Elizabeth _?_; b 1693; Cambridge
NYE, Benjamin (?1620-) & Katherine TUPPER (-1694, 1676?); 19 Oct 1640; ?Sandwich
NYE, Benjamin (1673-1715) & Hannah BACKHOUSE/BACKUS; 23 Feb 1698/9, 1699 (m in Sandwich 23 Feb 1698/9); Falmouth, MA/Sandwich
NYE, Caleb (?1658-1704) & Elizabeth [WOOD?/ATWOOD?]; b 1685?; Sandwich/Hardwick
NIE, Ebenezer & Sarah GIBBS; 17 Dec 1675, 1674?; Sandwich
NIE, John, Jr. (?1647-1722) & Esther [SHEDD]; b 1673; Sandwich
NYE, Jonathan (1649-1747?) & 1/wf Hannah _?_; b 1683, ca 1679; Sandwich/Hardwick
NYE, Jonathan (1649-1747) & 2/wf Patience [BURGESS]; b 1691; Sandwich/Hardwick
NIE, Nathan (?1660-) & [Mary/Mercy] _?_; b 1687; Sandwich

OAKES, Edward (-1687) & Jane _?_ (1603-); in Eng, b 1631; Cambridge/Concord
OAKES, Edward & Bethia BAKER, m int 2 Jun 1696; Boston
OAKES, George (-1688) & Jennet/Janet _?_; b 1661?, b 1664; Lynn
OAKES, John & Sarah MARTIN; 24 Oct 1689; Marblehead/Lynn
OAKES, Nathaniel & 1/wf Mehitable REDIAT (1646-1702); 14 Dec 1686, no issue; Marlboro
OAKES, Richard (-1748) & Hannah PHILLIPS (-1742); m int 4 Dec 1697; Lynn
OAKE, Samuel & Joanna PHILLIPS; 4 Oct 1693; Boston
OAKES, Thomas (-1658) & Elizabeth _?_ (-1686), m/2 Seth SWEITZER 1661, m/3 Samuel HAYWARD 1662, 1663; b 1646; Cambridge
OAKES, Thomas (1644-1720, 1719, Wellfleet) & Martha _?_ (-1719, ae 70); b 1687?, b 1689; Boston
OAKES, Thomas (1659-1732) & Sarah TUFTS (-1749); 22 May 1689; Malden/Charlestown
OKES, Thomas & Elizabeth DANSON, w George; 2 Feb 1692; Boston
OAKES, Urian (1631/2-1681) & [Ruth AMES]?; in Eng, b 1657; Cambridge
OAKEMAN, Elias & Joanna [ALGER], m/2 John MILLS b 1686; b 1680; Boston
OAKMAN, Josiah & ?Mary _?_; Spurwent
OAKMAN, Samuel (-1676?) & Mary [BRADEN], m/2 Walter ADAMS; b 1664, b 1660?; Marshfield/Scarborough, ME
OAKMAN, Samuel & Grace (BRIARS) [CHILSON], w William; aft 1 Jul 1676, b 1677
OAKSMAN, Tobias (1664-1750) & Elizabeth [DOTY] (1673-1745); b 3 Dec 1696; Marshfield
OBBIT, John & Elizabeth _?_; b 1685(6?); Ipswich

OBER, John & Hannah **WOODBARY/WOODBURY** (1672-); 5 Jul 1694; Beverly/Ipswich
OBER, Richard (1641-) & Abigail **WOODBERRY/WOODBURY** (1655-); 26 Dec 1671; Beverly/Concord
OCKINGTON, Matthew/Mathias & Lydia __?__ ; b 1694; Dedham
OCKINGTON, Thomas & Rebecca **MASON**; 5 Feb 1682/3; Dedham
OKINGTON, William & Mary __?__ ; b 1666(7?); Boston
OCKONELL/O'CONNELL, Tego & Philipa **KING**; 1 May 1662; Boston
ODDING, George & Margaret __?__ (?d in N. E.?), m/2 John **PORTER**
ODELL, John[2] (-1707) & Mary [**WALKER**?] (-1711/12); b 1666; Fairfield, CT
ODELL, John[3] (1666-) & Sarah [**WHEELER**] (1665-1743); b 1689; Fairfield, CT
ODELL, John[3] & Joanna/Hannah [**TURNER**]; b 1688; Fordham, NY/?Westchester, NY
ODAL, Regnal/Reginald & Priscilla [**MESSENGER**] (bpt 12 Jun 1659), dau Henry & Sarah; b 1686(7?); Boston
ODELL, Richard (1605-) & Ursula **FRANKLYN**; 12 Nov 1627; Southampton
ODELL, ?Samuel & Patience __?__ ; b 1697; ?Rye, NY
ODELL, Thomas & Hannah [**SMITH**] (1673-), m/2 Ebenezer **FOLSOM**; b 1701?
ODLE, William (1603-1676) & Agnes/?Rebecca **FRANKLYN**; 4 May 1629; Concord/Southampton/ Fairfield, CT
ODELL, William[2] (1630-) & Mary [**VOWLES**]; b 1656?; Rye, NY/?Greenwich
ODIORNE, Isaiah & Judith __?__ ; b 1656?; Isles of Shoals
ODIORNE, John (ca 1627-) & Mary **JOHNSON**; b 1675, b 1694; Rye, NH
ODIORNE, Jotham & Sarah (**BARSHAM**)/[**BASSUM**] **BICKFORD**, w Benjamin; b 1700, aft 1697, b 1701; Newcastle
ODIORNE, Philip & ?[Elizabeth **SEAVEY**?] (1652); Portsmouth, NH
AUDLEY, Edmund & __?__ ; b Dec 1642; ?Lynn
ODLIN, Elisha (1640-1705) & Abigail **BRIGHT** (1637-); Aug 1659; Boston
ODLEN, Elisha & Mary **COLBURN**; 30 Dec 1697; Boston
ODLIN, John (1602-1685) & Margaret __?__ ; b 1635; Boston
ODLIN, John & Elizabeth __?__ ; b 1656; Newport
ODLIN/AUDLEY, John (1642-1711) & Martha [**HOLMES**] (1640-1711); ca 1665?; Newport
ODLIN/AUDLEY, John (1666-) & Lydia [**TILLINGHAST**] (1665-1707); ca 1687; Newport
ODLIN, Peter (1646-) & Hannah [**SHARP**]; b 1672; Boston
AFFLEY, David & Elizabeth [**WOLCOTT**]; 26 Sep 1639; Boston
OGDEN, David (?1668-1715) & Abigail **SHERWOOD** (1670-1744); b 1695; Fairfield, CT
OGDEN, David & __?__ ; b 1701?; White Plains, NY
OGDEN, John (-1683?) & Judith/Jane? [**BUDD**], m/2 Francis **BROWN** 1683?; ?ca 1640/55; Stanford, CT/Rye, NY
OGDEN, Joseph (?1666±-1715±) & Mary __?__ ; Southampton/Rye, NY
OGDEN, Richard & Mary [?**HALL**]; 1631, 1639?, b 1655; Stanford, CT/Fairfield, CT
OGDEN, Richard (?1655-1698) & Sarah [?**STAPLES**]; b 1680; Fairfield, CT
OGDEN, Richard (?1674-) & __?__ ; Rye, NY?
OGDEN, ?John (-1745) & 1/wf [Mary **DIMON**]?; Cohansey, NJ
OHOGEN, Patrick & __?__ (-1694); Boston
OKILLE/O'KELLEY, David (-1697) & Jane [**POWELL**] (-1711); b 1668; Yarmouth
OKILLE, David, Jr. (-1715+) & Anna **BILLES/BILLS**; 10 Mar 1692; Yarmouth
OCELEY, Jeremiah (-1728) & Sarah [**CHASE**]; b 1689?; Yarmouth
OKILLY, John (-1693) & Bersua/Bathsua/Bethia **LEWES** (did she m/2 Thomas **BAKER** ca 1700?); 10 Aug 1690; Yarmouth
O KALLY, Peter & __?__ ; b 1686; Dorchester
OKEY?/OAKEY, John & Mary __?__ ; b 1686; Boston
OLCOTT, John (1649-1712) & Mary (**BLACKLEACH**) [**WELLS**], w Thomas, m/3 Joseph **WADSWORTH**; ca 1695; Wethersfield, CT/Hartford
OLCOTT, Samuel (?1643-1704) & Sarah [**STOCKING**]; ca 1665-70?, b 15 Jul 1673; Hartford
OLCOTT, Thomas (1613-1654) & Abigail [**HOARE?/PORTER?**] (1615-1693); ca 1635; Hartford
OLCOTT, Thomas (?1637-1719+) & Mary [?**CULLICK**] (-1721, Windsor, CT); ca 1660?; Hartford
OLCOTT, Thomas (-1719+) & Sarah **FOOTE** (-1756); 30 Nov 1691; Wethersfield, CT
OLCOTT, Thomas (-1712?) & Hannah **BRAINARD** (1670-); 13 Nov 1695; Hartford
OLD, Robert[1] (?1645-1728) & 1/wf Susanna/Susan [**HANFORD**] (-1688); 31 Dec 1669; Windsor, CT/Suffield, CT

OLDS, Robert[1] (?1645-1728) & 2/wf Dorothy GRANGER; 1 Apr 1689; Suffield, CT
OLD, Robert[2] (1670-) & Elizabeth (ATKINSON) LAMB (1672-), w Daniel; 28 Jan 1696/7; Springfield
OLDAGE, Richard (-1661) & __?__; b 1629; Windsor, CT
OLDAM, Isaac & Hannah CANE/KEEN; 21 Nov 1695; Duxbury/Pembroke
OLDHAM, John (-1636) & __?__; Plymouth/Watertown/etc.
OLDHAM, John (-1719) & 1/wf Abigail WOOD; 22 Jul 1675; Cambridge
OLDHAM, John (-1719), Cambridge & 2/wf Elizabeth (HALL) PIERCE, Medford, MA, w Thomas; 9 Aug 1694; ?Woburn
OLDHAM, Richard (-1655) & Martha [EATON] (1636-), m/2 Thomas BROWN 1656; b 1649; Cambridge
OLDHAM, Samuel & Hannah DANA (1651-); 5 Jan 1670, 1670/1?; Cambridge
OLDAM, Thomas (-1711) & Mary WITHERELL; 20 Nov 1656; Scituate
OLDAM, Thomas & Mercy SPROUT (1662-);27 Jun 1683; Scituate
OLDHAM, __?__ & Frances __?__, m/2 David CARWITHEN 1660; Boston?
OLIVER, Daniel (1664-1732) & Elizabeth BELCHER (1678-1736); 23 Apr 1696; Charlestown
OLIVER, David & Grace [PARKER]; b 1672; Pemaquid
OLIVER, David & Sarah (PEDRICK) BRENTNALL, w Henry; 3 Mar 1691/2; Marblehead
OLIVER, James (ae 64 in 1682) (son-in-law of George CARR) & Mary (DEXTER) [FREND/FRIEND], w John; b Aug 1655; Barnstable
OLIVER, James (1659-1703) & Mercy [BRADSTREET] (1667-1710); b 1695; Cambridge
OLIVER, John (1616-1646) & Elizabeth [NEWGATE] (-1709), m/2 Edward JACKSON 1649; b 1638; Boston
OLIVER, John (1613-1642), Bristol, Eng, & Joanna [LOWELL], m/2 William GERRISH 1645; b 1639; Newbury
OLIVER, John (1644-1683) & Susanna [SWEET], dau John; b 1668; Boston
OLIVER, John (had son Hammond) & Sarah [?HAMMOND]; ca 1685; Boston
OLIVER, John & Hannah MATHER (1680-1700); 28 Jan 1697; Boston
OLIVER, Joseph & __?__
OLIVER, Nathaniel (1652-1704) & Elizabeth BRATTLE (1660-1719); 3 Jan 1676/7, 3 Jan 1677; Cambridge/Boston
OLIVER, Peter (?1618-1670) & Sarah [NEWGATE] (1621-1692); b 1642; Boston
OLIVER, Richard & Wilmot [?FRYER]; b 1668; Isles of Shoals
OLIVER, Robert & Elizabeth BUREY; 14 Sep 1693; Boston
OLIVER, Samuel (-1652) & Lydia [ALDIS], m/2 Joshua FISHER 1654; b 1647; Boston
OLIVER, Samuel & Annock SIMMONS; 10 Feb 1691/2; Huntington, LI
OLIVER, Thomas (?1582-1658) & 1/wf Ann __?__ (-1635?, 1637?; in Eng, b 1616; Boston
OLIVER, Thomas (1601-1670+), Norwich, Eng, & Mary __?__ (1602?-); b 1637, b 1632?; Salem
OLIVER, Thomas (-1658) & 2/wf Ann (SQUIRE) [PURCHASE] (1591-1662), w Aquila; aft 1637, aft 1635; Boston
OLIVER, Thomas (-bef 14 Jun 1681, 1679) & 2/wf (1/wf?) Bridget MASSELBE, m Edward BISHOP; 26 Jul 1666; Salem
OLIVER, Thomas (1646-1715) & 1/wf Grace PRENTICE (1648?-1681); 27 Nov 1667; Cambridge/Roxbury/Newton
OLIVER, Thomas (1646-1715) & 2/wf Mary WILSON (1661-1741); 19 Apr 1682; Cambridge/Newton
OLIVER, Thomas & Bethiah CLAPPE (1675-); 11 Nov 1696; Scituate
OLIVER, William & Mary (AKERLY) [SIMKINS], w Vincent?; aft 1653, bef 1657; Stanford, CT
OLIVER, William (1620-) & Elizabeth __?__; b 1673, b 1672; Isles of Shoals
OLIVER, __?__ & [Elizabeth ELIOT] (1680-), dau Asaph, m Isaac ROYAL 1 Jul 1697; b 1697; Boston
OLMSTEAD, James (-1640) & Joyce CORNISH (-1621, in Eng); Great Leigha, Eng, 26 Oct 1605; Boston/Hartford
OLMSTEAD, James (-1731), Norwalk & Phebe BARLOW (1651-); 1673?, ?1 May 1673, ?26 Jun 1673; Norwalk
OLMSTEAD, John (1617, ?1626-1686) & Elizabeth [MARVIN] (1622-1708); b 1650?, no issue; ?Norwich, CT
OLMSTEAD, John (1640-) & 1/wf Mary BENEDICT; 17 Jul 1673, 11 Nov 1670; Norwalk, CT

OLMSTED, John (-1704) & 2/wf Elizabeth (PARDEE) [GREGORY] (1660-), w Thomas; b 1696; Norwalk, CT

OLMSTED, Joseph (-1726) & Elizabeth [BUTLER]; b 1673-4?; Hartford, CT

OLMSTED, Joseph (1677-1748) & Mehitable [WARNER] (1673±-); b 1700; Norwalk, CT

OLMSTEAD, Nehemiah (1618-1657) & Elizabeth [BURR], m/2 Obadiah GILBERT 1660±, m/3 Nathaniel SEELEY 1674?; ca 1648/53; Fairfield, CT

OLMSTEAD, Nicholas (1612-1689) & 1/wf Sarah LOOMIS (1617-1687); by 28 Sep 1640; Windsor, CT/Hartford, CT

OLMSTEAD, Nicholas & Mary (THURSTON) LORD?, w Thomas (Thomas LORD m Hannah THURSTON); aft 1667; Windsor, CT

OLMSTEAD, Richard (1612, 1608?-) & 1/wf _?_; b 1646?; Cambridge/Hartford/Norwalk, CT

OLMSTEAD, Richard (-1684) & 2/wf [?Magdalen SMITH], w William; [by 1676]; Hartford/Norwalk, CT

OLMSTED, Samuel (1653-1726) & Mary [LORD] (1649-1736) (Lydia FITCH ca 1682?); b 1677; Lyme, CT/Haddam, CT/E. Haddam, CT

OLMSTEAD, Samuel (-1726) & Mary ROWLEY, dau Moses; 1697, b 1699; E. Haddam, CT

OLMSTEAD, Thomas (-1741) & ?2/wf Hannah MIX; 25 Jun 1691, 26 Jun; Hartford

OLMSTED, _?_ & Joanna (ROSE) [FLEMMING], w Robert; aft 18 Jul 1681, bef 15 Sep 1687; ?Stonington, CT/Preston, CT

OLNEY, Epenitus (1634-1698) & Mary WHIPPLE (1648-1698); 9 Mar 1666, 1665/6; Providence

OLNEY, Epenitus (1675-1740) & Mary/Mercy? [WILLIAMS] (-1740+); b 1709, b 1701?; Providence/Foster, RI

OLNEY, John (1678-1734) & Rachel COGGESHALL (-1760); 11 Aug 1699; Providence

OLNEY, Thomas (1600-1682) & Mary ASHTON (not SMALL) (1605-1679(-)); St. Albans Abbey, 16 Sep 1629; Salem/Providence

OLNEY, Thomas (1632-1722) & Elizabeth MARSH (-1722(-)); 3 Jul 1660, ?31 Jul; Providence

OLNEY, Thomas & Lydia [BARNES]; 13 Jul 1687; Providence

OLNEY, William (1663-) & Catherine SAYLES (1671-1751); 28 Dec 1692; Providence

ONG, Edmund (-1630) & Frances REED (1583-1638); Brent Eleigh, Suffolk, Eng, 8 Apr 1602; Watertown

ONG, Isaac (-(169-)) & 1/wf Mary UNDERWOOD; 18 May 1670; Shrewsbury, NJ

ONG, Jacob & ?Sarah _?_, m/2 Abraham BYAM 1689; b 1671; Chelmsford/Groton

ONION, Benjamin (1659-1718, 1719?), Dedham & Deborah WOODCOCK, Rehoboth; 24 May 1683; Rehoboth/Dedham

ONION, Robert[1] (1609-1673) & 1/wf Mary _?_ (-1643); Roxbury

ONION, Robert & 2/wf Grace EBREW (-1647); 3 Dec 1643; Dedham

ONION, Robert (ca 1610-1673) & 3/wf Sarah [METCALF] (1624-1676); b 1649; Dedham

ONION, Thomas & Margaret _?_; b 1645?, b 1615?; Kittery, ME

OORSON, William & Mary ELLIS; 27 Jun 1699; Boston

ORCHARD, Robert & Sarah [BLISH] (1641-); b 1668; Boston

ORCUTT, Andrew & Frances [WARD] (1671-1737); b 1693; Weymouth

ORCUTT, John (-1753, ae ca 86) (nephew of John WHITMAN) & 1/wf _?_ [PRATT?]; b 1695; Bridgewater

ORCUTT, Joseph (1672-) & Sarah SMITH (1672-); Stafford, CT

ORCUTT, William[1] (-1693) & 1/wf Mary LANE; 24 Jan 1663/4; Hingham

ORCUTT, William[1] (-1693) & 2/wf Martha _?_ (-1712?); ca 1668?; Weymouth

ORCUTT, William (1664-1739) & 1/wf Jane [WASHBURN]; b 1694; Bridgewater

URROHART, William (1664-1739) & 2/wf Hannah SMITH (-1751, in 71st , 72nd y); 21 Sep 1698; Bridgewater

ORDWAY, Abner & Sarah DENNIS, w Edmund/Edward; 15 Aug 1656; Boston

ORDWAY, Edward (1653-) & 1/wf Mary WOOD; 12 Dec 1678; Newbury

ORDWAY, Hananiah (1665-) & [Abigail MERRILL] (1665-1708); b 1690; Newbury

ORDWAY, James[1] (1624-1704+?, 1692+, 1711+?) & 1/wf Anne EMERY (1633-31 Mar 1687, ae 56); 25 Nov 1648; Newbury

ORDWAY, James & 2/wf Joanna CORLEY/CORLIAS, w George; 4 Oct 1687; Newbury

ORDWAY, James[2] (1651-) & 1/wf Tirzah (TITCOMB) [BARTLETT] (1658-1696), w Thomas; aft 6 Apr 1689, b 1691; Newbury

ORDWAY, James[2] (1651-1722) & 2/wf Sarah CLARK (1677-), m/2 William MOULTON, m/3 Samuel DRESSER 1733; 19 Jun 1696; Newbury/Rowley

ORDWAY, John (1655-1717/18) & Mary GODFREY (1661-); 5 Dec 1681; Newbury
ORDWAY, Samuel (-1694) & Sarah ORDWAY (1656-); ?25 Feb [1678/9?]; ?21 Feb; Ipswich/Newbury
ORIO, Eley & Ann _?_ ; b 1701; Boston
ORMES, John & Mary _?_ (-1694+); b 1656; Salem
ORMS, John (1658-) & Ann _?_ ; b 1687; Salem
ORMES, Richard & Rebecca _?_ ; b 1682; Boston
ORMES, Richard (-1712) & Rebecca (LONG) RAWLINCE/RAWLINS, w Nicholas; 5 Nov 1700; Newbury
ORMSBY/ARMSBY, Edmund?/Edward? & _?_ ; b 1638; Boston
ORMSBY, Jacob/Isaiah (1648-1677) & Mary PERREN (1649-), m/2 Nicholas IDE 1677; 2 Dec 1670; Rehoboth
ORMSBEY, John (?1641-1718) & Grace MARTIN (1640-1710); 5 Jan 1664; Rehoboth
ORMSBY, John & Susannah _?_ ; b 1696; Rehoboth
ORMSBY, Lemuel/Samuel? & Martha FREEMAN (1655-); 27 Dec 1686; Rehoboth
ORMSBY, Richard (1608-1664) & Sarah _?_ ; b 1641; Saco, ME/Haverhill/Salisbury/Rehoboth
ORMSBEY, Thomas (1645-1716) & Mary FITCH, dau John; 11 May 1667; Taunton
ORMSBY, Thomas (-1724) & Rebecca WHITAKER (-1721); 14 Nov 1698; Rehoboth
ORMSBY, _?_ & Ann _?_ ; Boston/Ipswich
ORIS, Elias & Ann _?_ ; b 1698(9?); Boston
ORRIS, Experience & Abigail [LEADER]; b 1677(8?); Boston/Braintree
ORRYS, George & Elizabeth _?_ (-1673); b 1645; Boston
ORRIS, John (1647-1699/1700) & 1/wf Sarah _?_ ; b 1672; Boston
ORRIS, John (1647-1699/1700) & 2/wf Hannah [LOWDEN]?; b 1684; Boston
ORRIS, Jonathan (1656-) & Deborah _?_ ; Falmouth, ME/Gloucester
ORRISE, Nathaniel (1664-1696) & Mary IVET, m/2 Samuel STURGIS 1697; 11 Sep 1690; Boston/Barnstable
ORTON, Ebenezer (1663-1694) & Abigail FURBUR (-1691); 28 Oct 1687; Charlestown
ORTON, John (-1695) & 1/wf _?_ [?HAWLEY/SMITH], dau Arthur?; ca 1670; Farmington, CT
ORTON, John (-1695) & 2/wf Anna/Hannah [ORVIS?] (1655-1694); ca 1686; Farmington, CT
ORTON, John (-1695) & 3/wf Mary [TUDOR], m/2 John JUDSON 1699; 1694, 1695; Farmington, CT
ORTON, Rosaman & Elizabeth _?_ ; b 1696; Westchester, NY
ORTON, Thomas & Margaret PELL?/PALL/PAUL/PRATT?; Jun 1641, 1 Jun 1641; Windsor, CT
ORTON, Thomas (-1687) & Mary [EDDY] (-1693); b 1648; Charlestown
ORTON, Thomas & Anna/An[n] BUCKINGHAM; 9 May 1698; Farmington
ORVIS, George (-1664) & Elizabeth (WELBOURNE)? [CARPENTER], w David, m/3 Richard BRONSON aft 27 Apr 1664; ca 1661; Farmington, CT
ORVICE, Roger (1657-) & Miriam HANDERSON/HENNISON?, Hartford; 15 Dec 1692; Farmington, CT
ORVICE, Samuel & Deborah _?_ ; ca 1680; Farmington, CT
OSBORN, Alexander & Sarah (WARREN) [PRINCE] (-1692), w Robert; aft 4 Jun 1674, aft 30 Jun 1674; Salem
OSBORN, Alexander & Ruth (CANTERBURY) (SMELL) SILSEBEY/SIBLEY, w Thomas, w William; 1 Dec 1692; Marblehead/Salem
OSBORN, Benjamin (1647-1722) & _?_ ; (-1718); East Hampton
OSBORN, Bezaleel (?1649-1687, 1686?) & Elizabeth _?_ ; East Hampton, LI
OSBOND, Daniel (-1712, ae 48); & _?_ ; b 1700 East Hampton, LI
OSBORN, David (-1679) & Abigail PINCKNEY, m/2 _?_ ; ca 1670; Eastchester, NY
OSBORN, Ephraim (1657-1734) & Jane MATSON; 21 Oct 1697; Cambridge
OSBORN, Henry & 1/wf Mary MARCHENT (-1679); 1 May 1661; Ipswich
OSBORN, Henry & Mary GAMAGE; aft 1681; Ipswich
OSBORN, James (-1676) & Joyce SMITH (-1684+), m/2 Gregory GIBBS 1676+; 1645, 1646; Springfield/Hartford
OSBORN, Jeremiah (1625-1676) & Mary _?_ ; b 1652; New Haven
OSBORN, Jeremiah (-1673) & _?_ ; b 1664, b 1660?; Newport
OSBORN, Jeremiah (-1709) & Mercy DAVIS (-1733); b 1684; Bristol, RI
OSBORN, Jeremiah (1656-) & Sarah (COE) [GIBBARD], w Timothy; ca 1687, b 1689; New Haven

OSBORN, John (1607-) & Mary [?KNIGHT] (-1678 at Charlestown?; b 1639(40?), ?31 May 1637?; Weymouth
OSBORN, John (1624, 1617-1686) & Ann OLDAGE (-1689); 19 May 1645; Windsor, CT
OSBORN, John (1631-1687?) & Mary/Mariam [JONES], w John?; b 1655?, b 1653?; New Haven
OSBORN, John (1646-) & 1/wf Abigail EGGLESTON (1648-1689, Windsor, CT); 14 Oct 1669, 4? Oct; Westford/Windsor, CT/LI?
OSBORN, John & ?2/wf Elizabeth RUCK; 5 Oct 1670, b 1672; Salem/Boston
OSBORN, John (?1652-1709) & Sarah [BENNETT]; bef 9 Jan 1673; Fairfield, CT
OSBORN, John & Mehitable ADDAMS (1665-); 11 Oct 1685; Ipswich
OSBORN, John & Lydia ROGERS; 12 Nov 1687, Nov 1687; Kittery, ME/York Co., ME
OSBORN, John & Grace (SHIPPIE) [PRATT], w Timothy; b 1688; Charlestown
OSBORN, John & 1/wf _?_ ; b 1689; Stratford, CT
OSBORN, John & Martha _?_ ; b 1692(3?); Windsor, CT
OSBORN, John (?1668-1740) & Elizabeth GIBBS (1672-1735); 7 Dec 1696; Windsor, CT
OSBORN, John & Mercy SOUTHWICK (1676-); b 1701?; Salem
OSBORN, Joseph (1667, 1660?-1743?) & [Mary BENNETT] (1673?, 1671-1737, 1752?); b 1692; New Haven
OSBORN, Joseph & Elizabeth [BLUX?]; b 1696; Easthampton
OSBORN, Richard (-1685±, 1684) & 1/wf _?_ ; b 1641; Hingham/Windsor, CT/New Haven/Fairfield, CT/etc.
OSBORN, Richard & Mary (LENINGTON?) (BEDIENT) TOWNSEND, w Mordecai, w Roger, m John WHARFORD; by 12 Jun 1677; Westchester, NY
OSBORN, Richard, Hempstead, LI, & Jane COATS; 5 Jan 1698/9; Hempstead, LI
OSBORN, Richard (1676-1779, 1778) & 1/wf Sarah [ANDREWS] (-1719); by 1699; Fairfield, CT/Eastchester, NY
OSBORN, Samuel (1660-1736) & 1/wf Mary BROOKS (1665-1690); 14 Nov 1683; Windsor, CT
OSBORN, Samuel (1660-) & 1/wf _?_ (-1685); b 1685; Springfield
OSBORN, Samuel & Sarah FITCH; 7 Sep 1691; Windsor
OSBORN, Samuel (1660-1736) & 2/wf Rebecca DENSLOW (1663-1751); 7 Feb -, aft Aug 1690; Windsor, CT
OSBORN, Samuel (-1715) & Hannah _?_, m/2 _?_ HALE; Springfield
OSBORN, Samuel & Eleanor SOUTHWICK (1674-1719+); 5 Jun 1695, b 1697; Salem
OSBORN, Samuel & Abigail [RUMSEY?] (ca 1680-1724); ca 1700; Fairfield, CT
OSBORN, Stephen (1634) (d Elizabeth, NJ) & Sarah [STANBOROUGH]
OSBORN, Thomas & Mary GOATLY; 18 Jan 1621/2, b 1630; Hingham/New Haven/Easthampton
OSBORN, Thomas & Sarah _?_, m/2 Joshua BRODBENT 1685; b 1647; Charlestown
OSBORN, Thomas & Hannah _?_ ; b 23 Feb 1661/2; Malden
OSBORN, Thomas (-1712, ae 89) & Mary BOND (1642-); b 1666; Easthampton, LI
OSBORN, Thomas & Margaret (FOWLER) (ROWELL) COLEMAN, w Thomas, w Thomas; b 25 Oct 1682; Nantucket
OSBORN, Thomas, Jr. & _?_ ; b 1694; East Hampton, LI
OSBORN, William (-1662) & Frezund?/Fridswide/Freesweed/Friedeswude _?_, m/2 John MULFORD 1663; b 1644; Dorchester/Braintree/Boston/Weymouth/New Haven/East Hampton, LI
OSBORN, William[1] (1646?-) (ae 33 in 1679) & Hannah BURTON; 17 Mar 1672/3; Salem
OSBORN, William & Alice (STILLWELL) HOLMES, w Samuel, m/3 Daniel LAKE 1684?; 1680?; Gravesend, LI
OSGOOD, Christopher[1] (-1650) & 1/wf Mary EVERATT; 21 Apr 1632, St. Mary, Marlborough, Eng; Ipswich
OSGOOD, Christopher[1] (-1650) & 2/wf Margery FOWLER, dau of Philip, m/2 Thomas ROWELL 1651, m/3 Thomas COLEMAN bef 1670, m/4 Thomas OSBORNE by 1682; 28 Jul 1633, St. Mary, Marlborough, Eng; Ipswich
OSGOOD, Christopher (1643-1723) & 1/wf Hannah BELKNAP (-1679), Lynn; 6 Dec 1663; Salem
OSGOOD, Christopher (1643-1723) & 2/wf Hannah BARKER (-1687); 27 May 1680; Andover
OSGOOD, Christopher (1643-1723) & 3/wf Sarah REDINGTON (1659-Jul 1689); 21 Dec 1687; Topsfield
OSGOOD, Christopher (1643-1723) & 4/wf Sarah _?_ ; aft Jul 1689, bef 1692; Andover
OSGOOD, Hooker (1668-1748) & Dorothy WOODMAN (1669-); 13 Apr 1692; Andover/Lancaster
OSGOOD, John (?1595-1651) & Sarah [BOOTH] (-1667); ca 1627, in Eng; Andover
OSGOOD, John (ca 1631-1693) & Mary CLEMENT; 15 Nov 1653; Andover

OSGOOD, John & Mary STEVENS, m/2 Nathaniel WHITTIER 1685; 5 Nov 1668; Salisbury

OSGOOD, John (1654-1725) & Hannah EIRES/AYRES (1662-1731); 17 Oct 1681; Andover

OSGOOD, Joseph (1673-) & Mary MARBLE (1678-); 8 May 1700; Andover

OSGOOD, Peter (1663-1753) & Martha AYRE/AYRES/AYERS (1668-1700), Haverhill; 19 May 1690; Salem

OSGOOD, Robert & Sarah DODSON; 14 Dec 1699; Scituate

OSGOOD, Stephen (ca 1638-1691) & Mary HOOKER; 24 Oct 1663; Andover

OSGOOD, Stephen (1670-) & Hannah BLANCHARD; 24 May 1699; Andover

OSGOOD, Thomas & Susannah LORD; 22 May 1674; Andover

OSGOOD, Timothy (1659-1748) & 1/wf Deborah POOR; 29 May 1689; Andover

OSGOOD, William (1609-1700) & Elizabeth [?CLEER/?CORLISS]; b 1637; Salisbury

OSGOOD, William & Abigail AMBROSE/?SEVERANCE (1654-); Oct 1672; Salisbury

OSGOOD, William & Hannah COLEBY/COLBY; 8 Jun 1693; Amesbury

OSLAND, Humphrey (-1720) & Elizabeth HIDE/HYDE (-1723); 7 Mar 1666/7, 7 Mar 1667; Cambridge/Newton

OSLAND, John (1669-) & Sarah HIDE/HYDE (1679-); 14 Oct 1697; Boston

OZLAND, Richard (-1716) & Mary _?_; Hempstead, LI

OSMAN, Abraham & Martha _?_ (-1706, wid); Southold, LI

OSMAN, Jacob (1670-) & Sarah [CORWIN] (1660±-); b 1690; Southold

OSMAN, John & Mary/Katherine [YOUNGS], wid in 169-; ca 1681; Southold, LI

OSMAN, Thomas & Martha [PURRIER] (1636?-); ?Jan 1653; Southold

OSMENT/?OSMAN/?OSMINT, John & Lydia _?_; b 1692; Boston

OSMENT, John & Mary PROCTER; 14 Jan 1700; Boston

OSWELL, William & Eleanor _?_; b 1667; Charlestown

OTIS, Job (1677-1758) & Mercy [LITTLE] (1678-1755); ca 1699, 1 Oct 1699; Plymouth

OTIS, John[1] (1581-1657) & 1/wf Margaret _?_ (-1653); in Eng, b 1604, ?Glastonbury; Hingham/Weymouth

OTIS, John[2] (-1684, 1683) & Mary [JACOB] (1637-), m/2 John HOLBROOK; ca 10 May 1649, b 1653; Hingham/Scituate/etc.

OTIS, John[1] (1581-1657) & 2/wf Elizabeth (WHITMAN) STREAM, w Thomas; aft 1653; Hingham/Scituate

OTIS, John (1657-1727) & Mercy BACON (1660-1737); Barnstable, 18 Jul 1683; Barnstable/Hingham

OTIS, Joseph (1663-1754) & Dorothy THOMAS (1670-); 20 Nov 1688; Scituate/Marshfield

OTIS, Nicholas (?1665-1696) & [Joyce] _?_, m/2 Henry TIBBETTS 1700; Dover, NH

OTIS, Richard (?1626-1689) & 1/wf Rose [STOUGHTON] (?1629-); by 1650?; Dover, NH

OTIS, Richard (-1689) & 2/wf Shuah (STARBUCK) HEARD, w James; b 5 Nov 1677, nr 1676, ca 1677; Dover, NH

OTIS, Richard (-1689) & 3/wf Grizel/Grizzel/Grizet WARREN (1662-1750), m/2 Philip ROBITAILLE; nr 1686, ca 1685; Dover, NH

OTIS, Richard (?1650-1701) & 2/wf? Susanna [HUSSEY] (1667-), m/2 John VARNEY 1703; nr 1690; Dover, NH

OTIS, Stephen (-1689) & Mary PITTMAN; 16 Apr 1674; Dover, NH

OATICE, Stephen (-1733, ae 72) & Hannah ENSINE/ENSIGN (1669-1729, ae 60); 16 Jan 1685, Jun; Scituate

OVERMAN, Jacob & Hannah _?_ (-1692, ae 38); 25 Oct 1677; Wethersfield, CT

OVERMAN, Thomas & Hannah (WISWELL) (MUNNINGS) [READ] (-1694), w Mahahaleel, w William; aft 23 Sep 1667, bef 27 May 1672; Boston

OVIATT, Roger & _?_; b 1660; Milford, CT

OVIATT, Samuel (1672-1749) & Mary _?_; Milford

OVIATT, Thomas & Frances ?BRYAN; b 1664; Milford, CT

OWEN, Daniel (1658-1683) & Mary BISSELL (1659-1690), m/2 Joseph BIRGE/BURGE; 24 Jan 1681; Windsor, CT

OWEN, Daniel/Josiah? & Hannah LINCOLN (1666-); 23 Dec 1689; Taunton/Braintree

OWEN, Ebenezer (1657-) & [Hannah] _?_; b 1681; Braintree

OWEN, Even/Edwin (-1684) & Martha _?_; b 1687; Brookhaven, NY

OWEN, George & _?_

OWEN, George, Jr. & _?_

OWEN, Isaac (1670-1736) & Sarah HOLCOMB (1673-1763), m/2 John CASE; 20 Dec 1694; Windsor, CT

OWEN, John (1624, ?1616-1697/8,1692) & Rebecca WADE (-1711); 3 Oct 1650; Windsor, CT

OWENS, John & Mary TUCKSBURY/TEWKESBURY; 13 Jun 1687; Manchester/Marblehead

OWEN, Jonathan (-1750) & Mary BREWSTER; Brookhaven, NY

OWEN, Joseph (1660-1735/40) & Esther [OSBORN/?OSGOOD] (1662-); b 1683; Windsor/Simsbury

OWEN, Josiah/Josias? (1651-) & 1/wf Mary OSBORN (1655-1689); 22 Oct 1674; Windsor, CT

OWEN, Josiah/Josias (-1722) & 2/wf Sarah __?__, m/2 Nathaniel HOLCOMB 1725; b 1692; Windsor, CT

OWEN, Josiah & Hannah __?__; b 1694; Braintree

OWEN, Josiah/Josias (1675-1763, Hebron) & Mary HOSFORD (1674-1753); 3 Dec 1698; Windsor, CT

OWEN, Morgan & Elizabeth DICKASON, m/2 Walter MOUNTJOY 167-; Jul 1670; Salem

OWEN, Moses & __?__

OWEN, Nathaniel (?1656-) & Mary __?__; b 1683?, b 1684?; Braintree

OWEN, Nathaniel (1656-) & 1/wf Mary GAYLORD (-1696); 14 Jun 1694; Windsor, CT

OWEN, Nathaniel & 2/wf Sarah PALMER (1675-1731); 2 Feb 1697 (not 22 Feb 1697/8; Windsor, CT

OWEN, Obadiah (1667-) & Christiana/Christian? WINCHELL (1672-1762); 21 Sep 1693, b 1691?; Windsor, CT

OWEN, Richard (-1695) & Martha [SMITH], w James; b 7 Mar 1662; Newtown, LI

OWENS, Samuel & Ann (CANNING) PETTY/PETEE, w John; 5 Sep 1681; Deerfield

OWEN, [Thomas] & Martha MERRITT (-1725); b 1681; Salem/Marblehead

OWEN, Thomas & Elizabeth CHINNY/CHENERY; 10 Sep 1694; Boston

OWEN, William (-1702) & Elizabeth DAVIES/DAVIS? (-1702) (her mother, Margery DAVIS, m/2 Charles GRICE); 29 Sep 1650; Braintree

OWEN, William & Sarah VITTERELL; 28 Apr 1693; Boston

OXENBRIDGE, John (1606-1674) & 1/wf Jane [BUTLER] (-1655); Boston

OXENBRIDGE, John & 2/wf Frances [WOODWARD] (-1659); in Eng, ca 1658, 1656?

OXENBRIDGE, John & 3/wf Mary HACKSHAW; lic 26 Feb 1660/1

OXENBRIDGE, John & Susanna [ABBIT/ABBOT]; ca 1666-7; Boston

OXFORD, Thomas & Grace (PITTS) [POTTER], w William; 30 Apr 1679; ?Boston

PABODIE, John (1590-1667) & Isabel [BRITTAINE?] (-1667+); in Eng, b 1620; Duxbury

PABODIE, William (1620-1707) & Elizabeth ALDEN (?1624-1717); 23 Dec 1644, 26 Dec; Duxbury/Little Compton, RI

PABODIE, William (1664-1744) & 1/wf Judith [?TILDON] (1669/70-1714); b 1698; Little Compton, RI

PACEY, Nicholas & Katherine __?__; b 29 Dec 1640, b 28 Dec 1640; Salem

PACEY, Thomas & Sarah (DUDLEY) KEAYNE (1620-1659, Boston), div wf of Benjamin; b 1655; Boston

PACKARD, Daniel & Mary [HARRIS]; b 1701?, 1713

PACKARD, John[2] (1655-1741) & Judith WINSLOW (1672-1761, in 90th y); 12 Apr 1688; Taunton

PACKARD, Nathaniel[2] (see Samuel) & [Lydia SMITH]/KINGMAN?, dau John; b 1694, ca 1682, b 1696; Bridgewater, CT

PACKARD, Samuel[1] (-1684) & Elizabeth __?__, m/2 John WASHBURN; in Eng, b 1657; Hingham/Weymouth

PACKARD, Samuel[2] (-1716) (see Nathaniel) & Elizabeth [LATHROP]/Lydia [SMITH] (1662-1716); ca 1681, 1678?; Bridgewater/Duxbury

PACKARD, Col. Thomas[2] & Elizabeth (SMITH) [HALL], w Joseph; 7 Aug 1687, 1686?; Greenland, NH/Portsmouth, NH?/Bridgewater

PACKARD, Zaccheus[2] (1651-1723, ae 80) & Sarah [HOWARD]; b 1680; Bridgewater

PACKARD, _?_ & Joanna [TUTTLE] (1664-); 1679; Ipswich?
PACKER, John (-1689) & 1/wf Elizabeth [FRIEND] (-1674); ca 1652/60?; New London, CT
PACKER, John (-1689) & 2/wf Rebecca (WELLS) LATHAM, w Thomas, m/3 _?_ WATSON; 24 Jun 1678; New London, CT
PACKER, John (-1701) & [Lydia LATHAM]/?Elizabeth MILLER/Sarah _?_ MILLER ?10 Mar 1686, w Thomas; ?ca 1690/95?, b 1680, 24 Jun 1678; New London, CT/Groton, CT
PACKER, Samuel (-1755) & Mary [WILLIAMS]; b 1701?; New London
PACKER, Thomas & 1/wf Hepzibah [DRAKE] (1659-1685); 23 Aug 1681; Marblehead/Salem
PACKER, Thomas (-1728), Portsmouth, NH, & 2/wf Elizabeth (SMITH/?WALDRON) HALL (-1717), w Joseph; 7 Aug 1687; Dover, NH (see Thomas PACKARD)
PADDLEFORD/PADLFOOT, Jonathan (-1661) & Mary BLANFORD (-1676), m/2 Thomas EAMES ca 1661; 5 Oct 1652; Cambridge
PADELFORD, Jonathan (1656-1710) & Hannah (THAYER) [HAYDEN] (not Hannah FLINT), w Samuel; b 1679(80?); Braintree/Taunton
PADDOCK, John (1643-1718) & Anna JONES; 21 Dec 1673; Swansea
PADDOCK, John (1669-1718) & Priscilla [HALL] (1671-1725); b 1695, pub 1694; Yarmouth
PADDOCK, Joseph (1674-) & Sarah GARDNER; 5 Mar 1696; Nantucket
PADDOCK, Robert (-1650) & 1/wf _?_ ; b 1636, b 1634?; Plymouth/Duxbury
PADDOCK, Robert (-1650, Plymouth) & 2/wf Mary [PALMER], w William, Sr., m/3 Thomas ROBERTS 1650/1; aft 1637, aft 1638?, aft 1640, betw 1644 & 1646; Plymouth/Duxbury
PADDOCK, Zachary/Zachariah? (1636, 1640-1727) & Deborah SEARS (1639-1732); 1659; Yarmouth
PADDOCK, Zachary (1664-1717, 1718?) & Bethia [HULL] (1664-1708); b 1687; Yarmouth
PADDY, Thomas (1647-1690) & Deborah [WAITE] (1644-1697); b 1671; Boston
PADDY, William (-1658), Plymouth & 1/wf Alice FREEMAN (1619-1651), Sandwich; 24 Nov 1639; ?Plymouth/?Sandwich
PADDY, William (-1658) & 2/wf Mary (GREENOUGH) PAITON/PEYTON (-1675, ae 60), w Bezaleel, m/? Philip BULLIS?; 3 Dec 1651; Boston
PAGE, Abraham & Mary _?_ ; b 1647, b 1646; Boston
PAGE, Amos (1677-) & Hannah?/Joanna? _?_ ; b 1698; Salisbury
PAGE, Benjamin (1644, 1640?-) & Mary WHITTIER (1647-1698); 21 Sep 1666; Haverhill
PAGE, Christopher (1670-1751) & Abigail TILTON (1670-1759); 14 Nov 1689; Hampton, NH
PAGE, Cornelius & 1/wf Martha CLOUGH; 13 Nov 1674; Haverhill
PAGE, Cornelius & 2/wf Mary MASH/MARSH; 16 Jan 1684; Haverhill
PAGE, Edward & Elizabeth [BEAMSLEY]/BUSHNELL (1632-); b 1653; Boston
PAGE, Edward (1658-1693) & Abial [THORNTON], m/2 _?_ LAWRENCE/LORESON 1693+; b 1682(3?); Boston
PAGE, Francis (1633-1706) & Meribah SMITH; 2 Dec 1669; Hampton, NH
PAGE, Francis (1676-1755) & Hannah NUDD (1678-1751); 27 Jan 1698; Hampton, NH
PAGE, George & Mary EDGECOMB, m/2 John ASHTON 1691; Sep/Oct 1664; Saco, ME/Marblehead
PAGE, George & Sarah LINDSLEY; b 1664, 1664(5?); Branford, CT
PAGE, George (1672-) & Mary [HALL] (1675-); b 1701?, b 1705; Bramford, CT/Wallingford, CT?
PAGE, Isaac/Samuel & Damaris SHATTOCK/SHATTUCK; 30 Sep 1653; Boston
PAGE, Jeremiah (1667-1749) & Deborah HENDRICKS; 2 Jul 1696; Haverhill
PAGE, John (1586-1676) & Phebe [PAYEN] (1594-1677); in Eng, ca 1620?, b 1633, 5 Jun 1621, Lanenham, Eng; Watertown
PAGE, John (-1687) & Mary [MARSH] (-1697); b 1641; Hingham/Haverhill
PAGE, John, Jr. (1641-) & Sarah DAVIS; 18 Jun 1663; Haverhill
PAGE, John (?1630-1712) & Faith DUNSTER (1640/1-1699); 12 May 1664, b 1685 Roxbury?; Groton/Watertown
PAGE, John & 2/wf Emory LAMB, wid; m cont 5 Sep 1699; Watertown
PAGE, John & Sarah SINGLETARY; 21 May 1700; Haverhill
PAGE, Joseph (1647-1684) & 1/wf Judith GILLE/GILL?/GILE/GOULD (1650-1672); 21 Jun 1671; Amesbury/Haverhill
PAGE, Joseph (1647-1684) & 2/wf Martha (DOW) HEATH, w Joseph, m/3 Samuel PARKER 1689; 2 Dec 1673; Haverhill
PAGE, Joseph & 1/wf Sarah SMITH (-1691); 12 Mar 1690/1; Salisbury
PAGE, Joseph & 2/wf Elizabeth _?_ ; aft 21 Oct 1691, [prob Jan 1691/2]; Salisbury

PAGE, Joseph & Margaret RULE, m/2 Thomas JOHNSON, m/3 Benjamin SNELLING; m int 13 Nov 1695; Boston

PAGE, Nathaniel (?1645-1692, Boston) & Joanna [MORRISON] (-1744); in Eng?, b 1679, 1677?; Billerica/Rowley

PAIGE, Nicholaus & Ann/Anna/?Hannah (KEAYNE/KEANIES) LANE, w Edward; aft 1664; Boston/Cambridge

PAGE, Onesiphorus & Mary HAUXWORTH; 22 Nov 1664, 1665?, prob 1664; Salisbury

PAGE, Onesiphorus & 2/wf Sarah (MORRILL) POWELL, wid, m/3 Daniel MERRILL 1708; 31 Jul 1695; Salisbury

PAGE, Robert (1604-1679) & Lucy [?WADD]/[?NUDD] (1607-1665); in Eng, b 1629; Salem/Hampton, NH/Salisbury

PAGE, Samuel (1633-1691) & Hannah [?DEAN] (1646-); b 1668, b 1667; Watertown/Concord

PAGE, Samuel (1671-) & 1/wf Sarah [LAWRENCE] (1672-); b or ca 1691; Watertown

PAGE, Samuel (1671-1769) & 1/wf Hannah WILLIAMS (-1700); 9 Jan 1696; Hampton, NH

PAGE, Samuel & Mindwell _?_ ; b 1700; Branford, CT

PAGE, Thomas (1697-) & Elizabeth _?_ (1598-); b 1633; Saco, ME/Salisbury

PAGE, Thomas (1639, 1633?-1686) & Mary HUSSEY (1638-1733, ae 95), m/2 Henry GREEN 1691, m/3 Henry DOW; 2 Feb 1664; Hampton, NH

PAGE, Thomas & _?_ ; Cape Elizabeth, ME

PAGE, William (-1664, 1665) & Anna/Hannah [BABCOCK]? (-1686), m/2 Nicholas WOOD, m/3 Edward WINN; b 1664, b 1642; Watertown

PAGE, _?_ & Mary [HADLEY] (1657-); b 18 Sep 1684

PAINE, Anthony[1] (-1650) & 1/wf [?Susannah] [?POTTER] (-1643); ?b 1622; Portsmouth, RI

PAINE, Anthony (-1650) & 2/wf Rose (_?_) GRINNELL (-1673), w Matthew, m/3 James WEIDEN 1650; 10 Nov 1643, agreement; Portsmouth, RI

PAINE, Daniel & Bethiah [BLANCHARD] (1668-); b 1697; Woburn

PAINE, Edward (returned to Eng) & _?_ ; b 1627; Charlestown

PAINE, Edward (-1691) & Bethia [SWEETSER] (1663-), m/2 Isaac WHEELER 1700; b 1682; Charlestown

PAINE, Elisha (1659-1735/6) & Rebecca DOANE (1668-1758); 20 Jan 1685; Eastham/Canterbury, CT

PAINE, Henry & Love [MAYER] (1674-)

PAINE, James & Amy _?_ ; b 1659/60; Newport, RI

PAINE, James & Martha _?_ ; Isles of Shoals

PAINE, James (1665-1728) & Bethia THACHER (1671-1734); 9 Apr 1691; Barnstable/Yarmouth

PAINE, Job & Susanna EGLESTONE (-1702); 11 Jan 1699; Middletown, CT

PAINE, John (-1677) & Elizabeth BURR, m/2 John WHIPPLE 1680; 21 Sep 1657: Ipswich

PAINE, John (1632-1675?) & Sarah PARKER; Mar 1659, ca 15 Mar 1658/9; Boston

PAINE, John (1620-) & _?_ ; b 1651?; Southold, LI

PAINE, John (-1665) & Agnes _?_ ; ?Boston

PAINE, John (1649-1729) & 1/wf Abigail BROCKETT (1650-); 22 Jan 1673; New Haven

PAINE, John (-1681) & Mary (HALL) MARTIN, w Anthony; 1 Aug 1676; Middletown, CT

PAINE, John (1646-) & Mary DAY; 7 Feb 1677, 1676/7; Dedham

PAINE, John & Elizabeth _?_ ; b 1679; Boston

PAINE, John & 1/wf Mary _?_ (1661-1690); b 1679; Southold, LI

PAINE, John (-1704, ae 62) & 1/wf _?_ ; b 1680; Newport, RI

PAINE, John (1656-) & Elizabeth [BELCHER] (1663-); b 1682; Rehoboth/Swansea

PAINE, John (-1704, ae 62) & 2/wf Mary [BROWN?]; aft 1683; Newport, RI

PAINE, John (1666-1706) & Deborah NEAL; 20 Jan 1688/9, 22 Jan 1688; Braintree/Milton

PAINE, John (1661-1731) & 1/wf Bennett FREEMAN; 14 Mar 1689, 1688/9; Eastham

PAINE, John & Jemima ALSOP (1670-1713); 24 Mar 1691/2; New Haven/Southold

PAINE, John (1649-1729) & 2/wf Mary [LITTLE]; ca 1694; New Haven

PAINE, John & Bethiah HODGE; 5 Jul 1698; Boston

PAINE, Joseph (-1712) & Patience SPARROW (-1715), m/2 John JENKINS; 27 May 1691; Eastham/Harwich

PAINE, Moses (1581-1643) & 1/wf Mary BENISON (-1617/18); 2 Nov 1615, Tenterden, Eng, m lic; Braintree

PAINE, Moses[1] (1581-1643) & 2/wf Elizabeth (SHEAFE) [COLLIER] (-1632); 1618; Braintree

PAINE, Moses[1] (1581-1643) & 3/wf Judith (PARES) [QUINCY] (-1654), w Edmund, m/3 Robert HALL; ca 1642/3; Braintree

PAINE, Moses (1623-1690) & Elizabeth [COLBURN] (-1704); b 1646; Braintree/Boston

PAYNE, Moses & Jane (WEEKS) BATES, w Benjamin; 18 Jun 1679; Roxbury

PAINE, Moses (1660-1746) & Mary [PIERCE] (1665-1743); b 1689; Braintree

PAINE, Nathaniel (-1678) & Elizabeth _?_ (-1704±); b 1661; Rehoboth/Boston

PAINE, Nathaniel (1661-1723/4) & Dorothy [RAINSFORD] (1663-1755); b 1681; Rehoboth/Bristol, RI

PAINE, Nathaniel (1667-1718) & Dorothy CHAFFEE (-1718); 1 May 1694; Rehoboth

PAINE, Nathaniel (-1731) & Ann _?_ ; b 1693; Southold, LI

PAINE, Nicholas (-1733) & Hannah [HIGGINS] (1672-1732); b 1700; Eastham

PAINE, Peter (?1617-1668) & Mary [FOLGER], m/2 Jeremiah VAIL 1660; b 1650, b 1645?; Southold, LI

PAYNE, Peter (?1645±-1697/8?, 1696?) & Abigail _?_ (-1716, ae 68?); ca 1670/80?, ca 1670?; Southold, LI

PAYN, Peter & Hannah COURSER; m int 27 Nov 1696; Boston

PAINE, Philip & Mary NASH (1652-); 1 Jan 1679; New Haven/Northampton

PAINE, Ralph (-1722) & Dorothy _?_ (see Nathaniel); b 1685; Freetown/Portsmouth, RI

PAINE, Richard (-1708, ae 72) & Sarah (TAYLOR) (CANNEY) [WINGATE] (-1707, ae 72, Boston), w Thomas, w John; aft 9 Dec 1687?, b 1701?, b - Jul 1693; Boston/Charlestown

PAINE, Robert (±1601-1684) & 1/wf Ann [WHITING]; in Eng, b 1624?; Ipswich

PAINE, Robert (±1601-1684) & 2/wf Dorcas _?_ (-1681); ca 1630?, b 1637?, ca 1640?; Ipswich

PAINE, Robert & Elizabeth REINER/REYNER/REYNOR; 10 Jul 1666, 11? Jul; Ipswich/Wells, ME

PAINE, Samuel & Elizabeth _?_ ; b 1670; Boston

PAINE, Samuel (1654-1739) & Mary PENNIMAN (1653-1704?); 4 Apr 1678; Braintree

PAINE, Samuel (-1712) & Patience FREEMAN; 31 Jan 1682, 1682/3; Eastham

PAINE, Samuel (1662-) & 1/wf Anna/Anne PECK (1667-1703); 16 Dec 1685?; Rehoboth

PAINE, Stephen[1] (-1679) & 1/wf Rose/Niobe _?_ (-1660/1); Great Ellingham?, Shropham?, Norfolk, in Eng, b 1629?; Hingham/Rehoboth

PAINE, Stephen (1626-1691) & Hannah BASS, m/2 Shadrack WILBUR 1692; 15 Nov 1651; Braintree

PAINE, Stephen (1629-1678) (son Stephen, Jeremiah NORCROSS his uncle) & Ann/Anne CHICKERING, m/2 Thomas METCALF 1679; 3 Nov 1652, 3 Nov 1659; Dedham/Rehoboth

PAINE, Stephen (?1634-1693?) & Elizabeth [CARRINGTON] (1639-1711), m/2 David CARWITHEN b 1688/9?; b 1658; Charlestown/Malden

PAINE, Stephen[1] (-1679?) & 2/wf Alice?/?Elizabeth [PARKER] (-5 Dec 1682), w William of Taunton; bef 3 Sep 1662, ca 20 Jan 1660/1, ca 1662; Taunton?/Rehoboth?

PAINE, Stephen (1654-1710) & 1/wf Elizabeth [WILLIAMS] (1660, 1659-); ca 1679; Rehoboth/Stonington, CT

PAINE, Stephen (1653-1690) & Ellen VEAZIE (1652-), m/2 Joseph CROSBY 1693; 20 Feb 1681; Braintree

PAINE, Thomas (1586-1644, Salem) & Elizabeth [?TUTHILL] (1584-1657); Eng, 22 Nov 1610; Salem/Southold, LI

PAINE, Thomas & _?_ ; ca 1620?; Yarmouth

PAYNE, Thomas & Jane [GALLION?], m/2 Thomas MAYHEW by 1638; London?, b 1629?, ca 1632?

PAINE, Thomas (1613-) & Rebecca [WARE]; ca 17 Oct 1640; Boston?/Dedham/Wrentham

PAINE, Thomas (-1706) & Mary [SNOW] (-1704); ca 1650; Eastham

PAINE, Thomas (-1667) & Hannah [BRAY/BRACEY] (-1682), New Haven; 25 Aug 1659, d Wethersfield, CT; Boston

PAINE, Thomas & _?_ ; b 1669; York Co., ME

PAINE, Thomas (1644-1726) & 1/wf Rebecca PECK (-1682); 25 Apr 1671; Dedham

PAINE, Thomas (1657-1721, in 65th y, Truro) & 1/wf Hannah SHAW (?1658-1713, ae 52); 5 Aug 1678; Eastham

PAINE, Thomas (-1700) & Elizabeth [MILBURY], m/2 Richard BEAZER; ca 1680; Dover, NH

PAINE, Thomas (-1715) & Mercy [CARR] (1661-1717), no issue; ca 1680/5?, b 8 Mar 1694, b May 1685; Newport

PAINE, Thomas (1644-1726) & 2/wf Margaret _?_ (-1688?); aft 28 Nov 1682+, ca 1683/4; Dedham

PAINE, Thomas (1644-1726) & 3/wf Mary LAWSON?/LAWSON (-1718); 20 Aug 1689, 30 Aug; Dedham

PAINE, Tobias (-1669) & Sarah (WINSLOW) STANDISH, w Myles, m/3 Richard MIDDLECOTT 1672; ?Nov 1666, 1667, 1665, ?Nov 1667; Boston

PAINE, William (1598-1660) & Ann _?_ (-1695); b 1624 in Eng; Watertown

PAYNE, William (-1684) & _?_ ; b 1650, b 1649; New Haven

PAINE, William (-1654) & Martha _?_ ; b 1645?

PAYNE, William & Mary (EDWARDS) BROWN (-1693), w Francis; aft 1668; New Haven

PAINE, William & Catharine _?_ ; b 1679; Boston

PAINE, William & Sarah [?SANFORD]; b 1680; Boston

PAINE, William (1664-1741) & 1/wf Ruth GROVER (1667-1722); 9 Mar 1691/2; Malden/Charlestown

PAINE, William (1669-1735, 1736) & 1/wf Mary TAYLOR (-1700); 11 Oct 1694; Boston

PAINE, William & Elizabeth [GEORGE] (1670-); b 1701?; Boston?

PAINTER, Daniel & Johanna _?_ ; b 1697; Stonington, CT

PAINTER, John & Sarah [TILTON] (1644-); ca 1666?, b 15 Jul 1687; ?Gravesend, LI

PAINTER, Shubael & Mercy [LAMBERTON] (1641-bef 1677); ca 1661/3?; Westerly, RI/Newport/New Haven

PAINTER, Thomas (-1706) & 1/wf Katherine _?_ (-1691); b 1639, b 1634?; Boston/Newport/Westerly, RI

PAINTER, Thomas & _?_ ; b 1644

PAINTER, Thomas (1670±-) & Rebecca [CANDEE] (1671-1739); b 1695; New Haven/West Haven

PAINTER, William (-1666) & Elizabeth [WADLOE]?; Charlestown

PAINTER, William & Mary MESSINGER (1672-); 28 May 1691; Boston

PALFREY, John (-1689) & Rebecca BOARDMAN; 4 Aug 1664; Cambridge

PALFREY, Peter (-1663) & 1/wf Edith _?_ ; b 1636; Salem/Reading

PALFREY, Peter (-1663) & 2/wf Elizabeth (?KNIGHT) [FAIRFIELD], w John; aft 22 Dec 1646; Salem

PALFREY, Peter (-1663) & 3/wf Alice _?_ (-1677); b 21 Oct 1662; Reading

PALFRAY, Walter (-1713) & Margaret MANNING (1657-1720+); 7 May 1680; Salem

PALFREY, William & Constant/Constance? _?_ ; b 1676; Boston

PALFREY, _?_ & Jane _?_ , m/2 George WILLIS b 1637; b 1632; Cambridge

PALSGRAVE, John (1634-) & Mary MAVERICK (-1706), m/2 Francis HOOKE 1660; 8 Feb 1655/6; Boston

PALGRAVE, Richard (-1651) & Ann/Anna? _?_ (-1609, ae 75); in Eng, b 1621?, b 1619; Charlestown/Roxbury

PAULGRAVE, Richard (-1631 in Eng) & Joan HARRIS, m/2 Rev. John YOUNGS; Great Yarmouth, Eng, 24 Jan 1625/6; Southold, LI

PALK, Samuel & Sarah BRABROOK; 13 Feb 1689/90; Concord

PALMER, Abraham (-1653, Barbados) & Grace _?_ (-1660); b 1632; Charlestown

PALMER, Benjamin (1642-1716) & _?_ ; b 10 Aug 1681, no issue; Stonington, CT

PALMER, Benjamin & Mary _?_ ; b 1695; Newport, RI

PALMER, Christopher (1626-1699) & Susanna HILTON (1635-1717); 7 Nov 1650; Hampton, NH

PALMER, Daniel & Elizabeth _?_ ; b 1701; Branford, CT

PALMER, Daniel & Margaret SMITH; 25 Mar 1700; Stonington, CT

PALMER, Edwardward? & Lucy [READE] (-1676); 1660; New London

PALMER, Elias & Frances _?_ ; ca 1685/90; Flushing, LI

PALMER, Elnathan (1665/6-) & Mercy/?Mary CLARKE; 25 Dec 1695; Scituate

PALMER, Ephraim (-1684) & Sarah [MESSENGER], m/2 _?_ GREGORY; ca 1668; ?Jamaica, LI/Greenwich, CT

PALMER, Ephraim, Jr. & _?_ ; b 1697

PALMER, Francis & 1/wf Elizabeth HUNT (1661-1689); 3 Dec 1682; Rowley

PALMER, Francis & Ann JEWETT; 10 Jun 1690; Rowley

PALMER, George (1620-1670) & Elizabeth [?NORTON]; b 31 Dec 1650; Kittery, ME

PALMER, George & Bethia MOREY/MOWRY (1638-1686); 30 Sep 1662; Warwick, RI

PALMER, Gershom (1645-1718, 1719) & 1/wf Ann DENISON (1649-1694); 28 Nov 1667; Stonington, CT
PALMER, Gershom (1672-) & Sarah [FENNER]; ca 1700; Stonington, CT/Saybrook, CT
PALMER, Henry & Elizabeth _?_ (-1664); b 1634; Newbury/Haverhill
PALMER, Henry & Catherine _?_ ; b 1642(3?); Watertown
PALMER, Henry & _?_ ; b 1663; Newport, RI
PALMER, Ichabod (1677-1752) & Hannah [PALMER] (1680-1757); b 1699; Stonington, CT
PALMER, James & Sarah [DUNHAM/DENHAM?]; b 1670, b 1688
PALMER, James & Elizabeth GROWTH/GROTH; 31 Dec 1690; Bradford
PALMER, John (?1600-) & _?_ ; b 1640, ca 1635; Hingham
PALMER, John & 1/wf Ruth ACY/ACIE (-1649); 17 Sep 1645; Rowley
PALMER, John & 2/wf Margaret (?NORTHEND) ?CROSS; 14 Jul 1650; Rowley
PALMER, John (-1689+) & _?_ ; b 1650?; Monhegan/etc.
PALMER, John & Sarah [RANDALL] (1640-1693+); b 1666; Hingham/Scituate
PALMER, John & Elizabeth [ALGER]; b 1666; Scarboro, ME/Boston
PALMER, John (-1692) & Bridget [BAXTER], div wf of Thomas; by May 1666; Westchester, NY
PALMER, John & Mary [?MUNJOY] (1652-1734); ca 1670/75; Marblehead
PALMER, John (?1665-1753) & Elizabeth [RICHMOND]; [1686]; Little Compton, RI/?Kingston, RI/?Westerly, RI
PALMER, John (1666-) & Phebe [POTTER] (-1738); b 1691; Branford, CT
PALMER, John & Hannah _?_ ; b 1694; Westerly, RI
PALMER, John & Mary ROSE; 20 Dec 1694; Scituate
PALMER, John (1673-) & Sarah MUDGE; 14 Jan 1695/6, 4 Jan 1695?; Windsor, CT/Northampton
PALMER, John & Rebecca BAXTER; 31 Oct 1700; Westchester, NY
PALMER, Jonah (-1709) & 1/wf Elizabeth GRISELL (-1692); 3 May 1655; Charlestown/Rehoboth
PALMER, Jonah (1662-) & Elizabeth KENDRICK/?KENRICK; 28 May 1689; Rehoboth
PALMER, Jonah (-1709) & 2/wf Abigail (CARPENTER) TITUS (-1710), w John; 9 Nov 1692; Rehoboth
PALMER, Joseph (-1715) & Sarah JACKMAN; 1 Mar 1664; Newbury/Branford
PALMER, Joseph (-1726) & Sarah [MARSH] (-1711); b 1666; Westchester, NY/Flushing, LI
PALMER, Joseph & Deborah BATCHELDER (1657-); 25 Jan 1677, 1676/7; Hampton, NH
PALMER, Joseph (1663-1710) & Frances PRENTICE (-1710+), Cambridge; 13 Nov 1687, 12? Nov; Newton/Stonington, CT
PALMER, Joseph (-1716+) & Elizabeth [TYLER]? (ca 1663); Greenwich, CT/Westchester, NY
PALMER, Joseph (1670-) & 1/wf Hannah _?_ ; b 1696; Newbury
PALMER, Joseph (1670-) & 2/wf Hester _?_ ; b 1700?; Newbury
PALMER, Joshua (1677-) & Mercy [STANFORD] (1679-); b 1701; Milford, CT/Branfford, CT
PALMER, Josiah (1643-) & _?_ ; b 1685; Hingham/Scituate
PALMER, Lisle & Esther [GANNETT]; b 1679; Boston
PAMER, Micah/Michael & Elizabeth BULKELEY; 2 Dec 1662; Branford, CT
PAMER, Micah (1664-) & Damaris WHITEHEAD (1670-); 14 Feb 1693, 1693/4; Branford, CT
PALMER, Moses (1640-1701) & Dorothy [GILBERT] (-1717); ca 1672; Stonington, CT
PALMER, Nathan & Mary BROWNE; 15 Dec 1675; Newbury
PALMER, Nehemiah (1637-1717/18) & Hannah STANTON (1644-1727); 20 Nov 1662; Stonington, CT
PALMER, Nehemiah (1677-1735) & Jerusha SAXTON (1683-), m/2 James DEAN 1735, m/3 William BUELL 1751; 17 Jan 1699, 1699/1700, 1700; Stonington, CT
PALMER, Nicholas (1607-1689) & 1/wf ?[Elizabeth KEMP]; b 1637, 15 Dec 1636?; Windsor, CT
PALMER/PAMMER, Nicholas (-1689) & Joan/Jane PURKES/PURCHASE (-1683), w John; 29 Oct 1646; Hartford, CT/Windsor
PALMER, Richard & 2/wf? Grace (SAMSONS) [TURK], w John; b 4 Apr 1671; Cape Porpoise
PALMER, Richard (-1689?) & Mary GILBERT; 24 Nov 1672; Salem
PALMER, Samuel (1644-) & Mary PEARSON (1651-); 20 Dec 1671; Rowley
PALMER, Samuel (-1716) & Mery _?_ (-1728); b 1675?; Westchester/Mamaroneck, NY/Flushing, LI
PALMER, Samuel (1659-) & 1/wf Elizabeth KINGSLEY/KINGSBURY; 12 Jan 1680, 13 Jan; Rehoboth
PALMER, Samuel (1652-) & Ann [SANBORN] (1662/3?-1745); ca 1684; Hampton, NH/Rye
PALMER, Stephen & Elizabeth CHEEVER (1665-); 19 Jan 1692; Boston/Cambridge

PALMER, Thomas (-1669) & Ann __?__ (-1686); - Aug 1643; Rowley
PALMER, [Thomas?] (-1689) & Elizabeth __?__; ca 1665, b 1665; Scituate
PALMER, Thomas (ca 1639-1689) & Elizabeth [RUSSELL] (1642-), dau Geo; b 28 Jun 1681; Tingley
PALMER, Thomas & Hannah JOHNSON; 9 Jan 1677, 1677/8; Rowley
PALMER, Thomas & Dorothy [COTTON]; b 1685; Charlestown/Boston
PALMER, Thomas & Abigail HUTCHINSON (1677-); 29 Jan 1696; Boston
PALMER, Thomas (-1743) & Elizabeth STEVENS (-1740); 9 Jan 1698/9; Hingham/Middleborough
PALMER, Timothy (-1713, ae 71) & 1/wf Hannah BUELL (1646-1704); 17 Sep 1663; Windsor, CT
PALMER, Timothy (-1697) & Elizabeth HUGGINS (-1716); 3 Jun 1670; Rowley/Suffield, CT
PALMER, Walter (1585?, 1598?-1661) & 1/wf Ann/Elizabeth? __?__; in Eng, b 1615, b 1608?; ?Charlestown
PALMER, Walter (1585-1662, 1661?) & 2/wf Rebecca [SHORT] (-1671); by Jan/Jun 1633, b 1 Jun 1633, 1 Jun 1632; Charlestown/Roxbury
PALMER, William (-1637/8) & 1/wf Frances __?__ (-1627+); in Eng, ca 1610/12; Plymouth
PALMER, William (1590-1650+?) & [Ann] __?__/?Mary [STAMFORD] (1608-), m/2 Francis PLUMER; b 1618, 30 Jan 1608?; Hampton, NH
PALMER, William (-1637?) & 2/wf [Mary?] __?__, m/2 Robert PADDOCK 1637?, b 1638, m/3 Thomas ROBERTS 1650; ca 1628/34; Plymouth
PALMER, William, Jr. (1612?-1636?, b 7 Nov 1637) & Elizabeth HODGSKINS, m/2 John WILLIS; 27 Mar 1634; Plymouth?/Duxbury
PALMER, William (-bef 1659) & Judith [FISKE], m/2 Jeffrey FERRIS b 6 Jan 1664, m/3 John BOWERS ca 1666-7; ca 1637?, 1639?; Yarmouth/Dartmouth/Newtown, LI
PALMER, William (-1670) & Martha [PADDOCK?/BOWNE?]; b 1642; Westchester, NY, Westchester Co., NY
PALMER, William & __?__; Obadiah b 1650; Branford, CT
PALMER, [William?] & 2/wf Ann __?__, m/2 Francis PLUMER 1649; b 1648; Newbury/Salisbury
PALMER, William & __?__; bef 1653; Kittery
PALMER, William (?1638, 1634?-1675, 1679) & Susanna (CLARK?)/HATHAWAY?, dau John; b 1663; ?Scituate/Dartmouth
PALMER, William (-1685) & Abisag/Abyshag LUX, m/2 Thomas MARSHALL 1687; May 1683; ?Portsmouth, NH/Hadley
PALMER, William (1663-) & Mary RICHMOND (1668-); ?Feb 1685?, 1685, ca 1684/6, b 1686(7?); Little Compton, RI/Kingston?, RI/Westerly, RI
PALMER, William & Mary [TYLER] (±1660-); b 1694; Greenwich/Westchester Co., NY
PALMER, William & __?__; b 1701?, ?Mamaroneck, NY; Flushing, LI
PALMER, __?__ & Rhoda HUDSON, dau John; b 1683
PALMES, Edward (-1715 in 78th y) & 1/wf Lucy [WINTHROP] (1640-1676); 1663/4, no issue; New Haven/New London, CT
PALMES, Edward (-1715 in 78th y) & 2/wf Sarah (FARMER) [DAVIS], w Capt. William, ca 1677, 13 Sep 1677; New London, CT
PANGBORN, Richard & Johanna [TUTTLE] (1675-); b 1701?, at Woodbridge?; CT?/Woodbridge, NJ/Munson
PANTON, Alexander & Mary MOODY, dau Samuel, m/2 James MUNN 1698; 30 Jun 1689; Hadley/Deerfield
PANTON, Richard & Mary __?__; b 25 Jul 1687; Westchester, NY
PANTRY, John (1629±-1653) & Hannah [TUTTLE], dau Richard, m/2 Thomas WELLES, Jr. 1654; ca 1649; Hartford
PANTRY, John (1650-1736) & Abigail [MIX] (1659-); ca 1676?; ?Hartford
PANTRY, William (?1597-1649) & Margaret [WELBOURNE/WYBURN], sister of Richard BRONSON's wf; 25 Nov 1619, Willsborough; Cambridge/Hartford
PAPILLON/PAPILLAUS/?PAPPILONS/PAPILLIO/PAMPILLO, Peter & Joane __?__; b 1679, b 1680; Boston/Bristol, RI
PAPLEY, James & Barbara __?__; b 1678; Hingham
PARDEE, George[1] (?1624-1700) & 1/wf Martha MILES (ca 1633-); 20 Oct 1650; New Haven
PARDEE, George[1] (1624-1700) & 2/wf Catherine LANE; 29 Dec 1662; New Haven
PARDEE, George[2] (1656-1723) & 1/wf Mercy BALL (-1684); 10 Feb 1675, 1675/6; New Haven
PARDEE, George[2] & 2/wf Mary DENISON (1668-1757); 11 Feb 1685, 1685/6; New Haven
PARDEE, George[1] (-1700) & 3/wf Rebecca __?__; b 1689; New Haven

PARDEE, Joseph (1664-1742+) & 1/wf Elizabeth YALE (1668-1702); 30 Jan 1688/9; New Haven
PARDICE, _?_ & Maria [MELYN], m/2 Matthias HITFIELD 1664
PARE, John (-1681 in France) & Marie [TISSAU]; b 1664?, in France; Boston/New York
PARENTS?/PARENCE, John (-1686) & Elizabeth _?_ ; b 1679; Haddam, CT
PARISH, John (see John PARRIS) & 1/wf Hannah JUELL/JEWELL; 30 Aug 1664; Braintree/
  Woodbury
PARISH, John (-1715, Preston, CT), Groton & 2/wf Mary WATTLE/WATTLES; 29 Dec 1685;
  Chelmsford/Groton
PARISH, Samuel & Martha/Mary? METAFOR/MADDIVER; 24 May 1699; Ipswich
PARISH, Thomas (1613-) (returned to Eng) & [Mary DANFORTH]; b 1638; Watertown/Cam-
  bridge
PARISH, Thomas (1641-1707?) & Mary _?_ (1651-1674, ae 23); Groton
PARKE, Edward & Deliverance FRENCH; 25 Dec 1667, 1669, 21 Dec 1669; Killingworth,
  CT/Guilford, CT
PARK, Edward (1661-1745), Newton & Martha FISKE (1671-), Watertown; 13 Mar 1694/5, 1695;
  Charlestown/Newton
PARK, John (1656-1718) & (1/wf) [?Sarah KNAPP]; b 1686; Watertown
PARK, John (?1660-1716) & Mary [WITTER] (1665-), m/2 Rev. Salmon TREAT; b 1686;
  Stonington, CT/Norwich, CT/Preston, CT
PARK, John (1656-1718) & 2/wf Elizabeth MILLER (ca 1670-); 5 Apr 1694; Watertown
PARKES, John & Deliverance [JACKSON]; b 1698; Cambridge/Weston?/Stonington, CT/Killingly,
  CT
PARK, Jonathan (1670-1719) & 1/wf Anna SPRING (-2 Apr 1691); 18 Mar 1690; Watertown
PARK, Jonathan (1670-1719) & 2/wf Elizabeth _?_ (-1713); b 1695; Watertown
PARK, Nathaniel (-1718), Groton/Preston & Sarah GEER (1659-); 28 Feb 1676/7; Preston, CT
PARKS, Richard (1602-1665) & 1/wf Margery [?CRANE] (?1595-ca 1650); b 1628, in Eng;
  Cambridge
PARK, Richard (-1665) & 2/wf Sarah (COLLIER) [BREWSTER] (-1691), w Love; ?aft 1 Sep
  1656; Cambridge
PARK, Richard & Mary _?_ (ae 39 in 1682); b 1665?, 1667; Cambridge/Concord/Sherborn
PARK, Richard (1663-1738, 1739) & Sarah [KING] (not CUTLER) (-1727); b 5 Nov 1684;
  Newton
PARKES, Richard (1667-1725) & Elizabeth BILLING (1669-); 14 Jul 1690; Concord
PARK, Robert (1580-1665) & 1/wf Martha CHAPLIN (bpt 4 Feb 1683/4), St. Edmunds, Bury,
  Eng, dau Robert; Semer Eng, 19 Feb 1601, 9 Feb, 1601/2; Wethersfield, CT/Stonington, CT
PARK, Robert (1580-1665) & 2/wf Alice (FREEMAN) [THOMPSON], w John; ca 30 May 1644;
  Roxbury/Stonington, CT
PARK, Robert (1651-1707) & 1/wf Rachel LEFFINGWELL (1648-1693±); 24 Nov 1681; Norwich,
  CT
PARK, Robert (1651-1707) & 2/wf Mary [ROSE]; ca 1693?; Stonington, CT
PARK, Robert & Tamzon (PACKER/PARKER?) BROMLEY, w Luke; 17 Jan 1698; Stonington, CT
PARK, Roger & Sophia CLASS/JANES, m/2 Joseph HORTON ca 1695; b 1686; Rye, NY
PARK, Samuel (?1621-) & Hannah _?_ ; b 1674; Stonington, CT
PARK, Samuel & Elizabeth EDDY/PEDDEY; 22 Feb 1695, 1694/5; Stonington, CT
PARK, Thomas (1615-1709) & Dorothy [THOMPSON] (1624-1709+); b 1646; Wethersfield,
  CT/New London/CT
PARKES, Thomas (?1628-1690) & Abigail DEEKES/DIX (1637-1691); 1 Dec 1653; Cambridge/
  Newton
PARKE, Thomas (1648-) & Mary ALLEN/ALLYN (1648-); 4 Jan 1672; Newton
PARKES, William (1607-1685, Roxbury), Roxbury & Martha [HOLGRAVE] (1615-1708), Salem; b
  1637; Roxbury
PARK, William (1654-) & 1/wf Hannah FRINK (-1705, Preston); 3 Dec 1684; Stonington,
  CT/Groton/Preston, CT
PARK, William & Jane BORDWYN/BORDWIN; 9 May 1699; Stonington, CT
PARKES, _?_ (Joshua bpt 7d 1mo 1652, Caleb bpt 26d 12mo 1653), Watertown & _?_ ; b 1652;
  Boston
PARK, _?_ & Hannah [PLYMPTON] (1670?-); aft 1697, b 1701?, no issue; ?Sudbury
PARKER, Abraham (-1685) & Rose WHITLOCK (-1691); 18 Nov 1644; Woburn/Chelmsford
PARKER, Abraham & Sarah PREBLE, m/2 Henry COOMBS; ca 1679; York, ME

PARKER, Abraham (1652-1732) & Martha LIVERMORE (-1740); 15 Jul 1682; Chelmsford/Bradford

PARKER, Benjamin (-1672) & Sarah HARTWELL (-1674); 18 Apr 1661; Billerica

PARKER, Benjamin (1662-) & Mary TRULL (-1694); 11 Oct 1684; Billerica

PARKER, Benjamin (1663-) & Sarah [HOWARD]/HAWARD (1667-); 14 Jan 1690/1; Chelmsford

PARKER, Benjamin & Abigail FRENCH (1665-); 10 Nov 1697; Billerica

PARKER, Benjamin, Yarmouth & Rebecca LUMBART; 8 Dec 1698; Barnstable

CARPENTER, Daniel (1667-1694) & Anna [ERRINGTON], m/2 John MAY, m/3 Thomas COPPIN; b 1687; Charlestown

PARKER, Daniel & Mary LUMBER/LUMBART; 11 Dec 1689; Barnstable

PARKER, David/John & Jane MALBY; 4 Mar 1689/90; New Haven

PARKER, Ebenezer (1674-) & Mary SMITH; 3 Sep 1694; Saybrook, CT

PARKER, Ebenezer (1676-1749) & Rebecca NEWHALL (1675-1737); 22 May 1697; Reading

PARKER, Edmund (-1694) & Elizabeth HOWE (-1657); 31 May 1647; Roxbury/Lancaster

PARKER, Edward (-1662) & Elizabeth (?WOODS) POTTER (-1677), w John, m/3 Robert ROSE 1664?; b Jul 1646, Jun 1646?, ca 1 Jul 1646; New Haven

PARKER, Eleazer (1660-) & 1/wf, 2/wf Mehitable [BARRON] (1668-living in 1711); aft 1704; Groton/Watertown

PARKER, Eleazer & Mary [WOODS] (1670-), m/2 John NUTTING 170-; b 1695; Groton

PARKER, Elisha (-1717) & Elizabeth HINCKLEY/HINCHLEY (1635-); 15 Jul 1657; Barnstable

PARKER, George & Hannah [JOHNSON], w William

PARKER, George (?1614, ?1612-1656?) & Frances _?_/JOHNSON?, m/2 Nicholas BROWN 1656, b 1656?; [b 1660]; Portsmouth, RI

PARKER, Hananiah[2] (?1638-1724) & 1/wf Elizabeth BROWNE (-1697); 30 Sep 1663; Reading/Watertown

PARKER, Hananiah[2] (?1638-1724) & 2/wf Mary (BARSHAM) BRIGHT (1648-1736, ae 87), w John; 17 Dec 1700, 12 Dec; Reading

PARKER, Isaac (1660-1689) & Esther FLETCHER (1664-), m/2 James PROCTOR 1691; 11 Apr 1681; Chelmsford

PARKER, Isaac & Mary PARKER; 4 May 1687; Cambridge/Lexington

PARKER, Jacob (-1669±) & Sarah _?_ (-1708, ae 81), m/2 John WAITE 1675; ca 1651/3, 1651?; Chelmsford

PARKER, Jacob (1652-1694, ae 42, Malden) & Joanna CALL (1660-1737, Malden), m/2 John STEARNS 1696; b 1681, ca 1676-7; Malden/Watertown

PARKER, Jacob & Thankful HEMENWAY (1668-); 3 May 1687; Roxbury

PARKER, Jacob & Anne RENDALL; m int 13 Feb 1695/6; Boston

PARKER, James (-1652) & Mary [MAVERICK] (1610-1652+); ca 1635; Weymouth/Portsmouth, NH/Barbados

PARKER, James (?1617-1700?) & 1/wf Elizabeth LONG (1621-); 23 May 1643; Woburn/Chelmsford/Groton

PARKER, James (-1694) & Mary PARKER (1655-); 11 Dec 1678; Chelmsford

PARKER, James (-1700, 1701?) & 2/wf Eunice (BROOKS) [CARTER] (1655-), w Samuel, m/3 John KENDALL; aft 1693, b 1697; Charlestown/Groton

PARKER, James & Martha _?_ ; b 1693; Lynn

PARKER, John (-1651+) & Mary _?_ (-1671+); b 1633; Saco, ME/Kennebec, ME

PARKER, John & ?Joan HELLYER?; 29 Sep 1628; Marlboro, Wilt.

PARKER, John (-1644?) & Jane [KEMBER?], m/2 Richard THAYER; 29 Sep 1628, b 1635, Marlboro?, Wiltshire?; Boston

PARKER, John (-1668) & Sarah [SUMMERS?]; b 1644; Hingham/Boston/Taunton

PARKER, John & _?_ ; b 1644/5; Marblehead/York, ME

PARKER, John (1615-1686) & Joanna _?_ (-1688); b 1648; Cambridge/Hingham

PARKER, John (-1685) & Sarah _?_ (-1685+); ca 1655/6; Roxbury/Boston, ME/Boston

PARKER, John (-1667) & Mary POULTER (1604-1692), w John, m/3 Thomas CHAMBERLAIN 1674; aft 22 Nov 1654, b 14 Jun 1667; Lexington

PARKER, John (-1690, 1700?) & Mary/Margaret? FAIRSFIELD; 20 Aug 1660; Boston/Kennebec, ME

PARKER, John & Margaret _?_ ; b 17 Dec 1661; Sagadahoc, ME

PARKES/PARKER?, John & Mary [ROWLES]; b 10 Nov 1662; Watertown

PARKER, John & Esther [?MANN]; b 1665?; Newport

PARKER, John (1642-1706) & Mary BUCKINGHAM; 24 Dec 1666; Saybrook, CT
PARKER, John[2] (1640±-1699) & 1/wf Hannah KENDALL (1650-1689); 13 Nov 1667; Reading
PARKER, John (1648-) & Hannah BASSETT (1650-); 8 Nov 1670; New Haven/Wallingford, CT
PAKER/PARKER, John & Mary/Alice? COREE/COREY/?HOLLINGWORTH; 29 May 1673; Salem
PARKER, John (-1723) & Sarah [GREEN] (see below) (-1727); ca ?1673/4
PARKER, John (1647-1699) & Mary DAMFORTH/DANFORTH (1658-); 4 Jun 1678; Billerica/
Chelmsford
PARKER, John (1649(-)-1679) & _?_ ; b 1679; ?Groton/Malden
PARKER, John (1651-1713?, 1720?) & Mary [TURNER] (1658-1715); b 1687; Newton/Medfield
PARKER, John, Boston & Elizabeth WOODWARD, Boston; 15 Apr 1687; ?Cambridge
PARKER, John (1653-1738), Andover & Hannah BROWNE (-1734), Reading; 24 May 1687;
Andover
PARKER, John (1664-1741) & 1/wf Deliverance DODGE (1661-1718); 2 Oct 1689; Reading/Lex-
ington
PARKER, John (?1640-1699) & 2/wf Thankful _?_ (-1699+); 28 Jan 1689/90; Feb?; Reading
PARKER, John/David & Jane MALBY; 4 Mar 1689/90; New Haven
PARKER, John (1667-1709) & Mary JONES (-1710+); 11 Dec 1690; Saybrook, CT/Norwich, CT
PARKER, John (1668-1741) & Elizabeth [GOODWIN] (1673-1731); 15 Jul 1691; Reading
PARKER, John & Sarah [GREEN]; b 1692, ca 1673/4; York, ME (anc of Lydia HARMON, see
above)
PARKER, John & Hannah HAVEN; 18 Jul 1693; Lynn
PARKER, John & Priscilla CHUBBS; 13 Sep 1694; Lynn
PARKER, John & 1/wf Sarah [VERING]; b 1695; Boston
PARKER, John & Abigail WHITTAKER; 15 Dec 1696; Billerica/Concord
PARKER/PACKER, John (1657-1727) & 1/wf Abigail (TUTHILL) [CONKLIN] (1670-1705), w
Joseph; aft 23 Nov 1698, b 1703; Southampton, LI/Southold, LI/Riverhead
PARKER, John & Mary KIBBE/KIBBY; 1 Nov 1699; Wallingford, CT
PARKER, John & Mehitable [BANCROFT?] (1678-); 2 Jan 1699/1700; Reading
PARKER, Jonathan (1665-) & Deliverance [ALEXANDER] (1672-); b 1701; Newton/(?Needham)
PARKER, Joseph (-1685) & _?_ ; b 1626; Portsmouth, RI/Shrewsbury, NJ
PARKER, Joseph (1614-1678) & Mary [?STEVENS] (-1695?; b 1642; Newbury/Andover
PARKER, Joseph (-1690) & Margaret/Maryetta? [BARETT?]; b 1653; Groton/Dunstable
PARKER, Joseph (-1690) & 2/wf? Rebecca REED; 24 Jun 1655
PARKER, Joseph (1647-1725) & Hannah GILBERT (1653-); 3 Jun 1673, 1672; New
Haven/Saybrook
PARKER, Joseph (1651?, 1653-) (ae 40 in 1691) & 1/wf [Elizabeth]/Hannah? [BLOOD?]; b
1679; Groton
PARKER, Joseph (1642-1684) & Elizabeth BRIDGES (-1703+), w Obadiah, m/3 Samuel
HUTCHINSON 1686?; 7 Oct 1680; Andover
PARKER, Joseph (1653?-) & Hannah [JENKINS] BAKE?/BAKER?/BANK?/BAUK? (?1646-), w
John, m/3 Robert BLOOD 1696; 19 Nov 1683, 1684?; Chelmsford/Groton
PARKER, Joseph (1658-1723) & [Mary WHITCOMB] (1665?-), dau Robert?; b 1684; Scituate
PACKER/PARCKE/PARKER, & Mary/Mercy WHITSTONE/WHISTON; 30 Jun 1698, 1 Jul 1697;
Barnstable
PARKER, Joseph & Lydia [FRYE]; b 1700; Andover
PARKER, Joseph & Elizabeth [ALEXANDER] (1670-); b 1701?; Deerfield/Needham
PARKER, Joshua (1658-1691) & Abigail (SHATTUCK) MORSE (-1694), w Jonathan; 22 Sep 1690;
Groton
PARKER, Josiah (1652?-) (ae 36 in 1691) & Elizabeth SAXTON (1661-1731+), Boston; 8 May
1678; Chelmsford/Woburn/Cambridge
PARKER, Kendall (1677-1755) & Ruth JOHNSON (1677-), dau of Samuel; m int 26 Oct 1699;
Lynn
PARKER, Moses (?1658-1732) & Abigail HILDRETH (1656±-); 19 Jun 1684; Chelmsford
PARKER, Nathan (-1685) & 1/wf ?Susanna [SHORT] (-1651, Andover); 20 Nov 1648;
Newbury/Andover
PARKER, Nathan (-1685) & 2/wf Mary [AYER] (?1635-1692, condemned as a witch); b 1653;
Andover
PARKER, Nathan (-1679) & Mary BROWNE, m/2 William ELIOT 1681; 15 Dec 1675; Newbury
PARKER, Nathaniel (1651-1737) & Bethiah POLLEY (1659-1748); 24 Sep 1677; Reading

PARKER, Nathaniel (-1690) & [Lois **ROGERS**]; ca 1688, aft 13 Jun; Plymouth
PARKER, Nathaniel (1670-1747) & Margaret [**WISWALL**] (1672-1736); b 1694, ca 1692-3; Newton/(?Charlestown)
PARKER, Nicholas[1] & Anne _?_ ; ca 1629; Boston
PARKER, Peter & Sarah [**COOKE**] (1633-); b 1664; Portsmouth, RI?
PARKER, Ralph (-1683) & 1/wf _?_ ; b 1646/7; Gloucester/New London, CT
PARKER, Ralph & 2/wf [Susanna] [**KEENY**] (1628-); b 1670; Gloucester
PARKER, Richard & Jane _?_ ; Boston
PARKER, Richard (-1673) & Anne _?_ ; b 1638; Boston
PARKER, Robert (1602-1685) (ae 82 in 1684) & Judith [**BUGBEE**], w Richard; b 1636; Cambridge
PARKER, Robert & 1/wf Sarah **JAMES** (-1664); 28 Jan 1656; Barnstable
PARKER, Robert (-1682?, 1680?) & 2/wf Patience **COB/COBB**, m/2 William **CROCKER**; beginning Aug 1667; Barnstable
PARKER, Samuel & Sarah **HOMAN/HOLMAN** (-1675); 9 Apr 1657; Dedham
PARKER, Samuel (1656?-1712) & Abigail [**LAKIN**]/**LAKE** (1667-1722+), m/2 Robert **DICKSON**/**DIXON** 1722; b 1686; Groton
PARKER, Samuel (1666-), Reading & Martha **BROWNE** (1668-1727), Cambridge; 3 Jan 1688/9; Cambridge/Lynn/Reading/Watertown
PARKER, Samuel (-1690) & Martha (**DOW**) (**HEATH**) **PAGE**, w Joseph, w Joseph; 19 Mar 1688/9; Haverhill
PARKER, Samuel (1659-1724) & Ruth [**DUNCKLEY**]?/Ruth **ELLIS**?/**MacKENY**? (1662-1698); b 1695; Newton
PARKER, Samuel (-1717) & Hannah **BUMPS/BUMPAS** (1680-); 12 Dec 1695, 14 Dec 1695; Barnstable/Sandwich
PARKER, Samuel & Hannah **FELCH** (1672-); 16 Apr 1700; Reading/Woburn
PARKER, Samuel (1659-) & 2/wf Mercy [**KINGSBURY**] (1677-); b 1701(2?), b 1701?; Newton
PARKER, Stephen (1652-1718) & 1/wf Mary **MARSTONE/MARSTON** (1655-1693); 1 Dec 1680; Andover
PARKER, Stephen (1652-1718) & 2/wf Susanna (**HARTSHORN**) **DEVEREUX** (1655-1718), w John; 10 Jan 1694/5; Andover/Watertown/Marblehead
PARKER, Thomas & Jane [**SANDERS**]; b 1635
PARKER, Thomas (1614, 1615-1683) (from Reading, Eng?), London? & Amy _?_ (-1690); b 1635, 1636; Lynn/Reading
PARKER, Thomas & [Mary **SHAW**?] (1645-); b 1665; Kenebec, ME
PARKER, Thomas (?1636-1699) & Deborah [**KIBBY**] (?1647-1699), dau Edward; 13 Nov 1667; Reading
PARKER, Thomas (1656-1698) & Mary **FLETCHER** (1658-); 21 Oct 1678; Chelmsford
PARKER, Thomas (1657-1679) & Margaret [**CLEAVES**], m/2 James **ATKINS** by 1682; b 6 Aug 1679; Newton
PARKER, Thomas, Salem & Elizabeth **HALL**, Greenland, NH, wid; m b 2 Aug 1687
PARKER, Thomas & Rachel [**MOORE**] (1664-1732), m/2 Thomas **HUNT** 1709; ca 1692, b 1693(4?); Boston
PARKER, Thomas & Mary **JENKINS/JUCKENE** (1662-); 5 Dec 1693; Falmouth, MA/Barnstable
PARKER, Thomas & _?_ ; b 1696; New Haven
PARKER, William (alias **OTWAY**) (1599-1662) (ae 60 on 15 Mar 1659) (uncle of James **PHILLIPS**) & Alice/Allis/(Eliz.?) _?_ m/2 Stephen **PAINE** bef 7 Sep 1662; Taunton
PARKER, William (-1686) & 1/wf Margery [**PRITCHARD**]/**ALLEN**? (1608-1685; b 1636; Hartford/Saybrook, CT
PARKER, William (-1684) & 1/wf Mary **RAWLINGS** (-1651); Apr 1639; Scituate
PARKER, William & Elizabeth/Margaret? _?_ ; b 1640; Watertown/Boston?
PARKER, William (-1684) & 2/wf Mary **TURNER** (-1684+); 13 Nov 1651; Scituate
PARKER, William (1645-1725) & 1/wf Hannah? _?_ (-1673); ca 1672, b 1672(3?), b 1659?; Saybrook, CT
PARKER, William & Elizabeth _?_ ; b 1672; Boston
PARKER, William (1643-) & 1/wf [?Mary] [?**CLARK**]; b 1675; Scituate
PARKER, William (1645-1725) (called James **BROWN** "uncle") & 2/wf Lydia **BROWN** (1650-1728); 7 Sep 1676, 6? Sep; Saybrook, CT

PARKER, William (-1686) & 2/wf Elizabeth (CLARKE) [PRATT], w Wm.; ca 1681, b 31 May 1682; Saybrook, CT
PARKER, William & Rachel CLARKE; 2 Mar 1696/7; Scituate
PARKER, Zachariah & Elizabeth PAGE; b 1686; Groton
PARKER, _?_ & Beatrice TOMPSON (1647); CT
PARKER, _?_ & Thankful WEEKS (1660); ?Dorchester
PARKER, _?_ & Margaret _?_, m/2 Jonathan CARY; Charlestown
PARKER, _?_ & Judith _?_ (-bef 11 Jun 1651); b 1645; Charlestown
PARKER, John & Sarah [CLEVES], w William; by 3 Feb 1684/5; Roxbury
PARKER, _?_ & Mary SHIPMAN; Saybrook
PARKHURST, Ebenezer & Mary _?_; b 1695; Chelmsford
PARKHURST, George & 1/wf Phebe [DALTON?] (sis of Mrs. Ruth DALTON); in Eng, b 1612?, b 1618?; ?Ipswich/Watertown
PARKHURST, George (1628-1699) & 1/wf Sarah BROWNE; 16 Dec 1643; Chelmsford
PARKHURST, George & 2/wf Susanna (_?_) [SIMPSON], w John; aft 24 Apr 1645?; Watertown/Boston
PARKHURST, George (-1699, ae 81) & 2/wf Mary PHEZA/VEAZEY? (-1681); 24 Sep 1650; Watertown
PURKIS/PARKHYRST?, George & Elizabeth/?Sarah [PEMBERTON], m/2 _?_ ELATSON; b 1678; Boston
PARKHURST, John (1644-1725) & Abigail [GARFIELD] (1646-1726); ca 1670; Watertown
PARKHURST, John (1672-) & Abigail [MORSE] (1677-); b 1695; Watertown
PARKIS, Joseph (1629-1709, Westford) & Rebecca READ (1627-); 24 Jun 1656, 26 Jun 1656, 16? Jun, 24 Jun; Chelmsford/Concord
PERKIS, Joseph (1661-1720, Plainfield, CT) & Eunice SPAULDEN/SPALDING (1661-1744); 4 Nov 1686; Chelmsford/Concord
PARKMAN, Deliverance (1651-1715) & 1/wf Sarah VEREN (-1682); 9 Dec 1673; Salem
PARKMAN, Deliverance (1651-1715) & 2/wf Mehitable [WAITE] (1658-1684); aft 14 Jan 1681/2; Salem
PARKMAN, Deliverance (1651-1715) & 3/wf Margaret GARDNER (1664-1689); 3 Jun 1685; Marblehead
PARKMAN, Deliverance (1651-1715) & 4/wf Susanna (CLARK) [GEDNEY] (1643-), w John; aft 25 Mar 1689; Salem
PARKMAN, Elias (-1662) & Bridget ?CONNER/?CONNAUGHT, m/2 Sylvester EVELETH 1662?, 1672?; b 1635; Dorchester/Windsor, CT/Saybrook, CT/Boston
PARKMAN, Elias (1635-London 1691) & Sarah TRASK (1634-1696); 13 Oct 1656; ?Salem
PARKMAN, Nathaniel (1655-) & Hannah [HETT]; b 1686; Boston
PARKMAN, William (1657, 1658?-1730) & Elizabeth ADAMS (1660-1749); 18 May 1680; ?Boston
PARLIN, John (1666-1722) & Mary HARTWELL (1668-); 1 Nov 1688; Concord
PARLEN, Nicholas & Sarah HAMNORE/HAMMER; 30 Nov 1665; Cambridge
PARLER/PARLOR, Thomas (-1705) & Elizabeth [LUSCOMB], ?m/2 James LEWIS 1716?; b 1679; Beverly/Middleboro
PARLER/PARLOW, ?William & Susanna [WING]? (1647-1717)
PARMELEE, Caleb (1663-1714) & 1/wf Abigail JOHNSON (-1692); 11 Apr 1690; Guilford, CT
PARMELEE, Caleb (1663-1714) & 2/wf Abigail HILL (-1737); 23 Apr 1693; Guilford/CT
PARMELEE, Isaac (1665-1749) & Elizabeth HIGHLAND/HILAND? (1666-); 30 Dec 1689; Guilford, CT/?Milford, CT
PARMELEE, Job (1673-1765) & Betsey EDWARDS, LI; 11 Mar 1699; Guilford, CT
PARMELEE, John (-1659) & 1/wf Hannah _?_ (-1650); in Eng, ?b 1620; Guilford, CT
PARMELEE, John[2] (?1620-1688, 1687?) & 1/wf Rebecca _?_ (-1651, 1650?); b 1645; Guilford, CT
PARMELEE, John[2] (?1620-1688) & 2/wf Anna (_?_) [PLAINE] (-1658), w William; aft 24 Sep 1651, 1651; Guilford, CT
PARMELEE, John[1] (-1659) & 2/wf Elizabeth (_?_) BRADLEY, wid, m/3 John EVARTS 1663; 8 Nov 1653; ?Guilford, CT
PARMELEE, John[2] (1620-) & 3/wf Hannah _?_; Feb 1658/9; Guilford, CT
PARMELEE, John (1659-1725) & Mary MASON; 29 Jun 1681, 27 Jun; Guilford, CT
PARMELEE, Joshua (1664-) & 1/wf Elsie/Alse/Alice? EDWARDS (-1714); ca 10 Jul 1696; Guilford, CT

PARMELEE, Nathaniel (1645-1676) & Sarah FRENCH, m/2 Nathaniel HAYDEN 1678; 24 Oct 1668; Killingworth, CT
PARMELEE, Nathaniel (1672-) & Esther [HALSEY] (not WARD) (1675-); ca 1696; Killingworth, CT
PARMELEE, Stephen (1669-1749) & Elizabeth BALDWIN (1673-); 30 Jun 1693; ?Guilford, CT
PALMITER, Benjamin (1610-1689) & Mary __?__ (1610-); b 1667; Marblehead
PARMINTER, Benjamin (-1737) & Tamisen/Thomasine RICE (1661-1748); 22 Sep 1680; Sudbury
PARMINTER, George (-1727) & Hannah JOHNSON; 20 Jan 1678; Sudbury
PARMENTER, John[1] (1671, ae 83) & 1/wf Bridget __?__ (-6 Apr 1660); in Eng, ca 1609?; Sudbury/Roxbury/Framingham
PARMENTER, John[2] (?1615±-1666) & Amy __?__ (-1681); b 1639; Sudbury/Framingham
PARMENTER, John[1] (-1671) (called Bartholomew CHEEVER "cousin" in 1671) & 2/wf Ann/Amis (BAYFORD) (CHANDLER) DANE (-1683?), w William, w John; 9 Aug 1660; Roxbury
PARMENTER, John & 1/wf Judith __?__ ; b 1666; Boston
PARMENTER, John & 1/wf Elizabeth [CUTLER] (1646-1685+); b 1668; Sudbury/Cambridge
PARMETER, John & 2/wf Hannah [WILLIAMS] (1649-1693); b 1688; Boston
PARMINTER, John & Elizabeth EAST; 1 Nov 1694; Boston
PARMENTER, Joseph (1655-1737) & 1/wf? Mary MARSH; 17 Nov 1675; Braintree
PARMENTER, Robert (1622-1696) & Leah (SANDERS) WHEATLY (?1620, ?1625-1700), w John; 13 Apr 1648; Braintree
PARNEL, Benjamin & Mary JONSON; 18 Jan 1699/1700; Beverly/Salem
PARNALL, Francis (-1698/9) & Mary STACY; 13 Jan 1667, 1666/7; Salem
PARNELL, Francis (-1724) & Dorothy FOWLES; 15 Aug 1692; Boston
PARNELL, Moses (1670-) & Joanna HOAR; 25 Apr 1694; Salem
PARIS, John & __?__ ; b 1645; Charlestown
PARRIS/PARISH, John (see PARISH) & Hannah/Mary JEWELL; 30 Aug 1664; Braintree/Boston
PARRIS, Robert (-1709) & 1/wf Seaborne (BATCHELDER) CROMWELL (-1664), w John; 22 May 1663; Chelmsford/Groton/Dunstable/Chelsea
PARRIS, Robert (-1709) & 2/wf Mary CRISPE; 11 Apr 1667; Chelmsford
PARRIS, Robert (-1709) & 3/wf Elizabeth [BLANCHARD], m/2 Thomas BURRAGE; ca 1685?
PARRIS, Samuel (-1720) & 1/wf Elizabeth [?ELDRED] (-1696); b 1681; Boston/Danvers/Newton/Watertown/Concord/Sudbury
PARRIS, Samuel (-1720) & 2/wf Dorothy [NOYES] (-1719); b 1699; Newton/etc.
PARRIS, Thomas & 1/wf Mary __?__ ; b 1686; LI/Boston/Pembroke
PARRIS, Thomas & 2/wf Abigail [ROGERS] (-1713), dau Joseph; b 1697; Pembroke
PARROT, Bryant & Hannah [MARSHALL]; b 1690(1?); Boston
PARROT, Francis (-1656) & Elizabeth (?NORTHEND), m/2 Thomas TENNEY; b 1640; Rowley
PARROTT, John & Sarah [CROCKETT]; by 1675; Kittery, ME
PARROT, John & ?Mary/?Ann [PEDRICK]; b 1686; Marblehead
PARROTT, Simon (1634-1718) & Elizabeth __?__ (1627-1705); b 1663; Newport, RI
PARRUCK, John (-1683) & Sarah SMITH (-1722); 17 Jul 1673; Charlestown
PARRUCK, John (1679-) & Hannah [BEARDSLEY] (1682-); b 1706, b 1701?; Stratford, CT
PARRY, Samuel & Hannah (WHEELER) SMEDLY; 8 Nov 1676; Concord
PARRY, Samuel & Esther (HARVEY) COMY/MACOMY, w David; 27 Nov 1682, 7 Nov; Concord
PARSELL, John & Judith __?__ ; Masketh, LI
PARSHALL, James (-1701) & Elizabeth [GARDINER]; b 1690, ca 1678; Southold, LI
PARSHALL, James & 2/wf Margaret __?__ ; ?b 1698; Southold, LI
PARCELL, Nicholas (-1691) & Sarah __?__ ; Flushing, LI
PARSLOW, William & Susanna [WING] (1647-1717); Harwich
PARSONS, Benjamin (?1629-1689) & 1/wf Sarah VORE (-1 Jan 1666(67?), 1676?); 6 Oct 1653, 3? Oct; Windsor, CT/Springfield
PARSONS, Benjamin (-1689) & 2/wf Sarah (HEALD) LEONARD (-1711), w John, m/3 Peter TILTON 3 Nov 1690; 26 Feb 1677, 1676?; Springfield
PARSONS, Benjamin (1658-1728) & Sarah KEEP (1666-1729); 17 Jan 1683, 1683/4; Springfield
PARSONS, Ebenezer & __?__ ; b 1672, b 1675; Simsbury, CT/Windsor, CT/Hartford
PARSONS, Ebenezer (1668-1752) & Margaret MARSHFIELD (1670-1758, ae 87); 10 Apr 1690; Springfield
PERSON/PIERSON, George & Elizabeth [WHEELWRIGHT] (1634-) (had son Wheelwright); b 1663?, b 1662, b 1667; Boston

PARSONS, Hugh (1613-1684) & Elizabeth [ENGLAND] (1613-1684), w Wm.; ca 1635/40?, ?aft 1641; Portsmouth, RI
PARSONS, Hugh (-1675) & 1/wf Mary LEWIS; 27 Oct 1645; Springfield/Watertown
PASSANT/PARSONS, Hugh (-1675) & 2/wf? Ruth _?_ (-1676); aft 1651?; Watertown
PERSONS, James (-1733) & Hannah YOUNGLOVE; 18 Dec 1688; Gloucester
PARSON, James & Elizabeth JUDD; 23 Dec 1700; Boston
PARSONS, Jeffrey (1631-1689) & Sarah VINSON/VASNEY (-1701), dau Wm. VINCENT?; 11 Nov 1657; Gloucester
PARSONS, Jeffrey & Abigail YOUNGLOVE; 5 May 1686; Gloucester
PARSONS, John (1650-1728), Northampton & Sarah CLARKE (1659-1728); 23 Dec 1675, 3 Dec; Springfield
PARSONS, John (-1692) & Elizabeth _?_, m/2 Peter HINKSON 1698; b 1677; York
PARSONS, John (-1686, 1694) & ?Lydia (HARDY?)/?Elizabeth [GARLICK?], w Joshua, m/3 John FISH ca 1694; 1679, b 1666?; East Hampton, LI/Cape May, NJ
PARSONS, John (1666-1715?) & Elizabeth [GARLICK]/SHAW?; ca 1696; East Hampton, LI
PERSONS, John & Isabella HAYNES; 19 Jan 1692/3; Gloucester
PARSONS, John (1673, 1673/4-) & 1/wf Sarah ATHERTON (1676-1729), Hatfield; 23 Dec 1696; ?Northampton
PARSONS/PASONS, John & Phillis HILLS (?1669-1712); 1 Dec 1698; Hartford
PARSONS, John (-1701) & Sarah LUDLAM (ca 1684-1743), East Hampton, LI, m/2 Ichabod LEEKE; b 1701; East Hampton, LI
PARSONS, Jonathan (1657-1694) & Mary CLARK, m/2 Benjamin HASTINGS ca 1696; 5 Apr 1682; Springfield
PARSONS, Joseph (?1619-1683) & Mary BLISS (1628-1712); 2 Nov 1646, 20 Nov 1646, 26 Nov 1646, 28 Nov 1646?; Springfield/Northampton
PARSONS, Joseph (1647-1729) & Elizabeth STRONG (1648-1736, 1737); 17 Mar 1669, 1668/9; ?Northampton
PARSONS, Joseph (-15 Apr 1687) & Mehitable BARTLETT; last week Dec 1676, b 1683; Simsbury, CT/Windsor, CT
PARSON, Joseph (-1720+) & Bethia [BRATTLE] (1665-1690); b 1684; Boston
PARSONS, Joseph & Abigail PHELPS (1679-); m int 1698?, 26 Mar 1697/8, ?15 Sep 1697; ?Northampton
PARSONS, Mark & Elizabeth _?_, m/2 John SPENCER; b 1672; Parker's Is.
PARSONS, Nathaniel (1658-1722) & Abigail HASKELL (1671-), m/2 Isaac EVELETH 1722; 27 Dec 1697; Gloucester
PARSON, Nicholas & _?_; b 1675; Flushing, LI
PARSONS, Robert & _?_; b 1630; East Hampton, LI
PASONS, Robet & 1/wf Mary DOMINY (-1717); 6 Mar 1700, prob 1700/1701; East Hampton, LI
PARSONS, Samuel (1630-1714) & Hannah [?TALMAGE] (1645-1728); ca 1662?; East Hampton, LI
PARSONS, Samuel (1653-1734) & 1/wf Elizabeth COOKE (1653?-2 Sep 1690); ca 1677; Northampton/Durham, CT
PARSONS, Samuel (1666-1736) & Hannah HITCHCOCK (1667-1748); 18 Mar 1683, 1688?; Springfield/Enfield
PARSONS, Samuel (1653-1734) & 2/wf Rhoda [TAYLOR] (1669-1711); aft 3 Sep 1690; Northampton/Durham, CT
PARSONS, Samuel & ?Phebe/?Deborah LUDLAM?; b 1693; East Hampton, LI
PARSONS, Seth (1665-1725) & Sarah _?_ (-1740 in 67th y); b 1701; East Hampton, LI
PARSONS, Thomas (-1661) & Lydia BROWN (-1674, bef 1671?), m/2 Eltweed POMEROY 1664; 28 Jun 1641; Windsor, CT
PARSON, Thomas & Priscilla DENISON, m/2 Samuel SMITH 1701, adopted Nathaniel AUSTIN; 9 Oct 1666, no issue; Ipswich/Suffield, CT
PARSONS, Thomas (1645-1680?) & Sarah DARE (-1674); 24 Dec 1668, ?6 Dec; Windsor, CT
PARSONS, Thomas (1674-) & Sarah _?_; b 1699; Enfield, CT
PARSONS, William (-1702 in 87th y) & Ruth _?_; b 1645; Boston
PARSONS, William & Hannah [PARKES?/?PARKER]; 26 Oct 1666; Windsor, CT
PARSONS/PERSON, William & Mary CARRINGTON/CARRIONTON; 26 Oct 1696, b 1695; Simsbury, CT/Windsor, CT

PARSONS, William & Hannah [WHEELWRIGHT], m/2 Philip ROLLINS; b 1697, Jan 1696/7; Wells, ME/Salisbury

PARSONS, William & Martha BALDWIN; 15 Sep 1697; Boston

PARSONS, _?_ & Bridget _?_, m/2 William VARNEY ca 1635; ca 1625

PARSONS, [?John] & Elizabeth [HARDY], dau Richard; b 21 Jul 1683; Stamford, CT

PARSONS, _?_ & Margaret _?_ ; in Eng; ?Oyster Bay, LI

PARTRIDGE, Alexander (-1654) & _?_ ; b 1645; Boston/Newport

PARTRIDG, Eleazer & 1/wf Elizabeth SMITH (-1704); 25 Apr 1692; Medfield

PARTRIDGE, George (-1695), Duxbury & Sarah TRACY, Plymouth; 28 Nov 1638, - Nov 1638, ?16 Nov; Plymouth

PARTRIDGE, John (-1706) & Magdalen BULLARD (-1677); 18 Dec 1655; Medfield

PARTRIDGE, John (-1722), Portsmouth, NH, & Mary FERNALD (-1722); 11 Dec 1660; Salisbury

PARTRIDGE, John & 1/wf Elizabeth ROCKETT/ROCKWOOD (-1688); 24 Dec 1678; Medfield

PARTRIDGE, John (-1731) & 1/wf Hannah SEABURY (1668-); 24 Dec 1684; Duxbury

PARTRIDGE, John & 2/wf Elizabeth ADAMS (1666-1719); aft 22 Jul 1688, b 1693; Medfield

PARTRIDGE, John (1659-by 1699) & Abigail [PLAISTED], dau Roger; b 1695?; ?Portsmouth, NH

PARTRIDGE, John & 2/wf Mary (_?_) BREWSTER (1661-1742), w Wrestling; 23 May 1700; Duxbury

PARTRIDGE, Nathaniel & Ellen [LEATHERLAND?]; bef 23 Apr 1643; Boston

PARTRIDGE, Nathaniel & Lydia WIGHT; 24 Nov 1686; Medfield

PARTRIDGE, Nehemiah ("brother" of Edward GOVE) & Sarah [ELLINS], m/2 James LEVITT/LEAVITT 1691, 1692; b 1671; Medfield

PARTRIDGE, Ralph (-1658, Duxbury) & Patience _?_ ; in Eng, b 1615?; Weymouth

PARTRIDGE, Samuel (1645-) & 1/wf Mehitable CROW; 24 Sep 1668; ?Hadley/?Hatfield

PARTRIDGE, Samuel (1672-1740) & Maria/Mary (COTTON) ATWATER? (1670-1729), w John?; 2 May 1695, where?; Hampton, NH/Hadley/Hatfield

PARTRIDGE, William (-1654) & Ann _?_ (-1689), m/2 Anthony STANYAN 1656; b 1638, b 1639; Salisbury

PARTRIDGE, William (-1668) & Mary SMITH (1625-1680); 12 Dec 1644, 10 Dec, [24?] Dec; Hartford/Hadley/Westfield

PARTRIDGE, William & 1/wf Sarah PRICE (-1656), Dedham; - Nov 1654, 23 Nov; Medfield

PARTRIDGE, William (-1692) & 2/wf Sarah COLBURN (-1715); 19 Nov 1656; ?Medfield

PARTRIDGE, William (-1729 in 75th y), Portsmouth, NH, & Mary BROWN (-1739); - Dec 1680, 8 Dec 1680; Newbury

PARTRIDGE, William & Abigail READING/RIDDAN (1671-); 11 Jan 1692/3; Portsmouth, NH

PARTRIDGE, William (1670-1750), Medfield & 1/wf Hannah FISHER (1674-1726), Medfield; 15 Nov 1693; ?Sherborn/Medfield

PASCO, Hugh & 1/wf Sarah WOOLAND (-1676); 20 Apr 1670; Salem

PASCO, Hugh & 2/wf Mary PEASE; 16 Dec 1678; Salem

PASCO, John (-1706) & Rachel (NEIGHBORS) [CODMAN?]/CODNER?, ?w Peter; b 1685; Boston/Enfield, CT

PASCO, John (-1697) & Elizabeth LOFT; 25 May 1691; Boston

PASCO, William & Ruth HETCHBONE; 20 Oct 1690; Boston

PASMER, Bartholomew & _?_ ; b 1641; Boston

PASMORE, William & Rebecca _?_, m/2 Robert EDMUNDS 1695; b 1674; Boston

PATCH, Abraham (1649-) & Eunice FRAILE; 13 Mar 1670, 1670/1; Ipswich

PATCH, Benjamin (-1730) & Susanna/Susan LEGROWE (now GROVES) (-1733); 16 Jul 1694; Salem

PATCH, Edmund & _?_ ; b 1649; Salem/Wenham/Ipswich

PATCH, James (?1626-1658) & Hannah [WOODBURY], m/2 Mark HASKELL; ca 1645; Salem

PATCH, James (1655-) & 1/wf Sarah BALCH/GARDINER; 24 Dec 1680, 29 Dec 1680; Beverly/Ipswich

PATCH, James (1678-) & Rebecca BILES; m int 22 Dec 1700; Beverly

PATCH, John (1623-1694) & Elizabeth [BRACKENBURY] (-1715); b 1648; Salem/Beverly

PATCH, Nicholas (1597-1673) & Elizabeth OWLEY; South Petherton, 17 Sep 1623; Salem/Beverly

PATCH, Richard & 1/wf Marie/Mary GOLDSMITH; 8 Feb 1672, 1672/3; Beverly

PATCH, Stephen (1680-) & Ruth _?_ ; b 1701; Wenham

PATCH, Thomas (-1722, ae 83) (son Nicholas) & Mary [SCOTT] (1642?-1723); b 1666; Wenham

PATCH, _?_ & _?_ [LEIGH]; 166-?; ?Ipswich

PATCH, Thomas & Mary LOVETTS (1650-), dau John; 8 Nov 1686; ?Beverly
PATCHEN, Jacob (1663-1749) & Mary (HUBBARD) [GRUMMAN], w Samuel; ca 1690?, 1691+?; Fairfield, CT
PATCHING, Joseph (1610-1689+) & 1/wf Elizabeth (BENNETT) INGULDEN/IGGLEDEN, w Stephen; 18 Apr 1642; Roxbury
PATCHEN, Joseph (1610-1689+) & 2/wf Mary [?MOREHOUSE]; b 1663; Fairfield
PATEFIELD, John & Amy _?_ (-1691, ae 76); b 1653; Charlestown
PATIENCE, Thomas & _?_ ; b 1642; Lynn
PATRICK, Daniel (-1644) & Anneke/Aelbrights/(Albertse) vanBEYEREN/VanBEYERON, m/2 Tobias FEAKE 1644/49?; b 1643, 3 Mar 1630, b 1645; Cambridge/Stamford, CT/Watertown/Flushing/Hartford
PATRICK/(KIRK)PATRICK, Daniel (-1721) & [Dinah YATES]; b 1675; Flushing, LI
PATRICK, Moses & Hannah _?_ ; b 1680; Boston
PATRICK, Moses & 2/wf? Catharine _?_ ; 1683
PATTEN, David & Mary [LAWRENCE]; b 1692; Dorchester
PATTIN, John & Margaret LUXFORD (1673-); 13 Mar 1699/1700; Cambridge
PATTEN, Nathaniel (-1671/2) & Justina [PIKE] (-1675); b 1640?; Dorchester
PATTEN, Nathaniel (-1725) & 1/wf Rebecca ADAMS (-1677); 24 Nov 1669; Cambridge/Lexington
PATTEN, Nathaniel (-1725) & 2/wf Sarah (MORSE) COOPER, w Timothy; 8 Oct 1678; Cambridge
PATTEN, Nathaniel & Hannah ROSS, m/2 Joseph EMERSON; 6 Dec 1695; Billerica
PATTIN/PATTEN/PADDEN, Thomas (1631-1690) & 1/wf Rebecca PAINE (1642-); 1 Apr 1662; Billerica/Dedham
PATTEN, Thomas ((163-)-1690) & 2/wf Sarah (KENDALL) DUNTON (1653-), w Samuel, m/3 Thomas RICHARDSON 1690; 20 May 1686; Billerica
PATTEN, Thomas (1666-1752) & Hannah FOSTER (-1742); 21 Dec 1699; Billerica
PATTEN, William (-1668) & Mary _?_ (-1673); in Eng, b 1632, b 1622?; Cambridge
PATTEN, William & Mary [?ROGERS], dau John?; b 1694; Billerica
PATTERSON, Andrew & Elizabeth PEAT (1669-); 19 Feb 1690; Stratford, CT
PATTERSON, Andrew (1672-1707) & Elizabeth KEBBE/KIBBEY (1681-); 8 Nov 1697; Charlestown
PATTERSON, Edward (?1615-1670) & ?Elizabeth _?_ ; b 1644; New Haven
PATTERSON, Edward (-1672) & Faith [CHAMBERLAIN], dau Henry[1], m/2 Thomas HUET/HEWETT?; b 1655(6?); Hingham/Rehoboth/Freehold, NJ
PATTERSON, James (1633-1701) & Rebecca STEVENSON/?STIMPSON (-1701+); 29 May 1662; Billerica/Cambridge
PATTERSON, John (-1710) & Keziah [BRACKETT], m/2 Joseph MAYLEM; b 1701/; Boston
PATERSON, Peter, Lyme & Elizabeth RITHWAY, Lyme, CT; 11 Jun 1678; Saybrook, CT/Lyme, CT
PATESHALL/?PADESHALL, Edmund (-1675+) & Martha DENHAM (1611-); m lic 29 Dec 1634; Pemaquid
PATTESHAL, Richard (1636-1689) & 1/wf Abigail _?_ ; b 1664; Boston
PATTESHALL, Richard & 2/wf Martha [WOODY] (1652-1713); b 1673(4?); Boston
PAUL, Daniel & Elizabeth [?LEVER]; ?Ipswich, Eng, ?9 Feb 1617, b 26 Aug 1640, b 24 Aug 1640; Kittery, ME
PAUL, Daniel & Sarah BRAGDON; 30 Mar 1700, 30 Mar 1701; York, ME
PAUL, Edward & Esther BOBBIT; 23 Aug 1693; Taunton
PAUL, James (1657-1724) & Mary _?_ ; b 1685; Taunton
PAUL, John & Lydia JENKINS; 3 May 1657; Malden
PAUL, John (1660-1718) & Dorothy WALKER; 26 May 1692; Taunton
PAUL, Richard & Margaret TURNER (-1673), m/2 Henry WITHINGTON 1662; 8 Nov 1638; Taunton
PAUL, Samuel (-1690) & Mary BRECK (1648-1720), m/2 John TOLMAN 1692; 9 Jan 1666/7; Dorchester/Roxbury
PAUL, Samuel & Hannah/Mary? [ROYAL]; b 1695; Dorchester
PAUL, Stephen (-1695±) & Katharine [MAVERICK] (-1706+); b 7 Jun 1682, ca 1672, aft 18 Jul 1668; Kittery, ME
PAULE, William (-1704, ae 80) & Mary [RICHMOND] (1639-1715); b 1657; Taunton
PAULING, Matthew & _?_ [WALLIS]
PAULING, Matthew & 2/wf Sarah/Susanna WALKER; 15 Jun 1698; Boston/Saco, ME

PAYSON, Edward (?1613-) & 1/wf Ann PARKES/PARKE (-1641); 20 Aug 1640, ?10 Aug; Roxbury

PAYSON, Edward (1613-) & 2/wf Mary ELLIOTT (1621-1697); 1 Jan 1642, 1641/2?; Roxbury

PAYSON, Edward (1657-1732) & 1/wf Elizabeth PHILLIPS (-1724); 1 Nov 1683; Rowley/Roxbury/Dorchester

PASON, Ephraim (1658-1732) & 1/wf Katherine LEADBETTER (1662-); 12 Jun 1684; Dorchester

PAYSON, Giles (?1609-1689) & Elizabeth DOWELL (-1678); Apr 1637; Roxbury

PASON, John (-1719) & 1/wf Bathsheba [TILESTON] (1649-20 Feb 1681); b 1670; Roxbury

PAYSON, John (-1719) & 2/wf Hannah _?_ (-1724, Roxbury); aft 20 Feb 1681, b 1686; Roxbury

PAYSON, Samuel (-1697) & Prudence LINCOLN, w William, m/3 Benjamin THOMPSON 1698; 31 Mar 1677, no issue; Roxbury

PASON, Samuel (1662-1721) & Mary PHILLIPS; 14 Jun 1688; Rowley/Dorchester

PEABODY, Francis (1614, ca 1612-1698) & 1/wf Lydia _?_ ; b 1640; Hampton, NH/Topsfield, MA

PEABODY, Francis (1612/14-1698?) & 2/wf Mary (FOSTER) [WOOD] (1618-1705), w Daniell; aft 1650; Hampton, NH

PEABODY, Isaac (1648+-1727) & 1/wf Sarah [ESTES]?; b 1694; Topsfield

PEABODY, Jacob (1664-1689) & Abigail TOWNE (1664-), m/2 Thomas PERLEY 1696; 12 Jan 1686; Topsfield

PEABODY, John (1612-1687) & 1/wf [Dorothy TOOLEY]?/TULLEY/TULLY; b 1655; Newport

PEABODY, John (1643, ?1642-1720) & 1/wf Hannah ANDREWS; 23 Nov 1665; Boxford/Topsfield

PEABODY, John (1612-1687) & 2/wf [Mary (_?_) ROGERS], w James; ca 1677; Newport

PEABODY, John & Rachel [NICHOLSON] (1658-1711); ca 1680?; Newport

PEABODY, Joseph (?1644-1721) & 1/wf Bethia BRIDGES; 26 Oct 1668; Boxford/Topsfield

PEABODY, Joseph (1671-1714) & Mary SYMONDS (1669-); - Mar 1693/4; Boxford

PEABODY, Nathaniel (1669-1715) & Francis [HOYT] (1674/5?-), no ch, m/2 Samuel SHACKFORD 1716; b 1701?; Salisbury

PEABODY, William (1646-1699) & Hannah HALE (1663-1733); 14 Aug 1684; Boxford

PEACH, John (1612-1683?) (ae ca 80 in 1684) & [?Margaret HINDS] (1605-); aft 1635, no issue; Marblehead

PEACH, John, Jr. (1614-1694) (brother of above John) & Alice _?_, "cousin" of Margaret SNOOK; ca 1639?; Marblehead

PEACH, John & Sarah STACEY; 30 Nov 1700; Marblehead

PEACH, William (1650-1713) (nephew of John, Sr.) & Emma [DEVEREAUX] (1657-1737); b 1680; Marblehead

PEACHIE/PEACHY, Thomas (-1683) & Mary ROBINSON (-1691); 3 May 1665; Charlestown

PEACOCK, Edward & Roby _?_ ; b 1699(1700?); Rehoboth

PEACOCK, John (-1670) & Joyce _?_ ; b 1641/2; New Haven/Stratford, CT/Milford, CT

PEACOCK, Jonathan (1673-) & Martha WILLIAMS; m int 23 Jun 1696; Boston

PEACOCK, Richard (-1669) & 1/wf Jane _?_ (-1653); b 1639(40?); Roxbury/Boston

PEACOCK, Richard (-1669) & 2/wf Margery SHOVE (-1680), wid; 17 Aug 1654; Boston

PEACOCK, Samuel (-1691) & Mary [BEVER?]; b 1662(3?); Charlestown/Boston

PEACOCK, William (1623-1660) & Mary WILLIS; 12 Apr 1653; Roxbury

PEACOCK, William (1655-) & Sarah EDSALL, ?dau Thomas; 3 Aug 1681; Roxbury

PEACOCK?/PECAKE?, _?_ & Ann _?_ (-1687)

PEAKE, Christopher (-1666) & Dorcas FRENCH (-1697), m/2 Griffin CRAFTS; 3 Jan 1636, 1636/7; Roxbury/Cranberry

PEEK, George & Hannah _?_ ; bef 1688; Salem

PEAKS, Israel (1655/6-) & [Tabitha NAYLOR] (1667-); b 1687; Scituate

PEAKE, Jonathan (1637-1700) & Sarah FRENCH (1638-1694); 15 Aug 1660; Roxbury

PEAKE, Jonathan (1663-) & Hannah [LEAVINS] (1666-1756); b 1691; Woodstock, CT

PEAKS, William & Judith (?DENNIS) LICHFIELD/(LITCHFIELD), w Lawrence; Oct 1650, 20 Oct 1650, 1649, 2 Oct; Scituate

PEAKES, William (1662-1717) & Joan/Jean _?_ ; b 1692; Scituate

PEAL, George & _?_ ; b 1674; Salem

PEAL, George (-1733) & Abigail AGUR; 28 Jul [bef 1697], 169[6?]; Salem

PEARD, Robert & Margaret/Mary _?_ , m Richard SMITH; b 1669; Boston

PEARD, Richard & Jane (HOBBS) NOSSITER, w Michael; 8 Jul 1669, 166-, [born]; Saco, ME

PEARL, John & Elizabeth [?HOLMES] (1662-); b 1683, b 1687; Boxford/Baseford

PEARL, Nicholas (-1706) & 1/wf Elizabeth BOSWORTH (-1702); 25 Oct 1686, 5 Oct, by 1690; Ipswich

PEARSALL/PARCELL/?PESHALL, Nicholas (-1691) & Sarah __?__; b 1649; Flushing, LI

PEARSALL, Henry[1] (-1668, 1667?) & Anne HALSTEAD?/Anne MOYLE? WILLIAMS/?Dorcas WILLIAMS (?GILDERSLEEVE), w Richard; b 24 Jul 1667, ca 1647; LI

PEARSALL, Nathaniel (-1703) & [Martha SEAMANS] (-1712); 4 Feb 1674/5, 1674; Hempstead, LI

PEARSALL, Thomas & Mary [SEAMAN]; b 1701?, b 1697, ca 1682, b 1699; Hempstead, LI

PEARSALL, George & __?__; b 1701?; LI

PEARSALL, Daniel (1653±-1698+) & __?__/Emma/Amy [BASSETT] (1658±-), dau Robert; b 6 Dec 1685, 1680±; Hempstead, LI

PEASE, Abraham (1662-1735) & Jane [MENTOR]; no issue; Enfield, CT

PEASE, Benjamin & Jean AREY; 17 Jun 1697; Edgartown

PEASE, David & __?__; b 1676; Martha's Vineyard

PEASE, Henry (-1647) & 1/wf Susan __?__ (-1645); b 1629, b 1628?; Boston

PEASE, Henry (-1648, 1649) & 2/wf Bridget __?__; aft Aug 1645, aft 25 Dec 1645; Boston

PEASE, Henry & Gertrude __?__; b 1649; Marblehead/Boston

PEASE, Isaac (1672-1731) & Mindwell OSBORN (1673-); 9 Jun 1692; Enfield, CT

PEASE, Isaac & Elizabeth THOMAS (1673-); 20 Apr 1696-7, 22 Apr 1697; Salem

PEASE, James (1627, 1637-1719) & 1/wf Elizabeth [NORTON]; b 1664; Martha's Vineyard

PEASE, James & Hannah [DUNHAM] (ca 1666, 1667-), m/2 Elisha PARKER; 1687; Edgartown

PEASE, James/Thomas (1670-) & Hannah HARMON; 17 Oct 1695, 18 Oct; Enfield, CT

PEASE, John & 1/wf Lucy [WESTON] (-1639+); b 1627(8?); Martha's Vineyard

PEASE, John & 1/wf Martha __?__; b 1648; Boston

PEASE, John & 2/wf Mary __?__, m/2 Thomas CREBER; b 1649; Martha's Vineyard

PEASE, John (-1689) & 1/wf Mary [GOODELL] (-1668, 1669); b 1654; Salem

PEASE, John & Ruth __?__; b 1665(6?); Boston

PEASE, John (-1689, in 60th y) & 2/wf Ann CUMMINS (-1689); 8 Dec 1669; Salem/Enfield, CT

PEASE, John (1654-1734) & Margaret ADAMS (1654-1737), Ipswich?; 30 Jan 1676/7; Salem/Enfield, CT

PEASE, John & Hannah __?__; b 1677(8?); Boston

PEASE, John & Abigail [MERRY] (1662-); b 1684; Martha's Vineyard

PEASE, John & 3/wf Ann __?__; b 1692; Enfield, CT

PEISE, John & Abigail THOMPSON; 5 Jan 1693; Braintree

PEASE, Jonathan (1669-1711) & Elizabeth BOOTH (ca 1668-1723); 11 Oct 1693; Enfield, CT

PEASE, Matthew & Mary GREEN; - Apr 1699; Edgartown

PEASE, Nathaniel & Mary HOBBS; 15 Mar 1667, 1668; Salem

PEASE, Nathaniel & Abigail VINSON/VINCENT?; 11 Oct 1700; Edgartown

PEASE, Robert & Margaret __?__ (-1644); in Eng, b 1607; Salem

PEASE, Robert (1608-1644) & Marish?/Mary [?FRENCH], m/2 Richard HAYNES 1644+; in Eng, b 1628; Salem

PEASE, Robert (1628?-) & Sarah __?__; b 1660; Salem

PEASE, Robert (1656-1744) & Abigail RANDALL (-aft 22 Sep 1743); 16 Dec 1678; Salem/Enfield, CT

PEASE, Robert, Jr. (-1744+) & Hannah WARRINER; 24 Dec 1691; Enfield, CT

PEASE, Samuel (-1689) & Mary __?__, m/2 Thomas WHITTEMORE; b 1679; Martha's Vineyard

PEASE, Samuel & Elizabeth __?__, m/2 Samuel SMITH; ca 1690/5?; Exeter, NH

PEASE, Stephen & 1/wf Deborah (MACY) [GARDNER]; b 1694, aft 1691; Martha's Vineyard

PEASE, Thomas (1656-) & Bathsheba [MERRY] (1665-); b 1685(6?), ca 1684; Edgartown

PEASE, William (1673?-) & Judith [PARRET], m/2 Samuel CRANSTON; ca 1694-5; Newport, RI

PEASLEE, Joseph (-1660) & 1/wf __?__; b 1630; Salisbury

PEASLY, Joseph (-1660) & 2/wf Mary [?JOHNSON] (-1694); b 1642?; Newbury

PEASLEY, Joseph (1646-1735) (ae 69 in 1716) & 1/wf Ruth BARNARD (-1723); 21 Jan 1671, 1671/2; Amesbury/Haverhill

PEASELY, Joseph & Elizabeth HASTINGS; 18 Sep 1699; Haverhill

PEAT, Benjamin (1640-1704) & Phebe [BUTLER]; b 1663; Stratford, CT

PEET, Benjamin (1665-) & 1/wf Priscilla [FAIRCHILD] (1669-); b 1687; Stratford, CT

PEAT, John (1597-1684) & [Mary?] __?__/?Margaret ALCOCK?; in Eng, ca 1618/20?, 16 Feb 1621/2; Stratford, CT

PEET, John & _?_ [CHARLES]/?Ann PEAKE (-bef 1673); Stratford, CT
PEET, John (?1638-1678) & Sarah [OSBORNE], m/2 John BROOKS 1685; b 1663; Stratford, CT
PEAT, John (1672-1710) & Mary MOREHOUSE, m/2 John CORBETT, m/3 Benjamin PEAT; 12 May
    1696; Fairfield, CT
PEAT, Samuel (1663-) & 1/wf Mary (HICKS) [JUDSON], w Isaac; b 1689; Straftord, CT
PEET, Samuel (1670-1748) & Abigail [HARVEY] (1671-); by 1698, bef 27 Mar 1698; Stratford,
    CT
PEAT, Samuel (1663-) & 2/wf Elizabeth SMITH; 1 Jun 1698, - Jun 1698; Fairfield/Stratford, CT
PEAKE?/PEAT?/PEACOCK, _?_ & Ann _?_ (-1687)
PEET, _?_ & Rachel [PIERCE] (1678-); b 1701?; RI
PEATHER, Nathaniel & Ann SALTER, m int 13 Jul 1695; Boston
PECK, Benjamin & Mary SPERRY; 29 Mar 1670; New Haven
PECK, Benjamin & Mary _?_ ; b 1687; Boston
PECK, Benjamin (1671-1742) & Mary SPERRY (-1728), New Haven; 2 May 1700; Derby,
    CT/Norwich, CT
PECK, Daniel & Dorcas _?_ ; b 1694(5?); Boston
PECK, David & _?_ ; b 1696(7?); RI
PECK, Ebenezer & Elizabeth _?_ ; b 1696; Boston
PECK, Eleazer (1643-1734) & Mary BUNNELL (1650-1724); 31 Oct 1671; New Haven/Walling-
    ford, CT
PECK, Henry (-1651) & [Joan] [?ALLEN], m/2 Andrew LOW 1651+; b 1643; New Haven
PECK, Hezekiah (1662-1723) & Deborah [COOPER]; b 1687; Swansea/Rehoboth
PECK, Israel (1644-1723) & Bethiah BOSWORTH (1644-1718); 15 Jul 1670; Swansea
PECK, Jothmieal/Jathniel (1660-1742) & Sarah SMITH (1670-1717); 28 Jan 1688/9, 28 Feb;
    Rehoboth
PECK, Jeremiah (1623-1699, Waterbury, CT) & Joanna KITCHELL; 12 Nov 1656, 12 Jan 1656?;
    Guilford, CT/New Haven
PECK, John (1627-1713) & Elizabeth [HUNTING] (-1667); b 1657; Rehoboth
PECK, John & _?_ ; b 1664; Hartford
PECK, John (-1724) & Mary MOSS (-1725, ae 78); 3 Nov 1664; New Haven/Wallingford, CT
PECK, John (-1713) & Elizabeth PRESTON (-1687); 30 Dec 1668; Rehoboth
PECK, John & Elizabeth _?_ (will 1697); b 1674(5?); Boston
PECK, John & _?_ ; b 1681; Milford, CT
PECK, John & 3/wf Rebecca? _?_ ; ca 21 Apr 1687, b 1708; Rehoboth
PECK, John & Martha _?_ (-1705, ae 55 y); Southold, LI
PECK, John & Millicent (HOLBROOK) [SPRAGUE]; b 1694; Mendon
PECK, John & Susanna STREET (1675-1704); 23 May 1694; Wallingford, CT
PECK, Jonathan (1666-) & Elizabeth THROOP (-1729); 31 Mar 1695; Bristol, RI
PECK, Joseph (1587-1663) (called Thomas COOPER "brother") & 1/wf Rebecca CLARKE
    (-1637); Hingham, Eng, 21 May 1617; Hingham
PECK, Joseph (1587-1663) & 2/wf [Deliverance?] _?_ ; 1637, 1638; Hingham/Rehoboth
PECK, Joseph & Hannah/?Joanna [ALLEN]; b 1650; Rehoboth
PECK, Joseph (-1700/1) & 1/wf Alice (HEATH) BURWELL (-1666), w John; [12 Sep] 1650, at
    Milford; Milford/New Haven
PECK, Joseph (1641-1718) & Sarah [PARKER] (1636-ae 90?); b 1663; Lyme, CT
PECK, Joseph (-1700/1) & 2/wf Mary [RICHARDS] (1631?-); 1669; Milford, CT
PECK, Joseph & Sarah ALLING (1649-); 28 Nov 1672; New Haven
PECK, Joseph (?1653-) & Mary CAMP (1660-); 27 Jan 1678, 1678/9; Milford, CT
PECK, Joseph & Sarah [NORTH?]; b 1689(80?); Boston/Rehoboth?
PECK, Joseph (1650, 1656-1720) & Elizabeth SMITH (1663-); 11 Dec 1684; Rehoboth
PECK, Joseph (1650-1698) & Ruth [ATKINS?] (doubtful), m/2 John HOSKINS 1699; b 1686;
    Windsor, CT
PECK, Joseph (1675-1746) & Lydia [BALL] (-1742); b 1702, b 1701?; Newark, NJ
PECK, Lemuel & Rachel [PIERCE]; b 1697; Rehoboth
PECKE, Nathaniel (1641-1676) & Deliverance BOSWORTH (1650-1675); b 1670; Swansea
PECK, Nathaniel & Tabitha _?_ ; ca 11 Jan 1686/7; Boston
PECK, Nathaniel & 1/wf Christian ALLEN (-1702); 18 Mar 1695/6, 8 Mar; Swansea/Rehoboth
PECK, Nicholas (1630-1710) & 1/wf Mary [WINCHESTER] (bpt 1637-1657); b 1650; Rehoboth
PECK, Nicholas (1630-1710) & 2/wf Rebecca [BOSWORTH] (1641?-1704); b 1660; Rehoboth

PECK, Paul (-1695) & Martha [HALE]/[H—E]; b 1639(?); Hartford
PECK, Paul (1639-1725) & Elizabeth [BAISEY]/BAYSEY (1645-); b 1666; Hartford
PECK, Richard (1602-) & Margaret _?_ (1595-); in Eng, b 1628
PECK, Rev. Robert (-1658) & 1/wf Anne LAWRENCE (-1648); in Eng, b 1620, b 1607; Hingham
PECK, Rev. Robert (-1658) & 2/wf (Martha (HONEYWOOD) BACON), w James
PECK, Samuel & 1/wf Sarah HUNT (-1673); 1 Jun 1666; Rehoboth
PECK, Samuel (1648/9?-1696) & Elizabeth _?_ ; b 1672; Hartford
PECKE, Samuel (1639-1708) & 2/wf Rebecca (PAINE) HUNT (1656-), w Peter; 21 Nov 1677; Rehoboth
PECK, Samuel (1659-1746) & Ruth FERRIS (1662-1745, ae 83); 27 Nov 1686; Greenwich, CT
PECK, Samuel (1672-1736) & Rachel _?_ (1676-1756, in 81st y); b 1697; Rehoboth
PECK, Samuel & Elizabeth LEE (1681-); 28 Dec 1699; Lyme, CT
PECK, Samuel (1677-) & Abigail [HITCHCOCK]; b 1701?, b 1701/2?, 1703?; Hartford
PECK, Simon & 1/wf Hannah [FARNSWORTH] (1638-1659); b 1659; Hingham
PECK, Simon & 2/wf Prudence CLAPP (1637-); Dorchester, 13 Feb 1659/60; Hingham
PECK, Stephen & 2/wf Theoda (PARKE) [WILLIAMS] (1627-1718, ae 81), w Rev./Dea. Samuel; ?aft 28 Sep 1698; Roxbury
PECKE, Thomas & Elizabeth _?_ ; b 1652(3?); Boston
PECK, Thomas & Elizabeth [COGGESHALL] (1650-); b 11 Mar 1677; Providence
PECKE, Thomas & Hannah _?_ ; b 1694; Boston
PECK, Thomas & Joanna POWELL; m int 12 Jul 1695; Boston
PECK, William (1604-1694, ae 93) & 1/wf Elizabeth _?_ (-1683); in Eng, b? 1622; Boston/New Haven/Lyme, CT
PECK, William (-1694) & 2/wf Sarah [HOLT] (-1717), w William; aft 5 Dec 1683; New London, CT
PECK, _?_ & Elizabeth BEERS, dau Anthony, did she m/2 Henry GOODIN? 1663
PECKER, James & Elizabeth [FRIEND]; b 1652; Salem/Haverhill/Salisbury
PECKER, James (-1734) & Ann DAVIS (1655-); b 1682(3?); Haverhill/Salisbury
PECKHAM, Clement & Lydia _?_ ; b 1692; Newport
PECKHAM, John[1] & 1/wf Mary [CLARKE] (1607-1648, ?b 30 May 1651); b 1637; Newport
PECKHAM, John[1] & 2/wf Eleanor _?_ ; aft 1648; Newport
PECKHAM, John (±1645-1712±) & Sarah _?_ ; b 1666, b 1668; Newport/Little Compton, RI
PECKHAM, John & Dorothy GOODENOW; 9 Dec 1687; Sudbury/Bristol, RI
PECKHAM, John (1672-1723) & Mary/?Mercy BENNETT (-1756); 1695?, 1696?, ?6 Jun 1696; Newport/Little Compton
PECKHAM, Joseph & Dorothy [HYDE]; b 1701?; Newton
PECKHAM, Stephen (-1724) & Mary _?_ (-1724+); b 1683, 1682±; Newport/Dartmouth
PECKHAM, Thomas (-1709) & 1/wf _?_ ; b 1680; E. Greenwich, RI/Newport
PECKHAM, Thomas (-1709) & 2/wf Hannah (WEEDEN) [CLARK], w William, m/3 Joseph CLARK; aft 30 Sep 1683, b 1692; Newport
PECKHAM, William (1647-1734) & 1/wf ?Elizabeth/?Susannah [CLARKE]; b 1675; Newport
PECKHAM, William (1647-1734) & 2/wf Phebe [WEEDEN] (1660-1745); ca 1680/5?, b 1701?; Newport
PEDLEY/PEDLY, Roger & Sarah [THORNE?]; LI?
PEDERICK, John (-1686) & Miriam _?_ , m/2 Richard GROSS 1688, m/3 Samuel WALDERNE?; by 1652; Marblehead
PETHERICK, John & Phillis _?_ ; b 1673; Salem
PEDERICK, John & Susanna LATEMORE/LATIMER; 29 Nov 1682; Marblehead
PEDERICK, John & Mary BROWNE; 10 Jan 1688/9; Marblehead
PEDERICK, John & Joanna/?Johanna HAWLEY (-1717?); 3 Dec 1691; Marblehead
PEDERICK, Joseph & Mary WHITE; 3 Nov 1696; Marblehead
PEDERICK, _?_ & Dorcas _?_ (-1686); b 1685; Marblehead (Joseph & Samuel bpt 8 Mar 1684/5)
PEGG/PEGGE, Robert & Rose _?_ ; b 1664; Boston
PELHAM, Edward (ca 1652-1730, ae 77) & 1/wf Freelove [ARNOLD] (1661-1711); 18 Apr 1682; Newport
PELHAM, Herbert (1601, 1600?-1674 in Eng) & 1/wf Jemima WALDEGRAVE; m lic 18 Oct 1626, London; Cambridge
PELHAM, Herbert (?1600-1674) & 2/wf Elizabeth (BASSEVILLE/BOSVILE?/BOSVILLE) [HAR-LACKENDEN] (-1659, Marshfield), w Roger; aft Nov 1638, bef 1643; Cambridge

PEELOW/PEELEY/PEDOW/PERRIN, John (see John PERRIN) & Mary [POLLY] (1650-), dau John; b 17 Dec 1686, ca 1675?, ca 1667; Rehoboth

PELHAM, John & Abigail _?_ ; ca 1690?, 4 ch in 1699; Woburn

PELHAM, Joseph & Rebecca BARBER (?1676-); 19 Mar 1697, 1696/7; Boston

PELL, Edward (-1700) & Elizabeth _?_ ; b 1687; Boston

PELL, John (1632-) & Mary/Maria [MAYNARD] (1644?-), dau John; b 1664; Boston

PELL, John (1643-1702) & Rachel [PINCKNEY]; [1684], b 1675?; Eastchester, NY

PELL, Joseph (did they come to New Eng?) & 1/wf? Johana/Hannah COCKETT/COUSHETT; Boston, Eng, 5 Oct 1637; ?Lynn

PELL, Joseph (-1650) & ?2/wf Elizabeth (_?_) [EATON/HEATON], w Nathaniel of Boston, m/3 John MAYNARD/John MINORET; Boston

PELL, Samuel & Deborah _?_ ; b 1664; Boston

PELL, Thomas (?1612-1669) & Lucy [BREWSTER], w Francis; ca 1647; New Haven

PELL, William (-1672) & Alice _?_ (-1672+); b 1634; Boston

PELLETT, Richard (1673-) & Ann [BROOKS]; b 1701; Canterbury, CT

PELLATE, Thomas (-1694) & Mary DANE; 5 Mar 1659/60; Concord

PELLET, Thomas & Phelice _?_ ; b 1690; Concord

PELLET, _?_ & Sarah _?_ , m/2 William UNDERWOOD 1639

PELTON, John (-1681) & Susanna _?_ (-1706); b 1645; Dorchester

PELTON, John (1645-) & Susanna _?_ ; b 1675(6?); Dorchester

PELTON, Robert (1675-1745), Dorchester & Rebecca CREHORE (1674-1747), Milton; 2 Sep 1697; Milton/Stoughton

PELTON, Samuel (1646/7-) & Mary SMITH (1655-); 16 Jul 1673; Dorchester/Bristol, RI

PEMBER, Thomas & Agnes (WAY) [HARRIS], w Samuel; ca 1686, b 1696; New London, CT

PEMBERTON, Benjamin (-1709) & Elizabeth [DIXIE/DIXEY] (1669-), m/2 Edward WINSLOW 1712; b 1689; Boston

PEMBERTON, James (-1662) & 1/wf Alice _?_ ; b 1633; Boston/Hull?/Malden

PEMBERTON, James (1622-1696) & Sarah [WILLEY?] (-1709) (dau of Alice, Thomas MARSHALL's wf); b 1647; Newbury/Boston

PEMBERTON, James (-1662) & 2/wf Margaret _?_ (1612-); b 1653; Charlestown

PEMBERTON, John (-1654 in Eng) & 1/wf Elizabeth [GOFF?] (-22 Feb 1645), wid?; Newbury

PEMBERTON, John (1640-1691) & Deborah [BLAKE]; b 1668; Malden

PEMBERTON, Joseph (1655-1702) & Marie (LORD) MINER (-1717, New London), w Samuel; 19 Mar 1683, 1682/3; Stonington, CT

PEMBERTON, Thomas (1653-1693) & Hannah [PHILLIPS] (1654-); b 1676; Boston

PENDER, John & Temperance _?_ (-1732); b 1659; Westfield

PENDERSON, John & _?_ ; b 1691; New Haven

PENDLETON, Bryan (1599-1681) & Eleanor PRICE (-1688?); Birmingham, Eng, 22 Apr 1619; Watertown/Portsmouth, NH

PENDLETON, Caleb (-bef 1677) & Judith _?_ , m/2 Thomas SNOWSELL; b 1662; Boston/?Westerly, RI

PENDLETON, Caleb (1669-1746) & Elizabeth _?_ ; ?ca 1689/90; ?Stonington, CT

PENDLETON, Edmund (1665-1750) & Mary _?_ ; b 1700; Stonington, CT?

PENDLETON, James (1628-1709) & 1/wf Mary PALMER (-1655); 22 Oct 1647; Sudbury/Stonington, CT/etc.

PENDLETON, James (1628-1709) & 2/wf Hannah GOODENOW (1639-1725+, 1709+); 29 Apr 1656; Sudbury/Portsmouth, NH

PENDLETON, Joseph (1661-1706) & 1/wf Deborah MINER (-1697); 8 Jul 1696; Stonington, CT/Westerly, RI

PENDLETON, Joseph (1661-1706) & 2/wf Patience POTTS (1683-), m/2 Samuel ROGERS; 17 Dec 1700; Westerly, RI

PENFIELD, Samuel (-1711) & 1/wf Mary LEWIS (1653-1741, ca 90), m/2 William STONE; last of Nov 1675; Lynn/Rehoboth/Bristol, RI

PENFIELD, Samuel (-1711) & Anne _?_ (no); b 1692; Bristol, RI

PENFIELD, Samuel (-1711) & Mary [FRISBIE?] (no); b 1696; Bristol, RI

PENFIELD, Samuel[2] (1676-1714) & Hannah _?_ ; b 1700; Bristol, RI

PENGILLY, John & Mary _?_ ; b 1684; Suffield, CT

PENHALLOW, Samuel (1665-) & 1/wf Mary CUTTS (1669-1713); 1 Jul 1687; Portsmouth, NH

PENN, James (-1671) (kinsman James ALLEN: Penn TOWNSEND) & Katharine _?_ ; Boston

PENN, William (-1688) (he did not marry); Boston
PENANT/PENNANT, James & Amy _?_ ; b 1682; Boston
PENNELL, Clement & _?_ ; b 1643
PENWELL, John (?1622-1673, bef 1675, ae ca 55) & _?_ ; b 1647; Isles of Shoals, NH
PENWELL, John & Sarah [PURINGTON]/PUDDINGTON?/DAVIS?, ?m/2 Alexander MAXWELL; b Nov 1674, b 1673; Salem/York/Boston
PENEWELL, Joseph (1629-1690) & Ann _?_ (-1688±, ae 60); b 1665(6?); Boston
PENNYWELL, Joseph & Mercy _?_ , m/2 William PERHAM 1693; b 1687(8?); Boston
PENEWELL, Peter & Phebe [NEWMARCH], m/2? Samuel CHAPMAN 1702, m/2? _?_ BALCH 1700, 1701?; Ipswich?
PENNEL, Walter (-1683, 1682) & Mary [BOOTH] (1627-1683+); b 1647, by 1649; Saco, ME/Newbury
PENNEL, Walter (?1649-) & 2/wf? Anne (GREEN) BASTON (1656-), w William; 15 Apr 1700; Newbury/York, ME
PENNIMAN, James & Lydia [ELIOT], m/2 Thomas WIGHT; ca 1630, b Mar 1632; Boston/Braintree
PENNIMAN, James (1633-1679) & Mary CROSSE; 10 May 1659; Boston
PENNIMAN, James (1661-) & Thomasin [MARION] (1660-); b 1684; Boston
PENNIMAN, John (1637-) & Hannah BILLINGS (-1678); 24 Feb 1664/5; Braintree
PENNIMAN, Joseph (-1705, ae 65) & 1/wf Waiting ROBINSON (1646-1690); 25 Sep 1666; Braintree
PENNIMAN, Joseph (-1705) & 2/wf Sarah (BASS) STONE (?1640-1739+), w John; 10 May 1693, 11 May; Braintree
PENNIMAN, Moses (1678-1718) & Mary _?_ ; b 1699; Braintree
PENNIMAN, Samuel (1645-) & Elizabeth PARMENTER; 6 Jan 1673/4, not 11 Aug 1673; Braintree
PENNINGTON, Ephraim & Mary _?_ ; b 1645; New Haven
PENNINGTON, Ephraim (1645-) & Mary BROCKET (1646-), Wallingford; 25 Oct 1667, at Milford?, 25? Sep; New Haven/Newark, NJ
PENOYER, Robert (1614-1677+) & 1/wf _?_ (-bef 6 Mar 1671); b 1652; Gravesend, LI/Stamford, CT/Rye, NY
PENOYER, Robert & 2/wf Elizabeth (_?_) [SCOFIELD], w Richard, m/3 Richard LOUNSBURY; b 6 May 1671, b 1684; Stamford, CT/Mamaroneck, NY
PENNOYER, Thomas (1658-1724, 1723) & Lydia KNAPP (ca 1670-1710); 22 May 1685; Stamford, CT
PENNOYER, William & Mary _?_ ; b 1681; Mamaroneck, NY
PENNY, Christopher & Elizabeth WALLERC?/?OLSRA; 8 Jan 1695, 1694; Taunton/Bristol, RI
PENNY, Henry (-1706) & _?_ ; Portsmouth, NH
PENNY, John & Elizabeth RAND (1662-), m/2 William SHEAF 1704; 4 Jul 1682; Charlestown
PENEY, Thomas (-1658) & Ann _?_ (-1667); b 1640; Gloucester
PENNY, Thomas & 2/wf Agnes CLARKE (-1681); 15 Aug 1668; Gloucester
PENY, Thomas & 3/wf Joan (_?_) BRAFUCK/BRABROOK, w Richard; 17 May 1682; Gloucester
PENNY, Thomas & 1/wf Joanna [LITTLEFIELD]; b 1701?, b 1707; Wells, ME
PENNY, William & Sarah GRINWICH/GREENWICH; 15 May 1676; Salem/Boston?
PENNEY, William (-1683) & Ruth [HOLLARD]; b 1681; Boston
PENTICOST, John & 1/wf? Joanna [LARKIN], sis Edward; b 1639; Charlestown
PENTICOST, John (-1697, ae 90) & 2/wf Joanna (HALL) LARKIN (1615-1685, ae 70), w Edward; aft 1652, b 1674, b 1659, aft 1656/7; Charlestown
PENYON, Nicholas & _?_ ; b 30 Dec 1647; Lynn
PIPER, Isaac (1659-) & Apphia FREEMAN (1666-); 7 Oct 1685; Eastham
PIPPER, Jacob (1661-) & Elizabeth PAINE (1664-); 15 Feb 1684, 15 Feb 1685; Rehoboth/Roxbury
PIPPER, John (1647-1670) & Bethia FISHER; 25 Oct 1669; Dedham/Roxbury
PIPPER, Joseph (1649-1676) & Mary [MAY], m/2 Joshua [SEAVER] 1678; ?4 Nov 1675, b 1676; Roxbury
PIPPER, Richard (1607-) & Mary _?_ (1605-); ca 1630; Roxbury
PEPPER, Robert (ca 1620-1684) & Elizabeth JOHNSON (?1622-1684); 14 Mar 1642, 1642/3; Roxbury
PEPPERELL, William & _?_ ; b 1694; Deerfield

PEPPERELL, William (1646, 1641-1733?, 1734?) & Margery [BRAY] (?1660-1741), w Joseph PIERCE; b 1685, b 1681, ca 1678, ca 1680?; Kittery, ME

PERSEVALL/PERCIVAL, James (-1692) & Mary (RAINSFORD) [BASSETT], w William; [1670], ?Jun 1671?; Sandwich

PARSEUAH, James (1671-1728) & 1/wf Abigail ROBINSON (1674-); 27 Feb 1695/6, 18 Feb 1695/6; Falmouth, MA/E. Haddom, CT/Sandwich/Barnstable

PERCIVAH, Theodore & Elizabeth MORSS; 12 Jan 1698; Boston

PERCY, Marmaduke & Mary _?_ ; in Eng, b 1637; Salem

PERCY, [?Robert], New London & Ruth (CROOKE) READ, w William; b 7 Jun 1681; ?New London, CT

PERDUE/PURDUE, Nathaniel & Hannah _?_ ; b 1694; Boston/Milton

PERUM, John (-1721, ae 88) & Lydia SHIPLE/SHEPLEY (-1710); 15 Dec 1664; Chelmsford

PERRAM, John & Lydia FLECHER; 27 Dec 1692; Chelmsford

PIRHAM, Joseph (1669-) & Dorothy [HYDE] (1675-); b 1694; Chelmsford/Groton

PARUM, William & Frances _?_ (-1695); b 1657; Boston

PERRAM, William & Mercy/Martha PENEWELL, w Joseph; 16 Nov 1693; Boston

PERIE, Daniel & Johanah COTTLE; 9 Feb 1687; Newbury

PERIGO, Robert (-1683) & Mary _?_ (-1701+), m/2 Henry PETERSON 1685; by 1659, b 1674, b 1667; Boston/Lyme, CT

PERKINS, Abraham (?1603-1683) & Mary [WYETH] (-1706, ae 88); b 1639; Hampton, NH

PERKINS, Abraham (1640-1732) & Hannah BEAMSLEY (1643-1732), Boston; 16 Oct 1661; Ipswich/Gloucester/Weymouth

PERKINS, Abraham (1639-1677) & Elizabeth SLEEPER, m/2 Alexander DENHAM, m/3 Richard SMITH; 27 Aug 1668; Hampton, NH

PERKINS, Abraham & _?_ [WEST]; b 1676; Ipswich

PERKINS, Beamsley (1673-1720) & Hannah (EMERSON) GLAZIER, w Zechariah; Sep 1697?, 1698?

PERKINS, Benjamin & Hannah _?_ ; b 1684; Newbury

PERKINS, Caleb (-1724+) & Bethia PHILBRICK (-1724+); 24 Apr 1677; Hampton, NH

PERKINS, David (-1736) & 1/wf Elizabeth [BROWN]; b 1677; Beverly/Newbury/Bridgewater

PERKINS, David & Deliverance BLISS; 8 Jun 1682; New Haven

PERKINS, David & Martha HAYWARD/[HOWARD]; 1 Feb 1698/9; Bridgewater

PERKINS, Ebenezer (1659-1703) & Mercy _?_ ; b 1683, b 1685; Hampton, NH/DE

PERKINS, Edmund (-d in Eng) & Alice _?_ ; 1624, 1625

PERKINS, Edmund (-1693) & Susanna (HUDSON) [HOWLETT] (±1645-), m/3 Christopher SLEG; b 1678; Boston

PERKINS, Edward & Elizabeth BUTCHER; 20 Mar 1649; New Haven

PERKINS, Elisha (1656±, 1654-) & 1/wf Catherine TOWNE (1662-1714); 23 Feb 1680; Topsfield/Newbury

PERKINS, Francis (1672-1706?) & Elizabeth [EVELETH] (1670-), m/2 George GIDDINGS 1706; b 1698; Ipswich/Gloucester

PERKINS, George & _?_ ; ca 1690; Isles of Shoals

PERKINS, Humphrey (1661-) & Martha [MOULTON] (?1666, ?1668-); b 1688; Hampton, NH

PERKINS, Isaac[1] (-bef 1639) & Alice _?_ (-1639+); Ipswich

PERKINS, Isaac & Susanna _?_ ; b 1639; Hampton, NH

PERKINS, Isaac (ca 1650-1726) & Hannah [KNIGHT]; ca 1669; Ipswich

PERKINS, Jabez (1671-) & 1/wf Hannah LATHROP (1677-1721); 30 Jun 1698; Norwich, CT

PERKINS, Jacob (1624-1700) & 1/wf Elizabeth [WHIPPLE] (ca 1629-1686); ca 1648; Ipswich

PERKINS, Jacob (-1719) & 1/wf Sarah [MAINWRIGHT] (-1688); [1667]; Ipswich

PERKINS, Jacob & Mary PHILBROOK; 30 Dec 1669; Hampton, NH

PERKINS, Jacob (1662-1705) (calls Thomas TREADWELL "brother") & 1/wf Elizabeth SPARKS (-1692); 25 Dec 1684, 27 Dec, 1698; Ipswich

PERKINS, Jacob (1624-1700, ae 76) & 2/wf Damaris (_?_) [ROBINSON] (-1716, ae 80), w Nathaniel; aft 2 Feb 1685/6, aft 12 Feb 1685/6, aft Feb 1685; Salisbury

PERKINS, Jacob (1641-1719) & 2/wf Sarah [KINSMAN] (1659-); b 1690; Ipswich

PERKINS, Jacob (1662-1705?) & 2/wf Sarah [TREADWELL] (1673-1738); ?5 Jan 1693, aft 1692; Ipswich

PERKINS, James (1647-) & 1/wf Mary _?_ ; [1675], b 1675

PERKINS, James (1647-1731?) & 2/wf Leah COX (1661-1749, ae 88); 13 Dec 1681; Hampton, NH
PERKINS, John[1] (1583±, 1590-1654) & Judith GATER (-1654+); 9 Oct 1608, Hillmorton, Warwick, Eng; Boston/Ipswich
PERKINS, John (?1609-1686) & Elizabeth _?_ (-1684); b 1636; Ipswich/Salisbury
PERKINS, John (1636-1699, 1659?) & Lydia _?_ ; ca 1656; Ipswich/Newbury/Salisbury
PERKINS, John & Keziah _?_ ; b 1662; Boston
PERKINS, John (-1668) & Deborah BROWNING (1647-1704), m/2 Isaac MEACHAM 1669; 28 Nov 1666; Topsfield
PERKINS, John (1652-1718) & 1/wf [Mary FISKE]; ca 1677?; Salisbury
PERKINS, John & [Mary] _?_ ; 16 May 1677, b 1679; New Haven
PERKINS, John (1655-1712) & Anna HUCHASON/HUTCHINSON (-1717); 29 Aug 1695; Lynn
PERKINS, John (-1717) & 2/wf Elizabeth PRYTHATCH/PRYTHOLD?; m int 18 Sep 1696, 13 Oct 1696; Wenham/Salisbury
PERKINS, John & 1/wf Mary (CHECKLEY) MACKFARLAND/McFARLAND (1613-), w Duncan; 11 Dec 1697; Boston
PERKINS, John & Mary [CHECKLEY?] (1673-); b 1699; Ipswich
PERKINS, Jonathan & Mary ELLCOCK/ALCOCK/ELCOCK/ELLIOT; 14 Jun 1682; New Haven
PERKINS, Jonathan (1650-1689) & Sarah _?_ , m/2 Josiah SANBORN 1690; Exeter?, 20 Dec 1682; Hampton, NH
PERKINS, Joseph (1661-1707) & Martha _?_ ; b 1689; Hampton, NH/DE
PERKINS, Joseph (1674-1726) & Martha MORGAN (1680-1754), m/2 Joseph LOTHROP 1727; 22 May 1700; Norwich, CT
PERKINS, Luke (ca 1641-1710) & Hannah (LONG) COOKERY/COOKEY? (-1715), w Henry; 9 Mar 1663; Charlestown/Hampton, NH
PERKINS, Luke (1649?-1694+) & 1/wf Elizabeth JAGO/JAQUITH?/JAQUES (-1690+); 26 Apr 1677; Ipswich
PERKINS, Luke (1667-) & Martha CONANT (1664-); 31 May 1688; Salem/Beverly/Plympton
PERKINS, Luke & 2/wf Sarah _?_ ; b 1693, ca 1692; Ipswich
PERKINS, Mark (-1739) & Mary _?_ ; ca 1685/88?; ?Stow
PERKINS, Matthew (1665-1755) & Esther [BURNHAM]; b 1687, ca 23 Mar 1685/6; Ipswich
PERKINS, Nathaniel & Hannah [TIBBITTS] (1651-); bef 1680, ca 1676; Dover
PERKINS, Nathaniel (1652-) & Judith _?_ ; b 1685; Ipswich
PERKINS, Samuel (1655-1700) & Hannah [WEST] (-1732); 1677; Ipswich
PERKINS, Stephen & Elizabeth FORD; 27 Aug 1700; New Haven
PERKINS, Thomas & _?_ ; in Eng, b 1628; Scarborough, ME/Cape Porpoise, ME
PERKINS/PERKS, Thomas (1623, 1616-1686) & Phebe [GOULD] (1620-); ca 1640; Topsfield
PERKINS, Thomas (?1622, ?1628-) & Frances _?_ , m/2 Miles GILES 1680; b 1660; Dover, NH
PERKINS, Thomas (-1722) & Sarah WALLIS; 6 Jun 1683; Topsfield
PERKINS, Thomas (1667-) & Sarah [RICHARDS]; b 1694; Enfield, CT
PERKINS, Thomas & Remember WOODMAN (1673-); 26 Jul 1694; Boston
PERKINS, Thomas & Mary [BANFIELD]; b 1701?; Arundel, ME
PERKINS, Timothy (1658-1728±) & Edna HAZEN (1667-1727+); 2 Aug 1686; Topsfield
PERKINS, Timothy (1661-1738) & 1/wf Hannah _?_ (-1690); ca 1688; Topsfield
PERKINS, Timothy (1661-1738) & 2/wf Abigail _?_ ; ca 1694?, ca 1692; Topsfield
PERKINS, Tolyah (1646-1723) & Sarah DENISON; 5 Nov 1680; Topsfield
PERKINS, William (1607-1682) & Elizabeth WOOTTON; in Eng?, 30 Aug 1636; Roxbury/Weymouth/Gloucester
PERKINS, William (?1639-1732?) & Elizabeth [AULT], dau John; b 28 Jan 1669; Dover, NH
PERKINS, William (1641-1695) & Elizabeth CLARK; 24 Oct 1669; Topsfield
PERKINS, William & _?_
PERKINS, William & ?Ann _?_ ; Southampton, LI
PERKINS, _?_ & Frances _?_ , m/2 Mark PERKINS
PERKINS, _?_ & [Mary REED]; b 1688?; Salem
PERLEY, Allan/Allen (1608-1675) & Susanna [BOKESON?/?BOKENSON/?BOLDERSON] (-1692); b 1636?; Ipswich
PERLY, Jacob & Lydia PABODY/PEABODY (1673-); 3 Dec 1696; Topsfield/Boxford
PERLEY, John (ca 1635/6-1729, Boxford) & Mary [HOWLETT] (?1642, 1644-1718); ca 1661; Boxford

PERLEY, John & Jane DRESSER; 13 Jul 1698; Rowley
PERLY, Samuel & Ruth TRUMBALL (1645-); 15 Jul 1664; Ipswich
PERLEY, Samuel & Abigail CUMINGS; 28 Mar 1694; Topsfield
PERLEY, Thomas (1641-1709) & 1/wf Lydia HOWLETT/HORSLEY/HOULEY (-1615); 8 Jul 1667, 1668?; Rowley
PERLEY, Thomas (1641-1709) & 2/wf Lydia (PEABODY) [HOWLETT] (-1715), w Thomas; b 8 Jan 1677, 1668?
PERLEY, Thomas (1668-) & 1/wf Sarah [OSGOOD] (1675-); b 1696; Boxford
PARLY, Thomas & Abigail (TOWNE) PABODY/PEABODY (1664-), w Jacob; 14 Jan 1695/6; Topsfield
PEARLY, Timothy (-1719, ae 64) & Deborah/Dorothy _?_ (-1735?); b 1682; Ipswich
PERRIMAN, _?_ & Elizabeth _?_ ; b 1640; Cambridge
PERREN, Abraham (1647-1694) & Sarah WALKER (1657-1694, 1693); 27 Dec 1677; Rehoboth
PERRIN, Hugh & Mary _?_ ; b 1679(80?); Boston
PERREN, John (1614-1674) & Ann/Anna/Hannah [HUBERT?] (-1689); b 1645; Braintree/Rehoboth
PERRIN, John (-1694) & Mary [POLLEY]/PEELOM/PELOM/PERRIN, dau John; b 1668; Rehoboth
PERRIN, John (1668-1694) & Sarah [BREMER] (1670-), Roxbury, dau Nathaniel; b 1693, b 1692, b 14 Sep 1692; Rehoboth
PERRIN, Peter & Ann [HOLMES]; ?Gravesend, LI
PERRIN, Samuel (1671-1743) & Mehitable [CHILD] (1669-); b 1695; Woodstock, CT
PERRIN, Thomas & Susan ROBERDS; 28 Feb 1666; Ipswich
PERRIN, Thomas & Elizabeth (EMERSON) [FULLER], w John; aft 25 Sep 1666, bef 31 Dec 1672; Ipswich
PERRIN, _?_ & Dorothy (PORTLAND) ROWLANDSON, w Thomas; b 1689
PERRY, Anthony & Elizabeth _?_ ; b 1648; Rehoboth
PERRY, Arthur & Elizabeth [?CROWELL], m/2 John GILLETT 1653, m/3 William WARDWELL; b 1635(?); Charlestown/Boston
PERRY, Arthur (?1651-1709) & Ann/Anna [JUDSON]; b 1677; Stratford, CT
PERRY, Benjamin (1670-) & Dinah [SWIFT] (ca 1672-); b 1695; Sandwich
PERRY, Charles & Ann SHEFFIELD; 1 Aug 1679; Boston
PERRY, David & Mary _?_ ; b 1696; Boston
PERRY, Edward[1] (1630-1695) & Mary ?FAIRMONT (1636-); ca 1653; Sandwich
PERRY, Edward & Elizabeth _?_ ; b 1686; Boston
PERRY, Ezra (-1689) & Elizabeth BURGE/BURGESS (?1629-1717); 12 Feb 1651, 1651/2; Sandwich
PERRY, Ezra, Jr. (-1729/30) & Rebecca [FREEMAN] (?1650-1738); b 1673; Sandwich
PERRY, Francis & Jane _?_ ; b 1637?; Salem/Barbados
PERRY, Henry & Susanna _?_ ; b 1685?; Marshfield
PERRY, Henry & Mary/?Mercy PRATT; 26 Nov 1700; Plymouth/Pembroke
PERRY, James & Mary [BAILEY] (1677-); 1700; Scituate?
PERRY, John (-1642) & Anna/Ann [NEWMAN]; 9 Jul 1628, b 1634?, Sabridgeworth, Eng; Roxbury
PERRY, John (-1674+) & Johanna [HOLLAND]; b 1644; Watertown/N. Brookfield
PERRY, John & Damaris _?_ ; b 1651?, b 26 Mar 1650; Newbury
PERRY, John (1639-1713) & Bethia MOSS/MORSE (1648-1717); 23 May 1665; Sudbury/Medfield
PERRY, John (1644?-) & Sarah CLARY; 13 Dec 1667; Watertown
PERRY, John (1657-1732?) & Elizabeth _?_ ; b 1684; Sandwich
PERRY, John & Sarah HIL/HILL (1670?-); 28 Jul 1691; Sherborn/Cambridge
PERRY, John, Watertown & Sarah PRICE, Watertown; 19 Jul 1693; Watertown
PERRY, John & [Priscilla GETCHELL]; b 1601; Portsmouth, RI
PERRY, John & [Rebecca CURTIS] (1674, 1675?-); b 21 May 1707, b 1707, b 1701?; Roxbury?
PERRY, Jonah & Susanna/Rebecca? SHAW; 9 Jun 1698; Boston
PERRY, Joseph (1674-) & Martha LOVET/LEVETT; 26 Apr 1698; Sherborn
PERRY, Matthew & Elizabeth BLAKE; 27 Mar 1665; Ipswich
PERRY, Michael & Joanna (?MASON) BRECK, w Robert; 12 Jul 1694; Boston
PERRY, Nathaniel (-1681(2?)) & ?Hester/[Esther LYON] (ca 1658-), m/2 John GRUMMAN b 1694; b 1678, b 1675?, b 12 Apr 1678, b 1676; Fairfield, CT
PERRY, Nathaniel (1660-) & Sarah CARPENTER (1664-); 17 May 1683; Rehoboth

PERRY, Obadiah (-1691) & Esther/Hester HASSELL (1648-); 21 Auq 1667; Watertown/Dunstable
PERRY, Obadiah & Mary _?_; b 1696; Boston
PERRY, Richard & 1/wf ?[Martha] [MALBON]; b 1640; New Haven
PERRY, Richard (-1658) & Grace (_?_) NICHOLS, w John; aft Jun 1653, aft 1655, b 4 Jun 1659, ca 1656; Fairfield, CT
PERRY, Richard & Joanna HAWLEY, m/2 Thomas MARSHALL?; Jun 1688
PERRY, Samuel (1640-1706) & Sarah STEDMAN; 26 Jan 1668; Roxbury
PERRY, Samuel & Mary MILLER/(MILLARD); 12 Dec 1678, 1676; Rehoboth
PERRY, Samuel & Esther TABOR of Dartmouth; 23 Oct 1689; Sandwich
PERRY, Samuel, Sandwich, Newport, etc. & Mary TUCKER, Dartmouth; 9 May 1690; ?Kingston, RI
PERRY, Samuel & Joanna LOVET/LOVETT; 26 Apr 1698; Sherborn
PERRY, Samuel & Mary MILLER/MILLARD; 12 Dec 1698, 1696; Rehoboth
PERRY, Seth & Mehitable [ELIOT] (1645-[1662/3?]); b 1662(3?); Boston
PERRY, Seth & Dorothy (Abigail wrong) CROWELL?/YELVERTON?, had son Yelverton (see YELVERTON, CROWELL, or CROW); b 1666; Boston
PERRY, Thomas (1591-1677) & Alice _?_; ca 1630?; Ipswich
PERRY, Thomas & Sarah [STEDMAN]; b 1643?, b 1650; Scituate
PERRY, Thomas & Susanna WHESTON/WHISTON (ca 1650-); 2 May 1671; Scituate
PERRY, Thomas & Ruth RIPLEY; 29 Jan 1699; Boston/Rehoboth/Hingham
PERRY, William (1606-) & Anna _?_ (1611-); b 1641; Watertown
PERRY, William (-1695) & Susan [BARSTOW]; Scituate/Marshfield
PERRY, William & Elizabeth LOBDELL; 31 May 1681; Scituate
PERRY, William & [Sarah] [STILES] (1677-1738/9); b 1701?; Windsor, CT/Stratford, CT
PERRY, _?_ & Elizabeth _?_, m/2 Edmund FREEMAN
PERRY, _?_ & _?_ GREGORY; b 1651
PESTER, William & Dorothy [?STRATTON]; b 1643; Salem
PETERS, Andrew (ca 1635-1713) & Mercy (BEAMSLEY) [WILBORNE] (1637-1726), w Michael; ca 1658; Ipswich/Andover
PETERS, Andrew (?1664-1689) & Elizabeth FARNUM/FARNHAM, m/2 James JOHNSON 1692; 8 Feb 1685, 1685/6?; Andover
PEETERS, Gilbert (-ca 1691) & Elizabeth HELLIARD/HILLIARD; 14 Sep 1669; Salem
PETER, Hugh (1599, 1598-) & 1/wf Elizabeth (COOKE?) [READ?] (-1637), w Edmund; in Eng, ca 1623?, ca 1628?; Salem
PETER, Hugh & 2/wf Deliverance [SHEFFIELD]; 1639, b Aug or Sep 1638; Salem
PEETERS, John (-1689) & Mary EDWARDS (1661-1733); 28 May 1680, 12 Apr 1680; Ipswich
PETERS, Richard & Bethia [ALLEN], w Joseph; b 1686, b 5 Dec 1684; Salem
PEETERS, Samuel & Phoebe FRIE/FRYE (1680-); 15 Dec 1696; Andover
PETERS, William (-1635/7) (ret'd to Eng) & Ann [WILLIAMS]; ca 1620/6?; Pemaquid, ME
PETERS, William (-1696) & Margaret [RUSS] (1673-), m/2 James WILSON 1704; b 1695; Andover
PETERSON, Benjamin (-1760) & Hannah WADSWORTH (-1733); 9 Feb 1698, 1698/9; Duxbury
PETERSON, Henry & Marah/Mary [PERIGO], w Robert; 15 Apr 1683, 25 Apr, 1685?; Lyme, CT
PETERSON, John (-1720) & Mary [SOULE]; b 1665; Duxbury
PETERSON/PETERS, John & _?_; b 1679(80?); Lyme, CT
PETERSON, Jonathan & Lydia [WADSWORTH] (-1756, ae 77-3-3); aft 23 Apr 1700, b 1701; Duxbury
PETTY, Edward (?1633-1697) & 1/wf Mary [YOUNGS]; b 1658; Southold, LI
PETTY, Edward (-1697) & 2/wf Mercy [YOUNGS] (1631-1727); aft 1658; Southold, LI
PETTY, Edward & Abigail TOPPING; 4 Oct 1688; Southampton, NY
PETTY, James & Mary LAWTON; 15 Jun 1683; Springfield/Brookfield
PETTY, James (-1705) & Experience _?_ (-1706+); by 1686; Southold, LI
PETTY, John & Ann CANNING, m/2 Samuel OWEN 1681; 30 May 1662; Boston/Springfield
PETTY, John (-1698) & Mary CHATFIELD (-1733); 12 Mar 1688/9; Southold, LI
PETTY, John & Mary/?Mercy TAYLOR (1671-1702?), m/2 Thomas RICH 1697, m/3 Joseph JENNINGS; 13 Apr 1693; Springfield/?Northampton
PETTEE, Joseph (1640-1692) & Sarah [?WHITMARSH]; b 1672; Weymouth
PETTY, Joseph (1672-) & 1/wf? Elizabeth [EDWARDS]; ca 1695?, 14 Feb 1701; Springfield
PETTY, Joseph (1667-) & Mary [SALMON] (1677-1753); ca 1695?; Southold, LI

PATRE/PATTEE/etc., Peter & Sarah GILL/GUILD/GUILE; 8 Nov 1682, 3 Nov 1682; Haverhill
PETTY, Robert & Sarah _?_ ; b 1670; Boston
PETTES?/[PITTEY], Samuel & Mary [SMITH] (1662-); b 1685; Weymouth
PATTE?/PATEY, Thomas (-1695) & Elizabeth (BILLINGTON) (BULLOCK) [BEERE]/BOONE, w
    Richard, w Robert; aft 1676; Providence
PITTEY, William (-1679) & Mary _?_ ; b 1638; Weymouth
PITTEY, William & Mary [PORTER] (1662-); b 1686; Weymouth
PETTY, _?_ & Sarah HERRICK, dau James; b 1687?; Southampton (Daniel DOANE m Rebecca
    PETTEE)
PETTIBONE, John (-1713) & Sarah EGGLESTON (1643-1713); 16 Feb 1664, 1664/5; Windsor,
    CT/Simsbury, CT
PETTIBONE, John (1665-1741) & Mary BISSELL (1666-); 18 Dec 1690; Simsbury, CT
PETTIBONE, Samuel (-1747) & Judith SHEPARD; 8 Nov 1699; Concord/Simsbury, CT
PATTEFOR/PETTIFORD, Samuel & Mary BAKER (1640-); 7 Feb 1666/7, 7 Feb 1666;
    Charlestown
PETENGALL, Daniel (1680-) & Mary STICKNEY; 13 Nov 1699; Newbury/Abington
PETTINGALE, Matthew & 1/wf Sarah NOYES (1658-); 13 Apr 1674; Newbury
PETTINGELL, Nathaniel (1654-) & 1/wf [?Mary] _?_ ; b 1694; Newbury
PETTENGAILE, Richard (1620/1-) & Joanna [INGERSOLL]; b 1645; Salem/Wenham/Newbury
PETTINGALE, Samuel (1645-) & Sarah POORE; 13 Feb 1673, 1673/4; Newbury
PETTIT, John (?1608-) & Mary _?_ (-1657); b 1638?; Roxbury/Stamford, CT
PETTIT, John (-1676) & Sarah SCOFIELD (-1684); 13 Jul 1665; Stamford, CT
PETTIT, John (1668-1715) & Mary BATES (-1702); 4 Oct 1693; Stamford, CT
PETTIT, John (-1726) & Margaret [OSBORN]; b 18 Sep 1695; Newtown, LI
PETTIT, Jonathan (1656-1720/1) & Elizabeth [FINCH] (1669-); b 1688; Stamford, CT
PETTIT, Nathaniel (1646-) & Mary _?_ ; ca 1667/72?, b 20 Jul 1695; Newtown, LI/Hopewell, NJ
PETTIT, Thomas (1610-living 1686) & 1/wf Christian ?MELLOWES; b 1636?, b 1647/8;
    Boston/Exeter, NH
PETTIT, Thomas (-1686+) & 2/wf Mary _?_ ; by 1654; Exeter, NH/Newtown, LI
PETTIT, [Thomas?] & 1/wf Sarah [MEACOCK], dau Peter; b 1659; Newtown, LI
PETTIT, Thomas & 2/wf Hannah [MOORE], w John; b 8 Jan 1685/6; Newtown, LI
PETTIT, Thomas & Mary [WAY], dau James; b 9 Mar 1690; Newtown, LI
PETTIT, Thomas & Cathrine BRANCH, m lic 26 Nov 1698
PEVERLY, John (1649-) & _?_ ; b 1688; Portsmouth, NH
PEVERLY, Thomas (-1670) & Jane WALFORD/WOOLFORD, m/2 Richard GOSS; ca 1644;
    Kittery, ME/Portsmouth, NH/Weymouth
PAITON/PEYTON/PAYTON, Bezaleel & Mary GREENOUGH, m/2 William PADDY 1651; 9 Oct
    1642; ?Boston/?Sandwich
PHARUS/?PHARISS/?PHAREZ, ?Zachariah & Jane _?_ (-1686, ae 82); b 1686; Charlestown
PHELPS, Abraham (-1728) & Mary PINNEY (1644-1725); 6 Jul 1665, not 1663; Windsor, CT
PHELPS, Christopher & 1/wf Elizabeth SHARP/Jane _?_ (-bef 1685); 9 Jul 1658, 9 May 1658;
    Salem
PHELPS, Edward (-1689) & Elizabeth [ADAMS] (1627-1718, ae 91); b 1651, b 1646, [b1657];
    Newbury/Andover
PHELPS, Edward & Ruth ANDREWS (1664-); 9 Mar 1682/3, 1683, 1682, 19 Mar 1682;
    Andover/Lancaster?
PHELPS, Ephraim (1663-1697) & Mary JAGGERS/JOGGERS/JAGGES, m/2 John COPP 1698; 24
    May 1691; Windsor, CT/Stamford, CT
PHELPS, George (?1610-1678) & 1/wf Philury [RANDALL] (-29 Apr 1648); ca 1637; Windsor,
    CT
PHELPS, George (1610-1678) & 2/wf Frances (_?_) (CLARK) DEWEY (1613-), w _?_, w
    Thomas; 2 Nov 1648, Nov 1648, 30 Nov, 16 Nov, 2 Nov; Windsor, CT
PHELPS, [Henry?] & Eleanor BATTER?/[MEALTON?], m/2 Thomas TRESLER; b 1632; Salem
    (prob BATTER)
PHELPS, Henry (see Nicholas) & [Hannah BASSETT]/[BASKET?]; b 1652; Salem?
PHELPS, Isaac (1638-1725) & 1/wf Ann/Anna? GAYLORD (1645-1690, 1689?); 11 Mar 1662/3,
    11 May 1663; Windsor, CT/Westfield
PHELPS, Isaac (1666-1698) & 2/wf Mary MOSLEY, Windsor, CT, w John, m/2 Eleazer WALLER;
    17 Dec 1690; Westfield

PHELPS, Jacob (1650-1689) & Dorothy INGERSOLL, m/2 _?_ ROOT; 2 May 1672; Westfield
PHELPS, John (-1685) (kinsman of Edmund BATTER) & Abigail [UPTON?/?AUTASOM]; b 1669; Salem/Reading
PHELPS, John (1652-ca 1741/2) & Sarah [BUCKLAND] (1649-); b 1675(6?), 1673; Windsor, CT
PHELPS, John & Rebecca THORFTS/THOITS; 2 Dec 1686; Boston
PHELPS, John & Jane LOVERIN, w John LOVERING; m int 17 Oct 1695; Boston
PHELPS, Joseph (1629±-1684) & 1/wf Hannah NEWTON (-1675, 1671?); 20 Sep 1660, 2 Sep, 20 Sep; Windsor, CT/Simsbury, CT
PHELPS, Joseph (1647-) & 1/wf Mary PORTER (1653-1682); 26 Jun 1673; Windsor, CT
PHELPS, Joseph (-1684) & 2/wf Mary (_?_) SALMON (-1682?), w Thomas; 19 Dec 1676, 9 Jan 1676; Northampton
PHELPS, Joseph (1666-1716) & Sarah HORSFORD/HOSFORD (1666-); 18 Nov 1686; Windsor, CT
PHELPS, Joseph (1647-1695?) & 2/wf Hester/Esther [HOSFORD] (1669-), m/2 Samuel KENT 1700, Suffield, CT; ca 1688; Windsor, CT
PHELPS, Joseph (1667-1750) & 1/wf Mary COLLIER (1669-1697/8); b 1689; Hartford?/Simsbury, CT
PHELPS, Joseph (1667-) & 2/wf Sarah CASE (1676-1704); 9 Nov 1699, 9 Nov; Simsbury, CT
PHELPS, Josiah/Josias? (1667-) & Sarah WINCHELL (1674-1733); 26 Apr 1690; Windsor, CT
PHELPS, Nathaniel (1627-1702, 1690?) & Elizabeth COPLEY (?1622-1702, 1712?), wid; 17 Sep 1650; Windsor, CT
PHELPS, Nathaniel (1653-1719) & Grace MARTIN (1656-1727); 27 Aug 1676, 11? Aug; Northampton
PHELPS, Nathaniel (-1723) & Eunice _?_ (-1738); b 1678, ca 1773?; Westfield
PHELPS, Nathaniel & Hannah BISSELL (1682-1717); 28 Mar 1700, 20 Mar 1700; Windsor, CT
PHELPS, Nicholas (see Henry), Quaker & [Hannah BASSETT?/BASKET?/BASKEL?]; b 1658?, b 28 Sep 1652; Salem
PHELPS, Samuel (1625-1669) & Sarah GRISWOLD (1631-1715), m/2 Nathaniel PENNEY 1670; 10 Nov 1650, 10 Jan 1650; Windsor, CT/Simsbury, CT
PHELPS, Samuel (1652-1741) & 1/wf Abiall WILLIAMS (1655-); 21 Jun 1678; Windsor, CT
PHELPS, Samuel & Elizabeth _?_; b 1681; Boston
PHELPS, Samuel (1657-1745/6) & Sarah CHANDLER (1661-1757); 29 May 1682; Andover
PHELPS, Samuel (-1741) & 2/wf? 3/wf? Sarah (ENO) [HOLCOMB], w Benajah; b 1701; Windsor, CT
PHELPS/PHILLIPS, ?Thomas (-1667) & _?_ ; Yarmouth
PHELPS, Timothy (1639-1719) & Mary GRISWOLD (1644-); 19 Mar 1661; Windsor, CT
PHELPS, Timothy & Martha CROW; 4 Nov 1686; Windsor, CT/Hebron, CT
PHELPS, Timothy (1656-1712) & 1/wf Sarah GAYLORD (1665-1689); 18 Nov 1686, 1680; Windsor, CT
PHELPS, Timothy (1656-1712) & 2/wf Sarah PRATT (-1758, in 96th y), Hartford; 13 Nov 1690; Windsor, CT/Hartford?/Simsbury?
PHELPS, William (?1599-1672) & 1/wf Elizabeth _?_ (-1635); b 1620, b 1619; Dorchester/Windsor, CT
PHELPS, William (?1599-1672) & 2/wf Mary [DOVER]?/?DYER (-1675); 1638±; Windsor, CT
PHELPS, William (1620-1681/2) & 1/wf Isabel WILSON (-1674); 4 Jun 1645, 1646, 16 Jun 1645, 4 Jun 1646, no issue; Windsor, CT
PHELPS, William (1620-1681/2) & 2/wf Sarah PINNEY (1648-1711); 20 Dec 1676, no issue; Windsor, CT
PHELPS, William (1657-) & Abigail STEBBINS (1660-1748); 30 May 1678; Northampton
PHELPS, William & 1/wf _?_ ; b 1690; Boston
PHELPS, William & 2/wf Jane BUTTERFIELD, w Henry; m cont ca 1 Apr 1691; Boston
PHELPS, William (1660-1711) & Hannah HAYDEN (1668-); 4 Jan 1693; Windsor, CT
PHELPS, William (1668-) & Abigail MUDGE (-1705); 7 Dec 1699; Northampton/Windsor
PHETTEPLACE, Philip (1687+) & _?_ ; b 1684; Portsmouth, RI
PHILBRICK, Elias (1680-) (ae 68 in 1749) & 1/wf Rhoda PERKINS (1677-); 24 May 1700, ?21 May; Hampton, NH
PHILBRICK, Ephraim (1656-) & Elizabeth [BARRON] (1660-); b 1687; Hampton, NH
PHILBRICK, James (-1674) (m/1 Jane ROBERTS? ca 1644) & Ann [ROBERTS], m/2 William MARSTON 1675, 1678; b 1651; Hampton, NH

PHILBRICK, James (1651-1723) & Hannah PERKINS (1656-1734, 1739?); 1 Dec 1674; Hampton, NH

PHILBRICK, John (1616-1657, drowned) & Ann?/Anna? [PALMER?/KNAPP?] (-1657, drowned); b 1648?, b 1650; Hampton, NH

PHILBRICK, John (1650-1737) & 1/wf Prudence SWAIN (1648-1717±); 28 Feb 1667/8, 26? Feb; Hampton, NH

PHILBRICK, John (1650-) & 2/wf Sabina (LOCKE) LEWIS; b 1701?, 7 Mar 1716/17; Hampton, NH

PHILBRICK, Jonathan (1657-1747) & _?_ SHAW, wid? or dau Benj.?; no issue; Hampton, NH

PHILBRICK, Joseph (1663-1755) & Triphena [MARSTON] (1663-); 1685, 1686; Hampton, NH

PHILBRICK, Samuel (1660-1694) & Jane _?_ ; b 1684?, b 1688; Hampton, NH

PHILBRICK, Thomas (-1667) & Elizabeth [?KNAPP] (-1664); in Eng, b 1624, b 1623?, b 1622?; Hampton, NH

PHILBRICK, Thomas (1624-1700) (see John) & 1/wf Anne?/Ann? [KNAPP?] (prob wrong); b 1647?, b 1651; Hampton, NH

PHILBRICK, Thomas (1624-1700) & 2/wf Hannah (FRENCH) WHITE, w John; 22 Sep 1669; Hampton, NH

PHILBRICK, Thomas (1659-1712) & Mehitable AYRES (1658?-1723), m/2 Timothy HILLIARD 1712; 14 Apr 1681; Hampton, NH

PHILBRICK, William (1670-) & Mary NEAL; 10 Oct 1689; Hampton, NH

PHILLIPS, Andrew & Elizabeth _?_ ; b 1657, b 1659; Charlestown

PHILLIPS, Andrew (1661?-1717) & Sarah SMITH (1669-), m/2 Nathaniel LAWRENCE; 11 Nov 1683; Malden/Charlestown

PHILLIPS, Benjamin (-1688, 1687/8) & Anne/Anna? _?_ (-1716), m/2 Benjamin LAWRENCE 1696; b 1680; Charlestown

PHILLIPS, Benjamin & Sarah THOMAS; 12 Jan 1681; Marshfield

PHILLIPS, Benjamin & _?_ [COVEL]; ca 1696; Chatham

PHILLIPS, Caleb & Elizabeth [POLLEY]; 16 Oct 1681; Roxbury

PHILLIPS, Caleb & _?_ [PACKARD]; b 29 Oct 1684

PHILLIPS, Charles & _?_ ; b 1656; Lynn

PHILLIPS, David & Bethia [KELSEY]; b 1664; Cambridge/Milford, CT

PHILLIPS, Edward & Susanna _?_ ; b 1692; Boston

PHILLIPS, Eleazer (1654-1709) & 1/wf Ann/Anna? [FOSTER] (1658-1695); b 1680; Charlestown

PHILLIPS, Eleazer (1654-1709) & 2/wf Sarah CUTLER (1655-1705); 10 Feb 1695/6; Charlestown

PHILLIPS, Ephraim & Mary _?_ (his pretended wife); 1680; Taunton/Plymouth

PHILLIPS, George (1593-1644) & 1/wf [?Elizabeth] [SERGENT] (-1630), ?w Robert WELDEN; ?Boxted, Co. Suffolk, in Eng, b 1625, b 1622; Watertown

PHILLIPS, George (-1678, Windsor) & Sarah _?_ (-1662); ca 1631?; Dorchester/Windsor, CT (no issue)

PHILLIPS, George (-1644) & 2/wf Elizabeth STEWART [WELDEN?] (-1681), w Robert; b 1632; Watertown

PHILLIPS, George (-1691) & _?_ ; Middletown, CT/Hartford

PHILLIPS, George (1664-1739) & Sarah [HALLETT] (1673-); b 1698, ca 1697; Watertown

PHILLIPS, George & Hope [STOW]; b 1701?; Middletown, CT

PHILLIPS, Henry (-1686) & 1/wf Mary BROCK (-1 Aug 1640); 5 Mar 1638/9; Dedham

PHILLIPS, Henry (-1686) & 2/wf Ann HUNTING; 1 May 1641; Dedham/Charlestown

PHILLIPS, Henry (-1686) & 3/wf Mary DWIGHT (1635-1693+); m cont 24 Jun 1653; Boston

PHILLIPS, Israel & Elizabeth [LEWIS], m/2 _?_ EBURNE/(ABORN)

PHILLIPS, Jacob (-1690) & Sarah [REA], m/2 James PRINCE bef 1693; b 1690?; Salem

PHILLIPS, James (nephew Wm. PARKER) & [Mary] _?_, m/2 Richard GODFREY 1684; b 1661(2?); Taunton

PHILLIPS, James & Abigail HATHAWAY (-1690?); 9 Dec 1685; Taunton

PHILLIPS, James & 2/wf Elizabeth FRENCH; 7 May 1690, 1691; Taunton

PHILLIPS, James (-1742) & Sarah STEVENS (1674(+)-); 12 Feb 1693/4; Salem

PHILLIPS, James (-1742) & 1/wf Mary [MOWRY]; Providence/Smithfield

PHILLIPS, John & Elizabeth AMES (-1659); in Eng, 6 Jan 1611/12; Salem

PHILLIPS, John (1605-1682) & 1/wf Joanna _?_ (-1675, ae 80?); b 1633; Dorchester/Boston

PHILLIPS, John (1602-1691/2) & 1/wf Mary? _?_ ; in Eng, b 1634; Duxbury

PHILLIPS, John & Mary _?_ ; b 1652; Boston

PHILLIPS, John (1602-1691/2) & 2/wf Grace HOLLAWAY (-1666), w William; 6 Jul 1654; Marshfield
PHILLIPS, John (-1726) & 1/wf Katherine/Catharine ANDERSON (-1699); 19 Jul 1655; Charlestown
PHILLIPS, John & Sarah _?_ ; b 1662; Boston
PHILLIPS, John (1602-1691/2) & 3/wf Faith (CLARK) DOTY (-1675), w Edward; 14 Mar 1666/7, 14 Mar 1666; Plymouth
PHILLIPS, John (-1726, ae 90) & Joanna _?_ ; b 1668; Boston/Charlestown
PHILLIPS, John & _?_ ; b 1672(3?); Bradford
PHILLIPS, John (1605-1682) & 2/wf Sarah MINOR, wid; Jan 1675/6; Boston
PHILLIPS, John (1602-1691/2) & 4/wf Ann (HATCH) TORREY, w James; 3 Apr 1677; Marshfield
PHILLIPS, John & Elizabeth [TOTMAN]; b 1696?; N. Kingston, RI
PHILLIPS, John & Ruth [BURDICK]; ca 1682; RI
PHILLIPS, John & Rebecca _?_ ; b 1688, b 1687; Newport
PHILLIPS, John (-1694) & Hannah _?_ ; b 1689; Lynn
PHILLIPS, John & Elizabeth [DRAKE?] (?1670-1748); b 1692(3?); Weymouth
PHILLIPS, John (-1756) & 1/wf Mary HAYMAN (-1702); 15 Aug 1694; Charlestown
PHILLIPS, John (1670-) & Mary GROSS; 25 Jun 1697; Charlestown
PHILLIPS, John & Sarah (STEDMAN) (BRACKETT) (ALCOCK) GRAVES (1644-1730), w John, w Samuel, w Thomas; aft 2 Mar 1698/9; Charlestown
PHILLIPS, Jonathan (1633-1704) & Sarah HOLLAND (1662-), m/2 John BEMIS 1717; 26 Jan 1680, 1680/1; Watertown
PHILLIPS, Joseph & Bridget [BOSWORTH?] (1660-); b 1684; Boston
PHILLIPS, Joseph & Mary COLLIER; b 1681
PHILLIPS, Joseph & Patience [HIGBY]; Huntington, LI
PHILLIPS, Joseph & Elizabeth [MALAVERY]; b 1701?; Providence
PHILLIPS, Joseph/Joshua (-1689) & Amy [DRAKE?]; b 1687; Weymouth
PHILLIPS, Michael & Barbara _?_ , m/2 Edward INMAN by 1689, 1686; b 1667, b 1670; Newport, RI
PHILLIPS, Moses & Mehitable WHITE; 5 Jul 1692; Marblehead
PHILLIPS, Nicholas (-1672) & Elizabeth [JENSON]/JEWSON; 26 Jun 1631, ca 1636, b 1641?; Wendover, Eng/Weymouth
PHILLIPS, Nicholas (-1670) & Hannah SALTER, m/2 John RUGGLES 1670?; 4 Dec 1651, 4 Jan 1652; Boston
PHILLIPS, Nicholas & Philippa _?_ ; b 1665; Boston
PHILLIPS, Nicholas (1664-1751) & Mary [RANDALL] (1668-1749); b 1690
PHILLIPS, Philip & Rachel _?_ ; b 1651, b 1656; Boston/LI
PHILLIPS, Richard (-1695) & 1/wf Mary [PACKARD] (-29 Oct 1684+); b 1657, 1659, b 1660; Weymouth
PHILLIPS, Richard (-1695) & 2/wf Elizabeth BYRAM? [KINGMAN] (1643-), w John; betw 1690 & 1695; Bridgewater
PHILLIPS, Richard (1667-1747) & Sarah [MOWRY]; Providence/Smithfield, RI
PHILLIPS, Samuel (1625-1696) & Sarah APPLETON (1627/9-1714, ae 86); Oct 1651, 15 Oct; Ipswich
PHILLIPS, Samuel & Mary (HOSKINS) COBB, w Edward; 15 May 1676; Taunton
PHILLIPS, Samuel (-1720, ae 58) & Hannah [GILLAM] (1662-1755); b 1681(2?); Boston/Charlestown
PHILLIPS, Samuel & Sarah [MASON] (1657-); b 1681(2?), b 1688, ca 1680; Boston/Charlestown
PHILLIPS, Samuel & Mary EMERSON (1665-1703); 26 May 1687, 22 May 1687/8, 26 Mar 1687; Watertown
PHILLIPS, Samuel & Elizabeth (WATSON) [WILLIAMS]; aft 17 Aug 1642, bef 1676; Taunton
PHILLIPS, Seth (1671?-) & Abigail _?_ (1680-1744); 1699; Little Compton, RI
PHILLIPS, Theophilus & Bethia KEEDELL/KETTLE?/KENDALL?/BEDELL?; 3 Nov 1666; Watertown
PHILLIPS, Theophilus (1636-) & 2/wf Mary BENNET/BENNETT (-1733); 21 Nov 1667, ?11 Nov 1677?; Watertown
PHILLIPS, Theophilus & 1/wf Ann/Anna [HUNT] (-1683); b 1670, b 1673; Newtown, LI
PHILLIPS, Theophilus & 2/wf Patience _?_ ; 15 Mar 1682/3

PHILLIPS, Theophilus (-1689) & 3/wf Elizabeth TOWNSENDS, m/2 Thomas POWELL, 1685, 18 Feb 1684; Oyster Bay, LI/Newtown

PHILLIPS, Theophilus & Frances _?_ ; b 1694; Newtown, LI

PHILLIPS, Thomas & _?_ ; b 1653?; Pemaquid

PHILLIPS, Thomas (-1673) & Agnes/[Annes] _?_ ; b 1673; Yarmouth

PHILLIPS, Thomas & Mary _?_ ; b 1678; Plymouth

PHILLIPS, Thomas & Hannah (LEAGER) [WALKER] (1655-), w John; b Feb 1682/3; Boston

PHILLIPS, Thomas (-1688?), Philadelphia & Mercy/Mary? JEFFERSON, Newport; 26 Feb 1684/5, 1685; Newport?/RI

PHILLIPS, Thomas & 2/wf Mary HOWARD; 1 Mar 1692, 1692/3; Boston

PHILLIPS, ?Thomas & [?Elizabeth DREW]; b 1701?; ?Ipswich

PHILLIPS, Timothy (-1711, 1712) & 1/wf _?_ ; b 1681; Boston/Charlestown

PHILLIPS, Timothy (-1711, 1712) & 2/wf Mary (FOSTER) SMITH (-1755), w James; 18 Apr 1681; Charlestown

PHILLIPS, Walter (-1704?) & Margaret _?_ (-1708?); b 1691?, b 1670?; Damariscotta, ME/Lynn?

PHILLIPS, William (-1654) & Elizabeth [PARKER?]/[WALKER?]; in Eng, b 1619; Duxbury

PHILLIPS, William (1607-1683) & 1/wf Mary _?_ (-1646); b 1631; Charlestown/Saco, ME

PHILLIPS, William (-1655) & Ann [ROGERS?]; ca 1639?; Hartford

PHILLIPS, William (?1607-1683) & 2/wf Susanna [STANLEY] (-1655), w Christopher; 1647 (b 10 Sep 1650); Charlestown

PHILLIPS, William & 1/wf Martha FRANKLIN; 24 Oct 1650; Boston

PHILLIPS, William (?1607-1683) & 3/wf Bridget (HUTCHINSON) SANFORD (1618-1698), w John; bef 10 Mar 1657, Dec 1655, ca 1655; Boston/Charlestown

PHILLIPS, William & Jane/Joan _?_ ; b 1671; Boston

PHILLIPS, William & _?_

PHILLIPS, William (1660-1705) & Deborah LONG (1670-), m/2 William SKINNER; 13 Nov 1689; Charlestown/Boston

PHILLIPS, William (1667?-) & Jane BUTTERFIELD, ?w Henry; 2 Apr 1691; Boston

PHILLIPS, William & Elizabeth/(Betty) _?_ ; b 1696(7?); Weymouth

PHILLIPS, William (-1705, ae 35?) & Hannah [GILBERT] (1677-1705); b 1699, b 1697?; Taunton

PHILLIPS, William & Christiana BARKER; b 1701?; Newport, RI

PHILLIPS, Zechary/Zachariah? (-1675) & Elizabeth [WILLIS]?/[SKIPPER] (ca 1626-); b 1652, b 1647, b 1650; Boston

PHILLIPS, Zerubabel (1632-1682+, 1686?) & Ann (COOPER) WHITE, w John; b 1663?; Southampton, LI

PHILLIPS, Zerubbabel (-1687) & Martha [HERRICK]; 1687; Southampton

PHILPOTT, James & Rachel [HASKINS], m/2 James CHADDOCK 1709; b 1701?, 1699?; Great Island

PHILPOT, Theophilus & Rebecca CHONOR; 22 Sep 1697; Boston

PHILPOT, William & Ann (_?_) HUNN, w George; 16 Dec 1651; Boston

PHINNEY, Ebenezer (1674-1754?) & Susannah LINNELL; 14 Nov 1695; Barnstable

FINNEY, Jeremiah (1662-1748) & Esther LEWIS (?1664-1743); 7 Jan 1684; Bristol, RI

FINNEY, John (-1687?, 1687/8) & 1/wf Christian _?_ (-9 Sep 1649); in Eng, b 1638; Plymouth

FINNEY, John (-1687?) & 2/wf Abigail (BISHOP) COGGIN (-1653), w Henry; 10 Jun 1650; Barnstable

FINNEY, John (-1687/8) & 3/wf Elizabeth BAYLEY (-1683/4); 26 Jun 1654; Barnstable/Bristol, RI/Swansea

FINNEY, John, Jr. (1638-1719) & Mary ROGERS (1644-1718+); 10 Aug 1664, 16 Aug 1664; Barnstable

PHINNEY, John (1665-1746) & Sarah LUMBERT (?1666, 1672/3-1753); 30 May 1689; Barnstable

FINNEY, Jonathan (1655-1728) & Joanna KINNICUTT (-1739); int? 18 Oct 1682; Bristol, RI/Swansea

FINNEY, Joseph (1668-1726) & Mercy/Mary? BRYANT; 15 Jan 1693, 14 Jun 1693; Plymouth

FINNEY, Joshua (1665-1714) & Mercy WATTS (-1724); 31 May 1688, ?int; Bristol, RI/Swansea

FINNEY, Josiah (1661-) & 1/wf Elizabeth WARREN (1662-); 19 Jan 1687, 1686/7, 1688; Plymouth

PHINNEY/FINNAH, Philip & Hannah _?_ ; b 1689; Boston

FINNEY, Robert (1608-1688?) & Phebe RIPLEY (1620?-9 Dec 1710 in 92nd y); 1 Sep 1641, no issue; Plymouth

PHINY, Samuel (1676-) & Bethia __?__ ; b 1701?; Barnstable?
PHINNEY, Thomas (1672-) & Sarah (LOCKWOOD) BEETLE?/BEDELL?/BEEDLE, w Christopher; 25 Aug 1698; Barnstable
FINNEY __?__ & __?__ (-22 Apr 1650, Plymouth, ae over 80)
PHIPENY, Benjamin² (-1678) & 1/wf Wilmot [EWER/YEO]; b 1651; Boston
PHIPPEN, Benjamin² (-1678) & 2/wf Eleanor __?__, m/2 Nathaniel JEWELL by 1685; b 1671; Boston/Stratford, CT
PHIPPEN, Daniel & Sarah __?__ ; b 1668; Boston
PHIPENY, Daniel (1671-) & Elizabeth [?ENGLISH] (1671-); b 1696; Boston
PHIPPEN, David¹ (-1650) & Sarah __?__ (-1659), m/2 George HULL 1650?; in Eng, b 1620; Hingham/Boston
PHIPPEN, David² (1647-1703) & Ann/Anna (CROMWELL) EGER/AGER/AUGER, w Benjamin; 26 Jun 1672; Salem
PHIPENY, Gamaliel² (?1625-1672) & Sarah [PURCHASE]? (ca 1627/8-?17 Jan 1683, ae 55); b 1649; Boston
PHIPPEN, George² (-1704) & Elizabeth __?__ (1643-1714); b 1659; Boston/Hull
PHIPPENY, James (?1663-1717) & Joanna __?__, m/2 Lemuel SHERWOOD; b 1696, b 1693; Hull/Stratford, CT
PHIPPENY, James³ (-1735) (son George) & Joanna CHAMBERLAIN? (-1735), dau Henry; b 1701?, b 1695?, m June 1691?; Hull
PHIPPEN, Joseph² (-1687) & 1/wf Dorothy [WOOD?]; b 1641?; Hingham/Boston/Salem/Falmouth, ME
PHIPPEN, Joseph² (-1687) & 2/wf Dorcas [WOOD?] (-1689+); aft 1653, b 1667; Boston
PHIPPEN, Joseph³ (1642-1710) & 1/wf Mary [STANDFORD]/[STANFORD]; ca 1663?; ?Boston/Falmouth, ME
PHIPPEN, Joseph³ (1642-1710) & 2/wf Seaborne GOODEN/GOODING?/GOODWIN?; 22 Dec 1670; Salem
PHIPPEN, Joseph⁴ ([1665+]-1733) & Elizabeth (PHIPPEN) SPENCER (1659-), dau Gamaliel, w Abraham; b 1686, b 12 Jun 1684; Salem
PHIPPEN, Joseph³ (1642-1710) & 3/wf Damaris (BARTLETT) SEARL (1647-) (ae 59 in 1706), w Thomas; 14 Apr 1686; Salem
PHIPPEN, Samuel² (1649-1718, ae 68) & Rachel GUPPY (-1711); 1 Feb 1676/7; Salem
PHIPS, Benjamin & Hannah DEAN; m bond 10 Oct 1693; ?New York
PHIPS, James & Mary __?__, m/2 John WHITE by 1661, m/3 __?__ HOWARD; ?Kennebec Bay, ME
PHIPS, John (-1688/93) & Rebecca __?__ (-1688+); ca 1670?; ME
PHIPS, John & [Elizabeth GENT]
PHIPPS, John (1669-) & Mary __?__ (1672-1754, ae 82); b 1686; Wrentham/Woburn/Duxbury
PHIPPS, Joseph & Mary KETTELL (1666-1729); 12 May 1689; Charlestown
PHIPPS, Samuel (-1725) & 1/wf Mary PHILLIPS (1660-); 8 Aug 1676; Charlestown
PHIPPS, Samuel (-1725) & 2/wf Katherine BRACKENBURY; 16 Feb 1680/1; Charlestown
PHIPPS, Samuel & Elizabeth STEVENS, m/2 Benjamin WELLINGTON 1712; 26 Dec 1700; Charlestown
PHIPPS, Solomon (1619-1671) & Elizabeth __?__ (-1688); b 1642; Charlestown
PHIPPS, Solomon, Jr. (1645-1693) & 1/wf Rebecca PICKARD (1645-1668); 13 Nov 1667; Charlestown
PHIPPS, Solomon (1645-1693) & 2/wf Mary [DANFORTH] (1650-), m/2 Thomas BROWN 1704; Jul 1669, b 1669; Charlestown
PHIPPS, Solomon (1675-) & Sarah (WILLIAMS) (SHARPE) [NOWELL] (1667-1707), w Thomas; b 7 Mar 1694/5; Charlestown
PHIPPS, Thomas (1676-1737) & 1/wf Eleanor (HARVEY) CUTTS/CUBBS, w Samuel, m/3 John PRAY; 4 May 1699; Charlestown
PHIPP, William (1650/1-1695), Boston & Mary (SPENCER)? HULL, w John, m/2 Peter SARGENT 1701; aft 1693; Sherborn
PHOENIX, Alexander & 1/wf __?__ ; b 1651; N. Kings Town, RI
PHOENIX, Alexander (-1679+, bef 1687) & 2/wf Abigail [SEWELL] (1650-1718+); b 16--; nr Warwick, RI/Wickford, RI
PHENIX, John (1646?, 1643?-1721+) & Deborah [LOCKWOOD] (ca 1648-1740, ae 92); b 1684?, b 1671; Kittery, ME
PICKARD, John (-1683) & Jane CROSBY (1627-1716); 29 Oct 1644; Rowley

PICKARD, John (-1697) & 1/wf Sarah SMITH (-1689); 11 Feb 1679, 1679/80; Rowley
PICKARD, John (-1697) & 2/wf Joanna (TUTTLE) BISHOP, w Job, m/3 Edmund POTTER, m/4 John WHIPPLE; 5 Mar 1690/1; Rowley
PICKARD, Samuel (1663-) & 1/wf Elizabeth BRODSTREET/BRADSTREET (-1686); 22 Jun 1685, 2 Jun; Rowley
PICKARD, Samuel (1663-) & 2/wf Elizabeth HALE (1668-1730); 31 May 1687; Rowley
PICKARD, _?_ & Ann _?_ (-1662), m/2 _?_ LUME; in Eng, b 1624; Rowley
PICKERAM?/PICKRAM?PICKERING?/PICKARAM, John (1570-1630) & Esther _?_ ; in Eng, b 1610?; Watertown
PICKERING, Benjamin (1665-1718) & Jane HOBBY (-1751); 27 Apr 1695; Salem
PICKERING, John (?1600-1659) & Elizabeth _?_ (-1662), m/2 John DEACON; b 1636?; Salem
PICKERING, John (-1669) & Mary _?_ ; b 1638; Cambridge/Portsmouth, NH
PICKERING, John (1637-1694) & Alice (FLINT) [BULLOCK], w Henry; aft 22 Aug 1657; Salem
PICKERING, John (1640-1721) & Mary STANYAN, Hampton; 10 Jan 1665, 1665/6; Portsmouth, NH
PICKERING, John & Sarah BURRELL/BURRILL (1661-); 14 Jun 1683; Salem
PICKERING, John (1666-1715) & Elizabeth MUNDEN; 17 Jul 1688; Dover
PICKERING, Jonathan (1639-) & Jane CROMWELL; 14 Mar 1665, 19? Mar; Salem
PICKERING, Thomas (-1719/20) & Mary [GEE]?; by 1680, by 1686; Dover
PICKERING, Thomas & Hannah PINKNEY; b 9 Jan 1688/9; Eastchester, NY
PICKERIN, William & Elizabeth _?_ ; b 1669; Boston
PICKRING, William & Hannah BROWNE; 19 Jun 1695; Salem
PICKETT, Adam (1658-1691) & Hannah WETHERALL (1660-1689); 26 May 1680; New London, CT
PICKET, Christopher (ae ca 60 in 1675) & Elizabeth STONE/STOW?/STOWE; - Jun 1647; Roxbury/Scarboro, ME
PICKET, Christopher & Elizabeth _?_ ; b 1657; Boston
PICKET, Daniel (-1688) & Mary UFFORD/UFFORT (1661, 1662-); 13 Sep 1683; Stratford, CT
PICKET, Henry & Mary HORTON; 3 Oct 1700; Boston
PICKETT, James & Elizabeth KEELER, ?m/2 Samuel HAYES; 17 Jul 1673; Stratford, CT
PICKETT, John (-1684) & Margaret _?_ (1622-1683); ca 1639?; Salem/Stratford, CT
PICKET, John (-1667) & Ruth BREWSTER (1631-1677), m/2 Charles HILL 1668; 14 Mar 1651; New London
PICKETT, John & Mary CROSSE/CROSS (-1687); 19 Jan 1672/3; Stratford, CT
PICKETT, Nicholas & ?Dorothy/Demoris? [?NORTHEY]; ?Jul 1670; ?Marblehead
PICKETT, Thomas & 1/wf Abigail SEYMOUR (1656-); 16 Nov 1676; Norwalk, CT/Stratford, CT
PICKETT, Thomas & 2/wf Sarah [BARNUM], ?m/2 Samuel HAYES; b 1686?, b 1695; Danbury, CT
PICKLES, Jonas (-1664, 1665) & Alice HATCH/HATTEE, m/2 Thomas ROVER 1665, 1666; 23 Dec 1657, 23 Sep 1657; Scituate
PICKLES, Jonas & Lydia (UTLEY) HEWITT, w Thomas; 15 Sep 1690; Stonington, CT
PICKLES, Nathan/Nathaniel (1662-) & Miriam TURNER (1658-); 3 Aug 1687; Scituate
PICKMAN, Benjamin (1645-1748) & Elizabeth HARDY (1650-1727); 27 Jul 1667; Salem
PICKMAN, Benjamin & 1/wf Elizabeth/Mary? [HACKETT]; ca 1696?, b 1699; Salem
PICKMAN, Benjamin & Elizabeth WARDWELL/WOODWELL?; 14 Nov 1700; Marblehead
PICKMAN, John (-1684, 1683?) & Hannah WEEKES (-1670); 27 Aug 1667; Salem
PICKMAN, Nathaniel (1616-1684) & 1/wf _?_ ; b 1636 (doubtful); Salem
PICKMAN, Nathaniel (1616-1684) & 2/wf Tabitha [DIKE] (-1668), w Anthony; aft 25 Jul 1639 (perhaps 1/wf); Salem
PICKMAN, Nathaniel & Parina _?_ ; b 1670; Salem
PITMAN/PICKMAN, Nathaniel & Mary GEORGE; 11 Dec 1695, at Boston; Watertown
PICKMAN, Samuel (-1691,1687?) & Lydia [PALFREY[? (-1694+); b 1659; Salem
PITCHMAN, Samuel & Elizabeth ASHWOOD 6 Feb 1684/5; Marblehead/Salem
PICKMAN, William (-1676) & Elizabeth EASTWICK, m/2 Edward BUSH 1678; 24 Jun 1673; Salem
PICKWORTH, Benjamin (1648-1681) & Elizabeth _?_ ; no issue; Salem
PICKWORTH, Elias & Anna KILLEGRIFF; 1 Mar 1682/3; Beverly
PICKWORTH, John (-1663) & Ann [?CHANDLER]; ca 1631-32; Plymouth/Salem
PICKWORTH, John & Mary BRIMBELCOMBE; 17 Oct 1692; Marblehead

PICKWORTH, Joseph (1643-1681+) & Abigail [ELITHORP] (ca 1645-); b 1668?; Manchester/
Marblehead
PICKWORTH, Samuel (-1675) & Sarah MASTONE/MARSTON (1648-), m/2 Joseph MASURY
1680; 3 Nov 1667; Salem
PICTON/PICKTON?, Thomas (-1677) & Ann [LAMBERT] (-1683, ae 84), wid; Salem
PIDCOCK, George & Sarah RICARD/RICHARD; 16 May 1640; Plymouth?/Scituate/Duxbury
PIER, Thomas & _?_; b 1678; Lyme, CT
PIERCE, Abraham (-1673) & Rebecca _?_; b 1638; Plymouth/Duxbury
PIERCE, Abraham (1638-1718) & 1/wf [?Hannah BAKER], dau Francis; ca 1660/70?; Duxbury
PIERCE, Abraham, Boston & Isabella/Isabel WHITERSPOONE, Boston; 11 Mar 1686/7; Salem
PIERCE, Abraham (1638-1718) & 2/wf Hannah [GLASS], Marshfield, Duxbury; 29 Oct 1695;
Scituate
PIERCE, Anthony^2 (1609-1678) & 1/wf Sarah _?_ (-1633); ca 1630?; Watertown
PIERCE, Anthony^2 (1609-1678) & 2/wf Ann _?_ (-1682/3); 1633+?; Watertown
PIERCE, Azrikim (1672-) & 1/wf Sarah HOWARD/HAYWARD (1676-1712); 31 Dec 1691;
Swansea/Rehoboth
PIERCE, Benjamin & Hannah BROOKS; 15 Jan 1678, 1677/8; Watertown
PEARCE, Benjamin (-1730) & Marth ADAMS; 5 Feb 1678; Scituate
PIERCE, Benjamin (-1739) & Mary REED (1670-1746); 10 Oct 1688; Woburn
PIERCE, Benjamin (1669-1711) & Lydia [FROST] (1674-1752), m/2 John GREENLEAF 1716; b
1693; Newbury
PIERCE, Benjamin (1667-1715) & Hannah BOWERS, m/2 William WILSON; 3 Apr 1693; Woburn
PIERCE, Daniel (1611-1677) (had nephew John SPENCER in 1651) & 1/wf [Sarah] _?_ (-1654);
b 1638; Salisbury/Newbury/Watertown?
PIERCE, Daniel & Katherine _?_; b 1651; Newbury
PIERCE/PEIRCE, Daniel (-1677) & Anne (BOODALE?/?LOWELL) MILWARD/MILLER (-1690),
w Thomas; 26 Dec 1654; Newbury
PEIRCE, Daniel (1642-) & Elizabeth MILLWARD (1644-1709); 5 Dec 1660; Newbury
PIERCE, Daniel (1640-1723) & Elizabeth _?_ (1642-1723+); b 1665; Groton/Watertown
PEARCE, Daniel (1658-1731+) & 1/wf _?_; b 1687; Portsmouth, RI/(Prudence Isl.)/N. Kings
Town, RI
PIERCE, Daniel (1663-1690) & Joanna _?_ (-1690); b 1690; Newbury/Salisbury
PIERCE, Daniel (1666-) & Abigail [WOODS] (1672-), m/2 Samuel BARRON; b 1698(9?); Groton
PEARCE, Ephraim (-1719) & Hannah [HOLBROOK] (-1719+); b 1671(2?); Weymouth
PIERCE, Ephraim (1673-1741) & Mary [WHITNEY] (1675-1749); b 1696; Groton/Lexington
PIERCE, Ephraim, Jr. & Mary LOW; 16 Apr 1697; Swansea
PEIRCE, Francis & Hannah JOHNSON, m/2 Joseph LOVEWELL 1730; 7 Dec 1694, 17 Dec;
Watertown
PERCE, Francis & Lydia [BISHOP] (1673-); b 1700; Manchester
PEARSE, George (-1662?) & Mary WOODHOUSE, m/2 Joseph MORSE b 1669, m/3 Francis
BROWN 1679; 1659; Boston
PEARCE, George (1662-1752) & 1/wf Alice HART (1664, 1669?-1708; 7 Apr 1687; Little
Compton, RI/Portsmouth, RI
PEARCE, George (1666-1746) & Rebecca _?_; b 1701; Beverly
PEARCE, Giles (1651-1698) & Elizabeth HALL (-1698+); 13 Apr 1676; East Yarmouth,
RI/Portsmouth, RI
PIERCE, Isaac (1661-1732) & Alice [CHARTLEY?]; b 1682; Middleborough
PIERCE, Jacob & Mary _?_, m/2 Isaac DENHAM 1694?; b 1695, b 7 or 8 Dec 1694; Westchester
Co., NY
PEIRCE, Jacob (-Medford) & Rachel _?_; b 1699; Boston
PIERCE, James (1659-1742) & Elizabeth RUSSELL?/PARKER (1663-1688); b 1688; Woburn/Lex-
ington/Framingham
PEIRCE, Jeremiah & Abigail _?_; b 1701; E. Greenwich, RI
PIERCE, John^1 (1588-1661) & Elizabeth _?_ (?1591, 1598-1667?, 1667/8); b 1609; Watertown
PEARCE, John (-1661) & 1/wf Parnell _?_ (-1639, prob 1637); b 1631; Dorchester
PIERCE, John (-1661) & 2/wf Mary _?_ (-1647); b 1638; Dorchester
PIERCE, John & Elizabeth _?_; b 1643; Boston/Woburn/Wethersfield
PEIRCE, John (ae 40 in 1660) & 1/wf Elizabeth _?_ (-1673); 4 Nov 1643; Gloucester
PEIRCE, John (-1661) & 3/wf Rebecca WHEELER (-1674), w Thomas; 10 Aug 1654; Boston

PEARCE, John (?1632-1692) & Mary __?__ (-1711); ca 1655; Portsmouth, RI/(Prudence Is.), RI

PIERCE, John (1615-1673) & Eleanor __?__ ; ca 1655?, ca 1645?; Kittery, ME

PEIRCE, John (-1682) & Ruth BISHOP (1639-), m/2 William FULLER [?1683]; 15 Apr 1656; Boston/Watertown

PIERCE, John (-1690?) & Isabel __?__ ; b 1659(60?), b 1669; Boston/Charlestown

PIERCE, John & Deborah CONVERSE; 1 Jul 1663; Woburn

PEARCE, John (1647-1707) & Mary TALLMAN (ca 1651-1720); ca 1668; Portsmouth, RI/Tiverton, RI

PEARCE, John (-1695) [1/wf d 3 Jul 1673] & 2/wf Jane STAINWOOD/STANWOOD, w Philip; ?17 Jul 1673, ?12 Sep 1673; Gloucester

PEARCE, John (-1653) & Mary [RATCHELL/ROCHELL] (1652-); b 1677, b 1691; Gloucester/Manchester

PEIRCE, John (-1696) & Lydia MORGAN (1654-1737), m/2 Edmond MARSHALL 1700; (27?) Aug 1677; Springfield/Enfield, CT

PIERCE, John (-1692) & 2/wf Phebe [NASH], w Isaac; ca 1680, b 1678?, by 7 Jul 1663; York, ME

PEARCE, John (1658-1715+) & Martha BRAYTON; b 1682; Portsmouth, RI/(Prudence Is.)

PIERCE, John & Elizabeth BROOKES; 24 May 1682; Simsbury, CT

PIERCE, John & Mary __?__ , m Josiah d 5 Dec 1706; Concord

PIERCE, John (1644-1731) & Ann [HUTHWITT]; b 1683; Wethersfield, CT/Woodbury, CT

PEIRCE, John & Patience DODSON; 12 Dec 1683; Scituate

PEARSE, John & Elizabeth __?__ ; b 1687; Boston

PIERCE, John (1664-1716) & Elizabeth MUDGE (1674-1748); 4 Feb 1691/2; Charlestown

PIERCE, John (1668-1744), Dorchester & Abigail THOMPSON (1667-1747), Braintree; 6 Jan 1693/4, 1692/3, 5 Jan 1692/3, 25 Jan; Braintree

PEIRC/PRIOR?, John & Eleanor CHILDS; 16 Aug 1695; Duxbury

PEIRCE, John (1671-1735) & Mary [PARKER] (1680-); b 1697; Woburn

PEIRCE, John & Mary COBET/COBHAM?; 9 Nov 1698; Boston

PIERCE, Jonathan (1661-1722) & Mary/Martha LOBDELL (1663-1744); 4 Dec 1683; Charlestown/Cambridge

PIERCE, Jonathan (1663-1694) & Hannah WILSON (1672-1726), m/2 James PROCTOR; 19 Nov 1689; Woburn/Cambridge?

PEARCE, Jonathan (1657-1713) & Elizabeth __?__ ; b 1700, b 1692, prob b 1685; Bristol, RI

PEIRS, Joseph (ca 1647-) & 1/wf Martha __?__ /BRAYTON?; b 1669; Watertown

PIERCE, Joseph (-1676?) & [Margery BRAY], m/2 William PEPPERELL 1680

PEARCE, Joseph & Lydia [FERNSIDE] (1653-), dau John; b 1676; Boston

PIERCE, Joseph (1649-1716) & Mary RICHARDSON (1651-1720, 1721), dau Theopholus (will 20 Jan 1716/17, probate 16 Jun 1721); 22 Jun 1681, 24 Jun; Woburn

PIERCE, Joseph (1669-1736+) & 1/wf Ruth HOLLAND (1666-); 20 Mar 1688/9, 20 May 1688/9; Watertown/Lexington

PEIRCE, Joseph (1669-1736+) & 2/wf Hannah MUNROW/MUNROE; 21 Dec 1692; Cambridge/Lexington

PIERCE, Joseph & 2/wf Elizabeth (KENDALL) WINSHIP (1652-1715), w Ephraim; 15 Jun 1698; Cambridge/Watertown

PEIRCE, Joseph & Mary WARRIN/WARREN (1675-); 30 Dec 1698; Watertown

PIERCE, Joshua (1642-1670) & Dorothy PIKE (1645-), m/2 John LIGHT 1674; 7 May 1668; Salisbury/Woodbridge, NJ

PIERCE, Joshua (1671-) & 1/wf Elizabeth HALL (1673-1717); 24 Jan 1694/5; Portsmouth, NH

PIERCE, Launcelot & Ann/Nan STEVENS (-1708, Milton, MA, ae 83); b 30 Jun 1676; Pejepscot/Pegypscot

PIERCE/PEERCE/PERCY?, Marmaluke & Mary __?__ ; b 1637; Salem

PIERCE, Michael (1615-1676) & 1/wf [Persis?] [EAMES] (1621-31 Dec 1662); b 1644, b 1646; Charlestown/Hingham/Scituate

PEIRCE, Michael (1615-1676) & Ann (JAMES) [ALLEN], w John; aft 1662, b 1 Jun 1663; Scituate/Hingham

PEIRSE, Moses & Mary __?__ ; b 1680; Boston

PIERCE, Nathaniel (1655-1692) & 1/wf Hannah CONVERSE (1660-1679); 27 Dec 1677; Woburn/Charlestown

PIERCE, Nathaniel (1655-1692) & 2/wf Elizabeth (PIERCE) (WHITTEMORE) FOSTER (1646-), w Thomas, w Hopestill; 23 Mar 1680, 1680/1, 22 Mar 1680/1; Woburn/Charlestown
PIERCE, Nathaniel & Christian [STODDARD] (1657, 1658-), m/2 Samuel BRIDGE 1690; b 1681; Boston
PEARSE, Nehemiah (1639, 1641?-1691) & 1/wf Phoebe [PLANTAINE], dau Wm. & Phebe; b 1663; Boston
PIERCE, Nehemiah (1639/41-1691) & 2/wf Anne (ADDINGTON) [MANLEY] (1646-), w Samuel; 1684?, aft 18 Sep 1684; Boston
PEARSE, Richard (1590-) & Martha __?__ ; in Eng, b 1615; Swansea
PEARSE/PEARCE, Richard (1615-1678) & Susannah [WRIGHT] (?1627-); Waldham Abbey, 5 May 1642, b 1643+; Portsmouth, RI/Swansea
PIERCE, Richard & Elizabeth BROWN; b 1647, ca 1642/6, b 1653; Pemaquid, ME
PEARCE, Richard/Wm?, Boston & Sarah COTTON (1663-1690); at Portsmouth?, 27 Aug 1680, 1689; Hampton, NH
PEARSE, Richard (1649-) & Experience __?__ ; ca 1680/4; Portsmouth, RI/Bristol, RI
PIERCE, Richard & Mary __?__ ; b 1690; Smelt Cove/Marblehead
PEARCE, Robert (-1664) & Anne [GREENWAY] (1591-1695?); ca 1625/30?; Dorchester
PEIRCE, Robert (1620-1706) & Mary [KNIGHT] (1620-1701, 1701/2); ca 1645/50, b 16 Oct 1646?; Woburn/Charlestown
PEARSE, Robert (ca 1612-1679) & Abigail [SYMONDS] (?ca 1622-1680); b 1656, ca 1644; Ipswich/Salisbury
PIERCE, Robert & Sarah EYRE/AYER?; 18 Feb 1657; Charlestown
PIERCE, Samuel (-1678) & Mary __?__ ; (1631-1705/6); b 1656; Malden/Charleston
PIERCE, Samuel (-1716) & Mary __?__ ; b 1673; Boston
PIERCE, Samuel (1648-1691) & Mary [ORTON] (1648-); b 1683; Charlestown/Boston?
PIERCE, Samuel (1656-1721) & Lydia BACON (1636-1717); 9 Dec 1680; Woburn
PEACE, Samuel & Mary [GIDDINGS?], ?m/2 William HUBBARD, 1697; b 1685, b 1697; Ipswich/Marblehead
PEARCE, Samuel (1664); & __?__ ; Portsmouth, RI/Prudence Isl.
PIERCE, Stephen (1651-1733), Woburn & Tabitha PARKER (1658-1742); 18 Nov 1676, 8 Nov 1676; Woburn
PEIRCE, Thomas (?1583-1666) & Elizabeth __?__ (1595/6-1666+, 1667+); in Eng, b 1619, b 1608, ca 1612?; Charlestown
PIERCE, Thomas[2] (1608?, 1613?-1683) & Elizabeth [COLE] (-1688); b 1639, 6 May 1635?; Charlestown/Woburn
PEIRCE, Thomas (1635-1706) & Mary [FRYE]? (1641/2, 1642-1704, 1701, ae 62); 3 Oct 1661[60?]; Dorchester
PIERCE, Thomas & Ann __?__ (-1668); b 1668; Gloucester
PIERCE, Thomas (1645-1717) & 1/wf [Eliza] __?__ ; b 1670, b 1671/2, b 1671(2?); Woburn
PEIRCE, Thomas (1645-1717) & 2/wf Rachel BACON (1652-1717+); 24 Mar 1680; Woburn
PIERCE, Thomas (1658-1693) & Elizabeth [HALL] (1658-), m/2 John OLDHAM 1694; b 1693; Charlestown
PIERCE, Thomas (-1714) & Mary WYMAN (1674-), m/2 John HUTCHINS; 27 Feb 1693, 1692/3?, 27 Feb 1692/3; Woburn/Plainfield, CT
PEIRCE, Thomas & Mehitable FROST; 5 Jan 1697/8; Newbury/Portsmouth
PIERCE, Timothy (1673-) & 1/wf Lydia SPALDING (-1706); 27 May 1696; Plainfield, CT
PEARCE, William (1595-1641) & Jane __?__ ; b 1633; Boston/Providence/Bahama Is./VA
PIERCE, William (-1661) & Sarah [COLBRON]; ca 1633/36?; Boston
PEIRCE, William (-1669, 1661) & Esther [WEBB]?; b 1656; Boston
PEARSE, William & Elizabeth __?__ ; b 1661(2?); Boston
PIERCE/TYER, William (-1666/7, ae 26, Copp's Hill) & Sarah KEIN/KINT?, dau Arthur?; m/2 Robert BRICKENTON, m/3 William ROUSE; 13 Jul 1666, 3 Jul 1666; Charlestown
PIERCE, William & Esther SPENCER; 9 Jan 1687/8; Suffield, CT
PIERCE, William (-1720) & Abigail SOMES/SOMERS (-1726), alias WARREN, born WARREN; 8 Apr 1690; Woburn/Charlestown
PEIRSE, William & Sarah [JEFFS?]; b 1691; Charlestown
PEARCE, William (1664-) & Hannah __?__ ; b 1700, ca 1690?; Mamaroneck
PIERCE, William & Miriam __?__ ; b 1701?, b 1703; Milton
PIERCE, William (-1733) & __?__

PIERCE, _?_ & Sarah **MITCHELL**; b 1701?
PIERCE, _?_ & Sarah [**HUMPHREY**] (1679–); Barrington, RI
PIERPONT, Ebenezer (1661–1696, Roxbury) & Mary **RUGGLES** (1666–), m/2 Isaac **MORRIS**; 20 Oct 1692; Roxbury
PIERPONT, James (–d in Ipswich?) & Margaret _?_ (–1664, London); in Eng, b 1619?; Ipswich
PIERPONT, James (1660–1714) & 1/wf Abigail **DAVENPORT** (1672–1692); 27 Oct 1691; New Haven
PIERPONT, James (1660–1714) & 2/wf Sarah **HAYNES** (–1696); 30 May 1694, at Hartford; New Haven
PIERPONT, James (1660–1714) & 3/wf Mary **HOOKER** (1673–1740); 26 Jul 1698; New Haven/?Farmington, CT
PIERPONT, John (–1682, ae 64 or 65) & Thankful [**STOWE**] (1629–); b 1649; Ipswich/Roxbury
PIERPONT, Jonathan (1665–1709) & Elizabeth **ANGIER** (1667–); 29 Oct 1691; Reading/Cambridge
PIERPONT, Robert (1622–1694) & Sarah **LYNDE** (1641–); 18 Feb 1656/7; Charlestown/Roxbury
PIERSON, Abraham[1] (1609 Bradford, Eng, ?1612–1678) & 2/wf? Abigail **MITCHELL** (1618–); b 1641; Boston/Lynn/Southampton, LI/Branford, CT/Newark, NJ
PIERSON, Rev. Abraham (1645, 1646–1707) & Abigail [**CLARK**] (1654–1727); ca 1671/2; Milford, CT/Newark, NJ/Killingworth, CT
PEARSONS, Bartholomew (–1687) & Ursula?/Azlee? _?_ (–1694); b 1640; Watertown/Woburn
PEARSON, Benjamin (1658–1731) & Hannah **THORSTON/THURSTON**; 20 Jan 1679, 1679/80?; Rowley/Newbury
PEIRSON/PEARSON/PARSONS?/PERSON?, George (1630–) (ae 38 in 1669) & Elizabeth [**WHEELWRIGHT**] (1634–1703+) (had son Wheelwright); b 1663, b 1662; Boston
PEASON/PERSON?, George & Ann (**WYETH**)/[**WARE**] **TAYLOR**, w William; 2 Apr 1677; Exeter, NH
PEARSON, Henry? (–1680/1) & Mary [**COOPER**] (1622–), m/2 Rev. Seth **FLETCHER**; b 1642?; Stamford, CT
PIERSON, Henry (?1652–1701) & Susannah [**HOWELL**] (1658–1715 will); b 1685, 1685; Southampton
PEARSON, James & Hepzibah **SWAYNE**, dau Jeremiah; 15 Feb 1697; Reading
PEARSON, Jeremiah (1653–1737) & Priscilla **HAZEN** (1664–1752); 21 Jul 1681; Rowley/Newbury
PEARSON, John (1615–1679) & Maudlin/Madeline _?_ (1619–1690) (not Maudlin **BULLARD** m John **PARTRIDGE**); b 1643; Reading/Lynn
PEARSON, John (–1693) & Dorcas _?_ (–1703); b 1643; Rowley
PEARSON, John & Ann **WISE/WYETH** (see George **PEARSON**); Piscataqua
PEARSON, John & Mary **PACKARD**/[**PICKARD**]; 14 Feb 1670; Rowley
PIERSON, John (–1677) & _?_ ; b 1674; Middletown, CT
PEARSON, John (1650–1728) & 1/wf Tabitha [**KENDALL**] (1660–1711); b 1678; Reading/Lynn
PEARSON, Joseph & 1/wf Amy **BARNES** (–1692); 17 Nov 1675; Southampton, LI
PEARSON, Joseph & Joanna [**COOPER**], w Thomas; aft 3 Oct 1692; ?Southampton
PEARSON, Samuel (1648–) & 1/wf Mary **POORE** (–1671); 6 Dec 1670; Newbury/Haverhill
PEARSON, Samuel (1648–) & 2/wf Dorcas **JOHNSON**; 16 Apr 1672; Haverhill/Newbury
PIERSON, Stephen (1645–1739) & Mary [**TOMLINSON**] (–1715); ca 1670; Stratford/Derby, CT
PEARSON, Stephen (1663–1706) & Mary **FRENCH** (–1730); 11 Nov 1684; Rowley
PIERSON, Stephen, Jr. (–1744) & 1/wf Mehitable **CANFIELD** (1671–); 12 Oct 1697; Milford, CT/?Derby, CT
PIERSON, Theodore (bef 1659–) & _?_ ; b 1697; Southampton
PIERSON, Theophilus (1659–1717)
PEARSON, Thomas (–1701) & Mary **HARRISON**; 27 Nov 1662; Branford, CT/Newark, NJ
PIERSON, Thomas (1641/2–1701) & Mary **BROWN** (1653–1684); b 1676, Nov 1662; Branford, CT/Newark, NJ
PEARSON, Thomas & Elizabeth **HAMMOND** (1672–); 19 Oct 1691; Charlestown/Boston
PIERSON, _?_ & [Rebecca **EMMONS**] (1673–), Boston; b 1710, b 1701?
PEARSON/PARSONS?, ?John & [Elizabeth **HARDY**], dau Richard; b 1683; Stamford, CT
PIDGE, John (ca 1640–1691) & 1/wf Mary **FARRINGTON** (1650–1676); 27 Apr 1667; Dedham
PIDGE, John & 2/wf Elizabeth **NEWCOMB** (1658–), m/2 James **EMERY** 1695; 3 Jul 1677; Dedham
PIGG, Robert (–1660?) & Margaret _?_, m/2 William **THORPE**; b 1632; New Haven

PIGG/PIDGE, Thomas[1] (-1643, 1644) & Mary/?Mercy SOTHY, m/2 Michael METCALF 1645; in Eng, 1 Nov 1619, ca 1624, ca 1620; Roxbury

PIKE, George (-1716) & [Hester ATKINS]; b 1684?; Marblehead/Mendon

PICKE, George & Hannah TRAVETT; 23 Oct 1684; Marblehead

PIKE, George, Cape Cod & Tabitha __?__ ; b 1694; Charlestown

PIKE, Hugh & 1/wf Sarah BROWN; 17 Jun 1685; Newbury

PIKE, Hugh & 2/wf Mary [WOODIES?]; ca 1692?, b 19 Dec 1692; Salisbury

PIKE/SPIKE?, James (-1699) & [Naomi?]/Sarah? __?__ (-1693?, 1692?); b 1647(8?), b 1647; Charlestown/Reading/Framingham

PIKE, James & 1/wf Hannah CUTLER (1662-); 25 Nov 1681; Reading

PIKE, James (-1727) & Sarah MARSH/MARCH (-1738); 23 May 1700; Newbury/Framingham/Weston

PIKE, Jeremiah (-1711) & Rachel LIPINGWELL/LEFFINGWELL (1653-); 15 Nov 1671; Reading/Framingham

PIKE, John (-1654) & Dorothy DAYE, Langford?/Landford; Whiteparish, Eng, Wiltshire, 17 Jan 1612/13; Newbury/Ipswich/Salisbury

PIKE, John (-1689) & 1/wf Mary TURREL?/TARVILLE?/TARBELL?; b 1638; Newbury/Woodbridge, NJ

PICKE, John & Mary __?__ ; b 1642; Cambridge

PIKE, John (-1709) & Elizabeth ENGLESHIE/ENGLEBY (-1609); 29 Mar 1671; Charlestown/Roxbury

PIKE, John (-1714) & Elizabeth STOUT; 2 Feb 1675; ?Middleton, NJ/?Woodbridge, NJ

PIKE, Rev. John (1653-1710) & Sarah MOODY (-1703); 5 May 1681; Dover, NH/Portsmouth, NH/Hampton, NH/etc.

PIKE, John (-1688/9) & 2/wf Elizabeth FitzRANDOLPH, w Edward; 30 Jun 1685; ?Woodbridge, NJ

PIKE/PEAKE?, John (-1699) & Elizabeth __?__ ; b 1690; New London, CT

PIKE, John & Lydia (COFFIN) LITTLE, w Moses; 18 Mar 1694/5; Newbury

PIKE, Joseph (-1694) & Susanna KINSBURY/KINGSBURY (-1718); 29 Jan 1661, 1661/2; Newbury

PIKE, Joseph & 1/wf Susanna SMITH (-1688?); 10 Nov 1680; Charlestown/Boston

PIKE, Joseph & Prudence EDMINSTER (1668-); 1 Jul 1689; ?Charlestown

PIKE, Joseph (1674-1757) & Hannah SMITH (1675-); m int 4 Dec 1695; Newbury

PIKE, Moses (1658-) & Susanna [WORCESTER] (1672-); b 1688; Salisbury

PIKE, Philip & Rebecca LEWIS?; b 1701?, b 3 Dec 1712/13; Wells, ME/Kittery, ME//Portsmouth, NH

PIKE, Richard & Elizabeth [ANDREWS], m/2 Thomas PURCHASE 1656?, m/3 John BLANEY 1678; ca 1653; Falmouth, ME

PIKE, Robert (-1674±) & Catherine __?__ (-1679+); in Eng?, b 1630; Providence

PIKE, Robert (1617-1706) & 1/wf Sarah SAUNDERS?/SANDERS (1615-1679); 3 Apr 1641; Salisbury

PIKE, Robert (-1690) & Martha (MOYCE) GOLDWYER, w George; 30 Oct 1684; Salisbury

PIKE, Robert (1655-1690) & Mary FOLLINSBY, m/2 William HOOKE ca 1691; 1 Dec 1686, ?1 Feb; Newbury/Salisbury

PIKE, Robert (-by 1718) & Mary [WALLACE] (see below); b 1686; Beverly/Portland, ME

PIKE, Samuel & Mary WALLIS (see above) (-1718+); b 1677; Salem/etc.

PIKE, Thomas (1654-) & 1/wf Elizabeth PARKER; 25 Jan 1686; Boston

PIKE, Thomas & 2/wf Hester BUNN; 4 Aug 1689; Woodbridge, NJ

PIKE, Thomas & 3/wf Mary PHILLIPS; 30 Jun 1699; Woodbridge, NJ

PIKE, William[1] & __?__ ; b 1655; New London

PIKE/PEAKE?, William (-1717) & Abigail COMSTOCK (-1745); 24 Jun 1679; Lyme, CT/Southold, LI

PILGRIM, [?John] & [Elizabeth BARTHOLOMEW] (1654-); b 26 Aug 1681; Salem

PILKINTON/PILKINGTON, Mark & Faith (BELCHER) CROSS, wid; 18 Nov 1691; Boston

PILSBURY, Abel & Mary __?__ ; b 1679; Newbury

PILSBURY, Job (1643-1716) & Katherine GAVET/GAVETT (-1718); 5 Apr 1677, 8 Apr; Newbury

PILSBURY, Joseph (1670-) & 1/wf Sarah __?__ ; b 1694?, b 1695; Newbury

PILSBURY, Moses (-1701) & 1/wf Susanna (__?__) WORTH (1649?-), w Lionel; - Mar 1668; Newbury

PILSBURY, Moses & Abigail ROLF/ROLFE; m int 5 Feb 1697/8; Newbury
PILSBERRY, Moses (-1701) & 2/wf Priscilla __?__; b 1701, ca 1690/4?; Newbury
PILSBURY, William (-1686, ae 71) & Dorothy [CROSBY]; betw 1 Jun & 29 Jul 1641; Dorchester/Newbury
PILSBURY, William & Mary KENNY; 13 Dec 1677; Newbury
PINCKNEY, John & Abigail [HUNT]; ca 1690; Eastchester, NY
PINCKNEY, Philip (1618-1689) & Jane __?__, niece of George HULL or of his 2nd wf; b Aug 1659; Fairfield, CT/Eastchester, NY
PINCKNEY, Thomas (1662-1732) & Hannah __?__; b 1680; Eastchester, NY
PINCKNEY, William & __?__; b 1682; Eastchester, NY
PINKNEY, Philip & Margaret GOUGH; 16? Oct 1610, The Cathedral; Salisbury, Eng
PINDAR, Henry (-1661) & 1/wf Mary __?__ (1582-); in Eng, b 1615; Gloucester
PINDAR, Henry & Elizabeth (__?__) ANDREWS, w Robert
PINDER, Jacob & __?__; Newport/Kings Town, RI
PINDAR, John (1627-1662) & Elizabeth [WILSON]; by 1658; Ipswich/Watertown
PINDER, John (1649-) & 1/wf 2/wf? Sarah [OTIS]/MERROW? (-1704+); b 1688; Durham, NH
PINDAR, Simon (-1725) & Hannah [BROWN] (1676-); b 1700(01?); Ipswich
PINE, James[1] (1631-1686) & __?__
PINE, James (-1687) & ?Edith WILLIAMS; in Eng, Sep 1630; ?Hempstead, LI
PINE, John & __?__ OGDEN (-bef 28 Apr 1687); ?Fairfield, CT
PYNE, John (-1703) & Abigail/Hester __?__; Hempstead, LI
PINE, Samuel (-1695) & Rachel __?__
PINE, William & [Sarah SMITH]; 1729, 1698
PINGREY, Aaron (-1696) & Jennet [STARKWEATHER], w Robert; aft 1674, no issue; Salisbury
PENGRY, Aaron (1652-1714) & Ann PICKARD; 22 Mar 1681/2; Ipswich/Rowley
PINGRY, John (1654-1723) & Faith JEWETT; 20 May 1678; Ipswich
PENGRY, Moses (1610/11-1696) & Lydia [CLEMENT] (?1618-1676); ca 1644, b 1646; Salisbury
PENGRY, Moses & 1/wf Sarah CONVERSE (-1692); 29 Jun 1680; Ipswich
PINGRY, Moses & 2/wf Abigail (MORSE) [HENDRICK] (1652-), w John; aft 1692, bef 1695; Newbury
PINKHAM, John (1643?-) & 1/wf __?__; ca 1668?; Dover, NH
PINKHAM, John & Martha [OTIS?] (-1699+); by 1688, b Jun 1674; Dover, NH
PINKHAM, Richard (1613-) & ?Julia/?Jellia/?Gylian __?__; b 1643; Dover, NH
PINKHAM, Richard (-1718) & Mary [COFFIN] (1665-1741), m/2 James GARDNER; b 1684; Nantucket
PINKHAM, Richard (?1672-1757+) & 1/wf Elizabeth [LEIGHTON], dau Thomas; b 1696, by 1699; Dover, NH
PINKHAM, Thomas & Mary ALLEN; 2 Dec 1700; Dover, NH
PINNER, John (-bef 1674) & Sarah [CLARKE] (1651-1706+), m/2 Caleb CARR ca 1677; no issue; RI
PINNEY, Humphrey (-1683) & Mary [HULL] (?1616, 1618-1684, 1685); ca 1632/4; Dorchester/Windsor, CT
PINNEY, Isaac (-1709) & Sarah CLARKE, m/2 __?__; 6 Oct 1685; Windsor, CT
PINNEY, Nathaniel (-1676) & Sarah (GRISWOLD) PHELPS (-1715?), w Samuel; 21 Jul 1670; Windsor, CT
PINNEY, Nathaniel (1671-1764) & Martha THRALL; 21 Sep 1693; Windsor, CT
PINNEY, Samuel & Joyce BISSELL; 17 Nov 1665; Windsor, CT/Simsbury, CT
PINNEY, Samuel (1668-) & Sarah PHELPS (-1712); 24 Oct 1698; Windsor, CT
PINION/PINNION, Nicholas (1608-1676) & 1/wf Elizabeth __?__ (-1667); b 1641; Lynn/New Haven
PINION, Nicholas (1608-1676) & 2/wf Mary (__?__) (DICKERSON) FINCH, w Thomas, w Daniel; aft 1667; Fairfield, CT?
PINION, Thomas (-1710) & Mercy __?__; b 1675; New Haven
PINSON, Andrew (-1697) & Jane JACKSON; 13 Sep 1681; Wethersfield, CT
PINSON, Edmund & 1/wf Anna COOPER (1643-1666); 2 Aug 1664; Cambridge
PINSON, Edmund, London & 2/wf Sarah DEXTER; m int 24 Jul 1666; Charlestown
PINSON, Thomas (1609-1694) & Joan/?Joanna [STANLEY]/STANDLAKE?; 10 Nov 1639; Scituate
PINSON/PINCHEN?, Thomas, Jr. (1640-) & 1/wf Elizabeth WHITE (1642-); 18 Sep 1662; Scituate

PINCEN, Thomas & ?2/wf Sarah TURNER; 26 Dec 1693; Scituate
PINSON, Thomas & Mary [GOULD]; b 1694; Salem
PINSENT, William (-1695) & Rebecca GREENE, dau of Thomas ROBBINS' sister, m/2 Joseph BOOBIER, m/3 Robert BARTLETT; 27 Feb 1675/6; Salem
PIPER, John (1663-) & Lydia _?_ ; b 1695; Wenham
PIPER, Jonathan (-1752) & 1/wf Sarah LEACH (-1700); 7 May 1695; Topsfield
PIPER, Jonathan (-1752) & 2/wf Alice DARBY (1679-1758); m int 21 Sep 1700; Beverly/Concord/Ipswich
PIPER, Nathaniel & Sarah [?EDWARDS], dau Rice, m/2 Ezekiel WOODWARD; b 1656, b 1658?; Ipswich
PIPER, Samuel & Abigail CHURCH; 23 Apr 1694; ?Dover, NH
PIPER, Thomas & Grace HAWLEY; 21 Nov 1692; Marblehead/Wenham
PITCHER, Andrew (-1661) & Margaret [RUSSELL] (-1681); b 1641; Dorchester
PITCHER, John (1650-) & Hannah _?_ ; b 1684(5?); Boston
PITCHER, Nathaniel (1652-1736) & Mary CLAP (-1709); 8 Jul 1685, 1684; Milton
PITCHER, Richard & Grace [MATTONE]; b 1701?; ?Boston
PITCHER, Samuel & 1/wf Alice CAIG (-1680); 30 Nov 1671; Milton
PITCHER, Samuel & 2/wf Mary BLAKE; 3 Aug 1681; Milton
PITKIN, Nathaniel & 1/wf Esther/Hester [HOSMER] (-1709); b 1699; Hartford
PITKIN, Roger (1662-1748) & Hannah [STANLEY] (1666-1703); b 1684; Hartford
PITKIN, William (?1635-1694, ae 58) & Hannah [GOODWIN] (?1637-1724); ca 1660-1; Hartford
PITKIN, William (1664-1723) & Elizabeth [STANLEY] (1669-); b 1687; Hartford
PITMAN, Ezekiel & 1/wf _?_ ; b 1691
PITMAN, Ezekiel (1658-1706) & 2/wf? Elizabeth [DERRY], w James, m John PINDER; by 1695; Dover, NH
PITMAN, James & Mary _?_ ; b 1676; Manchester
PITMAN, Jeremiah & Martha BAND; 2 Jul 1686; Salem
PITTMAN, John & Charity GALE (1644-), m/2 Mark HASKELL 1697; 5 May 1681; Marblehead
PITMAN (?1663-) & Mary [SAUNDERS] (-1711, ae 45); b 1690; Newport
PITMAN, John & Margaret WARD; 14 Jun 1696; Marblehead
PITMAN, Jonathan (ca 1642-173(-)) & Temperance WELLS (ca 1654-1728); 29 Nov 1681, 21 Nov; Stratford, CT
PITMAN, Joseph (-1704) & Elizabeth _?_ , m/2 Barnaby SANDERS; ca 1692?; Durham, NH
PITMAN, Joseph & Elizabeth _?_ ; b 1697; Marblehead
PITMAN, Mark (1622-1690) & Sarah [SHAPLEIGH?]; Marblehead
PITMAN, Mark & Sarah BASEE; 29 Oct 1696; Manchester
PITMAN, Moses & Remember [PARKER]; b 1683; Marblehead
PITMAN/PICKMAN?, Nathaniel, Boston & Mary GEORGE, Boston; in Boston, 11 Dec 1695; Watertown
PITMAN, Nathaniel & Deliverance DERRY, w John; b 1697?, nr 1700, b 17 Nov 1697; ?Durham, NH
PITMAN, Nicholas & Elizabeth PITMAN; 3 Jul 1685; Marblehead
PITCHMAN/PICKMAN?, Samuel & Elizabeth ASHWOOD; 6 Feb 1684/5; Marblehead/Salem
PITMAN, Thomas & ?Mary DENNIS; b 1675?; Marblehead
PITMAN, Thomas & Margaret (GOULD) STILSON, w James; 30 Mar 1696; Marblehead
PITMAN, Thomas & Sarah _?_ ; b 1701; Manchester
PITTMAN, William (?1632-1682), Dover, NH, & 1/wf Barbary EVONS/Barbara EVANS; 29 Nov 1653; Boston/Piscataway
PITMAN, William (-1682) & 2/wf Ann [ROBERTS]?; by 1665, b 1661?; Dover, NH/Durham
PITMAN, William & 3/wf Dorothy _?_ ; b 1673
PITMAN, William (-1676) & Elizabeth [ESTWICK], m/2 Edward BUCKMAN 1678
PITMAN, William & Elizabeth (BOLLES)/BOWLES LOCKE, w Philip?/John?; aft 14 Aug 1679, aft 1683; Portsmouth, NH
PITTNEY/PITNEY, James (1583-1663, Marchfield) & Sarah _?_ (1613-); in Eng, b 1628; Plymouth/Boston
PITTUM/PITTAM/?PITMAN, John & Mary _?_ ; b 1678, b 1674?; Boston
PITTS, Ebenezer (1671±-) & Elizabeth HOSKINS; ca 1692; ?Taunton
PITTS, Edmund (-1685, ae 72), Hingham, Eng, & Ann _?_ (-1686); b 1639, b 1637; Hingham
PITTS, James & Elizabeth HOUGH; 10 Mar 1691; Boston

PITTICE/PETTIS/PITTS?, John (-1651) & Margaret _?_ ; ca 1640, 5 dau in 1651; ?Ipswich
PITTS, John (1656-) & Christian _?_ ; b 1692; Boston
PITTS, John & Elizabeth _?_ ; b 1696; Boston
PITTS, John & Elizabeth LINDALL; 10 Sep 1697; Boston
PITTS, Peter (-1692?) & Mary (ANDREWS) [HODGES], w William; soon aft 2 Apr 1654; Taunton
PITTS, Peter & Bethiah [ROBINSON], dau Increase, Jr.; Taunton
PITTS, Samuel (-1696?) & Sarah BOBITT, m/2 Samuel BLAKE; 25 Mar 1680; Taunton
PITTS, William & _?_ ; in Eng, b 1632; Marblehead
PITTS, William & Susan/Susanna AEALY/ALLEY (-1668), w Philip; 7 Dec 1655; Boston
PITTS, William & Ann PARTRIDGE; 29 Jul 1664; Charlestown
PITTS, William & Hopestill (VIALL) SHUTE (1639-), w William; b 1669(70?); Boston
PITTS, _?_ /William? & Elizabeth _?_ (-1655); b 1639, b 1634?; Dorchester
PIXLEY, Joseph & Abigail CLARKE, Farmington, CT; 23 Aug 1699; Westfield/Sheffield, CT
PIXLY, Thomas & Lydia [DIBBLE]; 20 Jan 1697/8; Westfield
PIXLEY, William & Sarah LAWRENCE; 24 Nov 1663; Hadley/Northampton/Westfield
PLACE, Enoch (1631-) & 1/wf? Dinah _?_ (-28 Jul 1657; Dorchester
PLACE, Enoch (1631-1695) & 2/wf? Sarah _?_ ; 5 Nov 1657; Dorchester/Kings Town, RI
PLACE, Enoch[2] (-1703) & Mary [SWEET] (1660-1746), m/2 Samuel WICKHAM 1707; b 1697; N.
    Kings Town, RI
PLACE, John & 1/wf _?_ ; b 1668; Portsmouth, NH/Newington, NH
PLACE, John & Sarah [LOVERING], m/2 John BUSHNELL b 1687; b 1674; Boston
PLACE, John & 2/wf? [?Phebe MUZEET] (doubtful); Portsmouth, NH
PLACE, Joseph & Joannah [PLACE] (1681-), dau John & Sarah (LOVERING) PLACE; 9 Nov
    1698; N. Kings Town, RI
PLAISE, Peter (1615-) & Alice _?_ ; b 1642?, b 1643?; Boston
PLACE, Peter (-1735) & 1/wf Sarah STEERE; 24 Dec 1685; Providence/Glocester, RI
PLACE, Richard (?1668-) & Abigail _?_ /?Martha LEIGHTON (-1722+); b 1695?; Portsmouth,
    NH/Newington, NH/Casco Bay, ME
PLACE, Thomas (1663-1727) & Hannah [COLE] (1668-); b 1695?; N. Kings Town, RI
PLASSE, William (1571-1646) & 2/wf Phebe (MANNING) [WATERS], w James; in Eng, ca 18
    Feb 1618/19, 8 Feb; Salem
PLAINE, William & Anne/Anna _?_ , m/2 John PARMELEE; b 1652?; Guilford, CT
PLAISTED, Elisha (?1660-1690) & Elizabeth HARVEY, m/2 Elisha ILSLEY aft 6 Jul 1693, m/3
    Robert RUTHERFORD; 11 Oct 1689; Dover/Portsmouth, NH
PLAISTED, Ichabod (1663/4-1715) & Mary JOSE (1666-), m/2 John BROWN; 5 Jan 1692/3;
    Portsmouth, NH
PLAISTED, James & 1/wf Lydia [HITCHCOCK] (1658-11 Feb 1692?); ca 1680/4, b 1680, b 12
    Oct 1681, 12 Oct 1680; ?Saco, ME/York, ME
PLAISTED, James & 2/wf Mary (RISHWORTH) (WHITE) (SAYWORTH) (HULL), w John, w
    Phineas; aft 26 Dec 1689, b 1692?, b 25 Jan 1691/2; York, ME
PLAYSTEAD, John & Elizabeth _?_ ; b 1678, b 1674?; Boston
PLAISTED, John & Mary [PICKERING] (1668-); b 1682/3; Portsmouth, NH
PLAISTED, John & Sarah WORTHILAKE; 25 Mar 1698; Boston
PLAISTED, Roger[1] (1627-1675) & Olive COLMAN, m/2 John WINCOLL; Preshute, Wilts, 25 Mar
    1648; Kittery, ME
PLAISTED, Roger[2] (-1675) & 1/wf Hannah TARBOT? (doubtful); 1669; Kittery, ME
PLAISTED, Roger[2] (-1675) & Hannah [FURBER]; 19 Sep 1671; Kittery, ME
PLAISTED, William (1652-) & _?_ ; b 1683; Boston
PLANT, John (-1691) & Betty [ROUNDBOTTLE]; in Eng, b 1678/9; Branford, CT/Stratford, CT
PLATT, Epenetus (?1640-1693) & Phebe WOOD; Mar 1667; ?Huntington, LI
PLATT, Epenetus (1674-) & 1/wf Hannah MARVIN; ca 1698?, ca 1703; Huntington, LI
PLATT, Francis & Dorothy BLAKEMAN; 31 Oct 1665; Stratford, CT
PLATT, Frederick & Elizabeth FOX (1677-), New London; ca 1700; Killingworth, CT
PLATT, Isaac (ca 1638-1691) & Elizabeth [WOOD]; ?1660, b 1665?; ?Huntington, LI
PLATT, John & Hannah/Meriam? CLARK (?1640-); 6 Jun 1660; Milford, CT
PLATT, John (1664-) & Sarah LOCKWOOD; - May 1695, May 1696, May 1695; Norwalk, CT
PLATT, Jonas (1667-) & Sarah [SCUDDER]; ?Huntington, LI
PLATT, Joseph (1649-1704), Norwalk & Mary KELLOGG (1662-); 5 May 1680; Milford, CT
PLATT, Joseph & 1/wf Elizabeth MARVIN (-1703); 6 Nov 1700; Norwalk, CT

PLATT, Josiah (1645-1724/5) & Sarah CAMFIELD/CANFIELD (1647-); 2 Dec 1669; Milford, CT

PLATT, Richard (1604-1684, 1685) & Mary WOOD (1605-), in Eng; b 1633, 26 Jan 1682/9; New Haven/Milford, CT

PLATTS, Abel (-1690) & Lydia BALLEY/BAILEY (1644-1722), m/2 Daniel WICOM; 8 May 1672, 18 May; Rowley

PLATTS, James (1661-1742) & Lydia HALE (1666-1740); 10 Sep 1691; Rowley

PLATTS, John & Judith FOSTER (1664-); 13 Apr 1693; Rowley

PLATS, Jonathan[1] (1630-1680) (ae 40 in 1674) & Elizabeth JOHNSON (?1634-1721), cousin of Gershom LAMBERT; 6 Dec 1655; Rowley

PLATTS, Jonathan (1661-) & Elizabeth [BROCKLEBANK??]/[NELSON?]; b 1698; Rowley/Boxford

PLATTS, Moses (1673-1739) & Hannah PLATTS (1676-1755); 22 Nov 1693; Rowley

PLATS, Samuel[1] (James father of Samuel) & 1/wf Sarah __?__ (-1681); in Eng, b 1649, ca 1647; Rowley

PLATS, Samuel[2] (1647?-) & Mary LAW; 4 Apr 1678; Rowley

PLATS, Samuel[1] & 2/wf Phillipa (ANDREWS) FELT, w George, m/3 Thomas NELSON 1690; 19 Dec 1682, 19 Nov 1682; Rowley/Salem

PLATTS, Thomas (1641-1686) & Esther [CRABTREE], m/2 Thomas HAMLIN ca 1687?; b 1670(1?); Boston

PLATT, Thomas & Hannah SIMONS; m int 28 Sep 1696; Boston

PLIMLY/PLIMBLY/?PLUMBLEY, Thomas & [Susannah] __?__ ; b 1678; Boston/Dorchester

PLIMPTON, John & Jane DUMMIN/DAMON, m/2 Nicholas HIDE/IDE? 1680; 13 Mar 1643/4; Dedham

PLIMPTON, John (-1704) & 1/wf Elizabeth FISHER (-1694); 2 Jan 1677/8; Medfield

PLIMPTON, John (-1704) & 2/wf Sarah TURNER; 28 Feb 1695/6; Dedham

PLIMPTON, Joseph (-1702) & Mary MORSE, dau Joseph; 3 Nov 1675; Medfield

PLIMPTON, Joseph & 1/wf Priscilla PARTERAGE/PARTRIDGE (1672-); 22 Aug 1699; Boston

PLIMPTON, Peter (1652-1717) & Mary MUNDEN; 2 Jul 1677; Hatfield

PLIMPTON, Thomas (-1676) & Abigail [NOYES]; b 1653, ca 1650?; Sudbury

PLUMB, Ebenezer & Sarah __?__ ; b 1687; Boston

PLUMB, Green & Mary HEMPSTEAD; 3 May 1694; New London, CT

PLUMB, John (1594-1648) & Dorothy __?__ ; in Eng, b 1616; Dorchester/Branford, CT/Wethersfield, CT

PLUMB, John (1630-1706+) & Mary __?__ (1629-1706+); b 1655; Dorchester

PLUMB, John & __?__ [GREENE?] (had son Greene); ca 1660?; Hartford/New London

PLUMB, John (1646-1728) & Elizabeth NORTON (?1645-), Farmington; 24 Nov 1668; Milford, CT

PLUMB, John & Elizabeth HEMPSTEAD; 13 Feb 1688/9; New London

PLUM, John & Hannah [CRANE], dau Azariah; ?b 1696; Milford, CT

PLUMB, Joseph, ?New London & Susanna [NEWTON] (1671-); ?1700; Milford, CT

PLUME, Robert (1617-1655) & Mary BALDWIN (1625-1708), m/2 William EAST 1676; ?aft? 9 Jan 1642, 1642/3; Milford, CT

PLUMB, Robert (1648-1703) & Ruth (CLARK) [FITCH] (1642-), w Thomas; aft 1684, b 14 Aug 1698; Branford, CT

PLUMB, Samuel (1626-) & __?__ ; b 1650, 1650/1?; Branford, CT/Newark, NJ

PLUMLY, Joseph & Jane __?__ ; b 1672; Braintree

PLUMLEY, Timothy & Hester WINTER?; b 1676

PLUMER, Benjamin & 1/wf Ann WOOD (1660-); 15 Jan 1678, ?17 Jan, 1678/9; Rowley

PLUMER, Ephraim (1654-1715) & Hannah JAQUES (-1731); 15 Jan 1679, 1679/80; Newbury

PLUMER, Francis[1] (-1673) & 1/wf Ruth __?__ (-1647, Tulyor, Eng); in Eng, b 1619; Newbury

PLUMER, Francis[1] (-1673) & 2/wf Ann PALMER (-1665), w William; bef 6 Oct 1647, 21 Mar 1649, 31? Mar, b 6 Oct 1647; Newbury

PLUMER, Francis (-1673) & 3/wf Beatrix/Beatrice (BURT) CANTERBURY, w William, m/3 Edward BERRY ca 1675/6; 29 Nov 1665; Newbury

PLUMMER, Francis & Mary ELITHORP; 27 May 1700; Ipswich

PLUMER, Jonathan (-1726 in 59th y) & Sarah PEARSON; 16 Jun 1696; Newbury/Rowley

PLUMER, Joseph (?1630-1706+) & Sarah CHENEY (1636-1692+); 23 Dec 1652; Newbury/Rowley

PLUMER, Joseph (-1728) & Hannah JEWET; 20 Jan 1684, 1684/5; Newbury

PLUMER, Joshua (1668-) & Elizabeth DOLE (1679-); 6 Nov 1699; Newbury

PLUMER, Samuel (?1619-1702, 1701) & Mary [BITFIELD]/?BEDFIELD (-1704); b 1647; Newbury

PLUMER, Samuel (1647-) & 1/wf Joanna WOODBERY/WOODBURY (1653-1714); 5 Dec 1670; Newbury

PLUMER, Sylvanus (1658-1733) & 1/wf Sarah MOODY (1658-); 18 Jan 1681, 1681/2; Newbury

PLUMER, Sylvanus (1658-1733) & 2/wf Emma (JEPSON) KELLY; 5 Nov 1700; Boston/Newbury

POCOCKE, John & Mary (COLE) ALMY (1639-), w John; b 28 Jun 1677; Newport

POCOCK, John & Rebecca _?_ ; b 1689; Newport

POCOCK, Robert & _?_ ; b 13 Oct 1700; Newport

PODD, Samuel & Grace? _?_ (-1695, Ipswich); b 1687, ca 1641-5?; Ipswich

POD, Thomas & Sarah WARE; m int 22 Sep 1696; Boston

PODGER/PODYER?/PODYEARD?, John? & Jane _?_ ; b 1644, b 1646; Hingham

POLAND, James (ca 1632-) & 1/wf Mary BARNES, w Thomas; Salem

POLAND, James (-1695/6) & 2/wf Austice MANNING (-1704); Salem

POLAND, James & Rebecca KIMBOLE/KIMBALL; 12 Apr 1694, at Ipswich; Wenham/Ipswich

POLAND, John & Bethiah _?_ ; b 28 Nov 1656; Wenham

POLAND, John & Mary _?_ ; b 1671; Gravesend, LI

POLIN, John & Margery [DIKE], w Anthony; 1680; Salem

POLL/?POOLE, Edward & Elizabeth DAWES (1661-), dau John, m/2 Thomas HOLMES bef 1698/9; Boston

POLLARD, John (1644-) & 1/wf Deliverance [?WILLIS]; b 1666; Boston

POLLARD, John (1644-) & 2/wf Mary LEANARD/LEONARD, Bridgewater, Braintree; 24 Dec 1673; Taunton

POLLARD, Jonathan (1666-) & Mary WINSLOW; 26 Dec 1693; Boston

POLLARD, Samuel (1646-) & Mary [TAINTOR?]; b 1673; Boston

POLLARD, Thomas (-1724) & Sarah FARMER (-1725); - Nov 1692; Billerica

POLLARD, William (-1686) & Anne _?_ (1620/2-1725, in 105th y?); b 1644; Boston

POLLARD, William (1653-1690/1) & Margaret _?_ , ?m/2 Thomas POWELL ca 1691?; b 1687; Boston

POLEY/POLLE/POLLY, Edward & Mary [MERROW] (1673-), m/2 Edmund WOOLET; b 1696; Reading/Portsmouth, NH

POLLY, George & Elizabeth WINN; 21 May 1649; Woburn

POLLY, George & Mary KNIGHT; 24 Oct 1677; Woburn

POLLY, John (?1618-1689) & 1/wf Susanna [BACON]? (-30 Apr 1664); b 1650; Roxbury

POLLY, John (1618-1689) & 2/wf Mary [IVES] (1641-1666); b 1665; Roxbury

POLLY, John (1618-1689) & 3/wf Hannah COWDREY (-8 Jun 1684); 18 Sep 1667; Reading

POLLEY, John & Mary (EDWARDS) EVERETT, w Francis; 16 May 1681; Reading/Woburn

POLLY, John (1618-1689) & 4/wf Jane (METCALF)/BUTTERWORTH? WALKER (-1701), w Philip; 2 Jun 1684; Roxbury

POLLY, Samuel (1661/2-) & Priscilla [EAMES] (1663-); b 1689; Woburn

POMROY, Caleb (1641-1691), Northampton & Hepzibah BAKER (1646-1711), Windsor, CT, m/2 Walter LEE; 8 Mar 1664, 1664/5; Windsor, CT/Northampton

POMEROY, Ebenezer & 1/wf Hannah STRONG (1669-29 Nov 1691); 4 May 1691, 4 Mar 1690, 4 Mar 1691, 4 May 1690; Northampton

POMEROY, Ebenezer (1661-1754) & 2/wf Sarah KING (1671-1747); 26 Dec 1692, 22? Dec; Northampton

POMEROY, Eltweed (1585-1673) & 1/wf Joanna KEECH (1586-1620); Basminster, Eng, 4 May 1617, 1616; Dorchester/Windsor, CT

POMEROY, Eltweed & 2/wf Margery/Mary? ROCKETT (-5 Jul 1655); Crewhorne, Eng, 7 May 1629; Dorchester/Windsor, CT

POMROY, Eltweed (1585-1673) & 3/wf Lydia (BROWN) PARSONS (ca 1628, 1618-), w Thomas; 30 Nov 1660/1, 1661; Windsor, CT

PUMEROY, Francis & Mehitable ORCHARD; 7 Feb 1694; Boston

POMEREE, John (-1691) & Mary COWES, m John FOSTER 1696; 22 Jul 1674; Salem

POMREY, John & Sarah _?_ ; b 1684; Boston

POMROY, John (1662-1686) & Mindwell SHELDON, m John LYMAN 1687; 30 Apr 168[1?]; Northampton

POMEROY, Joseph (-1674) & Elizabeth _?_ (-1674); b 1672; Dover, NH

POMROY, Joseph (1652-), Lebanon, CT/Colchester & Hannah LYMAN (1660-1736); 20 Jun 1677, 26 Jun; Westfield

POMEROY, Joseph (1672-1712) & Hannah SEYMOUR, m/2 Josiah HALE 1713, 1715?; 29 Nov 1692; Suffield, CT/Colchester, CT/Northampton/Suffield, CT

POMROY, Joshua (1646-1689) & 1/wf Elizabeth LYMAN (-22 May?, 22 Mar? 1676); 20 Aug 1672; Northampton

PUMRY, Joshua (-1689) & 2/wf Abigail COOK, m/2 David HOYT bef 1691, m/3 Nathaniel ROYCE 1708; 9 Jan 1676, 1676/7; Northampton/Deerfield

PUMRY, Joshua (-1714 & 1/wf Sarah LENNARD (-1702); 1 May 1700, 1701?; Deerfield/Dorchester

POMROY, Medad (1638-1716) & 1/wf Experience WOODWARD (-1686); 21 Nov 1661, 26? Nov, 13? Nov; Northampton/Deerfield

POMROY, Medad (-1716) & 2/wf Abigail (STRONG) CHAUNCEY (?1645-1704), w Nathaniel; 8 Sep 1686; ?Northampton/Windsor, CT

POMERY, Orpheus (-1683) & Mary __?__; Portsmouth, RI

POMEROY, Richard & Deliverance BERRY; 14 Feb 1697/8; Dover, NH

POMEROY, Samuel (1669-1748) & 1/wf Elizabeth FRENCH (1669-); ca 1690; Deerfield

PUMMERY, Thomas & Rebecca BROOKING, m/2 Clement RUMMERILL 1687, m/3 Thomas ROUSE, m/4 George ALSTON; b 1700, b 1679, by 1679, b 4 Jun 1679; Portsmouth, NH

POMEROY, William & Elizabeth __?__; b Oct 1683; Isles of Shoals

POMEROY, __?__ & [Agnes GERRISH], m/2 __?__ MATHES

POMFRET, William & 1/wf Hosanna __?__; b 1640, b 1630?; Dover, NH

POMFRET, William (-1680) & Rose __?__ (-living in 1675); aft 1640; Dover, NH

POND, Caleb & Priscilla [COLBURN]; b 1696; Dedham

POND, Daniel[2] (-1698) & 1/wf Abigail [SHEPARD] (1631-1661); b 1652; Dedham

POND, Daniel (-1698) & 2/wf Ann EDWARDS (-1732, ae 92 y); 18 Sep 1661; Dedham

POND, Daniel (1663-) & Tabitha [EDWARDS] (1673-), Reading; b 1690; Dedham

POND, Ephraim & Deborah HAWS/HAWES (1666-), m/2 Thomas BACON; 6 Jan 1685, 1685/6; Wrentham

POND, Isaac (1645-1669) & Hannah GRIFFEN (1649-); 10 May 1667, 20 May, 1 May; Windsor, CT

POND, Jabez (1677-1749) & 1/wf Mary GAY (1677-1731); 11 Jan 1698/9; Dedham

POND, John, Wrentham & 1/wf Hannah HILL (-1692, 1691?), Sherborn; 30 Sep 1686; Wrentham

POND, John & 2/wf Rachel [STOW] (-1695?); b 1693(4?); Wrentham

POND, John & 3/wf Judith __?__; b 1699; Wrentham

POND, Nathaniel (1676-1716) & 1/wf Elizabeth [SLASON]/SLAWSON (1673-1711); b 1698; Branford, CT

POND, Robert[1] (-1637) & Mary __?__, m/2 Edward SHEPARD; b 1631?; Dorchester

POND, Robert (-1660/3) & Mary [BALL]/BULL? (-1719), m/2 Nicholas ELLEN 1663, m/3 Daniel HENSHAW b 1671; b 1651, b 1657; Milton/Dorchester

POND, Robert (1667-1750) & 1/wf Joanna [LAWRENCE]? (-1726+); b 1689; Wrentham

POND, Samuel (-1655) & Sarah [WARE] (no), m/2 John LINSLEY 1655; 18 Nov 1642; Windsor, CT

POND, Samuel (1648-) & Miriam BLAKESLEE/BLATCHLEY (1652-); 3 Feb 1669, 1669/70, 5 Jan 1669; Branford, CT

POND, William (-1690) & Mary [DYER] (-1711); ca 1640?, b 1657; Dorchester

PONDER, John (-1712) & Temperance BUCKLAND (1642-1732); 26 Jun 1668, at Hartford; Windsor, CT/Westfield

PONTUS, William (-1653, Plymouth) & Wybra HANSON; Leyden, Holland, 4 Dec 1610; Plymouth/Duxbury

POOLE, Daniel & Sarah [SOLART] (28 in 1682); 1682

POOLE, Edward & ?1/wf Mary [LANE]? (not certain that m took place); ca 1641?; Weymouth

POOLE, Edward (1609-1664) & ?2/wf Sarah [PINNEY]; betw 1641 & 1645, by 1635?, aft 1642?; Weymouth

POOLL, Isaac & 1/wf Elishama __?__; b 1669; Weymouth/Dighton

POOL, Isaac & 2/wf Margaret/Bethia __?__; aft 1680, b 1701

POOLE, John (-1667) & Margaret __?__ (-1662); b 1632-3(?), b 1634; Cambridge/Reading

POOLE/POLE, John (1630/39-1707/12) & Elizabeth BENTON/BRENTON (1650-1694); 28 Mar 1672; Taunton/Dorchester/Boston

POOLE, John & Elizabeth _?_ ; b 1679; Weymouth
POOLE, John (-1721, Lynn) & Mary GOODING/GOODWIN? (1671-1702), m/2 Timothy OSGOOD of Andover; 17 Nov 1686; Reading
POOLE, John & 2/wf Joanna [SMITH]; b 1687; Weymouth
POOL, John (1670-1727) & 1/wf Susan (HASKELL) [WOODBURY] (1661-1716), w Richard; b 1694; Beverly/Gloucester/Rockport
POOLL, Jonathan (1634-1678) & Judith JACOB/JACOBS (no) (-1704), m/2 William HASEY 1681, ?1678; b 1656; Reading
POOLL, Jonathan (-1723) & Bridget [FITCH] (1669-1723); 3 Dec 1692, 1691?; Reading
POOLL, Joseph (-1706) & 1/wf Elizabeth [SHAW] (1656-), m/2 Peter HOLBROOK, m/3 Robert WEARE; b 1674; Weymouth
POOLE, Joseph & 2/wf Mary _?_ ; b 1690; Weymouth
POOL, Matthew & Sarah (_?_) BLAKE, w John, m/3 James MIRICK 1711; 29 May 1694; Boston/Watertown
POOLE, Samuel (retd to Eng) & [Silence SAXTON]; b 1642; Boston
POOLL, Samuel (-1669) & Mary [FRENCH], m/2 John LAMB by 1677; b 1668; Weymouth
POOLL, Samuel (1671-) & Mary [PARKER] (1679?-), dau Hananiah, m/2 John SOUTHER 1705; 19 Nov 1690; Reading
POOL, Thomas (?1673-1732) & Rebecca BOUTWELL; 18 Jun 1695; Reading
POOLE, William (1595-1675) & [Jane/Mary? GREENE]; ca 1636/7; b 1639; Taunton
POOLE, William & Judith _?_, ?m/2 Robert GOULD 1687?, 1689+?; ca 1678; Hull
POOLE, William & Mary _?_
POER, Benjamin & Mary (FOGG) HARDY (-1707), w George; 13 Apr 1696; Newbury
PORE, Daniel (1624-1689) & Mary FARNUM (-1714, ae 85); 20 Oct 1650, at Boston; Andover
POOR, Daniel (1656-1735) & Mehitable OSGOOD (1671-); 25 Apr 1688; Andover
POER, Edward (-1743) & Elizabeth _?_ ; b 1688; Newbury
POORE, Henry (1650-) & Abigail HALE (1662-); 12 Sep 1679; Newbury
POOR, John[1] (-1684) & Sarah _?_ (-1702); b 1642; Newbury
POORE, John[2] (1642-1701) & Mary TITCOMB (1643-); 27 Feb 1665; Newbury
POOR, John (1636-1686) & 1/wf Sarah BROWN (-1677); 13 Mar 1660/1; Charlestown/Hampton, NH
POOR, John (1636-1686) & 2/wf Elizabeth (BURRAGE) DEANE, w Thomas; 12 Aug 1680; Charlestown
POORE, Joseph & 1/wf Mary WALLINGTON/WALLINGFORD (1663-); 6 Aug 1680; Newbury
POER, Joseph & Anna JOHNSON, Haverhill; 15 Mar 1677/8, m int; Newbury
POOR, Samuel (-1683) & [Rebecca?] _?_ (-mentioned in will); b 1649; Newbury
POORE, Samuel (1653-1727) & Rachel BAILEY (1662-living in 1754); 16 Feb 1679, 1679/80?; Newbury
POOR, Walter & Elizabeth [LANE] (1646-); b 1669; Hingham/Boston
POPE, Benjamin (1653-1702) & Damaris SHATTUCK (1653-); b 1682?; Salem
POPE, Ephraim (-1676/7) & ?Elizabeth/?Ann [HARONETT] [BACON]; ca 1649?, b 1655; Boston
POPE, Isaac & Alice [MIND] (1658-1755), Freeman; b 1687; Dartmouth
POPE, John, Sr. (-1649, 1646?) & Jane _?_ (-1662/3); b 1635, b 1630?; Dorchester
POPE, John, Jr. (-1686) & 1/wf Alice _?_ ; b 1643; Dorchester
POPE, John (-1686) & 2/wf Margaret _?_ (1628-1702); b 1658; Dorchester
POPE, John (-1713) & Elizabeth _?_ ; ca 1670/80?; Southampton, LI/Elizabeth, NJ
POPE, John (1658-1698) & Beatrice/Beatrix HAUGHTON (1665-1700+) (dau Beatrix m Elias SAWYER); 20 Sep 1683, 30 Sep; Lancaster
POPE, John (1675-) & 1/wf Elizabeth BOURNE (-1715); 2 Jan 1699/1700; Sandwich
POPE, Joseph (-1666/7) & 1/wf Damaris _?_ (-1653+); b 1643; Salem
POPE, Joseph (-1666/7) & 2/wf Gertrude [SHATTUCK?] (-1699+); b 1643?, aft 1653; Salem
POPE, Joseph (1650-1712) & Bathshua [FOLGER] (-1726+); b 1678, 1679?; Salem
POPE, Ralph (1674-), Dorchester & Rachel NEALE; ?24 Mar 1697/8, ?25 Mar 1698; Braintree
POPE, Richard (-1694) & Sarah _?_ ; b 1685?, by 1688; Winter Harbor, ME/ Saco, ME/Kittery, ME
POPE, Samuel & 1/wf Exercise SMITH; 28 Jan 1685, 1685/6; Salem
POPE, Seth (1648-1727) & 1/wf Deborah [PERRY] (1654-1711); b 1675; Sandwich/Dartmouth
POPE, Thomas[1] (1608-1683, ?Dartmouth) & 1/wf Anne FALLOWELL (-bef 29 May 1646); 28 Jul 1637; ?Plymouth

POPE, Thomas (-bef 1677?) & [Mary] _?_ ; b 1641?; Stamford, CT/Hempstead, LI/Southampton, LI/Elizabeth, NJ

POPE, Thomas[1] (1608-1683) & 2/wf Sarah JENNEY; 29 May 1646; ?Plymouth

POPE, Thomas (1643-) & 1/wf [Elizabeth MERRIFIELD], dau Henry; b 1670; Dorchester

POPE, Thomas & 2/wf Margaret LONG (-1688), wid; 18 Nov 1681; Dorchester/Suffield, CT

POPE, Thomas (?1677(wrong)-), mariner & 1/wf Elizabeth MANSER (1672-); 3 Dec 1687; Charlestown

POPE, Walter & Eleanor _?_ , m/2 Richard MILLER, ca 1639; b 1640, b 1631?; Charlestown

POPE, William & Mary _?_ ; b 1692; Marlborough

POPE, _?_ & Elizabeth (GEORGE) GLAZIER, w John; aft 7 Apr 1691, bef 1695, b 1 May 1693; Charlestown

POPLEY, James & Barbara LEGORWELL; 23 Oct 1675; Charlestown

PORDAGE, George & Elizabeth [LYNDE] (1662-1746); b 1684(5?); Boston

PORMORT/PERMORT?/PURMORT, Joseph (1650-bef 1691) & Hannah [WOODY]/[WOODIS]; by 1675/80?, b Jun 1681; New Castle, NH

PORMONT, Lazarus (1636-) & _?_ ; b 1676; Dover, NH

PORMORT, Philemon & 1/wf Susan BELLINGHAM (-1642); 11 Oct 1627; Boston/Exeter, NH/Wells, ME

PORMORT, Philemon & 2/wf Elizabeth _?_ ; b 1653, b 1650?; Boston

PORTER, Abel & Anne/Hannah [SIMMONS], wid; b 1643; Boston

PORTER, Benjamin & Sarah _?_ , m/2 Edmund SCOTT 1689; Waterbury, CT

PORTER, Daniel (-1690) & Mary _?_ ; Farmington, CT

PORTER, Daniel (-1726/7) & Deborah [HOLCOMB] (1674-1765); b 1699; Waterbury, CT

PORTER, Edward (-1677) & 1/wf Elizabeth/Anna? _?_ ; b 1633; Roxbury/Boston

PORTER, Edward (-1677) & Rhoda (_?_) (GORE) REMINGTON, w John, w John, m/4 Joshua TIDD

PORTER, Edward & Abigail/Abia/Abial ARNOLD/EARLY; m int 8 Jan 1695/6; Boston

PORTER, Experience (1676-1750) & Abigail WILLIAMS (1674-1765); 26 May 1698; Hadley/Roxbury/Mansfield, CT

PORTER, Hezekiah (1665-1752) & 1/wf Hannah COWLES; 20 May 1686; Hadley/E. Hartford, CT

PORTER, Hezekiah & Mary BUELL; 27 Jun 1700; Windsor, CT

PORTER, Ichabod (1678-) & Dorcas MARSH (-1746); 4 Jul 1700; Hadley

PORTER, Israel & Elizabeth HATHORNE; 20 Nov 1672; Salem

PORTER, James & Sarah TUDOR (1652-); 15 Jan 1679; Windsor, CT

PORTER, John (-1674) & Margaret [ODDING], w George; ca 1610/15, in Eng, div 1665; Roxbury

PORTER, John (1594-1648), Messing, Eng/Pelsted & Anna/Rose WHITE (1600-1647, 1648); 18 Oct 1620, Messing, Eng; Windsor, CT

PORTER, John (1696±-1676) & Mary [?GARDNER] (-1684, 1684/5); ca 1623-30?; Hingham/Salem

PORTER, John (1628-1688) & Mary [STANLEY] (1629-1688); b 1651; Windsor, CT/Hadley

PORTER, John (-1717) & Deliverance BIRAM/BYRAM (-1720); 9 Apr 1660, 9 Feb 1660; Weymouth/Marshfield

PORTER, John, Jr. (1651-1699) & Joanna GAYLORD (1653-1716?); 16 Dec 1669, 1669; Windsor, CT

PORTER, John & Joanna _?_ ; b 1670; Boston

PORTER, John & Herodias (LONG) (HICKS) [GARDINER], (div) w John, w George; b 1673, ca 1665; Kingston, RI/Weymouth

PORTER, John (1658-1733) & Lydia [HERRICK] (1661, 1666-1738); b 1687, b 1681?; Wenham/Salem

PORTER, John (1666-1747) & 1/wf Mary BUTLER (1670-1706+); 3 Apr 1690; Hadley/Lebanon, CT/Hebron, CT

PORTER, John & ?Mercy/Mary [CARVER] (1672-1709); b 1694; Weymouth/Marshfield

PORTER, John (1662-) & Rebecca WOODFORD; 2 Jan 1696, 1695/6; Farmington, CT

PORTER, John & Mary TITHARTON (1676-); 8 Oct 1696; Stratford, CT

PORTER, John & Mary DRAKE; 23 Sep 1697; Windsor, CT

PORTER, Jonathan (-1660) & Eunice _?_ , m/2 Giles SMITH; b 1632?; Beverly/Salem/Huntington, LI

PORTER, Joseph (1638-1714) & Anna/Ann?/Anne? HATORNE/HATHORNE (1643-1712?); 27 Jan 1664, 1664/5; Salem

PORTER, Joseph (-1741, ae 66) & Hannah BUELL (1674-1761), Killingworth; 5 Dec 1699; Killingworth, CT/Windsor, CT
PORTER, Joshua (-1675) & Mary FIELD; 2 Oct 1663; Hadley/Northampton
PORTER, Nathaniel (1640-) & 1/wf Hannah/Anna? GROVES (-1671?, 1672?); b 1667; Windsor, CT/Stratford, CT
PORTER, Nathaniel (-1679) & 2/wf Elizabeth BALDWIN (1649-1683(4?)); 1671?, aft 1673?, b 1674; Windsor, CT/Stratford
PORTER, Nathaniel/Nathan? (1660-1709, 1710?) & Deborah BUELL/BUSH (1665-1712); ?1700, ?18 Nov 1711, b 1704, 1700; Lebanon
PORTER, Nathaniel (1672-) & Rebecca (WHEELER)/Ruth WOODRUFF; b 1700, b 18 Jul 1699; Windsor, CT
PORTER, Nehemiah (1656-1722) & Hannah LUM (±1664-), Woodbury; 21 Jan 1686/7; Farmington, CT
PORTER, Nicholas (1672-) & Bathsheba [REED]; b 1699; Weymouth/Marshfield
PORTER, Richard (-1689) & [Ruth?] __?__ (no evidence); b 1639; Weymouth
PORTER, Richard (1658-) & Ruth [HOLCOMB] (-1710); b 1688, b 1686; Farmington, CT/Waterbury, CT
PORTER, Robert (-1689) & 1/wf Mary SCOTT; 7 Nov 1644; Hartford
PORTER, Robert (-1689) & 2/wf Hannah (ATWOOD/AUTWOOD) FREEMAN, w Stephen, m/3 [?John] CLARK by 1690; aft 1666; Farmington, CT
PORTER, Robert & Sarah BURT (-1689); 21 May 1688; Deerfield/Northampton
PORTER, Roger (1584-) & 1/wf __?__ ; b 1638, ca 1615/24?; Watertown
PORTER, Roger (1584-1654) & Grace (MAKEN) (SHERMAN) (ROGERS) ROGERS (1592-1662), wid, calls John COOLIDGE brother; aft 12 Nov 1638; Watertown
PORTER, Samuel (-1660) & Hannah [DODGE] (1642-1689), m/2 Thomas WOODBURY 1661; b 1658; Salem
PORTER, Samuel (1635-1689) & Hannah STANLEY (-1708); ca 1659; Hartford/Hadley/Hatfield
PORTER, Samuel (1660-1722) & 1/wf Joanna COOK (1665-1713); 22 Feb 1683, 1683/4?; Hadley
PORTER, Samuel & Martha FREEMAN (?1663-living 1715); 18 Feb 1685; Farmington, CT
PORTER, Samuel (1669-1749) & 1/wf Judith DORMAN (?1675-1721?); 14 Jan 1695/6; Salem/Topsfield
PORTER, Samuel & Mary [NASH] (1675-); b 1699, ca 1698; Weymouth
PORTER, Samuel & Martha FREEMAN; 18 Feb 1685; Farmington, CT
PORTER, Samuel & Love [HOWE]; b 1701?; Salem
PORTER, Thomas (-1697) & Sarah HART; 20 Nov 1644; Hartford/Farmington, CT
PORTER, Thomas (1648-1711) & Lois STANLEY (1645-1711+); b 1670, b 1 Dec 1670; Farmington, CT
PORTER, Thomas & Sarah [VINING]; b 1673; Weymouth
PORTER, Thomas (1650-1718?) & Abigail COWLES; May 1678; Farmington, CT
PORTER, Thomas & Abigail HOLBROOK (1675-); b 1696; Weymouth
PORTER, Timothy & Susanna/Juanah BULL (1679-1743); 22 Apr 1697; Farmington, CT/Deerfield
PORTER, William & Grace [PITTS], m/2 Thomas OXFORD; b 1670; ?Boston
PORTER, William & Elizabeth [HAWKINS]; b 1673; Boston
PORTER, William & Elizabeth GALE; 31 Jan 1694; Boston
PORTER, William (-1713), Haddam, CT, & Sarah CHURCH (1670-), m/2 __?__ VENTRUS; 3 Dec 1697; Hadley/Haddam, CT
PORTER, __?__ & Hannah __?__ , had Hannah b 12 Jul 1693; b 1693; Boston
PORTIS, Robert & Alice GREENWOOD; 3 Nov 1659; Boston
POSMORE, James & Alice __?__ ; b 1642; Concord
POST, Abraham (?1629, ?1640-1705) & Mary [JORDAN] (ca 1640-1684); 1663; Saybrook, CT
POST, Abraham (-1705) & 2/wf Lydia (BROWN) (LORD) DUNK (-in or bef 1699); aft 1684
POST, Abraham (1669-1748) & Hudah __?__ /Elizabeth STEPHENS (1672-); 1689(?), b 1691, 7 Apr 1692; Saybrook, CT
POST, Daniel & Mary [RUTTY] (1679-); 29 Aug 1699; Killingworth, CT?/Saybrook
POST, James (1671-) & Sarah DOUGLAS; 29 Jan 1700; Saybrook
POST, Jeremiah & __?__ (did he marry?); b 1701?; Southampton, LI/Hempstead
POST, John (1626, 1627-1710, ae 84) & Hester/Esther HYDE (-1703); March 1652, March the last, 10 Mar 1653; Saybrook, CT/Norwich, CT
POST, John (-1687) & Mary [HALSEY], dau Isaac; 3 Nov 1678; Southampton

POST, John (1657-1690) & Sarah REYNOLDS (1656-1703); 24 Dec 1685; Norwich, CT
POST, Joseph (1649-1723) & Sarah _?_ ; ca 1670-80?, no issue; Southampton, LI
POST, Richard (1617-1689±) & Dorothy [JOHNSON?]/ORGRAVE? (-1694); ca 1640-45?; New London, CT/Southampton, LI
POST, Richard (1627-) & 1/wf Susanna SUTTON; 27 Feb 1650, 1649/50, 27 Dec 1649 (wrong); Woburn
POST, Richard (1627-1675) & 2/wf Mary TYLER, m/2 John BRIDGES 1678; 18 Nov 1662; Woburn
POST, Samuel (1668-) & Ruth LATHROP; 17 Mar 1697/8; Norwich, CT
POST, Stephen (-1659) & Eleanor [CHANDLER]? (-1670); in Eng, b 1627; Cambridge/Hartford/Saybrook
POST, Stephen (1664-) & Hannah HOSMER (1670-); ca 1690, 14 Jun 1692; Hebron, CT
POST, Thomas (-1701) & 1/wf Mary ANDREWS (-1661); Jan 1656; Norwich, CT
POST, Thomas (-1691) & Elizabeth [BEAL]; b 1661; Cambridge
POST, Thomas (-1701) & 2/wf Rebecca BRUEN (-1721); Sep 1663, 2 Sep; Norwich, CT
POST, [Abraham] (-1708) & Lydia (BUCKLAND) (BROWN) LORD, w William BROWN, w William LORD; aft 1682, aft Mar 1684; Saybrook
POST, William (-1703) & Allshe _?_ ; Maspath Kill, LI
POST, _?_ & Judith _?_ (-1682, ae 57, Cambridge)
POTE/POTEY, Thomas & Elizabeth (BILLINGTON) (BULLOCH) BEERE
POAT, William (1640-) & Hannah GREENFEILD (-15 Oct 1688); 4 Oct 1688; Marblehead
POAT, William (1640-1696?) & Ann (GREENFIELD) HOOPER, w Robert; 7 Aug 1689; Marblehead
POTTER, Abel (-1692) & Rachel WARNER (-1724); 16 Nov 1669; Warwick, RI
POTTER, Anthony & 1/wf Elizabeth [WHIPPLE] (-1641)
POTTER, Anthony (1627/8-1690) & 2/wf Elizabeth [STONE] (1629-1712); b 1653; Cambridge/Ipswich
POTTER, Anthony & Martha DRESSER; 11 Jul 1695; Ipswich
POTTER, Edmund (1654-1702) & Abigail [WELLS] (1662-); b 1680; Ipswich
POTTER, Edmund & Elizabeth STONE?; b 1683
POTTER, George (-1640, Portsmouth) & _?_ , m/2 Nicholas NILES by 1640; ca 1638?; Portsmouth, RI
POTTER, Humphrey & _?_ ; b 1640; Salem
POTTER, Ichabod (?1639-1676) & Martha [HAZARD], m/2 Benjamin MOWRY 1676?; ca 1651?, b 1657; Portsmouth, RI
POTTER, Ichabod (?1657-1730) & Margaret [HOLME] (1679-1727(-)); ca 1700?; Portsmouth, RI
POTTER, Inigo (1636-) & Mary LAWRENCE (-1687); 25 Aug 1663; Charlestown
POTTER, John (-1643) & Elizabeth [?WOODS], m/2 Edward PARKER 1646, m/3 Robert ROSE 1664?; 14 Apr 1630?, b 1634, b 1636; New Haven
POTTER, John (1636-1706) & 1/wf Hannah [COOPER] (1638-1695); b 1662; New Haven
POTTER, John (1642±-1694), ?Portsmouth, RI, & 1/wf Ruth FISHER, ?Portsmouth, RI; 2 Jun 1664; Warwick, RI
POTTER, John (-1706, 1707, ae 70) & Mary (HITCHCOCK) RUSSELL (-1706), w Ralph; 29 Dec 1679; New Haven
POTTER, John (1652-1718) & Sarah [KIMBALL?/?FELLOWS] (1661-1724); b 1680; Ipswich/N. Brookfield
POTTER, John & Sarah (WRIGHT) COLLINS, w Eleazer; 7 Jan 1684/5; Warwick, RI
POTTER, John (1665-1715) & Sarah [WILSON] (1666-1739+); b 1692, ca 1690; Kings Town, RI/?N. Kingston, RI
POTTER, John & Elizabeth HOLT/HALL (-1718); 23 Feb 1691/2; New Haven
POTTER, John & Elizabeth NORWOOD; 27 May 1692, 24 May; Lynn/Lancaster
POTTER, John (1661-1711) & Jane [BURLINGAME]?, m/2 Edward POTTER; b 1698; Warwick, RI/?Boston
POTTER, John & Jane _?_ ; b 1695; Boston
POTTER, John & Sarah SELLICK (1670-); 30 Aug 1698; Stamford, CT
POTTER, Joseph (1635-1669) & [Phebe] [IVES]/?REACY, m/2 John ROSE 1670+; b 1631; New Haven
POTTER, Judah & 1/wf Grace BROOKS; 2 Dec 1686, 6 Dec; Concord
POTTER, Luke (-1697) & 1/wf Mary _?_ (-1644); b 1640; Concord

POTTER, Luke (-1696) & 2/wf Mary **EDMUNDS**; 19 Oct 1644; Concord/Charlestown

POTTER, Marmaduke & Abigail **CHATFIELD**; 18 Jan 1671; Killingworth, CT

POTTER, Nathaniel (-1644?) & Dorothy ? (1617-), m/2 John **ALBRO**; b 1637; Portsmouth, RI

POTTER, Nathaniel (1637-1704) & Elizabeth [**STOKES**] (-1704+); b 1665, b 1669; Portsmouth, RI

POTTER, Nathaniel & Elizabeth **HOWES/HAWES**; 1 Apr 1675; New Haven

POTTER, Nathaniel (1669?-1736) & [Joan **WILBUR**] (1668-1759); b 1689; Little Compton, RI

POTTER, Nicholas (-1677) & 1/wf Emma/[?Em]/Elizabeth [?**KNIGHT**]; b 1636; Salem/N. Brookfield

POTTER, Nicholas (-1677) & 2/wf Alice [**PLASSE**] **WEEKS** (1630-1658/9), w Thomas; aft Jun 1656; Salem/N. Brookfield

POTTER, Nicholas (-1677) & 3/wf Mary **GEDNEY**; aft 1659, b 1661, b 12 Jan 1661/2; Salem/Lynn

POTTER, Robert (-1653, Roxbury) & 1/wf Isabel [?**ANTHONY**]; b 1630; Lynn/Newport/Rowley/Warwick, RI/Boston

POTTER, Robert (-1656?) & 2/wf Sarah ? (-1686), m/2 John **SANFORD** 1657; aft 1643; Lynn/etc./RI

POTTER, Robert & 1/wf ? ; b 1657; Lynn

POTTER, Robert & 2/wf Ruth **DRIVER**; 25 Jan 1659/60; Lynn

POTTER, Robert & Martha **HALLE/HALL** (1660-1709); 9 Jan 1681, 1681/2; Lynn

POTTER, Robert & Elizabeth [**COLE**]; b 1688; RI

POTTER, Robert (?1676-1745) & [Elizabeth **WELLS**]; South Kings Town, RI/N. Kingston, RI

POTTER, Samuel, Wallingford, Branford, Newark, NJ, & 1/wf Anna **RUSSELL** (1650-1676, Wallingford); 21 Nov 1670; New Haven

POTTER, Samuel & 2/wf ? ; 4 Dec 1676; Wallingford, CT

POTTER, Samuel (1648-1676) & Sarah **RIGHT/WRIGHT** (1653-), m/2 Joshua **SKYRE/(SAWYER?)** 1677/8; 8 Jan 1673; Concord

POTTER, Samuel & 1/wf Joanna [**WOOD**]; b 1685; Ipswich

POTTER, Samuel & 2/wf Ruth **DUNTON** (-1706); 18 Apr 1692; Ipswich

POTTER, Samuel (1669-1693) & Rebecca [**TRASK**] (1674-), m/2 Joseph **BOYCE** 1694?, m/3 Benjamin **VERY**; b 1693; Salem

POTTER, Samuel (1675-1748) & Mary ? ; b 1701; Dartmouth

POTTER, Thomas & Ann ? ; b 1664; Newport

POTTER, Thomas (-1728) & Susanna **TRIPP** (1667-); 20 Jan 1686, 1687; S. Kingston, RI/Portsmouth, RI/N. Kingston, RI

POTTER, Thomas & Mary **KIMBALL**; 16 Jun 1696, m int 16 Jun 1695; Ipswich

POTTER, William (1608-1662) & Frances ? (1609-); in Eng, b 1633, b 1635; ?(Watertown)/New Haven

POTTER, William (1610-1654) & Judith (?**ALLARD**) **GRAVES** (-1683, Roxbury), w John; 2 Jun 1646; Roxbury

POTTER, William (-1685) & ? ; b 1650?, b 1627?; Stamford, CT

POTTER, William (-1720+) & Ann [**DURFEE**] (1661-1731); b 1692; ?Portsmouth, RI

POTTER, William & [?Ann **TALLMAN**] (1670?-); b 1701?; see Stephen **BRAYTON**

POTTER, ? & Hanna ? , m/2 ? **BEECHER**; in Eng

POTTER, ? & Rachel [**PECK**] (1655-), Boston

POTTER, ? & Mary [**TRIPP**] (1670-), Portsmouth, RI; b 1716, b 1701?

POTTER, ? & Mary [**SHERMAN**] (1670)

POTTLE, Christopher (1663-1710) & Hannah **GRAVES** (1668-1710+); 12 Mar 1693/4; Ipswich

POTTS, Richard (-1676), Casco Bay & Margaret [**DAVIS**], w William; b 1670, b 24 Jun 1661; Dover, NH

POTTS, Thomas (son Richard) & Joanna **ROBERTS**; 24 Mar 1689/90; Dover, NH

POTTS, William, Newcastle, Eng, & Rebecca **AVERY** (1756, 1656-); 5 Aug 1678; New London, CT/Groton, CT

POTWIN/POTWINE, John (-1700) & Sarah [**HILL/HULL**]; b 1698; Boston

POULTER, John[1] & Mary ? , m/2 John **PARKER** 1654+, m/3 Thomas **CHAMBERLAIN** 1674; in Eng, b 1633; Billerica

POULTER, John (1635-1676) & Rachel **ELIOT** (1643-1723), Braintree, m/2 John **WHITMORE** ca 1677; 29 Dec 1662; Billerica

POULTER, John (1666-1744) & Hannah [HAMMOND] (1669-), Watertown; b 1696; Cambridge/ Boston

POULTER, Jonathan (1669-1708) & Elizabeth [?COOLIDGE]; b 1692; Lexington

POWLLEN/? POLAND/? POWLAND/POWSLAND/POWSLEY/POWLTON/? POUSLAND/POUSLIN/ POUSLY, James & Mary BARNES, w Thomas; 2 Aug 1670; Salem

POULDON/POLAND, Maxmilian & Mary VODEN, ?m/2 Richard PALMER; 2 Jun 1694, 27 Jul 1694; Salem

POWLING/POUSLAND?/?POLAND/POLIN?, James & Austice MANNING (1651-29 Oct 1704+); Salem (did they live in New Eng?)

POWSLAND, Thoms & Grace STASEY alias COAZE; 27 Aug 1699; Marblehead

POWLLEN/POUSLAND?, James & Mary BARNES, w Thomas; 2 Aug 1670; Salem

POUSLAND/POWSLAND/POWSLEY/POUTLAND, Richard & Dorothy _?_ ; b 1674?, b 1693; Falmouth, ME

POWSLAND, Thomas & Grace STASEY alias COAZE, w Michael COWES; 27 Aug 1699; Marblehead

POWELL, Arthur & Sarah MEKUSETT; 18 Jan 1693/4, 17 Jan 1693?; Braintree/Boston

POWELL, John (-1668) & Sarah SALLIE, m/2 John BLANEY 1672; 20 May 1667; Charlestown

POWELL, Michael (-1673) & Abigail [BEDLE]; b 1637?, b 1641; Dedham/Boston

POWELL, Ralph & Martha (DEANE) CLEMENT, w James; 30 Oct 1676; Marshfield

POWELL, Robert (1636-) & Mary [MORE]/MOORE (1638±-); b 1660(1?), b 22 Jan 1660/[1?]; Ipswich/?Exeter, NH

POWELL, Rowland & Isabella _?_ ; b 1657(8?); Gloucester

POWELL, Rowland & Elizabeth [TRUEMAN?]; b 1685; Lebanon, CT

POWELL, Thomas (-1681) & Priscilla [?WHITSON]; b 1641; New Haven

POWELL, Thomas (1641-1721) & 1/wf [Abigail WOODS]; ca 1663/4; ?Westbury, LI/Bethpage, LI

POWELL, Thomas (-1685) & Alse GRAHAM/TRAHORN (-1687, Springfield); 25 Aug 1676, 1675?; Windsor, CT

POWELL, Thomas (1641-1721), Huntington & 2/wf Elizabeth (TOWNSEND) PHILIPS, w Theophilus; 2 Nov 1690; Westbury, LI

POWELL, Thomas (1670-1731) & Mary WILLETS (1671-); 6 Nov 1691; Bethpage, LI

POWELL, Thomas & Margaret [POLLARD], w William; b 1692; Boston

POWELL, Thomas (retd to Eng) & Elizabeth _?_ (-1644); b 1637; Charlestown

POWELL, William & Sarah FRANCIS; 26 Feb 1690/1; Wethersfield, CT

POWERS, Isaac (ca 1665-) & 1/wf Abigail [WHITMORE] (1678-); b 1700; Littleton

POWER, John & Sarah _?_ ; b 1643; Charlestown

POWER, Nicholas (-1657) & Jane _?_ (-1667+); b 1652; Providence

POWERS, Nicholas (-1675) & Rebecca RHODES, m/2 Daniel WILLIAMS 1676; 2 Feb 1671/2, 3 Feb; Providence

POWER, Nicholas (1673-1734) & 1/wf Mary [HALE]; b 1696; Swansea

POWER, Nicholas (1673-1734) & 2/wf Mercy [TILLINGHAST] (1680-1769); 1699(?)

POWER, Thomas (1667-1707+) & 1/wf Elizabeth _?_ (-1698); b 1690?, b 1692; Concord

POWER, Walter (ca 1639-1708?) & Trial SHEPARD (1641-1708+); 11 Mar 1659/60; Malden/Concord

POWER, Walter (1674-1738), Concord & Rebecca BARET/BARRETT (1673, 1670-1750); 16 Dec 1696; Chelmsford

POWER, William (1661-1710) & Mary BAUK?/?BANK (1670-); b 1694, ca 1688?; Concord

POWNALL, Henry & Rebecca (_?_) LEIGH, w John; b 1692; Charlestown

POWENING/POWNING, Henry & Elizabeth _?_ (-1724, ae 95); b 1651; Boston

PRATT, Aaron (?1654-1736) & 1/wf Sarah [PRATT] (1664-1700); ca 1685?; Hingham

PRATT, Abraham (-1644) & Joanna/Mary _?_ (-1644); ca 1628?, no ch; Roxbury/Charlestown/ etc.

PRATT, Benajah (-1682) & Persis DUNHAM (1641-1691+), m/2 Jonathan SHAW 1683; 29 Nov 1655; Plymouth

PRATT, Benajah & Mary [LASSELL], w Joshua; b 1695; Plymouth

PRATT, Daniel (-1691) & Hannah [WARNER] (1632-1682); ca 1648; Hartford

PRATT, Daniel & _?_ ;

PRATT, Daniel (-1703) & Elizabeth LEE, m/2 John SHELDON 1708; 10 Mar 1691/2; Hartford

PRATT, Daniel & Esther [WRIGHT]; b 1701; Plympton

PRATT, Ebenezer & Mary [FLAGG]; b 1693; Sherborn

PRATT, Ebenezer & Martha _?_ ; ca 1700; Weymouth
PRATT, Ebenezer (1669-1718) & Mehitable/?Mabel _?_ ; b 1701?; Oyster Bay, LI
PRATT, Eleazer & Hannah **KANEDY/KENNEDY**; 22 Sep 1697; Plymouth
PRATT, Ephraim (1675±-1748) & Phebe _?_ (-1736); b 1698, (ca 1695?); Weymouth
PRATT, Ephraim & Elizabeth _?_ ; b 1700(1?), [ca 1699]; Sudbury
PRATT, Jabez & Elizabeth **COBB**; 23 Feb 1697/8; Taunton
PRATT, John & _?_ ; in Eng, b 1629; Cambridge (retd to Eng, no ch)
PRATT, John (-1647?) & Mary? [**WHITMAN?**], dau John, m/2 William **TURNER** bef 1671; b
    1630; Dorchester
PRATT, John (-1655) & Elizabeth [?**TUCKER**]; b 1636; Hartford
PRATT, John (ca 1622-1716) & Elizabeth **WHITMAN** (-1716, ae 82); 22 Nov 1656, 9? Oct, 27
    Nov, no ch; Weymouth
PRATT, John (-1679, 1690?) & 1/wf Hannah [**BOOSEY**] (1641-); b 25 Nov 1658; Wethersfield,
    CT/Hartford
PRATT, John & Ann **DEXTER** (-bef 1660), Malden, 6 ch
PRATT, John (ancestor of Walter Merriam **PRATT**) (had Thomas b 1669) & Ann **DEXTER**; prob
    by 16 1659; Charlestown/Malden
PRATT, John (1630-1707?) & Rebecca **COLBURN** (1643-); 26 Jun 1661; Medfield
PRATT, John (-1698+) & Ann **BARKER** (?1643-1695+); b 1664; Kings Town, RI/Kingston, RI
PRATT, John (1644-1726+), Saybrook & Sarah **JONES** (-1726+, at Guilford), Guilford; 8 Jun 1669;
    Saybrook
PRATT, John & Mary _?_ , m/2 William **TURNER**; b 1 Apr 1671; Boston
PRATT, John & Mary **ALSOP**, wid; b 16 Feb 1675/6; Boston
PRATT, John & Mary **ANDREWS**; 10 Aug 1676; Saybrook, CT
PRATT, John (1638-1689) & 2/wf Hepzibah [**WYATT**] (1651?-1711), m/2 John **SADD** ca 1690;
    ca 1678, b 1661?; Hartford
PRATT, John (1655-1708, ae 53) & Mary _?_ (1655-1710, ae 55); b 1683, b 1678;
    Malden/Charlestown
PRATT, John & Margaret _?_ ; b 1686; Plymouth
PRATT, John (1663-1744) & 1/wf Mary [**NEWCOMB?**]; b 1686; Weymouth
PRATT, John (1660-1742) & Martha **PRATT** (1663-1742, ae 79); 18 Nov 1686; Malden
PRATT, John (1661-) & Hannah [**SANFORD**]; b 1687; Hartford
PRATT, John & Susanna [**GOODWIN**] (-1712); b 25 Jun 1689; CT
PRATT, John (1668-) & Mercy [**NEWCOMB**] (1665-1721); b 1690; Weymouth
PRATT, John (1665-) & Ruth [**STIMPSON**], dau James; b 1691; Sherborn/Framingham
PRATT, John & Sarah [**BATCHELDER**]; 2 Jul 1691; Reading/Medfield
PRATT, John (1665-1730, ae 65) & Margaret **MAVERICK** (?1672-1759); 29 Jul 1691;
    Boston/Salem
PRATT, John, Jr. & Hannah **WILLIAMS**; 10 Nov 1697; Saybrook, CT
PRATT, Jonathan (?1639-) & 1/wf Abigail **WOOD** (-1684?); 2 Nov 1664; Plymouth
PRATT, Jonathan (?1639-) & 2/wf Elizabeth (**WHITE**) **HALL** (-1707), w Samuel; 3 Mar 1689/90;
    Taunton
PRATT, Jonathan (?1668-) & Margaret **LOE/LOWE?/LOC?/LOOK?**; 8 Jan 1691/2; Scituate
PRATT, Jonathan & Sarah [**GALE**] (1681-); b 1701, ca 1700; Framingham
PRATT, Joseph (1639-1720) & Sarah **JUDKINS** (1645-1726); 7 May 1662; Weymouth
PRATT, Joseph (1648-1703) & 1/wf Margaret [**PARKER**] (-bef 1686); b 1671; Saybrook, CT
PRATT, Joseph (-1712) & Dorcas **FOLDGIER/FOLGER**; 12 Jan 1674/5, 12 Feb 1675, 12 Feb
    1674/5; Charlestown/Nantucket
PRATT, Joseph (1648-1703) & 2/wf Sarah **CHAPMAN** (1657-1703+); Sep 1686; Saybrook, CT
PRATT, Joseph (1665-1765) & Sarah [**BENSON**] (-bef 1721); b 1693, ca 1690?; Weymouth
PRATT, Joseph & Hannah **PROVENDER**; 19 Mar 1695/6; Sherborn/Framingham
PRATT, Joseph & 1/wf Elizabeth **MARSH** (-1696)
PRATT, Joseph & 2/wf Sarah **COLLIER**; 22 Jul 1697; Hartford
PRATT, Joshua (-1656) & Bathsheba _?_ , m/2 John **DOGGETT** 1667; b 1633, b 1667;
    Dartmouth/Charlestown
PRATT, Matthew (-1673?) & Elizabeth [**BATES?**]; in Eng, b 1628, b 1622, 1619?;
    Weymouth/Rehoboth
PRATT, Matthew (1628-) & Sarah **HUNT** (1640-1729); 1 Aug 1661; Weymouth
PRATT, Matthew & Susanna **PORTER/Mary** _?_ (1665-1761); b 1691; Weymouth/Abington

PRATT, Nathaniel (1660/1-1744?) & 1/wf Sarah BEAMENT (ca 1661-1716); 2 May 1688; Saybrook, CT
PRATT, Peter & ?
PRATT, Peter (-1688) & Elizabeth (GRISWOLD) ROGERS (-1737, Lyme), (div from John ROGERS), m/3 Matthew BECKWITH; 5 Aug 1679; Lyme, CT/New London
PRATT, Philip (-1739) & Rebecca [NEWTON] (-1728), w Isaac & Samuel NEWTON; b 1698; Framingham
PRATT, Phineas/Phinehas? (1590/93-1680, ae 90?) (ae 81 in 1674) & Mary (PRIEST) GOBERTSON/CUTHBERTSON (-1682+, 1689?); ca 1627/33; Plymouth/Charlestown
PRATT, Richard (?1615-1691) & Mary ? ; b 1643; Charlestown/Malden
PRATT, Richard (-1732) & 1/wf Mercy/Mary?   ?   (-1725); 16 Mar 1692, prob 1692/3; Boston/Chelsea/Malden
PRATT, Samuel (-1679) & Hannah RODGERS/ROGERS (-1721, ae 77), m/2 Thomas BAILEY b 1687; 19 Sep 1660, 19 Jul; Weymouth
PRATT, Samuel (-1676) & Mary [BARKER], m/2 Francis COOMBS 1678±, m/3 David WOOD 1684/5; betw 19 Dec 1667 & 2 Nov 1668; Middleboro
PRATT, Samuel (1655-1705) & Ruth HUNTINGDON (1658-1683/4); 26 May 1681, 1681; Norwich, CT
PRATT, Samuel & 2/wf Elizabeth PECK (1669-1688); 5 Dec 1686, 8 Dec 1686; Lyme, CT
PRATT, Samuel (1670-1728) & Patience [CHARLES] (1675-1735); b 1695; Weymouth/Taunton
PRATT, Samuel (1670-1745±) & [Hannah?] [MILLER]; b 1697; Middleborough
PRATT, Thomas (ca 1626-1676) & 1/wf Mary ? ; b 1653, b 1659; Weymouth
PRATT, Thomas (-1692) & Susannah ? ; b 1656; Sherborn
PRATT, Thomas & Sarah ? ; b 1661; Malden
PRATT, Thomas & Lydia [?BROWN], m/2 Josiah CHAPIN 1676; ca 1665, b 1676; Weymouth
PRATT, Thomas (1646-1720) & Alice ? ; b 1669; Charlestown/Chelsea
PRATT, Thomas (-1676) & Lydia (BROWN?) (1658?-) of Ipswich, m/2 Josiah CHAPIN 1676; ca 1665; Weymouth
PRATT, Thomas (1646-) & ? (had Mary 19 Apr 1680, Thomas 9 Dec 1682, Hannah 19 Jul 1685); b 1680; Concord (see Thomas & Alice)
PRATT, Thomas (1656-) & Lydia PARMENTER; 5 Jun 1681; Sherborn
PRATT, Thomas & Deborah LOVELL (1664/5-1727); ca 1690; Weymouth
PRATT, Thomas (1669-1732, Malden, ae 63) & Mary (DAVIS) [LEWIS] (1663-1732+), w Isaac? (line by Walter Merriam PRATT is wrong); aft 1691, b 1692/3?, bef 28 Jul 1691, aft 6 Apr 1691, aft 9 Jun 1691; Charlestown/Boston
PRATT, Thomas & Mary? ? (had Ann (see above), had Elizabeth 1692, Sarah); b 1694(5?), b 1700 wf Elizabeth, she d 1741, ae 63, Elizabeth EDMUNDS 1703 Boston; Boston
PRATT, Timothy & Deborah COOPER, dau Anthony, sister of Josiah; 9 Nov 1659; Boston
PRATT, Timothy (?1660-1683) & Grace SHIPPIE/SHIPPIN, m/2 John OSBORN 1683; 19 Nov 1679; Charlestown
PRATT, William ((?16--)-1678/9) & Elizabeth [CLARK], m/2 William PARKER 1681?; ca 1640, b Jun 1636/39; Hartford/Saybrook, CT
PRATT, William (1653-1718) & Hannah KIRTLAND (1652-1704+); 20 Feb 1678/9; Saybrook, CT
PRATT, William (1659-1713) & Elizabeth [BAKER]/[SWIFT?] (1656-); 26 Oct 1680; Dorchester
PRATT, William (ca 1620-) & Experience [KING]; b 1692; Weymouth/Dorchester
PRATT, William & Hannah ? ; ca 1700; Weymouth
PRATT, William (1674-) & Hannah HOUGH; 8? Oct 1700; Saybrook, CT
PRATT, ? & ?Ruth WARNER
PRATT, ? & Elizabeth SWIFT (1662-1717+); ?Milton
PRAY, Ephraim & Elizabeth [HAYDEN] (1663-); b 1681; Braintree
PRAY, Ephraim (-1727) & Sarah ? (-1726+); b 1682; Providence
PRAY, John (-1676) & Joanna DOWNHAM/DOWNAM, m/2 Daniel LIVINGSTONE bef 1680?; 7 May 1657; Braintree
PRAY, John (-1730, 1733) & Sarah BROWN (-1733+); 14 Nov 1678; Providence/Smithfield
PRAY, Quinton (1595-1667, 1677?) & Joan ? (-1667+); b 1630?, b 1634; Lynn/Braintree
PRAY, Richard (1630-1688, 1693?) & 1/wf Mary ? (-1686, 1688?); b 30 Dec 1647; Kittery, ME/Providence
PRAY, Richard (-1693) & 2/wf Elizabeth (WHITE) [HERENDEAN]/HEARNDEN, w Benjamin; 1688±; Providence

PRAY, Samuel (1669-) & Mary [FERNALD] (?1671-), dau Thomas; b 1 Sep 1697, b Sep; Kittery, ME

PREBLE, Abraham (1604-1663) & Judith [TILDEN] (1620-1663+); b 164-, 3 Jan 1641?, 3 Jun?; Scituate/York, ME

PREBLE, Abraham (1641-1714) & Hannah SAYWARD; 13 May 1685; Gloucester

PREBLE, Abraham (-1723) & 1/wf Mary [BRAGDON] (1675-1697); ?9 Aug 1694?; York Co., ME

PREBLE, Abraham (-1723) & 2/wf Hannah __?__ (-bef Apr 1699)

PREBLE, Benjamin (1657-1732) & Mary [BASTON]; b 1679; Charlestown/Cambridge

PREBLE, John (1659-1695, 1692) & Hannah __?__ (-1695); York, ME

PREBLE, Joseph (-1691) & Sarah [AUSTIN], m/2 Job YOUNG; York, ME

PREBLE, Nathaniel (?1648-1692) & Priscilla [MAINE], m/2 Joseph CARROLL 1695; ca 1670?; York, ME

PREBLE, Stephen (?1645-1696?) & Rachel [MAINE], m/2 Joseph CARLISLE 1695?; ca 1687?; York, ME

PRENCE, Thomas (1600-1673) & 1/wf Patience BREWSTER (-1634); 5 Aug 1624; Plymouth

PRENCE, Thomas (1600-1673) & 2/wf Mary COLLIER (-1644); 1 Apr 1635; ?Plymouth

PRENCE, Thomas (1600-1673) & 3/wf Apphia (QUICK) FREEMAN, w Samuel; bef 8 Dec 1662, aft 15 Oct 1646; ?Duxbury

PRENCE, Thomas (1600-1673) & 4/wf Mary (?BURR) HOWES (-1695, Yarmouth), w Thomas; aft 21 Feb 1665/6, bef 1 Aug 1668, ?9 Feb 1667/8

PRENTICE, Henry[1] (-1654) & 1/wf Elizabeth [WHITE]? (-13 May 1643); Stowkley, Co. Bucks, 26 Nov 1638, [b 1643?]; Cambridge

PRENTICE, Henry[1] (-1654) & 2/wf Jane/Joanna __?__, m/2 John GIBSON 1662; aft 13 May 1643; Cambridge

PRENTICE, Henry (?1651-1713+) & Mary GOVE; 7 Apr 1682; Cambridge

PRENTICE, James (-1710, ae 81) & Susannah [JOHNSON] (1627-), dau Capt. Edward; b 1656; Cambridge/Woburn

PRENTICE, James (?1656-1711+) & Elizabeth [?BARTLETT]; b 1701?, ca 1677/85?; Newton

PRENTICE, John[2] (?1629-1691) (Elizabeth, widow of Thomas BOWEN, m/2 Samuel FULLER, calls John PRENTICE, brother-in-law, 2 May 1667) & 1/wf Esther/Hester [WILLIAMS?]/?NICHOLS (-6 Jan 1679/80, ae 44?); b 1652; New London

PRENTICE, John[3] (1652-1715) & Sarah JONES (1659-1733); 23 Nov 1675; New London/?Stratford, CT

PRENTICE, John (1655-1689) & Elizabeth JACKSON (1658-1741), m/2 Jonas BOND 1699; 28 Jun 1677, no issue; Cambridge

PRENTISE, John & Esther NICHOLS, dau Caleb; aft 1680

PRENTIS, John[2] (-1691) & 3/wf Rebecca PARKER, dau Ralph; 19 Jun 1685, 12 Jun 1685; New London, CT

PRENTISS, John[2] (-1691) & 2/wf Esther [NICHOLS] (1655, 1653-); b 6 Aug 1690, prob ca 1682, ca 1676-1688; Stratford, CT

PRENTICE, John (-1721) & 1/wf Hannah OSLAND (-1704); 21 May 1696; Newton

PRENTICE, Jonathan (1657-1727) & Elizabeth [LATIMER] (1667-1759); b 1692; Newton

PRENTICE, Joseph (?1677-) & Hannah CHESEBROUGH (1674-); 25 Nov 1700, 26 Nov 1700, 25 Nov; Stonington, CT/Preston, CT

PRENTICE, Robert (-1665/6?) & __?__ ; in Eng, b 1629 (doubtful); Roxbury

PRENTICE, Solomon (1646-1719) & 1/wf Elizabeth __?__ (-bef 1678); b 1674; Cambridge

PRENTICE, Solomon (1646-1719) & 2/wf Hepzibah [DUNTON]/DUNN? (1654-1742), of Reading?; b 1678; Cambridge

PRENTICE, Solomon (1673-1758) & Lydia __?__ (1677-1758, ae 81); b 1697; Cambridge

PRENTICE, Stephen (1666-1756) & Elizabeth [ROGERS] (1671-1737); b 1693, 1689, 1690; New London, CT

PRENTICE, Thomas[1] (1621-1710) & Grace __?__ (-1692); in Eng, b 1648; Cambridge/Newton

PRENTICE, Thomas (1632, ?1629-1724?, 1722?) & Rebecca [JACKSON] (1636-); ca 1664/8?; Cambridge

PRENTICE, Thomas[2] (1650-1685) & Sarah STANTON (1655-1713), m/2 William DENNISON 1686; 20 Mar 1675; Cambridge/Newton

PRENTICE, Thomas (-1724?) & Elizabeth [?BOND]; b 1691; Newton

PRENTICE, Thomas (1674-1769) & 1/wf Mariah RUSSELL (1678-1701); 23 Dec 1696, 28 Dec 1696; Cambridge/Charlestown

PRENTICE, Valentine (-1633) & Alice B—, m/2 John WATSON 1634; 29 Jun 1696; Roxbury
PRESBURY, John (-1648?) & Catherine _?_, m/2 Richard CHADWELL; ca 1639?; Sandwich
PRESBURY, John (-1679) & Dorcas [BESSEY]; b 1664; Sandwich/Salisbury/Saco, ME
PRISBURY, Nathan/(Nathaniel wrong) & Elizabeth GANSON, m/2 Joseph LORD; 16 Feb 1698; Boston
PRESBURY, Stephen (-1730) & Deborah [SKIFF] (1668-1743); ca 1693; Edgartown/Martha's Vineyard
PRESBURY, William (1664-) & Priscilla [RANDALL] (-1752); Beverly
PRESCOTT, James (1643-1728) & Mary [BOULTER] (1648-1705); b 1668; Hampton, NH
PRESCOTT, James (1671-) & Maria MARSTON (1672-); 1 Mar 1695; Hampton, NH
PRESCOTT, John & Mary GAWKROGER; 11 Apr 1629, Halifax, Eng; Watertown/Lancaster
PRESCOTT, John (-1718+) & 1/wf Sarah HAYWARD (1645-1709); 11 Nov 1668; Lancaster/Concord
PRESCOTT, John & Joanna _?_ ; b 1671; Boston
PRESCOTT, Jonas (ca 1647/8-1723) & Mary [LOKER] (1653-1735); 14 Nov 1672; Lancaster/Groton
PRESCOTT, Jonas & Thankful WHEELER (1682-1716); 5 Oct 1699 at Concord; Groton
PRESCOTT, Jonathan (1645/6?-1721) & 1/wf Dorothy _?_ /?WATERS/?HOALD (-1674); 3 Aug 1670; Lancaster
PRESCOTT, Jonathan (1645/6?-1721) & 2/wf Elizabeth HOAR (ca 1650-1687); 23 Dec 1675; Concord
PRESCOTT, Jonathan (1645/6?-1721) & 3/wf Rebecca (WHEELER) BULKELEY (1645-1717, 1718), w Peter; 18 Dec 1689; Concord
PRESCOTT, Jonathan (1675-1755) & Elizabeth (PULSIFER) [CLIFFORD], w Isaac; b Jun 1696; Hampton, NH
PRESCOTT, Peter (-1712, 1713) & Edith/Elizabeth REDINGTON (-1695); 22 May 1679; Salem/Boxford
PRESCOTT, Samuel & Esther WHEELER; 5 May 1698; Concord/Lancaster
PRESSIE/PRESSEY, John (ae 55 in 1693) & Marah GOUGE (?1645-); 4 Dec 1663; Salisbury
PRESSE, William (1671-) & Susannah [JAMESON] (1672-); b 1691; Amesbury/Salisbury
PRESTON, Daniel (1621-1707, ae 85) & Mary _?_ (?Elizabeth doubtful) (-1695, in 75th y); b 1645; Dorchester
PRESTON, Daniel (1649-1726) & Abigail [JACKSON] (1647-1723); b 1675, ?Dec 1673; Newton
PRESTON, Edward (1619-1699) & Margaret [HURST] (-1690); b 1651; New Haven/Boston
PRESTON, Eliasaph (1643-1707) & 1/wf Mary WILCOXON (doubtful) (-1674); 9 Jul 1673, ?19 Jun 1673; Stratford, CT
PRESTON, Eliasaph (1643, 1642?-1705/7) & 2/wf Elizabeth [BEACH] (1652-1692); ca 1675; Stratford, CT/Wallingford, CT
PRESTON, Eliasaph (1643-) & 3/wf Martha (BRADLEY) [MUNSON], m/3 Matthew/Daniel? SHERMAN; ca 1694
PRESTON, Hackaliah & Emm/Emma FAIRCHILD (1653-1733); 20 Apr 1676; Stratford, CT/Woodbury, CT
PRESTON, Jehiel (1640-1684) & 1/wf Sarah [FAIRCHILD] (1642-); b 1663; New Haven/Stratford, CT
PRESTON, Jehiel (1640-1684) & 2/wf Temperance [NICHOLS], m/2 Samuel HUBBELL 1688; [1682?]
PRESTON/PRESSON, John (?1632-1668+) & Susanna (_?_) READ, w Robert; 28 May 1661; Boston
PRESTON, John (1651-) & Sarah GARDNER; 25 Mar 1678; Hadley
PRESSON, John & Jeane _?_ ; b 15 Apr 1681; Portsmouth, NH
PRESTON, John & Sarah (GARY) HOLT, w John; 2 Nov 1687; Andover/Windham, CT
PRESTON, John (1676-) & Susanna [POMEROY]; ca 1698?
PRESTON, Joseph (1646-1733) & Joanna (LEEK) STEVENS (1657-), w Henry; aft 1689, (no issue); New Haven
PRESTON, Levi & Abigail BROOKS; 16 Oct 1695; Swansea/Fairfield, NJ
PRESTON, Lewis & Abigail _?_ ; b 1697; Newport
PRESTON, Roger (1614-1666) & Martha _?_ (?1622-1703), m/2 Nicholas HOLT; b 1643; Ipswich/Salem
PRESTON, Samuel (-1738) & 1/wf Susanna GUTTERSON (ca 1654-1710); 27 May 1672; Andover

PRESTON, Samuel & Abigail THOMAS, m/2 Richard LOUNSBURY or John; b 1693
PRESTON, Samuel & Sarah BRIDGES (-1725+), m/2 William PRICE; 2 Apr 1694; Andover
PRESTON, Thomas (-1697) & Rebecca NURSE/NOURSE (-1719); 15 Apr 1669; Salem
PRESTON, William[1] (1591, ?1589-1647) & 1/wf Elizabeth SALE (1590-1634); Chisham, Eng, 11 Oct 1613; New Haven
PRESTON, William (1591, ?1589-1647) & 2/wf (doubtful) Marie/Mary [SAYBROOK]/[SEA-BROOK], m/2 Thomas KIMBERLY 1659+; ca 1635; Duxbury/New Haven
PRESSON, William & Priscilla _?_ ; b 169[5?]/[2?]; Beverly
PRETIONS, Charles & Rebecca MARTINE; 17 Nov 1653; Boston
PRICE, Benjamin & Mary [SAYRE]; b 1669; ?Southampton, LI
PRICE, Charles & Jane [LORD] (1668-), dau William; Salem
PRICE, David (-1660+) (uncle of John GURNELL) & [?Elizabeth HUMPHREY]; b 1636?; Dorchester
PRICE, Ebenezer & Sarah [ENSIGN] (1672-); Hartford
PRICE, Ephraim (doubtful) & Mary [WHITNEY] (1675-), Groton, dau Joshua; b 1701?
PRICE, Hugh (-bef 1691) & Mary [WRIGHT]; b 1685, b 1688, aft 9 Jun 1676; Boston/Middleborough
PRICE, Jacob & Rachel [GARFIELD]? (1656-); b 1698; Boston
PRICE, John (-1691), Salem & Sarah WOLCOTT (-1698), Windsor, CT; 6 Jun 1674, - Jan 1673/4 (wrong); Windsor, CT
PRICE, John (see Robert) & Mary [ROUSE?] (1640-), dau John & Annis; b 1679(80?); Boston
PRICE, John (-1710) & 1/wf Hannah (BAXTER) LUKE (-1698), w George; 3 Jun 1691; Charlestown
PRICE, Joyluffe & Rebecca CONEY (1670-); 7 Dec 1692; Boston
PRICE, Matthew (ae ca 31 in 1661) & Elizabeth _?_ ; b 1656; Charlestown
PRICE, Matthew (1660-) & _?_ ; b 1690; Barnstable
PRICE, Philip John & Susannah (HENDRICK) BROPHAM, w Robert; 6 Dec 1691; Fairfield, CT
PRICE, Richard & Elizabeth CRUMWELL/CROMWELL (-1674+), m/2 Isaac VICKARY/VICKARS, m/3 Joseph LOBDELL; 18 Aug 1659; Boston
PRICE, Richard & Grace WAITE (1639-); 6 May 1662; Boston
PRICE, Robert (?had Francis, see John PRICE) & Mary [ROUSE] (1640-) (doubtful); b 1674; Dorchester
PRICE, Robert & Sarah [?WEBB], w Zachariah?; b 1678; Northampton/Deerfield
PRICE, Robert, Boston & Hannah CHANLER/CHANDLER?, Boston; 16 Apr 1688; Charlestown
PRICE, Theodore (-1671) (ae ca 15 in 1659) & Anne WOOD/WHITE, m/2 Dudley BRADSTREET 1673; 1 Aug 1667; Salem/Andover
PRICE, Walter (1615-1674) (ae ca 46 in 1659) & Elizabeth [GERRISH?] (?1616-1688, 1674?); Bristol, Eng, b 1642(3?), b 1641?; Salem
PRICE, Walter (1676-1731) & 1/wf Freestone TURNER (1677-1714); 30 Mar 1699; Salem
PRICE/PRIEST, William (-1685) & Mary MAPELLHEAD/?MARPLEHEAD; 9 Apr 1657; Watertown
PRICE, William (1658-) & Leah [NEWCOMB] (1658-); b 1688; Braintree/Watertown/Groton
PRICE, _?_ & Mary _?_ (-1698); Little Compton, RI
PRIDE, John (-1647) & Edith _?_ ; 3 ch; Salem
PRIDE, John & Jane [LOVERING]; b 1675, 6 ch bpt 1686; Pemaquid/Beverly
PRID, (1675-1743) & Hannah THISTLE; m int 22 Dec 1700; Beverly
PRIDE, William & Hannah THORNDIK/THORNDIKE; m int 22 Jul 1699; Beverly/Norwich, CT
PRIDEUX/PRIDEAUX, John & Susanna PAGE; 3 Nov 1698; Marblehead
PRIEST, Degory (1576-1621) & Sarah (ALLERTON) VINCENT (-1633), w John, m/3 Cuthbert CUTHBERTSON/Godbert GODBERTSON 1621; Leyden, Holland, 4 Nov 1611; Plymouth
PRIEST, James (?1610-1676) & Elizabeth _?_ (-1676?); b 1638; Dorchester
PRIEST, John (-1708?) & 1/wf Elizabeth GRAY; 25 Feb 1672/3; Salem
PRIEST, John (-1704) & 1/wf Sarah _?_ (prob wrong); b 1679; Woburn/Lancaster
PRIEST, John (-1704) & 2/wf Rachel [GARFIELD] (1656-1737); aft 1680, 1678 prob; Woburn/Lancaster
PRIEST, John (-1708?) & 2/wf Hannah (MEACHAM) GILL, w William; 4 Mar 1699/1700; Salem
PRIEST, Joseph & Hannah [HAGER] (1649-1702, Watertown); b 1678(9?); Boston
PRIEST, William & Leah _?_ ; b 1685; Weymouth
PRIEST, William & Sarah (HILL) [FLETCHER] (1661-1722), w Pendleton, m/3 Andrew BROWN 1710, m/4 John TREWORGY; aft 24 Feb 1699/1700, b Oct 1702; Saco, ME

PRIME, James (-1685) & Mary? __?_ ; b 1633?; Milford, CT
PRIME, James (-1736) & Martha MERWIN (1666-); 20 Sep 1685; Milford, CT
PRIME, Mark (-1683) & Ann __?_ (-1672); b 1649; Rowley
PRIME, Samuel (1649-1684) & Sarah PLATS/PLATTS, m/2 Moses BRADSTREET; 1 Jan 1673, 1673/4; Rowley
PRENCE/PIERCE, Abraham & Isabel WHITHERSPOON; 11 Mar 1688/9, in Boston; Watertown
PRINCE, Isaac (1654-1718) & Mary TURNER (1658-1738); 23 Dec 1679, 28? Dec; Hull
PRINCE, James (1668-1724) & Sarah (REA) [PHILLIPS], w Jacob; b 1693; Salem
PRINCE, Job (1647-1693?, 1694?) & Rebecca [PHIPPENY] ?BALDWIN, w Samuel, m/3 George CLARK; b 1679; Boston
PRINCE, John (1610-1676) & 1/wf Alice HONOR (-1668); - May 1637; ?Charlestown/Watertown/ Hull/Hingham
PRINCE, John (-1690) & Margaret __?_ (-1703); b 1649; Hingham/Hull
PRINCE, John (-1670) & Elizabeth [COLLIER] (1648-), Hull, dau Thomas; b 1670, ca 1668?, no issue; Boston
PRINCE, John (1610-1676) & 2/wf Ann (HUBBARD) [BARSTOW], w William; 1670±; Hingham/Hull?
PRINCE, John (1638-1690) & Rebecca [VICKEROW?/?VICKEREY]; 1672(?); Scituate/Hull
PRINCE, Jonathan (-1685) & Mary __?_ , ?m/2 John WARNER; b 1685, b - May 1682; Ipswich
PRINCE, Joseph (-1695, Quebec), Hull & Joanna MORTON, Plymouth; 7 Dec 1670; Plymouth
PRINCE, Joseph & Elizabeth ROBINSON; 3 Jan 1698/9; Salem
PRINCE/PRANCE, ?Philip (-1691) & Rachel __?_ (-1691); Marblehead
PRINCE, Richard (-1675, ae 61) & __?_ ; b 1642; Salem
PRINCE, Richard & Sarah RIX (1651-); 25 Dec 1677; Salem
PRINCE, Robert (-1674) & Sarah WARREN, Watertown, m/2 Alexander OSBORNE 1674+; 5 Apr 1662; Salem
PRINCE, Samuel (1649-1728, Middleboro) & 1/wf Martha BARSTOW (1655-18 Dec 1684); 9 Dec 1674; Sandwich
PRINCE, Samuel (1651-1703) & Susanna __?_ (-1703); b 1685; Salem
PRINCE, Samuel (1649-1728) & 2/wf Mercy [HINCKLEY] (1663-1736); 1686; Sandwich
PRINCE, Thomas (1619/20-1690) & [Margaret] __?_ (1626-1705/6); b 1650; Gloucester
PRINCE, Thomas (1650-1705) & Elizabeth HARRDAINE/[HARRADEN] (-1716+); 27 Sep 1676; Gloucester
PRINCE, Thomas (1658-1696) & Ruth [TURNER] (1663-), m/2 Israel SYLBARE 1761 (1674-); ?Dec 1685; ?Scituate/Boston
PRINCE, ?James & Mary __?_ , m/2 John GEDNEY; in Eng; Salem
PRINGLE/PIERCE, Abraham & Isabella WITHERSPOON, Boston; 11 Mar 1686/7; Watertown
PRINDLE, Alexander & Sarah __?_ ; b 1687; Boston
PRINDLE, Ebenezer (1661-1740) & Elizabeth [HOBBY/HUBY]; ca 1690?; ?Greenwich, CT/Milford, CT/Newtown, CT
PRINGLE, John (1658-) & 1/wf Mary HULL (1666-1696); 23 Dec 1685; Derby, CT
PRINGLE/PRINDLE, John & 2/wf Abigail HAWKINS (1672?-1698); 1 Mar 1696, 1696/7; Derby, CT
PRINDLE, John & 3/wf Hannah BOTSFORD/BOXFORD, m/2 Joseph HULL; 21 Dec 1699; Derby, CT
PRINGLE, Joseph (1663-1738) & Mary BROWN (1664-); 19 Aug 1686; New Haven
PRINDLE, Samuel (1668-1750) & Dorothy PLUM; 1 Jan 1699; Milford, CT/New Milford, CT
PRINGLE, William (-1690) & Mary DISBURROW/DESBOROUGH; 7 Dec 1655; New Haven
PRYNGRYDAYS/PRINGRIDAYS/PRIMVADOES?/PRIMRADOES, Edmund (-1675) & Mary MORGAN, m/2 Nicholas RUST 1678; 1 Nov 1666; Springfield
PRIOR, Benjamin & Bethia PRATT; 9 Dec 1697; Duxbury
PRYOR, Daniel & Mary [HATCH]; b 1656; Scituate
PRIOR, Daniel (1667-) & 1/wf Sarah EGGLESTON (1670-1708); 8 Feb 1692/3, 9 Feb 1693; Windsor, CT/Middletown, CT
PRIOR, Humphrey (-1719) & 1/wf Ann OSBORN (1647-29 Sep 1682); 12 Nov 1663; Windsor, CT
PRIOR, Humphrey (-1719) & 2/wf Mary [WHITCOMB] (-1723), w Job; aft 1682, 1686?; Windsor, CT
PRYER, James & Susanna __?_ , ?m/2 Robert WATSON 1690[1]; b 1682(3?), b 1681; Boston

PRIOR, John (-2 Apr 1698) & Elizabeth **BOWNE** (1658-), m/2 Samuel **PETERS**; 2 Nov 1678; ?Flushing, LI

PRIOR, John & Mary **GEER**; 15 Apr 1686, 1685?; Enfield, CT

PRYOR, John (-1742) & Bethiah [**ALLEN**] (1669-); ca 1687/90?; Bridgewater

PRIOR?/PIERCE?/PEIRE, John & Elenor **CHILES**; 16 Aug 1695; Duxbury

PRIOR, Joseph (?1623-1692) & Hannah __?__ ; ca 1650/60?; Scituate/Duxbury/Bridgewater

PRIOR, Matthew (-1686/1692, aft 22 Nov 1687) & Mary (?**CLARK**) [?**BRYER**] (-1700, 9 Jul 1700); b 1651, b 1657; Salem/LI

PRYOR, Thomas (-1639) & __?__ ; in Eng, b 1610?; Scituate

PRIOR, Thomas & Sarah [**PRIME**]; b 1685?; Milford, CT?

PRISSON/?PRESSON/?PRESTON, Richard & Mary **HODGE** (1666-); 10 Sep 1688; Salem

PRITCHARD, Benjamin & Susanna (**NEWCOMB**) **BLAGUE**, w Philip; ca 1689/80

PRITCHARD, Benjamin (1657/8-) & Rebecca **JONES/JANES**?; 14 Nov 1683; Milford, CT

PRICHARD, Hugh & [Eleanor] __?__ ; b 1641; Gloucester/Roxbury (? went home)

PRITCHETT, John & 1/wf [?Mary/May?] [**DENISON**] (ca 1658-); b 1675; Ipswich

PRITCHETT, John & 2/wf Mary **TOWNE** (?1655-1717); 1 Mar 1680/1; Topsfield

PRITCHET, Joseph (1658-1732) & Frances [**COLBY**] (1662/3-1732+); ca 1682?; Amesbury

PRITCHARD, Nathaniel (-1710) & 1/wf Hannah **LAUGTON** (-1690); 4 Feb 1652, 4 Jun 1651; Springfield

PRITCHARD, Nathaniel & 2/wf Hannah ?(**HULL**) (**ALEXANDER**) [**DAVIS**], w Samuel; 9 Apr 1691; Northampton

PRICHARD, Richard (-1669) & 1/wf Anne __?__ (-1666); b 1624; Yarmouth/Charlestown

PRICHARD, Richard & Margary (__?__) (**ALCOTT**) (**BENHAM**)/**BONHAM**, w Thomas, w John; 20 Feb 1666/7, 20 Feb 1666; Charlestown

PRICHARD, Roger (-1670) & 1/wf Frances __?__ (-1651); in Eng, b 1629; Wethersfield, CT/Springfield/Milford, CT

PRICHARD, Roger (-1670/1) & Elizabeth (**PRUDDEN**) **SLOUGH** (-1669) w William; 18 Dec 1653; Milford/, CT/Waterbury, CT

PRITCHETT, Thomas & Mary [**MASH**]; 15 Feb 1682; Westchester, NY

PRITCHETT, William (-1675) & 2/wf? __?__ /?Hannah __?__ (-1705, Andover), m/2 John **LOVEJOY** 12 Feb 1676/7; ca 1652?; Lynn/Brookfield

PRICHARD/PRITCHETT, William (-1697) & 1/wf Elizabeth **ALLEN** (-1685); 14 Nov 1683, 15? Nov; Suffield, CT

PRICHARD/PRITCHETT, William & 2/wf Elizabeth **PALMER**; 20 Oct 1688; Suffield, CT

PRICHARD/PRITCHETT, William (-1698?) & 3/wf Rebecca **TAYLOR**, m/2 Ebenezer **BURBANK** 1699; 22 Jan 1696, 1695/6; Suffield, CT

PROCTER, Benjamin (1651-) & Deborah **HART**; Feb 1673, 15 Feb; Ipswich

PROCTER, Benjamin (1662-) & Mary (**BUCKLEY**) **WHITRIDGE**, w Sylvester; 18 Dec 1694; Lynn

PROCTER, Edward & Elizabeth **COCK/COX** (1671-); 24 Nov 1691, 1690; Boston

PROCTOR, George (-1662) & Edith __?__ ; b 1636, prob; Charlestown/Dorchester

PROCTER, Gershom (1648-1714) & Sarah **WHITTAWS/WHITTACRES**; 4 Jul 1690; Chelmsford

PROCTER, Israel & Margaret **HILDRETH** (1660-); 10 Jun 1689; Chelmsford

PROCTER, James & 1/wf Esther (**FLETCHER**) **PARKER** (1658-1693), w Isaac; 3 Dec 1691; Chelmsford

PROCTOR, James & 2/wf Hannah (**WILSON**) [**PIERCE**?] (1672-), w Jonathan; b 1696; Woburn

PROCTOR, John[1] (1595-1672) & 1/wf Martha __?__ (-1659); in Eng, b 1632; Ipswich/Salem

PROCTOR, John[1] (-1672) & 2/wf Martha __?__ ; aft 13 Jun 1659; Salem

PROCKTER, John[2] (ae 50 in 1684) & 1/wf Elizabeth **THORNDICK/THORNDIKE** (-1672); - Dec 1662; Ipswich/Salem

PROCTOR, John[2] (-1692) & 2/wf Elizabeth **BASSETT**, m/2 Daniel **RICHARDS** 1699; 1 Apr 1674; Salem

PROCTOR, John & Miriam/?Mary [?**MARSHALL**] (1670-1767, ae 99); b 1694; Chelmsford

PROCTOR, John & __?__ ; b 1701

PROCTOR, Joseph & Martha [**WAINWRIGHT**]; b 1677(8?); Ipswich

PROCTOR, Joseph & Sarah (__?__) [**INGERSOLL**], w Richard; aft 27 Nov 1683, b 24 Dec 1701; Ipswich/Salem

PROCTER, Obadiah & Margaret **GARDNER**; 24 Aug 1699; Boston

PROCTOR, Peter, Chelmsford & Mary **PATTERSON** (1666-), Billerica; 30 Jan 1688, prob 1688/9; Billerica/Framingham, CT

PROCTER, Richard & Rachel __?__ ; b 1689; Boston
PROCTER, Robert (?1624-1697) & Jane HILDRETH (?1625-living 1697); last of Dec 1645; Concord/Chelmsford
PROKTER, Samuel (1640-) & Mary __?__ ; b 1671(2?); Boston
PROCTOR, Samuel & Sarah __?__ ; b 1694; Chelmsford
PROCTOR, Samuel & Mary PHILLIPS; m int 4 Sep 1695; Boston
PROCTER, Thomas & Elizabeth __?__ ; b 1696; Boston
PROCTOR, Thorndike (1672-1758) & 1/wf Hannah (FELTON) ENDICOTT (1663-), w Samuel; 15 Dec 1697; Salem
PROCTER, [?John] & Mary/Miriam? MARSHALL (1670-); b 1693; Charlestown
PROUSE, John & Hannah BARNES (1644-1688); b 1666; Salisbury
PROUSE, Roger & Hannah __?__ ; b 1686; Boston
PROUT, Ebenezer (1656-1735) & 1/wf Elizabeth WHEELER (-11 Oct 1683); 28 May 1678; Concord/Watertown
PROUT, Ebenezer (1656-1735) & 2/wf Grace [SHERMAN] (1659-); b 1690; Watertown
PROUT, John (1648-1719) & Mary (RUTHERFORD) HALL (-1723), w Daniel; 23 Aug 1681; New Haven
PROUT, Timothy (1620-1702) & 1/wf Margaret __?__ (-1685); b 1645; Boston
PROUT, Timothy (1645-) & Deborah SYMMES (1642-1715); 13 Dec 1664; Charlestown/Boston
PROUT, Timothy (1620-1702) & 2/wf Elizabeth (UPSHALL) [GREENOUGH] (1627-1694), w William; aft 29 Oct 1688; Boston
PROUT, William (1653-) & Love [GIBBONS], m/2 John FOWLE aft 1675; b 1673; Charlestown/Boston
PROUTY, Richard (-1708) & Damaris [TORREY] (1657-1714+); b 1677, ca Dec 1676; Scituate
PROVENDER, John & __?__ ; b 1680; Malden
PRUDDEN, James (-1648) & [?Elizabeth __?__]/Sybil MITCHELL (-1618?); in Eng, 7 Apr 1608; Milford, CT
PRUDDEN, John (1646, 1645?-1725) & Grace __?__ ; b 1675; Jamaica, LI/Newark, NJ
PRUDDEN, Peter (1601-1656) & 2/wf Joanna [BOYSE] (-1683?), m/2 Thomas WILLETT 1670, m/3 Rev. John BISHOP 1683; ca 1637, b 1640; Milford, CT
PRUDDEN, Samuel (1644-1685) & Grace JUDSON (1651-1724), m/2 Thomas CLARK; 30 Dec 1669; Stratford, CT/Milford, CT
PUDEATER/?POINDEXTER, Jacob & 1/wf Isabel MOSIER (-1677); 28 Oct 1666; Salem
PUDEATOR, Jacob (-1682) & 2/wf Ann [GREENSLIT]/GREENSLADE (-1692/3), w Thomas; aft 1677; Salem
PUDNEY, John (-1712) & Judith COOK; 18 Nov 1662; Salem
PUDNEY, John (1663-1712/13) & Mary JONES (-1725+); 1 Jan 1683/4; Salem
PUDNEY, Joseph (1673-) & Sarah MACKINTIRE; 18 May 1697; Salem
PUFFER, George (-1639) & __?__ (-1676/7); in Eng, b 1624?; Boston/Braintree
PUFFER, James (-1692) & Mary SWALDEN/LUDDEN? (?1636-1709), dau James; 14 Feb 1655/6; Braintree
PUFFER/DUFFER, James (-1749), Braintree & Mary ELLIS (-1751, ae 80 y), Dedham; 18 Sep 1690, 25 Sep 1690; Braintree
PUFFER, James & Abigail NEWTON; 3 Dec 1695, 17 Dec 1695; Milton/Dorchester
PUFFER, John & Mary HOLBROOK (-1736, ae 62); 17 Dec 1695; Dorchester
PUFFER, Matthias & 1/wf Rachel FARNSWORTH (1642-1675); 18 Mar 1662, 1661/2; Braintree
PUFFER, Matthias & 2/wf Abigail EVERARD/EVERETT (1647-1685); 11 Apr 1677; Dedham
PUFFER, Matthias, Milton & 3/wf Mary (SPURR) CREHORE, Milton, w Teague; 14 May 1697; Milton
PUFFER, Richard & Ruth EVERET/EVERETT (1653-); 23 Mar 1681; Dorchester/Wrentham
PUE/PUGH, Peter & Mary __?__ ; b 1661; Boston
PULLEN, Edward (1607-) & __?__ ; Hingham
PULLIN, Edward & Elizabeth __?__ ; b 1669; Boston
PULLING, Simon & __?__ [TOSH]; b 1684
PULMAN/PULLMAN, Jasper (1633-) & Ann __?__ ; ca 1655/60; York, ME
PULMAN, Nathaniel & Mary __?__ ; b 1686(7?); Boston
PULSIFER, Benedict (?1635-1710) & __?__ (-1673); ca 1659?; Ipswich
PULSIPHER, Benedict (?1635-1710) & 2/wf Susannah WATTERS/WATERS (1649-1726); - Feb 1673, 1673/4; Ipswich

PULSEVER, John & Joanna KENT (1666-1755); 31 Dec 1684; Gloucester

PULSEFER, Richard (1675-1762) & 1/wf Ruth [GOLD]; b 28 Mar 1698/9, b 5 Jan 1698/9; Ipswich

PUMP, Philip & Sarah __?__; b 1687(8?); Bristol, RI

PUNCHARD, William & Abigail WATERS (1645-); 26 Oct 1669; Salem

PUNDERSON, John (-1681?) & Margaret __?__; b 1642; New Haven

PUNDERSON, John (1644-1730) & Damaris ATWATER (1649-1711); 5 Nov 1667; New Haven

PONDERSON, John (1673-1742) & 1/wf Abigail ALLING (1673-1739); 3 Aug 1699; New Haven

PURCHASE, Abraham & Ruth WILLIAMS; 22 Oct 1694; Beverly

PURCHASE, Aquila (-1633) & Ann SQUIRE (1591-1662), m/3 Thomas OLIVER 1635?, bef 1637; Kingweston, Eng, 28 Jan 1613/14; Dorchester?

PURCHASE, John (-1645) & Jane __?__ (-1683), m/2 Nicholas PALMER 1646; Hartford, CT

PURCHASE, John (-1667) & 1/wf Elizabeth __?__ (-16 Mar 1663); b 1652; Boston

PURCHASE, Oliver & 2/wf Elizabeth __?__

PURCHASE, Oliver (1613-1701, ae 88 y, Concord) & 1/wf Sarah __?__ (-1671); b 1640; Dorchester/Taunton/Lynn

PURCHASE, Oliver (-1701) & 2/wf Mary PERKINS (1651-); 17 Sep 1672; Lynn/Concord

PURCHASE, Thomas (1576-1678) (uncle of Eleazer WAY) & 1/wf Mary [GOVE/GROVE] (-7 Jan 1655/6); Lynn

PURCHASE, Thomas (1576-1678) & 2/wf Elizabeth (ANDREWS) [PIKE] (1633-), w Richard, m/3 John BLANY, Sr. 1678; ca 1656

PURCHAS, Thomas & Elizabeth WILLIAMES, m/2 John BLENEY, Jr. (?), m/3 ?Jonathan FELT 1695?; 3 Dec 1679, ?1683; Salem

PURDY, Francis[1] (-1658) & Mary [BRUNDISH/BRUNDAGE?], m/2 John HOYT ca 1659; b 1644?; Fairfield, CT

PURDY, Francis (1650-1722+) & ?Mary LANE/?Sarah BROWNE; Rye, NY

PURDY, John (-1678) & Elizabeth [BROWN] (1647-); Fairfield, CT/Rye, NY

PURDY, Joseph (-1709) & Elizabeth [?OGDEN] (1662±-); ca 1690?; Fairfield

PURRINGTON, Elias (-1720) & Sarah ORRIS; 7 Jul 1694; Boston

PURINGTON/PUDDINGTON, George (-1647/49) & Mary POOKE, m/2 John DAVIS by 1662; Tiverton, Eng, 5 Feb 1630; Salisbury

PURINGTON, James (1664±-1718) & 1/wf Elizabeth __?__; ca 1689/90?; Salisbury

PURINGTON, James (-1718) & 2/wf Lydia (MUZZEY) [RANDALL] (1671-1737), w John; b 1693; Salisbury

PURINGTON, John (1635-) & Mary [SCAMMON]?; b 1660?; Salisbury

PURINGTON, John & Sarah [?BARTON]; b 1690(1?); Salisbury

PURINGTON, Robert & __?__; b 1634?; Portsmouth

PURINGTON, Robert & ?Amy [DAVIS?]/[ONION?], m/2 Francis GRAVES 1689; b 1665; Portsmouth

PURINGTON/PUDDINGTON, Thomas & Rachel WILLIAMS; 20 Sep 1689; Dover

PURINGTON, __?__ & Agnes __?__ (-1655+); b 1605/8?

PURPLE, Edward (-1720?) & Hannah [ACKLEY]; 1675; Haddam, CT

PURRIER/PURRYER, William (1594-1675?), Olney, Bucks, & Alice __?__; in Eng, b 1628; Ipswich

PURSLY/PURSLEY, Garrot & Sarah __?__; b 1697; Boston

PUTNAM, Benjamin (1664-1715) & 1/wf Sarah/(not Hannah) [TARRANT?] (-1705), had son Tarrant; 25 Aug 1686?, b 1686; Salem

PUTNAM, Edward (1664-1747/8) & Mary HALE/HALL?; 14 Jun 1681; Salem

PUTNAM, Eleazer & 1/wf Hannah [BOREMAN]/[BOARDMAN?] (1670/1-); b 1693; Salem

PUTNAM, James (-1727) & 1/wf Sarah [BROCKLEBANK] (1664-1717, ae 53); b 1686; Salem

PUTNAM, John (1579/80-1662) & Priscilla [GOULD]?/?[DEACON]; in Eng, b 1605; Salem

PUTNAM, John (1630-1710) (ae ca 30 in 1660) & Rebecca PRINCE; 3 Sep 1652; Salem

PUTNAM, John (1657-) & Hannah CUTLER (1655-); 2 Dec 1678; Salem

PUTNAM, John (1667-1737) & Hannah __?__; b 1691(2?), b 1694; Salem

PUTNAM, Jonathan (1660-1739) & 1/wf Elizabeth [WHIPPLE] (1660, 1661-1682); b 1682; Salem

PUTNAM, Jonathan (1660-1739) & 2/wf Lydia [POTTER]; b 1684, ca 1683; Salem

PUTNAM, Joseph (1669-1725) & Elizabeth PORTER (1673-1746); 21 Apr 1690; Salem

PUTNAM, Nathaniel (1619-1700, ae 79?) & Elizabeth PRINCE?/[HUTCHINSON] (1629-1688); b 1648, ca 1656, b 1652; Salem

PUTNAM, Samuel (1653-1676) & Elizabeth [LEACH?], m/2 Benjamin COLLINS 1677; Salem

PUTNAM, Thomas (1615-1686) & 1/wf Ann HOLYOKE (-1665); 17 Oct 1643; Salem
PUTNAM, Thomas (1615-1686) & 2/wf Mary VEREN (-1695), w Nathaniel; 14 Nov 1666; Salem
PUTNAM, Thomas (-1699) & Ann CARR (1661-1699); 25 Nov 1678; Salem
PYGAN, Alexander (-1701) & 1/wf Judith REDFIN/?REDFIELD (-1678); 17 Jun 1667, 1668; New London, CT
PYGAN, Alexander (-1701) & 2/wf Lydia (BEAMAN/BEAMOND) BOYES, w Samuel; 15 Apr 1684; Saybrook, CT/New London, CT
PIMM/PYM, Charles & Elizabeth [RANDOLPH]; b 1696; Boston
PYMM, John & Sarah DIKERSON, Boston; m bond 20 Jun 1688; Boston
PIM, John & Mary ORCHARD; 5 Feb 1690; Boston
PYNCHON, John (?1625-1703) & Amy/Ann WYLLYS (1625-1694, 1698/9?); ?6 Nov 1645, 30 Oct 1644, ?30 Oct 1645 at Hartford; Hartford/Springfield
PYCHON, John (1647-1721) & Margaret [HUBBARD] (1647-1716); ca 1672, b 18 Jan 1673; Ipswich/Springfield
PYNCHON, William (?1590, ?1585-1662) & 1/wf Ann/Anna [?ANDREWS] (-1630); in Eng, b 1625, b 1619?; Dorchester/Roxbury/Springfield
PYNCHON, William (1590-1662) & 2/wf Frances (_?_) (SMITH) [SANFORD] (-1657), w _?_, w Thomas; 1630 or later; Dorchester/Roxbury/Springfield
PINCHEON, William, Jr. & Martha ELKINS (1760-); 1780 (4 Mar 1680 wrong); Salem
PUNCHIN/PINCHEON, William, Boston & Joanna (EDGECOMB) ELKINS, w Henry; 1 May 1693; Marblehead

QUACKEY/?QUAKEE, Peter & Hannah BASH; 14 May 1700; Boston
QUARLES, William (1646-1689) & Martha DICKENSON (1649-); 9 Dec 1669; Ipswich
QUARLES, William & Sarah _?_ ; b 1696; Ipswich
QUELCH, Benjamin & Elizabeth _?_ ; b 1692; Boston
QUIDDINGTON, Abraham & Sarah [POLLARD], m/2 John DINCLAY ?bef 1695; b 1685, (1686?); Boston
QUILTER, Mark[1] (1602-1654) & 1/wf Elizabeth _?_ ; b 1629, b 1630; Ipswich
QUILTER, Mark[1] (-1654) & 2/wf Thamer/Tamar _?_ (1612-1679+); Ipswich
QUILTER, Mark[2] (?1630-1678) & Frances [SWAN] (1633-1694?, 1700?); ca 1653; Ipswich
QUINBY, John (-1709/10) & Deborah [HAIGHT?]; b 1654; Westchester, NY
QUENBY, John (1665-) & Mary [MUDGETT] (1667-1710); b 1688; Salisbury
QUINBY, John (1660-) & Anne/Anna [KIERSTADT], dau Hance; b 1680; Westchester, NY
QUENBY, Joseph (1676-) & 1/wf Elizabeth [GETCHELL]; b 1700; Amesbury
QUINBY, Josiah (ca 1663-1728) & Mary MULLINEX/MOLYNEAUX?/MULINEAUX; 17 Jun 1689, ?7 Aug; ?Westchester, NY
QUENBY, Robert (-1677) & Elizabeth [OSGOOD] (-1694±); ca 1656, 1653?; Salisbury
QUENBY, Robert & Mary [?ROWELL]; b 1685; Amesbury
QUINBY, William (?1600-) & Ann [?SMITH], m/2 George STUCKEY 1657; b 1625?; Stratford
QUENBY, William (1660-1705, 1694?) & Sarah _?_ ; b 1689(90?); Amesbury
QUINCY, Daniel (1651-1690) & Ann/Hannah?/Anna SHEPARD, m/2 Rev. Moses FISKE 1700, 1700/1; 9 Nov 1682, 8 Nov; Charlestown/Boston
QUINCY, Edmund (1602-1635?) & Judith PARES, m/2 Moses PAINE ca 1642/3, m/3 Robert HULL 1646+; Wigsthorpe, Eng, 14 Jul 1623; Braintree
QUINCY, Edmund (1627/8-1698) & 1/wf Joanna HOARE (1624, 1623?-1680); 26 Jul 1648; Braintree
QUINCY, Edmund (1627/8-1698) & 2/wf Elizabeth/Mary? (GOOKIN) ELLIOT (-1700), w John; 8 Dec 1680; Braintree
QUINCY, Edmund (1681-1738) & Dorothy FLINT (1678-); - Oct 1700
QUINCY, _?_ & Mary TAPPAN/TOPPING; Wethersfield, CT (see QUINNEY)
QUINNY _?_ & Mary TOPPING; Southampton, LI?

RACKET, John & Anna __?__, m/2 John CARTWRIGHT/CARTRITH/CARTERET 1686; b 1681; Southold, LI

RACKET, John & Elizabeth? __?__; b 1698?; Southold, LI

RACKLIFF/RACKLEFF, John & Elizabeth [TRAFTON], York, m/2 Joseph JOHNSON 1691+; 1690±; Kittery, ME

RACKLIFF, William (1668-) & 1/wf Mary NELSON; Portsmouth, NH/Kittery, ME

RACKLEY/RACHLIFFE, William & 2/wf Dorothy LORD, wid; 18 Oct 1689; Kittery, ME?/Dover, NH

RACKLIFF, William[1] & 1/wf __?__; Portsmouth, NH

RACKLIFF, William[1] & 2/wf Jane __?__, ?m/2 Anthony LIBBY; bef 1699; Portsmouth, NH

RATCLIFFE/RADCLIFF, John & Alice __?__; b 1664; Boston

RADLEY, John & Mary [HAYWARD] (1677-); b 1701?; Huntington, LI/Elizabeth, NJ

RAINSBORO/RAINSBOROUGH, William (-1648 in Eng) & Margery [COYTMORE?]; b 1648, [b 1626], b 1617; Charlestown/Watertown

RAINSFORD, David (1644-1691) & 1/wf Abigail __?__; b 1674; Boston

RAINSFORD, David (1644-1691) & 2/wf Abigail [GRIGGS], m/2 Joshua FULLER 1691+; b 1688(9?); Boston

RAINSFORD, Edward (-1682, 1680?, ae 71) & 1/wf Mary __?__ (-June 1632); b 1632; Boston

RAINSFORD, Edward (-1682?, ae 71) & 2/wf Elizabeth [?DILLER/DILLOS] (-1688, ae 81); b 1634; Boston

RAINSFORD, Edward (-1717, ae 48) & Huldah [DAVIS] (1659-); b 1686; Boston

RAINSFORD, John (1634-) (ae 25 in 1660) & Susanna [VERGOOSE], dau Peter; b 1661(2?); Boston

RAINSFORD, John & Rebecca __?__; b 1695; Boston

RAINSFORD, Jonathan (1636-1671) & Mary SUNDERLAND (1642-1698), m/2 Joshua HOBART 1672; 29 Nov 1656; Boston

RAINSFORD, Jonathan (1661-) & Martha [RAYMOND]; b 1686; Boston

RAINSFORD, Joseph & Martha __?__; b 1693; Boston

RAINSFORD, Nathan (1641-) & Mary ALLEN (1644-1672); 28 Nov 1665; Charlestown/Boston

RAINSFORD, Ralph & Martha [CORNISH]?, dau Richard; b 1695, b 1694; Boston

RAINSFORD, Solomon (-1693) & Priscilla [GOTSHELL] (1649-); b 1670; Boston

RAYSON/RAISIN/REASON?, George & Elizabeth DYER, m/2 Newcomb BLAGUE; 21 May 1689; Boston

RAMBLE, Thomas (-bef 1652) & __?__; Stratford, CT

RAMSDELL, Aquila & Hannah __?__ (-1688); b 1672; Lynn

RAMSDELL/RAMSDEN?, Daniel (1649-) & ?Hannah/Sarah CASWELL; b 1690; Plymouth

RAMSDELL, Isaac (-1713+) & Eleanor VINTON (1648-1713+); 12 Jul 1666; Lynn/Concord

RAMSDELL, Isaac & Abigail __?__; b 1690; Lynn

RAMSDEN, John (-1687) & Hannah (ADAMS) MUNCY/MUNSEY, w Francis; 1675+; Newtown, LI

RAMSDELL, John (-1688, ae 86) & Priscilla __?__ (-1675/6); b 1653, b 1648?; Lynn

RAMSDELL, John & Elizabeth PERKINS (1643-); 31 May 1671; Salem/Boxford

RAMSDELL, Jonathan (1672-1743) & Anna CHADWELL (1679-1745+); m int 27 Nov 1699; Lynn

RAMSDEN/RAMSDELL?, Joseph (-1674) & 1/wf Rachel EATON (ae 23 in 1648); 2 Mar 1645; Plymouth

RAMSDELL/?RAMSDEN, Joseph (-1674) & 2/wf Mary SAVORY; 16 Oct 1661; Plymouth

RAMSDELL, Nathaniel (-1748) & Elizabeth MANSFIELD; 2 Nov 1698; Lynn

RAND, Francis (1616-1691) & [Christina]/Christian __?__ (-1689+); b 1645; Strawberry Bank, Sandy Beach/?Great Island, NH

RAND, Henry & Mary/?Sarah CRANE; 29 Sep 1682; Stow

RAND, John (1645±-1690, 1695?) & Remembrance [AULT] (-1695?); b 1672; Dover, NH

RAND, John (-1698) & Elizabeth __?__, m/2 William GLINES; Dover, NH

RAND, John (-1737) & 1/wf Mehitable CALL (1668-1727); 2 Dec 1685; Charlestown

RAND, Nathaniel (-1696) & 1/wf Mary CARTER (ca 1645-13 Apr 1678); 2 Sep 1664; Charlestown

RAND, Nathaniel (-1696) & 2/wf Abigail (DAMON) [CARTER] (-1695), w Samuel; b 1680; Charlestown
RAND, Nathaniel (of age in 1686) & Elizabeth [MARDEN]; b 1703, b 1701?, 1701; NH
RAND, Robert (-ca 1639) & Alice [SHARP] (-1691, ae 97?, 87?); b 1624; Charlestown
RAND, Robert (-1694) & Elizabeth _?_ (-1693); b 1653, b 1657; Lynn
RAND, Robert & Talithacumy/Tabitha/Jedbatha? IVERY; - Jan 1683; Lynn
RAND, Samuel, Dover, NH, & 1/wf Mary WALTON; 14 Aug 1679; Sandy Beach
RAND, Samuel & Susanna _?_, m/2 William WEBSTER; aft 1689; Sandy Beach
RAND, Thomas (-1683) & Sarah EDENDEN/IDAMS (-1699, in 63rd y); 25 Mar 1656, 12 Mar 1655/6; Charlestown
RAND, Thomas (-1695) & Sarah LONGLEY, m/2 Benjamin WATTS 1701; 17 Jun 1679; Charlestown
RAND, Thomas (-1732) & 2/wf? Hannah _?_ ; b 1680?, b 1690?; Rye, NH
RAND, William (1674-1747) & Persis (PIERSE) [SHAEPHERD] (1669-1748), w John; b 1695; Charlestown
RAND, Zachariah & Ann/?Anna/?Hannah IVERY, m/2 Samuel BAXTER; 2 Apr 1684; Lynn
RANDALL, Abraham (-1690) & Mary [PHELPS]/WARE (-1677); 8 Dec 1690, no issue; Windsor, CT
RANDALL, Abraham (-1690) & Elizabeth (BOOTH)? ?HINDS/KIRBY (-1697+), w John; 27 Oct 1681, bef 25 Oct 1680?, no issue; Windsor, CT
RANDALL, Edward & ?Mary _?_ (1649-); b 1679, b 1663; Newcastle
RANDALL, Isaac (-1684) & Abigail LOVETT (1655-); bef 1684; b 1655; ?Beverly
RANDALL, Isaac (1658-1760) & 1/wf Susannah BERSTOW/BARSTOW; 19 Nov 1684; Scituate
RANDALL, Isaac (1658-1760, ae 102) & 2/wf Deborah BUCK (1670-); 29 Nov 1693; Scituate
RANDALL, Jacob & Katherine? EASTWICK, m/2 _?_ TUCKER; Newcastle, ca 1693?
RANDALL, James & Elizabeth _?_ ; b 1700; Newcastle
RANDALL, Job (see John RANDALL) (1654/5-1727) & ?Elizabeth [DOTY?] (1648?-), dau Wm. PARKER; b 1680; Scituate
RANDALL, John (-1680) (called John KENDALL "brother") & Susan/Susanna [KIMBALL/KIMBELL] (1632-1673); b 1651?; Watertown
RANDALL, John (-1685?) & Elizabeth [MARTIN?] (doubtful) (-1685+); b 1666, b 1665?; Newport/Westerly, RI/Stonington, CT
RANDALL, John & 1/wf Mary _?_ (-1666); b 1666; Weymouth/Braintree
RANDALL, John (-1718) & 2/wf Mary/Mercy ALDRICH (1650-1702); 27 Aug 1667; Medfield/Weymouth
RANDALL, John (see Job RANDALL 1650-1728?) & ?[Patience PARKER] (1649-1711/12), dau William; b 1677; Rochester/Scituate
RANDALL, John & Mary/?Rachel WAIT; 13 Jul 1688; Watertown
RANDALL, John & Lydia MUZZY, m/2 James PURINGTON by 1693; 23 Jul 1689; Amesbury
RANDALL, John (1666-) & 1/wf Abigail [BILLINGS] (-1705); b 1696, b 1 Sep 1695; Stonington, CT
RANDALL, John & Susanna [BENSON] (?1676-1761); b 1697; Weymouth
RANDALL, Joseph (?1642-1723) & Hannah MAYCUMBER/MACOMBER, Marshfield, - Oct 1672; Scituate
RANDALL, Joseph & Elizabeth GARMINE/GERMAN?/JARMINE?, m/2 Samuel WILLEY; 20 Oct 1692; Dover, NH
RANDALL, Matthew (1668, 1671-1736) & Eleanor _?_ (-1735+); ca 1693, b 1694; Stonington, CT/Hopkinton, RI
RANDALL, Peter (doubtful) & Rebecca [WARREN] (1677-1740?), dau Joseph; b 1701?; Medfield
RANDALL, Philip (-1662) & [Joane FUSH] (clue) (?1578-1665, ae 87); 10 Apr 1608, in Eng, b 1620; Dorchester/Windsor, CT
RANDALL, Richard & Elizabeth _?_ (-1701); b 1659; Saco, ME/Dover, NH
RANDALL, Richard (1659-) & 1/wf Elizabeth TOZIER (-1704); b 1693; Durham/Dover, NH
RANDALL, Robert (1608-1691) & 1/wf Mary _?_ (-Sep 1640); ca 1634; Weymouth
RANDALL, Robert (-1691) & 2/wf Mary [FRENCH]; ca 1741; Weymouth
RANDALL, Samuel (1675-) & Mary BAILEY/GURNEY, m/2 Isaac LEONARD by 1701?; b 1697; Bridgewater
RANDALL, Stephen (-1708) & Susan/Susanna BARRON (ca 1635-); 14 Dec 1653; Watertown
RANDALL, Stephen (-1737) & Mehitable BUCK?/[CRANE]; b 1694; Stow

RANDALL, Stephen, Stonington, CT, & Abigail **SABEN/SABIN**; 29 Dec 1697, 24 Dec; Rehoboth/Stonington, CT

RANDALL, Thomas (-1711) & 1/wf Joan [**DRAKE**]? (1628-); b 1659; Weymouth

RANDALL, Thomas (-1667), Marblehead & Sarah **LANGDON**, Boston; Feb 1665, aft 2 Feb 1664; ?Boston/Marblehead

RANDALL, Thomas (-1711) & 2/wf Hannah (**PACKARD**) [**BRIGGS**], w Clement; ca 1671; Weymouth/Bridgewater

RANDALL, Thomas & Rachel **LINCOLN** (-1715); 20 Jan 1696/7; Taunton

RANDALL, Walter (1646-1692) & 1/wf _?_ **WALLIS**; b 1675?, b 1685; Isles of Shoals

RANDALL, Walter (1646-1692) & 2/wf Joanna _?_, m/2 Philip **SYLAND** 1694

RANDALL, William (-1693) & [Elizabeth **BARSTOW**?] (-1672?); b 1640; Scituate

RANDALL, William (1621-1688+) & Elizabeth _?_ ; 2 Oct 1649; Newbury

RANDALL, William (?1647-1712) & Rebecca [**FOWLER**] (-1730); b 1675; Providence

RANDALL, William (1653-ca 1727/8) & 1/wf Rebecca _?_ (-1677); b 1676; Newbury

RANDALL, William (-1720+) & Mary _?_ ; b 1682, b 1678?; Westfield/Enfield, CT

RANDALL, William (-1684) & Mary [**GRANT**], w Peter; aft 1 Nov 1681; Hartford

RANDALL, William & Elizabeth **HILL**; 10 Dec 1691; Boston

RANDAL, William & Elizabeth **SHERRY**; 21 Dec 1699; Boston

RANDALL, William (1675-1742) & Abiah/Abial [**WIGHT**?] (-1740?); ca 1695/8?, ca 1694?; RI

RANDALL, _?_ & Elizabeth _?_ (-1672, ae 80); in Eng; Watertown

RANDALL, _?_ & Rebecca _?_ ; Taunton

RANGER, Edmund & 1/wf Sarah [**FULLER**], dau Robert; b 1672; Boston

RANGER, Edmund & 2/wf Anna [**SMITH**] (1651-); b 1676

RANGER, Edmund & 3/wf Mary [?**PEARSE**]/**GATLINE** (1655-); b 1681; Boston/Bristol, RI

RAINGER, John (1674-) & Elizabeth **WYLLYS**; m int 9 Oct 1695; Boston

RANKIN, Andrew (-1677/8) & Martha **MERRY/?MERROW**, m/2 Philip **FROST** 1678+; 4 Dec 1667; Kittery, ME/York, ME

RANKIN, Andrew & Grace (**NEWCOMB**) **BUTLER** (1664-), w James; 5 Apr 1692; Boston

RANKIN, Constant (1667±-) & Hannah [**WITTEM/WITTUM**] (1669±-); b 1688; Kittery, ME

RANKIN, Joseph & Sarah **HACKET**, m/2 Samuel **CANNEY/KENNEY** 1699; m int 11 Oct 1695; Boston

RANNEY, Ebenezer (-1754) & Sarah **WARNER** (-1741); 4 Aug 1698; Middletown, CT

RANNEY, John (1662-) & Hannah **TURNER**; 28 Dec 1693; Middletown, CT

RANNEY, Joseph (1663-1745) & Mary **STARR** (1671-); - Jan 1693; Middletown, CT

RANNEY, Thomas (-1713) & Mary **HUBBARD** (1642-1721); - May 1659; Middletown, CT

RANNEY, Thomas (1661-1727) & Rebecca **WILLETT**, m/2 Jacob **WHITE**; 29 Mar 1691, May 1690; Middletown, CT

RANSOM, Joshua & 1/wf Mary **GIFFORD** (1669-1689); 21 Feb 1686; Plymouth

RANSOM, Joshua & 2/wf Susannah **GARNER** (-1735, Halifax); 10 Mar 1691/2; Plymouth

RANSOM, Matthew & Hannah **JONES**; 7 Mar 1682/3; Saybrook, CT

RANSOM, Robert[1] (-1697) (perhaps had 2/wf Susannah or Hannah _?_) & Abigail _?_ (1637-living 1673) (ae 36 in 1673); ca 1660; Plymouth/Sandwich

RANSOM, Robert (-1723, Plympton) & Ann/Anna [**WATERMAN**] (1671-); b 1691; Plymouth

RAPER, Thomas & Martha/Mercy [**ANDREWS**] (1660-); b 1680; Boston

RASER/RAZOR, Richard & Exercise **BLACKLEECH** (1637/8-), m/2 Thomas **HODGES** 1663; 24 Aug 1660; Boston/Charlestown

RASHLEY/RASLEIGH, Thomas & _?_ ; b 1645; Exeter, NH/Boston

RATCHELL, Robert & Judith/Rachel [**HART**], m/2 Thomas **REAPE** 1660, m/3 Philip **BULLIS** 1663; b 1652; Boston/Charlestown

RATHBONE, John[1] (?1634-1702) & Margaret [**DODGE**?]; ca 1656; New Shoreham, RI

RATHBONE, John (1658-1723) (1/wf _?_ 20 Jun 1680) & 1/wf Ann **DODGE** (-1723+?); 10 Jan 1688; New Shoreham, RI

RATHBONE, Joseph (1670-) & Mary **MOSHER**; 19 May 1691; New Shoreham, RI/Kings Town/Exeter, RI

RATHBONE, Samuel (1672-) & Patience **COGGESHALL** (1670-); 3 Nov 1692; New Shoreham, RI

RATHBONE, Thomas (1657-1733) & Mary **DICKENS**; 21 Apr 1685; New Shoreham, RI

RATHBONE, William (1661-1727) & Sarah _?_ ; 18 Dec 1680; ?New Shoreham, RI/Westerly, RI

RATTLIFE/RATLIFE, Robert & _?_ ; b 1623; Plymouth

RATLIFFE, William (-1676) & Elizabeth **THELE**; 29 Oct 1659; Stamford, CT/Greenwich, CT

RAtTOON?/RATTONE, Thomas & Margaret [THORNE]; LI?
RAUNCE, John (-bef 1 Jan 1694/5) & Mary [COLEMAN]; Scituate/Boxford
RAVEN, Charles & Mary _?_; b 1686(7?); Boston
RAVENSCROFT, Samuel & Dyonisia [SAVAGE] (1649-), m/2 Thomas HADLEY; b 1681; Boston
RAWDON, John & Elizabeth [HAMMOND], w Richard; aft 1676
RAWLINS, Benjamin & Eunice _?_; b 1691?, b 1684; Boston
RAWLINS, Benjamin (1678-1740) & 1/wf Sarah _?_
RAWLINS, Benjamin (1678-1740) & 2/wf Elizabeth _?_; b June 1701?, b 1696?; Exeter, NH
RAWLINS, Caleb (1645-1693) & Elizabeth [WILMOT] (1657-), m/2 Richard NEWLAND by 1695;
    b 1673; Boston
ROLLINS, Ichabod (1640±-1707) & 1/wf Mary TIBBETTS (1658-?bef 1688), m/2 Thomas ASH ca
    1698?; b 5 May, by 1677; Dover, NH
RAWLINS, James (-1691) & Hannah _?_; b 1640?; Ipswich/Newbury/Dover, NH
RAWLINS, Jasper (-1667) (left ch in Eng) & 1/wf Jeane _?_ (1600-); ca 1630?:
    Roxbury/Wethersfield, CT/Windsor, CT
RAWLINS, Jasper (-1667) & 2/wf [Mary] (GREEN) GRIGGS, w John, w Thomas; 8 Jun 1651;
    Roxbury
RAWLINS, John & Judah _?_; b 1685(6?); Boston
RAWLINGS, Joshua & Abigail _?_; b 1671; Boston
RAWLINGS, Nathaniel (?1626-1662) & Lydia SYLVESTER, m/2 Edward WRIGHT 1664; 4 Sep
    1652; Scituate
RAWLINS, Nicholas & Rebecca LONG, m/2 Richard ORMES 1700; 31 Oct 1679; Newbury
RAWLINS, Richard & Mary _?_; b 1641; Boston
RAWLINS, Robert & Mary [BLAISDELL], dau Robert; b 1686, ca 1685; Amesbury
ROLLINS, Samuel (1649-1694) & Rebecca [PICKERING]; by 1675; Dover, NH
RAWLINS, Thomas[1] (-1660) & 1/wf Mary _?_ (-1639, 1643?); in Eng, b 1620; Roxbury/Wey-
    mouth/Scituate/Boston
RAWLINS, Thomas (1608-1670) & Hannah/Anna (FRYE?) (-1691/2) (sister of William); b 1640;
    Weymouth
RAWLINS, Thomas[1] (-1660) & 2/wf Emma _?_ (-27 Dec 1655, Boston); aft 1639, b 1655; Boston
RAWLINS, Thomas[1] (-1660) & 3/wf Sarah MADOCKS/MATTOCKS (-1660+), w David; 2 May
    1656; Boston
RAWLINS, Thomas & Sarah _?_; b 1666(7?); Boston
RAWLINS, Thomas (1641±-1706) & Rachel [COX]; ca 1670; Dover, NH/Exeter, NH
ROLLINS, Thomas & 1/wf Phebe LAWRENCE; 29 Nov 1696; Hampton, NH
RAWLINS, Thomas (1623-1693) & Abigail (LINDELL) [WADSWORTH] (-1711/12, ae 72), w
    Samuel; b 1667; Milton
RAWLINS, _?_, Exeter, Sanbornton & Sarah PALMER (1665-1713); b 1701?; Salisbury
RAWLINS, _?_ & Alice _?_; Southold
RAWSON, Edward[1] (1615-1693) & Rachel [PERNE] (-1677); in Eng, ca 1635; Newbury/Boston
    (Edward RAWSON, son of David & Margaret (WILSON) RAWSON (she m/2 William
    TAYLOR) and gr-son of Edward & Bridget (?WARD) RAWSON; Rachel PERNE dau of
    Thomas PERNE, gr-dau of John & _?_ (GRINDALL) HOOKER; Edward RAWSON called
    "cousin" by Rev. John WILSON)
RAWSON, Grindall[2] (1659-1715) & Susanna WILSON (1664-1748); 30 Aug 1682; Medfield
RAWSON, William (1651-1728) & Ann/Anna GLOVER (-1730); 11 Jul 1673; Boston/Dorchester
RAWSON, William & Sarah CROSBEY; 26 Oct 1700; Billerica
RAY, Caleb (1654-) & Hannah [GEORGE] (21 Jan 1660-); b 1682(3?); Boston/Sheepscott,
    ME/Pemaquid
REA, Daniel (-1662) & Bethiah _?_ (-1663); in Eng, b 1629, b 1628?; Plymouth/Salem
REA, Daniel & Hepzibah PEBODY/PEABODY (1652-); 10 Apr 1678; Salem/Danvers
RAY, David & Hannah BERRY; m int 8 Jan 1695/6; Boston/Charlestown
RAY, James & Elizabeth (FOSTER) HUET, w Ephraim HUETT; 17 Jan 1681/2; Hingham
RAE, John & Ruth _?_; b 1691, b 1690?; Salem
RAY/REA, Joshua & Sarah WALTERS (?) (1630-1700); 26 Feb 1651; Salem
RAE, Joshua (1664-1710) & Elizabeth LEACH (1668-); Oct 168[?], 1685?, 1686; Salem
RAY, Samuel (-1717/18) & Mary _?_; b 1685/8; Salem
RAY, Simon (1610-1641, 1642?) & Mary [ROWNING] (1616-), m/2 Peter GEORGE 1642(?); in
    Eng, ca 1632, 1635; Marshfield/etc.

RAY, Simon^2 (1638-1737) & 1/wf Mary [THOMAS]; b 1665; Salem
RAY, Simon^2 (1638-1737) & 2/wf Elizabeth (_?_) TIFFANY (1645-), w Humphrey; aft 27 Oct 1655, aft 15 July 1685, bef 18 Oct 1690; New Shoreham, RI
RAY, Simon (1672-) & 1/wf Judith MANWARING (1676-1706); 17 Jan 1694, 1694/5; New London, CT
RAY, _?_ & Anna [WILSON], m/2 William MUMFORD
RAYLY?/RALEIGH, John & Jane _?_; b 1694; Boston
RAYMOND, Daniel (1653-1696) & 1/wf Elizabeth [HARRIS] (1656-1683); ca 1678(?); New London, CT
RAYMENT, Daniel (1653-1696) & 2/wf Rebecca LAY/SAGE (1665, ?1666-), m Samuel GAGER of Norwich 169-; 15 Apr 1684; Lyme, CT/Saybrook
RAIMENT, Edward (1668-1727) & Mary HERRICK; 1 May 1695; Beverly
RAYMENT, George & Jerusha WOODBERY/WOODBURY (1680-); 28 Mar 1698; Beverly
RAYMENT, John (1619, 1622?-) & 1/wf Rachel [SCRUGGS] (1627-1666?); b 1650, b 1648?; Salem/Beverly
RAYMOND, John (ca 1633-1695) & Mary BETTS (ca 1642?-); 10 Dec 1664; Norwalk, CT
RAYMENT, John (1616-1703, ae 87) & Judith (_?_) [WOODBURY] (-1702, ae 75), w William; b 1670, ?20 Aug 1668; Beverly
RAYMENT, John (-1725, ae 74, Middleboro) & Martha [WOODIN/?WEARE] (1655-); b 1677; Beverly
RAYMOND, John, Jr. (1665-) & Elizabeth St.JOHN; 7 Mar 1690, 1690/1; Norwalk
RAYMENT, John & 1/wf Deborah PERRY; 23 Jan 1698/9; Beverly
RAYMOND, Jonathan (1666-1745) & Sarah WOODBERRY/WOODBURY (1668-1747); 6 Feb 1688/9, 20 Feb; Beverly
RAYMOND, Joshua (1639-1670, Taunton) & Elizabeth SMITH (1645-1712), m/2 George DENNIS 1681; 10 Dec 1659; ?New London
RAYMOND, Joshua (1660-1704) & Mercy SANDS (1663-1744); 29 Apr 1683; New London, CT/New Shoreham, RI
RAYMENT, Nathaniel (1670-1749) & Rebecca [CONANT] (1671-1760); b 1692; Beverly
RAYMOND, Richard (1602?-1692) & Judith _?_; b 1633; Salem/Saybrook, CT/New London, CT/Norwalk, CT
RAYMOND, Samuel (1645-1700+) & Mary SMITH (1645-1700+?, 1705); New London, CT/Saybrook, CT
RAYMOND, Samuel (1673-) & Judith PALMER (1673-); 1 Apr 1696; Norwalk, CT
RAIMENT, Thomas (1652/3-1732) & [Mary] _?_ (?1659-); b 1682, b 1684; Beverly
RAIMENT, William (1637-1709) (ae 60 in 1697) & 1/wf Hannah [BISHOP] (1646-); ca 1665, b 1668, ca 1661?; Beverly
RAYMOND, William (1637-1709) & 2/wf [Ruth HULL/HILL]; b 1682; ?Salem/?Beverly
RAIMENT, William, Jr. (1666, 1662?-1701) & Mary [KETTLE], dau John?; b 1688; Beverly
RAYNES, Francis & Eleanor _?_; b 1676, b 1651; York, ME
RANES, John & Mary RODGERS (1631-) (ae 28 in 1669); 24 Nov 1659; Weymouth
RAYNES, Nathaniel (1651?-1734) & Joanna _?_ (-1732); York, ME
RAYNOR, Edward (will 1681) & _?_; Hempstead, LI
RAYNOR, Henry & Joanna EDWARDS, wid; 9 Jun 1662; Boston
REYNER, Humphrey (-1660) & Mary _?_ (-1672); in Eng, ca 1630/34; Rowley
RAYNER, Jachim/Jachin (-1718) & Elizabeth DENISON, Roxbury; 12 Nov 1662; Rowley
RAYNER, James & Elizabeth ANDREWS; 25 Oct 1692; Boston
RENER, John (1600-1669) & 1/wf Anna [BOYCE/BOYSE] (-1647?); 12 Aug 1633, b 1625?, by 1632; Plymouth
REYNER, John (-1669) & 2/wf Frances/?Elizabeth [CLARK] (-1676+); by 1642?; Plymouth
RAYNER, John (-1675/6?, 1676) & Judith [QUINCY] (1655-1679/80); ca 1673?; ?Braintree
RAYNER, John & 1/wf Katharine ADAMS (1638-1682); 7 Sep 1681; Charlestown
RAYNER, John & 2/wf Abigail HATHORNE (-1714); 3 Jul 1685; Charlestown
RAYNOR, Jonathan & Sarah PIERSON; 2 Jun 1680; Southampton, LI
RAYNOR, Joseph (1623-1682?) & Mary _?_ (-1686?); b 1660?; Southampton, LI
RAYNER, Joseph & Sarah DAVIS; 3 Feb 1696; Boston
RAYNOR, Josiah & Sarah [HIGBY?] (1665-); ca 1687?; Hartford/Huntington, LI/Lyme, CT/?Southold, LI
RAINIER, Samuel (-1669) & Mary _?_; b 1654; Cambridge

RAYNOR, Samuel (1656±-1703) & Mary _?_; 1688±; Hempstead, LI
RAYNOR, Thurston[1] (1594-1667) & 1/wf Elizabeth _?_ (1598-); in Eng, b 1621, b 1620; Watertown
RAYNOR, Thurston[2] (1621-1667) (no) & 2/wf Martha [?WOOD] (1612-); b 1650; Southampton
RAYNOR, Thurston (1594-1667) & 2/wf Martha [?WOOD]; b 1667; Southampton
RAYNOR, Thurston & Sarah (_?_) JOHNES; Jul 1693; Cape May, NJ
REINER, William (-1672) & Elizabeth (BLACK) GILBERT, w Humphrey, m/3 Henry KIMBALL 1673+, m/4 Daniel KILHAM ca 1678; 24 Sep 1658; Ipswich
RAYNOR, _?_ & Susannah (HARDY) SHERMAN, w Edmund; aft 3 Nov 1683, bef 9 Jan 1694/5; Stratford, CT
RAYNOR, _?_ & Deborah _?_; b 1650/1; Southampton
READ, Adam & Margaret DENKIN; 11 Jan 1699; Boston
READ, Christopher (?1640-1696) & Katharine _?_ (-1710?), ?m/2 William GREEN 1696; b 1671; Boston/Cambridge/Dunstable
READ, Christopher & Elizabeth [HOUR]; b 1682; Beverly/?Cambridge
REED, Daniel (1655-1710) & Hannah PECKE/PECK; 20 Aug 1677, 20 Mar 1676/7; Rehoboth
REED, Daniel & Sarah JOHNSON (-1703); 17 Jan 1699/1700; Charlestown/Woburn
READ, Edward (1611/14-1690) & Margaret _?_; b 1650; Marblehead
READE, Esdras (-1680, Boston) & 1/wf Alice?/Elizabeth WATSON; b 1622, b 1637; Salem/Chelmsford/etc.
READE, Esdras (-1680, Boston) & 2/wf? Alice?; b 1677/8
READ, Esdras (-1680, Boston) & 2/wf Sarah _?_; b 1670; Woburn
REED, George (1629-1706) & 1/wf Elizabeth GINNINGS/JENNISON?/JENNINGS (1637-1665); 4 Oct 1652; Woburn
REED, George (1629-1706) & 2/wf Hannah ROCKWELL; 9 Nov 1665; Woburn/Charlestown
REED, George & Abigail PIERCE (-1719); 18 Feb 1684/5, 28 Jan; Woburn
READE, Giles & Judith MAYER; 10 Nov 1674; Saco, ME
REED, Hugh & 1/wf Sarah JONES
READ, Isaac & Joan STONE; 10 Mar 1673; Salem
REED, Israel (1642-1711) & Mary [KENDALL] (1651-1722); b 1670, ca 1669; Woburn/Cambridge
READ, Israel & Rebecca RUGELLS/RUGGLES; 6 Nov 1684; Rehoboth
READ, Jacob (1662, 1663?-1745) & Elizabeth GREEN (1668-); - Dec 1693; Salem/Southfield, RI
READ, Jacob (1673-1709) & Elizabeth LAW, m/2 William MOSES; 29 Apr 169[9?]; Concord/Simsbury, CT
REED, James & Susannah RICHMOND (1661-); 18 Apr 1683; Taunton
READ, James & Mercy/Mary/Merry COOPER (-1709+); 7 Jan 1696/7; Rehoboth
REED, John[1] (1598-1685) & Sarah [LESSIE] (-1702); b 1640; Weymouth/Dorchester/Braintree/Weymouth
READE, John (1610/15-) & _?_; Newport
REED, John (1640-1676) & Rachel _?_, m/2 Thomas WILMARTH, Sr. 1678; b 1664; Rehoboth/Attleborough
READE, John & Ann [DERBY], w Francis; b 1667; Warwick, RI/Norwalk, CT
REED, John (-1694) & Mary [WINTER]; 1668; Marshfield/Scituate
READE, John (-1728, ae 81, Windham, CT) & Hannah [HALLOWAY]; ca 1672, betw 1668 & 1673; Norwich, CT/Windham, CT
READE, John (-1728, ae 81, Windham, CT) & 2/wf Sarah _?_
REED, John (-1721, Dighton) & 1/wf? 2/wf? Bethia [FRYE] (-1730, ae 77); b 1674; Weymouth/Taunton
READ, John (-1690) & Mary _?_; b 1674, b 1670; Kittery, ME
REED, John & Elizabeth HOLDEN (-1703); 21 Mar 1682, 1681/2; Woburn
READ, John & 2/wf Sarah _?_; b 1685, b 1680?; Windham, CT
REED, John (-1721) & Hannah [PEABODY?] (-1727); b 1687, b 1670?; Newport/Freetown
REED, John, Jr. & Elizabeth TUTTLE (1666-); 28 Mar 1687; Norwalk, CT
READE, John & Mary [TALLMAN] (1674-1726); ca 1689; Freetown
READ, John & Mary [PEARCE] (-1735); b 1690; Freetown/Fall River
REED, John & Sarah _?_; b 1695; Rehoboth
REED, John & _?_; b 1697; Kittery, ME
REED, John & Ruth JOHNSON (1675-); 10 Jan 1697; Woburn
READ, John (1679/80-1749, Boston) & Ruth [TALCOTT] (1677-1759); b 1699; Fairfield, CT

REED, John & Hester _?_ ; b 1700; Bridgewater
REED, John & Deborah NILES; Jan 1700, 1700/1701; Lyme, CT
READ, John (1674-1739) & Bethia COBB (1678-); b 1701, 15 Jun 1697
READ, John & Elizabeth [DANA]?; b 1701?
REED, John & Susanna [BROWNELL] (1676-); b 1701?; Freetown
REED, John (-1730) & _?_ [SCOFIELD]; ?Stamford, CT
REED, Joseph (1670?-1743) & Phebe [WALKER] (-1743); ca 1694 (b 1695); Woburn
READE, Josiah (-1717) & Grace HALLOWAY (-1727); Nov 1666; Marshfield/Norwich, CT
READ, Josiah & Elizabeth AMSDEN (1678-); 3 Jun 1697, 3 Jul 1697; Marlborough/Norwich, CT
REED, Micah & _?_ ; b 1691?; Bridgewater
READ, Moses (1650-1716) & Rebecca FITCH (-1724); 6 Dec 1677; Rehoboth
REED, Obadiah (1640-1722) & 1/wf Anna SWIFT (1647-1680); 19 Aug 1664; Dorchester
READ, Obadiah (1640-1722) & 2/wf Elizabeth [BROUGHTON] (1646-1713, 1726+?); b 1683, ca 1682; Boston
REED, Philip (-1676) & Mary [DYER?] (?sister of Thomas); b 1641; Weymouth
REED, Philip (-1715) & 1/wf Hannah _?_ ; b 1669/70?; Weymouth/Bridgewater/Abington
READ, Philip (1624-1696) & Abigail [RICE] (-1709), dau Richard; b 1671, b 1670; Concord/Cambridge
REED, Philip (-1715) & 2/wf Abigail _?_ ; b 1681; Weymouth/Bridgewater/Abington
REED, Philip & Thanks/?Thankful DILL; 6 Dec 169[9?], 1698; Concord
REED, Ralph (1630-1712) & Mary [PIERCE] (1636-1701); ca 1654; Cambridge/Woburn
REED, Richard (?1632-1698/1700) & 1/wf Esther/Hester [JAMES]; b 1661; Marblehead/Salem
READ, Richard & Joanna _?_ ; b 1687; Boston
REED, Richard (-1698) & Sarah SANLIN; 17 Jul 1690; Marblehead
READ, Richard & 2/wf Prudence HICKS, Boston; m cont 18 Aug 1691; Marblehead?/Boston
READ, Robert (-1657) & 1/wf Hannah _?_ (-1655); b 1646; Boston/Exeter, NH/Hampton, NH
READ, Robert (-1657) & 2/wf Susanna _?_ , m/2 John PRESSON/?PRESTON 1661; aft 24 Jun 1655; Boston/Hampton, NH
READ, Samuel[2] (-1717) & 1/wf Hopestill HOLBROOK (-1706), dau Wm.; 10 May 1668, 5 May; Rehoboth/Mendon
READ, Samuel (1656-1709) & Elizabeth MOUSAL (-1729); 19 Jun 1679; Charlestown/Cambridge
READ, Samuel (1661-) & 1/wf Abigail ROWLAND (1664-); 17 Apr 1684; Marblehead
REED, Samuel (1635/40-1716) & Wilmot _?_ , sister of Samuel CONDY's wife; b 1692, ca 1655/60; Salem
REDD, Samuel (-1716) & Jane STACEY/STACY, w Henry; 4 Nov 1692; Marblehead
READ, Samuel (1661-) & 2/wf Mary BRIDGES; 11 Dec 1692; Lynn
READ, Samuel[3] (1669-1725) & 1/wf Deborah CHAPIN (1675-1702); 8 Jul 1693, 8 Jun 1693; Milford/Mendon/Cambridge
READ, Thomas & Priscilla [BANKS] (1613-); in Eng, b 1630; Salem (returned to Eng)
READ, Thomas & 1/wf Sarah? _?_ (-ca 1645); b 1637; Salem
READ, Thomas (-1667) & 2/wf Mary _?_ ; ca 1646; Salem
READE, Thomas (1627-1701) (nephew of Edmund BROWN?, nephew of Richard SMITH) & 1/wf Katharine _?_ (?1628-1667) (?sister of Elizabeth, wf of John GOODRICH); b 1649; Sudbury
REED, Thomas & Elizabeth _?_ ; b 1651; Newtown, LI/?Milford, CT
READ, Thomas (-1659) & Mary _?_ , m/2 Thomas MATSON 1660; b 1656/(7?), b 1656; Boston
REED, Thomas (1641-1696) & 1/wf Elizabeth CLARKE (-1674/5); 29 Mar 1665; Rehoboth
REED, Thomas (1645-1719) & Sarah [BICKNELL]; b 1671; Weymouth
READ, Thomas (1641-1696) & 2/wf Anna/Anne?/Hannah/Hanna PERREN (1645-1710); 16 Jun 1675; Rehoboth
READ, Thomas (1627-1701) & 2/wf Mary (_?_) WOOD, w Michael; 7 Mar 1677; Sudbury
READ, Thomas, Jr. (ca 1653-1726+, 1733?) & Mary GOODRIDGE/GOODRICH; 30 May 1677; Sudbury
READ, Thomas (1656-) & Hannah BLANCHARD (1659-), dau John; b 14 Jun 1679; Dunstable
REED, Thomas & Elizabeth _?_ ; Stratham, b 1680
READ, Thomas (1665-) & Anna/Hannah _?_ ; b 1687; Chelmsford?
READ, Thomas (1627-1701) & 3/wf Arabella (_?_) THONG/TONG/TONGUE (1646, ?1654-1717), wid; 29 Dec 1689; Sudbury
REED, Thomas & Mary OLMSTEAD; 9 May 1694; Norwalk
READ, Thomas & Sarah BUTTERWORTH (1675-); 21 Jun 1699; Rehoboth

REED, Timothy & Martha **BOYDEN**; 27 Dec 1688; Woburn/Holden/Charlestown

READ, William (1587-1656, in Eng) & Mabel **KENDALL** (1605-1690), m/2 Henry **SUMMERS** 1660; in Eng, b 1629; Dorchester/Woburn/etc./Roxbury

REED, William (?1606-1679) & Susannah **HAYME** (?1606-1653); in Eng, 12 Oct 1629; Weymouth

REED, William (1605?-1657?) & Avis **CHAPMAN/CHEPMAN** (1610-1676+); in Eng, 26 Oct 1635; Weymouth

READ, William & Ruth **CROOKE** (-1674+); 20 Mar 1653/4, 20 May; Boston/New London, CT

READE, William (?1631-1667) & Hannah **(WIGWALL)** [**MUNNING**] (1635-), w Mahalaleel, m/3 Thomas **OVERMAN** by 1672; b 1665, ca 1661; Boston

REED, William (-1697) & 1/wf Deborah [**BALDWIN**] (1657±-); ca 1673; Fairfield, CT

REED, William (1656, 1639?-1706) & Esther [**THOMPSON/TOMSON**] (1652-1706); 1675; Weymouth

REED, William (-1688) & Elizabeth [?**PIERCE**]; b 1682; Woburn

READE, William (1662-1718) & Abigail **KENDALL** (1666-1734); 24 May 1686; Woburn/Cambridge

READ, William (not John) (-1697) & 2/wf Mary **(BRINSMEDE)** [**BOSTWICK**] (1640-1704), w John; ca 4 Dec 1688, aft 5 Nov 1689; Fairfield, CT

READE, William & Anna **STARK**; 4 May 1699; Norwich, CT

REAPE, Samuel & Joanna **(ARNOLD) RHODES**, w Zachariah; 11 Jan 1666, 1666/7; Providence

REAPE, Thomas & Judith **(HART) RATCHEL**, w Robert, m/3 Philip **BULLIS** 1663; 30 Nov 1660; Charlestown/Boston

REAPE, William (1628-1670, ae 42) & Sarah __?__ (-1716±); b 1664; Newport

RECORD, John & Hannah **(BURR) HOBART** (-1683), w John; 26 Aug 1677, Jul?; Hingham

RECORD, John (-1713) & Grace __?__, m/2 Thomas **PARRIS**; b 1692; Pembroke

RECORDS, __?__ & Sarah **SIMMONS** (1672-); b 11 Mar 1707/8, b 1701?; Salisbury

REDDING, John (-1716, ae 62) & Mary **BASSETT** (1654-); 22 Oct 1676; Sandwich

REDING, John (1660-) & 2/wf? Jane **HAWKINS**, m/2 Richard **BABSON**; 12 Mar 1692/3; Gloucester

REDDING, Joseph (-1674) & ?Agnes/?Annis __?__; b 1640; Boston/Cambridge/Ipswich

REDDING, Richard & Mary [**BROWN**]; b 1670?, b 1690

REDDING/RIDDAN/now **RADDAN**, Thaddeus & Elizabeth [**KING**]; b 1655; Marblehead

RIDDING, Thomas (-1673) & Eleanor **PENNY/PENNOYER** (1623-); 20 Jul 1639; Plymouth/Casco Bay/Scituate/Saco, ME/Weymouth

REDINGTON, Abraham (1618-1697) & Margaret __?__ (-1697+, 1694?); b 1645(6?); Topsfield

REDINGTON, Abraham[2] (1647-1713) & Martha __?__ (-1695); ca 1675; Boxford

REDINGTON, Daniel (1657-1732) & Elizabeth **DAVISON**; 23 Mar 1680/1; Topsfield

REDINGTON, John (-1690) & 1/wf Mary [**GOULD**] (1621-); b 1649, ca 1647; Topsfield

REDINGTON, John & 2/wf Sarah __?__, m Edward **BRAGG** 1691; b 1690; Ipswich

REDINGTON, Thomas (1649-) & Mary **KIMBLE/KIMBALL**; 22 Mar 1682/3; Boxford/Topsfield

REDDOCK/?**REDDOUGH**, Henry (-1672/3?) & 2/wf Mabel **BURROWES/BURROUGHS**; 2 Jun 1656; Providence/Warwick, RI

REDFIELD, James & 1/wf Elizabeth **HOW** (1645-); - May 1669; New Haven/Saybrook, CT/Fairfield, CT

REDFIELD, James & 2/wf Deborah **(STURGES) SEELEY**, w Benjamin; b 1694; Fairfield, CT

REDFIELD, William (-1662) & Rebecca __?__ (-1667+); ca 1636?; Cambridge/New London, CT

REDFORD, Charles & Elizabeth **(ROBERTS) TURNER**, w John; 19 Jun 1684; Marblehead/Salem

REDFORD, William (-1697?) & 1/wf Sarah **(FROST) SHIPWAY** (-1695, ae 29), w John; b 1695

REDFORD, William & Elizabeth [**DEW**], m/2 Richard **WIBIRD** b 1701; ca 1696; Portsmouth, NH

REDYATE, John (-1687) & Anne **DOLT**; 26 Aug 1643; Sudbury

REDIAT, John (1644-) & Susannah [**GOODENOUGH/GOODNOW**], m/2 John **MILES** 1679, m/3 John **WILSON** 1698; b 1670; Marlborough

REDKNAP, Benjamin & Sarah **TOMPSON**; 19 Mar 1673, 1673/4; Charlestown

REDNAP, Joseph (-1685) & Sarah [**LAUGHTON**]; b 1644; Lynn

REDMAN, Charles (1666-), Milton & Martha **HILL**, Dorchester; 10 Feb 1688, 1688/9; Milton/Stoughton

REDMAN, John (1615-1700) & 1/wf Margaret [**KNIGHT**] (-1658), dau Richard; b 1637, b 1642; Hampton

REDMAN, John & Martha **CASS** (1649-); 27 Mar 1667; Hampton, NH

REDMAN, John (1615-1700) & 2/wf Sabina **(?LOCKE/?HEMING/?PAGE) MARSTON** (-1689), w William; 23 Jul 1673; Hampton, NH

REDMAN, John (1672-1718) & Joanna BICKFORD, m/2 Samuel HEALEY; 12 Nov 1696; Dover, NH

REDMAN, Robert (1611-1679) & Lucy _?_; b 1658; Dorchester/Milton

REDMAN, [?John] & Ann [PARSONS], m/2 John RICHBELL b 1670, m/3 John EMERSON b 1686; b 1654?; Mamaroneck, NY?

REDWAY/REDEWAY, James (-1684) & _?_ (-1654+); b 1644, b 1642; Rehoboth

REDWAY/REDEWAY, John (1644-1718) & Mary (IDY) FULLER, w Samuel; 27 Dec 1677; Rehoboth

REDWOOD, Abraham & Mehitable [LANGFORD] (-1715); b 1697, b 1696; Newport

REEVES, Isaac & Annis [RIDER] (-1722), wid in 1686; aft 1671, b 16 Feb 1677; Southold, LI

REEVES, James (-1697?, 1698) & ?Mary [TERRY] (-bef 1692); b 1672, b 26 Nov 1671; Southold, LI

REEVES, James (?1672-1732, ae 69) & Deborah [?HOWELL]/?[SATTERLY] (?1676-1754, ae 78) [?dau Wm., Brookhaven]?; Southold, LI

REEVES, John (?1609-1681) & 1/wf Jane _?_; b 1640; Salem

REEVES, John (-1681) & 2/wf Elizabeth _?_; b 1658; Salem

REEVES, John (?1652-1712) & 1/wf Hannah [BROWN]; b 1675?; Southold, LI

REEVES, John (?1652-1712) & 2/wf Martha _?_ (?1676-16 May 1762); ca 1700?; Southold, LI

REEVES, John (1673-1753) & Rachel _?_; b 1701?; Southampton, LI

REEVES, Jonathan (-1708) & Martha _?_ (-1728, 1729); ca 1691?, b 1683?; Southold, LI

REEVES, Joseph (1656-1736) & 1/wf Abigail _?_ (-1708); ca 1678; Southold, LI

REEVE, Robert (-1681) & 1/wf Mary [SKINNER] (1633-); ca 1655; Hartford

REEVE, Robert (-1681) & 2/wf Elizabeth [NOTT]; b 1663?; Hartford

REEVE, Robert (1675-) & 1/wf Elizabeth _?_; b 1701?; Hartford

REEVES, Thomas (-1650) & Hannah ROE, m/2 Richard EXELL 1651; 15 Apr 1645; Roxbury

REEVES, Thomas (-bef 22 May 1666) & Mary [PURRIER] (1628-1707), dau William; ca 1644-6; Southold, LI

REEVES, Thomas (-1685) & Rebecca [?RIDER], m/2 Benjamin DAVIS 1685+; by 1672?; Southampton, LI

REEVES, William (?1646-1718) & Elizabeth COLLINS; 14 Mar 1669/70; Salem

REEVES, William (?1649-1697) & Mary [?TERRY]; ca 1670/74; Southold, LI

REITH, Richard (-1708) & Elizabeth GORGE; 16 Feb 1664/5; Lynn/Marblehead

REITH, Richard & Ann ORMES; 29 Apr 1691; Marblehead

RELZEA, Thomas & Rachel [PARKER] (1680-); b 1700; Wallingford, CT?

REMICK, Abraham (1667-) & Elizabeth [FREEMAN] (1671-), m/2 Joseph MERRICK/MYRICK 1712; b 1692; Eastham

REMICK, Christian (1631-1718+) & Hannah [?THOMPSON] (-1703+); b 1656; Kittery, ME

REMICK, Isaac (1665-) & Elizabeth _?_; Kittery, ME/SC

REMICK, Jacob (1660-1745) & 1/wf Lydia _?_; b 1684; Kittery, ME

REMICK, Jacob (1660-1745) & 2/wf? Mary [SHAPLEIGH?]; b 1692; Kittery, ME

REMICK, Joshua (1672-) & 1/wf Anna LANKESTER/LANCASTER; 21 Dec 1693; Amesbury

REMICK, William & _?_; b 1652 (wife in Eng); Marblehead

REMINGTON, Daniel & Hannah _?_; b 1671; Boston

REMINGTON, Daniel (1661-) & _?_ (?COOKE); b 1686, b 1697; Jamestown, RI

REMINGTON, John[1] (-1667) & 1/wf Elizabeth _?_ (-1657); b 1630?, b 1629; Rowley/Roxbury

REMINGTON, John[2] (-1709+) & Abigail [ACRE/ACY]; b 1650(1?); Rowley/Haverhill/Andover

REMINGTON, John[1] (-1667) & Rhoda (_?_) [GORE], w John, m/3 Edward PORTER aft 1675, m/4 Joshua TIDD 1677+; aft 2 Jun 1657, bef Jun 1659; Rowley/Roxbury

REMINGTON, John (1650/1-1688) & Abigail [RICHMOND] (1656-1744), m/2 Henry GARDINER; b 1681; Newport/Kings Town, RI

REMINGTON, John (1661-) & 1/wf Margaret SCOTT (1671-1693); 6 Dec 1687; Suffield, CT

REMINGTON, John (1661-) & 2/wf Hannah HALE (-1768); 19 Dec 1700, 29 Dec; Suffield, CT

REMINGTON, Jonathan (1639-1700) & Martha BELCHER (1644-1711); 13 Jul 1664; Cambridge

REMINGTON, Joseph & _?_; b 1680; Jamestown, RI

REMINGTON, Stephen (-1738) & Penelope _?_; b 1686; Jamestown, RI

REMINGTON, Thomas (ca 1636-1721) & Mehitable WALKER (-1718); 19 Mar 1657/8; Rowley/Windsor, CT/Suffield, CT

REMINGTON, Thomas (-1710) & Mary [ALLEN] (-1710+); b 1682; Portsmouth, RI/Warwick, RI

REMINGTON, Thomas & Remember STOWELL (1662-1694); 16 Mar 1687/8, m bond 15 Mar 1687/[8]; Hingham

REMINGTON, [?Daniel] & Elizabeth (SANFORD) [DYER] (1655-1718), w Henry, m/3 _?_ SIMPSON; aft Feb 1690; ?Portsmouth, RI

REVEDLY, George & Catharine HOLMES; 28 Aug 1696; Gravesend, LI?

RUE, Abraham & Elizabeth _?_ ; b 1687(8?); Boston

REW, Edward (-1678) & Sarah [RICHMOND] (?2638-1691), m/2 James WALKER 1678, m/3 Nicholas STOUGHTON 1691?; b 14 Dec 1663, no issue; Taunton

REW/RUE?, John (-1717) & Hannah (NORTON) [NORTH], w Samuel; ca 1683/5; Farmington, CT

REW, Thomas & Rachel [BROUGHTON] (1670-); by 1701; Boston

REYLEAN, John & Margaret BRENE; 15 Mar 1661; Boston

RENALDS, Alexander & Mary PEASE; 16 Jul 1686, 6 Jul; Salem

RENALS, Elistius (1653-1738) & Mary _?_ (same?); b 1687(8?), b 1693; Manchester/Middleborough

REYNOLDS, Francis (1662-1722) & Elizabeth [GREENE] (1668, 1669-1722), ?m/2 _?_ HILL?; b 1689; North Kingston, RI

REYNOLDS, Henry (-1693) & [Sarah] _?_ ; b 1642; Salem/Lynn

REYNOLDS, Henry (1656-1716) & Sarah [GREENE] (1664-1716+); b 1686; Kings Town, RI/E. Greenwich, RI

REYNOLDS, James (-1700) & Deborah _?_ ; b 1648; Providence/N. Kingston, RI

REYNOLDS/RENALS, James (1650-) & 1/wf Mary GREENE (1660-); 19 Feb 1684/5, 16 Feb 1684/5; Warwick/Kingston, RI

REYNOLDS, James (1674-) & 1/wf _?_ ; 1697?; ?Greenwich, CT (had 2/wf Sarah HOLMES b 1686?)

REYNOLDS, James (1650-) & 2/wf Joanna _?_ ; b 22 Mar 1699; Kings Town, RI

REYNOLDS, Job & _?_ /Sarah CRAWFORD, wid?; b 1674, b 1692; Portsmouth, NH

REYNOLDS, John (-1662) & [Sarah] _?_ (?1614-1657); b 1634?; Watertown/Wethersfield, CT

REYNOLDS, John & _?_ ; b 1646?, b 1647; Portsmouth, NH/Isles of Shoals

RENOLDS, John (-1691) & Ann [HOLBROOK] (1629/30?-), dau Thomas; b 1652?; Weymouth/Westerly, RI/Stonington, CT

REYNOLDS, John (-1702) & Sarah [BACKUS] (-1702+); b 1655; Saybrook, CT/Norwich, CT

REYNOLDS, John (-1682) & Naomi [LATIMER], wid called Mary, m/2 Philip GOFF ca 1683; b 1666?, b 1668; Wethersfield

REYNOLDS, John & Judith [PALMER] (dau Wm. P. & Judith FISKE); ca 1667/8?, 1668; ?Greenwich, CT

REYNOLDS, John (1648-1675) & _?_ ; ca 1670?; Kings Town, RI

REYNOLDS, John (1651-1722) & Sarah _?_ ; ca 1675; ?Kennebunk, ME/Portsmouth, NH

REYNOLDS, John & Mary _?_ ; b 1682; Watertown/Wethersfield, CT

REYNOLDS, John (?1662-1734) & Abigail _?_ ; b 1686; ?Stonington, CT

REYNOLDS, John & Rebecca [COGGESHALL] (1669-); b 1687?; ?Newport, RI

REYNOLDS, John (1674-) & Hannah DIX (-1733, in 65th y); 16 Nov 1693; Wethersfield, CT

REYNOLDS, John (?1662-1736) & Ruth [KNAPP] (1666?, 1667?-1736+?); b 1694, b 1696; Greenwich, CT

REYNOLDS, John (1670-1732) & [Lydia FERRIS]; b 1695; Greenwich, CT

REYNOLDS, Jonathan (1635/7-1674) & Rebecca [HEUSTED] (?1645-); ca 1656?, ca 1658, b 1660?; Greenwich, CT

REYNOLDS, Jonathan (1660-1728) & Nevill RIDEWARE/RIDEWERE/Newell RICE?/RIDE?; 7 Dec 1682, 4 Dec 1682; Greenwich, CT

REYNOLDS, Jonathan (-1704) & Elizabeth COULTMAN/COLTMAN?/COLEMAN?, m/2 Stephen HOLLISTER; 4 Nov 1697; Wethersfield, CT

REYNOLDS, Joseph (1652-1739) & 1/wf _?_ ; b 1672/3; N. Kings Town, RI

REYNOLDS, Joseph (?1660-1728/9) & Sarah EDGERTON (1667-1714); 10 Jan 1688; Norwich, CT

REYNOLDS, Joseph (1672/3-1722) & Susanna [BABCOCK], sister Job, m/2 Robert SPENCER 1723; b 1697; N. Kings Town, RI

REYNOLDS, Joseph & 1/wf Abigail [FINCH]; 1698, b 1699; Greenwich, CT

REYNOLDS, Joseph (1652-1739) & 2/wf Mercy _?_ ; b 1701?; N. Kingston, RI

REYNOLDS, Nathaniel (-1708) & 1/wf Sarah DWITE/DWIGHT (1638-24 Jan 1664/5); 30 Dec 1657, 1 Jan 1657, 7 Jan 1657, 30 Dec 1657, 7 Jan 1657/8; Boston

REYNOLDS, Nathaniel (-1708) & 2/wf Priscilla [BRACKETT] (-bef 1738); aft 24 Jan 1664/5, bef 21 Feb 1666; Boston/Bristol, RI
REYNOLDS, Nathaniel & Sarah/Ruth? _?_; b 1687; Boston
REYNOLDS, Nathaniel (1663-) & Ruth [?LOWELL] (1665-1716); b 1689, ca 1685?; Boston
RAYNOLL/REYNELL, Nicholas & _?_
REYNOLDS, Owen & _?_
REYNOLDS, Peter (1670-1740) & Mary GILES; b 1700, ca 1699; Bristol, RI
REYNOLDS, Robert (1585-1659) & Mary _?_ (-1663); b 1620?; Boston/Watertown/Wethersfield, CT
REYNOLDS, Robert (-1662) & _?_; Wethersfield, CT
REYNOLDS, Robert & Elizabeth _?_; b 1669(70?); Boston/Pulling Point
REYNOLDS, Robert (1676/7-1715) & Deliverance [SMITH] (1684?-1715+); ca 1700; Kings Town, LI
REYNOLDS, Thomas (?1652-1723) & Sarah CLARKE (1663-1726); 11 Oct 1683, 29 Oct 1683; Newport/Westerly, RI/Stonington, CT/New London
REYNOLDS, William (-1646+) & _?_; b 1628; Providence
RENOLDS, William & Alice KITSON; 30 Aug 1638, 3? Aug; ?Plymouth/?Duxbury/Cape Porpoise, ME?
REYNOLDS, William & Elizabeth [FROST] (1673-), m/2 William HOADLEY; b 1695(6?), div, b 1695; New Haven
REYNOLDS, William & 1/wf _?_; ca 1660/78?; Pemaquid
REYNOLDS, _?_ (-by 1688) & Alice _?_; Charlestown
RHODES, Eleazer (1641-) & _?_; b 1670?; Lynn
ROADS, Henry (1608-) & Elizabeth [?WHITE] (-1700); b 1641, b 1640; Lynn
ROADS, Henry & Elizabeth PAUL; 27 Feb 1694; Boston/Lynn
RHODES, Jeremiah (1647-) & Madeline [HAWKINS]; b 1676; Providence
RHODES, John, Sr. (-1685) & _?_ CARPENTER?/[HUBBARD], w Benj.?, had son Jeremiah; b 1665, ca 1660?; Jamaica, LI
ROADS, John (1658-1716) & Wait WATERMAN (1668±-1711+); 12 Feb 1684/5; Warwick, RI
RHODES, John & Dinah/Diana _?_; b 1686; Oyster Bay, LI
RHODES, John & Susanna EDGECOMB/BRADEN?; 5 Aug 1696; Marblehead
RHODES, John & Tabitha BODIN; 31 Oct 1700; Marblehead
ROODS, Joseph (1645-) & Jane COOTTS/COATES; 25 May 1674; Lynn
ROODS, Joshua (1648-1725) & Ann GRAVS/GRAVES; 12 Jun 1678; Lynn
ROODS, Josiah & 1/wf Elizabeth COOTS/COATES; 23 Jul 1673; Lynn
RHODES, Josiah & Anna BURRELL (1666-); 24 Jul 1695; Lynn
ROADS, Malachi (-1682), Providence & Mary CARDER (-1698); 27 May 1673; Warwick, RI
RHODES, Malachi (-1714), Warwick & Dorothy WHIPPLE; 8 Mar 1699/1700; Providence, RI/Warwick, RI
RHODES, Peleg (1660-1724±) & Sarah _?_; ca 1690/5?; Providence
ROAD, Richard & 1/wf _?_/Prudence HICKS, Boston; m cont 7 Aug 1691; Marblehead
ROODS, Samuel (1642-1718) & Abigail COOTS/COATS (1663-); 16 Jan 1681, 1681/2; Lynn
RHODES, Thomas & Mary [THOMPSON]; b 1680; Kittery, ME
RHODES, Thomas & Elizabeth PEDERICK, ?m/2 Joseph ABORN; 26 May 1695; Marblehead
RHODES, Walter & _?_; b 1682, b 1668?; Providence/Newport
RHODES, William & _?_; by 1676?; Newport
RHODES, William & Sarah MANSFIELD, m/2 John ALLEN ca 1707?, ca 1700; 1 Jun 1698; New Haven/Newport
RHODES, Zachariah/Zachary? (1603±-1665?, 1666) & [Joanna ARNOLD] (1617-1692?, 1668?), m/2 Samuel REAPE 1667; b 1647, b 29 Jun 1647, by 7 Mar 1646; Rehoboth/Providence/Weymouth
RHODES, John & _?_ CARPENTER, dau John (had Hannah, Abigail); b 10 Nov 1694; Jamaica, RI/LI?
RICE, Benjamin (1640-1713) & 1/wf Mary BROWN (-1691); ca 1662; Sudbury
RICE, Benjamin (1640-1713) & 2/wf Mary (CHAMBERLAIN) GRAVES, w John; 1 Apr 1691; Sudbury
RICE, Benjamin (1666-1748, 1748/9) & Mary RICE (1669-1736), dau Samuel; 15 Nov 1692; Marlborough
RICE, Caleb (1668-1739) & Mary WARD (1676-1742); 21 May 1696; Marlborough

RICE, Daniel (1655-1737) & 1/wf Bethiah WARD (ca 1658-1721); 10 Jan 1681; Marlborough
RICE, David (1659-1723) & Hannah WALKER (1670-1704); 7 Apr 1687; Sudbury/Framingham
RICE, Ebenezer (-1724) & Bethiah WILLIAMS (1676-1721); 17 May 1698; Dorchester/Sudbury
RICE, Edmund (-1663) & Thomasine FROST (1600-1659); Bury, Eng, 15 Oct 1618; Sudbury
RICE, Edmund (1594-1663) & 2/wf Mercy (?HURD) BRIGHAM (-1693), w Thomas, m/3 William HUNT; 1 Mar 1655, 1654/5?; Sudbury
RICE, Edmund (1653-) & Joyce RUSSELL (1660-); 13 Oct 1680; Sudbury
RICE, Edmund (1663-1726) & Ruth PARKER, Roxbury; 15 Nov 1692; Marlborough
RICE, Edward (1622-1712) & Agnes BENT (-1713); b 1647; Sudbury
RICE, Ephraim (1665-1732) & 1/wf Hannah LIVERMORE (1670-1724); 21 Feb 1688/9, 22 Feb, 21 Feb; Watertown/Sudbury
RICE, Gershom (1667-1768) & Elizabeth [BALCOM] (1672-1752); b 1698, b 1696?; Charlestown/ New London, CT
RICE, Henry² (1621-1711) & Elizabeth MOORE (-1705); 1 Jan 1643, 1 Feb 1643, 1644; Sudbury
RICE, Henry & Jane [JACKSON], wid; aft 1683
RICE, Isaac (1668-) & Sybil/Sybella COLLINGS/COLLINS (1671, 1670-), m/2 George REED; 27 Sep 1690; Concord/Sudbury
RICE, Jacob (1660-1741) & Mary __?__ (1672?-1752); b 1693; Marlborough
RICE, James (1669-1730) & Sarah [STONE] (1675-); b 1695; Marlborough/Worcester
RICE, John & Ann HACKLEY; 27 Nov 1649; Dedham
RICE, John & Mary __?__; b 1669; Boston
RICE, John (1646-1731) & Elizabeth HOLDEN (1652-); 16 Jul 1674; Warwick, RI
RICE, John (?1647-1719) & Tabitha STONE (1655-1719+); 2 Nov 1674, 2 Nov, 27 Nov; Sudbury
RICE, John & Elizabeth WILSON; 4 Dec 1684; Dedham
RICE, John (1675-) & Elnathan WHIPPLE (1675-); 25 Jul 1695; Providence
RICE, John (1675-1733) & 1/wf Elizabeth CLAP (1682-1705); 13 Mar 1700; Milton/Sudbury
RICE, Jonathan (1654-1725) & 1/wf Martha EAMES/AMES (-1675, 1676?); 23 Mar 1675/6, should be [1674/5]; Sudbury
RICE, Jonathan (1654-1725) & 2/wf Rebecca WATSON (-1689); 1 Nov 1677; Cambridge/Sudbury
RICE, Jonathan (1654-1725) & 3/wf Elizabeth WHEELER; 12 Feb 1690/1; Sudbury
RICE, Joseph (1637-1711) & 1/wf Martha KING (1641-1669); 4 May 1658; Sudbury
RICE, Joseph (1637-1711) & 2/wf Mary [BEERS] (1643-1677); b 1671; Sudbury/Watertown
RICE, Joseph (1637-1711) & Sarah (PRESCOTT) WHEELER (1637-), w Richard; 22 Feb 1677/8; Dedham
RICE, Joshua (1632-) & Bathsheba PRATT (1639-); b 1664, Dec 1662; Boston
RICE, Joshua (1661-1734) & Mary [SAWYER] (1671-1766?, ae 95); b 1693
RICE, Leonard & Mary __?__; b 5 Jul 1700
RICE, Matthew (1629/30-1717) & Martha LAMSON (1634-1717+); 7 Jul 1654, 2 Nov; Sudbury
RICE, Nathaniel (1660-) & 1/wf Sarah __?__; ca 1685/90?; Sudbury
RICE/RIST?, Nicholas & Sarah (CLARK) [DAVIS], w George; b 1668, ca 1671; Reading
RICE, Paul & Hannah __?__ (-1709); Concord
RICE, Peter & Mary FORD; 29 Oct 1683; Concord
RICE, Peter (1658-1753) & Rebecca [HOWE] (1668-1749); b 1690; Marlborough
RYCE, Peter & __?__; b 1701, 1688; Simsbury, CT
RICE, Richard (-1709) & 1/wf Elizabeth __?__; b 1641
RICE, Richard (-1709) & 2/wf [Mary] __?__; b 1698; Concord/Cambridge
RICE, Samuel (1634-1684, 1685?) & 1/wf Elizabeth KING (ca 1635-1667); 8 Nov 1655; Sudbury
RICE, Samuel (1634-) & 2/wf Mary (DIX) BROWN (-1675), w Abraham; ?Sep 1668, Aug?/Sep 1668, 2 Sep; Sudbury/Watertown
RICE, Samuel (-1685) & 3/wf Sarah (WHITE) HOSMER, w James; 13 Dec 1676, 31 Dec; Concord
RICE, Samuel & Rebecca MILLS; 5 Dec 1682; Dedham
RICE, Samuel (alias KING) (1667-1713) & Abigail CLAPP (-1713); 30 Oct 1693, prob 1695; Milton
RICE, Thomas (1626-1681) & [Mary KING]? (-1715); b 1654, b 1652, betw 1665 & 1677?; Sudbury
RICE, Thomas (1654-1748) & 1/wf Mary __?__ (-1677); b 1677; Sudbury/Watertown
RICE, Thomas & Mary [WITHERS] (1660-); ca 1676, ca 1675, b 22 Jul 1675; Kittery, ME
RICE, Thomas (1654-1748) & 2/wf Anna RICE (1661-1731); 10 Jan 1681/2, 1681; Marlborough
RICE, Timothy & Abigail MARRET, m/2 Joseph CRACKBONE; 27 Apr 1687; Cambridge/Concord

RICE, _?_ & _?_ RICE, wid; Feb 1639/40
RICH, Edward & Anna/Ann [BALCH], m/2 Nathaniel WALLIS 1698; b 1695; Beverly
RICH, Henry (1654-), Greenwich & Martha PENOIR/PENOYER (1664-); m cont 21 Dec 1680, 1682?; Stamford, CT
RICH, John (1665-1747) & 1/wf Mary TREAT (1682-1723); 12 Dec 1700; Eastham
RICH, Nicholas & Abigail [GREEN] (1661-); b 1687; Wenham/Wallingford, CT
RICH, Obadiah (1678) & Bethiah WILLIAMS, m/2 Benjamin GANSON bef 1682; 3 Jul 1661; Salem
RICH, Richard (-1692, Eastham) & Sarah [ROBERTS]; b 1665, b 1671; Portsmouth, NH/Eastham
RICH, Richard (1674-1743) & Ann/Anna/Anne _?_ (-1753, ae 63); b 1696; Eastham
RICH/?LARICH, Thomas & Mary (TAYLOR) PETTY/(PETTEE), m/3 Joseph JENNINGS; 6 Apr 1697; Springfield/Brookfield
RICH, Thomas & Mary MACKINTER/McINTIRE; 30 Jun 1699; Salem/Reading
RICH, Richard² (-1692) & Mary ROBERTSON? (1647-); b 1685; Eastham
RICH, _?_ & Mary (?BASSETT)/(?HOOD) DERICH (1657-1701+), w Michael; aft 1690
RICH, _?_ & Martha _?_ (-1692), m/2 Giles COREY
RICHARDS, Benjamin (-1665, 1666) & Hannah HUDSON, m/2 Richard CRISP 1666?; 10 Oct 1661; Boston
RICHARDS, Daniel & Elizabeth (BARRETT) PROCTOR, w John; m int 22 Sep 1699; Lynn
RICHARDS, David & Elizabeth RAYMOND (1662-); 14 Dec 1698; New London, CT
RICHARDS, Edward (1610-1684) & Susan/Susanna HUNTING; 10 Sep 1638; Dedham
RICHARDS, Edward (1616-1690) (called "bro." by Matthias FARNSWORTH, settlement of William KNIGHT's estate) & Ann KNIGHT (-1690+); b 1651; Lynn
RICHARDS, Humphrey & Mehitable [RUGGLES] (1650-); b 1666(7?); Boston
RICHARDS, Humphrey (-1727, ae 61) & Susanna WAKEFIELD (-1728); 25 Oct 1695; [Boston]/Watertown
RICHARDS, Israel (ca 1668/70?-) (see RICHARDSON) & ?Hannah WOODRUFF; b 1701?, 5 Dec 1697; New London, CT/Waterbury, CT
RICHARDS, James (1631?-1680) & Sarah [GIBBONS] (1645-), m/2 Humphry DAVY by 1686; b 1662; Boston/Hartford
RICHARDS, James (-1711) & Ruth [BICKNELL] (1660-1728); b 1683(4?); Weymouth
RICHARDS, John (1631-) & Lydia [STOCKING] (Lydia BEMAN not same John); b 1652; Plymouth/Hartford
RICHARDS, John² (1615?, 1625?-1694) & Elizabeth (HAWKINS) (LONG) WINTHROP, w Nathaniel, w Adam; 3 May 1654; Boston
RICHARDS, John (-1695) & Sarah [PRATT] (-1727); b 1672; Weymouth
RICHARDS, John (-1689) & Mary COLEBORNE/COLBURN (-1685); 1 Oct 1672; Dedham
RICHARDS, John & Elizabeth WOODBERIE/WOODBURY; 16 Jun 1674; Beverly
RICHARDS, John & Mary BRUER/BREWER; 18 Nov 1674; Lynn
RICHARDS, John & Mary _?_; b 1677; Plymouth
RICHARDS, John & 2/wf Mary FULLER (-1715), dau Robert, m/2 Boaz SIMS, Sr. 1695; aft 1685, b 1688; Dedham
RICHARDS, John & Abigail (PARSONS) MUNN, w John; 7 Oct 1686; Deerfield/Westfield
RICHARDS, John & Elizabeth _?_; b 1689; Boston
RICHARDS, John (1661-1705±) & Mary WALTON; 17 Aug 1692; Wallingford, CT
RICHARDS, John (-1694) & 2/wf Anne WINTHROP (-1704); 1 Sep 1692
RICHARDS, John & 1/wf Hannah GOODRIDG/GUTTERIG (1665-1695); 22 Mar 1693/4; Newbury
RICHARDS, John (1666-1720) & Love [MANWAING] (1670-1743); b 1691(2?), b 1695, ca 1686?, b 1693; New London, CT
RICHARDS, John, Jr. & 2/wf Sarah CHENY (1666-); 16 Jul 1696; Newbury/Rochester, NH
RICHARDS, John & Judith [FULLER]?/FAIRBANKS? (1673?-); b 1698; Dedham
RICHARDS, Joseph & 1/wf Susan/Susanna _?_ (-1680?); b 1676, b 1680; Weymouth
RICHARDS, Joseph & 2/wf Sarah _?_; b 1684, aft 28 Sep 1680; Weymouth
RICHARDS, Joseph & Abigail ROLLINS; 12 Aug 1697; Dover, NH
RICHARDS, Joseph (-1710) & Anna CARVER (1670-), m/2 Joseph PRATT; b 1701; Weymouth
RICHARDS, Justinian & _?_; b 1670; Greenland
RICHARDS, Nathaniel & 1/wf _?_ (?)HAYES, wid; Norwalk
RICHARDS, Nathaniel (-1682, Norwalk) (ae 77 in 1681), Norwalk & [Rosamond] LINDON/LINDALL? (-1683, Norwalk), w Henry L-; 15 Mar 1663/4; New Haven/Fairfield
RICHARDS, Nathaniel (1648-1727) & Mary ALDIS (1657-1727); 21 Feb 1678/9; Dedham

RICHARDS, Obadiah (-1702) & 1/wf Hannah [ANDREWS] (1647-); ca 1666, b 1668; Farmington, CT/Waterbury, CT
RICHARDS, Obadiah, Jr.? (-1702, Waterbury) & 2/wf Rachel _?_; Hartford/Waterbury, CT
RICHARDS, Philip & Alice _?_; b 1690; Boston
RICHARDS, Richard (-1678?) & Elizabeth REEVES (-1681+); 16 Jan 1660/1; Salem
RICHARDS, Samuel & 1/wf _?_; b 1696(7?); Hartford
RICHARDS, Samuel (-1732/3) & 2/wf? Hannah HENBURY; 14 Jun 1697, 1694?; Hartford
RICHARDS, Thomas (?1590-1650?, 1651?) & Welthean [LORING]? (-1679?); in Eng, b 1615; Boston/Weymouth/Hull
RICHARDS, Thomas (-bef 1639, 1659?) & Priscilla WAKEMAN (-1671?); 23 Jan 1630, b 1631; Hartford
RICHARDS, Thomas (1666-1749) & Mary PARSONS; 1 Oct 1691, 2? Oct, 21 Oct; Hartford
RICHARDS, William (-1682) & Grace [SHAW] (?1621-1682?); b 1656; Weymouth
RICHARDS, William (-1694) & Mary [BATCHELDER] (1652-); by 26 Mar 1673
RICHARDS, William & Mary _?_; b 1680; Lexington
RICHARDS, William (1656?, 1658?-1683) & Mary [WILLIAMS]; ca 1680?; Weymouth
RICHARDS, William (-1693) & _?_; [b 1691?]; Salem
RICHARDS, William & Mary DOW/DOE?; 23 Aug 1694; Salisbury
RICHARDS, _?_ & Mary DUNGAN
RICHARDSON, Amos (-1683) & Mary [?SMITH]/?TINKER; b 1645; Boston/Stonington, CT/Westerly, RI
RICHARDSON, Benjamin & Lydia (DRAPER) WHITTEMORE, w Samuel, m/3 _?_ PARKER; 11 Mar 1699/1700; Charlestown
RICHARDSON, Caleb (1652-1725) & Mary LADD; 31 Jul 1682; Newbury
RICHARDSON, Edward & _?_; b 1647; Newbury
RICHARDSON, Edward (1649-1682) & Anne BARTLETT, m/2 John WEED; 28 Oct 1673; Newbury
RICHARDSON, Edward (1674-) & Elizabeth HALE; 11 Dec 1696; Newbury
RICHARDSON, Ezekiel (-1647, Woburn) & Susanna _?_, m/2 Henry BROOKS; b 1632; Boston/Charlestown
RICHARDSON, Ezekiel (1655-1734), Woburn & Elizabeth SWAN; 27 Jul 1687; Cambridge/Woburn
RICHARDSON, Ezekiel (1667-1696) & Mary [BUNKER] (1669-), m/2 Moses BARRON, m/3 Thomas HOWE; b 1688(9?); Charlestown
RICHARDSON, Francis (-1688) & Rebecca [?LAYWARDS], m/2 Edward SHIPPEN; Jan 1680?, London; RI/NY?
RICHARDSON, Francis & Susanna POWSLAND; 20 Oct 1698; Marblehead
RICHARDSON, George (1605, 1607?-) & _?_; aft 1635, b 1642; Watertown
RICHARDSON, Henry & Mary _?_; ca 1622/6?; 5 ch in 1635 or 1636
RICHARDSON/RICHARDS?, Isaac (1643-1689) & Deborah FULLER, m/2 _?_ SHAW; 19 Jun 1667; Woburn/Charlestown
RICHARDSON, Israel (-1712) & Hannah WOODRUFF (-1713); 5 Dec 1697; Waterbury, CT
RICHARDSON, Jacob & Hannah CONVERSE; 9 Nov 1697; Woburn
RITCHESON, James (?1641-1677) & Bridget HINCKSMAN/HENCHMAN (-1731), m/2 William CHANDLER 1679; 28 Nov 1660; Chelmsford/Charlestown
RICHARDSON, James (-1722) & 1/wf Rebecca EATON (-1699); 1698; Woburn
RICHARDSON, James (-1722) & 2/wf Elizabeth ARNOLD; 22 Dec 1699; Reading/Woburn-/Charlestown
RICHARDSON, John & Elizabeth FRYAR/TRUAIR?/TRYER?, ?m/2 John CLIFFORD (no, see William RICHARDSON); ?12 Oct 1643, declared void; Watertown/Wells, ME
RICHARDSON, John (-1679?) & Martha [MEAD] (-1690?), m Thomas WILLIAMS; b 1656; Westchester, NY
RICHARDSON, John (1639-1697) & 1/wf Elizabeth BACON; 22 Oct 1658; Woburn
RICHARDSON, John & Sarah [BREEDON?]; b 1662; Boston?
RICHARDSON, John & 2/wf Mary PEIRSON/PIERSON/?REASONS; 28 Oct 1673, 1672?; Cambridge/Woburn
RICHARDSON, John (-1696) & [Mary] HALLAM?; b 1674, ca 12 Oct 1673; Newbury
RICHARDSON, John & Rebecca CLARKE (1660-), m/2 John HILL; 1 Ma- 1679, 1 May 1679; Medfield

RICHARDSON, John (-1715) & Susanna DAVIS (1662-), m/2 David ROBERTSON, m/3 Peter HAY; 22 Oct 1680; Woburn

RICHARDSON, John (1668-1749) & 1/wf Deborah [BROOKS] (1669-1704); b 1689; Woburn

RICHARDSON, John & 3/wf Margaret WILLING; 25 Jun 1689; Woburn

RICHARDSON, John (1670-1746) & Elizabeth FAREWELL/FARWELL (-1722); 31 Jan 1693/4; Chelmsford

RICHARDSON, John (1670-) & Margaret WOODMANSEY; 22 Jun 1699; Boston

RICHARDSON, John (1679-) & Esther BRICK/BRECK; 8 Nov 1699; Sherborn

RICHARDSON, Jonathan (1667-1758) & 1/wf Elizabeth BATS/BATES (1671-3 Jul 1693); 8 Nov 1692; Chelmsford/Charlestown

RICHARDSON, Jonathan (1674?-1700) & Ann [EDWARDS] (1678-), m/2 William DAVENPORT 1702; b 1697; ?Hartford/Stonington, CT

RICHARDSON, Jonathan (1669-) & Mary [CUTLER]/[ISAAC?]; b 1701; Mendon

RICHARDSON, Joseph (1643-1715) & Hannah GREEN; 5 Nov 1666; Woburn

RICHARDSON, Joseph (1655-1724) & Margaret GODFREY (1663-); 12 Jul 1681; Newbury

RICHARDSON, Joseph & Mary BLOCKHEAD/BLODGET (1673-); 24 Oct 1693; Woburn/at Charlestown

RICHARDSON, Joshua (1651-) & Mary PARKER (-1685); 31 Jan 1678; Newbury

RICHARDSON, Joshua (1651-) & Jeane/Jane ORDIWAY/ORDWAY; 4 Jan 1687/8; Newbury

RICHESON, Josiah (1635-1695) & Remembrance UNDERWOOD (1640-1719); 6 Jun 1659; Chelmsford/Charlestown

RICHARDSON, Josiah (1665-1711), Chelmsford & Mary PARRIS/PARISH? (1668-1743), m/2 Jonathan BUTTERWORTH; 14 Dec 1687; Dunstable

RICHARDSON, Nathaniel (1651-1714) & Mary _?_ (-1719); b 1675; Woburn

RICHARDSON, Nathaniel (1673-) & Abigail REED (1679-); 18 Sep 1694; Woburn/Lancaster

RICHARDSON, Pierson & Mary PERRING/PERRIN (1673-1772); 17 Apr 1695; Woburn

RICHARDSON, Richard (-1677) & Joanna _?_ ; ca 1635; Boston

RICHARDSON, Richard (-1681) & Amy GRAVES, m/2 John LINDSEY 1682; 20 Jun 1665; Lynn

RICHARDSON, Samuel (1610, 1602?, 1604?-1658) & Joanna THAKE/OHAKE (-1666?); b 1638, 1622; Charlestown

RICHARDSON, Samuel (1646-) & 1/wf Martha _?_ (-1673); b 1670; Woburn

RICHARDSON, Samuel (1646-) & 2/wf Hannah KINGSLEY (-1676); 30 Sep 1674, 20 Sep; Woburn

RICHARDSON, Samuel (1646-) & 3/wf Phebe BALDWIN (-1679); 7 Nov 1676; Woburn

RICHARDSON, Samuel (1646-1712) & 4/wf Sarah HAYWARD/HAYWOOD? (1656, 1655-1717); 8 Sep 1680; Woburn

RICHARDSON, Samuel (-1712/13) & Anne/Anna [CHESEBROUGH] (1660-); ?1685, b 1686; Stonington, CT

RICHARDSON, Stephen & Lydia [GILBERT] (Oct 1654-), m/2 John CHAPMAN 1696+; b 25 Sep 1673; Hartford/Stonington, CT

RICHARDSON, Stephen (1649-1717/18) & Abigail WYMAN (-1720); 31 Dec 1674, 2 Jan 1675, 1674/5; Billerica/Woburn/Charlestown

RICHARDSON, Stephen (1674-) & Bridget RICHARDSON (1674-); 21 Nov 1695; Woburn

RICHARDSON, Stephen & Susanna [WILSON]; b 1700; Billerica

RICHARDSON, Stephen & Joanna MINER (bpt 1680-); 1 Oct, b 1702, b 1701?; CT

RICHARDSON, Theophilus (1633-1674) & Mary CHAMPNEY (-1704), m/2 John BROOKS 1684; 2 May 1654; Woburn

RICHARDSON, Thomas (1608-1651) & Mary _?_ (-1670), m/2 Michael BACON 1655; b 21 Feb 1635/6; Charlestown/Woburn

RICHARDSON, Thomas (-1712) & Mary [SENIOR] (-1712); b 1667; Farmington, CT/Waterbury, CT

RICHARDSON, Thomas (1645-1721) & 1/wf Mary STIMSON (-1690); 5 Jan 1669/70; Billerica

RICHARDSON, Thomas (1661-1700) & Hannah COBORN/COLBURN? (1656-); 28 Sep 1682; Chelmsford

RICHARDSON, Thomas (1645-1721) & 2/wf Sarah (KENDALL) (DUNTON) PATTEN (-1734), w Samuel, w Thomas; 29 Dec 1690; Billerica

RICHARDSON, Thomas (1675-1718) & Abigail [RUGGLES] (1675-1758); b 1698(9?); Roxbury/Billerica

RICHARDSON, Thomas & [Rachel PARKER] (1680-); 1700; Wallingford, CT

RICHARDSON, Thomas (1674-) & _?_ ; b 1701?; Boston
RICHARDSON, William & Ann _?_ (1625-1659); ca 1638/45?; Newport/Flushing, LI
RICHARDSON, William (-1657) & Elizabeth WISEMAN; 23 Aug 1654; Newbury
RICHARDSON, William, Newport & ?2/wf Deliverance SCOTT (-1676); 30 Aug 1670; Providence/Flushing, LI/Newport
RICHARDSON, William & ?3/wf Amy BORDEN (1654-1684); 27 Mar 1678; Newport/Flushing, LI
RICHARDSON, William (see RICKETSON) & Elizabeth MOTT; 14 May 1679; ?Newport/Flushing, LI
RICHARDSON, Zachariah & Mehitable PERRING/PERRIN; 14 Feb 1700, prob 1699/1700; Woburn
RICHBELL, John (-1684) & [Ann] REDMAN, wid, m/3 John EMERSON 1685?; b 1670; Charlestown
RICHBELL, _?_ & _?_ (PARSONS); b 1651; Oyster Bay, LI
RICHMOND, Ebenezer (1676-) & Anna [SPROUT/SPROAT] (1671-); b 1701; Middleboro
RICHMOND, Edward (?1632-1696) & 1/wf Abigail [DAVIS] (1635-); b 1656, ?aft 20 May 1657; Taunton/Newport/Little Compton, RI
RICHMOND, Edward (?1632-1696) & 2/wf Amy [BULL]; ca 1680?, aft 1672; Newport/Little Compton, RI
RICHMOND, Edward (1658-) & Sarah _?_ ; b 1684; ?Newport/Little Compton, RI
RICHMOND, Edward (1665-1741) & 1/wf Mercy _?_ (-by 1711); b 1693; Taunton
RICHMOND, John[1] (?1594-1664) & _?_ ; in Eng, b 1627; Taunton/Newport
RICHMOND, John (?1627-1715) & 1/wf Susanna HAYWARD (-1662?); b 1654; Bridgewater-/Taunton
RICHMOND, John[2] (?1627-1715) & 2/wf Abigail [ROGERS] (1641-1727); b 1663?; Taunton
RICHMOND, John (?1660-1740, 1738?) & Elizabeth _?_ ; ca 1694?; Westerly, RI
RICHMOND, Joseph (1663-) & Mary ANDREWS; 26 Jun 1685; Taunton
RICHMOND, Samuel (1668-1736), ?Freetown & 1/wf Mehitable ANDREWS; 20 Dec 1694; Taunton/Middleboro
RICHMOND, Sylvester (1672-1754) & Elizabeth [ROGERS] (1672?, 1673-1724); b 1694; Little Compton, RI/Dartmouth
RICKARD, Eleazer & Sarah _?_ ; b 1688; Plymouth
RICKARD, Giles[1] (1597-1684) & 1/wf Judith (COGAN) [KING] (-1661, 1661/2?), w William; in Eng, b 1622; Plymouth/Middleboro
RICKARD, Giles[2] (1623-1710) & Hannah DUNHAM (-1709); 31 Oct 1651; Plymouth
RICKARD, Giles[1], Sr. (1597-1684) & 2/wf Joane TILSON, w Edmund; 20 May 1662; Plymouth
RICKARD, Giles[1], Sr. (1597-1684) & 3/wf Hannah (PONTUS) CHURCHILL (-1690), w John; 25 Jun 1669; Plymouth
RICKARD, Giles[3], Jr. & Hannah SNOW, dau Wm., m/2 Joseph HOWES b 1701?; 7 Nov 1683, no issue; Plymouth
RICKARD, John (-1678) & Esther/Hester? BARNES; 31 Oct 1651; Plymouth
RICKARD, John (?1652-1726, Plympton) & Hester [DUNHAM]; b 1677; Plymouth
RICKARD, John & Mary [?COOKE]/?SNOW (-1775+), Pilgrim; ca 1677, 1676?; Plymouth
RICKARD, John & Grace _?_ ; ca 1688
RICKARD, Josiah (-1765, Plympton) & Rebecca EATON (-1770, Plympton); 21 Nov 1699; Plymouth
RICKARD, Samuel (1663-1727, Plympton) & Rebecca SNOW (-1740, ae 67); 31 Dec 1689; Plymouth
RICKER, George (-1706) & Eleanor [EVANS]; b 1681; Dover, NH
RICKER, Maturen (-1706) & _?_ (4 ch); ca 1690/95?, 1692?; Dover, NH
RICKER, William & _?_ ; b 1654; Boston
RICKETSON, William (-1691) & Elizabeth MOTT (1659-1723+), m/2 Matthew WING 1696; 14 May 1679; Portsmouth, RI
RIDDAN/REDDEN/REDDING/now RADDAN, John (1665-) & Joan HAWKINS; 12 Mar 1692/3; Marblehead
RIDDIN/REDDING?, Thaddeus (1624-1691) & Elizabeth [KING]; b 1660, b 1655; Lynn/Marblehead
RYDER, Benjamin & Mary GRAY; 10 Jun 1680, ?13 Jun 1670; Yarmouth
RIDER, John (-1706) & _?_ (-1691); b 1664; Yarmouth
RYDER, John & _?_ ; b 1665?; Newtown, LI
RIDER, John & _?_ ; b 1675; E. Casco Bay, ME/Charlestown

RIDER, John (1664-1719) & Hester/Esther [HALL?]; b 1692; Yarmouth
RIDER, John (ca 1663, ca 1664-) & 1/wf Hannah [BARNES] (1672-1703); b 1694, ca 1692; Plymouth
RIDER, Joseph (?1644-1718) & 1/wf _?_ ; b 1676?; Yarmouth
RIDER, Joseph (?1644-1718) & 2/wf Sarah [MATTHEWES], w Thomas; Yarmouth
RIDER, Phineas (-1681) & Alice _?_ ; Casco, ME
RYDER, Samuel (1601-1679) & Anne _?_ (-1695); b 1630?, b 1636; Plymouth/Yarmouth
RIDER, Samuel & _?_ (see above); b 1647; ?Yarmouth
RIDER, Samuel[2] (?1630-1715) & 1/wf Sarah BARTLETT (1635±-bef 1680); 23 Dec 1656; Plymouth/Yarmouth
RIDER, Samuel (called "cousin" by John CROW 1684) & 2/wf Lydia TILDEN (1658-1740), Plymouth; 14 Jun 1680; Taunton
RIDER, Thomas (-1655) & Elizabeth [LANE], m/2 Henry GUERNSEY; b 1649; Boston/Dorchester
RIDER, Thomas & ?Mary/?Abigail _?_ /TERRY?; b 1650?; Southold, LI
RIDER, Thomas (-1699) & Abigail [TERRY] (1 Mar 1650/1-); b 1672?; Southold, LI
RIDER, Thomas & Sarah [LAWRENCE] (-1714, ae ca 40); b 1694; Dorchester/Roxbury
RIDER, William (-1724) & Hannah LOVET/LOVETT (?1656-1715); 11 Aug 1674; Watertown/Cambridge/Sherborn
RYDER, Zechariah (?1638-1685) & Mary _?_ , m/2 Edward STURGIS 1692; b 1670?; Yarmouth
RYDER, _?_ & [Elizabeth WATERMAN]; ?Plymouth
RIGDALE/RIDGDALE, John (-1621) & Alice _?_ (-1621); b 1620; Plymouth
RIDGEWAY, John (1623-) & Mary [BRACKINBURY] (1634-1670); b 1652; Charlestown/Pemaquid
RIDGEWAY, John (-1721, ae 68) & Hannah/?Anna _?_ ; b 1688(9?); Boston
RIDGEWAY, Solomon & Bethiah WIT/WITT; 25 Apr 1698; Boston
RIDLEY, Mark & _?_ ; Truro
RIDLEY, William (-1720) (?son of William RIDLAND/RIDLON) & _?_ ; b 1701?; Charlestown
RIDLON/RIDLAND/REDLAND?, William (-1694) & Patience [DAVIS] (1640-); b 1663; Charlestown
RIGBY, John (-1647) & Isabel _?_ (1610-), m/2 Edward BRECK ca 1647, m/3 Anthony FISHER 1663; ca 1636?, b 1640; Dorchester
RIGBY, John (-1690) & Elizabeth _?_ (-1701); 30 Aug 1662; Lancaster/Concord
RIGBY, John (1663-1710) & Mary CRISP (-1755); 13 Dec 1695; Concord
RIGBY, Samuel (1640-1691) & 1/wf Elizabeth [GEORGE] (1641-); ca 1660; Dorchester
RIGBY, Samuel (1640-1691) & 2/wf Hannah _?_ (-1691); b 1670?, b 1676; Dorchester
RIGGS, Edward[1] (-1672) & 1/wf Elizabeth _?_ (-Oct 1635); in Eng, b 1614; Roxbury
RIGGS, Edward[2] (-1668) & Elizabeth ROOKE?/ROOSA?, m/2 Caleb CARWITHIE; 5 Apr 1635; Roxbury/Milford, CT
RIGGS, Edward[1] (-1672) & 2/wf Elizabeth _?_ (-1669); aft Oct 1635; Roxbury
RIGGS, Edward[3] & Mary [MUNN]?; b 1662; Derby, CT/Newark, NJ
RIGGS, John & Ruth WHEELAR/WHEELER; 1 Jan 1689/90; Gloucester
RIGGS, John & Elizabeth TOMLINSON; 23 Feb 1699, 1699/1700; ?Derby, CT
RIGGS, Joseph (ca 1642-1699) & Hannah BROWNE, m/2 Aaron THOMPSON; ca 1676
RIGGS, Samuel (-1734) & 1/wf Sarah BALDWIN (1649-1712); 14 Jun 1667; Milford, CT/Derby, CT
RIGES, Thomas (-1722) & 1/wf Mary MILLET/MILLETT (1639-); 7 Jun 1658; Gloucester
RIGGS, Thomas & Anne/Ann WHEELER; 22 Nov 1687, at Amesbury; Gloucester
RIGGS, Thomas (-1722) & 2/wf Elizabeth FRESE, w James; 30 Oct 1695; Gloucester
RYLEY, Henry (-1710) & 1/wf Mary ELETROPE/ELITHORP (1635-1700); 12 Oct 1656; Rowley
RIELIE, Henry (-1710) & 2/wf Elizabeth (PALMER) (WALLINGFORD) BENNETT (-1741), w Nicholas, w Anthony; 12 Dec 1700; Rowley
RILEY, Isaac (-1738) & Ann BUTLER; 17 Dec 1696; Wethersfield, CT
RILEY, James & [Abiah BAILEY]; b 5 Mar 1688/9; Queens Co., NY
RILEY, John (-1679) & Grace [BUCK?] (1624-1703); b 1646; Wethersfield, CT
RILEY, John (-1684) & Margaret [O'DEA?] (-1689); b 1660; Springfield
RILEY, John (1646-1711) & Lydia [GILBERT] (1656-1705+); Wethersfield, CT
RILEY, John & Mary _?_ ; ca 1685?; Kennebec/Charlestown
RYLEE, John & Bridget _?_ ; b 1693; Boston

RILEY, Jonathan (1653-1712) & Sarah DEMING (1663-); 13 Jul 1681, 31? Jul; Wethersfield, CT

RILEY, _?_ & Mary FROST; Fairfield

RINDGE, Daniel[1] (-1661) & 2/wf? Mary [KINSMAN], m/2 Uzel WARDWELL 1664; b 1648, b 1654; Roxbury/Ipswich

RINDGE, Daniel (1654-) & 1/wf Hannah [PERKINS] (-Jul 1684); b 1684; Ipswich

RINDGE, Daniel (1654-) & 2/wf [Hannah RUST] (1664-); aft Jul 1684; Ipswich

RINDGE/RING, Isaac & 1/wf Elizabeth [DUTCH] (-1700); ca 1692, b 29 Mar 1692; Ipswich

RINDGE, Isaac & 2/wf Elizabeth (BURNHAM) KINSMAN, w Thomas; m int 27 Jul 1700; Ipswich

RINDGE, Roger (1657-) & Sarah SHATSWELL (1658-); 9 Jun 1684; Ipswich

RINGE, Andrew (?1615-1693), Plymouth/Middleboro & 1/wf Deborah [HOPKINS] (-1669); ca 23 Apr 1646; ?Plymouth

RING, Andrew (?1615, ?1618/19-1693) & 2/wf Lettice [MORTON] (-1691), w John; aft 3 Oct 1673, ca 1674; Middleboro

RING, Eleazer (-1749) & Mary SHAW (ca 1665-1730); 11 Jan 1687, 1686/7?, 1687/8?; Plymouth

RING, Jarvis & Hannah FOWLER; 24 Dec 1685; Salisbury

RING, John (-1684?) & Mary BRAY (-1725, ae 77); 18 Nov 1664; Ipswich/Gloucester

RING, John (1662-) & Priscilla [NORTON] (1667-); b 1691; Salisbury

RING, John & Mary [BROWN] (1676-1726+); b 1701?; Salisbury

RING, Joseph (1664-) & Mary [BRACKET]?, m/2 Nathaniel WHITTIER; [ca 168-90?]; Salisbury

RING, Robert (-1691) (had son Jarvis) & Elizabeth [JARVIS?]; b 1654; Salisbury

RING, Robert & Ruth _?_ ; b 1691; Amesbury

RING, Samuel & Sarah _?_ ; b 1670; Plymouth

RING, Samuel & Bethiah [KING]; b 1697; Plymouth

RING, Thomas & Elizabeth CLAPP; 20 Apr 1669; Scituate

RING, William (-1731) & Hannah SHERMAN; 13 Jul 1693; Plymouth

RING, William & Sarah SAWYER; 5 Dec 1699; Gloucester

RING, [?William] & Mary _?_ (-1631, 1633); in Eng, b 1611?; Plymouth

RIPLEY, Abraham (1624-1683) & Mary [FARNSWORTH] (1637-1705), m/2 Edward JENKINS 1684; b 1660?, b 1661?, b 2 Jan 1659; Hingham

RIPLEY, Abraham (1661-1697) & Ruth _?_ ; b 1690; Hingham

RIPLEY, George (1644?-) & Sarah _?_ ; b 1680; Boston/Marlboro

RIPLEY, Jeremiah (1662-1737) & 1/wf Mary GAGER (1671-1731); 7 Apr 1690, 1 Apr 1690; Windham, CT

RIPLEY, John (?1622-1684) & Elizabeth [HOBART] (1632-1692); b 1656, ca 1654; Hingham

RIPLEY, John (?1656-1720) & Jane [?CHAMBERLAIN (no)]/?WHITMARSH (1664 at Weymouth-); 13 Oct 1686; Hingham

RIPLEY, Joshua (1658-1739) & Hannah BRADFORD (1662-1738); Plymouth, 28 Nov 1682; Hingham/Windham, CT

RIPLEY, Josiah (1667-1742) & Joanna SMITH (-1743) (sister of Joshua); b 1695(6?); Weymouth

RIPLEY, Peter (1668-1742) & Sarah LASELL (1666-1736); 17 Apr 1693; Hingham

RIPLEY, William[1] (-1656) & 1/wf _?_ ; in Eng, b 1620; Hingham

RIPLEY, William[1] (-1656) & 2/wf Elizabeth FLAXTER (-1660), w William, m/3 John DWIGHT 1658; 29 Sep 1654; Hingham

RIPLEY, William & Mary CORBISON, m/2 Benjamin HANKS; 11 Oct 1693; Taunton/Bridgewater

RISBY, William & Sarah _?_ ; b 1668, 1660; Dover/Oyster River, NH

RISBY, William & _?_ ; Oyster Bay

RISDON, Robert (-1666) & Beatrice _?_ ; b 1654(5?); Boston/Fairfield, CT

RISHWORTH, Edward (ca 1617-1690) & Susanna/Susan? [WHEELWRIGHT]/?HUTCHINSON; b 20 Jan 1656; Salisbury

RISING, James (-1688) & 1/wf Elizabeth HINSDALE/ENSDELL (1638-1669); 7 Jul 1657; Boston/Salem/Windsor, CT/Suffield, CT

RISING, James (-1688, Suffield, CT) & 2/wf Martha BARTLETT (-1674), w John; 13 Aug 1673; Windsor, CT

RISING, John (ca 1660-1719/20) & 1/wf Sarah HALE (1665-1698); 27 Nov 1684; Suffield, CT

RISING, John (ca 1660-1719/20) & 2/wf Mary MACKCLAFLIN (1678-1764), m/2 Jonathan REMINGTON 1723; 22 Sep 1699; Suffield, CT

RISLEY, John (1678-1755) & Mary [ARNOLD]; b 1701?, ca 1699; Hockanum, CT

RISLEY, Richard (-1648?) & Mary _?_ , m/2 William HILLS 1648; ca 1640?; Hartford

RISLEY, Richard (1648-) & Rebecca [ADAMS]; b 1668; Hartford

RIX, James (1651-) & ?Margaret __?__ ; b 1685; Salem/Wenham/Preston, CT
RICKS, John (1648-) & Charity [SILVESTER?] (?1648-); b 1673?, b 1674, aft 1 Sep 1673; Boston
RIX, Theophilus (1665-1726) & 1/wf Elizabeth __?__ (-1708); b 1696; Wenham
RIX, Thomas[1] & 1/wf Margaret [WARD] (-1660), w Miles; b 1650?, aft 3 Mar 1650/1?; Salem
RIX, Thomas[1] & 2/wf Bridget (MUSKET) FISK, w William; 3 Nov 1661; Salem
RICKS, Thomas & Sarah BLITHE, m/2 Joseph GOODALE ca 1680; 31 Dec 1673; Charlestown/ Boston
RIX, Thomas[1] (-1684) & 3/wf Susanna (SKELTON) [MARSH] (1627-1684+), w John; aft 1680; Salem
RIX, Thomas (-1690) & Abigail [INGERSOLL], m/2 Joshua WILLS; Wethersfield, CT
RIX, William & Grace __?__, m/2 Andrew NEWCOMB by 1664; b 1645; Boston
ROECH, John & Mary PRINGLE/PRINDLE; 23 Jan 1683; New Haven/Milford, CT
ROACH, Thomas (-1708+) & Rebecca REDFIN/REDFIELD (-1670); 12 Dec 1661; New London, CT
ROCH, William & Jael __?__ ; b 1661; Braintree
ROACHE/ROTCH?, William (-1705) & Hannah [POTTER] (1666-), m/2 Daniel DARLING 1717; b 1692; Salem
ROBINS, Benjamin & Sarah BROOKS, m/2 Nathaniel THORPE; 29 Aug 1687; New Haven
ROBINS, Edmund & Barbara __?__ ; b 1688; Boston
ROBBINS, George (-1689) & 1/wf Mary __?__ (-1672); b 1667; Chelmsford
ROBBINS, George (-1689) & 2/wf Alice __?__ (-1686); b 1675(?), b 1682(?); Chelmsford
ROBBINS, George (-1689) & 3/wf Mary BARET (1658-); 21 Jan 1686, 1686/7; Chelmsford
ROBBINS, George (1675-1747, Stow) & 1/wf Elizabeth WOOD (1678-); 19 Oct 1697; Concord/Stow
ROBBINS, Jeduthan (-1721, Plympton) & Hannah PRATT; 13 Jan 1693/4; Plymouth/Plympton
ROBBINS, John (-1660) & Mary [WELLES] (1616-Sep 1659), niece of Gov. Thomas WELLES; b 1639, Sep, ca 1641; Wethersfield, CT
ROBBINS, John & Maria/Mary ABBOTT, w Robert; 4 Nov 1659; Branford, CT
ROBBINS, John (-1670), Bridgewater & Jehosabath/Jehosabeth JOURDAINE (-1723, ae 83, Plympton; 14 Dec 1665; Plymouth
ROBBINS, John & Jane (EVANS) TILLESON, w John; 23 Jun 1670; Branford, CT
ROBBINS, John & __?__ LATTING (?1649/50-), dau Richard; [ca 1672?], by 1666?; Stratford, CT
ROBBINS, John (?1649-10 Jul 1689) & Mary BOREMAN/BOARDMAN (-1721), m/2 __?__ DENISON b 7 Mar 1698/9; 24 Apr 1675; Wethersfield, CT
ROBINS, John (-1717+) & Sarah CHILD; 13 Oct 1680; Marblehead/?Warwick
ROBINS, John & Elizabeth __?__ ; 20 Sep 1692; Lyme, CT
ROBINS, John & Dorothy HILDRETH (-1757, ae 83); 30 Nov 1699, 1698?, 169-; Chelmsford
ROBINS, Joseph & Sarah [WATROUS]; 10 Jun 1697; Lyme, CT
ROBBINS, Joshua (1652/4-1738) & Elizabeth [BUTLER] (no)/ROSE? (yes) (1655-1737); 24 Dec 1680; Wethersfield, CT
ROBBINS, Nathaniel (1649-1719) & Mary BRASIER; 4 Aug 1669; Cambridge/Lexington
ROBBINS, Nathaniel (-1741) & Hannah [CHANDLER] (1673(4?)-); b 1696; Cambridge/Charlestown
ROBBINS, Nicholas (-1650) & Anne __?__ ; b 1645, b 1643?; Duxbury/Bridgewater
ROBBINS, Richard (?1610-1683+) & 1/wf Rebecca __?__ ; b 1650; Charlestown/Boston/Cambridge
ROBBINS, Richard & 2/wf Elizabeth (COOLIDGE) CRACKBONE, w Gilbert; 26 Mar 1673; Cambridge
ROBINS, Robert & Mary [MAXWELL?]; b 1671; Concord
ROBBINS, Robert & 1/wf Mary DILL; 27 Mar 1697; Chelmsford
ROBBINS, Samuel & Mary BROWN; 2 Sep 1663
ROBBINS, Samuel (1643-) & Ebenezer __?__ ; b 1676(7?); Cambridge
ROBINS, Thomas (1617, ?1620-1688) & 1/wf Elizabeth?/Isabel? [WEST] (-1674), wid, w Michael SPENCER; aft 1657?, b Mar 1657; ?Duxbury/Salem
ROBBINS, Thomas & 2/wf Mary (__?__) (GOULD)/GAULT BISHOP, w William, w Richard; 11 Mar 1674/5; Salem
ROBBINS, William & Elizabeth __?__ ; b 1669; Boston
ROBBINS, William (-1725) & Priscilla GOING/GOWING; 2 Jul 1680; Reading/Walpole
ROBERTS, Abraham (-1731, Reading) & Sarah [BURNAP] (1653-1696); b 1681; Reading/Lynn

ROBERTS, Abraham (-1731, Reading) & 2/wf Susannah **THOMPSON** (1661-); 7 Mar 1700; Reading/Woburn

ROBERTS, Archibald & Sarah __?__ ; b 1690; Woburn

ROBERTS, Charles & Mary [**WEARE**] (1660-), of York, m/2 Peter **BROWN**; b 1695, 1690; Boston

ROBERTS, David (-1724) & Joanna **BROOKS** (1659-1724); 2 Oct 1678, 3 Oct; Woburn

ROBERTS, Ely/Eli? & [Mary **MALLORY**], m/2 Samuel **COOK** 1696, m/3 Jeremiah **HOW** 1705; b 1679; New Haven

ROBERTS, Ephraim & 1/wf Dorothy **HENDRICKS?**/**HENDRICK** (1659-1702); 28 Aug 1684, 24 Aug; Haverhill

ROBERTS, George & Mary **JONES**, m/2 Nathaniel **FOLSOM** by 1696, m/3 Nicholas **NORRIS** 1725+

ROBERTS, Gyles (-1667) & __?__ [**SHELDON**]; ca 1652?, ca 1658?; Scarboro, ME

ROBERTS, Gyles & Margaret [**BARRETT**] (1676-); b 1699; Boston

ROBERTS, Hatevil & Lydia [**ROBERTS**]; ca 1686; Dover, NH

ROBERTS, Henry & __?__ ; b 1677; Dorchester

ROBERTS, Hugh & Mary **CALKINS**; 8 Nov 1649; Gloucester/Duxbury?

ROBERTS, John (-1650/1) & Elizabeth __?__ ; in Eng, b 1615?, [came 1636 with 7 ch]; Duxbury

ROBERTS, John (1629-1695) & Abigail [**NUTTER**]; b 1655, ca 1654; Dover, NH/Durham, NH

ROBERTS, John & Elizabeth (**STONE**) **SEDGWICK**, div wf of William **SEDGWICK**; aft 1 Jan 1674/5; Hartford/NJ/Newtown, LI

ROBERTS, John (-1714) & Hannah **BRAY** (1661-1717); 4 Feb 1677/8; Gloucester

ROBERTS, John & Mary __?__ ; b 1681; Boston

ROBERTS, John & Experience __?__ ; b 1684, b 1686; Boston

ROBERTS, John & Patience [**SAXTON**] (1658-); b 24 Jan 1688, 1687?; Windsor, CT/Simsbury,CT

ROBERTS, John (-1721) & Sarah **BLAKE** (1675-); 27 Dec 1693; Middletown, CT

ROBERTS, Joseph & Elizabeth [**JONES**] (1672±-); b 1692, b 1694; Dover, NH

ROBERTS, Joseph & Esther [**DRAPER?**] (1669-); b 1696, b 1694; Boston/Sheepscot, ME

ROBERTS, Mark & Mary **BAKER**; 1 Jan 1682; Warwick, RI

ROBERTS, Nicholas & Mary __?__ ; b 1701; Boston

ROBERTS/**ROBERTSON?**, Peter (-1706+) & Sarah **BAKER**; 27 Apr 1685; Warwick, RI

ROBERTS, Richard (ca 1662/3?-) & Elizabeth __?__ ; ca 1690?; Ipswich

ROBERTS, Robert (1619?, 1617?-1663) (ae ca 40 in 1659) & Susanna [**DOWNING?**]; b 1641?; Ipswich

ROBERTS/**ROBINS?**, Robert & __?__ ; b 1676; Rowley

ROBERTS, Samuel & Elizabeth __?__ (-1692); 9 Dec 1680; Norwalk, CT

ROBERTS, Samuel (-1740) & Mercy **BLAKE** (1673-1724); 22 Sep 1691; Middletown, CT

ROBERTS, Simon (-1680?) & Christian **BAKER** (1634-); 18 Jul 1654; Boston

ROBERTS, Thomas (-1673/4) & [Rebecca] __?__ ; b 1629, b 1628; Dover, NH

ROBERTS, Thomas (-1654) & Eunice **COLE** (1628-), m/2 Moses **MAVERICK** 1656; b 1646; Boston

ROBERTS, Thomas & Mary (__?__) (**PALMER**) **PADDUK/PADDOCK**, w William, w Robert; 24 Mar 1650, 1650/1; Plymouth

ROBERTS, Thomas (-1676) & [?Parnell **HARRIS**], sister of Wm. **HARRIS**; ca 1655?; Providence (no ch)

ROBERTS, Thomas & Sarah **ELLIOT**; 27 Jan 1658/9; Stamford, CT

ROBERTS, Thomas (1636-1679) & Sarah [**STRICKLAND**], m/2 Jonathan **FREEMAN**; ?Newtown, LI

ROBERTS, Thomas (1633, 1636?-) & Mary [**LEIGHTON**]; ca 1660?, by 1664; Dover, NH

ROBERTS, Thomas & Sarah [**CANNEY**]; by 1687

ROBERTS, Thomas & Elizabeth [**HOPLEY**]; nr 1700, aft 1703; Dover, NH

ROBERTS, William & Anne/Anna [**AVERY**], w Matthew; b 1646; Weymouth/Charlestown

ROBERTS, William (-1676?, 1675?) (Quaker) & Dorothy __?__ ; ca 1647/50?, by 1655; Oyster River, NH

ROBERTS, William (1617-1689, Milford) & Joanna __?__ (-1693); b 1650; New Haven/Milford, CT

ROBERTS/**ROBBINS**, William & Susanna **LANE**; 23 Dec 1665; Hingham

ROBERTS, William, Boston & Elizabeth **TOWER** (1648-); 9 Oct 1667; Hingham

ROBERTS, William (1640-) & Anna/Nan? **CROCKETT**, dau Thomas; ca 1668/75?, by 1673, b 1671?; Isles of Shoals/Kittery, ME

ROBERTS, William & Sarah [**HINMAN**] (1653-); b 1677; Stratford, CT

ROBERTS, William & ?Mary/[?Abigail **ABBOTT**], dau Robert; b 1681; New Haven

ROBERTS, William (1663-) & Elizabeth [LOBDELL] (1664 at Springfield-); ca 1690?; Durham, CT

ROBERTS, William & Dorothy [FORBES]; b 1690; Hartford

ROBERTS, William (-1689) & Joanna __?_ (-1693); b 1653; Milford, CT

ROBERTS, William & Sarah [CRESSEY]; ca 1700; Kittery, ME

ROBERTS, Zachariah (1653-) & Mary LAWRENCE; 8 Feb 1676/7; Milford, CT/Bedford, NY

ROBERTS, __?_ & __?_ (-7 Jan 1645/6, ae 102), mother of John; Roxbury

ROBERTS, __?_ & Annis LAKEMAN, dau Wm.; b 1701?; Ipswich?

ROBERTSON, David (1662-) & Elizabeth BUD, Boston; 23 Jun 1684; Charlestown

ROBERTSON, James (-1720, ae 88 y) & Elizabeth [FARNSWORTH?] (-1729); 16 Jan 1667; Groton/?Charlestown

ROBINS/?ROBINEAU, Stephen & Judith [PARE], dau Stephen?/John?; b 1685, b 1680; Boston/Narrangett, RI?

ROBINSON, Abraham (-1645±) & Mary __?_ (-1690), m/2 William BROWNE 1646, m/3 Henry WALKER 1662; b 1644; Gloucester

ROBINSON, Abraham & Mary HARRANDINE/HARRENDON/HARRADUN (1649-1725); 7 Jul 1668; Gloucester

ROBINSON, Andrew & Elizabeth WHAFE/WAFFE; 23 Sep 1674; Charlestown

ROBINSON, Benjamin & Rebecca INGRAHAM; 30 Jul 1693; Rehoboth

ROBINSON, Dane & Mary/Jane CHADWICK; 18 Jan 1693/4; Andover

ROBINSON, Daniel & Hope POTTER; 10 Feb 1663, 3 Feb 1663; New Haven/Monmouth Co., NJ

ROBINSON, David & 1/wf Sarah TAYLOR; 24 May 1680; Exeter, NH

ROBINSON, David (1660-1748) & 1/wf Abigail [KIRBY] (1666-1694); ca 1689; Guilford, CT/Durham, CT

ROBINSON/ROBERTSON, David (see ROBERTSON) & Elizabeth BUDD (1668-); b 1694, 23 Jun 1684; Boston/Charlestown

ROBINSON, David (1660-1748) & 2/wf Mercy (ATWATER) [STOW] (1662-), w Ichabod; ca 25 Jan 1694/5, b 1698; Durham, CT/Guilford, CT

ROBINSON, George (-1699) & Joanna INGRAHAM (-1699); 18 Jun 1651, 18 Apr; Rehoboth

ROBINSON, George & Mary BUSHNELL/BEAMSLEY?, m/2 Thomas DENNIS 1668; 3 Oct 1657; Boston

ROBINSON, George (1659-) & 1/wf Elizabeth __?_ (-1697); b 1680; Boston

ROBINSON, George & Elizabeth GAILLE/GALE?/GUILD? (?1660-); 17 Nov 1680, 12? Nov, 1-Nov 1680; Rehoboth

ROBINSON, George & Sarah [REED] (1665-); b 1683(4?), Dec 1685?, ?12 Dec 1685; Watertown/Cambridge/Woburn?/Lexington

ROBINSON, George & Elizabeth __?_ (1657-1697); b 1695(6?); Boston

ROBINSON, George (1659-b 1702) & 2/wf Sarah (SMITH) MAVERICK, w Elias; 7 Apr 1698; Boston

ROBINSON, Increase (1642-1699) & Sarah PENNIMAN; 19 Jan 1663/4, 19 Feb 1663; Dorchester/Taunton

ROBINSON, Increase (-1738) & Mehitable WILLIAMS (1676-); b 1701?, 11 Feb 1695, 1694/5; Taunton

ROBINSON, Isaac (1610-1704) (ae 92 in 1702) & 1/wf Margaret HANFORD (1619-1649); Scituate

ROBINSON, Isaac (1610-1704) & 2/wf Mary __?_ ; 1650; Duxbury

ROBINSON, Isaac (1642-1668) & [Ann]? __?_ ; b Jun 1666; Falmouth, MA

ROBINSON, Isaac (1670-) & 1/wf Hannah [HARPER] (1670-); ?1 Mar 1690; Falmouth

ROBINSON, Isaac & Sarah [EVERTON] (1667-); b 1693; Charlestown

ROBINSON, Isaac (1651-1728) (previous to 1668 Israel) & Ann [COTTLE] (1673-1727?); b 1701?; Martha's Vineyard

ROBINSON, Jacob & Sarah HITCOCK/[HITCHCOCK] (1669-); b 1691; New Haven

ROBINSON, Jacob (1653-1728?, 1733?) & 1/wf Mary __?_

ROBINSON, Jacob (1653-1728?, 1733?) & 2/wf Experience [ROGERS] (1673-); b 1714, b 1688?, b 1700; Falmouth/Martha's Vineyard

ROBINSON, James (-1673+) & Martha BUCK; 21 Feb 1653/4; Boston

ROBINSON, James (-1694) & Mary ALCOCK/ALCOTT? (1645, 1644-1718), dau Thomas; 27 Sep 1664; Dorchester

ROBINSON/ROBERTSON?, James (see ROBERTSON) & Elizabeth FARNSWORTH (1647-); 16 Jan 1667; Groton/Chelmsford?

ROBINSON, James (-1710?) & Lucretia [FOXWELL] (1644-); ca 1667/70?; Blue Point/Scarborough, ME/Newcastle, NH

ROBINSON, John (-1675) & [Ellen]/Elizabeth? _?_; b 1641, ca 1639; Newbury/Haverhill/Exeter, NH/Dover, NH

ROBINSON, John & Sarah MASON; 16 Oct 1665; Salem

ROBINSON, John (1640-1714+) & Elizabeth WEEKS; about middle of May 1667, 1? May; Barnstable

ROBINSON, John & [Dorothy] [PERKINS]; b 1668; Topsfield

ROBINSON, John & Jeane _?_; ca 1675/80; Oyster Bay, LI/Hempstead, LI

ROBINSON, John & Eunice/Annis (1694) _?_; b 1683(4?); Boston

ROBINSON, John (1661-) & Mary [WHITE]; b 1688(9?); Boston

ROBINSON/ROBERTSON?, John & Susanna _?_; b 1690; Newbury

ROBINSON, John/Isaac? (-1726) & Hannah [HARPER?] (1666-1755); 1690, b 1692; Barnstable?/Rehoboth

ROBINSON, John & Margaret WOODWELL (1671-); 18 Jun 1694; Topsfield

ROBINSON, John & Judith COOPER (Elizabeth is wrong) (1673-1750); 10 Jan 1698, 8 Aug 1698; Rehoboth

ROBINSON, John (1671-1749) & [Mehitable STANYAN] (1676-); b 1701?; ?Exeter, NH

ROBINSON, Jonathan (1648-1716, 1675?) & 1/wf _?_; b 1671; Exeter, NH

ROBINSON, Jonathan (1648-1716, 1675?) & 2/wf [Sarah? (BRADLEY) BEAN]

ROBINSON, Joseph & Phebe DANE; 30 May 1671; Andover

ROBINSON, Joseph (1657-) & Sarah _?_; b 1690; Boston

ROBINSON, Joseph (1679-) & 1/wf Bethia GALL/GALE? (had son Rowland 1701 m Thankful DIMICK 1723); 22 Oct 1700; Falmouth, MA/Martha's Vineyard

ROBINSON, Joseph (1679-) & 2/wf Bethia LAMBERT; 7 Dec 1701

ROBINSON, Nathaniel & Damaris _?_, m/2 Jacob PERKINS ca 1687, b 1655; Boston

ROBINSON/ROBERTSON?, Nicholas (1605-) & Elizabeth _?_ (1603-); in Eng, b 1623?

ROBINSON, Peter (1665-1740) & 1/wf Mary [MENTER] (1665-bef 1698); ca 1687; Martha's Vineyard

ROBINSON, Peter (1665-1740) & 2/wf? Experience MANTON; b 1699

ROBINSON, Robert & Mary SILVER; 26 Oct 1664; Newbury

ROBINSON, Robert & Mary [DAVIS]; b 1701?; Brookhaven, LI

ROBINSON, Rowland (1654-1716) & Mary [ALLEN/ALLING] (1653-1716+); b 1682, ca 1677?; Portsmouth, RI/Newport/Naragansett, RI/Kings Town, RI/Kingstown?

ROBINSON, Samuel & 1/wf Jane? _?_; b 1660?; Salem

ROBINSON, Samuel (-1723) & 2/wf Martha HAUKINS; 15 Aug 1664; Salem

ROBINSON, Samuel (-1682) & [Mary] _?_; b 1665; Hartford

ROBINSON, Samuel (1640-1718) & Mary [BAKER] (1641-1714); 1664?, b 1666; Dorchester

ROBINSON, Samuel (-1674) & Comfort CABLE; ca 1665/70?; Fairfield, CT

ROBINSON, Samuel (-1699) & Mary [WHITTEMORE] (1668-), m/2 John BLITHEN; 1688 or bef; Salem/Charlestown

ROBINSON, Samuel (Daniel in wrong) (1654-1724) & Mehitable REED (-1719); 10 Oct 1688, ?15 Oct; Rehoboth/Attleboro

ROBINSON, Samuel (-1698) & Abigail LOCKWOOD, dau Daniel; 20 Aug 1691; Fairfield, CT

ROBINSON, Thomas & _?_; b 1637?; LI

ROBINSON, Thomas (-1665) & 1/wf Silence _?_; b 1638; at sea/Roxbury/Scituate

ROBINSON, Thomas & 1/wf Margaret _?_; b 1646; Boston

ROBINSON, Thomas (-1689) & Mary _?_ (-1668); b 1650; Hartford/Guilford, CT

ROBINSON, Thomas (-1665) & 2/wf Mary (COGAN) WOODEY/BEAMSLEY? (-1661); 10 Jan 1652, 10 Jan 1652/3; Scituate/Boston

ROBINSON, Thomas (-1665) & 3/wf Elizabeth (LOCK?) [SHERMAN] (-1667), w Richard; aft 26 Oct 1661; Charlestown/Boston

ROBINSON, Thomas & Mary [WELLS] (1650-); b 1665?; New London, CT

ROBINSON, Thomas (-1700) & Sarah [DENNISON] (1657-); ca 1676; Charlestown/Roxbury/Boston

ROBINSON, Thomas (1650-1712) & 1/wf Sarah [CRUTTENDEN] (1665-1692); 3 Oct 1686; Guilford, CT

ROBINSON, Thomas, Salem & Rebecca LAWRENCE, Dorchester; 23 Feb 1686/7; Middlesex, CT
ROBINSON, Thomas (1666-) & Sarah GRAVE/[GRAVES]; 17 Jan 1692; Guilford, CT
ROBINSON, Thomas (-1725) & Lydia [ACKLEY]; b 1695?; E. Haddam, CT
ROBINSON, Thomas & Hannah DORMAN; 20 Nov 1695; Topsfield
ROBINSON, Thomas & Hannah [HORTON], m/2 Miles OAKLEY; b 25 Nov 1696, b 1699/1700; Rye, NY
ROBINSON, Thomas (1650-1712) & 2/wf Sarah [GRAVES] (1668-1715); b 1701?, 17 Jan 1695, 13 Jan 1692, 17 Jan 1693/4; Guilford, CT
ROBINSON, Timothy (-1668) & Mary KITCHEN, m/2 Thomas HANSON 1669; 20 Feb 1665; Salem
ROBINSON, Timothy & Mary [ROBERTS?]/ALLEN?; 1682; Kittery, ME/Dover, NH
ROBINSON, Timothy (1671-) & Mehitable/Experience WEEKS (1671-); 3 May 1699; Falmouth, MA/Martha's Vineyard
ROBINSON, William (-d in Eng) & Constance (_?_), m/2 Jonas AUSTIN 1627
ROBINSON, William & Isabelle _?_; b 1636, b 1637; Salem
ROBINSON, William & 1/wf Prudence _?_; b 1637?; Dorchester
ROBINSON, William (?1615-1668) & 1/wf Margaret _?_/[Margaret BUCK]? (-1664+); in Eng, 14 Oct 1637?; Dorchester
ROBINSON, William (1615-1668) & 2/wf Ursula (ADAMS) (STREETER) HOSIER (1619-), w Stephen, w Samuel, m/4 Griffin CRAFT 1673; aft Jul 1665, ca 1666, 21 Aug 1666; Charlestown/Dorchester/Watertown
ROBINSON, William (-1693) & Elizabeth [CUTTER]; b 1669, 1667 or bef; Concord/Cambridge/Framingham
ROBINSON, William & _?_; b 1674; Watertown
ROBINSON, William & _?_; b 1677; Lyme, CT
ROBINSON, William & _?_; b 1683; Lynn
ROBINSON, William & Elizabeth [UPHAM]; b 1696; Boston
ROBINSON, _?_ & Dorothy _?_, m/2 Edmund FAULKNER 1647; in Eng, ?1705+
ROBINSON, _?_ & Eleanor [WALDRON]; b 1671; Salem
ROBINSON, _?_ & Mary [BARTLETT] (1672/3-); ?Newton, MA
ROBINSON, _?_ & Mary [GREEN]; New London
ROBINSON, _?_ & _?_; b 1669; Kittery, ME
ROVE, Andrew & 1/wf Abigail CURTICE/CURTIS (-1700), w James; 19 Nov 1691; Hartford
ROBY, Henry (1619-1688) & 1/wf Ruth [MOORE] (-1673); b 1645; Hampton, NH
ROBY, Henry (1619-1688) & 2/wf Elizabeth (PHILBRICK) (CHASE) GARLAND (-1677), w Thomas, w John; 19 Jan 1674; Hampton, NH
ROBY, Henry (-1688) & 3/wf Sarah [SHAW] (-1703); aft 11 Feb 1677; Hampton, NH
ROBY, Ichabod (1664-) & 1/wf Lucy PAGE (1672-); 4 Jan 1694; Hampton, NH
ROBE, James & Sarah _?_; b 1687(8?); Boston
ROBIE, John & 1/wf Mary _?_
ROBIE, John (1649-1691) & 2/wf Ann CORLIS/CORLISS (1657-1691); 1 Nov 1677; Haverhill
ROBIE, Samuel (1629-) & Mary [WALTON] (1646?-); ca 1663?; Great Island, NH
ROBIE, Samuel (1659-1733) & Mary [PAGE] (1665-1750); b 1686?; Hampton, NH
ROBY, Thomas (1657-1720); 8 Dec 1687; Hampton, NH & Martha EATON
ROBIE, William (1648-1718) & Elizabeth [GREENOUGH] (1664-); b 1687; Boston
ROCKE, Joseph & Elizabeth [COGAN], sister of Thomas ROBINSON's 1/wf?, 2/wf?; b 1652; Boston
ROCKE, Joseph (-1683) & Mary (WILSON) [DANFORTH] (1633-1713, ae 81), w Samuel; aft 19 Nov 1674; Cambridge/Boston/Roxbury
ROCKWELL, Abraham (-1677) & Mary _?_; 4 Dec 1640, no issue; Windsor, CT
ROCKWELL, John (1588-1662) & Wilmet/Wilmoth CADE (-1662); Fitzhead, Eng, 22 Feb 1619/20; Windsor, CT
ROCKWELL, John (-1676) & _?_; by 1641?; Stamford, CT/Greenwich, CT?/Rye, NY/etc.
ROCKWELL, John[2] (1627-1673, ae 46); & 1/wf Sarah ENSIGN (-1659); 6 May 1651; Windsor, CT
ROCKWELL, John[2] (-1673, ae 46) & Deliverance HAWES (1640-), m/2 Robert WARNER 1674; 18 Aug 1662; Windsor, CT
ROCKWELL, John (-1673/4) & Elizabeth [WEED] (ca 1637-); ca 1660/4?, ca 1658?; ?Rye, NY
ROCKWELL, John & Anne [SKINNER] (1684-); ca 1700, b 1701; Windsor, CT
ROCKWELL, Jonathan (?1665-) & Abigail CANFIELD; April last week, 1700; Norwalk, CT
ROCKWELL, Joseph (?1670-1733) & Elizabeth [DRAKE] (1675-); 23 Jan 1694; Windsor, CT

ROCKWELL, Joseph (-1742) & Elizabeth FOSTER (-1753); 1 Feb 1693/4; Middletown, CT
ROCKWELL, Josiah (-1675?, 1676?) & [Rebecca LOOMIS]; b 1661?, b 1658?; Norwich, CT
ROCKWELL, Josiah (1662-1729) & Ann BLISS (-1715); 8 Apr 1686, 1688; Norwich, CT
ROCKWELL, Samuel (1631-1711) & Mary NORTON (ca 1635-); 7 Apr 1660, 9? Apr 1658?; Windsor, CT
ROCKWELL, Samuel (-1725) & Elizabeth (GAYLORD) HUBBELL (1649-); 10 Jan 1694; Windsor, CT
ROCKWELL, William (1591-1640/1, 1640) & Susanna CAPEN (1602-1666), m/2 Matthew GRANT 1645; Holy Trinity, Dorchester, Eng, 14 Apr 1624; Dorchester/Windsor, CT
ROCKETT, Benjamin (1651-1747) & Judith ELLICE/ELLIS; 27 Sep 1678; Medfield/Wrentham
ROCKETT, John[2] (1641-1725) (m/2 Rebecca bef 3 Jun 1724) & Joanna FORD; 15 Sep 1662; Braintree/Wrentham/Medfield
ROCKETT, John & 1/wf Bethiah TWICHELL/TWITCHELL (-1707); 19 Jul 1688; Medfield
ROCKETT, Joseph (?1659-1693) & 1/wf Hannah PARTRIDGE (-1680); 2 Apr 1679; Medfield/Swansea
ROCKETT, Joseph (-1683) & Mary WILMOUTH/WILMARTH, m/2 Gyles GILBERT 1686, m/3 Jeremiah WHEATON 1723; 5 Jan 1680, 1680/1; Rehoboth
ROCKET, Joseph[3] ((166-), ?1671-) & Mary [HAYWARD]; b 1690; Mendon
ROCKETT, Josiah & 1/wf Mary TWICHELL (-1699); 9 May 1677; Medfield
ROCKETT, Nathaniel (1665-1721) & Joanna ELLICE/ELLIS (1677-1716+); 7 Dec 1698; Medfield/Wrentham
ROCKWOOD, Nicholas (?1628-) & 1/wf Jane/Joan? [ADAMS?] (-1654); b 1651, b 1646; Medfield
ROCKWOOD, Nicholas & 2/wf Margaret HOLLOCK/HOLBORN? (-1670; 16 Jul 1656; Medfield
ROCKETT, Nicholas (-1680) & 3/wf Silence (BOWERS) DUNTHING/DUNCKLEE? (-1677), w Elnathan; 25 May 1675, 16? May; Medfield
ROCKWOOD, Richard (?1598-1660) & 1/wf __?__ ; b 1628?; Dorchester/Braintree
ROCKWOOD, Richard[1] (-1660?) & 2/wf Agnes (?LOVELL) [BICKNELL] (-9 Jul 1643), w Zachary; ca 1636?; Dorchester/Braintree
ROCKWOOD, Richard (1598-1660) & 3/wf Ann __?__ (-1664); aft 9 Jul 1643; Dorchester
ROCKETT, Samuel (-1728) & 1/wf Hannah ELLIS (1651-1717); 15 Dec 1671; Medfield
REDMAN, John & 1/wf Christina GIBSON (-1682); 15 May 1676; Barbados
RODMAN, John & 2/wf Mary [SCAMMON] (-1748); aft 25 Oct 1682; Barbados/Newport/Block Island/Flushing, LI
RODMAN, Thomas (1640-1728) & 1/wf Sarah PEAD (-1682); 9 Mar 1671/2; Barbados
RODMAN, Thomas (1640-1728) & Patience (EASTON) MALINS/MALINES (1655-1690, ae 35), w Robert; 7 Jun 1682; Newport
RODMAN, Thomas (1640-1728) & 3/wf Hannah CLARKE (-1732); 26 Nov 1691, 6 Nov 1691; Newport
ROGERS, Daniel, Billerica & Mary RUSSELL, Concord; 28 Dec 1686; Billerica
ROGERS, Daniel (1667-1722) & Sarah [APPLETON] (-1755, ae 82); b 1694; Ipswich
ROGERS, David & __?__ ; b 1641; Braintree
ROGERS, Edward & Mehitable __?__ ; b 1698; Mamaraneck, NY
ROGERS, Eleazer & Elizabeth (KNOWLES) FORD, w Thomas; 16 Mar 1663, 27 Mar 1663; Milford, CT
ROGERS, Eleazer (1673-1739+) & Ruhamah [WILLIS?] (-1739+), had son Willis; b 1698; Plymouth
ROGERS, Ezekiel & 1/wf Sarah [EVERARD] (no)
ROGERS, Ezekiel & Joane [HARTOPP] (-1649); b 1649; Rowley
ROGERS, Ezekiel (-1660/1) & Elizabeth [WILSON] (-1651); 1650; Rowley/Braintree
ROGERS, Ezekiel (-1660/1) & Mary (__?__) BARKER (-1679), w Thomas, sister of Francis LAMBERT or his wife; 16 Jul 1651; Newbury/Rowley
ROGERS, Ezekiel (-1674, ae 36) & Margaret (HUBBARD) [SCOTT] (-1678), w Thomas; ca 1658?, 1659?, 1661?; Ipswich
ROGERS, Ezekiel (1667-) & Lois (IVORY) BLIGH, w Samuel, m/3 Joseph BASS 1708; 20 Sep 1694; Lynn
ROGERS, Gamaliel (1657-) (had 2/wf Sarah BROWN) & Mary __?__ ; b 1688/[9]?, by 1689; Boston
ROGERS, George & __?__ ; Kittery, ME
ROGERS, Henry & Mary EXELL; 30 Dec 1675; Springfield
ROGERS, Hezekiah & __?__ ; b 1688; East Hampton, LI

ROGERS, Ichabod (1659-) & Sarah **CURRIER**, m/2 Amos **SINGLETARY** 1690+; 13 Jan 1689/90; Haverhill/Salisbury

ROGERS, Israel & Mary [**LOUNSBURY**]; b 11 Aug 1701

ROGERS, Jabez (1649-) & Sarah _?_/**WARD**?; Milford, CT

ROGERS, James (ca 1609-1676) & Mary _?_, m/2 John **PEABODY** 1677; b 1630?; Newport

ROGERS, James (?1615-1688?) & Elizabeth [**ROWLAND**]; b 1640; Stratford, CT/Saybrook, CT/Milford, CT/New London, CT

ROGERS, James (1648-1678) & Mary **PAINE** (-1710+), m/2 Israel **COLE** 1679; 11 Jan 1670; Eastham

ROGERS, James & Mary **JORDAN** (-1713); 5 Nov 1674; New London, CT

ROGERS, James (1673-1751) & Susannah **TRACY/TREACY**; 17 Feb 1697/8; Eastham

ROGERS, James & Sarah **STEVENS** (1680-); 27 Mar 1699; New London, CT

ROGERS, James (1675-1735, Norwalk) & 1/wf Elizabeth _?_ (1681-1713); b 1700; New London, CT/Norwalk, CT

ROGERS, James & Elizabeth _?_; b 1704, b 1701?; Newport, RI

ROGERS, Jehoshophat (1663-) & Sarah [**REED**] (1665-); b 1694?; Salem/Topsfield

ROGERS, Jeremiah (-1676) & Abiah [**PIERCE**] (not Mehitable) (-1678/9); b 1652; Dorchester/Lancaster

ROGERS, Jeremiah (-1717) & 1/wf Dorcas _?_; 11 Dec 1672; Lancaster

ROGERS, Jeremiah (-1717) & 2/wf Abigail (**TRESCOTT**) [**WEEKS**], w Ammiel; b 1693; Salem

ROGERS, John (1594-1674, ae 80) & 1/wf _?_; in Eng, b 1618; Watertown

ROGERS, John (-1661?) & Frances [?**WATSON**] (-1657?), m/2 Walter **BRIGGS** ca 1661; ca 1630/32; Duxbury/Marshfield/Scituate

ROGERS, John (-1661) & Judith? _?_ (left wid Judith, perhaps 2/wf, ?Judith **FRENCH** ae 20 in 1636); b 1636; Weymouth

ROGERS, John² (-1692) & Ann **CHURCHMAN** (-bef 26 Aug 1691); 16 Apr 1639; ?Duxbury

ROGERS, John¹ (-1683/4) & Ruth _?_; ca 1640; Milford, CT

ROGERS, John & Priscilla [**DAWES**]; b 22 Nov 1640; Watertown/Billerica

ROGERS, John (1594-1674) & 2/wf Abigail **MARTIN**; 3 Nov 1653; Watertown

ROGERS, John & _?_; b 1654; Wenham

ROGERS, John (1632-1717) & 1/wf Rhoda **KING** (1639-1662); 8 Oct 1656; Scituate/Marshfield/Boston

ROGERS, John (1630-1684) & Elizabeth **DENNISON** (1645-1723, ae 82); 14 Nov 1660; Ipswich/Cambridge

ROGERS, John (-1710, ae 71) & 1/wf Mary **BATES**; 8 Jan 1662, ?8 Feb 1663?; Weymouth

ROGERS, John (1632-1717) & 2/wf Elizabeth _?_ (-1692); 1662/3; Scituate/Marshfield

ROGERS, John (?1640-1732) & Elizabeth **PABODIE** (1647-1679?); - Nov 1666; Duxbury

ROGERS, John & Mary **SHEDD** (-1688); 10 Oct 1667; Billerica

ROGERS, John (1641-1716) & Elizabeth _?_ (-1676); 1667?; Newport, RI

ROGERS, John & Ann (**GREGORY**) [**CROAKER**], w William; aft 2 Mar 1667, b 14 Dec 1670; Oyster Bay, LI

ROGERS, John & Elizabeth (**RUGGLES**) **BROWN**, Boston, w William; 6 Jul 1669; Billerica

ROGERS, John & Naomi **BURDECK**

ROGERS, John (1642-1714) & Elizabeth **TWINING** (-1724/5); 19 Aug 1669; Eastham

ROGERS, John (1648-1721) & 1/wf Elizabeth **GRISWOLD**, m/2 Peter **PRATT** 1679, m/3 Matthew **BECKWITH**; 17 Oct 1670, div 1676; New London, CT

ROGERS, John (-25 Apr 1672) & Elizabeth _?_; b 25 Apr 1672; Boston

ROGERS, John (-1715) & Elizabeth **BAXTER** (1644-1714); 29 Oct 1674; Salem

ROGERS, John (1640-1732), Duxbury & 2/wf Hannah (**HOBART**) **BROWN** (1638-1691), w John; 21 Oct 1679; Hingham/Bristol, RI

ROGERS, John & Hannah **CHISKE**; 7 Nov 1679; Ipswich

ROGERS, John & Mary [**FORD**] (1658-); ca 1679?; Milford, CT

ROGERS, John (1657-1738) (had 2/wf Hannah 1701) & 1/wf _?_; b 1683; Scituate

ROGERS, John & Martha [**SMITH**] (1670-1740), m/2 Jacob **BOARDMAN** 1699; - Jan 1687, ?12 Jan; Ipswich

ROGERS, John (-1698) & Eleanor _?_; b 1688; Charlestown

ROGERS, John (1641-1695), Billerica & Abigail (**GOULD**) **ROGERS**, Billerica, w William; 7 Feb 1688, [1688/9]; ?Billerica

ROGERS, John (1638-1710), Weymouth & 2/wf Judith STERNS (-1709+), Dedham; 3 Jul 1690; Braintree

ROGERS, John (1666-1745) & Martha WHITINGHAM (1670-1759), m/2 _?_ BOREMAN; 4 Mar 1690/1; Ipswich

ROGERS, John (1640-1732) & 3/wf Marah (COBHAM) BROWNING/BRUNING (?1651-1739), w Joseph; 1693?; Duxbury/Boston/Barrington, RI

ROGERS, John (1632-1717) & 3/wf Elizabeth _?_ (-1705); aft 13 Sep 1692; Marshfield

ROGERS, John, Eastham, Harwich & Priscilla HAMLIN (1670-); 23 Apr 1696; Eastham

ROGERS, John & Elizabeth WILLIAMS; 24 Jun 1696, 1696; Barnstable

ROGERS, John (1668-1727) & Sarah LAWTON (1676-); 4 Nov 1698; Newport, RI

ROGERS, John (1648-) & 2/wf Mary RANSFORD, m/2 Robert JONES 1710; 6 Jun 1699, div; New London, CT

ROGERS, John & Bathsheba SMITH; 2 Jan 1700, 1699/1700; New London, CT

ROGERS, John & 1/wf Hannah SPRAGUE; 11 Dec 1700; Marshfield

ROGERS, John (1677-1761) & Jane [BROWN] (1677-1769); ca 1700; Newport, RI

ROGERS, Jonah & Phebe [LUDLAM] (ca 1673-); b 1691; Bridgehampton, LI

ROGERS, Jonathan & Rebecca [?WILKES/?WICKES]; b 1668; Huntington, LI

ROGERS, Jonathan (1656-1697) & Naomi BURDICK, m/2 _?_ KING; 2 Mar 1678; New London, CT

ROGERS, Jonathan (-1749, ae 82) & 1/wf Mary _?_ ; b 1698; Huntington, LI

ROGERS, Joseph (-1678) & Hannah _?_ (-1678+); b 1633; Duxbury/Sandwich/Eastham

ROGERS, Joseph (1635-1660/1) & Susanna DEAN, m/2 Stephen SNOW 1663; 4 Apr 1660; Eastham

ROGERS, Joseph (1646-1697) & Sarah _?_ (-1728?); ca 1670?; ?Waterford, CT/New London, CT

ROGERS, Joseph (-1716?) & Abigail [BARKER] (-1718?); b 3 May 1677; Duxbury/Pembroke

ROGERS, Joseph (son of Simon) & Elizabeth _?_ ; b 1686; Boston

ROGERS, Joseph (-1696) & ?Prudence _?_, m/2 Machiel ATWOOD 1700; b 1691; Eastham

ROGERS, Joseph & 1/wf Elizabeth [SMITH] (-1704); b 1699; Newport/Tiverton, RI

ROGERS, Joseph & Sarah [CLARK]; b 1701?; Milford, CT

ROGERS, Joshua & Ann FISON/?FINSON; 12 Oct 1653; Boston

ROGERS, Judah & Hannah SKINNER; 3 May 1694; Salem

ROGERS, Nathaniel (1598-1655) & Margaret [CRANE] (-1675); 23 Jan 1625; Ipswich

ROGERS, Nathaniel & Martha CLOYES (1654-); 25 Nov 1685; Billerica

ROGERS, Nathaniel & Margaret WOODMANSEY; 22 Jun 1699; Boston

ROGERS, Nathaniel (1669/70-1735) & Sarah (PEMBERTON) PURKESS/PURKIS; 26 Oct 1699; Boston

ROGERS, Nehemiah & Hannah MORGAN; 20 Nov 1660; New London, CT

ROGERS, Noah (1646-1725) & Elizabeth TAINTOR (1655-1732); 8 Apr 1673; Branford, CT

ROGERS, Obadiah (-1689/90) & Mary [?RUSSELL]; b 1655; Southampton, LI/Southold, LI

ROGERS, Obadiah & 1/wf Sarah HOWELL (-1685); 20 Dec 1683; Southampton, LI

ROGERS, Obadiah & 2/wf Mary [CLARK], w Edmond; aft 1685, bef 1699, by 1687; Southampton, LI

ROGERS, Richard (ca 1643-) & 1/wf Esther _?_ ; bef 1665; Eliot, ME

ROGERS, Richard (ca 1643-) & 2/wf Sarah (LIBBY) TIDY, m/3 Christopher BANFIELD; b 11 Jan 1700/01; Kittery, ME

ROGERS, Richard, Jr. & Eleanor (MOORE); b 1694; Kittery, ME

ROGERS, Robert & _?_ ; b 1640; New London, CT

ROGERS, Robert & Susanna _?_ ; b 1650; Newbury

ROGERS, Robert & Dorothy [SMITH]; b 1701?

ROGERS, Samuel (1635-1693) & 1/wf Judith APPLETON (-1659); 24 Dec 1657; Ipswich

ROGERS, Samuel (1635-1693) & 2/wf Sarah WADE, m/2 Henry WOODHOUSE 1694; 13 Nov 1661; Ipswich

ROGERS, Samuel (1640-1713) & Mary STANTON; 17 Nov 1662; New London, CT/Milford, CT

ROGERS, Samuel & Abigail PLUMB; 16 Jan 1694, 1694/5; New London, CT

ROGERS, Samuel & Grace ROGERS (1679-); 2 Jan 1695, prob 1695/6; Billerica

ROGERS, Samuel (?1670-1747) & Jael HUET/HEWITT (1674-); 3 Dec 1697; Hingham/Scituate/Marshfield

ROGERS, Samuel & 1/wf _?_ ; b 1701; Westerly, RI

ROGERS, Simon & 1/wf Mary _?_ (-1640); b 1640; Concord

ROGERS, Simon & 2/wf Susanna/Susan _?_; b 1643; Boston
ROGERS, Thomas (-1621) & _?_; ca 1600?, b 1612; Plymouth
ROGERS, Thomas (-1638) & Grace (MAKIN) SHERMAN, m/3 Roger PORTER; in Eng, aft 24 Jan 1616; Watertown
ROGERS, Thomas & _?_; b 1634; Saco, ME
ROGERS, Thomas (-1677) & Esther FOXWELL; Jul 1657; Kittery, ME/Saco, ME
ROGERS, Thomas (1638-) & Elizabeth SNOW (?1642-1678); 13 Dec 1665; Eastham
ROGERS, Thomas (1639-1719) & Sarah _?_; ca 1665/70; Newport/Dartmouth/Portsmouth, RI
ROGERS, Thomas & Hannah SHED; 30 Sep 1672; Billerica
ROGERS, Thomas & Ruth BROWN; 18 May 1677; Newbury
ROGERS, Thomas & Mary BROWN; 16 Mar 1680/1; Billerica
ROGERS, Thomas (1672-) & Sarah TREAT (1678-1728); 10 Dec 1700; Eastham/Truro
ROGERS, Timothy (-1728) & Eunice [STETSON] (1650-); ca 1669; Scituate
ROGERS, William (1613-) & Ann/Anna HALL?; ca 1640?, 2 Feb 1630/1?; Wethersfield, CT/Hempstead, LI/Southampton/Huntington, LI
ROGERS, William & ?1/wf [?Sarah LYNN] (1636-); ca 1658?; Salisbury
ROGERS, William & Susanna _?_; b 1667; Boston
ROGERS, William (-1683) & Abigail GOULD, m/2 John ROGERS; 1 Apr 1669; Charlestown/Reading
ROGERS, William & Lydia [GUTCH] (1645-); by 1670; Kennebec
ROGERS, William & Martha [BARNARD]; ca 1670; Martha's Vineyard
ROGERS, William (-1676) & Margaret [SCOTT], m/2 William SNELLING; ca 1672; Boston
ROGERS, William & 2/wf Rebecca (MASHWORTH) [WHARFE], w Nathaniel; b 20 May 1676; Kittery, ME
ROGERS, William & Elizabeth PERKINS, m int 15 Apr 1698; Wenham
ROGERS, Zachariah & _?_; Bridgehampton, LI/Southampton
ROAFE, Benjamin (?1640-1710) & Apphia HALE (1642-1708); 3 Nov 1659; Newbury
ROLF, Benjamin (1662-1708) & Mehitable ATWATER; 12 Mar 1693/4; Haverhill
ROLFE, Benjamin (1674-) & Margaret [HOLLAND]; b 1701?; Salisbury
ROLFE, Daniel (-1654) & Hannah [BRADSTREET] (1625-1665), m/2 Nicholas HOLT 1658; b 1651, b 1650?; ?Andover/?Ipswich
ROFFE, Daniel (-1748, Bedford, MA, nearly 100) & Mary KNIGHTS; 5 Jun 1677; Salem/Chelmsford/Concord
ROLFE, Ezra (-1652) & Hester (FOWLER) [BIRD], w Jathnell, m/3 Robert COLLINS by 1657; b 1652; Salisbury
ROLF, Ezra (-1689) & Abigail BOND, m/2 Thomas FOLLANSBEE 1694; 2 Mar 1675/6; Haverhill/Ipswich?
ROLFE, Ezra & Sarah _?_; b 1691; Newbury
ROLFE, Henry/John & Honour ROLFE (-1656); Whiteparish, Wiltshire, 28 May 1621; Charlestown/Newbury
ROLFE, John (1588-1664) & 1/wf Joane COLES; Whiteparish, Wiltshire, 2 Nov 1612; Salisbury
ROLFE, John (-1664) & 2/wf Hester _?_ (-1647); betw 1638 & 1647; Salisbury
ROAFE, John & Mary SCULLARD; 4 Dec 1656; Newbury/Newtown, LI
ROLFE, John (1664-) & Sarah MOORES; 18 Jul 1688; Nantucket/Woodbridge, NJ
ROLF, John (1660-) & Dorothy [NELSON] (1660-); b 1691; Newbury
RALPH, Samuel (-1723) & Mary _?_ (-1723+); b 1699; Providence
ROLFE, Samuel (1673-) & Martha GIBSON (1671-); 14 Jan 1698/9; Cambridge/Newbury
RALPH, Thomas (-1682) & 1/wf Elizabeth [DESBROUGH], m/2 John JOHNSON; b 1648, div 1 Oct 1651; Guilford, CT/Warwick, RI
RALPH, Thomas (-1682) & 2/wf Mary [COOKE], w John; b 1656(7?); Warwick, RI
ROLFE, Thomas (-1657) & _?_; Salisbury
RALPH, Thomas (1658-1696±) & Eleanor _?_ (-1696+); ca 1685?; Providence
ROLLO, Alexander (-1709) & Hannah (KIRBY) [ANDREWS], w Thomas, m/3 William STONE; b 1693, 1693, betw 3 Nov 1693 & 3 Dec 1693; Haddam/Middletown, CT
ROLLO, Alexander & 1/wf _?_; b 1677 in Scotland
ROLLS/ROLLES?/?ROWELL/?ROWLE/?ROWLES, Thomas?/?Timothy/?Robert & Mary _?_; b 1694; Marblehead
ROOD, Benjamin (1663-) & Mary WILLIAMS; 7 Jun 1690; Norwich, CT
RUDE, John (?1658-1705) & Mary EDDY (1667-); 24 Jun 1687; Preston, CT

ROOD, Micah (1653-1728) & Sarah (PIKE) DAYNS, w Abraham; 15 Jan 1691; Norwich, CT
ROOD, Samuel (1666-) & Mary MARINER; 20 May 1690; Norwich, CT
ROOD, Thomas (-1672) & Sarah _?_ (-1668); b 1649; Norwich, CT
ROOD, Thomas (1651-) & Hannah BENNUM/BENHAM (-1695), Wallingford, CT; 5 May 1684; Norwich, CT
ROOKER/ROCKER?, William & Dorothy SMITH; 30 May 1687; Hadley
ROOT, Caleb (-1712) & 1/wf Elizabeth SALMON, Westfield; 9 Aug 1693; Farmington, CT
ROOT, Darius & Dorothy [ABBOTT]; b 1689?; ?Norwalk, CT
ROOT, Hezekiah (-1690) & Mehitable FRARY, m/2 Jeremiah ALVORD; 12 Jul 1682; Deerfield
ROOT, Hope (1675-1750) & Sarah WRIGHT; - Jul 1699; Deerfield
ROOT, Jacob (ca 1661-1731) & Mary/?Mercy FRARY (1662-1744); 2 Feb 1681, 1680/1?; Deerfield/Northampton
ROOTES, Jerwin (-1697?) & Willmet [COATES], wid; Queens Co., NY
ROOT, John & Mary [KILBOURN] (1619-); ca 1640; Farmington, CT
ROOT, John (1642-1687) & Mary ASHLEY (1644-1702); 18 Oct 1664; Deerfield/Westfield/Wethersfield, CT/Farmington
ROOT, John & Mehitable (JOHNSON) HINSDALE, w Samuel, m/3 John COLEMAN; ca 1676; Deerfield
ROOT, John (?1646-1723) & Dorcas ABBOTT (1661-1720, Woodbury); ca 1677; Beverly/Woodbury, CT
ROOT, John (1669-1710) & Mary [WOODRUFF], m/2 Nathaniel WINCHELL; b 1690; Northampton/Farmington, CT
ROOT, Jonathan (-1741) & Ann GULL (-1746); 22 Mar 1680; Northampton
ROOT, Jonathan (?1666-) & Abigail [?GAIL]; Beverly/Marblehead
ROOT, Joseph (1640-1711) & 1/wf Hannah HAYNES (-1691); 30 Dec 1660; Northampton
ROOT, Joseph (1664-1690) & Hannah [BENTON]; b 1686; Deerfield
ROOT, Joseph & 1/wf Elizabeth WARNER; 17 Sep 1691, b 1692; Farmington, CT
ROOT, Joseph (-1711) & 2/wf Mary (HOLTON) [BURT] (-1713), w David; aft 28 Jan 1691, 1692, 1593, by 1692; Deerfield
ROOT, Josiah (-1683) & Susanna _?_ (-1683+); b 1640?, b 1642, 4 ch bpt 24 Sep 1648; Salem/Beverly
ROOT, Josiah (1642?-) & _?_ [ALLEN?], dau Bozoan?; ?Boston/Beverly
ROOT, Ralph[1] (1585-) & 1/wf Ann _?_; ca 1615/20?, [b 1639]; Boston
ROOTE, Ralph & 2/wf Mary RUG (-15 Nov 1655, Boston); Boston
ROOT, Ralph & Mary (CURTIS) [RUGGLES] (-1675, ae 88), w Thomas; 1644+; Roxbury
ROOTS, Richard (-1653?) & Margaret _?_, m/2 Michael FRY ca 1653; b 1640; Lynn/Salem
ROOT, Samuel (?1644-1711) & Mary [ORTON] (1650-1730), m/2 Mark WARNER 1713; b 1680, no ch; Westfield
ROOT, Stephen (-1717) & Sarah [WADSWORTH] (1667-1740); b 1681?, (3 ch bpt 1691); Farmington, CT
ROOTES, Thomas & 1/wf Katharine _?_ (-living 1681); ca 1636/40?; Salem
ROOT, Thomas (?1605, ?1606-1694) & _?_; b 1640, b 1646; Hartford/Deerfield/Northampton
ROOT, Thomas (1644-) & 1/wf Abigail ALVORD (1647-1699); 3 Jul 1666; Northampton
ROOT, Thomas (1648-1709) & 1/wf Mary [GRIDLEY] (1652-1673); 1670?; Westfield
ROOT, Thomas (1648-1709) & 2/wf Mary SPENCER (1655-1690); 7 Oct 1675; Westfield
ROOT, Thomas & Sarah [?CLARK]; b 1677, b 1678; Boston/Salem/Beverly/?Deerfield
ROOT, Thomas (1651-1683?) & Elizabeth [GALE] (bpt 1663-); ca 1680?, b 1682; Boston
ROOT, Thomas, Manchester & 1/wf Sarah (_?_) (STANDISH) [HUTCHINSON], w James, w Richard; aft 1682, b 7 Nov 1683; Salem
ROOT, Thomas (1667-1756) & Thankful STRONG (1672-1742); 4 Mar 1691; Northampton/Coventry, CT
ROOT, Thomas (1667-1726) & Sarah [CLARK], Farmington; b 1692; Northampton
ROOT, Thomas (1648-1709) & 3/wf Sarah (DUMBLETON) LEONARD (-1694), w Josiah; 25 Jan 1692, 1692/3; ?Westfield
ROOT, _?_ & _?_, m/2 _?_ MASON bef 1636?, had son Thomas ROOT; b 1615?; Salem
ROOTS, _?_ & Emma _?_; b 1628 in Eng; Salem
ROOT, _?_ & Dorothy (INGERSOLL) PHELPS, w Jacob; aft 6 Oct 1689; Westfield
ROOTEN, Richard (-1663) & _?_; no ch in will; Lynn
ROPER, Ephraim (1644-) & 1/wf Priscilla _?_ (-1676); b 1672; Dedham/Lancaster

ROPAR, Ephraim (-1697) & Hannah (BREWER) GOBLE (-1697), w Daniel; 20 Nov 1677; Concord

ROPER, John (1611-1676) & Alice _?_ (1614-1687), m/2 John DICKINSON 1681, m/3 William ALLEN 1684?; in Eng, ca 1633; Dedham/Charlestown

ROPER, John (1649-1709) & Anna [CALDWELL] (1661-1721); ca 1690; Ipswich

ROPER, Walter (1612-1680) (ae ca 46 in 1659) & Susan _?_ (1616-); b 1639; Haverhill/Ipswich

ROPES, Benjamin (1670-1717) & Ann PHIPPEN, m/2 John GREEN; 10 Mar 1694/5; Salem

ROPES, George (-1670) & Mary _?_ ; b 1642; Salem

ROPES, James & Sarah _?_ ; b 1680; Boston

ROPES, John (1647-) & Lydia WELLS; 25 Sep 1669; Salem

ROAPES, William (1651-) & Sarah INGERSON/INGERSOLL; 26 Jul 1676; Salem

ROSBOTHAM/?ROTHBOTHAM, Joseph (-by 1717) & Elizabeth [CHURCH] (1684-1757), m/2 James SAMPSON 1717, m/3 Samuel WOODBURY 1739; ca 1700-1701, ?1700, b 1701; Bristol, RI

RUSCOE, John & Rebecca BEEBE (1630-); 2 Jan 1650, 1650/1; Hartford/Norwalk, CT

RESCO/RUSCOE, Nathaniel (-1673) & Johanna/Joanna/Joane? CORLET; 11 Nov 1645; Hartford/LI

RESCOE/RUSCOE, Nathaniel (1650+-) & Elizabeth [HALSEY] (1655-1686); 3 Aug 1688, b 1684; Southampton, LI

ROSCOE, Robert & Anna [WILLIX], m/2 James BLUNT, m/3 _?_ SOUTHWELL/_?_ LEARE, m/4 Robert SMITH; Exeter, NH/VA?/NC

RUSCO, Samuel (1648-) & Mercy _?_ ; b 1693; Jamaica, LI

RUSCO, William (1594-) & 1/wf Rebecca _?_ (1595-); in Eng, ca 1620/6, b 1610/14?; Cambridge/Hartford

RUSKEW, William & 2/wf Hester/Esther [MUZZEY], w ?Edward; Feb or Mar 1635/6; Cambridge/Hartford

ROSE, Daniel (1631?, 1630-) & Elizabeth [GOODRICH] (1645-); b 1665; Wethersfield, CT

ROSE, Edward & [Rebecca BURGESS] (1667/8-1711+); b 1693; Rochester

ROSE, Gideon & _?_ ; b 1679

ROSE, Jeremiah (-1699) & Elizabeth [COLLAMORE]; b 1699, 1698; Scituate

ROSE, John[2] (?1616-1683) & 1/wf _?_ ; ca 1636/40?; Watertown/Branford, CT

ROSE, John[2] (-1683) & 2/wf Ellen (NORTHROP) [LUDINGTON], w William; aft 3 Mar 1662/3, bef 5 May 1663; New Haven

ROSE, John[3] & 1/wf Deborah [USHER?] (-living in 1669); b 1668; Branford, CT

ROSE, John & [Abigail] [RAYNOR]; Southampton

ROSE, John[3] & Phebe (IVES)/BASSETT? [POTTER], w Joseph; Aug 1670; New Haven

ROSE, John[2] (-1683) & 3/wf Phebe (BRACEY) [DICKINSON], w Joseph, m/3 Samuel HALE; aft 1675

ROSE, John[3] & 3/wf Elizabeth (CURTIS) [MOSS] (1654-1720), w Mercy (sic); b 1690, b 1687; Branford, CT

ROSE, John (1675-1751) & Sarah BUCK (1678-1763); 8 Jul 1697; Wethersfield, CT

ROSE, John (1678-1720) & Mary DODGE (1682-1720+); 28 Dec 1698; New Shoreham, RI

ROSE, John & Mary LEE; 26 Jul 1700; Charlestown

ROSE, Jonathan & Charity WARD?; 5 Jan 1669; Branford, CT

ROSE, Jonathan (-1684) & Delivered/Deliverance [CHARLES], m/2 John JAMES 1684+; (see record above) 1669, b 1671; Branford, CT

ROSE, Jonathan (-1736) & Abigail (BARKER) FOOTE, w Samuel; 15 Aug 1697; Branford, CT

ROSE, Joseph & Elizabeth BUMPUS; Jun 1653, 5 Jun, 6 Jun 1653; Marshfield

ROSE, Joseph, Jr. & Hannah [FORD?] (-1711); b 1688; Marshfield

ROSE, Martyn & _?_ ; b 1700; Southampton, LI

ROSE, Richard (-1684) & Ruth INGERSON/INGERSOLL, m/2 Jeremiah NEALE 1684+; 7 Jun 1670; Salem

ROSE, Robert[1] (1594-1665) & 1/wf Margery _?_ (1594-); b 1619; Watertown/Wethersfield, CT/Branford, CT/Stratford, CT

ROSE, Robert & Dorothy _?_, m/2 Thomas CONCKLYNE by 1654; by 1634?; Easthampton, LI

ROSE, Robert (?1619-1683) & Rebecca _?_, m/2 Henry ALLYN 1685?; b 1655, b 7 Oct 1651; Branford, CT

ROSE, Robert[1] (-1665) & 2/wf Elizabeth (_?_) (POTTER) [PARKER] (-28 Jul 1677), m/1 John POTTER 1630?, m/2 Edward PARKER 1646; aft 7 Jun 1664, b 1665; Branford, CT

ROSE, Ro₁ er (?1638-) & Abigail [GRANT] (1635-); ca 1661, b 1670; Watertown/Boston
ROSE, Samuel (?1625-1698?) & Mary [TOMPKINS]; CT?/Newark, NJ
ROSE, Thomas & 1/wf _?_; b 1660; Scituate
ROOSE/ROUSE?, Thomas & 2/wf Alice (HATCH) PICKLES, w Jonas; - Dec 1666, 1665?; Scituate
ROSE, Thomas (1653-1744) & Hannah [ALLEN]/ALLYN (-1746); 16 Sep 1680?, b 1681?; ?New London/Preston, CT
ROSE, Tourmet/Dormet/Tourmot? (-1684) & Hannah [GEORGE] (1648-1693±), m/2 James DANIELSON 1685; b 1678, 22 Jul 1676; Block Island, RI
ROSE, [Thomas?] & Joanna _?_ (-1693+), m/2 Robert FLEMMING by 1674, m/3 _?_ OLMSTEAD bef 1687; b 1659; ?CT
ROES, _?_ & Sarah _?_; b Nov 1673; Boston
ROSE, _?_ & _?_ CONKLIN, dau Ananias; ca 1645/51; (had John, Thomas, Samuel, Mary, Jonathan ROSE)
ROSEBOROUGH, George & Mary LOVELL; 6 Aug 1686; ?Worcester/?Marlborough
ROSEMORGAN, Benjamin (called Benjamin MORGAN); New London
ROSEMORGIE/ROSMORGAN, Richard (-1698) & Hopestill MIRICK (-1712); 7 Oct 1664; Charlestown
ROSEWELL, Richard (1652-1702) & Lydia TROWBRIDGE (-1731); 22 Dec 1681, b 1684; New Haven
ROSEWELL, William (-1696, 1694?) & 1/wf _?_; b 1652; New Haven/Branford, CT
ROSEWELL, William (-1694, ae 64) & 2/wf Katharine RUSSELL (-1698); b 1688, 29 Nov 1654; New Haven/Branford, CT
ROSEWELL, _?_ & _?_; 29-2-1654, 29-9 mo; Charlestown
ROSS, Funell (-1683) & Hannah BULL, m/2 Robert SWAN 1690; 16 Mar 1664; Ipswich
ROSS, George & Constance LITTLE; 7 Dec 1658; New Haven/Albany/Elizabeth, NJ
ROSS, James (-1690) & Mary GOODENOW (1640-); 5 Dec 1658; Sudbury
ROSS, James (-1676) & Ann [LEWIS] (-1676); b 1662, 1660?, b 1667; Casco Bay, ME/Falmouth, ME
ROSS, James & 1/wf Sarah FORGESON/FERGUSON, Berwick, ME; 19 Dec 1695; York Co., ME
ROSSE, John & Mary OSBORNE, Weymouth; 7 May 1659; Boston
ROSS, John & _?_; b 1664; Ipswich
ROSS, John & Mary [BARRETT], dau James; b 1675; Charlestown/Malden
ROSS, Kiticris (-1683/4) & Mary GALLY (-1720, ae 80); 9 May 1661; Ipswich
ROSS, Thomas & Seeth HOLMAN (-1695); 16 Jan 1661; Cambridge/Billerica
ROSS, Thomas (1663-) & Sarah _?_; b 1693; Billerica
ROSS, William (-1712) & [Hannah HUNGERFORD] (1659-); b 1694(5?); Westerly, RI
ROSS?, _?_ & Rebecca [BURGESS] (1667-); b 3 Oct 1695; Sandwich/Rochester, MA
ROSSITER, Bryan/Bray (-1672) & Elizabeth [?ALSOP] (-1669); ca 1639; Dorchester/Windsor, CT/Guilford, CT
ROSSITER, Edward (?1585-1630) & _?_; b 1615; Dorchester
ROSSITER, Hugh & [?Jane] _?_ (1614-1691), m/2 Thomas GILBERT 1639; Dorchester
ROSSITER, John (-Sep 1670), Guilford & Mary [GILBERT] (1649-), m/2 Samuel HOLTON 1673; ca 1669; Hartford/Killingworth, CT
ROSSITER, Josiah (-1716) & Sarah [SHERMAN] (1654-1712); b 1677; Stratford, CT/Guilford, CT
ROSSITOR, Peter & Rebecca MAYER; 19 May 1688, at Marblehead; Salem
ROST, Walter & Anna HARRIS; 29 Dec 1698; Boston
ROUNDS, John[1] (-1716) & Elizabeth _?_; ca 1674?, b 1676; Swansea
ROUNDS, John[2] & 1/wf Abigail [BOWEN]; b 1699; Swansea
ROUND, Mark (-1729) & Sarah LARIFORD; m int 11 Nov 1696; Boston
ROUNDY, Philip & 1/wf _?_; b 1656
ROUNDAY, Philip & 2/wf Ann BUSH; - Nov 1691; Salem
ROUNDIE, Robert (-1715) & Deborah PLUMB (1655-1740); 13 Jul 1678; Beverly
ROUSE, Alexander & Judith [CADY]; 15 May 1672; Groton
ROUSE, Edward (-1672) & Jane [SMITH] (-1701+), w John, m/3 Robert COE 1675; aft 1643, aft 1659; Mespat, LI
ROUSE, Faithful (-1664, ae 75) & Sinetinot [STARR] (1599-1686); 9? Dec 1618, Ashford, Eng; Charlestown
ROWSE, John (-1684) & Annis [PABODIE]/(PEABODY) (-1688); b 1640; Duxbury/Marshfield

ROUSE, John & 1/wf Mary [ROGERS?]
ROUSE, John (1643-1717) & 2/wf Elizabeth DOETY/DOTY; 13 Jan 1674, 1674/5?; Marshfield
ROUSE, Simon (1645, 1645/6?-) & 1/wf _?_ (-1706?); b 1676?; Marshfield/?Little Compton, RI
ROUSE, Thomas (see Thomas ROSE/ROUSE) & Alice (HATCH) [PICKLES], w Jonas; ?Dec 1665, 1666?; Scituate
ROUSE, Thomas & Eva _?_; b 19 Apr 1686; Eastchester, NY
ROUSE, Thomas & 1/wf _?_
ROUSE, Thomas & 2/wf Rebecca (BROOKINGS) (POMEROY) RUMMERELL, m/4 George ALSTON; 2 Sep 1689; Dover, NH
ROUSE, William (1640/1-1705) & Sarah (KIND) (TYER) [BUCKANDEN], w William, w Robert; b 1676; Boston
ROUSE, William (-1721) & 1/wf Mary PEACHE/PEACHIE (1674-); 31 Dec 1691, 19 Jan 1691/2; Charlestown
ROWDEN/ROWDON, John (1611-1683) & 1/wf Mary _?_; b 1643; Salem
ROWDEN, John (1611?-1683) & 2/wf Elizabeth (_?_) (SMITH) [HAMMOND] (-1687+), w James, w Richard; aft 1676; Salem
ROE, Anthony (1636-) (did he marry) & _?_; b 1661; Falmouth, ME
ROWE, Anthony & Martha ?WESTBROOK/?BREWSTER; b 1692?; Portsmouth, NH
ROE, David & Mary _?_; b 166-; Flushing, LI
ROE, David (alias MUNROE/MunROE) & Elizabeth TED; 27 May 1690; Huntington, LI/Norwalk, CT
ROWE, Edward & Mary _?_; b 1701?; Newington
ROW/ROE, Elias (1629/30-1687) & Rebecca LONG (ca 1627-1680); 17 Jul 1656; Charlestown
ROE, Hugh (1615?, 1617-1689, Suffield, CT) & Abigail _?_ (1626-1689); b 1645?, b 1655, b 1643?; Weymouth/Hartford/Suffield, CT
ROW, Hugh/John (ca 1645-1694) & 1/wf Rachel LANGTON (ca 1651-1674), dau Joseph (see William VINSON); 10 Jun 1667, no sons mentioned; Gloucester
ROW, Hugh & 2/wf Mary PRINCE, m/2 Isaac ELWELL 1699+; 16 Sep 1674, 10 Sep 1675; Gloucester
ROWE, John (-1662) & Bridget [JIGGLES]? (?1619-), m/2 William COLEMAN 1662; b 1643; Gloucester
ROE, John (-1714) & 1/wf Elizabeth _?_; ca 1660; Newtown, LI/Brookhaven, LI
ROE, John (son of John) & 1/wf Mary DICKKEESONNE/DICKINSON (-1684); 27 Sep 1663; Gloucester
ROE, John (-1714) & 2/wf? Alice _?_/Elizabeth? [RAWLINGS?]; b 1671; Brookhaven, LI
ROW, John (1659-1724) & Abigail ALLSUP/ALSOP (1656-); 14 Jul 1681, 1680?; New Haven
ROW, John (?1643-1700) & 2/wf Sarah REDINGTON (-1701); 1 Sep 1684; Gloucester
ROW, John (1662-1698) & Ruth KNIL (1670-1731); 15 Sep 1687; Charlestown
ROE, John & _?_ [HEDGER]; b 1694?; Flushing, LI
ROE, John & Jemima _?_; b 1695?; Brookhaven, LI
ROE, John[1] (-1714) & 3/wf Sarah _?_; b 1701?; Brookhaven, LI
ROWE, Mark & _?_; b 1670, b 1665?; Isles of Shoals
ROW, Matthew (-1662) & [Sarah ABBOTT] (-1693); b 1650; ?Gloucester/New Haven
ROW, Michael & [Mary MUSSELL?], m/- Digory JEFFREY by 1662; Newcastle
ROE, Nathaniel & Elizabeth _?_; b 169-; Flushing, LI
ROE, Nathaniel & Hannah [REEVE] (1678-1759); b 1698; Brookhaven, LI
ROWE, Nicholas[1] & Elizabeth _?_; b 1648, b 1640?; Portsmouth, NH
ROE/ROWE, Peter (ca 1661-1739) & Sarah PEMINGTON (1668-); 24 Jan 1688/9; Suffield, CT
ROWE, Richard (-1705, 1703) & Susanna _?_; by 1645, bef 1677; Dover, NH
ROWE, Richard (-1684) & Ann _?_ (1637-); Kittery, ME
ROE, Richard & Margery BENBOW; 30 Jun 1695; Boston
ROWE, Robert & Mehitable LEAVITT (1682-); b 1701?, 19 Dec 1707; ?Hampton
ROW, Stephen (-1718) & Martha [LOW]; b 1700, 6 Jul 1699; Gloucester
ROWE, Thomas & Mary _?_; b 1686; Boston/?Dover, NH
ROWE, Thomas & Elizabeth _?_; b 1701; Portsmouth, NH
ROW, Thomas & Sarah B-/[BROWN], ?m/2 William MANNING; 8 Jan 1695/6; Gloucester
ROW, William (1645-) & Sarah WOODWARD; - Nov 1671; Ipswich
ROWELL, Jacob (-1701) & 1/wf Mary YOUNGLOVE (-1691); 29 Apr 1690; Ipswich
ROWELL, Jacob (-1701) & 2/wf Elizabeth WARDELL (1666-); 21 Sep 1691, ?11 Sep; Ipswich

ROWELL, Jacob (1672-1747) & Hannah BARNARD; 1 Dec 1693; Amesbury

ROWELL, Philip (1648-1690) & Sarah MORRILL, m/2 Onesiphorus PAGE 1695, m/3 Daniel MERRILL 1708; 5 Jan 1670; Amesbury

ROWELL, Thomas (-1662) & 1/wf __?__ ; b 1623; Salisbury/Ipswich/Andover

ROWELL, Thomas (-1662) & 2/wf Margery/Margaret (FOWLER) OSGOOD, w Christopher, m/3 Thomas COLEMAN bef 1670, m/4 Thomas OSBORNE 1682; m cont 24 Feb 1650/1; Salisbury

ROWELL, Thomas (-1684) & Sarah BARNS/BARNES (1650-), m/2 John HARVEY 1685?, m/3 Daniel HOYT; 8 Sep 1670; Amesbury

ROWELL, Valentine (-1662) & Joanna PINDOR (1621-1692), m/2 William SARGENT 1670, m/3 Richard CURRIER 1676; 14 Nov 1643; Salisbury

ROWLAND, Henry (-1691/2) & Rebecca __?__ (-1694); b 1647; Windsor, CT

ROWLAND, Henry, Lyme & Elizabeth [DOUGLAS] (1677-); b 1701?; ?New London, CT

ROLAND, Hugh & Hannah [SMITH] (1651-), m/2 __?__ ANDREWS/ANDRUS; Lyme, CT

ROWLAND, Israel & Elizabeth [TURNEY?] (1668-), m/2 John STAPLES?; ca 1690?; Fairfield, CT

ROWLAND, John & Elizabeth [GOODALE], m/2 Jeremiah TOWER 1670; b 1665; Boston

ROWLAND, John (-1693) & Abigail [TRASK] (1664-), m/2 Thomas LARRIMORE by 1696, m/3 William JACOBS; b 1687; Salem

ROWLAND, Jonathan (-1691) & Abigail [BARLOW], m/2 Samuel DENTON; b 28 Jan 1690, ?18 Jan 1690; Fairfield, CT

ROWLAND, Joseph (1647?-) & Sarah [WILSON] (1650?-); ca 1672; Stratford, CT

ROWLAND, Richard (-1685) & Mary [SMITH] (1627?-); ca 1648?; Salem

ROWLAND, Richard & Lucy BAND, m/2 Gregory CODNER 1692; 7 Jun 1686; Salem

ROWLAND, Samuel & __?__ ; b 1624?; Stratford, CT

ROWLAND, Samuel & Mary __?__ ; b 1700; Swansea

ROWLANDSON, Joseph (?1631-1678) & Mary WHITE; 1656; Lancaster

ROWLANDSON, Joseph (1661/2-1712) & Hannah [WILSON] (-1704, ae 29); b 1696; Wethersfield, CT

ROWLANDSON, Thomas & 1/wf __?__ ; b 1633, b 1631; Salisbury

ROWLANDSON, Thomas & Bridget ?(BRADSTREET) [MUSSEY], w Robert, m/3 William KERLEY 1659; ca 1644-48, b 26 Sep 1648; Salisbury

ROWLESON, Thomas (-1682) (see ROWLESON) & Dorothy PORTLAND, m/2 __?__ PERRIN by 1689; 17 May 1654, 1653?; Salisbury

ROWLANDSON, Thomas & Martha BRADSTREET; pretended marriage

ROWLANDSON, William & 1/wf Elizabeth (LYON) [BANKS], w Benjamin; aft 2 May 1692, b 12 Mar 1694/5; Fairfield, CT

ROWLSTONE, John & Mercy [BOSWORTH?]; b 1682(3?); Boston

ROLESON, Thomas & Dorothy PORTLAND; 17 May 1654; Salisbury

ROWLEY, Aaron (1666-) & Mary WEEKS (1670-); 7 Mar 1690, 1689/90?; Falmouth

ROWLEY, Henry & 1/wf __?__ /?Bridget/?Sarah [PALMER?]; b 1630?; Plymouth

ROWLEY, Henry & 2/wf Ann/Anna? (?PALMER/ELSDON?/HARLSDON) BLOSSOM, w Thomas; 17 Oct 1633; Plymouth

ROWLEY, Matthew (-1705+) & Joanna __?__ ; E. Haddam, CT

ROWLEY, Moses (-1705) & Elizabeth FULLER (-1714+); 22 Apr 1652; Barnstable/Haddam, CT

ROWLEY, Moses (1654-1735) & 1/wf Mary [?FLETCHER]/[?TROOP]; b 1681; E. Haddam CT

ROWLEY, Nathan & Mercy [HATCH] (1667-); b 1691; Falmouth, MA

ROWLEY, Shubael (1660/1-1714) & Catherine [CRIPPEN] (-1719); b 1694; Falmouth/Colchester, CT

ROWLEY, Thomas (-1708) & Mary DENSLOW (1651-1739); 5 May 1669; Windsor, CT/Simsbury?, CT

ROWLEY, Thomas (1671-1741) & Violet STEDMAN (1681-1751); 16 Mar 1699, 15 Mar 1699/1700; Windsor, CT

ROWSLEY, Robert (-1693+) & Abigail (PAUL) ALCOCK (-1693+), w Joseph; b 1681, ca 1679; Portsmouth, NH

ROY, John & Elizabeth PHIPPS (1643-); b 1662(3?); Charlestown

RYAL, Isaac (-1729) & 1/wf Ruth [TOLMAN] (1644-1681); b 1668; Dorchester

RIALL, Isaac (-1729) & 2/wf Waitstill [SPURR] (-1732); 1681; Dorchester

ROYAL, Isaac (1672-1739, Dorchester) & Elizabeth (ELIOT) OLIVER (1680-), wid; 1 Jul 1697; Charlestown

ROYALL, John & Elizabeth [DODD] (1657-), m/2 Thomas SOUTHERIN; by 1680?; Casco Bay, ME

ROYAL, Joseph (1645-1728, ae 83) (called "uncle" in 1693 by John COOMBS, Jr.) & Mary _?_; b 1673; Charlestown

ROYALL, Joseph (1673-1702) & Elizabeth COLEMAN, m/2 Thomas BARLOW, m/3 John COOMBS, m/4 John WARREN; 29 Jul 1697; Watertown/Boston

RYALL, Samuel (-1675) & Sarah [MARSHALL]; b 1663; Boston/Scarboro, ME

RIALL, William (-1676, Dorchester) & Phebe [GREEN] (-1678), m/2 Samuel COLE; b 1640; Medford/Casco Bay

ROYAL, William (1640-1724) & Mary _?_; b 1672; N. Yarmouth/Dorchester/Charlestown

ROYALL, _?_ & _?_ LEWIS?

ROYCE, Daniel & Ruth [DAVIS] (1662-); b 1666(7?); Boston

ROYCE, Isaac (-1682) & Elizabeth LOTHROP (1648-1690±), m/2 Joseph THOMPSON 1682?; 15 Dec 1669; New London, CT/Wallingford, CT

ROYCE, John (1668-1724) & Sarah PERIGOE; 29 Nov 1683; Norwich, CT

ROYCE, Jonathan (-1690) & Mary [SPINNING] (-1658?); ca 1657; CT

ROYCE, Jonathan (-1690) & Deborah CAULKINS (1643-), m/2 John WOODWARD/WOODWORTH; - Jun 1660; Norwich, CT

ROYCE, Jonathan (-1725) & Ruth BECKWITH; - Mar 1700; Norwich, CT

ROUCE, Joseph (-1701) & Mary PORTER; 1 Oct 1684; Wallingford, CT

ROYCE/RICE?, Joshua (?1637-) & Barsheba/Bathsheba PRATT; Dec 1662; Charlestown/Boston

ROYCE, Josiah & Elizabeth PARKER, m/2 Ebenezer CLARK 1696, m/3 Nathaniel ANDREWS 1721; 24 Mar 1693; Wallingford, CT

ROYCE, Nathaniel (1639-) & 1/wf Esther [MOSS?] (-19 Jun 1677); ca 27 Oct 1673; Wallingford, CT

ROYCE, Nathaniel (1639-1739) & 2/wf Sarah LOTHROP; 21 Apr 1681; Wallingford, CT

ROYCE, Nehemiah (ca 1635-1706) & Hannah MORGAN (1642-1706); 20 Nov 1660; New London, CT/Wallingford, CT

ROYCE, Robert[1] (-1676) & Mary [SIMS] (-1688+, 1697); ?Mertock, Eng, ?4 Jun 1634, 1624; Stratford, CT

ROYCE/RICE?, Robert & Elizabeth _?_, m/2 Michael TARNE by 1652; b 1637; Boston

ROYCE, Robert (1670-) & Mary PORTER; 2 Jun 1692; Wallingford, CT

ROYCE, Samuel & 1/wf Hannah CHURCHWOOD/CHURCHILL (1644-); 9 Jan 1666, 1666/7; New London, CT/Wallingford, CT

ROYCE, Samuel (-1711) & 2/wf Sarah BALDWIN; 5 Jun 1690; Wallingford, CT

ROYCE, Samuel & Hannah BENEDICT (1670, 1676?-), Norwalk, 12 Dec 1695, ?24 Mar 1693; Wallingford, CT

RUBTON, John & _?_; b 1663; Salem

RUCK, John (1627-1697) & 1/wf Hannah [SPOONER] (-1661); ca 1650; Salem

RUCK, John (1627-1697) & 2/wf Sarah FLINT (-1672); 17 Sep 1661; Salem

RUCK, John (1627-1697) & 3/wf Elizabeth (PRICE) CROAD, w John; 26 Dec 1672; Salem

RUCK, John & Damaris [BUFFUM]? (1677-) (see Thomas RUCK); b 1693(4?); Salem

RUCK/RUSH, John & Hannah HUTCHINSON (1672-1740±); 29 Apr 1697; Boston

RUCK, Samuel & Margaret CLARKE (niece of Elizabeth, widow of Thomas SPOONER in 1664; Elizabeth had brother Thomas of Cambridge); 22 Jul 1656; Boston

RUCK, Samuel & Hannah/Ann/Anne? _?_; b 1685(6?); Boston

RUCK, Samuel & Hannah NICHOLSON; 4 Apr 1693; Boston

RUCK, Samuel & Elizabeth TAWLEY; 30 Jun 1699; Salem

RUCK, Thomas (-1668) & Elizabeth [SHEAFE] (1597-1670); in Eng, 3 Oct 1616; Charlestown/Boston

RUCK, Thomas (-1705) & [Damaris BUFFAM]; b 1694; Salem

RUCKS, William & Mary ELLISSA; 29 Mar 1694; Boston

RUCK, _?_ & Mary [BASSETT] (1667-1701+), dau William

RUDD, Jonathan (-1658) & Mary? [?METCALF]; ca 1646; ?Saybrook, CT

RUDD, Jonathan (?1648-1689) & Mary/Marcy BUSHNELL (1657-1741), m/2 Joseph CARY by 1693; 19 Dec 1678; Norwich, CT/Preston, CT

RUD, Joseph & Deborah ARELAND; 19 May 1698; Boston

RUDD, Nathaniel (-1727) & 1/wf Mary POST (ca 1662-1705); 16 Apr 1685; Norwich, CT

RUDDOCK, John (1609-) & 1/wf Dorothy [GOODNOW] (-1686); b 1654; Marlborough

RUDDOCK, John & 2/wf Jane BRIMSMEAD (-9 Feb 1687/8); 30 Dec 1686; Marlborough
RUDDOCK, John & 3/wf Rebecca _?_ (-1694); b 28 Jan 1692/3; Marlborough
RUEL, John & Emma [SEELEY]; 1668 or later; Saco, ME
RUGG, John (-1696?) & 1/wf Martha _?_ (1632-1655); ?4 Nov 1654, 1654; ?Lancaster
RUGG, John (-1696?) & 2/wf Hannah _?_ (?1639-1697); 4 May 1660; Lancaster
RUGG, John (1662-1712) & Elizabeth _?_ ; ca 1690?; Framingham
RUGG, Joseph (1668-1697) & _?_ ; Lancaster
RUGG, Thomas & Elizabeth [MUNROE]; b 1690; Cambridge/Lexington/Mansfield, CT
RUGGLES, Benjamin (1676-1708) & Mercy WOODBRIDGE (1672-1707), Wethersfield, CT; 19 Nov 1696; Suffield, CT
RUGGLES, George (-1669) & Elizabeth _?_ (-1669+); b 1633; Boston/Branford
RUGGLES, Jeffrey (-1630) & Margaret _?_ ; b 1630; Boston
RUGGLES, John (-1656) & Frances _?_ ; in Eng, b 1620; Boston
RUGGLES, John (ca 1591-1663) & 1/wf Barbara _?_ (1605-1637); in Eng, b 1632, b 1633; Roxbury
RUGGLES, John (-1663) & 2/wf Margaret HAMMOND; aft 1636/7, 1638?; Roxbury
RUGGLES, John (1625-1658) & Abigail CRAFTS (1634-1707), m/2 Ralph DAY 1659, m/3 Edward ADAMS 1678; 24 Jan 1650, [1650/1]; Roxbury
RUGGLES, John (1633-1712) & 1/wf Mary GIBSON (-1674); 3 Apr 1655; Roxbury
RUGGLES, John (1637-1709) & Rebecca FARNSWORTH (1644-); 18 Mar 1661/2, 1-18-1662; Braintree
RUGGLES, John & Hannah (SALTER) PHILLIPS, w Nicholas; b 1671; Boston
RUGGLES, John (1658-1694) & Martha DEVOTION (1658-1714), m/2 John PAINE 1704; 2 Sep 1674; Roxbury
RUGGLES, John (1633-1712) & 2/wf Sarah DYER (?1649-1687); 15 Mar 1674, [1674/5]; Roxbury
RUGGLES, John & Hannah DEVOTION (-17 Dec 1700); 1 May 1679; Roxbury
RUGGLES, John (1633-1712), Roxbury & 3/wf Ruth SWAN, Roxbury; 12 Oct 1687; Cambridge
RUGGLES, John (-1778, in 56th y) & Mary/Mercy VEAZIE (-1741 in 72nd y); 24 Apr 1690; Braintree
RUGGLES, John & Martha MOSELY; m int 30 Mar 1692; Boston
RUGGLES, John & Elizabeth WARE?; 13 Feb 1700, prob 1700/01; Boston
RUGGLES, Joseph & Mary MAY; 4 Nov 1675; Roxbury
RUGGLES, Joseph & Susanna [TWALLS?]; b 1698; Braintree
RUGGLES, Samuel & _?_ ; ca 1645?; Boston
RUGGLES, Samuel (1629-1692) & 1/wf Hannah FOWLE/FOWLES (-1669); 10 Jan 1654/5, 10 Jan 1654; Charlestown/Roxbury
RUGGLES, Samuel (1629-1692) & 2/wf Ann/Anna BRIGHT (1643-1711); 26 May 1670; Roxbury
RUGGLES, Samuel (1648-1697) & Sarah [HOWARD], dau Samuel; b 1673; Boston
RUGGLES, Samuel (1658-1718) & Martha WOODBRIDGE (-1738); 3 Jul 1680; Roxbury
RUGGLES, Samuel & Jemima _?_ ; b 1681; Boston
RUGGLES, Thomas (?1584-1644) & Mary CUSTIS (1586-1675, ae 88), m/2 Ralph ROOTE; Nazing, Eng, 1 Nov 1620; Roxbury
RUGGLES, Rev. Thomas (1671-1728) & 1/wf Sarah [FISKE] (1674-1706); b 1698, b 1699; Guilford, CT
RUMBALL, Daniel & 1/wf _?_ ; Salem
RUMBALL, Daniel (1599-) & 2/wf Sarah [SMITH], w Samuel; ca 1643; Salem
RUMBALL, Thomas (1613-1649) & Rose [SHERWOOD] (1622±-), m/2 Thomas BARLOW 1651?, m/3 Edward NASH by 1673; ca 1640/44; Saybrook, CT/Stratford, CT
RUMMERY, Eleazer & Mehitable BRIARS; 4 Apr 1687; Marblehead
RUMERILL, Clement & Rebecca (BROOKINGS) POMEROY/POMMERY, w Thomas, m/3 Thomas ROUSE, m/4 George ALSTON; 6 Sep 1687; Dover, NH
RUMRILL, Simon & Sarah FIRMAN; Feb 1692, 3 Feb 1690; Enfield, CT
RUMSEY, Benjamin (ca 1667-1732) & 1/wf Hannah [MOREHOUSE]; b 1693; Fairfield, CT
RUMSEY, Benjamin (?1667-1732) & 2/wf Mary [HIDE] (1672-); by 1696; Fairfield, CT
RUMSEY, Isaac & Hannah [OSBORN] (1677-); by 1694; Fairfield, CT/Salem, NJ
RUMSEY, Robert (-1712) & Rachel [FROST] (-1717+); b 1667; Fairfield, CT
RUMSEY, Simon & Mary _?_ ; b 1698; Southold, LI
RUMSEY, Thomas & Rebecca RAWSON (-1692); 1 Jul 1679; Boston
RUNDELL, William & Abigail [TYLER]; b 1678, b 1690; Stamford, CT/Greenwich, CT

RUNLET/RUNDLETT, Charles & [Mary] SMITH, w Nicholas (Mary SATCHWELL, m/1 William DALE, m/2 Nicholas SMITH, m/3 Charles RUNLET); 10 Jan 1675/6; Exeter, NH

RUNLET, Charles (1676-) & [Lydia LADD]; b 1701

RUNDLET, James & Elizabeth [ROBINSON] (1674-), m/2 Abraham FOLSOM; 21 Nov 1699; Exeter, NH/Stratham/Hampton, NH

RUPLING, John & Sarah _?_; 14 Dec 1680; Charlestown

RUSH, Isaac & Mary (PITCHER) [MILLS?] (1644-)

RUSH, Jasper (1611-) & 1/wf Elizabeth _?_; b 1651; Dorchester

RUSH, Jasper (1611-1669) & 2/wf Judith _?_; 24 Mar 1663/4; Dorchester

RUSSE, John (1611/12-1692) & Margaret _?_ (1619/20-1689); b 1641; Newbury/Andover

RUSE, John (1641-) & Deborah OSGOOD (1640-); 28 Aug 1663; Andover

RUSS, John & Hannah ROSS; 6 May 1695; Andover/Pennycook, NH

RUSSELL, Benjamin & Rebecca/Elizabeth? _?_ (-1673?); b 1667; Cambridge/Charlestown/Concord

RUSSELL, Daniel (1642-1679?) & Mehitable [WYLLYS]/Margaret SPRINGER (1658?-1698), m/2 Isaac FOSTER 1679, m/3 Timothy WOODBRIDGE 1685?; 20 Jan 1675, ca 1676; Charlestown/New London

RUSSELL, Daniel & Hannah _?_; b 1694; Rowley

RUSSELL, David & Abigail [WINTER]; b 1701?; Cambridge

RUSSELL, George & 1/wf _?_; ca 1625/26?; Hingham

RUSSELL, George (1596-1694) & 2/wf Jane (_?_) JAMES (1605-1688, 1688/9), w Philip; 14 Feb 1640, 1639, 1639/40; Hingham/Scituate/Marshfield

RUSSELL, George (-1659?) & Ann [ROGERS], m/2 John JUDSON; b 1652?, ca 1656?; Hingham/Dorchester

RUSSELL, George & Ruth _?_; b 23 Jul 1687; Duxbury

RUSSELL, Henry (-1640) & Jane _?_; b 1630; Weymouth

RUSSELL, Henry (-1683) & Elizabeth [PITMAN], m/2 Jacob KNIGHT 1684; b 1664, b 1672; Ipswich

RUSSELL, Henry & _?_; b 1679; Great Island

RUSSELL, James (-1673) & Mary [BALL] (-1674); New Haven

RUSSELL, James (1640-) & 1/wf Mabel HAYNES (1646, 1645-1676); b 1665; Charlestown/Cambridge

RUSSELL, James (1640-1709) & 2/wf Mary HOLIOKE/HOLYOKE (1656-1678); 5 Feb 1676/7; Charlestown

RUSSELL, James (1640-) & 3/wf Mary WOLCOTT (1651-); 3 Jan 1679, 2 Jun 1679; Charlestown

RUSSELL, James (1640-1709) & 4/wf Abigail (CORWIN) HATHORNE (1643-), w Eleazer; 28 Aug 1684; Charlestown/Salem

RUSSELL, Jason (1658-1738) & Mary HUBBARD (1665-); 27 May 1684, 27 Jun; Cambridge/Lexington/Charlestown

RUSSELL, John (1595/7-1680) & 1/wf [Phebe COLLINS] (1605-1642); in Eng, b 1626; Cambridge?/Wethersfield, CT

RUSSELL, John (-1676) & 1/wf Elizabeth _?_ (-1644); b 1641; Woburn

RUSSELL, John & _?_; b 1643; Marblehead

RUSSELL, John[1] (1608-1695) & Dorothy _?_ (-1687, Dartmouth); b 1645; Marshfield/Dartmouth

RUSSELL, John & 2/wf Elizabeth BAKER; 13 May 1645; Woburn

RUSSELL, John (1595, 1598-1680) & 2/wf Dorothy [SMITH] (-1694), w Rev. Henry; ca 1648/9, 1645?; Wethersfield, CT/Hartford?/Hadley

RUSSELL, John & 1/wf Mary TALCOTT (-betw 1655 & 1660); 28 Jun 1649, 28 Jan 1649; Hartford/Hadley

RUSSELL, John (1626±-1692) & 2/wf Rebecca [NEWBERRY?] (-1688); ca 1650-60, prob 1651; Hadley

RUSSELL, Rev. John (-1680) & Sarah CHAMPNEY (-1696); 31 Oct 1661; Woburn

RUSSELL, John (1645-1733) & Elizabeth FRAKE/FISH/FISKE, dau David FISKE; b 1669; Boston/Cambridge/Lexington

RUSSELL, John (-1681) & Hannah _?_, m/2 Robert DAWSON bef 1687; b 1670; New Haven/East Haven, CT

RUSSELL, John & Elizabeth PALMER; 21 Dec 1682; Woburn

RUSSELL, John (-1696) & Mehitable SMITH, m/2 James BURRELL; 17 Sep 16-, 17 Jul 1685, 17 Jul 16-; Dartmouth

RUSSELL, John & Hannah MOULTHROP (1665-); 17 Aug 1687; New Haven
RUSSELL, John & Abigail [WHITING]; b 1689; Hadley/Branford, CT
RUSSELL, John & 1/wf Martha GRAVES (-1740); 9 Apr 1691; Wethersfield, CT
RUSSELL, John & Mary (POTTER) LIVERMORE, w Thomas; 12 Nov 1691; Charlestown/Boston
RUSSELL, John (?1626-1692) & 3/wf Phebe (GREGSON) [WHITING] (1643-1730), w John; aft 21 Nov 1688, 1692; Hadley/Hartford
RUSSELL, Jonathan (?1655-1711) & Martha [MOODY] (-1729, ae 67); b 1681; Barnstable
RUSSELL, Jonathan (-1727) & Hasediah SMITH (1650-); 5 Feb 1678, 5 Apr 1678; Dartmouth
RUSSELL, Joseph (-1694) & Mary BELCHER (-1691); 23 Jun 1662; Cambridge/Lexington
RUSSELL, Joseph[2] (1650-1739) & Elizabeth [FOBES/FORBES] (6 Mar 1657-25 Sep 1737); b 1679?; Dartmouth
RUSSELL, Joseph (-1713, ae 48) & Mary SKINNER? (1670-1705), dau Thomas SKINNER (prob), had sons Thomas & Skinner; b 1687; Boston
RUSSELL, Joseph (-1688) & Jane BLAKEMAN, m/2 Thomas GRIFFIN, m/3 James CLARK, m/4 Nathan ADAMS; 12 Jun 1687; New Haven
RUSSELL, Joseph (1664-) & Susanna CHEEVER (1660-1744); 5 Jun 1693; Boston
RUSSELL, Noadiah (1659-1713) & Mary HAMLIN (1662-1743); 20 Feb 1689/90; Middletown, CT
RUSSELL, Philip (-1693) & 1/wf Joanna SMITH (-1664); 4 Feb 1663/4; ?Hatfield/CT/Hadley
RUSSELL, Philip (-1693) & 2/wf Elizabeth TERRY (1642-1677); 10 Jan 1665, 1665/6, 1666, 1666/7, 1665; ?Hadley/Windsor, CT
RUSSELL, Philip (-1693) & 3/wf Mary CHURCH (1656-); 25 Dec 1679; Hadley
RUSSELL, Philip (-1731) & Joanna CUTLER/CUTTER (-1703); 19 Jun 1680; Charlestown/Danforth
RUSSELL, Ralph[1] & _?_ ; b 1608; Taunton
RUSSELL, Ralph (-1679, 1675?) & Mary HITCHCOCK, m/2 John POTTER 1679; 12 Oct 1663; New Haven
RUSSELL, Richard (1611-1676, 1674) & 1/wf Maud PITT? (-1652); in Eng, b 1638; Charlestown
RUSSELL, Richard (-1676) & Mary (?SHARPE/WADE?) CHESTER, w Linus; aft 1654, 1644, 1648; Charlestown
RUSSELL, Richard & Mary SOUDEN; 11 Oct 1680; Marblehead
RUSSELL, Robert & Mary MARSHALL; 6 Jul 1659; Andover
RUSSELL, Roger (-1687) & Elizabeth _?_ ; Marblehead
RUSSELL, Samuel & Mary DOUGHTY, m/2 Cornelius BRIGGS 1677/8; b 1677(8?); Scituate/Duxbury
RUSSELL, Samuel (?1645-) & Elizabeth ELDRIDGE/ELBRIDGE (1653-); 9 Nov 1682; Marblehead
RUSSELL, Samuel (1660-1731) & Abigail WHITING (1666-1733); ca 1685, b 1686/7, b 24 Jan 1686; Deerfield/Branford, CT
RUSSELL, Samuel & Esther TUTTLE; 27 Feb 1694/5; New Haven
RUSSELL, Samuel & Mary _?_ ; b 1701; Boston
RUSSELL, Thomas (-1676) & Prudence CHESTER (1643-1678); 30 Dec 1669; Charlestown/Cambridge
RUSSELL, Thomas & Mary _?_ ; b 1679, 4 ch bpt 1679; Salem
RUSSELL, Thomas & Phebe _?_ ; b 1687; Andover
RUSSELL, Thomas (-1713?) & _?_ ; b 1698; New Haven
RUSSELL, Thomas & Ann DAVENPORT; 5 Sep 1700; Boston
RUSSELL, Walter & 1/wf Mary PATTEN; 17 May 1699; Cambridge
RUSSELL, William (-1661/2) & Martha _?_ (-1695), m/2 Humphrey BRADSHAW 1665, m/3 Thomas HALL 1683; in Eng?, b 1636?, 1626?; Charlestown/Cambridge
RUSSELL, William[1] (-1665) & Sarah [DAVIS] (-1664); b 1645, b 1650; New Haven
RUSSELL, William & Alice SPARROW, wid; 7 Sep 1653; Boston
RUSSELL, William (-1678) & Elizabeth [ROGERS]; b 1670; Southampton
RUSSELL, William & Elizabeth NURSSE/NOURSE; 25 Oct 1678; Salem/Reading?
RUSSELL, William (1655-1744) & Abigail WINSHIP (-1709); 18 Mar 1682/3; Cambridge/Lexington
RUSSELL, William & Hannah ADAMS; 24 Apr 1688; Concord
RUSSELL, _?_ & Jane _?_ (1653-); b 1696?; Bedford, NY
RUST, Henry & _?_ ; b 1638; Hingham/Boston
RUST, Israel (1643-1712) & Rebecca CLARK (?1649-1733); 9 Dec 1669; Northampton
RUST, John & Sarah [FELLOWS] (1657-1722+), dau William, widow in 1722; Ipswich

RUST, John & Hannah [SWETT] (1664-), dau Benjamin; 12 May 1703; Hampton, NH
RUST, Nathaniel (1640-1713) & Mary [WARDWELL] (1642, 1644-1720); b 1664; Ipswich
RUST, Nathaniel (-1711) & Joanna KINSMAN (1665-); 22 Feb 1684; Ipswich
RUST, Nathaniel (1671-) & Mary?/Mercy? ATCHISON (1673-); 17 May 1692; Hadley
RUST, Nicholas & Mary (MORGAN) PRYNGRYDAYS/PRIN- (-1683), w Edmund; 23 Apr 1678; Springfield
RUST, Richard & Hannah [PRIEST], dau James; b 1676; Weymouth/?Boston
RUST, Samuel (1638-) & Elizabeth [ROGERS]; b 1672; Boston
RUST, _?_ & Mary [MUDGE] (1671-1706); b 1701?; ?Northampton
RUTHERFORD, Henry (-1668) & Sarah [?NEWMAN] (-1693), m/2 William LEETE 1670; b 1641, b 1649?; New Haven/Guilford, CT
RUTTER, John (1616-1695) (ae 37 in 1652) & 1/wf Elizabeth PLIMTON/PLIMPTON (-1689); 1 Nov 1641; Sudbury
RUTTER, John (1645-1692) & 2/wf Hannah (HUDSTON) BUSH, w John, m/3 James SMITH 1693, m/4 Joseph WATERS, m/5 Zechariah MAYNARD 1721; 12 Mar 1690; Sudbury
RUTTER, Thomas (1650-1703+) & Jemima STANHOP[E] (1665-1748); 15 Oct 1689; Sudbury
RUTTY, Edward (-1714) & Rebecca STEVENS; 6 May 1678; Killingworth, CT
RIAN/RYAN, Timothy & Jane SKELTON, w James; 17 Dec 1688; Marblehead
RYCROFT, Richard & Sarah _?_ ; b 1684; Boston
RYCROFT, _?_ & [Frances PITCHER] (-1638); b 1638
RYMES, Samuel (-1709) & Mary [WENTWORTH] (1674-1731+, 1743±), m/2 John CLIFTON; b 1694, 1 Jun 1691; Portsmouth, NH/Isles of Shoals

SABEERE, Stephen & Deborah ANGELL; 14 Nov 1668; Providence
SABIN, Benjamin (1646-1725) & 1/wf Sarah [POLLEY] (1650-); b 1669; Rehoboth/Roxbury
SABIN, Benjamin (1646-1725) & 2/wf Sarah PARKER (-1718); 5 Jul 1678; Roxbury/Pomfret, CT/Woodstock, CT
SABIN, Benjamin (1673-1750) & Elizabeth DAVIS (-1753); 4 Nov 1700, - - 1700; Roxbury/Woodstock, CT/Pomfret, CT
SABIN, Ebenezer (1671-1739) & Susanna _?_ ; b 1696; Pomfret, CT/Woodstock, CT
SABIN, Israel (1673-) & 1/wf Mary ORMSBY (-1715); 20 May 1696; Rehoboth/Swansea/Barrington, RI
SABIN, James (1665-1748) & Abigail BRASIER (1664-1746), Charlestown; 16 Oct 1689, 18 Oct; Rehoboth
SABIN, John (1666-1742) & Sarah PECK (1669-1738); 3 Sep 1689; Rehoboth/Pomfret, CT
SABIN, Joseph (1645-1690) & Waitstill (Hopestill wrong) _?_ , m/2 Jarrett INGRAHAM 1692; b 1674; Rehoboth
SABIN, Nehemiah (1647-1676) & Elizabeth FULLER; 1 Aug 1672; Rehoboth
SABIN, Samuel (?1640-1699) & Mary BILLINGTON; 20 Jan 1663/4; Rehoboth
SABIN, Samuel (1664-) & Grace [ORMSBY] (1669-); b 1696; Rehoboth
SABIN, William[1] (-1687) & 1/wf _?_ [WRIGHT]; b 1640?; Rehoboth
SABIN, William[1] (-1687) & 2/wf Martha ALLENS/ALLEN (1641-), m/2 Richard BOWEN 1690; 22 Dec 1663; Medfield/Rehoboth
SABLES/SABLE, John & Priscilla _?_ ; b 1701; Boston
SACKETT, John & _?_ ; in Eng, b 1628; Plymouth/Providence
SACKETT, John (?1629-1684) & Agnes TINCOME/TINKHAM; 20 May 1652; New Haven
SACKETT, John (-1719) & 1/wf Abigail HANNUM (-1690); 25 Nov 1659, 23? Nov; Northampton/Westfield
SACKETT, John (1653-) & Mary [WOODIN/WOODING] (-1719); b 1686?, b 1690; New Haven
SACKETT, John (1660-1745), Westfield & 1/wf Deborah FILLEY (1661-1701); 1 Dec 1686; Windsor, CT/Westfield
SACKET, John (-1719) & 2/wf Sarah (STILES) STEWARD/STEWART, w John; 15 Jan 1690/1; Windsor, CT

SACKETT, Joseph (1656-1719) & 1/wf Elizabeth [BETTS]; Newtown, LI
SACKETT, Samuel & Elizabeth [BISSELL]; b 1700; Westfield
SACKETT, Simon[1] (-1635) & Isabel __?__, m/2 William BLOOMFIELD; b 1630; Cambridge
SACKETT, Simon (?1630-1659) & Sarah [BLOOMFIELD], m/2 ?Lambert WOODWARD; ca 1652; Springfield
SACKETT, William (1662-1700) & 1/wf Sarah CRAM?; 27 Nov 1689, 26 Dec 1687; Westfield
SACKETT, William (1662-1700) & 2/wf Hannah GRAVES (1666-); 27 Nov 1689; Westfield
SADD, John (-1694) & 1/wf __?__ ; in Eng, b 1674; Hartford
SADD, John (-1694) & 2/wf Hepzibah (WYATT) [PRATT] (-1711); w John; ca 1690; Hartford
SADLER, Abiel (1650-1697) & Rebecca [DIKE?] (1668-), ?m/2 Josiah TARNER; b 1690(4?); Gloucester
SADLER, Anthony (1629-1650) & Martha [CHENEY] (1629-1658), m/2 Thomas BURPEE 1653?; ca 1649, b 1650; Newbury
SADLER, John (returned to Eng) & __?__ ; b 1631; Gloucester
SADLER, John (-1673) & Deborah __?__ (1610-); no issue; Wethersfield, CT
SADLER, Richard (?1610-1675) (?returned to Eng) & __?__ ; Lynn
SADLER, Thomas & Rebecca (EMERY) [WEYMOUTH], w Robert, m/3 Daniel EATON aft 1681; ca 1662/4?; Kittery, ME/Flushing, LI
SAWDY, John (-1674) & Ann __?__ ; b 1650; Boston
SADY, John & Elizabeth PEETERS, m/2 Walter WRIGHT ?1684; 25 Nov 1678; Ipswich/Boston
SAFFIN, John (?1634-1710) & 1/wf Martha WILLETT (1639-1678); 2 Dec 1658; Plymouth
SAFFIN, John (-1710) & 2/wf Elizabeth (SCAMMON) LIDGETT (-1681, 1682?), w Peter; 1680, m cont May 1680; Charlestown
SAFFIN, John (-1710) & 3/wf Rebecca [LEE] (-1713), m/2 Joseph BAXTER 1712; aft 1687; ?Charlestown/Bristol, RI
SAFFORD, John (?1636, 1633-) & Sarah [LOWE] (ca 1637-1708+, 1712+); ca 1661, b 1664; Ipswich
SAFFORD, John (1662-1736, ae 73) & 1/wf Hannah NEWMAN; 15 Sep 168[5?]; Ipswich/Preston, CT
SAFFORD, John (?1672-1739, 1736) & Abigail __?__ (1672-); b 1697; ?Norwich, CT
SAFFORD, Joseph (1631, 1633?-1701) & Mary BAKER (1641-1701+); 6 Mar 1660, 1660/1; Ipswich
SAFFORD, Joseph (1664-) & Hannah [CHALLIS] (1675-); b 1701?; Ipswich
SAFFORD, Thomas (-1667) & Elizabeth __?__ (-1670/71); b 1633, b 1631; Ipswich
SAMFORD/SANFORD, Thomas (1672-1754) & 1/wf Eleanor (CHENEY) SETCHWELL/SHATS-WELL (1679-1724), w Richard; 7 Oct 1698; Ipswich
SAGE, David (1639-1703) & 1/wf Elizabeth KIRBY (1645, ?1646-1669?, 1670?); Feb 1664, ?1 Feb 1664/5; Middletown, CT
SAGE, David (1639-1703) & 2/wf Mary/Mercy [WILEY] (8 Feb 1647/8, 13 Nov 1654, 1654, 1646-1711); ?Sep 1671, 1672?, 1673?; Middletown, CT
SAGE, David (1665-1712?) & Mary COULTMAN (1672-1744); 3 May 1693; Wethersfield, CT
SAGE, John (1668-) & Hannah STARR (1673-1753); 10 Jan 1693/4, 10 Jan 1693; Middletown, CT
St.JOHN, Daniel, Norwalk & Grace [SHERMAN] (1676-); Fairfield
St.JOHN, Ebenezer & Elizabeth COMSTOCK (1679-); CT
SENSION, James (ca 1649-1684) & Rebecca PICKET, m/2 Andrew MESSENGER 1684?; 31 Dec 1673, 18 Dec 1673; Stratford, CT
St.JOHN, James & Mary COMSTOCK (1672-); 18 Dec 1693; Norwalk, CT
St.JOHN, Joseph & Sarah BETTS (ca 1665-); 5 Mar 1695/6; Norwalk, CT
SENSION, Mark (ca 1634-) & 1/wf Elizabeth [STANLEY]; ca 1655, b Dec 1656; Norwalk, CT
SENSION, Mark (-Aug 1693) & 2/wf Dorothy (SMITH) (BLACKMAN) HALL, w John, w Francis, m/4 Isaac MOORE; Jan 1692/3, 21 Jan 1691/2, Jan 1690; Norwalk, CT/Fairfield, CT
St.JOHN, Matthew/Matthias[1] (-1669?) & __?__ ?HOYT/?SEELEY (see below)/Elizabeth? COM-STOCK (-ca 1714); b 1630?; Dorchester/Windsor, CT/Norwalk, CT
St.JOHN, Matthew/Matthias[2] (1630-1728) & Elizabeth [?SEELEY] (see above); ca 1655/60?; Norwalk, CT
St.JOHN, Matthew/Matthias (?1660-1740) & Rachel [BOUTON] (1667-); ca 1690; Norwalk, CT/Ridgefield, CT
SENCHION, Nicholas (-1698) & Isabel __?__ (1618-1689); 12 Jun 1645, no issue; Windsor, CT

SENSION, Samuel (-1685) & Elizabeth HAITE/HOYT (-1686) (see above); Sep 1663; Norwalk, CT
St.JOHN?, Thomas & _?_ ; b 1639; Windsor, CT
SAISE/?SUISE, William & Martha BARBER; 8 Jul 1675; Charlestown
SALISBURY, Cornelius & Mary _?_ ; b 1692(3?); Swansea
SALISBURY, John (-1708) & 1/wf Annabel _?_ (-1694); b 1690(1?); Boston
SALISBURY, John (-1708) & 2/wf Bridget WILLIAMS; m int 5 Sep 1695; Boston
SALLSBURY, Joseph & Mary PADDOCK; 16 May 1698; Rehoboth/Taunton/Little Compton, RI
SALISBURY, Nicholas (1637-) & 1/wf Elizabeth _?_ (1642-1708, ae 66); Charlestown/Boston
SALLSBURY, Samuel & 1/wf Mary [BROOKS]; b 1698; Rehoboth
SALLSBURY, Samuel & 2/wf Jemima MARTIN (1672-); m int 28 Oct 1699; Rehoboth
SALISBURY, William (-1678) & Susanna _?_ ; b 1659; Dorchester/Milton
SALISBURY, William (1659-) & Hannah/Ann/Anna/Anne COLE (1664-1704); 30 Jul 1684; Swansea
SALAS, John (?1627-1708) & Hannah WOOLFE; 9 Dec 1655; Salem
SALLOWES, John & 2/wf? Elizabeth _?_ ; b 1672; Beverly
SALLOWS, John & Sarah _?_ ; b 1679; Beverly
SALLOS, John (-1690) & Catharine [LOVETT?]; b 1690; Beverly
SALLOWS, Michael (-1646) & Ann [?WILSON]; ca 1620?; Salem
SALLOWS, Robert (-1663) & Freeborn [WOOLFE/WOLF] (?1635-1681?), m/2 John BLACK, Jr. 1664; b 27 Mar 1644; Salem
SALLOWES, Robert (1676-1758) & 1/wf Mary THISTLE (-1714); 14 Dec 1699; Beverly
SALLOWS, Thomas (-1663) & Grace [LEMON] (-1663); ca 1656?; Salem
SALLOWES, Thomas (-1747, ae ca 80) & Abigail [WALLACE]; b 1693; Beverly
SALLEE/SALLY, Manus (-1650) & Sarah [HEPBURNE]; ca 1648?; Charlestown
SALMON, Clement & Joanna RILAND; 13 Jun 1660; Boston
SALMON, Daniel (1610/12-) (ae ca 50 in 1660) & ?Margaret _?_ ; b 1641?; Lynn
SAMON, George (-1673) & Remember FELTON (-1678+); Oct 1654; Salem
SALMON, John (-1676) & Katharine _?_ (-1680+); b 1676; Southold, LI
SALMON, John & Sarah BARNES (1655-1738); 23 Aug 1683; Southold, LI
SALMON, Peter & Anna THOMPSON; 4 Jun 1677; Salem
SALMON, Peter & Mary MARSHALL; m int 22 Oct 1696; Boston
SALMON, Thomas (-1675) & Mary _?_ , m/2 Joseph PHELPS 1676; b 1660; Northampton
SALMON, William (1610-) & Katherine (?CURTIS) [SUNDERLAND]/SENDERLAND, w Matthew; Southold, LI
SALMON, William & 2/wf Sarah [HORTON], m/2 Joseph CONKLIN 1670±, 1687; 1649; Southold, LI
SALMON, William & Hannah [BUTTON], dau Matthew; b 1675; Amesbury
SALTER, Charles & Elizabeth _?_ ; b 1685; Boston
SALTER, Eneas & Joan/Joanna _?_ ; b 1673; Boston
SALTER, Henry & Hannah _?_ (1633-1686); ca 1653?; Charlestown
SALTER, Jabez (-1720) & Elizabeth _?_ (?1651-1726); b 1671; Boston
SALTER, John & Mary PITMAN; 3 Mar 1684; Marblehead
SALTER, John (1656-) & Mary ADAMS (1664-); 27 Feb 1684/5; Charlestown
SALTER, Joseph & Elizabeth _?_ ; b 1696; Boston
SALTER, Matthew & [Sarah PARKER], m/2 Samuel SMITH 1703; b 1679?, 5 ch in 1689; Charlestown
SALTER, Malachi & _?_ ; b 1690; Boston
SALTER, Nicholas & Rebecca _?_ ; b 1698; Braintree
SALTER, Simion & Joanna/Jane _?_ (-1684+); ca 1638/40?, b 1663; Newport
SALTER, Thomas & Mary HABBERFIELD; 4 May 1693; Boston/Roxbury
SALTER, William (?1607-1675) & Mary _?_ ; b 1635, b 1634; Boston
SALTER, _?_ & Ann CODY; b 1677
SALTONSTALL, Gurdon (1666-1724) & 1/wf Jerusha [RICHARDS] (1665-25 Jul 1697); b 1690; Boston/New London
SALTONSTALL, Gurdon (1666-1724) & 2/wf Elizabeth [ROSEWELL/ROSWELL] (1679-1710); b 1701?, b 1702?; Blanford, CT/New London, CT
SALTONSTALL, Nathaniel (1634, ?1633-1707) & Elizabeth WARD (1647-1714); 28 Dec 1663; Haverhill

SALTONSTALL, Richard (1586-) (ret'd to Eng) & 1/wf Grace [KAYE]; in Eng, b 1610; Watertown
SALTONSTALL, Richard (1610-1694) (ret'd to Eng) & Muriel/Merrell/Meriel GURDON (1613-); Jun 1633, 4 Jul 1633; Ipswich/Watertown
SAMES/SAMS/?SAMMS, Constantine (-1692) & Elizabeth _?_; b 1676; Boston
SAMIS, Ralph & Phillippi _?_; b 1689(90?); Boston
SAMMIS, John & Abigail [COREY]; ca 1692, b 1693, b 1673; Huntington, LI
SAMMIS, John & Mary (CORNISH) [COREY], w John; b 28 Nov 1693, aft 25 Jan 1695/6
SAMWAYS, Richard (-1650) & [Esther HOSFORD]; b 1642; Windsor, CT
SAMFIELD, Austin (-1661) & _?_; b 1661; Fairfield, CT
SAMPLE, Robert & Elizabeth BOWEN; 12 Oct 1696; Boston
SAMSON, Abraham & _?_ [NASH], dau Samuel; b 1646?; Duxbury
SAMPSON, Abraham & 2/wf _?_; bef 1658; Duxbury
SAMPSON, Abraham (1658-1727) & Lorah [STANDISH]; b 1682; Duxbury
SAMPSON, Andrew & _?_; b 1670; Portsmouth, NH
SAMPSON, Andrew (1670-) & Rachel (CODNER) [SHORES w John], m/1 John DARBY/DERBY, m/2 Andrew SAMPSON, m/3 John SHORES; m int 12 Dec 1695, Boston; Portsmouth, NH
SAMPSON, Caleb (1660±-1744+) & 1/wf Mercy [STANDISH] (-1704+); b 1685; Marshfield, Duxbury
SAMPSON, George (1655-1739) & Elizabeth _?_ (-1727 in 70th y); b 1679; Plympton
SAMSON, Henry (-1684) & Ann/Anne PLUMMER (-bef 1684) (called "cosen" by John BARNES in will 1668); 6 Feb 1635/6; Plymouth/?Duxbury
SAMPSON, Hugh (-by 1692?) & Mary [COTTA] (1668-), m/2 Samuel DYER of Newport; b 1688; Boston
SAMPSON, Isaac (?1660-1726) & Lydia [STANDISH] (-1734+); b 1688; Plymouth/Plympton
SAMPSON, James (-1718) & Hannah (_?_) [WAITE], w Samuel; aft Feb 1676/7, b 1679; Portsmouth, RI/Dartmouth
SAMPSON, John (?1627-) & 1/wf _?_; b 8 May 1660; Salem
SAMPSON, John (?1627-) & 2/wf Sarah PEASE; 22 Oct 1667; Beverly
SAMPSON, John & _?_ [STODDER], w John; betw 1672 & 1676; New London, CT
SAMPSON, Jonathan & Mary CHANDLER; 16 Nov 1695; Newbury
SAMPSON, Richard & Sarah _?_, m/2 Josiah CLARK 1677; ?Portsmouth, NH
SAMPSON, Samuel (?1646-1678) & Esther _?_ (-1733, ae 95), m/2 John SOULE 1678?; b 1678; Duxbury
SAMSON, Samuel (-1744, ae 75) (had 2/wf Mercy _?_) & 1/wf Assadiah EEDY/Hasadiah EDDY (1672-bef 1722; 29 May 1695; Duxbury/Middleboro
SAMPSON, Stephen (-1715?) & Elizabeth _?_; b 1675; Duxbury
SAMPSON, Thomas & _?_; b 10 Jul 1737; Richmond Isl.
SAMUEL, John (-1662) & Lucy WIGHT, w Thomas; 24 Dec 1652; Boston
SANBORN, Benjamin (1668-) & 1/wf Sarah [WORCESTER] (1666-1720); b 1690; Hampton, NH
SANBORN, John (-1692), Hampton & 1/wf Mary [TUCKE] (-1668); b 1649; Hampton, NH
SANBORN, John (-1692) & 2/wf Margaret (PAGE) MOULTON (1629-1699), w William; 2 Aug 1671; Hampton, NH
SANBORN, John (1649-1723) & Judith COFFIN (1653-); 19 Nov 1674; Hampton, NH
SANBORN, Jonathan (1672-1741) & Elizabeth SHERBURNE (1672-1741); 4 Feb 1691/2, Feb 1691; Dover, NH
SANBORN, Joseph (1659-1722+) & Mary GOVE (1666-), m/2 Moses MORRILL; 28 Dec 1682; Hampton, NH
SANBORN, Josiah & 1/wf Hannah MOULTON (1652-1687); 25 Aug 1681; Hampton, NH
SANBORN, Josiah & 2/wf Sarah (_?_) [PERKINS], w Jonathan; ca 1690; Hampton, NH
SANBORN, Mephibosheth (1663-1749) & Lydia [LEAVITT] (1668-); b 1695; Hampton, NH
SANBORN, Nathaniel (1666-1723) & 1/wf Rebecca PRESCOTT (-1704); 3 Dec 1691; Hampton, NH
SANBORN, Richard (1655-) & 1/wf Ruth MOULTON (-1685); 5 Dec 1678; Hampton, NH
SANBORN, Richard (1655-) & 2/wf Mary (DRAKE) BOULTER/BOLTER, w Nathaniel; 20 Dec 1693; Hampton, NH
SANBORN, Stephen & Sarah [BATCHELDER?]; b 1651; Hampton, NH
SANBORN, Stephen (1671-) & Hannah PHILBRICK (1676-); 26 Jul 1693; Hampton, NH
SANBORN, William (1622-1692) & Mary MOULTON; b 1652, b 1650, b Jan 1649; Hampton, NH

SANBORN, William (1650-1744) & Mary MARSTON (1661-1686); 1 Jan 1680, 1679-80?; Hampton, NH

SANBORN, _?_ & Ann BATCHELDER (1610-); (doubtful)

SANDERSON, Benjamin (1649-) & Mercy [VIAL]; b 1673(4?); Boston

SANDERSON/SANDERS?, Edward & ?Sarah LYNN/Mary EGELLSTON/EGGLESTON; 16 Oct 1645, ?15 Oct; Watertown/Cambridge?

SANDERSON/SANDERS?, Henry (-1685?) & _?_ ; b 1670(1?); Sandwich

SANDERS/SANDERSON?, Henry (?1676-) & Ann _?_/Anna [BATES]? (1675-); b 1701; Plymouth

SANDERSON, John & Mary _?_ ; b 1699; Boston

SANDERS/SANDERSON, Jonathan (1646-1735) & Abiah/Abial? BARTLETT (1651-1723); 24 Oct 1669; Cambridge/Watertown

SANDERSON, Jonathan (1673-1743) & Abigail FISK; 14 Jul 1699; Watertown

SANDERSON, Joseph (1643, 1642?-) & Mary _?_, sister of Mrs. Francis THOMPSON, m/2 Augustine LINDON (divorced), m/3 William ARDELL 1681, 1682; b 1666; Boston

SANDERSON, Robert[1] (-1693) & Lydia _?_ ; b 1639; Hampton

SANDERSON, Robert[1] (-1693) & 2/wf Mary [CROSS] (-1681), w John; b 1643; Watertown/Boston

SANDERSON, Robert[1] (see below) & Elizabeth _?_ (-1695, ae 78); aft 21 Jun 1681; Framingham

SANDERSON, Robert[1] (-1693) (see above) & 1/wf Elizabeth [KINGSWILL] (-1695, ae 78); b 1684, 24 Aug 1681; Boston

SANDERSON, Robert (1652-) & 2/wf Sarah CROW; 21 Dec 1693; Boston

SANDERSON, Robert (1652-) & 3/wf? Esther [WOODWARD]; b 1695; Boston

SANDERSON, William & Sarah _?_ ; 18 Dec 1666; Watertown/Groton

SANDIN, Arthur (-1666) & Margaret _?_ ; Marblehead

SANDIN, Ephraim (1654-1731) & Miriam [BASSETT?]/GALE? (1655-1731); ca 1675?; Marblehead

SANDIN, John (-1654) & Mary _?_ ; ca 1648?; Marblehead

SANDIN, Samuel (-1706) & Charity _?_ (-1706); b 1674; Marblehead

SANDS, Edward (1672-1708) & Mary WILLIAMS (-1708+), m/2 Robert MASTCOTT; ?12 Feb 1693, ?7 May 1693; New Shoreham, RI

SANDS, James (1622-1695) & Sarah [WALKER]? (-1709); b 1644; Portsmouth/Block Island/New Shoreham, RI

SANDS, James (-1731, 1733) & Mary [CORNELL] (1679-); b 1697?, b 1699; Cow Neck, LI

SANDS, John (1652-1712) & Sybil [RAY] (1665-1733); b 1681?, b 1684, b 1680; New Shoreham, RI/Cow Neck, LI

SANDS, Samuel (-1716) & 1/wf Mary (RAY) KENYON (1669-); ca 1688?; Cow Neck, LI

SANDS, _?_ & [Patience GIBBINS], m/2 John ANNABLE 1720; b 1694

SANDY/SAWDY/?SANDYS, John & Ann HOLMES; 7 Jul 1653; Boston

SANDY/SUNDYE, Joseph (1660-) & Bethia LUCAS; 18 Oct 1682; Bristol, RI

SANDEY, Winsor & Mehitable BULL; 12 Feb 1694; Boston

SANDY, _?_ & Christian BRANTON; b 9 Feb 1673; Newport, RI?

SANDYS, Henry (-1651) & Sybil _?_ ; b 1639, b 1640; Boston

SANDYS, John (1646-) & Ann [MANNING] (1652-); b 1671; Boston

SANFORD, Andrew[1] (1617-1684) & 1/wf Mary _?_ (-1662); b 1643; Hartford/Milford, CT

SANFORD, Andrew[1] (1617-1684) & 2/wf _?_ ; aft 13 Jun 1662, 4 ch bpt 4 Jun 1671; Hartford/Milford, CT

SANFORD, Andrew[2] (1643-) & 1/wf Mary BOTSFORD (1643-); 8 Jan 1667, 1667/8; Milford, CT

SANFORD, Andrew[2] & 2/wf Sarah [GIBBARD] (1648-); ca 1688; Hartford/Milford, CT

SANFORD, Andrew[3] (1673-) & Hannah [RAYMOND] (1679-); b 11 Dec 1699; Milford, CT

SANFORD, Ephraim (1646-1687) & Mary POWELL, m/2 Nathaniel BALDWIN; 18 Nov 1669; New Haven/Milford, CT

SANFORD, Esbon (1646-1666+, 1682) & Sarah _?_ ; RI

SANFORD, Ezekiel & Rebecca WIEPLE/WAKELEE/WHELPLEY?; 25 Apr 1665; Fairfield, CT

SANDFORD, Ezekiel (1697-1716) & Hannah [MITCHELL]; b 1680; Southampton, LI

SANFORD, Ezekiel (-1685/6) & Elizabeth [RATLIFF] (1666±-), m/2 Zachariah BALDWIN 1686/7; bef 11 Jan 1685/6; Milford, CT

SANFORD, Ezekiel (1668-1729) & Rebecca GREGORY (1673-1765); Mar 1696, by 1697; Fairfield, CT

SANFORD/SANDFORD, Henry & Mary LONG; 23 Jan 1676/7; Charlestown
SANFORD, James (-1661) & Elizabeth [SMITH], m/2 John/?George HUNNIBORN 1662?; 1656;
    Boston
SANFORD, John[1] (-1653) & 1/wf Elizabeth WEBB/EVERED; ca 1632; Boston/Portsmouth, RI
SANFORD, John[1] (-1653, Newport?) & 2/wf Bridget [HUTCHINSON] (1619-1696), m/2 William
    PHILLIPS 1658±; ca 1637; Boston/RI
SANFORD, John (1633-1687) & 1/wf Elizabeth SPATCHURST (-1661); 8 Aug 1654; Portsmouth,
    RI
SANFORD, John (1633-1677) & Sarah POTTER, w Robert; 19 Feb 1656/7; Boston
SANFORD, John (1633-) & 2/wf Mary (GORTON) GREEN, w Peter; 17 Apr 1663; Portsmouth,
    RI
SANFORD, John (1668-) & Frances CLARKE (1669-1703); 6 Sep 1689; Portsmouth, RI
SANFORD, John & Margery _?_ (1664-1721)
SANFORD, John (?1672-) & 1/wf Content [HOWLAND]; b 1699; Portsmouth, RI
SANFORD, Nathaniel & 1/wf _?_ ; b 1659
SANFORD, Nathaniel (-1687?) & 2/wf Susannah [CLARK?]/KELLY/[BLAKE?], m/2 John
    BUTTOLPH 1687+; b 1671, b 1666; Hartford
SANFORD, Peleg (1639-1701), Newport & 1/wf Mary [BRENTON] (-1684(-)); ca 1665-70;
    Newport, RI
SANFORD, Peleg (1639-1701) & 2/wf Mary CODDINGTON (1654-1693); 7 Dec 1674; Newport
SANFORD, Richard (1594-) & Margaret _?_ (-1640); in Eng, b 1626; Boston
SANFORD, Robert (1615-1675, 1676?) & Anne [ADAMS]? (-1682); b 1643?, b 1645(6?);
    Hartford
SANFORD, Robert & Elizabeth [SKELTON] (ca 1630-); b 1654; Boston
SANFORD/STANFORD/STANDFORD, Robert (see Robert STANFORD) & Mary (HOWLAND)
    WILLIAMSON, dau Arthur HOWLAND, wid Timothy WILLIAMSON; 22-1-1679, 22 Jan
    1679/80; ?Marshfield
SANFORD, [?Robert] (1656-1728) & Mary [PRATT]; aft 3 Mar 1686/7; Hartford
SANFORD, Samuel (1635-1713) & 1/wf Sarah WOODELL (1644-1680); Oct 1662; Portsmouth, RI
SANFORD, Samuel (1643-1691) & Hannah BRONSON, Farmington; 16 Apr 1674, 16 Aug; Milford,
    CT
SANFORD, Samuel (1635-1713) & 2/wf Susannah SPATCHURST (-1723); 13 Apr 1682, 13? Apr,
    23? Apr; Portsmouth, RI
SANFORD, Samuel & Hannah BALDWIN; Nov 1695, b 1696?
SANFORD, Thomas & Frances [SMITH], wid (had son Henry SMITH), m/3 William PYNCHON; b
    1630; Roxbury
SANFORD, Thomas (-1681) & Sarah _?_ (-1681); 1636, 1637, b 1641(2?); Dorchester/Milford,
    CT
SANFORD, Thomas (1617-1684) & 1/wf Mary _?_ (-1662); b 1648, b 1638; Hartford/Milford, CT
SANFORD, Thomas & 2/wf Sarah GIBBARD; ca 1662-3; Hartford/Milford, CT
SANFORD, Thomas (-1682/3) & Elizabeth [WILLIAMS] (1640-), dau Nathaniel, m/2 John
    CLARK; ca 1665?, no issue; ?Boston
SANFORD, Thomas (1644-1721) & 1/wf Elizabeth PAYNE; 11 Oct 1666; New Haven
SANFORD, Thomas (1673-1704, Medway) (2/wf Tabitha CLARK, Medfield; 1710) & 1/wf
    Christian _?_ ; b 1693; Swansea/Medway
SANFORD, Thomas (1675-) & Hannah [STEVENS] (1679, 1678-); ca 1699, ca 1700; Fairfield,
    CT
SANFORD, Thomas & Sarah _?_ ; b 1701; Southampton
SANFORD, William (1676-) & Hope SISSON; 26 Jan 1699, 1699/1700; Portsmouth, RI
SAMFORD, Zachary (-1668) & [Hannah] [ROCKWELL] (-1665); b 1653; Saybrook, CT
SANFORD, Zachary/Zachariah (?1644-1714) & Sarah [WILLETT]; b 1681, 1678?; Hartford
SANFORD, Zachariah/Zachary? (-1711) & Bethiah BENTON; 9 Oct 1694; Saybrook, CT
SANFORD, _?_ & Thomasine [SCOTLOW, wid]
SANFORD, William/?John & _?_ ; b 1642?, b 1625/32; Portsmouth, RI
SANGER, John (1657-) & Rebecca [PARK]; b 1685; Watertown
SANGER, Nathaniel (1652-1735±) & 1/wf Mary [CUTTER] (-1711); b 1680; Sherborn/Roxbury/
    Woodstock, CT
SANGER, Richard (-1691) & Mary [RANNALS/REYNOLDS] (-1611+); ?ca 1648, b 1652;
    Watertown

SANGER, Richard (1666/7-1731) & Elizabeth [MORSE] (1677-); b 1693; Sherborn
SARGENT, Andrew (1655-1691) & Mary __?__ (-1697?), m/2 __?__ INGALLS; b 1691; Ipswich?
SARGENT, Benjament (?1672-) & Abigail __?__; Sep 1694; Portsmouth, NH/etc.
SARGENT, Charles (1674-) & Hannah [FOOTE] (1680/1-); b 1696; Amesbury
SARGENT, Digory, Worcester & Constant JAMES; 13 Oct 1693; Boston
SARGENT, Digory (-1707) & 2/wf Mary __?__/[PARMENTER?]; b 1696; ?Boston
SARGENT, Edward & Elizabeth [?PLAISTED] (-1718, ae 56); b 1684; Newbury/Saco, ME
SARGENT, Edward (-1695) & Joanna HOMAN; 3 Jun 1695; Dover, NH
SARGENT, Jacob & Gertrude DAVIS; m int 2 Nov 1700; Amesbury
SARGENT, John & [?Ruth] __?__; b 1661 or 1662; ?Saco, ME/Hampton, NH
SARGENT, John (1639-1716) & Deborah HILLIER (1643-1669); 19 Mar 1662/3; Barnstable/Malden
SARGENT, John (1639-1716) & 2/wf Mary BENSE (-1671); 3 Sep 1669; Malden
SARGENT, John (1639-1716, nr 77) & 3/wf Lydia [CHIPMAN] (1654-1730/1); b 1675; Malden
SARGENT, John & Hannah/Anna HOWARD, m/2 Nathaniel COIT (int 1711); 24 Dec 1679; Gloucester
SARGENT, John (-1751) & Mary [LINNELL?]; b 1689; Malden/Reading/Mansfield, CT
SARGENT, Jonathan (-19 Dec 1652) & __?__ (-19 Dec 1651); b 1640?; Branford, CT/Deerfield
SARGENT, Jonathan (1677-1754) & 1/wf Mary LYNDE (1675-); 13 Mar 1700, 1699-1700; Malden
SARGENT, Joseph (1663-1717) & Mary [GREEN] (1668-); b 1685; Charlestown
SARGEANT, Nathaniel & 1/wf Sarah HARVEY (-1706); 24 Jan 1694/5; Gloucester
SARGEANT, Peter & 1/wf Mary Elizabeth SHRIMPTON (-1700); 14 Dec 1682; Boston
SARGENT, Philip & Mary TUXSBERRY/TEWKESBURY; 7 Dec 1693; Amesbury
SARGEANT, Samuel & Mary NORWOOD; 24 May 1689; Gloucester
SARGENT, Stephen (-1649) & __?__ (no wife?); ?b 1638/40; Richmond Isl./Winters Isl., ME
SARGENT, Stephen & Dorothy __?__ (try Dorothy HEALD); b 1670; Boston
SARGENT, Thomas (-1726) & Rachel BARNES; 2 Mar 1667/8, 2 Mar 1668; Salisbury/Amesbury
SEARJEANT, Thomas & [Ruth JOHNSON]; b 1690; Scituate
SARGENT, Thomas & Hannah __?__; b 1692; Gloucester
SARGENT, Rev. William (1602-) & 1/wf Hannah __?__ (-1632); in Eng, b 1629, ca 1627; Malden
SARGENT, William & 2/wf Marie __?__ (-ca 1637); ca 1633?; Malden
SARGENT, William (ca 1610-1675) & 1/wf Judith [PERKINS/SHATSWELL] (ca 1612-)
SARGENT, William (1602-1675, ae 73) & 2/wf? Elizabeth [PERKINS] (-1674); ca 1639 or 1640, b 1643, b 1634?; Salisbury
SARGENT, Rev. William (1602-1682) (see Theophilus SHATSWELL) & 3/wf Sarah (_?_) [MINSHALL] (-1681, ?1682), w William; in Eng, b 17 Mar 1638/9; Charlestown/Barnstable
SARGANTE, William (-1717, ae 92) & Abigail CLARK (-1711, ae 79); 10 Sep 1651; Gloucester
SARGENT, William (1646-) & Mary COLBY (1647-); 23 Sep 1668; Amesbury
SARGENT, William (-1675) & 3/wf, 2/wf Joanna (PINDOR) ROWELL, w Valentine, m/3 Richard CURRIER 1676; 18 Sep 1676; Amesbury
SARGENT, William & Mary DUNCAN; 21 Jun 1678; Gloucester
SARGENT, William & 1/wf Naomi STAINWOOD/STANWOOD (-1702); 26 Oct 1681; Gloucester
SARGENT, William & Mary BEEDLE/?BEDELL; 6 Apr 1689; Amesbury
SARSON, Richard & Jane MAYHEW; b 1667, ?aft Sep 1667; Martha's Vineyard
SARSON, Samuel & Ann/Anne (PLATTS) CLAY, w John, m/3 John WORTH; 3 Jan 1694; Boston
SATTERLEE, Benedict & Rebecca (BEMIS) (WINTER) DYMOND, w Tobias, w John; 2 Aug 1682; New London, CT/Killingworth, CT
SATTERLEE, Nicholas & Mary __?__; b 1698; Westerly, RI
SATTERLY, Robert & Dorothy __?__; b 1695; Kittery, ME
SATTERLEE, William (-1677/80?) & [?Mary JENNER WEEKS?] (-1679), dau John JENNER; b 1660, b 7 Mar 1674; Groton, CT/LI?/Setauket, LI
SATTERLY, William (1660-1722) & Mary [MOGER]; ca 1682; Brookhaven, LI
SANDERS, Christopher & Elizabeth __?__; b 1675; Windsor, CT/Bristol, RI/Rehoboth, MA
SANDERS, Ephraim & Charity SANDIN; 11 Jun 1694; Marblehead
SANDERS, George (-1690) & 1/wf Mary [SAXTON] (1651-); bef 8 Jul 1674; Windsor, CT/Simsbury, CT
SANDERS, George (-1690) & Mehitable [BARTLETT] (1651-), m/2 John BURBANK 1694; b 1688; Simsbury
SAUNDERS, George (-1697) & Abigail BISSELL; 17 Dec 1691, no issue; Windsor, CT

SANDERS, Henry (see Henry SANDERSON); Sandwich
SANDERS, James (1643/4-) & 1/wf Sarah PAGE; 14 Jan 1669; Haverhill
SANDERS, James & Hannah TEWKSBURY; 20 Oct 1687; Haverhill/Newbury
SANDERS, James & Elizabeth WHITTIER; 22 Jun 1699; Haverhill
SANDERS, John (-1670) & Ann __?__; b 1632; Salisbury/Hampton, NH
SANDERS, John (ret'd to Eng) & Hester [ROLFE], ?m/2 Charles GLOVER 1650; ca 1638; Salisbury
SAUNDERS, John (1613-1643) & Elizabeth [GRAFTON], m/2 John KITCHEN 1643+; b 1640; Salem
SAUNDERS, John (-1689) & 1/wf Mary MUNGY/MUNJOY; 9 Oct 1650; Braintree
SAUNDERS, John & __?__; b 1654; Boston/?Watertown
SANDERS, John (1640-1694) & Hannah PICKMAN (1642-1706, 1707?); 5 Nov 1661; Salem
SANDERS, John & Mary FARLEY; 16 Oct 1671; Billerica
SANDERS, John & Mary __?__ (-1717, Gloucester); b Oct 1673; Salisbury/Cape Porpoise
SANDERS, John & __?__; b 1677; Dorchester
SANDERS, John & Mary [DOLLIVER] (1662-); ca 1682?
SAUNDERS, John & Elizabeth LAWRENCE; m lic 26 Jul 1683; LI
SANDERS, John (-1689) & 2/wf Hannah __?__, m/2 Caleb HOBART 1704; b 1685; Braintree
SANDERS, John (1665-) & Return SHATTUCK; 24 Sep 1688; Salem
SANDERS, John & Elizabeth [WRIGHT], w Thomas; 1691, 1692; Scituate
SAUNDERS, John & Hannah PENNIMAN; 15 Dec 1692; Braintree
SAUNDERS, John (1672-) & Mary SARGENT; 26 Dec 1695; Haverhill
SANDERS/SAUNDERS, John (-1746) & 1/wf Silence [BELCHER] (1679-1721+); b 4 Mar 1696/[7?]; Westerly, RI
SAUNDERS/SANDERS, John & Susannah THOMPSON (1673-); 24 May 1698; Braintree/Boston
SAUNDERS, Josiah & 1/wf Rachel HOLMAN; 4 Dec 1693; Braintree/Boston
SANDERS, Josiah & Rebecca (ELBRIDGE) SMITH, w Thomas; 7 Apr 1697; Boston
SANDERS, Martin (1595-1658) & 1/wf Rachel [?WHEATLEY] (1595-1651), wid; in Eng, b 1625; Cambridge/Braintree
SANDERS/SAUNDERS, Martin, Jr. & Lydia HARDIER/HARDING? (-1711); 1 Apr 1651; Braintree
SANDERS, Martin, Sr. (1595-1658) & 2/wf Elizabeth BANCROFT, w Roger, m/3 John BRIDGE 1658, m/4 Edward TAYLOR 1673; 23 May 1654; Braintree
SAUNDERS, Nathaniel & Mary __?__; b 1687; Boston
SANDERS, Richard & Mary MORSE, m/2 Richard EBURNE/ABURN; 17 Jun 1697; Dover, NH/Portsmouth, NH
SANDERS, Robert & Joanna __?__; b 1659; Dorchester
SAUNDERS, Robert (ae 25 in 1683) & Mary __?__; b 1682/[3?]; Boston
SANDERS, Thomas & Hope REYNOLDS, m/2 John CLEG; 23 Oct 1664; Saco, ME
SAUNDERS, Tobias (-1695) & Mary [CLARK?] (-1695+); b 19 Dec 1674; Taunton/Newport/Westerly
SANDERS, William & Sarah __?__; 15 Dec 1660; Watertown
SANDERS, William & Mary VOKES; 30 Nov 1669; Salem
SANDERS, William & Sarah WITTUM, m/2 George BRAWN 1700; Dec 1687; Kittery, ME
SANDERS, __?__ & Mary __?__; b 1660?
SAVAGE, Ebenezer (-1684) & Martha [ALLEN]; b 1683; Boston
SAVAGE, Ephraim (1645-1731) & 1/wf Mary [QUINCY] (1650-1676); b 1671; Boston
SAVAGE, Ephraim (1645-1731) & 2/wf Sarah (HOUGH) WALKER (-1687), w Obadiah; 26 Feb 1677/8; ?Boston/Reading?
SAVAGE, Ephraim (1645-1731) & 3/wf Elizabeth (NORTON) SIMMES/SYMMES (-1710), w Timothy; 12 Apr 1688; Charlestown
SAVAGE, Habijah (1638-1669) & Hannah TYNG (1640-1688), m/2 Daniel GOOKINS 1685?; 8 May 1661; Boston/Charlestown
SAVAGE, Henry & Elizabeth [WALFORD]; b 1666?; Portsmouth, NH
SAVAGE, John (-1675) & Elizabeth DUBBLIN/D'AUBIN?; 10 Feb 1652, 1651/2; Middletown, CT
SAVAGE, John (-1678) & Sarah BOWEN, m/2 Joseph BRAYMAN/BRAMAN 1681; 16 May 1672; Rehoboth
SAVAGE, John (-1708) & Katherine __?__; b 1673; Eastham/Truro/Nantucket

SAVAGE, John (1652-1726) & Mary RANNEY (1665-1734); 30 May 1682; Middletown, CT/Cromwell, CT

SAVAGE, John & 1/wf _?_ ; ca 1680/2?; Portsmouth, NH

SAVAGE, Nathaniel (1671-173-) & Esther RANNEY (1673-1750, ae 76); 3 Nov 1696, 31 Dec, 3 Dec; Middletown, CT/Portland, CT

SAVAGE, Thomas (1607-1682, ae 75) & 1/wf Faith [HUTCHINSON] (1617-1652); ca 1637; Boston/Charlestown

SAVAGE, Thomas (-1682, ae 75) & 2/wf Mary SYMMES, m/2 Anthony STODDARD 1684?; 15 Sep 1652; Boston

SAVAGE, Thomas (-1705) & Elizabeth SCOTTO/SCOTTOW (1647-1715); ca 1664; Charlestown/ Boston

SAVAGE, Thomas & 1/wf Mehitable (PHILLIPS) HARWOOD, w Benjamin; 5 Feb 1690, 1689/90; Boston

SAVAGE, Thomas (-1720/[1]) & Margaret [LYNDE] (1669-); b 1694; Charlestown/Boston

SAVAGE, William (1668-1735, 1726?) & Christian MOULD (1677-1750, 1719?); 6 May 1696, 1696/7; Middletown, CT/Portland, CT

SAVERY, Aaron (-1717) & Hannah _?_ ; ?Dartmouth

SEVERY, Andrew (-1715) & Mary _?_ ; b 1685, b 1683; Marblehead

SEVERY, John (-1742 in 98th y) & Mary _?_ ; ca 1675/80?; Wenham

SEVERY, Peter (-1685) & Mary _?_ ; b 1684; Wenham

SEVERETT, Philip (-1690) & Joanna JOSE (-1691); 10 Oct 1680

SAVORY, Robert & Mary (SAWYER) MITCHELL, w William; 8 Dec 1656; Newbury

SAVORY, Samuel (1651-) (ae 22 in 1673) & _?_ ; b 1678, by 1676?; Plymouth/Rochester

SAVORY, Thomas & [Ann] _?_ ; ca 1643?; Plymouth

SEVERY, Thomas & Elizabeth BROWN; 1 Nov 1683; Marblehead

SAVORY, William (1659-1709+) & Hannah _?_ (-1751); b 1691(2?); Bradford

SAVIL, Benjamin (1645-) & Lydia BARNES; 30 Dec 1670; Braintree

SAVILLE, John (1642-) & Mehitable HANDS, m/2 Thomas METCALF 1689; 20 Oct 1668; Braintree

SAVIL, Samuel (1643-1700) & Hannah ADAMS (1652-1726, ae 74); 10 Apr 1673, 1672; Braintree

SAVIL, William[1] (-1669) & 1/wf Hannah [TIDD] (-14 Jun 1650); b 1642; Braintree

SAVILL, William[1] (-1669) & 2/wf Sarah _?_ (-13 Jul 1655); 1650, 1651; Braintree

SAVILL, William[1] (-1669) (calls Samuel BASS "brother" 1669) & 3/wf Sarah (MULLINS) GANNETT, w Thomas, m/3 Thomas FAXON 1670; 8 Nov 1655, 6 Nov 1655; Braintree

SAVIL, William (1652?-1700) & 1/wf Deborah FAXON (1654-1692); 1 Jan 1679, 1679/80?; Braintree

SAVIL, William (-1700) & ?2/wf Experience QUINCY; 24 Nov 1693; Braintree

SAWIN, John (-1690) & Abigail [MUNNING] (1627-); b 1647?, b 1650?; Watertown

SAWIN, John[2] (-1697+) & Judith PEIRSSE/PIERCE (?1650-1723); 16 Feb 1666/7, 1666, no issue; Watertown

SAWIN, Munning (1655-1722) & Sarah STONE (1663-); 15 Dec 1681; Watertown

SAWINE, Thomas & Deborah RICE; 23 Jan 1683, 1683/4; Sudbury

SAWTLE, Enoch[2] (-1741) & Susannah/Susan [RANDALL] (1659-); b 1687; Watertown

SATLE, Henry & Sarah [BAYLY], w Elias; b 13 Apr 1668; Newtown, LI

SARTEL, James (-1683)& _?_ ; Newtown, LI

SAWTELL, John (-bef 1700) & ?1/wf ?Elizabeth _?_

SAWTELL, John (-bef 1700) & 2wf? Anna/Ann [POST?] (-1711), dau Thomas; Cambridge

SAWTELL, Jonathan (1639-1690) & Mary [TARBELL]? (related to Abraham HOLMAN in some way); 3 Jul 1665; Groton

SAWTELLE, Obadiah (1649-1740, in 92nd y) & Hannah [LAWRENCE] (1662-1707+); b 1683; Groton

SAUTLE, Richard (-1694) (see clue below) & Elizabeth POPLE (-1694); b 1638, 5 Feb 1627/8; Watertown/Groton

SAWTELL, Richardus (-1694) (clue) & Elizabeth POPLE (-1694); High Dam, Somersetshire, 5 Feb 1627

SAWTELL, Zachariah (1643-1688/1692) & 1/wf Elizabeth HARRIS (1644-1679?, 1677/8?; - Apr 1668, 13 Apr 1669; Malden/Charlestown

SAWTELLE, Zachariah (1643-1688/1692) & 2/wf Anna [PARKER] (1663-1726+); b 13 Jul 1684, b 13 Jul 1683?; Groton

SAWTELL, Zachariah & 1/wf Mary [BLOOD?] (1678-1699?), dau Nathaniel?; b 1697 (only one wife); Groton

SAWTELL, Zachariah & 2/wf Mercy __?__; b 1700; Groton

SAWYER, Caleb (1659-) & Sarah HOUGHTON (1662-); 28 Dec 1687, 21 Dec; Lancaster

SAWYER, ?Edward & Mary [?PEASLEY], Rowley

SAWER, Edward (?1608-1674) & Mary __?__; b 1645; Ipswich/York/Rowley

SAWYER, Ephraim (1678-) & Elizabeth GEORGE (1671-); 4 Jul 1700; Marlborough/Mansfield, CT/Windham, CT

SAWYER, James & Martha __?__; b 1669; Salisbury

SAWYER, James (-1703) & Sarah [BRAY]; b 1670; Gloucester

SAYER, James (1657-1753), Lancaster & 1/wf Mary MARBEL (-1708); 4 Feb 1677, 4 Feb 1678; Concord/Pomfret, CT/Lancaster

SAWYER, John (-1711) & 1/wf Mercy LITTLE (-1693); last of Nov 1666; Marshfield

SAWIER, John & Mary [PARRAT?] (1647?-); b 1674(5?); Rowley

SAWYER, John (1648-1689) & Sarah POORE (1655-), m/2 Joseph BAILEY 1707; 18 Feb 1675, 1675/6; Newbury

SAWYER, John (1661-1705±) & Mary BRELL/BULL/BALL, m/2 William STERLING; 16 Jun 1686; Lancaster/Lyme, CT

SAWYER, John (-1711) & 2/wf Rebecca (BARKER) SNOW (-1711), w Josiah; 23 Nov 1694; Marshfield

SAWYER, John & Mary (BROWN) MERRILL (1673-), w Peter; 25 Dec 1700; Newbury

SAIRE, Joshua (1655-1738), Woburn & Sarah (WRIGHT?) POTTER (1653-), w Samuel; 2 Jan 1677, 1678; Concord/Lancaster

SAWYER, Nathaniel (1670-1756) & 1/wf Mary [?HOUGHTON] (-1709+); b 1693; Lancaster

SAWYER, Samuel (1646-1718) & Mary EMERY (1652-); 13 Mar 1670/1; Newbury

SAWYER, Stephen (1663-1753) & Anne TITCOMBE (-1750, ae 83); 10 Mar 1686/7; Newbury

SAWYER, Thomas (?1616-1706, ae ca 90?) & Mary [PRESCOTT] (1630-1716?) ; b 1648; Rowley/Lancaster

SAWYER, Thomas (1649-1736) & 1/wf Sarah [FAIRBANKS] (1645-1672); 11 Oct 1670; Lancaster

SAWYER, Thomas (1649-1736) & 2/wf Hannah [HOUGHTON?/LEWIS?/WELD?] (?1649-); 21 Nov 1672, b 1675; Lancaster/Marlborough

SAWYER/SAYER, Thomas (-1695?) (see SAYER) & Mary CHAMBERLAIN; 13 Oct 1685; Hingham/Middleboro

SAWYER, Thomas & Hannah MILLET (-1690); 17 Feb 1689/90; Gloucester

SAWYER, Thomas (-1711) & Hannah (VERRY) FOSTER (?1651-), w Bartholomew; 18 Nov 1691; Gloucester

SAWYER, William[1] (1613-1702) & Ruth [BENFORD?/BEDFIELD?/BEDFORD?/PERLEY]; ca 1643, b 1645; Newbury/Durham, NH

SAWYER, William (1656-) & 2/wf Sarah (LITTLEFIELD) WELLS, w John; b 16 Nov 1677, ca 1677; Salisbury

SAWYER, William & 1/wf Abigail [LILLEY] (1672-); ca 1696; Reading

SAWYER, William & 2/wf Dorcas BURNAP; 30 Apr 1700; Reading

SAWYER, William (1679-) & Hannah [HOUGHTON] (1680-); b 1701?: Bolton

SAXTON, John (1647-1686) & Mary [?CLARK] (had son Clark); b 1683; Boston

SAXTON, Joseph (1656-1715, Stonington) & Hannah (DENISON) CHESEBROUGH (1643- 1715+), w Nathaniel; ca 15 Jul 1680; Stonington, CT

SAXTON, Peter (ret'd to Eng, Leeds, Eng) & __?__; Scituate

SAXTON, Samuel (1653-1693) & Susanna [ADAMS] (1648-), dau Alexander, m/2 Thomas HUNT 1694; b 1678(9?); Boston

SAXTON, Thomas[1] (1612-1680) & 1/wf Lucy __?__; b 1645; Boston

SAXTON, Thomas[1] (1612-1680) & 2/wf Ann (COPP) ATWOOD (-1661), w Harmon; 10 Mar 1650/1, 1651/2; Boston

SAXTON, Thomas[1] (1612-1680) & Mary __?__, m Samuel GOFFE 1682; b 1664; Boston

SAXTON, Thomas[2] (-bef 1680) & Mary [WOODWARD] (-1740), m/2 John BALLANTINE; Boston

SAYS/SAITH?, Christopher & Hannah __?__; b 1676?; Malden

SAILS, Edward (1609-1693) & Margaret __?__ (-1664, Rehoboth); b 1638; ?Marblehead/Salem/Weymouth/Rehoboth

SALE, Ephraim (1638-1690) & 1/wf Alice __?__; b 1676, b 1673; Boston

SALE, Ephraim (1638-1690) & 2/wf Mary [FOSTER] (1656-), m/2 Samuel WARD 1691; b 1681; Boston

SALE, Ephraim & Joanna PRINCE; m int 29 Jun 1696; Boston

SAYLES, John[1] & _?_ ; b 1628; Charlestown/Providence, RI

SAYLES, John (?1627-1681) & Mary [WILLIAMS] (1633, 1632-1681); b 1652, 1650±; Providence

SAYLES, John (1654-1727) & 1/wf Elizabeth [OLNEY]? (1666-1699); b 1689; Providence

SALE, Michael & Hannah _?_ ; b 1693; Boston

SALE, Obadiah (1640-) & Sarah _?_ ; b 1680; Boston

SAYLES, Richard (1635) (did he marry?)

SAYRE, Caleb & Mary [EVANS]; b 1698; Southampton, LI/Newark, NJ

SAYRE, Daniel[2] (-1708) & 1/wf Hannah FOSTER; ?ca 1655/60, b 1666; Southampton, LI/Bridgehampton, LI

SAYRE, Daniel[2] (-1708) & 2/wf Sarah _?_ ; b 14 Apr 1690; Southampton, LI

SAYRE, Daniel (1666-1747/8) & Sarah _?_ (1667-1733); Southampton, LI

SAYRE, Daniel (1666-1747/8) & Mary [?CLARK] FORDHAM, w Joseph; aft 1688

SAYRE, David[3] (-1748) & [?Sarah RILEY]; b 1698; Southampton/Cohansey, NJ

SAYRE, Francis[2] (-1698) & Sarah WHEELER (wife in 1693); b 1665; Southampton, LI

SAYRE, Ichabod & Mary HUBBARD (1674, 1664?-); 31 Mar 1697, b 10 Apr 1697; New London

SAYRE, Job (1611-) & _?_ ; ca 1635? (did he marry?); Salem

SAYRE, Job[2] & 1/wf Sarah [LUM] (1652±-29 Oct 1684); 27 Oct 1670; Southampton, LI

SAYRE, Job[2] & 2/wf Hannah (RAYNOR) HOWELL, w Arthur; 18 Jun 1685; Southampton, LI

SAYRE, John (1665-1724) & Sarah _?_ ; 27 Sep 1689; Southampton, LI

SAYRE, Joseph[2] (-1695) & Martha _?_ ; b 1665?; Southampton, LI

SAYRE, Joseph[3] (-1710) & Priscilla _?_ ; ca 1686/90?; Southampton/Fairfield/Cohansey, NJ

SAYRE, Samuel[3] (-bef 21 Aug 1707) & _?_ ; Southampton, LI/Elizabeth, NJ

SAYRE, Thomas[1] (1597, 1590, 1594?-1670) & Margaret ALDRED (-23 Aug 1634); ca 1620/30 in Eng; Lynn/Southampton, LI

SAYRE/SAWYER?, Thomas & 1/wf Sarah PRINCE; 26 Nov 1673; Hingham

SAYER/SAWYER?, Thomas & 2/wf Mary CHAMBERLAIN; 13 Oct 1685; Hingham

SAYRE, Thomas (1667-1715) & Patience [FOSTER]; Southampton, LI

SAIR, William & Martha BARBER; 8 May 1685, 1675; Middlesex Co

SAYWARD, Edmund & _?_ ; Ipswich

SAYWARD, Henry & Mary [PEASLEY] (1633-); b 1655; Hampton, NH

SAYWARD, James (-1737, in 68th y) & 1/wf Deborah [STOVER] (-1734, ae 67); b 1694; Gloucester

SAYWARD, John & Mary (ROCKFORD) (WHITE) HULL, w Wm., w Phineas, m/4 James PLAISTED; 6 Apr 1681; Hampton, NH

SAYWARD, Jonathan & Mary AUSTIN, m/2 Lewis BANE; May 1686; York, ME

SAYWARD, ?Robert & _?_

SAYWELL, David (-1672) & Abigail BUTTOLPH, m/2 Thomas BINGLEY; 15 Aug 1660; Boston

SCADLOCK, Samuel & Ann _?_ ; b 1698; Boston

SCADLOCK, William & Eleanor _?_ , m/2 Stephen KENT 1663; ca 1636; Saco, ME

SCADLOCK, William (-1664?) & Ann (BULLY) BERRY, w Ambrose, m/3 John CARTER 1665; b 1661

SCAILS, James (-1685/6) & Sarah CURTIS (1654-); 7 Nov 1677; Rowley

SCALES, John (-1684) & Susanna [JARRAT]/?[Amy] RUSSELL? (-1683), w John; b 1650; Rowley

SCALES, William & Ann _?_ ; b 1657; Rowley

SCAMMON, Humphrey (1640-1727) & ?Elizabeth/_?_ _?_ ; b 1677; Kittery, ME/Cape Porpoise/Saco/Biddeford

SCAMMON, John & _?_ ; Kittery, ME

SCAMMON, Richard (-1691) & Prudence [WALDRON]; b 1661; Dover, NH/Exeter/Stratham, NH/?Hampton, NH

SCAMMON, Richard (?1662-) & Elizabeth [WAKELY] (1664-); b 1760; Kittery, ME

SCAMMON, William (1664/5-) & _?_ ; ?b 1694; Stratham, NH/Exeter, NH

SCAMPE/SCAMP, Robert & Joan/Jane? COLLINS (-1663); 25 Dec 1661; Gloucester

SCANT, William & Sarah BROWN; 29 Mar 1654; Braintree

SCARBOROUGH, John (-1646) & Mary [SMITH], m/2 Philip TORREY 1647; b 1642; Roxbury

SCARBOROUGH, John & Mehitable BUGBEE; 17 Oct 1695; Woodstock, CT

SCARBOROUGH, Samuel (1645-1715) & 1/wf ?Deborah/Rebecca [?PARKE] (-1679); b 3 Jan 1674/5; Roxbury
SCARBOROUGH, Samuel (1645-1715) & 2/wf Bethiah [WISE] (1654-1728, ae 75); ca 1680; Roxbury
SCARLET, John (-1688) & Thomasine __?__; b 1653; Boston
SCARLET, Samuel (-1675) & __?__; b 1660; Charlestown/Boston
SCARLET, Samuel & Ann/[?Hannah PAUL]; b 1690(1?); Boston
SCARLET, [?John] & Anne [GRAFTON]; b 1630?; Salem
SCARLET, __?__ & Sarah [ADAMS]/[WACUM], m/2 Peter GRANT 1694; ?Boston
SCATE/?SKEATH/SKATE, John (-1708) (see John SHAW) & Sarah WATERS (1636-); 7 Jun 1658; Weymouth/Boston
SCATE, John (1661-1697, killed by Indians) & __?__ (-1697); Lancaster
SKEATH, Joseph (1668-) & Hannah DAVISE; 18 Apr 1692; Boston
SCHELLENGER, Abraham (1659-1712) & 1/wf Joanna HEDGES (-1708); 15 Nov 1688; East Hampton, LI
SCHELLINGER, Cornelius & 1/wf Lydia __?__
SCHELLENGER, Jacob & Cornelia (MELYN) LOPER, w Jacob; 7 Apr 1653
SCHELLINGER, Jacob (1663) & Hannah __?__
SCHRICK, Paulus & Mary (VARLEET) AMBEEK, w Johannes; 30 Dec 1655; Hartford
SCOFIELD, Daniel (-1669) & Sarah __?__, m/2 Miles MERWIN 1670; b 1649; Stamford, CT
SCOFIELD, Daniel (-1714) & Abigail [MERWIN] (1652±-); ca 1670/2?; Stamford, CT
SCOFIELD, John (-1699) & Hannah MEAD (1661?-); 12 Jul 1677, 13 Jul; Stamford, CT
SCOFIELD, Richard (-1671) & [Elizabeth] __?__, m/2 Robert PENOYER 1671?, m/3 Richard LOUNSBURY by 1684; b 1653; Stamford, CT
SCOFIELD, Richard & Ruth BRUNDISH; 14 Sep 1689; Stamford, CT
SCOLLEY/SCOLLAY, John & Hannah BARRETT (1648, ?1647-); b 1665; Charlestown/Malden?/ Boston?
SCOLLY, John (1665-) & Lydia GROVER; 22 Dec 1690; Boston
SCONE, John (-1684) & Sarah HART (-1692), m/2 John BURBANK 1692; ca 1675; Westfield
SCONER, Paltiel & Lydia __?__; b 1668; Boston
SCOTCHFORD, John (-1696) & Susanna [MERRIAM] (-1707); b 1679; Concord/Charlestown
SCOTT, Benjamin (-1647) & Hannah __?__, m/2 John HARBOUR 1647; b 1638, b 1635?; Braintree
SCOTT, Benjamin (-1671) & Margaret [STEPHENSON] (-1692); ca 28 Jul 1642; Cambridge/Rowley
SCOTE, Benjamin (1646-) & Susannah [SCALES]; 28 Dec 1676; Rowley
SCOTT, Benjamin (1674-) & Mary DANIEL; 31 May 1699; Braintree/Milton
SCOTT, David & Sarah RICHARDS; 10 Jun 1698, 10 Nov; Waterbury, CT
SCOTT, Edmund (-1691) & 1/wf Hannah BIRD; b 1660; Farmington, CT
SCOTT, Edmund (-1691) & 2/wf Elizabeth (FULLER) [UPSON], w Thomas; Farmington, CT
SCOTT, Edmund (-1746) & Sarah PORTER (-1749), w Benjamin; Jun 1689; Waterbury, CT
SCOTT, Edward & 1/wf Elizabeth WEBSTER (-1689); 22 Nov 1670; Hadley/New Haven
SCOTT, Edward & 2/wf Mercy (BROOKS) [HILL], div wf Ebenezer HILL; ca 1693; New Haven
SCOTT, Edward & Martha __?__ (-1694); ca 1693; Suffield, CT
SCOTT, George (-1724) & Mary RICHARDS (1669-); Aug 1691; Waterbury, CT
SCOTT, Henry (-1634 in Eng) & Martha WHATLOCK (1568-1634+) (came to New Eng); Rattlesden, Eng, 25 Jul 1594
SCOTT, Jehomiah (-1739) & __?__ JACKSON; b 1698; Southampton
SCOTT, John (-1682, ae 75) & Elizabeth __?__ (-1676); ca 1635/38?; Charlestown
SCOTT, John (-1690) & Sarah BLISS (-1705), m/2 Samuel TERRY 1690; 20 Jul 1659, 26? Jul; Springfield
SCOTT, John (-1677) & Rebecca [BROWNE]?, m/2 John WHIPPLE; b 1662; Providence
SCOTT, John & Deborah [REYNOR], m/2 Charles STEVENS; b 1663; Southampton
SCOTT, John & Hannah DUNKEN/DUNCAN (1651-); 29 May 1672; Roxbury
SCOTT, John & Elizabeth __?__; b 1673; Boston
SCOTT, John (1664-1725) & Elizabeth [WANTON] (1668-); ca 1690?; Newport/Scituate
SCOTT, Jonathan & Hannah HANKS/HAWKS, Deerfield; Nov 1694; Deerfield/Waterbury, CT/Hadley
SCOTT, Joseph (-1708) & Mary [RISDEN?]; b 1657; Hempstead, LI
SCOTT, Joseph & Anna/Hannah/Susanna [BROWN?]; b 1678; Rowley

SCOTT, Joseph & Elizabeth WINSLOW (1674-), m/2 Samuel HINCKES; 18 Jan 1693; Boston
SCOTT, Josiah & Sarah [BARRETT]; b 1699; Hadley
SCOTT, Peter (-1693) & Abigail NEALE; 22 Jan 1673, 22 Dec 1673, 22 Jan 1673/4; Dorchester
SCOTT, Richard (1605-1680±) & Katherine MARBURY (1610+-1687); 7 Jun 1632, aft 1637; Ipswich/Providence
SCOTT, Richard & Bathshua [OXENBRIDGE], dau John; b 12 Jan 1673/4; ?Boston
SCOTT, Robert (-1654) & Elizabeth _?_ (1616-) (ae 47 in 1663); b 1638; Boston
SCOTT, Robert (-1690, ae 56) & Esther _?_ ; b 1677, b 1681; Charlestown/Boston
SCOTT, Robert (1624-) & 2/wf _?_ (MERCER) DRAPER, w Nathaniel; by 1680
SCOTT, Roger & Judith _?_ ; b 1698; Attleboro
SCOTT, Samuel (1663-1745) & Mary ORVIS (1663-1748); Feb 1686/7; Farmington, CT
SCOTT, Silvanus/Sylvanus (1672-1742) & Joanna [JENKS] (1672-1750); 1692±, b 1694, bef 1792 (wrong); Providence/Smithfield, RI
SCOTT, Stephen & Sarah LAMB; 27 Jul 1664; Braintree
SCOTT, Thomas (-1643) & Ann _?_ (1587-), m/2 Thomas FORD 1644; b 1618, b 1614?; Hartford
SCOTT, Thomas[1] (1595-1654) & Elizabeth STRUTT (1594-?1678, bef 1654?); Rattlesden, Eng, 20 Jul 1620; Ipswich
SCOTT, Thomas (1628-1657) & Margaret [HUBBARD], m/2 Ezekiel ROGERS; (had Margaret & Thomas); Ipswich/Stamford, CT
SCOTT, William, Hatfield & Hannah ALLIS (1654-); 28 Jan 1670, 28 Jun 1670; Hadley/Hatfield
SCOTT, William & Abigail (TITUS) WARNER (1650-), w Ralph; m lic 7 Feb 1678; Gravesend, LI
SCOTTOW, John (1644-1678) & Rebecca _?_ , ?m/2 Caleb CHURCH 1691; b 1668; Boston
SCOTTO, Joshua (1615-1698) (ae 47 in 1662/[3]?, ae 66 in 1682) & Lydia _?_ (-1707, ae 86); b 1641; Boston/Scarboro, ME
SCOTTOW, Joshua (1655?-) & 1/wf Sarah SYMMES (1672-1710); 25 May 1697; Charlestown/Bradford/Boston
SCOTTO, Thomas (1612-1661) & 1/wf Joan [?SANFORD] (see below); b 1639; Boston
SCOTTOW, Thomas (1612-1661) & 2/wf Sarah [?HARWOOD], ?m/2 John TUCKER; b 1655; Boston
SCOTTOW, _?_ & Thomasine _?_ , ?m/2 _?_ SANFORD; in Eng, b 1612
SOTTOW, _?_ & Elizabeth [DALTON?] (1661-), m/2 John FRENCH; by 1700
SCOVELL, Arthur & Joane/Jane _?_ ; b 1662; Boston/Middletown, CT
SCOVILLE, Arthur (1664-1692, 1694) & Rachel _?_ (-1707), m/2 Nathaniel HUDSON, m/3 James SMITH; 17 Dec 1690, 1689?; Lyme, CT/Middletown, CT
SCOVELL, Edward (-1703), Haddam, CT, & Hannah BENTON (±1676-1771), m/2 Benjamin SMITH; 21 Feb 1699/1700 at Hartford, ?20 Feb; Haddam, CT/Wethersfield, CT
SCOVIL, James (1670-1711) & Hannah [?SUMMERS]; b 1698; Middletown, CT
SCOVIL, John & Sarah BARNES; 29 Mar 1666, ?26 Mar; Farmington, CT/Waterbury/Haddam
SCOVIL, John (-1727) & Hannah RICHARDS (-1720); 6 Feb 1693/4, 6 Feb 1693; Waterbury, CT
SCOFIELD/SCOVILLE, John (-1712) & Mary LUCAS (1672-), m/2 _?_ CROWFOOT, m/3 Nathaniel BURT; 9 Feb 1697/8; Middletown, CT
SCRANTON, John[1] (?1601-1671) & 1/wf Joanna _?_ (-1651); b 1640?; Guilford, CT
SCRANTON, John[1] (?1601-1671) & 2/wf Adeline/"Addy" (_?_) (JOHNSON) HILL (Mercy JOHNSON) (-1685), w Robert; 22 May 1666; Guilford, CT
SCRANTON, John[2] (-1703) & 1/wf Mary SEWARD (1652-1690, 1688?); 12 Mar 1673, 1673/4; Guilford, CT
SCRANTON, John[2] (-1703) & Elizabeth (BISHOP) CLARK (-1727), w Thomas?; 16 Dec 1691; Guilford, CT
SCRANTON, John (1676-1723, 1758?) & 1/wf Mary NORTON (-living in 1712); 12 Dec 1699; Guilford, CT
SCRANTON, John & Sarah [STAFFORD] (1671-); b 1701?
SCRANTON, Thomas (1643±-1711) & 1/wf Deborah (DUDLEY) [THOMPSON] (1647-1681), w Ebenezer; [1681]; Guilford, CT
SCRANTON, [?Thomas] (1643±-1711) & 2/wf Hannah [ALLING] (1659-); b 6 May 1689, aft 1681; ?New Haven/Guilford, CT
SCRANTON, Thomas (1643±-1711) & 3/wf Elizabeth [GOODRICH?]/[GRISWOLD?]; aft 1689, b 1701?; Guilford, CT
SCRANTON, Thomas & _?_ ; b 1641; Warwick, RI
SCRANTON, Thomas (1641) & Mary _?_ ; Portsmouth (Prudence Island)/Warwick, RI

SCRIBNER/SCRIVENER, Benjamin (-1704) & Hannah CRAMPTON; 5 Mar 1679/80, 5 Mar 1680; ?Huntington, LI/Norwalk, CT
SCRIBNER, John (-1675) & Mary _?_; b 1664; ?Dover, NH
SCRIBNER, John (1664-) & Elizabeth [CLOICE]/CLOYES; ca 1688; ?Dover, NH
SCRIPTURE, Samuel[1] (1649?-1738/42) & Elizabeth KNAP (1655-); 11 Sep 1674; Cambridge/Groton
SCRIPTURE, Samuel (1675-1755) & Mary (PIERCE) GREEN, w John?; 8 Feb 1699/1700; Concord
SCRIVEN, William (1629-1713) & Bridgett CUTTS; 23 Jul 1674; Kittery, ME
SCRUGGS, Thomas (-1654) & Margaret/Margery _?_ (-1663); b 1634, b 1619; Salem
SCUDDER, Benjamin (-1739) & 1/wf Sarah _?_ ; b 1698; Huntington, LI
SCUDDER, David & Mary _?_ ; b 26 Jun 1686
SCUDDER, Henry (-1661) & Catharine [ESTY?/ESTEY], m/2 Thomas JONES 1661+; b 1657, b 1637?; Huntington, LI
SCUDDER, John (1619-) & Mary [KING] (?1623-); ca 1642/4?; Salem/Southold, LI/Huntington, LI
SCUDDER, John (1645-, Boston) & Elizabeth (_?_) LETHROP
SCUDDER, John (-1690) & [Hannah] _?_ (-1690+); b 1646; Barnstable
SCUDDER, John (-1732) & Joanna [BETTS]; ca 1669/79?, b 1671?; Newtown, LI/NJ
SCUDDER, John & Elizabeth HAMLIN; last Jul 1689, 31? Jul 1689; Barnstable
SCUDDER, Jonathan (1657-1691) & Sarah BROWN; 14 Nov 1680; Huntington, LI
SCUDDER, Richard B.? (1671-1754) & Hannah R-?/REEDER? [STILWELL] (1671-1734) ; b 1701, ca 1695?; Newtown, LI
SCUDDER, Samuel (-1688/9) & Phebe [TITUS] (1660-), m/2 Robert FIELD 1690; Waterbury, LI/Newtown, LI
SCUDDER, Thomas (-1658) & Elizabeth [LOWERS]? (-1666); in Eng, b 1622; Salem
SCUDDER, Thomas (-1690) (had dau Cleman) & Mary [LUDLAM]/CONKLIN?; ca 1654?; Southold, LI/Huntington, LI
SCUDDER, Thomas & Sarah PHILLIPS; 4 Nov 1689, 3 Nov; Boston
SCUDDER, Timothy & Sarah [?WOOD] (1658-1739); LI
SCUDDER, William (-1657) & Penelope _?_ ; b 1650; Salem
SCULLARD, Samuel (-1647, 1643, ae 30?) & Rebecca [KENT], m/2 John BISHOP 1647; in Eng, b 1641(2?); Newbury
SIBORNE/SIBBORN/SEABORNE, John & Mary _?_ ; b 1644; Boston
SEBER, John & Susanna SAWARD; 6 Jun 1700; Boston
SEABURN, Samuel & Patience KEMPE; 16 Nov 1660, 9 Nov 1660; Duxbury/Weymouth
SEABROOK, Robert[1] (ca 1565-aft 1650) & ?[Alice GOODSPEED]; 12 Sep 1596, b 1597; Stratford, CT
SEABROOK, Thomas & Mary _?_ ; b 1601
SEABROOK, Thomas & Mary [BRAY]; b 1667; Dover, NH
SEABURY, John & Grace _?_, m/2 Anthony/Anthonie LANE?; b 1639; Boston
SEABURY, John (ca 1674-1759) & Elizabeth ALDEN (ca 1676-1771); 9 Dec 1697; Duxbury/Stonington, CT
SEBURY, Samuel (1640-1681) & 1/wf Patience KEMP (-1676); 16 Nov 1660; Duxbury
SEBURY, Samuel (1640-1681) & 2/wf Martha PABODIE (1649, 1651?-1712), m/2 William FOBES; 4 Apr 1677; Duxbury
SEABURY, Samuel (1666-) & Abigail ALLEN (1669-); 13 Dec 1688; Duxbury
SEAGER, Henry[1] (1649-1724) (ae 24 in 1673) & Sarah BISHOP (1659-1733); 21 Jan 1673, 19 Apr 1671, 1673/4; Cambridge/Newton
SAGER, John (-1737) & _?_ ; b 1684; Newton/South Kingston, RI
SEAGER, Joseph (-1698) & Abigail TAYLOR; 27 Sep 1680; Suffield, CT/Windsor, CT
SEAGER, Richard (63 in 1658) & Elizabeth _?_ ; b 1650; Hartford
SEGAR, Richard (-1698) & Abigail GRIFFEN (-1698); 20 Mar 1682; Simsbury, CT
SEAMAN, Benjamin (?1650-1733) & Martha [TITUS] (1663-1732+); b 1685; ?Jerusalem, LI
SEAMAN, John[1] (SYMONDS alias SEAMAN) (?1610-ca 1695) & 1/wf Elizabeth [STRICKLAND]?; ca 1644; Hempstead, LI
SEAMAN, John[1] (?1610-ca 1695) & 2/wf [Martha MOORE] (1639-1698+); ca 1655; Hempstead, LI
SEAMAN, John[2] (?1645-1697±) & Hannah [WILLIAMS]/MOORE; ca 1665; ?Hempstead, LI
SEAMAN, Jonathan (?1647-) & Jane _?_ ; ca 1675?; Hempstead, LI

SEAMAN, Nathaniel (-1759) & Rachel WILLIS (-1759); 9 Oct 1695; Westbury, LI

SEAMAN, Richard (1673-1749) & Jane [MOTT] (1680-1759); ca 1694; Hempstead, LI

SEAMAN, Samuel (?1668-1732+) & Phoebe [HICKS] (1672-1732); ca 1695; Hempstead, LI

SEAMAN, Solomon (?1651-1733) & Elizabeth [LINNINGTON]; ca 1682; ?Hempstead, LI

SEAMAN, Thomas (-1724) & Mary _?_ ; ca 1675?; ?Hempstead, LI

SEAMANS, Thomas & Susannah [SALISBURY] (1662-); 1687?, b 1692; Swansea

SEARLE, Andrew (1614-1690) & _?_ ; ?b 1665, b 1655; Kittery, ME

SEARLE, Daniel & Deliverance [TYNG]; b 1666; Boston/Barbados

SEARLE, Ebenezer (1666-1740) & Margaret SEARLE; 14 Jan 1699; Stonington, CT

SEARLES, Edward (-1679+) & Joan (?CALVERLY) WHITE, wid; b 1647; Barbados?/Providence/
Warwick, RI

SEARLE, Edward, Jr. & Ann (GREEN/GROVE)? LIPPITT, w John; 21 Feb 1671, 1671/2?, 13 Feb
1670; Warwick, RI/Cranston, RI/Provicence

SEARLES, George (-1706) & Mary BLAKEMAN (1661-); ca 1680?, b 1686; Stratford,
CT/Fairfield

SEARLE, John (-1641) & Sarah BALDWIN, m/2 Alexander EDWARDS 1642; 19 Mar 1639,
1638/9; Springfield

SEARLE, John (1629-1711) & Katherine (?MITCHELL) WARNER (-1707), w Thomas; 26 Nov
1661; Boston/Stonington, CT

SEARLE, John & 1/wf Ruth JANES (-1672); 3 Jul 1667; Northampton/Springfield

SEARLE, John (-1675/6) & [?Joane ANDREWS], m/2 John FORD b 1679; Kittery

SEARLE, John & Mary [GREEN] (1651-); b 1675; Kittery, ME

SEARLE, John (-1691) & Mary [PETHERICK]; b Nov 1676; Marblehead/Salem

SEARLE, John (1641-1718) & 2/wf Mary NORTH (-1726); 30 May 1675; Springfeild/Northampton

SEARLE, John & 1/wf Mary RUGGLES (1656-); 6 Jun 1682; Roxbury

SEARLE, John & Margaret HINKSMAN/HENCHMAN; 14 Nov 1687; Charlestown

SEARL/SEARLE, John & Mary [PHIPPEN], m/2 Joseph ENGLISH 1693, 1694; b 1688; Salem

SEARLE, John (-1704) & Abigail POMEROY, m/2 Nathaniel ALEXANDER (?); 5 Apr 1694;
Springfield

SEARLE, John (1675?-) & Lydia GROSS; 10 Mar 1699/1700; Marblehead

SEARLE, Nathaniel (1662-1750) & Sarah [ROGERS] (1677-1770); b 1695; Dorchester/Little
Compton, RI/Tiverton, RI

SEARLE, Philip (1633-1710) & Hannah _?_ (-1691); b 1655/60; Roxbury

SEARLE, Philip (1660-1722) & Hannah ELLIS (1659-1722); 29 May 1690; Roxbury

SEARLE, Robert (-1717) & Deborah [SALTER?] (-1714) (had son Salter SEARLE); b 1662;
Dorchester

SEARLE, Robert (1671-) & Rebecca EVANS; 4 Dec 1695; Dorchester

SEARLE/SERLES, Samuel (-1691) & Deborah [BRAGG] (1658-); b 1685, ca 1682, 1690 (error);
Ipswich/Rowley

SERLL, Samuel (son of Daniel) & Sarah PERHAM; 26 Sep 1699; Chelmsford/Dunstable

SEARLE, Stephen (-1670?) & Mary (LEMON) [SEARS], w Alexander; 1669; Salem

SEARLE, Thomas & Damaris [BARTLETT?], m/2 Joseph PHIPPEN 1686; b 1666; Salem

SEARLE, Thomas & Elizabeth BUSH (1679-), m/2 William FROST; 14 Apr 1697; Salem

SEARLE, William (-1667) & [Grace] COLE (?1636-1686), m/2 Thomas DENNIS 1668; b 1665, ca
1660?, 12 Apr 1659; Ipswich

SEERS, Alexander (-1667?) & Mary [LEMON] (1639-), m/2 Stephen SEARLE; b 1657; Salem

SEERS, Alexander & Rebecca [STAINES]; b 1686; Boston

SEARS, Daniel (-9 Feb 1651/2 adm) & Mary _?_ ; b 9 Feb 1651/2; Boston

SEARS, John & 1/wf Susanna _?_ (-1677); b 1640; Charlestown

SEARS, John & 2/wf Hester/Esther (HOWE) MASON (-1680), w Henry; 20 Nov 1677; Woburn

SEARS, John & 3/wf Anna/Ann (_?_) FARRAR, w Jacob; 2 Nov 1680; Woburn

SEERS, Joseph & Hannah HALL (?1680-1753); 19 Sep 1700; ?Yarmouth

SEARS, Paul (ca 1637-1708) & Deborah [WILLARD] (1645-1721), dau George; b 1659;
Yarmouth

SEARS, Paul (1669-1740) & Mercy [FREEMAN] (1674-1747); b 1694, [ca 1693]; Yarmouth

SEARS, Richard (-1676) & Dorothy JONES (-1679); ca 1632, b 1635; Yarmouth

SEARS, Robert & Bashua/Bathsheba HARLOW; 21 Oct 1696; Plymouth

SEERS, Robert (not William) & Abigail _?_ ; b 1682(3?); Boston

SEARS, Samuel (1663-) & Mercy (LUMPKIN) [MAYO] (1664-), w Samuel; b 1685; Harwich, CT

SEARS, Silas (1639, 1637?-1698) & Anna [BURSALL?]; b 1661; Eastham/Yarmouth

SEARS, Silas (1661-) & Sarah [CROSBY] (1667-); b 1694, 1692?; Yarmouth

SEERS, Thomas (-1661) & Mary HILTON (alias DOWNER), m/2 or m/3 Abel HUSE 1663; 11 Dec 1656; Newbury

SEARS, _?_ & ?Alice HOWLAND; b 1701? (doubtful)

SEARS, Knyvit & Elizabeth DIMMOCK

SEAVER/SAVON, Caleb (-1713) & Sarah INGLESBY/ENGLESBIE/ENGLESHIE (-1708); 15 Dec 1671; Charlestown/Roxbury

SEAVER, John (-1671) & Sarah [GARDNER], dau Andrew; b 1696(7?); Roxbury

SEAVER, Joshua (-1730) & Mary (MAY) PEPPER, w Joseph; 28 Feb 1677; Roxbury

SEAVER, Nathaniel (1645-1676) & Sarah _?_, m/2 Benjamin WILSON ca 1677; b 1671; Roxbury

SEAVER, Robert[1] (1609-1683) & 1/wf Elizabeth [ALLARD?/BALLARD?] (-6 Jun 1657 bur?); 10 Dec 1634; Roxbury

SEAVER, Robert (1609-1683) & 2/wf Sarah [BURRELL] (-bur 18 Dec 1669), w John; aft 4 Mar 1662; Roxbury

SEAVER, Robert (1609-1683) & 3/wf _?_ ; b 16 Jan 1681; Roxbury

SEAVER, Shubael (1640-1730, ae 92?) & Hannah WILSON (1647-1722, ae 75); 7 Feb 1668, 1668/9?; Roxbury

SEAVEY, Benjamin & Mary _?_ ; b 1692; Rye, NH

SEAVEY, Henry (-bef 1697) & Sarah (PIERCE) [MATTOON], w George JONES & Hubertus MATTOON; b 8 Feb 1682

SEAVEY, John, Portsmouth, NH, & Hannah (PHILBROOK) WALKER, w Joseph; 29 Jul 1686; Hampton, NH

SEAVEY, Samuel (?1672-) & _?_ ; b 1691; Rye, NH

SEAVEY, Stephen & Anne [FERNALD]; Kittery, ME

SEAVEY, Thomas (1627-1708) & Tamsen _?_ (1641-); b 1667; Portsmouth, NH

SEAVEY, William (1601-1679+) & ?Elizabeth/?Mary _?_ ; b 1649, b 1648?; Portsmouth, NH

SEAVEY, William (1648±-) & Hannah [JACKSON] (1663-); Rye, NH

SEAVEY, _?_ & Susanna [BUTLER]; Bradford

SECCOMB, Richard & _?_ ; b 1678; Lynn

SECOMB, Thomas & Rebecca WILLIS/[?WILLOWES]; b 1701?

SEDENHAM/?SYDENHAM, William & ?Frances _?_ ; b 31 Mar 1691; Fairfield, CT

SEDGWICK, Robert (-1656) & Joanna [BLAKE] (-1667+), m/2 Rev. Thomas ALLEN; b 1631; Charlestown

SEDGWICK, Robert (1651-1683) & Sarah _?_ (1655-), m/2 _?_ WISSENDUNK; b 1676; Charlestown

SEDGWICK, Samuel (1639-1683) & Elizabeth [?HARWOOD] (1650-1684+); b 1667; Charleston/London

SEDGWICK, Samuel (ca 1667-1735) & Mary [HOPKINS] (1670±-1743); b 1690; Hartford

SEDGWICK, William (ca 1643-) & Elizabeth [STONE], m/2 John ROBERTS 1675; b 1667, div 1674; Charlestown/Hartford

SEELEY, Benjamin & [Deborah] STURGES, m/2 James REDFIELD by 1694; b 4 Oct 1681; Fairfield, CT/Southampton, LI

SEELEY, Cornelius (1649/50?-) & Priscilla [OSBORN] (1650-); ca 1672, b 1673, by 1674; Fairfield, CT/Stamford, CT/Bedford, NY

SEELEY, Cornelius (1673-) & Mary [JONES] (1678-); b 1700; Stamford/Bedford, NY

SELE, Edward & Elizabeth (WASHBURN) [HOWARD], w James; 1692; Bridgewater

SEELE, Fearnot & Bethiah _?_ ; b 1695; Boston

SELLY, John (1642±-) & Margaret _?_ ; b 1666(7?); Boston/Braintree

SEELEY, John (1661±-1710) & 1/wf Sarah SQUIRE (-1690±); b 1684?, ca 1685, b 1685; Fairfield, CT

SEELEY, John & 2/wf Rebecca SANFORD (1672-1720), m/2 Benjamin NICHOLS 1711, m/3 John MASON 1716; ca 1690; Fairfield, CT/Stratford, CT

SEELEY, John & Lydia _?_ ; b 1693(4?); Boston

SEELEY, John & Sarah GORY; 23 Sep 1700; Boston

SEELEY, Jonas & 1/wf _?_ ; b 1685; Stamford, CT

SEELEY, Jonas (?1653-1704?, 1703?) & 2/wf Mary (WEEKS?/WEED?/WICKS?) [WATERBURY], w John; ca 1689; Stamford, CT/Bedford, NY

SEELEY, Joseph & Mary/Sarah? (GODWIN) [JACKSON], w Joseph; b 1684; Stratford, CT/Fairfield, CT/Cohansey, NJ

SEELEY, Nathaniel[2] (1627-1675) & 1/wf Mary [TURNEY] (1631-); ca Oct 1649; Fairfield, CT

SEELEY, Nathaniel (-1675) & Elizabeth (BURR) (OLMSTED) [GILBERT], w Nehemiah, w Obadiah; aft 8 Mar 1674; Fairfield

SEELEY, Nathaniel (?1650-1688) & Hannah [BENNETT?] (1654?-); b 1678; Fairfield, CT

SEELEY, Nathaniel (1678-1703) & Hannah [ODELL] (1679-); ca 1697/8, ca 1700; Fairfield, CT

SEELEY, Obadiah (-1657) & Mary (?) MILLER, w John; b 1648?; Stamford, CT

SEELEY, Obadiah (-1680) & [Esther] [?STEVENS], m/2 Moses JACKSON by 1696; ca 1671; Stratford, CT

SEELEY, Obadiah & Susanna FINCH; 5 Dec 1692, 1 Dec; Stamford, CT/Bedford

SEELEY/SEALLY, Richard (1621-) & ? ; b 1642?, b 1670, b 1662; Isles of Shoals/Hampton, NH

SEELEY, Robert[1] (-1668) & 1/wf Mary MASON; 15 or 25 Dec 1626, b 1625; Watertown/Wethersfield, CT

SEELEY, Robert (-1668) & 2/wf Mary (MANNING) WALKER; NY m lic 22 Dec 1666; Fairfield

SEELEY, Robert (?1653-1690) & Sarah [OLMSTEAD]; bef 16 Mar 1675, by 16 Mar 1675; Fairfield, CT

SEALLY/CILLEY/SILLEY, Thomas & Ann [STANYAN]; b 1697, 2 Jul 1697; Hampton Falls, NH/Nottingham, NH/Andover, ME

SEALY, William & Elizabeth [GUNNISON?]/[LYNN?] (1638-), m/2 Thomas COWELL; b 1652/4?; Kittery, ME/Isles of Shoals/Saco, ME

SEELEY, ?Richard & Martha ? , m John CLOUGH 1687; b 1650?; Amesbury

SEELEY, Thomas & Martha (BLAISDELL) BOWDON, m/3 John CLOUGH 1687

SELDEN, John & Sarah HARRISON; 24 Mar 1698; Hadley

SELDEN, Joseph (bpt 1651-1724) & Rebecca CHURCH (1661, 1654?-1726); 11 Feb 1677; Hadley/Lyme, CT

SELDEN, Thomas (1617-1655) & Esther/Hester [?WAKEMAN] (1617-1693), m/2 Andrew WARNER by 1659; b 1640?, b 1645; Hartford

SELDEN, Thomas (1645-1734) & Felix [LEWIS] (1658-1738+); b 1675; Hadley

SELLICK, David (-1654) & Susanna [KIBBY], m/2 Robert TILLMAN; b 1638; Boston/VA

SELLECK, John (1643-) & Sarah LAW (-1732); 28 Oct 1669; Stamford, CT

SELLICK, John & Martha [GOLD] (1667?-1712), m/2 John DAVENPORT 1695; Stamford, CT

SELLICK, Jonathan (1641-1712/13) & Abigail LAW (1637-bef 1712, 1711); 11 May 1663; Stamford, CT

SELLICK, Jonathan (1664-1710) & Abigail GOLD; 5 Jan 1685; Stamford, CT

SELLICK, Nathaniel (1678-1712) & Sarah LOCKWOOD, m/2 Benjamin HICKOCK; 25 Jan 1699/1700; Stamford, CT

SEMOND/SIMMONS, William (-1642) & Anne [BARRELL]? (-1659), w George, m/1 ? GAWOOD, m/2 Abel PORTER (he d 1643); b 1640?; Boston

SENNET/SENATE, Walter & Mary ? ; b 1640; Boston

SENDALL, Samuel & Joanna ? ; b 1651; Boston/Newbury

SENDALL, Samuel & Elizabeth [WARREN], w John?, m/3 John HAYWARD 1684+, m/4 Phineas WILSON; m cont 29 Sep 1681; Boston

SENTER, John & Mary MUZZY (-1658); 27 Mar 1656; Boston

SCENTER, John (-1607) & Sarah [WEEDON]?, m/2 Jeremiah BELCHER 1667?; b 1663; Boston

SENTER, William (1654-) & Mary [MATTHEWS] (1652±-)

SERVANT, William & Sarah STOUR; 28 Nov 1695; Marblehead

SESSIONS, Alexander (-1688) & Elizabeth SPAFORD/SPAFFORD (1641-1724+), m/2 ? [LOWE]; 24 Apr 1672; Andover

SETT, Stephen & Mary ? ; b 1696; Newbury

SEVAN, John & Sarah ? ; b 1676; Westfield

SEVERANCE, Ebenezer (1673-) & Mary ? (-1761); 9 May 1695; Salisbury

SEVERANS, Ephraim (1656-) & Lydia MORRILL; 9 Nov 1682; Salisbury

SEVERANCE, John (-1682) & 1/wf Abigail [KIMBALL] (?1617-1658); b 1637; Salisbury

SEVERANCE, John (-1682) & 2/wf Susanna AMBROSE, w Henry; 2 Oct 1663; Salisbury

SEVERANCE, John (1647-) & Mary ? (1650-); 15 Aug 1672; Salisbury/Suffield, CT/Deerfield/Bedford, NY

SEVERANCE, Joseph (1650-) & Martha [WORDEN] (1643-1725); b 1676; Salisbury/Yarmouth

SEAVORNE/SEVERNS, John & Mary ? ; b 1642; Boston

SEAVERNS, John & Elizabeth FULLER; 10 Apr 1683; Lynn

SEVERNES, Samuel & Sarah GRANT (1643-), m/2 Thomas SYLVESTER; 23 Feb 1665, 1666?; Charlestown

SEUERINS, Samuel (1669-) & Rebecca STRATTON; 20 Dec 1699; Watertown

SEVOLLE, Joseph/Joshua (-1735) & Elizabeth [SWAINE] (1676-1760); Nantucket

SEAWELL, Edward (1640-1684) & Sarah HALE, m/2 Nicholas GORDON; 3 Jul 1671; Salem/Exeter, NH

SEWALL, Edward & Sarah [GORDON], m/2 Samuel LOVERING; ?b Aug 1697, b 1699; Exeter, NH

SEWELL, Henry (1576-1656) & 1/wf Mary [CAWARDEN] (d in Eng); ca 1696/1600?; Ipswich/Newbury/Rowley

SEWALL, Henry (1576-1656, 1657?) & 2/wf [Anne HUNT] (-1615); Coventry, Eng, b 1615 in Manchester, Eng; Ipswich/Newbury/Rowley

SEWALL, Henry & 3/wf Ellen (MOSLEY) NUGENT, w Walter; 16 Dec 1615, m lic Manchester, Eng; Ipswich/Newbury/Rowley

SEWALL, Henry (1615-1700) & Jane DUMMER (1627/[8?]-1701); 25 Mar 1646; Newbury

SEWALL, John (1654-1699) & Hannah FISSENDEN (1649-1723), m/2 Jacob TOPPAN 1705; 27 Oct 1674, 28 Oct 1674; Newbury/Cambridge

SHOWELL, Joseph & Sarah __?__; b 1674/[5?]; Boston

SEWALL, Samuel (1652-1730) & Hannah HULL (?1658-1717); 28 Feb 1675/6; Boston

SEWALL, Stephan (1657-1729) & Margaret MITCHELL (1664-1736); 13 Jun 1682;; Salem/Cambridge

SEWELL, Thomas & __?__; b 1648; Springfield

SEWARD, Caleb (1662-1728) & Lydia BUSHNELL (1661-1753), Saybrook; 14 Jul 1686; Guilford, CT

SEWARD, Henry (-1737) & Mary HUNTRESS; 23 Jun 1694, 21? Jun; Dover, NH/Newington, NH

SEWARD, James & Edith __?__; b 1693; Boston

SEWARD, John (?1646-1705) & Agnes?/Ann? __?__; b 1674; Portsmouth, NH

SEWARD, John (-1748) & Abigail BUSHNELL (1659-); 25 Jun 1678, 1679; ?Saybrook, CT/Deerfield, CT/Guilford, CT

SEAWARD, John & Joanna DOWNING; 1 Jan 1681/2; Marblehead

SEWARD, Joseph (1655-1731) & Judith BUSHNELL (1666-1740, ae 84 y); 7 Feb 1682, 1681, 5? Feb 1681/2; ?Guilford, CT/Durham, CT

SEWARD, Obadiah & Dinah [BIGGS]; b 1698?; Brookhaven, LI

SEWARD, Obed & Bethiah HAWES (1637-); 31 Oct 1660; Milford, CT

SEWARD, Richard (-1663) & __?__; by 1630; ?Portsmouth, NH

SEWARD, Richard (-1668) & Mary __?__; b 1652?, b 1658?; Portsmouth, NH/Boston

SEWARD, William (1627-1689) & Grace NORTON (-1704); 2 Apr 1651; Guilford, CT

SEXTON, Daniel & Sarah BANCROFT; ?28 Dec 1680, 9? Dec; Westfield

SEXTON, George[1] (?1618-1690?) & Katherine __?__ (-1689); b 1659, b 1650?; Westfield/Windsor, CT/Deerfield

SEXTON, George[2] & 1/wf Hannah SPENCER (1653-); b 1680; Hartford/Westfield

SEXTON, George[2] & 2/wf Hannah [SPENCER?] (1653-), m/2 Daniel BRAINERD 1698, m/3 Jonathan CHAPMAN; Westfield/Newtown, LI

SEXTON, George & Sarah [KNIGHT] (1680-); b 1701?, 25 Dec 1699; Colchester

SEXTON, James (-1741) & 1/wf Hannah FOWLER (1654-1700); 29 Apr 1680; Windsor, CT/Westfield

SEXTON, John (1650-1718) & Mary HILL; 30 Jul 1677; Windsor, CT/Simsbury, CT

SEXTON/SEXTUS, Joseph (?1666-1742) & Hannah WRIGHT (1669-1742); 20 Nov 1690; ?Westfield/Enfield, CT

SIXTON, Richard (-1662) & Sarah COOK (-1674); 15 Apr 1647, 16 Apr 1647, 16 Apr 1646, 1646?; Windsor, CT

SEYMOUR, John (1639-1713) & Mary [WATSON]; b 1666; Hartford/Wethersfield, CT

SEYMOUR, John (1666-1748) & Elizabeth WEBSTER (1673-1754); 19 Dec 1693; Hartford

SEYMOUR, Matthew (1669-) & Sarah [HAYES] (1673-1712+); b 1694; Norwalk, CT

SEYMOUR, Richard (-1655) & Mary RUSCOE (ca 1610-), m/2 John STEELE 1655; 18 Apr 1631; Sawbridgeworth, Co. Herts.; Hartford/Norwalk, CT/etc.

SEYMOUR, Richard (1645-1710) & Hannah [WOODRUFF] (ca 1648-1712); ca 1674; ?Hartford/Farmington, CT

SEYMOUR, Thomas (1632-1712?) & 1/wf Hannah MARVIN; 5 Jan 1654; Norwalk, CT
SEYMOUR, Thomas (1632-1712?) & 2/wf Sarah [WILDMAN], w Thomas; betw 1690 & 1697; Norwalk, CT
SEYMOUR, Thomas (1668/9-) & Ruth NORTON; 19/20/21/24 Feb 1700; Hartford
SEYMOUR, Zachariah (-1702) & Mary GRITT, m/2 John HOLLISTER; 9 Feb 1688; Wethersfield, CT
SHACKFORD, John & Sarah HUDSON; ca 1697; Portsmouth, NH
SHACKFORD, Samuel & 1/wf Abigail RICHARDS - Jun 1695; ?Portsmouth, NH
SHACKFORD, William (1640-) & Deborah [TRICKEY] (1646±-); by 1680, by 1671; Dover, NH
SHADDUCK/SHATTUCK/?CHADDOCK, Elias (-1676) & Hannah OSBORN (1657-), m/2 Benjamin EGGLESTON 1678; [26 Nov 167]5; Windsor, CT
SHAFFLIN, Michael (1605-) (ae ca 80 in 1685) & Elizabeth _?_; b 1639, b 1636; Salem
SHAFFLIN, Michael & Alice (?TEMPLE) [BOOTH], w George; Salem
SHALER, Abel (1673-) & 1/wf Elizabeth ACKLEY; b 20 Mar 1696
SHALER, Abel (1673-1744) & 2/wf Mary [PARENTS]; 5 Jan 1697/8; Haddam, CT/Bolton, CT
SHALLER, Michael & 1/wf Sarah _?_; b 1678; Boston
SHALLER, Michael & 2/wf Hannah (WEARE) JEWELL, w Nathaniel; m int 28 Jan 1696/7; Boston
SHALER, Thomas (-1692) & Marah (SPENCER) BROOKS (not Alice), w Thomas; bef 11 Apr 1670, aft 18 Oct 1668; Haddam, CT/Killingworth, CT
SHAYLOR, Thomas (1670-) & Catharine [CLARK]; 22 Oct 1696; Haddam, CT
SHALER, Timothy (ca 1675-1727) & 1/wf Elizabeth [ACKLEY?]; 28 Mar 1695/6; Haddam, CT
SHALER, _?_ & Sarah (GATES) FULLER (1670), w Timothy; doubtful
SHALEY/SHEELEY?/SHEELLEY?, Ebenezer (1666-) & _?_; ca 1691; Little Compton, RI/Tiverton, RI
SHALOTE, Samuel & Mary COLLINS, wid; 23 Nov 1696; Salem
SHANNON, Nathaniel (1655-1723) & Elizabeth _?_; b 1689; Boston
SHAPCOT/SHAPCOTE, Thomas & Ann _?_; b 1668(9?); Boston
SHAPLEIGH, Alexander (1585±-1650?) & 1/wf 2/wf Jane EGBEARE/EGBERE; St. Savior's, Dartmouth, 12 Dec 1602; Kittery, ME
SHAPLEIGH, Alexander (?1674-1701?) & Mary [ADAMS], m/2 John DENNOTT/DENNETT; Kittery, ME
SHAPLEY, Benjamin (-1706, in 56h y) & Mary PICKET (-1706+, 1735?); 10 Apr 1672; New London, CT
SHAPLEIGH/SHAPLEY, Benjamin (1675-) & Ruth [DIMOND] (1680-); 29 Feb 1699/1700; New London
SHAPLEY, John (1640-1706) & Sarah [WITHERS] (-1708/1723); ca 1673, aft 25 Apr 1671; Kittery, ME
SHAPLEY, Joseph & Abiel HOWARD (-1687); 8 Jun 1665; Charlestown
SHAPLEY, Nicholas (?1605, 1608-1663) & Ann _?_ (1607-1687); b 1631, ca 1635?, by 1651; Charlestown
SHAPLEIGH, Nicholas (1618-1682) & Alice [?MESANT] (-1685+); ca 1642/50?, by 1651, no issue; Kittery, ME
SHAPLEY, Nicholas & Margaret _?_; b 1671; Charlestown
SHAPLEY, _?_ & Sarah ATKINS, m/2 Samuel GURNEY 1693
SHAREL/SHARD?, _?_ & Elizabeth _?_, m/2 Henry MORE 1695; b 1695; Salem
SHARP, Henry & Elizabeth _?_; b 1695(6?); Boston
SHARP, James & Elizabeth [WENTWORTH] (1653-), m/2 Richard TOZER; by 1672?; Dover, NH
SHARP, James & Dorcas SEALY/SEELEY; m int 16 Oct 1696, did not marry; Boston
SHARPE, John (1643-1676) & Martha [VOSE], m/2 Jabez BUCKMINSTER betw 1676 & 1683; b 1665; Boston/Roxbury
SHARP, John & Elizabeth [GIBBONS] (1652-); 14 Nov 1667; Saco, ME
SHARP, John & Elizabeth (STEDMAN) (UPHAM) [THOMPSON], w Nathaniel, w Henry; ca 1677?, aft 1677?; Cambridge
SHARP, John & 1/wf Mary BROOKS (-1726); 6 Sep 1697; Boston
SHARP, Nathaniel (1644-) & Rebecca MARSHALL; 30 Dec 1658; Salem
SHARP, Richard (-1677?) & Hannah [GILLAM]; b 1671(2?); Boston
SHARP, Robert[1] (?1617-1656) & Abigail [WRIGHT] (?1622-), m/2 Thomas CLAPP 1656?, m/3 William HOLBROOK aft 1679, 1684+; b 1643; Roxbury

SHARPE, Robert (1665-) & Sarah [WILLIAMS] (1667-1707), m/2 Thomas NOWELL, m/3 Solomon PHIPPS 1694/5; b 1687?, b 1688?; Roxbury/Charlestown
SHARP, Robert, Billerica & Mary FRENCH (1670-1695/6?), m/2 Nathaniel DUNCKLER 1693; 20 Jun 1687; ?Woburn
SHARP, Samuel (-1647?) & Alice STILEMAN (-1667); b 1632?, b 1637, m lic 4 Apr 1629; Salem
SHARP, Thomas (ret'd to Eng) & _?_; b 1631; Boston
SHARP, Thomas & Abigail _?_; b 1680(1?); Braintree
SHARP, William (1674-1751) & Abigail [WHITE] (1676-1753); 1699?, b 1700; ?Pomfret, CT
SHARP, _?_ (had Benoni, Jun 1682) & Deborah COMBS, dau Henry, m Joseph GANNETT 15 Aug 1682, m/3 Joseph HOUSE 1723; Scituate
SHERRATT/SHARRATT, Hugh (-1678) & 1/wf Elizabeth _?_ (-29 May 1662; Haverhill
SHERRAT, Hugh (-1678) & 2/wf Elizabeth (?ANDREWS) GRIFFING/GRIFFIN (-1670), w Humphrey; 10 Feb 1662, 1662/3; Haverhill
SHARSWOOD, George (-1674) & Mary _?_, m/2 George DARROW ?1674, 1673?; b 1672, b 1671, ca 1667; New London, CT
SHARSWOOD, William (1671-ca 1704) & Abigail _?_, m/2 George POLLY; ca 1696; Cape May, NJ/New London, CT/Newcastle, DE
SHATSWELL, John (ca 1605-) & 1/wf _?_; ca 1625; Ipswich
SHATSWELL, John (ca 1605-1647) & 2/wf? Joanna _?_, m/2 John GREEN; Ipswich
SATCHEL, John & Sarah YOUNGLOFF/YOUNGLOVE; 20 Jun 1684; Ipswich
SATCHWELL, John & Lydia _?_; b 1701; Ipswich
SHATSWELL, Richard (ca 1626, 1625?-1694) & Rebecca [TUTTLE]; ca 11 Feb 1646; Ipswich
SACHELL, Richard (-1698) & Eleanor CHENY/CHENEY (1679-1724), m/2 Thomas SAFFORD 1698; 17 Dec 1696; Newbury/Ipswich
SHATSWELL, Theophilus (?1617, 1614?-1663) (called William SARGENT "brother") & Susanna [BOSWORTH]? (-1672); b 1650, ca 1640/2?; Haverhill/Ipswich
SHATTUCK, John (1647-1675) & Ruth WHETNY/WHITNEY (1645-), m/2 Enoch LAWRENCE 1676/7; 20 Jun 1664; Watertown
SHATTUCK, John (1666-1709) & Mary [BLOOD?]/[MORSE?]; b 1690(1?); Groton
SHATTACK, Philip (1648-1722) & 1/wf Deborah BAIRSTO/BARSTOW (1650-1679); 9 Nov 1670; Watertown/Scituate
SHATTACK, Philip (1648-1722) & 2/wf Rebecca CHAMBERLIN; 11 Feb 1679, 1679/80; Watertown
SHATTUCK, Samuel (1620-1689) & 1/wf Grace _?_; b 1649; Salem
SHATTOCK, Samuel (1620-1689) & 2/wf Hannah _?_ (-1701, ae 77); Salem
SHATTOCK, Samuel (1649-1723) & Sarah BUCKMAN/BUCKNAM (1650-); 24 Jul 1676; Salem
SHATTACK, Samuel (1666-) & Abigail _?_; b 1686; Watertown
SHATTUCK, Samuel (1673-) & Elizabeth [BLOOD] (1675-1759); b 1696; Groton
SHATTOCK, William (?1621, ?1614-1672) & Susan/Susanna _?_ (-1686), m/2 Richard NORCROSS 1673; b 1643?; Watertown
SHATTOCK, William & Hannah _?_; b 1654; Boston/NJ
SHATTACK, William (1653-1732) & Susannah [RANDALL] (-1723); ca 1678; Watertown
SHATTUCK, William (1670-1744), Groton & 1/wf Hannah UNDERWOOD (-ca 1717), Watertown; 19 Mar 1687/8; Cambridge/Watertown
SHATTUCK, _?_ & Damaris _?_ (-1674), m/2 Thomas GARDNER; in Eng, b 1620; Salem
SHAW, Abraham (1585-1638) & Bridget BEST (1592-); Halifax, Eng, 24 Jun 1616; Watertown/ Dedham
SHAW, Anthony (-1705) & Alice STANARE/STONARD; 8 Apr 1653; Boston/Portsmouth, RI/Little Compton, RI
SHAW, Benjamin (-1717, 1718) & Esther/Hester RICHARDSON (1645-1736); 25 May 1663; Hampton, NH
SHAW, Benjamin (1670-1728) & Hannah [?BICKNELL]? (see Samuel VINSON); b 1692?, b 1698; Weymouth/Taunton
SHAW, Benoni (1672-) & Lydia [WATERMAN] (1678-); b 1697; Plymouth
SHAW, Caleb (1671-) & Elizabeth [HILLIARD] (1679-), m/2 Joseph TILTON; ca 1695; Hampton, NH/Hampton Falls, NH
SHAW, Daniel & Ruth WILLIAMS; 17 Sep 1678; Stonington, CT
SHAW, Ebenezer (1674-1706) & 1/wf Susanna _?_; b 1698; Weymouth
SHAW, Ebenezer (1674-1706) & Hannah PRATT, prob m/2 _?_ HINES; 30 May 1699; Hingham

SHAW, Edmund (-1676) & _?_ ; East Hampton, LI
SHAW, Edward (-bef 1662) & Jane _?_ ; b 1632; Saco, ME/Duxbury
SHAW, Fearnot & Bethiah [LEAGER] (1651-); b 1672; Boston
SHAW, George (-1720) & Constant/?Constance DOANE (1670-1719+); 8 Jan 1690; Eastham
SHAW, Israel (1660-) & _?_ [TALLMAN] (ca 1674-); 1689, 1690; Little Compton, RI
SHAW, Israel & Elizabeth BOOTH (1674-); 26 Dec 1695; Salem
SHAW, James & Mary MICHELL/MITCHELL, m/2 John JENNEY by 1699; 24 Dec 1652; Plymouth
SHAW, John & Alice _?_ (-1654/5); ca 1625?; Plymouth
SHAW, John & Martha [KEENE]; b 1646; Boston
SHAW, John (ca 1630-1704) & Alice _?_ (-1704+); ca 1653; Weymouth
SHAW, John & 1/wf _?_ ; 1667; Malden
SHAW, John (-1687) & Elizabeth _?_ ; b 1670; Boston
SHAW, John (-1678) & Sarah [BRACKETT], m/2 _?_ ; b 1670?; Boston
SHAW, John & Elizabeth RAMSDEL; 12 Aug 1674; Malden
SHAW, John & Susannah WEST; 4 Oct [1677?]; Stonington, CT
SHAW, John & Hannah [?WHITMARSH]; b 1679; Weymouth
SHAW, John (-1696) & Hannah [BRACKETT] (1656-), dau Peter, m/2 John BENJAMIN; b 1680;
    Rehoboth/Swansea
SHAW, Jonathan & 1/wf Phebe WATSON; 22 Jan 1656, 1656/7?; Plymouth/?Duxbury
SHAW, Jonathan & 2/wf Persis (DUNHAM) [PRATT], w Benajah; Aug 1683; ?Plymouth
SHAW, Jonathan, Jr. (1663-1730) & Mehitable PRATT (1667-1712, Plympton); 29 Dec 1687;
    Plymouth
SHAW, Joseph (bpt 1618-1653) & [Mary] _?_ ; b 1643; Weymouth
SHAW, Joseph (1618-1653, 1654) & Mary SOUTHER/SOUTHOR, m/2 John BLAKE 1654; 1 Dec
    1653; Boston
SHAW, Joseph (-1720) & Elizabeth PARTRIDGE (1643-); 26 Jun 1661; Hampton, NH/Hampton
    Falls, NH
SHAW, Joseph & Sarah POTTARTON/POTTER; 16 Dec 1664; Charlestown
SHAW, Joseph & Ruth [BLAKE] (1659?-); b 1680(1?); Boston
SHAW, Joseph (1664-1718), Bridgewater & Judith [WHITMARSH]/WHITMAN (1669-1760); b
    1687; Weymouth
SHAW, Joseph & Mercy CROSS; 22 Feb 1699; Boston
SHAW, Josiah (-1700) & Meribah PAGE, m/2 Samuel TILTON 1703, m/3 Benjamin SANBORN
    1721; ca 31 May 1700; Hampton, NH
SHAW, Nathaniel & Margaret JACKSON; 12 Jul 1698; Boston
SHAW, Nicholas & Deborah [WHITMARSH] (1665-); b 1687; Weymouth
SHAW, Peter & Jane [ALLISON], m/2 William BRADFORD, m/3 Robert LEACH 1717; b 1675;
    Scarboro/Ipswich
SHAW, Richard (-1683) & Remember _?_ ; bef 1660; Easthampton, LI
SHAW, Richard (-1709), Easthampton, LI, & Rebecca BEEBE (wf Elizabeth 1698, no); ca 1688;
    Stonington, CT
SHAW, Roger (-1661) & 1/wf Anne _?_ ; b 1635, b 1624?; Cambridge/Hampton, NH
SHAW, Roger (-1661) & 2/wf Susanna [TILTON] (-1656), w William; aft 28 Jan 1655?, b 10 Nov
    1656; Hampton, NH
SHAW, Samuel (1661-) & 1/wf Esther [BATCHELDER?] (1664, 1664/5-1715); ca 1684/88?, no
    issue; Hampton, NH
SHAW, Thomas (-1701) & Mary _?_ ; b 1645; Charlestown/New London, CT/Stonington, CT
SHAW, Thomas & ?Susanna CLARK; b 1676; Southampton, LI
SHAW, Thomas & 2/wf Martha/Mary _?_ ; by 1698, b 1693; Newport
SHAW, Walter & Anna GALE, m/2 Jonathan WILLIAMS; 4 Dec 1696; Beverly
SHAW, William (-1726) & 1/wf Elizabeth FRAYLE/FRAILE; 23 Nov 1668; Salem
SHAW, William & 2/wf Mary _?_ ; b 1692; Salem
SHAW, William & Joanna [PUDLEY]; ?17 May 1694, ?1683; Salem
SHAW, William & Elizabeth _?_ ; b 1698; Westchester, NY
SHAW, William & Agnes/Annis [FROST]; ca 1700; York, ME
SHAW, _?_ & Deborah (FULLER) [RICHARDSON] (1650-), w Isaac (had Daniel, Ebenezer); b
    1698, aft 2 Apr 1689; Charlestown/?Woburn
SHEAFE, Edmund (-1626 in Eng) & 1/wf Elizabeth TAYLOR (-1598); 30 May 1596, Cranbrook,
    Eng

SHEAFE, Edmund (-1626) & 2/wf Jane DOWNE, wid; 15 Aug 1599, m lic Canterbury
SHEAFE, Edmund (-1626) & 3/wf Joan (JORDAN) [KITCHELL] [LAKE] (-1659), Guilford, CT), w John, w Richard; 17 Oct 1610, London
SHEAFE, Edmund (1605-1649, London?) & Elizabeth [?COTTON]/[?BARKER]; Boston
SHEAFE, Edward & Mary [CATER] (-1748)
SHEAFE, Jacob (1616-1659) & Margaret WEBB, m/2 Thomas THATCHER; 7 Sep 1643, spec. permit; Boston
SHEAFE, Sampson & Mehitable [SHEAFE]; b 1677; Boston
SHEAFE, William (ae 36 in 1685) & 1/wf Ruth WOOD (-1677); 15 Aug 1672; Charlestown
SHEAFE, William & 2/wf Mary _?_ (-1703); b 1679; Charlestown
SHEAR/SHEARE/SHARE, John & Sarah GIBBS (-1689); 5 Dec 1661; Windsor, CT
SHERER/SHERROD, Alexander & 1/wf Sarah WINSOR/SHERRARD (-1700/3); m int 13 Sep 1695; Boston
SHEARAR, John & Eleanor _?_ ; b 1667; Boston
SHEARER, Thomas & Hannah BUMSTEED; 18 Apr 1659; Boston
SHEARS, Jeremy & 1/wf Elizabeth _?_ ; Kittery, ME/York, ME
SHEARS, Jeremiah/Jeremy (-1664) & 2/wf Susanna [GREEN], w Nicholas; b 29 Mar 1663/4; ?York, ME
SHEARS, John, Sudbury & Alice MITCHELSON, Cambridge; 9 Apr 1688; Cambridge/Sudbury
SHEERES, Samuel & 1/wf Ann (COLE) GROSSE (-1660), w Edmond; 15 Aug 1658, m prob 1655, bef 29 Apr 1656; Boston/Dedham
SHEARS, Samuel & 2/wf Mary PEACOCK (-1704); 29 Jul 1663; Dedham
SHEARS, Samuel & Elizabeth HEATH (1657-), Roxbury; 27 Oct 1685; Wrentham
SHEARS, Robert & _?_ ; b 1670; Portsmouth, NH
SHEARS, Robert (?) & [Tamsen GOWELL], m/2 Thomas HANSCOMB by 1698; by Mar 1687/8; Falmouth, ME
SHEATHER, John (-1670) & Susanna _?_ (-1677+), m/2 Thomas GOLDSMITH; b 1651; Guilford, CT
SHEATHER, John (1651-1721) & Elizabeth WILLMAN; 9 Jan 1679, 1678; Killingworth, CT
SHEATHER, Samuel (1657-) & Mary [?DURANT], m/2 Robert CHAPMAN 1694; b 1694, ca 1683?; Killingworth, CT
SHEDD, Daniel & 1/wf Mary [GURNEY?], ?dau John; b 1647(8?); Braintree
SHEDD, Daniel & 2/wf Elizabeth [GURNEY?]; b 1659; Billerica
SHEDD, Daniel (1649-1690) & Ruth MOORE (-1730), m/2 Jacob FRENCH ca 1711; 5 Jul 1670; Billerica
SHEDD, John (1655-1737) & Sarah CHAMBERLAIN (1655-1736); 9 Jan 1676/7; Billerica
SHED, Nathan (-1736) & Mary FRENCH (1670-1740); 21 Feb 1693/4; Billerica
SHED, Samuel & Elizabeth [BOWERS]; b 1690, b 1688?; Chelmsford
SHED, Zachariah (1656-1735) & 1/wf Ann BRAY (-1692); 16 Jan 1677; Billerica
SHEDD, Zachariah (1656-1735) & 2/wf Lydia FARLEY (1670-1702); 9 Mar 1692/3; Billerica
SHEFFIELD, Amos (1673-1710) & 1/wf Anne PIERCE (1674-); 5 Mar [1695/6], 1696; Tiverton, RI
SHEFFIELD, Edmond (1612-1705) & 1/wf _?_ ; in Eng, ca 1634; Braintree
SHEFFIELD, Edmund (1612-1705) & 2/wf Mary WOODY/WOODIE (-1662), dau Richard; 17 Apr 1644; Roxbury/Braintree
SHEFFIELD, Edmund (1612-1705) & 3/wf Sarah (BEAL) MARSH (1624/6-1710), w Thomas; 5 Sep 1662; Braintree
SHEFFIELD, Ichabod (1635-1712) & Mary [PARKER]; 1660; Portsmouth, RI
SHEFFIELD, Ichabod (1670-1736) & Elizabeth MANCHESTER; 27 Dec 1694; Portsmouth, RI
SHEFFIELD, Isaac (1651/2-) & _?_ (doubtful); b 1690, wrong
SHEFFIELD, Joseph (1661-1700) & Mary SHERIFF/SHREVE?; 12 Feb 1684, 1684/5; Portsmouth, RI/Stonington, CT
SHEFFIELD, Nathaniel (1667-1729) & 1/wf Mary [CHAMBERLAIN] (1672-1707); ca 1691; Newport
SHEFFIELD, Thomas & Ann _?_ , m/2 _?_ PERRY; Boston
SHEFFIELD, William (?1619-1700) & Mary [WEBB] (-1714, ae 78), dau Christopher; by 1659; Dover/Hingham/Sherborn
SHEFFIELD, William (1667-) & Hannah BULLARD; 30 May 1692; Sherborn
SHELDON, Ephraim (-1694) & Rebecca _?_ ; by 1691, prob by 1682; Salem

SHELDON, Ephraim & Jane PEARD; 30 Apr 1694; Lynn/Salem/Norton/Attleboro
SHELDON, Godfrey (-1670) & Alice FROST; 11 Mar 1620/1, Bakewell, Derby; Scarboro, ME
SHELDON, Godfrey (-1690, 1691, ae 24) & __?__; b 1690; Salem or Danvers
SHELDON, Isaac (1629-1708, ae 79) & 1/wf Mary [WOODFORD] (1636-1684); ca 1653; Hartford/Northampton
SHELDON, Isaac (1656-1712) & Sarah WARNER; 25 Nov 1685; Northampton
SHELDON, Isaac (1629-1708) & 2/wf Mehitable (GUN) [ENSIGN] (1644-1720), div wf of David ENSIGN ca 1682; ca 1686; Northampton
SHELDON, John (-1690, ca 63) & Mary (CONVERSE) THOMPSON, w Simon; 1 Feb 1658/9; Billerica/Woburn
SHELDON, John & Joan VINCENT; m int 6 Mar 1659?, 1660?, 24 Mar 1660?, 26 Mar 1660?; Providence
SHELDON, John (-1706) & __?__; ca 1678?; Kings Town, RI
SHELDON, John (1658-1734) & 1/wf Hannah STEBBINS (1664-1704); 5 Nov 1679; Northampton/Deerfield
SHELDON, John (-1741) & ?Patience THORNTON; ca 1687?; Providence
SHELDON, John (-1724) & Deborah HILL (-1730); 20 Nov 1690, 29? Nov; Billerica
SHELDON, Joseph (1668-1708, Suffield, CT) & Mary [WHITING/?WHETNEY] (1672-), m/2 John ASHLEY; b 1695; Northampton/Suffield, CT
SHELDON, Nehemiah (1672-) & Rachel [MANN] (1679-); ca 1700?; Providence
SHELDON, Nicholas (-1747) & Abigail [TILLINGHAST] (1674-); 1691?; Providence
SHELDON, Samuel (1675-1745) & Mary [WARNER?] (?1672-); ca 1699?, by 26 Jan 1700; Hadley/Hatfield/New Marlboro, MA
SHELDON, Thomas (1661-1725) & Mary [HINSDALE]; ca 1685; Northampton
SHELDON, Timothy (1661-1744+) & Sarah [BALCOM]; b 1687; Providence
SHELDON, William (-1694) & Rebecca [SCARLET]? (-1716/20) (see below); ca 1655/65?; Salem/Scarboro, ME
SHELDON, William (1623-1691, ae 80?, Danvers) & Rebecca [SCADLOCK] (1642-1720?)
SHELLEY, Robert & Judith GARNETT, Boston; 26 Sep 1636; Scituate/Barnstable
SHELLEY, Robert (-1692) & ?Susanna [DIMMOCK?] (-1692+); b 1668(9?), b 1662?; Barnstable
SHELLEY, __?__ & Sarah __?__ (mentioned in James PENN's will 1671)
SHELLEY, Isaac & __?__
SHELSTONE/SHELSTON, Robert & Ann __?__; b 1676; Boston
SHELTON, Daniel (?1665-1728) & Elizabeth WELLS (1670-bef 6 May 1746, 1747); 4 Apr 1692; Stratford, CT
SHAPARD, Abraham (ca 1650-1716) & Judith FILLBROOK/PHILBRICK STILL?/SILL?, wid?; 2 Jan 1672, 1672/3; Concord
SHEPARD, Andrew (-1676) & __?__ (-1676); 1 Jan (wrong); Boston
SHEPHERD, Daniel & Mary BRICE; 21 Dec 1686; Portsmouth, RI
SHEPARD, David & Rebecca CURTICE (?1675-); 12 Apr 1699; Plymouth/Taunton
SHEPARD, Edward[1] (-1680?) & 1/wf Violet [?WOLTERTON] (-9 Jan 1648/9); in Eng, ca 1625; Cambridge
SHEPARD, Edward (-1680?) & 2/wf Mary [POND], w Robert; ca 1649; Cambridge
SHEPARD, Edward (1662-1711) & Abigail SAVAGE (1666-1719); 14 Apr 1687; Middletown, CT
SHEPHERD, Francis & Sarah OSBURNE/OSBORN (1647-); 28 Apr 1670; Charlestown
SHEPARD, Isaac (1634-12 Feb 1676) & Mary SMEDLEY (1648-), m/2 Nathaniel JEWELL 1676/7; 10 Dec 1667; Concord
SHEPHERD, Isaac, Jr. (-1748) & Hannah [SPALDING]; b 1694?; Plainfield, CT
SHEPPARD, Jacob (-1717) & Mary CHICKERING (1668-); 22 Nov 1699; Medford/Charlestown
SHEPARD, Jeremiah (1646, 1650-1720) & Mary [WAINWRIGHT] (-1710, ae 53); b 1676; Cambridge/Lynn
SHEPPARD, John (1599-1650) & Margaret [SQUIRE] (1604-1675); b 1641, b 1635; Braintree/Medfield, CT
SHEPARD, John (?1627-1707) & 1/wf Rebecca GRENHILL (1634-1689); 4 Oct 1649, 1 Oct 1649; Cambridge/Hartford/Middletown
SHEPERD, John (ca 1637-1699) & Sarah [GOBLE]/GLOBE? (1638-1717); b 1661; Concord
SHEAPARD, John (-1689) & 1/wf Rebecca (PUTNAM) FULLER (1653-1689), w John; 6 Dec 1677; Salem/Rowley
SHEPARD/SHEPHERD, John (1634±-) & __?__; ca 1677; Kittery, ME

SHEPARD, John, Jr. (1657-1736) & 1/wf Hannah PECK (1660±-); 12 May 1680; Hartford
SHEPHERD, John & Elizabeth CRAGGIN/CRAGIN; 19 Mar 1689/90; Concord
SHEPARD, John (-1691) & Persis PEIRCE (1669-), m/2 William RAND by 1695; 26 Mar 1690; Charlestown
SHEPARD, John (?1627-1707) & 2/wf Susan/Susanna (GARBRAND) (HOOKER) GOODWIN (-1698), w Thomas, w William; m cont 3 Aug 1691; Middletown, CT?
SHEPARD, John & 2/wf Hannah (GREEN) [ACY?]/ACRE (1656-), w John; b 1698; Rowley
SHEPARD, John (-1707) & 3/wf Martha (BEAMAN) HENBURY, w Arthur; 8 Sep 1698, aft 7 Mar 1698/9; Hartford
SHEPARD, John & 1/wf Elizabeth WOODRUFF (1679-); b 1701?, b 1706; ?Westfield, MA/CT
SHEPARD, Jonathan (1674-) & Annah GARRISON (1680-), Easthampton; 14 Jan 1699/1700; Bedford, NY
SHEPERD, Ralph (?1603, ?1606-1693, Malden) & Thanks/Thanklord _?_ (1612-1669+); b 1633; Watertown/Concord/Chelmsford/Charlestown/Weymouth/Rehoboth/Plymouth/Malden
SHEPHERD, Ralph (?1665, 1667-1722, Milton) & Marah?/Mary? _?_ ; ca 1690/5?; Charlestown/Brookline
SHEPHERD, Richard & Jane TALBY; 14 Oct 1663; Charlestown
SHEPARD, Samuel (1613, 1615-) & Hannah _?_ ; b 1638, b 1633?; Cambridge (returned to Eng)
SHEPARD, Samuel (1641-1668) & Dorothy FLINT (-1668); 30 Apr 1666; Rowley/Charlestown/Braintree
SHEPARD, Samuel (-1707) & Mary (PAGE) [DOW], w John; 14 Jul 1673; Haverhill
SHEPARD, Samuel (1667-1723) & Alice MASON (1668-); 14 Jul 1698; Boston/Woodbridge, NJ
SHEPHERD, Solomon, Towchester & Sarah (EASTMAN) FRENCH (1655-1745, 1748?), w Joseph; 4 Aug 1684, 2 Aug (no); Salisbury
SHEPARD, Thomas (1605-1649) & 1/wf Margaret [TOUTEVILLE] (-1636); in Eng, b 1632; Cambridge
SHEPARD, Thomas (1605-1649) & 2/wf Joanna [HOOKER] (-1646); ?Oct 1637, b 1641; Cambridge
SHEPARD, Thomas (1605-1649) & 3/wf Margaret BORODELL, m/2 Jonathan MITCHELL 1650; 8 Sep 1647; Cambridge
SHEPHERD, Thomas (1635-1677) & Anne/Hannah?/Anna? TYNG (1640-1709); 3 Nov 1656; Charlestown
SHEPARD, Thomas (?1633-1719, ae 87, Milton) & 1/wf Hannah ENSIGNE/ENSIGN (1639-1698); 19 Nov 1658; Malden/Hingham
SHEPARD, Thomas (1658-1685?) & Mary (ANDERSON) LYNDE (-1717), w Thomas, m Samuel HAYMAN 1686; 27 Jul 1682; Charlestown
SHEPHERD, Thomas (-1726) & Hannah BLANCHARD; 7 Dec 1682; Charlestown/Bristol, RI
SHEAPARD, Thomas & 1/wf? Susannah SCOTT; 5 Sep 1695; Hartford
SHEPARD, William (-1664) & _?_ [HATHAWAY?]; b 1650; Taunton
SHEPARD, William & _?_ ; b 1677; CT
SHEPARD, [Thomas?] & Ann _?_ , m/2 Benjamin STEVENS?; nr 1700; Dover, NH
SHEPHERD, _?_ & Mary _?_ (-15 Aug 1683, wid); Stamford, CT
SHEPARDSON, Daniel (-1644) & Joanna _?_ (-1661), m/2 Thomas CALL; b 1637; Charlestown
SHEPARDSON, Daniel (1640-) & Elizabeth (CALL) TINGLEY (1641-), w Samuel; - Apr 1667, 11 Apr 1668; Malden/Charlestown
SHEPARDSON, John (1671-1728) & Elizabeth FULLER, m/2 James TIFFANY; 9 Apr 1694; Rehoboth/Attleboro
SHIPPEE/SHEPPY, David (-1718+) & Margaret SCRANTON; 15 Aug 1664; Warwick, RI
SHIPPIE, Thomas (1620-1683) & 1/wf ?Elizabeth/?Thanklord _?_ ; b 1648; Charlestown
SHIPPIE, Thomas (1620-1683) & 2/wf Grace _?_ (-1696, a 1696) b 1656; Charlestown
SHIPPIE, Thomas (-1702) & Mabel MITCHELL, m/2 Nicholas HOPPIN; 17 Apr 1690; Charlestown
SHERBORN, Henry[1] (1612, 1611?-1680, 1681?) & 1/wf Rebecca GIBBONS (ca 1620-1667); 13 Nov 1637; Portsmouth, NH
SHERBURNE, Henry[1] (1612-1680, 1681) & 2/wf Sarah [ABBOTT], w Walter; ca 1667?; ?Kittery, ME
SHERBURNE, Henry (1666-1738) & Sarah [WIGGIN] (1669-); b 21 Oct 1691; Portsmouth, NH
SHERBURNE, Henry (1674-1757) & Dorothy [WENTWORTH] (1680-1754); b 1698; ?Portsmouth, NH
SHERBURNE, John (1615-1693) & Elizabeth [TUCK]; ca 1649?, b 1666, b 1646?; Hampton, NH

SHERBURNE, John (1649-1698) & Mary COWELL (-1736+); ca 29 Jan 1677; Great Island, NH/etc.

SHERBURNE, John (1650-1723/1731) & 1/wf Mary [JACKSON]; b 20 May 1700, b 1689, b 1673, by 1680?; Portsmouth, NH

SHERBURNE, John & Mary (LEACH) [MOSES], w Aaron

SHERBIN, Joseph & [Amy COWELL], m/2 Jethro FURBER 1678, m/3 Nathaniel AYRES b 1692; 19 Oct 1678

SHERBURN, Samuel (1638-1691) & Love HUTCHINS (1647-1739); 15 Dec 1668; Haverhill

SHERMAN, Abijah & Sarah FRANKS; 13 Jul 1694; Boston

SHERMAN, Benjamin (1650-1719) & Hannah MOWRY (1656-1718); 3 Dec 1674; Portsmouth, RI

SHERMAN, Benjamin (1662-1741) & Rebecca PHIPPEN (1666-1739); 6 Jun 1683; Stratford, CT

SHERMAN, Bezaleel (1640) & ? ; Watertown/Madras, East Indies

SHERMAN, Daniel (1642-1716) & 1/wf Abiah STREET (1642-); 28 Sep 1664; New Haven

SHERMAN, Daniel (1662-) & Sarah JENEE/JENNEY; 18 Apr 1693; Dartmouth

SHERMAN, Daniel (1668/9-1741) & Rebecca WHEELER (-1751); 19 Dec 1694; Stratford, CT

SHERMAN, David (1665-1753) & Mercy [WHEELER]; ca 1690; Stratford, CT

SHERMAN, Ebenezer & Margaret [DECROW] (-1726); b 1700[1701?]; Marshfield

SHERMAN, Eber (1634-1706) & Mary [WILCOX]; ca 1665/73?; Kingston, RI

SHERMAN, Eber (1674-) & Honora ? ; b 1700; Nantucket/Swansea

SHERMAN, Edmund (1572-1641) & Joan [MAKIN]; ca 1598, in Eng; Westhersfield, CT/New Haven

SHERMAN, Edmund^2 (1599-) & 1/wf ? ; Watertown (ret'd to Eng?)

SHERMAN, Edmund (1641-1719) & Dorcas ? ; b 1674; Portsmouth, RI/Dartmouth

SHERMAN, Edmund (1647-1683) & Susannah [HARDY]; b 1674; Stratford, CT

SHERMAN/SHEARMAN, Edward (1677-1728) & Sarah PARKHURST; 16 Oct 1700; Watertown/Wayland

SHERMAN, Rev. James (1645(6?), 1651-1718) (ae 26 in 1677) (son Rev. John) & Mary WALKER (1661-); 13 May 1680; Sudbury/Elizabeth, NJ

SHERMAN, John (1585-1616 in Eng) & Grace [MAKIN], m/2 Thomas ROGERS, m/3 Roger PORTER; in Eng, b 14 May 1610; Dedham, Eng

SHERMAN, Capt. John (?1612, 1615-1691, ae 76?) & Martha [PALMER] (-1701); b 1638; Watertown/Stratford, CT

SHERMAN, Rev. John (1613-1685) & 1/wf Mary [GIBBS] (-1644, New Haven); b 1639; Watertown/New Haven/Milford, CT

SHERMAN, Rev. John (1613-1685) & 2/wf Mary [LANNER] (-1710); ca 1645, b 1648; Watertown/Milford, CT

SHERMAN, John (1644-1734) & Sarah [SPOONER] (1653-1720+); ca 1675, ca 1670; Dartmouth

SHERMAN, John (1646-1728) & Jane HATCH (1656-1744); at Boston, 25 Oct 1677; Marshfield

SHERMAN, John (1651-1730) & Elizabeth [THORNE] (-1744); b 1680; Woodury, CT/Stratford, CT

SHERMAN, John (1675-1756) & Mary [BULLEN]; b 1699; Watertown/Marlboro

SHERMAN, John (1673-) & Dinah [THOMAS] (1678-); b 1699, b 1701?; New Haven

SHERMAN, Joseph (1650-1731) & Elizabeth WINSHIP (1652-); 18 Nov 1673; Watertown, CT

SHERMAN, Matthew (?1645-1698) & [Hannah BUCKLEY] (very doubtful) (-1713); b 1692, b 25 Mar 1691; Fairfield, CT

SHERMAN, Nathan (1678-) & Freelove ? ; b 1700/(01?); Dartmouth

SHERMAN, Nathaniel & 1/wf Grace ? ; b 1659; Boston

SHERMAN, Nathaniel & Mary ? , ?dau Alice THOMAS or dau Philip? KIRKLAND (see John COX); b 1664; Boston

SHERMAN, Nathaniel (1657-1712) & 1/wf Mary PHIPPENEY/PHIPPEN (1660?-); 13 Jun 1680, 1681?, 30 Jun; Stratford, CT

SHERMAN, Nathaniel & Sarah HUTCHINSON, m/2 John HARNDEN; m int 14 Dec 1696; Lynn

SHERMAN, Peleg (-1719) & Elizabeth LAWTON (1639-); 25 Jul 1657; Portsmouth, RI/Little Compton, RI/Tiverton, RI

SHERMAN, Peleg & Alice FISH; 16 Mar 1697, 16 Nov 1697; Portsmouth, RI

SHERMAN, Philip (?1610-1687) & Sarah [ODDING] (-1681); in Eng, ca 1633; Roxbury/RI

SHERMAN, Philip & Hannah [?WILCOX]/?Sarah JENNEY; b 1699; Dartmouth/?Portsmouth, RI

SHERMAN, [Philip] & Mary ANTHONY (1680-); 14 Apr 1699; Portsmouth, RI

SHERMAN, Richard (1577-1660, Boston) & 1/wf? ? ; in Eng, b ?

SHERMAN, Richard (1577-1660) & 2/wf? Elizabeth [?LOCKE]? (-1667), m/2 Thomas
ROBINSON 1661; b 1613?, b 1635 Boston; Boston
SHERMAN, Samson (1642-1720) & Isabel TRIPP (1651-bef 1716); 4 Mar 1674/5; Portsmouth, RI
SHERMAN, Samuel (-bef 1660) & _?_ ; ca 1636?; Ipswich
SHERMAN, Samuel & Mary [WHARTON]?; doubtful; ?Stratford, CT
SHERMAN, Samuel (1601-1645?, 1644?) & 1/wf? Grace [_?_]; b 1639, b 1637; Boston/Water-
town
SHERMAN, Samuel (1618-1700) & Sarah [MITCHELL?] (1621-); ca 1640; Watertown/Stratford,
CT
SHERMAN, Samuel & 2/wf? Naomi _?_ ; b 1661, b 1659; Boston
SHERMAN, Samuel (1641-1700) & 1/wf Mary TITHARTON/TITTERTON?; 19 Jun 1665;
Stratford, CT
SHERMAN, Samuel (-1718) & 1/wf Sarah [DOGGETT] (-1680); b 1673, ca 1668?; Marshfield/
Weymouth
SHERMAN, Samuel (-1718) & 2/wf Hannah _?_ ; aft Jul 1680, bef 1688/9; Marshfield
SHERMAN, Samuel (1648, 1658±-1717) & 2/wf? Martha TRIPP (1658-1717); 23 Feb 1680/1, 1680,
1681; Portsmouth, RI
SHERMAN, Samuel & Anne SHEFFIELD; 6 Nov 1694; Portsmouth, RI
SHERMAN, Samuel (1641-1719) & 2/wf Abigail (THOMPSON) (CURTISS) HUSE (-1731), w
Jonathan, w Nicholas; 1 Aug 1695; Stratford, CT
SHERMAN, Samuel & Sarah [PEARCE]; b 1701?; Swansea/Portsmouth, RI
SHERMAN, Theophilus (1643-1712) & 1/wf Comfort [ROBBINS] (1646-); ca 1665; New
Haven/Wethersfield, CT
SHERMAN, Theophilus & Mary [COULTMAN]/COLTMAN, w John; aft 10 Dec 1688, by 1697;
Wethersfield, CT
SHERMAN, Thomas (1658-) & Lydia WILCOX; b 1701?, 26 May 1701; RI
SHERMAN, William (-1679) & Prudence HILL; 23 Jan 1638; Plymouth Colony
SHERMAN, William (-1680) & Desire DOETY/DOTY, m/2 Israel HOLMES 1681, m/3 Alexander
STANDISH 1686?; 25 Dec 1667, 26? Dec; ?Duxbury/?Marshfield
SHERMAN, William (1659-) & Martha WILBORE/WILBUR (1662-); 12 May 1681; Portsmouth,
RI/Little Compton, RI/Tiverton, RI/Dartmouth
SHERMAN, William (1672-1739) & Mary/Merry WHITE (-1739), dau Peregrine; 3 Feb 1697;
Marshfield
SHERN, John & Eleanor _?_ ; b 1669; Boston
SHERRILL, Samuel (1649?-1719) & _?_ PARSONS; b 1678; Southampton, LI
SHEARIN/SHERRING/?SHERWIN, Ebenezer & Susannah HOWLET; 1 Feb 1699/1700; Boxford/
Topsfield
SHERRIN, John (1644-1726) & 1/wf Frances LOMASE; 25 Nov 1667; Ipswich
SHERRIN, John & Mary CHANLER/CHANDLER (1659-1745); 30 Sep 1691; Ipswich
SHERIN, Richard & Sarah _?_ ; b 1694; Boston
SHOERIN, Thomas & Sarah KETTLE (-1690); 12 Jun 1685; Charlestown
SHERRINGTON, Thomas (1625-1702) & 2/wf ?Mary _?_ ; Fairfield, CT
SHERWOOD, Benjamin[3] & Sarah _?_ ; b 1693; Stratford, CT
SHERWOOD, Isaac[2] (-1733+) & Elizabeth [JACKSON] (1662-1727+); b 1679?, b 1681; Stratford,
CT
SHERWOOD, Isaac (?1675-1748) & Mary _?_ ; b 1601(?); Stratford, CT
SHERWOOD, John (-1689) & Sarah HURD (1661-), m/2 Samuel BEECHER 1691; 23 Apr 1685;
Stratford, CT
SHERWOOD, John (-1696) & Johanna [BOOTH] (1678-), m/2 Thomas HAWLEY 1701; ca 1694;
Stratford, CT
SHERWOOD, Joseph &_?_ ; b 1701?
SHERWOOD, Matthew[2] (1644-1715) & 1/wf Sarah [TURNEY] (1641-); ca 1666; Stratford, CT
SHERWOOD, Matthew[2] (1644-1715) & 2/wf Mary [FITCH] (1644-1730); b 1670; Stratford, CT
SHERWOOD, Matthew[3] & Elizabeth [MOREHOUSE]; b 21 Dec 1696; Fairfield, CT
SHERWOOD, Nathaniel (-1733, Rye, NY) & Abigail _?_ ; b 1701?
SHERWOOD, Samuel &_?_ ; b 1696; Fairfield, CT/Stratford, CT
SHERWOOD, Stephen[2] & 1/wf Rebecca [TURNEY] (1641-); ca 1656-60, by 1661; Fairfield, CT
SHERWOOD, Stephen[2] & 2/wf Hannah (JACKSON) [GALKIN], w Philip; ca 1686/8; Fairfield,
CT

SHERWOOD, Stephen[2] & 3/wf Mary (ADAMS) (GUISE) MERWIN (1647-1712), w Luke, w _?_ ; betw 1697 & 1701; Fairfield, CT

SHERWOOD, Stephen (1663?-bef 1715) & Mary [HOYT?]; b 1701?, b 1697?; ?Rye, NY

SHERWOOD, Thomas[1] (1586-1655) & 1/wf Alice [SEABROOK?] (1587-); in Eng, b 1620; St. Michael's Parish, London/Wethersfield, CT/Fairfield, CT/Stamford, CT?

SHERWOOD, Thomas[1] (1586-1655) & 2/wf Mary [FITCH?] (-1694?), m/2 John BANKS by 1659; aft 1639, ca 1642?; Fairfield, CT

SHERWOOD, Thomas[1] (-1657/8) & Sarah [SEABROOK] (?1623-); by 1642; Stratford, CT

SHERWOOD, Thomas[2] (1624-) & 1/wf Sarah [WHEELER] (1628-); ca 1652; Fairfield, CT

SHERWOOD, Thomas[2] (1624-1698) & 2/wf Ann [TURNEY] (1637-); ca 1660?, "by 1659"; Fairfield, CT

SHERWOOD, Thomas[2] (1624-1698) & 3/wf Elizabeth [CABLE], w John; betw 7 Nov 1673 & 19 Dec 1683; Fairfield, CT

SHERWOOD, Thomas (?1653-1699) & Sarah _?_ ; ca 1676/80?; Fairfield, CT/Eastchester, NY/Fordham, NY

SHERWOOD, Thomas[2] (1624-1698) & 4/wf Sarah (HIDE) COLEY, w Peter; m contract 25 Jun 1695; Fairfield, CT

SHERWOOD, Thomas & Hannah BARNSTEAD

SHAVALLY/SHEVALLY/?SHAVALLEY, Nicholas & Rebecca [WHEELER] (1662-); b 1689; Concord

SHILLABER, John & _?_ ; b 1680; Brighton

SHILLABER, John & Mary [FRASK] (1661-); Salem

SHILLABER, John[1] & Blanche _?_

SHIPLY, John (-1694) & Susannah WHELER ((164-)-1694), Concord, dau Obadiah; 23 Sep 1672; Chelmsford

SHIPLEY, John[1] (-1678) & Ane? _?_ (-1685?); b 1637; Chelmsford

SHIPLE, John (1677?-1736) & Lydia [LAKIN], m/2 Jonathan BOYDEN; b 1700; Groton

SHIPMAN, Edward (-1697) & 1/wf Elizabeth COMSTOCK (-1659); beginning of Jan 1651, - Jan 1650/1; Saybrook, CT

SHIPTON, Edward (-1697) & 2/wf Mary ANDREWS (-1704), div wf William, m/2 _?_ ; 1 Jul 1663; Saybrook, CT

SHIPMAN, Edward (1654-) & _?_ ; Saybrook, CT/Chester

SHIPMAN, John (1664-) & Martha HUMPHRIES/HUMPHREY; 5 May 1686, May 1686; Saybrook, CT

SHIPMAN, William (1656-1725), Colchester/Hebron & Alice HAND; 26 Nov 1690; Saybrook, CT

SHIPPEN, Edward (-1712) & Elizabeth [LYBRAND] (-1686); b 1672(3?), 1671; Boston

SHIPPEN, Edward & 2/wf Rebecca (LAYWARD) RICHARDSON, w Francis of New York; 15 Jul 1688, 7 Jun, 4 Sep 1689, 4 Sep 1691; Newport/Boston

SHIPREVE, William & Jane _?_ ; b 1687; Boston

SHIPWAY, John (1626-1663) & Anne [CUTTS]; b 18 Mar 1658/9; Portsmouth, NH

SHIPWAY, John (-1694) & Sarah [FROST] (1666?-), m/2 William REDFORD by 1695; 1687; Portsmouth, NH

SHIRLEY, Robert (-1711) & Sarah [EASTON]; b 20 Jan 1687; Hartford

SHIVERICK, Samuel & _?_ ; b 1672; Portsmouth, NH

SHIVERICK, Samuel & _?_ ; b 1697; Barnstable

SHOOTER, Peter (-1654) & Anna/Hannah? _?_, m/2 Nathaniel MOTT 1656; b 1654; Braintree/Scituate?

SHORE, Edward & Abigail _?_ ; b 1682(3); Boston

SHORES, John & Rachel (CODNER) (DERBY) [SAMPSON], ?dau Rachel PASCO, ?dau James NAYBOURS, w John, w Andrew; Portsmouth, NH

SHORE, Jonathan (1649-) & Priscilla HAWTHORNE (1649-); 15 Jan 1668/9, 15 Jan 1668; Charlestown/Lynn/Woodbury, CT

SHORE/SHOREBORNE, Sampson/Samson[1] (1615-1687) & Abigail _?_ ; in Eng, b 1640; Boston

SHORE, Samson[2] (1645-1679) & 1/wf _?_ BENSON, dau John; b 1668; Boston

SHORE, Samson[2] (1645-1679) & 2/wf [Mary PAYTON], dau Bezaleel; b 10 May 1678, no issue; Boston

SHORE, Samson[3] (1668-) & Mary [HOLLAND] (dau John & Sarah); b 1694; Boston

SHORES/SHOVE?/SHOWERS, Nathaniel (1668-1693) & Mary [LINCOLN] (1679/80-); b 1701?; Taunton

SHORY/SHOREY, John & Mary __?__ ; b 1687; Boston
SHORT, Clement & Faith **MUNT** (-1689); 21 Nov 1660; Boston/Berwick, ME/Kittery, ME
SHORT, Henry (-1673) (nephew of James **JACKMAN**) & 1/wf Elizabeth __?__ (-1648); b 1647; Ipswich?
SHORT, Henry (-1673) & 2/wf Sarah **GLOVER** (-1697), m/2 Robert **ADAMS** 1677/8; 9 Oct 1648; Newbury
SHORT, Henry (1652-) & 1/wf Sarah **WHIPPLE** (-1691); 30 Mar 1674; Newbury
SHORT, Henry (1652-) & 2/wf Ann **(SEWALL) LONGFELLOW** (-1706), w William; 11 May 1692; Newbury
SHORT, Luke (-1746) & Susanna **STEWARD**; 13 Jun 1692; Marblehead/Middleboro
SHORTHUS/SHORTHOUSE/SHORTHOSE?, Robert & Katharine __?__ (?relative of Rachel **HICKS**, wf of John), m/2 Baptist **SMEDLEY** 1645; b 1637, b 1629; Charlestown
SHORTRIDGE, Richard (1631-) & Esther [**DEARBORN**]; b 1673, b 1661; Portsmouth, NH
SHORTRIDGE, Richard & Alice **CREBER**; 16 May 1687; Portsmouth, NH
SHORTRIGS, William & Mary [**GAMMON**] (-1709, 1703?); b 1686, b 1663; Boston
SHOVE, George (-1687) & 1/wf Hopestill **NEWMAN** (1641-1674), Rehoboth; 12 Jul 1664; Taunton/Rehoboth
SHOVE, George (-1687) & 2/wf Hannah **(BACON) WALLEY** (1643-1685), w Thomas; 16/17/18 Feb 1674/5; Taunton/Rehoboth
SHOVE, George (-1687) & 3/wf Sarah **(POOLE?) FARWELL**, w Thomas; 8 Dec 1686; Taunton
SHOVE, Nathaniel & [?Mary **LINCOLN**] (1679/80-); b 1701?; Taunton (see **SHORE**)
SHOVE, Samuel (1670-) & Dorothy **THOMPSON**, m/2 Samuel **BURR** 1700; 16 Nov 1692; Charlestown
SHOVE, Seth (1667-1735) & 1/wf Mary **DRAKE** (living 1 May 1699?)
SHOVE, Seth (1667-1735) & 2/wf? [Abigail **BUSHNELL**] (1676-); b 1695?; Simsbury/Danbury, CT
SHOVE, __?__ (dead in 1638) & Margery __?__ (-1680, Taunton), m/2 Richard **PEACOCK**; b 1638; Rowley
SHREVE, Caleb (1652?-) & Sarah [**ARESON**] of LI; ca 1680?; LI
SHREVE, Daniel & Jane __?__ ; 1688?, b 1690(1?); Little Compton, RI
SHREVE, John (-1739) & Jane **HAVENS**; last of Aug 1686; Portsmouth, RI
SHREVE/SHERIFF, Thomas (-1675) & Martha __?__ , m/2 Thomas **HAZARD**; b 1649; Plymouth/RI
SHERIFF, Daniel (-1737) & Jane __?__ (-1737+); 1688±; Little Compton, RI
SHRIEVE, John (-1739) & Jane **HAVENS**; last of Aug 1686; Portsmouth, RI
SHERIVE/SHERIFF, Thomas (-1675) & [Martha] __?__ (-1691+), m/2 Thomas **HAZARD** 1675, m/3 Lewis **HUES**; b 1649; Plymouth
SHRIMPTON, Epaphras (1654-) & Rebecca __?__ ; b 1687; Boston
SHRIMPTON, Henry (-1666) & 1/wf Eleanor __?__ ; b 1641; Boston
SHRIMPTON, Henry (-1666) & 2/wf Mary (_?_) **(HAWKINS) FENN**, w Thomas, w Robert; 27 Feb 1661; Boston
SHRIMPTON, Jonathan (-1673) & Mary [**OLIVER**] (1646-), m/2 Nathaniel **WILLIAMS** by 1675, b 1665; Boston
SHRIMPTON, Samuel (-1698) & Elizabeth **(ROBERTS?)** [**USHER**] (1645/6-1674+); b 1666; Boston/Cambridge
SHRIMPTON, Samuel & Abiel **(BURRILL)/[BURR?]** **BROWN**, w Jonathan; 11 Aug 1668; Hingham
SHRIMPTON, Samuel (-1698) & 2/wf Elizabeth [**BREEDON**], wid, m/2 Simion **STODDARD** 1709; 1672?, aft 1674?; Boston
SHRIMPTON, Samuel (-1703) & Elizabeth **RICHARDSON**, m/2 David **STODDARD** 1713; 7 May 1696; Boston
SHUMWAY, Joseph (see Peter) & Mariah **SMITH** (1677-); ?1700
SHUMWAY, Peter (-1695) & Frances __?__ ; b 1678; Topsfield
SHUMWAY, Peter & Mariah/Mary **SMITH** (1677-); 11 Feb 1700, 1700/1, 1701; Boxford
SHURTLEIF, Abiel (1666-1732) & Lydia **BARNES** (-1727); 14 Jan 1695/6; Plymouth/Plympton
SHIRTLY, William (1624-1666) & Elizabeth **LETTICE** (-1693), m/2 Jacob **COOKE** 1669, m/3 Hugh **COLE** 1689; 18 Oct 1655; Plymouth
SHIRTLEFF, William (1657-1730) & Susanna **LOTHROP** (1663/4-1726); ca 20 Oct 1683; Plymouth
SHUTE, John & Rebecca [**SEAVEY**]; b 1687; Smuttynose
SHUTE, John & Abigail [**FOWLER**]; b 1700; Eastchester, NY

SHUTE, Michael (-1702) & Mary VERMAY; b 1682; Boston
SHUTE, Richard (-1705?) & Sarah SANFORD; 14 Aug 1656; Milford, CT/Eastchester, NY
SHUTE, Richard (-1703, ae 72) & 1/wf Elizabeth _?_ (-1691, ae 63 1/2); b 1666; Boston
SHUTE, Richard (1667-1736) & Lydia [GREENLAND] (1673-); b 1693; Malden
SHUTE, Richard (-1703) & 2/wf Catharine/Katherine [GUTTERIDGE], w Thomas?; b 1703, b 1701?; Boston
SHUTE, Thomas (1659-1711+) & [?Susanna] _?_ (-1711+); Eastchester, NY
SHUTE/SHUTT, William & Hopestill VIALL, m/2 William PITTS by 1670; 1 Jul 1659; Boston
SHUTE, William & Rachel (ALLAN) DEDSON; Jamaica
SHUTE, William & Martha BUDD, dau Edward; 19 May 1690; Boston
SHUTLEWORTH, Vincent & Elizabeth LEONARD; 18 Feb 1677/8; Dedham/Medford
SIAS, John & Anne (ROBERTS) [PITMAN]; 1698, by 1700, Jan 1698/9; Wells, ME
SIAS, _?_ & _?_ ROBERTS, m/2 Selathiel DENBO, m/3 William GRAVES; b 1675; Oyster River, NH
SIBLEY, John (-1649) & Sarah [?HOWE], ?sister of Joseph, m/2 Francis CHICKERING 1650, m/3 John BOWLES aft 1658; b 1635?, b 21 (12) 1634/5; Charlestown
SIBLEY, John (-1661) & Rachel [LEACH], m/2 Thomas GOLDTHWAITE bef 1671; b 1642; Salem
SIBLEY, John (-1710) & Rachel [?PICKWORTH]; b 1675; Manchester
SIBLEY, John (1669-) & Elizabeth PEALE; 4 Jul 1695; Salem
SEBELL/SIBLEY?, John & Priscilla WHITE; 3 Sep 1700; Boston
SYBLY, Joseph (-1718) & 1/wf Susannah FOLLET (1662-); 4 Feb 1683, prob 1683/4; Salem
SIBLEY, Richard (-1676) & Hannah _?_ (-1700+); b 1656; Salem
SYBLY, Samuel & Mary [WOODROW]; b 1687; Salem
SIBLEY, Samuel (1659-1708) & Sarah WELLS/WELD, m/2 John SAWYER; 13 Sep 1695; Salem
SIBLEY, William (-1691) (He calls Mrs. (Robert PLUMER) BERRY "mother".) & Ruth (CANTERBURY) SMALE, w Thomas, m/3 Alexander OSBORN; 1 Nov 1676; Salem
SIGOURNEY, Andrew & Charlotte [PAIRAN]; in France, b [1673]; Oxford
SIGOURNEY, Andrew (1673-) & Mary [GERMAINE] (1684, 1680?-1704); b 1701?, b 1702, b 1702(3?), 1696/1700; [Boston]
SIGSWORTH, George & Esther _?_; b 1679; Boston
SILL, John & Joanna _?_ (-1671); in Eng, b 1635; Cambridge
SCILL, Joseph (-1696, ae 60) & 1/wf Jemima BELCHER (1642-); 5 Dec 1660; Cambridge/Lyme, CT
SILL, Capt. Joseph (-1696, ae 60) & 2/wf Sarah (CLARK) MARVIN (ca 1644-1715/16), w Reynold; 12 Feb 1677, 1677/8?; Lyme, CT
SYLE/SILL?, Richard & 1/wf _?_; Rowley
SYLE/SILL?, Richard & 2/wf Hannah (?BROWN) SCOTT (1657-1715), w Joseph; 31 Aug 1697; Newbury
SEALY/CILLEY?, Richard (see Richard SEELEY) & Martha _?_, m/2 John CLOUGH; b 1667, b 1650; Isles of Shoals/Hampton/Salisbury
SILLEY, Thomas & Ann STANYAN (see SEELEY); bef? 2 Jul 1697; Hampton/Salisbury
CILLEY, _?_ & _?_; b 1675
SILLIMAN, Daniel¹ (-1690/1) & 1/wf Peaceable (_?_) EGGLEDEN, w John; m cont Jul 1661; Fairfield, CT
SILLIMAN, Daniel¹ (-1690/1) & 2/wf Hannah/Hannica [HENDRICKSEN/HENDRICK?], w Hendrick/Henry; aft 18 Jun 1684; Fairfield, CT
SILLIMAN, Daniel² (-1697) & Abigail [OGDEN]; ca 1684, b 1687; Fairfield, CT
SILLIMAN, Robert² (-1748) & Sarah (HULL) [KNAPP], w John; by 1691; Fairfield, CT
SEALIS, Richard (?1581-1656?) & 1/wf Phebe CHRISFEILDE (-1612); Biddenden, Eng, 14 Apr 1604; Scituate
SEALIS, Richard (?1581-) & 2/wf Margery (?ASHENDEN) LEA; Biddenden, Eng, 4 May 1613; Scituate
SEALIS, Richard (-1656) & 3/wf Eglin (HATHERLY) (DOWNE) HANFORD, w _?_, w Jeffrey; 15 Dec 1637; Scituate
SELLIVANT/SILLIVANT, Daniel & 1/wf Abigail [COLE], dau James; b 1652; Hartford
SILLIVANT, Daniel (-1655) & 2/wf Elizabeth LAMBERTSON/LAMBERTON (1632-1716), m/2 William TROWBRIDGE 1657; 17 Oct 1654; New Haven
SILLAWAY, Daniel & Mary GRIFFIN; 7 Sep 1687; Newbury
SILSBEE, Ephraim & Rachel BASSET (1666-); 23 Jan 1693; Salem

SILSBE, Henry (?1608-1700) & 1/wf Dorothy ? (-1676); ca 1646?; Salem/Ipswich/Lynn
SILSBY, Henry (?1608-1700) & 2/wf Grace (?) EATON (-bef 17 Mar 1698/9, w Jonas; 18 Nov 1680; Lynn
SILSBY, John (-1676) & Bethia PITMAN/PICKMAN, m/2 Alexander COLE 1680; 15 Feb 1673, 1673/4?; Salem
SILSBY, Jonathan (-1714) & Bethiah MASH/MARSH (1650-1705); 1 Jan 1673; Lynn/Windham, CT
SILSBY, Nathaniel & 1/wf Deborah TOMPKINS (1651-); 5 Nov 1671; Salem
SILSBY, Nathaniel & 2/wf Elizabeth [PICKERING]; b 1697; Salem
SILSBIE, Ralph (seems doubtful) & ? (ABORN) FOSTER, wid; b 1670
SILSBY, Samuel (-1687) & Mary BISCOW/BISCOE, m/2 ? /?Jonathan JOHNSON 1689?; 4 Jul 1676; Lynn
SILVER, Samuel (1662-) & 1/wf Mary ? (-1701); b 1692; Rowley
SILVER, Thomas (-1682) & 1/wf ? ; b 1645; Newbury
SILVER, Thomas (-1682) & 2/wf Catharine/Katherine ? (-1665); 16 Aug 1649; Newbury
SILVER, Thomas (-1695) & Mary WILLIAMS, m/2 Simon WAINWRIGHT 1700, m/3 John BOYNTON, m/4 Joshua BOYNTON; 28 Dec 1681, 4 Jan 1681; Haverhill/Newbury
SIMCOCK/SIMCOOK?/SIMCOX, Thomas & Mary ? ; b 1684; Boston
SYMONS/SIMMONS, Aaron & Mary WOODWORTH (1651-); 24 Dec 1677; Scituate
SYMONDS, Benjamin (1654-) & Rebecca/Judith ? ; b 1678/[9]; Woburn
SYMONDS, Caleb (-1712) & Sarah BACON (1644-1727); 25 Sep 1677; Woburn
SYMONDS, Harlackenden (1627-) (ret'd to Eng) & Elizabeth [DAY?] (1641-); b 1668; Wells, ME/Gloucester/Ipswich
SIMONDS, Henry (-1643) & Susan ? , m/2 Isaac WALKER; by 1643; Boston/Lancaster
SIMMONS, Isaac & Martha [CHANDLER]; b 1696; Marshfield
SYMONDS, James (1633-1714) & Elizabeth BROWNING; 20 Nov 1661; Salem
SIMONDS, James (-1717) & Susanna BLODGETT (-1715); 29 Dec 1685; Woburn/Lexington
SYMONDS, James & Mary ROBINSON (1669-); 25 Mar 1697; Salem
SIMMONS, Job (1674-) & Hannah BUSHOP/BISHOP; 15 Jun 1700; Plymouth
SYMONDS, John & 1/wf Ruth [FOX]; b 1625; Salem
SYMONDS, John (-1671) & 2/wf Elizabeth [?BLOTE]; b 1630?, b 1637; Salem
SYMONDS, John & ?Ann ? ; b 1640; Braintree
SYMONDS, John (1614±-) & 1/wf ? ; b 1651; Kittery, ME
SIMMONS, John & Mary ? ; b 1663; Boston
SIMMONS, John (?1640-) & 1/wf Elizabeth BOYNTON (1642-1677); 9 Nov 1664; Rowley/Bradford
SYMONDS, John (1614±-) & 2/wf Welthen (?) GODDARD, w John; by 4 Jun 1668, aft 12 Nov 1666; Oyster River, NH
SIMONS, John (-1715, 1716) & Mercy PABODIE (1650-1728); 16 Nov 1669; Duxbury
SYMONS, John & Martha ?MOORE of Southold; b 1677?; Boston/Taunton
SIMMONS, John & 2/wf Mary PIERCE; 19 Jul 1678; Bradford
SYMONDS, John & Ann ? ; b 1686/[7?]; Boston
SYMONDS, John (1666-1728/9) & 1/wf Sarah WATERS; 3 Mar 1689/90; Salem
SIMMONS, John & Hannah HATHAWAY; 14 Dec 1697; Taunton
SIMMONS, ?John (1670) & Experience [PICKNELL?]; b 1701?; Plymouth
SYMONDS, Joseph (1652-1733) & Mary TEED/TIDD; 7 Mar 1680/1; Cambridge/Lexington
SYMONDS, Mark (1584-1659 & 1/wf ? ; b 1612?, b 1614; Ipswich
SYMONDS, Mark (?1584-1659) & 2/wf Joanna ? (-1666); b 1620; Ipswich
SIMMONS, Moses (-1689?, 1691?) & Sarah ? ; ca 1630; Duxbury/Bridgewater
SIMMONS, Moses (-1676?) & Patience [BARSTOW] (1643-), m/2 Samuel BAKER 1677; b 1660?, b 1662; Scituate
SYMONDS, Peter & Katherine BRADISH; m lic 30 Oct 1665; Southold, LI
SYMONDS, ?[Richard] & Hannah [MONE] (1644-1691+); Southold, LI
SIMONDS, Richard (-1682) & Hannah WELLS (-1682+); 16 Aug 1679; Salem
SIMONS, Robert (1645-1724, ae nearly 79) & Thomasin [WALDEN]; b 1678?; Windham, CT
SYMONDS, Samuel (1595-1678) & 1/wf Dorothy HARLAKENDEN (1596-1636); Great Yeldham, Eng, 2 Apr 1617; Salisbury
SYMONDS, Samuel (1595-1678) & 2/wf Martha (READE) [EPES] (-1662), w Daniel; ca 1637; Salisbury
SYMONDS, Samuel (1638-1722) & Elizabeth ANDREWS (-1725); 14 Apr 1662; Salem/Boxford

SYMONDS, Samuel (1595-1678) & 3/wf Rebecca (SWAYNE) (BYLEY) (HALL) (WORCESTER), w Henry, w John, w William; Apr or May 1663; Salisbury

SIMONS, ?Samuel (-1669) & Martha [MOORE]; Southold, NY (see John SYMONS)

SIMONS/SYMONDS, Samuel (-1711) & Elizabeth [WEBSTER]? (1646±-); ca 1668; Haverhill

SYMONDS, Samuel & _?_ ; b 1681; Ipswich

SYMONDS, Samuel (1672-) & 1/wf Abigail PORTER (1676-1716); 8 Jun 1698; Boxford/Salem/Topsfield

SIMONDS, Samuel & Hannah [JOHNSON] (1669-); b 1700; Woburn

SIMMONS, Simon & Tabitha BENTON; 27 Nov 1684, no issue; New Haven

SIMONS, Solomon & Elizabeth _?_ ; b 1686; Hempstead, LI

SYMONDS, Thomas (-1642) & _?_ ; b 1638; Braintree

SYMONS, William & 1/wf Sarah _?_ (-1641); b 1638?; Concord

SYMONDS, William (-1642) & Anne (GARWOOD) [BARRELL], m/3 Abel PORTER; b 1640; Boston

SIMONDS, William (-1672) (ae 41 in 1658) & 2/wf Judith (PHIPPEN) HAYWARD (-1689/90, w James; 18-1 mo. 1643, 18 Jan 1643, [1642/3]; Woburn

SYMONDS, William (-1667?) & Elizabeth _?_ ; b 1645; Ipswich/Haverhill

SYMONDS, William (1632-1679) & Mary [WADE]?, m/2 Francis LITTLEFIELD by 1689; b 1668/9; Ipswich/Wells, ME

SIMONS, William & Sarah [HADLOCK] (1659-); ca 1677?; Salisbury

SIMMONS, William (1672-1765) & Abigail [CHURCH] (1680-); ca 1696; Little Compton, RI/Tiverton/ RI

SIMKINS, Daniel (-1699) & ?1/wf _?_ ; wit 15 Jun 1672, b 1672?, b 1657?; Bedford, NY

SIMKINS, Daniel (-1699/1700) & ?2/wf Elizabeth (?HINES) [WEBB] (1669-), w Joshua; aft 1694, b 9 May 1694?; Bedford, NY

SIMPKINS, Daniel (-1710+) (son Nicholas) & _?_ ; b 1701?; Oyster Bay, LI

SIMKINS, Ezekiel (-1706+, 1717?) (son Nicholas) & Sarah _?_ ; b 1701?; Oyster Bay, LI/Hempstead, LI

SIMKINS, John (1671-1730+) & Elizabeth PAGE (1666-); 28 Dec 1698; Boston

SIMPKINS, Nicholas (-1656) (ae 54 in 1654) & Isabel _?_ (-1656+) (ae 44 in 1654); b 1638, b 1624?; Boston/Yarmouth

SIMPKINS, Nicholas (1627-1703+) (had nephew William) & Elizabeth [WEEKS] (1640?-) (bpt 1647); b 1659, ca 1666, b 1655?; Oyster Bay, LI

SIMPKINS, Pilgrim (1624-1720) & 1/wf Miriam _?_ (-10 Nov 1660); ca 1659?; Boston

SYMPKINS, Pilgrim (1624-1720) & 2/wf Katherine RICHARDSON (-1721, ae 86); 27 Nov 1661; Boston

SIMPKIN, Thomas (1670 (wrong), 1671-1706) & Margaret BASTON; m int 30 Jul 1696 (m lic date Am Gen wrong); Boston

SIMPKINS, Vincent (-1653) & Mary [AKERLY], dau Henry, m/2 William OLIVER; b 1641?, b 1627?; Stamford, CT

SIMPKINS, William & Mary WILLMAN (-1681); 16 May 1678; Southampton, LI/Oyster Bay

SIMSON, Alexander & Anne _?_ ; b 1665(6?); Boston

SIMPSON, Daniel (-1747) & Frances [PLAISTED] (-1747); ca 1690?, b 1697, ca 16 Oct 1696; ?York, ME

SIMPSON, Henry[1] & Jane [NORTON], m/2 Nicholas BOND by 1650; b 13 Mar 1638; York, ME

SIMPSON, Henry[2] (?1647, ?1644-1695) & Abigail [MOULTON]; b 6 Jul 1669; York, ME

SIMPSON, Henry & _?_ ; b 1701?; York, ME

SIMPSON, John (1605-1643) & Susan/Susanna _?_ , m/2 George PARKHURST by 1645; b 1634; Watertown

SIMPSON, John (1638-1695) & Abigail SMITH (-1746, Boston, ae 100 1/2); 1 Dec 1665; Charlestown

SIMPSON, John & _?_ ; ca 1676?; Scarborough, ME

SIMPSON, John (1668-) & Rely HOLMES (-1747); 4 Jun 1695 in Boston; Charlestown/Boston

SIMPSON, Jonathan (1640-1705) & Wayte/Wait CLAP (1649-1717); 3 Apr 1673; Charlestown

SIMPSON, Joseph & Hannah _?_ ; b 1687; Boston

SIMPSON, Joseph (1673-1738+) & Elizabeth COBHAM; 15 Dec 1698; Charlestown

SIMPSON, Laomi & Deborah _?_ ; b 1669; Boston

SIMPSON, Peter (-1685) & Mary [COLEY] (1651-1705), m/2 John STREAM, Jr., m/3 Joseph LOCKWOOD 1689+; Milford, CT

SIMPSON, Savil & Sarah __?__ ; b 1676; Boston
SIMSON, Simon/?Simeon & Tabitha BENTON; 27 Mar 1684; New Haven
SYMSON, Thomas & [Lydia JORDAN] (1644-), m/2 George WHITE 1671; b 1664; Salisbury
SIMPSON, William & __?__ ; Hempstead, LI/Matinecock, LI
SINCLAIR, James (1660-) & 2/wf? Mary [SCAMMON] (1673-); [b 1690]; Exeter, NH
SINCLAIR, John[1] (-1700) & 1/wf Mary __?__ ; b 1660; Exeter, NH
SINCLAIR, John[1] (-1700) & 2/wf Deborah __?__ (-1700+); aft 27 Apr 1667, b 14 Nov 1697; Exeter, NH
SINCLAIR, John (-1731) & Elizabeth [BEAN] (1678-1733+); b 1701?
SINGLETARY, Amos (1651-) & Sarah (CURRIER) [ROGERS], w Ichabod; aft 1690; Salisbury
SINGLETERY, Benjamin (1656-) & Mary STOCKBRIDGE; 4 Apr 1678; Haverhill
SINGLETARY, John (1675-) & 1/wf Mary GRELEE; 17 Dec 1700; Haverhill/Salisbury/Framingham
SINGLETERY, Jonathan (alias DUNHAM) (1640-) & Mary [BLOOMFIELD]; b 1661; Salisbury
SINGLETARY, Nathaniel (1644-1689) & Sarah BELKNAP; 22 Dec 1673; Haverhill
SINGLETARY, Richard (-1687) & 1/wf __?__ (-1638, 1639; Newbury
SINGLETARY, Richard (-1687) & 2/wf Susanna [COOKE]; ca 1639; Salisbury
SINGLETON/SINGLETARY?, Richard (-1711) & __?__ ; by 1686?; New London, CT
SIRKMAN, Henry & Bridget FULLER; 30 Sep 1641; Plymouth
SIRY, George & Jane FALL; 16 Mar 1697; Boston
SISSON, George (1644-1718) & Sarah LAWTON (-1718, in 71st y); 1 Aug 1667; Dartmouth/Portsmouth, RI
SISSON, James (-1734) & Lydia [HATHAWAY] (1662-1714); b 1682; Dartmouth
SISSON, John (-1687±) & Mary __?__ (-1687); Newport
SISSON, Richard (1608-1684) & Mary __?__ (-1692); b 1644; Portsmouth, RI/Dartmouth
SKEEL/SKEELS, John (-1721) & Hannah [TERRILL] (1645-1730); b 1678; Stratford, CT/Woodbury, CT
SKELTON, James & Jean __?__ , m/2 Timothy RYAN 1688; b 1683; Marblehead
SKELTON, Joseph & Deborah HOW; 25 Feb 1673; Dorchester/Woburn
SKELTON, Samuel (1584-1634) & 2/wf Susannah TRAVIS (1597-1631); Sempringham, Eng, 27 Apr 1619; Salem
SKILTON, Thomas & Mehitable (HETT) TURNER, w Increase TURNER; 2 Mar 1693/4; Charlestown
SKELTON, Thomas & Jane __?__ ; b 1698; Dorchester
SKERRY, Ephraim (1643-1676) & Martha MELLARD, m/2 Richard WELLS 1679; - Sep 1671; Salem
SKERRY, Francis (-1684) & Bridget __?__ (-1692); b 1658; Salem
SKERRY, Francis (1666-1734) & [?Mary HODGES]; Salem
SKERRY, Henry (1606, ?1613-1691) & Elizabeth __?__ (1612-1692/3; in Eng, b 1637; Salem
SKERRY, Henry (-1697) & Priscilla LUNT (-1736+); 9 Nov 1665; Salem
SKIDMORE, John[2] (1643-1680) & Susannah __?__ ; 1663; Stratford, CT/Jamaica, LI
SKIDMORE, John[3] (-1740/1) & Mary [?NORTON] (1665-1748); b 1693; Stratford, CT
SKIDMORE, John[3] & Sarah [?SMITH]; b 1701; Huntington, LI
SKIDMORE, Samuel[3] (?1665-1733) & 1/wf Susanna __?__ ; b 1701?; Jamaica, LI
SKIDMORE, Thomas[1] & 1/wf Ellen __?__ (-bef 1664); b 1625; Cambridge/Hartford/Fairfield/?New London
SKIDMORE, Thomas[2] (1628-1681) & __?__ ; ca 1655-60; Huntington, LI/Jamaica, LI
SKIDMORE, Thomas[1] & Joanna (?__) WESTCOTT [BALDWIN] (1612-), w Richard, w Nathaniel; bef 14 Feb 1664 (m cont)
SKIDMORE, Thomas[1] (-1684) & 3/wf Sarah (?__) (TREADWELL) (WHELPLEY) [KEELER] (-1684), w Ralph; aft 10 Sep 1672; Fairfield
SKIFF, Benjamin (1655-) & Hannah MERRY (1660-); 20 Feb 1679/80; Martha's Vineyard
SKIFF, James (-1688+) & Mary __?__ (-1673); b 1638; Lynn/Sandwich
SKIFF, James (1638-) & 1/wf Elizabeth NABOR/NEIGHBOR?/TABOR?; 18 Nov 1659, div 1670; Sandwich
SKIFF, James (1638-) & 2/wf Sarah BARNARD (?1648-1732); Mar 1677; Martha's Vineyard
SKIFF, Nathan (1658, 1655?-) & 1/wf Hepzibah [CODMAN] (-1696); ca 10 Jul 1678; Martha's Vineyard

SKIFF, Nathan (1655-1700), Chilmark & 2/wf Mercy **CHIPMAN** (1668/9-); 13 Dec 1699; Sandwich/Chilmark

SKIFF, Nathaniel (1645-1723, Windham) ("bro." of Thomas **WEST** 1698/9) & 1/wf Mary [**PARTRIDGE**], dau George; [?b 1679?], b 1669?; Sandwich

SKIFF, Nathaniel (1645-1723) & 2/wf Ruth [**WEST**] (1651-1741, Windham); aft 1683, b 1694; Falmouth, MA/Windham, CT

SKIFF, Stephen (1641-1710) & Lydia [**SNOW**] (ca 1639-1713, 1711, 1712) (had gr-dau Keziah _?_ b ca 1687-88); b 1666; Sandwich

SKIFF, Stephen (1685-) & Sarah **LOTHROP** (ca 1678-); b 1701?, prob aft 1705

SKIFT, Samuel & Elizabeth (?**WHITMAN**) [**EDENDEN/EDDENDEN**] (-1694, ae 88), w Edmund; 1630/40?; Charlestown

SKILLINGS, John & 1/wf Mary _?_; by 1673; Falmouth, ME

SKILLINGS, John (1644-1689) & 2/wf? Elizabeth [**INGERSOLL**], m/2 ?Elihu **GUNNISON** 1689, 1690; ca 1674/6?; Falmouth, ME

SKILLINGS, John (see Joseph) & Elizabeth _?_; b 1701?, b 1706; Portsmouth, NH/Boston

SKILLINGS, Joseph (see John) & Elizabeth _?_; b 1701?

SKILLEN, Thomas (-1667) & Deborah _?_, m/2 George **HADLEY** 1668; b 1640?, b 1643; Salem/Gloucester/Falmouth, ME

SKELLIN, Thomas (1643-1676, ?Wenham) & Mary [**LEWIS**] (1654-1732+), m/2 Jotham **LEWIS** by 1685, m/3 Henry **WILKINS**; 1671?; Salem/Gloucester

SKILLINGS, Thomas & Rebecca **STREETER**; 24 Dec 1698

SKILLION, Benjamin & Susanna _?_; b 1693; Ipswich

SKINNER, Abraham (1649-1726?, bef 1698?) & Hannah _?_ (-1726); b 1681; Malden

SKINNER, Abraham & Abigail [**CHAMBERLAIN**]; 20 Jun 1699; Lyme, CT

SKINNER, Christopher & Agnes _?_; b 1670; Boston

SKINNER, Francis & Mary _?_; b 1670; Boston

SKINNER, Gabriel & _?_; b 10 Nov 1660; Marblehead/Salem

SKINNER, James (1635-1701) & _?_; b 1656, b 1666?; Marblehead?

SKINNER, John (-1650) & Mary [**LOOMIS**] (?1620-1680), m/2 Owen **TUDOR** 1651; b 1638, b 1637?, b 1633; Hartford

SKINNER, John (1641-1690) & Mary [**EASTON**] (-1695); b 1664; Hartford

SKINNER, John & Elizabeth _?_; b 1666; Boston

SKINNER, John (1666, 1667?-1743) & Rachel **PRATT** (1671-1748); 22 Feb 1693, 1693/4; Hartford

SKINNER, John (1673-) & Sarah **GOVER/GLOVER/PORTER**? (1668?-1748), of Salem?; b 1697, bpt Wrentham; Boston

SKINNER, John (1675-1740) & Sarah [**PORTER**]; b 1697; Colchester, CT

SKINNER, Joseph (1643-1724) & Mary **FILLEY** (1651-1711?, 1734?); 5 Apr 1666; Windsor, CT

SKINNER, Joseph (1669-1748) & Mary **GRANT** (1676-1734, 1711?); 13 Mar 1694; Windsor, CT

SKINNER, Joseph & Elizabeth _?_; b 1696; Boston

SKINNER, Joseph & 1/wf Dorothy **HOSMER** (-1702); 1 Jan 1696; Hartford

SKINNER, Richard (-1727) & Alice **WOODS** (-1723); 30 Nov 1682; Marblehead

SKINNER, Richard & Rachel _?_; b 1687(8?); Boston

SKINNER, Richard & Thamasin (**SCARLET**) **TAYLOR**, w Joseph; 21 Apr 1692; Boston

SKINNER, Thomas[1] (1617-1704) & 1/wf Mary _?_ (-1671); in Eng, b 1645; Malden

SKINNER, Thomas (1645-) & Mary [**PRATT**] (1643-1704); b 1666; Charlestown

SKINNER, Thomas (1644-1690, ae 46) & 1/wf Mary **GOULD**; 22 Dec 1669; Charlestown

SKINNER, Thomas[1] (1617-1704) & 2/wf Lydia (**SHEPARDSON**) [**CALL**] (-1723), w Thomas; aft 9 Apr 1671, ca 1678; Charlestown

SKINNER, Thomas (ca 1644-1690) & 2/wf Elizabeth (**MAVERICK**) [**GRAFTON**] (1649-), w Nathaniel; ca 1676, ca 1677; Charlestown/Boston

SKINNER, Thomas (1668-) & Hannah [**CARPENTER**?]; b 1695; Wrentham

SKINNER, Walter (1630-) & Hannah _?_ (-1705+); b 1669(70?); Groton

SLACK, William (-1727) & Mary _?_ (-(17--?)); b 1683; Boston/Weymouth/Hingham/Attleboro

SLOUD, Joseph & Mercy **BUTTERWORTH** (1663/4-1711+), dau John, m/2 Samuel **THAYER** (no), m/3? _?_ **BLOOD** (prob error for **SLADE**); 12 Dec 1681; Swansea

SLADE, William & _?_; b 1659?; Newport

SLADE, William & Sarah [**HOLMES**] (1664-1761, ae 97); b 1689; Swansea

SLAFTER, John & _?_/?Elizabeth **BRADSTREET**; b 1688; ?Lynn/Mansfield, CT

SLATER/SLAUGHTER, John (-1713) & Abiah (GILLETT) [BARTLETT], w Isaiah; 15 Jul 1669, b 1669(70?); Windsor, CT/Simsbury, CT

SLATER, Leffelane/Loughlin & [Ruth] [DRAKE] (-1729+); b 1683, by 1682; Eastchester, NY

SLATTER, John (-1665) & Elizabeth _?_ ; b _?_ ; Marblehead

SLAUGHTER, ?George & [Elizabeth?] [GODDARD]; Pemaquid

SLAUGHTER, John (-1713) (see SLATER) & Abiah (GILLETT) BARTLETT, w Isaiah; 15 Jul 1669; Windsor, CT

SLAUGHTER, John & Mary [LIBBY]; [b 1690], b 1682?; Lynn/Mansfield, CT/Wallingford

SLAWSON, Eleazer & 1/wf Mary [CHAPMAN]; by 1672; Stamford, CT

SLAWSON, Eleazer & Susannah [?BELDING], ?m/2 Samuel HOYT 1700; [by 1680?]; Stamford, CT

SLASON, George (-1695) & 1/wf _?_ ; ca 1637?; Lynn/Sandwich/Stamford, CT

SLAWSON, George (-1695) & 2/wf Mary (WILLIAMS) JENNINGS (-1697±), w Joshua; 16 Dec 1686; Fairfield, CT

SLASON, John (?1641-1706) & 1/wf Sarah TUTTLE (1642-1676, murdered); 17 Nov 1663, 19? Nov, ?22 Nov; New Haven

SLAWSON, John & 2/wf Elizabeth [BENEDICT] (-1690+); aft 12 Nov 1676, by 1679; Stamford, CT

SLAWSON, John (-1706) & 3/wf Hannah (PUNDERSON) [GIBBS] (1642-1716), w John; aft 1690; Stamford, CT

SLASON, John, Jr. (1664-1745) & [Mary HOLMES]; b 1693(4?), b 1704, b 1699; Stamford, CT

SLASON, Jonathan (1670-) & Mary WATERBURY (1679-1710); 4 Feb 1699/1700; Stamford, CT

SLAWSON/CLAWSON, Josiah & Mary WILLIAMSON; 10 Mar 1678/9, 12? Mar; Marshfield

SLEEPER, Aaron (1661-) & [Elizabeth SHAW] (1664-1708); b 1686, b 1684, 23 May 1682; Salisbury/Hampton, NH

SLEEPER, Thomas (1616?-1696) & [Joanna] [LEE?] (1623-1703, Kingston, NH); b 1648, b 1658; Haverhill/Hampton, NH

SLEG, Christopher (-1697) & 1/wf Elizabeth _?_ (-10 Aug 1696); Boston

SLEG, Christopher (-1697) & 2/wf Susannah (HUDSON) (HOWLETT) PERKINS, w John, w Edmund; m int 30 Oct 1696; Boston

SLOAN, Thomas & Elizabeth [PALMER], m/2 William CHAPMAN 1677; b 1663, no issue; Stonington, CT

SLOCUM, Anthony (?1590-1690) & _?_ [HARVEY] (?1610-); b 1635?; Taunton/Albemarle Co., NC

SLOCUM, Ebenezer (1650-1715) & Mary [THURSTON] (1657-1732); b 1678; Portsmouth, RI/Jamestown, RI

SLOCUM, Eliezer (1664-1727) & Eliphal [FITZGERALD] (-1748); b 1689; Portsmouth RI/Dartmouth

SLOCUM, Giles (?1623-1683) & Joan [COOK?] (-1679); b 1642; Taunton/Portsmouth, RI

SLOCUM, Giles (1647-) & Anne [LAWTON]; 26 May 1669; Portsmouth, RI/Newport

SLOCUM, John (1645-1702) & Meribah [PARKER] (-1698+); bef 1674, no issue; Portsmouth, RI/NJ

SLOCUM, Nathaniel (1652-1703) & Hannah [TUCKER] (-1702+); b 1682; Portsmouth, RI/Shrewsbury, NJ

SLOCUM, Peleg (1654-1733) & Mary [HOLDER] (1661-1737); b 1681, 1680±; Portsmouth, RI/Dartmouth

SLOCUM, Samuel (1657±-) & _?_ ; living in 1681

SLOO/SLUE, Leonard & Tabitha _?_ ; b 1695; Beverly

SLEW/SLOW?, Tho & Elizabeth PAULMER/PAUME; 2 Jun 1665 m int, 2 Jun 1655 m int; Providence

SLOPER, John (-1693) & Sarah _?_ , m/2 Moses WORCESTER 1695; Kittery, ME

SLOPER, Richard (1630-1719, 1713?, 1716, ae 85 (no)) & Mary SHERBURN (1640-1718); 21 Oct 1658; ?Portsmouth, NH

SLOTH, John & Sarah _?_ ; b 1670; Boston

SLOW, Philip & Barbara HITCHEL; 24 Feb 1697; Boston

SLOW/SLOUGH, William & Elizabeth [PRUDDEN] (-1668), m/2 Roger PRITCHARD 1653; [1643], b 1648, b 1649(50?), by 1647; Milford, CT/New Haven

SLOWMAN, Symon & Hannah _?_ ; b 1691; Newbury

SLUMAN, Thomas & Sarah [BLISS] (1647-1730), m/2 Solomon TRACY 1686; - Dec 1668, 16?
   Dec 1668; Norwich, CT
SLY, Stephen (-1707) & Experience ABBEY; 10 Jul 1700; Providence, RI
SMALE, Benjamin & Martha FISK; - Jan 1671; Salem
SMALLEY, Benjamin (1669?-1721, Lebanon, CT) & Rebecca [SNOW] (1676-1753), m/2 John
   PORTER 1728; b 1695; Eastham
SMALL, Daniel (1672±?-1729+) & _?_ ; b 1695?; ME/Truro
SMALE, Edward[1] & Elizabeth _?_ ; in Eng, ca 1624; ME
SMALL, Edward[3] (?1654-1702) & Mary [WOODMAN] (-1742+); ca 1680/2?; Dover, NH/Chatham
SMALL, Francis (1625-1712+) & Elizabeth _?_ (1634-1712+); ca 1650; Kittery, ME
SMALE, Francis (1659?-1710) & Elizabeth [HICKS?] (had grandson Hix SMALLEY); b 1685?;
   ME/Truro
SMALL, John[1] & Ann [?GROVE] (1616-); b 1636; Salem
SMALEY, John (-1692) & Ann WALDEN (-1694); 29 Nov 1638; Plymouth/Eastham/Piscataway, NJ
SMALE, Joseph (-1676) & Lydia BUXTON (-1708+), m/2 Joseph HUTCHINSON 1678/[9?]; 26
   Dec 1672; Salem
SMALL, Robert & _?_ FARNS/FERNS, w John; b 1701?; Norwalk
SMALL, Samuel (?1666-) & Elizabeth (HEARD) [CHADBURNE], w James; aft 1686, bef 1695,
   bef 28 Aug 1688; Kittery, ME
SMALE, Stephen & Hannah SIBLEY; 25 Feb 1676/7; Salem
SMALE, Thomas (-1676) & Ruth CANTLEBURY/CANTERBURY, m/2 William SIBLEY 1676, m/3
   Alexander OSBORN 1692; 15 Mar 1662/3; Salem
SMALLBENT, Mark (-1696) & Mary BELLES; 12 Jul 1689; Norwich, CT
SMALEDGE/SMALLEDGE, William & Mary _?_ ; b 1653; Boston
SMALLAGE, William & Martha _?_ ; b 1686/7; Boston
SMALLPEICE/SMALLPIECE, John & Olive FURNEL; 7 Apr 1699; Boston
SMART, Francis (-1750) & Mary [CROCKETT]; b 1701?; Kittery, ME
SMART, John (-bef 1652) & Margaret _?_ (-1654+); ca 1630?, b 1635; Hingham/Exeter, NH
SMART, Robert & _?_ ; by 1654, b 1646; Exeter, NH
SMART, Robert, Jr. (1646-1703) & 1/wf Elnell/Hellena/Eleanor PRATTY/PRATLY; 25 Sep 1674;
   Exeter, NH
SMART, Robert (-1703) & 2/wf Rebecca [?HILTON]; b 1701?, b 1685; Exeter, NH
SMART, Robert & Mary _?_ ; b 1701?; Exeter, NH
SMEAD, Ebenezer (-1753) & Esther [CATLIN] (-1733); b 1695; Deerfield
SMEAD, John & 1/wf Anna WELD (-1712); 22 Nov 1699; Deerfield
SMEAD, Samuel (-1731) & 1/wf Mary PRICE; 17 Mar 1698/9; Deerfield
SMEAD, William (-d in Eng) & Judith (STOUGHTON) [DENMAN] (-1639), w John; b 1635;
   Deerfield
SMEAD, William (?1635-) & Elizabeth LAWRENCE (bpt 1642-1704); 31 Dec 1658; Dorchester/
   Northampton
SMEDLEY, Baptist (-1675) & Katherine (_?_) SHORTHOSE/SHORTHOUSE, w Robert; 27 Mar
   1645; Concord
SMEDLEY, James (1650-1724) & Mary BARRET/BARRETT (ca 1651-); 4 Dec 1671; Concord
SMEDLEY, John & Ann _?_ (-1697); b 1646; Concord
SMEDLEY, John & Sarah WHEELER; 5 May 1669; Concord
SMEDLEY, Samuel (-1675) & Hannah WHEELER; 11 Jul 1667; Concord
SMEDLEY, Samuel & 1/wf Abigail DIMON/DIMOND; 30 Nov 1700; Stratfield, CT
SMITH, Abraham & _?_/Jane _?_ ; b 1641; New Haven/?Hempstead, LI/Jamaica, LI
SMITH, Abraham (-1683) & Martha _?_ , m/2 Mark Athy 1685; b 1667; Charlestown
SMITH, Abraham & Hope STOW (1656-Nov 1678); 15 Feb 1678, 1677/8, 1677, 13? Feb;
   Middletown, CT
SMITH, Abraham & Mary PERKINS; 25 Apr 1694; Topsfield
SMITH, Abraham (-1696) & Mary _?_ ; b 1696, ?much earlier; Boston
SMITH, Abraham (-bef 1712) & Anna [?LANE], m/2 _?_ BASSETT; White Plains, NY
SMITH, Alexander & Mary _?_ ; b 1688; Jamaica, LI
SMITH, Amos (?1622-1712) & 1/wf Mary [?MOSS] (& 2/wf? Mary ROE);? ca 1694; Jamaica, LI
SMITH, Andrew & Mary BUNDEY/BUNDY (1653-); 5 Jan 1673; Taunton
SMITH, Andrew (1670-1727) & Sarah TOMLISON; 21 May 1696; Derby, CT
SMITH, Armstrong & Mehitable[3] [COFFIN]; ?b 1701; Nantucket

SMITH, Arthur (-1655) & Margaret _?_ (-1692?, 1693?), m/2 Joseph NASH, m/3 Stephen HART; b 1644/[5?]; Hartford
SMITH, Arthur & _?_; b 1659?, b 1650, (earlier?); Southold, LI/Brookhaven, LI
SMITH, Arthur & Sarah [?HUDSON]; b 1677; Boston
SMITH, Arthur (-1712, 1713) & Sarah [NEWELL] (1655-); b 1684; Hartford
SMITH, Arthur (-1713) & 2/wf Phebe _?_; b 1701; Hartford
SMITH, Asahel & Mary _?_; b 1671; Dedham
SMITH, Asahel & Elizabeth [?BREWER] (1661-), ?dau Nathaniel; ca 1677/80; Dedham/?Boston
SMITH, Bartholomew & Jane _?_, m/2 Edward ROUSE, m/3 Robert COE; b 1657?; Huntington, LI
SMITH, Benjamin & Mary CLARKE, dau Rowland; 10 Aug 1641; Dedham/Boston
SMITH, Benjamin & Martha _?_; b 27 Jun 1650; Essex Co, MA/?Lynn
SMITH, Benjamin (1631±-1713) & Lydia [CARPENTER] (1638-1711); b 1660; Providence/Warwick
SMITH, Benjamin & 1/wf Mary BALDWIN (1643-1680); 21 Oct 1660, 24 Oct, 26 Oct; Milford, CT/Huntington, LI
SMITH, Benjamin (1637-1691) & Jehoidan PALFREY (-1662); 27 Mar 1661; Reading
SMITH, Benjamin & Hannah _?_; b 1663; Boston
SMITH, Benjamin (1658-) & 1/wf Ruth [LOOMIS] (1660-1725); b 1682; Farmington, CT/Westfield, MA
SMITH, Benjamin (-1700+) & 2/wf Sarah (PHIPPEN) HOUGHTON (1649-), w Robert; 9 Feb 1682; Milford, CT
SMITH, Benjamin & _?_; b 1683 (?); Brookhaven, LI
SMITH, Benjamin (?1658-1720) & Jedidah [MAYHEW] (1666-1736); ca 1684; Martha's Vineyard
SMITH, Benjamin & Elizabeth _?_; b 1685[6?]; Sandwich
SMITH, Benjamin (-1723+) & Sarah GALE; m cont 3 Feb 1686, 1685/6; Jamaica, LI
SMITH, Benjamin & Hannah [TITUS] (1667-); ca 1687?; Hempstead, LI
SMITH, Benjamin & Phebe ARNOLD; 25 Dec 1691; Warwick, RI
SMITH, Benjamin (1672±-1751) & 1/wf Mary ANGELL (1675-1721); 12 Apr 1693; Providence
SMITH, Benjamin (-1764) & 1/wf [?Elizabeth WELLES]; b 1697; Haddam, CT
SMITH, Benjamin (ca 1655-1731) & 1/wf ?[Dorothy BENTON] (-by 1704); ca 1700; Wethersfield, CT/Glastonbury, CT
SMITH, Benjamin (1673-) & Ruth BUCK (1681-); 14 Mar 1699/1700; Wethersfield, CT
SMITH, Benjamin & Sarah PEABODY; 22 Oct 1700, 22 May 1700; Salem
SMITH, Benjamin & Sarah [?TOWNSEND]; b 1701?; ?Oyster Bay, LI
SMITH, Bryant (-1711) & Abigail [MORSE]; b 1688; Boston
SMITH, Chileab (1635±-1731) & Hannah HITCHCOCK (1645-1733); 2 Oct 1661; Wethersfield, CT
SMITH, Christopher (-1676) & Alice _?_ (-1681+); ca 1630-1; Providence
SMITH, Christopher (-1676) & Mary (FAIRBANKS) METCALF (1622-1684), w Michael; 2 Aug 1654; Dedham
SMITH, Christopher & Dorcas _?_; b 1672/[3?]; Boston
SMITH, Christopher & Mary _?_/Elizabeth ARNOLD?/Amity HARRIS? (-1726+), m _?_ MORSE; ca 1696; Providence
SMITH, Cornelius (1675-) & _?_ [CHICESTER], dau James; b 1701?; Queens Village, LI
SMITH, Daniel (-1650, 1660?) & Elizabeth [ROGERS] (1617-) (dau Thomas & Grace); b 1642; Watertown
SMITH, Daniel (-1692) & Esther CHICKERING (1643-1682); 20 Oct 1659; Rehoboth
SMITH, Daniel (1642-1681) & Mary GRANT; 22 Feb 1667/8, 27? Feb; Watertown
SMITH, Daniel (-1707) & Elizabeth WADLEN/WADLAND, w Crispen; 2 Jan 1671/[2]; Charlestown
SMITH, Daniel & Mary YOUNG; 3 Mar 1676/[7], 3 May 1676; Eastham
SMITH, Daniel (ca 1648-1740) & Hannah [KNAPP] (1660-1721?); ca 1678-9, 1675?; Greenwich, CT/Stamford, CT
SMITH, Daniel (ca 1663/4-1754) & Abigail [?BAYLESS]; ca 1688-92; Jamaica, LI
SMITH, Daniel (1656-1713±) & 1/wf Ruth [TOOKER]/[TOSKIN]?; b 1690
SMITH, Daniel & Hannah COOLIDGE, m/2 Nathan FISKE; 3 Nov 1693; Watertown
SMITH, Daniel (1673-1724) & Abigail PRESTON (-1732); 23 Jun 1696; Rehoboth
SMITH, Daniel & Ann MOORE; 12 Mar 1697/8

SMITH, Daniel & Ruhamah (JOHNSON) HAWKINS, w Timothy; 18 Jun 1700; Watertown/Smithtown, NY

SMITH, David (?1664-bef 1704) & _?_ ; ?East Haddam, CT

SMITH, Deliverance (-1729) & Mary [TRIPP]; b 1692; Dartmouth

SMITH, Dermit/Deuremont (see Jeremiah)

SMITH, Ebenezer (1653-1714) & Mary _?_ ; b 1686; New Haven

SMITH, Ebenezer (1668-1716) & Abigail BROUGHTON/BOUGHTON? (1670-); Oct 1691; Hadley/Norwalk, CT

SMITH, Ebenezer & Sarah (HUXLEY) [BARLOW], w James, m/3 Martin KELLOGG 1732; ca 1693; Northampton/Hadley/Suffield, CT

SMITH, Ebenezer (1675±-) & Clement [DENTON], m/2 John GREGORY; ca 1699?, 1700±; Jamaica, LI

SMITH, Edward & _?_ ; in Eng, b 1629; Weymouth/Rehoboth/Newport, RI

SMITH, Edward (-1703) & Amphillis ANGELL; 27 Apr 1663, 9 May 1663; Providence

SMITH, Edward (ca 1637-1689) & Elizabeth BLISS (1645-1689); 7 Jun 1663; New London, CT

SMITH, Edward (-1689+) & Mary HALL; 13 Jan 1668/9; Exeter, NH

SMITH, Edward & Mary _?_ ; b 1680; Boston

SMITH, Edward (1654-) & Sarah ALLEN; 21 Apr 1685; Deerfield, MA/Suffield, CT

SMITH, Edward (-1730) & 1/wf Elizabeth [LAWTON] (1675-1711); b 1699; Newport, RI

SMITH, Edward (-1726) & Mercy [MOWRY], m/2 William HALL 1741; b 1701?; Providence

SMITH, Eliezer & Ruth SPRAGUE (1658-); 12 Oct 1680; Dartmouth

SMITH, Elisha (-1676±) & Mary [BARKER/BACKER?] (1649-1723), m/2 Israel ARNOLD 1677; ?ca 1669, no issue; Newport, RI

SMITH, Elisha (-1714) & Elizabeth WHEELOCK; 15 Jan 1699/1700; Medfield/Windham, CT

SMITH, Elisha (1680-) & Experience [MOWRY]; 1700?, 1701?; Providence/Smithfield, RI

SMITH, Eluzar/Eluzer & Rebecca [ROWLAND]; ca 1685?; Fairfield, CT/Fairfield, NJ

SMITH, Ephraim (1644-1712) & Abigail [BRISCOE]?; ca 1666?; ?Milford, CT/Derby, CT

SMITH, Ephraim & Rachel COLE; Apr 1686; Farmington, CT

SMITH, Ephraim (-1712) & Susanna _?_ , m/2 _?_ SAMPSON; ?ca 1693; Derby, CT

SMITH, Ephraim (1663-) & Mary RAMSDELL (1674/5-); 6 Sep 1694; Boxford

SMITH, Ephraim & [?Sarah PERRY]; b 1695; Topsfield

SMITH, Francis (-1650) & Alice _?_ (-1650+, 1667, ae 84?); b 1621; Watertown/Reading

SMITH, Francis & Elizabeth _?_ ; aft 1630, b 1636?; Roxbury/Boston

SMITH, Francis (?1619-) & 1/wf Agnes _?_ (-1665/6); b 1639; Hingham/Taunton

SMITH, Francis & 2/wf Sarah _?_ ; aft 1666, by 1679; Taunton

SMITH, Francis (1658-1744, ae 86) & Ruth MAVERICK (-1717); 1 Mar 1679/80; Reading

SMITH, Francis (-1687?) & Mary [LONG] (1668-), m/2 John ATWOOD 1690; b 1688; Charlestown/Boston

SMITH, Francis (1657-1739) & Mary _?_ ; ca 1690/3; Lyme, CT

SMITH, Francis & Mary _?_ ; ca 1692; Boston

SMITH, George (ca 1637-) (did he have 2/wf Rachel in 1699?) & _?_ ; Salem

SMITH, George (-1662) & Sarah _?_ (-1680+, 1686+), m/2 John JACKSON 1668; b 1642; New Haven

SMITH, George (-1674) & Mary [FRENCH] (1624-) (dau Thomas & Susan); b 1644; ?Salem/Ipswich

SMITH, George & Jane _?_ ; ca 1670?

SMITH, George (-1744) & Hannah [GASKELL] (1669-); b 1691; Salem

SMITH, George (-1724) & Rachel (ROOD) BLAKE; b 1696; New London, CT/?Lyme

SMITH, Gershom (-1718) & Rebecca RIPLEY (1674-); 6 Jun 1695; Dartmouth

SMITH, Gershom & Hannah [JUDD] (1681-); b 1701?; Glastonbury, CT

SMITH, Giles (-1669) & 1/wf _?_ ; ca 1625/30?; Hartford/New London, CT

SMITH, Giles (-1669) & 2/wf Eunice [PORTER], wid?; ca 1660; Hartford/etc.

SMITH, Hazadiah (1657-1735) & Hannah GROVER; 27 May 1684; Beverly

SMITH, Henry (1588-1648) & _?_ ; ca 1620?; Wethersfield, CT

SMITH, Henry (-1649) (called Thomas COOPER "brother") & Judith _?_ (-1650); ca 1624; Hingham/Rehoboth

SMITH, Henry & Elizabeth _?_ ; b 1634?; Dedham/Medfield

SMITH, Henry (-1682 in Eng) (son of Mrs. Elizabeth SANFORD) & Ann [PYNCHON]; prob by 1635; Springfield

SMITH, Henry (1588, ca 1600-1648) & 2/wf Dorothy __?__ (ca 1590-1694), m/2 John RUSSELL 1649; ca 1636?, 1635?; Wethersfield, CT
SMITH, Henry (-1687) & 1/wf __?__ ; b 1645?; Stamford, CT
SMITH, Henry (-1655) & __?__ ; say ca 1650?; Rowley
SMITH, Henry (-1676?) & Elizabeth COOPER (-1690?); 29 Nov 1657; Rehoboth
SMITH, Henry (-1687) & 2/wf Ann [ANDREWS?] (-1685); ca 1664
SMITH, Henry (-1720, ae 75) & Lydia BUCKE; 3 Mar 1672/3; Cambridge/Lexington
SMITH, Henry (-1681) & Sarah ANDREWS; ca 1673; Hartford
SMITH, Henry (1644-) & __?__ ; b 1688; New Dartmouth
SMITH, Henry (-1702) & Mary [BROOKS]?/HUNGERFORD?; 15 Feb 1689; Lyme, CT
SMITH, Henry & Sarah FLOOD; m int 24 Jun 1696; Boston
SMITH, Henry & Anne __?__ ; b 1701?, b 7 Sep 1707; St. George's Manor, LI
SMITH, Hezekiah (1655?-) & Mary __?__ (1661?-); b 1682; Dartmouth
SMITH, Hugh (-1656) & Mary __?__ , m/2 Jeremiah ELLSWORTH 1657; b 1642; Rowley
SMITH, Ichabod (1660-1722) & __?__ ; ca 1685(?); Martha's Vineyard/Woodbridge, NJ/Barnstable, MA
SMITH, Ichabod & Mary [HUXLEY]; b 1693/[4?], 1692?; Hadley
SMITH, Ichabod (1675-1746) & Elizabeth COOK (1678-1751); 19 Jul 1698, 9 Jul; Hadley/Deerfield
SMITH, Isaac & Elizabeth [UNDERHILL] (1669-); b 1690
SMITH, Israel (1671-1723) & Hannah __?__ ; b 1701(?); Exeter, NH
SMITH, Jacob & Sarah __?__ ; b 1690; Sudbury
SMITH, Jacob (1673-) & Priscilla [ROGERS]; b 1701(?), b 12 Jan 1701/2; Kittery, ME
SMITH, Jacob (1674-) & Rebecca [SYMONDS] (1679-); b 1701(?); Boxford/Topsfield
SMITH, James (-1661, Marblehead) & Mary __?__ (-1662, 1663); in Eng, b 1625; Marblehead/Gloucester
SMITH, James (-1676) & Joane __?__ (-1676+); b 1635(?); Weymouth
SMITH, James & __?__ ; b 1644; Boston/Barbados
SMITH, James (-1662) & Martha __?__ , m/2 Richard OWEN; by 1642?, by 1646?; Smithtown, LI/Newtown, LI
SMITH, James & Elizabeth __?__ , m/2 Richard HAMMOND 1667?, m/3 John ROWDEN 1677+); b 1648; ME/Woolwich, ME
SMITH, James (ca 1634-1692) & 1/wf __?__ (-1659); ca 1658; Weymouth
SMITH, James (ca 1634-1692) & 2/wf Mary BRANDON (?1638-1748+); 11 Nov 1659; Weymouth
SMITH, James (-1674+) & __?__ ; b 1661; Marblehead?
SMITH, James (1645-1690) & Sarah COKER (1643-); 26 Jul 1667; Newbury
SMITH, James (-1687?) & Martha [MILLS] (1653-), m/2 Christopher GRANT; by 25 Apr 1671; Wells, ME/Berwick, ME
SMITH, James (-1690) & Sarah [DAVIS] (1649-1694); b 1672; Dover, NH
SMITH, James (-1703) & Margaret [PHILLIPS] (-1704+); b 1676(?); Salem/Damariscotta, ME
SMITH, James (-1678) & Mary FOSTER, m/2 Timothy PHILLIPS; 8 Aug 1676; Charlestown
SMITH, James (-1701) & Hannah GOODENOW (1657-); 25 Mar 1680; Sudbury
SMITH, James & Mary __?__ ; b 1684; Beverly/?Danvers
SMITH, James (-1693) (will 1690, 4 ch) & __?__ WOOD?/CONKLIN; ca 1682; Huntington, LI
SMITH, James & Mary (TRUMBULL) ADAMS, w Thomas, m/3 Thomas WALKER; b 1687; Boston
SMITH, James, Boston & Prudence HARRISON, Boston; 26 Apr 1688; Watertown/Boston
SMITH, James & Elizabeth HOLBROOK (1673-); 10 Nov 1691; Weymouth
SMITH, James (-1700, Lancaster) & Hannah (PENDLETON) BUSH RUTTER (1655-), w John, w John, m/4 Joseph WATERS, m/5 Zachariah MAYNARD 1721; 5 May 1693; Sudbury
SMITH, James & Martha [BRAGDON]; by 1694, Jul 1693; York, ME
SMITH, James & Jane [KENT]; ca 1695; Newbury
SMITH, James & Elizabeth SMITH; 26 Oct 1698; Hadley
SMITH, James & Mary __?__ ; b 1700; Canterbury, CT
SMITH, James & Elizabeth SOUTHER; 28 Nov 1700; Boston
SMITH, James (-1714, ca 52) & Mary (NOYES) [MUNJOY], w George; prob 1700; Sudbury/Roxbury
SMITH, James & Rachel __?__ ; b 1701?; ?Lyme, CT
SMITH, Jasper (-1696) (3 ch) & Margery __?__ ; b 1690?; Flushing, LI

SMITH, Jeremiah/Deuremont/Dermit & Abigail __?__ (-1720/1?), m/2 Zachariah EDDY aft 1692; b 1670; Milton/Swansea

SMITH, Jeremiah (-1720) & Mary GEREARDY (-1722+); 2 Jan 1672; Warwick, RI/Prudence Isl./Portsmouth, RI

SMITH, Jeremiah (-1706) & Hannah ATWOOD (1649-1729); 3 Jan 1677; Eastham

SMITH, Jeremiah (-1726) & Ann __?__; b 1689/90; Huntington, LI/Hempstead, LI

SMITH, Jeremiah & Mary __?__; b 1698; Boston

SMITH, Jeremiah & Ann PEATHER; 21 Dec 1699; Boston

SMITH, Job (-1719+) & Elizabeth [THOMPSON] (1658±-); b 1700

SMITH, John & Isabelle __?__ (-1639, ae 60); in Eng, b 1605; Watertown

SMITH, John (Rock) & __?__; in Eng, b 1615?, b 1630; Hempstead, LI/Stamford, CT

SMITH, John (-1669) & 1/wf Alice __?__ (1595-1629?); in Eng, b 1617; Lancaster

SMITH, John (-1674), tailor & Mercy __?__; in Eng, ca 1620; Boston

SMITH, John (1595-1648±), miller & Alice __?__ (-1650); in Eng, b 1621; Providence

SMITH, John (-1643) (called "Blue") & Jane? __?__, m/2 Edward ROUSE, m/3 Robert COE lic 15 Feb 1674/5; ca 1623/25?, ca 1633?; Taunton/Mespet, LI

SMITH, John (-1669?) & Mary __?__ (-1659); aft 1629; Lancaster

SMITH, John (-1618), Quartermaster & 1/wf Mary [?RYDER]; in Eng, b 1630; Dorchester

SMITH, John (-1663) & Ann COLLINS (-1678, Warwick, RI), wid; prob aft 1630; Providence

SMITH, John & Dorothy __?__; b 1630?, by 1636; Dorchester

SMITH, John & Joanna __?__ (1614-1687), wid; prob aft 1634; Boston

SMITH, John, mason & 1/wf __?__; b 1635, prob b 1630, prob earlier, say by 1625; Providence

SMITH, John & Bennett MOORECOCK; 7 Dec 1638; [Plymouth]

SMITH, John (-1674) & Deborah [PARKHURST] (?1619-1670+); ca 1638/40; Watertown/Hampton, NH/Martha's Vineyard

SMITH, John & Mary [ELIOT] (1622-) (no, should be Lydia ELIOT ca 1654); ?ca 1642?; Dedham

SMITH, John (-1684) & Grace HAWLEY? (-1689, 1690?); 1642, 1643?; Milford, CT

SMITH, Rev.? John & Susannah HINCKLEY; 13 Jun 1643; Barnstable

SMITH, John & Margaret __?__; b 1644 (doubtful); Dedham

SMITH, John (-1695) & Sarah WOODWARD; 8 May 1645; Hingham

SMITH, John (-1673) & Sarah __?__ (-1687); b 1646; Charlestown

SMITH, John & 1/wf Joan __?__ (?wid); b 1646; Cape Neddick

SMITH, John (-1678), Quartermaster & 2/wf Katherine __?__; b 1642?, b 1655; Dorchester

SMITH, John (1621-1706) & Catherine MORRILL (-1662); 1 Aug 1647; Roxbury/Reading/Boston

SMITH, John (1622±-1687) & Sarah HUNT; 13 Oct 1647; Sudbury

SMITH, John (1618-1692) & 1/wf Deborah HOWLAND (-1665); 4 Jan 1648/9; Plymouth/Dartmouth

SMITH, John (-1687) & Elizabeth __?__ (-1706+); ca 1650?; Providence

SMITH, John (-1710+) & [?Sarah STICKLAND]; ca 1650?; Hempstead, LI

SMITH, John (ca 1626-1694) & 1/wf Anna [GILDERSLEEVE] (ca 1627-), dau Richard; ca 1650?, ca 1646?; Nantucket/Hempstead, LI

SMITH, John (-bef 1677) & Margaret __?__, m/2 John SNOOK; ca 1650; Portsmouth, RI/Prudence Isl. RI

SMITH, John & Martha __?__ (prob COOLEY); b 1654; Ipswich

SMITH, John (-1678), Quartermaster & 2/wf Katherine __?__; by 1654; Dorchester

SMITH, John (-1660, 1694, 1668?), mason & 1/wf Anne [COMSTOCK], w Samuel; 1656±; Providence/Hempstead

SMITH, John & 1/wf Lydia [ELIOT] (1631-Jul 1672) (not Mary ELIOT ca 1642) (?Jael PACKARD 1672, 2/wf?); prob 1657, 1656?; Dedham/Medfield/Taunton

SMITH, John (-1661) & Faith PARROT, m/2 William LAW 1666; 24 Feb 1657/[8]; Rowley

SMITH, John (-1672) & Elizabeth [GOODALE], m/2 William BENNETT 1675; ca 1657-8; Salem

SMITH, John (-1676?, 1682) & Miriam [?DEAN] (1633-1706), m/2 Ellis WOOD; ca 1657-8; Boston/?Dorchester

SMITH, John (-1680) & Margaret [?THOMPSON] (-1678/9) (prob not BUFFUM); b 4 Jul 1659; Salem

SMITH, John & Rebecca [PAGE]; ca 1659(?); Salem

SMITH, John (-1682) & Sarah [WHIPPLE] (1642-1687); ca 1660; Providence, RI

SMITH, John & Barbara [CLARK], w Edward; aft 17 Sep 1661; ?Cape Porpoise

SMITH, John (-1691/2) & Elizabeth [TISDALL] (-1687, ae 40), m/2 _?_ JONES?; b 1663; Taunton

SMITH, John (-1706, ae 85) & 2/wf Martha BELL (?1645-1694, ae 48); 6 Jan 1662, 1662/3; Reading/Boston

SMITH, John, Quartermaster & Katherine [PELTON] (1620-1710), wid; b 1665, prob b Jun 1661, b 1655?; Dorchester

SMITH, John (ca 1637-1676) & Mary PARTRIDGE (-1683), m/2 Peter MONTAGUE 1679; 12 Nov 1663; Hatfield

SMITH, John & Mary BEACH (BEERS wrong) (1641-); 12 Apr 1665, 1664; Watertown

SMITH, John & 1/wf Sarah FOWLER (-1694); 19 Jul 1665; New Haven/Milford, CT

SMITH, John (1618-1692) & 2/wf Ruhamah [KIRBY] (-1707+); ca 1665-6; Dartmouth

SMITH, John & Huldah HUSSEY; 26 Feb 1666/7; Hampton, NH

SMITH, John (1644-) & Hannah WILLIAMS, m/2 Thomas MULFORD; 24 May 1667, 24 May 1670; Eastham

SMITH, John & Rebecca POORE; 26 Nov 1667; Newbury

SMITH, John & Mary ELDRIDGE; 30 Nov 1668?, "last of Nov"; Eastham

SMITH, John & Abigail DIXEY; 25 Feb 1669/70; Salem

SMITH, John & Sarah (RUGGLES) [WILMOT] (1645-), w John; 1670, aft 19 Apr; Boston

SMITH, John (-1694) & 2/wf Elizabeth (WICKES) [TOWNSEND], w Richard; aft 8 Apr 1671; ?Hempstead, LI

SMITH, John (1647-1711) & Grace WINSTON (1654-1695); 24 Oct 1672; New Haven

SMITH, John (-1691/2) & 2/wf? Jael PACKARD/PARKER (1651-), Bridgewater; 15 Nov 1672; Taunton

SMITH, John (-bef 12 Jan 1691/2) (had son Nicholas JONES b 21 Feb 1672/3, 1672) & 2/wf? _?_ JONES; aft 21 Feb 1672/3; Taunton

SMITH, John & Mary HAUGH (?1655-); by 1673; Boston

SMITH, John (1646-1732) & Phebe CANFIELD (1656-1730); 23 Jan 1672/3; Milford, CT

SMITH, John & _?_ ; b 1674?, b 1667?; York/Gloucester

SMITH, John (-1730) & Phillis GEREARDY (1654-1729+); ca 1674?; South Kingston, RI/Portsmouth/Prudence Isl. RI

SMITH, John (-1691) & 1/wf Abigail CARTER (1650-1676); 7 May 1674; Woburn

SMITH, John & 1/wf Rebecca ADAMS (-1675); 14 May 1675; Hampton, NH

SMITH, John & 2/wf Rebecca MARSTON; 3 Aug 1676, 23 Aug 1676; Hampton, NH

SMITH, John & Sarah PRENTICE (-1723), dau Henry, m/2 John WOODWARD 1699; 8 Jun 1676; Cambridge/Lexington

SMITH, John (-1691) & 2/wf Mary ORNE/HORNE (-1691); 22 Oct 1677; Charlestown/Salem

SMITH, John, York & Mary (FARROW) [CLARK], w Edward; ca 1677-79, (betw 13 Sep 1677 & 29 Mar 1679); ?Portsmouth, NH

SMITH, John & Susanna _?_ ; b 1678; b 1678 Portsmouth, RI/Newport/?Bristol, RI 1686

SMITH, John & Abigail DAY (1661-); 21 Dec 1677; Dedham

SMITH, John (1654-1737) & Elizabeth SMITH (-1736, ae 83); 13 Nov 1678; Ipswich

SMITH, John (-1683) & Mary (SMITH) TREAT [WRIGHT], w Matthias, w Anthony; aft 4 Dec 1679; Wethersfield, CT

SMITH, John (1653-1729) & 1/wf [Hannah] PARK (1658-1713, 1714); 6 Apr 1680; Hingham/Roxbury

SMITH, John & _?_ [MILLS]; bef 22 Jan 1682/3; Jamaica, LI

SMITH, John (1659-1727) & Mary _?_ (1661-1750); ?ca 1683; Middleborough

SMITH, John & Susannah MARYS; 1683, in Eng; NJ

SMITH, John, Haddam & Sarah [WHITE] (1663/4-, Middletown, CT); ?ca 1683; ?Middletown

SMITH, John (1661-1727) & Joanna KELLOGG (1664-); 29 Nov 1683; Hadley

SMITH, John (-?1688) & Sarah DODD; 18 Feb 1683/4; Marblehead

SMITH, John (1656-) & Mary [TINKER]; 26 Oct 1685; Lyme, CT

SMITH, John & Jane [INGLES], m/2 John STEVENS; b 1686; Boston

SMITH, John & Rebecca _?_ ; b 1686; Brookhaven, LI

SMITH, John (-1727) & Mary ?ELLINGWOOD/?HERRICK; b 1686; Beverly

SMITH, John & Mary ROOT; 23 Feb 1686, 1686/7?; Westfield/Hadley

SMITH, John (-1711) & 1/wf Elizabeth _?_ (-1703); b 1687; Stamford, CT

SMITH, John (-1737) & Hannah _?_ (-1756); ?ca 1687; Providence

SMITH, John & Ann _?_ ; b 1688; Boston

SMITH, John & 2/wf Damaris [**BABBITT**] (1663-1689); prob 1688; Taunton
SMITH, John (-1690) & Elizabeth [**JENNINGS**] (1662-1690); prob 1688; Fairfield, CT
SMITH, John & Abigail _?_ ; prob 1688; Gloucester
SMITH, John & Ann **SKERRY** (1669-); 6 Feb 1689; Salem
SMITH, John & Patience **SHATTUCK** (1666-); 29 Jul 1689; Salem
SMITH, John (-1712) & 1/wf Sarah [**WHITE**]; 1689 or bef; Haddam, CT
SMITH, John (1671-ca 1750) & Martha [**GOLDING**]; 1691, no issue; Wethersfield, CT/Hadley
SMITH, John (1667-) & Rachel **BLANCHARD** (ca 1670-); 18 Feb 1691; Charlestown/Killingworth, CT
SMITH, John & Sarah **SCUDDER**; 16 Sep 1691; Boston
SMITH, John (1661-) & Bathsheba **PECK**; 14 Oct 1691; Rehoboth
SMITH, John (1668-1748) & Martha _?_ ; prob 1691; Fairfield, CT/Greenfield
SMITH, John (?1660-) & Ruth _?_ ; ?ca 1690-2; Jamaica, LI
SMITH, John & Rebecca _?_ ; prob 1691; Gloucester
SMITH, John & Ann [**BENNETT**]; b 1692; Salem
SMITH, John & Sarah [**PHILLIPS**]; b 10 Feb 1692, [1692/3?]; Boston
SMITH, John & Rebecca _?_ ; b 20 Feb 1693, [1693/4]; Boston
SMITH, John (-1704) & Ruth **CUTLER**, m/2 Thomas **UPHAM**; 18 May 1693; Charlestown/Reading
SMITH, John & Sarah [?**JONES**]; b 1694; Charlestown
SMITH, John & Clemence (**HOSMER**) **HUNT** (-1698), w Jonathan; 2 Mar 1694 (prob 1694/5); Milford, CT
SMITH, John & Bethiah **SNOW**; 14 May 1694; Eastham
SMITH, John (1670-1744) & Susanna **CHESLEY** (-1746, ae 68); 17 Jun 1694; Dover, NH
SMITH, John & Susanna _?_ ; ?1694; Watertown/Newton
SMITH, John (-1739, in 67th y) & Susanna _?_ (-28 Sep 1746, in 78th y); ?1694; Newton/Preston, CT/Stonington, CT
SMITH, John & Mehitable _?_ ; ?1694; Sandwich
SMITH, John (?1668-) & Mary _?_ ; ?1694; Watertown/Lexington (see John m 1698?)
SMITH, John & Abigail **SHAW** (1671-); 11 Apr 1695; Hampton, NH
SMITH, John (-will 1742) & 1/wf Sarah [**COLLINS**] (1673-1713+); prob 1695; Eastham
SMITH, John & Mary **CLARK**; 3 Oct 1696, 1695?; Salem
SMITH, John (1669-) & [Phebe **FOBES**], ?m/2 Joseph **SEABURY** 1701?; ?1696; Little Compton, RI
SMITH, John (-1712) & 2/wf Lydia _?_ ; ?ca 1697; Haddam, CT
SMITH, John & 1/wf Mary _?_ (-1704); 1698(?); Cambridge (see John m 1694?)
SMITH, John (1674-1749) & Mary **BRACY/BRACE**; 1 Jun 1699; Milford, CT/Derby, CT
SMITH, John & Susanna **HALL**; 25 Jun 1699; Plainfield, CT
SMITH, John & Martha **EAMES**; 14 Dec 1699; Cambridge/Sherborn
SMITH, John (1679-1738) & Priscilla **BLAKE**; 30 May 1700; Taunton
SMITH, John & Elizabeth **GROSS**; 15 Aug 1700; Marblehead
SMITH, John (-1729) & Elizabeth [**BUSS**]; b 1701(?); Oyster River
SMITH, Jonathan (?1635-1711+) & 1/wf Hannah [**ADAMS**], dau Jeremy; ca 1660(?); Hartford, CT
SMITH, Jonathan (?1635-1711+) & 2/wf Martha **BUSHNELL** (ca 1644-1705+); 1 Jan 1663, 1663/4; Saybrook, CT
SMITH, Jonathan & Mehitable **HOLDRIDGE**; 25 Jan 1669, 1669/70; Haverhill/Exeter, NH/Hampton, NH
SMITH, Jonathan, Jr. & Grace [**MOTT**] (1653-); ca 1673?; Hempstead, LI
SMITH, Jonathan (1646-) & 1/wf Rachel [**STEELE**] (1654-); ca 1673?; Farmington, CT
SMITH, Jonathan & Sarah [**BREWSTER**] (1656±-); ca 1673?; Smithtown, NY
SMITH, Jonathan (-1718) & Mehitable **TAYLOR** (1654-1718+); 29 Dec 1681; Yarmouth
SMITH, Jonathan (1659-1724) & Jane **PEABODY**; 16 Mar 1682, 1682/3; Watertown
SMITH, Jonathan & Abigail **KELLOGG** (1671-); 14 Nov 1688; Hadley
SMITH, Jonathan (1646-1721) & 2/wf Mary [**BIRD**] (ca 1660-); aft 2 Jan 1689, bef 13 Jan 1695/6; Farmington, CT
SMITH, Jonathan (1663-1728) & Hannah **PAINE**; 8 Sep 1692; Wethersfield, CT
SMITH, Jonathan & Alice **LEEK**; 25 Dec 1695; Middletown, CT
SMITH, Jonathan & Elizabeth [**PLATT**] (1682-); ?b 1701; Huntington, LI
SMITH, Joseph (ca 1629-1673) & Lydia [**WRIGHT**], m/2 William **HARRIS** aft 1685; ca 1653; Wethersfield, CT

SMITH, Joseph (-1689/90) & Lydia HEWITT/HUIT; 20 Apr 1656; Hartford
SMITH, Joseph (?1637-) & 1/wf Ruth [BEARDSLEY] (ca 1635-); by 1665; Stratford, CT/Jamaica, LI/Norwalk
SMITH, Joseph (?1640-1727) & Elizabeth [BICKFORD] (-1727); ca 1668; Durham, NH
SMITH, Joseph (1643-1711) & Hannah TIDD (1652-1704+); 1 Dec 1674; Watertown
SMITH, Joseph & Rebecca _?_; b 1677; Boston
SMITH, Joseph (1655-1697) & Lydia BRISTOL (1657-1752), m/2 John PLUMB; 6 May 1680; New Haven
SMITH, Joseph & Rebecca DICKINSON; 11 Feb 1681, 1680/1; Hadley
SMITH, Joseph (1660-1687) & Mary DEMING; 26 Nov 1685; Wethersfield, CT
SMITH, Joseph (bef 1658-1735+) & Deborah [WHITMAN]; ?ca 1688; ?Providence
SMITH, Joseph & Lydia GARDINER; 4 Apr 1689; Providence
SMITH, Joseph (1667-) & Ann FULLER (1669-1722); 29 Apr 1689; Barnstable
SMITH, Joseph (ca 1665-1732) & Mary [MATTHEWS]; ca 1690; Jamaica, LI
SMITH, Joseph & Maria BEDLOO; m lic 3 Nov 1690
SMITH, Joseph (1655-1718) & 2/wf Joanna LOOMIS (1663-); 20 Nov 1691; Farmington, CT
SMITH, Joseph (?1667-1713) & Hannah [MORRIS] (1671-), m/2 Joseph SACKETT 1718; ca 1692(?); New Haven
SMITH, Joseph (?1653-1717) & 1/wf Dorothy [COTTON] (1656-1706); bef 1694; Hampton, NH
SMITH, Joseph & Anna HATCH (1677-); 28 Aug 1695; Swansea
SMITH, Joseph (1672-) & Sarah HOUSE (1675-); 2 Jan 1695/6; Glastonbury, CT
SMITH, Joseph (1670-) & Canada WAITE (1678-1749); 15 Dec 1696; Hadley
SMITH, Rev. Joseph (1674-1736) & Esther PARSONS (1672-1760); 15 Sep 1698; Hadley
SMITH, Joseph & Susannah FISHER; 17 Aug 1698; Dedham
SMITH, Joseph (1669-1739) & Elizabeth HAWKINS; 4 Apr 1699; Providence/Glocester, RI
SMITH, Joseph & Hannah (_?_) (SMITH) HODSHON, w Nicholas, w Timothy; b 1700; York, ME
SMITH, Joseph (1677-) & Mary [RICHARDS] (1680-); [1700]; Lexington
SMITH, Joseph & Mary [BURSLEY] (1679-); ?b 1701; Barnstable
SMITH, Joshua (-1669) & Ruth [FRYE]?, m/2 Jonathan TORREY; [1667?]; Weymouth
SMITH, Joshua (-1719) & Mary PECK (1664-1755); 9 Feb 1687/8; Rehoboth
SMITH, Josiah (1657-) & Mary PRATT, Dartmouth; 25 May 1687; Taunton
SMITH, Judah & Mary _?_; [1696?]; Dartmouth
SMITH, Lawrence (-1665) & Mary _?_; ?ca 1640; Dorchester
SMITH, Luke (1666-) & Mary CROW (1672-); 9 Apr 1690; Hadley
SMITH, Martin (-1704) & Mary PHELPS; 25 Dec 1684; Deerfield/?Northampton
SMITH, Matthew[1] (1610-1681) & Jane _?_; in Eng, ca 1630; Charlestown
SMITH, Matthew[2] (1630-) & 1/wf _?_; b 1658; Woburn
SMITH, Matthew[2] & 2/wf Alice LOADER/LEADER; 14 Jul 1665; Charlestown
SMITH, Matthew[3] (1659-1690) & 1/wf Elizabeth _?_ (-1680, Reading); 1679(?); Reading
SMITH, Matthew[3] (1659-1690) & 2/wf Mary CUTLER (1663-), m/2 Joseph DUTTON; 2 Mar 1681/2; Charlestown
SMITH, Matthew[2]) (1630-) & 3/wf Mary (VERY) CUTTER, w Thomas; 20 Jun 1684; Reading/Woburn
SMITH, Matthias & Elizabeth [?BREWER]?, dau Nathaniel; b 1686/[7?]; Boston
SMITH, Matthias & Hannah [?WARREN]; ca 1700; Hartford
SMITH, Micah (will 1647) & Phebe _?_; Huntington, LI (4 ch)
SMITH, Michael & Joan [ATKINS]? (-1692, ae 73); b 22 Dec 1639; Charlestown/Reading
SMITH, Morris & Bethia _?_; b 1664; Jamaica, LI/Flushing, LI
SMITH, Morris & Sarah (LEECH) MILLETT, w John; 4 Nov 1681; Gloucester
SMITH, Nathan (1656-1726) & 1/wf Esther GOODYEAR (1654-1691); 10 Aug 1682; New Haven
SMITH, Nathan (1656-1726) & 2/wf Hannah [BROWN] (1669-1729); b 1698; New Haven
SMITH, Nathan (?1672-1755) & Martha _?_; b 1701(?); Jamaica, LI
SMITH, Nathaniel & Elizabeth LADD; 14 May 1663; Haverhill
SMITH, Nathaniel (-1700/1703) & 1/wf Experience _?_; ca 1670; Weymouth
SMITH, Nathaniel & Mary DICKINSON; 6 Feb 1696, 1695/6; Hadley
SMITH, Nathaniel (-1711) & Esther DICKINSON, m/2 Hezekiah PORTER; 9 Jul 1696, 1686 (wrong); Hartford
SMITH, Nathaniel (1639-1700/1703) & 2/wf Deliverance OWEN [EDDY]; aft 27 Jun 1696; Taunton

SMITH, Nathaniel & Anne [HASKINS] (1677/8-); ca 1697?; Rehoboth
SMITH, Nathaniel (1674-) & Sarah HASKINS (1679-); 20 Sep 1699; Rehoboth
SMITH, Nehemiah (ca 1605-1686, Norwich, CT) & Ann BOURNE (?1620, ?1615-1684+); 21 Jan 1639/[40]; Marshfield/Norwich, CT
SMITH, Nehemiah & 1/wf Sarah PUDDINGTON; 3 Feb 1667/8; Hempstead, LI
SMITH, Nehemiah (1646-1727, Groton, CT) & Lydia WINCHESTER (1645-1723?, Groton, CT); 24 Oct 1669, 28 Oct; Rehoboth/New London, CT
SMITH, Nehemiah (1641-1723+) & 2/wf Elizabeth (SMITH) [LUDLAM], w William; by 24 Feb 1687/8; Jamaica, LI
SMITH, Nehemiah (1673-1724) & Dorothy WHEELER (1679-1736), m/2 Samuel FISH; 22 Apr 1696; ?New London/Groton, CT
SMITH, Nehemiah & Ann [?WATERS]; ?b 1701; Jamaica, LI
SMITH, Nicholas (ca 1629-1673) & 1/wf _?_ ; b 1660; Exeter, NH
SMITH, Nicholas (-1681+) & Mary TIBBALS (1644-); 12 Jul 1664; Milford, CT/Huntington, LI
SMITH, Nicholas (ca 1629-1673) & 2/wf Mary (SATCHWELL) [DALE], w William, m/3 Charles RUNLETT 1676; aft Oct 1665; Exeter, NH
SMITH, Nicholas & Grace _?_ ; b 1690; Watertown
SMITH, Nicholas (1661-) & Mary [GORDON] (1668-); ca 1692(?)
SMITH, Nicholas (-1697) & Hannah HODSHON, ?w Timothy, m/3? Joseph SMITH; 25 Jun 1695; Kittery, ME
SMITH/[JONES?], Nicholas (1672-) & Mercy [NEWLAND]?; b 1700; Norton
SMITH, Obadiah (-1727) & Martha ABELL (1683-1751), m/2 William BUELL 1730; 7 Feb 1699/1700; Norwich, CT
SMITH, P. & _?_ ; b 1695; Fairfield, CT
SMITH, Pelatiah (1657-) & 1/wf Sarah _?_ ; b 1683, [1683/4?]; Malden
SMITH, Pelatiah (1657-) & 2/wf Jane (HARRIS) [DUNBAR], w James, m/3 Zuriel HALL int 1742; ca 1691; Bridgewater
SMITH, Peter (-1688) & Mary [DENTON]; Hempstead, LI
SMITH, Philip (?1633±-1685) & Rebecca [FOOTE] (1634-1701), m/2 Aaron COOKE 1688; ca 1657; Wethersfield, CT/Deerfield/Hadley
SMITH, Philip (1634-1700) & Mary _?_ (1644-1700); ca 1664?; Newport/?Tiverton
SMITH, Philip & Dorcas [STEWART]; b 1685; Martha's Vineyard
SMITH, Philip (1665-1725) & 1/wf Mary BLISS (1670-1707); 1 Feb 1687/8, 9 Jul 1687?; Springfield
SMITH, Preserved (1677-1715) & Mary SMITH (1681-1746+, 1763?); 15 Dec 1697; Wethersfield, CT
SMITH, Ralph (1589-1661) & ?2/wf Mary (GOODALL) [MASTERSON]; 1634?; Plymouth/Boston
SMITH, Ralph (-1685) & 1/wf _?_ ; b 1641; Charlestown/Hingham/Eastham
SMITH, Ralph (-1685) & 2/wf Grace (LEWIS) [HATCH?], w Thomas; Eastham
SMITH, Richard (ca 1589-1669+) & Rebecca [?BUSWELL] (-1667+); b 1617; Wethersfield, CT
SMITH, Richard (ret'd to Eng (Shropham, Norfolk) 1651) & _?_ ; in Eng, b 1629, b 1625?; Ipswich
SMITH, Richard (?1596-1666) & _?_ (-1664?); b 1630; Taunton/Kings Town/Newport?
SMITH, Richard (ca 1617-1690) & Mary [WEED] (ca 1618-1704); b 1640; Wethersfield, CT/Glastonbury, CT
SMITH, Richard & Ruth BONUM/?BONHAM; 27 Mar 1646
SMITH, Richard (?1621-1680+) & 1/wf Mary KERBY/KERLEY/CARLEY? (-1654); 6 Oct 1647; Sudbury/Lancaster
SMITH, Richard (-1692) & Sarah [FOLGER] (-1708); by 1648(?); Southampton, LI/Setauket, LI/Smithtown, LI
SMITH, Richard (?1617-) & Rebecca [TREAT]?/Dorcas TREAT (1662-); b Oct 1649, b 20 Jan 1681; Wethersfield, CT
SMITH, Richard (1621-1680+) & 2/wf Joanna QUARLES; 2 Aug 1654; Boston/Lyme, CT/Lancaster/Saybrook, CT
SMITH, Richard (1630-1692) & Esther _?_ ; ?ca 1654-8, no issue; Kings Town, RI
SMITH, Richard & _?_ ; by 1659; Norwalk, CT
SMITH, Richard (?1640, 1629-1714) & Hannah CHENEY (1642-1722); Nov 1660, 16 Nov 1659, 16 Nov 1660; Ipswich/Newbury
SMITH, Richard & Sarah CHANDLER; 17 Oct 1666; Newbury/Salisbury

SMITH, Richard (-1682), Lyme & Bathsheba ROGERS (1650-), m/2 Samuel FOX; 4 Mar 1669/70; New London, CT/Wethersfield, CT
SMYTH, Richard & 1/wf Mary/?Mercy REEDMAN/REDMAN (-1698); 13 Jan 1676; Milton
SMITH, Richard & Margaret _?_ ; b 1676/[7?]; Boston
SMITH, Richard, Jr. (ca 1649-1702) & 1/wf Elizabeth LAY (-1690); 17 Nov 1677, 27 Nov; Lyme, CT
SMITH, Richard & Joyce _?_ ; b 1677; Boston/Bristol, RI
SMITH, Richard & Dorcas [TREAT] (1662-); b 20 Jan 1681; Wethersfield, CT
SMITH, Richard & Mary [?DAVIS] (1664-1731), m/2 Samuel WOOD; b 1684; Gloucester/Marblehead/Falmouth, ME
SMITH, Richard & Elizabeth (SLEEPER) (PERKINS) [DENHAM], w Abraham, w Alexander; ca 1685; Salisbury/Hampton, NH
SMITH, Richard (-1689) & _?_ ; Hartford
SMITH, Richard, Jr. (ca 1649-1702) & 2/wf Elizabeth (_?_) [HARRIS], w William; aft 3 Apr 1690; Lyme, CT
SMITH, Richard & _?_ WADE; ca 1691?
SMITH, Richard & Hannah [TOOKER], dau John; ?1690±; Smithtown, LI
SMITH, Richard & Mary CLAY; 9 Feb 1699; Boston
SMITH, Richard Suske & Hannah JOHNSON; 3 Sep 1669; Warwick, RI
SMITH, Robert (ret'd to Eng) & Susanna _?_ ; ca 1636/7?
SMITH, Robert (?1611-1706) & Susanna _?_ (-1680); ?ca 1637-8?; Exeter, NH/Hampton, NH
SMITH, Robert & Alice _?_ ; ?b 1652; Southold, LI/Brookhaven, LI
SMITH, Robert (1623±-1693) & Mary [FRENCH] (Boston 1634-1693+, 1719) (dau Thomas & Mary); b or ca 1656; Ipswich/Topsfield
SMITH, Robert & Elizabeth KELLY, w David; 4 Aug 1663; Charlestown
SMITH, Robert & Mehitable _?_ ; b 1676; Boston
SMITH, Robert, Charlestown & Margaret SWILLOWAY, Malden, w Henry; 15 Aug 1687 at Malden; Charlestown
SMITH, Robert & Elizabeth [?HUTCHINS], ?dau Thomas, m/2 John VENTEMAN 1699; b 1691/[2?]; Boston
SMITH, Robert & Deborah KING; 12 Jul 1694; Boston
SMITH, Roger (?1626-1672) & Rebecca _?_ , m/2 John HOPPING?; ca 1663?; East Hampton, LI
SMITH, Samuel (1602-1642) & Sarah _?_ (1602-1650); in Eng, b 1617?, ca 1636?; Salem/Wenham
SMITH, Samuel (1602-1680) & Elizabeth SMITH (not CHILIAD) (1602-1686); in Eng, b 1625, 6 Oct 1624; Wethersfield, CT/Hadley/Hatfield/Deerfield
SMITH, Samuel (1625±-) (deserted wf Rebecca) & Rebecca SMITH, dau Henry, m/2 Nathaniel BOWMAN 1669; Wethersfield, CT
SMITH, Samuel & Susanna READ, dau William; 13 Dec 1659; Boston
SMITH, Samuel & Mary _?_ ; ca 1659; Jamaica, LI
SMITH, Samuel (1639/40, 1638/9-1703) & Mary [ENSIGN] (-1713); ca 1661; Wethersfield, CT/Northampton/Hadley
SMITH, Samuel & _?_ ; ca 1661; Taunton
SMITH, Samuel (-1690) & Mary HOPKINS (1640-1700); 3 Jan 1665, 1664/5?, 1665/6?; Eastham
SMITH, Samuel & Sarah FROST; ca 11 Mar 1664/5; Fairfield, CT
SMITH, Samuel & 1/wf Elizabeth TURNER; 22 Dec 1669; Medfield
SMITH, Samuel (-1723+, betw 1730 & 1745) & Rachel [MARVIN] (1649-1687±); ca 1670/1; Norwalk, CT
SMITH, Samuel & Mary BRIDGMAN; 8 Apr 1673; Salem
SMITH, Samuel (1651-1726) & Obedience LAMBERTON (1644-1734); 13 Jan 1675, 1675/6; New Haven
SMITH, Samuel & Sarah (CLARK) BOWERS, w John; 22 Feb 1676/7; Medfield
SMITH, Samuel (-1691) & Mary (Elizabeth wrong) ELITHORP; 21 Jun 1677; Rowley
SMITH, Samuel (-1727) & 1/wf Martha SMITH; 13 Nov 1678; Ipswich
SMITH, Samuel (1640-1732, Glastonbury) & Jane TUDOR (1657-1718, Glastonbury); 28 Oct 1680; Windsor, CT
SMITH, Samuel & 1/wf Mary CHURCH (1664-1700, 1701); 16 Nov 1682; Hadley/E. Hartford
SMITH, Samuel (-1685) & Mary [MAVERICK], m/2 Joshua ATWATER; prob 1682; Boston
SMITH, Samuel (1653-1723) & Joanna McLATHLIN/?MACKLATHLIN; 18 Nov 1685; Hadley/Northampton/Suffield, CT

SMITH, Samuel (1665-1724) & Sarah BLISS (-1742+); 9 Mar 1687, prob 1686/7; Hadley
SMITH, Samuel (-1725) & Ruth PORTER, m/2 Joseph ROOT 1727; 24 Mar 1687; Farmington, CT
SMITH, Samuel (1665-) & 1/wf Mary COREY (1668-); 14 Feb 1688/9; Huntington, LI
SMITH, Samuel (1665-1698) & Abigail [TURNER]; [ca 1689]; Medfield
SMITH, Samuel & Rebecca HOAR (-1694); 20 Feb 1690; Taunton
SMITH, Samuel, Jr. (1668-1692) & Bathshack LOTHROP (1673-), m/2 Samuel FREEMAN ca
   1693; 26 May 1690; Eastham
SMITH, Samuel & Abigail EMERSON; 30 Nov 1693; Haverhill
SMITH, Samuel (1666-) & Rebina (REYNOLDS) HALL (ca 1671-), w John; 28 Feb 1694, 1693/4;
   Wethersfield, CT
SMITH, Samuel (1672-) & Phebe DOW [not HOWE] (-1715+); 16 Jan 1694/5; Topsfield
SMITH, Samuel & Elizabeth ADAMS (1672-); 14 Aug 1695; Dedham
SMITH, Samuel & Anna/Ann? _?_; ca 1695; Boston
SMITH, Samuel & 1/wf Abigail LYON (ca 1673-1698); 9 Jan 1696, 1695/6; Fairfield, CT
SMITH, Samuel (1676-1732+) & Sarah ARMSTRONG (-1707+); 11 May 1696; Norwich, CT
SMITH, Samuel & Sarah CURTIS (1675/6-1718+); 12 May 1696; Salem/Topsfield
SMITH, Samuel & Hannah (MAYHEW) DOGGETT (1635-), w Thomas; betw 1695 & 1705;
   Martha's Vineyard
SMITH, Samuel & 1/wf Ruth HASKELL (-1700); 8 Dec 1696; Hampton, NH
SMITH, Samuel & 2/wf Deborah JACKSON; 27 Oct 1699; Fairfield, CT
SMITH, Samuel & Priscilla HOVEY; 23 Nov 1699; Malden/Reading/Mansfield, CT
SMITH, Samuel & Ruth HASKELL; 1699; Martha's Vineyard
SMITH, Samuel (1676-) & Mary COOPER (1669-); 14 Aug 1700; New Haven
SMITH, Samuel & Hannah [DENTON] (1677-); b 1701; Jamaica, LI
SMITH, Samuel (1676-) & Elizabeth ELY; b 1701; Lyme, CT
SMITH, Samuel & Esther [CASWELL] (1669-); ?b 1701; Taunton
SMITH, Seth & Mary THURSTON; 27 Dec 1660; Medfield
SMITH, Seth & Mehitable HEATH; 10 Jan 1693; Boston
SMITH, Shubael & 1/wf Mary SWIFT (-1689); 6 Feb 1677; Sandwich
SMITH, Shubael & 2/wf Abigail (not Lydia) [SKIFF] (1666-); aft 1 or 6 Mar 1689, 1684?;
   Martha's Vineyard (see Thomas SMITH)
SMITH, Silas & Eunice [PORTER]; ca 1660; Fairfield, CT
SMITH, Simon (1628-1688) & _?_; by 1660?; Haddam, CT
SMITH, Simon & Alice _?_; b 1689; Haddam, CT
SMITH, Simon (-1715+) & Hannah (BLISS) HALEY, w John; 1 May 1689; Hadley
SMITH, Simon (?1666-1712) & Mary ANDREWS (-1714+); 5 Jan 1698/9; Warwick, RI
SMITH, Stephen & Decline LAMB (1637-); 7 Dec 1663, not 1666; Charlestown
SMITH, Theophilus (1667-1731) & Mary STANYAN (1664-1718+); Exeter, NH/Hampton, NH
SMITH, Thomas & Joanna _?_; ca 1636?, b 1636?; Ipswich
SMITH, Thomas (-1666) & Rebecca _?_ (-1680), m/2 Thomas HOWLETT; ca 1636?;
   Ipswich/Newbury
SMITH, Thomas (1601-1693) & Mary [KNAPP]; ca 1636?; Watertown
SMITH, Thomas (-1662) & Mary _?_; ca 1636?; Salem
SMITH, Thomas & _?_; b 1643; Gloucester/?Newbury
SMITH, Thomas & Elizabeth _?_; b 1646; Boston
SMITH, Thomas & Grace _?_ (-1656), m/2 William CHARD; b 1648; Charlestown
SMITH, Thomas & Judith SMITH; 5 Nov 1651; Rehoboth
SMITH, Thomas & Hannah NETTLETON (ca 1639-); 10 Jul 1656; Branford, CT/Guilford
SMITH, Thomas & Temperance [HOWARD]; b 1657; Boston
SMITH, Thomas (-1670, drowned) & Ruth WICKENDEN (-1670, drowned); m int 27 Jan 1659;
   Providence/Warwick/Newport?
SMITH, Thomas (?1627-1689) & Patience [?MILLS]; ca 1660?, ca 1659; Jamaica, LI
SMITH, Thomas & Elizabeth [PATTERSON] (1644-); 1662; New Haven
SMITH, Thomas (1640-1727) & Mary HOSMER (1646-1719); 19 Jan 1663; Concord
SMITH, Thomas (-1690, 1691) & Sarah [BOYLSTON] (1642-1711); ca 1663; Charlestown
SMITH, Thomas & _?_; b 1670?; Brookhaven, LI
SMITH, Thomas (1648-1718) & 1/wf Joanna [?SMITH]; 25 Oct 1671; Ipswich
SMITH, Thomas & _?_; ca 1671; Groton
SMITH, Thomas, mariner & _?_; ca 1669-70?; Boston

SMITH, Thomas (-1688) & Rebecca [GLOVER] (1655-1711), m/2 Thomas CLARK 1691; prob at Feb 1671; Boston
SMITH, Thomas & Mary _?_; ca 1673?; Boston
SMITH, Thomas & Elizabeth _?_; ca 1673; Boston
SMITH, Thomas (1648-1718) & 2/wf Esther (MORSE) [HOLMES] (1651-1731), w Robert; ca 1675-6; Ipswich
SMITH, Thomas & Sarah _?_; ca 1677; Boston
SMITH, Thomas (1658-1718) & Abigail [RICE] (1657-1735); ca 1678; Sudbury
SMITH, Thomas (-1720) & Mary _?_ (-1720+); ca 1681; Eastham
SMITH, Thomas (ca 1657-1725/[6]), Junkolder & Martha [GILBERT] (?1656-1728); aft Mar 1683, 1682?; Ipswich
SMITH, Thomas & 1/wf Joanna BARBER (1667-1688); 18 Mar 1684/5; Suffield, CT
SMITH, Thomas, Cambridge & Mary RICHARDS, Weymouth; 11 Oct 1687; Milton
SMITH, Thomas (-1700) & Abigail _?_ (1666-1742+), m/2 Meletiah BOURNE aft 1705; ca 1686-7; Sandwich
SMITH, Thomas & 2/wf Mary YOUNGLOVE; 2 Dec 1689; Suffield, CT
SMITH, Thomas & Margaret _?_ (-7 Oct 1692); b 1692; Boston
SMITH, Thomas & Mary COOK; 20 Aug 1693, 30 Aug 1693; Reading
SMITH, Thomas (1664-) & _?_ /?Abigail _?_; ca 1693?; Watertown
SMITH, Thomas & Mary _?_; b 1694; Lynn
SMITH, Thomas & Rebecca [ELBRIDGE], m/2 Josiah SANDERS 1697; b 1694/[5?]; Boston
SMITH, Thomas & Mary SHURAH; 10 Mar 1696; Boston
SMITH, Thomas & Rachel _?_; Jamaica
SMITH, Thomas & Mary JEFFORD; m int 27 Apr 1696; Boston
SMITH, Thomas (ca 1666-) & 1/wf Sarah _?_; ?[by 1696]; Huntington, LI
SMITH, Thomas (1673-) & Sarah [DOW] (-1718); ?ca 1696; New Haven
SMITH, Thomas (1671-1741) & Phebe [ARNOLD] (1672-1741+); ca 1696; Providence/Smithfield
SMITH, Thomas & Deborah _?_; ca 1698; Boston
SMITH, Thomas (1677-1743) & Hannah CAMP (1677-); 2 Dec 1699; Milford, CT
SMITH, Thomas & Elizabeth _?_; ca 1699; Boston
SMITH, Wait (ca 1645-1709+) & 1/wf _?_; ca 1669; Jamaica, LI
SMITH, Wait (ca 1645-1709+, 1717?) & 2/wf Phebe [ASHMAN] (ca 1652-ca 1732); ca 1683; Jamaica, LI
SMITH, Walter (-1709) & 1/wf Elizabeth FARRAND (SEWARD wrong); 26 Sep 1676; Milford, CT
SMITH, Walter (-1709) & 2/wf Rebecca PRINE (-1702, 1703); 1 Apr 1677, 1678; Milford, CT
SMITH, William & Magdalen _?_, m/2 Richard OLMSTEAD; b 1627; Weymouth/Rehoboth/Huntington, LI
SMITH, William (-bef 1654) & Anna _?_; ca 1638; Charlestown
SMITH, William (-1670) & Elizabeth (IGLEDEN)? [STANLEY?] (-1678), w John; Aug 1644, 16 Aug 165-; Hartford/Middletown, CT/Farmington, CT
SMITH, William & Rebecca KEYES (1637/8-1699), m/2 Daniel KILHAM 1693; 6 Jul 1657; Topsfield
SMITH, William & Margaret _?_; ca 1664; Salem
SMITH, William & Martha [BAKER] (1644-); ca 1665; Charlestown/Boston
SMITH, William & Hannah GRAVES; 28 Jan 1665/6; Lynn
SMITH, William & Hannah SCUDDER; 4 Jan 1668, 1668/9; Huntington, LI
SMITH, William (-1686) & Elizabeth [HADDEN]; b 1671; Yonkers Plantation, NY
SMITH, William (1654-1705) & Martha TUNSTALL (-1709); Surrey Co., Eng, 26 Nov 1675; Brookhaven, LI
SMITH, William & _?_; b 1677/[8?]; Ipswich
SMITH, William & Hannah/Anna [PIERCE] (1660-) (dau John & Ruth (BISHOP)), m/2 _?_ EMERSON of Providence; b 1681; Boston
SMTIH, William (1658-) & Martha [?VARNEY] (ca 1664?-); b 1687; Topsfield
SMITH, William & Mary _?_; b 1689; Wethersfield, CT
SMITH, William & Mary [RUCK] (1665-); ca 1687; Salem/Newport, RI
SMITH, William & Mary _?_; ca 1689; Boston
SMITH, William & Abigail PAGE; 21 Apr 1693; Salisbury
SMITH, William & Hephzibah _?_; ca 1699; Eastham
SMITH, William & Mary PERRY; 8 Jan 1699; Boston

SMITH, William & Sarah [GOING/GOWEN/GOWAN?] (1684-); ?ca Oct 1699; ?Kittery, ME/Berwick, ME
SMITH, William & Abigail [FOWLE]; ca 1700; Charlestown
SMITH, William & Abigail [BLAKEMAN] (1680-); ca 1700; Stratford, CT/Stratfield
SMITH, _?_ & Sarah DICKINSON (1670)
SMITHSON, Richard & Dorothy _?_; b 1697; Boston
SMITHSON, Samuel & _?_; b 1693; Guilford, CT
SMITON, William[1] (-1671) & Sarah [LLOYD] (-1709); b 1658; Portsmouth, RI
SNAWSELL, Thomas & Judith [PENDLETON], w Caleb; b 1669; Boston
SNAWSELL, Thomas & [Martha LAWRENCE]; m lic 22 Aug 1695; Flushing, LI/NY
SNELL, Amos & Mary PACKARD; 2 May 1700; Bridgewater
SNELL, George & 1/wf _?_; Portsmouth, NH
SNELL, George & 2/wf? Agnes (?HARVEY) COWELL (-1681), w Edward; Portsmouth, NH
SNELL, George & Record (LITTLEJOHN?) HANKING (-1695), w John; Oct 1681, aft 7 Jun 1682
SNELL, George (-1708) & 3/wf? Hannah ?(ALCOCK) (FERNSIDE)? [HULL] (1650-), dau John FERNSIDE?, w Reuben; by June 1698, b 1687?; Portsmouth, NH?
SNELL, John & Phillip/?Phillippa _?_; b 1659; Boston
SNELL, John (-1668) & Hannah [SMITH] (dau James & Jone), m/2 Thomas NARRAMORE by 1671; b 1667; Boston
SNELL, John & Elizabeth [HULL] (1673-); b 1696?
SNELL, Josiah (1674-1753) & 1/wf Anna ALDEN (-1705); should be 1699, 21 Dec; Duxbury
SNELL, Samuel (-1690) & Hannah [HUBBARD], m/2 John DOANE 1694?; m bond 12 Jan 1687/[8], b 1689; Hingham
SNELL, Samuel & Mary [FICKETT]; b 1701?
SNELL, Thomas (ca 1625-1725) (nephew of Samuel EDSON) & Martha [HARRIS] (-1626+); b 1669; Bridgewater
SNELL, Thomas (1671-) & Abigail [KINGSLEY/KINTLEY]; b 1696; Bridgewater/Mansfield
SNELL, William (-1726) & Sarah [BURTON]; b 1675 (no issue); Boston
SNELL, _?_ & Martha [MATTHEWS], dau Francis, m/2 _?_ BROWN; b 1648; Dover, NH
SNELL, _?_ & Mary _?_, m/2 Alexander THOMPSON 3 Aug 1699; b 1699; Ipswich
SNELLING, Benjamin & 1/wf Jemima ANDREWS; 29 Jan 1694; Boston
SNELLING, John[1] (-1672) & Sarah _?_; b 1657; Saco, ME/Boston
SNELLING, John (1664-1700) & Jane [ADAMS], m/2 John CHAMBERLAIN; b 1689(90?); Boston
SNELLING, Joseph[2] & 1/wf Sarah SEDGWICK (d soon); 8 Jun 1693; Boston
SNELLING, Joseph[2] (1667-1726) & 2/wf Rebecca ADAMS (-1730); 19 Jul 1694; Boston
SNELLING, Nicholas & Mary HIBBERT/HIBBARD (1641-); 8 Nov 1660; Gloucester
SNELLING, William & Margaret _?_ (see below); Sep 1646; Newbury
SNELLING, William (-1674) (returned to Eng) & Margaret STAGGE (-1667, ae 46); 5 Jul 1648 at Boston; Newbury/Boston
SNELLING, William & Margaret (SCOTT)? [ROGERS] (-1678?), w William; aft 22 Apr 1676, bef 31 Jan 1676/7, prob in 1676; Boston
SNELLING, William & Mary TUCKER; 4 Jul 1692; Marblehead
SNOOKE, James (-1655) & Margaret _?_ (-1660+); Weymouth
SNOOK, John (-aft 1686, b 1695) & Margaret _?_, w John SMITH of Portsmouth, RI; Portsmouth, RI (Prudence Island)
SNOW, Anthony (-1692) & Abigail WARREN (-1693+); 8 Nov 1639; Plymouth
SNOW, Benjamin (-1743) & 1/wf Elizabeth ALDEN (-1705); 12 Dec 1693; Bridgewater
SNOW, Benjamin (1673-1748?) & Thankful BOORMAN/BOWERMAN?; 6 Jun 1700; Eastham
SNOW, Daniel & 1/wf Rachel JONES (-1715, ae 36); 5 Aug 1696; Woburn
SNOW, Ebenezer & Hope HORTON, m/2 Thomas ATKINS 1739; 22 Dec 1698; Eastham
SNOW, Edward (1672-1757±) & Sarah [FREEMAN] (1676-1739); ca 1695(?); Eastham/Harwich
SNOW, Jabez (ca 1642-1690) & Elizabeth [?SMITH], m/2 William MERRICK; 1670; Eastham
SNOW, Jabez (1670-1750) & Elizabeth [TREAT] (1676-1755); b 1696; Eastham
SNOW, James (1642-) & Sarah [JAQUITH]; ca 1670; Woburn
SNOW, John (-1692) & Mary SMALLEY, m/2 Ephraim DOANE; 19 Sep 1667; Eastham
SNOW, John (-1706) & Mary [GREEN]; ca 1667?; Woburn/Lexington
SNOW, John (1668-1735) & Sarah STEVENS; 13 Feb 1693, 13 Feb 1693/4; Woburn/Chelmsford
SNOW, John (1678-) & Elizabeth RIDLEY (1678-); 25 Feb 1700, ?1700/01; Eastham
SNOW, Joseph (-1723) & Mary _?_ (-1723+); ca 1670; Eastham

SNOW, Joseph (1668-) & Hopestill [?ALDEN]; ca 1689; Bridgewater
SNOW, Joseph (1671-1706) & Sarah SMITH, m/2 Daniel HAMILTON 1708; 15 Dec 1690; Eastham
SNOW, Josiah (-1692) & Rebecca [BARKER], m/2 John SAWYER 1694; ca 1669; Marshfield
SNOW, Mark (1628-1694/5) & 1/wf Ann/Anna COOK (-1656); 18 Jan 1654, 1654/5; Eastham
SNOW, Mark (1628-1694/5) & 2/wf Jane PRENCE (1637-1712, Harwich); 9 Jan 1660, 1660/1; Eastham
SNOW, Micajah (1669-) & Mercy YOUNG; 25 Nov 1697; Eastham
SNOW, Nicholas (?1600-1676) & Constance [HOPKINS] (-1677); bef 1 Jun 1627; Plymouth/Eastham
SNOW, Prence (1663-) & Lydia SHAW; 4 Apr 1689; Eastham/Harwich
SNOW, Prence (1674-1742) & Hannah [STORRS] (-1751); ca 1698; Harwich
SNOW, Richard (-1677) & Anis/?Avis ? ; ca 1639?; Woburn
SNOW, Samuel (1647-1717) & 1/wf Sarah [WILSON] (-1686); ca 1668; Woburn
SNOW, Samuel & Sarah ? ; b 1674; Boston
SNOW, Samuel & Mary [GOWING/GOING] (-1732); ca 1670-80; Reading/Wilmington
SNOW, Samuel (1647-1717) & 2/wf Sarah PARKER (1660-1695); 9 Aug 1686; Woburn
SNOW, Samuel (1670-) & Abigail [JONES] (1675-); ca 1691; Woburn/Ashford, CT
SNOW, Stephen (-1705) & 1/wf Susanna (DEANE) ROGERS, w Joseph; 28 Oct 1663; Eastham
SNOW, Thomas (-1668, 1669) & Milcah [KELWAY] (-1669+); ca 1637?; Boston
SNOW, Thomas (1668-1732+) & 1/wf Hannah SEARS (1672-1705?); 8 Feb 1692, 1692/3; Eastham/Harwich
SNOW, William (ca 1623-1708) & Rebecca [BROWN] (-1699+); ca 1652?; Duxbury
SNOW, William & Naomi WHITMAN; last of Nov 1686; Bridgewater
SNOW, Zerubbabel (1672-1733) & Jemima CUTLER (-1734); 22 Sep 1697; Woburn
SNOWTON/SNOWDEN, William & Rachel WOODWARD; 28 Jun 1699; Boston
SOLARO, Dennis & Elizabeth ? ; b 1688; Bristol, RI
SOLART, John[1] (-1672) & Elizabeth ? , m/2 Ezekiel WOODWARD 1672; b 1650; Wenham
SOLART/SOORLARD, John[2] & Sarah [COCK], m/2 Isaac HULL; b 1672; Wenham
SOLAS, John & Hannah WOLFE; 9 Dec 1655; Salem
SOLLAS, Thomas & Grace [LEMON] (1639-); b 1662; Salem
SALENDIN/SOLENDINE/SOLLENDINE, John & Elizabeth USHER, m/2 John CUMMINGS; 4 Apr 1679, 2 Aug 1680, 2 Apr 1679; Chelmsford
SOLEY, Matthew (-1684) & Sarah (PATEFIELD) STRAPEN (-1744, ae 93); 7 Dec 1671; Charlestown
SOLEY, John (-1696) & Abigail [SHUTE], m/2 Jeffery GRAY ca 1697; b 1683; Charlestown/New London
SOLEY, John & Anne ? ; b 1683(4?); Boston
SOLEY, John & 2/wf Mary SCOTT; 16 Feb 1696/7; ?Suffield, CT
SOLOMON/SALMAN?, William & ? ; b 1698; Southold, LI
SOMERBY, Abiel (?1641-1671) & Rebecca KNIGHT (1642-); 13 Nov 1661; Newbury
SOMERBY, Abiel & Jane BROCKLEBANK; 26 Jan 1692/3; Newbury
SOMERBY, Anthony (1610-1686) & Abigail ? (-1673); b 1641; Newbury
SOMERBY, Anthony & Elizabeth HEARD; m int 1 Mar 1696/7; Newbury
SOMERBY, Henry (1612-1652) & Judith [GREENLEAF] (1626/8-1705), m/2 Tristram COFFIN 1657; b 1644(5?); Newbury
SOMERBY, Henry & Mary MOODY; 26 Jun 1683; Newbury
SOMERS, Henry & 2/wf Mabel (?KENDALL) REED (-1690), w William; 21 Nov 1660; Woburn
SOMERS, Henry & Susanna [CARTER]; b 4 Dec 1675, b 1674; Charlestown
SOMERS, John & Elizabeth [BRANCH]; b 1696, b 1686; Rochester/Marshfield
SOAMES, John (-1700) & Hannah [SHATTUCK] (1651-); b 1671; Boston
SOMES, Morris (?1610-1689) & 1/wf Margaret/Margery ? (-1646/7); b 1642; Gloucester
SOMES, Morris & 2/wf Elizabeth KENDALL; 26 Jun 1647; Gloucester/?Cambridge
SOAN, Robert & Elizabeth [HATCH], m/2 John STOCKBRIDGE 1643
SOMES, Timothy (1648-1706) & Jane STAINWOOD/STANWOOD (-1696); 2 Apr 1673; Gloucester
SOAMES, Timothy & Elizabeth ROBINSON; 31 Dec 1695; Gloucester
SOAMES, Timothy & Hannah DESPER/DEEPAR?; 11 Mar 1696/7; Gloucester
SOAN, William (-1672) & Dorothy ? , m/2 William TUBBS 1672; b 1668; Scituate
SOPER/?SLOPER, John & Sarah [?REMICK], m/2 Moses WORSTER 1695; Kittery, ME
SOPER, John (-1713) & Mary [ROGERS?]; b 1685(6?); Hull

SOPER, Joseph (-1678) & Elizabeth **ALCOCKE** (1638-), m/2 ?Thomas **HILLMAN/HELMAN** bef 1685; 6 May 1656; Boston
SOPER, Joseph (1665-) & Margaret _?_ (-1704); b 1692; Boston
SOPER, Richard & Deborah **STEVENS**; 4 Mar 1686/7; Huntington, LI
SOPER, Thomas (?1668-) & Mary [**TILLMAN?/WHITE?**] (1670-), m/2 Richard **WOODWARD**; b 1695; Scituate
SOPER, _?_ & Mary **MILLS**; b 1701/2?
SOWDEN, Gregory & Eleanor **STACY**; 27 Nov 1680; Marblehead
SOUDEN, Thomas & _?_ ; ca 1680?; Marblehead
SOULE, Aaron & Mary [**WADSWORTH**] (1668-1741, Pembroke); b 1699; Marshfield
SOULE, Benjamin (1666, ca 1665-1729) & Sarah [**STANDISH**] (1667-1740); 1693?, b 1694(5?); Plymouth
SOWLE, George[1] (-1680?) & Mary [**BECKET?/BUCKET?**] (-1677, 1676?); b 1623?, b 1627?; Plymouth/Duxbury
SOULE, George[2] (-1704) & Deborah _?_ (-1708?, 1709, 1710); b 1670?, b 1684, ca 1668?; Dartmouth
SOULE, George (-bef 1697) & _?_
SOUL, James (-1744) & Lydia **TOMSON** (1659-1741/2); 14 Dec 1693; Duxbury/Middleboro
SOULE, John (ca 1632-1707) (ae 74 in 1706) & 1/wf Rebecca [**SIMMONS**] (-bef 1678); b 1657?; Duxbury?
SOULE, John (-1707) & 2/wf Hester/?Esther (**NASH**) **SAMPSON**? (-12 Sep 1735, ae 93-6-6), w Samuel; ca 1660?, ca 1678; Duxbury
SOUL, John & Ruth _?_ ; b 1687(8?); Boston
SOLLE, John & Lydia _?_ ; b 1700; Boston
SOULE, John (1674-1743) & Martha [**TINKHAM**] (1678-1758); b 1701?, 8 Dec 1701; Middleboro
SOULE, Nathaniel (-1699) & Rose [?**THORN**]; 12 Jan 1681; Dartmouth
SOULE, William (ca 1670-) & Hannah [?**BREWSTER**]; b 1692; Dartmouth
SOULE, Zachariah (?1627-1663) & Margaret [**FORD**]; b 1663?, no issue; Duxbury
SOUTHER, Daniel (1674-) & Elizabeth **BODEN**; 15 Jun 1697; Boston
SOWTHER, John & 1/wf Hannah **READ** (-1675); 11 Jan 1660?, 1660/1; Boston/Hampton, NH
SOUTHER, John & 2/wf Mary [**READ?**]; b 1678(9); Hampton, NH
SOUTHER, John (1660-1748) & 1/wf Sarah [**BURRILL**] (-1705), dau George; ca 1685; Boston/Reading/Stoneham
SOWTHER, Joseph & Elizabeth **FAIREFEILD**; 22 Oct 1657; Boston
SOUTHER, Joseph & Hannah [**HOLLAND**] (-1711, ae 53), dau Christopher; b 1685(6?); Boston
SOUTHER, Nathaniel (-1655, Boston) & 1/wf Alice _?_ (-1651); b 1624?; Plymouth/Boston
SOWTHER, Nathaniel (-1655) & 2/wf Sarah **HILL**, wid; 5 Jan 1653/4; Boston
SOUTHMAYD, John (1676-1755) & Susanna [**WARD**] (1674-1752); b 1701; Middletown, CT
SOUTHMATE, William (-1648/9) & Mellison/Millicent **ADDE**[?]/**ADDIS/ADDES**, m/2 William **ASH**, m/3 Thomas **BEEBE** b 1663; 28 Nov 1642; Gloucester
SOUTHMAYD, William (1643, ?1645-1702) & 1/wf Esther **HAMLIN** (-1682); - Oct 1673, 16 Oct 1673; Middletown, CT
SOUTHMAYD, William (1643-1702) & 2/wf Margaret [**ALLYN**] (1660-1733); ca 1684; Middletown, CT
SOUTHWELL, William & Sarah **STEBBINS** (1668-); 24 Feb 1686, 24 Feb 1687, 24 Feb 1686/7; Northampton
SOUTHWICK/SOUTHACK?, Cyprian & Elizabeth _?_ ; b 1692; Boston
SOUTHWICK, Daniel (?1637-1718/19) (ae 81 in 1717, ae 58 in 1695) & Hester **BOYES/BOYCE** (1641-1734+); 23 Feb 1663/4; Salem
SOUTHWICK, Daniel (1671-) & Jane _?_ ; b 1696; Salem
SOUTHERICK, Isaac (1671-) & Ann _?_ ; 5 May 1691; Reading
SOUTHWICK, John (1620-1672) & 1/wf Sarah (_?_) **TIDD**, w Samuel; b 1642?, aft May 1642; Salem
SOUTHWICK, John (1620-1672) & 2/wf Hannah/?Ann (_?_) [**FLINT**] (-1668), w Thomas; aft 15 Apr 1663, ?12 May 1658, ?1658; Salem
SOUTHWICK, John (1620-1672) & 3/wf Sarah **BURNETT/BURNAP**? (?1646-), dau Robert, m Thomas **COOPER** (div), m Cornelius **BROWN** 20 Nov 1684; 3 Feb 1668/9; Salem
SOUTHWICK, John (1669-1743) & Hannah (**BLACK**)? **FOLLETT**; 23 Dec 1687, 1688; Salem
SOUTHWICK, Joseph (1662-) & Ann _?_ ; b 1694; Salem

SOUTHWICK, Josiah (-1692/3) & Mary BOYCE (?1636-1694+); 13 Dec 1653; Salem
SOUTHWICK, Josiah (1660-) & Ruth [SYMONDS] (1664-); ca 1685; Salem/Northampton, NJ
SOTHWICK, Lawrence (-1660) & Cassandra _?_ (-1660?, Shelter Is.); in Eng, b 1620?; Salem/Shelter Island
SOUTHWICK, Samuel (1658-1709/10) & Mary ROSS; 24 Jun 1686; Ipswich/Salem
SOUTHWORTH, Constant (?1614-1679) & Elizabeth COLLYER/COLLIER (-1682); 2 Nov 1637; ?Duxbury
SOUTHWORTH, Edward (-1621, in Eng) & Alice CARPENTER (1590-1670), m/2 William BRADFORD 1623; Leyden, Holland, 28 May 1613; Plymouth
SOUTHWORTH, Edward (-1727) & Mary PABODY (1648-1727); 16 Nov 1671, 1669?; Duxbury
SOUTHWORTH, Nathaniel (-1710, 1710/11) & Desire GRAY (-1690); 10 Jan 1671, 1671/2; Plymouth/Middleboro
SOUTHWORTH/SOUTHERN, Thomas (?1616-1669, ae 53) & Elizabeth REYNOR; 1 Sep 1641; Plymouth
SOUTHWORTH, Thomas (?1676-1743) & Sarah [ALDEN] (1680-1738); b 1702, b 1701?; Duxbury
SOUTHWORTH, William (1659-1719, 1718?) & 1/wf Rebecca [PABODIE] (1660-1702); ca 1680; Duxbury/Little Compton, RI
SOWELL, Thomas & Elizabeth _?_ ; b 1652; Boston
SPARHAWK, John (?1673-1718) & 1/wf Elizabeth POOL (1674-); 22 Jun 1699; Boston/Bristol, RI
SPARHAWK, Nathaniel (?1598-1647) & 1/wf Mary [ANGIER] (1603-1643/4); in Eng, b 1623; Cambridge
SPARHAWKE, Nathaniel (-1647) & 2/wf Katharine [?HADDON] (-1647); b 1645; Cambridge
SPARHAWK, Nathaniel (-1687) & Patience NEWMAN (-1690); 3 Oct 1649; Cambridge
SPARHAWK, Nathaniel (1667-1734), Cambridge & Abigail GATES (-1775?), Muddy River, m/2 Joseph MAYO 1735; 2 Jan 1693/4; Braintree
SPARHAWK, Samuel (1664-1713) & Sarah WHITING (-1752); 2 Dec 1696; Cambridge
SPARKS, Henry (-1694), Exeter, NH, & Martha BARRETT (1656-), Concord; 10 Jul 1676; Chelmsford/Exeter, NH
SPARKE, John & Mary SENNET (1641, 1640?-); 26 Nov 1661; Boston/Ipswich
SPARKS, John (-1704?) & Mary/?Sarah [ROPER] (1641-1712); ca 1664; Ipswich
SPARKS, John (-1710) & Dorothy _?_ , m/2 John PARSONS 1712; b 1695, b 1692?; Windsor, CT
SPARKS, _?_ & Rebecca _?_ , m/2 Robert McKENNY 1692; NH
SPARKMAN, _?_ & _?_ ; b 1678; Salem
SPARROW, John (1656-1735) & Apphia TRASE/TRACEY (-1739); 5 Dec 1683; Eastham
SPARO, Jonathan (?1633-1707) & 1/wf Rebecca BANGS (-living 1665); 28 Oct 1654, 26 Oct 1654; Eastham
SPARROW, Jonathan (?1633-1707) & 2/wf Hannah (PRENCE) [MAYO], w Nathaniel; aft 1667, 1669?, b 1670?, b 1671; Eastham
SPARROW, Jonathan (1665-1740) & Rebecca [MERRICK] (1668-); ca 1690?; Eastham
SPARROW, Jonathan (?1665-1740) & 2/wf Sarah (LEWIS) COB/COBB, w James; 23 Nov 1698; Barnstable
SPARROW, Richard (-1661, 1660/1) & Pandora/?Theodora _?_ (-1660+, 1665+); in Eng, b 1632; Plymouth/Eastham
SPARROW, _?_ & Alice _?_ , m/2 William RUSSELL 1653, b 1653; Boston
SPARREY, John & Jane _?_ ; b 1677; Boston
SPARRY, Nicholas & Sarah SAMS; 20 Aug 1694; Boston
SPARTA, Philip & _?_ ; b 1678; Concord
SPALDING, Andrew (-1713) & Hannah JEFAS/JEFTS, Billerica; 30 Apr 1679; Chelmsford
SPALDING, Benjamin (1643-) & Olive FARWELL; 30 Oct 1668; Chelmsford/Canterbury, CT
SPALDING, Edward¹ (-1670) & 1/wf Margaret _?_ (-Aug 1640); b 1631?; Braintree/Chelmsford
SPALDING, Edward¹ (-1670) & 2/wf Rachel _?_ (-bef 5 Apr 1670); ca 1642; Braintree/Chelmsford
SPALDEN, Edward (-1708) & 1/wf Priscilla UNDERWAD/UNDERWOOD (?1647, 1646-); 6 Jul 1663; Chelmsford
SPALDIN, Edward (-1708) & 2/wf Margaret BARETT/BARRETT (1660-1748); 22 Nov 1681; Chelmsford
SPALDIN, Edward (1663-1725) & 1/wf Mary BRASKETT (1665-1704, Plainfield, CT), Billerica; 27 Nov 1683; Chelmsford/Plainfield, CT

SPAULDING, Edward (1672-) & Mary [ADAMS] (-1754, ae 78); b 1696; Canterbury, CT/Brooklyn, CT

SPALDING, Edward & Lydia ___?_; b 1700(01?); Chelmsford

SPALDEN, John (ca 1633-1721) & Hannah HALLE/[HEALD] (-1689); 18 May 1658; Chelmsford

SPAULDING, John (?1659-1709, Plainfield, CT) & Ann BALLARD (-1709+); 20 Sep 1681; Andover/Chelmsford

SPAULDYING, John (1633-1721) & Mary (_?_) (COTTON) FLETCHER, w John, w Samuel; 18 Nov 1700; Chelmsford

SPALDING, Joseph (1646-1740) & Mercy JEWELL (1653-1728); 9 Dec 1670, 1671?; Chelmsford/Plainfield, CT

SPALDING, Joseph (1671-) & Mary ___?_; b 1697; Chelmsford

SPAULDYNG, Joseph (1673-1728) & Elizabeth COLBURN (1679-); 10 Apr 1700; Chelmsford

SPALDING, Samuel (1673-1728) & Mary BUTTERFIELD; 30 Jun 1698; Chelmsford/Canterbury, CT

SPALDIN, Timothy & Rebecca WINN; 5 Mar 1700, prob 1699/1700; Chelmsford/Woburn

SPAULE, Thomas & 1/wf Alice [SHERMAN]; b 1644; Boston

SPAULE, Thomas & 2/wf Mary GUTTERIDGE; 18 Aug 1653; Boston

SPEAR, Ebenezer (1654-1719) & 1/wf Rachel DEERING (1659-1717); 16 Jul 1679; Braintree

SPEAR, George (ca 1612-1688?) & 1/wf Mary [HEATH] (-1674), dau William; b 1644, b 1647; Braintree

SPEAR, George & 2/wf Mary (NEWCOMB) DEERING (-1678), w Samuel; 27 Apr 1675; Braintree

SPEAR, George & 3/wf Elizabeth (_?_) GENT/JENT, w John; b 1688; Braintree

SPEAR, Nathaniel (1665-1728) & Hannah HOLMAN (-1751, ae 81); 8 Aug 1689; Braintree

SPEAR, Samuel (1659-1713) & 1/wf Sarah ___?_ (dismissed to Braintree 1684); b 1684; Billerica?

SPEAR, Samuel (1659-1713), Braintree & 2/wf Elizabeth DANIEL (1673-1727?), Milton; 7 Jun 1694, 5 Jun 1694; Braintree/Milton

SPECK/SQUEAK, Jeret/Jarah/Gerard & ___?_ [PURCHASE], dau John; Hartford, CT

SPELMAN, Richard & 2/wf Alice [FRENCH]; b 1701; Middletown, CT

SPENCER, Abraham (-1683) & 1/wf Abigail [WIBORNE]; b 5 Jan 1679; Boston

SPENCER, Abraham (-1683) & 2/wf Elizabeth [PHIPPEN], m/2 Joseph PHIPPEN; Boston

SPENCER, Benjamin (1670-) & 1/wf Martha ___?_; b 1698/[9?]; East Greenwich, RI

SPENCER, Ebenezer & 1/wf Mary BOOTH (1678-1724); 28 Feb 1699; Hartford

SPENCER, ?George & Brawn ___?_; b 6 Apr 1697; York, ME

SPENCER, Humphrey (ca 1646-1700) & 1/wf Elizabeth [SHEARS]; ca 1673; Kittery, ME/Great Isl.

SPENCER, Humphrey (1646-1700) & 2/wf Grace ___?_; by 1676; Kittery, ME/Great Isl.

SPENCER, Humphrey (?1674-1712) & Mary [CUTTS] (1675-), m/2 Joseph MOULTON; b 7 Jun 1701; Berwick

SPENCER, Jared/[Gerard] (1614-1685) & 1/wf Hannah ___?_; ca 1637; Lynn/Hartford/Haddam, CT

SPENCER, Jared/[Gerard] (1614-1685) & 2/wf Rebecca (PORTER) [CLARK], w John; aft 1677; Haddam, CT

SPENCER, Jared (ca 1650/1-1712) & Hannah PRATT (1658-1692); 22 Dec 1680; Hartford

SPENCER, Jared/Gerrard (1670-1744) & Deborah BIRGE (1671-); 12 Nov 1692, 12 Nov 1691; Windsor, CT/Haddam, CT

SPENCER, Dr. John (ca 1638-1684) & Susanna ___?_ (-1719); ca 1665; Newport/E. Greenwich, RI

SPENCER, John & ___?_ (PORTER) CLARK (1630-), w John?; aft 21 Sep 1677, d in 1682, ca 1667; Saybrook, CT

SPENCER, John (?1638-1682) & Rebecca [HAYWARD/HOWARD] (1648-), dau Robert; ca 1665; Haddam, CT

SPENCER, John & Rachel HICKS; 24 May 1676 m lic; New York (Province)

SPENCER, John & Elizabeth [PARSONS]?, w Mark; aft 1687; Saco, ME/etc.

SPENCER, John (-1712) & Mary [WORMWOOD], wid; aft 1690

SPENCER, John (1666-1743) & Audrey GREENE (1667-1733); b 1693, ca 1692; E. Greenwich, CT

SPENCER, John & Sarah SMITH; 4 Oct 1693; Hartford

SPENCER, Michael[1] (1611-1653) & 2/wf Isabel ___?_ (-1674), m/2 Thomas ROBBINS; b 1635?; Cambridge/Lynn

SPENCER, Michael (1648±-) & Rebecca SWETMAN/SWEETMAN (1649-); 7 Dec 1671; Salem

SPENCER, Michael (1668-1748) & Elizabeth ___?_; 16 Nov 1692; E. Greenwich, RI

SPENCER, Moses (1642-1719±) & Elizabeth (FREETHY?) BOTTS, w Isaac; - Jul 1679, bef 1 Jul 1679; S. Berwick, ME?
SPENCER, Nathaniel & 1/wf Lydia [BAILEY?]; b 1682; Haddam, CT
SPENCER, Obadiah (ca 1639-1712) & Mary [DISBROW?/DESBOROUGH]; b 1666; Hartford/Wallingford, CT
SPENCER, Obadiah (ca 1666-1741) & Ruth [KELSEY] (ca 1676-1733+); b 1695; Hartford
SPENCER, Robert (1674-1748), East Greenwich & 1/wf Theodosia WAITE/WHALEY?; 15 Jul 1697; Kingston, RI
SPENCER, Roger (-1675) & Gertrude __?__; b 1649; Charlestown/Saco, ME
SPENCER, Samuel (1639-1727, 1716) & Sarah [RICHARDS??] (-1706, Hartford); b 1668; Hartford
SPENCER, Samuel (ca 1650-1705) & 1/wf Hannah (WILLEY) (HUNGERFORD) BLATCHFORD (1642-1681±), w Thomas, w Peter; ca 1673; East Haddam, CT/Haddam, CT
SPENCER, Samuel (a nephew of Barnabas DERIFIELD/DORIFIELD of Braintree, prob of Windham, CT) & Sarah __?__; b 1686, b 1684, adm 8 Feb 1684/5; Braintree
SPENCER, Samuel & __?__; Mendon
SPENCER, Samuel (ca 1650-1705) & 2/wf Miriam (MOORE) [WILLEY] (-1706+), w John; 1689; East Haddam, CT
SPENCER, Samuel (ca 1668-1748) & Hepsibah CHURCH (1678, ca 1679-1745); Sep 1696, 16 Sep 1696; Hartford
SPENCER, Samuel & Deborah BECKLEY; 10 Oct 1696, ca 1695; Hartford/Middletown, CT
SPENCER, Samuel (ca 1674-1743) & Elizabeth MASCRAFT (1669-); 18 Mar 1700; Suffield, CT
SPENCER, Thomas (?1591, 1596-1681) & Patience CHADBURNE (1612-1683); b 1630; Kittery, ME/Piscataqua
SPENCER, Thomas[1] (1607-1687) & 1/wf [Ann DERIFIELD] (-1644); ca 1635?; Hartford
SPENCER, Thomas[1] (1607-1687) & 2/wf Sarah BEARDING; 11 Sep 1645; Hartford
SPENCER, Thomas (ca 1641-1689) & Esther [ANDREWS] (1641-1698, Suffield, CT); b 1670, by 1663; Hartford/Suffield, CT
SPENCER, Thomas (-1699/1700) & 1/wf [Elizabeth] [BATES]; ca 1673; Haddam, CT/Westbrook, CT
SPENCER, Thomas & 2/wf Elizabeth WALLER
SPENCER, Thomas (1666, ca 1668-1761, ae 95) & Sarah [MEADKIN] (1672, bpt 1674-1741); ca 1696, b 1695; Hartford
SPENCER, Timothy (ca 1652-1704) & [?Sarah CLARK] (-1704), dau Wm.; b 1679, by 1675; Haddam, CT
SPENCER, William (1601-1640) (Matthew ALLEN, a cousin) & Agnes PRATT?/TUCKER?/ [WAKEMAN]/HEANE?, m/2 William EDWARDS; b 1633; Cambridge/Hartford, CT
SPENCER, William, Jr. (-1711, 1712/13) & Sarah [ACKLY]; b 1693, b 1687, b 1695; East Haddam, CT
SPENCER, William (ca 1656-1731) & Margaret BATES (1664-); ca 1680/4, ca 1684, b 1680/1; Haddam, CT
SPENCER, William (1672-1748) & Elizabeth __?__; b 1698; East Greenwich, CT/North Kingston, RI
SPENCER, William & Margaret [CLARK]
SPENCER, William (-1698) & __?__
SPENCER, William & Susannah GRAVES
SPENCER, __?__ & Joanna __?__ (-20 Apr 1713, ae 88); Charlestown
SPENCER, __?__ (see John SPENCER) & Rebecca (PORTER) CLARKE (-1682?, 1683?), Saybrook, w John; aft 21 Sep 1667; Saybrook, CT
SPERRY, Daniel (1663-) & 1/wf Deborah PECK (1672-1711); 3 Apr 1694, ?3 Aug; Lyme, CT/New Haven
SPERRY, Ebenezer & Abigail DICKERMAN; 21 Jan 1689/90; New Haven
SPERRY, John (-1692) & Elizabeth POST (1655-1715), m/2 Benjamin BUNNELL, m/3 Edmund DORMAN 1700; 1 Sep 1676; New Haven
SPERRY, Nathaniel & 1/wf Sarah DICKERMAN; 2 Oct 1683; New Haven
SPERRY, Richard (-1698) & Dennis __?__ (-1707); b 1649(50?); New Haven
SPERRY, Richard (1652-1734) & Martha MANSFIELD; 16 Dec 1680; New Haven
SPERRY, Thomas & Elizabeth FERNES/FARNES; 18 Nov 1684; New Haven
SPICER, Peter (-1694) & Mary BUSICOTT; 15 Dec 1670; Warwick, RI/Norwich, CT/New London
SPICER, Edward & Catharine STONE (1674-); b 1698(9?); New London?

SPICER, Thomas & 2/wf Micall JENKINS, wid; 5 Feb 1635 m lic Canterbury; Gravesend, LI
SPICER, Thomas & Ann GRANT; 4 Feb 1626 m lic Canterbury, Eng
SPICER, Samuel & Esther TILTON (1647-); 21 May 1665; Gravesend, LI/NJ
SPILLER, Henry & Sarah (MOORE) WALCOM, w Zaccheus; b 1693; Ipswich
SPILLER, _?_ & Anne ROWE (1637-1684+), w Richard
SPINK/SPRIKE?/PITE?, Robert (1615?-1695) & Alice _?_ ; b 1680, b 1668?, b 1660?; Newport,
    RI/Kingston, RI/E. Greenwich, RI
SPICK/SPRECK?/PITE?, Jared & Mary PURCHAS; Hartford
SPINK, Robert² (-1709±) & _?_ ; Kings Town, RI
SPINK, Nicholas (-1733) & 1/wf Abigail _?_ ; b 1700; North Kings Town, RI
SPINNEY, James & Grace [DENNETT]; b 1697; Kittery, ME
SPINNEY, John (-1705±) & Mary [DIAMOND], m/2 Jeremiah BURNHAM; ca 1690/2; Kittery, ME
SPINNEY, Samuel & 1/wf Elizabeth KNIGHT; 26 Sep 1687; Kittery, ME
SPINNEY, Thomas¹ (-1701) & Margery [RANDALL], div wf of William NORMAN; ca 1651, aft
    14 Oct 1651; Kittery, ME
SPINNEY, Thomas² & Christiana/Christian _?_ (1675-); b 1701; Kittery, ME
SPINNING, Humphrey (-1656) & _?_ [ATRED?], wid; b 1640; New Haven/Milford, CT
SPINNING, Humphrey & Abigail HUBBARD (1640-); 14 Oct 1657; Guilford, CT/New
    Haven/Elizabeth, NJ
SPINNING, Humphrey & 2/wf Anne/Anna _?_ ; ca 1664
SPINNING, John & 1/wf Deborah BARTLETT (1668-1692); 16 Mar 1687; Guilford, CT
SPINNING, John (-1712) & 2/wf Rachel SAVAGE (1673-), m/2 Thomas HALL; 20 Aug 1694;
    Guilford, CT
SPOFFORD, John¹ (?1612-1678) & Elizabeth [SCOTT] (1623-1691); b 1647; Rowley
SPOFFORD, John (1648-1696) & Sarah WHEELER (-1732), m/2 Caleb HOPKINSON 1701; 9 Mar
    1675; Rowley
SPOFFORD, John & Dorcas HOPKINSON; 15 Feb 1699/1700; Rowley
SPOFFORD, Samuel (1653-1744) & Sarah BURKBEE/BURPEE (1661-1729); 5 Dec 1676; Rowley
SPOFFORD, Thomas (1650-1706) & Mary LITON/LEIGHTON (1654-1719), m/2 John HART-
    SHORN 1709; 23 May 1686, no issue; Rowley
SPOONER, Ebenezer (1666-1718) & Mercy [BRANCH] (1664-1746); b 1694; Plymouth
SPOONER, Isaac (-1709) & Alice [SIMPSON] (had son Simpson); b 1699(1700?); Dartmouth
SPOONER, John² (-1734+) & 1/wf _?_ ; b 1668; Dartmouth
SPOONER, John² (-1734+) & 2/wf Rebecca [PECKHAM]; b 1680; Dartmouth
SPOONER, Samuel (1655-) & [Experience WING] (?1668-); b 1688(9?); Dartmouth
SPOONER, Thomas (-1664) & Elizabeth _?_ (-1676, 1677?) (she called Margaret RUCK of
    Boston & Thomas CLARK of Cambridge "cousins" in 1664); b 1636, b 1632?; Salem
SPOONER, William (-1684) & 1/wf Elizabeth [PARTRIDGE] (-1648, 1647?); b 1648; Plymouth
SPOONER, William (-1684) & 2/wf Hannah PRATT; 18 Mar 1651, 1651/2; Plymouth/Dartmouth
SPOONER, William (?1660-1729) & Sarah _?_ ; b 1690; Dartmouth
SPOONER, William (1680-) & Alice [BLACKWELL]? (1681-); b 1700; Dartmouth
SPOONER, _?_ & Ann _?_ ; Salem
SPOWELL, William & Elizabeth [BUCKMASTER]; b 1652; Boston
SPOWELL, William & Mary _?_ ; b 1674; Boston
SPRAGUE, Anthony (1635-1719) & Elizabeth BARTLETT (-1713); 26 Dec 1661; Plymouth
SPRAGUE, Anthony (1663-) & Mary [TILDEN]; b 1691; Rehoboth/Providence/Attleboro
SPRAGG, Edward¹ & _?_ ; Hempstead, LI
SPRAGG, Edward & Mary _?_ ; b 4 Nov 1692; Hempstead, LI
SPRAGUE, Edward (-1711) & Dorothy LANE (1669-); 14 Nov 1693; Malden
SPRAGUE, Francis & [?Lydia]/?Anna _?_ ; b 1621 in Eng; Plymouth/Duxbury/Dartmouth
SPRAGUE, John & Lydia GOFFE; 2 May 1651; Malden
SPRAGUE, John (-1678) & Ruth (?BARSOTT)?; ca 1655; Plymouth/Marshfield
SPRAGUE, John (-1683) & Elizabeth HOLBROOK, m/2 James BICK by 1689; 13 Dec 1666;
    Hingham
SPRAGUE, John (1652-1703) & Elizabeth [STOWER] (1651-1736); ca 1676, b 1676?;
    Charlestown
SPRAGUE, John (1656-1728) & 1/wf Lydia _?_ (-1725); b 1685; Duxbury/Lebanon, CT
SPRAGUE, Jonathan & Elizabeth [?HARDING]; b 1670; Weymouth/RI

SPRAGUE, Jonathan (1648-1741) & Mehitable [HOLBROOK], dau Wm.; b 1672; Hingham/Providence/Smithfield, RI
SPRAGUE, Jonathan (1656-1731) & Mary [BUNKER] (1658-1714); b 1679; Charlestown
SPRAGUE, Jonathan & 1/wf Bethiah MANN (1683-1712); 28 Dec 1698?, 28 Nov 1699?; Providence/Smithfield, RI
SPRAGUE, Phineas (-1690/1) & 1/wf Mary CARRINGTON (1642-1667); 11 Dec 1661; Malden
SPRAGUE, Phineas (1637-1690/1) & 2/wf Sarah HASSE/[HASEY], m/2 Moses TYLER; 5 Jan 1669, 5 Jan 1670, 1669/70; Malden/Charlestown
SPRAGUE, Phineas (1670-1736) & Elizabeth [GREEN] (1673-1747); b 1690, b 1691; Malden/Charlestown
SPRAGUE, Ralph (ca 1599-1650) & Joan/Johane WARREN (-1680), m/2 Edward CONVERSE 1662; Fordington, St. George, 15 Aug 1623; Charlestown/Boston/Malden
SPRAGUE, Richard (-1668) & Mary [?MORTON]/[?SHARP]; b 1632, no issue; Charlestown
SPRAGUE, Richard (-1703) & 1/wf Eunice CHESTER (1645, ?1647-1676); 25 Feb 1672, 1672/3, 1 Feb 1672; Charlestown
SPRAGUE, Richard (-1703) & 2/wf Katharine (RICHARDSON/RICHESON) ANDERSON (-1701), w David; 7 May 1679; Charlestown
SPRAGUE, Samuel (1632-1696, Malden, ae 65) & Rebecca/Recuba CRAWFORD (1633?-1710), dau Winifred, m/2 John BROWN 1697; 23 Aug 1655; Malden/Boston
SPRAGUE, Samuel (1640-) & Sarah [CHILLINGWORTH]; b 1666; Marshfield
SPRAGUE, Samuel (1662-1738) & 1/wf Sarah _?_; b 1685, ca 1684; Malden/Charlestown
SPRAGUE, Samuel (1662-1738) & 2/wf Sarah [GREENE] (1677-1744); b 1694, ca 1693; Malden
SPRAGUE, Samuel & Ruth ALDEN (?1674-1758); 29 Nov 1694; Duxbury
SPRAGUE, Samuel (1659-1743) & 1/wf Lois BURRILL; 5 Jun 1695; Woburn
SPRAGUE, Samuel (1659-1743) & 2/wf Elizabeth _?_ ; aft 5 May 1696, b 1701?, b 4 Mar 1714; ?Woburn
SPRAGUE, William (1609/10-1675) & Millicent [EAMES] (-1696); b 1636; Charlestown/Hingham
SPRAGUE, William (1650-1723) & 1/wf Deborah LANE (1652-1707); 30 Dec 1674; Hingham/Providence
SPRAGUE, William & Hannah [HIDE]; b 1679, b 1680; Fairfield, CT
SPRAGUE, William (-1712) & Grace [WADSWORTH] (1679-1757), m/2 Josiah WORMELL; b 1702, ca 1700/1; Duxbury
SPRAGUE, _?_ & Millicent HOLBROOK, m/2 ?John PECK; ca 1694?
SPRAY/SPRY, Henry & Purchase _?_ ; b 1686; Boston
SPRING, Henry (1628-1697) & 1/wf Mehitable BARTLETT (1640-); 7 Jan 1657, 1657/8; Watertown
SPRING, Henry (1662-1749) & Lydia [CUTTING]; b 1686; Watertown
SPRING, Henry (1628-1697) & 2/wf Susana/Susanna (STOWERS) (WHEELER) (GOODWIN) COCKE/COOKE, w George, w Edward, w Gregory; 15 Sep 1691; Watertown
SPRING, John (1589-1664+) & 1/wf Eleanor _?_ (1588-); in Eng, b 1623; Watertown
SPRING, John (1589-1664+) & 2/wf Lydia [HATCH] (-1665+), Scituate, w Thomas; by 1654; Watertown
SPRING, John (1630-1717) & Hannah BARSHAM (1638-1710); 19 Dec 1656; Watertown/Newton
SPRING, William (1633-1695±) & _?_ ; b 1677; ?Watertown/Barbados
SPRINGER, Dennis, Ireland & Mary HUDSON, London; Oct 1667; New London, CT
SPRINGER, ?Edward & Desire [GORHAM] (1675-), m/2 Daniel HAMILTON 1715; b 1707, b 1701?; ?Newport
SPRINGER, James & Hannah [DICKINSON]; b 1701?; Oyster Bay, LI
SPRINGER, Jeremiah (-1716+) & _?_ ; b 1700?; Taunton/Scarborough, ME
SPRINGER, John & Elizabeth _?_ (?1675-); b 1697; Little Compton, RI
SPRINGER, Lawrence & Martha _?_ ; b 1684, b 1670?; Little Compton, RI
SPRINGFIELD, Emanuel (1635-) (returned to Eng 1655) & Mary MELLOWES (1638-); 13 Sep 1655; Boston
SPROUT/SPROAT, Robert (-1712) & Elizabeth [SAMSON] (-1712+); b 1661; Scituate/Middleborough
SPRY, Henry & Purchase _?_ ; b 1687(8?), b 1686; Boston/etc.
SPRY, John & Margaret _?_ ; b 1678; Boston
SPURHAM, Henry & Elizabeth _?_ ; b 1698/(9?); Boston
SPURRE/SPURR, John & Elizabeth _?_ ; b 1637(8?); Boston

SPURE, John & Mercy HOARE; 26 Dec 1676; Dorchester
SPURE, Robert (-1703, ae 93) & Ann _?_ (1624-1712); ca 1642?; Dorchester
SPUR, Robert (1661-1739) & Elizabeth TILESTONE (1666-1788); 24 Oct 1684; Dorchester
SPURWELL/?SPURRELL, Christopher & Jane/Julian? _?_ (1620-), m/2 John CLOYES; b 1656; Charlestown
SQUIRE, Barnard & 1/wf _?_; Portsmouth, NH/Oyster River
SQUIRE, Barnard & 2/wf Margaret [WILLEY], w Thomas; aft 1681
SQUIRE, Crispin/Crispus? & Elizabeth JACKSON; 25 Jul 1688; Marblehead/Newark, NJ
SQUIRE, George^1 (1618-1691) & [Ann] _?_; b 1643; Concord/Fairfield, CT
SQUIRE, George$^2_2$ & _?_; ca 1672/4; Fairfield, CT
SQUIRE, John (-1713, ae ca 83) & Sarah [FRANCIS] (1646-1713+); b 1667; Reading/Cambridge
SQUIRE, John & Mary [?CLIFFORD], ?w Mark DAY; b 1686(7?), bef 1683; Boston
SQUIRE, John (-1702) & Ann EDWARDS, m/2 Capt. Josiah HOBART 1705; b 1692, b 1681/2; East Hampton, NY
SQUIRE, John (1667-) & Rebecca [PATTEN]?/TAPPIN?; b 1697, 16 Apr 1694; Cambridge
SQUIRE, Jonathan & [Mary SEELEY]; b 1685; Woodbury, CT/Fairfield, CT
SQUIRE, Philip (1630-1693) & 1/wf Rachel [RUGGLES] (1643-); b 1665(6?); Boston
SQUIERE, Philip (-1693) & 2/wf Margaret THOMAS; 1 Mar 1682/3; Swansea
SQUIRE, Philip & Mary _?_; b 1686(7?); Newbury
SQUIER, Samuel & [Sarah SEELEY]; b 1689; Fairfield, CT
SQUIRE, Thomas & Bridget [?GYVER]; ca 1630/40?; Charlestown
SQUIRE, Thomas (-1712) & 1/wf _?_; b 1672; Fairfield, CT/Stratford, CT/Woodbury, CT
SQUIRE, Thomas & Martha [BLAQUE/BLAKE?]; b 1677; Boston
SQUIRE, Thomas & 2/wf? Elizabeth _?_ (-1743); ca 1679; Stratford, CT/Woodbury, CT
SQUIRE, Thomas (1672-) & Deborah [ROBBINS] (1674-); b 1701?; Cambridge
SQUIRE, William (-ca 1680?, 1679?) & Barbara _?_, m/2 John CLARK; b 1673; Eastchester, NY/Fairfield
STACKHOUSE, Richard (-1693+) & Susanna _?_ (?1617-); ca 1642?, [3 ch bpt May 1648]; Salem
STACKPOLE, James (1654-1736) & Margaret [WARREN] (1655-1749); b 1680; Kittery, ME/Dover, NH
STASEY, Benjamin & Anna HARDIN; 30 Nov 1688; Marblehead/Salem
STACY, Ephraim (1673-) & Elizabeth SAMMONS; 3 May 1695; Lynn
STACY, Henry & 1/wf Hannah INGALLS (-1684); 2 May 1673; Lynn/Ipswich/Providence/Rehoboth
STACY, Henry & _?_; b 1680; Dover, NH
STACY, Henry (-1689) & Jane _?_, m/2 Samuel REED 1692; b 1689; Salem
STACY, Henry & 2/wf Rebecca [BALLARD]; b 1700; Rehoboth/Attleboro
STACY, Hugh & Margaret _?_; b 1641, b 1624?; Dedham/Lynn?/Salem?
STACY, John (?1594-1672) & [Eleanor?] _?_; b 1642; Salem/Ipswich?
STACY, John (1646-1705) & Agnes [PEDRICK] (-1715); b 1674, 3 ch bpt 1678; Marblehead/Salem?
STASEY, John (see below) & Mary CLARKE; 26 Aug 1689; Marblehead/Watertown?/Salem
STASY, John (see above) & Mary SANDIN; 13 Sep 1696; Marblehead/Watertown?
STACEY, Joseph (-1711) & Elizabeth/?Rebecca ADAMS (-1709); 29 Jun 1682; Charlestown
STACEY, Richard (-1687) & Abigail _?_; b 1664; Hingham/?Taunton
STACY, Samuel & Elizabeth [READ] (1655-); ca 1678?; Salem?
STACY, Samuel & Ruth WRIGHT; 28 Oct 1698
STASEY, Samuel & Sarah SERVANT; 10 Dec 1699; Marblehead
STACEY, Simon (-1699?) & Elizabeth [CLARK] (-1670); ca 1620?, b 1634, 6 Nov 1620 m lic; Ipswich
STACE, Simon (-1699) & Sarah WALLIS; 19 Apr 1659; Ipswich
STACE, Thomas (-1690) & Susanna WOOSTER/WORCESTER (-1692+); 4 Oct 1653; Ipswich
STACIE, Thomas & Hannah HICKS (1666-); 20 Jun 1683; Cambridge
STACY, William (1656-) & Priscilla BUCKLEY; 28 Nov 1677; Salem
STACY, William & Mehitable [WEYMOUTH] (1669-1753); b 1690; Kittery, ME
STACY, _?_ & Margaret (PARTRIDGE) MASON (1628-1711); aft 1676, b 1695; Dedham
STADDIN/STADDEN?, [Andrew?]/Elias? & Hannah _?_; b 1685; Marblehead
STAFFORD, Amos (1665-1760) & Mary BURLINGAME (-1760); 19 Dec 1689; Warwick, RI

STAFFORD, Joseph (-1698) & [Sarah HOLDEN] (1658-1731); ca 1680?; Warwick, RI
STAFFORD, Josiah & [Sarah LAKE] (1678-); 1698; ?Tiverton, RI
STAFFORD, Samuel (1636-1718) & Mercy [WESCOTT] (-1700); b 1661; Warwick, RI
STAFFORD, Thomas (?1605-1677) & Elizabeth _?_ (-1677+); b 1635 Plymouth; Newport/War-
wick, RI
STAFFORD, Thomas (-1723) & 1/wf Jane DODGE; 28 Dec 1671, 20? Dec; Warwick, RI
STAFFORD, Thomas (-1723) & 2/wf Sarah _?_
STAYNER/STAINER, Roger & Elizabeth _?_ ; b 1683; Boston
STAINES, Richard & Joyce _?_ ; b 1655; Boston
STAINES, _?_ & Ann LEWIS (-1676) (ae 70 in 1665); b 1642; Farmington, CT (returned to Eng)
STANBOROUGH, John (1665-) & _?_ ; ca 1690?; Southampton, LI
STANBOROUGH, Josiah[1] (-1661) & 1/wf Frances [GRANDSDEN] (1618-); 1636; Lynn/South-
ampton, LI
STANBOROUGH, Josiah[1] (-1661) & Alice [WHEELER] (-1673), w Thomas; 1657; Southampton,
LI
STANBOROUGH, Josiah & Adnah/Admah?/Anne? CHATFIELD; 24 Jul 1670; Southampton,
LI/Elizabeth, NJ
STANBOROUGH, Peregrine (?1640-1702) & Sarah JAMES; 15 Dec 1664; Southampton, LI
STANBRIDGE, John (-1725) & Sarah [NORTON] (?1653-); b 1673; Newport, RI/Martha's
Vineyard
STANBURY, John & Sarah _?_ ; b 1668(9?); Boston
STANBERRY, Thomas (-1652) & Martha _?_ ; b 1642; Boston
STANBURY, Thomas & Susanna [WALKER]; b 1669(70?); Boston (will of Isaac[1] WALKER)
STANCLIFT/STANCLIFF, James (-1712) & Mary _?_ (-1712); b 1686; Middletown, CT
STANDISH, Alexander (ca 1626-1702) & 1/wf Sarah [ALDEN] (1629-1685?, d many years bef
1686?); ca 1650/2?; Duxbury?
STANDISH, Alexander (ca 1626-1702) & 2/wf Desire (DOTY) (SHERMAN) HOLMES (ca 1645-
1732), w William, w Israel; 1686?; Marshfield
STANDISH, Ebenezer (1672-1755) & Hannah [STURTEVANT] (ca 1679-1759); b 1698; Plympton
STANDISH, James (-1679) & Sarah _?_ , m/2 Richard HUTCHINSON, ?1670, 1679?, m/3 Thomas
ROOT 1682, 1683; ca 1638/40?; Salem/Manchester/Lynn
STANDISH, Josiah (-1690) & 1/wf Mary DINGLEY (-1655, 1665); 19 Dec 1654; Marshfield
STANDISH, Josiah (-1690) & 2/wf Sarah [ALLEN] (1639-); aft 1 Jul 1665; Duxbury/Preston, CT
STANDISH, Myles[1] (1584-1656) & 1/wf Rose _?_ (-1621); b 1620; Plymouth
STANDISH, Myles[1] (1584-1656) & 2/wf Barbara [ALLEN]? (-1659+); betw Jul 1623 & 3 Apr
1624; Plymouth/Duxbury
STANDISH, Myles (-1663) & Sarah WINSLOW (1638, 1636-1726), m/2 Tobias PAINE 1665, m/3
Richard MIDDLECOT 1673; 19 Jul 1660, no issue; Boston
STANDISH, Myles & Mehitable (CARY) ADAMS (1670-), w Eliashib; 5 Dec 1700; Bristol,
RI/Preston, CT
STANDISH, Thomas[1] (1612-1692) & 2/wf Susanna SMITH (1624-1692); b 1660; Wethersfield, CT
STANDISH, Thomas (1660-1735) & 1/wf Mary CHURCH (-1705); 20 Mar 1690, 1689/90?;
Wethersfield, CT
STANDLAKE, Daniel (-1638) & _?_ (-1638+); b 1638; Scituate
STANDLACK, Richard (-1691) & 1/wf _?_ ; b 1661; Scituate
STANDLAKE, Richard (-1691) & 2/wf Lydia (HATCH) [BARSTOW], w Jeremiah; ca 1677;
Scituate
STANFORD, John (1648-1730) & Margaret [HARRIS] (1657-1750); b 1678; Ipswich
STANDFORD, Robert (see Robert SANFORD) & 1/wf Mary (HOWLAND) WILLIAMSON
(-1690), w Timothy; 22 Jan 1679, 1679/80; Marshfield
STANFORD, Robert (-1709) & _?_ (-1721); Falmouth, ME/Gloucester
STANFORD, Robert & 2/wf Rebecca (BARTLETT) BRADFORD, w William; aft 1690, b 1693?, b
1709; Duxbury
STANFORD, Thomas (-1695) & Sarah (CROUCH) [JONES] (-1707), w Thomas; b 1681;
Charlestown
STANFORD, Thomas & Mary FLUENT; 2 Dec 1697; Marblehead
STANFORD, Thomas & _?_ ; b 1647?; Falmouth, ME/Purpooduck
STANOP, Jonathan (-1702) (ae 66 in 1699) & 1/wf Susanna AYRE; 16 Apr 1656; Sudbury
STANHOP, Jonathan (-1702) & 2/wf Sarah GRIFFIN (1642-); 11 May 1674; Sudbury

STANHOPE, Joseph & Hannah BRADDISH/BRADISH, m/2 Edward MARRETT bef 1694; 1 Jan 1684/5; Sudbury

STANLEY, Caleb[1] (1642-1718) & 1/wf Hannah [COWLES] (ca 1646-1689, 1690); ca 1665; Hartford

STANLEY, Caleb (1642-1718) & 2/wf Sarah (FOSTER) MOORE LONG (-1698, ae 44), w Benjamin, w Zachariah; 24 Sep 1690; Charlestown/Hartford

STANLEY, Caleb[2] (1674-1712) & 1/wf Hannah SPENCER (1679-1702); 13 May 1696, no issue; Hartford

STANLEY, Caleb[1] (1642-1718) & 3/wf Lydia (COLE) WILSON (-1732), w John; 14 Sep 1699; Hartford

STANLEY, Christopher (1603-1646) & Susanna __?__ (1604/10-), m/2 William PHILLIPS; b 1635; Charlestown

STANDLEY, George & Bethiah [LOVETT]; b 1671/[2?]; Beverly

STANDLEY/STANLEY, George & Jean STASY/Jane STACEY, m/2 John STONE 1726; 4 Nov 1692; Beverly/Marblehead

STANLEY, Isaac (1648-1671) & Mary __?__ ; no issue; Hadley

STANLEY, James & Esther CLIFFORD (1662-); 20 Jul 1686; Ipswich

STANLEY, John (1603-1634, d on ship) & [Ruth WERDEN?] (-1630/1); ?18 May 1624

STANLEY, John (1624-) & 1/wf Sarah SCOTT (-1661); 15 Dec 1645, 5 Dec; Hartford

STANLEY, John (1624-), Farmington & 2/wf Sarah FLETCHER, Milford; 20 Apr 1663

STANLEY/STANDLEY?, John (-1718) & Hester NEWELL (1652-1740); 18 Nov 1669, 1679?; ?Farmington, CT/?Waterbury, CT

STANLEY, John & Rebecca [LARCOM?]; b 1695, b 1700; Beverly

STANLEY, Matthew & Ruth ANDREWS?; ca 1649?, b 1656, b 1659; Topsfield

STANLEY, Nathaniel (1634-1712) & Sarah BOOSEY (1636-); 2 Jun 1659; Hartford

STANLEY, Samuel & Joanna __?__ ; b 1678; Topsfield/Attleboro

STANLEY, Thomas (1597-1663) & Benet/Benedicta? TRITTON (1609-1665) (1664, ae 55) (some say SHEPARD), m/2 Gregory WOLTERTON; Ashford, Kent, Eng, 3 Aug 1630; Lynn/Hartford/ Hadley

STANLEY, Thomas (1649-1713) & Anna/Anne PECK (1665-1718); May 1690, 1 May 1690; Farmington

STANLEY, Timothy (1600-1648) & Elizabeth [MORRICE?], m/2 Andrew BACON; b Jan 1632/3; ?Hartford/Farmington?

STANLEY, Timothy (?1653, 1653/4-1728) & Mary STRONG (1658-1722); 22 Nov 1676; Windham, CT/?Farmington, CT

STANARD, John (-1649) & Margaret __?__ ; b 1637; Roxbury

STANNARD, Joseph (-1688) & Elizabeth SPENCER (ca 1646-); b 1668; Saybrook, CT

STANNARD, Joseph (1668-1703) & Hannah BRACKETT, m/2 Andrew WARNER 1706; 4 Apr 1692 in Boston; Saybrook

STANNARD, Joseph & Elizabeth SPENCER?, ?m/2 Joseph POST 1717 Saybrook (see below); b 1701?; Haddam, CT?/?Saybrook

STANNARD, Samuel & Elizabeth __?__ , m/2? Joseph POST; ca 1697; ?Saybrook, CT

STANNARD, William & Mercy WRIGHT; 22 Mar 1699/1700; Saybrook, CT

STANTON, Benjamin & ?Joanna __?__ ; Pemaquid

STANTON, Daniel (?1648-1687) & [?Sarah WHEELER]; ?1 Jun 1671; Stonington, CT/Barbados

STANTON, Daniel (1648-1690±) & Elizabeth __?__ (-1690+); b 1676; Newport, RI/Westerly, RI

STANTON, John (1641-1713) & Hannah THOMPSON (1645-), dau Anthony (not William); b 1665; Stonington, CT

STANTON, John (1645-1713) & 1/wf Mary [HARNDELL] (1647-); b 1668; Newport

STANTON, John (1645-1713) & 2/wf Mary (CLARK) (JONES) [CRANSTON] (-1711), w Philip of NY, w John; aft 12 Mar 1680; Newport, RI

STANTON, John (1674-) & Elizabeth CLARKE (1680-1730); 9 Feb 1698; Newport, RI

STANTON, Joseph (1646/7-1714) & 1/wf Hannah MEAD (1655-1676); 19 Jun 1673; ?Roxbury

STANTON, Joseph (1646/7-1714) & 2/wf Hannah LORD (1656-1681); 13 Aug 1677; ?Hartford

STANTON, Joseph (1646/7-1714) & 3/wf __?__ ; b 13 Mar 1683; Stonington, CT

STANTON, Joseph (1646/7-1714) & 4/wf __?__ ; Stonington, CT/Westerly, RI

STANTON, Joseph & Margaret CHESEBROUGH; ?18 Jan 1696, ?18 Jul 1696, prob Jul; Stonington, CT

STANTON, Robert (1599-1672) & Avis __?__ ; b 1638; ?(Dorchester)/Newport, RI

STANTON, Robert (1653-1724) & Joanna GARDNER (1657-); 12 Sep 1677, ?12 Nov; Stonington, CT

STANTON, Samuel (1657, 1658?-1697+, 1711+?) & Borodell DENISON (1651-1702); 6 Jun 1680, 2 Jun; Stonington, CT

STANTON, Theophilus (1676-1705) & Elizabeth ROGERS (1673-), m/2 _?_ HARRIS; 5 Jan 1698; New London, CT

STANTON, Thomas (-1677) & Ann/Anna LORD (1614-1688); ca 1637; Hartford/Stonington, CT

STANTON, Thomas (1638-1718) & Sarah [DENISON] (1641/2-1701); b 1660; Stonington, CT

STANTON, Thomas (1670-) & Ann [STANTON] (1675-); b 1692?, b 1693; Preston, CT

STAINWOOD, John (1653-1706) & Lydia (MERCER) ?BUTLER/?CUTLER; 9 Dec 1680 in Boston; Gloucester/Falmouth, ME

STANWOOD, Jonathan (1661-) & Mary NICOLS/NICHOLS; 27 Dec 1688; Gloucester/Ipswich

STANWOOD, Philip^1 (-1672) & Jane _?_, m/2 John PEARCE 1673; ca 1648; Gloucester

STAINWOOD, Philip^2 (-1728) & 1/wf Mary BLACKWELL (-1678/79); 22 Nov 1677; Gloucester

STAINWOOD, Philip^2 (-1728) & 2/wf Esther BRAY; 30 Oct 1683; Gloucester

STANWOOD, Samuel (1658-) & Hannah PRESSEE/PRESSEY (1668-); 16 Nov 1686; Amesbury/Gloucester

STANION, Anthony^1 (-1689) & 1/wf Mary _?_ ; b 1642; Boston/Exeter, NH/Hampton, NH

STANIAN, Anthony (-1689) & 2/wf Ann PARTRIDGE (-1689), w William; 1 Jan 1655, 1655/6; Salisbury

STANYAN, James (1667-) & Ann HUSSEY (1669-); ca 1689

STANIAN, John^2 (1642-1718) & Mary BRADBURY; 17 Dec 1663, 15 Dec; Salisbury/Hampton, NH

STAPLEFORD, Thomas & Margaret _?_ ; b 1678; Boston

STAPLES, Abraham (1638-1703) & Mary RANDALL (1642-1712); 19 Sep 1660, 17 Sep; Weymouth/Mendon

STAPLES, Abraham (1663-) & Mehitable [HAYWARD] (1670-), m/2 Nicholas COOKE; b 1689; Mendon

STAPELLS, Benjamin & Mary COX; 26 May 1699; Boston

STAPLE, Ebenezer (1677-) & 1/wf Huldah ALDRICH; 15 Sep [1699?]; Mendon

STAPLES, Ephraim (1678-) & Elizabeth WEBSTER; 16 Aug 1699; Taunton

STAPLES, Jacob (1669-) & 1/wf Abigail WINTER; 28 Mar 1690; Mendon

STAPLE, Jacob & Mary (_?_) BRIGGS, w Remember; 15 Sep 1696; Taunton

STAPLES, Jeoffrey/Geoffrey? (-1646/7) & Margery _?_ ; b 1639(40?); Weymouth

STAPLES, John (-1683) & [Rebecca?] _?_ ; b 1637; Weymouth/Dorchester

STAPLE, John & Sarah ATKINS, m/2 Samuel BAILEY; b 1672; Weymouth/Braintree?

STAPLES, John (1663-1748) & Abigail [CANFIELD] (1665-); ca 1685/8; Fairfield, CT

STAPLES, John & Mary CRAFT (1671-); 24 Jul 1690; Cambridge/Newton

STAPLES, John, Braintree & Jemima JEWIT/JEWETT, Dorchester; 6 Jul 1693; Milton/Braintree

STAPLES, John (1671-1749) & Hannah _?_ (-1757); b 1699; Taunton

STAPLES, John & Mary [DIXON]; b 1700, Oct 1696; Kittery, ME

STAPLES, Joseph & [Mary MACOMBER?]; b 1670(1?); Taunton

STAPLES, Peter & Elizabeth (BEADLE?) [EDWARDS], w Stephen; b 1673; Kittery, ME

STAPLE, Peter (?1675-1721) & Mary LONG/LANG? (1678-); 8 Jan 1695/6; Kittery, ME

STAPLES, Samuel & 1/wf Mary COLE; 1644; Braintree

STAPLES, Samuel & 2/wf Mary BOLES/BOWLES?; 30 Aug 1652; Braintree

STAPLE, Samuel & Hannah LILLIKIN/LINCOLN; 9 Feb 1691/2, 9 Feb 1692-3; Taunton

STAPLES, Thomas (-1688?) & Mary _?_ (-1696?); b 1646?, b 1659?; Fairfield, CT

STAPLES, Thomas & Elizabeth GRIFFIN (1667-); 21 Apr 1694; Haverhill

STAPLES, Thomas, 2nd & 1/wf Sarah OYDEN, w Richard; late in 1700; Fairfield, CT

STAPLETON, Samuel (1640-1717), London & Mary WHYTT/WHITE (1636-1725), London; 7 Mar 1678, 1677/8 prob; Newport, RI

STARBIRD, Thomas & Abigail DAM (1663-); 4 Jan 1687/8; Dover, NH

STARBUCK, Edward (1605-) & [?Katherine] [?REYNOLD]?; b 1635; Dover, NH/Nantucket

STARBUCK, Jethro & Dorcas GAYER/GEYER? (1675-1747); 6 Dec 1694; Nantucket

STARBUCK, Nathaniel (?1635-1719) & Mary [COFFIN] (1645-1717); ca 1662; Nantucket

STARBUCK, Nathaniel (1668-1753) & Dinah/Dionis? COFFIN (-1750); 20 Nov 1690; Nantucket

STARK, Aaron (?1608-1685±) & [?Sarah] _?_ ; Hartford/New London, CT

STARK, Aaron (-1714+) & Mehitable SHAW (-1714); 27 Jan 1676; Stonington, CT/Groton, CT

STARK, John (-1689) & Elizabeth [?PACKER], m/2 John WEEKS; b 1685?; New London, CT
STARK, William & Elizabeth _?_; b 1690; Stonington, CT/Groton, CT
STARKEY, John (1638-) & Sarah _?_; b 1667; Boston/Malden/Pemaquid, ME
STARKEY, John (-living 1694) & Susannah PATTEN, m/2 John GUPPY 1700; 19 Jul 1686; Salem
STARKEY, Robert (-1705) & _?_; b 1684; Boston
STARKWEATHER, John (1646-1703) & Ann _?_ (-1727); b 1680; Ipswich/Preston, CT
STARKWEATHER, Robert (-1694) & Janet [ROBERTS]; b 1643; Roxbury/Ipswich
STARR, Benjamin (1648-1678) & Elizabeth ALLERTON (1653-), m/2 Simon AYRES 1679; 23 Dec 1675; New Haven
STARR, Comfort (?1590-1659/60) & Elizabeth _?_ (?1595-1658); b 1615, in Eng; Cambridge/Duxbury/Boston
STARR, Comfort (-1693) & Mary [WELD] (1646-1688); b 1666; Boston/New London
STARR, Comfort & Rachel _?_; b 1670?, b 1674; Middletown, CT
STARR, Comfort (1662-1729) & Mary STONE (1665-1735); 14 Nov 1683; Dedham
STARR, Comfort & Elizabeth [HOPSON] (1674-); b 1695; Guilford, CT
STARR, Eleazer & 1/wf Mary _?_; b 1664, b 1663?; Boston
STARR, Eleazer (-1712) & 2/wf Martha _?_; b 1681; Boston/Milton
STARR, John (1626-1704) & Martha [BUNKER]; b 1652; Charlestown
STARR, Jonathan (-1747) & Elizabeth MORGAN (1678-1763), m/2 Thomas ADGATE 1749; 12 Jan 1698, 1698/9; New London, CT
STARR, Joseph & Abigail BALDWIN; 24 Jun 1697; Middletown, CT
STARR, Josiah (1657-1715) & Rebecca _?_ (-1739, ae 74); by 1685; Scarsdale, NY/Danbury, CT
STARR, Josias & Elizabeth HICKS (-1691); Apr 1672; Hempstead, LI
STARR, Robert & 1/wf Susanna HOLLINGSWORTH (-1665); 24 Nov 1650; Salem
STARR, Robert & 2/wf Mary (ABORN)/ODIORNE? CONKLIN, w Cornelius, m/3 William NICK 1680, m/4 George JACKSON 1690; 30 Dec 1669; Salem
STARR, Samuel (1641) & Lydia _?_; Charlestown/Boston
STARR, Samuel (ca 1640-1688?) & Hannah BREWSTER (1648-1688+); 23 Dec 1664; New London, CT
STARR, Thomas & Susan _?_; b 1637; Boston
STARR, Thomas (1615-1658) & Rachel _?_, m/2 John HICKS 1662; b 1641, b 1640?; Charlestown/Scituate
STARR, Thomas (ca 1642-) & 1/wf Elizabeth [GILBERT]; b 1677?; Yarmouth/Newport?
STARR, Thomas (ca 1642-) & 2/wf Ruth _?_
STARR, Thomas (1668-1710) & Mary MORGAN (1670-), m/2 William PEABODY/PABODIE; 1 Jan 1693/4; New London, CT
STARR, _?_ & Mary (RICHARDSON) GATLIFFE (?1644-1681), w Jonathan; aft Feb 1675, bef Aug 1678
STARSE, Samuel & _?_; b 1683; Scituate
START, Edward (1614-1671) & Wilmot LAMSYTT, m/2 William ROANES; Brixham, Devonshire, 23 Jun 1645; York, ME (ch: Thomas, Sarah m [Henry] WRIGHT, Elizabeth m Moses WORCESTER, Mary m _?_ PORTADOE & Antonio FORTADO)
START, John (1633±) & _?_ TAYLOR (heir)?
STATHEM, Thomas & Ruth [UDELL]; 1671; Westchester, NY (moved to Cumberland Co., NJ)
STAY, Samuel & _?_; b 1680; Ipswich
STEARNS, Charles & 1/wf Hannah _?_ (-1651); Watertown
STEARNS, Charles & Rebecca GIBSON (1635-); 22 Jun 1654; Cambridge/Lynn/Lexington
STEARNS, Isaac (-1671) & Mary [BARKER]; 1622, Stoke-by Nayland, England; Watertown
STEARNS, Isaac (1633-1676) & Sarah BEERS, m/2 Thomas WHEELER 1677; 28 Jun 1660; Cambridge/Lexington
STEARNS, Isaac (1658-1692) & Hannah [BECKETT], m/2 John CHAPMAN 1694; b 1685; Salem
STEARNS, Isaac (1665-) & Elizabeth [STONE] (1670-); b 1690(1?); Cambridge
STEARNS, Isaac (1661-), Billerica & Mary [MERRIAM] (1664-); b 1700; Billerica
STEARNS, John (1623-1669), Billerica & 1/wf Sarah [MIXER] (-1656); b 1654; Billerica/Watertown
STEARNS, John (-1669) & 2/wf? Mary LATHROP (1640-), m/2 William FRENCH, m/3 Isaac MIXER; 20 Nov 1656, Dec 1656; Barnstable
STEARNS, John (1654-1728) & 1/wf Elizabeth BIGELOW (1657-1694); 6 Sep 1676?, where?
STEARNS, John (1657-1732) & Judith [LAWRENCE] (1660-); b 1682(3?); Watertown

STEARNS, John & Joanna (CALL) PARKER (-1737, ae 80), w Jacob; 22 Apr 1696; Malden
STEARNS, John (1675?) & Mercy DAVIS; 26 Apr 1699; Concord
STEARNS, Nathaniel & Mary [STONE] (?1632-1684); b 1661; Dedham
STEARNS, Nathaniel, Dedham & Mary RAINE, Weymouth; 25 Oct 1687; Milton
STEARNS, Nathaniel (1666-) & 1/wf Elizabeth [DIX] (1671-1712); b 1694; Watertown
STEARNS, Obadiah & Rebecca [ROSE] (1657-); Stratford, CT
STEARNS, Samuel (1638-1683), Watertown & Hannah MANNING (1642-1724); 1 Feb 1662, 1662/3; Cambridge
STEARNS, Samuel (1650-1694) & Mehitable _?_ ; b 1685/(6), b 1686; Watertown/Lexington
STEARNS, Samuel & Mary BROWN; 9 Jul 1696, b 1697; Concord/Dedham
STEARNS, Samuel & Phebe [WAITE] (1676-); b 1697; Watertown/Lexington/N. Brookfield
STEARNS, Samuel & Mary HAWKINS; 2 Mar 1697/8; Watertown
STEARNS, Shubael (1655-1734), Lynn & 1/wf _?_ ; b 1683; Watertown/Lynn
STEARNS, Shubael (1655-1734), Lynn & 2/wf? Mary UPTON; 1705, int 27 Apr 1705
STEARNS, Thomas (1665-1696) & Rebecca CHAMBERLAIN, m/2 George FARLEY 1699; 20 Jun 1688; Billerica
STEBBINS, Benjamin & Ruth WILLIAMS
STEBBINS, Benjamin (1658-1698) & 1/wf Abigail DENTON (-1689); 9 Oct 1682; Springfield
STEBBINS, Benjamin (1658-1698) & 2/wf Mary (GRAVES) BALL, w Samuel, m/3 James WARRINER 1704; 11 Apr 1690; Springfield
STEBBIN, Benoni (1655-1704) & 1/wf Mary (BROUGHTON) [BENNETT] (-1689), w James; ca 1676; Springfield
STEBBIN, Benoni (1655-1704) & 2/wf Hannah (ATKINSON) [EDWARDS], w Joseph, m/3 Thomas FRENCH; ca 1691; Springfield
STEBBINS, Daniel & ?Rebecca/?Bethiah COMSTOCK; 31 May 1675; New London, CT
STEBBINS, Edward (-1668) & Frances (TOUGH) (CHESTER) SMITH; b 1632, 1629?; Cambridge/Hartford
STEBBINS, Edward (1656-1712) & 1/wf Sarah GRAVES (1659-1700); Apr 1679; Springfield
STEBBIN, John & 1/wf Margaret/?Mary _?_ (-1678); b 1640; Watertown/Northampton
STEBBINS, John & 1/wf Ann MUNKE (-1680, ae 50); 17 Apr 1644; Roxbury
STEBBINS, John (ca 1626-1679) & 1/wf Anne (MUNSON) MUNDEN, w Abraham (-1656); 14 May 1646; Springfield
STEBBINS, John (ca 1626-1679) & 2/wf Abigail BARTLETT, m/2 Jedediah STRONG 1681; 17 Dec 1657; Northampton
STEBBINS, John (1640-1707) & Deborah [?MOORE], dau Miles?; 8 May 1663; New London, CT
STEBBIN, John & 2/wf Rebecca HAWKINS, wid; 4 Jun 1680; Roxbury
STEBBIN, John (1647-) & Dorothy ALEXANDER (?) (1660-); 4 Jan 1680, ca 1683 at Boston; Deerfield
STEBBINS, John & Phebe MINER (1679-); 17 Jun 1697, 17 or 16 Jun; New London, CT
STEBBINS, Joseph (1652-1728) & Sarah DORCHESTER (1653-1746); 27 Nov 1673; Springfield
STEBBINS, Joseph & Rebecca COLTON, m/2 John MERRICK 1725; 29 Feb 1700, 1699/1700; Springfield
STEBBIN, Martin (1589-1659) & Jane GREEN (-1659); 25 Dec 1639; Roxbury/Boston
STEBBIN, Rowland (1594, 1592?-1671) & Sarah WHITING (1591-1649); Bocking, Eng, 30 Nov 1618; Springfield/Northampton
STEBBINS, Samuel (1659-1732) & 1/wf Mary FRENCH (-1696), div 27 Dec 1692, 1695?; 4 Mar 1678, 14 Mar, 14 Mar 1677/8, 4 Mar; Northampton/Belchertown
STEBBINS, Samuel (1646-1708) & 1/wf Joanna LAMB (1657-1683); 2 Jul 1679, 22 Jul; Springfield
STEBBINS, Samuel (1646-1708) & 2/wf Abigail BROOKS (1665-1754); 10 Dec 1685; Springfield
STEBBINS, Samuel (1646-) & 2/wf Sarah WILLIAMS; 14 Mar 1692, 14 Mar 1692/3?, m in RI; Deerfield
STEBBINS, Thomas (?1620-1683) & 1/wf Hannah WRIGHT (-1660); Nov 1645, 14 Nov; Springfield
STEBBINS, Thomas (1648-1695) & 1/wf Abigail MUNN (1650-1692); 21 Dec 1672; Springfield
STEBBINS, Thomas (?1620-1683) & 2/wf Abigail (BURT) (BALL) MUNN (1621-1707), w Francis, w Benjamin; 14 Dec 1676; Springfield
STEBBINS, Thomas (1662-1712) & 1/wf Elizabeth WRIGHT (1666-), m/2 John HANNUM; 26 Sep 1684; Deerfield

STEBBINS, Thomas (1648-1695) & Mary (DAY) ELY, w Samuel, m/3 John COLEMAN 1696; 12 Apr 1694; Springfield
STEBBINS, Thomas (1662-) & Mary (PARSONS) ASHLEY, w Joseph; 2 Mar 1699
STEDMAN, Caleb (1671-1748) & Hannah WISAVEL/WISWALL (1674-1743, Roxbury); 1 Apr 1697; Newton/Brookline
STEDMAN, George (-1691) & Hannah OSBURN/OSBORN, m/2 Thomas BARBER 1693; 4 Apr 1674; Charlestown
STEADMAN, Isaac (?1605-1678) & Elizabeth _?_ (1609-); in Eng, b 1630, b 1631; Scituate/Boston
STEDMAN, Isaac (1635-) & Pilgrim (EDDY) BAKER (1644-), w William, m/3 Sylvester EVELETH 1678/9; b 1678, b 11 Jan 1677; Watertown
STEDMAN, John (-1693) & Alice _?_ (-1689?, 1690?); b 1641; Cambridge
STEDMAN, John (-1675) & Elizabeth _?_ (-by 21 Oct 1678); ca 1650; New London/Hartford/Wethersfield, CT
STEDMAN, John (-1678, not 1676) & Elizabeth REMINGTON (ca 1647-1680), m/2 Samuel GIBSON 1679; 14 May 1666; Cambridge/Roxbury
STEDMAN, John & 1/wf Violet SHEPARD (-1682); 10 Aug 1678; Wethersfield, CT
STEDMAN, John (1651-) & 2/wf Susannah (FRANCIS) NORTH (1651-), w John; 14 Apr 1683; Wethersfield, CT
STEDMAN, John (1668-1728) & Sarah GIBSON; 9 Apr 1691; Cambridge
STEDMAN, Joshua (-1762, ae 89) & 1/wf Margaret [?BRIDGE] (-1701, ae 28); b 1700; Brookline
STEDMAN, Nathaniel (-1678, ca 50) & 1/wf Sarah [HAMMOND] (1640-bef 1675); Watertown
STEDMAN, Nathaniel (-1678, ae ca 50) & 2/wf Temperance [WILLIS?] (1648-), dau Michael?; b 1667?, ?1669+; Boston/Brookline
STEDMAN, Robert (-1666) & Anne _?_ (-1675/6); b 1638; Cambridge
STEDMAN, Robert (1659-1736) & _?_ [FITCH] (-1740); ca 1683; Hartford/Lebanon, CT
STEDMAN, Thomas (1607-) & _?_ ; b 1640?; New London, CT
STEDMAN, Thomas (-1701?) & Hannah ISBEL/NICHOLLS? (1642-), m/2 John FOX ca 1690?; 6 Aug 1668; ?New London, CT
STEDMAN, Thomas & Mary [WATSON] (1644-); b 1669; Newton/Roxbury/Brookline
STEDMAN, Thomas & Jane [SCAMMON] (1667-), m/2 Thomas DEANE 1691; b 1687(8?); Boston
STEDMAN, Thomas & Mary [TROWBRIDGE] (1670-); b 1696; Brookline
STEDWELL, Joseph[2] (-1695+) & (Mary LYON) (1649-), m/2 John WILSON; b 1680; Stamford, CT
STUDWELL, Thomas (-1669) & _?_ ; Stamford, CT/Greenwich, CT
STEELE, Barrett (-1713) & Mary BROOKS (1677-); 30 Dec 1697; Springfield
STEELE, Francis & Elizabeth _?_ ; b 1701(?); Exeter, NH
STEELE, George & [?Margery] [?SORRELL]; 1608?, b 1629; Hartford
STEELE, James (1622-) & 1/wf Bethia BISHOP; 18 Oct 1651?; Guilford, CT
STEELE, James & 2/wf Bethia (HOPKINS) STOCKING, w Samuel; aft Dec 1683; ?Middletown, CT/Hartford
STEELE, James (-1712) & Sarah [BARNARD]; b 23 Apr 1685; Hartford
STEELE, James (1662-1713) & Anne WELLES, m/2 James JUDSON 1718; 19 Jul 1687; Wethersfield, CT
STEELE, John (1591-1665) & 1/wf Rachel TALCOTT (-1653); 10 Oct 1622, Fairsted, Eng; Cambridge/Hartford/Farmington, CT
STEELE, John[2] (-1653) & Mary WARNER, m/2 William HILLS; 22 Jan 1645, 1645/6; Hartford
STEELE, John[1] (-1665) & 2/wf Mercy (RUSCOE) SEYMOUR, w Richard; 25 Nov 1655; Farmington, CT
STEELE, John & Ruth [JUDD]; b 1678; Farmington, CT
STEELE, John (1660-1698, Hartford) & Melatiah [BRADFORD] (1664-1715+), m/2 Samuel STEVENS; b 1691; Norwich, CT
STEELE, John & Abigail LOBDEN; 25 May 1696 m int; Boston
STEELE, Samuel (?1626-1685) & Mary [BOOSEY] (1635-1702); b 1652; Farmington, CT
STEELE, Samuel (1652-1710?, 1709) & Mercy BRADFORD (1660-1720); 16 Sep 1680; Hartford
STEERE, John (1634-1724) & Hannah WICKENDEN (-1703+); 27 Oct 1660 m int; Providence
STEERE, John[2] (-1727) & Esther [WHITMAN] (-1748); b 1701?; Providence, RI
STEERE, Richard (-1721, in 78th y) & _?_ ; Southold, LI
STEERE, Richard & Elizabeth WHEELER, w John; ca 1692; New London

STEERE, Thomas (1674-1735) & 1/wf Mary [ARNOLD] (1668-1725); b 1701?; Providence/Smith-field

STEERE, _?_ & Bethiah _?_ (-11 Oct 1739, in 67th y); Southold, LI

STELLE, Ponett/(Poncet) & Eugene _?_/Eugenie LEGEREAU; b 1682; Boston

STENT, [?Eleazer] & Elizabeth? _?_, m/2 Thomas BEAMONT; b 1645; New Haven

STENT, Eleazer & Elizabeth [BUTLER] (-1712); b 1671; Branford, CT

STENT, _?_ & Elizabeth STENT, m/2 Thomas HARRISON 1666; ?Branford

STEPNEY, Francis & Catharine _?_; b 1687; Boston

STERLING, Daniel (1673-) & Mary (MARVIN) ELY (1666-1744), w Richard; 6 Jun 1699; Lyme, CT

STALLION, Edward & 1/wf Margaret _?_ (-1680+); b 1653; New London, CT

STALLION, Edward & 2/wf Elizabeth [MILLER], dau George; b 1685; New London, CT

STALLION, Edward & 3/wf Christian (BELL?) [CHAPEL], w William; 16 Mar 1692/3; New London, CT

STARLING, Nathaniel (1671-) & Mary STAR; m int 10 Feb 1695/6; Boston

STARLIN, Richard (1663-) & Grace _?_; b 1686; Bristol, RI

STARLING, William¹ & 1/wf Elizabeth [SAWTELLE] (?1638-1675); ca 1659; Bradford/Haverhill

STERLING, William¹ & 2/wf Mary (BLAISDELL) STOWERS (-1681), w Joseph; 19 Dec 1676; Haverhill

STARLING, William² (1660/1-1695) & Mary _?_; b 1684, ca 1682/3; Boston

STERLING, William & 3/wf Ann (NICHOLS) NEALE, w John; 24 Apr 1683; Haverhill/Lyme, CT

STERLING, _?_ & Mary SAWTELLE (1640)

STERRY, Roger & Hannah (PALMER) HEWITT (1634-), w Thomas, m/3 John FISH 1681; 27 Dec 1671; Stonington, CT

STERTT, William (-1645?) & Jane _?_; b 1643; Boston

STETSON, Benjamin (1641-1711) & Bethia HAWKE (not LINCOLN) (1643-); 15 Aug 1665; Hingham

STETSUN, Benjamin & Grace TURNER (1665-); 22 Jan 1690, prob 1689/90; Scituate

STUDSON, James (1670-) & Susanna TOWNSEND; 26 Nov 1696; Boston

STETSON, John (1648-1690) & Abigail [HUDSON] (-1691+), dau John; b 1677; Scituate

STETSON, Joseph (1639-1724?) & 1/wf Ruth [HILAND]; b 1667; Scituate

STETSON, Joseph (1639-1724?) & 2/wf [Prudence] _?_; b 1670; Scituate

STETSON, Joseph (1667-) & 1/wf Hannah OLDAM; 6 Nov 1688; Scituate

STETSON, Robert¹ (-1702, ae 90) & 1/wf [Honor] [?TUCKER]; b 1639, 2 May 1635; Scituate

STETSON, Robert² (1653-) & [Deborah BROOKS] (1654/5?-); ca 1675/8, 1670?; Scituate

STETSON, Robert¹ (-1702, ae 90) & 2/wf Mary (HILAND) [BRYANT], w John; aft 1684; Scituate

STETSON, Robert & Mary CALLOMER (1667-); 12 Jan 1692/3; Scituate

STETSON, Samuel (1646-1731+) & 1/wf ?Mercy/Mary _?_ (-1687?); b 1679; Scituate

STETSON, Samuel (1646-) & 2/wf [Lydia PICKLES]; b 1691; Scituate

STETSON, Thomas (1643-1729?) & Sarah [DODSON] (1652-); b 1671; Scituate

STETSON, William & Elizabeth (?WILLIAMS/THOMAS?/CUTTER?) [HARRIS] (-1670), w Thomas; betw 1631 & 1634, no issue; Charlestown

STEVENS, Amos & Margery SHEPARD; b 1682?; N. Yarmouth, ME

STEVENS, Benjamin & 1/wf Ann SHEPHERD, w Thomas; 8 Apr 1666, Apr 1666; N. Yarmouth, ME

STEVENS, Benjamin (1650-1690) & Hannah BARNARD; 28 Oct 1673; Salisbury

STEVENS, Benjamin & Hannah _?_; b 1673, ca 1680?; Stamford, CT/Bedford, NY

STEVENS, Caleb (-1675) & Ruth [GLANFIELD], m/2 Henry KIRKE 1675+

STEVENS, Caleb (-1706) & Grace [MOSES], wid; betw 1691 & 1706; Ipswich

STEEVENS, Cyprian (-1692+) & 1/wf Mary WILLARD (1653-prob 1685); 22 Jan 1671/2; Lancaster

STEVENS, Cyprian (-1692+) & 2/wf Ruth _?_ (-bef 1693); aft 1683, bef 9 Dec 1693; Lancaster

STEVENS, Daniel & Hannah RICH; m int 1 Aug 1695; Boston

STEVENS, David & Elizabeth WEBSTER, m/2 Peter HAWKSWORTH 1699/1700; 29 Jan 1690, 19 Jan 1690; Boston

STEVENS, Ebenezer & Mary [SANBORN] (1677-); b 1701?; Hampton, NH?/Kingston, NH

STEVENS, Ebenezer (1669/70-1738) & Jean/Jane REDFIELD; b 1701?, no issue, 27 Apr 1698; Killingworth, CT

STEEVENS, Edward (-1689) & ?Mary ADAMS?/_?_ SHERMAN (1698-1680?), sister of John SHERMAN; b 1666; Marshfield

STEVENS, Edward & Mary _?_; b 1669; Boston

STEVENS, Edward & Martha _?_; b 1678?, b 1683; Newbury/Ipswich

STEVENS, Edward & Esther _?_; b 1680; Boston

STEPHENS, Edward & Rebecca (JOSSELYN) (CROCUM/CROCKHAM?) HARRIS, w John, w Thomas; 8 Oct 1700; Boston

STEEVENS, Ephraim (-1718, ae 69) & Sarah ABBOTT (-1711); 11 Oct 1680; Andover

STEVENS, (Ephraim?) & Sarah (CHANDLER) WILSON?/[CLEAVES], w William (Sarah PARKER in 1683), m/4 _?_ ALLEN 17 Apr 1691?; (see above) b 4 Sep 1681, 11 Oct 1688, 1680?; Roxbury

STEVENS, Erasmus & Elizabeth [CLARK?], dau Thomas?, ?m/2 Thomas BLIGH/BLY by 1687; b 1671; Boston

STEVENS, Francis (-1669) & _?_; b 1641?, b 1639? (see below); Rehoboth?

STEVENS, Francis & Elizabeth [?BROOKS] (1645-1675); b 1663 (see above); Rehoboth

STEVENS, Henry (1611-1690) & 1/wf Alice _?_ (1613-ca 1649/50); b 1635; Boston

STEVENS, Henry (1611-1690) & 2/wf Mary [BUCKMASTER]; b 1652, b 15 Feb 1651; Boston/Framingham/Roxbury

STEVENS, Henry & Elizabeth _?_; b 1656; Newport

STEVENS, Henry & Joanna LEEKE, m/2 Joseph PRESTON 1689+; 6 Feb 1678, 1677; New Haven

STEVENS, Henry & Elizabeth [GALLUP]; b 1678; Stonington, CT

STEVENS, Henry & Mary?/Sarah? [WAKELY]; b 1689; Stratford, CT

STEVENS, Jacob & Anna/Hannah [WHIPPLE]/GREGORY? (-1675); ca Mar 1613/4; Stow

STEEVENS, James (ca 1630-1697) & Susanna EIVLEIGH/EVELETH; 31 Dec 1656; Gloucester

STEVENS, James (1640-) & Elizabeth?/[Sarah SMITH] (1646-); b 1665, b 1677; Hingham/New London, CT?/Norwich, CT?/Boston/Brewster

STEVENS, James & Mary [?WAKELEE]; b 1674; Killingworth, CT

STEVENS, James (1671-) & Hannah [?BARNES]? (?1670-); b 1701; West Haven, CT/Killingworth, CT

STEVENS, Jeremiah & Elizabeth STANYON/STANYAN; 6 Jan 1697/8 ; Salisbury

STEVENS, John (-1627) & Alice [ATKINS] (-1650, Newbury, MA); Caversham, Oxford, 27 Feb 1597/8

STEVENS, John (-1670) & [Mary?] _?_; in Eng, b 1624; Guilford, CT

STEVENS, John (1606-1662) & Elizabeth [PARKER?] (1614?-1694); b 1638; Newbury/Andover

STEVENS, John (-1689) & Catharine _?_ (-1682) (wf Abigail 1647); b 1639; Salisbury

STEEVENS, John & 1/wf Love HOLYROAD/HOLGROVE? (-1675), dau Joshua; 2 Jul 1661; Salem

STEEVENS, John (1639-1689) & 1/wf Hannah BARNARD (-1675, Andover); 13 Jun 1662; Andover

STEPHENS, John (1637-1691) & Elizabeth HILDRETH (1646-1717/18); 15 Dec 1664; Chelmsford

STEVENS, John & Mary COIT; b - Nov 1665; New London/New Haven

STEVENS, John & Mary CHASE (1651-); 9 Mar 1669, 1669/70; Newbury/Haverhill

STEVENS, John & Joanna THORN (-1692+) (2/wf Hannah? or same as Joanna?); 17 Feb 1669/70; Salisbury

STEEVENS, John (1639-1689) & 2/wf Esther BARKER (1651-1713); 10 Aug 1676; Andover

STEVENS, John & 2/wf Mary (WATERS) ENGLISH, w Clement; ca 1683/4, ca 23 Dec 1682, b 28 Sep 1685; Salem

STEVENS, John (1661-1722) & Abigail COLE (1661-), m/2 John FRENCH; 28 Apr 1684; Killingworth, CT/Wallingford, CT?

STEVENS, John & Mary _?_; b 1686; Boston

STEVENS, John & Mary GIMPSON/JAMESON; 10 May 1688; Amesbury

STEEVENS, John & Ruth POOR; 20 Dec 1689; Andover

STEEVENS, John (1670-) & Dorothy [HUBBARD] (1673-); b 1692; Salisbury

STEEVENS, John & Sarah SNOW (1672-), Woburn; 17 Jan 1692/3; Chelmsford

STEVENS, John & Grace GAMMON; 6 Jun 1694; Boston

STEEVENS, John & Hannah CURRIER; 18 May 1697; Haverhill

STEVENS, John & Mary BARTLET/BARTLETT; 30 May 1700; Haverhill

STEVENS, John & Abigail [LORD?]/[ALCOCK?] (1674-); ca 1700; Charlestown

STEVENS, Jonathan (-1689) & Mary _?_; Norwalk, CT

STEVENS, Jonathan (1675-) & Deborah [STILES] (1682-1748); b 1701?; CT

STEVENS, Joseph & Mary [BLAISDALE]; 1667; Salisbury
STEVENS, Joseph (-1677) & Sarah TAYER/THAYER (1654-); 2 Jul 1671; Mendon/Braintree
STEVENS, Joseph (1654-1742) & 1/wf Mary INGALLS (-1699); 28 May 1679; Andover
STEVENS, Joseph & Sarah BUXTON (1656±-); 24 Jun 1680; Stamford, CT
STEVENS, Joseph & _?_ ; b 1690; Beverly
STEVENS, Joseph & Joanna WINCHESTER (1674-); 5 Jun 1698; Roxbury
STEPHENS, Joseph (1654-1742) & 2/wf Elizabeth BROWNE; 13 Nov 1700; Salem/Andover
STEVENS, Joshua (widower) & Mary FRIE/FRY, m/2 _?_ BARKER; 22 Dec 1696; Andover
STEVENS, Josiah (1670-), Killingworth & 1/wf Sarah HUBBELL; 25 Jun 1699; Killingworth, CT/Fairfield, CT
STEVENS, Marmaluke & Elizabeth [WADE] (div); b 1679; Scituate
STEVENS, Moses (-1689) & Waitstill [FISKE]?; b 1685; Wenham
STEEVENS, Nathan & Elizabeth ABBOT (1673/4?-); 24 Oct 1692, 24 Nov; Andover
STEVENS, Nathaniel (1645-) & 1/wf Mary [LAWRENCE]?; b 1672; Dover, NH/Salisbury
STEVENS, Nathaniel & 2/wf Mehitable COLCORD (?1658-); 20 Dec 1677; Salisbury/Dover, NH?
STEVENS, Nathaniel (1661-) & Sarah _?_ ; ca 1686/8; Guilford, CT
STEVENS, N. & Abigail BARNUM?; b 1688
STEVENS, Nicholas & Elizabeth _?_ ; b 1669; Boston
STEPHENS, Nicholas & 1/wf Remember [TISDALE]; b 1698; Taunton
STEVENS, Obadiah (-1703) & Rebecca ROSE; 18 Dec 1678; Stamford
STEVENS, Richard (-1683) & _?_ ; Concord
STEVENS, Richard & ?Mary (LINCOLN) HACK, w William; ca 1666, ca 1667; Taunton
STEVENS, Richard & _?_ ; in Eng, b 1681; Marlboro/Framingham
STEVENS, Richard (1674-1753) & Hannah HALD/HEALD (1676-1755); 15 Nov 1699; Chelmsford
STEVENS, Robert & Mary _?_ (?1602-1692); b 1641; Braintree
STEVENS, Robert & _?_ ; b 1678?; Pemaquid, ME
STEPHENS, Robert & Elizabeth [ASPINWALL?], m/2 Daniel DRAPER b 1695; b 1693; Marblehead
STEPHENS, Roger & Elizabeth SOWDEN?/LOWDEN?; 24 Jul 1686; Marblehead
STEVENS, Roger (-1730) & Sarah NICHOLS; 24 Nov 1698; Amesbury/Brookfield/Salisbury
STEEVENS, Samuel (-1675) & Rebecca REA, m/2 Simon HORNE/ORNE 1675/6, m/3 Joseph BALLARD 1692; 17 Dec 1672; Salem
STEVENS, Samuel (1656-) & 1/wf Elizabeth [HILL?] (-1701?), wid; b 1683; Guilford, CT/Killingworth, CT
STEVENS, Samuel (1665-) & Mary ELLERY (1677-1758), m/2 Edmund GROVER 1758; 12 Jan 1692/3; Gloucester
STEVENS, Samuel (1657-1712) & Meletiah (BRADFORD) [STEELE] (1664-), w John; ca 1698; Killingworth, CT
STEVENS, Samuel & Abigail [CLARK] (1674-); b 1699; East Haven, CT
STEVENS, Thomas (-1658) & _?_ ; ca 1640/45?; Stamford, CT
STEVENS, Thomas & Sarah _?_ ; b 1648; Boston
STEPHENS, Thomas & _?_ ; in Eng, b 1649; Taunton
STEVENS, Thomas (-1685) & Mary [FLETCHER] (1634?-); b 1651; Guilford, CT/Killingworth, CT
STEVENS, Thomas (-1704) & Mary GREEN (1634-1695+); b 1662, b 1658; Charlestown/Sudbury?
STEVENS, Thomas (-1729) & Martha BARTLET/BARTLETT (1653-1718); 15 Apr 1670, 1671, 1672, 1673; Newbury/Salisbury
STEVENS, Thomas & Esther _?_ (6 ch bpt in Old South Ch, Boston, 14 Nov 1686)
STEVENS, Thomas & Elizabeth [LAWRENCE]; 1672; Flushing, LI/Newtown, LI
STEVENS, Thomas (1620-) & 2/wf Margaret (ROYAL?) [WATKINS] (1642-), w Thomas; b 1674, by Aug 1672?; Boston
STEVENS, Thomas & Joan _?_ , m/2 Thomas BARNES by 1696; Portsmouth, NH
STEVENS, Thomas (-1701, ae 51) & Elizabeth COOK; 20 Oct 1675; Southampton, LI
STEVENS, Thomas & Mary MYGHIL/MIGHILL, ?w Nathaniel; 13 Oct 1681; Newbury
STEPHENS, Thomas & 1/wf Hannah EVARTS (-1687); 3 Jun 1686; Killingworth, CT/Guilford?
STEVENS, Thomas (-1703) & 2/wf Sarah BUSHNELL (1668-1691(2?)); 9 Nov 1688, Guilford, CT; Guilford, CT/Killingworth
STEVENS, Thomas (1665-) & Ruth [HALL] (1670-); ca 1690/5?; Sudbury/Stow/Plainfield, CT
STEVENS, Thomas & _?_ ; b 1691; Scituate/etc.

STEEVENS, Thomas (-1703) & 3/wf Deborah __?__; aft 4 Feb 1691, b 1697; ?Killingworth, CT?
STEVENS, Thomas & ?Jane (HALL) ELTON, w John (his wife in 1714); ?b 1693; Middletown, CT
STEVENS, Thomas & Sarah __?__ (-1695); b 1684; Suffield, CT
STEVENS, Thomas (?1669-) & Sarah PLACE (-1725, Boston?); 9 Apr 1696 in Boston, 13 Jul 1695; Watertown/Boston/Charlestown
STEVENS, Thomas (-1711) & Hannah __?__; Southampton
STEPHENS, Thomas & Mary CASWELL; 28 Sep 1699; Taunton
STEVENS, Thomas (1678-1736) & Mary [HALL] (-1728+); ca 1700; Westerly, RI
STEVENS, Timothy (1640, 1641-1708) & Sarah DAVIS (1647-1695); 12 Mar 1664; Roxbury
STEVENS, Rev. Timothy (1666, 1665-1726) & 1/wf Eunice CHESTER (1668-1698); 17 May 1694; Wethersfield, CT/Glastonbury
STEEVENS, Timothy (1664-1712) & __?__; b 1697; Killingly, CT
STEEVENS, William (-1667+) & Philippa __?__ (-1681); ca 1634; Gloucester/Salem
STEVENS, William (-1653) & Elizabeth BIDFIELD/BITFIELD?, m/2 William TITCOMB; 19 May 1645; Newbury
STEVENS, William[1] & Mary MEIGS (1633-1703); 3 Mar 1653; Guilford, CT/Killingworth, CT
STEEVENS, William & Abigail GREENE; 7 Jul 1673, 1 Jul; Cambridge
STEVENS, William (-1704) & Sarah __?__; say ca 1675, say b 1670, b 1653?
STEEVENS, William & Abigail SARGAINT/SARGENT, m/2 Nathaniel COIT; 15 Jun 1682; Gloucester
STEVENS, William (-1685) & Ann/Anna [LAKE]; ca 1680/3; Salem
STEPHENS, William (1666-) & Hannah [TILDEN?]; b 1692; Marshfield
STEVENS, William & Elizabeth [?DRAPER]; b 1695; Rowley
STEVENS, William & Anna (_?_) NEWCOMB, w Michael; 18 Jan 1699/1700; Charlestown
STEVENS, __?__ see William CLEAVES
STEVENS, __?__ & Grace BARRON (1665-); b 1711
STEVENS, William & 2/wf Sarah [CARPENTER], w David
STEVENS, __?__ & Alice __?__; b 1623?; Newbury
STEVENS, Sarah & __?__; 14 May 1664
STEVENS, Sarah & __?__; 1 Feb 1680/7
STEVENSON, Bartholomew & Mary CLARK; 10 Oct 1680; Oyster River, NH
STEVENSON, Edward (-1662) & Ann __?__, m/2 William GRAVES; b 1640; Newtown, LI
STEVENSON, Edward (-1700) & Charity [FIELD] (?1653-); b 1682; LI
STEVENSON, James (-1711), Windsor, CT, & 1/wf Mary DENSLOW (1658-1688); 8 Jun 1682; Springfield
STEVENSON, James (-1711) & 2/wf Joanna (MILLER) BARBER (1659-1713), w John; 4 Jun 1691; Springfield
STEVENSON, John & Sarah __?__, m/2 Rev. William BLAXTON/BLACKSTONE? 1659; b 1643; Boston
STEVENSON, John & Emma __?__; b 1669; Boston
STEVENSON, Jonathan & Mary ?WHITEHEAD ALLEN, w Thomas, m/3 John BOWTON aft 1689?; 16 Jul 1684; Burlington, NJ/Norwalk, CT/Newtown, LI
STEVENSON, Thomas (-1663) & Margaret __?__ (-1663); ca 1640/43; Dover, NH/Oyster River, NH
STEVENSON, Thomas (1615-) & Maria/Mary (BULLOCK) BERNARD, w William; 15 Aug 1645; New York/Flushing, LI/Newtown, LI/Southold, LI
STEVENSON, Thomas (?1648-1725) & 1/wf Elizabeth LAWRENCE (-ca 1686); Feb 1672; LI
STEVENSON, Thomas (?1648-1725) & 2/wf Ann [FIELD] (-1725); ca 1687; Newtown, LI
STEWART, Alexander & Hannah TEMPLAR (1643-1674); 12 Oct 1662; Charlestown
STUART, Alexander (-1731) & Deborah (REDIAT) FARROWBUSH (1652-1720+), w Daniel FORBUSH/FORBES; 23 May 1688, 22 May 1688; Sudbury/Marlborough
STEWART, Charles (1661-1689) & __?__; b 1688; Salem
STEWART, Daniel (-1703) & Mary __?__ (-1702+); b 1663; Barnstable/Eastham/Tisbury/Edgartown
STEWART, Duncan (-1717) & Ann WINCHURST (-1729); Apr 1654; Ipswich/Newbury/Rowley
STEWART, Ebenezer (1676-1749) & Elizabeth JOHNSON (?1677-1749); 23 May 1698; Rowley
STUARD, Hugh & Wait __?__; b 1670; Falmouth/Yarmouth
STEWART, James & Anna [BATES]; b 1669; Weymouth
STUARD, James (-1727) & 1/wf Bennett/Benit BRIGGS; 20 Aug 1687; Rochester
STEWART, James (1664-1750) & 1/wf Elizabeth __?__ (-1732); b 1688; Newbury/Rowley

STEWART, James & Desire [?TOBEY]; b 1690; Sandwich
STUARD, James (-1727) & 2/wf Sarah WAIT; 4 Jun 1694; Rochester
STEWART, James (1663-) & Experience _?_; b 1691?, ca 1694; Norwalk, CT
STEWART, John (-1690) & Sarah [STILES], m/2 John SACKETT 1691; ca 1650-70?; Windsor, CT
STEWART, John & 1/wf Elizabeth _?_ (-1689); b 1686; Newbury/Wenham
STEWART, John (1668?-) & Elizabeth [?LUDLAM]; b 4 Jan 1694/5; Jamaica, LI
STEWART, John & 2/wf Elizabeth [DRESSER] (-1726); b 23 Jun 1695; Rowley
STEWART, Robert (-1688), Norwalk, CT, & Bethia RUMBALL/RUMBLE; 12 Jun 1661; Stratford, CT/Norwalk, CT
STEWART, William (-1664) & Sarah _?_; Lynn
STEWART, William (-1693) & Anne _?_ (-1697), m/2 Bartholomew GADNEY; b 1683; Ipswich
STICKNEY, Amos (-1678) & Sarah MORSE, m/2 Stephen ACREMAN/ACKERMAN 1684?; 24 Jun 1663; Newbury
STICKNEE, Andrew & 1/wf Edna (NORTHEND) LAMBERT (1649-1722), w Thomas; 22 Jan 1689, 1688/9; Rowley
STICKNEY, Andrew (-1717) & 1/wf Rebecca [SOMERBY?] (-Jan 1692/3); b 1693; Newbury
STICKNEY, Andrew (-1717) & 2/wf Elizabeth [CHUTE]?, m/2 Henry LUNT; aft Jan 1692/3, b 1695; Rowley
STICKNEY, John (1640-) & Hannah BROCKLEBANK; 9 Jun 1680; Rowley
STICKNEY, John (1666-1727) & Mary POER/POOR; 10 Dec 1689; Newbury
STICKNEY, Samuel (ca 1633-1709) & 1/wf Julian SWAN (-1674?, 1673?); 18 Apr 1653; Rowley
STICKNEY, Samuel (-1716) & 2/wf Prudence (LEAVER) GAGE (1644-), w Benjamin; 6 Apr 1674; Bradford
STICKNEY, Samuel (1663-1714) & Mary [HASELTON] (1672-1731), m/2 Joseph TIDD 1722; b 1690; Bradford
STICKNEY, Thomas (1646-1714) & Mehitable [KIMBALL]? (?1657-1689); b 1689; Bradford
STICKNEY, William (1592-1665) & Elizabeth _?_ (1608-1678+); in Eng, ca 1630/32; Rowley
STIFF, Elias & Mary _?_; b 1674; Boston
STILEMAN, Elias[1] (-1662) & Judith _?_ (-1663+); in Eng, b 1617; Salem
STILEMAN, Elias[2] (1616/17-1695) (ae 79 in 1695) & 1/wf ?Deborah/?Mary [WOLFE?] (-1684+) (in 1662 & 1672); b 1640; Salem/Portsmouth, NH/Newcastle, NH
STILEMAN, Elias[3] (1641-) & Ruth MANNYARD/MAYNARD; 13 Apr 1667; ?Portsmouth, NH
STILEMAN, Elias & 2/wf [Mary STILEMAN], w Richard; by 1684; Portsmouth, NH
STILEMAN, Elias[2] (1616/17-1695) & 3/wf Lucy (TREWORGY) (CHADBOURNE) [WELLS/WILLS?] (-1708), w Thomas; ca 1688?; Salem
STILEMAN, Richard[1] (1611-1678) & 1/wf Hannah _?_; b 1644; Cambridge/Salem/Portsmouth, NH
STILEMAN, Richard[1] (1611-1678) & 2/wf Mary _?_ (1634-), m/2 Elias STILEMAN; b 1657(8?); Portsmouth, NH
STILEMAN, Robert & Elizabeth FRY; 4 Oct 1660; Andover
STILER, John & Mary BULL; 9 Jun 1697; Boston
STILES, Benjamin (-1711), Woodbury & Abigail [ROGERS] (1654-1723), Milford; b 1681; Woodbury, CT
STILES, Ephraim (1645-1714) & 1/wf Ruth (ROGERS) GOODWIN WHEELER, w Thomas, w Obadiah; 28 Jul 1669; Stratford, CT
STILES, Ephraim (1645-1714) & 2/wf Bathseba [TOMLINSON] (1661/2-1735), m/2 Benjamin CURTIS; ca 1685?, b 15 Mar 1680/1?; Stratford, CT
STILES, Ephraim & Abigail NEAL; 2 Aug 1694; Springfield/Westfield
STILES, Francis[1] (1602-) & Sarah _?_ (1600-1682), m/2 Robert CLARK; b 1632, in Eng; Dorchester
STILES, Henry (1629/32-1724) & 1/wf _?_ [KETCH] (-1659?), wid; b 1658; Windsor, CT
STILES, Henry (1629/32-1724) & 2/wf Elizabeth WILCOXSON; 16 Apr 1663; Windsor, CT
STILES, Henry & _?_; b 1690; Windsor, CT
STILES, Henry & Sarah PARSONS; 1 Nov 1698; Windsor, CT
STILES, Isaac (-1715) & Hannah [PALMER]/Deborah JONES (1645-); b 1663; Wethersfield, CT
STILES, Isaac (1663-1691) & Hannah [ROSE], m/2 Samuel HARGER 1693, m/3 John TIBBALS 1700; ca 1686; Stratford, CT
STILES, John (1595-1662) & Rachel _?_ (1610-aft 10 Mar 1682/3); b 1629, in Eng; Dorchester
STILES, John (-1683) & Dorcas BURT; 28 Oct 1658; Springfield
STILES, John & Hannah [MORSE?] (1642-); b 1669; Boston

STILES, John & Deliverance **TOWN** (1664-); 24 Nov 1684; Boxford
STILES, John (1665-) & 1/wf Ruth **BANCROFT** (1670-1714); b 1691, b 1697; Windsor, CT
STILES/STILEMAN, Robert (-1710, ca 91) & Elizabeth **FRY** (1637-); 4 Oct 1660; Andover/Dorchester
STILES, Robert (-1721) & Ruth **BRIDGES**; 10 Nov 1699; Boxford/Salem/Hebron, CT
STILES, Samuel & Elizabeth **SHERWOOD**; last of Dec 1664, no issue; Stratford, CT
STILES, Thomas (1613-1675+) & ?Margaret __?__; Stratford, CT/Flushing, LI (? had 2 daughters)
STILES, Thomas (-1745) & Bethiah [**HANMER**]; ca 1698, no ch; Springfield
STILLMAN, George (-1728) & 1/wf Jane __?__/**PICKERING**? (-1684); b 1679; Wethersfield, CT
STILLMAN, George (-1728) & 2/wf Rebecca [**SMITH**] (1668-1750); b 1688, ca 1686; Hadley
STILWELL, Daniel & Mary **MOTT**; b 1678; Staten Island
STILWELL, Jasper (-1656) & Elizabeth __?__; b 1651; Guilford, CT
STILWELL, John & __?__; b 1693; NJ/Staten Island
STILLWELL, Joseph & Mary [**OGBORN**]
STILLWELL, Nicholas & Michal [**LAKE**]; b 1690; LI
STILLWELL, Nicholas & Rebecca [**BAYLIS/BAYLESS**]; b 1682; ?Jamaica, LI
STILWELL, Nicholas[1] & 1/wf Abigail [**HOPTON**]; in Eng b 1634; New York
STILWELL, Nicholas[2] (1636-1715) & 1/wf Catharine **MORGAN**, wid; 6 Nov 1671, 6 Feb 1671; Gravesend, LI
STILEWELL, Nicholas[2] & 2/wf Elizabeth [**CORWIN**]; Gravesend, LI
STILWELL, Nicholas[3] & Mary **MOORE**; b 1683(or5); Brooklyn
STILLWELL, Nichols[1] (1603-1671) & Ann **VanDYKE**; b 1648; Brooklyn/Staten Island, NY
STILLWELL, Richard (1634-1689?) & 1/wf? Mary **HOLMES**; May 1655; Gravesend, LI
STILLWELL, Richard (-1689) & 2/wf Freelove/Mercy [**COOKE**]; Gravesend, LI/Dover/Staten Island
STILLWELL, Thomas & Martha **BATIEU/BALEIN/CALORIC**; 8 Jan 1670; Gravesend, LI
STILWELL, Thomas (1671-) & Martha **POILLON**; ca 1695?; Staten Island
STILWELL, Thomas[3] & Ann **HUBBARD**; b 1696; Gravesend, LI
STILWELL, William & __?__; b 1678; Staten Island, NY/NJ
STILSON, James (-1686/8, 1689?) & Margaret [**GOULD**] (-1751?, ae 92), m/2 Thomas **PITMAN** 1696; b 1679?, 1675?; Marblehead
STILSON, Vincent & 1/wf Grace __?__ (-1676)
STILSON, Vincent (-1690) & Mary __?__, m/2 Simon **COUCH**; ca 1646/50?; Milford/Marblehead
STILSON, Vincent & Sarah __?__ (-1695?); b 1680; Milford, CT/Marblehead
STILLSON, Vinson/(Vincent) & 2/wf Susannah (**LANGDON**) **GRAY** (1677-), Boston, w Samuel, m/4 Joseph **VAJOLL** 1702; m int 4 May 1696; Marblehead
STILSON, William (1601-1691) & 1/wf Elizabeth (?**CUTTER**) [**HARRIS**] (-1670, ae 93?, 73?); b 22 Mar 1633; Charlestown
STILSON, William (1601-1691) & 2/wf Mary (**HOUGHTON**) (**PHILLIPS**) **NORTON** (-1691), w Francis; 22 Aug 1670; Charlestown
STIMSON/STEVENSON, Andrew (-1683) & Jane __?__; b 1637; Cambridge
STIMSON, Andrew (ca 1650-1721, ae 72) & Abigail **SWEETSER** (-1726); 9 Mar 1678, 1677/8?, ?9 Mar; Charlestown
STIMPSON, George (1645-) & Alice **PHILLIPS** (1656-); 22 Jul 1676; Ipswich
STIMSON/STEVENSON, James (-1691, 1690) & 1/wf Naomy **LEAPINWELL** (1638-1681); 18 Apr 1661; Reading, CT
STIMPSON, James (-1691) & 2/wf Patience (**COOK**) [**GOODALE**], w Isaac; b 1684; Reading
STIMPSON, James & Bethiah **MANSFIELD**; 4 Jan 1698/9; Watertown
STIMSON/STEVENSON, Jonathan (1644-1692) & Elizabeth **STUBBS** (1650?-1727), m/2 Richard **BARNES**, m/3 Jonathan **BULLARD**; 8 Jul 1669; Cambridge/Watertown
STIMPSON, Jonathan & Mehitable **SPRING**; 21 Mar 1698/9; Watertown
STIMSON, Thomas & Mary **TAYLOR**; 8 Jan 1696; Reading/Woburn
STITES, John (?1595-1717?) & __?__; b 1646, b 1640?; Hempstead, LI
STITES, Richard (1646, 1640?-1702) & Mary **NAYLOR**; 14 May 1668, b 1686?, b 1676; Hempstead, LI
STITES, Henry & [Hannah **GARLICK**]; ca 1692; in East Hampton, LI?
STOAKHAM, John & Mary/Elizabeth? [**KNIFFEN**]; b 1678; ?Rye, NY

STOCKBRIDGE, Charles (1634-1683) & Abigail [PIERCE?/ALLEN?/JAMES?] (-1710), (sister of Michael PIERCE's or of his 1/wf or 2/wf), m/2 Nathaniel TURNER; b 1659; Charlestown/Scituate/Boston

STOCKBRIDGE, Charles (-1731) & Abigail [TILDEN]; b 1690; Scituate

STOCKBRIDGE, John¹ (1608-1657) & 1/wf Ann [HATCH?] (1614-1642); in Eng, b 1634; Scituate/Boston

STOCKBRIDGE, John¹ (1608-1657) & 2/wf Elizabeth (HATCH) SONE, Scituate, w Robert; 9 Oct 1643; Scituate

STOCKBRIDGE, John¹ (1608-1657) & 3/wf Mary _?_, m/2 Daniel HENDRICK 1660; b 1655; Boston

STOCKBRIDGE, John (1657-) & Mary GODFREY, Hampton, NH; 23 Nov 1681; Haverhill

STOCKBRIDGE, Joseph & Margaret TURNER; 20 Oct 1697; Scituate/Pembroke

STOCKBRIDGE, Thomas (-1717) & Sarah REED (POOL wrong), dau Thomas; 28 Jul 1697; Hingham

STOCKER, Ebenezer (-1704) & Sarah MARSHALL (1654-); 15 Jul 1674; Lynn

STOCKER, Edward & 1/wf Mary _?_ (-1704); b 1701; Lyme

STOCKER, Joseph & Ann [SHEFFIELD] (1649-); b 1671; Boston

STOCKER, Samuel & Mary (DIVEN) WITT, w Jonathan; 6 Jun 1666; Lynn/Boston

STOCKER, Samuel & Dorcas _?_ ; b 1680; Boston

STOCKER, Samuel & Elizabeth _?_ ; b 1683; Boston

STOCKER, Thomas (?1620-) & Martha _?_ ; b 1655; Boston/Lynn

STOCKER, Thomas & Sarah BERRY, Boston; 29 Nov 1700; Lynn

STOCKING, Daniel (1677-1733) & Jane MOULD (-1758); 27 Aug 1700; Middletown, CT

STOCKING, George (-1683) & 2/wf? Anna/Anne/Agnes _?_ ; b 1630?, b 1633; Hartford

STOCKING, George (1665-1714) & Elizabeth _?_ (1674-1737), m/2 Samuel HALL; b 1694; Middletown, CT

STOCKING, Samuel (-1683) & Bethia HOPKINS (1629-), m/2 James STEELE 1683+; 27 May 1652; Hartford/Middletown, CT

STOCKMAN, John & Sarah (PIKE) BRADBURY (1641/2-), w Wymond; 10 May 1671; Salisbury

STOCKTON, Richard (-1675+) & Abigail _?_ (-1713+); b 1656?, b 1671; Flushing, LI

STOCKTON, Richard & Susanna (WITHAM) (ROBINSON); b 1693

STOCKWELL, Eleazer (1679-) & Sarah PEASE/PEARSE?; 21 Oct 1700; Suffield, CT/Deerfield/Branford, CT

STOCKWELL, Quintin & Abigail BULLER/BULLARD?; 11 Apr 1666; Medfield/Hatfield/Branford, CT/Suffield, CT

STOCKWELL, William & Sarah LAMBERT; 14 Apr 1685; Ipswich

STODDARD, Anthony (1617, ?1614-1687) ("cousin" of William PAYNE) & 1/wf Mary [DOWNING] (ca 1620-16 Jul 1647) (dau Emanuel & Ann); b 1640; Boston/Salem

STODDARD, Anthony (-1687) & 2/wf Barbara (CLAPP) WELD (-1654?), w Joseph; m cont 24 Jul 1647?, 24 Aug 1647?; Boston?/Cambridge

STODDARD, Anthony (-1687) & 3/wf Christian [EYRE?]; betw June & Sep 1655; ?Boston/?Roxbury

STODDARD, Anthony (1616-1687) & 4/wf Mary (SYNMES) [SAVAGE] (1628-), w Thomas; aft 7 Dec 1683, bef 10 Apr 1684; Charlestown/Boston

STODDARD, Anthony (1678-1760) & Prudence WELLS (1682-1715); 20 Oct 1700; Wethersfield, CT

STODDER, Daniel (-1737, ae 104) & Abigail LANE (did she m/1 John LOWE?); 27 Dec 1665; Hingham

STODDARD, Daniel & Elizabeth [BALLARD]; b 1686(7?); Boston

STODDER, Daniel & Margaret MACVARLO/?MACFARLAND; 26 May 1690; Hingham

STODDER, John (-1661/2) & Ann/Anna/Hannah _?_ (-1675); ca 1630/33; Hingham or Hull?

STODDARD, John (-1664) & Mary [FOOTE] (1623-), m/2 John GOODRICH 1674, m/3 Thomas TRACY; ca 1642; Wethersfield, CT

STODDER, John & Catherine _?_ ; b 1652; Hingham, CT

STODDER, John (-1708) & Hannah BRYANT (1645, ?1646-1702); 13 Dec 1665; Hingham

STODDARD, John (1646-1703) & Elizabeth CURTIS (?1649-1704+); 26 May 1674; Wethersfield, CT

STODDARD, John (1675-1728) & Sarah CAMP (1678-1742); 19 Nov 1696; Wethersfield, CT

STODDER, John & Mary JOY; 14 Nov 1699; Boston/Hingham

STODDARD, Joshua (1648-1725) & Bethia SMITH (ca 1660-1725), dau Richard; 15 Aug 1680?, 1684?, no issue; Wethersfield, CT

STODDARD, Nathaniel (1661-1714) & 1/wf Mary [MARSHALL?] (-1693); b 1692; Wethersfield, CT

STODDARD, Nathaniel (-1714) & 2/wf Eunice [STANDISH] (1664-1716); 7 Dec 1693; Wethersfield, CT

STODDARD, Ralph (1666-1753) & Mary [AMES] (1664-1728); ?ca 1696; ?Groton, CT/?New London, CT

STODDARD, Robert (?1652-1749) & Mary [MORTIMER]; b 1690; New London, CT

STODDARD, Samson (1645-1698) & Susanna [CLARK] (ca 1648-1707+); b 1672; Boston

STODDER, Samuel & 1/wf Elizabeth GILL (-1693); 6 Jan 1666/7, Feb 1667, 6 Jul 1666, 6 Feb 1667; Hingham

STODDER, Samuel (1670-1762) & 1/wf Elizabeth [OTIS?] (-1749, ae 79); 1 Mar 1692/3; Scituate

STODDARD, Samuel (-1731, ae 92 y) & 2/wf Martha (BEAL) CHUBBUCK (1646-), w John; 12 Jan 1698/9, 10? Jan; Hingham

STODDARD, Simeon (1651-1730) & 1/wf Mary __?__ (-1708) (wife called Mehitable in 1696); b 1676; Boston

STODDARD, Solomon (1643-1729) & Esther (WARHAM) MATHER (1644-1736), w Eleazer; 13 Mar 1670, 8? Mar; Northampton

STODDER, Stephen (1674-) & Hannah CANTERBURY; 1 Apr 1700; Hingham

STODDER, Thomas & Deborah ROISE/ROYCE; Dec 1699; Norwich, CT

STOKES, Anthony & Susanna __?__; b 1685; Boston

STOKES, Isaac & Rebecca [RAWLINS/ROLLINS]; b 1663/4; Dover, NH

STONE, Benajah (1649-1738) & Esther/Hester [KIRBY]; b 1676, ca 1673; Guilford, CT

STONE, Benjamin (see Daniel) & Joanna [HUNBOCK] (1633/4?); b 1680; Cambridge/Boston

STONE, Daniel[2] (1620-1687) & Mary __?__ (-1658, Boston); b 1644; Cambridge/Boston

STONE, Daniel (1644-) & 1/wf Mary (MOORE) WAD/WARD, w Richard; 22 Nov 1667, 2 Nov; Sudbury

STONE, Daniel (-1713) & Patience GOODWIN; 19 Sep 1670; Kittery, ME

STONE, Daniel (1651-) (see Benjamin above) & Joanna [PARKER] (1654-1727); ca 1678; 3 ch bpt 1687

STONE, Daniel (1668-1702) & Patience [BROWN] (1672-), m/2 Nathaniel RICE 1704; ca 1692; Sudbury/Lexington

STONE, Daniel (-1720) & Sarah WALLIS (1675-), m/2 John MACKMILLIAN; ?18 Jul 1699, ?20 Jul 1698; Salem

STONE, David (1622-1704) & Dorcas __?__; ca 1648; Cambridge

STONE, David (1650-1679) & Sarah HILDRETH (1648-); 31 Dec 1674; Cambridge/Lexington

STONE, David (1646-1737) & Susanna __?__; ca 1675; Sudbury

STONE, Ebenezer (1662/3-1754) & Margaret TROWBRIDGE (1666-1710); 11 Mar 1686, 18 Mar; Cambridge/Lexington

STONE, Elias & Abigail LONG (-1731); 10 May 1686; Charlestown

STONE, Gregory (1592-1672) & 1/wf Margaret GARRAD (1597-1626); Nayland, in Eng, 20 Jul 1617; Cambridge/Lexington

STONE, Gregory (1592-1672) & 2/wf Lydia [COOPER] (-1674), w Simon; in Eng, ca 1627; Cambridge

STONE, Hugh (1638-1732) & Abigail BUSECOT/BASSAKER?/BUSECOTT (-1723±); b 1667?, b 1672, ca 1668?, b 1669; Warwick, RI

STONE, Hugh & Hannah FOSTER; 15 Oct 1667; Andover

STONE, Hugh (1669-) & Mary [POTTER]; b 1692; Providence/Warwick, RI

STONE, James & Hannah LAPTHORNE; 3 Jan 1692/3; Salem

STONE, John & 1/wf __?__; in Eng, b 1625, b 1622; Gloucester/Salem

STONE, John & 2/wf [Ellen]/Eleanor/Elinor/Sarah [HASKELL], w William; b 1632; Beverly

STONE, John (1618-1683) & Ann/Anna ROGERS? [TREADWAY?] (1625?-1719), wid; b 1640; Sudbury

STONE, John (1610-1687) & Mary __?__; 1642, b 1644; Hartford/Guilford, CT

STONE, John (-1691) & Abigail [DIXEY] (1636-1703); b 1654; Salem/Beverly

STONE, John & Mary LATHROP; Oct 1656; Billerica

STONE, John (-1659?) & Mary __?__, m/2 Roger WHEELER; b 1659; Boston

STONE, John (-1664) & Jane?/Joan _?_ (-1674), cousin of Robert **GOULD**; b 1659; Boston/Farmingham

STONE, John (1635-1691) (brother of Lewis **JONES**) & Sarah [**BASS**] (ca 1640-1739+), m/2 Joseph **PENNIMAN**; b 1661, ca 1662; Boston/Watertown/Braintree

STONE, John (1644-1686) & Susanna [**NEWTON**] (1654-1703), m/2 Samuel **BURWELL** 1687; b 1674; Guilford, CT/Milford, CT

STONE, John (1661-) & 1/wf Esther/Hester **GAINES** (1660±-1689, 1690); 12 Apr 1683; Beverly/Salem/Ipswich

STONE, John & Rachel **SHEPARD**; 27 Apr 1687; Cambridge/Lexington

STONE, John (1661-) & 2/wf Sarah [**GALE**]; b 1690; Beverly

STONE, John & Mary **RUSS**; 14 Nov 1690; Andover

STONE, John (-1691) & Abigail _?_; Beverly

STONE, John (1654-) & Mary [**BARSHAM?**]/[**BIXBY?**] (1659/60?-); b 1694 (see Josiah **STONE**); Lexington/Watertown?

STONE, John (1666-) & Thankful [**CAPEN**] (1669-); b 1697; Watertown

STONE, John (1658-1735) & Sarah (**NUTTING**) **FARNSWORTH** (1663-), w Matthias; 7 Dec 1698, 16 Dec wrong; Concord/Groton

STON/STONE, Jonathan & 1/wf Ruth **EDDY** (1681-1702); 15 Nov 1699; Watertown

STONE, Jonathan & Sarah _?_; b 1699; Kittery, ME

STONE, Joseph & Hannah [**HILL**] (1664-); b _?_; Wells, ME

STONE, Joseph (1670-1703) & Sarah _?_/[**WAITE?**]; b 1693; Lexington/Cambridge

STONE, Joseph (1674-) & Mary **SCRANTON** (1678-); 9 Jul 1699; Guilford, CT

STONE, Josiah & Mary [?**BIXBY**]/?**GREENOUGH**; b 1686 (see John); Boston

STONE, Matthew & 1/wf Rachel **POND** (1658-1695/6?); - Jul 1681; Dedham

STONE, Matthew & 2/wf Mary **PLYMPTON** (1656-1727); b 1696?; Lancaster/Sudbury

STONE, Nathaniel & Elizabeth _?_; b 1656; Ipswich

STONE, Nathaniel (1631±-1718) & Remember [**CORNING**]; b 1659; Salem/Beverly

STONE, Nathaniel & Mary _?_; b 1664; Boston/Beverly

STONE, Nathaniel & Sarah _?_; b 1672; Beverly

STONE, Nathaniel (1648-1709) & Mary **BARTLETT** (1654-1724); 10 Jul 1673; Guilford, CT

STONE, Nathaniel (1660-1732) & Sarah **WAITE** (ca 1664-); 25 Apr 1684; Malden/Sudbury

STONE, Nathaniel (1663-1741) & Mary **BALSH/BALCH** (-1737); 26 Mar 1689; Beverly/Salem

STONE, Rev. Nathaniel (1667-1755), Harwich 1699+ & Reliance **HINCKLEY** (1675-1759); 15 Dec 1698; Barnstable

STONE, Nathaniel (1678-) & Hannah [**GRAVE**] (1680-); b 1701?

STONE, Nehemiah (1670-1732) & Lydia [**HART**] (1672-); b 1696; Beverly

STONE, Nicholas (-1689, ae 76) & Hannah _?_; b 1651(2?); Boston

STONE, Peter (1672-) & Elizabeth **SHAW**; 25 Jun 1696; Warwick, RI

STONE, Robert (-1694, 1690?) & Sarah [**SHAFFLIN**] (-1708); b 1657; Salem/Ipswich

STONE, Robert (-1688) & Hannah **EAGER/(AGER?**) (-1691, ae 29); 27 Aug 1685; Salem

STONE, Samuel (1602-1663) & 1/wf _?_ (-Oct 1640?); ca 1632; Cambridge/Hartford

STONE, Samuel (1602-1663) & 2/wf Mrs. Elizabeth [**ALLEN**] (-1681, 1689?), m/2 George **GARDNER** ca 1673; b Jul 1641; Cambridge/Hartford

STONE, Samuel (1631-1715) & Sarah **STERNE/(STEARNS**) (-1700); 7 Jun 1655; Cambridge/Lexington (at Watertown)

STONE, Samuel (1656-1743) & Dorcas **JONES** (1659-); 12 Jun 1679; Cambridge/Lexington

STONE, Samuel (1646-1708) & Sarah **TAINTOR** (1658-1732); 1 Nov 1683; Branford, CT?/Guilford, CT

STONE, Samuel (1657-1724) & Mary **TREDWELL** (1665-1731+); 28 Jan 1684, 1683/4?, 1674, 1674/5; Salem

STONE, Samuel (1658-1717) & Elizabeth **HERRICK** (1657-1730+); 11 Mar 1683/4; Beverly/Salem

STONE, Samuel (1656-) & Hannah _?_; ca 1689; Cambridge/Lincoln

STONE, Samuel (1666-1739) & Abiel/Abiah/Abial **GAINES** (1672-1754); 27 May 1690; Ipswich/Manchester

STONE, Simon (1586-1665) & 1/wf Joane **CLARK**; in Eng, 5 Aug 1616, Great Bromley; Watertown

STONE, Simon (?1630-1708) & Mary [**WHIPPLE**] (1634-1720); ca 1655; Watertown

STONE, Simon & 2/wf Sarah (**BAKER**) **LUMPKIN** (-1663), w Richard; ca 1655, b 1655; Cambridge/Salisbury

STONE, Simon (1658-) & Sarah [FARNSWORTH] (1663/4-1731); ca 1685; Groton
STONE, Thomas (1650-1683) & Mary JOHNSON (1657-1732); 13 Dec 1676, 23 Dec 1676; Guilford, CT
STONE, William & 1/wf Hannah __?_ ; b 1639; Guilford, CT
STONE, William & 2/wf Mary [HUGHES], w Richard; 1659, b 5 May 1659, 1657; Guilford, CT
STONE, William (1642-) & 1/wf Hannah WOLFE/DeWOLFE (-1712); 20 Feb 1664, 1673, 1674; Guilford, CT
STONE, William (1665-) & Hannah WALLEY, ?m/2 James LEONARD?; 2 Jun 1686; Bristol, RI
STONE, William & Esther (_?_) CROSS, w Thomas; m int 22 Oct 1698; Ipswich
STONE, William & Hannah KIRBY ANDREWS ROLLO, wid; b 1701?; Guilford, CT
STONE, _?_ & Sarah SHEPARD
STONARD/STONEHARD, John (-1649) & Margaret __?_ ; ca 1630-40?; Roxbury
STORER/STOARE, Augustine & Susannah HUTCHINSON (1601-); ?Alford, Eng, ?Belsby, 21 Nov 1623; Boston/Wells, ME
STORER, Jeremiah & Ruth [MASTERS] (-1701); b 1680; Wells, ME
STORER, Joseph (1648-) & Hannah [HILL]/HALL?; b 1680, b 23 May 1681; Charlestown/Wells, ME
STORER, Richard & __?_ ; b 1639; Braintree
STORER, [Samuel] (-1700) & Lydia [LITTLEFIELD]/AUSTIN? (-1701+); b 1690; Charlestown
STORER, William (-1660?) & Sarah STARBUCK, m/2 Joseph AUSTIN, m/3 Humphrey VARNEY 1665; ?23 Aug 1648; Charlestown/ME
STORER, _?_ & Elizabeth _?_, m/2 Robert HULL; in Eng, b 1615?; Braintree
STORES, Samuel (1640-1719) & 1/wf Mary HUCKENS (1646-1683); 6 Dec 1686; Barnstable
STORES, Samuel (1640-1719) & 2/wf Hester/Esther EGARD (-1730, Mansfield, CT), w John AGARD; 14 Dec 1685; Barnstable/Mansfield, CT
STORRS, Samuel (1677-1727) & Martha BURGESS (-1728); 31 Oct 1700; Windham, CT/Mansfield, CT
STORY, Charles (1664-1716) & Susannah __?_ ; b 1701?; Portsmouth, NH
STORY, Joshua & Alice HURST; 7 Sep 1692; Dorchester
STORY, Rowland & Bethiah __?_ ; b 1677; Boston
STORY, Rowland & Anne [BELCHER] (?1665-); b 16 Jul 1680, 1682?; Boston
STOREY, Samuel (-1726) & 1/wf Elizabeth _?_ (-by 1716); b 1685; Ipswich/Norwalk, CT
STOREY, Seth (1646-1732) & Elizabeth _?_ (-1736); b 1684(5?); Ipswich
STORY, William (ca 1613/14-1702, ae 79) & Sarah [FOSTER] (1620?-1703); ca 1642?, 1640?; Ipswich
STORY, William & 1/wf Susanna FULLER (1650-); 25 Oct 1671; Ipswich/Concord
STORY, William & 2/wf? [Mary] __?_ ; b 1698; Charlestown
STOUGHTON, Israel (1580?, ?1602-1644) (calls Tho. CLARK "brother", had sister CHAMBERLAIN, ret'd to Eng) & Elizabeth [?STARK]/KNIGHT, wid; 27 Mar, b 1631, b 1628?; Dorchester/Windsor, CT
STOUGHTON, John (1657-1712) & 1/wf Elizabeth BISSELL (1666-1688); 11 Aug 16--, [1682], 24 Aug 1682; Windsor, CT
STOUGHTON, John (1657-1712) & 2/wf Sarah FITCH, m/2 Joseph DRAKE; 23 Jan 1689, 1689/90?; Windsor, CT
STAUGHTON, Nicholas & 1/wf Elizabeth KNAPP (-1681); 17 Feb 1673; Taunton
STOUGHTON, Nicholas & 2/wf Sarah (RICHMOND) (REW) [WALKER] (1638-1691); ?b 1690 Taunton, ?m 1691; Taunton
STOUGHTON, Nicholas & 2/wf? 3/wf Sarah HOAR (1658-1713?); 25 Feb 1691/2, ?Saybrook, CT; Taunton/Boston
STOUGHTON, Samuel (1665-1702) & Dorothy [BISSELL] (1665-); b 15 Mar 1693/4, in Eng; Windsor, CT
STOUGHTON, Thomas[1] (-1661) & 1/wf _?_ MONTPESON; b 1624; Dorchester/Windsor, CT
STOUGHTON, Thomas[1] (-1661) & 2/wf Margaret (BARRETT) HUNTINGTON, w Simon; aft 1633; Dorchester/Windsor, CT
STOUGHTON, Thomas[2] (?1624-1684) & Mary WADSWORTH (-1712), Hartford; 30 Nov 1655; Windsor, CT
STOUGHTON, Thomas (1663-1749) & 1/wf Dorothy TALCOTT (1666-1696); 31 Dec 1691; Windsor, CT

STOUGHTQN, Thomas (1663-1749) & 2/wf Abigail (EDWARDS) LOTHROP (1671-), Hartford, w
Benjamin; 19 May 1697; Windsor, CT
STOVER, Charles & _?_ ; ME
STOVER, George & 1/wf Abigail ELWELL; 25 Jan 1692/3; Gloucester
STOVER, John & Abigail (ALCOTT)? (-1730); b 1701; Cape Neddick
STOVIER?, Josiah & Sarah _?_ ; b 1698(9?); Tiverton, RI
STOVER, Sylvester (-1687, 1690) & Elizabeth [NORTON]?; b 1653; York, ME
STOVER, _?_ & Sarah (VERY) COOKE; Boston?
STOWE, Benjamin & Mary _?_ ; b 1674(5?); Boston
STOW, Daniel (called "cousin" by Ebenezer HUBBARD) & Azuba _?_ ; b 1701?; Middletown, CT
STOW, Ebenezer & Abigail PARLING; 2 May 1700; Concord
STOW, Ichabod (1653, 1652/3-1695) & Mary ATWATER (1662-1700), m/2 David ROBINSON ca
1697; 22 Oct 1688; Middletown/New Haven
STOW, John (1582-1643) & Elizabeth BIGGE (1590-1638); Biddenden, Eng, 13 Sep 1608;
Charlestown
STOW, John & Mary _?_ ; b 1658(9?); Sudbury
STOW, John (1641-1688) & Mary WETMORE; 13 Nov 1668; Middletown, CT
STOW, John (1650-1732) & Esther (CORNWALL) WILCOX (1650-1733), w John; in 1677;
Middletown, CT
STOW, John (-1722, Middletown) & Bathsheba HOWE (-1759), m/2 Daniel HUBBARD;
Middletown, CT, May 1698; ?Middletown, CT
STOW, Nathaniel (?1621-1684) & 1/wf Elizabeth _?_ (-1661); b 1657; ?Concord
STOW, Nathaniel (-1684) & 2/wf Martha (METCALF) (BECKNAL) SMITH, m/1 William
BEGNALL/BECKNER, m/2 Christopher SMITH; 20 Aug 1662; Concord
STOWE, Nathaniel (-1705) & Hannah WETMORE (1653-1704); 4 Apr 1677; Middletown, CT (no
issue)
STOW, Nathaniel & Ruth MERRIAM (1670-); 3 Dec 1690; Concord
STOW, Samuel (1624-1704, ae 82) & Hope [FLETCHER] (ca 1624, ca 1625-); ca 1649;
Charlestown/Middletown, CT
STOW, Samuel (1645?-1721) & Elizabeth STONE (ca 1649-1737); 16 Nov 1669; Concord/Marlboro
STOW, Samuel & _?_ ; b 1673; Middletown, CT
STOW/STONE, Thomas (1615-1684) & Mary CRAGG/GRAGG?/GRIGGS? (-1680); 4 Dec 1639;
Roxbury/Braintree/Concord/Middletown, CT
STOWE, Thomas (ca 1650-1730) & Bethia STOCKING (1658-1732); 16 Oct 1675; Middletown, CT
STOW, Thomas (1674-1765) & Rebecca BOW (-1716); Feb 1700, 1 Feb 1700/1701, Feb the last
1700, Feb the last 1700/01; Middletown, CT
STOWE, _?_ & Abigail [HARVEY] (1664-), dau Richard; Salem (?removed to Southold, LI)
STOWELL, David (1660-) & 1/wf Mary CHAMPNEY (1662-1690); 4 Dec 1685; Cambridge
STOWELL, David (1660-) & 2/wf Mary STEDMAN; 7 Apr 1692; Cambridge
STOWELL, Israel (1670-1725) & Abigail [?FULLER] (doubtful) (-1718); b 1699; Hingham/New-
ton
STOWELL, John (1658-1691?) & Mary BEAL (1662-), m/2 Nathaniel HOBART 1695; 3 or 19 Sep
1683; Hingham
STOWELL, Samuel[1] (-1683) & Mary FARROW, m/2 Joshua BEAL 1689; 25 Oct 1649; Hingham
STOWELL, Samuel (1655-1695) & Rachel GILL (1661-1715); 13 Jan 1684/5; Hingham
STOWELL, William (1666-1693) & Sarah _?_ ; ca 1692; Hingham
STOWERS, John & 1/wf Jane _?_ ; b 1633?, b 1635; Watertown
STOWERS, John & 2/wf Phebe _?_ ; b 1650; Watertown/Newport
STOWERS/STOVER, John & Mary BLANCHARD, dau Samuel; m int 13 Aug 1696; Boston
STOWERS, Joseph (?1633-1672) & Mary [BLAISDELL/BLASDELL], m/2 William STERLING
1676; b 1661; Charlestown/Salisbury
STOWER, Nicholas (-1646) & Amy _?_ (-1668); b 1616; Charlestown
STOWERS, Richard (1616-1693) & Joanna _?_/Hannah FROST (-1698, ae 81); b 1647;
Charlestown
STOWERS, Samuel (1663-1721) & Hannah [SPRAGUE]; b 1692; Charlestown/Malden
STRAIGHT, Henry (1652-1728) & Mary [LONG] (-1757); b 1679?; Portsmouth, RI/E. Greenwich,
RI
STRAIGHT, Henry & Hannah _?_ ; 13 Feb 1696/7; E. Greenwich, RI

STRAIGHT, Thomas (1619-1681) & Elizabeth [KEMBALL] (-1719, ae 89, 80?, Waltham); b 1657; Watertown
STREIGHT, Thomas (1660-) & Mary SHEPARD (-1727, ae 75); 28 May 1683, no issue; Concord/Watertown
STRAKER, Ralph & Susanna _?_; b 1685; Boston
STRAND, _?_ & Rachel [BURROWS]; ca 1700?; Jamaica, LI?
STRANGE, George & _?_; b 1637; Dorchester/Hingham
STRANGE, John (-1657) & Sarah [HOWE], m/2 Richard CURTIS 1657; b 1651; Boston
STRANGE, John (-1687+) & Alice _?_ (-1687+); b 1652; Portsmouth, RI
STRANGE, John & Sarah [COBHAM], dau Josiah; b 1681; Boston
STRANGE, Lot (-1683) & Alice [PAINE] (-1690); in 1649 or 1650, no issue; Portsmouth, RI
STRANGE, Lot (-1699) & Mary [SHERMAN] (1664-1699+); b 1689; Portsmouth, RI
STRANGE, Robert & Katharine ELKIN; m int 18 Jan 1696/7; Boston
STRANGE, _?_ & Hannah _?_; b 1698; Marblehead
STRANGE, ?James & Alice [SHERMAN?]; b 1699; Portsmouth, RI
STRAPIN, John (-1671) & Sarah PATEFIELD, m/2 Matthew SOLEY 1671; 7 Jul 1669; Charlestown
STRATFORD, John & Elizabeth _?_; b 1694; Boston
STRATTON, Bartholomew (1628-1686/7) & Elizabeth [SANFORD] (1637-1724); b 1658; Boston
STRATTON, Benjamin (-1716) & Mary _?_; b 1698; East Hampton, LI
STRATTON, Caleb & Mary [ADAMS] (1645-); b 1662, b 1665(6?), b 1670; Boston/Hingham
STRATTON, Cornelius (-1704) & 1/wf _?_; b 1695; Fairfield, CT/East Hampton, LI
STRATTON, Cornelius (-1704) & 2/wf Martha (HULL) SMITH, m/3 _?_ ADAMS; b 16 Sep 1695; East Hampton, LI
STRATTON, Elias & Hannah WATERS; 25 May 1682; Marblehead
STRATTON, John (-1627 in Eng) & Anne [DEARBAUGH/BEARHAUGH?]; in Eng, b 1606(?); Salem
STRATTON, John (-1686) & [Sarah] ?BANCROFT; b 1645; Salem/East Hampton, LI
STRATTON, John (-1691) & Elizabeth TRAYNE/TRAINE (1640-1708); 10 Mar 1658, prob 1658/9; Watertown
STRATTON, John (-1691) & Mary SMITH; 26 Nov 1667, 20 Nov 1667; Watertown
STRATTON, John (1646-1736) & Mary [JAMES] (1654-1718); ca 1672?; East Hampton, LI
STRATTON, John (-1716) & [Priscilla?] _?_; b 1682?; Woodbury, CT
STRATTON, John (1669-1718) & Abigail [PRENTICE]?/BLANCHARD? (1666-1732); b 1689; Watertown
STRATTON, John & Mary BUTTERE/BUTTERS (-1695) (div wf of Wm.? or dau? [prob dau]); 15 Feb 1691; Watertown
STRATTON, John & Bethshuah APPLIN; 3 Jan 1697/8; Watertown
STRATTON, Joseph (1650±-1722/3, ae 72) & 1/wf _?_ (-bef 1714); ca 1671/80?; East Hampton, LI
STRATTON, Joseph & Sarah HOW/HOWE; 14 Nov 1695; Marlborough
STRATTON, Philip & Margaret _?_; b 1673; Boston
STRATTON, Richard (1619-1675?) & Elizabeth [EDWARDS], m/2 Thomas BAKER 1678?; b 1655; East Hampton, LI
STRATTON, Richard (1628-1658) & Susan/Susanna _?_ (-1708), m/2 Thomas DAKIN 1660; b 1658; Watertown
STRATTON, Richard & Sarah [STURGES], dau John; ca 1685?; Fairfield
STRATTON, Richard & 1/wf Naomi (HOYT) LOVEJOY (-1687), w John; 6 Jan 1686, prob 1686/7; Chelmsford
STRATTON, Richard & 2/wf Margaret SHEAFE, m/2 _?_ PARKER 1727+; 8 Apr 1699; Charlestown
STRATTON, Samuel (?1592-1672) & 1/wf Alice? _?_; b 1628?, b 1638?, b 1640?; Cambridge/Watertown
STRATTON, Samuel (-1707) & 1/wf Mary FRY (-1674); 25 Mar 1651, 1651; Watertown/Concord
STRATTON, Samuel (1633-) & Rebecca [GRAVES]; ca 1655/60?
STRATTON, Samuel (1592-1672) & Margaret (BOWLINS?) PARKER (-1676, ae 81), w Wm.; 27 Aug 1637; Boston
STRATEN, Samuel (-1707) & 2/wf Hannah WHEAT (1643-); 20 Oct 1675; Concord

STRATTON, Samuel (1661-1717) & Elizabeth FLETCHER (1663-1762); 28 Nov 1683, 28 Aug; Concord
STRATTON, Samuel & Ruth [GOBLE] (1663-), w John GARFIELD?, m/2 __?__ STONE; b 1690; Concord
STRATTON, Samuel (-1723) & Sarah/Mary PERRY (-1719?); 20 Dec 1699; Watertown
STRATTON, Stephen (-1697) & Hannah [REEVE/REEVES?], m/2 Isaac HALSEY 1699; ca 1684/8?; ?Hartford
STRATTON, Thomas & Mary [MILLER]; b 1699; East Hampton, LI
STRATTON, Thomas & Dorcas MAXWELL; 19 Jul 1699; Watertown
STRATTON, William & Elizabeth __?__ (1663/4-1727); b 1687, b 1685; Boston
STRAW, William & Mehitable [?HOYT]; ca 1683?, b 1686; Amesbury
STRAW, William & Margaret __?__; b 1692; Amesbury
STREAM, Thomas (-d in Eng) & Elizabeth WHITMAN, m/2 John OTIS; m lic 22 Feb 1619/20, London, m same day; Hingham
STREAM, John (-1685) & Martha BEARD (-1706); 20 Dec 1649 at Milford, CT; New Haven
STREAM, John (1657-1689) & Mary (COLEY) [SIMSON] (-1705), w Peter, m/3 Joseph LOCKWOOD 1689+; Milford, CT
STREAM, ?Ephraim & Mary [BUCKINGHAM] (1668); Milford, CT
STREEN, Patrick & Hannah NIEL; 4 Apr 1687; Glastonbury, CT
STREET, Daniel (1658-1738) & Hannah (WEST) [EAST]; b 1692
STREET, Francis (-1665) & Elizabeth (ANDREWS) [HARVEY] (-1717, ae 103), w Thomas, m/3 Thomas LINCOLN 1665; ca 1652-3; Taunton
STREET, John & Sarah MING; 10 Sep 1694; Boston
STREET, Nicholas (bpt 29 Jan 1603, 1603-1674) & 1/wf ?Alice __?__ /POOLE? (1607?-); b 1635?; Taunton/New Haven
STREET, Nicholas (1603-1674) & 2/wf Mary [NEWMAN], w Francis, m/3 William LEETE 1674+; aft Nov 1660; New Haven
STREET, Robert & Elizabeth __?__; b 1676; Boston
STREET, Samuel (1635-1717) & Anna MILES (1642-1730?); 3 Nov 1664; New Haven/Wallingford, CT
STREET, Samuel (-bef 1692) & Maudlin DANIEL, ?m/2 James FOUNTAIN, ?m/3 Luke HAYES, ?m/4 Dennis HIGGINS; 1 Nov 1684; Wallingford, CT
STREET, Samuel (?1667-1720±) & 1/wf Hannah GLOVER (1672-1715); 14 Jul 1690, 11 Jul 1690; Wallingford, CT
STREETER, Henry & Sarah [LARGIN]; b 1671(2?); Charlestown
STREETER, John (1651-1676) & Margaret DAVIS; 18 Apr 1671
STREETER, John (-1729?) & Mary WHETCOMB (-1716?); 9 Apr 1700; Cambridge/Attleboro
STREETER, Samuel (1647-1694) & Mary HORNE; 21 Jan 1666, 1666/7?; Cambridge
STREETER, Samuel & 1/wf Deborah __?__ (-1708); b 1693; Watertown/Cambridge/Attleboro
STREETER, Stephen (1600-1652) & Ursula ADAMS (1619-), m/2 Samuel HOSIER 1657, m/3 William ROBINSON, m/4 Griffin CRAFT 1673; 5 Oct 1640; ?Gloucester/Charlestown
STREETER, Stephen (1641-1689) & Deborah SMITH (-1689); 16 May 1666; ?Watertown/Cambridge
STREING, Daniel & Charlotte __?__; b 1688; Boston
STRICKLAND, Edward (?1610) & Hannah __?__, m/2 Richard FIDOE by 1674; Fairfield, CT
STRICKLAND, John (-1672) & __?__; b 1627?; Watertown/Wethersfield, CT/Fairfield, CT/Hempstead, LI/Huntington, LI/Jamaica, LI
STRICKLAND, John (1649-1719+) & Hester [SMITH] (ca 1653-); 1 Sep 1676; Wethersfield, CT
STRICKLAND, Jonathan (ca 1635-1691) & 1/wf __?__; Newtown, LI
STRICKLAND, Jonathan (ca 1635-1691) & 2/wf Margaret [LYNCH], w Gabriel; b 1686
STRICKLAND, Jonathan & Mary [STANBOROUGH] (1672-); b 1699; Southampton, LI
STRICKLAND, Joseph (1654-1703) & Elizabeth CHAPMAN (1667-); 11 Dec 1684; Windsor, CT/Hartford
STRICKLAND, Peter (1646-1723) & Elizabeth [COMSTOCK]; b 1675; New London, CT
STRICKLAND, Thwaite (-1670) & Elizabeth [?SHEPARD], m/2 Nicholas DESBOROUGH 1674; b 1647; Dedham/Stonington, CT
STRIDE/?STRADE/?STRODE/?STROUD, John & Elizabeth OKER; 26 Apr 1687; Charlestown
STRINGHAM, Peter & Susannah (HARCUTT) [HALSTEAD], w Joseph; b 1683?, b 4 Mar 1680/1; Jamaica, LI

STRONG, Adins (1676-) & Eunice [JOHNSON]; ca 1700?; Derby, CT/Southbury, CT/Woodbury, CT

STRONG, Asahel (1668-1739) & Mary HART; 11 Jun 1689; Farmington, CT/Northampton

STRONG, Ebenezer (?1643-1729) & Hannah CLAP/CLAPP (1646-); 14 Oct 1668; Northampton

STRONG, Ebenezer & 1/wf Mary HOLTON (1680-); 25 Oct 1695?; Northampton

STRONG, Jacob (1673-1749) & Abigail BISSELL (1677-1764); 10 Nov 1698; Windsor, CT

STRONG, Jedediah (1639-1733) & 1/wf Freedom WOODWARD (1642-1681); 18 Nov 1662?, 11 Dec 1662?; Northampton/Coventry, CT

STRONG, Jedediah (1639-1733) & 2/wf Abigail (BARTLETT) STEBBINS (-1689), w John; 19 Dec 1681?, 28 Dec 1681; Deerfield/Lebanon, CT

STRONG, Jedediah (1667-1709) & Abiah INGERSOLL (-1732); 1 Jan 1688, 8 Nov 1688?; Northampton/Lebanon, CT

STRONG, Jedediah (1639-1733) & 3/wf Mary (HART) LEE (-1710), w John; 5 Jan 1691/[2]; Windsor, CT

STRONG, Jerijah (1665-1754) & Thankful STEBBINS (1678-1744); 18 Jul 1700; Northampton

STRONG, John (-1699) & 1/wf Margaret [DEAN] (-1635?); ca 1629; Hingham/Taunton/Windsor, CT/Northampton

STRONG, John (-1699) & 2/wf Abigail [FORD] (1619-); ca 1655-6; Hingham/Taunton/Windsor, CT/Northampton

STRONG, John (-1698) & 1/wf Mary CLARK (-1663), dau wid Frances; 26 Nov 1656; Windsor, CT

STRONG, John (-1698) & 2/wf Elizabeth [WARRINER] (-1684); 1664?; Windsor, CT

STRONG, John (-1698) & 3/wf Hannah (SMITH) TRUMBULL, w Joseph, m/3 Nicholas BUCKLAND 1698; 26 Nov 1686; Windsor, CT/Suffield, CT

STRONG, John (1665-1749) & Mary [PINNEY] (1667-1747); b 1688

STRONG, Joseph (1672-) & 1/wf Sarah [ALLEN] (1672-); 1694; Northampton

STRONG, Josiah (1678-1759) & Joanna GILLET/GILLETT (1680-); 5 Jan 1698, 5 Jan 1698/9; Simsbury, CT/Colchester, CT/Windsor, CT

STRONG, Nathaniel (1673-) & Rebecca [STEBBINS] (1676-1712); 1697; Northampton

STRONG, Return (1640/1-1726) & 1/wf Sarah WARHAM (1642-1678); 11 May 1664; Windsor, CT

STRONG, Return (1640/1-1726) & 2/wf Margaret NEWBERRY (1662-); 23 May 1689; Windsor, CT

STRONG, Return (1669-) & Elizabeth BURRELL/BURETT/BURITT; 19 Jun 1700; Windsor, CT

STRONG, Samuel & 1/wf Esther CLAPP; 9 Jun 1684; Dorchester

STRONG, Samuel & 2/wf Ruth (SHELDON) WRIGHT (1663-), w Joseph; 28 Oct 1698, 27 Oct 1698; Deerfield/Northampton

STRONG, Samuel (1675-1742) & Martha BUCKLAND (1678-1770); 9 Nov 1669; Windsor, CT

STRONG, Thomas (?1637-1689) & 1/wf Mary HUIT/HEWETT (1640-1670/1); 5 Dec 1660; Windsor, CT

STRONG, Thomas (-1689) & Rachel HOLTON, m/2 Nathan BRADLEY 1698; 10 Oct 1671; Northampton/Windsor, CT

STRONG, Thomas (1661-) & Mary STEBBINS; 17 Nov 1683; Northampton/Durham, CT

STROUD, Robert & Mary _?_; b 1659; Boston

STROUT, Christopher (-1715) & Sarah PICKE/PIKE, m/2 Joseph COLLINS; 2 Dec 1680; Marblehead/Provincetown

STRIKER/STRYKER, Joseph & Hanna/Hannah WATERS (1652-); - Apr 1673, 10 Apr; Salem

STUBBS, Joshua (-1655±) & Abigail [BENJAMIN], m/2 John WOODWARD; b 1642; Watertown

STABBS/STUBBS, Richard (-1677) & Margaret READ; 3 Mar 1659; Boston/Hull

STUBBS, Richard & Rebecca [LOBDELL]; b 1692; Hull

STUCKEY, George (-1660) & 1/wf _?_; b 1645, b 1640?; Windsor, CT/Stamford, CT

STUKEY, George (-1660) & 2/wf Elizabeth [CLOSE] (-1656), wid; Stamford, CT

STUCKEY, George (-1660) & 3/wf Ann (_?_) QUEMBY/QUINBY, w William; 28 Nov 1657; Stamford, CT

STUDLIE, Benjamin (1661-1743) & Mary MERRETT; 7 Oct 1683; Scituate

STOODLEY, James & _?_; b 1695, in Eng; Portsmouth, NH

STUTLY, John & Elizabeth [LAPHAM?] (-1678); b 1659; Boston

STUDLEY, Joseph & Sarah [BROOKS] (1650), dau William; proof?; Scituate

STUDWELL, Thomas (-1669) & _?_; Stamford, CT

STURGES, Edward[1] (-1695, Sandwich) & 1/wf Elizabeth [HINCKLEY] (1617-1692); b 1642, b 1640?; Watertown/Yarmouth

STURGES, Edward[2] (-1678) & Temperance [GORHAM] (1646-1713), m/2 Thomas BAXTER 1679; ca 1663; Yarmouth

STURGES, Edward[1] (-1695, Sandwich) & Mary RIDER, w Zechariah; 20 Apr 1692 m cont; ?Yarmouth

STURGES, James (1668-1718) & Rebecca [THACHER] (1669-1734), m/2 Ebenezer LEWIS; b 1690; Yarmouth

STURGES, John (?1624-1700) & Deborah [BARLOW]; b 1650; Fairfield, CT

STURGES, John (-1744) & Abigail __?_; b 1687?; Fairfield, CT

STURGES, Jonathan (?1650-1711) & 1/wf Susannah [BANKS]; b 1679; Fairfield, CT

STURGES, Jonathan (?1650-1711) & Sarah OSBORN, m/2 Peter BURR, m/3 Jonathan LAW; 31 Jul 1692; Fairfield, CT

STURGES, Joseph (1654-1728) & 1/wf __?_; b 1680; Fairfield, CT

STURGES, Joseph (1654-1728) & 2/wf Sarah (JUDSON) [WATKINS] (1662-), w David; ca 1688/90?; Fairfield, CT

STURGES, Joseph (-1749) & Hope [TAYLOR] (1674-1705); b 1694; Yarmouth

STURGES, Joseph (1654-1728) & 3/wf Mary (HILL) [MOREHOUSE], w Thomas; 1700; Fairfield, CT

STURGES, Samuel (1640-1674) & Mary [HEDGE] (1648-), m/2 John COGGESHALL 1679; [1667]; Plymouth?

STURGES, Samuel & Mary (IVET) ORIS, w Nathaniel; 14 Oct 1697; Barnstable

STURGES, Samuel (1665-1737) & Mercy HOWES (ca 1682-1713); 17 Oct 1700; Yarmouth

STURGES, Thomas (1659-1708) & Abigail [LATHROP] (1660-); b 1681; Yarmouth/Barnstable

STURTEVANT, John (1658-1752) & 1/wf Hannah (WINSLOW) CROW (1644-1709), w William; b 1687; Plymouth

STIRTEVANT, Joseph (1666-) & Anna JONES; 5 Dec 1693; Plymouth

STURTEVANT, Samuel[1] (-1669) & Anne __?_, m/2 John BASS 1675; b 1647; Plymouth

STURTEVANT, Samuel (1654-1736, Halifax) & 1/wf Mercy [BENNETT?] (?1655-1714, Plympton); b 1676?; Plympton/Duxbury

STURDEVANT, William & Mary __?_; b 1676; Norwalk

STUCHE/STUTCHE, John & Sarah __?_; b 1662; Boston

SUAWSELL, Thomas (1634-) & Martha [LAWRENCE]

SUGARS/SUGAR, Gregory & Jane __?_; b 1688; Boston

SUMERS, Edward & Mary __?_ (-1724, ae 72); b 1684; Boston

SUMMERS, Henry (-1675) & 1/wf Elizabeth [WORDEN]; in Eng, b 1635; Woburn

SUMMERS/SIMMONS, Henry (-1675) & 2/wf Mabel (?KENDELL) REED (?1605-1690), w William; 21 Nov 1660; Charlestown

SUMMERS, Henry (-1717) & 1/wf [Sarah GREGORY] (-1690?); b 1669; Stratford, CT/Milford, CT/New Haven

SUMMERS, Henry (-1724) & 1/wf Susanna [CARTER] (-1708, ae 59); b 1674; Charlestown

SUMMERS, Henry & Mary (HOLBROOK) [WHEELER] (1650-), w Ephraim; b 1695; Milford, CT

SUMMERS, John & Mary [SAMSON], dau Henry; b 24 Dec 1684; Duxbury

SUMERS, John & 1/wf Elizabeth [BRANCH] (1656-); b 1686; Marshfield

SUMMERS, Samuel (?1669-1728) & Abigail [READ?] (-1767, in 89th y); ca 1697?; Stratford, CT

SUMNER, Clement (1671-) & Margaret HARRIS; 18 May 1698; Boston

SUMNER, Ebenezer (1666-1727+), Boston & Elizabeth [PAINE] (1667-); aft 1694; Charlestown/Boston

SUMNER, Ebenezer, Dorchester & 1/wf Elizabeth CLAPP (1676-); 14 Mar 1699/1700, 14 Mar 1700; Dorchester/Milton

SUMNER, Edward & Mary __?_; b 1687; Boston

SUMNER, George (-ca 1651?) & __?_; ca 1630/40?; Rowley

SUMNER, George (1635-1715), Milton & Mary BAKER (1642-1719); 7 Nov 1662; Northampton/Milton

SUMNER, George (1666-1732?) & Ann [TUCKER] (1673-); b 1695, [ca 1694]; Milton

SUMNER, Increase (1643-1683) & Sarah STAPLES; 26 Mar 1667; Dorchester/SC

SUMNER, Roger (1632-1698) & Mary JOSLIN (1634-1711); 1656; Lancaster/Milton

SUMNER, Samuel (1638-) & Rebecca [STAPLES] (1638-); 7 Mar 1658/9; Dorchester/SC

SUMNER, Samuel (1659-) & [Experience BLAKE] (1665-), m/2 Eleazer CARVER 1695; 15 Mar 1683, 1683/4; Milton

SUMNER, Thomas (son of George) & _?_ (1643?), m/2 _?_; Rowley

SUMNER, William (1605-1688) (brother-in-law of Thomas[1] SWIFT) & Mary SWIFT (-1676); Bicester, Eng, 22 Oct 1625; Dorchester

SUMNER, William (-1675) & Elizabeth CLEMENT; b 1652, b 1656(7?); Dorchester/Boston

SUMNER, William (1656-1703) & 1/wf Rachel AVERY (1657-); 22 May 1677, 1676?; Dedham

SUMNER, William (1656-1703) & 2/wf Hannah [HINCHMAN] (?1653-1719), m/2 John HALL 1705; b 1679; Boston/Middletown, CT

SUMNER, William & Esther PUFFER (-1748); 2 Jun 1697; Milton

SUMNER, _?_ & Ruth CLAPP

SYNDERLAND, John (1618-1703) & 1/wf Dorothy _?_ (-29 Jan 1663/4, Boston); b 1640; Boston

SUNDERLAND, John (1618-1703, 1704?) & 2/wf Thomasine (LUMPKIN) [MAYO] (-1709, in 84th y), w Samuel; bef 24 Jun 1654, aft Apr 1664; Boston/Eastham

SUNDERLAND, John & Mary VJALL/VIALL (1641-), m/2 Thomas BURROUGHS; 26 Jan 1658, 1658/9; Boston

SUNDERLAND, John (1660/1-1724) & Mary _?_; b 1691; Boston

SUNDERLAND/SINDERLAND, Matthew & Katherine [CURTIS?], m/2 William SALMON; LI

SUNDERLAND, Nathaniel (1667-) & Elizabeth MINOTT; 7 Feb 1695/6; Dorchester

SURT?, Martin & Cordine POCOCK; m int 7 Feb 1695/6; Boston

SUTLIFFE, Abraham & Sarah _?_; b 1659; Scituate

SUTLIFF, John (?1675-1752) & Hannah [BROCKETT] (1678-1760, 1761), dau Benjamin; b 1699, b 1695?, b 1697?; Branford, CT/Durham, CT/Waterbury, CT/Woodbury

SUTLIEFFE, Nathaniel & Hannah PLIMPTON, m/2 Samuel HARRINGTON 1676; 31 Jan 1664/5; Medfield

SUTLIFF, Nathaniel (-1732) & Sarah [SAVAGE?] (1673-1733); b 1694; Rehoboth

SUTTON, Bartholomew (-1700, ae 73) & Hannah [POLLARD] (-1700+, 1730, ae 83), m/2 Samuel JOHNSON; b 1665; Boston

SUTTON, Daniel & Mary COLE (1639-); 15 Apr 1667; Charlestown/Boston

SUTTON, George & Sarah [TILDEN] (1613-); b 25 May 1641, ?13 Mar 1636/7; Scituate

SUTTON, John[1] (-1672) & Julian _?_ (-1678); in Eng, b 1621; Hingham/Rehoboth

SUTTON, John[2] (1621-1691) (ae 70 in 1691) & Elizabeth HOUSE (1636-1679+); 1 Jan 1661; Scituate

SUTTON, John[3] & Abigail CLARKE; 6 Jun 1692; Plymouth

SUTTON, Joseph & Sarah _?_; b 1659; Boston

SUTTON, Lambert (-1649) & Elizabeth _?_; Charlestown/Woburn

SUTTON, Richard (1621?-) & 1/wf Rachel _?_ (-1672, Roxbury); b 1650?; Roxbury/Andover

SUTTON, Richard (1621?-) & 2/wf Faith [SWAN]; b 1674; Reading

SUTTON, Richard (1621?-) & 3/wf Katharine _?_; b 8 Jan 1679; Charlestown

SUTTON, Richard & Susannah [PULCIPHER], m/2 Jeremiah DOW; b 1697; Ipswich

SUTTON, William & Damaris BISHOP; 11 Jul 1666; Eastham/Piscataway, NJ

SUTTON, William (-1680) & Mary/Sarah? GAFFELL/GARFIELD?, wid Sarah m John GILD/ GUILD 1680/1; 27 Oct 1679; Newbury

SUTTON, William & Mary JOHNSON; 31 Jan 1694; Boston

SUTTON, _?_ & Agnes [HITCHESON] (-1684?), wid

SWAYNE, Benjamin & Margaret _?_; 26 Sep 1695; Reading

SWAYNE, Daniel (-1690) & Dorcas ROSE (1632-1708), m/2 _?_ WHEELER; b 1651, 26 Jul 1653; Bramford, CT

SWAIN, Francis (1621-1663?) & Martha _?_, m/2 Caleb LEVERICH; Exeter, NH

SWAIN, Henry (?1650, ?1647-) & 1/wf Mary SMITH (-1678); 16 Nov 1670; Charlestown

SWAIN, Henry & 2/wf Hannah LATHROP (1655-), m/2 Henry BERESFORD/BERRELFORD; 21 Aug 1679; Charlestown

SWAIN, Jeremiah/Jeremie? (-2 Apr 1658) & Mary _?_ (-living in 1709), m/2 Thomas CLARK 1658; b 1642; Charlestown/Reading

SWAYNE, Jeremiah (1643-1710) & Mary SMITH (1648-1714+); 5 Nov 1664; Reading

SWAIN, Jeremiah (1665-1696) & Elizabeth (PARKER) [COWDREY] (1668-1696), w Nathaniel; b 1693; Reading

SWAIN, John (-1715, 1717) & Mary WEARE/WYER? (ca 1633-1714); 15 Nov 1660, 15 Sep 1660; Hampton, NH

SWAIN, John & Mary MOORE, m/2 John CANDAGE/CANDIGE 1678?; 4 Aug 1669, bef 2 Oct 1677; Charlestown
SWAIN, John (1660-1694) & [?Judith PIERCE]; ?ca 1683/88; Bramford, CT
SWAIN, John (1664-1739) & Experience FOLGER (-1739); b 1689?; Nantucket
SWAIN, John (-1699) & Mary [ODIORNE], m/2 _?_; Piscataqua
SWAYNE, John & Jane WESTOVER (1672-), m/2 John BYINGTON; ?b 1692, b 1699; Bramford, CT
SWAIN, Joseph (1673-) & Mary [SIBLEY] (1671-); b 1699, 1695?; Nantucket
SWAYNE, Richard (?1606, 1597-1682) & 1/wf Basselle?/Elizabeth? _?_ (-1657); in Eng, b 1619?; Hampton, NH/Nantucket
SWAIN, Richard (-1682) & 2/wf Jane (GODFREY) BUNKER (-1662), w George; aft 29 May 1658, 15 Sep 1658; Hampton, NH
SWAIN, Richard, Jr. (1660-1707) & _?_; b 1684(5?); Nantucket
SWAIN, Roger & Margaret (CLARK) (JACKSON) [WHITE], w John, w Philip; b 4 Jan 1700/01; Portsmouth
SWAINE, Samuel (1622-) & Joanna [WARD], w Josiah; b 1649; Bramford, CT/Newark, NJ
SWAINE, Thomas & Deborah _?_; b 1684; Sudbury
SWAIN, William (1585?-) & _?_; Watertown/Wethersfield, CT
SWAIN, William (-1657) & Prudence [MARSTON], m/2 [Moses] COX 1658; ca 1642?; Hampton, NH
SWAIN, William & Mary WEBSTER (1658-), m/2 Joseph EMMONS 1694; 20 Oct 1676; Hampton, NH
SWALLOW/FEARLOW/FEARLON, Ambrose & Mary MARTIN, m/2 Samuel WARNER 1684; 2 Dec 1668; Chelmsford
SWALLOW, Ambrose & Sarah BARRETT; 8 Dec 1696; Chelmsford/Woburn
SWALLOW, John & Anna BARRETT (1668-); 3 Jan 1692/3; Chelmsford
SWAN, Ebenezer (1672-1740) & Elizabeth BRUCE (1672-1748); 2 Mar 1698, 1697/8; Woburn/Cambridge
SWANN, Gershom (1654-1708) & Sarah HOLDEN; 20 Dec 1677; Cambridge
SWAN, Henry & Joan [RUCK], m/2 Henry FARNHAM by 1662; b 1642(3?); Salem/Boston
SWAN, John (ca 1621-1708) & 1/wf Rebecca PALFORY/PALFREY (-1654); 1 Feb 1650, 1650/1?, 1 Jan 1650/1; Cambridge
SWAN, John (ca 1621-1708) & 2/wf Mary PRATT (ca 1633-1703); 1 Mar 1655, 1655/6, 2 Mar, 2 1st mo 1655; Cambridge
SWAN, John & Sarah THOMPSON (1670-); 11 Apr 1692; Woburn
SWAN, John (1668-1743, ae 75) & Susanna (EASTMAN) WOOD (1673-1772), w Thomas; 1 Aug 1699; Haverhill/Stonington, CT
SWAN, Richard (-1678) & 1/wf Ann _?_ (-Apr 1658); in Eng, b 1626; Boston/Rowley
SWAN, Richard (-1678) & 2/wf Ann (HOPKINSON) TRUMBLE/TRUMBULL (1665-1678) (ae 60 in 1676), w Michael, w John; 1 Mar 1658, 1658/9; Rowley
SWAN, Richard (1661-) & Hannah STORY?/STONE/STORER (1662-), m/2 Thomas JEWETT 1692; 3 Dec 1683; Rowley
SWAN, Robert (1626-1698) & 1/wf Elizabeth [ACIE] (1632-1689); ca 1650; Haverhill
SWAN, Robert (1657-) & Elizabeth STORIE/STORY; 20 Jul 1685; Haverhill
SWAN, Robert (1626-1698) & 2/wf Hannah (BULL) RUSS/ROSS (1649-), w Funell; 1 Apr 1690; Haverhill
SWAN, Samuel (1672-1751) & Dorothy AMES; 8 Mar 1693/4, 6? Mar; Haverhill
SWAN, Thomas (-1688) & Mary [LAMB] (1644-1717), m/2 Rev. James BAILEY; b 1665; Boston/Roxbury/Cambridge
SWAN, Thomas (1669-1710), Roxbury & Prudence WADE (1669-), Medford; 27 Dec 1692 in Charlestown; Medford/Milton
SWAN, Thomas & Rachel HUNT; 22 May 1699; Marblehead
SWARTON/?SWANTON, John & Hannah?/Joanna HIBBARD/HIBBERT? (1651-); 8 Jan 1671, 1670; Beverly
SWAZEY, John & _?_; in Eng, b 1611; Salem/Setauket, LI/Southold, LI
SWAYSEY, John (1619-1706) & Katherine [KING] (1625-1692); b 1650?; Salem/Aqueboque, LI
SWASEY, John (1651-1717) & Mary _?_; b 1685?; Southold, LI
SWACY, John (1666-) & Christian (LEGRO) GRAY; 22 Oct 1695; Salem
SWASE, Joseph & Mary _?_; b 1653; Salem

SWEZEY, Joseph (1653-bef 1717, 1713) & Mary [BETTS]; b 1678; Southld, LI

SWASY, Joseph (1653-1710) & Elizabeth LAMBERT; 16 Oct 1678; Salem

SWASY, [?Samuel] (?1664-) & Mary _?_ (-1737), m/2 Edward COYS; b 1694; Salem

SWAZEY, Samuel & Hannah (?BEARDSLEY) HULSE, w Richard

SWASY, Stephen & Esther _?_; b 1685; Boston

SWEET, Benoni (1663-1751) & Elizabeth _?_; b 1688; N. Kingstown, RI

SWEET, Daniel (1657-1728?) & Ethalenah/Ethelannah [CARPENTER]; b 1697; Warwick, RI

SWEET, Henry & Mary/?Margaret _?_; b 1682(3?); E. Greenwich, RI

SWEET, Henry (-1704) & Elizabeth WALKER; 29 Mar 1687, 31 Mar; Rehoboth/Attleboro

SWEET, James (?1622, ?1615-1695+) & Mary [GREENE] (1633-); b 1655; Warwick, RI/Providence

SWEET, James (-1719) & Jane [BROWNING] (1655±-1719+); ca 1676?; ?Prudence Island, RI

SWEET, James (1657-1725) & Mary (PEARCE) [HILL], w Robert; aft 23 Sep 1689, aft 1690, b 1711, no issue; Portsmouth, RI

SWEET, John (-1637) & Mary _?_ (-1681), m/2 Ezekiel HOLLIMAN 1638±; b 1622; Salem/Providence

SWEET, John & 1/wf Temperance _?_ (-Jan 1645); Boston

SWEET, John (?1603-1685) & Susanna _?_ (?1622-1666); b 1647; Boston

SWEET, John (-1677) & Elizabeth [SCOTT?] (ae 45 in 1684), wid, m/2 Samuel WILSON; b 1657?, ca Sep 1651; Warwick, RI/Newport

SWEET, John (-1716) & Deborah [REYNOLDS] (1658-1716(-)); RI

SWEET, Philip (1655-) & Elizabeth _?_; bef 1693

SWEET/SWAYT, Richard & 1/wf Mehitable LARKIN; 15 Dec 1673; Westerly, RI

SWEET, Richard & Priscilla [CARPENTER] (1661-); aft 13 Jun 1687; ?Prudence Isl., RI

SWEETING, Henry & Joan _?_ (-1687); b 1687; Rehoboth

SWEETING, Henry & Martha COLE (-1708); m bond 22 Jun 1688; Rehoboth

SWEETING, John & Eleanor EVANS; 7 Feb 1694; Boston

SWEETEN, John & Frances CHILD; 8 Aug 1700; Boston

SWEATLAND/SWEETLAND, John & Rebecca CLARK (1669-); 4 Aug 1684; Marblehead/Attleboro

SWETLAND, William & Agnes _?_, m/2 Simon LOVETT; b 1676; Salem/Salem, CT

SWETMAN, Samuel (1659-) & Margaret PEARD; 26 Oct 1693; Boston

SWEETMAN, Thomas (-1683) & Isabelle [CUTTER] (-1709+); b 1646(7?); Cambridge

SWEETMAN, Thomas (-1691) & Joyce _?_ (-1691); b 1687; Springfield

SWEETSER, Benjamin (1632-1718) & Abigail [WIGGLESWORTH] (1640-), m/2 Rev. Ellis CALLENDER 1719; by 1660?; Charlestown

SWEETSER, Benjamin (1666-1720) & Elizabeth [PHILLIPS] (1672-), m/2 William PAINE; b 1694; Charlestown

SWEETSER, Joseph (-1699+) & Elizabeth [WHITE]/EDWARDS?, m/2 Samuel BACHELDER 1701/2; b 1696; Charlestown

SWEETSER, Samuel (-1759, ae 83) & Elizabeth [SPRAGUE] (-1752); ca 1699; Charlestown/Malden

SWEETSER, Seth (1606-1662) & Bethia _?_; b 1632; Charlestown

SWEETSER, Seth (1606-1662) & Elizabeth OAKES, w Thomas, m/3 Samuel HAYWARD/HAYWOOD? 1662, 1663; - Apr 1661; Charlestown

SWEETSER, Seth (-1731) & Sarah (LYNDE) CLARK (1666-1739+), w Thomas; 12 Jan 1691/2, 1692; Charlestown/Woburn

SWITSER/SWEETSER, Wigglesworth & 1/wf Ursula COLES (-1727); 2 Feb 1699; Boston

SWETT, George (1653-) & Rebecca [SMART?]; by 1672

SWETT, Benjamin (1624-1677) & Hester WYRE/Esther WEARE, m/2 Stephen GREENLEAF 1678?; - Nov [164-?], 1 Nov 1647; Newbury/Hampton, NH

SWETT, Benjamin (1656-) & Theodale HUSSEY (1660-); 9 May 1682; Hampton, NH/Hampton Falls/New Castle, DE

SWETT, Clement/George & Sarah _?_

SWETT, John (-1651/2) & Phoebe/?Sarah _?_ (-1655); in Eng, b 1603?; Newbury

SWETT, John (?1603-1693) & 1/wf Mercy [ROUSE] (-1686); b 1659, b 1661; Charlestown

SWETT, John (1648-1718) & Mary PLUMER (1649/50-); 6 Dec 1670; Newbury

SWETT, John (?1603-1693) & 2/wf Jane [HODGES?]; b 1688; Charlestown

SWETT, John (1660-1753) & 1/wf Bethia PAGE (1679-1736); 3 Dec 1696; Hampton, NH/Kingston, NH

SWETT, John (1677-1725) & Susannah PAGE (1676-1739); m int 4 Jun 1698; Newbury

SWETT, Joseph & 1/wf Elizabeth [TAYLOR?]; Oct 1651?, b 1658; Newbury/Boston

SWETT, Joseph (-1695?) & 2/wf Mary (BAXTER) [BUTTOLPH], w Thomas; b 1673; Boston

SWETT, Joseph (-1720) & 1/wf Hannah [WARD] (1655-1701); b 1682; Hampton, NH

SWETT, Joseph & Hannah (DEVEREUX) (GREENFIELD) KNOTT, w Peter, w Richard; b 1689; Salem

SWETT, Moses (1661-1731) & Mary HUSSEY (1665-); 12 May 1689; Hampton, NH/Hampton Falls

SWETT, Stephen & 1/wf Hannah MERRILL (-1662); 24 May 164-?, 1647; Newbury

SWET, Stephen & 2/wf Rebecca SMITH; 4 Aug 1663; Newbury

SWETT, Stephen (1672-) & Mary KENT; m int 27 Dec 1695; Newbury

SWIFT, Ephraim (1656-1742) & Sarah [PERRY] (-1734), dau Ezra; b 1679; Sandwich

SWIFT, Jirch (-1749, Wareham) & 1/wf Abigail GIBBS (ca 1677-by 1741); 26 Nov 1697; Sandwich

SWIFT, Obadiah (1638-1690) & Rest [ATHERTON] (?1639-1708); 15 Mar 1660/1; Dorchester

SWIFT, Obadiah (1670-1747) & Abigail BLAKE (1663-1738); 31 Dec 1695; Dorchester

SWIFT, Samuel (1662-1733) & Mary _?_ (-1733+); ca 1688?; Sandwich

SWIFT, Thomas (-1675, ae 73) & Elizabeth CAPEN (1610-1678); 18 Oct 1630, Holy Trinity, Dorchester, Eng; Dorchester

SWIFT, Thomas (1635-1718) & 1/wf Elizabeth VOSE (-1676); 9 Dec 1657; Dorchester

SWIFT, Thomas (1635-1718) & 2/wf Sarah CLAP (-1718); 16 Oct 1676; Milton

SWIFT, Thomas (1659-), Weymouth & Elizabeth THOMPSON (1654-), Weymouth, sister of Mrs. William REED, Weymouth; 22 Sep 1687 m bond; Weymouth

SWIFT, William[1] (-1644) & Jane/Joan _?_ (-1663); b 1618; Watertown/Sudbury/Sandwich

SWIFT, William[2] (-1706) & 1/wf _?_ ; b 1651/[2?]; Sandwich

SWIFT, William[2] & 2/wf Ruth (PARSONS) YOUNGS, wid Giles (doubtful)

SWIFT, William[3] (1654-1701) & Elizabeth _?_ (not Elizabeth THOMPSON); b 1679/[80?]; Sandwich

SWILLOWAY, Henry (-1684?) & Margaret _?_, m/2 Robert SMITH 1687; b 1666; Malden/Charlestown

SWINERTON/SWINNERTON, Job[1] (1601-1689) & Elizabeth _?_ ; b 1630; Salem

SWINERTON, Job[2] & 1/wf Ruth SYMONS/SYMONDS (-1670); 19 Jul 1658; Salem

SWINERTON, Job[2] & 2/wf Hester BAKER; 2 Sep 1673; Salem

SWINERTON, John (-1691, ae 57) & Hannah (BARTHOLOMEW) BROWNE (-1713, ae 71), w James; 8 Mar 1679/80; Salem

SWINERTON, Joseph (1660-1731/2) & Mary [SUMNER] (1664-); b 1693, ca 1690?; Salem

SWITCHZER/SWITCHER, Seth & Elizabeth OAKES; - Apr 1661; Cambridge

SWODEL, William & _?_ ; b 1697; New London, CT

SYDENHAM, William & Anne _?_ ; b 1682(3?); Boston

SYKES/SIKES/SILES, Humphrey & _?_ ; Southampton, LI

SIKES, Increase (1644-1712) & Abigail FOWLER (1646-1733); 22 Mar 1671, 1670/1; Springfield

SIKES, Increase (1675-) & 1/wf Mary KNOWLTON (1677-); 28 Oct 1697; Springfield

SIKES, Nathaniel (1646-1681) & Hannah BAGG; 3 Feb 1680, 1680/1; Springfield

SIKES, Nathaniel (1673-) & Elizabeth [BALL] (1677-); 24 Dec 1696; Springfield

SIKES, Richard (-1676) & Phebe _?_ (-1687); b 1640; Dorchester/Springfield

SIKES, Victory/Vicary? (1649-1708) & 1/wf Elizabeth BURT (1652-1683); 22 Jan 1672, ?1672/3, 29 Jan 1673; Springfield/Suffield, CT

SIKES, Victory/Vicary? (1649-1708) & 2/wf Elizabeth GRANGER? (1662-1692); 16 Jan 1684, 16 Jul 1684; Suffield, CT

SIKES, Victory/Vicary? (1649-1708) & 3/wf Mary (PRICHARD) TRUMBLE/TRUMBULL, w Judah; 22 Dec 1692; Suffield, CT

SIKES, William & Susanna _?_ ; b 1687; Beverly

SILVESTER, Benjamin (1657-1733+) & Mary [STANDLAKE] (1666-); b 1687; Scituate

SILVESTER, Giles & Hannah (SAVAGE) GILLAM, w Benjamin; Sep 1685; ?Boston/?Shelter Isl., NY

SILVESTER, Israel (1646?-1727) & Martha _?_ (-1726+) (Martha BRYANT?, no proof, she was b 1652); b 1674; Scituate

SILVESTER, John (1635-1706) & Sarah _?_ (-1706+); ca 1658; ?Mashfield/Scituate

SILVESTER, Joseph (1638-1690) & Mary [BARSTOW] (1641-1715?); ca 1662?, 1663?; Scituate
SILVESTER, Joseph (1664-) & Hannah [BARTLETT]; ca 1689, ?Apr 1690; Scituate/Plymouth
SYLVESTER, Nathaniel (-1680) & Grizzell/Grissell [BRINLEY]; b 1656?, 1652, b 1661; Shelter
Island, NY
SYLVESTER, Nathaniel (1661-1705) & Margaret HOBART/SLATES?; b 3 Apr 1700; ?East
Hampton/Newport
SYLVESTER, Peter (-bef 1661) & Mary [BRINLEY]; ca 1690, Shelter Island; Shelter Island, NY
SILVESTER, Richard[1] (-1663) & 1/wf Naomi/?Emmeline _?_ (-1668); b 1633; Weymouth/Scitu-
ate/Marshfield
SILVESTER, Samuel (1676-) & Lucretia JOYCE (-1718); 9 Oct 1700; Marshfield
SYLVESTER, Thomas (-1696) & Sarah (GRANT) SEAVERNS (1643-) w Samuel; 1694±;
Watertown
SIMES, Peter & _?_ ; b 28 Feb 1642/3
SYMMES, Timothy (-1678) & 1/wf Mary NICHOLS (-1669); 10 Dec 1668; Charlestown
SYMMES, Timothy (-1678) & 2/wf Elizabeth NORTON, m/2 Ephraim SAVAGE 1688; 27 Sep 1671;
Charlestown
SYMMES, Capt. William (1627-1691) & 1/wf Mary [SPARHAWK] (had Sarah); b 1657;
Charlestown
SYMMES, Capt. William (1627-21, 22 Sep 1691) & 2/wf [Mary CHICKERING] (1648-), m/2 Rev.
Samuel TORREY; b 1676; Charlestown
SYMMES, Zachariah (1599-21 Sep 1671) (cousin of Thomas ADAMS, cousin of James
CUDWORTH) & Sarah BAKER (-1676); St. Saviour, Southwark, Eng, 13 Aug 1622;
Charlestown
SIMMES, Zachariah (1638-1708) & 1/wf Susannah GRAVES (-1681); 18 Nov 1669; Charlestown/
Bradford
SIMMES, Zechariah (1638-1708) & 2/wf Mehitable (PALMER) DOLTON/DALTON (ca 1630-), w
Samuel; 26 Nov 1683; Bradford/Charlestown
SYMMES, Zechariah (1674-) & Dorcas BRACKENBURY (1682-1727); 28 Nov 1700; Charlestown
SYMMES, _?_ & Anna _?_ ; b 1684; Marblehead

TABER, Philip[1] (1605-1672) & 1/wf Lydia [MASTERS]; 1633?, b 19 Dec 1639; Cambridge/Edgar-
town
TABER, Philip (1605-1672) & 2/wf Jane [?LATHAM]; b 1669; Portsmouth, RI/etc.
TABER, Philip[2] (1646-1693±) & Mary [COOK] (-1694+), m/2 _?_ DAVIS 1693; b 1668/[9?];
Dartmouth
TABER, Philip (1675-) & ?Susannah/Margaret ?WILCOX/?WOOD/?TUCKER (had son Tucker
1717); b 1700?, b 1711; Dartmouth
TABER, Thomas (1646-1730) & 1/wf Hester/Esther [COOK] (1650-1672); b 1668; Dartmouth
TABER, Thomas (1646-1730) & 2/wf Mary THOMPSON (1650-1734); Jun 1672; Dartmouth
TABER, Thomas & Rebecca HARLOW; 4 Jul 1700; Dartmouth
TADOURNEAU, _?_ & _?_ ; b 1697(8?); Boston
TAFT, Robert[1] (-1725) & Sarah _?_ (-1725); b 1671?; Mendon/Bristol, RI
TAFT, Robert (1674-1748) & Elizabeth [WOODWARD] (1671-); b 1696; Mendon
TAFT, Thomas (?1671-) & Deborah [GENERY/CHENERY] (1667-); b 1693; Medfield
TAINTOR/TAINTER, Benjamin (1651-) & Mary _?_ ; (doubtful); Sudbury
TAINTOR, Charles (-1658, 1659?, 1654?) & _?_ ; ca 1630?; Wethersfield, CT/Branford, CT
TAINTOR, John (1650-) & Dorcas [SWAIN], m/2 John COLLINS 1700; Wethersfield, CT
TAYNTOR, Jonathan (-1712) & 1/wf Elizabeth WARRIN/WARREN (-1692); 6 Dec 1681;
Watertown
TAINTOR, Joseph (1613-1690) & Mary [GUY?] (1619-); b 1644; Watertown
TAINTOR, Michael (-1673) & Elizabeth [ROSE] (-1659); b 1650; Branford, CT
TAINTOR, Michael (1652-1730) & 1/wf Mary LOOMIS (1660-1695); 3 Apr 1679; Windsor,
CT/Branford, CT/Colchester, CT

TAINTOR, Michael (1652-1730), Colchester & 2/wf Mabel (OLMSTED) BUTLER, w Daniel; Aug 1697, 26 Aug 1697; Windsor, CT/Wethersfield, CT

TAINTOR, Simon (1660-1739) & Joanna STONE (1665-1731); 9 May 1693; Boston/Watertown

TALBY/TALBOT, James & Martha BARSTOW; 24 May 1663, 14? Oct; Charlestown/Boston

TALBOT, James (1664-1700) & Elizabeth (GRIDLEY) BLORE, w Thomas, m/3 Thomas JEPSON 1708; 25 Dec 1699; Boston

TALBUTT, Jared/Garrett & Sarah ANDREWES; 1 Apr 1664; Taunton

TALBUT, Jared (1667-) & Rebecca HATHAWAY; 4 May 1687; Taunton/?Dighton

TALBUTT, Peter & 1/wf Mary (GOLD/GOULD) WADELL/WATTLES? (-1687), w John; 12 Jan 1677, 1677/8; Dorchester/Milton/Chelmsford

TALBOT, Peter, Chelmsford & 2/wf Hannah (CLARK) FRISSELL, Concord, William; 29 Dec 1687; ?Woburn/Chelmsford

TALBOT/TALBY?, Samuel & Priscilla SOUTHWORTH, m/2 John IRISH 1708; 1 Mar 1689; Bristol, RI

TALBOT, Samuel (1675-1738) & Mary [DYER]?; 1698?, b 1700(1?); Taunton

TALBOTT, William & Cicely [NOTT]?; in Eng, 7 Sep 1635; Boston

TALBY, James, Boston & Martha BARSTOW; 14 Oct 1663; Charlestown

TALBY, John (-1645) & Dorothy __?__ (-1638); b 1632?; Salem

TALBOT/TALBY, Samuel (son Stephen) & Priscilla SOUTHWORTH; 1 Mar 1689; Bristol, RI

TALBYE, Stephen (1633-1674) (son John of Salem) & Hannah __?__; b 1663; Boston

TALCOTT, Benjamin (1674-1727) & 1/wf Sarah HOLLISTER (1676-1715); 5 Jan 1699, 1698/9?; Wethersfield, CT/Springfield/Glastonbury, CT

TALCOTT, Elezur/Eleazer/Elizur (1669-) & Sarah [WEBSTER?] (1678?-); b 1695, b 1693?; Wethersfield, CT

TALCOTT, John (?1600-1660) & Dorothy [MOTT]/SMITH? (-1670); in Eng, b 18 Dec 1630; Cambridge/Hartford

TALCOTT, John (-1688) & 1/wf Helena WAKEMAN (1632-1674); 29 Oct 1650; Hartford

TALCOTT, John (-1688) & 2/wf Mary COOK; 9 Nov 1676; Hartford

TALCOTT, John (1653-1683) & Abigail [TIBBETTS/TIBBALS]? (1683); no issue

TALCOTT, Jonathan (-1711) & Martha MOODY; ca 1680

TALCOTT, Joseph (1669-1741?) & 1/wf Abigail [CLARKE] (1680-1704/5); b 1699; Hartford

TALCOTT, Samuel (?1635-1691) & 1/wf Hannah HOLYOKE/?PYNCHON (1644-1677/8); 7 Nov 1661; Wethersfield, CT

TALCOTT, Samuel (?1635-1691) & Mary __?__ (not ELLERY) (1638-1711); 6 Aug 1679; Wethersfield, CT

TALCOTT, Samuel (1662-1698) & Mary [ROWLANDSON]/[ELLERY?], m/2 James PATTERSON 1704; b 1691; Wethersfield, CT

TALEY, John & Elizabeth BOYDEN; 7 Dec 1676; Salem

TALLEY, Richard & 1/wf Sarah [BLAKE] (-5 Aug 1697); b 1684; Boston/Milton

TALLY, Richard & 2/wf Elizabeth GROSS, dau Isaac; 27 Jan 1697, 1697/8; Boston

TALLEY, Thomas & Mary __?__; b 1685; Boston

TALLMAN, James (1668-1724) & 1/wf Mary DAVOL; 18 Mar 1689/90, 1689; Portsmouth, RI

TALLMAN, John (-1709) & Mary __?__ (-1707+); ca 1690; Flushing, LI

TALLMAN, Jonathan (-1762) & Sarah __?__ (-1748+); b 1690; Dartmouth

TALLMAN, Peter (1623-1708) & 1/wf Ann [HILL?]; Barbados, 2 Jan 1649, div 1665; Portsmouth, RI

TALLMAN, Peter (1623-1708) & 2/wf Joan BRIGGS (-1685); m cont 24 Jul 1665; Portsmouth, RI

TALLMAN/TOLMAN?, Peter (1658-1728) & Ann (WRIGHT) WALSTONE (-1731), w John; 7 Nov 1683; Portsmouth, RI/Guilford, CT

TALLMAN, Peter (1623-1708) & 3/wf Esther __?__ (-bef 1708); 1686±; Portsmouth, RI/Newport

TALMAGE, David (-1708, ae 78) & __?__; b 1660; East Hampton, LI

TALLMADGE, Enos (1656-1690) & Hannah YALE (1662-1744), m/2 Samuel BISHOP 1695; 9 May 1682; New Haven

TALLMADGE, John (1654-1690) & Abigail BISHOP, m/2 William MALTBIE b 1693; 18 Nov 1686; New Haven

TALMAGE, Nathaniel & Rebecca __?__ (1658-1743); b 1676(7); East Hampton, LI

TALMAGE, Nathaniel & __?__; b 1701; East Hampton, LI/Southampton, LI

TALMAGE, Onesimus (1662-1723) & Rebecca [WHEELER] (-1751); ca 1693; East Hampton, LI

TALLMADGE, Robert (-1662) & Sarah [NASH] (-1691+); ca 1648, b 1650; New Haven

TALMAGE, Thomas & ? ; b 1610?; Charlestown/Lynn/Southampton, LI/East Hampton, LI
TALMAGE, Thomas (-1691) & Elizabeth ? ; b 1643; Lynn/East Hampton, LI
TALLMADGE, Thomas (1650-1733) & Elizabeth [ALSOP] (1650-1719); b 1677; New Haven
TALMAGE, Thomas & ? ; b 1698; East Hampton, LI
TALMAGE, William & 1/wf Elizabeth ? (-1660); ca 1630/4?; Roxbury/Boston/Lynn
TALMAGE, William & 2/wf Elizabeth [PEIRCE] (1643-); b 1666; Boston
TALMAGE, ? & Elizabeth [HULLS] (-1677), w Josiah; aft 1670; ?Killingworth, CT
TAMLIN, John & Sarah ? ; b 1663; Boston
TANKERSLY, George & Tabitha ? ; b 1673; Boston
TANNER, John (-1669) & ? ; in Eng?, b 1664?; Portsmouth, NH
TANNER, John (-1705+) & 1/wf Rachel [CHAMPION] ((165-)-); ?Lyme, CT
TANNER, John & 2/wf Rebecca (SPENCER) KENARD, w John d 1689; aft 1689, ca 1699?;
   Lyme, CT
TANNER, Nicholas (-1708) & Mary STURGES, sister of John, aunt of Margaret SQUIRE; 27 Jul
   1696; Swansea
TANNER, William & 1/wf ? TIBBETT, dau Henry; ca 1685?; ?Stonington, CT
TANNER, William & 2/wf Mary [BADCOCK]; b 1692(?); Stonington, CT
TAPLEY, Gilbert (-1714) & Thomasine ? (-1715); b 1665; Salem/Beverly
TAPLEY, Gilbert (1665-1710) & 1/wf Lydia SMALL; 10 Apr 1686; Salem
TAPLEY, John (?1639-1693+) & Elizabeth PRIDE (-1693+); 6 Dec 1663; Salem
TAPLEY, John (1669-) & Anne [LEWIS], Kittery, ME; b 1701?; Salem/Portsmouth, NH
TAPLEY, William & Elizabeth CASH (1672-); 7 Mar 1697, 1698/9, 1697/8; Salem
TAPP, ?Edmund (1653-) & Ann ? (-1673, 1660?); b 1614; Milford, CT
TAPP, William & ? ; CT
TAPPAN, Abraham (?1606/7-1672) & Susannah TAYLOR (1606-1688/9); Norwich, Eng, 28 May
   1632; Newbury
TAPPAN, Abraham (1644-1704) & Ruth PIKE; 9 Nov 1670; Salisbury/Newbury
TAPPING, Bartholomew (-1688+) & Lydia [DEAN], dau Walter; Boston/Taunton
TAPPAN, Christopher (1671-1747) & Sarah ANGIER (-1739); 13 Dec 1698; Watertown/Newbury
TOPPING, Elnathan (1640-1705) & Mary ? ; b 1664; Southampton, LI
TAPPAN, Isaac & 1/wf Hannah KENT (-1688); 29 Sep 1669; Salisbury
TAPPAN, Isaac & 2/wf Mary MARCH; 27 Mar 1691; Salisbury
TAPPAN, Jacob (1645-1717) & 1/wf Hannah SEWALL (1649-1699); 24 Aug 1670; Newbury
TAPPAN, Jacob (1671-1725) & 1/wf Sarah KENT (1667-1712); m int 15 May 1696; Newbury
TOPPING, James (-1712) & Hannah GARRETT; 5 Mar 1656; Guilford, CT/Milford, CT/Middle-
   town, CT
TOPPING, James (1665-1741) & Anne WARD? (1670-1755); 4 Feb 1691/2, 1692/3?; Middletown,
   CT
TOPPING, James (1670-1694) & Abigail [LUPTON] (1675±-), m/2 Christopher FOSTER 1697; b
   1694; Southampton, LI
TAPPINE, John (-1678) & Mary WOODMANSEY, m/2 William AVERY; 20 Aug 1654; Boston
TOPPING, John (1636±-1686) & 1/wf Sarah [WHITE]; b 1662; Southampton, LI
TOPPING, John (1636-1686) & 2/wf Deborah (LOCKWOOD) WARD, w William; aft 1676, bef 19
   Apr 1678; Southampton, LI
TAPPAN, John (1651-1743) & 1/wf Martha BROWNE; 3 Sep 1688; Andover
TAPPING, Joseph & Mariana/Marran ? ; b 1678; Boston
TOPPING, Josiah (1663-1726) & Hannah [SAYRE]; Southampton, LI
TAPPAN, Peter (1633-1707) & Jane BATT; 3 Apr 1661; Newbury
TAPPAN, Peter (1667-) & Sarah (?KENT) GREENLEAF, w Samuel; 28 Apr 1696; Newbury
TAPPING, Richard & 1/wf Judith ? (-1635); b 1633; Boston
TAPPING, Richard (-1654+) & Alice ? ; b 1645; Boston
TAPPAN, Samuel (1670-), Newbury & Abigail WIGGLESWORTH (1681-1702); 23 Dec 1700, ?3
   Jun 1701; Malden
TAPPING, Thomas[1] (-bef 1688) & 1/wf Emma ? ; b 1640; Wethersfield, CT
TOPPING, Thomas[2] (-1681) & Hannah [WHITE]; b 1661; Southampton, LI
[TOPPING], Thomas[1] (-1688±) & 2/wf Mary (?) (MAPHAM) BALDWIN (-1676), w John, w
   Timothy; m cont 20 Oct 1666; Milford, CT
[TOPPING], Thomas[1] & 3/wf Lydia [WILFORD] (-1694), w John; b 1678; Milford, CT/Branford,
   CT

TOPPING, Thomas (1661-) & Mary _?_ (-1688); Southampton, LI
TOPPING, [?Ephraim] & Deborah HOWELL, dau Edward; b 27 Jan 1697; Southampton
TAPPER, John & Hannah _?_ ; b 1688; Boston
TAPRILL, Robert (-1678) & Abishag/(Abishai) [WALTON]; b 1663; Great Island/Newcastle, NH
TARBELL, John (-1715) & Mary NURSE (-1749); 25 Oct 1678; Salem
TARBELL, Thomas[1] (?1618-1678) & 1/wf Mary _?_ (1620-1674); b 1645?; Watertown/Groton
TARBELL, Thomas[2] (-1678) & Anna/?Joanna/Hannah LONGLEY (-1680); 30 Jun 1666; Groton/Charlestown
TARBELL, Thomas[1] (1618-1678) & 2/wf Susanna LAWRENCE (-1691), w John; 15 Aug 1666, 1677, 1676; Charlestown
TARBELL, Thomas (1667-1715) (ae 25 in 1691) & Elizabeth WOODS/BLOOD (1665-1717); 1 Dec 1686; Groton
TARBELL, William & Mary [BOWER]/[HILDRETH?]; Bridgehampton, CT
TARBOX, Ebenezer (1678-1723) & Mary BREAN; 15 Apr 1700; Lynn
TARBOX, John (-1674) & [Rebecca?] _?_ (Samuel had wife Rebecca); b 1633?, left 2/wf; Lynn
TARBOX, John (ca 1645-1723+) & Mary HAVEN (1647-1690); 4 Jul 1667; Lynn
TARBOX, John (1668-1748) & Elizabeth _?_ ; b 1691; Lynn/E. Greenwich, RI
TARBOX, Jonathan (1668-1718) & Eleanor _?_ , m/2 John GOTT; ca 1693; Lynn
TARBOX, Samuel (?1647-1715) & 1/wf Rebecca ARMITAGE (-1676); 14 Nov 1665; Lynn
TARBOX, Samuel (?1647-1715) & 2/wf Experience LOOK; 16 Oct 1678; Lynn
TARBOX, ?William & _?_ ; (doubtful)
TARBOX, ?Godfrey (1670-1701) & _?_ ; b 1695; Lynn
TARLETON, Henry (-1680, ae 31) & 1/wf Mary _?_ (-1678, ae 22); b 1678; Boston
TARLETON, Henry (-1680, ae 31) & 2/wf Deborah CUSHING, m/2 Rev. Benjamin WOOD-BRIDGE 1686; 25 Sep 1679; Hingham
TARLTON, Richard (-1706) & 2/wf Ruth (STILEMAN) [BUSSELL], w William; b 1693, aft 1 Jun 1691, 1692±; ?New Castle, NH
TARNE/TERNE, Miles/Michael (-1676) & 1/wf Sarah _?_ (?relative of Charity WHITE); b 1638, b 1636?; Boston
TARNE, Miles/Michael (-1676) & 2/wf Elizabeth ROYCE/RICE?, w Robert; b 23 Oct 1652; Boston
TARR, Richard & 1/wf _?_ ; b 1687
TARR, Richard (ae 84 in 1730) & 2/wf Elizabeth [DICER] (1667-); b 1690, ca 1687?; Gloucester/Saco, ME
TARRIN/TARRING, John & Abigail ABBOTT; 1 Jul 1686; Marblehead
TART, Thomas & Elizabeth _?_ ; b 1641; Boston/Barbados/Scituate
TASKER, William (1656-1697±) & Mary [ADAMS] (-1700); b 1694, by 1688?, b 1683?; Dover, NH
TATENHAM, Elias (probably Eliah TOTTINGHAM) & Mary _?_ ; b 1683; Boston
TATTON, Robert & Anna PITMAN; 3 Jul 1685; Marblehead
TAUNTON, Matthew & Susanna _?_ ; b 1688; Boston
TAULEY, Thomas (-1686) & Mary _?_ ; b 1678; Boston
TAWLEY, John (-1690) & Elizabeth [EMERY?]/BOYDEN?; Salem
TAY, Jeremiah (1657-) & Mercy WOODWARD, dau Nathaniel; 14 Mar 1683; Boston
TAY, John (-1641) & Elizabeth ALLEN; Nazing, Eng, 28 Aug 1621; Boston
TAY, John (1647-1678) & [Elizabeth GANNETT]; ca 1670/2?; Billerica/Weymouth
TAY, Nathaniel (1655-) & Bathsheba WYMAN; 30 May 1677; Billerica/Woburn
TAY, William (1608-1683) & Grace NEWELL (-1712, in 91st y); 14 Sep 1644; Roxbury/Billerica/Boston
TAYLOR, Abraham & Hannah _?_ ; b 1673; Haverhill
TAYLOR, Abraham (1656-1729) & Mary WHITAKER (1662-1756); 16 Dec 1681; Concord
TAYLOR, Anthony (-1687) & Philippa _?_ (-1683); b 1646; Hampton, NH
TAYLOR, Benjamin (-1747) & Rachel [?LAWRENCE] (-1749); b 1696; Exeter, NH/Stratham, NH
TAYLOR, Edward (-1694) & 1/wf Christian _?_ (-1673); ca 1645?; Reading
TAYLOR, Edward & Hannah [?THROCKMORTON]; b 1655; Providence
TAYLOR, Edward (-1705) & Mary MERLL/MERRILL? (-1701); 19 Feb 1663; Barnstable
TAYLOR, Edward (-1694) & 2/wf Elizabeth BRIDGE (-1686), m/1 Roger BANCROFT, m/2 Martin SAUNDERS, m/3 John BRIDGE, m/4 Edward TAYLOR; 29 Jul 1673; Reading

TAYLOR, Rev. Edward (1642-1729) & 1/wf Elizabeth **FITCH** (1652-1689); 5 Nov 1674; Westfield

TAYLOR, Edward, Jr. & Rebecca **HUMPHREYS**; 24 May 1687, m in Boston; Watertown

TAYLOR, Edward (-1704) & Rebecca __?__, m/2 Thomas **DUDLEY**; b 1691; Exeter, NH/etc.

TAYLOR, Edward (1642-1729) & 2/wf Ruth **WYLLYS**; 2 Jun 1692; Hartford/Westfield

TAYLOR, Edward & Jane **PAYN**; 4 Aug 1692; Boston

TAYLOR, Eleazer & Lydia **BARRETT**; 18 Apr 1699; Marlboro

TAYLOR, Elisha (1664-1741) & Rebecca [?**WHEELER**]? (-1730); b 1689; Yarmouth

TAYLOR, George (1604-1667) & Elizabeth __?__; b 1646; Lynn

TAYLOR, George & Margaret [**HINKSON**], w Philip; aft 1653; Saco, ME

TAYLOR, Gregory & Alse/Asca/Achsah? __?__; b 1632; Watertown/Stamford, CT

TAYLOR, Henry & Lydia **HATCH**; 19 Dec 1650; Barnstable

TAYLOR, Henry & Mary __?__; b 1665; Boston

TAYLOR, Henry & Sarah __?__, m/2 Benjamin **FIELD**; ca 1693(?); Flushing, LI

TAYLOR, Hopestill & Mary **LOVETT**; 17 Feb 1668/9; Medfield

TAYLOR, Isaac (1659-), Concord & Elizabeth **KNIGHT**, Cambridge; 19 Dec 1688; Concord/[Bedford?]

TAYLOR, Isaac & Sarah __?__; b 1692; Boston/Scituate/etc.

TAYLOR, Jacob (1662-1705+) & Deborah **NUTTING** (-1705+); 29 Nov 1687; Concord

TAYLOR, Jacob & Rebecca **WEEKS**; 29 May 1693; Barnstable

TAILOR, James (-1690) & Isabella/(Elizabeth) **TOMKINS**; 19 Oct 1641; Concord/Marlboro/Cambridge

TAILER, James/?John & Elizabeth/Isabelle? [**FULLER**?] (see James of Boston); b 1656; Concord

TAYLOR, James & Mary **TAYLOR** (1649-); 17 Jan 1667, 1668; Springfield/Suffield, CT

TAILOR, James (-1713) & Sarah [?**NEWTON**] (?1652-1713+) (did she m/2 Benjamin **MILLS** 1718 of Dedham?); b 1671, ca 1670; Marlborough

TAYLOR, James (see Richard **TAYLOR**) & Elizabeth [**FULLER**?] (-bef 1679); b 1674; Boston/Dorchester

TAYLOR, James & Emma __?__; b 1683; Beverly

TAYLOR, James & Mary [**CHAPLIN**]; b 1683; Dorchester

TAYLOR, James & Rebecca [?**WHEELER**] (see Elisha); 1679; Boston

TAYLOR, James (-1690) & Catharine __?__ (-1690, ae 24); b 1689; Newport, RI

TAYLOR, James & Hannah **GREEN**; int 25 - 1696; Suffield, CT

TAILOR, James (1674-) & Elizabeth __?__ (-1710+); b 1696(7?); Marlborough

TAYLOR, James & __?__; b 1701; Colchester, CT

TAYLOR, Jasper (-1719) & Hannah **FITTSRANDLE/FITZRANDOLPH** (1648-); 6 Nov 1668; Barnstable

TAYLOR, John (-1646) (called Thomas **LORD** brother 17 Oct 1648) & 1/wf __?__ (-1630, 1639); in Eng, b 1630; Lynn/Windsor, CT

TAYLOR, John (-1668) & Rebecca __?__; b 1639; Weymouth

TAYLOR, John & __?__ **THROCKMORTON**; ca 1645?, b 1649; Damariscotta River

TAYLOR, John (-1645?) & 2/wf? Rhoda __?__, wid, m/2 or m/3 Walter **HOYT** bef 1652; b 1641?, betw 1630 & 1638; Windsor, CT

TAYLOR, John (1610-) & Katharine __?__; b 1651; Cambridge

TAYLOR, John & Phebe **ROCKWOOD**; b 1660, b 1664; Weymouth

TAYLOR, John (1641-1704) & Thankful **WOODWARD** (1646-1724+); 18 Dec 1662?, 18 Nov 1662?, b 1655?; Northampton

TAYLOR, John & Martha __?__; ca 1666?; Berwick, ME

TAYLOR, John & __?__; b 1673; CT

TAYLOR, John (?1639-1713) & Mary **SELDEN** (1648-1713); 12 Dec 1666; Hadley

TAYLOR, John & 1/wf Deborah **GODFREY** (-1699); 5 Dec 1667; Hampton, NH/Watertown

TAYLOR, John (?1647-), son Richard?, & Rebecca [**TAINTOR**] (1647-), dau Joseph; b 1674; Boston/Watertown

TALAR, John (ca 1652-1721, 1722) & Sarah **MATHUES/MATTHEWS** (1649-); 15 Dec 1674, 5 Sep; Yarmouth

TAILER, John (-1719) & Eunice **WOOLY/WOOLEY**; 26 Mar 1678; Concord

TAYLOR, John & Rebecca [?**REDDING**]; b 1680, by 1681; Boston/Weymouth

TAYLOR/TYLER, John & 1/wf Sarah **YOUNGLOVE** (-1683); 25 Sep 1682; Suffield, CT

TAYLOR, John & Mary [**BANKS**]; b 12 Jan 1685; Fairfield, CT

TAYLOR, John (-1724) & Katharine JOHNSON; 24 Dec 1685; Charlestown

TAYLOR/TYLER, John & 2/wf Elizabeth SPENCER (ca 1668-); 24 Mar 1686, 1685/6; Suffield, CT/Windsor, CT

TAYLOR, John (1667-1744) & 1/wf Wait [CLAPP] (1670-1722); b 1690; Norwalk, CT/Deerfield

TAYLOR, John (1659-1747) & 1/wf Abigal __?__ (-1720); b 1691, b 1682, 1681; Little Compton, RI

TAYLOR, John (1670-) & Hannah GILLET (1674-); 9 Feb 1694; Hadley

TAYLOR, John & Mary [WHITEHEAD], m/2 Thomas BURROUGHS, m/3 Rev. William URQUHART d 1709; b 1695; Oyster Bay, LI

TAYLOR, John & Elizabeth BELCHER; 5 Apr 1697; Newbury?/Cape May Co., NJ

TAYLOR, John & Sarah __?__ ; b 1698; Braintree/Little Compton

TAYLOR, John (1649-) & Sarah (HART) SCONE?, dau John?; 2 Mar 1699, [1698/9]; Wethersfield

TAYLOR, John & Susannah (DRAKE) BRACKETT, w Anthony; 30 Oct 1700; Hampton, NH

TAYLOR, John (1673-) & Mary [BUSHNELL] (1679-); b 1701?; ?Danbury, CT

TAYLOR, Jonathan (-1683, Suffield, CT) & Mary [?WRIGHT]/?Experience __?__ (-1683); b 1649; Springfield/Suffield, CT

TAYLOR, Jonathan & __?__ ; b 1658; Deerfield

TAYLOR, Jonathan & [Sarah BROOKS] (1658-), m/2 John HANCHET; 11 Jul 1678; Deerfield

TAYLOR, Jonathan (1675-) & Hannah [THOMAS] (1678-), div 1708; b 1701?; Deerfield/NJ/DE?

TAYLOR, Joseph & Bethia [BRUNDAGE?] (see Timothy KNABB); aft 1654; Rye, NY?/Westchester, NY

TAYLOR, Joseph (-4 Apr 1682) & Mary (BRYAN) MOLTBY, w John, m/3 John HOWELL 1690; aft 5 Nov 1677, ca 16 Jan 1677/8?; Cambridge/New Haven

TAYLOR, Joseph (1660-1727) & Experience WILLIAMSON (-1727+); 25 Apr 1684; Marshfield

TAYLOR, Joseph (-1699/1700) & 2/wf Ruth __?__ ; b 1698, b 1686?; Westchester, NY

TAILOR, Joseph & Thomasin [SCARLET], m/2 Richard SKINNER 1692; b 1686; Boston

TAYLOR, Joseph, Jr. & Elizabeth __?__ ; b 1686; Westchester, NY

TAYLOR, Joseph (-1709) & Ruth WOOLY/WOOLEY (-1709); 4 Dec 1691; Concord

TAYLOR, Joseph (?1639, 1670?-) & Rachel __?__ ; b 1694; Exeter, NH/Wells, ME

TAYLOR, Joseph (1677-) & 1/wf Mary MARSTON (1678-); ca 1690; Hampton, NH

TAYLOR, Joseph (1674-) & Sarah __?__ ; 28 Nov 1698?, b 1701?; Danbury/Deerfield

TAYLOR, Nathan (-1703) & Sarah [DRISCO]; Mar 1699-1700, b 3 Jun 1700, Jun 1700; Exeter, NH/Hampton?, NH

TAYLOR, Nathaniel? (-1652) & Jane __?__

TAYLOR, Nathaniel (1656-) & Abigail BISSELL (1658-); 17 Oct 1678; Windsor, CT

TAYLOR, Nathaniel & Sarah __?__ ; b 1698; Westchester, NY

TAYLOR, Peter (1661-1736) & 1/wf Elizabeth [PICKHAM] (-1714); b 1697, 1696, b 1697+; Little Compton, RI/Portsmouth, NH

TAYLOR, Richard (-1659) & Ann __?__ ; b 1643; ?Charlestown

TAYLOR, Richard (-1673) (tailor by trade) & Ruth WHELDEN (-1673?, 1693?); ca 27 Oct 1646, date of her father's consent; Yarmouth

TAYLOR, Richard (-1703) & Ruth [BURGESS] (-1673?); b 1652; Yarmouth

TAYLOR, Richard (-1673) & 1/wf Mary __?__ ; b 1647; Boston

TAYLOR, Richard (-1706) & Ann [WHELDEN] (-1694); b 1665, b 1663; Charlestown

TAYLOR, Richard (-1673) & 2/wf Elizabeth [?FULLER] (see James TAYLOR) (1/wf Mary); Boston

TAYLOR, Richard (1652-1732) & Hannah [RICE]? (see below); ca 1676/80; Yarmouth

TAYLOR, Richard & Hannah (RICE) WARD, w Eleazer; 17 Oct 1677; Sudbury

TAYLOR, Robert (-1688) & Mary HODGES; Nov 1646; Scituate, MA/Newport

TAYLOR, Robert & Sarah __?__ ; b 1660(1?); Boston

TAYLOR, Robert (1653-1707, ae 54?) & Deborah [PECKHAM] (-1707+); b 1682, b 1687; Newport?, RI/Portsmouth, RI

TAYLOR, Samuel & Mary [BANKS]/BRANKER?; 27 Oct 1670, b 1672; Windsor, CT/Springfield/Westfield

TAYLOR, Samuel (-1689) & Ruth COGAN (-1724), m/2 Thomas COPLEY 1693; 24 Jun 1675; Springfield/Suffield, CT

TAYLOR, Samuel (1651-1711) & Sarah (COLE) PERSONS (1654-1712); 10 Apr 1678; Wethersfield

TAYLOR, Samuel (1656-1695+) & Mary ROBINS/ROBBINS (-1695+); 9 Dec 1685; Concord
TAYLOR, Seabred (1643-1714) & Mary HARRINGTON; 21 Nov 1671; Reading
TAYLOR, Stephen (-1688) & 1/wf Sarah HOSFORD (-1649); 1 Nov 1642; Windsor, CT
TAYLOR, Stephen (-1688) & 2/wf Elizabeth NEWELL/NOWELL? (-1689?), wid(?); 25 Oct 1649; Windsor, CT
TAYLOR, Stephen (-1665) & Sarah [WHITE] (1641-1702), m/2 Barnabas HINSDALE 1666, m/3 Walter HICKSON/[HIXON] 1678/9; b 1665; Hadley/Deerfield
TAYLOR, Stephen & Hannah __?__ ; b 1668; Boston
TAYLOR, Stephen (-1707) & Joanna PORTER, Farmington; 8 Nov 1676; Farmington, CT?/Suffield, CT
TAYLOR, Stephen (-1719) & Patience BROWN; 27 Nov 1700; Deerfield/Hatfield/Colchester, CT
TAYLOR, Thomas (ca 1620-1691) & Elizabeth __?__ (-1650); b 1639; Charlestown/Watertown/Reading
TAYLOR, Thomas & Rebecca KETCHAM; 14 Feb 1667/[8], 1677 (error); Norwalk/Stratford, CT/Danbury, CT
TAYLOR, Thomas & Mary HUPPER/HOPPER?/HOOPER (1647-); 1 Oct 1671; Reading
TAYLOR, Thomas (1655-1741) & 1/wf Abigail ROE (-1691); 15 Jun 1678, 12 Jun; Suffield
TAYLOR, Thomas & Patience [BROOKS] (1661-); ca 1680, aft 8 Aug 1680; Deerfield/Springfield
TAYLOR, Thomas (-1691) & Mary PETTY, m/2 Thomas RICH; 29 Dec 1687; Deerfield
TAYLOR, Thomas (1655-1741) & 2/wf Hannah [GRANGER]; ca 1691, b 1697; Suffield, CT
TAYLOR, Thomas (1668-) & 1/wf Phebe [BENEDICT]; b 1701; Danbury
TAYLOR, Tobias & Sarah [HAM] (-1688), w Matthew; b 11 Nov 1667; Portsmouth, NH
TAYLOR, Walter & Alice [?WELLS]; b 1658; Salem?/Salisbury
TAYLOR, Walter & Deliverance GRAVES
TAYLOR, William (-1679) & Ann [JONES?] (WYETH aft 25 Mar 1648), m/2 George PEARSON 1677 (see below); b 1639; Exeter, NH
TAYLOR, William & Mary __?__ ; b 1647, b 1649, ca 1648, b 1649/50; Wethersfield
TAYLOR, William (-1696) & Mary [MERRIAM? (no)] (-1699); b 1650; Concord
TAYLOR, William (-1682) & Rebecca STOUGHTON (1641-); 25 Aug 1664, at Boston?; Dorchester
TAYLOR, William & 1/wf [Anne] [WYETH?], m/2 George PEARSON 1677 (see above); aft 25 Mar 1648, b 1667, b 27 May 1664; Exeter, NH
TAYLOR, William (-1682) & Rebecca __?__ ; b 1667; Boston
TAYLOR, William (-1706) & 1/wf Mary JOHNSON (-1672); 15 Nov 1671; Marlborough/Medfield
TAYLOR, William (-1706) & 2/wf Hannah [MERRIAM] AXTELL (1645(?)-), w Henry; 16 Jul 1677, 5 Jul; Marlborough
TAYLOR, William (-1706) & 3/wf Mary CHEEVERS (-1697); 28 Nov 1683; Cambridge
TAYLOR, William & Margaret [BEAN] (1670-); b 1688; Exeter, NH
TAYLOR, William & __?__ ; b 1689, b 1688; Scituate
TAYLOR, William (-1693) & __?__ ; b 1692, b 1683?; Portsmouth, NH
TAYLOR, William & Elizabeth BIGGS; 18 Dec 1693; Wethersfield
TAILOR, William (-1706) & 4/wf Sarah (WHEELER) LAKEIN (1666-1742+), w John; 3 Feb 1699; Marlborough
TAYLOR, William & 1/wf Sarah BYFIELD; 2 Mar 1699, 1699/1700; Boston
TAYLOR, John & __?__ ; ME
TAYLOR, __?__ & Hopestill [HOLMES]
TAYLOR, __?__ (-bef 13 Jun 1688) & Catherine __?__
TAYLOR, __?__ & Mary __?__ ; b 1688; Southampton
TAYNOUR/TAINER?, Elias & Mary POWELL; 19 Sep 1692; Marblehead
TAYNOUR, Humphrey & Mary MALLARD; 25 Feb 1699/1700; Marblehead
TAYNOUR, Thomas & __?__ ; b 1667; Marblehead
TEALE, William & 1/wf Mary __?__ ; b 1685(6?), b 1686; Malden/Charlestown
TEFF, Henry & Mary BASSETT; 6 Nov 1673; ?Windsor, CT
TEFFT, John[1] (-1676) & Mary [?BARBER]; b 1644; Portsmouth, RI/Kings Town
TEFFT, John (-1762) & Joanna [SPRAGUE] (-1757); b 1699; Richmond, RI/South Kingston, RI
TEFFT, Joshua (-1676) & Sarah __?__ ; b 1672; ?Warwick, RI/Kings Town, RI
TEFFT, Peter (-1725(-)) & Mary __?__ ; b 1699; Westerly, RI/Stonington, CT
TEFFT, Samuel[1] (1644-1725) & Elizabeth [JENCKES] (1658-1740); ca 1677; Kings Town/Westerly, RI

TEFFE, William (-1648) & 1/wf _?_ ; Boston
TEFFE/T&FT?, William (-1648) & 2/wf Anna _?_ (-1672), m/2 Henry ALLEN; Boston
TEMPLAR, Richard & Ann/Hannah [PRITCHARD], m/2 Nathaniel MORTON; b 1642(3?); Yarmouth
TEMPLE, Abraham & 1/wf [Abigail?] _?_ ; b 1623?; Salem
TEMPLE, Abraham & 2/wf Margaret _?_ , m/2 John GIFFORD; Salem
TEMPLE, Abraham (1652-1738) & Deborah HADLOCKE (-1743); 4 Dec 1673; Concord
TEMPLE, Christopher (-1691) & Alice [HASSELL], m/2 Jacob KENDALL 1695; 3 Dec 1685; Dunstable
TEMPLE, Isaac (1657-) & Prudence HOWELL; 9 Jul 1691; Concord
TEMPEL, Isaac (1678-1765) & Martha JOSLIN (-1768); 1 Mar 1698/9; Marlboro
TEMPLE, John & Martha _?_ ; b 1676/7; Boston
TEMPLE, Richard (?ca 1623-1689) & Joanna _?_ (-1688); b 1647; Salem/Charlestown/Concord
TEMPLE, Richard (1654-1698) & Sarah PARLING/PARLIN (1668-), m/2 Joseph BRABROOK 1698; 24 Apr 1688; Concord
TEMPLE, Richard (1667/8-1737) & Deborah [PARKER] (1674-1751); b 1695?; Reading/Woburn
TEMPLE, Richard (1674-1756) & 1/wf Mary BARKER; 2 May 1699; Concord/Stow
TEMPLE, Robert (-1675) & _?_ ; b 1668; Saco, ME
TENCH, Edward & Sarah _?_ ; b 1634; New Haven
TENNANT, Alexander (-1696+) & _?_ ; b 1680; Kings Town, RI/Jamestown, RI
TENNY, Daniel (1653-) & 1/wf Elizabeth STICKNEY (1661-1694); 21 Jul 1680, 17 Aug; Bradford
TENNEY, Daniel & 2/wf Mary HARDY; 22 May 1695; Haverhill
TENY, James (1650-1726) & Abigail LAMBERT (-1756); 3 Oct 1684; Rowley
TENEY, John (1640-) & 1/wf Mary/Mercy PARRAT (1646-1667); 26 Feb 1663, 1663/4; Rowley
TENNEY, John (1636-) & 1/wf Agnes [BOWDEN] (1639-); ca 1664; Kittery, ME
TENNY, John (1640-) & 2/wf Susanna WOODBERY; 2 Dec 1668; Bradford
TENNEY, John, Boston & Sarah ATKINS/?ADKINS, Boston, m/2 Alexander CHAMBERLAIN 1699; 9 May 1688; Charlestown
TENNEY, John (-1722) & Margaret [?WALLIS]/[WADOCK], wid; by 1693
TENNEY, John & Elizabeth [MITCHELL], m/2 Samuel JOHNSON; b 1695?, ca 1698; Kittery, ME
TENNEY, Samuel (1667-) & 1/wf Abigail [BAILEY] (1671/2-1689); b 1689; Bradford
TENNEY, Samuel (1667-) & 2/wf Sarah BOYNTON (-1709); 18 Dec 1690; Bradford
TENNEY, Thomas (1614/16-1700) & 1/wf Ann [MIGHILL] (-1657); b 1640; Rowley
TENNEY, Thomas & 2/wf Elizabeth (NORTHEND) PARRAT, w Francis; 24 Feb 1657, 1657/8; Rowley/Preston
TENY, Thomas (1648-) & Margaret HIDDEN; 8 Sep 1680; Rowley
TENY, William (-1680) & Catherine [MARSTON?]; b 1643, b 1640, ?10 May 1642; Rowley
TERNE, Miles & Sarah _?_ (?relative of Charity WHITE?); b 1638; Boston
TERRY, Daniel & Sarah _?_ (-1706); ca 1675/85; Southold, LI
TERRY, Ephraim (-1760) & Hannah EGGLESTON; 25 Jul 1695; Springfield/Lebanon, CT
TERRY, Gershom (?1652-1725) & Deborah [WELLS] (1662-1729); ca 1680/4?; Southold, LI
TERRY, John (1637-1691), Windsor & Elizabeth WADSWORTH (-1715), Hartford; 27 Nov 1662, ?at Hartford; Windsor, CT/Simsbury, CT
TERRY, John & _?_ ; b 1668; Portsmouth, NH
TERRY, John (1662-1733) & Hannah [MOORE] (-1753); b 1698, b 1691?; Southold, LI
TERRY, Nathaniel & Mary HORTON; 31 Nov 1682 [sic]; Southold, LI
TERRY, Richard (1618-1675/6) & Abigail LINES (-1686+); 22 May 1650, at Southold; New Haven/Southold, LI
TERRY, Richard (-1723, 1734, ae 64) & Prudence _?_ ; b 1698; Southold, LI
TERRY, Samuel (ca 1663/4-1730?) & 1/wf Ann LOBDELL (-1684); 3 Jan 1660, 1660/1, ?at Boston; Springfield
TERRY, Capt. Samuel (1661-2 Jan 1730/1) & 1/wf Hannah MORGAN (1656/7-1697); 17 May 1682; Springfield/Enfield, CT
TERRY, Samuel (-1730?, Lebanon?, Enfield?) & 2/wf Sarah (BLISS) SCOTT (-16 Nov 1705), w John; 19 Nov 1690; Springfield/Enfield, CT
TERRY, Capt. Samuel (1661-1730/1) & 2/wf Martha (BOARDMAN) CRANE, w Benjamin; 4 Jan 1697, 1697/8, 5 Jan, 6 Jan 1697/8; Enfield, CT/Springfield
TERRY, Stephen (1608-1668) & 1/wf _?_ (-1647); b 1633?, b 1635?, ?Symondsbury, Dorset, Mar 1633/4? (no); Dorchester

TERRY, Stephen (1608-1668) & 2/wf Elizabeth _?_ (-1683); aft 1647; Windsor, CT/Hadley
TERRY, Thomas (1607-1672) & 1/wf Marie _?_ (-1659); Southold, LI
TERRY, Thomas (1607-1672) & 2/wf _?_ (-1671+); Southold, LI
TERRY, Thomas (-1704?) & Hannah/?Anna (ROGERS) TISDALE, w John, m/3 Samuel
    WILLIAMS; aft 1677, bef 1679; Taunton/Freetown
TERRY, Thomas (-1724) & 1/wf Elizabeth _?_ (-1706); b 1680; Southold, LI
TERRY, Thomas (1665-1760) & 1/wf Martha COOLEY (1659-1720); 21 Apr 1687; Springfield
TERRY, Thomas & Abigail DEANE; 4 Jan 1699/1700; Taunton
TETHERLY, Gabriel (-1695) & Susanna [KING], w Richard; 1653+; Kittery, ME
TETHERLY, William (-1692) & Mary ROBY/ROBIE, m/2 John LYDSTON ca 1693?; 13 Aug 1683;
    Kittery, ME
TEW, Henry (1654-1718) & 1/wf Dorcas _?_ (-1694±); b 1680; Middletown, RI
TEW, Henry (1654-) & 2/wf Sarah _?_ (1668-1718+); aft 1694; (REW wrong)
TEW, Richard (-1674, 1673±) & Mary [CLARKE] (-1687+); in Eng, m cont 18 Oct 1633, in Eng,
    b 1640; Newport, RI
TEW, Richard & Ruth [SISSON] (1680-); b 1701?; Portsmouth, RI?
TEW, Richard & _?_ ; Flushing, LI
TEW, _?_ & Sarah _?_ ; b 1702; Newport
TEUXBURY/TEWKSBURY, Henry (?1626-) & Martha (COPP) HARVEY, w William; 10 Nov 1659;
    Boston/Newbury/Amesbury
TUKESBURY, Henry (1664-) & Hannah _?_ ; b 1694; Amesbury
TUXBERY, John (1674-) & Hannah [COLBY]; b 1696; Amesbury
TEUXBURY, Thomas & _?_ ; in Eng, ca 1665?
THATCHER, Anthony[1] (-1667) & 1/wf Mary _?_ (-1634 in Eng); in Eng, b 1619?;
    Marblehead/Yarmouth
THATCHER, Anthony[1] (-1667) & 2/wf Elizabeth [JONES] (-1670); in Eng, b 1635, 1635;
    Salem/Yarmouth
THACHER, John (1639-1713) & 1/wf Rebecca WINSLOW (1643, 1642-1683); ?6 Nov 1661,
    1664?: ?Marshfield/?Yarmouth
THATCHER, Capt. John (1639-1713) & 2/wf Lydia GOREHAM (1661-1744); 1 Jan 1683, 11? Jan
    1683/4; Yarmouth
THACHER, John (1675-) & Desire (STURGES) DIMOCK/DIMMOCK? (1666-), w Thomas; 10 Nov
    1698; Barnstable
THACHER, Josiah (1667-1702) & Mary HEADG/HEDGE, m/2 Zachariah PADDOCK 1708; 25 Feb
    1690/91; Yarmouth
THACHAR, Judah (-1676) & Mary [THORNTON] (-1708, ae 68); ca 1666; Yarmouth
THATCHER, Peter (bpt Salem 1651-1727, Milton) & 1/wf Theodora OXENBRIDGE (-1697); 2
    Nov 1677, 21 Nov 1677; Milton
THATCHER, Peter (1665-1736) & Thankful [STURGIS] (1675-1745); b 1694; Yarmouth
THATCHER, Peter (1651-1727) & 2/wf Susanna (WILKINS) BAYLEY/BAILEY (-1724, ae 59), w
    Rev. John; 25 Dec 1699; Milton/Boston
THACHER, Rodolphus & Ruth PARTERIDG/PARTRIDGE; 5 Jan 1669; Duxbury
THATCHER, Samuel (-1669) & Hannah _?_ ; b 1645; Watertown
THACHER, Samuel (1648-1726) & Mary FARNSWORTH; 11 Apr 1676; Lynn/?Watertown
THACHER, Thomas (1620-1678) & 1/wf Elizabeth (PARTRIDGE) KEMP (-1664), w William; 11
    May 1643; ?Duxbury
THATCHER, Thomas (1620-1678) & 2/wf Margaret (WEBB) [SHEAFE] (1625-1693, 1694, ae 68),
    w Jacob; ca 1665
THATCHER, Thomas (-1680) & Mary [SAVAGE] (1647-); b 1671; Boston
THAXTER, Benjamin (1663-1721) & Susanna MOLTON; 4 Dec 1693; Boston
THAXTER, David (1672-1760) & Alice CHUBBUCK (1671-1745); 24 Jun 1695; Hingham
THAXTER, John (?1626-1687) & Elizabeth JACOB (-1725), m/2 Daniel CUSHING 1691; 4 Dec
    1648; Hingham
THAXTER, Joseph (1656-) & Mary [BUTTOLPH] (1665-), m/2 Robert GUTTRIDGE/GOOD-
    RICH; b 1689; Boston
THAXTER, Samuel (1641-1725) & 1/wf Abigail CHURCH (1647-1677); 19 Dec 1666; Hingham
THAXTER, Samuel (1641-1725) & 2/wf Deborah LINCOLN (1645-1694); 13 Jun 1678; Hingham
THAXTER, Samuel (-1740) & Hannah GRIDLEY (-1756); 29 Dec 1691; Hingham

THAXTER, Thomas (-1654) & Elizabeth __?__ (-1660), m/2 William RIPLEY 1654, m/3 John DWIGHT 1658; in Eng, b 1626; Hingham

THAXTER, Thomas (1654-) & Lydia (COFFIN) LOGAN (1669-), w Robert; 31 Dec 1696, m int 26 Nov 1696; Hingham/Martha's Vineyard

TAYER/(THAYER?), Benjamin (-1716) & Susanna (MARTIN) [JAMES], w William; b 1675?, aft 1677; Newport

THAYER, Benjamin (-1729) & 1/wf Sarah HAYWARD (-1711); 15 Sep [1699?], 1698?; Mendon

TAYER/(THAYER?), Benjamin & Mary BOWMAN; 18 Nov 1700; Newport

THAYER, Bradick & __?__ ; b 1672; Boston

THAYER, Cornelius (1670-) & Abigail [HAYDEN]?/COPELAND? (-1731); b 1696?, b 1695?; Braintree

THAYER, Ebenezer (-1720), Braintree & Ruth NEAL/JACKSON; 2 Aug 1688; Taunton/Braintree

THAYER, Ebenezer, Mendon & Martha TOMSON/WHITE, Mendon; 13 Jun 1695; Milton/Mendon

THAYER, Ephraim (1670, ?1669-1757) & 1/wf Sarah BASS (1672-1751); 7 Jan 1691/2; Braintree

THAYER, Ferdinando (1625-1713) (m/2 Anna FREEBURG) & Huldah HAYWARD (1625-1690); 14 Jan 1652/3; Braintree/Mendon

THAYER, Isaac (-1755) & 1/wf Mercy WARD/ROCKWOOD (-1700), dau John; 1 Apr 1692, 1 Feb 1691?, 1 Apr 1691?; Billingham/Mendon

THAYER, John (-1746) & Mary [NEALE]/Mary BASS (1664/5-1724) (insane); Braintree

TAYER/?THAYER, John & Charity FORSTER/FOSTER?; 16 Jan 1700; Newport, RI

THARE, Jonathan, Mendon & Elizabeth FRENCH (-1703); 13 Jul 1680; Medfield

THAYER, Jonathan & Sarah [DARLING?]; b 1687(8?); Mendon

THAYER, Josiah (1668/9-) & Sarah [BASS?]; b 1691, ?7 Feb 1690; Mendon

THAYER, Nathaniel & Abigail [HARVEY] (1640-1691), dau Wm.; 1660?, b 1665; Taunton

THAYER, Nathaniel & Deborah [TOWNSEND] (1650-); b 1671; Boston

THAYER, Nathaniel (1658-1726) & Hannah HOIDEN/HAYDEN/HEIDEN (1661-); 27 May 1679; Braintree

THAYER, Nathaniel & Rebecca BRIGGS; 11 Feb 1690; Taunton

THAYER, Nathaniel & Sarah [WALES] (1680-); b 1713, b 1701?

THAYER, Richard (-by 1668) & 1/wf Dorothy MORTIMER (-1640/1); Thornbury, Eng, 5 Apr 1624; Braintree

THAYER/TARE/TARR, Richard & 2/wf? Jane [PARKER], w John; bef 15 Jul 1646, bef 1 Oct 1656, b 1652; Boston

THAYER, Richard (1625-1705) & Dorothy PRAY (1634-1705); 24 Dec 1651; Braintree

THAYER, Richard (1655-1729) & Rebecca MICALL (1659-1732); 16 Jul 1679; Braintree

THAYER, Samuel (-1721) & Mary/Mercy (BUTTERWORTH)/BASS? SLADE?/SLOUD (-1723/27?) w Joseph, m/2 __?__ BLOOD; 1690; Mendon

THAYER, Samuel (1667-1710) & Susanna SCANT; 18 Jan 1694, 17 Jan 1694; Braintree/Boston

THAYER, Shadrach (1629-1678) & 1/wf Mary BARRETT (-1658, 1657); 1 Jan 1654/5; Braintree

THAYER/RORE, Shadrack (1629-1678) & 2/wf Deliverance PRIEST (-1723, ae 78); 12 Jul 1661; Weymouth

THAYER, Thomas (?1596-1665) & Margery WHEELER (-1672/3); Thornbury, Eng, 13 Apr 1618; Braintree

THAYER, Thomas (1622-1693) & Hannah/Anna/Ann __?__ ; (-1698, ae 73); b 1647; Braintree

THAYER, Thomas (-1705) & Abigail VEAZIE (-1712); 25 Mar 1680; Braintree

THAYER, Thomas, Mendon & Mary/Alice? POOL/ADAMS, Braintree; 28 Oct 1687; Milton/Mendon

THAYER, William (1675-) & Hannah (NEWCOMB) HAYWARD/HAYWOOD, w William; 22 Sep 1699, 27? Sep; Braintree

THEALL, Joseph (1640) & __?__ ; Stamford, CT/Bedford, NY/Rye, NY

THEALE, Joseph (1640-), Bedford, NY, & Rebecca (JONES) HALL; aft 7 Oct 1695; Fairfield/Bedford, NY/Stamford, CT

THELE/THEAL, Nicholas (-1658?) & Elizabeth __?__ (-1660), m/2 Thomas UFFET; b 1640; Watertown/Stamford, CT

TEALE, William & 1/wf Mary __?__ ; b 1685?, b 1686; Malden/Charlestown

THEROLD/?THOROLD, George & Ann PECOCK, 22 Nov 1700; Boston

THING, Jonathan (1621-) & Joanne [WADLEIGH], m/2 Bartholomew TIPPING; b 1654; Ipswich/Hampton, NH/Wells, ME/Exter, NH

THING, Jonathan (?1654-1694) & 1/wf Mary GILMAN (1658-1691); 26 Jul 1677; Exeter, NH

THING, Jonathan (?1654-1694) & 2/wf Martha (DENISON) WIGGINS, m/3 Matthew WHIPPLE 1697; - Jul 1693; Exeter, NH

THING, Samuel (1667-) & 1/wf Abigail GILMAN (1674-1728); 8 Jul 1696; Exeter, NH

THISSELL/THISTLE, Richard & Elizabeth [PATCH]/?Mary THORNDIKE (1654-); b 1672, 1664?; Beverly

THOMAS, Benjamin (1653-) & Anna [BELDING]; b 1689; Springfield/Brookfield

THOMAS, Benjamin & Mary LEAVITT (1679-1747); 12 Sep 1700; Hampton, NH

THOMAS, Daniel & Mary [FRARY]; 1654?; Natick

THOMAS, Daniel (-1694) & Rebecca THOMPSON, m/2 John PERKINS; 3 Feb 1669; New Haven

THOMAS, Daniel & Experience TILDEN; 26 Apr 1698; Marshfield

THOMAS, David (-1689) & Joanna _?_ (-1689+); b 1649; Salem/Middleboro

THOMAS, David & Abigail [WOOD]; b 1678; Middleboro

THOMAS, David & Joanna _?_; b 1681(2?); Boston

THOMAS, Edward & Elizabeth WINSLOW; 4 Oct 1689; Charlestown/Boston

THOMAS, Edward (1669-1726) & [Lucy/Mary? NELSON]; b 1694; Middleboro

THOMAS, Ephraim & Alice CHURCH; 18 Dec 1696; Little Compton, RI

THOMAS, Evan (-1661) & 1/wf Jane _?_ (-12 Jan 1658/9); ca 1630/2?; Boston

THOMAS, Evan (-1661) & Alice [KIRTLAND] (-1697), w Philip; ?aft 14 Oct 1659, bef 8 Nov 1659; Lynn

THOMAS, Francis & Rebecca [IYANS]; b 1665; Boston

THOMAS, George & Mary GRAVES; 28 Dec 1667; Salem

THOMAS, George (-1696+) & Rebecca [MAVERICK] (1660-1696+); b 1681(2?); Boston/Charlestown

THOMAS, George & [?Susanna SHREVE]; b 1694; Newport/Portsmouth, RI

THOMAS, Hugh (-1683, ae 76) & Clement _?_ (-1683); b 1630?, no issue; Roxbury

THOMAS, Israel (1670-1755) & Bethiah SHERMAN (1678-1728); 23 Feb 1698; Marshfield

THOMAS, James & Martha [GODDARD], m/2 Elias CRITCHET; b 1672, by 1670; Dover, NH/Hampton, NH

THOMAS, James (1663-) & Mary TILDEN (1668-); 3 Jan 1692/3; Duxbury/Marshfield

THOMAS, James & Mary [SMITH] (1670-), m/2 Samuel PAGE, ca 1696?; Durham, NH

THOMAS, Jeremiah (?1659, 1660-1736) & 1//wf Lydia HOWLAND (-1717); 25 Feb 1684; Middleboro

THOMAS, John (-1671) & Tabitha _?_ (-1690); b 1640; New Haven

THOMAS, John (-1691?) & Sarah PITNEY (-1682); 21 Dec 1648; Marshfield

THOMAS, John (-1672, 1673) & _?_

THOMAS, John & Lydia PARKER (1652-); 12 Jan 1671, 1671/2?; New Haven

THOMAS, John (1649-1699) & Sarah [BALSTON], m/2 John FOSTER; b 1675; Marshfield

THOMAS, John (-1709) & Mary [BLAKESLEY] (1659-); b 1678; New Haven/Woodbury, CT

THOMAS, John & _?_; b 1681; Jamestown, RI/N. Kingstown

THOMAS, John & Selah COFELL, Boston?; int 25 Mar 1684; Marblehead/?Marshfield

THOMAS, John (-1725?) & Elizabeth VIALL (1670-); 30 Mar 1687; Swansea/Warren, RI

THOMAS, John (1672-1712) & Mary [FORD]?/?WALTER; b 1698; New Haven

THOMAS, Josiph & Mary _?_; b 1674/5; Springfield/Hatfield/Lebanon, CT

THOMAS, Josiph & Abigail PRESTON; 21 Mar 1687/8; New Haven

THOMAS, Nathaniel (1606-1675) & ?Mary _?_; in Eng, b 1638; Marshfield

THOMAS, Nathaniel (1643-1718) & 1/wf Deborah JACOB (-1696); 19 Jan 1663, 1663/4, 11 Feb 1663/4; Marshfield

THOMAS, Nathaniel (1664-1738) & Mary APPLETON (-1727); 20 Jun 1694, 1694; Marshfield/Ipswich

THOMAS, Nathaniel & 2/wf Elizabeth (WILKES) (CONDY) DOLBERRY (-1713), w William, w Abraham; 3 Nov 1696; Marshfield/Hingham/Charlestown

THOMAS, Rice (-1684) & Elizabeth [BILLING], w John; b 6 Mar 1647?, b 1656, aft 1647?, by 1647; Kittery, ME

THOMAS, Richard & Mary MASON; 16 Jul 1695; Boston/Watertown

THOMAS, Roger & Mary _?_; b 1686; Kittery, ME

THOMAS, Rowland (-1698) & Sarah CHAPIN (1628-1684); 14 Apr 1647; Springfield

THOMAS, Samuel (1656-1720) & Mercy FORD (-1741); 27 May 168-, 1680; Marshfield

THOMAS, Samuel & [Elizabeth OSBORNE] (1665-); b 1692(3?); New Haven

THOMAS, Walter & Hannah [BUCKNAM]; b 1673; Boston (prob of John BUCKMAN, Jr., 1676)

THOMAS, William (1574-1651) & _?_ ; in Eng, b 1606; Marshfield
THOMAS, William & Susanna ROGERS, w Robert; 8 Mar 1665, 1665/6; Newbury
THOMAS, William & Mary [BARRETT]; Jun 1680; Cape Porpoise/Arundel, ME
THOMAS, William (-1697, ae 41) & 1/wf Elizabeth (_?_/WOODS) [?STRATTON], w Mark; b 1687; Newton
THOMAS, William & 1/wf Sarah PRAT (-1702, Middleboro); 30 Jul 1691; Taunton/Middleboro
THOMAS, William (-1697) & 2/wf Anna (_?_) LOVERING, w Thomas; 29 Aug 1695; Newton/Watertown
THOMAS, William (1672-) & Ann [PADISHALL]; b 1702, b 1701?; Boston
THOMAS, [?George] (-1728) & [Susanna SHREVE] (-1714+), dau Thomas; ca 1690?
THOMAS, _?_ & Rebecca/?Ruth (BASSETT) SPRAGUE (1633-), w John; aft 26 Mar 1676; Duxbury
TOMPSON, Alexander & Deliverance HAGGETT; 19 Sep 1662; Ipswich
THOMPSON, Alexander & Mary SNELL, wid; 3 Aug 1699; Ipswich
THOMPSON, Alexander (1670-1720) & Anna/Anne [CURTIS]; ca 1700?; Kittery, ME
THOMPSON, Ambrose (-1742) & Sarah [WELLS] (-1730); by 1679; Stratford, CT
TOMPSON, Anthony (-1648) & 1/wf _?_ ; ca 1636/9, in Eng; New Haven
TOMPSON, Anthony (-1648) & 2/wf Katherine _?_, m/2 Nicholas CAMP; prob 1644; New Haven
THOMPSON, Anthony & Abigail _?_ ; b 25 Feb 1678/9; Brookhaven, LI
THOMPSON, Bartholomew & _?_ ; b 1689(90?); Kittery, ME
THOMPSON, Benjamin (1642-1714, Roxbury) & Susanna [KIRTLAND] (1652-1693); b 1670; Boston/Roxbury
THOMPSON, Benjamin & Amy BRIDGES; 7 Feb 1695/6, m int; Boston
THOMSON, Benjamin (1642-1714) & 2/wf Prudence (_?_) LINCOLN PACEN/PAYSON, w William, w Samuel; 13 Dec 1698; Dedham/Roxbury
THOMPSON, Caleb & Mehitable SCOVILLE; Feb 1685
THOMPSON, David (-1628) & Amyes COLLE/Amyas? COLE, m/2 Samuel MAVERICK; 18 Jul 1613, St. Andrew, Plymouth, Eng; Weymouth
TOMPSON, David (1664-) & Mary _?_ ; b 1694; Ipswich
THOMPSON, Ebenezer (1648-1674) & Deborah DUDLEY (1647-), m/2 Thomas SCRANTON 1681; [16?] Jun 1671, - Jun 1671; Guilford, CT
THOMSON, Ebenezer (1677-1747) & Susanna (ROCKWOOD) [HINSDALE], w Samuel; b 1698(9?); Medfield
TOMPSON, Edmund & Martha?/Mara FISKE; b 1643, 9 Aug 1637?; Salem
TOMPSON, Edward & _?_ ; b 1688; Simsbury, CT
TOMPSON, Edward (1665-1705) & Sarah WEBSTER (1659-), dau John; b 1691, b 1697; Newbury/Marshfield
TOMPSON, George (-1674) & Sarah _?_ (?1639-), ?m/2 John EDMINSTER 1681; b 1659; Lynn/Reading
THOMPSON, Henry & Elizabeth (STEDMAN) UPHAM, w Nathaniel, m/3 John SHARPE; 27 Apr 1669; Cambridge/Boston
TOMSON, Henry & Mary KEEFE; 8 Aug 1693; Boston
TOMSON, Henry & Mary VOCORY/VICKERY; 11 Sep 1693; Boston
THOMPSON, Isaac (-1738) & Mary [HOLMES] (-1751); 1696, (b 1697); Westerly, RI/Stonington
THOMSON, Jacob (1662-1726) & Abigail WADSWORTH (1670-1744, in 75th y); 28 Dec 1693; Middleborough
THOMPSON, Jacob & Mary [HAYWARD]; b 1701?; Brockton
THOMPSON, James (?1595-1682) & 1/wf Elizabeth _?_ (-1643, 1642?); in Eng, b 1623; Charlestown/Woburn
THOMPSON, James (-1682) & 2/wf Susanna BLODGETT (-1661), w Thomas; 15 Feb 1643/4; Woburn
THOMPSON, James (1649-1693) & 1/wf Hannah WALKER (1648-1686); 27 Jan 1674, 27 Jun 1675; Woburn/Charlestown
THOMPSON, James (1649-1693), Woburn & 2/wf Abigail GARDNER, Charlestown, m/2 Edward JOHNSON; 13 Apr 1687; Woburn/Charlestown
THOMPSON, James (1667-) & Sarah TRACK; 22 Oct 1695; Woburn
THOMSON, James & Katharine BROCKUS; m int 27 Jan 1696/7; Boston
THOMPSON, James & Elizabeth FRYE; 3 Mar 1701, 1700/01; ?Kittery, ME/York, ME

THOMPSON, John (-1626, in Eng) & Alice [FREEMAN], m/2 Robert PARK 1644; in Eng, b 1619; Roxbury/Stonington

THOMPSON, John (-1639) & Margaret _?_; b 1636; Watertown

THOMPSON, John (-1678, 1678/9) & Mirabel/Mirable _?_ (-1690); b 1641; Stratford, CT

THOMPSON, John (1619-1685) (ae 40 in 1659?) & Sarah [?HAYWARD]; b 1642, ca 1642; Concord?/Mendon?

THOMPSON, John (-1656, 1657) & Elizabeth _?_, m/2 Daniel FINCH 1657; b 1644; Windsor, CT/Fairfield, CT

TOMSON, John (ca 1616-1696, Middleboro) & Mary COOKE (-1714, in 88th y); 26 Dec 1645; Plymouth/Barnstable/Middleboro

THOMPSON, John (-1655) & 1/wf Dorothy _?_, m/2 Thomas HARRISON 1656; b 1646; New Haven/East Haven

THOMPSON, John (-1674) & Ellen/Helena HARRISON (-1690); 25 Feb 1650, 1651?; New Haven/Milford?

THOMPSON, John & _?_ STRONG; ca 1655; Brookhaven, LI

THOMPSON, John & Anne VICARIS/VICKERS/VICKERY?; 4 Aug 1656; Boston/New Haven

THOMPSON, John & Ann (FITCH) [HART], w Stephen; ca 1658/65?, b 1696, aft 1689?; Farmington, CT

TOMSON, John & Sarah _?_; b 1666; Boston

THOMPSON, John (-1693) & Priscilla POWELL (-1726); 22 May 1666, 29? Mar; New Haven?/Branford, CT

THOMSON, John (1642-1715) & Thankful [WOODLAND] (1646-); b 1667, ca 1665; Mendon

THOMSON, John (ca 1649-1712, 1711) & Mary STEELE (1646-); 24 Oct 1670; Farmington, CT

THOMPSON, John & Sarah? _?_, m/2 John SLOPER/SOPER; b 1675; Kittery, ME

THOMPSON, John & Sarah [WOODMAN]? (1663-); ca 1678/80, 1678?; Durham, NH/Oyster River, NH

TOMSON, John (1648-1725) & Mary [TINKHAM] (1661-1731, in 67th y?); b 1681; Middleboro

THOMPSON, John (1657-1711) & Rebecca DANIEL (1657-); 9 May 1682; New Haven

THOMPSON, John & Sarah SMITH; 19 Sep 1682; Rehoboth

THOMPSON, John (-1694) & Margaret _?_, m/2 Joseph LEONARD 1695; b 1683?; Middletown, CT

THOMPSON, John (1651-1734) & Sarah GOLD (-1741, 1747?); 25 Apr 1684; Fairfield, CT

THOMPSON, John (-bef 6 Mar 1702/3) & Sarah [EMERY], m/2 Gilbert WARREN; b 1679, ca 1688; Kittery, ME

THOMPSON, John (-1684) & Hannah [REMICK] (1656-), m/2 Richard GOWELL

THOMSON, John (1667-1739) & Hannah [WIGHT] (1667-1759); b 1689; Mendon/Medfield b 1698

TOMSON, John (1661-1725) & Elizabeth _?_; b 1690; Reading/?Rehoboth

TOMSON, John & Elizabeth [BRUER]/BREWER (1672-); b 1691, b 1689; Salisbury

THOMSON, John & Ann (FITCH) HART, w Stephen, Jr.; by 1696

THOMPSON, John & Elizabeth PAUL; Apr 1696; Kittery, ME

THOMPSON, John (1667-1721) & Mercy [MANSFIELD] (1667-1743), m/2 Nathaniel BRADLEY; b 1696, b 1694, ca 1691; New Haven/E. Haven?

THOMSON, John & Margaret ORTON; 2 Nov 1699; Farmington, CT

THOMSON, John (1661-1725) & Elizabeth _?_; b 1701; Rehoboth

THOMPSON, Jonathan & Susanna BLODGETT (1637-1698); 28 Nov 1655; Woburn

THOMPSON, Jonathan & Frances [WHITMORE] (1671-); b 1689/90, b 1690(1?); Cambridge/Woburn

TOMPSON, Jonathan & Mary BOUTALL/BOUTELLE; 25 Mar 1700; Reading

THOMPSON, Joseph (1640-1732) & 1/wf Mary BRACKET (-1679); 22 Jul 1662, 2 Jul, 24 Jul; Billerica

TOMPSON, Joseph (1640-) & 2/wf Mary DENISON (-1743, ae 91); 17 Mar 1680/1; Billerica

THOMPSON, Joseph & 1/wf Elizabeth (LATHROP) [ROYCE] (1648-), w Isaac; b 11 Jun 1690, b 1683; ?Wallingford, CT

THOMPSON, Joseph & 2/wf Mercy (BARNES) JACOBS, w Bartholomew; 22 Nov 1694; Wallingford, CT

THOMPSON, Joseph (1664-1711) & Elizabeth SMITH (1675-1743); 2 Feb 1695, 1696/7?; New Haven

THOMPSON, Miles & Ann [TETHERLY]? (1635-1717); ca 1655/60; Kittery, ME

TOMSON, Peter & Hannah GREEN; 1 Mar 1692/3; Marblehead/Attleboro

TOMSON, Peter (-1731?) & Sarah __?__ (1670-24 Oct 1742, in 73rd y); b 1699; Plymouth
THOMPSON, Peter & Rebecca [STURTEVANT] (doubtful); b 1699 (no)
TOMPSON, Peter & [Abigail] __?__; b 1700; Dorchester
THOMPSON, Robert (-1695) & __?__ HOPKINS?; b 1639?; Boston (returned to Eng)
THOMPSON, Samuel (ca 1631, 1630-1695) & 1/wf Sarah SHEPPARD (1636-1680, 1679/80); 25 Apr 1656, 27 Apr; Braintree
TOMPSON, Samuel & Abigail __?__; b 1670; Boston
THOMPSON, Samuel (ca 1631-1695) & 2/wf Elizabeth BILLINGS (-1706, ae 69); 4 Oct 1680; Braintree
THOMPSON, Samuel (1662-) & Hannah PARMENTER (1659-); 25 Dec 1684; Braintree
THOMPSON, Samuel (1669-1749) & Rebecca BISHOP (1673-1734); 14 Nov 1695; New Haven
TOMPSON, Samuel & Hannah __?__; b 1699; Marshfield
THOMSON, Samuel (1676, 1668?-1739, 1749) & Hannah (BREWSTER) [MUNCEY], w John; ?b 1701, aft 1691; Farmington, CT
THOMPSON, Samuel (1677-) & Abigail [POTTER] (1680-), m/2 Thomas SMITH; b 1701?, b 1699?; New Haven
THOMPSON, Simon (1610?-) (ae ca 50 in 1660) & __?__ WOOD?/SHORT?; b 1637; Ipswich/Salisbury
THOMPSON, Simon (-1658) & Mary CONVERSE, m/2 John SHELDON 1659; 19 Dec 1643; Woburn
THOMPSON, Simon (-1676) & Rachel GLOVER; 21 Aug 1656; Newbury
THOMPSON, Simon/(Thomas wrong) (1673-) & Hannah/Anna? BUTTERFIELD; 12 Dec 1700; Woburn/Chelmsford
THOMPSON, Thomas (-1655) & Ann WELLES (1625?, 1619?-1680), m/2 Anthony HAWKINS/ HOWKINS 1655?, 1656?; 14 Apr 1646; Hartford/Farmington
THOMPSON, Thomas & __?__; b 1651; Stratford
THOMPSON, Thomas & Mary __?__; b 1670; Boston
THOMSON, Thomas & Hannah __?__; b 1677; Hartford
THOMPSON, Thomas (?1651-1705/6) & 1/wf Elizabeth [SMITH] (-aft 1691, aft 7 Dec 1692); b 1679; Farmington, CT
THOMPSON, Thomas & Mary __?__; b 1686; Braintree
THOMPSON, Thomas (-1705/6) & 2/wf Abigail [THORPE]; aft 7 Dec 1692, aft 1691, b 1701?; Farmington, CT
THOMPSON, Thomas (-1715) & Sarah [FURBISH]/FURBISK; ca 1698; Kittery, ME
THOMPSON, Thomas & Elizabeth [COWLES] (1680-); b 1701?; CT
THOMPSON, William (1597-1666) & 1/wf Abigail [COLLINS? (no)] (-1643, 1644); in Eng, b 1627, b 1626; Braintree
THOMPSON, William (1597-1666) & 2/wf Anna/Anne (BRIGHAM) [CROSBY] (-1675, ae 68), w Simon; b 1646, b 1647; Braintree
THOMPSON, William (-1664+) & Catharine TREAT (1637-), ?m/2 __?__ JOHNSON?; 19 Nov 1655; Boston/Wethersfield/New London
THOMPSON, William (-1676) & __?__ [WHITE?]; b 1658, nr 1656, nr 1676?; Dover, NH
THOMPSON, William/Wry (ae 28 in 1677?) & Mary GRAVE; 3 Oct 1673; Ipswich
THOMPSON, William & Ruth [AVERY]; b 1676; Stonington, CT
THOMPSON, William & Philadelphia TILESTONE; 19 Jul 1678; Lyme, CT
THOMPSON, William & Mary LOVERING; 4 Sep 1682; Dover, NH/Portsmouth, NH
THOMPSON, William (1660-) & Johanna/Joanne (DANIEL) GLOUER/GLOVER (1652-), w John; 28 Dec 1682; New Haven
THOMPSON, William (b Lyme?) & __?__; b 1685; Fairfield, CT
THOMPSON, William & Sarah __?__; b 1687; Boston
THOMPSON, William (1664-1705) & Bridget CHESEBROUGH (1669-1720), m/2 Joseph MINER 1709; 7 Dec 1692; Stonington
TOMPSON, William & Abigail (KILLAM) ALLEE/ALLEY, w Thomas; 25 Jun 1700; Rowley
THOMPSON, __?__ & Elizabeth MANSFIELD; b 1660/70?, b 20 Apr 1667; ?Salem
THORNE, Barnard & Martha [BROWN]; b Dec 1673; Ipswich
THORN, Israel & Sarah __?__; bef 5 Apr 1686; Salem
THORN, John (-1681/2) & Ann __?__, m/2 __?__ WILSON; b 1660?; Cambridge
THORNE, John (1643-1709, 1707) & Mary PASSILL/PARCELL; m lic 9 Mar 1664, 1664/5?; ?Flushing, LI/Chesterfield, NJ
THORNE, John[3] (-1737) & Catherine __?__ (-1766); ca 1690/2; Flusing, LI/Crosswicks, NJ

THORN, John & Martha/Mercy? **WOOD**; 28 Jul 169-, 1698?; Ipswich
THORNE, Joseph[2] ((?165-)-) & ?1/wf Anna **LAWRENSON**; m lic 1 Feb 1672; ?Flushing, LI
THORNE, Joseph[2] (-1727) & 2/wf Mary [**BOWNE**] (1660/1-); b 1680; Flushing, LI
THORN, Joseph (**THOME** wrong) (-1732) & Joanna **PINCEN** (-1722); 16 May 1695; Scituate/ Hingham
THORNE, Joseph[3] (-1753) & Martha Joanna **BOWNE** (1673-1750); 9 Nov 1695; Flushing, LI
THORNE, Peter & Susanna [**FIELD**]; aft Jun 1699; Newtown, LI
THORNE, Richard (-1707) & Phebe **DENTON** (-1706); m lic 29 Aug 1699; ?Hempsted, LI
THORNE, Samuel (?1657, 1654?-1732) & Susannah __?__; by 1683, b 1675?; Flushing, LI
THORN, Samuel & Abigail **BARBER** (1659-); 17 Dec 1691; Boston
THORN, Thomas & Joanna __?__ (1649-), m/2 __?__ **CARR**; New London/Newtown, LI
THORN, William (left wid Susannah, see below) & 1/wf __?__; ca 1632/38?; Lynn/Sandwich/Flushing, LI/Gravesend, LI/Jamaica, LI
THORN, William & ?Hannah __?__; b 1643, b 1645; Roxbury/Boston
THORNE, William, Jr. (-1688?) & Winifred **LEMINGTON**?/**LENNINGTON**?/**KAY**? (?1632-1713); ca 1660/5?; ?Flushing, LI
THORN, William[1] & ?1/wf ?2/wf Susannah __?__ (see above), m/2 William **HALLETT** 1669 or earlier, bef 25 Apr 1674, bef Jun 1669; Flushing, LI
THORN, William & Mary __?__; b 1672; Boston
THORNE, William (1628?-) & Lydia (**REDFIELD**) [**BAILEY**], w Thomas; 28 Jul 1676; New London, CT
THORNBURY, James & Lydia **CURTICE/CURTIS**; 14 Sep 1699; Boston
THORNDIKE, John & Elizabeth [**STRATTON**]; ca 1640; Salem/Beverly
THORNDIKE, John & Joanna (**LARKIN**) **DODG/DODGE** (1675/6-), w Joshua; 20 Apr 1696; Beverly
THORNDIKE, Paul & Mary **PATCH**; 28 Apr 1668; Beverly
THORNYCRAFT/THORNEYCRAFT, Thomas (-1667?) & [Jean] __?__; Pawtuxet, RI/Massapague Kills, Marpeth
THORNICRAFT, William (1645?-) & [Hannah] [**CARPENTER**] (1662-); ca 1682; Pawtuxet, RI/Glen Cove, LI
THORING/THORNING, Anthony & Sarah **COURSER** (1677-); 3 Nov 1693; Boston
THORNTON, James & Sarah __?__; ?b 1701; Providence
THORNTON, John (-1695+) & Sarah __?__ (-1692+); b 1667?, by 1648?; Newport/Providence
THORNTON, John (-bef 16 Nov 1639) & Joane __?__, m/2 Matthias **BUTTON**; Ipswich
THORNTON, John (-1716) & Dinah [**STEERE**]; ca 1680?; Providence
THORNTON, Peter (1615-1652) & Mary __?__; b 1647; Boston
THORNTON, Robert (1624-) & 1/wf __?__; b 1656, by 1648?; Boston
THORNTON, Robert & 2/wf Mary (**DOLING**) **MERRY**, w Walter; 13 Nov 1657; Boston
THORNTON, Solomon (-1713) & __?__; ca 1695/1700; Providence
THORNTON, Theophilus & Hannah __?__; b 1677; Boston
THORNTON, Thomas (1607, 1609?-1700) & Mary? __?__; in Eng, ca 1630?; Yarmouth/Boston
THORNTON, Thomas & __?__ [?**PACKS**]; b 1640; Dorchester/Windsor, CT/Stratford, CT
THORNTON, Thomas (-1703) (calls George **GRAVES** "brother") & Hannah **FARRAND**; 5 Aug 1674; Milford, CT
THORNTON, Thomas & __?__ **MORE**, wid; 10 Jun 1683; Yarmouth
THORNTON, Thomas (-1712) & Margaret __?__ (-1712); ca 1693(?); Providence
THORNTON, Timothy (1647-1726) & 1/wf Experience [**BROOKING**?] (-1694?); b 1674; Boston
THORNTON, Timothy (-1726), Boston & 2/wf Sarah **GREENOUGH** (-1725), Boston; 9 Aug 1694; Braintree
THORNTON, Walter (1599-) & Joanna __?__ (1591-); b 1635; came 1635
THORNTON, William & Anna/Ann **HARRIS/HANET**, m/2 George **HALLARD**; 17 Aug 1693; Charlestown/Boston
THORPE, Henry (-1672) & Anne [**BULLARD**], w Robert; by 25 Nov 1639; Watertown
THORP, James & Hannah **NEWCOMB** (1637-); 8 Jan 1657/8; Dedham
THORP, John (-1633) & Alice __?__, ?m/2 William **DAVIS**; b 1633; ?Plymouth/?Duxbury
THORP, John (1643-1720) & 1/wf Hannah [**FROST**]; b 1679; Fairfield, CT
THORP, John & Mary (**MEEKER**) (**ADAMS**) [**LYON**], w Samuel, w Moses; aft 2 Mar 1697/8, b 1701?; Fairfield, CT
THORP, John & Mary **DAVIS**; 15 May 1699; Fairfield, CT

THORPE, Nathaniel & 1/wf Mary FORD (-1684); 20 Nov 1662; New Haven
THORP, Nathaniel (1665-) & Elizabeth [LITTLE] (1666-1735); b 1688; New Haven
THORP, Nathaniel & 2/wf Sarah (BROOKS) ROBBINS, w Benjamin; 10 Dec 1691; New Haven
THORP, Peter & 1/wf Bethiah [EVERETT] (-1694); b 1692; Dedham
THORP, Peter & Abigail WHITE (1674-); 29 Oct 1695; Dedham/Charlestown
THORP, Samuel (?1646, 1644-1728) & Mary BENTON (1642-1718); 6 Dec 1666; New Haven/Wallingford, CT
THORP, Samuel & Elizabeth WHIT/WHITE; 15 Feb 1699/1700; Dedham
THORP, Thomas & Rebecca MILLERARD, wid; 27 May 1656; Boston/Woodbridge, NJ
THORP, William (-1679) & 1/wf ?Elizabeth (no) __?__ (?1615-1660?); b 1640; New Haven
THORPE, William (-1679) & 2/wf Margaret PIGG, w Robert; 8 Oct 1661, 1662?; New Haven
THARPE, Zebulon (-1717) & Hannah [DILLINGHAM] (-1721); b 1687(8?), before; Yarmouth
THOYGHT, Jonathan & Hannah __?__ ; b 1691; Lynn
THRALL, John (1671-1732) & Mindwell MOSES (1676-); 6 Jan 1697; Windsor, CT
THRALL, Thomas (1676-) & Elizabeth HOSKINS (1682-); 2 Nov 1699; Windsor, CT
THRALL, Timothy (1641-1697) & Deborah GUNN (1641/2-1694/5); 10 Nov 1659, 5? Nov; Windsor, CT
THRALL, Timothy (1662-1724) & Sarah ALLYN; ?31 Dec 1699, ?21 Dec 1699; Windsor, CT
THRALL, William (1606-1679) & __?__ [GOODE]? (-1676); b 1639; Windsor, CT
THRESHER, Arthur & Mary GOODRIDG/GUTTERAGE? (1665-); 21 Apr 1684; Newbury
THRASHER, Christopher (-1679) & [?Katharine] __?__ ; b 1648; Taunton
THRESHER, Francis & Elizabeth HICKS/[HIGGS], w John; 9 Aug 1694; Boston/Watertown
THRESHER, [?Henry] & Deborah [SOUTHWICK] (1656-); ?Boston/Salem/Casco Bay
THRASHER, Israel (1648-) & Mary CASWELL (1654-); 15 Aug 1676; Taunton
THRASHER, John (1653-1733) & Mercy CROSMAN/CROSSMAN (1670-); 26 Jan 1687; Taunton
THRESHER, Samuel, Taunton & Bethia BROOKS (1662-), Rehoboth; 4 Dec 1683, 5 Dec 1683; Rehoboth/Taunton
THREENEDLE/THREEDNEDLE/THREENEEDLE, Bartholomew (-1702) & Damaris [HAWKINS], dau James; b 1660; Boston (John KNEELANDS calls him brother-in-law)
THROCKMORTON, John (1601-1687, 1684) & Rebecca [COVILL?]/COLVILLE; b 1630, b 1635; Salem/Providence
THROCKMORTON, John (-1690) & Alice STOUT (-1690+); 12 Dec 1670, NJ?; Providence/Middletown, NJ
THROW, David (-1710) & Priscilla (CORISH) HUNTER (-1725), w William; 7 Feb 1678, 7 Feb 1677; Springfield
THURBER, Edward & Margaret __?__ ; b 1699; Swansea
THURBER, James (1660-1736) & Elizabeth BLISS (1657-); 25 Jun 168-, 1684?; Rehoboth
THURBER, John (-1706) & Priscilla __?__ ; by 1650?; Rehoboth/Swansea
THURBER, John (1649-1717) & Mary __?__ (-1718, in 74th y); b 1674; Swansea/Warren, RI
THURBER, Thomas & Ruth BUZIGUT; 23 Feb 1677; Swansea
THURBER, Thomas & Ann __?__ ; b 1700(01?); Swansea
THURBER, __?__ & Mercy [STAFFORD] (1668-)
THARLAY/THORLEY/THURLOW, Francis (-1703) & Anne MORSE; 5 Feb 1654; Newbury
THURLOE, George & Mary ADAMS (1672-); 26 Nov 1694; Newbury
THARLAY, John & Sarah HOW; 2 Mar 1684/5; Newbury
THARLAY, Jonathan & Mary MERRILL (1667-); 22 Dec 1685; Newbury
THORLA, Richard (-1685) & Jane __?__ (-1684); b 1630; Rowley
THARLAY, Thomas & Judith MARCH; 13 Apr 1670; Newbury
TURLOW, William & Jane [TYER?]/[DYER?]; b 1687; Boston
THURSTON, Benjamin (-1678) & Elishua WALKER; 12 Dec 1660; Boston/Stratford, CT
THURSTON, Benjamin & Sarah __?__ ; by 1693?, b 1701?; Jamaica, LI
THURSTON, Daniel (-1666) & 1/wf __?__ (-25 May 1648); Newbury
THURSTON, Daniel (-1666) & 2/wf Anne LIGHTFOOT, w Francis?; 29 Aug 1648, no issue; Newbury
THIRSTON, Daniel (-1693) & Anna/Ann/Anne PELL; 20 Oct 1655; Newbury
THURSTON, Daniel (1646-) & 1/wf Mary STEDMAN (-1680); 1 Apr 1674; Cambridge/Medfield
THURSTON, Daniel & 2/wf Hannah MILLER, prob m/2 Silas TITUS; 6 Dec 1681, 16 Dec; Rehoboth
THURSTON, Daniel (1661-1712) & Mary [EASTON] (1668-); b 1687?, b 1689; Newport

THURSTON, Daniel (1661-) & Mary [DRESSER]; b 1690; Newbury
THURSTUN, Daniel & Experience WARREN; 28 Dec 1699; Medfield/Uxbridge
THURSTON, Daniel & _?_; b 1700; Hempstead, LI
THURSTON, Edward (1617-1707) & Elizabeth MOTT (1629-1694); - Jun 1647; Newport
THURSTON, Edward (1652-1690) & Susanna JEFFERAY (-1738, ae 82), m/2 John RHODES; b
    1678; Newport, RI
THURSTON, Edward & Elizabeth GARDNER; 16 Jan 1699; ?Newport
THIRSTON, James & Mary PEARSON; 24 Jan 1693/4; Rowley/Newbury
THURSTON, John¹ (1601, ?1607-1685) & Margaret _?_ (1605-1662); in Eng, b 1633, ?Wrentham;
    Dedham/Medfield
THURSTON, John² (1635-1712) & Mary WOODE (1642-1726?); 4 Oct 1660, 8 Aug; Medfield
THURSTUN, John (1656-), Kittery, ME, & Hannah CARY, Kittery, ME; 15 Aug 1688, York Co.,
    ME; Medfield/Rehoboth
THURSTON, John (1664-1690) & Elizabeth _?_ (-1690, ae 21); b 1690; Newport
THURSTON, Jonathan (1650-1740) & Sarah _?_; b 1679; Newport/Little Compton, RI/Dartmouth
THURSTON, Joseph (1640, 1636?-1691) & Anne _?_ (-1721); ca 1662/5?; Dedham/Jamaica, LI
THURSTON, Joseph & 1/wf Mehitable KIMBALL; m int 21 Nov 1695; Newbury
THURSTON, Richard & Martha/Mary [STANLEY?]; b 1652; Boston
THURSTON, Samuel (1669-1747) & Abigail [CLARKE] (1674-1731); b 1696; Newport
THURSTON, Thomas (1633-1704) & Sarah THAXTER (-1678), Hingham; 13 Dec 1655, 10 Nov;
    Medfield
THURSTON, Thomas & 1/wf Mehitable MASON (-1692); 23 Jul 1685; Medfield/Wrentham
THURSTON, Thomas (-1704) & 2/wf Esther CLARK (-1713); 15 Jun 1693; ?Sherborn/Wrentham/
    Medfield
THURSTON, Thomas (1671-1730), Freetown & Mehitable TRIPP (-1730+), dau Peleg; 23 Jul
    1695?; Newport?
THURSTON, _?_ (had David) & _?_ FAIRBANKS
THURSTON, _?_ & _?_ GAUNT; b 1691
THWAITS, Alexander (1615-) & Anne _?_; ca 1640?; Concord/Casco Bay, ME
THWAITES, Jonathan (1665-) & Hannah _?_; b 1691; ?Lynn
THWING, Benjamin (1619-1673) & Deborah _?_; b 1642; Boston
THWING, Benjamin (1647-1681/2) & Abigail [?DICKAM]/DIXON (1648-bef 31 Aug 1632); b
    1670; Boston/Cambridge
THWING, Edward (1652-1707) & Elizabeth [LAWSON] (1645-); b 1675; Boston
THWING, John (1644-1690) & Mary/Maria [MESSENGER] (?1647-1705, 1706) (dau Henry &
    Sarah); ?6 Jan 1669; Boston
THWING, John & Martha [DREW] (1671-) (bpt 7 May 1620, Boston); 14 Aug 1692; Boston
THWING, William (1656-1707) & Mary [BARRETT] (1663-); b 1686; Boston
TWING/THWING, William (1675-1705) & Ruth CHAPIN (1672-); 26 Jan 1698; Boston
TIBBALS/TIBBALLS, John (1645-) & Margaret (TOMLINSON) HARGER (-1698), w Jabez; aft
    1678; Derby, CT
TIBBALS, John & Hannah (ROSE) (STILES) HARGER, w Isaac, w Samuel; 28 Mar 1700; Derby,
    CT
TIBBALS, Josiah & Mary SHERWOOD; 13 Jul 1670; Milford, CT
TIBBALS, Thomas (1615-1703) & 1/wf [Mary] _?_ (-1644); b 1643; Milford, CT
TIBBALS, Thomas (1615-1703) & 2/wf _?_; aft Jun 1644; Milford, CT
TIBBALS, Thomas (1651-1703) & Abigail STREAME (1655-); 12 Dec 1672; Milford, CT
TIBBETTS, Benjamin (-1713) & Elizabeth _?_
TIBBETS, Ephraim (?1596-1678, 1676) & 1/wf Elizabeth _?_ (?1596-); nr 1631; Dover
TIBBETS, Ephraim & Rose [AUSTIN] (1678-1755); ca 1693; Dover
TIPPETT, George & Mehitable [BETTS], m/2 Louis VITREY/VITTERY, m/3 Samuel HITCH-
    COCK; ca 1660/1?; ?Eastchester, NY
TIPPET, George & Joane _?_; b 1697; Fadham, NY
TIBBETS, Henry (-1678, 1676) & 2/wf? (no) Mary [?AUSTIN]
TIBBETS, Henry (-1713) & [Sarah STANTON] (?1640-1708+); Dec 1661; Kings Town, RI/N.
    Kingstown, RI
TIBBITTS, Henry (-1702) & Rebecca _?_ (-1752); ca 1688/90?; Kingston, RI
TIBBETTS, Henry & Joyce OTIS, w Nicholas; 25 Feb 1699/1700; Dover, NH

TIBBETS, Jeremy (1631-1677) & Mary [CANNEY] (now KENNEY), m/2 John LOOMS/LOOME; b 1656, ca 1654-5; Dover, NH
TIBBETS, Jeremy/Jeremiah (1656-1743) & Mary [TWOMBLEY] (1663-); by 1686, b 28 Feb 1684, ca 1678; Dover
TIBBETTS, Joseph (1663-1748, 1745, 1746) & 1/wf Elizabeth _?_ (1672-1707); b 1697; Dover, NH
TIBBETS, Nathaniel & Elizabeth _?_ (-1717+), m/2 Francis PITTMAN; by 1700; Dover, NH
TIBBETS, Samuel (1666-1738) & 1/wf Dorothy TUTTLE; 2 Sep 1686; Dover, NH
TIBBETTS, Thomas (1660-1748+) & 1/wf Judith DAM (1666-1728); 6 Jul 1684; Dover, NH
TYBBET, Walter (1584-1651) & Mary _?_, m/2 John HARDING 1652; in Eng, b 1622; Gloucester
TICE, William & Mary _?_ ; b 1667; Boston
TICHENOR/TICHENER, Martin & Mary CHARLES; 16 May 1651; New Haven/Newark, NJ
TICKNOR, William & Hannah STOCKBRIDGE (-1665); 29 Oct 1656; Boston
TICKNOR, William & Deborah [HYLAND] (-1693); 1666(?); Scituate
TICKNER, William, Jr. & Lydia TILDEN (1666-); 2 Nov 1696; Scituate/Lebanon, CT
TIDD, Daniel & Lydia CARTER/CARLEY/KERLEY (1672-1727); 21 Dec 1694; Cambridge/Woburn
TIDD, John[1] (-1656) & 1/wf Margaret [GREENLEAF?] (-1651); in Eng, b 1621?; Charlestown/Woburn
TIDD, John (1625-1703) & Rebecca WOOD (ca 1625-1717); 14 Apr 1650; Woburn/Lexington
TIDD, John[1] (-1657) & 2/wf Alice [TEEL], m/2 William MANN 1657; b 1656; Charlestown
TIDD, John (1655-1743) & Elizabeth FIFIELD (1657-1732); 12 Jun 1678; Charlestown/Woburn
TEED, John (-1687) & ?Mary JENNINGS?; Huntington, LI
TIDD, Joseph (1662-1730) & 1/wf Mary _?_ (-1694/5, ae 23); b 1694?; Lexington
TIDD, Joshua (1607-1678) & 1/wf Sarah _?_ (-1677); b 1639; Charlestown
TIDD, Joshua (1607-1678) & 2/wf Rhoda (_?_) (GORE) (REMINGTON) [PORTER] (-1693, ae 86), w John, w John, w Edward; aft 15 Oct 1677; Charlestown
TID, Samuel (-1642) & Sarah _?_ (-1658), m/2 John SOUTHWICK aft May 1642; b 1642; Salem
TIDMARSH, Richard & Mary FELMINGAME/FELMINGHAM/FILMINGHAM; 20 Jun 1659; Salem
TIFFANY, Consider (1675-1708) & Abigail NILES; 27 May 1696; New Shoreham, RI
TIFFINY, Ebenezer (?1663-1747) & Elizabeth _?_ (1665-1749); b 1695(6?); Swansea/Barrington, RI
TIFFANY, Ephraim (1677-1727) & Bethia _?_ ; b 1701; New Shoreham, RI
TIFFENY, Humphrey (?1630-1685) & Elizabeth _?_ (1645-1708+), m/2 Simon RAY 1685+; ca 1662?; Rehoboth/Milton/Swansea
TIFFINY, James (?1666-1732) & 1/wf Bethia _?_ (-1711); b 1689; Swansea/Attleboro
TIFFINY, Thomas (1668-) & Hannah _?_ (-1734); b 1690; Swansea/Bristol, RI
TILDEN, Joseph (1615-1670) & Elizabeth/Ellice/Alice TWISDEN (bpt 1633-1694+); 20 Nov 1649; Scituate
TILDEN, Nathaniel (1583-1641) & Lydia [HUCKSTEP] (1588-), m/2 Timothy HATHERBY; in Eng, b 1608; Duxbury
TILDEN, Nathaniel (1650-1731) & 1/wf Mary SHARPE (1652-19 Feb 1689; 5 Nov 1673; Scituate
TILDEN, Nathaniel (1650-1731) & 2/wf Margaret DODSON (1656-), Hingham; 3 Jan 1693/4 (1673/4 wrong); Scituate
TILDEN, Nathaniel, Jr. (1678-) & Ruth TILDEN (1676-), m/2 Ebenezer PIERCE 1752; 18 Dec 1700; Scituate
TILDEN, Samuel (1660-1739), Scituate/Marshfield & Sarah CURTICE; 25 Jul 1694; Scituate
TILDEN, Stephen (1629-1711) & Hannah LITTELL/LITTLE (-1710); 25 Jan 1661, 15 Jan 1660/1, 1661/2; Scituate/Marshfield
TILDEN, Stephen (?1664-1732) & Abigail [CLAPP]? (?1659, 29 Jan 1659/60, Scituate-1736), dau Thomas; b 1686; Marshfield
TILDEN, Stephen (1659, 1663-1729) & Mary _?_ (-1727+); ca 1688/9; Scituate/Lebanon, CT
TILDEN, Thomas (?ret'd to Eng) & Ann _?_ ; in Eng, b 1623; Plymouth
TILDEN, Thomas (1619, ?1616-1705) (ae ca 50 in 1671) & Elizabeth (BOURNE) WATERMAN (-1663), w Robert; b 1654; Marshfield
TILDEN, Thomas (1619-1705) & Mary HOLMES; 24 Jan 1664, 1664/5; Marshfield
TILDEN, Thomas (ca 1670-1719) & Hannah MENDALL (1670-); 20 Dec 1692; Marshfield
TILESTON, Onesiphorus (1651-1699) & Sarah _?_ (admin. his estate 1699); b 1690; Dorchester

TILESTONE, Thomas (?1611-1694, ae 83) & Elizabeth _?_ (2/wf Sarah in his will of 1694); b 1633; Dorchester

TILESTON, Thomas (1675-) & Mary GARDNER; 30 May 1700; Roxbury

TILESTON, Timothy (1636-1697) & Sarah BRIDGMAN (1643-1712); 28 Apr 1659, ?3 May?; Dorchester

TYLSTONE, Timothy (1664-1736/7), Dorchester & Hannah [STETSON]; 5 Jan 1697; Scituate

TILL, Peter (-1697) & Elizabeth NICK; 26 Feb 1651/2; Boston

TILLETT/TILLET, James & Sarah [LAWRENCE]; LI?

TILESON/TILLETSON, James (1652-1694) & Elizabeth _?_ ; 20 Apr 1692; Lyme, CT

TILETSON, John (-1670) & 1/wf Dorcas COLEMAN (-1654/5); 4 Jul 1648, 14? Jul; Newbury

TILLOTSON, John (-1670) & 2/wf Jane EVANS, m/2 John ROBBINS 1670 Branford; 24 May 1655; Newbury/Lyme, CT

TILLOTSON, John (1651-1719) & Mary MORRIS; 25 Nov 1680; Saybrook, CT

TILLOTSON, Jonathan (1659-1709, Lyme) & Mary JONES; 10 Jan 1683; Saybrook, CT/Lyme, CT

TILLEY, Edward (-1621) & Ann _?_ (-1621); Plymouth

TILLY?/TILLEAR, Hugh & Rose _?_ , m/2 Thomas HIGGINS/HUSKINS?/HUCKINS? 1648; b 1643?; Yarmouth

LETELIER, Jan & Christina [PETERS]; 1665

TILLEY, John (-1621) & Elizabeth COMYNGS (-1621); 2 Feb 1605, St. Andrew, Undershaft, London; Plymouth

TILLEY, John & _?_ ; Salem

TILLEY, John & _?_ ; by 1630?; Dorchester

TILLEY, John (-1636) & Edith _?_ , m/2 Nicholas CAMP 1640; b 1636; Windsor, CT

TILLEY, John & _?_ BLOWER, Boston; m int 6 Jul 1640; Plymouth

TILLEY, Samuel & Ann GILLETT; 29 Oct 1663; Deerfield

TILLEAR, Samuel & Mary SIMPKINS; m lic 26 Sep 1678; Oyster Bay, LI

TILLEY, Thomas & Hannah _?_ ; b 1657; Boston

TILLEY, William & Alice _?_ (1603-); Boston/Dorchester

TILLEY, William & Abigail MELLEN?/WOODMANCY?, m/2 Samuel SEWELL; b 1701?; Boston

TILLEAR/TILLIAR/?TILLEY, Samuel & Mary SIMKINS; 26 Sep 1678; Oyster Bay, LI

TILLINGHAST, Benjamin (1672-1726) & Sarah [RHODES] (-1743); ca 1698; Providence

TILLINGHAST, John (1657-1690) & Isabel [SAYLES] (1658-), m/2 Robert HICKS 1690+; ca 1678; Providence/Newport

TILLINGHAST, Joseph (1677-1763) & 1/wf Freelove [STAFFORD]; ca 1700/1703; Providence/Newport

TILLINGHAST, Pardon[1] (1622-1718) & 1/wf [Sarah BUTTERWORTH] (1623-1660?); ca 1653; Providence

TILLINGHAST, Pardon[1] (1622-1718) & 2/wf Lydia TABER, m/2 Samuel MASON; 16 Apr 1664; Providence

TILLINGHAST, Pardon (1668-1713), Providence, E. Greenwich, & 1/wf Mary [KEECH] (-1726); ca 1688/93; E. Greenwich, CT

TILLINGHAST, Philip (1669-1732) & Martha HOLMES (1675-1729); 3 May 1692; Providence

TILSON, Edmund/Edward? (-1660, 1661?) & Joane/Jane _?_ , m/2 Giles RICKARD 1662; ca 1628/30?; Plymouth/Scituate

TILSON, Edmund & 1/wf Elizabeth WATERMAN (1668-); 28 Jan 1691, 1691/2; Plymouth

TILSON, Ephraim (?1636-1715, 1716, Plympton) & Elizabeth HOSKINS (?1646-); 7 Jul 1666; Plymouth

TILTON, Abraham (?1639, 1642?-1728) & 1/wf Mary CRAM; 25 Jan 1665/6; Hampton, NH

TILTON, Abraham (ca 1639, 1642?-1728) & 2/wf Deliverance [LITTLEFIELD] (1655-1733); ca 1676; Ipswich

TILTON, Abraham (ca 1666-1756) & Mary JACOBS; 11 Dec 1693; Ipswich

TILTON, Daniel (-1715) & Mehitable SANBORN; 23 Dec 1669; Hampton, NH

TILTON, John (-1688, Gravesend, LI) & Mary _?_ (-1683); b 1640; Lynn/Flushing, LI/Oyster Bay, LI/NJ

TILTON, John (1640-1704?) & 1/wf Mary COATS; 10 Oct 1670; Oyster Bay, LI

TILTON, John (1640-1704) & 2/wf Rebecca TERRY; 12 May 1674; Flushing, LI

TILTON, John (1670-) & Sarah MAYHEW; ca 1699; Martha's Vineyard

TILTON, Joseph (1677-1744) & 1/wf Margaret SHERBURNE (-1717); 26 Dec 1698, 6? Dec; Hampton, NH

TILTON, Peter (-1696) & 1/wf Elizabeth _?_ ; 10 May 1641; Windsor, CT
TILTON, Peter (1643-1700) & Rebecca BRAZIER; 22 Apr 1663; Gravesend, LI
TILTON, Peter (-1696) & 2/wf Mary _?_ (-1689); Hadley
TILTON, Peter (-1696) & 3/wf Sarah (HEATH/HEALD) (LEONARD) PARSONS (-1711), w John,
    w Benjamin; 3 Nov 1690; Hadley
TILTON, Samuel (-1731, Chilmark) & Hannah MOULTON (-1720, Chilmark); 17 Dec 1662;
    Hampton, NH
TILTON, William (-1653) & 1/wf _?_ ; ca 1618?; Lynn
TILTON, William (-1653) & 2/wf Susanna _?_ (-1655), m/2 Roger SHAW 1655; Hampton, NH
TILTON, William (1668-1750) & Abiah [MAYHEW] (1673?-1739); Mar 1696; Martha's Vineyard
TIMBERLAKE, Henry₂ & Mary _?_ ; b 1653; Newport
TIMBERLAKE, Henry² (-1687) & Sarah _?_ (-1687+); Newport
TIMBERLAKE, John (-bef 1706) & _?_
TIMBERLAKE, Joseph & Mary (EARLE) COREY? (-1718, w William; b 1682, 1683±; Portsmouth,
    RI/Little Compton, RI
TIMBERLAKE, William (-1678) & Mary _?_ ; b 1673; Newport/Boston
TINGLEY, ?Palmer (1614-) & Anna [FOSDICK] (-1681), m/2 James BARRETT b 1642; Ipswich?
TINGLE/DINGLES, Samuel (-1666) & Elizabeth CALL (1641-), m/2 Daniel SHEPARDSON 1668,
    1667; 20 Sep 1663; Charlestown/Malden
TINGLEY, Samuel (1666-1714) & Martha _?_ ; b 1688?; Rehoboth
TINGLEY, Thomas (1667-1724) & Hester/Esther STEVENS (1671-); 14 Aug 1694; Rehoboth/At-
    tleboro
TINKER, Amos (1657-1730) & Sarah DURANT/DUREN; 1 Jun 1682; Lyme, CT
TINKER, John (-1662) & 1/wf Sarah (WILSHIRE) [BARNES] (-1648), div wf of William
    BARNES; betw 6 Jun 1646 & 22 Jul 1648, aft 6 Apr ?; Boston/Lancaster
TINKER, John (-1662) & 2/wf Alice [SMITH], m/2 William MESURE [1664]; ca 1649;
    Boston/Lancaster
TINKER, Samuel (1659-1733) & Abigail [DURANT]; Lyme, CT
TINKER, Thomas (-1620/1) & _?_ (-1620/1); Plymouth
TINKHAM, Ebenezer (1651-1718) & Elizabeth [BURROWES]/LISCOM? (-1718); b 1676;
    Middleboro
TINKHAM, Ephraim¹ (-1685?, 1684?) & Mary BROWN (-1685); ?27 Oct 1647; ?Plymouth
TINKHAM, Ephraim (1649-1714) & Esther/?Hester [WRIGHT] (ca 1649-1713); b 1678;
    Middleboro
TINCOM, Helkiah (1656-bef 1716) & Ruth _?_ ; b 1685; Plymouth
TINCOM, Isaac (1666-1732) & Sarah KING (1670-1732+); 17 Nov 1692, no issue; Plymouth
TINKHAM, John (1663) & Hannah _?_ (-4 Oct 1694?); ?Dartmouth
TINKHAM, Peter (1653-1709) & Mercy [MENDALL] (1666-); [b 1696]; Middleboro
TIRRELL/TERRILL, Daniel (1660-) & 1/wf Mary [FITCH] (1668±-1712); Milford, CT
TERRILL, Gideon (1664-1730) & Hannah [SHAW] (1668-); b 1689; Weymouth
TERRILL, John (-1712) & Sarah [WILLEY] (1644-1712); b 1671; New London, CT
TERRILL, John (?1644-1723?) & Abigail _?_ ; b 1676; Milford, CT/Wallingford, CT
TERRILL, Roger (-1682) & [Abigail UFFORD]; b 3 Nov 1644; Stratford, CT/New
    Haven/Milford, CT
TERRILL, Roger (1650-1722) & Sarah [RISDEN?]/[SCOTT?] (?1662-1728); b 1681; Woodbury,
    CT
TERRILL, Samuel (1647-) & Abigail _?_ ; Brookhaven, LI
TERALL, Thomas (-1698+) & Mary REEVE (-bef 1698); 5 Sep 1665; Southold, LI
TERRILL, Thomas & Abigail [REEVE]; b 23 Aug 1686; Southold, LI
TERRILL, Thomas (1656-1725) & 1/wf Margaret [DAYTON] (-1684); Milford, CT/Easthampton,
    LI/Rahway, NJ
TERRILL, Thomas (1656-1725) & 2/wf Mary _?_
TERRILL, Thomas, Jr. (-1746) & 2/wf? Sarah _?_ (-1706); ca 1693, 2 ch in 1698; Southold, LI
TERRILL, William & Rebecca SIMPKINS; 29 Jan 1654/5; Boston
TERRILL, William & Abigail [PRATT] (1662-); b 1683; Weymouth/Abington
TISDELL, James (ca 1644-1715, ae 71) & Mary AVERY (1645-1713?); 5 Nov 1666;
    Dedham/Middleboro
TISDALE, James (?1670-1727) & Abigail [COLEMAN] (?1676, 1677-1726, in 45th y), Nantucket;
    b 1701?; ?Nantucket/Lebanon, CT

TISDALL, John (?1620-1675) (called "cosen" by John **BROWN**) & Sarah [**WALKER**] (?1618-1676); b 1644; Taunton

TISDALL, John (-1677) & Hannah/Anna **ROGERS**, Duxbury, m/2 Thomas **TERRY** ca 1678, m/3 Samuel **WILLIAMS**; 23 Nov 1664; Taunton

TISDALE, John (1669-1728) & 1/wf Deborah [**DEANE**] (-1703/4); b 1701?; Taunton

TISDALE, Joseph (1656-1722) & Mary **LEONARD** (1663-1726); - Aug 1681, 2 Aug?; Taunton

TISDALE, Joshua (-1728) & Abigail **ANDREWS** (-1741); 5 Jul 1688; Taunton/Freetown

TITCHBORN/TITCHBORNE, John & Sarah **ALLIN**; 12 Aug 1699; Boston

TITCOMB, Benaiah & Sarah **BROWN**; 24 Dec 1678; Newbury

TITCOMB, Penuel (1650-1718) & Lydia **POORE**; 8 Jan 1683, 1683/4?; Newbury

TITCOMB, Thomas & Mary **DAM**; - Nov 1693, 30 Nov?; Newbury

TITCOMB, William[1] (-1676) & 1/wf Joanna [**BARTLETT**] (1611-1653); b 1640(1?); Newbury

TITCOMB, William[1] (-1676) & 2/wf Elizabeth (**BITFIELD**) **STEVENS**, w William; 3 Mar 1653/4; Newbury

TITCOMB, William & Anne **COTTLE**; 15 May 1683; Newbury

TITE, Henry & Sarah **WALTON**; 11 Feb 1656/7; Boston

TITE, Henry & Ann **GILARD**; 20 Feb 1700, [1700/1701]; Boston

TITERTON/TITTERTON, Daniel & Jane? __?__; b 1639; Stratford, CT

TITHARTON, Daniel (-1709) & __?__; b 1673; Stratford, CT

TITHARTON, Samuel (-1711) & Hannah **HURD** (1667-); 14 Jul 1693; Stratford, CT

TITHARTON, Timothy (1651-1740) & Patience **WAKELEY/WAKELEE**?; 3 Oct 1692; Stratford, CT

TITUS, Abiel (1641, 1640-1736?) & ?Rebecca [?**SCUDDER**]; b 1674; Huntington, LI

TITUS, Content (1643-1730) & [Elizabeth **MOORE**]; Huntington, LI/Newtown, LI

TITUS, Edmund/Edward (1630-1715) & Martha [**WASHBURNE**] (1637, 1639-1727, ae 84?, ae 90?); b 1658; Westbury, LI/Hempstead, LI

TITUS, John (1627-1689) & 1/wf ?Rachel __?__; b 1650; Rehoboth

TITUS, John (1627-1689) & ?2/wf Abigail [**CARPENTER**] (?1643-1710), m/2 Jonah **PALMER** 1692; b 1661, 1659?; Rehoboth/Attleboro

TITUS, John (1650-1697) & 1/wf Lydia **REDWAY** (1653-1676); 17 July 1673; Rehoboth

TITUS, John (1650-1697) & 2/wf Sarah **MILLER** (-1752); 3 Jul 1677, 1678?; Rehoboth

TITUS, John (1672-) & 1/wf Sarah **WILLIS** (1671-); 9 Oct 1695; Westbury, LI

TITUS, John (?1678-) & Hannah __?__ (-1709); b 1701; Rehoboth

TITUS, Joseph (1666-) & Martha **PALMER** (1666-); 19 Jan 1687/8; Rehoboth

TITUS, Peter (1674-1753) & Martha [**JACKSON**] (-1753); b 1701?; Hempstead, LI

TITUS, Robert (1600-) & Hannah __?__ (1604-1679); in Eng, b 1627; Weymouth/Rehoboth/Huntington, LI

TITUS, Samuel (1635-) & Elizabeth [**ROGERS**]?; b 1669; Huntington, LI

TITUS, Samuel (1658-1732) & 1/wf Elizabeth **POWELL** (-1704); 6 Nov 1691; Bethpage, LI/Westbury, LI

TITUS, Samuel (1661-) & Elizabeth **JOHNSON** (-1726); 21 Nov 1693, 27 Nov; Rehoboth/Attleboro

TITUS, Silas & 1/wf Sarah **BATTELLE** (-1689); 23 Oct 1679; Dedham

TITUS, Silas & 2/wf Hannah (**MILLER**?) **THURSTON**, w Daniel; 4 Jul 1689; Rehoboth

TITUS, __?__ & __?__ **WANDELL**; Maspeth Kills, LI

TOBIE, Ephraim (-1693) & Hannah [**SWIFT**] (1651(2?)-1714, 1713?); b 1689?, b 1691(2?); Sandwich

TOBEY, Gershom & 1/wf Mehitable **FISH** (1680-1720); 29 Apr 1697; Sandwich

TOBEY, James (-1705) & 1/wf Katherine __?__; by 1668; Kittery, ME

TOBEY, James (-1705) & 2/wf Ann [**HANSCOMB**] (-1719+), w Thomas; Kittery, ME

TOBEY, John (?1660-1738) & Jane __?__; b 1684(5?); Sandwich

TOBEY, John & __?__; b 1700; Kittery, ME

TOBEY, Jonathan (-1741) & Remember/?Remembrance __?__ (1674-1732); b 1694; Sandwich

TOBIE/TOBY, Nathan (1656/7?-) & 1/wf Mary [**SARGENT**] (1667-); b 1686(7?); Sandwich

TOBEY, Nathan & 2/wf Sarah [**FALLOWELL**]; ca 1696?; Sandwich

TOBEY, Richard & Grace [**DIAMOND**], m/2 Richard **TUCKER**; b 1695; Newcastle?/Isles of Shoales

TOBEY, Samuel (1664/6-) & Abiah [**FISH**] (1678-); b 1697; Sandwich

TOBY, Stephen (1665-) & Hannah **NELSON**; 29 Nov 1688; Kittery, ME

TOBIE, Thomas (-1714) & 1/wf Martha KNOTT (-1689); 18 Nov 1650; Sandwich

TOOBE, Thomas (1651-1677) & Mehitable [CROWELL]/CROWE?, Yarmouth; b 1676(7?); ?Sandwich/Yarmouth

TOBEY, Thomas (-1714) & 2/wf Hannah (SWIFT) [FISH] (-1721), w Ambrose; aft 1689, aft 1691; Sandwich

TOBEY, Thomas & Rebecca [KNOWLES]? (1675-1758); ca 1700; ?Eastham/Yarmouth

TODD, Christopher (1617-1686) & Grace [MIDDLEBROOK]; b 1642; New Haven

TODD, James & Mary HOPKINSON; 22 Jun 1699; Rowley

TODD, John (-1690) (called "bro" by Thomas WOOD 1675) & Susan/Susanna [HUNT?]? (-1710); b 1650; Rowley

TODD, John (1642-) & 1/wf Sarah GILBERT (-1672); 26 Nov 1668; New Haven

TODD, John & 2/wf Sarah BLAKEMAN (1658-1688); 20 Aug 1677; New Haven

TODD, John, Woburn & Elizabeth FIFIELD (1657-); - Jun 1678, 12 Jun; Hampton, NH

TOD, John & 1/wf Elizabeth BROCKLEBANK; 14 Mar 1685, 1684/5, 1685/6?; Ipswich

TODD, Michael (1653-1713) & Elizabeth [BROWN], m/2 Samuel STREET, m/3 John MERRIMAN; b 1690(1?); New Haven

TOD, Samuel (1645-1714) & Mary BRADLEY (1653-); 26 Nov 1668; New Haven

TODD, Samuel & Priscilla BRADSTREET, wid; 26 Apr 1694; Rowley

TODD, Samuel (1672-1742) & 1/wf Susanna TUTTLE; 16 Sep 1698; New Haven/Waterbury, CT

TODD, Thomas & Rachel [BOWLES?]?, m/2 Joseph GOODHUE; b 1683; Boston

TODD, Walter (-1673+) & Margaret [BARTON], w Rufus; aft 1648, no issue; Warwick, RI

TOLLES/TOWLE, Henry & Sarah _?_; b 1669; Saybrook, CT

TOLES, Henry (1664-1750) & Dorothy THOMAS (?1664-1727); 13 Apr 1693; New Haven

TOLEMAN, John (?1642-1725) & 1/wf Elizabeth COLLINS (1648-1690); - Nov 1666, 30 Nov 1666; Lynn

TOALMAN, John (1642-1725) & 2/wf Mary (BRECK) PAUL (-1720), w Samuel; 15 Jun 1692; Dorchester

TOALMAN, John (1671-1759) & 1/wf Susanna BRECK (1678-1713); - Feb 1696/7; Dorchester

TOLMAN, Thomas[1] (1608/9-1690) & 2/wf Sarah _?_ (-1677); b 1633?, b 1642; Dorchester

TOLMAN, Thomas (?1633-1718) & Elizabeth JOHNSON (1638-1720, 1726?, Dorchester); 4 Nov 1664; Lynn

TOLMAN, Thomas[1] (-1690) & 2/wf Katharine _?_ (-1677); b 1677; Dorchester

TOLMAN, Thomas (-1738) & Experience [BLISS?] (1663/4-1762) (had son Bliss TOLMAN; b 1689; Dorchester/Bridgewater/Stoughton/Canton

TOLMAN, _?_ & [Rebecca] BURROUGHS (1674-); ?b 1701

TOMLINS, Edward & _?_; b 1630?, b 1605?; Lynn

TOMBLIN, Isaac & Mary WAIT; 10 Dec 1696; Marlboro

TOMLINE, John & Sarah BARNES; 26 Dec 1660; Boston

TOMBLIN, Matthew & Esther _?_; b 1691; Marlboro

TOMBLIN, Matthew & Sarah BULLARD; 20 Jan 1700, ?7 May 1701; Dedham

TOMLIN, Nathaniel (1668-, Boston) & _?_; Chatham

TOMLIN, Thomas & Sarah SREET [sic]/STREET?; 30 Dec 1697; Boston

TOMLINS, Timothy & _?_; Lynn

TOMLIN, _?_ & Grace [DIAMOND], m/2 Richard TUCKER b 1701?; Kittery, ME

TOMLINS, _?_ & Elizabeth SPENCER (1602-)

TOMLINSON, Agur (1658-1728) & 1/wf Elizabeth JUDSON; 13 Dec 1681; Stratford, CT

TOMLINSON, Agur (1658-1728) & 2/wf Sarah (WELLES) HAWLEY (1664-1694); 19 Oct 1692; Stamford, CT/Stratford, CT

TOMLINSON, Henry (1606-1681) & Alice _?_, m/2 John BIRDSEY 1688; ca 1634; Milford, CT/Stratford, CT

TOMLINSON, Jonas & Hannah [?GUNN]; b 1676; Derby, CT

TOMLINSON, Robert & _?_; b 1648; Milford, CT/Stratford, CT

TOMLINSON, Thomas (-1685) & Elizabeth _?_; b 1665; Hartford, CT

TOMLINSON, William (1643±-1711) & _?_; ca 1680?; Derby

TOMLINSON, _?_ & Ellen _?_, m/2 Arthur BOSTWICK

TOMPKINS, John (-1681) & 1/wf Margaret GOODMAN (-1672); Adlesborough, Bucks, 27 Aug 1632; Salem

TOMPKINS, John & _?_, m/2 William HAYDEN bef 1661; b 1640; Concord/Fairfield, CT

TOMPKINS, John (1642-) & Mary _?_; Fairfield, CT/Eastchester, NY

TOMKINS, John (1645-) & 1/wf Rebecca KNIGHTS (-1688); 26 Jun 1672; Salem
TOMKINS, John (-1681) & 2/wf Mary READ, w Thomas?; Sep 1673; Salem
TOMKINS, John & Mary _?_; b 1683; Portsmouth, RI
TOMKINS, John & 2/wf Mary REED (1653-); 20 Nov 1693; Salem
TOMPKINS, Jonathan (1643-) & Mary PENNINGTON (1646-); 12 Apr 1666; New Haven/Newark, NJ
TOMPKINS, Micah/Michael & Mary _?_; b 12 Dec 1643; Milford, CT/Newark, NJ
TOMPKINS, Nathaniel (-1724) & Elizabeth ALLEN/WATERS (1651, 1655?-1714); 15 Jan 1670, 1670/1; Newport/Little Compton, RI
TOMPKINS, Nathaniel (-1684/5) & Elizabeth _?_; ca 1672?; Eastchester, NY
TOMPKINS, Nathaniel & Elizabeth [HANNA]; b 1701?; Eastchester, NY
TOMPKINS, Ralph (1585-1666) & 1/wf Katharine FOSTER (1577-); in Eng, 6 Nov 1608; Dorchester/Bridgewater/Salem
TOMPKINS, Ralph (1585-1666) & 2/wf Hannah [ABORNE]; aft 1635; Salem
TOMPKINS, Samuel (1617-1695, 1653?) & Lettice FOSTER; 11 Oct 1639, no issue; ?Duxbury/Bridgewater
TONGUE, George (?1600-1674) & Margary/Margery _?_; b 1652; New London, CT
TONGUE, George (1658-) & _?_; b 1682; Stonington, CT
TOUNG, James (-1656) & Elizabeth HAGBORNE; 8 Sep 1654; Boston
TONGUE, Stephen & Mary PAYNE (-1700); 31 May 1688; Amesbury/Salisbury
TOOGOOD, Edward & 1/wf Elizabeth (EVERITT) GRANT (1641-1695?), w James; aft 1683; Salmon Falls/?Berwick
TOOGOOD, Edward & 2/wf Gertrude (URIN) [?MERCER]; by 1695; Boston
TOOGOOD, Edward & Cartwright _?_; b 5 Oct 1699 (seems doubtful); Portsmouth, NH
TOOGOOD, Nathaniel & Elizabeth _?_; b 1679; Boston/Swansea
TOOGOOD, Nathaniel & Martha _?_ (-1735), m/2 Benjamin CARPENTER 1706; b 1693; Swansea
TOOKER, John[1] (-1658) & Ann _?_, m/2 Benjamin HORTON 22 Feb 1659; Southold, LI/Brookhaven?
TOOKER, John[2] & 1/wf Sarah _?_ (-1685); [b 1655]; Southold/Brookhaven, LI
TOOKER, John[2] & Ann WINES NICHOLS ELTON (-bef 1698), w Francis, w John, m/4 John YOUNG ca 1691; 1683, m cont 3 Jun 1686; Setauket, LI
TOOKER, Joseph (ca 1655-) & Dinah BRUSTER/BREWSTER; 6 Apr 1685; Brookhaven, LI
TOOCKIE/TOOKIE, Nicholas & Mary _?_ (-1678, ae 27); b 1678; Charlestown
TOOLY, Christopher/Cristanda (-1718) & ?Elizabeth _?_ (wf in 1705); b 1684; Killingworth, CT
TOLLY, Thomas & _?_; b 1665; Lynn
TULLY, Thomas & Rebecca _?_
TOOTHAKER, Andrew & _?_; b 1700; York, ME
TOOTHAKER, Roger (1613-) & Margaret _?_, m/2 Ralph HILL 1638; b 1635; Billerica
TOOTHAKER, Roger & Mary ALLIN (-1695); 9 Jun 1665; Billerica
TAPLIF, Clement (1603-1672) & Sarah _?_ (1605-1693); b 1637; Dorchester
TOPLIFE, Samuel (1646-1722) & Patience SOMES (1652-1728), Boston; ca 5 Oct 1671; Dorchester
TORREY, Angel (1657-1725) & Hannah _?_; b 1690; Weymouth/Bristol, RI
TORREY, James[1] (1616/17-1665) & Ann HATCH (1626-), m/2 John PHILLIPS 1677; 2 Nov 1643; Scituate
TORREY, James[2] (1644, ?1643-1719) (ae 44 in 1657) & 1/wf Lydia WELLES/WILLS (1645-1679); 1 Jun 1666; Scituate
TORREY, James (1644-1719) & 2/wf Elizabeth RALLINGS/RAWLINS (1661-1700); 29 Sep 1679, 24 Sep 1679; Scituate
TORREY, John (1673-1729) & Mary SIMMES/SYMMES (-1758); 26 Dec 1700; Weymouth
TORREY, Jonathan (1654-1718) & Ruth (FRY) [SMITH] (1650-1724, ca 74), w Joshua; b 1676, b 1675?; Weymouth
TORREY, Jonathan (1651-1703) & Abigail _?_, m/2 William STORY; b 1689; Boston
TORREY, Joseph (1621-1676) & _?_; b 1650; Rehoboth/Newport
TORIE, Josiah (1650-1732) & Sarah (WILSON) BATT, w Paul; 5 May 1680; Medfield/Boston/Mansfield, CT
TORRY, Josiah (1658/9-1722) & 1/wf Isabell (_?_) (HYLAND) WITHERLEE/WETHERELL (-1699), w Samuel, w Samuel; 6 Oct 1684; Scituate
TORRY, Josiah (1658/9-) & Sarah MENDALL (1668-); 12 Jan 1692; Scituate

TORREY, Micajah (1643-1710/11) & Susanna __?__ (-1720); b 1673; Weymouth

TORY, Philip (?1615-1686) (ae 52 in 1674) & Mary (SMITH) SCARBOROUGH, w John; 1 Oct 1647; Roxbury

TORREY, Samuel (-1707, ae 75) & 1/wf Mary RAWSON (-1692, ae 50); 15 May 1657; Boston/Weymouth

TORREY, Samuel (-1707, ae 75) & 2/wf Mary (CHICKERING) SYMMES (-1721), w William; 30 Jul 1695; Braintree

TORREY, Samuel (1675-1746) & Abigail BRIDGE; 29 Jun 1699; Boston

TORREY, William[1] & 1/wf Agnes COMBE (-1630); Combe, St. Nicholas, Eng,. 17 Mar 1629; Weymouth

TORREY, William[1] & 2/wf Jane [HAVILAND] (-1639); in Eng, ca 1630; Weymouth

TORREY, William[1] & 3/wf Elizabeth [FRYE]; in Eng, b 1641; Weymouth

TORREY, William & Deborah [GREENE] (1649-1729); b 1670; Weymouth

TOSH, Daniel & Margaret ACRES (1665-); 19 Oct 1686, 1685?; Newport/Block Island

TOSH, William (-1685) & Jael SWILVAN/SULLIVAN?; 7 Feb 1660/1; Braintree/New Shoreham, RI

TOSH, William (1665-1691) & Penelope NILES, m/2 Edward MOTT 1695; ca 1685; New Shoreham, RI

TOSH, William (-1691) & Mary __?__, m/2 James DANIELSON 1700 (conflicting statements); RI

TOTMAN, Jabez (1641-1705) & 1/wf Deborah TURNER (-1689); 18 Nov 1668; Medfield/Roxbury

TOTMAN, Jabez (1641-1705) & 2/wf Elizabeth [DAVIS]; aft 1689, b Feb 1695/6; Roxbury

TOTMAN, John (-1670) & Johannah __?__ (-1668); b 1641; Roxbury

TOTMAN, Stephen & Dorothy [STODDARD] (1660-), dau Anthony; b 1691; Scituate/Plymouth/Truro

TOTMAN, Thomas (-1678) & Mary [PARKER] (1639/40-1666); b 1666, b 1665; Plymouth/Scituate

TOTTINGHAM, Eliah (1652-) & Mary [PALMER]; b 1683; Boston/Woburn

TOTTINGHAM, Henry (1608-1679) & 1/wf Anna __?__ (-1654); b 1646; Woburn

TOTTINGHAM, Henry & 2/wf Alice [EAGER/ALGIER/AGER?], w William?; 13 Jul 1654; Woburn

TOUSEY/TOUCEY, Richard & 1/wf __?__ ; b 1650; Saybrook

TOUSEY, Richard & Dorothy (MOULTON) (FINCH) [EDWARDS], w John; 1667; Saybrook

TOUSEY, Thomas (1650-1712) & Arminell? __?__ ; b 1680; Ipswich

TOUGH/TOUGHE, Thomas & Mary __?__ ; b 1679/80; Boston

TOURTELLOT, Abraham & 2/wf? Mary [BERNON]; b 1694; Roxbury

TOUT, Benjamin (1668-1743) & Mary/Mercy WINSOR; 29 Aug 1691; Boston

TOUT, Richard & Elizabeth __?__ ; b 1661; Boston

TOUT, Richard (1665-) & Hannah [WATERS] (1666-); b 1688; Boston

TOUT/TROUT, William (-1698) & Mary/Elizabeth __?__ ; b 1677(8?); Boston

TOVY/TOVIE, John (-1686) & Mary HERRICK; 5 Nov 1684; Beverly

TOWER, Benjamin (1654-1722) & Deborah GARNET (1657-1728); - Sep 1680; Hingham

TOWER, Benjamin (1674-1743?) & Deborah WHIPPLE (1681-1755); m int - - 1697; Rehoboth/Cumberland, RI

TOWER, Ibrook (1644-1732) & 1/wf Margaret HARDIN/HARDING (-1705); 24 Apr 1668; Hingham

TOWER, Jeremiah (1646-) & Elizabeth (GOODALE) ROWLAND, w John; 28 Oct 1670; Hingham

TOWER, Jeremiah (1671-) & Hannah HOBART; 3 Jan 1698/9; Hingham

TOWER, John (1609-1702) & Margaret IBROOK (1620-1700); 13 Feb 1638/9, Feb 1639; Hingham

TOWER, John (1639-1693) & Sarah HARDIN/HARDING (-1729); 14 May 1669; Hingham/Braintree

TOWER, John (1673-1711) & Hester CANTERBURY (1671-1729); 15 Jan 1695/6; Hingham

TOWER, Richard (-1702) & Abigail [FARROW] (1670-), m/2 Francis HORSWELL, m/3 John ORCUTT; b 1694; Hingham

TOWER, Samuel (1662-1724) & 1/wf Silence DAMON (1664-1702); 14 Dec 1683; Hingham

TOWER, Thomas (-1684) & Hannah DASTIN/DUSTIN? (1645-), m/2 Thomas JACKSON (called Hannah TAYLOR, wrong); 30 Oct 1662; Reading

TOWERS, William & Sarah __?__ ; b 1665; Boston

TOWERS, William & Leah [WARDWELL] (1646-); b 1668; Boston

TOLE, Benjamin (1669-1759) & Sarah BOWDEN/BORDEN? (1671-1759); 7 Nov 1693; Amesbury

TOWLE, Caleb (1678-1763) & Zipporah BRACKETT (1680-1756); 19 Apr 1698; Hampton, NH

TOWLE, Francis (see DOWELL)

TOLL, John (-1690) & Katherine _?_ (-1675, [1675/6?]); b 1641; Sudbury

TOWLE, Joseph (1669-1757) & 1/wf Mehetabel HOBBS (1673-); 14 Dec 1693, 17 Dec; Hampton, NH

TOWLE, Joshua (1663-1715) & Sarah REED; 2 Dec 1686; Hampton, NH

TOWLE, Philip (1616-1696) & Isabella ASTEN/AUSTIN (ca 1633-1719); 19 Nov 1657; Hampton, NH

TOWNE, Edmund (?1629, 1628-1678) & Mary [BROWNING] (1638-1717); b 1655, b 1657, ca 1652; Topsfield

TOWNE, Jacob (1632/33-1704) & Catharine SYMONS/SYMONDS; 26 Jun 1657; Topsfield

TOWNE, Jacob (1660-1741) & Phebe SMITH (1661-1740); 24 Jun 1684, 1683?; Topsfield

TOWNE, John & Phebe [LAMSON] (1652?); doubtful; ?Ipswich

TOWNE, John (1658-1740) & Mary SMITH (1658-); 2 Feb 1680; Topsfield/Framingham

TOWNE, Joseph (1639, bpt 1648-1713) & Phebe [PERKINS] (?1644-1715+); b 1666, ca 1665; Topsfield

TOWNE, Joseph (1661-1717) & Ruhama/Amy? SMITH (1668-1756); 10 Aug 1687; Topsfield

TOWNE, Joseph (1673-) & 1/wf Margaret CASE; 9 Nov 1699; Topsfield

TOWNE, Peter (?1633-1705, ae 72 y 10 m) & 1/wf Joanna _?_ ; Cambridge

TOWNE, Peter (?1633-1705), Cambridge & 2/wf Elizabeth PAYN (-1724+); 8 Apr 1697, 6 Apr 1697, 1 Apr 1697; Braintree/Cambridge

TOWNE, Samuel & Abigail _?_ ; b 1661; Boston

TOWNE, Samuel (1673-1714) & Elizabeth KNIGHT, m/2 Elisha PERKINS; 20 Oct 1696; Topsfield

TOWNE, Thomas & Sarah FRENCH; 17 Mar 1684/5; Topsfield

TOWNE, William (1599-1672, 1673) (ae 60 in 1660) & Joanna/Jone BLESSING; Yarmouth, Eng, 25 Mar 1620, 25 Apr 1620; Salem/Topsfield

TOWNE, William (-1685, ae 80) & Martha _?_ (-1674); b 1632; Cambridge

TOWN, William (1659-) & 1/wf Eliza/Elizabeth? _?_ ; Topsfield

TOWNE, William & Margaret (_?_) WILLARD, w John; 22 Aug 1694; Topsfield

TOWNER, Richard (-1727) & 1/wf Mary _?_ ; b 1686?; Branford

TOWNLEY, Richard (-1711) & Elizabeth (SMITH) (LAWRENCE) CARDERET, w William, w Philip; aft 1682, b 1691, ca 1685; NJ

TOWNSEND, Andrew (?1654-1693) & Abigail COLLINS (1661-1693); 18 Jul 1678; Lynn

TOWNSEND, Daniel (-1702) & Susannah [FORMAN]; ca 1697?; ?Oyster Bay, LI

TOWNSEND, George (1661-1697/8) & Mary/Meribah? HAWXHURST, m/2 Abraham ALLING; 17 Nov 1684; ?Matinecock, LI/Oyster Bay, LI

TOWNSEND, George & 1/wf Rebecca COWDRY (1663-1704?); 27 Feb 1688/9; Charlestown/Reading

TOWNSEND, George, Portsmouth, NH, & Bethia [DAM] (1675-); b 1701?

TOWNSEND, Henry (-1695) & Ann [COLES] (?1635-1695+); b 1649?, 1653?; Warwick, RI/Jamaica, LI/Oyster Bay

TOWNSEND, Henry (1654?, 1649/53-bef 1717, aft 30 Mar 1709) & Deborah [UNDERHILL] (1659-30 Mar 1698); ca 1676, b 1684, by 1676; Oyster Bay, LI

TOWNSEND, ?Henry (ca 1660-) & Elizabeth [WRIGHT] (1667-)

TOWNSEND, James (1646-1689?) & 1/wf Elizabeth [LIVERMORE]; b 1671; Boston

TOWNSEND, James (1646-) & 1/wf Elizabeth [WRIGHT] (1653/4-1677?); b 1673?, b 1671?; Oyster Bay, LI

TOWNSEND, James (-1698) & 2/wf Jean/Jane REDDOUGH; 16 Oct 1677; Oyster Bay, LI

TOWNSEND, James & 2/wf Elizabeth [PRICE] (1664-), m/2 Joseph LOBDELL 1692; b 1684; Boston

TOWNSEND, James & Audrey [ALMY] (1669-); b 1692; ?Oyster Bay, LI

TOWNSEND, James & Mary LYNCH; 7 Nov 1693; Boston

TOWNSEND, James (1671-1705) & Rebecca MOSELY/MOSELEY, m/2 Jonathan WILLIAMS; 22 Jan 1694, 1694/5; Boston/Cohansey, NJ

TOWNSEND, James (-1697/8) & 3/wf Delivered/Deliverance? [PRATT] (1664-1699); b 1698, b 11 Feb 1698; Oyster Bay, LI

TOWNSEND, James (-1744) & Alice NEWEL; 7 Jun 1700; Boston

TOWNSEND, James (?1674-) & Hannah HALSTEAD (1675-); b 1701?, ca 1692?; ?Oyster Bay, LI

TOWNSEND, John[1] (1608/10-1668?) & Elizabeth [?MONTGOMERY]/?COLE (-1684); in Eng, 1630/36; Warwick, RI/Flushing, LI/etc.

TOWNSEND, John (-1705) (?see John TOWNSEND m Phebe WILLIAMS ca 1690) & 1/wf Phebe
__?__ (-1698, bef 1696); ca 1664; Oyster Bay/Jericho, LI
TOWNSEND, John (-1726) & 1/wf (no) Sarah PEARSON (1647-1689); 27 Jan 1668/9; Lynn
TOWNSEND, John (-1705) & 1/wf Johannah (TOWNSEND?) FORMAN? (-6 Oct 1680); ca 1679;
Oyster Bay, LI
TOWNSEND, John (-1705) & 2/wf Esther [SMITH] (-1749+); aft 6 Oct 1680; Hempstead,
LI/Oyster Bay, LI
TOWNSEND, John, son of Richard & 1/wf Phebe [WILLIAMS] (-1698+), dau Robert; ca 1690?, b
14 Feb 1692/3, ca 1665?; ?Oyster Bay, LI/Cape May Co., NJ
TOWNSEND, John (-1726) & 2/wf Mehitable BROWN (1661-1735), Cambridge, dau Thomas; 23
Apr 1690; Lynn
TOWNSEND, John & 1/wf Rebecca ALMY (1671-(17--)); 28 Apr 1692; Portsmouth, RI
TOWNSEND, John (-1705) & 2/wf Phebe [?WILLIAMS]; ca 1696?, b 14 Feb 1692/3; Oyster Bay,
LI
TOWNSEND, John (1675-1757) & Sarah BOUTEL (-1737); 28 Apr 1698; Lynn/Reading
TOWNSEND, John & Catharine [WILLITS?]; b 1701?
TOWNSEND, Jonathan (1668-1718) & Elizabeth WALTON/WALTHAM? (-1749); 22 Mar 1695;
Boston
TOWNSEND, Joseph (-1698) & Dorothy [CLARKE]; b 1672; Boston/Falmouth, ME
TOWNSEND, Joseph (1665-) & 1/wf Elizabeth BERRY (1665-1693); 22 May 1690; Charlestown/
Boston
TOWNSEND, Joseph (1665-) & 2/wf Judith WOODMAN (1667-1701); 9 Aug 1694; Charlestown
TOWNSEND, Martin (1596-) & Martha __?__ (1603-); b 1634
TOWNSEND, Martin (ae 47 in 1691) & 1/wf Abigail TRAYNE/TRAINE (-1691); 11 Apr 1668, 10
Apr; Watertown
TOWNSEND, Martin & 2/wf Esther/Hester (HESSELE) PERRY, Woburn, w Obadiah; 30 Aug
1693; Watertown
TOWNSEND, Nathaniel & [?Elizabeth BIRDSALL]; b 1701?
TOWNSEND, Penn (1651-1727) & 1/wf Sarah [ADDINGTON] (1653-1692); b 1674; Boston
TOWNSEND, Penn (-1727) & 2/wf Mary (LEVERETT) DUDLEY (-1699, ?living 1707?), w Paul;
aft 11 Mar 1691/2; Boston
TOWNSEND, Peter (1642-1696) & 1/wf Lydia [DASSETT?]; b 1666; Boston
TOWNSEND, Peter (1642-1696) & 2/wf Margaret __?__ ; b 1677; Boston
TOWNSEND, Peter (1642-1696) & 2/wf Ann __?__, m/2 Abraham COLE 1697; by 1680; Boston
TOWNSEND, Peter (1671-1720) & Mary WELCOME; 15 Nov 1694; Boston
TOWNSEND, Richard (-1670) & 1/wf Deliverance [COLE]/COLES (?1631-); b 1651, b 1650?;
Warwick, RI/Oyster Bay/etc.
TOWNSEND, Richard (-1670) & 2/wf Elizabeth [WICKS]?/WEEKS, dau John, m/2 John SMITH;
ca 1660; Warwick, RI/Hempstead, LI/etc.
TOWNSEND, Robert (?1636-1669+) & __?__ [?FITTS]; b 1661; Portsmouth, NH
TOWNSEND, Roger & Mary [BEDIENT], w Mordecai, m/3 Richard OSBORN; b 1677, b
1670/75?, by 1677; Westchester, NY
TOWNSEND, Samuel (?1638-1704) & Abigail [DAVIS] (-1729, ae 87 y 8 m); b 1662, b 1661?;
Charlestown/Boston
TOWNSEND, Samuel (?1662-1723) & 1/wf Elizabeth (MELLINS) BARLOW (-1699), w Thomas;
15 Mar 1693; Charlestown/Boston
TOWNSEND, Solomon & Catharine [ALMY] (1674)
TOWNSEND, Solomon (1676-) & 1/wf Elizabeth (STRATTON)? JARVIS (1665-1713, ae 47), w
William; 20 Jun 1698; Boston
TOWNSEND, Thomas (1595/1601?-1677) (bro-in-law of John NEWGATE) & Mary __?__ (-1693);
ca 1630?; Lynn
TOWNSEND, Thomas (?1635-1700) & Mary [DAVIS] (1646-1700+); b 1665; Boston
TOWNSEND, Thomas (1642-1715) & 1/wf Sarah [COLE]/[COLES] (?1644-); ca 1665, ca 1666?,
b 1672; Oyster Bay, LI/Portsmouth, RI
TOWNSEND, Thomas (1642-1715) & 2/wf Mary (UNTHANK) ALMY (-1724+), w Job; aft 1 Mar
1684; Portsmouth, RI
TOWNSEND, Thomas & 1/wf Elizabeth __?__ ; b 1691?; Boston
TOWNSEND, Thomas & Sarah [PEARSALL]; b 1701?
TOWNSEND, Thomas & Elizabeth [ORRIS]; 24 Dec 1702; Boston

TOWNSEND, William (1601-1669, 1668) & Hannah [PENN] (-1700, in 93rd y), sister of James PENN; b 1636, b 1635; Boston

TOWSLEY, Michael (-1712) & Mary HUSSE/HUSSEY, m/2 Jonathan WINCHELL; 4 Jun 1678; Salisbury/Suffield, CT

TOWSEY, Richard & 1/wf _?_ ; b 1662; Wethersfield, CT

TOWLEY/TOUSEY?, Richard & 2/wf Dorothy (MOULTON) (FINCH) EDWARDS, w Abraham, w John; May 1667, see TOWNLEY; ?Wethersfield, CT

TOWSEY, Thomas (-1712, ae 62) & _?_ ; Wethersfield, CT

TOZER/TOZIER?, Richard (-1675) & Judith SMITH (-1683); 3 Jul 1656; Boston

TOZER, Richard & Elizabeth (WENTWORTH) [SHARP] (?1669-), w James; ca 1690; Kittery, ME

TOZER, Richard & Mary [BEEBE]; New London

TOZER, Simon (-1718) & Mary [KNAPP] (1666-); b 1693; Watertown/Weston

TOZER, William & Damaris [MANSFIELD] (1658-); Salem

TOZER, [Richard] & [?Mary] (BLOTT) GREEN, w Ralph?, had son John GREEN; b 27 May 1662

TRACY, Daniel (1652-1728) & 1/wf Abigail ADGATE (1661-1710); 19 Sep 1682; Norwich, CT

TRACY, John (?1633-1718) & 1/wf Mary [PRENCE] (-by 1697); ca 1660; ?Plymouth/Windham, CT/?Duxbury

TRACY, John (?1643-1702) & Mary WINSLOW (?1646-1721); 17 Jun 1670; Norwich, CT

TRACY, John (1673-1726) & Elizabeth LEFFINGWELL (1676-1739); 10 May 1697; Norwich, CT

TRACY, John (ca 1661-1701) & Deborah _?_ ; ca 1682; Duxbury

TRACY, Jonathan (?1640-1709) & 1/wf Mary GRISWOLD (1656-1711); 11 Jul 1672; Norwich, CT/Saybrook, CT/Preston, CT

TRACY, Jonathan (1675-) & Anna [PALMER]; ca 1700?, 11 Feb 1700/01; Preston, CT

TRACY, Solomon (ca 1650-1732) & 1/wf Sarah [HUNTINGTON] (1654-1683); 23 Nov 1676; Norwich, CT/Saybrook

TRACY, Solomon (ca 1650-1732) & 2/wf Sarah (BLISS) SLUMAN (-1730), w Thomas; 8 Apr 1686; Norwich, CT

TRACY, Stephen (ret'd to Eng) & Tryphosa LEE; 2 Jan 1620/1, Leyden, Holland; Plymouth/Duxbury

TRACY, Thomas (?1610-1685) & 1/wf _?_ ; ca 1641; Wethersfield, CT/Saybrook, CT

TRACY, Thomas (1644-1721) & Sarah _?_ ; b 1675; Preston, CT

TRACY, Thomas & 2/wf Martha (BOURNE) [BRADFORD] (-1689), w John; ca 1678/9, b 20 Feb 1679/80; Wethersfield

TRACY, Thomas (-1685, ae 76) & 3/wf Mary (FOOTE) (STODDARD) GOODRICH, w John, w John; 1683; Norwich, CT

TRAIN, John (1610-1681) & 1/wf Margaret [DIX]? (-1660); b 1640; Watertown

TRAINE, John (1651-1718) & Mary STUBBS; 24 Mar 1674, 1674/5; Watertown

TRAIN, John (1610-1681) & 2/wf Abigail BENT (-1691); 12 Oct 1675; Watertown

TRAIN, Thomas (1653-1739) & Rebecca STEARNS (1661-1746); 25 Jan 1692/3; Watertown

TRANTER/TRANTON, Thomas & _?_ ; b 1688; Freetown

TRAPP, Thomas (1639-1719?) (ae ca 20 in 1659) & Mary _?_ ; b 1675; Martha's Vineyard (related to Thomas BIRCHARD's wf?)

TRASK, Benjamin & Mercy/?Mary (SHATTUCK) ELLIOTT (1655-1710, ae 52?), w Andrew; aft 12 Sep 1688; Salem

TRASK, Edward & Deborah ROUNDEY; m int 21 Apr 1700; Beverly

TRASK, Henry (-1689±) & Mary [SOUTHWICK?] (1630-), m/2 William NICHOLS; b 1652; Salem

TRASK, John (1642-1700) (ae 53 in 1695) & 1/wf Abigail PARKMAN; 14 Feb 1662/3; Salem

TRASK, John & Florence [HART], Marblehead; betw 1668 & 1672

TRASK, John & 1/wf Christian WOODBERRIE/WOODBURY (-1689); 9 Apr 1679; Beverly

TRASK, John (-1729+) & Hannah [SOLART] (1658-); b 1681, b 1687/8; Beverly/Lexington

TRASK, John & 2/wf Mary/?Elizabeth DODG/DODGE; 30 Oct 1690; Beverly

TRASK, Joseph & Elizabeth SALLOES/SALLOWS; 20 Dec 1693; Salem

TRASK, Osmond (1625-1676) & 1/wf Mary _?_ (-1663?); 1 Jan 1649/50; Salem

TRASK, Osmand (1625-1676) & 2/wf Elizabeth GALLY/GALLEY, m/2 John GILES 1679; 22 May 1663; Salem

TRASK, Samuel (-1741/2) & Susanna _?_ (-1739+); b 1690; Salem

TRASK, William[1] (1589-1666, ae 77) & Sarah _?_ ; b 1636; Salem

TRASK, William (1640-1691) & 1/wf Ann PUTNAM (1645-1676); 18 Jan 1666, 1666/7?; Salem

TRASK, William² (1640-1691) & 2/wf Anna/Hannah _?_; ca 1677; Salem
TRASK, William (1671-1723) & Sarah MARSTONE; 11 Jun 1696; Beverly
TRASK, William (-1745) & 1/wf Ann [WHITE]; b 15 Jul 1697, b 1699; Salem/Weymouth/Braintree
TRAVERS, Henry (-1659?) & Bridget (?FITTS) GOODWIN, w Richard, m/3 Richard WINDOW; b 1636; Newbury
TRAVERS, Samuel & Frances ALLERTON
TRAVIS, Daniel (-1683) & Esther _?_; b 1652; Boston
TRAVERIS, Francis & Mary BURGESS; 27 Jan 1699; Boston
TRAVIS, Garret (-1705+) & Katherine _?_ (-1705+); ca 1655?; Rye, NY
TRAVERS, Henry (-1659?) & Bridget (FITTS) GOODWIN, w Richard, m/3 Richard WINDOW; b 1636; Newbury
TRAVIS, James (1645-) & Mercy PEARCE; 8 Apr 1667; Gloucester/Brookfield
TRAVIS, James & 1/wf Mercy [LELAND]; b 1700; Framingham
TRAVIS, Richard & Grace CLEMENTS; 22 Dec 1657, 1656?; Boston
TRAVIS, Richard & Anna _?_; b 1674; Boston
TRAVIS, Robert & _?_ [GALPIN], dau Philip; b 22 May 1686; ?Rye, NY
TRAY, John & Deliverance _?_; b 1673; Boston
TREADWAY, Jonathan (1640-1710) & Judith THURSTANE/THURSTON (-1726); 1 Mar 1665, 1665/6; Medfield/Sudbury
TREADAWAY, Josiah (?1652-1732) & 1/wf Sarah SWEETMAN (1654-1697); 9 Jan 1673/4, 9 Jun 1674; Charlestown
TREADWAY, Josiah (-1732) & 2/wf Dorothy (BELL) CUTLER, w Samuel (-1740); 3 Feb 1697/8; Charlestown
TREADWAY, Nathaniel (-1689) & Sufferance [HAYNES] (ca 1617-1682); b 1640; Watertown
TREADWELL, Edward (-1660/1), Huntington, LI, & Sarah _?_ (-1684), m/2 Henry WHELPLEY, m/3 Ralph KEELER, m/4 Thomas SKIDMORE; b 1644; Ipswich/Branford, CT/Southold, LI/Huntington, LI
TREADWELL, Edward & Mary [TURNEY] (1673-); b 1695; Fairfield
TREADWELL, John & 1/wf Elizabeth [STARR] (1646?-), m lic 6 Mar 1666/7, m same day?; ?Hempstead, LI
TREADWELL, John & 2/wf Hannah [SMITH]; b 5 Jul 1682; Hempstead, LI
TREADWELL, John & Phebe [PLATT] (1669-); b 12 Jan 1696/7; ?Huntington, LI
TREADWELL, John (1670-) & Mary [FOWLER]; b 1699; Ipswich
TREADWELL, John (1675-1716) & Abigail MINOR (1681-), m/2 Richard MILES; 8 Feb 1699, ?1699/1700; ?Stratford, CT
TREADWELL, Nathaniel (1638-1727) & 1/wf Abigail WELLS (-1677); 19 Jun 1661; Ipswich
TREDWELL, Nathaniel (1638-1727) & 2/wf Rebecca TITCOMB; 25 Mar 1678; Ipswich
TREADWELL, Nathaniel (1677-) & Hannah _?_, m/2 George HART; b 1698; Ipswich
TREADWELL, Samuel (-1718) & Ruth [WHEELER] (-1719); ca 1670, b 1669?; Stratford, CT
TREADWELL, Samuel & Martha [TURNEY] (1676-), m/2 Samuel SMEDLEY 1721; b 1698; ?Stratfield
TREADWELL, Samuel & Mary [HAMMOND]; b 1701?; Wells, ME
TREADWELL, Thomas (1605-1671) & Mary [TAYLOR]; in Eng, b 1634; Dorchester/Ipswich
TREDWELL, Thomas & Sarah TITCOMB; 1664, 16 Mar 1664/5; Ipswich
TREADWELL, Thomas (1666-1744) (called "brother" by Jacob PERKINS 1705) & 1/wf Mary _?_; b 1691; Ipswich
TREDWELL, Thomas (1666-1744) & 2/wf Frances [SAWYER] (1670-1744); b 19 May 1693; Ipswich
TREADWELL, Thomas & Hannah [DENTON] (1673-1748); b 1698; Hempstead, LI
TREADWELL, Timothy & Mary [PLATT] (1672-); b 12 Jan 1696/7
TREAT, Henry (?1649-1681) & Sarah [ANDREWS], m/2 David FORBES?; 1673; Hartford
TREAT, James (1634-1709) & Rebecca LATIMER (1646-1734); 26 Jan 1664/5; Wethersfield, CT
TREAT, James (1666-1742) & Prudence CHESTER (1666-1727); 17 Dec 1691; Wethersfield, CT
TREAT, John (1650-1714) & 1/wf Abigail TITCHENER/TICHENOR? (-1713?), Newark; Newark, NJ
TREAT, Joseph (1662-1721) & 1/wf Frances BRYAN (1668-1703); b 1690; Milford, CT
TREAT, Matthias (-1662) & Mary [SMITH], m/2 Anthony WRIGHT, m/3 John SMITH; ca 1648; Wethersfield, CT

TREAT, Richard (1584-1669/70) & Alice GAYLORD (1594-1670+); Pitminster, Eng, 27 Apr 1615; Watertown/Wethersfield, CT

TREAT, Richard (1623-1693±) & Sarah [COLEMAN] (?1639, ?1642-1734); ca 1661; Wethersfield, CT

TREAT, Robert (1625, 1621?-1710) & 1/wf Jane TAPP (1628-1703); aft 19 Apr 1649?, ca 1647; Milford, CT

TREAT, Robert (1654-) & 1/wf Elizabeth _?_ ; b 3 Jul 1679; Milford, CT

TREAT, Robert & Abigail [CAMP] (1667-1742); ca 1691/3?; Milford, CT

TREAT, Salmon (1673?-1762) & 1/wf Dorothy NOYES (1675-1714), Stonington; 12 Apr 1698, 28? Apr; Preston, CT

TREAT, Samuel & Mary _?_ ; b 1661; Wethersfield, CT

TREAT, Samuel (1648-1717) & 1/wf Elizabeth MAYO (-1696, ae 44); 16 Mar 1674; Eastham

TREAT, Samuel (1648-1717) & Abigail (WILLARD) EASTERBROOK/ESTABROOK (-1746), w Benjamin; 29 Aug 1700; Eastham

TREAT, Thomas (1668-1713) & Dorothy BULKELEY (-1757); 5 Jul 1693; Wethersfield/Glastonbury

TREAT, [Richard] (1668-bef 1694) & Hannah STEELE (1668-), dau Samuel, m/2 John HART 12 Apr 1694

TREBE, John (-1675) & Mary _?_

TREBY, Peter & Ruth _?_ ; b 1688; Newport

TREBY, Peter & Mehitable SHEPARD; b 5 Apr 1714, b 1701?

TREE, Joseph & Mercy CHUBB; 2 Mar 1695/6; Beverly

TREE, Richard & Joanna ROGERS; 21 Sep 1669; Lynn/Salem?

TREVY/TREFRY, Thomas & Agnes/Annas DENNIS; 14 Oct 1692; Marblehead

TREHERN, Edward (-1715) & Sarah (WATERBURY) (DIBBLE) WEBSTER, w _?_, w Nicholas; aft 1687; ?Stamford, CT

TRELANCE/?TRANANCE/?TRENANCE/?TRENANTS, John (-1704) & Martha _?_ (-1718, ae 55); b 1692; Beverly

TRERICE, John & Hannah LYNDE/LINES (1642-), m/2 James KILLING 1679; 3 Sep 1663; Charlestown

TRARICE, Nicholas (1598-1652) & Rebecca _?_ (1606-), m/2 Thomas LYNDE 1665; b 1638, b 1636?; Charlestown/Woburn

TRERICE, Nicholas (1668, ?1669-) & Hannah [TRECOTHERICK]/?TREOTHIC, ?m/2 Roger TALBOT; b 1695(6?); Boston

TRESCOTT, John (1651-1741) & Rebecca _?_ (-1741, ae 88) (called Mary 1694); b 1678(9?); Dorchester

TRESCOTT, Joseph (1668-) & Miriam _?_ ; b 1689; Dorchester

TRESCOTT, Samuel (1646-1730) & Margaret [ROGERS] (-1742, ae 90?); b 1673; Dorchester/Milton

TRESCOTT, Thomas (-1654) & Ann _?_ (-1654); Boston

TRESCOTT, William (1615-1699) & Elizabeth [DYER] (1625-1699), relative of Philip EDWARDS; b 1646; Dorchester

TRESWELL/TRESSWELL/?TRUSSELL, Henry & Martha [RING]; b 1686; Salisbury

TREVETT/TREVET, Henry & 1/wf Elizabeth NEWHALL (-23 Oct 1694); 14 Jun 1688; Lynn

TREVETT, Henry & 2/wf Mary HALLOWAY; 31 May 1695; Lynn

TREVETT, Richard & Martha JOHNSON; 13 Oct 1685; Marblehead

TRIBAH, Nicholas & Christian _?_ ; b 1680; Boston

TRICKER/?TUCKER, Mark & Mary _?_ ; b 1685; Manchester

TRICKEY, Ephraim & Mary [NASON]/, m/2 William WITTUM b 1694, nr 1680; Dover, NH

TRICKEY, Francis & Sarah _?_ ; b 1668, b 1652; Kittery, ME

TRICKEY, Isaac (1647-) & _?_

TRICKEY, Joseph (-1695?) & Rebecca [ROGERS], m/2 Joshua DOWNING; Dover, NH

TRICKEY, Thomas (-1675) & Elizabeth _?_ (-1680+); by 1646; Dover, NH

TRICKEY, Zachariah (1651±-) & Elizabeth [WITTUM]; b 1693, b 1696; Dover, NH

TRIM, Christopher & Alice/?Mary REDDING; 27 Sep 1700; Dorchester

TRIMMINGS, Oliver & Susanna _?_ ; b 1656, b 1655; NH?

TRIPE, Sylvanus (-1716) & Margaret [DIAMOND] (-1742); 1695±; Kittery, ME

TRIPP, Abiel (1653±-1684) & Deliverance HALL (-1721, m/2 Thomas DURFEE; 30 Jan 1679; Portsmouth, RI

TRIPP, James[2] (1656±-1730) & 1/wf Mercy **LAWTON** (-bef 1685); 19 Jan 1681/2; Portsmouth/ Dartmouth

TRIPP, James[2] (ca 1656-1730) & 2/wf Lydia _?_ (-bef 1702); b 1685; Portsmouth, RI/Dartmouth

TRIPP, John[1] (1610-1678) & Mary [**PAINE**] (-1687?), m/2 Benjamin **ENGELL/INGALL**? 1682; b 1640; Portsmouth, RI

TRIPP, John (1640±-1719) & Susanna **ANTHONY** (-1716+); 7 Sep 1665; Portsmouth, RI

TRIPP, John (-1687) & Sarah [**MOTT**] (1657-)

TRIPP, John (1673-) & Mary **HART**; 6 Sep 1693; Portsmouth, RI

TRIPP, Jonathan (1671-) & Martha **BROWNELL** (1678-), m/2 Samuel **HART**; 22 Aug 1695; ?Little Compton, RI

TRIPP, Joseph[1] (1644-1718) & Mehitable **FISH**; 6 Aug 1667; Dartmouth

TRIPP, Peleg[2] (1642±-1714) & Anne **SISSON** (-1713±); ca 1664?; Dartmouth/Portsmouth, RI

TRIPP, Peleg (1663-) & _?_, had Othniel 1697; b 1697

TRIPP/TRIPE, Silvanus & Margaret [**DIAMOND**]; b 1699, 1695±; Ipswich

TRIPP, _?_ & Phebe **PECKHAM**, m/2 William **WEEDEN**; b 1701?

TRISTRAM, Ralph (-1678) & _?_ **LACY**, w Morgan; b 1644; Biddeford, ME

TROWBRIDGE, James (?1626-1717, Newton) & 1/wf Margaret **ATHERTON** (1638-1672, Newton); 30 Dec 1659; Dorchester/Cambridge/Wilton

TROWBRIDGE, James (?1636-1717) & 2/wf Margaret **JACKSON** (1649-1727); 30 Jan 1674, 2 Jan, 20 Jan?; Newton

TROWBRIDGE, James (1664-1732) & 1/wf Lydia **ALSOP** (1665-1690); 8 Nov 1688; New Haven

TROWBRIDGE, James (1664-1732) & 2/wf Hester **HOW** (1671-1697); 29 Sep 1691, 1692?; New Haven

TROWBRIDGE, James & Mary **BELDING/BELDEN** (1677-), Hatfield; 19 Apr 1698; Wilton, CT

TROWBRIDGE, John (1661-1689) & Ann **LEET** (1661-1747), m/2 Ebenezer **COLLINS** 1696; 19 Nov 1683; New Haven

TROWBRIDGE, John (1664-) & 1/wf _?_, b 1701?; Cambridge

TROWBRIDGE, Samuel (1670-1742) & Sarah **LACEY**, m/2 Edward **TREADWELL** 1713; 30 Dec 1697; Stratfield, CT

TROWBRIDGE, Samuel & Sarah [**BELDING**?] (1682-); b 1699; Hadley

TROWBRIDGE, Thomas (-1672) (ret'd to Eng) & Elizabeth **MARSHALL** (1602/3-16[41]?); St. Mary Arches Exeter, Eng, 26 Mar 1627; Dorchester/New Haven

TROWBRIDGE, Thomas (1631-1702) & 1/wf Sarah **RUTHERFORD** (1641-1687); 24 Jun 1657; New Haven

TROWBRIDGE, Thomas & Abigail **BEARDSLEY**; 26 May 1684, 28? May; New Haven

THROOP, Daniel/Dan (1670-1737) & 1/wf Dorcas **BARNEY** (1671-1697); 23 Aug 1689; Bristol, RI

THROOP, Daniel/Dan & 2/wf Deborah **MACEY/MARCY**; 5 Jan 1697, 1697/8; Bristol, RI

THROOP, John & Rebecca **SMITH**; 25 Nov 1697, 26 Nov 1697; Bristol, RI

TROOP, Jonathan (1670-) & Martha **BROWNELL** (1678-); 22 Aug 1695; Little Compton, RI/Tiverton, RI

TROOP, William (?1637, ?1638-1704) & Mary **CHAPMAN** (1643-1705+); 14 May 1666; Barnstable

THROOP, William & Martha **COLLYE/COBLEY**; 20 Mar 1698, 1698/9; Bristol, RI

TROTT, Bernard & Mary [**EVANS**]; aft 9 Feb 1664; Boston

TROTT, John & Anne _?_; b 1679; Nantucket

TROTT, John (1664-1719) & 1/wf Mehitable **RIGBY** (-1703); 3 Apr 1696; Dorchester

TROTT, Samuel (1660-1724) & ?Mary/?Mercy [?**BEAL**]/**BALE**; b 1691, ca 1690; Dorchester

TROTT, Thomas (1614-1696) & Sarah [**PROCTOR**] (-1712); b 1644; Dorchester

TROT, Thomas (-1694) & Ann _?_ (-1694+); b 25 Jul 1677; Dorchester/Roxbury

TROTT, Thomas & Abigail _?_; b 1699; Dorchester/Boston

TROTT, Simon & 1/wf _?_ [**BATSON**]; Cape Porpoise

TROTT, _?_ & 2/wf Elizabeth _?_

TROTT, _?_ & _?_ **STANTON**, dau Robert; b 1679

TROTTER, [William] & Cutbury **GIBBS**; 9 Dec 1652; Newbury/Boston

TROWTE, William (-1698) & Mary/Elizabeth _?_; b 1677(8?); Boston

TROW, George & Sarah [**CONANT**] (1667-1751); b 1686; Beverly

TROUGH, John & Mary (**SUMNER**) [**HOWE**] (-1706), w Nicholas; b 1678; Boston/Newport

TROW, Tobias & Mary [**GREEN**] (1664-); b 1685; Beverly

TROWBRIDGE, Thomas (1664-1711) & Mary **WINSTON** (1667-1742); 16 Oct 1685; New Haven

TROWBRIDGE, Thomas (1631-1702) & 2/wf Hannah (NASH) BALL (1655-1708), w Eliphalet; 2 Apr 1689; New Haven

TROWBRIDGE, Thomas (1677-) & 1/wf ?Mary WINCHESTER?/WHITE (1676-); ca 1700, b 1702

TROWBRIDGE, William (1633-1690) & Elizabeth (LAMBERTSON/LAMBERTON) SILLIVANT, w Daniel; 9 Mar 1656/7, ?at Milford, CT, ?9 Jun; New Haven/Milford, CT

TROWBRIDGE, William (1657-1704) & Thankful [STOW] (1664-1719+); ca 1686, 1687?; New Haven

TRUANT, John (1655-1730) & Silence _?_ (1643-1718) (bur in "Little" Cemetery, Marshfield); Marshfield

TRUANT/TREUANT, Joseph & Hannah BARNES; 6 Jan 1674; Marshfield

TRUANT, Morris (-1685) & Jane _?_ (-1678+); 16 Oct 1639; Plymouth Colony/?Duxbury/Marshfield

TREW, Henry & Israel/?Jeeral [PIKE], m/2 Joseph FLETCHER 1660; b 1645; Salem/Salisbury

TRUE, Henry & Jane BRADBURY; 15 Mar 1667/8; Salisbury

TRUE, Henry & Abigail FRENCH; 20 Dec 1699; Salisbury

TRUE, Joseph & Ruth WHITTIER; 20 Apr 1675; Salisbury

TRUE, William (1670-) & Eleanor [STEVENS]; b 1694; Salisbury

TRUEMAN, David & Mary _?_ ; b 1684; Rehoboth

TRUMAN, Joseph (-1697) & _?_ ; b 1666; New London, CT

TRUESDALE, Richard (bpt 11 Oct 1607, Boston, Eng-1671) & Mary [HOOD] (-1679?); b 1640, no issue; Cambridge

TRUESDALE, Richard & Katherine HATTON/?HALTON/?KALTON/?KELTON, m/2 Enoch GREENLEAF 1712; 29 May 1673, in Eng; Cambridge

TRUSDELL, Richard (1672-) & Mary (RICHARDS) FAIERBANK (1675-), w Benjamin, m/3 Samuel GATES 1710; 24 Feb 1696/7; Dedham

TRUESDALL, Samuel & Mary [JACKSON] (-1700+); b 1672; Cambridge/?Branford, CT

TREWORGY/TRUEWORTHY, James (-1650?) & Catherine/Katherine SHAPLEIGH (-1676), m/2 Edward HILTON ca 1654; Kingswear, Eng, 16 Mar 1616, 1616/17; Kittery, ME

TREWORGY, James & 1/wf Mary FERGUSON (-1696); 16 Jul 1693; Kittery, ME

TREWORGYE, James (-1699) & Mary [WATTS]; b 1697; Boston

TREWORGY, James & 2/wf Sarah [BRADY], w John; b 1698; Kittery, ME

TREWORGY, John (1618-) & Penelope SPENSER; 15 Jan 1646, 164-; Newbury

TREWORGY, Samuel (1628-), (ae 33 in 1661) & Dorcas [WALTON]; aft 1666; Portsmouth, NH

TREAUANT, Joseph & Hannah BARNES; 6 Jan 1674; Marshfield

TREWANT, Morris (-1685) & Jane _?_ ; 16 Oct 1639; ?Plymouth/Marshfield

TRUFANT, Morris (-1685) & Mary [BICKWELL] (1678-); b 1701, b 1705; Weymouth

TRULL, John (-1704, ae 70) & Sarah FRENCH (1637-1710); 11 Dec 1657; Billerica/Woburn

TRULL, John (1665-) & Elizabeth HOOPER (1665-1698); 22 Apr 1692; Billerica

TRULL, Samuel (-1714) & Ann HAILE (-1692); 15 Jun 1668; Billerica

TRULL, Samuel (1673-1706) & Hannah [HOGGETT], Andover; ca 1699, b 1702; Billerica

TRUMBALL, Daniel & Sarah [NORTON?]; b 30 Jan 1643; ?Wenham/?Lynn

TRUMBLE, John & 1/wf Elinor CHANDLER (-1648/9); Newcastle-on-Tyne, Eng, 7 Jul 1635; Rowley

TRUMBLE, John & Elizabeth [KING?] (-1696, ae 86); b 1638; Cambridge/Charlestown

TRUMBULL, John (-1657) & 2/wf Ann (?GOTT) [HOPKINSON], w Mighill, m/3 Richard SWAN 1658; Aug 1650; Rowley

TRUMBLE, John (1639-1691) & Deborah JACKSON; 14 May 1662; Rowley

TRUMBULL, John (1641-1731) & Mary JONES (1636/7-1721); 26 Sep 1665; Charlestown

TRUMBULL, John (1674-) & 1/wf Elizabeth WINCHELL; 3 Sep 1696; Suffield, CT

TRUMBULL, Joseph (1647-1684) & Hannah SMITH (1647-1719?), m/2 John STRONG 1686, m/3 Nicholas BUCKLAND 1698; 6 May 1669; Rowley/Suffield, CT

TRUMBULL, Joseph & Mary [CLOYES] (bpt 1669), dau Peter CLOYES; ca 1692?, b 1697(8?); Framingham

TRUMBULL, Judah (1643-1692) & Mary PRITCHARD, m/2 Vickary/Victory SIKES 1692; 19 Sep 1672; Suffield, CT

TRUMBLE, Judah & 1/wf Elizabeth ACIE/ACY; 11 Nov 1698; Rowley

TRUSLER, Thomas (-1654) & Eleanor (?BATTER) PHELPS (-1655), w Henry; b 1644, b 1654; Salem

TRY, Michael (-1677) & 1/wf _?_ PHILLIPS (-1646), sister of George; Windsor, CT/Fairfield, CT

TRY, Michael (-1677) & 2/wf Margery (_?_) [ROOT], w Richard; by 1653; Fairfield, CT
TRY, Stephen & _?_ (5 Jun 1647); Windsor, CT
TRIANS, Ananias & Abigail NORTON (1642-); 6 Aug 1667; Saybrook, CT/Killingworth, CT
TRYAN, David (ca 1673-1730) & Hannah WADHAMS (1680-); 25 Aug 1698; Wethersfield, CT
TRYHERN, Edward & Sarah _?_ (-1702); ?ca 1684; Stamford, CT
TRYON, Joseph (ca 1671-1738) & Lydia _?_ ; b 1695; Glastonbury, CT
TRYON, William (ca 1645-1711) & 1/wf _?_ ; b 1671; CT
TRYON, William (ca 1645-1711) & 2/wf Saint (ROBINSON) LATIMER (1656-1711), w Bezaleel;
    ca 1688, b 17 Jan 1688/9; ?Guilford, CT
TU, ?John & _?_ [?LEATHERLAND]; b 1692; Boston
TUBBS, Benjamin & Elizabeth KIM, w William; 12 Jan 1698/9; Dover, NH
TUBBS, Joseph & Hannah TREWANT; 4 Apr 1698
TUBBS, Samuel (?1638-1696) & Mary [WILLEY] (1648±-1725+); ca 1668; New London, CT
TUBBS, Samuel (1672-) & Elizabeth [LAY] (1681-); b 1699; Lyme, CT
TUBBS, William[1] (-1688) & 1/wf Mercy SPRAGUE; 9 Nov 1637, div 1668; ?Duxbury
TUBBS, William[1] (-1688) & 2/wf Dorothy [SOANE]/SOAMES, w William; m cont 23 Mar 1671/2;
    ?Duxbury
TUBBS, William[2] (1655-1718) & 1/wf Hannah _?_ ; b 1686; ?Duxbury
TUBBS, William[2] (1655-1718, ae 63) & 2/wf Judith (PRINCE) [BARKER], w Isaac; aft 1693?,
    1691?; Duxbury/Penbroke
TUBBS, ?William (1674-) & Lydia ROACH?; 27 Sep 1698; New London?
TUCK, Edward (-1652) & Mary [PHILBRICK] (-1699), m/2 James WALL; ca 1648; Hampton, NH
TUCK, George (-1751) & Mary [MORRELL]; b 1701; Beverly
TUCK, John & Rachel _?_ ; b 1678; Beverly
TUCK, John (1652-) (cousin of Philip LEWIS) & Bethia HOBBS (1659-); 9 Jan 1677/8; Hampton,
    NH
TUCK, John & Sarah SHAW; 8 Nov 1694; Beverly
TUCK, Joseph (-1718) & Sarah REITH; 27 Oct 1698; Marblehead/Beverly
TUCKE, Robert (-1664) & [Joanna] _?_ (-1674); in Eng, b 1624; Watertown/Salem/Hampton,
    NH
TUCK, Thomas (1611-) & 1/wf _?_ ; b 1643; Salem
TUCK, Thomas & _?_ /[Joan?] [HARRIS] (-living 1679), w George; b 1650; Salem
TUCK, Thomas (-1687) & Elizabeth NICHOLS (-1713); 21 May 1663; Charlestown
TUCK, _?_ & Mary [COLE]; b 1675
TUCKER, Abraham[2] (1653-1725) & 1/wf Mary [SLOCUM] (1660-1689); 30 Oct 1679; Dartmouth
TUCKER, Abraham (1653-1725) & 2/wf Hannah MOTT (1663-1730); 26 Nov 1690, 6? Nov;
    Dartmouth
TUCKER, Andrew (-1691?) & Mary _?_ ; b 1688; Marblehead
TUCKER, Andrew & Elizabeth DIMON/DIAMOND (1672-); 6 Nov 1690; Marblehead
TUCKER, Benjamin (1644/5-1714) & 1/wf Ann [PAYSON] (1651-1689+); ca 1670; Roxbury
TUCKER, Benjamin & 2/wf Elizabeth (WELD) [GORE], w Samuel; aft 4 Jul 1692, b 1696?;
    Roxbury
TUCKER, Benjamin & 1/wf Sarah _?_ ; b 1696; Milton
TUCKER, Benjamin/John (1671-1728) & 2/wf Elizabeth COE? (?1672-); b 1696?, b 1698; Roxbury
TUCKER, Benoni (1662-1735) & Ebenezer NIOLS/NICHOLS (1684-); Jun 168[6], 1685?;
    Salisbury
TUCKER, Edmund & Ruth WILLIAMS; 8 Feb 1688/9; Marblehead
TUCKER, Ephraim (-1736), Milton & Hannah GOULIVER/GULLIVER, Milton; 27 Sep 1688;
    Milton
TUCKER, George & Mary [?BRIMBLECOME]; b 1676; Boston
TUCKER, Henry[1] (-1694) & Martha _?_ (-1697); Feb 1651, 1651/2?, ?9 Jan; ?Sandwich/Dart-
    mouth
TUCKER, Hugh & 1/wf Bridget _?_ ; b 1701?, b 1707/8, by Jul 1698; Kittery, ME
TUCKER, Jabez (1674-) & Rebecca [KNIGHT], m/2 Roger LARKIN; b 1701?; ?Tiverton,
    RI/?Westerly, RI
TUCKER, James (1640-1718) & [Rebecca TOLMAN] (bpt 1647-1688+); b 1673; Milton
TUCKER, James (1667-1749) & [Mary BRANCH]; b 1701?, aft 6 Jul 1699, aft 1 May 1701, int 25
    May 1703; Tiverton, RI
TUCKER, John & 1/wf _?_ (-1644); b 1638, b 1635?; Watertown/Hingham

TUCKER/TOOKER, John & __?__ BEAMONT/DEAMENT, wid; aft 1647?; Salem
TUCKER, John (-1661) & Ann NORTON (-1675), w William; 11 Jun 1649; Hingham
TUCKER/TOOKER?, John? (-1658) & Ann __?__, m/2 Benjamin[2] HORTON 1659; 165-?; Southold, LI (see John TOOKER)
TUCKER, John & Elizabeth HOBART; 12 Mar 1657/8; Boston/Hingham
TUCKER, John & Ursula __?__; b 1669?; Portsmouth, NH
TUCKER, John & Sarah (HARWARD/HARWOOD?) [SCOTTO?], ?w Thomas; b 1670; Boston
TUCKER, John & Keziah [ASTEN] (bpt 1641-); b 1674; Boston
TUCKER, John & Mary RICHARDSON; 11 Jul 1676, in Salem?; Newbury
TUCKER, John & Sarah RIGGS; 9 May 1681; Salem/Falmouth, ME/Gloucester
TUCKER, John (-1681?) & Susanna __?__; b 1686, b 1675?; Tisbury
TUCKER, John (1656-1751) & Ruth WOOLLEY (1664-1759); 25 Apr 1688; Dartmouth/NJ
TUCKER, John & Mary [NORTON], dau William; b 1692; Boston
TUCKER, John (1664-) & 1/wf Tryphena [HAM]; nr 1700; Dover, NH
TUCKER, Joseph & __?__; b 1678; Milton
TUCKER, Joseph (1621/2-1743) & Phebe PAGE (1674-1736); m int 14 Oct 1695; Salisbury
TUCKER, Joseph & Hannah WILKINSON; 6 Dec 1695, 7 Dec 1695; Taunton
TUCKER, Joshua & Hannah CLEVERLY; 2 Nov 1697; Hingham/Boston
TUCKER, Lewis & 1/wf? 2/wf Sarah [GUNNISON] (1637-1666?); b 1680, b 1653?; Casco Bay, ME
TUCKER, Manasseh (1654-1743) & Waitstill SUMNER (1661-1748); 29 Dec 1679; Milton
TUCKER, Morris & 1/wf Elizabeth STEVENS (1639-1662); Oct 1661, 14 Oct 1661; Salisbury
TUCKER, Morris & 2/wf Elizabeth [GILL] (1646-); b 1664; Salisbury
TUCKER, Morris (-1711) & 3/wf Grace (WOOLLEY) LIPPENCOTT, w Jacob; b 1701?; Salisbury
TUCKER, Nicholas (1653-1717) & Jane __?__; b 1690?; Kittery, ME
TUCKER, Nicholas & Priscilla BICKFORD; 30 Oct 1689; Marblehead
TUCKER, Philip & Elizabeth __?__; b 1679, by 1687; Isles of Shoals/ Portsmouth, NH/?Concord, NH
TUCKER, Richard (1594?, ?1608-1678/9) & [Margaret] __?__ (?1612-), sister of Arnold ALLEN's wf; b 1646, no ch (same as below?); Portsmouth, NH/Casco Bay, ME
TUCKER, Richard & Margaret [REYNOLDS]; b 23 May 1661; Salisbury/Casco Bay, ME
TUCKER, Richard & __?__ [?BROAD]; b 1691 Newcastle
TUCKER, Richard & Grace (DIAMOND) [TOMLIN], wid; b 1701?; Kittery
TUCKER, Robert[1] (1662/4-1682) (had bro-in-law Henry ALLEN) & Elizabeth [ALLEN?]; b 1639; Weymouth/Milton/?Gloucester
TUCKER, Robert & __?__; b 1652; Gloucester
TUCKER, Robert & Mehitable [HUNT]; b 1701; Norton
TUCKER, Thomas & Joanna (MANNING) LEE, w Henry; 13 Apr 1696; Marblehead
TUCKER, William (-1666) & Grace __?__, m/2 Hugh ALLARD; b 1648/9; Isles of Shoals
TUCKER, William & Mary OLIVER, w Richard? (Richard OLIVER & Wilmot FRYER); 7 Jul 1684; Marblehead
TUCKER, William & Elizabeth __?__; b 1694; Newton/Boston
TUCKERMAN, Abraham (1670-) & Constance WORSTER, m/2 John NOILES; 15 Jul 1692, no issue; Boston
TUCKERMAN, John[1] (-1712) & Sarah __?__ (-1713); b 1652; Boston
TUCKERMAN, John[2] (1655-1735+) & 1/wf Mary __?__ (ae 28 in 1685); b 1680?; Boston
TUCKERMAN, John[2] (1655-1735+) & 2/wf Susanna CHAMBERLINE/CHAMBERLAIN (?1671-1737+); 14 Nov 1693; Boston
TUCKERMAN, Nathaniel & Martha __?__; b 1684; Ipswich/Portsmouth, NH
TUCKERMAN, Otho (-1664) & Emma __?__; b 1660; Portsmouth, NH
TUDOR, John & Elizabeth __?__; b 1673; Boston
TUDOR, Owen (-1690) & Mary (LOOMIS) SKINNER (-1680), w John; 13 Nov 1651; Windsor, CT
TUDOR, Samuel (1652-1727) & Abigail (FILLEY) BISSELL (1658-1707), w John; ?30 Oct 1685, 20 Oct 1685; Windsor, CT
TUFTON, Robert[2] (afterward MASON) (-1696) & ?Catherine WIGGIN?; b 1699; NH
TUFTS, James (?1674-1733) & Hannah WOODIN (1669-1748); 1 Jul 1696; Beverly/Medford/Wells, ME
TUFTS, John (1665-1728) & Mary [PUTNAM] (1668-1758); b 1688; Charlestown/Malden
TUFTS, Jonathan (1660-1722) & Rebecca WAITE (1662-1756); 31 Mar 1681; Malden/Medford

TUFTS, Peter (1617-1700) (called bro. by William BRIDGES) & Mary [PIERCE] (1628-1703); b 1648; Charlestown/Malden

TUFTS, Peter (?1649-1721) & 1/wf Elizabeth LYNDE (1650-1684); 26 Aug 1670; Charlestown/ Medford

TUFTS, Peter (-1721) & Mary/Mercy COTTON (1666-1715); 16 Dec 1684, 11 Dec; Medford

TULLER, John & Elizabeth (CASE) [LEWIS] (1658-1718), [w Joseph]; ?1684, b 1685; Simsbury, CT

TULLY, John (-d in Eng), Horley, Surrey, & Sarah [FENNER] (1615-1676), m/2 Robert LAY 1647; 17 Oct 1637, b 1638; Saybrook, CT

TULLY, John (1638-1701) & Mary BEAMONT; 3 Jan 1671, 1671/2; Saybrook, CT

TULLY, John (1672-) & Elizabeth ELDRIDG/ELDREDGE; 20 Jan 1696; Boston

TULLEY, Samuel & Hannah _?_ ; b 1693(4?); Boston

TUPPER, Eldad & Martha WHEATON; 30 Dec 1700/01

TUPPER, Israel (1666-1730+) & 1/wf Elizabeth [GIFFORD] (1665-1701); b 1692; Sandwich

TUPPER, Robert[1] (ret'd to Eng) & Deborah PERRY?; 9 May 1654; Sandwich?

TUPPER, Thomas (1578-1676) & Ann _?_ (1587-1676); ca 1620; Lynn/Sandwich

TUPPER, Thomas[1] & 1/wf Katharine GATOR; Chelmsford, Eng, 29 Apr 1622

TUPPER, Thomas[1] & Susan TURNER? (-1634), wid; 25 Jan 1628; Topsfield, MA?

TUPPER, Thomas[1] & Ann HODGSON ?; 21 Dec 1634; Ipswich?

TUPPER, Thomas (1638/9-1706) & Martha MAYHEW (?1642-1717); 27 Dec 1661; Sandwich

TUPPER, Thomas (1664-1706+) & Mary _?_ ; b 1688(9?); Sandwich/Stoughton

TURBEFEILD, Henry & Mary [PRIEST]; b 1673; Weymouth

TURBERFIELD/TRUBERFEELD, James & Mercy CAMPBELL/CAMPBALL; 6 Dec 1699; Braintree/Boston

TURBET/TURBAT, John (?1651-) & Mary [KENDALL/YOUNG], m/2 Emanuel DAVIS; ?ca 1674; Arundel, ME

TURBET, John (-1704) & Abigail CASE/(CASS); 17 Nov 1698, no issue; Dedham

TURBET, Nicholas & Elizabeth (SPENCER) [CHICK]; by 1693; Berwick, ME

TURBET, Peter (-1670) & Sarah [SANDERS], m/2 Daniel GOODWIN; ca 1648/50?; Cape Porpoise

TURFS/TUFTS?, James (not FROST) & Hannah [WOODIN]; b 1697, ?1 Jul 1696, Wells, ME; Beverly/Medford (see James TUFTS)

TURHAND/TIRHAND, Thomas & Mary (MANSFIELD) [WISE] (1658-), w Henry, m/3 John HILL Aug 1703; ca 1686

TOURNEUR/TURNER?, Daniel & Ann WOODHULL (1659-); m lic 5 Feb 1683; Harlem (NY City)

TURNER, Amos (-1739, ae 68) & Mary HILAND (-1722); 6 Apr 1695; Scituate

TURNER, Benjamin & Elizabeth HAWKINS; 14 Apr 1692; Scituate

TURNER, Charles & Rachel _?_ ; b 1643; Salem

TURNER, Charles & Mercy CURTIS; 25 Dec 1700; Scituate

TURNER, Daniel & Hannah RANDALL; 20 Jun 1665; Scituate

TURNER, Daniel (-1705) & Margaret _?_ ; b 1698; Westchester, NY

TURNER, David (1670-1698?) & Elizabeth [STOCKBRIDGE] (1670-); b 1693; Plymouth

TURNER, Edward (-1717, ae 84) & Mary SANFORD; 25 Oct 1656; Boston/Milford, CT/Middletown, CT

TURNER, Edward (1664-1717) & Sarah (HALL) BLAKE (-1726), w John; b 1694; Milford, CT/Middletown, CT

TURNER, Eliab & Elnathan HINKSMAN; 22 Nov 1694; Scituate

TURNER, Elisha & Elizabeth JACOB; 6 Jun 1687; Scituate/Hingham

TURNER, Ephraim (1639-) & Sarah [PHILLIPS] (-1673+); b 1663; Boston

TURNER, Ephraim (-1705) & Mary NICOLS/NICHOLS; 2 May 1700; Hartford

TURNER, Ezekiel (-1704) & Susanna KEENEY (1662-1748), m/2 Joseph MINER; 26 Dec 1678; New London, CT

TURNER, George (-1695) (had "brother" John ROBBINS 1668) & Mary [ROBBINS]; b 1660?, b 1663; Bridgewater

TURNER, Habakkuk (-1685) & Mary GARDNER, m/2 John MARSTON 1686; 30 Apr 1670; Salem

TURNER, Humphrey[1] (?1593-1673) & Lydia [GAMER?]; ca 1622; Scituate

TURNER, Humphrey & Mary [HALL]?; b 1694; Plymouth

TURNER, Increase (1642-) & Mehitable HETT (1648-), m/2 Thomas SKELTON 1694; 3 Oct 1673; Charlestown

TURNER, Isaac (-1699) & Mary TODD (-1676); 19 Aug 1668; New Haven

TURNER, Isaac & Rebecca [CRAFTS], m/2 John ROCKWOOD; 1682; Medfield

TURNER, Isaac (1669-) & Abigail __?__; b 1701; New Haven

TURNER, Israel (1654-1689) & Sarah [STOCKBRIDGE] (1665-); b 1689; Scituate

TURNER, Jacob (1667-1723) & Jane [VINING] (1672-), m/2 Samuel ALLEN 1728; b 1693; Weymouth

TURNER, James & 1/wf Mehitable [CHENEY] (-1690); b 1689; Charlestown

TURNER, James (-1704) & Hannah [LAZELL], m/2 William JOHNSON; b 1692; Charlestown

TURNER, Japhet (1650-1690) & Hannah [HUDSON], dau John; b 1673; Duxbury

TURNER, Jeffrey (-1654) & Isabella [GILL] (-1660); b 1640; Dorchester

TURNER, John (-1621) & __?__; b 1615?; Plymouth

TURNER, John & 1/wf __?__; b 1620; Lynn/Taunton

TURNER, John & Mary BREWSTER; ca 1645/50, 10 Nov 1645, 12 Nov 1645; Plymouth

TURNER, John & Elizabeth [?MARSH] (-1647); b 1647; Roxbury

TURNER, John (-1705) & 2/wf Deborah [WILLIAMS] (-1675); b 1649; ?Roxbury/Medfield/Deerfield

TURNER, John (ca 1627-1687) & Ann JAMES; 25 Apr 1649; Scituate

TURNER, John & 2/wf 3/wf Jane [GODFREY], wid; aft 1654; Taunton

TURNER, John & Joanna [BOWMAN] (1642-1669+); b 1666; Boston/Cambridge

TURNER, John (-1680) & Elizabeth ROBERTS, m/2 Charles REDFORD 1684; 21 Dec 166[7?]; Salem

TURNER, John & Lucy [GARDNER] (1654-), m/2 George MONK; b 1673; Boston

TURNER, John (-1710) & Sarah ADAMS (1660-); 10 Jan 1677/8; Medfield

TURNER, John & Sarah __?__; 1680, b 1680, b 1678; Westchester, NY

TURNER, John (-1728) (see James TURNER) & Hannah [LASELL?] (1662-1728); b 1686; Bridgewater

TURNER, John & Joanna BENTON (1660-1692); 16 Dec 1686; CT

TURNER, John (1654?-1706) & Abigail [PEARSHALL] (1664-); b 1690; Scituate/Boston

TURNER, John (-1696) & Elizabeth BARBER, Killingworth; in Jun 1694; Guilford, CT

TURNER, John (prob was Richard) & Susanna KENNET; 14 Feb 1693, 1693/4; Boston

TURNER, John & Elizabeth (GRANT) LANDERS, w James, m/2 William HEARD; 28 Nov 1694; Berwick, ME

TURNER, John (1669-) & Susanna [MERRILL] (1677-); b 1 Jan 1698/9, ca 1695; Milford, CT

TURNER, Jonathan (1646-) & 1/wf Martha BISBEE (-1687); b 1677, ca 1678?; Scituate

TURNER, Jonathan (1646-) & 2/wf Mercy [HATCH] (1665-); aft 24 Mar 1687, ca 1690; Scituate

TURNER, Joseph (1649-1724) & Bathsheba (HOBART) LEAVITT (1640-1724), w John; 19 Nov 1674; Hingham

TURNER, Josiah, Scituate & Hannah HOLEBROOK (1679-), Scituate); 24 Jan 1700, prob 1699/1700; Scituate

TURNER, Lawrence & 1/wf Sarah __?__; b 1650; Exeter/Newport, RI/Greenwich, RI

TURNER, Lawrence (1620-1668, Westchester Co.) & 2/wf? Martha __?__, m/2 Edward HUBBARD; Westchester Co., NY

TURNER, Lawrence & Mary Martha __?__, m/2 Edward HUBBARD 1676; ca 1690/1700?

TURNER, Michael & __?__; b 1637?, b 1643?; Lynn/Sandwich

TURNER, Nathan (-1693) & Osiah/Osia/[Ozia WANG] (-1696+); b 1680; Scituate/Litchfield

TURNER, Nathaniel (-1646, at sea) & [Elizabeth?] __?__, m/2 Samuel VanGOODENHOUSEN/ GOODENHOUSE?; ca 1630/2?; Lynn/New Haven

TURNER, Nathaniel (-1715) & 1/wf Mehitable RIGBEE/RUGBY/BUGBEE? (1643-1680); 29 Mar 1664, 1664/5; Scituate/Dorchester

TURNER, Nathaniel & 2/wf Abigail JAMES STOCKBRIDGE (-1710), w Charles; bef 31 Mar 1691; Scituate

TURNER, Philip (1673-) & Elizabeth [NASH]; b 1701; Scituate

TURNER, Peregrin & Naomi [WINTERS]?, dau Christopher; b 5 May 1678; Westchester, NY

TURNER, Praisever (-1675) & Elizabeth COOLY/COPLEY?, m/2 Samuel LANGTON 1676, m/3 David ALEXANDER; 26 Jan 1664; Northampton

TURNER, Ralph & __?__; b 1693; Falmouth, ME

TURNER, Robert (-1664) & Penelope __?__ (-1674+); b 1639; Boston

TURNER, Robert (1611-1651) (see John TURNER, Roxbury) & Elizabeth [FREESTONE] (1619-1662+); b 1644, b 1643, b 1647, b 9 Mar; Boston

TURNER, Samuel (-1759, ae 89), Scituate & Desire BARKER/BAKER, Scituate; 20 Nov 1700; Scituate

TURNER, Thomas[2] (-1688) & Sarah HYLAND/HILAND; 6 Jan 1652, 6 Jan 1651; Scituate

TURNER, Thomas & Mary (?) (BEEDLE) BATCHELDER, div wf of Rev. Stephen; Scituate

TURNER, Thomas (-aft 26 Feb 1727/8), tailor & [Lydia] _?_ (-1708+); b 1682; Scituate/Swansea

TURNER, Thomas & Hannah JENKENS; 9 Feb 1693, prob 1692/3, 1695 prob wrong; Scituate

TURNER, Capt. William (-1676) & 1/wf Frances _?_ (-bef 1 Apr 1671); b 1644; Dorchester/Boston

TURNER, Capt. William (-1676) & 2/wf Mary [PRATT], wid; b 1 Apr 1671; Boston

TURNER, Capt. William (-1676) & 3/wf Mary [ALSOP], w Key; 16 Feb 1675/6; Boston

TURNER, William & 1/wf Ruth _?_ ; b 1679; Boston

TURNER, William & 2/wf Hannah JACKLIN; 28 Aug 1689; Boston

TURNER, Lawrence? & Susanna WINDSOR

TURNER, _?_ & Prudence [BALSTON] (1655-), m/2 John MARION 1700; Boston

TURNER?/URNAR?, _?_ & _?_ ; 19 Feb 1691; Yarmouth

TURNER, _?_ & Elizabeth _?_ , wid in 1636, had land in Salem, a wit 23 Nov 1635; Salem

TURNEY, Benjamin (-1648) & Mary ODELL (1604-), m/2 Joseph MIDDLEBROOK; Salford, Bedfordshire, 12 Jul 1630, b 1631; Concord/Fairfield, CT

TURNEY, Benjamin (1645-1694) & Rebecca KEELER, m/2 John HULL 1699; 16 Nov 1671; Fairfield, CT

TURNEY, Joseph & 1/wf _?_ ; b 1680?; Stamford, CT

TURNEY, Joseph & Mary (BELL) HOYT (1646-1724), w Joshua; m cont 23 Mar 1691; Stamford, CT

TURNEY, Robert (1633-1690+) & Elizabeth [HOLLY] (-1690+), dau John; b 1661; Stamford, CT

TURPIN, Thomas & Jane _?_ , m/2 Thomas FURSON; b 1636?; Kittery, ME/Portsmouth, NH?

TURPIN, William (-1709) & 1/wf Elizabeth [HOARE] (1660-bef 1692); b 1690; Tiverton?/Providence

TURPIN, William (-1709) & 2/wf Ann _?_ (-1746+); Providence

TURELL, Daniel (-1693) & 1/wf Lydia [BLOTT] (-1659); b 1646; Boston

TURELL, Daniel (-1693) & 2/wf Mary (COLBRON) BARRELL (-1697/8), w John; 10 Nov 1659, ?at Roxbury; Boston

TURELL, Daniel (1646-1699) & Anna [?BARRELL] (1651-); b 1672; Boston

TURELL, Joseph & Sarah [SUMNER] (1662-), m/2 Joseph WEEKS; b 1679; Boston

TURELL, Samuel (1659-1738) & Lydia [STODDARD] (1660-); b 1687; Boston

TURRIL/TURVIL?, Thomas & Judith _?_ ; b 1677, no issue; Newbury

TUTTLE, Caleb & Mary HOTCHKISS (1680-); 1 Mar 1699, 1698/9; New Haven

TUTTLE, Daniel (1664-1700) & Hannah [SANFORD] (1670-); b 1694; Milford, CT

TUTTLE, David & Mary REED; 24 Nov 1698; Norwalk, CT

TUTTLE, Edward & Abigail [?BAKER]; b 1677/(8?); Boston

TUTHILL, Henry (1612-1644/50) & [Bridget] _?_ , m/2 William WELLS; b 1637, b 1635?; Hingham/Southold, LI

TUTHILL, Henry (1665-1750) & Bethiah [HORTON]; b 1690; Southold, LI

TUTTLE, John (1596-1656, Ireland) & Joan (ANTROBUS) LAWRENCE (1596-1656+, 1661/1674), w Thomas; ca 1627; Ipswich

TUTTLE, John (1618-1663) & Dorothy _?_ ; ca 1642?; Dover, NH

TUTTLE, John (?1625-1687) & Mary HOLYOKE (ca 1624-); 10 Feb 1646, 1646/7; Boston/?Lynn

TUTTLE, John (1631-1683) & Katharine LANE; 8 Nov 1653; New Haven

TUTHILL, John (1635-1717) & Deliverance KING (1641-25 Jan 1688/90 [sic]); 17 Feb 1657, 1657/8; Southold, LI

TUTHILL, John & Mary [LEIGH] (1638-1705); b 1660; Boston

TUTTLE, John (1646-1720) & [?Mary] _?_ (left wid Mary); ca 1668; Dover, NH

TUTHILL, John (1658-1754) & Mehitable [WELLS] (1666-1742); by 1685; Southold, LI

TUTTLE, John & Martha _?_ ; b 1685/6?; Boston

TUTHILL, John & Mary [BROWNE]; b 11 Feb 1686; Southold, LI

TUTTLE, John (1669-) & Mary BURROUGHS (1672-); 29 May 1689, at New London; New Haven/Lebanon, CT

TUTTELL, John (1666-1716) & Martha WARD (1672-1723), m/2 George HART 1722; 3 Dec 1689; Ipswich

TUTHILL, John (1635-1717) & 2/wf Sarah (WINES) YOUNGS (-1727), w John; 28 May 1690; Southold, LI

TUTTLE, John (1671-1712) & Judith [OTIS] (1667-); b 1698; Dover, NH

TUTTLE, Jonathan (1637-1705) & Rebecca [BELL] (1643-1676); b 1664?, b 1669; New Haven

TUTTLE, Jonathan & Anne SMITH? (-1714+); 10 May 1692; Chelsea

TUTTLE, Joseph (1640-1690) & Hannah MUNSON (1648-1695), m/2 Nathan BRADLEY 1694; 2 May 1667; New Haven

TUTTLE, Joseph (1668-) & Elizabeth SANFORD (1671-); 10 Nov 1691, 20 Nov, at Milford; New Haven

TUTTLE, Nathaniel (1653-1721) & Sarah HOW (1654-1783); 10 Aug 1682; New Haven/Woodbury, CT

TUTTLE, Nathaniel (1675/6-) & Esther [DOOLITTLE] (1683-1756); ca 1700; New Haven

TUTTLE, Richard (1593-1640) & Anne TAYLOR (1591-), m/2 Edward HOLYOKE bef 1648; 19 Jun 1622, in Eng; Boston

TUTTLE, Samuel (1659-1733) & 1/wf Sarah NEWMAN (1665-); Jun 1684; New Haven

TUTTLE, Samuel (-1709) & Sarah HART, Farmington, CT; 11 Dec 1695; New Haven

TUTTLE, Simon (1631-1692) & 1/wf Joan _?_; ca 1660?/2, 1659 (no); Ipswich

TUTTLE, Simon (1631-1692) (ae 44 in 1676) & 1/wf Sarah [COGSWELL] (1645-1732); b 1664; Ipswich

TUTTLE, Simon (1647-1719) & Abigail _?_; b 1680; New Haven/Wallingford, CT

TUTTLE, Simon (1667-1747) & Mary ROGERS (1672-1736); 16 Jan 16[95/6], 1697; Ipswich

TUTTLE, Simon (1671-1725) & Elizabeth [ABERNATHY] (1673-); b 1698; North Haven, CT

TUTTLE, Thomas (1634, 1635?-1710) & Hannah POWELL (1641-1710); 21 May 1661; New Haven

TUTTLE, Thomas (1667-1703) & Mary SANFORD (1668-), m/2 Daniel JOHNSON 1707; 28 Jun 1692; New Haven

TUTTLE, William (1609-1673) & Elizabeth _?_ (1612-1684); in Eng, b 1631; Boston/New Haven

TUTTLE, William (1673-) & Mary [ABERNATHY] (1679-); b 1698; New Haven

TUTTLE, _?_ & Isabel _?_ (1565-), ?mo of Richard; b 1593

TEWELL, Richard & Margaret _?_; b 1695(6?); Boston

TWELLS, Robert (-1691, ae 80, 1697, ae 77?) & Martha BRACKETT; 23 Nov 1655, 22 Nov 1655; Braintree/Boston

TUELL, Samuel, Scituate & Mehitable JAMES, Scituate; 24 Oct 1700; Scituate

TWINNING, Stephen (1659, 1659/[60]-1720) & Abigail YOUNG (1660-1715); 3 Jan 1683, 1682, 1682/3?; Eastham/Newtown, PA

TWINING, William[1] (-1659) & 1/wf Ann _?_; b 1625; Yarmouth/Eastham

TWINING, William[1] (-1659) & 2/wf Ann/Anna [DOANE]? (-1680/1); (doubtful); Eastham

TWINING, William[2] (-1703) & Elizabeth [DEAN] ca 1650/4; Eastham/Newtown, PA

TWINING, William, Jr. (-1735) & Ruth COLE (1668-1735+); 21 Mar 1688/9; Eastham

TWISDELL, James & Mary _?_ (Sarah 1682); b 1680; Boston

TWISDEN, Christopher (see Thomas TWISDEN) & Sarah _?_; b 1699; Marblehead (?had Christopher 29 Sep 1699)

TWISDEN, John (1592-1660) (?cousin of James CUSHMAN) & Susanna STUPPELL; in Eng, 8 May 1620; Scituate/York, ME

TWISDEN, Peter (1624-) & Mary [ALCOCK] (-1698?); Kittery, ME

TWISDEN, Thomas (see Christopher TWISDEN) & Sarah REED, wid; 13 Jun 1699; Marblehead

TWIST/TWISS, Peter (-aft 1734) & Anna KELLUM/CALLUM? (1659-aft 6 Apr 1634); 26 Oct 1680; Marblehead/Salem

TWIST, Peter (1681-) & Sarah NURSE (1680-1737); 20 Dec 1699; Salem

TWITCHELL, Benjamin (-1680) & Mary [RIGGS]; b 1640?, ca 1649/51; Dorchester/Medfield

TWITCHELL, Benjamin & Mary WHITE; 5 Apr 1683, (1685 wrong); Medfield/Sherborn/Charlestown

TWITCHELL, John & Sarah PIERSO. (26 Jan 1698/9, 21 Jan; Derby, CT

TWITCHELL, Joseph (1582-1657) & Elizabeth [LOVETT]; Dorchester

TWITCHELL, Joseph (-1710) & Lydia [JOHNSON?] (-1725); b 1678; Sherborn

TWOMBLY, John & 1/wf Mary KENNEY/CANNEY; 16 Apr 1687, 18 Apr; Dover, NH

TROMBLY, John & 2/wf Rachel ALLEN; 3 Oct 1692; Dover, NH

TROMBLEY, Joseph (1661-) & Jane _?_; b 1701?, no ch

TWOMBLY, Ralph (-1686) & Elizabeth __?__; b 1661, by 1660; Dover, NH

TWOMBLY, Ralph (-1700) & __?__; b 1700, no issue

TIDY/TYDEY, Robert & Sarah [LIBBY] (1653-), m/2 Richard ROGERS, m/3 Christopher BANFIELD; b 1692; Kittery, ME/Scarborough, ME

TYER/PEIRE, William (-Jan 1666/7) & Sarah KEIN/KIND, dau Arthur KIND, m/2 Robert BRICKENDON b 1669, m/3 William ROUSE b 1676; 13 Jul 1666; Charlestown

TYLER, Abraham (-1673) & Hannah VARNUM/FARNUM/FARNUN, m/2 Edward BRUMIDGE; 26 Dec 1650; Haverhill

TYLER, Charles (-1738) & Rebecca (POTTER) [FRISBIE] (1663-), w Samuel; Branford, CT

TYLER, Daniel & Ann/Anne? GEER (1679-); 28 May 1700; ?Preston, CT

TILER, Ebenezer & Elizabeth [WALKER] (1668-1745); b 1694; Boxford

TYLER, Francis (-1712) & 1/wf __?__; b 1681; Branford, CT

TYLER, Francis (-1712) & Sarah [PAGE] (1666-); Branford, CT

TYLER, George & 1/wf Hannah [LUDDINGTON]; b 1680, b 1679(80); Branford, CT

TYLER, George (-1731) & 2/wf Mary __?__; b 1694; Branford, CT

TYLER, Hopestill (1646-1734) & Mary LOVETT (1653-1732); 20 Jan 1668; Mendon/Roxbury/Preston, CT

TYLER, James & Phebe [ROYALL]; b 1701?; Casco Bay, ME/Arundel, ME/Scarboro, ME

TYLER, Job (1619-1700) & Mary [HORTON]? (1620?-) [wid]?; ca 1640; Andover/Mendon/etc.

TYLER, Job (1675-) & Margaret [BRADSTREET] (1680-); b 1701; Boxford

TYLER, John (-1700) & Sarah [HAVENS] (-1718+); b 1662; Portsmouth, RI

TYLER, John & Ann __?__ (-30 Apr 1694, ae 40); ca 1674/80?; Boston

TYLER, John (-1742) & Hannah PARKER; 14 Sep 1682; Andover/Mendon

TYLER, John & 1/wf Sarah __?__; ca 1688/92?; Charlestown

TYLER, John (ca 1667-1741) & Abigail HALL (1674-1741); 14 Jan 1694; Wallingford, CT

TYLER, John & 2/wf Joanna __?__; b 1695?, aft 1700?; Charlestown

TYLER, John & Anna MESSENGER (?1677-1745); m int 14 Nov 1695; Boston/?Charlestown/Boxford

TYLER, John & Deborah LEATHERLAND (1678-); 2 Nov 1699; Boston

TYLER, John (1674-) & Hannah STENT; ca 1700

TYLER, Joseph (1671-1699) & Martha __?__ (-1745, ae 71); ?Salem

TYLER, Lazarus & __?__; b 1698; ?Preston, CT

TYLER, Moses & 1/wf Prudence BLAKE (-1689); 6 Jul 1666; Andover/Rowley/Boxford

TYLER, Moses (1641/2-1727) & 2/wf Sarah (HASEY) [SPRAGUE] (1647-1718), w Phineas; b 1693, 1691?; Boxford

TILER, Moses & Ruth PERLEY; 3 Jan 1693/4; Topsfield

TYLER, Nathaniel (-1652) & Jane __?__; b 1652; Lynn

TYLER, Peter (-1712) & 1/wf Deborah SWAYNE (1654-1684+); 20 Nov 1671; Branford, CT

TYLER, Peter (-1712) & 2/wf Hannah WHITEHEAD; 25 Dec 1688; Branford, CT

TYLER, Peter (1673-) & Elizabeth [STENT] (1676-); b 1701; Bramford, CT

TYLER, Roger (-1674, 1673?) & Ann __?__; New Haven

TYLER, Roger & Sarah (TUTTLE) HUMISTON, w John (see HUMBERTSON); 10 Jan 1698/9, 1698; Wallingford, CT

TYLER, Samuel (1655-1695) (bro. of Hopestill) & Hannah __?__; b 1687(8?), b 1685; Mendon

TYLER, Thomas (-1704, 1722) & Miriam [SIMPKINS] (1662-); b 1685; Boston/Weymouth/?Derby, CT

TYLER, William (-1693) & Abigail [TERRILL] (1644-); b 1660; Milford, CT

TYLER, William (1665-) & Mary LOTHROP; 3 Jun 1692; Derby, CT

TYLER, __?__/Roger[1] & Joan __?__, ?m/2 Nathaniel DICKINSON; b 1619; Providence

TYLER, __?__ & Sarah WINSOR, dau Joshua; ca 1670/85?

TYLER, __?__ & __?__ LEWIS, dau John

TYLEY/TELY, Samuel & Sarah __?__; b 1689, b 1687; Boston

TILEE, Thomas & Hannah __?__; b 1657; Boston

TYLLY, William & Isabella __?__; b 1691; Boston

TING, Edward (1610-1681, ae 81) & Mary [SEARS?]; b 1640; Boston/Dunstable

TYNG, Edward (1649-ca 1700) & Elizabeth [CLARKE] (-1690); ca 1680, by 1682; Falmouth, ME

TINGE, Jonathan (1642-1724) & 1/wf Sarah [USHER] (1650-); b 1669; Boston/Dunstable/Woburn

TING, William (1602, 1602/3?-1653) & 1/wf [Ann BROWN]/Ann DERSLEY; in Eng, b Jun 1634; Boston/Braintree

TING, William (-1653) & 2/wf Elizabeth COTYMORE/COYTMORE; b 1638; Boston/Braintree
TING, William (-1653) & 3/wf Jane [HUNT?] (-3 Oct 1652, in Eng), w Richard; b 1652, b 10 Feb 1648/9, aft 30 Jan 1643/4, 10 Jan 1648/9; Boston
TYNG, William & Lucy CLARK (1679-); 19 Sep 1700; Chelmsford

UDALL, Philip & _?_ ; ?b 1650; Flusing, LI
UDALL, Philip & Mary BAILEY (1653-); 16? Dec 1681; b ca 1675?, b 1675?; Huntington, LI
UFFORD, John (OFFIT in early records) (?1626-1692) & 1/wf Hannah/Anna? [HAWLEY], m/2 John BEARD 1654?; ca 1654?, div; Milford, CT
UFFORD, John & 2/wf Martha [NETTLETON]; ca Jun 1659; Milford, CT
UFFORD, John (1667-1712) & Abigail [?MERWIN]/[SHORE]; b 1701?; Milford, CT
UFFORD, Samuel (1670-1746) & Elizabeth CURTISS; 5 Dec 1694; Stratford, CT
OFFITT/UFFORD, Thomas[1] (-1660) & 1/wf Isabel _?_ ; in Eng, b 1621; Roxbury/Springfield/ Stratford, CT/Milford, CT
UFFORD, Thomas[2] (-1683) & Frances [KILBORNE] (1621-1683); ca 1640/5?, no issue; Stratford, CT
UFFORD, Thomas[1] (-1660) & 2/wf Elizabeth (_?_) THEALE (-1660), w Nicholas; ca 1658?, ca 1659; Stamford, CT
HUMPHREVILLE/HUMPHREYVILLE/UMPHERVILE, John & _?_ ; b 1666; West Haven, CT
UMPRAVILLE, John & Alice _?_ ; b 1673(4?); Charlestown
UMBERFIELD, Samuel (-1748) & 1/wf Sarah [GRAY]; b 1695; New Haven
UNDERHILL, David (1672-1708) & 1/wf _?_ [WRIGHT?]; LI
UNDERHILL, David & 2/wf? Hannah [FORMAN]; LI
UNDERHILL, Giles & _?_ ; b 1668; NH
UNDERHILL, Humphrey (-1722) & [Sarah SMITH], Jamaica, LI, wid; b 1678, ca 1665/70?; LI/Rye, NY
UNDERHILL, John[1] (-7 Sep 1672) & 1/wf Helena deHOOCH; The Hague, 12 Dec 1628; Boston/Oyster Bay, LI/etc.
UNDERHILL, John[1] (-1672) & 2/wf Elizabeth FEAKE; ca 1658
UNDERHILL, John (1642-1692/3) & Mary PRIOR (1637-9/29? Jul 1698); 11 Oct 1668; ?Oyster Bay, LI
UNDERHILL, John (1670-) & Elizabeth [WILLETTS] (1674-), Jericho, LI; ca 1695; ?Matinecock, LI
UNDERHILL, Nathaniel (1663-1710) & Mary FERRIS?; 10 Dec 1685; ?Westchester, NY
UNDERHILL, Samuel (1675-) & Hannah WILLETS (-1753), Jericho, LI; 28 Feb 1700, 1699/1700; Oyster Bay, LI
UNDERWOOD, Henry & Jane _?_ ; b 1667; Newport/Jamestown, RI
UNDERWOOD, James (1611-) & _?_ ; b 1652; Salem
UNDERWOOD, John (-1706, ae 59) & Elizabeth _?_ ; b 1680; Boston
UNDERWOOD, John & Sarah [PECKHAM]; b 1699; Jamestown, RI
UNDERWOOD, Joseph (1614-1676/7) & 1/wf Mary [WILDER] (-1658/9); b 1645, ca 1638?; Hingham/Watertown
UNDERWOOD, Joseph (1614-1676/7) & 2/wf Mary HOW (-1668); 26 Apr 1665; Dorchester
UNDERWOOD, Joseph (1649-1691) & Elizabeth _?_ , ?m/2 William BULL 1693; b 1673; Reading/Watertown
UNDERWOOD, Martin (1596-1675) & Martha [FISK] (1602-1684); ca 1625/35?, no issue, b 11 May 1629?; Watertown
UNDERWOOD, Samuel (1656-1735) & Sarah _?_ (-1734); b 1693, b 1681?; Litchfield, NH
UNDERWOOD, Thomas (-1680) & 1/wf _?_ [TILSON]; in Eng?, b 1645; Hingham
UNDERWOOD, Thomas (-1668) & Magdalen _?_ (1607-1687), m/2 Thomas UNDERWOOD 1669 (she called Mehitable (DEMICK) CHILD, a "kinswoman"); no issue; Hingham/Watertown
UNDERWOOD, Thomas (-1680) & 2/wf Magdalen UNDERWOOD (1607-1687), wid; 7 Sep 1669; Watertown

UNDERWOOD, Thomas (1658-1691) & Mary PALMER; 19 Nov 1679; Watertown
UNDERWOOD, Thomas (1655-1743) & Mary _?_ (-1742); ca 1680-90?; Lincoln/Lexington
UNDERWOOD, William (-1697) & 1/wf Sarah [PELLET]? (-1684); b 1640; Concord/Chelmsford
UNDERWOOD, William (-1697) & 2/wf Ann/?Anna KIDDER, Billerica; 17 Mar 1684/5; Billerica/Chelmsford
UNDERWOOD, William & Sarah _?_ ; b 1694; Jamestown, RI/Newport
UNDERWOOD, _?_ & Elizabeth HERRICK (1647-), m/2 Arthur CROUCH 1682
UNTHANK, Christopher (-1680+) & Susanna _?_ (-1680+); b 1648; Providence/Warwick, RI
UPDIKE, James & Elizabeth _?_ ; b 1693; Boston
UPDIKE, Lodowick (1646-1736±) & Abigail [NEWTON]/SMITH (1654-1736, 1745); Fairfield
UPDIKE, Gilbert & Katharine SMITH; 24 Sep 1643; Kingston, RI/etc.
UPHAM, John (-1681/2, ae 84) & 1/wf Elizabeth SLADE (1608-1670); Bicton, Devonshire, 1 Nov 1626; Weymouth/Malden
UPHAM, John (-1681/2, ae 84) & 2/wf Catherine (RICHARDS) HOLLARD, w Angel; m cont 14 Aug 1671; Malden/Charlestown
UPHAM, John (1666-1733) & 1/wf Abigail HOWARD/HAYWARD (1662-1717); 31 Oct 1688; Malden/Charlestown
UPHAM, Nathaniel (-1662) & Elizabeth STEDMAN, m/2 Henry THOMPSON 1669, m/3 John SHARPE; 5 Mar 1661/2; Cambridge
UPHAM, Nathaniel (1661-1717) & Sarah [FLOYD] (1662-1713); ca 1684; Malden/Charlestown
UPHAM, Phinehas/Phineas (-1676) & Ruth WOOD (?1636-1697, Malden); 14 Apr 1658; Malden/Charlestown
UPHAM, Phinehas/Phineas (1659-1720/1) & Mary [MELLENS] (1664±-); b 1682; Charlestown
UPHAM, Richard & Abigail HOVEY; 19 May 1698; Topsfield/Malden/Charlestown
UPHAM, Thomas (1668-1758) & 1/wf Elizabeth HOVEY (-1704); 21 Apr 1693; Topsfield/Charlestown
UPHAM, _?_ & _?_ BRACKETT, dau Peter; b Feb 1666
UPSAL/UPSALL, Nicholas (-1666, ca 70) & Dorothy [CAPIN] (1606-1675, ca 75, Boston); Dorchester, Eng, 17 Jan 1629/[30]; Dorchester
UPSHALL, William & _?_ ; b 1651; Boston
UPSON, Stephen & Mary LEE (1664-), Farmington; 28 Dec 1682, 29? Dec; Waterbury, CT
UPSON, Thomas (-1655) & Elizabeth FULLER, m/2 Edmund SCOTT; 23 Jan 1646; Hartford/Farmington
UPSON, _?_/?Stephen & Elizabeth _?_ (-1688), m/2 Hugh GRIFFIN ca 1639, m/3 Philemon WHALE 1657; b 1638?; Sudbury
UPTON, Ezekiel (1668-), Redding & 1/wf Rebecca PRESTON (1670-), Salem Village; 28 Dec 1693; Reading
UPTON, John (-1699) & Eleanor [?STEWART]?; b 1650; Salem/Reading
UPTON, John & Sarah TOMSON/THOMPSON (-1719); 14 Dec 1680, 19? Dec; Reading
UPTON, Joseph & Abigail [PHELPS]; 12 Feb 1691, 1691/2; Reading
URIN, Edward (-1676) & Jane _?_ ; b 6 Nov 1668; Boston/Star Isl.
URINE, Francis (-1713) & Alice _?_ ; b 1681; Ipswich
URANN, John (ca 1663-) & 1/wf? Abigail [WESTBROOK]; ?Portsmouth, NH
VRIN, John & 2/wf Rebecca CATE (-1745); 12 Nov 1686
URIN, William (-1664) & Eleanor _?_ , m/2 Richard WELCOM; by 1650?; Star Isl./Portsmouth, NH
URQUHART/URQUAHART/URQUEHART, John (-1716) & _?_ ; b 1695; Oyster Bay, LI/NJ
URQUHART, William (-1709) & Mary (WHITEHEAD) TAYLOR, w John; Jamaica, LI
UYYOHART/URROHART?, William & Hannah SMITH; 21 Sep 1698; Bridgewater
USE, Valentine & Susanna _?_ ; b 1691; Boston
USHER, Hezekiah (1616-1676) (mentions brother Willis & wf in his will) & 1/wf Frances _?_ (-1652); b 1639; Cambridge/Boston
USHER, Hezekiah (1616-1676) & 2/wf Elizabeth SYMMES (1630-); 2 Nov 1652; Boston/Salem
USHER, Hezekiah (1616-1676) & 3/wf Mary (ALFORD) [BUTLER] (-1693), w Peter, m/3 Samuel NOWELL 1676+; Charlestown
USHER, Hezekiah (1639-1697) & Bridget (LISLE) HOAR (-1723), w Leonard; 29 Nov 1676; Boston
USHER, John (-1726) & 1/wf Elizabeth LIDGETT (-1698); 24 Apr 1668; Charlestown
USHER, John (-1726) & 2/wf Elizabeth ALLEN (-1732+); 11 Mar 1699; Cambridge

USHER, Robert (-1669) & Elizabeth JAGGER, w Jeremy; 12 May 1659; Stamford, CT
USHER, Robert, Dunstable & Sarah BLANCHARD, Dunstable; 23 Jan 1693/4; Chelmsford/Dunstable
USSELL, Richard & Abigail [DAVIS], m Edward RICHMOND; b 1656, b 20 May 1657, m declared unlawful; Newport?
URSELTON/USSELTON, Frances/Francis & Sarah BARNES; 25 Nov 1655; Wenham/Topsfield/ Martha's Vineyard
UTLEY, Samuel (-1662) & Hannah HATCH; 6 Dec 1658; Scituate
UTLEY, Samuel & Sarah ASHBY/ASSBE; 9 Apr 1691; ?Stonington, CT/Windham, CT
UTTER, Jabez & Mary _?_; b 1685; Stow/Canterbury, CT
UTTER, Nicholas (-1722) & 1/wf _?_; b 1665; Kingstown, RI/Westerly, RI/Stonington, CT
UTTER, Nicholas (-1722) & 2/wf Elizabeth _?_ (-1722+); b 1701?; Stonington, CT/RI
UTTER, Thomas & _?_; ?Stonington, CT (b 1703)

VALE, Christopher & Joanna HEIFERNAN; 21 Sep 1692; Boston
VAILE, Jeremiah[1] (1617-1687) & 1/wf Catherine _?_; b 1644; Salem/Southold, LI
VAIL, Jeremiah[1] (1617-1687) & 2/wf Mary (FOLGER) PAINE (-1689?), w Peter; 24 May 1660; Southold, LI
VAIL, Jeremiah[2] (1649-1726) & 1/wf _?_; ca 1660/5?; Southold
VAIL, Jeremiah[1] (1617-1687) & 3/wf Joyce _?_; b 1685; Southold, LI
VAIL, Jeremiah[2] (1649-1726) & 2/wf Anne (HAMPTON) [MOORE] (-1726), w Benjamin; 1691, 1690?; Southold, LI
VAIL, Jeremiah & Mary _?_; b 1698; Southold, LI
VAIL, John (-1684) & Eunice _?_; no issue; Westchester Co., NY
VAIL, John (1663-1737) & Grace [?BRADDOCK (no)]/[?BURGESS] (1666-1751); b 18 Jul 1684; Southold, LI
VAIL, Joseph (-1698) & _?_; Huntington, LI
VAIL, Philip & Mary _?_; b 1688; Huntington, LI
VAIL, Samuel (-1695) & Elizabeth [?HUNT] (1657-1747, Woodbridge, NJ), m/2 Thomas GACH/(GAUGE), m/3 John GRIFFITH 1709; b 1678; Westchester Co., NY
VAIL, Thomas[1] (-1687/8, living 1691?) & 1/wf Sarah (?WENTWORTH) (-living 1691); b 1650; Southampton, LI/Westchester Co., NY
VAIL/VEALE, Thomas & Sarah _?_; b 1 Mar 1691/2, b 1686, b 20 Nov 1701; Eastchester, NY
VALENTINE, Benjamin & 1/wf _?_; b 1698?; Westchester Co., NY
VALENTINE, Ephraim & _?_; b 1685, b 1670?; Hempstead, LI
VALENTINE, John & _?_ ?RICHARDSON; b 18 Apr 1702
VALENTINE, Jonah & _?_; b 1679?; Hempstead
VALENTINE, Obadiah (1660-1743) & 1/wf? Martha _?_; b 1683?, b 1695, b 1670?; Hempstead, LI
VALENTINE, Richard (1620?-bef 1684) & [Rachel] _?_; Hempstead, LI
VALENTINE, Richard (1651, 1676?-1725) & Sarah HALSTEAD (2 Oct 1660-); ca 1682-4?, 1681; Hempstead, LI
VALENTINE, William & _?_; b 1685, b 1670?; Hempstead
VALENTINE, _?_ & _?_ ODELL; b 1698
VEIN/VANE, Edward & _?_; b 1676; Boston
VanGOODENHAUSEN, Samuel & 2/wf _?_ TURNER, w Nathaniel; ca 1647; New Haven
VANGOODENHOUSE/VANGOODENHOUSEN?/VanGOODENHOUSEN, Samuel, Jr.? & Elizabeth PARRIS?; 11 Nov 1662; New Haven
VARNEY, Ebenezer (1672-) & Mary [OTIS]; nr 1692; Dover
VARNEY, Humphrey (-1714) & Esther [STARBUCK]/AUSTIN; Gloucester/Dover, NH
VARNEY, Humphrey (-1714) & ?2/wf Sarah (STARBUCK)/(STORER?) AUSTIN, w Joseph; 2 Mar 1664; Dover, NH
VARNEY, Peter (1666-1702) & 1/wf Elizabeth _?_; ca 1689; Dover, NH

VERNEY, Thomas & Ann BROWN; 23 Dec 1667; Charlestown
VARNEY, Thomas & Abigail [PROCTOR] (1639-1732, ae 92); b 1669; Ipswich
VARNEY, Thomas & Mary _?_ (-1696); b 1672; Boston
VARNEY, William (-1654, Salem) & Bridget PARSONS [KNIGHT?] (-1672, Gloucester), wid?; b 1641?, b 1644, 4 May 1629?, b 1634; Ipswich/Gloucester/Salem
VARNAM, George (-1649) & ?Hannah _?_ (not certain-1649+); b 1619; Gloucester/Ipswich
VARNUM, John (1669-1715) & Dorothy PRESCOTT (1681-); 13 Nov 1700; Dracut
VARNUM, Joseph (1672/3-1749) & 1/wf Ruth JEWETT (1681-1728); 3 Oct 1697; Rowley
VARNAM, Samuel (?1619-) & Sarah [LANGTON] (-1698+?); b 1659, ca 1645/50?, say ca 1656; Ipswich/Chelmsford
VARNUM, Thomas (1662-) & Joanna JEWETT; 10 Nov 1697; Rowley/Chelmsford
VASSALL, William (1592-1655) & Anna/Anne? KING (?1593-); ?Cold Norton, Essex, ?lic 9 Jun 1613; Roxbury/Scituate/Barbados
VAUGHAN, Daniel (1653-1715(-)), Newport & Susanna GRIMES/JENNEY (1657-1715+), Plymouth; 27 Mar 1678; Newport
VAUGHAN, Daniel (1656-1730) & Hepzibah _?_ (1666?-1726); Middleboro
VAUGHAN, David (1646-1678) & Mary _?_, m/2 Thomas JOSLIN; ca 1676/80?; Newport/Portsmouth, RI
VAUGHAN, David & Mary [ALCOCK]; b 1687; Boston
VAUGHAN, George (1622-1694, Middleboro), Scituate & Elizabeth [HINCKSMAN]/HINKSMAN? (1634-1693); 1652; Marshfield/Middleboro
VAUGHAN, George (1650-1704) & Margery SPINK (-1704+); 26 Jul 1680, Newport, etc.; E. Greenwich, RI
VAUGHAN, George (1676-), Portsmouth, NH, & 1/wf Mary BELCHER (1680-1700); 8 Dec 1698; Boston/Charlestown
VAUGHAN, John (-1687+) & Gillian _?_ ; b 1644; Boston/Newport
VAUGHAN, John & Elizabeth BULL; 24 Nov 1648; Portsmouth, RI
VAUGHAN, Joseph (1654-1734) & 1/wf Joanna THOMAS (-1718); 7 May 1680; Middleboro
VAUGHAN, William (-1677) & Frances (LATHAM)/(WESTON) (DUNGAN) [CLARK] (1611-1677), w William, w Jeremiah; betw Jan 1652 & 18 Jan 1656; Newport, RI
VAUGHAN, William (1640-1719) & Margaret CUTTS/(CULT) (?1650-1693, 1690?); 8 Dec 1668; Portsmouth, NH
VEECH, Andrew & Elizabeth [WILLIAMS]; b 1690; Boston/Lebanon, CT
VEASEY, George, Dover & Mary WIGGIN, m/2 William MOORE 1673; 23 Jan 1664; Exeter, NH
VEASEY, George (1655-1752) & Martha (HARVEY) [WILSON], w John; b 13 Feb 1699/1700; Stratham, NH
VEAZEY, Robert & Mary _?_, m/2 George PARKHURST; b 1636(7?), b 1648/9; Watertown, CT
VEAZY, Samuel (1656-) & 1/wf Mary _?_ ; b 1687; Boston
VEAZY, Samuel (1656-) & 2/wf Mary VIRGOOSE; 25 Nov 1691; Boston
VEASEY, Solomon (1651-) & Elizabeth SANDERS; 23 Nov 1680; Braintree
VEASEY, Thomas (1669/70-1750) & Mary [LEAVITT] (1667-); ca 1690?; Stratham, NH
VEAZY, William (-1681, ae 65) & Eleanor/?Helen [THOMPSON] (1627-1711), m/2 John FRENCH 1683; b 1644(5?); Braintree
VEAZY, William (1647-) & Mary [SANDERS]; b 1674, b 1672; Braintree
VEALEE/VELEY, Thomas (-1718) & Mary LADDEN; 22 Jul 1672; Salem
VELLER/VELLERS/?VILER, John & Mary HARDING; 3 Sep 1700; Boston
VENNER, Thomas & Alice _?_ ; b 1641; Salem/Boston (retd to London)
VENNY, Thomas & Elizabeth PEASE; 28 Oct 1697; Marblehead
VENTEMAN, John & 1/wf Elizabeth (HUTCHINS) SMITH (-14 Feb 1709/10); 13 Jul 1699; Boston
VENTROUS/VENTRES, John (1657-1737) & 1/wf Lydia [SPENCER?] (1673-); 1694, b 1695, div; Haddam, CT
VENTRIS, Moses[1] (-1697) & Grace _?_ ; 14 Jan 1646, 1646/7; Hartford
VENTRIS, Moses & [?Mary] [BIRGE]; b 1696; Haddam, CT
VENTRIS, William (-1701, ae 78) & 1/wf Elizabeth _?_ (1632-1708, ae 76, Haddam); b 1654; Farmington/Haddam, CT
VENTRIS, William (-1701, ae 78) & 1/wf? 2/wf Elizabeth _?_ ; b 1700?; Haddam, CT
VENUS, [William] & _?_ ; b 1651; Salem
VEREN, Hilliard (1622-1683) (brother-in-law of Edmond BATTER) & Mary CONANT (-1692); 12 Apr 1641; Salem

VEREN, Hilliard (1649-1680) & Hannah PRICE (1648-1683); 4 May 1670, no issue; Salem
VEREN, John (-1713) & Mercy/Mary WISEMAN (-1713+); 12 Jun 1660; Boston
VERIN, John (1661-) & Penelope COOKE, ?m/2 William WAY; 30 Aug 1683; Bristol, RI/Boston
VERRIN, Joshua (-1695, Barbados) & 1/wf Jane __?__; b 1638, no issue; Salem/Providence/Barbados
VERIN, Joshua (-1695) & 2/wf Agnes __?__, m/2 John DRAKE?, m/3 Thomas KING; no issue; Providence/Barbados
VEREN, Nathaniel (1623-) & Mary __?__, m/2 Joseph PUTNAM 1666; b 1648; Salem
VEREN, Philip (-1649?) & Dorcas [?HILLIARD] (-1659+); in Eng, ca 1615?; Salem
VEREN, Philip (1619-) & Joanna __?__ (-1664); b 1641; Salem
VEREN, Robert & __?__; b 1639; Salem
VEREIN, Thomas (1663-) & Hannah [FITCH] (1664-), Reading, dau Joseph; b 1689(90?); Boston
(Note: Eleanor, 2nd wf of Anthony GULLIVER of Milton, had grand daughter Eleanor VEREN, bapt 1693, she m John DANIEL 1707)
VERGOOSE, Isaac (1637-1710) & 1/wf Mary [BALSTON] (-1690, ae 42); b 1669; Boston
VERGOOSE, Isaac (1637-1710) & 2/wf Elizabeth FOSTER (1665-); 5 Jul 1692; Charlestown
VERGOOSE, Peter (-1667) & Susanna VERMAYES (-1684/5) (called Joshua BUFFMAN "cousin" in 1677); in Eng?, b 1637; Boston
VERMAYES/VERMAGES, Capt. Benjamin, Boston & Mercy BRADFORD (-bef 1661); 21 Dec 1648, 15 Jun 1648; Plymouth
VERMAES, Mark? & Alice [BLESSING?] (-1656), of Boston, wid in 1655; Salem (Mark VERMAES, Jr. returned to Eng)
VERNON, Daniel (1643-1715) & Ann (HUTCHINSON) [DYER] (1643-1717), w Samuel; b 18 Oct 1687, 22 Sep 1679; Kingston, RI
VERY, Benjamin (-1730+) & Jemima NEWHALL (1678-1725+); 9 Jun 1698; Lynn
VERY, Samuel (1619-1683/4) & Alice [WOODIS] (-1716+); ?ca 1640; Salem
VERY, Samuel & Abigail [ARCHER] (1668-1697+); ca 1683, ca 1682?; Salem
VERY, Samuel (1659-) & Elizabeth [TOY] (1660-); ca 1685, b 1688; Boston
VERREY, Thomas (1626-1694) & Hannah GYLES (-1683); 6 Jul 1650; Gloucester
VERY, Thomas (-1717) & Elizabeth PROCTER; 28 Mar 1681; Salem
VERY, __?__ & Bridget __?__ (1600-1680), m/2 Edward GILES; in Eng, b 1619; Salem
VETCH, Andrew (1655-1742), Boston/Lebanon, CT, & Elizabeth [WILLIAMS]; b 1690, b 1701?, b 1703; Boston/Lebanon, CT
VIALL, Benjamin (1672-1750) & 1/wf Rachel BROWN (1679-); 5 May 1697; Swansea
VIALL, John (1619-1686) & 1/wf Mary __?__; b 1639; Boston/Swansea
VIALL, John (1619-1686) & Elizabeth [SMITH], m/2 Samuel NEWMAN 1687, 1688; b 1664, b 1663?; Boston/Swansea
VIALL, John (1644-1720) & Mary [WILLIAMS] (1646-); b 1672; Boston
VIAL, John (1672-) & Mary ADAMS, m/2 Daniel WEAR/WYER 1705; 27 Dec 1694; Boston
VIALL, Jonathan & ?Mary/?Mercy __?__; b 1699; Swansea/Barrington, RI
VICKERS/VICARS, Philip & Abigail __?__; b 2 Jun 1695; Fairfield
VICARS, [Philip?] & Hannah PARDEE (1672-); b 1700; New Haven/Fairfield, CT/Fairfield, NJ
VICARS, Roger & Mary __?__ (1635-); b 1664; Black Point
VICKERIE, Benjamin (-1718) & Dorcas [PAINE] (-1707); ca 1689; Hull
VICARS, Edward (-1684) & Hannah __?__; New Haven
VICKERY, George (-1679) & Rebecca [PHIPPEN]; ca 1647?; Hingham
VICKERY, George (-1721) & Lucy [HODSDON] (-1725); b 24 Jun 1673, 1683; Hull/Boston
VICKERY, Isaac (-1726) & 1/wf Elizabeth (CROMWELL) [PRICE] (-1697), w Richard; b 1677
VICKERY, Isaac (-1726) & 2/wf Lydia [JONES]; aft 14 Apr 1697, b 1701?
VICKARS, John & Sarah [CROAKUM] (1660-1717+); b 1688; Boston
VICKERY, Jonathan (?1648-1702) & Elizabeth [HUDSON], dau John; ca 1675?, b 1683; ?Marshfield/Chatham
VICKERY, Roger & 1/wf Grace __?__ (-1693); b 1685; Marblehead
VICARY, Roger & Amy WILLEN/WOOLEN/WILLING, w Richard; 4 Dec 1694; Marblehead
VILLAROCK, Phillip & Eliza/Elizabeth? WILCOT; 3 May 1694; Boston
VINALL/VINAL, Jacob (1670-) & Mary CUDWORTH (-1755, ae 77); 12 Feb 1695/6; Scituate
VINALL, John (-1698, ae 62) & Elizabeth BACKER/BAKER; 2 Feb 1664; Scituate
VINALL, John (-1728) & Mary [GODDARD] (-1723 in 53rd y); b 1691; Scituate
VINALL, Stephen (1630-) & Mary BAKER; 26 Feb 1661, 1661/2, 26 Feb 1662; Scituate

VINALL, _?_ & Anna/Ann _?_ (-1664); in Eng, ca 1627; Scituate
VINSENT, Henry (-1722) & Mary MATTHEWES; 15 Dec 1657; Sandwich
VINCENT, Humphrey (-1664) & Joane/Joanna _?_ (-1657); Ipswich
VINCENT, John (-d in Holland) & Sarah [ALLERTON], m/2 Degory PRIEST 1611, m/3 Cuthbert CUTHBERTSON 1621; b 1611
VINCENT, John (-1663+) & _?_ ; b 1633; Lynn/Sandwich
VINCENT, John (-1659) & Rebecca _?_ (-1679); b 1639; New Haven
VINCENT, Thomas & Sarah [POST]; ca 1676
VINCENT, William (1638-1695) & 1/wf Priscilla CARPENTER (1643-1690+); 31 May 1670; Providence
VINCENT, William (-1695) & 2/wf Jemima _?_ ; aft 15 Nov 1690, b 21 Dec 1695; Providence
VINCENT, [?Nicholas] & Elizabeth DIX; b 1697?; Wethersfield, CT
VINCENT, _?_ /Thomas & Fridgswith CARPENTER; b 1649
VINE, William (-ca 1708) & Elizabeth ARRINGTON/HARRINGTON? (1643-1717); 15 Oct 1674; Charlestown
VINING, George & Hannah JUDKINS; 10 Oct 1700; Weymouth
VINING, John[1] (1636-1685/6) & 1/wf Margaret REED (1636-1659); 11 May 1657; Weymouth
VINING, John[1] (1636-1685/6) & 2/wf Mary REED (-1717); 22 Jan 1659, 1659/60; Weymouth
VINING, John (1662-) & Naomi _?_ (-1719); b 1687(8?); Weymouth
VINING, Samuel (1670-) & Sarah _?_ ; b 1701; Weymouth/Enfield, CT
VINING, William & ?Joanna _?_ ; b 1683, b 1686?; Portsmouth, NH/Boston?
UINSON, Charles & Elizabeth _?_ ; ca 1690?; Fordham, NY
VINSON, John (-1718) & Sarah [GURNEY?]/?WHITMARSH (-1729), m/2 John CANTERBURY 1721; b 1676; Weymouth
VINSON, John & Sarah [KINGMAN]; b 1697; Weymouth
VINSON, Samuel & Hannah [BICKNELL?] (doubtful), m/2 Joseph NASH; b 1698(9?); Weymouth
VINSON, Thomas & Martha [SHAW] (bpt 1632-); doubtful; Weymouth
VINSON/(now VINCENT), Thomas (1656-) & Sarah [POST] (1657-); ca 1676; Martha's Vineyard
VINCEN/VINSON, William (1611-1691) (cousin of Anthony BUXTON) & 1/wf Sarah _?_ (1620?- 4 Feb 1660/1); ca 1639; Gloucester
VINSON/(now VINCENT), William (?1626-1697?) & 1/wf Susannah [BROWNING] (?1636-1722); b Dec 1655; Martha's Vineyard
VINCEN, William (-1690) & 2/wf Rachel (PARSONS) COOKE (-1707), w Thomas; 10 Jun 1661, 17 Oct 1660; Gloucester
VINTON, Blaze/Blaise (-1716) & Lydia [HAYDEN], m/2 Jonathan TURNER; ca 1693; Hingham
VINTON, John (-1664) & Ann/Eleanor? (no) _?_ (-1664); b 1648; Lynn/New Haven
VINTON, John (1650-1727) & Hannah GREEN (1660-1741); 16 Aug 1677; Malden
VIRGIN, Richard & Frances SPARKES; 1 May 1696; Chelmsford
VIRGUE/?VIRGO, Peter & Sarah JOHNSON; 21 Jan 1690; Boston
VOEDEN/?VOUDEN/?VODIN, John & Colete MASTERS; 2 Dec 1669; Salem/Swansea
VOWDEN, Moses (-1681) & Mary ORMES (1656-1716+); 1 Mar 1674, [1674/5]; Salem
VODEN, Philip & Abigail KEMBALL, m/2 Isaac JARVIS 1698; 22 Dec 1692; Boston
VORE, Richard (-1683) & Ann _?_ (-1683); in Eng, b 1630, m lic 25 Jul; Dorchester/Windsor, CT
VOSE, Edward[2] (1636-1716) & Abigail [SHARP]/[?WATER] (-1712, ae 65); b 1666; Milton
VOSE, Henry (1663-1752) & 1/wf Elizabeth BADCOCK (1666-1732); 18 May 1686; ?Boston/Milton
VOSE, John (1676-), Milton & Sarah CLAP (1677-), Milton; 1 Jul 1700; Milton
VOSE, Nathaniel[3] (1672-1753), Milton & Mary BELSHER/BELCHER (1670-1758), Milton; 16 Dec 1696; Milton
VOSE, Robert[1] (1599-1683) & Jane MOSS (-1675), Childwall, Eng; in Eng, m lic 25 Jul 1629; Dorchester/Milton
VOSE, Thomas (1641-1708) & Waitstill [WYATT] (1645-1727/8); b 1661; Dorchester/Milton
VOSE, Thomas, Jr., Milton & Hannah BADCOCK (1675-), Milton; 28 May 1695; Milton
VOSE, William (1674-1717), Milton & Mary BADCOCK (1680-), Milton; 3 Apr 1700; Milton
VOWLES/?FOWLES, Richard & Mary [SADLER] (1628-); ?b 1647; ?Fairfield, CT/Rye, NY
VOWLES, Jonathan (1647-1713+) (called John ODELL "cousin") & Deborah _?_ ; b 1698; Rye, NY

WADE, John & Elizabeth [DURANT] (-1704); b 1693; Lyme, CT

WADE, John (1675-1703) & Elizabeth GERRISH (1674-), m/2 Joshua PIERCE; 3 Sep 1696; Dover, NH

WADE, Jonathan (-1683) & Susanna ___?___ (-1678); b 1632; Charlestown/Ipswich

WADE, Jonathan (-1689) & 1/wf Dorothy BUCKLEY/BULKLEY (?1640-), ?dau of Rev. Peter (probably yes); 9 Dec 1660; Ipswich

WADE, Jonathan (-1689), Medford & 2/wf Deborah [DUDLEY] (1645-1683); b 5 Feb 1664/5; Charlestown

WADE, Jonathan & Sarah ___?___ ; b 1681; Boston

WADE, Jonathan (-1689) & 3/wf Elizabeth [DUNSTER] (1656-1729), m/2 Nathaniel THOMAS ca 1714; b 1687; Charlestown/Cambridge

WADE, Nathaniel (1648-1707) & Mercy BRADSTREET (-1714, 1715); 31 Oct 1672, 29 Oct; Andover

WADE, Nathaniel (1673-) & Mary DAVENPORT (1676-); 21 May 1694, 22 May; New Haven

WADE, Nicholas & Elizabeth [HANFORD] (ca 1621-1717?, 1672+); b 1652, b 1648; Scituate

WADE, Nicholas (1660-1723) & Mary [RIPLEY] (1660-); b 1688; Scituate

WADE, Richard (1575-) & Elizabeth ___?___ (1579-); in Eng, b 1613; Dorchester/Sandwich

WADE, Robert & ?Joane ___?___ ; div 1657; Dorchester/Hartford/Saybrook/Norwich, CT

WADE, Robert & Abijah/Abiah ROYCE; 11 Mar 1691, 1690/1?; Norwich, CT

WADE, Thomas (1650-1696) & Elizabeth COGSWELL (?1650-1721); 22 Feb 1670; Ipswich

WEAD, Thomas & Elizabeth [CURTIS]; b 1673; Scituate

WADE, Thomas (1673-) & Elizabeth THORNTON; 4 Apr 1700; Ipswich

WADE, William, Middletown, CT, & Sarah PHELPS (-1659); 9 Jun 1658; Windsor, CT

WADDAMS/WADHAMS, John (-1676) & Susannah ___?___ (-1683), m/2 ?Samuel BUSHNELL; b 1655; Wethersfield, CT

WADDAMS, John (1655-1718) & 1/wf Hannah BIDWELL (-1696); 20 Dec 1677; Wethersfield, CT

WADDAMS, John (1655-1718) & 2/wf Abigail (BALDWIN) BALDWIN, w Samuel; 13 Apr 1697; Wethersfield, CT

WADLAND, Amos (1654?-) & Elizabeth ___?___ ; b 1693; Boston

WADLAND, Crispin[1] (-1668) & Agnes ___?___ (1610-1683); Charlestown

WADLAND, Crispin (-1671) & Elizabeth ___?___ , m/2 Daniel SMITH; b 1671; Charlestown

WADLAND, Daniel & Sarah CROCKER; 29 Mar 1682; Marblehead

WADLON, Moses & Ruth CHEEVER (1672-), m/2 ___?___ STACEY; 29 Jun 1699; Marblehead

WADLIN, William & Elizabeth [GATTENSBY]; b 1701?

WADLEIGH, Henry (-1732) & Elizabeth (GILMAN) LADD (1661-), w Nathaniel; 3 Dec 1693; Exeter, NH

WADLEIGH, John[1] (-1671) & Mary ___?___ ; b 1629, ca 1625; Saco, ME/Wells, ME

WADLEIGH, John (-1728) & Abigail [MARSTON]? (1658-); b 1684; ?Kittery, ME/Exeter, NH

WADLEIGH, Jonathan & 1/wf Sarah/Hannah? WEARE; by 1698?

WADLEIGH, Jonathan & 2/wf Anna ?WILSON/?BEALS [HILTON], w William; ca 1717, b 1701?; Salisbury

WADLEY, Joseph & Rachel BRACKETT; 3 Dec 1688; Braintree

WADLEIGH, Robert (1628?-) & Sarah ___?___ ; ca 1655?, ca 1648?, b 17 Jun 1654; Salisbury/Wells/Kittery/Exeter

WADLEIGH, Robert & Sarah NELSON (1673-); 8 Sep 1696; Rowley/Stratham, NH

WADSWORTH, Benjamin (1669/70-1737) & Ruth BORDMAN/BOARDMAN; 30 Dec 1696, no issue; Cambridge

WADSWORTH, Christopher (-1687) & Grace [COLE?] (-1688); b 1636; Duxbury

WADSWORTH, Christopher (1663-1687) & ___?___ [DAVIS] (-1687); Milton

WADSWORTH, Ebenezer (1660-1717) & Mary ___?___ (-1737, ae 77); b 1684; Milton

WADSWORTH, Elisha (-1741) & Elizabeth WISEWALL/WISWALL (1670-); 9 Dec 1694; Duxbury

WADSWORTH, James (1677-1756) & Ruth [NOYES]; b 1700?; Farmington, CT

WADSWORTH, John (-1689) & Sarah [STANLEY] (-1718); ca 1656; Farmington, CT

WADSWORTH, John (1638-1700) & Abigail ANDREWS (-1723), dau Henry; 25 Jul 1667; Duxbury

WADSWORTH, John (1662-1718) & 1/wf Elizabeth STANLEY (1672-); 20 Aug 1696; Farmington, CT
WADSWORTH, John (1674-1734) & Elizabeth VOSE (1678-1766); 28 Dec 1698; Milton
WADSWORTH, Joseph (?1648-1731) & Elizabeth [TALCOTT]; 1682; Hartford
WADSWORTH, Joseph (1636-1689) & 1/wf Abigail [WAITE]; ca 1655/65?; Duxbury
WADSWORTH, Joseph (-1689?, 1690?) & 2/wf Mary __?__; Duxbury
WODSWORTH, Joseph (1667-1750) & Hannah MOUNTFORD; m int 18 Jul 1695; Boston
WANTSWORTH, Nicholas & Rebecca HACKETT; m int 13 Jan 1696/7; Boston
WADSWORTH, Samuel (-1676), Milton & Abigail [LINDALL] (-1687), Marshfield, m/2 Thomas RAWLINS; b 1660; Marshfield/Dorchester/Milton
WADSWORTH, Samuel (1660-1731) & Hannah JUDSON (1657-), Woodbury; 12 Jun 1689; Farmington, CT/Stratford, CT
WADSWORTH, Samuel & __?__ [HUNT]; b 1700; Lebanon, CT?
WADSWORTH, Thomas (see Joseph) (1651-1725) & Elizabeth [BARNARD]; b 14 Nov 1677; Hartford
WADSWORTH, Timothy (1662-1717) & Susanna [COX]/COCKS (1666-1737); b 1687; Boston/Newport
WADSWORTH, William (1595-1675) & 1/wf [Sarah TALCOTT] (-betw 1636 & 1644); in Eng, ca 1625; Cambridge/Hartford
WADSWORTH, William (1595-1675) & 2/wf Elizabeth STONE (1621-1682); 2 Jul 1644; Hartford
WADSWORTH, William (1671-1751) & 1/wf Abigail LEWIS (1678-1707); 10 Dec 1696; Farmington, CT
WAFFE, John & Katharine __?__, m/2 Abraham BELL b 1652; b 1645; Charlestown
WAFFE, Thomas (1646-) & Alice __?__; b 1685, b 1682?; Charlestown
WAGGET/WAGGETT, Thomas & Susanna [WHITE], dau William; b 1670; Boston
WAGGET, Thomas & ?2/wf Elizabeth __?__; b 1688; Boston
WAINWRIGHT, Francis (-1692) & 1/wf Phillippa [SEWALL] (-1669); b 1648; Ipswich
WAINWRIGHT, Francis (-1692, Salem) & 2/wf Hannah __?__, m/2 Daniel EPES 1693?; 1669?; Ipswich
WAINWRIGHT, Francis (1664-1711) & Sarah WHIPPLE (1671-1709); 12 Mar [1689/90?], 1686?; Ipswich
WAINWRIGHT, John (1648/9-1708) & Elizabeth NORTON (-1742), m/2 Isaac ADDINGTON 1713; 10 Mar 1674; Ipswich
WAINWRIGHT, Simon (?1660-1708) & 1/wf Sarah GILBERT (?1658-1688); 6 Oct 1681; Haverhill
WAINWRIGHT, Simon (?1660-1708) & 2/wf Ann PEIRCE (1666-1697); 2 Oct 1688; Haverhill
WAINWRIGHT, Simon (?1660-1708) & 3/wf Mary (WILLIAMS) SILVER, w Thomas, m/3 John BOYNTON, m/4 Joshua BOYNTON; 7 Aug 1700; Haverhill
WAINWRIGHT, Thomas & __?__; b 1659; Dorchester
WAITE, Alexander (-1681) & Damaris __?__ (1651-), m/2 John MARSHALL 1681, m/3 Thomas JOHNSON; Billerica/Malden
WAITE, Benjamin (ca 1645-1704) & Martha LEONARD (1649-); 8 Jun 1670; Hadley/Hatfield/Deerfield/Springfield?
WAITE, Gamaliel (?1598-1685) & Grace __?__ (ae ca 61 in 1671); b 1637; Boston
WAITE, Jeremiah (1646?, 1648?-1677(-)) & Martha [BROWNELL] (1643-1744), m/2 Charles DYER aft 8 Mar 1690/1; no issue; Portsmouth, RI
WAITE, Capt. John (1618?-1693, Malden) & 1/wf Mary HILLS (?1625-1674), dau Joseph; b 1650, b 1656; Malden/Charlestown
WAIGHT, John (1639-1722) & Mary WOODWARD (1641-1718); 13 Jan 1663, 1663/4; Watertown/Weston
WAYTE, John (1646-1702) (?ae 26 in 1670?) & 1/wf Mary __?__; b 1674; Boston
WAITE, John (-1722) & Sarah MUZZY; 12 Jun 1674, 4 Jun; Malden
WAITE, Capt. John (?1618-1693) & 2/wf Sarah PARKER (1627-1708, ae 81), w Jacob; 4 Aug 1675, 4 Jun; Malden
WAYT, John (-1702) & 2/wf Eunice [ROBERTS] (-1702+) (wf called Anna 1696, Sarah 1697); b 1677; Boston
WAITE, John (1658-) & Katherine/Catherine CARRELL; 14 Aug 1685; Ipswich
WAITE, John (1660-1705) & Ruth EDMANDS (1669-1721); 28 Apr 1687; Charlestown
WAITE, John (-1693, ae 78) & 2/wf Sarah __?__ (-1708, ae 81) (see above); b 1693
WAITE, John & Mary __?__; b 1694; Watertown

WAITE, Jonadab & Hannah DOLE (1677-); m int 13 Dec 1699; Newbury
WAITE, Joseph (1643-1665) & Sarah _?_ (-1665+); b 1665; Portsmouth, RI/Kingston, RI
WAITE, Joseph (-1692) & 1/wf Hannah OAKES (1657-); 7 Aug 1672, 12 Jul; Malden
WAITE, Joseph (1643-) & Ruhamah [HAGAR] (1647-); ca 1674/5; Watertown/Marlborough
WAITE, Joseph, Malden & 2/wf Mercy TUFTS (-1736), Charlestown, m/2 Lemuel JENKINS 1694; 24 Oct 1688, 24 Dec; Malden/Charlestown
WAIT, Nathaniel (1667-) & Elizabeth [LYNDE] (-1734+); b 1700; Malden/Charlestown
WAITE, Return (1639-1702) & Martha [MARCH] (1657-1735, Plymouth, in 79th y); b 1679; Charlestown/Boston
WAITE, Reuben (-1707) & Tabitha [LOUNDERS]? (-1707+); b 1681, b 1683; Dartmouth/E. Greenwich, RI
WAITE, Richard (?1596-1680, ae 84) & Elizabeth _?_ (-1651?); b 1637; Boston/Charlestown
WAIGHT, Richard (1609?, 1610?-) (ae 55 in 1655) & Mary _?_ (-1678, ae 72); b 1638, b 1632?; Watertown
WAITE, Richard (-1680) & 2/wf Rebecca HEPBURN; b 1653; Boston
WAITE, Richard & Sarah (CLARKE) BARNARD (1649-), w Richard; 16 Sep 1686; Springfield/Danbury, CT
WAITE, Richard (1658-) & 1/wf Lydia HALE (1677-1700, 1700/1701, ae 31); 9 Dec 1686; Charlestown
WAITE, Samuel (?1640-1677?) & Hannah [?WHITMAN], m/2 James SAMPSON bef 12 Oct 1694; ca 1659; Kingston, RI/Exeter, RI
WAITE, Samuel (1650-1720) & Mehitable BUCKNAM (1654-1734); b 1680, b 1679?; Charlestown/Malden
WAIT, Samuel (-1752) & Alice WIGHTMAN (1666-1747); b 1697; N. Kingston, RI/Wickford, RI/Exeter, RI
WAITE, Thomas (?1601, 1615?-1665, 1669?, 1677(-)) & Eleanor? _?_ (-1669+), m/2 Ralph COWLAND ca 1668; b 1640; Portsmouth, RI
WAITE, Thomas (-1713+) & _?_ ; b 1654; Ipswich
WAIGHT, Thomas & Sarah [CUTLER] (1653?-1744); b 1675; Watertown/Cambridge
WAITE, Thomas & Susan AYRES; 21 Nov 1677; Ipswich
WAIT, Thomas (-1733) & Sarah COOK (?1654, ?1658-1733+); b 1680; Tiverton, RI/Portsmouth, RI/?Dartmouth
WAIGHT, Thomas & Abigail STANLEY; 27 Feb 1688/9; Topsfield
WAIT, Thomas & Mary [EDWARDS] (1662-); b 1694; Salisbury
WAITE, Thomas (1660-1742) & Mary [PARKER] (1667-1763); b 1696; Malden
WAITE, William (-1732) & 1/wf Sarah KINGSLEY (1666-1691); b 1687, 22 Mar 1680/1; Northampton/?Rochester
WAIT, William (-1732) & 2/wf Ann WEBB (1671-1748); 29 Jul 1691, 29 Jul 1692, b 1693, 5 Jan 1691/2?; Northampton
WAIT, William & Elizabeth _?_ ; b 1696; Rochester, MA
WAIT, William & Abiah/Abiel/Abial TOMBLIN; 22 Apr 1700; Dedham
WAKE, William (-1654) & _?_ ; in Eng, b 1637; Salem
WAKE, _?_ & Elizabeth [BARNARD], [wid]; aft 20 Sep 1675, bef 1691; Fairfield, CT
WAKEFIELD, James, Biddeford, ME, & Rebecca [GIBBINS]; b 1699; Wells, ME
WAKEFIELD, John (ca 1615-1667) & Ann _?_ (?1623-1703), m/2 John CHILD 1667+; b 1638; Boston
WAKEFIELD, John (-1660) & Ann/Anna? _?_ (-1695), m/2 James CLARK 1661; b 1643?, b 1644; New Haven
WAKEFIELD, John (-1674), Biddeford, ME, & Elizabeth [LITTLEFIELD] (1627-); ca 1644/8?, by 1661; ?Wells, ME
WAKEFIELD, John (ca 1640-1703) & Deliverance [TARNE] (-1716), m/2 William HAYWARD; b 1664; Boston
WAKEFIELD, John & Hester [HARBOR] (1663); Mendon
WAKEFIELD, John (1669-1735) & Elizabeth WALKER (1673-1738); 23 Nov 1693; Boston
WAKEFIELD, Obadiah (ca 1642-1733) & 1/wf Susanna _?_ (1655-1709, ae 54); b 1674; Boston
WAKEFIELD, Samuel (ca 1644-1728) & Elizabeth DOVE; 2 Jun 1675; Salem
WAKEFIELD, William (-1707) & Rebecca LITTLEFIELD, m/2 William KING; 13 Mar 1698/9; Salem
WAKEFIELD, William (returned to Eng) & Anne _?_ ; b 1638; Hampton, NH

WAKEHAM, Edward & Sarah MEADER; 16 Mar 1691/2; Dover, NH
WALCOM, James & Elizabeth HOPKINS; 27 May 1695; Boston
WAKEHAM, John (-1692) & Martha [BROOKINGS] (1669±-), m/2 John LEWIS 1699, m/2 Joseph RANDALL 1709; ca 1688; Portsmouth, NH
WAKUM, Robert & Elizabeth [?BLANCHARD]; b 1665; Boston
WACOMB, Thomas (-1709) & Mary [HUNKING] (-1711+); b 1667?; Portsmouth, NH
WAKEHAM/WAKUM, Robert (-1677) & Hannah __?__ ; ca 1665?; Boston
WAKELEY, Deliverance (?1651-1707) & Hannah NASH; 3 Dec 1678; Stratford, CT
WAKELEY, Henry (-1692, 1690) & Sarah (BURT) GREGORY (1621-1711+), w Judah;'4 Sep 1649, 4 d 7 mo; Springfield/Hartford/Stratford, CT
WAKELEY, Jacob & 1/wf __?__ [WALLIS], w Richard; by 1677
WAKELEE, James & 1/wf __?__ ; in Eng, b 1620?; Hartford/Wethersfield, CT
WAKELY, James (-1690+?) & Alice BOOSEY (-1683), w James; 5 Oct 1652; Hartford/?Wethersfield, CT
WAKELEE, James & 1/wf Hannah [PEAT] (1667-); b 1688; Stratford, CT
WAKELEY, John (-1675) & Elizabeth SOWARS (-1675); 10 Jun 1657, 10 May 16--; Gloucester/Falmouth, ME/Salem
WAKELEY/WAKELIN, Luke (-1683) & Catherine __?__ (-1683); Topsfield
WAKELEY/?WALKLEY, Richard (?1634-1681) & Rebecca __?__ , m/2 Daniel CONE by 1692; b 1672; Hartford/E. Haddam, CT/Haddam, CT
WAKLY, Thomas (-1675) & Elizabeth __?__ (-1675); b 1631; Gloucester/Falmouth, ME
WAKELEY, ?Joseph/?Samuel & Mary [CORNWALL] (?1677-); b 1701?; Middletown, CT
WAKEMAN, Ezbon (ca 1634/5-1683) & Hannah JORDAN (ca 1648-1697?), m/2 Joseph BASTARD 1684; ?28 Jun 1666, ?1 Apr 1669; Stratford, CT
WAKEMAN, Gregory & Sarah __?__ ; b 1685; Boston
WAKEMAN, John (1601-1661?) & Elizabeth HOPKINS (1610-1658); in Eng, 28 Jan 1628/9; New Haven
WAKEMAN, John (?1660-1709) & Martha HUBBELL (-1710); ?24 Apr 1687; Fairfield, CT
WAKEMAN, Joseph (1670-1726) & Elizabeth [HAWLEY] (1679-1753), m/2 John BURR 1727; ca 1697/8; Fairfield, CT
WAKEMAN, Samuel (1603-1641) & Elizabeth __?__ , m/2 Nathaniel WILLETT; in Eng, b 1631; Cambridge/Hartford
WAKEMAN, Samuel (1635-1692) & Hannah GOODYEAR (?1637-1721), m/2 Nathaniel BURR; 29 Oct 1656; New Haven
WAKEMAN, Samuel (1657-1691) & 1/wf Mary [BURR] (ca 1666-1688±); b 1688; Fairfield, CT
WAKEMAN, Samuel (1657-1691) & 2/wf Sarah [KNOWLES], m/2 Dugal MACKENZIE 1696; ca 1689; Fairfield, CT
WALLBRIDGE/WALBRIDGE, Henry (-1751) & Anna AMES/AMOS (1666-1729); 25 Dec 1688; Preston, CT
WALDIN, [?John] & Elizabeth (SANDERS) BATSON, w John, m/2 John GOVE 1700; ?b 26 May 1697; Cambridge/Salisbury
WALDO, Cornelius (ca 1624-1700/01) & Hannah [COGSWELL] (ca 1624-1704); b 2 Jan 1651/2; Ipswich/Chelmsford
WALDO, Cornelius (1659-) & Faith (PECK) [JACKSON] (1658-), w Jeremiah; b 1684; Boston/Dunstable
WALLDOW, Daniel & Susannah ADAMS; 20 Nov 1683; Chelmsford/Pomfret, CT
WALDO, John (1659-1700, Windham) & Rebecca ADAMS (1654-1727, 1724?), m/2 Eliezer BROWN 1710; 16 Mar 16[73-4?], 1677?, 1676/7; Chelmsford/Boston/Windham, CT
WALDO, Jonathan (-1731) & 1/wf Hannah MASON (-1726); 28 Nov 1692; Boston
WALDERNE/WALDEN?, Edward (-1679) & __?__ ; b 1666, b 1656?; Wenham
WALDERNE, George (1603-1680+) & Bridget RICE; Alcester, Eng, in Eng, 21 May 1635; ?Dover, NH
WALDRON, George & Rachel [BAKER] (wife Constant 1678); b 1676; Boston/Bristol, RI
WALDRON, Isaac (-1683) & Priscilla BYFIELD, m/2 Ebenezer BRENTON by 1687; London, 24 Feb 1674, 25 Feb; York, ME/Boston
WALDRON, John (1625-1702) & Dorothy DOLLEVER (1635-); - Nov 1653; Marblehead
WALDRON, John & __?__ ; b 1675; Dover
WALDERN/WALDEN?, John & Dorcas RISE/RICE?; 25 Sep 1679, 22 Sep 1680; Salem/Wenham
WALDERNE, John & Deliverance BROWNE; 22 Nov 1694, 25 Nov 1694; Marblehead

WALDRON, John (1675±-) & Mary (HAM) HORNE (1668-), w John; 29 Aug 1698; ?Dover, NH

WALDERNE, Nathaniel (-1751, ae 91 1/2) & Abigail _?_ (-1733, ae 73); b 1695; Wenham

WALDRON, Nicholas & Mary _?_ ; Dec 1693, b 1681?; Portsmouth, NH

WALDRON, Richard[1] (1615-1689) & 1/wf? _?_ ; ca 1637; Dover

WALDREN, Richard[1] (-1689) & 2/wf [Ann SCAMMON] (-1686?, 1680?); ca 1650; Boston

WALDRON, Richard[2] (1650-1730) & 1/wf Hannah CUTT (1666-1682); 16 Feb 1681, 1681/2; Portsmouth, NH

WALDRON, Richard (1650-1730) & 2/wf Eleanor [VAUGHAN] (1670-1727); 6 Feb 1692/3; Portsmouth, NH

WALDERNE, Samuel (-1691) & Miriam PEDERICK, m/2 Benjamin HENLEY 1694, m/3 Abraham LASHERE; 2 Jan 1689/90; Marblehead

WALDRON, Samuel (-1729) & Hannah BRIGGS; 17 Apr 1693; Taunton

WALDRON, William (1601-1646?) & _?_ ; by 1625; Dover, NH

WALES, John (-1707) & Elizabeth _?_ (-1701); b 1659; Dorchester

WALES, [John?] & Ruth [BATHERICK]; b 1701; Cambridge

WALES, Jonathan & Sarah _?_ ; b 1687; Boston

WALES, Nathaniel (1586-1661) (Humphrey ATHERTON his brother-in-law?; see below 1649) & _?_ , in Eng, b 1613; Dorchester

WALES, Nathaniel (1586-1661) & 2/wf _?_ ; Dorchester

WALES, Nathaniel (1586-1661) & 3/wf Susannah [GREENWAY] (-1662+); b 1648?, b 1650; Dorchester/Boston

WALES, Nathaniel (1623-1662) & Isabel [?ATHERTON]? (1630-); b 1649; Boston/Dorchester

WALES, Nathaniel (?1649-1718) & 1/wf Elizabeth [BILLINGS] (1659-Oct 1676); b 1675(6?); Dorchester

WALES, Nathaniel (?1649-1718) & 2/wf Joanna [FAXOM] (1660-1704); b 1679; ?Braintree

WALES, Nathaniel (1662-1744), Milton & 1/wf Susannah BLAKE (1661, 1670-1729), Milton; 29 Aug 1688, 30 Aug; Milton/Windham, CT

WALE, Richard & Hannah SKERRY; 21 Dec 1699; Boston

WALES, Samuel (-1712) & 1/wf Mary _?_ (-Apr 1700); b 1678(9?); Dorchester

WALES, Samuel (-1712) & 2/wf Hannah PEAKE (-1731); 19 Dec 1700; Roxbury

WALES, Thomas & Elizabeth _?_ ; b 1668; Boston

WALES, Timothy (?1616-1690) & _?_ ; b 1651; Dorchester

WALES, Timothy (1651-1720+, 1722) & 1/wf _?_ ; Boston

WALES, Timothy (1651-1722) & 2/wf Sarah [WRIGHT] (1670-3 May 1726); b 1701?, no issue; Boston

WALFORD, Ham & 1/wf Mary (GODDARD) (BENNETT) (FIELD), dau John, w Arthur, w John/Joseph; by 1698

WOLFORD, Jeremiah (-1662?, 1660) & Mary [BATCHELDER], m/2 John AMENSENE/AMAZEAN; b 1653?, b 1661, b 1656; Portsmouth, RI?, NH?

WOLFORD, Thomas (-1666, 1667?) & Jane _?_ (1598-1670+); b 1631; Charlestown/Portsmouth, NH

WALK, John (-1694?) & Abigail _?_ ; b 1689; Salem

WALKER/WAKER/WAGER, Andrew & Elizabeth ALLEN (1672-); 8 Aug 1689; Boston

WALKER, Archibald & Mary GARDNER/GARDINER?; 18 Jul 1690; Providence

WALKER, Augustine (-1653) & 1/wf Anna/Hannah _?_ ; b 1640; Charlestown

WALKER, Augustine (-1653) & 2/wf Mary _?_ ; b 1653(4?); Charlestown

WALKER, Benjamin & Palgrave [EDWARDS]; in London?, 8 Jan 1671/2, Stepney, Eng; Boston

WALKER, Ebenezer (1676-) & Mehitable WILMARTH (-1702); 19 Nov 1700; Rehoboth

WALKER, Edward & _?_ ; 1690 or bef; Newington, NH

WALKER, Edward & Elizabeth [DEAN] (1671-); b 1690; Charlestown/N. Brookfield

WALKER, Francis & Elizabeth [SOULE]; betw 1650 & 1668, aft 1662?, b 1663?, b 1668; Middleborough/Bridgewater

WALKER, George & _?_ ; New Haven

WALKER, George (1662-) & Mary JACKSON; 25 Dec 1689; Portsmouth, NH

WALKER, George (see George WALKUP) & Naomi [STIMSON]; b 24 Jul 1690; Reading

WALKER, George & Rebecca DAVENPORT; 5 Oct 1699; Boston

WALKER, Henry (-1693) & Mary (_?_) (ROBINSON) BROWNE (-1690), w Abraham, w William; 26 Sep 1662; Gloucester

WALKER, Henry (-1726+) & Ruth (KENDALL) WALKER, w John; 15 Oct 1700; Woburn

WALKER, Isaac (-1674) & 1/wf Sarah __?__ ; Boston

WALKER, Isaac (-1674) & 2/wf 3/wf Susannah [SYMONDS] (-living in 1688); b 1646; Boston

WALKER, Isaac[2] (1647-1688) & Hannah [FRARY], m/2 Andrew BELCHER 1690; no ch; Boston

WALKER, Israel (1648-1719, Woburn) & Susanna [BALDWIN] (1652-1694); b 1672; Woburn/Lexington

WALKER, Israel (-1719) & Hannah (LEFFINGWELL) FLAGG (-1724), w Gershom; 10 Dec 1696; Woburn

WALKER, Jabez (1668-1742) & Elizabeth __?__ ; b 1695; Eastham

WALKER, Jacob (1644-) & Elizabeth (WHEELER) BLAKEMAN/BLACKMAN? (1642-), w Samuel; 6 Dec 1670; Stratford, CT/Huntington, LI

WALKER, James (1618-1691/[2]?) & 1/wf Elizabeth [PHILLIPS]? (1619-1678); b 1646, ca 1643?; Taunton

WALKER, James & Lydia __?__ ; b 1658

WALKER, James & Elizabeth __?__ ; b 1659; Chelmsford

WALKER, James (-1718, ae 72) & Barsheba BRUKES/BROOKS (1655-1738); 23 Dec 1673; Taunton

WALKER, James (1618-1691/2?) & 2/wf Sarah (RICHMOND) REW, w Edward; 4 Nov 1678; Taunton

WALKER, James (1674-) & 1/wf Sarah RICHMOND (1670-1727); 6 Oct 1699; Taunton

WALKER, John (-1647) & ?[Katherine]/?Hannah __?__ (not HUTCHINSON); b 1630?, b 1638?, b 1625?; Roxbury/Portsmouth, RI

WALKER, John (-1652) & Grace __?__ , m/2 Edward WATSON 1652; b 1641; New Haven, CT

WALKER, John (-1663) & Lydia REED; 20 Oct 1654; Marshfield

WALKER, John (-1711) (see John b 1656, Robert m ca 1636) & 1/wf Anna/Hannah [?LEAGER]? (-1672, ae 41); b 1667?; Charlestown

WALKER, John (-1711) & Hannah MIRICK (-1714) (see __?__ MERCER); 1 Aug 1672; Charlestown

WALKER, John (1656-1678/9) & Hannah [LEAGER] (1655-), m/2 Thomas PHILLIPS; b 1677, 1673 (see m 1667); Boston

WALKER, John (1650-1724) & 1/wf Mary PIERCE (1654-1695); 14 Oct 1672; Woburn

WAKER/WALKER, John & Elizabeth WOODBERRIE/WOODBURY (1657-); 12 Mar 1678/9; Beverly/Boston

WAKER/WALKER, John & Elizabeth __?__ ; b 1681; Wethersfield, CT

WALKER, John (?1657-1747?) & Mary KNOLES/KNOWLES; 22 Jul 1684; Taunton

WALKER, John (ca 1665-) & Lydia [?COLBURN]/COBURN (1668-); b 1688(9?), b 1686?; Chelmsford

WALKER, John (1665-1699) & Ruth KENDALL (1675-), m/2 Henry WALKER 1700, Woburn; 9 Nov 1691; Woburn

WALKER, John & Abigail [GRAFTON] (1667-), m/2 Joseph ANDREW 1704; b 1693, b 1689; Salem

WALKER, John & [?Hannah] __?__ ; b 1696; Chelmsford

WALKER, John (1667-) & Elizabeth __?__ ; b 1701, b 1696?; Portsmouth, NH/etc.

WALKER, John & 2/wf Bethiah SIMONDS; 13 Aug 1696; Woburn

WALKER, Joseph & Elizabeth [MOSES] (ca 1640-); b 1662, ca 1660; ?Portsmouth, NH

WALKER/WALTERS, Joseph (-1687, 1686?) & Abigail PRUDDEN (1647/8-1718), m/2 Richard HUBBELL 1688; 14 Nov 1667, at Milford; Stratford, CT

WALKER, Joseph (1645-1729, Billerica) & Sarah WYMAN (-1729); 15 Dec 1669; Billerica/Woburn

WALKER, Joseph & Hannah [PHILBROOK] (1651-), m/2 John SEAVEY 1686; 1670?; Hampton, NH/Portsmouth, NH

WALKER, Joseph & Abigail __?__ ; b 1674; Boston

WALKER, Nathaniel (son of Capt. Richard) & __?__ [DYER?]; ?Lynn

WALKER, Obadiah (son Capt. Richard) & Sarah [HAUGH]/[HOUGH], m/2 Ephraim SAVAGE 1678; b 1674, b 1673; Lynn/Reading

WALKER, Obadiah & Mary __?__ ; b 1674

WALKER, Peter (1649?-1711) & Hannah [HUTCHINSON] (1659-1704, ae 44!); b 1689; Taunton

WALKER, Philip (-1679) & Jane (?BUTTERWORTH)/[METCALF] (1632-1707), m/2 John POLLEY; b 1655; Rehoboth

WALKER, Philip (1661-) & 1/wf Mary BOWEN (-1694); 31 Dec 1687, 31 Dec 168-, -ember 1689; Rehoboth

WALKER, Philip & 2/wf Sarah __?__ (-1739, 6 Feb 1739, in 68th y); b 1696; Rehoboth
WALKER, Capt. Richard¹ (1593, 1611-1687, ae 95) & 2/wf? Sarah __?__ (-1687+, at E. Cambridge) (signed deed 1646) (see below); ca 1640, b 1611 or 1612?, ca 1638?; Lynn
WALKER, Richard & Anne [BOLTON] HOLDON, w Richard?; b 1637, aft 1634; Boston
WALKER, Richard² & 1/wf Jane [TALMAGE]; ca 1639?; Reading
WALKER, Richard² & 2/wf? Persis __?__; b 1639; Salem/Reading (same man?)
WALKER, Richard (ca 1638?-) & Sarah STORY (ca 1641-); 29 Oct 1661; Ipswich
WALKER, Richard & Sarah __?__; b 1697; Newbury
WALKER, Richard & Hannah __?__; b 1695; Newport
WALKER, Robert (1606-1687) (ae ca 72 in 1679) (see John WALKER m ca 1667) & __?__ (wf Sarah LEAGER? 1636+) (-1695); b 1636, Manchester, Eng, b 1623; Boston
WALKER, Robert & Hannah __?__; b 1640; Charlestown
WALKER, Robert & Ruth WILCOXSON (1677-); 1 Aug 1695; Stratford, CT
WALKER, Samuel (?1617-1684) (ae 44 in 1661) & 1/wf __?__; b 1643; Reading/Woburn
WALKER, Samuel (1642?-1703, Woburn) & 1/wf Sarah REED (-1681, living in 1693); 10 Sep 1662, 23 Oct, 10 Sep 1661(2?); Woburn
WALKER, Samuel & Sarah [SCOTTO]; b 24 Sep 1672, b 1672; Boston
WALKER, Samuel (-1684) & 2/wf Ann/Agnes? SHELDON [ALGER] (-1716), w Arthur; aft 14 Oct 1675, b 1677; Woburn
WALKER, Samuel (1655-1712) & Martha IYDE/[IDE] (1654-1700); 11 Nov 1681; Rehoboth
WALKER, Samuel & Hannah __?__ (1642-); aft 1 Nov 1681; Woburn
WALKER, Samuel, Woburn & Judith HOWARD (-1724), Concord; 1 Jun 1688, 1689?; Woburn/moved to Burlington, NJ
WALKER, Samuel (-1703, ae 61) & Abigail (CARTER) FOWLE (1640-1718), w James, m/3 Samuel STONE; 18 Apr 1692; Woburn
WALKER, Samuel & Abigail (BUTLER) CRANE, m/3 Samuel WRIGHT; 23 Feb 1697; Wethersfield, CT/Stratford, CT
WALKER, Shubael (-1689) (son Capt. Richard) & Patience JUETT/JEWETT (1645-), m/2 Richard DOLE 1690; 29 May 1666; Lynn/Bradford/Reading
WALKER, Thomas & 1/wf __?__
WALKER, Thomas (ca 1605-1659) & 2/wf? Anne __?__ (-1664+); b 1650; Boston
WALKER, Thomas (-1697) & Mary [STONE] (1644-1731), m/2 John GOODENOW 1705; b 1661; Boston/Sudbury
WALKER, Thomas (ca 1638-1726?) & Susanna COLLINS (1643?-bef Jul 1724); 25 Mar 1662; Boston
WALKER, Thomas & Elizabeth PARRIS; 4 Nov 1684; Bristol, RI
WALKER, Thomas & Martha HOW (1669-); 7 Dec 1687; Sudbury
WALKER, Thomas (1665-) & Rebecca [PAINE] (dau Moses & Elizabeth (COLBURN)); b 1687(8?); Boston
WALKER, Thomas & Mary (?BLACKMORE) (?ADAMS) SMITH, ?w Thomas, ?w John/w James; b 1699, b 1698?; Charlestown
WALKER, Thomas & Elizabeth __?__; b 1701?
WALKER, Timothy (-1706, ae 34) & Elizabeth FOWLE (1681-), m/2 Stephen HALL; 2 Mar 1699, prob 1698/9; Woburn/Charlestown
WALKER, William (-1720+) & 1/wf Alice __?__ (1630-); ca 1640/5?, by 1670, no ch?; Portsmouth, NH
WALKER, William (1620-1703) & Sarah SNOW (?1632-1703+); 25 Jan 1654, 25 Feb 1654; Eastham
WALKER, William & Sarah GOODENOW/GOODNOW; 6 May 1686; Sudbury
WALKER, William (1659-1744) & Susanna __?__; b 1692; Eastham
WALKER, William (-1720+) & Mary (WALFORD) [BROOKIN] (1635±-), w William; 1695?, 1698+; Portsmouth, NH
WALKER, Zachariah (1637-1700) & Mary [PRUDDENS] (1641-bef Nov 1681); b 1670, b 1668, aft 1687; Fairfield/Stratford, CT/Woodbury, CT
WALKER, Zachariah (1637-1700) & 2/wf Susannah ROSSITER? (1652-1710); b 4 Jul 1675
WALKER, Zachariah (1670?-1753) & [Elizabeth MINER]/BULL (1668-1749); b 1690; Woodbury, CT
WALKER, William & Eleanor [PENDLETON]; b 1711, b 1701?
WALKER __?__ & Katherine [BARTHOLOMEW] (adopted)

WALKER _?_ & _?_ ; b 1618?; Rehoboth (widow had James, Sarah & Philip, m John **BROWNE**, bro or brother-in-law)

WALKER, _?_ & Mary **MANNING**, m/2 Robert **SEELEY** 1666

WALCUP/WALKUP, George (?1668-1748), Reading (see George **WALKER**) & Naomi **STEVEN-SON/STIMSON**, Reading; 4 Nov 1688; Billerica/Framingham

WALL, James & 1/wf Margaret _?_ ; Hampton, NH

WALL, James (-1659) (Thomas **SPENCER** his son-in-law 1652) & 2/wf Mary **(PHILBRICK) TUCK** (-1699, 1702?); b 1656(7?), b 1656; Hampton, NH

WALLICE, & 1/wf Elizabeth **MORGAN** (-1703); 23 Mar 1695/6; Beverly

WALLIS, Caleb (1657-1714, 1715?) & Sarah **STONE** (1669-); 12 Dec 1687; Beverly

WALLIS, George (1619-1685) & Eleanor _?_ ; Portsmouth, NH

WALLIS, George & Ann **SHORTRIDGE**; 18 Nov 1686; Portsmouth, NH

WALLIS, James & Martha [**STANFORD**]; b 1694; Beverly/Gloucester

WALLIS, John (-1690) & Mary **PHIPPEN** (1644-); b 1662; Gloucester/?Falmouth, ME

WALLAS, John & Bridget [**SHEPARD**]; b 1675; Salem

WALLIS, Joshua & Abiah/Abial? **CONANT** (-1696); 1 Jun 1691; Beverly/Windham, CT

WALLIS, Joshua & Hannah **WELLS**; 11 Nov 1697; Windham, CT/Wenham

WALLIS, Josiah & Elizabeth [**WOODMAN**?] (1661-); b 1694; Beverly

WALLIS, Josiah & 1/wf Mary [**STANFORD**]; b 1696; Gloucester/Falmouth, ME

WALLIS, Nathaniel (?1630-1709, ae 77), Scarboro, ME, & Margaret [**WALLIS**?] (- 1711, ae ca 84); ca 1654; Portland, ME/Beverly

WALLICE, Nathaniel & Anna **(BALCH) RICH**, w Edward; m int 31 Mar 1698, m 20 Apr 1698; Beverly

WALLACE, Nicholas (1634-) & Jane [**LINDES**], m/2 Henry **MERROW** 1660, 1661; 1655; Charlestown

WALLIS, Nicholas (1634-) & Sarah **BRADSTREET**; 13 Apr 1657; Ipswich

WALLIS, Nicholas & Rebecca **SUMMERSBIE/SOMERBY**; 28 Apr 1691; Ipswich/Newbury

WALLIS, Richard, Norwich, CT, & _?_ , m/2 Jacob **WAKELEE** by 1677; b 1670

WALLIS, Robert & _?_ ; b 1637, b 1634?; Ipswich

WALLACE, Robert & Susanna [**LAWRENCE**]; b 1681; Charlestown

WALLIS, Samuel & Sarah **WATSON**; 30 Dec 1690; Ipswich

WALLIS, Samuel & Anna/Ann? **PORTER**; 7 Jul 1696; Ipswich/Topsfield

WALLIS, Thomas (he or his wife related to the **KELLY**s; he was called cousin in 1698 by Sarah **KELLY**, Sr. ae 55) & Sarah _?_ ; b 1696; Boston

WALLIS, Thomas & Christian _?_ ; b 1698(9?); Boston

WALLIS, William & Jane **DRAKE**; 15 Dec 1673; Hampton, NH

WALLEN, Ralph & Joyce _?_ ; b 1627, b 1623; Plymouth

WALLER, Christopher (1620-1676) & Margaret [**FELTON**]/**INGERSOLL**? (-1700), m/2 Robert **FULLER**; no issue; Salem/Ipswich

WALLER, John & Mary **DURINE/?DURANT**; 28 Dec 1678; Lyme, CT

WALER, Joseph (-1672?) & Lydia _?_ , m/2 John **DAVIS** 1672; b 1669(70?); Boston/Fairfield, CT

WALLER, Joseph (1670-) & Abigail _?_ , m/2 Israel **CURTIS** 1728); b 1695?; Woodbury, CT

WALLER, Matthew & ?Sarah _?_ ; ca 1637?; Salem/Providence/New London

WALLER, Samuall & Mary **DANIELS/DANNIEL**; 26 Dec 1685; New London

WALLER, Samuel (-1742) & Hannah **(HEMPSTEAD) MOORE**; b 1701?; New London, CT

WALER, Thomas & 1/wf Martha/Mary? _?_ (see below); b 1667; Boston

WALLER, Thomas & 2/wf Mary [**PHILLIPS**]; b 1670, pledged 1665, b 1667; Boston

WALLER, William[1] & Elizabeth [**MARVIN**]/[?**WOLTERTON**]; ca 1648; Saybrook, CT/Lyme, CT

WALLER, William (?1650-1681?) & Mary [**TINKER**] (1653-), m/2 John **SMITH**; ca 1673/76?; Saybrook, CT/Lyme, CT

WALLER, [Thomas], Sr. & Joan _?_ , m/2 Francis **CRONKHAM** 1669+; Boston

WALLER, _?_ & Rebecca **GARUET/GARVET**; b 7 Oct 1681; Norwalk?

WALLEY, John & Elizabeth **WING** (1644-); 3 Apr 1661; Boston

WALLEY, John (?1644-1712) & Sarah _?_ ; b 1677; Boston/Barnstable

WALLEY, John & Sarah _?_ ; b 1685; Bristol, RI

WALLEY, John & Elizabeth [**ALDEN**] (1665-), m/2 Simon **WILLARD** 1702; b 1693; Boston

WALLEY, Rev. Thomas[1] (-1677/8) & _?_ ; in Eng, [b 1640]; Barnstable

WALLEY, Thomas[2] (-1672) & Hannah [**BACON**] (1643-1685), m/2 George **SHOVE** 1675; ca 1660; Taunton

WALLEY, Thomas & Christian JOHNSON; 22 Sep 1692; Boston
WALLEY, William & Ruth [LONG] (1639-1682+), m/2 John BAKER 1670; b 1659; Charlestown
WALLEY, William (1659-) & Sarah MARSHALL (1667-); 18 Feb 1685, 1684; Charlestown
WALLING, James (-1753) & 1/wf _?_; Providence/Smithfield
WALLING, Thomas (-1674) & 1/wf Mary [ABBOT] (-1669); b 1651; Providence
WALLING, Thomas & Margaret (WHITE) COLWELL, div wf Robert, m/3 Daniel ABBOTT 1678; 19 Jun 1669; Providence
WALLING, Thomas & Sarah ELWELL; 20 May 1695, 10 May; East Greenwich, RI/Providence/Cohansey, NJ
WALLINGFORD, James (1665-) & Deborah [HAZELTON]; b 1693; Bradford
WALLINGFORD, John (1659-) & Mary TUTTLE; 6 Dec 1687; Dover, NH/Bradford
WALLINGFORD, Nicholas (-1682) & Sarah TRAVERS, m/2 Onesipherous MARSH; 30 Aug 1654; Newbury/Bradford
WALLINGFORD, Nicholas (-1682) & Elizabeth PALMER, m/2 Anthony BENNETT 1686/[7?], m/3 Henry RILEY 1700; 4 Dec 1678; Bradford
WALSBEE, David & 1/wf Hannah [MANNING]? (-1655/6); b 1651; Braintree
WALSBY, David & 2/wf Ruth BASS (-1659); 24 Sep 1656; Braintree
WALSBY, David & 3/wf Ruth _?_; b 1667, aft 1659; Braintree
WALSTON?/WALDSTONE/?WALSTONE/?WALTON, John (-1680?) & Ann/Anna WRIGHT, m/2 Peter TALLMAN 1683; 6 Feb 1677; Killingworth, CT
WALTER, Nehemiah (1663-1750) & Sarah [MATHER] (1671-1746); ca 1691; Roxbury
WALTER, Richard & Sarah _?_ (returned to Eng), m/2 Thomas LUCK 1659
WALTER, Thomas & 1/wf _?_; b 1663; Roxbury
WALTER, Thomas (-1724) & Hannah [GRAY] (1657-1734); b 1680; Charlestown
WALTER, Thomas & 2/wf Abigail (PHILLIPS) (WOODBURY) EAST, w Jonathan, w David; 17 Aug 1687, 19 Sep 1687; Charlestown/Boston
WALTERS, Timothy & Ruth BATES; b 6 Oct 1714, b 1701?; Hempstead, LI?/Haddam, CT
WALTHAM/WALTON, Henry (-1656) & Ann _?_ (-living 1659); b 1640, b 1619?; Weymouth
WALTHAM, John & Rebecca _?_; b 1687; Beverly
WALTON, George (1615-1686?) & Alice [?HILTON] (ca 1617-); by 1641; Dover, NH/Great Island
WALTON, George (1649-1678?, 1679?) & Mary _?_, m/2 Samuel RAND 1679; Great Island, NH
WALTON, Henry & Mary _?_; b 1639; Boston
WALTON, John & _?_; b 1638; Portsmouth, NH (sailed for Eng)
WALTON/WALSTON?, John & Ann/Anna? [WRIGHT], m/2 Peter TALLMAN; 6 Feb 1677 (see WALSTON); Guilford, CT/Killingworth, CT
WALTON, Lawrence & Margaret SMITH; 10 Aug 1693; Preston, CT
WALTON, Samuel (1639-1718) & Sarah [MAVERICK] (1641-1714); ca 1663; Marblehead
WALTON, Shadrack (-1741, ae 83) & Mary [NUTTER]; b 1684; Newcastle, NH
WALTON, William (-1669?, 1668?) & Elizabeth [COOKE]; in Eng, b 1627; Lynn/Hingham
WALTON, Richard & _?_ [GALPIN]; b 1683, Rye, NY
WALTON, Thomas & _?_ LAWRENCE; m lic 16+ Dec 1671; Staten Is., NY
WALSWORTH/WALWORTH, William (-1703) & Mary [SEATON] (-1752); b 1694, aft 1689, b 1692; Groton, CT/Fishers Island
WAN, John (Indian) & Lucretia _?_ (-1665); New Haven
WANNERTON, Thomas & Ann _?_ (-1671+), m/2 Thomas WILLIAMS; b 5 Jul 1643; Strawberry Bank
WANTON, Edward (1632, 1629-1716) & 1/wf Elizabeth/?Margaret _?_ (-1674); b 1658, 1663?; Boston/Scituate
WANTON, Edward (-1716) & 2/wf Mary _?_; b 1677; Scituate
WANTON, John & Mary [STAFFORD]/STOVER; b 1697, int 15 Nov 1695 Boston?; Newport
WANTON, Joseph (1664-1754), Scituate, RI, & Sarah FREEBORN (1667-1737), Portsmouth; 29 Jan 1690, 1689; Scituate, MA/Tiverton, RI
WANTON, William (1670-) & 1/wf Ruth BRIANT (1673-), Scituate, MA; 1 Jun 1691; Portsmouth, RI
WARD, Andrew & 1/wf _?_ [?BARKER]; ?ca 1623; Watertown/Fairfield, CT
WARD, Andrew (?1597-1659) & 2/wf Hester SHERMAN (1606-); ca 1624-5?; Watertown/Fairfield, CT
WARD, Andrew (?1643-1690) & Tryal/Trial MEIGS; ca 1667/8; Guilford, CT/Killingworth, CT

WARD, Andrew & Deborah **JOY** (**GAY** wrong); 19 Nov 1691; Killingworth, CT
WARD, Benjamin (-1666) & Mary [**BUTLER**], wid, had son Stephen; b 1621; Boston
WARD, Edmund & Mary [**HOYT**]; b 1694; Eastchester, NY/Westchester, NY
WARD, Edward (-1749) & Grace [**LOVERING**] (ca 1677-1754); b 1699; Newton
WARD, Eleazer (-1676) & Hannah **RICE**, m/2 Richard **TAYLOR** 1677; 10 Jul 1675; Marlborough
WARD, George (-1653) & _?_ ; b 1631; Branford, CT
WARD, Henry (1635±-1715) & Remember **FARROW** (1642-1715); 3 Feb 1659/60; Hingham
WARD, Henry & Ruth **BAILEY**; 25 May 1694; Hingham
WARD, Increase (1645-1690) & Record **WHEELOCKE** (1644-1726); 3 Oct 1672; Medfield
WARD, Israel (-1734) & _?_ ; LI/Greenwich, NJ
WARD, James (-1712) & Elizabeth **ROCKWELL** (1670-1721); 1 Feb 1693/4; Middletown, CT
WARD, John (1606-1693) & Alice **EDMUNDS**; 24 May 1636 m lic; Haverhill
WARD, John (-1698) & Phebe _?_ [not **FENNER**]; b 1641; Newport
WARD, John (1626-1708) & Hannah [**JACKSON**] (1631-1704); ca 1649-50; Cambridge/Newton
WARD, John & Sarah [**HILLS**] (ca 1633-1691), m/2 Stephen **DAVIS**; by 1651; Branford, CT/Newark, NJ
WARD, John (?1639-1684) & Mary **HARRIS** (1645-), m/2 Josiah **GILBERT** 1688; 18 Apr 1664; Middletown, CT
WARD, John (1658-1727) & Mary **SPRING** (1659-1731); 30 Nov 1681; Cambridge/Newton
WARD, John (-1694) & Hannah (**CRANE**) [**HUNTINGTON**], w Thomas; aft 1684; Branford, CT
WARD, John (-1705) & Sarah [**NICHOLSON**] (1653-1705+); ca 1685; Portsmouth, RI
WARD, John & Jehoadan **HARVEY**; 22 Aug 1689; Mablehead/Gloucester
WARD, John & Hannah **BEAL**; 24 May 1698; Hingham/Weymouth
WARD, Jonathan & Abigail **HALL**; 31 Dec 1700; Cambridge/Newton
WARD, Joseph & Abiah **WHEELOCK**; 5 Jun 1700; Marlborough
WARD, Joshua (-1680) & Hannah **FLINT** (1647?-), m/2 Eleazer **KEYSER** 1680+; 18 Jan 1668/9; Salem
WARD, Josiah & Elizabeth [**SWAINE**] (1654-), m/2 David **OGDEN**; NJ?
WARD, Lawrence & _?_ ; New Haven/Branford, CT/NJ
WARD, Marmaluke & _?_ ; Newport
WARD, Miles (-1650) & Margaret [**UGGS**], m/2 Thomas **RIX**; b 1641, b 1639, Co. Kent, Eng; Salem/VA
WARD, Miles (-1764, ae 92) & 1/wf Sarah **MASSEY** (1669-1728); 16 Sep 1697; Salem
WARD, Nathaniel (1570-) & _?_ ; in Eng, b 1606; Ipswich
WARD, Nathaniel (will 1664) (William **MARKHAM**, a kinsman) & 2/wf? Jane [**HOPKINS**], w John, m/3 Gregory **WOLTERTON** by 1670; aft 1654, b 1664; Hadley/Hartford
WARD, Nathaniel & Mary **BRADSTREET**; 11 Nov 1672
WARD, Nathaniel & Christian [**SWAYNE**] (1659-); NJ?
WARD, Obadiah (1632±-1718) & Mary _?_ , (-1706); 28 Nov 1667; Marlborough
WARD, Obadiah (1663-1717) & Joanna (**MIXER**) **HARRINGTON** (1666-1725+), w Joseph; 20 Dec 1693; Sudbury
WARD, Peter & Mary **JOY**; 30 Nov 1698, 1698; Killingworth, CT
WARD, Richard (1635±-1666) & Mary **MOORES/MOORE** (-1703), m/2 Daniel **STONE** 1667; 8 Sep 1661; Sudbury
WARD, Richard & Mary [**FOWLER**]; ca 1680/90?, b 1692, b 25 Nov 1691, b 11 Oct 1683; Mamaraneck, NY/Eastchester
WARD, Richard (1666-1739) & Thankful **TROWBRIDGE** (1668-1742); 15 Dec 1690; Newton/Cambridge
WARD, Richard & Mary **GUSTIEN**; 22 Oct 1697; Boston
WARD, Robert & Sarah _?_ ; b 1660; Boston
WARD, Robert (-1731) & Margaret **PEACHIE** (1668-1736); 22 Dec 1692; Charleston
WARD, Robert & Lucy _?_ ; b 1694; Boston
WARD, Samuel (1593-1682) & 1/wf Mary **HILLIARD**?; b 1635; Charlestown/Hingham
WARD, Samuel (-1682) & 2/wf? (no) Frances (**PITCHER**) [**REYCROFT**]; ca 28 Nov 1638; Hingham/Charlestown
WARD, Samuel & Mary **CARTER**; 1 Jan 1658, 1658/9?; Branford, CT
WARD, Samuel (1638-1690) & 1/wf Abigail [**MAVERICK**] (1645-1674+?); b 1663 (Samuel bpt 1674); Salem/Charlestown
WARD, Samuel & Joanna _?_ (Hannah 1673); b 1665; Boston

WARD, Samuel (1641-1729) & 1/wf Sarah [HOW] (1644-1707); 6 Jun 1667; Marlborough
WARD, Samuel (?1648-1693) & 1/wf ?Hannah [OGDEN] (-1687+); ca 1672/4, [b 1671?]; Fairfield, CT
WARD, Samuel (1638-1690) & 2/wf? Sarah (BRADSTREET) [HUBBARD], w Richard; b 24 Jun 1684; Marblehead/Charlestown
WARD, Samuel (?1648-1693) & Hannah (HAWKINS) [NICHOLS] (±1661-1698), w Jonathan, m/3 John JUDSON 1693?; aft 30 Apr 1691; Fairfield, CT
WARD, Samuel (-1702) & Mary (FOSTER) SALE; 10 Dec 1691; Boston
WARD, Samuel & Hannah? _?_; b 1698; Eastchester, NY/New York, NY
WARD, Samuel (1674-) & Sarah TUTTLE (1672-1703); 13 Nov 1699; Ipswich
WARD, Samuel (-1715) & _?_; b 1701?; Middletown, CT
WARD, Thomas & [Margaret SHAW]? (1634?, 1624?-); b 1652, b 1651; Hampton, NH
WARD, Thomas (1641-1689) & 1/wf ?Mary _?_; Newport
WARD, Thomas (1641-1689) & 2/wf Amy/Ammi? [BILLINGS]/SMITH (1658-1732), m/2 Arnold COLLINS 1692, 1691/2; b 1683, b 1689; Newport
WARD, Thomas (1661-1728) & Anna/Hannah TAPPIN (1662-1712); 6 Dec 1683; Middletown, CT
WARD, Thomas (1666/7-1743) & Sarah _?_; b 1692; Hampton, NH
WARD, William (?1603-1687) & 1/wf [Eleanor?] _?_; in Eng, b 1626; Cambridge/Newton
WARD, William (?1603-1687) & 2/wf Elizabeth [STOREY?] (1613-1700); b 1641, b 1639; Cambridge/Newton
WARD, William (?1631-1676) & Deborah [LOCKWOOD] (1636-), m/2 John TOPPING ca 1677; ca 1656, b 20 Oct 1658; Fairfield, CT
WARD, William (1632-1690) & 1/wf Sarah _?_; b 1659; Middletown, CT
WARD, Ens. William (1632-1690) & 2/wf Phebe [FENNER] (1633/4-1691); 28 Mar 1660; Middletown, CT
WARD, William (1640-) & Hannah WARD/BRIGHAM? EAMES (1656-1720), w Gershom; 4 Aug 1679; Marlborough
WARD, William (1664-1752) & Abigail SPRING (1667-1742); b 1683, 31 Dec 1689, Dec ult.; Newton/Cambridge
WARD, William (1670-) & Judith _?_; b 1691; Marlborough
WARD, William & ?Grace [?MILLS]; b 1683; Flushing, LI/Upton, NJ
WARD, William (1677-1767) & Leatis/Lettis [BEACH?]; b 1701?, ?14 Dec 1701; Wallingford, CT
WARD, [Richard] (-1635, in Eng) & Joyce [TRAFORD] (-1641); Wethersfield, CT
WORDEN, Isaac (1673-) & Rebecca _?_; b 1701?; Kings Town, RI
WORDEN, James & Mary _?_; b 1670(1?); Boston
WORDEN, Peter (-1639) (John LEWIS a grandson) & _?_; in Eng, ca 1607; Lynn/Yarmouth
WORDEN, Peter (?1609±-1681) & Mary [?WINSLOW]/SEARS? (1610-1687); b 1639; Yarmouth
WORDEN, Peter (-1732) & Mary HOLLY (-1733); 20 Feb 1693; Yarmouth
WORDEN, Samuel (-1716, ae 71) & Hopestill [HOLLEY]; b 1665; Yarmouth/Kings Town, RI/Stonington, CT
WORDEN, Samuel & Mehitable [HINCKLEY] (1659-), m/2 William AVERY 1698; b 1682; Dedham/Boston
WARDEN/WORDEN?, Thomas (-1730) & Elizabeth [SERGEANT?/?SARGENT]/?Mary JOHNSON (-1718, ae 72?); b 1691, b 1687?; Scituate/Boston
WARDWELL, Eliakim (1634-) & Lydia PERKINS; 17 Oct 1659; Hampton, NH/LI/NY
WARDELL, Elihu (1641-) & Elizabeth WADE (-27 May 1665); 26 May 1665, 27 May 1665; Ipswich/Charlestown
WORDELE, Elihu & Sarah (ADAMS) WEST (1666-), wid; 15 Oct 1700; Boston/Ipswich
WARDELL, Jonathan (1672-Ipswich) & 1/wf Catharine/Katharine CHICKRIN/CHICKERING (1669-); 12 Dec 1695, 12 Dec 1696, at Charlestown; Ipswich/Charlestown
WARDLE, Samuel (1643-1692) & Sarah (HOOPER) HAWKES, w Adam; 9 Jan 1672, 1672/3; Andover
WERDALL, Thomas (-10 Dec 1646) & Elizabeth _?_; in Eng, b 1634; Boston/Exeter, NH
WARDALL, Uzell[2]/Usal? (1639-1732) & 1/wf Mary (KINSMAN) RING/RINDGE, w Daniel; 3 May 1664; Ipswich
WARDWELL, Uzel[2]/Uzal (1639-1732) & 2/wf Grace _?_ (-1741); b 1684; Bristol, RI
WERDALL, William[1] (-1670) & 1/wf Alice _?_; b 1637; Boston/Exeter, NH/Wells, ME
WARDELL, William (-1670) & 2/wf Elizabeth (?CROWELL) PERRY JELLET/GILLETT, w Arthur, w John; 5 Dec 1656, cont 4 Dec 1657; Boston

WARDWELL, _?_ & Susannah [ELLERY] (1673-), Gloucester, m/2 John HARRIS 1700; Ipswich
WARHAM, John[1] (-1670) & 1/wf _?_ (-?Dec 1634); Dorchester
WARHAM, John[1] (-1670) & 2/wf Jane (DABINOTT) [NEWBERRY] (-1655?), w Thomas; ca 1637; Windsor, CT
WARHAM, John (-1670) & 3/wf Abigail (_?_) BRANKER (-1684), w John; 9 Oct 1662, 16 Oct?; Windsor, CT
WAREHAM, William & Hannah ADAMS (1650-); 10 Feb 1681, 1681/2; Newbury
WARFIELD, John & 1/wf Elizabeth SHEPPARD (-1669); 3 Aug 1661; Medfield
WARFIELD, John & 2/wf Peregrina WHEELOCKE (-1671); 26 Oct 1669; Medfield
WARFIELD, John & 3/wf Hannah RANDALL; 26 Dec 1671; Medfield/Mendon
WARING, Edmund (1674-1749) & Elizabeth BOUTON (1681-1760); 6 Oct 1698; Norwalk, CT/Oyster Bay, LI
WARING, John & Elizabeth [WHITE]; Southampton, LI/Lloyd's Neck/Brookhaven, LI
WAREING, John (-1687) & Joyce _?_ ; Salem
WARING, Richard & _?_ ; Brookhaven, LI/Oyster Bay, LI
WARKMAN, Samuel & Martha WHITE; 3 Aug 1693; Boston
WARLAND, Owen & Hannah GUY/GAY?, ?dau John; 3 Apr 1679; Cambridge
WARLY/WARLEY, _?_ & Abigail _?_ ; b 1683; Salem
WARNER, Andrew[1] (1595-1684) & 1/wf Mary HUMPHREY (1602/3-); 5 Oct 1624; Cambridge/ Hartford
WARNER, Andrew[2] (-1682) & Rebecca FLETCHER (1638-1715), m/2 Jeremy ADAMS; 10 Oct 1653, Milford, CT; Hartford/Hatfield/Middletown, CT
WARNER, Andrew[1] (1595-1684) & 2/wf Esther (WAKEMAN) [SELDEN] (-1693), w Thomas; ca 1656?; Hadley/Deerfield
WARNER, Andrew & Deborah (LEFFINGWELL) [CROW], w Nathaniel; aft 2 Jul 1695, by 1697; Hadley/Hartford/Windham
WARNER, Daniel (-1688) & 1/wf Elizabeth [DENNE]/DENNY?/DANE?; b 1640; Ipswich
WARNER, Daniel (-1688) & Faith [?LORD/?WATSON] BROWNE, w Edward; 1 Jul 1660; Ipswich
WARNER, Daniel (-1692) & 1/wf Mary _?_ ; b 1663(?4); Hadley
WARNER, Daniel (-1679) & 1/wf 2/wf Sarah? ROE?, dau Hugh; b 1667, b 1671; Farmington, CT
WARNER, Daniel (-1696) & Sarah DANE (1645-1701); 23 Sep 1668; Ipswich
WARNER, Daniel (-1692) & 2/wf Martha BOLTWOOD (-1710); 1 Apr 1674; Hatfield/Hadley
WARNER, Daniel & Ellen (PELL) (BOYNTON) JEWETT, w John, w Maxmilian; 1 Jun 1686; Ipswich
WARNER, Daniel (-1754) & 1/wf Mary HUBBARD (1669-); 12 Dec 1688; Hadley/Hatfield
WARNER, Daniel (-1713) & Mary ANDRUSS (1675-1709); Apr 1693; Waterbury, CT
WARNER, Daniel (-1754) & Dorcas ADAMS (1678-1701); 29 Feb 1699/1700; Ipswich
WARNER, Ebenezer & Waitstill SMEAD; 5 Jan 1698/9; Deerfield
WARNER, Eleazer (-1728, 1729) & Hester/Esther TAYLOR (-1748, ae 82); 27 May 1689, 29 May; Hadley
WARNER, Ephraim (1670-1753) & Esther RICHARDS (1673-); 16 Aug 1692; Waterbury, CT/Woodbury, CT
WARNER, Gabriel & Mary _?_ ; b 1681; Boston
WARNER, George (-1681) & _?_ ; b 1681; New Haven
WARNER, Isaac & Sarah BOLTWOOD, m/2 John LOOMIS 1696; 31 May 1666; Hadley/Northampton
WARNER, Isaac (1670-1754) & Hope NASH (1670-); 24 Jan 1694, 1693/4; Hadley/Northfield
WARNER, Jacob (-1711) & 1/wf Rebecca _?_ (-1687); b 1687; Hadley
WARNER, Jacob (-1711) & 2/wf Elizabeth [GOODWIN]; ca 1689(?); Hadley
WARNER, John (1616-1692) & Priscilla [SYMONDS] (1620-); ca 1639, not 1655; Ipswich/Hadley
WARNER, John (1615-1654±) & Priscilla HOLLIMAN (-1652+); b 1645; Providence/Warwick, RI/Salem
WARNER, John (-1700) & Anna NORTON (1625-1679); 28 Jun 1649, ?Branford, CT, 1655, 1657; Guilford, CT/Farmington/Middletown/Hartford
WARNER, John (ca 1642-1712) & 1/wf Hannah BACHELOUR/BATCHELDER (1644-1688); 20 Apr 1665; Ipswich
WARNER, John (1645-1712) & Ann/Anna GORTON; 7 Aug 1670, 4 Aug 1670, 4 Aug; Warwick, RI

WARNER, John (-1701 Waterbury, CT) & _?_ (d at Farmington); b 1670(1?); Waterbury
WARNER, John (1648-1724) & 1/wf Lydia BOLTWOOD (-1682/3); 2 Apr 1674, 1 Apr; Hadley/Springfield
WARNER, John (-1722) & Sarah WOOD; 12 Jun 1677, b 1684; Cambridge/Charlestown
WARNER, John (-1679) & Margaret _?_; bef 1649; Farmington, CT
WARNER, John (1648-1724) & 2/wf Sarah WARNER (-1687); 31 Aug 1683, ?3 Aug; Springfield
WARNER, John (1648-1724) & 3/wf Sarah FERRY (1668-1689); 30 Jun 1687; Springfield
WARNER, John, Marlboro & Elizabeth NEWBY, Marlboro; 9 Feb 1687/8; Marlboro
WARNER, John (ca 1642-1712) & 2/wf Mary (_?_) [PRINCE], w Jonathan; b 1691; Ipswich
WARNER, John (1648-1724) & 4/wf Rebecca (WILLIAMS) COOLEY (1649-1715), w Obadiah; 26 Nov 1691; Springfield/Farmington
WARNER, John (?1673-1732) & 1/wf Elizabeth COGGERSHALL/COGGESHALL (1677-1711); 27 Nov 1694; Warwick
WARNER, John & Elizabeth MIGHEL; b 1698; Suffield, CT
WARNER, John (-1751) & Rebecca RICHARDSON (1679-1745); 28 Sep 1698; Waterbury, CT
WARNER, John, Sr. (1671-) & Ann WARD; 14 Dec 1699; Middletown, CT
WARNER, Jonathan (-1733) & Elizabeth RANNEY (1668-1757); 4 Aug 1698; Middletown, CT/E. Middletown
WARNER, Mark (1646-1738) & 1/wf Abigail MONTAGUE (1653-1705); 8 Dec 1671; Hadley/Northampton
WARNER, Nathaniel (-1684) (son Daniel) & Hannah BOYNTON (-1694), m/2 John BATCHEL-DER 1687; 24 Nov 1673, 29 Nov; Ipswich
WARNER, Nathaniel (ca 1650-1714) & Joanna GARDNER (-1729); 3 Feb 1680, 1681, prob 1680/1; Hadley
WARNER, Philemon (1675-1741) & Abigail TUTTLE (1673-); 27 Apr 16[97?], 1696?, 1690; Ipswich
WARNER, Ralph & Mary TILTON; 15 May 1669 m lic; ?Gravesend, LI?
WARNER, Robert (ca 1632-1690) & 1/wf Elizabeth GRANT (-1673); Feb 1654; Middletown, CT
WARNER/WARRINAH, Robert (-1690), Middletown & 2/wf Deliverance (HAWES) ROCKWELL (-1718), w John, m/3 _?_ BISELL; 2 Feb 1674; Middletown, CT/Mendon, CT
WARNER, Samuel & _?_; b 1659?; Ipswich
WARNER, Samuel (1640-1703) & 1/wf Mercy/Mary SWAN (-1683); 21 Oct 1662; Ipswich/Dunstable
WARNER, Samuel (1640-) & 2/wf Marah/Mary (MARTIN) SWALLOW, w Ambrose; 4 May 1684, should be 1685, aft 3 Nov 1684; Dunstable
WARNER, Samuel (1668-1752) & Mehitable SABIN (1677-); 2 Jan 1694/5; Woodstock, CT
WARNER, Seth (1658-1713) & Mary WARD (-1729); 25 Dec 16[--], 1686?; Middletown, CT
WARNER, Thomas (-1660) & Katherine [MITCHELL?], m John SEARLE 1661; b 1658, b 1655; Boston/Cape Porpoise, ME
WARNER, Thomas (-1714) & Elizabeth _?_; ca 1675?; Waterbury, CT
WARNER, William (1586-1647) & [Abigail?]/Susanna? BAKER; Boxted, Eng?, ca 1611, b 1606?, ca 1613; Ipswich/Salisbury
WARNER, William (?1646-1714) (ae 57 in 1703) & Hannah ROBBINS (1643-1714); 1 Nov 1667; Wethersfield, CT
WARNER, William (-1726) & 1/wf Mary CRANE (1673-1714); 21 May 1696; Wethersfield, CT
WARNER, _?_ & Abigail TITUS, m/2 William SCOTT 1678
WARREN, Abraham (-1682) & Isabel _?_ (-1672); b 1642; Salem
WARREN, Arthur & [Mary] _?_; b 1639; Weymouth
WARREN, Arthur (1639-1671) & Abigail [ROGERS] (-1671); 1667?; Chelmsford
WARREN, Benjamin (1670-) & 1/wf Hannah MORTON (1677-1715); 22 Apr 1697; Plymouth
WARIN, Daniel (1627-1703) & Mary BARRON (ca 1631-1716); 10 Dec 1650; Watertown
WARIN, Daniel & 1/wf Elizabeth WHITNY (1656-); 19 Dec 1678; Watertown
WARREN, Ebenezer, Milton & Mary RYDER, Milton; 2 Jun 1697; Milton
WARREN, Edmund (1673-1717+) & Elizabeth BOUTON; 6 Oct 1698; Norwalk, CT/Oyster Bay, LI
WARREN, Ephraim & Elizabeth _?_ (?1663-1727), m/2? Thomas CHEEVER/[CENTER?] 1707; b 1685; Boston
WARREN, Ephraim & Abigail _?_; b 1700; Plainfield CT
WARREN, Gilbert (1656±-1733) & Sarah (EMERY) [THOMPSON]; b 1698?; Kittery, ME

WARREN, Humphrey (-1680) & Mehitable (CLARK) [DOWNE] (1640-), w Edmund; b 1674?, by 1674; Boston

WARREN, Jacob (1642-1722) & Mary HILDERITH/HILDRITH (-1730, 17 Dec 1730); 27 Jun 1667; Chelmsford/Canterbury, CT/Plainfield, CT

WARIN, Jacob, Jr. & Sarah __?__ (1667-1759); b 1689, b 1684?; Chelmsford/Plainfield, CT

WARREN, James (1621-1702) & Margaret __?__ (-1713); b 1654; Kittery, ME/Berwick, ME

WARREN, James (1665-1715) & Sarah DOTY (1666-), m/2 John BACON; 21 Jun 1687; Plymouth

WARREN, James & Mary [FOST] (1667-); 1691, ca 1692, [1 Nov 1692]; Kittery, ME

WARREN, John (ca 1585-1667) & Margaret __?__ (-1662); in Eng, b 1615; Watertown

WARREN, John & 1/wf Deborah WILSON (-1668); 21 Oct 1650; Exeter, NH/Hingham/Boston

WARREN, John (1622-1703) & Michal/Michel? (JENNISON) BLOYSS/BLOSS (-1713), w Richard; 11 Jul 1667; Watertown

WARREN, John (see John HAYWARD m 1684+) & 2/wf Elizabeth (?ROYALL) (BARLOW) [COOMBS] (-1672?), w Thomas, w John; b 1670; Boston

WARREN, John & 3/wf Elizabeth __?__, m Samuel SENDALL 1681, m John HAYWARD, m Phineas WILSON; b 1676; Boston

WARREN, John (-1703) & Mary BROWNE (1662-), m/2 Samuel HARRINGTON 1704; 22 Mar 1682; Watertown

WARREN, John & 1/wf Abigaile [HASTINGS] (1679-1710); 1699?, b 1701; Lexington

WARREN, John & __?__ ; b 1701?; Hartford

WARREN, Joseph (?1626, 1627-1689) & Priscilla [FAUNCE] (1633-1707); ca 1650; Plymouth

WARREN, Joseph & Experience WHEALOCK/WHEELOCK (1648-); 21 May 1668; Medfield

WARREN, Joseph (1663-1729, Roxbury) & Deborah [WILLIAMS] (1668-1743); ca 1690/3; Roxbury/Deerfield

WARRIN, Joseph (1657-1696) & Mehitable WILDER; 20 Dec 1692; Plymouth

WARREN, Joseph & Ruth WHEELER; 11 Mar 1696, prob 1695/6; Chelmsford

WARREN, Joshua & Rebecca [CHURCH] (1678-); b 1696; Watertown

WARREN, Nathaniel (?1624, ?1621-1667) & Sarah WALKER; 19 Nov 1645; Plymouth

WARREN, Nathaniel (1662-1707) & Phebe PECKHAM?/[MURDOCK], m/2 Thomas GRAY; no issue; Plymouth

WARREN, Peter & 1/wf Sarah TUCKER; 1 Aug 1660; Boston/Dorchester

WARREN, Peter & 2/wf Hannah [WILLIAMS?]; b 1675, b 1680; Boston

WARREN, Peter & 3/wf Esther [WOODWARD]; b 11 Oct 1687; Boston

WARREN, Richard[1] (1628-) & Elizabeth __?__ (-1673, ae ca 90); in Eng, b 1661; Plymouth

WARREN, Richard (1646-1697) & Sarah [TORREY] (1661-1722+), m/2 Thomas EWER 1712; b 1679; Middleboro

WARREN, Richard (1672-) & Lydia __?__ (1675-); b 1700; Bedford, NY

WARREN, Robert & Elizabeth BENNIT/BENNETT; 11 Dec 1700; Manchester

WARREN, Thomas & Sarah __?__ ; b 1693; Boston

WARREN, Thomas & Sarah FITCH (1661-); 14 Dec 1694; Boston

WARREN, William & __?__ ; b 1674, b 1670?; York, ME

WARREN, William & Elizabeth [CROW], m/2 Phineas WILSON (no, 2 wives); b 1676, b 1667; Hadley

WARREN, William (-1706) & Abiel ROGERS (1666-); 1 Nov 1690; Boston

WARRINER, James (1641-1727) & 1/wf Elizabeth BALDWIN (1645-1687), Milford, CT; 31 Mar 1664; Hadley?

WARRINER, James (-1727) & 2/wf Sarah ALVORD (1660-1704); 10 Jul 1687; Springfield

WARRINER, James (1668-1736) & Sarah THOMAS (1666-), dau Rowland; 20 Jan 1691/2; Springfield

WARRINER, Joseph (1645-1697) & 1/wf Mary MONTAGUE (1642-1689); 25 Nov 1668; Hadley/Enfield, CT

WARRINER, Joseph (1645-1697) & Sarah (TIBBALS) COLLINS, w Daniel, m/3 Obadiah ABBEE; 15 Jul 1691; Enfield, CT

WARRINER, William (-1676) & 1/wf Joanna SEARLE (-1660); 31 Jul 1639; Springfield

WARRINER, William (-1676) & 2/wf Elizabeth (GIBBONS) [HITCHCOCK] (-1696), w Luke, m/3 Joseph BALDWIN 1678); 2 Oct 1661; Springfield/Hadley?/Deerfield

WARRINER, William (1672-1738/9) & 1/wf Elizabeth WELLER; 5 Feb 1697; Deerfield

WARRINER, William & Abigail [LAY]; aft 1686, bef 1700

WASHBURN, Hope (-1696) & Mary [STILES] (-1712), Windsor, CT; ca 1660; Stratford, CT/Derby, CT

WASHBURN, James (1672-1749) & Mary BOWDEN (-1747); 20 Dec 1693; Bridgewater

WASHBURNE, John (1597-1670) & Margaret MOORE (1586, bpt 1588-); Bengeworth, Eng, 23 Nov 1618; Duxbury/Bridgewater

WASHBORNE, John (1620-1686, Bridgewater) & 1/wf Elizabeth MICHELL/MITCHELL (?1628-); 6 Dec 1645, Dec; ?Duxbury

WASHBURN, John (-1658), Stratford, CT, Hempstead, CT, & Mary BUTLER (-1713), m/2 Thomas HICKS by 1660; 17 Jun 1655; Stratford, CT

WASHBURN, John (1657-) & Sarah [CORNELL] (1657-), m/2 Isaac ARNOLD 1691; b 1679; LI

WASHBURNE, John (1646-1724?) & Rebecca LAPHAM; 16 Apr 1679; Bridgewater

WASHBURN, John (1620-1686) & 2/wf Elizabeth [PACKARD], w Samuel; betw 7 Nov 1684 & 30 Oct 1686; Bridgewater

WASHBURN, John (1672-1750) & 1/wf Lydia [BILLINGTON] (-1716); b 1699; Plymouth/Kingston

WASHBORNE, John & Hannah [HALLETT]; b 1701?, doubtful; LI

WASHBURN, Jonathan (-1725/6) & Mary [VAUGHN]; ca 1683; Bridgewater

WASHBURN, Joseph (?1653-1733) & Hannah [LATHAM] (1645-); ca 1676?, ca 1671?; Bridgewater/Plympton

WASHBURN, Philip (-1700+) & Elizabeth [IRISH]; b 1680, b 1664?; Bridgewater

WASHBOURN, Samuel (ca 1651-1720) & 1/wf Deborah [PACKARD]; b 1678; Bridgewater

WASHBURN, Thomas (-1732) & 1/wf Deliverance [PACKARD] (1652-); b 1684; Bridgewater

WASHBURN, William (1601-1659) & Jane/Mary? _?_; in Eng, b 1629; Stratford, CT/Hempstead, LI

WASHBURN, William (1668-1742) & Hannah WOOSTER (-1743), Derby; 20 Aug 1696; Stratford, CT/Derby, CT

WASS, John & _?_; Martha's Vineyard

WASS/WASE?, Thomas & Ann BRINLEY; b 1630?, in Eng

WATERBURY, David (ca 1655-1706) & 1/wf [Sarah NEWMAN]; b 1682; Stamford, CT

WATERBURY, David (ca 1655-1706) & 2/wf Sarah WEED (1675-), m/2 Benjamin FERRIS, m/3 Nathaniel POND; 11 Aug 1698; Stamford, CT

WATERBURY, John (-1659, 1658) & Rose (TAYLOR?)/[LOCKWOOD?], m/2 Joseph GARNSEY 1659; ca 1650, 1645?; Watertown/Stamford, CT

WATERBURY, John (-1688) & Mary WEEKS?/WEED?/WICKES?, m/2 Jonas SEELEY ca 1689; ca 1672; Stamford, CT

WATERBURY, Jonathan (-1702) & Eunice _?_; b 1677; Stamford, CT

WATERBURY, William & Alice _?_; in Eng, b 1630; Boston

WATERHOUSE, Abraham (ca 1650, ca 1644-1718+) & Rebecca [CLARK] (1653-1704); ca 1673, 1674; Saybrook, CT

WATERHOUSE, Abraham (1674-1750) & 1/wf Hannah STARKIE; 12 Nov 1697; Saybrook, CT/New London, CT

WATERHOUSE, Isaac (ca 1645, 1641-1713) & Sarah PRATT (?1657, 1652-1725); 20 Apr 1671, 1670; Lyme, CT

WATROUS, Isaac & Elizabeth [LORD] (1683-); ca 1700; Lyme, CT

WATERHOUSE, Jacob (?1618-1676) & Hannah _?_; b 1648?, b 1645?, b 1635?; Wethersfield, CT/New London, CT

WATERHOUSE, Jacob (-1728) & Ann [DOUGLAS] (1669-1713); ca 1690; New London, CT

WATERHOUSE, John (-1687) & Mary _?_, m/2 John HAYDEN 1687+; New London, CT

WATERHOUSE, Richard (-1718) & 1/wf Sarah (FERNALD) LYDE, w Allen; 29 Jun 1672; Kittery, ME

WATERHOUSE, Samuel (1675-1732?) (Sarah LIBBY was 2/wf) & 1/wf Sarah _?_; by 1700; Portsmouth, NH

WATERHOUSE, Thomas & Anna [MAHEW]; Coddenham, Co. Suffolk, Eng, b 1639; Dorchester

WATERHOUSE, Timothy & Ruth [MOSES], m/2 Joseph MEAD, m/3 Thomas SKINNER; - Jan 1700; Portsmouth, NH

WATERMAN, Benjamin (-1762) & ?Sarah KNIGHT/?Mary/?Mercy WILLIAMS; b 1701?, b 1705; Johnston, RI

WATERMAN, John (1642-1718, Plympton) & Anna/Ann STURTEVANT (1647, 1648-1720, Plympton); 7 Dec 1665; Plymouth/Marshfield

WATERMAN, John (1666-1728) & Anne [OLNEY] (1668-1745); b 1692; Warwick, RI
WATERMAN, Joseph (1643, ?1649-1712, 1711/12, 1708?, 1715?) & Sarah [SNOW] (1651-1741, ae 90); b 1674; Marshfield
WATERMAN, Nathaniel (1637-1712) & Susanna CARDER (-1711, 1712); 14 Mar 1663, 1662/3; ?Providence
WATERMAN, Nathaniel/Nathan? (-1725) & Mary OLNEY (1672-1725(-)); 9 May 1692; Providence
WATERMAN, Resolved (1638-1670) & Mercy [WILLIAMS] (1640-1705+), m/2 Samuel WINSOR 1677, m/3 John RHODES?; ca 1659; Providence
WATERMAN, Resolved (1667±-1719) & 1/wf Anne [HARRIS] (1673-); ca 1695?; Providence
WATERMAN, Richard (1590?-1673) & Bethiah __?__ (-1680); b 1634?; Salem/Providence
WATERMAN, Richard (-1744) & Abigail ANGELL (1679-1742(-)); 1 Apr 1697; Providence
WATERMAN, Robert (-1652) & Elizabeth BOURNE (ca 1613-1663), m/2 Thomas TILDEN 1653; 11 Dec 1638; Plymouth/Marshfield
WATERMAN, Robert & 1/wf Susanna LINCOLN (-1696); 30 Sep 1675, ?1 Oct; Hingham
WATERMAN, Robert (-1741, ae 88) & 2/wf Sarah (LEWIS) LINCOLN, w Thomas; 20 Feb 1698/9; Hingham
WATERMAN, Samuel & 1/wf Marsy RANSOME; 26 Jul 1692; Taunton/Plymouth
WATERMAN, Thomas & 1/wf Hannah/Ann __?__ (-1641); Roxbury
WATERMAN, Thomas & 2/wf Margaret MILLER, sister of Mrs. Robert[1] BURNAP; aft 1641, b 1670, ca 1650, prob ca 1642; Roxbury
WATERMAN, Thomas (1644-1708) & Miriam TRACY (1648-); Nov 1668; Norwich, CT
WATERMAN, Thomas (1670-1755) & Elizabeth ALLYN (1669-1755); 29 Jun 1691; Norwich, CT
WATERMAN, __?__ (-1632?) & Susannah __?__, m/2 Anthony COLBY, m/3 William WHITRIDGE; Boston
WATERS, Anthony (-1675) & Rachel [DAYTON?]/ROSE (-1675+); by Oct 1634; Marshfield/Southampton, LI/Jamaica, LI/Hempstead, LI
WATERS, Anthony & Elizabeth [WHITEHEAD]; b 1694; ?Jamaica, LI
WATERS, Bevil (-1730, in 97th y) & 1/wf ?Sarah __?__ (had 2/wf Sarah (WATERS) MYGATE, w Joseph, 1698+); b 1677; Hartford
WATERS, David (-1742) & Hannah [SMITH], dau Thomas; b 1701?; Jamaica, LI
WATERS, Edward & Bridget __?__; b 1688; Westchester, NY
WATERS, Ezekiel (1647-1721) & [Mary] __?__; b 1673; Salem
WATERS, Jacob (1650-1714) & 1/wf Sarah [HUTSON]/[HUDSON] (1656-1709); b 1676; Charlestown/Cambridge
WATERS, James (-1617 in Eng) & Phebe [MANNING], m/2 William PLASSE; in Eng, b 1600; Salem
WATERS, James & 1/wf Mary STALWORTHIE; 24 Mar 1669/70, 1668/9; Topsfield
WATERS, James (-1704) & 2/wf Rachel HART; 22 May 1695; Topsfield
WATERS, John & Frances __?__; ?b 1630; Boston
WATERS, John[2] (1640-1708) & Sarah TOMPKINS (1642-1707+); 1 Aug 1663; Salem
WATERS, John & __?__; b 1670?; Kittery, ME
WATER, John & Sarah __?__; b 1678(9?); Sudbury
WATERS, John (1665-1742) & Mary __?__; ca 1694/6, 3 ch bpt 1702; Salem
WATERS, Jonathan & __?__; Jamaica, LI
WATERS, Joseph & Martha MELLOWES (1636-); 13 Sep 1655; Boston/Milford, CT?
WATERS, Joseph (1647-1720) (left wid Hannah) & 1/wf Elizabeth __?__; b 1679; Lancaster/Groton
WATERS, Lawrence (1602-1687) & Anne [LINTON] (-1680, Charlestown); ca 1632, b 1635?; Watertown/Lancaster/Charlestown
WATERS, Lawrence (1635, ?1634-1693) & Hannah __?__ (-1693); b 1663; Boston
WATTERS, Nathaniel[3] (1671-1718) & Elizabeth KING (1671-1744+); 12 Dec 1699; Salem
WATERS, Richard (1604-1677) & Joyce?/Rejoice? [PLASSE?] (-1687+); b 1630; Salem
WALTERS/WATERS, Richard[3] (1669-1726, Oxford) & Martha REED (-1726+); 3 Mar 1697/8; Salem/Sutton
WATERS, Sampson (-1693) & Rebecca __?__, m/2 Thomas BARKER; b 1667; Boston
WATERS, Samuel (1652-1728 (not 1729)) Woburn & Mary [HUTSON]/HUDSON (1653-1721); 21 Mar 1671/2; Charlestown/Lancaster/Cambridge
WATERS, Samuel (1674-1729) & 1/wf Bethiah ARCHER (1668?-); 1 Jan 1694/5, no issue; Salem
WALTERS/WATERS, Samuel & Mary HAWKINS; 2 Aug 1698; Salem

WATERS, Samuel (1675-) & _?_ [TURRELL], m/2 Nathaniel MAUDLEY; b 1701?; Woburn/Easton
WATERS, Stephen (1643-1720) & Sarah CARTER (ca 1648-1724); 12 Jun 1674; Charlestown
WATERS, Thomas & Anna COMBS; 9 Jul 1685; E. Greenwich, RI
WATERS, Thomas (-1728) & Alice BARTOLL (1669-); 7 Oct 1687; Marblehead
WATERS, Thomas, Marblehead & Mary ROUNDELL/ROUNDY/ROUNDEE?; 19 Apr 1695; Beverly/Salem
WATERS, Thomas (-1719?) & Sarah FENN, Milford; 19 May 1696?; Hartford
WATERS, Thomas (-1713) & Mary [FOSTER]; Jamaica, LI
WATERS, William (-1690) & Elizabeth? _?_; b 1632?; Boston
WATERS, William (-1684) & Hannah (PEACH) [BRADSTREET], w John; aft 14 Jun 1660; Rowley/Marblehead
WATERS, William & AbigaiL _?_; b 1673; Damariscove
WATERS, William & Elizabeth LATIMER (-1699, ae 35); 4 Aug 1686; Marblehead
WATERS, William & Abigail [CLOYES]/CHASE (1676, 1677-); m int 7 Jul 1696; Boston/Framingham
WATERS, William & Mary (WARD) DOLLIBER/DOLLIVER (1669-), w Peter; 17 Jul 1699; Marblehead
WATKINS, Andrew & _?_; ca 1674?, 5 ch bpt in 1686; Roxbury
WATKINS, David (-1688) & Sarah [JUDSON] (1662-), m/2 Joseph STURGES; ca 1686?; Stratford, CT
WADKINS, Edward (1662-1701) & Sarah _?_; b 1683(4?); Boston
WATKINS, John & 1/wf Mary RUSSELL (1670-1701); 22 Jul 1691; Charlestown
WATKINS, Joseph (-1711) & Johannah BLAKEMAN/BUCKINGHAM (1667-), m/2 Jesse LAMBERT, m/3 Samuel CAMP 1723; in Milford, 4 Dec 1688; Stratford, CT
WATKINS, Thomas & Elizabeth [BAKER] (1632-); b 1652; Boston
WATKINS, Thomas (-bef 1674, bef 26 Nov 1674) & Margaret [?ROYAL], m/2 Thomas STEVENS; b 1669; Boston/?Kennebunk, ME
WATKINS, Thomas & Elizabeth FELTON (1652-); 29 Nov 1678; Salem
WATSON, Abraham (1661-1705/6) & Mary BUTTERFIELD (-1730), m/2 Samuel WHITMORE; 13 Mar 1688/9; Watertown/Cambridge
WATSON, Benjamin & Ann DRUE/DREW; 15 Sep 1694; Boston/Watertown
WATSON, Caleb (1641-1725, 1726?) & Mary HYDE, Boston; 15 Dec 1665, no issue; Roxbury/Hadley/Hartford
WATSON, Edward (-1660) & Grace (_?_) WALKER (-1660), w John; 1 Jul 1652; New Haven/Wallingford, CT
WATSON, Elkanah (1659, 1655/6-1690) & ?Mercy/?Mary [HEDGE?] (1659-1721), m/2 John FRIEMAN ca 1697?, 1696+; b 1676?, b 1678; Plymouth
WATSON, George (1603-1689) & Phebe [HICKS] (-1663); ca 1635; Plymouth
WATSON, Jedediah (1666-1741) & Mary (CLARK) GAYLORD (1658-1738), w John; [ca 1700], b 7 Mar 1699/1700; Windsor, CT
WATSON, John (-1672) & _?_; b 1619?
WATSON, John (1592-1672, 1671, ae 77?) & Alice (B-) PRENTISS, w Valentine; 3 Apr 1634; Roxbury
WATSON, John (1610-1650) & Margaret [SMITH] (-1683); b 1642?; Hartford
WATSON, John (1619-1711) & Rebecca [ERRINGTON] (1625-1690); b 1650; Cambridge
WATSON, John (-1693, ae 59) & Mary [?ECCLES], m/2 Benj. FITCH of Reading 1697+; b 22 Sep 1661, no issue; Boston/Roxbury
WATSON, John (1646-1730) & 1/wf Ann/Anna [?NICHOLLS]; ca 1668/75?; Hartford
WATSON, John (-1685) & Eunice [BARKER] (1645-); b 1671; Rowley/Bradford
WATSON, John (-1728) & 1/wf Dorcas [GARDINER] (-bef 1702); b 1673; ?Newport/S. Kingston, RI
WATSON, John (-1725?) & Sarah _?_; b 1680; Hartford
WATSON, John (1656-1714) & Elizabeth HUDSON/HODSHON?; 30 Mar 1681; New Haven
WATSON, John & Ruth GRIFFEN; 22 Mar 1687/8; Amesbury/Salisbury
WATSON, John (1671-) & Ruth HARTSHORN/HARRIS? (?1674-); 25 Feb 1691/2, 2 Feb 1691/2; Bradford/Cape Porpoise
WATSON, John & 2/wf Rebecca [GARDINER]; b 4 Aug 1702, b 1701?; ?Newport/?Swansea
WATSON, Jonathan & Elizabeth [BEARD]; b 16 Dec 1678; Dover, NH

WATSON, Jonathan (-1714+) & 1/wf Abigail [DUDLEY] (doubtful); Dover, NH

WATSON, Nathaniel (1663-1690) & Dorothy BISSELL (1665-); 21 Jan 1685; Windsor, CT

WATSON, Robert & Elizabeth __?__ ; b 1602

WATSON, Robert (-1689) & Mary ROCKWELL (-1684); 10 Dec 1646; Windsor, CT

WATSON, Robert & Hannah [KENT?], m/2 John AMBLER; b 1680; Oyster River, NH/Durham, NH

WATSON, Robert & Susanna PRIOR, w? James?; 13 Feb 1690; Boston

WATSON, Robert & Mary [ORR]; Londonderry, Ireland, 1695; Providence

WATSON, Thomas (-1673) & Joane/Joan __?__ (-1674); b 1636; Salem

WATSON, Thomas & Mary HUBBARD; 19 May 1687; Salisbury

WATSON, William & 1/wf Sarah PERLY/PERLEY; 15 Jan 1670, 6 Dec 1670, Newbury; Ipswich

WATSON, William & 2/wf Mary (HUTCHINSON) HALE, w Thomas; 5 Feb 1694/5; Topsfield/Boxford

WATSON, __?__ & Hannah/Susannah MILBURNE, w William; aft Aug 1694; ?Boston

WATSON, __?__ & Elizabeth __?__ ; b 17 Jul 1638, she deeded land; Plymouth

WATSON, __?__ & Elizabeth [FROST], m/2 John GRAY ?ca 1640, m/3 John RAMSDEN; ca 1632; Boston?

WATSON, __?__ & Sarah __?__ , m/2 Samuel DUNHAM 1694; Plymouth

WATSON, __?__ & Rebecca (WELLS) (LATHAM) PACKER; aft 1689; Kingston, RI

WADDELL, John (-1676) & Mary GOOLE/GOULD (1651-), m/2 Peter TALBOT 1678; 25 Dec 1666; Chelmsford

WATTLES, Richard & Mary __?__ ; b 1655?, b 1661?; Ipswich

WATTLES, William (1672-1737) & Abigail BELCHER (-1744); 28 Apr 1697, 29? Apr; Milton

WATTS, Henry (1604-) (did he marry?) & __?__ ; b 1665, ?ca 1630/5?; Saco/Scarborough, ME

WATTS, Henry (1604-) & 2/wf Cicely BARLOW, w George; 1665/70, by 1670

WATTS, James (1625-) (ae ca 35 in 1660) & Elizabeth BOWDEN; 26 Jul 1661; Salem

WATTS, Jeremiah & Eleanor __?__ (1630-), m/2 Jonathan HUDSON 1698; 1665(6?); Wenham

WATTS, John & Lydia [GOODYEAR] (-1700, ae 55); b 1668(9?), 1668±; Boston

WATTS, John & Mary CARYL; 20 Feb 1693/4; Marblehead/Bristol, RI/Salem

WATTS, Richard (-1654) & 2/wf? Elizabeth __?__ (-1666); in Eng, b 1616; Hartford

WATS, Samuel (alias MERCER) & 1/wf Elizabeth AYERS (-1695); 28 Oct 1684; Haverhill

WATTS, Samuel (alias MERCER) & 2/wf Elizabeth (AYER) CLEMENT, w John; 8 Mar 1696/7; Haverhill

WATTS, Thomas (ca 1626-1683) & Elizabeth STEEL (-1685); 1 May 1645, no issue; Hartford

WATTS, Thomas & 1/wf __?__ ; in Eng; Charlestown

WATTS, Thomas & 2/wf Elizabeth [HAYDEN] (-1699), w Ferman; b 1664; Charlestown

WATTS, __?__ & Mary __?__ ; see Samuel BRABROOK

WAY, Aaron (-1695) & Joan/Jane/Joanne [SUMNER]; b 1650; Dorchester/Boston/Salem

WAY, Aaron (1650-1696+) & Mary [MAVERICK]; b 1674(5?); Salem/Charlestown/Dorchester

WAY, Ebenezer (1673-) & Irene [HOBART] (1676, 1674?-1753); b 1696?, b 2 Nov 1699, b 1698; Hartford/Southold, LI

WAY, Eleazer (-1687) (called Thomas PURCHASE "uncle") & Mary __?__ ; (-1701); b 1662; Boston/Hartford

WAY, Francis & Elizabeth __?__ , m/2 Peter BUCKHOUT 1713; b 5 Oct 1685; Newtown, LI

WAY, George (1619-), Saybrook & Elizabeth __?__ (dau of Joanna, wf of John SMITH); b 1651; Boston/Providence/Saybrook, CT

WAY, George (-1717) (m/2 Susannah (TILLMAN) BECKWITH bef 10 May 1713, aft 11 Jan 1710/11) & 1/wf Sarah [NEST]; say ca 1689; New London, CT/?Lyme

WAY, Henry (-1667, ae 89) (James GREEN his uncle) & Elizabeth __?__ (-1665, ae 84); in Eng, b 1615; Dorchester

WAY, James (-1663, 1665?) & Ede __?__ ; Newtown, LI

WAY, James (-1715) & __?__ ; Newtown, LI

WAY, John (-1715) & Sarah DEAN; 22 Nov 1687; Newtown, LI/Jericho, LI

WAY, Moses & Sarah __?__ ; 5 Apr 1694; Boston

WAY, Richard (?1624-1697) & 1/wf Hester/Esther [JONES]; b 1651; Salem/Boston

WAY, Richard (-1697) & 2/wf Bethia [HARLOCK?]/[MAYHEW?] (1636-1678); b 2 Jun 1675; Boston

WAY, Richard (-1697) & 3/wf Katharine __?__ (-28 Apr 1689, ae ca 55); aft 1678; Boston

WAY, Richard (-1697) & Hannah (TOWNSEND) (HULL) (ALLEN) KNIGHT, w Thomas, w Hope, w Richard; 13 Aug 1689; Boston

WAY, Richard & Hannah PERKINS (1673-); 4 Dec 1694; Charlestown

WAY, Samuel & Mary _?_ ; b 1696; Boston

WAY, Thomas & _?_ ; b 1652, in Eng; Marblehead

WAY, Thomas (-1726) & Ann [LESTER]; b 1688; New London/East Haven, CT

WAY, William & Persis _?_ ; b 1676; Dorchester/Boston/Salem

WAY, William & Penelope (COOKE?) VEREN, w John?; m int 25 Dec 1695; Boston

WAY, _?_ & _?_ , wid; mentioned 23 Feb 1646/7; Dorchester

WAYMAN, Thomas & _?_ ; b 1690?; Boston

WAR, Abraham & 1/wf _?_ ; Ipswich

WAR, Abraham (-1654) & 2/wf _?_ ; Ipswich

WARE/WEAR/WIRE, Daniel (-1736, Cambridge) & 1/wf Hannah [BOADEN] (1658-1697); b 1692; Boston

WEAR, Daniel & 2/wf Lydia HILLIER (-1705); 31 Oct 1698; Boston

WARE, Ebenezer (1667-1765) & 1/wf Martha HERRING (1668-1710); 18 Mar 1689/90; Dedham

WEARE, Elias (-1707) & Magdalen (HILTON) ADAMS, w Nathaniel, m/3 John WEBBER; 6 Jan 1696?, Apr 1697; York, ME

WARE, Ephraim (1659-1753) & Hannah HERRING (-1738); 13 Jul 1685; Dedham/Needham

WARE, Jacob, Southampton, LI, & Elizabeth OSBORN; m lic 3 Oct 1692

WARE, John (1648-) & 1/wf Mary METCALF (1646-1677); 10 Dec 1668; Dedham/Wrentham

WEARE/WARE, John (1646-1718) & Joanna (GAY) WHITEING/WHITING (1645-1708), w Nathaniel; 24 Mar 1678/9; Dedham/Wrentham

WARE, John (-1694) & Sarah _?_ ; b 1683; Boston

WARE, John & Elizabeth _?_ ; b 1698; Southampton, LI

WARE, John (1670-1719) & Mehitable CHAPEN/CHAPLIN (1675-1750, ae 76), Dorchester; 14 Jan 1695/6; Wrentham

WEARE, Joseph (?1668-1700) (cousin of John PURINGTON) & Hannah [PENWILL]?; York, ME

WEARE, Nathaniel (-1681) & Sarah _?_ (-1682+); b 1629; Newbury/Nantucket

WEARE, Nathaniel (1631?-1718, ae nearly 87) & Elizabeth SWAYNE (1638-1712/13, Seabrook, NH); 3 Dec 1656; Newbury/Hampton, NH

WEARE, Nathaniel (1669-1692) & 1/wf Huldah HUSSEY (1670-1701); 17 Nov 1692; Hampton, NH

WARE, Nathaniel (-1724) & Mary WHEELOCK (-1750), m/2 Cornelius FISHER 1727, m/3 Thomas BACON 1746; 12 Oct 1696; Wrentham

WARE, Nicholas & Anna [VASSALL]; by 18 Jul 1657; ?Scituate/VA

WEARE, Peter (1618-1692) & 1/wf Ruth [GOOCH] (-1664?); b 1644; Salisbury

WEARE, Peter (1618-1692) & 2/wf Mary PURINGTON/PUDDINGTON (1633-1715+) (?step-dau Maj. John DAVIS); 1666; York, ME

WEARE, Peter (1650±-) & 1/wf Elizabeth _?_ ; b 1682; Boston

WEARE, Peter (1650±-) & 2/wf Abigail; 1684/5?, b 1684

WEARE, Peter & 1/wf Elizabeth WILSON (1665-1692); 6 Jan 1691/2; Dover, NH

WEARE, Peter & 2/wf Elizabeth (TOTHERLY) WEST, w John; 30 Dec 1698; Hampton, NH

WARES, Robert (-1699) & 1/wf Margaret HUNTING (-1670); 24 Mar 1644/5; Dedham

WEARE, Robert (-1699) & 2/wf Hannah JONES (1636-1721, Dorchester); 3 May 1676; Dedham

WEARE, Robert (1653-1724) & 1/wf Sarah METCALF (1648-1718); 4 Jun 1677; Dedham/Wrentham

WARE, Samuel (1657-1731) & 1/wf Elizabeth RICE (-1719); 21 Jul 1690; Dedham

WARE, William (-1658) & Elizabeth [PRENTICE?]; b 1631?, 1637; Dorchester/Boston

WEIRR, William (-1689) & Deborah _?_ ; Maadorcus Neck, LI

WETHERBY, John[1] (-1711) & 1/wf Mary HOW (1653-1684); ?13 Aug 1672, ?18 Sep 1672; Marlboro/Sudbury/Stow

WHITERBY, John[1] (-1711) & 2/wf Lydia MOORE; 16 Sep 1684; Stow

WEATHERBY, John[2] (1675-1720) & Catherine WHITCOMB (-1715+); 2 Jun 1698, in Concord; Stow

WITHERBY, Joseph (-1720) & Elizabeth JOHNSON (-1726); 9 Feb 1699; Marlboro

WETHERBY, Thomas (1678-1713) & Hannah WOODS; 20 Feb 1698/9; Marlboro

WEATHERBY, William & _?_ DAYTON; b 11 Apr 1699; Brookhaven, LI

WEAVER, Clement (?1590-) & Rebecca **HOLBROOK** (1597-); St. John's, Glastonbury, Eng, 19 May 1617; Weymouth/Newport, RI

WEAVER, Clement (-1683) & Mary [**FREEBORN**] (1627-); ca 1645/7; Newport, RI

WEAVER, Clement (-1691) & 1/wf _?_ (-bef Sep 1677); b 1669; Newport

WEAVER, Clement (-1691) & 2/wf Rachel **ANDREW**, m/2 William **BENNETT** ca 1693; ?26 Sep 1677; Newport/E. Greenwich, RI

WEAVER, Clement (1669-1738) & Hannah **LONG** (-1759); 1 Jan 1690/1; E. Greenwich, RI

WEAVER, John (-1703) & Catherine _?_; b 1672; Newport/E. Greenwich, RI

WEAVER, Samuel & Elizabeth **CRAVATH**; 27 Mar 1697, 24 Mar 1696/7; Boston/Watertown

WEAVER, Thomas & Elizabeth _?_; b 1674; Boston

WEAVER, Thomas (?1657-) & Mary [**VAUGHAN**?]? (1658?-); ?16 Jun 1681, b 1684; RI

WEAVER, Thomas (1672±-1753) & Mary _?_, m/2 Thomas **FRANCIS**?; b 1694; Newport/Freetown, MA

WEAVER, William & Elizabeth **HARRIS**; 17 Dec 1693; E. Greenwich, RI

WEBB, Benjamin & Mercy **BUCKNAM** (1648-); 7 Dec 1669; Malden

WEBB, Benjamin (1667-1739) & Susanna **BALLENTINE** (1668-); 21 Nov 1692; Boston/Braintree?

WEBB, Caleb (-1704) & _?_; b 1701?; Stamford, CT

WEBB, Christopher (-1671) & [?Humility] _?_ (1588-1687); in Eng, ca 1615-20, b 1630; Braintree

WEBB, Christopher (1630-1694) & Hannah **SCOTT** (1635-1718); 18 Jan 1654/5; Braintree

WEBB, Christopher (1663-1690) & Mary **BASS** (1670-), dau John, m/2 William **COPELAND** 1694, m/3 Ebenezer **SPEAR** 1718; 24 May 1686; Braintree

WEBB, Daniel (ae 64 in 1716) & Mercy **BECKETT**; 20 Jul 1675; Salem

WEBB, Elisha (1676-1710) & Lydia **SCOTTO**, m/2 Thomas **DAVIS**; 18 Nov 1697; Charlestown

WEBB, Henry (-1660) & 3/wf Dosabell _?_ /[Dowsabel **SMITH**]; in Eng, b 1625?, 11 Aug 1633, St. Edmund, Salisbury, Eng, Wiltshire; Boston

WEBB, Henry (1668-) & Mary **HURLBURT**; 10 Oct 1695; Wethersfield, CT

WEBB, Jeremiah (1668-1734) & 1/wf Priscilla **MACKCLAFLIN/McLATHLIN** (1672-1716/17); b 1694; Northampton

WEBB, John & Ann [?**BASSETT**] (-1667); b 1647(8?); Hartford

WEBB, John & Anna _?_; b 1651; Boston

WEBB, John (alias EVERED) (-1668) & Mary (**OSBORN**?) **FAIRWEATHER**, w Thomas, m/3 William **GOODHUE** 1669; ca 1651/60?; Boston/Chelmsford

WEBB, John & (?Sarah) **BASSETT**; b Jun 1653; Stratford, CT

WEBB, John (?1642-1720) & Susannah (**CUNLIFFE**) **COLE** (1644-1735), w Matthew; 12 Dec 1665; Northampton

WEBB, John (1642-1670) & 2/wf Elizabeth **SWIFT**, m/2 Robert **DANKS**; ?16 Oct 1667, b 1668; Northampton

WEBB, John & Bridget **WHITFORD**; b [1678]; Salem

WEBB, John & 1/wf Bethiah **ADAMS** (1661-); - May 1680; Braintree

WEBB, John & Elizabeth _?_; b 1689; Boston

WEBB, John & Mary (**HOLLOWAY**) **ASHLEY**, w Edward; betw 1689 & 1703; ?Boston/?Charlestown

WEBB, John (1667-1712) & Hannah/Anna _?_ (-1719); ca 1695?; ?Northampton

WEBB, John (-1712) & Ruth **GRAVES**?; 25 Jan 1699/1700

WEBB, Joseph (-1698?) & Grace **DIPPLE**; 16 Apr 1666; Scituate/Boston

WEBB, Joseph (-1684) & Hannah **SCOFIELD** (-1710), m/2 John **FINCH**; 8 Jan 1672, 1672/3; Stamford, CT

WEBB, Joseph (1666/7-1732) & 1/wf Elizabeth **NICHOLS** (-1718); 8 Jul 1691, 9 Jul; Fairfield, CT

WEBB, Joseph & Mary **HOYT/HART**; 23 Feb 1698, ?25 Feb 1698/9; Stamford, CT

WEBB, Joseph & Lydia _?_; b 1698(9?); Boston

WEBB, Joseph & Deborah **BASS**; 29 Nov 1699; Braintree

WEBB, Joshua, Bedford, NY, & Elizabeth [?**HINES**] (1657-), m/2 Daniel **SIMKINS**; b 1694; Bedford, NY

WEBB, Peter (1657-1718?) & 1/wf Ruth [**BASS**] (1662-1699), niece of Mrs. Sarah **FAXON**; b 1684; Braintree

WEBB, Richard (1580-1665) & 1/wf Grace **WILSON**; in Eng, May 1610; Cambridge/Boston

WEBB, Richard (-1665) & 2/wf Elizabeth [**GREGORY**]/**BUCHARD**?/**GRANT** (-1680); b 1635; Cambridge/etc.

WEBB, Richard (1611-1676) & Margery [MOYER?]; b 1636; Stratford, CT/Stamford, CT

WEBB, Richard (-1659) & Mary [FAIRWEATHER?]?/?Sarah UPHAM?; b 1640; Weymouth/Boston

WEBB, Richard (-1680) & Elizabeth [GRANT], w Seth; aft 1646

WEBB, Richard (-1700) & Patience _?_ (ca 1658-1704); b 1684, ca 1680; Northampton

WEBB, Samuel (-living 23 Oct 1694, 1739, Windham, CT) & Mary ADAMS (1664-1744), dau Samuel; 16 Dec 1686; Chelmsford/Braintree/Windham, CT

WEBB, Samuel (1662-) & Hannah JAGGER (1668±-); b 1691; Stamford, CT

WEBB, Thomas & Mary [FOSDICK] (1630-); b 1666; Charlestown

WEBB, Thomas & Sarah [GREEN?] (1671?-); b 1691; Boston

WEBB, William (-1644) & Rebecca _?_ (-1654); b [1628], b 1644; Boston/Roxbury

WEBB, William & Charity [LITTLEFIELD]; b 1694(5?), b 1680?, by May 1685; Boston

WEBB, _?_ & Sarah GILLETTE (1673/4-); b 1701?; Windham, CT

WEBB, _?_ & Amy HAYDEN (1672-); ?Braintree

WEBBER, Benedict & Sarah RICE; 14 May 1694; Boston

WEBBER, James (-1729, in 64th y) & Patience [LITTLEFIELD] (-1748+); b 1697; Charlestown

WEBBER, John & Sarah _?_ ; b 1650; Marblehead

WEBBER, John (1656?-) & Elizabeth _?_ ; b 1674(5?); Boston

WEBBER, Joseph & _?_ ; b 1699?; Kittery, ME

WEBBER, Josiah & _?_ ; b 1668; Reading

WEBBER, Michael (-1729, ae ca 90) & _?_ ; ca 1660/5?; Gloucester

WEBBER, Michael & Deborah BEDFORD; 14 Aug 1686; York Co., ME/Gloucester

WEBBER, Nathaniel (1671-) & Elizabeth _?_ (-1732); b 1697; Charlestown

WEBBER, Richard (1641±-) & Lydia (TRICKEY) [GREEN], w Edmund; by 1682, by 1674; Dover, NH

WEBBER, Richard (-1726+) & Damaris [BOWDORN]/[BOADEN] (1652±-1752+); b 1695; Casco Bay/Marblehead

WEBBER, Robert/Robin? & _?_ ; b 1697; Cambridge

WEBBER/WEBB, Samuel (?1656-1716) & Deborah [LITTLEFIELD] (-1747); b 1695, b 1690?, b 1685; Gloucester

WEBBER, Thomas & Sarah _?_ ; b 1643; Boston

WEBBER, Thomas (-bef 1692), Falmouth, ME, & Mary [PARKER] (ae 53 in 1692); b 1656; Charlestown

WEBBER, William & Mary SUMER; 19 Sep 1699; Boston

WEBLY, George & Ann CARPENTER; 16 Jul 1667; Charlestown

WEBSTER, George (-1721) & Sarah BLISS; 13 Dec 1695; Longmeadow/Lebanon, CT

WEBSTER, Henry & Esther _?_ (-1731, ae 75), m/2 Richard HENCHMAN 1697; b 1682/[3?]; Boston

WEBSTER, Isaac (1670-), Kingston & 1/wf Mary HUTCHINS; 1 Apr 1697; Hampton, NH

WEBSTER, Israel (-1683) & 1/wf Elizabeth BROWNE (-1668); 3 Jan 1665; Newbury

WEBSTER, Israel (-1683) & 2/wf Elizabeth LUNT (-1688); 9 Nov 1669; Newbury

WEBSTER, James (-1689) & Mary HAY; 14 Feb 1658; Boston

WEBSTER, James (1659-1711) & Mary [DAWES] (1664-); by 1680?, b 1686; Boston

WEBSTER, John (-1661) & Agnes SMITH; 7 Nov 1609, Cossington, Eng; Hartford/Hadley

WEBSTER, John (-1646) & Mary [SHATSWELL] (-1694), m/2 John EMERY 1649); ca 1627?, in Eng; Ipswich

WEBSTER, John (-by 1662) & 1/wf _?_ ; ca 1628?; Portsmouth, NH/Strawberry Bank

WEBSTER, John & Anne BATT; 13 Jun 1653; Newbury

WEBSTER, John (-by 1662) & 2/wf Rachel _?_ ; by 16 Dec 1658; Portsmouth, NH/Strawberry Bank

WEBSTER, John (-1694) & Sarah [MYGATT], m/2 Benjamin GRAHAM/GRIMES; ?ca 1674; Middletown, CT

WEBSTER, John (-1737) & Bridget HUGGINS (1651-); 9 Mar 1680/1; Newbury

WEBSTER, John (1668-1742) & Tryphena LOCKE (-1739); 14 Jun 1693; Haverhill

WEBSTER, John & Elizabeth DEWEY (1677-); b 1699; Northampton/Lebanon, CT

WEBSTER, Jonathan (1657-1735) & 1/wf Dorcas HOPKINS (-1695+); 11 May 1681; Hartford

WEBSTER, Jonathan & 2/wf Mary JUDD; 2 Jan 1696, 23 Jan 1695; ?Farmington, CT/Hartford

WEBSTER, Joseph & 1/wf Mary JUDD; 23 Jan 1695, 1695/6?; Hartford/Farmington, CT

WEBSTER, Matthew (1610-1675) & [?Elizabeth _?_] (-11 Feb 1656); ca 1652?; Farmington, CT

WEBSTER, Nathan (1646-1694) & Mary HAZELTINE (1648-1735); 30 Jun 1673; Salisbury

WEBSTER, Nicholas (-1687) & Sarah (WATERBURY) DIBBLE, divorcee, m/1 Zachariah DIBBLE, m/3 Edward TREHEARNE; aft 1672; Stamford, CT

WEBSTER, Rev. Nicholas (1673-1717) & Mary [WOODMAN] (1678-); b 1701?; Salisbury

WEBSTER, Robert (1627-1676, 1677?) & Susannah [TREAT] (1629-1705); ca 1652; Hartford/Middletown, CT

WEBSTER, Robert (1662-1744) & 1/wf Hannah BEKLEY/BECKLEY (-1715); 10 Sep 1689; Hartford

WEBSTER, Samuel (-1744) & Elizabeth [REEVE] (1668-1747); ca 1688/95?, no issue; Hartford

WEBSTER, Stephen (ca 1637-1694) & 1/wf Hannah AYER (1644-1676); 24 Mar 1662/3; Haverhill

WEBSTER, Stephen (-1694) & 2/wf Judith BROAD, w William; 26 May 1678; Haverhill

WEBSTER, Stephen & Sarah CLARK; 1 Nov 1698; Newbury

WEBSTER, Stephen & Mary (GOODWIN) COOK, w Barnabas; 23 Oct 1700; Charlestown

WEBSTER, Thomas (-1634, in Eng) & Margaret _?_ (-1686), m/2 William GODFREY ca 1638, m/3 John MARRIAN/MARION/MARIAN 1671; in Eng, b 1631; Salisbury

WEBSTER, Thomas (1631-1715, ae 83) & Sarah BREWER; 2 Nov 1657, 29? Nov; Hampton, NH

WEBSTER, Thomas & Mary _?_ ; b 1661(2?); Boston

WEBSTER, Thomas (1616-1686) & Abigail ALEXANDER; 16 Jun 1663; Northampton/Hadley/Northfield

WEBSTER, Thomas (1665-1733) & Sarah (?GODFREY) (-1718); b 1690; Hampton, NH/Kingston, NH

WEBSTER, Thomas (1661-) & Deborah _?_ ; ca 1690/1700?, b1701; Exeter, NH

WEBSTER, William (1614-1676) & Mary REEVE (-1698); 17 Feb 1670, no issue; Hadley

WEBSTER, William (1666-1720) & Mary MOSELY (1677-); 25 Nov 1696; Boston

WEBSTER, William (1671-1722) & Sarah NICHOLS, m/2 Samuel CATLIN; ?20 Nov 1700, ?28 Nov 1700; Hartford?, CT

WEBSTER, [?Benjamin] & Grace _?_ , m/2 Christopher BROWN 13 Dec 1700; Beverly/Salem

WEBSTER, [?Thomas]/?John (-1695) & Sarah EDWARDS (1671-), dau Joseph; b 1697; Wethersfield, CT

WADGE, Isaac & Hannah HAMLET; 11 Dec 1699; Charlestown

WEDGE, John (1667-) & 1/wf Sarah HALL (-1725); 30 Nov 1694; Stow/Attleboro

WEDGE, Thomas & _?_ ; b 1661

WEDGE, Thomas (-1685) & Deborah [STEVENS] (1645-1703, Norwich, CT); b 1667; Lancaster/Sudbury

WEDGEWOOD, David & Hannah HOBBS (1662-); 4 Jan 1683; Hampton, NH

WEDGEWOOD, John[1] (-1654) & Mary [?SMART] (1618-1670); b 1639; Hampton, NH

WEDGEWOOD, John[2] (1640±-) & _?_ ; Exeter, NH

WEDGEWOOD, Jonathan (?1649-) & 1/wf Sarah _?_ (-1680); Hampton, NH

WEDGEWOOD, Jonathan & Rachel (DAVIS) HAINES (1661-1749), w Robert; 9 Feb 1700; Hampton, NH

WEED, Daniel (ca 1652-1697) & ?Ruth/(not Mary) _?_ (-1709), m/2 Peter FERRIS 1705, m/3 John CLAPP 1708; ca 1673; Rye, NY

WEED, Daniel & Mary WEBB; 23 Sep 1697; Stamford, CT

WEED, Ephraim (1666-) & Elizabeth [COLBY]; b 1689; Amesbury

WEED, George (1661-) & Margaret [WORTHEN]; b 1700; Amesbury

WEED, John[1] (-1689) & Deborah WINSLEY; 14 Nov 1650; Salisbury/Amesbury

WEED, John (ca 1643-1690) & 1/wf Joanna [WESTCOTT] (-by 1678); by 1665, b Feb 1664?; Wethersfield, CT

WEED, John (ca 1643-1690) & 2/wf Mary _?_ (-1714), m/2 Josiah FORMAN; b 1679; Stamford, CT

WEED, John & 1/wf Anne (BARTLETT) RICHARDSON, w Edward; ca 1683/5, b 1685; Salisbury

WEED, Jonas (1610-1676) & Mary _?_ (-1690); ca 1637; Watertown/Wethersfield/Stamford, CT

WEED, Jonas (ca 1647-1704) & Bethia HOLLY (-1713); 16 Nov 1676?, 1677?, 1670; Stamford, CT

WEED, Jonas (-1706) & Mary [SCOFIELD], m/2 Samuel HOYT; b 1695; Stamford, CT

WEED, Joseph & Rachel HOYT; 29 Nov 1693; Amesbury

WEED, Samuel & Bethia MORGAN (1653-); 12 Mar 1675/6; Amesbury

WEED, Samuel (?1645-1708) & Mary _?_ (-1714); ca 1680/4?; Stamford, CT/Danbury, CT

WEED, Thomas & Joanna _?_ ; b 1698; Amesbury

WEEDEN, Edward (1613-1679) & Elizabeth [COLE] (-1696); b 1644; Boston

WEEDEN, Edward & Jane __?__; b 1687; Boston
WEEDEN, James (1585-1673(-)) & 1/wf Phillip/?Phillipa COCK (1588-living 1632); Chesham, Bucks, 11 Sep 1615; Boston/Newport
WEEDEN, James (-1673(-)) & 2/wf Rose (_?_) (GRINNELL) PAINE, w Matthew, w Anthony; ca 1650; Portsmouth, RI
WEEDEN, James (-1711+) & Mary __?__ (-1725±); b 1674, by 1670?; Newport
WEEDEN, James & Elizabeth [PECKHAM] (1668-); Newport
WEEDEN, Jeremiah (-1756) & 1/wf Mary [CLARKE]; ca 1694?; Newport
WEEDEN, John & Ruth __?__; b 1687; Boston
WEEDEN, John (-1710) & Jane [UNDERWOOD] (1669-1736); b 1687; Jamestown, RI
WEEDEN, Philip (-1727+) & Ann [SISSON] (1672-1750); b 1698; Newport/Portsmouth, RI
WEEDEN, William (1619-1676) & ?Sarah __?__; b 1657; Portsmouth, RI
WEEDEN, William (-1722+) & Sarah [PECKHAM]; ca 1680/5?; Newport
WEEDEN/WEEDE?, [Samuel] & Hannah [PROCTOR], Salem; b 1672; Ipswich?
WEEKES, Ammiel (?1633-1679) & Elizabeth [HARRIS] (1634-1723); b 18 Jan 1655; Dorchester
WEEKS, Ammiel (1662-) & Abigail TRESCOTT, m/2 Jeremiah ROGERS by 1693; 2 Mar 1682; Dorchester
WEEKS, Christopher & Mary __?__; b 1695; Boston
WEEKES, Daniel (-1698) & Mary [ALLING?]/ALLEN; b 1691; Oyster Bay, LI
WEEKS, Ebenezer (1665-), Dorchester & Deliverance SUMNER (-1712), Boston; 8 May 1689; Milton/Boston
WICKES, Edward & Sarah [MANCHESTER]; prob 1700; Tiverton, RI
WEEKES, Francis (1615/20-1689) & Elizabeth/Alice? __?__; ca 1638, b 1640; Providence/Gravesend, LI/Hempstead, LI/Oyster Bay, LI
WEEKS, George (-1650, 1659) & Jane [CLAPP] (-1668), m/2 Jonas HUMPHREY; b 1628/9; Dorchester
WEEKES, James (bpt 1652-1704+) & __?__; ca 1673/77; Oyster Bay, LI
WEEKES, James & Elizabeth [?CARPENTER (no)], dau Wm.? (no); ca 1692/5, b 1696; ?Oyster Bay, LI
WICKES, John (1609-1675) & Mary __?__; b 1634; Plymouth/Warwick, RI/ Portsmouth, RI
WICKES, John (1652/3-) & Hester KETCHAM; m lic 25 Apr 1673; ?Huntington, LI
WEEKS, John (1652-1714) & Sarah HAMMON/HAMMOND?/HAMANT?, Medfield; 4 Nov 1674; Dorchester
WEEKS, John & Mary ROWLEY (1653-); 7 Jan 1675, 1675/6; Falmouth, MA
WICKS, John (-1689) & Rose [TOWNSEND], m/2 Samuel HAYDON; b 1677; Warwick, RI/Oyster Bay, LI
WEEKS, John & Richard __?__; b 1688(9?); Boston
WEEKS, John (1647-) & Hannah [TOWNSEND]; Oyster Bay, LI
WICK, John (1661-1719) & Temperance BARNES (1679-); ca 1695?, ca 1689/92?; Southampton, LI/Bridgehampton, LI
WEEKS/WICKES?, John & Jemima? __?__; b 1696?, doubtful; Huntington, LI
WEEKS, John (1668-1711±) & __?__; ca 1696?; Portsmouth, NH
WEEKES, John (-18 Dec 1756, ae 86 y) (?son Joseph) & Mercy [FORMAN]?; ?b 1695; Oyster Bay, LI
WICKES, John (1677-1741) & Sarah GORTON (-1753); 15 Dec 1698; Warwick, RI
WICKS, John (-1718) & Rebecca __?__; b 1689; Little Compton, RI
WEEKS, Joseph (ca 1635-1690) & Mary ATHERTON (-1692); 9 Apr 1667; Dorchester
WEEKES, Joseph (1645?-) & 1/wf Hannah [REDDOCK]; ca 1667, b 1674; Oyster Bay, LI
WEEKS, Joseph (1667-) & Sarah (SUMNER) [TURELL] (1662-1736, ae 74), w Joseph; b 1691, b 1689?; Dorchester
WEEKS, Joseph (1672-1735) & 1/wf Eadah/Adah [BRIAR]; b 1696; Kittery, ME
WEEKES, Joseph[2] (-1714+) & 2/wf Hannah (CROOKER) [FORMAN], m/1 Moses F-; ca 1698, b 1699; Oyster Bay, LI
WEEKS, Joseph[3] (doubtful, see Samuel WEEKS) & Ann [CARPENTER] (1676-), dau Joseph; ca 1696/99?
WEEKS, Joseph (1670-) & Deliverance __?__; doubtful
WEEK, Joshua (1674-) & Comfort HUBBERD; 7 Nov 1699; Boston
WEEKS, Leonard (1639?-) & 1/wf Mary [REDMAN]? (1649-); b 1667, b 1668; Portsmouth, NH/Greenland, NH

WEEKS, Leonard (1635-1707) & 2/wf Elizabeth HAYNES/HAINES; aft 1679, b 1679?; Portsmouth, NH

WEEKS, Nicholas (-1694) & Judith [?MENDUM]; by 1666; Kittery, ME

WEEKS, Nicholas & Priscilla GUNNISON; 8 May 1700, 7? May; Kittery, ME

WEEKES, Philip & Martha __?__; b 1701; Oyster Bay, LI

WICKS, Richard (-1724?) & Mercy (?CALL) LEE (-1729 called Mary), w Samuel; 2 Dec 1686; Malden/?Attleboro

WEEKS, [?Richard] & 1/wf Abigail [NORTON] (1666-1723+); ca 1690/5; Attleboro

WEEKS, Samuel (-1699?) & Elizabeth [REDDOCK] (-1701+); b 1674, b 1670?; Oyster Bay

WEEKS, Samuel (1670-1746) & Eleanor HAINES (1675-1736, ae 61); 23 Aug 1695; Portsmouth, NH/Greenland, NH

WEEKES, Samuel (see Joseph) (-1729?) & Anna [CARPENTER]? (1676-); b 1701?, ca 1696?-99?; Oyster Bay, LI

WEEKES, Supply & Susannah BARNES (-1712); 4 Jun 1699; Marlboro

WEEKES/WICKS, Thomas & Alice [PLASSE?]?, m/2 Nicholas POTTER; b 1637; Charlestown/Salem

WICKES, Thomas (-1671) & __?__; Wethersfield, CT/Hadley/Huntington, LI/Stratford, CT

WICKES, Thomas & Deborah [WOOD?]; b 1671?; Huntington, LI

WEEKS, Thomas (bpt 1652, 1651?-) & 1/wf __?__; ca 1675?; Oyster Bay, LI

WEEKS, Thomas (1651-1716+) & 2/wf Isabella [HARCUTT?]/HARCOURT (1662-); 1679, b 1701?; Oyster Bay, LI

WICKES, Thomas & Margaret [BRUSH]; b 1701?; ?Huntington, LI

WEEKS, William (-1688/9) & 1/wf __?__ (-1655+); b 1645; Martha's Vineyard

WEEKS, William (1628/9-1677) & Elizabeth [ATHERTON]? (no) (1631-1710), m/2 Timothy MATHER ?1679 (she was 1/wf of Timothy MATHER); b 1652; Dorchester

WEEKS/WICKS, William (-1688/9) & 2/wf Mary (LYNDE) [BUTLER] (-1693+), w John; aft 1658; Charlestown/Falmouth

WEEKES, William (-1690, ae 60) & Joan __?__ (-1690, ae 62); ca 1660/70?, b 1686; Enfield, CT/?Portsmouth, NH/?Kittery, ME

WEEKS, William (1645-1716+) & 1/wf Mercy ROBINSON (1647-); 16 Mar 1669, 1662?; Falmouth, MA

WEEKS, William & Martha PHILLIPS; 31 Aug 1687 m bond

WEEKS, William (1645-1716+) & 2/wf Mary [HATCH] (1648, 1647?-); ca 1689; Martha's Vinehard

WELCH, James, Swansea & Mercy SABIN (1666-), Rehoboth; 9 Nov 1683; Rehoboth/Bristol, RI/Swansea/Plainfield, CT

WELCH, John & Elizabeth [WHITE]; b 1682; Boston

WELTCH, John (1670-1728) & Sarah [?HODGE] (-1731); b 1693, b 1686?; Ipswich/Beverly/Norwich, CT/Preston, CT

WELCH, Jonathan (1670-) & 1/wf Katharine [WYER] (1666-1709?); b 1697; Charlestown

WELCH/WELLS, Philip & Hannah HAGGET/HAGGERT; 20 Feb 1666; Ipswich/Wenham/Portsmouth, NH/Topsfield

WELCH, Philip (1668-) & Elizabeth [CAME]; b 1694; York, ME

WELCH, Thomas (-1701, ae 79) & Elizabeth [UPHAM] (1630, ?1632-1706); ca 1650; Charlestown

WELCH, Thomas (-1681) & Hannah [BUCKINGHAM] (-1684); b 1655; Milford, CT

WELCH, Thomas (-1701) & Hannah MOUSAL (1662-1713), m/2 Joseph LAMSON; 21 Jan 1679; Charlestown

WELCH, Thomas (1658-1705) & Elizabeth [PECK], m/2 Eleazer BUCHER; by 1696; Milford, CT

WELCH, __?__ & Mary [BUTLER], wid?

WELD, Daniel (-1666) & 1/wf Alice __?__ (-1647); b 1643; Braintree

WELD, Daniel & 2/wf Ann HIDE, w George; 30 Jul 1647; Braintree/Roxbury

WELD, Daniel (1642-1690?) & Bethiah [MITCHELSON] (1642-1719, 1712?); b 1663; Cambridge/Salem/Roxbury

WELD, Daniel (1642-1699) & Mary HINSDELL/HINSDALE (1644-); 8 Jun 1664; Medfield

WELD, Edmund (1659-1747?) & Elizabeth WHITE (1667/8-1721); 10 Nov 1687; Roxbury

WELD, Edward (-1702) & Mary (HIGGINSON) GARDNER, w Thomas, m/3 James LINDALL; 25 Apr 1699; Salem

WELD, John (1623-1691) & Margaret BOWEN (1629-1692); 24 Dec 1647; Roxbury

WELD, John (-1739) & Hannah PORTIS; 22 Jan 1678; Roxbury

WELD, Joseph (1595-1646) & 1/wf Elizabeth [?DEVOTION]/WISE (ca 1600-1638); in Eng, 11 Oct 1620; Cambridge/Roxbury

WELD, Joseph (1595-1646) & 2/wf Barbara CLAP (-1655), m/2 Anthony STODDARD 1647?; 20 Apr 1639; Roxbury

WELD, Joseph & 1/wf Elizabeth DEVOTION (1651-1679); 2 Sep 1674; Roxbury

WELD, Joseph (-1712, ae 63) & 2/wf Sarah FAXON (1659-1745), m/2 Jacob CHAMBERLAIN 1719; 27 Nov 1679; Roxbury

WELD, Samuel (1655-1737) & Susannah POLLY (-1729, ae 67); 28 Jun 1683; Roxbury

WELD, Thomas (-1660, 1661) & 1/wf Margaret [?DORSELYE]/DERESLYE (-1637); ?Terling, Essex, in Eng, b 1625; Roxbury

WELD, Thomas (1590-1661) (returned to Eng) & 2/wf Judith __?__ (-1656), wid; ca 1638; Roxbury

WELD, Thomas (1626, 1627-1683) & Dorothy WHITING (1628-1694); 4 Jun 1650; Roxbury

WELD, Thomas (1653-1702) & 1/wf Elizabeth WILSON (1656-1687); 9 Nov 1681; Medfield/Dunstable

WELD, Thomas (1653-1702) & 2/wf Mary SAVAGE (1667-1731); 22 May 1700; Cambridge/Deerfield/Dunstable

WELDON, Robert (-1631) & Elizabeth __?__, ?m/2 Rev. George PHILLIPS 1631; b 1630; Charlestown

WELDON, __?__ & Elizabeth [HIGGINS], w John; aft Apr 1683, b 1694; Boston?

WELLCOMB, Daniel (see Zaccheus) & Sarah [?MOORE]?; b 1691?; Portsmouth, NH

WELLCOMB, Peter & Mehitable HODSHON/HOGGESDELL (1641-1694); 3 Nov 1665; Salem/Boston

WELLCOMB, Peter & Mehitable [HOWARD] (-1694), w Jeremiah; aft 1677; Boston

WELLCOMB, Richard & Eleanor [URIN]/[URANN] (-1699), w William; 1664?, by 1667; Isles of Shoals

WELLCOMB, William (1643-1674+) & [?Susanna WADE] (1652-), m/2 Joseph WHITE bef 1683; Pemaquid, ME

WELLCOMB, Zaccheus (see Daniel) & Sarah [MOORE], m/2 Henry SPILLER by 1693; b 1686; Isles of Shoals/Ipswich

WELLER, Eliezer (1650-1684) & Hannah PRICHARD (-1682); 14 Nov 1674; Westfield/Deerfield

WELLER, John (1645-1686) & Mary ALVORD (1651-); 24 Mar 1669, 1669/70; Northampton

WELLER, John (1671-1734) & Rebecca COOLEY, Springfield; 22 Mar 1693/4; Deerfield/New Milford, CT

WELLER, Nathaniel (1648-) & Deliverance [HANCHETT]; b 1677, b 1674; Westfield

WELLER, Richard & 1/wf Ann WILSON (-1655); 17 Sep 1640; Windsor, CT/Farmington, CT/Northampton

WELLER, Richard & 2/wf Elizabeth (ABELL) CURTIS, w Henry; 22 Jun 1662; Northampton

WELLINGTON, Benjamin (-1710) & Elizabeth SWOETMAN/SWEETMAN (1647-); 7 Dec 1671; Cambridge

WELLINGTON, Benjamin (1676-) & 1/wf Lydia BROWN (1677-1711); 18 Jan 1698/9; Watertown

WILLINGTON, John (1638-1726) & Susannah STRAYTE/STRAIGHT; 9 Jun 1681; Cambridge

WELLINGTON, John & Hannah MORSE; 19 May 1699; Watertown

WELLINGTON, Joseph (1643-1714) & 1/wf Sarah __?__ (-5 Feb 1683/4); Watertown

WELLINGTON, Joseph (1643-1714) & 2/wf Elizabeth STRAIGHT; 6 Jun 1684, 6 Jul 1684; Watertown

WELLINGTON, Oliver (1648-1707) & Anna (BRIDGE) [LIVERMORE] (-1727), w Samuel; aft 5 Dec 1690, no issue; Cambridge

WELLINGTON, Palgrave (-1715) & Sarah BOND; 29 Jan 1688/9, no issue, 1689/90?; Watertown

WELLINGTON, Roger (-1698) & Mary [PALGRAVE] (1619-1695); ca 1636, b 1638; Watertown

WELLMAN, Abraham (?1643-1717) & Elizabeth [COGSWELL] (1648-1739, 1736?); b 1669; Lynn

WILLMAN, Abraham & Hannah __?__; b 1686?; Southampton, LI

WILLMAN, Isaac & [?Mary] __?__ (-1688?); b 1657; Southampton, LI

WELLMAN, Isaac & Hannah ADAMS; 13 Mar 1678/9; Lynn

WILLMAN, Isaac [Jr.] & Mary WINES (-1688?), Southold; 7 Oct 1686; Southampton, LI

WILLMAN, Isaac & 2/wf Susannah __?__; b 1689; Southampton

WELLMAN, Thomas (-1672) & Elizabeth __?__; ca 1642; Lynn

WELLMONE, Thomas (1669-) & Sarah BROWN (1670-); 6 Jan 1696/7; Reading

WELLMAN, William (-(9 Aug 167-), 1672, 1670?, 1671) & Elizabeth [SPENCER] (1633-), m/2 Jacob JOY 1671, 23 May 1672; 1640, 1653, 1649?; Hartford/Killingworth, CT/etc.

WELLMAN, William (1661-) & [Elizabeth **JOY**]; b 1692; Killingworth, CT
WELLS, Ebenezer (1669-) & 1/wf Mary **WAITE** (1672-); 4 Dec 1690; Hatfield
WELLS, Edward & Sarah __?__ ; b 1645; Boston
WELLS, Edward & Deborah [**SAVAGE**]; by 1694; Portsmouth, NH
WELLS, Ephraim (1671-) & Abigail **ALLIS** (1672-); 23 Jan 1695/6; Hatfield
WELLS, Hugh & Frances __?__ (-1678), m/2 Thomas **COLEMAN** (disproved); in Eng, ca 1619; Hartford
WELLS, Hugh (-1678) & Mary **ROSCOE** (1628-); 19 Aug 1647; Hartford
WELLS, Ichabod (1660-) & Sarah **WAY** (1662-); 4 Sep 1684; Hartford
WELLS, Isaac (-1673) & Margaret __?__ (-1675); b 1620; Scituate/Barnstable
WELLS, James (-1697) & Elizabeth [**CLARK**]; b 1668; Haddam, CT
WELLS, James & Sarah [**POTTER**] (1661-1704); Portsmouth, RI?
WELLS, James (1668-1744) & Rebecca [**SELDEN**] (1678-); b 1699; Deerfield
WELLS, John (-1659) & Elizabeth [**BOURNE**], m/2 John **WILKINSON** 1663; by 1647; Wethersfield, CT
WELLS, John (-1692) & Sarah [**CURTIS**] (1642-), m/2 Samuel **BELDEN**; b 1659; Stratford, CT
WELLS, John (-1677) & Sarah [?**LITTLEFIELD**] (1649-), m/2 William **SAWYER** 1677; b 31 Jul 1666, ca 1664; Salisbury
WELLS, John & Mary **GREENLEAFE**; 5 Mar 1668, 1668/9?; Newbury/Boston
WELLS, John (1648-1714, 1713) & Mary [**HOLLISTER**] (ca 1650-); ca 1668-9; Stratford, CT
WELLS, John (1648-) & Margaret [**ALLEN?**] (had a son Allyn); 10 Dec 1678; Wethersfield, CT
WELLS, John & Mary **PECK**; 18 Feb 1697, 1696/7; Boston/Wells, ME
WELLS, John & Elizabeth **BICKFORD**; 31 Oct 1698; Boston
WELLS, John & Mary **JUDSON** (1679-1743); 15 Dec 1698; Stratford, CT
WELLS, John (1670-1720), Hatfield & Rachel [**MARSH**] (1674-); b 1700(1?); Hadley
WELLS, John & Mary __?__ ; b 1 Apr 1701; Westerly, RI
WELLS, John (1676-1732) & Elizabeth [**CONGDON**] (-1732); b 1701?; N. Kingstown, RI
WELLS, Jonathan (?1659-1739) & 1/wf Hepzibah **COLTON** (1656-1697); 13 Dec 1682, 29 Mar 1683?; Hadley
WELLS, Jonathan (?1659-1739) & 2/wf Sarah (**STRONG**) **BERNARD** (?1656-1733?, 1734?), w Joseph; 23 Sep 1698; Deerfield
WELLS, Joseph (1595-) & __?__ ; ca 1617
WELLS, Joseph (1656-1711) & Hannah **REYNOLDS** (-1711+); 28 Dec 1681; ?Westerly, RI/?Groton, CT/?Stonington, CT
WELLS, Joseph (1667-1698) & Elizabeth [**WAY**] (-1744+); ca 1689; ?Hartford
WELLES, Joshua (ca 1647-1721) & 1/wf Azuba/"Asubaty" **LAMSON** (-1676); 5 May 1670; Windsor, CT
WELLS, Joshua (?1647-1721) & 2/wf Hannah **BUCKLAND** (1654-1694); 11 Aug 1681; Windsor, CT
WELLS, Joshua (1664-1744) & Hannah **TUTHILL** (1667-); 19 Jan 1686; Southold, LI
WELLS, Joshua & Ruth [?**BATHRICK**]; b 1696; Boston
WELLS, Joshua & Elizabeth (**SKINNER**) **GRANT** (-1707), w John; 12 May 1697; Windsor, CT
WELLS, Joshua & Sarah **SAVAGE**; 25 Dec 1699; Boston
WELLS, Nathaniel (-1681, 1682) & Lydia **THURLEY/THURLO**, m/2 Nathaniel **EMERSON**; 29 Oct 1661; Ipswich
WELLS, Nathaniel (-1721) & Mary __?__ (1669-); b 1693; Ipswich
WELLS, Noah (1666-1714) & Mary [?**WHITE**] (1664-); b 1686; Hatfield/Hadley/Deerfield/New London, CT/Colchester, CT
WELLS, Peter (-1715, ae 85) & __?__ ; b 1667; Jamestown, RI/Kings Town
WELLS, Peter & Mary (**SAVAGE**) [**LEAR**], w Hugh; by 1694
WELLS, Richard (-1672, ae 63) & Elizabeth [**ROWLANDSON**], m/2 John **HARRIS** 1677; Lynn
WELLS, Richard & Martha (**MELLARD**) **SKERRY**, w Ephraim; 1 Jan 1678/9; Salem/Boston
WELLS, Robert (ca 1651-1714) & 1/wf Elizabeth **GOODRICH** (?1658-1698); 9 Jun 1675; Wethersfield, CT
WELLS/WELLES, Robert (1651-1714) & 2/wf Mary **STODDARD** (1668-1740?), dau Anthony; 13 Oct 1698; Boston
WELLS, Samuel (?1630, ?1629-1675) & 1/wf [?Elizabeth **HOLLISTER**] (?1640-); ca 1659; Wethersfield, CT

WELLS, Samuel (?1629, 1630-1675) & 2/wf Hannah [LAMBERTON] (1634-), m/2 John ALLYN 1676?; ca 1670; Wethersfield, CT

WELLS, Samuel (1662-1690) & Sarah CLARK, m/2 Thomas MEEKINS ca 1693/5?; 11 Dec 1684; Northampton

WELLS, Samuel (1660-1731) & Ruth RICE (1659-1742, Glastonbury, CT?); 20 Jun 1683, b 1689; Marlboro

WELLS, Samuel (1656±-1729) & Abigail [WHEELER]; ca 1685; Stratford, CT

WELLES, Samuel (1662-1733), Hartford & Ruth [JUDSON] (1664-1744); b 1689; CT/Hartford

WELLS, Thomas (ca 1590-1660) & 1/wf Alice TOMES; in Eng, ca 5 Jul 1615; Hartford/Wethersfield, CT

WELLS, Thomas (1605-1666) & Abigail [WARNER] (1614-1671); aft 23 Jul 1630, b 1641; Ipswich

WELLES, Thomas (-1659) & 2/wf Elizabeth (DEMING) FOOTE (-1683), w Nathaniel; ca 1646; Wethersfield, CT

WELLES, Thomas (-1676) & Mary BEARDSLEY (-1691), m/2 Samuel BELDING/BELDEN 1678; - May 1651; Wethersfield, CT

WELLS, Thomas (?1627-1668) & Hannah (TUTTLE) PANTRY (1632±-1683), w John; 23 Jun 1654; Hartford/New Haven

WELLS, Thomas (-1700) & Naomi [MARSHALL] (1637-1700+); b 1656; Boston/Ipswich/Westerly, RI

WELLS, Thomas (1647-1734) & Mary PERKINS (-1727, ae 75); 10 Jan 1669; Ipswich/Amesbury

WELLS, Thomas (-1691) & Hepzibah BUELL (1649-1704), m/2 Daniel BELDING 1699; 12 Jan 1672, [1672/3]; Windsor, CT

WELLS, Thomas & Mary PECKAR/PARKER?; 3 Mar 1672; Newbury

WELLS, Thomas (ca 1651, 1650-1720/1, 1719/20) & Elizabeth [TITHERTON] (-ca 1729); ca 1675/80?, no issue; Stratford, CT

WELLES, Thomas (1657-1695) & Mary [BLACKLEDGE], m/2 John OLCOTT 1695, m/3 Joseph WADSWORTH; b 1690, b 1689, ca 1689; Hartford

WELLS, Thomas (1663-1716) & Sarah ? ; b 1692?, b 1697; Westerly, RI

WELLS, Thomas (1673-) & Elizabeth [MACKCLAFLIN] (1670-), Wenham; b 1696; Ipswich

WELLS, Thomas & 1/wf Sarah BROWNE; 14 May 1696; Newbury/Wells, ME

WELLS, Thomas (1662-1711) (ae 41 in 1703) & 1/wf Thankful ROOT (-1704), Northampton; 7 Jan 1697, 1696/7; Deerfield

WELLS, Thomas (1676-1741) & Hannah WARNER (1678-1738); 28 Sep 1699; Wethersfield, CT

WELLS, Thomas & Rebecca ? ; b 1700; Boston

WELLS, Thomas (-1750) & Sarah BARNARD (-1754); 29 Mar 1700, 27? Mar; Deerfield

WELLS, Thomas (1669-1727) & Sarah [ROGERS] (-1716+); b 1701?; E. Greenwich, RI

WELLS, Titus (1675-) & Joanna [ROWELL]; b 1698; Amesbury

WELLS, William (-1671, ae 63) & Mary [?YOUNGS] (-1709), m/2 Thomas MAPES?; Southold, LI

WELLS, William & Bridget [TUTTLE], w John; Southold, LI

WELLS, William (1660-1696) & Elizabeth TUTHILL (1661-), m/2 John GOLDSMITH 1697; 1 Jun 1681; Southold, LI

WELLSTEAD, William & Mehitable CARY?/CORY (-1712, ae 72); 24 Nov 1665; Charlestown

WELLSTEAD, William (1666-1729) & 1/wf Katharine/Katherine LONG; 24 May 1694; Charlestown

WELTON, John (-1726) & Mary [UPSON] (-1716); b 1672, b 1666; Farmington, CT/Waterbury, CT

WELTON, Richard (1680-) & Mary [UPSON]; b 1701, 5 Nov 1701; Waterbury, CT

WEN/WENBOURNE, William & Elizabeth ? ; b 1635; Boston

WENTWORTH, Benjamin (-1728) & Sarah [?ALLEN] (1680±-); b 1698; Dover, NH

WENTWORTH, Ephraim (-1748) & 1/wf Mary [MILLER]; b 22 Oct 1696 & Jul 1699; Dover, NH

WENTWORTH, Ezekiel (see William WENTWORTH) (-1714) & Elizabeth [?KNIGHT]; b 1670; Dover

WENTWORTH, Gershom (-1731) & Hannah FRENCH; 18 Mar 1695/6; Salisbury/Dover, NH

WENTWORTH, John & Martha [?STEWART]/MILLER? (1659?-); b 1676; Dover, NH/York, ME/Canton, MA

WENTWORTH, John (1672-1730, Portsmouth, NH) & Sarah HUNKING (-1741, in 68th y); 12 Oct 1693; Kittery, ME

WENTWORTH, Paul (uncle of Benjamin BARNARD b 1694) & Catherine [?STEWART] (1658-); b 1680; Dover, NH/Rowley, MA/Norwich, CT/New London, CT

WENTWORTH, Samuel (1641-1690) & Mary [BENNING] (-1725, ae 77), m/2 Richard MARTIN/MARTYN; b 1666, by 1666; Dover, NH/Portsmouth, NH

WENTWORTH, Samuel (1666-1736) & 1/wf Hannah WIGGIN (1666-1691); 21 Feb 1689; Exeter, NH/Hampton, NH

WENTWORTH, Samuel (1666-1736) & 2/wf Elizabeth HOPSON; 12 Nov 1691; Boston

WENTWORTH, Samuel (1666-1736) & 3/wf Abigail (PHILLIPS) GOFFE, w Christopher; 28 Oct 1699; Boston

WENTWORTH, Sylvanus & Elizabeth STEWART (1662-); 7 Nov 1685; Dover, NH

WENTWORTH, Timothy (-1719) & Sarah [CROMWELL]?; b 1698; Dover, NH/Berwick, ME

WENTWORTH, William (1616-1698, 1697?) & 1/wf _?_; b 1640?; Dover, NH

WENTWORTH, William (-1698, 1697?) (see Ezekiel WENTWORTH) & 2/wf Elizabeth KNIGHT; bef 1653; Exeter, NH/Dover, NH

WENTWORTH, _?_ & [Mary KEY]; b 13 Apr 1710, b 1701?; Kittery, ME

WERNEY, Thomas & Ann BROWN; 23 Dec 1667; Charlestown

WESSELBEE, Samuel & Bridget _?_, m/2 Thomas OLIVER 1666; in Eng, b 1665(6?); Boston

WESSON, John (-1723?) (ae 63 in 1685) & Sarah FITCH (-1698); 18 Apr 1653; Reading/Salem

WESSON, John (1661-1719) & Mary BRIANTT (1666-); 26 Nov 1684, 26 Sep 1684; Reading

WESSON, Samuel (1665-), Reading & Abigail EAMES (1666-), Woburn, m/2 Jonathan BARRETT 1696; 29 Aug 1688; Woburn/Reading

WESSON/WESTON?, Stephen (1667-1753) & Sarah TOWNSEND (?1673-1739/40), Lynn; 22 Mar 1694; Reading

WESSON, Thomas (1670-1720) & Elizabeth BROWN (-1715); 13 Nov 1694; Reading

WEST, Bartholomew & Catharine [ALMY]; b 1654?, b 1647?; Portsmouth, RI/Monmouth, NJ

WEST, Benjamin (-1733) & Hannah WEST; 14 Mar 1691/2; Middletown, CT

WEST, Edward (-1677) & Martha [WALTON]; b 1665; Great Island, NH/Newcastle, NH

WEST, Edward (-1694, ae 57) & Mary [MORSE] (1650-1736); Medfield

WEST, Edward & Alice [LEAVITT]; Newcastle, NH/Hampton, NH

WEST/WESTON, Francis (-1645) & 1/wf _?_; Salem

WEST/WESTON, Francis (see WESTON) & Margaret REEVES; 27 Feb 1639; Duxbury/?Plymouth

WEST, Francis & Susanna [SOULE]; ca 1655?, b 1661, ca 1650?; Kingston, RI

WEST, Francis, Jr. & _?_; b 1681, Stonington, CT

WEST, Francis (?1669-) & Mercy MINER; 20 Dec 1696; Preston, CT/Tolland, CT

WEST, Francis & Sarah MILLARD; 12 May 1699; E. Greenwich, RI

WEST, Henry (-1703) (ae ca 57 in 1686) & Elizabeth MERRIAM (1641-1691); 7 Sep 1664; Ipswich/Salem

WEST, John (1589-1663) & Edith _?_; ca 1625?; Saco, ME

WEST, John & Mary LEE (-1691, 1690?), w Henry; 1 Jun 1675; Beverly/Manchester

WEST, John & Mehitable _?_; b 1679; Swansea/Rehoboth

WEST, John (1661-) & 1/wf Sarah TENNEY; 22 Jul 1687; Rowley/Ipswich

WEST, John (?1664-1695) & Elizabeth [TETHERLY], m/2 Peter WEARE; ?ca 1688; Newcastle, NH

WEST, John & Mary WEBSTER; 25 Mar 1696; Bradford/Salem

WEST, John & 2/wf Elizabeth ATWOOD, w Thomas; 9 Sep 1697; Ipswich

WEST, Matthew & _?_; ca 1628/31?, b 1627; Lynn/Newport

WEST, Nathaniel & _?_; b 12 Oct 1648; Newport

WEST, Nathaniel & Elizabeth [DUNGAN] (1652)

WEST, Peter (-1721, Plympton) & Patience _?_ (-1725, Plympton); b 1675; Duxbury

WEST, Peter & [?Ruth] _?_; b 1692; Kingston, RI

WEST, Richard (-1701, ae 67) & Hannah/Ann?/Anne?/Anna? [SANDERSON]? (-1723, Rehoboth), m/2 Preserved ABEL 1706; b 1674; Boston

WASTE, Richard & Mary SAMSON; 26 Oct 1693; Duxbury

WEST, Robert & 1/wf Elizabeth _?_ (-1663+); b 1645?; Providence/?Portsmouth, RI/Monmouth, NJ

WEST, Samuel (-1689) & Tryphosa PARTRIDGE (-1701); 16 Dec 1668; Duxbury

WEST, Samuel (-1685) & Rhoda MEACHAM; b 1685; Salem/Bradford?/Boston

WEST, Samuel & Mary POORE; 29 Jan 1690; Salem

WEST, Stephen & Mercy COOK (1654-); b 1684, b 1682?, 1682?; Dartmouth

WEST, Thomas & 1/wf Phebe **WATERS** (-1674); 11 Oct 1658; Salem
WEST, Thomas & Elizabeth **JACKSON**; 12 Dec 1661; Beverly
WEST, Thomas & 2/wf Mary **TENNEY** (1646-1731); 14 Oct 1674; Salem
WEST, Thomas & Mary [**LEE**], wid; 1675
WEST, Thomas & Elizabeth _?_ (-1689); 10 May 1677; Wethersfield, CT
WEST, Thomas (?1646-1706) & Elizabeth _?_ (-1728, ae 75); b 1678; Tisbury
WEST, Twyford/Twiford (-1683/4) & Mary [?**CROSS**]; b 1656, ca 1650?; Rowley/Ipswich
WEST, William (-1673) & Mary (**OLIVER**) **HILLIARD**, w Job; 30 Aug 1672; Salem
WEST, ?William & Jane **TANNER**, dau Francis; b 1701?
WEST, _?_ (doubtful) & Abigail **STONE**, dau Hugh
WESTALL/WASHULL, John (-1682) & Susannah [**KIRTLAND**] (-1684); b 1650; Wethersfield,
    CT/Saybrook, CT
WESTBROOK, George & Sarah [**JUDSON**], m/2 John **WOODCOCK**; b 1672; Dedham
WESTBROOK, John & Martha (**WALFORD**) [**HINKSON**], w Thomas; b 1666; Weymouth
WESTBROOK, John (-1697) & Alice [**CATE**] (-1697+), w James; Portsmouth, NH
WESTBROOK, Thomas & Mary [**SHERBURNE**]; ca 1700; ?Portsmouth, NH
WESTCARR, John & Hannah **BARNARD**, m/2 Simon **BRAMAN** 1680; 17 Oct 1667; Hadley
WESTCOTT/WESCOTT, Amos (1631-1685) & 1/wf Sarah [**STAFFORD**] (-1669); 13 Jul 1667;
    Warwick, RI
WESTCOTT, Amos (1631-1685) & 2/wf Deborah **STAFFORD** (1651-1706); 9 Jun 1670; Warwick,
    RI
WESTCOTT, Daniel & Maria _?_ ; b 1646; Marblehead
WESTCOTT, Daniel & Esther _?_ ; b 1670 in Eng; Portsmouth, NH
WESTCOTT, Daniel (1643?-1704) & Abigail [**GAYLORD**] (1653-); ca 1673?; Stamford, CT
WESTCOTT, Jeremiah/Jeremy (-1686) & Eleanor/Ellen **ENGLAND** (-1686); 27 Jul 1665, 27 Feb
    1665; Warwick, RI
WESTCOTT, John & Ruth [**HYATT**] (1650-1710+); b 1668; Bedford, NY
WESTCOTT, Richard (-1651) & Joanna _?_ , sister of Robert **SANFORD**'s wife, m/2 Nathaniel
    BALDWIN 1651?, m/3 Thomas **SKIDMORE** by 1667; b 1641; Wethersfield, CT/Fairfield, CT
WESTCOTT, Richard & Rachel [**HOLMES**]; b 1695; Bedford, NY
WESTCOTT, Richard & Anna [**HALEY**] (ca 1670-); b 1701?; Kittery, ME
WESTCOTT, Robert (-1676) & 1/wf? Catherine/?Elizabeth [?**RATHBURN**], m James **HAZLE-
TON** 1678; b 1664; Warwick, RI
WESTCOTT, Samuel (-1742) & Elizabeth [**COLEY**] (1680-); b 19 Jun 1705, b 1701?;
    CT/Cohansey, NJ
WESTCOTT, Stukeley (1592-1677) (uncle of John **COOKE** 1652) & ?Julian **MARCHANTE**; Yeovil,
    Somerset, in Eng, b 1618, 5 Oct 1619; Salem/Providence/etc.
WESTCOTT, Stukeley (1672-1750), Providence & Priscilla **BENNETT** (-1754), E. Greenwich; 21
    Dec 1693; Providence/Warwick, RI
WESTCOTT, Thomas & Joan _?_ ; Scarborough, ME
WESTCOTT, Zerubbabel (1666-) & 1/wf Jane _?_ ; b 1700, b 1695?; N. Kingstown, RI
WESTCOTT, Zerubbabel (1666-) & 2/wf Mary [**DAVIS**] (-1743); b 1701?
WESTEAD/?WELSTEAD, William & _?_ ; b 1683; Saybrook, CT
WESTERHOUSEN, William & _?_ ; b 1650; New Haven
WESTFIELD, George & Sarah [**BISHOP**] (-1657); Guilford, CT
WESTGATE, Adam & Mary _?_ ; b 1647; Marblehead
WESTGATE, John (1663-) & Elizabeth _?_ ; b 1690; Salem
WESTGATE, Robert (?1647-1717) & Sarah _?_ (-1723); b 1684; Newport/Warwick, RI
WESTGATE, Thomas (1654-) & Ruth **ROSE**; 4 Apr 1685; Marblehead
WESTON, Edmund (?1605-1686) & _?_ [**DELANO?**]; b 1657; Boston/Duxbury
WESTON, Edmund (1660-1727) & Rebecca **SOULE** (1657-1732); 13 Dec 1688; Plymouth
WESTON, Elnathan (-1724, 1729?) (m 1715) & Jane _?_ ; b 1687; Duxbury
WESTON, Francis (-1645) & Margaret [**PEASE**]?, sister of John, she was wid with dau Lucy who
    m John **PEASE**; b 5 Jun 1638, no issue; Salem
WESTON/?WEST, Francis (-1692) (see **WEST**) & Margery **REEVES**; 27 Feb 1639; Plymouth/Provi-
    dence
WESTON, John (1662-1736) & Deborah [?**DELANO**]; ca 1696; Duxbury
WESTOVER, Jonas (-1709) & Hannah **GRISWOLD** (1642-1714); 19 Nov 1663; Windsor,
    CT/Simsbury/Killingworth, CT

WESTWOOD, James (-1707) & Mary EDWARDS; 13 Jun 1687; Wallingford, CT
WESTWOOD, William (1606-1669) & Bridget _?_ (1602-1676); b 1634; Hartford/Hadley
WETHERELL, Daniel (1630-1719) & Grace BREWSTER (1639-1689); 4 Aug 1659; ?New London, CT
WETHERELL, John & Grace [FOSDICK?]; b 1635; Sudbury/Watertown
WETHERLEE, John (-1691, 1690?) & Hannah (PINSON) [YOUNG] (1642-), w George, m/3 Jonathan MOWRY by 1694; b 1675; Scituate
WETHERELL, John & Susannah [NEWLAND]?; ca 1687; Taunton
WETHEREL, Samuel (-1683) & Isabel [HILAND]/[HYLAND] (-1689), w Samuel, m/3 Josiah TORREY 1684; b 1678; Scituate
WETHERELL, Samuel (1678-) & Eunice ROGGERS/ROGERS (1677-); 26 May 1698; Marshfield
WITHERELEE, Theophilus & Lydia PARKER (1640-1719); 9 Nov 1675; Scituate
WETHERELL, William (-1684) & Mary FISHER; m lic 26 Mar 1627, in Eng; Cambridge/Scituate
WETHERELL, William (-1691) & Dorothy _?_ ; ca 1650?; Taunton
WETHERELL, William & Elizabeth NEWLAND; 14 Mar 1681; Taunton
WEYMOUTH, Benjamin & Mary _?_ ; b 1694, by 1693; Dover, NH
WEYMOUTH, Edward (1639±-) & Esther HODSDON (1640-); 25 Dec 1663; Dover, NH
WAYMOUTH, James (-1678) & Mary _?_ , m/2 Thomas DIAMOND by 1685; by 1660; Isles of Shoals
WEYMOUTH, James (-1710) & Katharine (?CHADBOURNE) LIDDEN, w Edward; aft 1691; Kittery, ME/Newcastle, NH
WEYMOUTH, Robert (-1661?) & Rebecca [EMERY] (-1719), m/2 Thomas SADLER ca 1663/4, m/3 Daniel EATON 1681+; Kittery, ME
WEYMOUTH, Thomas & 1/wf Rachel _?_ ; b 1701?; Kittery, ME
WEYMOUTH, William (alias SADLER) & Sarah _?_ (-1705); b 1686; Dover, NH
WHALE, Philemon (-1676) & 1/wf Elizabeth _?_ (-1647); ca 1619?, ca 1615; Sudbury
WHALE, Philemon (-1676) & 2/wf Sarah (_?_) CAKEBREAD, w Thomas; 7 Nov 1649; Sudbury
WHALE, Philemon (-1676) & 3/wf Elizabeth (UPSON) GRIFFINE (-1688), w Hugh; 9 Nov 1657; Sudbury
WHALEY, George & Katherine _?_ ; b 1650; Cambridge
WHALEY, Theophilus (1616-1720±) & Elizabeth [MILLS] (1645±-1715±); Virginia/Kings Town, RI
WHAPLES, Joseph & _?_ ; b 1687; Middletown, CT/Hartford
WHAPLES, Thomas (-1671) & _?_ ; b 1653
WHAPLES, Thomas (-1713) & [Mary] _?_ ; Hartford
WHARFE/WHARF, John & Martha _?_ ; b 1695; Boston
WHARFE, Nathaniel & Rebecca MACWORTH, m/2 William ROGERS by 1676; b 1662, b 1661; Gloucester/Falmouth, ME
WHARFFE, Nathaniel (1662-) & Anna RIGGS; 30 Jan 1683; Gloucester
WHARTON, John & Sarah BALLENTINE; 14 Oct 1698; Boston
WHARTON, Philip & Mary [BRIDLEY] (1632-1699); ca 1651, b 1660; Boston
WHARTON, Richard (-1690) & 1/wf Bethia [TING] (1641-); b 1663, ca 1659?; Charlestown/Boston
WHARTON, Richard (-1690) & 2/wf Sarah [HIGGINSON] (-1675?); b 1671, 1670; Boston
WHARTON, Richard & 3/wf Martha [WINTHROP] (1646-1712); b 1679, b 1675?; Charlestown/Boston
WHEAT, Joshua (-1708) & Elizabeth MANSFIELD (-1704); 10 Jun 1675; Lynn/Concord/Groton
WHEAT, Moses (-1700) & Tamzen [BROOKS?] (-1689); b 1640; Concord (Samuel RAYNER in will 1669 mentions bro. WHEATE; Moses W-, a witness)
WHEATLEY, Gabriel (-1645) & _?_ ; b 1637; Watertown
WHEATLEY, John & [?Leah SANDERS] (1623-), m/2 Robert PARMENTER 1648; b 1643; Braintree
WHEATLEY, John (-1723?) & Sarah _?_ ; b 1684; Boston
WHEATLEY, Lionel (-1677) & 1/wf Eleanor _?_ (Mary wrong); b 1654; Boston
WHEATLEY, Lionel (-1677) & 2/wf Abigail [MATTSON]; b 1671; Boston
WHEATLEY, Thomas (doubtful; prob John & Sarah) & Sarah _?_ ; b 1685(6?); Boston
WHEATON, Benjamin[2] (1661-1726?) & Margaret _?_ ; b 1693; Rehoboth/Mendon
WHEATON, Christopher & Martha [PRINCE]; 1674, b Oct 1671; Hingham
WHEATON, Rev. Ephraim (1659-1734) & Mary MASON (1660-1727); 7 Jan 1684; Rehoboth

WHEATON, Jeremiah & Hannah [AMIDOWN] (-1719); b 1666; Rehoboth
WHEATON, John (1650-) & Elizabeth [CARPENTER]/THURBER (doubtful); b 1679(80?); Swansea
WHEATON, John & Mary _?_ ; b 1696; Branford, CT
WHEATON, Obadiah & Sarah _?_ ; b 1684; Scituate/Milton
WHEATON, Robert (1605-1695/6) & Alice [BOWEN], m/2 _?_ DARLING; ca 1636?; Rehoboth
WHEATON, Samuel (-1684, 1683, [1683/4]) & Elizabeth WOOD, ?m/2 Richard BOWEN; 5 Dec 1678; Swansea
WHEATON, Thomas & _?_ ; b 1671; Branford, CT
WHEADEN, John (1671-1710) & Mary [FROST] (1679-), m/2 Henry COOKE; b 1696; Branford, CT?
WHEDON, Thomas (-1691) & Ann (SMALL) HARVEY (-1692); 24 May 1661; New Haven/Branford, CT
WHEDON, Thomas & Hannah [SUTLIFF], m/2 _?_ BARNES; b 1686; Branford, CT
WHEELER, Abraham (1659-) & Tabitha _?_ ; b 1683(4)?, ca 1682; Lancaster
WHEELER, Benjamin & Sarah _?_ ; b 1700; Boston
WHEELER, David (-1700+) & Sarah WISE (-1702+); 11 May 1650; Newbury/Rowley
WHEELER, Deliverance (1663-1716) & Mary DAVIS (1663-1748); 28 May 1691; Concord/Groton/Stow
WHEELER, Edward (1669-1734) & Sarah MIRIAM/(MERRIAM) (1675-1738); 23 Nov 1697; Concord
WHEELER, Ephraim & Ann _?_ (not Ann TURNEY); b 1638; Concord/Fairfield, CT
WHEELER, Ephraim & Mary HOLBROOK (1650-), m/2 Henry SUMMERS; 8 Sep 1675; Milford, CT
WHEELER, Ephraim & 1/wf Abigail _?_ (-1687); b 1687; Newton
WHEELER, Epharim, Newton & 2/wf Sarah SPRING (1662/3-), Newton; 1 Jan 1688, prob 1688/9; Newton
WHEELER, Ephraim (-1705) & 1/wf Sarah [TURNEY] (1663-bef 1689); Stratford, CT
WHEELER, Ephraim (-1705) & 2/wf Sarah [SHERWOOD] (ca 1676-1743), m/2 Benjamin FAIRWEATHER, m/3 Anthony NOUGUIER; b 1694; Stratford, CT
WHEELER, Ephraim (1678-1725) & Elizabeth SPALDING (1680-1724); 20 Apr 1698; Concord/Plainfield, CT
WHEELER, George (-1687) & 1/wf Mary STUDD; 12 May 1628, Cranfield, Eng; Concord
WHEELER, George (-1687) & 2/wf Katherine [WHEELER]? (1609-1684); b 1640, b 1630?; Concord
WHEELER, George (-1667/8) (brother-in-law of Matthias BUTTON) & Susanna STOWERES/(STOWERS), m/2 Edward GOODWIN 1668, m/3 Gregory COOKE 1681, m/4 Henry SPRING 1691; 30 Apr 1660; Newbury
WHEELER, George (-1737) & 1/wf Abigail HOSMER (1669-1717); 14 Aug 1695; Concord
WHEELER, Henry (1635-) & Abigail [ALLEN] (1640-); b 1659; Salisbury
WHEELER, Henry (1659-1684) & Rachel [SQUIRE] (1665-), m/2 Benjamin ALLEN 1686; b 1684; Salisbury/Boston/Attleboro
WHEELER, Isaac & Frances _?_ (1608-), m/2 Richard COOK, m/3 Thomas GREEN 1659; b 1641; Charlestown
WHEELER, Isaac (1642-) & 1/wf _?_ ; ca 1663/5?; Fairfield, CT/Stratford, CT
WHEELER, Isaac (?1646-1712) & Martha PARK (1646-1717); 10 Jan 1667, 10 Jan 1668, 16 Jan 1667/8; Stonington, CT
WHEELER, Isaac (1661-1731) & Experience [METCALF] (-1731); b 1684, 1682, 1683; Lancaster/Medfield
WHEELER, Isaac (-1698) & Rebecca [WHEELER], m/2 Nathaniel PORTER; b 1692, ca 1693; Fairfield, CT/Stratford, CT
WHEELER, Isaac (1673-1737) & Mary SHEPHERD (1679-1761); 9 Dec 1697; Stonington, CT
WHEELER, Isaac & 2/wf Susannah [HALL], w Samuel; b 18 Sep 1699?; Fairfield, CT
WHEELER, Isaac & Sarah HOW; b 19 Jan 1699/1700; Concord
WHEELER, Isaac (1678-1755) & Bethia (SWEETSER) PAINE (1663-1747), w Edward; 3 Apr 1700, 30 Apr 1700; Cambridge/Charlestown
WHEELER, James & Sarah RANDALL; 24 Jun 1682; Stow/Watertown?
WHEELER, James (1667-1753) & Grisel [SQUIRE] (1668-); b 1691; Rehoboth/Salisbury
WHEELER, James & _?_ ; ca 1696?; Fordham, NY
WHEELER, Jethro (1664-1725) & Hannah/Anna? FRENCH (1666-); 2 Jul 1690; Rowley

WHEELER, John (-1670) & Ann **YEOMAN** (-1662); in Eng, ca 1618, 1 Dec 1611; Salisbury/Newbury/Hampton, NH

WHEELER, John & _?_ ; b 1640?; CT/Southampton, LI

WHEELER, John (1624-1690) & 1/wf Judith [**TURNEY**] (1635-1672?); b 1660, b 1679; Fairfield, CT/Stratford, CT

WHEELER, John (1630-1716) & 1/wf Sarah **SHERWOOD** (-1704); ?5 Nov 1662?, 16 Dec 1662, beginning Dec; Fairfield/Milford, CT/Stratford, CT

WHEELER, John (1643-1713) & Sarah **LARKEN/(LARKIN)** (1647-1725); 25 Mar 1663; Concord/Charlestown

WHEELER, John (-1728, 1718, ae ca 80) & Sarah [?**TALMAGE**]?, had dau Rebecca **TALMAGE**; 9 Dec 1669; Southampton, LI/East Hampton, LI

WHEELER, John (see Jonathan) (1653-) & Mary [?**SINCLAIR**] (see Mary **GILES** m 1700); b 1679; Beverly

WHEELER, John (1624-1690) & 2/wf Elizabeth [**ROWLAND**]; by 1673; Fairfield/?New London

WHEELER, John (-1691) & Elizabeth _?_ , m/2 Richard **STEER** 1692?; b 1675; New London

WHEELER, John (1653-) (son of David?) & Mary _?_ ; ca 1777?, b 1679; Salisbury (see John & Mary of Beverly/Rowley; prob moved to Beverly, see above)

WHEELER, John (1655-1713, 1736?) & Sarah **STARNES/STEARNS** (1662-); 27 Dec 1678; Concord

WHEELER, John (1640-1704) & 2/wf [Ruth?] _?_ ; b 1679, b 1666?; Woodbury, CT/Milford, CT?

WHEELER, John & Elizabeth **WELLS**, m/2 Daniel **RICE** 1725; 25 Jun 1684, 25 Apr 1684; Concord/Marlboro

WHEELER, Sergt. John & 1/wf Elizabeth **ROWLAND**; ca 1685?, b 1690; ?New London/Fairfield, CT

WHEELER, John (1664-1754) & 2/wf Abigail **BURR** (-1712); 18 Mar 1692, 22 Mar 1693, 22 Mar 1692; Fairfield, CT/Stratford, CT

WHEELER, John (1668-1706) & Elizabeth **PERKINS**; b 1696, by 1700, 10 Jun 1694; Oyster River (Durham), NH

WHELLER/WHEELER, John (1679, Rowley-) & Mary **GILES**; m int 29 Jun 1700; Beverly/Preston, CT

WHEELER, Jonathan (see John WHEELER m Mary) (1658-) & Mary _?_ /SINKLER/[SINCLAIR] (1663-); 15 Mar 1683, 1683/4; Rowley

WHEELER, Jonathan & Susanna **GREEN**; 27 Jun 1700; Boston

WHEELER, Lt. Joseph (bpt 18 Feb 1609/10-1678+) (ae 68 in 1698?) & 1/wf Elizabeth _?_ (bur 19 Jul 1642); b 1640; Concord

WHEELER, Lt. Joseph (1610-1678+) & 2/wf Sarah (**GOLDSTONE**) [**MERRIAM**] (?1606±- 1671), w Joseph (will proved 26 Oct 1642, d 1 Jan 1640/1); 1642?, aft 26 Oct 1642?, aft Jan 1640/1, aft 9 Jul 1641, had Mary b 20 Sep 1643; Concord

WHEELER, Joseph & Mary _?_ ; b 1665; Boston

WHEELER, Joseph & Lydia _?_ ; b 1667; Boston

WHEELER, Joseph & Patience **HOLBROOK**; Jun 1678; Milford, CT/Newark, NJ

WHEELER, Joseph (ca 1660-1698) & Mary **POWERS** (1653-1740); 1 Mar 1680/1, 1 Mar 1681; Concord/Stow/Chelmsford/Stratford, CT

WHEELER, Joseph & Sarah **BADGER**; 24 Dec 1685; Newbury

WHEELER, Joseph & Jane **HODGES**; 1 Jul 1695; Boston

WHEELER, Joseph & Elizabeth **PELL**; 14 Dec 1697; Boston

WHEELER, Joshua & Elizabeth [?**HAYWARD**]; b 1663; Concord

WHEELER, Josiah (1669-) & Elizabeth _?_ ; b 1693; Salisbury

WHEELER, Moses (1598?-) & (Miriam [**HAWLEY**?]) (1600?-) (doubtful); b 1642; New Haven/Stratford

WHEELER, Moses (1651-1724) & 1/wf Sarah **NICHOLS** (1650-); 20 Oct 1674, 28 Oct 1674, 20 Oct; Stratford, CT

WHEELER, Moses & Ruth **BOUTON**; Dec 1698; Stratford, CT

WHEELER, Nathan (1659-) & Elizabeth **SAFFORD** (1667-1755) (prob should be Rebecca); 13 Jan 1689/90; Ipswich/Rowley

WHEELER, Nathan (1659-) & Rebecca [**SAFFORD**] (1667-1755); 13 Jan 1689/90; Newbury

WHEELER, Nathaniel (1642-) & Esther **BOTSFORD** (1647-); 27 Jun 1665, 21 Jun 1676; Milford, CT/Newark, NJ/Stratford, CT

WHEELER, Nathaniel & Mary [**MUNN**]?; ca 1676-80?; Deerfield

WHEELER, Nathaniel & Mary **BRIDGES**; 9 Nov 1697; Boston
WHEELER, Obadiah (1609-1671) & 1/wf Susanna **WHEELER** (1607-1649); b 1640?, b 1641, 20 Jan 1633, Cranfield, Eng; Concord
WHEELER, Obadiah (1609-1671) & 2/wf ? ; aft 24 Mar 1649; Concord
WHEELER, Obadiah (1644-1668?) & Ruth **(ROGERS) [GOODWIN]** (1643-), w Thomas; ca 1666/7; Stratford
WHEELER, Obadiah & Elizabeth **WHITE** (1652-); 17 Jul 1672; Concord
WHEELER, Richard (John called son of Richard WHEELOCK in Dedham records error) & 1/wf Elizabeth **TURNER**; 4 May 1644; Dedham/Lancaster
WHEELER, Richard (-1676) & Sarah **PRESCOTT** (1637-), m/2 Joseph **RICE** 1678; 2 Aug 1658; Lancaster
WHEELER, Richard & Prudence **PAYSON**; 2 Dec 1702; Roxbury
WHEELER, Roger (-1661) & 1/wf Mary **WILSON** (-1658); 7 Dec 1653; Newbury
WHEELER, Roger (-1661) & 2/wf Mary **STONE**, w John; 23 Nov 1659; Boston
WHEELER, Samuel & Mary **PERRY**; 10 Nov 1673; Concord
WHEELER, Samuel & Elizabeth **HARRIS**, m/2 Hugh **NESBITT**; 29 May 1678, no issue; Stratford, CT
WHEELER, Samuel & Sarah **[GRANT]** (1664-); b 2 Jul 1687; ?Hartford
WHEELER, Samuel (-1717) & Mary **HOSMER** (1668-), m/2 John **BELLOWS** 1721; 27 Jan 1689/90; Concord
WHEELER, Samuel (-1708) & Hannah **WHEELER** (ca 1676-), m/2 Dr. John **WHEELER** 1708; b 1700, b 1701; Stratford, CT
WHEELER, Thomas (?1591-1654) & Ann **HALSEY** (-1659); Cranfield, Eng, ca 5 May 1613; Stratford, CT/Fairfield, CT
WHEELER, Thomas (-1672/3) & ? ; in Eng, b 1625; New Haven
WHEELER, Thomas (-1654) & Rebecca ? , m/2 John **PIERCE** 1654; b 1637; Boston
WHEELER, Thomas[1] (?1606-1672, Milford) & Joan **[BRYAN** (doubtful)]**/SEABROOK**? (no) (-1673); b 1640, b 1638?, b 1636?; Milford/Stratford
WHEELER, Capt. Thomas[2] (1603, 1620?-1676) & Ruth **[WOOD]**; b 1640, by 1644; Concord/Charlestown/Fairfield, CT
WHEELER, Thomas[2] (-1656) & Alice ? /**SEABROOK**? (-1673), m/2 Josiah **STANBOROUGH** 1657; b 1647; New Haven
WHEELER, Thomas (1603, 1606-1686) & [Mary] ? ; b 1648, b 1646; Lynn?/Salem?/Stonington, CT
WHEELER, Sergt. Thomas[2] (1621-1704) & 1/wf Sarah **[MERRIAM]** (-1676) (doubtful); b 1649; Concord/Fairfield, CT
WHEELER, Thomas (-1687) & Hannah **HARROD/HARWOOD**; 10 Oct 1657; Concord/Fairfield
WHEELER, Thomas & Hannah **PELL**; b 1663; Boston
WHEELER, Thomas (-1678) & Elizabeth **CHAMBERLIN** (1652-1678+); 5 May 1673; Charlestown
WHEELER, Thomas (1650-1727) & ? ; ca 1677?; Milford, CT/Stratford, CT
WHEELER, Sergt. Thomas (1621-1704) & 2/wf Sarah **(BEERS) STARNS/STEARNS**, wid; 23 Jul 1677; Concord/Watertown
WHEELER, Thomas, Milford & Anna **FRENCH** (1666-), Derby; 1 Jun 1685?; Milford, CT
WHEELER, Thomas & Mary ? ; ca 1690; Milford, CT/Durham
WHEELER, Thomas & Sarah **[HAUGH?]**; b 1687(8?); Boston
WHEELER, Thomas & Sarah **DAVIS**; 13 Nov 1695; Concord
WHEELER, Timothy & 1/wf Susan **KNIGHT** (-1633); 30 Apr 1632, Cranfield, Eng
WHEELER, Timothy (1601, 1604-1687) & 2/wf Jane ? (-1643); b 1640, ca 1638; Concord
WHEELER, Timothy (1601-1687) & 2/wf Mary **BROOKS** (-1693); b 1657, ca 1655; Concord/Watertown
WHEELER, Timothy (-1678) (son Capt. Thomas?) & Ruth **FULLER** (1648-), m/2 Henry **WILKINS**; 29 Jun 1670; Concord
WHEELER, Timothy (1660-1730) & 1/wf Rebecca **TURNEY**; 11 Apr 1689; Stratford, CT/Fairfield
WHEELER, Timothy (1667-1718) & Lydia **WHEELER** (1675-); 19 May 1692; Concord
WHEELER, William (1616?, 1618-1666) & Sarah **[DELL?]**, m/2 William **BROOKS** [1666]; ca 1645/52?; Stratford, CT/Norwalk, CT
WHEELER, William (-1683) & Hannah **BUSSE/BUSS** (1642-); 30 Oct 1659, 20? Oct; Concord
WHEELER, William (-1705) & Ruth **SMITH**; 12 Apr 1682; Milford, CT
WHEELER, William & Ann **PHIPPEN**; 16 May 1686; Boston/Fairfield

WHEELER, William (1671-) & Elizabeth __?__; b 1693; Boston
WHEELER, William (1665-) & Sarah [FLETCHER] (1668-); b 1694; Concord
WHEELER, Zebediah (1665-1729) (son Richard) & Mary [LAWRENCE?] (1610-1728); b 1696; Concord/Stow
WHEELER, ?Samuel & Johanna __?__, m/2 Henry FEAKE d 1657; Newtown, LI?
WHEELOCKE, Benjamin (1640-) & 1/wf Elizabeth BULLIN/BULLEN (1646-1689); 21 May 1668; Medfield/Mendon
WHEELOCK, Benjamin & 2/wf Elizabeth [FRENCH] (1655-); 1692; Mendon
WHEELOCK, Benjamin & Huldah THAYER (1682-); 9 Dec 1700; Mendon
WHEELOCK, Eleazer (1654-1731) & 1/wf Elizabeth FULLER (-1689); 17 Apr 1678; Rehoboth/Medfield/Mendon
WHEELOCK, Eleazer (1654-1731) & 2/wf Mary [CHENERY]; b 1690; Medfield/Mendon
WHELLOCK, Gershom (ca 1637-1684) & Hannah STODER/STODDARD, Hingham; 18 May 1658; Medfield
WHEELOCK, Joseph (-1752) & Elizabeth __?__; b 1695; Lancaster
WHEELOCK, Ralph (1600-1684) (m/2 Hannah __?__ (very doubtful)) & Rebecca [?BARBOUR]/WILKINSON?, ?sister of George; ca 1632?; Watertown/Dedham/Medfield/Deerfield
WHEELOCKE, Samuel (1642-) & Sarah KENRICKE/KENDRICK; 3 Apr 1676; Medfield
WHEELOCK, Samuel (-1756) & Lydia [RICE] (1668-); ca 1692, b 1696; Marlboro
WHEELWRIGHT, Rev. John (?1592-1679) & 1/wf Marie STORRE (-1629?); Bolsby, Eng, 8 Nov 1621; Braintree/Exeter, NH/etc.
WHEELWRIGHT, John (-1679) & 2/wf Mary [HUTCHINSON]? (1605-); 1630?, in Eng; Salisbury
WHEELWRIGHT, John (-1745) & Mary SNELL; 28 Jan 1688/9, Wells, ME; Salisbury/Wells, ME
WHEELWRIGHT, Samuel (1637-1700), Wells, ME, & Esther [HOUCHIN] (-1699+); b 1664; Salisbury
WHELDON, Gabriel (-1654) & 1/wf __?__; ca 1620?, 1610?; Yarmouth/Malden
WHELDON, Gabriel (-1654) & 2/wf Margaret __?__; Yarmouth/Lynn/Malden
WILDEN, Henry (-1694) & Eed __?__; ?25 Jan 16[47-8]; Yarmouth
WHELDEN, John (of age in 1653) & Mary [FOLLAND], dau Thomas; ca 1655/58?, b 1 Oct 1686; Yarmouth
WHELDON, John & __?__; b 1681; Salem
WHELDEN, Jonathan & Mercy __?__; b 1700(?1701); Yarmouth
WHEELDING, Joseph & Hannah [GORHAM] (1663-); ?bef 3 Aug 1683; Yarmouth/Cape May, NJ
WHELDON, Ralph & __?__; Yarmouth
WHILDING, Thomas & Elizabeth MARCHANT (?1681-); 21 Oct 1698; Martha's Vineyard/Yarmouth
WHELPLEY, Henry (-1662) & 1/wf __?__; Stratford, CT
WHELPLEY, Henry (-1662) & 2/wf [?Sarah] WHITLOCK, w John; ?1660; Fairfield, CT
WHELPLEY, Henry (-1662) & 3/wf Sarah [TREADWELL], w Edward, m/3 Ralph KEELER, m/4 Thomas SKIDMORE; ?bef 1 May 1661; Stratford, CT
WHELPLEY, Jonathan (-1713) & Sarah __?__; ca 1691; Greenwich, CT
WHELPLEY, Joseph (-1682) & Rebecca [BULKELEY] (1646-1690); b 1676; Fairfield, CT
WHELPLEY, __?__ & Mary __?__, m/2 George KNIFFEN
WHERRY, Jeremiah & Jane WAY; 21 Apr 1685; Charlestown
WHIDDEN, John (-1681) & Elizabeth __?__; Portsmouth, NH
WHIDDEN, Jonathan & 2/wf? Rebecca HACKETT; 5 Aug 1695; ?Salisbury
WHIDDEN, Michael, Portsmouth & Elizabeth MESERVE; 6 Jun 1694; Dover, NH
WHIDDEN, Richard (-1690) & Sarah HILL (-1697); 15 Apr 1686; Fairfield, CT
WHIDDEN, Samuel (-1718) & Mary [CATE]; b 1675; Greenland, NH
WHIDDEN, Samuel & Sarah [JONES], m/2 John SAVAGE; ca 1700; ?Portsmouth, NH
WHIPPLE, Benjamin (1654-1704) & Ruth MATHEWSON (-1704+); 1 Apr 1686; Providence
WHIPPLE, Cyprian & Dorothy SYMONDS; 19 Dec 1695; Ipswich/Stonington, CT/Stow, MA
WHIPPLE, David & __?__; ca 1634/40?; Rehoboth
WHIPPLE, David (1656-1710) & 1/wf Sarah HEARNDEN/HEARNDON (-1677); 15 May 1675; Providence/Rehoboth
WHIPPLE, David (-1710) & 2/wf Hannah TOWER/COWELL? (1652-1722); 13 Dec 1677, 11 Nov 1677, 13? Nov; Hingham/Attleboro/Providence
WHIPPLE, Eleazer (1645-1719) & Alice ANGELL (1649-1743); 26 Jan 1669, 1669/70?, 1668/9; Providence

WHIPPLE, Israel (1678-1720) & Mary WILMARTH; m int 1697; Rehoboth/Attleboro
WHIPPLE, James & 1/wf Experience HINCKLEY (1664/5-); b 27 Jul 1688; Barnstable?/Boston
WHIPPLE, James & 2/wf Abigail (HAMMON) GREEN; 25 Feb 1692
WHIPPLE, Jeremiah & _?_ [SHOPPY]?/[SHOPPEN]?; b 1684?; Rehoboth?/Cumberland, RI
WHIPPLE, John (1596-1669) & Susanna [(STACY/CLARK)] (-aft 13 Jul 1661); in Eng, b 1622; Ipswich
WHIPPLE, John (?1617-1685) & 1/wf Sarah _?_ (?1624-1666); b 1641, 1639?; Dorchester/Providence
WHIPPLE, John (1628-1683) & 1/wf Martha [REYNER] (-1679/80); ca 1653, b 1655; Ipswich
WHIPPLE, John (?1633, 1632-1695) & 1/wf Sarah [KENT] (-1658); ca 1656; Rowley
WHIPPLE, John (?1633-1695) & 2/wf Elizabeth WOODMAN (-ca 1662); 5 May 1659, 6 May; Ipswich
WHIPPLE, John (?1633-1695) & 3/wf Mary STEVENS (1640?-); 21 Jul 1663; Charlestown
WHIPPLE, John (1640±-1700) & 1/wf Mary OLNEY (-1676±); 4 Dec 1663; Providence
WHIPPLE, John (-1669) & 2/wf Jennet (_?_) [DICKINSON] (-1687), w Thomas; aft Apr 1662, ca 1667; Rowley/Ipswich
WHIPPLE, John (1640-1700) & 2/wf Rebecca (?BROWN) SCOTT (-1701), w John?; 15 Apr 1678; Providence
WHIPPLE, John (-1683) & 2/wf Elizabeth (BURR) PAINE, w John; 28 Jun 1680; Ipswich
WHIPPLE, John (1657-1722?) & Catharine LAYTON/LEIGHTON (-1721); 16 Jun 1681; Ipswich
WHIPPLE, John (?1660-1722?) & 1/wf Hannah [ROLFE] (1664?-1701); b 1687; Ipswich
WHIPPLE, John (1640, 1664?-1700) & Lydia HOAR; 9 Nov 1688, 16 Nov 1688; Providence/Bristol, RI/Taunton
WHIPPLE, Jonathan (1664-1721) & 1/wf Margaret [ANGELL]; b 1692, b 1691(2?); Providence
WHIPPLE, Jonathan (1664-1721) & 2/wf Anna/Hannah [DARLING]?; b 1701?; Providence
WHIPPLE, Joseph (1640-1707) & 1/wf Sarah _?_ (-1676); b 1665; Ipswich
WHIPPLE, Joseph & 2/wf Sarah _?_, m/2 Walter FAIRFIELD?; ca 18 Jul 1676, ca 1678; Ipswich
WHIPPLE, Joseph (1662-1746) & Alice SMITH (1664-1739); 20 May 1684; Providence, RI
WHIPPLE, Joseph (1666-1734+) & Sarah [HUTCHINSON] (-1734+); b 1692, b 1691?; Ipswich/Salem
WHIPPLE, Joseph & Mary [ADAMS] (1670-1734); b 1692, ca 4 Aug 1688; Ipswich
WHIPPLE, Joseph (1666-) & Mary SYMONDS (1674-1703); 10 Dec 1697; Ipswich
WHIPPLE, Matthew[1] (-1647) & 1/wf Anna HAWKINS (ca 1600-1643); Bucking, Eng, 7 May 1622; Ipswich
WHIPPLE, Mathew[1] (-1647) & 2/wf Rose [(?BARKER/?BAKER)] CHUTE, w Lionel; bef 13 Nov 1646, aft 7 May 1645; Ipswich
WHIPPLE, Matthew (1635-1658) & Mary BARTHOULMUE, m/2 Jacob GREEN 1660?; 24 Dec 1657; Gloucester
WHIPPLE, Matthew (1663?-) & 1/wf Jemima [LANE] (1666-); b 1685; Ipswich
WHIPPLE, Matthew (1663?-) & 2/wf Joanna [APPLETON?]/[COGSWELL?] (ca 1670-); ca 1688, b 1685, b 1696; Ipswich
WHIPPLE, Matthew (1664-1736) & Dorcas [PAINE] (?1666-1735); ?Ipswich
WHIPPLE, Matthew (?1663-) & 3/wf Martha (DENISON) (WIGGIN/WIGGEN) [THING] (1668-), w Thomas, w Jonathan; 11 Jun 1697, 11 Jan; Ipswich/Stonington, CT
WHIPPLE, Matthew (-1742) & Bethia _?_; b 1701; Ipswich
WHIPPLE, Noah (-1703) & 1/wf Susannah _?_; ca 1680/90?, b 1696, b 1697; Providence
WHIPPLE, Noah (-1703) & 2/wf Anphillis [SMITH] (-1703+); b 1701?; Providence
WHIPPLE, Samuel (1644-1711) & Mary [HARRIS] (?1639-1722); b 1669; Providence
WHIPPLE, Samuel (1669-1728) & Elizabeth EDDY (1670-); 26 Feb 1690, 1690/1; Providence/Groton, CT
WHIPPLE, Thomas & Abigail JENKS, b 1701?; Providence
WHIPPLE, William (1652-1712) & Mary _?_ (-1712+); b 1685; Providence
WHIPPO, James & Abigail (HAMMOND) GREENE/GREENOUGH, w Luke; 25 Feb 1691/2, 25 Feb 1692; Boston/Barnstable/Charlestown
WHIPPEY, James & Mary _?_; b 1701; Roxbury
WHITSTONE, John (-1664) & Susanna [HANFORD], m/2 William BROOKS ?1665, 1666; b 1640?, b 1645; Scituate
WHITSTON/WHETSTONE, John (1648-1693) & 1/wf Abigail LUMBART (-1754), ?dau Joshua, m/2 Benjamin/Jedediah? LUMBART 1694; b 1678; Scituate

WHITHEARE/?WHITAKER/WHITTIER?, Abraham/Abram? (1604-) & _?_ b 1639; Marblehead/ Manchester

WHITHEARE/?WHITAKER/WHITTIER?, Abraham/Abram? (1604-) & ?2/wf Mary _?_, m/2 John KNIGHT

WHITAKER/WHITTICKER, Abraham (1609-1701) & Elizabeth SIMMONS (-1683); 19 Mar 1655/6; Haverhill

WHITICKER, Abraham (-1691, 1692) & Hannah BEANE (-1692); 6 Apr 1682; Haverhill

WHITTAKER, Abraham & Sarah (TRASK) ARCHER, ?w John; 7 Sep 1694; Lynn

WHITAKER, Isaac? ([166-]-) & Elizabeth _?_; Salem

WHITAKER, Jacob & Mary WEBSTER; 14 Jun 1693; Manchester/Salem/Haverhill ·

WHITAKER, James & _?_; b 1683; Flushing, LI

WHITAKER, John (1641-) & Elizabeth _?_ (1642-); b 1661(2?); Watertown/Billerica

WHITAKER, John (Nathaniel wrong) (-1744) & Mehitable PECK (-1718); m int 1696/7; Rehoboth

WHITTAKER, Jonathan & Sarah TOOTHAKER; 15 Nov 1694; Boston/Chelmsford

WHITTAKER, Nathaniel (-1703) & Elizabeth SQUIER (-1703); 14 May 1687; Rehoboth

WHITTAKER, Richard & [Rebecca] (Bathsheba wrong) COOPER (-1707); last of Nov 1659; Rehoboth

WHITTAKER, Samuel & Mary SQUARE/SQUIRE?; 5 May 1697; Rehoboth

WHITTIKER, Thomas & _?_; b 1675; Flushing, LI

WHITICKER, William (1659-) & 1/wf Sarah EMERSON (-1702); 15 Jan 1684; Haverhill

WHITCOMB, David (1668-1730) & Mary (HAYWARD) FAIRBANKS (1667-1734), w Jonathan; 31 May 1700; Concord/Lancaster

WHITCOMB, Israel, Scituate & Mary STODDER/STODDARD; 28 May 1700; Hingham

WHITCOMBE, James (1632-1686) & 1/wf Rebecca _?_; b 1662; Boston

WHITCOMB, James & 2/wf Elizabeth [DAVIS] (1655-), dau William; b 1680; Boston

WHITCOMB, James (1668-1730) & Mary PARKER (1667-1729); 22 Nov 1694; Scituate

WHITCOMB, Job (?1636-8 Nov 1683) (see John, had Mary 27 Dec 1671) & Mary _?_, m/2 Humphrey BRIOR; 19 May 1669; Lancaster/Cambridge

WHITCOMB, Job & [?Ann LOOMIS]; b 1697; CT

WHITCOMB, John[1] (-1662) & Frances COGGAN (-1671); St. Mary Magdalene, Taunton, Eng, 26 Nov 1623; Hingham/Scituate/Lexington

WHITCOMB, John (see Job) (1626-7 Apr 1683) & Mary _?_ (-1692); 16 Mar 1670/1; Lancaster

WHITCOMBE, Jonathan (1628-1691) & Hannah _?_ (-1692); 25 Nov 1667; Lancaster

WHITCOMB, Jonathan (1669-1715) & Mary/(Hannah in 1699) [BLOOD?]/JOSLIN?/FARRAR? (no), dau John, Jr.?; b 1690

WHITCOMBE, Josiah (?1638-1718) & Rebecca WATERS (1640, ca 1644-1726); 4 Jan 1664/5; Lancaster

WHITCOMB, Josiah (1667-1718) & 1/wf Mary [BROWN] (1672-); b 1690; Lancaster

WHITCOMB, Robert (1629-1671+) & 1/wf Mary CUDWORTH (1617, 1637-bef 1682); 1659 Quebec, 9 Mar 1660; Hingham/Scituate/Cohanset

WHITCOMB, Robert (1629-) & 2/wf Mary _?_; Scituate

WHITCOMB, Robert (-1704) & Elizabeth [BUCK]; b 1695; Scituate/Hingham

WHITE, Agnes & Patience _?_; b 1674; Boston

WHITE, Andrew & Elizabeth _?_; b 1687(8?); Boston

WHITE, Andrew & Sarah SANDERSON; 4 Feb 1696, prob 1695/6; Woburn

WHITE, Anthony & Grace HALL; 8 Sep 1645; Watertown

WHITE, Benjamin (-1723) & Susannah COGSWELL (?1658-1701+); 21 Jan 1681; Ipswich/Brookline/Boston

WHITE, Cornelius (1646-1685) & Priscilla [DAVIS]; b 1673; Boston

WHITE, Daniel (-1713) & Sarah CROW; 1 Nov 1661; Hatfield/Hadley

WHITE, Daniel (-1724) & Hannah HUNT; 19 Aug 1674; Marshfield

WHITE, Daniel (1662-1739) & Susannah MOULD (1663-); - Mar 1682/3; Middletown, CT

WHITE, Daniel (1671-) & 1/wf Sarah [BISSELL] (1672-1703); b 1693; Hadley/Hatfield

WHITE, Daniel (1668-) & 1/wf Mary WINTER (1675-1727?), Watertown; 25 May 1694; Cambridge/Lexington

WHITE, Domingo & Sarah ALLIN (1644-); 15 Jan 1666/7; Medfield/Lynn

WHITE, Ebenezer (1648-1703) & Hannah [PHILLIPS] (1654-); b 2 Jun 1671; Weymouth

WHITE, Ebenezer (1672-1756) & Hannah [PIERSON]; b 1701?, b 1695; ?Weymouth

WHITE, Edward & Martha [KING]; 1616 Cranbrook, in Eng, b 1625; Dorchester

WHITE, Edward & Mary COOPER (1669-), m/2 Harvey COLES; 15 Mar 1685/6; Oyster Bay, LI

WHITE, Edwin & Elizabeth [WARD]; b 1659; ?Scituate

WHITE, Elius (-1679+) & Mary/Joane (BENNETT) CODNER (1638-), w Christopher, m/3 Richard DOWNING; div?, 26 Jun 1661, same?, annulled 1663; Marblehead/New London

WHITE, Emanuel & Katherine _?_; b 1636; Watertown

WHITE, George & Lydia (JORDAN) SANSON/SIMSON (1643/4-1722/3), w Thomas; 5 Apr 1671; Ipswich

WHITE, Gowin/Gawen (-1665, 1664), Scituate & Elizabeth [WARD]? (1597?-); 15 Oct 1638; Scituate

WHITE, Henry & Martha (MONTAGUE) HARRISON, w Isaac; 3 Apr 1677; Deerfield

WHITE, Henry (-1713) & Mary WEEKS (1656-); b [1680]; Dorchester

WHITE, Henry & Mary (ALEXANDER) BARRETT, w Benjamin; 25 Feb 1691, 1691/2; Deerfield

WHITE, Ignatius & Ruth BURRAGE (1665-); 4 Jun 1683; Charlestown

WHITE, Isaac (son Wm.) & Susanna _?_; b 1672(3?), b 1690 same?; Boston

WHITE, Jacob (1645-1701?) & Elizabeth [BUNCE] (-1716); b 2 Aug 1683, no surviving ch; Hadley/Hartford

WHITE, Jacob (1665-1738) & Deborah SHEPARD (ca 1670-1721); 4 Feb 1692; Middletown, CT/Hadley

WHITE, James (-1713) (called "son-in-law" in George DYER's will) & 1/wf _?_, dau of George DYER; b 1665; Dorchester

WHITE, [James?] & Martha [PROCTOR]; ca 1663?, b 1672, betw 1665 & 1672; ?Salem

WHITE, James (1637-1713) & 2/wf Sarah BAKER (1645-1688); 22 Feb 1664/5, 12? Feb; Dorchester/Roxbury

WHITE, James (-1694) & Ruth STRATTON; 24 Nov 1675; Southampton/?Easthampton

WHITE, James & Esther _?_; b 1690, ca 1682; Boston

WHITE, James & Sarah _?_; ca 1690?; ?Huntington, LI

WHITE, James (-1713) & 3/wf Elizabeth (PRESTON) WITHINGTON, w John; 13 Feb 1695/6; Dorchester

WHITE, James & Sarah HAWKINS; m int 9 Nov 1696, 10 Nov 1696; Boston

WHITE, John (-1684) & Mary [LEAVITT?] (-1666/7); in Eng, 26 Dec 1622; Cambridge/Hartford/Hadley

WHITE, John & _?_; b 1656?; Scituate/Boston/etc.

WHITE, John (?1602-1673) & Joan WEST (1606-1654, Lancaster); Drayton, Eng, Somerset, 28 May 1627, 3 Mar; Salem/Wenham/Lancaster

WHITE, John (-1662) & Ann [COOPER], Southampton, m/2 Zerubbabel PHILLIPS; b 1630?; Lynn/Southampton, LI

WHITE, John (d in Eng) & Elizabeth (HERBERT), m/2 George CORWIN

WHITE, John (-1691) & Francis GAYN/ONGE?; m int 10 Apr 1640; Boston/Watertown/Brookline/Roxbury

WHITE, John & 1/wf Lucy _?_; b 1640?, b 1660; York Co., ME

WHITE, John & 2/wf Mary [PHIPPS], w James, m/3 _?_ HOWARD; b 4 Oct 1679, by 1661; Pemaquid, ME

WHITE, John (1628-1676) (ae ca 40 in 1668) & Elizabeth [GOBLE], m/2 Thomas CARTER 1682; b 1653; Sudbury/Charlestown

WHITE, John (-1665) & Sarah [BUNCE] (1642-), m/2 Nicholas WORTHINGTON; b 1662, b 1661?, b 1659; Hadley

WHITE, John (1639/40-1669) & Hannah FRENCH, m/2 Thomas PHILBRICK 1669; 25 Nov 1662, 26 Nov 1662; Haverhill/Salisbury

WHITE, John (-1691/2, 1690?) & Mary SWIFT; 11 Jan 1663/4; Dorchester/Roxbury

WHITE, John (-1670?) & Hannah _?_; b 1665?; Southampton, LI?

WHITE, John (1642-1695, Roxbury) & Elizabeth BOWLES (1652-1700); b 1667/(8?); Roxbury/Dorchester

WHITE, John & Hannah SMITH; 24 Feb 1679, 1679/80; Taunton

WHITE, John (-1684) & Rebecca BEMIS (1654-), m/2 Thomas HARRINGTON 1686; 11 Apr 1684, no issue, 1 Apr 1684; Watertown

WHITE, John (1657-1748) & Mary [PIERCE?]; b 1687; Hartford

WHITE, John, Hatfield & Hannah WELLS (1668-1733); 7 Jul 1687; Hadley/Bolton/Hardwick

WHITE, John (-1727) & Lydia GILMAN (1668-); 24 Oct 1687; Haverhill/?Exeter, NH

WHITE, John & Sarah _?_; b 1688; Andover

WHITE, John & Elizabeth TREVY/[TREFRY]; 7 Jun 1694; Marblehead
WHITE, John & Elizabeth (METCALF) IVES, w Thomas; 16 Jan 1695, 1695/6; Salem
WHITE, John & Miriam GALE (1671-); 9 Apr 1696; Beverly/Ipswich
WHITE, John & Salome _?_, m/2 Francis JENNERS; Portsmouth, NH
WHITE, John (1668-1725) & Sarah _?_ ; b 1700; Mendon
WHITE, John (1675-1753) & Susanna SHERMAN (-1766); 18 Feb 1700, 1700/1?; Marshfield
WHITE, John (1669-) & Martha [DOTY] (ca 1672-); b 1701(2?), b 1689, aft 17 Mar 1691, b 1696; Rochester
WHITE, Jonathan (1658-1737?) & 1/wf Hester NICKERSON (-1703); 2 Feb 1682, 2 Feb 1682/3; Yarmouth
WHITE, Joseph (-1706) & Lydia ROGERS (1642-1727); 19 Sep 1660; Weymouth/Mendon
WHITE, Joseph & Hannah [SCARBOROUGH?] (1643-1720/1); b 1670; Roxbury
WHITE, Joseph (-1711) & 1/wf [Mary] _?_ (-1677); b 1677; Scituate
WHITE, Joseph (-1724) & Mary _?_ ; b 1682; Taunton
WHITE, Joseph, Jr. (1662-1757) & Lydia [?COPELAND] (1661-1727); b 1683; Mendon
WHITE, Joseph (1667-1725) & Mary MOULD (1665?-1730); 3 Apr 1693; Middletown, CT
WHITE, Joseph, Jr. (1674-1715) & Oseeth/Osah/Osiah (WING) TURNER; 16 Sep 1696; Scituate
WHITE, Joseph (ca 1644-1711) & 2/wf Susannah (WADE) WELCOME? (?1652-1698), w William; b 1698, aft May 1699; Scituate
WHITE, Joseph, Sr. (-1711) & 3/wf Elizabeth VINALL; 7 Jun 1699; Scituate
WHITE Joseph & Sarah TALLEY; 11 Apr 1700; Boston/?Weymouth
WHITE, Josiah (1643-1714) & 1/wf Mary LEWIS (1646-); b (ca 1666/70?); Lancaster
WHITE, Josiah (1643-1714) & 2/wf Mary/Keziah? RICE (1656-1733), m/2 Thomas SAWYER 1718; 28 Nov 1678; Malborough/Lancaster
WHITE, Josiah (1654-1710) & Remember [READ] (1657-); b 30 Dec 1680; ?Boxford
WHITE, Josiah & _?_ ; b 1690?, b 1688?; Purpooduck
WHITE, Lawrence & Margaret _?_ (-1713); no issue; Boston
WHITE, Malatiah/Melatiah (-1709) & Mercy [WINSLOW] (1676?-), m/2 Thomas JENKINS 1715; b 1699; Rochester
WHITE, Nathan & Salome (JACKSON) WYATT, w John, m/3 Zacheus JENNERS; aft Jun 1670; Portsmouth, NH
WHITE, Nathaniel (1629-1711) & 1/wf Elizabeth _?_ (1625-1690); b 1652; Middletown, CT/Hadley
WHITE, Nathaniel (1652-) & Elizabeth SAVAGE (1655-); 28 Mar 1678, 1677/8; Middletown, CT
WHITE, Nathaniel (-1698?) & _?_ DRAKE; b 1684; Eastchester, NY
WHITE, Nathaniel & _?_ ; ca 1685?; Purpooduck
WHITE, Nathaniel (1629-1711) & 2/wf Martha (COIT) MOULD (-1730), w Hugh; aft 19 Jul 1694; Middletown, CT/Hadley
WHITE, Nicholas & Margery _?_, m/2 William HAYNES
WHITE, Nicholas (-1697/8) & Susan/Susanna HUMPHREY (1615±-); ca 1642?; Dorchester/Taunton
WHITE, Nicholas & Ursula MACOMBER; 9 Dec 1673; Taunton
WHITE, Paul (1590-1679) & 1/wf Bridget _?_ (-1664); Pemaquid/Bristol, ME
WHITE, Paul (-1679) & 2/wf Anne JONES, w Thomas; 14 Mar 1664/[5]; Newbury
WHITE, Peragrine[2] (1620-1704) & Sarah BASSETT (1630-1711); ?24 Dec 1646, b 16 Mar 1649, ca 1646 or 1647?; ?Duxbury/Marshfield
WHITE, Peregrine[3] (1660-1727) & 1/wf Susanna _?_ ; b 1685(6?); Weymouth/Middleborough
WHITE, Peregrine[3] (1660-1727) & 2/wf Mary _?_, m/2 Cornelius JUDEWINE; by 1698
WHITE, Peter (1660-1743, 1737) & Rachel [BABCOCK] (1660-1732); b 1683; Milton
WHITE, Philip & Deborah [MANSFIELD]; b 1686; Beverly
WHITE, Philip & Margaret (CLERK) JACKSON, w John, m/3 Roger SWAIN by 1701; 1693±; ?Portsmouth, NH
WHITE, Resolved (1614-1685+, 1690+) & 1/wf Judith VASSALL (1619-1670?, Marshfield); 5 Nov 1640, 8 Apr 1640; Scituate/Marshfield
WHITE, Resolved (1614-1682+) & 2/wf Abigail (_?_) LORD (-1682), w William; 15 Oct 1674, 5 Oct 1674; Salem
WHITE, Richard & Frances [HILTON], w William; ca/bef 30 Jun 1656; Kittery, ME
WHITE, Richard & Lydia [HIGBY]; b 1 Mar 1682; Huntington, LI

WHITE, Richard & Mary [NORDEN] (?1669-), dau Samuel, m/2 Samuel HOOPER, m/3 John PERKINS; b 1691; Boston
WHITE, Richard & Elizabeth RUST; 4 Jan 1699, 1699/1700; Boston
WHITE, Robert (-1617, in Eng) & Bridget ALLGAR/APGAR; in Eng, b 24 Jun 1585, ?24 Jun 1585; CT
WHITE, Robert & _?_; in Eng, b 1652; Saco, ME
WHITE, Robert & Elizabeth _?_; b 1700; Boston
WHITE, Samuel (?1642-1698/9, ae 57) & Mary DYER (1641-1716) (no issue); ca 1666?; Weymouth
WHITE, Samuel (1646-1694) & Rebecca [GREEN?] (1646-1711); b 1669; Rochester
WHITE, Samuel & Mary [JAY?]/[BUCKNER?]; b 1681; Boston
WHITE, Samuel & Ann/Hannah SNELL; b 1686; Boston
WHITE, Samuel (1667-), Weymouth & Anna BINGLEY/DINGLEY? (-1738?), Weymouth; 6 Dec 1687; Milton
WHITE, Samuel (?1676-1760) & Anna/Ann [PRATT] (1682-1757), dau Matthew, Jr.?; b 1696, ca 1700?, b 1700; Weymouth
WHITE, Samuel & Arabella [POTE]; 2 Nov 1692?, b 1698; Mablehead
WHITE, Samuel & 1/wf Mary _?_; b 1699; Rochester
WHITE, Stephen & Sarah HARRIS; m int 25 Sep 1695; Boston
WHITE, Sylvanus (-1688) & Deborah _?_; b _?_; Plymouth/Scituate
WHITE, Thomas (-1664) & 1/wf Susanna?/Margaret [MILLER?] (-1649, Sudbury); b 1628; Charlestown/Framingham/Sudbury
WHITE, Thomas (-1664) & 2/wf _?_ (-1687, ae 89); aft 1649
WHITE, Thomas (1599-1679) & _?_; ca 1629? (3 ch in 1636); Weymouth/Braintree
WHITE, Thomas (1630-1672) & 1/wf Martha _?_; b 1658; ?Wenham
WHITE, Thomas (1636-1716) & Mary FROTHINGHAM (1638-); 17 Nov 1663; Charlestown
WHYTE, Thomas (1630-1672) & 2/wf Ruth [HAFFIELD] (1632-1713); b 1664(5?), ca 1660; Wenham
WHITE, Thomas (?1642-1714) & Remember _?_ (-1719?); b 1667; Marblehead
WHITE, Thomas (ca 1644-1706) & Mary [PRATT] (-1706+); b 1672; Braintree/Weymouth
WHITE, Thomas & Sarah [MANN]?; b 1679; Charlestown
WHITE, Thomas (1664-1730) & Sarah RAND (1666-1749); 4 Mar 1684/5; Charlestown
WHITE, Thomas (1665-) & 1/wf Mehitable THORNTON (-1704); - Dec 1687; Boston/Mendon
WHITE, Thomas & Susanna GRANT; 4 Jul 1692; Marblehead
WHITE, Thomas & Martha [FISKE]; b 1696; Wenham
WHITE, Thomas (-1765) & 1/wf Mehitable ADAMS (1678-1713); 21 Jul 1697; Braintree
WHITE, Thomas (1673-1752) & Mary [WHITE] (1677-1710), dau James; b 1701; Weymouth
WHITE, Timothy (-1704) & Abigail ROGERS; 1 Jan 1678/9; Scituate
WHITE, William (-1621) & Susanna/Ann/Anna FULLER (1594-1680), m/2 Edward WINSLOW 1621; 11 Feb 1612; Plymouth
WHITE, William (-1690, ae 80) & 1/wf? Mary [WARE] (-1681); b 1639?; Newbury/Ipswich-/Haverhill/Watertown
WHITE, William & Elizabeth _?_; b 1647; Boston
WHITE, William (1610-1684) & Catherine [JACKSON] (-1671), w John; aft 18 Sep 1648, b 28 Jun 1649; Ipswich
WHITE, William (-1656) & _?_; Fairfield, CT
WHITE, William & Philippa WOOD (-1654); 4 Aug 1653; Boston
WHITE, William & Katharine DOWNS; 28 Aug 1669; Gravesend, LI
WHITE, William (1610-1690) & Sarah (?LARRIFAL) (MARTIN) FOSTER, w John, w Reginald; 21 Sep 1682; Haverhill/Watertown
WHITE, William & Margaret [JOSE] (1666-1691); bef Oct 1689, 1690?
WHITE, William & Elizabeth HODGES (1674-); 28 Nov 1700; Boston
WHITE, William & Abigail [WHIDDEN]; b 1701?; Portsmouth, NH
WHITE, Zachariah (-1721) & Sarah RUMERY; 23 Oct 1678; Salem/Haverhill
WHITE, _?_ & Deborah ROGERS (1670-), m/2 John BURNETT 1695; b 1690/1
WHITE, _?_ & _?_ [BREWSTER]; b 1660?, ca 1655?; Fairfield
WHITE, _?_ & Margaret [SPARKS] (1670-); b 1701; Ipswich
WHITE, ?William & Mary [RISKWORTH], m/2 John SAYWARD ca 1682, m/3 Phineas HULL 1690, m/4 James PLAISTED 1691; b 1679, b 1675?; Salisbury

WHITFOOT/WHITEFOOT/(BLANCPIED)?, John & Elizabeth [SWASEY]; b 1683; Salem

WHITHAM, Henry & Sarah SOMES; 15 Jun 1665; Gloucester

WHITEHAM, John & Mehitable [BISHOP]; Guilford, CT

WHITEHAND, George & Alice _?_ ; b 1633; Charlestown

WHITEHART, John & Martha LADD; 6 Jun 1695; Boston

WHITEHEAD, [?Adam]/Daniel & Jane [SKIDMORE], m/2 John INGERSOLL ca 1673?; ca 1660?; Huntington, LI

WHITEHEAD, Daniel (1603-1668) & _?_ ARMITAGE; ca 1638?; Newtown, LI/Huntington, LI/Oyster Bay, LI

WHITEHEAD, Daniel (1647-1704) & 1/wf? Abigail (STEVENSON) [DENTON], former wf Daniel; 1672?; Jamaica, LI/Newtown, LI/etc.

WHITEHEAD, Daniel (?1647-) & 2/wf? Abigail (CARMAN) [COE] (-1717?), w Benjamin; b 1701; Jamaica, LI

WHITEHEAD, Eliphalet (1674-) & _?_ ; b 1701?; Branford, CT

WHITEHEAD, Isaac & Susanna _?_ ; b 1650; New Haven/Elizabeth, NJ

WHITEHEAD, John (-1695) & Martha/Maria? BRADFIELD (-1695+, 1709+); 9 Mar 1661, 25 May 1660?; Branford

WHITEHEAD, Jonathan & Sarah FIELD; m lic 23 Jul 1696, 1697?; Jamaica, LI

WHITEHEAD, Richard & Mary [HOPKINS] (-1670+), w William; ca 1644-5; Windsor, CT

WHITEHEAD, Samuel (-1690) & Sarah (GREYSON) GILBERT (-1697), w John; 9 May 1676; New Haven

WHITEHEAD, Samuel & Mary COOPER (-20 Apr 1687); 12 Sep 1682; Southampton

WHITEHEAD, Samuel & Joanah BEEBE; 24 Oct 1689, 1689?; Southampton

WHITEHEAD, ?Thomas & Mary [FORDHAM]; b 1688; Southampton, LI?/?Huntington, LI

WHITEHEAD, _?_ & Sarah [UPDIKE] (1650-1704+) (had son Richard & dau Sarah)

WHITHEARE, Abraham (1607-1674) & 1/wf _?_ ; Salem

WHITEHEARE, Abraham (1607-1674) & Mary _?_ ; Salem

WHITHEARE, Isaac ((166-)-) & Elizabeth _?_ ; Manchester

WHITHEARE, William (-1712?, 1707, ae 44?) & Deliverance HOMAN; Southold?/Brookhaven, LI

WHITEHOUSE, Peter & Rachel [FANCY]; b 27 Oct 1684; Brookhaven, LI

WHITEHOUSE, Thomas & Elizabeth [DAM], dau John; Dover, NH

WHITFIELD/WHITEFIELD, Henry (returned to Eng) & Dorothy [SHEAFE]; in Eng, b 1619; Guilford, CT

WHITFORD, Walter (-1692) & Bridget _?_ ; b 1668; Salem

WHITFORD, Pasco & _?_ ; b 1675; Newport/E. Greenwich, RI/Kings Town, RI

WHITING, James (-1708) & Elizabeth [BARLOW]; b 1693, ?19 Sep 1686; Malden

WHITING, John (?1633-1689) & 1/wf Sybil [COLLINS] (-1672); ca 1654?; Salem/Hartford

WHITING, John (1637-1689) (he returned to Eng) & Esther _?_ (-1689); probably in Eng

WHITING, John & 2/wf Phebe [GREGSON] (1643-1730), m/2 John RUSSEL ca 1688/92; bef 27 Sep 1673; ?Hartford/?New Haven

WHITING, John, Wrentham & 1/wf Mary BILLINGS (-1728), Dorchester; 24 Dec 1688, 25 Dec, 4 Dec; Wrentham

WHITING, John (1664-1697) & Alice [COOK], m/2 Rev. Timothy STEVENS 1701; b 1694?, ca 1694?; Lancaster/Cambridge/Lynn

WHITING, Jonathan (-1728) & Rachel THORP (1671-1728+); 3 Dec 1689; Dedham

WHITING, Joseph (1645-1717) & 1/wf Mary PYNCHON (1650-1674?, 1676?); 5 Oct 1669, 6 Aug 1670?; ?Hartford/Springfield/?Westfield

WHITING, Rev. Joseph (1641-1723) & 1/wf Sarah DANFORTH (1646-1682+); b 1674; Lynn/Cambridge?/Southampton, LI

WHITING, Joseph (1645-1717) & 2/wf Anna?/Ann [ALLYN] (1654-1735); ca 1676?; Hartford

WHITING, Joseph (1641-1723) & 2/wf Rebecca PRESCOTT? [BISHOP] (-1726, ae 63 y 2 m), w Jonathan, Jr.? (no, in my opinion); aft 1684, bef 16 Nov 1694; Stamford, CT/Southampton, LI

WHITING, Nathaniel (-1683) & Hannah DWIGHT (1625-1714); 4 Nov 1643; Dedham

WHITING, Nathaniel (1644-1676) & Joanna GAY (1645-), m/2 John WARE 1679; 29 Mar 1664; Dedham/Boston

WHITING, Oliver (1665-1736) & Anna DANFORTH (-1737); 22 Jan 1689/90, 22 Dec 1689; Billerica/Cambridge

WHITING, Samuel (1597-1679) & 1/wf _?_ ; in Eng, ca 1624; Lynn

WHITING, Samuel (1597-1679) & 2/wf Elizabeth St.JOHN (1605-1677, ae 72); Boston, Eng, 6 Aug 1629; Lynn/Billerica
WHITING, Samuel (1633-1713) & Dorcas CHESTER (1637-1713); 12 Nov 1656; Lynn/Charlestown/Billerica
WHITING, Samuel (-1727) & 1/wf Sarah METCALF (1658-1701); 23 Nov 1676; Dedham
WHITING, Samuel (1662-1714/15), Billerica & Elizabeth READ; 27 Jan 1686/7; ?Billerica/Dunstable
WHITING, Samuel (1674-) & _?_ FITCH
WHITING, Samuel (1670-1725) & Elizabeth ADAMS (1681-1766?, 1760?), m/2 Rev. Samuel NILES 1737; 4 Sep 1696, 14 Sep; Windham, CT
WHITING, Samuel (-1705) & Mary [CLARK], m/2 _?_ DARLING; b 1699; Wrentham
WHITING, Timothy (-1728) & Sarah [BULLARD] (1659-1732); b 1680; Dedham
WHITING, William (-1647) & Susanna _?_ (-1673), m/2 Samuel FITCH 1650, m/3 Alexander BRYAN 1662; b 1633; Hartford/Newport
WHITING, William & 1/wf Mary ALLYN; Oct 1686, 6 Oct 1686; Hartford/Newport/Windsor, CT
WHITLOCK, David (-1722) & Mary [SHERWOOD]; b 1681; Fairfield, CT
WHITLOCK, John & [Sarah?] _?_, m/2 Henry WHELPLEY; b 1645; Fairfield, CT
WHITLOCK, John (-1698) & Sarah [SHERWOOD]; ca 1682; Fairfield, CT
WHITLOCK, ?Thomas & Mary _?_ ; Westchester Co., NY
WHITLOCK, _?_ & Mary BRAY, w Richard; aft 1665, bef 1689
WHITMAN, Abiah (-1728) & Mary [FORD] (-1715); b 1673; Weymouth/Abington
WHITMAN, Ebenezer (-1713) & Abigail BARNAM/BURNHAM (-1746), m/2 Edmund HOBART; 17 Nov 1699; Bridgewater
WHITMAN, Francis & Mary _?_ ; b 1685; Boston
WHITMAN, John (-1692, ae 90) & ?Mary/?Ruth _?_ (-1662); in Eng, b 1629; Weymouth/Abington
WHITMAN/WEIGHTMAN, John (-1684, ae 80) & Susanna _?_ ; b 1641; Boston/Charlestown
WHITEMAN, John[2] & 1/wf Ruth REED (-1663), probably dau William; 19 Dec 1662; Weymouth
WHITMAN, John & 2/wf Abigail [HOLLIS]; [1663]; Weymouth
WHITMAN, John (-1727) (see Samuel WHITMARSH m Hannah PRATT; John ORCUTT a nephew) & Mary?/[?Hannah PRATT]; 10 Jun 1686; Bridgewater
WHITMAN, John & 1/wf Dorothy PRATT (-1733); 13 Aug 1700; Weymouth
WHITMAN, John & Deborah _?_ ; b 1701?; Huntington, LI
WHITMAN, Joseph & Sarah [KETCHAM]; ca 1660; Huntington, LI
WHITMAN, Joseph & Hannah _?_ ; b 1701?; Huntington, LI?
WHITMAN, Nicholas & 1/wf Sarah VINING (-1713); 19 Nov 1700; Bridgewater
WHITMAN, Robert & 1/wf Susanna _?_ (-1664); 1648; Ipswich
WHITMAN, Robert & 2/wf Hannah (TUTTY) KNIGHT, w Alexander; 9 Nov 1664; Ipswich
WHITMAN, Thomas (ca 1629-1712) & Abigail BIRON/BYRAM; 22 Nov 1656; Weymouth/Bridgewater
WHITMAN, Valentine[1] (-1701) & Mary _?_ (-1718); b 1652, ca 1650; Providence
WHITMAN, Valentine (1668-1750) & Sarah BARTLETT; 12 Dec 1694; Providence
WHITMAN, Zachariah (-1666) & Sarah BISCOE (1616-1671); Chesham, Eng, 10 Jun 1630; Dorchester/Milford, CT
WHITMAN, Zachariah (1644-1726) & Sarah ALCOCK (1650-); m cont 26 Oct 1670; Hull?
WHITMAN, _?_ & Catherine HOLMES, dau Jonathan; RI?
WHITMARSH, Ebenezer & Christian [BAYLEY] (1662-1732); b 1683; Weymouth/Bridgewater/Abington
WHITMARSH, Ezra (1670-1754) & Bathsheba RICHARDS (1674-1752); 20 Jan 1693; Boston
WHITMARSH, John (1596-by 1644) & Alice _?_ (1600-); in Eng, b 1624, b 1619?; Weymouth
WHITMARSH, John (-1709) & Sarah?/Mary? [HARDING] (-bef 22 May 1693); ca 1654; Weymouth
WHITMARSH, Nicholas & Hannah REED; 2 Dec 1658; Weymouth
WHITMARSH, Nicholas & Mercy [REED]; b 1699; Weymouth
WHITMARSH, Samuel & Hannah [BARKER/PRATT], dau Matthew; b 1691, 1686?; Weymouth/Dighton
WHITMARSH, Simon (-1708) & 1/wf Sarah [HOLBROOK]; b 1667; Weymouth
WHITMARSH, Simon (-1708) & 2/wf Elizabeth [BICKNELL] (1673-); b 1695; Weymouth
WETMORE, Beriah (1658-1756) & 1/wf Margaret STOW (-1710); 1 Sep 1692, 2 Sep 169-, 1 Apr 1691, 1 Sep 169[-], 1691?, 1692?; Middletown, CT

WHITMORE, Francis (1625-1685) & 1/wf Isabel [PARKE]/HALE? (?1628-1665); ca 1648; Cambridge/Lexington
WHITMORE, Francis (-1685, Cambridge) & 2/wf Margaret HARTY (-1686); 10 Nov 1666; Lexington
WHITMORE, Francis (-1700) & Hannah [HARRIS]; 8 Feb 1674, 1674/5?; Middletown, CT
WHITMORE, Francis & Mary CORNWELL; 30 May 1698; Middletown, CT
WHITMORE, Francis & 1/wf Anna PEIRCE/Ann PIERCE; 7 Dec 1699; Boston
WETMORE, Izrahiah (1656/7-) & Rachel STOWE (1667-1723); 13 May 1692; Middletown, CT/Stratford, CT
WHITMORE, John (-1648) & 1/wf _?_; in Eng, b 1615?; Wethersfield, CT/Stamford, CT
WHITMORE, John (-1648) & 2/wf Joanna [JESSUP], w John; aft Feb 1637/8, b 1647; Hartford
WHITMORE, John (1654-1739) & Rachel (ELIOT) POULTER (1643-1723), w John; aft 20 May 1676, b 1678; ?Cambridge/Milford
WETMORE, John (1646-1696) & 1/wf Abigail WARNER (-1685); 30 Dec 1680; Middletown
WHITMORE/WETMORE, John (1646-1696) & 2/wf Mary SAVAGE (SANDERS wrong) (-1723), m/2 Obadiah ALLEN, m/3? Benjamin ANDREWS; 1 Apr 1686; Middletown, CT/Windsor, CT
WHITMORE, Joseph & Mary KENDALL (1681-1760, ae 82); 13 Feb 1699, 1698/9; Woburn
WHITMORE, Samuel (-1724) & 1/wf Rebecca GARDNER (-1709); 31 Mar 1686; Charlestown/Lexington
WETMORE, Samuel (1655-1746) & Mary BACON (-1709); 13 Dec 1687; Middletown
WHITMORE/WETMORE, Thomas (1615-1681) & 1/wf Sarah HALL (-1664); 11 Dec 1645; Hartford
WHITMORE/WETMORE, Thomas (-1681) & 2/wf Mary (PLATT) ATKINSON/ALLENSON (-1669), w Luke; 3 Jan 1666, 3 Feb, 1666/7; Middletown
WETMORE, Thomas (-1681) & 3/wf Katherine (ROBERTS) LEEKE/LEETE/LEEFS/LOCKE/ROBERTS? (-1693); 8 Oct 1673; Middletown, CT
WETMORE, Thomas (1652-1711, 1690?) & Elizabeth HUBBARD (1659-1725); 20 Feb 1684, 1684/5; Middletown, CT
WHITMORE, Thomas (?1673-) & Mary [WATERS] (1675-), Woburn; b 1694; Lexington/Billerica/Killingly, CT
WHITNELL, Jeremiah (-1682) & Elizath MITCHELL (-1683), w Thomas; Jan 1663; New Haven
WHITNEY, Benjamin (1643-1723) & 1/wf Jane _?_ (-14 Nov 1690); b 1669; Watertown/Sherborn
WHITNEY, Benjamin (1660-1736) & 1/wf Abigail HAGER; 31 Mar 1687; Watertown
WHITNEY, Benjamin (1643-1723) & 2/wf Mary POOR/POORE; 13 Apr 1696, 11 Apr 1695?; Malboro
WHITNEY, Benjamin (-1718) & Mercy TRAVIS/TRAVERS (1668-), m/2 Thomas FRINK; 24 Oct 1700; Sherborn
WHITNEY, Eleazer (1672-) & Anna _?_, m/2 _?_; Stow/Pomfret, CT
WHITNEY, Eleazer (-1735) & Dorothy ROSSE/ROSS (-1731); 11 Aug 1687; Watertown/Sudbury
WHITNEY, Henry (?1620-1673) & 1/wf _?_; b 1644; Southold, LI/Huntington, LI/Jamaica, LI/Norwalk, CT/etc.
WHITNEY, Henry (-1673) & 2/wf [Sarah KETCHAM], w Edward; b 1660; Southold, LI/etc.
WHITNEY, Isaiah (1671-1712) & Sarah (WOODWARD) EDDY (1675-1715), w John; b 1698, 1695?; Cambridge
WHITNEY, John[1] (?1592-1673) & Eleanor _?_ (-1659, ae 54); in Eng, b 1619; Watertown
WHITNEY, John (1621-1692) & Ruth [REYNOLDS]; b 1643; Watertown
WHITNEY, John (-1673) & Judah/Judith? CLEMENT (-1673+), w Robert; 29 Sep 1659; Watertown
WHITNEY, John (1643-1727) & Elizabeth [HARRIS] (1644-); ca 1669; Roxbury
WHITNEY, John (?1644-1720, Norwalk) & Elizabeth SMITH (-1741+); 17 Mar 1674/5; Norwalk, CT/Fairfield, CT
WHITNEY, John (1662-), Sherborn & 1/wf Mary HAPGOOD (1661-), Sherborn; 10 Apr 1688; Watertown/Sherborn
WHITNEY, John & 2/wf Sarah [?HAVEN] (1655-1718); b 1695; Sherborn
WHITNEY, Jonathan (1634-1702/3) & Lydia JONES; 30 Oct 1656; Watertown
WHITNEY, Jonathan (1658-1735) & Sarah [HAPGOOD?] (1672-); b 1693; Sherborn/Watertown
WHITNEY/WIDNEY, Joseph & Mary BUCKMASTER; 20 Nov 1664; Charlestown
WHITNEY, Joseph (1652-1702) & Martha BEECH/BEACH (ca 1650-); 24 Jan 1674, 1674/5?; Watertown
WHITNEY, Joshua (1635-1719) & 1/wf Lydia _?_; b 1666; Groton

WHITNEY, Joshua (1635-1719) & 2/wf Mary __?__ (-17 Mar 1672); aft 10 Oct 1668, b 1671/2; Watertown

WHITNY, Joshua (1635-1719) & 3/wf Abigail TARBELL; b st of Sep 1672; Watertown/Groton/etc.

WHITNEY, Joshua (1666-) & 1/wf Mary __?__ ; Plainfield, CT

WHITNEY, Josiah (-1718) & 1?/wf 2?/wf Abigail __?__ (-1718+); b 1698, b 1696; Wrentham

WHETNEY, Moses (1655-), Stow & Sarah KNIGHT (-1755), Cambridge; 30 Sep 1686; Stow

WHITNEY, Nathaniel (1646-1733) & Sarah HAGAR (1661-1746); 12 Mar 1673, 1673/4?; Watertown/Weston

WHITTNY, Nathaniel & Mercy/Mary? ROBINSON; 7 Nov 1695; Watertown/Weston

WHETNY, Richard (?1624-) & Martha COLDAM; 19 Mar 1649/50, 19 (1 mo) 1650, 1650/1?; Watertown

WHITNEY, Richard (1661-1723) & Elizabeth [?SAWTELLE] (1668-1723, ae 56); b 1694; Watertown/Stow

WHITNEY, Samuel (1648-1730) & Mary BEMIS (1644-); 16 Feb 1683/4; Watertown

WHETNY, Thomas (-1719, ae 90) & Mary KEDELL/KETTLE?/KEDALL; 11 Jan 1654/5; Watertown

WHITNEY, Thomas (should be WHITTEN) & Winifred HARDING (-1660); 22 Nov 1659; Plymouth

WHITNEY, Thomas & Patience (MORTON) [FAUNCE] (-1691), w Thomas; b 1 Mar 1669?; Plymouth

WHITNEY, Thomas (1656-) & Elizabeth LAWRENCE (1659-); 29 Jan 1678, 1678/9?; Watertown/Stow

WHITNEY, William (1678-) & 1/wf Lydia PERHAM (1673-1716); - Mar [1700?]; Chelmsford/Watertown

WHITPIN/?WHITPAIN, John & Content [GOULD] (1671-1720); 1692; ?Newport, RI/Philadelphia

WHITSON, Thomas & Martha [?JONES], dau Thomas; b 18 Apr 1684; ?Huntington, LI

WHITTEMORE, Benjamin (1640-1726) & Elizabeth [BUCKMAN] (1644-1726); b 1668; Malden

WHITTEMORE, Benjamin (1669-1734) & Esther BROOKES; 17 Aug 1692; Concord

WHITTEMORE, Daniel (1633-1683), Watertown, Malden, & Mary MELLINS (-1691+, 1693+); 7 Mar 1662; Charlestown

WHITTEMORE, Daniel (1663-1756) & Lydia [BASSETT] (ca 1671-1755); b 1690, 1692?; Charlestown

WHITTEMORE, John (1639-1694) & 1/wf Mary [UPHAM] (-1677); b 1662; Charlestown

WHITTEMORE, John (1639-1694) & 2/wf Mary MILLER (-1732, 1731); 8 Nov 1677; Charlestown

WHITTEMORE, John, Jr. (ca 1662-1702) & 1/wf Elizabeth ANABEL (-1686); 26 May 1684; Charlestown

WHITTEMORE, John (-1702) & 2/wf Sarah [HALL], m/2 Joseph FROST; b 1690; Charlestown

WHITEMORE, John (1665-1730) & Ruth BASSETT (1671-1750); 22 Dec 1692; Bridgewater

WHITTEMORE, Joseph (1666-) & 1/wf Joanna MOUSAL (-1691); 30 Mar 1687/8; Charlestown

WHITTEMORE, Joseph (1666-) & 2/wf Susanna [FROST] (1669-); ca 1693; Charlestown

WHITTEMORE, Lawrence (-1644, ae 80) & Elizabeth __?__ (-1643); b 1635; Roxbury

WHITTEMORE, Nathaniel (-1671) & Mary [KNOWER], m/2 John MARBLE 1673; b 1668; Charlestown

WHITTEMORE/WHITMAN, Nathaniel (1671-), Boston & Elizabeth RHOADS; m int 4 Nov 1695, m int 5 Nov; Lynn

WHITTEMORE, Samuel (-1726) & Hannah [?RIX/RICE?] (1652-1728); b 1672; Dover, NH

WHITTEMORE, Samuel (-1694) & Lydia [SCOTT/DRAPER] (1674?-), m/2 Benjamin RICHARD-SON, m/3 __?__ PARKER; b 1693; Charlestown

WHITTEMORE, Thomas (1593-1661) & 1/wf __?__ (-1616); in Eng, b 1616; Charlestown

WHITTEMORE, Thomas (1593-1661) & 2/wf Sarah DEARDES (-1628), wid; in Eng, 14 Apr 1623; Charlestown

WHITTEMORE, Thomas (-1661) & 3/wf Hannah CHAWKLEY, m/2 Benjamin BUTTERFIELD 1663; b 1633, 26 Oct 1632 m lic; Charlestown/Chelmsford

WHITTEMORE, Thomas (-1670) & Elizabeth PIERCE (1646-1692), m/2 Hopestill FOSTER 1671, m/3 Nathaniel PIERCE 1680/1; 9 Nov 1666; Woburn/Charlestown

WHITTEMORE, Thomas (1664-1717) & Mary [PEASE], w Samuel; b 1694; Cambridge

WHITTEMORE, Thomas & Hannah MAKMALLIN; 10 Jul 1700; Salem

WHITON, Enoch (1660-1714) & Mary LINCOLN (1662-1716); 11 Jan 1687/8, 1687; Hingham

WHITON/WHITING?, James (?1624-1710) & Mary BEAL (1622-1696/7); 30 Dec 1647; Hingham

WHITON, James (1651-1725) & Abigail [RICKARD] (1656-1740); b 1676; Hingham
WHITTON, Jeremiah (1627-) & Elizabeth [DAGGETT] (?1638-); Sandwich/Martha's Vineyard
WHITIN/WHITING?/WHIDDON?, Jonathan & Rebecca HACKET; 5 Aug 1695; Salisbury/?Portsmouth, NH
WHITTEN, Josiah & Ruth TUCKER; 12 Jun 1684
WHITON, Matthew (-1725) & Deborah (PITTS) HOWARD/HAYWARD?, w Daniel; 22 Dec 1677; Hingham
WHITTEN/WHITNEY, Thomas (-1674) & 1/wf Adrian (CORK) MOORECOCK, w Henry; Egerton, Co. Kent, 1 Oct 1625; Plymouth
WHITTEN, Thomas (-1674) & 2/wf Winifred HARDING (-1660); 22 Nov 1639; Plymouth
WHITNEY/WHITTON, Thomas (-1674) & 3/wf? Patience (MORTON) [FAUNCE] (-1691, ae 76); b 1 Mar 1669; Plymouth
WHITON, Thomas & Joanna (MAY) GARDNER?/GARNET, w Francis, m/3 Nathan FARROW; 26 Jan 1689/90; Hingham
WHITTIER/WHITAKER?, Abraham (1607-1674) & 1/wf _?_ ; b 31 Dec 1639; Salem/Mablehead/Manchester
WHITTIER/WHITAKER?, Abraham (-1674) & 2/wf Mary _?_, m/2 John KNIGHT; ca 1650/3; Marblehead/Manchester
WHITTIER, John & Mary HOIT/HOYT; 14 Jan 1685, 1685/6; Haverhill
WHITTIER, Joseph (1669-) & Mary PEASLY; 24 May 1694, 29 May; Haverhill
WHITCHER/WHITTIER?, Nathaniel (1658-) & 1/wf Mary (STEVENS) OSGOOD, w John; 26 Aug 1685; Salisbury
WHITTIER, Thomas (1620-1696) & Ruth [GREEN] (-1710); b 1647; Salisbury
WHITTINGHAM, John (1616-1649) (son of Baruch, gr-son of Rev. William of Durham) & Martha [HUBBARD] (1613-), m/2 Simon EYRE/AYRES? ca 1651; b 1637(8?); Ipswich
WHITTINGHAM, William (-1672) & Mary [LAWRENCE]? (-1671, Boston); [ca 1660?]; Boston
WHITTLESEY, John[1] (-1704) & Ruth DUDLEY (1645-1714); 20 Jun 1664; Saybrook, CT
WHITTLESEY, John[2] (1665-1735) & Hannah (LONG) LARGE (1665-1752), w Simon; 9 May 1693; Saybrook, CT
WHITTLESEY, Stephen[2] (1667-1760) & Rebecca WATERUS/WATERHOUSE (1677-1716); 14 Oct 1696; Saybrook, CT
WHITTLESEY, _?_ & Martha [JONES] (1672-), m/2 Samuel COMSTOCK; b 28 Feb 1703/4, b 1701?; ?Saybrook, CT
WHITREDGE, Richard & Phoebe _?_ ; b 1687; Boston
WHITTERAGE, Sylvester & Mary BUCKLEY, m/2 Benjamin PROCTOR; 17 Nov 1684; Marblehead/Salem
WHITTREDGE, Thomas (-1672) & Florence (NORMAN) [HART] (-1672), w John; ca 1656, ca 1657; Salisbury
WHITRIDGE, Thomas (1656-1717) & 1/wf Charity [LIVERMORE]; b 1683; Beverly
WHITRIDGE, William (1599-1668) & 1/wf Elizabeth _?_ (1605-); b 1625; Salisbury
WHITRED, William & Frances _?_ ; b 1658; Ipswich
WHITRIDGE, William (1599-1668) & 2/wf Susanna [COLBY] (-1691), w Anthony; ca 1663; Salisbury
WHITRIDGE, William (1658-1695) & Hannah ROBERTS; 4 Mar 1683/4; Gloucester/Ipswich
WHITWAY, Thomas & _?_ ; Wethersfield, CT/Branford
WHITWAY, William & Ureth [WATERS], m/2 John NICKS by 1684; b 1673; Boston
WHITWELL, Bartholomew & Amy _?_ ; b 1667; Boston
WHITWELL, William & 1/wf Joanna _?_ ; b 1653(4?); Boston
WHITWELL, William (-1686) & 2/wf Mary _?_ ; b 1669; Boston
WIARD/?WYART, John (?1646-) & Sarah STANDISH; 7 Apr 1681; Wethersfield, CT
WIARD/WYAR, Robert (-1682) & Mary _?_ ; b 1646; Boston
WIBORN, James & Mary GRAFORD; 11 Jan 1699; Boston
WEYBURN, John & Mary [HINCKLEY]? (1644-1688+); b 1671; Boston
WIBORN, John (-1748) & Esther RIPPLE/RIPLEY; 10 May 1694; Boston/Scituate/Lebanon, CT/Norwich, CT
WIBORNE, Thomas (-1656) & Elizabeth _?_, m/2 Henry FELCH ca 1657; b 1637; Boston
WIBORNE, Thomas (-1697+) & 1/wf Abigail ELIOT (1639-1660, Boston); 16 Dec 1657; Boston
WYBORNE, Thomas (-1697+) & 2/wf Ruth _?_ (-1672+); b 1663; Boston/?Scituate
WYBORNE, Thomas (-1697+) & 3/wf Mary [LOWELL]; aft 1672, b 1687; Boston

WICKENDEN, William (-1670) & 1/wf __?__ ; by 1653, by 1643; Salem/Providence

WICKENDEN, William (-1670) & 2/wf Eleanor SHERRINGHAM; m int 23 Dec 1663; Providence

WICOME, Daniel (?1641-) & Mary SMITH; 14 Oct 1658; Rowley

WICOME, Daniel (-1724+) & 1/wf Sarah HAZEN (1672, 1673?-); 27 Jun 1690; Rowley

WICOM, Daniel & Lydia (BAILEY) PLATTS, w Abel; 11 Nov 1691; Rowley

WYCOME, John & Abigail KIMBLE/KIMBALL (ca 1652-); 14 May 1673; Rowley

WICKHAM, Joseph (-1734) & Sarah [DYMOND] (1676-1700?); b 1701, b 1698; Killingworth, CT/Southold, LI

WICOM, Richard (-1664) & Ann __?__ (-1674); b 1635; Rowley

WICKHAM, Samuel (1664-1712±) & 1/wf Ann __?__ ; 2 Aug 1688; Warwick, RI

WICKHAM, Samuel (1664-1712±) & 2/wf Barbara HOLDEN (1668-1707); 4 Jun 1691; Warwick, RI

WICKHAM, Thomas (ca 1623-1688/9) & Sarah __?__ (ca 1628-1700); b 1648; Wethersfield, CT

WICKHAM, Thomas (1651-) & Mary __?__ ; 11 Jun 1673; Wethersfield, CT

WICKHAM, Thomas (1674-1706) & __?__ ; b 1700

WICKHAM, William (1657-1730+) & [Sarah CHURCHILL] (1657-); b 1690, b 17 Nov 1683; Wethersfield, CT/Glastonbury, CT

WICKWARE, John & Mary TONGE/TONGUE (1656-); 6 Nov 1676; New London

WIDGIER, John & Bethia SWEET; 12 Nov 1685; Marblehead

WIDGIER, John & Hannah __?__ ; Hannah WIDGER sister of Mercy DUE ae 32 in 1683

WIDGER, James (-1715, ae 89) & Mary [PHIPPS] (1637±-1721, ae 84)

WICKIN, Andrew & Hannah/Ann BRADSTREET; 3 Jun 1659, 8 Jun; Andover/Exeter, NH

WIGGIN, Andrew & 1/wf Abigail FOLLET; 2 Sep 1697; Dover, NH

WIGGIN, Bradstreet (1676-) & Ann CHASE, m/2 John SINCLAIR; 25 Aug 1697; Salisbury

WIGGIN, James & Magdelen [?HILTON], m/2 Henry KENNING 1698; by 1646, by Jun 1656

WIGGIN, James & Rachel [BROOKS] (1650-); b 1672; Rehoboth/Southold, LI

WIGGIN, James (1658±-) & Sarah [?WINNOCK], m/2 James DAVIS 1693; ca 1687?; Newbury

WIGGIN, James & Annis [CONKLIN]? (very doubtful); b 1698?; Southold, LI

WIGGINS, John & Hannah [RIDER] (-1738); b 1672; Southold, LI

WIGGINS, John & Ruhaman MARBLE (?1644-); 1668/9; Medford

WIGGIN, Josias (-1720) & Isabella __?__ ; LI

WIGGIN, Simon (1664-1720?) & 1/wf [?Judith WILSON]; ca 1690?; Exeter, NH

WIGGIN, Thomas (ae 46 in 1633) (widower) & Catharine [WHITING?] (ae ca 32 in 1633); ca 11 Jul 1633, Mar 1635; Hampton, NH

WIGGIN, Thomas (-1683) & __?__ ; Jamaica, LI

WIGGINS, Thomas & Sarah [BAREFOOT]; 27 Aug 1649, 1659?; Reading

WIGGINS, Thomas & Rebecca [WOOLSEY] (1661-); b 2 Nov 1691

WIGGIN, Thomas (1664-1727) & Sarah __?__ ; ca 1685/8?; Stratham, NH

WIGGIN, Thomas & Martha [DENISON] (1669-), m/2 Jonathan THING 1693, m/3 Matthew WHIPPLE 1697; ca 1690

WIGGLESWORTH, Edward (1604-1653) & [?Esther RAYNER?]/[?Hester MIDDLEBROOK?]; in Eng, b 1631; Charlestown/New Haven

WIGGLESWORTH, Michael (1631-) & 1/wf Mary [RAYNER]/REYNIA? (-1657), Rowley; 18 May 1655, b 1655(6); Charlestown/Malden

WIGGLESWORTH, Michael (1631-) & 2/wf Martha [?MUDGE] (?1662-1690, Malden); aft 8 May 1679, b 1682; Malden/Charlestown

WIGGLESWORTH, Michael (1631-1705), Malden & 3/wf Sylvia/Sybil/Lydia (SPARHAWK) AVERY, w Jonathan (-1708); Dedham, 23 Jun 1691; Braintree

WIGHT, Benjamin (-1739) & Elizabeth NEWELL (-1743); 10 Apr 1690; Sudbury

WIGHT, Benjamin & Sarah [BARNES]; b 1701?; Providence

WIGHT, Daniel (1656-1719) & Anna DUEING/[DEWING]; 17 Feb 1686/7, 1685/6?; Dedham

WIGHT, Eleazer & Relief [WARREN] (-1730); b 1697(8?); Medfield

WIGHT, Ephraim (-1723) & Lydia MORSE (-1722); 2 Mar 1667/8; Medfield

WIGHT, Henry (-1681) & Jane [GOODNOW] (-1684); b 1652; Dedham

WIGHT, John (-1653) & Ann [BURNAP] (1632-), m/2 Isaac BULLARD 1655, m/3 David JONES, Sr., 1685; ca 1652, she is called cousin by Mrs. Margaret WATERMAN; Medfield

WIGHT, Jonathan (-1718) & Elizabeth [FISHER]/HAWS, dau Thomas FISHER; 19 Apr 1687; Wrentham

WITE, Joseph & 1/wf Deborah COLBORNE/COLBURN (1657-1684); 15 Jan 1679/80; Dedham

WIGHT, Joseph (-1729) & 2/wf Mary STEARNES (-1733); 22 Apr 1685; Dedham
WIGHT, Joshua & Abigail ROCKWOOD (1679-); 30 Nov 1696; Dedham
WIGHT, Joshua & Elizabeth SPOWEL; 4 Oct 1699; Boston/Windham, CT
WIGHT, Samuel (-1716) & Hannah ALBIE/ALBEE (1641-); 25 Mar 1662/3, 1663; Medfield
WIGHT, Samuel (-1745) & Marie/Mary PRATT (-1743); 12 May 1687; Medfield
WIGHT, Thomas[1] & 1/wf Alice _?_ (-1665); ca 1630?; Dedham/Wrentham
WIGHT, Thomas (-1690) & Mehitable [CHENEY] (1643-1693); b 1663; Medfield
WIGHT, Thomas[1] (-1674) & 2/wf Lydia (ELIOT) PENIMAN (-1676), w James; [?]7 Dec 1665; Medfield
WIGHT, Thomas (1607?-1648?) & Lucy _?_, m/2 John SAMUEL 1652; ca 1640/2; Exeter, NH
WIGHTMAN, Daniel (1668-1750) & 1/wf Catharine [HOLMES] (1671-1699); ca 1694?; Kings Town, RI/Newport
WIGHTMAN, George (1632-1722) & Elizabeth [UPDIKE] (1644-); b 1664; Kings Town, RI
WIGHTMAN, George (1673-1761) & 1/wf Elizabeth _?_ ; ca 1698?; Warwick, RI
WEIGHTMAN, John (1674-1750) & 1/wf Jane BENTLEY; 6 Jan 1700; Kings Town, RI/Exeter, RI
WIGLEY, Edmund & Mary [MILES] (1640-1708), m/2 Joseph LEE 1697; ca 1660?, ca 1667?, b 1693; Concord
WILLBORNE/WILBORNE, Michael & Mary BEAMSLEY (1637-1726), m/2 Andrew PETERS 1658, 1659; 17 Oct 1656; Boston
WILBORE, Benjamin (-1729), Portsmouth, RI, Dartmouth, MA, & 1/wf Mary KINNECUT (-1708); 22 Jun 1700; Little Compton, RI
WILBORE, Daniel & Ann [BARNEY]; b 1694, 1692?; Little Compton, RI/Swansea
WILBUR, John (1658-) & Hannah _?_ ; 1682, b 1683; Little Compton, RI
WILBORE, Joseph (-1691) & Elizabeth [FARWELL?]/DEAN? (-1670); b 1652; Taunton
WILBORE, Joseph (-1691) & 2/wf _?_ ; b 1672
WILBUR, Joseph (1656-1729) & Ann [BROWNELL] (1654-1747); 1683, b 1684, ?4 May 1683; Little Compton, RI
WILBORE, Joseph (1670-1720) & Mehitable [DEANE] (1671-); b 1696; Taunton
WILDBORE, Samuel (-1656), Boston, Portsmouth, RI, Taunton, & 1/wf Ann [SMITH]; in Eng, b 1625?, b 1614?, 1621; Taunton
WILDBORE, Samuel (-1656) & Elizabeth [LECHFORD], w Thomas, m/3 Henry BISHOP 1657; b 1645, b 29 Nov 1645; Boston
WILBUR, Samuel (-1679±) & Hannah [PORTER] (-1722); b 1650; Boston/Portsmouth, RI
WILBUR, Samuel & Mary SHERMAN; 1674
WILBUR, Samuel (1663-1695) & Sarah PHILLIPS; 19 Dec 1688; Taunton
WILBUR, Samuel (1663, 1664-1696?, 1740) & Mary [POTTER]/SHERMAN?; b 1696, seems doubtful, 1689, b 1690; Taunton, RI/Little Compton, RI
WILBORE, Shadrack (-1698) & 1/wf Mary [DEAN] (-1691); b 1659; Taunton
WILBOR, Shadrack (?1632-1698), Taunton & Hannah (BASS) PAYNE (-1696+, 1710), Braintree, w Stephen; 13 Sep 1692, 14 Sep 1692; Taunton/Braintree
WILBOR, Shadrack (1672-1749), Tanton, Raynham & Joanna NEALE (1680-); 20 Mar 1700, 21 Mar 1700; Braintree
WILDBORE, Thomas (?1659-) & Mary _?_
WILBUR, William (1630-1710) & Martha _?_ ; 1653, b 1654; Portsmouth, RI/Tiverton, RI
WILBUR, William (1660-1738) & 1/wf _?_ TALLMAN (-1732); 18 Dec 1680; New Shoreham, RI/Little Compton, RI
WILCOX, Daniel (-1702) & 1/wf _?_ (-bef 1 Aug 1661); by 1657?; Portsmouth, RI
WILCOX, Daniel (-1702) & 2/wf Elizabeth COOKE (-1715, Tiverton, RI); 28 Nov 1661; Plymouth
WILCOX, Daniel (-bef 1692) & Hannah [COOK] (1660-1736), m/2 Enoch BRIGGS; ca 1680/2?, by 1681; Portsmouth, RI
WILCOX, Daniel (-1717+) & Mary [WODELL?]/[WARDELL?] (-1717+); b 23 Mar 1697; Portsmouth, RI
WILCOX, Edward & _?_ ; b 1633; Kingston, RI
WILCOX, Edward (1662-1715) & 1/wf Mary [HAZARD]; b 1689?; Westerly, RI
WILCOX, Edward (1662-1713) & 2/wf Thomasin STEPHENS (1677-); 1 May 1698, 5? May; Westerly, RI/Taunton
WILCOX, Edward (ca 1675/6-1718) & Sarah [MANCHESTER]; b 1701; Tiverton, RI
WILCOX, Ephraim (1672-1712/13) & Silence HAND (1680-1725?), m/2 John WARNER 1715; 23 Aug 1698; Middletown, CT

WILCOX, Israel (1656-1689) & Sarah **SAVAGE** (1657-1724); 28 Mar 1677/8; Middletown, CT
WILCOX, John (-1651) & Mary __?__ (-1668); ca 1615; Hartford
WILCOX, John (-1676) & 1/wf Sarah **WADSWORTH** (ca 1626-1698); 17 Sep 1646; Hartford/Middletown, CT
WILCOX, John (-1676) & 2/wf Katharine/Catharine **STOUGHTON**; 18 Jan 1649, 1649/50; Hartford/Middletown, CT
WILCOX, John (-1676) & 3/wf Mary **(LANE) (LONG)** [**FARNSWORTH**] (-1671), w Joseph/John, w Joseph; ca 1660; Middletown, CT
WILCOX, John (-1676) & 4/wf Esther [**CORNWALL**] (1650-1733), m/2 John **STOW** 1677; 1671, b 1672; Hartford, CT/Middletown, CT
WILCOX, John (1670-1718) & Rebecca [**MOSHIER**]; 1698, b 1699; Little Compton, RI
WILCOX, Samuel (-1702?) & Mary [**WOOD**] (1664-1721), m/2 Thomas **MALLET** by 1697, m/3 John **SANFORD**; b 1683; Dartmouth
WILCOX, Samuel (-1714) & Abigail **WHITMORE** (1660-1687); 9 May 1683; Middletown, CT
WILCOX, Stephen (1633?-1690±) & Hannah [**HAZARD**]; ca 1657?, b 1662, 1658?; Portsmouth, RI/Westerly, RI
WILLCOX, Stephen (-1736) & 1/wf Susannah **BRIGGS** (1672-1719+); 9 Feb 169-, 1695?, 1690?; Westerly, RI/Portsmouth
WILCOX, Stephen & Elizabeth [**CRANDALL**]; ca 1691?
WILCOX, Thomas (-1728) & Martha [**HAZARD**]; b 1687; Exeter, RI
WILCOX, William (-1653) & Mary **POWELL**, m/2 Jacob **ELLIOT** 1655; 20 Feb 1650, 1650/1, 22 Jan 1650; Cambridge
WILCOX, William & Dorothy **PALMER**; 25 Jan 1697/8; Stonington, CT
WILCOX, __?__ & Grace __?__ (-1657/8, Guilford, CT)
WILCOXSON, John (1633-) & 1/wf [Joanna] **TITHERTON/TITTERTON**; b 1657; Hartford, CT
WILCOCKSON, John (1633-) & Elizabeth **(BOURNE) WELLES**, w John; 19 Mar 1663, 1662/3; Stratford, CT
WILCOXSON, John (1657-) & Elizabeth **(JONES) BUSS**, w Joseph; 14 Mar 1682/3; Concord/Stratford, CT
WILCOCKSON, Joseph (-1684) & Ann/Anna __?__ ; b 1659; Killingworth, CT
WILCOX/WILCOXSON, Joseph & Hannah **KELSEY**; 14 Feb 1693, 1693/4, 14 Feb 1695, 1693 prob OK; Killingworth, CT
WILCOXSON, Nathaniel (1668-1712) & Hannah **LANE**; 21 Nov 1695; Killingworth, CT
WILCOX/WILCOXSON, Obadiah & 1/wf Mary [**GRISWOLD**] (1650-1670); Killingworth, CT/Guilford, CT
WILCOXSON, Obadiah (1648-) & 2/wf Lydia [**ALLING**] (1656-); b 1676; Guilford, CT
WILCOCKSON, Obadiah (1646-1713) & 3/wf Silence [**MANSFIELD**] (1664-), m/2 George **CHATFIELD**; b 1690; Guilford, CT
WILCOCKSON, Samuel (1640-1713?) & Hannah [**RICE**], Cambridge, MA, dau Richard; b 1666; Windsor, CT
WILCOXEN, Samuel (1663-1713?) & Mindwell [**GRIFFIN**] (1664-); ca 1691; Sinsbury, CT
WILCOXSON, Samuel & Ruth **WASCOT/WESTCOTT**; 1 Jan 1696; Killingworth, CT
WILCOCKSON, Timothy (ca 1637-1711) & Joanna **BIRDSEYE** (1642-); 28 Dec 1664; Stratford, CT
WILCOCKSON, William (-1652) & Margaret __?__ (1612-), m/2 William **HAYDEN**; b 1633, b 1630?; Concord/Stratford, CT
WILCOXSON, William (-1733) & Elizabeth **WILSON** (1674-), Windsor, CT; 18 Jan 1699/1700; Simsbury
WILDE, Ephraim (1665-1725) & Mary **HOWLET** (1671, 1671/2-1758); 18 Mar 1689, 1689/90; Topsfield
WILES, John (1618?-1705) (ae 40 in 1660) & 1/wf Priscilla [**GOULD**] (1625-1663); 1645?; Topsfield
WILD, John (-1705) & 2/wf Sarah **AVERILL** (ca 1627-1692?); 23 Nov 1663; Topsfield
WILD, John (-1721) & 1/wf Sarah [**HAYDEN**] (1667-1725); 1691; Braintree
WILDES, John (-1705) & 3/wf Mary **JACOBS**, Salem, w George?; 26 Jun 1693; Topsfield
WILES, Michael & __?__ ; b 1695(6?); Ipswich
WILDE, Richard & __?__ ; b 1675; Flushing, LI
WILD, Richard & Margaret **DOLLIN/DOLLING**; 22 Aug 1687; Middlesex Co.

WILDES, William (-1662) & 2/wf? Elizabeth _?_, m/2 Richard MOORE 1662; b 1649, no issue; Topsfield/Ipswich/Rowley

WILDER, Edward (-1690) & Elizabeth [EAMES] (?1624-1692); ca 1650; Hingham

WILDER, Ephraim (1677-1769) & Elizabeth [STEVENS] (?1681-1769); 1698; Lancaster

WILDER, Isaac (1656-1690) & Mary WHITON, m/2 Baruch JORDAN, m/3 Thomas SAYER; 3 Jan 1688/9; Hingham

WILDER, Jabez (1658-1731) & Mary [FORD] (1671-1748); b 1695, ca 1692?; Hingham

WILDER, John (?1651, ?1646-1722) & Hannah [?ATHERTON] (1657-), dau Richard?, m/2 John HOUGHT 1725; 17 Jul 1672; Lancaster/Marlborough

WILDER, John (-1724) & Rebecca DOGGETT (-1728); 30 Nov 1675; Hingham

WILDER, John & Sarah [WHITE] (1680-); 1699; Lancaster

WILDER, Nathaniel (1655-1704, ae 54?) & Mary SAWYER (1652-1711); 24 Jan 1673/4; Lancaster/Sudbury

WILDER, Thomas (1618/19-1667) & Anna [JOHNSON?]/?Hannah MEARS?/EAMES (-1692); b 1642; Charlestown/Lancaster

WILDER, Thomas (1644-1716) & Mary [WHEELER] (1646-); 25 Jun 1668; Lancaster/Marlboro

WILDER, [Thomas?] & Martha _?_ (-1652); in Eng, b 1616; Hingham

WILDMAN, Thomas (-1689) & [Sarah?] BROOKS?, m/2 Thomas SEYMOUR 1690+; ca 1670/75?; Bedford, NY

WILLY/WILEY, John (-1680?) & Elizabeth CLOUGH; 21 Jun 1644; Watertown/Reading

WILE, John & Elizabeth SWIFT; 16 Oct 1667; Northampton

WEYLY, Timothy (1653-1728) & 1/wf Elizabeth DAVIS (-1695), dau George; 4 Dec 1677, 4 Jan 1678/9, 22 Jan 1678/9; Cambridge/Reading

WILLY, Timothy (1653-1728) & 2/wf Susannah (KENDALL) [CONDREY] (1658-31 Aug 1732, ae 74-2-4), w Nathaniel; b 1697, b 26 Oct 1696; Reading

WILFORD, Gilbert & Mary [DOW], m/2 Matthew CLARK 1679; b 1667; Bradford

WILLFORD, John & Bridget _?_; b 1656; Boston

WILFORD, _?_ & Lydia _?_ (-1694), m/2 _?_ TOPPING; Branford

WILKES, Thomas (-1662) & Mary _?_; b 1 Oct 1656, b 1650; Salem

WILKES, William & ?Joan/Jean _?_ (-1646); b 1633; Boston/New Haven

WILKIE, Jacob (1669-) & _?_ CRAW, dau Richard; 1694; Little Compton, RI

WILKIE, Jeremiah (1670-1711) & Dinah [WESTCOTT] (1670-1711+); no issue; Kings Town, RI

WILKEY, John & Elizabeth _?_, m/2 Jeremiah CUSHING by 1661, b 1653; Boston

WILKINS, Benjamin (-1715) & Priscilla BAXTER; 3 Jun 1677; Salem

WILKINS, Bray (-1702) (brother-in-law John GINGLE) & Anna/Hannah? [GRINGELL]/GINGILL; b 1636; Lynn/Dorchester/Salem

WILKINS, Henry (bpt 1651-) & 1/wf Rebecca _?_ (-1689, ae 40); ca 1670; Salem

WILKINS, Henry & 2/wf Ruth (FULLER) WHEELER, w Timothy; 1689?; Concord/Salem

WILKINS/WILKINSON?, Jacob & Mary _?_; b 1678(9?); Boston

WILKINS, James & Margaret BRAYE; 20 Apr 1684; Salem

WILKINS, John (bpt 1642-1672) & Mary _?_ (-1672+); b 1665; Salem

WILKINS, John & Anstis (GOLD) [BISSETT], w Thomas; b 1671; Boston/Bristol, RI

WILKINS, John & Susanna _?_, m/2 John BAILEY 1695, m/3 Peter THATCHER; b 1674; Boston

WILKINS, John & 1/wf Lydia _?_ (-?27 Jan 1688/9?, 1686/7?); Salem

WILKINS, John (-1723) & 2/wf Betty SOUTHWICK (1668-1718+); - Aug 1687?, note dates; Salem

WILKINS, John & Elizabeth HOW; 27 Apr 1697; Boston

WILKINS/WILKINSON?, John & Abigail [GOWING], dau Robert; Reading

WILKINS, Richard (-1704) & _?_; b 1670; Boston/Milton

WILKINS, Samuel (1636-1688) & Jane _?_ (-1696+); Salem

WILKINS, Samuel & 1/wf Sarah _?_; b 1693; Salem

WILKINS, Samuel & 2/wf Priscilla PARKER; 1 Feb 1698, 1698/9; Salem/Newport

WILKINS, Thomas (bpt 1647-1717) & Hannah NICHOLS; - May 1667; Salem

WILKINS, Thomas (1673-) & Elizabeth TOWNE (1669-); 19 Dec 1694; Topsfield/Boxford

WILKINS, William (-1694) & Ann STILLWELL, wid; 29 Dec 1672; Gravesend, LI

WILKINS, William & Alse _?_/[?Alice BARNES]; b 10 Feb 1697/8, b 8 Apr 1687; Gravesend, LI

WILKINSON, Edward (-1698) & Rebecca SMITH; 2 Jul 1672; Milford, CT

WILKINSON/WILKINS & Mary _?_; b 1678; Boston

WILKINSON, John (-1675) & _?_; Malden

WILKINSON/WILKINS?, John & Abigail [GOING]
WILKENSON, John & Elizabeth READ; 10 Dec 1675; Salem
WILKINSON, John (1654-1708) & Deborah WHIPPLE (1670-1748); 16 Apr 1689; Providence
WILKINSON, Josias (-1692) & Hannah [TYLER], m/2 Joseph TUCKER; Providence
WILKINSON, Lawrence[1] (-1692) & Susannah [SMITH] (-bef 1692); b 1646?, b 1651(2!); Providence
WILKINSON, Philip & Helena TILLER; m lic 11 Oct 1694; ?NY/LI?
WILKINSEN, Philip & Mary BRAZIER; m lic 16 Sep 1697; NY/LI?
WILKINSON, Samuel (-1727) & Plain [WICKENDEN]; b 1674, 1672; Providence
WILKINSON, Samuel (1674-) & Huldah ALDRICH (1682-); 13 Apr 1697; Providence
WILKESON, Thomas & Ann _?_ ; 5 Feb 1657/8; Dorchester
WILKINSON, _?_ & Ann _?_ (-1684, ae ca 94); Billerica
WILKINSON, _?_ & Isabel _?_ (-1655/6), cousin of Wm. & Rachel CUTTER; in Eng, b 1622; Cambridge
WILKINSON, _?_ & Prudence _?_ ; b 1630; Charlestown/Malden
WILLARD, Benjamin (ca 1664-1732), Sudbury, Grafton & Sarah [LAKIN] (-1662); ca 1691; Sudbury/Framingham
WILLARD, Daniel (1658-1708) & 1/wf Hannah CUTLER (1654-1691); 6 Dec 1683; Charlestown
WILLARD, Daniel (1658-1708) & 2/wf Mary MILLS, m/2 David MELVILLE; 4 Jan 1692/3; Braintree/Boston
WILLARD, Daniel (1645-1712) & Esther MATTHEWS (1651-); 10 Jun 1695, no issue; Yarmouth
WILLARD, George (1614-) & Deborah [?DUNSTER]; ca 1640; Scituate/MD
WILLARD, Henry (1655-) & 1/wf Mary LAKIN (-1688); 18 Jul 1674; Groton
WILLARD, Henry (1655-1701) & Dorcas [CUTLER], m/2 Benjamin BELLOWS 1704; 1689; Lancaster
WILLARD, Henry & 1/wf Abigail TEMPLE (1677-); 21 Jul 1698; Concord/Lancaster
WILLARD, Jacob (-1678) & Mary WHITE; 23 Oct 1677; Watertown
WILLARD, John & Margaret _?_, m/2 William TOWNE 1694; b 1690?; Salem
WILLARD, John (-1726) & Mary HAYWARD (1677-); 31 Oct 1698; Concord/Lancaster
WILLARD, Jonathan (1669-1706) & Mary BROWN (1668-1720); 8 Jan 1690/1; Sudbury/Roxbury
WILLARD, Joseph (1661-bef 1721) & _?_ ; ?London
WILLARD, Josiah (ca 1635-1674), Wethersfield, CT, & Hannah HOSMER, m/2 William MALTBY by 1686; 20 Mar 1656; Concord/Hartford, CT
WILLARD, Samuel (1640-1707) & 1/wf Abigail SHERMAN (1648-1679); 8 Aug 1664; Groton
WILLARD, Samuel (1640-1707) & 2/wf Eunice [TYNG] (1655-1720); [1679], ?29 Jul 1679; Boston
WILLARD, Samuel (1658-1716) & Sarah CLARK ([ca 1662]-1723), m/2 Nathaniel PRATT; 6 Jun 1683; Saybrook, CT
WILLARD, Simon (1605-1676) & 1/wf Mary [SHARPE]; ca 1630; Cambridge/Lancaster
WILLARD, Simon & 2/wf Elizabeth [DUNSTER] (1619-); ca 1643; Charlestown
WILLARD, Simon (1605-1676) & 3/wf Mary [DUNSTER], m/2 Joseph NOYES 1680; 1652?; Lancaster
WILLARD, Simon (1649-1731) & 1/wf Martha [JACOB] (-1721); ca 1679; Ipswich
WILLARD, Simon (?1661-1727) & Mary GILBERT (1674-); 12 Feb 1690; Wethersfield, CT
WILLARD, Simon (1676-1706) & Mary WHITCOMB (1676-), m/2 Samuel FARNSWORTH 1706; 1700; Lancaster
WILLARD, Thomas & Abigail BRADLEY; 8 Jul 1689; Guilford, CT
WILLETTS, Andrew (1655-1712) & Ann CODDINGTON (1663-1751); 30 May 1682; Newport/Kings Town, RI
WILLETT, Andrew, Boston & Susannah HOLBROOK; 6 Mar 1693/4; Braintree
WILLET, Francis & Martha SILVER; 20 Dec 1669; Newbury
WILLET, Francil & Elizabeth LOWLE/LOWELL; 29 Jan 1695/6; Newbury
WILLETT, Hezekiah (-1676) & Ann/Anna/Andra BROWN; 7 Jan 1675; Swansea
WILLETS, Hope (1652-) & Mercy [LANGDON]; b 1677; Jerusalem, LI
WILLETT, James (1549-) & 1/wf Elizabeth HUNT (-1676); 17 Apr 1673; Rehoboth
WILLETT, James (1649-) & 2/wf Grace FRINK; Jun 1677; Stonington
WILLETT, John (1641-1664) & Abigail [COLLINS] (1644-1673), m/2 Lawrence HAMMOND 1665; b 1663; Charlestown
WILLITS, John & Margaret [HALLOCK]

WILLETT, Nathaniel (-1698) & 1/wf Elizabeth [WAKEMAN], w Samuel; b 4 Dec 1645; ?Hartford

WILLETT, Nathaniel (-1698) & 2/wf Hannah [ADAMS]; Hartford

WILLITS, Richard (?1612-1664/5) & Mary [WASHBURNE] (1629-1713); ca 1650; Hempstead, LI

WILLETS, Richard (1660-1703) & 1/wf Abigail BOWNE (1662-1688); 25 Mar 1686; Flushing, LI/Jericho, LI

WILLITS, Richard (1660-1703) & 2/wf Abigail POWELL (1668-1757); 15 May 1690; Huntington, LI

WILLETT, Richard & 1/wf? Mary WILLETT (-1701); 22 Dec 1697; ?New York

WILLET, Robert & _?_; b 1697; Topsfield

WILLETT, Samuel & _?_; b 1701; Flushing, LI

WILLET, Thomas[1] (-1674) & 1/wf Mary BROWNE (1614-1669); 6 Jul 1636; Plymouth

WILLETT, Thomas (-1647), Bristol, Eng, & Sarah CORNELL, m/2 Charles BRIDGES 1647, m/3 John LAWRENCE 1682; 1 Sep 1643; New York

WILLETT, Thomas & _?_; b 1655

WILLETT, Thomas (1645-1722) & 1/wf Helena/Eleanor [STOOTHOFF] (-1704); b 1668; LI

WILLETT, Thomas (-1674, in 64th y, at Swansea) & 2/wf Joanna (BOYES) PRUDDEN, w Peter, m/3 John BISHOP 1683; 19 Sep 1671, 20? Sep; Milford, CT

WILLITS, Thomas (1650-1714) & Dinah [TOWNSEND] (1651-1732); ca 1672/3?, ca 1670?; ?Jericho, LI/Islip, LI

WILLETT, Thomas (ca 1672-1724) & 1/wf Sarah HENCHMAN; 24 Aug 1695; ?Jamaica, LI

WILLETT, William (?1670-1733) & 1/wf Anna [?FIELD]; b 1692; Westchester, NY/LI?

WILLEY, Abraham (-1692) & Elizabeth [MORTIMER]; b 1684; New London, CT/Haddam, CT

WILLEY, Allen & Alice _?_, m/2 Thomas MARSHALL; b 1634; Boston

WILLEY, Isaac[1] (-1685) & 1/wf Joanna _?_; b 1640; Boston/New London, CT

WILLEY, Isaac[2] (1640-1662) & Frances BURCHAM, m/2 Clement MINER 1662; 8 Jun 1660; Boston

WILLEY, Isaac[1] & 2/wf Ann/?Hannah/Anna? (BROOKS) (FOX) [LESTER] (-1692), w Thomas, w Andrew; ca 1670?, ?24 Apr 1672; New London, CT

WILLEY, Isaac (1673-) & 1/wf Rose BENNETT; 14 Dec 1697; Lyme, CT/New London, CT

WILLEY, John (-1688) & Miriam MOORE, m/2 Samuel SPENCER 1689; ?18 Mar 1669/70, ?1668/9, 1668; New London, CT

WILLEY, John (?1659, 1655?±-1639?) & Alice/Dorcas _?_; ca 1688/90?; Durham, NH

WILLEY, John (1675-) & Elizabeth HARVEY, New London, CT; Oct 1698; Lyme, CT/East Haddam, CT

WILLEE, Richard & Elizabeth [WILLIS]; b 1687; Boston

WILLEY, Stephen (1649-1700) & Abigail [PITMAN], m/2 Edward deFLECHEUR; b 1671, by 1671; Durham, NH

WILLEY, Thomas (±1617-1681) & Margaret [CRAWFORD] (1615-), w Stephen; ca 1649, b 6 Oct 1649; Durham, NH

WILLEY, William (-1706) & Rebecca [NOCK] (ca 1660-), m/2 Samuel TIBBETS; ca 1680?; Durham, NH

WILLEY?/WILEY, _?_ & Hannah [BRASIER]; b 1687; Charlestown

WILLIAMS, Abraham (?1628-1712) & Joanna [WARD] (ca 1628-1718); ca 1659; Watertown/Cambridge/Newton/Marlboro

WILLIAMS, Amos (-1683) & Elizabeth _?_, m/2 Thomas HOLLISTER ca 1690; 29 Jun 1670, 27 Jun; Wethersfield, CT

WILLIAMS, Anthony & Mary SOLARE; 25 Sep 1676; Beverly

WILLIAMS, Arthur (-1673/4) & Catherine (_?_) CARTER, w Joshua, m/3 William BLANCH 1673; 30 Nov 1647; Windsor, CT/Northampton

WILLIAMS, Augustine & Hannah [NORTON] (1648-), m/2 [John] BROWN b 1700, ca 1693; b 1680; Stonington, CT/Killingworth, CT

WILLIAMS, Benjamin & Rachel _?_; b 1670; Boston

WILLIAMS, Benjamin & Ruth _?_; b 1672; Boston

WILLIAMS, Benjamin & Rebecca _?_; b 1678; Boston

WILLIAMS, Benjamin & Rachel _?_; b 1687; Boston

WILLIAMS, Benjamin (ca 1651-1701) & Rebecca MARY, m/2 James LEONARD; 12 Mar 1689/90, ?18 Mar; Taunton

WILLIAMS, Charles (-1740, ae 88), Worcester & Elizabeth **WEEKS** (-1725), Worcester; 11 Jan 1686; ?Marlboro/Hadley/Middlesex

WILLIAMS, Charles & ?Hannah/?Sarah [**GREER**] (1666-); b 1689, b 1688/9?; Preston, CT

WILLIAMS, Charles & Mary **GLADDING**; 13 Feb 1695/6; Taunton

WILLIAMS, Daniel (1642-1712) & Rebecca **(RHODES) POWER** (-1727), w Nicholas; 1 Dec 1676, 7 Dec 1676, 2 Dec; Providence

WILLIAMS, Daniel & Alice [**ALLEN**] (1674-); b 1695; Manchester

WILLIAMS, Ebenezer (1649-1718) & Martha **HALL** (1648-); 18 Sep 1674; Dorchester

WILLIAMS, Ebenezer & Sarah **BEAMAN** (-1681); 28 Dec 1680; Dorchester

WILLIAMS, Ebenezer & Deborah **(WISWALL) CHENEY**, w William; aft Sep 1681, b 1688?; Medfield/Dorchester

WILLIAMS, Ebenezer (1666-1747) & Mary **WHEELER** (1668-1709); 24 Jan [1686/7], 1687; Stonington, CT

WILLIAMS, Ebenezer (1675-) & Elizabeth **TROTT**; 26 Dec 1698; Salem

WILLIAMS, Ebenezer & Mary **PALFREY**; 1 Oct 1700; Cambridge

WILLIAMS, Eleazer (1669-1725) & 1/wf? Mary [**HOBART**]/?**HYDE** (1682-); b 1696; Newton/Mansfield, CT

WILLIAMS, Elias & Mary **(JENNINGS) HAMERY** (- bef 13 Feb 1678/9); b 13 Nov 1635; Kittery, ME

WILLIAMS, Francis & Helen __?__

WILLIAMS, Francis & Mary __?__; b 1686; Boston

WILLIAMS, Freeborn (woman?) & __?__ [**HART**]; b 1663; Providence

WILLIAMS, Gabriel & __?__; b 1695(6?); ?Hartford

WILLIAMS, George (-1654) & [Mary] __?__ (-1654); b 1636; Salem

WILLIAMS, Griffin & Sarah __?__; b 1685(6?); Boston

WILLIAMS, Henry & Deborah [**COLLINS**]; ca 1685/90?, ca 1665?; Saco/Scarboro/Boston/Hampton, NH

WILLIAMS, Henry & 2/wf Christian [**HASKINS**], w William; b 1701?, b 1712; Hampton, NH

WILLIAMS, Hilliard (1668-1699) & Abigail [**MASSEY**]/**MANCY?** (1671-), m/2 Jonathan **ARCHER** 1699; b 1699; Salem

WILLIAMS, Hugh & Sarah [**COITMORE**]; b 1650; Charlestown

WILLIAMS, Isaac (1638-1707) & 1/wf Martha [**PARK**] (1641-1675, Newton); b 1660; Cambridge/Roxbury?/Newton

WILLIAMS, Isaac (?1629-1696) & Margery/Margaret [?**COLLINS**] (1633-1702); b 1660; Salem

WILLIAMS, Isaac (1638-1708, Newton) & 2/wf Judith **(HUNT) COOPER** (-1724, Newton, MA), w Nathaniel; 13 Nov 1677; Rehoboth

WILLIAMS, Isaac (1662-) & Mary **ENDICOT**; 2 Aug 1685; Salem

WILLIAMS, Isaac (1661?-1739) & 1/wf Elizabeth [**HYDE**] (1659-1699); b 1686; Newton/(?Roxbury)

WILLIAMS, Isaac & 2/wf Mary **(GRIFFIN)** [**HAMMOND**], w Nathaniel; aft 26 Jun 1699, b 6 May 1702, b 1701?; Newton

WILLIAMS, Jacob (1665-1712) & Sarah **GILBERT** (1661-bef 1705); 10 Dec 1685; Wethersfield, CT

WILLIAMS, James & Sarah **RICHARDSON**; 2 Oct 1691; Hartford/Wallingford, CT

WILLIAMS, James & Sarah **SALISBURY**; 7 Aug 1694; Boston

WILLIAMS, James & Sarah **SHIPPY** (1667-); 12 Aug 1700; Boston

WILLIAMS, Jenkins/Jenkin? (-1675) & Abigail [**CLOYSE**] (ca 1645-); ca 1670/3?, b 1 Oct 1667; Framingham

WILLIAMS, John (-1667) & Ann/?Anna __?__ (-1658); b [1624], b [1616?]; Scituate

WILLIAMS, John (-1667) & 2/wf? Jane __?__ (-1680); b 1630; Haverhill/Salisbury

WILLIAMS, John & 1/wf __?__; b 1630; Newbury/Haverhill

WILLIAMS, John (-1712) & 1/wf Mary **BURLEY/BURKLY** (-1665, 1681?); 29 Jun 1644; Windsor, CT

WILLIAMS, John (-1685) & Mary __?__; b 1659; Boston

WILLIAMS, John (-1698) & 1/wf Rebecca **COLBY** (-1672); 9 Sep 1661; Haverhill

WILLIAMS, John & Elizabeth [?**SKERRY**]; b 1663; Salem

WILLIAMS, John & Jane __?__; b 1665; Boston

WILLIAMS, John & Elizabeth **SMITH**; 23 Nov 1665; Salem

WILLIAMS, John (will 1691) & Elizabeth **LATHROP**; b 1666 (div); Barnstable/Scituate

WILLIAMS, John (1644-1687/8, Newport) & Anna ALCOCK (1650-1723), m/2 Robert GUTT-REDGE/GUTHRIE 1689, Newport; 24 Feb 1669/[70]; Watertown/Roxbury?/New Shoreham, RI

WILLIAMS, John (-1712) & 1/wf Bethia (PARSONS) MASKELL/?MASCALL (-1681), w Thomas; 8 Aug 1672, 18? Aug; Windsor, CT

WILLIAMS, John & Sarah __?_; b 1673 (div); Barnstable/Scituate

WILLIAMS, John & Martha KNIGHT; 9 Dec 1674; Beverly

WILLIAMS, John (-1698) & 2/wf Esther/Hester (BLAKELEY) BOND, w John; ·5 May 1675; Haverhill

WILLIAMS, John & Leah [TOWNSEND] (1652?-); ca 1676?; LI

WILLIAMS, John & Elizabeth [MOORE?]/[ALLEN?]; by Apr 1674?, b 1677(8?); Exeter, NH/Boston

WILLIAMS, John (-1705) & Thomasine/Tamsen? CARPENTER (1664-); b 13 Feb 1682(3?); Glen Cove, LI/Musketa Cove, LI/Madnin's Neck

WILLIAMS, John & Hannah __?_; b 1683; Boston

WILLIAMS, John (-1698) & Mary __?_; Hempstead, LI

WILLIAMS, John (-1741) & Jane (LATHAM) HUBBARD (1648-1739, ae 91 y), w Hugh; 1685/6; New London, CT

WILLIAMS, John, Sr. (-1712) & 2/wf Esther (WILLIAMS)? (EGGLESTONE) ENO (-1720), w James, w James; 10 Jun 1686; Windsor, CT

WILLIAMS, John & 1/wf Sarah MANNING (1667-); 8 Dec 1686; Salem

WILLIAMS, Rev. John (1664-1729) & 1/wf Eunice MATHER (1664-1704); 21 Jul 1687; Northampton/Deerfield

WILLIAMS, John (1667-) & Martha WHEELER (1670-); 24 Jan 1687/[8]; Stonington, CT/Newton/Deerfield

WILLIAMS, John & 1/wf Mary (DEMING) [SMITH] (1665-); ca 1688, aft 9 Apr 1687; Wethersfield, CT

WILLIAMS, John & __?_; b 1692; Hartford

WILLIAMS, John & [Humilis] __?_; b 1694; Boston

WILLIAMS, John & Abigail [?HOBART]; b 1694; Westchester, NY

WILLIAMS, John (1668-1752) & Mary __?_ (-1772, ae 102!); b 1694; Boston

WILLIAMS, John (1662-1735) & 2/wf Sarah HOLLISTER (ca 1670-); 24 Jan 1694/5; Wethersfield, CT

WILLIAMS, John & Sarah TRASK; 15 Feb 1694/5; Beverly

WILLIAMS, John & Mary BIGELOW; 11 Jan 1700; Hartford

WILLIAMS, John (1664-1745) & Ruth __?_; ca 1700(?); Durham, NH

WILLIAMS, John (1675-) & Hannah [ROBINSON]; b 1702, b 1701?; Taunton

WILLIAMS, Jonas & Mary __?_; b 1693; Hartford

WILLIAMS, Jonathan & 1/wf Mary HUNLOCK; 12 Jul 1697; Boston

WILLIAMS, Joseph (-1682) & Sarah BROWNING (-1719+); 20 Nov 1661; Salem

WILLIAMS, Joseph (ca 1642-1693, 1692?), Taunton & Elizabeth WATSON (1648-), m/2? Samuel PHILIPS 1716; 28 Nov 1667; Plymouth

WILLIAMS, Joseph & Lydia __?_; b 1669; Boston

WILLIAMS, Joseph (1643-1724) & Lydia OLNEY (1645-1724); 17 Dec 1669, 26 Nov 1669; Providence/Salem

WILLIAMS, Joseph (1647-1720, 1722+) & Mary FULLER (1644-1720); 18 Nov 1674; Haverhill/Norwich, CT

WILLIAMS, Joseph (1673-1752) & Lydia HEARDEN (-1763); ca 1697?; Providence

WILLIAMS, Joseph & Sarah LAYTON; 9 Dec 1698; Boston

WILLIAMS, Lewis (-1696?) & Christian [HARRIS], w Samuel, m/3 __?_ CARR by 1698, m/4 John WYETH; b 24 Sep 1681; ?Portsmouth, NH

WILLIAMS, Matthew (-1664) & 2/wf? Susannah [COLE?]; b 1645(6?); Wethersfield, CT

WILLIAMS, Matthew & Elizabeth [GILES]? (-1722+?); ?b 1658?; Salisbury

WILLIAMS, Matthew (1651-1732) & Ruth [WHEELER] (1657-1724); b 1686, ca 1675?; NJ?

WILLIAMS, Michael/Miles/Moyles, (-1644) & Anne [VALENTINE] (no), m/2 Henry PEARSALL; Hempstead, LI

WILLIAMS, Nathaniel (-1661) & Mary __?_, m/2 Peter BRACKETT; b 1638; Boston

WILLIAMS, Nathaniel (?1639, 1641-1692) & Elizabeth ROGERS (-1724); 17 Nov 1668; Taunton

WILLIAMS, Nathaniel (1642-1714?) & 1/wf? Lydia __?_; b 1670; Boston

WILLIAMS, Nathaniel & Sarah [COREY](?); ca 1670?; Southold, LI

WILLIAMS, Nathaniel (1642-1714?) & 2/wf? Mary (OLIVER) [SHRIMPTON], w Jonathan; b 1675; Boston/Cambridge

WILLIAMS, Nathaniel (-1711) & Mary OWEN; 30 Oct 1681, 3 Oct; Windsor, CT/Westfield, MA

WILLIAMS, Nathaniel (1675-1738) & Anne BRADSTREET; 21 Nov 1700; Cambridge/Boston

WILLIAMS, Park & Priscilla [PAYSON]; b 1699; Roxbury/Deerfield/Stonington, CT

WILLIAMS, Paul & Catherine LECORNAH; 1684

WILLIAMS, Paul & Joanna (CROCKER) [GASKIN]; aft 2 May 1690, b 1692(3?); Kittery, ME

WILLIAMS, Peleg (1678-) & Elizabeth [CARPENTER] (1676-); b 1701?; RI

WILLIAMS, Peter & Naomi CLARK; m int 12 Dec 1695; Boston

WILLIAMS, Richard (1606-1693) & Frances DIGHTON/DEIGHTON (1611-1700?); Witcomb Magna, Gloucester, Eng, 11 Feb 1632; Taunton

WILLIAMS, Richard & _?_ ; ca 1635/45?; ?Southold, LI/?Huntington, LI

WILLIAMS, Richard & _?_ (same as above?); b 1655; Branford, CT/Fairfield, CT/New London, CT

WILLIAMS, Richard & Bathsheba _?_ ; b 1672; Boston

WILLIAMS, Richard & _?_ ; b 1696?; New London, CT

WILLIAMS, Richard & Elizabeth _?_ ; b 1700; Salem

WILLIAMS, Robert (1608-1693) & 1/wf Elizabeth [STALHAM]/?STRATTON (1609-1674, ae 80?); b 1632, b 1630, 4 ch in 1637, in Eng; Roxbury

WILLIAMS, Robert (-1678) & _?_ ; b 1641; Boston

WILLIAMS, Robert (-1684) & Sarah [WASHBURN] (1625-1693, 1695); b 1660; Hempstead, LI

WILLIAMS, Robert & _?_ ; b 1671; Killingworth, CT

WILLIAMS, Robert & Margaret/Margery _?_ (1647-1727); b 1672; Boston

WILLIAMS, Robert (1608-1693), Roxbury & 2/wf Margaret FEARING (-1690), w John; 3 Nov 1675; Hingham/Roxbury

WILLIAMS, Roger (-1683) & Mary BARNARD (1609-1676+); High Laver, Essex, in Eng, 15 Dec 1629; Plymouth/Salem/Providence

WILLIAMS, Roger & 1/wf [Frances?] DIGHTON (-1645); Dorchester/Windsor, CT

WILLIAMS, Roger & 2/wf Lydia [BATES] (1615-); ca 1647-8, ca 1649?; Dorchester

WILLIAMS, Samuel (1633-1698) & Theoda PARK (1637-1718), m/2 Stephen PECK; 2 Mar 1653, 1653/4; Roxbury

WILLIAMS, Samuel (-1689) & Mary VEREN; 2 Apr 1662; Salem

WILLIAMS, Samuel (?1639, 1637-1697) & 1/wf Mary GILBERT, dau Thomas (Jane wrong); ca 1662; Taunton

WILLIAMS, Samuel & _?_ ; b 1674; Boston

WILLIAMS, Samuel & 1/wf Sarah MAY (1659-1712); 24 Feb 1679, 1679/[80]; Roxbury

WILLIAMS, Samuel (1639, ca 1637-1697) & 2/wf Anna (ROGERS/TISDALE) TERRY, w Thomas; aft 25 Jul 1686, bef 6 Aug 1697; Taunton

WILLIAMS, Samuel & Margaret RUST; 24 Oct 1694; Salem

WILLIAMS, Samuel & 1/wf Mary STEBBINS; 24 Jun 1697; Wethersfield, CT

WILLIAMS, Samuel & Mary _?_ ; b 1701; Roxbury

WILLIAMS, Stephen (1640-1720) & Sarah/Mary [WISE] (1647-1728); Apr 1666?, b 1667; Roxbury/Stonington, CT

WILLIAMS, Stephen & Bethiah CARTER (1672-); b 1697; Woburn/Charlestown

WILLIAMS, Stephen (1678-) & 1/wf Mary CAPEN; 18 Jun 1700; Dorchester

WILLIAMS, Thomas & _?_ (-1674+); Saco, ME?

WILLIAMS, Thomas (-1696) & Elizabeth TART/TATE?; 30 Nov 1638; ?Plymouth/Scituate?

WILLIAMS, Thomas (-1675+) & Ann [WANNERTON] (-1671+), w Thomas

WILLIAMS, Thomas & 1/wf Elizabeth [BLISS?] (1615-); b 1650, b 8 Jun 1649; Boston/Exeter, NH

WILLIAMS, Thomas (-1692) & [Rebecca] WATERHOUSE; b 1656(7?); Wethersfield, CT

WILLIAMS, Thomas & 2/wf Anne _?_ ; b 1661; Boston

WILLIAMS, Thomas (-1705) & Mary HOLDEN; 11 Aug 1666, 11 Jul; Groton/Charlestown

WILLIAMS, Thomas (1644-1705) & Joanna _?_ (-1744), m/2 Samuel ROGERS; b 1672; New London, CT

WILLIAMS, Thomas & _?_ ; b 1675; Flushing, LI

WILLIAMS, Thomas & 2/wf? Elizabeth _?_ (see Thomas & Anne above); b 1676; Boston

WILLIAMS, Thomas & Hannah _?_ ; 20 Oct 1678, 26 Oct 1678; Wethersfield, CT

WILLIAMS, Thomas & Mary [MACY] (-1719, ae 76), m/2 Rev. James KEITH; ca 1679; Taunton
WILLIAMS, Thomas & Ruth [BRADLEY]; ca 1681; Fairfield, CT
WILLIAMS, Capt. Thomas (-1703) & Martha (MEAD) [RICHARDSON] (-ca 1695, ca 1694), w John; aft 26 Jun 1683; Westchester, NY
WILLIAMS, Thomas & __?__; b 1686; Woburn
WILLIAMS, Thomas (-1723, ae 58) & Sarah FOSTER (1667-); 22 Sep 1686, 23 Sep 1686; Stow/Sudbury/Plainfield, CT
WILLIAMS, Thomas & Hannah [?DUNTON] (1650-); b 1690; Reading/Boston
WILLIAMS, Thomas (1667-) & Elizabeth [BLOOD] (?1673-); b 1692; Groton
WILLIAMS, Thomas & Susannah __?__; b 1694; Dorchester
WILLIAMS, Thomas & 1/wf Mary LOWELL; 15 Jan 1695/6; Newbury
WILLIAMS, Thomas & Experience HAYDEN? (1669, 1669?-); 24 Sep 1698, 28 Sep 1704; Killingworth, CT
WILLIAMS, Thomas (1672-1724) & 1/wf Mary BLACKMAN/BLACKMAR (-1717); ca 1700; Providence
WILLIAMS, Walter & Mary LEGROUE/LEGROS?; 13 Aug 1685; Marblehead
WILLIAMS, William (1597-) & Alice __?__ (1599-); b 1628; Salem/?Watertown
WILLIAMS, William & [Agnes] [NEWTON?]; Taunton, Eng, 4 Feb 1628?, b 1636, as early as 1635; Dover, NH
WILLIAMS, William (-1689) & Jane WESTAVHOR/WESTOVER (-1690); 25 Nov 1647, 20 Nov, 24 Nov; Hartford
WILLIAMS, William (-1676) & Joanna LINN, m/2 George ABBOTT of Norwalk, CT; 19 Jul 1660; Boston
WILLYAMS, William & Margaret [STEVENSON]; b 1662, as early as 1662; Salisbury
WILLIAMS, William (-1704) & Arabella [THOMPSON]; ca 1663/1675; New London, CT
WILLIAMS, William & Agnes [FIELD], w Darby; aft 1651, b 18 Jun 1674; Durham, NH
WILLIAMS, William & Jane HEARN; 9 Nov 1678; Gravesend, LI
WILLIAMS, William & 2/wf Mary [BEARD], w William; by 1680; Dover, NH/Kittery, ME
WILLIAMS, William & Martha TUFTS; - Jun 1681; Lynn
WILLIAMS, William & Sarah HURD; 21 Jan 1685; Charlestown/Boston
WILLIAMS, William (1665-1741, Hatfield) & 1/wf Elizabeth COTTON (1665-1698); 8 Jul 1686; Hadley/Deerfield
WILLIAMS, William (1662±-1702) & Elizabeth [LARKIN] (1671-); b 1692; Malborough/Charlestown
WILLIAMS, William (1662-) & Mary __?__; as early as 1696; Dover, NH
WILLIAMS, William & Joanna MOWER, wid; m int 31 Jul 1699; Lynn
WILLIAMS, William (1665-1741) & 2/wf Christian STODDARD (1676-); 9 Aug 1699; Hadley
WILLIAMS, Zebediah (1649-1675) & Mary MILLER (-1688), m/2 Godfrey NIMS 1677; 18 Dec 1672; Northampton/Deerfield
WILLIAMS, Zebadiah & Sarah ARMS, m/2 Samuel JONES, m/3 Thomas ALLEN; 2 May 1700; Deerfield/?Northampton
WILLIAMS, ?Robert & Martha [STORY] (-in 92nd y)
WILLIAMS, __?__ & Sarah [OLCOTT]; b 1 Dec 1703; ?Hartford, CT
WILLIAMS, __?__ & Elizabeth [JONES] (1664-), m/2 John MORGAN; b 1690
WILLIAMSON, Caleb (1662-1738, 1737) & Mary COB/COBB (1664-1737); 3 May 1687; Barnstable/Hartford
WILLIAMSON, George (1675-) & Mary CRISP (1681-); 5 Dec 1700; Eastham
WILLIAMSON, Gustavus & Phila __?__; b 1688; Providence
WILLIAMSON, Michael (1605) & Anne [PANCKHURST]; Ipswich/?Newport, RI
WILLIAMSON, Nathan (-1718) & Mary [SPRAGUE]; b 1693(4?); Marshfield
WILLIAMSON, Paul & __?__, m/2 Thomas LAMPSON 1650; ?ca 1635; Ipswich
WILLIAMSON, Timothy (-1676) & Mary HOWLAND (-1690), m/2 Robert STANFORD/SANFORD; 6 Jun 1653, - Jun 1653, ?6-6-1653; Marshfield
WILLIAMSON, William (1600-) & Mary __?__ (1602-); b 1635
WILLIAMSON, __?__ & [Ruhanah CLARK]; b 17 Nov 1700; Boston
WILLIS/WILETT, Andrew & Susanna HOLBROOK; 6 Mar 1693/4; Braintree/Boston
WILLIS, Benjamin (1657-1696) & Susanna [WHITMAN]; b 1690?; Bridgewater
WILLIS, Comfort & [?Mary BLAKE] (1655-); ?ca 1685, ca 19 Oct 1692; Bridgewater/Milton
WILLIS, Edward (-1698) & Ruth SYMMES (1635-); 15 Jun 1668; Charlestown/Boston

WILLIS, Elkanah (-1711) & Mercy [**HILL**] (1643-1709); b [1678]; Bridgewater

WILLIS, Experience (1646-1709) & Elizabeth _?_; b 1670; Boston

WILLIS, Experience & 2/wf? Elizabeth **BOTTON**?/**BOLTON** (-1720), m/2 _?_ **SIMON**?/**LEMON**; 25 Oct 1676; Dorchester/Boston

WYLLYS, George[1] (?1590-1644/5) & 1/wf Bridget **YOUNG** (-11 Mar 1629); Stratford-on-Avon, 2 Nov 1609; Hartford

WYLLYS, George[1] (1689/90-1644/5) & 2/wf Mary (**SMITH**) **BYSBIE** (-1669+), w Alexander; in Eng, aft 11 Mar 1629, b 1631(2?); Hartford/Stow

WILLIS/WILLOWES/etc., George (-1690) & 1/wf _?_; in Eng, b 1630?; Cambridge

WILLIS, George (1602-) & 2/wf? Jane [**PALFREY**], wid; b 1637?; Cambridge

WILLIS, George (1602-) & 3/wf? Sarah _?_

WILLIS, Henry & Elizabeth [**OTIS**]; 1642; ?Bridgewater

WILLIS, Henry & Mary [**HUTCHINSON**?]; b 1653; Boston/?Windsor, CT

WILLIS, Henry (1628-1714) & Mary [**PEACE**] (1632-1714); in Eng, b 1654; Oyster Bay, LI/Hempstead, LI/Huntington, LI/?Westbury

WILLIS, Hope & Mary _?_; b 1677; Hempstead, LI

WILLIS, John (-21 Nov 1634) & Jane _?_; b 1632; Boston

WILLIS, John & 1/wf Hannah _?_ (doubtful); b _?_; Duxbury/Bridgewater

WILLIS, John & 2/wf? Elizabeth (**HODGKINS**) [**PALMER**], w William; b 12 Jan 1637/8; ?Plymouth/?Duxbury

WILLIS, John (?1630-) & Hannah **ELSSE/ELSE**; 11 Jan 1654/5; Boston

WILLIS, John (-1712) & Experience [**BYRAM**] (-ca 1712); b 1671/2, [1654?]; Bridgewater

WYLLS, John & Ann _?_; b 1688(9?); Boston

WILLIS/WILLOWES, John & Hester/Esther [**GARDNER**]; b 1694; Medford/Charlestown

WILLIS, John (1671/2-) & Mary [**BRETT**] (1678/9-); b 1699; Bridgewater

WILLIS, Joseph (?1645-1705, Taunton) & Sarah [**LINCOLN**] (1645-); b 1683, b 1675?; Bridgewater

WILLIS, Joseph (-1734?) & Mary (**BLAKE**) [**LEONARD**] (1655-1721+), w Joseph; b 20 Dec 1699, 1692/96; Tanton

WILLES, Joshua (-1722) & Abigail _?_; b 1690, by 1687?; Windsor, CT

WILLIS, Josiah & Hannah [**MUNNINGS**] (1657-); 8 Oct 1675; Boston/England

WILLIS, Lawrence & _?_; b 1648; Sandwich

WILLIS, Lawrence & Mary **MAKEPEACE**; 5 Sep 1656; Boston

WILLIS, Michael (-1669) & 1/wf Joan _?_; b 1639, b 1633?; Dorchester/Boston

WILLIS, Michael (-1669) & 2/wf Mildred _?_, wid?; b 1648?, b 1652; Boston

WILLIS, Nathaniel (1652-1712) & Elizabeth [**LOWDEN**] (1656-); b 1680; Charlestown/Boston/London

WILLIS, Nathaniel (-1686) & [?Bridget **HUTCHINSON**]; b 1639; Sandwich/Bridgewater

WILLIS, Nathaniel (-1716) & Lydia _?_ (-1716+); b 1680; Bridgewater

WILLIS, Nathaniel & Ruth [**PORTER**] (-1676); b 1701?, b 1708; Bridgewater

WILLIS, Nicholas[1] (-1650) & Ann _?_; b 1634; Boston

WILLIS, Richard & Amy **GLASSE**, m/2 Edward **HOLMAN** b 1645; 11 Oct 1639; ?Duxbury/?Plymouth

WILLIS, Richard & Patience **BONUM/BONHAM**, m/2 _?_ **HOLMES**; 28 Dec 1670; Plymouth

WILLIS, Robert & Sarah _?_; b 1643; Boston

WILLES, Robert & Eunice **STIELS/STILES**; 15 Dec 1688[9?], prob 1692, b 13 Dec 16[93?], [had Sarah], bpt 30 Apr 1696; Boxford

WILLIS, Roger & Ruth **HILL** (-1736); 19 Jul 1664; Dorchester/Sudbury

WILLYS, Samuel (?1634-1709) & Ruth [**HAYNES**] (1639?-1680+, 1680/1688); ca 1655?; Cambridge/Hartford

WILLIS/WELLS, Samuel & _?_; b 1676; Scituate

WILLIS/WYLLYS, Samuel (?1631-1709), Hartford & Mrs. Mary (**TAYLOR**) **LOVE**, Berwick, ME, w William; 28 Nov 1688, 28 Dec 1688; York Co., ME/?Berwick

WILLIS, Samuel & Experience **NEWELL**; 23 May 1700; Roxbury

WILLIS/WILLOWES?, Stephen (1644-1718) & Hannah **ELLIOT** (1651-1732); 3 Aug 1670; Braintree/Charlestown

WILLIS/WILLOWES?, Stephen (-1718) & Susanna **WADE** (1677-); 18 Dec 1698; Medford

WILLIS, Thomas & _?_; in Eng, ca 1610/30?; Lynn/Sandwich

WILLIS/WILLOWES, Thomas (1638-1724) & Grace [TAY] (1645-[1715, ae 70 y 8 m]), sister of Dea. John WHITMORE's wf; b 1664, - Jan 1662; Billerica/Charlestown/Medford
WILLIS, Thomas & Ruth [NOYES]; b 1685; Taunton
WILLIS/WILLS?, William (-1688, ae 90) & Lucy _?_; Sep 1638; Scituate
WILLIS, William (1663-1736) & Mary TITUS (1665-1747); 10 Aug 1687; Westbury, LI
WILLIS, _?_ & Mary _?_, m/2 John MANN; Boston?
WILLASTON, Ichabod (1677-) & Dorothy GARDNER; 28 Mar 1700; Boston
WILLISTON, John & Abigail SALSBURY; 9 Jun 1676; Milton
WILLISTON, Joseph (?1667-1747) & 1/wf Mary (PARSONS) ASHLEY (1661-), w Joseph; 2 Mar 1698/9; Windsor, CT
WILLIX, Belshazzar (1595-1655) & 1/wf Hannah/Anna _?_ (-1648); b 1636; Salisbury/Exeter, NH
WILLIX, Belshazzar (1595-1655) & 2/wf Mary HAUXWORTH; aft 1648; Salisbury
WILLOUGHBY, Francis (?1613-1671) & 1/wf Mary _?_ (-1640); in Eng, b 1639, b 1635; Charlestown
WILLOUGHBY, Francis (?1613-1671) & 2/wf Sarah [TAYLOR] (-1654); 1640?, in Eng; Charlestown
WILLOUGHBY, Francis (?1613-1671) & 3/wf Margaret (LOCKE) TAYLOR, w Daniel, m Lawrence HAMMOND 1675; ca 1658-9, in Eng; Charlestown
WILLOUGHBY, Jonathan (ca 1635-) & Griszel GOLDESBOROUGH; in Eng, - Dec 1661, lic 3 Dec 1661; Charlestown/Wethersfield, CT
WILLOUGHBY, Nehemiah (1644-1702) & Abigail BARTHOLOMEW (1650-1702); 2 Jan 1671/2, 2 Jan 1671; Charlestown/Salem
WILLOUGHBY, William (1588-1651, in Eng) & Elizabeth _?_ (-1662, Charlestown); in Eng, b 1613; Charlestown
WILLOUGHBY, William & Abigail _?_; Greenland, NH
WILLS, Edward & Deborah [SAVAGE]; b 1697; Portsmouth, NH
WILLS, Samuel (1640-) & Rebecca [PIERCE] (-1724); b 1676, b 1673; Scituate/Marshfield
WILLS, Thomas & Sarah [ABBOTT] (?1641-bef 1709); b 1667, by 1662; Kittery
WILLS, Thomas & 2/wf Lucia (TREWORGY) [CHADBOURNE], m/3 Elias STILEMAN; aft 13 Sep 1667, ca 1 Apr 1669; Kittery
WILLS, William (-1688) & Lucy _?_ (-1697); Sep 1638, 4 or 5 Sep; Scituate
WILLS, William & _?_; b 1670; Isles of Shoals
WILMOTH/WILMARTH, John (-1719) & Ruth KENDRICK (-1706); 6 Feb 1671; Rehoboth
WILLMOUTH, Jonathan & Esther PECKE (1658-); 29 Dec 1680; Rehoboth
WILLMARTH, Thomas[1] (-1694) & 1/wf Elizabeth [BLISS] (1615-Feb 1676), sister of Jonathan; b 1647; Braintree/Rehoboth
WILMOUTH, Thomas[2] (-1690) & Mary ROBINSON; 7 Jun 1674; Rehoboth
WILMOTH, Thomas[1], Sr. (-1694) & 2/wf Rachel (_?_) READ (-1710), w John; 27 Jun 1678; Rehoboth
WILMOT, Alexander (1672-1721) & 1/wf Sarah [BROWN] (-1697?); b 1696; New Haven/Southampton, LI/Southold?
WILMOT, Alexander (1672-1721) & 2/wf Mary [NORRIS], m/2 James LANDON; b 1701?; Southampton, LI
WILMOT, Benjamin (?1589-1669) & Ann _?_ (-1668); in Eng, b 1620; New Haven
WILMOT, Benjamin (-1651) & Elizabeth [HEATON] (-1685), wid, m/3 William JUDSON 1660; ca 1644; New Haven
WILMOT, John (-1670) & Sarah [RUGGLES] (1645-), m/2 John SMITH; ?Boston
WILMOT, John (1668-ca 1731) & Sarah [CLARK] (1671-), m/2 Daniel SPERRY; b 1695; New Haven
WILMOT, Nicholas & [Mary] _?_ ca 1650?; Boston/Charlestown
WILMOT, William (-1689) & Sarah THOMAS (-1711); 14 Oct 1658; New Haven
WILLMOT, William (1665-1714) & Mary CHIDSEY; 20 Oct 1692; New Haven
WILSON, Andrew & Bethia _?_ (1656-1702); b 1689; Boston/Roxbury
WILSON, Andrew (1670-1722) & Hannah [WILLIAMS]; b 1696; Cambridge
WILSON, Anthony (-1662) & 1/wf Rachel (HUBBARD) [BRUNDISH] (-?1648), w John; 5 Aug 1642 agreement; Fairfield, CT
WILSON, Anthony (-1662) & Elizabeth [HILL] (-?1658); by 1650; Fairfield, CT

WILSON, Anthony (-1662) & Sarah (JONES) [BULKELEY] (1620-1683), w Thomas; ca 1659; Fairfield, CT

WILSON, Benjamin (-1667) & Ann/Anna _?_ (1634-1692), m/2 George CANNOWAY 1671; b 1655; Charlestown

WILSON, Benjamin (1656-1694) & Sarah [SEAVER] (-1689), w Nathaniel; ca 1677; Newton/ Roxbury

WILSON, Benjamin (1670-) & Elizabeth _?_/?COOKE/?FULLER; b 1694; Woburn/Rehoboth

WILSON, Benjamin & Jane [OLMSTED]; b 1698; Norwalk, CT

WILSON, Edward (-1684) & _?_ ; b 1661, b 1656?; Salem

WILSON, Edward (-1706) & 1/wf Mary HALE (1639-1696); 6 Nov 1656; Charlestown

WILSON, Edward (-1706) & 2/wf Rebecca (EDINGTON) LORD, w Samuel; 5 Nov 1696; Charlestown

WILSON, Ephraim & Rebecca SUMNER; 10 May 1681; Dedham

WILSON, Francis (1660-1724) & Ruth DUNTLIN; 6 Mar 1683; Woburn/Warren, RI

WILSON, Gowen (1618-1686) & _?_ ; b 1647; Exeter, NH/Kittery, ME

WILSON, Henry (-1686) & Mary METCALF (1618, 1619-1686+); 24 Nov 1642; Dedham

WILSON, Humphrey (-1698) & Judith HERSEY (-1716); 21 Dec 1663; Hingham/Exeter, NH

WILSON, Isaac (1658-1709) & Susanna ANDREWS (-1740); 9 Jul 1685; Cambridge/Newton

WILSON, Jacob & _?_ (-1663?); b 1641; Braintree

WILSON, Jacob & Susanna [?ROSS]; 20 May 1696; Malden

WILSON, James & 1/wf Deborah PIERCE (1666-1703); 19 Jan 1687, 1686/7; Woburn/Lexington

WILSON, James (-1706) & Alice [SABEERE] (-1706); Kings Town, RI

WILSON, Jeremiah, Lancaster & Hannah BEMAN, Lancaster; 27 Dec 1687; Lancaster

WILSON, Jeremiah (-1740) & 1/wf Ann MANOXEN/MAINWARING (1682-); 8 Dec 1700; New Shoreham/Block Isl., RI

WILSON, Rev. John (1592-1677) & Elizabeth [MANSFIELD]; b 1618, in Eng; Charlestown/Boston

WILSON, John & _?_ ; ?ca 1645; Fairfield, CT

WILSON, Rev. John (1621-1691) & Sarah [HOOKER] (1630-); ca 1648; Medfield/Cambridge

WILSON, John (-1687) & Hannah [JAMES] (ae 58 in 1687), m/2 Thomas FULLER; ca 1650, in Eng; Woburn

WILSON, John (-1735, Bedford) & 1/wf Joanna [CARTER]; b 1673; Woburn/Billerica/Bedford, MA

WILSON, John & Hester (CHANDLER) [GAGE], w Jonathan; ca 1675; Elizabeth, NJ

WILSON, John (1650-1698) & Lydia [COLE], m/2 Caleb STANLEY 1699; ca 1675/8?; Hartford

WILSON, John (1660-) & Sarah NEWTON (1662-); 4 Jul 1683; New Haven/Braintree/Marshfield

WILSON, John & Esther _?_ ; b 1689; Bristol, RI

WILSON, John & Mary [LYON]; b 1691; Bedford, NY/Rye, NY

WILSON, John (1664-) & Abigail [?OSGOOD]; b 1691; Charlestown/Boston

WILSON, John & Elizabeth FOSTER (1673-); 27 Nov 1694; Billerica

WILSON, John & Martha [HARVEY], m/2 George VEASEY; aft 1695

WILSON, John (-1735, Bedford) & 2/wf Susannah (GOODENOUGH) (REDIAT) MILES, w John, w John; 10 Nov 1698; Billerica/Concord

WILSON, Joseph & Dorcas RANDALL; 2 May 1670; Lynn

WILSON, Joseph & Mary LOVEJOY; 4 Jul 1670; Andover

WILSON, Joseph (-1705, ae 58) & _?_ ; b 1673; Malden

WILSON, Joseph & Sarah LORD; 24 Apr 1678; Andover

WILSON, Joseph & Hannah ENDLE; b 1683; Kittery, ME

WILSON, Joseph (1655/6-1725) & Deliverance [JACKSON] (1657-1718); b 1683?, b 1685, ca 1684; Roxbury/Newton

WILSON, Joseph & Marah/Mary RICHARDSON (1660?-); 25 Jan 1699/1700; Andover

WILSON, Michael & Mary HAMMON/HAMANT; 4 Nov 1674; Medfield

WILSON, Nathaniel[1] (1621-1692) & Hannah CRAFTS (?1628-1692); 2 Apr 1645; Roxbury/Newton

WILSON, Nathaniel & _?_ ; b 1649; Hingham (same as above)

WILSON, Nathaniel[2] (1653-1721) & 1/wf Hannah [JACKSON] (1661-); b 1680, b 1681; Newton

WILSON, Nathaniel (-1733) & Thankful BEAMONT/BEAMAN/BEAUMONT (1663-1732); 27 Sep 1683; Charlestown

WILSON, Nathaniel & Elizabeth [HENDRICK]/[HENDRICKSON]; ca 1691, b 1685, b 1687; Fairfield, CT

WILSON, Nathaniel[2] (1653-1721) & 2/wf Elizabeth OSLAND; 11 Mar 1692/3; Newton/Framingham

WILSON, Nathaniel & Susanna JONES (1675-); Apr 1700; New Haven/Hartford

WILSON, Paul (?1632-1714, in 82nd y) & Mary __?__ (-1716, ae 60); b 1671(2?); Charlestown

WILSON, Phineas (-1691) & 1/wf Mary [SANFORD]; b 1688?, b 14 Oct 1687, b 1670?; Hartford

WILSON, Phineas (-1691) & 2/wf Elizabeth (CROW) [WARREN?] (1650?-), wid (see John HAYWARD); Hartford

WILSON, Richard (-1654) & 2/wf? Sarah HARST, m/2 John BENHAM 1655; 7 Apr 1654; Boston/New Haven

WILSON, Robert (-1655, 1656?) & Elizabeth [STEBBINS], m/2 Thomas CADWELL 1658?; b 1650; Windsor, CT/Farmington, CT

WILSON, Robert (-1675) & Deborah BUFFAM; 12 Aug 1658; Salem

WILSON, Robert (-1685?) & Deborah [STEVENSON]/STIMSON (1637?-), m/2 Matthew ABDY 1688; b 1666; Cambridge/Sudbury

WILSON, Robert (-1681) & Anna/Ann [TRASK] (1654-), m/2 Joseph FOSTER 1683; b 1681; Salem

WILSON, Robert (1663-1716/17) & Elizabeth [COOKE]; ca 1685; Salem

WILSON, Samuel (1622-1682) & 1/wf [?Mary] TEFFT (-1674+)?; b 1661?; Portsmouth, RI/Kingston, RI

WILSON, Samuel (1622-1682) & 2/wf Elizabeth [SWEET] (1629-1684), w John; aft 1677; Portsmouth, RI/Kingston, RI

WILSON, Samuel (see Thomas WILSON) & Jane __?__ ; b 1654; Boston/Rowley

WILSON, Samuel (-1697) & Mary GRIFFIN (1651-1728), m/2 Anthony HOSKINS; 1 May 1672; Windsor, CT

WILSON, Samuel & Phebe MIDDLEBROOK; m cont 1679, b 2 Jun 1679?, ca 12 Jun 1679; Fairfield, CT (He is called bro-in-law by Robert TURNEY 1689)

WILSON, Samuel (1658-1729) (son John) & Elizabeth PIERCE (1658-); 24 Feb 1682, 1681/2, 1681; Woburn

WILSON, Samuel & Sarah BAXTER (1665-1689); 10 Sep 1685; Charlestown

WILSON, Samuel (1666-) & Experience [TROWBRIDGE] (1675-1705); b 1697; Newton/Cambridge

WILSON, Samuel & Rebecca [CARPENTER]; b 1701?; Pawtuxet, RI?/Norton, MA

WILSON, Shoreborn & Abigail OSGOOD; 9 Sep 1657, 9? Apr; Ipswich/Salisbury

WILSON, Theophilus (1601-1689) & Elizabeth [KNOWLTON?]/KENNING? (-1688, 1681?), sister of Mrs. Jane KENNING; b 1637, b 1634; Lexington

WILSON, Thomas (-1643) & 2/wf Ann __?__, m/2 John LEGGETT; in Eng, ca 1627; Roxbury/Boston/Hampton, NH

WILSON, Thomas (1634-1703) & Jane [SWAN] (-1709+); b 1657; Ipswich

WILSON, Thomas (-1691) & Hannah __?__ (-1694); b 1673; Milford, CT (Did he move to Fairfield, CT?)

WILSON, William & Patience __?__ ; b 1635; Boston

WILSON, William & Priscilla PURCHASE; 26 Oct 1663; Lynn

WILSON, William (?1660-1732) & Remember WARD (-1684); 1 May 1679; Charlestown

WILSON, William (?1660-1732) & 2/wf Mary PEARCE/PIERCE (1661-); 1 Oct 1685, b 1681?; Charlestown/Boston

WILSON, William (1664-1745) & 1/wf Sarah BLOOD (-1717); 1 Jul 1686; Concord/CT

WILSON, William & Sarah SIMPKINS/[SIMKINS]; Musketa Cove, LI

WILSON, William, Ipswich & Elizabeth ANDREWS, Boxford; 19 Apr 1693; Topsfield

WILSON, William & Elizabeth __?__ ; b 1694; Hampton, NH

WILSON, William & Mehitable ELIOT (1676-1723); b 1701?, at Saybrook, CT, 1703; Guilford, CT/Killingworth, CT

WILSON, __?__ & Anne THORNE, w John; aft 1683; Cambridge

WILSON, __?__ & Ann __?__, m/1 Anthony WHITING, Dedham, Eng, m/2 Thomas WILSON; (see John BARNARD)

WILTON, David (-1678) & Catherine [?TYLER]/HOSKINS?, m/2 Thomas HOSMER 1679; b 1636; Dorchester/Windham, CT/Northampton

WILTON, Edward & Elizabeth __?__ ; b 1690; Boston

WILTON, Nicholas (-1683) & Mary STANIFORD/STANFORD (-1683); 20 Nov 1656; Windsor, CT

WILTSHIRE, Thomas & Sarah [ABERNATHY] (1677-); b 1701?; Wallingford, CT

WINBOURNE, John Rossiter? & Elizabeth HART; 11 Apr 1667; Malden
WINBORNE, William & Elizabeth _?_; b 1638; Boston
WINCH, Samuel & Hannah GIBS/GIBBS (?1654-); 11 Feb 1672; Sudbury
WINCH, Samuel & Susannah PARKER; 30 Sep 1698
WINCH, Samuel (-1718) & Sarah (?WENTWORTH)? BARNARD, w Benjamin, ?m/2 Joshua
    PARMENTER; 11 Jan 1698/9, 17 Jan; Watertown/Framingham
WINCHCOMB, John & Mary [HARRIS]; b 1676; Boston/Bridgewater
WINCHELL, Benjamin (1674-) & Sarah (MOORE) WINCHELL (1672-), w Thomas; 18 Jul 1700;
    Suffield, CT
WINCHELL, David (1643-1723) & 1/wf Elizabeth FILLEY (1650-1728?); 17 Nov 1669; Windsor,
    CT
WINCHELL, David (1643-1723) & 2/wf Mary GRIFFIN; 1 May 1672; Windsor, CT
WINCHELL, Jonathan (-1714) & 1/wf Abigail BRUNSON/BRONSON (-1710); 16 May 1666, at
    Farmington; Windsor, CT/Suffield, CT
WINCHELL, Joseph (1670-) & Sarah TAYLOR; 2 Jan 1700, prob 1700/01; Suffield, CT
WINCHELL, Nathaniel (-1699/1700) & Sarah PORTER (1646-1725), Farmington; 8 Apr 1664;
    Windsor, CT
WINCHELL, Nathaniel (1665-), Windsor & ?Mary/?Mercy GRAVES, Hartford; 15 Mar 1693/4;
    Windsor, CT
WINCHELL, Robert (-1667) & _?_ (-1655); ca 1631?; Dorchester/Windsor, CT
WINCHELL, Stephen (1677-1726, Simsbury) & Abigail (PHELPS) MARSHALL? (1676-), w David
    MARSHALL; 10 Mar 1697/8; Windsor, CT
WINCHELL, Thomas (1669-1697) & Sarah MOORE, m/2 Benjamin WINCHELL 1700; 26 Apr 1690;
    Windsor, CT
WINCHESTER, Alexander (-1647) & _?_ ; b 1637; Boston/Braintree/Rehoboth
WINCHESTER, John (?1611, 1616-1694), Hingham & Hannah SILLIS/SEALIS (1615-1697),
    Scituate; 15 Oct 1638; Scituate/Boston
WINCHESTER, John (?1644, 1642-1718) & Joanna [STEVENS] (1652-1718+); b 1674; Roxbury/
    Boston
WINCHESTER, John (1676-1751) & 1/wf Sarah [WHITE] (1680-1716); b 1701; Roxbury
WINCHESTER, Jonathan (-1679) & Mary _?_, m/2 John ALDIS 1682; b 1677; Roxbury
WINCHESTER, Josiah (1655-1728) & Mary [LYON]? (1650-1730); 1678?, ?10 Dec 1678,
    ?evidence; Roxbury/Brookline
WINCHESTER, Robert & Elizabeth _?_, m/2 John CARD 1684; York Shoals
WINCOLL, John (-1694) (called Thomas BROUGHTON "brother-in-law" in 1671) & 1/wf
    Elizabeth _?_ (-1673); no issue; Watertown/Piscataqua, ME/Kittery, ME
WINCOLL, John (-1694) & 2/wf Mary ETHERINGTON (-1679?); m cont 29 Feb 1675/6; Kittery,
    ME
WINCOLL, John (-1694) & 3/wf Olive (COLMAN) [PLAISTED], w Roger; b 16 Sep 1682
WINCOLL, John (-by 1713) & Deborah [MORSE] (1679-), m/2 _?_ DENNETT 1716; b 5 Apr
    1699; Portsmouth, NH
WINCOLL, Thomas[1] (-1657, ca 70) & Beatrix _?_ (-1655, ca 80); in Eng, b 1615; Watertown
WINCOLL, _?_ & Elizabeth _?_ (ae 52 in 1635); came in 1635 with son John, aged 16
WINDOW, Richard & 1/wf _?_ (-bef 20 Feb 1648/9, in Eng); Gloucester
WINDOW, Richard & 2/wf Ellen/Eleanor [BENNETT] (-1658), wid; b 1654; Gloucester
WINDOE, Richard (-1665) & 3/wf Bridget (FITTS) (GOODWIN) TRAVIS (-1673), w Henry; 30
    Mar 1659; Gloucester/Salem
WINSOR, John (-1667) & Mary NEIBOURS, m/2 Daniel MATTHEWS 1668?; 21 Sep 1665, 22 Sep;
    Charlestown
WINSOR, Joshua (-1679) & _?_ (-1655); b 1644; Providence
WINSOR, Joshua (1648-1717) & Sarah _?_; b 1672; Boston
WINDSORE, Robert & Rebecca _?_; b 1645; Boston
WINSOR, Samuel (1644-1705) & Mercy (WILLIAMS) WATERMAN, w Resolved, m/3 John
    RHOADES?; 2 Jan 1677, 1676/7; Providence
WINSOR, Thomas (1659-) & Rachel [BUCKLAND]; b 1692; Boston
WINES, Barnabas & Ann [EDDY] (1603-); b 1646, b 1630?; Watertown
WINES, Barnabes[2] (1636-1711?) & Mary _?_ (-1727, ae 89); Southold, LI
WINES, Barnabas (1675-1762) & 1/wf Anna _?_ (-1707); b 1701?; Southold, LI
WINES, Faintnot (-1664/5) & Bridget _?_; b 1645; Charlestown

WINES, Samuel & Mary [MAPES]; b 23 Aug 1686, b 1671; Southold, LI

WING, Ananias (-1718) & Hannah [?FREEMAN]? (-1730); 1687; Harwich

WING, Bachelor (1671-1740) & Joanna [HATCH] (-1761); b 1694; Sandwich/Scituate/Hanover

WING, Daniel (-1659) & ?1/wf Hannah [SWIFT] (-1664); b 1642?, ?5 Nov 1641, ?5 Nov 1642; Sandwich

WING, Daniel (-1698) & ?2/wf Anna EWER, ?w Thomas; ?2 Jun 1666, ?2 Sep 1666, 2 Aug, 6 m. 2 1666

WING, Daniel (1664-1740) & Deborah [DILLINGHAM] (1660-); 1686; Sandwich

WING, Ebenezer (1671-1738) & Elizabeth BACKHOUSE/BACKUS (-1758); 23 Feb 1698/9; Sandwich

WING, Elisha & Mehitable BUTLER; 1 Mar 1689; Rochester

WING, John (d in Eng) & Deborah [BACHELOR]/[BATCHELDOR] (1592-); ca 1610; Sandwich

WING, John (?1613-1699) & 1/wf Elizabeth [?DILLINGHAM] (-1692); b 1647; Yarmouth

WING, John (1637-1703) & Joshabeth [DAVIS] (1642-); b 1660; Boston

WING, John (-1683) (see Samuel WING) & Mary ?DILLINGHAM; b 1680; Sandwich?

WING, John (1656-1717) & Martha [SPOONER] (-1717+); b 1684; Rochester

WING, John (1661-) & 1/wf Mary PERRY ((166-)-1714); ?22 Sep 1685; Sandwich

WING, John (-1699) & 2/wf Miriam [DEAN] (-1703, 1702?); ca 1693; Sandwich/Harwich

WING, Joseph & Joanna _?_ ; b 1673(4?); Boston

WING, Joseph (-1679) & Jerusha [MAYHUE], m/2 Thomas EATON 1684; 12 Apr 1682, 1676?; Yarmouth

WING, Matthew (1674, 1673/4-1724) & Elizabeth (MOTT) RICKKETSON (?1659-), w William; 4 Sep 1696; Dartmouth

WING, Nathaniel (?1647-1730+, 1738+) & Sarah [HATCH] (1664-1731); b 1688; Falmouth

WING, Nathaniel & Hannah [TILTON] (1663-1718+) (doubtful); Martha's Vineyard

WING, Robert (1584-1651) & 1/wf Judith _?_ ; b 1634; Boston

WING, Robert (-1651) & 2/wf Joanna _?_ (-1651+); b 1637; Boston/?Watertown

WING, Samuel (1652-1701) (see John WING) & Mary [DILLINGHAM]? (1653-); b 1676; Sandwich?

WING, Stephen (?1621-1710) & 1/wf Oseth/Oziah [DILLINGHAM] (1622-1654); ca 1646; Sandwich

WING, Stephen (?1621-1710) & 2/wf Sarah BRIDGGS/BRIGGS (-1689); 7 Jan 1654/5; Sandwich

WING, _?_ & Mary KING (1676/7-), m/2 John LANGLEY, m/3 William LEA/LEE; b 1699; ?Boston

WINGATE, John (-1687) & 1/wf Mary [NUTTER] (-1674+); b 1668; Dover, NH

WINGATE, John (-1687) & 2/wf Sarah (TAYLOR) [CANNEY], w Thomas, m/3 Richard PAINE; aft 1678?, b May 1677?, nr 1676; Dover, NH

WINGATE, John (1670-1715) & Ann [HODSHON], m/2 John HEARD; nr 1691, by 1691; Dover, NH

WINKLEY, Samuel & Sarah [TRICKEY]; b 1687; Portsmouth, NH

WINN, Edward[1] (-1682) & 1/wf Joanna _?_ (-1649); b 1629?; Woburn

WINN, Edward[1] (-1682) & 2/wf Sarah BEAL (-1680); 10 Aug 1649; Woburn

WINN, Edward[1] (-1682) & 3/wf Anna/Hannah PAGE [WOOD], w Nicholas; ca 1681; Watertown

WINN, Edward (1668-) & Mary STRATTON; 3 Jan 1697/8, 3 Jan 1698; Watertown/Woburn

WINN, Increase (1641-1690) & Hannah SATALL/SAWTELLE (1642-1723); 13 Jul 1665; Woburn

WINN, Joseph (-1715) & Rebecca [READ] (1647-); b 1665; Woburn/Cambridge

WINN, Joseph (1671-) & Martha BLODGETT (1673-); 7 Apr 1696; Woburn

WINSHIP, Edward (1613-1688) & 1/wf Jane [?WILKINSON] (-1648/1651); b 1638; Cambridge

WINSHIP, Edward (1613-1688) & 2/wf Elizabeth [PARKE]/WHITTEMORE? (1631-1690); b 1652; Cambridge

WINSHIP, Edward (1654-1718) & Rebecca BARSHAM (1657-1717); 14 May 1683; Cambridge/Lexington

WINSHIP, Ephraim (1643-) & 1/wf Hannah REYNER (-1674); 7 Apr 1670, no issue; Cambridge/Lexington

WINSHIP, Ephraim (1643-) & 2/wf Elizabeth KENDALL (1655-), m/2 Joseph PIERCE 1698; 9 Nov 1675 no issue; Cambridge/Lexington

WINSHIP, Joseph (1661-1725) & Sarah HARRINGTON (1671-1710); 24 Nov 1687; Watertown/Cambridge

WINSHIP, Samuel (1658-1696) & Mary POWTER/POULTER, m/2 Isaac POWERS 1701; 12 Apr 1687; Cambridge/Lexington/Medford

WINSLADE/WINSLAD/WINSLEAD/?WINSTEAD, Jacob & Elizabeth WHITTEMORE (1669-); 16 May 1690, 26 May; Malden/Charlestown

WINSLOW/?WINSLADE, John & Sarah MOULTON; 5 May 1652; Malden

WINSLEY, Ephraim (1641-1709) & Mary GRELE/GREELEY (-1697); 26 Mar 1668; Salisbury

WINSLEY, John & Elizabeth [PADDY] (1641-1711); b 1664; Boston

WINSLEY, Nathaniel & Mary JONES; 14 Oct 1661; Salisbury/Block Island

WINSLEY, Samuel[1] (-1663) & 1/wf Elizabeth _?_ (-1649); b 1634; Salisbury

WINSLEY, Samuel[1] (-1663) & Ann BOAD/BOYD?/BODE, Wells, ME, w Henry; m cont 5 Oct 1657; Salem

WINSLEY, Samuel & Catharine STEVENS; 29 Apr 1696; Salisbury

WINSLEY, _?_ & Esther/Ellen JENNER, w Thomas, a widow in 1686; Boston

WINSLOW, Edward (1595-1655) & 1/wf Elizabeth BARKER (-1621); Leyden, Holland, aft 12 May 1618; Leyden/Plymouth

WINSLOW, Edward (1595-1655) & Susanna (FULLER) WHITE, w William; 12 May 1621; Plymouth/Marshfield

WINSLOW, Edward (1634-1681/2) & 1/wf Sarah [HILTON] (1641-1667); b 1661; Boston

WINSLOW, Edward (1634-1681/2) & 2/wf Elizabeth HUTCHINSON, m/2 _?_ ; 8 Feb 1668; [Boston]

WINSLOW, Edward (1669-1753) & Hannah [MOODY] (-1711); b 1693, ?30 Jun 1692, ?ca 1691; Boston

WINSLOW, Edward & Sarah [?CLARK] (-1767, in 85th y); b 1701?, b 1703; Rochester

WINSLOW, Gilbert (1673-1731) & Mercy SNOW; 7 Feb 1698; Marshfield

WINSLOW, Isaac (1644-1670) & Mary NOWELL, m/2 John LONG 1674; 14 Aug 1666; Charlestown

WINSLOW, Col. Isaac (1670-1738) & Sarah WENSLEY (-1753, ae 80); 11 Jul 1700; Marshfield/Boston

WINSLOW, James (1669-) & 1/wf Mary [?SNOW] (-4 Dec 1717, ae 43); b 1699; Plymouth/Rochester

WINSLOW, Job (1641-1720, Freetown) & Ruth [?COLE]/[?HOPKINS] (1653-); b 1674; Swansea/Freetown

WINSLOW, John (1597-1674) & Mary CHILTON; betw Jul 1623 & 1 Jun 1627, ?12 Oct 1624; Plymouth

WINSLOW/WINSLEAD, John & Sarah MOULTON; 5 May 1652; Malden

WINSLOW, John (?1633-1683) & 1/wf Elizabeth _?_ ; b 1669; Boston

WINSLOW, John (-1683) & 2/wf Judith _?_/[?SMITH very doubtful] (-1714, ae ca 90); Boston

WINSLOW, John (1669-1695) & Abigail ATKINSON, m/2 James OBORNE/OSBORN 1702, m/3 Samuel PINHALLOW 1714; 18 Jun 1689; Boston

WINSLOW, Jonathan (1638-1676) & Ruth [SARGENT] (-1713), m/2 Richard BOURNE 1677, m/3 Samuel PINHALLOW 1714; ca 1663; Marshfield

WINSLOW, Joseph (-1679) & Sarah [LAWRENCE], m/2 Charles LeBROS; b 1672(?); Boston/LI

WINSLOW, Joseph & Martha ROBISON/[ROBINSON], m/2 William BEAN 1702, m/3 Samuel POPE; 14 May 1695; Salem

WINSLOW, Josiah (1606-1674) & Margaret [BOURNE] (-1683); b 1637; Scituate/Marshfield

WINSLOW, Josiah (1629-1680) & Penelope [PELHAM] (-1706?); 1651?, 1657?; Marshfield

WINSLOW, Josiah (1669-1761) & 1/wf Margaret TISDALE (1675-1737); m int 13 Jun 1691; Freetown/Taunton

WINSLOW, Kenelm[1] (1599-1672) & Ellen (NEWTON) ADAMS (1598-1681), w John; - Jun 1634; Plymouth/Salem

WINSLOW, Kenelm (1635-1715) & 1/wf Mercy [WORDEN] (-1688); 1664?, ?23 Sep 1667; Scituate/Yarmouth

WINSLOW, Kenelm (1635-1715) & 2/wf Damaris [EAMES]; aft 22 Sep 1688, bef 12 Jul 1693; Harwich

WINSLOW, Kenelm (1668-1729) & Bethiah HALL, m/2 Joseph HOWES/HAWES; 3 Jan 1689; Yarmouth

WINSLOW, Nathaniel (1639-1719) & Faith MILLER (-1729, in 85th y); 3 Aug 1664; Marshfield

WINSLOW, Nathaniel (1667-1736) & 1/wf Lydia [SNOW] (1672-1716); ca 1692; Marshfield/Swansea

WINSLOW, Samuel (1641-1680) & Hannah [BRIGGS], m/2 Thomas JOLLS; ca 1675, b 16 Jan 1676; Scituate/Boston

WINSLOW, Samuel & Amy [?FURBER], ?w Moses; b 1692; Boston

WINSLOW, Samuel (ca 1674-1760) & 1/wf Bethiah HOLBROOK; 26 Sep 1700; Scituate/Rochester

WINSLOW, _?_ & Mercy BURGESS; b 1701?; Sandwich/Yarmouth

WINSTON, John (1621-1697) & Elizabeth [AUSTIN] (-1680); b 1649; New Haven

WINSTON, John & Elizabeth DANIEL; 9 May 1682; New Haven

WINSWORTH, Robert & Rebecca _?_; b 1645; Boston

WINTER, Christopher (?1606-1683, Marshfield) & Jane COOPER; ca 4 Sep 1638; ?Plymouth/Scituate/Marshfield

WINTER, Edward & Deborah GOLT/GAULT; 17 Nov 1669; Salem

WINTER, John & Joan BOWDON; Halberton, Devon, 29 Jan 1609/10; Scarboro, ME

WINTER, John (-1662, ae ca 90?) & _?_; in Eng, ca 1610?, b 1634; Watertown

WINTER, John (-1651) & _?_, m/2 [?James] TURNER; ca 1633?; Scituate

WINTER, John & Posthume [?BRUNDAGE]/[?BRUNDISH]; ?Rye, NY/Westchester, NY

WINTER, John (1634-1690) & Hannah HARRINGTON? (?1638-); b 1655; Cambridge/Watertown

WINTER, John (1677-) & Abigail ?[SMITH] (1670-); b 1688; Lexington

WINTER, John & Ann PHENIX; 2 Apr 1697; Boston

WINTER, Timothy (?1641-) & Esther/Hester PLUMLY; 16 Dec 1670; Braintree

WINTER, Tobias (-1674) & Rebecca BEMIS, m/2 John DYMOND 1674, m/3 Benedict SATTERLEE 1682; 3 Apr 1672

WINTER, William (-1685) & Deborah _?_; b 1644; ?Lynn

WINTHROP, Adam (-1652) & 1/wf Elizabeth [GLOVER] (-1648); ca Feb 1642, Feb 1641/2; Cambridge

WINTHROP, Adam (-1652) & Elizabeth (HAWKINS) [LOUEY]/(LONGE), m/3 John RICHARDS 1654; aft 1648; Dorchester

WINTHROP, Adam (1647-1700) & Mary [LUTRELL] (-1706), m/2 Joseph LYNDE 1705/6; b 1676, by 1676; Charlestown/Boston

WINTHROP, Adam (1676-1743) & Anne WAINWRIGHT (1682-); 7 Nov 1700; Ipswich

WINTHROP, Deane (1623-1704) & 1/wf Sarah [GLOVER]; b 1651, b 1648; Cambridge/Boston/Chelsea

WINTHROP, Deane (1623-1704) & 2/wf Martha [MELLOWES] (-1716), w John; by 1678; Boston

WINTHROP, Fitz. John (1638/9)-1707) & Elizabeth [TONGUE] (1653-1731); New London, CT

WINTHROP, Henry (1607-1630) & Elizabeth FONES, m/2 Robert FISKE, m/3 William HALLETT; in Eng, 25 Apr 1629; [Boston]

WINTHROP, John[1] (1587, 1587/8-1649) & 1/wf Mary FORTH (-1615, in Eng); in Eng, 16 Apr 1605; Charlestown/Boston

WINTHROP, John[1] & 2/wf Thomasine CLOPTON (-1616, in Eng); in Eng, 6 Dec 1615; Charlestown/Boston

WINTHROP, John[1] & 3/wf Margaret TYNDAL (-1647); in Eng, 29 Apr 1618; Charlestown/Boston

WINTHROP, John[2] (1606-1676) & 1/wf Martha FONES (-1634); in Eng, 8 Feb 1630/1, Groton, Eng; Charlestown

WINTHROP, John[2] (1606-1676) & 2/wf Elizabeth READE (1614-1672); in Eng, 12 Feb 1635; Charlestown/New London, CT

WINTHROP, John[1] (1587-1649) & Martha (RAINSBOROUGH) COYTMAN (-1660), w Thomas, m/3 John COGGAN 1652; 4 Dec 1647; Charlestown

WINTHROP, Stephen (1619-1658) (ret'd to Eng) & Judith [RAINSBOROUGH] (1624-), m/2 John RALSTON 1687; b 1644; Boston

WINTHROP, Wait Still (1642-1717) & 1/wf Mary [BROWNE] (1656-1690); b 1679; Boston

WINTON, [Andrew?] & Hannah/Susannah _?_, m/2 Aaron FOUNTAIN by 1690?; ca 1679?, b Dec 1681?; New London? (She had son John b ca 1680?, bpt 22 May 1698; he m Susanna ADAMS ca 1711; Joseph HILL's will mentions gr-dau Hannah WINTON, said to be VINTON)

WINUS/(WINANS), John (-1699) & 1/wf Susannah MELYEN/MELYN, m/2? Jacob SCHILLINGER; 25 Aug 1664; New Haven

WINANS, John & 2/wf? Ann [ROBERTSON]?; b 1694; New Haven (prob wrong)

WISE, Henry (-1684) & Mary [MANSFIELD] (1658-1712), m/2 Thomas TURLAND, m/3 John HILL; ?Guilford, CT

WISE/WYETH?, Humphrey (-1638) & Susan/Susanna (TIDD?), m/2 Samuel GREENFIELD; b 1626, b 1634, b 1610?; Ipswich

WISE, James & Elizabeth [CLARK]; b 1681; Ipswich/Newbury

WISE, John (1652-1725) & Abigail GARDNER (1652-); 5 Dec 1678; Hatfield/Ipswich

WISE, Joseph (-1684) & Mary THOMPSON (?1619-1693); 3 Dec 1641; Roxbury

WISE, Thomas & Elizabeth [?DAMERILL], w John; b 1691; York, ME/etc.

WISE, _?_ & Elizabeth _?_; b 1634, widow: member of Church; Roxbury

WISE, _?_ & Jane _?_ (-1637, widow); Roxbury

WISEMAN, James & Dorothy _?_ ; b 1655; Boston

WISSENDUNK/?WISENDONK, ?Warner (-1689?) & Sarah [SEDGWICK], w Robert; b 1693, b 1689, aft 1683; Charlestown/Boston

WISWALL, Ebenezer (1646-1691) & Sarah (PAYSON) FOSTER (1648-1714), w Elisha; 26 Mar 1685; Dorchester

WISWALL, Enoch (1633-1706) & Elizabeth OLIVER (1639, 1639/40-1712); 25 Nov 1657; Dorchester/Roxbury

WISWALL, Ichabod (?1637-1700) & 1/wf Remember _?_ ; b 1670; ?Duxbury

WISWALL, Ichabod (?1637-1700) & Priscilla PABODIE (1653-1724, Kingston); 2 Dec 167[9?], 1677?, 24 Dec 1677?; Duxbury

WISWALL, John (1601-1687) & Margaret [SMITH]?; b 1634; Dorchester

WISWALL, John & 1/wf Millicent _?_ ; b 1663; Boston

WISWALL, John & 2/wf Hannah HAUBURY?/HANBURY; b 1666; Boston

WISWALL, John (1658-) & 1/wf Hannah BAKER (1662-1690, ae 28); 5 May 1685, 6 May; Dorchester

WISWALL, John & 2/wf Mary _?_, m _?_ WHITE; aft 1690; Dorchester

WISWALL, Noah (1638-1690) & Theodosiah/Theodosia JACKSON (1643-1725), m/2 Samuel NEWMAN 1693+; 14 Dec 1664; Cambridge/Newton

WISWALL, Oliver (1665-1746) & Sarah BAKER (1668-1755); 1 Jan 1690; Dorchester

WISWALL, Thomas (1602-1683) & 1/wf Elizabeth _?_ (-1657+); b 1633; Dorchester/Cambridge/Newton

WISWALL, Thomas (1602-1683) & 2/wf Isabella (?BARBAGE)/?(MUSTON) [FARMER] (-1686), w John; Cambridge/Newton

WISWALL, Thomas (1666-1709) (kinsman of John MERRICK) & Hannah CHENY (1673-1752), m/2 David NEWMAN 1719, 17 Dec 1696; Newbury

WISWALL, _?_ (1666-1709) & _?_, m/2 William BRADFORD (doubtful)

WITCHFIELD, John & _?_ (-1659); Windsor, CT

WITCHFEILD, John & Margaret (?WILKINSON) GOFFE (-1669?), w Edward; - Dec 1662; Cambridge

WITHAM, Henry & Sarah SOMES; 15 Jun 1685; Gloucester/Salem

WITHAM, Henry & Lydia (YOUNGLOVE) GRIFFIN, w Samuel; 23 Oct 1691; Gloucester

WITHAM, Thomas & Abigail BABSON; 8 Jul 1691; Gloucester

WITHAM, William & Hannah?/?Mary [FOLLETT]/NASON (-1694) (see Ephraim TRICKEY); by 1694; Dover, NH

WITHERLY/WITHERLEY/?WEATHERBEE, Nathaniel & Sarah BURGIS; 10 Dec 1699, 27 Dec 1700; Boston

WITHERS, Thomas (±1606-1685) & Jane _?_, m/2 William GODSOE 1691; ca 1640/50?; Kittery, ME

WITHINGTON, Ebenezer (-1729) & 1/wf Mary _?_ (-1691); b 29 Jul 1677, no issue; Dorchester

WITHENTON, Ebenezer & 2/wf Mary ROYAL (1670-1736), Taunton; 2 Feb 1692/3; ?Dorchester

WITHINGTON, Henry (1588-1666) (ae ca 76 in 1665) & 1/wf Anne LEECH (-1621); Leigh, Co. Lancaster, Sep 1615; Dorchester

WITHINGTON, Henry (1588-1666) & 2/wf Elizabeth SMITH (-1660/1); Leigh, Eng, 30 Sep 1622; Dorchester

WITHINGTON, Henry (1588-1666) & 3/wf Margaret (TURNER) PAUL (-1676), w Richard; m cont 25 Jun 1662; Dorchester

WITHINGTON, Henry (-1688) & Sarah LEADBETTER (?1660, 1659-1696), m/2 Ebenezer HOLMES 1692/[3]; 29 May 1684; Dorchester

WITHINGTON, John (1649-1690) & Elizabeth [PRESTON] (-1722, ae 69), m/2 James WHITE 1696; b 1673; Dorchester

WITHENTON, Joseph (1668-1698) & Deliverance LEADBETTER (1667-1747), m/2 John TROTT 1703; 29 Mar 1693; Boston

WITHINGTON, Philip (-1736) & 1/wf Thankful POND (?1661-1711); 17 Nov 1682; Dorchester

WITHINTON, Richard (?1618-1701) & Elizabeth [ELIOT] (1627-1714); ca 1648; Dorchester

WITHERINGTON, William & ? GOULD

WITSHALL, Emanuel & Joanna ? ; b 1674; Marblehead

WITT, John & 1/wf ? ; ca 1638

WITT, John (-1675) & Sarah ? ; b 1643; Lynn/Groton

WITT, John (ca 1650-) & Elizabeth BAKER; 14 Jun 1676; Lynn

WITT, Jonathan (ca 1640-1665) & Mary DIVEN; 23 Mar 1663; Lynn

WITT, Thomas (1661-1690, 1691?) & Bethia POTTER (1668-); 26 Feb 1685; Lynn

WITTECOM, Alexander & Mary DAVIS; 31 May 1688; Swansea/?Rehoboth

WITTER, Ebenezer (1668-1712) & Dorothy MORGAN, ?m/2 Daniel BREWSTER; 5 May 1693; Preston, CT/Norwich, CT

WITTER, Josiah/Josias (1638-) & 1/wf Elizabeth WHEELER (-1672); 25 Feb 1661/2; Lynn

WITTER, Josiah (1638-1690) & 2/wf Sarah [CRANDALL] (1650±-), m/2 Peter BUTTON b 1689?; aft 5 Aug 1672, b 1677; New London, CT

WITTER, William (1584-1659) & Annis [CHURCHMAN?]; b 1630?; Lynn

WITTOMS, Peter & Redgon/Redigan/Redigon CLARKE (1627-1700+); 17 Jun 1652; Boston

WITTUM, Peter (1656-) & Agnes/Annis?/Eunice? ? ; b 1684; Kittery, ME

WITTY, George & Sarah SPEAR (1647-); 19 Jun 1672, 17 Jun 1672, 19 Jun 1678; Braintree

WIXOM/?WICKSON/?WIXON, Robert (-1686) & [Alice] ? (-living 1686); b 1655; Cape Cod/Barnstable/Eastham

WIXAM, Barnabas & Sarah (REMICK) GREENE, w John; b 1683?, b 1687, b 1693; Cape Cod

WIXAM/HICKSON/VIXEN, Robert & Sarah [BREWSTER]?, w Nathaniel; 26 Sep 1679; Eastham

WODELL, Gershom (1642-) & Mary [TRIPP] (1646±-1716+), m/2 Jonathan GETCHELL 1683/4; ?18 Jul 1662, b 1663; Portsmouth

WODELL, Richard (-1710(-)) & Susanna [PEARCE] (1672±-1710(-)); b 1691; Tiverton, RI

WODELL, William (-1693) & Mary ? (-1676); b 1640; Boston/Portsmouth, RI/Tiverton, RI

WODELL, William (1663-1699, ae 36) & Ruth LAWTON (-1726); 10 Feb 1681, 1681/2?; Portsmouth, RI

WODELL, ?Samuel & Sarah ?

WALCUTT, Abraham & 1/wf Ruth HOOPER (1653-1688); 22 Nov 1682; Salem

WALCUTT, Abraham & Abigail BRIGS/BRIGHT?, Reading; 30 Apr 1689; Salem

WOLCOTT, George (-1662) & Elizabeth [TREAT]? (prob correct) (1627-) (did she m/2 ? JOHNSON?); ca 1649, b 20 Jun 1650; Wethersfield, CT

WOLCOTT, George (1652-1726) & Elizabeth [CURTIS] (-1741); 30 Aug 1691; Windsor, CT

WOLCOTT, Henry[1] (1578-1655) & Elizabeth SAUNDERS (1584-1655); in Eng, 19 Jan 1606; Windsor, CT

WOLCOTT, Henry (1611-1680) & Sarah NEWBERRY (ca 1622-1684); 8 Nov 1641, 1640?, ?18 Nov; Windsor, CT

WOLCOTT, Henry (-1710) & Abiah GOFFE (-1717), Cambridge, MA; 12 Oct 1664; Windsor, CT

WOLCOTT, Henry[3] (1670-1747) & 1/wf Jane ALLEN/ALLYN (1670-1702); 1 Apr 1696; Windsor, CT

WOLCOTT, John (-1638?) & 1/wf Mary [VAYLE?]/ATKINS?; ?Glaston, Eng, b 1622; Watertown/Salem

WOLCOTT, John (-1638) & 2/wf Winifred [CRAWFORD], w John?, m/2 Thomas ALLEN b 1644, ?10 Nov 1646; ca 1634; ?Watertown

WOOLCUTT, John (-1690?) & Mary THARLY/THURLOW; 20 Nov 1653; Newbury/?Brookfield

WOLCOTT, John (1645-1712) & Mary CHESTER (1654-1689); 14 Feb 1676, 13 Feb 1677, 14 Feb [1676/7]; Wethersfield, CT

WOOLCOT, John (-1725) & Sarah JOHNSON, m/2 Benjamin BRADLEY, m/3 David PERKINS; 8 Feb 1683; New Haven

WOOLLCUTT, John & Hannah/Joanna? EMERSON; 4 Jan 1684; Newbury

WOLCOTT, John (-1713, 1712?) & 2/wf Hannah (HAWLEY) NICHOLAS?/NICHOLS, w Josiah, m/3 Samuel POTTER, m/4 Henry WOLCOTT 1727; 22 Jun 1692; Windsor, CT

WOLCOTT, John (-1737/8) & 1/wf Mary ? (-1711+); b 1693; Salem

WALCOT, Jonathan (?1640-1699) & 1/wf Mary SIBLY/SIBLEY (-1683); 26 Jan 1664/5; Salem

WALCUTT, Jonathan (-1699) & 2/wf Deliverance PUTNAM (-1723+); 23 Apr 1685; Salem

WALCOTT, Jonathan (1670-1745, Windham, CT) & Priscilla BAYLEY (1676-1770); b 1696; Newburyport/Windham, CT

WOLCOTT, Joseph & Rebecca GRANGER (-1693); 4 Mar 1686, 1685/6; Springfield/Suffield, CT/Brookfield

WOLCOTT, Joseph & _?_ ; aft 27 Jul 1693; Suffield, CT

WOOLCOTT, Joseph & Bethiah (JOHNSON) KNIGHT (?1660-), w Jonathan 1693+; in or bef 1697; Woburn

WOLCOT, Josiah (-1721) & Penelope CORWINE (1670-1690); 19 Feb 1684/5, 1686; Salem

WALCOTT/WILCOT, Josiah (-1721) & 2/wf Mary FREKE, Boston; 1 May 1694; Salem

WOLCOTT, Samuel (1656-1695) & Judith APPLETON (ca 1653-1741), Ipswich; 6 Mar 1678; Wethersfield, CT

WOLCOTT, Simon^2 (1625-1687) & 1/wf Joanna COOKE (1638-Apr 1657); 19 Mar 1657, 1656/7; Windsor, CT

WOLCOTT, Simon^2 (1625-1687) & 2/wf Martha PITKIN (1639-1719), m/2 Daniel CLARK 1688?, 1689?; 17 Oct 1661; Windsor, CT

WOLCOTT, Simon (1666-1732) & Sarah CHESTER (1657-1723), Wethersfield, CT; 5 Dec 1689; Windsor, CT

WOLCOTT, William & Alice [INGERSOLL]; b 1643; Salem

WOLFE, Peter (-1675) & Martha _?_ ; b 1644; Salem/Beverly

WOLTERTON, Gregory (1583-1674) & 1/wf Susanna [?SHEPARD] (1587-1662); ?Hartford

WOLTERTON, Gregory (1583-1674) & 2/wf Benet/Benedicta (TRITTON) [STANLEY] (1609-1665), w Thomas; 1663, 1664; Hadley

WOLTERTON, Gregory (1583-1674) & Jane (HOPKINS) [WARD], w John, w Nathaniel; b 24 Oct 1670

WOOD, Abiel (-1719) & Abijah BOWEN (-1746); Dec 1683; Middleborough

WOOD, Abraham (-1746, 1747) & Sarah [DAKIN] (1659-1748); b 1684; Concord/Sudbury

WOOD, Andrew & Dorothy _?_ ; b 1687(8?); Boston

WOOD, Anthony (-1684) & Mary GROVER; 11 Jun 1666; Ipswich/Beverly

WOOD, Anthony & Mary PACK; 22 - 1692; Lynn

WOOD, Caleb & _?_ ; LI

WOOD, Daniel (-1649) & Mary [FOSTER], m/2 Francis PEABODY; b 1646?; Ipswich

WOOD, Daniel & Sarah [ANDREWS] (-1714); b 1670; Topsfield/Boxford

WOOD, David & Mary (BARKER) (PRATT) COMBS, w Samuel, w Francis; 5 Mar 1684/5; Middleborough

WOOD, Ebenezer (1671-) & Rachel NICHOLS; 5 Apr 1695; Rowley/Mendon

WOOD, Edmund (1578-1662) & 2/wf Martha LUM; 21 May 1611, Halifax, Eng; Springfield/Wethersfield, CT

WOOD, Edward (-1642) & Ruth _?_ ; b 1636; Charlestown

WOOD, Edward (-1659+) & Elizabeth _?_ ; b 1644; Charlestown/Boston

WOOD, Eleazer (1662-1704) & Dorothy _?_ (not BABCOCK), m/2 John WARE 1709; b 1688/[9?]; Sherborn

WOOD, Ellis & Katharine _?_ (-1663); b 1658; Dedham

WOOD, Ellis (-1696) & Miriam [SMITH] (-1706, ae 93), w John; ca 1680, aft 1676; Dedham/Dorchester

WOOD, Gabriel & Nancy _?_?; b 1690; Beverly

WOOD, Gabriel & Mercy _?_?; b 1693; Beverly

WOOD, George & [?Ann ROGERS?], w William; 16 Jul 1660, Jul 1660, 1? Jul; Saybrook, CT

WOOD/ATWOOD?, Henry (-1670) & Abigail JENNEY; 28 Apr 1644; Yarmouth?/Middlebury

WHOD/HOOD, Henry & Hannah _?_ ; b 1670, b 1671; Newport

WOODS, Isaac (1655-1720) & 1/wf Mary [MAYNARD] (-1689), dau John^2; b 1683; Marlborough

WOOD, Isaac (1660?-1741) & Elizabeth [MERRIAM] (1660-1717); ca 1687, [b 1690]; Concord/Lexington

WOODS, Isaac (1655-1720) & 2/wf Mary FAIRBANKS; 8 May 1700; Sherborn/Dedham?

WOOD, Isaiah & Mercy THOMPSON; 26 Jan 1653; Ipswich?

WOOD, Isaiah & Hannah WHEELER; 23 Jun 1684, 23 Apr 1684?, 23 Dec; Ipswich

WOOD, Israel & Anna WOODBERY; m int 15 Oct 1697; Beverly

WOOD, ?Jacob & _?_ ; did he marry?; Southampton, LI

WOOD, Jacob (1662-1723) & Mary FLETCHER/WHEELER? (1673-); 15 Apr 1697; Concord

WOOD, James (1647-1718) & Hopestill WARD (1646-1718); 22 Apr 1678; Marlborough

WOOD, James (-1728) & Experience FULLER (-living in 1725); 12 Apr 1693, 2 Apr; Middleborough/Bridgewater

WOOD, Jeremiah (1614, 1620-1686) & [Elizabeth] _?_/GILDERSLEEVE?; b 1650; Stamford, CT/Hempstead, LI

WOOD, Jeremiah (1641-1710) & ?Elizabeth GILDERSLEEVE? (Susannah in 1709) (1650-); b 1678; Hempstead, LI

WOOD, Jeremiah & Mary [SHERRINGTON]; b 21 Nov 1702; Fairfield

WOOD, John (-1655) & 1/wf Elizabeth _?_; Portsmouth, RI

WOOD, John (?1610-1678) & Mary [PARMENTER?] (1610-1690); b 1641; Sudbury/Framingham

WOOD, John (alias ATWOOD) (?1610-1675) & Sarah [MASTERSON]; b 1643?; Plymouth

WOOD, John & Mary [?PEABODY]; ca 1656?; Newport

WOOD, John & _?_; b 1658; Springfield

WOOD, John & Anna _?_; b 1662; RI

WOOD, John & _?_; by 1665; Dover, NH

WOODS, John (1641-1716) & Lydia [RICE]? (1649-1723); b 1670, bef; Marlborough

WOOD, John & Elizabeth [HALL] (1653-); ca 1671/5?; Dorchester

WOOD, John (-1684) & Mary HELY; 1 May 1676; Ipswich

WOOD, John (son Timothy?) & _?_ [RHODES]; b 1677(8?); Huntington, LI/Southampton

WOOD, John (son Timothy?) & Elizabeth CONKLIN?

WOOD, John (-1728) & Elizabeth VINTON (-1728); 13 Nov 1677; Concord

WOOD, John & Martha [WICKES]; b 1677(8?); ?Huntington, LI

WOOD, John (1656-1729+) & Isabel [HAZEN] (1662-1726+); 16 Jan 1680; Rowley/Bradford/CT/Littleton

WOOD, John, Jr. & _?_; by 1686?; Dover, NH

WOOD, John & Tabitha FAIRFIELD; 27 Oct 1687; Wenham

WOOD, John & Elizabeth PLATT (no) (1685-); ca 1687?, b 1687; Huntington, LI

WOOD, John (-1738) & Mary CHAPELL?/BUDDINGTON? (1669-1744); b 1688?; New London

WOOD, John (1663-) & Bethiah MASON; 23 May 1688; Swansea

WOOD, John (-1740) & Mary [CHURCH] (1668-1748); b 1689, 1688; Little Compton, RI?

WOOD, John & Elizabeth _?_; b 1690; Dorchester

WOODS, John/Obadiah & Martha [BISELOW]/SAWYER? (1662-); b 1696; Marlboro/E. Hartford, CT

WOOD, John & _?_; b 1697; Salisbury

WOOD, John & Alice _?_; b 1698; E. Greenwich, RI

WOOD, Jonas (1616?-1689), Oram & [Elizabeth?] STRICKLAND? (1619-1650?); b 1636?; Wethersifeld, CT/Stamford, CT/Huntington, LI/Hempstead, LI/Southampton, LI

WOOD, Jonas, Jr. & _?_

WOOD, Jonas, Halifax & Joanna STRICKLAND, Southampton; b 1650; Stamford, CT/Huntington, LI

WOOD, Jonas[3] & Elizabeth CONKLIN (1649-); b 1684, b 1668

WOOD, Jonas & Deborah WILTSEE; b 1687

WOOD, Jonas & Lydia SMITH; by 1692; Hempstead

WOOD, Jonathan & Anne _?_; b 1658; RI

WOOD, Jonathan & Mary DANIEL; 26 May 1674; Milton/Dorchester

WOOD/ATWOOD?, Joseph & Hester/Esther? WALKER (1650-1696); 1 Jan 1679; Taunton

WOOD, Joseph & Eunice JARVIS/Mary MATTHEWS; 15 Dec 1681; Huntington, LI

WOOD/ATWOOD?, Joseph (-1696) & 2/wf? Abigail PAUL (1673-); 18 Oct 1697; Taunton

WOOD, Joseph & Judith HELY/HEALEY; 20 Oct 1697; Boston

WOOD, Joseph (-1725) & Mary BLANEY (1679-1743); 19 Apr 1699; Charlestown

WOOD, Joshua & Elizabeth BUCK; 28 Aug 1678, 20 Aug; Cambridge

WOOD, Josiah (1635-1691) (bro of Obadiah) & Lydia BACON (-1712, ae 74); 28 Oct 1657; Charlestown

WOOD, Josiah (1664-1728) & 1/wf Sarah ELITHORP (ca 1668-1689); 5 Mar 1685?; Rowley/Concord/Enfield, CT/Somers, CT

WOOD, Josiah, Woburn & Abigail BACON, Billerica; 13 Dec 1686; Billerica/Woburn

WOOD, Josiah (?1665-1728?) & 2/wf Mary FELT/BLANEY? (-1753?); 17 Oct 1689, 12 Dec; Rowley/Concord/Enfield, CT/Somers, CT

WOOD, Josiah (1664-) & Margaret [HOPKINS]; b 1692, b 1689, 23 Dec 1686; Topsfield/Rowley

WOOD, Mark & Elizabeth HANCOCK (1645-); 2 Feb 1664/5, 1664; Charlestown

WOOD, Michael (-1674) & Mary [**THOMPSON?**], m/2 Thomas **READ** 1678; b 1642, b 1638; Concord

WOOD, Nathaniel & Lucy _?_ ; b 1693; Topsfield

WOODS, Nathaniel & Eleanor/Alice? [**WHITNEY?**] (-1711?, 1718) (m/1 Eleanor?, m/2 Alice?); b 1694; Groton

WOOD, Nehemiah & Susannah **LOW**; m int 16 Mar 1695/6; Beverly

WOOD, Nicholas[1] (-1670) & 1/wf Mary **PIGG/PIDGE/WILLIAMS?** (-1663), ?dau Thomas; b 1642; Roxbury/Braintree/Dorchester

WOOD, Nicholas (-1670) & 2/wf Ann/Anna/Hannah **BABCOCK? PAGE**, w William, m/3 Edward **WINN** ca 1681; m cont 16 Nov 1665; Watertown

WOOD, Obadiah (-1694) (bro of Thomas) & 1/wf Margaret [**SPARK?**]; b 1665, b 26 Mar 1650; Charlestown/Ipswich

WOOD, Obadiah (-1694) & 2/wf Hazelelpony/Hasabelponah? (**WILLIX**) [**GEE**] (1636?-), w John; aft 1667, b 1675, aft 1676, ca 1672?, aft 19 Nov 1671; Ipswich

WOOD, Obadiah (-1712) & _?_ [**KING**]; b 1687; Hartford

WOOD, Obadiah (-1712) & 2/wf Martha **BIGELOW?/SAWYER** (-1712+)

WOOD, Peter & Abigail _?_ ; b 1688; Dorchester/Boston

WOOD, Richard & Sarah _?_ ; b 1650; Cambridge

WOOD, Richard & Dorothy _?_ ; b 1677; York, ME

WOOD, Richard & Hannah _?_ ; b 1690; Roxbury/Boston

WOOD, Richard (-1705) & Sarah **CLARK**, m/2 Matthew **BELLANY** 1705; 20 Dec 1699; Wallingford, CT

WOODS, Samuel (?1636-1718?) & Alice **RUSHTON** (?1636-1712); 28 Sep 1659; Cambridge/Groton

WOOD, Samuel (?1640-) & Deborah _?_ ; ca 1665/72?; Huntington, LI

WOOD, Samuel (-1718) & Rebecca [**MORTON?**]/**TUFFES?** (-1718); b 1679(80?); Middleborough

WOOD, Samuel & Judith _?_ ; b 1682(3?); Ipswich

WOOD, Samuel & Rebecca [**BENEDICT**] (1660?-); ca 1683?, b 28 Feb 1690; Norwalk, CT/Danbury, CT

WOOD, Samuel & Mary **BOLTON**; 27 May 1684; Ipswich

WOODS, Samuel (-1712) & Hannah **FARWELL** (1668-1739), m/2 Peter **JOSLIN**; 30 Dec 1685; Chelmsford

WOOD, Samuel (1666-1690) & Margaret **ELLITHORPE** (1672-), m/2 Jonathan **HARRIMAN** 1691; 21 Jan 1689, 1688/9; Rowley

WOOD, Simon & Elizabeth **FOSTER**; 8 Aug 1674; Ipswich

WOOD, Solomon (1669-1752) & Mary **HASELTINE** (1671-1749); 15 Oct 1690; Rowley/Bradford/Mendon/Uxbridge

WOOD, Thomas (?1634, 1635?-1687) (ae 41 in May 1674, 40 in Mar 1675) (called _?_ **TODD** brother) & Ann [_?_] (-1714?); 7 Jun 1654; Rowley

WOOD, Thomas & Rebecca _?_ ; b 1679, b 1663; Swansea

WOOD, Thomas, Jr. (1658-1702) & Mary **HUNT**, m/2 Simon **DAVIS**, Concord, 19 Oct 1714; 26 Jun 1683; Rowley

WOODS, Thomas & 1/wf Elizabeth _?_ (-1688); b 1688; Groton

WOOD, Thomas & Hannah **RIDER**; 1 May 1690; Swansea/Little Compton, RI

WOOD, Thomas & Content _?_ ; b 1692; Socsonett

WOOD, Thomas (-1697) & Susanna/Susan? **EASTMAN** (1673-1772), m/2 John **SWAN** 1699; 19 May 1693, 13? May; Haverhill

WOODS, Thomas & Hannah [**WHITNEY**]; b 1697, prob b 1694; Groton

WOOD, Thompson & Martha **FOSTER** (1672-); 8 Dec 1691; Ipswich/Framingham

WOOD, Timothy (1622-1659?) & _?_ ; Southampton, LI

WHOD/HOOD?, Walter & Amy _?_ ; b 1676; Newport

WOOD, William (1582-1671) (called "uncle" by Thomas **FLINT** 1652) & Margaret? _?_ /**HATCH?** (-1659); in Eng, b 1622?, b 1642, b 1618; Concord

WOOD, William (1610-) & Elizabeth _?_ (1611-); in Eng, b 1635; Lynn/Sandwich

WOOD, William (-1708) & [?Mary **PEACH**] (-1711+, bef 31 Jan 1714/15); 19 Oct 1663; Marblehead

WOOD, William (-1696?, 1697) & Martha [**EARLE**]; ca 1666/7, ca 1675, b 19 Nov 1673; Dartmouth/Portsmouth, RI

WOOD, William & Dorothy (**WETHERELL**) **IRISH**, w Elias; 1 Apr 1686; Taunton

WOOD, William & _?_ COOKE?; b 1689; Dartmouth
WOOD, William & Susannah _?_ ; b 1696; Swansea
WOOD, William & Elizabeth _?_ ; b 1695; Beverly
WOOD, _?_ & _?_ [ROCKWELL]
WOOD, _?_ & Joane _?_ ; b 1640; Charlestown
WOOD, _?_ & Deborah SMITH
WOODBRIDGE, Benjamin (-1710), Medford & 1/wf Mary WARD (1649-1685); 3 Jun, 5 Jun, 13 Jun 1672; Stonington, CT
WOODBRIDGE, Benjamin (-1717, Medford) & 2/wf Deborah (CUSHING) TARLTON (1651-), w Henry; 31 Aug 1686; Hingham/Bristol, RI/Kittery, ME/Windsor, CT/etc.
WOODBRIDGE, John (1613-1695) & Mercy [DUDLEY] (1621-1691); b 1640; Newbury/Cambridge
WOODBRIDGE, John (1644-1691) & Abigail LEETE (-1711, 1710?); 26 Oct 1671, Guilford, CT; Killingworth, CT
WOODBRIDGE, John (1678-1718) & Jemima ELIOT (1679-), m/2 _?_ WHEELER; 14 Nov 1699; Guilford, CT
WOODBRIDGE, Joseph (-1727) & Martha ROGERS (?1661-1736); 20 May 1686; Newbury/Lynn
WOODBRIDGE, Thomas (1649-1681) & Mary JONES, m/2 Joseph COKER; 4 Jun 1672?, 12? Jun, 1671?; Newbury/Stonington, CT
WOODBRIDGE, Timothy (1656-1732) & 1/wf Mehitable/Mabel (WYLLAS) (RUSSELL) FOSTER (?1658-1698), w Daniel, w Isaac; aft 20 Aug 1682, ca 1685; Hartford?/Stonington, CT
WOODBRIDGE, _?_ & _?_ TAYLOR; ?evidence
WOODBERY, Andrew (1623-1685) & Mary [COCKERELL]; b 1657; Salem
WOODBERY, Andrew (1665-1698?, 1695?) & Emma [ELLIOTT], m Thomas BLOWERS 1702; b 1689; Beverly
WOODBURY, Benjamin & Mary _?_ (-1685); b 1683; Bristol, RI
WOODBERY, Benjamin (1668-) & Mary WOODBERY, m/2 Michael FARLEY; 23 Mar 1693/4; Beverly
WOODBERY, Ebenezer (1657-1714) & Hannah DODGE (1671-1757); 15 May 1690; Beverly
WOODBERY, Hugh (-1702) & Mary DIXY (-1705); - Dec 1650; Salem/Bristol, RI
WOODBERRIE, Humphrey (1608-1686) (ae 72 in 1680) & Elizabeth [?HUNTER] (-1689); b 1639, b 1636?, ?11 Apr 1639; Salem
WOODBERRIE, Humphrey (1646-1727) & Anna WINDER/WINDOW? (1653-1728); 10 Oct 1671; Beverly
WOODBERRY, Isaac (1644-1725/6?) & Mary WILKES; 9 Oct 1671; Beverly
WOODBERRY, Isaac (1661-) & Elizabeth [HERRICK] (1668-); b 1688; Beverly
WOODBURY, John (-1643) & Joanna HUMPHREY; Burlescombe, Eng, 21 Jun 1596, doubtful; Salem
WOODBERY, John (-1643, 1641?) & ?Agnes _?_ ; b Aug 1629; Salem
WOODBURY, John (?1630-1673) & Elizabeth _?_, m/2 John DODGE 1675?; b 1655, b 1654?; Salem
WOODBERRIE, John (1641-) & 1/wf Elizabeth [TENNEY] (1643-1689); b 1670; Beverly
WOODBERY, John (1641-) & 2/wf Alice DARBYE, w John; 2 Jul 1690; Beverly
WOODBURY, John & Mary REYNOLDS (-1718); 18 May 1694; Bristol, RI
WOODBERRY, Jonathan (-1677) & Abigail [PHILLIPS] (1645-), m/2 David EAST, m/3 Thomas WALTER 1687; b 1672(3?); Boston
WOODBURY, Joseph (1659-1714) & Elizabeth WEST; 19 Dec 1687; Beverly/Manchester
WOODBERY, Nicholas (1618-1686, ae 70?) & Anna/Anne? [PALGRAVE] (1625-1701); b 1653, b 1651?; Salem
WOODBURIE, Nicholas (1657-1691) & Mary ELLIOTT (1662-), m/2 Kinsley HALL; 4 Jun 1684; Beverly
WOODBERRY, Peter (1640-1709) & 1/wf Abigail BATHELOUR/BATCHELDER (1643-1666); Sep 166[5?], 1664?; Beverly
WOODBERY, Peter (1640-1709) & 2/wf Sarah DODGE (1644-1726); - Jul 1667; Beverly
WOODBERY, Peter (1666, 1663-1707) & Mary DODGE (1675-1763); 18 Nov 1692; Ipswich
WOODBERRIE, Richard (1655-1690) (see Edward HARADEN) & Sarah HASCOLL/HASKELL, ?m/2 John POOLE; 16 Dec 1679; Beverly
WOODBERY, Robert (-1746) & Mary WEST (1676-1754); 11 Dec 1693; Beverly/Ipswich
WOODBURY, Samuel & Mary _?_ ; b 1685; Bristol, RI

WOODBERRIE, Thomas & 1/wf Hannah (DODGE) PORTER (1642-), w Samuel; 2 Dec 1661; Salem/Beverly

WOODBURIE, Thomas & Abigail [LOVETT?], m/2 Thomas LARCOM 1700; b 1688; Beverly

WOODBERY, Thomas & 2/wf Elizabeth COURTIS/CURTIS, w Samuel; 28 Apr 1690; Beverly

WOODBURY, William (1589-1677) & Elizabeth PATCH (1594-), m/2 John WALKER?; South Petherton, Eng, 29 Jan 1616, 1616/17?, 1617/18?; Salem

WOODBURY, William (1620-1667/8) & Jude/Judith _?_ (-1702, ae 75), m/2 John RAYMOND 1668?; b 1665(6?); Salem

WOODBERRIE, William (1651-1711) & Hannah HASCALL/HASKELL (1658-1740); 20 Nov 1676; Beverly

WOODBERRY, William (1662-1725) & Joanna WHEELER, Concord; 29 Sep 1689; Beverly

WOODCOCK, Israel (-1718) & Elizabeth GATCHELL; 5 Nov 1682; Dedham/Attleboro

WOODCOCK, Jeremiah & Mary METCALF (1676-); 5 Jan 1698/9; Dedham

WOODCOCK, John[1] (-1700, 1701?) & 1/wf Sarah [?CURTIS] (-1676); ca 1649; Rehoboth

WOODCOCK, John[2] (-1718) & 1/wf Sarah SMITH; 26 Feb 1673; Rehoboth

WOODCOCK, John[1] (-1700, 1701) & 2/wf Joanna _?_, m James FOWLER; aft 1676, bef 1692

WOODCOCK, John (-1718) & 2/wf Sarah (JUDSON) WESTBROKE (1651-1718), w George; 5 Nov 1682; Dedham

WOODCOCK, John & Martha [COOKE]; b 1683; Newport

WOODCOCK, Jonathan (-1736) & 1/wf Rebecca MARTIN; 23 Aug 1694; Rehoboth/Attleboro

WOODCOCK, Jonathan & 2/wf Mary/Mercy WILLIAMS; 14 Dec 1698; Rehoboth/Attleboro

WOODCOCK, Thomas & Mary _?_; b 1690; Rehoboth/Swansea

WOODCOCK, William[1] (-1703) & 1/wf Sarah COOPER; Oct 1648; Hingham

WOODCOCK, William (-1669) & Hannah _?_; b 1663; Salem

WOODCOCK, William[1] (-1703, Attleboro) & Mary _?_; 10 Dec 1663; Hingham/Attleboro

WOODCOCK, _?_ & Jane _?_/(DEY?) (-1666)

WOODING, Benjamin & Hannah (BROWN) JONES (1667/8-), w Benjamin; 1694; New Haven

WOODEN, Ithamar & Bethia _?_; b 1685; Beverly/?Haverhill/Ipswich

WOODEN, Jeremiah (1653-) & [Esther ANGUR] (1677-); b 1696; New Haven

WOODIN, John (-1721) & _?_; b 1652/3; Rowley/Beverly/etc.

WOODIN/WOODHAM/WOODAM, John (-1678) & Mary _?_ (-1681); b 1634?, by 12 Feb 1644/5; Haverhill/Salisbury/Rowley/Windham/Hampton, NH

WOODEN, John (1659-1713+, 1721, 1725+) & Katherine (HEARD) [LITTLEFIELD] (-1713+, 1725+), w James; ca 1680/5?, b 25 Feb 1690/1; Wells. ME/Salem/Beverly

WOODEN, Nathll. & Martha SACKET/SACKETT; Dec 1687; New Haven

WOODING, Peter (1674-) & Elizabeth MALLOT/MALLETT; 15 Oct 1696; Beverly

WOODEN, Samuel (-1685) & Martha _?_, had bro-in-law John EDWARDS; Wenham

WOODEN/WOODING, William (-1684) & Sarah OLARD/CLARK (-1693); 25 Oct 1650; New Haven

WOODEN, William (1651-1711) & Jane HOLMES; 26 Jun 1695; New Haven

WOODFIELD, John (-1669) & Esther _?_ (-1672); b 1669; Scituate

WOODFORD, Joseph (-1710) & Rebecca [NEWELL] (1643-); ca 1668; Farmington, CT/Northfield

WOODFORD, Joseph (-1760) & 1/wf Lydia SMITH; 23 Jan 1699, 1699/1700; Farmington, CT

WOODFORD, Thomas (ca 1612-1667) & Mary [BLOTT] (?1618-); ca 1632/5, ca 1633, ?4 Mar 1635?; Roxbury/Hartford/Northampton

WOODGATE, James & Prudence _?_ (lived in Eng in 1698); b 1690; Charlestown

WOODHAM/WOODAM?/WOODDAM, John (-1678) & Mary _?_; b 1647; Ipswich

WOODHEAD, William & Mary BROWNE, m/2 John GOVE 1677; 21 Jun 1669; Chelmsford

WOODIS, Henry (-1700) & 1/wf Eleanor/Ellen [HOPKINSON] (-1693); b 1651; Concord

WOODIS, Henry (-1700) & 2/wf Sarah (WADE) ROGERS, w Samuel; 29 Jun 1694; Concord?

WOODIS, John (-1659) & Frances _?_ (-1658); b 1630; Salem

WOODHOUSE, Richard (-1676) & 1/wf Mary _?_; b 1638; Boston

WOODHOUSE, Richard (-1676) & 2/wf Sarah _?_; b 1661(2?); Boston

WOODHULL, Richard & Deborah/Dorothy [?CREWE]; b 1649; Southold, LI?

WOODHULL, Richard (1649-1699) & Temperance TOPPING; 20 Nov 1684; Southampton, LI

WOODLAND, John & Martha _?_; b 1651, b 1646; Braintree/Dorchester/Mendon

WOODLEY, William & Elizabeth [?RUSSELL] (-1692); b 1687; Marblehead

WOODMAN, Archelaus (1614-1702) & 1/wf Elizabeth _?_ (-1677); b 1641?; Newbury

WOODMAN, Archelaus (1614-1702) & 2/wf Dorothy (SWAN) (ABBOTT) CHAPMAN (-1710), w Thomas, w Edward; 13 Nov 1678; Newbury

WOODMAN, Archelaus (1672-1766) & Hannah __?__ (-1749); b 1696; Newbury

WOODMAN, Edward (1606-1688+, 1692?) & Joanna [SALWAY?]/BARTELL? (?1614-1688+); b 1628?; Newbury

WOODMAN, Edward (?1628-1694) & Mary GOODRIDG/GOODRIDGE (1634-); 20 Dec 1653; Newbury

WOODMAN, Edward (-1693/98) & Remember [MAVERICK] (1652-1686/1691, bef 12 Apr 1691); ca 1670?; Boston?/Marblehead

WOODMAN, John (1630-1707±) & 1/wf Mary FIELD (-1698); 15 Jul 1656; Newbury

WOODMAN, John (1637-1713) & Hannah [TIMBERLAKE] (1656-1713); b 1677; Little Compton, RI/?Tiverton, LI

WOODMAN, John (-1705) & 1/wf Mary [RAYNES]; b 1693, by Aug 1693; ?Dover, NH/Kittery, ME/York, ME

WOODMAN, John (?1630-1707±) & 2/wf Sarah (BURNHAM) HUCKINS (1654-), w James; 17 Oct 1700; Salisbury

WOODMAN, Jonathan (1643-1706) (called Stephen GREENLEAF "uncle" in 1681) & Hannah/ Anna? HILTON; 2 Jul 1668; Newbury

WOODMAN, Jonathan & 1/wf Abigail ATKINSON (1673-); m int 1 Jan 1695/6; Newbury

WOODMAN, Jonathan (1665-1729) & Elizabeth [DOWNING] (1669-); ca 1698, by 1699; Durham, NH

WOODMAN, Jonathan (1674-1744) & Sarah MIGHILL; 24 Jun 1700; Rowley/Bradford

WOODMAN, Joshua (?1636-1703) & Elizabeth STEVENS (-1714); 22 Jan 1665, 1665/6, 23? Jan; Andover

WOODMANCY, Gabriel (-1685) & Sarah __?__, m/2 __?__ REX; b 1670; New London, CT

WOODMANSEY, James (1665-) & Abigail MELLEN/MELYEN (-1720), m/2 William TILLEY, m/3 Samuel SEWALL 1719; 17 May 1686; Boston

WOODMANSEY, John (son of Robert) & 1/wf Margaret __?__ (-1660); b 1660; Boston

WOODMANCY, John & 2/wf Elizabeth CARR (1642-); 1 May 1662; Boston

WOODMANCY, John & 3/wf Elizabeth CLARKE, m George MONK 1686+; 23 Jul 1672; Cambridge

WOODMANCY, Joseph & Sarah [LESTER] (1671-); b 1701?; CT

WOODMANSEY, Robert[1] (-1667) & 1/wf 2/wf Margaret __?__ (-1670); b 1630?, b 1634; Ipswich/Boston

WOODROW/WOODRUFF?, Benjamin (-1697+) & Rebecca [CANTLEBURY] (-1663); b 1660, 1659; Salem

WOODRUFF, John (-1611, in Eng) & Elizabeth [CARTWRIGHT], m/2 John GOSMER; in Eng, 1601?

WOODRUFF, John (1604-1670) & Ann __?__; in Eng, b 1637; Southampton, LI

WOODRUFF, John (1637-1691) & Mary [OGDEN]; b 1661; Southampton, LI/Elizabeth, NJ

WOODRUFF, John (1643-1692) & Mary WINCHELL; b 1667; Farmington, CT

WOODRUFF, John & Hannah [NEWTON]; 1670 or later; Southampton, LI

WOODRUFF, John & Sarah COOPER (1666-1727); 25 Oct 1683; New Haven

WOODRUFF, John (1669-) & 1/wf Elizabeth [THOMPSON] (-1705); b 1697; ?Farmington, CT

WOODRUFF, John (-1726) & Mary PLATT; 22 Dec 1698; Milford, CT

WOODRUFF, Joseph & 1/wf Lydia SMITH; 23 Jan 1699/1700; Farmington, CT

WOODRUFF, Mathew (-1682) & Hannah __?__; b 1642; Hartford/Farmington, CT

WOODRUFF, Matthew (1646-1691) & 1/wf Mary PLUMB; 16 Jun 1668; Milford, CT/Farmington, CT

WOODRUFF, Matthew (-1691) & 2/wf Sarah [NORTH] (1653-1691/2); b 24 Nov 1686; Farmington, CT

WOODRUFF, Matthew (1669-1751) & 1/wf Elizabeth BALDWIN (1673-1728/9); 15 Sep 1694; Farmington, CT

WOODRUFF, Samuel (1661-1742) & Rebecca [CLARK] (?1667-1737); ca 1685-6; Farmington, CT/Southington, CT

WOODRUFF, Samuel & Mary [JUDD] (1681-); b 1701?; Farmington, CT

WOODWARD, Amos (?1645-1679) & Sarah [PATTEN] (-1677); b 1677; Cambridge

WOODWARD, Daniel (1653-1713, Preston, CT) & Elizabeth DANA (1662-), m/2 Jonathan JENNINGS of Wenham; 14 Jan 1679; Medford

WOODWARD, Daniel & Elizabeth (SMITH) [GREELEY], w Benjamin; b 1697?, ca 1692?, seems doubtful; ?Cambridge

WOODWARD, Ezekiel (1622, ?1624-1699, 1698?) & 1/wf Anne [BEAMSLEY] (1633-1671); b 1651; Boston/Ipswich

WOODWARD, Ezekiel (1622-1699, 1698?) (ae 58 in 1680) & 2/wf Elizabeth (_?_) SOLART, w John; 20 Dec 1672; Wenham

WOODWARD, Ezekiel (1622-1699) & 3/wf Sarah [PIPER], w Nathaniel; aft 26 Sep 1676, ?Jun 1679; ?Ipswich/Wenham

WOODWARD, Ezekiel (1666-) & 1/wf Hannah [PERKINS]; b 1697; Gloucester

WOODWARD, George (?1619-1676) & 1/wf Mary _?_ (-1658?); b 1641; Watertown

WOODWARD, George (1619-1676) & 2/wf Elizabeth HAMMOND (?1634-1700); 17 Aug 1659; Watertown

WOODWARD, George (1660-1696) & Lydia BROWNE (1663-1711+); 31 Dec 1686, 30 Dec 1686; Watertown

WOODWARD, Henry (?1607-) & Elizabeth [MATHER?] (-1690); b 1642; Dorchester/Northampton/Deerfield

WOODWARD, Israel (-1674) & Jane GODFREY (-1736, ae 85), m/2 John COBB 1676; 4 Aug 1670; Taunton

WOODWARD, Israel (1674-) & Bennet EDY/EDDY; 28 Dec 1698; Taunton

WOODWARD, James (-1732) & Hannah [STACY]; b 1698; Taunton

WOODWARD, John (?1621-1696) & 1/wf Mary [WHITE] (-1654, Sudbury); b 1650; Watertown

WOODWARD, John (?1621-1696) & 2/wf Abigail (BENJAMIN) [STUBBS] (-1704), w Joshua; aft 9 Mar 1655/6, b 1658?; Watertown/Sudbury

WOODWARD, John (?1645, 1647-1723, 1724, ae 77) & 1/wf Ann DEWEY (1643-1707); 18 May 1671; Northampton/Westfield/Lebanon, CT

WOODWARD, John (1649-1732) & 1/wf Rebecca [ROBBINS] (-1696); b 1674, ca 1672; Cambridge/Newton/Reading

WOODWORD, John (-1688) & Sarah CROSSMAN (ca 1653-); 11 Nov 1675, 1676?; Rehoboth

WOODARD, John & 1/wf Sarah BANCROFT (1665-1697); 7 Jul 1686; Reading

WOODWARD, John (1661-1736) & Susannah [GROUT] (1664-1727); b 1692; Sudbury

WOODERD, John (1675-) & Hannah HIDE (-1725); 11 Apr 1698; Boston/Newton/Canterbury, CT

WOODWARD, John (1649-1732) & 2/wf Sarah (PRENTICE) SMITH (-1723), w John; 16 Mar 1698/9; Cambridge

WOODWARD, John (-1744) & 2/wf Margaret (HUTCHINSON) LEAMON, w Samuel LEMAN?; 29 Jan 1699/1700; Reading

WOODWARD, John (1676-1759+) & [Deborah THAYER]; b 1701?; Taunton?

WOODWARD, Joseph (-1726) & 1/wf Mary PRAY; 15 Jan 1677; ?Providence

WOODWARD, Joseph (-1726) & 2/wf Ruth [GOODSELL] (1658-1729) (div wf of Thomas GOODSELL); aft 1683, no issue

WOODWARD, Joseph & Lydia [SMITH]; b 1702, b 1701?; Worthington, CT

WOODWARD, Lambert & ?Sarah (BLOOMFIELD) [SACKETT]?, w Simon; Newtown, LI

WOODWARD, Nathaniel & Margaret _?_; in Eng, b 1615; Boston

WOODWARD, Nathaniel (-1675?) & Mary [JACKSON]; b 1644; Boston

WOODWARD, Nathaniel (-1686+) & 2/wf Katherine _?_; b 21 Mar 1664/5; Taunton

WOODWARD, Nathaniel (1646-) & Elizabeth _?_; b 1667; Boston/Taunton

WOODWARD, Nathaniel (-1675) & Mary _?_; b 1667(8?); Boston

WOODWARD, Peter (1604-1685) & _?_; ca 1622?; Dedham

WOODWARD, Peter (1638-) & Mehitable _?_; b 1668(9?); Dedham/?Roxbury

WOODWARD, Ralph (-1662) & _?_; ?ca 1625; Hingham

WOODWARD, Ralph & 2/wf Mary _?_; 12 Feb 1639; Hingham

WOODWARD, Richard (1589-1663) & 1/wf Rose _?_ (1584-6 Oct 1662, ae ca 80); in Eng, b 1619; Watertown

WOODWARD, Richard (1589-1663) & 2/wf Ann (VEARE) GATES (-1683), w Stephen; m cont 18 Apr 1663; Watertown

WOODWARD, Robert (-1653, Boston) & Rachel [SMITH], m/2 Thomas HARWOOD 1654; b 1641; Boston

WOODWARD, Robert (1646-1675) & _?_; ca 1670?

WOODARD, Robert & 1/wf Bethia [TORREY] (1665-1714+); b 1685; Scituate

WOODWARD, Smith (-1737) & Thankful POOP/POPE (1672-1738); 29 Jul 1691; Dorchester

WOODARD, Thomas (-1685) & Mary GUNS/GOOSE; 7 Mar 1659/60; Boston/Roxbury

WOODWARD, Thomas & Esther __?__; b 1663; Boston

WOODWARD, Thomas, Muddy River & Tryphena FAIRFIELD (1667-), Ipswich; 30 May 1688; Watertown/Boston/Brookline

WOODWARD/WOODWORTH, John?, Lebanon, CT, & Deborah (CALKINS) [ROYCE] (1643, 1645-1723, 1724), w Jonathan; aft 1690, b 14 Dec 1709, aft 1707

WOODWARD, Ezekiel & Hannah [PERKINS] (1673/4-); b 1701?; Ipswich?

WOODWARD, Smith & Deliverance HOPPIN, m/2 Richard BUTTS b 1670; Dorchester

WOODWELL, John (1665-) & Elizabeth [STACEY], dau Thomas; b 1697, b 9 Feb 1690; Salem

WOODWELL, Matthew (-1691) (called John ARCHER "son" in 1669) & Mary [ARCHER?]; b 1659; Salem

WOODWELL, Matthew (1668-1702) & Ann __?__; Salem

WOODWELL, Samuel (-1697) & Thomasine [STACY], m/2 __?__ HILL; b 1687, b 1685(6?); Salem

WOODWORTH, Benjamin[2] (son Walter) & 1/wf Deborah __?__ (see Thomas?); b 1660?, ca 1678?, ca 1677?; Scituate

WOODWARD/WOODWORTH, Benjamin[2] (-22 Apr 1629, 1728, Lebanon) & 2/wf Hannah __?__ m John MAY 1695?, m/2 Preserved HALL (wrong); b 24 Jun 1691; Little Compton, RI

WOODWORTH, Benjamin & Mary SWIFT; 19 Jul 1699; Lebanon, CT? (doubtful)

WOODWORTH, Hezekiah (1670/1-) & Hannah CLAP (1671, 1673?-1734); 23 Dec 1697; Scituate/Little Compton, RI

WOODWORTH/WOODWARD?, Isaac (1659?-) & Lydia [STANLAKE], dau Richard; ca 1680/90, ca 1686?; Scituate/Little Compton, RI/Norwich, CT

WOODWORTH, Joseph (ca 1644-) & 2/wf? Sarah STOCKBRIDGE; 6 Jan 1669, 1669/70, 6 Jan 1666; Scituate

WOODWORTH, Joseph (1671-) & Rebecca __?__; b 1694; Little Compton, RI

WOODWORTH, Thomas (ca 1640-1718) & Deborah DAMEN/DAMON (1645-1696+); 8 Feb 1666; Scituate

WOODWORTH, Walter[1] & __?__; b 1636, b 1631?; Scituate

WOODWORTH, Walter & __?__; 1669; Little Compton, RI

WOODY, Isaac (-1670) & Dorcas HARPER; 20 Mar 1655/6; Boston

WOODY, John (-1650) & Mary [COGGAN], m/2 Thomas ROBINSON 1653; b 1649; Scituate/Boston

WOODDEE, John (1659-) & Mary __?__; b 1687; Boston

WOODY, Richard[1] (-1658) & 1/wf Anna __?__ (-1656); b 1626; Roxbury/Boston

WOODY, Richard[2] & Frances DEXTER; 29 Dec 1646; Roxbury/Boston

WOODY, Richard[1] (-1658) & 2/wf __?__ [PAUL], wid; b 1658; Roxbury

WOOLEN, Richard (-1694) & Amy __?__, m/2 Roger VICARY

WOOLLEN, Thomas & Mary [NORTON]; ca 1686; Martha's Vineyard/Weymouth

WOOLLEY, Adam (1653/4-1676) & Mary __?__; b 1674; Newport

WOOLLY, Christopher (-1701) & 1/wf Ursula WODELL/?ODELL (1628-1674); 26 Feb 1646/7; Concord

WOOLLIE, Christopher (-1701) & 2/wf Mary HOW (-1695), w William; 10 Apr 1677; Concord

WOOLLEY, Edward (1655-) & Lydia/Lelia? [ALLEN] (1660-); b 1685; Sandwich/Newport/Monmouth, NJ

WOOLLEY, Emanuel & Elizabeth __?__; b 1653(4?); ?Sandwich/Newport

WOOLEY, John (?1659-) & Elizabeth [ISBELL]; b 1689; ?Killingworth, CT

WOOLLY, Joseph (-1745), Concord & Rachel BRACKET (1669-), Chelmsford; 3 Dec 1688, ?10 Mar 1688/9; ?Chelmsford

WOOLLY, Robert & Ann [WOODRUFF]; Southampton, LI

WOOLLY, Thomas (-1710, 1701?) & Rebecca FRENCH, m/2 John BLYTHE; 19 Dec 1697; Concord

WOOLRYCH/WOOLRICH, John & Sarah [KETCHAM]; b 1633; Charlestown

WOOLLRIGE, ?Mihill (Did he marry?) & __?__; CT

WOOLSEY, George (?1610-1698) & Rebecca CORNELL? (-1718, ae 91); 19? Dec, 9 Dec 1647; New York/Flushing, LI/Jamaica, LI

WOOLSEY, George (1652-1740) & [Hannah] __?__; b 1682, ca 1679; NY/Jamaica, LI/Dosorus, LI

WOOLSEY, John (1661-1727) & Abigail __?__; Jamaica, LI

WOOLSEY, Thomas (1655-) & Ruth __?__; Jamaica, LI/Bedford, NY

WOOLSON, Joseph (1677-1755) & Hannah __?__ (-1721); b 1699; Watertown/Weston

WOOLSON, Thomas (-1713) & Sarah HIDE/(HYDE) (1644-1721); 20 Nov 1660; Cambridge/Sudbury

WOOLSON, Thomas (1667-1723) & Elizabeth [CHADWICK] (1673-); b 1694; Watertown/Cambridge

WOOLERY/WOOLWORTH, Richard & Hannah HUGGINS; 24 Dec 1678; Newbury/Suffield, CT

WOOREY, Ralph & Margaret __?__; b 1641; Charlestown

WOOSTER, Abraham (1673-1743) & Mary WALKER; 22 Nov 1699, 1697?; Stratford, CT

WOOSTER, Edward[1] & 1/wf Dorothy [LANGTON?]/LANGDON?; b 1652?; Milford, CT

WOOSTER, Edward (-1689, ae 67) & 2/wf Tabitha [TOMLINSON] (-1691), m/2 John HULL 1690; b 1666?; Stratford, CT

WOOSTER, Sylvester (-1712) & Susanna __?__, m/2 Samuel WASHBURN; b 1699, b 1701; Derby, CT

WOOSTER, Thomas (?1656-1713), Derby, CT, & Phebe [TOMLINSON] (1656-1740); b 1679; Stratford, CT

WOOSTER, Timothy (1670-) & Ann/Anna PERRY (1680-); 23 May 1699; Milford, CT/Derby, CT

WOSTER, Francis (-1717) & Mary CHEYNY/CHENEY, m/2 Joseph EATON; 29 Jan 1690/1, 20? Jan; Bradford

WOOSTER, Joseph (-1746) & 1/wf Sarah ROSS (-1728); 17 May 1699; Concord/Bradford

WORCESTER, Moses (1643-1731+) & 1/wf Elizabeth [START]; b 1676, b 4 Jul 1676; Kittery, ME

WORCESTER, Moses (1643-1731+) & 2/wf Sarah SOPER, w John; 4 Apr 1695; Kittery, ME

WORCESTER, Samuel (-1681) & Elizabeth PARRAT (1640-), m/2 Onesiphorus MARSH 1686; 29 Nov 1659; Rowley/Bradford

WORCESTER, Timothy (1642-1672) & Susanna __?__, m/2 Henry AMBROSE 1672; b 1667; Salisbury

WOSTER, Timothy (-1706) & Huldah CHEYNEY/CHENEY, m/2 Simon DAKIN?; 29 Jan 1690/1, 20? Jan; Bradford/Salem/Newbury

WORCESTER, William (-1662) & 1/wf Sarah __?__ (-1650); in Eng, b 1637, ca 1632?; Salisbury

WORCESTER, William (-1662) & Rebecca (SWAYNE) (BYLEY) HALL (-1695), w Henry, w John, m/4 Samuel SYMONDS 1663; 22 Jul 1650; Salisbury

WOSTER, William (-1683) & Constant/Constance __?__; b 1666; Rowley/Boston

WOSTER, William (-1706) & Martha CHEYNY (1673-1739), m/2 John PEMBERTON 1711; 29 Jan 1690/1; Bradford

WORMELL, Daniel & 1/wf Sarah __?__; b 1701; Boston

WORMELL, John & Mary BURROWS; 9 Jan 1698; Duxbury/Bridgewater

WORMELL, Joseph (-1662) & Miriam __?__; b 1642; Rowley/Boston/Scituate

WORMALL, Josiah (1642-) & [?Remember BROWN?] (-1684), dau John; b 1674; Duxbury

WORMALL, Josiah & 1/wf Patience SHERMAN; 15 Jan 1695; Duxbury

WORMESTALL, Arthur & Susanna [SCADLOCK]; b 1658, b 1663; Saco, ME/Winter Harbor, ME

WORMSTALL, Michael & Rebecca DIMON, m/2 Edward HAMMOND 1709; 5 Jul 1696; Mablehead

WORMWOOD, Henry & Mary [KNIGHT]?; b 1666; Reading/Lynn/Concord/Andover

WORMWOOD, Jacob & __?__ [REYNOLDS?]; Saco, ME/Durham, NH/etc.

WORMWOOD, Joseph/?Henry & Mary __?__; b 1669(70?); Concord

WORMWOOD, Thomas & Jane [REYNOLDS]; Durham, NH/Kittery, ME

WORMWOOD?/WORNAL?/WORNAN?, William & Christian [TALMAGE], m/2 Edward BELCHER; b 1635; Boston

WORMWOOD, William (-1690) & 1/wf Catherine __?__; b 1650?, b 1647; Kittery, ME/Isles of Shoals

WORMWOOD, William & Mary __?__, m/2 John SPENCER 1690+; York, ME

WORMWOOD, William (1666-) & Sarah BALLARD (1669-); 25 Mar 1690; Lynn

WORMWOOD, [John?] & Alice [SMALL], m/2 Beriah SMITH 1711; b 1709, b 1701?; ME/Truro

WORMWOOD?, __?__ & Hope [?REYNOLDS]

WORRELL, John (alias JOHNSON) & Mary DOWNE; 7 Dec 1668; Warwick, RI

WORTH, James & Elizabeth __?__; b 1686(7?); Boston/Dorchester

WORTH, John (1666-1732) & 1/wf Miriam GARDNER (-1700); 22 Sep 1684; Nantucket/Edgartown

WORTH, John & Elizabeth WEBSTER; 17 Mar 1686/7; Newbury

WORTH, Lionel (-1667) & Susanna [WHIPPLE] (1622-), m/2 Moses PILSBURY 1668; ca 1648, b 1650; Newbury

WORTH, Richard & Mary PIKE; 11 Sep 1667; Newbury

WORTH, William (1640±-1724) & 1/wf Sarah MACY (1646-1701); 11 Apr 1665; Nantucket
WATHEN/WORTHEN, Ezekiel (±1636-1716) & Hannah MARTYN/MARTIN (-1730); 4 Dec 1661; Salisbury/Amesbury
WATHEN, George (-1642/3?) & Margaret _?_ (-1644); in Eng, b 1625; Salem
WOTHEN, George (1669-) & Ann [ANNIS] (1681-), Newbury; b 1700; Amesbury
WATHEN, John (1665-) & Mary HADLOCK; 30 Dec 1689; Amesbury
WATHEN, Thomas (1667-1702) & Hannah ANNIS (1679-), m/2 Ephraim WEAD 1704; m int 11 May 1700; Amesbury
WORTHILAKE/WORTHLAKE?, Benjamin & Susanna _?_ ; b 1688(9?); Boston
WORTHYLAKE, George & Ann _?_ ; b 1701?; Boston
WORTHELIKE, Peter & Alice? _?_ ; b 1676; Scituate
WORTHINGTON, Nicholas (-1683) & 1/wf Sarah (BUNCE) [WHITE] (-1676), w John; ca 1668, b 12 Feb 1669/76; Hartford
WORTHINGTON, Nicholas (-1683) & 2/wf Susanna? _?_ (-1727), wid, m/3 Jonathan BALL; b 1679, 1677?; Hadley/Hartford
WORTHINGTON, William (1670±-1753) & Mehitable (GRAVES) MORTON (1671-1742), w Richard; b 1695; Hartford/Colchester, CT
WRIGHT, Abel (?1632-1725) & Martha KRITCHWELL/KITCHERELL (-1708); 1 Dec 1659; Springfield/Westfield
WRIGHT, Abel (1664-1745) & Rebecca TERRY (1673-1745); 16 Sep 1691; Springfield
WRIGHT, Adam (-1724) & 1/wf Sarah [SOULE] (-1691+); ?ca 1665/75?; Duxbury/Bridgewater
WRIGHT, Adam & Mary [DENNIS]; b 1673; Oyster Bay, LI
WRIGHT, Adam (-1724) & 2/wf Mehitabel [BARROWS]; b 1699; Middleboro
WRIGHT, Anthony (-1679) & Mary (SMITH) [TREAT], w Matthias, m/3 John SMITH; b 1670; Wethersfield, CT
WRIGHT, Benjamin (-1677) & Jane _?_ (-1684); b 1644; Guilford, CT/Killingworth, CT
WRIGHT, Benjamin (1660-1743) & 1/wf Thankful TAYLOR (1663-1701); 22 Mar 1680; Deerfield/Northampton
WRIGHT, Benjamin (1667-1704) & Mary CHAPIN (?1668-1708); 24 Jan 1695, 1694/5; Springfield
WRIGHT, Benoni (1675-1702) & Rebecca [BARRETT], m/2 Samuel DICKINSON; ca 1700; Northampton
WRIGHT, Caleb (1645-1695) & Elizabeth DICKINSON (1652-1695); 167-; Oyster Bay, LI
WRIGHT, David & Hannah _?_ ; b 1695; Flushing, LI
WRIGHT, David (1677-) & 1/wf Rebecca GOODRICH (1680-1703); 28 Dec 1699; Wethersfield, CT
WRIGHT, Dennis & Susanna [HAUXHURST]; 1699; Oyster Bay, LI/Huntington, LI
WRIGHT, Ebenezer (1663-) & 1/wf Elizabeth STRONG (-1691?); 16 Sep 1684, 26 Sep 1684; Northampton
WRIGHT, Ebenezer (1663-) & Hannah HUNT; 19 Dec 1691, 1692?; Northampton
WRIGHT, Ebenezer & Hannah FLETCHER; 14 May 1697; Chelmsford
WRIGHT, Edmund (1640-1703) & Sarah [WRIGHT] (1648-); b 1666?, b 1670; Oyster Bay, LI
WRIGHT, Edmund (1670-) & Sarah [TOWNSEND]; by 1690?, b 1695; Oyster Bay, LI
WRIGHT, Edward (?1627-1691) & Elizabeth (MELLOWES) [BARRETT] (1625-1691), w Thomas; ca 1654-6; Concord
WRIGHT, Edward & 1/wf Mary POWELL; 27 May 1657, 1656?; Boston
WRIGHT, Edward (-1703) & Hannah/Axtell? EPSON/[UPSON]; 18 Jun 1659; Sudbury
WRIGHT, Edward & Lydia (SYLVESTER) RAWLINS, w Nathaniel; 25 May 1664; Scituate/Hull
WRIGHT, Edward & _?_ [?COLES]; b 1674; Matinicock, LI
WRIGHT, Edward (1657-1725) & Lydia [DANFORTH] (1664-1725+); b 1693; Concord
WRIGHT, Eleazer (1668-) & Mary _?_ [probably not PARDEE]; b 1689; ?Northfield
WRIGHT, George & _?_ ; b 1620?, b 1626; Newport, RI
WRIGHT, George & Mary HANNISON; 18 Oct 1694; Hartford
WRIGHT, Gideon & Elizabeth [TOWNSEND], m/2 Gershom LOCKWOOD; b 1671; Oyster Bay, LI
WRIGHT, Henry & Elizabeth _?_ ; b 1635; Dorchester
WRIGHT, Henry (-1720+) & Sarah [START]; Jul 1673; Boston
WRIGHT, Henry & Mary _?_ ; b 1698; Flushing, LI
WRIGHT, James (-1705) & 1/wf Mary _?_ (-1659); b 1659; Wethersfield, CT
WRIGHT, James (-1705) & 2/wf Dorcas [WEED] (ca 1641-1692); 20 Nov 1660; Wethersfield, CT
WRIGHT, James (-1723) & Abigail JESS; 18 Jan 1664/[5]; Northampton

WRIGHT, James (ca 1661-1748) & Mercy/?Mary ROSE (1670-1740); 17 July 1690; Wethersfield, CT

WRIGHT, James & Mary [?DUDLEY]; aft 1692; Wethersfield, CT

WRIGHT, James & Hannah [SANFORD] (1675-); ca 1696/7; ?Milford, CT/Durham, CT

WRIGHT, James & 1/wf Sarah [WISE]; b 1701; Saybrook, CT

WRIGHT, Job & Rachel [TOWNSEND]; b 1680?; Oyster Bay, LI

WRIGHT, John (1601-1688) & Priscilla _?_ (-1687); b 1630?; Woburn

WRIGHT, John (-1658/9) & [?Alice _?_]; b 1650; Newbury

WRIGHT, John (?1631-1714) & Abigail WARREN (-1726, ae 84); 10 May 1661; Chelmsford

WRIGHT, John & Mary [TOWNSEND]; b 1670?, b 1686, b 1691; ?Oyster Bay, LI

WRIGHT, John & Marie/Mary STEPHENS/STEVENS; 13 Apr 1692; Chelmsford

WRIGHT, John & Mercy/Mary [WARDWELL] (1673-); 1697; Andover

WRIGHT, John (1672-) & Lydia KENDALL (1674-1711); 21 Sep 1698; Woburn

WRIGHT, Jonathan (-1698) & Sarah _?_; b 1670?; Flushing, LI

WRIGHT, Jonathan, Jr. & Wine _?_; by 1694-5?; Flushing, LI

WRIGHT, Joseph & Elizabeth HASSELL (-1713); 1 Nov 1661; Woburn

WRIGHT, Joseph (1639-1711) & 1/wf Mary [STODDARD] (1643-1683); 10 Dec 1663; Wethersfield, CT

WRIGHT, Joseph (1657-1697) & Ruth SHELDON, m/2 Samuel STRONG 1698; 6 Nov 1679; Deerfield/Northampton

WRIGHT, Joseph (1639-1714) & 2/wf Mercy (DEMING) CURTIS (-1715), w Joseph; 10 Mar 1685, 1685/6?; Wethersfield, CT

WRIGHT, Joseph (1660-) & Sarah OSBORN (1666/7(?)-1733+); 29 Dec 1687; Springfield/Palmer

WRIGHT, Joseph & 1/wf Elizabeth BATEMAN (-1704); 7 Jul 1692; Woburn

WRIGHT, Joseph & Ann HENRY; m lic 11 Jan 1694; Oyster Bay, LI

WRIGHT, Joseph & Elizabeth _?_ (-1702); b 1696; Killingworth, CT

WRIGHT, Joseph & Deborah [?STEVENS]; b 1700; Chelmsford

WRIGHT, Josiah (1674-1747) & Ruth CARTER (1681-); 17 Sep 1700; Woburn

WRIGHT, Judah (1642-1705) & 1/wf Mercy BURT (1647-1705?); 7 Jan 1666/[7]; Northampton

WRIGHT, Nicholas (1609-1682) & Ann [BEAUPRE]; b 1630; Lynn/Sandwich/Oyster Bay, LI

WRIGHT, Peter & Alice _?_, m/2 Richard CRABB; b 1634; Sandwich/Oyster Bay, LI

WRIGHT, Peter (1665-1718) & Elizabeth LAMSON, m/2 Enoch CLEVELAND 1719; 5 May 1684, no issue; Concord

WRIGHT, Richard[1] & Margaret _?_; b 1620?; Saugus/Boston/Braintree

WRIGHT, Richard (1608-1681) & Hester/Esther COOKE; 21 Nov 1644; Plymouth

WRIGHT, Robert & Mary _?_; b 1645; Boston

WRIGHT, Samuel (-1661) & Margaret _?_ (-1681, Northampton); in Eng, b 1627; Springfield

WRIGHT, Samuel & Elizabeth BURT, m/2 Nathaniel DICKINSON; 24 Nov 1653; Springfield

WRIGHT, Samuel (-1690) & Mary [BUTLER] (-1689); 29 Sep 1659; Wethersfield, CT

WRIGHT, Samuel & Hannah ALBEE; 25 Mar 1663; Medfield

WRIGHT, Samuel (-1664) & Lydia MOORES/MOORE (1643-1723), m/2 James CUTTER 1665; 3 May 1664; Sudbury

WRIGHT, Samuel (1654-1734) & Sarah LYMAN (1658-); 3 Jan 1678, 1677/8?; Northampton

WRIGHT, Samuel (1661-1741) & 1/wf Mary [HOSMER] (1664-1725); ca 1680/6?, 1690; Concord

WRIGHT, Samuel (-1734) & 1/wf Rebecca CRAFT (1671-1711); 11 May 1686, 12 May 1686; Roxbury/Wethersfield, CT

WRIGHT, Samuel (1670-1740) & Mary [STEVENS] (1672-1739); b 1698; Braintree/Sudbury?/Rutland

WRIGHT, Samuel & Rebecca [SYKES] (1678-); 3 Nov 1697; Lebanon, CT

WRIGHT, Thomas (1610-1670) & 1/wf _?_ CRANBROKE; in Eng, b 1630; Wethersfield, CT

WRIGHT, Thomas (1610-1670) & 2/wf Margaret (HILLIARD?) [ELSON] (-1671), w Hugh?/Benjamin?, w John; aft 1648; Wethersfield, CT

WRIGHT, Thomas (1632-1680) & Elizabeth [CHITTENDEN]/DEMING? (1637?-1683, 1675?); 16 Jun 1657; Wethersfield, CT

WRIGHT, Thomas & Hannah _?_; b 1670; Sudbury

WRIGHT, Thomas (1660-1692) & Sarah BENTON (1650-1692); 9 Dec 1673, 1673; Guilford, CT

RIGHT, Thomas (-1691) & Elizabeth _?_, m/2 John SANDERS 1691, 1692; b 1683; Scituate

WRIGHT, Thomas & Mary [GREENWOOD] (1673-), m/2 Thomas POTTS 1713; b 1701; Boston

WRIGHT, Walter & 1/wf Susanna JOHNSON; 26 Feb 1667, 1668; Andover

WRIGHT, Walter & 2/wf Elizabeth (PETERS) SADIE/SADIR?, w John; 9 Sep 1684, 1687?; Andover

WRIGHT, William (-1633) & Priscilla/Dille? [CARPENTER], m/2 John COOPER 1634; in Eng, b 1621?; Plymouth

WRIGHT, William & Melcha [SNOW] (-1678), wid; aft 28 Apr 1669, b 1672; Boston

WRIGHT, William & Abigail [SNOW]; b 1671; Boston

WRIGHT, William & Sarah BROWNE; 5 Oct 1692; Newbury

WRIGHT, _?_ & Dorothy _?_, m/2 John BLANDFORD 1642; Sudbury

WRIGHT, _?_ & Elizabeth [STODDARD] (1656); doubtful

WRIGHT/(DAVIS?), William & Mary (DAVIS) (DODD) AUSTIN

WRONG, Michael & Judith _?_; b 1685; Boston

ROATH/WROTH, John & Sarah WILLIAMS; 6 Aug 1695; Norwich, CT

ROATH, Robert & Sarah SAXTON (-1688); - Oct 1668; Norwich, CT

WROTHAM, Simon (-1689) & [?Sarah] _?_ (-1684); b 1663; ?Farmington

WYAT, Edward (-1681) & Mary _?_ (1614-1706, ae 92); b 1649; Dorchester/Milton

WYATT, George (-1720+) & Elizabeth _?_; b 1702, 2 ch bpt, b 1701?; Salem

WYATT, Israel (1668-) & Sarah PRATT; 10 Dec 1690; Hadley/Hatfield/(Northampton, etc.)

WYATT, James (-1664) & Mary _?_; ca 1643?; Taunton

WYATT, John (-1665) & 1/wf _?_; b 1624?, b 1616?; Ipswich

WYATT, John & 2/wf 3/wf Mary [?JACKSON] (-1684), m/2 James BARKER 1666; Ipswich

WYATT, John (-1668) & Mary [BRONSON], m/2 John GRAVES 1671?, m/3 William ALLIS 1678, m/4 Samuel GAYLORD 1681; b 1647; Hartford/Farmington/Haddam, CT

WYATT, John & Elizabeth LONG, w Samuel?; 8 Oct 1674; Cambridge/Charlestown

WYATT, John & Salome [JACKSON], m/2 Nathan WHITE, m/3 Francis JENNERS; by 1669; Portsmouth, NH

WYAT, John (1650-) & Elizabeth _?_; b 1680; Woodbury, CT

WIAT, John & Hannah/Ann/Anna GARRET; 7 Feb 1694, 7 Feb 1694/5; Boston/Watertown

WYATE, John & Anna [CHRISTOPHERS], dau Richard; b 1701; Boston

WYATT, John (-1747) & Mary BADGER; 15 Dec 1700; Newbury

WYAT, Nathaniel & 1/wf Johanna SPUR (-1687/8); 8 Jan 1668/9; Dorchester

WIET, Nathaniel, Dorchester & 2/wf Mary CORBIN, New Cambridge, w John; 13 Dec 1688; Milton

WEAT, Nathaniel & _?_/(Rachel WEBSTER) (not married); b 1697; Stamford, CT

WIETT, William & Elizabeth _?_; b 1696(7?); Rochester

WYATT, ?Richard & Hannah (PARKER)? BROMSFIELD, w John; 28 Dec 1704

WYER, Edward (-1693, ae 71) & Elizabeth JOHNSON (1639-1715), m/2 William MONROE; 5 Jan 1658/9, 5 Dec 1658, 5 Jan 1659?, 5-11-1658; Charlestown

WYER, Edward (?1661-1700?, 1688?) & Abigail LAWRENCE, m/2 Nicholas LAWRENCE ?1689, m/3 Edward CLIFFORD ?1711+; 1 Sep 1684; Charlestown/Cambridge

WIER, Eleazer (1672-) & Katherine [WADE] (1673-); b 1696; Charlestown/Medford

WYAR, Robert & Mary _?_ (see WIARD); b 1646; Boston

WYER, Robert (1644-1709) & 1/wf Elizabeth FOWLE (-1689); 26 Jun 1688; Charlestown

WYER, Robert (1644-1709) & 2/wf Ruth [JOHNSON] (1670-1742, in 74th y?); b 1693; Charlestown

WYER, Zachariah (1676-1717) & Marah JONES; 7 Jun 1698, at Concord; Charlestown/Boston

WYETH, John (1655-) & Deborah WARD (1662-); 2 Jan 1682/3; Cambridge

WYETH, Nicholas (1595-1680) & 1/wf Margaret [CLARKE] (1608-); ca 1630/4; Cambridge

WITHE, Nicholas & 2/wf Rebecca [ANDREWS], w Thomas, m/3 Thomas FOX 1685; ca 1648; Cambridge

WITHE, Nicholas & 1/wf Lydia FISK (1648-); 6 Sep 1681; Cambridge/Lexington

WYETH, Nicholas & 2/wf Deborah PARKER; 30 Jun 1698; Watertown

WYTHE, William & Ruth SHEPARD; 16 Oct 1683; Cambridge

WYMAN, David (-1678) & Isabel FARMER?, m/2 James BLOOD 1679, m/3 William GREEN 1695; 8 Feb 1674/5, Apr 27 1675; Charlestown

WYMAN, Francis (1619, 1617-1699) & 1/wf Judith PIERCE; 30 Jan 1644, 1644/5, 30 Dec 1644; Woburn

WYMAN, Francis (1617-1699) & 2/wf Abigail REED (bpt 1638-); 2 Oct 1650; Woburn

WYMAN, Jacob (-1742), Woburn & 1/wf Elizabeth RICHARDSON (-1739), Woburn; 23 Nov 1687; Woburn

WYMAN, John (1621-1684) & Sarah NUTT (-1688), m/2 Thomas FULLER 1684; 5 Nov 1644; Woburn
WYMAN, John (1648-1675) & Mary [CARTER] (1648-1688), m/2 Nathaniel BATCHELDER 1676; b 1672; Woburn
WYMAN, John (-1728) & Hannah FARRAR (1668-); 14 Dec 1685; Woburn
WYMAN, John & Rebecca REED; 28 Jan 1696; Woburn
WYMAN, Jonathan (1661-1736) & 1/wf Abigail FOWLE (-1690); 29 Jul 1689; Woburn/Charlestown
WYMAN, Jonathan (1661-1736) & 2/wf Hannah FOWLE (1671-); 31 Jul 1690; Woburn/Charlestown
WYMAN, Nathaniel (1665-1717) & Mary WINN, m/2 John LOCKE 1720; 28 Jun 1692, 1691?; Woburn
WYMAN, Samuel (1667-1725) & Rebecca JOHNSON (1665-); 1692; Woburn
WYMAN, Seth (1663-1715) & Hesther/?Esther JOHNSON (-1742); 17 Dec 1685; Woburn
WYMAN, Thomas (1671-1731) & Mary RICHARDSON (-1774), m/2 Josiah WINN 1733; 5 May 1696; Woburn/Charlestown
WYMAN, Timothy (1661-1709) & Hannah __?__ (not WISWALL); b 1688; Woburn
WYMAN, William (1656±-1705) & Prudence [PUTNAM] (1652-), m/2 Peter TUFTS 1717; ca 1682/3; Woburn
WYNYARD/WHINYARD, Thomas & Anna [GOULD]; Charlestown

YALE, David (1613-) & Ursula __?__; b 1644; Boston/London, Eng
YALE, John (-1711) & Rebecca [MIX] (-1734); b 1694; New Haven
YALE, Nathaniel (-1730) & Ruth BISHOP; 11 Oct 1692, 21 Oct; New Haven
YALE, Thomas (-d in Wales) & Anne [LLOYD] (-1659), m/2 Theophilus EATON; ca 1610; New Haven
YALE, Thomas (1615-1683) & Mary [TURNER] (-1704); b 1646; New Haven
YALE, Thomas, Wallingford & 1/wf Rebecca GIBBARD; 11 Dec 1667; New Haven
YALE, Thomas (-1736) & 2/wf Sarah NASH (1649-1716); 8 Feb 1688/9; New Haven/Wallingford, CT
YEALE/YEALES, Timothy & Naomi [FRY]; b 1674(5?), b 1673; Boston/Weymouth
YARROW, Joseph & Sarah __?__, m/2 Thomas WHITE 1709; b 1698; Salem
YATES, Francis & __?__; Wethersfield, CT/Stamford, CT
YATES, Francis (-1682) & Dorothy MARSH; m lic 22 Jul 1669; Westchester, NY
YATES, John (-1651) & Mary __?__, m/2 Richard HIGGINS 1651, m/3 Isaac WHITEHEAD 1689; b 1650; Eastham
YATES, John (1650-bef 2 Jul 1682) & Deborah (?KENDRICK) (1646-1717+), m/2 John HURD; ca 1673; Eastham
YATES, John & Abigail ROGERS (1678-); 11 Jan 1698/9; Eastham
YEATES, John & Edey WILDE; NY m lic 5 Jul 1699; ?Flushing
YEATES, Thomas (mother's name Mary, had William, Benjamin, Jane) & Mary __?__; Flushing
YATES, William & [?Mary] __?__; b 1670?; Flushing
YELL, John & Joanna SMITH; 27 Jul 1690; Ipswich
YELLINGS, John & Tryphena __?__; by 1684; Isles of Shoals
YELINGS, Roger & Elizabeth [BALLANTINE/BALLENTINE], m/2 John COOMB; b 1680; Boston
YES, Thomas (-1658) & Sarah [PHIPPEN], m/2 Nathan GOLD; b 1652, b Nov 1650; Boston/Salem/Stratford, CT/Fairfield/Hingham
YOE, Samuel (1657) & Rebecca __?__
YEOMANS, Christopher & Hannah __?__; New Haven/Hempstead, LI
YEOMANS, Edward & Susannah __?__; b 1650; Charlestown
YEOMANS, Edward & Elizabeth JOSLIN (1629-), m/2 Edward KILBY 1662; 21 Jun 1652; Boston
YEOMAN, Edward & Mary BUTTON (1634-); 6 Dec 1652; Haverhill/?Plainfield, CT
YEOMANS, Edward (1663-) & Mary __?__; b 1692; Stonington, CT

YEOMANS, John (?1671, 1670-) & Millicent [UTTER]; ca 1693; Stonington, CT
YEOMANS, Samuel (1655-1704) & Mary ELLIS; 9 Oct 1684, 1º Oct 1684; ?Stonington, CT
YARRINTON/YERRINGTON, Peter & Abiel __?__ ; b 1696, (ca 1693?); Beverly
YORK, Benjamin (1654-) & [Abigail FOOTMAN], m/2 Thomas MEAKINS 1713±; b 27 Jun 1676; Dover, NH
YORK, James (1614-1683) & Joanna __?__ (-1685); ca 1637?; Braintree
YORK, James (1648-1676) & Deborah BELL, m/2 Henry ELIOT 1679; 19 Jan 1669, 17 Jan 1669; Stonington, CT
YORK, James (1672-1759) & Hannah STANTON; 13 Nov 1695; Westerly, RI
YORK, John (1642-1690), North Yarmouth, ME, & Ruth [GRAVES?] (doubtful); b Jun 1676; Dover, NH
YORK, Joseph & Abigail ROBINSON (-1720); 10 Jan 1699/1700, 10 Jan 1700; Gloucester
YORK, Richard (-1674) & Elizabeth __?__ (1618-), m/2 William GRAVES; b 1645; Dover, NH
YORK, Samuel (1645-1718) & Hannah __?__ (-1724); b Jun 1676, b 1677, b 1678; N. Yarmouth, ME/etc.
YORK, William (-1697) & Mary UTLEY/ALLEY; 18 Dec 1695; Stonington, CT
YOUNG, Benjamin & Sarah SNOW (1677-); 15 Feb 1699/1700; Eastham
YOUNGE, David (1662-1700) & Ann DOANE (1666-1758); 20 Jan 1687, 1687/8?; Eastham
YOUNG/TOUNG, Edward (-1743) & Hannah WHITTIER; 20 May 1683; Haverhill/Newbury
YOUNG, Francis & Rebecca (SMITH) CHAPMAN, w John; 4 Dec 1678; Ipswich
YOUNGE, George (-1672) & Hannah PINSON (1642-), m/2 John WETHERELL, m/3 Jonathan MOWRY by 1694; 15 Jan 1661; Scituate
YOUNG, George & Ann MURFY; 16 Jun 1696; Marblehead
YOUNG, Giles & Ruth [PARSONS] (1646-), ?m/2 William/Wm.? SWIFT; b 1672, by 1695; Boston
YOUNG, Henry (1672-1706) & Sarah [SNOW?] (?1673-1716), m/2 Jonathan SPARROW; b 1695; Eastham
YOUNGE, Henry & Elizabeth CONCORD?; b 1696; Charlestown
YOUNG, Job (1664-) & Sarah (AUSTIN) PREBLE (-1720), w Joseph; aft Oct 1691; York, ME
YOUNG, John (-1661) & Alice/?Achsah __?__ (-1647); b 1641?; Windosr, CT
YOUNG, John (-1691) & Abigail HOWLAND (?1630-1692); 13 Dec 1648, 1647?; Plymouth
YOUNG, John & __?__ ; b 1649 (doubtful); Portsmouth
YOUNG, John (1649-1718) & Ruth [COLE] (1651-), m/2 Jonathan BANGS 1720; ca 1674; Eastham
YOUNG, John (-1697) & Sarah [WADLEIGH] (-1697+); b 1675, int Feb 1671/2, b Mar 1671/2; Exeter, NH
YOUNG, John & Sarah RUNNALS; 16 Mar 1698 (doubtful); Northwood, NH
YOUNG, Joseph (1654-1721, 1722) & Sarah DAVIS (1660-1721+); 23 Oct 1679; Eastham
YOUNG, Joseph (ca 1672-1734) & Abigail [DONNELL]; b 1697; York, ME
YONG, Matthew/Matthews? & Eleanor HAYES/HAYNES (1673/4-); 23 Apr 1696; Newbury/York, ME
YOUNG, Nathaniel (1656-1706) & Mercy [DAVIS] (1662?-), m/2 Nathaniel MAYO 1708; ca 1680; Eastham
YOUNG, Richard (-1673) & Margaret (BATSON) KENDALL, w Wm., m/3 Robert ELLIOTT; b 1656; Kittery, ME
YOUNG, Robert (?1658-1690) & Mary [SAYWARD], m/2 Richard BRAY 1691?; b 4 Jul 1676, Jul 1676; York, ME
YOUNG, Robert (1667-1742) & Joanna HIX/HICKS (-1739+); 22 Mar 1693/4; Eastham
YOUNG, Rowland & 1/wf __?__ ; b 1649; York, ME
YOUNG, Rowland & 2/wf Joane [KNIGHT]; b 1668, ca 1648; York, ME
YOUNG, Rowland (1649-1721) & Susanna [MATTHEWS] (1652-); ca 167-; York, ME
YOUNG, Samuel (?1662-) & Elizabeth [MASTERSON]; b 1701?; York, ME
YOUNG, Thomas & Jane __?__ ; b 1658; Boston
YOUNG, Thomas (-1732, ae 69) & Sarah WHITE (1663-9 Aug 1755, ae 92), dau Peregrine; Jan 1688/9; Scituate
YOUNG, Thomas & Mary __?__/[ROBERTS?]; b 1691; N. Kingston, RI (prob not same Thomas)
YOUNG, William & Sarah [IRISH]?; b 1659; Andover
YOUNG, William & Sarah WHITEACHE; 11 Oct 1694; Boston
YOUNG, __?__ & __?__, widow had grant; b 1638; Cambridge
YOUNGLOVE, John[2] (-1690) & Sarah __?__ (-1710/11); b 1666; Hadley/Suffield, CT

YOUNGLOVE, John[3] & _?_ ; b 1700; Killingly, CT
YOUNGLOVE, Joseph[2] & Jane [PETTIS?]; Salisbury
YOUNGLOVE, Samuel[1] (1605-) (ae 62 in 1668) & Margaret _?_ (1607-); in Eng, b 1634; Ipswich
YOUNGLOVE, Samuel[2] (-1707) & 1/wf Sarah KINSMAN; 1 Aug 1660; Ipswich
YOUNGLOVE, Samuel[2] (-1707) & 2/wf Sarah (HADDON) [ELLIOT], w Edmund; b - Sep 1685; Salisbury
YOUNGLOVE, Samuel[3] & Abilene HUNTER; 28 Jul 1696; ?Suffield, CT
YOUNGLOVE, Samuel[2] (-1707) & 3/wf Mary [ROE]; aft 1695; Salisbury
YOUNGMAN, Francis (-1712) & Ann/Anna? (FISHER) HEATH, w Isaac; 2 Dec 1685; Roxbury
YOUNGS, Benjamin (1640-1697) & Elizabeth _?_ ; b 1676; Southold, LI
YOUNGS, Benjamin (1668-1742) & 1/wf Mary GROVER (1675-1706); 16 Sep 1695; Southold, LI
YONGS, Christopher (-1647) & Prisca [ELVIN] (-1646±); b 1639(40?), ca 1635; Salem/Wenham
YOUNGS, Christopher (-1695) & 1/wf Mary _?_ ; b 1668; Southold, LI
YOUNGS, Christopher (-1695) & 2/wf Mary [BUDD] (1654-1723/4+), dau John; ?ca 1675; Southold, LI
YOUNGS, Christopher (1643-1698), Southold, LI, & 1/wf Ann/?Hannah [NICHOLS]; b 4 Feb 1677; Stratford, CT
YOUNGS, Christopher & 2/wf Mercy (HORTON) [YOUNGS], w John; betw 1689 & 1698; Southold, LI
YOUNGS, Christopher (1677-1727) & Elizabeth [MOORE] (1679-1748); ca 1698; Southold, LI/Aquebogue
YOUNGS, Daniel & Judith FRINK (1680-); 12 Jan 1699; New London, CT
YOUNGS, Ephraim & ?Mary _?_ ; b 1698; Southold, LI
YOUNGS, Gideon (1638-1699) & Sarah _?_ (-1699+); b 1673, ca 1660/5?; Southold, LI/Orient, LI
YOUNGS, Gideon (1673-1749) & Hannah [REEVE] (1679-1738), dau John; b 1698; Southold, LI/Oyster Pond, LI/Orient, LI
YOUNGS, John (-1672, in 74th y) & 1/wf Joan (JENTELMAN)/?LOVINGTON/?PALGRAVE HARRINGTON (-1630?); Southwold, Eng, 25 Jul 1622; Southold, LI
YOUNGS, Rev. John (1598-1672) & 2/wf Joan (HARRIS) [PALGRAVE], w Richard; aft 30 March 1630, in Eng; Southold, LI
YOUNGS, Rev. John (1598-1672) & 3/wf Mary (WARREN) [GARDNER]; ca 1639, b 1641; Southold, LI
YOUNGS, Col. John (1623-1698) & 1/wf Mary [GARDNER]/GARDINER? (1630-1689, ae 59); ca 1653, b 1655; Southold, LI
YOUNGS, John & Mercy [HORTON]/NICHOLS, m/2 Christopher YOUNGS; b 1676; Southold, LI
YOUNGS, John (1654-1684/5) & Mary [WELLS] (1661-1729); b 1680, ca 1678; Southold, LI
YOUNGS, John (1668-1728) & 1/wf Ruth HIAT/HYATT (-1713); 30 Dec 1690; Stamford, CT
YOUNGS, Col. John (1623-1698) & Anne/Hannah (WINES) (NICHOLS (ELTON) [TOOKER]; ca 1691; 30 Dec 1690 m cont; Southold, LI
YOUNGS, Joseph & Margaret WARREN; 5 Feb 1632; Salem/Southold, LI
YOUNGS, Joseph (-1675) & 2/wf? Sarah WINES, ?m/2 John TUTHILL?; 16 Oct 1660; Southold, LI
YOUNGS, Joseph & 1/wf Rebecca [MAPES]
YOUNGS, Joseph & 2/wf Elizabeth [HARCUTT] (1654?-); ca 1660/70?, b 1660?, 1673; Southold, LI
YOUNGS, Josiah & Mary _?_ ; b 1698; Southold, LI/Aquebogue
YOUNGS, Samuel & 1/wf _?_ [COMSTOCK]; b 1675; Southold, LI
YOUNGS, Thomas (1645±-1720) & 1/wf Rebecca [MAPES]?; b 1668; Greenwich, CT/Oyster Bay, LI
YOUNGS, Thomas (1645+-1720) & 2/wf Elizabeth [HACUTT] (-1698+); b 1674?, b 4 Aug 1685
YOUNGS, Thomas (1655-1714) & 1/wf Mary _?_ (1668-1687, ae 19-9-13); ca 1686; Southold, LI
YOUNGS, Thomas (1655-1714) & 2/wf Mary (CHRISTOPHERS) BRADLEY (-1724), m/3 Nathaniel LYNDE; b 1693, aft 25 Aug 1687; Southold, LI
YOURES, William & Juda _?_ ; b 1686; Boston

ZELLICK/ZULLISH, David (-1658?) & Susanna __?__
ZALLETH, Joseph & __?__ ; b 1687(8?); Ipswich

--- A ---

Aball, Joanna 408
Aball, Robert 408
ABBE 1
Abbe, Mary 498
Abbe, Obadiah 172
Abbe, Rebecca 438
Abbe, Samuel 512
Abbe, Thomas 530
Abbee, Obadiah 782
ABBEY 1
Abbey, Experience 679
ABBIE 1
Abbit, Susanna 549
Abbot, Elizabeth 708
Abbot, Mary 384, 777
Abbot, Susanna 549
ABBOTT 1, 2
Abbott, Abigail 628, 728
Abbott, Daniel 131, 777
Abbott, Deborah 17
Abbott, Dorcas 636
Abbott, Dorothy 636
Abbott, Elizabeth 127, 232, 345
Abbott, Geo. 412
Abbott, George 202, 409, 822
Abbott, Hannah 144, 278, 409
Abbott, John 468
Abbott, Lydia 144
Abbott, Maria 627
Abbott, Mary 41, 140, 331, 345, 412, 627, 628
Abbott, Mercy 142
Abbott, Priscilla 160
Abbott, Richard 316
Abbott, Robert 627, 628
Abbott, Sarah 144, 260, 639, 668, 707, 824
Abbott, Thomas 145, 838
Abbott, Walter 668
ABBY 1
Abby, Mary 437
Abbye, Rebecca 438
ABDA 2
ABDY 2
Abdy, Matthew 826
Abel, Preserved 796
ABELL 2
Abell, Caleb 472
Abell, Elizabeth 197, 793
Abell, Experience 35, 408
Abell, Martha 687
Abell, Mary 479
Abernathy, Elizabeth 761
Abernathy, Mary 761
Abernathy, Sarah 826
ABERNETHY 2
Able, Mary 309
ABORN 2
Aborn, --- 674
Aborn, Elizabeth Lewis Phillips 577
Aborn, Joseph 619
Aborn, Mary 176, 412, 536, 703
ABORNE 2
Aborne, Hannah 385, 747
Aborne, Rebecca 61
Aborne, Sarah 166, 388

ABOURN 2
ABOURNE 2
Abraham, Sarah 118
Aburn, Richard 652
Accee, Hannah 118
Acie, Elizabeth 722, 755
Acie, Hannah 118
Acie, Mary 104
Acie, Ruth 554
ACKERMAN 2
Ackerman, Stephen 710
ACKERS 3
Ackers, Mercy 266
ACKLEY 3
Ackley, Elizabeth 663
Ackley, Hannah 607
Ackley, Lydia 631
Ackley, Mary 191
Ackly, Sarah 696
Acre, Abigail 617
Acre, John 668
Acreman, Stephen 710
ACRES 3
Acres, Catherine 367
Acres, Katharine 367
Acres, Margaret 748
Acres, Martha 133
ACY 3
Acy, Abigail 617
Acy, Elizabeth 755
Acy, Hannah 118
Acy, John 668
Acy, Mary 104
Acy, Ruth 554
ADAMS 3, 4, 5, 6
Adams, Abigail 49, 130, 369
Adams, Abraham 473, 517
Adams, Alexander 654
Adams, Alice 734
Adams, Anna 237, 328
Adams, Anne 186, 299, 328, 650
Adams, Aphra 63
Adams, Apphia 63
Adams, Archelaus 284, 487
Adams, Bethiah 788
Adams, Deborah 63
Adams, Dorcas 780
Adams, Dorothy 26
Adams, Edward 58, 211, 642
Adams, Eliashib 700
Adams, Elizabeth 100, 144, 237, 281, 342, 343, 423, 441, 449, 524, 560, 563, 575, 689, 699, 809
Adams, George 90
Adams, Hannah 34, 237, 267, 517, 527, 609, 644, 653, 685, 780, 793, 818
Adams, Henry 290, 367
Adams, Jane 632, 691
Adams, Jeremy 323, 780
Adams, Joan 632
Adams, Joanna 316
Adams, John 66, 101, 236, 342, 349, 829
Adams, Jonathan 148, 375
Adams, Joseph 49
Adams, Katharine 613
Adams, Lucy 365

Adams, Lydia 10, 203
Adams, Margaret 566
Adams, Marth 582
Adams, Martha Hull Smith Stratton 717
Adams, Mary 50, 163, 182, 238, 256, 285, 310, 330, 451, 506, 647, 663, 671, 695, 707, 717, 728, 734, 740, 767, 789, 803
Adams, Mehitable 260, 807
Adams, Nathan 155, 326, 644
Adams, Nathaniel 787
Adams, Rachel 256
Adams, Rebecca 53, 162, 564, 626, 684, 691, 699, 772
Adams, Richard 278
Adams, Robert 672
Adams, Ruth 77, 267, 329
Adams, Samuel 304, 481, 739
Adams, Sarah 74, 111, 140, 186, 188, 257, 317, 403, 446, 656, 759, 779
Adams, Susanna 404, 654, 830
Adams, Susannah 772
Adams, Temference 539
Adams, Temperance 539
Adams, Thomas 682, 725, 775
Adams, Ursula 389, 631, 718
Adams, Walter 542
Adams, William 269, 368
Addams, Elizabeth 524
Addams, Mary 256
Addams, Mehitable 547
Adde, Mellison 693
Adde, Millicent 693
ADDES 6
Addes, Mellison 693
Addes, Millicent 693
ADDINGTON 6
Addington, Anne 523, 584
Addington, Isaac 770
Addington, Rebecca 205
Addington, Sarah 750
ADDIS 6
Addis, Ann 96
Addis, Anne 204
Addis, Mellison 693
Addis, Millicent 22, 58, 693
ADEWITTE 6
ADFORD 6
Adford, Mary 338, 416
ADGATE 6
Adgate, Abigail 751
Adgate, Elizabeth 126
Adgate, Hannah 475
Adgate, Rebecca 405
Adgate, Sarah 405
Adgate, Thomas 126, 703
ADJET 6
ADJETT 6
ADKINS 6, 24 see ATKINS
Adkins, Ann 16
Adkins, Elizabeth 255, 305
Adkins, Jane 249
Adkins, Mary 249
Adkins, Sarah 141, 732
Adkins, Thomas 373
ADKINSON 24
Adkinson, Elizabeth 454

Adkinson, Jane 149
Adkinson, Rebecca 132, 133
ADLINGTON 6
ADONIS 6
ADVARD 6
ADVERD 6
Adverd, Experience 129
Adverd, Mary 416
ADY 242
AEALY 14
Aealy, Philip 589
Aealy, Susan 589
Aealy, Susanna 589
AFFLEY 543
Afford, John 132
Afford, Martha 132
AGARD 6
Agard, John 715
AGER 6 see ALGER, EAGER, HAGAR
Ager, Abigail 436, 441
Ager, Alice 748
Ager, Benjamin 580
Ager, Hannah 714
Ager, William 748
AGNEW 7
Agnew, Niven 47
AGUR 6
Agur, Abigail 565
Ahdel, Mary 65
AHHAYRES 28
AIKEN 7
AINSWORTH 7
AIRES 27
AIRS 28
AKAS 3
AKERLY 2
Akerly, Henry 675
Akerly, Mary 544, 675
AKERS 3
Akers, Priscilla 443
Akers, Sarah 526
Akers, Thomas 443, 526
AKORS 3
Alabaster, Thomas 440
Alban, Alice 170
ALBARDSON 7
ALBEE 7
Albee, Hannah 814, 843
Albee, Lydia 475
Albee, Sarah 48
ALBERRY 7
ALBERSON 7
ALBERTSON 7
Albertson, Elizabeth 170
ALBERTUS 7
Albertus, John 14
ALBESON 7
ALBIE 7
Albie, Hannah 814
Albie, Prudence 44
ALBINS 24
Albone, Elizabeth 479
Albree, Sarah 169
Albright, Margaret 27
ALBRO 7
Albro, Elizabeth 176
Albro, John 597
Albro, Mary 368
Albro, Susanna 19
ALBROUGH 7
Alburtes, John 455
Alby, Lydia 475
ALCOCK 7 see ELCOCK
Alcock, Abigail 707
Alcock, Anmer 144
Alcock, Ann 144, 311, 331
Alcock, Anna 820

Alcock, Annis 144
Alcock, Elizabeth 39, 236, 292, 373
Alcock, George 221
Alcock, Grace 139
Alcock, Hannah 144, 401, 691
Alcock, Joanna 403
Alcock, Joseph 640
Alcock, Lydia 233
Alcock, Margaret 566
Alcock, Margery 62
Alcock, Mary 448, 572, 629, 761, 766
Alcock, Samuel 89, 319, 578
Alcock, Sarah 301, 366, 809
Alcock, Thomas 62, 82, 629
Alcocke, Anne 19
Alcocke, Elizabeth 693
Alcord, Anne 19
ALCOTT 7
Alcott, Abigail 716
Alcott, Margery 62
Alcott, Mary 629
Alcott, Philip 127
Alcott, Thomas 62, 82, 605, 629
ALDEN 7, 8
Alden, Anna 691
Alden, Elizabeth 144, 549, 658, 691, 776
Alden, Gideon 63
Alden, Hopestill 692
Alden, John 255
Alden, Mary 13
Alden, Matthew 13
Alden, Mercy 123
Alden, Priscilla 149
Alden, Rebecca 214
Alden, Ruth 49, 698
Alden, Sarah 694, 700
ALDERMAN 8
Alderman, William 372
Aldersey, --- 457
Aldersey, Eleanor 201
Aldin, Sarah 194
ALDIS 8
Aldis, Hannah 258
Aldis, John 827
Aldis, Lydia 544
Aldis, Mary 267, 621
Aldis, Sarah 377
Aldred, Margaret 655
ALDRICH 8
Aldrich, Catherine 179
Aldrich, Experience 81
Aldrich, Henry 359, 429
Aldrich, Huldah 702, 817
Aldrich, Mary 359, 429, 610
Aldrich, Mercy 610
Aldrich, Sarah 48, 358
ALDRIDG 8
ALDRIDGE 8
Aldridge, Experience 81
Aldridge, Henry 429
Aldridge, Martha 233
Aldridge, Mary 429
Aldridge, Mattithia 233
ALEWELL 8
ALEXANDER 8
Alexander, Abigail 790
Alexander, David 451, 759
Alexander, Deliverance 558
Alexander, Dorothy 704
Alexander, Elizabeth 558
Alexander, Hannah Hull 208, 605
Alexander, Martha 286
Alexander, Mary 45, 526, 805
Alexander, Nathaniel 659
Alexander, Sarah 198

ALFORD 8, 9
Alford, Elizabeth 399
Alford, Mary 127, 191, 541, 764
Alford, William 399
ALFRED 9
ALGER 9
Alger, --- 23
Alger, Andrew 208
Alger, Arthur 775
Alger, Deliverance 453
Alger, Elizabeth 510, 526, 554
Alger, Joanna 510, 542
Alger, Matthew 139
Alger, Roger 347
Alger, Thomas 453
Algier, Alice 748
Algier, William 748
ALIACK 7
ALIBON 9
ALIE 14
Alin, Ann 419
Alin, Bozoan 419
Alin, James 199
Aline, Mary 342
ALKIN 9
ALLABEN 9
ALLAIRE 9
Allan, Alice 20
Allan, Dorothy 174
Allan, Rachel 673
ALLARD 9
Allard, Elizabeth 660
Allard, Hugh 757
Allard, Judith 318, 597
Allbins, Abigail 357
Allee, Thomas 738
ALLEN 9, 10, 11, 12, 13, 14, 26
Allen, Abiah 417
Allen, Abigail 134, 154, 658, 712, 799
Allen, Alice 218, 819
Allen, Amey 352
Allen, Anme 352
Allen, Ann 406, 419
Allen, Anne 4
Allen, Arnold 757
Allen, Barbara 700
Allen, Benjamin 799
Allen, Bethia 574
Allen, Bethiah 605
Allen, Bogan 377
Allen, Bozoan 419, 420, 636
Allen, Catherine 173
Allen, Christian 567
Allen, Daniel 138
Allen, Daniel (Dr.) 480
Allen, Deborah 113, 212, 456
Allen, Eleazer 208
Allen, Elizabeth 75, 90, 98, 119, 138, 169, 183, 195, 223, 257, 258, 293, 357, 435, 540, 605, 714, 728, 747, 757, 764, 773, 820
Allen, Esther 116
Allen, Experience 264
Allen, Frances 335
Allen, George 173, 382, 533
Allen, Gideon 371
Allen, Hannah 8, 27, 104, 203, 233, 268, 385, 414, 567, 638
Allen, Henry 732, 757
Allen, Hester 11, 17, 116
Allen, Hope 211, 401, 445, 787
Allen, Ichobod 162
Allen, Isaac 417
Allen, James 203, 252, 569
Allen, James (Rev.) 95
Allen, Jane 115, 490, 832

Allen, Joan 98, 226, 476, 567
Allen, Joanna 93, 567
Allen, John 17, 332, 374, 459, 494, 583, 619
Allen, Joseph 379, 574
Allen, Joshua 517
Allen, Leah 133
Allen, Lelia 840
Allen, Lewis 9, 283
Allen, Lydia 62, 97, 140, 840
Allen, Margaret 397, 794
Allen, Margery 559
Allen, Martha 87, 137, 397, 434, 645, 652
Allen, Mary 4, 88, 157, 160, 280, 281, 310, 324, 342, 366, 400, 453, 482, 556, 587, 609, 617, 630, 631, 791
Allen, Mary Parmenter Burke 120
Allen, Matthew 696
Allen, Mehitable 8
Allen, Mercy 233
Allen, Miriam 240
Allen, Nehemiah 120
Allen, Nicholas 365
Allen, Obadiah 810
Allen, Patience 254
Allen, Priscilla 377
Allen, Rachel 211, 373, 761
Allen, Rebecca 212, 310, 344
Allen, Richard 318
Allen, Robert 121, 453
Allen, Rose 382, 394, 533
Allen, Ruth 39
Allen, Samuel 448, 469, 759
Allen, Sarah 134, 313, 385, 460, 477, 508, 681, 700, 719, 795
Allen, Sarah Chandler 161, 707
Allen, Thomas 85, 234, 709, 822, 832
Allen, Thomas (Rev.) 349, 660
Allen, William 59, 91, 220, 268, 533, 637
Allens, Martha 645
Allenson, Luke 810
ALLERTON 14
Allerton, Elizabeth 256, 703
Allerton, Frances 752
Allerton, Mary 200, 383
Allerton, Remember 498
Allerton, Sarah 307, 603, 768
Alles, William 297, 318
ALLEY 14
Alley, Martha 510
Alley, Mary 466, 846
Alley, Philip 589
Alley, Susan 589
Alley, Susanna 589
Alley, Thomas 738
ALLEYN 11
Allgar, Bridget 807
ALLIBONE 9
Allice, Hannah 104
ALLIEN 9, 13
ALLIN 9, 10, 11, 12, 13
Allin, Jane 490
Allin, John (Rev.) 232
Allin, Leah 433
Allin, Mary 747
Allin, Richard 443
Allin, Ruth 443
Allin, Sarah 351, 745, 804
ALLING 14
Alling, Abigail 607
Alling, Abraham 749
Alling, Elizabeth 388
Alling, Hannah 657
Alling, James 199

Alling, Joan 226
Alling, Lydia 815
Alling, Mary 310, 311, 523, 630, 791
Alling, Sarah 24, 567
ALLIS 14
Allis, Abigail 794
Allis, Hannah 104, 127, 657
Allis, Ichabod 60
Allis, John 60, 157
Allis, Mehitable 515
Allis, Samuel 355
Allis, William 844
ALLISET 14
ALLISON 14 see ELLISON, ELLISTON
Allison, Ann 104
Allison, Christian 288
Allison, Jane 665
Allison, Mary 489
Allison, Sarah 440
ALLISTON 14
Allme, William 24
Allsaebrook, Elizabeth 176
Allsup, Abigail 639
Allsup, Mary 507
ALLY 14
Ally, Sarah 466
ALLYN 9, 10, 11, 12, 13
Allyn, Abigail 73
Allyn, Ann 808
Allyn, Anna 808
Allyn, Deborah 291
Allyn, Elizabeth 784
Allyn, Esther 301
Allyn, Frances 335
Allyn, Hannah 638
Allyn, Henry 637
Allyn, Hester 301
Allyn, Jane 832
Allyn, John 17
Allyn, Margaret 693
Allyn, Martha 177
Allyn, Mary 531, 556, 809
Allyn, Mehitable 19, 98
Allyn, Sarah 298, 740
Allyn, Thomas 191, 300, 474
ALMARY 14
ALMY 14, 15
Almy, Ann 235, 321
Almy, Audrey 749
Almy, Catharine 750, 796
Almy, Elizabeth 461, 519
Almy, Job 293, 750
Almy, John 591
Almy, Rebecca 750
Almy, Sarah 130, 504
Almy, Susannah 539
Almy, William 24
Alsbee, John 436
Alsbee, Sarah 169
ALSOP 15
Alsop, Abigail 639
Alsop, Elizabeth 36, 280, 638, 727
Alsop, Jemima 551
Alsop, Joseph 507
Alsop, Key 760
Alsop, Lydia 754
Alsop, Mary 507, 599, 760
Alston, George 592, 642
ALTHERTON 24
ALTON 15
ALVORD 8, 15 see ALFORD
Alvord, Abigail 636
Alvord, Elizabeth 124, 230
Alvord, Jane 279
Alvord, Jeremiah 636

Alvord, Joan 279
Alvord, Joanna 279
Alvord, Mary 793
Alvord, Sarah 782
Alvord, Thomas 439
Alward, Judith 318
ALWAY 15
ALWAYS 15
Alwood, Sarah 53
ALYSWORTH 28
AMADOWNE 16
Amazean, John 773
AMAZEEN 15
AMBECK 15
Ambeek, Johannes 656
AMBERY 16
AMBLER 15
Ambler, Abraham 17
Ambler, John 242, 786
Ambler, Mary 107
AMBREY 16
AMBROSE 15
Ambrose, Abigail 156, 548
Ambrose, Dorothy 168
Ambrose, Henry 661, 841
Ambrose, Samuel 149, 365
Ambrose, Susanna 661
AMBROSS 15
AMBRUSS 15
AMEE 16
Amensene, John 773
Ameredith, Joanna 7
AMERIDETH 15
AMES 16, 238 see AMOS, EAMES
Ames, Anna 772
Ames, Dorothy 722
Ames, Elizabeth 264, 577
Ames, Hannah 277, 356
Ames, Martha 620
Ames, Mary 713
Ames, Millicent 441
Ames, Robert 277
Ames, Ruth 19, 542
Ames, Sarah 360
Ames, William 537
AMEY 16
Amidown, Hannah 799
AMLET 16
AMMIDOWNE 16
AMORY 16, 251 see EMERY
Amory, Mary 251
AMOS 16
Amos, Anna 772
Amos, Mary 358
AMSBERY 16
AMSDEN 16
Amsden, Elizabeth 615
Amsden, Isaac 201, 282
AMY 16
Anabel, Elizabeth 811
ANDERSON 16
Anderson, Amy 89
Anderson, Catharine 578
Anderson, David 698
Anderson, Emma 89, 480
Anderson, Jane 5
Anderson, Joanna 534
Anderson, John 378
Anderson, Katherine 578
Anderson, Mary 357, 481, 668
ANDREW 16
Andrew, Joseph 774
Andrew, Rachel 64, 788
Andrew, Samuel 54, 432
Andrew, William 286, 414
Andrewes, Sarah 726
ANDREWS 16, 17, 18, 19
Andrews, Abigail 40, 41, 77, 391,

Andrews, Abigail (cont.) 745, 769
Andrews, Abigail Coale Norman 538
Andrews, Alice 282
Andrews, Ann 69, 608, 682
Andrews, Anna 608
Andrews, Benjamin 12, 190, 810
Andrews, Catherine 70
Andrews, Christyan 70
Andrews, Christian 70
Andrews, Dorcas 205
Andrews, Edward 6
Andrews, Elisha 281
Andrews, Elizabeth 5, 6, 77, 238, 238, 290, 301, 316, 326, 350, 400, 428, 466, 586, 607, 613, 664, 674, 718, 826
Andrews, Esther 696
Andrews, Grace 124
Andrews, Hannah 190, 292, 387, 530, 565, 622
Andrews, Hannah Kirby 715
Andrews, Hannah Smith Roland 640
Andrews, Hepzibah 485
Andrews, James 338
Andrews, Jane 9, 208, 483, 498, 529
Andrews, Jedidiah 11
Andrews, Jemima 691
Andrews, Jeremiah 15
Andrews, Joan 25
Andrews, Joane 659
Andrews, Joanna 275, 372
Andrews, John 11, 55, 131, 175, 186, 220, 487
Andrews, Katerin 70
Andrews, Margaret 314
Andrews, Margaret Palmer Boobyer 82
Andrews, Margery 392
Andrews, Martha 611
Andrews, Mary 44, 56, 101, 112, 121, 186, 187, 196, 326, 378, 401, 540, 589, 596, 599, 624, 671, 689
Andrews, Mehitable 624
Andrews, Mercy 611
Andrews, Nathaniel 155, 641
Andrews, Philippa 261
Andrews, Phillipa 590
Andrews, Phillipp 531
Andrews, Rachel 112
Andrews, Rebecca 4, 61, 88, 286, 368, 414, 487, 844
Andrews, Robert 121, 175, 587
Andrews, Ruth 476, 575, 701
Andrews, Samuel 478, 529
Andrews, Sarah 133, 175, 318, 512, 547, 682, 752, 833
Andrews, Susanna 825
Andrews, Susannah 387
Andrews, Thomas 20, 175, 281, 635, 844
Andrews, William 203, 218, 299, 671
Andrews, Wm. 355
ANDROS 16, 17
Andros, Elizabeth 300
Andros, Jedidiah 11
Andros, Joanna 372
Andross, Elizabeth 300
Andross, Margaret 314
ANDRUESON 16
ANDRUS 16
Andrus, Elizabeth 300
Andrus, Hanna Smith Roland 640

Andrus, Mary 112
ANDRUSS 16
Andruss, Mary 780
ANGELL 19
Angell, Abigail 784
Angell, Alice 802
Angell, Amphillis 681
Angell, Deborah 645
Angell, Margaret 803
Angell, Mary 22, 680
ANGER 6, 19
ANGIER 19
Angier, Bridget 345
Angier, Elizabeth 585
Angier, Mary 488, 694
Angier, Ruth 148
Angier, Sampson 400
Angier, Sarah 400, 727
Angin, Elizabeth 110
Angur, Esther 837
Angur, Martha 495
ANNABLE 19
Annable, Anna 23, 33
Annable, Desire 41
Annable, Elizabeth 132
Annable, Hannah 80, 87
Annable, John 649
Annable, Samuel 98
Annable, Sarah 256
Annable, Susanna 353
Anniball, Anna 23
Anniball, Susanna 353
ANNIS 19
Annis, Ann 842
Annis, Hannah 842
Annis, Priscilla 307
Ansel, Mary 474
ANSELL 19
Anter, Hannah 361
Anter, Jane 361
Anter, Joan 361
ANTHONY 19
Anthony, Elizabeth 321
Anthony, Isabel 597
Anthony, Mary 669
Anthony, Susanna 754
ANTRIM 20
Antrim, Obadiah 18
Antrobus, Joan 760
Antrome, Obadiah 18
ANTRUM 20
Antrum, Hannah 120
Apgar, Bridget 807
APLEBEE 20
Apleton, Elizabeth 233
APPLEBY 20
APPLEGATE 20
APPLETON 20
Appleton, Hannah 229
Appleton, Joanna 803
Appleton, John 236
Appleton, Judith 634, 833
Appleton, Martha 414
Appleton, Mary 735
Appleton, Priscilla 133
Appleton, Sarah 578, 632
APPLEY 20
APPLIN 20
Applin, Bethshuah 717
APPLY 20
Apsley, Alice 262
ARCHARD 20
ARCHER 20
Archer, Abigail 767
Archer, Alice 233
Archer, Bethiah 784
Archer, Hannah 93, 228, 416
Archer, John 804, 840

Archer, Jonathan 819
Archer, Mary 370, 840
Archer, Samuel 407
Archer, Sarah Holbrook 209
ARDELL 20
Ardell, William 649
ARDEN 20
Areland, Deborah 641
Areson, Sarah 672
AREY 20
Arey, Jean 566
Arey, Richard 344
Ariens, Janneken 502
Ariens, Jannetie 502
ARMITAGE 21
Armitage, --- 808
Armitage, Eleazer 222
Armitage, Joanna 331
Armitage, Katrina 23
Armitage, Rebecca 728
ARMS 21
Arms, Margaret 60
Arms, Sarah 822
ARMSBY 546
ARMSTRONG 21
Armstrong, Gregory 70
Armstrong, Mary 419, 448
Armstrong, Sarah 419, 689
ARNOLD 21, 22
Arnold, Abia 594
Arnold, Abial 594
Arnold, Abigail 594
Arnold, Content 165
Arnold, Damaris 78, 136
Arnold, Elizabeth 136, 175, 322, 383, 387, 441, 622, 680
Arnold, Ephraim 182
Arnold, Esther 19, 218, 355
Arnold, Freelove 568
Arnold, Godsgift 116, 493
Arnold, Hannah 494
Arnold, Hester 19
Arnold, Isaac 783
Arnold, Israel 681
Arnold, Joanna 616, 619
Arnold, John 112, 276
Arnold, Joseph 93, 197, 325
Arnold, Josiah 99
Arnold, Mary 160, 182, 218, 339, 437, 626, 706
Arnold, Oliver 489
Arnold, Penelope 308, 360
Arnold, Phebe 680, 690
Arnold, Sarah 112, 136, 218
Arnold, Susanna 258
Arnold, Susannah 103
ARNOLL 22
ARRINGTON 345
Arrington, Elizabeth 768
Arthur, Alse 99
ASBURY 22
Asbury, John 326
ASCRAFT 22
ASH 22
Ash, Martha 484
Ash, Mary 334, 396
Ash, Thomas 612
Ash, William 58, 693
ASHBOURNE 22
ASHBURY 22
ASHBY 22
Ashby, Anthony 448
Ashby, Sarah 765
ASHCRAFT 22
ASHCROFTE 22
Ashenden, Margery 673
ASHFIELD 22
ASHLEY 22, 23

Ashley, Abigail 463
Ashley, Edward 788
Ashley, Hannah 245
Ashley, John 667
Ashley, Joseph 705, 824
Ashley, Mary 540, 636
Ashley, Robert 389
Ashley, Sarah 410, 464
Ashley, Thomas 103
ASHMAN 23
Ashman, Deborah 216
Ashman, Elizabeth 216
Ashman, Mary 135
Ashman, Phebe 690
ASHTON 23, 26
Ashton, Alice 19
Ashton, Deliverance 223
Ashton, John 550
Ashton, Mary 464, 545
Ashton, Susanna 165
Ashwood, Elizabeth 581, 588
Ashwood, Hannah 156
ASLET 23
Aslet, John 436
ASLETT 23
Aslett, Abigail 107
Aslett, Anna 107
Aslett, Hannah 107
Aslett, Mary 287
Aslett, Rebecca 423
Aslett, Sarah 169
ASPINWALL 23
Aspinwall, Anna 19
Aspinwall, Elizabeth 230, 708
Aspinwall, Hannah 19
Aspinwall, Mary 316
Aspinwall, Peter 458
Assbe, Sarah 765
Asselbie, Abigail 107
Asselbie, Anna 107
Asselbie, Hannah 107
Aste, Jemima 445
Asten, Isabella 749
Asten, Keziah 757
ASTIN 25, 26
Astin, Joan 492
Astin, Joanna 492
Aston, Francis 458
ASTWOOD 23
Astwood, Hannah 283
Astwood, John 36
ATCHET 6
ATCHINSON 23, 24
Atchinson, Elizabeth 448
ATCHISON 23
Atchison, Elizabeth 448
Atchison, Mary 645
Atchison, Mercy 645
ATHEARN 23
Athearn, Samuel 140
ATHERTON 23, 24
Atherton, Catherine 496
Atherton, Deborah 117
Atherton, Elizabeth 328, 496, 792
Atherton, Hannah 816
Atherton, Hope 34
Atherton, Humphrey 773
Atherton, Isabel 773
Atherton, Margaret 754
Atherton, Mary 70, 791
Atherton, Patience 402
Atherton, Rest 724
Atherton, Richard 816
Atherton, Sarah 562
Atherton, Thankful 71
ATHY 24
Atkens, James 161
ATKINS 24 see ADKINS,

ATKINS (cont.) see ELKINS
Atkins, Abigail 357
Atkins, Alice 707
Atkins, Anne 158
Atkins, Elizabeth 207
Atkins, Hester 586
Atkins, James 559
Atkins, Jane 213
Atkins, Joan 686
Atkins, Mary 331, 832
Atkins, Rachel 65, 230
Atkins, Robert 254
Atkins, Ruth 389, 567
Atkins, Sarah 331, 663, 702, 732
Atkins, Thomas 331, 427, 691
ATKINSON 24
Atkinson, Abigail 829, 838
Atkinson, Elizabeth 235, 454, 544
Atkinson, Hannah 102, 244, 490, 704
Atkinson, Helen 373
Atkinson, Jane 149
Atkinson, John 149
Atkinson, Luke 810
Atkinson, Marmaduke 179, 188
Atkinson, Mary 179
Atkinson, Rebecca 359
Atkinson, Sarah 166
Atkinson, Susannah 102
Atkinson, Susan 102
Atkinson, Theodore 213, 480, 496
Atred, --- 697
Atred, Lettice 483
Attwood, Abigail 436
Atty, Mary 239
ATWATER 24, 25
Atwater, Abigail 426
Atwater, Ann 130, 233
Atwater, Damaris 607
Atwater, John 54, 563
Atwater, Joshua 369, 688
Atwater, Mary 156, 176, 716
Atwater, Mehitable 635
Atwater, Mercy 25, 629
ATWELL 25
Atwell, Benjamin 492
Atwell, Dorothy 492
Atwell, Lydia 183
Atwell, Mary 175, 410
Atwell, Philip 17
ATWOOD 25, 833, 834 see WOOD
Atwood, Abigail 432, 461, 512
Atwood, Alice 438
Atwood, Elizabeth 186, 279, 542, 796
Atwood, Hannah 181, 595, 683
Atwood, Harmon 654
Atwood, John 195, 459, 681
Atwood, Machiel 634
Atwood, Margaret 223
Atwood, Mary 91, 383, 459
Atwood, Mehitable 182
Atwood, Philip 329
Atwood, Sarah 257
Atwood, Stephen 446
Auber, Sarah 129
AUBREY 25
AUBUR 6
AUDLEY 543
Audley, --- 206
Audley, Ann 156
AUGER 6, 19, 238
Auger, Benjamin 580
Augur, Hester 185
AULGAR 9
AULT 25
Ault, Elizabeth 572

Ault, John 572
Ault, Rebecca 242, 337
Ault, Remembrance 609
AUSTIN 25, 26
Austin, Abigail 435
Austin, Agnes 468
Austin, Annis 468
Austin, Catherine 398
Austin, Deborah 165
Austin, Ebenzer 62
Austin, Elizabeth 164, 222, 266, 372, 474, 830
Austin, Esther 533, 765
Austin, Francis 458
Austin, Isabella 93, 749
Austin, Jemima 445
Austin, John 101, 119, 386, 398
Austin, Jonas 370, 631
Austin, Joseph 715, 765
Austin, Lydia 715
Austin, Mary 56, 294, 390, 466, 655, 741
Austin, Mary Davis Dodd 844
Austin, Matthew 223
Austin, Nathaniel 562
Austin, Richard 300
Austin, Rose 741
Austin, Sarah 443, 601, 846
AUSTINS 26
Autasom, Abigail 576
Auter, Hannah 361
Auter, Jane 361
Auter, Joan 361
Autwood, Hannah 595
Avelly, Joan 18
Avelly, Thomas 18
Averad, Israel 427
Averell, Sarah 478
AVERIL 26
AVERILL 26
Averill, Abigail 72
Averill, Sarah 815
AVERY 26, 27
Avery, Abigail 72
Avery, Anna 628
Avery, Anne 628
Avery, Deborah 12
Avery, Elizabeth 117
Avery, Hannah 237, 511
Avery, James 149
Avery, John 209
Avery, Jonathan 813
Avery, Margaret 518
Avery, Mary 215, 267, 511, 744
Avery, Matthew 628
Avery, Rachel 721
Avery, Rebecca 597
Avery, Ruth 738
Avery, Sarah 507
Avery, Thomas 115, 181
Avery, William 727, 779
AVES 27
AVIS 27
Avis, Sarah 158
AWARDS 360
AWBREY 25
AWKLEY 27
Awood, Alice 438
AXALL 27
Axall, Humphrey 321
AXDELL 27
Axdell, Mary 310, 499
Axdell, Thomas 499
AXEY 27
AXTEL 27
AXTELL 27
Axtell, Henry 731
Axtell, Mary 499, 534

Axtell, Thomas 499
AYARS 28
AYER 27, 28
Ayer, Elizabeth 60, 161, 786
Ayer, Hannah 60, 790
Ayer, Mary 131, 168, 558
Ayer, Rebecca 23, 436
Ayer, Ruth 215
Ayer, Sarah 584
Ayer, Timothy 228
AYERS 27, 28
Ayers, Elizabeth 470, 786
Ayers, Love 441
Ayers, Martha 548
Ayers, Mary 261
Ayers, Rebecca 436
AYLETT 28
Aylett, Mary 245
AYRAULT 28
Ayre, Martha 548
Ayre, Susanna 700
AYRES 27, 28
Ayres, Abigail 473
Ayres, Ann 456
Ayres, Anne 542
Ayres, Edward 428
Ayres, Elizabeth 161
Ayres, Hannah 548
Ayres, John 210
Ayres, Joseph 236
Ayres, Martha 548
Ayres, Mary 206, 530
Ayres, Mehitable 577
Ayres, Nathaniel 290, 669
Ayres, Rebecca 23
Ayres, Sarah 173, 349, 449
Ayres, Simon 703, 812
Ayres, Susan 771
Ayres, Susanna 210

--- B ---

B-, Alice 602, 785
B-, Sarah 639
BABADGE 28
BABB 28
Babbadg, Hester 493
Babbage, Christopher 134
Babbert, Martha 256
BABBET 28
Babbett, John 67
BABBIDGE 28
Babbidge, Hester 493
BABBITT 28
Babbitt, Damaris 685
Babbitt, Deliverance 382
Babbitt, Elizabeth 29
Babbitt, Erasmus 29, 345
Babbitt, Experience 98
Babbitt, Ruth 140
BABCOCK 28, 29
Babcock, Abigail 40, 521
Babcock, Ann 835
Babcock, Anna 551, 835
Babcock, Dorothy 833
Babcock, Elizabeth 423, 462
Babcock, Hannah 521, 551, 835
Babcock, James 423
Babcock, Jane 93, 463
Babcock, Joanna 463
Babcock, Job 618
Babcock, John 28
Babcock, Margaret 460
Babcock, Mary 9, 105, 143, 190, 483
Babcock, Rachel 806

Babcock, Robert 460
Babcock, Sarah 463
Babcock, Susanna 618
BABEL 29
Baber, Martha 647
BABSON 29
Babson, Abigail 831
Babson, Richard 616
BACHELDER 51
Bachelder, Abigail 26
Bachelder, Mary 186
Bachelder, Nathaniel 443
Bachelder, Rebecca 193
Bachelder, Samuel 723
Bachelder, Seaborn 193
BACHELER 51
BACHELLER 51
BACHELOR 51
Bachelor, Abigail 240
Bachelor, Deborah 828
Bachelour, Hannah 780
Bachiler, Theodate 406
BACHILLER 51
BACK 39
Back, Elizabeth 347
Backaway, Mary 363
Backer, Deborah 151
Backer, Elizabeth 767
Backer, Mary 681
Backer, Sarah 467
BACKHOUSE 29
Backhouse, Elizabeth 61, 828
Backhouse, Hannah 542
BACKSTER 53
BACKUS 29
Backus, Elizabeth 61, 405, 828
Backus, Frances 299
Backus, Hannah 70, 542
Backus, Lydia 31
Backus, Mary 190, 408
Backus, Ruth 322
Backus, Sarah 196, 444, 618
Backus, William 70
BACON 29, 30
Bacon, --- 202
Bacon, Abigail 834
Bacon, Alice 39
Bacon, Andrew 701
Bacon, Daniel 287, 291
Bacon, Elizabeth 11, 74, 622
Bacon, Elizabeth Haronett 593
Bacon, Hanna 85
Bacon, Hannah 672, 776
Bacon, James 568
Bacon, John 184, 782
Bacon, Lydia 584, 834
Bacon, Margaret 314
Bacon, Martha 328
Bacon, Mary 132, 199, 288, 291, 441, 447, 450, 810
Bacon, Mercy 447, 548
Bacon, Michael 541, 623
Bacon, Nathaniel 207
Bacon, Patience 510
Bacon, Peter 202
Bacon, Rachel 584
Bacon, Rebecca 27, 297
Bacon, Samuel 71
Bacon, Sarah 248, 288, 396, 674
Bacon, Susanna 591
Bacon, Susannah 218
Bacon, Thomas 592, 787
Bacor, Eleanor 384
BADCOCK 28, 29
Badcock, Dorothy 203
Badcock, Elizabeth 94, 423, 768
Badcock, George 228
Badcock, Hannah 452, 521, 768

Badcock, James 423, 452
Badcock, Mary 143, 247, 483, 727, 768
Badcock, Ruth 217
Badcock, Sarah 334
Badcock, Thankful 481
Badg, Priscilla 91
BADGER 30, 31
Badger, Giles 108
Badger, John 89
Badger, Mary 844
Badger, Sarah 800
BADLAM 31
BADMAN 31
Badson, Elizabeth 257
BAGG 31
Bagg, Abigail 179
Bagg, Hannah 724
Bagg, Mercy 425
BAGGERLEY 31 see BICKLEY
BAGGS 31
BAGLEY 31
Bagley, John 481
Bagley, Sarah 482
Bagley, Timothy 427
Bagly, Sarah 482
BAGNELL 67
BAGWORTH 31
Bagworth, Benjamin 331
Bagworth, Jane 331
Bailes, Elizabeth 397
BAILEY 31, 32
Bailey, Abiah 625
Bailey, Abigail 364, 732
Bailey, Damaris 458
Bailey, Elizabeth 159, 345
Bailey, Guido 491
Bailey, Guydo 118, 331
Bailey, Hannah 361, 496
Bailey, James (Rev.) 722
Bailey, Joanna 405
Bailey, John 301, 459, 816
Bailey, John (Rev.) 733
Bailey, Jonas 41, 213, 413
Bailey, Joseph 654
Bailey, Lydia 462, 590, 696, 813
Bailey, Mary 205, 461, 573, 610, 763
Bailey, Rachel 593
Bailey, Rebecca 105, 224
Bailey, Richard 539
Bailey, Ruth 370, 778
Bailey, Samuel 702
Bailey, Sarah 148, 254, 370
Bailey, Susannah 396
Bailey, Thomas 110, 462, 600, 739
Bailey, William 456
Bailey, Wilmot 252
BAILY 31, 32
BAINBRIDGE 32
Bainbridge, Jane 322
Baines, Joshua 247
Bainton, Ann 53
Bairsto, Deborah 664
BAIRSTOW 47
Bairstow, Mary 411
Baisey, Elizabeth 568
Baisie, Mary 122
BAITMAN 52
Bake, John 558
BAKEN 30
BAKER 30, 32, 33, 34
Baker, Abigail 441, 760, 781
Baker, Ann 54
Baker, Anna 54
Baker, Bethia 542
Baker, Bethiah 238
Baker, Catherine 420

Baker, Christian 628
Baker, Deborah 151
Baker, Desire 760
Baker, Eleanor 384
Baker, Elizabeth 20, 44, 147, 159,
   204, 236, 402, 413, 438, 537,
   600, 643, 767, 785, 832
Baker, Francis 582
Baker, Geoffery 410
Baker, Hannah 9, 29, 182, 460,
   464, 582, 831
Baker, Hannah Buckland 473
Baker, Hepzibah 591
Baker, Hester 724
Baker, Jane 302
Baker, Jeffrey 410
Baker, John 217, 411, 558, 777
Baker, Joseph 113, 480
Baker, Joshua 512
Baker, Joyce 127
Baker, Katherine 420
Baker, Lydia 253, 430
Baker, Margery 529
Baker, Martha 18, 20, 64, 690
Baker, Mary 5, 21, 110, 279, 351,
   397, 406, 417, 424, 474, 512,
   575, 628, 630, 646, 720, 767
Baker, Mercy 242
Baker, Nicholas 222
Baker, Priscilla 20, 387
Baker, Rachel 772
Baker, Rose 153, 803
Baker, Ruth 15
Baker, Samuel 245, 309, 405, 674
Baker, Sarah 216, 275, 315, 353,
   407, 414, 467, 479, 529, 628,
   714, 725, 805, 831
Baker, Silence 247
Baker, Susanna 200, 781
Baker, Thankful 327
Baker, Thomas 543, 717
Baker, Timothy 23
Baker, William 126, 255, 417, 705
BALAAM 34
BALCH 34, 35
Balch, Abigail 452
Balch, Ann 621, 776
Balch, Anna 621
Balch, Benjamin 157, 484
Balch, Elizabeth 446
Balch, Freeborn 51
Balch, John 224
Balch, Joshua 316
Balch, Martha 392
Balch, Mary 714
Balch, Phebe Newmarch Penewell
   570
Balch, Rebecca 224
Balch, Ruth 231
Balch, Samuel 33
Balch, Sarah 563
Balch, Seith 175
BALCOM 35
Balcom, Catherine 10
Balcom, Elizabeth 620
Balcom, Katharine 417
Balcom, Sarah 667
BALDEN 35
Balden, Elizabeth 302
Balden, Hannah 20
Balden, Joanna 297
Balden, John 297, 457
Balden, Samuel 157
Balden, Sarah 192
Baldin, George 92
Baldin, Hannah 92
Baldwicke, Joanna 297
Baldwicke, John 297

BALDWIN 35, 36, 37, 86
Baldwin, --- 139
Baldwin, Abigail 36, 703, 769
Baldwin, Ann 111
Baldwin, Deborah 616
Baldwin, Elizabeth 125, 561, 595,
   782, 838
Baldwin, George 92, 250
Baldwin, Hannah 2, 85, 92, 268,
   400, 650
Baldwin, Hannah Norman 457
Baldwin, John 149
Baldwin, Joseph 140, 375, 782
Baldwin, Martha 531, 563
Baldwin, Mary 12, 132, 140, 175,
   239, 355, 417, 535, 590, 680
Baldwin, Nathaniel 649, 676, 797
Baldwin, Peter 214
Baldwin, Phebe 623
Baldwin, Rebecca 511
Baldwin, Richard 280
Baldwin, Samuel 155, 604, 769
Baldwin, Sarah 49, 50, 112, 243,
   262, 625, 641, 659
Baldwin, Susanna 774
Baldwin, Sylvester 23
Baldwin, Temperance 71, 125
Baldwin, Timothy 503, 727
Baldwin, Zachariah 649
BALE 31, 54
Bale, Benjamin 489
Bale, Mary 754
Bale, Mercy 754
Balein, Martha 711
Balies, Elizabeth 397
Balke, Hannah Jenkins 79
BALL 37
Ball, --- 288
Ball, Abigail 237
Ball, Eleazer 271
Ball, Eliphalet 755
Ball, Elizabeth 335, 724
Ball, Ellen 365
Ball, Francis 527, 704
Ball, Jane 219
Ball, Joanna 219
Ball, Jonathan 842
Ball, Lydia 567
Ball, Margaret 425
Ball, Mary 192, 247, 334, 335,
   365, 375, 514, 592, 643, 654
Ball, Mercy 555
Ball, Nathaniel 52, 445
Ball, Priscilla 508
Ball, Rachel 505
Ball, Samuel 704
Ball, Sarah 142, 270, 411
Ball, Susanna 78, 100
BALLANTINE 37
Ballantine, Elizabeth 323, 845
Ballantine, John 654
Ballantine, William 471
BALLARD 37, 38 see BOLLARD
Ballard, Ann 128, 424, 695
Ballard, Eleanor 422
Ballard, Elizabeth 1, 79, 95, 660,
   712
Ballard, Esther 418
Ballard, Hannah Snell 468
Ballard, Jarvis 304
Ballard, John 468
Ballard, Joseph 388, 708
Ballard, Lydia 128
Ballard, Mary 128, 354, 480
Ballard, Rachel 505
Ballard, Rebecca 699
Ballard, Sarah 385, 841
Ballard, Susanna 288

Ballard, William 445
BALLATT 38
Ballatt, Elizabeth 229
Ballatt, Samuel 333, 491
Ballentine, Benjamin 180
Ballentine, Elizabeth 180, 845
Ballentine, Sarah 798
Ballentine, Susanna 788
Ballerd, Sarah 385
BALLETT 38
BALLEY 31
Balley, Damaris 458
Balley, Lydia 590
Ballington, Martha 194
Ballott, Lydia 303
BALLOU 38
Ballou, Lydia 293, 356
Balls, Elizabeth 339
BALLY 31
Balsh, Mary 714
Balsomon, Deliverence 15
BALSTON 38
Balston, Elizabeth 315
Balston, John 38
Balston, Jonathan 9, 488
Balston, Lydia 9
Balston, Mary 239, 767
Balston, Prudence 488, 760
Balston, Sarah 278, 735
Balstone, Abigail 288
Balticome, Elizabeth 340
Bamon, Abigail 138
BANBRIDGE 32
Banbridge, Jane 322
Banbury, --- 127
BANCROFT 38, 39
Bancroft, Anna 303, 326
Bancroft, Elizabeth 107, 652
Bancroft, Hannah 326
Bancroft, Jane 40
Bancroft, John 471
Bancroft, Mehitable 558
Bancroft, Rebecca 304
Bancroft, Roger 97, 652, 728
Bancroft, Ruth 711
Bancroft, Samuel 318
Bancroft, Sarah 111, 662, 717,
   839
Bancroft, Thomas 40, 387
Band, Agnes Thorne 76
Band, Lucy 165, 640
Band, Martha 588
Bandouin, Pierre 214
BANE 56
Bane, Lewis 655
BANEBE 42
BANFIELD 39 BENFIELD
Banfield, Abigail 271
Banfield, Agnes 271
Banfield, Christopher 509, 634,
   762
Banfield, Mary 572
Banford, Hannah 222
Banges, Hannah 223
BANGS 39
Bangs, Apphia 25, 446
Bangs, Bethia 334
Bangs, Jonathan 846
Bangs, Lydia 369
Bangs, Mary 537
Bangs, Mercy 504
Bangs, Rebecca 694
Bangs, Sarah 394
Bangs, Thomasine 120
BANISTER 39
Banister, --- 164
Banister, Christopher 69
BANK 39

Bank, Hannah 33
Bank, John 558
Bank, Mary 598
Banker, Hannah 533
Bankes, Elizabeth 74
BANKS 39
Banks, Abigail 490
Banks, Benjamin 640
Banks, Elizabeth 117
Banks, Hannah 121
Banks, John 126, 671
Banks, Lydia 253, 526
Banks, Mary 729, 730
Banks, Priscilla 615
Banks, Sarah 318
Banks, Susannah 720
Banning, John 537
BANOE 39
BANT 40 see BENT
Bant, Martha 318
Banthy, Sarah 393
Barbage, Isabella 258, 831
BARBANT 45
Barbant, Mary Bishop 204
BARBER 40
Barber, Abigail 342, 739
Barber, Deborah 141
Barber, Dorothy 521
Barber, Elizabeth 45, 101, 121,
    213, 498, 759
Barber, Hannah 531
Barber, Joanna 690
Barber, John 39, 521, 709
Barber, Josiah 230
Barber, Martha 655
Barber, Mary 21, 98, 108, 286,
    304, 540, 731
Barber, Mercy 304, 540
Barber, Patience 169
Barber, Rebecca 569
Barber, Ruth 154
Barber, Sarah 333, 336
Barber, Thomas 38, 705
Barber, William 59, 531
Barbor, Elizabeth 360
Barbour, Elizabeth 520
Barbour, George 802
Barbour, Hannah 28
Barbour, Mary 521
Barbour, Rebecca 802
Barbraum, Hannah 405
Barby, Mary 529
BARCLAY 40
BARD 40 see BEARD
Barday, --- 134
BARDEN 40 see BORDEN
Barden, Abraham 83
Barden, William 119
Bardin, Abraham 83
BARDING 40
Barding, Nathaniel 18
BARE 59
Bareden, Anne 71
Barefoot, Sarah 813
BARENCE 44
Barensz, John 396
Baret, Mary 627
Baret, Rebecca 598
Barett, Hannah 87
Barett, Margaret 558, 694
Barett, Maryetta 558
Barge, Giles 32
Barge, Gyles 413
BARIT 45, 46
BARKER 42, 93
Barker, --- 777
Barker, Abigail 274, 634, 637
Barker, Ann 19, 599

Barker, Christian 58, 240
Barker, Christiana 58, 181, 579
Barker, Deborah 41
Barker, Desire 760
Barker, Dorothy 403, 439
Barker, Elizabeth 111, 240, 282,
    436, 666, 829
Barker, Ester 217
Barker, Esther 707
Barker, Eunice 785
Barker, Grace 132
Barker, Hannah 19, 422, 547, 809
Barker, Henry 255
Barker, Isaac 194, 756
Barker, James 436, 844
Barker, Jane 448
Barker, John 78, 199
Barker, Joseph 407
Barker, Judith 342
Barker, Mary 180, 194, 436, 449,
    531, 600, 681, 703, 732, 833
Barker, Mary Frie Stevens 708
Barker, Matthew 809
Barker, Rebecca 430, 654, 692
Barker, Robert 22, 489
Barker, Rose 153, 803
Barker, Sarah 1, 27, 272
Barker, Susanna 363
Barker, Susannah 86
Barker, Thomas 448, 632, 784
BARKLY 40
BARLEY 42
Barley, Mary 529
BARLOW 42
Barlow, Abigail 216, 234, 640
Barlow, Ann 230
Barlow, Audrey 15
Barlow, Cicely 786
Barlow, Deborah 122, 123, 391,
    720
Barlow, Elizabeth 279, 286, 353,
    808
Barlow, George 66, 786
Barlow, Isabella 153
Barlow, James 681
Barlow, Jane 391
Barlow, John 230
Barlow, Joseph 263
Barlow, Martha 59
Barlow, Mary 10, 141, 529
Barlow, Phebe 544
Barlow, Ruth 91, 517
Barlow, Thomas 180, 528, 641,
    642, 750, 782
BARLY 120
BARNABE 42
BARNABY 42
Barnaby, James 530
Barnam, Abigail 809
BARNARD 42, 43
Barnard, Abigail 261
Barnard, Ann 105
Barnard, Anna 88, 308, 476
Barnard, Anne 88
Barnard, Benjamin 796, 827
Barnard, Deborah 48
Barnard, Dorothy 197
Barnard, Edith 85
Barnard, Eleanor 165, 467
Barnard, Elizabeth 112, 173, 222,
    770, 771
Barnard, Frances 220
Barnard, Hannah 55, 308, 487,
    640, 706, 707, 797
Barnard, John 168, 358, 826
Barnard, Martha 43, 114, 358, 635
Barnard, Mary 43, 46, 58, 118,
    178, 240, 273, 520, 821

Barnard, Nathaniel 166, 273
Barnard, Phebe 88
Barnard, Richard 771
Barnard, Ruth 566
Barnard, Sarah 197, 331, 676,
    705, 795
Barnard, Thomas 467
Barne, Sarah 422
Barned, Dorothy 197
BARNELL 43
Barnerd, Abigail 261
BARNES 43, 44, 45, 46
Barnes, Abigail 286, 345, 426
Barnes, Alice 816
Barnes, Amy 585
Barnes, Anna 13, 94, 101
Barnes, Anne 13
Barnes, Benjamin 484
Barnes, Deborah 208, 325
Barnes, Dorothy 369
Barnes, Elizabeth 4, 25, 101, 117,
    319, 474
Barnes, Elizabeth Harris 345
Barnes, Esther 624
Barnes, Hannah 94, 101, 345, 606,
    625, 707, 755
Barnes, Hannah Sutliff Whedon
    799
Barnes, Henry 81
Barnes, Hester 624
Barnes, Jane 37
Barnes, Joanna 256, 363
Barnes, John 270, 648
Barnes, Joshua 363, 428, 459
Barnes, Lydia 545, 653, 672
Barnes, Mary 139, 337, 357, 395,
    405, 490, 591, 598
Barnes, Mary Linsley 44
Barnes, Matthew 272, 404
Barnes, Mercy 414, 737
Barnes, Patience 478
Barnes, Rachel 651
Barnes, Rebecca 469, 519
Barnes, Richard 77, 223, 711
Barnes, Sarah 222, 349, 640, 647,
    657, 746, 765, 813
Barnes, Susanna 469
Barnes, Susannah 792
Barnes, Temperance 791
Barnes, Thomas 58, 94, 101, 438,
    591, 598, 708
Barnes, William 744
BARNET 45
Barnet, Mary Bishop 204
BARNETT 45
Barnett, Hannah 89
Barnett, Mary Bishop 204
BARNEY 45
Barney, Abigail 490
Barney, Ann 814
Barney, Dorcas 754
Barney, Hannah 89, 193
Barney, Mary Bishop 204
Barney, Sarah 329, 340
Barnham, Sarah 398
BARNS 44
Barns, Sarah 640
BARNSDALE 45
BARNSDELL 45
Barnstead, Hannah 671
BARNUM 45
Barnum, Abigail 708
Barnum, Sarah 581
Barnum, Thomas 405
Barnwell, Richard 517
BARNY 45
BARON 47
BAROW 47

Barras, Elizabeth 45
BARRAT 46
BARREL 45
BARRELL 45
Barrell, Anna 760
Barrell, Anne 661
Barrell, Anne Garwood 675
Barrell, George 661
Barrell, John 760
Barrell, William 415
BARRENCE 44
BARRET 46
Barret, Agnes Dennen 225
Barret, Margaret 303, 405
Barret, Mary 79, 679
BARRETT 45, 46
Barrett, Anna 722
Barrett, Benjamin 805
Barrett, Easter 61
Barrett, Elizabeth 45, 215, 409, 468, 621
Barrett, Esther 61
Barrett, Grace 125
Barrett, Hannah 87, 656
Barrett, James 638, 744
Barrett, John 74, 447
Barrett, Jonathan 108, 370, 796
Barrett, Lydia 37, 148, 350, 729
Barrett, Margaret 628, 694, 715
Barrett, Martha 694
Barrett, Mary 45, 172, 238, 447, 638, 679, 734, 736, 741
Barrett, Mehitable 315
Barrett, Rebecca 598, 842
Barrett, Sarah 97, 280, 305, 329, 336, 469, 657, 722
Barrett, Stephen 502
Barrett, Thankful 117
Barrett, Thomas 168, 238, 842
BARRILL 45
BARRON 46, 47
Barron, Abigail 391
Barron, Elias 256
Barron, Elizabeth 576
Barron, Ellis 355
Barron, Grace 709
Barron, Hannah 130, 180
Barron, Margery 360
Barron, Mary 69, 350, 781
Barron, Mehitable 557
Barron, Moses 622
Barron, Samuel 582
Barron, Sarah 253
Barron, Susan 610
Barron, Susanna 610
BARRONS 43
BARROW 47
Barrow, Deborah 113
Barrow, James 7
Barrow, Rebecca 320
BARROWS 47 see BARRUS, BARRY
Barrows, Deborah 266
Barrows, Elizabeth 45
Barrows, Mehitabel 842
BARRUS 47
BARRY 47, 66
Barry, James 7, 230
BARSHAM 47
Barsham, Dorothy 10
Barsham, Elizabeth 255
Barsham, Hannah 698
Barsham, Mary 99, 557, 714
Barsham, Rebecca 828
Barsham, Sarah 67, 107, 109, 486, 543
Barsham, Susanna 133
Barsott, Ruth 697

BARSTOW 47, 66
Barstow, Deborah 664
Barstow, Elizabeth 611
Barstow, Jeremiah 700
Barstow, Margaret 296
Barstow, Martha 604, 726
Barstow, Mary 411, 725
Barstow, Patience 34, 674
Barstow, Sarah 152
Barstow, Susan 574
Barstow, Susannah 610
Barstow, William 604
Bartell, Joanna 838
BARTELLS 49
BARTER 47
BARTHOLOMEW 47
Bartholomew, --- 291
Bartholomew, Abigail 286, 824
Bartholomew, Elizabeth 142, 586
Bartholomew, Hannah 106, 724
Bartholomew, Henry 233, 415
Bartholomew, John 285
Bartholomew, Katherine 775
Bartholomew, Mary 310
Bartholomew, Sarah 293
Bartholmue, Mary 803
BARTLES 49
BARTLET 48, 49
Bartlet, Martha 708
Bartlet, Mary 707
Bartlet, Rebecca 31
Bartlet, Sarah 383
BARTLETT 47, 48, 49
Bartlett, Abiah 306, 649
Bartlett, Abial 649
Bartlett, Abigail 251, 504, 704, 719
Bartlett, Abraham 425
Bartlett, Anna 383, 385
Bartlett, Anne 622, 790
Bartlett, Bathsheba 20, 85
Bartlett, Bethia 493
Bartlett, Christopher 493
Bartlett, Damaris 580, 659
Bartlett, Daniel 473
Bartlett, Deborah 5, 187, 304, 697
Bartlett, Ebenezer 214
Bartlett, Elizabeth 108, 279, 312, 601, 697
Bartlett, Elizabeth Spurwink 33
Bartlett, Hannah 72, 437, 725
Bartlett, Hepzibah 219
Bartlett, Isaiah 678
Bartlett, Jane 81
Bartlett, Joanna 745
Bartlett, John 142, 626
Bartlett, Lydia 42, 530
Bartlett, Margaret 46
Bartlett, Martha 536, 626, 708
Bartlett, Mary 22, 32, 43, 54, 228, 231, 278, 525, 631, 707, 714
Bartlett, Mehitable 118, 562, 651, 698
Bartlett, Mercy 412
Bartlett, Moses 342
Bartlett, Rebecca 91, 344, 700
Bartlett, Robert 588
Bartlett, Sarah 49, 153, 154, 383, 625, 809
Bartlett, Thomas 545
Bartlitt, Bethshuah 20
BARTOL 49
Bartol, Joan 165
Bartol, John 523
BARTOLL 49
Bartoll, Alice 785

Bartoll, Joan 145
Bartoll, Mary 223, 444, 465
BARTON 49
Barton, Ann 157
Barton, Margaret 131, 746
Barton, Martha 350
Barton, Mary 321, 383
Barton, Matthew 221
Barton, Phebe 165
Barton, Rufus 746
Barton, Ruth 179
Barton, Sarah 607
BARTRAM 66
Bartram, Esther 533
Bartram, John 91, 320
Bartram, Sarah 320
Barttey, Sarah 393
BASCOM 49
Bascom, Abigail 410
Bascom, Hannah 104
Bascomb, Hepzibah 480
Basee, Sarah 588
BASFORD 49
Bash, Hannah 608
BASHFORD 49
Baskel, Hannah 576
Basket, Hannah 576
BASON 84
BASS 49, 50
Bass, Deborah 788
Bass, Hannah 4, 552, 814
Bass, John 720
Bass, Joseph 80, 632
Bass, Mary 133, 182, 288, 734, 788
Bass, Mercy 734
Bass, Ruth 777, 788
Bass, Samuel 425, 653
Bass, Sarah 570, 714, 734
Bass, Thomas 77
Bassaker, Abigail 713
Basset, Mary 85, 526
Basset, Nathaniel 526
Basset, Rachel 673
BASSETT 50, 51
Bassett, Abiah 467
Bassett, Amy 566
Bassett, Ann 788
Bassett, Anna Lane Smith 679
Bassett, Deborah 517
Bassett, Elizabeth 120, 262, 265, 605
Bassett, Emma 566
Bassett, Hannah 465, 558, 576
Bassett, Lydia 811
Bassett, Maria 251
Bassett, Mary 217, 418, 526, 616, 621, 641, 731
Bassett, Miriam 649
Bassett, Nathaniel 526
Bassett, Phebe 637
Bassett, Rachel 278
Bassett, Rebecca 736
Bassett, Robert 566
Bassett, Roger 124
Bassett, Ruth 736, 811
Bassett, Sarah 76, 250, 326, 370, 376, 464, 537, 788, 806
Bassett, Thomas 56
Bassett, William 451, 571
Basseville, Elizabeth 568
BASSON 51, 84 see BOSSON
Basson, Hannah 415
Bassum, Sarah 67, 543
Bastar, Elizabeth 245
BASTARD 51
Bastard, Joseph 772
BASTER 51

Baster, Sarah 404
Baster, Susanna 320
BASTON 51
Baston, Margaret 675
Baston, Mary 601
Baston, William 570
BASTOW 47
Basum, John 536
Basum, Walter 536
Batchaler, Elizabeth 510
BATCHELDER 51, 52
Batchelder, Abigail 213, 446, 836
Batchelder, Agnes 69
Batchelder, Ann 649
Batchelder, Deborah 554
Batchelder, Elizabeth 510
Batchelder, Esther 257, 665
Batchelder, Hannah 183, 780
Batchelder, Jane 449
Batchelder, John 781
Batchelder, Joseph 35, 304
Batchelder, Mary 186, 191, 622, 773
Batchelder, Mercy 213
Batchelder, Nathaniel 845
Batchelder, Rachel 25
Batchelder, Rebecca 349
Batchelder, Ruth 75
Batchelder, Sarah 599, 648
Batchelder, Seaborne 561
Batchelder, Stephen 57
Batchelder, Stephen (Rev.) 760
Batchelder, Susannah 454
Batcheldor, Deborah 828
Batcheller, Elizabeth 206
BATCHELOUR 51
Bate, --- 51
Bate, Rachel 465
BATEMAN 52
Bateman, --- 507
Bateman, Elizabeth 21, 325, 328, 481, 843
Bateman, Hannah 177
Bateman, John 325
Bateman, Martha 212
Bateman, Mary 425, 481
Bateman, Rachel 383
Bateman, Sarah 129, 245, 321, 538
Bateman, Thomas 37, 444, 445
BATES 52, 53
Bates, Anna 649, 709
Bates, Benjamin 552
Bates, Edward 257, 271
Bates, Elizabeth 32, 391, 455, 599, 623, 696
Bates, Esther 164
Bates, Hannah 145, 372
Bates, James 300
Bates, Joanna 242, 500
Bates, John 298
Bates, Judith 300
Bates, Lydia 185, 821
Bates, Margaret 300, 696
Bates, Mary 15, 162, 277, 391, 575, 633
Bates, Rachel 465
Bates, Robert 194, 396
Bates, Ruth 777
Bates, Sarah 128
Bates, Susanna 500
Bates, Susannah 50, 77
Bathelour, Abigail 836
Batherick, Ruth 773
Batherick, Thomas 59
BATHRICK 53
Bathrick, Ruth 794
Batieu, Martha 711

Batrap, Eleanor 182
Bats, Elizabeth 623
Bats, Sarah 128
BATSON 53
Batson, --- 754
Batson, Elizabeth 23, 257
Batson, John 316, 772
Batson, Margaret 846
Batson, Margery 247
Batson, Mary 102, 160
BATT 53
Batt, Ann 19
Batt, Anna 19
Batt, Anne 19, 789
Batt, Jane 727
Batt, Mary 247
Batt, Paul 747
Batt, Sarah 507
BATTALY 53
BATTELEE 53
BATTELL 53
Battelle, Mary 111
Battelle, Sarah 745
BATTEN 53
Batten, John 445, 506
Batten, Susannah 330
BATTER 53
Batter, Edmond 766
Batter, Edmund 576
Batter, Eleanor 576, 755
Batter, Jane 20
Batter, Mary 250
Batters, Mary 250
BATTEY 53
BATTIS 53
BAUDEN 86
BAUDOUIN 36, 86
BAUK 39
Bauk, Hannah 33
Bauk, Hannah Jenkins 79
Bauk, John 558
Bauk, Mary 598
Bauke, Sarah 318
BAULSTON 38
Baulstone, Elizabeth 166
BAVRICK 53
Bawke, Sarah 318
BAXTER 53, 54
Baxter, Abigail 4
Baxter, Alice 403
Baxter, Anne 373
Baxter, Bethia 213
Baxter, Bridget 554
Baxter, Elizabeth 633
Baxter, Elsje 403
Baxter, Hannah 237, 478, 603
Baxter, John 483, 541
Baxter, Joseph 646
Baxter, Mary 116, 128, 724
Baxter, Priscilla 816
Baxter, Rebecca 554
Baxter, Samuel 610
Baxter, Susanna 203, 294, 408
Baxter, Thomas 554, 720
Baycon, Jarvis 244
Baycon, Sarah 244
Bayer, John 89
BAYES 54
Bayes, Abigail 53
Bayes, Anne 532
Bayes, Hannah 97
Bayes, Mary 540
Bayes, Ruth 540
Bayford, Agnes 202
Bayford, Amis 561
Bayford, Ann 202, 561
Bayford, Annis 202

Bayford, Hannah 202
Bayless, Abigail 680
Bayless, Mary 367
Bayless, Rebecca 711
BAYLEY 31, 32
Bayley, Christian 809
Bayley, Elizabeth 579
Bayley, Esther 439
Bayley, John (Rev.) 733
Bayley, Priscilla 833
BAYLIE 31, 32
BAYLIES 54
Baylis, Rebecca 711
BAYLY 32
Bayly, Elias 653
Bayly, Sarah 653
Baynton, Ann 53
BAYSE 54
BAYSEY 54
Baysey, Adrian 473
Baysey, Elizabeth 568
Baysey, Lydia 33
Baysey, Mary 122
Baysey, Mercy 122
BEACH 54
Beach, Benjamin 257
Beach, Bethia 67
Beach, Elizabeth 602
Beach, Hannah 257, 540
Beach, Leatis 779
Beach, Lettis 779
Beach, Martha 810
Beach, Mary 198, 401, 484, 684
Beach, Richard 400
Beach, Sarah 481
Beach, Thomas 506
BEACHAM 54
Beacham, --- 470
Beacham, Edward 506
Beacham, Robert 419
BEACHAMP 54
BEACHUM 54
Beachum, Elizabeth 309
BEACON 30
BEADLE 57
Beadle, Dorothy 474
Beadle, Elizabeth 702
Beadle, Joseph 212
Beadle, Mary 319
Beadle, Nathaniel 438
Beadle, Susanna 366
Beadley, Elizabeth 244
BEADON 58
BEAL 54, 55
Beal, Abigail 285
Beal, Christian 34
Beal, Elizabeth 596
Beal, George 375
Beal, Hannah 261, 778
Beal, John 414
Beal, Joseph 17
Beal, Joshua 716
Beal, Martha 152, 234, 713
Beal, Mary 252, 377, 383, 411, 459, 716, 754, 811
Beal, Mercy 754
Beal, Sarah 324, 450, 489, 666, 828
Beal, Susanna 424
BEALE 54, 55
Beale, Abishag 43
Beale, Anne 374
Beale, Martha 194, 257
Beale, William 412
BEALES 55
BEALL 55
Beall, Sarah 450
Beals, Anna 769

Beals, Eleazer 201
Beals, Mary 53
BEAMAN 55
Beaman, Abigail 36
Beaman, Elizabeth 145
Beaman, Lydia 88, 608
Beaman, Martha 364, 668
Beaman, Mary 179
Beaman, Rebecca 156
Beaman, Sarah 819
Beaman, Thankful 825
Beament, Sarah 600
BEAMON 55
Beamon, Mary 509
Beamon, Ruth 509
Beamond, Lydia 608
BEAMONT 55
Beamont, --- 757
Beamont, Deborah 303
Beamont, Mary 758
Beamont, Thankful 825
Beamont, Thomas 706
BEAMSLEY 55, 56
Beamsley, Anne 839
Beamsley, Elizabeth 550
Beamsley, Grace 319
Beamsley, Hannah 571
Beamsley, Mary 629, 814
Beamsley, Mary Cogan 630
Beamsley, Mercy 574
Beamsley, William 126
BEAN 56
Bean, Abigail 265
Bean, Catherine 226
Bean, Elizabeth 134, 676
Bean, Lewis 100
Bean, Margaret 731
Bean, Mary 429
Bean, Sarah Bradley 630
Bean, Tamosen 523
Bean, William 829
Beane, Hannah 804
Beane, Mary 154
BEANS 56
Beans, Elizabeth 131
BEAR 58, 59
Bear, Sarah 86
BEARD 56 see BARD
Beard, Anna 280
Beard, Elizabeth 785
Beard, George 128
Beard, John 763
Beard, Martha 93, 334, 718
Beard, Mary 36, 163, 399, 822
Beard, Sarah 100, 112
Beard, William 398, 822
Bearding, Nathaniel 18
Bearding, Sarah 696
BEARDSLEY 56
Beardsley, Abigail 754
Beardsley, Elizabeth 211
Beardsley, Hannah 220, 400, 401,
  418, 561, 723
Beardsley, Mary 60, 211, 795
Beardsley, Rebecca 58, 197
Beardsley, Ruth 686
Beardsley, Sarah 45, 220, 501
Beardsley, Thomas 50, 211
BEARE 59
Bearhaugh, Anne 717
BEARSE 59
Bearse, Priscilla 334
Bearse, Sarah 339
BEARSTOW 47
Beaton, Grace 380
BEAUCHAMP 54
Beauchamp, Elizabeth 309
Beaumond, Patience 353

Beaumont, Patience 353
Beaumont, Rebecca 156
Beaumont, Thankful 825
BEAUMOUNT 55
Beaupre, Ann 843
BEAVERLY 56
Beazer, Richard 552
BEAZLEY 56
Bech, Bethiah 507
Bech, Bethuah 507
BECK 56, 57
Beck, Elizabeth 253
Beck, Henry 253
Beck, Mary 322
Becker, Elizabeth 233
BECKET 57
Becket, Hannah 145
Becket, Mary 88, 693
BECKETT 57
Beckett, Hannah 703
Beckett, John 193
Beckett, Margaret 193
Beckett, Mercy 788
Beckett, Sarah 49
BECKLEY 57
Beckley, Abigail 130
Beckley, Deborah 696
Beckley, Hannah 790
Beckley, Nathaniel 522
Beckley, Sarah 152
Becknal, Martha Metcalf 716
Beckner, William 716
Beckwich, Elizabeth 52
BECKWITH 57
Beckwith, Anna 511
Beckwith, Elizabeth 70, 113, 298
Beckwith, Hannah Cogswell 167
Beckwith, Mary 113, 203, 317
Beckwith, Mathew 114
Beckwith, Matthew 113, 600, 633
Beckwith, Mercy 203
Beckwith, Ruth 641
Beckwith, Sarah 317, 511
Beckwith, Susannah Tillman 786
BEDELL 57
Bedell, Bethia 578
Bedell, Christopher 580
Bedell, Mary 651
Bedfield, Mary 591
Bedfield, Ruth 654
BEDFORD 57, 58
Bedford, Deborah 789
Bedford, Margaret Piere 418
Bedford, Nathan 131
Bedford, Ruth 654
BEDICT 61
BEDIENT 58
Bedient, Mary 750
Bedient, Mordecai 547, 750
BEDLE 57
Bedle, Abigail 598
Bedloo, Maria 686
BEDORTHA 58
Bedortha, Joseph 233
Bedortha, Samuel 461
BEDWELL 68
BEE 58
Bee, Thomas 44
BEEBE 58
Beebe, --- 61
Beebe, Agnes 203
Beebe, Ann 192
Beebe, Hannah 355
Beebe, James 197
Beebe, Joanah 808
Beebe, Mary 279, 751
Beebe, Rachel 112
Beebe, Rebecca 385, 637, 665

Beebe, Thomas 22, 693
Beech, Martha 810
BEECHER 58
Beecher, --- 597
Beecher, Hannah 155
Beecher, Isaac 506
Beecher, Samuel 670
Beecher, Sarah 62
Beecher, Thomas 181, 240
BEEDE 58
Beedel, Susanna 366
BEEDLE 57
Beedle, Christopher 580
Beedle, Henry 221
Beedle, Mary 51, 651, 760
Beedle, Robert 51
Beedle, Susanna 371
BEEDON 58
BEEFORD 58
Beeks, John 1
BEELS 54
BEER 58
BEERE 59
Beere, Elizabeth Billington Bulloch
  596
Beere, John 13
Beere, Robert 575
BEERES 58, 59, 82
Beeres, Hester 421
BEERS 58, 59
Beers, Alice 266
Beers, Anthony 3, 568
Beers, Bethiah 507
Beers, Bethuah 507
Beers, Deborah 401
Beers, Elizabeth 204, 307, 311,
  568
Beers, Esther 421
Beers, Jabez 40
Beers, Joseph 233
Beers, Judith 10
Beers, Martha 115
Beers, Mary 620, 684
Beers, Robert 117
Beers, Sarah 429, 703, 801
Beese, Ann 337
Beese, Anna 337
Beese, Anne 337
Beetle, Christopher 580
BEGAR 59
Begelow, Mary 110
Beggarly, Alice 203
Begnall, William 716
BEHONEY 59 see BOHOMON,
  BONOMIE
BEIGHTON 59
Beighton, Lydia 197
BEIRSE 56
Bekley, Hannah 790
BELCHER 59, 60
Belcher, Abigail 315, 786
Belcher, Andrew 774
Belcher, Ann 121
Belcher, Anna 38, 422
Belcher, Anne 715
Belcher, Dorcas 314
Belcher, Dorothy 328
Belcher, Edward 841
Belcher, Elizabeth 79, 285, 302,
  544, 551, 730
Belcher, Faith 194, 586
Belcher, Hannah 38
Belcher, Jemima 673
Belcher, Jeremiah 141, 529, 661
Belcher, John 204, 459
Belcher, Judith 17
Belcher, Martha 617
Belcher, Mary 18, 50, 262, 489,

Belcher, Mary (cont.) 644, 766, 768
Belcher, Mercy 435
Belcher, Rebecca 289, 509
Belcher, Samuel 89, 537
Belcher, Sarah 225, 281, 411, 480
Belcher, Silence 652
BELCONGER 60
BELDEN 60
Belden, --- 71
Belden, Daniel 160
Belden, George 92
Belden, Hannah 92
Belden, Margaret 431
Belden, Mary 14, 754
Belden, Samuel 14, 794, 795
BELDIN 60
BELDING 60
Belding, Anna 735
Belding, Daniel 795
Belding, Elizabeth 102
Belding, Lydia 431
Belding, Mary 14, 214, 754
Belding, Samuel 69, 795
Belding, Sarah 754
Belding, Susannah 678
BELFLOURE 61
Belfloure, Anna 200
Belfloure, Hannah 200
BELKNAP 60, 61
Belknap, Abraham 409
Belknap, Hannah 547
Belknap, Mary 316, 409
Belknap, Ruth 501
Belknap, Sarah 676
BELL 61
Bell, Abraham 770
Bell, Ann 526
Bell, Catherine 501
Bell, Christian 146, 706
Bell, Deborah 246, 846
Bell, Dorothy 200, 752
Bell, Elizabeth 66, 194
Bell, Esther 335
Bell, Grace 519
Bell, Hannah 66, 67
Bell, James 490
Bell, Jane 247
Bell, Joanna 252
Bell, Martha 684
Bell, Mary 184, 340, 396, 537, 760
Bell, Nathaniel 525
Bell, Rebecca 761
Bell, Sarah 173, 487
Bell, Thomas 526, 535
BELLAMY 61
Bellamy, Bridget 84
Bellany, Matthew 835
Bellard, William 95
Belles, Mary 679
BELLFLOUR 61
BELLFLOWER 61
Bellflower, Deliverance 505
BELLINGHAM 61
Bellingham, Anne 367
Bellingham, Hester 367
Bellingham, Susan 594
BELLOWS 61
Bellows, Abigail 454
Bellows, Benjamin 817
Bellows, John 801
BELOUSE 61
Belsher, Mary 262, 768
Belt, Grace 519
BELVELE 61
BELVILLE 61
BEMAN 55

Beman, Hannah 825
Beman, Lydia 621
Beman, Mary 179
Bemas, Rebecca 512
Bemas, Sarah 327
BEMENT 55
Bement, Martha 364
BEMIS 61
Bemis, John 42, 578
Bemis, Mary 328, 332, 811
Bemis, Mercy 328
Bemis, Rebecca 218, 345, 512, 651, 805, 830
Bemis, Sarah 68
BEMISH 61
BEMOND 55
Benbow, Margery 639
BENDALL 61
Bendall, Mariana 9
Bendall, Mary 9, 480
BENDER see PINDAR
BENEDICT 61, 62
Benedict, Elizabeth 678
Benedict, Esther 411
Benedict, Hannah 641
Benedict, James 16
Benedict, Mary 544
Benedict, Mary Messenger 401
Benedict, Phebe 731
Benedict, Rebecca 835
Benedict, Sarah 58, 470
Benet, Priscilla 136
Benffield, Mary 295
BENFIELD 62 see BANFIELD
Benfield, Mary 295
Benford, Ruth 654
BENHAM 62, 82
Benham, Anna 422
Benham, Hannah 636
Benham, John 7, 605, 826
Benham, Joseph 411
Benham, Sarah 421
Benison, Mary 551
BENJAMIN 62
Benjamin, Abigail 373, 530, 719, 839
Benjamin, Caleb 347
Benjamin, Hannah 296
Benjamin, Jemima 296
Benjamin, John 138, 665
Benjamin, Joshua 25
Benjamin, Lydia 53
Benjamin, Mary 157, 219, 296
Benjamin, Mercy 296
Benjamin, Sarah 332
Benmet, John 501
BENMORE 62
Benmore, Philip 446
Benmore, Temperance 3
Bennet, Mary 578
Bennet, Susanna 183
BENNETT 62, 63, 64
Bennett, Abigail 72
Bennett, Alice 407
Bennett, Ann 685
Bennett, Anthony 625, 777
Bennett, Arthur 264
Bennett, Benjamin 318
Bennett, Constance 374
Bennett, David 148
Bennett, David (Dr.) 117
Bennett, Deliverance 195
Bennett, Eleanor 827
Bennett, Elizabeth 193, 206, 245, 365, 409, 411, 564, 782
Bennett, Ellen 827
Bennett, Francis 407
Bennett, George 105, 367, 400

Bennett, Hannah 661
Bennett, Henry 122, 131
Bennett, Jacob 93
Bennett, James 83, 329, 507, 704
Bennett, Joane 229, 805
Bennett, John 319, 377, 501, 773
Bennett, Mary 165, 229, 264, 547, 568, 578, 805
Bennett, Mercy 568, 720
Bennett, Peter 475
Bennett, Priscilla 797
Bennett, Richard 331
Bennett, Rose 818
Bennett, Ruth 496
Bennett, Samuel 276
Bennett, Sarah 547
Bennett, Susanna 157, 475
Bennett, William 683, 788
BENNICKE 62
Benniman, Abigail 530
BENNING 64
Benning, Ann 213
Benning, Elizabeth 275
Benning, Mary 493, 796
Bennit, Elizabeth 782
Bennum, Hannah 636
Bense, Mary 651
BENSON 64
Benson, Elizabeth 42
Benson, Henry 424
Benson, John 671
Benson, Mary 181, 331
Benson, Sarah 599
Benson, Susanna 610
BENT 64, 65 see BANT
Bent, Abigail 751
Bent, Agnes 44, 77, 420, 620
Bent, Ann 77
Bent, Hannah 4
Bent, Martha 393
BENTLEY 65
Bentley, Jane 814
BENTON 65
Benton, Bethiah 650
Benton, Dorothy 68, 680
Benton, Elizabeth 592
Benton, Hannah 2, 132, 636, 657
Benton, James 452
Benton, Joanna 759
Benton, Lydia 459
Benton, Mary 29, 68, 170, 740
Benton, Rebecca 80, 338
Benton, Sarah 76, 843
Benton, Tabitha 675, 676
BERAT 45
Berat, John 46
Berbeane, Mary 391
Berdet, Hannah 142
Beresford, Henry 721
Bergen, Rachel 397
BERNARD 43, 65
Bernard, Joseph 794
Bernard, William 709
BERNARDS 65
BERNON 65
Bernon, Mary 748
Berre, Abigail 535
Berrelford, Henry 721
BERRIEN 65
Berrien, Cornelius J. 243
BERRY 65, 66
Berry, --- 673
Berry, Aetheldred 503
Berry, Ambrose 137, 655
Berry, Athildred 503
Berry, Benjamin 197
Berry, Deliverance 592
Berry, Desire 64

Berry, Edward 133, 351, 590
Berry, Elizabeth 109, 426, 469, 750
Berry, Ethelred 503
Berry, Hannah 9, 386, 612
Berry, James 230
Berry, Jane 230, 314
Berry, Mary 152, 276
Berry, Mercy 338
Berry, Rachel 462, 488
Berry, Samuel 488
Berry, Sarah 230, 712
Berry, Thomas 462
Berry, Wm. 230
Berrye, Agnes 187
Berse, Ann 337
Berse, Anna 337
Berse, Anne 337
BERSTOW 47
Berstow, Susannah 610
BERTEAU 66
BERTLES 49
BERTRAM 66
Bertram, John 320
Bertram, Sarah 320
BERVERS 67
Berwick, Grace 38
Besbege, Ales 85
Besbege, Alice 85
Besbege, Allis 85
Besboth, Mary 109
Besbye, Hopestill 465
BESHEAU 66
BESSE 66
Besse, Anthony 42
Besse, Elizabeth 80
Besse, Jane 42
Besse, Rebecca 404
Bessee, Mary 197
Bessett, William 412
Bessey, Dorcas 602
Bessie, Ann 337
Bessie, Anna 337
Bessie, Anne 337
BEST 66
Best, Bridget 664
Best, Susannah 506
BETHUEN 129 see BUTTON
BETHUNE 66
BETSCOME 66
BETTELLE 53
BETTS 66, 67
Betts, Ann 130
Betts, Anna 25
Betts, Elizabeth 646
Betts, Joanna 658
Betts, John 4, 99, 276, 467
Betts, Martha 319, 435
Betts, Mary 80, 613, 723
Betts, Mehitabel 376
Betts, Mehitable 741
Betts, Mercy 43
Betts, Pity 211
Betts, Richard 191
Betts, Roger 130
Betts, Sarah 280, 403, 646
BEUFORD 67
BEUKER 112
BEVANS 67
Bever, Mary 565
BEVERLY 56
Beverly, Mary 383
BEVIL 67
BEVIN 67
Bevin, Mary 333
Bevin, Mercy 509
BEVINS 67
BEWFORD 67

BIAM 129
BIBBELL 67
Bibble, Anna 426
Bibble, John 226
Bibble, John 542
Bibble, Sybil 542
Bibble, Thomas 5
BICK 67
Bick, James 697
Bickerstaff, Hannah 88
BICKFORD 67
Bickford, Benjamin 543
Bickford, Deborah 427
Bickford, Elizabeth 686
Bickford, Elizabeth 794
Bickford, Joanna 617
Bickford, Lydia 231
Bickford, Mary 348
Bickford, Priscilla 757
Bickford, Temperance 121
BICKLEY 67
BICKNELL 67, 68 see
  BRICKNELL
Bicknell, Edward 391
Bicknell, Elizabeth 809
Bicknell, Hannah 664, 768
Bicknell, Joanna 275
Bicknell, John 370
Bicknell, Mary 237
Bicknell, Ruth 621
Bicknell, Sarah 615
Bicknell, Zachary 632
BICKNER 67
Bickner, Anna 487
Bickner, Hannah 67
BICKNOF 67
Bickwell, Mary 755
BIDDLE 68
Biddle, Joseph 212
BIDFIELD 73
Bidfield, Elizabeth 709
BIDGOOD 68
BIDLAKE 68
Bidlake, Christopher 392
Bidle, Dorothy 88
BIDLOACK 68
BIDWELL 68
Bidwell, Ann 253
Bidwell, Hannah 769
Bidwell, Mary 222, 501
Bidwell, Richard 253
Bidwell, Sarah 93, 391
Bierse, Sarah 339
Bigalow, Sarah 458
BIGELOW 67, 68
Bigelow, Abigail 345
Bigelow, Elizabeth 127, 703
Bigelow, Jonathan 170
Bigelow, Martha 835
Bigelow, Mary 110, 270, 820
Bigelow, Sarah 458
BIGG 68
Bigg, Elizabeth 211
Bigg, John 307, 513
Bigg, Patience 278
Bigge, Elizabeth 716
BIGGISBY 73
BIGGS 68, 99
Biggs, Ann 268
Biggs, Anna 416
Biggs, Annie 416
Biggs, Dinah 662
Biggs, Elizabeth 731
Biggs, John 512
Biggs, Mary 356
Bignall, Martha 37
BIGSBE 73
BIGSBEE 73

BIGSBY 73
BIGSBYE 73
BIGULA 68
BIGULAH 68
Bigulah, Mary 270
BILES 129
Biles, Rebecca 563
BILEY 129
Biley, Mary 232
Biley, Rebecca 332
BILL 68, 69
Bill, Elizabeth 146
Bill, Hannah 59, 327, 434
Bill, Martha 303
Bill, Mary 396
Bill, Philip 113, 114, 154
Bill, Sarah 148
Bill, Susanna 189, 433
Bill, Thomas 74, 457
Bille, Thomas 114
BILLENS 69
Billes, Anna 543
BILLING 69, 70
Billing, Daniel 497
Billing, Elizabeth 556, 735
Billing, Hannah 330
Billing, John 449, 735
Billing, Mary 390
Billing, Nathaniel 39
BILLINGS 69
Billings, Abigail 610
Billings, Ammi 779
Billings, Amy 172, 779
Billings, Ann 303
Billings, Dorothy 483
Billings, Elizabeth 738, 773
Billings, Hannah 570
Billings, Lydia 101
Billings, Margaret 257
Billings, Mary 60, 390, 537, 808
Billings, Nathaniel 168, 479
Billings, Samuel 60, 369, 509
Billings, Sarah 221
BILLINGTON 70
Billington, Desire 82
Billington, Dorcas 498
Billington, Eleanor 21
Billington, Elizabeth 59, 117, 575, 596
Billington, Francis 117, 240
Billington, Lydia 783
Billington, Martha 241
Billington, Mary 492, 645
Billington, Mercy 492
BILLS 69
Bills, Anna 543
Bills, Elizabeth 445
Bilton, Sarah 508
Binding, Sarah 113
BINEY 70
Bing, Sarah 185
BINGHAM 70
Bingham, Ann 494
Bingham, Mary 29
Bingham, Thomas 29
BINGLEY 70
Bingley, Anna 807
Bingley, Elizabeth 147
Bingley, Thomas 655
BINNING 64
Biram, Deliverance 594
Birch, Mary 244
Bircham, Anna 356
Bircham, Edward 356
Bircham, Hannah 356
BIRCHARD 70
Birchard, Elizabeth 78
Birchard, Hannah 35

Birchard, Thomas 751
BIRCK 119
BIRD 70, 71
Bird, Abiel 154
Bird, Anne 157
Bird, Damaris 354
Bird, Dorothy 473
Bird, Hannah 212, 518, 538, 656
Bird, Hester 173
Bird, Jathnell 173, 635
Bird, Lydia 518
Bird, Margaret 186
Bird, Mary 417, 538, 539, 685
Bird, Mehitable 76
Bird, Rebecca 448
Bird, Simon 417
Bird, Thankful 288
Birdley, Giles 378
Birdley, Gyles 270
Birdley, Rebecca 270
BIRDLY 120
BIRDSALE 71
Birdsale, Judith 178
BIRDSALL 71
Birdsall, Elizabeth 750
Birdsall, Samuel 170
BIRDSEY 71
Birdsey, Catherine 356
Birdsey, Hannah 54
Birdsey, John 54, 746
Birdseye, Joanna 815
BIRGE 71 see BURGE, BURGESS
Birge, Deborah 695
Birge, Elizabeth 304
Birge, Joseph 548
Birge, Mary 766
Birge, Richard 390
Biron, Abigail 809
Births, Bietnes 258
Births, Christian 258
Births, Hannah 417
BISBE 71
BISBEE 71
Bisbee, Ales 85
Bisbee, Alice 85
Bisbee, Allis 85
Bisbee, Elisha 30
Bisbee, Hannah 103
Bisbee, Hopestill 465
Bisbee, Martha 759
Bisbee, Mary 54, 109
Bisbie, Phebe 493
BISBORN 73
Bisby, Mary 109
Bisby, Phebe 90
BISCOE 100
Biscoe, Elizabeth 412
Biscoe, Mary 104, 113, 308, 674
Biscoe, Sarah 82, 809
BISCON 71
Biscow, Mary 674
Bisell, Deliverance Hawes
    Rockwell Warner 781
Biselow, Martha 834
BISHOP 71, 72, 73
Bishop, --- 340
Bishop, Abigail 82, 166, 485, 579,
    726
Bishop, Alice 392, 463
Bishop, Ann 126
Bishop, Anna 427
Bishop, Anne 158, 264, 383, 427
Bishop, Annis 504
Bishop, Bethia 705
Bishop, Damaris 721
Bishop, Edward 139, 544
Bishop, Elizabeth 82, 232, 303,
    657

Bishop, Hannah 210, 211, 449,
    469, 519, 613, 674
Bishop, Henry 458, 814
Bishop, Hester 121
Bishop, James 199
Bishop, Job 581
Bishop, John 103, 658, 818
Bishop, John (Rev.) 606
Bishop, Jonathan (Jr.) 808
Bishop, Lucy 447
Bishop, Lydia 582
Bishop, Mary 45, 125, 168, 204,
    265, 378, 390, 421, 453
Bishop, Mehitable 808
Bishop, Rebecca 381, 738
Bishop, Richard 155, 296, 439,
    627
Bishop, Ruth 290, 583, 690, 845
Bishop, Samuel 121, 726
Bishop, Sarah 114, 147, 421, 658,
    797
Bishop, Susanna 77
Bishop, Tabitha 274
Bishop, Thomas 108, 295, 469
BISPHAM 73
BISS 73
Biss, Lydia 452
BISSELL 73
Bissell, Abigail 253, 297, 651,
    719, 730
Bissell, Daniel 71
Bissell, Dorothy 715, 786
Bissell, Elizabeth 646, 715
Bissell, Hannah 318, 576
Bissell, Jacob 114
Bissell, John 472, 757
Bissell, Joseph 369
Bissell, Joyce 587
Bissell, Mary 230, 548, 575
Bissell, Mindwell 327
Bissell, Samuel 511
Bissell, Sarah 804
Bissett, --- 64
Bissett, Thomas 816
BITFIELD 73
Bitfield, Elizabeth 709, 745
Bitfield, Mary 591
BITNER 73
BITTLESTONE 73
Bittlestone, Elizabeth 100
BIXBE 73
BIXBEE 73
BIXBY 73
Bixby, Joseph 362
Bixby, Mary 714
Bixby, Phebe 493
BLABER 74
Blaber, Robert 129
BLABOUR 74
BLACHLEY 77, 78
Blachley, Aaron 274
Blachley, Abigail 37
BLACK 74, 75
Black, Abraham 216
Black, Elizabeth 302, 437, 614
Black, Hannah 460, 693
Black, Jane 302
Black, John 79, 647
Black, Lydia 206
Black, Martha 84
Black, Persis 273
BLACKALER 74
BLACKBURN 74
Blackburn, Mary 391
BLACKDEN 74
Blacke, Anna 302
Blacket, Mary 737
Blackhealth, Benjamin 69

Blackington, Pentacost 45
BLACKINTON 74
Blackinton, Pentecost 263
BLACKLEACH 74
Blackleach, Benjamin 114, 487
Blackleach, Exercise 378
Blackleach, John 386, 416
Blackleach, Mary 416, 543
Blackleath, Sarah 148
BLACKLEDGE 74
Blackledge, Elizabeth 346
Blackledge, John 416
Blackledge, Mary 416, 795
Blackledge, Nathaniel 282
Blackledge, Sarah 148
BLACKLEECH 74
Blackleech, Exercise 611
BLACKLER 74
BLACKLEY 74, 76
BLACKLY 76
BLACKMAN 74, 76
Blackman, Abigail 220
Blackman, Hannah 302
Blackman, James 328
Blackman, Jane 326
Blackman, Joan 326
Blackman, John 646
Blackman, Martha 37
Blackman, Mary 24, 369, 822
Blackman, Miriam 539
Blackman, Rebecca 152
Blackman, Samuel 774
Blackmar, Mary 822
BLACKMER 74
Blackmer, Phebe 383
Blackmor, William 117
BLACKMORE 74
Blackmore, H. 6
Blackmore, Mary 5, 6, 775
Blackmore, Phebe 383
Blackmur, Phebe 383
BLACKSTONE 74, 75
Blackstone, William (Rev.) 709
BLACKWELL 75
Blackwell, Alice 697
Blackwell, Desire 418
Blackwell, Jane 300
Blackwell, Mary 702
Blackwell, Michael 300
Blademan, Jane 326
Blademan, Joan 326
BLADGET 79
BLAGDEN 75
BLAGDON 75
Blagdon, James 137, 219
Blagdon, Samuel 400
BLAGGE 75
Blagge, Martha 213
BLAGROVE 75
BLAGUE 75, 76
Blague, Newcomb 609
Blague, Philip 605
Blaids, Sarah 418
Blaisdale, Mary 708
BLAISDELL 75
Blaisdell, Elizabeth 405
Blaisdell, Henry 168
Blaisdell, John 395
Blaisdell, Martha 86, 661
Blaisdell, Mary 612, 706
Blaisdell, Robert 612
BLAKE 74, 75, 76
Blake, Abigail 128, 724
Blake, Ann 457
Blake, Anne 337
Blake, Deborah 247, 518, 569,
    469
Blake, Elizabeth 235, 288, 422,

Blake, Elizabeth (cont.) 573
Blake, Experience 138, 721
Blake, James 404
Blake, Jane 432
Blake, Joanna 660
Blake, John 593, 665, 758
Blake, Martha 699
Blake, Mary 422, 461, 588, 822, 823
Blake, Mehitable 99
Blake, Mercy 628
Blake, Priscilla 685
Blake, Prudence 762
Blake, Rachel Rood 681
Blake, Rebecca 16
Blake, Ruth 665
Blake, Samuel 589
Blake, Sarah 484, 628, 726
Blake, Susannah 650, 773
BLAKELEY 76
Blakeley, Esther 820
Blakeley, Hester 820
Blakely, Esther 81
Blakely, Hester 81
Blakely, Samuel 102
BLAKEMAN 76 see BLACKMAN
Blakeman, Abigail 220, 691
Blakeman, Dorothy 589
Blakeman, Hannah 302
Blakeman, James 328
Blakeman, Jane 155, 644
Blakeman, Johannah 785
Blakeman, John 334, 515
Blakeman, Mary 369, 659
Blakeman, Miriam 539
Blakeman, Samuel 774
Blakeman, Sarah 176, 746
BLAKESLEE 76
Blakeslee, Miriam 592
Blakeslee, Samuel 104
BLAKESLEY 76
Blakesley, Mary 735
Blakesley, Samuel 102
Blakey, Anna 302
BLAKSLEY 76
BLANCH 76
Blanch, Elizabeth 302
Blanch, William 818
BLANCHANT 76
BLANCHARD 76, 77
Blanchard, --- 295
Blanchard, Abigail 717
Blanchard, Ann 294
Blanchard, Anna 294
Blanchard, Bethiah 6, 551
Blanchard, Elizabeth 327, 561, 772
Blanchard, Hannah 548, 615, 668
Blanchard, John 441, 615
Blanchard, Joshua 243
Blanchard, Mary 103, 181, 204, 260, 716
Blanchard, Mehitable 177
Blanchard, Nathaniel 50
Blanchard, Rachel 685
Blanchard, Samuel 716
Blanchard, Sarah 212, 765
Blanchard, Thomas 44, 294
Blanchard, William 485
BLANCHART 77
BLANCHER 77
BLANCHETT 77
BLANCPIED 808
BLAND 77
Bland, Annabelle 47
Bland, Isabel 25
Bland, Isabella 25, 458
BLANDFORD 77

Blandford, John 844
Blandford, Sarah 499
BLANDING 77
BLANEY 77
Blaney, Anna 287
Blaney, Elizabeth 261
Blaney, John 586, 598
Blaney, Mary 834
Blaney, Susanna 279
Blanford, Hannah 105
Blanford, Mary 239, 550
Blanford, Sarah 435
BLANO 77
BLANTON 77
Blanton, Mary 383
Blanton, Phebe 383
Blanton, Wm. 383
BLANY 77
Blany, Hannah 217
Blany, John (Sr.) 607
Blany, Sarah 243
Blaque, Martha 699
Blasdell, Mary 716
BLASHFIELD 77
BLASHFORD 77
Blaskledge, Benjamin 69
BLATCHFORD 77
Blatchford, Peter 402, 696
BLATCHLEY 77
Blatchley, Miriam 592
Blatchley, Susannah 284
Blatchley, Thomas 100
Blaxton, William (Rev.) 709
BLAYNFORD 77
Bleake, Mary 199
Bleney, John (Jr.) 607
Bless, Experience 141
Blessing, Alice 767
Blessing, Joanna 749
Blessing, Jone 749
BLETHEN 78
BLETSOE 78
BLEVIN 78
BLIGH 79, 80
Bligh, Mary 33
Bligh, Samuel 632
Bligh, Thomas 255, 276, 707
Blighe, Sarah 309
BLIN 78
Blin, Margaret 60
Blin, Mary 406
BLINCO 78
BLINMAN 78
Blinn, Margaret 160
Blinn, Mary 406
BLISH 78
Blish, Abraham 41
Blish, Lydia 452
Blish, Sarah 545
BLISS 78
Bliss, Ann 145, 632
Bliss, Bethiah 135
Bliss, Deliverance 571
Bliss, Dorothy 135
Bliss, Elizabeth 518, 681, 740, 821, 824
Bliss, Experience 746
Bliss, Freelove 41, 500
Bliss, Hannah 174, 333, 689
Bliss, Hester 277
Bliss, Jonathan 824
Bliss, Lawrence 174, 448, 540
Bliss, Lydia 452
Bliss, Margaret 274
Bliss, Martha 250, 409
Bliss, Mary 140, 344, 380, 562, 687
Bliss, Nathaniel 302, 491

Bliss, Rachel 485, 486
Bliss, Rebecca 474
Bliss, Sarah 274, 656, 679, 689, 732, 751, 789
Blith, Ann 145
Blithe, Sarah 309, 627
Blithen, John 630
BLIVEN 78
BLOCKED 78
BLOCKHEAD 78
Blockhead, Mary 623
BLOD 79
BLODGET 78
Blodget, Mary 623
BLODGETT 78, 79
Blodgett, Martha 828
Blodgett, Ruth 433
Blodgett, Sarah 359
Blodgett, Susanna 674, 736, 737
Blodgett, Thomas 736
BLODGHEAD 78
BLOGED 78
BLOGGET 78
BLOGGETT 78, 79
Bloice, Michall 4
BLOIS 79
BLOMFIELD 79
BLOOD 79
Blood, Anna 76
Blood, Elizabeth 129, 558, 664, 728, 822
Blood, Hannah 558, 804
Blood, James 323, 844
Blood, John (Jr.) 804
Blood, Mary 129, 208, 654, 664, 804
Blood, Mercy Butterworth Sloud Thayer 677, 734
Blood, Robert 39, 558
Blood, Sarah 167, 305, 826
BLOOMFIELD 79
Bloomfield, Mary 234, 676
Bloomfield, Sarah 646, 839
Bloomfield, William 646
Blore, Thomas 726
BLOSS 79
Bloss, Richard 782
BLOSSE 79
BLOSSOM 79
Blossom, Elizabeth 270
Blossom, Mercy 395
Blossom, Thankful 289
Blossom, Thomas 640
BLOTE 79
Blote, Elizabeth 674
BLOTT 79
Blott, --- 322, 323
Blott, Joanna 476
Blott, Lydia 760
Blott, Mary 751, 837
Blott, Robert 476
Blott, Sarah 248
BLOUD 79
Blouds, Sarah 263
BLOUNT 79
BLOWER 79
Blower, --- 79, 743
Blower, Tabitha 127
Blowers, Mary 411
Blowers, Thomas 836
BLOYCE 79
Bloyss, Richard 782
BLUMFORD 79
BLUNT 79
Blunt, Esther 477
Blunt, Hester 477
Blunt, James 637
Blunt, Mary 319

Blux, Elizabeth 547
Blux, Katharine 415
Blux, Mary 526
Blux, Return 415
BLY 79, 80
Bly, Rebecca 304
Bly, Thomas 707
Blyth, Margaret 440
Blythe, John 840
Boad, Ann 829
Boad, Henry 829
BOADEN 86
Boaden, Damaris 789
Boaden, Elizabeth 207
Boaden, Hannah 787
Boaden, Rebecca 107
Boaden, Susanna 242
BOADIN 86
BOAG 80
Boals, Mary Call 473
BOARDMAN 80, 88
Boardman, Elizabeth 181
Boardman, Hannah 607
Boardman, Jacob 633
Boardman, Joanna 261
Boardman, Martha 190, 253, 732
Boardman, Mary 215, 442, 627
Boardman, Rebecca 553
Boardman, Rebecca Wright 211
Boardman, Ruth 769
Boardman, Sarah 270, 281
Boardman, Thomas 169, 436
Boardman, William 218
BOARNE 85
BOASON 84
Boasum, Walter 536
Bobbett, Deliverance 382
Bobbit, Esther 564
Bobbit, Hannah 483
BOBET 28
Bobitt, Sarah 589
BOCKFORD 80
Boddington, Sarah 531
BODE 80
Bode, Ann 829
Bode, Henry 829
BODEE 80
BODEN 82, 86
Boden, Elizabeth 693
BODERITT 80
BODFISH 80
Bodfish, Mary 192
Bodfish, Robert 374
Bodfish, Sarah 79
BODGE 80, 81
Bodge, Henry 43
Bodge, Priscilla 95
BODIN 86
Bodin, Tabitha 619
BODINGTON 81
BODKYN 81
BODMAN 81
BODWELL 81
Boffee, Elizabeth 346
BOGLE 81
BOGUE 80
BOHOMON see BEHONEY,
  BONAMIE
Boice, Joanna 72
BOILES 129
Bokenson, Susanna 572
Bokeson, Susanna 572
Bolderson, Susanna 572
Boles, Mary 353, 702
BOLITHAR 81
BOLLARD 81 see BALLARD
BOLLES 81 see BOWLES
Bolles, Elizabeth 469, 588

Bolles, Hannah 57, 371
Bolles, Joseph 473
Bolles, Mary 286
Bolles, Sarah 141, 371
Bolles, Thomas 146, 174
BOLLS 81
BOLT 81
Bolt, Alice 218
BOLTEN 81
BOLTER 81
Bolter, Hannah 539
Bolter, Nathaniel 648
BOLTON 81
Bolton, Anne 775
Bolton, Elizabeth 823
Bolton, Mary 835
Bolton, Ruth 400
BOLTWOOD 81
Boltwood, Lydia 701
Boltwood, Martha 780
Boltwood, Mary 58
Boltwood, Sarah 431, 472, 780
BOMAN 88
BOMER 82
BONAMIE 81 see BEHONEY,
  BEHONON
BOND 81, 82, 86
Bond, Abigail 273, 635
Bond, Agnes Thorne 76
Bond, Dorothy 31
Bond, Elizabeth 47, 150, 601
Bond, Esther 146
Bond, John 351, 820
Bond, Jonas 601
Bond, Margaret 180
Bond, Mary 180, 328, 367, 547
Bond, Nicholas 675
Bond, Penticost 497
Bond, Rachel 283
Bond, Sarah 793
Bond, William 531
BONDE 81
BONDFEILD 82
Bondfeild, Mary 263
Bondfeild, Sarah 305
Bondfield, Rebecca 265
BONDMAN 80
Bonds, Sarah 263
Bonet, Thankful 117
BONEY 82
Boney, Mary 512
BONFIELD 82
Bonfield, Jemima 261, 477
Bonfield, Martha 194
Bonfield, Mary 263
BONHAM 82
Bonham, John 605
Bonham, Patience 823
Bonham, Ruth 47, 687
Bonham, Sarah 111
Bonker, Edmund 380
BONNELL 82
BONNER 82
Bonner, John 322
Bonner, Mary 497
Bonnett, Elizabeth 45
Bonnett, Priscilla 136
BONNEY 82
Bonney, Mary 512
Bontel, Mary 75
Bonum, Patience 385, 823
Bonum, Ruth 47, 687
BONYOT 82
BONYTHON 82
Bonython, Eleanor 153
Bonython, Elizabeth 196
Bonython, Sarah 281
Bonython, Susannah 281

Bonython, Winnifret 536
BOOBIER 82
Boobier, Joseph 588
BOOBYER 82
Boodale, Ann 582
BOODEY 82
BOODY 82
BOOGE 80
BOOMER 82
Boomer, Elizabeth 128
Boomer, Mary 283, 456
BOONE 82
Boone, Robert 575
Boorman, Thankful 691
BOOSEY 82
Boosey, Alice 772
Boosey, Hannah 599
Boosey, James 772
Boosey, Joseph 122
Boosey, Mary 705
Boosey, Sarah 701
BOOTEMAN 128
BOOTH 82, 83
Booth, Abiah 54
Booth, Alice 489
Booth, Bridget 11
Booth, Catherine 356
Booth, Ebenezer 426
Booth, Elizabeth 441, 511, 566,
  610, 665
Booth, Ellen 117, 364
Booth, Ephraim 63
Booth, George 663
Booth, Johanna 670
Booth, John 158, 260
Booth, Martha 456
Booth, Mary 40, 64, 488, 516,
  570, 695
Booth, Robert 447
Booth, Sarah 547
Booth, Simeon 249
Booth, Simon 249
Booth, William 123
Boothe, Bethia 198
Boradell, Margaret 513
BORDEN 83, 84 see BARDEN
Borden, Amy 147, 624
Borden, Dinah 262
Borden, Elizabeth 424
Borden, Elizabeth Cooke 99
Borden, Joanna 50
Borden, Mary 178
Borden, Sarah 379, 384
BORDMAN 80
Bordman, Ruth 769
Bordman, Sarah 376
Bordman, William 376
Bordwin, Jane 556
Bordwyn, Jane 556
BOREMAN 80, 88
Boreman, Hannah 607
Boreman, Joanna 261
Boreman, Martha 190
Boreman, Martha Whitingham
  Rogers 634
Boreman, Mary 441, 627
BORG 119
BORLAND 84
BORMAN 80
Borman, Joanna 534
Born, Ann 87
Born, Joanna 261
BORNE 85
Borodell, Ann 214
Borodell, Margaret 513, 668
Borston, Hannah 66
Bosman, Martha 477
BOSS 84

Boss, Mary 141
BOSSINGER 84
BOSSON 51, 84 see BARSHAM, BASSON
Bosson, John 536
Bosson, Walter 536
Bostick, Mary 429
BOSTON 84
BOSTWICK 84
Bostwick, Arthur 746
Bostwick, Ellen 423
Bostwick, John 616
Bostwicke, Mary 223
Bosvile, Elizabeth 568
Bosville, Elizabeth 344, 568
BOSWELL 126
Boswell, Elizabeth 129
Boswell, Isaac 290
BOSWORTH 84, 85, 425
Bosworth, Abigail 245
Bosworth, Alice 272, 407
Bosworth, Ann 181
Bosworth, Bathsheba 424
Bosworth, Benjamin 428
Bosworth, Bethiah 567
Bosworth, Bridget 578
Bosworth, Deliverance 567
Bosworth, Dorcas 155
Bosworth, Elizabeth 90, 315, 520, 566
Bosworth, Experience 315
Bosworth, Hannah 197, 414, 418, 469
Bosworth, Joseph 509
Bosworth, Judith 152
Bosworth, Mary 113, 164
Bosworth, Mehitable 315
Bosworth, Mercy 640
Bosworth, Rebecca 567
Bosworth, Sarah 469
Bosworth, Susanna 664
Boteler, John 262
Both, Mary 516
Bots, Pity 211
BOTSFORD 85
Botsford, Elizabeth 35, 36
Botsford, Esther 392, 800
Botsford, Hannah 36, 604
Botsford, Mary 35, 649
Botsford, Ruth 35
Botton, Elizabeth 823
BOTTS 85
Botts, Elizabeth 90
Botts, Hannah 132
Botts, Isaac 696
BOUCHER 85, 295
BOUDEN 86
BOUDESART 85
BOUENTON 115
Boughey, Elizabeth 346
BOUGHTON 85
Boughton, Abigail 681
BOULDERSON 85
BOULL 114
BOULTER 81
Boulter, Elizabeth 257
Boulter, Mary 602
Boulter, Nathaniel 648
Boulton, Ruth 400
BOUND 85
BOUNDS 85
Bouney, Sarah 170
BOURMAN 80, 87
BOURNE 85, 86
Bourne, Alice 485
Bourne, Ann 31, 110, 687
Bourne, Elizabeth 64, 336, 593, 742, 784, 794, 815

Bourne, Hannah 31, 525
Bourne, Job 366
Bourne, John 130
Bourne, Margaret 829
Bourne, Martha 90, 213, 751
Bourne, Mary 10
Bourne, Meletiah 690
Bourne, Richard 151, 829
Boutall, Mary 737
Boutel, Sarah 750
BOUTELL 86
BOUTELLE 86
Boutelle, Hannah 465
Boutelle, Mary 737
BOUTON 85
Bouton, Alice 493
Bouton, Bridget 431
Bouton, Elizabeth 780, 781
Bouton, John 13, 493
Bouton, Rachel 646
Bouton, Ruth 800
BOUTWELL 86
Boutwell, Alice 187
Boutwell, Alse 187
Boutwell, Henry 87
Boutwell, James 187
Boutwell, Rebecca 593
BOW 86
Bow, Alexander 266, 276
Bow, Anna 254
Bow, Elizabeth 254
Bow, Mary 160, 254
Bow, Rebecca 716
Bow, Sarah 214
BOWD 86 see BOADE, BOND
BOWDE 81
BOWDEN 82, 86
Bowden, Agnes 732
Bowden, Elizabeth 786
Bowden, Mary 783
BOWDEY 82
BOWDIGE 86
BOWDISH 86
BOWDITCH 86
Bowditch, --- 234
Bowditch, Sarah 116
BOWDOIN 36, 82, 86 see BOODY
Bowdoin, Margaret 281
Bowdon, Joan 830
Bowdon, Mary Blaisdell 661
Bowdorn, Damaris 789
BOWEN 86, 87, 88
Bowen, Abigail 23, 638
Bowen, Abijah 833
Bowen, Alice 799
Bowen, Elizabeth 6, 289, 519, 648
Bowen, Ester 509
Bowen, Hannah 103
Bowen, Hester 28, 509
Bowen, Lydia 494
Bowen, Margaret 30, 792
Bowen, Mary 10, 150, 214, 774
Bowen, Richard 645, 799
Bowen, Ruth 433
Bowen, Sarah 2, 93, 289, 652
Bowen, Thomas 601
BOWER 87
Bower, Mary 728
Bower, Ruth 446
BOWERMAN 80, 87
Bowerman, Thankful 691
BOWERS 87
Bowers, --- 393
Bowers, Ann 199
Bowers, Barbara 342
Bowers, Elizabeth 506, 666
Bowers, Esther 115

Bowers, George 86, 403
Bowers, Hannah 582
Bowers, John 263, 443, 555, 688
Bowers, Jonas 370
Bowers, Marie 506
Bowers, Mary 506, 536
Bowers, Patience 92
Bowers, Ruth 285, 446
Bowers, Sarah 506
Bowers, Silence 233, 632
BOWES 87
Bowes, Sarah 87
BOWHONNO 81
Bowiger, Mary 154
BOWKER 88
Bowker, Elizabeth 479
Bowker, Margaret 380
Bowker, Mary 380
Bowland, Elizabeth 459
BOWLES 88 see BOLLE
Bowles, Elizabeth 469, 588, 805
Bowles, Hannah 57, 371
Bowles, John 673
Bowles, Mary 294, 702
Bowles, Rachel 746
Bowles, Sarah 371
Bowley, Mary 21
Bowlins, Margaret 717
BOWMAN 80, 88
Bowman, Dorcas 74, 487
Bowman, Joanna 759
Bowman, Mary 255, 734
Bowman, Nathaniel 74, 688
BOWNE 88
Bowne, --- 523
Bowne, Abigail 818
Bowne, Dorothy 259, 282
Bowne, Eliza 275
Bowne, Elizabeth 605
Bowne, Hannah 264
Bowne, Joanna 739
Bowne, Martha 555
Bowne, Mary 739
Bowne, Sarah 275
BOWREY 88
BOWRY 88
Bowstred, Elizabeth 534
Bowstreet, Elizabeth 534
BOWTELL 86
Bowton, John 709
Bowyer, Frances 202
Boxford, Hannah 604
BOYCE 88
Boyce, Anna 613
Boyce, Dorothy 136
Boyce, Elizabeth 342
Boyce, Hester 693
Boyce, Joseph 597
Boyce, Mary 694
Boyd, Ann 829
Boyd, Henry 829
Boyde, Esther 308
BOYDEN 88
Boyden, Elizabeth 726, 728
Boyden, Jonathan 671
Boyden, Martha 616
Boyden, Mary 154
Boyden, Thomas 521
BOYEN 88
BOYER 89
Boyer, Hannah 527
Boyer, Johanna 527
Boyer, Sarah 450
Boyer, Simon 454, 456, 527
BOYES 88
Boyes, Hester 693
Boyes, Joanna 72, 818
Boyes, Samuel 608

BOYKIM 89
Boykin, Bethiah 215
Boykin, Jarvis 244
Boykin, Sarah 244
BOYLE 89
BOYLES 89
Boylsonn, Sarah 151
Boylsonn, Thomas 151
BOYLSTON 89
Boylston, Abigail 102, 288
Boylston, Elizabeth 267
Boylston, Mary 450
Boylston, Sarah 103, 151, 689
Boylston, Thomas 151
BOYNTON 89
Boynton, Elizabeth 674
Boynton, Hannah 51, 781
Boynton, John 420, 674, 770, 780
Boynton, Joshua 674, 770
Boynton, Mary 240
Boynton, Mercy 157, 309
Boynton, Sarah 206, 732
BOYS 88
Boyse, Anna 613
Boyse, Joanna 72, 606
Brabrick, Rachel 288
BRABROOK 89
Brabrook, Elizabeth 196
Brabrook, Joseph 732
Brabrook, Mehitable 229
Brabrook, Rachel 288
Brabrook, Rebecca 230, 236
Brabrook, Richard 570
Brabrook, Samuel 786
Brabrook, Sarah 553
BRACE 90
Brace, Mary 685
Brace, Phebe 220
BRACER 94
Bracey, Constance 518
Bracey, Hannah 552
Bracey, Phebe 220, 637
Bracey, Thomas 493
Brachembury, --- 129
BRACHETT 90
Brachett, Eleanor 17
Brachett, Hannah 50, 76, 441
BRACKENBURY 89
Brackenbury, Anne 279
Brackenbury, Catherine 442
Brackenbury, Dorcas 725
Brackenbury, Elizabeth 563
Brackenbury, John 480
Brackenbury, Katherine 580
Brackenbury, Samuel 60
Brackenbury, Susanna 279
BRACKET 90
Bracket, Elizabeth 230
Bracket, Mary 626
Bracket, Rachel 840
BRACKETT 89, 90 see
   BRECKETT, BROCKETT
Brackett, Anthony 730
Brackett, Eleanor 281, 421
Brackett, Elizabeth 87, 134
Brackett, Hannah 62, 488, 665,
   701
Brackett, Jane 358, 491
Brackett, John 7, 248, 491, 578
Brackett, Keziah 564
Brackett, Martha 761
Brackett, Mary 512
Brackett, Peter 278, 665, 764,
   820
Brackett, Priscilla 619
Brackett, Rachel 193, 769
Brackett, Sarah 62, 193, 201,
   371, 473, 665

Brackett, Silence 91
Brackinbury, Mary 625
BRACY 90
Bracy, John 135
Bracy, Mary 685
Bracy, Mercy 338
BRADBURY 90
Bradbury, Ann 10
Bradbury, Elizabeth 126
Bradbury, Jane 755
Bradbury, Judith 514
Bradbury, Mary 702
Bradbury, Sarah 519
Bradbury, William 498
Bradbury, Wymond 712
BRADDEN 95
BRADDICK 90
Braddish, Hannah 701
BRADDOCK 90
Braddock, Grace 765
Braden, Mary 6, 542
Braden, Susanna 619
BRADFIELD 90
Bradfield, Leslie 3
Bradfield, Lesly 3
Bradfield, Maria 808
Bradfield, Martha 808
Bradfield, Mary 3
BRADFORD 90, 91
Bradford, Alice 6, 269
Bradford, Hannah 626
Bradford, James 269
Bradford, John 751
Bradford, Martha 498
Bradford, Mary 404
Bradford, Melatiah 705
Bradford, Meletiah 708
Bradford, Mercy 705, 767
Bradford, Sarah 33
Bradford, Susanna 102
Bradford, William 383, 665, 694,
   700, 831
BRADHERSE 91
BRADHURST 91
Bradhurst, Dorothy 30
BRADING 91
Brading, Elizabeth 101
Brading, James 101
BRADISH 91
Bradish, Hannah 701
Bradish, Katherine 674
Bradish, Mary 300, 322
Bradish, Robert 519
BRADLEY 91, 92
Bradley, Abigail 302, 524, 817
Bradley, Ann 528
Bradley, Anna 528
Bradley, Benjamin 832
Bradley, Daniel 227
Bradley, Deliverance 184, 299
Bradley, Elizabeth 13, 218, 254,
   275, 327, 560
Bradley, Ellen 14, 227
Bradley, Hannah 71, 363, 462
Bradley, Henry 209
Bradley, John 13
Bradley, Lucretia 152
Bradley, Martha 330, 514, 602
Bradley, Mary 362, 369, 458, 461,
   513, 746
Bradley, Mary Christophers 847
Bradley, Nathan 719, 761
Bradley, Nathaniel 737
Bradley, Peter 152
Bradley, Richard 35
Bradley, Ruth 822
Bradley, Sarah 56, 101, 328, 630
Bradley, Stephen 460

Bradley, Susanna 306
Bradley, Susannah 339
Bradly, Rebecca 337
BRADSHAW 92
Bradshaw, Elizabeth 195
Bradshaw, Humphrey 336, 644
Bradshaw, Mary 513
Bradshaw, Ruth 63
BRADSTREET 92
Bradstreet, Ann 813
Bradstreet, Anne 821
Bradstreet, Bridget 434, 528, 640
Bradstreet, Dorothy 185
Bradstreet, Dudley 603
Bradstreet, Elizabeth 581, 677
Bradstreet, Hannah 385, 635, 813
Bradstreet, John 247, 785
Bradstreet, Margaret 762
Bradstreet, Martha 55, 640
Bradstreet, Mary 437, 544, 778
Bradstreet, Mercy 769
Bradstreet, Moses 539, 604
Bradstreet, Priscilla 746
Bradstreet, Rebecca 82
Bradstreet, Sarah 397, 776, 779
Bradstreet, Simon 253, 294
Brady, John 755
Brady, Sarah 755
Brafuck, Richard 570
BRAG 94
BRAGDON 93
Bragdon, Lydia 28
Bragdon, Martha 682
Bragdon, Mary 601
Bragdon, Patience 131
Bragdon, Samuel 358, 374
Bragdon, Sarah 564
BRAGG 93
Bragg, Deborah 659
Bragg, Edward 616
Bragg, Thomas 268
Bragge, Mary 255
BRAIDEN 91, 95
Brainard, Hannah 543
BRAINERD 93
Brainerd, Daniel 21, 662
Brainerd, Hannah 296
BRALEY 93
BRAMAN 93
Braman, Experience 479
Braman, Joseph 652
Braman, Simon 797
Brame, Benjamin 163
BRAMHALL 93
Brampas, Mary 64
Brampos, Mary 64
BRAN 93 BRAND, BRYAN
Bran, Sarah 95
BRANCH 93
Branch, Anna 74
Branch, Cathrine 575
Branch, Elizabeth 692, 720
Branch, Mary 756
Branch, Mercy 697
Branch, William 137
BRANCKER 94
BRANCUM 94
BRAND 93, 94 see BRAN,
   BRYAN
Brandish, Bethia 443
Brandish, Hannah 488
BRANDON 94
Brandon, Mary 682
Brandon, William 287
Branhall, George 334
BRANKE 94
Branker, John 780
Branker, Mary 730

Brans, Elizabeth 174
BRANSCOMB 94
BRANSON 94
Branson, Henry 276
Branson, Mary 23
Branton, Christian 649
BRASIER 94
Brasier, Abigail 645
Brasier, Hannah 818
Brasier, Mary 627
Braskett, Mary 694
BRATLE 94
BRATTLE 94
Brattle, Bethia 562
Brattle, Catharine 256
Brattle, Elizabeth 544
Brattle, Mary 507
Brattle, William 322
BRAWN 94
Brawn, George 652
BRAY 94
Bray, Ann 666
Bray, Esther 702
Bray, Hannah 282, 552, 628
Bray, Joan 213
Bray, Margery 571, 583
Bray, Mary 213, 626, 658, 809
Bray, Priscilla 372
Bray, Richard 846
Bray, Sarah 654
Braye, Margaret 816
Braylie, Elinora 324
BRAYMAN 93
Brayman, Jane 382
Brayman, Joseph 652
BRAYTON 94
Brayton, Elizabeth 85
Brayton, Martha 583
Brayton, Mary 210
Brayton, Sarah 299
Brayton, Stephen 597
BRAZER 94
BRAZIER 94
Brazier, Ann 11
Brazier, Mary 817
Brazier, Rebecca 744
BREAD 95
Bread, Allen 445
Bread, Elizabeth 122
Bread, Mary 464
BREAM 94
Bream, Benjamin 101, 163
Brean, Mary 728
Breard, Sarah 132
BRECK 94, 95
Breck, --- 75
Breck, Bethia 203
Breck, Edward 267, 625
Breck, Elizabeth 129, 512
Breck, Esther 623
Breck, Mary 564, 746
Breck, Robert 573
Breck, Sarah 370
Breck, Susanna 4, 346, 746
BRECKETT 95 see BRACKETT,
   BROCKETT
BREDEAN 95
BREDING 95
Bredshaw, Mary 386
BREED 95
Breed, Allen 38, 503
Breed, Elizabeth 122, 503
Breed, Mary 464
Breed, Sarah 386
BREEDEN 83, 95, 100 see
   BORDEN, BRADDEN
Breedon, Elizabeth 672
Breedon, Sarah 622

BREEME 94
Brell, Mary 654
Bremer, Sarah 573
Brene, Margaret 618
BRENTNALL 100
Brentnall, Esther 498
Brentnall, Henry 544
BRENTON 95
Brenton, Abigail 124
Brenton, Ebenezer 772
Brenton, Elizabeth 592
Brenton, Martha 292
Brenton, Mary 650
Brenton, Mehitable 107
Brenton, Sarah 247
Bretoun, Marian 28
BRETT 95
Brett, Alice 359
Brett, Elihu 359
Brett, Hannah 134
Brett, Mary 823
Bretton, James 245
Bretton, William 518
BREUER 96
BREWER 95, 96
Brewer, Abigail 479
Brewer, Ann 144
Brewer, Dorothy 507
Brewer, Elizabeth 463, 478, 680,
   686, 737
Brewer, Hannah 35, 87, 144, 306,
   470, 637
Brewer, Joanna 144, 345
Brewer, John 378, 409
Brewer, Mary 146, 450, 621
Brewer, Nathaniel 680, 686
Brewer, Sarah 96, 319, 499, 790
BREWSTER 96
Brewster, --- 807
Brewster, Abigail 121
Brewster, Ann 188
Brewster, Benjamin 204
Brewster, Daniel 832
Brewster, Dinah 747
Brewster, Elizabeth 92, 152, 251,
   289
Brewster, Fear 14
Brewster, Francis 569
Brewster, Grace 798
Brewster, Hannah 527, 693, 703,
   738
Brewster, Love 556
Brewster, Lucy 569
Brewster, Martha 639
Brewster, Mary 269, 384, 549,
   759
Brewster, Nathaniel 376, 832
Brewster, Patience 601
Brewster, Ruth 6, 370, 581
Brewster, Sarah 47, 374, 376,
   685, 832
Brewster, Wrestling 563
Briant, Hannah 58
Briant, Lydia 153
Briant, Ruth 777
Briantt, Mary 796
BRIAR 97
Briar, Adah 791
Briar, Eadah 791
Briar, Grace 151
Briar, Richard 153, 285
BRIARD 97
Briars, Eleanor 137
Briars, Grace 542
Briars, Mehitable 642
Brice, Mary 667
BRICK 94, 112
Brick, Eleanor 190

Brick, Esther 623
Brick, Jemima 74
Brick, Mary 481
Brick, Robert 10
BRICKENDEN 96
Brickendon, Robert 762
BRICKENTON 96
Brickenton, Robert 584
BRICKET 96
BRICKETT 96
Brickford, Elizabeth 40
BRICKINDINE 96
BRICKNALL 96 see BICKNELL
BRICKNELL 67
Bricknell, Edward 391
BRIDG 97
BRIDGAM 99
BRIDGE 97
Bridge, Abigail 748
Bridge, Anna 469, 793
Bridge, Dorcas 143
Bridge, Elizabeth 66, 294, 728
Bridge, Hannah 469
Bridge, John 38, 66, 652, 728
Bridge, Margaret 705
Bridge, Mary 297, 444, 481
Bridge, Prudence 499
Bridge, Samuel 584
Bridge, William 347
Bridgeman, Joseph 188
BRIDGES 96, 97
Bridges, Amy 736
Bridges, Bethia 565
Bridges, Charles 455, 818
Bridges, Edmund 163, 448, 468
Bridges, Elizabeth 54, 419, 558
Bridges, Faith 74
Bridges, Hannah 49
Bridges, John 596
Bridges, Mary 224, 615, 801
Bridges, Obadiah 407, 558
Bridges, Ruth 711
Bridges, Sarah 603
Bridges, William 758
BRIDGEWATER 97
Bridggs, Sarah 828
BRIDGHAM 97
Bridgham, Ann 128
Bridgham, Hannah 128
Bridgham, Henry 128
Bridgham, Mary 49
Bridgman, Deliverance 439
Bridgman, Martha 221
Bridgman, Mary 49, 407, 688
Bridgman, Sarah 743
Bridgum, Mary 61
BRIDGWATER 97
Bridley, Mary 798
BRIER 97
Brier, Grace 151
Brier, Richard 153, 285
BRIERS 97
Briers, Grace 151
BRIGDEN 97
Brigden, Mary 432
BRIGGAM 99
BRIGGS 98, 99
Briggs, Benit 709
Briggs, Bennett 709
Briggs, Clement 611
Briggs, Cornelius 19, 644
Briggs, Deborah 394
Briggs, Elizabeth 28, 64
Briggs, Enoch 814
Briggs, Experience 465
Briggs, Hannah 47, 101, 101, 345,
   366, 424, 773, 830
Briggs, Ireane 183

Briggs, Joan 726
Briggs, John 37, 183, 272, 440
Briggs, Mary 7
Briggs, Peace 83
Briggs, Peter 516
Briggs, Rebecca 183, 734
Briggs, Remember 702
Briggs, Sarah 450, 828
Briggs, Susanna 178, 216, 539
Briggs, Susannah 815
Briggs, Walter 633
BRIGHAM 97, 99
Brigham, Anna 193, 738
Brigham, Anne 193, 738
Brigham, Constance 193
Brigham, David 534
Brigham, Hannah 238, 779
Brigham, Johannah 415
Brigham, John 105
Brigham, Mary 260
Brigham, Sarah 310
Brigham, Thomas 260, 404, 521, 620
BRIGHT 99
Bright, Abigail 543, 832
Bright, Ann 642
Bright, Anna 642
Bright, Beriah 279
Bright, Elizabeth 352
Bright, John 557
Bright, Mary 180
Bright, Susannah 64
BRIGHTMAN 99
Brightman, Esther 7
Brightman, Hester 144
BRIGNALL 99 see BICKNELL
BRIGNELL 67
BRIGS 68
Brigs, Abigail 832
Brimbelcomb, Philip 290
Brimbelcombe, Mary 581
BRIMBLECOM 99
BRIMBLECOMBE 99
Brimblecome, John 141, 206
Brimblecome, Mary 756
Brimblecome, Richard 382
Brimsmead, Jane 642
BRINK 99
Brinkham, Cornelius 322
BRINLEY 99
Brinley, Ann 165, 783
Brinley, Grissell 725
Brinley, Grizzell 725
Brinley, Mary 725
Brinley, Wm. 21
BRINSDON 101
BRINSMADE 99
Brinsmade, Mary 460
BRINSMEAD 99
Brinsmead, Ebbett 403
Brinsmead, Mary 84, 616
BRINTNALL 100
Brior, Humphrey 804
BRISCO 100
Brisco, Joseph 125
Brisco, Rebecca 278
Brisco, Robert 232
BRISCOE 100
Briscoe, Abigail 681
Briscoe, Mary 104
Briscoe, Nathaniel 132, 262
BRISSON 100
Brisson, Charles 56
BRISTOL 100 see BRISTOW
Bristol, Daniel 378
Bristol, Hannah 375
Bristol, Lydia 686
Bristol, Mary 330

Bristol, Rebecca 132
Bristol, Richard 78
Bristol, Sarah 374
BRISTOW 100 see BRISTOL
Bristow, Richard 78
Brite, Mary 184
BRITNALL 99
BRITT 95
BRITTAIN 100
BRITTAINE 100
Brittaine, Isabel 549
BRITTEN 100
BRITTON 100
Britton, James 169
Britton, William 194, 518
Britz, Mary 184
BROAD 100
Broad, --- 757
Broad, Judith 790
Broad, William 790
BROADBENT 100
BROADBROOK 100
BROADBROOKS 100
BROADISH 91
Broadish, Mary 286
BROADLEY 91
Broadley, Martha 330
Broadly, Mary 362
BROADRIDGE 100
Broadway, Mary 11
BROCK 100, 101, 102
Brock, Ann 257
Brock, Elizabeth 316, 347
Brock, Jane 249
Brock, John (Rev.) 391
Brock, Mary 214, 577
Brocket, Mary 570
BROCKETT 101 see BRACKETT, BRECKETT
Brockett, Abigail 551
Brockett, Benjamin 25, 721
Brockett, Hannah 721
Brockett, Mary 524
Brockett, Samuel 266
Brockett, Silence 91
Brocklbanck, Mary 225
BROCKLEBANK 101
Brocklebank, Elizabeth 590, 746
Brocklebank, Hannah 710
Brocklebank, Jane 1, 692
Brocklebank, John 4
Brocklebank, Sarah 166, 225, 607
BROCKUS 102
Brockus, Katharine 736
Brockus, William 160
BROCKWAY 101
Brockway, Bridget 58
Brockway, Elizabeth 347
Brockway, Hannah 143
Brockway, Mary 524
Brockway, Wolston 345
Brodbent, Joshua 547
BRODGE 101
BRODHURST 91
Brodstreet, Elizabeth 581
Broklebank, Samuel 225
BROMEFIELD 101
BROMFIELD 101
BROMLEY 101
Bromley, Luke 556
Bromsfield, John 844
BROMSON 102
Bromson, Mary 297
BRONSDON 101
Bronsdon, Elizabeth 325
Bronsdon, Mary 84, 254
Bronsdon, Robert 84, 94, 180
BRONSON 101, 102

Bronson, Abigail 827
Bronson, Dorcas 387
Bronson, Dorothy 432
Bronson, Elizabeth 347
Bronson, Hannah 650
Bronson, Jacob 44
Bronson, John 147
Bronson, Mary 14, 222, 318, 368, 373, 844
Bronson, Rebecca 220
Bronson, Richard 135, 546, 555
Bronson, Sarah 112, 436
Brook, Richard 181
BROOKE 102
BROOKER 102
Brookes, Elizabeth 583
Brookes, Esther 811
Brookes, Mary 37, 538
Brookes, Robert 184
BROOKHOUSE 102
BROOKIN 102
Brookin, William 775
BROOKING 102
Brooking, Experience 739
Brooking, Godfrey 273
Brooking, Hannah 471
Brooking, John 328
Brooking, Rebecca 592
BROOKINGS 102
Brookings, Henry 444
Brookings, Martha 463
Brookings, Mary 477
Brookings, Martha 772
Brookings, Rebecca 639, 642
Brookings, Sarah 106
Brookins, Grace 450
BROOKS 102, 103
Brooks, --- 363
Brooks, Abigail 602, 704
Brooks, Ann 71, 281, 462, 569, 818
Brooks, Anna 462, 818
Brooks, Barsheba 774
Brooks, Bethia 740
Brooks, Deborah 623, 706
Brooks, Deliverance 124
Brooks, Elizabeth 117, 201, 270, 464, 486, 707
Brooks, Eunice 138, 557
Brooks, Gershom 97
Brooks, Gilbert 136, 481
Brooks, Grace 596
Brooks, Hannah 1, 71, 194, 281, 462, 582, 818
Brooks, Henry 52, 76, 415, 622
Brooks, Hepzibah 495
Brooks, Hepzibeth 495
Brooks, Joanna 71, 628
Brooks, John 191, 567, 623
Brooks, Lydia 178
Brooks, Martha 52
Brooks, Mary 97, 168, 275, 452, 539, 547, 647, 663, 682, 705, 801
Brooks, Mercy 138, 370, 656
Brooks, Miriam 198, 505
Brooks, Patience 731
Brooks, Phoebe 485
Brooks, Rachel 813
Brooks, Rebecca 390, 422, 492
Brooks, Remembrance 106
Brooks, Ruth 37
Brooks, Sarah 112, 318, 410, 461, 474, 481, 525, 627, 719, 730, 740, 816
Brooks, Tamzen 798
Brooks, Thankful 152.
Brooks, Thomas 663

Brooks, Timothy 441
Brooks, William 801, 803
BROOM 103
BROOMAN 93
BROOME 103
Broome, Hannah 23
Bropham, Robert 603
Brotherton, --- 224
BROUCE 110
BROUGH 104
BROUGHTON 104
Broughton, Abigail 681
Broughton, Elizabeth 615
Broughton, John 415, 433
Broughton, Mary 63, 704
Broughton, Rachel 618
Broughton, Sarah 384, 424
Broughton, Thomas 827
Browen, Hannah 35
BROWN 104, 105, 106, 107, 108,
  109, 110
Brown, Abigail 107, 280, 284,
  285, 349
Brown, Abraham 620
Brown, Andra 817
Brown, Andrew 271, 603
Brown, Ann 762, 766, 796, 817
Brown, Anna 251, 656, 817
Brown, Christopher 790
Brown, Cornelius 156, 174, 182,
  693
Brown, Deborah 389, 500
Brown, Deliverance 184, 299
Brown, Dorothy 434
Brown, Edmund 277, 476, 615
Brown, Edward 454, 456
Brown, Eleanor 189
Brown, Eliezer 772
Brown, Elizabeth 49, 56, 62, 64,
  127, 163, 268, 283, 294, 349,
  436, 464, 491, 519, 540, 571,
  584, 607, 653, 746, 796
Brown, Elizabeth Simpson
  Nicholson 536
Brown, Eme 215
Brown, Emma 214, 215
Brown, Esther 40
Brown, Eunice 498
Brown, Francis 63, 145, 455, 521,
  543, 553
Brown, Hannah 9, 15, 254, 354,
  392, 424, 431, 450, 587, 617,
  656, 673, 686, 837
Brown, Henry 497
Brown, Isabel 389, 394
Brown, Isabella 410
Brown, Jabez 99
Brown, James 19, 153, 293, 362,
  487, 536, 559
Brown, Jane 29, 479, 634
Brown, Jeremiah 179
Brown, Joanna 188
Brown, Joannah 345
Brown, John 156, 234, 353, 392,
  473, 589, 633, 698, 745, 818
Brown, John (Capt.) 250
Brown, Jonathan 672
Brown, Josiah 268
Brown, Judith 91, 209
Brown, Katherine 114
Brown, Lydia 100, 144, 447, 559,
  562, 591, 595, 600, 793
Brown, Margaret 143, 314, 430
Brown, Martha 137, 418, 526,
  559, 738
Brown, Martha Matthews Snell
  691
Brown, Mary 28, 158, 217, 231,

Brown, Mary (cont.) 247, 273,
  316, 362, 396, 406, 436, 458,
  463, 477, 493, 501, 504, 505,
  523, 541, 551, 563, 585, 604,
  616, 619, 626, 627, 635, 654,
  704, 744, 804, 817
Brown, Mehitable 750
Brown, Nathaniel 161
Brown, Nem 215
Brown, Nicholas 557
Brown, Patience 68, 713, 731
Brown, Peter 129, 275, 443, 628
Brown, Phebe 183, 347, 452, 459
Brown, Priscilla 13
Brown, Rachel 101, 767
Brown, Rebecca 158, 292, 504,
  692, 803
Brown, Remember 841
Brown, Richard 413, 489
Brown, Ruth 27, 353, 426, 499,
  635
Brown, Sarah 4, 19, 26, 104, 177,
  212, 226, 228, 318, 320, 349,
  362, 440, 530, 541, 586, 593,
  600, 632, 639, 655, 658, 745,
  793, 824
Brown, Susan 268
Brown, Susanna 268, 656
Brown, Susannah 326, 339
Brown, Thankful 397
Brown, Thomas 219, 323, 425,
  515, 544, 580, 750
Brown, William 32, 328, 343, 596,
  633
Brown, Wm. 396
Browne, Abigail 440, 519
Browne, Abraham 378
Browne, Anna 142
Browne, Anne 142
Browne, Deliverance 772
Browne, Dinah 205
Browne, Edward 780
Browne, Eleanor 195
Browne, Elizabeth 316, 331, 378,
  557, 708, 789
Browne, George 23, 361
Browne, Hannah 491, 558, 581,
  625
Browne, Isaac 224
Browne, James 724
Browne, John 125, 259, 293, 491,
  776
Browne, Lydia 378, 839
Browne, Margaret 130, 448
Browne, Martha 259, 727
Browne, Mary 200, 241, 271, 307,
  351, 473, 480, 554, 558, 568,
  760, 782, 818, 830, 837
Browne, Mercy 255
Browne, Phebe 223
Browne, Rebecca 30, 398, 656
Browne, Richard 30
Browne, Sarah 67, 120, 402, 414,
  477, 560, 607, 795, 844
Browne, William 629, 773
BROWNELL 110
Brownell, Ann 814
Brownell, Martha 237, 754, 770
Brownell, Mary 176, 361
Brownell, Sarah 83, 282
Brownell, Susanna 615
BROWNING 110
Browning, Deborah 500, 572
Browning, Elizabeth 674
Browning, Jane 723
Browning, Joseph 634
Browning, Mary 485, 532, 749
Browning, Sarah 820

Browning, Susannah 768
BRUCE 110
Bruce, Elizabeth 722
Bruce, Mary 103, 191
Bruce, Sarah 499
Bruce, William 315
BRUCKEN 110 see BROOKIN
BRUEN 110
Bruen, Hannah 35
Bruen, Mary 35
Bruen, Rebecca 596
Bruen, Sarah 23, 36
Bruer, Elizabeth 463, 737
Bruer, Hannah 409
Bruer, Mary 621
Bruer, Sarah 319
BRUFF 104
BRUGGE 110
Brukes, Barsheba 774
BRUMIDGE 110
Brumidge, Edward 762
Brundage, Bethia 730
Brundage, Mary 607
Brundage, Posthume 830
BRUNDISH 111
Brundish, Bethia 443
Brundish, John 824
Brundish, Mary 395, 607
Brundish, Posthume 830
Brundish, Ruth 656
Bruning, Joseph 634
BRUNNING 110
BRUNO 111
Brunson, Abigail 827
Brunson, Joanna 488
BRUSH 110, 111
Brush, Hester 111
Brush, John 326
Brush, Margaret 792
Brush, Mary 176
Bruskett, Christobel 292
BRUSTER 96
Bruster, Dinah 747
BRYAN 111 see BRAN, BRAND
Bryan, Alexander 269, 809
Bryan, Elizabeth 235
Bryan, Frances 548, 752
Bryan, Hannah 344
Bryan, Joan 518, 801
Bryan, Mary 393, 484, 730
Bryan, Robert 381
Bryan, Samuel 245
Bryan, Sarah 23, 36, 269, 531
BRYANT 111, 112
Bryant, Abigail 111
Bryant, Abraham 241, 287
Bryant, Anna 45
Bryant, David 153
Bryant, Elizabeth 439
Bryant, Hannah 58, 712
Bryant, John 706
Bryant, Lydia 153
Bryant, Martha 724
Bryant, Mary 153, 579
Bryant, Mehitable 439
Bryant, Mercy 579
Bryant, Sarah 469
Bryant, Stephen 484
Bryant, William 222
BRYER 97
Bryer, Mary Clark 605
BUBIER 82
Bucanan, John 448
BUCHANAN 112
Buchard, Elizabeth 788
BUCHER 85, 112
Bucher, Eleazer 792
BUCK 112, 120

Buck, --- 128
Buck, Deborah 505, 610
Buck, Elizabeth 143, 232, 804,
Buck, Elizabeth (cont.) 834
Buck, Grace 625
Buck, Hannah 280, 540
Buck, Isaac 212
Buck, James 344
Buck, John 227
Buck, Jonathan 308
Buck, Joseph 311
Buck, Margaret 631
Buck, Martha 214, 629
Buck, Mary 214
Buck, Mehitable 610
Buck, Rachel 102, 103, 236
Buck, Ruth 53, 295, 680
Buck, Sarah 214, 329, 637
Buck, Susanna 295
Buck, Susannah 349
Buckanden, Robert 639
Buckaway, Mary 363
Bucke, Lydia 682
Bucke, Mehitable 151
Bucket, Mary 693
Buckett, Elizabeth 87
Buckhout, Peter 786
BUCKINGHAM 112, 113
Buckingham, Ann 546
Buckingham, Anna 546
Buckingham, Esther 55
Buckingham, Hannah 451, 792
Buckingham, Johannah 785
Buckingham, Mary 558, 718
Buckingham, Samuel 394
Buckingham, Sarah 35
Buckingham, Thomas 386
BUCKITT 113
BUCKLAND 113, 114
Buckland, Benjamin 474
Buckland, Deborah 168
Buckland, Elizabeth 3, 508
Buckland, Hannah 473, 794
Buckland, Leah 474
Buckland, Lydia 106, 234, 473,
596
Buckland, Martha 719
Buckland, Nicholas 719, 755
Buckland, Rachel 827
Buckland, Samuel 69
Buckland, Sarah 576
Buckland, Temperance 592
Buckland, Thomas 33
BUCKLEN 113
Bucklend, Samuel 57
BUCKLEY 113
Buckley, Dorothy 769
Buckley, Hannah 669
Buckley, Joseph 535
Buckley, Mary 605, 812
Buckley, Priscilla 699
BUCKMAN 114
Buckman, Edward 588
Buckman, Elizabeth 811
Buckman, John (Jr.) 735
Buckman, Joses 480
Buckman, Sarah 144, 664
Buckman, William 351
BUCKMASTER 114
Buckmaster, Abigail 331
Buckmaster, Dorcas 182, 183
Buckmaster, Elizabeth 697
Buckmaster, Mary 202, 707
Buckmaster, Mary 810
Buckmaster, Sarah 144, 454
Buckmaster, Thomas 294
BUCKMINSTER 113
Buckminster, Elizabeth 437

Buckminster, Jabez 663
Buckminster, Joseph 448
Buckminster, Lydia 156
Buckminster, Mary 202
Buckminster, Thomas 294
BUCKNAM 114
Bucknam, Elizabeth 502
Bucknam, Hannah 735
Bucknam, Judith 372
Bucknam, Mehitable 771
Bucknam, Mercy 788
Bucknam, Samuel 358, 502
Bucknam, Sarah 218, 664
Bucknam, William 351
BUCKNELL 113, 114 see
BUCKNER
Bucknell, Hannah 65
Bucknell, Samuel 69, 74
BUCKNER 114 see BUCKNELL
Buckner, Charles 416
Buckner, Mary 807
Buckner, Samuel 74
Buclan, Elizabeth 508
BUCLAND 113
Bud, Dorothy 203
Bud, Elizabeth 629
BUDD 114
Budd, Alice 467
Budd, Ann 388
Budd, Edward 673
Budd, Elizabeth 629
Budd, Hannah 348
Budd, Jane 306, 389, 543
Budd, John 407
Budd, Judith 105, 543
Budd, Martha 673
Budd, Mary 536, 847
Budd, Mercy 536
Budd, Sarah 176
Buddington, Mary 834
BUDESANT 85
BUDEZERT 85
Budezert, John 326
BUDLONG 114
Budlong, Francis 359
BUEL 114
Buel, Hannah 538
Buel, Mary 511, 538
BUELL 114
Buell, Abigail 40
Buell, Deborah 595
Buell, Hannah 555, 595
Buell, Hepzibah 60, 795
Buell, Martha 380
Buell, Mary 73, 594
Buell, Peter 73
Buell, Sarah 313
Buell, William 554, 687
BUERLY 114
BUERS 67
BUFF 115
BUFFAM 115
Buffam, Damaris 641
Buffam, Deborah 826
BUFFET 115
BUFFINGTON 115
Buffman, Joshua 767
BUFFUM 115
Buffum, Damaris 641
Buffum, Lydia 371, 469
Buffum, Margaret 683
Buffum, Mary 530
Buffum, Sarah 56
BUGBEE 115
Bugbee, John 182
Bugbee, Judith 559
Bugbee, Mehitable 655, 759
Bugbee, Rebecca 30

Bugbee, Sarah 142
Bugbey, Rebecca 30
BUGBY 115
Bugby, Elizabeth 163
BUKER 112
BUKLIN 113
BULFINCH 115
Bulfinch, Katherine 61
BULGAR 115
Bulkeley, Dorothy 753
Bulkeley, Edward (Rev.) 447
Bulkeley, Elizabeth 107, 250, 390,
554
Bulkeley, Grace 436
Bulkeley, Jane 272
Bulkeley, Joseph 512
Bulkeley, Lucian 447
Bulkeley, Martha 502
Bulkeley, Mary 159
Bulkeley, Peter 602
Bulkeley, Rebecca 802
Bulkeley, Sarah 105
Bulkeley, Thomas 825
BULKLEY 115
Bulkley, Charles 27
Bulkley, Dorothy 769
Bulkley, Margaret 293
BULL 115, 116
Bull, --- 266
Bull, Abigail 43, 112
Bull, Amy 624
Bull, Elizabeth 11, 766, 775
Bull, Ellen 365
Bull, Hannah 234, 638, 722
Bull, Henry 240
Bull, Juanah 595
Bull, Katherine 155
Bull, Margaret 425
Bull, Mary 166, 184, 247, 365,
592, 654, 710
Bull, Mehitable 649
Bull, Phebe 141
Bull, Rebecca 184
Bull, Robert 168
Bull, Ruth 80
Bull, Susana 595
Bull, Susannah 118
Bull, Thomas 112, 464
Bull, William 763
BULLARD 116, 117
Bullard, Abigail 712
Bullard, Ann 202
Bullard, Anna 426
Bullard, Anne 739
Bullard, Augustus 237
Bullard, Benjamin 371
Bullard, Eleazer 460
Bullard, Elizabeth 172
Bullard, George 248, 487
Bullard, Hannah 9, 666
Bullard, Isaac 424, 813
Bullard, Joanna 361
Bullard, John 219
Bullard, Jonathan 711
Bullard, Magdalen 563
Bullard, Mary 259, 297, 354, 376,
384, 445
Bullard, Maudlin 585
Bullard, Robert 739
Bullard, Sarah 37, 498, 746, 809
Bullard, Susanna 182
Bullard, William 327, 445
BULLEN 117
Bullen, Bethia 167
Bullen, Elizabeth 802
Bullen, Mary 521, 669
Bullen, Meletiah 267
BULLER 117

Buller, Abigail 712
Buller, Rebecca Spencer 63
BULLEY 117
Bulley, John 63
BULLIER 117
Bullier, Julian 270
BULLIN 117
Bullin, Elizabeth 802
Bullin, Mary 155
Bullin, Meletiah 267
BULLINE 117
BULLIS 117
Bullis, Philip 550, 611, 616
BULLIVANT 117
Bulloch, Elizabeth Billington 596
BULLOCK 117
Bullock, Abigail 87
Bullock, Elizabeth 82, 242, 538
Bullock, Henry 581
Bullock, Hopestill 471
Bullock, Maria 65, 709
Bullock, Mary 333, 709
Bullock, Richard 575
Bullock, Thankful 492
Bullock, Thomasin 130
Bulluck, Richard 59
BULLUCKE 117
BULLUK 117
BULLY 117
Bully, Abigail 364
Bully, Ann 65, 655
Bully, Anne 137
Bully, Elizabeth 227
Bully, Grace 86
Bully, Nicholas 364
BULMAN 117
BULUK 117
BUMPAS 117, 118
Bumpas, Hannah 559
Bumpas, John 153
Bumphis, Sarah 234
Bumps, Hannah 559
Bumpus, Elizabeth 637
Bumpus, Jacob 74
Bumpus, Mary 192, 193
Bumpus, Sarah 235
BUMSTEAD 118
Bumstead, Hannah 209
Bumstead, Mary 210
Bumstead, Mercy 84
Bumstead, Peter 209
BUMSTED 118
BUMSTEED 118
Bumsteed, Hannah 666
BUNCE 118
Bunce, Catherine 159
Bunce, Elizabeth 805
Bunce, Mary 229, 501
Bunce, Sarah 805, 842
Bunce, Susanna 360
BUNDEY 118
Bundey, Mary 679
BUNDY 118
Bundy, John 144, 331
Bundy, Mary 679
BUNKER 88, 118
Bunker, Ann 171
Bunker, Elizabeth 124, 360, 472
Bunker, George 392, 722
Bunker, Hannah 533
Bunker, Jonathan 476
Bunker, Martha 406, 703
Bunker, Mary 47, 166, 231, 331,
  479, 622, 698
Bunkhead, Elizabeth 394
BUNN 118
Bunn, Edward 392
Bunn, Hester 586

BUNNELL 118, 125
Bunnell, Benjamin 226, 696
Bunnell, Judith 378
Bunnell, Lydia 284
Bunnell, Mary 567
Bunnell, Rebecca 125
BURBANK 118, 119
Burbank, Caleb 343
Burbank, Ebenezer 605
Burbank, John 651, 656
Burbank, Lydia 276
Burbank, Martha 290
Burbank, Mary 343, 509
BURBEEN 119
Burbeen, Mary 391
BURCH 119
Burch, Elizabeth 170
Burch, George 170
BURCHAM 70, 119
Burcham, Frances 511, 818
BURCHARD 70
Burchard, Abigail 140
Burchard, John 408
Burchard, Sarah 42
Burche, Mary 173
BURCHSTED 119
Burchsted, J. H. 442
Burchwood, Sarah 42
Burckard, Mary 349
Burdeck, Naomi 633
BURDEN 40, 119 see BURDETT
Burden, Robert 142
Burden, Sarah 500
BURDETT 119 see BURDEN
Burdett, Anne 307
Burdett, Hannah 142
Burdett, Robert 142
BURDICK 119
Burdick, Deborah 190
Burdick, Naomi 634
Burdick, Ruth 578
Burdick, Tacy 498
BURDITT 119
Burditt, Ruth 526
Burett, Elizabeth 719
Burey, Elizabeth 544
BURFE 119 see BROUGH,
  BURPH
BURGE 119 see BIRGE,
  BURGESS
Burge, Elizabeth 573
Burge, John 313, 327, 331, 419,
  436, 458
Burge, Joseph 548
Burge, Margaret Cheney 149
BURGES 120
Burges, Elizabeth 433
BURGESS 119, 120 see BIRGE,
  BURGE
Burgess, --- 16
Burgess, Dorothy 162
Burgess, Elizabeth 243, 573
Burgess, Grace 765
Burgess, Jane 109
Burgess, Margaret Cheney 149
Burgess, Martha 715
Burgess, Mary 248, 752
Burgess, Mercy 830
Burgess, Patience 542
Burgess, Rebecca 637, 638
Burgess, Roger 440
Burgess, Ruth 730
BURGESSE 119
BURGIS 119, 120
Burgis, Jane 109, 334
Burgis, Sarah 831
Burill, Elizabeth 259
Buritt, Elizabeth 719

BURKBEE 121
Burkbee, Mary 231
Burkbee, Sarah 697
BURKE 120
Burke, Richard 12, 14
Burkly, Mary 819
Burlea, John 442
BURLEIGH 120
Burleigh, Gyles 270
Burleigh, Rebecca 270
Burley, Giles 378
Burley, Mary 819
BURLING 120
BURLINGAME 120
Burlingame, Jane 596
Burlingame, Mary 699
Burlingame, Mercy 313
BURLISON 120
BURNAM 121
Burnam, Sarah 258
BURNAP 120
Burnap, Ann 116, 813
Burnap, Anne 424
Burnap, Bethia 329
Burnap, Dorcas 654
Burnap, Elizabeth 241
Burnap, Lydia 222
Burnap, Mary 241
Burnap, Robert 693, 784
Burnap, Sarah 86, 182, 627, 693
Burnard, Mary 178
Burnass, Sarah 104
BURNE 85
BURNELL 120, 121
Burnell, Benjamin 318
BURNET 120, 121
Burnet, Hannah 89
Burnet, Mary 241
BURNETT 120, 121
Burnett, Aaron 388
Burnett, Benjamin 318
Burnett, Elizabeth 388
Burnett, John 807
Burnett, Lois 173
Burnett, Robert 693
Burnett, Sarah 104, 693
BURNHAM 121
Burnham, Abigail 809
Burnham, Ann 382
Burnham, Anna 291, 477
Burnham, Elizabeth 207, 328, 441,
  517, 626
Burnham, Esther 572
Burnham, Jeremiah 697
Burnham, Joanna 534
Burnham, Mary 156, 522
Burnham, Rebecca 485
Burnham, Ruth 137
Burnham, Sarah 159, 398, 838
Burnham, Thomas 72
BURNS 121
BURNUM 121
Burnum, Elizabeth 441
BURPBE 121
BURPEE 121
Burpee, Hannah 399
Burpee, Mary 231
Burpee, Sarah 697
Burpee, Thomas 646
BURPH 104, 121 see BROUGH,
  BURFE
BURR 118, 121, 122
Burr, Abiel 107, 672
Burr, Abigail 341, 470, 800
Burr, Ann 10, 66, 84
Burr, Anna 10
Burr, Elizabeth 159, 302, 398,
  545, 551, 661, 803

Burr, Esther 115
Burr, Frances 63, 233
Burr, Grace 519
Burr, Hannah 198, 372, 377, 616
Burr, Jehu 82
Burr, Johannah 198
Burr, John 63, 82, 131, 772
Burr, Mary 154, 157, 195, 394, 471, 601, 772
Burr, Nathaniel 772
Burr, Peter 720
Burr, Samuel 672
Burr, Sarah 130, 147, 308
BURRAGE 122
Burrage, Elizabeth 212, 593
Burrage, John 470
Burrage, Mary 490
Burrage, Robert 178
Burrage, Ruth 805
Burrage, Sarah 423
Burrage, Susanna 512
Burrage, Thomas 561
BURRELL 123
Burrell, Anna 619
Burrell, Elizabeth 259, 719
Burrell, James 643
Burrell, Lydia 222
Burrell, Sarah 581, 660
BURREN 122
Burren, Mary 272
Burridge, Hannah 284
BURRILL 122, 123
Burrill, Abiel 107, 672
Burrill, Elizabeth 313
Burrill, Esther 187
Burrill, George 693
Burrill, Lois 698
Burrill, Sarah 144, 208, 581, 693
BURRINGTON 123
BURRITT 123
Burritt, John 257
BURROUGHS 123
Burroughs, Edward 379, 399
Burroughs, Elizabeth 7
Burroughs, Francis 246, 328, 363
Burroughs, George 107, 353
Burroughs, George (Rev.) 123
Burroughs, Hannah 13, 375
Burroughs, John 83
Burroughs, Mabel 616
Burroughs, Margaret 217
Burroughs, Mary 193, 386, 760
Burroughs, Rebecca 279, 746
Burroughs, Robert 411
Burroughs, Thomas 721, 730
Burrowes, Elizabeth 744
Burrowes, Mabel 616
BURROWS 123
Burrows, --- 204
Burrows, Mary 841
Burrows, Rachel 717
Burrows, Robert 411
Bursall, Ann 660
BURSELL 123
BURSLEY 123
Bursley, Elizabeth 153
Bursley, Joanna 221
Bursley, John 205
Bursley, Mary 192, 686
Bursley, Temperance 192
Bursley, Elizabeth 311
BURT 120, 124
Burt, Abigail 37, 527, 704
Burt, Beatrice 65, 133, 590
Burt, Beatrix 590
Burt, David 13, 636
Burt, Dorcas 710
Burt, Elizabeth 220, 724, 843

Burt, Hannah 31, 353
Burt, Henry 15
Burt, James 292
Burt, Jonathan 341
Burt, Mary 50, 103, 164, 484
Burt, Mercy 843
Burt, Nathaniel 657
Burt, Patience 78
Burt, Rachel 442
Burt, Rebecca 263
Burt, Richard 292
Burt, Sarah 66, 226, 325, 375, 389, 442, 444, 595, 772
BURTLES 49
BURTON 124
Burton, Dorothy 95
Burton, Elizabeth 363
Burton, Ethalannah 155
Burton, Hannah 136, 365, 547
Burton, Martha 95
Burton, Phebe 423
Burton, Rose 279, 280
Burton, Sarah 440, 691
Burton, Susannah 313
Burton, William 523
Burtt, Sarah 444
BURWELL 118, 124, 125
Burwell, Elizabeth 162
Burwell, Esther 215
Burwell, John 107, 341, 567
Burwell, Mary 106, 107, 469
Burwell, Samuel 714
Busbeem, James 298
BUSBY 125
Busby, Abraham 100
Busby, Ann 537
Busby, Sarah 328
BUSBYE 125
BUSECOT 125
Busecot, Abigail 713
Busecott, Abigail 713
Busey, Dorcas 254
BUSH 125
Bush, Ann 638
Bush, Deborah 483, 595
Bush, Edward 581
Bush, Elizabeth 485, 659
Bush, John 485, 645, 682
Bush, Lydia 452
Bush, Mary 48
Bush, Mehitable 151
Bush, Reynold 336
BUSHELL 125
BUSHNELL 125, 126
Bushnell, Abigail 452, 662, 672
Bushnell, Ann 408
Bushnell, Anne 408
Bushnell, Edmund 55
Bushnell, Elizabeth 423, 550
Bushnell, Francis 540
Bushnell, Hannah 390, 443, 452
Bushnell, Jane 252, 371, 373, 589
Bushnell, Judith 662
Bushnell, Lydia 662
Bushnell, Marcy 641
Bushnell, Martha 685
Bushnell, Mary 93, 216, 426, 460, 510, 629, 641, 730
Bushnell, Mercy 134
Bushnell, Rebecca 340, 473
Bushnell, Richard 6
Bushnell, Ruth 513
Bushnell, Samuel 769
Bushnell, Sarah 186, 376, 410, 708
Bushnell, William 116
Bushnell, Wm. 216
Bushop, Hannah 674

BUSHROD 126
Busicott, Mary 696
Busketh, Sarah 286
BUSS 126
Buss, Ann 84
Buss, Dorcas 144
Buss, Elizabeth 685
Buss, Hannah 801
Buss, Joseph 815
Buss, William 425
BUSSE 126
Busse, Hannah 801
BUSSELL 126
Bussell, William 728
BUSSEY 126
Bussill, Samuel 416
BUSSY 122, 126
Bussy, Rachel 191
BUSTED 119
BUSWELL 126
Buswell, Isaac 290
Buswell, Mary 108
Buswell, Phoebe 303
Buswell, Rebecca 687
Buswell, Robert 162
Buswell, Sarah 276
BUTCHER 126
Butcher, Elizabeth 571
Butcher, Mary 53
Butcher, Sarah 242, 343, 523
BUTERFILD 128
BUTLAND 126
BUTLER 126, 127, 128, 200
Butler, Abigail 190, 443, 775
Butler, Ann 625
Butler, Anna 371
Butler, Daniel 726
Butler, Dorothy 436
Butler, Elizabeth 130, 252, 442, 545, 627, 706
Butler, Hannah 12, 130, 139, 141, 322, 323, 371
Butler, Henry (Rev.) 383
Butler, James 374, 611
Butler, Jane 549
Butler, Joan 193
Butler, John 470, 792
Butler, Joseph 510
Butler, Lydia 512
Butler, Lydia Mercer 702
Butler, Mary 23, 100, 231, 368, 387, 470, 519, 594, 778, 783, 792, 843
Butler, Mehitable 828
Butler, Nathaniel 139
Butler, Patience 300
Butler, Peter 541, 764
Butler, Phebe 566
Butler, Prudence 344
Butler, Rebecca 405
Butler, Richard 323
Butler, Ruth 311
Butler, Sarah 7, 112, 210, 301
Butler, Susanna 474, 660
BUTMAN 128
Butman, Jeremiah 173
Butman, Joseph 346
BUTREKE 129
BUTT 129
Butt, John 74
BUTTALL 128
BUTTELL 128
BUTTELS 128
Buttere, Mary 717
Buttere, Wm. 717
BUTTERFEILD 128
BUTTERFIELD 128
Butterfield, Anna 738

Butterfield, Benjamin 811
Butterfield, Deborah 472
Butterfield, Hannah 738
Butterfield, Henry 576, 579
Butterfield, Jane 576, 579
Butterfield, Mary 78
Butterfield, Margaret 311
Butterfield, Mary 695, 785
Butterfield, Thomas 513
Butterice, Grace 362
Butterick, Tabitha 268
BUTTERS 128, 129 see
    BUTTREY
Butters, Mary 717
Butters, Wm. 717
BUTTERWORTH 128
Butterworth, Anne 289
Butterworth, Deborah 417
Butterworth, Hopestill 479
Butterworth, Jane 591
Butterworth, Jonathan 623
Butterworth, John 677
Butterworth, Mary 162, 418, 495,
    734
Butterworth, Mercy 79, 677, 734
Butterworth, Sarah 360, 479, 615,
    743
BUTTERY 129
BUTTOLPH 128
Buttolph, Abigail 60, 70, 655
Buttolph, George 453
Buttolph, John 650
Buttolph, Mary 733
Buttolph, Thomas 56, 97, 724
BUTTON 128, 129
Button, Abigail 233, 474
Button, Elizabeth 285
Button, Hannah 341, 647
Button, Mary 285, 845
Button, Matthew 647
Button, Matthias 236, 739, 799
Button, Peter 832
Button, Robert 407
Button, Samuel 520
Button, Thomas 230
BUTTRICE 129
Buttrice, Grace 362
Buttrice, Martha 412
BUTTRICK 129
Buttrick, William 310
Buttrik, Sarah 46
BUTTRY see BUTTERS
BUTTS 129
Butts, Grace 519
Butts, Hepzibah 239
Butts, Richard 840
Buxstone, Elizabeth 178
BUXTON 129
Buxton, Anthony 768
Buxton, Clement 108, 443
Buxton, Elizabeth 178, 290, 399,
    400
Buxton, Hannah 277
Buxton, Lydia 407, 679
Buxton, Mary 178, 309
Buxton, Sarah 708
BUZELL 126
Buzigut, Ruth 740
Buzzell, Isaac 290
BYAM 129
Byam, Abraham 545
BYFIELD 129
Byfield, Deborah 480
Byfield, Priscilla 95, 772
Byfield, Sarah 731
BYINGTON 129
Byington, John 722
BYLES 129

Byles, Jonathan 161
Byles, Josiah 324
BYLEY 129
Byley, Henry 334, 675, 841
Byley, Rebecca 332
BYRAM 130
Byram, Abigail 809
Byram, Deliverance 594
Byram, Elizabeth 440, 578
Byram, Experience 823
Byram, Mary 457
Byram, Susanna 243
BYRUM 130
Bysbie, Alexander 823

--- C ---

Caball, Mary 10
CABLE 130
Cable, Comfort 630
Cable, Elizabeth 671
Cable, John 66, 671
Cable, Mary 10
Cable, Rebecca 446
Cable, Sarah 153
CADE 130
Cade, Wilmet 631
Cade, Wilmoth 631
CADMAN 130
Cadman, Richard 504
Cadwalles, Bertha 286
CADWELL 130
Cadwell, Hannah 78
Cadwell, Mary 121
Cadwell, Mehitable 80
Cadwell, Thomas 826
CADY 130 see KADE
Cady, Judith 638
CADYE 130
CAFFINCH 130
CAHOON 130
CAHOONE 130
Caig, Alice 588
CAIN 130 see KEAYNE, KEEN
CAINE 130
CAIRNESS 135
CAKEBREAD 131
Cakebread, Anna 200
Cakebread, Anne 200
Cakebread, Isaac 17
Cakebread, Mary 328
Cakebread, Thomas 328, 798
CALDWELL 131
Caldwell, Anna 637
Caldwell, Mary 221, 277
Caldwell, Robert 1
Caldwell, Sarah 27
Calee, Mary 209
CALEF 131
Calef, Martha 366
Calendar, George 255
Calendar, Sarah 255
Calender, Elizabeth 133
CALFE 131
Calkin, Sarah 391
CALKINS 140
Calkins, Deborah 840
Calkins, Mary 301, 628
CALL 131, 169
Call, Elizabeth 668, 744
Call, Esther 287
Call, Hannah 406
Call, Joanna 557, 704
Call, Margaret 323
Call, Mary 81, 473, 792
Call, Mehitable 609

Call, Mercy 11, 459, 792
Call, Philip 122
Call, Thomas 668, 677
Callam, Sarah 273
CALLENDER 131
Callender, Ellis (Rev.) 723
CALLEY 131 see KELLEY
Calley, Austice 486
Calley, Richard 57
CALLO 131
Callomer, Mary 706
CALLOW 131
CALLOWAY 131
CALLOWE 131
Callowe, Olive 163
CALLUM 131, 173, 483 see
    McINTIRE, McMILLAN
Callum, Anna 761
Callum, John 174, 331
Callum, Martha 273
Callum, Sarah 273
Caloric, Martha 711
CALTIL 140
Calverly, Joan 659
Caly, Sarah 221
CAMBALL 132
CAMDEN 131
CAME 131
Came, Arthur 93
Came, Elizabeth 792
Came, Mary 453
Came, Sarah 93
CAMER 131
CAMFIELD 131
Camfield, Elizabeth 36
Camfield, Sarah 590
CAMLER 131
CAMMOCK 132
Cammock, Margaret 428
Cammock, Thomas 428
CAMP 132
Camp, Abigail 36, 753
Camp, Edward 292, 450
Camp, Hannah 690
Camp, Mary 35, 100, 132, 567
Camp, Nicholas 35, 100, 736, 743
Camp, Nicholas (Jr.) 262
Camp, Samuel 133, 137, 785
Camp, Sarah 35, 712
Campball, Mercy 758
CAMPBELL 132
Campbell, John 332
Campbell, Mercy 758
CAMPENALL 132
Campenall, Judith 361
CAN 435
CANADA see KENNEDY
CANDAGE 132
Candage, Elizabeth 76
Candage, John 722
Candage, Mary 239
CANDEE 132
Candee, Hannah 389
Candee, Rebecca 553
Candee, Zaccheus 389
CANDIDGE 132
CANDIGE 132
Candige, John 722
CANE 130, 131 see KEAYNE,
    KEEN
Cane, Eliza 511
Cane, Elizabeth 511
Cane, Esther 374
Cane, Hannah 544
Cane, Joanna Dore 85
Cane, Ruth 422
CANFIELD 133
Canfield, Abigail 631, 702

Canfield, Elizabeth 36
Canfield, Hannah 302
Canfield, Mary 132
Canfield, Mehitable 585
Canfield, Phebe 684
Canfield, Sarah 590
Canfield, Thomas 132
CANIBALL 197
Canliff, Susanna 169
CANN 133, 435
CANNADIE 132
CANNADY 132
Canne, Lydia 342
CANNEDY 132
Canner, Henry 200
CANNEY 133, 433
Canney, --- 26
Canney, Hannah 377
Canney, Lydia 342
Canney, Martha 529
Canney, Mary 742, 761
Canney, Samuel 611
Canney, Sarah 628
Canney, Thomas 552, 828
Canning, Ann 549, 574
CANNON 133
Cannon, Sarah 239
CANNOWAY 133
Cannoway, George 825
CANNY 133
CANON 133
CANSTINE 140
CANTERBURY 133
Canterbury, Anna 44
Canterbury, Hannah 713
Canterbury, Hester 748
Canterbury, John 768
Canterbury, Ruth 546, 673, 679
Canterbury, Sarah 500
Canterbury, William 65, 590
CANTLEBURY 133
Cantlebury, Mary 388
Cantlebury, Rebecca 838
Cantlebury, Ruth 679
Capan, Bernard 237
CAPEN 133
Capen, Dorothy 77
Capen, Elizabeth 724
Capen, Honour 341
Capen, Mary 277, 821
Capen, Susan 333
Capen, Susanna 317, 632
Capen, Susannah 333
Capen, Thankful 714
Caper, Mary 305
Caper, Timothy 305
Capin, Dorothy 764
CAPRIL 133
CAPRILL 133
CAPRON 133
Capron, Banfield 224
CARD 133
Card, Agnes 188
Card, John 827
Card, Rebecca 351
Card, Richard 351
Card, William 167
CARDER 133, 134, 146, 183 see
CHARDER, CORDAY
Carder, Mary 322, 322, 619
Carder, Sarah 313
Carder, Susanna 784
Carderet, Philip 749
CARDIS 134
CAREW 134 see CARROW
CAREY 134
Carey, Rebecca 12
Carey, Sarah 418

Carinon, Timothy 339
Carinton, Phebe 350, 352
CARKEET 134
CARL 134 see CARROLL
Carl, Elizabeth 52
Carl, Hannah 52
CARLE 134
Carle, Amy 445
Carles, Catherine 20
CARLETON 134
Carleton, John 28
CARLEY 435 see KERLEY
Carley, Joseph 241
Carley, Lydia 742
Carley, Mary 422, 687
Carley, William 422
CARLILE 134
CARLISLE 134, 135
Carlisle, Joseph 601
CARLL 134
CARLTON 134
Carly, Ruth 469
CARMAN 135
Carman, Abigail 165, 338, 808
Carman, Florence 368
Carman, Frances 43
Carman, John 368
CARMEN 135
Carmen, Abigail 338
CARMICHAEL 135
Carmichael, John 90
CARNES 135 see KERNS
Carnes, Thomas 44, 228
Carow, Peter 132
CARPENTER 135, 136, 557
Carpenter, --- 220, 619
Carpenter, Abigail 554, 745
Carpenter, Agnes 289
Carpenter, Alice 91, 694
Carpenter, Ann 789, 791
Carpenter, Anna 792
Carpenter, Benjamin 747
Carpenter, David 102, 403, 546,
   709
Carpenter, Dille 844
Carpenter, Elizabeth 146, 370,
   426, 791, 799, 821
Carpenter, Ethalenah 723
Carpenter, Ethelannah 723
Carpenter, Fridgsworth 768
Carpenter, Hannah 135, 368, 677,
   739
Carpenter, Hester 100
Carpenter, John 211, 619
Carpenter, Joseph 791
Carpenter, Juliana 432, 522
Carpenter, Lydia 680
Carpenter, Margaret 141
Carpenter, Mary 192, 368, 375
Carpenter, Miriam 78
Carpenter, Nathaniel 181
Carpenter, Priscilla 181, 521, 723,
   768, 844
Carpenter, Rebecca 826
Carpenter, Ruth 478
Carpenter, Samuel 102
Carpenter, Sarah 573, 709
Carpenter, Susanna 21
Carpenter, Tamsen 820
Carpenter, Thomasine 820
Carpenter, Wm. 791
CARR 136, 137, 435
Carr, Ann 608
Carr, Caleb 220, 587
Carr, Christian Harris Williams
   346, 820
Carr, Dorothy 284
Carr, Elizabeth 106, 293, 838

Carr, George 424, 544
Carr, Hannah 99
Carr, Joanna 161
Carr, Joanna Thorn 739
Carr, Margaret 349
Carr, Mary 31, 239, 368, 458
Carr, Mercy 552
Carr, Peter 132
Carr, Richard 333
Carr, Robert 197
Carr, Rosannah 137
Carr, Sarah 34, 398
Carr, Thomas 14
CARRE 136
Carrell, Catherine 770
Carrell, Hannah 20
Carrell, Katherine 770
Carrell, Mary 281
Carrell, Priscilla 92
CARRIER 137
CARRINGTON 137
Carrington, Elizabeth 139, 552
Carrington, Hannah 380
Carrington, Mary 562, 698
Carrington, Peter 467
Carrington, Rebecca 16
Carrionton, Mary 562
CARROL 137
CARROLL 134, 137 see CARL
Carroll, Elizabeth 52
Carroll, Hannah 52
Carroll, Joseph 601
CARROW 137 see CAREW
Carrow, Peter 132
CARSELEY 137
CARSLEY 137
Carsly, John 538
Carsly, Sarah 538
Carson, Elizabeth 339
CARTE 137
Cartee, Alice 458
CARTER 137, 138
Carter, Abigail 271, 279, 684, 775
Carter, Agnes 484
Carter, Ama 185
Carter, Anna 185, 279
Carter, Anne 185
Carter, Bethiah 426, 821
Carter, Edward 219
Carter, Eleanor 301
Carter, Elizabeth 136, 200, 270
Carter, Hannah 46, 109, 177, 323
Carter, Joanna 825
Carter, John 65, 250, 486, 655
Carter, Joseph 241
Carter, Joshua 93, 265, 818
Carter, Judith 177, 265
Carter, Lettice 520
Carter, Lydia 742
Carter, Mary 51, 99, 144, 187,
   279, 404, 449, 609, 778, 845
Carter, Miriam 411
Carter, Richard 403
Carter, Ruth 843
Carter, Samuel 105, 557, 610
Carter, Sarah 207, 486, 785
Carter, Susanna 326, 692, 720
Carter, Thomas 423, 805
Carter, Ursula 221
Carter, William 75
CARTERET 137, 138
Carteret, John 609
Carteret, Philip 455
Cartes, Mary 171
CARTHEW 138
CARTHRICK 138
Carthrick, Mildred 97
Cartie, Alice 304

CARTRITH 138
Cartrith, John 609
CARTWRIGHT 138
Cartwright, Bethia 540
Cartwright, Elizabeth 838
Cartwright, John 609
CARVER 138, 139
Carver, Anna 621
Carver, David 128
Carver, Eleazer 315, 721
Carver, Elizabeth 402
Carver, John 230
Carver, Martha 9
Carver, Mary 594
Carver, Mercy 594
Carwin, John 485
CARWITHEN 139 see CORWIN
Carwithen, David 544, 552
Carwithen, Elizabeth 178
Carwithen, Sarah 198
Carwithie, Caleb 625
CARWITHY 139
Carwithy, Elizabeth 525
Carwithy, Joshua 527
Carwithy, Mary 303
CARY 134
Cary, Anna 436
Cary, Elizabeth 95, 510
Cary, Hannah 436, 741
Cary, John 97
Cary, Jonathan 560
Cary, Joseph 641
Cary, Martha 370
Cary, Mehitable 3, 700, 795
Caryl, Mary 786
CARYLL 137
CASE 139
Case, Abigail 758
Case, Ann 481
Case, Anna 333
Case, Elizabeth 377, 463, 758
Case, Henry 407
Case, John 472, 549
Case, Margaret 749
Case, Mary 8, 372, 536
Case, Sarah 576
Case, Thomas 483
CASELEY 139
CASELY 137
Casewell, Sarah 390
CASEY 139
CASH 139
Cash, Elizabeth 727
Cash, Hester 270
Cash, Mary 500
Cash, William 71
Casly, John 538
Casly, Sarah 538
Cason, Elizabeth 339
CASS 139, 140
Cass, Abigail 758
Cass, Ann 481
Cass, Elizabeth 327
Cass, Haercy 321
Cass, John 481
Cass, Joseph 147
Cass, Martha 616
Cass, Mary 321, 464
Cass, Mery 321
Cassell, Sarah 160
CASTEL 140
Caster, Mary 254
CASTINE 140
CASTLE 140
Castle, Elizabeth 219, 220
Castle, Mary 291, 406
Castle, Samuel 257, 536
CASWEL 140

Caswel, Abigail 426
CASWELL 140 see CASTEL
Caswell, Benjamin 98
Caswell, Elizabeth 219, 220, 462
Caswell, Esther 689
Caswell, Hannah 609
Caswell, Mary 709, 740
Caswell, Mary Hudson 531
Caswell, Sarah 390, 609
CATE 140
Cate, Alice 797
Cate, Elizabeth 67
Cate, Isabel 419
Cate, Isabella 419
Cate, Mary 802
Cate, Rebecca 764
Cate, Sarah 28
CATER 138, 140
Cater, John 138, 666
CATES 140
CATHCART 140
CATLIN 140
Catlin, Elizabeth 184
Catlin, Esther 679
Catlin, Hannah 49
Catlin, John 36, 539
Catlin, Mary 153, 222, 285
Catlin, Samuel 790
Catlin, Thomas 249
CATON 140
Cator, Richard 67
CAULEY 131
CAULKINS 140
Caulkins, Ann 70
Caulkins, David 2
Caulkins, Deborah 641
Caulkins, Elizabeth 408
Caulkins, Sarah 36, 391
CAULY 131
CAVE 140
Cave, Elizabeth 234
Cave, Hannah 234
Cave, Sarah 392
CAVERLY 140
Caverly, William 331
Caves, Abigell 113
Caves, Sarah 392
Cawarden, Mary 662
CAYTE 140
Celley, Agnes Card Cox 188
Celley, Sarah 190
CEN see SENTER
CENTER 141
Center, Thomas 781
Cerley, Sarah 190
CERLILE 134
CETILL 435
CHADBOURNE 141
Chadbourne, Alice 226
Chadbourne, Elizabeth 7
Chadbourne, Katharine 798
Chadbourne, Katherine 465
Chadbourne, Lucy 368, 463
Chadbourne, Lucy Treworgy 710
Chadbourne, Lucia Treworgy 824
Chadbourne, Mary 276
Chadburne, James 679
Chadburne, Mary 276
Chadburne, Patience 696
Chaddack, Hannah 455
CHADDOCK 141, 663
Chaddock, James 579
CHADWELL 141
Chadwell, Anna 609
Chadwell, Benjamin 420
Chadwell, Mary 229
Chadwell, Richard 602
Chadwell, Ruth 348, 530

Chadwell, Thomas 99, 206, 427
CHADWICK 141
Chadwick, Charles 281, 538
Chadwick, Elizabeth 373, 841
Chadwick, Hannah 358, 360
Chadwick, Jane 629
Chadwick, Mary 629
Chadwick, Mercy 417
Chadwick, Sarah 329
CHAFEY 141
CHAFFEE 141
Chaffee, Dorothy 552
Chaffer, John 282
Chalice, Lydia 147
CHALIS 141
CHALKER 141
Chalker, Alexander 371
Chalker, Jane 432
Chalker, Mary 186
CHALKLEY 141
Challinge, Jane 171
Challinge, John 171
Challis, Elizabeth 75, 395
Challis, Hannah 228, 646
Challis, Lydia 147
Challis, Mary 228
CHAMBERLAIN 141, 142, 143
Chamberlain, --- 715
Chamberlain, Abigail 677
Chamberlain, Alexander 732
Chamberlain, Benjamin 48
Chamberlain, Dorothy 6
Chamberlain, Edmund 1, 119
Chamberlain, Elizabeth 204
Chamberlain, Faith 564
Chamberlain, Henry 564
Chamberlain, Jane 439, 626
Chamberlain, Jacob 793
Chamberlain, John 508
Chamberlain, Joanna 580
Chamberlain, John 691
Chamberlain, Mary 318, 458, 619, 654, 655, 666
Chamberlain, Rebecca 258, 704
Chamberlain, Richard 47
Chamberlain, Sarah 207, 502, 511, 666
Chamberlain, Susanna 137, 757
Chamberlain, Thomas 557, 597
Chamberlain, Ursula 169
CHAMBERLIN 141, 142
Chamberlin, Elizabeth 801
Chamberlin, Rebecca 664
CHAMBERLINE 142
Chamberline, Susanna 757
CHAMBERLING 142
Chamberling, Mary 47, 318
CHAMBERLYN 142
Chamberlyne, Joanna 66
CHAMBERS 143
Chambers, Thomas 198, 413
CHAMBLET 143
CHAMBLET see CHAMPNOIS
Chamblet, Morris 314
CHAMBLETT 143
Chamerlain, Susanna 241
CHAMPANELL 143
CHAMPERNOWNE 143
Champernowne, Francis 201
Champian, Mary 416
CHAMPION 143
Champion, Hannah 421
Champion, Henry 426
Champion, Martha 249
Champion, Mary 405
Champion, Rachel 727
Champion, Sarah 63
Champlain, Ann 158

CHAMPLIN 143
Champlin, Amy 361
Champlin, Ann 158
Champlin, Christopher 210
Champlin, Mary 29
CHAMPNEY 143
Champney, Daniel 512
Champney, Dorcas 87
Champney, Esther 177, 203
Champney, Jane 515
Champney, Joan 515
Champney, Joanna 515
Champney, John 515
Champney, Lydia 351
Champney, Mary 103, 284, 623, 716
Champney, Sarah 46, 155, 643
CHAMPNEYS 143
CHAMPNOIS 143 see CHAMBLET
CHAMVERLAIN 415
CHANCY 147
CHANDLER 143, 144
Chandler, Abigail 105
Chandler, Ann 581
Chandler, Eleanor 596
Chandler, Elinor 755
Chandler, Elizabeth 495
Chandler, Hannah 1, 73, 202, 231, 603, 627
Chandler, Hester 290, 825
Chandler, John 7
Chandler, Lydia 369
Chandler, Margaret 215
Chandler, Martha 118, 674
Chandler, Mary 18, 362, 462, 477, 648, 670
Chandler, Mehitable 167
Chandler, Phoebe 461
Chandler, Samuel 208
Chandler, Sarah 13, 161, 167, 461, 576, 687, 707
Chandler, William 202, 561, 622
Chaney, Martha 121
Chaney, Mehitable 520
Chanler, Hannah 325, 603
Chanler, Mary 670
CHANNECK 146
Channon, Tamson 496
Channon, Thomasine 496
CHANTERELL 144
Chantrell, John 144
Chantril, Mary 491
CHANTRILL 144
Chapel, William 706
Chapell, Abigail 405
Chapell, Mary 834
Chapen, Mehitable 787
CHAPIN 144, 145
Chapin, Catherine 78, 302, 491
Chapin, Deborah 615
Chapin, Ebenezer 264
Chapin, Hannah 375
Chapin, Josiah 507, 600
Chapin, Mary 4, 842
Chapin, Ruth 741
Chapin, Sarah 527, 735
CHAPLEMAN 145
CHAPLEY 145
CHAPLIMAN 145
CHAPLIN 145
Chaplin, Ann 306
Chaplin, Barbara 425
Chaplin, Elizabeth 413
Chaplin, Martha 556
Chaplin, Mary 729
Chaplin, Mehitable 787
Chaplin, Robert 556
CHAPMAN 145, 146

Chapman, Avis 616
Chapman, Edmond 165
Chapman, Edward 2, 165, 194, 838
Chapman, Elizabeth 295, 367, 429, 718
Chapman, Hannah 115, 317
Chapman, John 105, 455, 623, 703, 846
Chapman, Jonathan 662
Chapman, Lydia 221
Chapman, Margaret 55
Chapman, Martha 226, 442
Chapman, Mary 52, 65, 190, 678, 754
Chapman, Ralph 314
Chapman, Rebecca 126
Chapman, Robert 666
Chapman, Ruth 241
Chapman, Samuel 570
Chapman, Sarah 539, 599
Chapman, Susanna 248, 248
Chapman, Susannah 248
Chapman, William 678
CHAPPEL 146
Chappel, Rachel 192
CHAPPELL 146
Chappell, Abigail 175
Chappell, Experience 187
Chappell, John 426
Chappell, Mary 203
CHARD 146
Chard, Elizabeth 275
Chard, Joanna 238
Chard, William 689
CHARDER 134, 146 see CARDER
CHARDON 146
CHARLES 146
Charles, --- 567
Charles, Deliverance 415, 637
Charles, Delivered 637
Charles, John 523
Charles, Mary 215, 742
Charles, Patience 600
Charles, Rebecca 372
Charles, Sarah 29
Charlet, Katherine 353
Charlet, Nicholas 353
CHARNOCK 146
Charteris, William 64
Chartley, Alice 582
CHASE 146, 147
Chase, Abigail 147, 785
Chase, Ann 813
Chase, Anna 40
Chase, Anne 40
Chase, Aquila 528
Chase, Elizabeth 28, 32
Chase, Esther 504
Chase, James 140
Chase, Mary 484, 707
Chase, Philip 353
Chase, Phillippa 353
Chase, Priscilla 504
Chase, Rachel 445
Chase, Sara 19
Chase, Sarah 19, 327, 484, 543
Chase, Thomas 295, 631
CHATER 147
Chater, Hannah 509
CHATFIELD 147
Chatfield, Abigail 597
Chatfield, Admah 700
Chatfield, Adnah 700
Chatfield, Anne 700
Chatfield, Elizabeth 424
Chatfield, George 815

Chatfield, Mary 574
Chatham, Catherine 142
Chather, Katherine 428
CHATTERTON 147
Chatterton, Mary 282, 390
Chatterton, Mercy 282
Chatterton, Sarah 65
Chatterton, Susanna 390
CHATWELL 147
Chatwell, Mary 229
CHAUNCEY 147, 148
Chauncey, Abigail 379
Chauncey, Katherine 95
Chauncey, Nathaniel 592
Chauncey, Sarah 115
Chaunsey, Abigail 399
Chauntrell, Mary 491
Chawkley, Hannah 128, 811
Cheame, Mary 5
Cheany, Hannah 144
CHEARLS 146
CHEATER 147
CHEAVERS 148
CHECKLEY 148
Checkley, Elizabeth 471
Checkley, Mary 482, 572
CHEECKLEY 148
Cheeney, Jane 61
Cheeney, Mary 379
CHEESEBROOK 149
CHEESEHOLME 148
CHEEVER 148
Cheever, Bartholomew 561
Cheever, Elizabeth 308, 554
Cheever, Hannah 46
Cheever, Mary 116, 464
Cheever, Ruth 769
Cheever, Sarah 359
Cheever, Susanna 644
Cheever, Thomas 781
CHEEVERS 148
Cheevers, Mary 731
CHELSTON 148
CHENERY 151
Chenery, Deborah 725
Chenery, Elizabeth 549
Chenery, Mary 802
CHENEY 148, 149
Cheney, Eleanor 646, 664
Cheney, Elizabeth 194
Cheney, Ellen 420
Cheney, Hannah 687
Cheney, Huldah 841
Cheney, Jane 61
Cheney, John 63
Cheney, Joseph 375
Cheney, Judith 250
Cheney, Margaret 117, 263, 352
Cheney, Martha 456, 646
Cheney, Mary 148, 436, 454, 841
Cheney, Mehitable 520, 759, 814
Cheney, Peter 24
Cheney, Sarah 590
Cheney, William 15, 365, 819
Cheny, Eleanor 664
Cheny, Hannah 831
Cheny, Lydia 433
Cheny, Sarah 621
Chepman, Avis 616
CHERRY 149
Cherry, John 399
CHESEBROUGH 149
Chesebrough, Abigail 26
Chesebrough, Anna 623
Chesebrough, Anne 623
Chesebrough, Bridget 738
Chesebrough, Elisha 35
Chesebrough, Elizabeth 411

Chesebrough, Hannah 601
Chesebrough, Margaret 701
Chesebrough, Nathaniel 654
Chesebrough, Samuel 26, 384
Chesebrough, Sarah 81, 292
CHESEMORE 151
CHESLEY 149
Chesley, Elizabeth 206
Chesley, Esther 335
Chesley, Hannah 22, 62
Chesley, Mary 335, 427
Chesley, Susanna 685
Chesley, Thomas 203
CHESTER 149
Chester, Dorcas 809
Chester, Eunice 698, 709
Chester, Frances Tought 704
Chester, Leonard 386
Chester, Linus 644
Chester, Mary 832
Chester, Mercy 123
Chester, Prudence 644, 752
Chester, Sarah 833
Chetwood, Grace 115
CHEVARLY 149
CHEVERLEY 149
CHEVERS 148
CHEW 149, 150
Cheyney, Huldah 841
Cheyny, Martha 841
Cheyny, Mary 841
CHICHESTER 150
Chichester, James 680
Chichester, Mary 491
CHICHLEY 148
CHICK 150
Chick, Elizabeth Spencer 758
Chick, Winifred 24
CHICKERING 150
Chickering, Agnes 520
Chickering, Ann 89, 506, 552
Chickering, Anne 552
Chickering, Annis 520
Chickering, Bathsheba 533
Chickering, Bethia 533
Chickering, Bethshua 533
Chickering, Catherine 779
Chickering, Esther 680
Chickering, Francis 88, 520, 673
Chickering, Hannah 520
Chickering, John 319
Chickering, Katharine 779
Chickering, Mary 506, 667, 725, 748
Chickery, John 319
Chickley, Anthony 299
Chickley, Hannah 4
Chickrin, Catharine 779
Chickrin, Katharine 779
CHIDSEY 150
Chidsey, Hannah 513
Chidsey, Mary 824
Chidsey, Sarah 14
CHILD 150, 151
Child, Abigail 474
Child, Ann 282
Child, Experience 270
Child, Frances 723
Child, Henry 395
Child, John 268, 771
Child, Joseph 497
Child, Mary 142
Child, Mehitable 294, 573
Child, Mehitable Demick 763
Child, Sarah 627
CHILDS 150
Childs, Eleanor 583
Childs, Elizabeth 68

Childs, Hannah 169
Chiles, Elenor 605
Chiliad, Elizabeth 688
CHILLINGWORTH 151
Chillingworth, Jane 225
Chillingworth, Joane 225
Chillingworth, Mary 278
Chillingworth, Mehitable 238
Chillingworth, Sarah 222, 698
Chillingworth, Thomas 225
Chillson, Sarah 120
CHILSON 151
Chilson, Mary 169
Chilson, William 542
CHILTON 151
Chilton, Isabella 144
Chilton, Mary 829
CHINERY 151
Chinery, John 89
Chinery, Lambert 264
Chinery, Mary 264
CHINN 151
Chinn, Elizabeth 138
Chinn, Mary 109, 328
Chinny, Elizabeth 549
CHIPMAN 151
Chipman, Bethia 221, 291
Chipman, Desire 85
Chipman, Elizabeth 429
Chipman, Hannah 398
Chipman, Hope 164, 398
Chipman, John 85, 221
Chipman, Lydia 651
Chipman, Mercy 677
Chipman, Ruth 192
CHISEMORE 151
CHISHOLM 151
CHISIMORE 151
Chiske, Hannah 633
CHITTENDEN 151
Chittenden, Elizabeth 843
Chittenden, Mary 80, 282, 460
Chittenden, Mercy 282
Chittenden, Sarah 172
Chittenden, William 196
CHOATE 151
Choate, John 301, 489
Choate, Margaret 270
Choate, Sarah 121
Choate, Thomas 131
Chonor, Rebecca 579
CHOTE 151
Chrisfeilde, Phebe 673
CHRISMAS 152
CHRISTEN 152
CHRISTMAS 152
CHRISTOPHERS 152
Christophers, Anna 844
Christophers, Joanna 499
Christophers, Margaret 184
Christophers, Mary 92, 847
Christophers, Richard 844
CHUBB 152
Chubb, Mercy 753
Chubb, Susanna 335
Chubbock, Mary 466
Chubbock, Rebecca 366
Chubbs, Priscilla 558
CHUBBUCK 152
Chubbuck, Alice 733
Chubbuck, John 713
Chubbuck, Martha 465
Chubbuck, Nathaniel 293, 295
Chubbuck, Sarah 269
CHURCH 152, 153
Church, Abigail 112, 344, 588, 675, 733
Church, Alice 735

Church, Benjamin 397
Church, Caesar 165
Church, Caleb 657
Church, Deborah 320
Church, Elizabeth 74, 157, 376, 637
Church, Hannah 69, 82
Church, Hepsibah 696
Church, Lydia 352
Church, Mary 159, 318, 644, 688, 700, 834
Church, Mehitable 220
Church, Naomi 81
Church, Naomy 80
Church, Rebecca 661, 782
Church, Ruth 497
Church, Sarah 123, 200, 273, 384, 444, 595
CHURCHER 153
CHURCHILL 153
Churchill, --- 502
Churchill, Benjamin 214
Churchill, Elizabeth 112, 127
Churchill, Hannah 231, 641
Churchill, Henry 227
Churchill, John 624
Churchill, Mary 153, 227, 244
Churchill, Prudence 310
Churchill, Sarah 813
CHURCHMAN 153
Churchman Ann 633
Churchman, Annis 832
CHURCHWELL 153
Churchwell, Sarah 457
CHURCHWOOD 153
Churchwood, Hannah 641
Churchwood, Humphrey 97
CHUTE 153
Chute, Elizabeth 710
Chute, Lionel 803
Chute, Mary 148
CILLEY 661, 673
Cilley, Elizabeth 207
Cilley, John 163
Cilley, Martha 163
Cilley, Richard 163
Cilley, Sarah 190
CINTTENDEN 151
Claes, Sophia 389
Claessen, Nealtje 447
CLAFLIN 483
CLAGHORN 153
Claghorn, Mary 207
Claghorn, Robert 475
CLAP 153, 154
Clap, Abigail 32, 439
Clap, Barbara 793
Clap, Elizabeth 620
Clap, Hannah 719, 840
Clap, Mary 254, 588
Clap, Prudence 153
Clap, Sarah 154, 496, 724, 768
Clap, Wait 675
Clap, Wayte 675
CLAPHAM 153
Clapham, Abigail 506
Clapham, Peter 106
CLAPP 153, 154
Clapp, Abigail 620, 742
Clapp, Ann 354
Clapp, Barbara 712
Clapp, Charity 64
Clapp, Elizabeth 75, 384, 440, 626, 720
Clapp, Esther 719
Clapp, Hannah 508, 719
Clapp, Increase .311
Clapp, Jane 402, 791

Clapp, John 248, 263, 790
Clapp, Nehemiah 393
Clapp, Prudence 568
Clapp, Radigon 133
Clapp, Robert 100, 493
Clapp, Roger 493
Clapp, Ruth 721
Clapp, Thomas 380, 663, 742
Clapp, Wait 730
Clappe, Bethiah 544
Clarck, Anne 19
CLARK 154, 155, 156, 157, 158,
   159, 160
Clark, ‒‒‒ 137, 227
Clark, Abigail 56, 128, 153, 481,
   585, 651, 708
Clark, Ann 106
Clark, Anne 324
Clark, Arich 438
Clark, Barbara 683
Clark, Bridget 53
Clark, Catharine 663
Clark, Catherine 297
Clark, Charity 455
Clark, Charles 210
Clark, Cicely 404
Clark, Content 350
Clark, Daniel 44, 217, 833
Clark, Deborah 129, 425
Clark, Deliverance 183
Clark, Ebenezer 641
Clark, Edmond 634
Clark, Edmund 238
Clark, Edward 206, 683, 684
Clark, Eleanor 202, 386
Clark, Elizabeth 22, 80, 110, 112,
   157, 178, 230, 290, 325, 333,
   340, 397, 407, 448, 452, 494,
   514, 525, 540, 572, 600, 613,
   699, 707, 794, 831
Clark, Esther 328, 477, 535, 741
Clark, Faith 227, 578
Clark, Frances 217, 576, 613, 719
Clark, George 72, 158, 443, 604
Clark, George (Sr.) 454
Clark, Hannah 357, 403, 494, 522,
   589, 726
Clark, Henry 281
Clark, Hester 328, 477
Clark, James 23, 47, 260, 521,
   644, 771
Clark, James (Jr.) 326
Clark, Jane 170, 177
Clark, Jeremiah 766
Clark, Joane 714
Clark, Joanna 309, 384
Clark, John 104, 106, 176, 208,
   268, 271, 283, 347, 473, 555,
   595, 650, 695, 699
Clark, Joseph 160, 568
Clark, Josiah 195, 648
Clark, Latham 532
Clark, Leah 34
Clark, Lucy 763
Clark, Lydia 314
Clark, Margaret 181, 413, 696,
   722
Clark, Marie 88
Clark, Martha 123, 134, 296, 341,
   516
Clark, Mary 70, 82, 88, 143, 145,
   147, 158, 196, 200, 234, 254,
   275, 297, 304, 351, 405, 469,
   512, 518, 520, 559, 562, 605,
   634, 652, 654, 655, 685, 701,
   709, 719, 785, 809
Clark, Matthew 816
Clark, Mehitable 228, 782

Clark, Meletiah 338
Clark, Mercy 47, 196, 521
Clark, Meriam 589
Clark, Naomi 821
Clark, Nathaniel 14, 60, 218, 319,
   333
Clark, Nicholas 462
Clark, Percival 112
Clark, Peter 255
Clark, Rachel 424
Clark, Rebecca 106, 644, 723,
   783, 838
Clark, Robert 710
Clark, Ruhanah 822
Clark, Ruth 270, 590
Clark, Samuel 257, 275, 375, 467,
   484, 539
Clark, Sarah 43, 56, 62, 97, 147,
   188, 206, 217, 262, 267, 305,
   344, 395, 405, 454, 484, 495,
   501, 514, 545, 620, 634, 636,
   637, 673, 688, 696, 790, 795,
   817, 824, 829, 835, 837
Clark, Susan 407, 431
Clark, Susanna 474, 484, 518,
   555, 560, 665, 713, 803
Clark, Susanna Wood Morton 522
Clark, Susannah 650
Clark, Tabitha 650
Clark, Theophilus 203
Clark, Tho. 715
Clark, Thomas 118, 258, 427, 430,
   535, 606, 657, 690, 697, 707,
   721, 723
Clark, Walter 315
Clark, Weston 240
Clark, William 181, 206, 262, 452,
   568
CLARKE 154, 155, 156, 157, 158,
   159, 160
Clarke, Abigail 589, 721, 726, 741
Clarke, Agnes 570
Clarke, Catharine 314
Clarke, Dorothy 750
Clarke, Elizabeth 40, 113, 134,
   282, 473, 560, 568, 615, 701,
   762, 838
Clarke, Frances 348, 650
Clarke, Hannah 286, 632
Clarke, Hester 387
Clarke, Hugh 113
Clarke, Jemima 231
Clarke, Jeremiah 233
Clarke, John 696
Clarke, Josiah 309
Clarke, Judith 498
Clarke, Margaret 281, 641, 844
Clarke, Mary 191, 282, 314, 348,
   388, 396, 521, 553, 568, 680,
   699, 733, 791
Clarke, Matthew 34
Clarke, Mercy 553
Clarke, Phebe 288
Clarke, Priscilla 167
Clarke, Rachel 560
Clarke, Rebecca 345, 567, 622
Clarke, Redgon 832
Clarke, Redigan 832
Clarke, Redigon 832
Clarke, Rose 373
Clarke, Rowland 680
Clarke, Ruth 360
Clarke, Sarah 87, 136, 184, 322,
   375, 415, 467, 493, 562, 587,
   619, 771
Clarke, Susanna 320
Clarke, Susannah 87, 184, 568
Clarke, Walter 349

CLARY 160
Clary, Hannah 144
Clary, John 441
Clary, Mary 407
Clary, Sarah 573
CLASON 160
Clason, Elizabeth 202
Class, Sophia 556
CLATTERY 160
CLAWSON 678
CLAY 160
Clay, John 651
Clay, Jonas 102
Clay, Mary 116, 688
Clay, Miles 235, 472
Clay, Rebecca 322
CLAYDON 160
CLAYTON 160
Clayton, Ann 116, 240
Clayton, Sarah 83, 524
CLEABEY 161
CLEAFLAND 162
CLEAR 162
CLEARE 161, 162
Cleare, Dorothy 281
Cleark, Hannah 297
Clearke, Lydia 314
Clearke, Susanna 297
CLEASBIE see CLISBY
CLEASBY 160, 161
Cleasby, John 311
Cleasby, Mary 482
CLEAVES 161
Cleaves, Margaret 24, 559
Cleaves, Martha 175
Cleaves, William 707, 709
Cleaves, Wm. 13
CLEEMY 163
Cleer, Elizabeth 548
CLEEVE 161
Cleeve, Elizabeth 513
Cleeveland, Dorcas 444
Cleeves, Elizabeth 350
Cleg, John 652
CLEMANCE 161
Clemans, Rebecca 172
CLEMENCE 161
Clemence, Elizabeth 497
Clemence, Hester 320
CLEMENS 161
CLEMENT 161
Clement, Elizabeth 721
Clement, Fawne 284
Clement, James 598
Clement, John 786
Clement, Judah 810
Clement, Judith 810
Clement, Lydia 422, 587
Clement, Margaret 528
Clement, Mary 133, 147, 547
Clement, Rebecca 172
Clement, Robert 810
Clement, Sarah 364, 519, 526
CLEMENTS 161
Clements, Elizabeth 81, 114
Clements, Grace 752
Clements, Hannah 192, 443
Clements, Hester 320
Clements, Jasper 108
Clements, Job 457
Clements, Mary 127, 444
Clements, Sarah 219
CLEMMONS 161
Clemmons, Elizabeth 81
Clemmons, Mary 127
CLEMONS 161
Clemons, Margaret 479
CLEMY 163

Clemy, Alexander 94
CLERE 161
Clerk, Margaret 806
CLESSON 163
Clesson, Elizabeth 341
Clesson, Mary 48
Clesson, Thankful 208
CLEVELAND 162
Cleveland, Anna 61
Cleveland, Dorcas 444
Cleveland, Enoch 843
Cleveland, Hannah 365
Cleveland, Isaac 198
Cleveland, Joanna 435
Cleveland, Miriam 276
Cleveland, Samuel 266
CLEVERLY 162
Cleverly, Elizabeth 390
Cleverly, Hannah 757
Cleverly, John 187, 306, 498
Cleverly, Mary 377
Cleverly, Sarah 376, 429
Cleves, Sarah 560
Cleves, William 560
CLIFFORD 162
Clifford, Edward 455, 844
Clifford, Elizabeth 10, 49
Clifford, Esther 701
Clifford, Hannah 484
Clifford, Isaac 602
Clifford, John 399, 622
Clifford, Mary 59, 699
CLIFFT 162
CLIFT 162
CLIFTON 162
Clifton, Hope 380
Clifton, John 645
Clifton, Mary 87
Clifton, Patience 13, 59
Clifton, Thomas 128
Clinton, Arabella (Lady) 420
Clinton, Lawrence 520
Clinton, Susan 402
CLISBY 162
CLISSON 162 see CLOSSON
CLOAD 163
CLOCKE 163
Clocke, Judith 131
Cloice, Elizabeth 658
CLOIS 163
CLOISE 163
Cloise, Sarah 197
CLOMY 163
Clomy, Alexander 94
Clopton, Thomasine 830
CLOSE 163
Close, Elizabeth 719
Close, Hannah 87, 236, 443
Close, Joane 4
Close, Mary 381
CLOSSON 163
Clothier, Ruth 32
CLOUDMAN 163
CLOUGH 163
Clough, Elizabeth 388, 816
Clough, John 86, 661, 673
Clough, Martha 550
Clough, Mary 454
Clough, Sarah 504
Clough, William 399
CLOUTEMAN 163
CLOUTMAN 163
CLOW 163
CLOYCE 163
CLOYES 163
Cloyes, Abigail 785
Cloyes, Elizabeth 658
Cloyes, Hannah 246, 337

Cloyes, John 699
Cloyes, Martha 634
Cloyes, Mary 123, 755
Cloyes, Peter 755
Cloyes, Sarah 391
CLOYSE 163
Cloyse, Abigail 819
Cloyse, Peter 58, 96, 201
Cloyse, Sarah 197
CLUGSTON 163
CLUNGEN 163
CLUNGER 163
CLUTTERBUCK 163
COALBURN 167
COALBURNE 168
Coale, Abigail 538
Coale, Mary 286, 468
Coalt, Mary 468
COARES 163
COARS 163
COATES 163
Coates, Elizabeth 619
Coates, Jane 619
Coates, Willmet 636
COATS 163
Coats, Abigail 619
Coats, Jane 547
Coats, Mary 743
Coaze, Grace 598
Cob, Elizabeth 443
Cob, James 694
Cob, Mary 822
Cob, Patience 559
COBB 164
Cobb, Bethia 615
Cobb, Edward 578
Cobb, Elizabeth 443, 599
Cobb, Hannah 207, 462
Cobb, James 694
Cobb, John 839
Cobb, Jonathan 398
Cobb, Lucy 505
Cobb, Mary 234, 259, 822
Cobb, Patience 63, 171, 192, 559
Cobb, Sarah 151, 374
COBBETT 164
Cobbott, Mary 60
Cobertson, Mary Priest 600
Cobet, Mary 583
COBHAM 164
Cobham, Elizabeth 675
Cobham, Joshua 372
Cobham, Josiah 717
Cobham, Marah 110, 634
Cobham, Mary 63, 110, 501, 583
Cobham, Sarah 717
COBLEIGH 164
Cobleigh, Elizabeth 290
COBLEY 164
Cobley, Elizabeth 290
Cobley, Martha 754
COBORN 167, 168
Coborn, Hannah 623
COBURN 167, 168
Coburn, Lydia 774
Cochet, Dorothy 429
COCHRANE 164 see
  COCKERELL
COCK 188
Cock, Bridgett 125
Cock, Elizabeth 605
Cock, Mary 525
Cock, Phillip 791
Cock, Phillipa 791
Cock, Sarah 282, 400, 692
COCKCROFT 164
COCKE 188
Cocke, Gregory 698

Cocke, Mary 88
COCKER 164
COCKERELL see COCHRANE
Cockerell, Hannah 173
Cockerell, Mary 836
Cockerell, Susanna 153
COCKERILL 164
Cockerill, Elizabeth 173
Cockerill, Susanna 153
COCKERUN 164
COCKES 188
Cockett, Hannah 569
Cockett, Johana 569
COCKRANE 164
Cocks, Susanna 770
COCKSHALL 166
COCKSHOTT 164
CODDALE 165
CODDINGTON 164, 165
Coddington, Ann 817
Coddington, Emm 419
Coddington, Emma 419
Coddington, Mary 650
Coddington, Thomas 519
CODLE 165
CODMAN 165
Codman, Abigail 352
Codman, Deborah 183
Codman, Hepzibah 676
Codman, Peter 563
CODNER 165
Codner, Christopher 229, 805
Codner, Deliverance 291
Codner, Edward 340
Codner, Gregory 640
Codner, Jane 74
Codner, Joane 82
Codner, Mary 100
Codner, Peter 563
Codner, Rachel 216, 648, 671
Codner, Sarah 64
Codnor, Edward 340
CODRY 187
Cody, Ann 647
COE 165
Coe, Benjamin 808
Coe, Elizabeth 756
Coe, Hannah 375, 393
Coe, Martha 258
Coe, Robert 188, 249, 638, 680, 683
Coe, Sarah 299
Coe, Sarah 410
Coe, Sarah 546
Coe, Susanna 14
COES 187
Coes, Agnes 536
Cofell, Selah 735
COFFIN 165, 166
Coffin, Abigail 209, 294
Coffin, Deborah 118, 444
Coffin, Dinah 540, 702
Coffin, Dionis 702
Coffin, Eliphalet 541
Coffin, Elizabeth 305, 324
Coffin, Eunice 127
Coffin, Judith 273, 648
Coffin, Lydia 468, 470, 586, 734
Coffin, Mary 3, 468, 587, 702
Coffin, Mehitable 679
Coffin, Nathaniel 225
Coffin, Peter 175
Coffin, Susanna 118
Coffin, Tristram 692
Coffley, Agnes 445
Cogan, Eleanor 212
Cogan, Elizabeth 252, 301, 631
Cogan, Judith 624

Cogan, Martha 114
Cogan, Mary 630
Cogan, Ruth 182, 730
Cogan, William 212
Cogens, Mary 478
COGGAN 166
Coggan, Frances 804
Coggan, Joanna 509
Coggan, John 167, 830
Coggan, Mary 840
Coggan, Thomas 509
Coggens, Martha 114
Coggershall, Elizabeth 781
COGGESHALL 166, 167
Coggeshall, Ann 240
Coggeshall, Content 540
Coggeshall, Elizabeth 568, 781
Coggeshall, Humility 320
Coggeshall, John 315, 720
Coggeshall, Mary 19, 115
Coggeshall, Patience 611
Coggeshall, Rachel 545
Coggeshall, Rebecca 618
Coggeshall, Wait 314
COGGIN 166
Coggin, Abigail 284
Coggin, Bathsheba 40
Coggin, Henry 579
Coggins, Mary 40
Coggswell, Elizabeth 495
Cogshall, Sarah 541
COGSWELL 167
Cogswell, Abigail 159
Cogswell, Elizabeth 769, 793
Cogswell, Esther 121
Cogswell, Hannah 219, 772
Cogswell, Hester 72, 121
Cogswell, Joanna 803
Cogswell, Margaret 355
Cogswell, Mary 21, 121
Cogswell, Samuel 215
Cogswell, Sarah 541, 761
Cogswell, Susannah 804
COHAR 172
COHOUN 130
COIT 167
Coit, Abigail 510
Coit, John 269
Coit, Martha 524, 806
Coit, Mary 247, 707
Coit, Nathaniel 651, 709
Coite, John 133
COITMORE 167
Coitmore, Rowland 320
Coitmore, Sarah 819
COKER 167
Coker, Hannah 479
Coker, Joseph 836
Coker, Sarah 3, 487, 682
COLAMER 172
Colard, Shuah 227
COLBORN 167
Colborn, Hannah 260
Colborne, Deborah 813
COLBOURN 167
COLBRON 168
Colbron William 45
Colbron, Margaret 45
Colbron, Mary 45, 760
Colbron, Sarah 584
COLBURN 167, 168
Colburn, Deborah 482, 813
Colburn, Elizabeth 552, 695, 775
Colburn, Hannah 8, 260, 623
Colburn, Lydia 774
Colburn, Mary 33, 543, 621
Colburn, Priscilla 521, 592
Colburn, Rebecca 599

Colburn, Sarah 563
COLBY 168
Colby, Anthony 784, 812
Colby, Dorothy 396
Colby, Elizabeth 228, 790
Colby, Frances 605
Colby, Hannah 548, 733
Colby, Mary 141, 651
Colby, Rebecca 819
Colby, Sarah 31, 75, 190
Colby, Susanna 812
Colby, Thomas 75
Colclough, Elizabeth 14
COLCORD 168
Colcord, Deborah 166
Colcord, Elizabeth 254
Colcord, Hannah 213
Colcord, Mary 265
Colcord, Mehitable 708
Colcord, Sarah 377
Colcord, Shuah 529
Coldam, Martha 811
COLDFAX 172
COLDHAM 168
Coldham, Elizabeth 541
COLDOM 168
Coldom, Elizabeth 541
Coldwell, Abigail 152
COLE 131, 168, 169, 170
Cole, Abigail 19, 67, 107, 276, 538, 673, 707
Cole, Abraham 750
Cole, Alexander 674
Cole, Amias 498
Cole, Amyas 498, 736
Cole, Ann 29, 328, 420, 647, 666
Cole, Anna 423, 647
Cole, Anne 65, 116, 647
Cole, Arthur 46, 238, 479
Cole, Daniel 25
Cole, Deliverance 750
Cole, Elizabeth 199, 340, 384, 416, 584, 597, 749, 790
Cole, Elizabeth Albone Luxford 479
Cole, Elizabeth Foote Burch 119
Cole, Esther 25
Cole, Eunice 498, 628
Cole, Grace 659, 769
Cole, Hannah 90, 307, 395, 499, 589, 647
Cole, Henry 116, 423
Cole, Hepzibah 192, 223
Cole, Hester 25
Cole, Hugh 178, 344, 522, 672
Cole, Isaac 100, 245
Cole, Israel 633
Cole, James 244, 526, 673
Cole, Jane 362, 468
Cole, Joanna 111, 395
Cole, John 80, 369
Cole, Lydia 701, 825
Cole, Margaret 228, 438
Cole, Martha 103, 395, 723
Cole, Mary 15, 286, 296, 309, 354, 387, 412, 441, 474, 476, 591, 702, 721, 756
Cole, Matthew 788
Cole, Nathaniel 68
Cole, Nicholas 468
Cole, Phillip 520
Cole, Rachel 681
Cole, Rebecca 125, 537
Cole, Robert 350, 520
Cole, Ruth 479, 526, 761, 829, 846
Cole, Samuel 430, 641
Cole, Sarah 504, 730, 750

Cole, Saraj 504
Cole, Susannah 246, 820
COLEBORNE 167, 168
Coleborne, Mary 621
COLEBOURNE 167
COLEBROOK 170
COLEBURNE 168
COLEBY 168
Coleby, Hannah 548
Coleby, Sarah 31
Colefax, Mary 68
COLEGROVE 172
COLEMAN 170, 171
Coleman, --- 56
Coleman, Abigail 744
Coleman, Ann 10, 210
Coleman, Benjamin 347
Coleman, Deborah 330
Coleman, Dorcas 743
Coleman, Elizabeth 353, 618, 641
Coleman, Esther 208
Coleman, Hannah 317, 529
Coleman, John 250, 375, 636, 705
Coleman, Mary 612
Coleman, Noah 514
Coleman, Phebe 140
Coleman, Sarah 179, 264, 388, 753
Coleman, Thomas 420, 507, 547, 640, 794
Coleman, William 148, 639
COLER 172
COLES 169, 170
Coles, --- 842
Coles, Ann 467, 749
Coles, Deliverance 750
Coles, Dinah 7
Coles, Harvey 805
Coles, Joane 635
Coles, John 467
Coles, Martha 483
Coles, Mary 229
Coles, Robert 350
Coles, Sarah 312, 387, 750
Coles, Susanna 453
Coles, Tamar 136
Coles, Ursula 723
Coleson, Mary 135
COLESWORTHY 168, 171
COLEY 171, 172
Coley, Abilena 144
Coley, Elizabeth 156, 797
Coley, Frances 402
Coley, Hannah 329
Coley, Mary 155, 156, 422, 470, 675, 718
Coley, Peter 671
Coley, Sarah 36
COLFAX 172
Colfax, Elizabeth 21
COLGROVE 172
Collacot, Experience 508
COLLAMER 172
COLLAMORE 172
Collamore, Elizabeth 637
COLLAR 172
Collard, Alice 353
Colle, Amyes 736
COLLEDGE 180
Colleham, Annover 494
Colleham, Annver 494
COLLER 172
Coller, Hannah 201
Coller, Mary 381
COLLES 170
Collever, Elizabeth 492
COLLICOT 172
Collicot, Elizabeth 335

COLLICOTT 172
Collicott, Experience 508
Collicut, Bethiah 312
COLLICUTT 172
COLLIER 172
Collier, Abel 518
Collier, Elizabeth 251, 604, 694
Collier, Elizabeth Sheafe 551
Collier, Experience 33
Collier, Joseph 116
Collier, Mary 110, 576, 578, 601
Collier, Rebecca 169
Collier, Ruth 168
Collier, Sarah 96, 556, 599
Collier, Thomas 199, 426, 604
Colliham, Annover 494
Colliham, Annver 494
Collihan, Annover 494
Collihan, Annver 494
COLLINGS 173
Collings, Frances 26
Collings, Sarah 468
Collings, Sybella 620
Collings, Sybil 620
COLLINS 172, 173, 174
Collins, Abigail 259, 339, 530,
  738, 749, 817
Collins, Ann 439, 683
Collins, Anna 409, 414
Collins, Anne 157, 409, 532
Collins, Arnold 779
Collins, Benjamin 270, 607
Collins, Christian 94
Collins, Christiana 94
Collins, Daniel 1, 782
Collins, Deborah 819
Collins, Dorothy 320
Collins, Ebenezer 754
Collins, Eleazer 596
Collins, Elizabeth 50, 284, 314,
  617, 746
Collins, Felix 464
Collins, Hannah 107, 109, 343,
  410
Collins, Jane 172, 655
Collins, Jane Andrews Neale 529
Collins, Joan 655
Collins, John 10, 128, 331, 441
Collins, Joseph 719
Collins, Lois 3
Collins, Loues 3
Collins, Lydia 369
Collins, Margaret 819
Collins, Margery 819
Collins, Martha 347, 515
Collins, Mary 145, 178, 206, 222,
  250, 301, 339, 386, 423, 435,
  516, 538, 663
Collins, Naomi 402
Collins, Phebe 643
Collins, Rebecca 81, 533
Collins, Robert 70, 635
Collins, Rose 506
Collins, Samuel 394
Collins, Sarah 223, 247, 399, 468,
  478, 685
Collins, Susanna 339, 473, 775
Collins, Susannah 122
Collins, Sybella 620
Collins, Sybil 620, 808
COLLIS 174
COLLISHAWE 174
Collman, Sarah 388
Collox, Alice 430
Collox, William 430
COLLRIM 173
Collye, Martha 754
Collyer, Elizabeth 694

Colman, Elizabeth 377
Colman, Olive 589, 827
Colman, William 299
COLON 174
COLOR 172
Colson, Adam 104
Colson, Ann 394
Colson, Anne 394
COLSTON 174
COLT 174
Colt, Esther 472
Colt, John 456
Colt, Sarah 206
Coltman, Elizabeth 618
Coltman, John 670
Coltman, Mary 670
COLTON 174
Colton, Dorothy 78
Colton, George 540
Colton, Hepzibah 794
Colton, Hester 104
Colton, Mary 43, 318
Colton, Rebecca 704
Colton, Sarah 179, 319, 431
COLVER 196
Colville, Rebecca 740
COLVIN 174
Colwell, Robert 777
COLYER 172
COMAN 174 see COMER
Coman, Richard 131
COMAR 174
Combe, Agnes 748
Combe, Jane 302
Combe, Winifred Rossiter 302
COMBEY 196
COMBS 180
Combs, Anna 785
Combs, Deborah 292, 664
Combs, Elizabeth 402
Combs, Francis 833
Combs, Henry 292, 402, 664
Combs, Mary 529
Combs, Mercy 47
Combs, Susanna 317
COMER 174 see COMAN
Comer, Richard 131
Comer, Ruth 300
Comer, Sarah 225
COMES 180, 181
Comey, Elizabeth 433
Comey, Mary 436
COMINGS 196
COMMINGS 196
Commings, Mary 74
COMPTON 175
Compton, Abigail 100, 125
COMSTOCK 175
Comstock, --- 847
Comstock, Abigail 586
Comstock, Anne 69, 683
Comstock, Bethiah 704
Comstock, Daniel 535
Comstock, Elizabeth 511, 646,
  671, 718
Comstock, Hannah 276, 502
Comstock, Hope 337
Comstock, John 405
Comstock, Mary 646
Comstock, Rebecca 704
Comstock, Samuel 683, 812
COMY 175
Comy, David 561
Comyngs, Elizabeth 743
CONANT 175
Conant, Abiah 776
Conant, Abial 776
Conant, Bethiah 12

Conant, Elizabeth 167, 341
Conant, Jane 494, 525
Conant, Joshua 316
Conant, Lot 486
Conant, Martha 572
Conant, Mary 35, 120, 224, 766
Conant, Rebecca 613
Conant, Roger 381
Conant, Sarah 524, 754
Concklyne, Thomas 637
Concord, Elizabeth 846
Condage, Mary 239
CONDEY 175
Condey, William 225
Condrey, Nathaniel 816
CONDY 175
Condy, Christian 386
Condy, Mary 149
Condy, Samuel 615
Condy, William 166, 735
CONE 175, 176
Cone, Daniel 772
Conet, Bethiah 12
CONEY 176
Coney, Elizabeth 83
Coney, John 156, 484, 502
Coney, Mary 215
Coney, Rebecca 603
CONGDIL 176
CONGDON 176
Congdon, Elizabeth 794
Congdon, Susanna 539
Conger, Sarah 170
CONKLIN 176
Conklin, --- 682
Conklin, Ananias 638
Conklin, Annis 813
Conklin, Bethia 389
Conklin, Cornelius 536, 703
Conklin, Elizabeth 834
Conklin, Esther 526
Conklin, Hester 526
Conklin, Jane 109
Conklin, John 332
Conklin, Joseph 558, 647
Conklin, Mary 658
Conklin, Rebecca 537
Conklin, Sarah 129, 456
CONKLING 176
Conkling, Hester 508
Conkling, Mary 508, 526
Conkling, Rebecca 111
Conkling, Sarah 454
CONLEY 176, 177
Conley, Abraham 255, 528
CONLIFFE 197
Conly, --- 473
CONNANT 175
Connant, Mary 120
Connatt, Lot 486
Connaught, Bridget 560
CONNAWAY 177
Connell, Hannah 226
CONNER 177
Conner, Bridget 560
Conner, Ruth 163
CONNETT 177
CONNEY 176
CONNIARS 177
CONNOR 177
CONNOWAY 177
Connoway, Sarah Hilliard
  Hollingsworth 381
CONOWAY 177
CONSTABLE 177
Constable, Anne 471
Constable, Marmaluke 508
Constable, Mary 178

Constable, Thomas 471
CONVERS 177
CONVERSE 177
Converse, Abigail 435
Converse, Deborah 583
Converse, Edward 373, 698
Converse, Hannah 583, 622
Converse, James 181
Converse, Josiah 203
Converse, Mary 207, 284, 667, 738
Converse, Rebecca 515
Converse, Ruth 202
Converse, Samuel 265
Converse, Sarah 587
CONWAY 177
CONYERS 177
Coock, Sarah 48
COOK 170, 177, 178, 179
Cook, --- 13
Cook, Abigail 316, 592
Cook, Alice 808
Cook, Ann 692
Cook, Anna 692
Cook, Barnabas 790
Cook, Bethiah 343
Cook, Catharine 54
Cook, Catherine 400
Cook, Deborah 15, 307
Cook, Elizabeth 157, 682
Cook, Esther 725
Cook, Experience 5
Cook, Hannah 440, 814
Cook, Hester 725
Cook, Jacob 168
Cook, Jane 512
Cook, Joan 678
Cook, Joanna 595
Cook, John 206, 250
Cook, Judith 606
Cook, Katharine 400
Cook, Martha 185
Cook, Mary 41, 199, 211, 323, 412, 424, 485, 690, 725, 726
Cook, Mercy 796
Cook, Miriam 460
Cook, Patience 711
Cook, Phebe 12
Cook, Phoebe 22
Cook, Richard 799
Cook, Samuel 628
Cook, Sara 34
Cook, Sarah 34, 336, 392, 662, 771
Cook, Thomas 106, 279, 451
COOKE 177, 178, 179
Cooke, --- 617, 836
Cooke, Aaron 275, 687
Cooke, Abigail 395
Cooke, Amy 160
Cooke, Ann 160
Cooke, Deborah 307
Cooke, Elizabeth 8, 62, 99, 227, 327, 336, 350, 384, 454, 532, 562, 574, 777, 814, 825, 826
Cooke, Esther 843
Cooke, Freelove 711
Cooke, Gregory 311, 698, 799
Cooke, Hannah 7, 33, 98, 113, 132
Cooke, Henry 799
Cooke, Hester 843
Cooke, Jacob 672
Cooke, Joanna 833
Cooke, John 98, 522, 635, 797
Cooke, Josiah 212
Cooke, Martha 199, 837
Cooke, Mary 209, 451, 525, 624,

Cooke, Mary (cont.) 635, 737
Cooke, Mercy 711
Cooke, Ellen 306
Cooke, Miriam 212
Cooke, Moses 230
Cooke, Nicholas 702
Cooke, Patience 309
Cooke, Penelope 767, 787
Cooke, Phebe 489
Cooke, Rachel 436
Cooke, Richard 323
Cooke, Robert 24
Cooke, Ruth 267
Cooke, Samuel 57
Cooke, Sarah 49, 308, 353, 559
Cooke, Sarah Very 716
Cooke, Susanna 676
Cooke, Thomas 768
Cooker, Joseph 364
COOKERY 179
Cookery, Henry 572
COOKEY 179
COOKSAY 182
COOLE 180
Coole, Martha 395
Cooledg, Mary 99
COOLEDGE 180
Cooledge, Hannah 81
Cooledge, Mary 513
COOLEY 179, 180
Cooley, Bethia 144
Cooley, Daniel 124
Cooley, Elizabeth 8, 290, 451
Cooley, Frances 402
Cooley, Henry 101
Cooley, John 189
Cooley, Martha 683, 733
Cooley, Mary 263
Cooley, Obadiah 781
Cooley, Rebecca 793
Cooley, Sarah 504, 518
COOLIDGE 180
Coolidge, Anna 5
Coolidge, Elizabeth 189, 598, 627
Coolidge, Grace 81
Coolidge, Hannah 680
Coolidge, John 497, 595
Coolidge, Mary 99, 468
Coolidge, Sarah 268
COOLLEDGE 180
COOLLIDGE 180
Cooly, Elizabeth 759
Coomb, John 845
Coombes, John 42
COOMBS 180
Coombs, Abigail 27
Coombs, Deborah 426
Coombs, Elizabeth 199, 359, 442
Coombs, Francis 600
Coombs, Henry 556
Coombs, John 641, 782
Coombs, John (Jr.) 641
Coombs, Lydia 509
Coombs, Margaret 346
Coombs, Mary 240
COOMER 174
COOMES 180
Coomes, Mary 410
COOMS 180, 181
Cooms, Margaret 346
COOPER 181, 182
Cooper, --- 265
Cooper, Abigail 421
Cooper, Ann 522, 579, 805
Cooper, Anna 419, 587
Cooper, Anthony 600
Cooper, Bathsheba 804
Cooper, Deborah 361, 567, 600
Cooper, Elizabeth 164, 409, 630,

Cooper, Elizabeth (cont.) 682
Cooper, Ellen 306
Cooper, Hannah 467, 596
Cooper, Helena 306
Cooper, Jane 830
Cooper, Joanna 585
Cooper, John 177, 226, 334, 340, 844
Cooper, Josiah 103, 164, 216, 600
Cooper, Judith 630
Cooper, Lydia 268, 282, 522, 713
Cooper, Martha 177
Cooper, Mary 122, 174, 219, 226, 271, 305, 392, 503, 523, 585, 614, 689, 805, 808
Cooper, Mercy 614
Cooper, Merry 614
Cooper, Nathaniel 819
Cooper, Rachel 136
Cooper, Rebecca 156, 314, 804
Cooper, Sarah 211, 364, 370, 514, 517, 837, 838
Cooper, Sarah Mew 467
Cooper, Simon 713
Cooper, Tacy 397
Cooper, Tase 397
Cooper, Thomas 58, 85, 104, 160, 182, 240, 567, 585, 681, 693
Cooper, Timothy 305, 369, 564
Coopper, Sarah 517
COOTS 163, 164
Coots, Abigail 619
Coots, Elizabeth 619
COOTSAY 182
Cootts, Jane 619
COOZENS 186
COPE 182
COPELAND 182
Copeland, Abigail 734
Copeland, Lydia 806
Copeland, Thomas 21, 25
Copeland, William 788
COPLEY 182
Copley, Elizabeth 8, 451, 576, 759
Copley, Mary 232
Copley, Thomas 730
COPP 182
Copp, Ann 25, 654
Copp, Joanna 538
Copp, John 60, 575
Copp, Martha 350, 733
Copp, Ruth 527
Copper, Thomas 58, 240
COPPERTHWAITE 187, 188
Coppin, Thomas 557
COPS 182
Copsey, Mary 232
CORAM 182
CORBE 183
CORBEE 183
CORBET 182
CORBETT 182
Corbett, Abiah 115
Corbett, Abigail 115
Corbett, John 567
Corbett, Robert 115
Corbett, William 17, 530
CORBIN 183
Corbin, Margaret 207
Corbin, Mary 294, 844
Corbison, Mary 626
Corbit, Abiah 115
Corbit, Abigail 115
Corbit, Robert 115
CORCKFORD 192
CORDAY 183
Cordener, Elizabeth 498

CORDEY 183
COREE 184
Coree, Alice 558
Coree, Mary 558
COREY 184, 185
Corey, Abigail 648
Corey, Alice 558
Corey, Deliverance 193
Corey, Elizabeth 407
Corey, Giles 621
Corey, Isaac 478
Corey, Margaret 161
Corey, Martha 161
Corey, Mary 92, 179, 558, 689
Corey, Mercy 424
Corey, Sarah 821
Corey, William 744
Corish, Priscilla 286, 404, 740
Corish, Scissilla 404
Cork, Adrian 812
Corles, Martha 447
Corles, Sarah 27
CORLET 183
Corlet, Hepzibah 143
Corlet, Joane 637
Corlet, Joanna 637
Corlet, Johanna 637
Corlett, Hepzibah 512
Corley, George 545
Corley, Joanna 545
Corlias, George 545
Corlias, Joanna 545
Corlin, Sarah 244
CORLIS 183
Corlis, Ann 631
Corlis, Deborah 240
Corlis, Huldah 441
Corlis, Mary 530
Corliss, Ann 631
Corliss, Deborah 441
Corliss, Elizabeth 548
Corliss, Huldah 441
Corliss, Johana 406
Corliss, Martha 447
Corliss, Mary 530
Corliss, Sarah 27
CORNELIUS 183
Cornelius, Anne Gridley 325
CORNELL 183
Cornell, Ann 434
Cornell, Elizabeth 14, 334, 455
Cornell, Innocent 84
Cornell, Martha 397
Cornell, Mary 191, 649
Cornell, Rebecca 840
Cornell, Sarah 21, 96, 98, 455,
  783, 818
Cornell, Thomas 447
CORNETH 191
CORNEY 197
CORNING 183
Corning, Elizabeth 359
Corning, Remember 714
Corning, Samuel 435
CORNISH 183, 184
Cornish, James 452, 459
Cornish, Joyce 544
Cornish, Martha 609
Cornish, Mary 185, 648
Cornish, Richard 609
CORNWALL 184
Cornwall, Esther 716, 815
Cornwall, Hannah 226
Cornwall, Mary 226, 772
CORNWELL 184
Cornwell, Elizabeth 334, 519
Cornwell, Martha 397
Cornwell, Mary 810

Cornwell, Sarah 396
CORP 184
Corp, John 299
CORPS 184
CORRELL 184
CORSE 184
CORSER 186
CORTAS 198
Corwell, Lydia 311
CORWIN 184 see CARWITHEN
Corwin, Abigail 353, 643
Corwin, Elizabeth 711
Corwin, George 103, 805
Corwin, Hannah 109
Corwin, Jonathan 300
Corwin, Lucy 249
Corwin, Martha 139, 407
Corwin, Mary 487
Corwin, Sarah 548
Corwine, Penelope 833
Corwine, Susannah 480
CORWITH 139 see CORWIN
Corwithey, Mary 150
CORY 185
Cory, Anne 64
Cory, Elizabeth 524
Cory, John 648
Cory, Mary 161
Cory, Mehitable 795
COSIER 185
Coss, George 343
COSTA 185
COSTIE 185
COSTIN 185
COSTONE 185
Cotler, Hannah 201
Cotlin, Sarah 513
Coton, Maria 271
COTTA 185
Cotta, Mary 237, 648
Cotten, John 271
Cotten, Mary 271
COTTER 185
Cotterell, Martha 505
Cotterell, Mary 127
COTTLE 185
Cottle, Ann 629
Cottle, Anne 745
Cottle, Hannah 373
Cottle, Johanah 571
Cottle, Mary 67
Cottle, William 332
COTTON 185
Cotton, Anne 136, 423
Cotton, Dorothy 555, 686
Cotton, Elizabeth 14, 199, 245,
  666, 822
Cotton, George 448
Cotton, Hester 104
Cotton, John 271, 496, 695
Cotton, John (Rev.) 19
Cotton, Maria 25, 90, 271, 496,
  563
Cotton, Mary 271, 496, 563, 758
Cotton, Mercy 758
Cotton, Roland 215
Cotton, Rowland 215
Cotton, Sarah 54, 90, 584
Cotton, Seaborn 193, 339
Cotton, Theophilus 218
Cotton, William 496
COTTRELL 186
Cotymore, Elizabeth 763
Cotymore, Rowland 320
COUCH 186
Couch, Hannah 171
Couch, Martha 265
Couch, Mary 63, 329

Couch, Rebecca 291
Couch, Samuel 301
Couch, Sarah 513
Couch, Simon 711
COULDUM 168
COULLY 180
Coulson, Elizabeth 62
Coult, Joseph 206
COULTMAN 186
Coultman, Elizabeth 618
Coultman, John 670
Coultman, Mary 646, 670
COUNCE 186
COUNTS 186
Counts, Elizabeth 162
Counts, Sarah 454
COURSER 186
Courser, Hannah 552
Courser, Sarah 739
Courtis, Elizabeth 837
Courtis, Samuel 837
COURTNEY 186
Cousens, Isaac 404
Coushett, Hannah 569
Coushett, Johana 569
COUSINS 186
Cousins, Elizabeth 309
Cousins, Isaac 244, 273
Cousons, Elizabeth 45
COUSSENS 186
COUSSINS 186
COUVEY 186
COVEE 186
COVEL 186
Covel, --- 577
COVELL 186
Covell, Elizabeth 246
COVILL 187
Covill, Rebecca 740
COVWELL 187
Cowan, John 485
COWDALL 186
Cowdall, John 209
Cowdrey, Bethiah 138
Cowdrey, Hannah 591
Cowdrey, Nathaniel 721
COWDRY 186, 187
Cowdry, Mary 241
Cowdry, Rebecca 749
Cowdry, William 86
COWEL 187
COWELL 187
Cowell, Amy 27, 290, 669
Cowell, Edward 162, 691
Cowell, Hannah 802
Cowell, Joseph 404
Cowell, Margaret 391, 422
Cowell, Mary 200, 669
Cowell, Sarah 410
Cowell, Thomas 661
COWEN 187
Cowen, Rebecca 354
COWES 187
Cowes, Agnes 536
Cowes, Mary 278, 591
Cowes, Michael 598
COWIN 187
COWING 187
Cowing, John 485
Cowing, Rebecca 354
COWLAN 187
COWLAND 187
Cowland, Ralph 771
COWLES 187
Cowles, Abigail 595
Cowles, Elizabeth 480, 738
Cowles, Esther 116
Cowles, Hannah 594, 701

Cowles, Mary 220
Cowles, Sarah 220, 312, 349
COWLEY 180
COWLISHHAWE 174
Cowper, Jane 51
COX 188
Cox, Alice 2
Cox, Ann 520
Cox, Elizabeth 605
Cox, Gowen 497
Cox, Hannah 418
Cox, John 372, 449, 669
Cox, Leah 572
Cox, Martha 307
Cox, Mary 329, 702
Cox, Moses 418, 722
Cox, Rachel 612
Cox, Sarah 515, 538
Cox, Susanna 97, 770
Cox, William 24
COXE 188
COY 188, 482
Coy, Mary 447
Coy, Sarah 459
Coye, Samuel 101
Coys, Edward 723
Coyt, Abigail 255
Coyt, Mary 247
Coytman, Thomas 830
Coytmore, Elizabeth 763
Coytmore, Margery 609
Coytmore, Thomas 166
Cozan, Eleanor 212
COZENS 186
COZIER 185
Cozzens, Mary 40
CRABB 188, 189
Crabb, Richard 165, 843
CRABTREE 189
Crabtree, Alice 366
Crabtree, Esther 339, 590
Crabtree, John 366
CRACKBONE 189
Crackbone, Gilbert 180, 627
Crackbone, Joseph 620
Crackbone, Sarah 34
Cracker, Agnes 213
CRACKSTON 189
CRADDICK 189
CRADOCK 189
Cradock, Matthew 306
CRAFFORD 189, 191
Crafford, Mungo 433
CRAFORD 189
Craford, Hester 390
CRAFT 189 see CRAFTS
Craft, Abigail 379
Craft, Griffin 631, 718
Craft, Hannah 286
Craft, Mary 702
Craft, Nathaniel 205
Craft, Rebecca 843
Craft, Richard 536
CRAFTS 189
Crafts, Abigail 3, 211, 310, 642
Crafts, Elizabeth 158
Crafts, Griffin 389, 565
Crafts, Hannah 423, 825
Crafts, Mary 327
Crafts, Rebecca 759
Crafts, William 213, 412
CRAGE 189
Cragen, Abigail 444
CRAGG 189
Cragg, Catharine 429
Cragg, Katharine 257
Cragg, Mary 716
CRAGGEN 189

Craggen, Abigail 444
CRAGGENE 189
Craggin, Elizabeth 668
Craghead, Katharine 386
CRAGIN 189
Cragin, Elizabeth 668
Cragin, Sarah 541
CRAIG 189
Craig, Catharine 429
Craig, Katharine 257
Craigg, Katharine 257
Craighead, Katharine 386
CRAIGIE 189
CRAIN 190
CRAM 189
Cram, Elizabeth 502
Cram, Hannah 265
Cram, John 51
Cram, Mary 743
Cram, Sarah 646
Cramphorne, Mary 363
CRAMPTON 189, 190
Crampton, Dennis 527
Crampton, Elizabeth 459
Crampton, Hannah 658
Cranbroke, --- 843
CRANDALL 190
Crandall, Charity 105
Crandall, Elizabeth 815
Crandall, Elizabeth Witter
    Langworthy 451
Crandall, Jane 29
Crandall, Joanna 464
Crandall, Sarah 832
CRANDILL 190
CRANE 190, 318
Crane, Abigail Butler 775
Crane, Azariah 590
Crane, Benjamin 732
Crane, Concurrence 48
Crane, Elijah 130
Crane, Elizabeth 301
Crane, Hannah 405, 590, 778
Crane, Henry 143
Crane, Jasper 405
Crane, Margaret 634
Crane, Margery 556
Crane, Mary 61, 132, 194, 331,
    400, 450, 609, 781
Crane, Mehitable 610
Crane, Mercy 61
Crane, Phebe 133, 432
Crane, Sarah 519, 609
Crane, Stephen 60
Cranfield, Mary 450
CRANIVER 190
CRANMER 190
CRANNEVER 190
Cranniwell, Susan 488
Cranniwell, Susanna 488
Cransden, Alice 165
CRANSTON 190, 191
Cranston, Elizabeth 107
Cranston, John 701
Cranston, Samuel 191, 566
Cranston, Walter 103
Cranston, William 300
CRARY 191
Cratey, Mary 247
CRAVATH 191
Cravath, Elizabeth 788
Cravath, Ezekiel 501
CRAW 191
Craw, Richard 816
CRAWFORD 189, 191 see
    CRAFFORD
Crawford, John 9, 832
Crawford, Margaret 818

Crawford, Rebecca 107, 698
Crawford, Recuba 698
Crawford, Sarah 160, 618
Crawford, Stephen 818
Crawford, Winifred 13, 698, 832
Crawith, Ezekiel 434
CRAWLEY 191
CRAY 191
Creasee, Mighill 388
CREASSON 191
CREATTY 191
Creatty, Andrew 224
Creatty, Mary 224
CREBER 191
Creber, Alice 672
Creber, Thomas 566
CREDIFORD 191
CREEBER 191
CREED 191
Creed, --- 478
Creel, Elizabeth 523
CREESEY 191
CREHORE 191
Crehore, Mary 306
Crehore, Rebecca 569
Crehore, Teague 606
CRESE 191
CRESEE 191
CRESEY 191
CRESIE 191
CRESSEE 191
Cressey, Mary 369
Cressey, Mighill 388
Cressey, Sarah 629
CRESSONS 191
CRESSY 191
Cressy, Mary 381
Cresttenden, Mary 48
CREW 191
Crewe, Deborah 837
Crewe, Dorothy 837
CRIPPEN 191
Crippen, Catherine 640
Crippen, Mary 183
CRISP 191, 192
Crisp, Elizabeth 454
Crisp, George 223
Crisp, Mary 315, 625, 822
Crisp, Richard 621
Crisp, Sarah 347
CRISPE 192
Crispe, Benjamin 472
Crispe, Deliverance 472
Crispe, Mary 323, 561
Crissy, Elizabeth 443
CRITCHET 192
Critchet, Elias 735
CRITCHETT 192
CRITCHFIELD 192
CRITCHLEY 192
Critchley, Richard 221
Crittenden, Isaac 502
CROAD 192
Croad, John 641
Croad, Judith 530
Croad, Sarah 310, 371
Croade, Abigail 525
Croade, Elizabeth 96, 448
Croade, Sarah 371
Croaker, William 633
CROAKHAM 193
Croakham, John 347
CROAKUM 193
Croakum, Sarah 767
CROCKER 192 see CROOKER
Crocker, Elizabeth 150
Crocker, Hannah 475
Crocker, Joan 242

Crocker, Joanna 821
Crocker, Michael 296
Crocker, Sarah 399, 483, 769
Crocker, Thankful Trot Hinkley 374
Crocker, Thomas 474
Crocker, William 559
Crocket, Mary 49
Crocket, Sarah 47
CROCKETT 192
Crockett, Ann 416
Crockett, Anna 628
Crockett, Mary 679
Crockett, Nan 628
Crockett, Sarah 561
Crockett, Thomas 416, 628
Crockham, John 707
CROCUM 193
Crocum, Hannah 70
Crocum, John 707
Crocum, Mary 457
CROE 195
Croel, Abigail 210
Crofert, Daniel 482
Croft, William 412
CROKER 192
CROMBE 195
CROMLON 193
CROMLONE 193
Crommeth, Sarah 274
CROMMETT 193
CROMPTON 189, 195
CROMWELL 193
Cromwell, Ann 6, 445, 580
Cromwell, Anna 580
Cromwell, Argentine 189
Cromwell, Elizabeth 293, 603, 767
Cromwell, Hannah 518
Cromwell, Jane 581
Cromwell, Joanna 377
Cromwell, John 561
Cromwell, Philip 57, 433, 461
Cromwell, Rebecca 196
Cromwell, Sarah 274, 456, 796
Cromwell, Thomas 424, 445
Cronkham, Francis 776
Crooke, Elizabeth 330
Crooke, Rebecca 294
Crooke, Ruth 571, 616
CROOKER 192, 193 see CROCKER
Crooker, Hannah 276, 791
Crooker, Sarah 483
CROOKSON 193
Crosbey, Rachel 436
Crosbey, Sarah 612
Crosbie, Hannah 421
CROSBY 193, 194
Crosby, Anthony 185, 339
Crosby, Dorothy 587
Crosby, Hannah 203, 421
Crosby, Jane 580
Crosby, Joseph 552
Crosby, Mary 451
Crosby, Sarah 660
Crosby, Simon 738
Crosby, Thomas 171
Crose, Martha 236
Crose, Robert 236
CROSMAN 194
Crosman, Elizabeth 360
Crosman, Mercy 740
CROSS 194
Cross, Albert 55
Cross, Anna 491
Cross, Anne 261
Cross, Elizabeth 29, 119, 531
Cross, Faith Belcher 586

Cross, Hannah 339, 414
Cross, John 317
Cross, Joseph 100, 518
Cross, Margaret Northend 554
Cross, Martha 236
Cross, Mary 33, 365, 371, 581, 649, 797
Cross, Mercy 665
Cross, Robert 236
Cross, Samuel 145
Cross, Sarah 52, 127
Cross, Stephen 455, 527
Cross, Thomas 715
Cross, William 52
CROSSE 194
Crosse, Elizabeth 84
Crosse, Mary 570, 581
CROSSMAN 194
Crossman, Bartholomew 505
Crossman, Mary 315
Crossman, Mercy 740
Crossman, Robert 241
Crossman, Sarah 839
CROSSWELL 194
Crosswell, Elizabeth 131
Crosswell, Hepzibah 347
Crosswell, Priscilla 326
CROSTHWAITE 194
Croswell, Naomi 202
Croswell, Priscilla 326
Croswell, Silence 335
CROUCH 194, 195
Crouch, Arthur 764
Crouch, Elizabeth 20
Crouch, Mercy 311
Crouch, Richard 20
Crouch, Sarah 423, 427, 700
CROW 195 see CROWELL
Crow, --- 574
Crow, Anna 221
Crow, Catharine 84
Crow, Cathrin 84
Crow, Elizabeth 159, 220, 782, 826
Crow, Esther 339
Crow, Hannah 221
Crow, John 625
Crow, Lydia 311
Crow, Martha 576
Crow, Mary 171, 514, 686
Crow, Mehitable 563, 746
Crow, Nathaniel 780
Crow, Ruth 297, 333
Crow, Samuel 489
Crow, Sarah 649, 804
Crow, William 720
Crowe, Christopher 157
Crowe, Mary 156
Crowe, Sarah 25
Crowe, William 25
CROWEL 195
CROWELL 195
Crowell, Abigail 210, 574
Crowell, Dorothy 574
Crowell, Edward 215
Crowell, Elishua 301
Crowell, Elizabeth 497, 573, 779
Crowell, Mehitable 746
Crowell, Susanna 65
CROWFOOT 195
Crowfoot, Joseph 497
Crowfoot, Mary Lucas Scofield 657
Crowfoot, Samuel 189
CROWINSHEL 195
CROWKHAM 193
CROWN 195
CROWNINSHIELD 195

CROWNSHIELD 195
CROYCHLEY 192
Crucy, Patience 82
CRUFF 195
CRUFFS 189
CRUFT 195 see CRAFTS
CRUMB 195
Crumb, Daniel 353
Crump, Lydia 144
Crumpton, Samuel 516
CRUMWELL 193
Crumwell, Elizabeth 603
CRUNMELL 197
CRUTTENDEN 195, 196
Cruttenden, Abraham 151
Cruttenden, Deborah 540
Cruttenden, Elizabeth 318, 396
Cruttenden, Hannah 390, 408
Cruttenden, Sarah 630
Cubbs, Samuel 580
Cubby, Experience 483
Cubby, Patience 483
CUDDINGTON 164
CUDWORTH 196
Cudworth, Ann 427
Cudworth, Hannah 352, 425
Cudworth, James 725
Cudworth, Joanna 171
Cudworth, Mary 767, 804
CUE 196
Cue, Robert 366
Culipher, Lydia 461
CULLAMORE 172
Culler, Joanna 414
CULLICK 196
Cullick, Elizabeth 53
Cullick, Hannah 306
Cullick, John 250
Cullick, Mary 543
Culliver, Elizabeth 492
Cullpeper, Susanna 466
Culpepper, Hannah 285
Cult, Margaret 766
CULVER 196
Culver, Margaret 257
Culver, Mary 123
Culver, Samuel 266
Cumbers, Mary 434
CUMBY 196
Cumings, Abigail 573
Cumings, Rebecca 395
CUMMINGS 196
Cummings, Elizabeth 315, 344, 420
Cummings, Jane 428
Cummings, John 692
Cummings, Mary 85
Cummings, Rebecca 395
Cummings, Sarah 285
CUMMINS 196
Cummins, Ann 566
CUMPTON 175
Cunliff, Susanna 169
CUNLIFFE 197
Cunliffe, Susannah 788
CUNLITH 197
CUNNABELL 197
CUNNELL 197
Cunnell, Elizabeth 506
CUNNIBILL 197
CUNNINGHAM 197
Cunningham, John 180
Cunningham, Timothy 243
Curier, Hannah 274
Curlos, Mary 171
CURNEY 197
CURRIER 183, 197
Currier, Ann 43

Currier, Anne 43
Currier, Elizabeth 450
Currier, Hannah 707
Currier, Mary 412
Currier, Richard 640, 651
Currier, Sarah 633, 676
CURRY 197
Curry, Sarah 14
CURTES 197
Curtes, Anna 285
Curtes, Hannah 285
CURTICE 197, 198, 199
Curtice, Abigail 324, 631
Curtice, Anna 285
Curtice, Elizabeth 477
Curtice, Hannah 285
Curtice, James 631
Curtice, John 162
Curtice, Lydia 739
Curtice, Martha 159
Curtice, Mary 335
Curtice, Mehitable 467
Curtice, Rebecca 667
Curtice, Sarah 742
CURTIS 197, 198, 199
Curtis, Abiel 30
Curtis, Abigail 30, 76, 324, 378,
    495, 631
Curtis, Abigail Thompson 400
Curtis, Anna 736
Curtis, Anne 736
Curtis, Barnabas 176
Curtis, Benjamin 710
Curtis, Deliverance 233
Curtis, Dodavah 65
Curtis, Dorothy 97
Curtis, Elizabeth 39, 103, 335,
    393, 426, 469, 477, 523, 532,
    637, 712, 769, 832, 837
Curtis, Hannah 296, 417, 462,
    511, 529
Curtis, Henry 793
Curtis, Israel 776
Curtis, James 631
Curtis, Jane 172, 426
Curtis, John 87, 438
Curtis, Joseph 843
Curtis, Katherine 647, 721
Curtis, Lydia 178, 739
Curtis, Martha 159
Curtis, Mary 29, 171, 190, 217,
    362, 382, 397, 413, 433, 472,
    636
Curtis, Mercy 758
Curtis, Philip 292
Curtis, Rebecca 21, 573
Curtis, Richard 717
Curtis, Richarden 143
Curtis, Ruth 438
Curtis, Samuel 87, 837
Curtis, Sarah 98, 176, 254, 365,
    655, 689, 794, 837
Curtis, Thomas 72
Curtis, William 311
CURTISS 198
Curtiss, Elizabeth 763
Curtiss, Jonathan 406, 670
Curtiss, Sarah 325
CURWEN 184
Cushen, Deborah 474
CUSHING 199
Cushing, Caleb (Rev.) 14
Cushing, Daniel 733
Cushing, Deborah 98, 474, 728,
    836
Cushing, Jeremiah 816
Cushing, John 384
Cushing, Sarah 414

Cushing, Thomas 97
CUSHMAN 199, 200
Cushman, James 263, 761
Cushman, Lydia 344
Cushman, Mary 407
Cushman, Sarah 355, 376, 390
Custis, Joseph 502
Custis, Mary 642
CUTHBERTSON 307
Cuthbertson, Cuthbert 603, 768
Cuthbertson, Mary Priest 600
Cutheridge, Margaret 400
CUTLER 128, 200
Cutler, Abigail 353, 503
Cutler, Anne 79
Cutler, Dorcas 817
Cutler, Elizabeth 561
Cutler, Hannah 152, 172, 326,
    489, 586, 607, 817
Cutler, James 143, 440
Cutler, Jemima 692
Cutler, Joanna 644
Cutler, John 367, 374, 463
Cutler, Lydia Mercer 702
Cutler, Mary 172, 236, 367, 488,
    514, 623, 686
Cutler, Penelope Arnold Goulding
    308
Cutler, Rebecca 64, 253
Cutler, Ruth 685
Cutler, Samuel 752
Cutler, Sarah 254, 300, 556, 577,
    771
Cutler, Susanna 122, 470
CUTT 200
Cutt, Hannah 773
Cutt, Joseph 332
Cutt, Mary 97, 153
Cutt, Robert 143
Cutt, Sarah 516
CUTTER 201
Cutter, Barbara 183
Cutter, Elizabeth 335, 631, 706,
    711
Cutter, Hannah 326
Cutter, Hepzibah 103
Cutter, Isabelle 723
Cutter, James 843
Cutter, Joanna 333, 414, 644
Cutter, Joyce 307
Cutter, Mary 650
Cutter, Rachel 817
Cutter, Rebecca 265
Cutter, Richard 16
Cutter, Sarah 265, 469
Cutter, Thomas 686
Cutter, Wm. 817
CUTTING 201
Cutting, John 58, 509
Cutting, Judith 106
Cutting, Lydia 698
Cutting, Mary 479, 515, 541
Cutting, Sarah 106, 362, 487
Cutting, Susan 532
Cutting, Susanna 532
Cutting, Susanna Stone 437
Cutting, Susannah Stone 477
Cuttinge, Susan 532
Cuttinge, Susanna 532
Cuttler, Mary 514
CUTTS 200, 201
Cutts, Anne 671
Cutts, Bridget 203, 316
Cutts, Bridgett 658
Cutts, Elizabeth 246
Cutts, Margaret 766
Cutts, Mary 569, 695
Cutts, Samuel 580

--- D ---

Da-, Em 249
Dabinott, Jane 531
Dabinott, Joane 531
Dabinott, John 780
DABY 217
DADEY 201
Dadey, William 488
Dady, Nathaniel 243, 478
DAFFORN 201
DAGAN 201
Daget, Anna 494
DAGGETT 225
Daggett, Elizabeth 812
Daggett, Esther 185
Daggett, Hepzibah 242
Daggett, Jemima 127
Daggett, Martha 190
Daggett, Mary 394
Daggle, Hannah 503
Dailie, Mary 259
DAIN 202
DAINES 202
Daines, Anne 229
Daines, Stepney 229
DAINS 202
DAKEN 201
DAKIN 201
Dakin, Sarah 833
Dakin, Simon 841
Dakin, Thomas 717
DALE 201, 212 see DEAL,
    DOYLE
Dale, Benjamin 428
Dale, Bridget 528
Dale, William 643, 687
DALEY 202
DALLEBAR 226
Dalling, Mary Natt Huntress 405
DALLISON 201
DALLY 201 see DALY
DALTIN 201
DALTON 201, 202
Dalton, Abiah 361
Dalton, Abigail 336
Dalton, Deborah 75
Dalton, Dorothy 212
Dalton, Elizabeth 657
Dalton, Mary 161
Dalton, Phebe 560
Dalton, Ruth 560
Dalton, Samuel 436, 725
Dalton, Timothy 372
DALY 202 see DALLY
DAM 202
Dam, Abigail 702
Dam, Bethia 749
Dam, Elizabeth 808
Dam, John 531, 808
Dam, Judith 742
Dam, Mary 133, 745
Damarill, Sarah 355
DAME 202
DAMEERE 214
DAMEN 202
Damen, Deborah 840
Damerill, Elizabeth 831
Damerill, John 831
DAMFARD 203
DAMFORD 203
Damforth, Mary 558
Dammon, Martha 194
DAMMOND 202
DAMON 202
Damon, Abigail 610
Damon, Deborah 840

Damon, Hannah 499
Damon, Henry 240
Damon, Jane 408, 590
Damon, John 30, 305
Damon, Margaret 116
Damon, Samuel 329
Damon, Silence 748
DAN 202
DANA 202
Dana, Deliverance 408
Dana, Elizabeth 615, 838
Dana, Hannah 544
DANE 202, 203, 212 see DEAN
Dane, Abigail 260
Dane, Elizabeth 278, 392, 423, 780
Dane, Francis 1
Dane, Hannah 309
Dane, John 144, 500, 533, 561
Dane, Mary 144, 569
Dane, Phebe 630
Dane, Rebecca 391
Dane, Sarah 362, 780
Danell, Elizabeth 143
DANEY 202
DANFORTH 203
Danforth, Abiel 270
Danforth, Ann 426
Danforth, Anna 97, 808
Danforth, Anne 97
Danforth, Elizabeth 59, 281, 360
Danforth, Jonathan 177
Danforth, Lydia 55, 842
Danforth, Mary 101, 556, 558, 580
Danforth, Samuel 631
Danforth, Sarah 285, 808
Dangan, Frances 380
DANIEL 203, 204
Daniel, Alice 31, 321
Daniel, Elizabeth 175, 257, 517, 695, 830
Daniel, Joanna 306, 738
Daniel, Johanna 738
Daniel, John 767
Daniel, Mary 281, 656, 776, 834
Daniel, Maudlin 718
Daniel, Rebecca 737
Daniel, Robert 18, 286, 414
Daniel, Samuel 275
Daniel, Stephen 294, 408
Daniel, Susanna 441
Daniel, Thomas 316
DANIELL 203
Daniell, Hannah 28
Daniell, Mary 281
DANIELLS 203
DANIELS 203
Daniels, Joseph 10, 149
Daniels, Mary 776
Daniels, Miriam 102
Daniels, Samuel 317
Daniels, Sarah 421, 516
DANIELSON 204
Danielson, James 638, 748
DANKS 204
Danks, Mehitable 346
Danks, Robert 788
DANSON 210
Danson, Elizabeth 542
Danson, George 542
DARBEY 216, 217
DARBY 216, 217
Darby, Alice 588
Darby, Elizabeth 471
Darby, Experience 272
Darby, John 648
Darby, Robert 266, 285

Darbye, Alice 836
Darbye, John 836
DARBYSHIRE 204
DARE 204
Dare, Sarah 562
DARELING 204
DARLEY 204, 217
DARLING 204
Darling, Alice Bowen Wheaton 799
Darling, Anna 803
Darling, Daniel 627
Darling, Ebenezer 485
Darling, Elizabeth 418
Darling, Hannah 492, 803
Darling, James 500
Darling, John 45, 331
Darling, Mary Clark Whiting 809
Darling, Mary Natt Huntress 405
Darling, Patience 485
Darling, Rebecca 119
Darling, Richard 511
Darling, Sarah 734
DARNTON 204
Darnton, William 59, 459
DARRELL 227
DARROW 204
Darrow, George 664
DART 204
Dart, Ann 518
Dart, Richard 232
Darte, Ambrose 96
Darte, Dinah 353
DARVALL 204
Darvell, Elizabeth 541
Darvell, Mary 541
DARVILL 204
DARWIN 204
Dassert, Mary 68
Dasset, Mary 89
Dasset, Sarah 525
DASSETT 204
Dassett, Hannah 317
Dassett, John 317
Dassett, Lydia 750
Dassett, Mary 68, 512
DASSITT 204
Dastin, Hannah 748
Dastin, Mary 174
D'Aubin, Elizabeth 652
Dauice, Rachel 307
Daulton, Elizabeth 257
DAVENISH 217
DAVENPORT 204, 205
Davenport, Abigail 169, 585
Davenport, Ann 644
Davenport, Elizabeth 246, 496
Davenport, John 485, 661
Davenport, Margaret 311
Davenport, Mary 498, 769
Davenport, Nathaniel 208
Davenport, Rebecca 773
Davenport, Sarah 426
Davenport, Truecross 512
Davenport, William 375, 623
Daves, Sarah 86
Davey, Ann 508
Davice, Mary 129, 412
DAVID see DICKWELL
David, Jeremiah 428
DAVIDS 205
Davids, David 223
DAVIE 209, 210
Davie, Alice 155
Davie, Mary 210
Davie, William 374
DAVIES 206, 208, 209
Davies, Elizabeth 549

DAVIS 205, 206, 207, 208, 209, 844
Davis, --- 769
Davis, Abigail 172, 236, 351, 624, 750, 765
Davis, Alice 155
Davis, Amy 318, 607
Davis, Ann 568
Davis, Anna 235
Davis, Benjamin 617
Davis, Constance 45
Davis, Cornelius 369
Davis, David 235
Davis, Deborah 298
Davis, Dolor 123
Davis, Ebenezer 285
Davis, Eleanor 404
Davis, Elizabeth 153, 167, 215, 352, 403, 468, 476, 500, 549, 645, 748, 804, 816
Davis, Ellen 306
Davis, Emanuel 758
Davis, Ephraim 155, 445
Davis, Fulk 211, 357
Davis, George 99, 141, 159, 620
Davis, Gertrude 651
Davis, Hannah 86, 95, 157, 218, 318, 327, 425, 436
Davis, Helena 306
Davis, Huldah 609
Davis, James 178, 250, 813
Davis, Joanna 183
Davis, John 30, 330, 459, 505, 607, 776
Davis, John (Maj.) 787
Davis, Joshabeth 828
Davis, Judith 251, 330
Davis, Lydia 170, 455, 507
Davis, Margaret 64, 240, 331, 597, 718
Davis, Margery 325, 549
Davis, Mary 26, 30, 43, 129, 157, 202, 209, 223, 286, 287, 301, 311, 329, 363, 374, 412, 463, 464, 477, 600, 630, 688, 739, 750, 797, 799, 832, 844
Davis, Mary Cook Taber 725
Davis, Mercy 546, 704, 846
Davis, Moses 149
Davis, Nichoas 469
Davis, Nicholas 42, 43, 411, 468
Davis, Patience 322, 625
Davis, Priscilla 321, 804
Davis, Rachel 307, 358, 790
Davis, Rebecca 5, 431, 455
Davis, Richard 144
Davis, Robert 9, 64, 440
Davis, Ruth 145, 336, 467, 641
Davis, Samuel 205, 605
Davis, Sarah 86, 99, 129, 130, 156, 168, 467, 507, 519, 550, 570, 613, 644, 682, 709, 801, 846
Davis, Simon 835
Davis, Stephen 778
Davis, Susanna 212, 235, 623
Davis, Thomas 10, 788
Davis, Tristam 20
Davis, William 186, 597, 739, 804
Davis, William (Capt.) 555
Davis, Zachary 91
Davise, Elizabeth 28
Davise, Hannah 656
DAVISON 209
Davison, Elizabeth 616
Davison, Mary 16, 378
Davison, Nicholas 16, 434
Davison, Sarah 222, 238, 480

DAVOL 209, 210
Davol, Mary 726
DAVOY 210
DAVY 210
Davy, Humphry 621
Davy, Thomas 517
DAWBY 216
DAWES 210
Dawes, Elizabeth 385, 591
Dawes, John 591
Dawes, Jonathan 325
Dawes, Mary 789
Dawes, Priscilla 633
Dawes, Rebecca 490, 522
Dawes, Samuel 154
Dawes, Sarah 189
Dawes, Susanna 206, 535
DAWSON 210
Dawson, George 194
Dawson, Judith 194
Dawson, Robert 643
DAY 210, 211
Day, Abigail 684
Day, Anna 478
Day, Bridget 428
Day, Elizabeth 674
Day, Hannah 250, 473
Day, John 196
Day, Lydia 438
Day, Mark 699
Day, Mary 160, 171, 250, 501,
   503, 551, 705
Day, Mehitable 438
Day, Ralph 3, 135, 642
Day, Robert 385, 499
Day, Sarah 124, 268, 330, 431,
   509
Day, Stephen 80
Day, Thomas 501
Daye, Dorothy 586
Daye, Mary 172
DAYLY 202
DAYNE 202
Dayns, Abraham 636
DAYTON 211
Dayton, --- 787
Dayton, Abigail 56
Dayton, Alice 34, 245
Dayton, Elizabeth 460
Dayton, Margaret 744
Dayton, Mary 210
Dayton, Rachel 784
Dayton, Ralph 68, 206, 357
Dayton, Samuel 56, 108
DEACON 211
Deacon, John 581
Deacon, Phebe 315
Deacon, Priscilla 607
Deacon, Prudence 492
DEAL 211 see DALE, DOYLE
Deal, Pity 186
DEALE 211, 212
Deament, --- 757
DEAN 202, 212
Dean, Abigail 243
Dean, Daniel 4
Dean, Elizabeth 243, 448, 761,
   773, 814
Dean, Grace 259
Dean, Hannah 23, 551, 580
Dean, James 554
Dean, John 342
Dean, Lydia 727
Dean, Margaret 329, 719
Dean, Mary 17, 814
Dean, Miriam 683, 828
Dean, Sarah 256, 342, 359, 786
Dean, Stephen 178

Dean, Susanna 634
Dean, Thomas 57
Dean, Walter 727
DEANE 202
Deane, Abigail 733
Deane, Alice 439
Deane, Deborah 745
Deane, Jonas 112
Deane, Martha 161, 598
Deane, Mary 126
Deane, Mehitable 814
Deane, Rachel 57, 68
Deane, Susanna 692
Deane, Thomas 593, 705
DEAR 213, 237
Dear, Elizabeth 228
Dear, Susanna 228
Dearbaugh, Anne 717
DEARBORN 212, 213
Dearborn, Esther 672
Dearborn, Godfrey 201
Dearborn, Mary 51
Dearborn, Sarah 76, 542
Deardes, Sarah 811
DEARE 213
DEARING 213
DEARLOVE 213
Dearnford, Eleanor 160
Dearseford, Eleanor 160
Dearslay, Anna 165
Dearslay, Hannah 165
DEAS 213
DEASE 213
DEATH 213
Death, Hepzibah 392
Death, John 238
Death, Mary 238
DEBELL 219
DEBLE 219
Deble, Hepzibah 300
DECKER 213
DeCOSTA 213
DECOSTER 213
DECREECHY 213
DECRO 213
DECROW 213
Decrow, Margaret 669
DEDICOT 213
Dedson, Rachel Allan 673
DEE 213
DEEBLE 219
DEEDBLE 219
Deekes, Abigail 556
Deengrine, Henry 7
DEEPAR 217
Deepar, Hannah 692
DEER 237
DEERE 213
DEERING 213
Deering, Bethiah 537
Deering, Elizabeth 32
Deering, George 32
Deering, Henry 64
Deering, Joanna 186, 515
Deering, Rachel 695
Deering, Roger 189
Deering, Samuel 695
Deering, Sarah 354, 368, 513
DEEX 222
deFlecheur, Edward 818
DeFOREST 213
DEGRISHA 213
deHooch, Helena 763
Deighton, Frances 821
Deighton, Jane 478
DeKAY 213
DELAND 213
DELANE 213

DELANO 213, 214
Delano, --- 797
Delano, Deborah 797
Delano, Mary 234
Delano, Philip 305
Delano, Sarah 231
Delano, Thomas 48, 49
DELANOE 213
Delanoy, Mary 234
Delans, Rebecca 153
DELAROCK 214
DELL 214, 221
Dell, George 341
Dell, Sarah 103, 801
Dellens, Rebecca 153
DELLOCLOCE 214
Dellocloce, Rachel 36
deLovel, Mary 169
DELVER 214
Deman, Mary 405
DEMANZADAY 214
DEMEN 214, 218
DEMERIT 214
DEMERITT 214
DEMERRETT 214
DEMERRY 214
Demick, Mehitable 763
DEMING 214, 218
Deming, Abigail 479
Deming, Comfort 57, 522
Deming, Elizabeth 57, 274, 510,
   795, 843
Deming, Hannah 57
Deming, Mary 405, 686, 820
Deming, Mercy 198, 843
Deming, Rachel 518
Deming, Sarah 515, 626
Demming, Ruth 211
DEMONSEDAY 214
DEMSDALL 214
DENBO 214
Denbo, Richard 118
Denbo, Salathial 319
Denbo, Selathiel 673
DENBOW 214
Dengayne, Henry 7
DENHAM 214, 234, 235
Denham, Alexander 571, 688
Denham, Hannah 160
Denham, Isaac 582
Denham, Martha 564
Denham, Rebecca 210, 374
Denham, Sarah 365, 554
Denham, Thomas 234, 365
DENING 215
DENISON 214, 215
Denison, Ann 554
Denison, Borodell 702
Denison, Elizabeth 613
Denison, George 347
Denison, Hannah 91, 107, 149,
   654
Denison, John 185
Denison, Margaret 106, 494
Denison, Martha 735, 803, 813
Denison, Mary 81, 190, 555, 605,
   737
Denison, Mary Boreman Robbins
   627
Denison, May 605
Denison, Priscilla 562
Denison, Robert 480
Denison, Sarah 29, 345, 572, 702
Denkin, Margaret 614
DENMAN 215, 298
Denman, John 679
Denman, Mary 498
DENMARK 215

Denmark, James 468
Dennatt, Sarah 338
Denne, Elizabeth 780
Dennen, Agnes 46, 225
Dennen, Annis 46, 225
Dennen, Em 249
DENNETT 215
Dennett, Alexander 194
Dennett, Amy 4
Dennett, Deborah Morse Wincoll 827
Dennett, Grace 697
Dennett, John 663
DENNING 215
Denning, Agnes 225
Denning, Annis 225
Denning, Em 249
Denning, Mary 211
DENNIS 215, 216
Dennis, Agnes 753
Dennis, Ann 106
Dennis, Annas 753
Dennis, Edmund 545
Dennis, Edward 545
Dennis, George 613
Dennis, James 195
Dennis, Judith 467, 565
Dennis, Marah 51
Dennis, Martha 55
Dennis, Mary 51, 414, 441, 456, 588, 842
Dennis, Sarah 314, 545
Dennis, Susanna 373
Dennis, Thomas 629, 659
Dennis, Waitawhile Makepeace Cooper 181
DENNISON 214
Dennison, Elizabeth 633
Dennison, John 351, 493
Dennison, Margaret 78
Dennison, Sarah 630
Dennison, William 601
Dennott, John 663
DENNY 216
Denny, Elizabeth 780
DENSLOW 216
Denslow, Deborah 389
Denslow, Elizabeth 440
Denslow, Hannah 124
Denslow, Joan 177
Denslow, Mary 640, 709
Denslow, Rebecca 547
Denslow, Ruth 182
Denslow, Susanna 378
Denslow, Temperance 113
DENTON 216
Denton, Abigail 704
Denton, Clement 681
Denton, Daniel 453, 470, 808
Denton, Hannah 689, 752
Denton, Mary 687
Denton, Phebe 739
Denton, Richard 278
Denton, Samuel 640
Denton, Sarah 511
Derbey, Alice 78
Derbey, John 78
DERBY 216, 217
Derby, Ann 614
Derby, Christopher 151
Derby, Edward 376
Derby, Elizabeth 471
Derby, Experience 272
Derby, Francis 614
Derby, John 151, 648, 671
Derby, Mary 537
Derby, Sarah 470
Dereslye, Margaret 793

DERICH 217
Derich, Michael 621
Derifield, Ann 696
Derifield, Barnabas 696
DERRICK 217
Derrick, Ann 103
Derrick, Anne 103
Derring, Elizabeth 424
DERRY 217
Derry, Deliverance 588
Derry, Elizabeth 588
Derry, James 588
Derry, John 588
Dersley, Ann 762
Desborough, Abigail 44
Desborough, Hannah 432
Desborough, Mary 604, 696
Desborough, Nicholas 718
Desborough, Phebe 432
Desborough, Thomas 536
Desbrough, Elizabeth 421, 635
Desbrow, Thomas 536
DESCHAMPS 217
DESPARD 217
Desper, Hannah 692
DEUALL 222
DEUCE 217
DEUING 217
Deurcant, Mary 293
DEUSBERRY 217
DEVAULX 217
DEVEL 210
DEVENISH 217
DEVEREAUX 217
Devereaux, Emma 565
Devereaux, Hannah 323
DEVEREUX 217
Devereux, Ann 536
Devereux, Anne 84, 536
Devereux, Bethia 48
Devereux, Hannah 445, 724
Devereux, John 559
Devereux, Sarah 1
DEVERSON 217
DEVOL 209, 217
DEVOTION 217
Devotion, Elizabeth 793
Devotion, Hannah 642
Devotion, Martha 642
Devotion, Mary 207
Devotion, Sarah 326
DEW 217 see DEWEY
Dew, Elizabeth 616
Dew, Thomas 33
Deweh, Hannah 537
DEWER 235
DEWEY 217
Dewey, Abigail 23
Dewey, Ann 839
Dewey, Elizabeth 538, 789
Dewey, Experience 304
Dewey, Israel 372
Dewey, Margaret 73, 376
Dewey, Mary 22
Dewey, Sarah 23
Dewey, Thomas 23, 160, 531, 576
DEWING 218
Dewing, Anna 813
Dewing, Deborah 354
Dewing, Lydia 30
DeWOLF 218
DeWolf, Alea 175
DeWolf, Alice 175
DeWolf, Mary 459
DeWolf, Simon 158
DeWolf, Susanna 143
DeWolfe, Hannah 715
Dewsbury, Esther 213

Dewsbury, Hester 213
DEXTER 218
Dexter, Abigail 19, 264, 337
Dexter, Alice 528
Dexter, Ann 599
Dexter, Elizabeth 46, 136, 502
Dexter, Frances 840
Dexter, James 19, 339, 355
Dexter, John 80
Dexter, Mary 9, 42, 285, 544
Dexter, Sarah 80, 107, 587
Dexter, Stephen 387
Dey, Jane 837
Diament, Mary 388
DIAMOND 218, 219
Diamond, Aholiab 375
Diamond, Andrew 317
Diamond, Edward 75
Diamond, Elizabeth 756
Diamond, Grace 463, 745, 746, 757
Diamond, Joan 137
Diamond, Margaret 753, 754
Diamond, Mary 697
Diamond, Thomas 798
Diamond, William 137
DIBBLE 219
Dibble, Abigail 265, 357
Dibble, Ebenezer 372
Dibble, Hepzibah 300
Dibble, Joanna 13
Dibble, Lydia 589
Dibble, Mary 253
Dibble, Miriam 304
Dibble, Sarah 319
Dibble, Sarah Waterbury 753
Dibble, Susanna 13
Dibble, Thomas 355, 375
Dibble, Zachariah 790
DIBBS 219
DIBELL 219
DIBOL 219
DICER 222
Dicer, Elizabeth 728
Dicer, Honor 415
Dickam, Abigail 741
DICKARSON 219
Dickason, Elizabeth 549
DICKENS 219
Dickens, Dorcas 224
Dickens, Mary 611
Dickens, Mercy 488
Dickens, Nathaniel 109
Dickens, Sarah 109
DICKENSON 219
Dickenson, Lydia 135
Dickenson, Martha 608
Dickenson, Obadiah 373
Dickenson, Phebe 406
DICKERMAN 219
Dickerman, Abigail 696
Dickerman, Abraham 390
Dickerman, Ellen 116
Dickerman, Hannah 50, 150, 262, 412
Dickerman, Mary 50
Dickerman, Ruth 92
Dickerman, Sarah 696
Dickerman, Thomas 116
DICKERSON 220
Dickerson, Abigail 140
Dickerson, Charles 136
Dickerson, Elizabeth 443
Dickerson, John 136
Dickerson, Mary 265, 415
Dickerson, Sybil 443, 536
Dickerson, Thomas 265, 587
DICKESON 219, 220

DICKINSON 219, 219, 220, 221
Dickinson, Abigail 189
Dickinson, Ann 160
Dickinson, Anna 441
Dickinson, Azariah 489
Dickinson, Charles 136
Dickinson, Elizabeth 3, 51, 342, 842
Dickinson, Elizabeth Tapley 49
Dickinson, Esther 686
Dickinson, Frances 42
Dickinson, Hannah 160, 300, 304, 397, 419, 431, 441, 460, 698
Dickinson, Isabel 342
Dickinson, John 13, 17, 136, 368, 637
Dickinson, Joseph 637
Dickinson, Mary 17, 451, 539, 639, 686
Dickinson, Mehitable 410
Dickinson, Mercy 5, 142, 231, 342
Dickinson, Nathaniel 211, 304, 330, 762, 843
Dickinson, Rebecca 686
Dickinson, Samuel 842
Dickinson, Sarah 17, 420, 431, 450, 691
Dickinson, Thomas 803
DICKISON 220
Dickkeesonne, Mary 639
Dicks, Deborah 44
Dicks, Edward 44
Dicksey, John 257
DICKSON 219, 220, 223
Dickson, Hannah 282
Dickson, Robert 559
Dicson, Mary 128
DIER 237, 238
DIGGENS 221
DIGGER 221
DIGGINS 221
Dighton, Catharine 232
Dighton, Catherine 332
Dighton, Frances 821
Dighton, Jane 478, 530
Dighton, Katharine 11
DIKE 222, 238
Dike, Agnes 155
Dike, Anthony 581, 591
Dike, Charity 8
Dike, Elizabeth 372
Dike, Margery 591
Dike, Mary 46, 67
Dike, Rebecca 646
Dike, Tabitha 581
Dikerson, Sarah 608
Dikes, Rebecca 270
Dikes, Sarah 403
DILL 214, 221 see DELL
Dill, George 341
Dill, Mary 627
Dill, Thankful 615
Dill, Thanks 615
Diller, Elizabeth 609
DILLINGHAM 221
Dillingham, Deborah 828
Dillingham, Dorcas 239
Dillingham, Elizabeth 42, 828
Dillingham, Hannah 740
Dillingham, John 320
Dillingham, Mary 828
Dillingham, Oseth 828
Dillingham, Oziah 828
Dillingham, Rebecca 320
Dillingham, Sarah 131, 425, 427
DILLOROCK 214
Dillos, Elizabeth 609
Dimick, Mehitable 150

Dimick, Thankful 630
Dimmock, Elizabeth 660
Dimmock, Susanna 667
Dimmock, Thomas 733
Dimmock, Timothy 291
DIMOCK 221
Dimock, Thmas 733
DIMON 218
Dimon, Abigail 679
Dimon, Elizabeth 756
Dimon, Elizabeth Norman 375
Dimon, Mary 543
Dimon, Moses 302
Dimon, Rebecca 841
Dimon, Ruth 211
Dimond, Abigail 679
Dimond, Elizabeth 453
Dimond, Moses 358, 371
Dimond, Ruth 663
Dinclay, John 608
DINELEY 221
DINELY 221
Dinely, Alice 192
DINGE 221
DINGHAM 221
Dingham, Henry 7
Dingle, Mary 211
DINGLES 744
DINGLEY 221, 222
Dingley, Anna 807
Dingley, Hannah 275, 430
Dingley, Mary 700
Dingley, Sarah 271, 275
DINGLY 222
DINHAM 234
Dinley, Mary 314
Dinnis, Mary 414
DINSDALE 222
Dinsdale, Adam 486
Dinsdale, Thomas 501
Dinsdale, William 479
DINSDALL 222
Dinsdell, Mary 469
Dinsley, Mary 314
DIONS 222
DIPPLE 222
Dipple, Grace 33, 788
Dircks, Jane 302
DIRGEY 235
DIRKYE 236
DISBOROUGH 222
Disborough, Abigail 272
Disbro, Thomas 536
DISBROW 222
Disbrow, Mary 696
Disbrow, Rebecca 108
Disbrow, Sarah 245
Disburrow, Mary 604
DISER 222
Disiter, Edward 112
Disiter, Hannah 112
DISPAU 222
DISPAW 222
DISSATER 222
Dissater, Edward 112
Dissater, Hannah 112
DISSPAW 222
DITCHFIELD 222
DITSON 222
Divall, Mary 454
Divan, Elizabeth 66
DIVEN 222
Diven, John 21
Diven, Mary 712, 832
DIVOL 222 see DAVOL
DIVOLL 222
Divoll, Hannah 435
Divoll, John 478

DIX 222, 223, 238 see DYKE
Dix, Abigail 556
Dix, Deborah 44
Dix, Edson 436
Dix, Edward 44
Dix, Elizabeth 704, 768
Dix, Hannah 618
Dix, John 269
Dix, Margaret 751
Dix, Mary 41, 104, 620
Dix, Mercy 308
Dix, Rebecca 270
Dix, Samuel 464
Dix, Sarah 105, 282, 403, 454, 456
Dixcy, Anna 429
Dixcy, Elizabeth 359
Dixcy, Hannah 86, 429
Dixcy, John 257
DIXEY 223
Dixey, Abigail 684, 713
Dixey, Elizabeth 569
Dixey, Mary 382
Dixey, Sarah 291, 331
Dixey, Thomas 350
DIXI 223
Dixie, Elizabeth 569
DIXON 223
Dixon, Abigail 741
Dixon, Ann 94
Dixon, Anne 14
Dixon, Hannah 282
Dixon, Mary 128, 702
Dixon, Robert 559
Dixon, Susannah 287
Dixon, William 287, 517
DIXWELL 205, 223 see DAVID
Dixwell, John 467
Dixwell, Mary 173
DIXY 223
Dixy, Ann 360
Dixy, Elizabeth 518
Dixy, Mary 836
DOAK 223
DOAN 223
DOANE 223
Doane, Abigail 221, 475
Doane, Ann 761, 846
Doane, Anna 761
Doane, Constance 665
Doane, Constant 665
Doane, Daniel 192, 575
Doane, Ephraim 691
Doane, John 691
Doane, Lydia 368
Doane, Martha 343, 343
Doane, Rebecca 503, 551
DOBSON 223
DOBYSON 223
Dockum, John 67
DOD 223
DODD 223
Dodd, Ann 541
Dodd, Anne 279
Dodd, Anne 424
Dodd, Elizabeth 641
Dodd, George 26, 468
Dodd, Hannah 280
Dodd, Joseph 444
Dodd, Mary Davis 844
Dodd, Mehitable 468
Dodd, Mercy 77
Dodd, Sarah 684
DODDRIDGE 227
Dodg, Elizabeth 751
Dodg, Joshua 739
Dodg, Mary 751
Dodg, Sarah 209

DODGE 223, 224
Dodge, Ann 611
Dodge, Anna 244
Dodge, Deliverance 558
Dodge, Elizabeth 335, 366, 751
Dodge, Hannah 322, 595, 836, 837
Dodge, Jane 700
Dodge, John 836
Dodge, Joshua 739
Dodge, Margaret 611
Dodge, Martha 209, 302
Dodge, Mary 366, 366, 446, 637, 751, 836
Dodge, Prudence 476
Dodge, Ruth 410
Dodge, Sarah 209, 219, 291, 836
Dodge, William 35, 191, 452
DODSON 224
Dodson, Bethiah 249
Dodson, Margaret 742
Dodson, Mary 83
Dodson, Patience 583
Dodson, Sarah 548, 706
DOE 224
Doe, Mary 622
Doety, Desire 670
Doety, Elizabeth 639
DOGED 224
DOGETT 224, 225
DOGGED 225
Dogged, Patience 19
Dogged, Thomas 19
Dogget, Ruth 30
DOGGETT 224, 225
Doggett, Amy 242
Doggett, Anna 494
Doggett, Hannah 77
Doggett, John 105, 599
Doggett, Martha 266
Doggett, Patience 19
Doggett, Rebecca 816
Doggett, Sarah 670
Doggett, Thomas 19, 151, 287, 689
DOGOOD 225
DOLBEAR 225
DOLBEARE 225
DOLBERRY 225
Dolberry, Abraham 735
Dolberry, Andrew 175
Dolberry, Susannah 195
Dolberson, Mary 304
DOLBERY 225
Dolbison, Mary 304
DOLE 225
Dole, Apphia 166
Dole, Elizabeth 590
Dole, Hannah 515, 771
Dole, Henry 166
Dole, Richard 101, 775
Dole, Sarah 324
DOLEBEAR 225
Dolens, Mary 505
DOLEVER 225
Dolever, Rebecca 238
Dolever, Samuel 293
Doling, Elizabeth 216
Doling, Mary 505, 739
DOLITTLE 226
DOLLABER 225
Dollen, Joanna 432, 485
Dollenger, Mary 312
Dollever, Dorothy 772
Dolliber, Peter 785
Dollin, Margaret 815
Dollin, Patience 485
Dolling, Margaret 815

Dolling, Mary 312
Dollins, Edward 515
Dollins, John 725
DOLLIVER 225, 226
Dolliver, Joseph 255
Dolliver, Mary 29, 652
Dolliver, Peter 785
Dolliver, Rebecca 238
Dolliver, Richard 46
DOLLOFF 226
Dolloff, Mary 305
Dolman, Elizabeth 265
DOLOVER 225
Dolover, Mary 400
Dolt, Anne 616
Dolteris, --- 16
Dolton, Samuel 725
Doman, Abigail Bachelor 51
Dominy, Mary 562
DONELL 226
DONELSON 204
DONHAM 234
Donice, Mary 441
Donier, Mary 441
DONNELL 226
Donnell, Abigail 846
Donnell, John 102
Donnell, Joseph 260
Donnell, Sarah 39
Donner, Sarah 475
Donstall, Ann 217
DOOLITTLE 226
Doolittle, Abigail 282
Doolittle, Abraham 474
Doolittle, Elizabeth 101
Doolittle, Esther 761
Doolittle, John 67, 76, 542
Doolittle, Sarah 2, 272
Door, Bryan 81
Dorby, Elizabeth 84, 509
DORCHESTER 226, 442
Dorchester, Anthony 344, 442
Dorchester, Benjamin 375
Dorchester, Mary 344
Dorchester, Sarah 704
DORE 226 see DORY
Dore, Joanna 85, 130
Dore, Mary 391
DOREY 226
DORIFIELD 226
Dorifield, Barnabas 696
DORMAN 226, 227
Dorman, Damaris 154
Dorman, Edmund 118, 696
Dorman, Hannah 420, 438, 631
Dorman, John 181, 392
Dorman, Judith 595
Dorman, Mary 253, 279, 458
Dorman, Thomas (Jr.) 332
DORR 227
Dorr, Mary 391
DORRELL 227
Dorselye, Margaret 793
DORY 227 see DORE
DOTEN 227
Doten, Edward 112
Doten, Hannah 213
Dotey, Martha 522
DOTTERIDGE 227
DOTY 227
Doty, Desire 383, 670, 700
Doty, Edward 112, 578
Doty, Elizabeth 521, 542, 610, 639
Doty, Hannah 213
Doty, Joseph 244
Doty, Martha 522, 806
Doty, Mary 11, 352

Doty, Sarah 782
Doty, Thomas 153
DOUBLEDAY 227
DOUGHTEY 227
Doughton, Mary 272
DOUGHTY 227
Doughty, Elizabeth 170
Doughty, Francis (Rev.) 516
Doughty, Mary 98, 368, 644
DOUGLAS 227, 228
Douglas, Ann 73, 295, 366, 783
Douglas, Anne 295
Douglas, Elizabeth 144, 204, 640
Douglas, Hannah 406
Douglas, John 529
Douglas, Sarah 175, 430, 595
Dounton, Mary 272
DOUSE 229, 230
Douse, Elizabeth 237
Douse, John 278
DOUTY 227
DOVE 228
Dove, Deborah 495
Dove, Elizabeth 771
Dove, Hannah 346
Dover, Mary 576
DOW 228
Dow, Hannah 91, 213, 280, 325
Dow, Henry 321, 438, 542, 551
Dow, Jeremiah 721
Dow, John 668
Dow, Martha 291, 363, 550, 559
Dow, Mary 157, 622, 816
Dow, Phebe 241, 689
Dow, Ruhamah 207
Dow, Samuel 28, 295
Dow, Sarah 690
DOWD 228
Dowd, Mary 400
Dowd, Rebecca 254
Dowd, Samuel 254
Dowd, Sarah 87
DOWDING 228
DOWELL 228, 749
Dowell, Elizabeth 565
Dowling, Mary 505
Dowman, Joanna 469
DOWN 228, 229
Down, John 28
Down, Thomas 377
Downam, Elizabeth 204
Downam, Joanna 600
DOWNE 228, 229
Downe, Edmund 782
Downe, Eglin Hatherly 341, 673
Downe, Elizabeth 109
Downe, Jane 666
Downe, Mary 421, 841
Downe, Mary Ann 421
Downe, Rebecca 186
DOWNER 229
Downer, Mary 660
Downer, Sarah 475
DOWNES 228, 229
Downes, Hannah 438
Downes, Thomas 377
DOWNHAM 229 see DUNNING
Downham, Elizabeth 204
Downham, Joanna 600
Downham, John 234
Downham, Sarah 200
DOWNING 229
Downing, Abigail 514
Downing, Amy 131
Downing, Ann 294, 712
Downing, Anne 92
Downing, Elizabeth 838
Downing, Emanuel 712

Downing, Hannah 277
Downing, Joanna 381, 662
Downing, John 381, 403, 501
Downing, Joshua 753
Downing, Lucy 540
Downing, Margaret 173, 533
Downing, Mary 712
Downing, Priscilla 137
Downing, Richard 165, 805
Downing, Sarah 478, 502
Downing, Susanna 628
DOWNS 228, 229
Downs, Ebenezer 484
Downs, Katharine 807
Downs, Mary 178
Downs, Thomas 334
DOWNTON 229
DOWSE 229, 230
Dowse, Deborah 172
Dowse, Elizabeth 12, 336, 452, 508
Dowse, Hannah 386
Dowse, John 278, 457
Dowse, Lydia 410
Dowse, Mary 372
Dowse, Naomi 173
Dowse, Relief 303
Dowse, Sarah 234, 237
Dowsett, Thomasin 333
DOWSO 230
DOXEY 230
Doxey, Katherine 449
Doxey, Thomas 449
DOYLE 230 see DALE, DEAL
DRAGHADY 230
DRAKE 230
Drake, --- 376, 806
Drake, Abigail 217, 372
Drake, Amy 578
Drake, Elizabeth 57, 113, 246, 279, 297, 338, 578, 631
Drake, Esther 328
Drake, Gillian 264
Drake, Hannah 361, 369, 395
Drake, Hepzibah 550
Drake, Hester 328
Drake, Jane 776
Drake, Joan 611
Drake, Job 178
Drake, John 65, 395, 767
Drake, Joseph 715
Drake, Lydia 472
Drake, Mary 73, 81, 174, 280, 297, 426, 491, 594, 648, 672
Drake, Mindwell 472
Drake, Nathaniel 66
Drake, Rebecca 160, 425
Drake, Ruth 40, 678
Drake, Samuel 42
Drake, Sarah 464
Drake, Susanna 89
Drake, Susannah 730
Drake, Thomas 139
DRAKELY 230
DRAPER 230, 231
Draper, Adam 236
Draper, Bridget 203
Draper, Daniel 708
Draper, Deborah 485
Draper, Elizabeth 709
Draper, Esther 628
Draper, Hannah Hunt 532
Draper, Lydia 454, 622, 811
Draper, Mary 470
Draper, Miriam 379, 420
Draper, Nathaniel 657
Draper, Patience 139
Draper, Roger 332

Draper, Sarah 332
Draper, Susanna 30
DRESSER 231
Dresser, Elizabeth 387, 710
Dresser, Jane 573
Dresser, John 220
Dresser, Martha 596
Dresser, Mary 277, 741
Dresser, Samuel 545
DREW 231
Drew, Abigail 97, 248
Drew, Ann 785
Drew, Bethia Bullen Colburn 167
Drew, Deliverance 154
Drew, Elizabeth 154, 213, 579
Drew, Elizabeth Dowse Larkin 452
Drew, Erzoman 232
Drew, Hannah 102, 273
Drew, Martha 741
Drew, Mary 247
Drew, Rosemund 232
Drew, Samuel 413
Drew, Thomas 247
Drew, William 273
DRING 231
DRINKER 231
Drinker, Elizabeth 309
DRINKWATER 231
DRISCO 231
Drisco, Sarah 730
Drisco, Timothy 424
DRISCOLL 231
DRIVER 231, 232
Driver, Ruth 597
Driver, Sarah 494
Driver, William 317
DROWN 232
Drown, Leonard 131
DRUCE 231, 232
Drue, Ann 785
Drue, Erzoman 232
Drue, Rosemund 232
DRUMMOND 232
Drummond, John 337
DRURY 232
Drury, Hugh 271
Drury, Mary 8
DRUSE 231, 232
Druse, Mary 79, 231
DRY 232
Dry, Ann 483
DUBBLEDEE 227
Dubblin, Elizabeth 652
DUBLEDEE 227
Duce, Israel 372
DUDGEON 232
DUDLEY 232, 233, 235
Dudley, Abigail 398, 434, 786
Dudley, Ann 92
Dudley, Anne 373
Dudley, Deborah 93, 657, 736, 769
Dudley, Dorothy 458
Dudley, Elizabeth 335
Dudley, John 520
Dudley, Lucia 384
Dudley, Lucretia 384
Dudley, Mary 264, 271, 343, 494, 843
Dudley, Mercy 836
Dudley, Patience 214
Dudley, Paul 750
Dudley, Rebecca 480
Dudley, Ruth 812
Dudley, Samuel 439
Dudley, Sarah 430, 549
Dudley, Thomas 11, 332, 729

DUDSON 233
Dudson, Abigail 437
Dudson, Joseph 474
Dudson, Mary 378
DUE 217
Due, Elizabeth 367
Due, Mercy 813
DUEIN 218
Duein, Lydia 30
DUEING 218
Dueing, Anna 813
DUFFER 606
Duffy, Hannah 231
Dugald, Hannah 503
DUGGALL 233
DUGGELL 233
DUGLAS 227
DUING 217
DULEY 233
DUMBLETON 233
Dumbleton, Elizabeth 124
Dumbleton, Hannah 504
Dumbleton, John 58
Dumbleton, Lydia 124
Dumbleton, Marah 211
Dumbleton, Mary 58, 211
Dumbleton, Mercy 58
Dumbleton, Rebecca 461
Dumbleton, Sarah 461, 637
DUMER 233
DUMERY 214
DUMMER 233
Dummer, Hannah 10, 92, 247
Dummer, Jane 662
Dummer, Joan 531
Dummer, Margaret 161
Dummer, Richard 122
Dummin, Jane 590
DUNBAR 233
Dunbar, James 687
Dunbar, John 59
Dunbar, Mary 345
Dunbar, Sarah 293, 295
Dunbar, Thomas 233
DUNCAN 233
Duncan, Hannah 656
Duncan, John 236
Duncan, Mary 651
Duncan, Sarah 481
Dunck, Deborah 514
Duncklee, Elnathan 632
Dunckler, Nathaniel 664
DUNCKLEY 233
Dunckley, Ruth 559
DUNGAN 233
Dungan, Barbara 41
Dungan, Elizabeth 796
Dungan, Mary 622
Dungan, William 155, 766
DUNHAM 233, 234, 235, 676
Dunham, Abigail 25
Dunham, Hannah 8, 160, 566, 624
Dunham, Hester 624
Dunham, John 229
Dunham, Jonathan 408
Dunham, Lydia 47
Dunham, Mary 339
Dunham, Mehitable 359
Dunham, Mercy 352
Dunham, Persis 598, 665
Dunham, Rebecca 365
Dunham, Samuel 257, 786
Dunham, Sarah 200, 393, 439, 554
Dunham, Susannah 338
DUNK 234
Dunk, Lydia Brown Lord 595
Dunk, Thomas 106, 473, 539
Dunken, Hannah 656

Dunken, Johanna 167
DUNKIN 233
Dunkin, John 236
Dunkin, Sarah 481
DUNKLEE 233
DUNKLIN 234
DUNN 234
Dunn, Hepzibah 601
Dunn, Nicholas 13
DUNNELL 234
DUNNING 229, 234, 235 see DOWNHAM, DUNHAM
DUNSTER 235
Dunster, Deborah 817
Dunster, Elizabeth 87, 769, 817
Dunster, Faith 550
Dunster, Henry 306
Dunster, Jonathan 241, 442
Dunster, Mary 541, 817
Dunthing, Elnathan 632
DUNTLIN 235
Duntlin, Hannah 460
Duntlin, Ruth 825
DUNTON 235
Dunton, Elizabeth 254
Dunton, Hannah 822
Dunton, Hepzibah 601
Dunton, Mary 29
Dunton, Ruth 597
Dunton, Samuel 564, 623
Dunton, Sarah 287
Dunwell, Mary 391
DUNWILL 234
DUPERY 235
DURANT 235
Durant, Abigail 411, 744
Durant, Elizabeth 769
Durant, George 76
Durant, John 380
Durant, Mary 146, 666, 776
Durant, Sarah 744
DURE 235
Duren, Sarah 744
DURFEE 235
Durfee, Ann 597
Durfee, Thomas 753
DURFEY 235
DURGEE 235
DURGEN 235
DURGIN 235
Durgin, James 205
Durgin, William 274
Durgy, Martha 290
DURHAM 235
Durham, Sarah 203
Durin, Jane 250
Durin, Susana 66
Durine, Mary 776
DURKEE 235
Durkee, Martha 290
DURRAM 234, 235
Durrant, Abigail 411
DURRELL 235
DURRUM 204
DUSEBERRY 217
DUSTIN 236
Dustin, Elizabeth 322
Dustin, Hannah 148, 748
Dustin, Mary 104, 174
Duston, Elizabeth 251, 440
Duston, Thomas 129
DUTCH 236
Dutch, Alice 202, 500, 533
Dutch, Benjamin 20
Dutch, Elizabeth 626
Dutch, Esther 250
Dutch, Grace 378
Dutch, Hannah 173

Dutch, Hester 250
Dutch, Hezekiah 419
Dutch, Martha 460
Dutch, Mary 187, 250
Dutch, Samuel 408
Dutch, Susanna 441
DUTCHFIELD 222
duTrieux, Sarah 213
DUTTON 236
Dutton, Benjamin 233, 387
Dutton, Elizabeth 34, 189
Dutton, Joseph 269, 686
Dutton, Mary 338
Dutton, Sarah 223, 464
Dutton, Susan 235
Dutton, Susanna 235
Dutton, Susannah 380
Dutton, Thomas 387
DUTY 236
DWELLEY 236
DWELLY 236
DWIGHT 236, 237
Dwight, Hannah 808
Dwight, John 626, 734
Dwight, Mary 577
Dwight, Sarah 618
Dwight, Timothy 4, 7, 244, 267, 292
DWINELL 234
Dwinell, Mary 391
Dwite, Sarah 618
Dyble, Abigail 265
DYE 237
Dye, Ellen 393
DYER 237, 238
Dyer, --- 774
Dyer, Abigail 529
Dyer, Ann 154
Dyer, Charles 770
Dyer, Elizabeth 386, 401, 609, 753
Dyer, George 805
Dyer, Grace 14
Dyer, Henry 116, 166, 237, 618
Dyer, Jane 740
Dyer, John 231, 452
Dyer, Mary 81, 124, 292, 386, 576, 592, 615, 726, 807
Dyer, Rebecca 99
Dyer, Ruth 353
Dyer, Samuel 648, 767
Dyer, Sarah 642
Dyer, Thomas 281, 342
DYKE 237
Dyke, Jonathan 142
Dymond, Elizabeth 364
Dymond, John 512, 651, 830
Dymond, Rachel 518
Dymond, Sarah 813
DYMONT 218, 219
Dyne, Elizabeth 174
Dynn, Elizabeth 131, 174
Dynn, William 217

--- E ---

EADES 242
Eades, Mary 59
Eads, Nicholas 266
EAGER 6, 238 see AGER
Eager, Alice 748
Eager, Deborah 349
Eager, Hannah 714
Eager, Ruth 39
Eager, William 46, 168, 479, 748
EAGINS 369

Eagleston, William 325
EAME 239
EAMES 15, 16, 238, 239
Eames, Abigail 46, 796
Eames, Anna 270, 275
Eames, Anthony 275
Eames, Damaris 829
Eames, Elizabeth 77, 238, 449, 816
Eames, Gershom 779
Eames, Hannah 277, 816
Eames, Margaret 4
Eames, Margery 379, 414
Eames, Martha 620, 685
Eames, Mary 186, 435
Eames, Millicent 441, 698
Eames, Persis 583
Eames, Priscilla 591
Eames, Robert 277
Eames, Samuel 213
Eames, Thomas 550
EAMS 238
EARL 239
Earl, Dorcas 154
Earl, Sarah 185
EARLE 239
Earle, Caleb 368
Earle, Elizabeth 354
Earle, Martha 835
Earle, Mary 83, 185, 368, 397, 744
Earle, Prudence 235
Earle, Ralph 368
Earle, Sarah 183, 447
EARLL 239
EARLY 239
Early, Abia 594
Early, Abial 594
Early, Abigail 594
Earnes, Thomas 484
EARSE 28
EARTHY 239
EASDELL 239
EASMAN 239, 240
EAST 239
East, David 777, 836
East, Elizabeth 561
East, Hannah West 718
East, William 590
EASTCOURT 239
EASTERBROOK 239
Easterbrook, Benjamin 753
EASTMAN 239, 240
Eastman, Benjamin 105, 428
Eastman, Elizabeth 42
Eastman, Hannah 183
Eastman, Jemima 207
Eastman, Joseph 329
Eastman, Marah 428
Eastman, Philip 520
Eastman, Ruth 362
Eastman, Sarah 15, 284, 521, 668
Eastman, Susan 835
Eastman, Susanna 722, 835
Eastman, Thomas 441
EASTMEAD 240
EASTON 240
Easton, Ann 136
Easton, Hannah 508
Easton, Mary 159, 677, 740
Easton, Mercy 136
Easton, Nicholas 58, 116, 181
Easton, Patience 484, 632
Easton, Peter 159
Easton, Sarah 312, 671
Easton, Waite 136
Eastow, Mary 491
EASTWICK 253

Eastwick, Elizabeth 268, 581
Eastwick, Katherine 610
EASTY 253
EATON 241, 363
Eaton, Abby 515
Eaton, Abigail 38, 495
Eaton, Alba 515
Eaton, Albee 515
Eaton, Ann 105, 443
Eaton, Anna 443
Eaton, Audrey 339
Eaton, Benjamin 55
Eaton, Benoni 352
Eaton, Bethiah 50
Eaton, Daniel 646, 798
Eaton, Elizabeth 38, 43, 206, 329, 406, 449
Eaton, Francis 70
Eaton, Grace 86
Eaton, Hannah 427
Eaton, Hepzabeth 287
Eaton, John 51, 111, 228, 287, 463
Eaton, Jonas 674
Eaton, Joseph 841
Eaton, Joshua 442
Eaton, Leah 267
Eaton, Lydia 343
Eaton, Marah 224
Eaton, Martha 109, 172, 252, 270, 349, 515, 544, 631
Eaton, Mary 131, 169, 224, 302, 372, 444, 494
Eaton, Mercy 161, 289
Eaton, Nathaniel 511, 569
Eaton, Rachel 609
Eaton, Rebecca 118, 352, 536, 622, 624
Eaton, Ruth 409
Eaton, Samuel 194, 357
Eaton, Sarah 117, 224, 229
Eaton, Tabitha 120
Eaton, Theophilus 845
Eaton, Thomas 828
EATTON 241
EAVERSON 255
EBBORNE 2
Ebborne, Rebecca 61
EBERAL 241
Eborne, Hannah 385
Ebrew, Grace 545
EBURNE 2
Eburne, Elizabeth Lewis Phillips 577
Eburne, Richard 652
ECCLES 241
Eccles, Hannah 102
Eccles, Martha 18
Eccles, Mary 269, 785
Eccles, Richard 137
ECKLES 241
ECLES 241
EDDENDEN 241, 242
Eddenden, Edmund 677
Eddenden, Mary 34
Eddendin, Mehetabel 542
Eddington, Rebecca 473
EDDY 242
Eddy, Abigail 62
Eddy, Alice 352
Eddy, Amy 225
Eddy, Ann 827
Eddy, Bennet 839
Eddy, Beulah 165
Eddy, Deliverance Owen 686
Eddy, Eles 352
Eddy, Eliz. 352
Eddy, Elizabeth 10, 470, 556, 803

Eddy, Hannah 160, 267, 487
Eddy, Hasadiah 648
Eddy, Hepzibah 352
Eddy, John 479, 810
Eddy, Mary 546, 635
Eddy, Mercy 267
Eddy, Pilgrim 255, 705
Eddy, Ruth 293, 714
Eddy, Sarah 180, 488
Eddy, Zachariah 683
EDEES 242
Eden, Alice 491
Eden, Barbara 108
Eden, Sarah 491
Edenden, Edmund 677
Edenden, Hannah 161
Edenden, Sarah 610
Ederkin, Hannah 60
EDES 242
Edes, Mary 328
Edes, Nicholas 266
Edey, Elizabeth 570
EDGARTON 242
Edge, Ann 192
Edge, Patience 352
EDGECOMB 242
Edgecomb, Joanna 247, 296, 608
Edgecomb, John 364
Edgecomb, Mary 23, 550
Edgecomb, Sarah 81
Edgecomb, Susanna 619
EDGERLY 242
Edgerly, Thomas 337
EDGERTON 242
Edgerton, John 475
Edgerton, Lydia 29
Edgerton, Sarah 618
Edgewood, Mary 168
Edington, Mary 34
Edington, Mehetabel 542
Edington, Rebecca 825
EDLIN 242
EDLING 242
EDLINGTON 245
EDMANDS 243
Edmands, Bethia 446
Edmands, Dorothy 230
Edmands, John 478
Edmands, Mary 229
Edmands, Ruth 770
EDMESTER 242
EDMINSTER 243
Edminster, John 736
Edminster, Prudence 586
EDMONDS 243
Edmonds, Elizabeth 508
Edmonds, Sarah 195, 368
Edmonds, William 493
EDMUNDS 243
Edmunds, Alice 778
Edmunds, Dorothy 366, 435
Edmunds, Elizabeth 493, 600
Edmunds, John 201
Edmunds, Joshua 493
Edmunds, Mary 207, 376, 406, 597
Edmunds, Robert 563
EDSALL 243
Edsall, Anna 455
Edsall, Annetje 455
Edsall, Ruth 65
Edsall, Samuel 65
Edsall, Sarah 565
Edsall, Thomas 565
EDSELL 243
Edsell, Elizabeth 52
EDSON 240, 243
Edson, Anna 436
Edson, Bethia 212

Edson, Elizabeth 440
Edson, Hannah 436
Edson, Mary 130
Edson, Samuel 691
Edson, Sarah 212
Edson, Susanna 359, 431
EDWARDS 243, 244, 245
Edwards Jane 347
Edwards, Abigail 86, 474, 520, 716
Edwards, Agnes 169
Edwards, Alexander 659
Edwards, Alice 560
Edwards, Alse 560
Edwards, Ann 169, 186, 404, 592, 623, 699
Edwards, Anna 252
Edwards, Anne 252
Edwards, Bethia 446
Edwards, Betsey 560
Edwards, Daniel 109
Edwards, Elizabeth 11, 34, 119, 158, 188, 214, 352, 574, 717, 723
Edwards, Elsie 560
Edwards, George 197
Edwards, Hannah 208, 209, 252, 415
Edwards, Joanna 613
Edwards, John 265, 404, 748, 751, 837
Edwards, Joseph 704
Edwards, Lucy 437
Edwards, Mabel 68
Edwards, Mary 105, 106, 153, 176, 255, 264, 277, 395, 457, 553, 574, 591, 771, 798
Edwards, Matthew 237, 354
Edwards, Nathaniel 310
Edwards, Palgrave 773
Edwards, Philip 753
Edwards, Rice 588
Edwards, Richard 169
Edwards, Ruth 333
Edwards, Sarah 172, 219, 538, 588, 790
Edwards, Stephen 702
Edwards, Susanna 541
Edwards, Tabitha 592
Edwards, William 423, 696
Edwind, Matthew 237
Edy, Bennet 839
EDZALL 243
Eedy, Assadiah 648
EELLS 245
Eells, Mary 281
Eells, Samuel 36, 111, 538
Egard, Esther 715
Egard, Hester 715
EGBEAR 245
Egbeare, Jane 663
EGBEER 245
Egbere, Jane 663
Egellston, Mary 649
Eger, Benjamin 580
EGGINGTON 245
Eggleden, John 673
EGGLESFIELD 245
EGGLESTON 245
Eggleston, Abigail 55, 547
Eggleston, Benjamin 663
Eggleston, Edward 34
Eggleston, Hannah 732
Eggleston, Hester 305
Eggleston, Mary 216, 649
Eggleston, Ruth 78
Eggleston, Sarah 542, 575, 604
Egglestone, James 820

Eggleton, Jane 100
Eggleton, Jane Cole 169
Eggleton, Joanna 100
Eggleton, Ruth 78
Eggleton, Sarah 542
EGGLETTEN see IGGLEDEN
EGLESFIELD 245
Eglesfield, Mary 5
EGLESTON 245
Egleston, James 253
Eglestone, Susanna 551
EGLETON 245
EGLIN 245
Eglington, Edward 34
Eglon, Margaret 492
EIMES 15, 16
EIRES 28
Eires, Ann 148
Eires, Hannah 548
Eires, Mary 206
Eisdon, Ann 79
Eivleigh, Susanna 707
ELA 245
ELA see ELY 243
Eland, Martha 196, 266
ELATHORP 247
ELATSON 245
Elatson, Elizabeth Pemberton
    Purkis 560
ELBRIDGE 245
Elbridge, Elizabeth 644
Elbridge, Rebecca 652, 690
ELCOCK 246 see ALCOCK
Elcock, Anne 19
Elcock, Mary 572
ELDER 246
Elder, Mary 190
ELDERKIN 246
Elderkin, Abigail 66
Elderkin, Anne 78
Elderkin, Hannah 341
Elderkin, John 297
Elderkin, Paltiah 175
ELDING 246
ELDRED 246
Eldred, Elizabeth 561
Eldred, Mary 364
Eldred, Susanna 143
Eldredge, Bridget 471
Eldredge, Elizabeth 758
Eldredge, Joseph 328
Eldredge, Mary 364
Eldredge, Rebecca 483
Eldridg, Elizabeth 758
ELDRIDGE 246
Eldridge, Elizabeth 338, 644
Eldridge, Joseph 363
Eldridge, Mary 684
Eldridge, Sarah Osgood 168
Eldridge, William 175
ELENWOOD 247
ELERY 247
ELETHORPE 247
Eletrope, Mary 625
Elgar, Thomas 265
ELIOT 246, 247
Eliot, Abigail 209, 235, 812
Eliot, Ann 454
Eliot, Barsheba 477
Eliot, Bathsheba 477
Eliot, Elizabeth 544, 640, 832
Eliot, Hannah 281
Eliot, Henry 846
Eliot, Jemima 836
Eliot, John 68, 483
Eliot, Lydia 570, 683, 814
Eliot, Mary 335, 376, 385, 683
Eliot, Mehitable 574, 826

Eliot, Rachel 597, 810
Eliot, Richard 231
Eliot, Susanna 229
Eliot, William 558
ELIOTT 246
Eliott, Ann 306
Eliott, Hannah 306
ELITHORP 247
Elithorp, Abigail 530, 582
Elithorp, Elizabeth 688
Elithorp, Margaret 345
Elithorp, Mary 590, 625, 688
Elithorp, Nathaniel 92
Elithorp, Sarah 834
Elithorp, Thomas 427
Elithorpe, Abigail 530
Elithorpe, Catharine 508
ELKIN 247
Elkin, Katharine 717
ELKINS 247
Elkins, Henry 44, 428, 530, 608
Elkins, Lydia 148
Elkins, Martha 608
Elkins, Nathaniel 459
Elkins, Robert 254
Elkins, Sarah 500
Elkins, Thomas 500
ELLAIRE 247
ELLASSON 249
Ellcock, Mary 572
ELLEN 12, 247 see ALLEN,
    ELLINS
Ellen, Anna 4
Ellen, Daniel 9
Ellen, Nicholas 592
ELLENWOOD 248
Ellerton, Rebecca 260
ELLERY 247
Ellery, Hannah 133, 167
Ellery, Mary 708, 726
Ellery, Susannah 346, 780
ELLES 245
Elles, Abigail 267
ELLET 247
Ellet, Sarah 58
ELLETT 246
ELLICE 248
Ellice, Ann 196
Ellice, Elizabeth 116
Ellice, Joanna 632
Ellice, Joseph 89
Ellice, Judith 632
Ellice, Mary 267
Elline, Mary 198
ELLINGWOOD 247
Ellingwood, Mary 684
ELLINS 248 see ELLEN
Ellins, Anthony 231, 413
Ellins, Margaret 413
Ellins, Sarah 458, 563
ELLINWOOD 248
ELLIOT 247
Elliot, Alice 493
Elliot, Deborah 381
Elliot, Edmund 847
Elliot, Elizabeth 218
Elliot, Frances 535
Elliot, Hannah 823
Elliot, Jacob 815
Elliot, John 608
Elliot, Mary 572
Elliot, Richard 517
Elliot, Sarah 58, 88, 199, 628
ELLIOTT 246, 247
Elliott, Andrew 751
Elliott, Emma 836
Elliott, Hannah 281
Elliott, Mary 565, 836

Elliott, Robert 846
Elliott, Sarah 8
Elliott, Susanna 377
ELLIS 248
Ellis, --- 151
Ellis, Abiel 40
Ellis, Abigail 267
Ellis, Ann 196
Ellis, Bennett 98, 242
Ellis, Deborah 227
Ellis, Elizabeth 116, 275, 371
Ellis, Frances 257
Ellis, Hannah 632, 659
Ellis, Joanna 632
Ellis, John 153
Ellis, Joseph 89, 364, 462
Ellis, Judith 632
Ellis, Mary 4, 267, 545, 606, 846
Ellis, Patience 3
Ellis, Rebecca 267
Ellis, Roger 116
Ellis, Ruth 3, 559
Ellis, Sarah 406
Ellis, Susanna 254
Ellise, Joanna 435
ELLISON 249 see ALLISON,
    ELLISTON
Ellison, Catharine 467
Ellison, Experience 303
Ellison, Mary 37, 641
ELLISTON see ALLISON,
    ELLESON
Ellithorpe, Margaret 835
ELLSWORTH 249
Ellsworth, Elizabeth 472
Ellsworth, Jeremiah 682
Ellsworth, Job 157
Ellsworth, Mary 472
ELLWELL 250
Ellwyn, Sarah 506
ELMER 249
Elmer, Edward 140
Elmer, Elizabeth 377
Elmer, Mary 140, 295
Elmer, Samuel 83
Elmer, Sarah 471
ELMES 249
Elmes, Sarah 352
Elmore, Edward 140
Elmore, Elizabeth 244
Elmore, Mary 140
Elmore, Sarah 471
Elsdon, Ann 640
Elsdon, Anna 640
ELSE 14
Else, Hannah 823
Else, Roger 116
Elsen, Abraham 526
Elsen, Rebecca 526
Elsen, Thomasin 28
ELSEY 249
Elsey, Nicholas 165
ELSON 249
Elson, Dinah 409
Elson, John 373, 843
Elson, Margaret 346
Elson, Mary 376
Elson, Tamazin 345
Elson, Thomasin 28
Elsse, Hannah 823
Elten, John 371
ELTHAN 249
ELTON 249
Elton, Anne Wines Nichols 847
Elton, John 535, 709, 747
Elton, Lucy 449
ELVE 249.
ELVES 249

Elvie, Hannah 471
Elvie, Scicilia 471
Elvie, Siseliah 471
Elvin, Prisca 847
ELWELL 249, 250
Elwell, Abigail 716
Elwell, Dorcas 29
Elwell, Hannah 294
Elwell, Isaac 639
Elwell, Jane 249
Elwell, Jean 249
Elwell, Josiah 178, 206
Elwell, Mary 226, 293
Elwell, Rachel 351
Elwell, Robert 457
Elwell, Sarah 777
Elwill, Mary 122
Elwyn, Sarah 506
ELY 245, 250 see ELA
Ely, Ann 484
Ely, Elizabeth 689
Ely, Jane 396
Ely, Richard 196, 706
Ely, Ruth 389
Ely, Samuel 171, 705
ELYOTT 246, 247
Elyott, Abigail 235
EMANS 251, 252
Emans, Sarah 518
Emblen, Mary 115
EMBREE 250
Embree, Mary 35
Embree, Robert 35
EMBRY 250
EMERIE 251
EMERSON 250, 251
Emerson, --- 231
Emerson, Abigail 689
Emerson, Elizabeth 142, 288, 439, 467, 573
Emerson, Hannah 236, 305, 571, 832
Emerson, Hannah Pierce Smith 690
Emerson, Joanna 832
Emerson, John 137, 617, 624
Emerson, Joseph 107, 564
Emerson, Lydia 489
Emerson, Martha 167
Emerson, Mary 94, 496, 537, 578
Emerson, Nathaniel 794
Emerson, Ruth 533
Emerson, Sarah 804
EMERY 16, 251
Emery, Abigail 409
Emery, Alice 147
Emery, Anne 545
Emery, Bethia 81
Emery, Eleanor 31
Emery, Elizabeth 431, 446, 728
Emery, Hannah 48
Emery, James 276, 308, 314, 585
Emery, John 250, 487, 789
Emery, Judith 399, 406
Emery, Lydia 108
Emery, Mary 109, 654
Emery, Rebecca 646, 798
Emery, Robert 240
Emery, Sarah 31, 737, 781
Emery, Zachary 397
Emery, Ebenezer 376
EMES 238
Emes, Elizabeth 312
Emes, Hannah 29
EMETT 251
EMMERSON 251
Emmerson, Lucian 202
Emmerson, Lucy Ann 202

EMMONS 243, 251, 252
Emmons, Elizabeth 325, 364
Emmons, Hannah 188, 309, 314
Emmons, Joseph 722
Emmons, Mary 231
Emmons, Rebecca 585
Emmons, Sarah 518
EMMS 15, 238
EMONS 251, 252
EMOTT 251
EMRY 251
Emsden, Isaac 201
ENDALL 252
ENDICOT 252
Endicot, Elizabeth 302
Endicot, Mary 819
ENDICOTE 252
ENDICOTT 252
Endicott, Hannah 296
Endicott, John 10, 301, 478
Endicott, Mary 366
Endicott, Samuel 606
Endicott, Sarah 348
Endicott, ⁷eru⁻ʰ⁻ʰ⁻ˡ 533
ENDLE 252
Endle, Elizabeth 250
Endle, Hannah 825
ENGELL 252, 409
Engell, Benjamin 754
ENGLAND 252
England, Eleanor 797
England, Elizabeth 227, 562
England, Ellen 797
England, John 375, 423
England, Susannah 135
Engleby, Elizabeth 586
ENGLES 252
Englesbie, Sarah 660
Engleshie, Elizabeth 586
Engleshie, Sarah 660
ENGLISH 252 see ENGS
English, Clement 707
English, Elizabeth 94, 163, 580
English, Hannah 161
English, Hester 12
English, Joseph 659
English, Philip 410
ENGLYS 252
ENGS 252, 253, 411 see INGLES, INGLISH, INGS
Engs, Samuel 459
Ennis, Thomas 101
Enno, Ann 139
Enno, James 245, 380
Ennos, Sarah 380
ENO 253
Eno, Ann 139
Eno, James 68, 820
Eno, Sarah 380, 576
Enos, Elizabeth 347
Ensdell, Elizabeth 626
ENSIGN 253
Ensign, David 471, 667
Ensign, Hannah 240, 548, 668
Ensign, Mary 688
Ensign, Sarah 603, 631
Ensigne, Hannah 668
Ensine, Hannah 548
Enstance, Joan 492
Enstance, Joanna 492
EPES 253
Epes, Daniel 674, 770
Eppes, Mary 233
Epps, Daniel 92
Epps, Elizabeth 153
Epps, Martha 324
Epson, Axtell 842
Epson, Hannah 842

Erington, Hannah 28
ERLAND 253
ERRINGTON 253
Errington, Anna 557
Errington, Hannah 28
Errington, Rebecca 300, 785
Errington, Sarah 464
ESDELL 239
ESGATE 253, 411
ESLAND 253
ESTABROOK 239
Estabrook, Benjamin 753
Estabrook, Mary 322
ESTABROOKS 239
Estance, Bridget 343
Estance, Thomas 343
Este, Mary 126
Estebrook, Joseph 474
Estebrook, Thomas 150
ESTEN 253
Esten, Joan 492
Esten, Joanna 492
ESTERBROOK 239
ESTES 253
Estes, Elizabeth 352
Estes, Matthew 357
Estes, Philadelphia 183
Estes, Richard 57
Estes, Sarah 565
Estey, Catharine 658
ESTIE 253
Esto, Mary 491
ESTOW 253
Estow, Sarah 377
ESTOWE 253
ESTWICK 253
Estwick, Elizabeth 125, 588
ESTY 253
Esty, Catharine 427, 658
Esty, Joseph 381
Esty, Mary 126
Esty, Sarah 303
ESTYE 253
ETHERIDGE 253
ETHERINGTON 253
Etherington, Mary 827
Etherington, Patience 362
Eueley, Margaret 292
Eueritt, Sarah 267
EUSTACE 254
Eustace, Sarah 46
Eustance, Joan 492
Eustance, Joanna 492
EUSTIS 254
Eustis, Sarah 46
EUSTISS 253
EVANCE 254
EVANS 254
Evans, Anna 483
Evans, Barbara 588
Evans, Concurrence 48
Evans, Ebenezer 9, 24, 247
Evans, Eleanor 446, 624, 723
Evans, Hannah 368
Evans, Henry 519
Evans, Jane 627, 743
Evans, Joanna 364
Evans, John 375
Evans, Maria 271
Evans, Martha 8
Evans, Mary 91, 271, 348, 655, 754
Evans, Mercy 432
Evans, Rebecca 659
Evans, Robert 341, 379
EVARED 255
EVARTS 254, 255
Evarts, Elizabeth 2

Evarts, Hannah 49, 708
Evarts, John 91, 560
Evarts, Lydia 71
Evarts, Mary 527
Evarts, Mehitable 77
Evarts, Sarah 515
EVE 255
Eveleigh, Margaret 292
EVELETH 255
Eveleth, Elizabeth 571
Eveleth, Isaac 510, 562
Eveleth, Mary 510
Eveleth, Susanna 707
Eveleth, Sylvester 560, 705
Eveley, Margaret 292
Eveligh, Mary 510
Eveloth, Sylvester 34
EVENS 254
Everall, Hannah 485
EVERARD 255
Everard, Abigail 606
Everard, Judith 20
Everard, Sarah 632
Everatt, Mary 547
EVERDEN 255
Everden, Anna 276
Everden, Elizabeth 264
Everden, William 131
Everdin, Anna 64
EVERED 255, 788
Evered, Abigail 263
Evered, Elizabeth 650
Evered, Hannah 27
EVERELL 255
Everell, Ann 77
Everell, Elizabeth 317
Everell, Hannah 77
Everell, John 257
EVERENDEN 255
EVEREST 255
Everet, Ruth 606
EVERETT 255
Everett, Abigail 606
Everett, Bethiah 740
Everett, Elizabeth 532
Everett, Francis 591
Everett, Hannah 193
Everett, Israel 427
Everett, Jedediah 225
Everett, Jonathan 158
Everett, Martha 473
Everett, Mary 165, 238
Everett, Ruth 606
Everett, William 176, 528
EVERID 255
EVERILL 255
Everill, Abiell 8
EVERINDEN 255
EVERITT 255
Everitt, Elizabeth 747
Everitt, Mary 483
Everitt, Sarah 267
EVERRARD 255
EVERSON 255
Everson, Martha 98
EVERTON 255
Everton, John 41
Everton, Sarah 80, 629
Everton, William 80
EVERTS 254
Everts, Mary 527
Evetts, Sarah 515
Eville, Hannah 435
Evins, Eleanor 446
Evons, Barbary 588
Ewall, Eunice 142
EWELL 255, 256
Ewell, Sarah 539

EWER 256
Ewer, Anna 828
Ewer, John 417
Ewer, Sarah 79
Ewer, Thomas 475, 782, 828
Ewey, Wilmot 580
EXELL 256
Exell, Mary 632
Exell, Richard 617
Extell, Sarah 315
Eyers, Ann 456
EYRE 256
Eyre, Catharine 147
Eyre, Christian 712
Eyre, Mary 522
Eyre, Sarah 173, 584
Eyre, Simon 812
EYRES 28
Eyres, Ann 148
EZGATE 253

--- F ---

F-, Moses 791
FABES 256 see FABINS
Fabes, Deborah 380
Fabes, John 304
FABIAN 256 see FABES
FABYAN 256
Faierbank, Benjamin 755
FAIRBANK 256, 257
Fairbank, Anna 497
Fairbank, George 342
Fairbank, Habadiah 516
Fairbank, Hagadiah 516
Fairbank, Martha 213
Fairbank, Ruth 264
FAIRBANKS 256, 257
Fairbanks, --- 741
Fairbanks, Benjamin 296
Fairbanks, Constance 497
Fairbanks, Deborah 482
Fairbanks, Hannah 213
Fairbanks, Jonas 46
Fairbanks, Jonathan 804
Fairbanks, Judith 621
Fairbanks, Lydia 271
Fairbanks, Margaret 380
Fairbanks, Mary 5, 9, 506, 680,
   833
Fairbanks, Rachel 267
Fairbanks, Sarah 654
Fairbanks, Susan 211
FAIRCHILD 257
Fairchild, Emm 602
Fairchild, Emma 602
Fairchild, Margaret 535
Fairchild, Priscilla 566
Fairchild, Ruth 368
Fairchild, Sarah 602
Fairchild, Thomas 140, 429, 536
FAIREBANCK 256
Fairefeild, Elizabeth 693
FAIREFIELD 257
Fairefield, John 437
Fairer, Elizabeth 115
FAIREWEATHER 257
FAIRFEILD 257
FAIRFIELD 257
Fairfield, Daniel 490
Fairfield, Elizabeth 35, 307
Fairfield, Frances 245, 354
Fairfield, John 244, 553
Fairfield, Mary 18
Fairfield, Prudence 224
Fairfield, Ruth 241

Fairfield, Sarah 1, 530
Fairfield, Tabitha 834
Fairfield, Tryphena 840
Fairfield, Walter 803
Fairfield, William 314
FAIRIWEATHER 257
Fairman, Abigail 424
Fairmont, Mary 573
Fairsfield, Mary 557
Fairsfield, Margaret 557
FAIRWEATHER 257
Fairweather, Benjamin 799
Fairweather, Mary 789
Fairweather, Penelope 158, 255
Fairweather, Thomas 158, 309,
   788
FALCONER 260
FALE 257
FALES 257
Fales, Hannah 30
Fall, Jane 676
FALLAND 273
Fallet, Rebecca 24
FALLOWELL 257
Fallowell, Anne 593
Fallowell, Sarah 745
Fallowell, William 234
Fancy, Rachel 808
FANE 260
FANNIN 257
Fannin, Jane 510
FANNING 257, 258
Fanning, Mary 367, 458
FANTON 258
FAR 259
Far, Elizabeth 406
Farebanks, Hannah 213
Farewell, Elizabeth 623
Farewell, Sarah 425
FARGO 258
Fargo, Mary 11
FARINGTON 259
Farington, Sarah 307
FARLEY 258
Farley, Benjamin 235
Farley, George 704
Farley, Lydia 666
Farley, Mary 652
Farley, Meshech 159
Farley, Michael 836
Farley, Rebecca 287
Farlos, Meshech 159
Farman, Elizabeth 243
FARMER 258
Farmer, Bethia 334
Farmer, Isabel 79, 323, 844
Farmer, John 831
Farmer, Sarah 209, 555, 591
FARNAM 258
Farnam, Elizabeth 139
Farnam, Joanna 93
Farnam, Sarah 1
Farnes, Elizabeth 696
Farnes, Martha 514
FARNEY 258
FARNHAM 258
Farnham, Alice 493
Farnham, Elizabeth 401, 421, 527,
   574
Farnham, Hannah 385
Farnham, Henry 722
Farnham, Joanna 409
Farnham, Rachel 493
Farnham, Ralph 493
Farnham, Sarah 1, 409
Farnoll, Mary 52
Farns, John 679
FARNSWORTH 258, 259

Farnsworth, Agnes 450
Farnsworth, Elizabeth 486, 629, 630
Farnsworth, Hannah 568
Farnsworth, Joseph 471, 815
Farnsworth, Mary 417, 626, 733
Farnsworth, Matthias 621, 714
Farnsworth, Rachel 606
Farnsworth, Rebecca 642
Farnsworth, Samuel 817
Farnsworth, Sarah 715
FARNUM 258
Farnum, Alice 493
Farnum, Elizabeth 385, 574
Farnum, Hannah 110, 385, 762
Farnum, Joanna 252, 409
Farnum, Mary 475, 593
Farnum, Mehitable 422
Farnum, Ralph 493
Farnum, Sarah 1
Farnum, Tabitha 287
Farnum, Hannah 762
FAROUGH 259
FAROW 260
FARR 259, 260 see FAWER
Farr, Ann 212
Farr, Eleazer 417
Farr, Elizabeth 406
Farr, Martha 160
Farr, Mary 259, 507
Farr, Sarah 384, 431, 433
FARRABAS 274
FARRAND 259
Farrand, Elizabeth 690
Farrand, Hannah 739
FARRAR 259, 260 see FARROW
Farrar, Deborah 262
Farrar, Dorothy 262
Farrar, Elizabeth 115
Farrar, Hannah 66, 804, 845
Farrar, Jacob 382, 659
Farrar, Joanna 201
Farrar, John (Jr.) 804
Farrar, Mary 391, 804
Farrar, Sarah 475
Farrar, Susanna 533
FARRER 259
FARRETT 259
FARRINGTON 259
Farrington, Abigail 161, 376
Farrington, Elizabeth 288, 317, 322
Farrington, Hannah 1
Farrington, John 319, 376
Farrington, Mary 164, 262, 585
Farrington, Sarah 95
FARRIS 263
FARROW 260
Farrow, Abigail 748
Farrow, Hannah 273, 428
Farrow, John 259
Farrow, Martha 197
Farrow, Mary 55, 114, 155, 684, 716
Farrow, Nathan 293, 295, 812
Farrow, Phebe 172
Farrow, Remember 778
Farrowbush, Deborah Rediat 709
FARRY 263
FARWELL 260
Farwell, Elizabeth 623, 814
Farwell, Hannah 835
Farwell, Mary 168
Farwell, Olive 694
Farwell, Sarah 425
Farwell, Thomas 672
FASSETT 260
Fassett, William 347

FASSIT 260
FATHOM 260
FAUKNER 260
FAULKNER 260
Faulkner, Edmund 631
Faulkner, Hannah 152
Faulkner, Mary 487
FAUNCE 260
Faunce, Mary 344
Faunce, Mercy 384
Faunce, Patience 383
Faunce, Patience Morton 812
Faunce, Priscilla 782
Faunce, Sarah 112, 227
Faunce, Susan 112, 227
Faunce, Thomas 811
FAVOR 260
Favor, Daniel 28
Favor, Thomas 226
FAWER 260 see FARR
Fawer, Barnabas 421
Fawer, Eleazer 417
Fawer, Isaac 259
FAWKNER 260
Fawkner, Mary 487
FAWNE 260
Fawne, Elizabeth 161
FAWRE 260
Faxin, Joan 267
Faxin, Joanna 267
Faxom, Joanna 773
FAXON 260
Faxon, Deborah 653
Faxon, Joan 40, 267
Faxon, Joanna 40, 267
Faxon, Rebecca 50
Faxon, Richard 376
Faxon, Sarah 788, 793
Faxon, Thomas 292, 653
FAY 260
Fay, John 99, 521
Fay, Mary 99
FAYERBANK 257
Fayerweather, John 223
FAYRBANKS 256
Fayrbanks, Marie 203
Fayrbanks, Mary 203
Fayrefield, Elizabeth 307
Feahe, Hannah 88
FEAKE 260, 261
Feake, Elizabeth 221, 518, 763
Feake, Elizabeth Fones Winthrop 337
Feake, Henry 802
Feake, Judith 280
Feake, Robert 337
Feake, Tobias 564
FEARING 261
Fearing, John 821
Fearing, Margaret 821
Fearing, Mary 366
Fearing, Sarah 465
FEARLON 722
FEARLOW 722
Featley, Sybel 533
Featley, Sybil 533
Feeeman, Edmund 574
Feke, Hannah 188
FELCH 261
Felch, --- 151
Felch, Anna 235
Felch, Hannah 235, 323, 559
Felch, Henry 812
Felch, Isabel 360
Felch, Mary 323
Fellett, Nicholas 102
FELLOES 261
Fellowes, Sarah 60, 69

FELLOWS 261
Fellows, Abigail 28
Fellows, Elizabeth 503
Fellows, Ephraim 491
Fellows, Hannah 108
Fellows, Mary 107, 108, 392, 461
Fellows, Sarah 596, 644
Felmingame, Mary 742
FELMINGHAM 265
Felmingham, Mary 742
FELT 261
Felt, Elizabeth 453
Felt, George 477, 531, 590
Felt, Jonathan 607
Felt, Mary 535, 834
FELTCH 261
Feltch, Elizabeth 200
FELTON 261, 262
Felton, Eleanor 410
Felton, Elizabeth 785
Felton, Exercise 507
Felton, Hannah 252, 606
Felton, Judith 410
Felton, Margaret 776
Felton, Remember 647
Felton, Ruth 385
Felton, Susanna Tuck 20
FEN 262
Fenbread, Sarah 23
FENECUM 262
FENN 262
Fenn, Benjamin 132
Fenn, Martha 534
Fenn, Mary 92, 374, 460
Fenn, Mehitable Gunn 100
Fenn, Robert 355, 672
Fenn, Sarah 125, 785
Fenn, Susanna 74, 386
FENNER 262
Fenner, Bethiah 432
Fenner, Freelove 191
Fenner, Phebe 453, 778, 779
Fenner, Sarah 456, 554, 758
Fennix, Elizabeth 250
FENNO 262
Fenns, Rebecca 284
Fenold, Patience 24
FENSEM 262
FENSUM 262
FENTON 262
FENWICK 262
Fenwick, Elizabeth 196, 250
FEREFEILD 257
Fergusen, Bethia 404
FERGUSON 262
Ferguson, Deliverance 142
Ferguson, Elizabeth 380
Ferguson, Mary 455, 755
Ferguson, Sarah 638
Ferman, Abigail 291
Ferman, Elizabeth 243, 507
FERMIN 266
FERN 261
FERNALD 262, 263
Fernald, Anne 660
Fernald, Elizabeth 155
Fernald, Mary 563, 601
Fernald, Patience 247
Fernald, Sarah 364, 480, 783
Fernald, Thomas 601
Ferneley, Mary 540
FERNES 263
Fernes, Elizabeth 696
Fernold, Joanna 431
Fernold, Patience 254
Ferns, John 679
FERNSIDE 263
Fernside, Hannah Alcock 401, 691

Fernside, John 583, 691
Fernside, Lydia 583
Fernside, Mary 400
Fernside, Sarah 362
Ferres, Jeffery 87
FERRIS 290
Ferris, Benjamin 783
Ferris, Grace 399
Ferris, Hannah 443
Ferris, James (Jr.) 501
Ferris, Jeffrey 470, 555
Ferris, Lydia 618
Ferris, Mary 414, 470, 505, 763
Ferris, Peter 790
Ferris, Peter (Jr.) 414
Ferris, Phebe 120
Ferris, Ruth 568
Ferris, Sarah 338
Ferris, Zachariah 42
FERRY 263
Ferry, Mary 124
Ferry, Sarah 781
Ferry, Solomon 85
FERRYES 263
FESINDEN 263
Feske, Judith 87, 263
FESSENDEN 263
Feuens, Susanna 312
Feuster, Jane 389
FEVERSHAM 145
FEVERYEAR 263
Feveryear, Edmund 343
FEVERYEARE 263
Feye, Joanna 528
FICKETT 263, 264
Fickett, Mary 691
Fidoe, Richard 718
FIELD 264, 265
Field, --- 488
Field, Abigail 414
Field, Agnes 822
Field, Alexander 486
Field, Ann 709
Field, Anna 818
Field, Arthur 773
Field, Benjamin 729
Field, Charity 332, 396, 709
Field, Darby 822
Field, Dorcas 118
Field, Elizabeth 98, 405, 426
Field, Experience 243
Field, Hannah 105, 497
Field, John 62, 282
Field, Joseph 60, 62
Field, Martha 497
Field, Mary 138, 218, 595, 838
Field, Mary Bishop Hodgkin
    Johnson 378, 421
Field, Robert 658
Field, Ruth 19
Field, Sarah 161, 231, 808
Field, Susanna 739
FIELDER 265
FIELDS 264
Fields, Zachariah 331
FIFIELD 265
Fifield, Elizabeth 742, 746
Fifield, Giles 177, 320
Fifield, Lydia 483
Fifield, Mary 358
Fifield, Mary Giles 56
Fifield, Richard 320
Fifield, Sarah 377
FIGG 265
Fike, Mary 188
FILER 265
Filer, Ann 389
Filer, Jane 219

Fillabrown, Mary 201
Fillbrook, Judith 667
FILLEBROWN 265
Fillebrown, Sarah 255
FILLEY 265
Filley, Abigail 73, 757
Filley, Anna 317
Filley, Deborah 645
Filley, Elizabeth 827
Filley, Hannah 317, 344
Filley, Margaret 470
Filley, Mary 677
FILLINGHAM 265
FILLOW 261
Filly, Abigail 73
FILMINGHAM 265
Filmingham, Mary 742
FINCH 265, 266
Finch, --- 151
Finch, Abigail 77, 618
Finch, Abraham 244, 751
Finch, Daniel 219, 587, 737
Finch, Dorothy Moulton 748
Finch, Elizabeth 575
Finch, John 289, 321, 788
Finch, Martha 321, 501
Finch, Nathaniel 217, 285
Finch, Sarah 381
Finch, Susanna 661
FINNAH 579
FINNEY 579, 580
Finney, Ann 439
Finney, Catharine 257
Finney, Giles R. 439
Finney, John 166
FINSON 266
Finson, Ann 634
FIRMAN 266
Firman, Sarah 642
FIRMIN 266 see FORMAN
Firmin, Elizabeth 58, 59
Firnold, Patience 9
Fiscock, Elizabeth 183
FISH 266, 267, 268
Fish, Abiah 745
Fish, Alice 446, 669
Fish, Ambrose 746
Fish, Elizabeth 643
Fish, John 162, 196, 367, 706
Fish, Jonathan 515
Fish, Lydia 417
Fish, Mary 94, 515
Fish, Mehitable 745, 754
Fish, Samuel 687
Fish, Sarah 294
FISHER 267, 268
Fisher, Abiah 167
Fisher, Abiel 167
Fisher, Abigail 33, 259, 385
Fisher, Ann 363, 847
Fisher, Anna 363, 847
Fisher, Anthony 40, 625
Fisher, Bethia 570
Fisher, Cornelius 168, 787
Fisher, Deborah 257
Fisher, Elizabeth 248, 387, 590,
    813
Fisher, Esther 289
Fisher, Hannah 93, 98, 123, 298,
    563
Fisher, John 355
Fisher, Joshua 123, 544
Fisher, Judith 117
Fisher, Leah 307
Fisher, Lydia 150, 520
Fisher, Martha 98
Fisher, Mary 53, 98, 154, 297,
    405, 798

Fisher, Meletiah 506
Fisher, Nathaniel 237
Fisher, Rachel 88
Fisher, Rebecca 297
Fisher, Ruth 596
Fisher, Sarah 256, 330, 333
Fisher, Susannah 686
Fisher, Thomas 813
Fisher, Vigilance 481
FISHLOCK 268
FISK 268, 269
Fisk, Abigail 35, 649
Fisk, Anna 138
Fisk, Anne 150
Fisk, Elizabeth 37, 502
Fisk, Hannah 138
Fisk, Lydia 844
Fisk, Martha 679, 763
Fisk, Remember 310
Fisk, Samuel 65
Fisk, Sarah 224
Fisk, William 627
FISKE 268, 269
Fiske, Abigail 514
Fiske, Anna 107, 455
Fiske, David 643
Fiske, Elizabeth 108, 643
Fiske, Hannah 107, 223, 455
Fiske, John (Rev.) 364
Fiske, Judith 555, 618
Fiske, Mara 736
Fiske, Margery 27
Fiske, Martha 3, 224, 269, 556,
    736, 807
Fiske, Mary 53, 267, 494, 572
Fiske, Moses (Rev.) 608
Fiske, Nathan 680
Fiske, Nathaniel 150
Fiske, Remember 1
Fiske, Robert 830
Fiske, Samuel 13, 93
Fiske, Sarah 178, 256, 260, 642
Fiske, Thomas 269
Fiske, Waitstill 708
Fison, Ann 634
Fissenden, Hannah 662
FITCH 261, 269, 270
Fitch, --- 705, 809
Fitch, Abigail 438, 494
Fitch, Ann 90, 349, 737, 737
Fitch, Anne 462
Fitch, Benj. 785
Fitch, Bridget 593
Fitch, Deborah 60
Fitch, Dorothy 73
Fitch, Elizabeth 107, 729
Fitch, Hannah 107, 513, 767
Fitch, James 6
Fitch, Jeremiah 506
Fitch, John 167, 373, 546
Fitch, Joseph 222
Fitch, Lydia 545
Fitch, Mary 39, 112, 121, 174,
    399, 404, 481, 546, 670, 671,
    744
Fitch, Mary Stacy Mears 501
Fitch, Nathaniel 437, 484
Fitch, Rebecca 615
Fitch, Samuel 111, 236, 531, 809
Fitch, Sarah 122, 275, 494, 547,
    715, 782, 796
Fitch, Thomas 269, 590
FITCHEW 270
FITCHLOCK 268
FITCHUE 270
FITS 270
FITT 270
Fittrande, Mary 374

FITTS 270
Fitts, --- 750
Fitts, Abraham 120
Fitts, Bridget 312, 752, 827
Fitts, Rachel 44
Fitts, Sarah 34
Fitts, William 44
FITTSRANDLE 270
Fittsrandle, Hannah 729
FittsRANDLES 270
FITZFARRALD 270
FITZGERALD 270
Fitzgerald, Eliphal 678
Fitzgerald, James 117
FITZHUE 270
FITZHUGH 270
Fitzrandolph, Hannah 729
FitzRANDOLPH 270
FitzRandolph, Elizabeth 586
FitzRandolph, Edward 586
FitzRandolph, Mary 374
FIZE 270
FLACK 270
Flack, Eleazer 43
Flack, Hannah 100
FLACKE 270
FLAGG 270
Flagg, Abigail 200
Flagg, Eleazer 43
Flagg, Elizabeth 68
Flagg, Gershom 774
Flagg, Hannah 321
Flagg, Mary 68, 150, 598
Flagg, Michael 239
Flagg, Rebecca 179
FLANDERS 270, 271
Flanders, Naomi 204, 239
Flanders, Philip 172
Flanders, Sarah 533
Flatcher, Sarah 128
FLAVELL 271
Flaxter, Elizabeth 626
Flaxter, William 626
Flecher, Lydia 571
FLEG 270
Fleg, Elizabeth 68
FLEGE 270
FLEGG 270
Flegg, Mary 68
Flegg, Rebecca 179
Fleming, Margaret 86
Fleming, Sarah 42
FLEMINGE 271
FLEMMING 271
Flemming, Robert 545, 638
FLETCHER 271
Fletcher, Abigail 534
Fletcher, Anna 436
Fletcher, Edward 232
Fletcher, Elizabeth 80, 85, 386, 718
Fletcher, Esther 557, 605
Fletcher, Grezell 331
Fletcher, Grisell 119, 419
Fletcher, Grizel 436
Fletcher, Grizell 327
Fletcher, Hannah 151, 436, 842
Fletcher, Hope 716
Fletcher, Jane 156
Fletcher, Joanna 16
Fletcher, John 156
Fletcher, Joseph 138, 755
Fletcher, Lydia 268
Fletcher, Mary 64, 232, 559, 640, 708, 833
Fletcher, Nicholas 156
Fletcher, Pendleton 603
Fletcher, Rebecca 4, 780

Fletcher, Samuel 37, 695
Fletcher, Samuel (Sr.) 185
Fletcher, Sarah 701, 802
Fletcher, Seth (Rev.) 585
Fletcher, William 52, 257
FLINDER 271
Flinder, Sarah 139
FLINT 271, 272
Flint, Abigail 385
Flint, Alice 117, 581
Flint, Anna 204, 236
Flint, Deborah 459
Flint, Dorothy 608, 668
Flint, Elizabeth 212, 457
Flint, Hannah 204, 435, 550, 778
Flint, Joanna 533
Flint, Margaret 312, 538
Flint, Mary 359
Flint, Ruth 271
Flint, Sarah 641
Flint, Thomas 693, 835
FLINTT 272
Floid, Abigail 355
FLOOD 272 see FLOYD
Flood, --- 163
Flood, Lydia 239, 325
Flood, Richard 325
Flood, Robert 44
Flood, Sarah 682
FLOWER 272
Flower, Hannah 289
Flower, Margaret 440
FLOYD 272 see FLOOD
Floyd, Abigail 355
Floyd, Lydia 325
Floyd, Sarah 764
Fluent, Mary 700
Fluent, Sarah 99, 290
Flunt, Jane 302
Fluster, Jane 389
Flynt, Henry 497
FOBES 272, 274, 274
Fobes, Elizabeth 360, 431, 644
Fobes, John 98
Fobes, Phebe 685
Fobes, William 658
FOGG 272, 273
Fogg, Mary 343, 593
FOKES 280
Foldgier, Dorcas 599
FOLGER 273
Folger, Abiah 282
Folger, Bathshua 593
Folger, Dorcas 599
Folger, Experience 722
Folger, Joanna 171
Folger, Mary 552, 765
Folger, Patience 344
Folger, Sarah 687
FOLINSBEE 273
FOLKE 279
Folland, Elizabeth 336, 425
Folland, Margaret 462
Folland, Mary 802
Folland, Thomas 802
FOLLANSBEE 273
Follansbee, Anne 147
Follansbee, Jane 397
Follansbee, Mary 386
Follansbee, Rebecca 147
Follansbee, Thomas 635
FOLLEN 273
FOLLET 273
Follet, Abigail 813
Follet, Susannah 673
FOLLETT 273
Follett, Abigail 501, 529
Follett, Hannah 831

Follett, Hannah Black 693
Follett, Mary 365, 831
Follett, Sarah 501
Follett, William 231
FOLLINGSBY 273
Follinsby, Mary 586
Followay, William 234
FOLSOM 273
Folsom, Abigail 305
Folsom, Abraham 643
Folsom, Ann 418
Folsom, Ebenezer 543
Folsom, Mary 447, 487
Folsom, Nathaniel 628
Folsom, Peter 186
Folsom, Ruth 538
Folsom, Samuel 276
FONES 273
Fones, Elizabeth 261, 337, 830
Fones, Martha 830
Fones, Mary 321
Fookes, Jane 389
FOORD 275
Foorebush, Katherin 170
FOOT 273, 274
Foot, Abigail 239
Foot, Dorothy 197
Foot, Elizabeth 221, 262, 318
Foot, Pasco 357
Foot, Sarah 197
FOOTE 273, 274
Foote, Elizabeth 60, 119, 153, 190
Foote, Frances 42, 220
Foote, Hannah 651
Foote, Mary 310, 712, 751
Foote, Nathaniel 330, 795
Foote, Rebecca 177, 687
Foote, Robert 77
Foote, Samuel 637
Foote, Sarah 197, 429, 543
FOOTMAN 274
Footman, Abigail 846
Footman, Thomas 235
FOOTT 274
FORBASH 274
FORBEE 274
FORBES 272, 274
Forbes, Daniel 709
Forbes, David 752
Forbes, Dorothy 629
Forbes, Elizabeth 644
Forbes, John 98
Forbes, Mary 291
Forbes, Sarah 172
FORBUSH 274
Forbush, Daniel 709
Forbush, Katherin 167
Forbush, Rebecca 129
FORBY 274
FORCE 279
FORD 228, 274, 275
Ford, Abigail 327, 719
Ford, Ann 461, 531
Ford, Bethya 61
Ford, Catharine 4
Ford, Elizabeth 196, 235, 466, 518, 572
Ford, Esther 4
Ford, Experience 225
Ford, Hannah 637
Ford, Hepzibah 480, 489
Ford, Joanna 154, 632
Ford, John 659
Ford, Joseph 203
Ford, Katharine 4
Ford, Lydia 93, 379, 534
Ford, Margaret 95, 693

Ford, Martha 108
Ford, Mary 620, 633, 735, 740, 809, 816
Ford, Mercy 735
Ford, Millicent 139, 230
Ford, Prudence 465
Ford, Samuel 275
Ford, Sarah 425, 426, 484
Ford, Thomas 158, 534, 632, 657
Forde, Martha 531
FORDHAM 275
Fordham, Florence 135
Fordham, Hannah 158
Fordham, Joseph 655
Fordham, Mary 393, 808
Fordham, Phebe 366
Fordham, Robert (Rev.) 158
Fordham, Susannah 158
FORGASON 262
Forgeson, Sarah 638
FORGINSON 262
FORMAN 266, 275, 276 see FIRMAN
Forman, Hannah 535, 763
Forman, Hannah Crooker 791
Forman, Johannah Townsend 750
Forman, Josiah 790
Forman, Mary 71
Forman, Mercy 71, 791
Forman, Moses 64
Forman, Samuel 342, 391
Forman, Sarah 64, 342
Forman, Susannah 749
Forster, Charity 734
Forster, Mary 119
Forster, Rebecca 119
Forster, Susanna 453
Forster, Thomas 281
FORSYTH 276
Fortado, Antonio 703
Forth, Mary 830
FORTUNE 276
Fortune, Elizabeth 465
Fortune, Mary 395
FORWARD 276
FOSDICK 276
Fosdick, Anna 45, 79, 744
Fosdick, Damaris 332
Fosdick, Grace 798
Fosdick, Hannah 45
Fosdick, John 66, 80, 94, 467
Fosdick, Martha 380
Fosdick, Mary 23, 789
Fosdick, Thomas 332
FOSECAR 276
FOSKET 276
FOSKETT 276
Foskett, Elizabeth 194
FOSS 276
Foss, Elizabeth 51
Foss, Jane 530
Foss, John 314
Foss, Martha 314
FOSSECAR 276
Fossecar, John 422
FOSSET 276
FOSSETT 276
FOSSEY 276
FOSSY 276
FOST 276
Fost, John 314
Fost, Mary 782
Fost, Sarah Goffe 308
FOSTER 276, 277, 278, 279
Foster, --- 280, 674
Foster, Ann 113, 577
Foster, Anna 577
Foster, Bartholomew 19, 654

Foster, Charity 734
Foster, Chatfield 147
Foster, Christopher 727
Foster, Edward 509
Foster, Elisha 831
Foster, Elizabeth 139, 286, 367, 437, 442, 612, 632, 767, 825, 835
Foster, Esther 276
Foster, Experience 284
Foster, Hannah 26, 271, 564, 655, 713
Foster, Hopestill 105, 584, 811
Foster, Isaac 643, 836
Foster, John 5, 431, 516, 591, 735
Foster, Joseph 110, 203, 826
Foster, Judith 590
Foster, Katharine 747
Foster, Lettice 747
Foster, Martha 217, 835
Foster, Mary 89, 119, 317, 352, 425, 436, 447, 475, 529, 565, 579, 655, 682, 779, 785, 833
Foster, Mehitable 26
Foster, Naomi 205, 424
Foster, Patience 109, 655
Foster, Prudence 80
Foster, Rebecca 119
Foster, Reginald 492, 807
Foster, Richard 525
Foster, Ruth 329
Foster, Sarah 79, 131, 426, 432, 471, 515, 701, 715, 822
Foster, Silence 154
Foster, Susanna Parker 281
Foster, Thankful 33
Foster, Thomas 90, 335
Foster, Timothy 216, 229, 457
Foster, William 377
Fosters, Edward 417
FOTHERGILL 279
Foulgar, Abiah 282
FOULKE 279, 280
Foulsham, Mary 447
Foulsom, Mary 487
Founall, Sarah 432
FOUNELL 279
FOUNTAIN 279
Fountain, Aaron 830
Fountain, James 718
FOWER 280
FOWKES 280
Fowkes, Hannah 472
Fowl, Mary 372
FOWLE 279
Fowle, Abigail 118, 691, 845
Fowle, Anna 525
Fowle, Catharine 432
Fowle, Elizabeth 775, 844
Fowle, Hannah 642, 845
Fowle, James 775
Fowle, Joan 84
Fowle, John 606
Fowle, Katharine 432
Fowle, Sarah 442, 471
FOWLER 279, 280
Fowler, Abigail 246, 672, 724
Fowler, Ann 113
Fowler, Deborah 448
Fowler, Elizabeth 173, 438
Fowler, Grace 403
Fowler, Hannah 112, 626, 662
Fowler, Hester 70, 635
Fowler, James 837
Fowler, Jane 275
Fowler, John 424, 534, 540, 541
Fowler, Jonathan 480

Fowler, Joseph 443
Fowler, Margaret 141, 171, 547, 640
Fowler, Margery 171, 547, 640
Fowler, Martha 443
Fowler, Mary 20, 59, 130, 144, 312, 439, 752, 778
Fowler, Mercy 69
Fowler, Patience 344
Fowler, Philip 540, 547
Fowler, Rebecca 611
Fowler, Samuel 518
Fowler, Sarah 112, 312, 340, 684
Fowler, Temperance 125
Fowler, Thomas 336
Fowler, William 36
FOWLES 279, 768
Fowles, Dorothy 561
Fowles, Hannah 567
FOWNELL 279
Fownell, John 399
Fownell, Mary 399
FOX 280, 281
Fox, Eliphalet 168, 403
Fox, Elizabeth 37, 145, 194, 532, 589
Fox, Hannah 462, 472
Fox, John 278, 705
Fox, Mary 152, 314, 350
Fox, Ruth 674
Fox, Samuel 11, 688
Fox, Sarah 436
Fox, Thomas 141, 322, 462, 818, 844
FOXALLS 281
FOXCROFT 281
Foxe, Susanna 381, 382
Foxel, Ruth 531
FOXHALL 281
FOXWELL 281
Foxwell, Esther 635
Foxwell, John 344
Foxwell, Lucretia 630
Foxwell, Martha 30
Foxwell, Mary 168, 540
Foxwell, Ruth 531
Foxwell, Sarah 198
Foxwell, Susannah 23
Foxwells, Philip 17
FOY 281
Foy, John 480
FOYE 281
Fracy, John 342
FRAILE 281
Fraile, Elizabeth 665
Fraile, Eunice 563
Fraile, Ruth 261
FRAIRY 281
Frake, Elizabeth 643
FRAME 281
Frame, Elizabeth 298
Frame, Hannah 349
Frame, Sarah 141
Frame, Susanna 539
FRAMPTON 281
FRANCECO 282
FRANCIS 282
Francis, Abigail 505
Francis, Damaris 157
Francis, Hannah 204
Francis, Sarah 268, 598, 699
Francis, Susannah 539, 705
Francis, Thomas 788
FRANCKLIN 282
Franckline, Elizabeth 498
Frane, Sarah 467
FRANK 282
FRANKLIN 282

Franklin, Elizabeth 162, 498
Franklin, Jonathan 264
Franklin, Martha 579
Franklin, Phebe 466
Franklin, Sarah 259
Franklyn, Agnes 543
Franklyn, Rebecca 543
Franklyn, Ursula 543
Franks, Sarah 669
FRARLOW 258
FRARY 281
Frary, Abigail 21
Frary, Hannah 59, 237, 774
Frary, John 237
Frary, Mary 636, 735
Frary, Mehitable 15, 465, 636
Frary, Mercy 636
Frary, Prudence 3, 187
Frary, Samuel 363
Frask, Mary 671
FRAYE 281
FRAYLE 281
Frayle, Elizabeth 665
FRAZER 282
FREAM 281
Fream, Elizabeth 298
FREATHY 282
Freathy, Joanna 384
Frebray, Mary 204
FREDERICK 282
Frederick, William 462
FREEBORN 282, 283
Freeborn, Ann 235
Freeborn, Gideon 456
Freeborn, Martha 183
Freeborn, Mary 788
Freeborn, Patience 19
Freeborn, Sarah 110, 777
Freeburg, Anna 734
Freed, Ann 82
FREELOVE 283
FREEMAN 283, 284
Freeman, Alice 504, 550, 556,
  737
Freeman, Apphia 570
Freeman, Bennett 551
Freeman, Daniel 409
Freeman, Deborah 449
Freeman, Elizabeth 248, 296, 617
Freeman, Hannah 107, 500, 828
Freeman, Henry 12
Freeman, John 358
Freeman, Jonathan 628
Freeman, Margaret 162, 266
Freeman, Martha 546, 595
Freeman, Mary 109, 164, 380, 461
Freeman, Mercy 168, 446, 659
Freeman, Patience 120, 194, 552
Freeman, Rachel 449
Freeman, Rebecca 573
Freeman, Ruth 223
Freeman, Samuel 156, 601, 689
Freeman, Sarah 254, 429, 449,
  691
Freeman, Stephen 595
Freeman, William 369
Freese, Catharine 277
Freestone, Elizabeth 293, 760
Freestone, Frances 372
FREETHE 282
Freethe, Joane 384
Freethy, Elizabeth 85, 696
Freethy, James 74
Freethy, Mary 329
FREEZE 284
FREIND 285
Freind, Sarah 80
Freke, John 407

Freke, Mary 833
FRENCH 284, 285
French, Abigail 557, 755
French, Alice 395, 695
French, Ann 471, 526
French, Anna 471, 799, 801
French, Deliverance 556
French, Dorcas 189, 565
French, Elizabeth 248, 385, 411,
  577, 592, 734, 802
French, Hannah 89, 135, 150,
  431, 442, 531, 577, 795, 799,
  805
French, Jacob 666
French, John 442, 657, 707, 766
French, Joseph 668
French, Judith 633
French, Lydia 87, 355
French, Margaret 12, 448
French, Marish 566
French, Martha 232
French, Mary 31, 36, 233, 241,
  254, 358, 408, 448, 566, 585,
  593, 610, 664, 666, 681, 688,
  704
French, Phebe 315
French, Rebecca 840
French, Sarah 36, 193, 356, 379,
  561, 565, 749, 755
French, Stephen 474
French, Susan 681
French, Temperance 86
French, Thomas 244, 428, 681,
  688, 704
French, William 514, 703
FREND 285
Frend, John 544
Frese, Elizabeth 625
Frese, James 625
Friary, Theophilus 324
FRIE 287
Frie, Mary 708
Frie, Phoebe 574
Frieman, John 785
FRIEND 285
Friend, Elizabeth 550, 568
Friend, John 544
Friend, Mary 437
Friend, Rebecca 32
Friend, Rebecca 110
FRIERSON 285
FRINCKS 285
FRINK 285
Frink, Deborah 448
Frink, Grace 817
Frink, Hannah 556
Frink, John 97
Frink, Judith 847
Frink, Thomas 810
Frisall, Mary 12
FRISBIE 285
Frisbie, Abigail 376
Frisbie, Hannah 47, 348
Frisbie, Jonathan 217, 266
Frisbie, Mary 569
Frisbie, Rebecca 47
Frisbie, Samuel 762
Frisbie, Silence 26
FRISSELL 286
Frissell, William 726
FRISSIL 286
FRIZELL 286
Frizell, Mary 428
FRIZZELL 286
Frizzell, Mary 12
FRO 286 see THROW
FROE 286
Froe, David 404

Froed, Ann 82
FROST 286, 287, 758
Frost, Abigail 44, 288
Frost, Agnes 498, 665
Frost, Alice 79, 667
Frost, Ann 57, 110
Frost, Anna 57
Frost, Anne 498
Frost, Annis 498, 665
Frost, Catherine 457
Frost, Edmund 18, 203, 414
Frost, Elizabeth 316, 320, 619,
  786
Frost, Esther 172
Frost, Hannah 716, 739
Frost, John 414
Frost, Joseph 401, 811
Frost, Katherine 339
Frost, Lydia 319, 582
Frost, Mary 57, 91, 371, 626, 799
Frost, Mehitable 466, 584
Frost, Philip 611
Frost, Rachel 642
Frost, Rebecca 83, 180
Frost, Sarah 360, 616, 671, 688
Frost, Susanna 811
Frost, Thomas 310, 423
Frost, Thomasine 620
Frost, William 342, 462, 659
FROTHINGHAM 287
Frothingham, Anna 473
Frothingham, Elizabeth 86
Frothingham, Hannah 435
Frothingham, Mary 807
Frothingham, Nathaniel 435
Frothingham, Ruth 243
Frothingham, Samuel 111
Frow, David 404
FRUDE 287
Frude, Henery 30
Frude, James 30
FRY 287
Fry, Elizabeth 268, 345, 710, 711
Fry, George 94
Fry, Mary 708, 717
Fry, Michael 636
Fry, Naomi 845
Fry, Ruth 747
Fry, Tamazin 502
Fry, Tamazine 502
Fry, Tamsen 502
Fry, Thomasin 502
Fryar, Elizabeth 622
FRYE 287
Frye, Anna 612
Frye, Bethia 614
Frye, Eleanor 103
Frye, Elizabeth 736, 748
Frye, Hannah 612
Frye, Lydia 558
Frye, Mary 347, 481, 584
Frye, Phoebe 574
Frye, Ruth 686
Frye, Sarah 519
Frye, William 225
FRYER 287, 288
Fryer, Elizabeth 374
Fryer, Margaret 294
Fryer, Nathaniel 14
Fryer, Sarah 247
Fryer, Wilmot 544, 757
FRYERS 287
FUGILL 288
Fugill, Dorothy 37
FULERTON 290
FULFORD 288
Fulford, Elizabeth 493
FULHAM 288

Fulham, Frances 426
FULLAM 288
FULLER 288, 289, 290
Fuller, Abigail 200, 218, 716
Fuller, Ann 289, 686, 807
Fuller, Anna 289, 807
Fuller, Bethiah 81
Fuller, Bridget 676
Fuller, Deborah 622, 665
Fuller, Elizabeth 212, 241, 288,
  408, 439, 440, 506, 640, 645,
  656, 662, 668, 729, 730, 764,
  802, 825
Fuller, Experience 834
Fuller, Hannah 82, 267.462
Fuller, Hannah Morton 285
Fuller, Isabelle 729
Fuller, John 474, 573, 667
Fuller, Joshua 202, 609
Fuller, Judith 621
Fuller, Launcelot 266
Fuller, Lydia 221
Fuller, Mary 104, 267, 426, 621,
  820
Fuller, Mercy 168
Fuller, Rachel 65
Fuller, Robert 621, 776
Fuller, Ruth 801, 816
Fuller, Samuel 87, 601, 617
Fuller, Sarah 68, 135, 195, 195,
  211, 392, 457, 611
Fuller, Susanna 715, 807, 829
Fuller, Thomas 825, 845
Fuller, Timothy 663
Fuller, William 126, 583
FULLERTON 290
Fullerton, Abigail 218
Fulton, Martha 491
Funk, Samuel 480
FURBER 290
Furber, Amy 830
Furber, Bridget 67
Furber, Elizabeth 202
Furber, Hannah 589
Furber, Jethro 27, 669
Furber, Moses 830
Furber, Susanna 67
Furber, William 433, 542
Furber, Wm. 67
FURBISH 274
Furbish, Catherine 529
Furbish, Hopewell 406
Furbish, Katharine 529
Furbish, Sarah 738
Furbisk, Sarah 738
FURBOSH 274
Furbur, Abigail 546
FURBUSH 274
Furbush, Catherine 529
Furbush, Katharine 529
Furbush, Margaret 350
Furbush, Rebecca 343
FURMAN 266
Furman, John 242
Furman, Martha 123
Furman, Mary 242, 266
FURNACE 290
Furnace, David 99
Furnel, Olive 679
FURNELL 290
Furnell, Ann 421
Furnell, Eleanor 448
Furnell, Joanna 14
Furnell, Strong 448
FURNESS 290
Furness, David 99
Furnill, Joanna 14
FURS 290

FURSE 290
Furson, Thomas 760
Fush, Joane 610
FUSSELF 290
Fussell, John 3
Fyfield, Deborah 194
Fynes, Arabella (Lady) 420

--- G ---

GAAL 291
Gach, Thomas 765
Gadney, Bartholomew 710
Gaffell, Mary 721
Gaffell, Sarah 721
GAGE 291
Gage, Benjamin 710
Gage, Elizabeth 437
Gage, John 435
Gage, Jonathan 825
Gage, Naomi 57
Gage, Nathaniel 323
Gage, Susannah 440
Gage, Thomas 378, 507
GAGER 291, 414
Gager, Bethiah 2
Gager, Elizabeth 11
Gager, Hannah 96
Gager, Lydia 405
Gager, Mary 11, 626
Gager, Samuel 613
Gager, Sarah 272, 274
Gail, Abigail 636
Gaille, Elizabeth 629
GAINES 291
Gaines, Abiah 714
Gaines, Abial 714
Gaines, Abiel 714
Gaines, Esther 714
Gaines, Hester 714
Gaines, Martha 243
Gaines, Sarah 191
GAINS 291
GAISHET 296
GALE 291
Gale, Abigail 505
Gale, Ambrose 305
Gale, Ann 417
Gale, Anna 665
Gale, Bethia 630
Gale, Bethia Chipman 221
Gale, Charity 351, 588
Gale, Deliverance 414
Gale, Elizabeth 541, 595, 629,
  636
Gale, Mary 223, 270, 291
Gale, Miriam 649, 806
Gale, Sarah 295, 599, 680
Gale, Sary 295
Galkin, Philip 670
Gall, Bethia 630
GALLE 291
GALLEY 292
Galley, Dorcas 376
Galley, Elizabeth 303, 751
Gallion, Jane 499, 552
GALLISON 291, 330 see
  GUNNISON
GALLOP 292
Gallop, Esther 378
Gallop, Hannah 301, 321
Gallop, Hester 378
Gallop, Joan 428
Gallop, Joseph 7, 236
Gallop, Mary 169
GALLOWAY 291

GALLUP 292
Gallup, Christobel 191
Gallup, Elizabeth 707
Gallup, Humphrey 124
Gallup, John 124
Gallup, Margaret 196
Gallup, Susanna 126, 127
GALLY 292
Gally, Elizabeth 751
Gally, Mary 638
GALPIN 292
Galpin, --- 777
Galpin, Calvin 446
Galpin, Mary 3
Galpin, Philip 752
GALUSHA 292
GALUSIAH 292
GAMAGE 292
Gamage, Mary 546
GAMBLIN 292
Gamblin, Mary 30
Gamblin, Robert (Jr.) 500
Gamer, Lydia 758
Games, Martha 243
Gaming, Margaret 264
GAMLIN 292
Gamlin, Benjamin 198
Gamlin, Elizabeth 151
Gamline, Elizabeth 151
Gammon, Catherine 427
Gammon, Grace 707
Gammon, Katherine 427
Gammon, Mary 672
Gammon, Thomas 427
GAMNUNG 298
Ganners, Mary 167
GANNETT 292 see GARNETT,
  GARRETT
Gannett, Abigail 224
Gannett, Elizabeth 462, 728
Gannett, Esther 554
Gannett, Hannah 3
Gannett, Joseph 664
Gannett, Mary 152
Gannett, Matthew 462
Gannett, Thomas 260, 653
Gannugh, Jeremiah 298
Gannugh, Mary 215
Gano, Mary 215
Ganong, Hannah 363
Ganong, Susanna 363
GANSON 292
Ganson, Benjamin 621
Ganson, Elizabeth 602
GANT 296
GANUNG 298
Garbrand, Susan 386, 668
Garbrand, Susanna 312, 386, 668
Gard, Christian 166, 175
Gard, William 297
GARDE 292
Gardener, Richard 77
Gardener, Sarah 250
GARDINER 292, 293, 294
Gardiner, Ann 401
Gardiner, Dorcas 785
Gardiner, Elizabeth 393, 561
Gardiner, George 356, 368, 594
Gardiner, Henry 617
Gardiner, John 167
Gardiner, Joseph 92
Gardiner, Lydia 686
Gardiner, Mary 106, 176, 773, 847
Gardiner, Rebecca 785
Gardiner, Samuel 106
Gardiner, Sarah 34, 563
Gardiner, Seeth 316
Gardiner, William 293

GARDNER 293, 294, 295
Gardner, Abigail 518, 736, 831
Gardner, Amie 144
Gardner, Andrew 660
Gardner, Ann 165
Gardner, Anne 164
Gardner, Damaris 43
Gardner, Deborah 174, 484
Gardner, Deborah Macy 566
Gardner, Dorcas 139
Gardner, Dorothy 139, 824
Gardner, Eleanor 331
Gardner, Elizabeth 404, 410, 741
Gardner, Esther 423, 823
Gardner, Francis 812
Gardner, George 356, 714
Gardner, Hannah 39, 128, 164,
    298, 369
Gardner, Hester 823
Gardner, Hope 165
Gardner, James 107, 226, 587
Gardner, Joanna 702, 781
Gardner, John 167
Gardner, Joseph 92
Gardner, Love 165
Gardner, Lucy 514, 759
Gardner, Margaret 560, 606
Gardner, Mary 59, 86, 89, 152,
    165, 239, 260, 294, 365, 491,
    594, 743, 758, 773, 847
Gardner, Mary Warren 847
Gardner, Mehitable 177
Gardner, Miriam 371, 841
Gardner, Priscella 22
Gardner, Rachel 107, 293
Gardner, Rebecca 189, 810
Gardner, Ruth 165, 353, 419
Gardner, Samuel 203, 316, 408
Gardner, Sarah 250, 273, 313,
    550, 602, 660
Gardner, Seeth 316
Gardner, Seith 175
Gardner, Susannah 272
Gardner, Thomas 664, 792
Garets, Grete 518
GAREY 295, 296
GARFEILD 294
GARFFEILD 294
GARFIELD 295
Garfield, Abigail 305, 560
Garfield, Ann 413
Garfield, Anna 413
Garfield, Deborah 103
Garfield, Edward 113
Garfield, Elizabeth 537
Garfield, Hannah 413
Garfield, Jeruska 68
Garfield, John 718
Garfield, Lydia 118, 537
Garfield, Mary 330, 537, 721
Garfield, Mercy 66
Garfield, Rachel 603
Garfield, Rebecca 513
Garfield, Ruth 333, 537
Garfield, Samuel 66, 537
Garfield, Sarah 330, 721
GARFORD 295
GARLAND 295
Garland, Jane 479
Garland, John 147, 631
GARLICK 295
Garlick, Elizabeth 562
Garlick, Hannah 711
Garlick, Joshua 562
GARMAN 299
Garmine, Elizabeth 610
GARNER 293, 294
Garner, Susannah 611

GARNET 294, 295
Garnet, Christian 233
Garnet, Deborah 748
Garnet, Francis 812
Garnet, Mary 152, 260
GARNETT 293, 294, 295 see
    GANNATT, GARRETT
Garnett, Abigail 224
Garnett, Benjamin 293
Garnett, Francis 293
Garnett, Judith 667
GARNICK 295
GARNOCK 295
GARNSEY 329
Garnsey, Hannah 389
Garnsey, Joseph 783
Garnsey, Mehitable 389
GARRAD 295
Garrad, Mararet 713
GARRARD 295
GARRELL 295
GARRESON 295
GARRET 295
Garret, Ann 844
Garret, Anna 844
Garret, Hannah 38, 844
GARRETSON 295
Garretson, Martha 73
Garretson, Rehromy 73
GARRETT 295
Garrett, Hannah 727
Garrison, Annah 668
GARROD 295
Garton, Elizabeth 323
Garuet, Rebecca 776
GARVEN 295
Garvet, Rebecca 776
GARVIN 295
GARWOOD 295
Garwood, Anne 675
GARY 295, 296
Gary, Elizabeth 2
Gary, Nathaniel 73
Gary, Patience 273
Gary, Sarah 385, 602
GASCOYNE 296
GASKALL 296
GASKELL 296
Gaskell, Hannah 681
Gaskell, Preserved 448
Gaskell, Samuel 379, 399
Gaskell, Sarah 428
GASKILL 296
GASKIN 296
Gaskin, Joanna Crocker 821
Gaskin, John 242
Gaskin, Sarah 428
GASSETT 296
GATCH 296
Gatch, Rachel 65
GATCHEL 299
Gatchel, Bathiah 16
GATCHELL 299
Gatchell, Bethiah 16
Gatchell, Elizabeth 837
Gatchell, Susanna 540
Gater, Judith 572
GATES 296
Gates, Abigail 694
Gates, Elizabeth 384, 453
Gates, Isaac 259
Gates, Mary 175, 499
Gates, Rebecca 301
Gates, Samuel 256, 755
Gates, Sarah 290, 663
Gates, Stephen 839
Gathercole, Lydia 123
GATLIFFE 296

Gatliffe, Jonathan 703
GATLINE 296
Gatline, Mary 611
GATLIVE 296
Gatlive, Prudence 198
Gator, Katharine 758
GATTENSBY 296
Gattensby, Elizabeth 769
Gattensby, John 428
GATTINSBY 296
GAUD 296
Gauge, Elizabeth 210
Gauge, Thomas 765
GAULT 296
Gault, Deborah 830
Gault, Mary 72
Gault, Mehitable 240
Gault, Rebecka 79
Gault, Sarah 167
Gault, William 72
GAUNT 296
Gaunt, --- 368, 741
Gaunt, Lydia 120
Gaunt, Mary 193
Gaunt, Mehitable 240
Gaunt, Peter 120
Gaunt, Zackariah 120
Gaurd, William 297
Gaut, Mehitable 240
Gavet, Katherine 586
GAVETT 296
Gavett, Katherine 586
GAWDREN 296
Gawdren, Mary Cole 412
Gawkroger, Mary 602
Gawood, Anne 661
GAY 296, 331
Gay, Abiel 354
Gay, Deborah 778
Gay, Elizabeth 493
Gay, Hannah 780
Gay, Joanna 787, 808
Gay, John 35, 780
Gay, Judith 288
Gay, Lydia 241
Gay, Martha 164
Gay, Mary 197, 592
Gay, Mercy 197
GAYER 296 see GEER
Gayer, Damaris 166
Gayer, Dorcas 702
Gayer, William 292
GAYLOR 296
GAYLORD 296
Gaylord, Abigail 797
Gaylord, Alice 753
Gaylord, Ann 576
Gaylord, Anna 576
Gaylord, Elizabeth 71, 368, 390,
    398, 632
Gaylord, Hannah 190
Gaylord, Joanna 594
Gaylord, John 785
Gaylord, Martha 249
Gaylord, Mary 210, 328, 472, 549
Gaylord, Samuel 14, 318, 844
Gaylord, Sarah 8, 429, 576
Gaylord, William 333
Gaylord, Wm. 246
Gayn, Francis 805
GAZEAU 314
GEAFFALS 296
GEARE 298
GEARFFEILD 295
Gearffeild, Rebecca 513
GEARFFFIELD 294
Gearfield, Jeruska 68
Gearish, Ann 339

Gearish, William 339
GEDNEY 296, 298
Gedney, Bethiah 407
Gedney, Elizabeth 439
Gedney, John 159, 560, 604
Gedney, Lydia 184
Gedney, Mary 597
Gedney, Ruth 293
Gedney, Susanna 184
Gedny, Hannah 316
GEE 298
Gee, Anna 378
Gee, Hannah 378
Gee, Martha 164
Gee, Mary 581
Geen, John 835
GEER 298 see GAYER
Geer, Ann 762
Geer, Anne 762
Geer, Jonathan 278
Geer, Margaret 296
Geer, Mary 499, 605
Geer, Sarah 556
GEERE 298
Geery, Elizabeth 2
Geery, Sarah 385
GEFFEERE 314
GEFFREY 314
GELGRIS 298
Gellume, Hannah 516
Gendall, Walter 517
GENERY 151
Genery, Deborah 725
GENING 419
Genivere, Rosamund 249
Genney, Elizabeth 253
Gennung, Mary 215
Gent, Elizabeth 494, 580
Gent, John 695
Gent, Mary 11, 323, 494
Gentle, Noah 96
GENUNG 298
Genung, Hannah 363
Genung, Susanna 363
GEORGE 298
George, Elizabeth 305, 365, 553, 594, 625, 654
George, Hannah 204, 508, 612, 638
George, John 119, 308, 514
George, Martha 514
George, Mary 37, 70, 229, 243, 581, 588
George, Nicholas 383
George, Peter 613
George, Ruth 111, 287
George, Samuel 512
George, Sarah 166, 224
George, Susan 345
George, Susanna 345, 434
GERALD 295
GERARD 298
Gerard, Elizabeth 32
Gerard, Robert 52
Gerearay, John 184
GEREARDY 298, 299
Gereardy, Mary 683
Gereardy, Phillis 684
GERFFIELD 295
GERFILD 294
GERMAINE 299
Germaine, Mary 673
GERMAN 299
German, Elizabeth 610
German, Priscilla 80
GERRARD 298
Gerrard, Mary 485
GERRISH 299

Gerrish, Agnes 592
Gerrish, Ann 339
Gerrish, Anna 100
Gerrish, Benjamin 118
Gerrish, Elizabeth 322, 324, 603, 769
Gerrish, Mary 225
Gerrish, William 339, 486, 544
GERRY 295
GETCHELL 299
Getchell, Elizabeth 608
Getchell, Jonathan 832
Getchell, Priscilla 573
Gethercole, Lydia 123
Geyer, Dorcas 702
GIBB 299
GIBBARD 299
Gibbard, Abigail 312
Gibbard, Hannah 159
Gibbard, Mary 389
Gibbard, Phebe 18
Gibbard, Rebecca 845
Gibbard, Sarah 649, 650
Gibbard, Timothy 546
Gibbard, William 18
GIBBINS 299
Gibbins, Hannah 367
Gibbins, James 29
Gibbins, Patience 649
Gibbins, Rachel 242
Gibbins, Rebecca 771
GIBBONS 299
Gibbons, Ann 507
Gibbons, Elizabeth 36, 375, 663, 782
Gibbons, Hannah 482
Gibbons, Love 279, 606
Gibbons, Rebecca 668
Gibbons, Sarah 210, 621
GIBBS 299, 300
Gibbs, Abigail 44, 724
Gibbs, Benjamin 148
Gibbs, Cutbury 754
Gibbs, Elizabeth 547
Gibbs, Gregory 546
Gibbs, Hannah 827
Gibbs, Hepzibah 220
Gibbs, Joanna 472
Gibbs, John 678
Gibbs, Lydia 334
Gibbs, Mary 286, 310, 669
Gibbs, Matthew 519
Gibbs, Meribah 273
Gibbs, Patience 216
Gibbs, Rebecca 308
Gibbs, Robert 184
Gibbs, Samuel 191
Gibbs, Sarah 102, 542, 666
Giblet, Abia 48
Gibman, Lydia 199
GIBS 300
Gibs, Hannah 827
GIBSON 300, 301
Gibson, Benjamin 26
Gibson, Christina 632
Gibson, Christopher 205
Gibson, Elizabeth 346, 347
Gibson, Elizabeth Cogan 252
Gibson, John 601
Gibson, Martha 445, 465, 532, 635
Gibson, Mary 296, 642
Gibson, Priscilla 128
Gibson, Rebecca 703
Gibson, Roger 13
Gibson, Samuel 705
Gibson, Sarah 197, 705
GIDDENS 301
GIDDING 301, 311

Gidding, Abigail 236
GIDDINGS 301
Giddings, Elizabeth 215, 351
Giddings, George 571
Giddings, Jean 342
Giddings, John 366
Giddings, Mary 398, 486, 584
Giddings, Sarah 342
Giddings, Susanna 157
Giddings, Thomas 151
GIDINGS 301
Gidins, Elizabeth 351
GIDLEY 301
GIDNEY 296, 298
GIE 298
GIFART 301
GIFFORD 301
Gifford, Elizabeth 758
Gifford, Grace 395
Gifford, Hannah 140
Gifford, John 732
Gifford, Margaret 167
Gifford, Mary 611
Gifford, Patience 441
Gifford, Ruth 269
Gilard, Ann 745
GILBERT 299, 301, 302, 303
Gilbert, Abigail 2
Gilbert, Amy 161
Gilbert, Benjamin 186
Gilbert, Dorothy 554
Gilbert, Elizabeth 214, 703
Gilbert, Esther 220
Gilbert, Gyles 632
Gilbert, Hannah 142, 159, 350, 558, 579
Gilbert, Hester 220
Gilbert, Humphrey 437, 614
Gilbert, Jan 330
Gilbert, Jane 330
Gilbert, John 14, 24, 87, 808
Gilbert, Josiah 778
Gilbert, Katharine 347
Gilbert, Lydia 145, 623, 625
Gilbert, Martha 174, 690
Gilbert, Mary 6, 385, 538, 554, 638, 817, 821
Gilbert, Obadiah 545, 661
Gilbert, Prudence 518
Gilbert, Rachel 491
Gilbert, Sarah 59, 264, 393, 417, 746, 770, 819
Gilbert, Thomas 78, 491, 638, 821
Gilbord, Jane 330
Gilborn, Jan 330
GILD 330
Gild, John 721
Gilden, John 338
GILDERSLEEVE 303
Gildersleeve, Anna 683
Gildersleeve, Dorcas 462
Gildersleeve, Elizabeth 834, 834
Gildersleeve, Richard 566
Gildersleeve, Richard (Jr.) 462
Gildersleeve, Susannah 834
GILE 330
Gile, Hannah 163
Gile, Judith 550
GILES 303, 330
Giles, --- 83
Giles, Edward 767
Giles, Elizabeth 30, 33, 820
Giles, John 751
Giles, Mary 56, 200, 619, 800
Giles, Mehitable 128, 173
Giles, Miles 572
Giles, Remember 523
GILFORD 330

Gilford, Susanna 419
GILL 303
Gill, Deborah 450
Gill, Elizabeth 713, 757
Gill, Frances 88
Gill, Hannah 154
Gill, Isabella 759
Gill, Judith 550
Gill, Mary 55
Gill, Phebe 519
Gill, Rachel 716
Gill, Rebecca 59
Gill, Sarah 451, 575
Gill, William 603
GILLAM 303, 304
Gillam, Benjamin 507, 724
Gillam, Elizabeth 331
Gillam, Faith 507
Gillam, Hannah 578, 663
Gillam, Joseph 38
Gillam, Ruth 475
Gillame, Elizabeth 93
Gille, Judith 550
GILLET 304
Gillet, Ann 265
Gillet, Anna 265
Gillet, Hannah 730
Gillet, Jeremiah 5
Gillet, Joanna 719
Gillet, Sarah 370
GILLETT 304
Gillett, Abiah 678
Gillett, Ann 743
Gillett, Hannah 293
Gillett, Joanna 719
Gillett, John 573, 779
Gillett, Joseph 220
Gillett, Mary 108
Gillett, Samuel 419
Gillett, Sarah 789
Gillette, Abigail 71
Gillette, Hannah 112
Gillette, John 540
Gillette, Joseph 302
Gillette, Mary 73, 114, 389, 411
Gillette, Priscilla 327
GILLING 304
GILLINGHAM 304
Gillingham, Elizabeth 64
Gillingham, William 51
Gillo, John 421
GILLOW 304
Gillow, John 421
GILLOWAY 291, 304
GILLSON 305
GILMAN 304, 305
Gilman, Abigail 735
Gilman, Alice 152
Gilman, Daniel 458
Gilman, Edward 256
Gilman, Elizabeth 232, 447, 769
Gilman, Joanna 166
Gilman, John 333
Gilman, Judith 480
Gilman, Lydia 805
Gilman, Mary 55, 273, 414, 734
Gilman, Moses 96, 448
Gilman, Sarah 232, 306, 458
GILMORE 305
GILSMAN 305
GILSON 301, 305
Gilson, Mary 483
GILVIN 305
Gimpson, Mary 707
Gimson, Maria 297
Gimson, Mary 292
Gingill, Anna 816
Gingill, Hannah 816

Gingle, John 816
Gininingham, Elizabeth 64
Ginnings, Elizabeth 614
Ginnuarie, Rosamund 249
Gippes, Ann 268
Gipps, Ann 268
GIPSON 300
Gipson, Elizabeth 346
Gipson, Roger 13
GIRDLER 305
Girdler, Deborah 291
Girdler, Francis 291
Girdler, John 365
Girdler, Mary 17
GIRLING 305
GISBORNE 305
Gist, Phillipa 292
Gittey, Dorcas 299
GLADDING 305
Gladding, Mary 819
Gladding, Susannah 509
GLADING 305
Glaisdell, Mary 716
Glamfield, Abigail 100
Glamfield, Elizabeth 457
GLANFIELD 305
Glanfield, Lydia 134
Glanfield, Ruth 442, 706
Glansha, Margaret 214
GLANVILLE 305
Glascock, Alice 289
Glascock, Elsie 289
GLASIOR 305
GLASS 305
Glass, Amy 236
Glass, Eame 236
Glass, Hannah 70, 582
Glass, James 214
Glass, Mary 236
Glass, Wybra 117
GLASSE 305
Glasse, Amy 382, 823
Glavefeild, Lydia 134
GLAZER 305
GLAZIER 305
Glazier, John 594
Glazier, Zechariah 571
GLEALING 305
GLEASON 305, 306
Gleason, Ann 300
Gleason, Anna 300
Gleason, Anne 300
Gleason, Joice 532
Gleason, Joyce 532
Gleason, Sarah 520
GLEDEN 306
GLEISON 305
Glen, Hannah 519
Glezin, Joice 532
Glezin, Joyce 532
GLIDDEN 306
GLIDE 306
GLIDEN 306
Glines, William 609
Globe, Sarah 667
Glouer, John 738
GLOVER 306
Glover, Abigail 121
Glover, Alice 52
Glover, Ann 612
Glover, Anna 612
Glover, Charles 652
Glover, Elizabeth 219, 425, 830
Glover, Hannah 22, 56, 254, 364, 489, 718
Glover, Jesse 235
Glover, John 67, 162, 498, 738
Glover, Joseph 525

Glover, Mary 184, 232, 317, 357
Glover, Mercy 486
Glover, Nathaniel 374
Glover, Priscilla 20
Glover, Rachel 738
Glover, Rebecca 159, 690
Glover, Richard 189
Glover, Sarah 5, 37, 672, 677, 830
Goad, Abigail 525
Goad, Joseph 504
Goade, Abigail 525
GOARD see GORE, GOUD
Goard, Phebe 18
Goardin, Elizabeth 251
GOARDINER 294
Goatley, Mary 547
GOAVE 316
GOBLE 306, 307
Goble, Abigail 232
Goble, Daniel 637
Goble, Elizabeth 138, 805
Goble, Mary 202, 212, 407
Goble, Ruth 718
Goble, Sarah 667
GODARD 314
GODBERTSON 307
Godbertson, Godbert 603
GODDARD 307
Goddard, Elizabeth 305, 678
Goddard, John 674
Goddard, Martha 735
Goddard, Mary 62, 264, 264, 767
GODDEN 311
GODDIN 311
Goddin, Elizabeth 116
GODDING 307
Godding, Elizabeth 521
GODEN 312
GODFREY 307
Godfrey, Alice 379
Godfrey, Elizabeth 134, 285
Godfrey, Hannah 395
Godfrey, Jane 118, 164, 722, 759, 839
Godfrey, Margaret 623
Godfrey, Mary 178, 223, 546, 712
Godfrey, Richard 435, 577
Godfrey, Sarah 162, 190, 258, 790
Godfrey, Susanna 435
Godfrey, William 488, 790
GODSOE 307
Godsoe, William 831
GODWIN 311, 312
Godwin, Mary 413, 661
Godwin, Samuel 340
Godwin, Sarah 661
GOFF 307, 308
Goff, Edward 68
Goff, Elizabeth 569
Goff, Jacob 112
Goff, Joanna 192, 472
Goff, Philip 618
GOFFE 307, 308
Goffe, Abiah 832
Goffe, Christopher 796
Goffe, Edward 831
Goffe, Hannah 516
Goffe, James 276, 314
Goffe, Lydia 697
Goffe, Samuel 654
GOING 313
Going, Abigail 817
Going, Elizabeth 261, 262
Going, Mary 692
Going, Priscilla 627
Going, Robert 417
Going, Sarah 417, 691

GOIT 308
GOLD 308, 314, 315
Gold, Abigail 481, 661
Gold, Anstis 816
Gold, Deborah 155
Gold, Edward 30
Gold, Elizabeth 382
Gold, Hannah 15, 17, 377
Gold, Martha 205, 661
Gold, Mary 407, 470, 726
Gold, Nathan 349, 845
Gold, Ruth 607
Gold, Sarah 73, 130, 265, 266,
   737
GOLDEN 308
Goldesborough, Griszel 824
Goldham, Susannah 72
Goldhatch, Alice 211
GOLDING 308
Golding, Ann 384
Golding, Elizabeth 415, 419
Golding, Martha 685
GOLDSMITH 308
Goldsmith, Hannah Killam 1
Goldsmith, John 795
Goldsmith, Marie 563
Goldsmith, Mary 563
Goldsmith, Richard 1
Goldsmith, Thomas 666
Goldston, Mary 366
GOLDSTONE 308
Goldstone, Anne 99
Goldstone, Henry 298
Goldstone, Mary 366, 367
Goldstone, Sarah 503, 800
GOLDTHWAIT 309
Goldthwait, Marian 136
GOLDTHWAITE 309
Goldthwaite, Elizabeth 439
Goldthwaite, Thomas 673
GOLDWIER 309
GOLDWYER 309
Goldwyer, George 586
GOLE 314
Golham, Susannah 72
Golt, Deborah 830
Golt, Rebecka 79
Golt, Sarah 167
GOLTHITE 308
GOLTHRITE 309
GOLTHWRITE 308
GONES 426
Gonzales, Charles 424
GOOCH 309
Gooch, Elizabeth 26
Gooch, Francis 226
Gooch, Lydia 342
Gooch, Ruth 787
GOOD 309
GOODALE 309
Goodale, Ann 13, 509
Goodale, Elizabeth 64, 477, 640,
   683, 748
Goodale, Hannah 437
Goodale, Isaac 711
Goodale, Joseph 627
Goodale, Martha 303
Goodale, Mary 256
Goodale, Robert 437
Goodale, Sarah 51
GOODALL 309
Goodall, Mary 495, 687
Goodard, Mary 773
GOODDIN 307
Goode, --- 740
Goode, Abigail 525
GOODELL 309
Goodell, Elizabeth 63

Goodell, Hannah 437
Goodell, Mary 566
Goodell, Robert 437
Gooden, Seaborne 580
GOODENHOUS 309
GOODENHOUSE 309 see
   VANGOODENHOUSEN
Goodenhouse, Samuel 759
GOODENOUGH 310
Goodenough, Susannah 616, 825
GOODENOW 310
Goodenow, --- 234
Goodenow, Abigail 44
Goodenow, Dorothy 568
Goodenow, Elizabeth 356
Goodenow, Hannah 569, 682
Goodenow, Jane 39, 69
Goodenow, John 775
Goodenow, Mary 638
Goodenow, Sarah 775
GOODFELLOW 309
Goodfellow, Thomas 34
GOODFELOW 309
GOODHUE 309, 310
Goodhue, Hannah 167
Goodhue, Joseph 157, 746
Goodhue, Margaret 446
Goodhue, Mary 301, 539
Goodhue, Sarah 437
Goodhue, Susanna 438
Goodhue, William 257, 268, 316,
   475, 788
GOODIN 311, 312
Goodin, Henry 568
GOODING 311
Gooding, Elizabeth 521
Gooding, Mary 593
Gooding, Seaborne 580
GOODMAN 310
Goodman, Margaret 746
Goodman, Mary 537
GOODNEW 310
GOODNOW 310
Goodnow, Dorothy 641
Goodnow, Jane 129, 813
Goodnow, Lydia 217
Goodnow, Sarah 435, 775
Goodnow, Susannah 507, 616
Goodnow, Thomas 129
GOODRICH 310, 311
Goodrich, Abigail 270
Goodrich, Elizabeth 204, 637,
   657, 794
Goodrich, Hannah 499
Goodrich, John 615, 712, 751
Goodrich, Lydia 254
Goodrich, Mary 31, 127, 128, 615
Goodrich, Rachel 65
Goodrich, Rebecca 842
Goodrich, Richard 254
Goodrich, Robert 733
Goodrich, Sarah 382, 436
Goodrich, William 28, 199
Goodridg, Hannah 621
Goodridg, Mary 740, 838
GOODRIDGE 310
Goodridge, Hannah 499
Goodridge, John 286
Goodridge, Mary 615, 838
Goodridge, Sarah 317
Goodridge, Thomas 311
GOODSELL 311
Goodsell, Ruth 839
Goodsell, Thomas 839
GOODSPEED 311
Goodspeed, Alice 658
Goodspeed, Benjamin 374
Goodspeed, John 112

Goodspeed, Mary 374
Goodspeed, Mercy 426
Goodspeed, Nathaniel 153
Goodspeed, Rose 418
Goodspeed, Ruth 207
GOODWIN 311, 312 see
   GODWIN, GOODING
Goodwin, Bridget Fitts 827
Goodwin, Christopher 422
Goodwin, Daniel 758
Goodwin, Edward 161, 178, 698,
   799
Goodwin, Elizabeth 62, 195, 251,
   294, 397, 521, 558, 780
Goodwin, Hannah 349, 588
Goodwin, Joyce 253, 411
Goodwin, Margaret 379
Goodwin, Martha 163
Goodwin, Mary 109, 125, 177,
   593, 790
Goodwin, Mercy 276
Goodwin, Patience 713
Goodwin, Richard 752, 752
Goodwin, Robert 538
Goodwin, Ruth 56
Goodwin, Samuel 340
Goodwin, Sarah 46
Goodwin, Seaborne 580
Goodwin, Susanna 108, 599
Goodwin, Thomas 710, 801
Goodwin, Timothy 457
Goodwin, William 386, 668
GOODWING 312
GOODWYN 312
Goodwyn, Mary 398
GOODYEAR 312
Goodyear, Ann 122
Goodyear, Elizabeth 23
Goodyear, Esther 686
Goodyear, Hannah 122, 772
Goodyear, Lydia 786
Goodyear, Mary 447
Goodyear, Rebecca 72
Goodyear, Stephen 72, 449
GOOG 314
GOOGE 309
GOOKIN 312
Gookin, Elizabeth 247, 608
Gookin, Mary 53, 608
Gookin, Samuel 100
Gookins, Daniel 652
GOOLD 315
Goold, Abigail 295
Goold, Hannah 292
Goold, Leah 4
Goold, Mary 407
Goold, Mercy 268
GOOLE 314, 315
Goole, Abigail 185
Goole, Martha 46
Goole, Mary 786
Goole, Mercy 268
GOOLL 315
GOORDING 313
GOOSE 313 see VERGOOSE
Goose, Mary 413, 840
Goose, Susanna 194
Goose, William 323, 413
GOOSS 313
GORD 306
GORDEN 313
GORDON 313
Gordon, Elizabeth 251
Gordon, Mary 687
Gordon, Nicholas 662
Gordon, Sarah 662
GORE 313 see GOARD
Gore, Elizabeth 291

Gore, Hannah 91, 301
Gore, John 594, 617, 742
Gore, Mary 507
Gore, Samuel 756
Goreham, Lydia 733
GOREN 313
Gorge, Elizabeth 617
GORHAM 313
Gorham, Desire 354, 698
Gorham, Elizabeth 337
Gorham, Experience 475
Gorham, Hannah 802
Gorham, Jabez 320
Gorham, Mary 374
Gorham, Mercy 215
Gorham, Sarah 394
Gorham, Temperance 54, 154, 720
GORIN 313
GORING 313 see GOWEN
GORNELL 313
Gornell, Jane 119
GOROM 313
GORSLINE 314
GORTON 313, 314
Gorton, Alice 278
Gorton, Ann 780
Gorton, Anna 780
Gorton, Elizabeth 190
Gorton, Mahershallalhashbaz 168
Gorton, Mary 321, 322, 323, 493,
    650
Gorton, Sarah 482, 791
Gorton, Susanna 49
GOSARD 307, 314
GOSIER 314
GOSLEE 314
GOSLINE 314
GOSLING 314
Gosling, Agnes 65
Gosling, Annis 65
GOSMER 314
Gosmer, John 838
GOSS 308, 314
Goss, Elizabeth 276
Goss, Philip 391
Goss, Richard 575
Gosse, John 536
Gosse, Sarah 536
GOSSWELL 314
GOSWELL 314
Gotshell, Priscilla 609
GOTT 314
Gott, Ann 388, 755
Gott, Charles 437
Gott, Charles (Sr.) 486
Gott, John 728
Gott, Lydia 93
Gott, Mary 353
Gott, Remember 268
Gouch, Benedict 340
Gouch, Mary 339
GOUGE 314 see GOOCH
Gouge, Ann 220
Gouge, Elizabeth 210
Gouge, Marah 602
Gough, Hannah 220
Gough, Margaret 587
GOULD 314, 315
Gould, --- 832
Gould, Abigail 481, 633, 635
Gould, Alexander 143
Gould, Anna 845
Gould, Content 811
Gould, Daniel 145
Gould, Elizabeth 57, 110, 186,
    528
Gould, Hannah 247, 292, 377, 437
Gould, John 110, 348

Gould, Judith 550
Gould, Leah 4
Gould, Margaret 588, 711
Gould, Martha 46, 534
Gould, Mary 97, 368, 407, 416,
    426, 588, 616, 677, 726, 786
Gould, Mehitable 311
Gould, Phebe 572
Gould, Priscilla 198, 348, 607, 815
Gould, Robert 188, 351, 593, 714
Gould, Sarah 73, 119
Gould, Thomas 166, 360
Gould, William 627
GOULDER 315
GOULDING 308
Gouldsmith, Sarah 129
GOULIVER 330
Gouliver, Hannah 756
GOURD 306
Gourd, Phebe 18
GOURDEN 313
GOURDING 313
Gourney, Elizabeth 283
GOVE 315, 316
Gove, Abigail 202
Gove, Ann 177
Gove, Edward 563
Gove, Hannah 161
Gove, John 53, 336, 772, 837
Gove, Mary 601, 607, 648
Gove, Sarah 213
Gover, Sarah 677
GOWAN 313
Gowan, Sarah 691
GOWELL 316
Gowell, Richard 737
Gowell, Tamsen 666
Gowell, Tamsin 341
GOWEN 316 see GORING
Gowen, Elizabeth 262
Gowen, Margaret 251
Gowen, Sarah 691
Gower, Anna 252
Gowge, Hannah 252
GOWING 316
Gowing, Abigail 816
Gowing, Mary 692
Gowing, Priscilla 627
Gowing, Robert 816
GOWINGE 316
GOYTE 308
Goznee, Priscilla 423
Gozzard, Elizabeth 530
Grace, Sarah 437
GRAFFAM 316
Graffam, Mary 317
Graffam, Stephen 2
GRAFFORT 316
Graffort, Thomas 203
Graffton, Remember 445
Graford, Mary 812
GRAFTON 316
Grafton, Abigail 774
Grafton, Anne 656
Grafton, Elizabeth 366, 400, 442,
    652
Grafton, Hannah 229
Grafton, John 175
Grafton, Joseph 294, 310, 475
Grafton, Mary 2, 263, 317, 343
Grafton, Nathaniel 677
Grafton, Priscilla 294, 414
Grafton, Remember 445
GRAGE 291
Gragg, Mary 716
GRAHAM 316, 327 see GRIMES
Graham, Alse 598
Graham, Benjamin 789

Graham, Elizabeth 459
Graham, Sarah 493
Graham, Susannah 493
GRAMES 316
Grandfield, Ann 460
Grandfield, Anne 447, 460
Grandsden, Frances 700
GRANGER 316
Granger, Dorothy 544
Granger, Elizabeth 724
Granger, Hannah 731
Granger, Mary 119
Granger, Rebecca 833
Grangier, Martha 332
GRANIS 316
GRANNIS 316
Grannis, Abigail 14
Grannis, Hannah 371
Grannis, Mabel 421
Grannis, Mehitabel 421
Grannis, Sarah 72
GRANT 317, 318
Grant, Abigail 638
Grant, Ann 251, 697
Grant, Anne 90
Grant, Christopher 682
Grant, Daniel 232
Grant, Deborah 446
Grant, Elizabeth 449, 759, 781,
    788, 789
Grant, Frances 435
Grant, Grizzel 435
Grant, Hannah 39, 105, 145, 361,
    423
Grant, James 317, 423, 747
Grant, Joan 317
Grant, John 194, 794
Grant, Joseph 231
Grant, Mary 9, 34, 192, 223, 309,
    382, 611, 677, 680
Grant, Mary Beckwith 203
Grant, Matthew 632
Grant, Peter 309, 317, 611, 656
Grant, Priscilla 402
Grant, Rebecca 347
Grant, Roger 218
Grant, Sarah 214, 249, 384, 505,
    662, 725, 801
Grant, Susanna 364, 807
Grant, Tahan (Jr.) 39
Grant, Thomas 481
Grantam, Alice 251
GRANTHAM 318
Grath, John 406
GRAUES 318
GRAVE 318, 319
Grave, Abigail 65
Grave, Elizabeth 513
Grave, Hannah 714
Grave, Mary 738
Grave, Sarah 257, 631
GRAVEENOR 328
GRAVENER 318
Graver, Deborah 63
GRAVES 298, 318, 319
Graves, Abigail 18, 60, 65, 367
Graves, Amy 466, 623, 619
Graves, Deliverance 731
Graves, Dorcas 1
Graves, Elizabeth 14, 96, 151,
    249, 351, 367, 427, 512
Graves, Emma 81, 351
Graves, Francis 607
Graves, George 472, 739
Graves, Hannah 500, 597, 646,
    690
Graves, Isaac 319
Graves, John 14, 297, 597, 619,

Graves, John (cont.) 844
Graves, Jonathan 438
Graves, Katharine 446
Graves, Mark 259
Graves, Martha 644
Graves, Mary 14, 37, 102, 214, 228, 248, 281, 351, 704, 735, 827
Graves, Mehitable 522, 842
Graves, Mercy 827
Graves, Nathaniel 365
Graves, Priscilla 488
Graves, Rebecca 5, 717
Graves, Ruth 435, 788, 846
Graves, Samuel 318
Graves, Sarah 7, 45, 89, 90, 214, 472, 473, 631, 704
Graves, Susannah 696, 725
Graves, Thomas 7, 89, 150, 578
Graves, William 219, 673, 709, 846
Gravs, Ann 619
Gravs, Sarah 454
GRAY 319, 320
Gray, --- 312
Gray, Anna 458
Gray, Christian Legro 723
Gray, Desire 694
Gray, Edward 157
Gray, Elizabeth 22, 486, 603
Gray, Hannah 2, 146, 777
Gray, Henry 330
Gray, Hugh 111
Gray, Jacob 66
Gray, Jane 473
Gray, Jeffery 692
Gray, Jemima 1
Gray, John 313, 398, 786
Gray, Katharine 319
Gray, Lydia 474
Gray, Mary 402, 448, 624
Gray, Parnell 541
Gray, Rebecca 168
Gray, Ruth 445
Gray, Samuel 51, 711
Gray, Sarah 159, 344, 468, 763
Gray, Susanna 57, 245
Gray, Susannah 169
Gray, Thomas 167, 782
Graye, Joseph 381
GRAZILLIER 320
GREAMES 327
GRECIAN 325
GREELEY 320
Greeley, Benjamin 839
Greeley, Mary 829
GREEN 320, 321, 322, 323
Green, Abigail 420, 621
Green, Abigail Hammon 803
Green, Ann 467, 494, 659
Green, Anne 49, 570
Green, Barbara 417
Green, Bethia 368
Green, Dorcas 111
Green, Edmund 789
Green, Edward 354
Green, Elizabeth 2, 130, 140, 147, 331, 423, 474, 614, 698
Green, Esther 270, 287, 515
Green, Hannah 192, 322, 623, 668, 729, 737, 768
Green, Henry 265, 551
Green, Jacob 471, 803
Green, James 364, 786
Green, Jane 704
Green, Joan 332
Green, Joanna 332
Green, Johanna Lee 459

Green, John 27, 31, 143, 203, 265, 327, 612, 637, 658, 664, 751
Green, Lydia 353
Green, Mary 191, 322, 322, 402, 437, 443, 566, 631, 651, 659, 691, 708, 754
Green, Mehitable 228
Green, Mercy 449
Green, Nicholas 666
Green, Percival 281
Green, Peter 440, 650
Green, Phebe 641
Green, Priscilla 325
Green, Ralph 751
Green, Rebecca 82, 230, 358, 533, 807
Green, Richard 82
Green, Ruth 812
Green, Sarah 340, 451, 558, 789
Green, Solomon 313
Green, Susanna 294, 666, 800
Green, Thomas 179, 799
Green, William 79, 109, 227, 384, 464, 480, 614, 844
Greenaway, Mary 510
GREENE 321, 322, 323
Greene, --- 590
Greene, Abigail 709
Greene, Anne 323, 524
Greene, Audrey 695
Greene, Catharine 380
Greene, Deborah 748
Greene, Dorcas 45, 89
Greene, Elizabeth 323, 334, 457, 618
Greene, Hannah 446
Greene, Henry 388
Greene, Jane 593
Greene, John 457, 832
Greene, Luke 803
Greene, Margaret 170
Greene, Mary 130, 237, 593, 618, 723
Greene, Phebe 362
Greene, Phillip 136, 220
Greene, Phillippa 136
Greene, Phillis 136
Greene, Rebecca 588
Greene, Ruth 368
Greene, Sarah 430, 618, 698
Greene, Thomas 291
Greene, Weltham 287
Greene, Welthyan 287
GREENEWEY 324
Greenfeild, Hannah 596
GREENFIELD 323
Greenfield, Ann 460, 596
Greenfield, Anna 386
Greenfield, Anne 447, 460
Greenfield, Margaret 365
Greenfield, Peter 445, 724
Greenfield, Samuel 831
GREENHALGE 323
GREENHALGH 323
GREENHILL 323
Greenhill, Rebecca 4
GREENLAND 323, 324
Greenland, Elizabeth 176
Greenland, Lydia 673
GREENLEAF 324
Greenleaf, Bethiah 162
Greenleaf, Edmund 372
Greenleaf, Elizabeth 30, 108, 155, 541
Greenleaf, Enoch 755
Greenleaf, John 582
Greenleaf, Judith 166, 692

Greenleaf, Margaret 742
Greenleaf, Mary 127, 515
Greenleaf, Rooksby 191
Greenleaf, Ruth 178
Greenleaf, Samuel 727
Greenleaf, Sarah 225, 374
Greenleaf, Stephen 427, 723, 838
Greenleafe, Mary 794
Greenlefe, Sarah 225
Greenliefe, Ruth 178
GREENMAN 324
Greenman, Content 159
GREENOUGH 324
Greenough, Elizabeth 631
Greenough, Luke 803
Greenough, Mary 550, 575, 714
Greenough, Mercy 300
Greenough, Robert 507
Greenough, Sarah 739
Greenough, William 606
GREENOW 324
GREENSLAD 324
Greenslade 606
GREENSLADE 324
Greenslade, Joane 26
Greenslade, Joanna 26
Greenslade, John 495
Greenslade, Ruth 97
Greenslade, Thomas 606
Greensland, Abigail 411
GREENSLETT 324
Greenslit, Ann 606
Greenslit, Thomas 606
Greenslitt, John 495
GREENSMITH 324
GREENWAY 324
Greenway, Anne 584
Greenway, Catherine 203
Greenway, Elizabeth 11
Greenway, Katharine 203
Greenway, Susannah 773
Greenway, Ursula 53
Greenwich, Sarah 570
GREENWOOD 324, 325
Greenwood, Abigail 267
Greenwood, Alice 595
Greenwood, Ann 364
Greenwood, Anna 321, 364
Greenwood, Hannah 321, 364
Greenwood, Mary 843
Greenwood, Nathaniel 281
Greenwood, Samuel 137
Greer, Hannah 819
Greer, Sarah 819
GREET 325
Grefte, Hannah 286, 423
GREGORY 325, 482
Gregory, --- 574
Gregory, Ann 193, 633
Gregory, Anna 707
Gregory, Elizabeth 493, 788
Gregory, Hannah 707
Gregory, John 681
Gregory, Judah 772
Gregory, Lydia 276
Gregory, Mary 85
Gregory, Percy 195
Gregory, Perses 195
Gregory, Phebe 61
Gregory, Rebecca 649
Gregory, Sarah 61, 720
Gregory, Sarah Messenger Palmer 553
Gregory, Susannah 28
Gregory, Thomas 545
Gregson, Anna 203
Gregson, Phebe 644, 808
Gregson, Sarah 302

Gregson, Susanna 195
GRELE 320
Grele, Mary 829
GRELEE 320
Grelee, Mary 676
GRENAWAY 324
Grene, Anne 524
Grenhill, Rebecca 667
GRETIAN 325
Gretian, Anthony 245
Grey, Hannah 2
Grey, Joanna 85
Grey, Lydia 474
Grey, Mary 197
Grey, Mercy 197
Greyson, Sarah 302, 808
GRICE 325
Grice, Charles 209, 549
Gridgley, Katherine 204
GRIDLEY 325
Gridley, Believe 183
Gridley, Elizabeth 79, 726
Gridley, Elizabeth Bateman 21
Gridley, Hannah 205, 733
Gridley, Joseph 272, 364
Gridley, Mary 636
Gridley, Return 206
Gridley, Richard 210
Gridley, Thomas 451
Gridley, Tremble 328
GRIFETH 326
Griffen, Abigail 658
Griffen, Eleanor 22
Griffen, Elizabeth 213
Griffen, Hannah 592
Griffen, Ruth 785
GRIFFETH 326
GRIFFIN 325, 326
Griffin, Agnes 85
Griffin, Benjamin 166
Griffin, Elizabeth 111, 702
Griffin, Hannah 402, 466, 469,
  520, 536
Griffin, Hugh 540, 764
Griffin, Humphrey 664
Griffin, Lydia 275
Griffin, Mary 222, 274, 287, 339,
  673, 819, 826, 827
Griffin, Matthew 372
Griffin, Mindwell 815
Griffin, Samuel 831
Griffin, Sarah 304, 700
Griffin, Shimuel 19
Griffin, Thomas 155, 644
GRIFFINE 326
Griffine, Hugh 798
Griffing, Ebenezer 398
Griffing, Humphrey 664
Griffing, Lydia 275
GRIFFINGS 326
GRIFFITH 326
Griffith, James 513
Griffith, John 765
GRIFFYN 326
GRIGGS 327
Griggs, Abigail 179, 609
Griggs, Ann 426, 453
Griggs, Elizabeth 30
Griggs, George 103
Griggs, Grizel Fletcher Jewell
  436
Griggs, Hannah 289, 496
Griggs, Henry 119
Griggs, Humphrey 331, 419
Griggs, Mary 103, 265, 716
Griggs, Rachel 11
Griggs, Sarah 120, 351, 436, 440
Griggs, Stephen 180

Griggs, Thomas 321, 612
Grigs, Elizabeth 30
Grigs, Rachel 11
GRIGSON 327
Grigson, Rebecca 87
Grigson, Susanna 195
GRIMES 316, 327
Grimes, Benjamin 789
Grimes, Sarah 493
Grimes, Susanna 766
Grimman, Thomas 63
Grimshaw, Agnes 314
GRIMSTED 327
GRINAWAY 324
Grindall, --- 612
Grinfield, Anna 386
Gringell, Anna 816
Gringell, Hannah 816
GRINNELL 327
Grinnell, Matthew 551, 791
GRINNOWAY 324
GRINOWAY 324
Grinwich, Sarah 570
Grisell, Elizabeth 554
GRISSELL 327
Grissell, Hannah 434
GRISSWOLD 327
Grist, Charles 209
Gristram, Ralph 447
Griswald, Hannah 434
Griswell, Hannah 160
GRISWOLD 327, 328
Griswold, Abigail 454
Griswold, Ann 101
Griswold, Anna 101
Griswold, Deborah 114, 190, 517
Griswold, Edward 61
Griswold, Elizabeth 57, 600, 633,
  657
Griswold, Esther 92
Griswold, Francis 117
Griswold, Hannah 101, 160, 797
Griswold, Hester 92
Griswold, Lydia 48
Griswold, Margaret 113, 146
Griswold, Mary 26, 180, 304, 576,
  751, 815
Griswold, Matthew 101, 459
Griswold, Samuel 70
Griswold, Sarah 146, 174, 370,
  576, 587
Griswould, Mary 304
Gritt, Mary 663
Grizold, Hannah 434
Grizwel, Lydia 48
GROASS 328
GROCE 328
Grombridge, Mary 125
GRONSLEY 328
GROOM 328
Groom, Edward 76
Groome, Elizabeth 527
Gros, Mercy 300
Grose, Elizabeth 137
Grose, Hannah 423
Grose, Lydia 345
GROSS 328
Gross, Anna 311
Gross, Elizabeth 324, 685, 726
Gross, Hannah 286, 338, 423
Gross, Isaac 325, 726
Gross, Lydia 659
Gross, Mary 578
Gross, Richard 109, 568
Gross, Thomas 363
Gross, William 501
GROSSE 328
Grosse, Ann 150

Grosse, Edmond 666
Grosse, Ruth 330
Grosse, Thomas 246
GROSVENOR 318, 328 see
  GRAVENER
GROTH 329
Groth, Elizabeth 554
Groth, John 406
GROUE 328
Grout, Abigail 198
Grout, Anna 200, 469
Grout, Elizabeth 12, 469
Grout, Hannah 469
Grout, John 200
Grout, Mary 443
Grout, Rebecca 120
Grout, Susannah 839
GROVE 460 see GROW
Grove, Ann 467, 659, 679
Grove, Edward 102
Grove, Hannah 525
Grove, John 486
Grove, Mary 292, 362, 607
GROVEER 329
GROVER 328, 329
Grover, Abigail 83
Grover, Deborah 63
Grover, Edmund 708
Grover, Elizabeth 25, 36, 192,
  389, 418
Grover, Hannah 298, 681
Grover, Lydia 656
Grover, Mary 833, 847
Grover, Matthew 202
Grover, Priscilla 315
Grover, Ruth 224, 553
Grover, Sarah 241, 320, 519
Grover, Thomas 25
GROVES 328, 460
Groves, Abigail 60
Groves, Amy 81
Groves, Anna 595
Groves, Hannah 2, 595
Groves, Susan 563
Groves, Susanna 563
GROW 328, 329
GROWTH 329
Growth, Elizabeth 554
Growth, John 406
GRUBB 329
GRUBBE 329
Gruman, Sarah 419
GRUMMAN 329
Grumman, John 573
Grumman, Samuel 564
GRUNDY 329
GUARD 292
Guard, Christian 175
Guard, Elizabeth 360
Guard, William 297
GUELL 330
GUENON 298
GUERNSEY 329
Guernsey, Henry 625
Guernsey, James 240
Guernsey, Joseph 100
Guild, Ann 10
Guild, Elizabeth 629
Guild, John 721
Guild, Sarah 575
GUILDFORD 330
GUILE 330
Guile, Sarah 575
Guilford, Susanna 419
GUINON 298
GUIRE 330
Guire, Mary Adams 506
Guise, Luke 671

GULE 330
GULL 330
Gull, Ann 636
Gull, Esther 304
Gull, Mary 41
Gull, Mercy 15
Gull, William 220, 274
GULLEY 330
GULLIFER 330
GULLISON 330
Gullison, Sarah 16, 273
GULLIVER 330
Gulliver, Anthony 767
Gulliver, Elizabeth 492
Gulliver, Hannah 756
Gulliver, Lydia 461
Gulliver, Mary 23, 24
GULLY 330
GUMAER 330
GUMAR 330
GUMMER 330
Gun, Mehitable 667
GUNN 330
Gunn, Abel 207
Gunn, Christian 85
Gunn, Deborah 740
Gunn, Elizabeth 355
Gunn, Hannah 746
Gunn, Mehitable 100, 132, 253, 262
Gunn, Nathaniel 431
Gunn, Samuel 319
Gunn, Sarah 508
GUNNISON 330
Gunnison, Deborah 410, 470
Gunnison, Elihu 677
Gunnison, Elizabeth 187, 661
Gunnison, Hugh 481, 512, 518
Gunnison, Priscilla 792
Gunnison, Sarah 273, 757
Guns, Mary 840
GUPPY 330
Guppy, John 703
Guppy, Mary 306
Guppy, Rachel 580
GUPTILL 331
Guptill, Thomas 140
GURCHFIELD 331
Gurdon, Meriel 648
Gurdon, Merrell 648
Gurdon, Muriel 648
GURGEFIELD 331
Gurgsfield, Margaret Davis 64
GURLEY 331
Gurley, William 424
Gurne, Jane 119
GURNELL 313
Gurnell, John 603
Gurnellin, Jane 119
GURNEY 331
Gurney, Elizabeth 666
Gurney, John 31, 118, 119, 265, 327, 419, 436
Gurney, Mary 610, 666
Gurney, Ruth 31
Gurney, Samuel 663
Gurney, Sarah 768
Gustien, Mary 778
GUSTIN 331
GUTCH 331
Gutch, Lydia 635
Gutch, Margaret 476
Gutch, Sarah 247
GUTHRIE 311, 331
Guthrie, Robert 820
GUTRIDGE 311
Gutridge, Katharine 279
Gutridge, Lydia 254

Gutridge, Richard 254
Gutterage, Mary 740
GUTTERIDGE 310, 311
Gutteridge, Catharine 673
Gutteridge, Katherine 673
Gutteridge, Mary 695
Gutteridge, Robert 311
Gutteridge, Thomas 673
GUTTERIG 311
Gutterig, Hannah 621
GUTTERSON 331
Gutterson, Elizabeth 131, 173
Gutterson, Mary 155
Gutterson, Sarah 365
Gutterson, Susanna 602
Gutterson, William 173
GUTTERY 311
Guttredge, Robert 820
GUTTRIDGE 311, 331
Guttridge, Mary 128
Guttridge, Robert 733
GUY 296, 331
Guy, Elizabeth 438
Guy, Hannah 780
Guy, Joane 517
Guy, John 780
Guy, Mary 725
GWIN 331
Gwin, John 479
Gwin, Thomas 249
GWINN 331
Gwinne, Mehitable 256
Gye, Mary 498
GYELLS 303
GYLES 303
Gyles, Hannah 767
Gyllam, Joseph 38
GYPSON 300
Gyver, Bridget 699

--- H ---

H--e, Martha 568
HABBERFIELD 331
Habberfield, Mary 647
Habberfield, William 31
Habbey, Judith 171
HABGOOD 342
Haborne, George 457
Haborne, Susanna 457
Haburne, Jane 318
HACK 331
Hack, William 708
Hackborne, Hannah 405
Hackburn, Hannah 405
Hackburne, Elizabeth 150, 319
Hackburne, Samuel 232
HACKELTON 332
HACKER 331
Hacker, Bethia 270
Hacker, Sarah 201
HACKET 331
Hacket, Hannah 307
Hacket, Rebecca 812
Hacket, Sarah 611
HACKETT 331
Hackett, Elizabeth 581
Hackett, Mary 581
Hackett, Rebecca 770, 802
Hackett, Sarah 133, 164
HACKLETON 331
Hackleton, William 132
Hackley, Ann 620
Hackley, Peter 33
Hackshaw, Mary 549
Hacutt, Elizabeth 847

HADDEM 332
HADDEN see HAYDEN
Hadden, Elizabeth 690
Hadden, Mary 75
HADDON 332
Haddon, Katharine 694
Haddon, Sarah 246, 847
Haddon, Susanna 168
HADE 332
HADEN 356
HADEWAY 353
HADLEY 332
Hadley, Ellen 227
Hadley, George 227, 677
Hadley, Hannah 422
Hadley, Joseph 201
Hadley, Mary 551
Hadley, Thomas 612
HADLOCK 332
Hadlock, James 276
Hadlock, Mary 231, 275, 488, 842
Hadlock, Nathaniel 231
Hadlock, Rebecca 436
Hadlock, Sarah 488, 675
Hadlocke, Deborah 732
HADLY 332
HAELL 333
Haes, Mary 126
HAFFATT 357
HAFFIELD 357
Haffield, Mary 164
Haffield, Rachel 162
Haffield, Ruth 807
Haffield, Sarah 409
HAGAR 332
Hagar, Mehitable 538
Hagar, Rebecca 362
Hagar, Ruharnah 771
Hagar, Sarah 811
HAGBORNE 332
Hagborne, Elizabeth 747
HAGBOURNE 332
Hagbourne, Elizabeth 150, 319
Hagbourne, Samuel 11
Hagburne, Samuel 232
HAGER 332
Hager, Abigail 810
Hager, Hannah 603
Hager, Susanna 328
Haggert, Hannah 792
HAGGET 332
Hagget, Hannah 792
HAGGETT 332
Haggett, Deliverance 736
Haggett, Othniel 300
HAIELL 333
HAIES 357
HAIEWARD 360
HAIGHT 332, 395, 396 see HOYT
Haight, Abigail 263
Haight, Ann 538
Haight, Deborah 608
Haight, Susanna 326
Haile, Ann 755
HAILSTONE 332
Hailstone, Ann 254
Hailstone, Margaret 271
HAINE 357, 358
HAINES 357, 358
Haines, Eleanor 792
Haines, Elizabeth 35, 792
Haines, Hannah 363
Haines, James 206
Haines, John 241
Haines, Matthias 491
Haines, Robert 790
Haines, Ruth 354

Haines, Sarah 2, 399, 441
HAIT 395
Haite, Elizabeth 647
Haiton, Margaret 3
HALBIDGE 332
Halbrook, Elizabeth 67
Halce, Margaret 21
Hald, Hannah 708
Haldey, Joseph 176
HALE 332, 333, 334, 336
Hale, ---- 60
Hale, Abigail 593
Hale, Apphia 635
Hale, Bennizer 221
Hale, Dorothy 373
Hale, Elizabeth 28, 581, 622
Hale, Eunes 128
Hale, Eunice 128
Hale, Hannah 565, 617
Hale, Hannah Osborn 547
Hale, Isabel 810
Hale, Joanna 224, 452
Hale, John 185
Hale, John (Rev.) 157
Hale, Joseph 224
Hale, Josiah 592
Hale, Judith 515
Hale, Lydia 590, 771
Hale, Martha 277, 568
Hale, Mary 58, 62, 65,97, 144,
     347, 598, 607, 825
Hale, Naomi 291
Hale, Rebecca 403
Hale, Robert 414, 452
Hale, Samuel 38, 220, 491, 637
Hale, Sarah 313, 626, 662
Hale, Thomas 263, 786
Hales, Mary 210
HALEWELL 382
HALEY 333 see HEALEY
Haley, Anna 797
Haley, Elizabeth 531
Haley, John 297, 689
Halfield, Mary 164
Halfield, Rachel 162
HALL 333, 334, 335, 336, 337
Hall, Abigail 115, 762, 778
Hall, Ann 235, 494, 635
Hall, Anna 18, 635
Hall, Beatrice 116
Hall, Bethiah 829
Hall, Betsey 405
Hall, Charity 124, 292
Hall, Christopher 386
Hall, Daniel 606
Hall, Deliverance 235, 753
Hall, Easter 428
Hall, Edward 428, 494
Hall, Eleanor 501
Hall, Elizabeth 28, 140, 142, 263,
     411, 450, 452, 544, 559, 582,
     583, 584, 596, 834
Hall, Elizabeth Pollard 426
Hall, Esther 428, 433, 625
Hall, Experience 373
Hall, Francis 76, 515, 646
Hall, George 124, 292
Hall, Gershom 93
Hall, Grace 804
Hall, Hannah 76, 226, 235, 282,
     659, 715
Hall, Hester 625
Hall, Honor 4
Hall, Isaac 337
Hall, James 396
Hall, Jane 249, 709
Hall, Joanna 570
Hall, John 129, 181, 229, 397,

Hall, John (cont.) 675, 689, 721,
     841
Hall, Joseph 549, 550
Hall, Kinsley 836
Hall, Lydia 201
Hall, Martha 597, 819
Hall, Mary 71, 72,92,98, 109, 147,
     178, 267, 283, 435, 492, 500,
     543, 550, 551, 607, 681, 709,
     758
Hall, Mercy 147, 373
Hall, Preserved 499, 840
Hall, Priscilla 550
Hall, Rebecca 30
Hall, Rebecca Jones 734
Hall, Richard 379
Hall, Robert 422, 552
Hall, Ruth 708
Hall, Samuel 318, 599, 712, 799
Hall, Sarah 26, 75, 120, 190, 198,
     202, 256, 335, 412, 423, 466,
     527, 758, 790, 810, 811
Hall, Stephen 370, 775
Hall, Susanna 685
Hall, Susannah 799
Hall, Thankful 226
Hall, Thomas 92, 125, 425, 644,
     697
Hall, William 280, 316, 681
Hall, Zuriel 687
HALLADAY 337
Halladay, Sarah 120
HALLAM 337
Hallam, Alice 468
Hallam, Mary 622
Hallard, George 739
HALLAWAY 382
HALLAWELL 337, 382
Halle, Hannah 695
Halle, Martha 597
HALLECK 337
HALLET 334, 337
Hallet, Ann 198
Hallet, Elizabeth 164
Hallet, Hannah 353, 783
Hallet, Jane 523
Hallet, Jenne 523
Hallet, Lois 164
Hallet, Lydia 232
Hallet, Ruhamah 85
HALLETT 337
Hallett, Abigail 8
Hallett, Alice 159, 535
Hallett, Bathsheba 85
Hallett, Hannah 353
Hallett, Mary 288
Hallett, Mehitable 218
Hallett, Rebecca 412
Hallett, Ruhamah 85, 366
Hallett, Sarah 577
Hallett, William 54, 261, 739, 830
Hallewell, Mary 533
HALLIDAY 337
HALLOCK 337
Hallock, Abigail 388
Hallock, Elizabeth 350, 393
Hallock, Margaret 817
Hallock, Mary 389
Hallock, Peter 393
Hallock, Sarah 298
HALLOM 337
Hallor, Martha 55, 126
HALLOWAY 382
Halloway, Adam 259
Halloway, Grace 615
Halloway, Hannah 98, 614
Halloway, Mary 23, 753
HALLOWELL 337

HALLOWELL (cont.) see
     HOLLOWAY
Hallowell, Henry 242
Hallowell, Mary 272
Hallowell, William 457
Halls, Thomas 10
HALLWELL 337
Hally, Elizabeth 145
HALLYDAY 337
HALSALL 337
Halse, Margaret Phipps 17
Halseld, Rachel 162
HALSEY 337, 338 see HASEY
Halsey, Abigail 393
Halsey, Ann 801
Halsey, Elizabeth 338, 393, 637
Halsey, Esther 561
Halsey, Hannah 393
Halsey, Isaac 399, 718
Halsey, Jemima 453
Halsey, Lydia 432
Halsey, Margaret 21
Halsey, Margaret Phipps 17
Halsey, Mary 393, 595
Halsey, Priscilla 530
Halsey, Rachel 478
Halsey, Sarah 516
HALSTEAD 338
Halstead, Anne 566
Halstead, Edna 539
Halstead, Grace 47
Halstead, Hannah 749
Halstead, Joseph 718
Halstead, Sarah 134, 765
HALSTED 338
Halsted, Edna 32
Halton, Katherine 755
Halton, Rachel 92
Haly, Lydia 148
HAM 338
Ham, Elizabeth 185
Ham, Mary 388, 773
Ham, Sarah 731
Ham, Tryphena 757
HAMANT 338
Hamant, Elizabeth 520
Hamant, Mary 825
Hamant, Sarah 791
HAMARY 338
Hamblehurst, Mary 350
HAMBLEN 338, 339
Hamblen, Martha 223
Hamblen, Sarah 369
HAMBLETON 338
Hambleton, Sarah 277
HAMBLIN 338
Hamblin, Nathaniel 338
Hamburg, Margaret 3
Hamby, Catherine 407
Hamery, Mary Jennings 819
HAMES 340, 358
HAMILTON 338
Hamilton, Daniel 692, 698
Hamilton, Nathaniel 339
HAMLEN 339
HAMLET 338
Hamlet, Hannah 790
Hamlet, Jacob 416
Hamlet, Rebecca 286
Hamlet, William 397
HAMLIN 339
Hamlin, Elizabeth 658
Hamlin, Esther 693
Hamlin, Experience 417, 463
Hamlin, Ezekiel 177
Hamlin, Hannah 150
Hamlin, James 150
Hamlin, John 116

Hamlin, Mary 177, 207, 644
Hamlin, Mehitable 386
Hamlin, Melatiah 369
Hamlin, Mercy 352
Hamlin, Nathaniel 338
Hamlin, Priscilla 634
Hamlin, Sarah 369
Hamlin, Thomas 590
Hamman, Elizabeth 268
Hammer, Sarah 560
Hammett, Thomas 122
HAMMON 339
Hammon, Abigail 323, 803
Hammon, Mary 825
Hammon, Sarah 791
HAMMOND 339, 340
Hammond, --- 309
Hammond, Abigail 324, 351, 803
Hammond, Ann 221, 474
Hammond, Anna 355
Hammond, Dorcas 201
Hammond, Edward 841
Hammond, Elizabeth 142, 282, 391, 494, 585, 612, 839
Hammond, Hannah 46, 355, 598
Hammond, John 185, 193
Hammond, Joseph 457
Hammond, Lawrence 299, 817, 824
Hammond, Lydia 309
Hammond, Margaret 642
Hammond, Mary 752
Hammond, Mercy 316
Hammond, Nathan 218
Hammond, Nathaniel 819
Hammond, Philippa 343
Hammond, Richard 612, 639, 682
Hammond, Sarah 449, 544, 705, 791
Hammond, Thomas 471
Hammonde, Elizabeth 268
HAMMONS 339
Hamnor, Sarah 560
Hamons, Elizabeth 498
HAMOR 340, 358
Hampson, Beatrice 84, 428
HAMPTON 340
Hampton, Anna 515
Hampton, Anne 765
Hampton, Mary 503
HANBURY 340 see HENBURY
Hanbury, Hannah 831
Hanbury, William 420
HANCE 340
Hanchet, Hannah 472
Hanchet, John 730
HANCHETT 341
Hanchett, Deliverance 793
Hanchett, Ellen 316
Hanchett, Esther 316
Hanchett, John 344
Hanchett, Thomas 124
HANCOCK 340
Hancock, Edward 312
Hancock, Elizabeth 834
Hancock, Mary 73, 252
HAND 340, 341
Hand, Abigail 328
Hand, Alice 671
Hand, John 165
Hand, Mary 43
Hand, Mehitable 507
Hand, Rebecca 502
Hand, Sarah 527
Hand, Silence 814
HANDERSON 364
Handerson, Miriam 546
HANDFORD 341

Handford, Nathaniel 38, 533
HANDLEY 365
HANDS 340
Hands, Abigail 214, 341
Hands, Ann 390
Hands, Mehitable 653
HANDY 341
Handy, Hannah 60
Handy, Richard 60
Hanet, Ann 739
Hanet, Anna 739
HANFORD 341
Hanford, Elizabeth 122, 769
Hanford, Elnathan 470
Hanford, Eunice 115
Hanford, Jeffrey 673
Hanford, Lettice 277, 417
Hanford, Margaret 629
Hanford, Mary 244
Hanford, Susan 543
Hanford, Susanna 103, 543, 803
Hanford, Thomas 125, 409
Hanking, John 691
HANKS 341
Hanks, Benjamin 626
Hanks, Hannah 656
HANMER 341
Hanmer, Bethiah 711
Hanmer, Lydia 428
Hanmor, Rebecca 368
HANMORE 341
Hanmore, Rebecca 368
Hanmore, Susanna 103
Hanna, Elizabeth 747
Hannaford, Hannah 327
HANNAH 341
Hannah, Mary 537
Hannewall, Elizabeth 339
HANNIFORD 341
Hanniford, Elizabeth 214, 498
Hanniford, John 214, 520
Hanniford, Rose 520
Hanniford, Sarah 365
HANNISON 364
Hannison, Mary 842
HANNUM 341
Hannum, Abigail 113, 645
Hannum, Elizabeth 126
Hannum, John 704
Hannum, Mary 11
HANSCOM 341
HANSCOMB 341
Hanscomb, Ann 745
Hanscomb, Thomas 666, 745
HANSET 341
HANSETT 341
HANSON 341, 342
Hanson, Elizabeth 340
Hanson, Isaac 254
Hanson, Mary 464
Hanson, Mercy 152
Hanson, Thomas 631
Hanson, Wybra 592
HAPGOOD 342
Hapgood, Elizabeth 105
Hapgood, Mary 810
Hapgood, Sarah 810
Hapgood, Shadrack 359
Hapscott, Hannah 294
HARADEN 342
Haraden, Edward 836
HARBARD 365
Harberd, Henry 509
HARBERT 342, 365
Harbert, Elizabeth 74
Harbittle, Dorothy 448
HARBOR 342, 365
Harbor, Esther 360

Harbor, Hester 360, 771
Harbottle, Dorothy 356, 448
HARBOUR 342, 365 see HERBERT
Harbour, Comfort 60
Harbour, John 656
HARCOOT 342
Harcourt, Dorothy 188
Harcourt, Isabella 792
Harcourt, Mercy 435
Harcourt, Meribah 14
HARCURT 342
Harcurt, Mercy 435
Harcurt, Richard 276
Harcurt, Sarah 170
HARCUT 342
Harcutt, Elizabeth 847
Harcutt, Isabella 792
Harcutt, Susannah 338, 718
HARD 342
Hard, Sarah 58
HARDAY 343
HARDEN 342, 343
Harden, Sarah 386
Hardey, Sarah 406
HARDIE 343
Hardie, Mary 360
Hardie, Sarah 420
HARDIER 342, 343 see HARDING
Hardier, Lydia 652
HARDIN 342, 343
Hardin, Anna 699
Hardin, John 523
Hardin, Margaret 748
Hardin, Sarah 748
HARDING 342, 343
Harding, Abraham 48, 237, 256, 281
Harding, Ann 128
Harding, Anna 128
Harding, Deborah 48
Harding, Dorothy 37
Harding, Elizabeth 3,97, 236, 342, 697
Harding, Hannah 128
Harding, Israel 287, 309, 501
Harding, John 742
Harding, Lydia 652
Harding, Margaret 748
Harding, Martha 108
Harding, Mary 40, 766, 809
Harding, Phebe 106
Harding, Priscilla 253
Harding, Prudence 25
Harding, Robert 340
Harding, Sarah 253, 748, 809
Harding, Susannah 110
Harding, Winifred 811, 812
HARDISON 343
HARDMAN 343
HARDWOOD 350
HARDY 343
Hardy, Anna 343
Hardy, Elizabeth 65, 351, 563, 581, 585
Hardy, George 593
Hardy, Hannah 25, 343, 490
Hardy, John 118
Hardy, Joseph 263, 490
Hardy, Lydia 562
Hardy, Mary 197, 360, 448, 732
Hardy, Richard 25, 563, 585
Hardy, Ruth 500
Hardy, Sarah 163, 420
Hardy, Susannah 614, 669
HARE 343
Hare, Samuel 74, 129

Harffield, Mary 164
HARFORD 349
Harford, Thomas 166
Harford, William 133
HARGER 343, 344
Harger, Abigail 207
Harger, Anna 147
Harger, Jabez 741
Harger, Samuel 710, 741
Harges, Abigail 186
Harges, Elizabeth 156
Hargreve, Sarah 64
Harington, Mary 57
HARKER 344
Harker, John 510
Harker, Sarah 409
Harlackenden, Roger 568
HARLAKENDEN 344
Harlakenden, Dorothy 674
Harlakenden, Mabel 241, 357
HARLOCK 344
Harlock, Bethia 786
Harlock, Thomas 20
HARLOW 344
Harlow, Bashua 659
Harlow, Bathsheba 659
Harlow, Francis 319
Harlow, Joanna 42
Harlow, Mary 234, 383
Harlow, Nathaniel 112
Harlow, Rebecca 199, 725
Harlow, Repentance 477
Harlow, William 168, 522
Harlsdon, Ann 640
Harlsdon, Anna 640
Harman, Jane 227
Harman, Mary 388
HARMON 344
Harmon, Elizabeth 39, 226, 272
Harmon, Hannah 566
Harmon, John 226, 281
Harmon, Lydia 55
Harmon, Mary 83, 226
Harmon, Naomi 177
Harmon, Sarah 263
HARNDEL 344
Harndel, Rebecca 523
HARNDELL 344
Harndell, Mary 701
HARNDEN 344
Harnden, John 669
HARNETT 344
HARNY 344
Haronett, Ann 593
Haronett, Elizabeth 593
HARPER 344
Harper, Christian 368
Harper, Dorcas 840
Harper, Experience 401
Harper, Hannah 629, 630
Harper, Mary 80
HARRADAINE 342
HARRADAN 342
HARRADEN 342
Harraden, Ann 207
Harraden, Elizabeth 604
Harradun, Mary 629
Harrandine, Mary 629
Harrdaine, Elizabeth 604
Harrendon, Mary 629
HARRIDON 342
HARRIMAN 344
Harriman, Elizabeth 313, 507
Harriman, Hannah 89
Harriman, Jonathan 835
Harriman, Mary 181
Harringman, Aaron 292
Harringman, Mary 292

HARRINGTON 345
Harrington, Daniel 294
Harrington, Edward 117
Harrington, Elizabeth 768
Harrington, Hannah 830
Harrington, Joan 847
Harrington, Joseph 778
Harrington, Mary 61, 285, 731
Harrington, Samuel 721, 782
Harrington, Sarah 828
Harrington, Susan 201
Harrington, Susanna 58, 201
Harrington, Thomas 805
HARRIS 345, 346, 347
Harris, Abigail 121, 518
Harris, Amity 521, 680
Harris, Ann 498, 739
Harris, Anna 498, 739
Harris, Anne 381, 498, 784
Harris, Bridget 89
Harris, Christian 820
Harris, Daniel 57
Harris, David 28
Harris, Desire 440
Harris, Elizabeth 92, 156, 235,
    277, 292, 306, 403, 498, 613,
    653, 788, 791, 801, 810
Harris, Elizabeth Cutter 711
Harris, Elizabeth Rogers Stanton
    702
Harris, George 756
Harris, Hannah 178, 279, 377,
    517, 810
Harris, Howlong 262
Harris, Jane 233, 315, 687
Harris, Joan 553, 756, 847
Harris, John 44, 73, 101, 174,
    180, 392, 463, 780, 794
Harris, Joseph 128, 515
Harris, Margaret 700, 720
Harris, Martha 167, 264, 691
Harris, Mary 13, 84, 106, 125,
    261, 302, 315, 325, 360, 398,
    421, 455, 549, 778, 803, 827
Harris, Mercy 315
Harris, Parnell 628
Harris, Patience 488
Harris, Rebecca 638
Harris, Richard 33, 313
Harris, Ruth 785
Harris, Samuel 137, 569, 820
Harris, Sarah 64, 68, 68, 104,
    387, 450, 807
Harris, Susannah 135, 533
Harris, Thomas 193, 215, 498,
    509, 706, 707
Harris, Walter 62
Harris, William 685, 688
Harris, Wm. 628
Harrise, Elizabeth 298
HARRISON 347, 348
Harrison, Abigail 153
Harrison, Anna 488
Harrison, Bethia 295
Harrison, Elizabeth 42, 214, 449,
    467, 519
Harrison, Ellen 737
Harrison, Helena 737
Harrison, Isaac 805
Harrison, Joan 39
Harrison, John 97
Harrison, Katherine 389
Harrison, Mary 466, 585
Harrison, Prudence 682
Harrison, Rebecca 404
Harrison, Sarah 364, 661
Harrison, Susanna 319
Harrison, Thomas 706, 737

HARROD 350
Harrod, Hannah 801
Harrod, Henry 271
Harrod, Joanna 16
Harrod, Mary 326
Harrod, Winifred 138
HARRUD 350
HARRUDE 350
Harst, Sarah 826
HART 348, 349
Hart, --- 325, 819
Hart, Alice 582
Hart, Deborah 518, 605
Hart, Elizabeth 271, 516, 827
Hart, Florence 751
Hart, George 752, 761
Hart, Hannah 90
Hart, John 730, 753, 812
Hart, Judith 117, 611, 616
Hart, Lydia 714
Hart, Martha 529
Hart, Mary 131, 191, 371, 459,
    532, 719, 719, 754, 788
Hart, Mehitable 169
Hart, Rachel 611, 784
Hart, Samuel 392, 754
Hart, Sarah 35, 95, 530, 540, 595,
    656, 730, 761
Hart, Stephen 529, 680, 737
Hart, Stephen (Jr.) 737
Hart, Thomas 159
Harte, Mary 61
HARTFORD 349
Harthorne, Sarah 494
Harthorne, Thomas 494
Hartopp, Joane 632
HARTSHORN 349
Hartshorn, Hannah 208
Hartshorn, John 697
Hartshorn, Ruth 785
Hartshorn, Susanna 217, 559
HARTSHORNE 349
Hartshorne, Sarah 494
Hartshorne, Thomas 494
Hartt, Mary 55
Hartt, Samuel 55
HARTWED 349
HARTWELL 349
Hartwell, Hannah 390
Hartwell, Mary 371, 560
Hartwell, Sarah 449, 557
Harty, Margaret 810
HARVARD 349
Harvard, John 13
Harven, Elizabeth 409
HARVEY 349, 350
Harvey, --- 678
Harvey, Abigail 567, 716, 734
Harvey, Agnes 187, 691
Harvey, Ann 109
Harvey, Ann Small 799
Harvey, Edmund 308
Harvey, Eleanor 201, 580
Harvey, Eliza 428
Harvey, Elizabeth 56, 225, 408,
    428, 589, 818
Harvey, Esther 175, 561
Harvey, Experience 350
Harvey, Henry 4
Harvey, Hester 175
Harvey, Jehoadan 778
Harvey, Joanne 43
Harvey, John 516, 640
Harvey, Martha 766, 825
Harvey, Mary 327, 402, 416, 534
Harvey, Matthias 170
Harvey, Peter 513
Harvey, Richard 716

Harvey, Sarah 651
Harvey, Thomas 466, 718
Harvey, William 733
Harvy, Judith 315
Harward, Sarah 757
HARWOD 350
HARWOOD 350, 352
Harwood, Benjamin 653
Harwood, Elizabeth 660
Harwood, Esther 266
Harwood, Hannah 487, 801
Harwood, Joanna 16
Harwood, John 223
Harwood, Margaret 355
Harwood, Mary 503
Harwood, Sarah 657, 757
Harwood, Thomas 839
Harwood, Winifred 138
HASCALL 351
Hascall, Hannah 837
Hascoll, Ruth 329
Hascoll, Sarah 836
HASELTINE 361
Haseltine, Abraham 273
Haseltine, Ann 437
Haseltine, Anna 437
Haseltine, Anne 437
Haseltine, Deliverance 202
Haseltine, Elizabeth 406
Haseltine, Hannah 323, 437
Haseltine, Mary 835
HASELTON 361
Haselton, Mary 710
Haselton, Mercy 437
Haselton, Nathaniel 415
HASELWOOD 361
HASEY 350, 351 see HALSEY
Hasey, Esther 321
Hasey, Joseph 114
Hasey, Sarah 698, 762
Hasey, Susanna 466
Hasey, Susannah 414
Hasey, William 593
HASIE 351
HASKALL 351
HASKELL 351
Haskell, Abigail 562
Haskell, Benjamin 81
Haskell, Eleanor 327, 713
Haskell, Elinor 713
Haskell, Elizabeth 224, 231
Haskell, Ellen 713
Haskell, Hannah 837
Haskell, Mark 215, 563
Haskell, Mary 206, 224, 588
Haskell, Roger 65
Haskell, Ruth 329, 689
Haskell, Sarah 224, 342, 713, 836
Haskell, Susan 593
Haskell, William 713
HASKET 351
Hasket, Sarah 433
HASKETT 351
Haskett, Elizabeth 217
Haskett, Sarah 252, 410
HASKINS 389, 390
Haskins, Anne 687
Haskins, Christian 819
Haskins, Grace 245
Haskins, Mary 164
Haskins, Rachel 579
Haskins, Rebecca 98
Haskins, Sarah 296, 687
Haskins, Susanna 386
Haskins, William 819
HASLETON 361
Hasoden, Mary 485
Hasptorn, Thomas 449

HASSAM 351
Hasse, Hester 321
Hasse, Sarah 698
HASSELL 351
Hassell, Abiah 77
Hassell, Alice 432, 732
Hassell, Anna 476
Hassell, Elizabeth 843
Hassell, Esther 574
Hassell, George 133
Hassell, Hester 574
HASSELTONE 361
Hassey, Rebecca 174
Hast, Margaret 315
HASTINGS 351, 352
Hastings, Abigail 80
Hastings, Abigaile 782
Hastings, Benjamin 562
Hastings, Elizabeth 69, 281, 566
Hastings, Hannah 181, 304
Hastings, Hepzibah 82
Hastings, John 240, 501
Hastings, Katherine 208
Hastings, Lydia 9, 12
Hastings, Mary 129
HASWOOD 350, 352
HATCH 352, 353
Hatch, Abigail 98
Hatch, Alice 581, 638, 639
Hatch, Ann 578, 712, 747
Hatch, Anna 686
Hatch, Benjamin 206
Hatch, Bethiah 275
Hatch, Betty 196
Hatch, Elizabeth 352, 529, 692, 712
Hatch, Esther 262
Hatch, Hannah 233, 765
Hatch, Jane 475, 669
Hatch, Joanna 828
Hatch, Lydia 47, 221, 698, 700, 729
Hatch, Margaret 835
Hatch, Mary 242, 268, 365, 604, 792
Hatch, Mercy 85, 640, 759
Hatch, Moses 39
Hatch, Patience 229
Hatch, Sarah 828
Hatch, Thomas 47, 687, 698
Hatch, William 47, 439, 440
HATHAWAY 353
Hathaway, --- 668
Hathaway, Abigail 577
Hathaway, Arthur 165, 339
Hathaway, Hannah 130, 165, 674
Hathaway, John 237, 555
Hathaway, Lydia 676
Hathaway, Mary 339
Hathaway, Rebecca 726
Hathaway, Susanna 555
Hatherby, Timothy 742
HATHERLY 353
Hatherly, Eglin 341, 673
HATHORN 353
HATHORNE 353
Hathorne, Abigail 613
Hathorne, Ann 594
Hathorne, Anna 594
Hathorne, Anne 594
Hathorne, Eleazer 643
Hathorne, Elizabeth 594
Hathorne, Sarah 95, 167, 364
Hathorne, William 123
Hatorne, Ann 594
Hatorne, Anna 594
Hatorne, Anne 594
Hatsell, Henry 254

Hattee, Alice 581
Hatton, Katherine 755
Haubury, Hannah 831
HAUGH 390, 391 see HUFF
Haugh, Elizabeth 365
Haugh, Mary 34, 684
Haugh, Samuel 101, 422
Haugh, Sarah 774, 801
HAUGHTON 353, 354 see
   HORTON, HOUGHTON
Haughton, Abigail 457
Haughton, Alice 195
Haughton, Beatrice 593
Haughton, Beatrix 593
Haughton, Katherine 127
Haughton, Mary 539
Haughton, Mercy 69
Haughton, Richard 146, 195
Haughton, Sarah 539
HAUKES 355
Haukins, Martha 630
HAUKSIE 395
HAUL 335
Hause, Ruth 92
Hautley, John 143
HAUXHURST 354
Hauxhurst, Susanna 842
HAUXWORTH 356
Hauxworth, Mary 551, 824
HAVEN 354
Haven, Hannah 309, 558
Haven, Mary 126, 728
Haven, Moses 96
Haven, Sarah 810
Haven, Susannah 167
HAVENS 354
Havens, Desire 293
Havens, Dinah 53
Havens, Jane 672
Havens, Mary 179
Havens, Ruth 133
Havens, Sarah 762
Haverlad, Mary 85
HAVILAND 354
Haviland, Edward 343
Haviland, Jane 748
Haviland, Susannah 343
HAWARD 359, 360
Haward, Hannah 370
Haward, Mary 326
Haward, Sarah 167, 557
HAWES 354
Hawes, --- 45
Hawes, Abigail 257
Hawes, Bethiah 662
Hawes, Constance 217
Hawes, Deborah 592
Hawes, Deliverance 631, 781
Hawes, Elizabeth 141, 225, 597
Hawes, Hannah 494
Hawes, Joseph 387, 829
Hawes, Lydia 297
Hawes, Mary 30
Hawes, Obadiah 383
Hawes, Robert 245
Hawes, Ruth 92
HAWGHTON 354
HAWKE 355
Hawke, Bethia 706
Hawke, Deborah 98, 440
Hawke, Elizabeth 465
Hawke, Hannah 199
Hawke, Mary 474
Hawke, Sarah 199
HAWKENS 394
HAWKES 354, 355
Hawkes, Adam 407, 465, 779
Hawkes, Anne 352

Hawkes, Elizabeth 167, 220
Hawkes, John 375
Hawkes, Sarah 420
Hawkes, Sarah Bassett Griffin 326
Hawkes, Susannah 167
HAWKHURST 354
Hawking, Agnes 531
HAWKINS 355, 356 see HOWKINS
Hawkins, Abigail 278, 431, 516, 604
Hawkins, Anna 803
Hawkins, Anthony 738
Hawkins, Damaris 740
Hawkins, Edward 19, 218
Hawkins, Elizabeth 471, 503, 595, 621, 686, 758, 830
Hawkins, Esther 358
Hawkins, Hannah 46, 358, 407, 429, 535, 779
Hawkins, James 443, 740
Hawkins, Jane 616
Hawkins, Joan 624
Hawkins, Madeline 619
Hawkins, Mary 28, 74,96, 443, 704, 784
Hawkins, Mehitable 294
Hawkins, Rebecca 704
Hawkins, Ruth 257, 349, 490
Hawkins, Sarah 10,95, 417, 805
Hawkins, Thomas 262, 358, 672
Hawkins, Timothy 46, 267, 681
Hawkins, William 293
Hawkredd, Elizabeth 176, 484, 502
Hawkridge, Sarah 185, 496
HAWKS 355
Hawks, Elizabeth 304
Hawks, Hannah 656
Hawks, Joanna 21
Hawks, John 14, 219, 376
Hawks, Margaret 261
Hawks, Mary 254, 375
Hawks, Mercy 309
Hawks, Sarah 497
HAWKSWORTH 356
Hawksworth, Peter 706
HAWLEY 356
Hawley, Ann 328
Hawley, Anna 56, 763
Hawley, Arthur 546
Hawley, Dorothy 83
Hawley, Ebenezer 370, 535
Hawley, Elizabeth 83, 145, 227, 772
Hawley, Ephraim 473
Hawley, Grace 588, 683
Hawley, Hannah 56, 535, 763, 832
Hawley, Jane 76
Hawley, Joanna 491, 568, 574
Hawley, Johanna 568
Hawley, Mary 165
Hawley, Miriam 800
Hawley, Samuel 398
Hawley, Sarah Welles 746
Hawley, Thomas 448, 670
HAWOOD 359
HAWS 354
Haws, Deborah 592
Haws, Elizabeth 813
Haws, Mary 66
Hawthorn, Sarah 494
Hawthorn, Thomas 494
Hawthorne, Elizabeth 205
Hawthorne, Priscilla 671
Hawthorne, William 107

Hawxhurst, Jane 526
Hawxhurst, Mary 14, 170, 749
Hawxhurst, Meribah 749
Hawxhurst, Sarah 193
HAY 356, 357
Hay, Mary 789
Hay, Peter 103, 191, 241, 442, 623
Hay, Timothy 476
HAYDEN 332, 356, 357 see HADDON
Hayden, Abigail 734
Hayden, Amy 789
Hayden, Elizabeth 30, 600, 786
Hayden, Experience 822
Hayden, Hannah 432, 576, 734
Hayden, John 783
Hayden, Jonathan 59
Hayden, Lydia 768
Hayden, Margaret 59
Hayden, Mary 255
Hayden, Mercy 435
Hayden, Nathaniel 561
Hayden, Ruhamah 524
Hayden, Samuel 550
Hayden, Sarah 254, 415, 427, 815
Hayden, Susanna 413
Hayden, William 746, 815
Haydon, Samuel 791
HAYE 356
HAYES 356, 357
Hayes, --- 621
Hayes, Edward 253
Hayes, Eleanor 846
Hayes, Hannah 1
Hayes, Luke 718
Hayes, Mary 85
Hayes, Rachel 506
Hayes, Samuel 360, 581
Hayes, Sarah 662
Hayes, Thomas 114
Hayes, Thomasine 532
HAYFIELD 357
Hayfield, Martha 188
Hayford, Abigail 341
HAYMAN 357
Hayman, Elizabeth 94
Hayman, Grace 66
Hayman, Mary 578
Hayman, Nathan 75
Hayman, Samuel 481, 668
Hayman, Sarah 153, 249
Hayme, Susannah 616
HAYNE 357, 358
Hayne, Dorothy 440
Hayne, Elizabeth 88
Hayne, John 88
HAYNES 340, 357, 358 see HINDS
Haynes, Abigail 105
Haynes, Ann 390
Haynes, Benjamin 388
Haynes, Deborah 99, 105
Haynes, Dorothy 283
Haynes, Edmund 451
Haynes, Eleanor 846
Haynes, Elizabeth 35, 792
Haynes, Hannah 636
Haynes, Isabel 341
Haynes, Isabella 562
Haynes, James 211, 274
Haynes, Josiah 283, 448
Haynes, Mabel 643
Haynes, Mary 30, 392, 541
Haynes, Rachel 469
Haynes, Richard 566
Haynes, Ruth 354, 541, 823
Haynes, Sarah 388, 441, 585

Haynes, Sufferance 752
Haynes, William 385, 806
HAYTE 395
HAYTER 358
HAYWARD 358, 359, 360
Hayward, Abigail 272, 469, 764
Hayward, Anne 318
Hayward, Daniel 812
Hayward, Deborah 8, 377
Hayward, Dorothy 42
Hayward, Elizabeth 16, 435, 800
Hayward, George 259
Hayward, Hannah 133, 167, 233, 259, 370, 382
Hayward, Henry 42
Hayward, Huldah 53, 128, 734
Hayward, James 675
Hayward, John 8, 661, 782, 826
Hayward, Joseph 342
Hayward, Judith 314
Hayward, Lydia 42, 516
Hayward, Margaret 106
Hayward, Margery 8, 150
Hayward, Martha 359, 571
Hayward, Mary 16, 50, 118, 257, 289, 326, 328, 425, 436, 512, 609, 632, 736, 804, 817
Hayward, Mary Harris 315
Hayward, Mehitable 233, 702
Hayward, Mercy 391
Hayward, Nathaniel 9
Hayward, Patience 9
Hayward, Persis 432
Hayward, Rebecca 695
Hayward, Robert 425, 695
Hayward, Samuel 509, 542, 723
Hayward, Sarah 6, 95, 167, 582, 602, 623, 734, 737
Hayward, Susanna 624
Hayward, Tabitha 378
Hayward, William 489, 734, 771
Haywell, Margaret 236
Haywood, Hannah 370
Haywood, Margaret 171
Haywood, Mary 16, 280, 436
Haywood, Persis 432
Haywood, Samuel 280, 723
Haywood, Sarah 35, 623
Haywood, William 734
Hayworth, Abigail 243
Hayworth, Elizabeth 243
Hayworth, John 429
HAZARD 360, 361
Hazard, Elizabeth 136, 403, 456
Hazard, Hannah 815
Hazard, Martha 400, 525, 596, 815
Hazard, Mary 814
Hazard, Thomas 672
Hazeltine, Elizabeth 134
Hazeltine, Mary 789
Hazelton, Abraham 102
Hazelton, Deborah 777
Hazelton, Elizabeth 134
Hazelton, Nathaniel 349
Hazelton, Robert 282
HAZEN 361
Hazen, Edna 572
Hazen, Edward 105, 301
Hazen, Elizabeth 346
Hazen, Hannah 301
Hazen, Isabel 834
Hazen, Priscilla 585
Hazen, Sarah 813
HAZLETON 361
Hazleton, Charles 496
Hazleton, James 797
HAZLEWOOD 361

HEACOCK 368
Heacock, Elizabeth 6
HEAD 361
HEADEN 369
Headg, Mary 733
HEADLEY 361
HEADLY 361
HEALD 361, 362
Heald, Dorothy 651
Heald, Elizabeth 142
Heald, Eunes 128
Heald, Eunice 128
Heald, Hannah 695, 708
Heald, Sarah 461, 561, 744
HEALES 361
HEALEY 362 see HALY
Healey, Hannah 239
Healey, Judith 834
Healey, Samuel 617
Healey, Sarah 42
Healey, William 106
HEALY 362
Healy, Elizabeth 325
Healy, Grace 411
Healy, Martha 197
Healy, William 487
Heane, Agnes 696
HEARD 362 see HARD
Heard, --- 458
Heard, Abigail 161, 425
Heard, Ann 254, 305, 341
Heard, Dorcas 295
Heard, Elizabeth 141, 290, 542, 679, 692
Heard, Hannah 494, 529
Heard, Israel 417
Heard, James 548
Heard, John 90, 468, 472, 828
Heard, Katharine 468
Heard, Katherine 837
Heard, Luke 73
Heard, Lydia 538
Heard, Mary 254, 338, 341
Heard, Samuel 417
Heard, Sarah 80
Heard, William 759
Hearden, Lydia 820
HEARING 366
HEARL 239, 362
Hearl, Sarah 185
Hearl, William 311, 402
Hearle, William 449
HEARLS 362
HEARN 362
Hearn, Jane 822
Hearn, Susannah 167
HEARNDEN 362
Hearnden, Benjamin 600
Hearnden, Mary 243
Hearnden, Sarah 802
Hearndon, Alice 104
Hearndon, Dorothy 37
Hearndon, Sarah 802
HEARNES 362
HEARTWELL 349
HEATH 362, 363, 458
Heath, Abigail 268
Heath, Alice 124, 567
Heath, Elias 246, 328
Heath, Elizabeth 88, 666
Heath, Hannah 91, 155, 425
Heath, Isaac 526, 847
Heath, Joseph 550, 559
Heath, Josiah 147
Heath, Margaret 421
Heath, Martha 93
Heath, Mary 182, 695
Heath, Mathew 93

Heath, Mehitable 689
Heath, Peleg 86
Heath, Samuel 296
Heath, Sarah 744
Heath, Susanna 63
Heath, William 695
HEATON 240, 241, 363
Heaton, Abigail 24
Heaton, Anna 91
Heaton, Elizabeth 824
Heaton, Leah 267
Heaton, Nathaniel 569
Heaton, Susanna 7
HEAWARD 359
Heaward, Ann 318
Heaward, Anne 318
HEBARD 367
HEBBART 367
HEBBOURN 365
Hedden, Sarah Jewett 205
HEDGE 363
Hedge, Elizabeth 44, 474
Hedge, Mary 166, 720, 733, 785
Hedge, Mercy 283, 785
Hedge, Sarah 394
Hedge, William 67, 401
HEDGER 363
Hedger, --- 639
HEDGES 363, 378
Hedges, Dinah 343
Hedges, Elizabeth 246
Hedges, Joanna 656
Hedges, Sarah 264, 496, 526
Hedges, Wm. 526
HEDLEY 361
HEFFERLAND 363
Heiden, Hannah 734
Heifernan, Joanna 765
HEIFORD 357
Heiford, Abigail 341
Heires, Sarah 173
HEITER 358
Hejlsdon, Ann 79
HELD 361, 362
HELDERETH 370
HELDRETH 369
HELE 362
Helie, Hannah 239
Helliard, Elizabeth 574
Hellier, Mary 195
Hellyer, Joan 557
Helman, Mary 154
Helman, Thomas 693
HELME 364
Helme, Elizabeth 361
Helme, Thomas 540
HELWISE 364
Helwise, Edward 167
Hely, Elizabeth 325
Hely, Judith 834
Hely, Martha 197
Hely, Mary 834
HELYAR 373
Hemanway, Elizabeth 336
HEMENWAY 364
Hemenway, Hannah 392
Hemenway, Joanna 7
Hemenway, Thankful 557
Heming, Sabina 616
HEMINGWAY 364
Hemingway, Elizabeth 266, 379
Hemingway, Mary 266
Hemingway, Sarah 311
Hemins, Judith 469
Hemins, Sabina 469
Hempfeild, Elizabeth 508
HEMPSTEAD 364
Hempstead, Elizabeth 590

Hempstead, Hannah 242, 515, 776
Hempstead, Joshua 242
Hempstead, Mary 227, 590
Hempstead, Robert 462
HENBERY 364
HENBURY 364 see HANBURY
Henbury, Arthur 668
Henbury, Hannah 622
Henbury, Mary 471
HENCHMAN 364
Henchman, Bridget 144, 622
Henchman, Edmund 268
Henchman, Elizabeth 268
Henchman, Hannah 370
Henchman, Joanna 376
Henchman, Margaret 387, 659
Henchman, Nathaniel 321
Henchman, Richard 789
Henchman, Sarah 161, 818
Henchman, Susan 174
Henchman, Susanna 174
Hencrick, Dorothy 628
HENDEE 341
HENDERSON 364
Henderson, Abigail 306
Henderson, John 117
HENDREKES 365
HENDRICK 365
Hendrick, Daniel 712
Hendrick, Elizabeth 825
Hendrick, Hannah 219, 673
Hendrick, Hannica 673
Hendrick, Hendrick 673
Hendrick, Henry 673
Hendrick, John 587
Hendrick, Sarah 409
Hendrick, Susanna 73
Hendrick, Susannah 603
Hendricks, Deborah 550
Hendricks, Dorothy 628
Hendricksen, Hannah 673
Hendricksen, Hannica 673
Hendricksen, Hendrick 673
Hendricksen, Henry 673
HENDRICKSON 365
Hendrickson, Elizabeth 825
Hendrickson, John 214
HENDY 341
Henerig, Tryntie 423
HENFIELD 365
HENLEY 365
Henley, Alice 163
Henley, Benjamin 773
Henley, Mary 409
HENLY 365
Hennery, Mary 132
HENNING 365
Hennison, Miriam 546
HENNYSON 365
Henry, Ann 843
Henry, James 241
Henry, Samuel 522
HENRYSON 365
Hensha, Thankful 461
HENSHAW 365
Henshaw, Daniel 247, 592
Henshaw, Thankful 461
Hepburn, Anna 478
Hepburn, Hannah 478
Hepburn, Rebecca 771
HEPBURNE 365
Hepburne, Sarah 647
HEPPE 365
HEPWORTH 365
HERBERT 342, 365 see HARBOUR
Herbert, Alice 184
Herbert, Ann 369

INDEX

Herbert, Elizabeth 74, 184, 805
Herbert, Henry 298, 509
Herbert, Hope Lamberton 15
Herbert, John 319
Herbert, Wm. 149
HERD 362
Herendean, Benjamin 600
HERFORD 357
Heriman, Mary 181
HERING 366
HERINGTON 345
Hermins, Judith 469
Hermins, Sabine 469
HEROD 365
HERRICK 365, 366
Herrick, Elizabeth 51, 194, 280,
  714, 764, 836
Herrick, Henry 301
Herrick, James 575
Herrick, John 196
Herrick, Joseph 199, 487
Herrick, Lydia 594
Herrick, Martha 579
Herrick, Mary 51, 613, 684, 748
Herrick, Sarah 518, 524, 575
HERRIDGE 366
HERRIMAN 345
Herriman, Elizabeth 313
HERRING 366
Herring, Hannah 787
Herring, James 241, 463
Herring, Martha 787
Herring, Mary 248
HERRINGTON 345
HERSEY 366
Hersey, Deborah 465
Hersey, Elizabeth 55, 305
Hersey, Frances 192
Hersey, Hannah 450
Hersey, Judith 825
Hersey, Mary 152
Hersey, Rebecca 420
Hersey, Ruth 54
Hersey, William 85, 305, 499
HERSOME 351
HERST 362
Heruey, Elizabeth 56
Hervey, Judith 315
Heseltine, Abraham 102
Hesilrige, Katherine 262
Hessele, Esther 750
Hessele, Hester 750
Hester, Mary 465
Heston, Elizabeth Judson 430
Hetchbone, Ruth 563
HETHERINGTON 366
HETHERSAY 366
HETHERSEY 366
HETHRINGTON 366
HETT 366 see HITT
Hett, Dorothy 525
Hett, Hannah 406, 560
Hett, Mary 269, 435
Hett, Mehitable 676, 759
Hett, Rebecca 101, 180
Hett, Thomas 435
Heusted, Rebecca 618
HEWARD 359
Hewen, Jacob 3
HEWENS 367
Hewens, Hannah 481
HEWES 366, 367, 399, 400 see
  HUGHS
Hewes, Abigail 353, 439
Hewes, Arthur 19
Hewes, Deborah 120
Hewes, Elizabeth 5, 364
Hewes, George 63

Hewes, Hannah 225
Hewes, John 123
Hewes, Joshua 189
Hewes, Mary 257, 352, 386, 448
Hewes, Phebe 306
HEWETT 367
Hewett, Elizabeth 397
Hewett, John 123
Hewett, Mary 719
Hewett, Thomas 200, 266, 564
Hewing, Jacob 3
HEWINS 367
Hewins, Elizabeth 409
Hewins, Hannah 268
Hewins, Mary 229
HEWITT 367
Hewitt, Jael 634
Hewitt, Lydia 686
Hewitt, Thomas 581, 706
Hewlet, Jane 523
Hewlet, Jenne 523
HEWLETT 367
Hewlett, Elizabeth 10
HEWS 400
Hews, Deborah 112
Hews, Tamazin 151
Hewsdell, Sarah 336
Hewsome, Grissie 520
HEWSON 367
Hewson, Ursula 243
Heyborne, George 457
Heyborne, Susanna 457
HEYDEN 357
HEYLETT 367
Heyward, Margery 8
HEYWOOD 359, 360
Heywood, Rose 11
Heywood, Sarah 35
Hiat, Ruth 847
HIBBARD 367
Hibbard, Abigail 77
Hibbard, Hannah 722
Hibbard, Joanna 722
Hibbard, Mary 172, 190, 691
Hibbart, Hannah Gibbons 482
HIBBERT 367
Hibbert, Abigail 77
Hibbert, Christian 105
Hibbert, Dorcas 1
Hibbert, Hannah 722
Hibbert, Joanna 723
Hibbert, Mary 691
HIBBINS 367
Hiberd, Abigail 77
HICHBORN 368
HICHENS 376
HICKCOCKS 368, 376
HICKE 368
Hickes, Sarah 153
Hickins, Hannah 354
Hickman, John 325
HICKOCK 376
Hickock, Benjamin 661
Hickock, Joseph 375
HICKOCKS 368
HICKOK 368
Hickok, Elizabeth 6
HICKOX 368
Hickox, Hannah 429
Hickox, Mary 102, 297
HICKS 368, 368
Hicks, Elizabeth 530, 679, 703,
  740
Hicks, Ephraim 219, 220
Hicks, Hannah 354, 418, 699
Hicks, Herodias Long 293
Hicks, Joanna 846
Hicks, John 135, 239, 293, 594,

Hicks, John (cont.) 672, 703, 740
Hicks, Joseph 239
Hicks, Lydia 39
Hicks, Margaret 327, 412
Hicks, Mary 57, 104, 429, 567
Hicks, Michael 463
Hicks, Phebe 785
Hicks, Phoebe 659
Hicks, Prudence 615, 619
Hicks, Rachel 672, 695
Hicks, Robert 743
Hicks, Sarah 19, 153
Hicks, Zechariah 19
HICKSON 376, 832
Hickson, Mary 195
Hickson, Walter 375, 731
HIDDEN 369
Hidden, Anne 191
Hidden, Elizabeth 236
Hidden, John 205
Hidden, Margaret 732
Hidden, Sarah 191
HIDE 408
Hide, Ann 792
Hide, Dorothy 218
Hide, Elizabeth 40, 419, 548
Hide, George 792
Hide, Hannah 319, 698, 839
Hide, Isaac 203
Hide, Joan 187
Hide, Mary 125, 642
Hide, Nicholas 590
Hide, Rebecca 6
Hide, Sarah 171, 258, 548, 671,
  841
Hiden, Elizabeth 236
Hiet, Rebecca 375
Higbee, Jedidah 414
HIGBY 369
Higby, Lydia 806
Higby, Mary 123
Higby, Patience 578
Higby, Sarah 478, 613
Higens, Jemima 526
HIGGENS 369
Higgenson, Ann 226
Higginbotham, Richard 182
HIGGINBOTTOM 369
HIGGINS 369, 399
Higgins, Dennis 718
Higgins, Elizabeth 793
Higgins, Hannah 552
Higgins, Jemima 526
Higgins, John 399
Higgins, Jonathan 284
Higgins, Mehitable 499
Higgins, Owen 69
Higgins, Richard 845
Higgins, Thomas 743
HIGGINSON 369
Higginson, Ann 147
Higginson, Anna 147
Higginson, John 24
Higginson, Mary 294, 792
Higginson, Sarah 353, 798
HIGGISON 369
HIGGS 369
Higgs, Elizabeth 740
Highland, Elizabeth 560
HIGINSE 369
HIGLEY 369
Higley, John 73
Hil, Elner 29
Hil, Sarah 573
HILAND 408
Hiland, Deborah 334
Hiland, Elizabeth 415, 560
Hiland, Hannah 371

Hiland, Isabel 798
Hiland, Mary 111, 336, 706, 758
Hiland, Ruth 706
Hiland, Samuel 798
Hiland, Sarah 760
Hilderith, Mary 782
HILDETH 370
HILDRETH 369, 370
Hildreth, Abigail 558
Hildreth, Dorothy 627
Hildreth, Elizabeth 707
Hildreth, Hannah 87
Hildreth, Jane 606
Hildreth, Margaret 605
Hildreth, Mary 728
Hildreth, Perses 162
Hildreth, Richard 128
Hildreth, Sarah 713
Hildreth, Thomas 87
Hildrith, Abigail 46
Hildrith, Mary 782
HILL 370, 371, 372, 373
Hill, --- 507
Hill, Abigail 9, 11, 460, 560
Hill, Ann 494, 726
Hill, Bethiall 168
Hill, Charles 581
Hill, David 186
Hill, Deborah 667
Hill, Dorcas 520
Hill, Ebenezer 146, 656
Hill, Edward 494
Hill, Eleanor 29
Hill, Eliphalet 356, 473, 535
Hill, Elizabeth 5, 37, 113, 209, 232, 351, 473, 492, 611, 708, 824
Hill, Elizabeth Greene Reynolds 618
Hill, Frances 26, 121
Hill, Hannah 88, 267, 287, 592, 714, 715
Hill, Isaac 67
Hill, Jane 468
Hill, John 10, 116, 141, 469, 535, 622, 758, 830
Hill, Joseph 830
Hill, Lidia 364
Hill, Lydia 199
Hill, Lydia Fletcher Fiske 268
Hill, Margery 518
Hill, Martha 616
Hill, Mary 95, 126, 233, 248, 260, 468, 517, 662, 720
Hill, Mercy 468, 823
Hill, Miriam 351
Hill, Naomi 203
Hill, Prudence 670
Hill, Ralph 468, 747
Hill, Rebecca 258, 320, 330
Hill, Robert 657, 723
Hill, Ruth 6, 238, 613, 823
Hill, Samuel 164
Hill, Sarah 10, 271, 472, 518, 573, 597, 603, 693, 802
Hill, Tabitha 193
Hill, Tahan 504
Hill, Thankful 448
Hill, Thomas 528
Hill, Thomasine Stacy Woodwell 840
Hill, William 188, 258, 324
Hill, Zechary 326
HILLAND 409
Hillard, Hannah 213, 259
Hillard, Mary 259
HILLER 373
Hiller, Grace 241

HILLIARD 372, 373
Hilliard, Abigail 386
Hilliard, Benjamin 249, 843
Hilliard, Dorcas 767
Hilliard, Elizabeth 499, 574, 664
Hilliard, Emanuel 505
Hilliard, Esther 52
Hilliard, Hugh 843
Hilliard, James 8
Hilliard, Job 797
Hilliard, Margaret 249, 843
Hilliard, Mary 195, 260, 497, 778
Hilliard, Nicholas 531
Hilliard, Sarah 137, 177, 381
Hilliard, Timothy 577
HILLIER 372, 373
Hillier, Deborah 651
Hillier, James 219
Hillier, John 269
Hillier, Lydia 787
Hillier, Sarah 48
HILLMAN 373
Hillman, Lucretia 217
Hillman, Thomas 693
HILLS 371, 372, 373
Hills, Abraham 80
Hills, Amy 345
Hills, Dorothy 382
Hills, Ebenezer 177
Hills, Elizabeth 76, 113, 323, 324, 480
Hills, Hannah 127, 328, 430, 436, 437, 471
Hills, John 6, 125
Hills, Joseph 220, 479, 502, 770
Hills, Mary 6, 80, 770
Hills, Philip 249
Hills, Phillis 562
Hills, Rebecca 323
Hills, Sarah 141, 147, 778
Hills, Susana 436
Hills, Susannah 437
Hills, Valentine 444
Hills, William 626, 705
HILLYARD 373
Hillyer, Andrew 217
Hillyer, James 8
HILTON 373, 374
Hilton, Agnes 54
Hilton, Alice 777
Hilton, Anna 838
Hilton, Anne 54, 374
Hilton, Edward 755
Hilton, Elizabeth 200
Hilton, Frances 806
Hilton, Hannah 838
Hilton, Jane 335, 497
Hilton, Magdalen 433, 787, 813
Hilton, Mainwaring 93
Hilton, Margadelen 5
Hilton, Mary 184, 335, 399, 406, 491, 660
Hilton, Rebecca 679
Hilton, Sarah 829
Hilton, Sobriety 373, 524
Hilton, Susanna 553
Hilton, William 200, 769, 806
HIMES see HOLMES
HIMS 374, 383
Hinchaman, Joanna 376
Hinchley, Elizabeth 557
HINCHMAN 364
Hinchman, Edmund 268
Hinchman, Elizabeth 268, 370
Hinchman, Hannah 721
Hinckes, Samuel 657
HINCKESMAN 364
Hinckis, John 164

HINCKLEY 374
Hinckley, Abigail 473
Hinckley, Bashua 336
Hinckley, Bathsheba 336
Hinckley, Elizabeth 557, 720
Hinckley, Experience 803
Hinckley, Hannah 306
Hinckley, John 311
Hinckley, Jonathan 214
Hinckley, Mary 812
Hinckley, Mehitable 27, 779
Hinckley, Melatiah 192
Hinckley, Meletiah 192
Hinckley, Mercy 604
Hinckley, Reliance 714
Hinckley, Sarah 30, 164
Hinckley, Susannah 683
Hinckley, Thomas 306
Hinckly, Thankful 499
HINCKMAN 364
Hinckman, John 325
HINCKS 374
HINCKSMAN 364
Hincksman, Bridget 622
Hincksman, Edmund 268
Hincksman, Elizabeth 268, 766
Hincksman, Hannah 370
HINCKSON 374
Hinckson, Naomi 510
HINDES 374
HINDS 357, 358, 374, 375 see HAYNES
Hinds, Benjamin 388
Hinds, Elizabeth 57, 441
Hinds, John 126, 610
Hinds, Margaret 565
Hinds, Sarah 145, 388
HINE 374, 375
Hine, Alice 132
Hine, Mercy 450
Hine, Mercy Lane 36
Hine, William 218
HINES 375
Hines, Elizabeth 675, 788
Hines, Hannah Pratt Shaw 664
Hingeson, Hannah 432
HINKLEY 374
Hinkley, Samuel 80, 398
HINKS 374
HINKSMAN 364
Hinksman, Elizabeth 766
Hinksman, Elnathan 758
Hinksman, Margaret 659
Hinkson, Honor 464
Hinkson, Margaret 729
Hinkson, Naomi 510
Hinkson, Peter 562
Hinkson, Simon 209, 210
Hinkson, Thomas 797
HINMAN 375
Hinman, Hannah 418
Hinman, Mary 160
Hinman, Patience 123
Hinman, Samuel 368
Hinman, Sarah 628
HINSDALE 375
Hinsdale, Anna 431
Hinsdale, Barnabas 731
Hinsdale, Elizabeth 184, 626
Hinsdale, Ephraim 148
Hinsdale, Experience 254
Hinsdale, Mary 360, 667, 792
Hinsdale, Mehitable 171, 220, 294
Hinsdale, Robert 219, 355
Hinsdale, Samuel 171, 636, 736
Hinsdale, Sarah 336, 415
Hinsdale, Stephen 376
Hinsdel, Sarah 336

HINSDELL 375
Hinsdell, Mary 792
HINTON 375
Hinton, Abigail 26
Hipkins, Elizabeth 275
Hipsley, Bridget 256
HIRES 375
HIRST 362
Hirst, Jane 205
HISCOCK 375
HISCOT 375
HISCOX 375
Hiscox, Elizabeth 369
HISKET 375
HISKETT 375
Hit, Dorothy 525
HITCHBORN 368
HITCHBORNE 368
HITCHCOCK 375, 376
Hitchcock, Abigail 421, 568
Hitchcock, David 53
Hitchcock, Edward 252, 423
Hitchcock, Elizabeth 72, 78, 392,
    529
Hitchcock, Hannah 562, 680
Hitchcock, Jerusha 401
Hitchcock, John 467
Hitchcock, Lucretia 295
Hitchcock, Luke 226, 782
Hitchcock, Lydia 589
Hitchcock, Margaret 251
Hitchcock, Margery 514
Hitchcock, Mary 54, 205, 596,
    644
Hitchcock, Mercy 210
Hitchcock, Richard 295
Hitchcock, Samuel 368, 741
Hitchcock, Sarah 503, 629
Hitchcock, William 36
Hitchel, Barbara 678
Hitchens, Rebecca 419
HITCHESON 376
Hitcheson, Agnes 721
Hitcheson, Sarah 460
Hitchings, Daniel 355
Hitchings, Hannah 354
Hitchings, Sarah 301
HITCHINS 376
Hitchins, Daniel 80
Hitcock, Sarah 629
HITFIELD 376
Hitfield, Matthias 556
HITT 366, 376 see HETT
Hitt, Henry 469
HIX 368
Hix, Hannah 418
Hix, Joanna 846
Hix, Margaret 412
Hix, Mary 240
Hixat, Margaret 412
Hixon, Robert 96
Hixon, Walter 731
HIXSON 376
HOADLEY 376
Hoadley, Hannah 422
Hoadley, Marie 217
Hoadley, Mary 217, 266, 285
Hoadley, William 87, 259, 285,
    619
HOAG 376, 379 see HOGG
Hoald, Dorothy 602
HOAR 376
Hoar, Annie 439
Hoar, Annis 439
Hoar, Daniel 168
Hoar, Elizabeth 602
Hoar, Joanna 561
Hoar, Leonard 764

Hoar, Lydia 803
Hoar, Margaret 497
Hoar, Margery 272
Hoar, Mary 483
Hoar, Rebecca 689
Hoar, Sarah 715
HOARE 376
Hoare, Abigail 543
Hoare, Bridget 185
Hoare, Elizabeth 422, 760
Hoare, Joanna 520, 608
Hoare, Mary 318, 346
Hoare, Mercy 699
Hoase, Rebecca 276
Hobard, Hannah 223
Hobard, Mary 172
HOBART 376, 377
Hobart, Abigail 820
Hobart, Bathsheba 458, 759
Hobart, Caleb 260, 652
Hobart, Daniel 424
Hobart, David 429
Hobart, Deborah 465
Hobart, Edmund 480, 527, 809
Hobart, Elizabeth 180, 626, 757
Hobart, Frances 63
Hobart, Hannah 106, 316, 356,
    633, 748
Hobart, Irene 786
Hobart, Israel 101
Hobart, Jael 90
Hobart, John 616
Hobart, Joshua 316, 609
Hobart, Josiah (Capt.) 699
Hobart, Lydia 466
Hobart, Margaret 725
Hobart, Martha 50
Hobart, Mary 144, 400, 819
Hobart, Mehitable 450
Hobart, Nathaniel 716
Hobart, Nazareth 55
Hobart, Peter 229
Hobart, Rebecca 39, 484, 494
Hobart, Sarah 101, 102, 162, 187,
    356, 527
Hobarte, Hannah 359
HOBBERT 398
Hobbes, Sarah 299
Hobbey, Judith 171
HOBBS 377
Hobbs, Abigail 228
Hobbs, Bethia 756
Hobbs, Christopher 279
Hobbs, Hannah 790
Hobbs, Jane 541, 565
Hobbs, Mary 140, 377, 434, 566
Hobbs, Mehetabel 749
Hobbs, Robert 523
Hobbs, Sarah 230, 458
HOBBY 377, 378
Hobby, Dorothy 164
Hobby, Elizabeth 465, 604
Hobby, Hannah 322
Hobby, Jane 581
Hobby, Martha 517
Hobby, Mary 384
Hobby, Rebecca 343
HOBKINS 387
HOBS 377
HOBSON 378, 388 see HOPSON
Hobson, Humphrey 291, 507
Hobson, John 531
Hobson, Mary 465
HOCKINGTON 378
Hodder, Parnell 49
Hodder, Sarah 313
Hoddy, John 435
Hodg, Katherine 213

HODGDON 378
Hodgdon, Abigail 316
Hodgdon, Elizabeth 291
HODGE 378
Hodge, Bethiah 551
Hodge, Dorcas 442
Hodge, Hannah 449
Hodge, Mary 605
Hodge, Robert 95
Hodge, Sarah 792
HODGEKINS 390
HODGES 378
Hodges, Andrew 104, 120
Hodges, Dorcas 442
Hodges, Elizabeth 807
Hodges, Jane 723, 800
Hodges, Joanna 209, 434
Hodges, John 16
Hodges, Katherine 213
Hodges, Mary 431, 676, 730
Hodges, Sarah 20, 517
Hodges, Thomas 611
Hodges, William 589
HODGKIN 378
Hodgkin, John 421
Hodgkin, Mary 58, 163
HODGKINS 378, 390
Hodgkins, Elizabeth 823
Hodgkins, Hannah 65
Hodgkins, Martha 360
Hodgkins, Mary Bishop 265
Hodgkins, Sarah 240
Hodgkinson, Mary 68
HODGMAN 378
Hodgman, Josiah 86
Hodgman, Thomas 519
Hodgskins, Elizabeth 555
HODGSON 379
Hodgson, Ann 758
HODON 332
HODSDON 378, 379
Hodsdon, Abigail 316
Hodsdon, Elizabeth 262
Hodsdon, Esther 798
Hodsdon, Israel 254
Hodsdon, Lucy 767
Hodsdon, Nicholas 530
Hodsdon, Sarah 519
HODSHON 379, 399 see
    HUDSON
Hodshon, Abigail 74
Hodshon, Ann 828
Hodshon, Elizabeth 785
Hodshon, Hannah 687
Hodshon, Mehitable 793
Hodshon, Sarah 148
Hodshon, Timothy 686, 687
Hodsman, Edward 240
Hodsoll, Bennett 283
HODSON 379, 399
Hodson, Abigail 74
Hodson, Nicholas 530
Hodson, Sarah 148
Hoeghin, Joseph 484
Hoel, Mary 143, 201
HOG 379
HOGG 379
HOGGE 379
Hoggesdell, Mehitable 793
Hoggett, Hannah 755
HOIDEN 356
Hoiden, Hannah 734
HOIT 396
Hoit, Mary 812
Hoit, Naomi 475
Hoit, Rachel 389
Hoite, Hannah 325
Holbridge, Arthur 425

Holbridge, Susanna 425
HOLBROOK 379, 380
Holbrook, Abigail 355, 595
Holbrook, Ann 618
Holbrook, Bethiah 521, 830
Holbrook, Daniel 420
Holbrook, Dorothy 84
Holbrook, Elizabeth 112, 500,
   529, 682, 697
Holbrook, Eunice 478
Holbrook, Experience 243, 482
Holbrook, Hannah 53, 159, 370,
   420, 582
Holbrook, Hopestill 615
Holbrook, Israel 506
Holbrook, Jane 35, 230
Holbrook, Joanna 159
Holbrook, John 336, 548
Holbrook, Margaret 632
Holbrook, Mary 167, 508, 606,
   720, 799
Holbrook, Mary White Loring 474
Holbrook, Mehitable 698
Holbrook, Millicent 567, 698
Holbrook, Patience 460, 800
Holbrook, Persis 260
Holbrook, Peter 593
Holbrook, Rebecca 788
Holbrook, Samuel (Jr.) 237
Holbrook, Sarah 20, 209, 809
Holbrook, Susanna 520, 822
Holbrook, Susannah 817
Holbrook, Thomas 460, 618
Holbrook, William 154, 663
Holbrook, Wm. 35, 698
Holbrooke, Elizabeth 352
Holbrooke, Jane 7
HOLCOMB 380
Holcomb, Abigail 25, 73
Holcomb, Benajah 576
Holcomb, Deborah 71, 594
Holcomb, Elizabeth 139, 249, 253
Holcomb, Jonathan 304
Holcomb, Mary 327
Holcomb, Nathaniel 549
Holcomb, Ruth 595
Holcomb, Sarah 139, 549
Holcomb, Thomas 253
HOLDEN 380
Holden, Barbara 813
Holden, Elizabeth 614, 620
Holden, Frances 383
Holden, John 520
Holden, Justinian 235
Holden, Margaret 246
Holden, Martha 88
Holden, Mary 134, 821
Holden, Sarah 700, 722
Holden, Susanna 320
HOLDER 380
Holder, Mary 678
Holdon, Richard 775
HOLDRED 380
Holdred, Mary 432
HOLDRIDGE 380
Holdridge, Mary 432
Holdridge, Mehitable 685
Holdridge, Rebecca 518
Holdridge, William 217
HOLDSWORTH 381
Holdsworth, Arthur 425
Holdsworth, Susanna 425
HOLE 381
Hole, Mary 143, 201
Holebroke, Persis 260
Holebrook, Hannah 759
Holeman, Mary 495
HOLGRAVE 381

Holgrave, James 320
Holgrave, Joshua 494
Holgrave, Lydia 331
Holgrave, Martha 556
Holgrove, Joshua 707
Holgrove, Love 707
Holioke, Mary 643
HOLKINS 381
HOLLAND 381
Holland, Ann 124
Holland, Christopher 693
Holland, Elizabeth 454
Holland, Hannah 471, 693
Holland, Johanna 573
Holland, John 671
Holland, Judith 433
Holland, Margaret 635
Holland, Mary 671
Holland, Obedience 198, 292
Holland, Relief 229, 278, 457
Holland, Ruth 583
Holland, Sarah 578, 671
Hollansby, Jane Mortimore 522
HOLLARD 381
Hollard, Angel 764
Hollard, Elizabeth 102, 110, 328
Hollard, George 488
Hollard, Hannah 37
Hollard, Ruth 488, 570
Hollaway, Grace 578
Hollaway, William 578
Hollett, Hannah 353
HOLLEY 362, 381, 382
Holley, Experience 311
Holley, Hopestill 779
Holley, Mary 270
Holley, Richard 229
Holley, Samuel 433
Holley, Sarah 11
HOLLIMAN 381, 382
Holliman, Ezekiel 723
Holliman, Priscilla 780
HOLLINGSHEAD 381
HOLLINGSWORTH 381
Hollingsworth, Arthur 425
Hollingsworth, Mercy 536
Hollingsworth, Susanna 425, 703
Hollingworth, Alice 558
Hollingworth, Jane 516
Hollingworth, Lydia 331
Hollingworth, Mary 252, 558
Hollingworth, Mercy 222
Hollingworth, Richard 111
Holliocke, Susanna 492
HOLLIS 381
Hollis, --- 451
Hollis, Abigail 809
HOLLISTER 382
Hollister, Abiah 382
Hollister, Elizabeth 794
Hollister, John 663
Hollister, Mary 347, 794
Hollister, Sarah 23, 34, 726, 820
Hollister, Stephen 618
Hollister, Thomas 818
Hollock, Margaret 632
HOLLOWAY 337, 382 see
   HALLOWELL
Holloway, Joseph 533
Holloway, Mary 788
Hollowell, Mary 23
Hollworth, Joshua 444
HOLLY 381
Holly, Bethia 790
Holly, Elizabeth 760
Holly, Hannah 396
Holly, Joanna 491
Holly, Mary 779

HOLMAN 382, 383
Holman, --- 361
Holman, Abigail 278
Holman, Abraham 653
Holman, Deborah 295
Holman, Edward 823
Holman, Elizabeth 4
Holman, Hannah 54, 695
Holman, Jeremiah 295
Holman, John 126
Holman, Mary 69, 74, 114, 495
Holman, Phebe 34, 245
Holman, Rachel 466, 652
Holman, Sarah 559
Holman, Seeth 638
Holme, Margaret 596
HOLMES 383, 384, 385 see
   HOMES
Holmes, Ann 212, 573, 649
Holmes, Anna 212
Holmes, Bathsheba 225
Holmes, Catharine 618, 814
Holmes, Catherine 809
Holmes, Charity 209
Holmes, David 482
Holmes, Desire 153
Holmes, Ebenezer 298, 831
Holmes, Elizabeth 371, 565
Holmes, Hannah 261, 448
Holmes, Hopestill 731
Holmes, Israel 670, 700
Holmes, Jane 482, 837
Holmes, Joan 482
Holmes, John 323, 354, 431, 433
Holmes, John (Rev.) 91
Holmes, Jonathan 240, 809
Holmes, Joseph (Jr.) 48
Holmes, Joshua 26, 149
Holmes, Josiah 448, 449
Holmes, Katharine 293
Holmes, Lydia 88
Holmes, Martha 381, 543, 743
Holmes, Mary 13, 146, 149, 160,
   166, 240, 377, 678, 711, 736,
   742
Holmes, Mercy 164
Holmes, Patience Bonum Willis
   823
Holmes, Rachel 205, 466, 797
Holmes, Rebecca 414
Holmes, Rely 675
Holmes, Robert 690
Holmes, Rose 77
Holmes, Samuel 447, 547
Holmes, Sarah 248, 509, 618, 677
Holmes, Thomas 591
Holmes, William (Maj.) 355
Holoman, Hannah 423
HOLSWORTH 381
Holsworth, Joshua 444
HOLT 385
Holt, Eleazer 22
Holt, Elizabeth 258, 596
Holt, Hannah 258, 320
Holt, John 602
Holt, Katherine 496
Holt, Mary 423
Holt, Mercy 226
Holt, Nicholas 602, 635
Holt, Priscilla 258
Holt, Sarah 91, 488, 568
Holt, William 568
Holten, Lydia 268
HOLTON 385
Holton, Abigail 480
Holton, Elizabeth 129
Holton, Joseph 358, 530
Holton, Mary 124, 636, 719

Holton, Rachel 719
Holton, Ruth 33, 480
Holton, Sarah 439, 530
HOLWAY 382
Holway, Hannah 115
Holwaye, Julian 386
HOLYMAN 382
HOLYOKE 385
Holyoke, Ann 608
Holyoke, Edward 486, 520, 761
Holyoke, Eliza 499
Holyoke, Elizabeth 436
Holyoke, Elizur 211
Holyoke, Hannah 726
Holyoke, Mary 643, 760
Holyoke, Sarah 17
Holyoke, Susanna 492
Holyroad, Joshua 707
Holyroad, Love 707
HOMAN 382, 383, 385
Homan, Deliverance 808
Homan, Esther 389
Homan, Joanna 651
Homan, Mordecai 389
Homan, Sarah 559
Homans, Ann 242
Homans, Anna 242
HOMARY 338
HOMER 386
Homer, Mary 333
HOMES 383, 384, 386 see
  HOLMES
Homes, Jane 403
Homes, Lydia 246
Honeyman, James (Rev.) 107
HONEYWELL 403
Honeywood, Martha 568
Honnsell, Edward 337
Honor, Alice 604
Honorel, Scicilia Elvie Longley
  471
HONYWELL 403
HOOD 386, 833, 835
Hood, Anna 95
Hood, Anne 95
Hood, Elizabeth 259
Hood, Mary 217, 621, 755
Hood, Rebecca 14
Hood, Sarah 50
HOOG 376
HOOK 386
Hook, Elizabeth 191
HOOKE 386
Hooke, Florence 165
Hooke, Francis 553
Hooke, Susanna 216
Hooke, William 540, 586
HOOKER 386
Hooker, Anne 7
Hooker, Dorothy 149
Hooker, Joanna 668
Hooker, John 612
Hooker, Mary 534, 548, 585
Hooker, Ralph 64
Hooker, Sarah 113, 825
Hooker, Sibil 64
Hooker, Susanna Garbrand 312
Hooker, Thomas 473, 668
Hooker, William 74
HOOKEY 386
HOOKIE 386
HOOPER 386, 387 see HOPPER
Hooper, Abigail 32
Hooper, Ann 87
Hooper, Dorothy 73
Hooper, Elizabeth 128, 357, 755
Hooper, Hannah 38
Hooper, Henry 538

Hooper, Mary 731
Hooper, Rebecca 38
Hooper, Richard 382
Hooper, Robert 596
Hooper, Ruth 832
Hooper, Samuel 807
Hooper, Sarah 355, 779
Hooper, William 39, 236
Hopcott, Sarah 484
Hope, Hannah 135
Hopestill, --- 146
HOPKINS 387
Hopkins, --- 738
Hopkins, Abigail 264, 504
Hopkins, Alice 302
Hopkins, Ann 346, 442
Hopkins, Bethia 206, 432, 705,
  712
Hopkins, Constance 692
Hopkins, Damaris 178
Hopkins, Deborah 178, 626
Hopkins, Dorcas 789
Hopkins, Elizabeth 321, 471, 772
Hopkins, Experience 464
Hopkins, Frances 485
Hopkins, Francis 61
Hopkins, Hannah 314
Hopkins, Jane 778, 833
Hopkins, John 833
Hopkins, Joseph 441
Hopkins, Margaret 834
Hopkins, Mary 312, 464, 660, 688,
  808
Hopkins, Patience 313
Hopkins, Rachel 169
Hopkins, Ruth 500, 829
Hopkins, Stephen 24
Hopkins, William 218, 314
HOPKINSON 387, 388
Hopkinson, Caleb 697
Hopkinson, Dorcas 697
Hopkinson, Eleanor 837
Hopkinson, Ellen 837
Hopkinson, Hester 121
Hopkinson, Mary 746
Hopkinson, Michael 722
Hopkinson, Mighill 755
Hopley, Elizabeth 628
Hoppan, Hannah 413
HOPPER 386, 388
Hopper, Mary 731
HOPPIN 388
Hoppin, Deliverance 129, 840
Hoppin, Nicholas 668
Hoppin, Opportunity 450, 479
Hopping, John 688
Hopscott, Hannah 294
HOPSON 388 see HOBSON
Hopson, Elizabeth 703, 796
Hopton, Abigail 711
Hore, Mary 483
Horey, Hannah 142
HORN 388
Horn, Simon 38
Horn, Simond 38
HORNE 388
Horne, Ann 262
Horne, Elizabeth 294
Horne, Jehoidan 350
Horne, John 321, 773
Horne, Mary 357, 476, 684, 718
Horne, Simon 708
HORNER 388
Horrel, Sarah 309
HORRELL 388
Horrell, Sarah 309
Horrocks, Elizabeth 185
HORSELEY 388 see HOSLEY

Horseman, Elizabeth 526
Horsford, Sarah 576
Horsley, John 191
Horsley, Lydia 573
HORSSLEY 388
HORSWELL 388
Horswell, Francis 748
HORTMAN 388
HORTON 353, 354, 388, 389 see
  HAUGHTON
Horton, --- 83
Horton, Abigail 515
Horton, Ann 418
Horton, Barnabas 114, 176
Horton, Benjamin 499, 503, 757
Horton, Bethiah 760
Horton, Caleb 385, 487
Horton, Ellen 418
Horton, Esther 487
Horton, Hannah 83, 631
Horton, Hope 691
Horton, John 385
Horton, Jonathan 308
Horton, Joseph 556
Horton, Martha 44
Horton, Mary 23, 114, 308, 581,
  732, 762
Horton, Mehitable 91, 92
Horton, Mercy 847
Horton, Sarah 175, 176, 647
Horton, Thomas 385, 433, 495
Hosetin, Sarah 369
HOSFORD 389
Hosford, Esther 434, 576, 648
Hosford, Hester 434, 576
Hosford, Mary 549
Hosford, Sarah 576, 731
Hosford, William 280
HOSIER 389
Hosier, Samuel 631, 718
Hoskin, Joane 350
HOSKINS 389, 390
Hoskins, Anthony 826
Hoskins, Catherine 390, 826
Hoskins, Elizabeth 588, 740, 743
Hoskins, Elizabeth Knapp 442
Hoskins, Grace 245
Hoskins, Isabell 15
Hoskins, Jane 15
Hoskins, John 567
Hoskins, Mary 164, 578
Hoskins, Rebecca 98, 432
Hoskins, Samuel 334
Hoskins, Sarah 240
Hoskins, Thomas 71
HOSLEY 390 see HORSELEY
HOSMAN 390
HOSMER 390
Hosmer, Abigail 799
Hosmer, Clemence 403, 685
Hosmer, Dorothy 677
Hosmer, Esther 113, 588
Hosmer, Hannah 359, 485, 596,
  817
Hosmer, Hester 113, 588
Hosmer, James 620
Hosmer, Mary 689, 801, 843
Hosmer, Sarah 393
Hosmer, Thomas 826
HOTCHKIN 378
Hotchkins, Sarah 421
HOTCHKISS 390
Hotchkiss, Joshua 22
Hotchkiss, Mary 760
Hotchkiss, Samuel 524
Hotton, Judith 433
Houchin, Elizabeth 10, 252
Houchin, Esther 802

Houchin, Mary 322
Houchin, Rachel 9
HOUGH 355, 390, 391, 399 see
HUFF
Hough, Abiah 228
Hough, Ann 392
Hough, Anne 392
Hough, Elizabeth 588
Hough, Hannah 83, 600
Hough, Samuel 101
Hough, Sarah 135, 652, 774
Hough, William 67, 96
Hought, John 816
HOUGHTON 354, 391
Houghton, Abigail 399
Houghton, Experience 153
Houghton, Hannah 654
Houghton, John (Jr.) 314
Houghton, Mary 65, 346, 654, 711
Houghton, Robert 680
Houghton, Sarah 306, 462, 654
HOULDREDG 381
HOULDRIDGE 381
Houldridge, Rebecca 518
Houley, Lydia 573
Hoult, Priscilla 258
HOULTON 385
Houlton, Lydia 268
HOUPER 386
Hour, Elizabeth 614
Hous, Deborah 120
Hous, Thomas 276
HOUSE 354, 391
House, Abigail 174
House, Elizabeth 721
House, Hannah 106, 474
House, Jemima 467
House, Joseph 292, 664
House, Peninah 467
House, Pininna 467
House, Rebecca 86
House, Sarah 686
HOUSHA 365
HOUSING 391
Houstin, Sarah 369
HOUSTON 391
Hout, Mary 371
HOUTCHIN 392
Houtton, Martha 308
HOVEY 391, 392
Hovey, Abigail 27, 378, 764
Hovey, Dorcas 420
Hovey, Elizabeth 764
Hovey, John 157, 309
Hovey, Nathaniel 68, 107
Hovey, Priscilla 689
Hovey, Susannah 26
HOW 392, 393
How, Abraham 445
How, Bathsheba 223
How, Bathshua 205
How, Deborah 46, 676
How, Edward 118
How, Eleanor 525
How, Elizabeth 412, 435, 616, 816
How, Hannah 392
How, Hester 754
How, Jeremiah 179, 628
How, Martha 775
How, Mary 1, 44, 244, 259, 392, 763, 787, 840
How, Rebecca 43
How, Sarah 97, 534, 717, 740, 761, 779, 799
How, William 840
How, Zachariah 266
HOWARD 358, 359, 360

Howard, Abiel 663
Howard, Abigail 272, 764
Howard, Ann 433, 441
Howard, Anna 651
Howard, Anne 160
Howard, Bethiah 440, 506
Howard, Catherine 325
Howard, Daniel 812
Howard, Edward 218
Howard, Elizabeth 272
Howard, Hannah 370, 512, 651
Howard, Huldah 53
Howard, James 660
Howard, Jonathan 282
Howard, Joseph 114
Howard, Judith 775
Howard, Margery 150
Howard, Martha 571
Howard, Mary 6, 50, 118, 164, 289, 328, 406, 425, 476, 519, 579
Howard, Mary Harris 315
Howard, Mary Phipps White 805
Howard, Mary Phips White 580
Howard, Mehitable 793
Howard, Mercy 391
Howard, Nehemiah 429
Howard, Rebecca 695
Howard, Robert 160, 425, 506, 695
Howard, Rose 11
Howard, Samuel 509, 642
Howard, Sarah 6, 298, 349, 364, 549, 557, 582, 642
Howard, Tabitha 378
Howard, Temperance 689
Howard, Thomas 517
Howards, Sarah 237
HOWCHIN 392
Howchin, Elizabeth 252
HOWD 392
Howd, Anthony 529
HOWDE 392
HOWE 392, 393
Howe, Abraham 73, 346, 463
Howe, Bathsheba 716
Howe, Bethia 294
Howe, Deborah 392
Howe, Elizabeth 61, 99, 141, 420, 492, 557
Howe, Esther 494, 659
Howe, Hannah 43
Howe, Hester 659
Howe, John 216, 226, 354, 434
Howe, Joseph 118, 348, 673
Howe, Love 595
Howe, Mary 88, 104, 259
Howe, Nathaniel 197
Howe, Nicholas 754
Howe, Phebe 689
Howe, Rebecca 620
Howe, Samuel 154
Howe, Sarah 88, 107, 150, 198, 428, 534, 673, 717
Howe, Thomas 47, 622
HOWELL 393
Howell, --- 337
Howell, Abigail 337
Howell, Abraham 415
Howell, Arthur 655
Howell, David 453
Howell, Deborah 617, 728
Howell, Edward 728
Howell, Elizabeth 473, 490
Howell, John 730
Howell, John (Jr.) 484
Howell, Margaret 227, 337, 516
Howell, Phebe 337

Howell, Prudence 732
Howell, Ruth 87
Howell, Sarah 634
Howell, Susannah 585
Howell, Thomas 450
Howells, Mary 81
HOWEN 394
Howen, Mary 456
HOWES 366, 394
Howes, --- 350
Howes, Elizabeth 30, 126, 503, 597
Howes, Hannah 106, 126, 497
Howes, Joseph 624, 829
Howes, Mary 337, 354
Howes, Mercy 720
Howes, Phebe 306
Howes, Rebecca 394
Howes, Sarah 387, 500
Howes, Thomas 601
Howett, Martha 365
HOWKINS 394
Howkins, Anthony 112, 738
Howkins, Elizabeth 99
Howkins, Hannah 535
Howkins, Mary 429
HOWLAND 394, 395
Howland, --- 522
Howland, Abigail 82, 846
Howland, Alice 660
Howland, Anne 192
Howland, Arthur 477, 650
Howland, Content 650
Howland, Deborah 683
Howland, Desire 313313
Howland, Elizabeth 10, 123, 219, 220, 339, 368, 477
Howland, Experience 56
Howland, Hannah 84, 192
Howland, Hope 151
Howland, Joseph 174, 417
Howland, Lydia 106, 417, 735
Howland, Martha 30, 202
Howland, Mary 11, 196, 283, 307, 650, 700, 822
Howland, Priscilla 64
Howland, Ruth 200
Howland, Sarah 216
Howland, Zooth 442
HOWLET 395
Howlet, Alice 196
Howlet, Mary 361, 815
Howlet, Susannah 670
HOWLETT 395
Howlett, Alice 196
Howlett, John 678
Howlett, Lydia 573
Howlett, Mary 361, 572
Howlett, Sarah 26, 196
Howlett, Susanna Hudson 571
Howlett, Thomas 285, 573, 689
Howse, Mary 333
HOXIE 395
Hoxie, Bathena 9
HOXWORTH 356
HOYLE 395
Hoyle, Christian 523
HOYT 332, 395, 396 see
HAIGHT
Hoyt, Abigail 263, 279
Hoyt, Daniel 349, 640
Hoyt, David 592
Hoyt, Deborah 45
Hoyt, Dorothy 475
Hoyt, Elizabeth 449, 647
Hoyt, Frances 168
Hoyt, Francis 565
Hoyt, Hannah 325

Hoyt, John 75, 150, 607
Hoyt, Joshua 171, 760
Hoyt, Mary 48, 196, 263, 371, 481, 493, 671, 778, 788, 812
Hoyt, Mehitable 718
Hoyt, Mercy 196
Hoyt, Miriam 276, 342
Hoyt, Naomi 475, 717
Hoyt, Nicholas 429
Hoyt, Rachel 389, 790
Hoyt, Samuel 308, 678, 790
Hoyt, Sarah 161, 266
Hoyt, Simon 52
Hoyt, Thomas 334
Hoyt, Walter 729
Hoyt, William 531
Hoyt, Zerubbabel 430
Hoyte, Barsheba 395
Hoyte, Bathsheba 395
Hoyte, Mary 105
HUBBARD 396, 397, 398
Hubbard, Abigail 697
Hubbard, Ann 47, 604, 711
Hubbard, Benj. 619
Hubbard, Bethiah 157
Hubbard, Daniel 716
Hubbard, Dorothy 707
Hubbard, Ebenezer 716
Hubbard, Edward 759
Hubbard, Elizabeth 112, 540, 810
Hubbard, Esther 127
Hubbard, George 526
Hubbard, Hannah 103, 106, 241, 316, 422, 499, 502, 526, 691
Hubbard, Hugh 820
Hubbard, James 338
Hubbard, Joseph 412
Hubbard, Joshua 316
Hubbard, Lydia 123
Hubbard, Margaret 306, 608, 632, 657
Hubbard, Margery 306
Hubbard, Martha 256, 479, 812
Hubbard, Mary 44, 205, 279, 329, 406, 451, 460, 564, 611, 643, 655, 780, 786
Hubbard, Mercy 80
Hubbard, Philip 251
Hubbard, Rachel 111, 327, 451, 824
Hubbard, Richard 309, 779
Hubbard, Ruth 119
Hubbard, Samuel 444
Hubbard, Sarah 64, 87, 143, 185, 187, 348
Hubbard, Thomas 335
Hubbard, William 25, 584
HUBBELL 398
Hubbell, Abigail 285
Hubbell, Ebenezer 325
Hubbell, Elizabeth 286, 401
Hubbell, Elizabeth Gaylord 632
Hubbell, John 356
Hubbell, Martha 772
Hubbell, Mary 534
Hubbell, Richard 256, 774
Hubbell, Samuel 602
Hubbell, Sarah 708
HUBBERD 397
Hubberd, Comfort 791
Hubberd, Judith 251
HUBBERT 376, 397, 398
Hubbert, Sarah 102
HUBBEY 398
HUBBS 398
HUBERD 376
HUBERT 397
Hubert, Ann 573

Hubert, Anna 573
Hubert, Hannah 573
HUBS 398
Hubs, Robert 523
Huby, Elizabeth 604
HUCHASON 407
Huchason, Anna 572
HUCHENSON 407
HUCHESON 407
HUCHIN 406
HUCHINGS 376
Huchins, Elizabeth 463
HUCHINSON 407
HUCKENS 398
Huckens, Experience 464
Huckens, Hannah 313
Huckens, Mary 715
Hucker, Joane 350
HUCKINS 398
Huckins, Elizabeth 56
Huckins, Experience 464
Huckins, Hannah 313
Huckins, Hope 531
Huckins, James 838
Huckins, John 164
Huckins, Mary 50, 350
Huckins, Robert 56
Huckins, Thomas 372, 374, 743
HUCKLEY 398
Huckstep, Lydia 742
Huckstop, Lydia 353
HUDELSTON 398
HUDLESTON 398
HUDSON 398, 399
Hudson --- (Capt.) 371
Hudson, Abigail 23, 74, 706
Hudson, Ann 428
Hudson, Anna 428
Hudson, Anne Hills Elton 249
Hudson, Elizabeth 240, 767, 785
Hudson, Hannah 158, 192, 257, 462, 621, 759
Hudson, John 555, 759, 767
Hudson, Jonathan 149, 786
Hudson, Lydia 259
Hudson, Mary 72, 140, 189, 531, 698, 784
Hudson, Nathaniel 657
Hudson, Rebecca 38
Hudson, Rhoda 555
Hudson, Sarah 148, 243, 663, 680, 784
Hudson, Susanna 395, 571
Hudson, Susannah 678
Hudson, William 279
Hudston, Hannah 645
HUES 400
Hues, Lewis 672
HUESTED 399
Huested, Abigail 404
Huested, Ann 343
Huested, Mary Lockwood 443
HUET 367
Huet, Elizabeth Foster 612
Huet, Jael 634
Huet, Thomas 564
Huett, Ephraim 612
HUFF 399 see HOUGH
Huggines, Bridget 162
Huggines, John 162
HUGGINS 399
Huggins, Bridget 789
Huggins, Elizabeth 555
Huggins, Hannah 841
Huggins, Martha 497
Huggins, Nathaniel 66
Huggins, Susanna 9
HUGHES 366, 367, 400 see

HUGHES (cont.) HEWES, HUSE
Hughes, Martha 108
Hughes, Mary 72, 715
Hughes, Mercy 72
Hughes, Rebecca 266, 276
Hughes, Richard 367, 715
HUGHS 400
Hughs, Esther 355
Hughs, Nicholas 198
Hughs, Rebecca 86
Hughs, William 414
HUIT 367
Huit, Elizabeth 397
Huit, Lydia 686
Huit, Mary 719
HUKE 400
HUKLY 398
HULATE 367
HULBERD 406
HULBURD 406
Hulet, Jane 523
Hulet, Jenne 523
HULETT 367
Hulett, Elizabeth 10
HULING 400
HULL 400, 401
Hull, Abigail 151, 196
Hull, Andrew 54
Hull, Bethia 550
Hull, Blanche 553
Hull, Dodavah 75
Hull, Dorothy 434, 496
Hull, Edeth 66
Hull, Elizabeth 219, 297, 362, 691
Hull, Esther 147
Hull, George 580, 587
Hull, Hannah 78, 208, 226, 605, 662
Hull, Isaac 692
Hull, Jeremiah 537
Hull, Joanna 123, 205
Hull, John 311, 580, 760, 841
Hull, Joseph 497, 604
Hull, Martha 531, 717
Hull, Mary 194, 273, 317, 378, 382, 395, 413, 587, 604
Hull, Naomi 121
Hull, Phaltial 273
Hull, Phineas 589, 655, 807
Hull, Pholiel 273
Hull, Rebecca 481
Hull, Reuben 691
Hull, Robert 608, 715
Hull, Ruth 613
Hull, Samuel 286
Hull, Sarah 11, 120, 150, 190, 443, 597, 673
Hull, Temperance 67
Hull, Thomas 445, 787
Hull, Tristram 363
HULLING 400
Hulls, Elizabeth 727
Hulls, Josiah 727
Hulse, Richard 723
Hult, Grace 208
Hult, Jane 208
HUMBER 401
HUMBERSTON 401
Humbertson, John 762
Hume, Esther 183
HUMISTON 401
Humiston, Henry 468
Humiston, John 762
Humiston, Thomas 392
HUMMERSON 401
HUMMERSTON 401
Hummery, Elizabeth 287
Humphey, Elizabeth 287

Humphres, Sarah 121
HUMPHREVILLE 763
Humphreville, Mary 484
HUMPHREY 402
Humphrey, Abigail 316, 327
Humphrey, Ann 507
Humphrey, Anna 116, 507
Humphrey, Anne 507
Humphrey, Elizabeth 225, 603
Humphrey, Hannah 116
Humphrey, Joanna 836
Humphrey, John 510
Humphrey, Jonas 532, 791
Humphrey, Martha 671
Humphrey, Mary 139, 354, 463,
    780
Humphrey, Sarah 121, 585
Humphrey, Susan 806
Humphrey, Susanna 806
HUMPHREYS 402
Humphreys, Elizabeth 355
Humphreys, Hopestill 75
Humphreys, Mary 325
Humphreys, Rebecca 729
HUMPHREYVILLE 763
Humphries, Martha 671
HUMPHRIS 402
HUMPHRY 402
HUMRSTON 402
Hunbock, Joanna 713
Hunding, John 457
HUNGERFORD 402
Hungerford, Anna 459
Hungerford, Elizabeth 296
Hungerford, Hannah 638
Hungerford, Joanna 459
Hungerford, Mary 682
Hungerford, Sarah 176, 400
Hungerford, Susannah 153
Hungerford, Thomas 77, 696
HUNKING 402
Hunking, Beaton 362
Hunking, Elizabeth 263
Hunking, Mary 534, 772
Hunking, Sarah 795
Hunking, Temperance 263
HUNKINGS 402
Hunkings, Agnes 402
Hunkings, Ann 402
HUNKINS 402
HUNLOCK 402
Hunlock, Mary 820
HUNN 403
Hunn, George 579
Hunn, Priscilla 87
HUNNEWELL 403
Hunnewell, Bridget 516
Hunnewell, Patience 353
Hunnewell, Richard 59, 90
Hunnewell, Roger 516
HUNNIBORN 403
Hunniborn, George 650
Hunniborn, John 650
Hunsey, Elizabeth 76
HUNT 367, 403, 404
Hunt, --- 770
Hunt, Abigail 587
Hunt, Ann 578
Hunt, Ann Edwards 244
Hunt, Anna 578
Hunt, Anne 532, 662
Hunt, Christian 516
Hunt, Eleanor 171
Hunt, Elizabeth 44, 46, 405, 488,
    553, 765, 817
Hunt, Enoch 42, 363, 439
Hunt, Ephraim 7, 135
Hunt, Hannah 271, 532, 804, 842

Hunt, Isaac 280
Hunt, Jane 763
Hunt, John 138, 186
Hunt, Jonathan 685
Hunt, Joseph 515
Hunt, Josiah 403
Hunt, Judith 181, 819
Hunt, Margaret 497
Hunt, Mary 82, 410, 835
Hunt, Mehitable 757
Hunt, Naomi 456
Hunt, Nehemiah 404
Hunt, Peter 75, 568
Hunt, Priscilla 434
Hunt, Rachel 722
Hunt, Richard 763
Hunt, Ruth 41, 141
Hunt, Sarah 66, 118, 176, 568,
    599, 683
Hunt, Susan 746
Hunt, Susanna 746
Hunt, Thomas 44, 282, 559, 654
Hunt, William 99, 187, 620
HUNTER 404
Hunter, Abilene 847
Hunter, Elizabeth 836
Hunter, Katherine 337
Hunter, Mary 300
Hunter, Priscilla 434
Hunter, Sarah 229
Hunter, Susan 381
Hunter, William 187, 286, 740
HUNTING 404, 405
Hunting, Ann 577
Hunting, Easter 237
Hunting, Elizabeth 567
Hunting, Esther 27, 237, 267
Hunting, Hercules 362
Hunting, Margaret 787
Hunting, Mary 114, 416
Hunting, Susan 621
Hunting, Susanna 621
Huntingdon, Ruth 600
Huntingdon, Susannah 229
HUNTINGTON 405
Huntington, Anne 70
Huntington, Ann 70
Huntington, Christopher 96
Huntington, Elizabeth 29, 396
Huntington, Hannah 144
Huntington, Marah 272
Huntington, Mary 206, 272, 274,
    308, 428
Huntington, Sarah 751
Huntington, Simon 715
Huntington, Susannah 328
Huntington, Thomas 778
HUNTLEY 405
Huntley, Elizabeth 183, 463
Huntley, Moses 175
HUNTON 405
HUNTOON 405
HUNTRESS 405
Huntress, Ann 149, 203
Huntress, Mary 662
Hupper, Mary 731
HURD 405
Hurd, Abigail 425
Hurd, Dorcas 295
Hurd, Hannah 45, 187, 745
Hurd, John 45, 429, 845
Hurd, Mary 45
Hurd, Mercy 99, 404, 620
Hurd, Sarah 670, 822
HURDE 405
HURLBART 406
HURLBERT 406
HURLBURT 405, 406

Hurlburt, Adry 301
Hurlburt, Edree 301
Hurlburt, Mary 788
Hurlburt, William 12
HURLBUT 405, 406
Hurlbut, Edna 186
Hurlbut, Elizabeth 112
Hurley, Sarah 262
HURRY 406
Hurry, Hannah 532
Hurry, Temperance 131
Hursdale, Mehitabel 373
HURST 362
Hurst, Alice 715
Hurst, Margaret 602
Hurst, Patience 164
Hurst, Sarah 62
HURT see HEARD
Hurt, Elizabeth 54
HUSE 367, 399, 400, 406
Huse, Abel 660
Huse, Hannah 106
Huse, Martha 108
Huse, Nicholas 670
Huse, Rebecca 86, 266, 276
Huse, Ruth 107
Huskins, Thomas 743
Huson, Ursula 243
Husse, Mary 751
HUSSEY 406
Hussey, Abigail 394
Hussey, Ann 702
Hussey, Bathsheba 28
Hussey, Christopher 511
Hussey, Elizabeth 77, 358
Hussey, Huldah 684, 787
Hussey, Mary 321, 551, 724, 751
Hussey, Priscilla 313
Hussey, Rebecca 394
Hussey, Susanna 548
Hussey, Theodale 723
HUSTED 399
Husted, --- 419
Husted, Abigail 404
Husted, Angell 37
Husted, Elizabeth 37
Hustis, Abigail 404
HUTCHINGS 376, 398
Hutchings, Sarah 301
HUTCHINS 406
Hutchins, Elizabeth 28, 198, 348,
    688, 766
Hutchins, Frances 363
Hutchins, John 584
Hutchins, Love 669
Hutchins, Mary 228, 417, 789
Hutchins, Thomas 688
Hutchins, William 329
HUTCHINSON 407
Hutchinson, Abigail 11, 22, 448,
    555
Hutchinson, Ann 767
Hutchinson, Anna 572
Hutchinson, Anne 174, 237, 354
Hutchinson, Bridget 579, 650, 823
Hutchinson, Catherine 415
Hutchinson, Edward 66
Hutchinson, Edward (Jr.) 129
Hutchinson, Elisha 282
Hutchinson, Elizabeth 348, 607,
    829
Hutchinson, Faith 653
Hutchinson, Frances 407
Hutchinson, Hannah 80, 258, 641,
    774
Hutchinson, Hannah Raiement
    Howard 360
Hutchinson, Joseph 315, 679

Hutchinson, Katherine 47, 774
Hutchinson, Margaret 461, 839
Hutchinson, Mary 145, 301, 333, 786, 802, 823
Hutchinson, Ralph 63
Hutchinson, Rebecca 332
Hutchinson, Richard 20, 636, 700
Hutchinson, Samuel 97, 558
Hutchinson, Sarah 669, 803
Hutchinson, Susan 626
Hutchinson, Susanna 164, 169, 626
Hutchinson, Susannah 715
Hutchinson, Thomas 139
Hutheson, Rebecca 332
HUTHWITT 408
Huthwitt, Ann 583
HUTSON 398
Hutson, Mary 378, 784
Hutson, Rebecca 38
Hutson, Sarah 784
HUTTON 408
Hutton, Elizabeth 280
Hutton, Richard 236
HUXFORD 408
Huxford, Samuel 234
HUXLEY 408
Huxley, Elizabeth 439
Huxley, Mary 682
Huxley, Sarah 42, 681
HYATT 396, 408
Hyatt, Deborah 413
Hyatt, Rebecca 375
Hyatt, Ruth 797, 847
Hyatt, Thomas 424
HYDE 408
Hyde, Dorothy 568, 571
Hyde, Elizabeth 408, 419, 473, 548, 819
Hyde, Esther 595
Hyde, Hannah 408
Hyde, Hester 595
Hyde, John 433
Hyde, Katherine 384
Hyde, Mary 104, 785, 819
Hyde, Phebe 328
Hyde, Samuel 70
Hyde, Sarah 408, 548, 841
Hyde, Stephen 294
Hyde, William 2
HYES 357
HYLAND 409
Hyland, Deborah 742
Hyland, Elizabeth 505
Hyland, Isabel 798
Hyland, Samuel 747, 798
Hyland, Sarah 760
Hyllier, Hugh 398
Hynes, Ann 390

--- I ---

Iasard, Mary 485
IBROOK 409
Ibrook, Christian 164
Ibrook, Elizabeth 164, 377
Ibrook, Ellen 377
Ibrook, Margaret 748
Idams, Sarah 610
IDE 408, 409
Ide, Jane 433
Ide, Martha 775
Ide, Mary 289
Ide, Nicholas 546, 590
Ide, Patience 136
Idy, Mary 617
IGGLEDEN 409

Iggleden, Stephen 564
Iggledon, Ruth 78
Igguldon, Elizabeth 501
IGLEDEN see EGGLEDEN 402
IJONS 411
ILLSLEY 409
ILSLEY 409
Ilsley, Elisha 589
Ilsly, Mary 517
Ilsly, Sarah 320, 333
INCE 409
Ince, Jonathan 341
INDICOT 252
INDICUT 252
INES 411, 426
INGALL 252
Ingall, Benjamin 754
INGALLS 252, 409 see ENGELL
Ingalls, Anna 409
Ingalls, Anne 409
Ingalls, Benjamin 487
Ingalls, Elizabeth 202, 348
Ingalls, Faith 9
Ingalls, Francis 60
Ingalls, Hannah 699
Ingalls, Henry 1
Ingalls, Lydia 60
Ingalls, Martha Perkins Brewer 95
Ingalls, Mary 127, 240, 440, 708
Ingalls, Mary Sargent 651
Ingalls, Ruth 146
Ingalls, Sarah 73
INGELL 409
INGELLS 409
Ingersold, Elizabeth 330
INGERSOLL 409, 410
Ingersoll, Abiah 719
Ingersoll, Abigail 627
Ingersoll, Alice 833
Ingersoll, Bathshua 444
Ingersoll, Deborah 452, 458
Ingersoll, Dorothy 576, 637
Ingersoll, Elizabeth 424, 445, 677
Ingersoll, Esther 331, 424
Ingersoll, Hannah 432
Ingersoll, Joanna 575
Ingersoll, John 533, 808
Ingersoll, Margery 112, 308
Ingersoll, Margaret 776
Ingersoll, Martha 510
Ingersoll, Mary 188
Ingersoll, Richard 444, 606
Ingersoll, Ruth 279, 530, 637
Ingersoll, Samuel 252
Ingersoll, Sarah 43, 46, 250, 333, 358, 385, 637
Ingersoll, Thomas 220, 497
INGERSON 410
Ingerson, Ruth 637
Ingerson, Sarah 637
INGGS 252
INGHAM 410
Ingham, Samuel 474
Ingham, Sarah 141
Inghams, Joseph 25
Ingle, Benjamin 487
Ingle, Waitstill 487
Ingleden, Elizabeth 690
INGLEFIELD 410
INGLES 252, 409, 411
Ingles, Elizabeth 94, 163
Ingles, Jane 684
Ingles, Joanna 317
INGLESBY 410
Inglesby, Sarah 660
INGLESFEELD 410
Inglis, James 43
INGLISH 252, 411

Inglish, Hannah 161
INGLLS 409
INGOLDSBY 410
Ingoldsby, Olive 415
INGOLLS 409
INGOLSBY 410
Ingolsby, Elizabeth 308
INGRAHAM 410, 411
Ingraham, Abigail 26, 149, 384
Ingraham, Elizabeth 116, 117
Ingraham, Jarrett 645
Ingraham, Joanna 629
Ingraham, Margaret 283
Ingraham, Mary 149
Ingraham, Rebecca 629
Ingraham, Richard 33
INGRAM 410, 411
Ingram, Richard 33
Ingram, Samuel 474
INGS 252, 411
Ings, Hannah 161
Ings, Samuel 459
Ingulden, Elizabeth 501
Ingulden, Stephen 564
INMAN 411
Inman, Edward 578
Inman, Joanna 525
Inman, Mary 49
INNES see INGS, IRONS
Innis, Catherine 485
IRELAND 411
Ireland, Jean 454
Ireland, Joan 454
Ireland, Margaret 311, 331
Ireland, Mary 123
Ireland, Samuel 123
Ireland, Sarah Esty Gill 303
Ireland, Thomas 454
Ireland, William 33
IRESON 411
IRESTON 411
IRISH 411
Irish, Elias 835
Irish, Elizabeth 345, 783
Irish, John 726
Irish, Rebecca 327
Irish, Sarah 846
IRONS 411 see INGS, INNES
ISAAC 411
Isaac, Elizabeth 208
Isaac, Joseph 208
Isaac, Mary 623
Isaacke, Susannah 19
Isaacs, Elizabeth 208
Isaacs, Joseph 208
Isbel, Hannah 705
ISBELL 411
Isbell, Ann 536
Isbell, Elizabeth 840
Isboll, Hannah 280
ISGATE 411
ISHAM 411
ISSUM 411
Itchenor, Goodith 182
Itchenor, Judith 182
Ive, Hannah 397
Ivery, Ann 610
Ivery, Anna 610
Ivery, Hannah 610
Ivery, Jedbatha 610
Ivery, Lois 80
Ivery, Tabitha 610
Ivery, Talithacumy 610
IVES 411, 412
Ives, Grace 411
Ives, Hannah 50, 179, 397
Ives, John 62
Ives, Martha 54

Ives, Mary 302, 591
Ives, Miles 129
Ives, Phebe 596, 637
Ives, Sarah 12, 338, 397
Ives, Thomas 806
Ives, William 50
Ivet, Mary 546, 720
IVEY 412
IVIE 412
IVORY 412
Ivory, Lois 80, 122, 632
Ivory, Ruth 32
Ivory, Sarah 141
Ivory, Thomas 189
Ivorye, Dorcas 391
Iyans, Rebecca 735
IYDE 409
Iyde, Martha 775
Iyde, Mary 289
IYONS 411

--- J ---

JACKLIN 412
Jacklin, Hannah 760
Jacklin, Mary 110
Jacklin, Rosamond 528
Jacklin, Susanna 388
JACKMAN 412
Jackman, Esther 528
Jackman, James 672
Jackman, Joanna 285
Jackman, Mary 343
Jackman, Sarah 554
JACKSON 412, 413, 414
Jackson, --- 37, 656
Jackson, Abigail 91, 602
Jackson, Anna 338
Jackson, Catherine 807
Jackson, Deborah 56, 689, 755
Jackson, Deliverance 556, 825
Jackson, Edmund 296
Jackson, Edward 55, 544
Jackson, Eleanor 32
Jackson, Elizabeth 81, 89, 97,
    227, 392, 489, 601, 670, 699,
    797
Jackson, George 176, 536, 703
Jackson, Hannah 17, 26, 220, 292,
    408, 433, 465, 660, 670, 778,
    825
Jackson, Jane 587, 620
Jackson, Jeremiah 772
Jackson, John 32, 41, 231, 248,
    313, 681, 722, 806, 807
Jackson, Joseph 413, 661
Jackson, Joshua 413
Jackson, Lydia 171, 289, 335, 458
Jackson, Margaret 540, 665, 754
Jackson, Martha 81, 170
Jackson, Mary 31, 55, 263, 277,
    279, 408, 481, 523, 669, 755,
    773, 839, 844
Jackson, Moses 286, 661
Jackson, Nicholas 145
Jackson, Rebecca 56, 601
Jackson, Richard 108, 241, 489
Jackson, Ruth 734
Jackson, Salome 806, 844
Jackson, Samuel 482
Jackson, Sarah 91, 254, 377
Jackson, Susanna 481
Jackson, Tamsen 226
Jackson, Theodosia 533, 831
Jackson, Theodosiah 831
Jacksun, Jonathan 196

Jacksun, Sarah 196
Jackwon, Martha 745
Jaco, Deborah 142
JACOB 414
Jacob, Deborah 199, 735
Jacob, Elizabeth 199, 733, 758
Jacob, Hannah 285, 474
Jacob, Jael 199
Jacob, Judith 351, 593
Jacob, Lydia 315
Jacob, Martha 817
Jacob, Mary 30, 71, 379, 548
Jacob, Nicholas 55
Jacob, Richard 333
Jacob, Sarah 199, 355
JACOBS 414
Jacobs, Ann 515
Jacobs, Anna 515
Jacobs, Anne 17
Jacobs, Bartholomew 737
Jacobs, Elizabeth 465
Jacobs, George 286, 287
Jacobs, John 466
Jacobs, Judith 593
Jacobs, Margaret 278
Jacobs, Mary 401, 743, 815
Jacobs, Mercy 401
Jacobs, Samuel 515
Jacobs, William 453, 640
Jacobson, Rebecca 527
JAFFORD 416
Jaffrey, James 100
JAGGER 414
Jagger, Elizabeth 395, 765
Jagger, Hannah 789
Jagger, Jeremy 765
Jagger, Sarah 435
Jaggers, Mary 182, 575
Jagges, Mary 575
Jago, Elizabeth 572
JAMES 414, 415, 426
James, Abigail 712, 759
James, Ann 11, 583, 759
James, Constant 651
James, Edmund 18, 203, 286
James, Elizabeth 408, 456
James, Erastus 534
James, Esther 615
James, Hannah 218, 290, 825
James, Harnet 290
James, Hester 615
James, Jane 4
James, John 45, 637
James, Mary 5, 285, 502, 717
James, Mehitable 761
James, Nathaniel 393
James, Philip 643
James, Reana 18
James, Ruth 346
James, Sarah 559, 700
James, William 734
JAMESON 415
Jameson, Hannah 75
Jameson, Jane 536
Jameson, Maria 297
Jameson, Mary 292, 707
Jameson, Susannah 602
Jameson, Tomasin 541
JAMISON 415
Janco, Deborah 142
JANES 208, 415
Janes, Hepzibah 244
Janes, Mary 259, 438
Janes, Rebecca 605
Janes, Ruth 659
Janes, Sophia 556
Janes, William 104
Janness, Eleanor 65

Jans, Dievertje 491
JANVERIN 415
Janveron, Richard 47
JANVRIN 415
JAQUES 415
Jaques, Abigail 444
Jaques, Elizabeth 142, 445, 572
Jaques, Hannah 590
Jaques, Mary 108
Jaques, Richard 361
Jaques, Ruth 251
Jaques, Sarah 332
Jaquish, Richard 361
JAQUITH 415, 416
Jaquith, Abraham 102, 338
Jaquith, Elizabeth 235, 572
Jaquith, Lydia 280
Jaquith, Sarah 691
Jarmine, Elizabeth 610
Jarrad, Mary 485
JARRAT 416
Jarrat, Susanna 655
JARRATT 416
Jarret, Hannah 38
JARVIS 416
Jarvis, Elias 123
Jarvis, Elizabeth 626
Jarvis, Eunice 834
Jarvis, Isaac 768
Jarvis, Mary 172
Jarvis, William 750
Jarvise, Esther 281
Jasper, Elizabeth 521
JAVISE 416
JAY 416
Jay, Mary 807
Jay, William 114
JAYE 416
JAYNE 416
Jayne, Anna 96
Jayne, Anne 96
Jecocks, --- 143
Jefas, Hannah 694
JEFFARD 416
JEFFERAY 416
Jefferay, Priscilla 164
Jefferay, Sarah 41
Jefferay, Susanna 741
JEFFERAYS 416
Jefferaz, Sarah 41
JEFFEREYES 416
JEFFEREYS 416
Jefferies, Mary 14
Jefferson, Benjamin 235
Jefferson, Mary 579
Jefferson, Mercy 579
JEFFERY 416
JEFFORD 416
Jefford, Mary 690
JEFFORDS 416
Jeffray, Sarah 41
JEFFREY 416
Jeffrey, Digory 192, 639
Jeffrey, Gregory 479
JEFFREYS 416
Jeffreys, Mary 362
JEFFRIES 416
Jeffries, Mary 321
JEFFRY 416
Jeffs, Elizabeth 424
Jeffs, Sarah 584
Jeffts, Joanna 236
JEFTS 417
Jefts, Elizabeth 138, 423, 424
Jefts, Hannah 694
Jefts, Henry 34, 71
Jefts, Joanna 233
JEGGLES 417

Jeggles, Bridget 171
Jeggles, Elizabeth 322, 323
Jegles, Abigail 273
Jellet, John 779
JELLISON 417
JEMISON 419
JENCKES 418
Jenckes, Elizabeth 731
Jenckes, Esther 509
Jenckes, Joseph 218
JENCKS 418
Jencks, Sarah 108
Jenee, Sarah 669
JENISON 419
Jenison, Micael 79
Jenison, Michael 79
Jenison, Mychall 79
Jenison, Rachel 47
Jenkens, Hannah 760
Jenkes, --- 333
Jenkes, Sarah 151
JENKINS 417
Jenkins, David 458
Jenkins, Edward 277, 462, 626
Jenkins, Hannah 10, 39, 79, 558
Jenkins, John 256, 551
Jenkins, Joseph 362
Jenkins, Lemuel 771
Jenkins, Lydia 564
Jenkins, Margaret 170
Jenkins, Martha 241
Jenkins, Mary 24, 27, 179, 188,
  321, 559
Jenkins, Mehitable 338, 416
Jenkins, Micall 697
Jenkins, Obadiah 463
Jenkins, Philadelphia 253, 357
Jenkins, Rowland 362
Jenkins, Samuel 260
Jenkins, Sarah 30, 435, 462, 503,
  529
Jenkins, Stephen 438
Jenkins, Thomas 806
Jenkins, William 358
JENKS 417, 418
Jenks, Abigail 803
Jenks, Daniel 10
Jenks, Elizabeth Potter Floyd 272
Jenks, Joanna 657
Jenks, Sarah 151
Jenmerson, Sarah Brackett Shaw
  Benjamin 62
JENNE 418
JENNER 418
Jenner, Ellen 829
Jenner, Esther 829
Jenner, John 651
Jenner, Mary 651
Jenner, Rebecca 464, 478, 480
Jenner, Thomas 829
Jenners, Francis 806, 844
Jenners, Mary 167
Jenners, Rebecca 480
Jenners, Zacheus 806
Jennery, Lambert 264
Jennery, Mary 264
Jennery, Mary Clapp 154
JENNESS 418
Jenness, Hannah 469
JENNEY 418
Jenney, Abigail 833
Jenney, Elizabeth 82, 253
Jenney, Hix 418
Jenney, John 665
Jenney, Mehitable 301
Jenney, Remember 112, 311
Jenney, Remembrance 112, 311
Jenney, Ruth 413

Jenney, Sarah 594, 669
Jenney, Susanna 47, 766
Jenning, Remember 112, 311
Jenning, Remembrance 112, 311
JENNINGS 418, 419
Jennings, Ann 415
Jennings, Captivity 47
Jennings, Elizabeth 614, 685
Jennings, Johannah 357
Jennings, Jonathan 1, 838
Jennings, Joseph 574, 621
Jennings, Joshua 678
Jennings, Mary 197, 742, 819
Jennings, Nicholas 58
Jennings, Samuel 63, 329
Jennings, Stephen 304
JENNISON 419
Jennison, Elizabeth 614
Jennison, Grace 380
Jennison, Judith 42
Jennison, Michal 782
Jennison, Michel 782
Jenson, Elizabeth 578
Jent, John 695
Jent, Mary 11
Jentelman, Joan 847
Jephson, John 164
JEPSON 419
Jepson, Emma 591
Jepson, John 164
Jepson, Thomas 79, 726
Jerman, Jane 456
JERVISE 416
Jervise 416
JESS 419
Jess, Abigail 842
JESSE 419
JESSON 419
JESSONS 419
JESSUP 419
Jessup, --- 470
Jessup, Elizabeth 54, 404
Jessup, Hannah 370
Jessup, Joanna 123, 810
Jessup, John 810
Jessup, Mary 225
JEWELL 419
Jewell, Grissell 271
Jewell, Hannah 556, 561
Jewell, Mary 561
Jewell, Mercy 695
Jewell, Nathaniel 580, 663, 667
Jewell, Thomas 119, 327, 331, 436
Jewell, William 236
JEWET 420
Jewet, Hannah 590
JEWETT 419, 420
Jewett, Ann 553
Jewett, Anna 41
Jewett, Deborah 446
Jewett, Eleazer 448
Jewett, Elizabeth 361, 369
Jewett, Ezekiel 141, 420
Jewett, Faith 230, 587
Jewett, Hana 28
Jewett, Hannah 28, 134
Jewett, Jemima 702
Jewett, Joanna 766
Jewett, Johannah 258
Jewett, John 141
Jewett, Joseph 9, 291, 323, 479
Jewett, Mary 104, 225, 361
Jewett, Maxmilian 89, 780
Jewett, Patience 225, 775
Jewett, Ruth 766
Jewett, Sarah 205, 249, 378, 531
Jewett, Thomas 722
JEWIT 419, 420
Jewit, Jemima 702

Jewit, Mary 225
Jewson, Elizabeth 578
Jiggles, Bridget 639
JIMSON 415
JOANES 425, 426
Jobs, Mary 30
Jocelyn, Henry 132
JOEY 428
Joggers, Mary 575
JOHANNOT 424
JOHNES 425, 426
Johnes, Ann 338
Johnes, Edward 338
Johnes, Rice 338
Johnes, Sarah 614
Johns, Mercy 41
JOHNSON 420, 421, 422, 423,
  424, 841
Johnson, --- 50, 245
Johnson, Abigail 173, 274, 467,
  560
Johnson, Alice 478
Johnson, Ann 353, 484
Johnson, Anna 593, 816
Johnson, Bethia 444
Johnson, Bethiah 833
Johnson, Catharine Treat Thompson
  738
Johnson, Christian 777
Johnson, Cornelia 14
Johnson, Daniel 761
Johnson, Deborah 20, 281, 344
Johnson, Dorcas 585
Johnson, Dorothy 538, 596
Johnson, Edmund 171
Johnson, Edward 379, 736
Johnson, Edward (Capt.) 601
Johnson, Eleanor 463
Johnson, Elizabeth 31, 86, 272,
  276, 336, 412, 421, 482, 501,
  514, 541, 570, 590, 709, 745,
  746, 787, 844
Johnson, Elizabeth Treat Wolcott
  832
Johnson, Esther 845
Johnson, Eunice 719
Johnson, Frances 557, 340
Johnson, Hannah 45, 117, 238,
  367, 370, 401, 406, 414, 467,
  486, 555, 557, 561, 582, 675,
  688
Johnson, Hesther 845
Johnson, Humphrey 499
Johnson, Isaac 265, 378, 453
Johnson, James 574
Johnson, Jean 424
Johnson, Jemima 1
Johnson, Joanna 139, 140, 332
Johnson, Johannah 43
Johnson, John 260, 304, 332, 391,
  424, 498, 635
Johnson, Jonathan 674
Johnson, Joseph 609
Johnson, Kate 402
Johnson, Katharine 730
Johnson, Lydia 17, 39, 761
Johnson, Margaret 108, 458
Johnson, Martha 16, 521, 753
Johnson, Mary 28, 47, 81, 105,
  155, 206, 259, 422, 436, 441,
  463, 478, 497, 508, 526, 543,
  566, 715, 721, 731, 779
Johnson, Mehitable 171, 375, 636
Johnson, Mercy 355, 657
Johnson, Nathaniel 311
Johnson, Perseverance 321
Johnson, Peter 276
Johnson, Rebecca 13, 38, 845

Johnson, Richard 173
Johnson, Robert 371
Johnson, Rosamond 542
Johnson, Ruhamah 355, 444, 681
Johnson, Ruth 28, 226, 228, 558, 614, 651, 844
Johnson, Samuel 259, 317, 439, 721, 732
Johnson, Sarah 28, 136, 282, 348, 389, 519, 614, 768, 832
Johnson, Solomon 286
Johnson, Susanna 332, 420, 843
Johnson, Susannah 601
Johnson, Thomas 252, 375, 551, 770
Johnson, William 29, 136, 138, 557, 759
Johnston, Ann Dodd Norton 541
Johnston, Anne Dodd 279
Johnston, Hannah Dodd 280
Johnston, Joanna 332
Johnston, John 332
Johnston, Susanna 332
JOHONNOT 424
Johonnot, Daniel 422
Joliffe, John 445
JOLLS 424
Jolls, Thomas 830
Jomdaine, Elizabeth 233
JONES 424, 425, 426, 427, 687
Jones, --- 458
Jones, Abigail 39, 692
Jones, Alice 441
Jones, Ann 338, 467, 523, 550, 731
Jones, Anna 503, 720
Jones, Anne 467, 806
Jones, Benjamin 231, 331, 837
Jones, Cornelius 64, 91, 396, 408
Jones, David (Sr.) 116, 813
Jones, Deborah 143, 710
Jones, Dorcas 714
Jones, Dorcus 126
Jones, Dorothy 348, 659
Jones, Edward 338, 453
Jones, Elizabeth 47, 50, 83, 126, 172, 195, 246, 299, 372, 518, 628, 733, 815, 822
Jones, Elizabeth Tisdall Smith 684
Jones, Ephraim 109
Jones, Esther 786
Jones, Experience 399
Jones, George 660
Jones, Hannah 33, 95, 116, 260, 312, 463, 508, 512, 611, 787
Jones, Hepzibah 131
Jones, Hester 786
Jones, Isaac 50
Jones, James 47
Jones, Jane 130
Jones, Jeremiah 336
Jones, John 523, 547
Jones, John (Rev.) 332
Jones, Joseph 160
Jones, Lewis 714
Jones, Lydia 180, 767, 810
Jones, Marah 844
Jones, Margaret 101
Jones, Mariam 547
Jones, Martha 811, 812
Jones, Mary 5, 44, 64, 72, 95, 140, 167, 231, 273, 302, 393, 400, 401, 408, 417, 463, 547, 558, 606, 628, 660, 743, 755, 829, 836
Jones, Matthew 453
Jones, Mehitable 288
Jones, Mercy 41

Jones, Nicholas 684
Jones, Phebe 393
Jones, Philip 191, 701
Jones, Rachel 691
Jones, Rebecca 115, 128, 321, 400, 512, 605, 734
Jones, Remember 332
Jones, Rice 338, 453
Jones, Richard 146, 370
Jones, Robert 172, 199, 634
Jones, Ruhamah 537
Jones, Ruth 360, 415
Jones, Samuel 370, 822
Jones, Sarah 60, 81, 108, 115, 132, 142, 227, 416, 417, 465, 520, 599, 601, 614, 685, 802, 825
Jones, Sarah Blackman 74
Jones, Sarah Pearce 497
Jones, Susanna 313, 413, 826
Jones, Thomas 24, 81, 141, 247, 658, 700, 806, 811
Jones, William 255, 427
JONS 426
Jons, Hannah 312
Jonson, Mary 561
Jonson, Mehitable 375
Jonson, Sarah 136
Jonus, Anna 503
JORDAINE 428
JORDAN 427, 428
Jordan, Ann 118, 415
Jordan, Anna 194, 415
Jordan, Anne 415
Jordan, Annes 102
Jordan, Annis 415
Jordan, Baruch 816
Jordan, Deborah 310
Jordan, Elizabeth 396, 460
Jordan, Hannah 51, 194, 280, 772
Jordan, Henry 481
Jordan, Jane 17
Jordan, Joan 666
Jordan, John 158
Jordan, Lydia 676, 805
Jordan, Mary 310, 437, 595, 633
Jordan, Rebecca 189, 306
Jordan, Robert 225
Jordan, Sarah 298
Jordan, Stephen 504
Jordan, Thomas 334
Jordon, Hannah 280
JOSE 428
Jose, Jane 299
Jose, Joanna 653
Jose, John 44, 247, 459
Jose, Margaret 807
Jose, Mary 589
Jose, Phebe 116
JOSELIN 428
Joselin, Thomas 434
JOSELYN 428
JOSLEN 428
JOSLIN 428
Joslin, Abraham 84
Joslin, Dorothy 424
Joslin, Elizabeth 437, 845
Joslin, Hannah 804
Joslin, Henry 132
Joslin, John (Jr.) 804
Joslin, Martha 732
Joslin, Mary 720, 804
Joslin, Peter 835
Joslin, Rebecca 347, 392
Joslin, Thomas 766
JOSLINE 428
JOSLYN 428
JOSSELYN 428

Josselyn, Rebecca 193, 536, 707
Jossolyn, Elizabeth 437
Jourdain, Sarah 372
Jourdaine, Jehosabath 627
Jourdaine, Jehosabeth 627
Jourdan, Sarah 324, 372
JOY 428
Joy, Deborah 428, 778
Joy, Elizabeth 55, 794
Joy, Ephraim 296
Joy, Hannah 110
Joy, Jacob 793
Joy, Mary 63, 712, 778
Joy, Rachel 446
Joy, Ruth 477
Joy, Samuel 239
Joy, Sarah 227, 235
Joy, Walter 285
JOYCE 428, 429
Joyce, Dorcas 50, 394
Joyce, Hosea 307
Joyce, Lucretia 725
Joyce, Martha 307
Joyce, Mary 50
Joyce, Susanna 332
Joyce, William 376, 396
JOYE 428
Joye, Abraham 206
Joyleffe, John 193
JOYLIFFE 424
Joyliffe, John 445
Joyner, Isabel 516
Juckene, Mary 559
JUDD 429
Judd, Elizabeth 349, 464, 472, 562
Judd, Hannah 464, 681
Judd, Mary 415, 427, 464, 472, 789, 838
Judd, Ruth 705
Judd, Sarah 387
Judd, Thomas 495
Judewine, Cornelius 806
JUDKIN 429
JUDKINS 429
Judkins, Hannah 768
Judkins, Sarah 599
Judkins, Thomas 360
Judsin, Mercy 124
JUDSON 429, 430
Judson, Abigail 198
Judson, Ann 573
Judson, Anna 573
Judson, Elizabeth 83, 746
Judson, Esther 197, 440
Judson, Grace 159, 606
Judson, Hannah 770
Judson, Isaac 567
Judson, James 705
Judson, Jeremiah 257
Judson, John 535, 546, 643, 779
Judson, Joshua 405
Judson, Mary 150, 794
Judson, Ruth 795
Judson, Samuel 8, 359
Judson, Sarah 393, 720, 785, 797, 837
Judson, William 363, 824
JUELL 419
Juell, Hannah 556
Juell, Thomas 327
Juett, Patience 775
JUKIN 430
Jukin, Job Cooke 430
JUNE 430
JUNKINS 430
Jupe, Mary 520
Jupe, Mary 523

JYNKS 418

--- K ---

KADE 130, 430
KAIAS 435
KAINE 430
KAKEBREAD 131
Kallum, John 174
Kallum, Martha 273
Kally, Agnes Card Cox 188
Kalsoe, Joanna 258
Kalton, Katherine 755
Kanedy, Hannah 599
Karl, Elizabeth 52
Karl, Hannah 52
KARLE 134
KASE 139
KAY 430 see KEY
Kay, Charity 386
Kay, Dorothy 29
Kay, Mary 183
Kay, Winifred 739
Kaye, Elizabeth 156
Kaye, Grace 648
Kaye, Martha 156
KEACH 430
Keanies, Ann 551
Keanies, Anna 551
Keanies, Hannah 551
KEASER 435
Keaser, Sara 291
Keaser, Sarah 304, 421
KEAYNE 430
Keayne, Ann 450, 551
Keayne, Ann Mansfield 170
Keayne, Anna 450, 551
Keayne, Benjamin 549
Keayne, Hannah 450, 551
Kebbe, Elizabeth 564
Kebben, Mary 496
Kedall, Mary 811
Kedell, Mary 811
KEDGERER 442
KEECH 430
Keech, Joanna 591
Keech, Mary 743
Keedell, Bethia 578
Keefe, Mary 736
KEELER 430
Keeler, Elizabeth 357, 395, 581
Keeler, Ralph 517, 676, 752
Keeler, Rebecca 760
Keeley, Mary 422
KEELING 430
KEEN see CAINE, KEAYNE
Keen, Elizabeth 72
Keen, Hannah 348, 544
Keen, Joanna Dore 85
KEENE 430, 433
Keene, Martha 665
Keene, Mary 246
KEENEY 430, 431, 433
Keeney, Agnes 58
Keeney, Alexander 172
Keeney, John 384
Keeney, Mary 58
Keeney, Sarah 96
Keeney, Susanna 758
KEENY 430
Keeny, Susanna 559
KEEP 431
Keep, Hannah 508
Keep, Sarah 561
KEESE 435
KEET 431

KEETCH 430
KEGWIN 431
KEHOE 431
KEIES 435
Keies, Hannah 89
Keies, Jane 162
Keies, Judith 277
Keies, Sarah 126, 278
KEIGWIN 431
Kein, Arthur 584
Kein, Sarah 584, 762
KEISAR 436
KEITH 431
Keith, James (Rev.) 822
Keith, John 221
Keith, Margaret 404
Keith, Mary 358
Keith, Susanna 359
Kelle, Sarah 121
KELLEN 431 see KELLOND
Keller, Ralph 802
KELLEY 431
Kelley, Mary 53
Kelley, Sarah 121
KELLING see KELLOND
KELLOGG 431, 461
Kellogg, Abigail 685
Kellogg, Elizabeth 529
Kellogg, Joanna 684
Kellogg, Lydia 157
Kellogg, Martin 450, 681
Kellogg, Mary 589
Kellogg, Prudence 504
Kellogg, Rachel 534
Kellogg, Samuel 330
Kellogg, Sarah 23, 99
KELLON 431
KELLOND 431 see KELLEN
Kellond, Susanna 479
Kellond, Thomas 278, 479
KELLUM 437
Kellum, Anna 761
Kellum, Hannah 476
Kellum, Sarah 178
KELLY 431, 432 see CALLY
Kelly, David 641
Kelly, Elizabeth 350, 688
Kelly, Emma 591
Kelly, John 15
Kelly, Mary 60, 128, 209
Kelly, Rebecca 106
Kelly, Renold 485
Kelly, Richard 57
Kelly, Sarah 286, 332
Kelly, Sarah (Sr.) 776
Kelly, Susanna 128
Kelly, Susannah 650
Kelp, Philip 63
KELSEY 432
Kelsey, Abigail 400
Kelsey, Bethia 577
Kelsey, Hannah 815
Kelsey, Lydia 450
Kelsey, Mary 304
Kelsey, Priscilla 304
Kelsey, Rebecca 304, 506
Kelsey, Ruth 696
KELTON 432
Kelton, Katherine 755
Kelway, Margaret 514
Kelway, Mary 450
Kelway, Milcah 692
KEMBALL 438
Kemball, Abigail 768
Kemball, Elizabeth 420, 717
Kemball, Hannah 41
Kemball, Sarah 445
Kember, Jane 557

Kember, Joan 166
KEMBLE 432 see KIMBALL
Kemble, Abigail 416
Kemble, Mary 67, 96, 391
Kemble, Sarah 50
KEMP 432
Kemp, Abigail 79
Kemp, Elizabeth 554
Kemp, Esther 278
Kemp, Mehitable 435
Kemp, Patience 658
Kemp, William 733
Kempe, Patience 658
KEMPSTER 432
KEMPTHORN 432
KEMPTHORNE 432
KEMPTON 432
Kempton, Joanna 522
Kempton, Manassah 522
KEN 430, 435
Kenard, John 727
KENDALL 432, 433, 507
Kendall, Abigail 367, 535, 616
Kendall, Bethia 578
Kendall, Elizabeth 583, 692, 828
Kendall, Hannah 109, 323, 558
Kendall, Jacob 732
Kendall, John 138, 381, 557, 610
Kendall, Lydia 843
Kendall, Mabel 616, 692
Kendall, Margery Batson 247
Kendall, Mary 111, 205, 614, 758,
    810
Kendall, Ruth 773, 774
Kendall, Sarah 235, 564, 623
Kendall, Susanna 312
Kendall, Susannah 816
Kendall, Tabitha 585
Kendall, Thomas 104
Kendall, Wm. 846
Kendell, Elizabeth 241
Kendell, Mabel 720
Kendell, Rebecca 86
KENDRICK 433
Kendrick, Deborah 405, 845
Kendrick, Elijah 408
Kendrick, Elizabeth 554
Kendrick, Hannah 506
Kendrick, John 381
Kendrick, Lydia 107
Kendrick, Mary 78
Kendrick, Ruth 824
Kendrick, Sarah 802
Kene, John 384
KENEL 433
KENELINE 433
KENERICK 433
KENEY 433
Keney, John 389
Keney, Susannah 389
KENICOTT 433
KENISTON 433
Keniston, Allen 193
Keniston, Dorothy 193
KENNARD 433
KENNEDY 433 see CANADA
Kennedy, Hannah 599
KENNET 433
Kennet, Richard 189
Kennet, Susanna 759
KENNEY 133, 441 see CANNEY,
    KENNING, KINNE
Kenney, Joanna 504
Kenney, John 384, 389
Kenney, Martha 529
Kenney, Mary 742, 761
Kenney, Samuel 611
Kenney, Susan 234

Kenney, Susannah 389
KENNICUT 433
KENNING 433 see KENNEY
Kenning, Elizabeth 826
Kenning, Henry 813
Kenning, Jane 446, 826
Kenning, Margery 446
KENNISTON 433
Kenniston, Agnes 484
Kenniston, John 484
KENNY 433
Kenny, Mary 587
Kenny, Nathaniel 135
KENRICK 433
Kenrick, Ann 339
Kenrick, Elizabeth 554
Kenrick, Hannah 339, 506, 533
Kenrick, Margaret 364
KENRICKE 433
Kenricke, Sarah 802
Kensley, Mary 212
KENT 434
Kent, Hannah 15, 130, 504, 727, 786
Kent, Hannah Glover 489
Kent, Jane 682
Kent, Joanna 607
Kent, John 327, 343
Kent, Martha 241
Kent, Mary 275, 724
Kent, Oliver 496
Kent, Rebecca 72, 258, 658
Kent, Richard (Jr.) 209
Kent, Samuel 576
Kent, Sarah 188, 195, 324, 727, 803
Kent, Stephen 655
Kent, William 501
KENYON 434
Kenyon, Mary Ray 649
KER 435
KERBEY 441
Kerbie, Jane 449
Kerby, Jane 449
Kerby, Mary 687
KERLEY 434, 435 see CARLEY
Kerley, Elizabeth 392
Kerley, Hannah 238
Kerley, Henry 392
Kerley, Joseph 241
Kerley, Lydia 742
Kerley, Mary 687
Kerley, William 528, 640
KERLY 134, 434
KERR 435
KERTLAND 442
Kertland, Elizabeth 50
Kertland, Mary 95
Kertland, Nathaniel 119, 456
Kertland, Parnall 454, 456
KESKEYS 435
Kesler, Rebecca 401
KETCH 430
Ketch, --- 710
KETCHAM 435
Ketcham, Edward 810
Ketcham, Hester 791
Ketcham, Rebecca 731
Ketcham, Sarah 809, 810
KETCHUM 435
Ketham, Sarah 840
KETTELL 435
Kettell, Hannah 131
Kettell, Joseph 366
Kettell, Mary 580
Kettell, Mercy 31
Kettell, Samuel 287
KETTLE 435

Kettle, Bethia 578
Kettle, Hannah 169, 452
Kettle, John 183, 613
Kettle, Mary 613, 811
Kettle, Sarah 670
KETTOW 435
KEY 435 see KAY
Key, Dorothy 29
Key, Elizabeth 2
Key, John 529
Key, Mary 796
KEYES 435
Keyes, Elias 499
Keyes, Hannah 89
Keyes, Jane 162
Keyes, Judith 277
Keyes, Mary 290
Keyes, Phebe 284
Keyes, Rebecca 690
Keyes, Robert 290
Keyes, Sarah 126
Keyes, Sarah 278
KEYNE 435
KEYSER 436
Keyser, Eleazer 778
Keyser, George 23
Keyser, Mary 524
KEYZAR 436
KIBBE 436
Kibbe, Anna 269
Kibbe, Mary 558
Kibbee, Henry 331
Kibbee, Mary 356
KIBBEN 436
KIBBEY 436
Kibbey, Ann 222
Kibbey, Elizabeth 564
Kibbey, Lydia 367
KIBBY 436
Kibby, Anna 222
Kibby, Deborah 559
Kibby, Henry 419
Kibby, James 476
Kibby, Lydia 63, 400
Kibby, Mary 558
Kibby, Susanna 661
Kidbee, Girzell 148
KIDDER 436
Kidder, Ann 764
Kidder, Anna 764
Kidder, Dorothy 408
Kidder, Enoch 203
Kidder, Hannah 435
Kidder, Sarah 105
Kiene, Sarah 403
Kierstadt, Anna 608
Kierstadt, Anne 608
Kierstadt, Hance 608
KILBEY 437
Kilbey, Sarah 231
KILBORNE 436
Kilborne, Frances 763
Kilborne, Sarah 190
KILBOURN 436
Kilbourn, Mary 636
Kilbourn, Naomi 333
KILBOURNE 436, 437
Kilbourne, Elizabeth 197
Kilbourne, Lydia 360
Kilbourne, Margaret 454
KILBURN 436
KILBURNE 436
Kilburne, Mary 127
KILBY 437
Kilby, Edward 845
KILCUP 437
KILHAM 437
Kilham, Abigail 495

Kilham, Ann 495
Kilham, Daniel 257, 498, 614, 690
Kilham, Elizabeth 302, 408
Kilham, Hannah 476
Kilham, Katherine 309
Kilham, Lucretia 217
Kilham, Martha 251
Kilham, Ruth 482, 483
Kilham, Sarah 178
Kilhams, John 331
KILKUP 437
KILLAM 437
Killam, Abigail 738
Killam, Daniel 302, 437
Killam, Elizabeth 302
Killam, Hannah 1, 476
Killam, Sarah 178
Killegriff, Anna 581
Killem, Ruth 483
Killham, Abigail 14
Killham, Sarah 269
Killim, Abigail 14
Killim, Sarah 269
Killing, James 753
KILLIOWE 437
Killom, Thomas 516
KILLUM 437
Killum, Abigail 495
Killum, Ann 495
Killum, Martha 251
Kilson, Sarah 448
KILTON 432
Kim, Elizabeth 756
Kim, William 756
KIMBAL 438
KIMBALL 432, 437, 438 see KEMBLE
Kimball, Abigail 5, 253, 278, 661, 813
Kimball, Ann 492
Kimball, Anna 492
Kimball, Caleb 120
Kimball, Dorcas 228
Kimball, Elizabeth 134, 196, 420
Kimball, Hannah 41, 307, 492, 521
Kimball, Henry 302, 437, 477, 614
Kimball, Joanna 521
Kimball, John 48, 124, 433
Kimball, Martha 147, 280
Kimball, Mary 73, 96, 236, 437, 446, 597, 616
Kimball, Mehitable 710, 741
Kimball, Mercy 446
Kimball, Priscilla 16
Kimball, Rebecca 478, 591
Kimball, Richard 228, 275
Kimball, Richard (Capt.) 438
Kimball, Sarah 10, 279, 290, 366, 596
Kimball, Susan 610
Kimball, Susanna 610
Kimball, Thomas 196
Kimbell, Susan 610
Kimbell, Susanna 610
Kimberley, Sarah 76
KIMBERLY 438
Kimberly, Abiah 80, 441
Kimberly, Abraham 198
Kimberly, Elizabeth 484
Kimberly, Mary 76, 151, 210, 357
Kimberly, Sarah 405, 436
Kimberly, Thomas 603
Kimble, Abigail 813
Kimble, Martha 147
Kimble, Mary 616 .
Kimbol, Prisselah 16
Kimbole, Rebecca 478, 591

Kimmin, Moses 313
KIMRIGHT 433
KINCADE 438
Kincade, David 417
KINCAID 438
Kincaid, David 417
KINCUM 438
KIND 438
Kind, Arthur 762
Kind, Mary 96
Kind, Sarah 96, 639, 762
Kindall, Elizabeth 137
KINDE 438
Kindell, Rebecca 241
KINDRICK 433
KING 438, 439, 440, 444, 620
King, --- 835
King, Agnes 26
King, Anna 766
King, Anne 766
King, Bethiah 626
King, Clement 44
King, Deborah 688
King, Deliverance 760
King, Dorothy 108
King, Dulcebella 72
King, Dulzebella 72
King, Ebenezer 159
King, Edward 373
King, Elizabeth 335, 346, 408,
  616, 620, 624, 755, 784
King, Experience 600
King, Hanna 77
King, Hannah 83, 108, 434, 498,
  499, 507
King, James 472
King, Jane 274
King, Joanne 37
King, John 42, 47, 353, 363, 403,
  528
King, Katherine 723
King, Martha 620, 804
King, Mary 144, 146, 288, 293,
  313, 323, 373, 461, 620, 658,
  828
King, Mary Ingalls Eaton 240
King, Mehitable 82
King, Naomi Burdick Rogers 634
King, Peter 63
King, Philipa 543
King, Ralph 463
King, Rhoda 633
King, Richard 72
King, Ruth 61
King, Samuel 15
King, Sarah 71, 81, 130, 230,
  357, 428, 465, 469, 530, 556,
  591, 744
King, Susanna 363, 461, 733
King, Susannah 86
King, Thomas 98, 200, 353, 767
King, William 120, 624, 771
King, Winifred 62
Kinge, Mary 421
KINGMAN 440
Kingman, Alice 43
Kingman, Ann 411
Kingman, Anne 380
Kingman, Bridget 209
Kingman, Deliverance 512
Kingman, Elizabeth 513
Kingman, Joane 380
Kingman, Joanne 43
Kingman, John 549, 578
Kingman, Lydia 549
Kingman, Sarah 768
Kingman, Susanna 453
KINGSBERY 441

Kingsbery, Elizabeth 202
KINGSBURY 440, 441
Kingsbury, Amy 290
Kingsbury, Anna 290
Kingsbury, Elizabeth 99, 202, 206,
  554
Kingsbury, Huldah 240
Kingsbury, John 322, 506
Kingsbury, Margaret 181, 289
Kingsbury, Mary 170, 181
Kingsbury, Mercy 559
Kingsbury, Sarah 194
Kingsbury, Susanna 586
Kingsbury, Thomas 240
Kingslane, Abigail 246
KINGSLEY 441
Kingsley, Abigail 691
Kingsley, Elizabeth 554
Kingsley, Enos 160
Kingsley, Freedom 284
Kingsley, Hannah 331, 451, 623
Kingsley, John 426
Kingsley, Lydia 330
Kingsley, Samuel 76, 407
Kingsley, Sarah 771
Kingsley, Susannah 331
Kingsnorth, Henry 173
KINGSNOTH 441
Kingsnoth, Henry 173
KINGSTON 441
Kingswill, Elizabeth 649
Kingswill, Mary 140
KINGSWORTH 441
Kinman, Bridget 209
KINNE 441
Kinne, Elizabeth 212
Kinne, Henry 450
Kinnecut, Mary 814
Kinnecutt, Lydia 479
KINNEY 441 see KENE,
  KENNEY
Kinney, Elizabeth 212
Kinney, Joanna 504
Kinnicutt, Joanna 579
KINSBURY 441
Kinsbury, Elizabeth 95
Kinsbury, Susanna 586
KINSLEY 441
Kinsley, Eldad 103
Kinsley, Elizabeth 196
Kinsley, John 427, 526
Kinsley, Mary 212, 328, 495
Kinsley, Stephen 328, 495
Kinsley, Tabitha 190
KINSMAN 441
Kinsman, Eunice 121
Kinsman, Hannah 203
Kinsman, Joanna 645
Kinsman, Martha 277
Kinsman, Mary 626, 779
Kinsman, Sarah 571, 847
Kinsman, Tabitha 360
Kinsman, Thomas 626
Kint, Arthur 584
Kint, Sarah 584
Kintley, Abigail 691
Kinward, Joan 125
Kip, Tryntie 213
KIPPEN 436, 441
KIRBY 441, 442
Kirby, Abigail 629
Kirby, Bethiah 17
Kirby, Elizabeth 646
Kirby, Esther 713
Kirby, Experience 523
Kirby, Hannah 18, 635, 715
Kirby, Hester 713
Kirby, John 610

Kirby, Mary 112
Kirby, Richard 387, 395
Kirby, Ruhamah 684
Kirby, Sarah 12, 397, 504
Kirby, Susanna 196
KIRK 442
Kirk, Elizabeth 40
Kirk, Jasper 40
Kirk, Sarah 8
KIRKE 442
Kirke, Eleanor 464
Kirke, Elizabeth 464
Kirke, Henry 706
KIRKHAM 442
Kirkham, Thomas 378
KIRKLAND 442
Kirkland, Mary 95, 158
Kirkland, Nathaniel 456
Kirkland, Parnall 456
Kirkland, Philip 669
Kirkland, Sarah 459
KIRKOM 442
KIRKPATRICK 564
KIRTLAND 442
Kirtland, Alice 735
Kirtland, Elizabeth 457, 460
Kirtland, Hannah 131, 600
Kirtland, Martha 75
Kirtland, Mary 95, 158, 188
Kirtland, Nathaniel 456
Kirtland, Parnall 456
Kirtland, Philip 241, 735
Kirtland, Priscilla 172
Kirtland, Sarah 207, 459
Kirtland, Susanna 736
Kirtland, Susannah 797
Kirtlind, Mary 95
KISSAM 442
KITCHELL 442
Kitchell, Grace 61
Kitchell, Joanna 567
Kitchell, John 666
Kitchell, Susannah 36
KITCHEN 442
Kitchen, John 652
Kitchen, Mary 342, 631
Kitchen, Priscilla 87
KITCHERELL 442
Kitcherell, Martha 842
Kitcherell, Samuel 226
Kitchin, Abigail 330
Kitchin, Priscilla 403
Kitson, Alice 619
KITT 442
KITTERIDGE 442
KITTREDGE 442
Kittredge, John 284
KITTRIDGE 442
KLINE 442
Knabb, Timothy 730
KNAP 442, 443
Knap, Elizabeth 658
KNAPE 443
KNAPP 442, 443
Knapp, Aaron 389
Knapp, Abigail 191
Knapp, Ann 577
Knapp, Anna 577
Knapp, Anne 577
Knapp, Caleb 455
Knapp, Elizabeth 129, 449, 577,
  715
Knapp, Femy 222
Knapp, Hannah 194, 396, 680
Knapp, John 673
Knapp, Joseph 399
Knapp, Joshua 87
Knapp, Josiah 536

Knapp, Judith 130, 398
Knapp, Lydia 334, 510, 570
Knapp, Mary 689, 751
Knapp, Nicholas 108
Knapp, Ruth 263, 618
Knapp, Sarah 222, 399, 500, 556
Knapp, William 3
Kneale, Philip 12
KNEELAND 443
Kneelands, John 740
KNELL 443
Knell, Elizabeth 512
Knell, Nicholas 446
Knell, Philip 12
KNIFFEN 443
Kniffen, Elizabeth 711
Kniffen, George 802
Kniffen, Mary 711
KNIGHT 443, 444, 445
Knight, Abigail 460
Knight, Alexander 809
Knight, Ann 621
Knight, Anna 395, 415
Knight, Anne 357, 415
Knight, Bridget Parsons 766
Knight, Catherine 371
Knight, Dinah 520
Knight, Eleanor 386, 540
Knight, Eleanor 102
Knight, Elizabeth 30, 257, 259,
  284, 319, 338, 433, 441, 520,
  541, 553, 597, 697, 715, 729,
  749, 795, 796
Knight, Em 597
Knight, Emma 597
Knight, Ezekiel 372, 468, 476
Knight, George 102
Knight, Hannah 160, 314, 541,
  571
Knight, Jacob 643
Knight, Joane 846
Knight, Joanna 291
Knight, John 223, 381, 410, 804,
  812
Knight, Jonathan 52, 833
Knight, Joseph 465
Knight, Margaret 52, 616
Knight, Margery 37
Knight, Martha 38, 304, 820
Knight, Mary 96, 169, 229, 292,
  377, 541, 547, 584, 591, 841
Knight, Philip 37, 52
Knight, Rebecca 5, 259, 692, 756
Knight, Richard 10, 401, 424, 787
Knight, Robert 193, 424, 473
Knight, Ruth 281
Knight, Samuel 392
Knight, Sarah 48, 431, 460, 515,
  541, 662, 783, 811
Knight, Susan 801
Knight, William 38, 95, 621
KNIGHTS 444
Knights, Mary 635
Knights, Rebecca 747
Knil, Ruth 639
KNILL 443
Knill, Elizabeth 51
Knill, John 51
Knill, Nicholas 446
KNITE 444, 445
Knoles, Mary 774
KNOLLYS 445
Knot, Joan 336
Knot, Joanna 336
KNOTT 445 see NOTT
Knott, George 234
Knott, Martha 234, 746
Knott, Richard 323, 724

KNOWER 445
Knower, Ann 114
Knower, George 114
Knower, Hannah 114
Knower, Mary 487, 811
Knower, Sarah 114
KNOWES 445
KNOWLES 445, 446
Knowles, Barbara 500
Knowles, Edward 500
Knowles, Elizabeth 72, 115, 275,
  632
Knowles, Hannah 469
Knowles, John 25
Knowles, Martha 246
Knowles, Mary 223, 467, 774
Knowles, Mehitable 105
Knowles, Rebecca 517, 746
Knowles, Ruth 173
Knowles, Sarah 483, 534, 772
Knowles, Stephen 85, 130
Knowles, Thomas 443
KNOWLMAN 446
KNOWLTON 446
Knowlton, Abigail 195
Knowlton, Deborah 75
Knowlton, Elizabeth 227, 826
Knowlton, Hannah 35
Knowlton, Jane 441
Knowlton, John 236, 408
Knowlton, Marrah 425
Knowlton, Mary 1, 425, 512, 724
Knowlton, Sarah 498
Knowlton, Susanna 183
Knowlton, William 275
KNOX 446, 537
Knox, Sarah Mellows 502
Knox, Sylvanus 56
Knox, Thomas 62
Kornie, Abiah 270
Kritchwell, Martha 842
Kritchwell, Samuel 226
Kymball, Abigail 253
KYNDE 438

--- L ---

L'---, Ann 231
LABORIE 447
LABROS 447
Lacey, Sarah 754
LACKEY 447, 460 see LEEKEY
LACKIN 452
Lackington, Mary 449
LaCroix, Albert 55
LACY 447
Lacy, Dorothy 258
Lacy, Morgan 754
LAD 447
Lad, Lydia 291
Lad, Sarah 489
LADBROOK 447
Ladbrook, Thomas 45, 83
LADBROOKE 447
LADD 447
Ladd, Elizabeth 306, 356, 686
Ladd, Lydia 291, 643
Ladd, Martha 808
Ladd, Mary 622
Ladd, Nathaniel 769
Ladd, Rebecca 58
Ladd, Sarah 489
Ladden, Mary 766
Laffetra, Ann 142
LAGRO 460
LAGROE 460

LaGrove, Hannah 525
LaGROVES 328
LAHERNE 447
LAHORNE 447
Laicore, John 262
LAITON 454, 456
Laiton, John 442
LAKE 447
Lake, Abigail 11, 559
Lake, Alice 129
Lake, Ann 185, 709
Lake, Anna 185, 709
Lake, Anne 185
Lake, Daniel 384, 547
Lake, David 183
Lake, Elizabeth 129, 415
Lake, Hannah 292
Lake, Henry 129
Lake, John 115
Lake, Margaret 308
Lake, Martha 345, 346
Lake, Mary 404
Lake, Mary Richardson Carder
  134
Lake, Michal 711
Lake, Richard 666
Lake, Sarah 700
Lake, Thomas (Capt.) 507
Lakein, John 731
LAKEMAN 447
Lakeman, Annis 629
Lakeman, Elizabeth 229
Lakeman, Wm. 629
LAKIN 447
Lakin, Abigail 447, 559
Lakin, Elizabeth 88
Lakin, Lydia 671
Lakin, Mary 493, 542, 817
Lakin, Sarah 817
Lakin, William 493
LAMB 448
Lamb, Abiel 113
Lamb, Abigail 456
Lamb, Daniel 544
Lamb, Decline 689
Lamb, Dorothy 420
Lamb, Ebenezer 419
Lamb, Edward 12
Lamb, Elizabeth 471
Lamb, Emory 550
Lamb, Joanna 704
Lamb, John 78, 174, 540, 593
Lamb, Mary 31, 476, 722
Lamb, Sarah 125, 657
Lamb, Thomas 356
LAMBERT 448, 449, 470 see
  LOMBARD
Lambert, --- 188
Lambert, Abigail 348, 732
Lambert, Ann 531, 582
Lambert, Bethia 630
Lambert, Daniel 96
Lambert, Elizabeth 71, 139, 723
Lambert, Esther 128
Lambert, Francis 632
Lambert, Gershom 590
Lambert, Hannah 30
Lambert, Hester 128
Lambert, Jesse 785
Lambert, John 22
Lambert, Margaret 94
Lambert, Mary 428
Lambert, Micah 358
Lambert, Michael 290, 358
Lambert, Sarah 30, 270, 287, 712
Lambert, Thomas 41, 710
LAMBERTON 449
Lamberton, Desire 182

Lamberton, Elizabeth 673, 755
Lamberton, George 312
Lamberton, Hannah 11, 795
Lamberton, Hope 15, 149, 365
Lamberton, Mercy 553
Lamberton, Obedience 688
Lamberton, Patience 72
Lambertson, Elizabeth 673, 755
LAMBIRD 449
LAMERE 449
LAMOS 478
LAMPHEAR see LANPHERE
Lamphere, Mary 129
LAMPREY 449
Lamprey, Elizabeth 228
Lampry, Sarah 406
LAMPSON 449
Lampson, Thomas 467, 519, 822
LAMSON 449
Lamson, Asubaty 794
Lamson, Azuba 794
Lamson, Elizabeth 843
Lamson, Hannah 173
Lamson, Joseph 69, 525, 792
Lamson, Martha 620
Lamson, Mary 179, 553
Lamson, Phebe 269, 749
Lamson, Sarah 104, 195
Lamson, William 349
Lamsytt, Wilmot 703
LANCASTER 449
Lancaster, Ann 313
Lancaster, Anna 617
Lancaster, John 39
Lancaster, Mary 504
Lanchaster, Mary 504
Lanchester, John 126
Lancois, Anne 460
Lancton, Mary 468
LANDER 449
Lander, Mary 176
LANDERS 449
Landers, James 759
LANDFEAR 449
LANDMAN 449
LANDON 449, 451 see
    LANGDON
Landon, James 824
LANE 449, 450
Lane, Abigail 712
Lane, Ann 94
Lane, Anna 277, 679
Lane, Anne 441
Lane, Annis 466
Lane, Anthonie 658
Lane, Anthony 658
Lane, Avith 466
Lane, Catherine 555
Lane, Daniel 230, 517
Lane, Deborah 698
Lane, Dorothy 697
Lane, Edward 551
Lane, Eleanor 104
Lane, Elizabeth 27, 157, 270,
    293, 329, 593, 625
Lane, Hannah 54, 402, 815
Lane, James 441
Lane, Jemima 803
Lane, Job 393
Lane, John 132, 239
Lane, Katharine 760
Lane, Margaret 190
Lane, Mary 27, 52, 248, 258, 471,
    545, 592, 607, 815
Lane, Mercy 36
Lane, Robert 270
Lane, Samuel 431
Lane, Sarah 33, 269, 330, 405,

Lane, Sarah (cont.) 463, 515
Lane, Susanna 628
Lane, William 258
Lane, Wm. 471
LANES 450
LANG 450
Lang, Mary 702
LANGBURRO 451
LANGBURY 451
LANGDON 451 see LANDON,
    LANGTON
Langdon, --- 183
Langdon, Dorothy 841
Langdon, Elizabeth 263
Langdon, Esther 341
Langdon, Jane 71
Langdon, John 325
Langdon, Margaret 519
Langdon, Mercy 817
Langdon, Sarah 611
Langdon, Susanna 51, 320
Langdon, Susannah 711
Langdon, Tobias 458, 493, 519
Lange, Sarah 154
LANGER 451
Langer, Margaret 466
LANGFORD 451
Langford, Mehitable 617
Langhorne, Elizabeth 361
Langhorne, Sarah 528
LANGLEE 451
Langlee, Sarah 366, 499
LANGLEY 451
Langley, Agnes 410, 444
Langley, Ann 410, 444
Langley, Anna 94
Langley, Hannah 94
Langley, John 828
Langley, Sarah 80
LANGMAND 451
LANGSFORD 451
LANGSTAFF 449, 451
Langstaff, Sarah 542
LANGTON 451 see LANGTON
Langton, Deliverance 124, 341
Langton, Dorothy 841
Langton, Elizabeth 357
Langton, Esther 341
Langton, George 357
Langton, Honor 456
Langton, Joseph 179
Langton, Mary 96, 211, 388, 468
Langton, Oner 456
Langton, Rachel 639
Langton, Samuel 8, 759
Langton, Sarah 766
LANGWORTHY 451
LANKESTER 449
Lankester, Anna 617
Lanner, Mary 669
LANPHERE 451 see LAMPHEAR
Lantersee, Anna 268
LAPHAM 451, 452
Lapham, Elizabeth 719
Lapham, Lydia 52
Lapham, Mary 50
Lapham, Rebecca 783
Lapham, Thomas 50
LAPPINWALL 460
Lapthorne, Hannah 713
LARCKUM 452
LARCOM 452
Larcom, Mary 495
Larcom, Rebecca 701
Larcom, Thomas 837
LARCUM 452
Larcum, Mary 484
Larcum, Mordecai 160

LARGE 452
Large, Simon 812
LARGIN 452
Largin, Henry 516
Largin, Sarah 718
LARICH 621
LARIFORD 452
Lariford, Sarah 638
LARISON 453
Larison, Amy 337
Larken, Sarah 800
LARKHAM 452
LARKIN 452
Larkin, Edward 570
Larkin, Elizabeth 231, 534, 822
Larkin, Hannah 38, 423, 532
Larkin, Joanna 224, 534, 570, 739
Larkin, John 224
Larkin, Mary 312, 423
Larkin, Mehitable 723
Larkin, Roger 756
Larkin, Sarah 93, 260, 800
Larkin, Sarah Dowse 237
Larkin, Thomas 231, 237
LARKUM 452
Larned, Hannah 260
Larned, Mary Stearns 119
Larned, Sarah 46, 475
Laroke, Sarah 496
Laroy, Sarah 517
LARRABEE 452, 453
Larrabee, Elizabeth 242, 364
Larrabee, Greenfield 183, 459
Larrabee, Jane 22
Larrabee, Samuel 73
Larrabee, Sarah 280
Larrifal, Sarah 807
Larriford, Sarah 278, 492
LARRIMORE 453
Larrimore, Thomas 640
LARRISON 453
Larrison, John 393
LARY 453, 456
Lary, John 12
Lary, Sarah 517
LASELL 453
Lasell, Hannah 759
Lasell, Mary 122
Lasell, Sarah 626
Laselle, Isaac 421
LASENBY 453
LASH 453
Lash, Joanna 486
Lash, William 486
Lashere, Abraham 365, 773
LASKEY 453
Laskin, Constance 486
Laskin, Damaris 486
Laskin, Edith 365
Laskin, Timothy 486
LASOLL 453
LASSEE 453
Lassee, Gabriel 216
Lassell, Joshua 598
Lassell, Mary 598
Latemore, Susanna 568
LATHAM 453
Latham, Elizabeth 178, 430, 460
Latham, Frances 155, 233, 766
Latham, Hannah 783
Latham, Jane 397, 725, 820
Latham, Lydia 550
Latham, Mercy 345
Latham, Rebecca Wells 786
Latham, Susannah 359
Latham, Thomas 550
LATHLEY 453
LATHROP 474, 475

Lathrop, Abigail 720
Lathrop, Bathsheba 54
Lathrop, Bathshua 54
Lathrop, Bethia 310
Lathrop, Elizabeth 549, 737, 819
Lathrop, Hannah 571, 721
Lathrop, Hannah Morton Fuller 285
Lathrop, Jane 289
Lathrop, Martha 311, 374
Lathrop, Mary 110, 195, 215, 512, 514, 703, 713
Lathrop, Ruth 596
Lathrope, John 226
LATIMER 453
Latimer, Ann 62, 71
Latimer, Bezaleel 756
Latimer, Elizabeth 382, 601, 785
Latimer, Jane 538
Latimer, Joan 34
Latimer, John 520
Latimer, Mary 538
Latimer, Naomi 308, 618
Latimer, Rebecca 752
Latimer, Robert 128
Latimer, Susanna 568
Latomie, Esther 201
LATTAMORE 453
LATTEN 453, 454
Lattimer, Robert 426
LATTIN 454 see LETTON
Lattin, Hannah 207
Lattin, Richard 411
LATTING 453
Latting, Hannah 207
Latting, Richard 399, 627
Lauder, Mary 176
LAUGHTON 454, 456 see LAWTON, LAYTON
Laughton, Elizabeth 341
Laughton, John 89, 442, 527
Laughton, Mary 211
Laughton, Rebecca 409
Laughton, Sarah 616
Laughton, Thomas 105, 161
Laugton, Hannah 605
LAUNDERS 449
Launders, Richard 11
LAURANCE 454
LAURENSON 454
Laurenson, Hannah 361
Laurenson, James 361
Laurenson, Sarah 361
Lauronson, Hannah 361
Lauronson, James 361
Lauronson, Sarah 361
LAURRENSON see LAWRESON
Lautersee, Anna 268
LAVENUCK 454
LAVENUKE 454
Laverett, Hannah 208
LAVISE 454
LAVISTONE 462
LAVITT 458
LAW 454
Law, Abigail 661
Law, Elizabeth 614
Law, Jonathan 720
Law, Mary 590
Law, Rebecca 420
Law, Sarah 661
Law, William 683
LAWES 454
Lawes, Francis 530
Lawes, Mary 486, 530
Lawrance, Abigail 67
LAWRENCE 454, 455
Lawrence, --- 777

Lawrence, Abial Thornton Page 550
Lawrence, Abigail 455, 844
Lawrence, Anne 568
Lawrence, Benjamin 5, 64, 577
Lawrence, Elizabeth 305, 652, 679, 708, 709, 811
Lawrence, Enoch 664
Lawrence, Grace 242
Lawrence, Hannah 110, 133, 380, 653
Lawrence, Hephzebah 305
Lawrence, Jane 301
Lawrence, Jannetye 515
Lawrence, Joanna 592
Lawrence, John 96, 818
Lawrence, Judith 703
Lawrence, Martha 222, 425, 492, 691, 720
Lawrence, Mary 121, 239, 251, 523, 564, 596, 629, 708, 802, 812
Lawrence, Mary Tuttle 121
Lawrence, Mercy 34
Lawrence, Nathaniel 577
Lawrence, Nicholas 844
Lawrence, Phebe 612
Lawrence, Rachel 728
Lawrence, Rebecca 631
Lawrence, Robert 194, 527
Lawrence, Samuel 464
Lawrence, Sarah 447, 551, 589, 625, 743, 829
Lawrence, Susanna 432, 728, 776
Lawrence, Susannah 512
Lawrence, Thomas 105, 145, 443, 760
Lawrence, William 7, 138, 749
Lawrence, Zechariah 482
Lawrene, Mary 56
Lawrenson, Anna 739
LAWRESON 456 see LAURENSON
LAWRISON 455
LAWSON 456
Lawson, Elizabeth 741
Lawson, Mary 553
LAWTON 454, 456, 474 see LAUGHTON
Lawton, Ann 14
Lawton, Anne 678
Lawton, Benedicta 509
Lawton, Elizabeth 99, 137, 197, 234, 669, 681
Lawton, Isaac 456
Lawton, Isabel 7
Lawton, John 283, 527
Lawton, Mary 28, 29, 574
Lawton, Mercy 754
Lawton, Ruth 832
Lawton, Sarah 634, 676
Lawton, Susannah 183
Lawton, Thomas 32
Laxton, Jane 42
LAY 453, 456 see LEE
Lay, Abigail 36, 782
Lay, Elizabeth 688, 756
Lay, Marah 426
Lay, Phebe 215
Lay, Rebecca 291, 613
Lay, Robert 758
Lay, Sarah 158, 218
LAYDON 456 see LAYTON
Laye, Catherine 182
LAYTHORP 475
Laythrop, Abigail 155
Laythum, Elizabeth 178
LAYTON 454, 456, 457

LAYTON (cont.) see LAWTON, LAYDON
Layton, Alice 311
Layton, Catharine 803
Layton, Elizabeth 334
Layton, Sarah 820
Layward, Rebecca 671
Laywards, Rebecca 622
LAZELL 453
Lazell, Hannah 759
Lazenby, Margaret 309
Lea, Margery Ashenden 673
Lea, William 828
LEACH 457
Leach, --- 486
Leach, Abigail 210
Leach, Alice 250
Leach, Bethiah 206
Leach, Catharine 11
Leach, Caturn 11
Leach, Elizabeth 172, 607, 612
Leach, Hannah 276
Leach, James 526
Leach, John 312, 517
Leach, Mary 411, 523, 669
Leach, Rachel 309, 673
Leach, Robert 250, 665
Leach, Samuel 35
Leach, Sarah 8, 366, 446, 510, 588
Leache, Mary 264
LEACOCK 459
LEADBETTER 457
Leadbetter, Deliverance 832
Leadbetter, Henry 229, 278
Leadbetter, Katherine 565
Leadbetter, Ruth 402
Leadbetter, Sarah 383, 831
LEADBITTER 457
LEADER 457
Leader, Abigail 546
Leader, Alice 686
Leader, Anna 158
Leader, Elizabeth 381
Leader, John 69
Leader, Ruth 11
Leader, Sarah 158
Leagar, Jacob 337
LEAGER 457
Leager, Anna 774
Leager, Bethiah 665
Leager, Hannah 579, 774
Leager, Sarah 775
LEAKING 448
LEALAND 460
Lealand, Deborah 305
Lealand, Experience 167
LEAMAN 461
Leamon, Margaret Hutchinson 839
Leanard, Mary 591
LEAPINGWELL 460
Leapinwell, Naomy 711
LEAR 457, 458
Lear, Elizabeth 502
Lear, Hugh 794
Lear, Susanna 448
Lear, Tobias 451, 493
Leare, Anna Willix Roscoe Blunt 637
Learnad, Sarah 256
LEARNED 458
Learned, Elizabeth 334
Learned, Hannah 260
Learned, Isaac 119
Learned, Mary 46
Learned, Peter 119
Learned, Sarah 475
Leate, Ann 173

LEATH 458
Leatherland, --- 756
Leatherland, Deborah 762
Leatherland, Elizabeth 346
Leatherland, Ellen 563
Leatherland, Margaret 433
LEATHERS 458
LEAVENS 458
Leavens, John 23
LEAVENSWORTH 458
LEAVENWORTH 458
Leavenworth, Grace 417
Leavenworth, Thomas 417
LEAVER 458
Leaver, Mary 231
Leaver, Prudence 290, 710
Leaver, Sarah 231
Leavett, Nehemiah 304
LEAVINS 458
Leavins, Hannah 565
LEAVITT 458
Leavitt, Abial 453
Leavitt, Alice 796
Leavitt, Elizabeth 232, 429
Leavitt, Hannah 239, 469, 474
Leavitt, Israel 335
Leavitt, James 563
Leavitt, John 759
Leavitt, Lydia 648
Leavitt, Mary 52, 735, 766, 805
Leavitt, Mehitable 639
Leavitt, Sarah 154, 393
Leavitt, Thomas 25
Leawith, Abigah 421
Leazer, Jacob 321
LeBARON 458
LEBARON 458
LeBLOND 458
LeBLOUD 458
LeBRETTON 100
LeBros, Charles 829
LECH 457
LECHFORD 458
Lechford, Elizabeth 72, 814
Lechford, Thomas 72, 814
LECKY 460
LECOCK 459
LECOCKE 459
LeCODY 459
LECODY 459
Lecornah, Catherine 821
Lecraft, Hannah 500
LEE 456, 459, 460 see LAY
Lee, Abigail 125
Lee, Abraham 44, 247, 428
Lee, Ann 25
Lee, Bridget 289
Lee, Elizabeth 38, 356, 359, 445,
  568, 598
Lee, Esther 287
Lee, Hannah 109
Lee, Jane 70, 408
Lee, Joanna 678
Lee, John 719
Lee, Joseph 168, 814
Lee, Joshua 411
Lee, Lydia 298
Lee, Marah 57
Lee, Mary 57, 196, 394, 473, 637,
  764, 796, 797
Lee, Phebe 452, 493
Lee, Rebecca 646
Lee, Richard 757
Lee, Samuel 11, 792
Lee, Sarah 112, 452
Lee, Simon 59, 204
Lee, Thomas 183, 207, 452
Lee, Tryphosa 751

Lee, Walter 591
Lee, William 828
Leech, Anne 831
Leech, Elizabeth 250
Leech, Sarah 510, 686
LEEDS 460
Leeds, Hannah 154
Leeds, Johannah 70
Leefs, Katherine Roberts 810
LEEK 460
Leek, Alice 685
Leek, Hannah 13
Leek, Joanna 602
LEEKE 460
Leeke, Ichabod 562
Leeke, Joanna 707
Leeke, Katherine Roberts 810
Leeke, Mary 207
LEEKEY 460 see LACKEY
LEES 459, 460
Leet, Ann 754
LEETE 460
Leete, Abigail 836
Leete, Ann 173
Leete, Caleb 130
Leete, Katherine Roberts 810
Leete, Mary 386
Leete, William 92, 645, 718
Leete, Wm. 533
LEETH 458
LeGROS 460
LeRoy, Esther 65
LEFFINGWELL 460
Leffingwell, Abigail 148
Leffingwell, Deborah 195, 780
Leffingwell, Elizabeth 751
Leffingwell, Hannah 270, 774
Leffingwell, Mary 125
Leffingwell, Rachel 556, 586
Leffingwell, Sarah 296
Leffingwell, Thomas 365
Leffingwill, Ann 125
Leg, Ann 491
Leg, Anna 491
LEGARE 460
Legat, Elizabeth 232
Legereau, Eugenie 706
LEGG 460
Legg, Ann 491
Legg, Anna 491
Legg, Elizabeth 107
Legg, Isabella 45
Legg, Mary 94
Legg, Sabella 45, 46
Leggett, John 826
Legorge, Elizabeth 9
Legorwell, Barbara 594
Legro, Christian 723
LEGROE 460
Legros, Mary 822
Legroue, Mary 822
Legrow, John 343
Legrowe, Susan 563
Legrowe, Susanna 563
LEICHFIELD 467
LEIGH 459 see LAY
Leigh, --- 563
Leigh, John 598
Leigh, Lucretia 82
Leigh, Mary 760
Leigh, Penelope 274
Leigh, Sarah 402
LEIGHTON 454, 456, 457 see
  LAWTON, LAYDON
Leighton, Catharine 803
Leighton, Elizabeth 193, 532, 587
Leighton, John 442
Leighton, Martha 589

Leighton, Mary 402, 628, 697
Leighton, Rebecca 409
Leighton, Sarah 407
Leighton, Thomas 587
Leighton, William 339
Leithfield, Sarah 65
LELAND 460
Leland, Deborah 305
Leland, Ebenezer 380
Leland, Experience 167
Leland, Lydia 475
Leland, Mercy 752
LELLOCK 461 see KELLOGG
LEMAN 461
Leman, Samuel 839
Lemarcom, Jane 78
Leming, Jane 91
Lemington, Winifred 739
LEMMON 461
LEMON 461
Lemon, Elizabeth 81
Lemon, Elizabeth Bolton Willis
  823
Lemon, Grace 647, 692
Lemon, Hannah 57
Lemon, Martha 291
Lemon, Mary 193, 659, 659
Lemon, Sarah 444
Lenard, Mary 78
Lenardson, Hannah 534
Lendon, Henry 466
Lenerus, John 161
Lenington, Mary 547
Lennard, Sarah 592
Lennardson, Mary 534
Lennington, Winifred 739
LENTHAL 461
LENTHALL 461
Lenthall, Sarah 454
LEONARD 461, 462
Leonard, Abel 58
Leonard, Abigail 441
Leonard, Deborah 216, 470
Leonard, Elizabeth 673
Leonard, Eunice 124
Leonard, Experience 378
Leonard, Hannah 190, 212, 216,
  267, 534
Leonard, Hopestill 9
Leonard, Isaac 610
Leonard, James 715, 818
Leonard, John 519, 561, 744
Leonard, Joseph 190, 531, 737,
  823
Leonard, Josiah 637
Leonard, Lydia 58, 100, 233
Leonard, Martha 770
Leonard, Mary 591, 745
Leonard, Phebe 373
Leonard, Prudence 464
Leonard, Rachel 340
Leonard, Rebecca 69, 145, 509
Leonard, Sarah 431
LEPINGWELL 460
Lepingwell, Hannah 270
Lepingwell, Sarah 296
Leppingwell, Esther 391
LERVAY 462
LERVEY 462
LESENBY 453
Lessen, Elizabeth 484
Lessie, Sarah 402
Lessingwell, Tabitha 77
LESTER 462
Lester, --- 159
Lester, Andrew 281, 364, 818
Lester, Ann 510, 787
Lester, Elizabeth 69

Lester, Hannah 146
Lester, Mary 281
Lester, Sarah 838
LETELIER 743
Lethebridge, Marie 86
LETHERBEE 452
LETHERLAND 458
Lethrop, Elizabeth 658
LETTICE 462
Lettice, Anna 418
Lettice, Anne 418
Lettice, Dorothy 157, 319
Lettice, Elizabeth 168, 178, 672
LETTIS 462
Leuthal, Anna 245
Levar, Prudence 290
Leven, Rachel 112
Lever, Abigail 7
Lever, Elizabeth 564
LEVERAN 476
LEVERET 462
LEVERETT 462
Leverett, Ann 397
Leverett, Anne 6
Leverett, Elizabeth 177
Leverett, Hannah 10
Leverett, John 66
Leverett, Mary 232, 750
Leverett, Rebecca 469
Leverett, Sarah Crisp Harris 347
LEVERICH 462
Leverich, Caleb 721
Leverich, Eleazer 287
LEVERIT 462
Levermore, Grace 345
LEVESTON 462
LEVESTONE 462
LEVET 458
Levett, Martha 573
LEVINS 458
LEVISTONE 462
Levitt, James 563
Lewen, Margaret 312, 449
Lewes, Bathsua 543
Lewes, Bersua 543
Lewes, Bethia 543
Lewes, Hannah 470
LEWIN 464
LEWIS 462, 463, 464
Lewis, --- 641
Lewis, Abigail 770
Lewis, Abraham 66
Lewis, Alice 25
Lewis, Ann 521, 638, 700
Lewis, Anne 727
Lewis, Bethiah 483
Lewis, Blanch 58
Lewis, Christopher 415
Lewis, Dorcas 119
Lewis, Ebenezer 720
Lewis, Eliza 379
Lewis, Elizabeth 2, 83, 95, 360,
    379, 579
Lewis, Esther 579
Lewis, Ezekiel 437
Lewis, Felix 661
Lewis, George 363
Lewis, Grace 352, 687
Lewis, Hannah 195, 204, 288,
    421, 489, 500, 502, 517, 654
Lewis, Isaac 600
Lewis, James 560
Lewis, John 34, 73, 200, 241,
    392, 418, 439, 762, 772, 779
Lewis, John (Bishop) 346
Lewis, Joseph 417, 758
Lewis, Jotham 677
Lewis, Judith 299

Lewis, Lydia 483
Lewis, Margery 264
Lewis, Mary 34, 111, 164, 169,
    257, 300, 406, 429, 448, 463,
    465, 562, 569, 677, 806
Lewis, Melatiah 319
Lewis, Mercy 13
Lewis, Patience 297
Lewis, Peter 368
Lewis, Philip 756
Lewis, Priscella 441
Lewis, Priscilla 433
Lewis, Rebecca 586
Lewis, Ruth 339
Lewis, Sabina Locke 577
Lewis, Samuel 223
Lewis, Sarah 63, 81, 89, 146,
    164, 338, 465, 466, 694, 784
Lewis, Sibyl 360
Lewis, Susanna 55, 163
Lewis, William 116
Lews, Mary 448
LEWYN 464
Lewyn, John 455
Lewyn, Rebecca 455
L'HOMMEDIEN 464
LIBBY 464
Libby, Abigail 264
Libby, Anthony 609
Libby, George 355
Libby, Hannah 272
Libby, Joanna 67
Libby, John 323
Libby, Mary 678
Libby, Rebecca 108
Libby, Sarah 634, 762, 783
Licence, Joanna 187
Lichfield, Lawrence 565
LIDDEN 465
Lidden, Edward 798
Lidden, Mary 439
LIDGETT 465
Lidgett, Elizabeth 764
Lidgett, Peter 449, 646
Lie, Joshua 252
Ligett, George 139
LIGHT 444, 465
Light, John 583
LIGHTFOOT 465
Lightfoot, Anne 740
Lightfoot, Francis 740
Lightfoot, Joanna 350
LIGHTON 456
Liland, Mary Willard Hunt 403
LILLEY 465
Lilley, Abigail 654
Lilley, Reuben 445
LILLIBRIDGE 465
LILLIE 465
Lillie, Elizabeth 378
Lillikin, Hannah 702
LILLY 465
Lilly, Mary 17, 131
LINCFORD 467
LINCOLN 465, 466
Lincoln, Abigail 18
Lincoln, Bethia 706
Lincoln, Constance 99
Lincoln, Deborah 453, 733
Lincoln, Elizabeth 99, 465, 489
Lincoln, Hannah 93, 463, 477,
    548, 702
Lincoln, Joseph 71
Lincoln, Margaret 465
Lincoln, Mary 41, 52, 331, 671,
    672, 708, 811
Lincoln, Mercy 140

Lincoln, Mordecai 144
Lincoln, Prudence 565
Lincoln, Rachel 453, 611
Lincoln, Rebecca 157
Lincoln, Ruth 303
Lincoln, Samuel 449, 451
Lincoln, Sarah 489, 535, 823
Lincoln, Susan 402
Lincoln, Susanna 47, 784
Lincoln, Tamason 26
Lincoln, Thomas 350, 718, 784
Lincoln, William 565, 736
LINDALL 466
Lindall, Abigail 367, 770
Lindall, Elizabeth 589
Lindall, Grace 430
Lindall, Henry 466, 621
Lindall, James 294, 792
Lindall, Mary 298, 395
Lindall, Mercy 435
Lindall, Rebecca 269
Lindall, Rosamond 621
Linde, Anthony 184
Linde, Sarah 184
Lindell, Abigail 612
Lindell, James 414
Lindell, Thomas 323
Linder, James 414
Lindes, Jane 505, 776
Lindle, Marie 168
Lindley, Anthony 184
Lindley, Sarah 184
LINDON 466
Lindon, Augustine 20, 649
Lindon, Grace 430
Lindon, Hannah 179
Lindon, Henry 621
Lindon, Rachel 436
Lindon, Richard 63
Lindon, Rosamond 621
Lindsay, Naomy 497
Lindsay, Sarah 414
LINDSEY 466
Lindsey, Abigail 533
Lindsey, John 623
LINDSLEY 466
Lindsley, Sarah 550
Line, Sarah 541
LINERSON 467
LINES 467
Lines, Abigail 732
Lines, Benjamin 137
Lines, Hannah 504, 753
Lines, Henry 449, 519
Lines, Samuel 375
Lines, William 169
LINFIELD 467
LINFORTH see LINSFORD
LINFURTH 467
Linfurth, Elizabeth 96
Linfurth, Mary 108
LING 467
Ling, Benjamin 181, 205, 223, 467
Ling, Joanna 223
Linington, Susannah 398
Linkhorne, Susanna 47
LINN 481
Linn, Joanna 1, 822
LINNEL 467
Linnel, Abigail 470
Linnel, Experience 206
LINNELL 467
Linnell, Bethiah 24
Linnell, Experience 206
Linnell, Hannah 205, 206
Linnell, Mary 150, 651
Linnell, Sarah 475
Linnell, Susannah 579

LINNETT 467
Linnett, Abigail 470
Linnington, Elizabeth 659
LINSCOTT 467
Linscott, John 102
LINSFORD 467 see LINFORTH
Linsford, Elizabeth 82
LINSLEY 466
Linsley, Abigail 43
Linsley, Hannah 43
Linsley, John 592
Linsley, Mary 44
LINSLY 466
Linssey, Sarah 414
LINSY 466
LINTON 467
Linton, Anne 784
Linton, Augustine 282
Linwell, Sarah 256
LINZY 466
LION 481
Lipingwell, Rachel 586
Lippencott, Jacob 757
Lippet, Mary 237
Lippett, Martha 120
Lippett, Mary 120
LIPPINCOTT 467
LIPPITT 467
Lippitt, John 659
Lippitt, Rebecca 114, 359, 467
LIPSEY 467
Liscom, Elizabeth 744
LISCOMB 467
Liscomb, Mary 140
Lisham, Jane 116, 248
Lisle, Bridget 376, 764
LISLEY 467
Lisley, Robert 66, 276
LISSEN 467
LISSON 467
Lisson, Hannah 56
Lisson, Mary 313
Lister, Ann 510
LITCHFIELD 467
Litchfield, Hannah 187
Litchfield, Lawrence 565
Litchfield, Mary 386
Litchfield, Remember 477
LITON 456
Liton, Mary 697
Littell, Hannah 742
Litten, Sarah 453
LITTLE 467, 468
Little, Abigail 430
Little, Ann 320
Little, Anna 320
Little, Anne 320
Little, Constance 638
Little, Elizabeth 740
Little, George 43
Little, Hannah 302, 742
Little, Judith 514
Little, Martha 155
Little, Mary 551
Little, Mercy 548, 654
Little, Moses 586
Little, Patience 425
Little, Richard 401
Little, Sarah 409
LITTLEFIELD 468
Littlefield, --- 524
Littlefield, Abigail 245, 246
Littlefield, Charity 789
Littlefield, Deborah 789
Littlefield, Deliverance 743
Littlefield, Dependence 38
Littlefield, Dorothy 529
Littlefield, Elizabeth 54, 771

Littlefield, Francis 675
Littlefield, Hannah 163, 371
Littlefield, James 837
Littlefield, Joseph 362
Littlefield, Joanna 570
Littlefield, Lydia 715
Littlefield, Mary 26, 45, 284, 352,
    442
Littlefield, Mercy 478
Littlefield, Nathan 215
Littlefield, Patience 789
Littlefield, Phebe 362
Littlefield, Rachel 287
Littlefield, Rebecca 440, 771
Littlefield, Sarah 444, 654, 794
Littlefield, Tabitha 251
Littlefield, Thomas 444
LITTLEHALE 468
Littlehale, Richard 96
Littlejohn, Record 691
Litton, Sarah 12
LIVEEN 468
Liveen, John 337
Liveridge, Temperance 502
LIVERMORE 468, 469
Livermore, Charity 812
Livermore, Elizabeth 749
Livermore, Grace 345
Livermore, Hannah 180, 620
Livermore, Martha 557
Livermore, Samuel 793
Livermore, Sarah 288
Livermore, Thomas 644
LIVINGSTON 462 see
    LEVESTON
LIVINGSTONE 469
Livingstone, Daniel 600
LIVINGTON 467
LLOYD 469, 480 see LYDE
Lloyd, Ann 241
Lloyd, Anne 845
Lloyd, Jane 173
Lloyd, Sarah 691
LOADER 469, 477 see
    LOWTHER
Loader, Alice 686
LOBDALE 469
LOBDELL 469
Lobdell, Ann 449, 732
Lobdell, Anna 449
Lobdell, Elizabeth 124, 320, 574,
    629
Lobdell, Joseph 603, 749
Lobdell, Martha 583
Lobdell, Mary 583
Lobdell, Rebecca 228, 719
Lobdell, Sarah 425
Lobdell, Simon 376
Lobden, Abigail 705
Lobel, Mary 169
Loc, Margaret 599
LOCK 469
Lock, Elizabeth 630
Lock, Mary 365
LOCKARD 469
LOCKE 469
Locke, Elizabeth 488, 670
Locke, John 588, 845
Locke, Judith 66
Locke, Katherine Roberts 810
Locke, Margaret 824
Locke, Mary 198, 433
Locke, Philip 588
Locke, Sabina 66, 492, 577, 616
Locke, Sarah 198
Locke, Tryphena 789
Locke, William 208
LOCKER 469

Locker, Elizabeth 57
Locker, George 371
LOCKERSON 469
LOCKWOOD 469, 470
Lockwood, Abigail 42, 54, 630
Lockwood, Abraham 190
Lockwood, Ann 481
Lockwood, Daniel 341, 630
Lockwood, Deborah 580, 727, 779
Lockwood, Edmund 453
Lockwood, Eleanor 443
Lockwood, Elizabeth 52
Lockwood, Gershom 842
Lockwood, Hannah 125, 341
Lockwood, Jonathan 505
Lockwood, Joseph 675, 718
Lockwood, Mary 59, 329, 399,
    443
Lockwood, Robert 127, 263
Lockwood, Rose 329, 783
Lockwood, Sarah 3, 57, 580, 589,
    661
Lockwood, Susannah 122
Lodnell, Bridget Bellamy Bosworth
    84
Loe, Eleanor 456
Loe, Margaret 599
LOFFE see LOVE
LOFT 470
Loft, Elizabeth 563
LOGAN 470
Logan, Alexander 122
Logan, Robert 734
LOGIN 470
LOINES 467
LOJEE 475
LOKER 469, 470 see LOCKER
Loker, Anne 534
Loker, Bridget 203, 208, 440
Loker, Elizabeth 516
Loker, Hannah 534
Loker, Henry 95
Loker, Mary 602
Lomase, Frances 670
LOMBARD 448, 470 see
    LAMBERT
Lombard, Eliony 354
Lombard, Hannah 216
Lombard, Jemima 62
Lombard, Margaret 170
Lombard, Martha 487, 492
Lombard, Mary 124
Lombard, Mercy 119
Lombard, Thomas 171
LONDON 471
London, John 38
LONG 471
Long, Abigail 713
Long, Ann 177
Long, Anna 177
Long, Deborah 579
Long, Elizabeth 39, 557, 844
Long, Ellen 493
Long, Hannah 179, 343, 452, 572,
    788, 812
Long, Herodias 293, 368, 594
Long, Joanna 311, 422
Long, John 258, 815, 829
Long, Joseph 258, 815
Long, Katharine 795
Long, Katherine 795
Long, Margaret 594
Long, Mary 5, 25, 92, 125, 166,
    326, 432, 528, 650, 681, 702,
    716
Long, Nathaniel 621
Long, Philip 177
Long, Rebecca 459, 546, 612, 639

Long, Richard 526
Long, Robert 321
Long, Ruth 33, 387, 777
Long, Samuel 844
Long, Sarah 100, 370, 405
Long, Susannah 77
Long, William 37
Long, Zachariah 515, 701
LONGBOTTOM 471
LONGBOTTUM 471
Longe, Elizabeth Hawkins 830
LONGFELLOW 471
Longfellow, William 672
LONGHORN 451
Longhorn, Bethia 488
LONGHORNE 451
Longhorne, Constance 513, 517
Longhorne, Elizabeth 361
Longle, Sarah 499
LONGLEY 471, 472
Longley, Anna 728
Longley, Elizabeth 79
Longley, Hannah 728
Longley, Joanna 728
Longley, John 482
Longley, Lydia 542
Longley, Margaret 482, 483
Longley, Mary 454, 461, 474
Longley, Sarah 610
Longley, William 192
Longley, William (Jr.) 192
LONGWORTH 472
LOOK 472
Look, Elizabeth 185
Look, Experience 166, 728
Look, Jonathan 362
Look, Margaret 599
Look, Mary 198
Look, Sarah 198, 477
LOOKE 472
Looke, Elizabeth 433
Looke, Mary 198
Looke, Sarah 198
Looker, Bridget 208
Looker, Elizabeth 516
LOOMAN 472
Loome, John 742
LOOMER 472
LOOMIS 472, 473, 478
Loomis, Abigail 40
Loomis, Ann 804
Loomis, Deborah 265
Loomis, Elizabeth 107, 121, 341,
401, 459
Loomis, Hannah 174, 429
Loomis, Joanna 686
Loomis, John 33, 113, 780
Loomis, Joseph 71
Loomis, Mary 114, 219, 677, 725,
757
Loomis, Mehitable 169
Loomis, Mindwell 107
Loomis, Nathaniel 139
Loomis, Rebecca 632
Loomis, Ruth 174, 680
Loomis, Sarah 219, 545
Loomis, Thomas 73, 403, 464
Looms, John 742
LOPER 473
Loper, Jacob 656
Loran, Hannah 267
Loranse, Hannah 267
LORD 473, 474, 475
Lord, Abigail 277, 320, 707
Lord, Amy 302
Lord, Ann 702
Lord, Anna 702
Lord, Anne 47, 342

Lord, Dorothy 388, 410, 609
Lord, Elizabeth 235, 307, 783
Lord, Faith 105, 780
Lord, Grace 270
Lord, Hannah 329, 484, 701
Lord, Jane 333, 603
Lord, Joseph 3, 602
Lord, Lydia Brown 595
Lord, Margery 276
Lord, Marie 511, 569
Lord, Martha 208, 468
Lord, Mary 47, 52, 131, 144, 229,
511, 545
Lord, Nathaniel 81, 197
Lord, Rachel 44
Lord, Richard 386
Lord, Robert 356, 370, 535
Lord, Samuel 825
Lord, Sarah 174, 181, 358, 825
Lord, Susannah 548
Lord, Thomas 545, 729
Lord, William 106, 234, 410, 596,
806
LOREIN 474
LOREING 474
LORESON 474
Loreson, Abial Thornton Page 550
LORING 474
Loring, David 13
Loring, Deborah 199
Loring, Hannah 199
Loring, Jane 301
Loring, Joan 301
Loring, John 113
Loring, Joseph 239
Loring, Mary 427
Loring, Rachel 376
Loring, Thomas 285
Loring, Welthean 622
LORTHOM 474
LORTHON 474
LORTHORN 474
LORTON 454, 474 see LAWTON
LOTEN 474
Lotham, Cary 470
LOTHROP 474, 475
Lothrop, Abigail 405
Lothrop, Ann 391
Lothrop, Anna 462
Lothrop, Barbara 250
Lothrop, Barnabas 233
Lothrop, Bathsheba 31
Lothrop, Bathshack 689
Lothrop, Bathshua 283, 489
Lothrop, Benjamin 716
Lothrop, Bethiah 374
Lothrop, Elizabeth 289, 463, 474,
641
Lothrop, Ellen 148
Lothrop, John 288
Lothrop, Joseph 572
Lothrop, Martha 523
Lothrop, Mary 285, 394, 762
Lothrop, Samuel 47, 242
Lothrop, Sarah 641, 677
Lothrop, Susanna 672
Lothrop, Tabitha 221
Lothrop, Thankful 363
Lothrop, Thomas 256, 316
LOTT 475
Lott, Mary 523
Lott, Sarah 523
LOUD 475
Louey, Elizabeth Hawkins 830
LOUGEE 475
Lounders, Tabitha 771
LOUNSBERRY 475
LOUNSBERY 475

Lounsbury, Mary 633
Lounsbury, Richard 570, 603, 656
LOUREIN 474
LOVE 475 see LUFF
Love, Joanna 367
Love, Mary 160
Love, William 823
LOVEJOY 475
Lovejoy, Abigail 2
Lovejoy, Ann 77
Lovejoy, Anne 77
Lovejoy, John 605, 717
Lovejoy, Mary 825
Lovejoy, Sarah 423
LOVEKIN 478
LOVEL 475, 476
Lovel, Mary 169
Lovel, Phebe 118
Lovel, Sarah 296
LOVELAND 475
Loveland, --- 244
Loveland, Mary 221
LOVELL 475, 476
Lovell, Agnes 68, 632
Lovell, Deborah 248, 600
Lovell, Eleanor 274
Lovell, Elizabeth 256
Lovell, Ellen 274
Lovell, Hannah 161, 236
Lovell, Jane 153
Lovell, Lydia 248
Lovell, Margaret 244
Lovell, Mary 146, 229, 638
Lovell, Sarah 296
Lovell, Thomas 244
Loven, Phebe 177
Lovenom, --- 244
LOVERAN 476
LOVERELL 476
LOVERILL 476 see LOVERING
Loverin, Jane 576
Loverine, John 105
LOVERING 476
Lovering, Esther 444
Lovering, Grace 778
Lovering, Jane 603
Lovering, John 444, 576
Lovering, Mary 738
Lovering, Samuel 662
Lovering, Sarah 125, 589
Lovering, Thomas 736
LOVET 476
Lovet, Hannah 625
Lovet, Joanna 574
Lovet, Martha 573
LOVETT 476
Lovett, Abigail 452, 610, 837
Lovett, Bethiah 701
Lovett, Catharine 647
Lovett, Elizabeth 761
Lovett, Hannah 625
Lovett, Joanna 574
Lovett, Margaret 35
Lovett, Martha 256
Lovett, Mary 520, 729, 762
Lovett, Simon 723
Lovett, Susanna 125
Lovett, Susannah 336
Lovetts, John 564
Lovetts, Mary 564
LOVEWELL 476
Lovewell, Elizabeth 55
Lovewell, Joseph 582
Lovewell, Patience 55
Lovewell, Phebe 177
Lovill, Patience 55
Lovill, Susanna 125
Lovington, Joan 847

LOVITT 476
LOW 476, 477
Low, Andrew 567
Low, Ann 208
Low, Dorcas 250
Low, Joanna 224
Low, Johanna 224
Low, Margaret 209
Low, Martha 224, 639
Low, Mary 329, 582
Low, Sarah 329
Low, Susannah 835
LOWD 475
LOWDEN 476
Lowden, Elizabeth 708, 823
Lowden, Hannah 546
Lowden, James 118
Lowden, John 436
Lowden, Martha 131
Lowden, Mary 119, 287, 298, 310
Lowden, Sarah 483
LOWDER 476
LOWE 476, 477
Lowe, Eleanor 456
Lowe, Elizabeth Spaford Sessions
  661
Lowe, John 712
Lowe, Margaret 599
Lowe, Sarah 646
Lowe, Thomas 437
LOWEL 477
LOWELL 477
Lowell, Ann 509, 511
Lowell, Anne 582
Lowell, Elizabeth 531, 817
Lowell, Joanna 299, 544
Lowell, Margery 379
Lowell, Mary 812, 822
Lowell, Rebecca 332
Lowell, Ruth 619
Lowell, Sarah 446
Lowell, Susanna 125
Lowell, Susannah 336
Lowers, Elizabeth 658
LOWERY 477
LOWLE 477
Lowle, Elizabeth 817
Lowle, Rebecca 332
LOWTHER 477 see LOADER
LOWWELL 476
LOYALL 479
LOYD 469
Loyd, Jane 173
LUCAS 477
Lucas, Bethia 649
Lucas, Hannah 138
Lucas, Mary 657
Lucas, Oliver 261
LUCE 477
Luce, Remember 505
Luce, Remembrance 505
Luck, Thomas 777
LUCKEIS 477
Luckeis, Oliver 261
Luckes, Oliver 261
Lucumb, William 348
LUCY 477
LUDDEN 478 see LYDSTON
Ludden, Joseph 18
Ludden, Mary 606
Ludden, Sarah 257
LUDDINGTON 478
Luddington, Hannah 762
Ludekein, Aaron 201
Ludington, William 637
LUDKIN 478
Ludkin, Aaron 243
Ludkin, Anna 230

Ludkin, Hannah 230
Ludkin, Lydia 10
LUDLAM 478
Ludlam, Anthony 184
Ludlam, Deborah 562
Ludlam, Elizabeth 710
Ludlam, Frances 439
Ludlam, Grace 139
Ludlam, Jane 176
Ludlam, Mary 658
Ludlam, Phebe 562, 634
Ludlam, Sarah 184, 562
Ludlam, William 687
Ludle, Anthony 184
Ludle, Sarah 184
LUDLOW 478
Ludlow, Hannah 176
Ludlow, Sarah 96
LUEN 464
Luen, John 455
Luen, Rebecca 455
LUFF 470, 475
Luff, Joan 367
Luffe, Gabriel 216
LUFKIN 478
Lufkin, Mary 434
LUGG 478
Lugg, Easter 490
Lugg, Esther 61, 490
Lugg, John 530
Lugg, Mary 43
LUIST 464, 478
Luist, Robert 480
LUKE 478
Luke, George 603
LULL 478
LUM 478
Lum, Elizabeth 375
Lum, Hannah 595
Lum, Jonathan 102
Lum, Martha 833
Lum, Sarah 655
LUMAS 478
Lumas, Samuel 222
LUMBARD 470, 471
Lumbard, Abia 153
Lumbard, Abigail 153, 339
Lumbard, Elizabeth 290
Lumbard, Jemima 62
LUMBART 470, 471
Lumbart, Abigail 803
Lumbart, Benjamin 803
Lumbart, Deliverance 537
Lumbart, Jedediah 803
Lumbart, Joshua 803
Lumbart, Martha 487
Lumbart, Mary 463, 475, 557
Lumbart, Mehitable 476
Lumbart, Rebecca 557
Lumbart, Susannah 475
Lumbe, Judith 91
LUMBER 471
Lumber, Eliony 354
Lumber, Elizabeth 221
Lumber, Mary 557
Lumber, Susan 248
Lumber, Susanna 248
LUMBERT 471
Lumbert, Hannah 207, 470
Lumbert, Martha 492
Lumbert, Mercy 352
Lumbert, Sarah 579
LUME 472
Lume, --- 581
Lume, Judith 91
LUMIS 472
Lumm, Elizabeth 375
LUMMIS 478

LUMMUS 478
LUMPKIN 479
Lumpkin, Ann 246
Lumpkin, Anne 246
Lumpkin, Hannah 320
Lumpkin, Mercy 659
Lumpkin, Richard 714
Lumpkin, Thomasin 500
Lumpkin, Thomasine 500, 721
Lumpkin, William 500
LUN 479
LUND 479 see LUNN
LUNDEN 471
Lundon, John 38
Lunerns, John 161
LUNERUS 479
LUNN 479 see LUND
LUNT 479
Lunt, Ann 373
Lunt, Daniel 515
Lunt, Elizabeth 789
Lunt, Henry 373, 710
Lunt, John 420, 531
Lunt, Mary 31, 312
Lunt, Priscilla 676
Lunt, Sarah 51, 541
LUPTON 479
Lupton, Abigail 277, 727
Lupton, Hannah 76
LURVEY 479
LUSCOM 479
LUSCOMB 479
Luscomb, Elizabeth 560
LUSCOMBE 479
LUSHER 479
Lusher, Eleazer 331
LUSON 479
Luson, Anne 267
LUTHER 479
Luther, Elizabeth 433
Luther, Mary 239
Luther, Mehitable 168
Lutman, Jane 232
Lutrell, Mary 830
Lutterell, Ann 155
LUX 479
Lux, Abisag 555
Lux, Abizag 491
Lux, Abyshag 555
Lux, John 222, 416
LUXFORD 479
Luxford, Elizabeth 312
Luxford, Margaret 564
Luxford, Reuben 46, 168, 238
LYALL 479
Lyall, Mary 61
Lybrand, Elizabeth 671
LYDE 480
Lyde, Allen 783
Lyde, Anna 324
Lyde, Edward 24, 99
LYDSTON 480 see LUDDEN
Lydston, --- 338
Lydston, John 733
Lydston, Sarah 12, 453
LYFORD 480
Lyford, John (Rev.) 377
Lyford, Martha 465
Lyford, Ruth 52
LYMAN 480
Lyman, Dorothy 101
Lyman, Elizabeth 592
Lyman, Hannah 592
Lyman, Hepzibah 217
Lyman, John 591
Lyman, Mary 335
Lyman, Phillis 373
Lyman, Preserved 249

Lyman, Richard 489
Lyman, Samuel 280
Lyman, Sarah 97, 489, 843
Lyman, Thankful 334
Lyman, Thomas 33
Lyn, Eleanor 248
Lyn, Ellen 248
Lynch, Gabriel 718
Lynch, Margaret 266, 718
Lynch, Mary 266, 749
LYNDE 480, 481
Lynde, Anna 324
Lynde, Elizabeth 57, 594, 758, 771
Lynde, Hannah 68, 307, 431, 513, 753
Lynde, Joanna 255
Lynde, John 114, 323
Lynde, Joseph 89, 281, 830
Lynde, Margaret 653
Lynde, Mary 57, 127, 651, 792
Lynde, Nathaniel 92, 112, 847
Lynde, Samuel 9, 464, 478
Lynde, Sarah 159, 532, 585, 723
Lynde, Thomas 357, 428, 668, 753
LYNDON 466
Lyndon, Abigail 367
Lynian, Elizabeth 461
LYNN 481
Lynn, Elizabeth 59, 187, 661
Lynn, Henry 330, 512, 518
Lynn, Priscilla 129
Lynn, Sarah 635, 649
Lynnett, Hannah 206
Lynsey, Abigail 533
Lynsey, Naomy 497
LYNSSY 466
Lynzey, Sarah 414
LYON 481, 482
Lyon, Abigail 39, 689
Lyon, Deborah 165
Lyon, Elizabeth 39, 490, 640
Lyon, Esther 329, 573
Lyon, George 76
Lyon, Hannah 60, 418
Lyon, Hester 573
Lyon, Israel 268
Lyon, Joseph 31
Lyon, Katharine 283
Lyon, Mary 705, 825, 827
Lyon, Mehitable 367
Lyon, Moses 5, 739
Lyon, Samuel 318
Lyon, Sarah 198, 505
Lyon, Susanna 517
Lyon, William 140
LYSEUM 467
LYSOM 479
Lysson, Mary 313

--- M ---

MABER 482
Mable, Ann 228
MACALL 482
MACARTIE 482
MACCALUM 483
Maccame, Deborah 274
MACCANE 482
Maccane, Sarah 440
MACCARTY 482
MACCHONE 483
Macchone, Hannah 296
MACCOMB 483
MACCOON 483
MACCRANEY 482

MacDANIEL 501
MacDowell, Elizabeth 109
MIACE 482
Mace, Robert 367
Macey, Deborah 754
Macfarland, Margaret 712
MACGINNIS 482
Machenetine, Matthew 513
Machett, Susannah 210
Machias, Margaret 413
Machias, Mary 280, 540
MacIntosh, Marcy 524
MacIntosh, Mercy 524
MACK 482
MACKANETENE 483
Mackarta, Elizabeth 97
MACKCLAFFIN 483
MACKCLAFLIN 483
Mackclaflin, Elizabeth 795
Mackclaflin, Mary 626
Mackclaflin, Priscilla 788
MACKCLOTHAN 483
MACKDUGGELL 482
MACKENAB 483
MACKENSTINE 483
MACKENY 483
MacKeny, Ruth 559
MacKENZIE 483
Mackenzie, Dugal 772
MACKERWITHY 483
MACKEY 483
MACKFARLAND 482
Mackfarland, Duncan 572
MACKFASSEY 483
MACKFASSY 483
MACKGINNIS 482
MACKGUDY 483
MACKHIEW 483
MACKHOE 483
MACKHUE 483
MACKIN 482
MACKINAB 483
Mackinter, Mary 621
MACKINTIRE 482
Mackintire, Sarah 606
MACKINTOCK 482
MACKINTOSH 482
Macklathlin, Joanna 688
MACKLOAD 483
MACKMALLEN 483 see
   McINTIRE, McMILLAN
Mackmallien, Allester 53
MACKMALLIN 483
MACKMALLION 483
MACKMALLON 483
MACKMAN 483
Mackman, James 247
Mackmillan, Mary 148
MACKMILLEN 483
Mackmillian, John 713
Mackmillion, Joshua 496
Mackmollen, Elizabeth 93
Mackoneer, Alexander 482
MACKOON 483
MACKRANNEY 482
MACKREST 483
MACKROREY 483
MACKWORTH 483
Mackworth, Arthur 18
MACLOTHIAN 483
MACLOUGHLIN 483
MACOCK 483
Macock, Mary 139
MACOMB 483
MACOMBER 483
Macomber, Edith 465
Macomber, Hannah 610
Macomber, Mary 702

Macomber, Sarah 99
Macomber, Ursula 806
Macombs, Martha 430
MACOMEY 175
MACOONE 483
Macoone, Daniel 178
Macoone, Isabella 78
MACOUNE 483
MACOY 482, 483
MACQUARRING 483
MacQUEDDY 483
MACQUERRY 483
MACREST 483
MACROON 483
MACVARLO 482
Macvarlo, Margaret 712
MACWORTH 483
Macworth, Agnes 195
Macworth, Rebecca 798
Macworth, Sarah 3
MACY 484
Macy, Bethia 294
Macy, Deborah 566
Macy, Elizabeth 378
Macy, Hannah 75
Macy, Mary 118, 822
Macy, Sarah 76, 842
MADDIVER 484
Maddiver, --- 488, 499
Maddiver, Judith 410
Maddiver, Martha 556
Maddiver, Mary 556
MADDOCK 497
Maddock, Henry 180
MADDOCKS 497
Madever, Michael 138
MADIVER 484
MADOCKS 497
Madocks, David 612
Madocks, Sarah 612
Maeson, Hannah 341
MAGDANIEL 501
MAGER 484
MAGGRIGE 482
MAGGRIGGE 514
MAGINNAH 482
MAGOON 484
Magoon, Alexander 471, 526
Magoon, Hannah 475
Magoon, Henry 433
Magoon, Mary 157
MAGOUN 484
MAGREGOR 482
MAGVARLOW 482
Mahew, Anna 783
Mahien, Hester 177
MAHONE 484
MAHOON 484
MAHOONE 484
MAHOOUNE 484
Maims, Priscilla 137
MAIN 499, 500
Main, Gertrude 503
MAINARD 499
MAINE 499, 500
Maine, Elizabeth 25
Maine, Hannah Lewis 204
Maine, Priscilla 601
Maine, Rachel 601
MAINOR 499
MAINS 500
Mains, --- 452
Mains, Elizabeth 25
Mains, Hannah Lewis 204
Mains, John 261
Mains, Lydia 261
Mains, Rachel 135
Mains, Sarah 53

MAINWARING 484
Mainwaring, Ann 825
Mainwright, Sarah 571
MAISHFIELD 491
MAJER 484
MAJERY 496
MAJOR 484
Major, Hannah 312
Majore, Susanna 496
MAJORY 484
MAKALLUM 483
MAKARORY 483
MAKCUM 483
Maken, Grace 595
MAKENTIER 482
MAKEPEACE 484
Makepeace, Anne 242
Makepeace, Esther 106
Makepeace, Hannah 388
Makepeace, Mary 823
Makepeace, Sarah 451
Makepeace, Thomas 176, 502
Makepeace, Waitawhile 181, 216
Makepease, Mary 209
MAKERWITH 483
MAKEY 483
Makin, Grace 635, 669
Makin, Joan 669
MAKINAB 483
MAKINTIRE 482
Makmallin, Hannah 811
MAKOE 483
MALAVERY 484
Malavery, Deliverance 497
Malavery, Elizabeth 578
Malbon, Martha 574
Malby, Jane 557, 558
MALEM see MILAM
MALIN 484
Malines, Robert 632
MALINS 484
Malins, Robert 632
Mallard, Mary 731
MALLERY 484
MALLESIE 484
Mallet, Thomas 815
MALLETT 484
Mallett, Elizabeth 837
Mallinson, Mary 420
MALLOON 484
MALLORY 484
Mallory, Mary 179, 628
Mallory, Rebecca 118
Mallory, Thomas 228
Mallot, Elizabeth 837
Mallott, Grace 34
Mallott, Hosea 34
MALONE 484
MALOON 484
Maltbie, William 726
MALTBY 484, 485
Maltby, Elizabeth 376
Maltby, John 393
Maltby, Mary 275
Maltby, William 817
MAN 485
Man, Deborah 189
Man, Dorothy 310
Man, Hannah 270
Man, Priscilla 474
Man, Rebecca 187, 221
Man, Richard 187
Man, Thomas 204
MANCHESTER 485
Manchester, Elizabeth 666
Manchester, Sarah 791, 814
Mancy, Abigail 20, 819
MANDER 485

Mander, James 432
Mandesley, Thomas 495
MANE 500
Maner, Hannah 205
Maner, John 205
MANERING 487
MANLEY 485
Manley, Samuel 584
MANLY 485
MANN 485
Mann, Abraham 387
Mann, Bethiah 698
Mann, Dorothy 310
Mann, Esther 557
Mann, Hannah 270
Mann, John 824
Mann, Mary 451
Mann, Priscilla 474
Mann, Rachel 667
Mann, Robert 125
Mann, Sarah 807
Mann, Thomas 204
Mann, Thomas 486
Mann, William 742
MANNEL 485
MANNELL 485
MANNERING 487
MANNING 485, 486, 487, 527
Manning, --- 506
Manning, Ann 649
Manning, Austice 591, 598
Manning, George 77
Manning, Hannah 346, 439, 704, 777
Manning, Hannah Tarne 222
Manning, Joanna 459, 757
Manning, John 299, 453
Manning, Margaret 553
Manning, Mary 6, 282, 401, 661, 776
Manning, Nicholas 320
Manning, Phebe 589, 784
Manning, Sarah 46, 116, 820
Manning, Thomas 485
Manning, William 639
MANNINGS 485
Mannyard, Ruth 710
Manoxen, Ann 825
MANSELL 527
MANSER 486
Manser, Elizabeth 594
MANSFIELD 486, 487
Mansfield, Abigail 24, 387
Mansfield, Andrew 175, 314, 530
Mansfield, Ann 170, 430
Mansfield, Anna 170, 430
Mansfield, Anne 170
Mansfield, Bethia 175
Mansfield, Bethiah 711
Mansfield, Comfort 62
Mansfield, Damaris 751
Mansfield, Daniel 123, 416
Mansfield, Deborah 806
Mansfield, Elizabeth 424, 609, 738, 798, 825
Mansfield, Hannah 105, 175
Mansfield, John 314, 316, 385, 438
Mansfield, Lydia 259
Mansfield, Martha 696
Mansfield, Mary 385, 758, 830
Mansfield, Mercy 100, 737
Mansfield, Paul 137, 452
Mansfield, Richard 264
Mansfield, Ruth 451
Mansfield, Sarah 619
Mansfield, Silence 815
MANSON 487

Manson, Esther 194
Manson, Thomasine 6
MANTER 487
Manter, Desire 139
Manter, Elizabeth 477
Manter, Mercy 256
MANTON 487
Manton, Ann 435
Manton, Elizabeth 253
Manton, Experience 630
Mantor, Amy 225
Manuell, Mary 296
Manwaing, Love 621
MANWARING 484, 487 see MAINWARING
Manwaring, Elizabeth 346
Manwaring, Judith 613
Manwaring, Prudence 57
Mapellhead, Mary 603
MAPES 487
Mapes, Esther 389
Mapes, Hester 389
Mapes, Mary 171, 828
Mapes, Naomi 219
Mapes, Rebecca 847
Mapes, Sarah 171
Mapes, Thomas 308, 795
MAPHAM 503
Mapham, Abigail 83
Mapham, John 36, 388, 727
Mapham, Mary 36, 388, 479
MAPLEHEAD 487
Maplehead, Mary 116
Maplesdame, Bethiah 290
Maplet, Mary 313
Mappam, John 36
Mappam, Mary 36
Marbel, Mary 654
MARBLE 487
Marble, Gershom 409
Marble, John 811
Marble, Mary 548
Marble, Ruhaman 813
Marbury, Anne 407
Marbury, Katherine 657
MARCH 487, 488
March, Ann 497
March, Anna 497
March, Anne 497
March, Daniel 195
March, Frances 112
March, George 108
March, Hugh 3, 74, 106, 362
March, John 147
March, Judith 386, 740
March, Marah 418
March, Martha 113, 771
March, Mary 113, 200, 344, 727
March, Nicholas 201
March, Rachel 255
March, Sarah 586
MARCHANT 503
Marchant, Elizabeth 802
Marchant, Sarah 20, 344
Marchante, Julian 797
Marche, Eulalia 124
Marchent, Mary 546
MARCY 488
Marcy, Deborah 754
MARDEN 488
Marden, --- 177
Marden, Elizabeth 610
Marden, Mary 427
MARE 488, 499, 515 see MAYER, MAYS, MAZE, MOORE
Mare, Hannah 414
MAREAN 488
MARES 488

Marett, Sarah 174
Marian, John 790
MARINER 488
Mariner, Mary 636
Mariner, Susanna 225
MARION 488, 503
Marion, Elizabeth 212
Marion, Hannah 307
Marion, John 38, 307, 760, 790
Marion, Sarah 38
Marion, Thomasin 570
MARJERY 496
Marjery, Mary 278
MARK 488
MARKANDROS 488
MARKES 488
Markes, Jane 78
MARKHAM 488
Markham, Elizabeth 52
Markham, Lydia 240
Markham, Priscilla 333
Markham, Sarah 441
Markham, William 778
MARKS 488
MARLOW 519
Marlow, Esther 138
Marlowe, Rebecca 428, 434
MARLTON 488
MARPLEHEAD 487
Marplehead, Mary 603
MARR 488
MARRABLE 487
MARRE 488
Marret, Abigail 620
Marret, Susanna 16
MARRETT 488, 505
Marrett, Abigail 267
Marrett, Amos 241, 442
Marrett, Edward 701
Marrett, Hannah 352
Marrett, Susanna 47
MARRIAN 488
Marrian, Elizabeth 212
Marrian, Hannah 307
Marrian, John 790
MARRINER 488
MARSH 488, 489
Marsh, Abigail 503
Marsh, Alexander 31, 54
Marsh, Ann 179, 285
Marsh, Anna 285
Marsh, Bethiah 674
Marsh, Dorcas 594
Marsh, Dorothy 845
Marsh, Elizabeth 87, 298, 439,
   545, 599, 759
Marsh, Frances 112
Marsh, George 413
Marsh, Grace 34, 310
Marsh, Hannah 266, 285, 289,
   437, 472
Marsh, John 480, 627
Marsh, Jonathan 220
Marsh, Lydia 472
Marsh, Mary 200, 284, 522, 550,
   561
Marsh, Mercy 50
Marsh, Onesipherous 777
Marsh, Onesiphorus 841
Marsh, Phebe 529
Marsh, Rachel 794
Marsh, Ruth 343
Marsh, Sarah 89, 504, 554, 586
Marsh, Thomas 666
MARSHALL 489, 490, 491
Marshall, Benjamin 522
Marshall, David 827
Marshall, Edmond 583

Marshall, Elizabeth 204, 387, 464,
   754
Marshall, Hannah 463, 561
Marshall, Joanna 183, 525
Marshall, John 257, 510, 770
Marshall, Joseph 394
Marshall, Lydia 356
Marshall, Martha 505
Marshall, Mary 33, 140, 257, 537,
   605, 606, 644, 647, 713
Marshall, Mercy 537
Marshall, Miriam 605, 606
Marshall, Naomi 795
Marshall, Rebecca 663
Marshall, Richard 61
Marshall, Ruth 177, 236, 387
Marshall, Sarah 641, 712, 777
Marshall, Susannah 516, 525
Marshall, Thomas 139, 261, 555,
   569, 574, 818
Marshall, Thomas (Capt.) 387
Marshall, William 38, 333
MARSHCROFT 493
MARSHFIELD 491
Marshfield, Esther 174
Marshfield, Hannah 58
Marshfield, Margaret 561
Marshfield, Samuel 78, 302
Marshfield, Sarah 277, 385, 509
MARSTON 491, 492
Marston, Abial 322
Marston, Abiel 322
Marston, Abigail 769
Marston, Catherine 732
Marston, Deliverance 182
Marston, Elizabeth 31
Marston, Hannah 41, 273
Marston, Isaac 358
Marston, James 90
Marston, John 758
Marston, Lucy 524, 525
Marston, Maria 602
Marston, Martha 385
Marston, Mary 90, 94, 203, 559,
   649, 730
Marston, Prudence 188, 722
Marston, Rebecca 684
Marston, Sarah 97, 228, 496, 582
Marston, Triphena 577
Marston, William 469, 576, 616
MARSTONE 491
Marstone, Mary 559
Marstone, Sarah 97, 752
Mart, Mary 344
Martain, Mehetable 27
Martain, Richard 458
MARTEN 493
MARTIN 492, 493
Martin, --- 220, 461
Martin, Abigail 332, 336, 633
Martin, Agnes 141
Martin, Alice 72, 155
Martin, Anne 141
Martin, Annis 141
Martin, Anthony 551
Martin, Constant 518
Martin, Dorothy 392
Martin, Elizabeth 29, 234, 423,
   610
Martin, Grace 546, 576
Martin, Hannah 301, 842
Martin, Jane 154, 332
Martin, Jemima 647
Martin, John 278, 807
Martin, Katherine 347
Martin, Lydia 183
Martin, Marah 781
Martin, Margaret 276, 428, 481

Martin, Mary 18, 175, 258, 276,
   722, 781
Martin, Mehetable 27
Martin, Rachel 68, 375
Martin, Rebecca 837
Martin, Richard 25, 48, 243, 796
Martin, Robert 154
Martin, Samuel 90
Martin, Sarah 542
Martin, Solomon 258
Martin, Susanna 33, 734
Martin, Susannah 415
Martin, William 447
MARTINDALE 493
MARTINE 492, 493
Martine, Ann 243
Martine, Mary 105
Martine, Rebecca 603
MARTYN 492, 493
Martyn, Elizabeth 433
Martyn, Esther 415
Martyn, Hannah 428, 842
Martyn, Hester 415
Martyn, Richard 215, 451, 796
Martyn, Sarah 201
MARVIN 487, 493
Marvin, --- 459
Marvin, Abigail 85
Marvin, Christopher 306
Marvin, Elizabeth 544, 589, 776
Marvin, Hannah 589, 663
Marvin, Mary 6, 61, 126, 173,
   250, 706
Marvin, Matthew 85
Marvin, Rachel 688
Marvin, Rebecca 156
Marvin, Reynold 673
Marvin, Sarah 57, 67, 199, 311
Marwin, Hannah 379
Mary, Rebecca 818
Marys, Susannah 684
MASCALL 493
Mascall, Thomas 820
MASCOLL 493
Mascoll, Mehitable 279
Mascraft, Elizabeth 696
MASCROFT 493
MASERVEY 506
MASH 489
Mash, Abigail 503
Mash, Bethiah 674
Mash, Mary 550, 605
Mashfield, Abilene 303
Mashworth, Rebecca 635
MASKELL 494
Maskell, Thomas 820
MASON 494, 495, 757
Mason, --- 637
Mason, Abigail 99, 231
Mason, Alice 668
Mason, Ann 215
Mason, Anne 107
Mason, Bethiah 834
Mason, Elias 381
Mason, Elizabeth 109, 118, 269,
   392, 421, 540
Mason, Esther 253
Mason, Hannah 103, 241, 454, 772
Mason, Helena 51
Mason, Henry 659
Mason, Hester 253
Mason, Isabel 73
Mason, Jane 233
Mason, Joanna 95, 573
Mason, John 11, 660
Mason, Jonathan 435
Mason, Judith 509
Mason, Margaret Partridge 699

Mason, Mary 188, 233, 239, 342, 486, 540, 560, 661, 735, 798
Mason, Mehitable 741
Mason, Nicholas 116, 334
Mason, Priscilla 269
Mason, Rachel 370
Mason, Ralph 541
Mason, Rebecca 543
Mason, Samuel 743
Mason, Sarah 293, 578, 630
Mason, Stephen 523
Mason, Susanna 541
Mason, Thankful 87
Mason, Thomas 324, 429
Masse, Anthony 240
Masselbe, Bridget 544
MASSEY 495
Massey, Abigail 20, 819
Massey, Sarah 778
MASSON 494
Masson, Mary 179
MASSY 495
Mastcott, Robert 649
Master, Lydia 468
MASTERS 495 see MASTERSON
Masters, Colete 768
Masters, Elizabeth 453, 470
Masters, John 223
Masters, Katherine 151
Masters, Lydia 725
Masters, Rebecca 459
Masters, Ruth 715
Masters, Sarah 223
MASTERSON 495 see MASTERS
Masterson, Elizabeth 846
Masterson, Lydia 93
Masterson, Mary Goodall 687
Masterson, Sarah 25, 93, 834
Mastone, Sarah 582
MASURY 484, 496
Masury, Joseph 582
Matchet, Bridget 269
MATHER 496
Mather, Abigail 75
Mather, Cotton 298
Mather, Cotton (Rev.) 397
Mather, Eleazer 713
Mather, Elizabeth 324, 839
Mather, Eunice 820
Mather, Hannah 544
Mather, Increase 185
Mather, Maria 320
Mather, Richard 185
Mather, Sarah 368, 777
Mather, Timothy 792
Mathew, --- 592
MATHEWES 497
MATHEWS 496, 497
Mathewson, Isabel 107
Mathewson, Isabella 107
Mathewson, Ruth 802
MATHUE 484
MATHUES 496, 427
Mathues, Mary 394
Mathues, Sarah 729
Matlat, Ann 228
MATSON 496
Matson, Elizabeth 516
Matson, Hannah 341
Matson, Jane 546
Matson, Thomas 615
Mattall, Ann Winter Batson 53
Matten, Elizabeth 322
Matten, Margaret 528
MATTESON 496
Matteson, Henry 361
Matthewes, Mary 768
Matthewes, Sarah 625

Matthewes, Thomas 625
MATTHEWS 496, 497
Matthews, --- 139
Matthews, Benjamin 434
Matthews, Catharine 274
Matthews, Daniel 827
Matthews, Elizabeth 68, 166, 231, 273
Matthews, Esther 817
Matthews, Francis 691
Matthews, John 195, 272
Matthews, Katherine 235
Matthews, Marmaduke 137
Matthews, Martha 110, 691
Matthews, Mary 141, 394, 661, 686, 834
Matthews, Mehitable 333
Matthews, Mercy 358
Matthews, Peter 188
Matthews, Sarah 729
Matthews, Susanna 846
Matthews, Wm. 68
MATTHEWSON 497
Matthewson, James 105
Mattle, Ann 228
MATTOCK 497
Mattock, Elizabeth 15
Mattock, Henry 180
MATTOCKE 497
Mattocke, Mary 108
MATTOCKS 497
Mattocks, Alice 72, 73, 463
Mattocks, David 612
Mattocks, Sarah 612
MATTON 497
Matton, Richard 335
MATTONE 497
Mattone, Grace 588
MATTOON \497
Mattoon, Hubertus 425, 660
MATTOX 497
Mattox, Mahitable 39
Mattson, Abigail 798
MAUD 497
Maudley, Nathaniel 785
MAUDSLEY 522, 523
MAUL 497
Maul, Susannah 104
MAULE 497
Maule, Elizabeth 466
MAURELLE 512
Maury, Mary Johnson 441
Mauson, Thomasine 6
MAVERICK 498
Maverick, Abigail 34, 157, 305, 778
Maverick, Ann 423
Maverick, Anna 423
Maverick, Anne 423
Maverick, Elias 629
Maverick, Elizabeth 117, 316, 366, 421, 677
Maverick, John 421
Maverick, Katharine 564
Maverick, Margaret 599
Maverick, Mary 24, 117, 262, 386, 553, 557, 688, 786
Maverick, Moses 628
Maverick, Rebecca 355, 735
Maverick, Remember 838
Maverick, Ruth 681
Maverick, Samuel 90, 736
Maverick, Sarah 777
Mavericke, Sarah 538
Maverill, Abigail 485
MAXCY 498
Maxcy, Alexander 437
MAXE 498

Maxe, Margaret 25
MAXELL 494
MAXEY 498
Maxey, Alexander 437
MAXFIELD 498
MAXON 498
MAXSON 498
Maxson, Dorothy 157
Maxson, Mary 462
MAXWELL 498
Maxwell, Alexander 570
Maxwell, Dorcas 718
Maxwell, Mary 627
MAY 498, 499
May, Abigail 422
May, Ann 82
May, Anne 82
May, Dorothy 91
May, Elisha 250
May, Elizabeth 306
May, Joanna 293, 295, 812
May, John 557, 840
May, Jonathan 366
May, Mary 570, 642, 660
May, Mehitable 520
May, Samuel 420
May, Sarah 821
MAYCOMBER 483
MAYCOME 483
MAYCUMBER 483
Maycumber, Edith 465
Maycumber, Hannah 610
MAYER 488, 499 see MARE
Mayer, Judith 614
Mayer, Love 551
Mayer, Mary 65
Mayer, Rebecca 53, 541, 638
Mayer, Sarah 333
MAYFIELD 499
MAYHEW 499
Mayhew, Abiah 744
Mayhew, Bethia 344, 786
Mayhew, Elizabeth 162
Mayhew, Hannah 225, 689
Mayhew, Jane 651
Mayhew, Jedidah 680
Mayhew, Jerusha 241
Mayhew, Martha 758
Mayhew, Mary 468
Mayhew, Sarah 743
Mayhew, Thomas 552
Mayhoone, Margaret 528
Mayhue, Jerusha 828
MAYLEM 499
Maylem, Joseph 564
MAYLESS 499
MAYN 500
MAYNARD 499, 511
Maynard, Damaris 452
Maynard, Elizabeth 99, 319
Maynard, Hannah 205, 356
Maynard, John 27, 205, 211, 241, 363, 385, 435, 569
Maynard, Lydia 38, 333, 491, 516
Maynard, Maria 569
Maynard, Mary 210, 398, 569, 833
Maynard, Ruth 710
Maynard, Sarah 127, 210
Maynard, Zachariah 682
Maynard, Zechariah 125, 645
MAYO 500
Mayo, Elizabeth 292, 394, 753
Mayo, Hannah 30, 519
Mayo, John (Rev.) 479
Mayo, Joseph 479, 694
Mayo, Nathaniel 694, 846
Mayo, Samuel 659, 721
Mayo, Sarah 283

Mayo, Thomas 292
Mayplett, Mary 313
MAYS 488, 498
Mays, Mary 39
MAZE 488, 498
MAZURE 495, 496
MAZURY 495, 496
McALLS 482
McCALL 482
McCALLUM 131
McCallum, John 174
McCARTHY 482
McCARTY 482
McCAULEY 482
McClaflin, Abigail 507
McCock, Peter 139
McCOMB 483
McCOY 482, 483 see McKAY
McCRANNEY 482
McCranney, William 509
McDOUGALL 482
McDOWELL 482
McDowell, Mary 149
McEhrich, William 104
McEWEN 482
McFARLAND 482
McFarland, Duncan 572
McFarland, Martha 430
McGREGOR 482
McGREGORY 482
McGUINNIS 482
McINTIRE 482 see MACMALLEN
McIntire, Mary 621
McINTOSH 482
McIntosh, John 383
McIntosh, Sarah 524
McKAY 482, 483
McKEE 483
McKellum, Thomas 516
McKENNEY 483
McKenny, Robert 694
McKENZIE 483
McKUNE 482
McLaflin, Abigail 507
McLathlin, Joanna 688
McLathlin, Priscilla 788
McLAUGHLIN 483
McLEOD 483
McMILLAN 483
McMILLION 483
McMULLEN 483
Mcomy, David 561
MEACHAM 500
Meacham, Hannah 603
Meacham, Isaac 572
Meacham, Jeremiah 41, 202, 533
Meacham, Rebecca 501
Meacham, Rhoda 796
Meacham, Sarah 88
MEACHUM 500
Meachum, Bethiah 331
Meachum, Hannah 303
Meachum, Rebecca 501
Meachum, Sarah 88
MEACKENY 482
MEACOCK 483
Meacock, Margaret 165
Meacock, Mary 165
Meacock, Peter 575
Meacock, Sarah 575
MEAD 500, 501
Mead, Hannah 398, 656, 701
Mead, Joseph 783
Mead, Martha 622, 822
Mead, Mary 399
Mead, Richard 63
Mead, Sarah 440, 463
Meadall, --- 192

MEADE 501
Meade, Experience 240, 363
Meade, Gabriel 242
Meade, Lydia 119
Meade, Patience 254
Meade, Sarah 242
Meade, Thomas 211
MEADER 501
Meader, Godfrey 273
Meader, John 464
Meader, Sarah 772
MEADES 501
Meadkin, Sarah 696
Meadowes, Hannah 482
MEADOWS 501
Meads, David 202
Meads, Mary 171, 208
MEAKIN 501
Meakin, Mary 60
Meakin, Mercy 60
MEAKINS 501
Meakins, Hannah 60
Meakins, Thomas 846
MEALOY 502
Mean, Anne 351
Mean, Deborah 258
Mean, Dorothy 258
MEANE 501
Meane, Mary 352
MEANS 501
Means, Anne 351
Means, Mary 209, 352
Means, Sarah 352
MEARIFIELD 504
MEARS 488, 501 see MAYER,
    MAYS, MAZE, MOORE
Mears, Hannah 816
Mears, John 191, 501
Mears, Samuel 328
MEASURE 501
Meays, Mary 186
MECAINE 482
MECARTER 501
MECCARTY 482
MECHALLY 482
MECOME 483
MEDBERY 501
MEDBURY 501
Medbury, John 342
Medbury, Sarah 342
MEDCALF 506, 507
Medcalf, Elizabeth 54
MEDCALFE 506
Medcalfe, Hannah 117
Medcalfe, Marie 248, 267
Medcalfe, Mary 267
Medcalfe, Thomas 267
Meddowes, Mary 208
MEDDUP 507
Mede, Experience 240, 363
Medford, Hans 62
Medleigh, Mary 511
MEDSELFE 506
Medup, Bethiah 37
MEECH 501
Meed, Lydia 119
Meed, Sarah 463
MEEDES 500
MEEK 501
Meek, Mary 283
MEEKER 501
Meeker, Mary 5, 481, 739
Meeking, Mary 157
MEEKINS 501
Meekins, Mary 14, 463
Meekins, Mehitable 221
Meekins, Sarah 426
Meekins, Thomas 229, 795

Meen, Sarah 352
MEERES 501
MEERS 501
MEGDANIELL 501
MEIGS 501, 502
Meigs, Concurrence 190
Meigs, Elizabeth 398
Meigs, Hannah 277, 478
Meigs, John 196
Meigs, Mary 254, 709
Meigs, Sarah 48
Meigs, Trial 777
Meigs, Tryal 777
MEKUSETT 502
MELCHER 502
Melcher, Mary 414
Meline, Sarah 352
Mellard, Martha 676, 794
MELLEN 502
Mellen, Abigail 743, 838
Mellen, John 291
Mellen, William 114
MELLENS 502
Mellens, Mary 764
MELLESON 502
Mellins, Elizabeth 42, 750
Mellins, James 46
Mellins, Mary 811
Mellinson, Mary 420
MELLISON 502
Mellney, Joanna 453
Mellon, Mary 306
MELLOUS 502
MELLOWES 502
Mellowes, Christian 575
Mellowes, Elizabeth 46, 501, 506,
    842
Mellowes, Hannah 118
Mellowes, John 446
Mellowes, Martha 460, 506, 784,
    830
Mellowes, Mary 698
Mellowes, Oliver 484
Mellowes, Sarah 446
Mellowes, William 35
MELLOWS 502
Mellows, Edward 373
Mellows, Mary 144
Mellows, Oliver 176
MELOY 502
MELTEN 502 see MILTON
Melton, Eleanor 576
MELVILLE 502
Melville, David 817
MELVIN 502
MELVINE 502
MELYEN 502
Melyen, Susannah 830
MELYN 502
Melyn, Cornelia 473, 656
Melyn, Magdalene 473
Melyn, Maria 556
Melyn, Mariah 376
Melyn, Susannah 830
MEMORY 502
MEMRY 502
MENDALL 502
Mendall, Hannah 742
Mendall, Mercy 744
Mendall, Ruth 227
Mendall, Sarah 747
MENDUM 502
Mendum, Judith 792
Mendum, Sarah 526
Menter, Mary 630
MENTOR 502
Mentor, Jane 566
MEPHAM 503

Mepham, John 36
Mepham, Mary 36
MERCER 503, 786
Mercer, --- 231, 657, 774
Mercer, Eleanor 480
Mercer, Gertrude Urin 747
Mercer, Lydia 128, 200, 702
Mercer, Samuel 161
MERCHANT 503
MERCY 505
Mere, Mary 468
MEREHOE 504
MERIAM 503
Meriam, Elizabeth 259
Meriam, Sarah 37, 316
Meriam, Susanna 656
MERICK 505
MERIER 503, 506 see
  MESSENGER
MERIHEW 504
MERIT 505
MERITT 505
Merll, Mary 728
Meroh, Rachel 255
Merrell, Abraham 82
MERRELLS 504
MERRET 505
MERRETT 488
Merrett, Mary 347, 719
Merrett, Rebecca 151
MERREY 505
MERRIAM 503
Merriam, Abigail 52
Merriam, Ann 126
Merriam, Anna 102
Merriam, Anne 102
Merriam, Elizabeth 243, 364, 796,
  833
Merriam, Hannah 27, 731
Merriam, Joseph 800
Merriam, Mary 397, 703, 731
Merriam, Rebecca 236, 269
Merriam, Ruth 716
Merriam, Sarah 271, 336, 418,
  799, 801
Merriam, Susanna 210
MERRICK 503, 504
Merrick, Ann 503
Merrick, Elizabeth 211
Merrick, Hannah 446, 503
Merrick, John 704, 831
Merrick, Joseph 617
Merrick, Mary 274, 387
Merrick, Mercy 494
Merrick, Rebecca 694
Merrick, Ruth 283
Merrick, Sarah 283, 375
Merrick, William 691
Merricke, Amantha 62
Merricke, Amathia 62
Merricke, Amithy 62
Merrifield, Elizabeth 594
Merrifield, Henry 594
Merrifield, John 342
Merrifield, Sarah 256, 342
MERRIHEW 504
MERRILL 504
Merrill, Abigail 545
Merrill, Daniel 551, 640
Merrill, Elizabeth 251
Merrill, Hannah 42, 471, 525, 724
Merrill, Lydia 69
Merrill, Mary 284, 728, 740
Merrill, Nathaniel 428
Merrill, Peter 654
Merrill, Sarah 431, 521, 522
Merrill, Susanna 118, 520, 759
Merrill, Thomas 372

MERRIMAN 504, 505
Merriman, Abigail 375
Merriman, Elizabeth 462
Merriman, Hannah 62, 411
Merriman, John 217, 531, 746
Merriman, Mary 199
Merriman, Samuel 194
Merriott, Abigail 267
MERRIT 505
Merrit, Hannah 328
Merrit, Katherine 202
MERRITT 505
Merritt, Elizabeth 223, 350
Merritt, Martha 549
Merritt, Thomas 470
MERROW 505
Merrow, Deborah 506
Merrow, Eleanor 501
Merrow, Hannah 417
Merrow, Henry 776
Merrow, Martha 611
Merrow, Mary 591
Merrow, Sarah 587
MERRY 505, 506
Merry, Abigail 566
Merry, Bathsheba 566
Merry, Hannah 417, 676
Merry, Joseph 372
Merry, Martha 286, 611
Merry, Sarah 90
Merry, Walter 739
MERWIN 506
Merwin, Abigail 656, 763
Merwin, Deborah 125
Merwin, Elizabeth 133
Merwin, Hannah 379
Merwin, John 36, 379
Merwin, Martha 604
Merwin, Mary 401
Merwin, Mary Adams Guire 330
Merwin, Mary Adams Guise 671
Merwin, Miles 54, 656
Merwin, Miles (Jr.) 508
MERYFIELD 504
Mesant, Alice 663
Mesenger, Mary 62
MESERVE 506
Meserve, Elizabeth 802
Meskell, Abigail 30
Meskin, Mary 60
Messant, Anne Burdett 307
MESSENGER 503, 506
Messenger, --- 530
Messenger, Abigail 204, 511
Messenger, Andrew 646
Messenger, Anna 762
Messenger, Dorcas 510
Messenger, Henry 741
Messenger, John 269
Messenger, Maria 741
Messenger, Martha 269
Messenger, Mary 401, 741
Messenger, Priscilla 543
Messenger, Sarah 325, 553, 741
MESSINGER 506
Messinger, Ann 530
Messinger, Bethiah 322
Messinger, Henry 510, 530
Messinger, Lydia 530
Messinger, Mary 553
Messinger, Priscilla 530
Messinger, Rebecca 530
Messinger, Sarah 495
Mesure, William 744
Metafor, Martha 556
Metafor, Mary 556
METCALF 506, 507
Metcalf, Elizabeth 248, 412, 806

Metcalf, Experience 799
Metcalf, Hannah 117
Metcalf, Jane 591, 774
Metcalf, Joseph 267
Metcalf, Marie 267
Metcalf, Martha 67, 99, 716
Metcalf, Mary 267, 641, 787, 825,
  837
Metcalf, Michael 440, 586, 680
Metcalf, Sarah 545, 787, 809
Metcalf, Thomas 267, 552, 653
METCALFE 506
Metcalfe, Elizabeth 39
Metcalfe, Mary 248
Metcalfe, Rebecca 482
METHUP 507
Mett, Anna 297
METTUP 507
MEULS 508
MEW 507
Mew, Ellis 467
Mew, Joanna 514
Mew, Sarah 181, 467
MIALS 507
MICALL 507
Micall, Rebecca 734
MICHEL 512, 513
MICHELL 512, 513
Michell, Elizabeth 783
Michell, Mary 414, 440, 665
MICHELSON 513
Michelson, Ruth 321
MICHILL 513
MICO 507
Micrist, Mary 267
MIDDLEBROOK 507
Middlebrook, Grace 746
Middlebrook, Hester 813
Middlebrook, Joseph 63, 760
Middlebrook, Phebe 826
Middlebrook, Sarah 369
Middlecot, Richard 700
MIDDLECOTT 507
Middlecott, Mary 300
Middlecott, Richard 553
MIDDLETON 507
Middleton, Elizabeth 13
MIDLETON 507
MIENVILLE 512
MIGHEL 507
Mighel, Elizabeth 781
MIGHELL 507
Mighell, Elizabeth 53
Mighell, Mary 31
Mighell, Stephen 324
MIGHILL 507
Mighill, Ann 732
Mighill, Ezekiel 291, 378
Mighill, Mary 708
Mighill, Nathaniel 708
Mighill, Sarah 838
MILAM 507 see MAYLEM
Milam, Constance 7
Milam, Humphrey 447
MILBOURN 508
MILBURNE 508
Milburne, Hannah 786
Milburne, Susannah 786
Milburne, William 786
Milbury, Elizabeth 552
Milbury, Lydia 467
Milbury, Mary 74, 282
Milbury, Sarah 467
MILES 432, 507, 508, 510, 511
Miles, Abigail 374, 498
Miles, Anna 718
Miles, Elizabeth 18, 307
Miles, Hannah 336

Miles, John 15, 616, 825
Miles, Katherine 167, 320
Miles, Martha 555
Miles, Mary 341, 409, 430, 431, 459, 478, 540, 814
Miles, Richard 177, 752
Miles, Samuel 336, 506
MILK 508
MILLAM 507
MILLARD 508, 509, 511
Millard, Elizabeth 93
Millard, Mary 574
Millard, Obadiah 166
Millard, Robert 93
Millard, Sarah 796
Millard, Thomas 509
MILLAT 510
MILLBORNE 508
Millens, Sarah 40
MILLER 508, 509, 510
Miller, Abraham 142
Miller, Agnes 120
Miller, Ann 30, 120
Miller, Annis 120
Miller, Deborah 295
Miller, Eleanor 365
Miller, Elizabeth 93, 286, 363, 399, 495, 550, 556, 706
Miller, Experience 286
Miller, Faith 829
Miller, George 706
Miller, Hannah 118, 187, 201, 243, 286, 315, 335, 478, 600, 740, 745
Miller, Joanna 40, 209, 434, 709
Miller, John 193, 201, 661
Miller, Lydia 178, 267
Miller, Margaret 335, 421, 784, 807
Miller, Martha 263, 795
Miller, Martha Hobby Morehouse Adams 517
Miller, Mary 16, 218, 265, 378, 399, 472, 537, 574, 718, 795, 811, 822
Miller, Mehitable 161, 193, 195, 217, 397
Miller, Mercy 279, 535
Miller, Obadiah 166
Miller, Patience 541
Miller, Paul 84
Miller, Rebecca 159, 225
Miller, Richard 39, 594
Miller, Robert 93
Miller, Sarah 21, 37, 423, 745
Miller, Susanna 807
Miller, Susannah 159, 229
Miller, Tabitha 392
Miller, Thankful 15
Miller, Thomas 69, 277, 347, 511, 550
Millerard, Rebecca 740
Milles, Sarah 40
Millet, Elizabeth 278
Millet, Hannah 654
Millet, Mary 625
Millet, Mehitable 250
MILLETT 510
Millett, John 686
Millett, Mary 625
Millett, Thomas 255
MILLIKEN 510, 526 see MULLEKEN
MILLING 510
MILLINGTON 510
Millington, Ann 470
Millins, Mary 306
Millinton, Alice 96

Milliston, Joseph 23
MILLITE 510
MILLS 507, 508, 510, 511
Mills, --- 684
Mills, Bethiah 27
Mills, Dorothy 344
Mills, Edward 506
Mills, Elizabeth 390, 798
Mills, Esther 245
Mills, Grace 779
Mills, Hannah 230
Mills, Hester 245
Mills, John 402, 542
Mills, Jonathan 490
Mills, Leady 301
Mills, Lydia 220
Mills, Martha 304, 317, 682
Mills, Mary 56, 100, 135, 163, 301, 355, 364, 402, 540, 693, 817
Mills, Mary Pitcher 643
Mills, Patience 689
Mills, Phebe 121
Mills, Rebecca 620
Mills, Richard 540
Mills, Robert 344
Mills, Samuel 501
Mills, Sarah 21, 163, 249, 261, 288, 295, 423
Mills, Simon 73
Mills, Susanna 210, 273
Mills, Susannah 186, 506
Mills, Zachariah 204
Millward, Elizabeth 582
MILNER 511
Milner, Abigail 161
Milten, Anne 89
MILTON 511 see MELTON
Milton, Dorcas 17
Milton, Mary 90
Milton, Michael 350
MILWARD 511
Milward, Thomas 509, 582
Mind, Alice 593
MINER 511
Miner, Clement 818
Miner, Deborah 569
Miner, Elizabeth 107, 775
Miner, Elnathan 337
Miner, Hannah 149
Miner, Joanna 623
Miner, Joseph 738, 758
Miner, Mary 149
Miner, Mercy 796
Miner, Phebe 704
Miner, Samuel 569
Ming, Sarah 718
MINGAY 511
Mingay, Ann 406
MINGO 511
MINOR 511
Minor, Abigail 752
Minor, Grace 317
Minor, Hannah 27, 285
Minor, John 241, 363
Minor, Mary 457
Minor, Rebecca 317
Minor, Sarah 198, 578
Minoret, John 569
MINOT 511, 512
Minot, Elizabeth 203
Minot, James 115
Minot, John 68, 252
Minot, Mehitable 182, 506, 510
Minot, Philip 183
MINOTT 511, 512
Minott, Elizabeth 203, 721
Minott, James 143

Minsall, William 651
MINSHALL 512
MINTER 512
Minter, Tobias 218
Minter, Tristram 33
MINVIELLE 512
MIRIAM 503
Miriam, Sarah 799
MIRICK 503, 504
Mirick, Hannah 446, 774
Mirick, Hopestill 638
Mirick, James 593
Mirick, Mary 210, 486
Mirick, Mercy 525
Mirick, Sarah 146
Miriour, Mary 40
MIRRIAM 503
Mirricke, Sarah 24
MITCHELL 512, 513
Mitchell, Abigail 585
Mitchell, Abraham 1
Mitchell, Andrew 361
Mitchell, Constant 98, 272
Mitchell, Elizabeth 7, 449, 732, 783
Mitchell, Elizath 810
Mitchell, Grace 483
Mitchell, Hannah 165, 249, 359, 649
Mitchell, Jane 291
Mitchell, Jean 291
Mitchell, Joanna 204, 272
Mitchell, John 298, 330, 517, 518
Mitchell, John (Capt.) 481
Mitchell, Jonathan 68, 307, 668
Mitchell, Katherine 659, 781
Mitchell, Mabel 668
Mitchell, Margaret 662
Mitchell, Martha 36
Mitchell, Mary 248, 414, 418, 440, 665
Mitchell, Prudence 95
Mitchell, Sarah 204, 359, 585, 670
Mitchell, Susanna 393
Mitchell, Sybil 606
Mitchell, Tamsen 400
Mitchell, Thomasine 400
Mitchell, Thomas 810
Mitchell, William 653
MITCHELSON 513
Mitchelson, Alice 666
Mitchelson, Bethiah 792
Mitchelson, Edward 24
Mitchelson, Elizabeth 24, 213
Mitchelson, Ruth 143, 321
MITTON 513
Mitton, Elizabeth 158
Mitton, Martha 318, 328
MIX 513
Mix, Abigail 555
Mix, Esther 514
Mix, Hannah 545
Mix, Rebecca 845
MIXER 513, 514
Mixer, Abigail 393
Mixer, Isaac 703
Mixer, Joanna 345, 778
Mixer, Mary 527
Mixer, Rebecca 433
Mixer, Sarah 332, 703
Mixor, Isaac 285
MIXTER 513
Mixter, Abigail 393
Mixter, Mary 527
Mixtur, Mary 485
MOADSLIE 523
Moakes, Anne 457
MODESLEY 523

Modesley, Mary 309
MODSLEY 522
MOFFATT 514
Moger, Mary 651
MOGEY 523
MOGGRIDGE 514
MOGRIDGE 514
MOISER 523
MOLLES 524
MOLLINS 526
Moltby, John 730
MOLTON 524, 525
Molton, Mary 513
Molton, Susanna 733
Molyneaux, Mary 608
MOLYNES 526
MOLYNEUS 526
Momford, Jane 19
MONAMPS 514
Monck, Henry 215
Mone, Hannah 674
MONEY 514
MONJOYE 527
MONK 514
Monk, George 759, 838
MONROE 514
Monroe, William 844
MONROW 514
Monsall, Thomas 516
MONSON 514
MONTAGUE 514
Montague, Abigail 781
Montague, Martha 347, 805
Montague, Mary 782
Montague, Peter 171, 684
Montgomery, Elizabeth 749
Montisse, Jane 339
MONTJOY 527
Montpeson, --- 715
MONUMPS 514
MONUPS 514
MONY 514
MOODEY 515
Moodey, Mary 333
MOODY 514, 515
Moody, Frances 436
Moody, Hannah 829
Moody, Joshua 414
Moody, Martha 644, 726
Moody, Mary 335, 527, 555, 692
Moody, Samuel 479, 555
Moody, Sarah 431, 487, 586, 591
Moody, William 288
Mooer, Hannah 514
Mooers, Jonathan 513
MOON 515
Moon, Abel 404
MOONE 515
MOOR 515, 516, 517
Moor, Anna 369
Moor, Mary 406
MOORE 488, 499, 515, 516, 517
    see MARE, MAYER, MORE,
    MOWER
Moore, Abigail 73
Moore, Alice 452
Moore, Amy 121
Moore, Andrew 486
Moore, Ann 680
Moore, Anna 369, 436
Moore, Anne 121, 436
Moore, Benjamin 471, 701, 765
Moore, Deborah 704
Moore, Dorothy 221
Moore, Eleanor 634
Moore, Elizabeth 139, 300, 329,
    368, 403, 472, 521, 620, 745,
    820, 847

Moore, Gershom 266
Moore, Golden 143
Moore, Hannah 134, 230, 351,
    575, 658, 732
Moore, Hannah Hempstead 776
Moore, Isaac 76, 334, 646
Moore, James 98
Moore, Jane 335
Moore, Jeremiah 452
Moore, Joan 53
Moore, John 227, 525, 575
Moore, Joseph 346
Moore, Katharine 177
Moore, Lydia 200, 258, 441, 511,
    787, 843
Moore, Margaret 783
Moore, Martha 76, 658, 674, 675
Moore, Mary 132, 185, 222, 270,
    300, 305, 316, 348, 403, 525,
    598, 711, 713, 722, 778
Moore, Miles 704
Moore, Mindwell 73
Moore, Miriam 696, 818
Moore, Naomi 243
Moore, Nathaniel 515
Moore, Phebe 464
Moore, Rachel 559
Moore, Richard 222, 403, 816
Moore, Richard (Capt.) 195
Moore, Ruth 540, 631, 666
Moore, Samuel 278, 415, 431
Moore, Sarah 306, 464, 514, 697,
    793, 827
Moore, Thomas 230, 449
Moore, William 12, 360, 766
Moorecock, Bennett 683
Moorecock, Henry 812
MOORES 517
Moores, Jonathan 513
Moores, Lydia 843
Moores, Martha 310
Moores, Mary 89, 778
Moores, Sarah 635
Moorton, Mary 533
MOOSE 520
MORDOE 517
MORDOGH 517
MORDOW 528
MORE 515, 516, 517
More, --- 739
More, Christian 175
More, Deborah 276
More, Elizabeth 243
More, Henry 663
More, Jonathan 452
More, Katherin 378
More, Lydia 258, 511
More, Mary 598
More, Phebe 464
More, Ruth 357
More, Sarah 303
More, Susanna 236, 408
MORECOCK 517
MOREHOUSE 517
Morehouse, Elizabeth 670
Morehouse, Hannah 642
Morehouse, Mary 197, 564, 567
Morehouse, Rebecca 398
Morehouse, Thomas 720
MORELEY 522
Morell, Sarah 174
MORER 517
MOREY 517, 518 see MOWRY
Morey, Abigail 347
Morey, Bethia 553
Morey, Jonathan 278
Morey, Mary 25, 166
Morey, Nicholas 100, 194

Morey, Walter 186
MORFREY 528
MORGAN 137, 518, 519
Morgan, --- 216, 237
Morgan, Abigail 16
Morgan, Ann 209
Morgan, Benjamin 638
Morgan, Bethia 790
Morgan, Catharine 711
Morgan, Deborah 33
Morgan, Dorothy 832
Morgan, Elizabeth 368, 703, 776
Morgan, Francis 330, 512
Morgan, Francis (Dr.) 481
Morgan, Hannah 453, 634, 641,
    732
Morgan, John 822
Morgan, Lydia 490, 583
Morgan, Martha 572
Morgan, Mary 74, 292, 604, 645,
    703
Morgan, Owen 111
Morgan, Prudence 55
Morgan, Robert 280
Morgan, Sarah 16, 452
MORGIN 518
MORGRAGE 519
Morgrage, Hannah 285
MORGRIDGE 519
MORISON 520
MORLEY 519 see MOSELEY
Morman, Elizabeth 156
MORREL 519
MORRELL 519
Morrell, Elizabeth 127, 232
Morrell, Lydia 519
Morrell, Lysbell 519
Morrell, Margaret 442
Morrell, Mary 266, 378, 756
Morrell, Sarah 247
MORREY 525
MORRICE 519, 520
Morrice, Elizabeth 29, 701
MORRILL 519
Morrill, Abraham 526
Morrill, Alice 23
Morrill, Catherine 683
Morrill, Elizabeth 95
Morrill, Hannah 95
Morrill, Hepsibah 219
Morrill, Joanna 95
Morrill, Lydia 372, 661
Morrill, Mary 273
Morrill, Moses 648
Morrill, Sarah 174, 209, 551, 640
Morrill, Vashti 91
MORRIS 519, 520
Morris, Ann 174
Morris, Anthony 164
Morris, Elizabeth 138, 314, 485
Morris, Grace 150
Morris, Hannah 479, 686
Morris, Hester 254
Morris, Isaac 585
Morris, John 449, 461, 467
Morris, Margaret 422
Morris, Margaret Painter 162
Morris, Martha 13, 300
Morris, Mary 364, 438, 486, 743
Morris, Robert 453
Morris, Sarah 199
Morris, Thomas 278, 385, 486
Morris, Thos. 314
Morris, William 170
MORRISE 519
MORRISH 520
MORRISON 520
Morrison, Joanna 551

Morrison, Mary 397
Morriss, Elizabeth 150
MORS 520, 521
Mors, Abigail 520
Mors, Hannah 534
MORSE 520, 521, 522, 523
Morse, --- 680
Morse, Abigail 255, 267, 365, 427, 520, 560, 587, 680
Morse, Anne 740
Morse, Anthony 240, 533
Morse, Bethia 237, 573
Morse, Bethshua 268
Morse, Deborah 827
Morse, Dorcas 154
Morse, Elizabeth 203, 204, 254, 455, 651
Morse, Esther 117, 384, 428, 690
Morse, Hannah 210, 272, 325, 533, 534, 710, 793
Morse, Hester 117, 384
Morse, Joanna 267
Morse, John 129
Morse, Jonathan 558
Morse, Joseph 88, 99, 237, 260, 582, 590
Morse, Lydia 813
Morse, Margaret 11
Morse, Mary 117, 183, 379, 590, 652, 664, 796
Morse, Mehitable 95
Morse, Priscilla 317
Morse, Ruth 89, 248, 514
Morse, Samuel 40
Morse, Sarah 2, 182, 455, 564, 710
Morse, Susannah 534
Morse, Thomas 105
Morsly, Elizabeth 72
Morss, Elizabeth 571
MORTIMER 522
Mortimer, Dorothy 734
Mortimer, Edward 8
Mortimer, Elizabeth 818
Mortimer, Mary 713
Mortimor, Elizabeth 135
MORTIMORE 522
MORTON 522
Morton, Ann 230
Morton, Deborah 180
Morton, Eleazer 490
Morton, Elizabeth 84
Morton, Ephraim 168, 344
Morton, George 432
Morton, Hannah 84, 237, 285, 288, 474, 781
Morton, Joanna 320, 384, 604
Morton, John 626
Morton, Lettice 626
Morton, Lydia 249
Morton, Margaret 184
Morton, Mary 84, 174, 285, 529, 698
Morton, Mercy 234
Morton, Nathaniel 732
Morton, Patience 260, 531, 811, 812
Morton, Rebecca 835
Morton, Remember 412
Morton, Richard 842
Morton, Ruth 42
Morton, Sarah 82
Morton, Thomas 57
Mory, Elizabeth 75
Mory, Martha 76
MOSAMY 522
MOSE 521
MOSELEY 522, 523 see MORLEY

Moseley, Elizabeth 72
Moseley, Mary 165
Moseley, Rebecca 749
Moseley, Thomas 495
Mosely, Martha 642
Mosely, Mary 790
Mosely, Rebecca 749
MOSEMAN 523
MOSEMY 522
MOSES 523
Moses, --- 191
Moses, Aaron 669
Moses, Elizabeth 774
Moses, Grace 706
Moses, Joanna 208
Moses, John 425
Moses, Martha 195
Moses, Mary 259, 399
Moses, Mindwell 740
Moses, Ruth 783
Moses, Sarah 127
Moses, Timothy 233
Moses, William 614
MOSHER 523
Mosher, Hannah 183
Mosher, Hugh 343
Mosher, Mary 498, 611
Moshier, Mary 498
Moshier, Rebecca 815
Mosier, Isabel 606
MOSISES 523
Mosley, Ellen 662
Mosley, Mary 576
MOSLY 522
MOSMAN 523
Mosman, James 162, 306, 498
MOSS 520, 523
Moss, Abigail 226
Moss, Bethia 573
Moss, Elizabeth 375
Moss, Esther 428, 641
Moss, Hannah 11
Moss, Jane 768
Moss, John 521
Moss, Joseph 260, 302, 303
Moss, Mary 18, 567, 679
Moss, Mercy 637
Moss, Sarah 146, 455
Moss, Susannah 534
MOSSE 523
MOSSET see MUZEET
MOSSETT 523
MOSTMAN 523
Moth, Lidia Wing 2
Motley, Ann 228
MOTT 523, 524
Mott, Abigail 354, 363
Mott, Adam 398, 475
Mott, Bethiah 2
Mott, Dorothy 726
Mott, Edward 748
Mott, Elizabeth 315, 377, 442, 468, 624, 741, 828
Mott, Grace 685
Mott, Hannah 756
Mott, Jacob 179
Mott, Jane 659
Mott, Jeremiah 162, 520
Mott, Lydia 468
Mott, Mary 179, 711
Mott, Nathaniel 671
Mott, Sarah 315, 754
MOULD 524
Mould, Christian 653
Mould, Hugh 806
Mould, Jane 712
Mould, Martha 511
Mould, Mary 806

Mould, Susannah 804
MOULDER 524
Moulthorp, Elizabeth 325
Moulthorp, Ellen 478
Moulthorp, Helen 478
Moulthorp, Matthew 390
MOULTHROP 524
Moulthrop, Hannah 644
MOULTON 524, 525
Moulton, Abigail 459, 675
Moulton, Abigall 61
Moulton, Ann 491
Moulton, Dorothy 244, 265, 748, 751
Moulton, Hannah 6, 272, 648, 744
Moulton, Jeremiah 226
Moulton, Joseph 695
Moulton, Martha 491, 571
Moulton, Mary 93, 253, 285, 357, 374, 474, 482, 513, 536, 648
Moulton, Meriam 51
Moulton, Miriam 35, 51, 440
Moulton, Rachel 226
Moulton, Robert 265
Moulton, Ruth 422, 648
Moulton, Samuel 306
Moulton, Sarah 117, 358, 829, 829
Moulton, Thomas 432
Moulton, William 545, 648
Moumford, Jane 19
MOUNTFORD 525
Mountford, Ann 246
Mountford, Anne 246
Mountford, Hannah 770
Mountford, Ruth 138
MOUNTJOY 527
Mountjoy, Hepzibah 8
Mountjoy, Huldah 538
Mountjoy, Walter 549
MOUSAL 525
Mousal, Elizabeth 615
Mousal, Hannah 792
Mousal, Joanna 811
MOUSALL 525
Mousall, Eunice 103
Mousall, Mary 37, 421
Mousall, Ralph 37
Mousell, Mary 307
MOWER 516, 525 see MOORE
Mower, Christian 175
Mower, Joanna 822
Mowrey, Abigail 347
MOWRY 517, 525, 526 see MOREY
Mowry, Benjamin 596
Mowry, Bethia 553
Mowry, Experience 681
Mowry, Hannah 117, 669
Mowry, Jonathan 278, 798, 846
Mowry, Mary 21, 166, 577
Mowry, Mehitable 103, 441
Mowry, Mercy 681
Mowry, Roger 353, 363, 441
Mowry, Sarah 578
Mowry, Walter 186
MOXON 526
Moxy, Mary 485
MOYCE 526
Moyce, Hannah 362
Moyce, Martha 309, 586
Moyer, Margery 789
Moyle, Anne 566
Moyse, Mary 320
MUCCALL 482
Muchemore, Mary 433
MUCHMORE 526
Muchmore, Walter 457
MUDD 526

Mudd, Henry 169
MUDGE 526
Mudge, Abigail 576
Mudge, Elizabeth 11, 136, 583
Mudge, Jarvis 249
Mudge, Martha 813
Mudge, Mary 263, 492, 645
Mudge, Mercy 329
Mudge, Sarah 554
MUDGET 526
MUDGETT 526
Mudgett, Mary 608
Mudgett, Thomas 471, 519
MUFFET 514
Mukusett, Sarah 598
MULBERRY 526
MULBERY 526
MULENER 526
MULFORD 526
Mulford, Elizabeth 152
Mulford, Hannah 176
Mulford, John 547
Mulford, Mary 494, 508
Mulford, Rachel 219
Mulford, Thomas 684
Mulhuish, William 104
MULIGAN 526
Mulikin, Jone 213
Mulineaux, Mary 608
MULLEGAN 526
MULLEGIN 526
Mullein, Mary 154
MULLERY 526
MULLICAN 526
MULLICKEN 526
MULLIKEN 526
MULLINER 526
MULLINES 526
Mullinex, Mary 608
MULLINGS 526
Mullings, George 454, 456
Mullins, Priscilla 8
Mullins, Sarah 260, 292, 653
Mullins, William 61
MUMFORD 527
Mumford, Abigail 266
Mumford, Edmund 139
Mumford, Sarah 21
Mumford, William 613
Mumfort, Sarah 502
MUNCEY 527
Muncey, John 738
MUNCY 527
Muncy, Francis 609
MUNDAY 527 see MUNDEN
MUNDEN 527 see MUNDAY
Munden, Abraham 704
Munden, Anne 57, 131
Munden, Elizabeth 581
Munden, Mary 590
Muneford, Ann 246
Muneford, Anne 246
Munford, Elizabeth 109
MUNGER 527
Munger, Nicholas 190
Mungy, Mary 652
Munings, Rebecca 497
MUNJOY 527
Munjoy, George 194, 455, 682
Munjoy, Mary 554
Munjoy, Mary 652
Munke, Ann 704
Munkley, S. 445
MUNN 527
Munn, Abigail 704
Munn, Benjamin 37, 704
Munn, James 555
Munn, Jane 405

Munn, John 621
Munn, Mary 48, 625, 800
MUNNING 527
Munning, Abigail 653
Munning, Hannah 329
Munning, Mahalaleel 616
MUNNINGS 527
Munnings, George 89, 454, 456,
   485
Munnings, Hannah 823
Munnings, Mahahaleel 548
Munnings, Rebecca 497
MUNNION 527
Munro, Elizabeth 466
MunROE 639
MUNROE 514, 639
Munroe, Elizabeth 642
Munroe, Hannah 583
Munroe, Martha 175
Munroe, Mary 260
Munrow, Hannah 583
MUNSELL 527
Munsell, Mary 479
MUNSEY 528
Munsey, Francis 609
MUNSON 514
Munson, Anne 527, 704
Munson, Elizabeth 182, 369
Munson, Hannah 92, 761
Munson, Martha 246
Munson, Martha Bradley 602
Munson, Samuel 504
MUNT 528
Munt, Eleanor 372
Munt, Faith 672
Munt, Mary 40, 441
Munt, Thomas 372
Munter, Frances 169
Munter, Susan 420
Munter, Susannah 420
Munyon, Judah 496
Murcock, Mary 109
MURDOCK 528
Murdock, Mary 109
Murdock, Phebe 782
Murford, Elizabeth 109
Murfy, Ann 846
MURPHY 528
MURRAY 528
Murray, John 314
Murrel, Margaret 442
MURREY 528
MURRILL 519
Musal, Martha Huggins Mattone
   497
Muse, Esther 183
Mushamore, Mary 433
Musket, Bridget 627
Muskett, Bridget 269
MusseJl, Audrey 479
Mussell, Mary 416, 639
MUSSEY 528
Mussey, Mary 228
Mussey, Robert 434, 640
MUSSILOWAY 528
Mussiloway, Daniel 146
Must, Esther 183
Muston, Isabella 258, 831
MUZEET 528 see MOSSETT
Muzeet, Phebe 589
Muzeet, Thomas 464
MUZZEY 528
Muzzey, Edward 637
Muzzey, Elizabeth 204
Muzzey, Esther 637
Muzzey, Hester 637
Muzzey, Lydia 607
Muzzey, Robert 434

MUZZY 528
Muzzy, Lydia 610
Muzzy, Mary 140, 479, 661
Muzzy, Sarah 770
MYCALL 507
Mycall, Mary 537
MYGATE 528
Mygate, Jacob 439
Mygate, Joseph 784
Mygate, Mary 214
Mygatt, Mary 115, 214
Mygatt, Sarah 316, 789
Myghil, Nathaniel 708
Myghil, Mary 708
Mygood, Nicholas 450
Mylam, Constance 7
Mylam, Sarah 9
MYLES 507, 508
Myles, Ann 243
Myles, Elizabeth 243
Myles, John (Rev.) 243
Myles, Katherine 167
MYNARD 499
MYNGES 528
MYNGS 528
Myrick, Abigail 11
Myrick, Amantha 62
Myrick, Amathia 62
Myrick, Amithy 62
Myrick, James 75
Myrick, Joseph 617
Myrick, Sarah 24

--- N ---

Nabor, Elizabeth 676
NAILOR 529
Nam-a-tam-a-hansett 473
NANNEY 528
Nanney, Robert 529
Nanny, Joanna 504
Nanny, Mary 237
NAPTOLI 528
NARAMORE 528
NARRAMORE 528
Narramore, Thomas 691
NASH 528, 529
Nash, --- 349
Nash, Abigail 6
Nash, Edward 42, 642
Nash, Elizabeth 176, 177, 759
Nash, Esther 693
Nash, Francis 537
Nash, Hannah 37, 237, 755, 772
Nash, Hester 693
Nash, Hope 780
Nash, Isaac 176, 255, 583
Nash, John 392
Nash, Joseph 349, 680, 768
Nash, Martha 159
Nash, Mary 14, 59, 333, 552, 595
Nash, Phebe 583
Nash, Samuel 159, 395, 648
Nash, Sarah 178, 230, 726, 845
NASON 529
Nason, Abigail 1
Nason, Alice 1
Nason, Benjamin 433
Nason, Charity 251
Nason, Hannah 831
Nason, Mary 317, 753, 831
Nason, Richard 227, 273
Nason, Sarah 150, 395
Natt, Mary 403, 405
NAYBOUR 530
Naybours, James 671

NAYLOR 528, 529
Naylor, Lydia 16
Naylor, Mary 711
Naylor, Tabitha 565
NAZITER 541
NEADOM 530
NEAL 529, 530
Neal, Abigail 710
Neal, Deborah 551
Neal, Hannah 343
Neal, Jannet 235
Neal, Mary 577
Neal, Rose 482
Neal, Ruth 734
Neal, Sarah 22, 84, 486
Neal, Saray 20
NEALE 529, 530
Neale, Abigail 657
Neale, Elizabeth 49
Neale, Hannah 356
Neale, Jeremiah 474, 637
Neale, Joanna 814
Neale, John 486, 706
Neale, Lydia 199, 348
Neale, Mary 509, 734
Neale, Rachel 593
Neale, Rebecca 537
Neale, Sarah 504
NEALES 530
NEALS 530
Neals, Lydia 426
Neate, Ellenor 358
NECK 530, 536
NEEDHAM 530
Needham, Abigail 315
Needham, Ann 366
Needham, Edmund 386
Needham, Elizabeth 379, 438, 486
Needham, Hana 21
Needham, Hannah 21, 222
Needham, John 379
Needham, Judith 199
Needham, Mary 348, 392
Needham, Rebecca 145
Needham, Sarah Fairfield 1
NEFF 530
Neffe, Mary 129
NEGOOSE 530
Negoose, Grace 260
Negoose, Jonathan 478
Negro, Matthew 323
NEGUS 530
Negus, Benjamin 43
Negus, Elizabeth 43
Negus, Grace 421
Negus, Hannah Phillips 19
Negus, Jonathan 478
Neibours, Mary 827
NEIGHBOR 530
Neighbor, Elizabeth 676
Neighbors, James 403
Neighbors, Martha 403
Neighbors, Mary 496
Neighbors, Rachel 165, 563
Neighbors, Sarah 421
NEIGHBOUR 530
NEILL 530
NELAND 443
NELSON 530, 531
Nelson, Ann 41
Nelson, Dorothy 635
Nelson, Elizabeth 590
Nelson, Hannah 745
Nelson, Jane 260
Nelson, Jean 260
Nelson, John 42
Nelson, Lucy 735
Nelson, Martha 164, 318, 411

Nelson, Mary 361, 609, 735
Nelson, Mehitable 227
Nelson, Mercy 288
Nelson, Philip 378
Nelson, Sarah 769
Nelson, Thomas 261, 479, 590
Nesbett, Mungo 269
NESBIT 531
Nesbitt, Hugh 801
NEST 531
Nest, Sarah 786
Nethercoole, Christian 342
Nethercooll, Christian 342
Nethercott, Christian 342
NETTLETON 531
Nettleton, Hannah 689
Nettleton, Isabel 147
Nettleton, Martha 763
Nettleton, Sarah 347, 509
NEVERS 531
NEVIL 531
Nevil, John 140
NEVILLE 531
NEVINSON 531
Nevinson, Elizabeth 82, 352
Nevinson, John 82
Nevinson, Mary 352
NEVISON 531
NEWBERRY 531
Newberry, Benjamin 217
Newberry, Dorcas 123
Newberry, Hannah 341
Newberry, Margaret 719
Newberry, Mary 154, 323, 522
Newberry, Rebecca 490, 643
Newberry, Sarah 154, 832
Newberry, Thomas 461, 780
Newberry, Walter 157
NEWBURY 531, 532
Newbury, Abigail 358
Newbury, Dorcas 123
NEWBY 532
Newby, Elizabeth 781
Newcom, Mary 471
NEWCOMB 532
Newcomb, Andrew 627
Newcomb, Anna 499
Newcomb, Bethiah 440
Newcomb, Elizabeth 24, 251, 585
Newcomb, Francis 5
Newcomb, Grace 127, 611
Newcomb, Hannah 360, 734, 739
Newcomb, Judith 419
Newcomb, Leah 603
Newcomb, Mary 213, 471, 599, 695
Newcomb, Mary Arnold Copeland 21, 182
Newcomb, Mercy 599
Newcomb, Michael 709
Newcomb, Peter 402
Newcomb, Rachel 5, 262
Newcomb, Ruth 182
Newcomb, Susanna 76, 605
Newcomb, Susannah 75, 376
Newcome, Rachel 262
Newcome, Sarah 175
NEWDIGATE 532
Newdigate, Elizabeth 412
NEWEL 532
Newel, Alice 749
Newel, Hannah 384
Newel, Susanna 517
NEWELL 532
Newell, Elizabeth 731, 813
Newell, Experience 823
Newell, Faith 63, 456
Newell, Grace 728

Newell, Hannah 217, 539
Newell, Hester 701
Newell, Mary 49, 335, 503
Newell, Rebecca 149, 279, 837
Newell, Sarah 354, 680
Newell, Susanna 526
Newfold, Sarah Bassett Griffin 326
NEWGATE 532
Newgate, Elizabeth 544
Newgate, Hannah 480
Newgate, John 750
Newgate, Sarah 544
NEWHALL 532, 533
Newhall, Elizabeth 120, 753
Newhall, Jemima 767
Newhall, Mary 109, 386, 496
Newhall, Nathaniel 410
Newhall, Rebecca 173, 557
Newhall, Sarah 95
Newhall, Susannah 354
NEWLAND 533
Newland, Elizabeth 798
Newland, Mary 164, 394
Newland, Mercy 245, 687
Newland, Richard 612
Newland, Rose 112
Newland, Susanna 798
Newland, William 382
NEWMAN 533, 534
Newman, Alice 206
Newman, Ann 573
Newman, Anna 573
Newman, Antipas 252
Newman, David 831
Newman, Eleanor 400
Newman, Elizabeth 321, 381, 443, 446
Newman, Frances 206
Newman, Francis 460, 718
Newman, Hannah 381, 646
Newman, Hopestill 672
Newman, John 202, 500
Newman, Mary 205, 718
Newman, Patience 694
Newman, Samuel 767, 831
Newman, Samuel (Rev.) 376
Newman, Sarah 347, 404, 645, 761, 783
Newman, Sibella 244
NEWMARCH 534
Newmarch, John 402
Newmarch, Martha 35
Newmarch, Phebe 570
Newmarch, Sarah 65, 66
Newmarsh, John 415
Newmarth, Martha 35
NEWSHAM 534
NEWSOM 534
NEWSOME 534
NEWSON 534
NEWTON 534
Newton, Abigail 606, 764
Newton, Agnes 822
Newton, Alice 112
Newton, Eleanor 4
Newton, Elizabeth 221, 238
Newton, Ellen 4, 134, 829
Newton, Hannah 61, 499, 576, 838
Newton, Isaac 534, 600
Newton, Jane 15, 474
Newton, Mary 142, 412, 422
Newton, Rebecca 534, 600
Newton, Samuel 280, 534, 600
Newton, Sarah .729, 825
Newton, Susanna 590, 714
Newton, Susannah 125

Newwork, Sarah 482
Nicarson, Elizabeth 246
NICCOLET 534
Nicholas, Josiah 832
NICHOLLES 536
NICHOLLS 535
Nicholls, Ann 785
Nicholls, Anna 785
Nicholls, Hannah 705
NICHOLS 534, 535, 536
Nichols, Abigail 246, 383, 493
Nichols, Abraham 113
Nichols, Ann 530, 706, 847
Nichols, Anna 246
Nichols, Anne Devereux Bosson
  84
Nichols, Anne Wines 847
Nichols, Benjamin 660
Nichols, Caleb 601
Nichols, Catherine 409
Nichols, David 69
Nichols, Ebenezer 473, 756
Nichols, Elizabeth 87, 96, 322,
  438, 756, 788
Nichols, Ephraim 356, 370
Nichols, Esther 248, 601
Nichols, Francis 249, 747
Nichols, Hannah 16, 22, 816, 847
Nichols, Hester 601
Nichols, Hugh 371
Nichols, Isaac 175
Nichols, Israel 157
Nichols, John 17, 222, 511, 574
Nichols, Jonathan 429, 779
Nichols, Josiah 832
Nichols, Mary 140, 148, 401, 449,
  510, 702, 725, 758
Nichols, Mary Elwill Burrill 122
Nichols, Mercy 222, 847
Nichols, Mordecai 159
Nichols, Nathaniel 113
Nichols, Patience 17, 55, 356, 398
Nichols, Phebe 443
Nichols, Rachel 139, 158, 833
Nichols, Rebecca 108, 391
Nichols, Robert 314
Nichols, Samuel 106, 140, 257
Nichols, Sarah 123, 339, 465, 496,
  708, 790, 800
Nichols, Susanna 361
Nichols, Temperance 398, 602
Nichols, William 411, 751
NICHOLSON 536
Nicholson, Catherine 409
Nicholson, Dinah 122
Nicholson, Elizabeth 18, 54, 110
Nicholson, George 207
Nicholson, Hannah 641
Nicholson, James 443
Nicholson, Rachel 565
Nicholson, Rebecca 136
Nicholson, Sarah 778
Nicholson, Susanna 86
Nicholson, Thomas 189
NICK 536
Nick, Elizabeth 743
Nick, Rebecca 48
Nick, Susanna 279
Nick, William 176, 412, 703
Nickels, Mary 449
NICKERSON 537
Nickerson, Ann 363
Nickerson, Elizabeth 130, 246
Nickerson, Hester 806
Nickerson, Judith 186
Nickerson, Mary 193
Nickerson, Mercy 513
Nickerson, Sarah 119, 186

NICKOLET 534
Nickolles, Rebecca 391
NICKS 536
Nicks, John 812
NICOLL 535, 536
Nicolls, Margaret 272
Nicols, Mary 702, 758
NIE 542
NIEL 537
Niel, Hannah 718
NIGHTINGALE 537
Nightingale, Bethiah 50
NILES 537
Niles, Abigail 742
Niles, Deborah 615
Niles, Hannah 187
Niles, Increase 528
Niles, John 16
Niles, Naomi 175
Niles, Nicholas 596
Niles, Penelope 524, 748
Niles, Samuel (Rev.) 809
NIMS 537
Nims, Godfrey 400, 822
Ninian, Joanna 504
Ninny, Joanna 504
Niols, Ebenezer 756
NISBET 531
NISBIT 531
NIX 537
Nix, Eunice 537
NIXON 537
NOAKES 537 see KNOX, OAKES
NOAKS 537
Noaks, Elizabeth 103
NOBLE 537, 538
Noble, Elizabeth 152
Noble, Esther 275
Noble, Hannah 310
Noble, Mary 174, 185
NOCK 446
Nock, Rebecca 818
Nock, Sylvanus 56
Nock, Thomas 62
NOCKS 537
Noiles, John 757
NOKES 537
Nokes, Anne 457
Noll, Martha 530
Nollings, Nathaniel 46
Nolt, Hannah 332
NOLTON 540
Norcot, Lydia 425
NORCOTT 539
NORCROSS 538
Norcross, Anna 208
Norcross, Elizabeth 141, 281
Norcross, Jeremiah 141, 552
Norcross, Richard 664
Norcross, Sarah 150
NORCUT 539
NORDEN 538
Norden, Hannah 366
Norden, Mary 807
Norden, Nathaniel 94
Norden, Samuel 807
Norden, Susanna 367, 399
NORGRAVE 538
NORMAN 538
Norman, Abigail 322
Norman, Annie 322
Norman, Arabella 35, 457
Norman, Arrabella 35
Norman, Elizabeth 156, 218, 375
Norman, Florence 348, 812
Norman, Hannah 35, 263, 457
Norman, Joseph 386
Norman, Lydia 72

Norman, Margaret 280, 518
Norman, Mary 262
Norman, Rebecca 218
Norman, Samuel 137
Norman, Susanna 263, 470
Norman, Timothy 19
Norman, William 697
Norman, Wm. 312
Normanton, Elizabeth 532
Norminton, Elizabeth 532
NORRAWAY 538
NORRICE 538
NORRIS 538
Norris, Elizabeth 306, 525
Norris, Margery 434
Norris, Mary 14, 824
Norris, Nicholas 273, 628
Norris, Sarah 376
Norsiter, Agnes 198
NORTH 538, 539
North, Bathsheba 328
North, Edward 245
North, Hannah 539
North, Jane 332
North, John 705
North, Mary 426, 490, 659
North, Samuel 618
North, Sarah 567, 838
North, Susanna 492
North, Susannah 429
North, Thomas 234
NORTHAM 539
Northam, James 36, 140
NORTHCOTT 539
Northcott, Lydia 425
NORTHEND 539
Northend, Alice 384
Northend, Edna 449, 710
Northend, Elizabeth 291, 378,
  507, 561, 732
Northend, Ezekiel 32
Northend, Margaret 194, 554
Northends, Sarah 333
NORTHEY 539
Northey, Demoris 581
Northey, Dorothy 581
Northey, Sarah 492, 493
Northrop, Ellen 637
Northrop, Mary 132
NORTHRUP 539
Northrup, Rouse 246
NORTHWAY 539
NORTON 539, 540, 541
Norton, Abigail 59, 233, 471, 493,
  756, 792
Norton, Alice 438
Norton, Ann 757
Norton, Anna 780
Norton, Anne 279, 424
Norton, Deborah 326, 372
Norton, Dorothy 221
Norton, Elizabeth 97, 553, 566,
  590, 652, 716, 725, 770
Norton, Esther 234, 408
Norton, Francis 711
Norton, George 280, 304
Norton, Grace 662
Norton, Grace Wells 125
Norton, Hannah 107, 225, 539,
  618, 818
Norton, Jane 82, 675
Norton, John 78, 174, 280, 448
Norton, Mary 349, 539, 541, 632,
  657, 676, 757, 840
Norton, Mehitable 5
Norton, Nathaniel 364
Norton, Peter 326
Norton, Priscilla 127, 626

Norton, Ruth 162, 663
Norton, Samuel 28
Norton, Sarah 224, 348, 354, 700, 755
Norton, Susanna 254, 330
Norton, Temferance 539
Norton, Temperance 539
Norton, Walter 386
Norton, William 757
NORWOOD 541
Norwood, Deborah 342
Norwood, Elizabeth 596
Norwood, Mary 651
NOSSITER 541
Nossiter, Michael 565
Nossiter, Peter 53
NOSSITOR 541
Noster, Agnes 198
Nostock, Sarah 6
NOTT 541 see KNOTT
Nott, Cicely 726
Nott, Elizabeth 617
Nott, Mary 405
Nouguier, Anthony 799
NOURSE 541
Nourse, Benjamin 521
Nourse, Elizabeth 644
Nourse, Rebecca 603
NOWELL 541
Nowell, Elizabeth 731
Nowell, Lydia 44, 224
Nowell, Mary 209, 471, 829
Nowell, Mehitable 77, 200, 374
Nowell, Samuel 764
Nowell, Thomas 580, 664
NOWSHOM 534
Noyce, Mary 284
NOYES 541
Noyes, --- 434
Noyes, Abigail 285, 590
Noyes, Dorothy 357, 561, 753
Noyes, Elizabeth 283, 340, 358
Noyes, Hannah 24, 149
Noyes, Joseph 817
Noyes, Mary 284, 527, 541, 682
Noyes, Peter 342
Noyes, Rachel 412
Noyes, Rebecca 444
Noyes, Ruth 769, 824
Noyes, Sarah 159, 285, 299, 333, 357, 575
Noyes, Thomas 30
NUCOM 532
NUDD 542
Nudd, Ann 168
Nudd, Hannah 550
Nudd, Joan 228
Nudd, Lucy 551
Nudd, Roger 228
Nugent, Walter 662
NULAND 533
NURSE 541
Nurse, Elizabeth 227
Nurse, Mary 728
Nurse, Rebecca 603
Nurse, Sarah 86, 761
NURSS 541
Nursse, Elizabeth 644
NUTE 542
Nute, --- 458
Nute, James 290
Nute, Leah 444
Nute, Martha 202
Nute, Sarah 118, 290
NUTON 534
NUTT 542
Nutt, Jules 67
Nutt, Miles 226

Nutt, Sarah 289, 845
Nutten, Mary 393
NUTTER 542
Nutter, Abigail 628
Nutter, Elizabeth 457
Nutter, Mary 777, 828
Nutter, Sarah 371
NUTTING 542
Nutting, Abigail 142
Nutting, Deborah 729
Nutting, John 557
Nutting, Mary 393
Nutting, Sarah 259, 714
Nutting, Susanna 168
NYE 542
Nye, Abigail 221
Nye, Mary 119
Nye, Mercy 248
NYLES 537
Nyles, Jane 375
Nyles, Mary 529
Nyles, Naomi 175

--- O ---

Oake, Hannah 19
OAKEMAN 542
OAKES 537, 542
Oakes, Elizabeth 371, 417, 723, 724
Oakes, Hannah 19, 771
Oakes, Margaret 52
Oakes, Mary 272
Oakes, Thomas 360
Oakes, William 194
OAKEY 543
Oakley, Elizabeth 105
Oakley, Mary 193, 295
Oakley, Miles 104, 193, 279, 631
Oakley, Sarah 377, 480
Oakley, Thomas 123
OAKMAN 542
Oakman, --- 502
Oakman, Elias 510
Oakman, Samuel 6, 151
Oakman, Susanna 63
OAKSMAN 542
OBBIT 542
OBER 543
Ober, Ann 518
Ober, Anna 518
Ober, Elizabeth 35
Oborne, James 829
OCELEY 543
Ocington, Mary 345
OCKESON 442
OCKINGTON 543
Ockington, Mary 345
OCKONELL 543
O'CONNELL 543
ODAL 543
Oddihorn, Deliverance 161
ODDING 543
Odding, George 594
Odding, Margaret 594
Odding, Sarah 669
O'Dea, Margaret 625
ODELL 543 see WODELL
Odell, --- 765
Odell, Elizabeth 70
Odell, Hannah 661
Odell, John 768
Odell, Mary 507, 760
Odell, Rebecca 330, 517
Odell, Sarah 20
Odell, Ursula 840

ODIORNE 543
Odiorne, Deliverance 161
Odiorne, Jotham 67
Odiorne, Mary 53, 176, 703, 722 •
ODLE 543
ODLEN 543
ODLIN 543
Odlin, --- 206
Odlin, Anna 118
Odlin, Anne 118
Odlin, Hannah 118, 237
Odlin, John 157
Odlin, John (Rev.) 232
Odlyn, Ann 156
Offin, Margaret 80
OFFIT 763
OFFITT 763
Ogborn, Mary 711
OGDEN 543
Ogden, --- 587
Ogden, Abigail 481, 673
Ogden, David 778
Ogden, Elizabeth 501, 607
Ogden, Hannah 779
Ogden, John 105
Ogden, Mary 838
Ohake, Joanna 623
OHOGEN 543
O KALLY 543
O'KELLEY 543
O'Kelley, David 195
O'Kelley, Jane 195
O'Kelley, John 34
O'Kelley, Sarah 195
Oker, Elizabeth 718
OKES 542
OKESON 442
OKEY 543
OKILLE 543
OKILLY 543
OKINGTON 543
Olard, Sarah 837
OLCOTT 543 see ALCOCK, ALCOTT
Olcott, Elizabeth 408
Olcott, John 795
Olcott, Mary 68, 121, 139
Olcott, Sarah 822
OLD 543, 544
Old, Robert 448
OLDAGE 544 see ALDRICH
Oldage, Ann 547
OLDAM 544
Oldam, Frances 139
Oldam, Hannah 706
OLDHAM 544
Oldham, Ann 52
Oldham, John 584
Oldham, Lucretia 96
Oldham, Margaret 50
Oldham, Mary 97
Oldham, Richard 109, 515
OLDS 544
OLIVER 544
Oliver, Abigail 421
Oliver, Christian 495
Oliver, David 99
Oliver, Elizabeth 136, 307, 430, 831
Oliver, Elizabeth Eliot 640
Oliver, James 285
Oliver, James (Capt.) 136
Oliver, John 412
Oliver, Lydia 267
Oliver, Mary 20, 372, 672, 757, 797, 821
Oliver, Richard 757
Oliver, Samuel 267

Oliver, Sarah 541
Oliver, Thomas 71, 372, 607, 796
Oliver, William 510, 675
Olliver, John 299
OLMSTEAD 544, 545
Olmstead, Joanna Rose Flemming 638
Olmstead, Mary 127, 615
Olmstead, Nehemiah 302
Olmstead, Rebecca 532
Olmstead, Richard 690
Olmstead, Sarah 1, 296, 661
OLMSTED 545
Olmsted, Jane 825
Olmsted, Joanna Rose Flemming 271
Olmsted, John 325
Olmsted, Mabel 126, 726
Olmsted, Nehemiah 661
Olmsted, Rebecca 68
Olmsted, Sarah 175
OLNEY 545
Olney, Anne 784
Olney, Elizabeth 655
Olney, Lydia 820
Olney, Mary 784, 803
Olsley, Sarah 333
Olsra, Elizabeth 570
Oneal, Sarah 227
ONG 545
Ong, Sarah 129
Onge, Francis 805
ONION 545
Onion, Amy 318, 607
Onion, Mary 53
OORSON 545
ORCHARD 545
Orchard, Mary 608
Orchard, Mehitable 591
ORCUTT 545
Orcutt, John 748, 809
Orcutt, Martha 461
Orcutt, Mary 398
Orcutt, Susanna 243
Ordiway, Jane 623
Ordiway, Jeane 623
ORDWAY 545, 546
Ordway, Abner 215
Ordway, Anna 126
Ordway, Anne 125
Ordway, Hannah 366
Ordway, James 49, 183
Ordway, Jane 623
Ordway, Jeane 623
Ordway, Mary 310
Ordway, Sarah 270, 546
Orgrave, Ann 403
Orgrave, Anna 138
Orgrave, Anne 138
Orgrave, Dorothy 596
ORIO 546
ORIS 546
Oris, Nathaniel 720
ORMES 546
Ormes, Ann 617
Ormes, Elizabeth 495
Ormes, Mary 768
Ormes, Richard 612
ORMS 546
ORMSBEY 546
Ormsbey, Jacob 409
ORMSBY 546
Ormsby, Grace 645
Ormsby, John 450
Ormsby, Mary 288, 645
Ormsby, Sarah 450, 450
ORNE 388
Orne, Ann 262

Orne, Elizabeth 294
Orne, Jehoidan 350
Orne, John 321
Orne, Mary 476, 684
Orne, Simon 38, 708
Orne, Simond 38
Orr, Mary 786
ORRIS 345, 546
Orris, Elizabeth 750
Orris, Sarah 607
ORRISE 546
ORRYS 546
ORTON 546 see HORTON
Orton, Elizabeth 464
Orton, Hannah 464
Orton, Hepzabeth 287
Orton, John 287, 429
Orton, Margaret 737
Orton, Mary 584, 636
Orton, Sarah 217, 503
ORVICE 546
ORVIS 546
Orvis, Anna 546
Orvis, Deborah 43
Orvis, George 102, 135
Orvis, Hannah 546
Orvis, Margaret 391
Orvis, Mary 657
OSBORN 546, 547
Osborn, Abigail 280, 300, 372
Osborn, Alexander 673, 679
Osborn, Ann 604
Osborn, Anna 519
Osborn, Elizabeth 21, 787
Osborn, Esther 549
Osborn, Friediswude 526
Osborn, Hannah 40, 245, 642, 663, 705
Osborn, James 299, 829
Osborn, Jeremiah 299
Osborn, John 270, 302, 425, 600
Osborn, Margaret 575
Osborn, Mary 58, 63, 90, 257, 309, 549, 788
Osborn, Mindwell 566
Osborn, Patience 8
Osborn, Priscilla 660
Osborn, Richard 58, 750
Osborn, Sarah 103, 480, 667, 720, 843
Osborn, Thomas 171
Osborn, William 384, 451, 526
Osborne, Alexander 604
Osborne, Elizabeth 476, 735
Osborne, Hannah 22, 35
Osborne, Mary 83, 310, 638
Osborne, Sarah 100, 476, 567
Osborne, Thomas 100, 547, 640
Osborne, William 447
Osbourne, Bethia 186
Osburn, Hannah 705
Osburne, Mercy 25
Osburne, Sarah 667
OSGOOD 547, 548
Osgood, Abigail 134, 825, 826
Osgood, Christopher 171, 640
Osgood, Deborah 643
Osgood, Dorothy 19
Osgood, Elizabeth 106, 608
Osgood, Esther 549
Osgood, Hannah 19, 20, 134
Osgood, Joanna 426
Osgood, John 812
Osgood, Jone 426
Osgood, Lydia 287
Osgood, Mary 23, 197, 260, 409, 475, 491
Osgood, Mehitable 593

Osgood, Sarah 161, 168, 573
Osgood, Timothy 593
OSLAND 548
Osland, Elizabeth 826
Osland, Hannah 601
OSMAN 548
OSMENT 548
Osmer, Sarah 393
OSMINT 548
OSWELL 548
Othea, Sarah 317
OTIS 548
Otis, Ann 26
Otis, Deborah 506
Otis, Elizabeth 13, 474, 713, 823
Otis, Experience 362, 417
Otis, Hannah 303
Otis, John 379, 718
Otis, Joyce 741
Otis, Judith 761
Otis, Margaret 49, 124
Otis, Martha 587
Otis, Mary 313, 765
Otis, Mercy 313
Otis, Nicholas 741
Otis, Richard 362
Otis, Sarah 587
OTWAY 559
Ovenden, Nathaniel 513
OVERMAN 548
Overman, Thomas 527, 616
OVIATT 548
Oviatt, Abigail 6
Oviatt, Amy 36
Oviatt, Esther 245
Oviatt, Frances 245
Oviatt, Thomas 157
Oviatte, Anna Hawley 56
OWEN 548, 549
Owen, Deliverance 242, 686
Owen, Elizabeth 527
Owen, Mary 71, 821
Owen, Morgan 527
Owen, Rebecca 304
Owen, Richard 682
Owen, Samuel 574
Owen, William 325
OWENS 549
Owfield, Mary 38
Owfield, Sarah 306
Owley, Elizabeth 563
OXENBRIDGE 549
Oxenbridge, Bathshua 657
Oxenbridge, John 657
Oxenbridge, Theodora 733
OXFORD 549
Oxford, Thomas 595
Oxston, Susanna 381, 382
Oyden, Richard 702
Oyden, Sarah 702
OZLAND 548

--- P ---

PABODIE 549 see PEABODY
Pabodie, Annis 638
Pabodie, Elizabeth 633
Pabodie, Hannah 49
Pabodie, Lydia 327
Pabodie, Martha 272, 658
Pabodie, Mercy 674
Pabodie, Priscilla 831
Pabodie, Rebecca 694
Pabodie, Ruth 48
Pabodie, Sarah 165
Pabodie, William 703

Pabody, Jacob 573
Pabody, Lydia 572
Pabody, Mary 694
Pacen, Samuel 736
PACEY 549
Pacey, Thomas 430
Pack, Mary 833
PACKARD 549, 550 see PACKER
Packard, --- 577
Packard, Deborah 783
Packard, Deliverance 783
Packard, Elizabeth 9, 783
Packard, Hannah 98, 611
Packard, Jael 683, 684
Packard, Mary 578, 585, 691
Packard, Mehitable 112
Packard, Samuel 783
Packard, Thomas 550
PACKER 550, 558
Packer, Elizabeth 6, 9, 703
Packer, John 184, 453
Packer, Mary 196
Packer, Rebecca Wells Latham 786
Packer, Sarah 212
Packer, Tamsen 101
Packer, Tamzon 101, 556
Packer, Thomas 335
Packer, Thomasine 101
Packs, --- 739
PADDEN 564
Paddlefoot, Jonathan 239
PADDLEFORD 550
Paddleford, Jonathan 239, 356
PADDOCK 550
Paddock, Alice 242
Paddock, Elizabeth 394
Paddock, Martha 555
Paddock, Mary 647
Paddock, Robert 555, 628
Paddock, Zachariah 733
Padduck, Susannah 242
Padduk, Robert 628
PADDY 550
Paddy, Elizabeth 829
Paddy, Margaret 53
Paddy, Mercy 228
Paddy, William 53, 575
PADELFORD 550
PADESHALL 564
Padishall, Ann 736
PADLFOOT 550
PAGE 550, 551
Page, Abigail 690
Page, Anna 828
Page, Bethia 724
Page, Catherine 99
Page, Edward 455
Page, Elizabeth 423, 560, 675
Page, George 23
Page, Hannah 185, 228, 828
Page, Joseph 363, 511, 559
Page, Lucy 631
Page, Margaret 423, 525, 648
Page, Margery 172
Page, Martha 345
Page, Mary 23, 228, 273, 468, 505, 631, 668
Page, Mercy 148, 163
Page, Meribah 665
Page, Mildred 342
Page, Onesiphorus 228, 640
Page, Phebe 200, 757
Page, Rebecca 492, 683
Page, Ruth 241
Page, Sabina 492, 616
Page, Samuel 735
Page, Sarah 372, 373, 406, 652,

Page, Sarah (cont.) 762
Page, Susanna 51, 305, 603
Page, Susannah 724
Page, Thomas 45, 321
Page, William 835
Paig, Abiel 474
PAIGE 551
Paige, Nicholas 450
Paige, Sarah 506
Pain, Dorothy 256
Pain, Sarah 227
PAINE 551, 552, 553
Paine, Abigail 202
Paine, Alice 717
Paine, Anna 20, 299, 460
Paine, Anne 460
Paine, Anthony 327, 791
Paine, Dorcas 177, 767, 803
Paine, Edward 799
Paine, Elizabeth 3, 45, 162, 294, 404, 570, 720
Paine, Hannah 20, 158, 198, 246, 257, 336, 685
Paine, John 642, 803
Paine, Martha 139
Paine, Mary 169, 252, 403, 633, 754
Paine, Mercy 286
Paine, Moses 52, 162, 401, 608, 775
Paine, Peter 765
Paine, Rebecca 404, 433, 564, 568, 775
Paine, Richard 133, 828
Paine, Samuel 376
Paine, Sarah 69, 215
Paine, Stephen 139, 538, 559
Paine, Stephen (Jr.) 506
Paine, Thomas 482, 499
Paine, Tobias 507, 700
Paine, William 723
PAINTER 553
Painter, Margaret 162, 520
Painter, Mercy 10
Pairan, Charlotte 673
PAITON 575
Paiton, Bezaleel 550
PAKER 558
Palfory, Rebecca 722
Palfray, Elizabeth 404
PALFREY 553
Palfrey, Hannah 422
Palfrey, Jane 823
Palfrey, Jehoidan 680
Palfrey, Lydia 581
Palfrey, Martha 307
Palfrey, Mary 819
Palfrey, Peter 86, 257
Palfrey, Rebecca 722
Palfrey, Remember 23
PALGRAVE 553
Palgrave, Anna 836
Palgrave, Anne 836
Palgrave, Elizabeth 244
Palgrave, Joan 847
Palgrave, Lydia 367
Palgrave, Mary 793
Palgrave, Richard 847
PALK 553
Pall, Margaret 546
Pallard, Deliverance 400
PALMER 553, 554, 555
Palmer, Abigail 144, 259
Palmer, Alice 187
Palmer, Ann 79, 172, 577, 590, 640
Palmer, Ann Humphrey 507
Palmer, Anna 317, 577, 640, 751

Palmer, Anne 450
Palmer, Bridget 49, 640
Palmer, Daniel 215
Palmer, Deborah 426
Palmer, Deliverance 162
Palmer, Dorothy 815
Palmer, Elizabeth 28, 62, 146, 150, 274, 605, 625, 643, 678, 777
Palmer, Ephraim 325
Palmer, Esther 120
Palmer, Gershom 495
Palmer, Gift 314
Palmer, Grace 135, 511
Palmer, Hannah 44, 266, 284, 293, 317, 367, 389, 465, 554, 706, 710
Palmer, Hester 533
Palmer, Joan 189, 213
Palmer, John 53, 194
Palmer, Jonah 745
Palmer, Judith 613, 618
Palmer, Margaret 82
Palmer, Martha 333, 669, 745
Palmer, Mary 97, 225, 227, 274, 282, 284, 389, 501, 550, 569, 748, 764
Palmer, Mehitable 202, 725
Palmer, Mercy 95
Palmer, Nicholas 607
Palmer, Rebecca 35, 149
Palmer, Richard 125, 438, 598
Palmer, Samuel 194
Palmer, Sarah 308, 344, 413, 440, 549, 612, 640
Palmer, Susanna 492
Palmer, Susannah 510
Palmer, Timothy 304
Palmer, William 87, 263, 491, 507, 590, 628, 823
Palmer, William (Sr.) 550
Palmer, Wm. 618
PALMES 555
Palmes, Anne 450
Palmes, Edward 209
Palmes, Susannah 27
Palmes, William 507
PALMITER 561
PALSGRAVE 553
Palsgrave, John 386
Palsgrave, Sarah 7
PAMER 554
PAMMER 554
PAMPILLO 555
Panckhurst, Anne 822
PANGBORN 555
Panthern, Mary Moody 527
Pantheron, Mary Moody 527
PANTON 555
Panton, Elizabeth 317
Panton, Mary Moody 527
PANTRY 555
Pantry, Ann 429
Pantry, John 795
Pantry, Mary 111, 513
Pantry, William 102
PAPILLAUS 555
PAPILLIO 555
PAPILLON 555
Papillon, Mary 41
PAPLEY 555
PAPPILONS 555
PARCEL 561
PARCELL 566
Parcell, Mary 738
Parcell, Sarah 250
Parchment, Lydia 109
PARCKE 558

PARDEE 555, 556
Pardee, Elizabeth 325, 545
Pardee, Hannah 767
Pardee, Mary 390, 842
Pardee, Rebecca 513
PARDICE 556
Pardice, Mariah Melyn 376
Pardie, Mariah Melyn 376
PARE 556
Pare, John 629
Pare, Judith 629
Pare, Stephen 629
PARENCE 556
PARENTS 556
Parents, Mary 663
Pares, Judith 401, 552, 608
Parffer, Mary 397
PARIS 561
PARISH 556, 561 see PARIS,
    PARRES
Parish, Mary 623
PARK 556
Park, Abigail 268
Park, Alice 452
Park, Elizabeth 381
Park, Hannah 684
Park, Martha 799, 819
Park, Rebecca 650
Park, Richard 96
Park, Robert 101, 737
Park, Roger 389
Park, Sarah 443
Park, Theoda 821
PARKE 556
Parke, Ann 565
Parke, Deborah 157, 656
Parke, Dorothy 518
Parke, Elizabeth 63, 828
Parke, Isabel 810
Parke, Rebecca 452, 656
Parke, Theoda 568
PARKER 556, 557, 558, 559, 560
Parker, --- 50, 76
Parker, Abiah 497
Parker, Abraham 180
Parker, Alice 488, 552
Parker, Ann 299, 486
Parker, Anna 653
Parker, Deborah 732, 844
Parker, Edward 329, 596, 637
Parker, Elisha 566
Parker, Elizabeth 155, 187, 258,
    295, 296, 469, 552, 579, 582,
    586, 641, 707, 721
Parker, Experience 278
Parker, Frances 108, 333
Parker, George 423
Parker, Grace 544
Parker, Hananiah 99
Parker, Hannah 5, 19, 79, 101,
    338, 471, 562, 762, 844
Parker, Hope 179
Parker, Isaac 605
Parker, Jacob 704, 770
Parker, Jael 684
Parker, James 138, 295
Parker, Jane 411, 734
Parker, Joanna 390, 494, 713
Parker, John 13, 96, 142, 161,
    176, 177, 184, 390, 597, 734
Parker, Joseph 39, 79, 97, 407
Parker, Joshua 521
Parker, Lydia 436, 468, 735, 798
Parker, Lydia Draper Whittemore
    Richardson 622, 811
Parker, Margaret 134, 223, 599
Parker, Margaret Sheafe Stratton
    717

Parker, Martha 390
Parker, Mary 175, 209, 215, 224,
    287, 329, 334, 341, 350, 417,
    418, 557, 583, 593, 623, 666,
    748, 771, 789, 795, 804
Parker, Mary Brown 231
Parker, Meribah 678
Parker, Nathan 247
Parker, Nicholas 197
Parker, Parnell Gray 541
Parker, Patience 610
Parker, Priscilla 816
Parker, Rachel 272, 617, 623
Parker, Ralph 601
Parker, Rebecca 156, 203, 601
Parker, Remember 588
Parker, Richard 486
Parker, Robert 115, 192
Parker, Ruth 5, 40, 330, 620
Parker, Samuel 363, 550
Parker, Sarah 34, 90, 116, 192,
    278, 302, 359, 551, 567, 645,
    647, 692, 707, 770
Parker, Stephen 217
Parker, Susannah 278, 281, 827
Parker, Tabitha 584
Parker, Tamsen 101
Parker, Tamzon 101, 556
Parker, Thomas 24, 32, 161, 336
Parker, Thomasine 101
Parker, William 106, 600
Parker, Wm. 577, 610, 717
PARKES 556, 557
Parkes, Ann 565
Parkes, Hannah 562
PARKHURST 560
Parkhurst, Abigail 196
Parkhurst, Deborah 683
Parkhurst, Elizabeth 372, 505
Parkhurst, George 675, 766
Parkhurst, Mary 138
Parkhurst, Phebe 22
Parkhurst, Rachel 291
Parkhurst, Ruth 202
Parkhurst, Sarah 669
PARKHYRST 560
Parkhyrst, Mary 79
PARKIS 560
PARKMAN 560
Parkman, Abigail 751
Parkman, Bridget 255
Parkman, Deliverance 297
Parkman, Elias 189, 255
Parkman, Rebecca 416
Parkman, Sarah 189
PARKS 556
Parks, Abigail 268
Parks, Sarah 443
Parks, William 467
Parkus, Abigail 499
PARLEN 560
PARLIN 560
Parlin, Hannah 361
Parlin, Sarah 89, 732
Parling, Abigail 716
Parling, Elizabeth 436
Parling, Hannah 361
Parling, Sarah 732
PARLOR 560
PARLOW 560
PARLY 573
Parmalee, John 91
PARMELEE 560, 561
Parmelee, Hannah 371, 372, 421,
    504
Parmelee, John 254, 589
Parmelee, Mary 189
Parmelee, Nathaniel 356

PARMENTER 561
Parmenter, Elizabeth 295, 570
Parmenter, Hannah 738
Parmenter, John 64, 144, 148, 202
Parmenter, Joseph 532
Parmenter, Joshua 827
Parmenter, Judith 199
Parmenter, Lydia 600
Parmenter, Mary 14, 63, 64, 120,
    131, 177, 651, 834
Parmenter, Robert 798
Parmenter, Sarah 88
PARMETER 561
PARMINTER 561
Parminter, Judith 199
PARNALL 561
Parne, Samuel 286
PARNEL 561
Parnel, Dorothy 286
PARNELL 561
Parnell, Joanna 320
Parnell, Mary 5
Parrat, Elizabeth 841
Parrat, Francis 732
Parrat, Martha 168
Parrat, Mary 654, 732
Parrat, Mercy 732
Parratt, Ann 420
Parratt, Faith 454
Parret, Judith 566
PARRIS 561 see PARISH
Parris, Elizabeth 765, 775
Parris, John 556
Parris, Mary 623
Parris, Robert 193
Parris, Thomas 616
Parrish, Hannah 308
PARROT 561
Parrot, Ann 507
Parrot, Faith 420, 683
PARROTT 561
Parrott, Elizabeth 237, 489
Parrott, Judith 191
PARRUCK 561
Parruck, Sarah 373
PARRY 561
Parry, Samuel 175
PARSELL 561
PARSEUAH 571
PARSHALL 561
Parsley, Richard 271
PARSLOW 561
PARSON 562
Parson, George 74
Parson, Mary 74
PARSONS 561, 562, 563, 585
Parsons, --- 624, 670
Parsons, Abigail 174, 277, 527,
    621
Parsons, Ann 617
Parsons, Anne 374
Parsons, Benjamin 461, 744
Parsons, Bethia 494, 820
Parsons, Bridget 766
Parsons, Elizabeth 235, 303, 374,
    695
Parsons, Esther 686
Parsons, Grace 32, 456
Parsons, Hannah 277, 306, 361,
    496
Parsons, Hugh 252
Parsons, John 508, 694
Parsons, Jonathan 351
Parsons, Mark 695
Parsons, Mary 23, 188, 254, 622,
    705, 824
Parsons, Puah 207
Parsons, Rachel 451, 768

Parsons, Ruth 79, 724, 846
Parsons, Sarah 226, 318, 459, 710
Parsons, Thomas 591
Parterage, Priscilla 590
Parteridg, Ruth 733
Partride, Mary 517
PARTRIDG 563
PARTRIDGE 563
Partridge, Ann 589, 702
Partridge, Bethia 203
Partridge, Deborah 4
Partridge, Elizabeth 10, 432, 665, 697, 733
Partridge, George 677
Partridge, Hannah 14, 315, 632
Partridge, John 96, 585
Partridge, Lydia 96
Partridge, Margery 495
Partridge, Margaret 699
Partridge, Mary 168, 236, 436, 490, 514, 677, 684
Partridge, Mehitable 236
Partridge, Mercy 168
Partridge, Nehemiah 315, 458
Partridge, Priscilla 590
Partridge, Rachel 147, 158, 203
Partridge, Rebecca 268
Partridge, Ruth 733
Partridge, Samuel 25, 310
Partridge, Sarah 12, 363, 402
Partridge, Tryphosa 796
Partridge, William 338, 702
PARUM 571
Pary, Susanna 484
PASCO 563
Pasco, John 165, 530
Pasco, Rachel 530, 671
Pasco, Ruth 131
Pasco, Sarah 332
PASMER 563
PASMORE 563 see POSMORE
Pasmore, Rebecca 243
Pasmore, William 243
PASON 565
Pason, Mary 133
PASONS 562
Pasque, Sarah 332
PASSANT 562
Passill, Mary 738
PATCH 563, 564
Patch, Agnes 35
Patch, Amis 35
Patch, Elizabeth 129, 735, 837
Patch, James 351
Patch, Mary 739
PATCHEN 564
Patchen, Jacob 329
Patchen, Joseph 409
PATCHING 564
PATEFIELD 564
Patefield, Rebecca 143
Patefield, Sarah 692, 717
Pateridg, Mary 168
Pateridg, Mercy 168
PATESHALL 564
Pateshall, Mary 297
PATEY 575
Patey, Thomas 59, 117
PATIENCE 564
Paton, Elizabeth 532
PATRE 575
PATRICK 564
Patrick, Daniel 261
Patrick, Mary 261, 261
Pattashall, Mary 297
PATTE 575
Patte, Thomas 59
PATTEE 575

PATTEFOR 575
PATTEN 564
Patten, Anna 238
Patten, Anne 238
Patten, Mary 327, 644
Patten, Mary Moody 527
Patten, Nathaniel 54, 182
Patten, Rebecca 207, 699
Patten, Sarah 838
Patten, Susannah 703
Patten, Thomas 235, 623
PATTERSON 564
Patterson, Elizabeth 689
Patterson, James 726
Patterson, Mary 606
PATTESHAL 564
PATTIN 564
Patty, Thomas 117
PAUL 564
Paul, --- 840
Paul, Abigail 7, 640, 834
Paul, Ann 656
Paul, Elizabeth 619, 737
Paul, Hannah 656
Paul, Margaret 546
Paul, Mary 154, 427
Paul, Richard 831
Paul, Samuel 746
Paul, Susanna 263
PAULE 564
Pauley, Leonara 520
PAULGRAVE 553
PAULING 564
Paulmer, Elizabeth 678
Paume, Elizabeth 678
Paxton, Wentworth 507
Payen, Phebe 550
PAYN 552
Payn, Elizabeth 749
Payn, Jane 729
PAYNE 552, 553
Payne, Elizabeth 340, 650
Payne, John 492
Payne, Lydia 529
Payne, Mary 219, 220, 279, 747
Payne, Sarah 8
Payne, Stephen 193, 814
Payne, William 105, 712
Paynton, Elizabeth 531
PAYSON 565
Payson, Ann 756
Payson, Edward 20
Payson, Elizabeth 105, 277
Payson, Joanna 481
Payson, Mary 133
Payson, Priscilla 821
Payson, Prudence 801
Payson, Samuel 466, 736
Payson, Sarah 277, 831
Payson, Susanna 133
PAYTON 575
Payton, Bezaleel 671
Payton, Mary 671
Payton, Sarah 462
PEABODY 565 see PABODIE
Peabody, Ann 186
Peabody, Anna 186
Peabody, Annis 638
Peabody, Deborah 515
Peabody, Elizabeth 209
Peabody, Francis 833
Peabody, Hannah 114, 614
Peabody, Hepzibah 612
Peabody, Jacob 573
Peabody, Jane 685
Peabody, John 522, 633
Peabody, Lydia 395, 572, 573
Peabody, Mary 213, 361, 834

Peabody, Rebecca 515
Peabody, Sarah 392, 680
Peabody, William 703
PEACE 584
Peace, Deliverance 472
Peace, Mary 137, 823
PEACH 565
Peach, Elizabeth 460
Peach, Hannah 92, 785
Peach, John 225
Peach, Margaret 225
Peach, Mary 835
Peache, Mary 639
PEACHIE 565
Peachie, Margaret 778
Peachie, Mary 639
PEACHY 565
PEACOCK 565, 567
Peacock, Deborah 155
Peacock, Mary 54, 500, 666
Peacock, Phebe 120
Peacock, Richard 672
Pead, Sarah 632
Peak, Dorcas 198
PEAKE 565, 567, 586
Peake, Ann 567
Peake, Christian 22
Peake, Christopher 189
Peake, Elizabeth 22
Peake, Hannah 773
PEAKES 565
PEAKS 565
PEAL 565
Peale, Elizabeth 673
Peame, Mary 96
PEARCE 582, 583, 584
Pearce, Abigail 466
Pearce, Alice 348
Pearce, Anne 90
Pearce, Elizabeth 179
Pearce, Exercise 420
Pearce, John 528, 702
Pearce, Martha 237
Pearce, Mary 110, 366, 371, 614, 723, 826
Pearce, Mercy 491, 752
Pearce, Samuel 398
Pearce, Sarah 425, 497, 670
Pearce, Susanna 110, 832
PEARD 565
Peard, Jane 667
Peard, Margaret 723
Peard, Richard 541
PEARL 565, 566
PEARLY 573
Pearly, Martha 167
PEARSALL 566
Pearsall, Henry 303, 820
Pearsall, Sarah 750
PEARSE 582, 583, 584
Pearse, Mary 611
Pearse, Ruth 442
Pearse, Sarah 712
Pearshall, Abigail 759
PEARSON 585
Pearson, Bethiah 137
Pearson, Dorcas 241, 378
Pearson, Elizabeth 387
Pearson, George 74, 129, 731
Pearson, John 241
Pearson, John (Dea.) 311
Pearson, Mary 74, 129, 241, 554, 741
Pearson, Phebe 347
Pearson, Rebecca 422
Pearson, Sarah 590, 750
PEARSONS 585
PEASE 566

Pease, Abigail 359
Pease, Deliverance 192
Pease, Elizabeth 766
Pease, John 191, 797
Pease, Jonathan 417
Pease, Margaret 797
Pease, Martha 24, 159
Pease, Mary 191, 563, 618, 811
Pease, Robert 358
Pease, Samuel 811
Pease, Sarah 224, 648, 712
Pease, Stephen 484
Pease, Susan 412
Pease, Susanna 412
Pease, William 191
PEASLEE 566
PEASLEY 566
Peasley, Jane 206
Peasley, Joseph 208
Peasley, Mary 654, 655
Peasley, Sarah 43
PEASLY 566
Peasly, Mary 812
PEASON 585
PEAT 566, 567
Peat, Benjamin 567
Peat, Elizabeth 564
Peat, Hannah 772
Peat, John 103
Peat, Sarah 447
PEATHER 567
Peather, Ann 683
Peavis, Sarah 226
Pebody, Hepzibah 612
PECAKE 565
PECK 567, 568
Peck, Abigail 14, 25
Peck, Ann 494
Peck, Anna 494, 552, 701
Peck, Anne 494, 552, 701
Peck, Bathsheba 685
Peck, Deborah 696
Peck, Ebenezer 196
Peck, Elizabeth 18, 268, 309, 357,
    371, 390, 391, 392, 495, 505,
    600, 792
Peck, Elizabeth Beers Goodin 311
Peck, Esther 100
Peck, Faith 413, 772
Peck, Hannah 16, 387, 540, 614,
    668
Peck, Henry 476
Peck, John 698
Peck, Joseph 124, 181, 389
Peck, Martha 65, 184, 397
Peck, Mary 2, 16, 17, 147, 226,
    403, 539, 686
Peck, Mary 794
Peck, Mehitable 804
Peck, Patience 87, 477
Peck, Rachel 597
Peck, Rebecca 377, 552
Peck, Ruth 24, 40, 54, 326
Peck, Samuel 404
Peck, Sarah 155, 302, 303, 645
Peck, Stephen 514, 821
Peck, William 385
Peckar, Mary 795
PECKE 567, 568
Pecke, Esther 824
Pecke, Hannah 614
PECKER 568
PECKHAM 568
Peckham, Deborah 730
Peckham, Elizabeth 791
Peckham, Judith 155
Peckham, Mary 434
Peckham, Phebe 754, 782

Peckham, Rebecca 697
Peckham, Sarah 763, 791
Peckham, Thomas 160
Pecock, Ann 734
Peddy, Elizabeth 556
PEDERICK 568
Pederick, Elizabeth 619
Pederick, Joanna 177
Pederick, Miriam 365, 773
PEDLEY 568
PEDLY 568
PEDOM 569
Pedrick, Agnes 699
Pedrick, Ann 45, 74, 561
Pedrick, Mary 561
Pedrick, Sarah 544
Pedricke, Sarah 99
PEEK 565
PEELEY 569
PEELOM 569
Peelom, John 573
Peelom, Mary 573
PEERCE 583
Peerson, Mary 120
Peery, Elizabeth 307
PEET 566, 567
Peet, Sarah 447
PEETERS 574
Peeters, Andrew 421
Peeters, Elizabeth 646
PEGG 568
PEGGE 568
PEIRC 583
PEIRCE 582, 583, 584
Peirce, Ann 770
Peirce, Anna 810
Peirce, Daniel 511
Peirce, Elizabeth 514, 727
Peirce, Martha 541
Peirce, Mary 168, 338
Peirce, Persis 295, 668
Peirce, Rebecca 207
Peirce, Richard 89
Peirce, Sarah 514
PEIRE 605, 762
PEIRS 583
PEIRSE 583
PEIRSON 585
Peirson, Mary 622
Peirson, Tabitha 311
Peirsse, Judith 653
PEISE 566
PELHAM 568, 569
Pelham, Herbert 344
Pelham, Penelope 61, 829
PELL 569
Pell, Ann 740
Pell, Anna 740
Pell, Anne 740
Pell, Eleanor 89, 420
Pell, Elizabeth 800
Pell, Ellen 89, 780
Pell, Hannah 801
Pell, Joseph 241, 363, 511
Pell, Margaret 546
Pell, Mary 298
Pell, Thomas 96
PELLATE 569
PELLET 569
Pellet, Sarah 764
PELLETT 569
Pellot, Mary 78
Pelom, John 573
Pelom, Mary 573
PELTON 569
Pelton, Katherine 684
Pelud, Kertland 381
PEMBER 569

Pember, Thomas 346
PEMBERTON 569
Pemberton, Deborah 438
Pemberton, Elizabeth 245, 248,
    560
Pemberton, Hannah 246
Pemberton, John 308, 841
Pemberton, Joseph 511
Pemberton, Mary 42
Pemberton, Sarah 245, 300, 560,
    634
Pemington, Sarah 639
PENANT 570
PENDER 569
PENDERSON 569
PENDLETON 569
Pendleton, Ann 105
Pendleton, Caleb 691
Pendleton, Dorothy 186
Pendleton, Eleanor 775
Pendleton, Hannah 125, 682
Pendleton, Judith 691
Pendleton, Mary 100, 194, 271,
    518
PENEWELL 570
Penewell, Joseph 571
Penewell, Martha 571
Penewell, Mercy 571
PENEY 570
PENFIELD 569
Penfield, Jonathan 412
Penfield, Mary 256
PENGILLY 569
PENGRY 587
Pengry, Hannah 211
Pengry, Lydia 121
Pengry, Sarah 210
PENHALLOW 569
Peniman, Hannah 334
Peniman, James 814
Penley, Mary 31
PENN 569, 570
Penn, Christian 70, 240
Penn, Elizabeth 340
Penn, Hannah 751
Penn, James 667, 751
Pennan, Sarah Sibley 236
PENNANT 570
PENNEL 570
Pennel, Walter 49
PENNELL 570
Pennell, Alice 283
Pennell, Anne 516
Pennell, Mary 367
Penney, Nathaniel 576
Penniger, Robert 475
PENNIMAN 570
Penniman, Abigail 134
Penniman, Bethiah 11
Penniman, Elizabeth 521
Penniman, Hannah 652
Penniman, Joseph 714
Penniman, Lydia 3
Penniman, Mary 33, 552
Penniman, Rebecca 274
Penniman, Sarah 629
PENNINGTON 570
Pennington, Mary 747
PENNOYER 570
Pennoyer, Eleanor 616
PENNY 570
Penny, Cicely 144
Penny, Eleanor 616
Penny, Jane 434
Penny, Joane 434
Penny, Thomas 89
PENNYWELL 570
Penoir, Martha 621

PENOYER 570
Penoyer, Martha 621
Penoyer, Robert 656
Pense, Deborah 370
Penster, Jane 389
PENTICOST 570
Penticost, John 452
Penuel, Alice 283
Penwell, Alice 283
Penwell, Walter 49
Penwill, Anne 516
Penwill, Hannah 787
PENY 570
PENYON 570
PEPPER 570
Pepper, Alice 157
Pepper, Bethia 206
Pepper, Elizabeth 255
Pepper, Joseph 660
Pepper, Mary 255
Pepper, Sarah 494
PEPPERELL 570, 571
Pepperell, --- 247
Pepperell, William 583
PERCIVAH 571
PERCIVAL 573
Percival, James 50
Percival, Sarah 464
PERCY 571, 583 see PIERCE
PERDUE 571
Perham, Lydia 811
Perham, Sarah 659
Perham, William 570
PERIE 571
PERIGO 571
Perigo, Marah 574
Perigo, Mary 574
Perigo, Robert 574
Perigoe, Sarah 641
Periman, Elizabeth 515
Periment, Elizabeth 160
Perkin, Mary 79
PERKINS 571, 572
Perkins, Abigail 273
Perkins, Abraham 214, 688
Perkins, Ann 223
Perkins, Beamsley 305
Perkins, Catherine 33
Perkins, David 832
Perkins, Dorothy 630
Perkins, Edmund 395, 678
Perkins, Elisha 749
Perkins, Elizabeth 10, 80, 228,
  469, 528, 609, 635, 651, 800
Perkins, Frances 303
Perkins, Hannah 577, 626, 787,
  839, 840
Perkins, Jacob 630, 752
Perkins, John 386, 482, 500, 735,
  807
Perkins, Jonathan 648
Perkins, Judith 108, 651
Perkins, Luke 179
Perkins, Lydia 63, 779
Perkins, Marah 1
Perkins, Mark 572
Perkins, Martha 95, 409, 449
Perkins, Mary 1, 19, 90, 147, 265,
  292, 308, 395, 524, 607, 679,
  795
Perkins, Mercy 144
Perkins, Phebe 749
Perkins, Phillipa 251
Perkins, Phillis 251
Perkins, Rebecca 269, 406
Perkins, Rhoda 576
Perkins, Sarah 92
Perkins, Susanna 290

Perkins, Susannah 126
Perkins, Thomas 303
PERKS 572
PERLEY 572, 573
Perley, Martha 167
Perley, Ruth 654, 762
Perley, Sarah 17, 786
Perley, Thomas 167, 395, 565
PERLY 572, 573
Perly, Sarah 786
Perman, Sarah Sibley 236
Perme, Mary 96
PERMORT 594
Perne, Rachel 612
Perne, Thomas 612
PERRAM 571
Perre, Margaret 418
Perre, Margart 58
PERREN 573
Perren, Anna 615
Perren, Anne 615
Perren, Hanna 615
Perren, Hannah 615
Perren, Mary 546
Perrey, Mary 433
PERRIMAN 573
Perriman, Frances 16, 201
Perriman, Rebecca 274
PERRIN 569, 573
Perrin, Dorothy Rowleson 640
Perrin, John 569, 573
Perrin, Mary 409, 573, 623
Perrin, Mehitable 624
Perrin, Mehittabel 16
Perrin, Thomas 288
Perring, Mary 623
Perring, Mehitable 624
PERRY 573, 574
Perry, Abiah 116
Perry, Ann 841
Perry, Ann Sheffield 666
Perry, Anna 351, 841
Perry, Arthur 304, 779
Perry, Deborah 301, 344, 485,
  593, 613, 758
Perry, Dorcas 240
Perry, Elizabeth 104, 121, 307,
  341, 380, 495
Perry, Esther 122, 350
Perry, Hannah 221
Perry, Margaret 283
Perry, Mary 228, 351, 483, 690,
  718, 801, 828
Perry, Michael 95
Perry, Nathaniel 329
Perry, Obadiah 750
Perry, Peace 526, 527
Perry, Richard 535
Perry, Sarah 209, 681, 718, 724
PERSEVALL 571
PERSON 561, 562, 585
Person, Mary 36
PERSONS 562
Persons, Sarah Cole 730
PERUM 571
PESHALL 566
PESTER 574
Petee, John 549
PETENGALL 575
Petengall, Joanna 528
PETERS 574
Peters, Andrew 421, 814
Peters, Christina 743
Peters, Elizabeth 844
Peters, Mary 144
Peters, Mercy 11
Peters, Richard 11
Peters, Samuel 605

Petersfield, Philip 539
PETERSON 574
Peterson, --- 174
Petersoh, Henry 571
Peterson, Joseph 227
PETHERICK 568
Petherick, Mary 659
Pett, Margaret 253
Pette, Rebecca 223
Pettee, Mary Taylor 621
Pettee, Rebecca 223, 575
PETTENGAILE 575
PETTES 575
PETTIBONE 575
Pettibone, Rebecca 380
Pettibone, Sarah 402, 510
PETTIFORD 575
Pettigrew, Francis 339
PETTINGALE 575
PETTINGELL 575
Pettingill, Joanna 528
Pettingill, Mary 3
PETTIS 589
Pettis, Jane 847
Pettis, Peter 332
PETTIT 575
Pettit, Bethia 508
Pettit, Hannah 266
Pettit, Martha 56
Pettit, Mary 56, 516
Pettit, Mercy 56
Pettit, Thomas 516
PETTY 574, 575
Petty, John 549
Petty, Mary 731
Petty, Mary Taylor 621
PEVERLY 575
Peverly, Martha 537
PEYTON 575
Peyton, Bezaleel 550
PHAREZ 575
PHARISS 575
PHARUS 575
Phele, Sarah 525
PHELPS 575, 576
Phelps, Abigail 15, 490, 562, 764,
  827
Phelps, Dorothy 436
Phelps, Eleanor 144
Phelps, Elizabeth 8, 38
Phelps, Ephraim 182
Phelps, George 160, 217
Phelps, Hannah 31, 436
Phelps, Henry 755
Phelps, Isaac 522
Phelps, Jacob 637
Phelps, John 476
Phelps, Joseph 434, 647
Phelps, Mary 3, 40, 162, 163, 389,
  610, 686
Phelps, Mercy 40
Phelps, Nathaniel 182
Phelps, Samuel 587
Phelps, Sarah 371, 486, 515, 587,
  769
PHENIX 580
Phenix, Abigail 104
Phenix, Ann 830
PHETTEPLACE 576
Phetteplace, Sarah 123
Pheza, Mary 560
Phiffen, Sarah 36
Philberd, Mary 364
Philbrack, Martha 89
PHILBRICK 576, 577
Philbrick, Apphia 373
Philbrick, Bethia 571
Philbrick, Elizabeth 66, 147, 295,

Philbrick, Elizabeth (cont.) 631
Philbrick, Esther 56
Philbrick, Hannah 463, 648
Philbrick, James 492
Philbrick, Jane 189
Philbrick, Judith 667
Philbrick, Martha 140, 481
Philbrick, Mary 463, 756, 776
Philbrick, Thomas 805
Philbrook, --- 335
Philbrook, Hannah 660, 774
Philbrook, Martha 89
Philbrook, Mary 571
Philips, Samuel 499, 820
Philips, Sarah 507
Philips, Theophilus 598
Philley, Hannah 344.
PHILLIPS 576, 577, 578, 579
Phillips, --- 359
Phillips, Abiell 42
Phillips, Abigail 77, 239, 307, 496,
    777, 796, 836
Phillips, Alice 157, 711
Phillips, Ann 454, 521
Phillips, Anna 454
Phillips, Anne 88, 521
Phillips, Annis 521
Phillips, Barbara 411
Phillips, Eleazer 69
Phillips, Elizabeth 8, 38, 72, 246,
    255, 328, 363, 565, 723, 774
Phillips, Experience 439
Phillips, George 755
Phillips, George (Rev.) 793
Phillips, Hannah 16, 19, 88, 521,
    530, 542, 569, 804
Phillips, Henry 19, 255
Phillips, Israel 2
Phillips, Jacob 604
Phillips, James 307, 559
Phillips, Jane 407
Phillips, Jemima 124
Phillips, Joanna 542
Phillips, John 89, 227, 319, 324,
    382, 511, 747
Phillips, John (Hon.) 7
Phillips, Margaret 682
Phillips, Martha 792
Phillips, Mary 194, 246, 264, 292,
    307, 402, 415, 455, 527, 532,
    565, 580, 586, 606, 776
Phillips, Mary Haughton 539
Phillips, Mary Houghton 711
Phillips, Mehitable 350, 653
Phillips, Michael 411
Phillips, Moses 313
Phillips, Nicholas 642
Phillips, Phebe 304
Phillips, Rebecca 473
Phillips, Richard 440
Phillips, Samuel 164
Phillips, Sarah 324, 415, 658, 685,
    758, 814
Phillips, Thomas 38, 774
Phillips, Timothy 682
Phillips, William 650, 701
Phillips, Zerubbabel 805
Philly, Margaret 470
PHILPOT 579
Philpot, William 403
PHILPOTT 579
PHINNEY 579, 580
Phinney, Hannah 522
Phinney, John 166
Phinney, Thomas 57
PHINY 580
PHIPENY 580
PHIPP 580

PHIPPEN 580
Phippen, Ann 6, 637, 801
Phippen, Benjamin 419
Phippen, David 6, 400
Phippen, Elizabeth 181, 580, 695
Phippen, Gamaliel 580
Phippen, Hannah 301
Phippen, Joseph 659, 695
Phippen, Judith 358, 675
Phippen, Mary 252, 659, 669, 776
Phippen, Mehitable 158, 275
Phippen, Rebecca 36, 155, 669,
    767
Phippen, Sarah 252, 308, 354,
    378, 680, 845
Phippen, Thomas 298, 308
Phippeney, Mary 669
PHIPPENY 580
Phippeny, Elizabeth 181
Phippeny, Mehitable 158
Phippeny, Rebecca 604
Phippeny, Sarah 36
PHIPPS 580
Phipps, Anne 381
Phipps, Bethiah 143
Phipps, Elizabeth 640
Phipps, James 805
Phipps, Jane 250
Phipps, Joane 250
Phipps, Margaret 17, 338
Phipps, Mary 805, 813
Phipps, Samuel 164, 461
Phipps, Solomon 541, 664
Phipps, Thomas 201
PHIPS 580
Phips, William 401
PHOENIX 580
Phoenix, Abigail 104
Phoenix, Elizabeth 250
Pichon, Mary 79
Pick, Obadiah 292
Pick, Sarah 712
PICKARAM 581
PICKARD 580, 581
Pickard, Ann 478, 587
Pickard, Hannah 92
Pickard, Jane 361
Pickard, John 72
Pickard, Mary 585
Pickard, Rebecca 580
Pickard, Samuel 420
Pickard, Sarah 340
PICKE 586
Picke, Sarah 719
PICKERAM 581
PICKERIN 581
PICKERING 581 see PICKERAM
Pickering, Abigail 185, 496
Pickering, Amy 496
Pickering, Ann 496
Pickering, Elizabeth 106, 211,
    438, 536, 674
Pickering, Jane 711
Pickering, John 117
Pickering, Mary 39, 589
Pickering, Rebecca 269, 612
Pickering, Sarah 128
PICKET 581
Picket, John 370
Picket, Mary 276, 663
Picket, Mercy 276
Picket, Rebecca 646
Picket, Sarah 396
PICKETT 581
Pickett, Elizabeth 357
Pickett, Elizabeth Keeler 357
Pickett, James 357
Pickett, John 152, 541

Pickett, Mary 396
Pickett, Rebecca 506
Pickett, Ruth 541
Pickett, Sarah 450
Pickham, Elizabeth 730
Pickham, Sarah 322
Pickham, Susanna 41
Pickham, Susannah 41
PICKLES 581
Pickles, Jonas 367, 638, 639
Pickles, Lydia 706
PICKMAN 581, 588 see PITMAN
Pickman, Bethia 674
Pickman, Hannah 652
Pickman, Martha 53
Pickman, Mary 95, 378
Pickman, Nathaniel 222, 238
Pickman, Sarah 499
Pickman, Susannah 272
Pickman, Tabitha 33, 263
Pickman, William 125
Picknell, Experience 674
PICKRAM 581
PICKRING 581
Pickring, Rebecca 269
PICKTON 582
Pickwith, Hannah 437
PICKWORTH 581, 582
Pickworth, Abigail 223
Pickworth, Ann 62
Pickworth, Hannah 437
Pickworth, Mary 51, 84
Pickworth, Rachel 673
Pickworth, Ruth 495
Pickworth, Samuel 496
Pickworth, Sarah 530
PICTON 582
PIDCOCK 582
PIDGE 585, 586
Pidge, Elizabeth Newcomb 251
Pidge, Martha 116
Pidge, Mary 835
Pidge, Sarah 506
Pidge, Thomas 835
PIER 582
PIERCE 582, 583, 584, 585, 604,
    605
Pierce, Abiah 633
Pierce, Abigail 379, 614, 712
Pierce, Alice 33
Pierce, Ann 810
Pierce, Anna 690
Pierce, Anne 135, 666
Pierce, Benjamin 335
Pierce, Bridget 469
Pierce, Christian 97
Pierce, Daniel 509
Pierce, Deborah 825
Pierce, Dorothy 482
Pierce, Ebenezer 742
Pierce, Elizabeth 37, 162, 198,
    277, 288, 536, 584, 616, 811,
    826
Pierce, Esther 521
Pierce, Exercise 420
Pierce, George 105, 521
Pierce, Hannah 186, 493, 690
Pierce, Hester 521
Pierce, Jacob 214, 234
Pierce, Joanna 319
Pierce, John 290, 490, 528, 690,
    801
Pierce, Jonathan 605
Pierce, Joseph 571, 828
Pierce, Joshua 444, 465, 769
Pierce, Judith 653, 722, 844
Pierce, Margaret 471
Pierce, Margery 238

Pierce, Mary 33, 214, 234, 322, 339, 366, 379, 417, 480, 552, 615, 658, 674, 758, 774, 805, 826
Pierce, Mehitable 633
Pierce, Mercy 491
Pierce, Michael 379, 712
Pierce, Michael (Capt.) 11
Pierce, Nathaniel 277, 811
Pierce, Nehemiah 523
Pierce, Perses 347
Pierce, Persis 97, 469
Pierce, Rachel 567
Pierce, Rebecca 207, 824
Pierce, Ruth 241, 442
Pierce, Sarah 92, 380, 660
Pierce, Thomas 544
Piere, Margaret 418
PIERPONT 585
Pierpont, Elizabeth 30
Pierpont, Experience 359
Pierrepont, Mary 354
Pierse, Persis 610
PIERSON 561, 585
Pierson, --- 340
Pierson, Abigail 205
Pierson, Deborah 356
Pierson, Grace 442
Pierson, Hannah 277, 481, 804
Pierson, Henry 271
Pierson, Joseph 182
Pierson, Mary 36, 196, 622
Pierson, Mercy 72
Pierson, Sarah 613, 761
Pierson, Stephen 390
Pierson, Susanna 61, 71
Pierson, Susannah 37
PIGG 585, 586
Pigg, Alice 418
Pigg, John 251
Pigg, Margaret 740
Pigg, Mary 835
Pigg, Robert 418, 740
Pigg, Thomas 835
PIKE 586
Pike, Anna 268
Pike, Dorothy 365, 444, 465, 583
Pike, Elizabeth 137
Pike, Hannah 27, 38, 268
Pike, Isadel 271
Pike, Israel 755
Pike, Ja-- 271
Pike, Jeeral 755
Pike, Jeremiah 42
Pike, John 270, 468
Pike, Justina 564
Pike, Martha 25
Pike, Mary 11, 17, 520, 841
Pike, Richard 77, 607
Pike, Robert 309, 386
Pike, Ruth 727
Pike, Sarah 90, 202, 440, 520, 636, 719
PILGRIM 586
Pilkenton, Elizabeth 412
PILKINGTON 586
Pilkington, Elizabeth 412
Pilkington, Mark 194
PILKINTON 586
Pillsbury, Deborah 254
Pillsbury, Mary 109
PILSBERRY 587
PILSBURY 586, 587
Pilsbury, Moses 841
Pilsbury, Susannah 391
Pimbrook, Frances 510
PIMM 608
PINCEN 588

Pincen, Joanna 739
PINCHEN 587
PINCHEON 608
Pincheon, William 247
PINCKNEY 587
Pinckney, Abigail 546
Pinckney, Elizabeth 122
Pinckney, Jane 218
Pinckney, Rachel 569
Pinckney, Sarah 263
PINDAR 587 see PENDER
Pindar, Mary 493
PINDER 587
Pinder, Ann 170
Pinder, Elizabeth 476
Pinder, John 217, 588
Pindor, Joanna 197, 640, 651
PINE 587
PINGREY 587
PINGRY 587
Pingry, Moses 365
Pinhallow, Samuel 829
PINION 587
Pinion, Christian 229
Pinion, Mercy 484
Pinion, Ruth · 98, 516
PINKHAM 587
Pinkham, Amos 149
Pinkham, Elizabeth 471
PINKNEY 587
Pinkney, Hannah 581
PINNER 587
Pinner, John 136
PINNEY 587
Pinney, Abigail 4
Pinney, Mary 575, 719, 719
Pinney, Sarah 318, 576, 592
PINNION 587
Pinnion, Nicholas 219, 265
Pinnion, Ruth 516
Pinsen, Bathsheba 535
PINSENT 588
PINSON 587, 588
Pinson, Hannah 525, 798, 846
Pinson, Rebecca 67, 82
Pinson, Sarah 391
Pinson, William 82
PIPER 570, 588
Piper, Margaret 324
Piper, Nathaniel 839
Piper, Sarah 839
PIPPER 570
PIRHAM 571
PITCHER 588
Pitcher, Andrew 534
Pitcher, Experience 115
Pitcher, Frances 645, 778
Pitcher, Joanna 462
Pitcher, Johanah 462
Pitcher, Mary 511, 643
Pitcher, Nazareth 199
Pitcher, Ruth 534
PITCHMAN 581, 588
PITE 697
PITKIN 588
Pitkin, Elizabeth 489
Pitkin, Hannah 188
Pitkin, Martha 154, 833
PITMAN 581, 588 see PICKMAN
Pitman, --- 359
Pitman, Abigail 818
Pitman, Anna 728
Pitman, Anne Roberts 673
Pitman, Bethia 168, 674
Pitman, Elizabeth 149, 417, 444, 588, 643
Pitman, Ezekiel 217
Pitman, John 351

Pitman, Mary 95, 276, 378, 647
Pitman, Nathaniel 217, 222
Pitman, Sarah 215, 223, 231, 424, 499
Pitman, Tabitha 263
Pitman, Thomas 223, 276, 711
Pitman, William 125, 469
PITNEY 588
Pitney, Sarah 735
Pitt, Mary 453, 532
Pitt, Maud 644
PITTAM 588
PITTEY 575
Pittey, Mary 3
PITTICE 589
Pittington, Elizabeth 55
Pittis, Susanna 332
PITTMAN 588
Pittman, Francis 742
Pittman, Mary 548
Pittman, Susannah 272
PITTNEY 588
Pittom, Mary 174
PITTS 588, 589
Pitts, Ann 428
Pitts, Anne 239
Pitts, Deborah 358, 812
Pitts, Edmund 382
Pitts, Elizabeth 26, 380, 427
Pitts, Grace 549, 595
Pitts, Mary 116, 353, 453
Pitts, Peter 378
Pitts, Sarah 382
Pitts, William 14, 673
Pittsfield, Philip 234
PITTUM 588
Piverly, Thomas 314
PIXLEY 589
Pixley, Sarah 459
PIXLY 589
PLACE 589
Place, Joannah 589
Place, John 125, 589
Place, Sarah 178, 709
PLAINE 589
Plaine, William 560
PLAISE 589
PLAISTED 589
Plaisted, Abigail 563
Plaisted, Elizabeth 651
Plaisted, Frances 675
Plaisted, James 401, 655, 807
Plaisted, Mehitable 312
Plaisted, Roger 563, 827
PLANT 589
Plantaine, Phoebe 584
Planter, Elisha 409
PLASSE 589
Plasse, Alice 597, 792
Plasse, Joyce 784
Plasse, Rejoice 784
Plasse, William 784
PLATS 590
Plats, Elizabeth 101
Plats, Sarah 604
PLATT 589, 590
Platt, Elizabeth 111, 326, 685, 834
Platt, Hannah 175, 176
Platt, Martha 54
Platt, Mary 24, 134, 752, 810, 838
Platt, Phebe 752
Platt, Sarah 54, 111, 506
PLATTS 590
Platts, Abel 813
Platts, Ann 160, 651
Platts, Anna 160

Platts, Anne 651
Platts, Elizabeth 101, 221
Platts, Hannah 590
Platts, Mary 241
Platts, Samuel 261, 531
Platts, Sarah 92, 150, 604
Platts, Thomas 160, 339
PLAYSTEAD 589
PLIMBLY 590
PLIMLY 590
PLIMPTON 590
Plimpton, Elizabeth 645
Plimpton, Hannah 721
Plimpton, Jane 216
Plimpton, John 408
Plimpton, Mary 422
Plimpton, Mehitable 375
Plimton, Elizabeth 645
Plomer, Anne 377
Plomer, Hannah 82
Plomer, Jan 82
Plott, Mary 24
Plott, Robert 74
PLUM 590
Plum, Dorothy 604
Plum, Mercy 152
Plum, Robert 239
PLUMB 590
Plumb, Abigail 634
Plumb, Deborah 638
Plumb, Dorcas 480
Plumb, Elizabeth 368, 376
Plumb, John 686
Plumb, Mary 838
Plumb, Robert 270
PLUMBLEY 590
PLUMBLY see PLIMBLY
PLUME 590
PLUMER 590, 591
Plumer, Benjamin 261
Plumer, Deborah 415
Plumer, Elizabeth 412
Plumer, Francis 65, 133, 555
Plumer, Hannah 517
Plumer, Mary 43, 63, 148, 723
Plumer, Robert 673
Plumer, Ruth 361, 415
Plumer, Silvanna 431
Plumer, Thomas 251
PLUMLEY 590
PLUMLY 590
Plumly, Alexander 467
Plumly, Esther 830
Plumly, Hannah 467
Plumly, Hester 830
PLUMMER 590
Plummer, Ann 648
Plummer, Anne 648
Plummer, Lydia 521
Plympton, Elizabeth 469
Plympton, Hannah 345, 556
Plympton, Mary 714
Plympton, Mehitable 148
POAT 596
POCOCK 591
Pocock, Cordine 721
POCOCKE 591
Pococke, John 15
POD 591
PODD 591
PODGER 591
Podington, Elizabeth 177
PODYEARD 591
PODYER 591
POER 593
Poer, Mary 710
Poignes, Agnes 375
Poillon, Martha 711

POINDEXTER 606
Poke, Mary 206
POLAND 591, 598 see
    POULDON, POUSLAND
Poland, Hannah 34
Poland, James 44
Poland, John 222, 238
POLE 592
Pole, Bethesda 265
Pole, Mary 364
Polen, John 222
POLEY 591
POLIN 591, 598
Polin, John 238
POLL 591
Poll, Edward 385
Polland, Elizabeth 425
POLLARD 591
Pollard, Elizabeth 426
Pollard, Hannah 721
Pollard, Margaret 598
Pollard, Mary 443, 476
Pollard, Mercy 476
Pollard, Sarah 221, 222, 608
Pollard, William 598
POLLE 591
POLLEY 591
Polley, Bethiah 558
Polley, Elizabeth 577
Polley, John 573, 774
Polley, Mary 573
Polley, Sarah 307, 645
POLLY 591
Polly, Abigail 481
Polly, Elizabeth 107
Polly, George 664
Polly, Hannah 33, 197
Polly, John 255, 569
Polly, Mary 569
Polly, Susannah 793
Polter, Elizabeth 203
POMEREE 591
POMEROY 591, 592
Pomeroy, Abigail 659
Pomeroy, Eltweed 562
Pomeroy, Francis 59, 204, 459
Pomeroy, John 278, 480
Pomeroy, Joshua 35
Pomeroy, Medad 148, 537
Pomeroy, Mehitable 439
Pomeroy, Mindwell 439
Pomeroy, Rebecca Brookings 639
Pomeroy, Sarah 65
Pomeroy, Susanna 602
Pomeroy, Thankful 480
Pomeroy, Thomas 642
POMERY 592
POMFRET 592
Pomfret, Elizabeth 202
Pomfret, Martha 202
Pomfret, Thomas 195
Pommery, Thomas 642
Pomphret, Elizabeth 202
POMROY 591, 592
Pomry, Mary 27
POND 592
Pond, Abigail 153, 210
Pond, Hannah 217
Pond, Hannah Griffin 466
Pond, Mary 45, 74, 667
Pond, Mercy 511
Pond, Nathaniel 783
Pond, Rachel 714
Pond, Robert 247, 365, 667
Pond, Samuel 466
Pond, Sarah 153, 379, 396
Pond, Thankful 72, 832
PONDER 592

PONDERSON 607
Ponton, --- 259
Ponton, Mary 262
PONTUS 592
Pontus, Hannah 153, 624
Pontus, Mary 214, 305
Pooke, Mary 607
POOL 592, 593
Pool, Alice 734
Pool, Elizabeth 172, 475, 694
Pool, Mary 734
Pool, Sarah 230, 712
POOLE 591, 592, 593 see POLL
Poole, Alice 718
Poole, Ann 57
Poole, Bethesda 265
Poole, Elizabeth Dawes 385
Poole, John 836
Poole, Margaret 46
Poole, Mary 237, 364, 535
Poole, Matthew 75
Poole, Samuel 448
Poole, Sarah 39, 260, 672
Poole, William 253
POOLL 592, 593
Pooll, Jonathan 351
Pooll, Mary 244
Poop, Thankful 839
POOR 593
Poor, Abigail 409
Poor, Benjamin 343
Poor, Deborah 548
Poor, Elizabeth 491, 521
Poor, Hannah 202
Poor, John 212
Poor, Lucy 26
Poor, Martha 316
Poor, Mary 156, 710, 810
Poor, Priscilla 515
Poor, Ruth 707
POORE 593
Poore, Elizabeth 413
Poore, Hannah 409
Poore, Lydia 745
Poore, Mary 541, 585, 796, 810
Poore, Rebecca 684
Poore, Sarah 51, 575, 654
Pootter, Christian 498
POPE 593, 594
Pope, Alice 339
Pope, Damaris 115
Pope, Eleanor 509
Pope, Elizabeth George Glazer
    305
Pope, Hanna 115
Pope, Hannah 48
Pope, Jane 514, 527
Pope, Joanna 353
Pope, Mary 188, 509
Pope, Patience 75, 353
Pope, Samuel 829
Pope, Sarah 374, 398
Pope, Susanna 188, 512
Pope, Thankful 839
Pope, Thomas 471
Pope, Walter 509
Pople, Elizabeth 653
POPLEY 594
PORDAGE 594
Poretiers, Alice 526
PORMONT 594
PORMORT 594
Pormort, Elizabeth 538
Pormott, Elizabeth 5, 538
Pormott, Mary 5
Portadoe, Mary 703
PORTER 594, 595
Porter, --- 695

Porter, Abel 661, 675
Porter, Abigail 543, 675
Porter, Ann 107, 297, 776
Porter, Anna 297, 416, 776
Porter, Anne 297
Porter, Benjamin 656
Porter, Edward 313, 617, 742
Porter, Elizabeth 18, 281, 420, 529, 607
Porter, Eunice 150, 344, 681, 689
Porter, Ginger 457
Porter, Hannah 107, 171, 199, 221, 416, 473, 529, 814
Porter, Hezekiah 686
Porter, Joanna 510, 731
Porter, John 293, 368, 387, 543, 679
Porter, Lois 312
Porter, Mary 64, 67, 224, 294, 317, 397, 416, 472, 575, 576, 641, 641
Porter, Mehitable 312
Porter, Nathaniel 799
Porter, Rachel 187
Porter, Rebecca 73, 156, 473, 695, 696
Porter, Robert 283
Porter, Roger 669
Porter, Ruth 32, 197, 472, 689, 823
Porter, Samuel 535, 837
Porter, Sarah 16, 54, 230, 293, 429, 539, 656, 677, 827
Porter, Susanna 132, 599
PORTIS 595
Portis, Hannah 792
Portland, Dorothy 573, 640
Posbey, Cicely 404
POSMORE 595 see PASMORE
POST 595, 596
Post, Abraham 106, 234, 473
Post, Ann 653
Post, Anna 653
Post, Catharine 141, 371
Post Elizabeth 118, 226, 696
Post, Hannah 145
Post, Joseph 701
Post, Lydia 404, 515
Post, Margaret 2
Post, Martha 277
Post, Mary 114, 117, 327, 641
Post, Richard 97
Post, Sarah 327, 390, 768
Post, Thomas 653
Post, William 362
POTE 596
Pote, Arabella 807
Pote, Margaret 253
Pote, William 386
Poter, Roger 635
POTEY 596
Pottarton, Sarah 665
POTTER 596, 597
Potter, --- 445
Potter, Abigail 738
Potter, Ann 530
Potter, Bethia 832
Potter, Deliverance 321
Potter, Dorothy 7, 103
Potter, Edmund 72, 581
Potter, Edward 596
Potter, Elizabeth 272, 299, 342, 426, 438, 533
Potter, Emma 445
Potter, Eunice 287
Potter, George 537
Potter, Hannah 58, 76, 102, 127, 500, 627

Potter, Hope 629
Potter, Ichabod 525
Potter, Isabel 114, 523
Potter, John 173, 557, 637, 644
Potter, Joseph 637
Potter, Judith 266
Potter, Luke 103
Potter, Lydia 607
Potter, Mary 45, 53, 58, 88, 249, 469, 486, 644, 713, 814
Potter, Nicholas 792
Potter, Phebe 554
Potter, Rebecca 5, 30, 285, 299, 442, 762
Potter, Robert 650
Potter, Ruth 412
Potter, Samuel 88, 654, 832
Potter, Sarah 77, 259, 274, 650, 665, 794
Potter, Susanna 19, 328
Potter, Susannah 551
Potter, William 94, 318, 549
POTTLE 597
POTTS 597
Potts, Joanna 69
Potts, Patience 569
Potts, Richard 209
Potts, Thomas 417, 438, 843
POTWIN 597
POTWINE 597
POULDON 598 see POLAND
POULTER 597, 598
Poulter, --- 142
Poulter, Hannah 232
Poulter, John 557, 810
Poulter, Mary 557, 829
Poulter, Rachel 109
POUSLAND 598
POUSLIN 598
POUSLY 598
Pously, Dorothy 191
Pously, Richard 191
POUTLAN 598
Pow, Elizabeth 225
POWELL 598
Powell, Abigail 395, 818
Powell, Ann 57
Powell, Elizabeth 111, 276, 381, 745
Powell, Hannah 761
Powell, Jane 543
Powell, Joanna 568
Powell, John 77
Powell, Margaret 358
Powell, Mary 246, 649, 731, 815, 842
Powell, Michael 358, 381
Powell, Priscilla 737
Powell, Ralph 161
Powell, Sarah 236
Powell, Sarah Morrill 551
Powell, Thomas 579, 591
POWENING 598
POWER 598
Power, Hope 155
Power, Hopestill 155
Power, Nicholas 819
Power, Sarah 156
POWERS 598
Powers, Isaac 829
Powers, Mary 800
POWLAND 598
Powle, Ann 57
POWLING 598
POWLLEN 598 see POLAND, POULDON
Powllen, James 44
POWLTON 598

POWNALL 598
Pownell, Henry 459
POWNING 598
Powning, Elizabeth 97
POWSLAND 598
Powsland, Dorothy 191
Powsland, Elizabeth 155
Powsland, Mary 225
Powsland, Richard 191
Powsland, Susanna 622
Powsland, Thomas 187
POWSLEY 598
Powter, Mary 829
Powyes, Jane 380
Powys, Jane 380
PRANCE 604
Pranket, Thomas 514
Prat, Hannah 132
Prat, Sarah 736
Pratly, Eleanor 679
Pratly, Elnell 679
Pratly, Hellena 679
PRATT 598, 599, 600
Pratt, --- 545
Pratt, Aaron 196
Pratt, Abial 68
Pratt, Abigail 68, 336, 744
Pratt, Agnes 696
Pratt, Ann 807
Pratt, Anna 807
Pratt, Anne 78
Pratt, Barsheba 641
Pratt, Bathsheba 620, 641
Pratt, Benajah 453, 665
Pratt, Bethia 604
Pratt, Bethiah 138
Pratt, Deliverance 749
Pratt, Delivered 749
Pratt, Dorothy 809
Pratt, Elizabeth 29, 69, 146, 159, 312, 355, 465, 473
Pratt, Experience 53
Pratt, Grace 236
Pratt, Hannah 154, 241, 375, 391, 627, 664, 695, 697, 809
Pratt, Hepzibah 286
Pratt, John 78, 295, 646
Pratt, Jonathan 336
Pratt, Joseph 621
Pratt, Joshua 224
Pratt, Lydia 442
Pratt, Mabel 489
Pratt, Margaret 546
Pratt, Marie 814
Pratt, Martha 54, 599
Pratt, Mary 13, 329, 573, 650, 677, 686, 722, 760, 807, 809, 814
Pratt, Matthew 13, 809
Pratt, Matthew (Jr.) 807
Pratt, Mehitable 665
Pratt, Mercy 382, 573
Pratt, Merriam 600
Pratt, Nathaniel 817
Pratt, Persis 200
Pratt, Peter 57, 633
Pratt, Philip 534
Pratt, Phineas 382
Pratt, Priscilla 126
Pratt, Rachel 677
Pratt, Samuel 32, 180, 833
Pratt, Sara 275
Pratt, Sarah 232, 275, 576, 598, 621, 783, 844
Pratt, Susanna 504
Pratt, Thomas 144, 463
Pratt, Timothy 547
Pratt, Wm. 560

Pratty, Eleanor 679
Pratty, Elnell 679
Pratty, Hellena 679
PRAY 600, 601
Pray, Dorothy 274, 734
Pray, Hannah 61, 530
Pray, Joanna 61
Pray, John 201, 469, 580
Pray, Mary 839
Pray, Richard 362
Prebble, Mary 241
Prebble, Nathaniel 137
PREBLE 601
Preble, Hannah 123
Preble, Joseph 846
Preble, Nathaniel 137
Preble, Sarah 180, 556
Preble, Stephen 135
Precious, Mary 386
Predy, Elizabeth 298
PRENCE 601, 604
Prence, Elizabeth 394
Prence, Hannah 694
Prence, Jane 692
Prence, Mary 751
Prence, Mercy 283
Prence, Rebecca 283
Prence, Sarah 394
Prence, Thomas 283, 394
PRENTICE 601, 602
Prentice, Abigail 717
Prentice, Elizabeth 8, 175, 787
Prentice, Esther 292
Prentice, Frances 554
Prentice, Grace 544
Prentice, Hannah 285
Prentice, Henry 300
Prentice, Hester 292
Prentice, John 81, 87
Prentice, Mary 340
Prentice, Sarah 684, 839
Prentice, Thomas 215
PRENTIS 601
PRENTISE 601
PRENTISS 601
Prentiss, Ann 390
Prentiss, Valentine 785
Presberry, John 141
Presberry, Katherine 141
PRESBURY 602
Presbury, John 141
Presbury, Katherine 141
Presbury, Mary 395
Prescot, Mary 314
PRESCOTT 602
Prescott, Abigail 85
Prescott, Dorothy 766
Prescott, Elizabeth 279, 320
Prescott, James 202
Prescott, John 392
Prescott, Jonathan 109, 115, 162, 425
Prescott, Lydia 46, 256
Prescott, Mary 171, 258, 391, 654
Prescott, Rebecca 648, 808
Prescott, Sarah 620, 801
PRESSE 602
Pressee, Hannah 702
PRESSEY 602
Pressey, Hannah 702
PRESSIE 602
PRESSON 602, 603, 605
Presson, John 615
PRESTON 602, 603, 605
Preston, Abigail 680, 735
Preston, Eliaseph 514
Preston, Elizabeth 15, 23, 70, 365, 431, 458, 567, 805, 831

Preston, Hannah 198, 431, 438
Preston, Jehiel 398
Preston, John 385, 615
Preston, Joseph 707
Preston, Mary 136, 163, 260, 410, 412, 417, 484, 504
Preston, Rebecca 764
Preston, Roger 385
Preston, Samuel 78, 475
Preston, Sarah 257, 501
Preston, William 438
PRETIONS 603
PRICE 603
Price, Anne 167
Price, Eleanor 569
Price, Elizabeth 43, 192, 469, 641, 749
Price, Hannah 767
Price, Joan 161
Price, John 276, 478
Price, Mary 234, 539, 679
Price, Philip 73
Price, Philip John 73
Price, Richard 767
Price, Robert 265
Price, Sarah 563, 573
Price, Susannah 326
Price, Theodore 92
Price, William 603
PRICHARD 605
Prichard, Alice 92
Prichard, Benjamin 75
Prichard, Elizabeth 11
Prichard, Hannah 475, 793
Prichard, Jane 470
Prichard, Joan 470
Prichard, Joanna 470
Prichard, Mary 724
Prichard, Richard 82
Prichard, Sarah 475
Prichard, William 118
PRID 603
PRIDE 603
Pride, Elizabeth 175, 727
Pride, Mary 476
PRIDEAUX 603
PRIDEUX 603
Prier, Hannah 287
PRIEST 603
Priest, Degory 307, 768
Priest, Deliverance 734
Priest, Elizabeth 22, 381
Priest, Hannah 645
Priest, James 645
Priest, John 303
Priest, Martha Stanbury 186
Priest, Mary 600, 758
Priest, Sarah 180
Priest, William 271
PRIME 604
Prime, Samuel 92
Prime, Sarah 605
PRIMRADOES 604
PRIMVADOES 604
Prin-, Edmund 645
PRINCE 604
Prince, Ann 409
Prince, Bethiah 407
Prince, Deborah 440
Prince, Elizabeth 474, 607
Prince, Hannah 500
Prince, James 577
Prince, Joanna 474, 655
Prince, Job 36, 155
Prince, John 47
Prince, Jonathan 781
Prince, Judith 41, 756
Prince, Martha 85, 798

Prince, Mary 203, 212, 250, 297, 428, 639
Prince, Rebecca 607
Prince, Robert 546
Prince, Sarah 655
Prince, Thomas (Gov.) 158
PRINDLE 604
Prindle, Hannah 401, 507
Prindle, Mary 627
Prindle, Phebe 58
Prine, Rebecca 690
PRINGLE 604
Pringle, Mary 627
PRINGRIDAYS 604
PRIOR 583, 604, 605
Prior, Daniel 268
Prior, Elizabeth 261
Prior, Hannah 287
Prior, Marry 512
Prior, Mary 512, 763
Prior, Sarah 315
Prior, Susanna 786
Prise, Sarah 415
Prisse, Margery 238
PRISSON 605
PRITCHARD 605
Pritchard, Ann 732
Pritchard, Anne 522
Pritchard, Hannah 732
Pritchard, Jane 470
Pritchard, Joan 470
Pritchard, Joanna 470
Pritchard, Margery 559
Pritchard, Mary 755
Pritchard, Nathaniel 208
Pritchard, Richard 7, 62
Pritchard, Roger 678
PRITCHET 605
PRITCHETT 605
Pritchett, Esther 341
Pritchett, Hester 341
Proby, William 165
PROCKTER 605
PROCTER 605, 606
Procter, Elizabeth 767
Procter, Joseph 410
Procter, Martha 316
Procter, Mary 51, 548
Procter, Sarah 527
PROCTOR 605, 606
Proctor, Abigail 477, 766
Proctor, Benjamin 812
Proctor, Dorothy 45
Proctor, Elizabeth 12
Proctor, Hannah 477, 791
Proctor, James 557, 583
Proctor, John 621
Proctor, Martha 332, 805
Proctor, Mary 306
Proctor, Sarah 142, 224, 228, 527, 754
Proctor, Thorndike 252
PROUSE 606
PROUT 606
Prout, John 334
Prout, Love 252, 409
Prout, Mary 470
Prout, Timothy 324
Prout, William 279
PROUTY 606
PROVENDER 606
Provender, Hannah 599
Prower, Marie 492
Prowse, Abiell 218
Prowse, Abigail 218
Prowse, Abihail 218
PRUDDEN 606
Prudden, Abigail 398, 774

Prudden, Ann 171
Prudden, Anne 171
Prudden, Elizabeth 122, 605, 678
Prudden, Hasadiah 215
Prudden, Joanna 151, 262
Prudden, Mildred 36
Prudden, Peter 72, 818
Prudden, Peter (Rev.) 72
Prudden, Samuel 159
Prudden, Sarah 10
Pruddens, Mary 775
Prunchin, William 247
Prusent, Rebecca 67
PRYER 604
Pryer, Elizabeth 261
PRYNGRYDAYS 604
Pryngrydays, Edmund 645
PRYOR 604, 605
Pryor, Martha 181
Prythatch, Elizabeth 572
Prythold, Elizabeth 572
Pucke, Joanna 258
PUDDINGTON 607
Puddington, Agnes 413
Puddington, Mary 787
Puddington, Robert 318
Puddington, Sarah 570, 687
PUDEATER 606
Pudeater, Jacob 324
PUDEATOR 606
Pudester, Jane 194
Pudestor, Jacob 324
Pudley, Joanna 665
PUDNEY 606
Pudney, Judith 482
PUE 606
PUFFER 606
Puffer, Esther 721
Puffer, Jane 8
Puffer, Mary 74
Puffer, Matthias 191
Puffer, Rachel 253, 411
PUGH 606
Pulcefer, Elizabeth 162
Pulcipher, Susannah 721
PULLEN 606
Pullen, Joan 295
Pullen, Joane 295
Pullen, Richard 17, 281
Pullen, Susannah 330
PULLIN 606
PULLING 606
Pulling, Richard 17
PULLMAN 606
PULMAN 606
Pulman, Mary 524
Pulmmer, Hannah 51
PULSEFER 607
PULSEVER 607
PULSIFER 606
Pulsifer, Elizabeth 162, 602
PULSIPHER 606
PUMMERY 592
Pummery, John 278
PUMP 607
PUMRY 592
PUNCHARD 607 see PUNCHIN
PUNCHIN 608
PUNDERSON 607
Punderson, Hannah 300, 678
PURCHAS 607
Purchas, Elizabeth 261
Purchas, Mary 697
PURCHASE 607
Purchase, Aquila 544
Purchase, Elizabeth 139, 261
Purchase, Jane 554
Purchase, Joan 133, 554

Purchase, John 554, 695
Purchase, Mary 528, 537
Purchase, Priscilla 826
Purchase, Sarah 49, 301, 580
Purchase, Thomas 77, 261, 586, 786
Purches, Hannah 79
Purchis, Hannah 79
Purchis, Thomas 77
Purden, Alice 65
PURDUE 571
PURDY 607
Purdy, Francis 395
Purdy, Mary 104, 443
Purdy, Samuel 114
PURINGTON 607
Purington, Elizabeth 177
Purington, George 206
Purington, James 610
Purington, John 787
Purington, Mary 787
Purington, Robert 318
Purington, Sarah 570
Purkes, Jane 554
Purkes, Joan 554
Purkes, John 554
Purkess, Sarah Pemberton 634
PURKIS 560
Purkis, Sarah Pemberton 634
Purkis, Warner 245
PURMORT 594
Purmott, Elizabeth 5
Purmott, Mary 5
PURPLE 607
PURRIER 607
Purrier, Martha 548
Purrier, Mary 617
Purrier, Sarah 487
Purrier, William 617
PURRINGTON 607
PURRYER 607
PURSLEY 607
PURSLY 607
Pusey, Susanna 240
PUTNAM 607, 608
Putnam, Ann 751
Putnam, Benjamin 385
Putnam, Deliverance 832
Putnam, Elizabeth 32, 272
Putnam, Hannah 105
Putnam, Joseph 767
Putnam, Mary 757
Putnam, Pricilla 32
Putnam, Prudence 845
Putnam, Rebecca 288, 667
Putnam, Samuel 172
Putnam, Sarah 407
Putnam, Susannah 71
Putt, Henry 487
PYCHON 608
PYGAN 608
Pygan, Alexander 88
Pygan, Jane 322
Pygan, Sarah 337
PYM 608
PYNCHON 608
Pynchon, Ann 681
Pynchon, Hannah 726
Pynchon, Mary 385, 808
Pynchon, William 247, 650
PYNE 587
Pynshon, Margaret 209
Pynson, Rebecca 67

--- Q ---

QUACKEY 608
QUAKEE 608
QUARLES 608
Quarles, Joanna 456, 687
Quarles, Mary 268
QUELCH 608
Quemby, Lydia 381
Quemby, William 719
QUENBY 608
Quick, Apphia 283, 601
Quick, Elizabeth 159
QUIDDINGTON 608
Quillington, Abraham 221
QUILTER 608
Quilter, Mary 191, 388
Quilter, Sarah 451
Quimby, Deborah 308
Quimby, Lydia 217
QUINBY 608
Quinby, Elizabeth 15
Quinby, Lydia 381
Quinby, Martha 145
Quinby, William 719
QUINCY 608
Quincy, Edmund 247, 401, 552
Quincy, Elizabeth 312
Quincy, Experience 653
Quincy, Joanna 376
Quincy, Judith 400, 613
Quincy, Mary 652
Quincy, Ruth 403
QUINEY see QUINCY
QUINNEY 608
Quinsey, Daniel 268
Quynell, Ferris 125

--- R ---

R-, Hannah 658
Racer, Eleanor 384
RACHLIFFE 609
RACKET 609
Racket, Anna 138
RACKLEFF 609
RACKLEY 609
RACKLIFF 609
Rackliff, John 422
Rackliff, William 474
RADCLIFF 609
RADDAN 616, 624
RADLEY 609
RAE 612
Rae, Jemima 360
Raebourn, John 513
Raiement, Hannah 360
Raiment, Mary 175
Raine, Mary 704
Raine, Stephen 193
RAINGER 611
RAINSBORO 609
RAINSBOROUGH 609
Rainsborough, Judith 38, 830
Rainsborough, Martha 166, 167, 830
RAINSFORD 609
Rainsford, Ann 391
Rainsford, Anna 391
Rainsford, David 289
Rainsford, Dorothy 552
Rainsford, Elizabeth 265, 324
Rainsford, Jonathan 377
Rainsford, Mary 571
Rainsford, Ranis 59

Rainstorpe, Esther 519
RAISIN 609
RALCOME 35
RALEIGH 613
Rallings, Elizabeth 747
Rallock, Cecilia 266
RALPH 635
Ralph, Alice 262
Ralph, Elizabeth 65
Ralph, Sarah 62
Ralph, Thomas 421
Ralston, John 84, 830
RAMBLE 609
Ramesden, Hannah 494
Ramsay, Hannah 184
Ramsdel, Elizabeth 665
RAMSDELL 609
Ramsdell, Mary 681
RAMSDEN 609
Ramsden, Hannah 494
Ramsden, John 320, 527, 786
Ramsden, Priscilla 4
Ramsey, Mary 184
RAND 609, 610
Rand, Alice 473
Rand, Christian 458
Rand, Elizabeth 96, 334, 335, 570
Rand, Hannah 287, 444
Rand, Hannah Hett Hurry 406
Rand, Margaret 230
Rand, Mary 44, 119, 442
Rand, Nathaniel 138
Rand, Samuel 777
Rand, Sarah 334, 366, 807
Rand, Susanna 532
Rand, William 668
RANDALL 610, 611
Randall, Abigail 566
Randall, Anne 133
Randall, Dorcas 825
Randall, Elizabeth 165, 206, 483
Randall, Hannah 758, 780
Randall, Joanna 411
Randall, John 607
Randall, Joseph 772
Randall, Margery 538, 697
Randall, Mary 141, 578, 702
Randall, Mercy 440
Randall, Patience 341
Randall, Philury 575
Randall, Priscilla 602
Randall, Richard 76, 77
Randall, Sarah 169, 554, 799
Randall, Susan 653
Randall, Susannah 653, 664
Randall, Thomas 98
Randall, Walter 411
Randall, William 156, 317
Randalls, Abraham 441
Randell, Mary 47
Randell, Wilmot 242
Randolph, Elizabeth 608
RANES 613
RANGER 611
Ranger, Prudence 162
RANIER 613
RANKIN 611
Rankin, Andrew 127, 286
Rankin, Joseph 133, 433
Rankin, Mary 499
Rannals, Mary 650
RANNEY 611
Ranney, Elizabeth 781
Ranney, Esther 653
Ranney, Mary 653
Ranney, Mercy 347
Ransden, Mary 140
Ransford, Mary 634

RANSOM 611
Ransom, Mary 66
Ransome, Marsy 784
Ranson, Hannah 412
Ranstop, Esther 519
Ranstrope, Esther 488
RAPER 611
RASER 611
Raser, Richard 378
RASHLEY 611
RASLEIGH 611
Ratchel, Robert 616
RATCHELL 611
Ratchell, Ann 333
Ratchell, Mary 583
Ratchell, Robert 117
Ratchell, Ruth 118
Ratchell, Temperance 423
Ratcliff, Elizabeth 37
RATCLIFFE 609
RATHBONE 611
Rathbone, Margaret 513
Rathbone, Sarah 298, 512, 513
Rathbourn, Catherine 361
Rathburn, Catherine 797
Rathburn, Elizabeth 797
Ratleff, Elizabeth 37
RATLIFE 611
Ratlife, Elizabeth 37
Ratliff, Elizabeth 649
RATLIFFE 611
RATTLIFE 611
RATTONE 612
RATTOON 612
RAUNCE 612
RAVEN 612
Raven, Susan 503
Raven, Susanna 503
RAVENSCROFT 612
RAWDON 612
Rawlince, Nicholas 546
RAWLINGS 612
Rawlings, Caleb 533
Rawlings, Elizabeth 242, 639
Rawlings, Hannah 432
Rawlings, Jane 531
Rawlings, Joan 432
Rawlings, Joanna 432
Rawlings, John 252, 409
Rawlings, Mary 559
RAWLINS 612
Rawlins, Abigail 442
Rawlins, Elizabeth 747
Rawlins, Jasper 327
Rawlins, Nathaniel 842
Rawlins, Nicholas 546
Rawlins, Patience 202
Rawlins, Rebecca 713
Rawlins, Ruth 490
Rawlins, Sarah 444
Rawlins, Thomas 497, 770
RAWSON 612
Rawson, Mary 748
Rawson, Perne 104
Rawson, Rachel 25
Rawson, Rebecca 642
RAY 612, 613
Ray, Bethiah 316
Ray, Daniel 154
Ray, Dorothy 154
Ray, James 367
Ray, Mary 213, 434, 649
Ray, Sarah 358
Ray, Simeon 298
Ray, Simon 742
Ray, Sybil 649
Raye, Bethia 315
RAYLY 613

RAYMENT 613
Rayment, Bathsheba 180
Rayment, Hannah 487
Rayment, Mary 51
Rayment, Rachel 91
RAYMOND 613
Raymond, Abigail 303
Raymond, Anne 91
Raymond, Bathsheba 180
Raymond, Daniel 291
Raymond, Elizabeth 621
Raymond, Hannah 27, 115, 360,
    484, 487, 649
Raymond, Joshua 215
Raymond, Martha 609
Raymond, Mary 51, 144, 175
Raymond, Rachel 91
RAYNER 613
Rayner, Abigail 433
Rayner, Elizabeth 276, 420
Rayner, Esther 813
Rayner, Judith 280
Rayner, Mary 181, 813
Rayner, Samuel 798
Rayner, Thurston 158, 393
Rayner, William 302
RAYNES 613
Raynes, --- 497
Raynes, Francis 218
Raynes, Mary 502, 838
Raynes, Sarah 201, 332
Raynes, Tabitha 379
Raynolds, Mary 119
RAYNOLL 619
RAYNOR 613, 614
Raynor, Abigail 479, 637
Raynor, Eleanor 393
Raynor, Elizabeth 450
Raynor, Hannah 393, 655
Raynor, Joseph 393
Raynor, Mary 239
Raynsford, Mary 50
RAYSON 609
RAZOR 611
Razor, Richard 378
REA 612
Rea, Bethia 310, 475
Rea, Bethiah 316
Rea, Daniel 475
Rea, John 385
Rea, Rebecca 38, 388, 708
Rea, Sarah 358, 577, 604
Reacy, Phebe 596
READ 614, 615, 616
Read, Abigail 208, 720
Read, Christopher 323
Read, Edmund 574
Read, Elizabeth 96, 123, 135,
    699, 809, 817
Read, Esther 133
Read, Experience 451
Read, Hannah 189, 693
Read, John 216, 824
Read, Katherine 323
Read, Margaret 719
Read, Martha 253
Read, Mary 145, 496, 693, 747
Read, Rebecca 560, 828
Read, Remember 806
Read, Robert 602
Read, Sarah 41, 42, 179, 263, 337
Read, Susanna 688
Read, Susannah 167
Read, Thomas 496, 747, 835
Read, Thomas (Jr.) 110
Read, William 527, 548, 571, 688
Readaway, Rebecca 135
Readaway, Sarah 102

READE 614, 615, 616
Reade, Elizabeth 830
Reade, Lucy 553
Reade, Martha 674
Reading, Abigail 563
Reafes, Sarah 489
Reap, Thomas 117
REAPE 616
Reape, Samuel 619
Reape, Thomas 611
Reape, William 99
REASON 609
Reasons, Mary 622
Rebenson, Elizabeth 136
RECORD 616
Record, John 377
RECORDS 616
Redaway, John 289
Redaway, Martha 2
Redaway, Sarah 136
REDD 615
Redd, Thomas 310
REDDEN 624
REDDING 616, 624
Redding, Alice 753
Redding, Eleanor 463
Redding, Elizabeth 404
Redding, Mary 753
Redding, Rebecca 729
Redding, Ruth 226, 260
REDDINGTON 616
Reddington, John 93
Reddington, Mary 366
Reddington, Phebe 93
Reddit, Mary 426
Reddit, Susannah 259
REDDOCK 616
Reddock, Elizabeth 792
Reddock, Hannah 791
Reddock, Mary 354
REDDOUGH 616
Reddough, Jane 749
Reddough, Jean 749
Reder, Sarah 200
Rederick, John 328
Rederick, Miriam 328
REDEWAY 617
REDFIELD 616
Redfield, James 660
Redfield, Jane 706
Redfield, Jean 706
Redfield, Judith 608
Redfield, Lydia 32, 739
Redfield, Rebecca 627
Redfin, Judith 608
Redfin, Lydia 32
Redfin, Rebecca 627
REDFORD 616
Redford, Charles 759
Redford, William 671
REDIAT 616
Rediat, Deborah 709
Rediat, John 507, 825
Rediat, Mary 408
Rediat, Mehitable 542
Rediate, Susannah 259
REDING 616
REDINGTON 616
Redington, Edith 602
Redington, Elizabeth 602
Redington, Martha 315
Redington, Mary 196, 366
Redington, Phebe 267, 268
Redington, Sarah 547, 639
REDKNAP 616
Redknap, Hanna 536
REDLAND 625
Redland, Patience 130

REDMAN 616, 617, 632
Redman, Abial 313
Redman, Abiel 313
Redman, Ann 398, 624
Redman, Elizabeth 523
Redman, John 469, 492
Redman, Maria · 495
Redman, Mariah 495
Redman, Marie 495
Redman, Marion 495
Redman, Mary 495, 524, 688, 791
Redman, Marya 495
Redman, Mercy 688
REDNAP 616
Rednap, Sarah 454
REDWAY 617
Redway, Lydia 745
Redway, Martha 2
Redway, Mary 135
Redway, Rebecca 135
REDWOOD 617
REDYATE 616
REED 614, 615, 616
Reed, Abigail 623, 844
Reed, Agnes 237
Reed, Alice 237
Reed, Ann 252
Reed, Bathsheba 595
Reed, Bethiah 421
Reed, Elizabeth 200, 235, 268
Reed, Experience 449
Reed, Frances 545
Reed, George 620
Reed, Hannah 249, 809
Reed, Jane 537
Reed, Lydia 774
Reed, Margaret 447, 768
Reed, Martha 784
Reed, Mary 29, 237, 422, 475, 516, 572, 582, 747, 760, 768
Reed, Mehitable 135, 630
Reed, Mercy 809
Reed, Rebecca 558, 845
Reed, Ruth 809
Reed, Samuel 699
Reed, Sarah 334, 629, 633, 712, 749, 761, 775
Reed, Thomas 712
Reed, William 692, 720, 724
Reeder, Hannah 658
Reeder, Jacob 123
Reedman, Mary 688
Reedman, Mercy 688
Reese, Nicholas 206
REEVE 617
Reeve, ─── 219
Reeve, Abigail 744
Reeve, Anne 269
Reeve, Elizabeth 790
Reeve, Hannah 639, 718, 847
Reeve, Jane 540
Reeve, John 847
Reeve, Mary 432, 744, 790
Reeve, Sarah 504
Reeve, Thomas 205
REEVES 617
Reeves, Abraham 505
Reeves, Elizabeth 622
Reeves, Hannah 337, 718
Reeves, Margaret 796
Reeves, Margery 797
Reeves, Thomas 256
Reich, Elizabeth 40
Reich, Jasper 40
REINER 614
Reiner, Elizabeth 552
REITH 617
Reith, Abigail 499

Reith, Sarah 756
Relph, Elizabeth 65
RELZEA 617
REMICK 617
Remick, Hannah 316, 737
Remick, Jacob 377
Remick, Lydia 170
Remick, Mary 223
Remick, Sarah 321, 692, 832
REMINGTON 617, 618
Remington, Abigail 293
Remington, Daniel 237
Remington, Elizabeth 300, 705
Remington, Hannah 452
Remington, John 293, 313, 594, 742
Remington, Jonathan 626
Remington, Mary 58, 461
RENALDS 618
RENALS 618
Rendall, Anne 557
Rendle, Joseph 439, 463
Reneff, Thankful 117
RENER 613
Rennolds, Judith 66
RENOLDS 618, 619
RESCO 637
RESCOE 637
Resley, Mary 373
Resley, Richard 373
Resseguie, Jane 447
Rest, Nicholas 206
Retchell, Ruth 331
REVEDLY 618
REW 618, 733
Rew, Edward 774
Rew, John 539
Rew, Sarah Richmond 715
Rewe, Martha 174
Rex, Sarah Woodmancy 838
Rex, Thomas 269
Reycroft, Frances Pitcher 778
REYLEAN 618
Reyley, Sarah 260
Reynar, Mary 334
REYNELL 619
REYNER 613
Reyner, Abigail 104
Reyner, Ann 378
Reyner, Anna 450
Reyner, Dorothy 7
Reyner, Elizabeth 420, 552
Reyner, Hannah 450, 828
Reyner, Martha 803
Reyner, William 437
Reynes, Abigail 96
Reynia, Mary 813
Reynold, Katherine 702
REYNOLDS 618, 619
Reynolds, ─── 841
Reynolds, Ann 171
Reynolds, Deborah 29, 723
Reynolds, Elizabeth 263, 280, 418, 443, 480
Reynolds, Hannah 794
Reynolds, Hope 214, 652, 841
Reynolds, Hopestill 214
Reynolds, Jane Reeve 540
Reynolds, Jane 841
Reynolds, John 308
Reynolds, Judith 66
Reynolds, Lydia 508
Reynolds, Margaret 757
Reynolds, Mary 242, 475, 536, 650, 836
Reynolds, Mary Beach Mallory 484
Reynolds, Mercy 536

Reynolds, Rebecca 106, 127, 153, 378
Reynolds, Rebina 689
Reynolds, Ruth 810
Reynolds, Sarah 28, 80, 276, 495, 501, 596
Reynolds, Seaborn 378
Reynolds, Tabitha 2
Reynolds, William 214
Reynor, Deborah 656
Reynor, Elizabeth 552, 694
Rhoades, Abigail 532
Rhoades, John 827
Rhoads, Elizabeth 811
Rhoads, Jane 151
RHODES 619
Rhodes, --- 834
Rhodes, Dorothy 135
Rhodes, John 135, 396, 741, 784
Rhodes, Mary 108, 135, 477
Rhodes, Rebecca 598, 819
Rhodes, Ruth 180
Rhodes, Sarah 743
Rhodes, Zachariah 616
RIALL 640, 641
RIAN 645
Ricard, Sarah 582
RICE 206, 439, 619, 620, 621, 641
Rice, --- 621
Rice, Abigail 189, 274, 615, 690
Rice, Ann 295
Rice, Anna 117, 620
Rice, Bridget 772
Rice, Daniel 800
Rice, Deborah 653
Rice, Deliverance 149
Rice, Dorcas 274, 772
Rice, Edmund 99, 404
Rice, Elizabeth 69, 95, 358, 449, 787
Rice, Esther 396
Rice, Frances 9
Rice, Gernow 81
Rice, Hannah 355, 397, 730, 778, 811, 815
Rice, Henry 414
Rice, Hester 396
Rice, Joseph 801
Rice, Keziah 806
Rice, Lydia 232, 355, 802, 834
Rice, Martha 64, 180
Rice, Mary 10, 99, 120, 619, 806
Rice, Mercy 10
Rice, Nathaniel 713
Rice, Newell 618
Rice, Patience 460
Rice, Rachel 225, 232, 255
Rice, Richard 182, 449, 815
Rice, Robert 728
Rice, Ruth 352, 795
Rice, Samuel 104, 390
Rice, Sarah 6, 182, 413, 439, 470, 789
Rice, Tamisen 561
Rice, Thomasine 561
RICH 621
Rich, Edward 776
Rich, Hannah 706
Rich, Martha 184
Rich, Mary Bassett Derich 217
Rich, Thomas 574, 731
Richard, John 86
Richard, Sarah 30, 582
Richard, Thomas 85
RICHARDS 621, 622
Richards, --- 33
Richards, Abigail 663

Richards, Alice 91
Richards, Bathsheba 101, 809
Richards, Benjamin 192, 291
Richards, Catherine 381, 764
Richards, Daniel 605
Richards, Elizabeth 207, 210, 387, 432
Richards, Esther 780
Richards, Giles 394
Richards, Hannah 268, 657
Richards, James 210
Richards, Jerusha 647
Richards, John 104, 471, 527, 830
Richards, Lydia 499
Richards, Mary 8, 62, 116, 117, 204, 256, 296, 374, 487, 530, 536, 567, 656, 686, 690, 755
Richards, Nathaniel 466
Richards, Rosamond Street Lindall 466
Richards, Sarah 205, 366, 572, 656, 696
RICHARDSON 621, 622, 623, 624
Richardson, --- 765
Richardson, Abigail 52, 488
Richardson, Benjamin 811
Richardson, Bethia 435
Richardson, Bridget 623
Richardson, Edward 790
Richardson, Elizabeth 9, 166, 167, 525, 672, 844
Richardson, Esther 664
Richardson, Ezekiel 47, 102
Richardson, Francis 671
Richardson, Hannah 35
Richardson, Hester 664
Richardson, Isaac 665
Richardson, James 144
Richardson, Joanna 21
Richardson, John 480, 822
Richardson, Katharine 16, 698
Richardson, Katherine 675
Richardson, Marah 825
Richardson, Mary 30, 35, 81, 134, 168, 279, 296, 332, 338, 339, 525, 540, 583, 703, 757, 825, 845
Richardson, Mary Bendall 9
Richardson, Phebe 35
Richardson, Prudence 337
Richardson, Rebecca 781
Richardson, Richard 466
Richardson, Ruth 289
Richardson, Samuel 335
Richardson, Sarah 159, 271, 278, 819
Richardson, Stephen 145
Richardson, Susannah 260
Richardson, Theophilus 103
Richardson, Theopholus 583
Richardson, Thomas 235, 564
Richardson, William 162
RICHBELL 624
Richbell, Ann 250, 398
Richbell, Anne 250
Richbell, John 617
Richeson, Katharine 16, 698
Richman, Henry 498
RICHMOND 624
Richmond, Abigail 293, 617
Richmond, Edward 765
Richmond, Elizabeth 554
Richmond, Esther 120
Richmond, Hannah 140
Richmond, Henry 498
Richmond, Mary 307, 555, 564
Richmond, Sarah 618, 715, 774
Richmond, Susannah 614

Richmond, Sylvester 474
Richworth, Mary 233
RICKARD 624
Rickard, Abigail 812
Rickard, Giles 153, 743
Rickard, Judith 260
Rickard, Mary 242
RICKER 624
Ricker, Judith 388
RICKETSON 624
Rickketson, William 828
RICKS 627
Ricks, Grace 532
Ricks, Thomas 309
Ricks, William 532
Ricord, Mary 140
Ricraft, Hannah 500
RIDDAN 616, 624 see REDDING
Riddan, Abigail 563
Riddan, Hannah 237, 116
RIDDIN 624
RIDDING 616
RIDDLESDALE 470
Riddlesdale, Anne 534
Riddlesdale, Hannah 534
Riddlesdale, Susan 285
Riddon, Mary 435
Ride, Newell 618
RIDER 624, 625
Rider, Abigail 229
Rider, Annis 617
Rider, Elizabeth 197
Rider, Hannah 424, 496, 813, 835
Rider, Joseph 497
Rider, Mary 375, 720
Rider, Patience 336
Rider, Rebecca 205, 617
Rider, Thomas 197, 329
Rider, Zechariah 720
Rideware, Nevill 618
Ridewere, Nevill 618
Ridgaway, Hannah 229
RIDGDALE 625
Ridge, Thomas 506
RIDGEWAY 625
Ridgly, Mary 17
Ridgway, Sarah 26
Ridiatt, Deborah 274
RIDLAND 625
Ridland, Patience 130
RIDLEY 625 see RIDLON
Ridley, Ann 445
Ridley, Elizabeth 691
RIDLON 625 see RIDLEY
RIELIE 625
Rifel, Mary 86
Rigbee, Elizabeth 24
Rigbee, Mehitable 759
Rigbie, Susannah 523
RIGBY 625
Rigby, Abigail 383
Rigby, Isabel 94
Rigby, John 267
Rigby, Mehitable 754
Rigby, Silence 129
Rigby, Susannah 523
RIGDALE 625
RIGGS 625
Riggs, Anna 798
Riggs, Elizabeth 50, 173
Riggs, John (Capt.) 57
Riggs, Mary 351, 761
Riggs, Sarah 478, 757
Riggs, Thomas 284
RIGHT 843
Right, Deborah 43
Right, Sarah 597
Riland, Joanna 647

RILEY 625, 626
Riley, Grace 311
Riley, Henry 62, 777
Riley, Lydia 60
Riley, Margaret 482
Riley, Mary 250, 301
Riley, Sarah 112, 413, 655
RINDGE 626 see RING
Rindge, Daniel 779
Rindge, Isaac 441
Rindge, Susanna 301
RING 626
Ring, Andrew 522
Ring, Daniel 779
Ring, Elizabeth 178, 212, 326, 500
Ring, Hannah 348
Ring, Martha 753
Ring, Mary 288, 522
Ring, Robert 348
Ring, Sarah 17, 332
Ring, Susanna 158
Ring, Susannah 210
RINGE 626
Ringe, Susanna 301
Riol, Ruth 191
RIPLEY 626
Ripley, Abraham 417
Ripley, Esther 812
Ripley, Frances 54
Ripley, Jeremiah 209
Ripley, Mary 769
Ripley, Phebe 579
Ripley, Rebecca 681
Ripley, Ruth 574
Ripley, Sarah 54
Ripley, William 236, 734
Ripple, Esther 812
RISBY 626
Risden, Mary 656
Risden, Sarah 744
RISDON 626
Rise, Dorcas 772
Rise, Patience 380
Risely, Mary 373
Risely, Richard 373
RISHWORTH 626
Rishworth, Mary 401, 589
RISING 626
Rising, James 48
Riskworth, Mary 807
RISLEY 626
Risley, Sarah 358
RIST 620
Rithway, Elizabeth 564
RIX 627
Rix, Grace 532
Rix, Hannah 811
Rix, Sarah 604
Rix, Thomas 309, 778
Rix, William 532
ROACH 627
Roach, Lydia 756
ROACHE 627
ROAD 619
ROADS 619
Roads, Abigail 337
Roads, Joanna 499
Roads, Josiah 155
Roads, Ruth 180
ROAFE 635
Roafe, Ezra 273
Roanes, William 703
ROAPES 637
ROATH 844
ROBBINS 627, 628
Robbins, Abigail 257
Robbins, Benjamin 740

Robbins, Comfort 670
Robbins, Deborah 699
Robbins, Elizabeth 12
Robbins, Hannah 781
Robbins, John 2, 215, 743, 758
Robbins, Mary 236, 438, 731, 758
Robbins, Rebecca 148, 839, 180, 189
Robbins, Samuel 45
Robbins, Thomas 72, 588
Robee, Deliverance 361
Roberds, Susan 573
Robernson, Mary 330
ROBERTS 628, 629
Roberts, --- 214, 319, 673
Roberts, Abigail 229, 334
Roberts, Ann 9, 492, 576, 588
Roberts, Anne 673
Roberts, Eli 179
Roberts, Elizabeth 13, 58, 93, 188, 234, 266, 362, 471, 616, 672, 759
Roberts, Ephraim 392
Roberts, Eunice 770
Roberts, George 273
Roberts, Giles 9
Roberts, Grace 233
Roberts, Hannah 188, 372, 812
Roberts, Hester 492
Roberts, Jane 576
Roberts, Janet 703
Roberts, Joanna 58, 597
Roberts, John 265, 660
Roberts, Katherine 810
Roberts, Lidia 49, 58, 628
Roberts, Mary 37, 189, 631, 846
Roberts, Ruth 206
Roberts, Sarah 160, 265, 344, 621
Roberts, Susanna 320
Roberts, Thomas 266, 498, 550, 555
Roberts, William 27
ROBERTSON 628, 629, 630 see ROBINSON
Robertson, Ann 830
Robertson, David 623
Robertson, Elizabeth 448
Robertson, Mary 621
Robey, Deliverance 361
Robey, Mary 273
ROBIE 631
Robie, Mary 733
ROBINEAU 629
ROBINS 627, 628, 629
Robins, Mary 731
ROBINSON 629, 630, 631
Robinson, Abigail 571, 846
Robinson, Abraham 109, 773
Robinson, Ann 232
Robinson, Anna 232
Robinson, Bethiah 589
Robinson, Catharine 274
Robinson, Constance 26
Robinson, Damaris 215
Robinson, David 429, 716
Robinson, Dorothy 260
Robinson, Elizabeth 136, 295, 314, 448, 482, 514, 604, 643, 692
Robinson, Fear 34, 79
Robinson, Francis 315
Robinson, George 216, 498
Robinson, Hannah 820
Robinson, Increase (Jr.) 589
Robinson, Jonathan 56
Robinson, Kat 274
Robinson, Martha 829
Robinson, Mary 250, 276, 321,

Robinson, Mary (cont.) 330, 453, 458, 565, 674, 811, 824
Robinson, Mercy 792, 811
Robinson, Nathaniel 571
Robinson, Prudence 97
Robinson, Saint 453, 756
Robinson, Sarah 128, 212, 531
Robinson, Sarah Bradley Bean 56
Robinson, Susanna Witham 712
Robinson, Thomas 631, 670, 840
Robinson, Timothy 342
Robinson, Ursula 189
Robinson, Waiting 570
Robinson, William 389, 718
Robiohn, Hannah 392
Robison, George 216
Robison, Martha 829
Robison, Timothy 342
Robisson, Mary 313
Robitaille, Philip 548
ROBY 631
Roby, Andrew 197
Roby, Henry 147, 295
Roby, Judith 362
Roby, Mary 480, 733
ROCH 627
Roch, Joseph 161
Roch, Mary 161
Rochell, Mary 583
Rochett, Richard 68
Rock, Hannah 91
Rock, Joseph 203
ROCKE 631
Rocke, Hannah 95
ROCKER 636
Rocket, Ann 204
Rocket, Anna 204
Rocket, Anne 204
Rocket, Joane 204
Rocket, Joanna 178
Rocket, Johannah 178
Rocket, Samuel 354
ROCKETT 632
Rockett, Elizabeth 563
Rockett, Joseph 302
Rockett, Margery 591
Rockett, Mary 591
Rockett, Nicholas 233
Rockett, Priscilla 182
Rockford, Mary 655
ROCKWELL 631, 632
Rockwell, --- 490, 836
Rockwell, Elizabeth 778
Rockwell, Hannah 228, 614, 650
Rockwell, Jane 33
Rockwell, Joan 33, 410
Rockwell, John 781
Rockwell, Josiah 70
Rockwell, Lydia 24
Rockwell, Mary 472, 786
Rockwell, Mehitable 430
Rockwell, Ruth 405, 513
Rockwell, Sarah 190, 297, 334
Rockwell, William 317
ROCKWOOD 632
Rockwood, Abigail 814
Rockwood, Ann 204
Rockwood, Anna 204
Rockwood, Anne 204
Rockwood, Elizabeth 563
Rockwood, Hannah 371
Rockwood, Joane 204
Rockwood, Joanna 178
Rockwood, Johannah 178
Rockwood, John 734, 759
Rockwood, Lydia 3
Rockwood, Mercy 734
Rockwood, Phebe 729

Rockwood, Richard 68
Rockwood, Samuel 354
Rockwood, Susanna 375, 736
Rockwood, Trial 359
Rodgers, Hannah 600
Rodgers, Mary 613
RODMAN 632
Rodman, Thomas 484
ROE 514, 639
Roe, Abigail 731
Roe, Elizabeth 452, 487, 504
Roe, Hannah 617
Roe, Hugh 780
Roe, John 171
Roe, Martha 175
Roe, Mary 184, 232, 679, 847
Roe, Rachel 211
Roe, Sarah 780
ROECH 627
ROES 638
Rofe, Daniel 385
Rofe, Hannah 225
ROGERS 632, 633, 634, 635
Rogers, --- 362, 362
Rogers, Abiel 782
Rogers, Abigail 13, 142, 306, 439,
  561, 624, 710, 781, 807, 845
Rogers, Alice 195, 341
Rogers, Ann 182, 399, 579, 643,
  713, 833
Rogers, Anna 713, 733, 745, 821
Rogers, Bathsheba 688
Rogers, Bathshua 281
Rogers, Deborah 121, 807
Rogers, Eleazer 132, 275
Rogers, Elizabeth 20, 32, 58, 188,
  230, 305, 347, 369, 375, 601,
  624, 644, 645, 680, 702, 745,
  820
Rogers, Eunice 490, 798
Rogers, Experience 629
Rogers, Ezekiel 80, 657
Rogers, Ezekiel (Rev.) 41, 449,
  531
Rogers, Grace 39, 509, 634, 680
Rogers, Grace Maken Sherman
  595
Rogers, Hannah 32, 91, 132, 343,
  369, 600, 733, 745
Rogers, Ichabod 676
Rogers, James 169, 565
Rogers, Jeremiah 791
Rogers, Joanna 753
Rogers, John 57, 80, 99, 106,
  109, 110, 170, 193, 399, 456,
  537, 564, 600, 635
Rogers, Joseph 25, 692
Rogers, Lois 559
Rogers, Lydia 122, 547, 806
Rogers, Margaret 66, 398, 462,
  753
Rogers, Martha 836
Rogers, Mary 45, 111, 169, 206,
  225, 280, 284, 302, 380, 398,
  504, 564, 579, 639, 692, 761
Rogers, Obadiah 155, 332
Rogers, Orange 138
Rogers, Patience 491
Rogers, Priscilla 180, 682
Rogers, Rebecca 229, 753
Rogers, Rebecca Drake Jones
  160, 425
Rogers, Richard 281, 762
Rogers, Robert 736
Rogers, Ruth 63, 312, 710, 801
Rogers, Samuel 569, 821, 837
Rogers, Sarah 113, 132, 332, 345,
  358, 445, 659, 795

Rogers, Susanna 736
Rogers, Susannah 506
Rogers, Thomas 380, 669, 680
Rogers, William 633, 691, 798,
  833
Roggers, Eunice 798
Roggers, Mary 225
Roice, Ruth 146
Roise, Deborah 713
ROLAND 640
Rolendson, Mary 78
ROLESON 640
ROLF 635
Rolf, Abigail 587
Rolf, Ezra 173
ROLFE 635
Rolfe, Abigail 587
Rolfe, Ann 77
Rolfe, Apphia 419
Rolfe, Daniel 385
Rolfe, Esther 306
Rolfe, Ezra 70, 273
Rolfe, Hannah 167, 168, 803
Rolfe, Henry 77
Rolfe, Hester 306, 652
Rolfe, Honour 77, 635
Rolfe, Rebecca 201
Rolfe, Thomas 178
ROLLES 635
ROLLINS 612
Rollins, Abigail 621
Rollins, Elizabeth 521
Rollins, Ichabod 22
Rollins, Joseph 538
Rollins, Philip 563
Rollins, Rebecca 713
Rollins, Sarah 149
ROLLO 635
Rollo, Alexander 18
Rollo, Hannah Kirby Andrews 715
ROLLS 635
Rolls, Thomas 291
Rolph, Alice 262
Romeyn, Geertye 251
ROOD 635, 636
Rood, Rachel 681
ROODS 619
Rooke, Elizabeth 625
ROOKER 636
Roosa, Elizabeth 625
ROOSE 638
Roose, Elizabeth 180
ROOT 636
Root, Abigail 522
Root, Dorothy Ingersoll Phelps
  576
Root, Hannah 207, 407
Root, Hezekiah 15
Root, Jane 128
Root, John 171, 375
Root, Joseph 124, 689
Root, Mary 101, 500, 684
Root, Richard 756
Root, Sarah 38, 217, 407, 431
Root, Susannah 451
Root, Thankful 795
Root, Thomas 188, 407, 461, 700
Roote, Ralph 642
ROOTEN 636
ROOTES 636
Rootes, Jerwin 170
Rootes, Josiah 390
Rootes, Susanna 390
ROOTS 636
Roots, Bethia 476
Roots, Emma 495
Roots, Mary 291
ROPAR 637

ROPER 636, 637
Roper, Alice 5, 220, 310
Roper, Elizabeth 236
Roper, Ephraim 306
Roper, Hannah 40
Roper, John 13, 220
Roper, Mary 694
Roper, Rachel 186
Roper, Ruth 357
Roper, Sarah 483, 694
ROPES 637
Ropes, Lydia 291
Ropes, Mary 538
RORE 734
RORING 474
ROSBOTHAM 637
ROSCOE 637
Roscoe, Mary 794
Rosdoe, William 528
ROSE 637, 638, 639
Rose, Deborah 35, 428
Rose, Dorcas 721
Rose, Elizabeth 63, 180, 533,
  627, 725
Rose, Fourmot 204
Rose, Hannah 285, 285, 344, 499,
  540, 710, 741
Rose, Joanna 26, 271, 545
Rose, John 220, 523, 596
Rose, John (Sr.) 478
Rose, Jonathan 274, 415
Rose, Martha 478
Rose, Mary 53, 422, 554, 556,
  843
Rose, Mercy 843
Rose, Rachel 784
Rose, Rebecca 10, 704, 708
Rose, Richard 530
Rose, Robert 176, 557, 596
Rose, Ruth 367, 797
Rose, Sarah 511
Rose, Tourmet 204
ROSEBOROUGH 638
Rosecrans, Johanna 205
ROSEMORGAN 638 see
  MORGAN
ROSEMORGIE 638
ROSEWELL 638
Rosewell, Elizabeth 647
ROSMORGAN 638
ROSS 638
Ross, Deborah 35
Ross, Dorothy 810
Ross, Elizabeth 471
Ross, Funell 722
Ross, Hannah 115, 564, 643
Ross, Jane 12
Ross, Lydia 275
Ross, Margaret 462
Ross, Mary 270, 305, 319, 694
Ross, Sarah 222, 376, 841
Ross, Susanna 825
ROSSE 638
Rosse, Dorothy 810
ROSSITER 638
Rossiter, Hannah 185
Rossiter, Hugh 302
Rossiter, Jane 348
Rossiter, Joan 348
Rossiter, Joanna 185
Rossiter, John 385
Rossiter, Susannah 775
Rossiter, Winifred 302
ROST 638
Roswell, Elizabeth 647
ROTCH 627
ROTHBOTHAM 637
Rothchild, Susan 137

Rotherford, Henry 460
Rouf, Hannah 168
ROUND 638
Round, Ruth 494
ROUNDAY 638
Roundbottle, Betty 589
Roundee, Mary 785
Roundell, Mary 785
Roundey, Deborah 751
ROUNDIE 638
ROUNDS 638
Rounds, Elizabeth 87
Rounds, Thankful 117
ROUNDY 638 see ROUNDS
Roundy, Mary 785
Roupes, Lydia 291
ROUSE 638, 639
Rouse, Ann 394
Rouse, Anna 383
Rouse, Anne 394
Rouse, Edward 165, 680, 683
Rouse, Elizabeth 86, 180
Rouse, Mary 246, 347, 603
Rouse, Mercy 723
Rouse, Thankful 117
Rouse, Thomas 592, 642
Rouse, William 96, 347, 584, 762
ROVE 631
Rover, Thomas 581
ROW 639
Row, Alexander 276
Row, Margaret 495
Row, Martha 358
Row, Mary 188
Row, Ruth 210
Row, Sarah 452
ROWDEN 639
Rowden, John 339
Rowden, John 682
ROWDON 639
ROWE 639
Rowe, Anne 697
Rowe, Elizabeth 452
Rowe, Hannah 256
Rowe, Hugh 250
Rowe, Jane 202
Rowe, John 171
Rowe, Mary 210, 416
Rowe, Micah 202
Rowe, Michael 416, 479
Rowe, Rachel 211
Rowe, Richard 697
ROWELL 635, 639, 640
Rowell, --- 304
Rowell, Hannah 75, 168
Rowell, Joanna 795
Rowell, Mary 168, 281, 509, 608
Rowell, Sarah 315, 350
Rowell, Thomas 171, 349, 547
Rowell, Valentine 197, 651
ROWLAND 640
Rowland, Abigail 427, 615
Rowland, Elizabeth 159, 459, 633,
  800
Rowland, Jane 473
Rowland, John 453, 748
Rowland, Jonathan 216
Rowland, Mary 286, 415
Rowland, Rebecca 681
Rowland, Richard 165
ROWLANDSON 640 see
  ROWLESON
Rowlandson, Elizabeth 247, 346,
  794
Rowlandson, Mary 78
Rowlandson, Martha 241, 248
Rowlandson, Sarah 82
Rowlandson, Thomas 434, 528,

Rowlandson, Thomas (cont.) 573
Rowlandson, William 39
Rowlanson, Sarah 82
ROWLE 635
Rowles, Mary 557
ROWLESON 640
Rowleston, John 84
ROWLESTONE see
  ROWLANDSON
ROWLEY 640
Rowley, Elizabeth 477
Rowley, Henry 79
Rowley, Mary 545, 791
Rowley, Mehitable 288
Rowley, Moses 183, 545
Rowley, Sarah 352
Rowlins, Sarah 381
ROWLSTONE 640
Rowning, Mary 298, 613
Rowse, Anna 383
Rowse, Elizabeth 86
ROWSLEY 640
Rowsley, Robert 7
Rowter, Elizabeth 203
ROY 640
ROYAL 640, 641
Royal, Hannah 564
Royal, Isaac 544
Royal, Margaret 708, 785
Royal, Mary 70, 564, 831
Royal, Ruth 191
Royal, Sarah 393
ROYALL 641
Royall, Benson 180
Royall, Elizabeth 42, 180, 782
Royall, Phebe 762
ROYCE 641
Royce, Abiah 769
Royce, Abigail 169, 187
Royce, Abijah 769
Royce, Deborah 713
Royce, Elizabeth 29, 459, 728
Royce, Esther 116
Royce, Isaac 737
Royce, Joanna 423
Royce, Jonathan 840
Royce, Josiah 155
Royce, Martha 539
Royce, Mary 54, 120
Royce, Nathaniel 258, 395, 592
Royce, Ruth 146, 226, 474
Royce, Sarah 140, 465
Royle, Dorothy 362
Ruble, Mary 26
RUBTON 641
RUCK 641
Ruck, Abigail 364
Ruck, Ann 182
Ruck, Elizabeth 40, 547
Ruck, Hannah 299
Ruck, Jasper 40
Ruck, Joan 337, 722
Ruck, John 192
Ruck, Margaret 123, 416, 697
Ruck, Mary 690
Ruck, Rebecca 20
Ruck, Sarah 107, 123, 353
Rucke, Elizabeth 401
Rucker, John 540
RUCKS 641
RUD 641
RUDD 641
Rudd, Jonathan 134
Rudd, Mary 70
Rudd, Patience 126
RUDDOCK 641, 642
Ruddock, Mary 326

RUDE 635
Rudkin, Sarah 492
RUE 618
Rue, John 372
RUEL 642
Rug, Mary 636
Rugby, Mehitable 759
Rugells, Rebecca 614
RUGG 642
Rugg, Hannah 37
Rugg, Rebecca 399
RUGGLES 642
Ruggles, Abigail 623
Ruggles, Ann 363
Ruggles, Anna 363
Ruggles, Elizabeth 31, 59, 109,
  633
Ruggles, John 3, 211, 578
Ruggles, Mary 585, 659
Ruggles, Mehitable 621
Ruggles, Rachel 699
Ruggles, Rebecca 425, 614
Ruggles, Ruth 28, 228
Ruggles, Sarah 481, 684, 824
Ruggles, Thomas 636
Rule, John 423
Rule, Margaret 551
Rulfe, Hannah 225
RUMBALL 642
Rumball, Alice 199
Rumball, Bethia 710
Rumball, Thomas 42
Rumble, Bethia 710
Rumble, Thomas 528
Rumbull, Thomas 528
RUMERILL 642
Rumery, Sarah 807
Rummerell, Rebecca Brookings
  Pomeroy 639
Rummerill, Clement 592
RUMMERY 642
RUMRILL 642
RUMSEY 642
Rumsey, Abigail 547
Rumsey, Rachel 408
RUNDELL 642
Rundell, Sarah 443
RUNDLET 643
RUNDLETT 643
Rundlett, Charles 19
Rundlett, Jane 19
Runket, Charles 19
Runket, Jane 19
RUNLET 643
Runlett, Charles 212, 687
Runnals, Sarah 846
Runnells, Hope 214
Runnells, Hopestill 214
Runnels, Mary 451
RUPLING 643
RUSCO 637
Rusco, Margaret 460
Rusco, Ruth 54
Rusco, Sarah 116, 168
RUSCOE 637, 637
Ruscoe, Adera 63, 105
Ruscoe, Adey 63
Ruscoe, Andrey 63
Ruscoe, Audery 105
Ruscoe, Mary 662
Ruscoe, Mercy 705
Ruscoe, Rebecca 153
Ruscoe, Ruth 1
RUSE 643
Ruse, Mary 277
RUSH 641, 643
Rush, Elizabeth 40, 59
Rush, Isaac 511

Rush, Jasper 40, 59
Rush, Mary 48
Rushmore, Thomas 146
Rushton, Alice 835
RUSKEW 637
RUSS 643
Russ, Funell 722
Russ, Margaret 574
Russ, Mary 277, 714
Russ, Sarah 475
RUSSE 643
Russel, John 808
Russel, Mary 414
RUSSELL 643, 644
Russell, Abigail 97
Russell, Amy 655
Russell, Ann 416
Russell, Anna 597
Russell, Anne 406
Russell, Daniel 277, 836
Russell, Elizabeth 215, 319, 365,
  396, 555, 582, 837
Russell, Ellen 306
Russell, George 399, 415
Russell, Hannah 210, 385, 438,
  444
Russell, Helena 306
Russell, Henry 444
Russell, James 353
Russell, John 408, 469, 682
Russell, Joseph 155, 326
Russell, Joyce 620
Russell, Katharine 638
Russell, Mabel 418
Russell, Margaret 588
Russell, Mariah 601
Russell, Martha 92, 305
Russell, Mary 103, 183, 385, 451,
  632, 634, 785
Russell, Miriam 341
Russell, Patience 482
Russell, Prudence 228, 340
Russell, Ralph 596
Russell, Rebecca 9, 166
Russell, Richard 149
Russell, Samuel 98
Russell, Sarah 185, 316, 409
Russell, William 92, 316, 336, 694
RUST 644, 645
Rust, Elizabeth 261, 807
Rust, Hannah 239, 626
Rust, Margaret 821
Rust, Mary 48
Rust, Mercy 540
Rust, Nicholas 604
Rust, Sarah 13
Rustorp, Ann 212
Rustorp, Hannah 212
RUTHERFORD 645
Rutherford, Mary 334, 606
Rutherford, Robert 409, 589
Rutherford, Sarah 754
RUTTER 645
Rutter, Hannah 455
Rutter, Jane 16
Rutter, John 125, 682
Rutter, Mary 380
Rutter, Rebecca 455
RUTTY 645
Rutty, Mary 595
RYAL 640
Ryal, Martha 148
RYALL 641
Ryall, Martha 148
Ryall, Mary 70
RYAN 645
Ryan, Timothy 676
RYCROFT 645

RYDER 624, 625
Ryder, Elizabeth 80, 94, 169, 478
Ryder, Mary 683, 781
Ryder, Rebecca 326
RYLEE 625
RYLEY 625
RYMES 645

--- S ---

SABEERE 645
Sabeere, Alice 825
Saben, Abigail 611
Saben, Mehitable 113
Saben, William 87
SABIN 645
Sabin, Abigail 611
Sabin, Abigaill 117
Sabin, Elizabeth 509
Sabin, Experience 117
Sabin, Hannah 11
Sabin, Joseph 410
Sabin, Josiah 149
Sabin, Mary 12, 181
Sabin, Mehitable 781
Sabin, Mercy 792
Sabin, Patience 202
Sabin, Sarah 441
Sabin, William 87
SABLE 645
SABLES 645
SACHELL 664
Sacket, Martha 837
SACKETT 645, 646
Sackett, Abigail 537
Sackett, Hannah 217, 531
Sackett, John 710
Sackett, Joseph 67, 686
Sackett, Martha 837
Sackett, Mary 522
Sackett, Sarah 14
Sackett, Simon 79, 839
SADD 646
Sadd, John 599
Sadie, Ann 337
Sadie, John 844
Sadir, John 844
SADLER 646, 798
Sadler, Ann 349
Sadler, Anna 13
Sadler, Anthony 121
Sadler, Mary 768
Sadler, Thomas 240, 798
SADY 646
SAFFIN 646
Saffin, John 465
SAFFORD 646
Safford, Elizabeth 107, 475, 800
Safford, Mary 437
Safford, Rebecca 800
Safford, Sarah 437
Safford, Thomas 664
SAGE 646
Sage, Elizabeth 115, 305
Sage, Mary 423
Sage, Rebecca 613
Sage, Susanna 8
SAGER 658
SAILS 654
St.JOHN 646, 647
St.John; Anna 61
St.John; Elizabeth 292, 396, 613,
  809
St.John; James 506
St.John; Mark 76, 334, 515
St.John; Mary 396, 408

St.John; Mercy 470
St.John; Rachel 429
St.John; Rhoda 493
St.John; Sarah 430
St.John; Sarah Reynolds Mead 501
SAIR 655
SAIRE 654
SAISE 647
SAITH 654
Saith, Hannah 299
Salait, Bethiah 366
SALAS 647
SALDERN 772
SALE 654, 655
Sale, Elizabeth 603
Sale, Hannah 182
Sale, Mary 486
Sale, Mary Foster 779
Sale, Miriam 136
Sale, Rebecca 410
Sale, Sarah 300
SALENDIN 692
SALISBURY 647
Salisbury, Sarah 819
Salisbury, Susannah 659
Salleck, John 205
SALLEE 647
Sallie, Sarah 77, 598
Salliman, Robert 443
Sallman, Hannah 228
Salloes, Elizabeth 751
SALLOS 647
SALLOWES 647
SALLOWS 647
Sallows, Abigail 32
Sallows, Catherine 476
Sallows, Elizabeth 751
Sallows, Hannah 328, 460
Sallows, Robert 74
SALLY 647
Sally, Rebecca 425
SALMAN 692
SALMON 647
Salmon, Ann 185
Salmon, Elizabeth 636
Salmon, Hannah 228
Salmon, Margaret 185
Salmon, Mary 225, 451, 574
Salmon, Ruth 406
Salmon, Sarah 232
Salmon, Thomas 576
Salmon, William 176, 721
Salos, Mary 239
Salsbury, Abigail 824
SALTER 647
Salter, Abigail 37, 339
Salter, Ann 567
Salter, Anne 329
Salter, Deborah 659
Salter, Elizabeth 416, 492
Salter, Hannah 578, 642
Salter, Mary 413
SALTONSTALL 647, 648
Saltonstall, --- 286
Saltonstall, Elizabeth 156, 185,
  215
Saltonstall, Gurdon 160
Saltonstall, Martha 156
Salway, Joanna 838
SAMES 648 see SAMIS
SAMFIELD 648
SAMFORD 646, 650
Samford, Elizabeth 402
SAMIS 648
SAMMIS 648 see SAMES
Sammis, Joanna 111
Sammis, Johanah 111
Sammis, John 185

Sammon, Grace 218
Sammons, Elizabeth 699
SAMMS 648
SAMON 647
Samp, Mary 309
SAMPLE 648
Sample, Elizabeth 301
SAMPSON 648
Sampson, Abraham 214, 395
Sampson, Andrew 216, 671
Sampson, Cyprian 151
Sampson, Dorcas 82
Sampson, Elizabeth 214
Sampson, Henry 43, 341
Sampson, Hugh 237
Sampson, James 637, 771
Sampson, Mary 309, 394, 395
Sampson, Richard 157
Sampson, Samuel 693
Sampson, Sarah 235
Sampson, Susanna Smith 681
SAMS 648
Sams, Mary 244
Sams, Sarah 694
SAMSON 648
Samson, Dorothia 502
Samson, Elizabeth 698
Samson, Hannah 384
Samson, Henry 720
Samson, Judith 394
Samson, Mary 720, 796
Samson, Sarah 229
Samsons, Grace 554
SAMUEL 648
Samuel, John 814
SAMWAYS 648
SANBORN 648, 649
Sanborn, Abial 491
Sanborn, Abiel 491
Sanborn, Abigail 491
Sanborn, Ann 554
Sanborn, Benjamin 202, 665
Sanborn, Deborah 261
Sanborn, Dinah 90, 491
Sanborn, John 525
Sanborn, Josiah 572
Sanborn, Judith 315
Sanborn, Mary 228, 706
Sanborn, Mehitable 743
Sanborn, Mercy 140
Sanborn, Richard 81
Sanborn, Sarah 491
Sanden, Mary 23
Sander, Elizabeth 316
SANDERS 649, 651, 652 see
  SANDERSON
Sanders, Abiah 56
Sanders, Abiel 56
Sanders, Abigail 56
Sanders, Anna 218
Sanders, Barnaby 588
Sanders, Elizabeth 53, 188, 766,
  772
Sanders, George 118
Sanders, Grace 125
Sanders, Hannah 271, 538
Sanders, Jane 559
Sanders, John 843
Sanders, Josiah 690
Sanders, Leah 561, 798
Sanders, Martin 97
Sanders, Mary 22, 246, 271, 766,
  810
Sanders, Sarah 241, 311, 586, 758
Sanders, William 94
SANDERSON 649
Sanderson, Abiah 128
Sanderson, Abiel 128

Sanderson, Ann 796
Sanderson, Anna 796
Sanderson, Anne 796
Sanderson, Hannah 796
Sanderson, Henry 652
Sanderson, Jonathan 306
Sanderson, Joseph 20, 466
Sanderson, Lydia 427
Sanderson, Mary 20, 140, 466
Sanderson, Robert 194
Sanderson, Sarah 216, 804
SANDEY 649
SANDFORD 649, 650
SANDIN 649
Sandin, Charity 651
Sandin, Mary 505, 699
SANDS 649
Sands, Ann 228, 426
Sands, Mercy 613
Sands, Samuel 434
Sands, Sarah 537
SANDY 649
SANDYS 649 see SANDS,
  SANDY
Sandys, Ann 228
Sandys, Mercy 191, 501
SANFORD 646, 649, 650
Sanford, Anna 1
Sanford, Bathsheba 119
Sanford, Deborah 426
Sanford, Elizabeth 12, 13, 172,
  237, 402, 413, 475, 618, 681,
  717, 761
Sanford, Ezekiel 37
Sanford, Frances 407
Sanford, Hannah 141, 319, 330,
  599, 760, 843
Sanford, James 403
Sanford, Joan 657
Sanford, John 322, 484, 579, 597,
  815
Sanford, Martha 379
Sanford, Mary 21, 22, 99, 132,
  235, 401, 758, 761, 826
Sanford, Nathaniel 128, 431
Sanford, Rebecca 660
Sanford, Robert 700, 797, 822
Sanford, Ruth 126
Sanford, Sarah 400, 553, 673
Sanford, Thomas 156, 427, 608
Sanford, Thomasine Scottow 657
SANGER 650, 651
Sanlin, Sarah 615
Sanson, Thomas 805
Sargaint, Abigail 709
SARGANTE 651
SARGEANT 651
Sargeant, Elizabeth 779
Sargeant, Peter 401
Sargeant, Sarah 132
SARGENT 651
Sargent, --- 359
Sargent, Abigail 709
Sargent, Andrew 409
Sargent, Edward 92
Sargent, Elizabeth 69, 168, 195,
  270, 519, 535, 779
Sargent, Hannah 35, 261
Sargent, Mary 95, 141, 409, 413,
  652, 745
Sargent, Peter 182, 580
Sargent, Ruth 85, 151, 829
Sargent, Sarah 31
Sargent, Susanna 168
Sargent, William 95, 197, 512,
  640, 664
SARSON 651
Sarson, Mehitable 475

Sarson, Richard 499
Sarson, Samuel 160
SARTEL 653
Satall, Hannah 828
SATCHEL 664
SATCHWELL 664
Satchwell, Hannah 503
Satchwell, Lydia 326
Satchwell, Mary 212, 643, 687
SATLE 653
Satle, Sarah 200
Satte, Henry 31
SATTERLEE 651
Satterlee, Benedict 218, 830
SATTERLY 651
Satterly, Benedict 512
Satterly, Deborah 617
Satterly, Wm. 617
Sauger, Mary 345
SAUNDERS 651, 652 see
  SANDERSON
Saunders, Abiah 128
Saunders, Abiel 128
Saunders, Abigail 151
Saunders, Anna 218
Saunders, Elizabeth 29, 832
Saunders, George 118
Saunders, John 306, 442
Saunders, Martin 38, 728
Saunders, Mary 246, 588
Saunders, Mercy 195
Saunders, Sarah 311, 586
Saunders, Susanna 41
Saunders, Susannah 41
Saunders, William 94
Saunderson, Robert 194
SAUTLE 653
SAVAGE 652, 653
Savage, Abigail 667
Savage, Deborah 794, 824
Savage, Dyonisia 612
Savage, Elizabeth 806
Savage, Ephraim 127, 725, 774
Savage, Habijah 16
Savage, Habyah 312
Savage, Hannah 304, 312, 724
Savage, Joan 239
Savage, John 93, 802
Savage, Mary 12, 457, 733, 793,
  794, 810
Savage, Rachel 697
Savage, Sarah 369, 721, 794, 815
Savage, Sarah Walford Hicks 368
Savage, Thomas 350, 712
Savell, Ann 50
Savell, Anne 50
SAVERY 653
Savery, Rebecca 526
Savery, Robert 513
Savil, Hannah 162, 530
Savil, John 507
Savil, Rebecca 49
SAVILL 653
Savill, William 260, 292
SAVILLE 653
SAVON 660
SAVORY 653
Savory, Elizabeth 242
Savory, Mary 609
Savory, Rebecca 526
Savory, Sarah 517
Saward, Susanna 658
SAWDY 646, 649
SAWER 654
Sawford, Elizabeth 475
SAWIER 654
SAWIN 653
SAWINE 653

Sawtel, Elizabeth 521
SAWTELL 653,SAWTELL 654
Sawtell, Ruth 366
SAWTELLE 653
Sawtelle, --- 454
Sawtelle, Abigail 120
Sawtelle, Elizabeth 706, 811
Sawtelle, Hannah 336, 828
Sawtelle, Mary 706
Sawtelle, Sarah 200
SAWTLE 653
SAWYER 654, 655 see SAYRE
Sawyer, Abigail 177
Sawyer, Elias 593
Sawyer, Elizabeth 390
Sawyer, Frances 752
Sawyer, Hannah 516
Sawyer, John 504, 673, 692
Sawyer, Joshua 597
Sawyer, Martha 834, 835
Sawyer, Mary 177, 188, 194, 251, 513, 620, 653, 816
Sawyer, Mercy 238
Sawyer, Ruth 520
Sawyer, Sarah 108, 626
Sawyer, Susanna 506
Sawyer, Thomas 277, 806
Sawyer, William 794
SAXTON 654 see SEXTON
Saxton, Elizabeth 558
Saxton, Jerusha 554
Saxton, Joseph 149
Saxton, Mary 304, 511, 651
Saxton, Patience 628
Saxton, Samuel 404
Saxton, Sarah 844
Saxton, Silence 593
Saxton, Thomas 25, 37, 308
Saybrook, Marie 603
Saybrook, Mary 603
SAYER 654
Sayer, Mary 513
Sayer, Thomas 816
Sayers, Joanna 191
Sayers, Robert 191
SAYLES 655
Sayles, Catherine 545
Sayles, Deborah 136
Sayles, Eleanor 322
Sayles, Ellen 322
Sayles, Isabel 368, 743
Sayles, Mary 323, 384
Sayles, Phebe 321
Sayles, Rebecca 410
SAYRE 655 see SAWYER
Sayre, --- 393
Sayre, Damaris 24, 393
Sayre, Daniel 275
Sayre, Hannah 727
Sayre, Mary 603
Sayre, Sarah 480
SAYS 654
SAYWARD 655
Sayward, Hannah 601
Sayward, Joanna 191
Sayward, John 807
Sayward, Mary 94, 846
Sayward, Robert 191
SAYWELL 655
Saywell, David 70
Saywell, Elizabeth 207
Sayworth, John 589
Scadding, --- 111
Scadding, Elizabeth 111
SCADLOCK 655
Scadlock, Rebecca 667
Scadlock, Sarah 292
Scadlock, Susanna 841

Scadlock, William 137, 434
SCAILS 655
SCALES 655
Scales, John 416
Scales, Susannah 656
SCAMMON 655
Scammon, Ann 773
Scammon, Elizabeth 24, 333, 465, 646
Scammon, Jane 212, 705
Scammon, Mary 607, 632, 676
Scammon, Rebecca 69
Scammon, Sarah 226
SCAMP 655
Scamp, Mary 301
SCAMPE 655
SCANT 655
Scant, Ruth 537
Scant, Susanna 734
SCARBOROUGH 655, 656
Scarborough, Hannah 806
Scarborough, John 748
Scarborough, Sarah 229
SCARLET 656
Scarlet, Elizabeth 303
Scarlet, Jane 287
Scarlet, Rebecca 667
Scarlet, Sarah Adams Wacum 317
Scarlet, Thamasin 677
Scarlet, Thomasin 730
SCATE 656
Scate, Rebecca 10
Scate, Sarah 92
Scell, Elizabeth 368
SCENTER 661
SCHELLENGER 656
Schellinger, Catharine 33
Schillinger, Jacob 830
Schofield, Daniel 506
SCHRICK 656
Schrick, Paulus 15
SCILL 673
SCOFIELD 656, 657
Scofield, --- 615
Scofield, Hannah 266, 788
Scofield, Mary 396, 790
Scofield, Richard 475, 570
Scofield, Sarah 575
Scofield, Thamasine 4
Scofield, Thomasine 4
SCOLLAY 656
SCOLLEY 656
Scolley, Sarah 254
SCOLLY 656
SCONE 656
Scone, John 118
Scone, Sarah Hart 730
SCONER 656
Scorch, William 278
SCOTCHFORD 656
SCOTE 656
Scotlow, Thomasine 650
SCOTT 656, 657
Scott, Abigail 84, 203
Scott, Ann 101
Scott, Anna 101
Scott, Benjamin 342
Scott, Deliverance 624
Scott, Edmund 594, 764
Scott, Edward 370
Scott, Elizabeth 209, 472, 697, 723
Scott, Hannah 101, 102, 104, 159, 280, 470, 788
Scott, John 193, 732, 803
Scott, Joseph 673
Scott, Lydia 811
Scott, Margaret 617, 635, 691

Scott, Mary 207, 213, 252, 380, 563, 595, 692
Scott, Patience 59
Scott, Robert 231
Scott, Sarah 461, 701, 744
Scott, Susannah 668
Scott, Thomas 275, 632
Scott, Ursula 438
Scott, William 781
SCOTTO 657
Scotto, Elizabeth 653
Scotto, Lydia 788
Scotto, Mehitable 154
Scotto, Sarah 775
Scotto, Thomas 757
SCOTTOW 657
Scottow, Elizabeth 653
Scottow, Lydia 148, 299
Scottow, Mary 148
Scottow, Rebecca 76, 152
SCOVELL 657
SCOVIL 657
Scovill, Mercy 132
SCOVILLE 657
Scoville, Arthur 399
Scoville, Mehitable 736
Scoville, Rachel 399
SCRANTON 657
Scranton, Elizabeth 459
Scranton, John 371, 422
Scranton, Margaret 668
Scranton, Mary 714
Scranton, Sarah 125, 254
Scranton, Thomas 736
Screven, Elizabeth 240
SCRIBNER 658 see SCRIVEN
Scribner, Elizabeth 240
Scripton, Samuel 322
SCRIPTURE 658
Scripture, Mary 454
SCRIVEN 658
SCRIVENER 658
SCRUGGS 658
Scruggs, Rachel 613
SCUDDER 658
Scudder, Clemons 494
Scudder, Elizabeth 7, 47, 242, 455, 475, 537
Scudder, Hannah 39, 319, 690
Scudder, Henry 427
Scudder, Margaret 421
Scudder, Mehitable 223
Scudder, Mercy 474
Scudder, Rebecca 745
Scudder, Samuel 264
Scudder, Sarah 176, 589, 685
Scudemore, Mary 285
Scuder, Mehitable 223
SCULLARD 658
Scullard, Mary 635
Scullard, Samuel 72
Scullard, Sarah 216
Scuthock, William 65
Seaborn, Elizabeth 258
Seaborn, Esther 404
Seaborn, Hester 404
SEABORNE 658
SEABROOK 658
Seabrook, Alice 671, 801
Seabrook, Damaris 169
Seabrook, Emma 257
Seabrook, Joan 801
Seabrook, Marie 603
Seabrook, Mary 438, 603
Seabrook, Sarah 257, 671
SEABURN 658
SEABURY 658
Seabury, Elizabeth 150

Seabury, Hannah 563
Seabury, Joseph 685
Seabury, Samuel 272
SEAGER 658
Seager, Elizabeth Butler Knapp 442
Sealey, Edward 359
Sealey, John 163
Sealey, Martha 163
Sealey, Richard 163
SEALIS 673
Sealis, Hannah 827
Sealis, Hester 414
Sealis, Richard 341
SEALLY 661
SEALY 661, 673
Sealy, Dorcas 299, 663
SEAMAN 658, 659
Seaman, Deborah 442
Seaman, Elizabeth 413
Seaman, Hannah 135
Seaman, Mary 566
Seaman, Sarah 524
SEAMANS 659
Seamans, Martha 566
Seamore, Elizabeth 443
Seamore, Mary 325
Seares, Bethia 195
SEARJEANT 651
SEARL 659
Searl, Joanna 530
Searl, John 252
Searl, Thomas 580
SEARLE 659
Searle, Anna 19
Searle, Anne 19
Searle, Benjamin 124
Searle, Edward 467
Searle, Grace 346
Searle, Joanna 782
Searle, John 243, 265, 275, 781
Searle, Margaret 659
Searle, Sarah 116
Searle, Stephen 659
Searle, William 216
SEARLES 659
Searles, Rebecca 410
SEARS 659, 660
Sears, Alexander 659
Sears, Deborah 550
Sears, Hannah 692
Sears, John 259, 494
Sears, Lydia 338
Sears, Mary 136, 446, 762, 779
Sears, Rebecca 295
Sears, Thomas 399, 406
Seaton, Mary 777
SEAVER 660
Seaver, Elizabeth 189, 379
Seaver, Joshua 570
Seaver, Nathaniel 825
Seaver, Robert 122
Seaver, Sarah 825
Seavern, Elizabeth 258
SEAVERNS 662
Seaverns, Samuel 725
SEAVEY 660
Seavey, Elizabeth 543
Seavey, Henry 425, 497
Seavey, John 774
Seavey, Rebecca 672
SEAVORNE 661
Seawall, Dorothy 539
SEAWARD 662
SEAWELL 662
SEBELL 673
SEBER 658
SEBURY 658

SECCOMB 660
SECOMB 660
SEDENHAM 660
SEDGWICK 660
Sedgwick, Robert 831
Sedgwick, Sarah 691, 831
Sedgwick, William 462, 628
SEELE 660
SEELEY 660, 661, 673 see SEALE, SILLEY
Seeley, --- 506
Seeley, Benjamin 616
Seeley, Dorcas 29, 186, 663
Seeley, Edward 359
Seeley, Elizabeth 76, 404, 646
Seeley, Emma 642
Seeley, John 163
Seeley, Jonas 783
Seeley, Joseph 413
Seeley, Martha 163
Seeley, Mary 235, 699
Seeley, Nathaniel 302, 545
Seeley, Obadiah 413, 508
Seeley, Richard 163, 673
Seeley, Robert 776
Seeley, Sarah 699
Seeley, William 187
SEERS 659
SEGAR 658
Segouche, Elizabeth 9
SELDEN 661
Selden, Mary 729
Selden, Rebecca 794
Selden, Thomas 780
SELE 660
Selley, Thomas 86
SELLICK 661
Sellick, Sarah 596
SELLIVANT 673 see SILLIMAN
Sellman, Hannah 228
SELLY 660
Selly, Dorcas 186
Selsby, Henry 168
SEMOND 661
SENATE 661
SENCHION 646
SENDALL 661
Sendall, Joanna 402
Sendall, Samuel 359, 782
Senderland, Matthew 647
Senior, Mary 623
SENNET 661
Sennet, Mary 694
SENSION 646, 647
Sension, Dorothy Smith 515
Sension, Mary 408
SENTER 140, 141, 661 see CENTER
Senter, John 59
Sention, Sarah 430
Seold, Catherine 8
Sergent, Elizabeth 577
SERLES 659
SERLL 659
SERVANT 661
Servant, Sarah 699
SESSIONS 661
Sessions, Alexander 477
Sessions, Elizabeth 137
Setchwell, Richard 646
SETT 661
SEUERINS 662
SEVAN 661
SEVERANCE 661
Severance, Abigail 100, 152, 548
Severance, John 15
Severance, Mary 165, 219
SEVERANS 661

SEVERETT 653
SEVERNES 662
SEVERNS 661
SEVERY 653
SEVOLLE 662
Sewal, Elizabeth 362
SEWALL 662
Sewall, Ann 672
Sewall, Anne 471
Sewall, Edward 313
Sewall, Hannah 515, 727
Sewall, Jane 299
Sewall, Mehitable 515
Sewall, Phillippa 770
Sewall, Samuel 300, 838
Sewall, Sarah 313
Sewall, Tabitha 126
SEWARD 662 see SAYWARD
Seward, Elizabeth 690
Seward, Hannah 340
Seward, Joan 413
Seward, Joanna 191
Seward, Margaret 335
Seward, Mary 75, 400, 657
Seward, Mercy 132
Seward, Robert 191
SEWELL 662
Sewell, Abigail 580
Sewell, Dorothy 539
Sewell, Samuel 743
SEXTON 662 see SAXTON
Sexton, George 93
Sexton, James 303, 509
SEXTUS 662
Seyanche, Elizabeth 9
Seymone, Elizabeth 9
SEYMOUR 662, 663
Seymour, Abigail 581
Seymour, Hannah 125, 592
Seymour, Mary 125, 325, 451, 451, 539
Seymour, Richard 705
Seymour, Thomas 816
Seymoure, Elizabeth 443
Seyward, Jonathan 56
Seywood, Jonathan 56
SHACKFORD 663
Shackford, Jane 378
Shackford, Samuel 565
Shaddock, Elias 245
SHADDUCK 663
Shaepherd, John 610
Shaff, Mary 214, 218
SHAFFLIN 663
Shafflin, Katherine 440
Shafflin, Michael 83
Shafflin, Sarah 714
SHALER 663
Shaler, Anna 157
Shaler, Michael 419
Shaler, Thomas 103
SHALEY 663
SHALLER 663
SHALOTE 663
Shalote, John 174
Shane, Phebe 522
Shanesberg, Margaret 502
SHANNON 663
SHAPARD 667
SHAPCOT 663
SHAPCOTE 663
SHAPLEIGH 663
Shapleigh, Alice 27
Shapleigh, Ann 276
Shapleigh, Anna 94, 276
Shapleigh, Catherine 755
Shapleigh, Katherine 755
Shapleigh, Mary 617

Shapleigh, Ruth 518
Shapleigh, Sarah 588
SHAPLEY 663
Shapley, Abial 52
Shapley, Mary 403
Shapley, Sarah Atkins 331
Shapman, Abigail 452
Shapman, Hannah 452
SHARD 663
Shard, Elizabeth 515
Shard, Mary 316
SHARE 666
SHAREL 663
Sharel, Elizabeth 515
SHARP 663, 664
Sharp, Abigail 227, 417, 768
Sharp, Alice 23, 251, 610
Sharp, Ann 447
Sharp, Elizabeth 57, 189, 575
Sharp, Hannah 292, 543
Sharp, James 751
Sharp, John 113
Sharp, Martha 113
Sharp, Mary 235, 540, 698
Sharp, Rebecca 503
Sharp, Robert 233, 380
Sharparowe, Elizabeth 104
SHARPE 663, 664
Sharpe, Deborah 292
Sharpe, Elizabeth 302
Sharpe, Henry 292
Sharpe, John 736, 764
Sharpe, Mary 149, 644, 742, 817
Sharpe, Robert 154, 541
Sharpe, Sarah 302
Sharpe, Sarah Williams 580
Sharpe, Thomas 220
SHARRATT 664
Sharratt, Hugh 326
SHARSWOOD 664
Sharswood, Elizabeth 204
Sharswood, George 204
Sharswood, Mary 204, 371
Shart, Mary 486
Sharwood, Mary 472
SHATSWELL 664
Shatswell, Hannah 503
Shatswell, Joanna 321
Shatswell, Judith 651
Shatswell, Lydia 326
Shatswell, Margaret 184
Shatswell, Mary 212, 251, 789
Shatswell, Richard 646
Shatswell, Sarah 626
Shatswell, Theophilus 651
SHATTACK 664
SHATTOCK 664
Shattock, Damaris 550
SHATTUCK 663, 664 see
    SHADDUCK
Shattuck, Abigail 521, 558
Shattuck, Damaris 294, 550, 593
Shattuck, Gertrude 593
Shattuck, Hannah 293, 692
Shattuck, John 454
Shattuck, Mary 107, 246, 338,
    340, 358, 751
Shattuck, Mercy 246, 751
Shattuck, Patience 685
Shattuck, Priscilla 371, 535
Shattuck, Rebecca 153
Shattuck, Return 652
Shattuck, Ruth 258
Shattuck, Samuel 340
Shattuck, Sarah 294
Shattuck, Susan 521
Shattuck, Susanna 99, 380, 521
Shattuck, Susannah 260

Shattuck, William 538
SHAVALLEY 671
SHAVALLY 671
SHAW 664, 665
Shaw, --- 478, 577
Shaw, Abial 109
Shaw, Abigail 112, 205, 685
Shaw, Alice 17
Shaw, Anne 273
Shaw, Benjamin 261
Shaw, Deborah Fuller Richardson
    622
Shaw, Edmund 278
Shaw, Elizabeth 562, 593, 678,
    714
Shaw, Emden 278
Shaw, Grace 130, 152, 205, 622
Shaw, Hannah 552, 744
Shaw, James 418
Shaw, John 62, 205, 488, 656
Shaw, John (Jr.) 62
Shaw, Jonathan 204, 598
Shaw, Joseph 62, 75
Shaw, Lydia 692
Shaw, Margaret 779
Shaw, Martha 78, 768
Shaw, Mary 16, 67, 134, 289, 439,
    476, 559, 626
Shaw, Mehitable 702
Shaw, Rebecca 573
Shaw, Roger 744
Shaw, Ruth 178
Shaw, Sarah 189, 273, 631, 756
Shaw, Susanna 573
Shaw, Susannah 130
SHAYLOR 663
Shaylor, Anna 157
Sheader, Mary 284
Sheaf, William 570
SHEAFE 665, 666
Sheafe, Dorothy 808
Sheafe, Elizabeth 184, 551, 641
Sheafe, Jacob 733
Sheafe, Jane 196
Sheafe, Joanna 151, 196
Sheafe, Margaret 442, 717
Sheafe, Mary 214, 218, 397, 503
Sheafe, Mehitable 666
Shealy, Hannah 467
SHEAPARD 667, 668
SHEAR 666 see SHEARS
SHEARAR 666
SHEARE 666 see SHEARS
Sheares, Jeremiah 322
SHEARIN 670
SHEARMAN 669
Shearman, Mary 43
Shearman, Mercy 43
SHEARS 666 see SHEAR
Shears, Elizabeth 695
Shears, Mehitable 20
Shears, Robert 341
Shears, Samuel 328
Sheatha, Mary 284
SHEATHER 666
Sheather, Elizabeth 432
Sheather, Hannah 336, 401
Sheather, Samuel 146
SHED 666
Shed, Abigail 258
Shed, Elizabeth 258
Shed, Hannah 635
Shed, James 189
Shed, Sarah 236
Shed, Susanna 236
SHEDD 666
Shedd, Esther 542
Shedd, Mary 633

Shedd, Mehitable 207
Shedd, Susannah 387
SHEELEY 663
SHEELLEY 663
SHEERES 666
SHEFFIELD 666
Sheffield, Ann 573, 712
Sheffield, Anne 670
Sheffield, Deliverance 574
Sheffield, Edmund 489, 490
Sheffield, Mary 156, 490, 510
Sheffield, Nathaniel 314
Sheffield, Rachel 203
Sheffield, Sarah 532
Sheffield, Susanna 336
SHELDON 666, 667
Sheldon, --- 628
Sheldon, Agnes 775
Sheldon, Ann 9, 775
Sheldon, Hannah 145
Sheldon, Isaac 253
Sheldon, John 598, 738
Sheldon, Lydia 86
Sheldon, Mary 22, 97
Sheldon, Mindwell 480, 591
Sheldon, Ruth 719, 843
Sheldon, Thankful 243
SHELLEY 667 see SHALEY
Shelley, Ann 281
Shelley, Hannah 467
Shelley, Mary 168, 344, 522
Shelley, Rebecca 142
Shelley, Susanna 294
SHELSTON 667
SHELSTONE 667
Sheltin, Elizabeth 132
SHELTON 667
SHEPARD 667, 668
Shepard, Abigail 127, 592
Shepard, Ann 268, 608
Shepard, Anna 608
Shepard, Benedicta 701
Shepard, Benet 701
Shepard, Bridget 776
Shepard, Deborah 256, 805
Shepard, Edward 592
Shepard, Elizabeth 222, 260, 312,
    376, 718
Shepard, Hannah 77, 229, 253,
    608
Shepard, Isaac 419
Shepard, John 3, 68, 288, 312,
    312, 364, 386
Shepard, Judith 575
Shepard, Margery 706
Shepard, Mary 717
Shepard, Mehitable 753
Shepard, Rachel 714
Shepard, Rebecca 68
Shepard, Ruth 844
Shepard, Samuel 228
Shepard, Sarah 307, 715
Shepard, Solomon 284
Shepard, Susanna 833
Shepard, Thomas 513
Shepard, Thomas (Rev.) 481
Shepard, Trial 598
Shepard, Violet 705
SHEPARDSON 668
Shepardson, Daniel 744
Shepardson, Elizabeth 289
Shepardson, Joanna 131, 433
Shepardson, Lydia 131, 677
Shepardson, Mary 410
SHEPERD 667, 668
Sheperd, Thankes 221
Sheperson, Joanna 433
Shepheard, Martha 352

SHEPHERD 667, 668
Shepherd, Ann 471, 706
Shepherd, Anna 471
Shepherd, Elizabeth 104
Shepherd, Martha 353
Shepherd, Mary 208, 347, 799
Shepherd, Sarah 349
Shepherd, Thomas 357, 706
Shepleigh, Catherine 373
Shepley, Abiel 99
Shepley, Lydia 571
SHEPPARD 667
Sheppard, Elizabeth 780
Sheppard, Hannah 380
Sheppard, Sarah 738
SHEPPY 668
SHERBIN 669
SHERBORN 668, 669
Sherburn, Henry 2
Sherburn, Joseph 27
Sherburn, Mary 678
Sherburn, Ruth 523
SHERBURNE 668, 669
Sherburne, Catharine 121
Sherburne, Elizabeth 140, 451,
    493, 648
Sherburne, Frances 225
Sherburne, Joseph 290
Sherburne, Margaret 743
Sherburne, Mary 96, 188, 797
Sherburne, Sarah 402
SHERER 666
SHERIFF 672
Sheriff, Elizabeth 137
Sheriff, Martha 361
Sheriff, Mary 666
Sheriff, Sarah 515
SHERIN 670
SHERIVE 672
SHERMAN 669, 670
Sherman, Abigail 202, 422, 817
Sherman, Alice 695, 717
Sherman, Amy 293, 294
Sherman, Bethiah 735
Sherman, Daniel 514, 602
Sherman, Edmund 614
Sherman, Elizabeth 296
Sherman, Grace 468, 606, 635,
    646
Sherman, Grace Maken 595
Sherman, Hannah 147, 275, 626
Sherman, Hester 777
Sherman, John 707
Sherman, John (Rev.) 46
Sherman, Margaret 535
Sherman, Martha 88, 105
Sherman, Mary 9, 12, 29, 46, 190,
    267, 283, 355, 597, 717, 814
Sherman, Matthew 602
Sherman, Nathaniel 188, 341, 470
Sherman, Patience 841
Sherman, Phillip 147
Sherman, Phillopa 147
Sherman, Richard 324, 630
Sherman, Samuel 198
Sherman, Sarah 147, 278, 379,
    527, 638
Sherman, Susanna 512, 806
Sherman, Theophilus 186
Sherman, William 383, 700
SHERN 670
Sherrar, Hannah 322
Sherrard, Sarah 666
SHERRAT 664
Sherrat, Hugh 326
SHERRATT 664
SHERRILL 670
SHERRIN 670

SHERRING 670
Sherringham, Eleanor 813
SHERRINGTON 670
Sherrington, Mary 834
SHERROD 666
Sherry, Elizabeth 611
SHERWIN 670
Sherwin, Frances 196
Sherwoo, Stephen 506
SHERWOOD 670, 671
Sherwood, Abigail 130, 470, 543
Sherwood, Elizabeth 395, 711
Sherwood, Hannah 91, 473
Sherwood, Jane 505
Sherwood, John 58
Sherwood, Lemuel 580
Sherwood, Margaret 498
Sherwood, Mary 121, 269, 741,
    809
Sherwood, Phebe 92
Sherwood, Rebecca 399
Sherwood, Rose 42, 528, 642
Sherwood, Ruth 42, 230, 380, 505
Sherwood, Sarah 56, 799, 800,
    809
Sherwood, Stephen 292, 330
Sherwood, Thomas 39, 130, 171
Sherwood, Thomasine 60
Shether, Samuel 146
SHEVALLY 671
Shiaffe, Elizabeth 300
Shiff, Bathsheba 85
Shiff, Sarah 283
SHILLABER 671
SHIPLE 671
Shiple, Lydia 571
SHIPLY 671
SHIPMAN 671
Shipman, Abigail 452
Shipman, Elizabeth 388
Shipman, Hannah 452
Shipman, Mary 560
SHIPPEE 668
Shippee, Elizabeth 181
Shippee, Martha 496
SHIPPEN 671
Shippen, Edward 622
Shippen, Sarah 257
SHIPPIE 668
Shippie, Elizabeth 526
Shippie, Grace 547, 600
Shippin, Grace 600
Shippy, Sarah 819
SHIPREVE 671
SHIPTON 671
Shipton, Elizabeth 388
SHIPWAY 671
Shipway, John 616
Shirburne, Elizabeth 458
SHIRLEY 671
Shirley, Hannah 467
SHIRTLEFF 672
SHIRTLY 672
SHIVERICK 671
Shoar, Mary 16
SHOERIN 670
Shofeld, Tamerson 4
Sholer, Elizabeth 477
SHOOTER 671
Shooter, Hannah 524
Shooter, Peter 524
Shoppen, --- 803
Shoppy, --- 803
SHORE 671, 672
Shore, Abigail 355, 399, 763
Shore, Eunice 306
Shore, Phebe 509
Shore, Priscilla 4

Shore, Samuel 122
SHOREBORNE 671
SHORES 671
Shores, John 216, 530, 648
SHOREY 672
SHORT 672
Short, --- 738
Short, Alice 471
Short, Elizabeth 89, 385
Short, Henry 5, 89, 412, 471
Short, Mary 320, 490
Short, Mercy 490
Short, Patience 182
Short, Rachel 163
Short, Rebecca 555
Short, Sarah 500
Short, Susanna 558
SHORTHOSE 672
Shorthose, Robert 679
SHORTHOUSE 672
Shorthouse, Robert 679
SHORTHUS 672
SHORTRIDGE 672
Shortridge, --- 359
Shortridge, Ann 776
Shortridge, Mary 207
SHORTRIGS 672
SHORY 672
Shotten, Rachel 379
Shotton, Alice 187
Shotton, Samson 187
SHOVE 671, 672 see SHORES
Shove, Elizabeth 382, 510
Shove, George 260, 776
Shove, Margery 565
Shove, Mary 289
Shove, Phebe 509
Shove, Samuel 122
Shove, Sarah 324
Show, Esther 228
Show, Sarah 324
SHOWELL 662
SHOWERS 671
Shrather, Susanna 308
SHREVE 672 see SHERIFF
Shreve, Elizabeth 137
Shreve, Martha 361
Shreve, Mary 666
Shreve, Sarah 515
Shreve, Susanna 735, 736
Shreve, Thomas 736
SHRIEVE 672
SHRIMPTON 672
Shrimpton, Bethia 465
Shrimpton, Elizabeth 651
Shrimpton, Henry 262, 271, 355
Shrimpton, Jonathan 821
Shrimpton, Mary 300
Shrimpton, Samuel 107
Shrimpton, Sarah 156, 407
Shuller, Michael 419
Shuman, Margaret 535
SHUMWAY 672
Shurah, Mary 690
Shurtleff, William 168, 178
SHURTLEIF 672
SHUTE 672, 673
Shute, Abigail 320, 692
Shute, Joanna 113, 535
Shute, Mary 230
Shute, Richard 311
Shute, William 211, 589
SHUTLEWORTH 673
SHUTT 673
SIAS 673
Sias, --- Roberts 214, 319
Sibberance, Joan 282
SIBBORN 658

Sibborn, Elizabeth 258
Sibborns, Elizabeth 258
SIBLEY 673
Sibley, Abigail 182
Sibley, Hannah 57, 679
Sibley, John 88, 163, 309
Sibley, Martha 163
Sibley, Mary 722, 832
Sibley, Rachel 468
Sibley, Richard 163
Sibley, Sarah 236
Sibley, Sarah Howe 150
Sibley, William 546, 679
Sibly, Hannah 95
Sibly, Mary 832
SIBORNE 658
SIGOURNEY 673
Sigourney, Susan 422
Sigourney, Susanna 424
SIGSWORTH 673
SIKES 724
Sikes, Rebecca 124
Sikes, Vickary 755
Sikes, Victory 755
SILES 724
SILL 673
Sill, Elizabeth 323, 368
Sill, Jemimah 335
Sill, Joseph 493
Sill, Judith Fillbrook Shapard 667
Sillavan, Mary 325
SILLAWAY 673
SILLES see SALE, SEALE
SILLEY 661, 673
Silley, John 163
Silley, Martha 163
Silley, Richard 163
SILLIMAN 673 see SILLIVANT
Silliman, Daniel 245, 365
Sillis, Hannah 827
Sillis, Hester 414
SILLIVANT 673 see SILLIMAN
Sillivant, Daniel 755
SILLOWAY 528 see
    MUSSILOWAY
Silloway, Daniel 146
Silloway, Hannah 398
Sills, Elizabeth 368
Sillyar, Mary 380
SILSBE 674
Silsbe, Mary 173
SILSBEE 673
Silsbee, Hannah 454
Silsbee, Henry 168, 241
Silsbee, Sarah 173
SILSBIE 674
SILSBY 674
Silsby, Hannah 457
Silsby, Joanna 457
Silsby, Mary 489
Silsebey, William 546
SILVER 674
Silver, Hannah 3
Silver, Martha 817
Silver, Mary 630
Silver, Sarah 14
Silver, Thomas 770
SILVESTER 724, 725
Silvester, Charity 627
Silvester, Eliza 107
Silvester, Elizabeth 476
Silvester, Mary 197
SIMCOCK 674
SIMCOOK 674
SIMCOX 674
SIMES 725
Simes, Frances 451
Simes, Sarah 322

SIMKINS 675
Simkins, Ann 135
Simkins, Anna 135
Simkins, Barbara 7
Simkins, Daniel 788
Simkins, Mary 743
Simkins, Sarah 437
Simkins, Sarah 826
Simkins, Vincent 544
SIMMES 725
Simmes, Mary 747
Simmes, Timothy 652
SIMMONS 661, 674, 675, 720
Simmons, Anne 594
Simmons, Annock 544
Simmons, Elizabeth 102, 236, 804
Simmons, Hannah 594
Simmons, Jane 126
Simmons, Martha 213
Simmons, Mary 8, 129, 488, 505
Simmons, Moses 34
Simmons, Patience 47
Simmons, Rebecca 374, 693
Simmons, Sarah 529, 616
Simon, Elizabeth Bolton Willis 823
SIMONDS 674, 675
Simonds, Bethiah 774
Simonds, Elizabeth 410
Simonds, Huldah 78
Simonds, Judda 41
Simonds, Judith 41
Simonds, Mary 144
Simonds, Sarah 359
Simonds, William 358, 468
SIMONS 674, 675
Simons, Benjamin 533
Simons, Grace 252
Simons, Hannah 590
Simons, Mary 62, 240
SIMPKINS 675
Simpkins, Deborah 122
Simpkins, Mary 743
Simpkins, Miriam 762
Simpkins, Rebecca 437, 744
Simpkins, Sarah 826
SIMPSON 675, 676
Simpson, --- 86
Simpson, Abigail 468
Simpson, Alice 697
Simpson, Elizabeth 536
Simpson, Elizabeth Sanford Dyer
    Remington 237, 618
Simpson, Henry 82
Simpson, John 560
Simpson, Mary 60
Simpson, Peter 470
Simpson, Susanna 363
Sims, Boaz (Sr.) 621
Sims, Mary 641
SIMSON 676
Simson, Peter 718
Simson, Thomas 805
SINCLAIR 676
Sinclair, John 813
Sinclair, Mary 800
Sinclair, Meribah 478
Sinclear, Sarah 424
SINDERLAND 721
Singletary 550
SINGLETARY 234, 676
Singletary, Amos 633
Singletary, Eunice 241
Singletary, Mary 249
Singletary, Unity 241
SINGLETERY 676
Singletery, Lydia 447
Singletery, Mary 241
SINGLETON 676

Singleton, Thomas 200
Sinkler, Mary 800
Sipperance, Joan 282
SIRKMAN 676
SIRY 676
Sisseton, Alice 224
SISSON 676
Sisson, Ann 791
Sisson, Anne 754
Sisson, Elizabeth 9, 156
Sisson, Hope 650
Sisson, Mary 456
Sisson, Ruth 733
Sith, Elizabeth 303
SIXTON 662
Skamp, Mary 301
SKATE 656
SKEATH 656
Skeath, Rebecca 10
Skeath, Sarah 92
SKEEL 676
Skeel, Hannah 368
SKEELS 676
SKELLIN 677
SKELTON 676
Skelton, Deborah 189
Skelton, Elizabeth 650
Skelton, James 645
Skelton, Jane 645
Skelton, Mary 262
Skelton, Susan 489
Skelton, Susanna 627
Skelton, Susannah 489
Skelton, Thomas 759
Skeper, Catherine 421, 498
SKERRY 676
Skerry, Ann 685
Skerry, Elizabeth 269, 819
Skerry, Ephraim 794
Skerry, Hannah 773
Skerry, Martha 530
Skerry, Mary 479, 531
Sketman, Jane 212
SKIDMORE 676
Skidmore, Dorothy 326
Skidmore, Grace 308
Skidmore, Jane 410, 808
Skidmore, Jedidah 369
Skidmore, Thomas 36, 430, 752,
    797, 802
SKIFF 676, 677
Skiff, Abigail 689
Skiff, Bethiah 288
Skiff, Deborah 602
Skiff, Lydia 689
Skiff, Mary 151
Skiff, Sarah 224
Skiffe, Hepzibah 540
Skiffe, Lydia 75
Skiffe, Mary 499
Skiffe, Patience 85
Skiffe, Sarah 471, 499
Skift, Samuel 242
SKILLEN 677
Skilling, Abigail 197
Skilling, Deborah 332
Skilling, Thomas 332
SKILLINGS 677
Skillings, Deborah 410
Skillings, John 330
Skillings, Thomas 463
Skillins, Abigail 197
SKILLION 677
SKILTON 676
SKINNER 677
Skinner, Ann 174
Skinner, Anne 631
Skinner, Elizabeth 317, 794

Skinner, Hannah 634
Skinner, John 757
Skinner, Mary 138, 344, 538, 617, 644
Skinner, Richard 730
Skinner, Sarah 311
Skinner, Thomas 316, 644, 783
Skinner, William 579
Skippen, Sarah 257
Skipper, Catherine 421, 498
Skipper, Elizabeth 579
Skipper, Jane 104
Skipperary, Sarah 257
Skuder, Hannah 39
Skyre, Joshua 597
SLACK 677
SLADE 79, 677
Slade, Elizabeth 764
Slade, Joseph 734
SLAFTER 677
Slamy, Elizabeth 54
SLASON 678
Slason, Eleazer 396
Slason, Elizabeth 592
Slason, Sarah 71
SLATER 678 see SLAUGHTER
Slater, Elias 313
Slater, John 139
Slates, Margaret 725
SLATTER 678
SLAUGHTER 678 see SLATER
Slaughter, John 48
Slaughter, Sarah 293
SLAWSON 678
Slawson, Eleazer 396
Slawson, Elizabeth 592
Slawson, George 418
Slawson, Hannah 308
Slawson, John 300
Slawson, Sarah 71
SLEEPER 678
Sleeper, Abigail 265
Sleeper, Elizabeth 214, 571, 688
Sleeper, Mary 247
Sleeper, Naomi 76
Sleeper, Ruth 458
SLEG 678
Sleg, Christopher 395, 571
Slett, Mary 287
SLEW 678
SLOAN 678
Sloan, Thomas 146
SLOCUM 678
Slocum, --- 302
Slocum, Elizabeth 322
Slocum, Joanna 14, 524
Slocum, Mary 166, 179, 320, 361, 756
SLOO 678 see SLOW
SLOPER 678, 692 see SOPER
Sloper, Bridget 444
Sloper, Elizabeth 338
Sloper, John 737
Sloper, Mary 96
Sloper, Rebecca 139
SLOTH 678
SLOUD 677
Sloud, Joseph 734
SLOUGH 678
Slough, Hasadiah 215
Slough, William 605
SLOW see SLOO
SLOWMAN 678
SLUE 678
SLUMAN 679
Sluman, Elizabeth 2
Sluman, Sarah 140
Sluman, Thomas 751

SLY 679
Slye, Sarah 160
Slye, Sarah 181
SMALE 679
Smale, Thomas 673
SMALEDGE 679
SMALEY 679
Smaley, Mary 223
SMALL 88, 679
Small, Alice 841
Small, Ann 349, 799
Small, Elizabeth 13, 387
Small, Joseph 407
Small, Lydia 727
Small, Mary 129, 286, 545
Small, Robert 263, 263
Small, Samuel 141
SMALLAGE 679
SMALLBENT 679
SMALLEDGE 679
SMALLEY 679
Smalley, Hannah 39
Smalley, Hix 679
Smalley, Mary 691
Smallidge, Joanna 335
SMALLPEICE 679
SMALLPIECE 679
Smally, Hannah 39
Smaly, Hannah 39
SMART 679
Smart, Mary 790
Smart, Rebecca 723
SMEAD 679
Smead, Elizabeth 208
Smead, Judith 355
Smead, Mehitable 400, 537
Smead, Thankful 355
Smead, Waitstill 780
Smead, William 215
SMEDLEY 679
Smedley, Baptist 672
Smedley, Hannah 143
Smedley, Mary 419, 667
Smedley, Samuel 752
Smedley, Sarah 349
Smedly, Hannah Wheeler 561
Smell, Thomas 546
Smethurst, Mary 12
SMITH 280, 316, 679, 680, 681, 682, 683, 684, 685, 686, 687, 688, 689, 690, 691
Smith, --- 72, 189, 412, 503
Smith, Abigail 4, 66, 186, 242, 352, 675, 764, 830
Smith, Abraham 24
Smith, Adrean 538
Smith, Adrian 538
Smith, Agnes 789
Smith, Alice 218, 501, 744, 803
Smith, Ammi 779
Smith, Amy 172, 749, 779
Smith, Andria 538
Smith, Ann 11, 46, 162, 328, 388, 516, 608, 814
Smith, Anna 46, 199, 433, 611
Smith, Annabelle 47
Smith, Anne 520, 761
Smith, Anphillis 803
Smith, Arthur 349, 529, 546
Smith, Barbara 87
Smith, Bathsheba 328, 634
Smith, Benjamin 354, 657
Smith, Beriah 280, 841
Smith, Bethia 713
Smith, Bethiah 312
Smith, Catherine 2
Smith, Christopher 506, 716
Smith, Content 394

Smith, Daniel 123, 355, 769
Smith, Deborah 51, 64, 455, 718, 836
Smith, Deliverance 32, 619
Smith, Dermit 242
Smith, Dorothy 76, 334, 515, 634, 636, 643, 646, 726
Smith, Dowsabel 788
Smith, Ebenezer 42
Smith, Eleanor 21
Smith, Elisha 21
Smith, Elizabeth 18, 21
Smith, Elizabeth 75, 88, 121, 132, 138, 146, 149, 154, 181, 183, 215, 219, 250, 256, 262, 274, 292, 302, 304, 313, 320, 330, 334, 335, 339, 369, 388, 402, 403, 404, 413, 455, 459, 478, 480, 487, 501, 508, 533, 541, 549, 550, 563, 567, 613, 634, 650, 682, 684, 687, 688, 691, 707, 737, 738, 749, 767, 810, 819, 831, 839
Smith, Elizabeth Goodell 63
Smith, Elizabeth Hutchins 766
Smith, Ellen 311
Smith, Esther 84, 110, 410, 750
Smith, Exercise 593
Smith, Frances 608, 650
Smith, Frances Tough Chester 704
Smith, Francis 25
Smith, George 413
Smith, Giles 413, 594
Smith, Grace 146, 256
Smith, Hannah 11, 46, 68, 85, 92, 113, 135, 139, 141, 183, 197, 223, 242, 251, 269, 273, 299, 362, 373, 443, 455, 465, 493, 501, 502, 514, 519, 528, 543, 545, 586, 640, 691, 719, 752, 755, 764, 784, 805
Smith, Hannah Hodsdon 379
Smith, Hasediah 644
Smith, Henry 17, 181, 650, 688
Smith, Henry (Rev.) 76
Smith, Hester 718
Smith, Hopestill 539
Smith, Hugh 249
Smith, Isabel 25
Smith, Isabella 25
Smith, J. 6
Smith, James 89, 125, 317, 399, 549, 579, 639, 645, 657, 691, 775
Smith, Jane 638
Smith, Jemima 498
Smith, Jeremiah 170, 242
Smith, Joan 534
Smith, Joanna 456, 593, 626, 644, 689, 845
Smith, Johanna 320
Smith, John 64, 77, 85, 155, 165, 175, 315, 403, 438, 454, 514, 526, 527, 539, 549, 638, 691, 750, 752, 775, 776, 786, 824, 839, 842
Smith, Jonathan 480
Smith, Jone 691
Smith, Joseph 347, 687
Smith, Joshua 626, 747
Smith, Joyce 299, 546
Smith, Judith 288, 495, 689, 751, 829
Smith, Katharine 764
Smith, Lucy 294
Smith, Lucy Marston 525
Smith, Lydia 31, 170, 272, 273, 369, 549, 834, 837, 838, 839

Smith, Magdalen 545
Smith, Marah 210
Smith, Margaret 251, 529, 553, 777, 785, 831
Smith, Margaret Hackett 331
Smith, Maria Catharine 328
Smith, Mariah 173, 672
Smith, Mariah Catherine 501
Smith, Marian 524
Smith, Martha 24, 80, 118, 146, 343, 375, 471, 549, 633, 688
Smith, Martha Hull 717
Smith, Mary 16, 21, 45, 63, 84, 96, 97, 102, 103, 122, 131, 132, 154, 160, 176, 182, 207, 210, 216, 234, 249, 252, 262, 263, 291, 306, 318, 319, 330, 333, 338, 348, 351, 366, 367, 374, 386, 387, 400, 422, 437, 438, 460, 469, 473, 483, 524, 541, 557, 563, 569, 575, 613, 622, 640, 643, 655, 672, 684, 687, 717, 721, 735, 748, 749, 752, 813, 823, 842
Smith, Mary Deming 820
Smith, Matthew 182, 200, 236
Smith, Mehitable 2, 132, 643
Smith, Mercy 62, 154, 330, 532
Smith, Meribah 550
Smith, Miriam 306, 833
Smith, Morris 510
Smith, Nehemiah 478
Smith, Nicholas 212, 643, 686
Smith, Pelatiah 233
Smith, Phebe 100, 749
Smith, Philip 177
Smith, Philippa 71
Smith, Rachel 62, 350, 839
Smith, Ralph 352
Smith, Rebecca 3, 80, 88, 145, 197, 376, 388, 395, 437, 529, 688, 711, 724, 754, 816, 846
Smith, Richard 132, 214, 281, 347, 481, 565, 571, 615
Smith, Robert 431, 433, 637, 724
Smith, Roger 388
Smith, Ruhama 749
Smith, Ruth 801
Smith, Samuel 24, 80, 87, 225, 502, 562, 566, 642, 647
Smith, Samuel (Jr.) 283
Smith, Sarah 20, 22, 73, 97, 109, 113, 156, 161, 240, 264, 268, 282, 308, 318, 341, 360, 402, 430, 432, 434, 455, 478, 497, 498, 510, 533, 545, 550, 561, 567, 577, 581, 587, 629, 642, 676, 692, 695, 707, 737, 763, 837
Smith, Simeon 333
Smith, Simon 333
Smith, Susanna 21, 52, 220, 396, 586, 700
Smith, Susannah 404, 466, 817
Smith, Thomas 159, 384, 395, 438, 652, 738
Smith, Tomasin 541
Smith, Waitstill 204
Smith, William 349, 396, 512, 545
Smithe, Martha 148
SMITHSON 691
SMITON 691
Smiton, Sarah 110
Smyne, Rebecca 334
Smyth, Christopher 67
Smyth, John 174
Smythe, Elizabeth 150
Snasher, Mary 475

SNAWSELL 691
Sneden, Gretie 298
Sneden, Margareta 298
Sneden, Margarita 298
SNELL 691
Snell, Ann 807
Snell, George 187, 401, 402
Snell, Hannah 38, 468, 807
Snell, Martha Snell 110
Snell, Mary 736, 802
Snell, Samuel 223
Snell, Susannah 350
Snell, Thomas 243
SNELLING 691
Snelling, Abigail 373
Snelling, Ann 205
Snelling, Anne 205
Snelling, Benjamin 423, 551
Snelling, William 635
SNOOK 691
Snook, John 683
Snook, Margaret 565
SNOOKE 691
SNOW 691, 692
Snow, Abigail 275, 426, 447, 844
Snow, Alice 41
Snow, Anna 25
Snow, Bashua 439
Snow, Benjamin 134
Snow, Bethiah 685
Snow, Elizabeth 504, 635
Snow, Grace 363
Snow, Hannah 170, 200, 223, 394, 624
Snow, John 223
Snow, Josiah 654
Snow, Lydia 127, 677, 829
Snow, Mary 537, 552, 624, 829
Snow, Melatiah 268
Snow, Melcha 844
Snow, Meletiah 268
Snow, Mercy 829
Snow, Milcha 268
Snow, Rebecca 624, 679
Snow, Ruth 169
Snow, Sarah 34, 309, 707, 775, 784, 846
Snow, Stephen 67, 634
Snow, Thomas 338
Snow, Wm. 624
SNOWDEN 692
Snowsell, Thomas 569
SNOWTON 692
SOAMES 692
Soames, Dorothy 756
Soames, William 756
SOAN 692
Soane, Dorothy 756
Soane, Elizabeth 426
Soane, William 756
Soatlie, Mary 422
Sodder, Margaret 365
Solard, Abigail 452
Solard, Bethiah 366
Solard, John 400
Solard, Martha 437
Solard, Sarah 592
Solare, Mary 244, 818
SOLARO 692
Solarre, Mary 244
SOLART 692
Solart, Elizabeth 476
Solart, Hannah 751
Solart, Mary 244
SOLAS 692
Sole, Patience 351
SOLENDINE 692
SOLEY 692

Soley, John 320
Soley, Matthew 717
SOLLAS 692
SOLLE 693
SOLLENDINE 692
SOLOMON 692
Solsby, Joanna 161
SOMERBY 692
Somerby, Elizabeth 157, 333, 514
Somerby, Henry 166
Somerby, Rebecca 434, 710, 776
Somerby, Sarah 332
Somerly, Abigail 324
SOMERS 692 see SUMMERS
Somers, Abigail 584
SOMES 692
Somes, Abigail 584
Somes, Mary 339
Somes, Patience 747
Somes, Sarah 808, 831
Sone, Robert 365, 712
Soole, Sarah 374
SOORLARD 692
SOPER 692, 693 see SLOPER
Soper, Elizabeth 490
Soper, John 737, 841
Soper, Joseph 373
Soper, Sarah 841
Sorrell, Margery 705
Sotheron, Jane 193
SOTHWICK 694
Sothwick, Sara 115
Sothwick, Sarah 115
Sothwicke, Provided 296
Sothy, Mary 506, 586
Sothy, Mercy 586
SOTTOW 657
SOUDEN 693
Souden, Mary 644
SOUL 693
SOULE 693 see SOWELL
Soule, Elizabeth 773
Soule, John 648
Soule, Mary 210, 574
Soule, Patience 351
Soule, Rachel 164
Soule, Rebecca 797
Soule, Sarah 374, 842
Soule, Susanna 796
Soulsby, Anne 119
South, Ann 189, 412
South, Joseph 445
SOUTHACK 693
Southard, Abigail 279
Southard, Eunice 279
Southard, Sarah 57
SOUTHER 693
Souther, Diana 497
Souther, Elizabeth 682
Souther, Hannah 340, 420
Souther, John 593
Souther, Mary 65, 75, 665
Souther, Nathaniel 372
SOUTHERICK 693
Southerick, John 104
Southerin, Thomas 641
SOUTHERN 694
Southerne, Mercy 283
SOUTHMATE 693
SOUTHMAYD 693
Southmayd, William 22, 58
Southmeade, William 22
Southor, Mary 665
SOUTHWELL 693
Southwell, Anna Willix Roscoe Blunt 637
Southwich, Cassandra 524
Southwich, Mary 536

SOUTHWICK 693, 694
Southwick, Betty 816
Southwick, Deborah 740
Southwick, Eleanor 547
Southwick, Esther 129
Southwick, John 104, 182, 272, 742
Southwick, Mary 124, 751
Southwick, Mercy 547
Southwick, Provided 296
Southwick, Sara 115
Southwick, Sarah 115, 365
SOUTHWORTH 694
Southworth, Alice 152
Southworth, Edward 91
Southworth, Eliz. 272
Southworth, Elizabeth 292, 394
Southworth, Mary 7
Southworth, Mercy 283
Southworth, Priscilla 726
Sowars, Elizabeth 772
SOWDEN 693
Sowden, Elizabeth 708
Sowdin, Susanna 208
SOWELL 694 see SOULE
SOWLE 693
SOWTHER 693
Sowther, Hannah 340
Spafford, Elizabeth 477, 661
Spafford, Hannah 512
Spaford, Elizabeth 661
Spaford, Hannah 512
SPALDEN 694, 695
Spalden, Sarah 503
SPALDIN 694, 695
SPALDING 694, 695
Spalding, Deborah 52, 486
Spalding, Dorothy 245, 248
Spalding, Elizabeth 799
Spalding, Eunice 560
Spalding, Hannah 667
Spalding, Lydia 584
Spalding, Mary 441
Spalding, Sarah 486, 503
SPARHAWK 694
Sparhawk, Anna 177, 181
Sparhawk, Anne 181
Sparhawk, Esther 5
Sparhawk, John 357
Sparhawk, Lydia 813
Sparhawk, Mary 46, 725
Sparhawk, Sybil 813
Sparhawk, Sylvia 813
SPARHAWKE 694
Sparhawke, Sybil 26
Spark, Margaret 835
Spark, Rose 533
SPARKE 694
Sparkes, Frances 768
SPARKMAN 694
SPARKS 694
Sparks, Elizabeth 571
Sparks, Margaret 807
Sparks, Mary 346
Sparks, Rebecca 483
Sparks, Susanna 19
SPARO 694
SPARREY 694
Sparro, Jonathan 500
SPARROW 694
Sparrow, Alice 644
Sparrow, Elizabeth 283
Sparrow, Jonathan 164, 846
Sparrow, Lydia 284, 369
Sparrow, Patience 551
Sparrow, Priscilla 319
Sparrow, Rebecca 283
SPARRY 694

SPARTA 694
Spatchurst, Elizabeth 650
Spatchurst, Susannah 650
Spaulden, Eunice 560
SPAULDING 695
Spaulding, Dinah 105
Spaulding, Edward 42
Spaulding, John 185, 185, 271
Spaulding, Mary 518
SPAULDYING 695
SPAULDYNG 695
SPAULE 695
Spaule, Mary 444
SPEAR 695
Spear, Ebenezer 788
Spear, George 213
Spear, Hannah 111
Spear, Mary Cramphorne 363
Spear, Sarah 832
SPECK 695
SPECKS see SPINK
Speed, Mary 93
SPELMAN 695
SPENCER 695, 696
Spencer, Abraham 580
Spencer, Alice 663
Spencer, Elizabeth 18, 150, 428, 701, 730, 746, 758, 793
Spencer, Esther 584
Spencer, Grace 210
Spencer, Hannah 93, 220, 424, 662, 701
Spencer, Jared 232
Spencer, John 562, 582, 841
Spencer, Lydia 539, 766
Spencer, Marah 103, 663
Spencer, Margaret 311
Spencer, Martha 65
Spencer, Mary 253, 401, 440, 580, 636
Spencer, Mehitable 175
Spencer, Michael 627
Spencer, Moses 85
Spencer, Rebecca 3, 63, 117, 433, 727
Spencer, Robert 618
Spencer, Ruth 157
Spencer, Samuel 77, 226, 402, 818
Spencer, Sarah 29, 139, 145, 240, 408
Spencer, Susan 29
Spencer, Susanna 29, 98, 296, 428
Spencer, Thomas 432, 776
Spencer, William 12, 245
Spenser, Elizabeth 476
Spenser, Penelope 755
Spenser, Richard 476
SPERRY 696
Sperry, Daniel 390, 824
Sperry, Esther 100, 390
Sperry, John 118, 226, 318
Sperry, Mary 567
Sperry, Nathaniel 519
SPICER 696, 697
Spicer, Anne 447
SPIKE 586
SPILLER 697
Spiller, Henry 793
SPINK 697 see SPECKS
Spink, Margery 766
Spinner, Thomas 131
SPINNEY 697
Spinney, Hannah 263
Spinney, Thomas 538
SPINNING 697
Spinning, Mary 641
Spinser, Gerard 156
Spinser, Jared 156

SPOFFORD 697
Spofford, Mary 403
Spofford, Sarah 438
SPOONER 697
Spooner, Hannah 641
Spooner, Martha 828
Spooner, Sarah 669
Spooner, Thomas 641
Spoor, Prudence Mitchell Bardden Tapley 95
Spoore, Catharine 508
Spoore, Mary 497
Spowel, Elizabeth 814
SPOWELL 697
SPRAGG 697
SPRAGUE 697, 698
Sprague, --- 455
Sprague, Ann 455
Sprague, Deborah 114, 502
Sprague, Desire 301
Sprague, Dorcas 239
Sprague, Elizabeth 723
Sprague, Hannah 634, 716
Sprague, Joanna 152, 731
Sprague, John 67, 736
Sprague, Jonathan 178
Sprague, Lydia 324
Sprague, Mary 243, 255, 440, 455, 822
Sprague, Mercy 756
Sprague, Millicent Holbrook 567
Sprague, Patience 418
Sprague, Persis 224
Sprague, Phineas 762
Sprague, Ralph 177
Sprague, Rebecca 25
Sprague, Ruth 681
Sprague, Samuel 107
Sprague, Sarah 159, 276, 384
Sprague, Winifred 218
SPRAY 698
SPRECK 697
SPRIKE 697
SPRING 698
Spring, Abigail 779
Spring, Anna 556
Spring, Elizabeth 291, 494
Spring, Hanery 799
Spring, Henry 178, 311
Spring, John 352
Spring, Mary 206, 778
Spring, Mehitable 711
Spring, Sarah 799
SPRINGER 698
Springer, Margaret 643
SPRINGFIELD 698
SPROAT 698
Sproat, Anna 624
SPROUT 698
Sprout, Anna 624
Sprout, Mercy 544
SPRY 698 see SPRAY
SPUR 699
Spur, Johanna 844
Spur, Patience 249
SPURE 699
SPURHAM 698
SPURR 698
Spurr, Mary 191, 606
Spurr, Waitstill 640
SPURRE 698
SPURRELL 699
SPURWELL 699
Spurwell, Abigail 53
Spurwell, Christopher 163
Spurwell, Julian 163
Spurwink, Elizabeth 33
Square, Mary 804

SQUEAK 695
SQUIER 699
Squier, Elizabeth 804
SQUIERE 699
SQUIRE 699
Squire, Ann 544, 607
Squire, Barbara 156
Squire, Edith 3, 290
Squire, Grisel 799
Squire, Hannah 140
Squire, John 210
Squire, Margaret 667, 727
Squire, Mary 32, 351, 804
Squire, Rachel 9, 799
Squire, Sarah 660
Squire, William 156
Squyre, Elizabeth 467
Sreet, Sarah 746
STABBS 719
Stable, Mary Boles 353
STACE 699
STACEY 699
Stacey, Abigail 390
Stacey, Anna 269
Stacey, Elizabeth 840
Stacey, Esther 349
Stacey, Grace 187
Stacey, Henry 615
Stacey, Hester 349
Stacey, Jane 615, 701
Stacey, Mary 466
Stacey, Ruth Cheever Wadlon 769
Stacey, Sarah 126, 565
Stacey, Susanna 284
Stacey, Thomas 840
Stacia, Anna 269
STACIE 699
STACKHOUSE 699
Stackhouse, Ruth 390
STACKPOLE 699
Stackpole, Catherine 430
Stackpole, Hannah 346
STACY 699
Stacy, Ann 228
Stacy, Anne 228
Stacy, Eleanor 693
Stacy, Elizabeth 6
Stacy, Hannah 839
Stacy, Henry 615
Stacy, Jane 615
Stacy, Margery Partridge Mason 495
Stacy, Mary 42, 174, 501, 561
Stacy, Mary Moore 270
Stacy, Priscilla 491
Stacy, Rebecka 120
Stacy, Simon 5
Stacy, Susanna 131, 803
Stacy, Susannah 491
Stacy, Thomas 174
Stacy, Thomasine 840
STADDEN 699
STADDIN 699
STAFFORD 699, 700
Stafford, Deborah 797
Stafford, Freelove 743
Stafford, Hannah 101
Stafford, Mary 777
Stafford, Mercy 740
Stafford, Patience 394
Stafford, Sarah 657, 797
Stagge, Margaret 691
STAINER 700
STAINES 700
Staines, Anne 170
Staines, Rebecca 659
STAINWOOD 702
Stainwood, Jane 583, 692

Stainwood, Naomi 651
Stainwood, Philip 583
Stalham, Elizabeth 821
STALLION 706
Stallion, Deborah 26
Stallion, Edward 146
Stallion, Margaret 274, 357
Stallion, Sarah 242
Stalworthie, Mary 784
Stambury, Abigail 282
Stamfield, Abigail 499
Stamford, Mary 555
Stamford, Thomas 423
STANARD 701
Stanare, Alice 664
STANBERRY 700
STANBOROUGH 700
Stanborough, Hannah 479
Stanborough, Josiah 801
Stanborough, Mary 244, 718
Stanborough, Sarah 547
STANBRIDGE 700 see
    STANBURY
Stanbrough, Sarah 366
STANBURY 700 see
    STANBRIDGE
Stanbury, Martha 186
STANCLIFF 700
STANCLIFT 700
STANDFORD 650, 700
Standford, Mary 580
STANDISH 700
Standish, Alexander 383, 670
Standish, Elizabeth 214
Standish, Elizabeth Thatcher Fuller 289
Standish, Eunice 713
Standish, James 407, 636
Standish, Lorah 648
Standish, Lydia 648
Standish, Mary 134
Standish, Mehitable 112
Standish, Mercy 648
Standish, Miles 507
Standish, Myles 3, 553
Standish, Sarah 407, 693, 812
STANDLACK 700
Standlake, Joanna 502
Standlake, Joan 587
Standlake, Joanna 587
Standlake, Mary 724
Standlake, Richard 47
STANDLEY 701
Standley, Abigail 386
Stanffull, Abigail 499
STANFORD 650, 700
Stanford, Joseph 225
Stanford, Martha 776
Stanford, Mary 580, 776, 826
Stanford, Mercy 554
Stanford, Robert 91, 822
Stanford, William 225
STANHOP 700
Stanhop, Hannah 419
Stanhop, Jemima 645
STANHOPE 701
Stanhope, Hannah 419
Stanhope, Jemima 645
Stanhope, Joseph 488
STANIAN 702
Staniford, Mary 826
STANION 702
Stanlake, Lydia 840
Stanlake, Richard 840
STANLEY 701
Stanley, Abigail 187, 386, 771
Stanley, Caleb 471, 515, 825
Stanley, Christopher 579

Stanley, Elizabeth 23, 588, 646, 770
Stanley, Hannah 156, 588, 595
Stanley, Joan 587
Stanley, Joanna 587
Stanley, John 690
Stanley, Lois 595
Stanley, Martha 741
Stanley, Mary 264, 265, 386, 594, 741
Stanley, Rebecca 473
Stanley, Ruth 515
Stanley, Sarah 297, 769
Stanley, Susanna 579
Stanley, Thomas 833
Stanley, Timothy 29
STANNARD 701 see
    STONEHARD
Stannard, Elizabeth 153
STANOP 700
Stansfield, Abigail 420
Stansfield, Miriam 230
STANTON 701, 702
Stanton, Ann 702
Stanton, Content 540
Stanton, Dorothy 480, 541
Stanton, Hannah 136, 554, 846
Stanton, Joanna 215
Stanton, John 191
Stanton, Mary 166, 191, 300, 456, 634
Stanton, Mercy 191, 300
Stanton, Robert 754
Stanton, Sarah 149, 215, 601, 741
STANWOOD 702
Stanwood, Jane 583, 692
Stanwood, John 128, 200
Stanwood, Naomi 651
Stanwood, Philip 583
Stanwood, Ruth 339
STANYAN 702
Stanyan, Ann 661, 673
Stanyan, Anthony 563
Stanyan, Elizabeth 707
Stanyan, Mary 581, 689
Stanyan, Mehitable 630
Stanyon, Elizabeth 707
STAPELLS 702
STAPLE 702
STAPLEFORD 702
STAPLES 702
Staples, Hannah 54
Staples, Jacob 98
Staples, John 640
Staples, Mary 350
Staples, Mary Boles 353
Staples, Mehitable 258
Staples, Peter 244
Staples, Rebecca 720
Staples, Sarah 543, 720
Staples, Sarah Atkins 331
STAPLETON 702
Star, Elizabeth 28
Star, Mary 385, 706
STARBIRD 702
Starborough, Ann 338
STARBUCK 702
Starbuck, Abigail 166
Starbuck, Dorcas 297
Starbuck, Elizabeth 166
Starbuck, Esther 290, 765
Starbuck, Eunice 293
Starbuck, Hepzibah 353
Starbuck, Mary 293
Starbuck, Priscilla 171
Starbuck, Sarah 26, 715, 765
Starbuck, Shuah 362, 548
Starbuck, William 26

STARK 702, 703
Stark, Anna 616
Stark, Elizabeth 358, 448, 715
Stark, Martha 266
Stark, Sarah 267
Starkes, Catherine 10
STARKEY 703
Starkey, John 330
Starkey, Mary 139
Starkie, Hannah 783
STARKWEATHER 703
Starkweather, Jennet 587
Starkweather, Robert 587
STARLIN 706
STARLING 706
Starling, Daniel 250
Starling, Hannah 363
Starnes, Sarah 800
Starns, Sarah Beers 801
STARR 703
Starr, Benjamin 256
Starr, Constant 519
Starr, Elizabeth 263, 752
Starr, Hannah 200, 273, 646
Starr, Lydia 256, 297
Starr, Mary 385, 499, 611
Starr, Mary Symonds Norrice 538
Starr, Rachel 368
Starr, Robert 176, 536
Starr, Ruth 516
Starr, Sinetinot 638
Starr, Thomas 368
STARSE 703
START 703 see STERT
Start, Elizabeth 841
Start, Sarah 842
STASEY 699
Stasey, Grace 598
STASY 699
Stasy, Jean 701
STATHEM 703
STAY 703
Stay, Ann 228
Stay, Anne 228
STAYNER 700
Steadford, Elizabeth 262
STEADMAN 705
Steadman, Sarah 366
Stearnes, Mary 814
STEARNS 703, 704
Stearns, Abigail 349, 520
Stearns, Elizabeth 486
Stearns, Hannah 283
Stearns, Isaac 145
Stearns, John 285, 514, 557
Stearns, Martha 407
Stearns, Mary 119, 200, 419, 458
Stearns, Rebecca 751
Stearns, Sarah 714, 800
Stearns, Sarah Beers 801
Stearns, Thomas 258
STEBBIN 704
STEBBINS 704, 705
Stebbins, Abigail 23, 576
Stebbins, Benjamin 37
Stebbins, Benoni 63, 244
Stebbins, Deborah 15, 327
Stebbins, Editha 211, 385, 499
Stebbins, Edward 174
Stebbins, Elizabeth 130, 156, 826
Stebbins, Hannah 537, 667
Stebbins, John 527, 719
Stebbins, Mary 297, 490, 719, 821
Stebbins, Rebecca 719
Stebbins, Sarah 78, 504, 693
Stebbins, Thankful 719
Stebbins, Thomas 37, 171, 250,
    527

Stebman, Damaris 452
STEDMAN 705
Stedman, Ann 462
Stedman, Elizabeth 234, 340, 663,
    736, 764
Stedman, George 40
Stedman, Hannah 408, 528
Stedman, Isaac 34, 255
Stedman, John 6, 300, 539
Stedman, Martha 178
Stedman, Mary 716, 740
Stedman, Sarah 7, 89, 319, 574,
    578
Stedman, Thomas 280
Stedman, Violet 640
STEDWELL see STUDWELL
Steel, Elizabeth 786
Steel, Martha 365
STEELE 705
Steele, Hannah 348, 753
Steele, James 712
Steele, John 373, 662, 708
Steele, Lydia 70
Steele, Martha 364
Steele, Mary 70, 336, 429, 737
Steele, Rachel 10, 685
Steele, Samuel 753
Steele, Sarah 80, 429
Steer, Richard 308, 800
STEERE 705, 706
Steere, Dinah 739
Steere, Jane 77
Steere, Sarah 589
STEEVENS 706, 707, 708, 709
Steevinson, Hannah 120
STELLE 706
STENT 706
Stent, Dorothy 44
Stent, Eleazer 55, 348
Stent, Elizabeth 55, 706, 762
Stent, Hannah 762
Stent, Margaret 348
Stenton, Anna 70
Stenton, Anne 29, 70
STEPHENS 707, 708, 709
Stephens, David 356
Stephens, Elizabeth 595
Stephens, Esther 426
Stephens, Honour 338
Stephens, Jane 383
Stephens, Margery 26, 386
Stephens, Marie 843
Stephens, Mary 346, 843
Stephens, Rebecca 444, 495
Stephens, Thomasin 814
Stephenson, Margaret 313, 656
Stephson, Sarah 75
STEPNEY 706
STERLING 706
Sterling, Daniel 57, 250
Sterling, Deborah 26
Sterling, Elizabeth 213
Sterling, Hannah 363
Sterling, Sarah 258
Sterling, William 530, 654, 716
Sterne, Sarah 714
Sterns, Hannah 100
Sterns, Judith 634
STERRY 706
Sterry, Hannah 70
Sterry, Roger 266, 367
STERT see START
Stertevant, Anne 49
Stertevant, Hannah 49
STERTT 706
STETSON 706
Stetson, Anne 29
Stetson, Bethia 18

Stetson, Eunice 415, 635
Stetson, Hannah 278, 743
Stetson, Lois 275
Stetson, Robert 111
Stetson, William 346
STETSUN 706
Stevenes, Joanna 44
Stevenes, Thomas 44
STEVENS 706, 707, 708, 709
Stèvens, Abigail 459, 504
Stevens, Alice 471
Stevens, Ann 583
Stevens, Benjamin 150, 668
Stevens, Caleb 442
Stevens, Catharine 829
Stevens, Charles 656
Stevens, Deborah 693, 790, 843
Stevens, Deliverance 218
Stevens, Dionis 166
Stevens, Dunie 399
Stevens, Ebenezer 211
Stevens, Edward 193, 347
Stevens, Eleanor 755
Stevens, Elizabeth 151, 555, 580,
    757, 816, 838
Stevens, Erasmus 80
Stevens, Esther 413, 661, 744
Stevens, Frances 277
Stevens, Grace 285
Stevens, Hannah 342, 650
Stevens, Henry 602
Stevens, Hester 744
Stevens, James 173, 264, 282
Stevens, Joanna 827
Stevens, John 90, 148, 165, 252,
    684
Stevens, Josiah 372
Stevens, Judith 96
Stevens, Katherine 212
Stevens, Marie 843
Stevens, Mary 41, 146, 167, 173,
    207, 223, 269, 289, 346, 423,
    432, 441, 511, 541, 548, 558,
    803, 812, 843
Stevens, Nan 522
Stevens, Naomi 346
Stevens, Rebecca 523, 645
Stevens, Richard 331
Stevens, Robert 230
Stevens, Ruth 306
Stevens, Samon 38
Stevens, Samuel 388, 705
Stevens, Sarah 23, 46, 75, 147,
    162, 223, 453, 519, 577, 633,
    691
Stevens, Sarah Chandler Cleaves
    13, 161
Stevens, Thomas 249, 424, 507,
    785
Stevens, Timothy (Rev.) 808
Stevens, William 135, 532, 745
STEVENSON 709, 711
Stevenson, Abigail 216, 808
Stevenson, Ann 319
Stevenson, Anna 149
Stevenson, Anne 149, 319
Stevenson, Deborah 826
Stevenson, Edward 319
Stevenson, Elizabeth 145, 255
Stevenson, James 40
Stevenson, Janetie 455
Stevenson, Jonathan 13, 85
Stevenson, Margaret 822
Stevenson, Mary 85, 406
Stevenson, Naomi 776
Stevenson, Rebecca 564
Stevenson, Richard 478
Stevenson, Sarah 75, 375, 476

Stevenson, Susannah 264
Stevins, Juliett 114
Steward, Jane 253
Steward, John 645
Steward, Sarah 2, 278
Steward, Susanna 672
STEWART 709, 710
Stewart, Abigail 185
Stewart, Anne 297
Stewart, Catherine 796
Stewart, Dorcas 687
Stewart, Eleanor 764
Stewart, Elizabeth 577, 796
Stewart, Hannah 237
Stewart, John 645
Stewart, Lydia 186
Stewart, Martha 795
Stewart, Sarah 2
STICKNEE 710
STICKNEY 710
Stickney, Amos 2
Stickney, Andrew 141, 420, 449
Stickney, Elizabeth 732
Stickney, Faith 291
Stickney, Mary 41, 575
Stickney, Samuel 290
Stiels, Eunice 823
STIFF 710
STILEMAN 710, 711
Stileman, Alice 664
Stileman, Elias 141, 824
Stileman, Elizabeth 427
Stileman, Mary 280, 710
Stileman, Richard 710
Stileman, Ruth 126, 728
STILER 710
STILES 710, 711
Stiles, Deborah 707
Stiles, Elizabeth 126
Stiles, Ephraim 312
Stiles, Eunice 823
Stiles, Francis 76, 158, 356
Stiles, Hannah 78, 375
Stiles, Isaac 344, 741
Stiles, Mary 245, 783
Stiles, Miriam 76
Stiles, Sarah 38, 158, 574, 645,
    710
STILEWELL 711
Still, Judith Fillbrook Shapard 667
STILLMAN 711
STILLSON 711
Stillson, Mary 186
Stillson, Vincent 186
STILLWELL 711
Stillwell, Alice 447, 547
Stillwell, Ann 816
Stillwell, Elizabeth 318
Stillwell, Mary 523
STILSON 711
Stilson, James 53, 588
Stilson, Margaret 374
Stilson, Mary 37, 42
Stilson, Vincent 51
Stilson, William 539
STILWELL 711
Stilwell, Abigail 384
Stilwell, Ales 384
Stilwell, Alice 384
Stilwell, Hannah Reeder 658
Stilwell, Rebecca 251, 318
STIMPSON 711
Stimpson, Abigail 62, 194
Stimpson, Deborah 2
Stimpson, Elizabeth 505
Stimpson, James 599
Stimpson, Rebecca 564
Stimpson, Ruth 599

Stimpson, Sarah 436, 476
STIMSON 711
Stimson, Abigail 86
Stimson, Deborah 826
Stimson, Hannah 120
Stimson, James 309
Stimson, Mary 623
Stimson, Naomi 773, 776
STIRTEVANT 720
STITES 711
STOAKHAM 711
STOARE 715
STOCKBRIDGE 712
Stockbridge, Abigail 428
Stockbridge, Charles 759
Stockbridge, Elizabeth 409, 758
Stockbridge, Hannah 742
Stockbridge, John 365, 692
Stockbridge, Mary 676
Stockbridge, Sarah 759, 840
STOCKER 712
Stocker, Martha 4, 95
Stocker, Mary 141, 337, 382
STOCKING 712
Stocking, Bethia 716
Stocking, Hannah 65
Stocking, Lydia 393, 621
Stocking, Samuel 705
Stocking, Sarah 543
STOCKMAN 712
Stockman, Elizabeth 90
Stockman, John 90
STOCKTON 712
Stockton, Prudence 385
STOCKWELL 712
STODDARD 712, 713
Stoddard, Anthony 653, 793
Stoddard, Caleb 312
Stoddard, Christian 584, 822
Stoddard, David 672
Stoddard, Dorothy 748
Stoddard, Elizabeth 428, 477, 844
Stoddard, Esther 244
Stoddard, Hannah 802
Stoddard, John 310, 751
Stoddard, Lydia 760
Stoddard, Mary 513, 794, 804, 843
Stoddard, Simeon 182
Stoddard, Simion 672
Stoddard, Solomon (Rev.) 496
Stoddard, Tabitha 450
STODDER 712, 713
Stodder, Elizabeth 428, 477
Stodder, John 648
Stodder, Mary 804
Stodder, Samuel 152
Stodder, Tabitha 450
Stoder, Hannah 802
STOKES 713
Stokes, Deborah 133, 433
Stokes, Elizabeth 597
Stokes, Mary 7, 520
STON 714
STONARD 715 see STANNARD
Stonard, Alice 664
STONE 713, 714, 715, 716
Stone, Abigail 100, 430
Stone, Ann 133, 228
Stone, Anna 426
Stone, Anne 228, 319
Stone, Bridget 227
Stone, Catharine 696
Stone, Daniel 778
Stone, Elizabeth 127, 160, 469,
    581, 596, 628, 660, 703, 716,
    770
Stone, Frances 321, 388
Stone, Gregory 182

Stone, Hannah 64, 460, 540, 722
Stone, Hannah Walley 461
Stone, Hester 100
Stone, Hugh 797
Stone, Joan 614
Stone, Joanna 726
Stone, John 125, 259, 351, 570,
    701, 801
Stone, Lydia 88
Stone, Margaret 110, 315
Stone, Mary 184, 185, 269, 280,
    403, 421, 493, 703, 704, 775,
    801
Stone, Phebe 452
Stone, Rebecca 346, 529
Stone, Rebekah 128
Stone, Ruth Goble Stratton 718
Stone, Samuel 14, 155, 279, 293,
    775
Stone, Sarah 44, 127, 155, 177,
    210, 244, 358, 370, 373, 485,
    503, 620, 653, 776
Stone, Sarah Ward Bradley 92
Stone, Simon 426, 479
Stone, Susanna 437
Stone, Susannah 307, 477
Stone, Tabitha 357, 620
Stone, William 194, 400, 569, 635
STONEHARD 715 see
    STANNARD
STOODLEY 719
Stoothoff, Eleanor 818
Stoothoff, Helena 818
Storce, Ann 228
Storce, Anne 228
STORER 715
Storer, Elizabeth 401
Storer, Hannah 339, 722
Storer, Paul 401
Storer, Sarah 26, 765
STORES 715
STOREY 715
Storey, Elizabeth 779
Storie, Ann 228
Storie, Anne 228
Storie, Elizabeth 722
Storre, Marie 802
STORRS 715
Storrs, Hannah 692
Storrs, Sarah 120
STORY 715
Story, Eleanor 381
Story, Elizabeth 138, 163, 211,
    423, 722
Story, Ellen 381
Story, Hannah 420, 722
Story, Margaret 201
Story, Martha 822
Story, Samuel 151
Story, Sarah 775
Story, Susanna 38
Story, Susannah 104, 156
Story, William 185, 496, 747
STOUGHTON 715, 716
Stoughton, --- (Capt.) 158
Stoughton, --- (Gen.) 531
Stoughton, Catharine 815
Stoughton, Christian 143
Stoughton, Elizabeth 247, 483
Stoughton, Hannah 511
Stoughton, Judith 215, 679
Stoughton, Katharine 815
Stoughton, Mary 259
Stoughton, Nicholas 618
Stoughton, Rebecca 496, 731
Stoughton, Rose 548
Stoughton, Thomas 405, 474
Stour, Sarah 661

Stout, Alice 740
Stout, Elizabeth 586
Stout, Mary 88
STOVER 716 see STOWERS
Stover, Deborah 655
Stover, Elizabeth 403
Stover, Hannah 153
Stover, Mary 777
Stover, Sarah 39, 126
STOVIER 716
STOW 716
Stow, Dorothy 302
Stow, Elizabeth 20, 68, 332, 581
Stow, Hope 577, 679
Stow, Ichabod 629
Stow, John 815
Stow, Margaret 809
Stow, Mary 185
Stow, Nathaniel 67, 99
Stow, Rachel 592
Stow, Samuel 155
Stow, Sarah 155
Stow, Thankful 25, 62, 755
STOWE 716
Stowe, Elizabeth 44, 581
Stowe, Jane 391
Stowe, Rachel 810
Stowe, Thankful 371, 585
STOWELL 716
Stowell, Elizabeth 450
Stowell, John 377
Stowell, Mary 294, 295
Stowell, Remember 618
Stowell, Samuel 55
STOWER see STOVER
Stower, --- 259
Stower, Elizabeth 259, 697
Stower, Hannah 370
Stower, Joanna 122
Stoweres, Susanna 799
STOWERS 716
Stowers, Abigail 444
Stowers, Ann 417
Stowers, Anna 417
Stowers, Deborah 396, 408
Stowers, Joseph 706
Stowers, Martha 360
Stowers, Mary 122, 140
Stowers, Sarah 137, 250, 360
Stowers, Susana 698
Stowers, Susanna 178, 311, 698, 799
Stows, Samuel 6
STRADE 718
STRAIGHT 716, 717
Straight, Elizabeth 793
Straight, Susannah 793
STRAKER 717
STRAND 717
STRANGE 717
Strange, Grizzel 267
Strange, John 198
Strapen, Sarah Patefield 692
STRAPIN 717
STRATEN 717
Straten, Mary 376
STRATFORD 717
Stratford, Clement 162, 198
Stratford, Elizabeth 262
Straton, Anna 360
Straton, Richard 201
STRATTON 717, 718
Stratton, --- 363
Stratton, Abigail 538
Stratton, Ann 287, 447
Stratton, Anna 360
Stratton, Anne 24
Stratton, Bridget 447

Stratton, Dorothy 574
Stratton, Elizabeth 151, 416, 448, 739, 750, 821
Stratton, Hannah 419
Stratton, Mark 736
Stratton, Martha 176
Stratton, Mary 376, 828
Stratton, Rebecca 126, 340, 662
Stratton, Richard 34, 201, 475
Stratton, Ruth 363, 805
Stratton, Stephen 337
STRAW 718
Strayte, Susannah 793
STREAM 718
Stream, Elizabeth 379
Stream, John 470
Stream, John (Jr.) 675
Stream, Mary 35
Stream, Thomas 548
Streame, Abigail 741
Streame, Martha 172
Streame, Sarah 124
STREEN 718
STREET 718
Street, Abiah 669
Street, Anna 194, 505
Street, Francis 350, 466
Street, Hannah 17, 19
Street, Mary 302
Street, Nicholas 460
Street, Nicholas (Rev.) 533
Street, Rosamond 466
Street, Samuel 746
Street, Sarah 363, 746
Street, Susanna 484, 567
STREETER 718
Streeter, Rebecca 677
Streeter, Sarah 316, 381
Streeter, Stephen 389, 631
Streetter, Sarah 316
STREING 718
STRICKLAND 718
Strickland, --- 478, 497
Strickland, Elizabeth 17, 204, 658, 834
Strickland, Joanna 834
Strickland, Sarah 266, 628, 683
Strickland, Thwaite 222
STRIDE 718
STRIKER 719
STRINGHAM 718
Stringham, Peter 338
STRODE 718
STRONG 719
Strong, --- 66, 737
Strong, Abigail 148, 440, 516, 592
Strong, Elizabeth 370, 562, 842
Strong, Esther 73
Strong, Experience 265
Strong, Hannah 135, 160, 387, 387, 591
Strong, Hester 73
Strong, Jedediah 459, 704
Strong, John 113, 755
Strong, Lydia 459
Strong, Maria 429
Strong, Mary 114, 156, 701
Strong, Mercy 114
Strong, Samuel 843
Strong, Sarah 73, 200, 369, 794
Strong, Thankful 36, 636
Strong, Thomas 92
STROUD 718, 719 see STRIDE
STROUT 719
Strutt, Elizabeth 657
STRYKER 719
Stryker, Jannetie 243
Stryker, Jannetye 243

STUARD 709, 710
Stuard, Anna 282
Stuard, Hannah 282
Stuard, Mary 278
STUART 709
Stuart, Anna 282
Stuart, Hannah 282
STUBBS 719
Stubbs, Elizabeth 711
Stubbs, Joshua 839
Stubbs, Mary 751
STUCHE 720
STUCKEY 719
Stuckey, George 163, 608
Studd, Mary 799
STUDLEY 719
Studley, Sarah 82
STUDLIE 719
STUDSON 706
Studson, Hannah 278
STUDWELL 705, 719 see STEDWELL
STUKEY 719
Stuppell, Susanna 761
STURDEVANT 720
Sturdevant, Mary 467
STURGES 720
Sturges, Deborah 616, 660
Sturges, Desire 221, 733
Sturges, Edward 54
Sturges, Elizabeth 363
Sturges, Hannah 320
Sturges, John 717, 727
Sturges, Joseph 517, 785
Sturges, Mary 363, 727
Sturges, Samuel 166
Sturges, Sarah 313, 717
Sturgis, Edward 625
Sturgis, Fear 384
Sturgis, Hannah 313
Sturgis, Samuel 546
Sturgis, Thankful 733
STURTEVANT 720
Sturtevant, Ann 783
Sturtevant, Anna 783
Sturtevant, Hannah 700
Sturtevant, John 195, 414
Sturtevant, Mary 467
Sturtevant, Mercy 84
Sturtevant, Rebecca 738
Sturtevant, Samuel 388
STUTCHE 720
STUTLY 719
Styker, Jannster 65
Styleman, Elizabeth 427
SUAWSELL 720
Sudham, Elizabeth 135
Sudham, William 135
SUGAR 720
SUGARS 720
SUISE 647
Suleavan, Margaret 229
Suller, Anna 13
Sullivan, Jael 748
Sullivan, Margaret 229
Sumer, Mary 789
SUMERS 720
Summer, Abigail 247
Summer, Thomas 247
SUMMERS 720 see SOMERS
Summers, Abigail 335
Summers, Hannah 657
Summers, Henry 616, 799
Summers, Sarah 557
Summersbie, Rebecca 776
SUMNER 720, 721
Sumner, Deliverance 791
Sumner, Elizabeth 365

Sumner, Experience 315
Sumner, Hannah 308
Sumner, Jane 163, 786
Sumner, Joan 786
Sumner, Joanne 786
Sumner, Mary 313, 393, 535, 724, 754
Sumner, Mercy 315
Sumner, Rebecca 376, 825
Sumner, Samuel 138
Sumner, Sarah 760, 791
Sumner, Thomas 427
Sumner, Waitstill 757
SUNDERLAND 721
Sunderland, --- 313
Sunderland, John 500
Sunderland, Mary 377, 609
Sunderland, Matthew 647
SUNDYE 649
Surrey, Grace 325
SURT 721
Sutleff, Nathaniel 345
Sutleffe, Anna 440
Sutleffe, Anne 440
SUTLIEFFE 721
SUTLIFF 721
Sutliff, Hannah 799
SUTLIFFE 721
Sutrobus, Joan 455
SUTTON 721
Sutton, Agnes Hitcheson 376
Sutton, Anna 224
Sutton, Anne 224
Sutton, Elizabeth 485
Sutton, Ester 87
Sutton, John 83
Sutton, Margaret 135
Sutton, Mary 83, 269
Sutton, Susanna 596
Sutton, William 330
SWACY 722
Swacy, Mary 188
Swadlock, Ann 298
SWAIN 721, 722
Swain, Benjamin 86
Swain, Dorcas 173, 725
Swain, Francis 462
Swain, Hannah 81, 418
Swain, Jeremiah 187, 241
Swain, John 132
Swain, Martha 462
Swain, Mary 241, 529
Swain, Prudence 577
Swain, Richard 118
Swain, Roger 806
Swain, Sarah 540
Swain, William 188, 405
SWAINE 722
Swaine, Elizabeth 662, 778
Swaine, Grace 81
Swaine, Mary 524
Swaine, Richard 118
Swaine, Sarah 423
Swaine, William 251
Swalden, Mary 606
SWALLOW 722
Swallow, Mary 781
SWAN 722
Swan, Ann 27
Swan, Dorothy 2, 145, 202, 838
Swan, Elizabeth 345, 622
Swan, Faith 721
Swan, Frances 608
Swan, Henry 258
Swan, Jane 826
Swan, John 835
Swan, Julian 710
Swan, Mary 781

Swan, Mercy 781
Swan, Richard 388, 420, 755
Swan, Robert 638
Swan, Roger 413
Swan, Ruth 349, 642
Swan, Sarah 89, 349
Swan, Thomas 31
SWANN 722
Swansey, Abigail 496
SWANTON 722
SWARTON 722
SWASE 722
SWASEY 722
Swasey, Elizabeth 465, 808
Swasey, Mary 188, 494
SWASY 723
SWAYNE 721, 722
Swayne, Ann 284
Swayne, Bethiah 524
Swayne, Christian 778
Swayne, Deborah 762
Swayne, Elizabeth 787
Swayne, Hepzibah 585
Swayne, Jeremiah 585
Swayne, Jeremy 158
Swayne, Joanna 190
Swayne, John 129
Swayne, Rebecca 129, 675, 841
Swaynes, Mary 490
SWAYSEY 722
SWAYT 723
SWAZEY 722, 723
Swazey, Abigail 337
Swazey, Mehitable 8
SWEATLAND 723
Sweatman, Margaret 416
SWEET 723
Sweet, Bethia 813
Sweet, Elizabeth 826
Sweet, James 371
Sweet, John 381, 382, 544, 826
Sweet, Martha 13
Sweet, Mary 243, 381, 382, 589
Sweet, Renewed 298
Sweet, Samuel 190
Sweet, Susanna 544
SWEETEN 723
SWEETING 723
SWEETLAND 723
Sweetland, Sarah 51
SWEETMAN 723
Sweetman, Bethiah 367
Sweetman, Elizabeth 793
Sweetman, Rebecca 695
Sweetman, Sarah 752
SWEETSER 723
Sweetser, Abigail 711
Sweetser, Bethia 551, 799
Sweetser, Hannah 269
Sweetser, Mary 77
Sweetser, Seth 159, 360
Sweezy, Abigail 337
Sweitzer, Seth 542
Swell, John 528
SWET 724
Swet, Hannah 30
SWETLAND 723
Swetland, Agnes 476
Swetland, Annis 476
Swetland, William 476
SWETMAN 723
Swetman, Bethiah 367, 400
Swetman, Rebecca 695
SWETT 723, 724
Swett, Benjamin 324
Swett, Esther 320
Swett, Hannah 30, 335, 645
Swett, John 323

Swett, Joseph 128
Swett, Mary 477
Swett, Miriam 477
Swett, Rebecca 291
Swett, Sarah 377
SWEZEY 723
Swezey, Samuel 401
SWIFT 724
Swift, Abigail 20
Swift, Anna 615
Swift, Dinah 573
Swift, Elizabeth 204, 600, 788, 816
Swift, Esther 12
Swift, Hannah 266, 745, 746, 828
Swift, Hester 300
Swift, Jane 33
Swift, Joan 33
Swift, Mary 689, 721, 805, 840
Swift, Merible 273
Swift, Ruth 324
Swift, Susanna 153
Swift, Temperance 86
Swift, Thomas 721
Swift, William 846
Swift, Wm. 846
Swillaway, Mary 325
SWILLOWAY 724
Swilloway, Hannah 398
Swilloway, Henry 688
Swilloway, Margaret 688
Swilvan, Jael 748
SWINERTON 724
Swinerton, Mary 530
SWINNERTON 724
Swinnerton, Elizabeth 407
Swinnerton, John 106
SWITCHER 724
Switcher, Hannah 89
SWITCHZER 724
SWITSER 723
SWODEL 724
Swoetman, Elizabeth 793
SYBLY 673
Sybthorpe, Elizabeth 247
SYDENHAM 660, 724 see SEDENHAM
SYKES 724
Sykes, Rebecca 843
Syland, Philip 611
Sylbare, Israel 604
SYLE 673
SYLVESTER 725
Sylvester, --- 21
Sylvester, Anna 52, 87
Sylvester, Anne 52, 87
Sylvester, Giles 304
Sylvester, Griselda 469
Sylvester, Grizzell 469
Sylvester, Joseph 52
Sylvester, Lydia 612, 842
Sylvester, Mary 134, 242
Sylvester, Patience 464
Sylvester, Thomas 662
Symes, Zachariah (Rev.) 5
Symes, Zechariah (Rev.) 196
SYMMES 725
Symmes, Deborah 606
Symmes, Elizabeth 203, 285, 764
Symmes, Frances 451
Symmes, Huldah 209
Symmes, Mary 653, 747
Symmes, Rebecca 83
Symmes, Ruth 822
Symmes, Sarah 101, 268, 322, 391, 657
Symmes, Susanna 150
Symmes, Timothy 652

Symmes, William 748
Symmes, Zachariah 202
Symmes, Zechariah (Rev.) 196
Symmons, Rebecca 374
Symms, Zachariah (Rev.) 5
SYMONDS 658, 674, 675
Symonds, Abigail 584
Symonds, Catharine 749
Symonds, Dorothy 348, 802
Symonds, Elizabeth 253, 533
Symonds, Grace 252
Symonds, John 307
Symonds, Martha 215, 493
Symonds, Mary 145, 468, 538,
    565, 803
Symonds, Priscilla 34, 780
Symonds, Rebecca 374, 682
Symonds, Ruth 250, 694, 724
Symonds, Samuel 129, 253, 841
Symonds, Sarah 477
Symonds, Susanna 27, 414
Symonds, Susannah 774
Symones, Samuel 334
SYMONS 674, 675
Symons, Catharine 749
Symons, Elizabeth 102
Symons, John 675
Symons, Ruth 724
SYMPKINS 675
SYMSON 676
SYNDERLAND 721
Synmes, Mary 712

--- T ---

Tabbot, Barbara 155
Tabbot, Elizabeth 353
Taber, Esther 110
Taber, Lydia 523, 743
Taber, Mary 239
Tabor, Elizabeth 676
Tabor, Esther 574
Tabor, Lydia 433, 441
Tabor, Philip 209
Tabson, Emma 431
TAILER 729
Tailer, Mary 259
TAILOR 729, 731
Tailor, Hannah 448
TAINER 731
Tainter, Sarah 59
TAINTOR 728
Taintor, Charles 39
Taintor, Elizabeth 634
Taintor, Joanna 304
Taintor, John 173
Taintor, Mary 591
Taintor, Michael 126
Taintor, Rebecca 729
Taintor, Sarah 714
TALAR 729
TALBOT 726 see TALBY
Talbot, Elizabeth 353
Talbot, James 79
Talbot, Jane 31
Talbot, Mary 252
Talbot, Peter 286, 786
Talbot, Roger 753
TALBUT 726
TALBUTT 726
TALBY 726 see TALBOT
Talby, Jane 668
TALCOTT 726
Talcott, Dorothy 715
Talcott, Elizabeth 770
Talcott, Hannah 149, 308

Talcott, Helena 535
Talcott, Mary 244, 245, 643
Talcott, Rachel 115, 705
Talcott, Ruth 614
Talcott, Sarah 770
TALEY 726
TALLEY 726
Talley, Jane 338
Talley, Sarah 806
TALLMADGE 726, 727
TALLMAN 726
Tallman, --- 665, 814
Tallman, Ann 94, 597
Tallman, Elizabeth 456
Tallman, Hannah 228
Tallman, Mary 583, 614
Tallman, Peter 777
Tallman, Susanna 57
TALLY 726
Tally, Hannah 113
TALMAGE 726, 727
Talmage, Christian 59, 841
Talmage, Elizabeth Hull 401
Talmage, Enos 72
Talmage, Hannah 562
Talmage, Jane 775
Talmage, John 485
Talmage, Mary 341
Talmage, Rebecca 800
Talmage, Sarah 44, 58, 390, 800
Taly, Jane 338
TAMLIN 727
TANKERSLY 727
TANNER 727
Tanner, Francis 797
Tanner, Jane 797
Taplease, Mary 105
TAPLEY 727
Tapley, Elizabeth 49, 221
Tapley, Mary 105
Tapley, Robert 95
TAPLIF 747
TAPP 727
Tapp, Anna 18, 299
Tapp, Elizabeth 529
Tapp, Jane 753
Tapp, Mary 280
TAPPAN 727
Tappan, Elizabeth 157, 507
Tappan, John 362
Tappan, Martha 366
Tappan, Mary 608
Tappen, Mary 43
TAPPER 728
Tappin, Anna 779
Tappin, Hannah 779
Tappin, Rebecca 699
TAPPINE 727
TAPPING 727
Tapping, Thomas 503
Tappley, Gilbert 20
Tapril, Priscilla 140
TAPRILL 728
Taprill, Priscilla 140
Tarball, Martha 513
Tarball, Sarah 352
Tarball, Thomas 454
TARBELL 728
Tarbell, Abigail 811
Tarbell, Anna 455
Tarbell, Elizabeth 63
Tarbell, Hannah 455
Tarbell, Martha 513
Tarbell, Mary 586, 653
Tarbell, Sarah 152
Tarbell, Susanna 382
Tarbell, Thomas 382
Tarbot, Elizabeth 39

Tarbot, Hannah 589
Tarbot, John 205
Tarbot, Sarah 352
TARBOX 728
Tarbox, Martha 420
Tarbox, Rebecca 314, 316
Tarbox, Ruth 51
Tarbox, Sarah 51
TARE 734
TARLETON 728
Tarleton, Ruth 24
TARLTON 728
Tarlton, Henry 836
Tarlton, Richard 126
TARNE 728 see FERNE
Tarne, Deliverance 771
Tarne, Hannah 222
Tarne, Michael 641
Tarne, Miles 222
Tarne, Sarah 28
Tarner, Josiah 646
TARR 728, 734
Tarr, Ann 212
Tarr, Benedictus 444
Tarrant, Hannah 607
Tarrant, Sarah 607
TARRIN 728
TARRING 728
TART 728
Tart, Elizabeth 821
Tarville, Mary 586
TASKER 728
Tatchell, Mary 541
Tate, Elizabeth 821
TATENHAM 728 see TOTMAN,
    TOTTINGHAM
Tattersall, Joan 321
TATTON 728
TAULEY 728
TAUNTON 728
TAWLEY 728
Tawley, Elizabeth 641
TAY 728
Tay, Grace 824
Tay, John 462
TAYER 734
Tayer, Benjamin 415
Tayer, Mary 384
Tayer, Sarah 708
Tayler, Experience 19
Tayler, Kerziah 246
Tayler, Keziah 246
TAYLOR 728, 729, 730, 731
Taylor, --- 273, 703, 836
Taylor, Abigail 312, 430, 658
Taylor, Alex 468
Taylor, Alice 421
Taylor, Ann 161, 207, 385, 394
Taylor, Anna 109
Taylor, Anne 761
Taylor, Barnabas 376
Taylor, Catherine 130
Taylor, Daniel 824
Taylor, Deborah 66
Taylor, Deliverance 312
Taylor, Edward 38, 97, 652
Taylor, Elizabeth 164, 264, 309,
    495, 531, 665, 724
Taylor, Esther 780
Taylor, Experience 19
Taylor, George 374
Taylor, Hannah 192, 414, 417,
    448
Taylor, Hester 423, 780
Taylor, Hope 720
Taylor, Joanna 15, 439
Taylor, Johannah 15
Taylor, John 63, 89, 123, 261,

Taylor, John (cont.) 396, 473, 764
Taylor, Joseph 393, 443, 484, 677
Taylor, Lydia 524
Taylor, Margaret 117
Taylor, Martha 56, 458
Taylor, Mary 24, 125, 206, 238, 259, 343, 367, 369, 454, 475, 503, 553, 574, 621, 711, 729, 752, 823
Taylor, Mehitable 685
Taylor, Mercy 574
Taylor, Mindwell 124, 316
Taylor, Rebecca 118, 331, 605
Taylor, Rhoda 562
Taylor, Richard 778
Taylor, Rose 783
Taylor, Samuel 182
Taylor, Sarah 41, 133, 155, 255, 295, 471, 552, 629, 824, 827, 828
Taylor, Stephen 375
Taylor, Susannah 727
Taylor, Thankful 842
Taylor, Tobias 338
Taylor, William 447, 585, 612
TAYNOUR 731
Taynour, Elizabeth 76, 143
Taynour, Joanna 110
TEAL see THEALE
TEALE 731, 734
Ted, Elizabeth 473, 514, 639
Teddeman, Alice 401
TEED 742
Teed, Mary 509, 674
Teel, Alice 485, 742
Teel, John 485
TEFF 731
TEFFE 732
Teffe, Anne 10
TEFFT 731
Tefft, Elizabeth 136
Tefft, Lydia 219
Tefft, Mary 826
Tefft, Tabitha 293
TEFT 732
Teleston, Ruth 278
TELY 762
Tempel, Abigail 89
TEMPLAR 732
Templar, Deborah 142, 508
Templar, Hannah 709
Templar, Richard 522
TEMPLE 732
Temple, Abigail 89, 817
Temple, Alice 83, 663
Temple, Christopher 432
Temple, Margaret 301
Temple, Mary 213
Temple, Phebe 539
Temple, Richard 89
Temple, Sarah 239, 530
TENCH 732
TENEY 732
TENNANT 732
TENNEY 732
Tenney, Elizabeth 836
Tenney, Hannah 422
Tenney, John 141
Tenney, Mary 797
Tenney, Mercy 343
Tenney, Ruth 343
Tenney, Sarah 25, 796
Tenney, Thomas 561
TENNY 732
Tenny, Agnes 339
Tenny, Annis 339
Tenny, Ruth 343
TENY 732

Teny, Mercy 343
TERNE 728, 732 see FERNE, TARNE
TERRILL 744
Terrill, Abigail 762
Terrill, Hannah 676
TERRY 732, 733
Terry, Abigail 431, 625
Terry, Ann 78
Terry, Anna 78
Terry, Bethiah 308
Terry, Elizabeth 380, 644
Terry, Mary 82, 310, 389, 617, 625
Terry, Rebecca 743, 842
Terry, Samuel 190, 656
Terry, Thomas 354, 500, 745, 821
TETHERLY 733
Tetherly, --- 292
Tetherly, Ann 737
Tetherly, Elizabeth 796
Tetherly, Gabriel 439
Tetherly, Mary Roby 480
Tetherly, Mehitable 215
TEUXBURY 733
TEW 733 see TU
Tew, Elnathan 346
Tew, Mary 345
Tew, Seaborn 69, 369
TEWELL 761
Tewell, Alice 284
Tewkesbury, Henry 350
Tewkesbury, Mary 549, 651
TEWKSBURY 733
Tewksbury, Hannah 652
Tey, John 412
Teyler, Hannah 476
THACHAR 733
THACHER 733
Thacher, Ann 53
Thacher, Bethia 551
Thacher, Elizabeth 205
Thacher, John 221
Thacher, Oxenbridge 465
Thacher, Peter 32, 298
Thacher, Rebecca 720
Thacher, Seaborn 378
Thaine, Rachel 47
Thaiur, Sarah 485
Thake, Joanna 623
Thamsin, Jane 510
THARE 734
Thare, Huldah 8
Thare, Trail 119
Thare, Triall 119
THARLAY 740
Tharly, Mary 832
THATCHER 733
Thatcher, Alice 228
Thatcher, Bethiah 394
Thatcher, Elizabeth 205, 208, 289, 298, 352
Thatcher, Hannah 383
Thatcher, Mary 231
Thatcher, Peter 816
Thatcher, Susannah 14
Thatcher, Thomas 666
Thatcher, Thomas (Rev.) 432
Thather, Bethiah 394
THAXTER 733, 734
Thaxter, Deborah 199
Thaxter, Elizabeth 199
Thaxter, John 199
Thaxter, Mary 199
Thaxter, Sarah 233, 384, 741
Thaxter, Thomas 236
THAYER 357, 734
Thayer, Abigail 99

Thayer, Benjamin 415
Thayer, Cicely 206
Thayer, Deborah 260, 839
Thayer, Elizabeth 28
Thayer, Esther 320
Thayer, Experience 284
Thayer, Hannah 356, 550
Thayer, Hester 320
Thayer, Huldah 8, 802
Thayer, Jael 342
Thayer, Joanna 194
Thayer, Josiah 380
Thayer, Margery 360
Thayer, Mary 31, 124, 384, 412, 431
Thayer, Naomi 178
Thayer, Richard 557
Thayer, Samuel 677
Thayer, Sarah 208, 359, 485, 708
Thayer, Trial 119
Thayer, Triall 119
Thayer, William 360
THEAL 734
THEALE 734 see TEAL
Theale, Nicholas 763
THEALL 734
THELE 734
Thele, Elizabeth 611
Theole, --- 20
THEROLD 734
Thickston, Katherine 362
THING 734, 735
Thing, Elizabeth 232
Thing, Jonathan 803, 813
Thing, Samuel 232
THIRSTON 741
THISSELL 735
THISTLE 735
Thistle, Hannah 603
Thistle, Joan 353
Thistle, Mary 647
Thoits, Mary 304
Thoits, Rebecca 576
THOMAS 735, 736
Thomas, --- 496
Thomas, Abigail 475, 603
Thomas, Alice 669
Thomas, Ann 475
Thomas, Anne 118
Thomas, Bethiah 467
Thomas, Deborah 192
Thomas, Dinah 669
Thomas, Dorothy 548, 746
Thomas, Elizabeth 66, 138, 149, 193, 276, 385, 467, 486, 566, 706
Thomas, Evan 188, 442
Thomas, Ewins 188
Thomas, Hannah 730
Thomas, Jane 413
Thomas, Jeremiah 235
Thomas, Joanna 766
Thomas, John 278
Thomas, Margaret 699
Thomas, Martha 224
Thomas, Mary 79, 114, 202, 309, 317, 539, 613
Thomas, Mary Kirtland 188
Thomas, Mercy 31
Thomas, Nathaniel 175, 225, 461, 769
Thomas, Rice 69
Thomas, Sarah 170, 181, 226, 384, 577, 782, 824
Thomas, Tabitha 385
Thomas, Welthean 398
Thomas, William 364, 476
THOME 739

Thomppsons, Jane 273
THOMPSON 736, 737, 738
Thompson, Aaron 625
Thompson, Abigail 15, 59, 173, 198, 400, 406, 507, 566, 583, 670
Thompson, Alexander 691
Thompson, Amy 311
Thompson, Ann 254, 379
Thompson, Anna 388, 647
Thompson, Anne 150
Thompson, Anthony 132
Thompson, Arabella 822
Thompson, Benjamin 466, 565
Thompson, Bridget 87
Thompson, David 498
Thompson, Dorothy 122, 348, 556, 672
Thompson, Ebenezer 375, 657
Thompson, Eleanor 284, 766
Thompson, Elizabeth 64, 73, 91, 167, 204, 265, 334, 683, 724, 838
Thompson, Esther 292, 325, 329, 616
Thompson, Francis 649
Thompson, Hannah 91, 252, 357, 390, 524, 617, 701
Thompson, Helen 766
Thompson, Henry 663, 764
Thompson, James 78
Thompson, Joanna 525
Thompson, Joanna Treat 424
Thompson, John 115, 213, 316, 349, 556
Thompson, Joseph 414, 641
Thompson, Lydia 196, 502
Thompson, Margaret 461, 683
Thompson, Martha 252, 297
Thompson, Mary 63, 181, 184, 202, 263, 349, 356, 375, 467, 513, 619, 725, 831, 835
Thompson, Mercy 833
Thompson, Olive 200
Thompson, Priscilla 150
Thompson, Rebecca 735
Thompson, Samuel 527
Thompson, Sarah 8, 37, 45, 270, 311, 365, 405, 722, 764
Thompson, Sarah Emery 781
Thompson, Simon 667
Thompson, Susannah 628, 652
Thompson, Thomas 394
Thompson, William 306, 424
Thompson, William (Rev.) 193
Thompsons, Samuel 69
THOMSON 736, 737, 738
Thomson, Bridget 214
Thomson, Mary 477
Thomson, William 14
Thong, Arabella 615
Thorfts, Rebecca 576
THORING 739
THORLA 740
Thorla, Martha 231
THORLEY 740
Thorley, Martha 231
THORN 738, 739
Thorn, Joanna 707
Thorn, Rose 693
Thorn, Susannah 337
Thorn, William 32
THORNBURY 739
Thorndick, Elizabeth 605
Thorndick, Sarah 477
Thorndik, Hannah 603
THORNDIKE 739
Thorndike, Elizabeth 315, 605

Thorndike, Hannah 603
Thorndike, John 224
Thorndike, Mary 735
Thorndike, Sarah 477
THORNE 738, 739
Thorne, Agnes 76
Thorne, Anne 826
Thorne, Desiretruth 3
Thorne, Desire ye Truth 3
Thorne, Elizabeth 524, 669
Thorne, Joan 172
Thorne, Joanna 172
Thorne, John 826
Thorne, Margaret 612
Thorne, Mary 280, 510
Thorne, Sarah 183, 270, 568
Thorne, Susannah 442, 469
THORNEYCRAFT 739
Thorneycraft, Anne 135
Thorneycraft, Thomas 135
THORNICRAFT 739
THORNING 739
THORNTON 739
Thornton, Abial 455, 550
Thornton, Abiel 455
Thornton, Ann 335
Thornton, Elizabeth 487, 769
Thornton, Joan 128
Thornton, Joane 129
Thornton, Katherine 133
Thornton, Mary 260, 325, 357, 733
Thornton, Mehitable 807
Thornton, Patience 667
Thornton, Priscilla 55
Thornton, Robert 505
Thornton, Sarah 46, 265, 331
Thornton, William 381
THORNYCRAFT 739
Thorogood, Alice 144
THOROLD 734
THORP 739, 740
Thorp, Elizabeth 226
Thorp, Hannah 117, 178
Thorp, Henry 117
Thorp, Mary 150
Thorp, Rachel 808
THORPE 739, 740
Thorpe, Abigail 738
Thorpe, Alice 209
Thorpe, John 5, 481
Thorpe, Mary 262, 483
Thorpe, Nathaniel 627
Thorpe, William 585
Thorston, Hannah 585
Thortes, Mary 304
THOYGHT 740
Thrale, Joseph 400
THRALL 740
Thrall, Deborah 523
Thrall, Elizabeth 183
Thrall, Martha 587
Thrall, Mehitable 158
Thrall, Phillipa 389
Thrasher, Francis 369
Thrasher, Hannah 140
Thredneedle, Mary 502
THREEDNEDLE 740
THREENEDLE 740
THREENEEDLE 740
THRESHER 740
Thresher, Sarah 461
Throckmarton, Deliverance 23
THROCKMORTON 740
Throckmorton, --- 729
Throckmorton, Deliverance 23
Throckmorton, Hannah 728
Throckmorton, Patience 166

Throckmorton, Sarah 467
THROOP 754
Throop, Daniel 320
Throop, Elizabeth 567
Throop, Mary 45
THROW 740
Throw, David 404
Thrumball, Mary 74
THRUSTON 741
THURBER 740
Thurber, Charity 509
Thurber, Elizabeth 150, 799
Thurber, Mary 117
Thurley, Lydia 794
Thurlo, Lydia 794
THURLOE 740
THURLOW 740
Thurlow, Lydia 251
Thurlow, Mary 832
Thurlow, Sarah 203
Thurlow, Tamasin 27
Thurogood, Ann 489
Thurstane, Judith 752
THURSTON 740
Thurston, Abigail 147
Thurston, Bethiah 145
Thurston, Daniel 465, 745
Thurston, Eleanor 354
Thurston, Elizabeth 281
Thurston, Hannah 148, 473, 475, 545, 585
Thurston, Judith 752
Thurston, Katherine 362
Thurston, Mary 265, 545, 678, 689
Thurston, Mehitable 248
Thurston, Rebecca 159, 240
Thurston, Sarah 513, 521
THURSTUN 741
Thurstun, Sarah 521
Thwaite, Mary 304
THWAITES 741
THWAITS 741
Thwaits, Anne 379
THWING 741
Thwing, Deborah 386
Thwing, Mary 399
TIBBALLS 741
Tibballs, Sarah 1
TIBBALS 741
Tibbals, Abigail 343, 726
Tibbals, Hannah 180
Tibbals, John 344, 710
Tibbals, Josiah 508
Tibbals, Mary 687
Tibbals, Mercy 10
Tibbals, Sarah 172, 539, 782
Tibbells, Abigail 207
TIBBETS 741, 742
Tibbets, Agnes 238
Tibbets, Elizabeth 67
Tibbets, Jeremy 67
Tibbets, Mary 22
Tibbets, Samuel 818
Tibbets, Walter 238
Tibbett, Henry 727
TIBBETTS 741, 742
Tibbetts, Abigail 726
Tibbetts, Henry 548
Tibbetts, Louis 376
Tibbetts, Mary 320, 351, 612
Tibbetts, Rebecca 62, 446
Tibbetts, Remembrance 25
Tibbetts, Sarah 336
TIBBITTS 741
Tibbitts, Ann 273
Tibbitts, Hannah 572
TICE 742
TICHENER 742

INDEX

TICHENOR 742
Tichenor, Abigail 752
TICKNOR 742
TID 742
TIDD 742
Tidd, Elizabeth 289, 303, 473
Tidd, Hannah 653, 686
Tidd, John 485
Tidd, Joseph 710
Tidd, Joshua 594, 617
Tidd, Mary 432, 674
Tidd, Rebecca 79
Tidd, Samuel 693
Tidd, Sarah 471
Tidd, Susan 831
Tidd, Susanna 831
TIDMARSH 742
TIDY 762
Tidy, Sarah Libby 634
TIFFANY 742
Tiffany, Humphrey 613
Tiffany, James 668
TIFFENY 742
TIFFINY 742
TILDEN 742
Tilden, Abigail 712
Tilden, Elizabeth 50, 198
Tilden, Experience 735
Tilden, Hannah 709
Tilden, Judith 601
Tilden, Lydia 295, 625, 742
Tilden, Mary 451, 697, 735
Tilden, Nathaniel 353
Tilden, Rebecca 98
Tilden, Ruth 742
Tilden, Sarah 721
Tilden, Thomas 784
Tildon, Judith 549
Tildon, Mary 50
TILEE 762
TILER 762
Tiler, Joan 219
TILESON 743
TILESTON 742, 743
Tileston, Bathsheba 565
TILESTONE 743
Tilestone, Elizabeth 699
Tilestone, Philadelphia 738
Tilestone, Ruth 216
TILETSON 743
TILL 743
TILLEAR 743
Tiller, Helena 817
Tilleson, John 627
TILLET 743
TILLETSON 743
TILLETT 743
TILLEY 743 see TILLIAR
Tilley, Edith 132
Tilley, Elizabeth 394, 504
Tilley, Sarah 330, 512
Tilley, William 838
TILLIAR 743
TILLINGHAST 743
Tillinghast, Abigail 667
Tillinghast, Isabel Sayles 368
Tillinghast, Lydia 543
Tillinghast, Mary 135
Tillinghast, Mercy 598
Tillman, Mary 693
Tillman, Robert 661
Tillman, Susannah 786
TILLOTSON 743
TILLY 743
Tilly, John 79
Tilly, Sarah 481, 518
Tilly, Wm. 481
Tillye, Hugh 398

Tillye, Rose 372
TILSON 743
Tilson, --- 763
Tilson, Edmund 624
Tilson, Elizabeth 233
Tilson, Joane 624
Tilson, Mary 169, 234
TILTON 743, 744
Tilton, Abigail 550
Tilton, Esther 697
Tilton, Hannah 828
Tilton, Joseph 664
Tilton, Mary 88, 147, 174, 240, 329, 781
Tilton, Mercy 247
Tilton, Peter 461, 561
Tilton, Samuel 665
Tilton, Sarah 553
Tilton, Susanna 665
Tilton, William 665
TIMBERLAKE 744
Timberlake, Elizabeth 166
Timberlake, Hannah 838
Timberlake, Joseph 185
Timberlake, Mary 527
Timberlake, Sarah 416
Tincknell, Sibell 67
Tincknell, Sybil 67
TINCOM 744
Tincome, Agnes 645
Tinesdale, Rebecca 303
TING 762, 763
Ting, Bethia 798
TINGE 762
TINGLE 744
TINGLEY 744
Tingley, Palmer 45
Tingley, Samuel 668
TINKER 744
Tinker, John 44, 501
Tinker, Mary 622, 684, 776
TINKHAM 744
Tinkham, Agnes 645
Tinkham, Martha 693
Tinkham, Mary 737
Tinney, John 141
Tippet, Mary 205
Tippets, Hiltabell 332
Tippets, Mehitable 332
Tippett, Mehitable 176
Tipping, Bartholomew 734
TIRHAND 758
TIRRELL 744 see TURRELL
TISDALE 744, 745
Tisdale, Abigail 28, 484
Tisdale, Anna 461, 821
Tisdale, John 106, 484, 733
Tisdale, Margaret 829
Tisdale, Mary 284
Tisdale, Mercy 378
Tisdale, Remember 708
Tisdale, Sarah 212, 422
TISDALL 745
Tisdall, Elizabeth 684
Tisdall, James 389
Tisdall, Mary 389
TISDELL 744
Tissau, Marie 556
TITCHBORN 745
TITCHBORNE 745
Titchener, Abigail 752
TITCOMB 745
Titcomb, Elizabeth 49
Titcomb, Hannah 315
Titcomb, Lydia 157
Titcomb, Mary 593
Titcomb, Rebecca 752
Titcomb, Sarah 752

Titcomb, Tirza 49
Titcomb, Tirzah 49, 545
Titcomb, William 709
Titcombe, Anne 654
TITE 745
TITERTON 745
TITHARTON 745
Titharton, Mary 594, 670
Titherton, Elizabeth 795
Titherton, Joanna 815
Titherton, Sarah 156
TITTERTON 745
Titterton, Joanna 815
Titterton, Mary 670
TITUS 745
Titus, Abigail 288, 290, 657, 781
Titus, Experience 534
Titus, Hannah 115, 680
Titus, Jane 216
Titus, John 554
Titus, Martha 658
Titus, Mary 87, 435, 824
Titus, Mercy 87
Titus, Patience 332
Titus, Phebe 264, 404, 658
Titus, Silas 740
TOALMAN 746
TOBEY 745, 746
Tobey, Alice 218
Tobey, Desire 710
Tobey, Ealse 218
Tobey, Elizabeth 218, 339
Tobey, James 341
Tobey, Thomas 266
TOBIE 745, 746
TOBY 745
Toby, Thomas 234
TOD 746
Tod, Grace 497
Tod, Mary 404
TODD 746
Todd, --- 835
Todd, Margaret 477
Todd, Mary 247, 363, 404, 507, 759
Todd, Mercy 50
Todd, Rachel 309
Todd, Walter 49
Tohnan, Mary 173
TOLE 748
TOLEMAN 746
TOLES 746
TOLL 749
Toll, Mary 404
Toll, Rebecca 328
Tolland, Elizabeth 7
TOLLES 746
TOLLY 747
TOLMAN 726, 746
Tolman, Ebenezer 279
Tolman, Elizabeth 27
Tolman, Hannah 481
Tolman, John 564
Tolman, Mary 190
Tolman, Rebecca 756
Tolman, Ruth 640
Tolman, Sarah 457
TOMBLIN 746
Tomblin, Abiah 771
Tomblin, Abial 771
Tomblin, Abiel 771
Tomes, Alice 795
TOMKINS 747
Tomkins, Elizabeth 729
Tomkins, Isabella 729
TOMLIN 746
Tomlin, Grace Diamond 757
TOMLINE 746

TOMLINS 746
Tomlins, Elizabeth 72
TOMLINSON 746
Tomlinson, Alice 71
Tomlinson, Ayer 356
Tomlinson, Bathseba 710
Tomlinson, Elizabeth 72, 342, 625
Tomlinson, Ellen 84
Tomlinson, Henry 71
Tomlinson, Margaret 344, 741
Tomlinson, Mary 585
Tomlinson, Phebe 841
Tomlinson, Sarah 73
Tomlinson, Tabitha 401, 841
Tomlison, Sarah 679
TOMPKINS 746, 747
Tompkins, Deborah 674
Tompkins, Elizabeth 72, 447
Tompkins, Hannah 408, 425
Tompkins, John 357
Tompkins, Martha 5, 278
Tompkins, Mary 261, 638
Tompkins, Priscilla 489
Tompkins, Sarah 784
TOMPSON 736, 737, 738
Tompson, Abigail 59
Tompson, Beatrice 560
Tompson, George 243
Tompson, Mary 78
Tompson, Sarah 8, 243, 616
TOMSON 736, 737, 738
Tomson, Anna 388
Tomson, Esther 616
Tomson, Lydia 693
Tomson, Martha 734
Tomson, Mary 349
Tomson, Mehitable 360
Tomson, Sarah 270, 764
Tong, Arabella 615
Tonge, Mary 813
TONGUE 747
Tongue, Arabella 615
Tongue, Elizabeth 830
Tongue, Hannah 33, 512
Tongue, Mary 813
TOOBE 746
TOOCKIE 747
TOOGOOD 747
Toogood, Deborah 262
Toogood, Edward 317, 503
TOOKER 747, 757 see TUCKER
Tooker, Ann 388
Tooker, Anna 388
Tooker, Anne Wines Nichols Elton
  847
Tooker, Hannah 688
Tooker, John 249, 388, 535, 688
Tooker, Ruth 680
TOOKIE 747
Tooley, Dorothy 565
Tooll, Mary 404
TOOLY 747 see TULLY
TOOTHAKER 747
Toothaker, Margaret 371
Toothaker, Martha 250, 371
Toothaker, Roger 142, 371
Toothaker, Sarah 804
Topleff, Clement 363
TOPLIFE 747
Topliff, Patience 384
Topliff, Sarah 424
Topliffe, Obedience 182
Toppan, Jacob 662
Toppans, Peter 324
TOPPING 727, 728
Topping, Abigail 574
Topping, Ann 34
Topping, Hester 275

Topping, James 277
Topping, John 27, 779
Topping, Lydia Wilford 816
Topping, Martha 366
Topping, Mary 608
Topping, Sarah 338
Topping, Temperance 837
Topping, Thomas 36, 503
Topsfield, Judith 118
Torbet, Elizabeth 481
TORIE 747
Torr, Benedictus 444
Torre, Philip 655
TORREY 747, 748
Torrey, Bethia 839
Torrey, Damaris 606
Torrey, James 112, 212, 578
Torrey, Joanna 404
Torrey, Jonathan 686
Torrey, Josiah 53, 408
Torrey, Judith 404
Torrey, Mary 207, 229, 402, 540
Torrey, Naomi 477
Torrey, Samuel (Rev.) 725
Torrey, Sarah 782
Torrey, Silence 359
TORRY 747
TORY 748
Tory, Mary 79
TOSH 748
Tosh, --- 606
Tosh, Marcy 524
Tosh, Mary 204
Tosh, Mercy 524
Tosh, Sarah 524
Tosh, William 524
Toskin, Ruth 680
Totherly, Elizabeth 787
Totingham, Henry 6
TOTMAN 748 see TATENHAM,
  TOTTINGHAM
Totman, Elizabeth 578
TOTTINGHAM 748 see
  TATENHAM, TOTMAN
Tottingham, Eliah 728
TOUCEY 748
TOUGH 748
Tough, Frances 704
TOUGHE 748
TOUNG 747, 846
TOURNEUR 758
TOURTELLOT 748
TOUSEY 748, 751
TOUT 748
Touteville, Margaret 668
TOVIE 748
TOVY 748
TOWER 748
Tower, Elizabeth 628
Tower, Hannah 187, 802
Tower, Ibrook 424
Tower, Jeremiah 640
Tower, John 187
Tower, Rachel 52
Tower, Sarah 199
TOWERS 748
Towers, Abigail 313
TOWLE 746, 748, 749 see
  TOLLES
Towle, Margaret 355
Towle, Mary 404
Towle, Philip 81
Towle, Sarah 446
TOWLEY 751
TOWN 749
Town, --- 452
Town, Deliverance 711
Town, Mary 253

Town, Susanna 360
TOWNE 749
Towne, Abigail 565, 573
Towne, Catherine 571
Towne, Elizabeth 816
Towne, Joanna 536
Towne, Mary 605
Towne, Peter 360
Towne, Rebecca 445, 541
Towne, Sarah 96, 163, 392
Towne, Susanna 196, 360
Towne, William 817
TOWNER 749
TOWNLEY 749, 751 see
  TOWSLEY
Townley, Richard 138
TOWNSEND 749, 750, 751
Townsend, Ann 168
Townsend, Bethiah 486
Townsend, Deborah 734
Townsend, Dinah 818
Townsend, Elizabeth 470, 503,
  598, 842
Townsend, Freelove 427
Townsend, George 14
Townsend, Hannah 10, 354, 401,
  445, 787, 791
Townsend, James 469
Townsend, Johannah 750
Townsend, John 170
Townsend, Leah 820
Townsend, Lydia 182
Townsend, Mary 843
Townsend, Penn 232, 416, 569
Townsend, Rachel 843
Townsend, Richard 684
Townsend, Roger 58, 547
Townsend, Rose 220, 791
Townsend, Samuel 42, 502
Townsend, Sarah 680, 796, 842
Townsend, Solomon 416
Townsend, Susanna 706
Townsend, Susannah 275
Townsend, Thomas 14
Townsends, Elizabeth 579
Townsends, George 301
Townsley, Richard 455
Towrey, Mary 153
TOWSEY 751
TOWSLEY 751
Towsley, Mercy 9
Towsley, Richard 244, 265
Towzey, Mary 153
Toy, Elizabeth 767
TOZER 751
Tozer, Richard 663
TOZIER 751
Tozier, Ann 417
Tozier, Anne 417, 438
Tozier, Elizabeth 610
Tozier, Martha 473
Tozier, Richard 322
Tracey, Apphia 694
Tracey, Lydia 460
Tracey, Thomas 310
Track, Sarah 736
TRACY 751
Tracy, Daniel 70
Tracy, Hannah 209
Tracy, Miriam 784
Tracy, Rebecca 504
Tracy, Sarah 511, 563
Tracy, Solomon 679
Tracy, Susannah 633
Tracy, Thomas 90, 712
Traffick, Deborah 53
Traford, Joyce 779
Trafton, Dorothy 500

Trafton, Elizabeth 422, 609
Trafton, Jane 55
Trahorn, Alse 598
TRAIN 751
Train, Mary 502
Train, Rachel 47
TRAINE 751
Traine, Abigail 750
Traine, Elizabeth 717
Traine, Hannah 150
Traine, Sarah 169
TRANANCE 753
TRANTER 751
TRANTON 751
TRAPP 751
Trapp, John 252
TRARICE 753
Trase, Apphia 694
TRASK 751, 752
Trask, Abigail 453, 640
Trask, Ann 278, 826
Trask, Anna 103, 278, 826
Trask, Benjamin 246
Trask, Elizabeth 366
Trask, Hannah 103
Trask, Henry 536
Trask, Mary 472, 478, 500
Trask, Osmund 303
Trask, Rebecca 88, 597
Trask, Sarah 20, 560, 804, 820
Trask, Susan 289
Trask, Susanna 2, 289
TRAVERIS 752
TRAVERS 752 see TRAVIS
Travers, Elizabeth 354
Travers, Hannah 27
Travers, Henry 312
Travers, Mercy 810
Travers, Sarah 489, 777
Travett, Hannah 586
TRAVIS 752 see TRAVERS
Travis, Hannah 27
Travis, Henry 312, 827
Travis, Mercy 810
Travis, Susannah 676
Travise, Lydia 239
Traxter, Thomas 470
TRAY 752
Trayne, Abigail 750
Trayne, Elizabeth 717
Trayne, Rachel 47
Treacy, Susannah 633
TREADAWAY 752
Treadaway, Deborah 307
Treadaway, Elizabeth 342
TREADWAY 752
Treadway, Ann Rogers 713
Treadway, Deborah 307
Treadway, Elizabeth 359
Treadway, Josiah 200
Treadway, Lydia 426
Treadway, Mary 267, 355
TREADWELL 752
Treadwell, Edward 430, 754, 802
Treadwell, Esther 391
Treadwell, Hannah 4
Treadwell, Hester 391
Treadwell, Martha 194
Treadwell, Mary 291
Treadwell, Rebecca 369
Treadwell, Sarah 108, 571, 676, 802
Treadwell, Thomas 571
TREAT 752, 753
Treat, Abigail 18, 382
Treat, Catharine 738
Treat, Dorcas 687, 688
Treat, Elizabeth 424, 691, 832

Treat, Hannah 496
Treat, Hannah Steele 348
Treat, Honor 214
Treat, James 80
Treat, Jane 283
Treat, Jemima 149
Treat, Joanna 382, 424
Treat, Mary 149, 190, 621
Treat, Matthias 684, 842
Treat, Rebecca 687
Treat, Robert 111, 381
Treat, Salmon (Rev.) 556
Treat, Sarah 132, 274, 310, 635
Treat, Susannah 160, 790
TREAUANT 755
TREBE 753
TREBY 753
Treby, Sarah 383
Trecotherick, Hannah 753
Tredaway, Mary 267
TREDWELL 752
Tredwell, Mary 714
Tredwill, Mary 291
TREE 753
TREFRY 753
Trefry, Elizabeth 806
Trehearne, Edward 790
TREHERN 753
Treherne, Edward 219
TRELANCE 753
Tremaine, Sarah 179
TRENANCE 753
TRENANTS 753
Treothic, Hannah 753
TRERICE 753
Trerice, Elizabeth 432
Trerice, Hannah 26
Trerice, John 431
Trerice, Rebecca 418, 481
Trerice, Sarah 313
Trerise, John 480
Trescote, Patience 55
TRESCOTT 753
Trescott, Abigail 633, 791
Trescott, Elizabeth 522
Trescott, Martha 367
Trescott, Mary 364
Trescott, Patience 55
Tresler, Thomas 576
TRESSWELL 753
TRESWELL 753
TREUANT 755
Treuant, Mary 150
TREVET 753
TREVETT 753
Trevoroye, Joanna 15
Trevoroye, Joan 15
TREVY 753
Trevy, Elizabeth 806
Trevy, Sarah 482
TREW 755
TREWANT 755
Trewant, Hannah 756
Trewant, Mehitable 224
Treworgie, James 373
TREWORGY 755
Treworgy, Elizabeth 264, 305
Treworgy, John 603
Treworgy, Lucia 824
Treworgy, Lucy 141, 710
TREWORGYE 755
TRIANS 755
TRIBAH 753
Trickee, Martha 330
TRICKER 753
TRICKEY 753
Trickey, Deborah 663
Trickey, Ephraim 831

Trickey, Joseph 229
Trickey, Lydia 789
Trickey, Martha 330
Trickey, Sarah 828
Triggs, Agnes 28
TRIM 753
TRIMMINGS 753
TRIPE 753, 754 see TRIPP
TRIPP 753, 754
Tripp, Abiel 235
Tripp, Alice 336
Tripp, Elizabeth 336
Tripp, Isabel 670
Tripp, Martha 670
Tripp, Mary 299, 409, 597, 681, 832
Tripp, Mehitable 741
Tripp, Susanna 597
Triscott, Martha 3
Triskey, Sarah 192
TRISTRAM 754
Tristram, Hannah 427
Tristram, Ralph 427
Tritton, Alice Goldhatch 211
Tritton, Benedicta 701, 833
Tritton, Benet 701, 833
TROMBLEY 761
TROMBLY 761
Trombridge, Thomas 37
TROOP 754
Troop, Mary 640
Troope, Daniel 320
TROT 754
Trot, Sarah 133
Trot, Thankful 374
TROTT 754
Trott, Elizabeth 138, 819
Trott, Mary 328
Trott, Preserved 33
Trott, Thankful 374
TROTTER 754
TROUGH 754
TROUT 748 see TOUT
TROW 754
Trow, John 393
TROWBRIDGE 754, 755
Trowbridge, Abigail 490
Trowbridge, Benjamin 3
Trowbridge, Elizabeth 85, 379, 399, 484, 503
Trowbridge, Experience 826
Trowbridge, Hannah 324, 413
Trowbridge, John 173
Trowbridge, Lydia 638
Trowbridge, Margaret 312, 713
Trowbridge, Mary 173, 705
Trowbridge, Mindwell 288
Trowbridge, Thankful 778
Trowbridge, William 673
TROWTE 754
Truair, Elizabeth 622
TRUANT 755 see TRUFANT
Truant, Hannah 238
Truant, Mary 150
Truant, Mehitable 224
TRUBERFEELD 758
TRUE 755
True, Henry 271
True, Jemima 90, 487
True, Mary 240
TRUEMAN 755
Trueman, Ann 415
Trueman, Elizabeth 598
Trueman, Hannah 415
TRUESDALE 755
Truesdale, Catherine 324
Truesdale, Elizabeth 80
Truesdale, Kate 324

Truesdale, Mary 274
Truesdale, Richard 296
Truesdell, Elizabeth 80
TRUEWORTHY 755
Trueworthy, Elizabeth 305
TRUFANT 755 see TRUANT
TRULL 755
Trull, Hannah 286
Trull, Mary 557
TRUMAN 755
Truman, Mary 353
TRUMBALL 755
Trumball, Hannah 357
Trumball, Ruth 573
TRUMBLE 755
Trumble, John 388, 722
Trumble, Judah 724
Trumble, Mary 436, 531
Trumbull, Abigail 32
Trumbull, Elizabeth 493
Trumbull, Hannah 53, 378
Trumbull, John 722
Trumbull, Joseph 113, 719
Trumbull, Judah 724
Trumbull, Mary 74, 249, 436, 682
TRUSDELL 755
TRUSLER 755
Trusons, Elizabeth 65
Trusons, Henry 65
TRUSSELL 753
TRY 755, 756
Try, Sarah 329
TRYAN 756
Tryan, Sarah 304
Tryer, Elizabeth 622
TRYHERN 756
TRYON 756
Tryon, Sarah 304
Tryon, William 453
TU 756 see TEW
TUBBS 756
Tubbs, Mary 192
Tubbs, William 41, 692
Tubs, Bethiah 341
TUCK 756
Tuck, Elizabeth 532, 668
Tuck, John 463
Tuck, Katharine 255
Tuck, Mary Philbrick 776
Tuck, Sarah 12
Tuck, Susanna 20
TUCKE 756
Tucke, Mary 648
TUCKER 753, 756, 757 see
    TOOKER, TRICKER
Tucker, Agnes 696
Tucker, Ann 175, 388, 720
Tucker, Anna 388
Tucker, Elizabeth 140, 153, 599
Tucker, Elizabeth Weld Gore 313
Tucker, Grace 9
Tucker, Hannah 678
Tucker, Honor 706
Tucker, John 388, 657
Tucker, Joseph 817
Tucker, Katherine Eastwick
    Randall 610
Tucker, Margaret 725
Tucker, Mary 152, 181, 208, 219,
    395, 426, 574, 691
Tucker, Rebecca 262
Tucker, Richard 109, 745, 746
Tucker, Ruth 812
Tucker, Sarah 395, 782
Tucker, Susannah 725
Tucker, Thomas 459
Tucker, William 9
TUCKERMAN 757

Tuckey, Lydia 320
Tucksbury, Mary 549
Tudman, Sarah 53
TUDOR 757
Tudor, Jane 688
Tudor, Mary 429, 546
Tudor, Owen 677
Tudor, Samuel 73
Tudor, Sarah 594
TUELL 761
Tuell, Martha 264
Tuffes, Rebecca 835
TUFTON 757
TUFTS 757, 758 see TURFS
Tufts, Anna 102
Tufts, Elizabeth 405, 480, 481
Tufts, Martha 822
Tufts, Mary 242
Tufts, Mercy 417, 771
Tufts, Peter 845
Tufts, Sarah 542
TUKESBURY 733
TULLER 758
Tuller, John 463
TULLEY 758
Tulley, Dorothy 565
TULLY 747, 758
Tully, Dorothy 565
Tully, John 456
Tulman, Hannah 76
Tulston, Elizabeth 501
Tumbers, Mary 434
Tunstall, Martha 690
TUPPER 758
Tupper, Ann 299
Tupper, Katherine 542
TURBAT 758
Turbat, Elizabeth 39
TURBEFEILD 758
TURBERFIELD 758
Turberfield, Susan 501
TURBET 758
Turbet, Elizabeth 481
Turbet, John 205
Turbet, Nicholas 150
Turbet, Peter 311
Turbet, Sarah 352
TURELL 760
Turell, Joseph 791
Turell, Lydia 278
Turfrey, Katharine 37
TURFS 286, 758
TURHAND 758
Turk, John 554
Turland, Tamasin 27
Turland, Thomas 830
Turloar, Tamasin 27
TURLOW 740
Turneer, Elizabeth 233
TURNER 758, 759, 760
Turner, --- 309
Turner, Abigail 379, 399, 689
Turner, Ann 95, 322
Turner, Anna 67
Turner, Bathshua 277
Turner, David 262
Turner, Deborah 748
Turner, Edward 75
Turner, Elizabeth 297, 299, 383,
    483, 509, 688, 801
Turner, Elizabeth Freestone 293
Turner, Eunice 109, 112, 212
Turner, Freestone 603
Turner, Grace 152, 706
Turner, Habakuck 491
Turner, Hannah 95, 387, 484, 543,
    611
Turner, Increase 676

Turner, James 830
Turner, Joanna 543
Turner, John 379, 449, 514, 616
Turner, Jonathan 768
Turner, Joseph 458
Turner, Laurence 396
Turner, Lydah 45
Turner, Lydia 45, 227, 415
Turner, Margaret 564, 712, 831
Turner, Martha 396
Turner, Mary 21, 86, 112, 142,
    243, 262, 267, 558, 559, 604,
    845
Turner, Miriam 581
Turner, Nathaniel 712, 765
Turner, Oseeth Wing 806
Turner, Praisever 8, 451
Turner, Prudence Balston 488
Turner, Rachel 418, 482
Turner, Rebecca 513
Turner, Robert 55, 370
Turner, Ruth 604
Turner, Sarah 140, 257, 379, 588,
    590
Turner, Susan 758
Turner, Thomas 51, 57
Turner, William 599
Turner, William (Capt.) 15
TURNEY 760
Turney, Abigail 418
Turney, Ann 671, 799
Turney, Benjamin 401, 507
Turney, Elizabeth 640
Turney, Joseph 396
Turney, Judith 800
Turney, Martha 752
Turney, Mary 661, 752
Turney, Rebecca 670, 801
Turney, Robert 330, 826
Turney, Ruth 85
Turney, Sarah 670, 799
TURPIN 760
Turpin, Agnes 252
Turpin, Elizabeth 5
Turpin, Jane 457, 526
Turrel, Mary 586
TURRELL see TIRRELL
Turrell, --- 785
Turrell, Daniel 45
TURRIL 760
TURVIL 760
Tustin, John 340
Tutheld, Mary 397
TUTHILL 760, 761
Tuthill, Abigail 176, 558
Tuthill, Ann 185
Tuthill, Daniel 91
Tuthill, Elizabeth 244, 308, 552,
    795
Tuthill, Hannah 794
Tuthill, John 847
TUTTELL 761
TUTTLE 760, 761
Tuttle, Abigail 46, 501, 781
Tuttle, Ann 405
Tuttle, Bridget 795
Tuttle, Dorothy 69, 742
Tuttle, Elizabeth 28, 193, 242,
    244, 423, 614
Tuttle, Esther 644
Tuttle, Hannah 158, 390, 555, 795
Tuttle, Joahanna 555
Tuttle, Joanna 72, 550, 581
Tuttle, John 193
Tuttle, Joseph 92
Tuttle, Joshua 513
Tuttle, Mary 121, 121, 137, 282,
    389, 777

Tuttle, Mercy 108
Tuttle, Rebecca 211, 664
Tuttle, Richard 385, 555
Tuttle, Samuel 44
Tuttle, Sarah 163, 401, 492, 532, 678, 762, 779
Tuttle, Susanna 746
Tutty, Anne 443
Tutty, Hannah 443, 809
Tuxberry, Frances 395
TUXBERY 733
Tuxbury, Naomi 247
Tuxsberry, Mary 651
Twalls, Susanna 642
TWELLS 761
Twells, Mary 159, 438
Twells, Rachel 285
Twelve, Rachel 285
Twelves, Martha 264
Twichell, Bethiah 632
Twichell, Elizabeth 13
Twichell, Hannah 372
Twichell, Mary 508, 632
TWING 741
TWINING 761
Twining, Anna 69
Twining, Elizabeth 633
Twining, Isabel 33
Twining, Joanna 69
Twining, Mehitable 223
TWINNING 761
TWISDELL 761
TWISDEN 761
Twisden, Alice 742
Twisden, Elizabeth 742
Twisden, Ellice 742
Twisden, Lydia 93
TWISS 761
Twiss, Rebecca 350
TWIST 761
TWITCHELL 761
Twitchell, Bethiah 632
Twitchell, Mary 508, 511
Twitchell, Patience 238
Twitchill, Hannah 372
Twombley, Mary 742
Twombley, Sarah 303
TWOMBLY 761, 762
TYBBET 742
Tybbot, Elizabeth 343
Tybbot, Mary 342, 351
Tybott, Agnes 155
TYDEY 762
TYER 584, 762
Tyer, Jane 740
Tyer, William 639
TYLER 729, 730, 762
Tyler, Abigail 642
Tyler, Abraham 110
Tyler, Catherine 826
Tyler, Charles 285
Tyler, Elizabeth 554
Tyler, Hannah 18, 126, 126, 476, 817
Tyler, Joan 219
Tyler, Martha 298
Tyler, Mary 97, 258, 555, 596
Tyler, Moses 698
Tyler, Roger 401
Tyler, Tamar 179
Tyler, William 96
Tylestone, Sarah 151
TYLLY 762
TYLSTONE 743
Tyndal, Margaret 830
TYNG 762, 763
Tyng, Anna 668
Tyng, Anne 668

Tyng, Deliverance 659
Tyng, Elizabeth 94
Tyng, Eunice 817
Tyng, Hannah 312, 652, 668
Tyng, Jonathan 280
Tyng, Mercy 92
Tyng, Rebecca 232
Tyrrell, Sarah 397

--- U ---

UDALL 763
Udall, Mary 10
Udell, Ruth 703
Uffet, Thomas 734
UFFORD 763
Ufford, --- 20
Ufford, Abigail 744
Ufford, Anna Hawley 56
Ufford, Martha 137
Ufford, Mary 581
Uffort, Mary 581
Uggs, Margaret 778
UINSON 768
Umberfeild, Mary 228
UMBERFIELD 763
Umberfield, Mary 484
UMPHERVILE 763
UMPRAVILLE 763
UNDERHILL 763
Underhill, Deborah 749
Underhill, Elizabeth 505, 682
Underhill, Hannah 15, 44
Underhill, John 520
Underhill, Lettice 115
Underhill, Mary 287, 404
Underhill, Sarah 114, 505
Underwad, Priscilla 694
Underwod, Sarah 78
UNDERWOOD 763, 764
Underwood, Deborah 128
Underwood, Elizabeth 116, 194, 200
Underwood, Hannah 300, 664
Underwood, Jane 791
Underwood, Joseph 116, 196, 378
Underwood, Magdalen 150, 763
Underwood, Mary 545
Underwood, Priscilla 694
Underwood, Remembrance 623
Underwood, Sarah 78
Underwood, Thomas 763
Underwood, William 569
UNTHANK 764
Unthank, Mary 14, 750
UPDIKE 764
Updike, Elizabeth 814
Updike, Sarah 808
UPHAM 764
Upham, Elizabeth 323, 631, 792
Upham, Hannah 471
Upham, Joane 493
Upham, John 381, 471, 493
Upham, Mary 811
Upham, Nathaniel 663, 736
Upham, Priscilla 194
Upham, Sarah 789
Upham, Thomas 685
UPSAL 764
UPSALL 764
UPSHALL 764
Upshall, Elizabeth 324, 606
Upshall, Nicholas 188
Upshall, Susanna 188
UPSON 764
Upson, Axtell 842

Upson, Elizabeth 325, 798
Upson, Hannah 368, 842
Upson, Mary 795
Upson, Thomas 656
UPTON 764
Upton, Abigail 576
Upton, Ann 281
Upton, Elizabeth 343
Upton, Mary 704
URANN 764
Urann, Eleanor 793
Urann, William 793
Urquhart, William (Rev.) 123
URIN 764
Urin, Eleanor 793
Urin, Gertrude 747
Urin, William 793
URINE 764
URNAR 760
URQUAHART 764
URQUEHART 764
URQUHART 764
Urquhart, William (Rev.) 730
URROHART 545, 764
URSELTON 765
USE 764
USHER 764, 765
Usher, Deborah 637
Usher, Elizabeth 350, 416, 692
Usher, Elizabeth Roberts 672
Usher, Hezekiah 104, 127, 376, 541
Usher, Rebecca 104
Usher, Robert 414
Usher, Sarah 762
USSELL 765
USSELTON 765
UTLEY 765
Utley, Lydia 367, 581
Utley, Mary 846
UTTER 765
Utter, Millicent 846
UYYOHART 764

--- V ---

VAIL 765
Vail, Jeremiah 515
Vail, Jeremiah 552
Vail, Sarah 515
Vail, Sarah 516
VAILE 765
Vajoll, Joseph 711
VALE 765
VALENTINE 765
Valentine, Anne 820
VALES 257
VanBeyeren, Anneke 261
vanBeyeren, Aelbrights 564
vanBeyeren, Albertse 564
vanBeyeren, Anneke 564
VanBeyeron, Aelbrights 564
VanBeyeron, Albertse 564
VanBeyeron, Anneke 564
VanCleefe, Rebecca 251
VanderSpigel, Lysbeth 213
VanDriest, Jaunetie 396
VanDyke, Ann 711
VANE 765
VanFlaisbeen, Frainettia 213
VanFlaisbeen, Phebe 213
VanGOODENHAUSEN 765
VANGOODENHOUSE 765 see GOODENHOUSE
VanGoodenhousen, Samuel 759
VANGOODENHOUSEN 765

VanGOODENHOUSEN 765
VanRensselaer, Anna 536
Varden, Sarah 386
Varleet, Mary 15, 656
VARNAM 766
Varnam, Hannah 167
VARNEY 765
Varney, Abigail 75, 121
Varney, Humphrey 26, 715
Varney, John 548
Varney, Martha 690
Varney, Mary 151, 270
Varney, Rachel 179, 261
Varney, William 563
Varnhum, Alice 493
Varnhum, Ralph 493
VARNUM 766
Varnum, Hannah 762
Varnum, Sarah 378, 531
Vary, Elizabeth 381
Vase, Ann 165
Vasney, Sarah 562
VASSALL 766
Vassall, Anna 787
Vassall, Frances 4
Vassall, Judith 806
Vassall, Margaret 377
VAUGHAN 766
Vaughan, David 428
Vaughan, Eleanor 773
Vaughan, Elizabeth 394
Vaughan, George 217
Vaughan, Mary 15, 238, 788
Vaughan, Mercy 136, 217
Vaughan, William 155, 233
Vaughn, Ann 136
Vaughn, Bridget 299
Vaughn, Mary 438, 783
Vaughn, Mercy 136
Vayle, Mary 832
VEACH see VETCH
VEALE 765
VEALLEE 766
Veare, Ann 296, 839
VEASEY 766
Veasey, George 517, 825
VEAZEY 766
Veazey, Mary 560
Veazie, Abigail 734
Veazie, Anna 324
Veazie, Elizabeth 14
Veazie, Ellen 552
Veazie, Hannah 324
Veazie, Mary 642
Veazie, Mercy 642
Veazie, William 284
VEAZY 766
VEECH 766
Veering, John 330
VEIN 765
VELEY 766
VELLER 766
VELLERS 766
VENNER 766
VENNY 766
Vensey, William 179
VENTEMAN 766
Venteman, John 688
VENTRES 766
Ventres, Elizabeth 318
Ventres, Susannah 93
VENTRIS 766
Ventris, Sarah 102
Ventriss, Elizabeth 318
VENTROUS 766
Ventrus, Grace 76
Ventrus, Sarah 102
Ventrus, Sarah Church Porter 595

Ventrus, Susannah 93
VENUS 766
Veray, Mehitable 340
VEREIN 767
VEREN 766, 767
Veren, Abigail 491
Veren, Dorcas 368
Veren, Eleanor 767
Veren, Hilliard 53
Veren, John 787
Veren, Mary 466, 608, 821
Veren, Nathaniel 608
Veren, Sarah 560
VERGOOSE 767 see GOOSE
Vergoose, Susanna 609
VERIN 767
Vering, Sarah 558
Verlet, Susannah 213
VERMAES 767
Vermaes, Abigail 129, 407
Vermaes, Alice 451
Vermaes, Sarah 451
VERMAGES 767
Vermais, Abigail 66
Vermay, Mary 673
Vermaye, Esther 253
Vermaye, Hester 253
VERMAYES 767
Vermayes, Susanna 767
VERNEY 766
VERNON 767
Vernon, Daniel 237
VERREY 767
VERRIN 767
Verry, Elizabeth 541
Verry, Hannah 56, 654
Verry, Mary 489
Versey, Eleanor 193
Versey, Ellen 193
VERY 767
Very, Abigail 18
Very, Benjamin 88, 597
Very, Bridget 303
Very, Hannah 277
Very, Mary 200, 686
Very, Mehitable 340
Very, Sarah 716
VETCH 767 see VEACH
VIAL 767
Vial, Mercy 649
VIALL 767
Viall, Abigail 498
Viall, Elizabeth 735
Viall, Hopestill 589, 673
Viall, John 533
Viall, Mary 8, 123, 721
Viall, Sarah 515
Vicaris, Anne 737
VICARS 767
Vicars, Jane 83
VICARY 767
Vicary, Roger 840
Vickars, Isaac 603
Vickary, Isaac 603
Vickerey, Rebecca 604
VICKERIE 767
Vickerow, Rebecca 604
VICKERS 767 see VICKERY
Vickers, Anne 737
VICKERY 767 see VICKERS
Vickery, Anne 737
Vickery, Mary 736
VILER 767
VILLAROCK 767
VINAL 767
VINALL 767, 768
Vinall, Elizabeth 806
Vinall, Grace 523

Vinall, Martha 151
VINCEN 768
Vincen, Elizabeth 293
VINCENT 768 see VINSON
Vincent, Abigail 250, 566
Vincent, Elizabeth 218
Vincent, Hannah 104
Vincent, Joan 667
Vincent, John 603
Vincent, Mary 339, 394
Vincent, Sarah 218, 394
Vincent, William 129
Vincent, Wm. 562
VINE 768
Vine, Hannah 213
Vine, Mary 518
VINING 768
Vining, Jane 759
Vining, Sarah 595, 809
Vinsen, Sarah 218
VINSENT 768
Vinsentt, Mary 394
VINSON see VINCENT
Vinson, Abigail 250, 566
Vinson, Elizabeth 293
Vinson, Hannah 247
Vinson, Samuel 664
Vinson, Sarah 562
Vinson, William 129, 179, 451, 639
VINTON 768
Vinton, Ann 361
Vinton, Eleanor 609
Vinton, Elizabeth 834
Vinton, Hannah 323, 830
Vinton, John 177
Vinton, Sarah 345
VIRGIN 768
VIRGO 768
Virgoose, Mary 766
VIRGUE 768
Vitrey, George 376
Vitrey, Louis 741
Vitterell, Sarah 549
Vittery, Louis 741
Vivion, Mary 246
VIXEN 832
Vjall, Mary 721
Vnderwood, Hannah 300
Voaker, Mary 159
Vocory, Mary 736
VODEN 768
Voden, Mary 598
VODIN 768
VOEDEN 768
Vokes, Mary 652
Volden, Philip 416
VORE 768
Vore, Abigail 113
Vore, Lydia 178
Vore, Mary 15
Vore, Sarah 561
VOSE 768
Vose, Elizabeth 190, 724, 770
Vose, Jane 391, 481
Vose, Martha 663
Vose, Thomas 190
Vosw, Martha 113
VOUDEN 768
VOWDEN 82, 768
Vowden, Philip 416
VOWLES 768
Vowles, Jonathan 389
Vowles, Mary 543
VRIN 764
Vringe, Sarah 111
Vyoll, Joseph 51

--- W ---

W-, Moses 798
WACOMB 772
Wacum, Sarah 656
Wacum, Sarah Adams 317
Wad, Richard 713
Wadd, Ann 168
Wadd, Lucy 551
Waddames, John 126
Waddames, Susannah 126
Waddames, William 126
WADDAMS 769
WADDELL 786
Waddell, Mary 456
Waddock, Joan 249
Waddock, Joanna 249
Waddock, Margaret 134
WADE 769
Wade, --- 688
Wade, Deborah 235
Wade, Elizabeth 708, 779
Wade, John 143
Wade, Jonathan 115
Wade, Katherine 844
Wade, Mary 149, 194, 468, 644, 675
Wade, Mercy 92
Wade, Prudence 185, 193, 339, 722
Wade, Rebecca 549
Wade, Robert 194
Wade, Sarah 634, 837
Wade, Susanna 793, 823
Wade, Susannah 806
Wadell, John 726
Wadell, Mary 511
WADGE 790
WADHAMS 769
Wadhams, Hannah 756
Wadhams, John 36, 126
Wadhams, Susannah 126
Wadhams, William 126
Wadin, Martha 94
Wadin, Marthew 94
Wadkins, Margaret 376
WADLAND 769
Wadland, Agnes 51, 304
Wadland, Crispen 680
Wadland, Elizabeth 680
WADLEIGH 769
Wadleigh, Henry 447
Wadleigh, Joanne 734
Wadleigh, Jonathan 374
Wadleigh, Mary 189
Wadleigh, Sarah 846
Wadlen, Agnes 304
Wadlen, Crispen 680
Wadlen, Elizabeth 680
WADLEY 769
WADLIN 769
Wadloe, Elizabeth 553
WADLON 769
Wadock, Margaret 732
WADSWORTH 769, 770
Wadsworth, Abigail 208, 736
Wadsworth, Elizabeth 732
Wadsworth, Grace 698
Wadsworth, Hannah 574
Wadsworth, John 325
Wadsworth, Joseph 543, 795
Wadsworth, Lydia 574
Wadsworth, Mary 17, 693, 715
Wadsworth, Samuel 612
Wadsworth, Sarah 23, 477, 636, 815
WAFFE 770

Waffe, Ann 131
Waffe, Elizabeth 97, 629
Waffe, John 61
WAGER 773
Waget, Esther 112
WAGGET 770
WAGGETT 770
Waggett, Esther 112
WAIGHT 770, 771
WAINWRIGHT 770
Wainwright, Anne 830
Wainwright, Elizabeth 167, 204
Wainwright, Martha 605
Wainwright, Mary 667
Wainwright, Mehitable 24
Wainwright, Sarah 286
Wainwright, Simon 674
WAIT 771
Wait, Eunice 182
Wait, Jeremiah 237
Wait, Mary 19, 239, 610, 746
Wait, Rachel 610
Wait, Sarah 710
Wait, Thomas 187
WAITE 770, 771
Waite, Abigail 24, 427, 770
Waite, Anne 69, 114
Waite, Canada 686
Waite, Damaris 490
Waite, Deborah 550
Waite, Eunice 182
Waite, Grace 603
Waite, Hannah 113, 114, 351
Waite, John 266, 557
Waite, Joseph 417
Waite, Mary 473, 794
Waite, Mehitable 371, 560
Waite, Phebe 704
Waite, Rebecca 757
Waite, Return 458
Waite, Richard 43
Waite, Samuel 648
Waite, Sarah 60, 714, 714
Waite, Theodosia 696
Waitt, Elizabeth 446
WAKE 771
WAKEFIELD 771
Wakefield, Ann 150, 155
Wakefield, Deliverance 69
Wakefield, Elizabeth 286, 410
Wakefield, Hannah 316
Wakefield, John 150
Wakefield, Martha 113
Wakefield, Mary 219, 287, 342, 372
Wakefield, Rebecca 440
Wakefield, Susanna 621
WAKEHAM 772
Wakeham, John 463
WAKELEE 772
Wakelee, Abigail 56
Wakelee, Henry 325
Wakelee, Jacob 776
Wakelee, Mary 454, 707
Wakelee, Mercy 454
Wakelee, Patience 745
Wakelee, Rebecca 80, 649
WAKELEY 772
Wakeley, Elizabeth 165
Wakeley, James 82
Wakeley, Patience 745
WAKELIN 772
WAKELY 772
Wakely, Elizabeth 655
Wakely, Henry 325
Wakely, Mary 707
Wakely, Sarah 707
WAKEMAN 772

Wakeman, Abigail 372
Wakeman, Agnes 696
Wakeman, Ann 415, 535
Wakeman, Anne 393
Wakeman, Elizabeth 21, 93, 216, 442, 818
Wakeman, Ellen 306
Wakeman, Esbon 51
Wakeman, Esther 661, 780
Wakeman, Ezbon 51
Wakeman, Grace 431
Wakeman, Hannah 331
Wakeman, Helena 306, 726
Wakeman, Hester 661
Wakeman, Joanna 331
Wakeman, Martha 209
Wakeman, Mary 163
Wakeman, Priscilla 622
Wakeman, Samuel 122, 483, 818
WAKER 773, 774
WAKLY 772
Wakly, Elizabeth 165
WAKUM 772
WALBRIDGE 772
WALCOM 772
Walcom, Zaccheus 697
WALCOT 832
WALCOTT 832, 833
Walcott, Mary 259, 260
WALCUP 776
WALCUTT 832
Waldegrave, Jemima 568
WALDEN 772 see WALDRON
Walden, Ann 679
Walden, Elizabeth 288
Walden, Elizabeth Sanders Batson 53
Walden, Hannah 259
Walden, John 316
Walden, Mary 367
Walden, Thomasin 674
WALDERNE 772, 773
Walderne, Ruth 367
Walderne, Samuel 568
WALDIN 772
Waldin, Edward 367
WALDO 772
Waldo, Cornelius 413
Waldo, Deborah 203, 275
Waldo, Elizabeth 90
Waldo, Rebecca 250
Waldon, John 316
WALDREN 773
Waldren, Sarah 164
WALDRON 772, 773 see WALDEN
Waldron, Ann 299
Waldron, Anna 299
Waldron, Edward 367
Waldron, Eleanor 631
Waldron, Elizabeth 299, 550
Waldron, Esther 44, 247, 428, 459
Waldron, Hester 247
Waldron, Isaac 95
Waldron, John 55, 316, 388
Waldron, Mary 100
Waldron, Priscilla 357
Waldron, Prudence 655
Waldron, Roger 528
Waldron, Samuel 365
Waldron, Sarah 312, 457
WALDSTONE 777
WALE 773
Waled, Mary 119
WALER 776
Walerne, Samuel 365
WALES 773
Wales, Constant 494

Wales, Hannah 69
Wales, Mary 23, 298, 383
Wales, Sarah 734
WALFORD 773
Walford, Elizabeth 652
Walford, Hannah 424
Walford, Hans 264
Walford, Jane 575
Walford, Jeremiah 15, 403
Walford, Martha 374, 383, 516, 797
Walford, Mary 15, 102, 528, 775
Walford, Sarah 368
WALK 773
WALKER 773, 774, 775, 776
Walker, Abigail 84
Walker, Ann 517
Walker, Deborah 311
Walker, Dorothy 564
Walker, Elishua 740
Walker, Elizabeth 116, 134, 244, 250, 269, 375, 416, 439, 463, 498, 579, 723, 762, 771
Walker, Esther 834
Walker, Eunice 32
Walker, Hannah 32, 336, 424, 620, 736
Walker, Henry 109, 351, 629, 774
Walker, Hester 25, 834
Walker, Isaac 59, 674, 700
Walker, Israel 270
Walker, Jacob 76
Walker, James 618
Walker, Jane 172, 320, 468
Walker, Joan 401
Walker, John 503, 579, 773, 785, 837
Walker, Joseph 398, 660
Walker, Lydia 268
Walker, Margaret 394
Walker, Mary 27, 106, 156, 230, 238, 239, 394, 452, 487, 514, 543, 669, 841
Walker, Mary Manning 661
Walker, Mehitable 617
Walker, Obadiah 652
Walker, Phebe 615
Walker, Philip 591
Walker, Rebecca 80
Walker, Richard 385
Walker, Samuel 9, 190, 279, 279
Walker, Sarah 13, 106, 383, 420, 420, 470, 564, 573, 649, 745, 782
Walker, Sarah Richmond Rew 715
Walker, Shubael 225, 487
Walker, Susanna 426, 469, 564, 700
Walker, Tabitha 438
Walker, Thomas 6, 426, 682
Walker, William 102
WALKLEY 772
Walkley, Rebecca 175
Walkley, Richard 175
WALKUP 773, 776
WALL 776
Wall, Elizabeth 350
Wall, Hannah 524
Wall, James 756
Wall, Mary 491
Wall, Sarah 217, 228
WALLACE 776
Wallace, Abigail 647
Wallace, Elizabeth 518
Wallace, Mary 586
Wallace, Nicholas 505
WALLAS 776
WALLBRIDGE 772

WALLDOW 772
WALLEN 776 see WALLING
Wallen, Thomas 131
WALLER 776
Waller, Eleazer 576
Waller, Elizabeth 696
Waller, Joan 193
Waller, Joseph 207
Waller, Margaret 289
Waller, Rebecca 81, 174
Waller, Samuel 515
Waller, Thomas 193
Wallerc, Elizabeth 570
WALLEY 776, 777
Walley, Elizabeth 3
Walley, Hannah 12, 461, 715
Walley, Mary 192
Walley, Sarah 147
Walley, Thomas 672
Walley, William 33
WALLICE 776
Wallice, Elizabeth 518
WALLING 777 see WALLEN
Walling, Thomas 1, 131
WALLINGFORD 777
Wallingford, Elizabeth 472
Wallingford, Mary 593
Wallingford, Nicholas 62, 489, 625
Wallingford, Sarah 387
Wallington, Mary 593
WALLIS 776
Wallis, --- 564, 611
Wallis, Abigail 405
Wallis, Dorcas 450
Wallis, Eleanor 65
Wallis, Honor 9
Wallis, Jane 450
Wallis, Margaret 732, 776
Wallis, Mary 586
Wallis, Nathaniel 621
Wallis, Nicholas 505
Wallis, Oner 9
Wallis, Richard 772
Wallis, Sarah 572, 699, 713
Wally, Ruth 255
Wally, Sarah 147
WALSBEE 777
WALSBY 777
WALSTON 777
WALSTONE 777
Walstone, John 726
WALSWORTH 777
WALTER 777
Walter, Hannah 119
Walter, Mary 735
Walter, Thomas 239, 836
WALTERS 774, 777, 784
Walters, Sarah 612
WALTHAM 777
Waltham, Deborah 285
Waltham, Elizabeth 750
WALTON 777 see WALSTON, WALTHAM
Walton, Abishag 728
Walton, Abishai 728
Walton, Dorcas 755
Walton, Elizabeth 175, 486, 750
Walton, Martha 527, 796
Walton, Mary 49, 610, 621, 631
Walton, Sarah 120, 745
WALWORTH 777
WAN 777
Wandell, --- 745
Wang, Osia 759
Wang, Osiah 759
Wang, Ozia 759
WANNERTON 777
Wannerton, Ann 821

Wannerton, Thomas 821
Wanten, Elizabeth 372
Wanton, Elizabeth 656
Wanton, Hannah 41
Wanwright, Francis 253
Wanwright, Hannah 253
WAR 787
War, Joseph 57
Warburton, Joanna 263
WARD 777, 778, 779
Ward, Abigail 218, 358, 375, 540
Ward, Alice 90, 396
Ward, Ann 781
Ward, Anne 535, 727
Ward, Bethiah 620
Ward, Bridget 612
Ward, Charity 637
Ward, Deborah 420, 421, 844
Ward, Dorothy 181
Ward, Eleazer 730
Ward, Elizabeth 289, 293, 295, 342, 392, 434, 435, 494, 647, 805
Ward, Esther 82, 122, 184, 356, 370, 435, 473, 535, 561
Ward, Frances 545
Ward, Hannah 36, 325, 392, 523, 724, 779
Ward, Hester 356, 435
Ward, Hopestill 833
Ward, Isabel 36
Ward, Isabella 140, 539
Ward, Joanna 722, 818
Ward, John 302
Ward, Joshua 435
Ward, Josiah 722
Ward, Lucy 505
Ward, Lydia 499
Ward, Marcie 66
Ward, Margaret 91, 370, 588, 627
Ward, Martha 161, 469, 761
Ward, Mary 21, 22, 41, 122, 156, 201, 212, 225, 271, 291, 382, 509, 619, 781, 785, 836
Ward, Mercy 131, 734
Ward, Miles 627
Ward, Nathaniel 387, 488, 833
Ward, Obadiah 345
Ward, Phebe 336
Ward, Record 534
Ward, Remember 826
Ward, Richard 713
Ward, Ruth 479
Ward, Samuel 135, 211, 397, 429, 535, 655
Ward, Sarah 92, 122, 252, 314, 340, 633
Ward, Sarah Clark Deverson 217
Ward, Susan 266
Ward, Susanna 262, 522, 693
Ward, Tabitha 260
Ward, Thomas 172
Ward, Thomasin 115
Ward, William 238, 335, 727
Ward, Wm. 356
WARDALL 779
Warde, Lydia 305
Warde, Martha 274
WARDELL 779
Wardell, Alice 305
Wardell, Elizabeth 639
Wardell, Innocent 84
Wardell, Mary 41, 456, 814
Wardell, Meribah 468
Wardell, William 304
WARDEN 779
Warden, Samuel 27
Wardin, Martha 94

Wardin, Marthew 94
WARDLE 779
Wardle, Samuel 355
WARDWELL 779, 780
Wardwell, Abigail 321
Wardwell, Elizabeth 581
Wardwell, Hannah 195
Wardwell, Mary 645, 843
Wardwell, Mercy 843
Wardwell, Meribah 468
Wardwell, Susannah Ellery 346
Wardwell, Uzel 626
Wardwell, William 573
WARE 787 see WYER
Ware, Ann 585
Ware, Anne 229
Ware, Elizabeth 303, 642
Ware, Esther 485
Ware, John 808, 833
Ware, Mary 610, 807
Ware, Rebecca 552
Ware, Samuel 211
Ware, Sarah 591
Ware, Sarah 592
WAREHAM 780
WAREING 780
WARES 787
WARFIELD 780
Warfield, Ithamar 16
WARHAM 780
Warham, Abigail 13
Warham, Esther 496, 713
Warham, John (Rev.) 94, 531
Warham, Sarah 719
WARIN 781, 782
Warin, Mary 68
WARING 780
WARKMAN 780
WARLAND 780
WARLEY 780
WARLY 780
Warmal, Mary 251
Warmall, Mary 251
Warman, Francis 295
Warne, Bridget 429
WARNER 780, 781
Warner, Abigail 202, 263, 459, 795, 810
Warner, Andrew 4, 195, 661, 701
Warner, Ann 397
Warner, Anna 397
Warner, Anne 397
Warner, Bethia 317
Warner, Daniel 89, 105, 420
Warner, Elizabeth 147, 314, 362, 636
Warner, Hannah 410, 598, 795
Warner, Isaac 472
Warner, Joanna 483
Warner, John 180, 604, 814
Warner, Lydia 55, 102, 103
Warner, Mark 636
Warner, Mary 47, 195, 373, 396, 539, 667, 705
Warner, Mehitable 545
Warner, Nathaniel 51
Warner, Priscilla 190, 196, 391
Warner, Rachel 596
Warner, Ralph 657
Warner, Rebecca 406
Warner, Richard 305
Warner, Robert 631
Warner, Ruth 431, 600
Warner, Samuel 722
Warner, Sarah 157, 284, 369, 438, 611, 667, 781
Warner, Susan 268
Warner, Susanna 95, 268

Warner, Thomas 659
Warr, Sarah 314
WARREN 781, 782
Warren, Abigail 473, 584, 691, 843
Warren, Alice 300
Warren, Amy 244
Warren, Ann 468
Warren, Deborah 373
Warren, Elizabeth 78, 152, 323, 376, 443, 579, 661, 725
Warren, Elizabeth Crow 826
Warren, Ellis 300
Warren, Experience 741
Warren, Gilbert 737
Warren, Grace 521
Warren, Grizel 548
Warren, Grizet 548
Warren, Grizzel 548
Warren, Hannah 48, 214, 500, 686
Warren, Humphrey 228
Warren, Jane 318, 470, 510, 698
Warren, Joanna 177
Warren, Johane 698
Warren, John 42, 79, 180, 359, 641, 661
Warren, Joseph 610
Warren, Margaret 699, 847
Warren, Mary 48, 68, 79, 122, 150, 268, 293, 321, 583, 847
Warren, Mercy 90, 213
Warren, Patience 477
Warren, Rebecca 610
Warren, Relief 813
Warren, Sarah 75, 178, 294, 295, 459, 546, 604
Warrin, Elizabeth 725
Warrin, Mary 583
WARRINAH 781
WARRINER 782
Warriner, Elizabeth 124, 719
Warriner, Hannah 318, 537, 566
Warriner, James 37, 704
Warriner, Joseph 1, 172
Warriner, Luke 36
Warriner, Mary 83
Warriner, William 375, 448
Warsilbe, Bridget 71
Wascot, Ruth 815
WASE 783
Wase, Ann 165
WASHBORNE 783
WASHBOURN 783
WASHBURN 783
Washburn, Elizabeth 16, 251, 359, 660
Washburn, Jane 545
Washburn, John 21, 368, 549
Washburn, Margaret 535
Washburn, Marjoram 461
Washburn, Mary 422, 441
Washburn, Phebe 23
Washburn, Samuel 841
Washburn, Sarah 16, 821
Washburn, Thomas 357
WASHBURNE 783
Washburne, Agnes 413
Washburne, Martha 745
Washburne, Mary 818
Washington, Margaret 497
Washington, Temperance 263
WASHULL 797
WASS 783
Wastall, Susannah 354
WASTE 796
Water, Abigail 768
WATERBURY 783
Waterbury, John 329, 660

Waterbury, Mary 678
Waterbury, Rachel 383
Waterbury, Sarah 219, 500, 753, 790
WATERHOUSE 783
Waterhouse, Elizabeth 33, 475
Waterhouse, Jacob 33
Waterhouse, John 356
Waterhouse, Mary 356
Waterhouse, Rebecca 812, 821
Waterhouse, Richard 480
Waterhouse, Samuel 464
WATERMAN 783, 784
Waterman, Ann 611
Waterman, Anna 611
Waterman, Bethiah 380
Waterman, Elizabeth 48, 269, 625, 743
Waterman, Lydia 664
Waterman, Margaret 813
Waterman, Mehitable 262
Waterman, Resolved 827
Waterman, Robert 466, 742
Waterman, Sarah 367
Waterman, Susanna Colby 168
Waterman, Wade 105
Waterman, Wait 105, 619
WATERS 784, 785
Waters, Abigail 23, 607
Waters, Ann 528, 687
Waters, Bevil 528
Waters, Dorothy 602
Waters, Eleanor 146
Waters, Elizabeth 747
Waters, Eunice 537
Waters, Hanna 719
Waters, Hannah 717, 719, 748
Waters, James 589
Waters, Joseph 125, 645, 682
Waters, Judith 386
Waters, Lawrence 467
Waters, Mary 64, 104, 208, 252, 416, 424, 707, 810
Waters, Penelope 416
Waters, Phebe 797
Waters, Rebecca 804
Waters, Sarah 65, 656, 674, 784
Waters, Susannah 606
Waters, Ureth 812
Waters, Urith 536, 537
Waters, William 3, 92, 225
Waterus, Rebecca 812
Wathem, Margaret 255
WATHEN 842
Wathen, Hannah 280
Wathen, Margaret 176
Watken, Deborah 428
WATKINS 785
Watkins, Bridget 205
Watkins, David 720
Watkins, Elizabeth 398
Watkins, Margaret 376
Watkins, Thomas 708
WATROUS 783
Watrous, Sarah 627
WATS 786
WATSON 141, 785, 786
Watson, Alice 614
Watson, Dorcas 4, 236
Watson, Ebenezer 432
Watson, Edward 774
Watson, Elizabeth 476, 578, 614, 820
Watson, Elizabeth Frost 320
Watson, Elkanah 283
Watson, Faith 105, 780
Watson, Frances 99, 633
Watson, Grace 336

Watson, Hannah 71
Watson, Hannah Millborne 508
Watson, Jedediah 297
Watson, John 269, 602
Watson, Margery 309
Watson, Mary 230, 234, 333, 462, 662, 705
Watson, Phebe 665
Watson, Rebecca 620
Watson, Rebecca Wells Latham Packer 453, 550
Watson, Robert 15, 604
Watson, Sarah 234, 504, 776
Watson, William 333
Watte, Mary 48
WATTERS 784
Watters, Susanna 606
Wattle, Mary 556
Wattle, Rose 110
WATTLES 786
Wattles, John 726
Wattles, Mary 556
WATTS 786
Watts, Anne 223
Watts, Benjamin 610
Watts, Eleanor 108, 161
Watts, Elinor 399
Watts, Elizabeth 397, 540
Watts, Henry 42
Watts, Jeremiah 89
Watts, Lydia 299
Watts, Margaret 6
Watts, Mary 89, 755
Watts, Mercy 579
Watts, Samuel 161
Watts, Thomas 332, 356
WAY 786, 787
Way, Agnes 346, 569
Way, Alice 146
Way, Eleazer 607
Way, Elizabeth 794
Way, George 57
Way, Henry 321
Way, James 575
Way, Jane 802
Way, Joan 275
Way, Joanna 142, 281
Way, Martha 10
Way, Mary 575
Way, Richard 10, 401, 445
Way, Sarah 794
Way, Susannah 509
Way, William 767
Waye, Martha 10
WAYMAN 787
Waymoth, Elizabeth 197
Wayne, Mary 37
WAYT 770
Wayt, Katherine 424
WAYTE 770
Wayte, Mary 48
WEAD 769
Wead, Ephraim 842
WEAR 787
Wear, Daniel 372, 767
WEARE 787 see WYER
Weare, Christian 51
Weare, Elias 5
Weare, Elizabeth 189, 303
Weare, Esther 324, 723
Weare, Hannah 419, 663, 769
Weare, Martha 613
Weare, Mary 232, 628, 721
Weare, Peter 197, 796
Weare, Phebe 488
Weare, Robert 593
Weare, Ruth 197, 243
Weare, Samuel 135

Weare, Sarah 317, 541, 769
WEAT 844
WEATHERBEE 831 see WEATHERLEY, WETHERLEY
WEATHERBY 787
Weatley, Jane 449
Weave, Elizabeth 226
WEAVER 788
Weaver, Clement 64, 283
Weaver, Elizabeth 233
Weaver, Judith 496
Weaver, Mary 277
WEBB 788, 789
Webb, Abigail 13
Webb, Ann 771
Webb, Christopher 182, 666
Webb, Elizabeth 37, 74, 323, 405, 650
Webb, Elizabeth Swift 204
Webb, Esther 584
Webb, George 341
Webb, Hannah 4, 27, 27
Webb, John 23, 257, 309
Webb, John (Jr.) 169
Webb, Joseph 266
Webb, Joshua 675
Webb, Margaret 666, 733
Webb, Mary 5, 239, 666, 790
Webb, Richard 127
Webb, Sarah 21, 114, 265, 406, 490, 603
Webb, Zachariah 603
WEBBER 789
Webber, --- 1
Webber, Elizabeth 117
Webber, John 5, 787
Webber, Josiah 378
Webber, Richard 320
Webber, Thomas 39
WEBLY 789
WEBSTER 789, 790
Webster, Abigail 488, 504, 525
Webster, Anne 489
Webster, Benjamin 104
Webster, Elizabeth 356, 488, 656, 662, 675, 702, 706, 841
Webster, Esther 364
Webster, Grace 104
Webster, Hannah 241, 250, 406
Webster, Henry 364
Webster, John 251, 316, 327, 736
Webster, Joseph 32
Webster, Lucy 504
Webster, Mary 39, 231, 251, 365, 440, 722, 796, 804
Webster, Nicholas 219, 753
Webster, Rachel 844
Webster, Robert 172
Webster, Sarah 450, 528, 726, 736
Webster, Stephen 100, 177
Webster, Susannah 318
Webster, Thankful 49
Webster, Thomas 307, 488
Webster, William 610
WEDGE 790
WEDGEWOOD 790
Wedgewood, Jonathan 358
Weeche, Margaret 194
WEED 790
Weed, Ann 403
Weed, Deborah 48
Weed, Dorcas 842
Weed, Elizabeth 631
Weed, Hannah 395
Weed, John 622
Weed, Mary 1, 55, 492, 660, 687, 783
Weed, Sarah 783

WEEDE 791
WEEDEN 790, 791
Weeden, --- 301
Weeden, Alice 42
Weeden, Elizabeth 170, 325, 328, 526
Weeden, Hannah 160, 568
Weeden, James 327
Weeden, John 325
Weeden, Margaret 313
Weeden, Martha 94
Weeden, Marthew 94
Weeden, Mary 170
Weeden, Phebe 568
Weeden, Sarah 59
Weeden, William 754
Weedin, Mary 324
Weedon, Sarah 141, 661
WEEK 791
Weeke, Alice 193
WEEKES 791, 792
Weekes, Hannah 581
Weekes, Jane 74
Weekes, Sarah 111
WEEKS 791, 792
Weeks, Abigail 352
Weeks, Ammiel 633
Weeks, Ann 135
Weeks, Anna 135
Weeks, Bethiah 20
Weeks, Elizabeth 14, 185, 365, 630, 675, 750, 819
Weeks, Experience 631
Weeks, George 402
Weeks, Jane 52, 552
Weeks, John 703, 750
Weeks, Joseph 276, 760
Weeks, Mary 90, 291, 322, 323, 460, 640, 660, 783, 805
Weeks, Mary Jenner 651
Weeks, Mehitable 631
Weeks, Mercy 501
Weeks, Nicholas 186, 333
Weeks, Rebecca 729
Weeks, Renew 135
Weeks, Richard 461
Weeks, Sarah 483
Weeks, Submit 179
Weeks, Thankful 560
Weeks, Thomas 597
Weeks, William 127, 496
Weiden, James 551
WEIGHTMAN 809, 814
WEIRR 787
Welbie, Olive 260
Welbourne, Elizabeth 546
Welbourne, Margaret 555
WELCH 792
Welch, Deborah 130
Welch, Dorcas 245, 325
Welch, Hannah 343
Welch, Mary 506
Welch, Sarah 280
Welcom, Amie 526
Welcom, Ann 526
Welcom, Richard 764
Welcomb, Amie 526
Welcomb, Ann 526
Welcome, Mary 750
Welcome, Peter 359
Welcome, Ruth 137
Welcome, William 806
WELD 792, 793
Weld, Anna 679
Weld, Bethia 442, 507
Weld, Bethula 507
Weld, Bethulia 507
Weld, Daniel 408

Weld, Dorothy 215
Weld, Edward 294
Weld, Elizabeth 189, 214, 313, 756
Weld, Hannah 363, 654
Weld, Joseph 712
Weld, Margaret 96
Weld, Mary 294, 345, 703
Weld, Sarah 282, 673
Welden, Elizabeth Higgins 369
Welden, Robert 577
WELDON 793 see WHELDON
Well, Sarah 33
WELLCOMB 793
Wellcome, Amie 526
Wellcome, Ann 526
Welld, Amy 464
Welld, Anne 464
WELLER 793
Weller, Elizabeth 241, 782
Weller, Mary 31
Weller, Richard 197
Weller, Sarah 217, 341, 376
Weller, Thankful 472
WELLES 794, 795
Welles, Ann 738
Welles, Anne 705
Welles, Elizabeth 680
Welles, John 815
Welles, Joshua 317
Welles, Lydia 747
Welles, Mary 333, 627
Welles, Rebecca 429
Welles, Richard 385
Welles, Samuel 11, 175
Welles, Sarah 68, 72, 149, 255, 746
Welles, Thomas 274, 555
Welles, Thomas (Gov.) 627
WELLINGTON 793
Wellington, Benjamin 580
Wellington, Elizabeth 260
Wellington, Mary 180, 497
Wellington, Oliver 469
Wellington, Ruhamah 108
WELLMAN 793, 794
Wellman, Elizabeth 400
Wellman, Martha 511
Wellman, Mary 360, 517
Wellman, William 327, 428
WELLMONE 793
WELLS 508, 792, 794, 795, 823
Wells, Abigail 146, 596, 752
Wells, Alice 731
Wells, Amy 464
Wells, Anne 308, 394, 464
Wells, Bethia 389
Wells, Deborah 732
Wells, Ebenezer 455
Wells, Elizabeth 7, 24, 53, 113, 121, 348, 597, 667, 800
Wells, Elizabeth Rowlandson 346
Wells, Esther 494
Wells, Frances 171
Wells, Grace 125, 540
Wells, Hannah 674, 776, 805
Wells, Hester 104
Wells, Irabelle 484
Wells, Izabell 484
Wells, Johanna 30
Wells, John 654
Wells, Lydia 145, 438, 637
Wells, Margaret 118, 392
Wells, Martha Skerry Neale 530
Wells, Mary 21, 36, 60, 302, 398, 429, 487, 499, 630, 847
Wells, Mehitable 760
Wells, Nathaniel 251

Wells, Patience 158
Wells, Peter 457
Wells, Prudence 712
Wells, Rebecca 397, 453, 550, 786
Wells, Richard 676
Wells, Ruth 434
Wells, Samuel 11
Wells, Sarah 54, 68, 149, 157, 210, 356, 395, 464, 495, 673, 736
Wells, Temperance 588
Wells, Thomas 60, 543, 710
Wells, William 308, 487, 760
WELLSTEAD 795
Welsh, Mary 379
Welsh, Sarah 534
WELSTEAD 797
WELSTED see WESTEAD
Welsted, Mehitable 26, 300
WELTCH 792
WELTON 795
Welton, Abigail 101
Welton, Elizabeth 326
WEN 795 see WINBORNE, WINBOURNE
WENBOURNE 795 see WINBORN, WINBOURNE
Wensley, Ann 377
Wensley, Ellen Jenner 418
Wensley, Mercy 97
Wensley, Sarah 829
Wenton, Persis 82
WENTWORTH 795, 796
Wentworth, Dorothy 668
Wentworth, Elizabeth 663, 751
Wentworth, Ezekiel 796
Wentworth, Mary 96, 645
Wentworth, Samuel 307, 493
Wentworth, Sarah 42, 765, 827
WERDALL 779
Werden, Ruth 701
Werdin, Jane 103
Werlidge, Esther 299
Werlidge, Hester 299
WERNEY 796
Wescoat, John 365
WESCOTT 797
Wescott, Katherine 230
Wescott, Mercy 700
Wescott, Thomas 230
Wesendock, Elizabeth 249
WESSELBEE 798
Wessels, Jannetie 243
Wessendank, George 245
WESSON 796 see WESTON
Wesson, Samuel 46
Wesson, Sarah 179
WEST 796, 797
West, --- 571
West, Ann 142
West, Elizabeth 145, 509, 627, 836
West, Hannah 572, 718, 796
West, Isabel 627
West, Joan 166, 805
West, John 25, 459, 787
West, Margaret 111, 368
West, Mary 20, 22, 111, 254, 333, 836
West, Peletiah 144
West, Ruth 351, 677
West, Samuel 213
West, Sarah Adams 779
West, Susannah 40, 665
West, Thankful 49
West, Thomas 169, 677
West, William 3, 372

West, Zachariah 368
WESTALL 797
Westavhor, Jane 822
Westbroke, George 837
WESTBROOK 797
Westbrook, Abigail 764
Westbrook, John 140, 374
Westbrook, Martha 639
Westbrook, Mary 445
WESTCARR 797
Westcarr, John 55
WESTCOTT 797
Westcott, Abigail 443
Westcott, Catherine 361
Westcott, Damaris 21
Westcott, Dinah 816
Westcott, Joanna 790
Westcott, John 365
Westcott, Richard 36, 676
Westcott, Robert 361
Westcott, Ruth 815
Westcott, Sarah 469
WESTEAD 797
WESTERHOUSEN 797
WESTFIELD 797
WESTGATE 797
Westland, Robert 254
Westoe, Susanna 369
WESTON 796, 797 see WESSON
Weston, Elizabeth 175
Weston, Lucy 566
Weston, Mary 213, 230, 417
Weston, Samuel 46
Weston, Sarah 508
Weston, William 766
WESTOVER 797
Westover, Elizabeth 34
Westover, Hannah 15
Westover, Jane 129, 722, 822
Westover, Mary 139
WESTWOOD 798
Westwood, Sarah 177
Wetherall, Hannah 581
WETHERBY 787
WETHEREL 798
WETHERELL 798
Wetherell, Dorothy 835
Wetherell, Elizabeth 111
Wetherell, John 525, 846
Wetherell, Mary 215, 347
Wetherell, Samuel 408, 747
Wetherell, Sarah 276, 377
WETHERLEE 798
Wethington, Ann 52
Wethington, Anna 52
Wethington, Hannah 52
Wethmer, Elizabeth 6
WETMORE 809, 810
Wetmore, Abigail 72
Wetmore, Hannah 716
Wetmore, Mary 716
Wetmore, Mehitable 29
Wetmore, Sarah 30
Wetmore, Thomas 24
WEYBURN 812
Weyeth, John 820
WEYLY 816
WEYMOUTH 798
Weymouth, Bridget 529
Weymouth, James 219, 465
Weymouth, Mary 219
Weymouth, Mehitable 699
Weymouth, Robert 646
Wezell, Susannah 94
Whafe, Elizabeth 629
Whaff, Ann 131
Whaff, Elizabeth 97
WHALE 798

Whale, Elizabeth 516
Whale, Philemon 131, 325, 764
WHALEY 798
Whaley, Elizabeth 361
Whaley, Martha 387
Whaley, Theodosia 696
Whalley, Francis 308
Whalley, Jane 386
Whaly, Sarah 488
WHAPLES 798
WHARF 798
WHARFE 798
Wharfe, Nathaniel 635
Wharfe, Rebecca 383
WHARFFE 798
Wharford, John 547
WHARTON 798
Wharton, Mary 670
Wharton, Sarah 185
Whatlock, Martha 656
Whattingham, John 256
WHEADEN 799
Wheaden, Esther 420
Wheadon, Sarah 250
Whealer, Ruth 56
Whealock, Experience 782
WHEAT 798
Wheat, Hannah 717
Wheat, Rebecca 281
Wheat, Samuel 34
Wheat, Sarah 67, 370
Wheate, --- 798
Wheatland, Rachel 113, 474
WHEATLEY 798
Wheatley, Lionel 536
Wheatley, Martha 536
Wheatley, Rachel 113, 474, 652
Wheatly, Dorothy 78
Wheatly, John 561
WHEATON 798, 799
Wheaton, Bathsheba 234
Wheaton, Bethia 77
Wheaton, Elizabeth 87
Wheaton, Esther 420
Wheaton, Hannah 128
Wheaton, Jeremiah 302, 632
Wheaton, Margaret 313
Wheaton, Martha 758
Wheaton, Mary 204, 485
Wheaton, Matthew 358
WHEDON 799
Whedon, Jane 242
Whedon, Thomas 349
Wheelar, Ruth 625
WHEELDING 802
WHEELER 455, 799, 800, 801, 802
Wheeler, Abigail 41, 373, 479, 795
Wheeler, Alice 700
Wheeler, Ann 146, 528, 625
Wheeler, Anne 625
Wheeler, Dorcas 79
Wheeler, Dorcas Rose Swayne 721
Wheeler, Dorothy 687
Wheeler, Elizabeth 58, 76, 95, 119, 120, 129, 175, 236, 271, 271, 323, 606, 620, 705, 774, 832
Wheeler, Ephraim 720
Wheeler, Esther 602
Wheeler, Frances 179
Wheeler, George 178, 311, 698
Wheeler, Grace 103
Wheeler, Hannah 58, 63, 271, 507, 561, 679, 801, 833
Wheeler, Henry 9

Wheeler, Isaac 179, 323, 551
Wheeler, James 165
Wheeler, Jamima Eliot Woodbridge 836
Wheeler, Joanna 261, 837
Wheeler, John 270
Wheeler, John (Dr.) 801
Wheeler, Joseph 503
Wheeler, Judanna 446
Wheeler, Katherine 799
Wheeler, Lydia 15, 801
Wheeler, Margery 734
Wheeler, Martha 820
Wheeler, Mary 6, 108, 223, 257, 280, 304, 323, 389, 503, 816, 819, 833
Wheeler, Mercy 669
Wheeler, Miriam 76, 328
Wheeler, Moses 454
Wheeler, Obadiah 312, 710
Wheeler, Rebecca 115, 198, 325, 512, 582, 595, 602, 669, 671, 726, 729, 799
Wheeler, Richard 447, 620
Wheeler, Roger 713
Wheeler, Ruth 109, 349, 425, 625, 752, 782, 820
Wheeler, Sarah 74, 100, 232, 260, 321, 447, 503, 512, 529, 543, 655, 671, 679, 697, 701, 731
Wheeler, Susanna 801
Wheeler, Thankful 602
Wheeler, Thomas 582, 700, 703
Wheeler, Timothy 816
Wheeler, William 103
Wheeler, Zapporah 81
WHEELOCK 802
Wheelock, Abiah 778
Wheelock, Elizabeth 681
Wheelock, Experience 782
Wheelock, Mary 787
Wheelock, Ralph 40
Wheelock, Rebecca 189
Wheelock, Sarah 329
WHEELOCKE 802
Wheelocke, Peregrina 780
Wheelocke, Record 778
WHEELWRIGHT 802
Wheelwright, --- 316
Wheelwright, Catherine 528
Wheelwright, Elizabeth 561, 585
Wheelwright, Hannah 148, 563
Wheelwright, Katharine 529
Wheelwright, Mary 24, 480
Wheelwright, Rebecca 90, 498
Wheelwright, Sarah 192
Wheelwright, Susan 626
Wheelwright, Susanna 626
Whelase, Mary 507
Whelden, Ann 730
Whelden, Ruth 730
WHELDON 802 see WELDON
Wheldon, Katharine 387
Wheler, Elizabeth 271
Wheler, Obadiah 671
Wheler, Susannah 671
WHELLER 800
Whelocke, Mary 507
WHELPLEY 802
Whelpley, Henry 430, 752, 809
Whelpley, Mary 443
Whelpley, Rebecca 649
Whelpley, Sarah Treadwell 676
WHERRY 802 see WOOREY
Wheston, Susanna 574
Whetcomb, Hannah 511
Whetcomb, Mary 718
WHETNEY 811

Whetney, Mary 667
WHETNY 811
Whetny, Ruth 664
Whetny, Sarah 345
Wheton, Matthew 358
WHETSTONE 803
Whetstone, John 470
WHIDDEN 802
Whidden, Abigail 807
Whidden, Alice 358
Whidden, Michael 395
WHIDDON 812
Whiddon, Jane 242
Whight, Martha 383
WHILDING 802
WHINYARD 845
WHIPPEY 803
Whipple, Abigail 218, 387
Whipple, Alice 525
Whipple, Anna 19, 154, 707
Whipple, Annable 154
Whipple, David 187
Whipple, Deborah 748, 817
Whipple, Dorothy 619
Whipple, Elizabeth 268, 571, 596, 607
Whipple, Elnathan 620
Whipple, Hannah 707
Whipple, John 72, 154, 551, 581, 656
Whipple, Mary 133, 251, 321, 414, 545, 714
Whipple, Matthew 153, 321, 735, 813
Whipple, Sarah 309, 672, 683, 770
Whipple, Susanna 450, 841
WHIPPO 803
Whippo, James 324
Whisson, Margaret 440
Whiston, John 103, 470
Whiston, Mary 558
Whiston, Mercy 558
Whiston, Sarah 536
Whiston, Susanna 574
Whit, Elizabeth 740
WHITAKER 804, 812 see WHITHEARE
Whitaker, Mary 728
Whitaker, Rebecca 546
WHITCHER 812
WHITCOMB 804
Whitcomb, Abigail 432
Whitcomb, Catherine 787
Whitcomb, David 257
Whitcomb, Hannah 463, 502, 511
Whitcomb, Jemima 472
Whitcomb, Joanna 428
Whitcomb, John 259, 516
Whitcomb, Mary 516, 558, 604, 817
Whitcomb, Rebecca 391
Whitcomb, Ruth 222
WHITCOMBE 804
Whitcombe, Catharine 249
WHITE 804, 805, 806, 807
White, --- 459, 738
White, Abigail 393, 664, 740
White, Ann 92, 450, 752
White, Anna 53, 359, 594
White, Anne 603
White, Charity 728, 732
White, Deborah 85
White, Elias 165, 229
White, Elizabeth 1, 18, 27, 156, 230, 312, 336, 362, 434, 472, 587, 599, 600, 601, 619, 723, 740, 780, 792, 801

White, Esther 158, 189, 249
White, George 676
White, Hannah 12, 53, 205, 220,
    222, 287, 478, 727
White, Hannah Farnum 110
White, Henry 45, 347
White, Hester 158, 189
White, Jacob 611
White, James 831
White, Joan Calverly 659
White, Joanna 269, 398
White, John 138, 184, 345, 412,
    492, 577, 579, 580, 842
White, Joseph 793
White, Kathrine 139
White, Lydia 179, 216
White, Margaret 1, 131, 777
White, Margery 358
White, Martha 224, 383, 393, 734,
    780
White, Mary 158, 184, 210, 294,
    302, 370, 380, 381, 460, 472,
    474, 568, 630, 640, 670, 693,
    702, 755, 761, 794, 807, 817,
    839
White, Mary Lawrence 455
White, Mary Rishworth 401, 589
White, Mary Wiswall 831
White, Mehitable 578
White, Merry 670
White, Nathan 844
White, Nathaniel 524
White, Nicholas 358
White, Patience 202
White, Paul 426
White, Peregrine 670, 846
White, Philip 413, 722
White, Phillipe 137
White, Phillip 137
White, Phillippa 137
White, Priscilla 673
White, Prudence 218
White, Resolved 473
White, Richard 374, 386
White, Rose 594
White, Ruth 216
White, Sarah 24, 31, 73, 174,
    287, 318, 375, 376, 390, 450,
    472, 492, 538, 620, 684, 685,
    727, 731, 816, 827, 846
White, Susanna 770
White, Thankful 402
White, Thomas 380, 845
White, Ursula 63
White, William 278, 492, 770, 829
White, Wm. 655
Whiteache, Sarah 846
WHITEFIELD 808
WHITEFOOT 808
WHITEHAM 808
WHITEHAND 808
WHITEHART 808
WHITEHEAD 808
Whitehead, --- 165
Whitehead, Adam 410
Whitehead, Amy 227
Whitehead, Damaris 554
Whitehead, Daniel 165, 216, 368
Whitehead, Deborah 368, 453
Whitehead, Elizabeth 784
Whitehead, Hannah 762
Whitehead, Isaac 369, 845
Whitehead, Jemima 463
Whitehead, Mary 67, 123, 709,
    730, 764
Whitehead, Mercy 67, 478
Whitehead, Richard 387
Whitehead, Samuel 302
Whitehead, Susanna 82

Whitehead, Susannah 118
WHITEHEARE 808 see
    WHITAKER, WHITTIER
WHITEHOUSE 808
Whiteing, Mary 256
Whiteing, Nathaniel 787
WHITEMAN 809
Whiteman, Elizabeth 242
WHITEMORE 811
Whitemore, Elizabeth 402
WHITERBY 787
Whiterig, Abigail 53
WHITFIELD 808
Whitfield, Abigail 269
Whitfield, Dorothy 428
Whitfield, Sarah 369
WHITFOOT 808
WHITFORD 808
Whitford, Bridget 788
WHITHAM 808
WHITHEARE 804, 808 see
    WHITAKER, WHITTIER
Whitherspoone, Isabel 582
Whitherspoone, Isabella 582
Whiticar, Abraham 20
WHITICKER 804
WHITIN 812
WHITING 808, 809, 811, 812
Whiting, Abigail 230, 644
Whiting, Abigial 53
Whiting, Ann 241, 463, 552
Whiting, Anna 241, 267, 476
Whiting, Anthony 826
Whiting, Catharine 813
Whiting, Dorothy 793
Whiting, Elizabeth 377
Whiting, Hannah 256, 267
Whiting, Joanna 75
Whiting, John 644
Whiting, Judith 462
Whiting, Martha 111, 245
Whiting, Mary 119, 173, 348, 442,
    667
Whiting, Nathaniel 787
Whiting, Phebe 42
Whiting, Sarah 116, 259, 439,
    528, 694, 704
Whiting, Sybil 111
Whiting, William 269
Whiting, Wm. 111
Whitingham, Elizabeth 20
Whitingham, Mary 155
Whitingham, Martha 634
WHITLOCK 809
Whitlock, Hannah 36
Whitlock, John 802
Whitlock, Mary 36
Whitlock, Mary Bray 94
Whitlock, Rose 556
Whitlock, Sarah 802
WHITMAN 809, 811
Whitman, Deborah 686
Whitman, Elizabeth 182, 242, 322,
    548, 599, 677, 718
Whitman, Esther 705
Whitman, Hannah 285, 457, 771
Whitman, John 545, 599
Whitman, Judith 439, 665
Whitman, Margaret 138
Whitman, Margery 138
Whitman, Mary 95, 411, 457, 599
Whitman, Naomi 692
Whitman, Robert 443
Whitman, Sarah 174, 188, 424
Whitman, Susanna 38, 822
Whitman, Zachary 155
WHITMARSH 809
Whitmarsh, Deborah 665

Whitmarsh, Hannah 665
Whitmarsh, Jane 626
Whitmarsh, Judith 665
Whitmarsh, Mary 52, 412
Whitmarsh, Ruth 138, 216
Whitmarsh, Samuel 809
Whitmarsh, Sarah 76, 574, 768
WHITMORE 810
Whitmore, Abigail 246, 598, 815
Whitmore, Ann 12, 259
Whitmore, Elizabeth 6, 488
Whitmore, Frances 737
Whitmore, John 12, 201, 419, 597
Whitmore, John (Dea.) 824
Whitmore, Margaret 138
Whitmore, Margery 138
Whitmore, Mary 95
Whitmore, Samuel 785
Whitmore, Sarah 469
Whitmore, Thomas 24
WHITNELL 810
Whitnell, Jeremy 513
WHITNEY 810, 811, 812
Whitney, Abigail 53, 406
Whitney, Alice 835
Whitney, Anna 267
Whitney, Benjamin 498
Whitney, Eleanor 835
Whitney, Hannah 267, 835
Whitney, Henry 435
Whitney, Isaiah 242
Whitney, Jane 521
Whitney, John 161
Whitney, Judith 462
Whitney, Lydia 5
Whitney, Mary 582, 603
Whitney, Ruth 454, 664
Whitney, Sarah 141, 345
Whitney, Sarah Shepard Goble
    307
Whitney, Thomas 260
WHITNY 811
Whitny, Elizabeth 781
Whitny, Mary 487
WHITON 811, 812
Whiton, Mary 816
Whiton, Thomas 293, 295
WHITPAIN 811
WHITPIN 811
WHITRED 812
Whitred, Elizabeth Roberts 93
WHITREDGE 812
WHITRIDGE 812
Whitridge, Elizabeth 538
Whitridge, Susannah 446
Whitridge, Sylvester 605
Whitridge, William 168, 784
Whitshcock, Benjamin 189
WHITSON 811
Whitson, Priscilla 598
WHITSTON 803
WHITSTONE 803
Whitstone, Mary 558
Whitstone, Mercy 558
Whittacres, Sarah 605
WHITTAKER 804
Whittaker, Abigail 558
Whittaker, John 37
Whittaker, William 183
Whittaws, Sarah 605
Whitte, Sarah 31
Whittel, Jane 84
Whittell, Lydia 3
WHITTEMORE 811
Whittemore, Elizabeth 155, 828,
    829
Whittemore, Hannah 535
Whittemore, Mary 630

Whittemore, Nathaniel 487
Whittemore, Samuel 622
Whittemore, Thomas 277, 566, 584
WHITTEN 811, 812
Whittene, Mary 487
Whitter, Susannah 119
WHITTERAGE 812
WHITTICKER 804
WHITTIER 804, 812
Whittier, Abraham 20, 444
Whittier, Elizabeth 652
Whittier, Hannah 846
Whittier, Mary 444, 550
Whittier, Nathaniel 548, 626
Whittier, Ruth 755
Whittier, Susanna 519
WHITTIKER 804
WHITTINGHAM 812
Whittingham, Mary 160
Whittingham, Richard 390
Whittler, Elizabeth 340
Whittleray, John 452
WHITTLESEY 812
Whittmore, Thomas 128
WHITTNY 811
WHITTON 812
WHITTREDGE 812
Whittredge, Thomas 518
Whittridge, Abigail 53
Whittridge, Elizabeth Roberts 93
Whittridge, Mary 348
Whittridge, Thomas 348
WHITWAY 812
Whitway, John 536
WHITWELL 812
Whitwell, Mercy 40
WHOD 833
WHYTE 807
Whytt, Mary 702
WIARD 812, 844 see WYER
Wiard, Mary 41
WIAT 844
Wiatt, John 41
Wiatt, Mary 41
Wibird, Richard 616
WIBORN 812
WIBORNE 812
Wiborne, Abigail 695
Wiborne, Elizabeth 261
Wiborne, Thomas 261
WICK 791
WICKENDEN 813
Wickenden, Hannah 705
Wickenden, Plain 817
Wickenden, Ruth 689
WICKES 791, 792
Wickes, Elizabeth 185, 684
Wickes, Hannah 124
Wickes, Martha 176, 834
Wickes, Mary 305, 783
Wickes, Rebecca 634
Wickes, Sarah 111
Wickes, Thomas 320
WICKHAM 813 see WIXAM
Wickham, Samuel 589
Wickham, Sarah 149, 399
WICKIN 813
Wickott, Benjamin 189
WICKS 791, 792
Wicks, Elizabeth 435, 750
Wicks, Mary 660
WICKSON 832 see WICKHAM
WICKWARE 813
WICOM 813
Wicom, Ann 282
Wicom, Daniel 590
Wicom, Mary 420

WICOME 813
Wicome, Francis 423
WIDGER 813
Widger, Hannah 813
WIDGIER 813
WIDNEY 810
Wieple, Rebecca 649
WIER 844
WIET 844
WIETT 844
Wiggen, Thomas 803
WIGGIN 813
Wiggin, Abigail 285
Wiggin, Catherine 757
Wiggin, Dorothy 305
Wiggin, Hannah 796
Wiggin, Katherine 495
Wiggin, Mary 305, 517, 766
Wiggin, Sarah 517, 668
Wiggin, Simon 495
Wiggin, Thomas 803
WIGGINS 813
Wiggins, James 206, 433
Wiggins, Martha Denison 735
Wiggins, Sarah 191
WIGGLESWORTH 813
Wigglesworth, Abigail 723, 727
Wigglesworth, Michael 26
Wigglesworth, Mary 60
Wigglesworth, Mercy 89
WIGHT 813, 814
Wight, Abiah 611
Wight, Abial 611
Wight, Abiel 486
Wight, Anna 121
Wight, Hannah 737
Wight, John 116
Wight, Joseph 507
Wight, Lucy 648
Wight, Lydia 179, 563
Wight, Mary 157, 248
Wight, Thomas 570
WIGHTMAN 814
Wightman, Alice 771
Wightman, Daniel 293
Wightman, Elizabeth 242, 400
WIGLEY 814
Wigley, Edmund 459
Wignall, Elizabeth 410
Wignol, Judith 278
Wigwall, Hannah 616
Wilamson, Mary 293
WILBOR 814
WILBORE 814
Wilbore, Anna 504
Wilbore, Martha 670
Wilbore, Samuel 72
Wilbore, Sarah 376
Wilborn, Anna 488
Wilborn, Mary 145
WILBORNE 814, 827 see WEN
Wilborne, Michael 574
Wilbourne, Abigail 102
Wilbourne, Elizabeth 102
WILBUR 814
Wilbur, Abigail 21
Wilbur, Anna 504
Wilbur, Elizabeth 283
Wilbur, Hannah 157
Wilbur, Joan 597
Wilbur, Martha 670
Wilbur, Mary 276, 525
Wilbur, Penelope 360
Wilbur, Rebecca 110, 353
Wilbur, Samuel 72, 458
Wilbur, Shadrack 552
WILCOCKSON 815
WILCOT 833

Wilcot, Eliza 767
Wilcot, Elizabeth 767
WILCOX 814, 815
Wilcox, Alice 282
Wilcox, Ann 334
Wilcox, Anna 334
Wilcox, Bethiah 186
Wilcox, Esther 340
Wilcox, Hannah 158, 669
Wilcox, John 258, 471, 716
Wilcox, Lydia 670
Wilcox, Margaret 725
Wilcox, Mary 239, 337, 340, 447, 669
Wilcox, Samuel 484
Wilcox, Sarah 68, 98, 253, 471
Wilcox, Stephen 273
Wilcox, Susannah 725
Wilcox, William 246
WILCOXEN 815
Wilcoxon, Mary 602
WILCOXSON 815
Wilcoxson, Elizabeth 58, 356, 710
Wilcoxson, Hannah 83, 258, 356
Wilcoxson, Johannah 257
Wilcoxson, John 126
Wilcoxson, Margaret 319, 356
Wilcoxson, Mary 514
Wilcoxson, Patience 76
Wilcoxson, Phebe 54, 71
Wilcoxson, Ruth 775
Wilcoxson, Sarah 482, 502
WILD 815
Wild, Elizabeth 525
Wild, John 414
Wild, William 525
WILDBORE 814
WILDE 815
Wilde, Edey 845
Wilde, Phebe 211
WILDEN 802
WILDER 816
Wilder, Abia 160
Wilder, Elizabeth 253, 261
Wilder, John 9
Wilder, Martha 102
Wilder, Mary 9, 56, 71, 196, 256, 427, 458, 763
Wilder, Mehitable 782
Wilder, Nathaniel 391
Wilder, Patience 9
Wilder, Sarah 71
WILDES 815, 816
Wildes, Elizabeth 424, 525
Wildes, Phebe 211
Wildes, Priscilla 447
Wildes, William 525
WILDMAN 816
Wildman, Martha 15
Wildman, Sarah 663
Wildman, Thomas 276, 663
WILE 816
WILES 815
Wiles, Elizabeth 150
Wiles, Phebe 211
Wiles, Priscilla 447
WILETT 822
WILEY 816, 818
Wiley, Mary 646
Wiley, Mercy 646
Wiley, Susan 202
Wiley, Susannah 202
Wiley, Timothy 312
WILFORD 816
Wilford, Amy 290
Wilford, Anna 290
Wilford, Gilbert 157
Wilford, Jane 314

Wilford, John 727
Wilford, Lydia 727
Wilford, Mary 183
Wilford, Ruth 28
Wilken, Elizabeth 225
WILKENSON 817
Wilkerson, Samuel 8
WILKES 816
Wilkes, Elizabeth 735
Wilkes, Mary 836
Wilkes, Rebecca 634
WILKESON 817
WILKEY 816
Wilkey, Elizabeth 175
WILKIE 816
Wilkie, Elizabeth 175, 199
Wilkie, John 199
WILKINS 816, 817
Wilkins, Abigail 247
Wilkins, Anna 277
Wilkins, Comfort 14
Wilkins, Eleanor 181
Wilkins, Elizabeth 32
Wilkins, Helena 181
Wilkins, Henry 463, 482, 677
Wilkins, Isaac 277
Wilkins, John 32
Wilkins, Lydia 511, 535
Wilkins, Margaret 445
Wilkins, Martha 98
Wilkins, Matthew 98
Wilkins, Rebecca 482
Wilkins, Sarah Neal Archer
  Tappley 20
Wilkins, Susanna 32, 733
Wilkins, William 181
WILKINSON 816, 817
Wilkinson, Elizabeth 261
Wilkinson, George 802
Wilkinson, Hannah 757
Wilkinson, Jane 222, 828
Wilkinson, John 794
Wilkinson, Margaret 308, 831
Wilkinson, Prudence 114, 261
Wilkinson, Rebecca 36, 802
Wilkinson, Ruth 173
Wilkinson, Sarah 114
Wilkinson, Susanna 84, 360
Wilkinson, Tabitha 72
Wilkison, Ruth 173
WILLARD 817
Willard, Abigail 239, 753
Willard, Deborah 659
Willard, Dorothy 60
Willard, Elizabeth 79
Willard, Esther 272
Willard, George 659
Willard, Hannah 100, 501
Willard, John 749
Willard, Josiah 485
Willard, Margery 205
Willard, Mary 60, 243, 403, 502,
  706
Willard, Mercy 60
Willard, Sarah 248, 359
Willard, Simon 541, 776
Willason, Rachel 50
WILLASTON 824
WILLBORNE 814
Willcox, Daniel 98
WILLEE 818
Willen, Amy 767
Willen, Richard 767
WILLET 817, 818
Willet, Hannah 32
Willet, Nathaniel 108
Willet, Sarah 247
WILLETS 817, 818

Willets, Hannah 763
Willets, Mary 287, 598
WILLETT 817, 818
Willett, Abigail 72
Willett, Elizabeth 21
Willett, Esther 272
Willett, John 339
Willett, Martha 646
Willett, Mary 386, 453, 818
Willett, Nathaniel 772
Willett, Rebecca 611
Willett, Sarah 213, 650
Willett, Thomas 72, 96, 455, 606
WILLETTS 817
Willetts, Elizabeth 763
WILLEY 818
Willey, Abigail 458
Willey, Alice 295, 490
Willey, Frances 392
Willey, Hannah 77, 402, 696
Willey, Isaac 281, 462, 511
Willey, Joanna 364, 462
Willey, John 696
Willey, Margaret 699
Willey, Mary 756
Willey, Samuel 610
Willey, Sarah 271, 569, 744
Willey, Thomas 189, 699
WILLFORD 816
Williames, Elizabeth 607
WILLIAMS 818, 819, 820, 821,
  822
Williams, Abiall 576
Williams, Abigail 12, 327, 338,
  495, 594
Williams, Alice 272
Williams, Amos 382
Williams, Ann 41, 64, 138, 450,
  574
Williams, Anna 41, 64, 138
Williams, Anne Moyle 566
Williams, Arthur 93, 137
Williams, Augustine 107
Williams, Bethiah 292, 620, 621
Williams, Bridget 647
Williams, Daniel 598
Williams, Deborah 320, 381, 759,
  782
Williams, Dorcas 303, 566
Williams, Edith 587
Williams, Elizabeth 55, 70, 77,
  156, 187, 201, 346, 372, 382,
  382, 408, 482, 486, 491, 552,
  634, 650, 706, 766, 767
Williams, Elizabeth Jones 518
Williams, Elizabeth Watson 578
Williams, Esther 188, 601, 820
Williams, Freeborn 159, 349
Williams, Hannah 38, 41, 78, 118,
  121, 338, 348, 408, 517, 521,
  526, 551, 561, 599, 658, 684,
  782, 824
Williams, Henry 390
Williams, Hester 188, 253, 601
Williams, Hilliard 20
Williams, Isaac 181, 339
Williams, Jane 165
Williams, Jemima 109
Williams, Jennings 109
Williams, Jinnus 109
Williams, Joanna 425
Williams, John 81, 156, 224, 245,
  253, 311, 331, 397, 494
Williams, John (Rev.) 73
Williams, Jonathan 665, 749
Williams, Lewis 140, 346
Williams, Lucretia 376
Williams, Lucy 41

Williams, Lydia 237
Williams, Martha 403, 404, 565
Williams, Mary 17, 28, 56, 68, 72,
  90, 91, 103, 151, 201, 214, 224,
  316, 330, 333, 387, 418, 419,
  500, 545, 550, 622, 635, 649,
  655, 674, 678, 767, 770, 783,
  835, 837
Williams, Mehitable 629
Williams, Mercy 537, 545, 783,
  784, 827, 837
Williams, Nathaniel 90, 111, 192,
  650, 672
Williams, Patience 44
Williams, Phebe 750750
Williams, Phoebe 245
Williams, Rachel 477, 607
Williams, Rebecca 180, 410, 482,
  487, 781
Williams, Robert 261, 750
Williams, Ruth 60, 297, 607, 664,
  704, 756
Williams, Samuel 133, 215, 733,
  745
Williams, Samuel (Dea.) 568
Williams, Samuel (Rev.) 568
Williams, Sarah 27, 81, 143, 212,
  274, 449, 537, 541, 580, 664,
  704, 844
Williams, Susanna 415
Williams, Temperance 113
Williams, Thomas 526, 622, 777,
  835
Williams, William 1, 56, 264
Williams, Zebediah 537
WILLIAMSON 822
Williamson, Abigail 40
Williamson, Experience 730
Williamson, Mary 163, 678
Williamson, Paul 449
Williamson, Timothy 650, 700
Willing, Amy 767
Willing, Margaret 623
Willing, Richard 767
WILLINGTON 793
WILLIS 822, 823, 824 see WILLS
Willis, Abigail 69, 457
Willis, Deliverance 591
Willis, Elizabeth 134, 336,
  350, 445, 579, 818
Willis, Esther 7
Willis, Experience 399
Willis, George 553
Willis, Grace 336
Willis, Hannah 359
Willis, Jane 335
Willis, Joanna 248
Willis, John 359, 555
Willis, Joseph 461
Willis, Lydia 541
Willis, Mary 485, 495, 565
Willis, Michael 705
Willis, Rachel 659
Willis, Rebecca 660
Willis, Richard 382
Willis, Roger 310
Willis, Ruhamah 632
Willis, Ruth 310
Willis, Sarah 16, 40, 745
Willis, Temperance 705
WILLISTON 824
WILLITS 817, 818
Willits, Catharine 750
WILLIX 824
Willix, Anna 637
Willix, Hasabelponah 835
Willix, Hazelelpony 835
Willix, Hazelpaneh 298

Willix, Susannah 425
WILLMAN 793
Willman, Elizabeth 666
Willman, Mary 7, 675
WILLMARTH 824
Willmarth, Elizabeth 288
Willmarth, Ruth 181
WILLMOT 824
Willmot, Elizabeth 288
Willmott, Benjamin 430
WILLMOUTH 824
Willott, Nathaniel 161
WILLOUGHBY 824
Willoughby, Elizabeth 14, 133
Willoughby, Francis 339
Willoughby, Margaret 339
Willoughby, Sarah 132
Willoughby, Susanna 480
WILLOWES 823, 824
Willowes, Elizabeth 336
Willowes, Jane 335
Willowes, Rebecca 660
WILLS 824
Wills, Joanna 201
Wills, Joshua 627
Wills, Lydia 145, 162, 747
Wills, Lydia Wilkins Nichols 535
Wills, Samuel 162
Wills, Sarah 298
Wills, Thomas 141, 710
Willsford, Martha 320
Willson, Abigail 370, 445
Willson, Elizabeth 369
WILLY 816
Willy, Sarah 40
Willyams, Elizabeth 372
WILLYS 823
Willys, Esther 343
Willys, Hester 343
WILMARTH 824
Wilmarth, Mary 138, 632, 803
Wilmarth, Mehitable 773
Wilmarth, Miriam 78
Wilmarth, Ruth 181
Wilmarth, Thomas (Sr.) 614
Wilmot, Abigail 3, 473
Wilmot, Ann 82, 118
Wilmot, Anna 137, 467
Wilmot, Anne 11
Wilmot, Benjamin 363
Wilmot, Eleanor 5
Wilmot, Elizabeth 513, 533, 612
Wilmot, Hannah 5, 506, 508
Wilmot, John 684
Wilmot, Mary 9, 111, 227
Wilmot, Mercy 111
Wilmot, Sarah 390
WILMOTH 824
Wilmoth, Mary 227
WILMOUTH 824
Wilmouth, Mary 302, 632
Wilshire, Sarah 44, 744
WILSON 824, 825, 826
Wilson, Abigail 370, 412, 445
Wilson, Ann 153, 647, 793
Wilson, Ann Thorn 738
Wilson, Anna 133, 177, 405, 613,
   769
Wilson, Anne 374, 476
Wilson, Anthony 111, 115
Wilson, Benjamin 177, 660
Wilson, Deborah 115, 277, 333,
   782
Wilson, Dorcas 162, 370
Wilson, Edward 473
Wilson, Elizabeth 326, 369, 398,
   587, 620, 632, 787, 793, 815
Wilson, Grace 788

Wilson, Hannah 211, 583, 605,
   640, 660
Wilson, Isabel 576
Wilson, James 574
Wilson, Jane 290, 427
Wilson, Joanna 97
Wilson, John 290, 359, 369, 481,
   507, 616, 701, 705, 766
Wilson, John (Rev.) 612
Wilson, Judith 813
Wilson, Katherine 43
Wilson, Margaret 612
Wilson, Margery 446
Wilson, Marie 94
Wilson, Martha 51
Wilson, Mary 94, 203, 341, 389,
   395, 419, 446, 488, 517, 544,
   631, 801
Wilson, Phineas 359, 419, 661,
   782
Wilson, Rebecca 43, 81
Wilson, Richard 62
Wilson, Robert 2, 130, 278
Wilson, Samuel 389, 723
Wilson, Sarah 53, 187, 191, 340,
   341, 596, 640, 692, 747
Wilson, Sarah Chandler 707
Wilson, Sarah Jourdan 372
Wilson, Seaborn 268
Wilson, Seaborne 268
Wilson, Susanna 303, 612, 623
Wilson, William 406, 582
Wilsted, Elizabeth 69
Wilterton, Susanna 428, 504
WILTON 826
Wilton, David 390
Wilton, Mary 490
Wiltsee, Deborah 834
WILTSHIRE 826
Wiltum, Ruth 82
Wily, Sarah 271
Wimes, Abigail 278
WINANS 830
WINBOURNE 827
WINCH 827
Winch, Mary 255
Winch, Samuel 42
WINCHCOMB 827
WINCHELL 827
Winchell, Benjamin 827
Winchell, Christian 549
Winchell, Christiana 549
Winchell, Elizabeth 755
Winchell, Jonathan 751
Winchell, Mary 838
Winchell, Nathaniel 636
Winchell, Sarah 576
Winchell, Stephen 490
Winchell, Thomas 827
WINCHESTER 827
Winchester, Alexander 53
Winchester, Elizabeth 51, 53, 133,
   487
Winchester, Ether 124
Winchester, Hannah 86
Winchester, Joanna 708
Winchester, John 487
Winchester, Lydia 687
Winchester, Martha 133
Winchester, Mary 8, 231, 232,
   567, 755
Winchester, Robert 133
Winchurst, Ann 709
WINCOLL 827
Wincoll, Elizabeth 379
Wincoll, John 379, 589
Winder, Anna 836
WINDOE 827

WINDOW 827
Window, Anna 836
Window, Richard 64, 312, 752
Windsor, Hannah 134
Windsor, John 496
Windsor, Susanna 760
WINDSORE 827
WINES 827, 828
Wines, Ann 747
Wines, Anne 249, 535, 847
Wines, Barnabas 477
Wines, Bethia 389
Wines, Elizabeth 404
Wines, Esther 379
Wines, Hannah 535, 847
Wines, Mary 793
Wines, Prudence 308
Wines, Sarah 477, 761, 847
WING 828
Wing, Beulah 42
Wing, Daniel 256
Wing, Elizabeth 228, 776
Wing, Experience 697
Wing, Hannah 42, 470
Wing, Joseph 241
Wing, Lidia 2
Wing, Lydia 338, 339, 524
Wing, Matthew 624
Wing, Osah 806
Wing, Oseeth 806
Wing, Osiah 806
Wing, Sarah 301
Wing, Susanna 560, 561
WINGATE 828
Wingate, Ann 379
Wingate, John 133, 552
WINKLEY 828
Winkley, Samuel 4, 263
WINN 828
Winn, Ann 162
Winn, Damares 189
Winn, Edward 551, 835
Winn, Elizabeth 591
Winn, Hannah 34
Winn, Joanna 444
Winn, Josiah 845
Winn, Mary 845
Winn, Rebecca 695
Winn, Sarah 279, 420
Winnock, Mary 192
Winnock, Sarah 206, 813
WINSHIP 828, 829
Winship, Abigail 644
Winship, Elizabeth 669
Winship, Ephraim 583
Winship, Margery 223
Winship, Mary 104
Winship, Sarah 397
WINSLAD 829
WINSLADE 829
WINSLEAD 829
WINSLEY 829
Winsley, --- 280
Winsley, Deborah 790
Winsley, Ellen Jenner 418
Winsley, Hepzibah 524
Winsley, Martha 280
Winsley, Mary 280, 284
Winsley, Samuel 80
Winsley, Sarah 126
WINSLOW 829, 830
Winslow, Ann 458
Winslow, Edward 569, 807
Winslow, Eleanor 34, 425
Winslow, Elizabeth 103, 124, 184,
   657, 735
Winslow, Ellen 34
Winslow, Hannah 195, 720

Winslow, Hepzibah 524
Winslow, Isaac 471
Winslow, Jonathan 85, 151
Winslow, Joseph 447
Winslow, Judith 549
Winslow, Katharine 365
Winslow, Kenelm 4
Winslow, Margaret 368, 509
Winslow, Martha 280, 345
Winslow, Mary 280, 319, 591, 751, 779
Winslow, Mercy 806
Winslow, Parnell 278
Winslow, Rebecca 733
Winslow, Samuel 290, 424
Winslow, Sarah 445, 507, 553, 700
Winslow, Susannah 453
WINSOR 827
Winsor, Joshua 762
Winsor, Mary 748
Winsor, Mercy 343, 748
Winsor, Samuel 784
Winsor, Sarah 666, 762
WINSTEAD 829
WINSTON 830
Winston, Elizabeth 14
Winston, Esther 519
Winston, Grace 684
Winston, Mary 754
WINSWORTH 830
WINTER 830
Winter, Abigail 643, 702
Winter, Ann 53
Winter, Anna 482
Winter, Anne 482
Winter, Elizabeth 181
Winter, Hannah 119, 142, 345
Winter, Hester 590
Winter, Martha 367
Winter, Mary 614, 804
Winter, Sarah 428
Winter, Tobias 651
Winters, Christopher 759
Winters, Naomi 759
Winters, Sarah 428
WINTHROP 830
Winthrop, Adam 471, 621
Winthrop, Anne 621
Winthrop, Deane 3, 502
Winthrop, Elizabeth 252, 533
Winthrop, Elizabeth Fones 337
Winthrop, Henry 261
Winthrop, Joanna 481
Winthrop, John 166, 167
Winthrop, Lucy 229, 555
Winthrop, Margaret 184, 196, 329
Winthrop, Martha 798
Winthrop, Mary 232
Winthrop, Mercy 390
Winthrop, Priscilla 3
Winthrop, Stephen 38
Winthrop, Waitstill 256
WINTON 830
Winton, Hannah 279
WINUS 830
WIRE 787
Wisavel, Hannah 705
WISE 830, 831 see WYETH
Wise, Abigail 314, 427
Wise, Ann 585
Wise, Bethiah 656
Wise, Elizabeth 793
Wise, Henry 78, 758
Wise, Humphrey 323
Wise, Katharine 496
Wise, Mary 237, 448, 821
Wise, Sarah 799, 821, 843
Wise, Susan 323

WISEMAN 831
Wiseman, Alice 193
Wiseman, Elizabeth 162, 624
Wiseman, Mary 767
Wiseman, Mercy 767
WISENDONK 831
Wisewall, Elizabeth 769
WISSENDUNK 831
Wissendunk, Sarah Sedgwick 660
Wiston, Bathsheba 234
Wiston, John 103
WISWALL 831
Wiswall, Deborah 149, 819
Wiswall, Ebenezer 277
Wiswall, Elizabeth 325, 769
Wiswall, Esther 13, 267, 423
Wiswall, Hannah 527, 705, 845
Wiswall, Hester 13, 423
Wiswall, Lydia 38
Wiswall, Margaret 559
Wiswall, Martha 200
Wiswall, Mary 243, 251, 251, 471
Wiswall, Noah 533
Wiswall, Rebecca 197, 422
Wiswall, Ruth 525
Wiswall, Sarah 354, 383, 384
Wiswall, Susannah 94
Wiswall, Thomas 258, 503
Wiswell, --- 91
Wiswell, Hannah 548
Wit, Bethiah 625
WITCHFEILD 831
WITCHFIELD 831
Witchfield, John 308
WITE 813
With, Nicholas 281
WITHAM 831 see WITTUM
Witham, Henry 326
Witham, Susanna 712
WITHE 844
Withe, Martha 412
WITHENTON 831, 832
WITHERBY 787
Witherdin, Mary 163
WITHERELEE 798
Witherell, Dorothy 411
Witherell, John 525
Witherell, Mary 544
Witherick, Robert 246
Witherick, Thomas 246
WITHERINGTON 832
Witherlee, Samuel 747
WITHERLEY 831
WITHERLY 831
WITHERS 831
Withers, Elizabeth 65, 197
Withers, Jane 307
Withers, Mary 620
Withers, Sarah 663
Withers, Thomas 307
Witherspoon, Isabel 604
Witherspoon, Isabella 604
WITHINGTON 831, 832
Withington, Ann 70
Withington, Constance 100
Withington, Elizabeth 335
Withington, Henry 383, 564
Withington, John 805
Withington, Mary 203
WITHINTON 832
Withinton, Faith 33
Witmore, Nathaniel 12
WITSHALL 832
WITT 832
Witt, Ann 45
Witt, Bethiah 382, 625
Witt, Elizabeth 446
Witt, Esther 353

Witt, Jonathan 712
Witt, Marah 438
Witt, Marey 438
Witt, Mary 438
Wittam, Abigail 423
WITTECOM 832
Wittem, Hannah 611
WITTER 832
Witter, Elizabeth 451
Witter, Hannah 40, 119, 142
Witter, Mary 556
Witterige, Mary 348
Witteston, Rachel 50
Wittingham, Martha 156
WITTOMS 832
WITTUM 832 see WITHAM
Wittum, Elizabeth 753
Wittum, Hannah 611
Wittum, Sarah 94, 652
Wittum, William 753
WITTY 832
WIXAM 832 see WICKHAM
Wixam, Barnabas 321
Wixam, Elizabeth 500
WIXOM 832
WIXON 832 see WICKHAM
Wodcoke, Mary 330
WODELL 832
Wodell, Alice 19
Wodell, Elizabeth 13, 485
Wodell, Frances 19
Wodell, Gershom 299
Wodell, Innocent 84
Wodell, Mary 327, 456, 814
Wodell, Ursula 840
Wofford, Henry 264
WOLCOT 833
WOLCOTT 832, 833
Wolcott, Ann 328
Wolcott, Anna 328
Wolcott, Elizabeth 12, 180, 183, 543
Wolcott, Elizabeth Treat 424
Wolcott, Hannah 192
Wolcott, Henry 115, 535, 832
Wolcott, Joanna 174
Wolcott, John 13, 191, 535
Wolcott, Joseph 444
Wolcott, Martha 13
Wolcott, Mary 230, 643
Wolcott, Sarah 147, 603
Wolcott, Simon 154
Wolf, Freeborn 647
Wolf, Freeborne 74
WOLFE 833
Wolfe, Deborah 710
Wolfe, Hannah 692, 715
Wolfe, Mary 710
WOLFORD 773
Wollerton, Susanna 504
Wolleston, Gregory 473
Wolley, Elizabeth 205
Wollidge, Philip 527
Wollrych, Sarah 28
WOLTERTON 833
Wolterton, Elizabeth 776
Wolterton, Gregory 387, 701, 778
Wolterton, Mary 524
Wolterton, Violet 667
Wombrey, Deborah 455
Wombrey, Martha 455
WOOD 25, 833, 834, 835, 836
Wood, --- 418, 682, 738
Wood, Abigail 390, 461, 544, 599, 735
Wood, Ann 92, 590
Wood, Anne 603
Wood, Bethia 201

Wood, Catherine 534
Wood, Daniell 565
Wood, David 180, 600
Wood, Deborah 792
Wood, Dorcas 580
Wood, Dorothy 580
Wood, Elizabeth 189, 289, 521, 526, 536, 542, 589, 627, 799
Wood, Ellis 683
Wood, Francis 386
Wood, Hannah 181, 342
Wood, Joanna 597
Wood, John 509
Wood, Judith 227
Wood, Margaret 223, 317, 485, 725
Wood, Martha 614, 739
Wood, Mary 61, 91, 97, 153, 285, 289, 383, 406, 484, 513, 545, 590, 815
Wood, Mehitable 212, 521
Wood, Mercy 739
Wood, Michael 615
Wood, Nicholas 50, 551, 828
Wood, Phebe 589
Wood, Philippa 807
Wood, Priscilla 37
Wood, Rebecca 742
Wood, Ruth 420, 666, 764, 801
Wood, Samuel 345, 688
Wood, Sarah 50, 257, 277, 483, 530, 658, 781
Wood, Silence 379
Wood, Stephen 446
Wood, Susan 513
Wood, Susanna 262, 522
Wood, Susannah 725
Wood, Thomas 317, 722, 746
Wood, William 272, 411
Woodall, Frances 434
WOODAM 837 see WOODEN
WOODARD 839, 840
Woodbary, Hannah 543
Woodberie, Elizabeth 621
WOODBERRIE 836, 837
Woodberrie, Christian 751
Woodberrie, Elizabeth 774
Woodberrie, Hannah 351
WOODBERRY 836, 837
Woodberry, Abigail 543
Woodberry, Judah 365
Woodberry, Judith 365
Woodberry, Sarah 613
WOODBERY 836, 837
Woodbery, Anna 833
Woodbery, Bethiah 51
Woodbery, Jerusha 613
Woodbery, Joanna 591
Woodbery, Mary 836
Woodbery, Susanna 732
Woodbridg, Dorothy 288
WOODBRIDGE 836
Woodbridge, Benjamin (Rev.) 728
Woodbridge, Dorothy 288
Woodbridge, Elizabeth 157
Woodbridge, Lucy 92, 253
Woodbridge, Mary 20, 185
Woodbridge, Martha 642
Woodbridge, Mercy 642
Woodbridge, Thomas 167
Woodbridge, Timothy 277, 473, 643
WOODBURIE 836, 837
Woodburn, Mary 97
WOODBURY 836, 837
Woodbury, Abigail 370, 448, 449, 543
Woodbury, Anna 366

Woodbury, Christian 751
Woodbury, Elizabeth 34, 366, 515, 621, 774
Woodbury, Hannah 32, 188, 224, 351, 543, 563
Woodbury, Jerusha 613
Woodbury, Joanna 591
Woodbury, John 175, 216, 224
Woodbury, Jonathan 239, 777
Woodbury, Lydia 365
Woodbury, Martha 105
Woodbury, Mary 175
Woodbury, Nicholas 335
Woodbury, Richard 342, 593
Woodbury, Samuel 637
Woodbury, Sarah 613
Woodbury, Susan 381
Woodbury, Susanna 49
Woodbury, Thomas 452, 595
Woodbury, William 613
WOODCOCK 837
Woodcock, Alice 113
Woodcock, Anne 290
Woodcock, Deborah 545
Woodcock, Ellis 113
Woodcock, John 797
Woodcock, Mary 97, 283, 330
Woodcock, Sarah 35, 239
Woodcok, Alice 113
Woodcok, Ellis 113
WOODDAM 837
Wooddam, Mary 27
WOODDEE 840
Wooddis, Hannah 149
Wooddis, Millicent 239
Woode, Mary 741
Woodell, Alice 19
Woodell, Elizabeth 485
Woodell, Frances 19
Woodell, Sarah 650
WOODEN 837
Wooden, Benjamin 227
Wooden, Dorcas 180, 187
Wooden, Hannah 286
Wooden, John 468
Wooden, Martha 94
Wooden, Marthew 94
Wooden, Mary 162
WOODERD 839
Woodey, Hannah 149
Woodey, Mary Cogan 630
WOODFIELD 837
WOODFORD 837
Woodford, Hannah 12, 539
Woodford, Mary 71, 667
Woodford, Rebecca 594
Woodford, Sarah 12, 71, 120
WOODGATE 837
WOODHAM 837 see WOODEN
Woodham, Mary 27
WOODHEAD 837
Woodhead, Bridget 148
Woodhead, Mary 227
Woodhead, William 316
WOODHOUSE 837
Woodhouse, Elizabeth 208
Woodhouse, Henry 634
Woodhouse, Mary 105, 459, 521, 582
Woodhouse, Millicent 239
WOODHULL 837
Woodhull, Ann 758
Woodhull, Deborah 455
Woodhull, Ruth 243
Woodie, Mary 201, 666
Woodie, Richard 666
Woodier, Grace 246
Woodies, Mary 459, 586

WOODIN 837
Woodin, Bethiah 296
Woodin, Grace 246
Woodin, Hannah 367, 757, 758
Woodin, Martha 613
Woodin, Mary 645
Woodin, Sarah 226, 227, 244
WOODING 837
Wooding, Abigail 370
Wooding, Benjamin 227, 424
Wooding, Mary 645
Wooding, Sarah 506
WOODIS 837
Woodis, Alice 767
Woodis, Elizabeth 208
Woodis, Hannah 524, 594
Woodis, Sarah 201
WOODLAND 837
Woodland, Thankful 737
Woodle, Nabbie 321
WOODLEY 837
WOODMAN 837, 838
Woodman, Archelaus 2, 145
Woodman, Bethia 324
Woodman, Dorothy 547
Woodman, Elizabeth 776, 803
Woodman, Hannah 395, 531
Woodman, John 398, 502
Woodman, Judith 750
Woodman, Margaret 48
Woodman, Mary 106, 251, 679, 790
Woodman, Mehitable 310
Woodman, Rebecca 456
Woodman, Remember 572
Woodman, Ruth 477
Woodman, Sarah 4, 24, 101, 434, 504, 737
WOODMANCY 838
Woodmancy, Abigail 743
Woodmancy, John 514
Woodmanse, Sarah 531
WOODMANSEY 838
Woodmansey, Ann 200
Woodmansey, Anna 200
Woodmansey, Elizabeth 250
Woodmansey, Margaret 623, 634
Woodmansey, Mary 27, 727
WOODROW 838
Woodrow, Mary 673
WOODRUFF 838
Woodruff, Ann 840
Woodruff, Elizabeth 104, 211, 314, 668
Woodruff, Hannah 621, 622, 662
Woodruff, Mary 65, 636
Woodruff, Matthew 539
Woodruff, Phebe 187
Woodruff, Ruth 595
Woodruff, Sarah 209
WOODS 833, 834, 835
Woods, Abigail 582, 598
Woods, Alice 677
Woods, Catherine 534
Woods, Elizabeth 557, 596, 728, 736
Woods, Frances 392
Woods, Francis 392
Woods, Grace 431
Woods, Hannah 458, 787
Woods, Lydia 238
Woods, Mary 557
Woods, Nathaniel 204
Woods, Obadiah 298
Woods, Sarah 458
WOODWARD 838, 839, 840 see WOODWORTH
Woodward, Abigail 520

Woodward, Ann 211
Woodward, Anne 211
Woodward, Daniel 320
Woodward, Elizabeth 242, 286, 459, 558, 725
Woodward, Esther 71, 649, 782
Woodward, Experience 592
Woodward, Ezekiel 206, 588, 692
Woodward, Frances 150, 549
Woodward, Freedom 719
Woodward, Israel 164
Woodward, John 461, 641, 684, 719
Woodward, Joseph 311
Woodward, Lambert 123, 646
Woodward, Margaret 18, 126
Woodward, Martha 251
Woodward, Mary 22, 37, 116, 239, 312, 480, 654, 770
Woodward, Mehitable 366
Woodward, Mercy 239, 728
Woodward, Nathaniel 728
Woodward, Priscilla 37
Woodward, Prudence 489, 520, 523
Woodward, Rachel 692
Woodward, Rebecca 268
Woodward, Richard 296, 693
Woodward, Robert 350
Woodward, Rose 538
Woodward, Sarah 242, 296, 364, 520, 639, 683, 810
Woodward, Smith 129
Woodward, Thankful 729
Woodward, Ursula 476
Woodward, William 316
WOODWELL 840
Woodwell, Elizabeth 581
Woodwell, Margaret 630
Woodwell, Matthew 20
WOODWORTH 840 see WOODWARD
Woodworth, Abigail 413
Woodworth, Caleb 527
Woodworth, Ezekiel 351
Woodworth, John 641
Woodworth, Margaret 267
Woodworth, Martha 202
Woodworth, Mary 674
Woodworth, Walter 202
WOODY 840
Woody, Hannah 594
Woody, Martha 564
Woody, Mary 201, 666
Woody, Richard 666
Wooland, Sarah 563
WOOLCOT 832
WOOLCOTT 833
Woolcott, Sarah 160
WOOLCUTT 832
Woolcutt, Sarah 141
Woolderson, Frances 46
WOOLEN 840
Woolen, Amy 767
Woolen, Jane 181, 334
Woolen, Jeane 334
Woolen, Richard 767
WOOLERY 841
Woolet, Edmund 591
WOOLEY 840
Wooley, Elizabeth 205
Wooley, Eunice 729
Wooley, Mary 393
Wooley, Ruth 730
Woolfe, Freeborn 647
Woolfe, Hannah 647
Woolford, Jane 575
Woolidge, Philip 505

Woolie, Mary 393
Woolland, Elizabeth 190
WOOLLCUTT 832
WOOLLEN 840
WOOLLEY 840
Woolley, Grace 757
Woolley, Ruth 757
Woolley, Sarah 271
WOOLLIE 840
WOOLLRIGE 840
WOOLLY 840
Woolman, Mary 360
WOOLRICH 840
Woolrich, Sarah 28
WOOLRYCH 840
WOOLSEY 840
Woolsey, Rebecca 813
Woolsey, Sarah 337
WOOLSON 840, 841
Woolson, Elizabeth 392
Woolson, Mary 426
Woolson, Sarah 82
Woolstone, Jane 260
WOOLWORTH 841
Wooly, Eunice 729
Wooly, Ruth 730
WOOREY 841 see WHERRY
WOOSTER 841
Wooster, Dorothy 201
Wooster, Edward 401, 451
Wooster, Elizabeth 420
Wooster, Hannah 783
Wooster, Ruth 87
Wooster, Susanna 699
Wooten, Jane 334
Wooten, Jeane 334
Wooten, Margaret 313
Wootton, Elizabeth 572
WORCESTER 841
Worcester, Moses 678, 703
Worcester, Samuel 489
Worcester, Sarah 648
Worcester, Susanna 586, 699
Worcester, Timothy 15
Worcester, William 284, 334, 675
Worchester, William (Rev.) 129
Word, Susanna 262
Wordden, Mary 119
WORDELE 779
WORDEN 779
Worden, Eleanor 4
Worden, Elizabeth 720
Worden, Ellen 4
Worden, Martha 661
Worden, Mary 119
Worden, Mercy 829
Worden, Samuel 27
Worin, Mary 79
WORMALL 841
Wormall, Esther 234
Wormall, Hester 234
Worman, Wm. 59
Wormbum, Ann 270
WORMELL 841
Wormell, Josiah 698
WORMESTALL 841
Wormlum, Wm. 59
WORMSTALL 841
Wormstall, Martha 217
Wormwell, Mary 514
WORMWOOD 841
Wormwood, Ann 270
Wormwood, Lydia 385
Wormwood, Margaret 126
Wormwood, Mary 59, 695
Wormwood, Wm. 59
WORNAL 841
Wornal, Ann 270

WORNAN 841
Wornan, Ann 270
WORRELL 421, 841
Worstall, Rebecca 225
Worster, Constance 757
Worster, Moses 692
WORTH 841, 842
Worth, John 160, 651
Worth, Judith 114, 480
Worth, Lionel 586
Worth, Sarah 303
WORTHELIKE 842
WORTHEN 842
Worthen, Hannah 280
Worthen, Margaret 790
WORTHILAKE 842
Worthilake, Sarah 589
Worthileg, Susanna 271
WORTHINGTON 842
Worthington, Elizabeth 23, 86, 87, 522, 524
Worthington, Nicholas 37, 522, 805
Worthington, Susannah 37
Worthington, William 522
WORTHLAKE 842
WORTHYLAKE 842
Worthylake, Elizabeth 143
Worthylake, Mary 476
WOSTER 841
WOTHEN 842
WRIGHT 842, 843, 844
Wright, --- 325, 645, 763
Wright, Abigail 154, 380, 663
Wright, Alice 189
Wright, Ann 291, 726, 777
Wright, Anna 121, 777
Wright, Anna 777
Wright, Anthony 684, 752
Wright, Deborah 43, 170, 270
Wright, Dorcas 12
Wright, Dorothy 77, 270, 515
Wright, Edward 46, 612
Wright, Eleanor 97, 155
Wright, Elizabeth 52, 155, 169, 198, 347, 349, 459, 652, 704, 749
Wright, Ellinar 97
Wright, Esther 491, 598, 744
Wright, Gideon 470
Wright, Hannah 69, 80, 171, 310, 376, 662, 704
Wright, Henry 703
Wright, Hester 491, 744
Wright, Jane 340
Wright, John 424
Wright, Joseph 198, 719
Wright, Josiah 141
Wright, Judah 12, 120
Wright, Lydia 78, 174, 190, 347, 388, 448, 540, 685
Wright, Margaret 39
Wright, Martha 361, 519
Wright, Mary 10, 18, 48, 60, 78, 142, 154, 328, 537, 603, 730
Wright, Mercy 13, 48, 142, 170, 701
Wright, Nathaniel 57
Wright, Peter 388
Wright, Priscilla 349
Wright, Rachel 458
Wright, Rebecca 80, 211, 287, 287, 462
Wright, Rose 170
Wright, Ruth 52, 128, 444, 699
Wright, Samuel 190, 200, 220, 775
Wright, Sarah 145, 173, 181, 196, 341, 453, 458, 596, 597, 636,

Wright, Sarah (cont.) 654, 773, 842
Wright, Stephen 200
Wright, Susannah 584
Wright, Thomas 249, 373, 652
Wright, Timothy 103
Wright, Walter 373, 646
Wright, William 26, 181, 223
WRONG 844
WROTH 844
WROTHAM 844
Wrotham, Elizabeth 532
Wrotham, Susanna 391
WYAR 812, 844
Wyard, Lois 214
WYART 812 see WYER
WYAT 844
WYATE 844
Wyath, Humphrey 323
Wyath, Sarah 268
Wyath, Susan 323
WYATT 844
Wyatt, Elizabeth 330
Wyatt, Hepzibah 599, 646
Wyatt, Joanna 264
Wyatt, John 14, 41, 137, 318, 346, 471, 806
Wyatt, Margaret 12
Wyatt, Mary 41, 437
Wyatt, Richard 101
Wyatt, Sarah 73, 318, 362
Wyatt, Susanna 253
Wyatt, Waitstill 768
Wyatts, John 297
WYBORNE 812
Wyborne, Elizabeth 505
Wyburn, Margaret 555
WYCOME 813
WYER 844 see WEARE, WIARD
Wyer, Daniel 767
Wyer, Edward 455, 514
Wyer, Eleazer 446
Wyer, Elizabeth 503
Wyer, Hannah 234
Wyer, Katharine 792
Wyer, Mary 721
Wyer, Ruhamah 371
Wyer, Sarah 265
WYETH 831, 844 see WISE
Wyeth, Abigail 141, 427
Wyeth, Amie 134
Wyeth, Ann 585, 731
Wyeth, Anne 731
Wyeth, Em 134
Wyeth, Martha 412
Wyeth, Mary 571
Wyeth, Mehitable 521
Wyeth, Nicholas 18, 281
Wyeth, Sarah 268
Wyeth, Susanna 123
Wygett, Sarah 327
Wyllas, Mabel 836
Wyllas, Mahitable 836
Wylles, Mehitable 277
WYLLS 823
WYLLYS 823
Wyllys, Amy 608
Wyllys, Ann 608

Wyllys, Elizabeth 611
Wyllys, Mary 247
Wyllys, Mehitable 643
Wyllys, Ruth 729
Wyllys, Samuel 475
WYMAN 844, 845
Wyman, Abigail 623
Wyman, Bathsheba 728
Wyman, David 79, 323
Wyman, Isabel 322
Wyman, John 51, 289
Wyman, Judith 30
Wyman, Mary 584
Wyman, Sarah 774
Wymonds, Wm. 468
WYNYARD 845
Wyott, Margaret 12
Wyre, Hester 723
WYTHE 844

--- Y ---

YALE 845
Yale, Abigail 486
Yale, Ann 387
Yale, Elizabeth 556
Yale, Hannah 72, 726
Yale, Mary 411
Yale, Thomas 241, 257
Yardley, Mary 381
YARRINTON 846
YARROW 845
YATES 845
Yates, Dinah 564
Yates, John 405
Yates, Marcy 315
Yates, Mary 183, 369
Yates, Mercy 315
YEALE 845
YEALES 845
YEATES 845
YELINGS 845
YELL 845
Yelling, Mary 68, 99
Yelling, Roger 180
Yelling, Triphena 282
YELLINGS 845
Yelverton, Abigail 574
Yelverton, Dorothy 574
Yeo, Esther 320
Yeo, Wilmot 580
YEOMAN 845
Yeoman, Ann 800
Yeoman, Hannah 501
YEOMANS 845, 846
Yeomans, Edward 437
Yeomans, Elizabeth 431
YERRINGTON 846
YES 845
YOE 845
YONG 846
YONGS 847
YORK 846
York, Abigail 58
York, Elizabeth 319, 417
York, Grace 305

York, Hannah 342
York, James 246
York, Mary 102
York, Rachel 400
York, Richard 319
Yorke, Dorothy 232
Yorke, Elizabeth 137
Yorke, Richard 137
YOUNG 846
Young, Abigail 761
Young, Alice 55
Young, Bridget 823
Young, Deborah 472
Young, Elizabeth 288
Young, Francis 145
Young, George 525, 798
Young, Jane 353, 440
Young, Job 601
Young, John 747
Young, Lydia 358, 528
Young, Mary 524, 680, 758
Young, Mercy 692
Young, Nathaniel 152
Young, Patience 289
Young, Rebecca 365
Young, Richard 247
Young, Robert 94
Young, Sarah 147, 165, 443, 474
Young, Susanna 165
YOUNGE 846
Younge, Sarah 443, 489
Youngloff, Sarah 664
YOUNGLOVE 846, 847
Younglove, Abigail 562
Younglove, Hannah 540, 562
Younglove, Lydia 316, 326, 831
Younglove, Mary 639, 690
Younglove, Samuel 246
Younglove, Sarah 664, 729
YOUNGMAN 847
Youngman, Francis 363
YOUNGS 847
Youngs, Bethia 303
Youngs, Christiana 389
Youngs, Christopher 388, 517, 536, 847
Youngs, Giles 724
Youngs, Hannah 217
Youngs, John 249, 535, 536, 761, 847
Youngs, John (Rev.) 553
Youngs, Katherine 548
Youngs, Margaret 337
Youngs, Martha 292, 517
Youngs, Mary 109, 176, 198, 548, 574, 795
Youngs, Mercy 574
Youngs, Thomas 92
YOURES 847

--- Z ---

ZALLETH 848
ZELLICK 848
ZULLISH 848
...eney, Anne 445